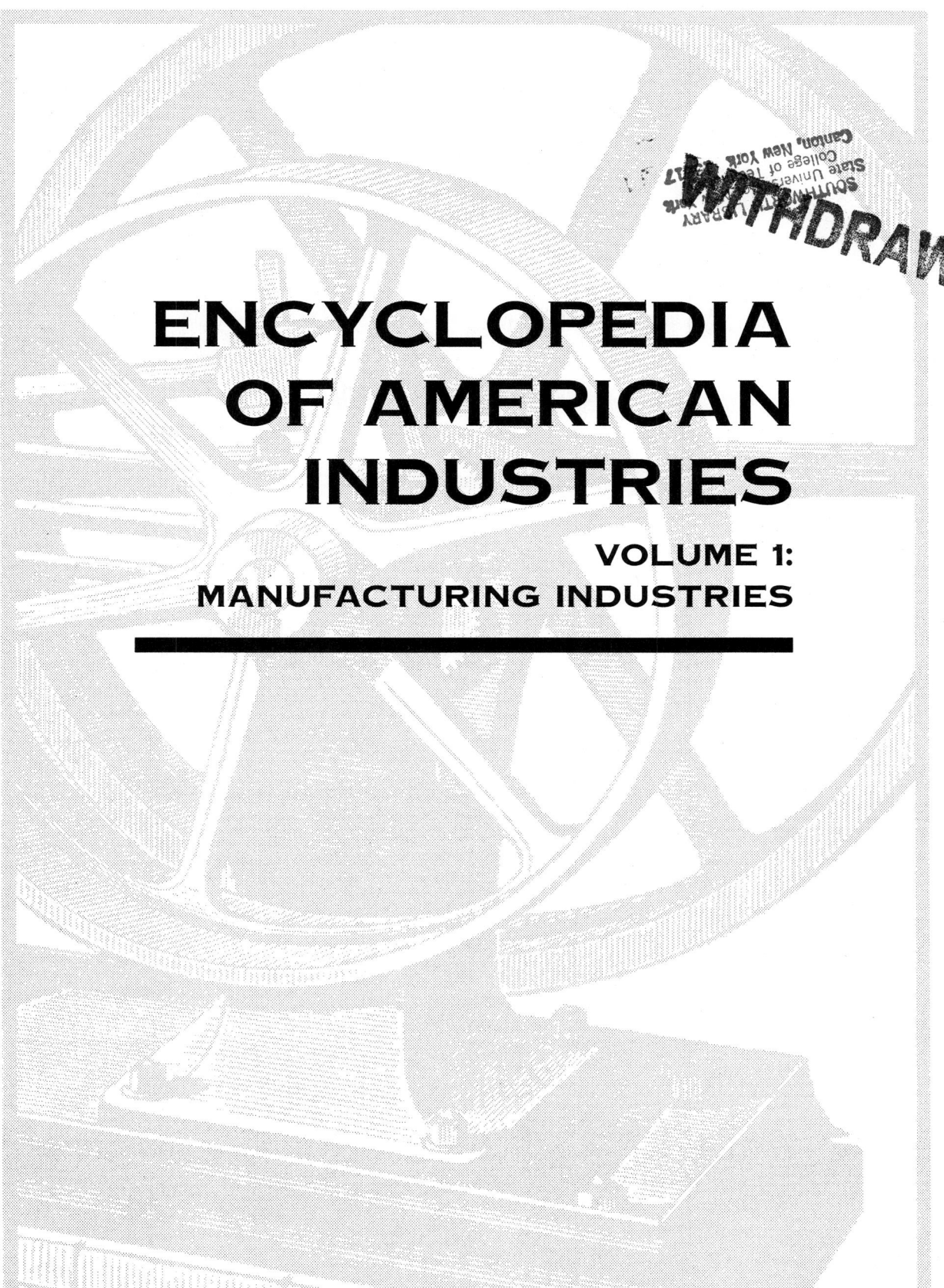

ENCYCLOPEDIA OF AMERICAN INDUSTRIES

VOLUME 1:
MANUFACTURING INDUSTRIES

ENCYCLOPEDIA OF AMERICAN INDUSTRIES

VOLUME 1:
MANUFACTURING INDUSTRIES

KEVIN HILLSTROM, EDITOR

MARY K. RUBY, ASSOCIATE EDITOR

Gale Research Inc.

An International Thomson Publishing Company

I(T)P

NEW YORK • LONDON • BONN • BOSTON • DETROIT • MADRID
MELBOURNE • MEXICO CITY • PARIS • SINGAPORE • TOKYO
TORONTO • WASHINGTON • ALBANY NY • BELMONT CA • CINCINNATI OH

STAFF

Kevin Hillstrom, *Editor*
Mary K. Ruby, *Associate Editor*
Marilyn Allen, *Editorial Associate*

Jennifer Arnold Mast, Suzanne M. Bourgoin, Shawn Brennan, David Collins, Sandra Doran,
Nicolet V. Elert, Kelly Hill, Janice Jorgensen, Paula Kepos, Mike Kroll, Camille Robinson,
Diane M. Sawinski, Kathleen Wilson *Contributing Editors*
Mark Berger, *Graphic Designer*

Peter M. Gareffa, *Senior Editor, Contemporary Biographies*

Mary Beth Trimper, *Production Director*
Shanna Heilveil, *Production Assistant*

Cynthia Baldwin, *Production Design Manager*
Pamela Galbreath, *Art Director*

Overview of Contents

Volume One: Manufacturing Industries

Volume Two: Service & Non-Manufacturing Industries

PREFACE

The *Encyclopedia of American Industries* (*EAI*) is a major new business reference tool that provides detailed, comprehensive information on a wide range of industries in every realm of American business. Volume One of the *Encyclopedia* provides coverage of 460 manufacturing industries, each discussed in its own essay. Manufacturing industries covered in this volume range from large ones, such as the automotive industry and the pharmaceutical industry, to smaller business sectors, such as the porcelain electrical supplies industry and the waterproof outerwear industry. Volume Two of the *Encyclopedia* presents 544 essays covering the vast array of service and other non-manufacturing industries in America. Industries covered in Volume Two range from major economic entities, such as the airline industry and the insurance industry, to smaller sectors, such as book stores and Irish potato farms. Combined, these two volumes provide individual essays on every manufacturing, nonmanufacturing, and service industry in America represented by a four-digit Standard Industrial Classification (SIC) code. Both volumes of the *Encyclopedia* are arranged numerically by SIC code for easy use.

CONTENT AND ARRANGEMENT

Essays. The *Encyclopedia*'s business coverage includes information on historical events of consequence as well as relevant trends and statistics entering the mid-1990s. Sections of coverage in an *EAI* essay may include the following:

Industry Snapshot. Provides an overview of the industry and its health in the mid-1990s.

Organization and Structure. Discusses the configuration and functional aspects of the industry.

Background and Development. Relates the industry's genesis and historical development, including major technological advances, scandals, pioneering companies, major products, important legislation, and other factors that shaped the industry.

Current Conditions. Provides information on the status of the industry in the mid-1990s, with an eye to industry challenges on the horizon.

Industry Leaders. Details specific industry leaders, the companies that reign in such areas as sales, market share, volume of production, and new product development.

Work Force. Contains information on the size, diversity, and characteristics of the industry's work force.

America and the World. Discusses the United States' place in the global marketplace in the industry, as well as trade issues and key international developments and competitors.

Research and Technology. Furnishes information on major technological advances, areas of research, and their potential impact on the industry.

Industry Information Sources. Provides users with suggested further reading on the industry. These sources, also used to compile the essays, are publicly accessible materials such as magazines, general and academic periodicals, books, annual reports, and government sources, as well as material supplied by industry associations.

Graphs. The *Encyclopedia of American Industries* includes hundreds of informative, easy-to-read graphs that detail a wide range of key economic and business information on the diverse industrial landscape of America.

Indexes. The *Encyclopedia of American Industries* provides two major indexes to aid the user:

General Index. Contains alphabetical references to all companies, associations, key government agencies, and specific legislation cited in the *Encyclopedia*. Using this index, users can easily locate all references in both volumes to: companies such as General Motors; pertinent government entities such as the Environmental Protection Agency; and key legislative measures such as the North American Free Trade Agreement.

Industry Index. Contains more than 19,000 alphabetical references to various types of business products and services currently offered in the United States. Each establishment reference is preceded by the four-digit Standard Industrial Classification code under which the U.S. government has placed the tracking of economic activity for that particular product or service. Utilizing this index, the user can easily determine which essay should be consulted in researching products as diverse as dog food and electric space heaters and services as varied as automotive repair shops and burglar alarm installation contractors. This index also includes inversions on significant keywords contained within product and service types.

BREADTH OF COVERAGE

All of the *Encyclopedia*'s features--the essays, the graphs, and the indexes--are expressly designed to provide the user with valuable information on an industry's status, both yesterday and today.

Developments discussed in *EAI* that have unfolded in the mid-1990s include:

- The introduction in 1994 of genetically modified tomatoes--the first genetically altered food approved for sale by the Food and Drug Administration--to the nation's produce stores (discussed in **SIC 0161: Vegetables and Melons**).

- The 1994 agreement reached by the HD Digital Conference, an international committee representing 50 companies worldwide, on a common standard for VCRs that use digital technology, an agreement deemed vital in order to avoid the format wars that took place in the industry in the early 1980s with analog VCRs (discussed in **SIC 3651: Household Audio and Video Equipment**).

- The May 1994 announcement by New World Communications Group that it was switching all 12 of its

affiliate television stations, including eight stations long affiliated with CBS, Inc., to the Fox Broadcasting Co., yet another development in the rapidly changing world of media and telecommunications (discussed in **SIC 4833: Television Broadcasting Stations**).

In addition to this coverage, however, the *Encyclopedia of American Industries* includes comprehensive information on notable historical events in the American business world, such as:

- The passage of the Food, Drug, and Cosmetic Act of 1938 in response to the deaths of more than 100 Americans who ingested an unsafe sore throat remedy; this legislation required that all new drugs be submitted to the newly created Food and Drug Administration for approval (discussed in **SIC 2834: Pharmaceutical Preparations**).

- The significant role played by the U.S. Post Office in the development of the American airline industry (discussed in **SIC 4512: Air Transportation, Scheduled**)

- The legal battles of the early 1900s that resulted in the anti-trust exemption granted to major league baseball, a favored legal status that remains unique among professional sports (discussed in **SIC 7941: Professional Sports Clubs and Promoters**).

STANDARD INDUSTRIAL CLASSIFICATIONS

The *Encyclopedia of American Industries* patterns its coverage after the U.S. government's Standard Industrial Classification (SIC) system, thus ensuring complete coverage of all major economic activity in the United States. The SIC is the statistical classification standard underlying all establishment-based federal economic statistics classified by industry. The classification covers the entire field of economic activities and defines industries in accordance with the composition and structure of the economy. It is revised periodically to reflect the economy's changing industrial organization. The *Encyclopedia of American Industries* is based on the 1987 update of the SIC system.

The Standard Industrial Classification (SIC) code system was established by the U.S. government to provide a uniform means for collecting, presenting, and analyzing economic data. It is currently maintained by the Office of Management and Budget. These codes are widely used by federal, state, and local government agencies; trade associations; private research organizations; and business professionals to promote comparability in the presentation of statistical data.

Each SIC code classifies what the government calls "establishments" by the types of activities in which they are engaged. An establishment is defined as an economic unit where a service is performed or a product is manufactured or sold (generally at a single physical location). To be recognized as a separate industry within the SIC system, a set of establishments must be statistically significant according to criteria such as the number of persons employed and the volume of business conducted. Each establishment is placed in a Standard Industrial Classification according to its primary activity, which is determined by the main product or group of products that it produces or distributes, or by the services it renders.

ACKNOWLEDGEMENTS

The staff of the *Encyclopedia of American Industries* would like to thank the members of the *EAI* Advisory Board for their invaluable help:

- **Dr. Raymond Genick,** Director, Small Business Development Center, Detroit, Michigan

- **Judith M. Nixon,** Librarian, Consumer & Family Sciences Library, Purdue University, West Lafayette, Indiana

- **Mark Patrick,** Librarian, Detroit Public Library, Detroit, Michigan

- **Janet M. Treichel,** Executive Director, National Business Education Association, Reston, Virginia

The editor would also like to thank the *EAI* editorial staff for their outstanding work on this *Encyclopedia*. The editor especially extends thanks to Mary Ruby for her considerable contributions to the production of *EAI*.

COMMENTS AND SUGGESTIONS

Questions, comments, and suggestions regarding the *Encyclopedia of American Industries* are welcomed. Please contact:

The Editor
Encyclopedia of American Industries
Gale Research Inc.
835 Penobscot Bldg.
Detroit, MI 48226-4094
Telephone: (313) 961-2242
Toll-Free: 800-347-GALE
FAX: (313) 961-6815

Contents:

Volume One:
Manufacturing Industries

TOBACCO PRODUCTS

TEXTILE MILL PRODUCTS

APPAREL & OTHER FINISHED PRODUCTS MADE FROM FABRICS & SIMILAR MATERIALS

LUMBER & WOOD PRODUCTS, EXCEPT FURNITURE

FURNITURE & FIXTURES

PAPER & ALLIED PRODUCTS

PRINTING, PUBLISHING & ALLIED INDUSTRIES

CHEMICALS & ALLIED PRODUCTS

PETROLEUM REFINING & RELATED INDUSTRIES

RUBBER & MISCELLANEOUS PLASTICS PRODUCTS

LEATHER & LEATHER PRODUCTS

STONE, CLAY, GLASS & CONCRETE PRODUCTS

PRIMARY METALS INDUSTRIES

FABRICATED METAL PRODUCTS, EXCEPT MACHINERY/ TRANSPORTATION EQUIPMENT

INDUSTRIAL & COMMERCIAL MACHINERY & COMPUTER EQUIPMENT

ELECTRONIC & OTHER ELECTRICAL EQUIPMENT & COMPONENTS, EXCEPT COMPUTER EQUIPMENT

TRANSPORTATION EQUIPMENT

MEASURING, ANALYZING & CONTROLLING INSTRUMENTS

Alphabetical Table of Contents:

Volume One: Manufacturing Industries

X

Y

ENCYCLOPEDIA
OF AMERICAN
INDUSTRIES

VOLUME 1:
MANUFACTURING INDUSTRIES

FOOD & KINDRED PRODUCTS

MEAT PACKING PLANTS

This industry includes establishments primarily engaged in the slaughtering (for their own account or on a contract basis for the trade) of cattle, hogs, sheep, lambs, and calves for meat to be sold or to be used on the same premises in canning, cooking, curing, and freezing, and in making sausage, lard, and other products. The industry also includes establishments primarily engaged in slaughtering horses for human consumption. Businesses primarily engaged in slaughtering, dressing, and packing poultry, rabbits, and other small game are classified in **SIC 2015: Poultry Slaughtering and Processing.** Those primarily engaged in slaughtering and processing animals not for human consumption are classified in **SIC 2048: Prepared Feeds and Feed Ingredients for Animals and Fowls, Except Dogs and Cats.** Businesses primarily involved in manufacturing sausages and meat specialties from purchased meats are classified in **SIC 2013: Sausages and Other Prepared Meat Products.**

INDUSTRY SNAPSHOT

With annual sales in the $70 billion range, meat packing is one of the largest agriculture-based industries in the United States in the 1990s. In recent years, however, changing consumer eating habits were having an impact on the beef and pork industries, by far the largest sectors in this industry category. As Americans ate less beef, the beef industry retrenched, eliminating smaller and inefficient plants and expanding their operations to incorporate poultry products. At the same time, the pork industry was striving to reposition

pork as "the meat of choice." Although technically a "red" meat, it was gaining acceptance as an alternative to white meat chicken.

ORGANIZATION AND STRUCTURE

The American Meat Institute (AMI) reported more than 1.25 million livestock operations in the early 1990s, raising beef cattle, hogs, and sheep destined for human consumption. According to U.S. government statistics, livestock on farms numbered 100.9 million cattle and calves, 10.2 million sheep and lambs, and 59.8 million hogs.

The meat packing plants that turned these animals into food and nonfood products ranged in size from those handling small numbers of livestock to operations processing millions of animals a year. According to the AMI, there were 4,021 slaughtering plants in operation in the United States in 1993. Federally inspected plants numbered 1,125, and 80 of these accounted for approximately 91 percent of commercial cattle slaughter, while 62 facilities accounted for almost 93 percent of all hog slaughtering in 1993. The dominance of a few major companies is further demonstrated by the fact that four packers processed approximately 70 percent of the beef and another four handled close to 60 percent of the pork. The processing of sheep and lambs accounted for only about seven percent of meat production.

Geography was an important factor not only in raising the livestock but in the location of slaughterhouses as well. Industry sources indicate that the North Central states raised almost 40 percent of the cattle and 78 percent of the hogs in the early 1990s, while South Central states raised more than 30 percent of the cattle and about six percent of the hogs. The top five cattle slaughtering states were Nebraska, Kansas, Texas, Colorado, and Iowa; the top five states in the slaughter of hogs were Iowa, Minnesota, Illinois, Nebraska, and South Dakota.

BACKGROUND AND DEVELOPMENT

Salt was used by the country's first meat packers, the colonial farmers of New England, to preserve meat. As the nation grew and moved westward, slaughterhouses were built near population centers so that meat could reach the table before it spoiled. The livestock herds were driven overland or barged to these early packing plants. So many hogs were slaughtered in Cincinnati, Ohio, that the city was called ''Porkopolis.''

Meat packing operations could only be carried out during the cold winter months, and ice was used for refrigeration. The development of mechanical refrigeration and the refrigerated railroad car in the second half of the nineteenth century changed this. From just after the Civil War until the 1920s, Chicago, a hub city for the railroads, became renowned for its a array of stockyards that collected and slaughtered livestock, often under harrowing working conditions.

With the turn of the century came mechanized disassembly and conveyor procedures in the plants, and the 1950s saw major improvements in plant sanitation and packaging. By the 1980s, the meat packing industry had again dispersed. Slaughterhouses moved closer to the feedlots where the animals were raised. Not having to ship them long distances reduced the stress, weight loss, and injury to the animals that was the inevitable effect of long journeys in crowded cattle cars and trucks.

Regulations. Under the 1906 Meat Inspection Act, Federal anti- and post-mortem inspection of meat that enters into interstate and foreign commerce became mandatory. Meat that will be used entirely within a single state may be inspected by that state's agriculture department. The Federal program was conducted by the Food Safety and Inspection Service (FSIS) of the U.S. Department of Agriculture (USDA). During the late 1980s and early 1990s, unfavorable media criticism of the inspection system spurred an overhaul of FSIS procedures.

In 1993, after four people died and hundreds more fell ill from ingestion of *e. coli* bacteria in undercooked hamburgers, food safety returned as a major industry issue. The USDA proposed a new labeling policy for red meat that was not ready to eat. Under the new policy, labels with safe-handling instructions would be attached to meat and meat products. In issuing the new labeling recommendations, USDA cited consumer surveys of 1985 and 1990 that revealed consumer ignorance of such basic food safety procedures.

Slaughter. The desirability of stunning animals prior to slaughter was recognized in both Europe and the United States before the end of the nineteenth century, but it wasn't until 1960—with the passage of the Humane Slaughter Act—that the practice became mandatory in the United States. The Act required that, before being slaughtered, animals must be rendered unconscious by mechanical, electrical, or chemical (carbon dioxide gas) means that cause the animal the minimum of excitement or discomfort. Captive-bolt pistols or pneumatic guns may be used on cattle. With sheep and pigs, pistols, electric shock, or anesthetization in a carbon dioxide chamber may be used. Compressed-air stunners came into use for cattle after World War II, and gas chambers for smaller animals. An exception could be made for ritual slaughter to satisfy the requirements of a particular faith. In kosher inspection, for example, a member of the Jewish faith cut the throat and bled the animal without first stunning it, and then examined it for abnormalities before approving it for food use.

After stunning, cattle would be suspended by one or both hindlegs while the carotid arteries and jugular veins were cut. Hides could then be removed by an automated process. A straight cut opened the center of the belly to remove the viscera. Next, the carcasses were split down the center of the backbone. Beef carcasses might then be shrouded, a procedure in which the carcasses were cooled for 24 hours after being tightly wrapped in muslin that had been soaked in warm water. The carcass fat would be smooth and trim when the shroud was removed. Specialty meat items like the brains, kidneys, tail, tongue, and sweetbreads did not accompany the carcass but were an important income source for packers. The procedures for veal carcasses were similar except that the hides were left on during chilling. Veal carcasses have very little fat and would shrink during chilling if the hides were removed.

In hog slaughter, the animals are bled after stunning by severing a large vein. The carcasses are then submerged in hot water to loosen the hair. After the removal of the hair, the carcass is eviscerated, split, and chilled.

Grading. While meat inspection is mandatory, grading is a voluntary program. Funded by fees paid by the packers, the service is offered by the USDA's Agricultural and Marketing Service. Grading establishes uniform trading standards and helps to determine the value of various meat cuts. Meat carcasses are graded by both quality and yield.

The quality grades for beef are prime, choice, good, standard, commercial, utility, cutter, and canner. Carcass characteristics that determine the grade include marbling (the streaks of fat in the lean portions); the color and texture of the lean; and maturity. Consumers tend to interpret grading as an indication of taste and tenderness, although it was not designed for this purpose. Growing consumer perceptions that lean meat is healthier have increased the demand for lower-fat grades. The ratio of usable meat to bone and fat determines a carcass's yield grade. Combined with the quality grade it is used to establish the monetary value of a carcass.

Working Conditions. The slaughterhouses of the United States in the early years of this century were grim and dangerous places to work. Low wages, coupled with unsafe conditions, made the stockyards of Chicago and other cities hazardous work sites. But it was not until reports on conditions there grew widespread—thanks in part to Upton Sinclair's novel *The Jungle,* which depicted in chilling detail the deplorable environment of the stockyards of Chicago—that the government turned its attention that way. This furthered the cause of fledgling unions, who grew in strength over the ensuing years.

Even in the 1990s, however, meat packing plants rank among the most hazardous work sites. *The Monthly Labor Review* noted that, even at the end of the twentieth century, automation had not replaced manual labor and the extensive use of sharp knives and other hand tools; workers were still lifting and lugging heavy carcasses; abattoir floors were slippery; workers suffered from exposure due to the need for continuous refrigeration systems. So long as there was no economical and reliable cutting machinery that could accommodate the physical variety of animal carcasses, processing them would continue to be a manual operation.

In the late 1980s, the industry's rate of cumulative trauma disorders (CTDs) was 75 times more than the average in other manufacturing industries. The illness usually took the form of carpal tunnel syndrome, in which repeated, rapid, and forceful motions pinch and compress the nerve that runs through the wrist to the hand. Lower back and various tendon disorders were also reported.

Two of the nation's largest meat packers, IBP Inc. and John Morrell, were cited by the Occupational Safety and Health Administration (OSHA) for underreporting or failing to record injuries and illnesses. Both companies contested the OSHA fines, which

were greatly reduced. More important, OSHA recognized that the CTDs plaguing meat industry workers needed a new approach. OSHA proposed improved ergonomics, or fitting the job to the employee rather than the other way round, and, after consultation with AMI and labor groups, issued ergonomic guidelines in 1990. The OSHA guidelines emphasized worker training in proper techniques, strengthened by refresher courses, and the importance for workers to report CTD symptoms early so as to prevent permanent injury. Medical management by trained health care providers was another program component.

OSHA offered special incentives to meat packers who entered into voluntary agreements with the agency to lessen their ergonomic hazards. While they would still be subject to OSHA inspections, they would not be cited or penalized on ergonomic grounds. Opinions on OSHA's voluntary guidelines were mixed. Jim Marsden, AMI vice-president for scientific and technical affairs, said in *Occupational Hazards,* that they were "especially effective because they're geared toward hazard prevention." Industry critics did not always agree. Phillip L. Immesote, president of the United Food and Commercial Workers (UFCW) Union, testified at a hearing of the House Employment and Housing Subcommittee that OSHA was about to repeat earlier disastrous experiences with "a new program of exemptions and voluntary compliance in the nation's packing houses" (*Occupational Hazards*).

Despite AMI, OSHA, and individual packers' efforts, the critics' negative comments appeared to have some truth. Injury and illness rates showed no improvement in the early 1990s, with reportable cases of injury, illness, and lost workdays actually increasing in 1990 and again in 1991.

CURRENT CONDITIONS

Per capita meat consumption has declined from 132.1 pounds in 1972 to 116.1 pounds in 1992, a change in eating habits commonly attributed to diet and health concerns. Industry observers, however, expect red meat consumption to remain stable for the next several years. At least for 1994, the USDA was forecasting larger meat supplies at lower wholesale prices, with resulting competition for consumer dollars at the retail level.

Beef. With demand for red meat declining, the number of companies producing it decreased by ten percent between 1982 and 1987, according to the *1987 Census of Manufactures*, and the number of federally inspected meat plants continued to decline after that. At the same time, meat processors sought to improve their business outlook by expanding into the fast-growing poultry market. The number of major meat producers who also engaged in production of poultry products rose from 11 in 1982 to 32 in 1992, almost a threefold increase.

There were reasons other than health concerns for beef's trend, according to Robert Adams, vice-president of Continental Grain Co.'s cattle feeding division. A 1994 article in *Feedstuffs* notes Adams' feeling that the beef industry is disorganized, divided among a great many operations that vary enormously in their size and in their handling of as many as 80 different breeds of cattle. Supermarket meat cases were overwhelming, too, said Adams, with a profusion of cuts creating confusion instead of convenience.

Meanwhile, enhanced genetics, the introduction of new feed additives and growth stimulants, and nutritional advances all played a part in the improvements to cattle growth rate over the last quarter of the twentieth century. Consumers who ate beef wanted it to be lean. This demand, as well as environmental concerns, were expected to continue to have an impact on the beef industry.

Pork. Nationwide, the number of hog enterprises has dwindled in recent years. In 1993 the number of hog farms was half of what it had been in 1980. Many of the smaller operations dropped out, while the larger outfits expanded. For pig-slaughtering operations, however, this consolidation of sources didn't adversely impact on their production.

Both the pork and poultry industries have become increasingly linked to high-output feed mills. North Carolina, a top turkey-producing state, saw a jump of 22 percent in its swine inventory at the end of 1993. Of the top ten hog companies, which accounted for ten percent of production, six were either based in North Carolina or had sow breeding units in the state. *Feedstuffs*, a weekly agribusiness paper, predicted that at that rate, North Carolina would rank second in the nation within a decade.

The National Pork Producers Council looked to the future in 1994, announcing a comprehensive plan to promote pork as the meat of choice both domestically and worldwide. The plan was the joint output of the NPPC, the National Pork Board, the National Live Stock and Meat Board's pork section, and hundreds of producers. Goals included building demand for pork by creating new products and expanding current uses; insuring that pork met or surpassed consumer expectations of safety, quality, value; and positioning the industry as socially responsible.

Whether the potential for larger herds and increased production could be parlayed into industry growth was dependent, however, on other factors such as cost competitiveness, exports, and the continued popularity of pork products. In the early 1990s that popularity remained stable. The United States in 1992 recorded a 2.8 percent increase in per capita pork consumption over 1991, accounting for the first significant increase in red meat consumption since 1988, another year in which increased pork sales made the difference. This continuing viability was due in part to new breeding techniques that produce pork lower in calories and cholesterol and with one-third less fat than ten years earlier.

INDUSTRY LEADERS

AMI ranked IBP, ConAgra, and Cargill as the top three beef slaughterers in 1992, while IBP, ConAgra, and John Morrell operated the country's top three pork slaughter operations.

IBP, Inc. Competition for the number one spot in the meat packing industry was strong, but Nebraska-based IBP Inc., a subsidiary of Occidental Petroleum Corp., held on with sales of $11.1 billion in 1992, a seven percent increase over the previous year. These posted earnings continued the company's growth pattern. Earnings from operations rose from $61 million in 1991 to $160 million, while share profits jumped from three cents to $1.34. The work force numbers increased as well, with 1,000 new employees joining IBP in a year when many companies were downsizing. Foreign exports accounted for 12 percent of sales, most of them to the Far East (Japan, Korea, Taiwan). Mexico was a strong beef market for IBP, and the company's sales of pork in Europe increased sevenfold in 1992. IBP continued to concentrate on beef and pork slaughter and processing, leaving the diversification into poultry products to competitors like ConAgra, Inc., and Cargill Meat Sector in Minneapolis.

By taking its slaughterhouses in 1961 to where the beef was, near Nebraska's and Iowa's cattle farms, IBP changed the meat-packing industry. At the company's plant in Dakota City, Nebraska, the animal carcasses were carried over 20 miles of conveyor systems. Within 48 hours, a 650-pound carcass could be broken, cut, and packed into 65- to 80-pound boxes for shipment to supermarkets. Pork became an important part of IBP's success starting in 1976, and by the late 1980s the company was planning six plants in Iowa and Nebraska, all within a 100-mile radius of the nation's largest hog-producing area.

ConAgra, Inc. Originally known as Nebraska Consolidated Mills, ConAgra's expansion to its present status as a leading food producer began in earnest with its development of Duncan Hines cake mix in the

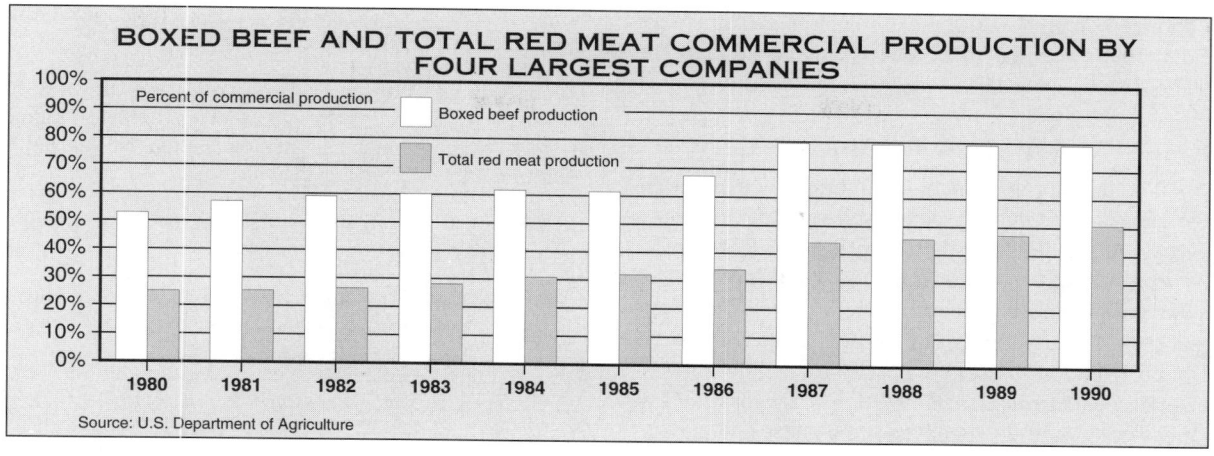

BOXED BEEF AND TOTAL RED MEAT COMMERCIAL PRODUCTION BY FOUR LARGEST COMPANIES
Source: U.S. Department of Agriculture

1950s. The company became a multifaceted food provider in the 1960s and 1970s, establishing a number of poultry processing plants to complement their growing flour mill business. In 1971 the company changed its name to ConAgra and continued its expansion into a variety of manufacturing industries. The company's purchases in recent years have included United Agri Products (1978), Banquet Frozen Foods (1980), Armour Food Company (1983), and Beatrice (1990), as well as a number of other businesses.

As *Hoover's Handbook of American Business 1994* notes, "ConAgra's primary division is its Prepared Food segment, which includes brands such as Hunt's, Wesson, Armour, and Butterball. . . . ConAgra's operations also include 208 retail stores."

Cargill. Founded in 1865, Cargill built its reputation in commodity trading, but by 1993 was one of the country's largest suppliers of raw foods and ingredients, with sales reaching $11 to $13 billion from diversified activities ranging from corn and flour milling to oilseed processing.

Although Cargill still regarded itself in 1993 primarily as an ingredient supplier, it had become the nation's third largest meat packer. Cargill had acquired Excel Corp., a leading name in boxed beef and pork, in 1979. When Cargill formed its Meat Sector in the early 1990s, it included the Excel Corp. and Cargill Meat Products (which further processed beef and pork). Excel distributed most of its products under private label. Estimated annual sales in the 1990s of $8 billion were split almost equally between retail and industrial/foodservice customers.

WORK FORCE

The number of employees in the meat packing industry began registering modest increases in the early 1990s, up to 141,500, after declining steadily from the 1965 count of 193,300. According to U.S. Department of Labor statistics, their weekly earnings averaged $378.90 in 1992, lagging well behind reported wages in meat processing ($399.78), in the food industry as a whole ($413.71), and for all manufacturing ($469.45). Meat packing is also a highly labor-intensive industry, and a higher proportion of total employees (84 percent) were production workers, compared to (72 percent) in all food preparation sectors and (67 percent) in all manufacturing.

Because of the low wages of the industry, employee turnover in the industry has increased. In 1977, the average pay in the meat packing industry was 17 percent higher than that for all manufacturing. By 1986, when the pay advantage had dropped to 15 percent below the factory average, growing numbers of workers quit the industry. Meat packing had traditionally recorded high layoff and recall rates, but until the sharp drop in pay scale, the number of workers who quit had been lower than in manufacturing as a whole.

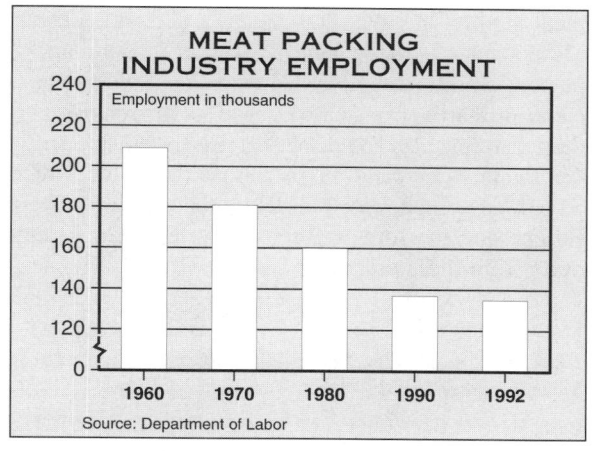

MEAT PACKING INDUSTRY EMPLOYMENT
Source: Department of Labor

Labor agreements with some of the large packers in the early 1990s seemed to be attempting to address the wage discrepancy, both to attract and hold workers.

AMERICA AND THE WORLD

The marketing of meat to American consumers in the supermarket lagged behind changes taking place elsewhere in the world, according to *Progressive Grocer* magazine. Centralized meat cutting that did away with the need for cutting operations in the supermarket was common in France, while retailers in the United Kingdom used new packaging technologies to extend product quality and shelf life. Across the Pacific, meat was often displayed in Japanese and Australian markets by its method of preparation rather than by animal, a system that exposed consumers to more varieties of meat.

International Trade. The United States enjoyed a favorable trade balance in red meat products, with exports increasing to more than $4.4 billion in 1992 from about $4.2 billion the year before. Pork made up only ten percent of exports. The major destination for beef exports was Japan, but increased sales to Mexico and South Korea, coupled with the weakness in the Japanese economy, eroded Japan's share. Japan, however, made up an estimated 73 percent of the export market for pork in 1992. This amount, a sudden increase over figures posted in previous years, was attributed to a scandal involving Taiwan's falsification of documents to avoid Japanese taxes. Even though high-end U.S. pork products were likely to remain competitively priced in Japan, Taiwan was expected to regain its market dominance.

As 1993 drew to a close, the USDA was predicting small improvement in meat trade, as Japan's economy remained slow. Both Canada and Mexico were expected to increase their exports.

Five countries accounted for 86 percent of all red meat imports in 1992: Australia (32 percent), Canada (24 percent), New Zealand (21 percent), Denmark (7 percent), and Argentina (2 percent). Pork imports came primarily from Canada and Denmark (60 percent). Strong pork prices in the European Economic Community compared to weaker pricing in the United States, combined with political upheavals in Eastern Europe and the former Yugoslavia, led to lower imports from these areas.

INDUSTRY INFORMATION SOURCES

1993 Meat & Poultry Facts, Washington, DC: American Meat Institute, 1993.

Bain, Herbert B., "The First 75 Years of the American Meat Institute," *American Meat Institute 75th Anniversary Com-*

memorative Magazine. Arlington, VA: American Meat Institute, 1980.

Baldo, Anthony, "Boxed In: For Two Decades, Iowa Beef Packing Prospered in the Rough-and-Tumble Meat-Cutting Business Without Much Fear of Competition. No Longer," *Financial World,* March 21, 1989.

Brown, Robert H., "AMI Testifies Against FDA Meat Inspection." *Feedstuffs,* November 22, 1993.

Carlson, Gordon S., "Larger Meat Supplies, Lower Prices on Tap," *Feedstuffs,* December 13, 1993.

Frazier, Frank, "Poultry Inspection History Shows New Tactics Tried Before," *Feedstuffs,* February 14, 1994.

Kushner, Gary Jay, "1994 Food Industry Legislative and Regulatory Outlook," *Food Processing,* January 1994.

LaBell, Fran, "Vegetarianism on the Rise," *Prepared Foods,* February 1994.

Lotterman, Ed, "The District Economy Grew on Agricultural Processing," *Fedgazette,* January 1993.

Marberry, Steve, "Pork Production 2000: Fewer Farms Doing More," *Feedstuffs,* February 28, 1994.

Pehanich, Mike, "The Quiet Giant Climbs the Value Chain," *Prepared Foods,* October 1993.

Personick, Martin E., Katherine Taylor-Shirley, "Profiles in Safety and Health," *Monthly Labor Review,* January 1989.

"Product Handbook: Pork," *ID,* September 15, 1993.

"Product Handbook: Processed Meats," *ID,* September 15, 1993.

Scheid, Jon F., "Beef Industry Striving to Be More Direct," *Feedstuffs,* February 21, 1994.

———, "Food Poisoning Cases Inspire New Policy," *Feedstuffs,* November 22, 1993.

Sheridan, Peter J., "Meatpackers Move to Cut Injury Rates," *Occupational Hazards,* May 1991.

Smith, Rod, "Pork Industry's Long-range Plan Ready to Go to Producers," *Feedstuffs,* January 24, 1994.

Spears, Jerry W., "Environment, Consumers, to Influence Beef Production, *Feedstuffs,* February 21, 1994.

U.S. Industrial Outlook 1993, Washington, DC: U.S. Department of Commerce, 1993.

Zbytniewski, Jo-Ann, "Marketing Methods: Meat products: Merchandising," *Progressive Grocer,* December 1992.

—Mary Ratcliffe

SIC 2013

SAUSAGES AND OTHER PREPARED MEAT PRODUCTS

Establishments in this category are primarily engaged in manufacturing sausages, cured meats, smoked meats, canned meats, frozen meats and other prepared meats and meat specialties, from purchased carcasses and other materials. Products include bologna, bacon, corned beef, frankfurters (except poultry), headcheese, luncheon meat, pigs' feet, sandwich spreads, stew, pastrami, and hams (except poultry). Prepared meat plants operated by packing houses as separate establishments are also included in this industry.

Establishments primarily engaged in canning or otherwise processing poultry, rabbits, or other small game are classified in **SIC 2015: Poultry Slaughtering and Processing**. Establishments primarily engaged in canning meat for baby food are classified in **SIC 2032: Canned Specialties**. Establishments primarily engaged in the cutting up and resale of purchased fresh carcasses, for the trade, are classified in **SIC 5147: Meats and Meat Products**, a wholesale trade industry.

INDUSTRY SNAPSHOT

The sausage and prepared meat industry is highly competitive, with national and regional brands vying for market share. The three national leaders in the industry are Sara Lee Corp., Hormel Food Corp., and Oscar Mayer Foods Corp., a subsidiary of Philip Morris Companies Inc.

Consumer concerns about fat, cholesterol, and salt intake have spurred big changes to the industry in recent years, as manufacturers have expanded their lines of meat to include "light" and "healthier" foods. Many companies have thus increasingly diversified into the production of prepared meats made from chicken and turkey; newly formulated beef- and pork-based lines of meat have also been introduced.

The prepared meat product industry, as well as other food industries, is also scrambling to meet federal timetables that require new product labels. These labels must conform to new government regulations that call for more complete information on product contents. The government has established definitions for many of the manufacturers' favorite claims—low-fat, low-salt, etc.—and these new regulations require that the product meet those definitions or drop the claim from the label.

In 1992 U.S. companies in this industry shipped products worth an estimated $40 billion; products shipped for all meat products was estimated at almost $90 billion. Imports of sausages and other prepared meats that year amounted to almost $2.9 billion of the total meat imports of just over $3 billion. Prepared meat exports were worth an estimated $4.4 billion, compared to $5.4 billion for all meat products. The red meat industry, which included meat-packing plants and establishments that produced processed pork and beef products, accounted for only 75 percent of the entire meat industry (which included poultry and poultry products) in 1992, compared to 80 percent in 1988. Sales of fish and poultry increased from 19 percent of all consumer meat spending in 1988 to 21 percent in 1992. The consensus among analysts is that this shifting market share is due to increasing consumer demand for healthier foods.

Although per capita consumption of red meat increased in 1992, consumption of pork was responsible for the 2.8 percent increase. Between 1982 and 1992 production of poultry and poultry products increased 70 percent.

Meats in the prepared meat product category are marketed to supermarkets and wholesale clubs, the pizza industry (for toppings), food services, and in-store delicatessens. Companies in this category also manufacture private label meats for restaurants and stores.

Costs and price in this industry are greatly affected by the hog commodities market. Some companies not only operate their own packing houses, they also raise hogs in order to avoid the price swings that often occur in the commodities market. When hog supplies increase, manufacturers' profit margins generally expand because only a small part of that savings is passed on to the consumer. When hog supplies decrease, forcing prices up, the manufacturers' profit margin narrows.

ORGANIZATION AND STRUCTURE

Many of the companies in this industry started out as meat-packing companies and sold nonbranded meat to stores, food services, and meat product manufacturers. They diversified, however, as it became clear that the food processing business was more profitable and less susceptible to swings in commodity prices and the cyclical nature of the fresh pork business. A company that processed pork earned 10 times as much on every dollar of sales as a company that derived most of its income from slaughtering.

Many of the establishments that produce prepared meat products also own and run packing houses that supply them with meat. Hormel, once a large meatpacking concern, severely limited its packing operations and concentrated most of its resources on processing hot dogs, cold cuts, sausages and other prepared meats. In some cases, meat manufacturing establishments have leased packing services or have exclusive contracts from meatpackers to supply only that manufacturer. Hormel leased one of its slaughter plants to a pork processing company to operate, but Hormel provided the hogs and purchased all of the plant's primal cut and processed product output.

Establishments that pack or process red meat have suffered to varying degrees as a result of the relatively recent consumer turn to poultry products. Between 1982 and 1987, the total number of companies in the red meat business fell 10 percent, leaving 2,562 companies, according to the *1987 Census of Manufacturers*. Between 1982 and 1992, the number of red meat processors also producing poultry products nearly tripled, from 11 companies to 32.

In addition, companies closed inefficient plants and introduced innovative new products. Red meat companies expanded into other product areas, especially poultry, through acquisitions or mergers. Meat packers diversified, shifting attention from meat packing to processing of low-fat cold cuts and other meat products. In 1980, half of all beef shipped in this country was shipped as non-carcass beef; in 1992, almost seven-eighths was non-carcass, or processed, beef.

Meat processors often work closely with vendors from other industries to develop innovative new packaging ideas, mindful of the importance of packaging from a marketing and a practical point of view. Because meat is a highly perishable item, packaging must ensure that the food inside will not spoil and that it will retain its flavor for long periods of time. The packaging must also be convenient and attractive to the consumer.

In addition to the large national brands, many regional brands of hams, sausage and other prepared meats were also available, many of them produced by family companies. A proliferation of processed meat products has put shelf and cooler space at a premium, forcing producers to create niches in the major markets and design more convenient and tasty products. The prepared meat industry's practice of creating products and then creating demand for those products which had never existed before was part of a larger food industry trend called differentiation. With differentiation, similar foods are altered enough to appear different either in preparation, flavor, or packaging, then marketed as a new product.

Prepared meat businesses owe much of their growth to the creation of new products such as premium, economy, flavored, low-salt, low-fat, high-protein, or more convenient versions of a basic meat product. The industry devised such creations as microwave bacon and sausages, shelf-stable stews and dinners, low-fat deli meats, frozen microwavable hamburgers, or cheese-filled hot dogs.

CURRENT CONDITIONS

Americans' quest for healthier eating habits has prompted many changes by leading manufacturers in the prepared meat industry. American consumption of beef has steadily decreased as cholesterol and fat content became important numbers on food labels. Meat processing companies introduced many new products that were "light" or "low-fat" versions of popular products. Chicken or turkey cold cuts and hot dogs also stole market share from beef and pork products.

It is likely, then, that processors will continue to diversify their product offerings. According to some estimates, by 1997 at least 70 percent of the top 25 poultry and meat producers will market both poultry and red meat products, compared to only 40 percent in 1992. Companies are also looking to fish and seafood products to further bolster their sales.

Sales of bacon have declined from a peak of $1 billion to about $800 million, in all probability because of bacon's fat and cholesterol content; sales of bacon in restaurants remained steady, however, suggesting that consumers allow themselves some leeway in their quest for a healthier diet.

In any event, the increased emphasis on healthy nutrition has revolutionized the prepared meat product industry. Philip Morris' Oscar Mayer Foods Corp. cut nearly 300 slow-selling products, dropped prices on bacon, hot dogs, and bologna and added light bologna and turkey bacon as part of an ambitious low-fat lunch meat line. In 1992 ConAgra's Armour Swift-Eckrich Inc. subsidiary introduced a full line of Healthy Choice lunch meats and hot dogs to go up against Oscar Mayer's Healthy Favorites and a Weight Watchers lunch meat line produced by Hillshire Farms, owned by Sara Lee Corp.

Oscar Mayer led the cold cuts or lunch meat market with a 33 percent share in 1991-92. While prepared luncheon meat products were the cornerstone of the company's stature, Oscar Mayer's Lunchables, a packaged meal of cheese, cold cuts, and crackers, was also a part of this success. This lunchtime fare was introduced in 1989, and by 1992 had reached sales of more than $130 million a year, with about 40 percent consumed by kids and the rest evenly split between men and women.

ConAgra, though, had high hopes for its Healthy Choice line, which included both beef, pork and poultry-based meats. It was being sold in pre-packaged form as well as at supermarket deli counters; the company also had plans to market it to food services. Company officials from Armour Swift-Eckrich predicted that its new line of 97-percent fat-free lunch meats would expand the existing market by turning light users of lunch meats into medium and heavy users, possibly reversing a trend away from sandwiches for lunch that hit the industry and sent processors looking for convenient substitutes to entice ''brown baggers.''

Lunch preferences. According to the *Wall Street Journal*, the number of people who brought their lunch to work every day had risen throughout the 1980s. That number rose to 11 percent of all Americans in 1992, a very lucrative market. While the nation's work force was bringing its lunch to work in record numbers, demand for sandwiches and sandwich meats was falling. The same *Journal* article, based on information from a consumer research firm, said that the average American carried 42 meals from home in 1984; 71 percent of those lunches included a sandwich. In 1991-92, the average working American brought 53 meals from home, but only 58 percent included a sandwich. During that same year, cold cut sales fell almost two percent to $2.4 billion. Sales of low-fat sandwich meats, however, rose 14 percent.

Package labeling. Nutrition labeling laws designed to enforce the 1990 Nutrition Labeling and Education Act were finally announced in 1992. The regulations required food processors to provide consumers with additional nutrition information on labels. The rules were due to go into effect in 1994 but some companies voluntarily switched their labels before the deadline.

The new labels require the manufacturer to list the total fat content, amount of saturated fat, number of calories derived from fat, and cholesterol, sodium, carbohydrates and protein content. According to the regulations, meat processors may use the term ''light in sodium'' if the meat product's sodium levels have been reduced 50 percent. In addition, the rules defined terms such as ''lite or light,'' ''low fat,'' ''fat-free,'' ''reduced calories,'' ''low in saturated fat,'' ''high fiber'' and other terms that manufacturers have been using to tout the ''healthiness'' of products. In order to use any of those terms on the label, food must meet the requirements of the definition. For example, a ''low-fat'' product must have only three grams of fat or less in a serving. The government also established standard serving sizes for many foods, so that food manufacturers could no longer shrink serving sizes so that they could claim products were low-calorie or low-sodium.

The new regulations are designed to eliminate much of the hype routinely utilized by food manufacturers. Companies that bring in less than $500,000 in annual sales were exempt from the laws. However, it was expected that the entire food industry, including prepared meat businesses, would spend about $2.8 billion on new labels and other related expenses.

Environmental concerns. Many highly processed or packaged meat products were providing convenience to consumers, but at a price to the environment. Disposable microwavable packages, such as microwave bacon, free up consumers from dirty dishes, but create more waste for overflowing landfills. Because of increasing public concern about the problem of garbage disposal, products packaged in disposable containers face growing criticism. Laws that call for recyclable packaging could have an impact on some processed meat products. Environmentalists and relief workers also continue to voice their criticism of the meat industry and its use of immense amounts of grain crops, water, energy, grazing areas, and other natural resources in the development of its product.

INDUSTRY LEADERS

Although most of the familiar processed meat brands are now owned by large conglomerates, many started out as small, regional, independent meatpacking and meat processing companies.

Sara Lee Corporation (known as Consolidated Foods until 1985) is one of the largest meat processing establishments in the United States. Sara Lee holds the number one position in sales of three of the major categories of packaged and processed meats. The company's Hillshire Farm smoked sausage product commanded a 38-percent share of the $1-billion retail market. It's Jimmy Dean breakfast sausage and Ball Park hot dog offerings each owned a 22-percent share of their respective billion-dollar markets. Sara Lee also boasts a number of very strong regional brands, such as Bryan, Kahn, and others.

With the acquisition of Kraft General Foods in 1988, Philip Morris brought the Oscar Mayer and Louis Rich meat products into its stable of goods. Oscar Mayer's genealogy dates back more than 100 years to a meat shop owned and run by three brothers, Oscar, Gottfried, and Max Mayer. In 1991 the Oscar

Mayer division of Philip Morris brought in revenues of $2.3 billion.

Conglomerate agribusiness ConAgra had total annual sales of more than $14.5 billion in 1992, with its Armour Swift-Eckrich meat packing plants and prepared meat operations bringing in $1.13 billion in 1991. ConAgra acquired Armour from Greyhound in 1983 and Swift-Eckrich from the Beatrice Co. in 1990. Armour and Swift-Eckrich became a single subsidiary of ConAgra, selling Sizzlean, Swift Premium Brown 'N Serve Sausage and Eckrich sausages and other Armour and Swift products. Before the acquisition, Swift had been the third-largest manufacturer of processed meat after Oscar Mayer and Sara Lee. ConAgra also owns meatpacking companies Swift Independent Packing and Monfort.

George A. Hormel & Company was founded in Austin, Minnesota in 1891 as a slaughterhouse and retail meat products shop. Its earnings for the first year were $220,000. About 100 years later, the company name was changed to Hormel Food Corporation, reflecting its change in focus from a packing and meat company to a food processing company with lines of meat products, frozen foods, and microwave products, as well as branded fresh pork and beef. Hormel was one of the few older meat companies that remained independent after a wave of takeovers in the 1980s. It had sales of $2.8 billion in 1991 and profits of $86 million.

Hormel became known as the industry's innovator in the late 1980s. Hormel was one of the largest meatpackers in the country, but its president, Richard Knowlton, closed many of its slaughtering facilities in the 1980s and began focusing on producing processed and branded meat products. Since the early 1980s, Hormel's hog slaughter capacity has been cut 75 percent. The portion of its revenues generated by prepared meat and other food products rose to between 65 and 75 percent.

In the first half of the decade, Hormel introduced two or three new products annually. In one 18-month period during the second half of the decade, however, it introduced 134 new products, including chicken, turkey, and fish products. The company achieved an industry breakthrough in 1987 with the debut of Top Shelf, a line of microwavable dinner entrees that stayed fresh unrefrigerated for 18 months. The company started development of the shelf-stable products three years earlier with a large investment in the equipment it needed to do the necessary research.

In 1992 Hormel's Cure 81 ham was the number one ham in the ''no-water-added'' category and ac-counted for 40 percent of the sales in the total retail ham market. Because there was little product differentiation in this market, consumers shopped largely on the basis of packaging and price.

Hormel's Black Label bacon is also a strong product, ranking second to Oscar Mayer in the retail bacon market. Hormel's market share in this area, however, was only about six or seven percent because the market was very fragmented, with numerous national and regional brands vying for consumer dollars.

Like Hormel, Smithfield Foods was an independent company—but on a smaller scale. It initially produced only pork products, and it spent but a fraction of the more than $70 million on advertising that Hormel spent. In 1992 the company had sales of more than $1 billion.

The name recognition of Smithfield canned hams enabled it to diversify into production of hot dogs, bacon, sausages and lunch meats from its main pork-packing operations. About half of its sales in 1988 were in nonbranded items—spareribs, pork chops or hot dogs packaged for other companies' for private labels.

Thorn Apple Valley, Inc., is one of the largest producers of customer-owned private label meat products and one of the largest regional producers of bacon, hot dogs, luncheon meats and smoked sausages. Its private label meats account for approximately 60 percent of its processed meat sales. It traditionally aimed its other products at the economy shopper; however, the company has begun to stress premium brands including its own brand and strong regional brands. In response to the healthy-eating trend, Thorn Apple also increased its sales of poultry-based products.

Other key prepared meat product industry forces include Chiquita Brands International Inc.'s subsidiary John Morrell and Co. Morrell earned $1.8 billion in revenue in 1991.

WORK FORCE

The meat industry has had its share of labor disputes in recent decades. Companies in the meatpacking and meat processing businesses have often been the targets of labor strikes, in part because of aggressive moves by industry leaders to contain labor costs.

One of the more notorious strikes of recent times involved Hormel. In 1985 base wages at a Hormel slaughter and processing plant were cut to $8.25 an hour, a 23 percent decrease. The company's 1,400 workers, represented by the United Food and Commercial Workers Union, walked out. The strike continued for 13 months, and tensions ran so high that the

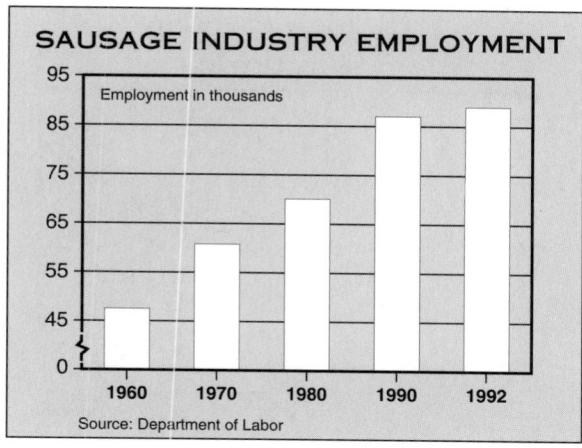

SAUSAGE INDUSTRY EMPLOYMENT

Employment in thousands

Source: Department of Labor

National Guard was called in to maintain order. The company continued to operate, earning record high profits despite the strike. The strike finally ended when the Hormel union was ejected from the international organization for refusing to settle. The workers finally agreed to a settlement negotiated by the international in which workers received a raise in the base wage to $10.70 an hour over the next three years. In the meantime, however, many strikers had been replaced.

Labor relations at Hormel apparently improved somewhat in the 1990s. An agreement with the United Food and Commercial Workers Union called for hourly wage rate hikes of 15 cents per hour the first two years and 25 cents the third year. The hourly base was $11.15, one of the highest in the industry. Sick leave, health insurance, and monthly pension benefits were improved also. However, Hormel had managed to reduce labor expenses by leasing out the more labor-intensive meatpacking operations at a lower rate and maintaining the processing operations that required fewer workers and generated higher profit margins. Machines were doing much of the work of ham preparation, for example, pouring pureed pork shoulder and ham mixture into cans, cooking those cans, and shipping about one million of them out weekly. According to *Financial World*, the company's labor costs dropped from 19 percent of sales in 1981 to almost 11 percent of sales in 1989.

When ConAgra made plans to acquire Armour in 1983, it made certain that 13 unionized plants were closed. When Conagra reopened the plants, they were staffed by nonunion labor.

John Morrell and Co. also had its share of controversy over its treatment and payment of workers. The company was fined a record $4.3 million by the Occupational Safety and Health Administration (OSHA) in 1988 for the high injury rate at one of its meatpacking plants. Morrell appealed the fine and finally settled in 1990. The agreement required Morrell to pay a fine of $990,000 and to establish a program to reduce repetitive motion injuries and other injuries. Morrell also cut base wages of $9.75 by $1.75 an hour at the same plant in 1989. The $9.75 rate was already $2 lower than the rate paid in 1982. Company officials said the lower pay scale was consistent with wages at other plants in the industry and reflected the fierce competition with non-union companies and the changing eating habits of consumers.

AMERICA AND THE WORLD

For many foreign companies, the new label laws were difficult to comply with because they were not accustomed to providing such complete analysis of content. Although the labels could be considered a barrier to trade and, as such, incompatible with the General Agreement on Tariffs and Trade (GATT), it was unlikely that any challenge would hold up, since both foreign and domestic companies had to observe the same regulations.

Imports from Canada of prepared meat products increased in 1992, but imports from Eastern Europe and the European Community (EC) declined. About 86 percent of imports came from Australia, Canada, New Zealand, Denmark and Argentina. On the other side of the ledger, exports of red meat products increased by 4.5 percent to more than $4.4 billion in 1992.

In 1993 Oscar Mayer prepared to compete in the Mexican market by signing an agreement insuring that Sigma Alimentos, Mexico's largest processed meat company, would be Oscar Mayer's sole distributor in Mexico. Like Oscar Mayer, Sigma Alimentos was a subsidiary of one of its country's largest corporations. Its share of the processed meat market in Mexico was 32 percent, reflecting a standing in the Mexican marketplace similar to that enjoyed by Oscar Mayer in the American market. Sigma Alimentos agreed to distribute Oscar Mayer meats, as well as Louis Rich turkey products and Claussen pickles. This was the first national distribution of Oscar Mayer products in Mexico. The company also exports products to the Caribbean, Asia, and the Middle East.

INDUSTRY INFORMATION SOURCES

Berss, Marcia, "This Isn't Ross Perot and GM," *Forbes* (June 8, 1992): 103-4.

Coletti, Richard, "Living Higher on the Hog," *Financial World* (November 27, 1990): 29.

Deveny, Kathleen, "Firms See a Fat Opportunity in Catering to Americans' Quest for 'Easy' Lunches, *Wall Street Journal* (November 3, 1992): B1.

Erickson, Julie Liesse, "Meatpacker's Makeover," *Advertising Age* (November 21, 1988): 53.

Gutfield, Rose, "Food Label 'Babel' to Fall as Uniform System Is Cleared," *Wall Street Journal* (December 3, 1992): B1.

Ingersoll, Bruce, "Food Concerns, Public in Limbo over Labeling," *Wall Street Journal* (November 9, 1992): B1.

Koselka, Rita, "$ Oink $ Oink," *Forbes* (February 3, 1992): 54-56.

Reier, Sharon, "High on the Hog," *Financial World* (June 28, 1988): 29-31.

Skislock, K.B., *George A. Hormel & Company: Company Report*, Dain, Bosworth, Inc., 1992.

Spencer, R., *Sara Lee Corporation: Company Report*, Painewebber Inc., 1992.

Strauss, R., *Thorn Apple Valley, Inc.: Company Report*, William Blair & Company, 1992.

1992 U.S. Industrial Outlook, Lanham, MD: U.S. Department of Commerce.

—Wendy J. Stein

SIC 2015

POULTRY SLAUGHTERING AND PROCESSING

Establishments primarily engaged in slaughtering, dressing, packing, freezing, and canning poultry, rabbits, and other small game, or in manufacturing products from such meats, for their own account or on a contract basis for the trade. This industry also includes the drying, freezing, and breaking of eggs.

INDUSTRY SNAPSHOT

Beginning in the 1930s, the U.S. poultry business evolved into a vertically integrated industry in which a few top companies accounted for most of the country's broiler (chicken) and turkey production. Vertical integration combined the previously independent and fragmented operations of the feedmills, hatcheries, farms, slaughterers, and processors into giant conglomerates that managed all stages of production. In 1990, for example, 20 companies accounted for 79 percent of broiler production, and the top four of these claimed 41 percent of the market. In the turkey sector, the top 20 companies accounted for 89 percent of production, while 29 percent came from the top four firms.

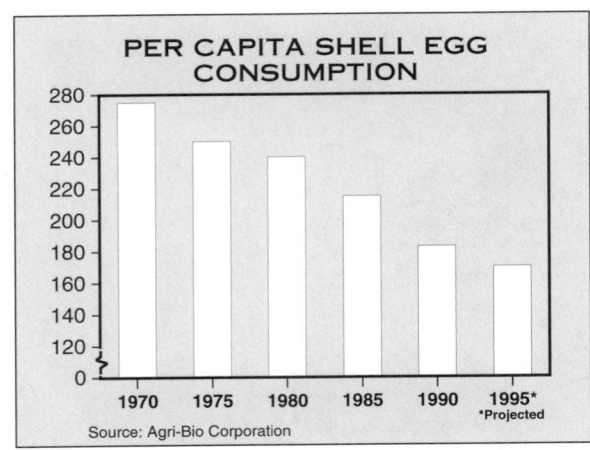

PER CAPITA SHELL EGG CONSUMPTION

Source: Agri-Bio Corporation

Broilers represented by far the largest component of the industry, with the value of production exceeding $10 billion in 1990, compared to $3 billion for turkey. Other poultry, such as ducks and geese, accounted for only about $300 million in industry sales. Broiler production was concentrated in seventeen southeastern states on the eastern seaboard and Gulf of Mexico. This so-called "broiler belt" was the source of 90 percent of production. No such regional concentration existed in the turkey sector. The top four turkey producing states were North Carolina, Minnesota, California, and Arkansas.

ORGANIZATION AND STRUCTURE

According to the U.S. Department of Agriculture (USDA), there were 508 federally inspected poultry slaughtering and processing plants in 1990, and 3,180 plants that slaughtered and/or processed both meat and poultry. Poultry processing firms totaled about 100 that year, with 54 of them being integrated broiler processors. The remainder encompassed 32 turkey processors and 14 processors of ducks, geese, and guineas.

Most broilers (99 percent) in the 1990s were produced under contractual arrangements in which the broiler company provided a grower with day-old chicks, and the grower then raised the birds in the carefully controlled environment of the grow-out house. Protected from disease and predators in an enclosed system, the birds would be fed mostly a diet of vitamin- and mineral-fortified corn and soybean meal during the six-and-a-half week period it took to bring them to market weight of about 4 pounds. Prior to being sent to the processing plant, the birds might be tested for traces of pesticides, toxins, or antibiotics in the ongoing USDA residue monitoring program.

The five primary product categories handled within the poultry processing industry were: chicken, turkeys, ducks, geese, and egg products. Available chicken types included young broilers/fryers weighing an average of 3 pounds; specially grown, 6-to-8 pound young roasters; capons, surgically de-sexed male birds weighing over 9 pounds; heavy hens (often called stewing hens), over a year old and weighing 4 to 6 pounds; and Rock Cornish or Cornish game hens, young chickens weighing about 1 to 2 pounds. About 18 percent of ready-to-cook chickens were sold as whole birds; the rest were sold as broiler parts, or as boneless chicken breasts or thighs.

Annual per capita consumption of turkey stabilized in the first half of the 1990s at about 18.1 pounds. The methods used in breeding, raising, slaughtering, and processing turkeys were almost identical with those used for chicken. Turkey hens reached maturity at about 16 weeks, with a market weight of from 16 to 18 pounds. Toms took 19 weeks to reach market weight of 28 to 30 pounds. Most turkeys were sold whole, either fresh or frozen.

The White Pekin was the most popular duck breed for mass production in the 1990s. Annual production was about 21 million ducks, which were generally packaged and sold whole and frozen. Duck feathers and down used by bedding manufacturers were valuable by-products. The total population of geese in the United States rarely exceeded 5 million; most were raised in Minnesota and Iowa.

Value-added egg products—including liquid, frozen, and dried—fell into two categories, commodities and branded products (such as Egg Beaters, Healthy Choice, and Simply Eggs). From 1980 to 1992, sales of value-added egg products rose from 24.1 to 41.4 million cases. Food manufacturers accounted for 24.6 million cases; 11.4 went for institutional use; 2.4 were sold at the retail level; and 3.0 million cases were exported.

BACKGROUND AND DEVELOPMENT

History. Poultry processing was one of the nation's first agribusinesses, characterized by many small farms. In the early days, raising meat-poultry was secondary to egg production. One of the first stages in the mechanization of poultry processing was the accelerated development in the 1920s of incubators that could hold thousands of eggs. Farmers could start with 500 chicks and no longer depended on hens to hatch them.

Prior to World War II, home cooks were likely to buy their chickens live. After the war, more and more

consumers purchased either "New York dressed" chickens—with only the blood and feathers removed—or in some areas, "dressed and drawn" birds—with head, feet, and intestines removed. The change had far-reaching effects, transferring the preparation of poultry to the processing plant, which consumers trusted to be as clean as their own kitchens.

Starting in the 1940s, the poultry industry went through three major changes: an increasing rate of vertical integration, which was largely completed by the mid-1950s; the phasing out of small operations and the concentration of production among a few large firms; and the movement of processing operations to the southeastern states to be closer to the broiler supply.

Regulations. Since mandatory Federal inspection began in 1957, all commercially produced chickens were inspected by USDA for wholesomeness before going to market. Traditionally, inspection took place in the processing plant, conducted by a USDA inspector who relied on sight, touch, and smell to determine the wholesomeness of each bird as it passed by on a swiftly moving conveyer line. In 1978, USDA introduced a faster, modified system in which three inspectors divided the task. One inspected the bird's exterior, another its viscera, and a third made a final inspection of the bird. A more scientific system, Hazard Analysis and Critical Control Points (HACCP), was proposed in the early 1990s. Under this program, inspectors would identify hazards, determine the points at which they could be controlled, and recommend corrective action.

In terms of processing, USDA regulations required that washed and eviscerated chickens be submerged in a water-filled chill tank that quickly reduced the birds' body temperatures to 40 degrees or less to prevent multiplication of salmonella and other microorganisms commonly found on chicken skin. The regulations further required that the water in continuous chill systems be replaced at a rate of one-half gallon per chicken as birds were added to the system.

Food safety continued to be an issue for poultry processors in the 1990s. Following an outbreak of foodborne illnesses, USDA proposed a new labeling policy under which safe-handling instructions would explain the need to refrigerate poultry until it was cooked, cook it thoroughly, refrigerate or discard leftovers immediately, and keep work areas clean. In issuing the new labeling recommendations, USDA cited surveys of 1985 and 1990 that revealed consumer ignorance of such basic food safety procedures. The government also cited data from the Centers for Disease Control (CDC) in Atlanta, Georgia, which showed that a third of at-home food poisoning inci-

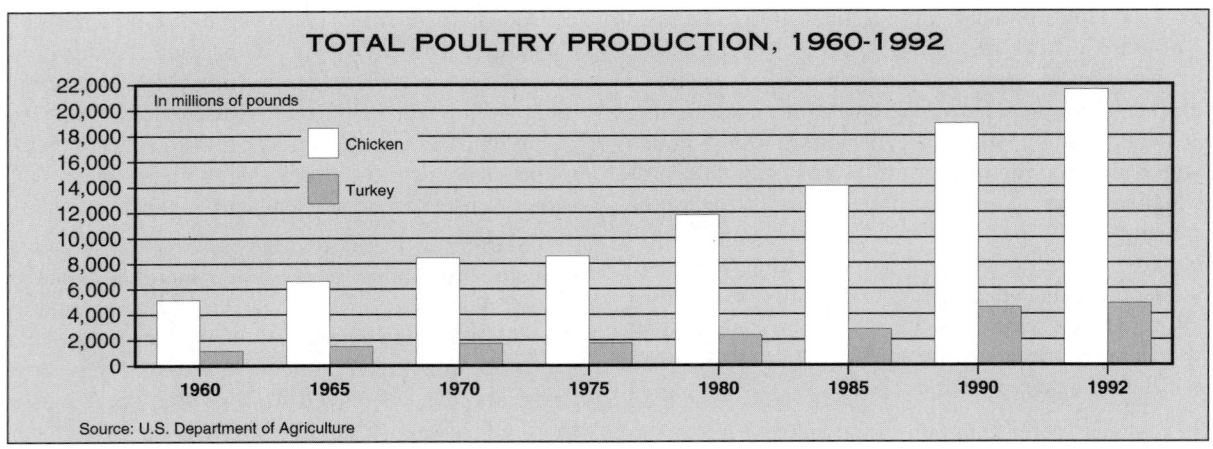

TOTAL POULTRY PRODUCTION, 1960-1992

Source: U.S. Department of Agriculture

dents were caused by undercooking, and another 12 percent resulted from holding pre-cooked food at unsafe temperatures. Safe-handling instructions were publicized by the leading industry associations, the National Broiler Council and the National Turkey Federation.

In 1992, USDA ruled that fresh or frozen uncooked whole carcasses or parts could be treated by irradiation. In 1993 irradiated, packaged poultry became commercially available, albeit in only four independently owned retail stores. Irradiation eliminated up to 99.9 percent of salmonella and 100 percent of campylobacter organisms, and probably any listeria bacteria as well. Given public concern over foodborne illnesses, the technology showed promise, but whether it would gain widespread consumer acceptance remained to be seen. The treatment was still controversial and even banned in some regions.

Another means of dealing with salmonella incidence levels in poultry was the use of trisodium phosphate (TSP) technology developed by Rhone-Poulenc Food Ingredients Inc. Immersion of birds for just seconds in a TSP solution near the end of production significantly reduced (but did not eliminate) salmonella and other pathogens such as e. coli and campylobacter. TSP application had no effect on further processing or packaging.

CURRENT CONDITIONS

A 1993 survey of the country's largest broiler companies, whose output of ready-to-cook product totaled 99 percent of U.S. production, showed a 6 percent production increase, slightly higher than in 1992 (5.3 percent) and 1991 (5.8 percent). Average weekly production for all companies was 475.81 million pounds.

From 1975 through 1992, Americans' annual per capita consumption (PCC) of chicken and turkey increased 81 percent to 86.5 pounds per person. In the same period, red meat PCC, which included beef, pork, veal, and lamb, dropped 14 percent to 122 pounds. In 1992, chicken consumption for the first time surpassed that of beef, Americans' former top meat choice. In addition, the top 50 companies in the combined meat and poultry industry included 19 poultry companies in 1992, up from just seven in 1982, and sales for the top meat packers increased only 2.3 percent for the period 1990-1991 compared to a 7 percent increase for the top ten poultry firms.

Forecasting the continuation of 4 percent annual growth in the industry, the nation's largest poultry processor, Tyson Foods, announced plans for a major expansion of its poultry production and processing capability with the addition of four new operating complexes. Each would include a feedmill, hatchery, and processing plant. Chairman Don Tyson also cited passage of the North American Free Trade Agreement

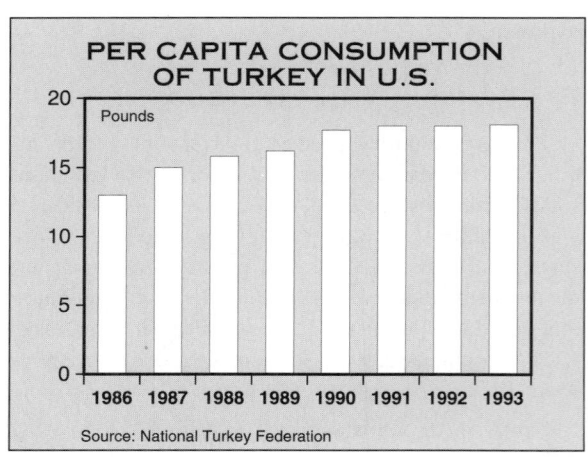

PER CAPITA CONSUMPTION OF TURKEY IN U.S.

Source: National Turkey Federation

and likely approval of the General Agreement on Tariffs and Trade as increasing demand for poultry.

Donald E. Wray, chief operating officer of Tyson Foods, Inc., predicted in *Consumer News* that demand for unadulterated (no filler) chicken products of high quality would increase, and that further-processed chicken would be even more important as sales of whole birds and cut-up parts continued to decline. Protein, including chicken, Wray claimed, "will be used more as an ingredient in foods, rather than as a center-of-the-plate feature." Product innovation would be the key to continued growth, especially the development of ethnic and regional foods offering new flavor combinations. By 2001, one-third of the U.S. population would be immigrants, and two-thirds would be in the 45-65 age bracket. These changing demographics would impact on the consumer-driven poultry industry.

INDUSTRY LEADERS

The nation's largest broiler company in the early 1990s was Arkansas-based Tyson Foods, Inc. Sales in fiscal 1993 reached $4.8 billion, up from $4.2 billion in fiscal 1992. Weekly production of ready-to-eat broiler meat reached 84.15 million pounds in 1993, making Tyson not only America's largest poultry producer but the third-largest in the world, after Brazil and China. Only 8 percent of Tyson's consumer poultry product sales were basic poultry; value-added products accounted for 73 percent. The company's 1989 purchase of Holly Farms resulted in an increase of 31.9 million ready-to-cook poultry pounds per week.

In 1993, Tyson operated 45 processing and further-processing plants and one fowl slaughter plant. Only sixteen of its plants were non-slaughter further-processing operations. The company derived only 19 percent of sales from its non-poultry operations, which included beef, pork, prepared foods, live swine operations, and other activities. The purchase in 1992 of the North Atlantic's largest catching and at-sea processing fleet, Arctic Alaska Fisheries Corporation, moved Tyson into yet another protein sector. Europe and Japan were the company's biggest foreign markets in the early 1990s, but John Tyson foresaw further growth potential in Southeast Asia.

Another Arkansas-based company, ConAgra, ranked second in broiler production in 1993, with weekly production of 40.53 million ready-to-cook pounds, based on slaughtering 11.25 million broilers a week weighing an average of 4.75 pounds. From 1988 to 1993, broiler production at ConAgra grew by 29 percent. The company's principal broiler operation was the ConAgra Broiler Company, with 14 process-

ing plants and fiscal 1993 sales of more than $1.5 billion. Products included Country Pride Roasted Chicken and a line of 20 premium boneless and bone-in Butterball products. The ConAgra Frozen Foods Co. added 5.7 million pounds per week in six processing plants.

Georgia-based Gold Kist, Inc. was the third-ranked poultry processor with 39.7 million ready-to-cook pounds of chicken in 1993, up 52 percent from 1988. Sales in 1992 reached $1.2 billion. The cooperative operated 11 processing plants in Georgia, Alabama, Florida, and the Carolinas. Other leading broiler companies in the United States included Perdue Farms, Inc., with average weekly ready-to-cook production of 28 million pounds; Pilgrim's Pride Corp. (24.5 million pounds); Wayne Poultry (16.4 million pounds); and Hudson Foods, Inc. (15.7 million pounds).

The largest turkey producers in 1993 were Butterball Turkey Corp., with 4 plants producing 700 million pounds of product; Jennie-O Foods Inc., with 5 plants producing 494 million pounds; and Rocco Turkeys, Inc., which operated 3 plants and produced 482 million pounds.

WORK FORCE

Between 1963 and 1985, the average annual rate of increase in employee output per hour at poultry processing plants was 2.9 percent, slightly greater than industry as a whole. Productivity gains were higher in the 1970s, when automated eviscerating and cutting machines were widely introduced. In the first half of the 1980s, productivity rose again to meet growing consumer demand for value-added poultry products and the requirements of an expanding number of fast food outlets.

Low wages were characteristic of the poultry industry; despite increases of 17 percent from 1986 to 1990, pay was usually lower than in any other sector of the food industry. While the industry employed a high proportion of low-wage production workers, it also required highly skilled personnel in research and development, and to manage and maintain the increasingly efficient and technologically advanced processing operations.

AMERICA AND THE WORLD

In 1990, the United States controlled about 30 percent of the world's poultry production. The country ranked as the world's largest producer and consumer of poultry products, as well as its second-leading exporter. Poultry exports in 1992 increased an estimated

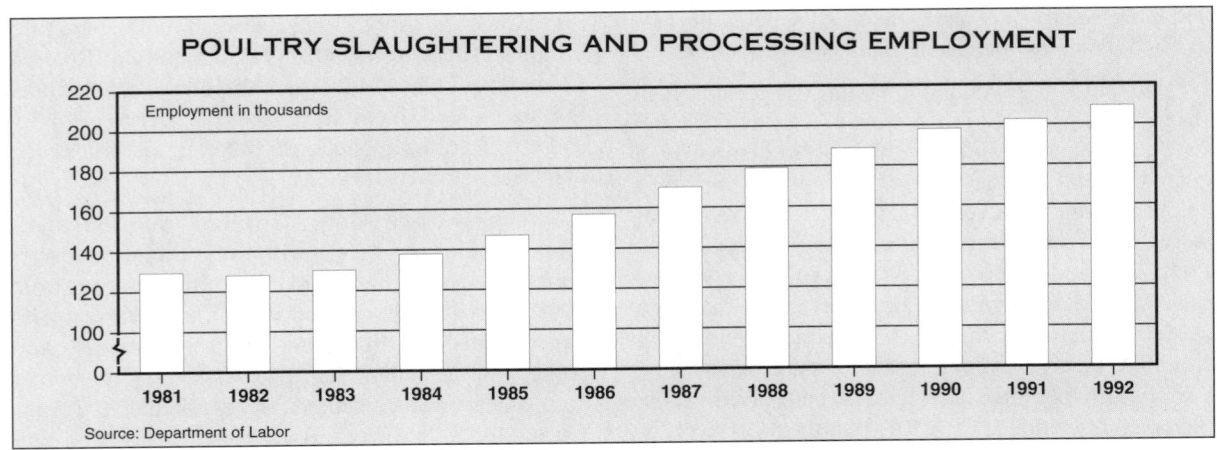

POULTRY SLAUGHTERING AND PROCESSING EMPLOYMENT

Employment in thousands

Source: Department of Labor

12 percent to $983 million. About 69 percent of U.S. exports went to four markets: Japan (23 percent), Mexico (17 percent), Canada (15 percent), and Hong Kong (14 percent). Chicken parts accounted for most poultry exports, but turkey exports rose 15 percent in 1992. Mexico and South Korea were the major markets for turkey products. U.S. poultry production supplied virtually all domestic consumption. Imports declined an estimated 8 percent in 1992; nearly half came from Canada and New Zealand.

RESEARCH AND TECHNOLOGY

New processing and packaging technologies facilitated the poultry industry's rapid growth in the last half of the twentieth century. Over the years, numerous automated processes took the place of manual labor at various stages of production. For example, mechanized killing machines capable of killing five birds per second—five times more than a skilled worker could accomplish with a sharp knife—were introduced in the 1960s. Defeathering operations were also automated.

Mechanical eviscerating machines came into use in the 1970s. At about the same time, mechanized cutting of the birds into parts was increasingly performed in processing plants rather than by meatcutters in retail outlets. The late 1970s also saw the introduction of automatic deboning machines capable of processing up to 800 pieces of chicken a minute and separating edible meat from bonier parts. The machines also collected meat scraps from partially defleshed carcasses; the scraps were used in the further processing of patties, soups, luncheon meats, and other products.

By the 1990s, as consumers began to expect the ready-to-cook convenience of portioned chicken, ultra-thin, high-pressure waterjet cutting and shaping delivered it. Video cameras sensed the changing pattern from a light projected on a partially prepared carcass. A computer received the information, calculated the best cutting patterns, and sent directions to waterjet nozzles, which then made precise cuts, trimming and portioning the chicken at the same time. Another machine used pistons to force chopped chicken through molds that created three-dimensional formed products. The possibilities included geometric shapes, concave patties, and pieces that looked like boneless breasts.

Since sanitation was always a concern, the poultry processing industry continued research into chemical cleansers and new dispensing techniques in the 1990s. For example, some firms experimented with low-cost robots that could transfer a variety of poultry products from conveyer belts to other processing areas.

INDUSTRY INFORMATION SOURCES

Ahmed, Ziaul Z., and Mark Sieling, "Two Decades of Productivity Growth in Poultry Dressing and Processing," *Monthly Labor Review,* April 1987.

Aho, Paul, "Poultry . . . More than a Meal," Gainesville, Georgia: Agri-Bio Corporation, 1992.

Berne, Steve, "Poultry Takes the Lead," *Prepared Foods,* January 1994.

Broiler Industry Reference Guide, Washington, DC: National Broiler Council, 1990.

Brown Robert H., "Tyson to Expand Poultry Output, Processing," *Feedstuffs,* January 10, 1994.

Frazier, Frank, "Poultry Inspection History Shows New Tactics Tried Before," *Feedstuffs,* February 14, 1994.

Industry and Trade Summary: Poultry, Washington, DC: U.S. International Trade Commission, June 1992.

Looper, Ken, "The Potential for Value-Added Egg Products," *Poultry Yearbook,* 1993.

Meyer, Ann, "The Leading 50: A Company/Family Man," *Prepared Foods,* July 1992.

"Raising Turkeys," Reston, Virginia: National Turkey Federation, 1993.

"Turkey Statistics 1993," Reston, Virginia: National Turkey Federation, 1993.

Pszczola, Donald, "Irradiated Poultry Makes U.S. Debut in Midwest and Florida Markets," *Food Technology,* November 1993.

"Salmonella Treatment Minimizes Liabilities," *Prepared Foods,* February 1993.

Smith, Rod, "Tyson Says Difficult Year 'Underscores' Its Strengths," *Feedstuffs,* January 3, 1994.

Thornton, Gary, "Nation's Broiler Industry," *Broiler Industry,* December 1993.

————, "Profiles of the Nation's Top 10 Broiler Companies," *Broiler Industry,* December 1993.

U.S. Industrial Outlook, Washington, D.C.: U.S. Department of Commerce, 1993.

Wray, Donald E., "Poultry Market Trends," *Consumer News,* Winter 1994.

—Mary Ratcliffe

SIC 2021

CREAMERY BUTTER

This industry consists of establishments primarily engaged in manufacturing creamery butter.

Despite our modern sanitary production methods, the butter we eat today is not much different from that enjoyed centuries ago by people who churned milk in animal skins slung from the backs of camels and horses. Butter manufacturing and marketing, a sector of the dairy industry, is extremely regionalized and competitive and the industry's quality standards and farm pricing are highly regulated by the U.S. government.

Commercial production of butter is a relatively recent development. In 1870 nearly all of the 514 million pounds of U.S. butter was produced on farms. In 1871 the first U.S. butter manufacturing creamery was built in Manchester, Iowa. Just 120 years later, in 1991, commercial production exceeded 1.3 billion pounds. Wisconsin and California were the leading butter producers in 1991, accounting for 654 million pounds of the national production. Approximately 17 percent of the milk produced on dairy farms in 1991 was used to make butter.

Under federal regulations, butter sold in the United States is made exclusively from milk or cream, or both, and must contain at least 80 percent milkfat by weight. Coloring or salt may be added. Butter is labelled by the U.S. Department of Agriculture (USDA) as Grade AA, A, or B according to flavor intensity, texture, color, and salt taste.

In the early 1990s, butter producers sold their butter products through supermarkets, club stores, and other retail outlets. In addition to individual consumers, butter producers served the foodservice industry (restaurants, fast-food operations), institutions (hospitals, schools), and industrial customers. At the retail level, Grade A butter was typically packaged in quarter-pound sticks packed four to a cardboard carton, and whipped butter, developed for easier spreadability, was packaged in tubs. Industrial and foodservice packaging ranged from 68-pound blocks to individually wrapped, single-serve pats. Butteroil, the anhydrous form of butter developed to use up surpluses during a period of lowered public consumption, has been used by the confectionery and baking industries and as a cooking oil.

From 1981 to 1991, annual per capita butter consumption increased only slightly from 3.7 to 3.9 pounds. In 1991, supermarket sales of butter were $917.48 million, of which $234 million was private label (store brand) butter. Total U.S. butter sales were $1.3 billion, or 2.1 percent of the $62.8 billion dairy industry in 1991.

The largest butter producers in the United States were also among the largest of the dairy cooperatives: Land O'Lakes and Mid-American Dairymen, Inc. These co-ops, which had originated to represent farmers in obtaining the best milk prices, had grown to become manufacturers and marketers of butter and other dairy products. With a 32-percent market share, Land O'Lakes, a 72-year old dairy co-operative, led the retail butter industry in the early 1990s. Mid-America Dairymen, Inc. sold its butter products to retailers under its Mid-Am name and to private label customers. Kraft sold butter made by Mid-Am under its Breakstone brand. Associated Milk Producers, Inc., and Darigold, Inc., were other major cooperatives with strong butter manufacturing operations.

INDUSTRY INFORMATION SOURCES

Butter, Springfield, MO: Mid-America Dairymen, Inc.

Butter Facts, California Manufacturing Milk Advisory Board, 1991.

Garrison, Bob, "Dynamic Duo," *Refrigerated & Frozen Foods,* May 1993.

"Market Stats and Data," *Dairy Field,* December 1992.

Milk Facts, Washington, DC: Milk Industry Foundation, 1992.

Reeves, James L., *The First 20 Years: The Story of Mid-America Dairymen,* Republic, MO: Western Printing Company, 1989.

Salvage, Bryan, "Private Label Renaissance," *Dairy Field,* August 1992.

"Rediscover the Values of Butter," Wisconsin Milk Marketing Board, 1993.

—Mary Ratcliffe

SIC 2022

NATURAL, PROCESSED AND IMITATION CHEESE

This industry encompasses establishments primarily engaged in manufacturing natural cheese (except cottage cheese), cheese foods, cheese spreads, and cheese analogues (imitations and substitutes). These establishments also produce byproducts, such as raw liquid whey.

INDUSTRY SNAPSHOT

Cheese is one of the principal product groups in the dairy industry and has become increasingly important to the growth of the entire dairy industry in the United States. Wisconsin has been the leading cheese producer of the 21 major cheese-producing states in the nation. The state accounted for 29 percent, or 2 billion of the 6.9 billion pounds of cheese produced in the United States in 1991. About 92 percent of the cheese Americans consume was made in the United States.

The United States has developed very few cheeses of its own. Processors have instead replicated European cheeses and used their European names, except for Roquefort, which is a protected name. Some of the cheeses created in this country are Monterey Jack, brick, colby, and Herkimer; all of these cheeses are firm, ripened Cheddar-type cheeses.

ORGANIZATION AND STRUCTURE

Kraft, the leading cheese producer, was part of a diversified conglomerate. In 1988, Kraft was purchased by the tobacco producer, Philip Morris Companies Inc., for $12.9 billion. Philip Morris combined Kraft with an 1985 acquisition to form Kraft General Foods, the largest coffee and cheese producer in the United States. Its strongest competition in the cheese area of its operations came from large dairy companies and dairy cooperatives like Land O'Lakes (LOL),

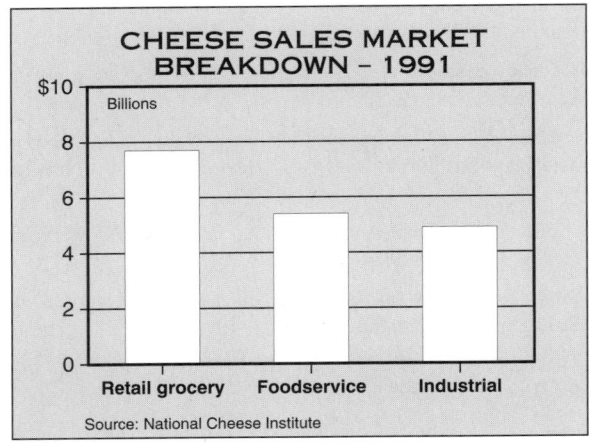

CHEESE SALES MARKET BREAKDOWN – 1991

Source: National Cheese Institute

Sargento, Inc., and Mid-America Dairymen, Inc. (Mid-Am).

As Americans' cheese palate became more adventurous in the early 1990s, there were growing numbers of small, regional cheesemakers sending their specialty products to market. U.S. cheese producers obtain the raw milk from which their products are made from thousands of commercial dairy farms. The number of farms has been dwindling steadily for decades, but they have grown larger in size, and milk production efficiency has been vastly improved. Many of the farmers were members of one of the several hundred regional dairy co-ops. These co-ops, formed to represent milk producers in price setting, were beginning to take over other dairy operations, including the manufacture and marketing of a broad range of cheese products and ingredients. Large food processors either owned their own farms or purchased raw milk from the co-ops and independent farmers. Approximately 30 percent of the 148,526 million pounds of raw milk produced by the country's 10 million dairy cows in 1991 was used to make cheese.

The dairy industry has been heavily regulated by the government. Cheese manufactured in the United States must meet Standards of Identity, which define such product characteristics as content levels of milkfat and manufacturing methods. Either Class I milk or milk of manufacturing grade may be used to make cheese. Class I fluid milk meets stricter standards, which include regular inspections of the herd, herd housing facilities, and dairy equipment and milk storage units to insure that they satisfy health and sanitation requirements. It is used for human consumption as a beverage, or in manufactured products such as cheese. Milk of manufacturing grade meets less stringent standards and may only be used for manufactured products.

The government has regulated milk pricing through the Federal Milk Marketing Orders authorized by the Agricultural Marketing Act of 1937, or the Agricultural Act of 1949, which established the ongoing dairy price support program. The complex pricing system affected all segments of the dairy industry.

Background and Development

Although there is no record of when cheese was first used as a food, its origins have been estimated to date back to 6000-7000 B.C. Its lasting quality made it a source of nourishment both at home and on journeys, and armies often carried cheese among their provisions. The first U.S. cheese plant was built in 1851 in Rome, New York, and the area remained the center of American cheesemaking for the next 50 years. The U.S. cheesemaking industry began shifting westward toward Wisconsin in the early 1900s.

There are hundreds of varieties of cheese worldwide and numerous ways of classifying them, usually according to the coagulating agent (rennet, acid, etc.) or texture (very hard, hard, semisoft, soft, acid). Natural cheeses are made directly from milk (or sometimes whey) by pressing the curd that forms when milk has been coagulated (or curdled), then heated and stirred, and finally by draining off the whey (the remaining liquid part of the milk). Processed cheeses are made from a combination of one or more batches of natural cheeses, heated to pasteurization temperatures. They were developed in the 1920s to extend shelf life, insure product uniformity, and make slicing easier, while simulating natural cheese. The first U.S. patent for processed cheese was issued to J. L. Kraft in 1916; it described a method of emulsifying the heated cheese mixture using alkaline salts.

Cheese analogues are made without butterfat and are designed to resemble natural or processed cheese in appearance, taste, texture and nutrition. The cost savings of using less expensive fats, such as vegetable oils instead of butterfat, provided the incentive to produce cheese analogues. Early examples were produced in the early 1900s by skimming butterfat from whole milk, replacing it with another fat, and then following regular cheesemaking procedures. Technology using dried milk protein, hydrogenated vegetable oil, emulsifiers and other ingredients was developed in the early 1970s to simulate processed American and mozzarella cheeses.

Some of the principal cheese products are: Cheddar, Swiss (hard); Parmesan, Romano (very hard); mozzarella, brick, Havarti, blue (semisoft); Brie, Bel Paese, Camembert (soft); powders and blends; and reduced-fat.

Current Conditions

The economic health of the cheese industry was varied at the start of the 1990s. Both sales and production of cheese hit record highs in 1991 as indicated by the following statistics: $18 billion in sales; 6.1 billion pounds of natural cheese; and 2.2 billion pounds of processed cheese. Overall industry growth, however, was flat, and in 1992, supermarket sales of $5.36 billion had dipped 3.06 percent from 1991. Sales were fairly evenly divided among three major markets: retail, foodservice (restaurants, fast-food outlets, institutions), and industrial (ingredients used by other food processors).

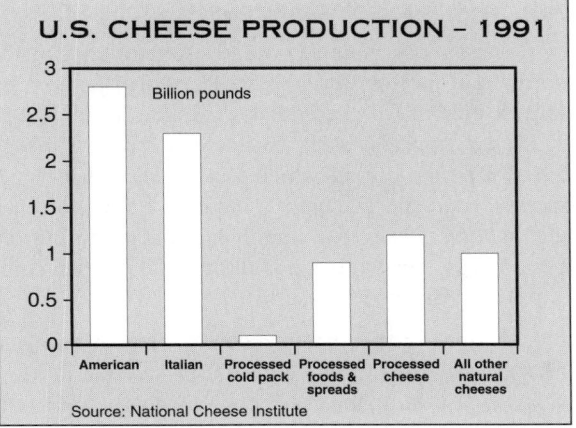

The biggest supermarket sellers were unshredded American and other natural cheeses. The biggest gains, however, were registered in natural (11.28 percent) and processed (72.6 percent) shredded cheeses. Sales of Italian cheeses in particular were projected to continue their upward curve in all areas. Although per capita consumption of cheese had hovered at a fairly steady amount of 11-12 pounds since the mid-1980s, annual Italian cheese consumption had surged by 50 percent, from 6.5 to 9.4 pounds per person in that period. Most of this increase was in mozzarella, with consumption exceeding 7 pounds per capita in 1991.

Pre-sliced, packaged process cheeses represented a healthy chunk of cheese sales, and processors followed up with packaged shredded cheese in such flavored varieties as "taco" and "pizza." Retailers also found that pre-sliced cheeses were popular among consumers at the deli counter as well. Vacuum-packed, pre-sliced cheese allowed deli counter staff to deal with other tasks instead of slicing cheese to order and reduced the time that customers spent waiting in line.

Industrial sales of cheese ingredients continued to grow. They accounted for about 28 percent of the industry's $18 billion sales figure for 1992. Here, too, much of the growth was in Italian-style cheeses, but processed cheeses, powders, and other natural cheeses were also big sellers. Industrial uses of cheese expanded as the country's changing demographics resulted in increased popularity of prepared and frozen foods. According to Jim Lauderdale of Mid-America Dairymen Inc. in *Dairy Field* magazine, "we're finding with both parents working, people want bigger variety. . . . Cheese plays a large part in adding variety and making a nutritious meal." Mid-Am offered mozzarella, provolone, Parmesan, Romano, ricotta, and such American-style cheeses as Colby and Monterey Jack, as well as cottage cheese.

Pizza's continuing popularity contributed to the strength of the foodservice market, which is the third largest market for cheesemakers. Italian cheese sales increased approximately 10 percent from 1987 to 1991, a period during which the segment as a whole grew 6.6 percent. The biggest increase was in hospitals and schools. The most significant change during the period was the waning popularity of Cheddar compared to processed cheese.

Portions of the cheese industry were suffering in the early 1990s. Declining cheese production in Minnesota was costing the state economy nearly $831 million annually and more than 12,000 jobs, according to a University of Minnesota study. Milk product sales of cheese (and ice cream) were down 10 percent from 1985. As production and sales dropped, so did dairy farm purchases from related industries. The milk production declines were triggered in part by sell-outs due to lower milk pricing and a relatively low per-cow production.

In a move that the industry hoped would alleviate erratic pricing, the New York Coffee, Sugar & Cocoa Exchange (CSCE) began trading in futures contracts for Cheddar cheese in June, 1993. Each contract was for 40,000 pounds of Cheddar in 40-pound blocks, with FOB delivery in the continental United States. In futures contracts, buyers and sellers agree to the price for a commodity on a fixed date. The contracts allowed cheese producers and processors a degree of control over the volatile pricing that had afflicted the industry in the 1980s, when the federal government reduced price supports and cheese became more subject to market forces. The first day of trading slightly exceeded the CSCE's pre-opening day estimate of 100 contracts, but whether the experiment would succeed over the long run was uncertain. Kraft General Foods supported the trading as did some dairy co-ops like Land O'Lakes, which had experienced some very wide swings in earnings for several years. Other producers, like Darigold, Inc., a Seattle co-op, planned to study the trading carefully before plunging into the unfamiliar CSCE market.

Legislation. The Nutritional Labeling Education Act (NLEA) mandated sweeping changes in labeling, emphasizing the relationship between nutrition and chronic disease over the vitamin/mineral content. The redesigned labels were meant to reduce consumer confusion by standardizing serving sizes (reference amounts), establishing rules for health claims, defining comparative nutritional claims, and relating them to U.S. Recommended Daily Intakes (RDIs) and U.S. Recommended Daily Allowances (RDAs) for vitamin/mineral percentages. The compliance date was set for 1994, but larger companies were expected to comply by mid-1993, putting pressure on smaller, regional processors as well as analytical testing laboratories and suppliers of packaging and printing.

Lowfat. Of the six billion pounds of cheese sold annually in the United States, some 5 percent consisted of lowfat products, but their flavor and texture couldn't match that of full-fat standard cheeses. A prime research effort of the cheese industry in the 1990s was to develop ways to improve the flavor of lowfat and fat-free products. Some success was achieved by using new adjunct cultures to enhance flavor. The development of new starter cultures created especially for lowfat cheeses also allowed for greater flavor with lower acidity.

INDUSTRY LEADERS

Kraft USA, long the country's top cheese producer, reported $2 billion in retail cheese sales in 1991 and an undisclosed share of the industrial cheese market, but it was suffering from the recession of the early 1990s. In a streamlining move, the company consolidated two cheese plants into one in Illinois and closed another in Michigan. By 1994, it hoped to have completed conversion of a 315,000 square-foot facility in Tulare, California, to bulk natural cheese manufacture. The converted Tulare plant was expected to process more than two million pounds of milk per day for a total daily cheese production of 200,000 pounds and an annual production total of 73 million pounds.

Kraft's Specialty Products Division planned strong promotional activity for its Italian and specialty cheeses in foodservice, in-store deli, and institutional markets. In the industrial market, Kraft Food Ingredients (KFI) sold a wide range of natural and processed cheeses and cheese substitutes to other food processors for use as food ingredients. The company that built its reputation on the pasteurized processed cheese it patented in 1916 continued to add to its consumer product line. "Marketers like Kraft are facing more competition than they ever have before," according to Robert Eckert, of Kraft USA's Retail Division, in *Dairy Field* magazine. In the fall of 1992, the company launched Kraft Healthy Favorites, a 23-item line of 50 percent reduced-fat cheese products.

Some of Kraft's competition was coming from Sargento Cheese Co., which knocked the giant from its number-one-in-the-market perch in the shredded cheese area. With its $320 million in sales versus Kraft's $2 billion, Wisconsin-based Sargento Cheese Co. wouldn't displace Kraft, but its 20 percent increase over 1991 sales made it a company to watch. Kraft sales had also dropped in the $1.5 billion processed cheese slices section of the dairy case as consumers opted for regional brand names or lower-priced private label brands. ConAgra's Beatrice Cheese unit also planned to do battle with Kraft's longstanding dominance with a line of 30 new fat-free cheeses under its Healthy Choice label.

Co-ops which processed the raw milk from their dairy farm membership were strong contenders in the competitive cheese industry. Mid-America Dairymen, Inc. (Mid-Am), the country's second-largest dairy co-op in the early 1990s, produced cheese from the milk of its member farms. Mid-Am used both milk of manufacturing grade and Class I (Grade A) milk that was not bottled for beverage use. It was one of the largest manufacturers of natural cheese in the country and also produced a range of specialty cheeses. Its output of mozzarella alone, largely destined for its fresh pizza customers, came to 180 million pounds a year. Under its Mid-America Farms label, it sold its cheese products to consumers, institutional and foodservice markets, and to food manufacturers for use as food ingredients.

Land O'Lakes (LOL), with a 72-year history and $2.6 billion in 1992 sales, half of which came from its dairy group, was a dairy co-op to be watched when it focused on increasing its cheese sales. The company backed its intention with a strong research and technical staff of 120 and an annual research investment nearing $10 million. A 30 percent increase in its 1993 advertising, promotion, and trade relations budget was established to reinforce LOL's message that it had a cheese business.

WORK FORCE

The U.S. Department of Commerce estimated that 33,300 people were employed in the cheese industry in 1992, down 2.3 percent from the 1991 estimate of 34,100. Of these employees, approximately 26,900 were production workers, earning an average hourly wage of $10.64.

AMERICA AND THE WORLD

U.S. cheese exports reached $37 million in 1991. Canada was the leading export market for the year, with shipments valued at more than $9 million, an increase of 6 percent over 1990. Mexico, America's number two market for cheese exports in 1991, was increasing its shipments rapidly; exports to Mexico were valued at nearly $8 million in 1991, up an astronomical 78 percent from 1990. Cheese imports, regulated by quotas, accounted for three-fifths of all dairy imports and were expected to increase. The forecast value of 1993 cheese imports was $480 million.

RESEARCH AND TECHNOLOGY

New technologies in the industry focused on product safety, automation, and quality controls. An increasing number of large Cheddar cheese plants operated non-stop, seven days a week, using sophisticated computer control systems that could pump 50,000 pounds of milk per hour. Many of these systems allowed a single operator to oversee the following processes: pasteurizing the milk, adding the starter culture, making the cheese, draining the whey, Cheddaring, and milling and salting. In 1991, there were less than one-tenth the number of U.S. cheese plants than there had been in 1940, but they were producing four times as much cheese.

INDUSTRY INFORMATION SOURCES

Campbell, Alta, Gary Hoover, and Patrick J. Spain, eds. *Hoover's Handbook of American Business 1993*. Austin, TX: The Reference Press, Inc., 1992.

"Cheese Sales Climb as Processors Diversify." *Dairy Field*, December, 1992.

"Cheese." *Institutional Distribution,* May 15, 1991.

Considine, Douglas M., P.E., ed. *Foods and Food Production Encyclopedia*. New York: Van Nostrand Reinhold Company, 1982.

Dexheimer, Ellen et al., "Navigators of the '90s." *Dairy Foods*, April 1993.

Doeff, Gail Rosenbaum. "Ready, Set, Hedge!" *Dairy Foods,* July 1993.

Dryer, Jerry. "Convenience: More Than Just a Fact of Life." *Dairy Field*, July 1992.

Fabricant, Florence. "Looking for Flavor? Say 'Cheese'." *The New York Times*, July 28, 1993.

Garrison, Bob. "Dynamic Duo." *Refrigerated and Frozen Foods,* May 1993.

Getler, Warren, and Scott Kilman. "Cheddar Lovers May Take a Slice of These Futures." *Wall Street Journal*, January 14, 1993.

Godfrey, Patricia, R.D., and Dan Best. "NLEA in a Nutshell." *Prepared Foods*, December 1992.

Honer, Clem. "Technology Update." *Dairy Field,* February 1993.

———. "Serious About Mozzarella." *Dairy Field*, August 1992.

"Infoscan Report, Full Year 1992 Figures." *Food & Beverage Marketing*, March 1993.

Janis, William V. "Dairy Products." *U.S. Industrial Outlook*. Washington, DC: U.S. Department of Commerce, 1992.

Kimbrell, Wendy. "Cheese Rap." *Dairy Field*, November 1992.

"Kraft Cheese Products." Memphis, TN: Kraft Food Ingredients.

LaBell, Fran. "Cultures Improve Low-fat Cheese." *Food Processing*, September 1992.

LaBell, Fran, et al. "Current Dairy Research Highlights Lowfat Cheese." *Food Processing,* September 1992.

Lenius, Pat Natschke. "Presliced Adds Up." *Supermarket News*, June 7, 1993.

Levitt, Alan. "Versatility Is Its Virtue." *Dairy Foods,* August 1993.

Liesse, Julie. "Brand Scorecard: Foes Poke Holes in Kraft Cheese Stranglehold." *Advertising Age,* December 7, 1992.

———. "ConAgra, Kraft Start Cheese War." *Advertising Age,* July 6, 1992.

Milk Facts. Washington, DC: Milk Industry Foundation, 1992.

"Milk Production Declines Expensive for Minnesota." *Feedstuffs*, June 14, 1993.

"More Than Just a Milk Check . . ." Mid-America Dairymen, Inc., 1991.

Ruland, Susan. "Bright Spot." *Dairy Field*, February 1993.

———. "Ready for Change." *Dairy Field*, August 1992.

—Mary Ratcliffe

SIC 2023

DRY, CONDENSED, AND EVAPORATED DAIRY PRODUCTS

This classification covers establishments primarily engaged in manufacturing dry, condensed, and evaporated diary products. Included in this industry are establishments primarily engaged in manufacturing mixes for the preparation of frozen ice cream and ice milk and dairy and nondairy base cream substitutes and dietary supplements.

INDUSTRY SNAPSHOT

The dry, condensed, and evaporated dairy products sector of the highly regionalized dairy industry embraces both small family operations and multinational giants, reporting sales in the billions of dollars. The spectrum of products produced by this industry is just as broad, ranging from retail staples like canned, evaporated milks, which have been familiar on market shelves for more than a century, to sophisticated milk protein ingredients which are constantly being refined in research laboratories for new food uses. With products as comforting as mother's milk and as baffling to consumers as the sodium caseinates that appear on the labels of the latest sports drinks, it was a $9,364 million industry by the 1990s.

From World War II, a dwindling number of dairy farms has supplied the raw milk from which dry, condensed, and evaporated milk products are processed, but the farms have become much larger. Huge dairy farm cooperatives combined with operations that processed the raw milk to produce branded consumer products and milk ingredients marketed to food and animal feed processors. Darigold Inc. was the largest Pacific Northwest cooperative in 1992. With 1400 dairy farmer members and its own processing plants and distribution centers, it was a top producer of powdered milk, projecting 1993 sales of $920 million.

The small companies that had pioneered condensed and evaporated milk technology and production in the 19th century were still in business more than 100 years later, producing the same products with which they had started out—and many, many others. Borden, Inc., and Pet, Inc., had grown into diversified giants ranked in the top 50 food companies nationwide. Pharmaceutical companies also reached into this dairy food category with their infant formulas. There was always room, though, for smaller companies, often specializing in milk ingredients like whey proteins and ice cream/yogurt/milkshake mixes.

BACKGROUND AND DEVELOPMENT

Removal of all or part of the water from milk not only reduces transportation costs and makes handling easier, it also allows unrefrigerated storage of sterilized or dried products for prolonged periods. Such products may be intended for consumer use or as ingredients in diverse processed foods.

The Federal Drug & Cosmetic Act has established Standards of Identity (SID) for milk products which define what can be packaged under a given product name. The Food and Drug Administration (FDA) designates food ingredients to be generally recognized as safe (GRAS) when extensive past use has not shown any harmful effects.

Dry Milk. Marco Polo, it is said, encountered sun-dried milk in his travels through Mongolia in the thirteenth century. It remained for later scientists to develop commercial production processes. An early patent for a commercial process to manufacture dried milk was granted in 1855. Technological advances since then have enabled a wide variety of manufactured milk products with applications in frozen dairy desserts, ice cream, frozen soft and hard yogurt, bakery goods, confectionery products, dry mixes, soups, animal feeds, and countless other nutritional and functional uses.

Nonfat dry milk (NDM) results when both fat and water are removed from milk. Lactose (milk sugar), milk proteins and milk minerals are present in the same relative proportions as in fresh milk. Moisture is not more than five percent by weight, and fat content is not over 1.5 percent by weight unless otherwise indicated. In the 1990s, nearly a billion pounds of NDM were being produced every year.

Dry whole milk results from the removal of water from milk. It contains not less than 26 percent milk fat and not more than four percent moisture. Dry buttermilk is made by removing the water from buttermilk derived from butter manufacture. It has not less than 4.5 percent milk fat content and not more than five percent moisture.

Milk Proteins. Derived through various processing steps from skim milk, milk proteins are used as ingredients in a wide range of food products both for their nutritional value and for their functionality. Casein, milk's principal protein, has been commercially isolated from skim milk since 1900. There are two basic types, depending on the coagulating agent used to precipitate the casein from the milk: lactic (acid) casein and rennet casein. Most acid caseins intended for food applications were converted to caseinates by dissolving the acid casein curd with water and dilute alkali and then drying the solution. Sodium caseinate is generally recognized as safe (GRAS).

Casein has a higher Protein Efficiency Ratio (PER) than vegetable proteins. Under the *Code of Federal Regulations,* "if the protein efficiency ratio of protein is equal to or better than that of casein, the U.S.

Recommended Daily Allowance (RDA) is 45 grams." However, if the PER is lower than that of casein (2.5), then 65 grams of protein are required to meet the USRDA. Because of its high protein quality and content, low lactose, and bland flavor, casein is used in nutritional supplements. Nutritional foods commonly formulated with casein include high-protein beverage powders, fortified cereals, infant formulas, and nutrition bars. Products incorporating casein for its functional properties of imparting texture, viscosity, emulsification, and opacity included coffee creamers, soups, sauces, ice cream, whipped toppings, yogurt, salad dressings.

Whey seemed to have been the "forgotten" milk protein until April 1971, when representatives of 56 firms gathered to consider the potential of these milk solids that remain after cheese manufacture. Warren S. Clark, Jr., executive director of the American Dairy Products Institute, wrote in the *Encyclopedia of Food Science and Technology,* "In no area of the modern dairy industry have changes of a technical nature been as innovative and rapid as in the whey products segment." The Food and Drug Administration affirmed the safety of whey products and their manufacture in 1984 with a declaration of common and usual names for diverse whey products ("Whey," "Reduced Minerals Whey," and "Whey Protein Concentrate") and by granting them GRAS status.

Evaporated Milk. When Gail Borden returned to the United States from England in 1851, it was on a ship that had to carry cows to provide milk for the immigrant children on board. There was no way to carry fresh milk on a long sea voyage without its spoiling. Five years later, in 1856, Borden was granted patents in the United States and England for the preservation of milk after it had been evaporated in a vacuum. The method used no added sugar, but sweetened condensed milk was to be Borden's first commercial product in 1861.

Thirty years later, the Helvetia Milk Condensing Company began production of the world's first unsweetened evaporated milk in 1885, calling it Highland Evaporated Cream after the plant's home in Highland, Illinois. The company was later to change its name to Pet, Inc.

Evaporated milk is a canned whole milk concentrate with a specified quantity of added vitamin D. Vitamin A may also be added. Related products are evaporated skimmed milk, evaporated low fat milk, evaporated filled milk, and evaporated goat milk.

Dairy and Non-Dairy Creamers. Health-conscious consumers in the 1990s regarded non-dairy creamers as cholesterol free and therefore better for you than milk-based products. Nestlé's Carnation, which introduced Coffee-Mate in 1961, added Coffee-Mate Lite in 1989, and again extended this top-selling non-dairy creamer line in 1992 with Hazelnut, Irish Creme, and Amaretto flavored powders. Pet, Inc. also marketed a non-dairy creamer.

Infant Formulas. Infant formulas that approximate human milk are fed to infants all over the world, sometimes as their sole source of nutrients during the first months of life. Such products were unknown until the 20th century, when they became a reliable alternative to breastfeeding. In the London of the early 1800s, only about ten percent of infants not breastfed lived past their first birthdays.

In the United States, the Infant Formula Act of 1980 and its 1986 amendments very specifically govern the manufacture of commercial infant formulas. The Act authorized the FDA to implement quality control regulations and recall procedures, labeling and nutrient requirements, and requirements for exempt infant formulas. Additionally, infant formulas must satisfy Federal Food, Drug and Cosmetic Act regulations dealing with foods for special dietary use, good manufacturing practices, and canned foods (for liquid infant formulas only).

The stringent regulations governing infant formulas have included setting maximum levels for 29 nutrients and minimum levels for 10. Labels were required to include a nutrient declaration; "use by" date information; a statement such as "use as directed by a physician"; a warning statement of the consequences of improper preparation; preparation and use directions that included pictograms if appropriate; and more. All of these requirements had long been standard practices of its member manufacturers, according to the Infant Formula Council.

Infant formulas were a $1.9 billion business in 1991, presenting their products as the best substitute for mother's milk. Yet the industry was mired in federal and state price-fixing investigations. Antitrust inquiries were directed at contracts awarded to the three top producers under the Special Supplemental Food Program for Women, Infants and Children (WIC), designed for low-income families. Although federally funded, WIC was administered by the states, which were paying full retail prices for formula because there was no competitive bidding.

In 1991, Abbott Laboratories, which marketed infant formulas through its Ross Laboratories unit, and Bristol-Myers Squibb, whose infant formulas were sold through its Mead Johnson Nutritional Group,

shared 85 percent of the market. American Home Products accounted for about nine percent of the market, selling through Wyeth-Ayerst Laboratories. The other major producers were Nestlé's Carnation unit and Gerber, which marketed a Bristol-Myers product. In the period between 1980 and 1991, wholesale formula prices had doubled, rising an average of 11 percent a year while milk prices were going up an average of only two percent annually.

In June, 1992, after a two-year investigation into the three biggest producers, the Federal Trade Commission charged them with price-rigging, contending that they had rigged contracts awarded under the federally-funded Special Supplemental Food Program for Women, Infants and Children. This program accounts for approximately one of every three cans of formula sold. The cost to the government was estimated at $25 million. Mead-Johnson and American Home, while admitting no wrongdoing, agreed to settle. Abbott Laboratories initially planned to fight the charges in federal court. The *Wall Street Journal* quoted Duane Burnham, Abbott's chairman and chief executive officer: "We have competed responsibly, aggressively, and completely within the law." In May 1993, however, Abbott Laboratories agreed to pay more than $140 million to settle a number of suits filed against the company nationwide and consolidated in Florida to simplify proceedings. The Federal Trade Commission's actions against Abbott remain in place.

CURRENT CONDITIONS

Value of shipments in this SIC category was expected to increase by 4.0 percent in 1993 over 1992, from $6,379 million to $6,632 million. Value of imports dropped from $345 million in 1989 to $247 million (forecast) in 1993. During the same period, exports jumped from $374 million to a forecast $876 million.

According to the American Dairy Products Institute, production of nonfat dry milk (NDM) was lower in 1992 than in 1991, but commercial sales were higher, representing 75.4 percent of the year's production. In previous years, commercial sales were 72.9 percent of 1991 production and 70.1 percent of 1990 production.

In terms of quantity, nonfat dry milk (NDM) production in 1992 totaled 873.0 million pounds, 4.5 million pounds (0.5 percent) below 1991. Most of it, 657.9 million pounds, was sold in the United States. Of this total, 417.7 million pounds (63.5 percent) went into dairy products, 94.1 million pounds (14.3 percent) went into bakery products, 55.3 million pounds (8.4 percent) were packaged for home use, and 26.3 million pounds (4.0 percent) were used for confectionery products. Some other applications using millions of pounds of NDM in 1992 were prepared dry mixes (20.4); chemicals and pharmaceuticals (11.9); animal feed (11.2); meat processing (7.9); dry blends (7.2); institutions (3.9); and soup manufacturers (0.7).

Dry whole milk production in 1992 climbed 38.0 percent over 1992 to 147.4 million pounds, while dry buttermilk production and sales figures were inconsistent for the year. This was apparently due to uncertainty relating to the definition of two separate products, dry buttermilk and dry buttermilk product. Production of dry buttermilk fell 3.2 percent to 58.0 million pounds; total domestic sales for the two products totaled 80.0 million pounds.

Whey products sold for human food in 1992 totaled 784.7 million pounds up 5.8 percent over 1991. Whey destined for animal feeds totaled 721 million pounds a decrease of 0.1 percent from 1991. The human-use whey products, including lactose, were incorporated in confectioneries, dry mixes, dairy and bakery products, and infant formulas. Whey solids were used in feeds for cattle, swine, pets, and poultry.

Industry Leaders

The top three companies in the industry, Nestlé USA (Carnation), Borden, Inc., and Pet, Inc., were all long-established producers of staple products for retail consumers. Nestlé USA (Carnation) claimed the top-selling non-dairy creamer, Carnation Coffee-Mate, and a full line of popular canned milks. Borden Inc., originator of sweetened condensed milk in the 19th century, continued to market the product under its Eagle brand name, while KLIM dried milk, sold in 85 countries, recorded record sales in 1991 of $275 million. The KLIM line was extended with KLIM Lite-line low fat milk powder, while KLIM Superkid fortified milk powder was formulated for children from three to seven. Pet, Inc., which introduced the first commercially produced evaporated milk in 1885, remained a leader. Its evaporated milk was still on market shelves nationwide, but the company had diversified to market many other food products. Ross Laboratories, a unit of Abbott Laboratories, was estimated to hold a 50 percent share of the $1.9 billion infant formula market.

Work Force

Employment declined steadily from 1987 through the early 1990s, but wages showed steady increases. Hourly earnings in 1987 were $11.47 compared to $12.75 (estimated) in 1992, but the number of hours worked dropped 1.0 percent in from 1980 (19.1 mil-

lion) to 1990 (18.1 million). Companies in the industry employed 12,100 workers in 1990, 8,500 of whom were involved in production processes.

America and the World

According to a 1993 National Dairy Promotion and Research Board market plan, nonfat dry milk (NDM) production in the United States decreased between 1987 and 1992 by 4.3 percent, from $480 million to $385 million, while consumption increased slightly from 329 to 339 million tons. During that same period, the European Community (EC) and Australasia produced far more NDM than they consumed, with most overproduction available for export. Underproducing countries were Mexico and Japan. U.S. exports of dry whole and nonfat dry milk to Mexico alone increased almost 165 percent in 1992, to $318 million.

Overall, 1992 exports of all dairy products in 1992 jumped 67 percent, marking the first trade surplus since 1972. Dry, evaporated and condensed milk exports, which accounted for almost 69 percent of dairy exports, more than doubled. The U.S. Government, through the Dairy Export Incentive Program (DEIP), continued to subsidize exports. The dairy industry was expected to profit from the historic North American Free Trade Agreement (NAFTA) passed in 1993, which combined Mexico, the United States, and Canada as the world's largest single consumer market, with a population topping 360 million people and an economy close to $6.5 trillion. American processors could look forward to barrier-free trade with the Mexican market, traditionally a major dairy importer.

Research and Technology

Evaporation and Drying. Water is removed from milk either by evaporation, in which heat is applied under a vacuum, or by drying. Spray drying has been the more widely used method for preparing dried milk products. In this process, the condensed fluid milk is pumped from the vacuum pan while it is still hot and atomized in the heated air of the spray dryer either by the centrifugal force of being discharged from a rapidly turning disk or by being forced through a narrow nozzle. Drying is almost instantaneous.

Roller drying has rarely been used to dry milk for human use. In this process, condensed milk is fed between a pair of heated rollers and adheres to them in a thin film. The dried milk is scraped off by a sharp blade and hammered into uniform, fine particles. In addition to roller and spray drying, these products could be made by foam or freeze drying. It was also possible to make them more readily soluble; such products were called "instantized."

Ultra-High Temperature Processing. Ultra-high temperature processing, which produced liquid soft-serve ice cream and yogurt mixes with a 90-day shelf life, six to nine times that of standard processing, enabled foodservice distributors in the 1990s to compete with local and regional dairies with a full line of dairy products. Until then, the dairies had a tight hold on this lucrative segment of the dairy industry, selling to giant fast food outlets like McDonald's as well as mom-and-pop stores.

INDUSTRY INFORMATION SOURCES

"All around the World, Borden Growth, Innovation Continue," *Borden Eagle,* April/May 1992.

Anderson, Sue Ann, Hermin I. Chinn, and Kenneth D. Fisher, "History and Current Status of Infant Formulas," *The American Journal of Clinical Nutrition,* February 1982.

Collins, James H., "The Story of Condensed Milk," Columbus, OH: The Borden Co., 1922.

"Creating a Masterpiece: The First 100 Years of Pet Incorporated," St. Louis: Pet Inc., 1985.

"Current Legislation and Regulations Regarding Infant Formulas," Atlanta: Infant Formula Council, 1992.

"Dairy Products," *Institutional Distribution,* 15 May 1993.

"Dry Milk and Whey Products Production & Markets—1992," Chicago: American Dairy Products Institute, 1992.

Encyclopedia Americana International Edition, 30 volumes. Danbury, CT: Grolier Incorporated, 1991. S.v. "Dairy Industry," by Harold E. Calbert.

Friedman, Marty, "Non-Dairy Creamers Build Their Case," *Dairy Foods,* April 1992.

Hui, Y. H., ed., *Encyclopedia of Food Science and Technology,* New York: John Wiley & Sons Inc., 1992. S.v. "Casein and Caseinates," by C. R. Southward and N. J. Walker.

Hui, Y. H., ed., *Encyclopedia of Food Science and Technology,* New York: John Wiley & Sons Inc., 1992. S.v. "Dry Milk," by Warren S. Clark, Jr.

Hui, Y. H., ed., *Encyclopedia of Food Science and Technology,* New York: John Wiley & Sons Inc., 1992. S.v. "Evaporated Milk," by Warren S. Clark, Jr. and J. C. Flake.

Hui, Y. H., ed., *Encyclopedia of Food Science and Technology,* New York: John Wiley & Sons Inc., 1992. S.v. "Whey Processing: History and Development," by Warren S. Clark, Jr.

Landa, Marinell, "A Look at America's Most Popular Non-Dairy Creamer," San Francisco, CA: Nestlé Beverage Products, 1992.

"Market Development Plan for the Pacific Rim and Latin America," Arlington, VA: National Dairy Promotion and Research Board, July 1992.

McGraw-Hill Encyclopedia of Science & Technology, Vol. 11. McGraw-Hill, Inc., 1992. S.v. "Milk," by Robert L. Bradley, Jr.

Meier, Barry. "Abbott Labs Settles in Florida Suits," *New York Times,* 25 May 1993.

———. "What Prompted Investigations Into Pricing of Baby Formula?" *The New York Times,* 19 January 1991.

"NAFTA Negotiations Conclude," *Dairy Field,* October 1992.

Noble, Barbara Presley. "Price-Fixing and Other Charges Roil a Once Placid Market," *The New York Times,* 28 July 1991.

Ruland, Susan. "Milk Shaker," *Dairy Field,* May 1992.

Salwen, Kevin G. "Firms Rigged Bids, U.S. Says," *Wall Street Journal,* 12 June 1992.

U.S. Industrial Outlook, Washington, DC: U.S. Department of Commerce, 1993.

Van Wagner, Lisa R. "Government Agencies," *Food Processing,* August 1992.

—Mary Ratcliffe

SIC 2024

ICE CREAM AND FROZEN DESSERTS

This industry classification encompasses establishments primarily engaged in manufacturing ice cream and other frozen desserts: frozen yogurt, ice milk, ices and sherbets, frozen custard, mellorine, frozen tofu, and pops (frozen desserts on sticks).

INDUSTRY SNAPSHOT

The ice cream and frozen desserts industry is an important sector of the American dairy industry. Its sales, ranked third behind the fluid milk and cheese sectors of the dairy industry, exceeded $9 billion in 1991 and represented over 15 percent of the dairy industry's overall sales of $62.8 billion. Measured by consumption, frozen desserts led the entire dairy industry segment in 1992. Increasing consumption of frozen desserts has been attributed to the introduction of products containing less milkfat, which were developed to address consumers' interests in healthier diets. Consumption of frozen yogurt, a lowfat alternative to ice cream, rose by 17 percent, and ice cream's 7.3 percent gain was attributed largely to reduced-fat products.

ORGANIZATION AND STRUCTURE

The production of ice cream begins with the milk produced by America's dairy farmers, many of whom belonged to large dairy cooperatives which marketed their milk to processors or, in some cases, operated their own processing facilities for the manufacture of ice cream and other dairy products. In 1991, America's 10 million dairy cows produced 148,526 million pounds of milk; approximately 8.6 percent of it, or 12.8 million pounds, was used to make frozen dairy products.

Manufacturers of ice cream and other frozen desserts ranged in size from small operations with sales under $1 million a year to subsidiaries or divisions of giant, diversified companies with annual sales in the billions of dollars and for which frozen desserts were only a portion of their total product lines. In 1991, there were 675 establishments making ice cream, 307 making ice milk, and 176 making water ice. Most of these plants made more than one type of frozen dessert product.

In the highly regionalized and extremely competitive dairy industry, many top producers' brand names were known only in the geographic areas in which they were distributed. Distribution to sales outlets was vital to the success of the frozen desserts, and competition for distributors was keen. Small producers trying to break into a market could be "frozen out" by leading producers who demanded absolute loyalty from their regional distributors.

Licensing agreements sometimes made partners of competitors. For example, in the San Francisco Bay Area, Dreyer's/Edy's Grand Ice Cream was a co-packer and distributor for Vermont-based Ben & Jerry's, and according to a filing with the Securities & Exchange Commission, 42 percent of Ben & Jerry's ice cream was being made by a Dreyer's plant in Fort Wayne, Indiana, using Vermont milk. Similarly, Steve's Homemade produced Yoplait frozen yogurts under an agreement with Yoplait's parent company, General Mills.

BACKGROUND AND DEVELOPMENT

Whether ice cream originated in China or Rome is a matter of debate, but there was little debate in the early 1990s that ice cream and its frozen dessert relatives had regained their position as one of Americans' favorite treats. Ice cream as we know it—smooth and creamy—was introduced in the United States early in the twentieth century as a result of two technological advances: homogenization, which reduced the fat particle size in milk; and a continuous freezing process that enabled a consistent ice crystal structure. Production and manufacturing advancements that have since been realized have centered primarily on formulation refinements and stabilizer and process systems.

Ice cream is a frozen, pasteurized mixture of milk, cream, nonfat milk solids, sugars, and stabilizers. Its contents and manufacture are regulated by the government and must meet Standards of Identity. To be called ice cream, a product must contain a minimum of 10 percent butterfat, which is dispersed throughout the mix to impart smooth texture. Fresh sweet cream is the best source of butterfat; unsalted butter, which is about 82.5 percent fat, can replace 50-75 percent of sweet cream fat. Other fat sources that can be used include anhydrous butter oil, concentrated sweet cream, and dried cream. French ice cream, or frozen custard, also contains more than 1.4 percent egg yolk solid. Consumer concerns about the negative health effects of fat in the diet, however, led to the popularity of lower-fat products such as ice milk, which contained between 2 percent and 7 percent butterfat. "Ice milk" as a product name, however, was headed for extinction with passage of the Nutrition Labeling and Education Act.

Other standard ice cream ingredients include sugars and sweeteners, milk proteins, stabilizers and emulsifiers. Sweetening agents can be natural (corn sweeteners, sucrose processed from cane and beet sugars, or fructose) or artificial (aspartame). The milk proteins used are whey proteins and casein. Milk and milk products themselves have some natural stabilizing and emulsifying properties that often eliminate the need for additional stabilizers and emulsifiers. Stabilizers help to prevent texture deterioration caused by inevitable temperature fluctuations that occur during distribution, which cause ice crystals to melt and then reform into larger crystals. Emulsifiers enhance the whipping qualities of the ice cream mix by creating a smoother texture and body.

Flavorings may be added before or after pasteurization, and may be pure flavor extracts, pure extracts with some synthetic or artificial components, or artificial flavors. As a general rule, premium ice creams use pure extracts, and use fruits, nuts and candies, and syrups to add flavor. In the 1990s, mix-in flavors like Chocolate Chip Cookie Mix, Carrot Cake Passion, and Cappuccino Commotion were very popular.

The luxury, or superpremium, ice creams that were regaining popularity in the 1990s were pioneered by Reuben Mattus in the early 1960s. Using all top quality, natural ingredients, and no artificial stabilizers or other additives, Mattus created Häagen-Dazs, a highly successful product that set the pattern for rich, clean-tasting ice creams. In the 1980s, such ice cream novelties as ice pops, fudgesicles, and ice cream sandwiches, which had been originally marketed at children, were becoming popular with adults. Häagen-Dazs entered this market with such products as Dove bars and Häagen-Dazs frozen yogurt bars.

Sherbets were defined by the Federal Code of Regulations to contain between 1 and 2 percent butterfat and between 2 and 5 percent total milk-derived solids. Ices contain no milk-derived ingredients or egg ingredients other than egg white; they can be made with non-pasteurized mixes because of their typically high acidity formulation. Mellorine products, although similar to ice cream, contained a combination of vegetable and animal fat in place of butterfat. Federal Standards of identity required mellorine products to contain at least 6 percent fat and no less than 3.5 percent protein.

Frozen yogurts are made using the bacteria cultures *Streptococcus thermophilus* and/or *Lactobacillus bulgaricus*. As most refrigerated yogurts were lowfat and had a healthy image with consumers, frozen yogurt was assumed to have the same health benefits as the refrigerated product. The Code of Federal Regulations, however, which required specific starting cultures and acidity levels for refrigerated yogurt, set no such product characteristic requirements for frozen yogurt. The National Yogurt Association (NYA) endorsed a 1991 International Ice Cream Association petition to the government that would standardize manufacturing procedures and require frozen yogurt to be made with specific characterizing yogurt cultures.

Nutrition Labeling and Education Act (NLEA). By defining terms that had been murky, the Food and Drug Administration's (FDA) Nutrition Labeling and Education Act, with its May 1994 compliance deadline, enabled many frozen food processors to call their products "lowfat ice cream." The act also separated the link between calories and fat, so that desserts getting more than half their calories from fat could be labeled "light" if its fat content had been reduced 50 percent from its reference product. The "light" label was also permitted on products getting less than half their calories from fat if the products had either a 50 percent fat reduction or a one-third reduction in calories.

A significant change in the new labeling would do away with the term "ice milk." Lower-fat ice creams, which previously had to be called "ice milk," could now be labeled as "reduced fat," "light," "lowfat," "nonfat," or "fat-free," depending on the product's fat content.

Although the definitions of the terms were clear, the actual fat content percentages were not, because they were tied to an indefinite term, "reference food." Thus, a "reduced fat" claim meant that a product had 25 percent less fat than its "reference food." "Light" referred to a product that had a 50 percent fat reduction from "the reference food," and a "lowfat" product was defined as having not more than 3 grams of total fat in a half-cup serving. "Nonfat" and "fat-free" were defined as products having less than 0.5 grams total fat per reference amount. The reference amount was a half-cup for ice cream and frozen yogurt products and 85 grams for flavored ices and juice bars.

To determine the "reference food," processors first had to find the marketplace average fat or calorie content by looking at the leading brands in the area where the product was to be sold. For example, a processor would have to compare its "light" Fudge Ripple with leading brands of Fudge Ripple to calculate how much of a reduction in fat or calories would satisfy the "50 percent less" requirement. If, on average, the leading brands contained 16 grams of fat, then a product containing 8 grams of fat could be labeled "light."

CURRENT CONDITIONS

With sales of $3.2 billion in 1991, ice cream was making a comeback as America's favorite dessert. Sales of other frozen desserts (ice milk, frozen yogurt nonfat/lowfat products, novelties, sherbets and sorbets, tofu-based products, mellorine and miscellaneous products) brought the industry total to $9.5 billion for the year. Overall, production increased 4 percent from 1990, with full-fat ice creams still leading the market at 61 percent. Frozen yogurt production, however, increased by 25 percent.

Americans spent $5 billion on frozen desserts to eat at home, and another $4.5 billion was spent on away-from-home purchases. Whether indulging in full-fat superpremium brands or following the trend to purchase healthier lowfat foods, Americans of all ages were purchasing more frozen desserts at supermarkets, restaurants, and ice cream shops. Per capita consumption rose 10 percent in 1991 and the outlook for future growth was encouraging.

While fat content continued to be of concern to many consumers, their buying patterns did not always reflect it. One survey found that nearly two-thirds of respondents regularly chose lowfat dairy foods. Older people and couples were more apt than single people to opt for lowfat regularly. The number of reduced-fat ice creams, which represented 54 percent of all reduced-fat product introductions in 1990, declined from 311 to only 94, or 23 percent of the market segment, in 1992.

At Ben & Jerry's Homemade, which built its success on full-fat, superpremium ice cream, efforts to develop a satisfactory lowfat ice cream yielded a 7 percent fat product. "This was lowfat according to Ben & Jerry's interpretation," said Peter Lind, the company's "primal ice cream therapist" (other companies called this research and development). The company did, however, develop a true lowfat frozen yogurt. The technical challenge for this was great, given B&J's requirement that the ingredients had to be easy to pronounce and not include "chemical sounding" words.

INDUSTRY LEADERS

Häagen-Dazs Co., whose parent company, Pillsbury, was in turn owned by the United Kingdom giant Grand Metropolitan PLC, set a course in the 1990s aimed at leaving the competition trailing. The company offered something for everyone in the frozen dessert segment: premium ice creams, frozen yogurt novelties on a stick, 98 percent fat-free frozen yogurts, and a new superpremium line of mix-in flavored frozen yogurts and ice creams that Häagen-Dazs dubbed Exträas. The new products were designed to meet increasingly stiff competition in the marketplace and to regain market share from Ben & Jerry's. Sales volume jumped 10 percent after the introduction of Exträas, and the company's market share jumped from 5.9 percent to 8.3 percent in just 12 weeks. Kate Boyle, marketing director of frozen novelties, said in *Dairy Foods* magazine that frozen yogurt stick bars were "somewhat of an afterthought." The afterthought had rewarding results. Overall, market sales of frozen yogurt novelties tripled after their introduction early in 1992, and Häagen-Dazs claimed 52 percent of that market niche.

Häagen-Dazs had taken its cue for mix-in flavored superpremium frozen yogurts from Ben & Jerry's Homemade, Inc., the successful Vermont ice cream maker. Ben & Jerry's is known for its social action programs as well as its unusual ice cream flavors. Their strategy of supporting charitable and political programs and introducing unique mix-in flavors paid off in 1992 with $6.7 million in profits, a 78 percent rise from the previous year, and nearly $132 million in sales, a 36 percent increase. In 1993, Ben & Jerry's followed its very successful vanilla-based Chocolate Chip Cookie Dough flavor with Peanut Butter Cookie dough and had ice cream lovers begging for more. Ben & Jerry's planned to increase its production capacity to 18 million gallons in 1993, up 63 percent, through co-packing agreements.

On the social action front, the company waived its usual $30,000 franchise free for a scoop shop in New York City's Harlem; 75 percent of the profits went to HARKhomes, an organization for homeless men, and the shop employed the homeless as well. Through the Children's Defense Fund, Ben & Jerry's also fought to give children's issues higher priority in the national agenda.

Dreyer's Grand Ice Cream of Oakland, California, with 1992 sales of $407 million, continued to expand its markets and its product line. Its acquisition of a New York dairy's premium ice cream brand and distribution brought it into the New York tri-state market, which includes New Jersey and Connecticut. The company also became the exclusive New York supermarket distributor for Dolly Madison ice creams and struck distribution agreements with Steve's Homemade Ice Cream, Inc. New products for the 1990s included low fat, sugar-free, and fat-free ice cream, Grand Delights frozen novelties, and a line of ice cream pies and mid-priced ice cream for food service companies. Additionally, Dreyer's and Ben & Jerry's were the only two companies that had mastered the art of making an ice cream stick bar with added-in chunks.

Gold Bond-Good Humor Ice Cream, a division of T. J. Lipton Co., specialized in high-sale frozen novelties. The company made up for the loss of its licensing rights to Walt Disney characters by acquiring the rights to Peanuts cartoon characters and launching a Snoopy ice cream bar. Gold Bond's plans included a full line of novelties, including a water ice Dinosaur Bar with a bubble gum ball in the center. The company's 1992 sales jumped from $200 million to $225 million.

Texas-based Blue Bell Creameries Inc. was a top-selling brand wherever it was sold. In 1992, the company was planning to expand its distribution into the Kansas/Missouri market and northern Florida. Blue Bell also looked to warehouse club stores for growth, and enjoyed considerable success with a family pack gallon of homemade vanilla ice cream. The company's $203 million in sales revenue in 1992, represented a 9.6 percent increase over the previous year.

Dannon, a subsidiary of BSN Groupe, a French company that in 1991 laid claim to being the world's largest dairy processor, introduced its first frozen yogurts in 1992. A leader in the U.S. refrigerated yogurt category, Dannon sent both sugar-free, nonfat products, and premium, full-fat, frozen yogurts to America's retail dairy cases. Frank Palantoni, Dannon's vice president for marketing, said in *Dairy Field* magazine, "In 1991, growth of frozen desserts was driven by frozen yogurt. [It was] up 26 percent." He added that, consistent with NYA guidelines, Dannon's frozen products would be "full of live active cultures . . . a true yogurt product."

WORK FORCE

Employment in the ice cream/frozen dessert industry declined slightly, from 20,700 in 1990 to a forecast of 20,100 in 1993. The lost jobs were apparently in management; the figure for production workers was expected to remain stable at 12,900. Production workers earned an average of $11.10 an hour in 1991, up 4.1 percent over the previous year. Although management salaries for the industry were undocumented, *Food Engineering* magazine's annual salary survey reported average 1992 increases of 4.7 percent.

AMERICA AND THE WORLD

The United States was the world's second largest ice cream exporter, sending 21,800 tons out of the country in 1991. This was a 76 percent increase over the previous year and three-and-a-half times the tonnage exported in 1988. Some of this share was taken from the European Community (EC). EC exports fell from 51 percent to 41 percent of the world total, and the U.S. share jumped from 13 percent to 27 percent. The value increase in that same period was over 700 percent, from $6,501,000 to $46,260,000, indicating the volume increase was higher in premium or superpremium products.

In terms of value, Japan led with imports of $13 million, followed by Mexico, then France and the United Kingdom (UK). The UK, France, and other European Community nations, however, were unlikely to continue importing premium ice cream at the same rate when the new Häagen-Dazs plant in France started production in 1992.

Worldwide production and consumption data for frozen dairy desserts were not very reliable, but based on available figures, the National Dairy Board estimated that the United States was by far the largest producer. Japan was the second largest producer, but its production was far less than that of the United States. The United States also led in per capita consumption, with Finland, New Zealand, and Australia close runners-up.

INDUSTRY INFORMATION SOURCES

Dexheimer, Ellen, et al. "Navigators of the '90s." *Dairy Foods*, April 1993.

Dillon, Patricia M. "Salary Survey: The High Price of an Average Raise." *Food Engineering*, December 1992.

Doeff, Gail Rosenbaum. "Competition for Ice Cream Distribution Heats Up." *Dairy Foods*, July 1993.

Dryer, Jerry. "Taking Lowfat Dairy Products Seriously." *Dairy Foods*, July 1993.

Fiscal Year 93 Market Development Plan. National Dairy Board.

Friday, Carolyn. "Cookies, Cream 'n' Controversy." *Newsweek*, July 5, 1993.

"Frozen Desserts Go Back to Basics With a Gusto." *Dairy Field*, December 1992.

Gerson, Vicki. "Fast and Furious." *Dairy Field*, March 1993.

Goerne, Carrie. "Häagen-Dazs Adds Flavors to Ice Its Superpremium Competitors." *Marketing News*, August 31, 1992.

Hui, Y. H., ed. "Ice Cream and Frozen Dessert," *Encyclopedia of Food Science and Technology*. 4 vols. New York: John Wiley & Sons, Inc., 1992.

Kimbrell, Wendy. "Healthy Culture." *Dairy Field*, April 1992.

"Land O'Lakes." *Results Technology*, February 1993.

"Market Stats and Data." *Dairy Field*, December 1992.

Milk Facts. Washington, DC: Milk Industry Foundation, 1992.

O'Donnell, Claudia Dziuk. "Cutting the Fat." *Dairy Foods*, July 1993.

———. "Benefiting from a Healthy Image." *Dairy Foods*, April 1993.

Ruland, Susan. "Exträa Energy." *Dairy Field*, September 1992.

U.S. Industrial Outlook 1993. Washington, DC: U.S. Department of Commerce, 1993.

—Mary Ratcliffe

SIC 2026

FLUID MILK

This industry encompasses establishments primarily engaged in processing fluid milk, cream and related products that included cottage cheese, yogurt (except frozen), and other cultured milk products.

INDUSTRY SNAPSHOT

The fluid milk industry is an important subsector of the nation's dairy business. In 1991, it accounted for 39.3 percent of all dairy industry sales: $24.7 billion out of a total of $62.8 billion for the entire dairy industry.

Fluid milk producers are often huge, sophisticated, diversified operations whose product lines cross industry boundaries. They manufactur and market a mix of fluid milk products, cheeses, ice creams, butter, dairy ingredients, and sometimes extensive lines of non-dairy products as well.

The 1990s brought a variety of changes and challenges for the industry. The pace of consolidation quickened. The number of dairy farms and dairy farm cooperatives was shrinking, and there were signs that the federal government would be reducing its price support role, forcing milk producers to deal with market fluctuations. In addition, although production was increasing, controversy concerning the introduction of scientific methodologies responsible for these increases was considerable. Consequently, the fragmented industry began an effort to pull together in order to address the changes on the horizon.

ORGANIZATION AND STRUCTURE

The highly regionalized fluid milk industry started on the dairy farm, where the raw milk was produced, and extended out to processors and manufacturing plants, which were owned by dairy farm cooperatives, general food processors, and even by supermarket chains that market out their own private label product lines. These processing plants made a variety of milk products destined for retail outlets, foodservice and institutional markets, and, to a lesser degree, other countries.

Milk is an extremely perishable commodity, and supply and demand can fluctuate unpredictably, depending on such variables as the output of individual cows, weather conditions, and even road conditions met by tank trucks. But, as pointed out in *Dairy Field* magazine by Don Blayney of the U.S. Department of Agriculture's (USDA) Agricultural Research Service, "Milk is produced every day. You can't store it on the farm. It has to move to someone who can do something with it."

In the 1990s, changes in the dairy industry were transforming the complex relationships between cooperatives and processors. Dairy cooperatives traditionally helped to reduce the impact of such fluctuations on milk handlers by coordinating supply arrangements and routing raw milk supplies not needed for fluid milk more efficiently. Dairy cooperatives that originated to represent the producers in price setting have in many cases taken over all stages of dairy operations, including: herd management and milking; management of

fluid milk supplies and surpluses; development of competitive new products; fluid milk processing; and the manufacture and marketing of a broad range of dairy products and ingredients.

Government pricing regulations were another means of insuring market stability. The government regulated milk pricing to farmers through Federal Milk Marketing Orders authorized by the Agricultural Marketing Act of 1937, or the Agricultural Act of 1949, which established the ongoing dairy price support program for areas where producers had agreed to abide by it. The pricing system was described in the *Wall Street Journal* as "so antiquated and complex that [it filled] three volumes of the Code of Federal Regulations." Supervised regionally by the USDA, prices were established geographically and according to the milk supply, fat content, weight, and the end use of the milk. From its inception, the support price fluctuated according to market conditions. In addition to the federal pricing structure, almost one-third of milk producing states also regulated milk pricing to farmers.

Milk Processing. Cow milk is the principal source of Americans' fluid milk supply. It contains about 87 percent water and 13 percent solids, which are comprised of solids-not-fat (SNF) and milk fat. Components of SNF are mostly protein (caseins and whey), lactose, and minerals important to human nutrition. An excellent source of calcium, phosphorous and vitamins A and B-2, and a good source of vitamins A, B-1 and B-12, milk's nutritional components earned it the label of "most perfect food." It is, however, a poor source for iron, copper, manganese, nicotinic acid, and vitamins C and D. Since the 1920s, most milk sold in the United States has been fortified with vitamin D.

Class I fluid milk meets strict standards, which include regular inspections of the herd and of herd housing facilities, dairy equipment, and milk storage units to insure that they satisfy health and sanitation requirements. It is used for human consumption or in manufactured milk products. Milk of manufacturing grade does not meet such strict standards and is priced lower than Class I milk.

In most dairy operations, raw milk is piped from a milking machine to a refrigerated bulk storage tank before it is transferred to a tank truck for delivery to a plant. There it undergoes the following processing operations:

Separation: The milk is split into cream (fat) and skim milk, and then cream is added back to the milk stream to achieve the desired fat content.

Pasteurization: The milk is heated to destroy pathogenic bacteria and other undesirable organisms that might lead to spoilage. In continuous high-temperature-short-time pasteurization (HTST), milk is heated to 161°F (72°C) for a minimum of 15 seconds. Since about 1970, ultrahigh temperature pasteurization (UHT), through which milk is heated at temperatures as high as 265°F (130°C) for three seconds, has been used with products such as heavy and light cream, and half-and-half. This process has extended their shelf life for several months.

Homogenization: This process breaks up the fat globules in milk, forming a stable emulsion that does not separate. Most fluid milk is homogenized.

Fresh Milk. The following products are included in the fresh milk category: whole milk, lowfat milk, skim or nonfat milk, cream, half-and-half, and buttermilk.

Whole milk contains not less than 3.25 percent milkfat and 8.25 percent SNF. Vitamins A and D may be added at levels of at least 2,000 International Units (IU) per quart for vitamin A and 400 IU for vitamin D. Flavoring ingredients may also be added. Lowfat milk contains milkfat at levels of 0.5, 1.5, or 2 percent, not less than 8.25 percent SNF, and at least 2,000 IU of vitamin A per quart. If vitamin D is added, it must be present at a level of 400 IU per quart. Flavoring ingredients are also permitted. Skim or nonfat milk contains less than 0.5 percent milkfat and not less than 8.25 percent SNF. It must contain 2,000 IU of vitamin A per quart. If vitamin D is added, it must be present at a level of 400 IU per quart. Flavoring ingredients are permitted.

Cream is made by separating out most of the skim milk and is rich in milkfat. Light (coffee) cream contains at least 18 percent and no more than 30 percent milk fat. Heavy (whipping) cream contains at least 36 percent milkfat. Half-and-half, a mixture of milk and cream, contains between 10.5 percent and 18 percent milkfat. It was often preferred over coffee cream for its lower fat and calorie content and lower cost. Buttermilk is a byproduct of churning cream into butter. Similar in composition to skim milk, it is condensed and dried for commercial use in baking and packaged cake mixes; it is not sold for consumption.

Cultured Milk Products. For centuries, people have known how to preserve the nutritional values of fresh milk for weeks or months by using bacterial cultures. Lactic-acid producing bacteria and certain characterizing ingredients may be added to fresh milk products and, depending on the level of milkfat, they may be labeled ''cultured buttermilk,'' ''cultured lowfat buttermilk,'' or ''cultured skim milk (or nonfat) buttermilk.'' Yogurt, sour cream, dry curd cottage cheese, and cottage cheese are included in the cultured milk products category.

Yogurt is made by culturing a mixture of milk and cream with lactic acid-producing bacteria, *Lactobacillus bulgaricus* and *Streptococcus thermophilus*, and contains not less than 3.25 percent milkfat and 8.25 percent SNF. Often sweeteners, flavorings, and other ingredients are added. Lowfat yogurt contains no more than 2 percent milkfat, and nonfat yogurt contains less than 0.5 percent milkfat. Sour cream results from the addition of lactic acid-producing bacteria to pasteurized cream containing not less than 18 percent milkfat.

Dry curd cottage cheese is made by adding either lactic-acid producing bacteria or acidifiers to skim milk and/or reconstituted nonfat dry milk. Rennet and/or other enzymes may also be added to help curd formation. The soft, unripened cheese contains less than 0.5 percent milkfat and no more than 80 percent moisture. Cottage cheese is made by the addition of a creaming mixture to dry curd cottage cheese. It contains at least 4 percent milkfat and no more than 80 percent moisture. Lowfat cottage cheese contains 2 percent or less milkfat and no more than 82.5 percent moisture.

BACKGROUND AND DEVELOPMENT

History. The first cows were landed at the Jamestown Colony in North America in 1611, and 13 years later, in 1624, cows were brought to Plymouth Colony. At that time, dairying was a family affair, and it was not until urbanization that dairy farms were established to supply nearby cities. In the industry's infancy, a large number of small, local producers provided the milk for their immediate areas. With the introduction of milk preservation and sanitation methods, it became possible for large dairy processors, often far removed from their raw milk sources, to supply ever more distant markets.

A creamery built in Goshen, Connecticut, in 1810, was one of the first formal business units established as a cooperative venture. Cooperative cheese rings and dairy cooperatives in eastern states soon followed, and the movement spread to Wisconsin and other midwestern states. It did not gain momentum, however, until after the Civil War, when the Grange and other farm organizations sponsored a number of experimental cooperatives. By 1900 there were approximately 1,000 farmer cooperatives. A period of dynamic growth occurred from 1915 to 1930 when cooperatives were placed under statute laws rather than common law. Passage of the Capper-Volstead Act in 1992 established the right of agricultural producers to band together in voluntary associations for their mutual benefit in collective processing, handling and marketing of agricultural products in interstate and foreign commerce.

In 1991 there were nearly 10 million dairy cows on cooperative farms or, on the increasingly rare, small and independent dairy farms, in the United States. They yielded an annual average of 14,867 pounds of milk per cow, for a total of 148,526 million pounds. *Holstein Association News* reported in 1993 that a 5-year-old cow, prophetically christened Royalty Maxima, had set a new world record by producing 58,952 pounds of milk, surpassing the previous record set in 1975. Breeding efficiency, the ability to improve the herds rapidly using artificial insemination techniques introduced in the 1940s, and the selection of superior sires, had brought milk production a long way from the mid-1800s, when cows produced an average of only 322 gallons annually.

Some milestones along the way: Louis Pasteur's experiments using heat to kill microorganisms in milk (1856); Gail Borden's first successful milk condensery in Burrville, Connecticut (1857); development of the milk bottle by Dr. Hervey D. Thatcher, Potsdam, New York (1884); introduction of tuberculin testing for dairy herds and the perfection, by Dr. S. M. Babcock, of a fat content test for milk and cream (1890); introduction of commercial pasteurizing machinery (1895); perfection of the automatic bottle filler and capper (1911); the first use of tank trucks for milk transport (1914); successful sale of homogenized milk in Torrington, Connecticut (1919); introduction of vitamin D-fortified milk (1932); perfection of a vacuum pasteurization process (1946); introduction of ultra-high temperature (UHT) pasteurization (1948); the start of nutrition labeling for fluid milk products (1974); widespread acceptance of UHT milks (1981); increased popularity of low fat and skim milk, with sales surpassing whole milk for the first time (1988); mandatory nutrition labeling under the Nutrition Labeling and Education Act (1991).

Record-breaking floods and drenching rains left tens of thousands of acres in the Mississippi River valley under water in the summer of 1993. Despite damage measured in tens of billions of dollars, it looked as if dairy farmers would be spared the worst of it. Minnesota farmers, for example, were unable to plant vast portions of acreage, but the cows responded to cooler-than-usual temperatures by giving more milk. A Land O'Lakes spokesman expected this to offset higher feed cost and increased risk of udder infections from the sloppy conditions.

Scandal in the Dairy Industry. Computerized bid-analysis techniques uncovered conspiracies in Florida in the mid-1980s, where the court said that illegal bid-rigging had raised the price of milk by as much as 14 percent. The U.S. Department of Justice and other states began their own investigations, and by mid-1987, signs of illegal bid-rigging extended into Georgia, Alabama, and Mississippi. Said Gina Talomona of the Justice Department in *The American School Board Journal*, these federal and state bid-rigging probes constituted the country's "biggest antitrust case in at least the last 10 years." The dollars involved were considerable. According to the Milk Industry Foundation, from 1981 to 1991 a steady 7 percent of fluid milk sales had been to schools. Fines and settlements had come to more than $100 million by 1993.

Even as investigations and prosecutions proceeded, a report from the General Accounting Office (GAO) criticized the government for its share of responsibility for the schemes. Once bid-rigging had been discovered, said the GAO, the USDA had the authority to halt federal funding to companies found guilty of bid-rigging and to bar their future participation in the federally financed programs. Under federal marketing and price-support programs, moreover, dairies were aware of competitors' minimum prices, creating a situation that provided opportunities for collusion.

The USDA countered that debarment of private companies was inappropriate if the companies paid the penalties imposed and satisfied the federal agencies that the problems leading to the problem had been solved.

Controversy. Monopolistic practices and political contributions have been the main controversies attached to dairy co-ops. Consumer advocate Ralph Nader accused the three largest dairy co-ops, Associated Milk Producers, Inc. (AMPI), Dairymen, Inc., and Mid-America Dairymen, Inc. (Mid-Am) of illegal contributions totaling $422,000 to President Richard Nixon's re-election campaign in order to influence the administration to enact higher price supports (enacted in 1971) and to drop antitrust suits against the three co-ops.

Eventually, AMPI pleaded guilty to having made illegal contributions in 1968, 1970, and 1970. This, however, was not the end of AMPI's legal battles; in 1989 the U.S. Supreme Court upheld an appeals court ruling, filed in 1971 by the National Farmers' Organization (NFO), which determined that AMPI had conspired to eliminate competitive milk producers.

CURRENT CONDITIONS

After decades of backing the industry through price support programs and the purchase of surpluses, the federal government was gradually reducing its role, although no one was predicting the elimination of supports in the near future. As with many issues in the dairy industry, opinions were divided as to whether supports protected the dairy farmers or whether a free market would serve them better.

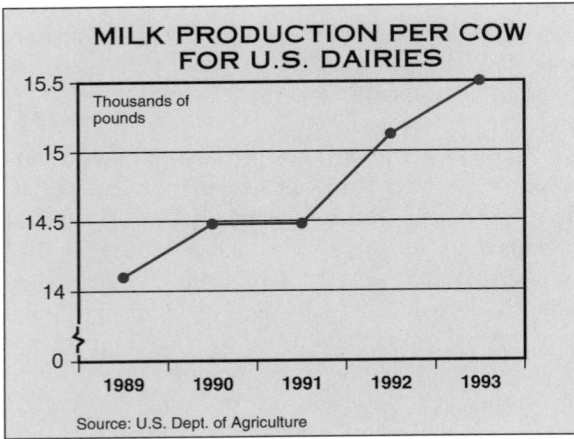

MILK PRODUCTION PER COW FOR U.S. DAIRIES

Source: U.S. Dept. of Agriculture

In the early 1990s, industry analysts forecasted that fluid milk sales were likely to drop between 1 and 1.5 percent annually. According to a 1992 *Supermarket Business* magazine Consumer Expenditures Study, sales declined in every major milk product except yogurt, which posted a 5.8 percent gain. The figures illustrated the trend reported by the Milk Industry Foundation (MIF), which said that from 1974 to 1991, total fluid milk product sales (plain whole milk, lowfat milk, skim milk, flavored milk and drinks, and buttermilk) had risen a scant 0.05 percent, from 52,476 million pounds to 55,227 pounds. Sales of whole milk had plummeted 43.7 percent in that period, from 36,765 million pounds to 20,680 pounds, while lowfat milk sales had jumped from 9,763 to 25,221 million pounds.

Consumers' health concerns about fat in the diet presented opportunities for the introduction of flavorful low-fat and skim milk products, and dairy companies were working to improve the taste of these products in order to compete with non-dairy beverages: soft drinks, bottled waters, beer, juices, sports drinks.

Per capita sales from 1974 to 1991 dropped 10.6 percent, from 245.9 pounds to 219.0 for all milk products, and from 172.3 to 82.0 for whole milk. During the same period, lowfat milk sales more than doubled, from 45.8 to 100.0 pounds per capita.

Dairy Field magazine quoted a report by Bozell Worldwide consultants with even worse statistics for the industry. The report detailed a 23 percent drop in per capita drop milk consumption was reported for the 35 years from 1955 to 1990, and noted a dramatic drop in milk drinking after age 17 at a time when 64 percent of the U.S. population was 25 or older. Still, nearly 95 percent of American households purchased milk, usually from supermarkets, where milk posted 1991 sales of nearly $6.8 billion and accounted for 31.06 percent of dairy case sales. It was the most frequently purchased supermarket item for the year ending March 1992, just ahead of bread.

Nevertheless, milk's image as the most perfect and nutritionally complete food was slipping. Studies linked it to diabetes and certain infant allergies. Consumers also expressed concern about the fat in milk, although a 1990 Pennsylvania State University study found that more than half of the survey's respondents didn't know the fat content of whole and skim milks, and 40 percent didn't know the fat content of lowfat milk. Even those who thought they knew milk's fat content tended to overstate it. A National Dairy Board study found that many Americans believed, erroneously, that reducing fat content also depleted milk's nutrients.

Facing slow sales growth and virtually no increase in consumption, fluid milk producers began to take aggressive steps to improve the industry's outlook. A combination of consumer education, advertising and promotion, and consumer-responsive new products were seen as imperatives to restoring consumer demand for and confidence in fluid milk and fluid milk products.

In 1993, the Milk Industry Foundation (MIF) took steps to set up a fund for a $55-million national consumer education program, the only strategy on which the fragmented industry was likely to unite. The money was to come from an assessment on Class I fluid milk sales. Said Bill Tinklepaugh, MIF vice president, in *Dairy Field* magazine, "Although the 1990 Farm Bill authorized a national advertising program, here we are in 1992 still trying to build a coalition of support for any program. That's because milk processors have so many divergent points of view." Howard Dean, chairman and chief executive officer of Dean Foods Co. and 1991-92 MIF chairman, said in the same article, ". . . we've never been able to get our act together and coordinate the industry."

As sales of fluid milk flattened out and cottage cheese sales plunged in the 1980s, sales of cultured milk products increased.

Yogurt sales soared by 88 percent, from 583 to 1,098 million pounds, from 1980 to 1991, and sour cream and dips jumped 61 percent, from 408 to 657 million pounds, in that same period. Growing popularity of ethnic foods, especially Mexican, in the late 1980s and early 1990s, spurred growth in the $750 million sour cream and dip market. Combined sales of cultured products reached $4 billion in 1991.

In 1992 the International Dairy Foods Association predicted that the number of fluid processing plants would decrease by as much as a third, to under 400, by the year 2000. They foresaw 90,000 dairy farms (in 1954, there had been 1,475,000) and 8.5 million cows, each producing an annual average of 18,000 pounds of milk for a total of 157 million pounds. Top dairy co-op executives expected that the number of national cooperatives would drop to four or five.

The industry appeared poised in the last decade of the twentieth century to tackle changes in the fluid milk market in united fashion and form a probable position of financial strength. On the heels of depressed profitability in 1990, Dun & Bradstreet reported median ratios on industry profitability in 1991 that showed a strong comeback: returns on sales were 1.6 percent in 1991, following a drop from 1.0 in 1989 to 0.8 percent in 1990; returns on assets were 5.3 percent, up from 1990's 2.9 percent; and returns on net worth were 12.5 percent, up from 7.4 percent in 1990. A return on net worth of 10 percent is generally considered desirable to provide for both dividends and future growth.

INDUSTRY LEADERS

The two major producers in the fluid milk industry were representative of the food industry as a whole in that their manufacturing activities were not limited to a single SIC category. Borden, Inc., which in the early 1990s was the leading maker of fluid milk products, was also a leading manufacturer of pastas and chemical adhesives. Dean Foods, second only to Borden, also made vegetable products.

Borden, Inc. Incorporated in 1899, this venerable U.S. company was founded by Gail Borden in the mid-nineteenth century, when it introduced condensed milk. By 1875 the company was producing fresh milk, which it sold door-to-door in New York City. Despite steady expansion into other food and chemical product lines, until 1956 management focus remained on the dairy business. Over the years, the company grew and prospered through a policy of aggressive acquisition.

In the late 1980s and early 1990s, the industry giant embarked on a major restructuring and consolidation of its business, including its dairy operations. Between 1988 and 1991, the company closed 15 dairy plants and sold off five more while folding its Dairy Division into its Grocery Products Division. Withdrawal from the fluid milk and cultured products markets in the East and Southeast was announced in 1989, due to market overcrowding and low profits. Borden continued to market its milk in southern, western and midwest states. The company also announced record capital expenditures for what it called "hyperplants." Three of the 11 planned state-of-the-art, high efficiency, mostly large-scale manufacturing facilities were slated to make dairy products.

Throughout this restructuring process, Borden, continued to hold the number one position in the dairy industry, even as its dairy business shrank. The company reported a $21.4 million operating loss in its dairy operations for 1992, compared to operating income of $85 million in 1991. The difference was attributed to the high cost of raw milk and the $47.3 million reorganization costs. At the same time, the company posted $1.5 billion in total dairy sales, a 1.5 percent increase and 25 percent of the company's 1992 income. "We probably don't have as much of a battle overcoming the commodity image of milk as many of our competitors do," said company spokesman John Rutan in *Dairy Field* magazine. "We have very strong regional brand equities . . . We're the #1 or #2 brand in all the markets we participate in." Borden planned in 1992 to reenforce its brand name with their Elsie the Cow trademark as advertising "spokescow." Elsie was also scheduled to make a strong reappearance on product packaging. Although she had been out of the limelight for nearly 20 years, Borden said more than half of all American adults still recognized Elsie.

Dean Foods. With 6 percent of the total market and sales of $1.1 billion in 1992, Dean Foods was catching up to Borden. The company appeared to be recovering from a slump that came after 40 years of uninterrupted earnings growth. Dean's 21 milk processing plants bought raw milk directly from farmers and processed it into skim milk, half-and-half, whipping cream, yogurt, sour cream, buttermilk, and cottage cheese. Typically, some 75 percent of plant output was marketed to supermarkets and other retail food outlets within a 250-mile radius of the plant. The rest was supplied to restaurants, hotels, schools, hospitals, military installations, and fast food chains. Industrial sales accounted for a relatively small portion of Dean's business.

The company's strategy for decades had been growth through acquisition, a policy Dean planned to continue through the 1990s as milk consumption flattened. Typically, Dean sought to purchase larger dairies with sales in the $25 million to $80 million dollar range, often retaining their strong regional brand names. In 1993 the company entered into negotiations to purchase the Flav-O-Rich, Inc. fluid milk and ice cream business. Flav-O-Rich, which operated nine fluid milk plants in the southeastern United States and had 1992 sales of approximately $400 million, was the milk-processing subsidiary of Dairymen, Inc., one of the country's largest dairy cooperatives. Dean was also looking to Mexico for growth. With half of the country's population under 18, the prime age group for milk drinking, and a chronic shortage of fresh milk, Mexico was an attractive new market for expansion.

Despite its emphasis on acquisitions, half of the company's growth over 20 years could be attributed to expanding markets and new product introductions. In 1992 the company continued to extend its line of lowfat products.

Cooperatives. The largest cooperative in the United States, the San Antonio-based Associated Milk Producers, Inc. (AMPI), was planning a reorganization of its management structure to allow it to react more quickly to the changes in consumer demands, milk supplies, and market opportunities. The co-op had registered 16,321 member farms in 20 states in 1991.

Other cooperatives were developing new strategies to deal with changing market conditions. Mid-America Dairymen, Inc. (Mid-Am), one of the largest of the dairy co-ops, with $1.85 billion in 1992 sales, said that approximately 50 percent of its milk production was sold as fluid milk. Mid-Am entered into joint ventures with other co-ops and processors and also bought into an independent dairy company, which handled no Mid-Am milk at all. The co-op's fluid milk operations were turned over to Prairie Farms, an Illinois cooperative, which managed Mid-Am plants profitably, something which had eluded Mid-Am, without sharing ownership in them.

Dairymen's sale of its Flav-O-Rich subsidiary, if successful, would take it out of the milk-processing business; it would revert to a raw-milk cooperative supplying other processors, including Dean. The sale would also catapult Dean Foods into the leading position in the dairy industry, over Borden.

Leaders in the burgeoning refrigerated yogurt category were Dannon, with close to a 33 percent market share and 1992 sales of $388.3 million, up 13.8 percent over 1991, and the General Mills subsidiary Yoplait, with its 17.8 percent market share and 1992 sales of $210.5 million. Private label brands ranked third in 1992, with sales of $153.3 million and a 13.3 percent market share.

WORK FORCE

Employment in the fluid milk industry declined 18 percent, from 84,000 to 69,000 jobs, from 1982 to 1991, according to the Bureau of the Census and MIF estimates. The number of production workers in the industry dropped from 37,900 to 33,400, while their wages rose from $693 million to $892 million. The average annual compensation for a production worker rose from $18,285 in 1982 to $26,707 in 1991.

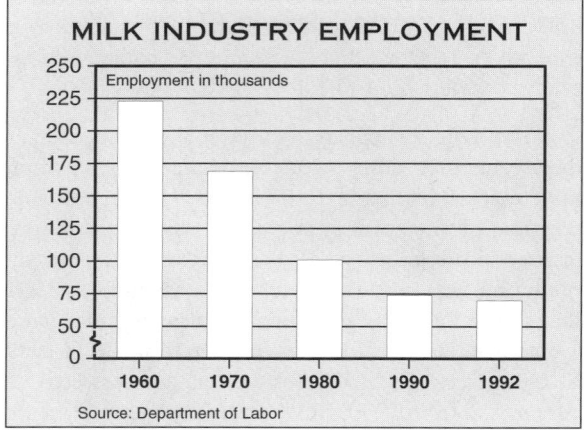

MILK INDUSTRY EMPLOYMENT
Employment in thousands
Source: Department of Labor

Jobs in the dairy industry which required a college degree included farm and processing plant management, quality control, and research. Training for herd management, milk production, processing, distribution, and sales could be obtained from secondary and vocational schools.

Many food industry companies were restructuring and reducing personnel in the early 1990s in response to the overall economic recession. Most of the job losses between 1991 and 1992 were in the supervisory (28.8 percent) and middle management (26.6 percent) areas; only 8.1 percent of professional/technical positions were lost.

AMERICA AND THE WORLD

NAFTA. The North American Free Trade Agreement (NAFTA) will do away with existing tariffs and other barriers to trade among the United States, Canada, and Mexico for the next fifteen years, creating the world's largest consumer market, with a population of more than 360 million people and a combined economy of nearly $6.5 trillion. Negotiations for the agreement concluded in 1992, and the legislation was passed by the U.S. Congress late in 1993.

The International Dairy Foods Association predicted that the treaty would be of overall benefit to the U.S. dairy industry, including the fluid milk sector. With or without NAFTA, Mexico was seen as a potential growth area by the dairy industry. Mexico, which had been a major importer of dry milk and cheese products, had also increased its imports of such fresh dairy products as fluid milk and yogurt. The impact of the treaty on dairymen was likely to be less in Canadian trade.

The opportunities NAFTA would create for fluid milk products in Mexico in the 1990s also presented many challenges for U.S. companies. Only about half of Mexico's households had refrigerators. Moreover, Mexican consumers often bought their food at small neighborhood stores that also had little refrigeration. Even some of the better equipped supermarkets turned off their electricity overnight. Quality controls for dairy products in Mexico were also much less stringent than those in the United States. As much as 40 percent of Mexican-produced milk went straight from the cow to the consumer, without being pasteurized.

Europe. The introduction of milk quotas to curtail surplus milk production in 1984, under the European Commission's Common Agriculture Policy (CAP), had apparently backfired by the 1990s. Production efficiency was suffering and competition was down. The industry was becoming polarized, as large producers were growing in size and smaller companies found it increasingly difficult to survive. Restrictive quotas also had an impact on available milk volumes in the domestic market. Processors, if they were strong enough, could purchase dairies in new markets to assure raw milk supply. Those unable to do this were threatened with takeover. Buying power, too, was becoming concentrated in a small number of powerful and aggressive retailing groups. The large, well-established international dairy suppliers were able to stand up to their demands, but smaller, national producers were at risk.

World Milk Production. There was very little international trade of fluid milk in the early 1990s. According to a National Dairy Board (NDB) market development plan for 1993, there was no change in the average rate of worldwide milk production from 1987 to 1991, but there was a significant drop in production in the USSR and Eastern Europe after the disintegration of communist rule. Much of the NDB data was drawn from the Foreign Agricultural Service (FAS) Dairy Livestock, Dairy and Poultry Division (DLP), so it does not include data from non-reporting countries.

The world's largest milk producer was the European Community, with an estimated production of 112.9 million tons in 1992. The USSR followed, with an estimated production of 95 million tons, and the United States ranked third, with an estimated 1992 production of 68.2 million tons. Worldwide, a production decline of 1 percent from 1991 to 1992 was predicted. Long range trends indicated that large, populous developing nations like Mexico, India, and China would increase their production capabilities.

RESEARCH AND TECHNOLOGY

Bovine Growth Hormone. There was consternation and divided opinion among dairy farmers and processors in the late 1980s and early 1990s on how, and whether, they would make use of bovine somatotropine (BST), even though it had been found safe for human consumption by the National Institutes of Health. The genetically engineered version of a hormone that occurs naturally in cows increases milk production by as much as 15 percent. Marketed by its producer, Monsanto, under the trade name Posilac, proponents argue that milk from BST-treated cows is indistinguishable from those produced by ordinary cows. Critics, however, note that cows that have been treated with BST (or BGH-bovine growth hormone, as its also known) are more likely to contract mastitis, an udder infection.

Approved by the U.S. Food and Drug Administration (FDA) only recently, the hormone was the subject of labeling debate as well. If milk products produced from BST-treated cows had to be labeled as such, it would open the door to similar requirements for other undisclosed substances in foods, such as pesticides and antibiotic residues.

INDUSTRY INFORMATION SOURCES

Baker, Stephen, and Lois Therrien. "Market Share Con Leche?" *Business Week/Reinventing America,* 1992.

Borden, Inc. "A History of Borden, Inc." Borden, Inc., (June 1992).

Bradley, Jr., Robert L. "Milk." *The Encyclopedia Americana International Edition,* 30 vols. Danbury, CT: Grolier Incorporated, 1991.

Burros, Marion. "Eating Well." *The New York Times* (May 12, 1993).

Calbert, Harold E. "Dairy Industry." *The Encyclopedia Americana International Edition,* 30 vols. Danbury, CT: Grolier Incorporated, 1991.

Campbell, Alta, Gary Hoover, and Patrick J. Spain, eds. *Hoover's Handbook of American Business 1993.* , TX: The Reference Press, Inc., 1992.

Considine, Douglas M., P.E., ed.-in-chief. *Foods and Food Production Encyclopedia.* New York: Van Nostrand Reinhold Company, 1982.

Corbett, David. "Milk Quotas - Benefit or Constraint?: Why a Common Agricultural Polich?" *British Food Journal* 94, No. 5, (1992).

Dairy Field. "NAFTA Negotiations Conclude; Dairy Industry Should Profit." (October, 1992).

Doeff, Gail Rosenbaum. "Cultured Comeback." *Dairy Foods* (April, 1993).

Dexheimer, Ellen. "Dean Dynasty." *Dairy Foods*, (November, 1991).

Dillon, Patricia M., Christopher Glenn, Leticia Mancini, and Charles E. Morris. "State of the Food Industry." *Food Engineering* (May, 1993).

Elmer-Dewitt, Philip, "Brave New World of Milk," *Time* (February 14, 1994): 31.

Feder, Barnaby J. "Beyond the Flood, Farmers Worry about Drought and an Early Frost." *The New York Times* (July 31, 1993).

Gatty, Bob. "The Regulatory Web." *Dairy Field* (April, 1993).

Gerson, Vicki and Susan Ruland. "Pouring It On." *Dairy Field* (November, 1992).

Getler, Warren, and Scott Kilmant. "Cheddar Lovers May Take a Slice of These Futures." *Wall Street Journal* (January 14, 1993).

Harbrecht, Douglas, William C. Symonds, and Geri Smith. "Why NAFTA Just Might Squeak Through." *Business Week* (August 30, 1993).

Henriques, Diana B. "Evidence Mounts of Rigged Bidding in Milk Industry." *The New York Times* (May 23, 1993).

Janis, William V. "Dairy Products." *U.S. Industrial Outlook.* Washington, DC: U.S. Department of Commerce, 1992.

Kimbrell, Wendy. "Fresh Focus." *Dairy Foods* (July, 1992).

"Market Stats and Data." *Dairy Field* (December, 1992).

Mid-American Dairymen, Inc. "News Update." *Mid-Am Reporter* (April, 1993).

————. "Mid-Am Resolutions." *Mid-Am Reporter* (April, 1993).

Milk Industry Foundation. *Milk Facts.* Washington, D.C.: Milk Industry Foundation, 1992.

"Milk Sales Inch On in the Face of Misconceptions." *Dairy Field* (December, 1992).

National Dairy Board. *NDB FY 93 Market Development Plan.*

Otolski, Greg. "Dairymen Hopes to Sell Flav-O-Rich to Dean Co." *The Courier Journal* (Louisville, KY), (June 10, 1993).

Palmer, Jay. "Growing Again." *Barron's* (July 6, 1992).

Pehanich, Mike. "Quality to the Core." *Dairy Foods* (November, 1991).

Progressive Grocer. "The 1992 Supermarket Sales Manual," (July, 1992).

Rist, Marilee C. "Cheating the Children." *The American School Board Journal* (May, 1993).

Rogers, Paul. "To BST or not to BST. . . ." *Dairy Foods* (July, 1993).

Salvage, Bryan. "Private Label Renaissance." *Dairy Field* (August, 1992).

Schmidt, Peter. "G.A.O. Says U.S. May Have Aided Milk Bid-rigging Schemes." *Education Week* (December 2, 1992).

Sole, Catherine. "The Changing Structure of Retailing: Consequent Impact on Players in the Dairy Industry." *British Food Journal* 94, No. 5, (1992).

"Some Cultured Products Experienced New Vitality." *Dairy Field* (December, 1992).

Wagner, Jim. "Borden: One Company, One R&D." *Dairy Field* (July, 1992).

—Mary Ratcliffe

SIC 2032

CANNED SPECIALTIES

This category covers establishments primarily engaged in canning specialty products, such as baby foods, nationality specialty foods, and soups, except seafood.

INDUSTRY SNAPSHOT

In 1990 the value of shipments in SIC 2032 was $5.2 billion and expected to rise only moderately over the next three years, with shipments of $5.3 billion forecast for 1992. Soup led the category in sales, with condensed soup in the position of best-selling canned food item on the shelf.

ORGANIZATION AND STRUCTURE

The canned specialties industry employed 23,900 workers in 1990, and compensation totaled $735.5 million. As is true with most industries, companies shipped products in more than one SIC category as well as generating additional income from other activities. Shipments classified under SIC 2032 totaled $4.1

billion, while secondary shipments came to $1.2 billion, and miscellaneous receipts were $105.4 million. Thus the specialization ratio, that is, the value of primary products compared to the total of primary, secondary, and miscellaneous income, was 78 percent. Geographically, California, Ohio, Pennsylvania, and Texas led in the number of people employed; the same states had led the 1982 census.

BACKGROUND AND DEVELOPMENT

Cans have unquestioned advantages as food containers. Hermetically sealed, they protect their contents from contamination by microorganisms or foreign matter as well as prevent undesirable fluctuations in moisture content, the absorption of oxygen, gases, or undesirable odors, and exposure to light. In addition, they allow for high-speed filling, sealing, and casing. Retailers can display them easily and attractively. For the consumer, their storage convenience is an added advantage.

Compared to other methods of food preservation, canning is a recent development. Freezing goes back to the ice ages, and even smoking and drying were used before recorded history. Canning did not come along until the first quarter of the nineteenth century.

Nicholas Appert, a French confectioner and chef, theorized in 1795 that if food is heated in a container with no air in it, the food will keep. He worked on his theorem for 14 years, cooking foods in cork-stoppered bottles in boiling water. Sent around the world on sailing ships, Appert's preserved fruits and vegetables remained wholesome. Eventually an English merchant, Peter Durand, would develop the use of tin canisters in 1810.

The first U.S. patent for tin containers was granted in 1825. At first, cans were made by hand; even an expert in the process could turn out only five or six in an hour. The term canning came to mean sterilizing food by heat and sealing it in airtight containers, either metal or glass, at an individual's home or in a processing plant.

The Civil War accelerated the need for canned foods, and by the war's end production of canned foods had increased six times, and Americans had learned to trust them. The importance of canned foods to the military was underscored again during World War II, when two-thirds of the food supplies for the U.S. and Allied forces came in cans. When the Japanese capture of Malaya cut off important sources of tin, conservation of the metal in the United States became critical. At the same time, glass containers, which had always been used for some foods, were used to replace tin cans.

CURRENT CONDITIONS

Canned Soups. "Healthy" was the hot word in canned soups in the early 1990s. There were 265 new soup products introduced in 1991, and the majority of them bore the word "healthy." Campbell Soup Company, long the industry leader, launched eleven new soups under its Healthy Request label. Almost simultaneously, ConAgra, Inc., entered the arena with its Healthy Choice line of soups. Even with no experience in soups, ConAgra, the second-largest food company in the country, was optimistic about its low-sodium, low-fat, low-cholesterol product.

Campbell Soup countered with a 41 percent increase in its advertising budget to a hefty $82 million and also lowered the fat and cholesterol content of its low-sodium Special Request soups. David A. Weiss, president of the New York-based market research firm Packaged Facts, was quoted in *Frozen Food Digest* as saying, "If [ConAgra is] planning on just rolling over Campbell, I know some people from Brooklyn who'd like to sell them a bridge."

Pet, Inc., maker of Progresso soups, lowered salt in its Sodium Watch Soups, while Pritikin Systems, a division of Quaker Oats, put out a line of Healthy Soups. Pet's Progresso brand continued to capitalize on eating trends in the 1990s with six new ready-to-serve canned soups, which contained pasta combined with a flavorful broth and plenty of vegetables. Campbell Soup Company added Dinosaur Vegetable and Souper Stars soups targeted to children.

Soup is an economical, versatile food service item. As canned soups improved in terms of fresh appearance and flavor, and formulations perceived as healthier (i.e., low-sodium, low-fat, no-MSG) were put on the market, they were more appealing than ever. The canned soup market is huge, comprising commercial outlets, including restaurants, cafeterias, fast-food chains, and non-commercial institutions, such as schools, hospitals, the military.

Baby Foods. Makers of baby foods launched 95 new products in 1991. The three-fold increase over 1990 was due to a mini baby boom, according to Peter Allen of FIND/SVP, a New York City market research company. Gerber Products Company, the leader in the category, introduced new vegetable and meat combinations and a line of Tropical Baby Foods targeting the Hispanic market. Beech-Nut, a division of St. Louis, Missouri-based Ralston-Purina, addressed consumer health concerns about chemical and pesticide residues with its 22-item Special Harvest line of fruits, vegetables, cereals, dinners, and juices from organic sources. H.J. Heinz Company weighed in with grape and pear/grape juices. By 1992 baby food sales in the United States reached nearly $1.1 billion, and per capita consumption during a child's first 12 months were reported at 612 jars, or 11.8 jars a week.

Ethnic Foods. As discounted and private label products, as well as new products geared toward niche markets, crowded supermarket shelves in the 1990s, many famous old brands began to disappear. La Choy and Chun King were typical of threatened brands, with competition coming from the increasing availability of fresh Chinese food. The volume of supermarket sales in 1992 was down by more than 12 percent from the previous year.

Campbell Soup Company staged a turnaround for its Spaghettios, sold under its Franco-American label, when the company became concerned that the product was being used as a generic term for any canned, shaped spaghetti. Campbell Soup obtained the license for the popular Where's Waldo cartoon character and created colorful labeling that emphasized its new mascot and reduced the prominence of the Franco-American name.

Canned Gravy. In a departure from its usual brand delineations, Campbell Soup Company in 1992 launched a line of bottled gravies in seasoned turkey, hearty beef, mushroom and wine, and golden chicken varieties under its Pepperidge Farm label. After considering its Campbell's and Franco-American brands, the company chose Pepperidge Farm, explained Campbell Soup manager of communications Judy Dagnoli in *Supermarket News,* "because it communicates authenticity, taste and high quality. Although it's 98 percent fat free, we also wanted to communicate the fact that it tastes really, really good." Campbell Soup Company was so confident that it did not even test market the product before rolling it out nationally. (Pepperidge Farm, a Campbell Soup brand usually reserved for baked goods, also offered a line of exotic canned soups in such flavors as bacon, lettuce, and tomato.)

Early in 1993, Heinz introduced a peppery, milk- and cream-based HomeStyle Gravy. The company promoted it with regional events and endorsements from local radio personalities in 37 markets, a strategy designed to "really get down to the personal level with consumers," noted Tom Becker, the associate product manager for the gravy in *Food Business.*

In summary, despite reduced sales in many canned food items, soup saw increased dollar volumes from 1992 supermarket sales, and industry leaders continued to extend their soup product lines. Baby food, too, showed respectable gains, but it was the canned gravy segment of the category that surged, with sales jumping 17 percent over the previous year. With the U.S. market for canned foods maturing, little growth was expected for domestic sales. Canned soups, though, were projected to increase at a rate of 5 to 6 percent annually from 1992 to 1996. Many companies looked overseas for future growth.

INDUSTRY LEADERS

Campbell Soup Company. The undisputed leader of the industry in the 1990s and indeed throughout its long history, Campbell Soup Company was selling 5 billion cans of soup a year, or close to half of all soup sales in a $2 billion market. Founded in 1869 by Joseph Campbell, a fruit merchant, and Abram Anderson, an ice box manufacturer, the company in 1992 ranked number ten among U.S. food manufacturers, with sales of $6,263 million and a 15 percent increase in operating income over the previous year.

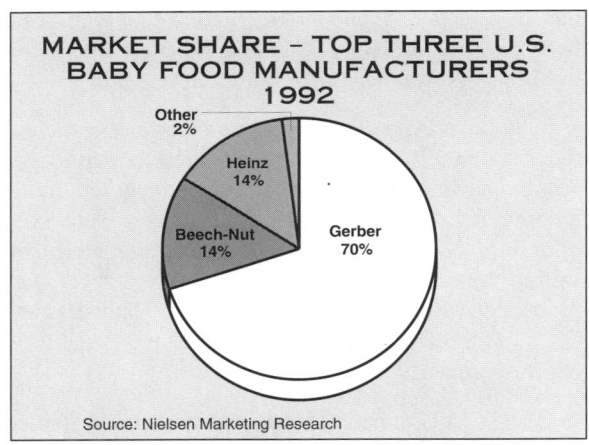

MARKET SHARE – TOP THREE U.S. BABY FOOD MANUFACTURERS 1992

Other 2%
Heinz 14%
Beech-Nut 14%
Gerber 70%

Source: Nielsen Marketing Research

Perhaps no event in the Campbell Soup Company's long history was more momentous than the arrival in 1897 of a 24-year-old chemist, Dr. John T. Dorrance, who signed on at a salary of $7.50. When he died 33 years later, he was sole owner of the Campbell Soup Company and had amassed a personal fortune of $115 million, an amount equal to $850 million in 1991.

Young Dorrance was a man with an idea: condensed soup. When he joined Campbell Soup Company, soup was sold in 32-ounce cans for about 30 cents. Since soup was made mostly of water, Dorrance reasoned, the removal of water would save on shipping, cans, and weight. Dorrance introduced condensed soups in ten and a half ounce cans selling for 10 cents. To win over consumers who tended not to trust the quality of such a low-cost product, he spent heavily on advertising and promotion. In 1990 Campbell produced its 20 billionth can of condensed tomato soup.

Campbell Soup Company's marketing high points include the 1904 introduction of the enduring image of the Campbell kids, created by Philadelphia artist Grace Gebbie Drayton. In the 1930s, the slogan ''M'm! M'm! Good!'' entered the nation's consciousness when Campbell sponsored the ''Amos 'n' Andy'' and the George Burns and Gracie Allen radio shows.

Gerber. A symbol of quality and trust, the Gerber baby was adopted as an official trademark in 1931, three years after Fremont Canning Company of Fremont, Michigan, began pureeing foods for babies. Commercial artist Dorothy Hope Smith created the unfinished charcoal sketch of a neighbor's child, who was the first Gerber baby.

Sales figures in the 1990s continued to support Gerber Products' dominance in baby food; it held a 72 percent share of the market. The highly focused company ranked number 41 among U.S. food manufacturers in 1992, with food sales up 23 percent over the previous year, from $707 million to $866 million. Being almost synonymous with baby food in the minds of American consumers, however, had occasional drawbacks. When it was revealed that competitor Beech-Nut was marketing an apple juice product without real juice, Gerber too lost sales.

AMERICA AND THE WORLD

NAFTA. The controversial North American Free Trade Agreement (NAFTA) did away with tariffs and other barriers to trade between the United States, Canada and Mexico for 15 years, creating the world's largest consumer market, with a population of more than 360 million people and a combined economy close to $6.5 trillion. Negotiations concluded in 1992, and by the end of 1993 the governments of the three nations had ratified the agreement. Even before a heated debate led to U.S. ratification of NAFTA in November of 1993, though, the country's food companies were becoming active in Mexico and Canada. Campbell Soup Company went so far as to reorganize the company, combining its North and South American units into one division.

Gerber in Poland. With its $25 million acquisition in 1991 of Alima S.A., a Polish infant food and juice company, Gerber ventured into the untapped Eastern European market. The venture presented hurdles, not all of them anticipated. Polish mothers were accustomed to making their own baby food, for example,

and distribution to small stores via treacherous roads was not as smooth as delivering to U.S. supermarkets. Production workers had to be trained in U.S. quality control standards.

Campbell Soup Company in a Global Market. When David Johnson became president and chief executive officer of Campbell Soup, his first moves were to refocus the company on the home front. By 1993 the company was ready to expand on a grander scale into the global marketplace. The purchase of Australian manufacturer Arnotts had given Campbell a Pacific base from which to penetrate China and the rest of the burgeoning Far East market. Campbell was already selling soup in China, South America, and Poland. Nevertheless, exports accounted for only 5 percent of the company's soup sales. Management proposed to capitalize on the lucrative potential in Poland, where per capita consumption of soup was 2.5 times more than in the United States, with exports of eight soup varieties then being manufactured at its Maxton, North Carolina, plant.

Heinz a Top Seller Overseas. After more than a century doing business in the United Kingdom, Heinz was hit hard by the recession in the early 1990s. Its best known product was baked beans, followed by baby food. ''In Third World countries,'' commented Barry Tilley, general manager of the company's Western Hemisphere Trading Division, in *Prepared Foods* magazine, ''baby food would top the list.'' Heinz still held 58 percent of the £208.4 million canned soup market, but that category was gradually shrinking. Only premium soups were experiencing growth, and Heinz sought to protect and revitalize its position with the introduction of a new, ''almost'' premium soup line, HJ Heinz.

Like many other companies in the years just after the breakdown of the Cold War, Heinz was looking to China and Russia to expand its global marketing activities, especially its baby food line. Tilley remarked, ''Heinz is building a platform at an early stage with baby food. Mothers today feed their babies Heinz baby food and then move onto other Heinz products. It's a natural progression.''

RESEARCH AND TECHNOLOGY

Processing. Technological advances in the canning industry accelerated after the Civil War. The invention of the retort, or pressure cooker, in 1874 made it possible to control cooking temperatures for the sealed cans. The invention of the so-called sanitary can in the early 1900s was another important technological advance. The new, cylindrical can had an open top, enabling canners to deposit larger food pieces without the damage that occurred when filling the old hole-and-cap can. The lid for the new can could be attached mechanically, and without the solder seal coming into contact with the food.

Near the end of the twentieth century, when consumers were concerned about lead in food, tin replaced lead in soldering. Other packaging developments included the flexible pouch for low-acid foods and cans made of aluminum and of steel.

Product Development. At Campbell Soup, research and development concentrated on products. ''Fat is our No. 1 area of concern,'' noted Herb Baum, then president of Campbell North and South America, in *Prepared Foods* magazine. Also, low sodium technology that was highly proprietary to Campbell Soup Company led to more flavorful low-sodium products.

INDUSTRY INFORMATION SOURCES

Amin, Melanie. ''Health Craze Settles on Soup.'' *Prepared Foods* (Mid-April, 1992).

Bivens, Terry, Carol Horner, and Jennifer Lin. ''The Dorrance Legacy of Control.'' *Philadelphia Inquirer* (March 18, 1981).

Bowens, Greg. ''Wiping the Mess Off Gerber's Chin.'' *Business Week* (February 1, 1993).

''A Brief History of Canning.'' *Guidelines for Evaluation and Disposition of Damaged Canned Food Containers.* Washington, DC: National Food Processors Association, December 1990.

''Campbell Hopes to Find Polish Market M-M-M Good.'' *Journal of Commerce* (November 3, 1992).

Campbell Soup Company Chronology. Campbell Soup Company.

Davis, Sue. ''You've Come a Long Way, Baby.'' *Prepared Foods* (Mid-April 1992).

Dyslin, John. ''The Leading 150.'' *Prepared Foods* (July 1993).

———. ''Globe Trotting.'' *Prepared Foods* (April 1993).

''The Ghost Brigade of the Future?'' *New York Times* (November 7, 1993).

''Healthy Soups Heat Up the Category.'' *Food Business* (November 23, 1992).

Heid, J. L., and Maynard A. Joslyn. *Fundamentals of Food Processing Operations: Ingredients, Methods and Packaging.* Westport, CT: The AVI Publishing Co., 1967.

''Importance of Canned Foods.'' *Guidelines for Evaluation and Disposition of Damaged Canned Food Containers.* Washington, DC: National Food Processors Association, December 1990.

Infoscan Report: Full Year 1992 Figures.'' *Food and Beverage Marketing* (March 1993).

Infoscan Report: Full Year 1992 Figures.'' *Food and Beverage Marketing* (June 1993).

Kanner, Bernice. ''Soupy Sales.'' *New York* (November 1, 1993).

Koranteng, Juliana. ''Heinz Finds New Niche.'' *Marketing* (December 3, 1992).

Kuhn, Mary Ellen. ''Heinz Goes Country for Promotion.'' *Food Business* (September 6 1993).

Littman, Margaret. ''Yes Sir, That's My Baby (Food).'' *Prepared Foods* (September 1992).

Meyer, Ann. ''Food Companies Make Post-NAFTA Plans.'' *Food Business* (November 1, 1993).

Pehanich, Mike. ''Brand Power.'' *Prepared Foods* (Mid-April 1993).

Perlez, Jane. ''In Poland, Gerber Learns Lessons of Tradition.'' *New York Times* (November 8, 1993).

''Preserved Fruits and Vegetables.'' *1987 Census of Manufactures.* Washington, DC: U.S. Department of Commerce, March 1990.

''Private Label's Tally.'' *Food & Beverage Marketing* (July 1993).

''Product Handbook: Soup.'' *ID* (September 15, 1993).

''Retail Sales of Soup Grew 6% in 1991.'' *Frozen Food Digest* (July 1992).

''Statistics for Industry Groups and Industries.'' *1990 Annual Survey of Manufactures.* Washington, DC: U.S. Department of Commerce, March 1992.

Turcsik, Richard. ''Campbell Soup Adding Pepperidge Farm Gravy.'' *Supermarket News* (August 31, 1992).

U.S. Industrial Outlook. Washington, DC: U.S. Department of Commerce, 1993.

Wagner, Jim. ''Campbell Soup Reshuffles, Strengthens Global Commitment.'' *Food Business* (July 26, 1993).

———. ''Landing the Big One.'' *Food Processing* (September 1992).

Wellman, David. ''New Products: Pass da Soup.'' *Food & Beverage Marketing* (September 1993).

—Mary Ratcliffe

SIC 2033

CANNED FRUITS AND VEGETABLES

Establishments primarily engaged in canning fruits, vegetables, and fruit and vegetable juices; and in manufacturing ketchup and similar tomato sauces or natural and imitation preserves, jams, and jellies. Establishments primarily engaged in canning seafood are classified in **SIC 2091: Canned and Cured Fish and Seafoods;** and those manufacturing canned specialties, such as baby foods and soups, except seafood, are classified in **SIC 2032: Canned Specialties.**

INDUSTRY SNAPSHOT

The $377 billion food industry was the nation's leading manufacturing business in 1992, and the canning industry was an important part of it. In the early 1990s, Americans consumed more than 110 pounds of canned foods per person per year. Canned food processors were the primary market for many of the nation's farmers. By contracting and paying in advance for a large part of the harvest, the industry guaranteed farmers and growers a cash income, helping to absorb the risks of marketing produce on the fresh market.

More than 80 percent of all tomatoes are processed into canned products, while almost 100 percent of table beets, 40 percent of sweet corn, 40 percent of Appalachian area apples, 60 percent of pears, and over 40 percent of peaches are canned.

Payments to farmers for fruits and vegetables accounted for 30 percent of the production cost of canned goods; 25 percent went for containers and labels. Labor took another 17 percent, while approximately three percent of production costs were attributable to fuel and energy. Miscellaneous costs such as machinery, overheads, rental and leasing payments, and insurance came to about 20 percent.

BACKGROUND AND DEVELOPMENT

Napoleon has been credited with saying, "An army marches on its stomach." Whether he did or not, he knew the importance to a successful military campaign of adequate, wholesome food for his troops. When the governing French Directorate offered a prize in 1795 to the citizen who found a way to keep food fresh during campaigns, Napoleon supported the project. Fourteen years later, in 1810, Emperor Napoleon would award the prize to Nicholas Appert, an obscure French confectioner and chef, whose accomplishment secured his place in history.

Appert theorized that if food is heated in a container with no air in it, the food will keep. He cooked foods in cork-stoppered bottles in boiling water, perfecting his methods. Proof of his success came when Appert's preserved fruits and vegetables were sent around the world on sailing ships and remained edible. Two months after Appert published his procedures, an English merchant, Peter Durand, applied to King George III for a patent for a "Method of Preserving Animal Food, Vegetable Food, or Other Perishable Articles a Long Time from Perishing or Becoming Useless." Durand's use of tin canisters in his process

revolutionized food packaging and launched the canning industry as we know it.

The popularity of the new "tinned foods" spread from the military to the civilian population. Captain Edward Perry took tinned foods on his Arctic expeditions in the first quarter of the nineteenth century. Tinned pea soup and beef left behind by his party were recovered and eaten in 1911, and tins of veal and carrots from Perry's 1824 expedition were found to have been safely preserved when they were opened more than 100 years later, in 1939.

Around 1822 tinned foods came to the United States; the first American patent for tin containers was granted in 1825. By the mid-1800s, vegetable processing in steel canisters coated with tin to protect against rust and erosion was becoming widespread, and the words "tin can" and "canning" entered the language. Canning came to mean sterilizing food by heat and sealing it in airtight containers, either metal or glass. Canning activities were undertaken both in food processing plants and in households across the country.

In 1861 canners began adding calcium chloride to the water in which they cooked their closed cans. This enabled canners to use higher temperatures; production time was thus shortened and production volume increased. The improved technology came just in time for the Civil War, which spurred a demand for canned products. By the time the war was over, production of canned foods had grown six times over, and Americans had learned to trust the quality of the products contained therein.

The importance of canned foods to the military was underlined during World War II, when fully two-thirds of the food supplies for the U.S. and allied forces came in cans. When the Japanese capture of Malaya cut off important sources of tin, conservation of the metal on the home front became critical. At the same time, glass containers, which had always been used for some foods, were used to replace tin cans.

The advent of a wide variety of food package choices in the 1980s led to a decline in the sales of canned food in metal cans. Microwave-safe plastic containers, high-barrier film pouches, and form-fill and seal cups were some of the choices offered to consumers. Furthermore, some advertising claimed superior freshness for foods packed in glass jars. In 1986 the Can Manufacturers Institute, the National Food Processors Association, and the American Steel Institute formed the Canned Food Information Council (CFIC) to restore canned foods' former level of acceptance and popularity and disseminate positive information about the nutritional quality and appetizing nature of foods in metal cans.

Regulations. The U.S. Department of Agriculture (USDA) grades canned vegetables on a point system, rating them on such characteristics as texture, size, variety, maturity, taste, odor, and absence of defects. Three more standards were applied to canned foods by the Food and Drug Administration (FDA). Standard of Quality referred to the permitted number of defects or foreign materials; Standard of Fill specified the minimum content for a particular size can or jar; Standard of Identity regulated what was in the container.

Nutritional Quality of Canned Foods. Because canned foods are heat sterilized in a sealed steel can, there is no need at all for preservatives. As consumer tastes changed, the levels of salt and sugar, which had been commonly added for flavor, were reduced to satisfy consumer demand for low-salt and low-sugar products. As for their nutritional qualities, CFIC reported a National Food Processors Association study conducted for the USDA. Because canned foods are already cooked, the comparison was made with home-cooked fresh lima beans, peas, spinach, sweet potatoes, carrots and squash, and with frozen vegetables that were boiled or microwaved according to package directions. Vitamin, mineral and fiber content were found to be similar and, in some cases, the canned product exceeded even the fresh in vitamin content. Studies comparing canned fruits to fresh and frozen counterparts achieved similar results. Canning actually protects foods from oxygen that can destroy vitamins A, B, C, D, and carotene. The process can also eliminate up to 99 percent of pesticide residues and destroy the bacteria that lead to spoilage.

Vegetables and Fruits. Most produce destined for canning goes directly from the growing fields to a nearby processing plant. Production methods allow vegetables to be canned within hours of harvest. It is in the plant that vegetables and fruit are chopped, sliced, peeled, or otherwise prepared for packing in cans. Blanching helps to preserve texture and flavor. Once they are in vacuum-packed cans and sealed, they are sent into the retort, or cooker, to be heat-processed. Cooling is the final step before the cans are labeled and prepared for distribution.

Juices. Traditionally, children have been the nation's juice drinkers. The 1990s, however, brought a decline in adult consumption of alcoholic beverages and a rise in adult juice consumption. Makers of bottled waters, soft drinks, and juices entered into spirited competition for these adult consumers. Blended fruit juices became increasingly popular, registering a 9.7

percent jump in volume in 1991 after double-digit growth in the previous two years.

While retail juice makers looked to expand their market with new blends, that old favorite, orange juice, held its number one position in foodservice, where it accounted for 65 percent of all juices sold. Juice was a staple in foodservice, where its use was not limited to breakfast. Seventy-four percent of restaurants in a 1990 survey reported that they served juices, and despite the burgeoning popularity of juice blends on the retail scene, old favorites maintained their dominance in restaurants. Among the commercial operations surveyed, 71 percent served orange juice, followed by tomato juice (52 percent), grapefruit juice (45 percent), cranberry juice (34 percent), pineapple juice (31 percent), apple juice (18 percent), and vegetable juice (18 percent). Grape, pink grapefruit, mixed, and prune juices were served in fewer than 10 percent of the establishments surveyed.

Some juice manufacturers have come under fire recently for misleading product labeling. A $2 million fine was levied by the federal government in 1987 on Beech-Nut Nutrition Corporation for selling a mix of sweetened water and chemicals as ''apple juice.'' Investigators estimated that as much as ten percent of juice sold, most of it orange juice, was adulterated, usually with sugar or watery orange byproducts. In a $12 billion industry, the cost to American consumers was estimated at $1.2 billion a year. Manufacturers cited in cases from 1987-1993 were mostly major wholesalers to important producers and grocery chains, not companies familiar to the public.

Adulteration cases were pursued haphazardly, in part because while labeling claims were misleading, they posed no threat to public safety. Furthermore, the FDA was hindered by its lack of the statutory powers to pursue the cases more aggressively. In 1993 the *New York Times* reported that some manufacturers were using preservatives not approved as safe for use in juice. The former general counsel for the Florida Department of Citrus, said in the *Times* that diluted juice had been around for a long time. Common dilutants were cheap but generally harmless ingredients such as beet sugar and the pulp wash from re-squeezing oranges that had been soaked in water. Such juice spoiled more readily, and the industry looked for less detectable preservatives, some of which had been banned by the Food and Drug Administration in the belief that they were potentially hazardous.

Jams, Jellies, and Preserves. This category is comprised of several distinct products. Jellies, a mixture of fruit juice, sugar, and pectin, are clear and bright with a tender but firm texture. Jams and preserves are thicker, made by cooking fruit, pectin, and sugar until the texture is almost a puree. In preserves, the fruit chunks are larger. Conserves, similar to jam, mix more than one kind of fruit and perhaps nuts. Marmalade contains citrus fruit rind, most often Seville oranges. Fruit butter is made by stewing fruit, sugar, and spices to a thick, smooth, spreadable consistency. Under federal guidelines, in order for a product to be called a jam or jelly it had to contain 55 percent sugar and be so labelled. Reduced-sugar products that catered to a health-conscious consumer were sweetened with fruit juice and had to be called something other than ''jam'' or ''jelly.''

Despite a more weight-conscious population in the late 1980s and 1990s, the category experienced some growth during the period, albeit slow. Supermarket sales alone reached $688.7 million in 1992, a year in which fruit butters registered the largest growth. Nine flavors made up nearly 80 percent of all products sold, with grape jelly and strawberry jam continuing to be the top favorites, followed by grape jam, red raspberry jam, orange marmalade, apple jelly, apricot jam, peach jam, and blackberry jam.

Most products of this kind (78 percent) were sold directly to consumers through retail outlets, with about 13 percent sold for industrial use and nine percent to the foodservice market. Industrial uses included baked goods, where the products were used as fillings for coffee cakes and donuts, and as flavor components for yogurt.

Spaghetti Sauces. Americans bought more than four billion pounds of pasta in 1992, and spaghetti sauces leapt in number and variety to keep up. Leaders in the field were Van den Bergh Food Co.'s Ragu and Campbell Soup Co.'s Prego, but in 1991 ConAgra jumped into the market by launching 20 new varieties under its Hunt's label. These ranged from traditional, meat- and mushroom-flavored sauces to a no-fat, no-cholesterol line of ''light'' sauces. Ragu and Prego countered with additions to their well-established lines. Van den Bergh Foods' Ragu Spaghetti Sauce managed to hang on to the top position with a 27 percent share of the $1 billion market.

Salsa. Salsa includes an array of sauces that includes picante, enchilada, taco, and other chili-based sauces. In 1991, when it outsold ketchup in retail stores by $40 million, David A. Weiss, president of the market research company Packaged Facts Inc., commented in *Supermarket Business* magazine that the taste for salsa had become as mainstream as apple pie. Retail sales in 1992 for salsa and other Mexican sauces were estimated at $730 million, and the first seven months of 1993 saw the introduction of 147 new salsa products on the market. While Pace Foods in San Antonio, Texas, which had introduced American consumers to salsa in 1947, still boasted the number one brand in 1993, other manufacturers had begun to extend their condiment lines with the spicy newcomer. Hormel, Nabisco, Frito-Lay, and Pet Incorporated all introduced Mexican-style products. H.J. Heinz Co., long dominant in the ketchup category, was so confident of its Salsa Style Ketchup that it introduced the product nationally in 1993 without any test marketing. At Campbell Soup Co., salsa appeared as V8 Picanta Vegetable Juice, a line extension of its V8 vegetable juice.

CURRENT CONDITIONS

Cost-conscious consumers and strong competition took a toll in the food industry overall in 1992. In *Prepared Foods* 1993 annual survey of the leading food manufacturers, 16 out of 70 publicly owned companies in the top 50 had declining sales in 1992 as compared to only three the previous year. The latter part of 1993, however, saw an upsurge in the overall American economy, a development that should help the food industry's membership.

In addition, widespread flooding in the prime Midwest growing region in 1993, coupled with crop damage from cool, wet weather, and planned-for reductions in planted acreage reduced the harvest by as much as 20 percent compared to 1992. U.S. canners hope that the resulting tightened inventories boost prices and contribute to a financial upswing for the industry.

The industry, though, does face a number of problems: the proliferation of warehouse club stores, which have induced retailers to look for ways to compete by forcing stronger competition among top brands; premiums on shelf space in retail outlets, combined with a stronger emphasis among retailers on their own private label products; nervous investors; and new, costly labeling laws.

Supermarket Sales. Supermarket sales results were mixed in the first half of the 1990s. Information Resources, Inc., a Chicago-based firm, compiled actual scanner data from 2,700 supermarkets having sales of more than $2 million. Canned fruit sales dropped in 1992, both in dollar and volume amounts, while vegetable sales registered fewer dollars but remained stable in volume. Juice sales remained relatively stable in 1992. Sales of canned tomato products showed a modest gain in volume, but with the exception of barbecue sauce, condiments posted reduced dollar and volume amounts.

Private Labels. Leading manufacturers of name brands have cause to be disturbed by the steady growth in private label (store brand) products. Private label fruits and vegetables accounted for a sizeable 30.83 percent and 27.02 percent dollar share, respectively, of supermarket sales in the canned food category.

Foodservice. Supermarket sales represent only a portion of the market for canned products. Foodservice establishments remain a huge outlet, although little data on this segment is available because of its size and diversity. *Food Processing* magazine reported in 1992 a total of 733,000 foodservice establishments. Of these, 614,000 were identified as commercial (fast-food restaurants, commercial cafeterias, family restaurants, supermarket delis, convenience stores, "white tablecloth" restaurants), compared to 119,000 non-commercial operators, which include hospitals, schools and universities, and the military. Many of these establishments are key customers for canned fruit and vegetable manufacturers.

Legislation. In the first half of the 1990s, the Nutritional Labeling Education Act (NLEA) mandated sweeping changes in labeling, with the emphasis more on the relationship between nutrition and chronic disease than on vitamin/mineral content. Intended to reduce consumer confusion and end the chaos of individual manufacturers' label definitions, the act called for standardized serving sizes (reference amounts) and established rules for health claims, defining comparative nutritional claims and relating them to U.S. Recommended Daily Intakes (RDIs) and U.S. Recommended Daily Allowances (RDAs) for vitamin/mineral percentages. This legislation calls for dramatic changes in some cases in the packaging for canned foods. Some manufacturers contend that meeting the requirements of the NLEA legislation will substantially increase their production costs.

Advertising and Promotion. With sales stagnant, media spending was down throughout the food industry in 1992, but nowhere was the decrease greater than in the canned fruit and vegetable segment, which reduced ad spending by 30 percent. Industry leader Del Monte's media spending plunged from $31 million in 1991 to only $8 million in 1992, and Dole juices reduced its advertising budget by 80 percent.

There were exceptions, however. H.J. Heinz Co. increased its marketing expenditures in 1992 from $550 million to $650 million, excluding trade promotions. Concentrating on consumer promotions and shelf pricing, the company sought to fend off challenges to its key brands. Campbell Soup Co., meanwhile, put $3 million of its $18 million V8 spending, double that of 1991, behind its new V8 Light 'n Tangy.

Smucker's increased ad spending for its jellies and preserves from $4 million to $6.8 million. Seagram Company Ltd., the top spender in the beverage category, poured $35 million into promoting its Tropicana brand. Ocean Spray Cranberries, Inc. was another juice producer that increased its 1992 ad dollars, from $18 million in 1991 to $23 million.

INDUSTRY LEADERS

Among the leading fruit and vegetable canners are H.J. Heinz Co., Del Monte Corporation, Stokely USA, Dole Food Co., Inc., and Ocean Spray Cranberries, Inc.

Following the Kohlberg Kravis Roberts & Co. purchase of Del Monte in a leveraged buyout from RJR Nabisco, the privately-owned company increased its leading share of the canned fruit and vegetable market. As a privately held company, it escaped the scrutiny applied to publicly traded firms, whose performance was closely watched by Wall street analysts and stockholders. Del Monte's food and beverage sales, reported at $1.43 billion in 1992, were stable during the economically tough early 1990s.

At the $6.6 billion H.J. Heinz Company, brand equity was a 1990s priority. Heinz ketchup managed to hold onto its 54 percent market share despite stiff competition from salsa. Chairman Anthony O'Reilly, in an interview with *Refrigerated & Frozen Foods* magazine, expressed his conviction that top brands needn't worry about private label products. The experience at Heinz was that its own top branded labels outsold the private label products it manufactured. "No. 1 and No. 2 brands" he said, "will retain their vitality if they behave themselves. But if they try and adopt positions where they are overpricing their products in conditions of zero inflation, you are not going to get a particularly sympathetic consumer."

Stokely USA, Inc., based in Oconomowoc, Wisconsin, produced the third-largest-selling canned vegetable brand in the country in the early 1900s. Founded in 1920 as Oconomowoc Canning and Products Co., the company over its 72-year history had established itself in both branded label and private label businesses, with sizable customer bases in both the foodservice and retail segments. Brand awareness for the Stokely name was strong in its core Southeast and Midwest markets, where the brand was almost synonymous with canned vegetables to consumers.

The company name went through some changes in the 1980s, first with the acquisition in 1983 of Stokely Van Camp Inc.; the 1984 acquisition of Stokely Van Camp by Quaker Oats, quickly followed by Stokely's outright purchase of the Stokely name in 1984; and the name change to Stokely USA, Inc., in 1985, the same year in which the company went public. Despite the changes in ownership, the brand name remained strong. Increased sales, which jumped from $139.7 million in 1986 to $272 million in 1990, demonstrated that strength. The five percent slump in 1991 to sales of $258 million was a result of the bad times affecting commodity markets, said *Prepared Foods*, and was not expected to improve until 1993.

AMERICA AND THE WORLD

Canned goods exports were up 10 percent in 1992, from $1.39 billion in 1991 to $1.53 billion, with fruit juices accounting for 16 percent and canned vegetables 11 percent of the total. Canada and Japan continued to be the top export markets, followed by Mexico, the United Kingdom, and Germany.

Imports outpaced exports, rising to $2 billion in 1992, compared to $1.7 billion the previous year. The steep increase was attributed to imports of apple juice concentrate from Germany. Fruit juices represented 23 percent of 1992 imports.

The 1993 North American Free Trade Agreement (NAFTA) did away with trade barriers between the United States, Canada, and Mexico for 15 years and created the world's largest consumer market, with a population of more than 360 million people and a combined economy close to $6.5 trillion in size. Even before NAFTA'S passage, canned food companies were expanding operations into Canada and Mexico.

RESEARCH AND TECHNOLOGY

Processing Advances. At the industrial level, the preservation of food in a sealed container by heating it to a temperature high enough to kill harmful bacteria is called retort processing; the cooker itself is referred to as a retort. Metal and glass, in part because of their long shelf life, remain the most important packaging forms for retorted products, but research efforts are in progress to develop new plastics capable of withstanding the high temperatures of the retort systems. Likely products for such plastic packaging include jams and jellies, soups, vegetables, tomato products, and fruit juices.

The 1990s saw the installation of new retort systems at a number of plants. Some automated systems were flexible enough to process food in glass jars, flexible pouches, plastic tubs, or irregular shapes. In batch retorting, a single operator can handle a system that automatically stacks cans in trays, conveys them

into the retort, removes them after sterilization and cooling, and carries them back to a de-stacker.

Packaging Advances. The 1990s saw the development of new, upscale cans to rival glass containers in style and sophistication. Not unlike the innovative changes in plastic packaging that had marked the 1980s, the new cans were designed to increase the containers' appeal and convenience to consumers.

Campbell launched Cianto pasta sauce in the United Kingdom in a Quantum can. Produced by the Foodcan Group of CarnaudMetalbox (CMB), the distinctive, vertically-fluted can with labeling graphics lithographed directly onto the metal won a 1992 Worldstar Award from the World Packaging Organization. CMB has also licensed the technology for its Ferrolite can to North American can makers. The Ferrolite can, a plastic-laminated, microwaveable, recyclable, fully retortable steel can, was another Worldstar Award winner for CMB.

INDUSTRY INFORMATION SOURCES

"A Brief History of Canning." *Guidelines for Evaluation and Disposition of Damaged Canned Food Containers.* Washington, DC: National Food Processors Association, December 1990.

Buss, Dale D. "Canners Set to Harvest Higher Profits." *Food Business*, September 6, 1993.

"Canned Vegetables." *Industrial Distribution*, May 15, 1991.

Davenport, Larry. "Jams and Jellies: Reaching Middle-age Spread." *Food Distribution Magazine*, June 1992.

Dyslin, John. "Globe Trotting." *Prepared Foods*, April 1993.

———. "The Leading 150." *Prepared Foods*, July 1993.

Friedman, Marty. "New Products Fuel Salsa's Fire." *Prepared Foods*, October 1993.

———. "New Sauces Heed Pastamania's Call." *Prepared Foods*, April 1993.

Furman, Phyllis. "Tin Tizzy: Public Image of Canned Food and Alternatives." *Madison Avenue*, June 1986.

"Gourmet Products and New Packaging Are Hot Topics in Jams and Jellies." *Fancy Food*, June 1991.

Henriques, Diana B. "10% of Fruit Juice Sold in U.S. Is Not All Juice, Regulators Say." *New York Times*, October 31, 1993.

"Infoscan Report: Full Year 1992 Figures." *Food and Beverage Marketing,* June 1993.

Kuhn, Mary Ellen. "The Top 10 New Products of 1993." *Food Business*, November 1, 1993.

Larson, Melissa. "New Ideas Come in Cans." *Packaging*, April 1993.

Littman, Margaret. "And the Brand Played On." *Prepared Foods*, August 1992.

McDermott, Michael J. "Juicing Up Adults." *Food & Beverage Marketing*, November 1992.

Meyer, Ann. "Food Companies Make Post-NAFTA Plans." *Food Business*, November 1, 1993.

Miller, Cyndee. "Moves by P&G, Heinz Rekindle Fears That Brands Are In Danger." *Marketing News*, June 8, 1992.

Morris, Charles E. "Shelf-Stable Convenience." *Food Engineering*, April 1993.

O'Neil, Molly. "New Mainstream: Hot Dogs, Apple Pie and Salsa." *Supermarket Business*, May 1992.

"Private Label's Tally." *Food & Beverage Marketing*, July 1993.

"Product Handbook: Canned Vegetables." *ID*, September 15 1993.

Rice, Judy. "Retortable Plastic Packaging Evolving." *Food Processing*, January 1993.

Sellers, Patricia. "H. J. Heinz: Has Cost Cutting Gone Too Far?" *Fortune*, November 2, 1992.

School Foodservice Factbook. Alexandria, VA: American School Food Service Association, 1993.

"Statistics for Industry Groups and Industries." *Annual Survey of Manufactures*. Washington, DC: U.S. Department of Commerce, 1992.

Swientek, Robert J. "Retorting Heats Up!" *Food Processing*, January 1993.

Therrien, Lois. "1993 Industry Outlook: Food - Tighter Belts, Wider Horizons." *Business Week*, January 11, 1933.

"Twelfth Annual Media Spending Guide." *Food & Beverage Marketing*, August 1993.

U.S. Industrial Outlook. Washington, DC: U.S. Department of Commerce, 1993.

Van Wagner, Lisa R. "1993 Food Industry Economic Outlook." *Food Processing*, February 1993.

Wellman, David. "New Products: Salsa Chugs On." *Food & Beverage Marketing*, October 1993.

—Mary Ratcliffe

SIC 2034

DRIED AND DEHYDRATED FRUITS, VEGETABLES, AND SOUP MIXES

Establishments primarily engaged in sun drying or artificially dehydrating fruits and vegetables, or in manufacturing packaged soup mixes from dehydrated ingredients. Establishments primarily engaged in the grading and marketing of farm dried fruits, such as prunes and raisins, are classified in **SIC 5149: Groceries and Related Products, Not Elsewhere Classified.**

Dried and dehydrated fruits, vegetables, and soups were a $2.9 billion business in 1991. California was the site of 90 percent of U.S. dried fruit production, although makers of dried potato products were mostly based in Idaho. Industry leaders included Sun-Diamond Growers of California, Basic American, Inc., and Dole Dried Fruit and Nut Co., with combined sales of $1.716 billion.

Sun drying, one of the oldest known methods of fruit preservation, originated thousands of years ago. Dehydration preserved foods by removing the moisture that microorganisms needed to thrive. Although the technique remained in use in the 1990s, mechanical drying methods increased beginning in the late nineteenth century. Besides preservation, reduction in bulk and weight were considerations in the drying of fruits and vegetables.

As consumer interest in healthy eating intensified in the 1980s, processors of dates, raisins, dried apricots, apples, cherries, and other fruits promoted their products as nutritious, year-round snacks as well as ingredients for home baking and cooking. By 1991, supermarket sales alone reached $594.25 million. Snack mixes posted the largest gain over the previous year at 10 percent. Dates and apricots also showed increases, but declining prune and raisin sales dragged the category down to a 2.52 percent increase for the year, compared to average annual gains of 5.32 percent for the previous five years. During the same period, supermarket sales of dried potato and other vegetable products reached $291.35 million.

Processors used dried fruits in a wide variety of food products. Dates—popular with retail shoppers—lent texture, flavor, and sweetness to processed cereals, baked goods, snack bars and confections, and frozen desserts. About 20 percent of California's annual 35 to 40 million pounds in date production was exported, mostly to Europe. California date producers were expected to benefit from continuing conflict in the Middle East, location of the world's largest date-producing countries, Iran and Iraq.

California-based Sun-Maid shipped 1,000 tons of raisins daily to more than 25 countries in 1991, making it the world's largest raisin producer. Like dates, raisins enjoyed a variety of uses in food processing. Products introduced in the early 1990s included donuts with raisins, fat-free raisin cookies and fruit bars, and even raisin salami.

Supermarket demand for individual dry soup mixes rose 15.30 percent in 1991, making it one of the top gaining products for the year. Aggressive marketing of ramen soups took market share from traditional brands. Campbell Soup Co. fought back by acquiring Sanwa Foods Inc., the third-largest U.S. ramen marketer.

Thomas J. Lipton, one of 63 food processing companies worldwide owned by the Anglo-Dutch giant Unilever, produced Cup-A-Soup and other soup mixes at its plant in Flemington, N.J. In 1990, Lipton introduced Single Serve Microwaveable Soup Mixes.

Due to increasing popularity, 99 of 159 new soups introduced in 1990 were dry mixes. Notable new products included a high protein, high fiber, no cholesterol Spanish Bean Soup Mix, as well as Creole Gumbo Reddi-mix, which required only the addition of water and seafood.

Internationally, dried fruits destined for Germany, Japan, the United Kingdom, and Canada comprised 27 percent of U.S. canned goods exports in 1991. The same year, imports of dried fruits and vegetables declined an average of 10 percent. With the fall of trade barriers in Western Europe and the gradual shift of Eastern European countries toward free market economies, American producers looked forward to greater international opportunities in the future.

INDUSTRY INFORMATION SOURCES

Crawford, Dawn, "Soup in a Snap," *Prepared Foods New Products Annual,* 1991.

Dillon, Patricia M., "Going Nuts . . . or Maybe a Little Fruity," *Food Engineering,* May 1991.

Hui, Y.H., *Encyclopedia of Food Science and Technology,* New York: John Wiley & Sons, 1992.

LaBell, Fran, "Dates Add Sweetness to Snacks, Cereals, Treats," *Food Processing,* October 1992.

Larson, Melissa, "Coding Upgrade Bears Fruit," *Packaging,* June 1991.

McClure, Barney H., "Sales Still Strong for Desert Dates, the World's First Cultivated Fruit," *Supermarket Business,* January 1991.

Neff, Jack, "Campbell Turns up the Heat in Ramen Market," *Food Business,* January 6, 1992.

"The 1992 Supermarket Sales Manual," *Progressive Grocer,* July 1992.

Sperber, Bob, "Lipton's Open Systems Foray: A Calculated RISC," *Food Processing,* November 1992.

U.S. Industrial Outlook, Washington, DC: U.S. Department of Commerce, 1992.

Ward's Business Directory of U.S. Private and Public Companies, Detroit: Gale Research, 1992.

—Mary Ratcliffe

SIC 2035

PICKLED FRUITS AND VEGETABLES, VEGETABLE SAUCES AND SEASONINGS, AND SALAD DRESSINGS

This category covers establishments primarily engaged in pickling and brining fruits and vegetables, and in manufacturing salad dressings, vegetable relishes, sauces, and seasonings. Establishments primarily engaged in manufacturing catsup and similar tomato sauces are classified in **SIC 2033: Canned Fruits, Vegetables, Preserves, Jams, and Jellies.** Establishments primarily engaged in manufacturing dry salad dressings and dry sauce mixes are classified in **SIC 2099: Food Preparations, Not Elsewhere Classified.**

Diversified multibillion dollar companies were the major producers of pickles, sauces and seasonings, and salad dressings in the late 1980s and 1990s, but small, regional independents accounted for many familiar products. H. J. Heinz, Kraft General Foods, Inc., Best Foods Division of CPC International, Inc., were the industry leaders.

The industry reflected the trends that were influencing other food processors: consumers' were concerned with healthier eating and had developed the taste for exotic flavors and ethnic cuisines. Overall, supermarkets rang up $4.5 million in sales of sauces and dressings in 1991, an increase of 5.35 percent that continued annual growth of 5.38 percent for the preceding five-year period. Pourable salad dressings outstripped all other products in the category, closely followed by mayonnaise and other sandwich spreads, and gravy and sauce mixes.

In 1950 the Food and Drug Administration established standards of identity for mayonnaise, salad dressing, and French dressing which regulated their ingredients and manufacture. Other dressings, though not regulated, had predictable flavors and characteristics. Italian, ranch, thousand island, French, and bleu cheese were America's favorite salad dressings in the 1990s, according to an Association for Dressings and Sauces (ADS) survey reported in *Institutional Distribution* magazine. Steady growth in the sector was in line with the findings of the same ADS survey that three out of four people ate a tossed salad every other day.

Low-fat, low-calorie dressings were introduced to meet consumers' dietary concerns, but achieving the flavor and texture to which people were accustomed was a challenge. "We were never able to reduce fat and keep the taste," said Jessie Ristic, spokesperson for Best Foods, maker of the top ranking Hellmann's mayonnaise line. But as suppliers "grew more sophisticated with fat replacers and low-fat flavor systems . . . we were finally able to come out with a reduced-fat mayonnaise that tasted good."

Ragu and General Mills emerged as industry leaders in the segment of simmer, or recipe, sauces. Offered in a variety of flavors, these sauces were added to meat—notably chicken—to create quick, more enticing meals. Such sauces were part of the "fastest-growing category in supermarkets" during the third quarter of 1992, according to Michael J. McDermott in *Food & Beverage Marketing*.

In the pickle segment of the industry, Richard Hentschel, executive vice- president of Pickle Packers International, Inc., reported that consumption of pickles had more than doubled from the mid-1940s to the early 1990s to an estimated nine pounds per person annually. Estimated sales at the consumer level were $1.45 billion. The industry association reported 50 known processors in the United States, but this figure did not include the many regional family producers. Heinz, Clausson, and Vlasic were the only national brands.

INDUSTRY INFORMATION SOURCES

Hui, Y. H., ed., *Encyclopedia of Food Science and Technology,* 4 vols. New York: John Wiley & Sons Inc., 1992.

"Ingredients," *Food & Beverage Marketing,* March 1993.

Lingle, Rick, "Four Packages You Wish You Had Introduced," *Prepared Foods,* April 1992.

McCormick, Richard D., "Demand for Dipping Sauces, Marinades Spurs Interest in Mustard," *Prepared Foods,* October 1986.

McDermott, Michael J., "Battle Simmering in Sauces," *Food & Beverage Marketing,* February 1993.

"The 1992 Supermarket Sales Manual," *Progressive Grocer,* July 1992.

Tanyeri, Dana, "Salad Dressings," *Institutional Distribution,* December 1991.

—Mary Ratcliffe

SIC 2037

FROZEN FRUITS, FRUIT JUICES, VEGETABLES

This classification covers establishments primarily engaged in freezing fruits, fruit juices, and vegeta-bles. These establishments also produce important by-products such as fresh or dried citrus pulp.

INDUSTRY SNAPSHOT

Frozen foods became available commercially beginning in 1930, making this category a comparative newcomer to the U.S. food industry. By 1991, all frozen foods combined had a retail and institutional value of $50.281 billion; of that total, frozen fruits, fruit juices, and vegetables accounted for $11.766 billion.

Consumers receive frozen fruits, fruit juices, and vegetables through two main sales outlets: grocery stores, which include supermarkets, other retail stores, and the emerging warehouse clubs; and foodservice, a highly fragmented market comprised of restaurants, lodging and recreation outlets, separate eating and drinking places, health care institutions, colleges and universities, primary and secondary schools, airlines, business and industry, the military, and more. The division of sales between retail and foodservice had once weighed in favor of retail, but that changed in the 1990s. Variation among the product groups was too great for easy generalization, but *Quick Frozen Foods International* indicated the split was approximately 45 percent retail to 55 percent institutional. For frozen fruits and vegetables, the difference was more pronounced: 38 percent retail and 62 percent institutional.

The frozen fruits, fruit juices, and vegetables industry has been greatly influenced by changes in the needs of the American consumer. Single parent families, two-income families, and growing numbers of women in the work force fueled the demand for convenience foods in convenient packaging. To compete in this changing marketplace, processors of commodity frozen vegetables extended their product lines with value-added items such as prepared meals, sauced vegetables, frozen entrees, pasta, and vegetable mixes. Changing demographics affected more than new product introductions. Single-serving frozen vegetables were an example of packaging that targeted changing demographic patterns, but they sold well only in stores with a high proportion of singles, and younger and elderly couples for customers.

ORGANIZATION AND STRUCTURE

The major producers of frozen fruits, fruit juices, and vegetables were subsidiaries or divisions of diversified, multinational, multibillion dollar conglomerates, with frozen fruits, juices, and vegetables being only one of their food operations. Ore-Ida, a leading producer of frozen potato products in the 1990s, was a subsidiary of H. J. Heinz. Minute-Maid, the top frozen orange juice concentrate, was produced by a division of Coca-Cola. Birds Eye, named for Clarence Birdseye, the "father" of the frozen food industry in the United States, was a Kraft General Foods (KGF) brand; KGF belonged to the Philip Morris family of companies. Green Giant was a subsidiary of Pillsbury Co. J. R. Simplot and its Food Group division were the lone privately held companies among the majors. Alongside these industry giants, smaller newcomers and regional processors carved out significant markets for themselves. McCain Foods USA, for example, laid claim to being the fastest growing frozen food company in the United States, increasing its business five-fold in six years and predicting sales of $1 billion by 1997.

David McDonald, president and chief executive officer of Curtice Burns Foods, said in *Refrigerated & Frozen Foods*: "At $1 billion in sales, I rate [us] a small company. Our main competitors average anywhere from $10 to $15 billion." He continued, "The frozen vegetable market is really in dramatic transition. In the last couple of years, the oversupply situation has been fueled by the overcapacity in the industry . . . It's harder to make money in this business." Nevertheless, Curtice Burns saw growth potential in foodservice and private label and targeted its efforts there.

BACKGROUND AND DEVELOPMENT

History. Humans have been using cold to preserve food quality for as long as they have been eating. Over 100,000 years ago, food was stored in caves where the temperatures were naturally low. Where ice and snow were available, they were used to preserve food. It was not until the twentieth century, however, that scientific research into freezing foods really began. The ability to deliver frozen food to consumers is generally dated from October 14, 1924, when Clarence Birdseye received a patent for his revolutionary new apparatus called a plate freezer. A few more years passed before M. A. Joslyn and W. V. Cruess reported the necessity of blanching vegetables prior to freezing, in 1929.

The industry has advanced steadily ever since. In 1930, June peas and spinach were the first commercially available frozen vegetables, making their debut in Massachusetts supermarkets. A shortage of tin for cans during World War II spurred the growth of frozen foods. Mechanically refrigerated railroad cars came into use in 1949, and the early 1960s saw the development of individually quick frozen (IQF) foods.

All food preservation systems are designed to prevent deterioration and spoilage during storage. Lowering food temperature decreases or inhibits the speed of chemical and physical reactions that result in spoilage. Microorganisms are also a factor in the deterioration of food quality; microbiologic growth stops when food temperature is reduced to less than -10°C. Foods frozen at temperatures as low as -40°C were not unusual towards the end of the 20th century.

Manufacturing. Processors used several methods of freezing foods. High quality could be achieved with individual quick freezing. Its advantages were rapid freezing rates and the fact that, because food pieces did not cohere into a solid block, individual portions could be stored in large containers. This made it particularly suitable for foodservice. In blast freezing, fans passed cold air over the food. Food could also be frozen between plates containing freezing coils, or by immersion into freezing liquid such as salt solutions, liquid nitrogen and liquid carbon dioxide.

CURRENT CONDITIONS

After a period of steady growth since 1986, the frozen food market dropped in the recessionary 1990s; even though poundage production was up slightly, production value was down for the first time since 1947. A surplus of vegetables had lowered prices, and sales in the frozen fruit and juice concentrate sectors were also down.

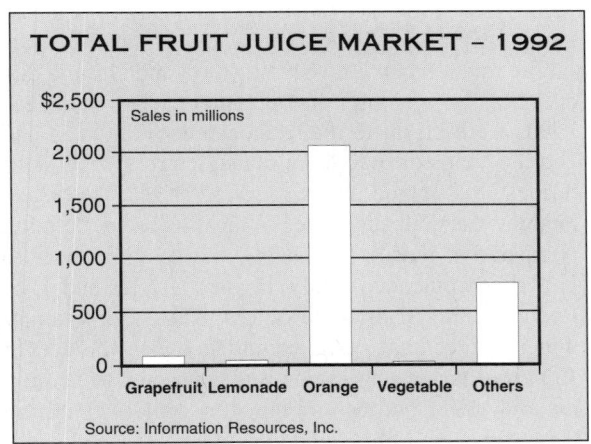

TOTAL FRUIT JUICE MARKET – 1992

Sales in millions

Grapefruit Lemonade Orange Vegetable Others

Source: Information Resources, Inc.

Despite a ten percent increase overall in frozen food industry shipments in 1992 over 1991, the increase was less than one percent for lower value-added frozen fruits and vegetables. Only frozen potato products reversed the trend, with 1991 supermarket sales up by 2.48 percent and 2.90 percent respectively for French fries and other potato products. Nielsen Marketing Research reported a slight increase in retail sales of frozen fruits for the 52 weeks ending June 27, 1992, up 1.9 percent to $149.9 million, but frozen vegetable sales for the same period were down 2.4 percent to $2.69 billion.

Increased supply tied to lower prices was particularly dramatic in concentrated juices. Frozen concentrated orange juice supply, for example, increased from 86,225 gallons for 1989-90 to 98,063 in 1990-91, but a 20-percent drop in average prices placed the product's value at $1.57 billion, down from $1.7 billion. *Progressive Grocer* reported supermarket sales in 1991 of $1.04 billion, down 7.20 percent from 1990. These figures did not include sales in warehouse clubs, which processors were anticipating to give a boost to sales of bulk packaged frozen fruits and vegetables. Club stores, characterized by membership fees, low prices, cash-only policies and limited selection, were a popular new marketing channel by the 1990s, posting annual sales in 1992 of $18.6 billion. Food consultant James Degen predicted in *Prepared Foods* that club store sales would reach $46.4 billion by 1996. An alternative to traditional retail and foodservice distribution channels, club stores were becoming more open to carrying regional brands, control label and private label products.

Some analysts predicted improving sales opportunities based on government recommendations of fruit and vegetable consumption and the Nutritional Labeling Education Act (NLEA). The NLEA mandated sweeping changes in labeling, with the emphasis more on the relationship between nutrition and chronic disease than on vitamin/mineral content. The redesigned labels were meant to reduce consumer confusion and end the chaos of individual manufacturers' label definitions by standardizing serving sizes (reference amounts), establishing rules for health claims, defining comparative nutritional claims and relating them to U.S. Recommended Daily Intakes (RDIs) and U.S. Recommended Daily Allowances (RDAs) for vitamin/mineral percentages. The compliance date was set for 1994, but larger companies were expected to comply by mid-1993, putting pressure on analytical testing laboratories and on suppliers of packaging and printing, as well as creating bottlenecks for smaller, regional processors.

Vegetables. The most popular frozen vegetable in both supermarket and foodservice markets has long been the potato. The average American consumed more than 127 pounds of potatoes annually by 1991. According to Gallup Organization data published in November 1991 and reported in *Institutional Distribution,* potatoes were the favorite side dish for 40 percent of Americans. French fries were second in popularity only to hamburgers as a restaurant choice.

Sales statistics compiled by the American Frozen Food Institute for 1990 listed green beans, corn (on the cob or cut), green peas, broccoli, spinach, sliced carrots, and vegetable mixes as the top frozen vegetable categories after potatoes. Since most frozen vegetables were individually quick frozen within hours of harvest, they offer home cooks and foodservice operations the advantages of labor-saving convenience plus nutrient value, no waste, speed and ease of preparation, and year-round availability. Total frozen vegetables sales in 1991 were $6,472 million; $1,949 in retail and $4,524 in institutional (foodservice) sales.

Fruits. The U.S. Department of Agriculture (USDA) provides voluntary grade standards for fruits and vegetables to help processors achieve uniform product quality. The best quality fruit is usually either sold as fresh produce or individually quick frozen, which results in a product close to fresh fruit. In the latter process, no sugar is added, and the speed of freezing minimizes ice crystal damage. Factors affecting fruit quality are color, size, blemishes, flavor, firmness, and unwanted portions such as skin, pits, or leaves. In bulk freezing, the fruit is filled into containers and then frozen. Such fruit can be frozen alone or with sugar or syrups added. Sometimes fruit is frozen in its own juice.

Frozen fruit sales in 1991 were $1,146 million; $1,010 million of that was institutional, compared to $137 million in retail sales. In both sectors, strawberries were the undisputed favorite. In 1990, California alone produced one billion pounds of strawberries, and more than 316 million pounds, or 32 percent, were frozen.

Fruit Juices. Citrus juices are regulated at the federal level by the Federal Food, Drug and Cosmetic Act, which established Standards of Identity under a grading system that considered flavor, color, absence of defects, and Brix, a designation which refers to the percent of solids, mostly dissolved sugar, in fruit juices and other fruit products having a high moisture content. The Florida Department of Citrus also imposes quality standards. The primary standard was also the Brix; it guaranteed that the strength of the Florida concentrates would be consistent regardless of the packer and flavor variations. Frozen juice concentrate sales in 1991 were $4,147 million; retail at $2,351 million surpassed institutional sales of $1,796 million.

INDUSTRY LEADERS

Simplot Food Group set its sights in 1993 on a 50 percent sales increase—to $1.5 billion over the next five years—by adding other vegetables as well as meat and dairy products to its potato line. Best known as a major supplier of French fries to the McDonald's restaurant chain, Simplot also processed 15 varieties of fruits and vegetables at plants in California, Washington, Iowa, and Mexico, with more than half of them destined for foodservice use. The company also offered pre-blended, pre-portioned vegetables as well as commodity bins of frozen vegetables to processors of prepared dinners and entrees. Simplot took the private label route into supermarkets, shipping frozen bulk product to facilities that would repack them for retail customers under their own brand names.

Industry leaders were not recession-proof in the 1990s. The Heinz subsidiary Ore-Ida, with a 54 percent share of retail frozen potato sales, experienced volume slippage and sought to come back with the introduction of Fast Fries, a shoestring fry designed to compete with fast-food fries in flavor and crisp texture. Ore-Ida executive Bob Ginkel told *Food Business*: "We've seen for several years that the category has been, if not flat, then just barely growing." Adding that there were 3.5 billion pounds of fast food restaurant fries being sold, Ginkel continued: "When you consider that Ore-Ida retail sales are about equal to that, I think you start to see the huge category-building potential [we can achieve]. . . ." The Boise, Idaho processor, reporting $900 million in sales in 1992, dominated supermarket freezer cases with 35 potato items. In 1992, Ore-Ida chairman Gerald Herrick told *Refrigerated & Frozen Foods,* "We already own the fried potato business and we think we can own a lot more, namely in side dishes." The company took aim at topping $1 billion in sales before 1995. A year later, Meg Carlson, vice president of business development, said in the same publication, "In the 1980s, it was appealing . . . to dabble in other businesses, but if you get too diversified, you take your eye off the ball. . . . We are definitely committed to our core product, which is potatoes of all kinds."

In 1991, Green Giant USA took first place in supermarket freezer units from longtime frozen vegetable leader, Birds Eye. Green Giant president Gary Klingl, quoted in *Food Business,* attributed the company's success against Birds Eye to selling frozen vegetables in plastic bags, which accounted for 50 percent of the frozen vegetable market. Green Giant's sales of bagged vegetables were seven million cases a year, up from one million ten years earlier.

AMERICA AND THE WORLD

In the 1990s, manufacturers of frozen fruits, fruit juices, and vegetables looked overseas for opportunities to expand. As the U.S. market for orange juice matured in the 1990s, the three leading producers, Coca-Cola's Minute Maid, Proctor & Gamble's Citrus Hill, and Seagram's Tropicana, were looking to Europe and Japan for increased sales. In 1992, frozen orange juice concentrate exports to Japan jumped an amazing 168 percent over 1991 sales.

Stiff competition from European-based giants like Unilever and Nestle SA encouraged American producers to explore the Americas for new markets and investment opportunities. Green Giant moved the broccoli and cauliflower growing and cutting operations from its Watsonville, California, plant to Irapuato, Mexico, where labor was cheaper. The Institute for Agriculture and Trade Policy, a Minneapolis-based labor-oriented research group, predicted that economic pressure would induce Green Giant to move more operations to Mexico. Simplot also looked to Irapuato, acquiring an equity interest in a leading Mexican processor which exported 100 percent of its frozen vegetables, most of them to the United States. In Canada, Simplot jointly owned a 210-million pound potato facility with Nestle Foodservice of Canada and predicted that it could import up to 150 million pounds of potatoes from Canada once the North American Free Trade Agreement (NAFTA) went into effect.

RESEARCH AND TECHNOLOGY

In 1989, the Chicago-based Institute of Food Technologists (IFT) named the ten most significant food science innovations to have taken place during its 50-year history. Third on their list was the development of frozen concentrated citrus juices at the U.S. Department of Agriculture research laboratories in the mid-1940s. The addition of approximately seven percent fresh juice to the concentrate was the key to the product's success. Since that time, processors have further refined the process with the addition of essential oils and natural flavors to the concentrate before it is packaged and frozen. Also making IFT's top ten list was the development of new freezing methods that enabled the prediction of optimal freezing and storage conditions, an important advance because nutrient loss is negligible when foods are properly frozen and stored.

Another breakthrough in the 20th century was the development of plastic packaging. Among plastic's advantages: it is heat sealable, microwavable, resistant to corrosion, and easily made. More than 80 percent of American households had microwave ovens by the early 1990s, and makers of frozen vegetables and fruits used dual-purpose plastics in packaging that enabled consumers to use either traditional top-of-the-stove cooking methods or the popular microwave ovens.

INDUSTRY INFORMATION SOURCES

Arble, Meade. ''Big-3 Orange Juice Firms Eyeing Europe for Growth.'' *Supermarket News*, 1 June 1992.

Best, Daniel and Patricia Godfrey. ''NLEA in a Nutshell.'' *Prepared Foods*, December 1992.

Blalock, Cecelia. ''Sharp Focus.'' *Refrigerated & Frozen Foods*, February 1993.

''Frozen Food Timeline.'' *Frozen Food Report*, January-February 1992.

Garrison, Bob. ''Market Maverick.'' *Refrigerated & Frozen Foods*, January 1993.

———. ''Potatoes Plus.'' *Refrigerated & Frozen Foods*, February 1992.

''Green Giant Squashing U.S. Labor?'' *Food Business*, 12 August 1991.

''How Frozen Vegetables Have Grown.'' *Frozen Food Report*, January-February 1992.

Hui, Y. H., ed. *Encyclopedia of Food Science and Technology*. New York: John Wiley & Sons, 1992.

Kimbrell, Wendy. ''Regional Edge.'' *Refrigerated & Frozen Foods*, July 1992.

Kuhn, Mary Ellen. ''Take-out Fry Taste Comes Home.'' *Food Business*, 4 January 1993.

Kuntz, Lynn A. ''Fruit Applications: From Down on the Farm to Up on the Shelf.'' *Food Product Design,* December 1992.

———. ''Fruit Applications: After the Harvest.'' *Food Product Design*, December 1992.

Liesse, Julie. ''Green Giant Heats Up in Freezer Case.'' *Advertising Age*, 11 November 1991.

Lingle, Rick. ''How to Gain Clout with Warehouse Clubs.'' *Prepared Foods*, September 1992.

''Looking Up.'' *Refrigerated & Frozen Foods*, November 1992.

Neff, Jack. ''McCain USA Hits the Big Time.'' *Food Business*, 20 July 1992.

''1992 Global Frozen Foods Almanac: Recession and Soft Commodity Prices Put Crimp on US Frozen Food Industry.'' *Quick Frozen Foods International*, October 1992.

''The 1992 Supermarket Sales Manual.'' *Progressive Grocer*, July 1992.

Pacyniak, Bernard. ''Filling the Food Service Order.'' *Prepared Foods*, April 1992.

Sender, Isabelle. ''Single Serve Caters to Single Shopper.'' *Supermarket News*, 23 September 1991.

Staff report. ''Top 10 Food Science Innovations 1939-1989.'' *Food Technology*, September 1989.

''A Strawberry Profile.'' *Frozen Food Report*, January-February 1993

Tanyeri, Dana. ''Any Way You Slice Them, Potatoes Mean Profit.'' *Institutional Distribution*, February 1993.

———. ''Frozen Vegetables.'' *Institutional Distribution*, 1 November 1991.

Van Wagner, Lisa R. ''1993 Food Industry Economic Outlook.'' *Food Processing*, February 1993.

———. ''Government Agencies.'' *Food Processing*, August 1992.

—Mary Ratcliffe

SIC 2038

FROZEN SPECIALTIES NOT ELSEWHERE CLASSIFIED

Establishments primarily engaged in manufacturing frozen food specialties, not elsewhere classified, such as frozen dinners and frozen pizza. The manufacture of some important frozen foods and specialties is classified elsewhere. For example, establishments primarily engaged in manufacturing frozen dairy specialties are classified in **SIC 2024: Ice Cream and Frozen Desserts;** those manufacturing frozen bakery products are classified in **SIC 2051: Bread and Other Bakery Products** and **SIC 2053: Frozen Bakery Products, Except Bread;** those manufacturing frozen fruits and vegetables are classified in **SIC 2037: Frozen Fruits, Fruit Juices, and Vegetables;** and those manufacturing frozen fish and seafood specialties are classified in **SIC 2092: Prepared Fresh or Frozen Fish and Seafood.**

INDUSTRY SNAPSHOT

Beginning in the 1980s, standard TV dinners gave way to a variety of meals and frozen specialty items that offered more choices and met specific dietary requirements. Frozen food manufacturers targeted their products at the needs of busy families who desired faster meal preparation and greater variety. They also developed new frozen entrees for children, as well as ethnic food specialties.

In 1992, dual-income households and the convenience of microwave ovens contributed to annual growth in the frozen food category. According to *Frozen Food Digest,* shipments of frozen foods increased 10 percent to $14.6 billion, which amounted to about 2 percent real growth after adjusting for price increases. Specialty frozen foods experienced 3 percent real growth, while frozen foods in general were anticipated to grow only 2 to 3 percent over the next three years.

Within the specialty frozen foods category, retail sales of frozen breakfast foods increased 7.5 percent to top $1 billion in 1992, and were projected to grow at 6 percent per year through 1997. Frozen waffles posted sales of $535 million in 1992, specialty breakfasts grew to $417 million, and french toast and pancakes garnered $127 million. Frozen dinners and meat pies posted total retail sales of $5.2 billion in 1991—an annual growth rate of 3.3 percent—and were expected to reach $6.1 billion by 1996. Low-cholesterol and low-fat frozen dinner entrees generated about $1.4 million in 1991 sales and were projected to increase to $2.4 million by 1996.

ORGANIZATION AND STRUCTURE

Frozen food grew from a $250 million retail business in 1947 to more than $50 billion by the early 1990s, according to the National Frozen Food Association. Frozen food specialties comprised $8.6 billion of the total sales in 1991, and required approximately $2.5 million worth of materials, ingredients, and supplies to produce. All of the top 75 leading food producers manufactured lines of frozen foods.

In terms of product share, 78 percent of the frozen food specialties category consisted of frozen dinners, pot pies, and ''nationality'' foods (mainly Italian, Chinese, and Mexican). The remainder included frozen whipped topping, breakfast foods, and other items.

BACKGROUND AND DEVELOPMENT

Clarence Birdseye was considered the ''father'' of the frozen food industry. He created the freezing process that preserved foods so they did not need to be cooked immediately. Birdseye formed Birds Eye Foods Ltd. in London in 1954, and it later became a subsidiary of Unilever. According to *Quick Frozen Foods International,* Birds Eye ''virtually held an umbrella over the industry during the squalls of its infancy.''

The frozen food industry evolved during the early 1960s, as the proliferation of supermarkets and self-service stores made mass marketing of frozen food products profitable. At the same time, refrigerator-freezers and stand-alone freezers gained in popularity. The first frozen food products were vegetables, poultry, fish, and fruit in boilable pouches. Items such as frozen juice concentrate, ice cream novelties, baked goods, variety dinners, seafood, breakfast items, and pizza gradually entered the industry from the mid-1960s through the 1990s.

But the explosive growth in the frozen food category could be attributed to the introduction of the microwave oven. In fact, *Quick Frozen Foods International* called the combination of the microwave oven and frozen food a ''marriage of convenience'': ''The microwave was made for frozen foods. There is no product—except for perhaps bacon—that performs better in a microwave oven.'' The magazine reported that microwave oven owners spent 34 percent more on pizza, 29 percent more on breakfast foods, 19 percent more on entrees, and 16 percent more on dinners than non-microwave owners. Improvements in taste over the past 40 years also made frozen food specialties increasingly attractive to busy families.

CURRENT CONDITIONS

Convenience in preparation was the primary appeal of frozen foods. Americans used fewer and fewer ingredients to make the main course of meals in the 1990s, and often substituted frozen foods for fresh produce. Concerns about health and nutrition also led consumers to reduce their intake of foods containing fat and sodium. The specialty frozen food industry responded by offering low-cholesterol and low-fat products. In 1992, *Supermarket News* predicted that ''Frozen foods should be able to grow faster than the total grocery industry because they offer convenience, health, and variety, three things consumers are now looking for.'' Industry analysts also anticipated that targeting products to specific demographic groups would help expand frozen food sales in the 1990s and beyond.

Due to tough economic conditions, the frozen food industry had to refine its marketing techniques to communicate value and quality to wary consumers. *Supermarket News* claimed that frozen food manufacturers should target the 40- to 54-year-old demographic group, which was expected to grow by about 20 percent through the mid-1990s, as well as the over 55-year-old group, which was projected to increase by about 7 percent. These two groups made up about 60 percent of the American population. Frozen food items heavily purchased by those in the over 55 group included pizzas, pies, and entrees.

Frozen food manufacturers also increased marketing efforts aimed at ethnic groups. The U.S. Hispanic population was expected to increase 27 percent by the year 2000, and the African-American population by 13 percent. In addition, the popularity of ethnic food was not confined to these groups alone. Mexican-style frozen food, for example, gained share in the overall frozen food market. According to *Supermarket News,* ''frozen Mexican and Tex-Mex foods have outgrown their purely regional appeal to gain acceptance in the diets of many Americans.'' Popular ethnic frozen food specialties included frozen tacos, burritos, and Mexican dinners.

Other analysts urged the frozen food industry to develop new prepared foods in order to avoid losing additional market share to ready-to-eat meals by the end of the 1990s. *Supermarket News* claimed that without drastic action, ready-to-eat meals—which included microwavable shelf-stable and refrigerated items—could erode the market share held by frozen foods from 66 percent in the mid-1990s to 34 percent by the year 2000.

Another challenge facing the industry was the strict product labeling guidelines proposed by the Nutrition Labeling and Education Act of 1990 and scheduled to take effect in 1994. The law required accuracy in labeling information, nutritional content claims, and definitions of serving sizes. An issue for the American Frozen Food Institute involved frozen food products that were packed and labeled before the deadline. According to the law, such products would have to be discarded. The American Frozen Food Institute planned to address this and other issues in an effort to develop consistent labeling standards.

Leading frozen food manufacturers engaged in damaging price wars and expensive trade promotions in the early 1990s. As a result, many companies began shifting their focus toward generating profits from existing products instead of launching new brands and line extensions. Advertising spending within the category declined 23 percent from 1992 to 1993, to $154.4 million.

Sales of frozen dinners and entrees declined 6 percent from 1990 to 1991, despite development of new, children-oriented and health-conscious lines by ConAgra, Tyson Foods, Campbell Soup, and others. For example, ConAgra's Healthy Choice brand experienced a 25 percent decline in sales from 1991 to 1992, which prompted the company to discount another brand that was intended to command premium prices. To counteract these declines, other manufacturers planned to boost marketing of children's frozen meal lines at the end of 1993.

INDUSTRY LEADERS

The leading manufacturers of frozen food specialties, in order of sales, were: Nestle USA, Inc., at $7.2 million; Campbell Soup Company, $6.58 million; Kellogg Co., $6.1 million; Tyson Foods Inc., $4.7 million; Pillsbury Co., $2.9 million; Campbell Taggart Inc., $1.6 million; J.R. Simplot, $1.5 million; ConAgra Consumer Frozen Food Co., $1.4 million; and Stouffer Corp., $1.2 million.

The top frozen dinner entrees were Campbell Soup's Swanson Frozen Foods, Weight Watchers, Stouffer's Lean Cuisine, and ConAgra's Healthy Choice lines. The highest concentration of frozen food manufacturers was in California, New York, Illinois, and Pennsylvania, followed by the Midwest states.

WORK FORCE

There were 285 establishments involved in producing frozen food specialties in 1989. These companies employed 44,700 workers at a total payroll of $852.5 million. Of the total employees, 36,300 performed production work at an average salary of $8.79 an hour.

INDUSTRY INFORMATION SOURCES

Darnay, Arsen, editor, *Gale's Service Industries USA,* Detroit: Gale Research, 1992.

DeNitto, Emily, "Frozen Food Results Chill Top 100," *Advertising Age,* September 29, 1993.

Dowdell, Stephen, "Increasing the Volume," *Supermarket News,* October 4, 1993.

"In Praise of Mighty Microwave Oven, FF Leaders Call for Standardization," *Quick Frozen Foods International,* January 1988.

Karolefski, John, "Industry Urged to Jazz Up Meal Offerings," *Supermarket News,* March 5, 1990.

Karolefski, "New Technology Expected to Increase Market Share," *Supermarket News,* March 5, 1990.

Klepacki, Laura, "Demographics, Value Stressed as Key to Frozen Food Growth," *Supermarket News,* November 9, 1992.

Klepacki, "Dollar Sales Rose 1.2 Percent in Frozen Food Month," *Supermarket News,* May 3, 1993.

Klepacki, "Mexican Style Fast Foods Securing Niche in Frozens," *Supermarket News,* April 19, 1993.

Predicasts Forecasts, Foster, California: Information Access Co., Fourth Quarter 1993.

Saxton, Lisa, "Meals on Deals," *Supermarket News,* October 4, 1993.

Sternman, Mike, "Would You Believe This Frozen Food Season," *Supermarket Business,* January 3, 1994.

Sternman, "Sorting Out the Labels," *Supermarket News,* October 4, 1993.

"Thirty Years around the World with Frozen Foods: 1959-1989," *Quick Frozen Foods International,* October 1989.

Turcsik, Richard, "Realignment at Campbell Splits Frozens, Condiments," *Supermarket News,* May 3, 1993.

Turcsik, "A Period of Cool Change," *Supermarket News,* December 28, 1992.

—Evelyn S. Dorman

SIC 2041

FLOUR AND OTHER GRAIN MILL PRODUCTS

This industry is comprised of establishments primarily engaged in milling flour from wheat, rye, and other grains except rice. Rice millers are categorized in **SIC 2044: Rice Milling.** Establishments involved in corn milling by the wet process are categorized in **SIC 2046: Wet Corn Milling.**

Products of this industry include plain flour or mixes and doughs prepared from milled ingredients. Establishments who supply mixes and doughs prepared from purchased ingredients are categorized in **SIC 2045: Prepared Flour Mixes and Doughs.**

INDUSTRY SNAPSHOT

In 1987, the flour and grain mill products industry shipped goods valued at $5.0 billion. Of this total, $4.6 billion represented products considered primary, $80.5 million represented secondary products, and $348.0 million represented miscellaneous transactions. These figures yielded a specialization ratio of 98 percent, an increase of 1 percent over the specialization ratio recorded in 1982. In 1990, states with the largest number of active mills were Pennsylvania, Kansas, New York, Minnesota, Ohio, and California.

Although any grain (rice, oats, barley, corn, millet, sorghum, and wheat) can be ground into flour, most of the world's flour was produced from wheat. Using standard milling procedures, 100 pounds of wheat yielded approximately 72 pounds of white flour. In addition to flour, the milling process produced millfeeds, which were made from pieces of bran and other portions of the wheat kernel. Millfeeds were used as ingredients in livestock food.

Flour could be packaged for sale to the household or bakery markets or used as an ingredient in bakery mixes, breads or doughs, or pastas. Different bread varieties were made with varying recipes, but on the average 100 pounds of flour could make about 150 one-pound loaves of bread. The bread and cake industry consumed approximately 72 percent of the flour milled in the United States. Other flour products included cookies, cereals, gravies, soups, whiskeys, and beers. Flour products were also used in non-food applications such as the manufacture of plywood adhesives, industrial starches, fertilizers, paving mixes, polishes, and cosmetics. Approximately 85 percent of the flour used by industrial users was milled from hard and durum wheat varieties.

BACKGROUND AND DEVELOPMENT

Milled grains have been used as principal food staples for thousands of years. Corn has been the predominant grain used by people in Latin America and the sub-Saharan regions of Africa, while many Asian nations have depended on rice. Inhabitants of Europe and North America relied primarily on wheat products.

The origins of wheat farming and milling are obscure. Historians estimate that wheat cultivation began between 10,000 and 15,000 years ago and marked the beginning of civilization. Because they could be stored, stocked, and transported, grains led to the evolution of trading practices. Documents in the form of artistic depictions and early writings chronicled the development of wheat grinding technologies and baking methods in ancient Egypt, Assyria, Greece, and China.

One of the oldest types of wheat known is bulgur wheat, and the earliest means employed to separate the parts of the wheat kernel involved rubbing the grain between the hands. Another method used the action of hoofed animals walking over grains which had been spread on hard ground. Winnowing was a process in which grains were tossed in the air so that the chaff would blow away. Removing the individual grains from the rest of the plant was necessary before milling could take place.

Wheat kernels are made up of three components: "endosperm," "bran," and "germ." The endosperm represents about 83 percent of the kernel and contains the starchy portion used to make white flour. The bran accounts for about 14.5 percent of the wheat kernel and is used in whole wheat flour and animal feeds. The smallest portion of the kernel, the germ, represents only about 2.5 percent of the kernel. The most common uses of wheat germ are in human food products and in animal feeds. Historically, the germ was separated from the rest of the wheat kernel because it contained fat and did not keep well in long term storage.

Grain milling practices were developed to separate the kernel components and make flour. The first types of milling procedures involved the use of rubbing stones, mortar and pestles, or querns. Querns were devices made from two stacked, disk-shaped stones. Wheat grains were poured into the quern through a hole in the top stone. As the two stones turned against each other with a rotary motion, the abrasive movement separated the parts of the wheat kernels and ground the endosperm into flour. The flour was then discharged between the stones.

More efficient methods of grinding grain progressed along with the development of alternative power supplies. Horses and oxen could turn millstones better than human power. Wind- and water-operated mills supplanted animal power. As the United States was settled, mills were constructed in almost every town. Typically the mill relied on water power and was, therefore, located near a source of running water.

The first continuous system for milling wheat into flour was developed during the last part of the eighteenth century by an American, Oliver Evans. Evans's mill design utilized steam technology and employed conveyors and bucket elevators to move the grain through a multi-phase milling process. Further advances in milling technology occurred during the nineteenth century. In 1865, Edmund La Croix developed a middlings purifier that separated the granular endosperm from the bran so that it could be reground to produce a better grade of flour. During the 1870s, the first roller mills in the United States were constructed. Roller mills possessed several advantages: they eliminated the need of dressing millstones; they were able to produce flour through a more gradual extraction process, which enabled millers to yield a larger percentage of better grade flour; and, they lent themselves to greater efficiency, thereby making the construction of larger mills more feasible.

As U.S. citizens moved westward, milling centers moved with them. Mills became larger in size but fewer in number. In 1870, an estimated 22,000 mills served the nation's population of about 30 million. One hundred and ten years later in 1980, the nation's population of 220 million was served by an estimated 150 to 250 mills. In Michigan the number of mills fell from 534 at the turn of the century to six in 1990. The consolidation of mills and the trend toward facilities with greater capacities led to the creation of giant corporations such as Pillsbury and General Mills. Millers began offering a wider variety of products during the early 1900s. Self-rising flour, biscuit and cake mixes, and prepared doughs were introduced during the 1920s and 1930s but failed to gain widespread popularity until after World War II.

During the middle of the twentieth century fundamental changes occurred in the primary location of mills. Prior to the 1950s, the cost of shipping wheat and the cost of shipping flour were approximately equal, and mills were frequently built close to wheat fields. During the early 1960s, the cost of shipping grain decreased following the introduction of hopper rail cars. At the same time, costs surrounding sanitation requirements increased the price of shipping flour. As a result, mills were constructed in close proximity to end markets rather than near the wheat fields.

Granular flour, a product made with particles of a uniform size with carefully controlled amounts of atomized moisture to reduce clumping, was introduced during the 1960s. Although granular flower was more expensive than regular flour, it offered several advantages. It had less dust, was easier to pour, did not require sifting, and dispersed in cold liquids.

During the 1970s, sales of household flour declined as society moved away from home baking and homemakers demonstrated a preference for the convenience and consistency of prepared mixes. In addition, many mixes were less expensive than individual ingredients. Baking from ''scratch'' ceased to be an activity of necessity and was relegated to hobby status. Demographic information revealed that households with higher incomes were more likely to use flour than lower income households. Flour volume losses within the household sector were partially offset by increases of flour sales to commercial bakers.

CURRENT CONDITIONS

Although overall flour consumption declined somewhat during the early 1970s, annual per capita flour consumption increased by 24 pounds between 1970 and 1990 to a total of 135 pounds. Industry analysts attributed gains to increased consumption of fiber, bran, and whole grain products along with growing consumption of such flour-based convenience foods as sandwiches and pizzas.

The diverse end uses of flours required a wide variety of milled grain products produced from different types of wheat. During the latter part of the twentieth century, 14 different wheat species were grown. The three most frequently used varieties were common wheat (*Triticum aestivum*), club wheat (*Triticum compactum*), and durum wheat (*Triticum durum*). Together, these three accounted for 90 percent of the wheat grown in the United States.

Different wheats were classified as ''hard,'' ''soft,'' or ''durum.'' Hard wheats were used to make flours for breads and rolls. Soft wheats were used primarily in cakes, cookies, crackers, and prepared mixes. Durum wheat was almost exclusively used to make pasta products. Although a single modern flour mill might offer more than one product, it typically ground only one class of wheat. Approximately 70 percent of the U.S. milling capacity during the late 1980s was devoted to hard wheat. Soft wheat mills accounted for 20 percent, durum wheat accounted for 8 percent, and mills dedicated to whole wheat production represented 2 percent of the nation's milling capacity.

A process called fractionation was used to separate the flour according to the fineness of its particles. Course fractions were reground. Intermediate fractions were used in applications requiring low amounts of protein, and fine fraction flour was blended with other flours or used alone in applications where high protein content was necessary. White flour was often bleached with agents such as potassium bromide, iodate, acetone peroxide, azodicarbonamide, ascorbic acid, and chlorine dioxide. In addition to providing consistent coloring, bleaching improved the condition of the flour gluten which improved its baking quality.

White flour is made only with the endosperm portion of the wheat kernel. Farina is also made from the endosperm, but it is ground to produce a granular product. The term "wheat germ" refers to the part of the wheat kernel from which a seed sprouts. It contains oil which was sometimes extracted for separate processing. Wheat germ was also used by breakfast cereal makers and in breads and other bakery products. Wheat germ is high in polyunsaturated fat and contains vitamin E. Whole wheat flour, also called graham flour, is made from the endosperm, bran, and germ combined. It has a higher protein content than regular white flour. Pastas such as spaghetti, macaroni, and noodles were made from durum wheat. A popular pasta ingredient, "semolina" was a granular grind of durum endosperm, comparable to farina.

As the grain mill products industry entered the 1990s, the number of mills continued declining and the capacity per mill continued to increase. Between 1973 and 1990, the average mill increased in size by 70 percent, but the total number of mills in the United States fell by 25 percent. Overall, between 1973 and 1990 the industry's capacity expanded by 28 percent.

In 1990, more than half of the nation's milling capacity was concentrated in mills with individual daily capacities exceeding a million pounds. The trend toward large mills was driven by economies of scale, which reduced labor and transportation costs. As a result of industry consolidation and expanding mill capacity, the top four milling companies owned approximately 58 percent of the nation's milling capacity in 1990. The top 12 establishments owned approximately 80 percent.

One of the biggest challenges facing the grain mill industry was the charge that flour performance was diminishing. Industry researchers speculated that one cause of deteriorating quality was a national grain breeding program that had emphasized increasing

yield per acre without paying sufficient attention to the quality of the end products produced with the grain. Other possible causes included: a drop in the amount of protein; a declining protein quality; an ever-increasing number of wheat varieties; the impact of agricultural practices such as irrigation and fertilizers; and, milling practices which improved efficiency but potentially produced inferior results.

INDUSTRY LEADERS

One of the leading companies within the flour and grain mill products classification was Pillsbury, a division of Grand Metropolitan PLC. Grand Metropolitan, a British firm, purchased Pillsbury in 1989 for $5.8 billion. In fiscal 1993, Grand Metropolitan reported that Pillsbury employed 16,000 workers worldwide, and its sales totaled $3.4 billion. Pillsbury operated three major groups: Pillsbury and Hungry Jack; Pizza; and Green Giant. The Pillsbury and Hungry Jack group offered flour to both the home and institutional markets, as well as pastries, prepared dough, baked goods, baking mixes, and specialty potatoes. The company also pioneered microwave products in the 1970s. Pizza products were sold under two brands, Jenos and Totinos. Vegetable products were marketed under the Green Giant label.

Pillsbury, originally a flour milling company, was established in 1869 in Minneapolis, Minnesota. In 1929, the company developed and patented a vented package that allowed dough to rise. The innovation enabled the company to boost its position in dough product sales. By 1993, the refrigerated dough product line represented the company's largest segment, and Pillsbury held the top position in U.S. refrigerated dough sales.

Though Pillsbury held the top position in refrigerated doughs, it lagged behind Duncan Hines and General Mills in overall bakery goods. In addition, the company relinquished its position as the nation's top flour miller in the late 1970s. Pillsbury's milling capacity grew by 39 percent between 1973 and 1987, but it was surpassed by three competitors: ConAgra, Archer Daniels Midland Milling, and Cargill. Between 1987 and 1990 Pillsbury's milling capacity decreased by nine percent, and in 1991 the company announced plans to sell four of its eight mills to Cargill.

In 1990, the nation's largest grain miller, as measured by capacity, was ConAgra. ConAgra moved into the top spot following its acquisition of Pevney and International Multifoods. In 1990 ConAgra's milling capacity totaled 27.6 million pounds per day and in fiscal year 1993, the company reported total flour production of 8.9 billion pounds.

ConAgra, a large, diverse food products organization, operated divisions in three areas: Prepared Foods, Trading and Processing, and Agri-Products. The company's total sales for fiscal 1993 totaled $21.5 billion. In addition to its wheat flour production mills, ConAgra operated oat, dry corn, and barley processing facilities. In the United States, the company's grain processing division operated 27 mills located in 14 states. An additional three U.S. mills were operated under joint venture agreements. ConAgra also operated mills in Canada and the United Kingdom.

Another industry leader was General Mills. In 1990, General Mills ranked sixth in U.S. flour milling capacity. The company's household flours, sold under the Gold Medal and Robin Hood labels, held a 34 percent share of the market. The company's Bisquick mix held a 73 percent market share within the baking mix category, and its Betty Crocker mixes held a 48 percent share of the dessert market.

WORK FORCE

According to the 1987 Census of Manufactures, employment within the U.S. flour and grain mills products industry totaled 13,300. Tennessee, Illinois, Texas, and Kansas were the top employers in the industry, employing 37 percent of the industry's workers. The statistics reported for 1987 represented a drop in employment of 1 percent from 1986 and a decline of 12 percent from 1982.

Safety issues within the industry included dust control, noise abatement, and controlling hazards that presented risks for fire and explosions. Concentrations of grain dust above certain limits were susceptible to burning rapidly if ignited. Dust control was also necessary to limit possible worker exposure to microorganisms, pesticide residues, toxins, insect parts, and animal hairs. Some studies suggested that workers with high levels of exposure to grain dust might be susceptible to respiratory diseases such as chronic bronchitis. Noise in mills was primarily attributed to pneumatic blowers and vehicles.

To control potential work place hazards, modern mills reduced dust generation by minimizing grain handling, reducing the velocity of grain movement, and installing enclosed conveyor systems. Protection from excessive noise was achieved by isolating work stations and limiting exposure.

INDUSTRY INFORMATION SOURCES

Blackwood, Alan. *Spotlight on Grain.* Vero Beach, FL: Rourke Enterprises, 1987.

Bush, Paul. "Pillsbury's Predictable Quality." *Prepared Foods* (January 1991).

ConAgra, Inc. Fiscal 1993 Annual Report. Omaha, NE: ConAgra, 1993.

General Mills 1993 Annual Report. Minneapolis, MN: General Mills, 1993.

Grand Metropolitan Annual Report 1992. London: Grand Metropolitan, 1992.

Harwood, Joy. "U.S. Flour Milling on the Rise." *Food Review* (April - June 1991).

Koeslka, Rita. "A Family Affair." *Forbes* (June 11, 1990).

Mutchler, John E. and Stephen W. Bell. "Grain Handling and Processing." *Industrial Hygiene Aspects of Plant Operations,* Lester V. Cralley and Lewis J. Cralley, eds. New York: Macmillan, 1985.

Otto, Alison. "Grand Met's Grand Plan." *Prepared Foods* (January 1991).

"Pillsbury Fact Sheet." Minneapolis: Grand Metropolitan, (February 1993).

U.S. Department of Commerce. *1987 Census of Manufactures.* Washington DC: Bureau of the Census, 1990.

Waldrop, Judith. "Scratch and Mix." *American Demographics* (October 1992).

Wheat Flour Institute. *From Wheat to Flour.* Washington, DC: Wheat Flour Institute, rev. ed., 1981.

—Karen Bellenir

SIC 2043

CEREAL BREAKFAST FOODS

This industry is comprised of establishments that manufacture cereal breakfast foods. Establishments that primarily manufacture granola and other types of breakfast bars are categorized in **SIC 2064: Candy and Other Confectionary Products.**

INDUSTRY SNAPSHOT

According to figures published by the U.S. Department of Commerce, the cereal breakfast foods industry shipped $6.6 billion worth of products in 1987. The total included $5.0 billion of products considered primary to the industry and $1.3 billion of secondary products. Miscellaneous transactions accounted for $319.0 million. These figures yielded a specialization ratio of 79 percent, an increase from the 77 percent specialization ratio recorded in 1982.

The largest and most rapidly growing segment within the industry consisted of ready-to-eat (RTE) cereals. By the end of the 1980s, the RTE market was estimated at $4.8 billion. By 1992, industry analysts valued it at $7.3 billion, and industry forecasters expected it to reach $8 billion in 1993.

A much smaller segment, hot cereals, experienced virtually no growth between 1982 and 1987. In 1988, however, the hot cereal market garnered sales of $600 million, a 20 percent increase over figures for the previous year. The sudden surge was attributed to a national focus on the reported health benefits of oat bran.

BACKGROUND AND DEVELOPMENT

Ready-to-eat cereals first appeared during the late 1800s. According to one account, John Kellogg, a doctor who belonged to a vegetarian group, developed wheat and corn flakes to extend the group's dietary choices. John's brother, William Kellogg, saw potential in the innovative grain products and initiated commercial production and marketing. Patients at the Battle Creek, Michigan Sanitarium were among Kellogg's first customers.

Another cereal producer with roots in the nineteenth century was the Quaker Oats Company. In 1873, the North Star Oatmeal Mill built an oatmeal plant in Cedar Rapids, Iowa. North Star reorganized with other enterprises and together they formed Quaker Oats in 1901.

The Washburn Crosby Company, a predecessor to General Mills, entered the market during the 1920s. The company's first ready-to-eat cereal, Wheaties, was introduced to the American public in 1924. According to General Mills, Wheaties was developed when a Minneapolis clinician spilled a mixture of gruel that he was making for his patients on a hot stove. The clinician approached the Washburn Crosby Company with his product and, following many tests and refinements, Wheaties was born. Other General Mills cereals followed in rapid succession. In 1937 Crispy Corn Kix was introduced. The company also launched the world's first ready-to-eat oat cereal in 1941. Originally named Cheerioats, the product later became "Cheerios."

During the 1940s cereal makers benefited from improved methods of puffing cereal products. Puffing methods employed a principle somewhat analogous to popping corn. Cereal ingredients were cooked and formed into pellets with precisely monitored amounts of water. The product was heated in an enclosed container called a "gun." As the heat increased, the water within the pellets turned to steam. The steam expanded and built up pressure within the gun until the intensity of the pressure caused the end of the gun to open. When the gun opened, the force of the escaping steam

propelled the pellets out of the gun into a receiving bin, and as the steam erupted from the pellets it left them permeated with thousands of air holes. These air holes caused the pellet to become larger and less dense. For example, one type of puffed product made with a pellet measuring 0.156 inches in diameter, measured 0.5 inches after puffing. During the first decade of the 1900s, before the development of modern puffing procedures, puffed products were actually shot from cannons.

Many kinds of cereal were manufactured with a device called a food extruder. The extruder mixed and cooked cereal ingredients in a process that also shaped and colored the mixture. Ingredients were added at one end of the extruder and conveyed through its inner mechanisms by spiraling screws. A die at the other end of the extruder squeezed out cereal shapes and a blade cut the pieces at a predetermined size.

These food extruder were similar in operation to meat grinders. The first extruders, used during the 1930s, had only a single screw and often had problems caused by dried pieces of food. The machines were improved by the development of twin screws. Twin screw extruders had two screws that intermeshed and cleaned each other as they propelled the cereal mixture.

The second half of the twentieth century brought rapid increases in brand offerings and growing national interest in ready-to-eat cereals. Many popular pre-sweetened cereals aimed at the children's market were introduced during the 1950s. Trix and Lucky Charms were launched in 1954. Cocoa Puffs made its first appearance in 1958. Adult cereals made an impact during the 1960s. Total, touted as a product containing 100 percent of the officially established U.S. RDA (recommended daily allowance) of vitamins and iron, was introduced in 1961. In 1970, the ready-to-eat cereal market was valued at $659 million, and it had reached $1.9 billion by 1979.

In the 1980s U.S. consumers became increasingly interested in health issues and consequently in improving their diets. In response, Kellogg introduced Nutri-Grain in 1981, the first line of flaked, whole grain ready-to-eat cereals with no sugar or preservatives. Other Kellogg offerings aimed at the health-conscious market included Crispix in 1983 and Just Right in 1985.

In 1985, Kellogg held a 40 percent share of the total ready-to-eat cereal market, which had grown to $4.35 billion. General Mills held a 22 percent share, followed by Post (14 percent), Quaker Oats (8 percent) and Ralston Purina (6 percent). All other cereal manufacturers combined held the remaining 10 percent. According to a report published by *Prepared Foods*, 92.4 percent of U.S. households used ready-to-eat cereal. The average household had four packages and the country consumed more than 20 billion bowls annually.

Much of the growth within the ready-to-eat cereal segment during the later part of the 1980s was attributed to interest in oat bran. Products specifically labeled "Oat Bran" were valued at $34.9 million in 1987, at $105.2 million in 1988, and at $328.2 million in 1989. Oat bran's popularity, however, was short-lived. A study published in the *New England Journal of Medicine* debunked advertising claims that oat bran possessed the ability to lower cholesterol levels. The study led to consumer skepticism and a downturn in the success of new products based on key ingredients. In 1990 ready-to-eat cereal sales increased only 0.2 percent.

Another ingredient to suffer from health controversies was psyllium. Psyllium, a grain grown mainly in India, was said to help reduce cholesterol and thereby reduce risks of heart disease. A study done by the University of Minnesota reporting a 9 percent reduction in cholesterol levels among people who ate a cereal containing psyllium was used to document the claims. Subsequently, General Mills incorporated it in "Benefit" and Kellogg used it in "Heartwise."

Psyllium had been previously approved by the Food and Drug Administration (FDA) for use as a laxative, but its use as a food had not been certified. The FDA expressed concern that it could result in damaging health consequences to the intestinal tract such as constipation, fecal impaction, depletion of necessary colon bacteria, and shifts in the body's ability to absorb nutrients. Allergic reaction posed another problem related to psyllium use. Consequently, General Mills discontinued Benefit in January 1990, and Kellogg encountered problems with regulatory challenges to its advertising. Six states—Iowa, California, Florida, Minnesota, Texas, and Wisconsin—brought suit against the company regarding the health benefit claims for Heartwise and other products including Special K, 40+, Bran Flakes, and Frosted Flakes. In addition, Texas banned Heartwise. The suits were settled in 1991 when Kellogg agreed to pay each of the six states $30,000 to use for consumer or nutritional education. In addition, the name "Heartwise" was changed to "Fiberwise."

CURRENT CONDITIONS

The early 1990s were notable for shifts in traditionally held markets. Kellogg's Frosted Flakes had lost its top position to General Mills's Cheerios in 1989, and the cereal giant's previous 40 percent market share slipped to 37.5 percent in 1991. At the same time, General Mills's market share increased to 25.1 percent. *Fortune* magazine estimated each percentage point was worth about $75 million dollars per year.

In addition, many of the country's major cereal manufacturers faced problems because of changing patterns regarding brand loyalty. Customers preferred purchasing a variety of cereals rather than one favorite. Another challenge was the growing percentage of market share being captured by private labels marketed by a supermarket or grocer. For a 12-week period that ended in January 1991, private labels accounted for 7 percent of the pound volume sales in the ready-to-eat cereal market and 4 percent based on dollar amount. The percentage varied by cereal type. For example, as measured in dollars, private labels captured 13 percent of the crisp rice segment and 11 percent of the frosted flakes segment. Many of these private label brands were manufactured by Ralston Purina.

Another change noted during the early 1990s was a shift away from products promoted solely on the basis of their health benefits. Although consumers continued to look at nutritional content, other factors such as taste, variety, convenience, and price were also important. The "all-family" cereal segment held almost half of the ready-to-eat market. All-family cereals were not as sweet as children's cereals but had more sugar than traditional adult cereals. Examples included General Mills's Wheaties Honey Gold and Kellogg's Frosted Bran.

The snack market, which was estimated to be more than three times larger than the ready-to-eat cereal market, represented an emerging growth area for cereal makers. Following the U.S. Department of Agriculture's release of its recommendation that Americans eat six to 11 servings of grain per day, cereal makers began promotions touting their products as tasty treats with positive health benefits. An estimated 7 percent of ready-to-eat cereals were consumed as snacks throughout the day. For example, Cheerios was promoted as a snack for toddlers, and an estimated one-third of all Chex cereal, made by Ralston Purina, was purchased for use as an ingredient in snack mixes rather than for breakfast consumption. Two new products aimed directly at the snack market were Kellogg's Rice Krispies Treats and General Mills's Fingos.

INDUSTRY LEADERS

The Kellogg Company was established in 1906, and throughout the twentieth century it was the world's market leader in ready-to-eat cereals. In 1992,

Kellogg operated manufacturing facilities in 17 nations, and the company's global distribution network reached 150 countries. Canada, the United Kingdom, and Australia represented Kellogg's three largest overseas markets.

In 1992, Kellogg reported total sales of almost $6.2 billion, an increase over the $5.79 billion reported for 1991. Global employment was reported to be 16,500. A few well-known Kellogg products were Corn Flakes, Frosted Mini-wheats, Corn Pops, and Froot Loops. In addition to its ready-to-eat cereal division, Kellogg also operated Mrs. Smith's Frozen Foods. The Mrs. Smith's division manufactured Eggo waffles and frozen pies.

General Mills was the second largest cereal manufacturer in terms of ready-to-eat market share. General Mills ranked as a larger corporation than the Kellogg Company, however, in terms of total assets and overall sales. General Mills's consumer foods division included its line of Big G cereals, Gold Medal Flour, Betty Crocker mixes, and Hamburger Helper. Outside its consumer foods division, the company also owned the Red Lobster and Olive Garden Restaurants. The restaurants accounted for approximately one-third of General Mills's total revenues.

In 1993, General Mills reported total sales of $8.13 billion. Of this total, consumer foods accounted for $5.4 billion. General Mills operated seven cereal manufacturing plants within the United States and an eighth in Toronto, Ontario and employed 121,000 people. Big G cereals included flaked products such as Total, Raisin Bran, and Country Corn Flakes; the company's puffed varieties included Kix, Trix, and Cocoa Puffs. Innovations undertaken during 1993 included the introduction of "Fingos" a dry, finger-food cereal aimed at the snack market and the addition of X's to Cheerios. The Cherrios and X's were packaged with a detachable game board on the back of the box.

Another leading cereal maker is the Quaker Oats Company. The company's first puffed product, "Puffed Rice," was introduced in 1905. In 1992, Quaker Oats held a 7.1 percent share of the ready-to-eat cereal market, and its principal product was Cap'n Crunch. Quaker Oats's market share within the ready-to-eat segment peaked in 1988 at 8 percent but slowly eroded in subsequent years. Within the smaller hot cereal segment, however, the company held approximately 60 percent of the market. In addition to cereal products, Quaker Oats produced Aunt Jemima Pancake mix and Gatorade sports drinks.

AMERICA AND THE WORLD

Kellogg was the first American company to enter the foreign market for ready-to-eat cereals. In 1914 the company began distribution in Ontario, Canada, and ten years later the company began operations in Australia. Kellogg opened its first plant in England in 1938 and began operations on the European continent in the 1950s. By the early 1990s Kellogg distributed its products to 150 nations and in some of these markets held a market share as large as 80 percent.

English-speaking nations represented the largest cereal markets. Consumption in non-English markets was estimated at only one-fourth the amount consumed by English speakers. For example, during the early 1990s per capita consumption of ready-to-eat cereal in England was 13.3 pounds per person, but in France it was only 1.8 pounds. On the European continent, consumption averaged 3.0 pounds per year. Shifting attention away from traditional breakfasts and focusing interest on low-cholesterol, convenient snack alternatives, cereal makers viewed low per capita consumption areas as potential growth fields. In Spain sales were growing at a rate of 20 percent per year; in Portugal they were growing at an annual rate of 50 percent. Some industry forecasters estimated that by the year 2000 the European cereal market would experience more than a four-fold increase and reach $6.5 billion.

In 1991, Kellogg announced a joint venture plan to build a cereal plant in Eastern Europe to supply the Baltic states and parts of the former Soviet Union. The plant, located in Riga, Latvia, was expected to be ready for production in 1994. Kellogg also announced plans to build plants in India and China. Ground-breaking for the production facility in Bombay, India was accomplished in October 1992 and the plant was also expected to begin production in 1994. The company's Chinese facility, to be located in the Guangdong Province, was scheduled for completion in 1995.

General Mills was also active in expanding its overseas operations. In Europe, General Mills and Nestle formed a joint venture called Cereal Partners Worldwide (CPW). In 1992, CPW claimed a 15 percent share of the United Kingdom market and planned an aggressive expansion campaign on the European continent. CPW also planned to enter the Mexican market and expand into Malaysia, Thailand, Philippines, Singapore, Indonesia, and Brunei.

INDUSTRY INFORMATION SOURCES

Austin, Beth. "Quaker in $45.6M Push." *Advertising Age* (July 13, 1987).

Biesada, Alexandra. "A Case of Heartburn." *Financial World* (June 11, 1991).

Biesada, Alexandra. "Life After Oat Bran." *Financial World* (June 11, 1991).

Brumback, Nancy. "Cereal's Sweeter Family." *Supermarket News* (May 31, 1993).

Dworetzky, Tom. "The Churn of the Screw." *Discover* (May 1988).

General Mills, Inc. "Big 'G' Cereals." Minneapolis, MN: General Mills, (January 1993).

General Mills, Inc. *1993 Annual Report*, Minneapolis, MN: General Mills, (June 1993).

"Going With the Grain." *Progressive Grocer* (August 1989).

Hammel, Frank. "Cereal." *Supermarket Business* (September 1990).

"How to Play With Cereal, But Without the Milk." *New York Times* (June 23, 1993).

Hunter, Beatrice Trum. "Foods or Drugs?" *Consumers' Research* (April 1990).

Kellogg. *1992 Annual Report* Battle Creek, MI: Kellogg, 1993.

"Kellogg Pays Six States." *New York Times* (October 4, 1991).

Knowlton, Christopher. "Europe Cooks Up a Cereal Brawl." *Fortune* (June 3, 1991).

Liesse, Julie. "Private-label Cereals Surge." *Advertising Age* (March 4, 1991).

Liesse, Julie. "Quaker's New Cereals Run Hot and Cold." *Advertising Age* (July 20, 1992).

Mans, Jack. "From Quaker's Tiny Oats, A Mighty Plant Grows." *Prepared Foods* (August 1988).

Messenger, Robert. "No More Blues in Battle Creek." *Prepared Foods* (February 1987).

Meyer, Ann. "Can't Catch Kellogg." *Prepared Foods* (February 1992).

Naude, Alice. "'Heartwise' Is Launched Amid Food Labeling Debate." *Chemical Marketing Reporter* (September 4, 1989).

Spethmann, Betsy. "Snack Time? Give Me My Cereal Bowl!" *Brandweek* (May 3, 1993).

Therrien, Lois, and Charlie Hoots. "Cafe Au Lait, A Croissant — and Trix." *Business Week* (August 24, 1992).

U.S. Department of Commerce. *1987 Census of Manufactures*. Washington DC: Bureau of the Census, 1990.

—Karen Bellenir

RICE MILLING

This industry is comprised of establishments that clean, polish, or process rice. Principle products include rice flour, rice meal, white rice, brown rice, and rice bran.

According to figures published by the U.S. Department of Commerce, in 1987 Rice Milling shipments totaled $1.2 billion. The industry's specialization ratio—a ratio of shipments considered primary to the industry to total shipments—was 98 percent.

In 1992, the Rice Council estimated that annual per capita rice consumption totaled 21 pounds. The amount was nearly twice the per capita consumption recorded during the 1970s. Increases reflected the diverse ways rice was available and trends toward health consciousness. Rice contained only trace amounts of fat and naturally provided protein, thiamin, riboflavin, niacin, phosphorous, iron, and potassium. It was cholesterol free, gluten free, and low in sodium. In addition, it came at a low price. In 1993, a serving of rice cost five cents.

Types of rice were classified according to grain size. Long grain rice was comprised of grains that were four to five times longer than their width. Medium grain rice was plumper than long grain rice, and short gain rice was almost round.

In the United States, fruitful rice production began near the end of the seventeenth century, following the importation of a variety of rice from Madagascar to the Carolinas. In 1726 rice exports through the port of Charleston, South Carolina, totaled 4,500 metric tons. California rice production began the following century in the aftermath of the Gold Rush of 1849. An estimated 40,000 Chinese immigrants demanded large amounts of rice which was originally imported from the Orient. California rice production began in the 1860s, but the first commercial crop was not produced until 1912. Rice growers on the east coast migrated westward and moved into Arkansas, Louisiana, Mississippi, Missouri, and Texas. These states, along with California, remained the centers of rice production in the United States throughout the twentieth century.

When workers harvested rice from the field it was first dried to help achieve stable storage conditions and then sold to a rice mill. At this stage, the rice was referred to as "paddy" or "rough" rice. Millers first removed the inedible hull surrounding each individual grain. After hull removal, rice grains still possessed seven natural bran layers. In this state, the rice could be sold as brown rice or it could be ''polished'' to remove the bran and produce white rice.

Because polishing rice removed some of the grain's natural ingredients, some millers turned to a procedure called ''parboiling'' to ameliorate nutrient losses. Parboiled rice was soaked in pressurized water, steamed, and dried before milling. In addition to helping grains preserve their nutrients, parboiling helped produce grains that fluffed better and were less sticky when cooked. Parboiled grains, however, took longer to cook.

Other rice mill products included brewers rice, enriched rice, and pre-cooked rice. Brewers rice was made of small, broken rice fragments and was primarily used by pet food manufacturers and brewers. Enriched rice contained artificially replaced nutrients. Pre-cooked rice was cooked and dehydrated after going through the milling process.

In 1987, the rice milling industry employed 4,500 workers. Arkansas, California, Texas, Louisiana, and Mississippi employed 93 percent of the industry's workers.

INDUSTRY INFORMATION SOURCES

Jaret, Peter. ''Bran News About Rice.'' *Health* (May/June 1993).

Rice Council. *U.S.A. Rice: A Guide the United States Rice Industry*. Houston: Rice Council, nd.

U.S. Department of Commerce. *1987 Census of Manufactures*. Washington DC: Bureau of the Census, 1990.

—Karen Bellenir

SIC 2045

PREPARED FLOUR MIXES AND DOUGHS

This industry classification is comprised of establishments primarily involved in manufacturing prepared mixes and doughs from purchased flours. Establishments primarily involved in milling flour from grain and manufacturing grain mill products, including prepared mixes and doughs, are classified in **SIC 2041: Flour and Other Grain Mill Products.**

In 1987 establishments classified in **SIC 2045: Prepared Flour Mixes and Doughs** shipped products totaling $2.6 billion. Of this amount, $2.2 billion represented products considered primary, $282.4 million represented secondary products, and $133.5 million represented miscellaneous transactions.

The concept of commercial mixes first developed when millers began adding a leavening agent and salt to flour products to make ''self-rising'' formulations. Self-rising flours became popular in the southeastern portion of the United States because traditional leavening agents, such as baking powder, had limited shelf lives in hot, humid climates.

The development of a stable shortening led to the introduction of the nation's first biscuit mix in the 1920s. Cake mixes tentatively appeared during the 1930s after the industry learned how to dehydrate eggs. Because mixes were convenience products rather than necessities, further commercial development was hampered by the economic hardships and product shortages associated with the Depression and World War II. Following World War II, however, the country embraced convenience. Cake mixes reappeared and began to find increasing popularity not only with homemakers but also among restaurants and institutional users.

During the early 1990s, mixes continued to enjoy widespread popularity. Many bakers preferred mixes to traditional ''from scratch'' recipes because in addition to offering convenience, they provided consistently favorable results, even for inexperienced cooks. Prepared mixes were available for a wide variety of products including breads, rolls, cakes, cookies, and pancakes. Mixes were generally one of two kinds. One type required only the addition of a specified amount of liquid. Another type required the addition of other ingredients such as eggs and shortening.

According to a report published by *Institutional Distribution* in 1990, the best selling cake mixes to food service establishments were chocolate, white, devil's food, spice, and pound cakes. In addition, carrot, crumb, gingerbread, lemon, sponge, angel food, applesauce, banana, and brownie mixes were also popular.

One of the leading companies in this industry was Chelsea Milling Co. Operated by the Holmes family in Chelsea, Michigan, Chelsea Milling began as a commercial flour mill. In 1957 the company refocused its energies to produce the Jiffy line of prepared mixes. In 1989 a writer for *Forbes* magazine estimated that Chelsea's sales approximated $65 million. In 1990 the company produced 1.25 million boxes of Jiffy mixes daily. The line included biscuit, muffin, and cake mixes. The nation's market for biscuit mixes, of which Jiffy held a 14 percent share, was estimated at $120 million annually.

According to government statistics, this industry employed 12,100 workers in 1987. The leading states in employment were Illinois, Tennessee, Indiana, and Missouri. Combined these four states accounted for 36 percent of the industry's employment. Small, single-establishment companies with 20 or fewer employees accounted for only three percent of the industry's total shipments.

INDUSTRY INFORMATION SOURCES

"Cake Mixes," *Institutional Distribution,* May 15, 1991.

From Wheat to Flour, Washington, DC: Wheat Flour Institute, 1981.

Koselka, Rita, "A Family Affair," *Forbes,* June 11, 1990.

Tanyeri, Dana, "Mixes Offer Fresh Benefits and Low Food Cost." *Institutional Distribution,* July 1990.

1987 Census of Manufactures, Washington DC: Bureau of the Census, 1990.

—Karen Bellenir

SIC 2046

WET CORN MILLING

Establishments primarily engaged in milling corn or sorghum grain (milo) by the wet process, and producing starch, syrup, oil, sugar, and byproducts, such as gluten feed and meal. Also included in this industry are establishments primarily engaged in manufacturing starch from other vegetable sources (e.g., potatoes, wheat). Establishments primarily engaged in manufacturing table syrups from corn syrup and other ingredients, and those manufacturing starch base dessert powders, are classified in **SIC 2099 Food Preparations, Not Elsewhere Classified.**

In 1987 the wet corn milling industry shipped $4.8 billion worth of products. Of this total, $4.2 billion were considered primary, $559.1 million were considered secondary, and $72.5 million represented miscellaneous transactions. These statistics yielded a specialization ratio of 88 percent.

Native Americans cultivated corn for thousands of years before European settlers came to the continent. Scientists estimate that early ears of corn were about the same size as ears of wheat. The development of hybrids and special varieties brought about the large plants and cobs known to the modern world.

Corn kernels are made up of several parts and every part has a use. The largest portion of the kernel is starch, which found utility in a variety of industries, including food products, paper, adhesives, textiles, and pharmaceuticals. Within the food processing industry,

corn starch was primarily made into sweeteners such as corn syrup, dextrose, and high fructose corn syrup (HFCS). According to one estimate, 400 million bushels of corn were used annually to make HFCS. In 1980 HFCS replaced sugar as the sweetener of choice for the United States' major soft drink manufacturers.

Starch can also be converted to ethanol. Wet corn millers advocated using ethanol as part of an overall national energy policy. Between 1981 and 1991 drivers around the world traveled almost one trillion miles on fuels made with ethanol blends.

Another important portion of a corn kernel is the germ, the portion of the kernel from which a seed would sprout. The germ contains oils used to make margarine, mayonnaise, salad dressings, and shortening. Other portions of the corn kernel are made up of protein and are used to produce corn gluten feed and corn gluten meal for animals and poultry.

During the early 1990s, the wet corn milling industry used approximately 28 million tons—almost one billion bushels—of corn annually. According to ADM Milling, one of the nation's leading wet corn millers, a typical bushel of corn yielded 31 pounds of starch; 12.3 pounds of 21 percent protein feed; 2.5 pounds of 60 percent gluten meal; and 1.5 pounds of corn oil.

In 1990 an estimated five billion pounds of industrial starches valued at $700 million were consumed. According to an account published in *Chemical Marketing Reporter,* "almost 4,000 individual items in a typical supermarket contain ingredients derived from corn, including new microwavable foods and fat replacers, of which starch is one of the most essential."

In 1987 the U.S. Department of the Census recorded 8,600 workers within the wet corn milling industry. Top states in employment were Iowa, Illinois, Indiana, and Tennessee. Employment figures indicated an increase of four percent from the previous year but a decrease of nine percent from the 9,500 workers employed in 1982.

INDUSTRY INFORMATION SOURCES

Archer Daniels Midland Company. *Amazing Grain: A Guide to the Wonders of Corn.* Decatur, IL: ADM, 1991.

Blackwood, Alan. *Spotlight on Grain.* Vero Beach, FL: Rourke Enterprises, 1987.

Singletary, Lynda. "Corn Refiners Are Finding Starches a Growing Niche." *Chemical Marketing Reporter* (October 14, 1991).

U.S. Department of Commerce. *1987 Census of Manufactures.* Washington, DC: Bureau of the Census, 1990.

—Karen Bellenir

SIC 2047

DOG AND CAT FOOD

This industry consists of establishments primarily engaged in manufacturing dog and cat food from cereal, meat, and other ingredients. These preparations may be canned, frozen, or dry. Establishments that manufacture feed for animals other than dogs and cats are classified in **SIC 2048: Prepared Feeds and Feed Ingredients for Animals and Fowls, Except Dogs and Cats.**

INDUSTRY SNAPSHOT

Retail sales of cat and dog food totaled $6.4 billion dollars in 1991 according to figures released by the Pet Food Institute, the association to which 95 percent of all U.S. pet food manufacturers belong. Of this total, dog food sales reached $3.9 billion, while cat food sales totalled $2.5 billion. The Packaged Facts research firm, however, estimated dog and cat food sales for 1992 at $8.9 billion, with continued dollar growth through the mid-1990s due to the proliferation of upscale products. The rate of growth for the industry in recent years has been relatively flat, with an average growth of one or two percent annually. As a vice-president for Quaker Oats told the *New York Times* in 1993, "This is a very competitive market. Unlike beverages where there is no limit to how much people will drink, dog food is driven by the change in dog population and we have only seen 1 to 2 percent (growth) a year."

This flat growth led to price wars in the early 1990s as the various manufacturers vied to take a larger share of a stagnant market. Flat growth in U.S. sales also led the U.S. pet industry to look to exports as a means of expanding the market. At the same time, the Pet Food Institute tried to expand the number of U.S. pet owners by targeting groups not usually associated with pet ownership, such as singles. Their success in this was primarily with promoting cat ownership since cats need less attention and are more adaptable to the lifestyle of the single person.

Another 1990s effort to overcome flat sales was the development of "upscale" healthy and gourmet pet food products. This paralleled a similar trend in the larger food industry. Established specialists in this area of the pet food market benefitted greatly. According to *Advertising Age,* pet food advertisers were generally among the top ten annual spenders in advertising during the 1980s, although this trend has diminished somewhat over the last few years. *Advertising Age* reported in 1993, for instance, that one of the effects of

the price wars was a cut-back on the advertising budgets of most pet food firms in order to sustain a profit. Downsizing product packages to sell more units of product was another tactic adopted by many of the manufacturers in the early 1990s to increase profits in a time of slow growth.

ORGANIZATION AND STRUCTURE

The dog and cat food segment of the pet food industry is comprised primarily of two types of firms. One is the large, general manufacturer that produces a variety of dog and cat foods and often also make other types of feed and/or food for humans in other divisions or subsidiaries. These manufacturers sell their product primarily through grocery stores. The other type is the specialty firm which produces exclusively pet food, usually a health or other specialized type of pet food. Traditionally, the general firms usually have sold their product in grocery stores while the specialty firms have sold their products through veterinary offices.

The pet food industry is subject to regulation at the federal and state levels. In 1958 the manufacturers of pet food formed The Pet Food Institute (PFI), a national trade association. PFI acts as a spokesman for the industry before the various regulatory agencies and bodies, sponsors research, represents the U.S. industry in international meetings, and works on uniform standards for pet food. PFI worked with the American Association of Feed Control Officials (AAFCO) to develop a uniform law on pet food standards that states may use as a model whenever they consider changes to their laws and regulations on the topic. Each state has its own set of laws and regulations which apply to pet food.

Regulation of the Pet Food Industry. At the federal level, pet food labeling and advertising claims are regulated by the Food and Drug Administration, by the Federal Trade Commission, and by the Department of Agriculture. All pet food plants are subject to FDA inspection and many of the FDA's canned food regulations apply to pet foods. Many manufacturers produce and/or sell products in more than one state, which means that their product and its labels much also meet the regulations of each state.

Sales Outlets/Product Distribution. Dog and cat food has traditionally been sold in grocery stores, pet stores, and by veterinarians. Veterinarian sales are especially prevalent for those brands that are marketed as a health specialty. Health consciousness for pets paralleled the general trend toward health consciousness in human consumption in recent years. This movement led to increased attention to labeling and awareness of obesity in pets, and the development of more specialized pet foods with greater emphasis on health in the marketing of the product. But still the grocery store remained the largest outlet for sales of pet food.

In the 1980s and early 1990s, the advent of the discount retailer as a major economic force in America began to change that trend. The biggest loser was the grocery store. The interest in health foods allowed those brands traditionally marketed through veterinarians and breeders to retain market share while the share of the grocery store fell to the discount chain. Efforts to stem the flow with in-house brands that were cheaper had only moderate success since people continued to prefer national brands, but wanted them at a lower price.

BACKGROUND AND DEVELOPMENT

The first commercially prepared dog food was a biscuit product introduced in England in about 1860, according to the Pet Food Institute. Dry dog foods were subsequently developed with formulas based on the nutritional knowledge of the day. After World War I, canned horse meat for dog food was introduced into the United States. In the 1930s canned cat food and dry meat meal dog foods came into use. These were succeeded by dry expanded type pet foods, which came onto the market during the 1950s. The 1960s, notes the Institute, "were marked with great diversification in the types of food available to the pet owner—dry cat food, many more varieties of canned products, and new soft-moist products. With the growth of the industry has come a greatly expanded use of by-products from the meat, poultry, and seafood processing industry. Approximately 1.1 million tons of these by-products . . . are now used annually in pet foods."

CURRENT CONDITIONS

Pet Food Industry Magazine notes that the Packaged Facts research firm has estimated continued growth in the dog and cat food manufacturing industry, with retail sales reaching more than $10 billion by 1995. This growth is predicated on the continued popularity of specialty brands, for, as *Pet Food Industry Magazine* commented at the end of 1992, although the country's cat population has increased by more than eight percent since 1987, the dog population in the United States has fallen by more than two percent.

INDUSTRY LEADERS

Leading companies involved in the manufacture of dog and cat food in the United States include the Ralston Purina Company, Alpo Petfoods Inc., Quaker Oats Pet Food Co., Friskies PetCare Company, Inc.,

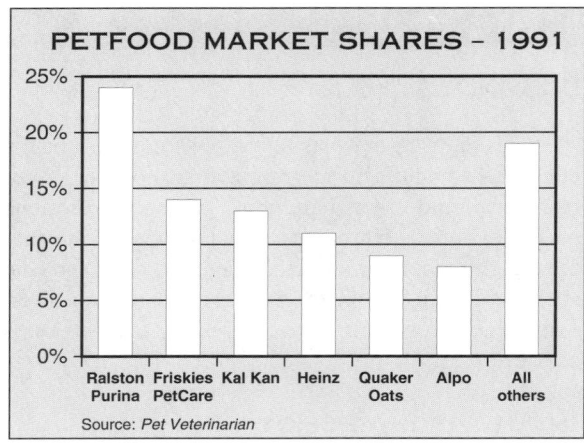

PETFOOD MARKET SHARES – 1991

Source: *Pet Veterinarian*

Hartz Corp., Kal Kan Foods Inc., Iams Co., and Heinz Pet Products Co.

According to A.C. Nielsen data, wet cat food sales were led in 1992 by Carnation's Friskies Buffet product line, with $221 million in sales and a 22 percent market share, while the leading brand of wet dog food was Kal Kan's Pedigree brand, with 1992 sales of $157 million and a 26 percent market share. The leading moist dog food that year was Ralston Purina's Moist & Meaty brand (33 percent market share), while the leading moist cat food in 1992 was Ralston Purina's Tender Vittles brand (50 percent). Friskies PetCare Company, Inc. led in the dry cat food category with its Friskies brand.

AMERICA AND THE WORLD

According to *Petfood Industry Magazine*, the United States has managed to maintain a favorable trade balance in the petfood industry. Exports amounted to $244 million in 1990 and have increased since 1980 at an annual rate of better than 13 percent. According to *FAS Agricultural Trade Highlights*, published in late 1991, world trade in pet food reached $715 million in 1990, with the United States accounting for approximately 25 percent of the world market share (with annual exports of almost 200,000 metric tons of pet food). While sales of pet food on the domestic front were flat, exports increased six-fold in a five-year period from 1986 to 1991.

During the 1980s pet food exports were around $50-60 million annually, but the size of the export market began to expand in the middle of that decade and has continued to grow since that time. Canada, Japan and the European Community are the three biggest markets for U.S. dog and cat food product exports. Products from Thailand are the biggest competitors with U.S. products on the world market, especially in the Common Market countries. Australia, meanwhile, provides the keenest competition for the Japanese market.

INDUSTRY INFORMATION SOURCES

Gibson, Rachel, ''Pet-Food Shoppers Watch their Pennies,'' *Wall Street Journal,* October 22, 1992.

''The Iams Company,'' Lewisburg, OH: Iams, 1992.

Liesse, Julie, ''Price War Bites at Pet Food Ad $,'' *Advertising Age,* April 5, 1993.

Pet Food Institute materials, Washington, DC: Pet Food Institute, 1993.

''Pet Foods—1992 Supermarket Sales Manual,'' *Progressive Grocer,* July 1992.

PFI Monitor, March 1993.

''Ten Insights,'' *Petfood Industry Magazine,* November/December 1992.

''Who's Who in Pet Food,'' *Petfood Industry Magazine,* January 1991.

—Joan Leotta

SIC 2048

PREPARED FEEDS AND FEED INGREDIENTS FOR ANIMALS AND FOWLS, EXCEPT DOGS AND CATS

This classification covers establishments primarily engaged in manufacturing prepared feeds and feed ingredients and adjuncts for animals and fowls, except dogs and cats. Included in this industry are poultry and livestock feed and feed ingredients such as alfalfa meal, feed supplements, and feed concentrates and feed pre-mixes. Also included are establishments primarily engaged in slaughtering animals for animal feed. Establishments primarily engaged in slaughtering animals for human consumption are classified in **SIC 2011: Meat Packing Plants, SIC 2013: Sausages and Other Prepared meat Products,** and **SIC 2015: Poultry Slaughtering and Processing.** Establishments primarily engaged in manufacturing cat and dog foods are classified in **SIC 2047: Dog and Cat Food.**

INDUSTRY SNAPSHOT

Feed is by far the largest input cost of producing food and fiber of animal origin, exceeding even the initial cost of the animals themselves. The cost of feed represents 50 to 70 percent of the cost of producing meat, milk and eggs at the farm level. For instance, the

United States Department of Agriculture calculates that it requires 88 pounds of feed to produce 100 pounds of milk, 9,523 pounds of feed to produce a steer, 1,273 pounds to produce a lamb, 50 pounds of feed for 100 eggs, 261 pounds of feed to produce 100 pounds of poultry and 629 pounds for 100 pounds of pork. In the case of grass-eating livestock such as cattle and sheep, a great deal of their nutrition may come from foraging pastureland, although the latter stages of their lives often include significant portions of prepared feeds; with poultry and hogs, however, nourishment is supplied primarily through prepared feed mixes.

According to the American Feed Industry Association, as much as $18 billion of feed ingredients are purchased each year. These products range from grain mixes to orange rinds to beet pulps. The feed is prepared in 3,000 primary feed manufacturing plants and 5,500 secondary or custom mix plants. Animal feed is manufactured in every state in the nation and is sold by 17,500 feed dealers; the feed industry as a whole employs 175,000 workers nationwide, with approximately 42,000 of those workers located in the manufacturing sector.

The feed industry is one of the most competitive businesses in the agricultural sector. The four largest feed dealers in the country produce less than 25 percent of the total animal feed consumed. Tens of thousands of farmers with feed mills on their own farms are able to compete with huge conglomerates with national distribution. The feed industry is by far the largest purchaser of U.S. corn, feed grains, and soybean meal.

ORGANIZATION AND STRUCTURE

Owning a feed mill is a capital extensive operation. Many modern feed mills increasingly rely on computer technology; human hands rarely touch the feed ingredients. Not only can the feed mill itself be a multi-million dollar investment (with attendant costs associated with maintaining a competitive position regarding machinery), but the feed manufacturer must also have an expensive commodIty inventory on hand at all times. Mill managers attempt to purchase their ingredients out front, often contracting for goods months in advance. To hedge the risks associated with fluctuating grain and commodity prices, many feed manufacturers utilize the option of futures trading. Most feed manufacturers also have a sizable investment in a truck fleet used to deliver bulk feed to dairies, poultry, and swine operations. Virtually all cattle feedlots in this country, however, prepare all their feed on the premises in bulk form. Many poultry processing companies own their own feed mills and sell the feed to contracting poultry producers who in turn sell their broilers back to the processor.

Another important aspect of the feed industry is the production of sacked feed which is sold through farm supply stores and feed dealers. This feed is often used for 4-H and FFA projects, backyard poultry projects, and for feeding of horses and small animals such as rabbits and guinea pigs. Retail outlets often will carry only one brand of feed. In return the feed companies do extensive advertising in the rural press, usually on a regional basis. The sacked feed sold in farm supply stores is prepared in the same manner as the feed delivered in bulk form, but it is more expensive because of the extra packaging.

Nutritional experts. Nutritionists are commonly employed in the feed manufacturing industry to determine the needs of domestic livestock. Animal nutritionists rely heavily on university research and industry publications for information on the chemical properties of various feed ingredients and their use and availability. More than 150 micro- and macro-ingredients are covered in a guide prepared by the Nutrition Council that has become the authoritative source for the feed industry.

There are thousands of professional nutritionists working for livestock feed suppliers, poultry feed manufacturers, feedlots, and poultry raising operations who spend a great deal of their time determining the needs of each animal for different phases of its productive life cycle. It is the role of the nutritionist to calculate a ration that fits the nutritional requirements for the least cost. This is known as a ''least cost ration'' and is the ultimate goal of all rations. Nutritionists use the most sophisticated computer hardware and software to make these calculations on a daily basis. Nutritionists either are employed ''in house'' or work on a consulting basis.

It is the role of the feed manufacturer to buy the commodities and blend them in the feed mill according to the specifications outlined by the nutritionist. There is little room for error because if the ration is not apportioned correctly it can manifest itself in lowered animal production and diminished outward appearance.

CURRENT CONDITIONS

The main ingredients used in commercially prepared feed are the feed grains. 137.2 million tons of corn, 23 million tons of soybeans, 9.7 million tons of sorghum, and 8.4 million tons of oats and barley were used in 1991 in the preparation of commercial feeds.

According to the USDA, In 1991 animals consumed 25 million tons of oil seeds, cakes, and meals; 3.3 million tons of animal proteins such as fish meal, meat, and bone meal; and 46.8 million tons of other by-products. This does not include liquid feeds, which are usually molasses-based supplements that are used on the range to supplement the grass diet of grazing cows and sheep.

The sale and manufacture of pre-mixes is an industry within an industry. Pre-mixes are micro-ingredients such as vitamins, minerals, chemical preservatives, antibiotics, fermentation products, and other essential ingredients that are purchased from pre-mix companies, usually in sacked form, for blending into commercial rations. Thanks to the advent of these products, a farmer who feeds his own grain can formulate his own rations and be assured that his animals are getting the minimum daily requirements of minerals and vitamins.

INDUSTRY LEADERS

Leading companies involved in prepared feeds production include ConAgra Inc., an Omaha, Nebraska-based firm; Ralston Purina Co., based in St. Louis, Missouri; and Purina Mills Inc., of St. Louis. Other significant industry players include SmithKline Beecham, Moorman Manufacturing Co., Hubbard Milling Co., Central Soya Company, Farmland Industries, and Baywood International Inc.

The merger in 1992 between the National Feed Ingredients Association (NFIA) and the American Feed Industry Association (AFIA) under the AFIA name brought the entire feed industry under representation by one single organization for the first time since 1909. The membership of the American Feed Industry Association includes companies that manufacture feed to sell, firms that manufacture feed for their own animals, and those who provide equipment, ingredients, services and supplies to feed manufacturers. AFIA headquarters are located in Arlington, Virginia.

One of the primary goals of the AFIA is to represent the interests of the feed industry on federal legislation and regulation. The AFIA meets often with Food and Drug Administration officials to coordinate such things as mill inspections, manufacturing practices, labeling requirements, feed additives, and the administration of laws and regulations. The association played a leading role in the development of the Uniform Sate Feed Law and other regulations that mandate uniform feed labels.

WORK FORCE

This industry, according to the Bureau of Labor Statistics, employed approximately 42,000 workers in 1992. This marks a significant drop from 1982, when the industry supported 53,600 employees. Of those employed in prepared feeds manufacturing, the bulk of them are engaged as production workers (nearly 27,000 in 1992). Average hourly earnings in the industry for production workers reached $9.83 in 1992, up from $9.07 in 1990 and $8.52 in 1988.

INDUSTRY INFORMATION SOURCES

Agricultural Statistics, U.S. Department of Agriculture, 1990, 1991.

American Feed Industry Association materials, Arlington, VA: AFIA, 1993.

Cattle and Beef Handbook, Englewood, CO: National Cattlemen's Association, 1992.

Cattle and Livestock Report, Washington, DC: Ag Statistics Board, NASS/USDA, 1992.

Factbook On U.S. Agriculture, USDA Office of Government and Public Affairs, 1991.

—Lee Pitts

SIC 2051

BREAD, CAKE, AND RELATED PRODUCTS

This industry is comprised of establishments that make fresh or frozen breads or rolls and perishable bakery products such as cakes, pies, and pastries. Manufacturers of dry bakery products such as cookies and crackers are classified in **SIC 2052: Cookies and Crackers**. Establishments involved in manufacturing frozen bakery products other than bread are classified in **SIC 2053: Frozen Bakery Products, Except Bread**. On-premises, retail bakeries are classified in **SIC 5461: Retail Bakeries**.

INDUSTRY SNAPSHOT

In the United States, 2,357 bread and cake plants operated during 1987. According to the U.S. Department of Commerce, total shipments for the bread, cake, and related products industry approximated $16.2 billion that year. Primary products represented $13.3 billion. Secondary products were valued at $411.8 million, and miscellaneous transactions represented $2.5 billion of the industry's total shipments.

According to figures for 1990, annual per capita consumption of bread products was increasing slightly. The average U.S. citizen consumed 28 pounds of white bread, 23 pounds of variety breads, 23 pounds of rolls, 15 pounds of cake, and four pounds of doughnuts and other sweet yeast products. Between 1991 and 1992 the value of the industry's shipments increased by 3.1 percent to $18.4 billion. Projections for 1993 anticipated that production would reach $19.2 billion. Forecasters predicted that annual per capita bread consumption would reach 60 pounds by the end of the century. One factor expected to drive the increase was the release of the Department of Agriculture's new four-tiered Food Guide Pyramid. The updated Food Guide Pyramid recommended six to 11 daily servings from the bread and grain food group.

Consumption increases varied by product, however, and overall industry growth was expected to be less than one percent in 1993 and only about 1.5 percent annually between 1993 and 1997. Industry watchers expected white bread to capture 58 percent of the total bread market. Demand for snack cakes was expected to increase 2 to 2.5 percent annually as manufacturers improved their quality and offered new packaging options such as individually wrapped, single-servings within larger boxes. Sales of sweet yeast doughnuts were expected to increase 2.5 percent per year, and increases of 3 to 3.5 percent were projected for bagels. Bagels benefited from their reputation as a convenient, healthy breakfast item.

A number of products, however, experienced declining consumption. Dinner roll consumption tapered off when pasta products gained popularity as bread substitutes. Sales of large pies, snack pies, full-size cakes, and cake-type doughnuts slackened as part of a national trend toward health consciousness. Some analysts noted that the increased consumption of sweet yeast doughnuts and snack cakes was contrary to the general trend toward more healthy products. They attributed the continuing popularity of these items to their convenience.

Recessionary conditions prevalent in the United States during the early 1990s also impacted the bread and cake products industry. Lower priced products, particularly white breads, attracted renewed interest. In 1992, white bread averaged $0.75 per pound. Whole wheat bread sold for $1.02 per pound, and French breads averaged $1.26 per pound.

ORGANIZATION AND STRUCTURE

Historically, the baking industry established itself close to population centers. Because bread and cake products were perishable, proximity to a customer base was a primary concern. One way growing bakeries overcame this geographic constraint was

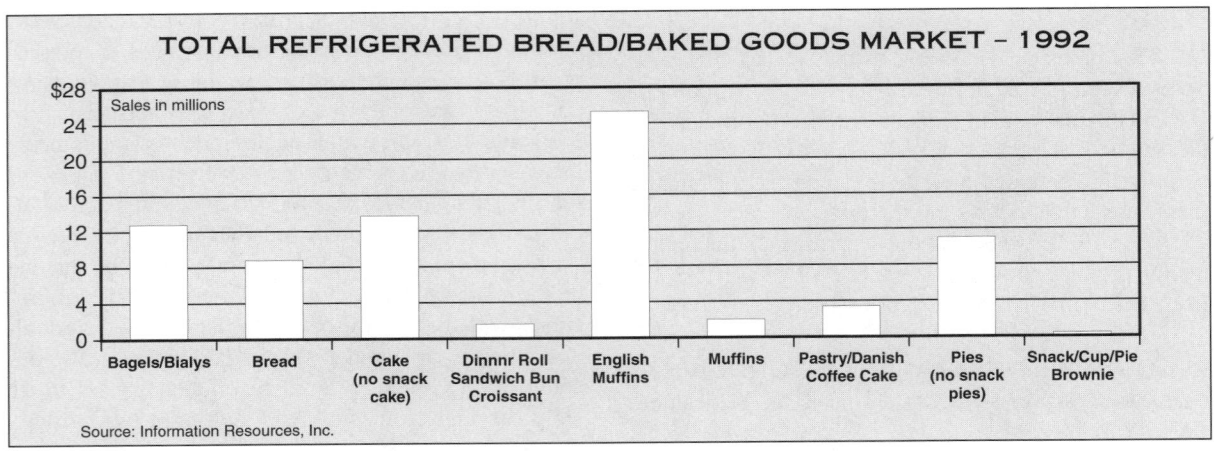

TOTAL REFRIGERATED BREAD/BAKED GOODS MARKET – 1992

Sales in millions

Bagels/Bialys | Bread | Cake (no snack cake) | Dinnnr Roll Sandwich Bun Croissant | English Muffins | Muffins | Pastry/Danish Coffee Cake | Pies (no snack pies) | Snack/Cup/Pie Brownie

Source: Information Resources, Inc.

through the purchase of companies in other areas. Many of the acquisitions and mergers within the industry during the last decades of the twentieth century transformed baking establishments with regional shipping systems into large conglomerates with national distribution networks. In addition, large baking establishments often attracted the attention of other investors. According to a report published in *Food Review*, since 1960 many of the nation's top wholesale bakeries were purchased by food processing companies. Joy Harwood, an agricultural economist writing for *Food Review*, stated that "control of every major wholesaler, except Flowers Industries, has changed."

The practice of buying or merging with existing firms had benefits in addition to overcoming the constraints related to delivering fresh products to the marketplace. Buying and refurbishing existing facilities was often less expensive than building new plants. Buying also helped avoid problems associated with creating excess capacity in specific geographic areas. Despite the trend toward building large corporations, many independent family-owned bakeries remained successful. In 1987 an estimated 56.3 percent of all wholesale bread and cake plants operated with less than 20 employees. These small establishments, however, captured only 2.3 percent of the industry's total sales.

The baking industry was monitored and regulated by several governmental agencies. For example, the United States Department of Health, Education and Welfare set the definitions and standards used to identify wheat and related products. The Food and Drug Administration (FDA) regulated product quality and mandated procedures by which food additives were to be approved prior to use. And, the National Research Council's Food and Nutritional Board (along with the American Medical Association's Council on

Foods and Nutrition) published guidelines for enriching bread products with nutrients.

BACKGROUND AND DEVELOPMENT

The oldest existing written record of a baked grain product dates back to about 2,600 B.C. The earliest known breads were flat, and people baked them on smooth stones or clay plates. According to a theory held by some historians, the ancient Egyptians created the world's first leavened breads. Leavened bread was made with ingredients possessing the chemical properties necessary to make dough rise. By contrast, unleavened breads were made from doughs that did not rise.

The ability to bake leavened breads may have been developed along with the ability to brew beer, as both processes relied on fermentation. Fermentation refers to a complex chemical process in which organic compounds are broken down into simpler substances. In alcoholic fermentation, the yeast converts a mixture's sugar or starch into carbon dioxide and alcohol. Recipes with sufficient liquid produced beer-like beverages. In mixtures with less liquid, the carbon dioxide produced by the fermentation process made the dough rise.

Fermentation of wheat and water mixtures was accomplished through the incorporation of yeast. Yeast is a member of the fungus family. Although an individual "yeast" is a single-celled organism, it lives and grows by multiplying into cultures consisting of thousands of cells. In order to grow, the cells eat the sugar and starch in dough mixtures. Early yeasts were incorporated into recipes by letting doughs sit out for a period of time to "sour." These wild yeast cultures, once established in a dough mixture, were carefully maintained through a process whereby some dough from each batch was saved to incorporate into the next batch. Before the development of commercial yeast, all leavened bread was made from sourdoughs. Sourdough breads are still made from flour, water, yeast, and bacteria.

Although many grains and other products could be fermented, wheat flours were the only ones to exhibit leavening. Wheat possessed a type of gluten (plant protein) unlike the gluten of other grains. Wheat gluten, when kneaded, formed an elastic structure that had the unique ability to trap the carbon dioxide given off by the yeast and to stretch and expand as more gas was created. When leavened doughs were baked, the heat killed the yeast but the dough's expanded structure remained. As a result, leavened breads were lighter and more airy than their unleavened counterparts.

The ancient Egyptians were also sometimes credited with inventing ovens. According to one theory, the first "ovens" were earthen pots. Early bakers discovered that when dough was placed inside preheated pots, it cooked more evenly than it did when placed on top of a heat source. The construction of permanent oven structures soon followed. Along with the development of ovens came the development of bread varieties as bakers experimented with different shapes and different ingredients. Sweet cakes first appeared in the twelfth century B.C. During the classical era, the Greeks modified oven designs and introduced the use of more innovative ingredients including milk, oil, wine, cheese, and honey.

Commercial bakeries first appeared within the Roman Empire. Under early Roman rule, baking progressed to an art form. As the Empire began to crumble, however, bakeries were taken over by the government and commercial baking became virtually non-existent. White flour was a luxury available only to royalty. During the Middle Ages, only monasteries and manor houses baked large quantities of leavened products. Monasteries were also credited with the development of pie crusts, an early pastry product. Although pie crusts were originally used only with meat dishes, they gained popularity for dessert items when sweetening ingredients were used.

Early sweeteners in baked goods consisted of honey, raisins, and other types of fried fruits. The use of sugar was introduced during the 1500s. Innovative bakers using sugared batters and doughs developed cakes and pastries. Commercial baking as a trade began to rise again during the urbanization that accompanied the early Industrial Revolution.

Innovations of the late nineteenth century and the early twentieth century enabled the mass-production of baked goods. As a result, large baking facilities began to supplant small local establishments. One of the most important innovations was the development of "tame" yeast, because these yeast cultures produced uniform, predictable results. Wild yeast cultures were too time consuming and too unpredictable to make automatic production feasible. The first yeasts used by commercial bakers were obtained from brewers, and in 1868 Charles Fleischmann made a compressed, distiller's yeast. The selective breeding of pure yeast cultures began in 1883, and by the early 1900s fast acting yeasts were well established.

Another innovation that helped shorten the time required to make bread was the mechanization of dough kneading. Kneading was necessary to develop gluten elasticity. The introduction of harder wheat hybrids that produced stronger flours enabled bakers to formulate doughs capable of withstanding the stress of mechanical kneading. The practice was introduced in the 1920s and had gained widespread acceptance by the 1950s .

The automation of milling and baking practices, however, did not produce uniformly beneficial results. In the 1930s, the U.S. Department of Agriculture (USDA) conducted nutritional surveys and found extensive thiamine and riboflavin deficiencies in some segments of the population. The deficiencies were attributed to milling methods which yielded finer white flours with diminished nutritional value. For example, stone-ground white flour contained 60 percent of the grain's original thiamine content, and roller-milled white flour contained only 12 to 20 percent of the wheat's original thiamine content. Concomitant with the surveys that identified these nutritional deficiencies, researchers developed the ability to synthesize vitamins.

During the 1940s efforts were made to restore the vitamins lost by milling practices. In 1941, the National Research Council recommended enriching white flour and white bread. Within a year, an estimated 75 to 80 percent of the nation's white bread was enriched on a voluntary basis. During World War II bread enrichment was mandated by the federal government, and to ensure continuation after the war, 27 individual states passed enrichment regulations. The Food, Drug, and Cosmetic Act, which became law in 1952, defined minimum and maximum levels for thiamine, riboflavin, and niacin enrichment.

Congress gave the Food and Drug Administration (FDA) the responsibility of establishing guidelines concerning the practice of adding nutrients to food products. According to recognized standards, the word "enriched" meant adding B-vitamins, iron, and optionally calcium to flour or cereal grain products. "Restored" referred to the practice of replacing natural nutrients which were lost during processing. "Fortification" involved the addition of nutrients not naturally present in a food. A few well known examples were the addition of vitamin D to milk or iodine to salt. During the early 1980s an estimated 90 percent of all standard commercial white bread was enriched.

Three bread-making techniques produced most of the commercial bread in the United States. These were called the straight dough process, the sponge method, and continuous production. In the straight dough process, all ingredients, including the yeast, were combined. The resulting dough rested during the fermentation process. Following fermentation, mechanical means were used to form loaves and the loaves were permitted to rise again before baking.

The sponge method was based on traditional bread making techniques but employed highly mechanized procedures. Recipes were based on ingredient weight rather than volume measurements. Flour was mixed with yeast and water to make a dough or "sponge," which was then permitted to ferment for several hours. After fermentation, other ingredients and additional flour were added and the dough was remixed. Following a time of rest, the dough was cut into pieces and placed in pans. After placement in pans, the dough was allowed to rise and was then moved to an oven for baking. Typical fermentation resulted in a five-fold volume increase. Resting times averaged 20 to 30 minutes, and rising times were approximately one hour.

The continuous production method was also highly automated. Flour and other ingredients were fed into a production line under carefully monitored conditions. The resulting dough was extruded through dies, pressed, or cut and placed in pans. The pans moved by conveyor through a large oven. Slicing machines cut finished loaves and packaging machines blew wrappers open with a puff of air to receive the finished product.

The commercial baking industry produced two basic types of breads—yeast breads and quick breads. Yeast breads were leavened with yeast. Quick breads used other leavening agents such as baking powder. Baking powder, which also worked by producing carbon dioxide, produced results more quickly than yeast. Quick breads included such products as muffins, loaves, and biscuits.

According to Ed Wood, a researcher of the history of bread making, 75 percent of the bread consumed in industrialized nations is produced by large commercial bakeries. The Wheat Flour Institute calculated that during the early 1980s U.S. bakers produced approximately 250 million pounds of bread every week. Bread products were available in many varieties and some individual bakers' lines exceeded 200 different products.

The most popular kind of bread was white bread made from white flour. French breads were made without milk, sugar, and shortening. Their characteristic texture was created by injecting steam into the oven during baking, and their flavor came from the wheat itself. "Whole wheat breads" were made from whole wheat flour, and "wheat bread" was made from a blend of white flour and whole wheat flour. Cracked wheat breads were made from white flour and crushed wheat meal. Other bread varieties were made with white flours of varying coarseness. Rye breads were with a mixture of rye flour and wheat flour, because rye flour, by itself does not possess the chemical properties necessary to produce a leavened product. Two types of rye flours were used to produce different rye breads. Light rye was made from the grain's endosperm; dark rye was made from the entire kernel.

In addition to its bread products, the baking industry also produced cakes. Cakes were typically made from pourable batters. Their basic ingredients were flour, liquid, eggs, and leavening agents plus flavorings and sometimes fat. The rising action of a baking cake was similar to the leavening action of bread. When a cake baked, steam and gasses caused the batter to expand. Different types of cakes were classified according to how they were leavened and whether they contained fat.

Two broad cake classifications were foam cakes and butter cakes. Foam cakes, typically airy and mild, were primarily leavened with air. One way in which this was accomplished was by beating egg whites and folding them into the mixture. Examples of foam cakes included angel food cake and sponge cake. Butter cakes relied on leavening agents such as baking powder, baking soda, or yeast. Butter cakes were typically more tender and possessed a smoother texture than foam cakes. Examples included layer cakes and pound cakes. Other types of cakes were created that did not easily fit these traditional distinctions. Chiffon cakes used egg whites and baking powder for leavening. Tortes were similar to sponge cakes but relied on ground nuts or crumbs to replace some or all of their flour.

CURRENT CONDITIONS

As the bread and cake industry entered the 1990s, its products were available virtually everywhere within the United States. Most of the products produced by commercial bakers were sold through grocery stores where breads and rolls represented the fifth largest selling category of grocery items. Additionally, the baking industry was the nation's largest consumer of nonfat dried milk. One industry analyst stated that nine million tons of bread, rolls, and buns were sold annually. Another report pointed out that U.S. commercial bakeries consumed 73 percent of the nation's milled flour in 1980.

Despite its ubiquitous presence, however, the bread and cake industry faced several challenges in the early 1990s. One challenge was increased competition from in-store bakeries. Supermarkets with large numbers of in-store bakeries in 1990 included Winn-Dixie (with 1,117), Kroger (946), and A&P (716). Although goods baked on the premises were often priced higher than pre-packaged goods, they held several advantages. Customers perceived them as fresher, and on-premises bakeries could offer specialty cakes and breads that were not available from mass producers. In-store bakeries often promoted their products as impulse items, placing them near the front of the store to take advantage of baking aromas.

To meet the competition from in-store bakeries, commercial wholesalers began offering more variety in single-serving packages and increasing their assortment of specialty products. Industry analysts disagreed about the long-term effect in-store bakeries would have on traditional distribution networks. Although sales from in-store bakeries increased from $4.9 billion in 1986 to $8 billion in 1990, the rate at which they were being developed slowed during the early 1990s.

In addition to the competition from in-store bakeries, wholesalers faced increased competition from prepared mixes. Prepared mixes were marketed to customers who wanted the convenience of purchased items and the freshness of newly baked goods. Competition from prepared mixes came not only within the household market, but also in the institutional market as users such as restaurants turned increasingly toward mixes.

Private label manufacturers also captured a growing portion of the bread and cake market. As the nation endured recessionary times during the early 1990s, consumers paid more attention to food prices. In order to retain their market share, major manufacturers increased their use of couponing and discounting.

Another challenge facing the industry during the early 1990s was increased concern about the environment. During the leavening process ethyl alcohol was released into the atmosphere. As a result, Southern California's South Coast Air Quality Management District Board ordered smog controls on the ovens of 24 large commercial bakeries. In addition, some environmental groups criticized the industry for its use of excess packaging. Officials countered the charges with claims that the packaging was necessary to prevent spoilage. To ameliorate the criticism, bakery wrapper recycling programs were instituted in some areas.

The bread and cake industry also faced the challenge of producing products for a nation caught up in a conflict between health consciousness and a desire for taste gratification. In 1989, many items were reformulated to eliminate ingredients viewed as unhealthy. These included such ingredients as tropical oils and other fat, sugar, and salt. The elimination of fat from many classes of bakery items was a difficult accomplishment because the fat incorporated in batters and doughs served many technical and aesthetic functions. Technically, it assisted the leavening process by incorporating air into mixtures, enabling the even transfer of heat during baking, and giving moisture to the final product. Aesthetically, the fat produced a favorable texture and added flavor.

To reformulate recipes without fat, different types of fat replacers were studied. Entenmann's Bakery was the first national company to offer a line of fat-free products. It began test marketing them in 1989 and reported sales of $200 million during the first full year of production. To honor Entenmann's achievement, the American Marketing Association awarded the company with the 1990 Edison Award for New Product Marketer of the Year. Entenmann's also received the grand prize from the Gorman's New Product Contest. The introduction of fat-free items helped increase consumption among consumers who traditionally skipped dessert items.

Following the launch of fat-free products during the early 1990s, many consumers reported that cholesterol and overall fat content were important in their purchasing decisions. As the trend expanded and many companies began bringing fat-free products to the marketplace, the FDA investigated merchandising practices and labeling regulations. The FDA also continued its efforts to regulate companies making unsubstantiated health claims about baked food products. For example, many products containing oat bran, touted as having the ability to reduce cholesterol levels, came under regulatory scrutiny. In a related incident, Campbell Taggart (Dallas) introduced an enriched bread with the name IronKids in 1989. The bread was made with the same fiber content as the company's whole wheat bread, and the FDA therefore challenged the product's name and marketing methods. Campbell Taggart and the FDA reached a compromise in 1992. Under the terms of the compromise, Campbell Taggart printed a disclaimer under the IronKids logo stating that the name ''refers only to a children's fitness program, and has no reference to either extra iron in this bread or to the bread resulting in superior strength or performance.''

Interest in healthy products, however, appeared to be waning in 1992. *Prepared Foods* published the results of a study conducted by the NPD Group of Port Washington, New York, which documented a shift toward snacking and diminished concern about calorie content. Consumers were also less likely to read labels. More emphasis was placed on upscale, indulgent products than on products aimed at health-conscious consumers. A similar trend was revealed by the results of a Gallup Poll published in *Progressive Grocer* in which consumer statements about health concerns contradicted consumer spending habits. Industry analysts theorized that low-fat sweet goods were of an inferior quality and priced higher than traditional formulas. One exception was noted within the bread category where multi-grain items with high-fiber and low-fat contents were doing well.

INDUSTRY LEADERS

One of the nation's largest bread and cake wholesalers was Continental Baking Company. In 1992, Continental reported sales of $2 billion. Its products were distributed throughout the country. The company's brands included Wonder Bread and Hostess Cakes. Ralston Purina purchased Continental Baking from ITT Corporation in 1984 for $475 million. In early 1992, Ralston Purina announced plans to study spinning off Continental, but abandoned the proposal because of its cost projections.

Another large bread and cake wholesaler was Interstate Bakeries. Interstate was formed in 1937 following the consolidation of two baking companies in Kansas City. Interstate operated two major divisions, the Bread Division and the Cake Division. Its major brands included Dolly Madison, Butternut, and Holsum. Interstate distributed products through more than 100,000 food outlets located along 4,200 routes. The distribution network covered all regions of the United States except the northeast. Interstate's thrift store network, which had 780 operating stores, was the industry's most extensive.

In 1992, Interstate Bakeries was the nation's largest independent and third largest baker and distributor of bakery products. According to company documents, Interstate's revenues totaled $1.1 billion. The com-

pany operated 30 bakeries and employed 14,000 workers. In fiscal 1993, Interstate reported that its Bread Division sales were up 2.9 percent but its Cake Division sales were down 1.1 percent from the previous year.

Another leading wholesale baking establishment was Flowers Industries. Flowers was founded in 1919 and operated predominantly in the nation's southeast. The company's products included white and variety breads, buns, rolls, snack cakes, pastries, pies, doughnuts, and brownies. It's major brands were Nature's Own, Cobblestone Mill, BeeBo, and Bluebird. In addition, the company manufactured products under regional brands and private labels. In fiscal 1992, Flowers reported total sales of $879 million and employed 8,200 full-time workers.

Many other major bread and cake establishments were owned by other corporations. For example Campbell-Taggart, with revenues of $1.5 billion reported for 1992, was owned by Anheuser Busch; and, Pepperidge Farm, with revenues of $600 million in 1992, was owned by Campbell Soup, Inc. Philip Morris owned Kraft-General Foods, and Kraft-General Foods owned Entenmann's, one of the nation's most widely distributed brands of pre-packaged bakery products.

Entenmann's was established in 1898 by William Entenmann. The company made its deliveries with a horse and buggy, but in 1957 a decision was made to switch from delivery routes to wholesale distribution through supermarkets. In 1978 the company was purchased by Warner-Lambert Company and was then sold, in 1982, to General Foods. The Entenmann's line included more than 200 different products in eight categories: danish, sweet cakes, pastry, cakes, cupcakes, pies, cookies, and doughnuts. According to a company narrative, its Bay Shore, New York bakery used 1.1 million pounds of flour, 1.2 million eggs, and 1.25 million pounds of sugar every week. In 1989, the company reported more than $500 million in sales and a total employment of 7,000 workers.

WORK FORCE

In 1987, the U.S. Department of Commerce reported that this industry employed a total of 161,600 workers. The number represented an increase over the employment reported for 1986 but a drop of five percent from 1982. States with the highest employment in the industry were California, New York, Texas, and Pennsylvania. Combined, these four states accounted for 32 percent of the industry's employment.

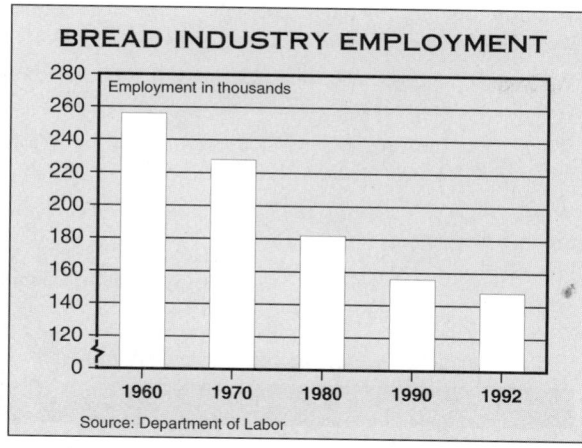

BREAD INDUSTRY EMPLOYMENT

Employment in thousands

Source: Department of Labor

The baking industry was highly automated and many jobs were done by machine. Jobs done by hand included decorating cake and pastry items and packaging fragile products.

AMERICA AND THE WORLD

Because bakery goods were perishable, international trade was limited. In 1992, exports of bread, cakes, and related products totaled $315 million. This represented only 1.3 percent of all bakery shipments. Five countries (Canada, Mexico, Bermuda, the United Kingdom, and Japan) received 81 percent of all U.S. exports. Imports in 1992 totaled $410 million, and seventy percent of these imports were received from Canada, Mexico, Denmark, Japan, and the United Kingdom.

Industry analysts expected increases in the international trade of bakery goods. According to government analysts export figures were expected to climb by 18 percent and imports by 5 percent. The largest growth was expected in East Asian nations where citizens were becoming more familiar with wheat-based product offerings. In addition, as a result of political activity, trade barriers were being dropped in Hong Kong, Singapore, South Korea, and Taiwan. Some analysts also expected that the ratification of the North American Free Trade Agreement would increase trade among the United States, Canada, and Mexico.

RESEARCH AND TECHNOLOGY

One of the most extensive areas of ongoing research within the industry involved investigating methods of extending shelf life and preserving product freshness. One method, Modified Atmosphere Packaging (MAP), involved introducing a predetermined atmosphere inside special barrier packaging materials at the time products were sealed for shipping. Nitrogen and carbon dioxide were the most frequently used gases in MAP. The technique was used to replace oxygen, a primary contributor to product staleness. According to published reports, MAP extended shelf life up to 30 days and increased freezer life up to six months.

Another, more advanced method of controlling the atmosphere within a product package was called Controlled Atmosphere Packaging (CAP). CAP relied on active means of manipulating the gas in a package's "headspace." Products were packed with chemical inserts to actively manipulate the environment within the package. For example, oxygen scavengers, frequently composed of iron compounds, would absorb any oxygen remaining after a package was sealed. Eliminating oxygen from packaging was important because it inhibited mold growth. Studies indicated that CAP extended the time period in which a product would remain mold-free by 300 percent.

MAP and CAP technologies presented many benefits. They eliminated the need for preservatives, and reduced distribution costs by eliminating the need for freezing and chilling during transportation. They also increased customer convenience because products did not require freezing following purchase. They also helped maintain appropriate moisture levels so products did not dry out. Two of the biggest problems surrounding MAP and CAP usage were customer perception and price. Customers did not view bakery products with extended shelf life as fresh, and products packaged with MAP and CAP were more expensive than those packaged with traditional methods. One industry analyst suggested that CAP and MAP technologies were best suited for wholesalers with large geographic distribution networks, rather than local baking operations.

INDUSTRY INFORMATION SOURCES

Amin, Melanie. "Baking Ingredients Offer the Right Mix." *Prepared Foods* (April 15, 1992).

"Anti-Staling Fat Mimetic: Too Good to be True?" *Prepared Foods* (August 1991).

Berger, Melvin. "Baking and Grain Processing." *Food Processing: Industry at Work.* New York: Franklin Watts, 1977.

Best, Daniel, Claudia Dziuk-O'Donnell, and Lisa Nelson. "Fat-busters for Bakery Foods." *Prepared Foods* (July 1992).

Blackwood, Alan. *Spotlight on Grain.* Vero Beach, FL: Rourke Enterprises, 1987.

Dornblaser, Lynn. "Have Your Cake and Eat It, Too." *Prepared Foods* (April 15, 1992).

Dornblaser, Lynn, and Marty Friedman. "New Product Numbers Down: Slow Down or Postponement?" *Prepared Foods* (February 1993).

Duff, Christina. "Ralston Abandons Proposal to Spin Off Its Continental Unit." *Wall Street Journal* (September 17, 1992).

Entenmann, Jackie. "Entenmann's." Bay Shore, NY: Entenmanns, nd.

Felgner, Brent H. "Baked Goods." *Supermarket Business* (September 1990).

Flowers Industries, Inc. 1992 Annual Report. Thomasville, GA: Flowers, 1992.

"Frozen Baked Goods: Nobody Does It Like Sara Lee." *Frozen Food Digest* (April/May 1993).

"Frozen Cake and Pastry." *Institutional Distribution* (May 15, 1991).

Harwood, Joy. "U.S. Baking Industry Responds to Customers." *Food Review* (April-June 1991).

———. "U.S. Flour Milling on the Rise." *Food Review* (April-June 1991).

"IBC: A Short Biographical Sketch." Kansas City, MO: Interstate Bakeries, nd.

"IBC: A Short Interview with Charles A. Sullivan." Kansas City, MO: Interstate Bakeries, nd.

"IBC Quick Facts." Kansas City, MO: Interstate Bakeries, nd.

"Interstate Bakeries Corp." *The Kansas City Business Journal* (February 7, 1992).

"Interstate Bakeries Corp." *The Kansas City Business Journal* (February 26, 1993).

Interstate Bakeries Corporation 1993 Annual Report. Kansas City, MO: 1993.

Lingle, Rick. "CAP for U.S. Bakery Products: To Be, or Not To Be?" *Prepared Foods* (March 1988).

Malovany, Dan and Bernard Pacyniak. "Projects Lightning and Thunder." *Bakery Production and Marketing* (September 24, 1991).

Pyler, Ernst John. *Our Daily Bread.* Chicago: Siebel Publishing, 1958.

Tanyeri, Dana. "Mixes Offer Fresh Benefits and Low Food Cost." *Institutional Distribution* (July 1990).

Tanyeri, Dana. "Top-Quality Baked Goods Start With High-Volume Staples and Mixes." *Institutional Distribution* (June 1992).

Turner, Dorothy. *Bread.* Minneapolis, MN: Carolrhoda Books, 1989.

U.S. Department of Commerce. *1987 Census of Manufactures.* Washington, DC: Bureau of the Census, 1990.

U.S. Department of Commerce. *U.S. Industrial Outlook 1993.* Washington, DC: U.S. Department of Commerce, 1993.

Waldrop, Judith. "Scratch and Mix." *American Demographics* (October 1992).

Weller, Ed. "Forget What the Consumer is Saying." *Progressive Grocer* (March 1992).

Wheat Flour Institute. *From Wheat to Flour,* rev. ed. Washington, DC: Wheat Flour Institute, 1981.

Wood, Ed. *World Sourdoughs from Antiquity.* Cascade, ID: Sinclair Publishing, 1989.

—Karen Bellenir

SIC 2052

COOKIES AND CRACKERS

This category includes establishments primarily engaged in manufacturing fresh cookies, crackers, pretzels, and similar "dry" bakery products. Secondary products that are part of this industry include biscuits, graham crackers, saltines, cracker meal and crumbs, cracker sandwiches made from crackers, wafers, and ice cream cones and cups.

INDUSTRY SNAPSHOT

Although mom is still America's favorite cookie maker, the bakeries that attempt to make cookies and crackers as good as mom's have become a huge industry. The U.S. Department of Agriculture estimates that the makers of bakery products constitute a $29.1 billion industry. The cookie and cracker segment of that industry is a significant one, as more than three billion pounds of cookies and 2.1 billion pounds of crackers were consumed in 1992, according to government estimations. Total supermarket sales of cookies and crackers is estimated to be approximately $5.5 billion, a figure that does not include sales in small retail outlets and discount stores. According to the U.S. Bureau of the Census, the cost of materials, services, fuels, and electric energy used by the cookies and crackers industry amounted to about $2.2 billion. The total value of shipments for establishments classified in this industry is estimated to be about $6.5 billion.

The U.S. Chamber of Commerce notes that cookie and cracker manufacturing is the fastest growing segment of the bakery industry. Shipments of all bakery products rose on the average of 1.3 percent per year from the years 1987 to 1992. But sales of cookies and crackers for the same years increased by rates of 2.3 percent. The primary reason given for the projected increase in sales is the recent introduction of low-fat, low-calorie, low-cholesterol cookies and crackers. Adult consumers have proven to be attracted to relatively new brands of items such as low-fat parmesan and romano cheese crackers now on the shelves. While sales of expensive national brand cookies declined somewhat, sales of lower-priced private labels rose. It is reasonable to assume that price, convenience, and health concerns will continue to influence the consumption of cookie and cracker goods in the near future.

ORGANIZATION AND STRUCTURE

According to *Ward's Business Directory of U.S. Private and Public Companies,* there are 87 cookie and cracker manufacturing companies listed under SIC 2052. In the major bakery companies, the cookies and crackers segment of business often operates as a separate division of the bakery division of the company. Many bakery companies today are often divisions of holding companies that are also involved with the diversification of products that include food, beverages, and, as is the case with RJR Nabisco company, tobacco.

Other manufacturers of cookies and crackers operate strictly under the bakery goods heading. Companies such as Mrs. Field's Cookies and Famous Amos at one time operated exclusively out of their own retail outlets. They later expanded to supermarkets and specialty stores. A number of these private label companies work through distributors, who can handle a number of varied products. Many of the larger companies handle their own distribution, working directly with supermarkets and retailers.

CURRENT CONDITIONS

The baked goods industry group has developed into three industries with three standard industry classifications. **SIC 2051** includes bread, cake, bagels, and related products, **SIC 2052** includes cookies and crackers, and **SIC 2053** includes frozen bakery items, except bread and rolls. Well into the late 1980s, bakery goods showed a consistent increase in sales. But consumption of sweet baked goods began to decline around 1992. Consumers were changing their buying habits and sought out bakery products that were lower in calories. Cookies and cracker sales also slowed by 1992, but showed signs of growth due to the availability of the new low-fat varieties. Sales of high-priced national brand cookies also declined, as consumers turned to lower-priced private labels.

The consumer segment most responsible for boosting the sales of baked goods is the 35- to 54-year-old age group, according to a survey compiled by the Bureau of Labor Statistics. The survey showed that people in this age group regularly spent more for bak-

ery products. Happily for cookie and cracker manufacturers, this consumer segment was growing at a rate of 2.7 percent yearly, and by 1997 it will represent 29.3 percent of the total U.S. population. One explanation for heightened consumption was that this group was at the peak of their earning potential, and therefore they had more disposable income. The consumption of cookies and crackers also went up due in part to manufacturers reacting to the health consciousness of the consumer. Many manufacturers replaced tropical oils and white flour with more health-oriented canola oil and whole wheat flour. Price and health concerns are expected to continue to be the prime influence in consumption changes.

In today's market, healthy cookies and crackers are what the consumer wants, and manufacturers are responding. Diana Morgan, writing in *In Health* magazine, accused the bakery industry of "the poisoning of America." Morgan lambasted Fruit and Fibre cereal, Triscuits crackers, Hydrox cookies, and Cracklin' Oat Bran as being laced with coconut palm or palm kernel oils that can clog arteries as badly as fatty pork chops and London broil. The food companies promptly promised to change their ways, but many of them are finding it difficult to make cookies with unsaturated oils unless they are resaturated. Dumping the high cholesterol tropical oils that do so much to enhance the product's flavor has not been easy. Unsaturated oils cause the product to lose the crunch that consumers favor, and usually result in premature staleness. While partially resaturated unsaturated products like "partially hydrogenated vegetable oil" help manufacturers solve the problem, the fact is that products are probably no healthier than they were before. According to Morgan, "partially hydrogenated oils can act even more saturated than they really are." But the experts are working at it, and they still hope to come up with the answer.

A number of companies have introduced products to suit this changing market. Nabisco introduced a new line of fat-free cookies and crackers called SnackWells. As reported in *Advertising Age,* Nabisco management insists that "the company is placing substantial corporate emphasis behind product categories that health-wise consumers are increasingly demanding." The company added that SnackWell cookies have one gram of fat compared with three grams in traditional cookies on the market. Nabisco predicted that SnackWell cookies could get half of the $500 million annual market for healthier cookies and crackers. The category accounted for about ten percent of the $5.5 billion cookie and cracker market in 1992.

Health Valley Foods and R. W. Frookies are also making a bid for the fat-free cookie market. Health Valley claims its cookie is the number one fat-free cookie. Frookies now has four flavors of fat-free cookies on the shelf. Frookies founder Richard Worth claims that Frookies shares equal shelf space with Nabisco in many supermarkets. He is convinced that Frookies is more of a health food than Nabisco's. Moreover, Campbell Soup Company's Pepperidge Farm division launched a low-fat cookie line called, Wholesome Choice. It claims it has no preservatives and no artificial flavors. Pepperidge Farm holds about six percent of the cookie market, according to Michael Wilke of *Advertising Age*.

The industry has also seen the merger and/or purchase of some major producers. *Business Week* reported the 1992 purchase of the Famous Amos brand of chocolate chip cookies by President Enterprises Corp., the Taiwanese food giant, for an estimated $60.6 million. George K. Liu, chief executive of President's U.S. division, implied that it will be the first of many acquisitions. President's corporate CEO, C. Y. Kao, promised that "in 25 years, we will be one of the biggest food companies in the world". At the same time, Campbell Soup Company made an unsolicited bid for Arnotts Ltd., an Australian maker of cookies and crackers.

Manufacturers have not hesitated to take legal action to protect their market share. The *Wall Street Journal* reported in 1992 that the Keebler Company sued RJR Nabisco Holding Corporation, claiming that Nabisco was copying the name and package design of its best selling cookie, Pecan Sandies. Nabisco's new cookie is called Pecan Supremes. In an effort to ease the situation, Nabisco agreed to change the package color of Pecan Supremes from yellow to tan, and plans to place a blue sticker on its packages with the words "new" and "Nabisco."

Nabisco also made efforts to reverse its losses in the cookie business. The *Wall Street Journal* noted that Nabisco sales have been slipping in part because baby boomers are giving up their old favorite high-fat, high-cholesterol cookies and discouraging their children from buying them. Another important reason for declines in Nabisco's cookie and cracker business is that, during the good years in the 80s, Nabisco aggressively increased its prices until the consumers started to fight back by not buying. Commenting on this strategy, Robert Urbain, a vice president with Pepperidge Farm, said, "Prices have gone beyond the levels that are justified." Nabisco still holds the lion's share of the business—28.2 percent, compared to total private labels of 13.7 percent, and Keebler's 12.4 percent. Private labels, however, have begun to cut heavily into Nabisco's market share. Nabisco is said to be working overtime to undercut its private label competition. In an effort to bolster its market, Nabisco is making an effort to gain market space in discount outlets and convenience stores. But private labels are slowly making inroads in all the major cookie and cracker markets.

Because it is the leader in the cookie and cracker industry, the private labels appear to be pointing their big guns at Nabisco. There are a number of upscale private lines available, including Sam's Choice, a line being sold at Wal-Mart stores, and Master Choice, sold at A & P stores. One of the front-runners, and a leader of the up-scale private label pack, is President's Choice. Produced by Canada's Loblaw Companies, the chocolate chip entry is beginning to chip away at Nabisco's Chips Ahoy! brand.

Concern for the environment has also affected the operations of bakery companies. Most are now spending more of their dollars on environmental protection. Many companies are introducing pollution abatement equipment, especially for their ovens, and will be introducing other pollution control measures. Many are converting their delivery vans so they can operate on cleaner-burning propane instead of gasoline. It is expected that environmental control efforts will eventually increase operating costs by as much as ten percent.

Bakery companies are also generally making changes in the ingredients they have been using for years. They are making efforts to minimize the use of chemical agents. Companies are beginning to phase out potassium bromate, which has always been a integral part of their recipes. Health conscious, label-reading consumers are turning from products with potassium bromate products that contain acceptable alternatives, such as barley malt. *U.S. Industrial Outlook* believes that the per capita consumption of crackers has edged up mainly due to bakery companies changing ingredients to satisfy consumer demands and tastes. The increase, it is believed, is due to cracker manufacturers eliminating questionable ingredients like tropical oils and white flour, and using canola oil and whole wheat flour in their place. This combination is preferred by health conscious adults who purchase crackers and examine ingredient labels.

Some manufacturers are employing extrusion used in other food industries. This engineering process permits continuous blending of ingredients. It results in a greater variety of products being made available to the consumer, and it results in less waste during production time, and also consumes less energy. Changes in ingredients and procedures are monitored carefully by the Food and Drug Administration.

Manufacturers of cookies and crackers are working harder at expanding their sources of sales. They are exploring non-traditional outlets such as toy retailers, drug stores, and children's stores to sell their products. They are incorporating the use of licensed characters for their cookies, hoping to increase consumption of cookies among children aged five to 14.

The inflation-adjusted prices of agricultural commodities are not expected to represent a factor in the cookies and crackers manufacturing industry. Although there have been periodic price increases, the average index of real prices of ingredients has actually shown a decline. This pattern should continue. Also, with the use of computers and better telecommunications, bakery companies today are more sophisticated and more easily able to protect themselves against sudden price increases of agricultural commodities.

INDUSTRY LEADERS

Ward's Business Directory lists the top ten cookie and cracker makers in the following order: Nabisco Foods Group, Keebler Company, Nabisco Foods Group Nabisco Biscuit Company, Lance Inc., Interbake Foods Inc., Sunshine Biscuits Inc., President Baking Company Inc., Mother's Cake and Cookie Company, Eagle Snacks Inc., and Mrs Field's Inc.

Nabisco is by far the leader of the group. According to the company overview, Nabisco Foods Group is one of the world's leading food companies, with annual sales amounting to $5.9 billion. The Nabisco Company produces, distributes, and markets a broad range of cookies, crackers, and snacks. Nabisco Biscuit has eight of the top ten cookies and crackers in the country, including Oreo Chocolate sandwich cookies, the world's largest-selling cookie brand, and Ritz crackers, the world's top-selling cracker. Nabisco markets its products through a direct store delivery system. Although Nabisco has a huge 44 percent share of the $3.2 billion cookie market, the company is making its heaviest bid ever for the fat-free cookie and cracker markets. It has already introduced its fat-free line extensions of Saltine crackers and Fig Newtons cookies.

Keebler, a subsidiary of United Biscuit Holding Corporation, based in Britain, is listed on the London Stock Exchange. Like Nabisco's, Keebler's products are represented in major supermarkets throughout the country. Keebler also produces and distributes a wide range of crackers and snacks.

Lance, Inc. manufactures and distributes a wide variety of packaged snack foods and bread basket items. They include crackers and cracker sandwiches, cookies and cookie sandwiches, peanuts, wafers, chips and bundled snack foods. They distribute to supermarkets, discount centers, convenience stores, schools, hospitals, restaurants, and similar institutions. A significant portion of their income is derived from vending machines, which are located in 35 states. Lance's line of snack items, under which cookies and crackers fall, accounts for 88 percent of their business.

WORK FORCE

According to the Bureau of the Census Annual Survey of Manufactures, the cookies and cracker industry employed approximately 46,000 people, 34,500 of whom fall into the category of production workers. *U.S. Industrial Outlook* figures showed that the average hourly wages for those workers came to about $12 per hour. Single-establishment companies in this industry with up to 20 employees were not surveyed or information was not received in time for the report. The leading states with the most employees in the cookies and crackers industry are North Carolina, Illinois, Pennsylvania, and Georgia.

AMERICA AND THE WORLD

The export trade of bakery goods has amounted to a small portion of the total bakery production in the United States, because of the problem of perishability and consumer preference in other countries. Nevertheless, bakery exports are growing. By 1992, bakery exports increased 35.2 percent to $315 million. The bakery exports consisted mainly of cookies, crackers, and specialty cakes that have adequate shelf life, attractive packaging, and competitive prices. On the other hand, bakery imports also rose by 7.6 percent to $410 million, which amounts to about 1.7 percent of the total U.S. consumption.

The United States shipped 81 percent of its bakery exports to five countries—Canada, Mexico, The United Kingdom, Bermuda, and Japan. Canada and Mexico, its closest neighbors, accounted for two-thirds of the total exports. People in foreign countries consumed many more cookies yearly than cookie eaters in the United States. For example, per capita yearly consumption of cookies in the Netherlands was 58.28 pounds, in Belgium and Luxembourg, 45.23 pounds, in the United Kingdom, 29.34 pounds, and in Canada, 16.51 pounds. In the United States, however, per capita consumption was a meager 12.93 pounds per year.

More American companies are jockeying for stakes in the foreign cookie and cracker market. As mentioned earlier, the Campbell Soup Company made a $590 million bid for Arnotts Ltd., the Australian maker of cookies and crackers. According to the *Wall*

Street Journal, Campbell's intentions are to make inroads in the lucrative Asian market. Although only two percent of Arnotts' sales come from Asia, Campbell's plans are to make Arnotts a premier brand name in Asia's $2 billion cookie market. Arnotts has also been in the middle of a heated take-over battle between Bond Corp. Holdings Ltd, and Nabisco Brands Inc. Although it has been considered the world's seventh largest maker of cookies and crackers, Arnotts has been having difficult times.

Campbell's bid for Arnotts is just the tip of the acquisitions iceberg. The *Wall Street Journal* also reported that the Philip Morris Companies have made a $1.5 billion bid for Scandinavian candy maker Freia Marabou AS, and H.J. Heinz Co. purchased New Zealand food company Wattie's Ltd. In another major purchase, PepsiCo purchased Empresas, the largest Mexican cookie maker, for $300 million. Taking advantage of the North American Free Trade Agreement (NAFTA), PepsiCo has plans to sell Mexican cookies in the United States.

For the near future, the real value of U.S. export shipments for all bakery items is not likely to grow more that 1.5 to 2.0 percent annually from 1993 to 1997. The fastest growth is expected to be from cookies and crackers exports which is expected to grow about two percent yearly. International competitiveness of bakery products is still a long way off. The value of bakery exports is around $250 million versus total imports of about $370 million. Since Mexico and South Korea have lowered their trade barriers against baked goods, they are receiving more U.S. exports. The most significant increase in exports is likely to come from the newly industrialized countries of East Asia, which are becoming more accustomed to our wheat-based foods. As far as the import of baked goods is concerned, Japan and Taiwan have now joined the circle of leading suppliers.

It is conceivable, however, that in the coming years exports and imports of bakery products, with cookies and crackers leading the way, will become more of a viable international fixture. According to *U.S. Industrial Outlook,* international trade in bakery products will continue to increase.

INDUSTRY INFORMATION SOURCES

"Campbell Soup Acquires Majority Stake in Arnotts." *Wall Street Journal,* 5 February 1993.

Hwang, Suein L. "Campbell Makes $590 Bid for Cookie Firm; Offer for Australia's Arnotts Is Aimed at Establishing Base for Asian Market." *Wall Street Journal,* 13 October 1992.

Hwang, Suein L. "Healthy Eating, Premium Private Labels Take a Bite Out of Nabisco's Cookie Sales." *Wall Street Journal,* 13 July 1992.

Konrad, Walecia. "Famous Amos Gets a Chinese Accent." *Business Week,* 28 September 1992.

Morgan, Diana. "Mixed-Up Munchies." *In Health,* April 1990.

"Nabisco Introduces Snack Products with Less Fat." *New York Times,* 15 July 1992.

Rice, Faye. "Eco-correct Crackers." *Fortune,* 9 September 1991.

U.S. Industrial Outlook 1993. Washington, DC: U.S. Department of Commerce, January 1993.

Wilke, Michael. "New Nabisco Line Joins Healthy Cookie Parade." *Advertising Age,* 13 July 1992.

—Ron Schultz

SIC 2053

FROZEN BAKERY PRODUCTS, EXCEPT BREAD

This industry is comprised of establishments primarily involved in manufacturing frozen bakery products other than bread and bread-type rolls. Products include frozen cakes, croissants, doughnuts, pies, and sweet yeast goods. Manufacturers of frozen bread products are classified in **SIC 2051: Bread, Cake and Related Products**.

According to figures released by the U.S. Department of Commerce, the Frozen Bakery Products industry made shipments totaling $1.2 billion in 1987. Industry employment for 1987 was 9,900. The states employing the largest number of the industry's workers were Michigan, Pennsylvania, Illinois, and California.

In 1992, the Frozen Bakery Products industry was experiencing declining conditions. According to government statistics, total shipments decreased 4.2 percent from the previous year. The reduction was attributed to consumer preferences for products that required no thawing or baking time. Another contributing factor was the limited amount of freezer space in retail supermarkets.

During the late 1980s, certain segments within the Frozen Bakery Products industry benefited from a trend toward increased consumption of breakfast food products. Survey data revealed that in 1987, 4 percent of Americans reported skipping breakfast. This number represented a drop from the 5 percent making a similar claim in 1983. As a result, sales of frozen breakfast foods were experiencing growth.

Industry forecasters during the early 1990s, however, expected more declines within industry. Sales during 1993 were expected to fall approximately 1.5 percent below sales for 1992. Forecasters also anticipated that industry sales would continue declining at a rate of about 0.5 percent annually between 1993 and 1997. Contributing factors were the industry's inability to compete with an ever-expanding number of convenience stores, discount retailers, and vending machine sales.

One of the first companies to offer frozen bakery products to the American marketplace was Sara Lee. Sara Lee Bakery was founded in 1949 by Charles Lubin. Originally the company offered a line of premium, fresh-baked products and made shipments within a 200 mile radius of its Chicago location. In 1953, in order to accommodate the needs of long-distance clients, the company pioneered freezing methods. In 1962, Sara Lee decided to switch its production exclusively to frozen products. Sara Lee products included more than 200 different items and were sold in supermarkets and restaurants throughout the United States.

Sara Lee's activities extended beyond the United States. In 1963, Sara Lee began marketing efforts in Canada and the company acquired plants in England and Australia in the 1970s. By the early 1990s, the company marketed its product line in 40 nations around the globe.

Another industry leader was Mrs. Smith's. Mrs. Smith's, a subsidiary of Kellogg, offered two product lines, Eggo frozen waffles and Mrs. Smith's frozen pies. Both were market leaders within their categories and sold predominantly to convenience-conscious customers. For example, Mrs. Smith's Pie in Minutes, a microwavable product introduced in 1985, was ready to serve in less than half the time normally required to bake a pie.

In addition to being promoted for their convenience, Eggo Waffles were also marketed at the health market. Nutri-gain Waffles were introduced in 1984 and Nutri-Grain Bran and Raisins appeared in 1985. According to Kellogg, waffles were consumed in 51 percent of U.S. households and frozen waffles were the fastest growing category of freezer products. In 1992, Mrs. Smith's expanded its market territory by offering products in Canada.

INDUSTRY INFORMATION SOURCES

Bridgford Foods Corporation 1992 Annual Report. Anaheim, CA: Bridgford, 1992.

Friedman, Marty. ''New Products Dawn on Breakfast Market.'' *Prepared Foods* (September 1987).

''Frozen Baked Goods: Nobody Does It Like Sara Lee.'' *Frozen Food Digest* (April/May 1993).

Kellogg 1992 Annual Report. Battle Creek, MI: Kellogg, 1993.

Messenger, Robert. ''No More Blues In Battle Creek.'' *Prepared Foods* (February 1987).

U.S. Department of Commerce. *1987 Census of Manufactures.* Washington, DC: Bureau of the Census, 1990.

U.S. Department of Commerce. *U.S. Industrial Outlook 1993.* Washington, DC: U.S. Department of Commerce, 1993.

—Karen Bellenir

SIC 2061

CANE SUGAR, EXCEPT REFINING

This classification includes establishments primarily engaged in manufacturing raw sugar, syrup, or finished (granulated or clarified) sugar from sugar cane. Establishments primarily engaged in refining sugar from purchased raw sugar or sugar syrup are classified in **SIC 2062: Cane Sugar Refining.**

INDUSTRY SNAPSHOT

The sugar cane industry is confined by the crop's growing conditions and the logistics of transporting sugar cane. Because sugar cane can grow only in a tropical climate, its production in the United States is limited to the weather conditions found in Florida, Hawaii, Louisiana, Texas and Puerto Rico. Mills that process the sugar cane into raw sugar must be located near the cane plantations since cut sugar cane is too bulky and heavy to ship. Mills in this category process the cane into crystals of raw sugar that can be transported in bulk, like grain, aboard ships or land transportation.

The profitability of milling sugar cane in the United States depends on federal government policies. Since the late 1700s, producing raw sugar has been a lucrative business for growers and millers because the price of domestic sugar has been government-controlled and foreign imports have been severely limited. Some members of Congress, as well as numerous critics of American agricultural policy, have been advocating less government involvement in the sugar industry. They have been pushing for a decrease in the price supports for domestic sugar cane and a lifting or easing of the quota on foreign sugar. Critics claim the American limitations on foreign raw sugar hurts small sugar-producing nations in the Caribbean, as well as the Philippines.

ORGANIZATION AND STRUCTURE

Sugar mills are located near the plantations on which sugarcane is grown and harvested. In many cases, the sugar mills are operated by the plantations or as cooperatives by the owners of several sugarcane plantations. United States Sugar Corporation in Clewiston, Florida, is both a grower and manufacturer of raw cane sugar, as is C. Brewer and Company Ltd, in Honolulu, Hawaii and Waialua Sugar Company, Inc. of Waialua, Hawaii. The Atlantic Sugar Association in Belle Glade, Florida, is a cooperative owned by area plantations. (Plantations primarily involved in production of sugarcane and sugar beets are classified under agricultural **SIC 0133**.)

Mills run continuously, day and night, from fall until spring, when the last cane is harvested. To facilitate the constant milling, growers cultivate a variety of sugar cane that they can harvest throughout the season. The variety of cane available, however, depends on the soil and climate on a particular plantation.

Government supports. The U.S. government has supported sugar prices for more than 200 years. In 1789, the federal government imposed an import tariff to raise revenue, and for the next 100 years, this sugar tariff yielded almost 20 percent of all import duties, the main source of government money before the Civil War. The Sugar Act of 1934 regulated domestic sugar production, imports, and prices. Import quotas were assigned to foreign sugar-growing countries. Price supports were applied sporadically during the 1970s, depending upon the price of sugar on the world market. Falling sugar prices resulted in the Agriculture and Food Act of 1981 in which the government agreed to purchase raw cane sugar and refined beet sugar for a specific price per pound if commercial prices were not high enough. But in order to avoid the outlay of any payments, the government imposed tariffs on imported sugar to discourage imports, limit the supply of sugar, and therefore keep the price of sugar at a level at or above the government's minimum price. Subsequent agricultural acts continued to provide price supports for sugar, keeping quotas low and prices high in the domestic market.

In recent decades, the United States has imposed strict quotas on import of foreign sugar, cutting imports 80 percent since 1975. The tariff on sugar imports in excess of the quota was also high enough to discourage imports. This quota has created great controversy regarding U.S. trade with developing nations. More than 110 countries grow sugar cane or sugar beets, and many of the developing nations have become dependent on sugar as a source of employment and income. In the early 1990s, the United States imported less than 1.5 million tons of sugar to make up the difference between the sugar cane produced domestically and the approximately nine million tons used.

Some critics of U.S. foreign trade policy blamed the federal sugar support program for the rise in cocaine traffic into the United States. These critics claimed that, not only did the sugar program hurt other countries financially, but the loss of the U.S. sugar market contributed to the increase in coca (from which cocaine is derived) production in Bolivia and Peru. U.S. sugar producers disputed this claim, maintaining that the nationalization of Peru's sugar industry was the major factor in its decline, not the cuts in U.S. sugar imports.

Price supports for sugar in the United States are provided in the form of nonrecourse loans, so that sugar growers can borrow money with the crop as collateral. The government sets the value of the collateral at a minimum price per pound, guaranteeing that the sugar producer will receive at least that price, even if the market drops. The loans are made to the sugar processor because the sugarcane (or sugar beets) must be milled before being sold or stored. When the raw sugar (or processed beet sugar) is sold, the growers receive payment too. In many cases the processor and the grower are the same concern.

Processing. The harvesting of sugar cane poses challenges to maintaining thoroughness while controlling cost-effectiveness. Harvesting is either carried out by hand-cutting or machine-cutting. While harvesting by machine costs half as much as harvesting by hand, mills complain that machine harvest includes too much debris, such as roots, dirt, leaves, and dead animals, according to Alec Wilkinson in his book *Big Sugar, Seasons in the Cane Fields of Florida.* He noted that mill owners estimated that machine-harvested sugar cane includes seven to ten percent trash, while hand-cut cane includes only about two percent. Mill owners complain that trash costs them money because it clogs the machines and absorbs juice during milling. According to Wilkinson, mill owners claim that machines leave too much sugar in the field because they cannot cut as close to the ground as the hand cutters and that every half inch of cane stubble left on an acre would have made another half ton of cane.

The tons of sugar cane stalks are transported to nearby mills in trucks or railroad cars to be washed and shredded, then placed in crushing machines or vats of hot water to dissolve the sugar. Crushing machines break open the cane and squeeze out the sugary juice. Water dissolves more of the sugar in the stalk, creating a sugary mixture called cane juice. The cane juice is heated, and lime is added to settle impurities; then carbon dioxide is used to remove the lime. The clear juice moves on to giant evaporator tanks. After removing most of the water, the thickened mixture is moved to a vacuum pan where it is heated to remove more water. When crystals form in the syrup, the mixture is transferred to a centrifuge, which spins the mixture at high speeds, separating the large sugar crystals from the thick syrup. The crystals, 97 to 99 percent sucrose, are called raw sugar. Producers may package the raw sugar, as turbinado, for consumer use or sell it to cane sugar refiners [classified under **SIC 2062: Cane Sugar Refining**] for the manufacture of granulated or powdered sugar. Any foreign sugar shipped to the United States is also transported in raw form.

CURRENT CONDITIONS

Sugar and other agricultural supports have been criticized by members of Congress and other government officials. Although cuts in price supports are likely, the government is unlikely to remove all supports. Sugar producers claimed that the federal sugar program protected U.S consumers from wild swings in world prices. Critics, however, contended that U.S. consumers spend an extra $3 billion annually because of the government program.

U.S. companies are among some of the critics of the sugar tariffs. In 1991, E. J. Brach's, a candy manufacturer, asked that a part of Chicago be declared a free trade zone so that Brach's could import sugar at the world price. The company said that if it had to continue to pay inflated U.S. sugar prices, the high cost would force it to move its operations out of the country. The sugar industry successfully blocked the company's application for free trade status.

The U.S. sugar industry and its very powerful lobby claimed that 80 percent of the sugar in the United States is consumed by food processors, who did not pass drops in sugar prices on to consumers. They cited government reports that said, from 1982 to 1992, the average cost of sweeteners (cane sugar, beet sugar and high fructose corn syrup) rose only about nine percent, less than the rate of inflation, however prices for products containing sugar rose 54 percent. The chairman of the American Sugar Alliance also claimed that U.S. consumers pay 25 percent less for sugar than consumers in other developed nations and that the U.S. price for sugar was ten percent less than the world average retail price.

The American Sugar Alliance also claimed that since the United States was not self-sufficient in sugar, it imported 27 percent of its sugar in 1991 and that exporters of sugar to the U.S. received the same level of price supports as United States sugar cane producers.

The North American Free Trade Agreement promised to open up the sugar market to Mexico; however, rather than increasing overall import of sugar, it would probably reduce U.S. purchases from the Philippines or Caribbean nations.

Pollution in the Everglades. According to environmentalists, agricultural run-off from sugar plantations and milling processes in southern Florida were responsible for damage to the Everglades. In 1991, United States Sugar Corporation was fined $3.75 million for improper disposal of hazardous materials from one of its Clewiston mills in the Everglades. The company pleaded guilty to knowingly allowing hazardous wastes into local landfills during three harvest years. Environmentalists continued to raise concerns about the effect of the sugar industry on the fragile ecosystem of the Everglades.

INDUSTRY LEADERS

According to the *Wall Street Journal,* one family supplies the United States with more than 15 percent of its cane sugar: the Fanjuls, through their Flo-Sun, Inc., own 160,000 acres of cane fields and milling facilities in southern Florida. According to the report, in 1959, after Fidel Castro took over Cuba, fifth-generation members of one of Cuba's largest sugar-growing families, the Fanjuls, bought a 25 percent share in a new sugar company. That company moved a Louisiana sugar mill to Florida, and the mill and sugar cane fields were established on 4,000 acres of land newly drained by the U.S. Army Corps of Engineers. In 1985, the Fanjuls bought Gulf & Western's sugar operations in Florida (and the Dominican Republic); although the price was not disclosed, experts estimated the acquisition cost between $200 million and $240 million.

Other large sugar cane concerns in Florida include: St. Joe Paper Co. (its $582 million in revenues includes diverse businesses in paperboard mills, communications, and transportation); U.S. Sugar Corp. ($360 million combined revenues from growing and processing sugar cane and sugar beets); Okleelanta Corp. ($200 million in revenues); Osceola Farms Company Inc. ($130 million); Atlantic Sugar Association ($65 million); and Talisman Sugar Corp. ($23 million).

Large sugar cane concerns in Hawaii include: Alexander and Baldwin (its $748 million in revenues includes diverse businesses in agriculture, real estate and transportation); C. Brewer and Company, Ltd. ($260 million); Hamakua Sugar Company, Inc. ($45 million); and Oahu Sugar Company, Ltd. ($36 million).

Sugar concerns in Louisiana include: Cora-Texas Manufacturing Company, Inc. ($30 million); Alma Plantation ($23 million); Cajun Sugar Cooperative, Inc. ($20 million); Sterling Sugars, Inc. ($18 million); and Iberia Sugar Cooperative ($16 million).

WORK FORCE

Although cutters are employed by the sugar growers, they are discussed here because many of the plantations in southern Florida are owned by the large sugar mills and are therefore part of this industry in the country's leading sugar-producing state. Sugar harvesters, called cane cutters, face one of the most grueling jobs imaginable. For decades, the Florida sugar cane industry had come under fire for the severe, even slave-like conditions in which the cutters lived and for illegal practices concerning wages. Most cane cutters in Florida were seasonal workers, coming from the Caribbean for the cutting season.

A 1991 congressional report accused the sugar cane industry of violating labor laws. In 1992, U.S. Sugar Corp., one of the largest sugar concerns in Florida, agreed to a wage increase and other improvements. Farm-worker advocacy groups were hoping to win reforms for cane cutters working at other sugar companies. However, southern Florida sugar concerns were increasingly turning to machine cutting because of the long history of controversy about the treatment of immigrant labor by the industry.

Employment in the fields and in the mills drops during the summer months and then picks up again between the fall and spring. According to the Bureau or Labor Statistics, in 1990, total employment of production workers classified under SIC 2061 was 3,500 in July and 6,400 in November.

INDUSTRY INFORMATION SOURCES

Bacon, Kenneth H. "U.S., Mexico Have Tentative Pact on Sugar Trade." *Wall Street Journal*, 29 July 1992, A2.

Barry, Robert D. "The U.S. Sugar Program in the 1980s." *National Food Review*, January-March 1990, 55-61.

Cheney, Carolyn. "Letter to the editor: Sugar Study's Sticky Trap." *Wall Street Journal*, 21 August 1991, A13.

Ingersoll, Bruce. "Sugar Subsidies Assailed for Drug, Environment Links." *Wall Street Journal*, 24 July 1990, 2A.

James, Canute. "Caribbean Nations Lose as U.S. Farms Automate." *Journal of Commerce and Commercial*, 31 August 1992, 4A.

Mayer, Jane, and Jose de Cordoba. "Sweet Life: First Family of Sugar Is Tough on Workers, Generous to Politicians." *Wall Street Journal*, 29 July 1991, A1.

Wilkinson, Alec. *Big Sugar, Seasons in the Cane Fields of Florida*. New York: Alfred A. Knopf, 1989.

—Wendy J. Stein

SIC 2062

CANE SUGAR REFINING

This entry includes establishments primarily engaged in refining purchased raw cane sugar and sugar syrup. Sugar cane is cut and milled into raw cane sugar, then shipped in that form to refiners to be processed into syrup, granulated sugar, powdered sugar, or brown sugar. Establishments that manufacture the raw cane sugar from sugar cane are included under **SIC 2061 Cane Sugar, Except Refining.**

The cane sugar refining industry has been facing heavy competition on many fronts. Manufacturers of beet sugar, high fructose corn syrup (HFCS) and artificial sweeteners have all taken large market shares away from cane sugar refiners. According to *National Food Review,* ten refineries out of twenty-one closed between 1981 and 1990. Soft drink manufacturers switched to HFCS from liquid cane sugar in the 1980s, striking a severe blow to the sugar industry. To compensate for the losses incurred from other sweeteners, many remaining cane sugar refiners diversified, adding sugar beet processing operations and/or wet-milling operations to produce HFCS and other corn sweeteners. Beet sugar's share of the sugar market increased from 30 percent in the 1970s to 40 percent in the 1980s, and its share continued to rise into the 1990s.

Besides the rise in HFCS, there were other problems for cane sugar refiners. Domestic production of sugar cane dropped, and a strict quota on imported raw cane sugar was imposed by the federal government. The drop in availability of imported raw sugar was especially serious to the industry since sugar refineries in the United States processed more imported raw sugar than domestically-milled raw sugar.

Price, in addition to new product competition, plagued the cane sugar refining industry in the 1990s. Federal programs kept the price of domestic sugar

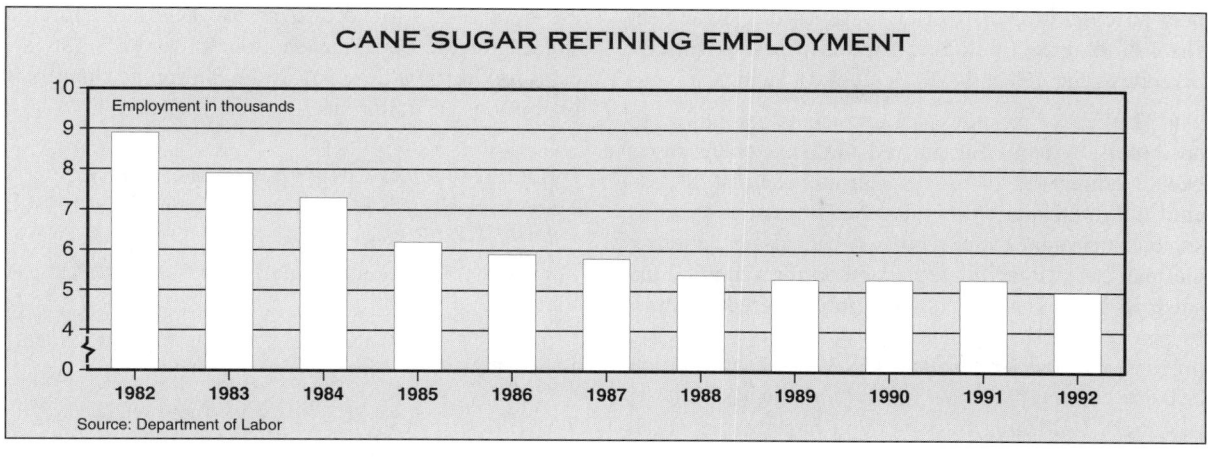

CANE SUGAR REFINING EMPLOYMENT

Employment in thousands

Source: Department of Labor

higher than world market prices. In 1992, for example, when the world price of sugar was ten cents a pound, the price in the United States was 21 cents a pound. The government also imposed a quota to prevent cheaper imported sugar from flooding the U.S. market. The United States continues to import some raw sugar, because it does not grow enough to meet U.S. demand. High fructose corn syrup producers have been able to undercut the sugar market—both beet sugar and cane sugar—and make HFCS a cheaper alternative in processed foods. Americans consumed more corn syrup than refined sugar in the early 1990s.

At least one market continued to prefer cane sugar to the competition. Candy and pastry makers were not impressed with substitutes for refined cane sugar. They insist that beet sugar is not suitable for their purposes and that they achieve better results with pure cane sugar. According to the U.S. government, cane sugar and beet sugar have the same chemical formula so refiners cannot claim any difference between them.

To produce refined sugar from raw sugar, the raw sugar crystals are transported, aboard ships or trains to refineries where first the yellow-brown film is rinsed off. The sugar crystals are dissolved in water and poured through a series of filters until the liquid is clear. The syrup is heated so the liquid evaporates leaving crystals again. The crystals are spun in a centrifuge, and then the white sugar is separated into a drying drum where any remaining moisture is eliminated. Syrup that does not form crystals is used to make brown sugar. Molasses is another by-product of the refining process.

Leading American sugar refiners include: Savannah Foods and Industries; Domino Sugar Corp.; Imperial Holly Corp. (which also processes beet sugar); and California and Hawaiian Sugar Co. (formerly a grower-owned cooperative, which was scheduled to be purchased by Alexander and Baldwin, a leader in manufacturing raw sugar from sugar cane); Tate and Lyle, Inc. (which also processes beet sugar); Colonial Sugars Inc.; Refined Sugars, Inc.; and Amstar Sugar Corp. (a subsidiary of Tate and Lyle, Inc.).

INDUSTRY INFORMATION SOURCES

Bacon, Kenneth. "Politics & Policy: U.S., Mexico Have Tentative Pact on Sugar Trade." *Wall Street Journal*, 29 July 1992, A2.

Carlsen, Clifford. "Business Is Sweet at C&H Sugar Co." *San Francisco Business Times*, 6 September 1991, 1.

Ingersoll, Bruce. "Range War: Small Minnesota Town Is Divided by Rancor over Sugar Policies." *Wall Street Journal*, 26 June 1990, 1A.

Kochilas, Diane. "Sweet Sense." *Restaurant Business*, 10 December 1990, 155.

Schontak, Judith. "Savannah Foods: Sweet on Profits." *Business Atlanta*, October 1988, 42.

—Wendy J. Stein

SIC 2063

BEET SUGAR

This entry includes establishments primarily engaged in manufacturing sugar from sugar beets.

Sugar beets are one of the world's main sugar sources and an important source of sugar for the United States. Reduced imports of raw cane sugar hurt U.S. refiners in the 1980s, and the sugar industry turned to sugar beets to make up the difference. The United States processes more sugar from domestically-grown sugar beets than from domestically-grown sugar cane. Many cane refiners also invested in sugar beet processing firms in the 1980s as the sugar beet share of total use (including imports) climbed from 30 percent in the 1970s to 40 percent in 1988.

The beet sugar industry can trace its beginnings to ancient Babylonia, Egypt, and Greece, where sugar beets were grown. In 1744, a German chemist discovered that the sugar from sugar beets was the same as sugar from sugar cane. About 50 years later, another German chemist developed a method for removing the sugar from the sugar beets. Sugar mills were soon built in Europe and Russia. In 1838, sugar beets were being processed in the United States as well. The first successful commercial beet sugar mill was built in Alvarado, California by American businessman E.H. Dyer.

Unlike sugarcane, which is processed into raw sugar (see **SIC 2061: Cane Sugar, except Refining**) to be marketed to cane refiners (see **SIC 2062: Cane Sugar Refining**), beets are processed directly into refined sugar. Beet sugar is produced from the root of the sugar beet plant, which is shipped to factories to be washed and cut into thin slices called cossettes. These cossettes are soaked in diffusers to remove the sugar and the pulp is dried and mixed with molasses to make feed for cattle. The sugar-water mixture goes through a series of purification processes in which lime, carbon dioxide, and filtration are used to remove impurities. Finally, the liquid is reheated until evaporation leaves a crystallized sugar product. Sugar products manufactured from sugar beets include dried beet pulp, beet sugar, molasses, granulated sugar, liquid sugar, invert sugar, powdered sugar, and syrup.

Leading sugar beet producing states are California, Idaho, Michigan, North Dakota and Wyoming. Leading beet sugar producers include Valhi Inc. of Dallas; Imperial Holly Corp. of Sugar Land, Texas; Holly Sugar Corp. of Colorado Springs; Spreckels Industries, Inc. of Pleasanton, California; Flo-Sun Inc. of Palm Beach, Florida; and Southern Minnesota Beet Sugar Cooperative of Renville, Minnesota.

The federal government has provided price supports to the U.S. sugar industry for almost 200 years. Nonrecourse loans to processors guarantee a minimum price for beet sugar. When processors sell the sugar, beet growers share in the returns, with the growers usually receiving about 60 percent of loan or sale proceeds and processors 40 percent. The government also imposes quotas on sugar imports to keep domestic prices higher than the loan rate. Many consumer groups and commentators are critical of the U.S. program that protects the sugar industry. In 1990, James Bovard, a policy analyst, wrote in *USA Today* that the sugar program results in American sugar prices that are double or triple world prices, keeps out foreign sugar to create "artificial shortages," and costs sugar-cane-producing allies such as the Philippines hundreds of millions of dollars in lost trade.

INDUSTRY INFORMATION SOURCES

Barry, Robert D. "The U.S. Sugar Program in the 1980s." *National Food Review*, January-March 1990, 55-61.

Bovard, James. "Farm Subsidy Follies." *USA Today*, November 1990, 15-18.

O'Rourke, P.J. "Manuregate." *Rolling Stone*, 12-26 July 1990, 45-48.

—Wendy J. Stein

SIC 2064

CANDY AND OTHER CONFECTIONERY PRODUCTS

This category includes establishments primarily engaged in manufacturing candy, including chocolate candy, other confections, and related products, including: chocolate-covered candy bars; breakfast bars; candy, except solid chocolate; chocolate bars made from purchased chocolate; chocolate candy, except solid chocolate; confectionery cake ornaments; fudge; granola bars; marshmallows; candy-covered nuts; candied, glazed or crystallized fruits; and popcorn balls and candy-covered popcorn products. Establishments engaged primarily in manufacturing solid chocolate bars from cacao beans are classified under **SIC 2066: Chocolate and Cocoa Products**. Establishments manufacturing chewing gum are included under **SIC 2067: Chewing Gum**, while those primarily engaged in roasting and salting nuts are classified in **SIC 2068: Salted and Roasted Nuts and Seeds**. Establishments primarily engaged in manufacturing confectionery for direct sale on the premises to household consumers are classified in **SIC 5441: Candy, Nut, and Confectionery Stores**.

INDUSTRY SNAPSHOT

America and the rest of the world have an appetite for candy. The $9 billion candy industry is very competitive and features a long rivalry between the two top manufacturers, Mars Inc. and Hershey Foods Corp., which together dominate the U.S. candy market.

Sales for candy rose in 1992, after a steep decline in 1990 and 1991. Manufacturers launched aggressive new product campaigns in 1992 and maintained the recent trend towards products with reduced fat and sugar content.

Candy exports were strong, especially with Mexico and Canada, and are expected to increase with the passage of the North American Free Trade Agreement. Candy makers, though, are also concerned about the ramifications of new environmental regulations that might require them to provide recyclable packaging.

BACKGROUND AND DEVELOPMENT

Many of the most popular candy bars sold today were developed between the 1890s and 1920 by various candy makers around the country. Rights to many of these candies have been bought and sold many times since they were developed and now are owned by large corporations such as Mars, Hershey Foods, Warner-Lambert, and RJR Nabisco.

Milton S. Hershey manufactured the first chocolate bar in the United States in 1894. Hershey Kisses were introduced in 1907. The Bunte Brothers are credited with manufacturing the first chocolate-covered candy bars in 1911. During World War I, Hershey and other candy makers shipped large blocks of chocolate to army training camps, where the blocks were cut into smaller chunks for distribution. This task became too time-consuming for military personnel, and the manufacturers started wrapping individual chocolate bars before shipping them. After the war, the candy makers continued to sell candy commercially in this form, and this method of selling candy became popular and convenient.

Many lines of candy bars were first sold for a dime, but sales did not catch on since consumers could buy a pound of loose candy for that same dime. Immediately after World War I, however, sugar and chocolate prices dropped and the price of most candy bars was dropped to a nickel. The price remained fairly constant until the late 1960s, when the price went back to a dime because of rising costs. Since then, prices have steadily climbed.

The forerunners of NECCO wafers and Canada Mints were first produced in 1847 by Chase and Company, with Canada Mints themselves introduced in Canada in the late 1880s and brought to the United States in 1908. NECCO wafers were introduced in 1912 by New England Confectionery Company, a company formed by Chase and two other candy companies; the NECCO brand name is derived from the company's initials. Cracker Jack entered the confectionery market in 1893 at Chicago's World's Fair but was not named until 1896.

Life Savers first rolled into production in 1912 in a small factory in Cleveland, Ohio, when Cornelius Crane, a chocolate maker, developed mint tablets as a summertime product to compensate for the drop-off in sales of chocolate during the hot summer months. Crane went to a pill manufacturer to produce the mints and a malfunctioning machine produced mints with a hole in the center, thus creating the first Life Savers product.

The first part of the twentieth century marked an explosive period of growth for the industry. Dozens of new candy products were introduced during this period, and many have endured. Ferrara Pan, a candy company formed in 1919 in Illinois, produced Jaw Breakers, Atomic Fireballs, and Boston Baked Beans. In 1919 the Oh Henry! bar was first manufactured by the Williamson Candy Company of Chicago. Charleston Chews! were first sold in 1922 by the Fox-Cross Candy Company near San Francisco. Goobers were first made by the Blumenthal Chocolate Company in 1925. Holloway Milk Duds were introduced in 1926 by the Holloway Company. During the 1920s and 1930s, the James O. Welch Company introduced several favorites that are still around today, including Sugar Daddy, Sugar Babies, Pom Poms, and Junior Mints. Heath Bars, manufactured by the L.S. Heath Company, went on the market in 1932. Chunky was developed in the mid-1930s by Philip Silverstein, a New York candy maker.

In 1930 the most popular candy bar in America was created—Snickers. Snickers is one of the few candy bars still produced by its originator—Mars Inc., which today is one of the largest private companies in the United States. Mars introduced the Milky Way bar in 1923, 3 Musketeers and the Mars Bar in the 1930s, and M&M's in 1941.

Peter Paul Candies was formed in 1919 and introduced its first candy bar, the Konabar. Three years later, the company introduced the dark chocolate-covered coconut bar that served as the cornerstone of the company's product line—Mounds. The first Mounds was a single bar for a nickel, but during the Depression, Peter Paul doubled the size of the package by adding a second bar without increasing the price. This two-for-one tactic increased sales, despite the hard times. Peter Paul replaced hand-wrapping with machine-wrapping by converting a machine designed to wrap soap bars. The company also became one of the first to venture into broadcast advertising. In 1948 the company combined almonds with coconut to launch Almond Joy. Peter Paul acquired York Peppermint Patty in 1972. Several years later, the company was acquired by Cadbury Schweppes PLC for $58 million and thus added to that empire.

The candy industry has gone through a period of consolidation during the past 20 to 30 years. In the 1960s Hershey acquired Reese's, maker of Reese's Peanut Butter Cups since 1923; in 1977 Hershey acquired Y&S Candies, which had marketed licorice Twizzlers and Nibs since the 1920s. Hershey's acquisition of Cadbury Schweppes' U.S. division in 1988 propelled Hershey past Mars to become the leading U.S. candy maker. The purchase gave Hershey the rights to Peter Paul Almond Joys and Mounds, as well as Cadbury and Caramello products, to buttress its already impressive product line.

Despite the presence of such corporate giants as Mars Inc. and Hershey Foods Corp., several independent companies have maintained a significant presence in the industry. Tootsie Roll Industries has remained an independent company since its founding in 1896. It markets a line of Tootsie Roll products, as well as several products, including Mason Dots and Bonomo Turkish Taffy, it acquired through the purchase of smaller companies. Another company that remained independent since its beginnings is PEZ Candy Inc., with its flavored rectangular sugar tablets and vast array of plastic, flip-top dispensers. PEZ was founded in 1952 and is based in Orange, Connecticut. The first PEZ tablets were invented in 1927 as a peppermint tablet and cigarette substitute. PEZ was an abbreviation for *pfefferminz*, the German word for peppermint.

CURRENT CONDITIONS

According to the *U.S. Industrial Outlook 1993*, industry shipments in 1992 reached approximately $8.9 billion, a 4.3 percent increase over 1991 levels. "Adjusted for inflation, the value of candy/confectionery shipments rose an estimated 3.2 percent for the year. Between 1987 and 1991, the inflation-adjusted value of industry shipments rose 2.2 percent annually."

Although sales of regular candy have been substantial, the candy makers have increasingly taken notice of the relatively recent nutritional health emphasis and used it as a source of growth. In 1992 sugar-free and other "healthier" candies accounted for only one percent of the confectionery market, but industry members anticipate the market will grow, especially as new low-fat or low-calorie ingredients improve the taste of the so-called "healthier" chocolate candies. Caprenin, developed by Procter & Gamble, combined the taste and consistency of ordinary fat, but contained half the calories. Mars used it in its reduced-fat, reduced-calorie Milky Way II, which contained half the calories of the original Milky Way and eight grams of fat. Smaller companies were also trying to capitalize on the health market. In 1992, 92 percent of supermarkets and other stores sold some kind of sugar-free candy. Although most retail outlets said that sugar-free candy sales represented a very small market share, 87 percent of the store buyers surveyed expected demand for sugar-free items to continue to increase well into the 1990s.

Candy makers are also cashing in on the holiday markets. Mars, Hershey, and Nestle had traditionally stayed away from the holiday candy market, but when candy consumption and sales remained flat, the candy giants saw great opportunity to capture a share of the $1.5 billion holiday sales. The three companies repackaged many of their most famous goodies in pastel colors for Easter. Their entry into the holiday market shoved aside many of the usual holiday candy manufacturers; within five years, the giants had gobbled up 40 percent of the Easter candy sales of almost half a billion dollars. In 1992 Hershey Easter candy sales rose 30 percent, to more than $124 million, while rival Mars was a distant second with $57 million in sales. That same year, Valentine's Day sales of candy increased 18 percent, while Halloween candy sales increased 14 percent, and Christmas candy 12 percent.

Many other confectioners are looking to the kids' market for growth. Industry experts and retailers note that over half the children in the United States between the ages of four and twelve possess an average of $4 a week to spend. Many candy makers are thus pitching their products directly to this market segment.

INDUSTRY LEADERS

At the beginning of 1993, all ten candy bars on the top-selling candy list in the United States were manufactured by Mars, Hershey, or Nestle. Snickers remained the number one candy bar with sales of more than $61 million annually; Hershey products were second and third on the list, with Reese's Peanut Butter Cups (sales of $41 million) and Kit Kat ($36 million). The rest of the list included M&M's Plain (Mars, almost $32 million); Butterfinger (Nestle, almost $32 million); M&M's Peanut (Mars, almost $30 billion); Crunch (Nestle, $26 million); Hershey Milk Chocolate ($24 million); Hershey Almond (24 million); and 3 Musketeers (Mars, $20 million).

Other leading candy companies include E.J. Brach Corp., Leaf Inc., Russell Stover Candies Inc., Archibald Candy Corp., and Midial U.S.A. Fanny Farmer Candy Shops Inc.

AMERICA AND THE WORLD

The value of U.S. candy and confectionery exports in 1992 was about $359 million, an increase of more than 32 percent over the previous year. The increase was due in part to a weak American dollar and aggressive marketing. Exports to Canada and Mexico accounted for about 64 percent of all U.S. candy exports, while exports to South Korea and Japan accounted for another 13 percent of export value.

Although Europeans consume a great amount of candy, Europe continued to be a poor market for U.S. candy. High duties have kept U.S. candy out of the European Community (EC), although some American companies have invested in European candy companies and avoided the duties. Hershey purchased its first European company in 1991 with the $31-million acquisition of Gubor Schokoladen, a chocolate company that manufactures pralines and chocolates. Warner-Lambert, a large pharmaceutical and consumer products manufacturer that also produces cough drops and other confectionery products, entered into a joint venture with Alivar S.p.A to sell cough drops and candies in Italy, a large confectionery market.

The value of candy imports rose by about 24 percent in 1992 to $420 million. The EC provides most of the United States' candy imports. In 1991 Germany, the United Kingdom, Italy, the Netherlands, France, and Spain accounted for more than 42 percent of U.S. candy imports. Canada was the single most important source of candy imports, though, providing 24 percent. Mexico provided four percent of import value.

INDUSTRY INFORMATION SOURCES

Broekel, Ray. *The Great American Candy Bar Book.* Boston: Houghton Mifflin Company, 1982.

Deveny, Kathleen. "Pushing Chocolate Chicks and Bunnies." *Wall Street Journal.* April 3, 1993: B1.

Moskowitz, Milton, Robert Levering, and Michael Katz. *Everybody's Business, A Field Guide to the 400 Leading Companies in America.* New York: Doubleday, 1990.

Rutherford, Andrea C. "Candy Firms Roll Out 'Healthy' Sweets." *Wall Street Journal.* August 10, 1992: B1.

Yoshihashi, Pauline. "New Candies for Kids May Seem Tasteless to Adults." *Wall Street Journal.* April 8, 1993: B1.

SIC 2066

CHOCOLATE AND COCOA PRODUCTS

Included in this industry classification are establishments primarily engaged in shelling, roasting, and grinding cacao beans for the purpose of making chocolate liquor—from which cocoa powder and cocoa butter are derived—and in the further manufacture of solid chocolate bars, chocolate coatings, and other chocolate and cocoa products. Also included is the manufacture of similar products, except candy, from purchased chocolate or cocoa. Establishments primarily engaged in manufacturing candy from purchased cocoa products are classified in **SIC 2064: Candy and Other Confectionery Products.**

INDUSTRY SNAPSHOT

Chocolate manufacturers import their raw material, cacao beans, by direct purchase or through the services of a broker. The beans are then processed to make chocolate liquor, which is in turn used to further manufacture such products as cocoa, chocolate syrup, and solid chocolate chips and baking bars. The chocolate liquor is also often sold to other manufacturers that combine it with additional ingredients to produce confections, bakery items, and dairy products. While the balance in trade for cocoa and chocolate has usually run at a deficit, in recent years exports have been growing steadily and closing the gap.

The industry has traditionally been subject to significant fluctuations in demand. Chocolate products tend to be seasonal in nature, with demand increasing sharply during the holidays. In addition, several consumer trends have also had an impact on demand. These include rising sales of premium-priced chocolates and the growing concern about the health risks associated with eating such high-fat foods as chocolate.

ORGANIZATION AND STRUCTURE

U.S. manufacturers must import all of their cacao beans because this nation's climate cannot support cacao trees, which need tropical conditions to survive. Growers are paid for the beans at market price, which is determined by the amount of crop available worldwide as well as the quality of farmers' crops in a number of countries. A number of other economic variables also determine this price. As a testament to cacao's importance as a commodity, cacao exchanges, similar to standard stock exchanges, have been established in such cities as New York, London, Hamburg, and Amsterdam.

There are approximately 12 companies involved in the production of chocolate in the United States. Manufacturers roast, shell, and grind the beans to produce unsweetened chocolate, the chocolate liquor that is the basic ingredient of all chocolate products. Further processing of chocolate liquor falls into two categories: cocoa manufacture and chocolate manufacture.

In cocoa production the fat is pressed from chocolate liquor, leaving cocoa cake which is crushed to form cocoa powder. The powder may be sweetened and sold as a cocoa beverage or left unsweetened for use in bakery and dairy products and for home cooking use. Cocoa butter, the fat removed from the chocolate liquor, is used mainly in sweetened chocolate, but it also is utilized as a moisturizer in such toilet articles as soaps and creams and in certain medications.

The production of chocolate requires the addition of sugar or other sweeteners and cocoa butter to chocolate liquor. Milk solids are also required in the manufacture of milk chocolate. Bulk quantities of sweetened chocolate (blocks of at least 4.5 kilograms) are called chocolate coating and are used for covering candy and baked goods. Chocolate coating is generally more expensive than the confectioners' coatings that are made from cocoa powder.

Chocolate manufacturers sell these semiprocessed cocoa products to other firms that use the items in the production of confectionery, bakery goods, and such dairy products as chocolate milk. In addition, some producers also manufacture their own confectionery. Exports of chocolate products were mainly confined to confectionery items rather than semiprocessed chocolate.

BACKGROUND AND DEVELOPMENT

Columbus returned from one of his trips to the Americas with some strange new beans for King Ferdinand of Spain. Those dark brown cocoa beans eventually became the basis of one of the most thriving industries in the world. Chocolate manufacture did not get its start in the United States, however, until 1765 when the first chocolate factory was established in New England, using beans shipped from the West Indies. Funding for the venture was provided by physician James Baker, and Baker's brand of chocolate continues to be produced by Kraft General Foods, Inc.

It was during World War I that the government realized how much chocolate could do to nourish the bodies and spirits of our troops. Space was made on cargo planes coming into the country so a sufficient supply of cocoa beans would be available to manufacture chocolate products. The U.S. Army D-rations still include 4-ounce chocolate bars and cocoa bean products are part of the rarified rations of NASA space travellers.

CURRENT CONDITIONS

The chocolate industry did not escape the effects of the recession of early 1990s. Few cocoa-based companies in North America have not experienced layoffs, mergers and consolidations, plant closings, shift cutbacks, advertising slashes, and operational streamlining that reflects poor sales figures and fiscal restraint. In fact, between 1989 and 1991 the industry experienced 50 acquisitions, mergers, licensing agreements, or joint ventures, and companies are intent on expanding and diversifying its product base.

The 1987 Census of Manufactures reported that there were 150 companies involved in the manufacture of chocolate that reported shipments of $100,000 or more. The Census also counted among that number 11 firms that produce chocolate candy from cocoa beans ground in the same company. The combined chocolate and confectionery industries counted 871 companies employing 57,000 persons. About 20 percent of those establishments employed at least 100 people or more, while 60 percent employed less than 20 persons.

INDUSTRY LEADERS

According to *Ward's Business Directory of U.S. Private and Public Companies 1994,* Nestlé USA Inc. of Glendale, California, was the industry's leading company, with $7.2 billion in sales. A subsidiary of the Swiss company Nestlé S.A., the U.S. firm employed approximately 43,000 people. Following Nestlé USA Inc. with a distant $3.2 billion in sales was Hershey Foods Corp. of Hershey, Pennsylvania. A Hershey Foods Corp. subsidiary, Hershey Chocolate USA, contributed $2.5 billion to the value of the industry, and the two Hershey companies together employed about 23,000 people.

In comparison to the top three companies, those rounding out the top five had substantially smaller sales and employed far fewer workers. They were Wilbur Chocolate Company Inc., located in Lititz, Pennsylvania, with sales of $105 million and 300 employees; World's Finest Chocolate Inc. of Chicago, Illinois, with $100 million in sales and 400 workers.

RESEARCH AND TECHNOLOGY

In an effort to compensate for lagging sales, a number of chocolate and cocoa-based companies have turned to technological advancements to increase efficiency and lower production costs. A case in point is Grace Cocoa's new Chocolate Americas Division headquarters. Hailed as somewhat of a miracle of modern engineering, the $95 million plant raised 335,000 square feet of computer-integrated manufacturing on a barren site in a Milwaukee, Wisconsin, industrial park. According to a *Candy Industry* interview with Dave Pollock, director of manufacturing at the new factory, "This really is the future."

Part of the new technology in the plant included computerization of a number of the production processes, and while this has helped facilitate more efficient productivity, it also engendered a number of challenges. One of these was retraining employees who were familiar with only rudimentary chocolate making procedures. The state of Wisconsin helped offset some of the costs of retraining by contributing half the cost of tuition at local technical colleges.

Cocoa has become such an intrinsic and valuable part of the U.S. economy that efforts by industry and science are underway to understand better the bean itself. The American Cocoa Research Institute contributed $1.5 million to Penn State University's Molecular Biology of Cocoa program. The main objective of the program is to increase understanding of the biology, botany, and genetics of the cocoa plant. The objectives of the study were revised January of 1992 and now include the study of disease resistance, quality, plant delivery, and tools.

INDUSTRY INFORMATION SOURCES

Hoover's Handbook of American Business 1993, Austin, TX: The Reference Press, Inc., 1992.

Mitchell, Dennis P., "An Industry in Turmoil," *Snack Food,* June 1992.

Office of Industries, *Industry & Trade Summary: Cocoa, Chocolate, and Confectionery,* Washington, DC: U.S. International Trade Commission, June 1993.

Tiffany, Susan, "Grace Cocoa unveils engineering marvel," *Candy Industry,* April 1993.

Ward's Business Directory of U.S. Private and Public Companies 1994, Detroit: Gale Research Inc., 1994.

SIC 2067

CHEWING GUM

This industry consists of establishments primarily engaged in manufacturing chewing gum or chewing gum base.

INDUSTRY SNAPSHOT

In 1992 there were an estimated 550 chewing gum companies around the world. Turkey had the most with 60 companies. Eight companies comprised the U.S. industry, which took in over $1.4 billion in sales in

1992. The two industry leaders, Wm. Wrigley Jr. Co. and Warner-Lambert Co., accounted for 75 percent of domestic chewing gum sales.

The American chewing gum industry has been marked by strong periods of growth and decline throughout the 20th century. Since the 1970s this industry has been growing at a faster pace overseas than within the United States. The industry's overall success has been the result of low manufacturing costs and aggressive marketing campaigns.

ORGANIZATION AND STRUCTURE

Chewing gum companies use two main channels of distribution. One channel is through wholesalers, who supply retail stores in the areas they serve. The other channel is the delivery of boxes of chewing gum directly to large retail outlets from the manufacturers' warehouses and factories. The retail distribution chain includes food, drug, variety, and convenience stores, gas stations, newsstands, and restaurants. Another important channel for these manufacturers has been distributors who stock vending machines.

BACKGROUND AND DEVELOPMENT

History. Though chewing gum bases are primarily synthetic today, gum was originally derived from natural sources such as tree resins and saps. The use of chewing gum made from tree resin dates back to ancient Greek and Mayan civilizations. In North America, Wampanoag Indians introduced gum chewing to European settlers. The gum was made from the resin of spruce trees.

Americans began manufacturing gum in the mid-1800s, adding paraffin wax, which was used to make the gum softer and more long lasting. At about this time flavors such as mint were added to the gum, helping to increase the product's popularity. In 1848 John Curtis of Maine started producing the first commercial spruce gum.

American settlers traveling west learned about chewing chicle, the hardened sap of sapodilla trees, from the Osage Indians. The sapodilla tree is found mainly in the tropical rain forests of the Yucatan Peninsula of Mexico and Guatemala. By 1869, the first commercial chicle was manufactured, and in 1906 paraffin was added to chicle.

During the late 1800s, companies that would become the industry leaders entered this business, making valuable contributions to the industry as a whole. In 1893 William Wrigley began making chewing gum and improved methods of manufacturing, packaging and marketing. Another industry leader, Franklin

Channing, invented the first dental gum, Dentyne, in 1899. About the same time, Henry Fleer created Chiclets, the first candy-coated chewing gum.

Bubble gum was first developed in 1906, but early batches were too sticky to sell and it was not until 1928 that bubble gum was first marketed. Another important development in this industry was the first sugarless gum, which was created in the late 1940s but not marketed until the 1950s. LifeSavers' CareFree and American Chicle's Trident appeared in the mid-1960s and dominated the sugarless gum market early on. In the 1980s, Wrigley's Extra gum was launched and by 1990 it controlled 40 percent of the $480 million sugar-free gum market.

Sugar-free gums began using xylitol, an artificial sweetener, in the late 1970s. However, in 1978, the U.S. Food and Drug Administration began investigating possible links between xylitol and cancer; though no link was ever established, products made with xylitol were reformulated using other artificial sweeteners. In the early 1990s, xylitol was reintroduced by Leaf Specialty Products, who manufactured XyliFresh, a chewing gum intended for fighting plaque.

Chewing gum manufacturers have also enjoyed heightened success brought on by wars. The Wm. Wrigley Jr. Co. recorded an increase in chewing gum demand during world wars I and II and during the 1990-91 conflict in the Persian Gulf. In fact, during World War II, when top-grade ingredients were scarce, production was limited to the armed forces and civilians were sold a lesser quality gum under the brand name Orbit.

Marketing and Product Trends. The chewing gum industry spends roughly ten percent of its revenues on marketing, primarily on television advertising. According to *Adweek's Marketing Week*, Amurol Products has brought roughly 12 new products to the market each year, eight of which last two years and only four of which last longer. Because of the short life span, companies have incentive to continue creating new products.

Since it was first sold in America, gum has been packaged with novelties, such as sports cards, toys, and comic strips. In the 20th century, companies launched novelty bubble gums, which were packaged in a variety of shapes and unusual forms, such as school lockers and toothpaste tubes.

In the early 1990s, sour gum became popular with children. These chewing gums have an extremely sour taste that becomes sweet and eventually has a neutral or tangy taste. Children often used these gums to play jokes on friends or to prove their mettle. In 1992 sour gum brought in an estimated $70 million in retail sales. Moreover, as the demand for sour gum caught suppliers by surprise, a "black market" for the product emerged.

In the 1980s, chewing gum sales were boosted by campaigns that promoted chewing gum as an alternative to smoking. Other advertisements have endorsed sugar-free gums as being good for teeth. In addition to advertisements on television, radio and in newspapers, companies in this industry use sales representatives to market their products. These representatives regularly visit retailers and assist them with display designs and layouts.

In 1993 LifeSavers made industry news with its innovative approach to selling bubble gum. Its Bubble Yum product was promoted through a traveling virtual reality arcade game, and LifeSavers was the first company to use the game as a marketing tool. The game, called Planet Bubble Yum, featured chunks of bubble gum flying around in three-dimensional animation. Bubble Yum charged proof of purchase seals for admission. The tour traveled to shopping malls in major U.S. cities, with an average attendance of 1,100 people per location.

Production. The cost of producing chewing gum has always been low. High demand for chewing gum, allowing for high volume production, and advances in automation have helped to reduce costs further. The price of ingredients, such as corn syrup and gum base, have also declined since the 1970s, thus reducing costs and increasing profit margins.

Modern methods and new materials have changed the character of chewing gum. Natural ingredients have become scarce due to changing climatic conditions, demand, and development in regions where the ingredients were harvested. Chicle and other products from trees are now used in conjunction with synthetic materials. Most chewing gums are made with five basic ingredients: chewing gum base, sugar, corn syrup, softeners (such as glycerin and other vegetable oils), and flavors (mostly extracted from mint plants). In sugar-free gums, sugar and corn syrup are usually replaced with aspartame, mannitol, and/or sorbitol.

Manufacturers typically employ food chemists to inspect and test all ingredients and materials. The Wm. Wrigley Jr. Company maintains a central quality assurance laboratory where samples from each factory are tested regularly so that flavor and texture are consistent in their products throughout the world.

Current Conditions

After a slump during the 1970s and early 1980s, chewing gum manufacturers entered the 1990s on a slight upswing. A new interest in chewing gum emerged in America since gum was promoted as an alternative to smoking when more public places began to prohibit smoking. Domestic per capita consumption of chewing gum increased from 168 sticks in 1986 to 183 in 1992, resulting in a 1.3 percent average annual rise in gum sales.

Companies that sell their gum through the sale of sports and entertainment cards have experienced sharp declines in their sales as a result of oversupply. In 1993 Topps Co. reported a 13 percent drop in their bubble gum card sales.

Industry Leaders

In 1993 Wm. Wrigley Jr. Co. controlled the industry's three leading companies. The parent company posted nearly $1.5 billion in sales that year, followed by two of its subsidiaries, L.A. Dreyfus Co. with $150 million and Amurol Products Co. with $66 million. The Wm. Wrigley Jr. Co., formed in 1893, manufactures and sells wholesale chewing gum throughout the United States and overseas.

William Wrigley, Jr., was a baking soda salesman who started offering two packages of chewing gum with each can of baking soda. When this promotion proved successful, Mr. Wrigley decided to enter the relatively undeveloped chewing gum business. His first two brands were Lotta and Vassar; later in 1893 he introduced Juicy Fruit and Wrigley's Spearmint. In the early days Wrigley used premiums to encourage merchants to stock his chewing gum. The success of this method of marketing led to a published catalog of premiums for retailers. Wrigley was also one of the pioneers in the use of advertising to promote brand name merchandise. Advertisements for Wrigley's gum ran in newspapers, magazines, and on outdoor posters. Even during industry slumps, Wrigley continued advertising.

By 1910, Wrigley's Spearmint gum was the largest selling chewing gum in the United States. Later that year, the company expanded by opening a factory in Canada. By 1927, Wrigley plants were built in Great Britain and Australia. The different preferences in international markets led to new types of products and flavors. Perhaps the most successful product for the company outside the United States was the pellet-shaped chewing gum sold under the PK brand.

In 1993 Wrigley owned 13 finished gum factories, four in the United States and the rest overseas, includ-

ing Australia, China and Europe. The company also operated two raw materials processing plants for gum production in the United States, along with one plant in France and another in Singapore.

Warner-Lambert Co. was the second ranked industry leader in 1992, with over $1.2 billion in chewing gum sales revenues. Its American Chicle Co., maker of Chiclets, was founded in 1856. The company also manufactures breath mints and other confectioneries. Its main chewing gum product, Chiclets, accounted for 12 percent of the company's worldwide sales in 1992. Other large sellers for Warner-Lambert have been Clorets and Trident brands.

Another industry leader, Topps Co., has also been a leader in commercial printing (see **SIC 2759: Commerical Printing, Gravure**) for their bubble gum sports cards, carrying over 30 percent of the market in sports and entertainment cards. In 1993 Topps' sales were over $263 million. This company has been most noted in the gum industry for producing Bazooka Bubble Gum. Despite the risky nature of the card end of their business, which relies on entertainment fads, some lines of cards developed in the early 1990s omitted the bubble gum.

America and the World

Much of American-produced chewing gum is sold overseas. Wrigley has operated in Europe since the 1910s and has had 80 percent of the chewing gum market in Britain and Germany. However, Wrigley did not position itself in Latin America, where many governments required joint ventures. In 1993 Wrigley's business abroad was rising over ten percent annually; in that year, the company opened a factory in China, where people had already been introduced to chewing gum through shipments from Singapore. In addition, 42 percent of Wrigley's 1993 earnings came from sales overseas, where the company has dominated most of its 109 markets.

Warner-Lambert has also done well in overseas markets. In 1993 about 50 percent of their sales were from overseas. Their markets have included Canada, Europe, Asia, the Middle East and Latin America. In 1993 this company launched an aggressive advertising campaign in Latin America, which included materials to help their products stand out in crowded street kiosks. According to the company, it held 79 percent of the Colombian market and 41 percent of the Brazilian market in 1993 chewing gum sales.

RESEARCH AND TECHNOLOGY

Companies in this industry are continually seeking ingredients and processes that can improve product quality and packaging. In the 1980s, new synthetic gum bases were developed to overcome the limitations of previously used natural ingredients. These new materials are aimed at increasing gum flavor, improving texture, and reducing stickiness.

The environmental impact of the packaging used for chewing gum has been of considerable concern for companies in this industry. These companies rely on the wrappers and plastic packaging to keep gum fresh, yet these materials result in considerable waste. Scientists at gum companies have been evaluating and making changes to packaging and researching materials to meet future disposal and recycling requirements.

In 1993 the *Wall Street Journal* reported that a dental scientist had developed a formula for gum that cleans and polishes teeth while being chewed. Two California businesses have acquired rights to the product, which has also garnered some interest from established gum companies.

INDUSTRY INFORMATION SOURCES

Aho, Debra, ''Bubble Yum Steps into Virtual Reality,'' *Advertising Age,* October 4, 1993.

Berry, Jon, ''From Wrigley's, Gum in a Tube,'' *Adweek's Marketing Week,* December 16, 1991.

''Candy and Gum,'' *Progressive Grocer,* July 1993.

Davis, Ricardo, ''Bubble Yum Kicks off Virtual Reality Game,'' *Advertising Age,* March 22, 1993.

''Don't Gouge the Customer,'' *Fortune,* autumn/winter, 1993.

Goldman, Kevin, ''Rapid-Fire Topps TV Ads Ignore Nostalgia,'' *Wall Street Journal,* December 10, 1993.

Khalaf, Roula, ''Card Glut,'' *Forbes,* December 21, 1992.

Klein, Carrie, ''Wm. Wrigley: Chew on This,'' *Financial World,* September 1, 1992.

Lesley, Elizabeth, ''A Burst Bubble at Topps,'' *Business Week,* August 23, 1993.

Liesse, Julie, ''Leaf Unwraps Gum with Xylitol,'' *Advertising Age,* October 8, 1990.

Malkin, Elizabeth, ''Chiclets Tries New Language,'' *Advertising Age,* April 19, 1993.

Quintanilla, Carl, ''If You Walk and Chew This Gum, You'll Stumble with a Smile,'' *Wall Street Journal,* June 8, 1993.

Rudnitsky, Howard, ''Chicle Is Chic,'' *Forbes,* November 8, 1993.

Young, Robert, *The Chewing Gum Book,* Minnesota: Dillion Press, 1989.

Zinn, Laura, and Sandra D. Atchison, ''Tastes Yucky, Sells Like Hotcakes,'' *Business Week,* May 18, 1992.

—Paola Trimarco

SIC 2068

SALTED AND ROASTED NUTS AND SEEDS

This category includes establishments primarily engaged in manufacturing salted, roasted, dried, cooked, or canned nuts or in processing grains or seeds in a similar manner for snack purposes. Establishments primarily engaged in manufacturing confectionery-coated nuts are classified under **SIC 2064: Candy and Confectionery Products** and those manufacturing peanut butter are classified under **SIC 2099: Food Preparations, Not Elsewhere Classified.**

Salted or dried peanuts account for about 53 percent of the snack-nut market. The rest of the snack-nut market is split among mixed nuts, cashews, walnuts, almonds, pistachios, and macadamia nuts. Salted or roasted sunflower seeds, pumpkin seeds, and other seeds are also included in this category. Nuts and seeds are sold both packaged and as bulk food in grocery stores.

The market for snack nuts has remained fairly level for a decade. Snack-food nuts have strong competition from potato chips, tortilla chips, pretzels, and microwave popcorn for the nation's snack dollars. The snack-nut and seed industry has handled its competition by introducing new flavors of seeds and nuts. Blue Diamond introduced lemon-chili and ranch flavor almonds in some parts of the country, and Planters introduced hot and mild versions of spicy peanuts.

Manufacturers have also tried more creative packaging. Planters brought out a line of snacks in small, narrow bags, calling the line Munch and Go Tube Nuts. But merchandising efforts for nut and seed snacks are minimal compared to the merchandising for chips. Manufacturers have been pushing for more shelf space and displays in grocery stores. While salted snack nuts and seeds showed flat sales, many producers and distributors were optimistic about sales of dried nuts because of their nutritional value.

Price has been another factor working against the industry. If prices are too high, consumers do not buy nuts. With peanut prices kept high by government quotas, restrictions against imports, and support prices, peanut snack manufacturers are somewhat restricted in their supply and prices. About 20 to 25 percent of domestic peanuts are used for snack nuts. While almond processors and processors of other nuts can buy foreign nuts, peanut processors must buy domestically-grown peanuts. A drought in 1990 sent peanut prices soaring, resulting in deep profit losses for peanut processors.

Peanuts for snack nuts are usually purchased raw by a nut sheller. Processors, such as Planters, purchase the shelled nuts and send them on to blanchers to have the skins removed. Finally the processing company receives them for roasting. Some snack nut companies, however, may do the shelling and blanching themselves.

Many non-peanut nuts are sold through grower-owned co-operatives; Blue Diamond Almonds and Diamond Walnuts are nationally known co-ops. In 1992, Blue Diamond marketed 40 percent of the almonds grown in California, the only state in which almonds are grown commercially. Ten years earlier, Blue Diamond was handling 55 percent of the crop, but some growers dropped out to sell their almonds to other California processors and out-of-state processors.

Some of the leading nut and seed snacks manufacturers are subsidiaries of America's largest corporations: Planters (a division of Nabisco), Dole Dried Fruit and Nut Co. (Dole Food Company Inc.), Sunmark (Nestle S.A.), Eagle Snacks (Anheuser-Busch) and Fisher Nut Co. (Proctor and Gamble). Independent roasted nut and seed companies include Lance, Inc., John B. Sanfilippos and Son, Inc., and Blue Diamond Growers.

INDUSTRY INFORMATION SOURCES

Bovard, James, ''Trade Nuttiness,'' *Wall Street Journal,* December 13, 1990, A14.

Graebner, Lynn, ''Blue Diamond Has Competition for Hearts of Farmers,'' *Business Journal Serving Greater Sacramento,* December 7, 1992, 1.

Ingersoll, Bruce, ''Shell Game: Peanut Quota System Comes Under Attack,'' *Wall Street Journal,* May 1, 1990, A1.

McClure, Barney H., ''Cooperating on Dried Fruit and Nuts,'' *Supermarket Business Magazine,* November 1990, 21-22.

Wold, Marjorie, ''Nuts Can't Crack the Snack Market,'' *Progressive Grocer,* May 1992, 179-180.

—Wendy J. Stein

SIC 2074

COTTONSEED OIL MILLS

This category covers establishments primarily engaged in manufacturing cottonseed oil, cake, meal, and linters, or in processing purchased cottonseed oil into forms other than edible cooking oils. Businesses primarily involved in refining cottonseed oil into edible cooking oils are covered in **SIC 2079: Shortening, Table Oils, Margarine, and Other Edible Fats and Oils, Not Elsewhere Classified.**

The first successful cottonseed oil mill began production in Natchez, Mississippi, in 1833. Up to that point, cottonseed left over from planting had been regarded as a hazard to health and a source of pollution. The cottonseed industry grew swiftly after the American Civil War, making the United States the largest consumer of cottonseed in the world.

The crushing of cottonseeds yields hulls (typically used as livestock feed) and kernels, which are then processed further by automated presses to yield oil and (representing up to about 80 percent of the total) cake. Aside from its role in the production of salad dressings, margarine, and shortening, the chief use for the oil is in the manufacture of lubricants, paint, and soap. The pressed cake is sometimes sold, broken into pieces, as cottonseed cake; but more commonly it is ground and sold as meal. Either way, its principal use is as a high-protein feed supplement for cattle, swine, and poultry; sometimes, too, it is used as a fertilizer. The output of meal from cottonseed (in thousands of metric tons) reached 1.476 million metric tons in 1990.

Any part of cottonseed intended for consumption by humans or by nonruminant animals has to be processed in such a way as to extract the gossypol, a pigment toxic to all nonruminants. Because this pigment is located in the tiny glands of cottonseed, the development of a glandless strain of cottonseed was seen as holding potentially great promise for the future of the cottonseed industry.

Linters. Before the crushing of cottonseeds, but after the removal from the seeds of the longer fibers processed in the manufacture of fabrics, the linters—shorter cotton fibers—are removed by a range of methods suited to their various uses in the production of sterile absorbent cotton, felt, and padding, in the manufacture of paper, film, explosives, plastics, and rayon, and as a source of essentially pure cellulose for the chemical industry.

Mill-run processing of linters is a one-step procedure used for smaller quantities than are handled in the alternative processing methods. Various production approaches yield both longer and shorter linters for use either in the chemical industry or for other purposes. A two-step processing method yields, at the first stage, the longer and softer first-cut linters well suited to the production of absorbent cotton, felt, and padding. At the second stage (the portion of the production process that generally represents the bulk of total linter production), the shorter and tougher second-cut linters usually reserved for use in the chemicals industry are garnered.

Leading manufacturers operating cottonseed oil mills in the United States include Southern Cotton Oil Co., Inc., located in Decatur, Illinois; Chickasha Cotton Oil Co., based in Chandler, Arizona; Yazoo Valley Oil Mill Inc., a privately-owned company in Greenwood, Missouri; Planter's Cotton Oil Mill Inc., a private company headquartered in Pine Bluff, Arkansas; and Plains Cooperative Oil Mill Inc. of Lubbock, Texas.

INDUSTRY INFORMATION SOURCES

"Feed Marketing and Distribution," *Feedstuffs,* July 16, 1992, 6-22.

"Global Outlook: Initial 1992/93 Projections," *Agricultural Outlook,* August 1992, 11.

McCormick, Ian, and Bengt Hyberg, "What's in the Future for Canola?" *Agricultural Outlook,* August 1992, 15-18.

U.S. Industrial Outlook 1994, Washington, DC: U.S. Department of Commerce, 1994.

—Richard Hillyer

SIC 2075

SOYBEAN OIL MILLS

This category covers establishments primarily engaged in manufacturing soybean oil, cake, and meal, and soybean protein isolates and concentrates, or in processing purchased soybean oil into forms other than edible cooking oils. Businesses primarily engaged in refining soybean oil into edible cooking oils are classified in **SIC 2079: Shortening, Table Oils, Margarine, and Other Edible Fats and OIls, Not Elsewhere Classified.**

Traditionally one of the largest U.S. crops, soybeans are especially valuable because the same automated presses yield two important products—oil and (representing more than 80 percent of the total) meal.

Soybean meal and oil are closely allied products with linked markets: growing demand for meal, partly reflecting the increasing desirability of high-protein animal feeds, and partly reflecting soy's enhanced status as a healthy ingredient in food, motivated a higher level of meal production, with accompanying gains in the volume of oil produced. This increased volume resulted in lower prices for oil and increased competition for other vegetable oils marketed along the same lines as that oil.

Output of soybean meal in thousands of metric tons rose from 20,464 in 1989 to 20,626 in 1990 to a forecast figure of 21,115 in 1991. U.S. exports of soybeans and soybean meal—dominant in the global meal market—were expected to be hampered in the early 1990s by a combination of increased foreign exports and tepid growth in product demand worldwide. The trend in the United States, however, appeared to be in favor of greater acceptance and more widespread use of soybean, especially in the form of isolated soy proteins and concentrates.

In the 1950s and 1960s, the only form of soy protein used in meat processing, its largest market by far, was soy flour. This product became outmoded as improved refining techniques yielded isolated soy proteins and concentrates having a wider range of applications and little or no independent flavor. These ingredients grew in popularity after legislation was passed that freed manufacturers of some meat products from regulations that insisted on prominent package labeling of the presence of such ingredients.

In recent years, soybean protein isolates and concentrates have garnered increased attention. Isolated soy proteins—ISPs—have been shown to equal the protein quality of milk and egg protein, to make logical substitutes for dairy protein because of their lack of fiber and 90 percent protein content, and to have uses in coffee creamers, protein-fortified beverages, both weight-loss products and body-building supplements, certain medical foods, and milk-free infant formulas.

Leading companies in this industry include Central Soya Company, Harvest States Cooperatives Honeymead Products Co., Cargill Inc.'s Soybean and Protein Processing division, Ralston Purina Co.'s Protein Technologies International, and Ag Processing Inc.

INDUSTRY INFORMATION SOURCES

"Feed Marketing and Distribution," *Feedstuffs,* July 16, 1992, 6-22.

"Global Outlook: Initial 1992/93 Projections," *Agricultural Outlook,* August 1992, 11.

Mancini, Leticia, "Giving Soy a Second Look," *Food Engineering,* August 1993, 94-95.

McCormick, Ian, and Bengt Hyberg, "What's in the Future for Canola?" *Agricultural Outlook,* August 1992, 15-18.

—Richard Hillyer

SIC 2076

VEGETABLE OIL MILLS, EXCEPT CORN, COTTONSEED, AND SOYBEAN

This category covers establishments primarily engaged in manufacturing vegetable oils, cake, and meal, with the exception of corn, cottonseed, and soybean, or in processing such vegetable oils into forms other than edible cooking oils. Businesses primarily engaged in manufacturing corn oil and its byproducts are classified in **SIC 2046: Wet Corn Milling;** those refining vegetable oils into edible cooking oils are covered in **SIC 2079: Shortening, Table Oils, Margarine, and Other Edible Fats and Oils, Not Elsewhere Classified;** and those primarily refining these oils for medicinal purposes are discussed in **SIC 2833: Medicinal Chemicals and Botanical Products.**

Meal output for several crops in this industry—including sunflower, linseed, and peanut—dropped from 1989 to 1990, but was forecast to rise in 1991. Over the same period, however, production of canola meal rose steadily. Industry analysts paid particular attention to sunflowers (along with soy beans and corn, one of the biggest U.S. crops) and to rapeseed, of which 160,000 acres were expected to be planted in 1992 (as compared to 6,383 acres just ten years earlier).

Sunflower Seed Oil. Sunflowers can be processed using the same automated presses as corn and soy beans, but use less water and are drought resistant. These advantages, together with the Sunflowerseed Oil Assistance Program (SOAP), which helps to offset the competitiveness of highly subsidized European Community vegetable oils, helped overcome reduced levels of production and the loss of two major export markets—Egypt and Russia—and boost U.S. sunflowerseed oil exports to a forecast figure for 1992-93 of 270,000 metric tons, the highest since the 319,000 tons of 1987-88. Meanwhile, domestic consumption of sunflowerseed oil was anticipated to rise from 90,000 tons to about 170,000 tons between 1991-92 and 1992-93. Industry leader National Sun Industries, Inc., the major American crusher of sunflowerseeds—with a plant in Enderlin, North Dakota, that processes 2,000 tons of sunflowers daily—saw sufficient future potential to open a new facility expected to double this level of production, with room for further expansion.

Canola. As a relatively new contender in the United States, canola in the early 1990s faced an uncertain future. The product was seen as one that might join the so-called specialty oils market—alongside such products as linseed oil, coconut oil, and walnut oil. Other observers, however, saw canola as a product as potentially lucrative as soy beans, corn, and sunflowers, with the potential to compete in the growing market for balanced feed concentrates. In addition, the granting of GRAS (Generally Recognized As Safe) approval to canola raised interest in its saturated fat content—the lowest among major vegetable oils—which suggested that it could play a significant role in food production targeted at increasingly health-conscious consumers.

Leading companies in this industry include National Sun Industries, Inc., Karlshamns USA Inc., Stevens Industries, Sessions Company Inc., and Colfax Inc.

INDUSTRY INFORMATION SOURCES

Bahner, Benedict, "Sunflowerseed Oil on Track for Exports," *Chemical Marketing Reporter,* April 12, 1993, 10.

Best, Annie, "U.S. Oilseed Crusher Sees Expanding Markets," *Feedstuffs,* December 7, 1992, 25.

"Feed Marketing and Distribution," *Feedstuffs,* July 16, 1992, 6-22.

McCormick, Ian, and Bengt Hyberg, "What's in the Future for Canola?" *Agricultural Outlook,* August 1992, 15-18.

Visser, Margaret, "Much Depends on Dinner," New York: Collier, 1988.

—Richard Hillyer

SIC 2077

ANIMAL AND MARINE FATS AND OILS

This category covers establishments primarily engaged in manufacturing animal oils (including fish oil and other marine animal oils) and fish and animal meal, together with those rendering inedible stearin, grease, and tallow from animal fat, bones, and meat scraps. Establishments primarily engaged in manufacturing lard and edible tallow and stearin are classified in meat-producing industries; those which refine marine animal oils for medicinal purposes are classified in **SIC 2833: Medicinal Chemicals and Botanical Products;** and those manufacturing fatty acids are classified in **SIC 2899: Chemicals and Chemical Preparations, Not Elsewhere Classified.**

Though the output quantities for meat meal and tankage were much larger than those for fish meal and oil in this industry entering the 1990s, and though fish meal typically constituted a small portion of the feeds given to poultry, pigs, and cattle (among such other ingredients as feather meal, meat meal, bone meal, and soybean meal), fish meal could make up over half the content of feeds manufactured for pond-raised salmon and trout.

In addition, fish meal represented a uniquely valuable source of nutrition because of its especially rich crude protein content and prominence of essential amino acids, and because its consumption was linked to faster growth and reproduction and larger quantities of eggs and milk. Moreover, fish oil—a natural by-product of fish meal manufacturing, released when steam-cooked fish are passed through large screw presses—had potential value in the domestic food industry, if, as expected, the GRAS (Generally Regarded As Safe) approval already granted to hydrogenated menhaden oil was then extended to refined menhaden oil.

Therefore losses in meal and oil production from menhaden—the industry staple—were of some concern. The reductions in metric tons for meal from 211,277 in 1991 to 175,155 in 1992 (and for oil over the same period from 123,040 to 80,347 metric tons) were attributed to reduced catches caused by bad weather. This led to anxiety that rising production in Latin America, especially Peru, would lead to dumping, and hence a drop in prices, further affecting U.S. profits on an already diminished yield. More alarmingly, such losses were part of a trend. The Gulf of Mexico, the prime menhaden-fishing area for the United States, has been yielding lower catches since 1984. The 1992 figure of roughly 425,000 metric tons marked a drop of about 23 percent from the catch of the previous year and amounted to about half the quantity harvested ten years earlier. Establishments in this industry, reliant on such product, have been impacted accordingly.

There are several companies of significant size engaged in this industry. The Darling-Delaware Company Inc., based in Irving, Texas, has annual sales of more than $650 million and employs 2,000 workers. Other leading members of the industry include American Proteins Inc., based in Roswell, Georgia; National By-Products Inc., of Des Moines, Iowa; Zapata Haynie Corp., headquartered in Hammond, Louisiana; and Baker Commodities, Inc., based in Los Angeles, California.

INDUSTRY INFORMATION SOURCES

Bahner, Benedict, ''Fish Oil, Meal Markets Look toward US Recovery.'' *Chemical Marketing Reporter,* April 19, 1993, 10.

''Feed Marketing and Distribution,'' *Feedstuffs,* July 16, 1992, 6-22.

House, Charles, ''Bad Weather Hinders Fishing,'' *Feedstuffs,* December 21, 1992, 7.

McCormick, Ian, and Bengt Hyberg, ''What's in the Future for Canola?'' *Agricultural Outlook,* August 1992, 15-18.

—Richard Hillyer

SIC 2079

SHORTENING, TABLE OILS, MARGARINE, AND OTHER EDIBLE FATS AND OILS, NOT ELSEWHERE CLASSIFIED

This category covers establishments primarily involved in manufacturing shortening, table oils, margarine, and other edible fats and oils that are not elsewhere classified. Companies primarily engaged in producing corn oil are discussed in **SIC 2046: Wet Corn Milling.**

Many of the goods classified in this industry are long-time staples of the American kitchen. Commonly utilized for cooking and baking purposes, products such as shortenings, vegetable oils, and margarine have become established presences in the marketplace.

Margarine is a key product in this industry. Invented in France in 1869, margarine's introduction to the United States was initially impeded by low quality and the efforts of a powerful butter lobby, which led to discriminatory taxes. With technical improvements and altered legislation margarine enjoyed increased acceptance. It came to be largely regarded as a healthier and cheaper alternative to butter. By the early 1990s, however, the $1.5 billion margarine industry began to falter while butter, which offered bargain prices, increased its market share. ''Consumer experts say softening margarine sales partly reflect shoppers' confusion about exactly what constitutes healthy eating,'' noted the *Wall Street Journal.* ''Admonished for years to cut back on animal fats, people by the millions switched from butter to margarine. Now, though, some who kicked the butter habit have become disillusioned after learning that vegetable shortenings may also raise the risk of cardiovascular disease.''

Margarine remains a major moneymaker for its producers, however. Unilever, with its I Can't Believe

It's Not Butter and Shedd's Country Crock brands, is the leading margarine manufacturer in the country. Nabisco is ranked second on the strength of its Fleischmann's label.

Vegetable oil remains the most popular pourable oil in America. Olive oil, meanwhile, has passed corn oil to secure the number two spot. As *Advertising Age* noted in 1993, "after more than three years of flat or minimal growth, sales volume gains are hitting double digits. The comeback is attributed to increased advertising that highlights [olive oil's] versatility, as well as a virtual freeze on prices." Leading olive oil manufacturers include Bertolli, Filippo Berio, and Pompeian.

Other leading companies in this industry include Van den Bergh Foods, Kraft Food, Borden Inc., and Schad Industries Inc.

INDUSTRY INFORMATION SOURCES

Davis, Riccardo A., "New Spread Formation," *Advertising Age,* August 2, 1992, 5.

DeNitto, Emily, "Olive Oil Sales Climb Out of the Pits," *Advertising Age,* September 6, 1993, 8.

Deveny, Kathleen, "Health Doubts Cut Into Margarine Sales," *Wall Street Journal,* June 24, 1993, B1, B10.

Mancini, Leticia, "Low Fat Comes of Age," *Food Engineering,* June 1993.

—Richard Hillyer

SIC 2082

MALT BEVERAGES

This category includes establishments primarily engaged in the manufacturing of malt beverages more commonly known as "beer."

INDUSTRY SNAPSHOT

Beer has been a part of the American lifestyle since the discovery of America and the creation of the United States. Records show that beer was brewed in colonial America and was made by American Indians. Throughout the years, beer has served cultural, spiritual, and even medicinal purposes. With nearly 80 million American beer drinkers, beer has become one of the most popular beverages, second only to water and tea.

Each year, the U.S. malt beverage (beer) industry has produced and sold more than 2.5 billion cases of beer, or about 190.2 million barrels. A barrel of beer is equal to two kegs or 31 gallons, which is roughly 13.8

24-unit cases of 12-ounce cans or bottles. The wholesale value of malt beverage shipments averages approximately $15 billion annually. According to the Beer Institute, the trade association for the malt beverage industry, the United States is the world's largest producer of beer, brewing more than 20 percent of the world's volume.

According to *Jobson's 1993 Handbook Advance,* beer consumption in the United States averages 2.6 billion cases annually. Although spending for alcoholic beverages has slowed in the late 1980s and early 1990s, total U.S. retail beer sales have reached more than $45 billion dollars annually. In the 1990s, the average American drank approximately 23 gallons of beer each year. California led all states in beer consumption with an annual rate of 306 million cases, with Texas in second place at 219 million cases. Other high consumption states have been Florida (164 million cases), Pennsylvania (130 million cases), and Illinois (126 million cases).

The top five leading domestic beers account for more than half of all U.S. beer sales. The top brand is Budweiser, manufactured by Anheuser-Busch, with 37 percent of market share. Bud, as it is popularly known, has been the best selling beer in the world and by itself has outsold the combined total of its four nearest competitors worldwide. Other leading beers include Miller Lite by the Miller Brewing Company, Bud Light by Anheuser-Busch, Coors Light by the Coors Brewing Company, and Busch by Anheuser-Busch. The two most popular kinds of beer have been premium beer with 36 percent market share and light beer at 34 percent market share. Heineken, imported by Van Munching & Co. from The Netherlands, has led in the consumption of imports with 30 million cases. Corona Extra, imported by Barton/Gambrinus from Mexico, has shipped 14 million cases, and Beck's, imported by Dribeck Importers from Germany, has sold ten million cases in the United States annually.

The American beer industry includes as many as 500 breweries, but three major companies hold nearly 78 percent of the market share. These breweries are Anheuser-Busch, located in St. Louis, Missouri; Miller Brewing Company in Milwaukee, Wisconsin; and Coors Brewing Company in Golden, Colorado. The U.S. beer industry, including brewers, wholesalers and retailers, employs more than 904,000 people who earn more than $13 billion in annual wages. Directly and indirectly, the U.S. beer industry supports more than 2.7 million jobs, providing more than $51 billion in wages to U.S. workers and over $167 billion in economic activity. The industry also pays approximately

$5 billion in excise taxes to federal, state, and local governments annually.

ORGANIZATION AND STRUCTURE

This industry includes only those companies that manufacture beer. The industry has been dominated by three major U.S. breweries, yet, regardless of size, all breweries have to sell their products through wholesalers and retailers. This distribution channel is the result of accommodating the variety of federal, state and local regulations regarding the sale of alcoholic beverages.

Federal and State Regulation. The Federal Alcohol Administration Act (FAA) was put into place at the end of Prohibition in 1933. Since that time, the Bureau of Alcohol, Tobacco and Firearms (ATF) has been responsible for administering and enforcing the FAA, including qualifying brewers, collecting brewer and wholesaler occupational taxes, and regulating trade practices, advertising and labeling.

Beyond the uniformity of the FAA, regulations have varied greatly among the 50 states, as the Beer Institute reported in their testimony to the U.S. Senate regarding the Malt Beverage Interbrand Competition Act. Probably the most dramatic example of regulatory diversity has been the way that states have allowed beer to be sold. States sell beer in one of two ways, either in a controlled environment or using an open, licensed method. "Open" states license retailers and wholesalers to handle the distribution and sale of alcoholic beverages. Thirty-two states and the District of Columbia are considered "open" states. The other 18 states operate under the control method, in which each state government buys and sells alcoholic beverages at the wholesale and retail levels.

In addition to federal regulations, some states have set up their own independent agencies that have been responsible for the administration, licensing, and enforcement of state laws, and the collection of state revenues. Additionally, some state legislatures have created their own Alcoholic Beverage Control (ABC) agencies with rule-making power, and 32 states have allowed their citizens to vote for or against the sale of liquor in various cities or counties.

Brewing Beer. Beyond the complexities of the regulations for producing and selling beer, brewing beer is a simple process. Beer is nothing more than a fermented alcoholic beverage made from malted barley and flavored with hops. Beer is produced by grinding barley, malt, and rice or corn and then mixing the combination with boiling water. The resulting "mash" is slowly cooked to convert the grain starches

to fermentable sugars. The mash then is strained and the clear amber liquid that remains is called "wort." The strained wort is piped to a brew kettle where it is boiled. Hops are added to give the brew the aroma and flavor associated with beer. The wort then is chilled and pumped to fermenting cellars, where yeast is added. This begins the fermentation process, producing the alcohol and carbonation in the beer. Upon completion, the yeast is filtered out and the brew is piped to aging tanks. There, the beer will age ten to 14 days prior to being packaged in bottles, cans or kegs.

Brand Segments. With 80 million American beer drinkers, the major brewing companies have created brand segments of beer, each presenting a different appeal to the consumer. These segments have been divided into super premium, premium, popular-priced, light, import, malt liquor, and the newly added non-alcoholic, dry brews, and bottled draft beer.

The highest priced and highest quality beers, super premiums, have been dominated by two brands, Michelob and Lowenbrau. This category has been in decline since the early 1990s as consumers have become more value-oriented and have traded down to lower-priced beers.

Premium beers have been the most popular kind of beer and are considered the standard of American brews. These brands are usually distributed nationally and have received the highest percentage of advertising dollars. Premium beers include Miller High Life, Budweiser, and Coors.

The popular-price beer segment was developed for the consumer interested in a full-bodied taste, but uninterested in paying a premium price. These beers fared well through the 1980s and the early 1990s due to weak economic conditions. Popular-priced beers include Miller's Meister Brau, and Milwaukee's Best. The light beer segment is the second most popular kind of beer in the United States. In the health conscious 1980s and 1990s, just as consumers demanded low calorie soft drinks, they also clamored for light beer. *Standard & Poor's Industry Survey* reported in 1992 that three of the four most popular beers in the United States were light beers: Miller Lite (number two), Coors Light (number three) and Bud Light (number four). Light beer generally has two-thirds to three-quarters of the calories of regular beers.

As consumers have spent more time and money at home during the 1990s, beer makers have taken a popular product associated with restaurants and bars—bottled draft beer—and effectively brought it into the home. Miller Genuine Draft was successfully introduced in 1985, and Miller Genuine Draft Light became the seventh-best-selling beer in 1991. Bottled draft beer, considered a premium beer, has been predicted to strengthen during the 1990s, as consumers move away from the more traditional premium brands. Another new type of beer is "dry" beer. Dry beer is brewed to produce a less sweet flavor that doesn't leave an aftertaste. This brand segment suffered a setback by 1991, as category sales volume fell by more than 19 percent. Even though dry beer has accounted for nearly 57 million cases sold, this category could become even weaker as other brand segments emerge. Dry beer brands have included Bud Dry and Michelob Dry.

Due to the consumer's increased awareness of health and fitness, non-alcoholic beers have continued to grow in popularity. In 1991, non-alcoholic beer sales volume increased about 33 percent, from 1.5 million barrels in 1990 to almost two million barrels. The early success of Miller's Sharp's and Anheuser-Busch's O'Doul's have propelled non-alcoholic beer as a strong brand segment. Malt liquors hold a very small percentage of total industry sales. Malt liquor is made like other beer but it contains 4.5 percent or more alcohol, compared to the 3.5 percent to 4 percent alcohol content in most other beers. This category has received a great deal of publicity during the past few years due to the its higher alcohol content. Nonetheless, *Standard & Poor's Industry Survey* predicted that the malt beverage industry will continue to grow at a strong pace, if only fueled by the notoriety it has received in the past.

BACKGROUND AND DEVELOPMENT

The foundation of the U.S. beer industry can be traced to the ancient times of kings and pharaohs. Babylonian clay tablets more than 8,000 years old depicted beer being brewed and gave detailed recipes. Other writings indicated that beer was brewed by the Egyptians as early as 3000 B.C. and by the Chinese in the 23rd century B.C. One of the world's oldest breweries still in existence is Brauerei Beck in Germany, where Beck's beer was first brewed in 1533.

Beer was first brewed in America in 1587 at Sir Walter Raleigh's colony in Roanoke, Virginia, and Puritan settlers brewed beer in Boston as early as 1620. In 1791, Congress levied the first tax on alcohol. By 1870, Adolphus Busch had pioneered the use of refrigerated railroad cars to ship beer over long distances. Following the steady development of temperance groups, the Pure Food and Drug Act, more commonly known as the Volstead Act, went into effect on January 16, 1920, ushering in the era of Prohibition. Prohibition, which banned the sale of alcoholic beverages, lasted 13 years and the production and distribution of millions of gallons of alcohol fell into the hands of gangsters called bootleggers.

After Prohibition was repealed in 1933, federal and state governments tightened regulations under the Federal Alcohol Act (FAA) and various state regulations. Brewers also adopted policies of self-regulation, such as the Distilled Spirits Council of the United States (DISCUS) voluntary "code of good practice." Following Prohibition, beer was produced in 750 locations throughout the country. It was distributed to wholesalers and retailers in limited geographic regions that seem extremely small when compared to current distribution areas. By the 1930s, the primary way to sell beer was in draft form and in refillable bottles.

In order for breweries to continue expansion, however, less costly containers were needed. The beer can, introduced in 1935, filled those needs perfectly. By the end of World War II, the beer can had become such a popular container that glass companies soon created the one-way bottle to keep up with the competition. Both of these less-expensive products allowed brewers to ship their products and expand their markets. By 1946, breweries served markets that were at one time only accessible to local and regional companies, and this expansion soon created the nationwide market of the major breweries.

CURRENT CONDITIONS

The beer industry, and the alcoholic beverage industry in general, seems always to be concerned with the same issues: taxation, regulation, alcohol abuse, and environmental policies. Future growth in the beer industry will depend on the development of competitive beers in the light beer and non-alcoholic beer segments, and development of niche beer markets.

Taxation. A major financial issue faced by the beer industry was the 1991 hike in the excise tax. As defined by the Beer Institute, an excise tax is a special form of tax levied on the production, sale, or distribution of a particular commodity, in this case, beer. The first federal excise tax on beer was imposed in the 1860s as a temporary measure to help pay for the Civil War, and it has yet to be repealed. In 1991, the excise tax was doubled to $18 per barrel, or from 16 cents to 32 cents per six-pack of 12-ounces bottles or cans. Brewers paid an estimated $5.2 billion in federal and state excise taxes on beer every year after 1991.

Advertising Regulation. With regulations differing greatly from state to state, nationwide advertising of beer has been a complicated issue. Even though all advertising must be approved by the Bureau of Alcohol, Tobacco and Firearms, some state agencies have demanded that advertising also meet their approval. The Beer Institute reported in their testimony before the U.S. Congress that the different regulatory structures of each state had tended to limit changes in advertising to fit each state system with its own peculiarities of its population, geography, and general drinking habits.

State regulatory variations have covered all kinds of selling tools, such as billboards, circulars, consumer and retailer novelties, product displays on retail premises, newspaper and magazine advertising, radio and TV, the use of premiums or other inducements, samples and signs. For example, in Vermont, Utah, and Oklahoma, billboard advertising of alcoholic beverages has been flatly prohibited, but many other states do not have any restrictions whatsoever. Nor does it seem that any of the regulations will change soon. "In an official study by the Joint Committee of the States to Study Alcoholic Beverage Laws, published in 1973, the Committee came to the conclusion, as it had twice previously, that it would be virtually impossible to recommend any uniformity or standardization of ABC laws, regulations or operations. This conclusion bore out of the innumerable differences between the advertising laws and regulations of the states," reported the Beer Institute. As decreed by the federal government, it is evident that the brewing industry will remain closely guarded regarding advertising and marketing issues.

Alcohol Abuse and Its Consequences. Beyond advertising regulations, the most visible and confrontational issue that breweries have faced has been alcohol abuse and related problems such as drunk driving, underage drinking, and other health-related problems. The tendency and consequences of abusing alcohol have been present since the first beer was brewed, and various groups of citizens have been fighting alcohol abuse and alcohol with varying success rates ever since. Lack of employee productivity, underage drinking, and the obvious health implications of abuse all have an associated cost to society. The National Institute of Alcohol Abuse and Alcoholism has estimated this cost at $136.3 billion annually.

Due to increase public awareness in the 1980s of these health and safety issues, Americans have seemed less tolerant of alcohol abuse, and have consumed fewer alcoholic beverages in the 1990s than in the 1980s. A 1992 Gallup Poll indicated that 64 percent of American adults drank alcohol at least occasionally, an increase from the previous two years, but still well below the late 1970s and early 1980s, when the figure regularly topped 70 percent. Consumption has de-

clined to the point that the *New York Times* dubbed this trend the "new temperance."

The beer industry has noticed and reacted to this consumer trend. Brewers have generated millions of dollars worth of advertising and promotional campaigns and have contributed to projects that fight alcoholism and study its consequences. "Underage drinking and drunk driving are black eyes for our industry," says Francine Katz, director of consumer awareness and education for Anheuser-Busch, in the *Dallas Morning News.* "We have invested over $100 million in the last ten years to promote personal responsibility among those who choose to drink, to discourage drunk driving and to fight underage drinking," Katz continued.

The Century Club, an industry-supported organization, was created in May 1991 to focus solely on drunk driving and underage consumption. Elizabeth Board, DISCUS's director of public relations, said in *Beverage Dynamics*: "We have to educate adults about the problem [of underage drinking], educate the youth in order to reduce their demand for beverage alcohol and back that up with enforcement and education of retailers, both on- and off-premise."

Falling Consumption. One consequence of alcohol awareness has been a steady decline in consumer consumption. As *Standard & Poor's Industry Survey* reported: "Health concerns and government attempts to rein in the enormous social costs of alcoholism and alcohol-related deaths have led to a domestic industry decline in recent years. The ability to increase [market] share in a mature industry will remain the key to growth." To combat a mature market, brewers have turned to new products to create consumer interest. The country's top five brewers introduced 15 new products in 1990 and 1991, with 12 out of the 15 showcased in 1991 alone. Categories of new products have included bottled draft, light beer, and non-alcoholic brews.

Environmental Awareness. The industry has taken a lead in environmental awareness in the 1980s and 1990s. According to the Beer Institute, the beer industry pioneered the production of recyclable aluminum cans for commercial use, and initiated the country's first aluminum can recycling effort. Brewers have been developing new methods to increase the amount of recycled materials in their glass bottles. Also, the companies have recycled spent grains from the brewing process into livestock feed to avoid further burdening America's overflowing landfills, and many breweries have created their own subsidiary recycling companies.

Future Trends. The future trends in the beer industry have been predicted to follow the consumer's interest in health and fitness, and personal safety issues. Also, consumers have been rediscovering regional beers, creating a steady growth in niche marketing.

Not only is the light beer segment predicted to grow, but continued interest in low-calorie, low-fat beverages also has precipitated the introduction of light-colored or translucent beer. Two companies already have begun test marketing ''clear'' beers: the Miller Brewing Company with Miller Clear and the Coors Brewing Company with Zima. John Zeu, brand development manager for Coors, explained in *Beverage Dynamics* that Zima's clear look emphasizes ''the product's light and refreshing positioning, as well as differentiating it from [wine] coolers.''

With fewer than half the calories of light beers and virtually none of the alcohol, non-alcoholic beers should continue to appeal to the American consumer. According to *Beverage Dynamics*, ''Without much fanfare, the category has grown almost 60 percent in the two years since . . . Anheuser-Busch's O'Doul's and Miller's Sharp's were introduced in 1990.'' Both the Stroh Brewing Company and Coors have launched their own successful non-alcoholic brews, which has created both competition and credibility for the brand segment. Unless consumer trends change dramatically, non-alcoholic beers have been predicted to grow into the 21st century.

Niche Beers. So-called ''niche'' beers from micro-breweries and brew-pubs across the country have also increased in popularity. Niche beers are meant to appeal to specific consumers who are attracted to that product's particular taste characteristics. Smaller breweries have become remarkably visible, especially considering that they have produced only a tiny fraction of the total U.S. beer consumed annually. Some well known specialty brews are Anchor Steam, produced in San Francisco, and Samuel Adams, produced by the Boston Beer Company.

Even the major breweries have become involved in niche marketing with the acquisition of brands and breweries. For example, Miller Brewing Company acquired Jacob Leinenkugel Brewing Company in 1987. Miller brewed Leinie Light and Leinie Limited, which started out as a fall beer, but was soon brewed year-round. Other companies involved in niche marketing include Coors, which has been brewing Killian Red since 1981. The brand went national in 1989, and has been experiencing annual growth of about 40 percent for several years. Coors also has found success with Winterfest. Originally available only in Colorado dur-

ing the holiday season, the brand went national in 1991. The acquisition of a micro-brewery by a major brewery has proved to be a good deal for both parties. The smaller, regional brewers have been able to continue to make niche products, and the larger breweries have found new products to market to the American consumer in the 1990s.

INDUSTRY LEADERS

Anheuser-Busch, Inc. Anheuser-Busch, Inc. is the world's largest brewer and the main subsidiary of the Anheuser-Busch Companies, based in St. Louis, Missouri. With 13 breweries, Anheuser-Busch produces 15 naturally brewed beers, one non-alcoholic beer and imports three beers for distribution in the United States. By 1992, Anheuser-Busch sold an all-time industry record of 86.8 million barrels of beer in one year.

Anheuser-Busch brands are exported to more than 40 countries and brewed under the company's supervision in five countries. Anheuser-Busch employs over 44,000 people and works with approximately 900 independent wholesale distributors. Anheuser-Busch also operates 11 company-owned distributorships. Other beer-related Anheuser-Busch subsidiaries are Anheuser-Busch International, Inc.; Busch Agricultural Resources, Inc.; Metal Container Corporation; Anheuser-Busch Recycling Corporation; Busch Media Group, Inc.; Busch Creative Services Corporation; St. Louis Refrigerator Car Company; Manufacturers Railway Company; and the International Label Company. Anheuser-Busch brands are Budweiser, Bud Light, Bud Dry Draft, Michelob, Michelob Light, Michelob Classic Dark, Michelob Dry, Michelob Golden Draft, Michelob Golden Draft Light, Busch, Busch Light, Natural Light, Natural Pilsner, O'Doul's, King Cobra, Carlsberg, Carlsberg Light, and Elephant Malt Liquor.

Adolphus Busch, founder of the Anheuser-Busch Brewing Company, immigrated to the United States in 1857, arriving in St. Louis via New Orleans. In 1861, Adolphus married Lilly Anheuser, and after serving a short time in the Union Army, he returned home and joined the management of his father-in-law's brewery. In 1869, Adolphus purchased half ownership of another brewery, called the Bavarian Brewery, which was restructured with his father-in-law, Eberhard Anheuser, as president and Busch as secretary. In 1879, the company was renamed Anheuser-Busch Brewing Association. Upon the death of Eberhard Anheuser, Adolphus Busch became president of the brewery. He continued in this position for the next 33 years until his death in 1913. Anheuser-Busch was the first brewer to use pasteurization to help keep beer

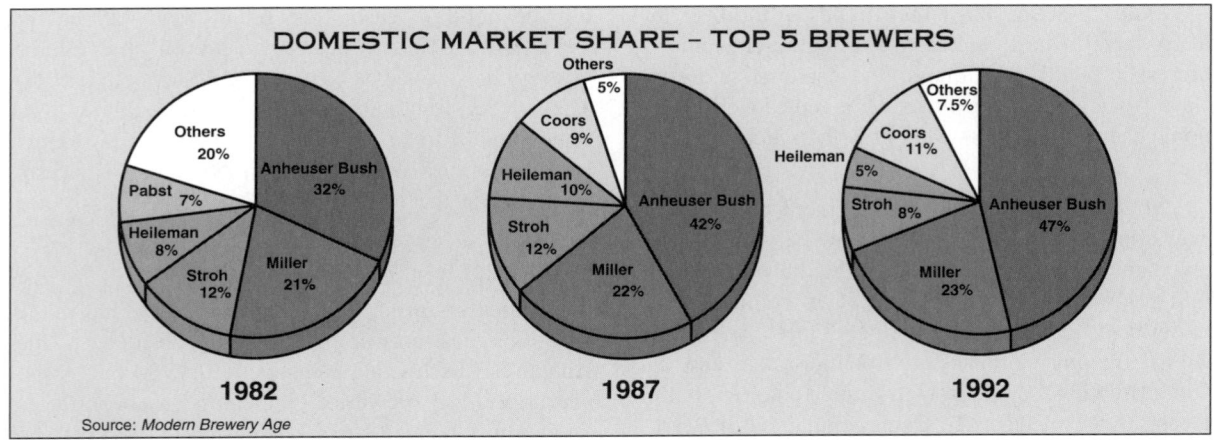

DOMESTIC MARKET SHARE – TOP 5 BREWERS

1982

Others 20%
Anheuser Bush 32%
Pabst 7%
Heileman 8%
Stroh 12%
Miller 21%

1987

Others 5%
Coors 9%
Heileman 10%
Stroh 12%
Anheuser Bush 42%
Miller 22%

1992

Others 7.5%
Coors 11%
Heileman 5%
Stroh 8%
Anheuser Bush 47%
Miller 23%

Source: *Modern Brewery Age*

fresh in transit and most packaged beer is still pasteurized.

Miller Brewing Company. The Miller Brewing Company is a wholly-owned subsidiary of Phillip Morris Companies Inc., with corporate headquarters in Milwaukee, Wisconsin. With approximately 10,000 employees, the company operates seven breweries, five manufacturing plants, a glass-bottling plant, a hops processing plant, a malting factory, and a packaging/printing plant. The Miller Brewing Company produces over 40 million barrels of beer each year. The company's major brands are Miller High Life, Miller Lite, Lowenbrau, Miller Genuine Draft, Meister Brau, Milwaukee's Best, Magnum Malt Liquor, Leinenkugal, and Sharp's non-alcohol. Miller products are distributed to retailers in the United States, Puerto Rico, and the Virgin Islands by a network of approximately 690 distributors. The company's products are also sold in approximately 50 foreign markets in Europe, Asia and the Caribbean, including U.S. military bases.

The Miller Brewing Company was founded by German immigrant Frederick Miller, who settled in Milwaukee after a brief stay in New York City. He bought the Plank Road Brewery in 1855, and soon after opened a 20-acre park or "sommer-garten." After Frederick's death, the Milwaukee Brewery was passed on to Miller's children. The W. R. Grace Co. purchased most of the children's stock in the Miller Brewing Company in 1966. Phillip Morris Inc. purchased the company in 1969 and the rest of the family's stock in 1970.

Coors Brewing Company. The Adolph Coors Company, founded in 1873, is America's third-largest brewer. Headquartered in Golden, Colorado, Coors sells approximately 17 million barrels of beer annually in 49 states and the District of Columbia. The Coors

Brewing Company employs 7,100 people, works with 597 independent distributors, and has seven company-owned distributorships. The Adolph Coors Company has three autonomous business units that are operated by fourth-generation Coors family members. These are the Coors Brewing Company, the Coors Ceramics Company, and the Coors Technology Companies. The Coors Brewing Company produces beer from all natural ingredients including pure Rocky Mountain water, and it is the only brewery that does not pasteurize any of its beer. Instead, it uses a sterile filtration process that the company developed in the late 1950s. Coors is the only company with a complete line of draft or non-pasteurized beers.

The Coors Brewing Company operates three breweries, including the world's largest single-site brewery. Coors products are exported to 12 foreign markets and to U.S. military bases in 16 countries worldwide. The company also has licensing agreements to brew and distribute Coors products in Japan, Canada, Scotland and Korea. Coors brands are original Coors, Coors Light, Coors Extra Gold, George Killian's Irish Red, Keystone and Keystone Light, Coors Winterfest (a seasonal beer), and Coors Cutter (a non-alcoholic beer).

German immigrant Adolph Coors founded the Coors Brewing Company. Upon his arrival in the United States in 1868, Adolph spent many years as a laborer and saved his money to fulfill his dream of owning a brewery. During one of his day's off from work, Adolph Coors found an abandoned tannery in the town of Golden at the base of Table Mountain. He and other investors remodeled the tannery and soon began brewing Coors beer. By 1880, Adolph was able to buy out his investors. The company was sustained during Prohibition by divesting into other industries, including a cement manufacturing facility and a porcelain plant. The Coors Ceramics Company has been one of the world's largest producers of industrial technical ceramics, and the sole supplier of chemical porcelain used in the United States, Mexico and Canada.

WORK FORCE

The U.S. beer industry consists of 54 leading breweries that employ approximately 97,000 people in all areas of the industry (including non-manufacturing areas). According to the Beer Institute, "Brewery workers' wages are among the highest of more than 350 industries annually surveyed by the U.S. Department of Labor. These men and women take home approximately $2.2 billion a year in salaries and wages with additional millions paid in the form of fringe benefits and retirement programs." Bureau of Labor Statistics data indicate, however, that the number of employees directly involved in the industry has dropped over the past several decades, from more than 71,000 workers in 1960 to a little over 40,000 employees at the end of the 1980s.

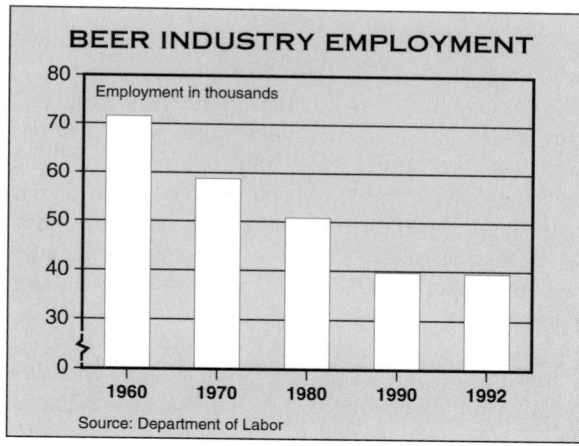

BEER INDUSTRY EMPLOYMENT

Employment in thousands

Source: Department of Labor

The top five states that are home to the largest number of brewery employees are New York, Wisconsin, Pennsylvania, California and Washington. The largest numbers of employees work as packaging and filling machine operators, driver-sales workers, salespeople, truck drivers, tractor operators, supervisors, and laborers. Estimates by the Bureau of Labor Statistics have shown that virtually all occupations within the beer industry will decline in the percentage of total employed by the year 2000. Those jobs that include "hands-on" involvement, such as freight, stock and material movers, hand packers, and testers, have been predicted to decline by at least 25 percent.

AMERICA AND THE WORLD

Exports. The growth rate for U.S. beer exports reached $195 million in the early 1990s. The top export market for beer has been Japan, with Canada in second and Mexico in third place. As noted in the 1992 Coors annual report, the international markets should provide significant potential for domestic brewers to advance their market share. Coors has predicted that by the end of the 1990s, the Far Eastern, Asian and South American markets will become the fastest-growing beer markets in the world. Business Week noted in April 1994, however, that trade disagreements between the United States and Canada regarding beer (and other goods) have grown increasingly heated, despite the passage of the North American Free Trade Agreement. In August 1993, *Business Week* states, "the U.S. and Canada agreed on a plan that would give U.S. brewers greater access to the Canada market. Nonetheless, U.S. beer exports to Canada plunged 40%" in 1993, "even while U.S. imports of Canadian beer soared 21%, to over 80 million gallons . . . The U.S. says it may impose punitive duties on Canadian beer, effectively closing the border."

Imports. Approximately 400 import brands have been marketed in the United States annually, but the top 20 brands have accounted for 90 percent of the total U.S. sales. During the mid-1980s, imports were quite successful, including standouts such as Corona, Foster's and Moosehead. In 1980 beer imports measured approximately 141 million gallons, according to *Beverage World;* by 1987 this amount had increased to 290 million gallons. But as the 1990s began, domestic companies fought back for market share with the emergence of new beer brands, such as dry and bottled draft. The non-alcoholic beverage category has been one example of domestic beer's re-emergence. "Before Sharp's and O'Doul's, imports were 33 percent of the category. Now they are around five percent. The whole category was redefined," said Paul Block, vice president of marketing for Guinness Imports, in *Beverage Dynamics.* Despite this sharp decline, the import category should return to stability by the end of the 1990s. As Ellis M. Goodman, Chairman and CEO of Barton Beers Ltd., concluded in *Beverage Dynamics:* "The main brands and leading importers have created a strong market presence, which they will be able to defend in the years to come. The 100 million case import category is likely to remain reasonably stable."

INDUSTRY INFORMATION SOURCES

"Adolph Coors 1992 Annual Report." Golden, CO: Coors Brewing Company, 1992.

"Anheuser-Busch 1992 Fact Book." St. Louis, MO: Anheuser-Busch, 1992.

Brandes, Richard. "Beverage Trends: The Shape of Drinks to Come." Beverage Dynamics, May 1993.

"Coors 1990 Facts & Figures." Golden: Coors Brewing Company.

"Economic Impact of the Beer Industry." Washington, DC: Beer Institute.

"Food, Beverages & Tobacco." Standard & Poor's Industry Surveys, 6 August 1992.

Goodman, Ellis M. "Trends and Opportunities in Imported Beer." Beverage Dynamics, September 1992.

"Facts About Beer, the Brewing Industry and Miller Brewing Company." Milwaukee, WI: Miller Brewing Company, 1990-91.

Henry, William L. "The Truth About Beer." Beverage Dynamics, September 1992.

"The History of Anheuser-Busch Companies: A Fact Sheet." St. Louis, MO: Anheuser-Busch.

Jobson's 1993 Handbook Advance. New York: Jobson's Publishing Corporation, 1993.

"The Malt Beverage Interbrand Competition Act." Washington, DC: United States Brewers Association, Inc., 21 June 1982.

"Miller History." Milwaukee, WI: Miller Brewing Company.

Morice, James L. "Anheuser-Busch Announces Record 1992 Beer Sales and Market Share Increase." Fleishman-Hillard, Inc. (press release), 19 January 1993.

Precker, Michael. "Alcohol's Tragic Toll." Dallas Morning News, 23 May 1993.

Sfiligoj, Eric. "Import-ant Gains," Beverage World, February 1993.

Sherer, Michael. "Specialty Brews." Beverage Dynamics, November/December 1992.

———. "Standing on Their Own." Beverage Dynamics, April 1993.

———. "The Year in Beer." Beverage Dynamics, September 1992.

"The Story Begins." Golden, CO: Adolph Coors Company.

Symonds, William C., "NAFTA Already Looks Frayed at the Northern Border," Business Week, April 11, 1994.

Wood, Donna Jean. "A Major Effort Against Minors." Beverage Dynamics, May 1993.

"The World of Beer." Beverage Dynamics, May 1993.

—Catherine A. Quagliana

SIC 2083

MALT

This classification covers establishments primarily engaged in manufacturing malt or malt by-products from barley or other grains.

Malt is a barley kernel that has been allowed to sprout and is used primarily for brewing and distilling. It has long been a central element in beer production. Approximately 123 million bushels of malt are produced in the United States on an annual basis. According to the American Malting Barley Association (AMBA), the largest barley crops for the malting market are traditionally garnered from barley growers in the Midwest. Growers in Minnesota, North Dakota, and South Dakota plant six-row malting barley varieties. Ninety percent of all malting barley grown is used by brewers, with the remainder used as feedstock. Barley is also grown in the western United States, but the primary market for barley from these states has traditionally been the feed industry.

Malt is created by germinating moistened barley under controlled conditions for a short period of time, usually four days. The germination process activates the enzyme systems, specialized proteins that break down the barley's starch and protein. Once germinated, the "green malt" must be kilned, or dried with heat. Essentially, the malt is cooked to stop its growth, although the enzyme activity continues. Prior to kilning, the rootlets that appear during germination are removed and discarded. What is left after kilning is considered to be malt.

Brewers create a mash with the malt by mixing it with water and heating it under controlled conditions. During the mashing process, the enzymes break down the starch into sugars and proteins, creating a soluble mixture or extract. The soluble product is filtered and yeast is added. Other starches such as corn or rice are added at this time, along with hops for flavor. All beer has some malt content. Budget beers usually are 50 percent malt and 50 percent corn or rice, while premium beer composition may be as high as 70 percent malt. Brewers generally specify to barley growers the variety of malt needed for their particular brands.

A number of the major American beer producers maintain in-house malt operations. Examples include Busch Agricultural Resources, Inc., a subsidiary of Anheuser-Busch Inc., which operates three malt plants that together supply the company with approximately one-third of Anheuser-Busch's malt needs, and Miller

Brewing Company's malt plant in Waterloo, Wisconsin.

Leading malt producers in America include the Great Western Malting Company, the largest producer of malt in the western United States with more than $120 million in annual sales. A subsidiary of Canada Malting Co., Ltd., the world's second largest producer of malted barley, Great Western is located in Vancouver, Washington. Other industry leaders include Fleischmann-Kurth Malting Company, the malt manufacturing subsidiary of the Archer Daniels Midland Company; Froedtert Malt Corp.; Schreier Malting Co.; Rahr Malting Co.; and Minnesota Malting Co.

Industry leaders such as Great Western have continued to post increasing export margins in the early 1990s. In 1992, for instance, Great Western's exports increased by 35 percent. Target markets are those countries where the demand for beer and malt has increased. Increased product interest has been particularly apparent in Japan and other areas of the Pacific Rim region. Another potentially profitable market is Mexico, where beer sales have increased by more than five percent annually. Mexico's importance as an export market may increase even more with the passage of the North American Free Trade Agreement (NAFTA). South America and China also have emerged as growing markets for malt and beer due to their large, young populations and growing economies.

INDUSTRY INFORMATION SOURCES

Anheuser-Busch Companies, Inc. 1992 Annual Report. St. Louis: Anheuser-Busch, 1992.

Archer Daniels Midland Company 1992 Annual Report. Decatur, IL: Archer Daniels Midland Company, 1992.

''Barley Research.'' Milwaukee: American Malting Barley Association, 1993.

Canada Malting Co. Limited Annual Reports. Toronto: Canada Malting Co., 1991, 1992.

Davis, Michael. ''Malting Barley Quality Factors.'' American Malting Barley Association, 1993.

Miller Brewing Company 1992 Annual Report. Milwaukee: Miller Brewing Company, 1992.

''Proceedings, 29th Barley Improvement Conference.'' Milwaukee: American Malting Barley Association. January, 1993.

—Catherine A. Quagliana

SIC 2084

WINES, BRANDY, AND BRANDY SPIRITS

This category includes establishments primarily engaged in manufacturing wines, brandy, and brandy spirits. This industry also includes bonded wine cellars which are engaged in blending wines. Establishments which primarily bottle purchased wines, brandy, and brandy spirits but which do not manufacture wines and brandy are classified in **SIC 5182: Wine and Distilled Alcoholic Beverages.**

INDUSTRY SNAPSHOT

The first commercial wine venture in the United States was in Pennsylvania in 1793. However, the majority of modern American wineries have been located in California, with Washington and New York coming in a distant second and third. California has accounted for over 90 percent of all U.S. wine production and over 70 percent of all wine sold in the United States. Wine is made in every region of the state. According to the Wine Institute, ''If viewed as a nation, California would rank sixth in worldwide wine production, following Spain but bigger than Germany.'' California also has been the leader in wine sales and consumption, accounting for over one-fifth of all wine consumed annually. In 1991, total wine consumption was 467 million gallons. Approximately 46 percent of the U.S. wine market has been in five states: California, New York, Florida, Texas and Illinois.

According to a five-year study of wine consumption patterns in the United States, wine is drunk in moderation and usually with a meal. The report found that 49 percent of wine drinkers are between the ages of 45 and 64, and 82 percent of wine consumption takes place with a meal, usually dinner. The study, conducted by two researchers at Washington University in St. Louis, Missouri, found that ''regardless of the setting, wine is most often consumed in moderation, one to two glasses per occasion and three to four glasses per week,'' according to a 1992 issue of *Beverage Dynamics.*

Table wine has been the most popular kind of wine sold in the United States. Varietals, table wine made predominately of one grape type, grew in popularity during the 1980s, following the trend that consumers are drinking less, but drinking more expensive wines.

ORGANIZATION AND STRUCTURE

All winemakers have to sell their products through wholesalers and retailers in order to accommodate various federal, state, and local regulations regarding the sale of alcoholic beverages. The Federal Alcohol Administration Act (FAA) was established after the 13-year Prohibition Era ended in 1933. The Bureau of Alcohol, Tobacco and Firearms (ATF) is responsible for administering and enforcing the FAA, including qualifying winemakers, collecting producer and wholesaler occupational taxes, and regulating trade practices, advertising and labeling. Beyond the uniformity of the FAA, regulations vary greatly among the 50 states.

States can sell wine in one of two ways, either in a controlled environment or using an open, licensed method. "Open" states have licensed retailers and wholesalers that handle the distribution and sale of alcoholic beverages. Thirty-two states and the District of Columbia are "open" states. The other 18 states operate under the control method, in which each state government buys and sells alcoholic beverages at the wholesale and retail levels. In addition to federal regulations, some states have set up their own independent agencies that are responsible for the administration, licensing, and enforcement of state laws and the collection of state revenues. Some state legislatures even have created their own Alcoholic Beverage Control (ABC) agencies with rule-making power, and 32 states allow their citizens to vote for or against the sale of liquor on a city or county-wide basis.

BACKGROUND AND DEVELOPMENT

California winegrowing began in 1769 when Father Junipero Serra planted vines at Mission San Diego. In September 1772, the grapes were harvested and pressed, creating California's first vintage. These early wines were produced for sacramental purposes and personal consumption at the missions.

The commercial era of wine production began in 1830 with the efforts of Frenchman Jean Louis Vignes from Bordeaux, France. His vineyard was located in what is now downtown Los Angeles, California. The wine industry boomed as an ancillary result of the discovery of gold in California in 1848. A surge of Europeans came to the state seeking their fortune. Immigrants from Italy, France, and Germany who had no luck finding gold turned to a trade they already knew: winemaking.

Between 1860 and 1880, the industry grew rapidly as numerous wineries were established. By 1890, several of the state's famous wine regions already had taken shape and the industry was producing 25 million gallons of wine per year. After suffering losses from a vine pest called phylloxera, the industry virtually disappeared with the passage of Prohibition in 1919. The repeal of Prohibition in 1933, however, prompted the industry to rebuild. Growth was steady between 1949 and 1960, with annual output increasing from 117 million gallons to 129 million gallons. By the 1970s, the demand for California table wines had doubled.

As the industry has evolved, so have consumer preferences. From 1933 to 1967, dessert wine was the most popular kind of wine in the United States. During the 1970s, generic table wines, like California Chablis and California Burgandy, dominated sales. By the late 1980s, varietal wines, those labeled with the name of the grape, had taken over. These wines have been projected to remain prominent throughout the 1990s.

Production. The making of wine begins with the grape harvest, which generally occurs from August through November depending upon the grape variety and the weather. The grapes are placed in a crusher that separates the stems from the fruit and breaks up the berries. The stems are then discarded, leaving a combination of juice, seeds, pulp, and skins, called "must." Juice from red or white winegrapes is colorless.

To make white wine, the skins and seeds usually are removed from the must after a few hours. The remaining juice is called "free-run." The discarded skins also are pressed to extract the "press juice." Both juices then are filtered, placed in storage, and given yeast to facilitate the fermentation process. White wine fermentation can last anywhere from three days to three weeks. Upon completion, the wine is filtered for solids or remaining yeast. The wine is then aged for a period of one week to a year in stainless steel, oak, or redwood containers. It can also be aged in the bottle. After aging, the wine can be blended with other wines to create a desired style or sent to be finished, a process that stabilizes and filters the wine before bottling.

Production of red wine is slightly different than the process of making white wine. Red wine is fermented at warmer temperatures than white wine. For red wine production, the skins are fermented with the crushed juice to give it color and flavor. The skins float to the top and are moistened regularly with juice to extract color and flavor. Red wine usually is fermented for five to ten days and then is filtered, clarified, and preserved with sulfites. Red wine commonly is aged in oak barrels for one to two years.

Types of Wines. Wines sold in the United States generally are divided into the following categories:

champagne, aperitifs, dessert, table, and varietal wines. Also included in SIC 2084 are brandy, other fortified wines and wine coolers. Wines can be named one of four ways; by variety, which tells the predominant type of grape; by a generic name describing the color, such as blush; by the region that originally inspired the wine, such as Chablis; or by a proprietary name created by the winery.

Champagne and sparkling wines are names used interchangeably in the United States for wines with effervescence. These wines range from very dry (Natural), to dry (Brut), to slightly sweet (Extra Dry), to sweet (Sec and Demi-Sec). Aperitifs are appetizer wines usually served prior to a meal and can include champagnes and sherries. Dessert wines are officially classified as those with an alcohol content of 17 percent to 21 percent. They can be sweet or dry and include sherries and port.

Table wine is a term commonly used to describe all red, white, blush, and rose wines that contain seven to 14 percent alcohol. These wines are still rather effervescent and are served mainly with meals. Table wines can be made from any grape or combination of grapes and in any style that the winemaker chooses. Varietal wines are table wines that are made from a minimum of 75 percent of a particular grape variety. They carry the name of the grape variety from which they are produced, such as Chardonnay or Merlot.

The red table wine category has been led by Cabernet Sauvignon, a full-bodied, rich, intense wine with noticeable tannins. Often aged for ten to 30 years, it has been one of the most widely available California wines. Two red varietals include Merlot and Petite Sirah. Merlot is a medium- to full-bodied wine that originally was made for the sole purpose of blending with Cabernet Sauvignon. Petite Sirah is a robust wine, often with peppery flavors.

White table wines have been dominated by Chardonnay, the most widely planted variety in California, making up more than 56,000 acres. It is a dry wine, which has a balance of fruit, acidity, and texture. Depending upon what the winemaker uses for storage, Chardonnay can range from clean and crisp wines to rich, complex oak-aged wines. A second popular California wine has been Chenin Blanc. It is made in dry to off-dry or slightly sweet styles.

Two white varietals include French Columbard and Sauvignon Blanc. French Columbard has been the second most widely planted varietal in California. Traditionally, this wine has been used in white wine blends to add acidity or crispness. Sauvignon Blanc has been one of the fastest growing varietals in Califor-

nia. Sometimes called Fume Blanc, it is best known for its grassy, herbal flavors and is often consumed with fish and shellfish.

Brandy is "burnt wine" or fruit wine that is boiled and aged in wood. Virtually any type of fruit can be used to make brandy, although grapes have been the most common. Brandy has been produced primarily in Spain, Italy, and France and most recently in the United States. Cognac has been considered to be the best of all brandies. Cognac's discerning characteristic has been its blending. "While other brandies . . . are sometimes unblended or vintage-dated, cognacs, from the most basic V.S. to the rarest X.O., are almost always the final product of tens of cognacs, which have been married to achieve the proper balance, flavor and style," according to the *New York Times Magazine.*

Fortified wines were the creation of the Spanish and Portuguese and included port, sherry, and madeira. Sherry is made by blending younger sherries with older sherries in oak casks. It varies in dryness levels, ranging from bone-dry to extremely sweet and in hues ranging from pale gold to chestnut. Harvey's Bristol Cream, imported by Hiram Walker & Sons, has been the top selling sherry in the United States, with a nearly 41 percent market share. The best-seller is a blend of aged oloroso, a fortified full-bodied sherry, and Pedro Ximines grapes, which sweetens the mixture.

Port is red wine fortified with grape brandy. It was created unintentionally in the seventeenth century when Portugal tried to ship its table wine to England. In order to stabilize the wine during its voyage over the Atlantic, the wine needed the addition of grape brandy. England has remained the most popular market for port.

Madeira comes from a tropical island of the same name and is a raisiny, sweet wine. Madeira has been closely linked with the history of the United States, according to the *New York Times Magazine.* It was considered to be the wine of choice for American Revolutionary notables such as Thomas Jefferson, George Washington, and Ben Franklin. One reason this wine became so popular in the New World was because, unlike other wines that soured during the long, hot voyage across the Atlantic, madeira has been the only wine known to improve dramatically with the introduction of heat.

A much more recent addition to the wine category have been wine coolers. The wine cooler craze began in the early 1980s with the introduction of Brown-Foreman's California Cooler. When first introduced, the wine cooler was a sweet, wine-based, single-serving bottle drink. But the cooler category has evolved beyond the wine-based products to both malt-based and spirits-based coolers. In fact, noted Donna Jean Hood in *Beverage Dynamics,* "Even the wine-based cooler lines are becoming more malt-based to gain additional distribution, and, in some states, to lower tax liability." The cooler category peaked in 1987 with 21 percent of the total U.S. wine sales volume. Consumption has since fallen but has remained second in sales volume after table wine. Despite its decline, coolers have been a $1 billion category that did not even exist prior to 1980.

CURRENT CONDITIONS

Americans have been consuming smaller amounts of wine each year. After a peak year in 1988, consumption fell to 467 million gallons in 1991. Table wines, including varietals, have grown to nearly 72 percent of the total wine market. Wine coolers have remained in second with 13.6 percent, while sparkling wines were at 6.9 percent, and desserts at 7.8 percent. Brandy and cognac are classified with distilled spirits, and maintained approximately four percent of that market. Total U.S. wine inventories have remained steady at approximately 596 million gallons, with 91 percent table wine.

In 1991, wine cooler sales accounted for nearly 61 million gallons. This was a 30 percent decrease from 1990 and indicative of the downward spiral of this category. The Seagram Company continued to dominate this category in 1991, with 46 percent market share, followed closely by E. & J. Gallo Wineries' Bartles & James brand. Some industry insiders believe that this decline will soon level off and that the category will maintain an established volume, according to *Beverage Dynamics.* New trends in low-alcohol and low-calorie varieties may help to create stability in this category.

Flavor remains the most important factor for the wine cooler market. "This is a product that is flavor-driven, rather than wine-driven," said Howard Jacobson, vice president of sales and marketing for Canandaigua Wine Company, the producer of Sun Country Wine Coolers, in *Beverage Dynamics.* Alfredo Piedra, assistant vice president of marketing at Barcardi, added, "The emerging trend in terms of flavor is that consumers are looking for the lighter, drier flavors as opposed to the syrupy-sweet flavors popular in the 1980s."

Sales of champagne and sparkling wines have been hurt by price-conscious consumers. Sales in the United States of imported French champagne were down in 1991 as were all imported sparkling wines, off a combined 16.6 percent, and the chief reason was price. "People are price-conscious," Bill Mayer, manager of Pacific Wine Merchants in San Francisco, told *Beverage Dynamics.* "We sell mainly French champagnes and find that we are selling less than before. The market is relatively steady and will stay that way until the economy changes."

"Although champagne still commands a superior image and still maintains the quality and complexity of the best sparkling wines, its pricing has reached the critical point, which has caused some loyal consumers to take a second look at less expensive alternatives," reported Gerold Boyd in *Beverage Dynamics.* Depending upon the occasion, consumers have been trading up or down with champagne and sparkling wines. Those trading up have been buying sporadically, usually for a special event. Those buying with more frequency have been trading down and looking for a high price/quality ratio. The upside to this trend is that some California producers of sparkling wine experienced increased sales, starting in 1992.

The dessert wine share of the U.S. market has decreased dramatically over the past three decades, according to the Wine Institute. In the mid-1950s, dessert wine accounted for over 60 percent of the U.S. wine market. In 1991, it was five percent. Brandy and cognac, measured as part of the distilled spirit market, have also been in decline. In 1992, 6.7 million 9-liter cases were sold, down from 7.5 million in 1990.

Beyond changing tastes, dessert wines are not sold because the consumer has little knowledge about these products, according to Berger in *Beverage Dynamics.* Berger wrote that "the least understood fine wine in the country is sherry, Spain's contribution to the first and last aspects of a great meal. The old view [has been] a little old lady sipping sherry at afternoon tea or of Aunt Gertrude taking a nip . . . before bedtime. This is far from the best way the product ought to be served."

In contrast, one strong area for the wine industry has been the success of California varietals. A five percent increased in domestic table wine growth in 1991 was fueled by the continued popularity of these premium wines, including Gallo Reserve Cellars (up 17.1 percent), Blossom Hill (up 59.1 percent) and Kendall-Jackson (up 22.7 percent). Relatively new to the industry, a "fighting" varietal has been defined as a value-priced, cork-finished 750ml varietal wine. The leader in fighting varietals has been Glen Ellen, followed by Fetzer's Bel Arbors, Sebastiani's Country Wines and Swan Cellar label, Beringer's Napa Valley, and Robert Mondavi's Woodbridge. Tim Wallace, a Glen Ellen executive, told *Beverage Dynamics* that "Fighting varietals are the foundation for the American wine industry in the future." He added that "Low-priced jugs and generics are on their way out and they are being replaced by affordable varietals." In 1991, Sutter Home shipped 4.5 million cases of fighting varietals, selling more white zinfandel and red zinfandel than anyone else. Stan Hock of Sutter Home Winery said, "People are looking for value, popular-priced brands they can trust. Value is the name of the game, and we see the future for fighting varietals as very positive."

The gradual decline in beverage alcohol consumption has been due largely to changes in the American lifestyle, with increased emphasis on diet, fitness, and health. The wine industry, however, may not be as greatly affected by Americans' quest for health due to its image of moderation and to the often-suggested health benefits of drinking wine. For example, publicity about the "French paradox" theory that red wine consumption may lower the rate of heart disease boosted red wine sales in 1992.

Even though wine is portrayed as healthier than other types of alcohol, Lefty Stern, director of marketing for the wine division of Brown-Forman, told *Beverage Dynamics* that "we already see a slowing in the rate of decline in consumption—it will go down at a slower rate." Changing demographics, however, could mean that although individuals may consume less in any given year they will be wine consumers for a longer period of time because life expectancy rates have increased. "We think consumption will stabilize at about 116 million cases" by the end of the century, Stern added.

INDUSTRY LEADERS

As dominant as the state of California is in the wine industry, so too are the wineries of California winemakers Ernest & Julio Gallo. Controlling nearly 40 percent of the U.S. wine market, E. & J. Gallo Wineries lead every wine category in which they compete. According to the *Wine Spectator,* one out of every three bottles of wine made in America is a Gallo product. E. & J. Gallo Wineries has been the world's largest winemaker, with annual sales of over $1 billion.

In 1933, brothers Ernest and Julio Gallo founded their original winery in Modesto, California. "Unable to obtain bank financing, they bought crushing and fermenting equipment on 90-day terms and rented a warehouse to make their first commercial wine." Using pamphlets on winemaking from the local library and grapes bought on a promise to pay from sales proceeds, the two brothers made their first batch of wine. By 1993, Gallo owned five separate vineyards

totaling more than 2,000 acres. The company has remained a private, family-owned business and is one of the largest organic farms in the United States.

The company's success has been due in part to the partnership of the Gallo brothers; Ernest marketed the wine that Julio made. Another part of Gallo's success has been its quest for improving the quality of the wine it produced. To this end, Gallo replanted its vineyard in Livingston in 1946 using grape varieties that had not been previously grown in the area. Various viticultural techniques were experimented, and in 1947 a formal research program was established to evaluate the results. Specific standards were developed for winemaking and have been used ever since.

In 1965, Julio Gallo established the first Growers Relations Department and shared their research finding with area growers. In 1967, Gallo offered long-term contracts to selected growers, giving economic security and incentive to replant vineyards with the better grapes varieties recommended by Gallo. During the 1970s, the winery shifted to producing premium varietal wines, and in 1991 introduced its first ultra-premium wine, 1991 Sonoma Estate Chardonnay. Leading brands for E. & J. Gallo Wineries have been Gallo, Andre, Bartles & James, and Carlo Rossi.

The Seagram Company, Ltd. has been one of the world's leading producers and marketers of distilled spirits and wines. Included in The Seagram Spirits and Wine Group are two specialized wine divisions: The Seagram Classics Wine Company and Seagram Chateau & Estates Wine Company. Based in San Mateo, California, the Classics Wine Company has produced, marketed and exported the wines of Sterling Vineyards, the Monterey Vineyard and Mumm Napa Valley. The division also has imported and marketed Mumm Champagnes and Barton & Guestier Wines from France and has acted as sales agent for select California and overseas wines. Based in New York, the Seagram Chateau & Estates Wine Company has imported many European wines, including 35 percent of all classified Bordeaux. The company also has imported Seagram-owned Perrier-Jouet Champagnes, the third best-selling champagne in the United States, and Sandeman Ports and Sherries and Janneau Armagnacs.

The Seagram Company has been dedicated to expanding its market around the world. In 1983, the United States accounted for the majority of its spirits and wine revenues. But by 1993, the Seagram Europe & Africa division had taken over as leader. Based in Paris, Seagram Global Brands has been responsible for all production and marketing of the company cognacs, champagnes, armagnacs, ports, and sherries.

Kentucky-based Brown-Forman has been well known for its collection of distilled spirits, especially bourbon. However, during the 1960s and 1970s the company expanded into the wine industry with the acquisition of Korbel champagne and brandy in 1965, and Bolla and Cella wines in 1968. By the early 1990s, Brown-Forman established a separate division for its wine operations and embarked on an aggressive plan to expand its business through long-term marketing and distribution contracts. Its base of wine products by 1991 included Bolla, Fontana, Candida, Brolio, Korbel, and Noilly Prat.

In late 1991, the company became the exclusive U.S. marketing, sales, and distribution agent for Fontanafredda wines. According to *Beverage Dynamics,* William Street, president and CEO of Brown-Forman Beverage Co. said, "The addition of Fontanafredda is another step in our strategy of becoming one of the largest premium wine suppliers to the trade and consumer."

WORK FORCE

The *Ward's Business Directory of U.S. Private and Public Companies 1993* lists 127 companies that have produced wine and brandy in the United States. Most of these companies are privately-held, with a handful of public companies such as Heublin, Hiram Walker, and the Seagram Company. In total, the winemaking industry employed over 17,000 workers. The majority of wineries have been family-owned, located predominately in California, and have created a tremendous impact on that state's economy. Los-Angeles-based Recon Research Corporation reported that the California wine industry has contributed nearly $1.5 billion annually to the Sonoma County economy, employing more than 3,600 people and creating secondary industrial employment of an additional 2,500 jobs.

AMERICA AND THE WORLD

Imports. Approximately 61 million gallons of wine was shipped to the United States in 1991, down nearly nine percent from 1990. Since 1984, when imported wines peaked at 142 million gallons, wine shipments have fallen an average of 11 percent annually. Dominating 78 percent of the market, table wine has been the largest amount of all wine imported to the United States. The two main suppliers of imported table wine have continued to be Italy, with nearly 41 percent market share, and France, with 29 percent. Italy, France, and Spain also have accounted for 97 percent of all imported champagne and sparkling wine. In addition to these countries, there have been a growing number of imported wines from the Southern Hemisphere, particularly Argentina, Australia and Brazil.

According to *Beverage Dynamics,* wines from Chile have sold well in the United States since 1986, with dramatic surges in 1992 and 1993. Sales in 1993 reached two million cases, up 50 percent over 1992 and up 100 percent since 1990. In April 1993, the Brown-Forman Beverage Company announced that it would import a line of Chilean wine with a brand name of Carmen. Seven premium varietals in this line have been made to specifications aimed at the U.S. market. According to Berger in *Beverage Dynamics,* "Carmen could become a major brand in the U.S. market because of Brown-Forman's influence."

An emerging South American competitor to Chilean wines has been the Argentinian wine industry, which produced nearly six times as much wine as Chile, noted Gerald Boyd in *Beverage Dynamics.* The company's largest winery, Trapiche, is located in the fertile land of Mendoza. This facility is so massive that the chairman of Trapiche, Carlos Pulenta, has claimed that it is the second largest winery in the world, after Gallo. Trapiche is owned by Penaflor Company, with headquarters in Buenos Aires. Annual exports have been 250,000 cases, a small part of the winery's total production. Its largest export market has been Scandinavia, although exports to the United States have grown annually since 1990.

Exports. According to the U.S. Department of Commerce, U.S. commercial wine exports increased to a record 31 million gallons in 1991, a gain of nearly 18 percent over 1990. The top three export markets have been Canada, Japan, and the United Kingdom. Sales to Canada alone reached 8.3 million gallons. However, a great deal was bulk wine for blending and bottling. Beyond these three main export markets have been an additional seven countries that have imported over 500,000 gallons of U.S. produced wine annually.

U.S. wine exports posted a value of $146.1 million in 1991, more than double the $60.8 million of U.S. wine exported in 1987. This increase in U.S. wine export values, combined with the decline in the value of wine imports, has led to a decline in the U.S. wine trade deficit, falling from $956 million in 1987 to $772 million in 1991.

INDUSTRY INFORMATION SOURCES
Berger, Dan. "Making the Most of Port and Sherry." *Beverage Dynamics*, November/December 1992.

———. "The Wines of Chile." *Beverage Dynamics*, July/August 1993.

Boyd, Gerald. "In This Corner . . ." *Beverage Dynamics*, March 1992.

———. "Selling the Sparkle." *Beverage Dynamics*, November/December 1992.

Boyd, Gerald. "Southern Exposure. Trapiche, Argentina's Largest Winery, Is Making a Mark in the U.S." *Beverage Dynamics*, June 1992.

"Brown-Forman Cultivates Its Growing Wine Business." *Beverage Dynamics*, March 1992.

"Distillations, Libations, and Celebrations: A Consumer Guide to Liqueurs, Cognac, Fortified Wines & Brandy." *New York Times Magazine*, December 13, 1992.

"E. & J. Gallo Winery History." Modesto, CA: E. & J. Gallo Wineries, 1993.

"Enjoying California Wine." San Francisco: Wine Institute, 1992.

"The Fine Wines of Ernest and Julio Gallo." Modesto, CA: E. & J. Gallo Wineries, 1993.

"Gallo Introduces First Sonoma Estate Wine." Modesto, CA: E. & J. Gallo Wineries, 1993.

Hood, Donna Jean. "From Sweet to Sophisticated." *Beverage Dynamics*, June 1992.

Jobson's Handbook Advance 1993. New York: Jobson Beverage Group, 1993.

"1991 Wine Industry Statistical Report." San Francisco: Wine Institute, October 1992.

"The Positive Power of the Press." *Beverage Dynamics*, March 1992.

The Seagram Company. *Seagram Company Annual Report*. New York: The Seagram Company Ltd., 1991-1992.

"A Scientific Look at Wine." San Francisco: Wine Institute, 1990.

"The Story of American Wines." San Francisco: Wine Institute, 1985.

"Wine Drinker Profiled." *Beverage Dynamics*, March 1992.

Ward's Business Directory of U.S. Private and Public Companies. Detroit: Gale Research Inc., 1993.

U.S. Department of Commerce. *U.S. Industrial Outlook 1993*. Washington, DC: U.S. Department of Commerce, 1993.

Standard & Poor's Industry Surveys. New York: Standard & Poors, 1993.

—Catherine A. Quagliana

SIC 2085

DISTILLED AND BLENDED LIQUORS

This category includes establishments primarily engaged in manufacturing alcoholic liquors by distillation and in manufacturing cordials and alcoholic cocktails by blending, processing, or mixing liquors and other ingredients. Establishments primarily engaged in manufacturing industrial alcohol are classified in **SIC 2869: Industrial Organic Chemicals, Not Elsewhere Classified,** and those bottling purchased liquors are classified in **SIC 5182: Wine and Distilled Alcoholic Beverages.**

INDUSTRY SNAPSHOT

Beverage alcohol consumption in the United States has been in perpetual decline since 1979, largely due to a changing American lifestyle that has increased emphasis on diet, fitness, and health. To combat the focus on diet, fitness, and health, the distilled spirits industry has promoted the value of its products rather than the volume, encouraging consumers to drink less, but drink better. Per capita consumption of distilled spirits has remained at 1.4 gallons, the smallest consumption level of all beverages, including soft drinks, beer, fruit juices, bottled water, and wine. However, retail receipts for spirits has ranked third, following beer and soft drinks, with nearly $31 billion in sales in 1992.

As American consumers have become interested in lighter tasting drinks, white goods—gin, vodka, rum, and tequila—have posted marginal gains. Three out of the five top selling brands in 1992 were white goods, Bacardi Rum, Smirnoff Vodka, and Seagram's Gin. Sales of brown goods—bourbon, scotch, or straight whiskey—have suffered the most in the United States; their sales are not growing at a rate comparable to white goods. Younger consumers have not been as interested in bourbon, scotch, or straight whiskey as their parents. Yet brown goods have maintained a 36 percent market share.

Market share statistics for the separate types of distilled spirits were reported by *Jobson's 1993 Handbook Advance*. Vodka held the top market share at 22.3 percent. Canadian whiskey followed with 12.4 percent, cordials and liqueurs 10.7 percent, straight whiskey 10.3 percent, gin 8.4 percent, rum 8.2 percent, scotch 7.5 percent, prepared cocktails 6.5 percent, blended whiskey 5.8 percent, brandy and cognac 4.6 percent, tequila 3.1 percent, and Irish whiskey 0.2 percent of the market. Ten states have accounted for nearly 54 percent of the total market for distilled spirits. They are California, Florida, New York, Illinois, Texas, Michigan, New Jersey, Pennsylvania, Massachusetts, and Georgia.

ORGANIZATION AND STRUCTURE

The distilled spirits industry has been dominated by a few large companies that offer a variety of alcoholic beverages. Most started with a flagship brand, such as Jim Beam Bourbon, and have diversified into a family of products that includes whiskey and non-whiskey items, such as gin, vodka, rum, tequila, cordials, mixed cocktails, and even fruit juices and other non-alcohol or low-alcohol beverages.

This category includes only those companies that produce distilled spirits. All distillers have to sell their products through wholesalers and retailers, in order to accommodate various federal, state, and local regulations regarding the sale of alcoholic beverages. The Federal Alcohol Administration Act (FAA) was established at the end of the 13-year Prohibition Era in 1933. The FAA, which is enforced by the Bureau of Alcohol, Tobacco and Firearms (ATF), qualifies distillers, collects producer and wholesaler occupational taxes, and regulates trade practices, advertising, and labeling.

Beyond the uniformity of the FAA, regulations vary greatly among the 50 states. States can sell distilled spirits in one of two ways, either in a controlled environment or using an "open," licensed method. Open states have licensed retailers and wholesalers that handle the distribution and sale of alcoholic beverages. Thirty-two states and the District of Columbia are open states. The other 18 states operate under the control method, in which each state government buys and sells alcoholic beverages at the wholesale and retail levels.

In addition to federal regulations, some states have set up their own independent agencies that are responsible for the administration, licensing, and enforcement of state laws, and the collection of state revenues. Some state legislatures have created their own Alcoholic Beverage Control (ABC) agencies with rule-making power, and 32 states allow their citizens to vote for or against the sale of liquor on a city or county-wide basis. In 1993, a large number of states were reviewing a variety of beverage alcohol industry issues, according to *Jobson's 1993 Handbook Advance*. At least 30 states considered state excise tax increases. Fifteen states looked at significant environmental legislation, while 13 states reviewed advertising and trade-practice legislation.

BACKGROUND AND DEVELOPMENT

Discussion of the alcoholic beverage industry generally has fallen into two categories: brown goods and white goods. The brown goods covers the whiskey group of straight and blended whiskey, bourbon, and scotch, including domestic and imported brands. The white goods are gin, vodka, rum, and tequila. Other major segments in the beverage alcohol market have been the growing cordials and liqueur category, and the assortment of ready-to-drink cocktails.

Whiskey is an all-encompassing term for any distilled liquor made from a fermented mash of grain. Many different types of whiskey make up the approximate 36 percent market share of alcoholic beverages consumed in the United States. However different in taste, all are similar in the distillation process. The four primary steps to make whiskey are mashing, fermenting, distilling and aging. The grains of corn, barley, rye, and/or wheat are ground into a fine meal, mixed with water, and cooked until the starches have been converted into sugars. This creates a "mash" that is mixed with yeast, converting the sugars into alcohol.

The fermented mixture is then pumped into a still where steam condensation allows the alcohol to separate from the water and by-products. Distillers use either a pot still or a continuous still to make whiskey. With a pot still, the heat is generated from beneath the still, causing the fermented mash to vaporize and to become trapped in a spiral pipe at the top of the still. With a continuous still, the heated mash is pumped into the top of the still, then filtered down through a series of baffle plates as the steam rises from the bottom of the still. Continuous stills have become the standard equipment for U.S. distillers.

Fresh from the still, the whiskey is colorless, harsh, and in need of aging. It is the aging process that enhances the spirit and refines the whiskey, giving it an amber color. Federal regulations specify that whiskey must be "produced at less than 190 proof and bottled at not less than 80 proof." American-distilled whiskeys include Tennessee, rye, and blended. Tennessee whiskey, such as Jack Daniel's and George Dickel, is a distinct product due to filtering the whiskey through charcoal prior to aging. Rye whiskey is made from at least 51 percent rye and distilled at no more than 160 proof. The whiskey then is stored at no more than 125 proof in new oak barrels. Blended whiskey, such as Seagram's Seven Crown, comes from at least 20 percent straight whiskey mixed with other whiskey grain neutral spirits. Blended whiskey became popular during World War II when whiskey was in short supply and distillers stretched its availability by adding grain neutral spirits.

Bourbon, part of the whiskey group, is a uniquely American product. The drink was created unintentionally in 1789 when a Bourbon County, Kentucky farmer sealed his whiskey in a charred barrel.

This aging process picked up the mellow smoky flavor of the wood, giving bourbon its distinctive taste. In 1964, the United States Congress officially named bourbon America's "Native Spirit," and has tightly regulated bourbon's production to ensure a consistent, quality product. Straight bourbon whiskey is required by law to contain at least 51 percent corn; to be distilled at no more than 160 proof; and to be aged a minimum of two years in new, charred oak containers. Jim Beam Kentucky Straight Bourbon Whiskey has been the best selling bourbon in the world, and has accounted for more than one-fifth of the bourbon market in the United States, according to *Market Watch* magazine.

Imported whiskeys have unique variations in their recipes as well. Canadian whiskey is a blend of mostly rye with corn, wheat, and barley malt. By Canadian law, no more than 9.09 percent of a Canadian label may include whiskey from other countries, and it has to age at in wood least three years.

Scotch whiskey is made from corn and barley and is processed in continuous stills. Distillers combine up to 40 true malt whiskeys with grain whiskeys to create the individual flavor of their brand. Scotch is matured for approximately four to five years in oak or sherry barrels. Irish whiskey, a cousin to scotch, is made with barley dried in a closed kiln and is distilled three times, unlike all other whiskeys which are distilled no more than twice.

Scotland distillers have been making single malt whisky for more than 500 years. Single malt whisky is the product of only malted barley distilled at one location, hence the name. The product is the outcome of an expensive, labor-intensive, five-step process which includes malting, mashing, fermenting, distilling, and maturing. Single malts are produced in pot stills. To make single malt whisky, barley is steeped in water, allowed to sprout, and dried over smoky peat fires, producing malting barley. Once dried, the malt is ground and soaked in large tanks, creating a product called "wort." After fermenting for two days, the wort becomes a liquid called "wash." Also known as "distiller's beer," this product contains ten percent alcohol. Using a copper pot still, the distiller's beer is distilled. The new, raw spirit is reduced with spring water to around 110 proof and is aged, by law, for at least three years in oak or sherry barrels. Most single malts are aged for period of ten to 15 years, which gives the malt whisky greater depth and character. The taste and consistency of single malts are derived from the region in Scotland in which they were made.

White goods command a sizable percent of the market in the United States. In 1993, they accounted for 42 percent of total U.S. distilled spirit sales and five of the top ten best-selling brands. Vodka is the most clean and crisp of the distilled spirits, making it a favorite for mixed drinks and one of the most popular spirits in the world. Vodka sales lead all other distilled spirit sales in 1993, giving it a 22 percent share of the U.S. market.

According to U.S. federal regulations, vodka lacks aroma, taste, and color. Originally produced in the twelfth century in Russia and Poland, vodka is a rye-based product that does not need to be aged. It is distilled at a high proof, extracting all of the congeners, or the natural compounds in the distillate that give the product its taste and aroma. It became popular in the United States after World War II with the introduction of a drink called the Moscow Mule.

Gin is the distilled product of juniper berries mixed with a clear grain-based spirit. First created in 1650 by a chemist in Holland, gin quickly became a popular drink in Britain and later in the United States. Government regulations require that gin be bottled at 80 proof or higher, have a juniper berry flavor, and be made either by distillation or compounding. Compound gin, a less costly method, is the combination of neutral spirits with the oil and extracts of the botanicals. Aging is not a factor with gin. Instead, each gin achieves its distinct taste through the distiller's specific combination of gin botanicals, such as cassia, anise, coriander, angelica, and juniper.

Rum, one of the all-time, best-selling alcoholic beverages in the United States, is a sweet, distilled spirit made from sugar cane. It was first created by Spaniards when Christopher Columbus brought sugar cane from the Canary Islands to Puerto Rico. Rum's production resembles the four-step process of making whiskey, and it usually is aged in wood for up to 15 years.

Newest to the white goods category is tequila. Produced in the town of Tequila in the central Mexican state of Jalisco, the drink is a distilled spirit made from the heart of the blue agave plant. The core of the plant, which resembles a large pineapple, is harvested, cut into chunks, and baked in steam ovens. The juice is extracted by steaming and compressing the core. After fermenting for several days, the juice is distilled at a low proof. The tequila then is double distilled to a powerful 110 proof and reduced to 80 proof with water before bottling.

Although tequila can be bottled as a clear product, the gold and "añejo" products are aged in wood. Gold tequila is kept in large oak vats for about nine months to a year, acquiring its pale gold color. By law, tequila designated asejo must be aged in a wood container for at least one year, although most asejo products are aged for three to seven years.

Originating in Europe, cordials and liqueurs are alcoholic beverages that are prepared by mixing or compounding various spirits with flavorings. The cordial category includes schnapps, liqueurs, cremes, and brandies. Cordials must contain at least 2.5 percent sugar by weight and incorporate natural flavorings. The most popular cordial has been Bailey's Irish Cream.

Cordials are produced by one of the following methods: percolation, maceration, or distillation. The percolation process starts putting the spirits in the bottom of a large tank with a basket-like container filled with fruit and spices near the top. The spirits then are "percolated" up through the basket, extracting the flavors of the fruit. With maceration, the fruit and other ingredients are mixed with the spirit and allowed to steep until all the flavors have been extracted. With the distillation process, all the ingredients are placed in the still with grain neutral spirits and gently heated.

Schnapps traditionally have been a clear, light tasting product used to mix in a drink or serve alone. A liqueur is sweeter than schnapps, drier than a creme, but not as potent as a flavored brandy. Cremes usually are the sweetest cordials and contain a higher sugar content, which gives them a creamy consistency.

CURRENT CONDITIONS

The distilled spirits industry has suffered as U.S. consumption of distilled spirits continues to fall. "In fact, excluding 1991, 1992 consumption was at its lowest level since 1967," according to *Jobson's 1993 Handbook Advance.* "Every major category, with the exception of tequila and prepared cocktails, suffered volume losses. And if the prepared cocktails category is excluded from the overall total, spirits consumption would have declined 1.5 percent." An eight percent increase in the federal excise tax (FET) and the recessionary economy of the United States added to the falling consumption rates with a 7.3 percent drop in sales in 1991.

The spirits industry recovered somewhat in 1992, posting a modest 0.3 percent gain. Volume increased from 349.3 million gallons in 1991 to just over 350 million gallons the next year. However, total whiskey consumption was down 1.2 percent in 1992, with a large drop in imported whiskey and a modest drop in American whiskey. Only the single malt category increased five percent in 1992. Even though brands such as Jim Beam, Jack Daniel's Black, and Early Times

posted healthy increases in 1992, the levels were still below those in 1990, according to *Jobson's 1993 Handbook Advance.*

Among the non-whiskey categories, the results were mixed as gin, vodka, rum, and cordials all posted declines ranging from 1.4 percent to 3.3 percent. Despite the decline of the overall segment, some individual brands performed well, including Seagram's Gin, Absolut Vodka, and Captain Morgan's Spiced Rum. Specific brands in the cordials segment also posted gains in 1992, including Jagermeister, Malibu, Rumple Mintz, Carolans, and Kamora.

Distillers have been combating declining consumption rates in the United States in a variety of ways. First, many companies have focused on promoting products to the younger generation of consumers. These products have been low-calorie, low-alcohol content, light-tasting and/or ready-to-serve. The mixability factor of the white goods has allowed them to keep up with changing consumer preferences. "All white goods have gained in share and have done extremely well relative to brown goods," Gary Clayton, marketing director for Beefeater Gin at Hiram Walker, told *Beverage Dynamics.* "Why? Because the consumer has shifted to lighter, sweeter, mixable drinks. And a lot of white spirits brands including Bacardi and Jose Cuervo have pursued mixability strategies."

Brown goods, however, have been a different situation. The younger generation has not turned to the brown goods as their parents did in the 1970s, the peak years of scotch consumption. In order to survive, this industry segment has consolidated, leaving a handful of companies—Jim Beam Brands, Brown-Forman, United Distillers Glenmore, and The House of Seagram—with a major presence in the market.

Beverage alcohol marketers also have turned to promoting both premium whiskey products and value-priced items. This strategy seems to be working as many of the premium scotch brands—Johnnie Walker Red, Black Label, Cutty Sark, and J&B Rare—all experienced increased sales in 1992. This increase starkly contrasted the declines of 1991 when the scotch category was down by more than 13 percent. Another example of promoting high-end products has been the introduction of the ultra premium bourbon. With prices as high as $50 a bottle, this tier of high-priced, specially-bottled products has become a category similar to single malt scotch. Jim Beam Brands Co.'s line of small-batch bourbons are ultra-premium, hand-bottled products, distilled in limited quantities and finished with hand-labeled packaging. With names like Baker's Bourbon, Basil Hayden's, and Knob Creek, the company has been promoting the rich history and tradition surrounding these bourbons. The value-priced brands also have seen growth. Benson Lilly, marketing director for Allied Brands Limited Scotch Portfolio, pointed out in *Beverage Dynamics,* "In this atmosphere, intrinsic value is what counts: quality, image, and price. As premium brands price themselves more aggressively, the bulk segment is adding image, package design, and advertising."

In stark contrast to the promotional image of traditional bourbons has been the explosion of high-alcohol content drinks that hit the market in 1992. The "shots" category or subcategory of the cordials segment was created with the successful introduction of the Jim Beam Brands Co. DeKuyper line of cordials. "After introducing the raft of exotic flavors and increasing promotional and ad dollars, DeKuyper has increased its share to almost 50 percent of the estimated 4-million case schnapps category," according to *Impact Databank.* "That's from about 37 percent of the market in 1988." "DeKuyper has become the brand name in the growing 'shots' market, attracting a varied audience to its line-up of 40 flavors," reported Fara Warner in *BrandWeek.* Once known as an after-beer chaser, potent unmixed shots have become the major force behind the recent schnapps category growth, led by products like Jagermeister and Rumple Mintz. At last count, 28 percent of the schnapps drinkers were under 29 years old, according to *Impact Databank,* making schnapps the most popular liquor of that age group.

Jim Beam's success with the DeKuyper line has attracted competitors, such as White Rock Distillers Co., of Lewiston, Maine. White Rock expects to sell at least 225,000 cases of its year-old 100 proof Firewater Cinnamon Schnapps annually. In addition, a new mint flavored Ice 101 (referring to the proof) entered the market in February 1993 and sold 75,000 cases in the first year.

Other areas of increased consumption were the continued growth of tequila and prepared cocktails. Tequila has become a well known beverage in several Western and Southwestern states and many metropolitan areas throughout the United States. Spurred by the continued popularity of Mexican cuisine and the ever-popular margarita, tequila sales have continued to rise.

Even though it has been one of the smallest spirits category with only three percent of total consumption, tequila sales have been projected to continue to grow far beyond 1993. Peter Bordeaux, president of Sazerac, the marketing company for Herradura Tequila, predicted a trend for drinkers to trade up to more expensive tequilas in *Beverage Dynamics.* "The tequila business is where the scotch business was in the early 1950s," Bordeaux said. "There was no malt scotch business, per se, and very little 12-year-old scotch. So tequila is still a very long-term market." The category has benefitted from the growth of its pre-eminent brand, Jose Cuervo, which has accounted for almost half of all tequila consumption, and has been the subject of successful line extensions using both margarita mix and premixed, ready-to-drink margaritas.

Ready-to-drink cocktails were not considered a large player in the overall distilled spirits market until the 1990 boom of Bacardi Breezer. In 1989, prepared cocktails represented just under three percent of total distilled spirits. In 1990, the share jumped to 4.5 percent and up to 6.5 percent in 1992. Although consumption of the Breezer cocktail has declined, other players have entered the market. Jack Daniel's Country Cocktails exploded onto the market in 1992, with sales of nearly two million cases, making it the 18th best selling spirit in America, according to the *Jobson Beverage Group.* The product uses Jack Daniel's whiskey and has "built-in equity" with the Jack Daniel's name. In 1993, Brown-Forman launched a second line of pre-mixed cocktails, Southern Comfort Cocktails, again borrowing brand equity from the Southern Comfort brand. Similarly, Heublein has used Jose Cuervo's brand name clout to help popularize its line of Jose Cuervo Ritas.

Several beverage alcohol executives have noted while the prepared cocktail category has been a healthy business in its own right, further advantages can be found for the parent brand. As John Shastid, vice-president and director of Southern Comfort development, explained in *Beverage Dynamics,* "The real jewel at the heart of this is the potential these products have to aid the parent brand." And with a stalled liquor industry, any assistance in creating brand awareness—especially for the brown goods—is considered to be a tremendous gain.

INDUSTRY LEADERS

International Distillers & Vinters (IDV) is the largest wine and spirits group in the world, and is the beverage division of Grand Metropolitan PLC, a London-based multinational company. IDV is known for its successful development of Smirnoff Vodka, J&B Whiskey, and Bailey's Irish Cream. IDV also is the parent company for Heublein, the marketer of Jose Cuervo Tequila.

Joseph Seagram & Sons is one of the world's leading producers and marketers of distilled spirits and wine. The business has been organized on a global basis, and has been conducted through subsidiaries and

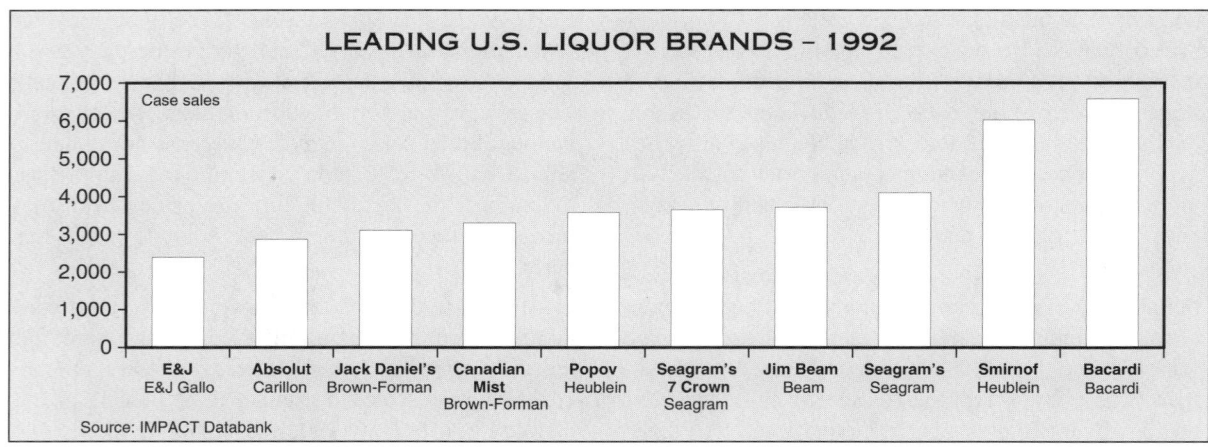

LEADING U.S. LIQUOR BRANDS – 1992

Source: IMPACT Databank

affiliates in 30 countries. Known as the Seagram Spirits and Wine Group, this division has been responsible for the production, brand management, business development, marketing, sales, and distribution of nearly all of Seagram's beverage alcohol business. The only exceptions have been Seagram's U.S. cooler business and the U.S.-based, specialized, premium wine operations. Focusing on premium and core brands, Seagram sold the trademark rights to seven distilled spirits brands in December 1991. A subsidiary of American Brands, Inc. purchased the trademark rights to Lord Calvert Canadian Whisky, Calvert Extra and Kessler Blended American Whiskeys, Calvert Gin, Wolfschmidt Vodka, Ronrico Rum and the Leroux line of cordials.

In 1988, Seagram acquired Martell, the world's second largest cognac producer. Other well known Seagram brands include Chivas Regal, Mumm, Crown Royal, Seagram's Gin, and V.O. With this portfolio of premium products, Seagram's has been successfully developing a worldwide market. As expected, the acquisition of Martell has delivered enhanced growth for Seagram in the Asia-Pacific market, the fastest growing area in the world for beverage alcohol products. In this market, cognac has been the most prestigious drink and Martell has been the pre-eminent cognac. This brand also has been popular in the markets of Singapore, Malaysia, and Hong Kong. With offices in New York and London, the Seagram Spirits and Wine Group revenues have been divided by region, with Europe/Asia leading at 43 percent, Asia Pacific/Duty Free Shops at 26 percent, North America at 22 percent, and Latin America at 9 percent.

The largest U.S. distilled spirit company is Kentucky-based Brown-Forman Corporation, which was created in 1870 when George C. Brown and John Forman opened their distillery in Louisville to pro-

ducer Old Forester bourbon. In 1902, Forman sold his interest in the company to the Brown family, which has remained in control of the business ever since. The company's first acquisition was Early Times in 1923. Brown-Forman went public prior to the onset of Prohibition and was allowed to remain open to produce alcohol for medicinal purposes. During World War II, alcoholic beverage production was curtailed in order to produce alcohol for the war effort. In 1941, Brown-Forman began the process for a new batch of bourbon to be complete by 1945. As a result, Early Times dominated the bourbon market following the end of World War II.

In 1956, the company purchased Jack Daniel's sour mash whiskey produced in Lynchburg, Tennessee. Brown-Forman retained the Jack Daniel's label and promoted the image of a small distillery. This product has become so popular that it sells at least four million cases annually throughout the world.

Brown-Forman continued its expansion during the 1970s, adding lines of wine, champagne, brandy, scotch, gin, whiskey and cordials. By the early 1990s, the company established a separate division for its wine operations and embarked on an aggressive expansion plan that included long-term marketing and distribution contracts.

Jim Beam Brands Company is the second largest distilled spirits company in the United States, producing and marketing more than 70 products, including six of the top 30 brands sold in the United States. Jim Beam Bourbon has been the company's flagship brand, and has been the best selling bourbon in the U.S. and worldwide. The company started up in 1795 when Jacob Beam, a Kentucky farmer, developed his recipe for Kentucky bourbon whiskey. His son, David, joined the business, and with the assistance of new roads the distillery business grew as distribution broadened into the surrounding counties. In the following years, the distillery was moved twice, first to take advantage of an abundance of spring water and again to be closer to the railroad lines. The company's distillery is located on 430 acres in Clermont, 30 miles south of Louisville. Booker Noe, grandson of Jim Beam, is the Master Distiller at Clermont.

Beyond the company's portfolio of bourbons, its other main brands include Gilbey's Gin, Canadian Supreme Whisky, Lord Calvert Canadian Blended Whisky, Kamchatka Vodka, and DeKuyper, the top selling cordial line in the United States. Jim Beam Brands Company operates its sales office and corporate headquarters in Deerfield, Illinois.

AMERICA AND THE WORLD

For 1992, the value of total U.S. alcoholic beverages exports (beer, wine, and liquor) reached nearly $800 million, almost 22 percent more than 1991. The value of distilled spirits exported rose an estimated 30 percent to $422 million, which represented 48.7 million gallons. Whiskey was the biggest seller, with nearly 33 percent share of the volume.

"International expansion represents a great opportunity for distillers. Leading spirit brands already enjoy worldwide cachet, especially within the whiskey and cognac categories," reported Jim Barrett in the *Value Line Investment Survey.* Export opportunities can be found in the fast-growing markets of the Asia Pacific region, Latin America, and the former Soviet Bloc. "Not only are these expanding markets, but the growth is generally occurring among higher-margin, deluxe brands. What's more, trade barriers have recently been lifted in a number of countries, such as India and Taiwan," added Barrett.

The Asia Pacific area has included some of the largest whiskey markets in world, with Japan at the top of the U.S. export list. The rapid ascent of a middle class in these countries bodes well for the future of beverage alcohol marketers. "Export is the hot spot," Barry M. Berish, president of Jim Beam Brands Co., noted in *Business Week.* From 1985 to 1990, total exports of Kentucky bourbon and Tennessee whiskey tripled to an estimated 11 million 100-proof gallons.

Growth for exports in Japanese markets is slowing, however. Japanese consumption rates have fallen, due to the country's weak economy and Japanese companies' decrease in expense accounts and entertainment budgets. Despite its continued success, bourbon's growth in Japan dropped in 1990, from 50 percent a year to the low teens. Most alcohol consumption in Japan has been on-premise, either in bars or restaurants. Of the 3,000 or so nightclubs in Tokyo's Ginza district, only ten have remained profitable, according to the *Economist.* To combat falling on-premise consumption rates, beverage alcohol marketers have begun to promote their wares as a beverage to be enjoyed at home.

Beverage alcohol marketers are beginning to focus on growth in other countries. After successful penetration of the Japanese market, whiskey advertising can be found in Australia, Britain, and other affluent markets. Latin America, for example, has become the second greatest growth opportunity, particularly for premium-priced scotch marketers like Seagram. Sales of scotch grew over 50 percent in 1991 in Venezuela, with much of the growth occurring among higher-priced brands, such as Chivas Regal Scotch. Scotch whisky has remained the most popular beverage in the world and has been sold in 190 countries.

Although U.S. consumption of imported beverages has fallen since the start of the 1990s, the U.S. market has continued to consume Canadian whiskey, scotch, and tequila. Brandy and cognac shipments have been one of the smallest volume import segments, but in dollar value they ranked third in 1992. The top six importers of beverages have been Canada, the United Kingdom, Mexico, France, Sweden, and Ireland.

INDUSTRY INFORMATION SOURCES

Brandes, Richard, "Beverage Trends: The Shape of Drinks to Come," *Beverage Dynamics,* May 1993.

Hood, Donna Jean, "The Value of Vodka," *Beverage Dynamics,* March 1992.

Jim Beam Brands Co. publicity materials, Deerfield, IL: Jim Beam.

Levin, Gary, "Liquor Sales Go Dry," *Advertising Age,* February 10, 1992.

Power, Christopher, "Sweet Sales for Sour Mash—Abroad," *Business Week,* July 1, 1991.

Prince, Greg W., and Eric Sfiligoj, "The Beverage Market Index for 1993," *Beverage World,* May 1993.

Riell, Howard, "Margarita Mania," *Beverage Dynamics,* April 1993.

"Thirst of the Lonely," *The Economist,* April 10, 1993.

"Top Selling Liquor Brands," *Advertising Age,* February 15, 1993.

Tougas, Jane Grant, "Scotch: Spirit of Tradition," *Beverage Dynamics,* May 1993.

U.S. Industrial Outlook 1994, Washington, DC: U.S. Department of Commerce, 1994.

Ursin, Cheryl, "Mixing It Up," *Beverage Dynamics,* July/August 1993.

Warner, Fara, ''Beam's Hot Shots,'' *Brandweek,* April 26, 1993.

—Catherine A. Quagliana

SIC 2086

BOTTLED AND CANNED SOFT DRINKS AND CARBONATED WATERS

This category includes establishments primarily engaged in manufacturing soft drinks and carbonated waters. Establishments primarily engaged in manufacturing fruit and vegetable juices are classified in various canned, frozen, and preserved food classifications. Those manufacturing fruit syrups for flavoring are classified in **SIC 2087: Flavoring Extracts and Flavoring Syrups, Not Elsewhere Classified;** those manufacturing nonalcoholic cider are classified in **SIC 2099: Food Preparations, Not Elsewhere Classified.** Establishments primarily engaged in bottling natural water are classified in **SIC 5149: Groceries and Related Products, Not Elsewhere Classified.**

INDUSTRY SNAPSHOT

The average American consumes more soft drinks than water, quaffing 49 gallons, or 296 eight-ounce servings, each year. The soft drink industry (excluding bottled water and fruit juices and drinks) generated $48.9 billion dollars in retail sales in 1992 and dominated total beverage consumption in the United States with 51.3 percent. Beer came in second place with 24.0 percent, fruit juices and drinks at 12.5 percent, bottled water at 8.7 percent, wine with 2.0 percent, and spirits at 1.5 percent.

Soft drinks have become intrinsically tied to the ''American way of life,'' and the leading soft drink, Coca-Cola, is a virtual icon of American culture. Close to 300 soft drinks manufacturers and bottling companies operate in the United States. Two companies, Coca-Cola and Pepsi-Cola, control nearly three-quarters of the U.S. market, with each company producing four of the top ten best-selling brands. Coca-Cola Classic continues to be the best selling brand in the United States and around the world, controlling nearly 20 percent of the domestic market and 46 percent of the worldwide market.

Some industry leaders have contended that the U.S. soft drink market has begun a slow, steady decline, citing its failure to post double-digit growth since the end of the 1980s. Pointing to an aging U.S. population and changing consumer tastes, industry an-

alysts have predicted that per capita consumption and the total consumption rate will not increase significantly in the near future. To combat a weak U.S. market, soft drink manufacturers have aggressively pursued overseas markets. Although no other country has a soft drink consumption rate as high as the United States, many areas have been targeted as potential for expansion, especially the underdeveloped and highly populated areas of China and India. The Coca-Cola Company has been the clear leader in overseas expansion with nearly 75 percent of its operating profits coming from areas outside the United States.

ORGANIZATION AND STRUCTURE

Soft drink companies manufacture and sell beverage syrups and bases to bottling operations, which add sweeteners and/or carbonated water to produce the final product. Independent bottlers work under contract with various soft drink manufacturers and are allotted specific territories to serve. The manufacturers provide the bottlers with syrups and bases, but also with a variety of business services, including product quality control, marketing, advertising, engineering, and financial and personnel training. In turn, the bottlers supply the required capital investment for land, buildings, machinery, equipment, trucks, bottles and cases.

During the past few years, the number of independent bottlers has declined as the major soft drink manufacturers have consolidated their bottling operations by acquiring independent companies and combining them into one large operation. Both Coke and Pepsi have such arrangements. Coca-Cola Enterprises (CCE) has become the world's largest soft drink bottler; their production accounted for 55 percent of all the bottled and canned Coke products sold in the United States. The company operates in 37 states, Washington, D.C. and the U.S. Virgin Islands. Meanwhile, Pepsi's company-owned bottling operations have been responsible for 52 percent of its bottling volume. Both companies have promoted the purchase of franchised bottling operations as a way of preparing for long-term strategic growth, domestically and internationally. As the economies of various countries have become more sophisticated and complex, so must soft drink manufacturers in their ability to produce, distribute and market their products.

The soft drink industry sells its product in two forms, packaged and fountain service. The packaged form of cans and bottles represented 75 percent of the total soft drink market, with 9.3 billion gallons sold in 1992. With fountain service, the soft drink product is dispensed and served in cups, typically in a restaurant or any location with a foodservice station. Fountain service volume increased 2.3 percent in 1992, reaching nearly 3.1 billion gallons or 25 percent of the market share.

Background and Development

The soft drink industry began in the mid-1880s, with the creation of a syrup that was mixed with carbonated water and served at drug store lunch counters. During the early years, soft drinks were sold only in stores that could provide fountain service. Increasing distribution was tied to building additional syrup manufacturing plants.

With the advent of bottling machinery, soft drinks began to be distributed beyond the town drug store. The first merchant to bottle Coca-Cola was Joseph A. Biedenharn of Vicksberg, Mississippi, who installed a bottling machine in his candy store in 1894. The development of large-scale bottling assisted the proliferation of Coca-Cola and by 1895 the drink was sold in nearly every part of the United States. An infrastructure of independent bottlers working under contract with Coca-Cola, producing the drink to exact specifications, and distributing it within a specific region soon became the model distribution method for Coke and was emulated by others.

The 1960s and 1970s brought acquisitions and diversification for Coca-Cola and Pepsi-Cola. In 1960, Coke purchased Minute Maid and later acquired Duncan Foods. The Coca-Cola Company Foods Division was created in 1967, and later renamed Coca-Cola Foods. Meanwhile, Pepsi-Cola merged with Frito-Lay in 1965, changing its name to PepsiCo but maintaining its beverage division under the name Pepsi-Cola. PepsiCo soon ventured into food service and snack foods with the acquisition of Pizza Hut, Taco Bell and Kentucky Fried Chicken restaurants.

During the 1980s, as consumers became more interested in health and fitness, the soft drink industry faced stiff competition from the makers of bottled water. In response, soft drink manufacturers developed low-calorie and caffeine-free beverages, such as Diet Coke and Diet Pepsi. The start of the 1990s ushered in a new kind of competition focussed on ''New Age'' beverages like ready-to-drink teas, fruit juice beverages, and flavored waters. Gatorade, the perennial leader among sports drinks, saw new competitors in the 1990s.

Current Conditions

From the simple beginnings of one cola, the soft drink industry has exploded into a kaleidoscope of traditional sodas, natural sodas, fruit juice drinks and various kinds of bottled water. Coca-Cola Classic was the best selling soft drink in the U.S. in 1992. Coke Classic controlled 19.3 percent of the soft drink market and posted a sales increase of 1.5 percent for the year. Pepsi-Cola was the second best-selling soft drink for the year, with 16.1 percent market share, down 0.8 percent over 1991. Diet Coke, Diet Pepsi and Dr Pepper completed the list of the top five soft drink brands for 1992.

The traditional cola producers were caught off-guard by the rise of generic store brands during the early 1990s, as the recession drove consumers to experiment with these lower-priced drinks. These colas are not expected to create a significant amount of brand loyalty, however, and therefore have not appeared as a substantial threat to the major soft drink manufacturers.

Despite their market dominance, traditional cola products have continued to lose market share. Total soft drink consumption grew roughly five percent annually between 1983 and 1989, but slowed to 3 percent

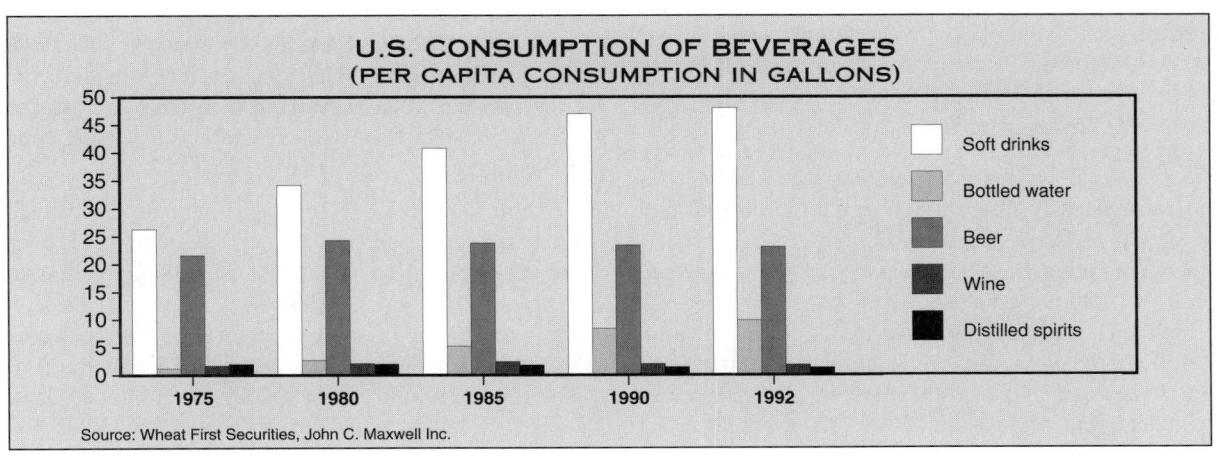

U.S. CONSUMPTION OF BEVERAGES
(PER CAPITA CONSUMPTION IN GALLONS)

Soft drinks
Bottled water
Beer
Wine
Distilled spirits

Source: Wheat First Securities, John C. Maxwell Inc.

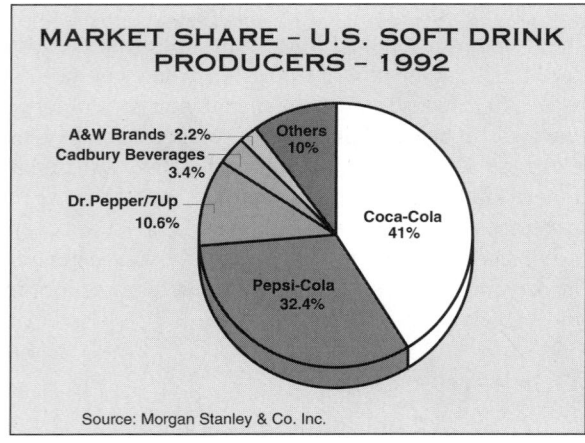

MARKET SHARE – U.S. SOFT DRINK
PRODUCERS – 1992

A&W Brands 2.2%
Cadbury Beverages
3.4%
Dr.Pepper/7Up
10.6%

Others
10%

Coca-Cola
41%

Pepsi-Cola
32.4%

Source: Morgan Stanley & Co. Inc.

in 1990 and only 1.6 percent by 1991. Even the diet cola market has faltered since 1990, losing ground to new drinks commonly called "New Age" beverages. In a category that had enjoyed a 10-20 percent growth rate during the 1980s, sales growth for diet colas was cut to approximately three percent a year. Industry analysts suggest that new drinks, including sodas and bottled water, are the most formidable opponents to traditional colas. This market segment began with the rise of the bottled water industry in the United States and has expanded into the creation of the "New Age" category.

Strongest during the 1980s, bottled water has remained a vibrant and growing segment of the beverage market into the 1990s. This industry can be divided into two segments, bulk water and refreshment beverages. Bulk water is nonsparkling water that is consumed instead of tap water, and has represented about 80 percent of the market. Refreshment beverages have ranged from still water such as Evian to flavored, vitamin-enriched sparkling mineral water from Crystal Geyser. While bulk water usually is bought through a delivery service and in five-gallon containers or larger, refreshment beverages are premium, image-driven brands, prepared in smaller containers, and are sold for both on- and off-premise consumption. These products compete directly with sodas and mixers.

Since 1980, the U.S. bottled water market has grown to nearly three billion gallons in annual consumption. After a decade of double-digit growth, the market faltered in 1991, showing only a 0.5 percent gain in volume. Analysts blamed the recession and concern over safety, prompted by the Perrier recall in 1990, for the downturn. The industry began to rebound in 1992 with a 3.7 percent increase in volume and a 3.2 percent increase in sales. By 1993, more than 700 brands of bottled water were produced in the United

States at 430 bottling facilities. Another 75 brands of water were imported.

The Perrier Group has been the largest bottled water company in the United States. Acquired in 1992 by Nestle, the Perrier Group includes a collection of strong regional domestic waters plus its flagship brand. The second largest bottled water company in the United States has been McKesson Water Products, with most of its business centered around home and office delivery. More than 80 percent of the company's sales have been in California with its Sparkletts brand. In a recent survey by Business Trends Analysts, consumers reported the most important reasons for drinking bottled water were health concerns and taste. "The more Americans learn about water the more they will drink it much the same way that Europeans do," Evian marketing director Ed Slade told *Beverage Dynamics.*

Beyond bottled water, an entirely new market segment has appeared, answering Americans' call for flavored drinks that are lighter, less filling, less sweet, "healthier" and more sophisticated than traditional sodas. The "New Age" beverages have covered everything from flavored sparkling waters to natural sodas to fruit juice drinks to flavored teas and bottled coffee products. A beverage fits in the New Age category if it is "relatively new to the market, considered by the consumer as 'good for me' and containing natural and/or healthy ingredients without preservatives," industry analyst Michael Bellas told *Beverage World.*

The all-natural soda division has been the most active New Age segment. Although sales slumped in 1990, "all-natural sodas stormed back to reach $309.8 million in sales in 1991, up a whopping 51 percent," reported Eric Sfiligoj in *Beverage World.* Consumption of all-natural sodas reached 81.3 million gallons annually by 1991, second in the category only to flavored waters. The healthy growth of all-natural sodas has been in direct response to the success of Vancouver-based Clearly Canadian. Launched in 1987, Clearly Canadian is Canadian water pumped from deep artesian wells and mixed with fruit flavors. The product is sweetened with fructose and does contain preservatives.

Sales of New Age beverages have been projected to grow at eight percent annually through 1995, with growth rates hitting 11 percent by 1996, according to *Beverage Dynamics.* With projections such as these, it was only a matter of time before the national cola brands added their own products to the plethora of New Age drinks. In early 1992, Pepsi introduced Crystal Pepsi, a clear, cola-flavored beverage that is 100 percent naturally flavored and contains no preservatives or caffeine. During its first year of national distribution in 1993, Crystal Pepsi captured more than two percent of the soft drink market or roughly $1 billion in sales.

Coca-Cola also launched its New Age soda, Nordic Mist, in 1992. The Coke product is a mixture of sparkling water, high fructose corn syrup, citric acid, potassium, and one of five natural fruit flavors. "New Age isn't our bread and butter," said Bob Bertini of Coca-Cola USA in *Beverage Dynamics,* "but it deserves a place at the table. We want to be fully represented in every category that makes sense for us. We're trying to respond to changes in the market, but our priority is still colas and traditional soft drinks."

In the face of rising competition from all fronts of the beverage market, both Coke and Pepsi have turned to joint ventures with other beverage companies. Pepsi-Cola has been working with Ocean Spray to provide all of their ready-to-drink beverages, including Ocean Spray Splash, a five-flavor line of fruit sparklers, and Ocean Spray Lemonade. In this alliance, Pepsi has become the exclusive distributor of all new Ocean Spray single-serve products.

In a joint venture with Nestle, Coca-Cola created the Coca-Cola Nestle Refreshment Company (CCNR) in 1991 to market ready-to-drink coffee, tea and chocolate beverages. Nestea Iced Tea, CCNR's first project, was introduced in the United States in March 1992. The bottled tea has no preservatives, artificial flavors or colors, and comes in regular and diet version.

Both cola manufacturers have also been test marketing sports drinks, such as All Sport by Pepsi and PowerAde by Coke. Sports drinks replenish fluids, minerals and energy lost during exercise, and the market for these drinks has grown into a billion-dollar retail segment. Gatorade has accounted for nearly 90 percent of nationwide sales, and will be the one brand for both Coke and Pepsi to beat. "Gatorade defines the category," says Jesse Meyers, publisher of *Beverage Digest,* in *Time.* "There is not a beverage category in any country in the world that is so dominated by one producer."

The movement of major players like Coke and Pepsi into nontraditional beverage markets has shown the affect of changing consumer preferences. Should the New Age category remain as a firmly established and viable drink alternative, these two manufacturers are likely to increase their domestic rivalry, possibly to the detriment of the smaller firms in the marketplace. Moreover, both Coca-Cola and Pepsi-Cola have set their sites on a much larger piece of the beverage market pie, overseas expansion. With improving distribution systems, these two giants have been preparing for what they do best, promoting worldwide consumption of their well-known and well-loved products.

INDUSTRY LEADERS

Coca-Cola has been the world's most popular soft drink, holding as high as 46 percent global market share. Using a franchise system for distribution, the company and its subsidiaries have sold the flagship brand and the other brands in the Sprite, Tab, and Diet Coke families in more than 195 countries and territories.

Coca-Cola originated in Atlanta, Georgia, on May 8, 1886, when pharmacist Dr. John Styth Pemberton created a caramel-colored syrup in his backyard. He took a jug of the syrup to Jacob's Pharmacy in Atlanta where the product debuted as a soda fountain drink for five cents a glass. Thinking that two C's would look good in advertising, Dr. Pemberton's partner and bookkeeper Frank M. Robinson suggested the name Coca-Cola and designed the now-famous script trademark. Dr. Pemberton, in poor health and in need of funds, soon sold portions of his company. Asa G. Candler, a druggist and Atlanta businessman, acquired complete control of the company for $2,300 in 1891.

In 1892, Candler, along with his brother John S. Candler and two other associates, formed "The Coca-Cola Company." In 1894, the first syrup manufacturing plant outside of Atlanta was opened in Dallas, Texas. The following year, two more were opened in Chicago and Los Angeles. By 1895, Coca-Cola was available in every state in the United States. Large-scale bottling began in 1899, when Benjamin F. Thomas and Joseph B. Whitehead of Chattanooga, Tennessee, obtained the exclusive rights to bottle and sell Coca-Cola. With the financial assistance of John T. Lupton, these men developed a regional franchise bottling system, engaging over 1,000 bottlers in 20 years.

In 1919, The Coca-Cola Company was sold to Atlanta banker Ernest Woodruff for $25 million. Ernest's son Robert was elected president of The Coca-Cola Company in 1923, when the business was reincorporated in Delaware and 500,000 shares of common stock were sold publicly for $40 per share. The new president led the company for six decades.

Coca-Cola's diversification into the food industry began with the purchase of Minute Maid Corporation in 1960, and the Minute Maid and Hi-C trademarks joined Coke's family of beverages. The company acquired Duncan Foods and formed The Coca-Cola Company and formed The Coca-Cola Company Foods Division in 1967, now known as Coca-Cola Foods. In 1986, the company consolidated its U.S. bottling operations, creating Coca-Cola Enterprises (CCE), 51 percent of which was sold to the public.

To sell its products throughout the world, The Coca-Cola Company has divided its operations into two sectors, the North America Soft Drink Business Sector and the International Soft Drink Business Sector. The North American division covers Coca-Cola USA, which operates in the United States, and Coca-Cola, Ltd., which operates in Canada. The International division has been divided into five operating units: EC Group, Northeast Europe/Middle East Group, Latin America Group, Pacific Group and the Africa Group. The Coca-Cola Company employs over 31,300 people.

Pepsi-Cola is the beverage division of PepsiCo, Inc., a worldwide consumer products company. The Pepsi brand, in addition to Diet Pepsi, Slice, Mountain Dew, Mug Root Beer and the new Crystal Pepsi, have accounted for as much as one-third of the soft drink market in the United States. Pepsi, a leading soft drink with nearly $17 billion in worldwide retail sales, was first created in 1898. Caleb D. Bradham, a druggist in New Bern, North Carolina, invented the drink and named it Pepsi-Cola, claiming that it cured dyspepsia or indigestion. Various owners operated the Pepsi-Cola Company from 1923 through 1963. Under the direction of Donald M. Kendall, who became company president in 1963, Pepsi acquired Frito-Lay, the largest snack chip company in the United States, and became PepsiCo, Inc. Additional acquisitions have included Pizza Hut (1977), Taco Bell (1978), and Kentucky Fried Chicken (1986).

Pepsi-Cola North America manufactures and sells soft drink concentrate to company-owned and independent franchised bottlers operating facilities throughout the United States and Canada. The company also provides fountain beverage syrups to restaurants, including the 18,000 kitchens at Taco Bell, KFC (formerly Kentucky Fried Chicken), and Pizza Hut. Pepsi-Cola International (PCI) controls the company's international soft drink operations. Through this division, Pepsi-Cola products are sold in 155 countries and territories throughout the world. PCI produces nearly 18 percent of all soft drinks sold internationally, including the business of Seven-Up International. World headquarters for PepsiCo, Inc. are located in Purchase, New York, and the company employs 370,000 people.

Dr Pepper/Seven-Up Companies, Inc. is the third largest soft drink manufacturer in the U.S. with an 11 percent market share. Dr Pepper and Seven-Up manufacture and market syrup to more than 750 licensed bottlers, and its products have been served in more than 100,000 foodservice outlets in the United States. Dr Pepper has remained the nation's fifth largest selling soft drink, behind the regular and diet versions of Coke and Pepsi. In addition to the family of Dr Pepper and Seven-Up brands, the company also sells IBC brand sodas and Welch's soft drinks.

The Dr Pepper Company was publicly traded on the NYSE from 1946 until February 1984, when it was taken private in a leveraged buyout. In November 1986, the company was sold to an owner equity group that included members of the management team and other investors. Later that year, the company management arranged a separate owner equity group to buy the domestic operations of The Seven-Up Company, then owned by Philip Morris, Inc.

The Dr Pepper brand was first sold at Morrison's Old Corner Drug Store in Waco, Texas in 1885. Created by pharmacist Charles Alderton and sold by store owner Wade Morrison, the new drink was named after one of Morrison's friends from Virginia. A bottler in Waco, Robert Lazenby, began producing the syrup and bottling the drink and soon formed a company with Morrison. In 1923, they moved the headquarters to Dallas, and in 1924 named their business the "Dr Pepper Company."

The Seven-Up Company began in 1929, when C. L. Grigg, owner of The Howdy Company in St. Louis, introduced his lemon-lime drink. In 1936, the company name was changed to The Seven-Up Company, in recognition of its popular drink. The company went public in 1967 and was bought by Philip Morris in 1978.

In August 1993, Cadbury Schweppes PLC, a British candy and soft drink maker, purchased 12.2 million Dr Pepper shares for $231.3 million, increasing its stake in the company to nearly 26 percent. Cadbury officials described the stock purchase as an excellent investment opportunity. However, industry analysts have speculated that Cadbury's increased ownership could help Dr Pepper expand into international markets. Cadbury sells its candy and soft drink products in 170 countries and posted $5 billion in worldwide sales in 1992.

The Dr Pepper/Seven-Up Companies operates one of the industry's most modern manufacturing plants near St. Louis, Missouri, which produces all of the company's concentrates, extracts and syrups. The plant also makes most of Cadbury's concentrate sold in North America. Dr Pepper/Seven-Up Companies' administrative headquarters is located in Dallas. Operating divisions are Dr Pepper USA, Seven-Up USA, Premier Beverages, Dr Pepper/Seven-Up Foodservice, and International. The company employs approximately 930 workers. President, chairman and CEO is John R. Albert.

WORK FORCE

According to *Ward's Business Directory of Public and Private Companies,* 292 soft drink manufacturers and bottling companies operate in the United States, employing approximately 207,300 workers. According to the U.S. Department of Labor, overall employment in food processing (which includes beverages) has been projected to decline six percent by the year 2005. Like other manufacturing industries, food processing has become less labor intensive, and occupational projections have reflected this predicted decline. According to *Manufacturing USA,* by the year 2000 employment for packaging and filling machine operations will drop 26.9 percent, industrial truck and tractor operators 23.4 percent, freight stock and materials movers (by hand) 23.8 percent, and hand packers and packagers 32.3 percent. Professional specialty occupations such as engineers and computer scientists have been expected to grow, which reflects the industry's continued emphasis on scientific research to improve food products and production processes. However, these jobs have comprised a very small proportion of industry employment.

AMERICA AND THE WORLD

Soft drinks have been produced or consumed in nearly every corner of the world. Growing consumption trends can be attributed to rising disposable incomes, falling trade barriers, universal product acceptance, and a rising demand for American consumer goods. Both Pepsi-Cola and Coca-Cola have company-owned franchised bottling plants in more than 120 countries that produce their respective brands within each country rather than exporting them from the United States.

Beverages that are exported from the United States include unsweetened bottled water, but these figures have remained relatively low as the worldwide market for bottled water has been dominated by a few well-established European producers. However, United States producers of sweetened water or New Age beverages have fared better in the export market. The international beverage market has seen the dominance and continued development of Coke and Pepsi in all parts of the world. These companies have taken their rivalry overseas and have been spending

millions to develop new markets for their products. One market that Pepsi-Cola has dominated has been Russia, controlling twice the market share of Coke. Establishing its presence in Russia during the Nixon administration, Pepsi gained entry into the country through a barter deal involving the exportation of vodka. By 1993, Pepsi-Cola controlled four percent of the market compared to Coke's two percent. The obvious market growth potential has made this former Soviet state a prime target for an American invasion of the cola wars.

In April 1993, Coke announced the construction of a $15 million production plant and training facility near Moscow. These facilities will serve the kiosks that have been installed in various Russian communities. Coca-Cola owns these kiosks, which are shaped like giant Coke cans, and rents them to a wholesaler, who in turns employs local citizens to operate the small soda stands. The acceptance of Russian rubles instead of American dollars differentiates this enterprise from the other American operations in Russia. "The idea," reported Laurie Hays in the *Wall Street Journal,* "is that such transactions will help the economy firm up and ultimately put more money into the pockets of citizens—more money they can use to buy Coke."

In August 1993, PepsiCo announced its plans to invest $500 million in Poland over the next five years, with $200 million expressly for the development of a Pepsi market among the country's 38 million consumers. This investment was the third such announcement made by Pepsi. The company previously revealed a $115 million, five-year investment plan for Hungary and a $750 million plan for Mexico.

With per-capita consumption second only to the United States, Mexico has been set up as another major battleground for the cola wars. The largest Pepsi bottler outside of the United States has been Grupo Embotellador de Mexico SA, or Gemex, located in Mexico City. Meanwhile, Fomento Economico Mexicano SA, or Femsa, owns the largest Coke franchise in the world and is located in Monterrey. Needless to say, Pepsi has dominated Mexico City while Coke has covered the southern Mexico market. With the assistance of market reforms enacted by Mexico's President Carlos Salinas de Gortari, both Coke and Pepsi have been working to compete in each other's established territories.

In the United States, imported unsweetened bottled waters, both still and carbonated, have continued to dominate their segment of the U.S. water and soft drink market. In 1991, France was responsible for 60 percent of unsweetened water imports and 34 percent of all water and soft drink imports. Canada had 24 percent of the unsweetened water imports, mainly with Clearly Canadian, and 42 percent of carbonated soft drinks. Due to the cost of shipping and distribution, imported products generally have been more expensive than domestically produced drinks and can be found at the luxury end of the U.S. market.

RESEARCH AND TECHNOLOGY

Advances in computer technology and automation have improved all aspects of the soft drink manufacturing industry from inventory control to ''smart'' vending machines. Those companies with computerized operations have found both increased profitability and improved product quality. One example of a computerized system is a plant-wide automated measurement system used in some syrup manufacturing plants. Working with a personal computer, the automated system can measure nearly every important segment of beverage production, including syrup usage, Brix count (per cent sugar) and beverage carbonation. Other system checks include monitoring the purification system for failures, and checking the warehouse temperature for the precise dew point. ''By keeping much closer control on all critical process variables, we [Abex Beverage Corporation] have been able over time to significantly improve yields, while also increasing the quality and consistency of our product,'' reported Randy Mostert, Abtex production manager, in *Beverage World.*

Another technological advancement can be found on the user-end of the soft drink industry with the ''smart'' vending machines. These products use computerized components that keep track of stock supplies, sales patterns, breakdowns, and other conditions. ''Bottlers are looking for ways to increase revenues and reduce their costs,'' Bill Astin, senior VP/sales and marketing at the Vendo Co., told *Beverage Industry.* ''This improved technology allows them to do just that.''

General Programming Inc. has introduced a wireless communications package called Vending Manager. This program allows vending machines to place orders as they are required, rather than have someone manually check the stock level. ''Loss of sales from a stock-out situation or out-of order situations will be eliminated, as machines will immediately notify the dispatcher of their status,'' said H.O. Bransom, president of General Programming Inc., in *Beverage Industry.*

Claiming that it could be the wave of the future, Coca-Cola USA already has begun to test market their own version of the smart vending machine called the Generation II, manufactured by Royal Vendors. ''With the GII, it [collecting data] is as simple as plugging a hand-held computer into the vendor controller, or keying the LED readout to deliver the information for the route person . . . ,'' said Ray Steeley, president of Royal Vendors, in *Beverage Industry.*

The final outcome of computerized operations eventually will be the paperless warehouse, where computers, robotics and electronic information transmission will control all operations. ''Computer control gives instant information on the whereabouts of any material within the system,'' said Jim Larsen, VP of Eaton-Kenway, the company that installed a real-time management system (along with Operations Management Inc.) in Coca-Cola Enterprises Market Service Center in Cincinnati, Ohio in 1991. ''Those who use a real-time communications system in the warehouse also report better inventory control, faster truck check-in and check-out, better stock rotation in the distribution center and elimination of truck load errors,'' added Norand Corporation executive Tom Miller in *Beverage Industry.*

INDUSTRY INFORMATION SOURCES

''Beverages—Pepsi (Fact Sheet).'' Somers, NY: PepsiCo, Inc., 1993.

''The Coca-Cola Company: A Brief Profile of a Worldwide Business.'' Atlanta: The Coca-Cola Company, 1993.

''The Coca-Cola Company Annual Report.'' Atlanta: The Coca-Cola Company, 1993.

''Crystal Pepsi to Roll in North America.'' Somers, NY: Pepsi-Cola Company, 8 December 1992.

''Dr Pepper/Seven Up Companies, Inc. Annual Report,'' Dallas: Dr Pepper/Seven Up Companies, 1992.

''Dr Pepper/Seven-Up Companies, Inc. Goes Public.'' *Clockdial*, Spring 1993.

Flaherty, Francis. ''Pepsi's $500 Million for Poland.'' *New York Times*, 15 August 1993.

Guyette, James E. ''Vending Smart, Bottlers Can Profit from High-Tech Breakthroughs.'' *Beverage Industry*, January 1993.

Hays, Laurie. ''Building a Market: Amid Russian Turmoil, Coca-Cola Is Placing a Bet on the Future.'' *Wall Street Journal*, April 6, 1993.

Jaroff, Leon. ''A Thirst for Competition.'' *Time*, June 1, 1992.

Moffett, Matt. ''A Mexican War Heats Up for Cola Giants.'' *Wall Street Journal*, April 20, 1993.

Mostert, Randy. ''Not by the Manual.'' *Beverage World*, October 1992.

''Nestea Ice Tea Launched.'' *Beverage Dynamics*, March 1992.

Oman, Bruce. "From the Bottom Up." *Beverage World,* January 1993.

"PepsiCo, An Overview." Somer, NY: PepsiCo, Inc., 1993.

Prince, Greg W., and Eric Sfiligoj. "The Beverage Market Index for 1993." *Beverage World,* May 1993.

———. "A League of Their Own," *Beverage World,* March 1993.

Sanborn, Stephen. "Soft Drink Industry." *Value Line Investment Survey,* August 20, 1993.

Sfiligoj, Eric. "Alive and Fizzing." *Beverage World,* August 1992.

———. "Is Gatorade a Sleeping Giant?" *Beverage World,* August 1992.

Standard & Poor's Industry Surveys 1993, New York: Standard & Poor's, 1993.

Tougas, Jane Grant. "Coke and Pepsi Go New Age." *Beverage Dynamics,* July/August 1993.

Tougas, Jane Grant. "Go With The Flow," *Beverage Dynamics,* June 1993.

———. "New Age Beverages Go Mainstream." *Beverage Dynamics,* July/August 1993.

U.S. Department of Commerce. *U.S. Industrial Outlook 1993.* Washington, DC: U.S. Department of Commerce, 1993.

Ursin, Cheryl. "Water, Water, Everywhere." *Beverage Dynamics,* March 1992.

Walker, Tracey L. "Warehousing . . . A Paperless Trek Through Time and Space." *Beverage Industry,* July 1992.

Zimmerman, Martin. "Cadbury Raises Dr Pepper Stake." *Dallas Morning News,* August 21, 1993.

—Catherine A. Quagliana

SIC 2087

FLAVORING EXTRACTS AND FLAVORING SYRUPS, NOT ELSEWHERE CLASSIFIED

This category includes establishments primarily engaged in manufacturing flavoring extracts, syrups, powders, and related products, not elsewhere classified. The products are generally used at soda fountains or during the manufacture of soft drinks, as well as adding color to baked products and confectioneries. Establishments primarily engaged in manufacturing chocolate syrup are classified in **SIC 2066: Chocolate and Cocoa Products.**

INDUSTRY SNAPSHOT

While most foods have some flavor, certain food agents can enhance foods. These products encompass a wide range of materials that can be used as a singular flavor or mixed into a blend. Substances used for flavoring "are those predominately purchased for flavoring contributions rather than functional characteristics," Kraft Food Ingredients marketing director Russ Williams told *Food Product Design.* Little formal classification for flavors exist, except broad categories like natural and artificial.

"As a group, flavors and enhancers are the fasting growing sector of the food additives industry," Dr. Charles Forman told *Chemical Marketing Reporter.* The $675 million industry should see annual growth of 6.2 percent until 1996. The development of new food products and new technology that makes foods faster or at lower costs has spurred the creation of new flavors for these products.

Approximately 100 companies produce flavors in the United States. Of these, about 11 have accounted for almost two-thirds of the flavor industry's sales to beverage and food processors. New York-based International Flavors & Fragrances has been the flavor industry leader in the United States and throughout the world.

The beverage industry has been the largest end-user of flavoring materials, claiming roughly 25 percent of the total flavor production, Arthur D. Little vice-president Nancy Smith told *Chemical Marketing Reporter.* Dairy products followed with 18 percent of the overall market, baked goods at 15 percent, and snacks and processed foods at 12 percent. Demand for new types of products continues to drive the industry's growth in the beverage industry. Due to the "greying" of North America, an increased interest in diet and health has prompted consumer demand for healthier beverages, including the usage of natural flavors. "Natural flavors and enhancers are enjoying the greatest growth, even though they are neither as strong or dependable as most synthetics," Forman told *Chemical Marketing Reporter.* "In fact, the natural to synthetic ratio has reached upwards of 75 percent natural, while only a decade ago this figure was reversed."

Colorants have continued to be one of the smallest segments of the food additives industry. With $245 million in annual sales in 1991, the segment has been projected to reach $268 million annually by 1996. The natural colorants, mainly caramel color used in cola drinks, have dominated the industry with $155 million in sales annually. Synthetic colorants also have been used largely by the beverage industry, followed by usage in pet food, confections and gums, and dry mixes. Financial concerns have led the colorant industry into major consolidations, leaving four major suppliers in the United States: Warner-Jenkinson, Colorcon, Hilton-Davis, and Compton & Knowles.

ORGANIZATION AND STRUCTURE

Flavoring manufacturers, sometimes called "flavor houses," create extracts, syrups, powders, and other forms of flavoring materials. These manufacturers work with natural base ingredients purchased from suppliers throughout the world. The manufacturers' dependence on natural sources leaves the flavor chemicals open to price fluctuation due to the availability and cost of the raw materials. Once processed, flavoring ingredients are sold to soft drink companies and other makers of processed foods.

Flavor manufacturers and food producers increasingly have worked together in research and development to create new food products. Flavor producers provide technical support on flavor issues, especially with the beverage industry. Flavor houses also custom tailor flavors, relying heavily on work in application laboratories. "Each flavor is so application-specific that flavor companies and product developers must work closely together with flavor chemists to make it work," Marcia Sprague, vice-president of Merlin Development, told *Prepared Foods.*

Although the starting materials must be of natural origin, all flavoring materials are processed in some manner. The distillation process uses hot water or steam to extract the aromatic materials from the flavoring materials. The quality of the flavor depends on the raw materials and the process. The product derived from this process is called a volatile or essential oil.

Extraction is used to obtain characteristic flavoring attributes provided by non-volatiles. Organic solvents are used to dissolve volatile and nonvolatile compounds from the natural starting material. After removing the solvent, usually with a high vacuum process, the flavoring compounds remain. An extracted flavor often is fractionated into many parts and only certain ones are selected for the final flavor.

Extraction and distillation have remained important methods for obtaining natural flavor components. Types of extracted/distilled flavor components have been essential oils, aromatic fractions of the plant, oleoresins (which are extracts without volatiles), standardized oleoresins (added with extra essential oils), and concentrated oils (which are essential oils fractionated to a specific degree of concentration).

The flavoring industry has worked closely with the Food and Drug Administration (FDA), primarily through the efforts of industry trade association Flavor Extract Manufacturers Association (FEMA). FEMA has been participating in the development of the Nutritional Labeling and Education Act of 1990. This legislation has mandated that producers detail the ingredients used in their processed food formulations. The Act was implemented in May 1993.

During the process of defining this legislation, FEMA made various arguments to exempt the flavoring industry from this legislation. First, FEMA argued that flavors shipped in bulk form to other companies should not be covered by the legislation because the purpose of the nutritional labeling is to provide the consumers, not the manufacturers, with information. FEMA based part of their argument on the FDA's regulation that defines flavors as those materials "whose significant function in food is flavoring rather than nutritional." The FDA also asked for opinions regarding if a rule should be enacted prohibiting companies from representing a food as "natural" if it contained any artificial ingredients or if it was more than "nominally processed." In reply, FEMA argued that the minimally processed criteria has never been applied to flavors, nor should it because flavors are processed by necessity.

BACKGROUND AND DEVELOPMENT

Development of the modern flavor industry has occurred only in the last 50 years. Some of the earliest flavors were manufactured by extraction during the 1940s, but by the 1950s and 1960s the industry had moved toward the use of synthetic flavor compounds as flavoring agents. By the 1970s, "natural" began to be a selling point and methods were sought to develop pure, natural chemicals. One problem with these natural extracts was the raw materials varied in taste and intensity. However, the modern flavor industry has resolved this issue by compounding natural flavor chemicals rather than using the extracts as final flavors. This procedure has provided food manufacturers with consistent flavors.

CURRENT CONDITIONS

Instead of one hot item, blended flavors dominated the drink market in 1992. "Everyone seemed to think that two flavors were better than one," said Michael duBois, vice president of sales and marketing for Sanofi-Bio Industries, in the April 1993 issue of *Beverage World.* "There was a definite increase in the number of blends our customers were requesting, particularly those that used at least one exotic or tropical flavor.''

Iced tea flavors have been in great demand due to the explosive growth of iced tea drinks such as Snapple. ''In the last year, every major soft drink company has entered the ice tea market. As a result, the majority of our customer requests the last few months have been for good-tasting ice teas,'' Joe Willoughby, manager of beverage application and technical services at Universal Flavors, told *Beverage World.* Ice tea and fruit drinks are only two examples of the growing market demand for drinks that are perceived to be healthy, prompting drink manufacturers to replace artificial ingredients with natural flavorings.

One supplier, Crompton and Knowles (C&K) Ingredient Technology Division, told *Beverage World,* ''We rarely get requests for artificial flavors. While they are still the trend internationally, because they're cheaper, the U.S. market is more interested in natural flavors, primarily because of labeling.'' Despite the preference for natural flavors, major obstacles regarding natural flavors still exist, according to *Beverage World.* Natural flavors can be expensive, costing up to ten times more than artificial ingredients. The lack of availability and consistency of natural materials only adds to the pricing dilemma, in addition to the issue of timeliness.

Fulfilling customers' demand for natural flavorings has necessitated that manufacturers find new sources for their raw material supply. ''The isolation of new basic materials will highlight flavor efforts in the 1990s,'' Frank Stebbins, president of Fritzsche Dodge & Olcott, told *Food Processing.* ''These building blocks of the future will have to support natural label specifications, increase stability demands, and attractive pricing.''

Hercules Inc. marketing director Chris Li described the flavor business as ''leaner, meaner and moving faster toward developing products on the fly. If guava and pineapple become popular, then the industry reacts within a month with their own flavor versions, whereas it once took a year or more for such reactions,'' Li told *Beverage World.*

The flavor industry has been fragmented, with many small companies working in highly specialized areas, such as creating flavors for cheese or beverages. Many of these smaller houses have merged with larger flavor manufacturers with the intent to broaden their flavor product line. ''This has created a conglomeration of flavors under one roof from which each producer tries to service all areas,'' Philip Katz, senior vice president of Herbert V. Shuster Inc., told *Chemical Marketing Reporter.* One of the most publicized mergers was the combination of IMCERA's Mallinckrodt Speciality Chemicals Company (Fries and Fries) and Hercules PFW Flavors and Citrus Speciality Business in a 50/50 joint venture. Becoming the fifth largest flavor house in the world, the new company adopted the name Tastemaker and is headquartered in Cincinnati, Ohio.

Despite the uncertain financial health of individual flavor houses, the industry in general has remained active and profitable as the major food processing companies have become more dependent on the flavor industry's research and development. According to *Business Week,* since several food processing companies have been carrying heavy debt loads from large acquisitions, they do not want the spend the money needed to design flavoring systems. ''With the advent of leveraged buyouts, [food] companies have chosen to reduce in-house staff in research and development,'' Frank J. Listi, president of Universal Flavor, told *Business Week.* ''The remaining companies are dependent on valuable suppliers.''

Industry Leaders

In the United States, International Flavors and Fragrances (IFF) has been the leader, followed by Givaudan-Roure Corporation, Fries & Fries and Universal Flavor. IFF is also the world's largest flavor company, followed by Givaudan-Roure, Quest, Haarmann & Reimer, Takasago, and Firmenich.

The flavor producing companies have become larger and more multinationally-based, while using a smaller sales force and a leaner corporate staff. Specific information related to job descriptions or other work force information is closely guarded due to the competitive and rather secretive nature of the flavor industry.

International Flavors and Fragrances (IFF) is a leading creator and manufacturer of flavors and fragrances used by other companies to impart or improve the flavor or fragrance of various consumer products. The company has more than 80,000 recipes on file, with most of the flavors sold primarily to the makers of dairy, meats, and other processed foods, beverages, snacks and savory foods.

As the makers of Halston and Calvin Klein's Eternity perfumes, IFF has been a well known leader within the fragrance market. However, with the growing demand for lighter, better-tasting and healthier foods, IFF has begun to concentrate more on the flavor side of its business. In 1993, the company completed a new fruit processing facility near its AuroTech facility in the midwest. These facilities have been expanded to encompass a variety of biotechnological flavors and food ingredient processes.

Approximately 69 percent of IFF sales has been from overseas, providing a strong position for the company in a growing global economy. IFF recently established new facilities in China, Korea, Argentina, and Japan. Flavor sales in Europe have grown especially well, with significant gains in France, Benelux, Germany, and Italy. Sales in former Eastern European countries are expected to gain in strength.

Universal Flavor manufactures beverage and food flavors in liquid and dry form, as well as fruit and speciality flavor ingredient systems for dairy and baking applications. In the North American flavor market, Universal Flavor has gained an 18 percent market share, compared to IFF's 13 percent. In the rest of the world, IFF is the industry leader, with an estimated 13 percent of the market, while Universal Flavor has a seven percent share, tieing it for fifth place in the industry. Universal Flavor has manufacturing and processing centers in three states in the United States. It also operates 14 color and flavor plants in 11 countries and has investments in 16 companies which operate yeast and allied product facilities in 12 foreign countries.

Universal Flavor's Color Division accounted for 14 percent of sales and 18 percent of operating income in 1993. The division supplied synthetic and natural colors to food processors (80 percent of sales) and cosmetic and pharmaceutical manufacturers (20 percent). In the color field, Universal Flavor holds a leading market share in North America, with a 44 percent share of the market, as well as holding an estimated 16 percent share internationally.

AMERICA AND THE WORLD

The flavoring of consumable products reflect current consumer trends in a specific country. Some U.S. drink producers, however, have attempted to export American trends, such as flavored bottled water and ice tea. Of the attempts, tropical drinks have gained the most international ground, especially in Latin America.

On the other hand, Japan has made inroads in the U.S. flavor market, especially with the presence of Takasago and Hosagawa. "They have hired some of the best technical, marketing and sales people in the industry. They have a stake in the ground and they are certainly making their presence felt," Smith told *Chemical Marketing Reporter*.

RESEARCH AND TECHNOLOGY

A popular area of research has relied on understanding and interpreting the basic effects of aroma and applying these findings to flavors that could possibly influence moods. Known as aromachology, this research involves the "effects of aromas on the mind and body, and a quantitative analysis of the sense of smell," Fran LaBell told *Food Processing*. Cosmetic and other personal care companies already use aromachology in the creation of their products for the American, European, and Japanese market. The makers of candy, chewing gum and beverages are the most likely candidates to use aromachology applications in their products.

Some of the substances tested, such as jasmine and caffeine, had a stimulating effect, as recorded through the use of EEG equipment that measures the voltage change in the brain when reacting to stimuli. Some essential oils and ylang ylang (a tropical Asian tree) were found to be stimulating, while oils of sandalwood, lemon, and chamomile had a relaxing effect.

INDUSTRY INFORMATION SOURCES

Best, Daniel. "Flavor Industry Survey Targets Customer Needs." *Prepared Foods*, April 1990.

"Colorful Growth." *Chemical Marketing Reporter*, June 15, 1992.

Cummins, R. J. "Universal Flavors Company Report." Wertheim Schroder & Co., October 30, 1992.

Fitzell, Phil. "Back To Nature." *Beverage World*, August 1990.

———. "A 'Berry' Exciting Flavor Forecast." *Beverage World*, April 1990.

———. "The Launching of McCormick and Wild." *Beverage World*, August 1990.

"Food Additives-Worldwide." *Speciality Chemicals, SRI International*, November 1988.

"International Flavors & Fragrances 1992 Annual Report." New York, NY: International Flavors & Fragrances, 1993.

Kuntz, Lynn A. "Flavors in Use and Practice: Tapping the Genie in the Bottle." *Food Product Design*, August 1993.

La Bell, Fran. "Beyond Refreshment: Flavors Influence Moods." *Food Processing*, October 1991.

———. "Past, Present and Future: 50 Years of Flavors & Spices." *Food Processing*, October 1990.

Roman, Monica. "Beef-Fat Flavor May Not Sound Glamorous, But . . ." *Business Week*, March 11, 1991.

Sfiligoj, Eric. "Fit to a Tea." *Beverage World*, December 1992.

———. "Shared Rule." *Beverage World*, April 1993.

Topfer, Kurt. "Adding Spice: Food Additives 92 Special Report." *Chemical Marketing Reporter*, June 15, 1992.

Wilkes, Ann Przybyla. "Flavor Development Combining Creativity with Modern Science." *Food Product Design*, September 1992.

Wittenburg, B. "Universal Flavors Corporation Company Report." Dain, Bosworth, Inc., 1992.

Wolf, A. E. "Colour My World." *Beverage World*, September 1991.

—Catherine A. Quagliana

SIC 2091

CANNED AND CURED FISH AND SEAFOODS

This category covers establishments primarily engaged in cooking and canning seafood products such as fish, shrimp, oysters, clams, and crab or in curing seafood products by means such as smoking, salting or drying. It also includes manufacturers of seafood soups, chowders, stews, broths, and juices. Establishments primarily engaged in preparing fresh fish or shucking and packing fresh oysters in nonsealed containers are classified in **SIC 2092: Prepared Fresh or Frozen Fish and Seafoods.**

INDUSTRY SNAPSHOT

According to figures released by the U.S. Department of Commerce, production for all establishments classified within the canned and cured fish and seafood industry was valued at $767.0 million. Of this amount $652.1 million represented products considered primary to the industry. The largest industry product was

tuna. The National Marine Fisheries Service, an agency of the U.S. Department of Commerce, reported that canned tuna production in 1990 equalled 581 million pounds. The second largest product, with production of 196 million pounds, was canned salmon. The third largest category, canned clam products, boasted production of 110 million pounds.

Six different species of clam were canned in the United States. East Coast production centers were located in Maine, Maryland, Massachusetts, and Florida. On the West Coast, primary clam production areas were located in Oregon, Washington, and Alaska. East Coast canners principally packed hard and soft shell clams, while most West Coast production involved razor clams, which were most often sold as minced clam meat. Other types of mollusks (soft-bodied shellfish) canned in the United States included oysters, mussels, abalone, cockles, donax, snails, and squid.

Per capita consumption of fisheries products peaked in 1987 at 16.2 pounds but fell to 14.9 pounds in 1991. Fresh and frozen products, the most popular form of seafood, represented 9.7 pounds, canned products represented 4.9 pounds, and cured products only 0.3 pounds. Although industry observers noted a slight increase in per capita consumption of fresh and frozen products in 1992 (up to 9.9 pounds), continued declines within the canned category, which fell to 4.6 pounds, led to an overall drop in per capita seafood consumption to 14.8 pounds, its lowest level since 1984. Per capita consumption of cured seafood products remained at 0.3 pounds per person, a level unchanged since 1980 but reduced from 0.4 pounds in the late 1970s and 0.5 pounds in 1974.

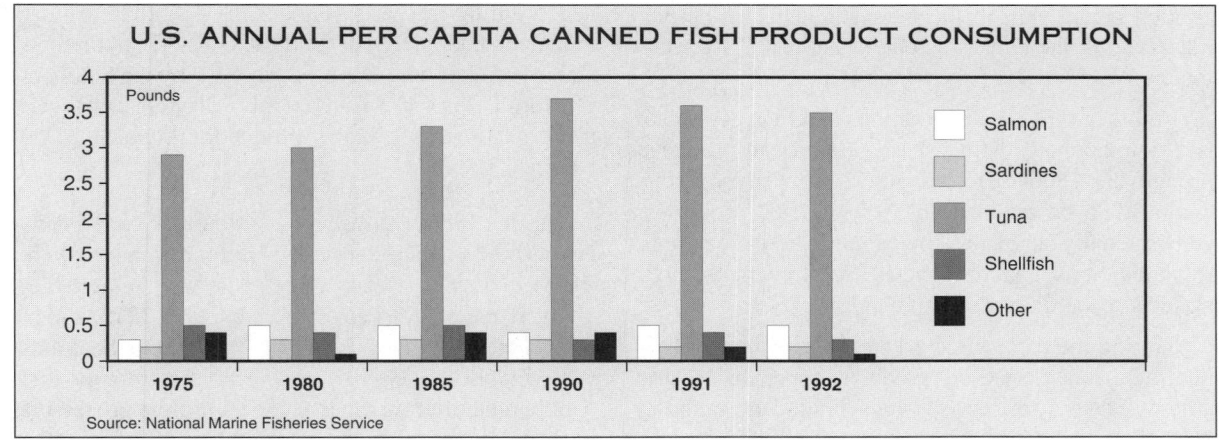

U.S. ANNUAL PER CAPITA CANNED FISH PRODUCT CONSUMPTION

Pounds

Legend: Salmon, Sardines, Tuna, Shellfish, Other

Years: 1975, 1980, 1985, 1990, 1991, 1992

Source: National Marine Fisheries Service

Although government projections anticipated stable catches for most commercial fisheries species through the middle years of the 1990s, problems attributed to overfishing were threatening some individual stocks. Tuna catches declined as did takes of some varieties of salmon. In 1992 Alaskan salmon fishermen reported reduced catches of pink salmon, but increased takes of sockeye salmon. In the Pacific Northwest region, the total 1993 salmon harvest was expected to surpass the 1992 catch by 20 million fish.

BACKGROUND AND DEVELOPMENT

Fish curing is one of the oldest industries in North America. Even before permanent European settlements had been established, fishermen were harvesting cod and other species off the northeastern coastline of the American continent. Fish were preserved and prepared for marketing by salting. According to Roy E. Martin of the National Fisheries Institute, ''As early as 1580 more than three hundred ships from Europe were salting cod in this area.''

New England colonists depended on salted cod and smoked herring as food and as trade items. During the seventeenth and eighteenth centuries, cured fish products made major contributions to the economies of New England and eastern Canada. Disputes over fishing rights and restraints on trade contributed to the political climate leading up to the Revolutionary War. Martin, writing in a volume he co-edited with George J. Flick titled *The Seafood Industry,* stated, ''The English Parliament in 1775 prohibited the New England colonies from trading directly with foreign countries and prevented New England vessels from fishing on the banks off Newfoundland, in the Gulf of St. Lawrence, and on the coasts of Labrador and Nova Scotia where they had been accustomed to fishing. This restriction meant ruin to the New England fish-curing industry, and the edict was one cause of the Revolutionary War.''

Another type of preservation, pickling, was also used commercially with fish and molluscan products through the 1800s. Pickled and cured fish products continued to be major industries until the processes were gradually supplanted by canning technology and by innovations enabling fresh and frozen seafood products to be delivered to inland markets.

During the early years of the nineteenth century, the first canned seafood products appeared in the United States. Initial offerings included salmon, lobsters, and oysters. Of these three, the most popular, and first to be canned on an industrial scale, was the Chesapeake Bay oyster. Canning technology enabled the sale of oysters to inland people who had previously been unable to purchase them. As canning technology improved, other products were added to the menu. Sardines, for example, were first successfully canned in Maine around the middle of the nineteenth century. As more products became available, consumer acceptance increased. The Civil War also helped the new industry gain favor by introducing many soldiers to canned products.

The 1860s saw the beginning and rapid expansion of canning operations for Pacific Salmon. From a small beginning in California, salmon canners spread north into Washington and Canada. The first canneries opened in Alaska in 1878. The 1870s also brought the first menhaden cannery. It opened on Long Island in 1872. Canned fish cakes (cod and haddock products) were introduced in 1878. By 1880, other canned items included mackerel, clams, and crabs. According to an estimate offered by Martin, U.S. (including Alaskan) production of canned products in 1880 was valued at $15 million. Finnan haddie (smoked haddock) was first offered commercially in 1890. ''Salad Fish'' which was canned flaked meat from cod and haddock was introduced in 1898. Other turn-of-the-century products included pickled sturgeon, carp, and shark meat.

During the early years of the twentieth century, the sardine canning industry moved from the East Coast to the West Coast. Canneries sprang up in the Monterey Bay area of California. As sardine canning operations expanded, demand for fish exceeded availability. To help increase catches, new fishing methods were developed using a special type of net, called a lampara net. Lampara nets encircled entire schools of fish and yielded large harvests. Canners also continued bringing new products to American consumers. Items added during the early years of the twentieth century included shad, alewives, and tuna. The first commercial offering of tuna was made in 1909 by the Southern California Fish Company. Only albacore tuna was used, and the first year's production equaled 2,000 cases.

In the following decade many major participants in the U.S. canned and cured seafood industry were founded. Ocean Beauty Seafoods was founded in 1910, Ward's Cove Packing Company in 1912, and in 1914 Peter Pan Seafoods and Van Camp Seafoods were established. By 1915, only six years after the first commercial offering of albacore, California processors packed 237,265 cases. In the Monterey Bay area, the sardine cannery industry was well established and continued growing. In 1918 nine sardine canning plants in Monterey packed a total of 1.4 million cases.

The 1920s saw expansion of Pacific mackerel canneries and increased activity in the Alaskan salmon industry. By the end of the decade, 159 canneries were operating in Alaska. Improvements in cold storage technology enabled canners to receive and process larger quantities of fish. Refined fishing techniques developed during the 1920s helped fishermen meet ever-growing demand. Purse seines, a type of large net closed by a drawstring-like apparatus, were capable of dropping to a depth of 100 feet and enclosing an area 100 feet across. Newer boats were built to operate hundreds of miles offshore and carry up to 150 tons of fish.

Catches of albacore, however, began decreasing during the 1920s and tuna canners consolidated. In 1926 albacore catches plummeted. As a substitute, Van Camp Seafood Company offered yellowfin tuna and marketed it as ''Fancy Light Meat Tuna.'' Sardine catches continued in large numbers and canneries prospered through the 1930s and early 1940s. Owners expanded operations by adding fish by-products such as poultry and livestock feed, fertilizer, and fish oil to their product lines.

During World War II the canning industry faced several challenges. Tuna boats were requisitioned by the Maritime Commission and by the U.S. Navy, primarily for use in delivering supplies. Fish harvests were reduced as fishermen enlisted or were drafted into armed service. Anti-submarine efforts along the Pacific coast restricted fleet movement. And inside the canneries, labor shortages persisted, intensified by a governmental policy of moving Japanese workers to internment camps. Despite the problems, however, the war years proved to be profitable ones for tuna and other fish packers because of the heavy demand spurred by government requisitions for canned products to feed troops.

During the second half of the 1940s, sardine catches began declining and forced canneries, one after another, to close. By 1952, Monterey's sardine era had ended. Industry analysts have attributed the declining sardine catches to various causes including pollution, climate and current changes, natural fish cycles, and fishing out stocks. Although the 1950s saw the demise of many sardine canners, other segments of the industry prospered. Larger fishing boats traveled greater distances from shore and some companies opened canneries in more distant locations. For example, in 1954, the Van Camp Seafood Company opened canning facilities in Pago Pago (Samoan Islands). The plant received fish from Japan, Korea, and Taiwan. It employed 600 people and averaged 145 tons of production daily. The modernization of fishing techniques continued to improve catches. By 1961, most commercial fishing vessels had shifted from hook-and-line gear to mechanized purse seining. By the 1980s, tuna fishermen were using seines measuring up to 4,800 feet by 702 feet and capable of hauling 200 ton catches.

These large nets, however, drew criticism because the seines indiscriminately captured all fish swimming in a school. For reasons not completely understood, dolphins (porpoises) often schooled with yellowfin tuna and reports of dolphin mortality increased. To help alleviate problems associated with dolphin mortality, the Marine Mammal Protection Act banned the importation of fish and fish products caught in ways that posed excessive risks to ocean mammals. Another piece of legislation, the Dolphin Protection Consumer Information Act, was passed to govern the conditions under which fishing operations could operate if their products carried a ''dolphin-safe'' label. In 1990 three major U.S. tuna canners, Star-Kist (owned by H. J. Heinz), Bumble Bee Seafoods, and Van Camp Seafood (''Chicken of the Sea'' brand) promised to provide dolphin-safe tuna.

CURRENT CONDITIONS

As the canned and cured fish and seafood industry entered the 1990s, tuna fish continued to be the top-selling product. Tuna consumption, which amounted to 3.5 pounds per person in 1992, accounted for 24 percent of the nation's total per capita fish consumption. Canned salmon, the second most important product of the industry, did not enjoy the same widespread acceptance. Per capita consumption of canned salmon was only 0.5 pounds in 1992, and, according to a report in *Supermarket News,* an analysis of the top 50 American markets found only 20 to 22 were good for canned salmon. Canned salmon products sold best in New England, the Carolinas, and along the lower Atlantic coast.

More than 90 percent of the salmon sold in the United States came from Alaska. Traditionally, half of the Alaskan catch was canned but in the late 1980s consumer preferences shifted away from canned salmon in favor of fresh and frozen alternatives. According to a report issued in 1989, approximately 65 percent of the Alaskan harvest was sold in fresh or frozen forms. Of the five species of salmon typically caught off Alaskan shores three were commonly used in canning: Red (Sockeye), Pink, and Chum. Two other types of salmon, Silver (Coho) and King (Chinook), were canned only in small quantities.

Per capita consumption of canned sardines was also declining. In 1972 it totaled 0.4 pounds. During much of the 1980s it stood at 0.3 pounds and in 1991 and 1992 measured only 0.2 pounds. In 1992 United Food Processors (UFP), a California sardine canning operation, declared bankruptcy. Company owners hoped to enter into a joint venture or partnership with investors who could provide the capital necessary to modernize their facility and install an oval-tin sardine processing line.

Technological advances in making fish products shelf stable enabled the development of new items such as smoked oysters and gourmet smoked salmon. Mackerel, another fish product offered as a smoked product, faced an uncertain future. California fish landings diminished during the early years of the 1990s. Fishermen and processors voiced concern about the possibility of reductions in quotas which would limit availability.

INDUSTRY LEADERS

According to *Ward's Business Directory of U.S. Private and Public Concerns* for 1994, the largest company involved in canning and curing fish and seafood products was Trident Seafoods Corp. Trident, a privately owned company headquartered in Seattle, Washington, was founded in 1973. Trident operated as a vertically integrated harvesting, processing, and marketing company. A corporate brochure stated that this style of organization enabled it ''to control its seafood products from the source to the plate.''

In 1991 Trident's sales were estimated at $371 million. The company employed 600 permanent employees and 3,000 during its peak season. Trident operated floating processing vessels and processing plants in Alaska and Washington. A company spokesman estimated that the company's product mix in 1993 was 80 percent frozen products and 20 percent canned. Trident's canned salmon was offered under several brands: Faust, Lily, Prelate, Rubinstein's, Sea-Alaska, Tulip and Whitney's. The highest-volume species canned was Pink salmon. According to information provided by Trident, most of the canned salmon produced in the United States was packed in 14.75 ounce cans. The second most popular size was 7.5 ounce cans. Other common sizes were 3.75 ounces and four pounds.

Another major participant in the seafood canning industry was Van Camp Seafoods Company. Van Camp was founded by a father and son team, Frank and Gilbert Van Camp. The company processed its first load of albacore tuna on June 6, 1914. Van Camp pioneered many of the technologies and practices that developed as the tuna industry evolved, including cold storage, advanced fishing methods, mechanized pro-

duction, and ''tendering,'' the practice of buying fish from boats at sea and ferrying them back to the cannery. Another Van Camp accomplishment was the establishment of Van Camp Laboratories to extract vitamins from fish scraps, organs, and oils. Van Camp adopted its ''Chicken of the Sea'' mermaid logo in 1953. During the 1960s the company was the largest canner of an advertised brand of tuna in the United States. In addition to its tuna line, the ''Chicken of the Sea'' brand includes canned salmon products. ''Chicken of the Sea'' was the first to offer skinless/boneless canned salmon.

WORK FORCE

According to figures released by the U.S. Department of Commerce, employment within the canned and cured fish and seafoods industry totaled 6,700 in 1987, a 52 percent drop from the 13,900 employed in 1982. The combined payroll for all establishments classified within the industry totaled $99.8 million. States with the highest employment were California, Maine, Alaska, and Washington.

INDUSTRY INFORMATION SOURCES

''Alaska Canned Salmon,'' Juneau, AK: Alaska Seafood Marketing Institute, 1988.

Chicken of the Sea Tuna and Salmon, St. Louis, MO: Van Camp Seafood Company, Inc., 1988.

Hutchinson, William, ''Net Gains,'' *Supermarket News,* September 20, 1993.

Kronman, Mick, ''Outlook: Wetfish Cannery Closure Bursts Sardine Bubble,'' *National Fisherman,* October 1992.

Lang, Linda, ''Seafood Processors,'' *Puget Sound Business Journal,* May 29, 1992.

Litwak, David, and Nancy Maline, ''Fifth Annual Seafood Operations Review,'' *Supermarket Business,* November 1992.

Martin, Roy E., and George J. Flick eds., *The Seafood Industry,* New York: Van Nostrand Reinhold, 1990.

McDowell, Eric, and Jim Calvin, *Alaska Seafood Industry Study: A Summary,* Juneau, AK: The McDowell Group, March 1989.

McMath, Robert, ''Fishy Snacks and Franks Swim Into Stores,'' *Adweek's Marketing Week,* July 30, 1990.

1987 Census of Manufactures, Washington, DC: Bureau of the Census, April 1990.

''Per Capita U.S. Consumption,'' Washington, DC: U.S. Department of Commerce (National Marine Fisheries Service), 1993.

Salmon 2000: Yearbook 1993, Juneau, AK: Alaska Seafood Marketing Institute, 1993.

Statistical Abstract of the United States: 1992, 112th edition, Washington, DC: U.S. Bureau of the Census. 1992.

''Trident Seafoods Corporation,'' *From the Source to the Plate,* Seattle, WA: Trident, nd.

''Tuna Without the Guilt,'' *Time,* April 23, 1990.

U.S. Industrial Outlook 1993, Washington, DC: U.S. Department of Commerce, 1993.

—Karen Bellenir

SIC 2092

PREPARED FRESH OR FROZEN FISH AND SEAFOODS

This category covers establishments that prepare fish, seafoods, and other seafood preparations (such as shrimpcakes, crabcakes, fishcakes, chowders, and stews), in fresh and raw or cooked frozen form. Prepared fresh fish are eviscerated or processed by removal of heads, fins, or scales. This industry also includes establishments primarily engaged in the shucking and packing of fresh oysters in nonsealed containers.

INDUSTRY SNAPSHOT

During the 1980s, health and diet concerns led American consumers to think about fish and seafoods in two ways. These years marked a significant trend towards higher levels of consumption of poultry, fish, and seafoods at the expense of red meat. But perennial worries about the quality of fish and seafoods, which swiftly lose their taste and freshness, were compounded by growing consumer knowledge about the potential harmful effects of pollution on fish and the consequences of improper handling and storage.

Heading into the 1990s, the American fish and seafoods industry sought to diversify the range of uses to which its processed products could be put (as in the case of surimi, manufactured as a filler in red meat or as a substitute for it), to prepare products to a higher and more consistent standard (as in the case of processed catfish, raised in ponds and net pens using the increasingly popular techniques of aquaculture), and to apply more rigorous standards of evaluation for every aspect of quality.

ORGANIZATION AND STRUCTURE

In an industry characterized by great fragmentation, the sheer length of the production line connecting harvesters, processors, and retailers made it difficult to keep consumers supplied with the desired quantity and quality of fish and seafoods.

Small-scale processing plants were tied to local fleets that were in turn tied to specific stocks of fish and seafoods that in many cases fluctuated dramatically, discouraging processors from expanding operations, developing new products, or adopting new technology. Those fleets not equipped for processing at sea were obliged to return to land at short intervals, rather than when full, so that their harvest could be processed when still fresh. The needs of processors and harvesters did not always agree: fleets were reluctant to take the effort to harvest such bottomfish species as Alaska pollock, Pacific cod, flounder, and sablefish, although processors regarded them as a potentially lucrative source. In addition to an expansion of at-sea processing operations and a greater use of fish and shellfish raised by aquacultural means, vertical integration was seen as the key to a profitable restructuring of the American fish and seafoods processing industry. Such restructuring, some industry observers say, is necessary to bring large-scale, sustained investment in underutilized species, greater speed and efficiency in bringing harvested and processed products to the consumer, and the overview necessary to respond to shortages and gluts, whether caused by changes in consumer demand or by fluctuations in the stock of a particular species.

A better and more far-reaching program of inspection was regarded as both a necessity for the future of the industry and a likely consequence of greater integration. While there was no mandatory inspection of fish and seafood by the federal government, processors, retailers, and wholesalers could at their own expense invite scrutiny of their working conditions by U.S. Department of Commerce Inspectors. Approximately ten percent of processors were participating in such voluntary inspection programs in 1992. But even in this restricted form there was no uniformity; three different seals were available, designating different levels of inspection.

Regulations at the state level differed from region to region but in general gave little protection to consumers. A majority of states required stores to keep records identifying the initial source and date of harvest of every batch of shellfish, and the company responsible for shipping it. But these records were often kept poorly or not at all.

BACKGROUND AND DEVELOPMENT

Beginning around the end of World War Two, American consumers began to rely increasingly on the convenience of fully or partially prepared fish and seafoods; often these products were made available in frozen form. These fish products were available with or without coatings of breading, while batter coatings were introduced in the 1960s. Dating from the same decade as batter coatings, batter-fried fish and seafood reached the consumer only after an extensive preparation in which the product was dusted with flour, encased in batter, and then lightly fried to fix the batter and achieve specified standards of texture and quality.

Fish and seafood constituted about half of the frozen battered and breaded products consumed in the United States, the largest consumer of breaded fish and seafood in the world. The most frequently consumed sorts of coated fish and seafood were precooked and raw portions of fish, followed by shrimp, fishcakes, and scallops. Among the breaded products most typically sold in frozen form were scallops, oysters, clam strips, clamcakes, and squid rings. But the majority of the clams that were frozen were intended for further processing and for the chowder market rather than for home consumption.

Freezing technology permitted great advances in an industry dependent on a product subject to rapid spoilage; but not all species of fish and seafood responded equally well to freezing, which had to be conducted in just the right way for each species if delicacies of texture and flavor were not to be lost. For instance, whereas crabmeat generally was found to freeze less well and have a briefer shelf life than many other types of fish and seafoods, king crab was discovered to lend itself rather well to freezing. Well-suited to shrimp, catfish, and halibut, the technique of rapid freezing proved especially effective because it minimized losses of texture and flavor by guaranteeing uniformity of freezing. The "I.Q.F." marking, which referred to individually quick frozen products, thus became a selling point for the American consumer. The equipment used for such freezing operations ranged from automated loading and unloading units, mechanically or electronically controlled to adapt to the specific requirements of each type of product, to straightforward and labor intensive batch-freezing units.

The United States was for a long period the world leader in terms of its versatility in processing, handling, distributing, and marketing frozen fish and seafoods. It was also an early leader in deploying techniques for freezing catches aboard ship but lost its edge in the commercial application of this technology, which allowed fishing vessels to remain at sea for greater periods of time. Ships could thus remain at sea until their load was full, the utilization of freezing technology putting to rest concerns about maintaining the freshness of the catch.

CURRENT CONDITIONS

Already appealing by virtue of their convenience, prepared fish and seafoods gained further appeal when dieticians began advising American consumers to eat less red meat and instead consume greater quantities of poultry and fish and seafoods. Some analysts felt that the increasing consumption of fish and seafoods in the United States during the 1980s had reached a plateau of roughly 15 pounds per person annually; others predicted that consumption would continue to increase into the next century. In its summary of a report by the National Fisheries Institute, *Prepared Foods* noted that annual per capita consumption of fish and seafoods in America was forecast to reach 20 pounds in the year 2000, with consumption of shrimp alone increasing to one billion pounds (from 567 million pounds in 1989). It furthermore noted that demographic trends within the United States indicated growing numbers of Asian and Hispanic consumers— consumers whose diets have traditionally favored relatively high levels of fish and seafood. In addition, the National Restaurant Association predicted that fish and seafood by the year 2000 would constitute about eight percent of total meat, poultry, and fish and seafood consumption in America, as compared with the equivalent figure of seven percent in 1960-1964. A Business Communications Company study summarized in *Frozen Food Digest* in 1989 observed that the American fish and seafood industry had grown stronger after 1985, both in itself and in its share of the global market, and concluded that "modernization of the U.S. fishery, particularly the Pacific trawl fishery, and policies recently instituted for management and conservation of U.S. fishery resources have returned harvesting in the U.S. Exclusive Economic Zone to U.S. fishermen." In its brief survey-pamphlet "Fisheries of the United States, 1992," the U.S. Department of Commerce noted that the proportion of domestic landings used for human food in 1992 increased by five percent between 1991 and 1992, a growth attributed to "the landings of Alaska pollock and other groundfish species used in surimi and other analog products."

An analysis undertaken by *Consumer Reports* in early 1992, however, found that much of the fish and seafood reaching American customers, whatever its supposed appeal from the point of view of health and diet issues, was of poor or inconsistent quality. Reactions in the industry ranged from concerns that the samples taken for the purposes of analysis were unrepresentative to genuine uncertainty as to what standards fish and seafood had to meet to offer reasonable guarantees to the consumer, and as to how best to achieve those standards. The lengthy chain of production separating harvested fish and seafoods from their arrival on the consumer's plate created difficulties in any attempt to determine which links in the chain were typically most culpable when the final end product was of poor quality, although *Consumer Reports* tentatively concluded that retailers were more to blame than the manufacturers. On the limited basis of visits to Mississippi plants responsible for "some 70 percent of the catfish sold in U.S. retail markets," *Consumer Reports*' investigator noted that the plants were "clean, modern, and operating under a voluntary inspection program run by the U.S. Department of Commerce," that the processors "appeared to follow good manufacturing practices" by "wearing gloves, hair covers, and aprons, and dipping their hands in a disinfectant whenever they entered the processing room," that "the catfish was hauled live to the plant from nearby ponds in tank trucks," and that it was "never out of water before it hit the conveyer belt that whisked it to the processing room."

INDUSTRY LEADERS

At the beginning of the 1990s, U.S. processors of fish and seafoods ranged in size from tiny operations, employing a handful of workers and concentrating on a single species or type of preparation, to large businesses engaged in many other areas. Major companies in this industry include Rich-Seapak Corp., a subsidiary of Rich Products Corp., with 1,100 employees and $210 million in sales, Icicle Seafoods (275 employees, $243 million in sales), Arctic Alaska Fisheries (2,000 employees, $224 million in sales), Coldwater Seafood Corp. (440 employees, $200 million in sales), Ocean Beauty Seafoods (300 employees, $200 million in sales), and Singleton Seafood Co., a subsidiary of ConAgra, Inc. (800 employees, $200 million in sales).

WORK FORCE

According to the U.S. Department of Labor's Bureau of Labor Statistics, little change in employment in the American fish and seafoods processing industry was expected through the year 2005, though there was likely to be a shift in the distribution of the work performed, with an increase in the amount of preparation undertaken by the typically semi-skilled workers in processing plants and a decrease in that undertaken by the typically skilled workers in markets and other retail centers.

The skills most important to processors include good eye-hand coordination, manual dexterity, depth perception, and color discrimination, and these were usually acquired in apprenticeship programs or on the job rather than in any more formal educational settings. Work environments often include extended periods of standing for employees, as well as low temperatures needed to keep product fresh.

Aside from promotion to a supervisory position, employment in processing of fish and seafoods offers few career prospects. In this area, as in other areas of the overall fishing industry, wages are typically low, although there are some variances in salary scales based on geographic location.

AMERICA AND THE WORLD

In 1966 the United States was heavily—perhaps too heavily—dependent on imported frozen fish and seafoods, which made up about half of its supply, both for sale directly to the consumer and for further processing. In the next few decades, however, the industry achieved a more equitable balance between imports and exports. Imports of processed fishery products reached $5.3 billion in 1992, while exports reached $3.2 billion.

RESEARCH AND TECHNOLOGY

According to *Frozen Food Digest,* between 1980 and 1990 the quantity of farm-raised processed catfish in the United States rose from 46 million pounds to 377 million pounds, and production of surimi likewise increased between 1987 and 1989 from 67 million pounds to 300 million pounds. Both products were formerly neglected ones whose increasing popularity was predicted to grow through the end of the century. The growth of catfish consumption partly reflected a substantial increase in aquaculture, which *Frozen Food Digest* noted was "outpacing all other types of farming" in the United States. The trend towards aquaculture was a significant one, not only because of the growing proportion of the U.S. supply of fish and seafood that it contributed, but also because it brought harvesting and processing into closer conjunction and thereby assured a higher and more consistent quality of product.

New processing and packaging technologies extending the shelf life of fresh and prepared fish and seafoods are keys to growth in the processing industry. Other challenges facing the U.S. fish and seafoods processing industry near the end of the twentieth century as it attempts to expand the consumption of batter-coated products include researching and developing products that can be microwaved without any loss of crispness, and utilizing new technologies to improve the overall quality of such products (which have been subject to unevenly distributed coatings and minor flaws in composition that substantially affect both cooking time and batter adhesion).

INDUSTRY INFORMATION SOURCES

Brown, Robert H. "Florida Has Its First Major Catfish Processor." *Feedstuffs,* September 30, 1991: 9.

Foodservice Industry Forecast. Washington, D.C.: National Restaurant Association, 1990.

Frozen Food Digest, October 1989: 68, 132.

Frozen Food Digest, March 1990: 34.

Frozen Food Digest, July 1991: 18, 42.

Garry, Michael. "Seafood Standoff." *Progressive Grocer,* March 1993: 85.

Gilbert, De Witt, ed. *The Future of the Fishing Industry of the United States.* University of Washington Publications in Fisheries, New Series, Vol. 4. Seattle: University of Washington, 1968.

"Is Our Fish Fit To Eat?" *Consumer Reports,* February 1992: 103-14.

Kummer, Corby. "Farmed Fish." *The Atlantic,* August 1992: 88-92.

Martin, Roy E., and George J. Flick, eds. *The Seafood Industry.* New York: Osprey, 1990.

McGoodwin, James R. *Crisis in the World's Fisheries.* Stanford, CA: Stanford University Press, 1990.

Prepared Foods, February 1991: 18.

Sullivan, Jeremiah J., and Per O. Heggelund. *Foreign Investment in the U.S. Fishing Industry.* Pacific Rim Research Series 3. Lexington, MA: D.C. Heath, 1979.

Wold, Marjorie. "FMI Probes Food Safety." *Progressive Grocer,* March 1992: 7.

"Why Doesn't the U.S. Inspect More Fish?" *Consumer Reports,* February 1992: 113.

—Richard Hillyer

SIC 2095

ROASTED COFFEE

This category covers establishments primarily engaged in roasting coffee and in manufacturing coffee concentrates and extracts in powdered, liquid, or frozen form, including freeze-dried. Coffee roasting by wholesale grocers is covered in **SIC 5149: Groceries and Related Products, Not Elsewhere Classified.**

INDUSTRY SNAPSHOT

Between 1970 and 1980, U.S. per capita consumption of coffee in gallons had dropped from 33.4 to 26.7, although it held steady at that approximate rate throughout the 1980s. At an estimated 1.75 cups, daily per capita consumption of coffee in 1991 was a far cry from that of the all-time high of 3.1 cups reached in 1962. According to a study summarized in *Advertising Age,* however, the retail coffee market at the end of the 1980s seemed headed for a period of modest growth as gourmet coffees and upscale versions of popular brands continued to increase their share of overall sales—from 10 percent in 1984, to 19 percent in 1989, to a projected 30 percent in 1994. Having in past decades exported a taste for instant coffee, the United States thus began importing a demand for specialty coffees and the European cafe lifestyle associated with them.

ORGANIZATION AND STRUCTURE

Due to a climate that cannot support coffee trees in areas other than Hawaii and Puerto Rico, U.S. production of coffee beans has been negligible. Instead the United States has become the largest importer of the beans, purchased from producing nations through traders. For this reason traders play an important role in the U.S. coffee industry, albeit one constrained by their obligation to serve the requirements of roasters. Thus the National Coffee Association, formed in the early 1970s, is dominated by the roasters.

Processing of coffee beans is performed by manufacturers that roast the beans for packaging. Also, roasters often further process the beans to be sold for brewing and instant coffee. At least until the mid-1980s, coffee produced in the United States was thought to be less superior than that of other countries. According to Michael Sivetz and Norman W. Desrosier in *Coffee Technology,* this can be explained by the fact that many of the leading manufacturers are owned by multinational conglomerates: "Most of the bad features in handling coffee in the U.S.A. (and elsewhere too) are due to mass production and centralized marketing and sales. The indicated particular treatment of green, roast ground coffees and their brewing is in conflict with corporate mass production and selling policies. . . . Commercial aspects, that is profit-making, invariably override technical considerations and process technology."

BACKGROUND AND DEVELOPMENT

The U.S. coffee industry can be traced back to the seventeenth century, when coffeehouses, already quite popular in Europe, began to open in the colonies.

Indeed, Revolutionary War strategy was often plotted in these establishments. At that point in time, only whole coffee beans were available, and these were sold from a barrel to be blended and ground in the home for boiling.

This method of preparing coffee proved its inconvenience during the Civil War, when transporting beans and grinders was quickly found to be unwieldy. As an alternative, coffee was made into a sort of concentrate by grinding it into a pulp that was fashioned into bricks and allowed to harden. This allowed soldiers to slice off an appropriate amount for boiling. In the meantime, however, entrepreneurs saw an opportunity. By roasting, blending, grinding, and packaging the coffee for sale, they offered consumers a welcome convenience.

Coffee beans are mainly categorized into two major varieties: arabica and robusta. Arabica beans are the most flavorful, and gourmet coffees are made with this type. Robusta beans are used in commercially packaged and instant coffees. Roasters store the purchased beans in silos until they are blended, which occurs immediately prior to roasting. Control of the blending process is usually done electronically, with preset percentages of the different varieties to go into the blend.

In addition to the type of bean used in a blend, roasting plays an important role in the resulting coffee's taste. Roasting eliminates the moisture from the bean, releasing the flavor. The color of the roasted beans determines the flavor, and consistency of color throughout a bean produces a high-quality brew. The beans should be dark enough to give the maximum amount of flavor, though not so dark that the coffee tastes scorched.

Until the end of World War II, robusta beans commanded a significantly lower price than arabica, not only because they are less flavorful, but also because they can be harvested more easily. Thereafter, the price differential was reduced by two developments: demand for robusta was boosted by coffee-consuming nations' shift toward blends that combined both kinds of beans and, on an even larger scale, the introduction and great success of soluble coffee (or "instant" as it would later be known) derived largely, though not exclusively, from robusta.

According to Richard L. Lucier, author of *The International Political Economy of Coffee,* "Only eight percent of world production was of robusta coffee in the late 1940s, but robusta's share more than tripled by the early 1970s. Over the same time period, soluble coffee's share of world consumption grew

from virtually zero (i.e. consumption was of regular coffee) to nearly 25 percent." Key points in the rapid development of the U.S. coffee industry during the decades after World War II included the pioneering of a soluble process by Hills Brothers in 1953, Nestlé's introduction in the same year of decaffeinated instant coffee, the emergence of freeze-dried coffee in 1965, and the creation of continuous freeze-drying systems in 1975.

The increasing demand for robusta had a sharp impact on the coffee-producing nations. Central and South America, where much of the world's arabica is grown, dominated coffee production before the 1950s. By the late 1980s, however, more than a third of world coffee production took place in the robusta-growing countries of Africa and Southeast Asia.

Latin America also suffered when the coffee boom, occurring from 1955 to 1962, was followed by a slump in prices triggered by over-production, a crisis that led in 1962 to the first of several International Coffee Agreements intended to stabilize prices. As M. Th. A. Pieterse and H. J. Silvis explained in *The World Coffee Market and the International Coffee Agreement,* "The instrument used is a system of export quotas, which—depending on price developments—limits producing members' exports to consuming members' markets. The role of consuming members is to police producing members' adherence to the quota provisions." According to Richard Lucier's analysis, the swift and concerted response by the U.S. coffee industry to the slump-induced crisis in Latin America reflected the political climate of the time (fear of Communist inroads into countries with deteriorating economies) as well as concern about the possible overall disruption of world coffee production and an attachment to neighbors and long-term trading partners.

CURRENT CONDITIONS

Despite numerous reports linking various health problems with coffee consumption, the results of such studies have been inconclusive and ambiguous, showing no clear reason to suppose that coffee drinkers are at risk of high cholesterol, heart disease, birth defects, cancer of the bladder or pancreas, and high blood pressure. Though the drop in coffee consumption through the 1960s and 1970s may have reflected anxiety induced by the sheer number of these reports, it may also have been prompted in part by dissatisfaction with the quality of the product. The increasing demand for specialty coffees suggested that consumers were attracted to higher quality brews, especially when accompanied by lower levels of caffeine—arabica beans are not only less bitter than robusta but also contain about half as much caffeine, the component of coffee most frequently cited in connection with potentially harmful side-effects.

While the specialty coffee market was estimated in 1994 to be growing at ten to 15 percent a year, the basic coffee industry was suffering. With less of a margin than such enterprises as Starbucks Corp. that have retail stores in addition to their manufacturing operations, producers found their profits being squeezed by bean shortages. Two factors that contributed to the bad harvests were the Rwandan civil war and pests that damaged the Colombian crop. In addition, manufacturers did not consider raising prices to be an option given that there was little growth in demand for mainstream coffee. By expanding their product line to include more specialty items, however, producers hoped to offset their shrinking margins.

INDUSTRY LEADERS

In a July 1993 ranking in *Advertising Age,* year-to-date leaders in sales of ground coffee were Procter and Gamble's Folgers with 28.2 percent of the market, followed by an 18.5 percent share for Kraft General Foods' Maxwell House. Folgers and Maxwell House were also second and third in sales of instant coffee (21.0 and 19.2 percent, respectively), led by the 24.2 percent share held by Nestlé Beverage's Taster's Choice.

According to an analysis by Bill Saporito that appeared in *Fortune,* Kraft General Foods became more aggressive in its promotion of Maxwell House when Philip Morris acquired the company in 1988, introducing a risk-taking mood. Saporito noted several reasons why such aggressiveness in the battle for market share in the ground and soluble coffee markets seemed ill-advised: with a profit of less than a penny per cup of coffee at stake, such coffee manufacturers had been competing against each other in expensive advertising campaigns, together with costly promotions aimed at supermarkets (in the form of incentives) and consumers (in the form of coupons), all the while neglecting opportunities to take advantage of a burgeoning taste for the more profitable specialty coffees, except by cautiously introducing upscale versions of already popular brands.

Because the giants in the U.S. coffee business imported in pre-roasted or even ready-soluble form so much of the coffee they used, much of the coffee processing actually done in this country was performed by smaller concerns, including those companies marketing the increasingly popular specialty coffees. Among such manufacturers, Starbucks Corp. led the way. The company opened its first store in Seattle

in 1971 and just over two decades later owned 100 stores in the Northwest, while steadily expanding into other areas of the United States and racking up weekly sales of $700,000.

AMERICA AND THE WORLD

With the exception of several countries in Latin America and a few in Africa that both produce and consume coffee, the world is divided between developed coffee-consuming nations and developing coffee-producing nations. In terms of kilograms of coffee per person consumed in 1985, the United States at 4.7 ranked tenth, behind Sweden (11.6), Denmark (11.0), Finland (10.1), Holland (9.5), Germany (6.8), France (5.5), and Italy (4.9) among the coffee-consuming nations, and behind Costa Rice (6.5) and Brazil (5.5) among the coffee-producing nations. Overall, in the decade between 1975 and 1985 European Community levels of imported coffee rose significantly, those of Japan doubled, while those of the United States remained steady despite increased population—an indication of a drop in per capita consumption.

Unlike other coffee-consuming nations, the United States imposed no import duty on this particular commodity. Another unique feature of the U.S. market is the nation's close cultural, geographical, political, and economic ties to Latin America, and thus to such major coffee producers as Brazil, Colombia, and Mexico. Although Mexico has been by far the least important of these in terms of output, its close proximity to roasters in the southern United States and its consequent ability to transport coffee overland have been advantageous.

Drawing parallels between America and most of Europe (roughly equivalent markets in terms of the sheer volume of their coffee imports), C. F. Marshall noted several contrasts in his 1983 study *The World Coffee Trade.* The quality of the coffee shipped to the United States appeared generally lower than that intended for Europe, and much of it was already roasted and ground or turned into soluble form, with a lighter roast than was customary in Europe, where "the higher roast forces the roaster to pay more attention to the regularity of bean and to avoid a large proportion of broken or thin textured shells which can scorch and spoil the taste." Marshall attributed these compromises on quality to the "intense competition" among coffee manufacturers in the United States, concluding that "some miracle is needed to switch the competition from one of price to one of quality."

Within just a few years of Marshall's analysis, the miracle in question had begun, driven by American consumers' increasing preference for precisely the kind of high-quality specialty coffees favored in Europe. However, a decade later Ted. R. Lingle, executive director of the Specialty Coffee Association of America, noted in the *Vending Times* that "the continued surplus of lower grades of coffee" meant that consumers in the United States were still faced with coffee that was "merely acceptable because it [contained] too high a proportion of low-grade coffees in the blend."

RESEARCH AND TECHNOLOGY

For several reasons, the leading manufacturers of coffee in the United States, despite their dependence on imported beans, managed to resist any competition from among the coffee-producing nations. One key advantage was that of patented technology, and consequently automated production on a huge (and therefore highly economical) scale. Eliminating much repetitive labor in loading and unloading, the introduction of the continuous roaster enabled a single person to operate two units continuously producing 5000 kilograms per hour, thereby doubling productivity to the level of 1600 bags per person-day. The developing coffee-producing nations could neither match this technological advantage nor afford to compete with U.S. manufacturers in a field characterized by heavy promotional and advertising costs.

Another obstacle preventing coffee-producing nations from manufacturing coffee for the U.S. market was that the industry leaders had used their technological advantage to shape local tastes to specific blends manufactured with great consistency. A single coffee-producing nation could not possibly draw on a sufficient variety of coffees to match these exact blends.

With the shift in national taste towards specialty coffees, quality of beans became a paramount concern for new producers entering the developing gourmet market. In response, the established American manufacturers began experimenting with refined versions of popular lines and researching possible new products, such as iced coffee. Based on its success in Japan, and given its potential appeal to younger consumers, iced coffee was regarded by a number of analysts as a probable strong seller in the American market during the 1990s. Others, however, remained skeptical of this product's ability to reproduce the success achieved by iced teas, diet sodas, or health drinks.

INDUSTRY INFORMATION SOURCES

Advertising Age, July 19, 1993, 16.

"Comeback Time for Coffee," *Time,* October 22, 1990, 59.

de Graaff, J., "The Economics of Coffee," *Economics of Crops in Developing Countries 1,* Wageningen, The Nether-

lands: Center for Agricultural Publishing and Documentation, 1986.

"Gourmet coffee stirs market," *Advertising Age,* October 1, 1990, 19.

Jorgensen, Janice, *Encyclopedia of Cosumer Brands* volume 1, Detroit: Gale Research Inc., 1994.

Lucier, Richard L., *The International Political Economy of Coffee,* New York: Praeger, 1988.

Marshall, C. F., *The World Coffee Trade,* Cambridge, England: Woodhead-Faulkner, 1983.

"No Break for Coffee Prices," *Fortune,* June 13, 1994, 13.

Pieterse, M. Th. A., and H. J. Silvis, *The World Coffee Market and the International Coffee Agreement,* Wageningen, The Netherlands: Wageningen Agricultural University, 1988.

Rothman, Howard, "You Love the Java, But Does It Love You?" *Nation's Business,* February 1992, 55.

Rothman, Matt, "Into the Black," *Inc.,* January 1993, 59-60, 62, 64-65.

Saporito, Bill, "Can Anyone Win the Coffee War?" *Fortune,* 21 May 1990, 97, 100.

Sivetz, Michael, and Norman W. Desrosier, *Coffee Technology,* second ed. Westport, CT: AVI, 1979.

Tantillo, L., "Iced Coffee Market Heats Up," *Beverage World Periscope Edition,* June 30, 1990, 10.

Vending Times, August 25-September 24, 1993, pp. 23, 41.

Willman, Michelle L., "Romancing the Bean," *Beverage Industry,* April 1993, 42-43.

—Richard Hillyer

SIC 2096

POTATO CHIPS, CORN CHIPS, AND SIMILAR SNACKS

Establishments primarily engaged in manufacturing potato chips, corn chips, and similar snacks. Establishments primarily engaged in manufacturing pretzels and crackers are classified in **SIC 2052: Cookies and Crackers;** those manufacturing candy covered popcorn are classified in **SIC 2064: Candy and Other Confectionery Products;** those manufacturing salted, roasted, cooked, or canned nuts and seeds are classified in **SIC 2068: Salted and Roasted Nuts and Seeds;** and those manufacturing packaged unpopped popcorn are classified in **SIC 2099: Food Preparations, Not Elsewhere Classified.**

INDUSTRY SNAPSHOT

The so-called "salty snack" industry included potato chips, corn chips, tortilla chips, ready-to-eat popcorn (except candy-coated), pork rinds, potato sticks, and extruded snacks such as cheese puffs. Dollar sales of savory snacks (in a broad category including pretzels and snack nuts) grew from $10.6 billion in 1987 to $13.8 billion in 1992—an increase of 30 percent. Per capita consumption jumped from 17.49 pounds in 1987 to 20.55 pounds in 1992. The field was dominated by Frito-Lay, a subsidiary of Pepsi Co., which claimed nearly half of the overall salty snack food market in 1992. But Americans' appetite for specialty and relatively "healthy" snacks kept the industry competitive. Over 400 new products were introduced in both 1991 and 1992, including several varieties of multigrain chips, flavored ready-to-eat popcorn, and diet cheese puffs.

The industry experienced steady sales growth, even during the recession of the early 1990s. But pound sales volume rose faster than dollar sales volume in both 1991 and 1992 due to the keen competition that characterized the industry. The decline in price per pound was also consistent with falling retail grocery prices nationwide. The issues described by snack food companies as posing the biggest challenges to profitability in the mid-1990s included: competitive pricing, government-mandated nutritional labeling, changing distribution patterns, and rising supermarket shelf fees.

ORGANIZATION AND STRUCTURE

The salty snack foods industry had a unique structure, since Frito-Lay controlled roughly half of the total market share with retail sales of about $5.6 billion in 1992. Its nearest competitor, Borden Snacks Group, had retail sales of just over $1 billion that same year.

Eagle Snacks, a unit of Anheuser-Busch breweries, was the third-largest maker of salty snacks with $600 million of retail sales. Several other companies showed retail sales from a quarter to half a billion dollars that same year. Although the industry had some elements of a monopoly, aggressive pricing and distribution policies among chip makers, along with the regional presence of many large and small manufacturers, kept it highly competitive.

Numerous companies of descending size made up the savory snack industry. Many competed only on a regional level, and some found it difficult to price their products competitively with the larger manufacturers. Others, however, created a market niche, sometimes with a specialty product such as kettle style potato chips or baked chips sold through health food stores. If their product met with success among customers, the smaller makers could often charge higher prices for their products than the biggest manufacturers. Larger manufacturers were generally full-service snack companies—those which offered a full range of products, including potato chips, tortilla chips, and other salty snacks. The smaller producers were more likely to specialize.

One such small manufacturer was Cape Cod Potato Chip Co., a Massachusetts-based firm that began frying chips over a kitchen stove before purchasing a storefront potato chip shop in 1980. The hand-operated frying kettles produced only 120 pounds of chips per hour, in contrast with the industry standard commercial cookers that produced 4,000 pounds. A decade after opening, Cape Cod employed 200 people—although the operation was purchased in 1985 by Eagle Snacks.

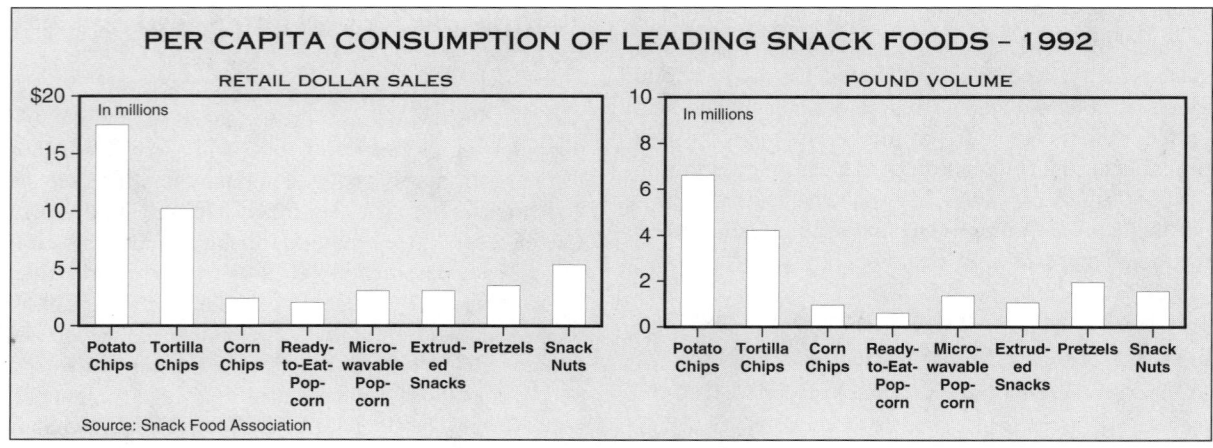

BACKGROUND AND DEVELOPMENT

The potato chip was born by accident in 1853, when railroad magnate and naval commodore Cornelius Vanderbilt was vacationing in a popular east coast inn. He ordered fried potatoes, but disliked them and returned the fries to the kitchen, complaining that they were "too thick." The cook, a Native American named George Crumm, reacted with indignation. He sliced a potato into slivers as thin as he could, fried them, and served them to Vanderbilt.

The newly invented snack gained popularity among other customers, but remained primarily a restaurant item for several decades. This style of potatoes became known as Saratoga chips, named after the town in which they were first consumed. In 1895, William Tappenden of Cleveland began manufacturing potato chips for home consumption. Snack food innovations included the introduction of ridged potato chips in 1966, and fabricated potato chips in the 1970s.

Popcorn was perhaps the oldest salty snack food still widely consumed. Indigenous peoples in what became Peru were known to toast corn kernels over flames until they burst. This tradition was recorded as early as the fifteenth century. North American natives also prepared popcorn, and a bag of it was believed to have been shared at the first Thanksgiving dinner in Plymouth, Massachusetts. The term popcorn became accepted around 1820. Early American settlers may have eaten it—sprinkled with sugar and doused in cream—as the first breakfast cereal. It was also used decoratively from the beginning of its history, having been strung and draped on Christmas trees during the 1800s.

The snack food received a boost from the invention of the first popping machine in 1885 by a Chicago inventor named Charles Cretors. His machine used oil to pop the corn, and was used for about a century until the development of the hot-air popper. In the mid-1960s the snack began to be manufactured on a mass scale by Orville Redenbacher, who then promoted his brand as a gourmet hybrid popcorn. The next major innovation came in 1986, when Pillsbury introduced microwavable popcorn.

CURRENT CONDITIONS

Industry analysts reported that the snack food industry fared well in the early 1990s, given the economic downturn. In fact, over time the industry developed a reputation for being recession-proof. However, stiff competition required increasingly aggressive promotions to grab the consumer dollar, so some viewed salty snacks as a no-growth industry. Profits for salty snack manufacturers were 7.5 percent in 1992, representing a slight drop from the previous year. These figures included additional snacks, such as pretzels and packaged nuts, which were made by "full-service" salty snack companies such as Frito-Lay and Borden. Pre-tax profit margins for this broad category of snacks slipped from 6.8 percent in 1991 to 4.2 percent in 1992. Domestic dollar sales in 1992 were $9.6 billion—up overall from 1991 sales. Consumers bought 3.56 billion pounds of salty snacks, or nearly 18 pounds per capita consumption.

Potato chips led the way in salty snack consumption in 1992, with a retail sales volume of $4.41 billion. This dollar amount represented the sale of over 1.66 billion pounds of potato chips, which claimed 32 percent of the market for all savory snacks, including popcorn, meat snacks, pretzels, and snack nuts. Tortilla chips were the second most consumed salty snack. Over $2.57 billion worth were sold in 1992—a volume of 1.06 billion pounds. This represented a 20.5 percent market share by pound volume, or 18.6 percent by dollar sales. Potato chips and tortilla chips combined to account for about half the savory snack market.

Over 40 percent of all purchases of salty snacks were made in supermarkets—food stores which reported annual sales of at least $2 million. Grocery stores—food stores with sales of under $2 million annually—accounted for between 10 percent and 20 percent of salty snack sales in 1992, depending on the product. The remaining salty snacks were sold in convenience stores, mass merchandisers (large general merchandise stores which also carried grocery items), warehouse club stores, drug stores, vending machines, and other retail outlets such as delicatessens, liquor stores, and sports stadiums.

Shifting Distribution Patterns. A market research study found that consumers paid an average price of $2.66 per pound of savory snacks in 1992, down 2.6 percent from $2.73 per pound the previous year. This was attributed to several factors—including the recession and the competitive nature of retail products—but another major factor was a shift in distribution patterns. Large warehouse club stores and mass merchandisers charged lower prices for snacks in order to attract customers from smaller supermarkets and grocery stores. While supermarkets accounted for nearly half of salty snack sales, sales by dollar volume rose only about 1 percent. By contrast, warehouse clubs saw an increase of over 50 percent in savory snack sales, and mass merchandisers also saw double digit growth. Since these larger outlets charged less per pound for snacks than supermarkets, the increased sales represented a decline in profitability.

Convenience stores charged the highest prices for both potato chips and corn chips. In 1992, average potato chip prices were $3.06 per pound—the only outlet where prices passed the $3 mark. By contrast, potato chips sold for $2.49 per pound in supermarkets and $2.44 at mass merchandisers. Corn chips in that same year sold for $2.74 per pound in convenience stores, compared with $2.44 in supermarkets and $2.00 in warehouse clubs.

Prices began a trend toward equalization in the early 1990s, however. Convenience store prices of tortilla chips, for instance, were $2.61 per pound in 1992—the highest of any outlet, though 10 percent lower than the previous year. Supermarkets, grocery stores, mass merchandisers, and drug stores saw only a modest shift in tortilla chip prices. However, the price at warehouse clubs jumped almost 30 percent to $2.27 per pound. This trend also reflected the fierce competition that kept profits low throughout the recession.

Moreover, savory snacks experienced intensely competitive pricing in supermarkets. Full-line snack companies reported spending 52 cents of each promotional dollar on price reductions. Another 25 percent of promotional expenses went toward advertising, and 16 percent was used for in-store promotions. On the whole, 72 percent of full-line manufacturers reported spending more money for advertising and other promotional endeavors in 1992 than in 1991. In addition, retail shelf space increased in price during the early 1990s. The average cost per section foot per store paid by salty snack manufacturers leaped from $283.33 in 1991 to $342.86 in 1992.

Health Implications. The salty snack industry adapted to shifting consumer demands and perceptions throughout the last several decades. During the late 1960s and 1970s, Americans learned from health experts that they were consuming salt in greater quantities than was necessary—or healthy. The average individual needed about one-third teaspoon of salt per day. High consumption of salty snacks and other prepared or processed foods resulted in an intake double that, or even higher.

In more recent years, university studies linked low-fat diets to reduced rates of cancer and heart disease. Research showed that low-fat diets, typical of those in the Far East, were associated with low or virtually nonexistent incidence of cancer. This was particularly true, for instance, in breast cancer for women, which was much more prevalent in the United States and other western nations than it was in China. Moreover, when women of Chinese descent lived in the United States and adopted the high-fat diet typical of Americans, the incidence of breast cancer jumped to the rate found among westerners. Consumers were advised to reduce their fat intake, and many began to do so. Whereas in the 1960s, Americans typically consumed about half of their calories in the form of fat, a healthy diet was said to be one in which a maximum of 30 percent of calories ought to be consumed through fats.

Thus, manufacturers of salty, high-fat foods battled public perception that their products were unhealthy. Salty snack makers responded to changing consumer tastes by creating potato chips, corn chips, and tortilla chips that were perceived as healthy—or at least not too harmful. No-salt potato chips were developed in response to consumer demand, although in 1992 they accounted for less than 1 percent of potato chip sales. Following the unspectacular success of no-salt chips, low-salt varieties were introduced and proved more successful, showing double-digit market share growth in the early 1990s.

Low-oil potato chips proved more successful, making up 3.7 percent of chip sales by volume. From 1991 to 1992 alone, this category of potato chip jumped by 24.3 percent. One low-oil chip maker claimed its product to contain only 4 grams of fat per one-ounce serving, and just 140 calories. Other specialty chips were baked rather than fried, and another manufacturer sold chips that were cooked in the potato's own juices, resulting in a fat-free chip. Similar innovations were found in the tortilla chip industry in the early 1990s. Low-salt and low-oil tortilla chips combined to make up about 9 percent of overall volume.

Despite the responsiveness of manufacturers to consumer demand for healthier products, the desire to eat foods lower in fat nevertheless affected the salty snack industry. Among industry products, popcorn consumption virtually exploded in the late 1980s and early 1990s. Multigrain snacks also showed remarkable growth for the first few years after their introduction. Other foods that competed with the potato chip and similar snacks included pretzels and snack nuts, both of which gained market share much more rapidly than potato chips and tortilla chips in the early 1990s. Double-digit growth was observed in both ready-to-eat popcorn and in pretzels from 1991 to 1992: 12 percent and 15.5 percent, respectively. This was due at least in part to consumer perception of pretzels and nuts as having more nutritive value than potato chips. Even low-oil chips contained more fat than pretzels, for instance, which were baked rather than fried. And snack nuts contained relatively little salt and oil, and featured nutrients such as protein and minerals not found in potato or tortilla chips.

Flavor Variety. The development of flavored chips and snacks throughout the 1980s and 1990s was generally successful in keeping snack consumption on the rise. Small manufacturers introduced kettle-style potato chips, cooked in kettles as in early chip history. Many larger manufacturers followed suit, either developing their own versions of kettle chips or buying smaller companies that developed them for regional markets. In 1992, kettle style chips made up 5.5 percent of pound volume consumed.

Regularly shaped chips made up 46.2 percent of pound volume, and ridged chips of all flavors accounted for 34.4 percent in 1992. Fabricated chips represented 13.9 percent of the market for potato chips in that same year. Flavored potato and corn chips also multiplied, accounting for much of the introduction of new products during the late 1980s and early 1990s. In addition to barbecue flavored potato chips, consumers purchased sour cream and onion, ranch, and other flavors.

Tortilla chips experienced the most success of any salty snack food with the introduction of flavor varieties. Regular flavored chips made up 61.4 percent of the tortilla chip market in 1992, while cheese flavored tortilla chips accounted for 26.3 percent of the market. The third most popular flavor that year was ranch, which represented just under 8 percent of the market. Other varieties included salsa, spicy hot, jalapeno, chili, and oat bran flavors. In addition, white corn tortilla chips were introduced in the early 1990s and apparently found favor with consumers.

Ready-to-Eat Popcorn. The ready-to-eat (RTE) popcorn category of snack grew in popularity during the late 1980s and early 1990s. Dollar sales jumped from $248 million in 1987 (including caramel coated) to over half a billion dollars in 1992. This was in contrast to more sluggish growth in the microwavable popcorn category, in which sales remained flat from 1990 to 1992 after booming during the 1980s. Analysts attributed this slowdown to market maturation—almost 90 percent of consumers owned a microwave oven by 1990.

While caramel coated RTE popcorn made up the largest market share of any individual type—39.2 percent in 1992—non-coated popcorn accounted for 60.8 percent of total RTE consumption. Regular flavor had the largest share of sales after caramel, with nearly 20 percent of the market. White cheddar and cheese combined made up over 17 percent of the market, with butter flavor accounting for nearly 12 percent, and cinnamon and other flavors combining to total about 2 percent. Sales of all varieties grew in double digits from 1991 to 1992, except for white cheddar flavored

popcorn, which dropped 13.2 percent in the latter year. Low salt RTE sold well, claiming 6.3 percent of pound volume in supermarkets.

Whereas total popcorn sales slid downward 4.2 percent to $1.358 billion in 1992, RTE popcorn sales (including caramel flavored) increased 12 percent to $510 billion that same year. Measured in pound volume, sales grew 15.4 percent between 1991 and 1992, with 154.2 million pounds consumed. Many RTE brands were air-popped, making them virtually fat-free. Moreover, RTE popcorn could be purchased and eaten immediately, making it even more convenient than its microwavable competitors. RTE varieties appeared to be causing the demise of a second competitor, unpopped popcorn, for which dollar sales slumped 11.3 percent to $117.4 million in 1992. This trend suggested that RTE popcorn would eventually split the market with microwavable brands, while unpopped popcorn would become a supermarket dinosaur.

Showing similar pricing and distribution patterns to potato and tortilla chips, RTE popcorn commanded the highest price in convenience stores in 1992—$3.46 per pound. The lowest price, $2.28 per pound, was found in the warehouse club stores, which nevertheless saw an 11.8 percent price increase over the previous year. As of the early 1990s, RTE popcorn was produced by only a few manufacturers, but as others took note of its popularity and profitability, new companies began marketing their own products.

Extruded Snacks. Extruded snacks was the industry term for cheese puffs, corn puffs, and onion rings. By far the largest segment of this snack category—about 96 percent—was controlled by cheese flavored products. Sales of extruded snacks remained flat relative to other salty snacks from 1987 to 1992. Dollar volume was $694.3 million in 1987, and $774.0 in 1992, having dropped from its peak of $813 million in 1991. Like other savory snacks, extruded snacks were characterized by the introduction, in the late 1980s and early 1990s, of many flavor varieties. A diet company even introduced individual serving-size low-calorie cheese curls. But the new varieties failed to bring as much growth as expected to the industry overall.

Extruded cheese snacks, although no higher in fat content than potato chips and corn chips, suffered from a consumer perception that they were highly processed and therefore not as healthful as related snack foods. Throughout the last decade, consumers showed a preference for more natural, less processed foods—including snack foods. Although consumers wanted convenience, there was nevertheless a trend toward the use of whole foods rather than refined foods, which might have implications for the extruded snack industry.

Pork Rinds. The pork rind segment of the salty snack industry grew steadily over the past five years, increasing in sales volume from $163.4 million in 1987 to $236 million in 1992. Double-digit sales growth in the late 1980s slowed to about 5 percent annually in the early 1990s. One reason for growth in this segment was that the industry leader, Frito-Lay, increased its focus on pork rinds in its promotions—particularly in the southern United States. The South represented over half of total pork rind consumption, with Pacific states totalling another 20 percent. The New England and mid-Atlantic states had virtually no market, with only 4 percent of national pork rind sales.

Supermarkets sold only 18 percent of pork rinds in 1992, while grocery stores—the smaller volume of the two types—saw 27 percent of the snack's sales. Convenience stores, which charged the highest price for pork rinds—$6.12 per pound—accounted for 18 percent of sales. Boosting this snack's popularity was the introduction of microwavable brands in 1992. The new product offered a 60 percent to 70 percent reduction in fat—undoubtedly a source of appeal to consumers. In addition, pork rinds, like other salty snacks, appeared in flavor varieties including cajun, jalapeno, barbecue, and chili.

A New and an Old Product. Of all the salty snacks manufactured and sold in the early 1990s, the type that demonstrated the greatest growth was the multigrain chip. Although only a $198 million industry in 1992, this sales volume represented a growth of 76.5 percent from the previous year. The first-year sales of Frito-Lay's multigrain product, Sunchips, totalled $115 million.

Introduced in 1990 by Frito-Lay, multigrain chips grew quickly enough that industry observers expected the product to become a substantial segment of the salty snack industry. Two competitors introduced their own versions of multigrain chips, but Frito-Lay still cornered the market in 1992 with $192 million in sales—nearly all of the product's volume. The success of multigrain chips was attributed to the perceived health value of the snack, which was made of grains and was relatively low in salt and oil.

By contrast, the decline in sales for four straight years signalled a maturing market for corn chips. In 1987, the corn chip industry saw $560 million in sales, but by 1992 that figure had grown to only $598 million. The introduction of flavor varieties did not boost sales, which peaked in 1989 at $668 million and slid each year thereafter. Efforts by Frito-Lay to bolster sales through redesigned packaging and new marketing campaigns met with consumer apathy. Nevertheless, corn chips represented 4.3 percent of the overall snack market.

Industry Challenges. In a 1993 survey of salty snack manufacturers, increased government regulations were cited most often as the biggest challenge facing the industry in the mid-1990s. This concern arose from the passage of the Nutrition Labeling and Education Act of 1990, which required that all food manufacturers list nutrients in greater detail beginning in May 1994. In addition, the NLEA required manufacturers to list nutritional components of foods by serving sizes determined at the discretion of the government. Previously, food makers determined portion size and listed vitamins, protein, minerals, fat, and calorie content accordingly.

The trend mentioned second most frequently in the survey was the increasing consolidation of the industry. Some snack makers expressed concern that the large, national companies steadily purchased successful smaller firms that cut into their profits. This trend was perceived as a possible threat to the healthy competitiveness of the industry provided by innovative regional and family-owned firms. Increasing consumer emphasis on the health value of foods was cited as the third most important trend in the mid-1990s. Other trends noted were increasing retail shelf space fees, continued intense pricing competition with other manufacturers, demographic changes, and rising environmental concerns.

INDUSTRY LEADERS

Because of its 45 to 50 percent market share, Frito-Lay's activities and innovations reverberated throughout the salty snack food industry. Profits from the manufacturer accounted for 39 percent of the total of its parent company, Pepsi Co. A competitive battle for market share during the early 1990s prompted Frito-Lay to carry out a reorganization, which included repricing products and laying off 1,800 executives. In addition, 2,000 employees were shifted from administrative positions into sales jobs.

The rising success of its nearest competitors—Borden, which controlled 8 percent market share in 1992, and Anheuser-Busch's Eagle Snacks, which claimed 6 percent—provided the impetus for the restructuring. In the late 1980s, Frito-Lay increased prices faster than the rate of inflation and allowed quality control to lapse, resulting in a higher rate of broken chips. In addition, Frito-Lay did not respond to aggressive product promotions by its competitors in certain cities.

The result was that Eagle's potato chips began to win taste test competitions with Lay's and were priced as much as 20 percent lower. Even though Eagle was still unprofitable, its market share gains left the larger manufacturer vulnerable. Frito-Lay responded in 1991 with price reductions, a new advertising campaign, and the reorganization. About 60 percent of its management and administrative positions were eliminated, and decision-making was dispersed throughout operations. Four out of 40 plants were closed or sold, and the product lineup was substantially streamlined. These changes brought about $100 million in cost savings in the first year, and Frito-Lay's operating profits rose 15 percent in the first six months of 1992. Frito-Lay gained one percentage point in market share, while Borden lost almost a percentage point.

AMERICA AND THE WORLD

Two snack food industry leaders exported their product, producing overseas sales of about $4 billion. Pepsi Co. Foods International, the overseas counterpart to Frito-Lay, reported selling $2.18 billion in salty snacks in 1992. Its nearest competitor, Borden, recorded non-domestic sales of $1.87 billion in that year. These figures encompassed the broad category of snacks, including pretzels and snack nuts. The international snack food market was more than one-quarter the size of the domestic market in 1992. The passage in fall 1993 of the North American Free Trade Agreement (NAFTA) was expected to result in increased sales of these products in Mexico and Canada. In addition, the ramifications of NAFTA on trade with European nations could expand the market overseas throughout the 1990s.

RESEARCH AND TECHNOLOGY

The salty snack food industry witnessed an innovative use of computer technology in the late 1980s, when Frito-Lay issued hand-held computers to each of its 10,000-member sales force. Prior to this change, the route salespeople tallied the inventory of product on supermarket shelves on paper. These data were returned manually to regional offices, compiled, and eventually sent to the company's headquarters in Dallas. The resulting reports were clumsy and slow to produce.

Following the issuance of the small computers, however, the sales staff punched in inventory counts while still in the stores. The figures were instantly transmitted via satellite to Frito-Lay's mainframe computer. This instantaneous sending of data allowed analysts in Dallas to see sales figures much more quickly. As a result, Frito-Lay sales people gained

discretion to lower prices on the spot if necessary to remain competitive with other products. Although this computer system, purchased from Fujitsu, cost $40 million in 1987, Frito-Lay maintained that the technology paid for itself several times over by eliminating stale product in stores. Following this innovation, Frito-Lay's major competitors introduced hand-held computers, and manufacturers in other packaged foods industries were expected to follow suit.

INDUSTRY INFORMATION SOURCES

Fink, Ronald, "Data Processing: Pepsi Co.," *Financial World,* September 29, 1992.

Gutner, Toddi, "Chip Mania," *Forbes,* July 19, 1993.

Kanner, Bernice, "Kernel Knowledge," *New York,* January 11, 1988.

Macnow, Glen, "A Taste of Old Cape Cod," *Nation's Business,* February 1990.

Main, Jeremy, "Frito-Lay Shorts Its Business Cycle," *Fortune,* January 15, 1990.

Manufacturing USA, Detroit: Gale Research, 1993.

1993 SFA State-of-the-Industry Report, Alexandria, Virginia: Snack Food Association, 1993.

Sellers, Patricia, "If It Ain't Broke, Fix It Anyway," *Fortune,* December 28, 1992.

Zellner, Wendy, "Frito-Lay is Munching on the Competition," *Business Week,* August 24, 1992.

—Karen Withem

SIC 2097

MANUFACTURED ICE

This category covers ice plants operated by public utilities and establishments manufacturing artificial ice for sale in the form of blocks or cubes; it excludes makers of dry ice, which are categorized in **SIC 2813: Industrial Gases.**

Technological advances freed consumers from their long dependence on the harvest of local, naturally occurring sources of ice by permitting first its export and then its manufacture. This production, whether by private companies or by public utilities, was based on developments that also heralded the era of domestic refrigeration, and the ice trays found in most American kitchens became the major rival of commercial ice manufacturers. In terms of volume, however, domestic refrigerators could not compete with ice plants, and manufactured ice has sold well in outlets where goods for parties, receptions, and other entertainments are routinely purchased.

Statistics prepared by the National Association of Convenience Stores indicated that in 1993 manufactured ice constituted 0.9 percent of merchandise purchases from convenience stores in 1992, up from 0.8 percent in 1991. In terms of the 1992 figures, purchases of manufactured ice were thus on a par with those of packaged delicatessen items (0.7 percent), cookies (0.8), and wine and liquor (0.8).

Domestic refrigerators also could not match the ice manufactured in plants for its clarity and purity. As Michael R. Enright explained in *Nation's Business,* many ice suppliers have learned to enhance the purity of their product by creating a hole in the center of each cube and then flushing it, rinsing away the sulphur, iron, and other impurities in water that had concentrated there during the formation of the cube.

Such purity concerned not only consumers but also businesses that required large quantities of ice to keep food cool and fresh. Despite the convenience and cheapness of ice produced in-house by such businesses, ice manufacturing specialists had the potential to create a product of greater purity. As Jordan Tatter, President of Southern Michigan Cold Storage, explained in *Frozen Food Digest* in 1989, "There is pending legislation at various levels of government to tighten controls on sanitation and the quality of standards in the ice industry. By approaching our ice product as a food stuff, we will be more keenly aware of the liability concerns facing food processors."

Both the continuing quest for purity and a heightened consciousness about ecological issues on the part of consumers have made one promising development of the 1990s the marketing of gourmet ice, as harvested from glaciers, springs, and other sources predating or little affected by human pollution—a return to the very origins of the ice industry, though with the probable addition of innovative packaging this time around.

Leading companies in the ice manufacturing business include the Union Ice Co., Jefferson Ice Company, Pelican Ice and Cold Storage Inc., Glacier Ice Co., Riverside Ice Company, and Crystal Ice and Cold Storage Inc.

INDUSTRY INFORMATION SOURCES

Cuneo, Alice Z., "California Warms Up to Spring-Water Ice," *Advertising Age,* October 7, 1989, 30MW.

Enright, Michael R., "Hot Ice." *Nation's Business,* July 1987, 57.

Frozen Food Digest, October 1989, 76.

Morris, David, *Self-Reliant Cities,* San Francisco: Sierra Club, 1982.

NPN: National Petroleum News, Mid-June 1993, 142.

—Richard Hillyer

SIC 2098

MACARONI, SPAGHETTI, VERMICELLI, AND NOODLES

Establishments primarily engaged in manufacturing dry macaroni, spaghetti, vermicelli, and noodles. Establishments primarily engaged in manufacturing canned macaroni and spaghetti are classified in **SIC 2032: Canned Specialties,** and those manufacturing fried noodles, such as Chinese noodles, are classified in **SIC 2099: Food Preparations, Not Elsewhere Classified.**

INDUSTRY SNAPSHOT

Americans consumed 4.8 billion pounds of pasta and noodle products in 1991, manufactured almost exclusively in the United States from durum semolina wheat. A growing consumer preference for nutritious, low-fat foods boosted the health of the industry, nearly doubling mean annual per capita consumption in the last two decades to 19 pounds. In addition, consumer perceptions of pasta shifted: it gained popularity among middle class and affluent adults and seniors, rather than being viewed as a meal for children or the working poor, as was the case during the 1960s.

Industry sales in 1991 totalled roughly $1.3 billion. Total employment was over 7,000 people in that same year. There were approximately 200 pasta manufacturers in the nation, more than double the number that existed in the early 1980s. The industry faced challenges entering the mid-1990s, however, in the form of increasing federal regulations. Tougher labeling requirements beginning in 1994 affected pasta industry profit levels, as did environmental protection and laws designed to protect employees, such as mandatory health care provisions.

ORGANIZATION AND STRUCTURE

The largest 32 companies produced virtually all the pasta made in the United States in the early 1990s. Of those firms, 15 were divisions or subsidiaries of larger companies, 15 were privately owned, and two were public entities. The 32 firms operated approximately 200 establishments throughout the United

States. New York, California, and New Jersey accounted for 2,200 workers, or one-third of those employed in the pasta industry.

In 1991, roughly 91 percent of dried pasta and noodles was sold through retail outlets such as supermarkets, convenience stores, and gourmet shops, for personal consumption. Nearly 5 percent was sold to restaurants. Just over 1 percent was exported, and the remainder was shipped to miscellaneous entities such as schools and hospitals.

As a whole, the pasta industry paid $395.3 million in material costs in 1987. Of that sum, $186.3 was for purchase of semolina wheat and durum flour. Packaging materials and other ingredients cost $195.8 million, and miscellaneous wheat flour, including farina, cost $13.2 million. Value added by manufacturing was $728.7 million, making the value of shipments $1.23 billion. Pasta manufacturers in 1990 had capital investments totalling $46.8 million.

Pasta Manufacturing. Dried pasta was manufactured from coarsely ground durum wheat, or "semolina." Durum was a hard, winter wheat, known for its high level of gluten, which made a stiff dough appropriate for pasta. Farina, a softer wheat, was sometimes added, as were powdered flavorings such as tomato or spinach. Gluten was also sometimes added to the dough, and "enriched" pasta received nutritional supplements such as thiamin, niacin, riboflavin, and iron. Most pasta was made without eggs, but noodles were formed by adding eggs to the dough before processing.

Prior to the formation of pasta into its characteristic shape, the wheat was harvested and tested for moisture content, volume, color, insects, chaff, and bran. Once the wheat was determined to meet sufficient standards, the process of milling began. Wheat was first "tempered," or soaked in water, to separate the bran from the berry. Tempering also gave the berry enough moisture to prevent shattering when it was ground—the next part of the process. Once ground, the wheat was sifted numerous times to create semolina—coarsely ground flour, with particles about the size of sugar crystals. A byproduct of this repeated sifting was durum flour, which was sold for other uses. The semolina was added to water and any other ingredients, such as dyes, to create dough, which was then extruded through machines that formed the pasta into its ultimate shape. The pasta was then dried, packaged, and distributed.

BACKGROUND AND DEVELOPMENT

Although pasta was generally associated with Italy, and indeed many of the varied shaped originated from that country, the first pasta was actually Chinese. The development of an agricultural civilization led to pasta, possibly around 3,000 B.C. Ancient Greeks considered pasta "marcus"—meaning "divine food." An Etruscan tomb created around 400 B.C. depicted the making of the grain product. Horace, a poet who lived in the first century B.C., described lasagna as one course of a Roman banquet.

Pasta was also a part of the cuisine of the Middle East. The Jewish and Arabic cultures, as well as that of Persia, discussed pasta as well as noodles. Germans consumed it, and the Genoese ate it in the thirteenth century. All of this took place before Marco Polo's legendary expedition to China, which led to the widespread consumption by Italians, who added red tomatoes to the recipe.

Noodles were consumed in the New World, prepared in the manner popular among the British—accompanied with a cream sauce and cheese. Thomas Jefferson was the first prominent American to embrace pasta, when he purchased a "macaroni" machine in Italy and shipped it to the United States. An Italian restaurateur in Richmond, Virginia, served pasta to his influential clientele, which included Jefferson.

By 1848, French miller Antoine Zerega opened the first macaroni factory. He followed both Chinese and Italian traditions, drying strands of spaghetti on the rooftop of his Brooklyn factory. The subsequent immigration of large numbers of Italians to New York helped bring pasta into the mainstream of American cuisine.

A subtle wheat flavor was considered the ideal taste for pasta, since blandness prevented the pasta noodle from competing with the flavor of the sauce. The ideal texture of pasta was obtained when it was cooked "al dente." This translated from Italian literally as "to the tooth," but it described a noodle that was firm when chewed.

CURRENT CONDITIONS

The value of sales of pasta (including frozen and canned) rose from $1.55 billion in 1980 to $3.47 billion in 1990—a 223 percent increase in a decade. Industry analysts estimated that sales volume would climb to $6.41 billion by the year 2000, with an average annual growth rate of 6.3 percent. Dry pasta sales volume in 1990 was $1.2 billion, up $57 million from the previous year. Dry pasta and noodles comprised 32 percent of total pasta sales. Purchases of dry pasta were expected to rise 5.6 percent annually throughout the remainder of the century.

Health Benefits of Consumption. Throughout the late 1970s and 1980s, the increased health consciousness of Americans caused pasta consumption to rise steadily. The mean annual per capita consumption was 11.3 pounds in 1975. That figure rose to 19.0 pounds in 1991, including 13.4 pounds of dry pasta. Between 1988 and 1993, the average adult increased his or her consumption of pasta by ten meals annually, making it second only to soft drinks among the fastest growing of all foods during this time period.

The reason for this dramatic trend was research about cancer and heart disease prevention combined with the nutritional qualities of pasta. Numerous public and private studies during the 1970s and 1980s linked diets high in fat content with various types of cancers and heart disease. During this same time period, separate research of individuals in developing countries demonstrated the benefits of a diet high in fiber—a non-nutritional substance found in whole grains, vegetables, and fruits. In addition, studies revealed the importance of complex carbohydrates, which were also found in grains such as durum wheat. Consuming complex carbohydrates helped to provide a steady flow of energy because they took longer to digest than simple carbohydrates.

All of these findings rippled throughout the food industry, causing consumer preference to shift away from meals high in fat toward foods low in fat. Americans reduced their consumption of meat and dairy products as part of a healthier overall diet. Simultaneously, consumers embraced diets with a higher percentage of whole grain foods—including pasta. In fact, the popularity of pasta among athletes led to the term "carbo-loading," which was frequently accomplished through the ingestion of pasta or other grains. The consumption of foods high in complex carbohydrates prior to a marathon or other athletic endurance event was widely believed to boost performance.

In addition to being high in carbohydrates, pasta products became widely recognized for their nutritional value and relatively low levels of fat. A 10-ounce serving of cooked pasta contained 420 calories, 14 grams of protein (although wheat protein was considered incomplete), and only 1 gram of fat. It also provided one-fifth of the iron, niacin, and riboflavin, and one-third of the thiamin, needed for one day.

The general perception of pasta also evolved in the last two decades. In the 1960s, consumers thought of "spaghetti and meatballs" as a children's meal, too unsophisticated for adults. With the introduction of pasta varieties—lasagna, fettucine, manicotti, linguine, ravioli, canneloni, tortellini, and angel's hair pasta—the age-old grain food gained acceptance among affluent adults, for both dining out and eating in. Moreover, the typical marinara, or tomato-based, sauce served with ground beef or meatballs gave way to a multitude of flavored toppings—ranging from basil and pine nuts to Alfredo or cream sauces. Another popular accompaniment to the noodle was a mixture of vegetables, often in a marinara sauce, known as "pasta primavera."

Other factors contributing to pasta's popularity included its convenience, durability, and economy. A box of dried pasta lasted up to seven years on the shelf. It was a relatively good food value, at a cost of about a quarter per 10-ounce serving. The nationwide availability of prepared sauces added to the ease with which a pasta meal could be prepared. Pasta could be cooked on the stovetop in about 10 to 15 minutes. It could be reheated—along with the accompanying sauce—in a microwave oven in a similar time. These factors had significant appeal to the increasing numbers of dual-income and single-parent households in the United States.

Frequency of Pasta Consumption. A five-year study conducted by a private research firm found that more than 85 percent of children ate pasta regularly, with those aged six to twelve consuming it more frequently than any other age group. Among young adults, pasta consumption was also high. One study indicated that 85 percent of women and 82 percent of men in the 18 to 34 age range ate pasta at least once every two weeks. Women in this age group increased the frequency of their pasta consumption 28 percent between 1988 and 1993, while men increased 33 percent.

The largest overall increase in pasta consumption was noted among working parents—a 50 percent increase in five years. Indeed, 90 percent of households with children prepared pasta at least once per two-week period. Young couples without children increased their consumption of pasta 40 percent during the same time frame. Seniors and couples whose children had left home also ate more pasta—over 30 percent in both cases.

Most pasta was served for dinner (76 percent in 1993), but the trend went toward more frequent pasta lunches, with a 20 percent increase in consumption at this meal. The most popular shapes were macaroni, which saw a 33 percent increase in consumption, and lasagna, which showed 31 percent growth.

Regulatory Challenges. Like much of the food industry, pasta manufacturers faced increased regulation under new federal laws. The Nutrition Labeling and Education Act of 1990, which took effect in May 1994, required that pasta packaging list nutrients in greater detail than in the past. In addition, the NLEA provided for the Food and Drug Administration to determine the serving size on which nutritional information was based—something which had previously been determined by the manufacturers themselves.

Another trend in regulation in the early 1990s was based on concern over the effects of fumigants on the ozone layer. Many pasta manufacturers employed methylbromide to rid storage areas of weevils and other pests that consumed wheat. One bill considered in 1993 declared methylbromide a class one ozone depleter and called for its production to be discontinued by the year 2000.

Competitive Challenges. The greatest challenge to the dry pasta and noodle industry was expected to come from competition with other types of pasta. For example, the sales volume of frozen pasta grew at an annual rate of 19.1 percent from 1980 to 1985 and 13.4 percent from 1986 to 1991. Although growth was expected to slow to about 6 percent per year in the latter part of the 1990s, the popularity of this pasta was expected to continue throughout the remainder of the decade.

This growth was attributable to the convenience of frozen pasta, which came with a variety of sauces and required nothing more than heating in the microwave or the conventional oven. While cooking dry pasta was simple and required little time, preparation of the sauce could be more complex, and working individuals were increasingly reluctant to create meals from intricate or lengthy recipes.

Shelf-stable pasta was yet another product that eroded market share of dry pasta, and was expected to continue to do so. The shelf-stable category included dry packages like macaroni and cheese, pasta and noodle side dish mixes, add-meat dinner mixes, and soups or other meals that came in microwaveable containers. Shelf-stable pasta sales grew 6.7 percent annually in the early 1980s, but its popularity grew during the latter part of the decade by about 10 percent. Sales of this product were expected to grow at an annual rate of better than 10 percent through the remainder of the 1990s.

The biggest gain in market share was expected to be captured by fresh pasta, which showed an increase in sales volume of 60 percent annually from 1988 to 1991. Sales volume was expected to increase at a 15 percent annual rate throughout the remainder of the 1990s. Fresh pasta was more costly than dry, but because of the food's relatively low price, this premium did not appear to inhibit sales. The drawback of fresh pasta was its perishability, which was a result of its high moisture content. This pasta gained market share among the affluent at the expense of its dry counterpart, as it was perceived to be more flavorful and nutritious. It was sold in gourmet shops, as well as restaurants and supermarkets. The greater ease of distribution enjoyed by dry pasta manufacturers was believed to be a primary reason that dry pasta held its own in market share.

An industry report published in 1990 found that dry pasta, including plain noodle and shelf-stable preparations, totalled $1.56 billion in sales in 1989. In the same year, consumers purchased $56 million in fresh pasta. Total pasta sales volume—including canned, fresh, frozen and dry—was $3.26 billion. Thus, dry pasta purchases represented nearly half of total consumption of the product.

Canned pasta posed no competitive threat to dry pasta and noodles. Despite attempts to upgrade its image to a premium food product, canned pasta was still perceived to be most appropriate for children or for lower income individuals. Canned food was also viewed as having depleted nutritional value, and the health value that drove much of the rise in pasta consumption was perceived to be lacking in canned dishes. Moreover, canned spaghetti with sauce was not believed by consumers to be as flavorful as that of either fresh, frozen, or dry pasta.

New Jersey-based Campbell Soup Company, a leader in the canned pasta market under the name Franco-American, introduced two new children's dishes in 1989—including teddy bear shaped pasta and sporty shapes, like bicycles, in sauces. Despite such innovations, canned pasta market analysts did not anticipate that this product would pose a threat to dry pasta's market share. After sales volume of this product grew 3.3 percent annually from 1980 to 1985, and 5.3 percent per year from 1986 to 1991, it was projected to increase less than 1 percent annually through the mid and late 1990s.

INDUSTRY LEADERS

Hershey Foods Corporation, located in Hershey, Pennsylvania, was the largest pasta manufacturer, with 1991 sales of $300 million and about 1,100 employees. Golden Grain Company, headquartered in California, tabulated $270 million in sales in the same year. Minneapolis' Borden Pasta Division, whose parent company was Borden Incorporated, manufactured and sold

$160 million worth of pasta and noodles in 1991. Sales volume of those three firms combined was $730 million, over half of the $1.28 billion in sales garnered by the largest 32 manufacturers. Although dry pasta was the staple of these leading manufacturers, sensitivity to market trends led to diversification in types of pasta made. Both Hershey and Borden introduced microwaveable pasta products in 1989.

WORK FORCE

Due to technological advances in the pasta industry, including the use of computers in the manufacturing process, the number of workers declined from the early 1980s to the early 1990s. About 8,400 people were employed in the manufacture of dry pasta in 1982; by 1990, that figure had dropped to 6,200. Over 77 percent of 1990 employees were involved in production activities.

Wages rose with worker productivity, from $7.15 per hour on average in 1982 to $10.07 in 1990. That figure was slightly lower than the manufacturing average hourly wage of $10.49 in 1989. Most pasta establishments were relatively small, employing an average of 28 people in 1989.

AMERICA AND THE WORLD

The United States consumed more pasta than any nation in the world. Moreover, U.S. sales grew faster than most of the world's other major consumers. In 1988, Americans purchased 3.62 billion pounds of pasta, while Italians bought 2.67 billion pounds, France followed with 772 million pounds sold, West Germans bought 650 million pounds, and the United Kingdom purchased 425 million pounds. Only the United Kingdom saw a significant increase in pasta sales—23 percent. This was just slightly less than the 25 percent sales growth that occurred in the United States during that same period. Of the 4.8 billion pounds of pasta consumed in the United States 1991, 275.7 million, or about 5 percent, were imported. Almost 60 percent of this total—or 164.8 million pounds—was imported from Italy. By comparison, only 20 percent of pasta imports in 1975 originated from Italy.

Although the U.S. imported and exported a negligible volume of manufactured pasta, the durum wheat from which it was made grew steadily as an export beginning with the 1959-60 growing season. Exports of this wheat variety were zero in that year, but climbed to peak annual levels of 80 million bushels during the 1980s. The quantity dipped to about 20 million bushels in the 1988-89 season, but rose again to about 55 million bushels in 1989-90 and again the

next harvest year. This jog in exports was due to variations in the amount of durum planted, as well as changing growing conditions.

Algeria was the largest importer of U.S. durum wheat, with Tunisia second. Trade with those countries was part of the Export Enhancement Program, an incentive program to facilitate U.S. exports to North African nations. The quantity of durum wheat grown for domestic manufacture roughly tracked that of export durum, although quantities did not fluctuate as widely for domestic use as for export. In 1959-60, more than 20 million bushels were produced, and that level grew to 68 million bushels in 1990-91.

The United States ranked fourth in the world in mean annual per capita pasta consumption. Italians consumed over 59 pounds per capita annually and Venezuelans nearly 28 pounds, while Americans ate 19 pounds apiece annually. With popularity of pasta on the increase due to its perceived convenience and nutritional value, however, per capita consumption in the United States was predicted to surpass that of every nation in the world except Italy by the year 2000.

INDUSTRY INFORMATION SOURCES

Business Trend Analysts, Inc., "The U.S. Pasta Market," *Pasta Journal,* November/December 1991.

Fisher, Neal, "Growth in Durum Markets Benefits Producers and Industry," *Pasta Journal,* November/December 1990.

"International Pasta," *Pasta Journal,* November/December 1990.

Kardong, Don, "Yankee Noodles," *Runner's World,* October 1992.

Manufacturing USA, Detroit: Gale Research, 1993.

National Pasta Association, "And on the Ninth Day There Was Pasta," *Pastahh,* Winter 1989-90.

"Pasta Is Growing Strong," *Pasta Journal,* May/June 1993.

"The Popularity of Pasta," *Pasta Journal,* January/February 1993.

"Spaghetti," *Consumer Reports,* August 1988.

—Karen Withem

SIC 2099

FOOD PREPARATIONS, NOT ELSEWHERE CLASSIFIED

This classification is comprised of establishments primarily engaged in manufacturing food preparations not classified under another category. It includes manufacturers of items such as syrups, leavening agents, dry mixes (for sauces and gravies), packaged mixes (made from pasta, rice, and potatoes), seasonings and spices, sugar, and ready-to-eat meals and salads. Also included are manufacturers of miscellaneous food specialties, such as fried Chinese noodles, sorghum, tortillas, bouillon cubes, nonalcoholic cider, honey, marshmallow creme, peanut butter, popcorn, tea, tofu, and vinegar.

Miscellaneous food preparations with separate classifications include: **SIC 2091: Canned and Cured Fish and Seafoods**; **SIC 2092: Fresh or Frozen Prepared Fish and Seafoods**; **SIC 2095: Roasted Coffee**; **SIC 2096: Potato Chips and Similar Snacks**; **SIC 2097: Manufactured Ice**; and **SIC 2098: Macaroni and Spaghetti**.

INDUSTRY SNAPSHOT

According to government statistics, the total value of goods shipped by establishments classified in SIC 2099 totaled $9.8 billion in 1987. In addition, some businesses with other classifications manufactured products considered primary to the industry. Combined, the value of all product shipments for items classified in the industry, irrespective of their source, totaled $10.7 billion. This number represented a 30 percent increase over the total of $8.1 billion recorded for 1982.

Not all product categories performed well, however. For example, shipments of vinegar and cider dropped from $187.8 million to $164.7 million, and shipments of blended honey dropped from $89.9 million to $79.4 million.

Despite these declines, many categories experienced substantial increases. Fast-growing classifications included: dry mix preparations (such as dip mixes, salad dressing mixes, gravy and sauce mixes, seasoning mixes, and frosting mixes), which increased from $1.2 billion to $2.2 billion; non-frozen, perishable prepared foods (such as salads, peeled vegetables, tortillas, and tofu), which increased from $769.1 million to more than $1.3 billion; tea packaged for consumers, which increased from $747.6 million to $936.3 million; and spices, which increased from $585.9 million to $888.8 million. Peanut butter sales rose slightly from $796.7 million in 1982 to $847.7 million in 1987. Consumption estimates for 1990 indicated that Americans ate enough peanut butter to make ten billion peanut butter and jelly sandwiches.

BACKGROUND AND DEVELOPMENT

Vinegar. One of oldest products classified within SIC 2099 is vinegar. Records of vinegar use date back 5,000 years, and some historians estimate it was known as long ago as 10,000 years. During the Civil War, vinegar was used to prevent scurvy, a disease caused by vitamin C deficiency. Throughout vinegar's long history, it has had a wide variety of applications, including use as a preservative and as a cleaning agent.

Vinegar, derived from two French words meaning ''sour wine,'' is a product of fermentation. When natural sugars ferment they produce alcohol, which after undergoing further acetic fermentation becomes vinegar. One of the best known types of vinegar is wine vinegar, but throughout history many other types of vinegar have been produced. These include vinegars made from naturally sweet products like molasses, sorghum, honey, and syrup, and vinegars made from fruits, potatoes, and grains.

Four different methods have evolved to control the fermentation process by which vinegars are made. Under the most labor-intensive method, called the solera system, vinegar is aged in different types of wood, a process that can take decades. Another technique, termed the Orleans method, uses a starter culture in a manner similar to the process by which bakers ferment bread dough in sourdough preparation. The Orleans method is implemented to produce vinegar in wooden barrels and takes up to six months. A faster method, termed the ''quick process,'' involves the aeration of wine along with organic materials to produce vinegar in about a week. The quickest vinegar production, however, occurs in a process called continuous production, which requires holding wine in a pressurized tank under carefully controlled conditions. Air is forced through the liquid to aid the fermentation process. Wine is continually added and finished vinegar taken off the top of the tank. Converting wine into vinegar using this process takes approximately one day.

In the United States, the vinegar industry formed alongside the apple industry. As a result, it was concentrated in areas with large harvests of apples. Called cider vinegar, vinegar in the United States was made from apples or apple juice. As the vinegar industry developed, it offered a variety of products to perform different functions. White vinegar, also called distilled vinegar, is primarily used in home canning and for making pickles, salsa, and relishes. Wine vinegar is an integral ingredient in vinaigrettes. Malt vinegar, a mildly sweet product, compliments salads and fish and chips. Rice vinegar, a particularly strong variety, is added to sushi rice. A rich, dark product, balsamic vinegar is used for vinaigrettes and as a condiment. Sherry vinegar, another variety with a strong flavor, is a cooking vinegar. In addition to the types of vinegar produced by using varying sources, infused vinegars are made by adding flavorings such as berries, garlic, or herbs.

Tofu. A product with a long history, tofu is a white, gelatinous substance made from soybean curd. It bears a slight resemblance to cream cheese but has a softer texture that has sometimes been described as "squishy." Although tofu by itself is considered bland, when cooked in a recipe it picks up flavors from other ingredients. To make tofu, manufacturers begin by soaking soybeans for 12 to 18 hours. After soaking, the beans are mashed and strained. The retained juice solidifies, is cut into portions, and packaged for sale.

Originating in China approximately 1,000 years ago, tofu was for centuries a staple in Oriental cooking. It began gaining popularity in the United States following World War II. Servicemen were introduced to tofu while they were overseas, and many returned to the United States with wives of Asian descent who were accustomed to cooking with it.

Tea. Another food product with historic ties to China is tea. Tea was originally made from the dried, processed leaves of an Asian shrub. One of the oldest companies in the U.S. tea industry was founded by Sir Thomas Lipton, a Scotsman, who began importing tea into the United States in 1890. The first instant tea was marketed by the Nestlé Beverage Company in 1948.

Peanut butter. One product native to the Americas is peanut butter. While not indigenous to North America, peanuts were grown by South Americans at least 1,000 years ago. Although the circumstances of their introduction to North America is unknown, historians believe that peanuts were grown by early European settlers, who used them as food for hogs. George Washington Carver is credited with developing more than 300 uses for peanuts and helping establish them as an important crop. Improvements made between the 1930s and the 1990s helped peanut farmers experience a fivefold increase in per acre yields. During the early 1990s, most U.S. peanut production came from Georgia. Other leading states were Alabama, Texas, North Carolina, and Virginia.

According to statistics, approximately half the peanuts eaten in the United States are consumed in the form of peanut butter. *Consumer Reports* calculated that on any given day peanut butter is consumed by one out of every six Americans. Although peanut butter is considered a good source of protein, dietary fiber, and B vitamins, it contains a high percentage of fat.

To make peanut butter, manufacturers remove peanut skins and grind the nuts into a thick, pasty substance. Frequently, hydrogenated vegetable oil is added as a stabilizer, and salt and sugar are added to improve flavor. Chunky varieties, containing pieces of peanuts, were also developed.

One of the problems associated with peanut butter is the presence of aflatoxin. Aflatoxin is a carcinogenic poison produced by *Aspergillus flavus,* a mold that grows on peanuts when they are not properly stored. Aflatoxin problems first appeared in the 1960s and led U.S. officials to establish limits on the amount of the substance allowable in peanut products. A 1990 *Consumer Reports* study noted that some peanut butter exceeded allowable levels of aflatoxin.

CURRENT CONDITIONS

During the early 1990s, the top U.S. peanut butter brands—Jif, Skippy, and Peter Pan—accounted for two-thirds of all peanut butter sales. Specialty and health food stores offered "natural" peanut butters that lacked sweeteners and stabilizers and some featured "grind your own" peanut butter options.

In 1993 industry watchers noted a decline in peanut butter sales. The drop was attributed to calorie-consciousness. Consumers also turned away from name brands in favor of private labels. According to a September 1993 report in the *Wall Street Journal,* peanut butter sales declined 12.2 percent during the 13-week period ending July 4, 1993. Chunky peanut butter sales fell the most, declining 15.7 percent, while creamy sales dropped 10.9 percent.

One of the fastest growing sectors within the industry during the early 1990s was prepackaged convenience foods, which were often sold as "kits" with premeasured ingredients that could be prepared quickly and easily by the consumer. Tofu was also experiencing rapid growth. Because it is a good protein source that is naturally low in saturated fat and has no cholesterol, its popularity was increasing particularly among vegetarians and health-conscious consumers. Tofu also benefited from a growing interest in ethnic cooking.

The tofu expansion could also attributed to improvements in packaging technology, giving products a longer shelf life. Most tofu was sold in packages of water and had a short shelf life of only about 10 days. In 1990 one producer, Mori-Nu, reported the development of innovative packaging that enabled its product to have a shelf life of 10 months without refrigeration.

One of the nation's largest tofu producers, Azumaya, Inc., of San Francisco, began producing tofu in 1927. In 1991 the company reported daily production of 3.5 tons of tofu. Some industry analysts predicted that as tofu gained in popularity it would become as popular as yogurt.

Another rapidly growing product during the early 1990s was tea; in 1991 sales of herbal teas in supermarkets passed the $100 million mark. The top three companies in herbal tea sales were Celestial Seasonings with 49.1 percent of the market, Lipton with 23.1 percent, and Bigelow with 14.6 percent. In 1992 enough herbal tea was sold in the United States to brew 58 million gallons. Sales represented a five percent increase over the previous year. According to a report in *Brandweek,* one of every eight cups of tea consumed in the United States is either decaffeinated or herbal, and approximately 80 percent of the tea is consumed as iced tea. In 1993 *Beverage World* estimated that iced tea sales would continue growing at an annual rate of 50 percent.

INDUSTRY LEADERS

A leader within the tea segment of SIC 2099 is the Thomas J. Lipton Company, a wholly owned subsidiary of Unilever PLC. Lipton, headquartered in Englewood Cliffs, New Jersey, reported sales of $1.4 billion in 1992, a 4.3 percent increase over 1991. According to one account, Lipton controlled about half of the black tea market, which was estimated at $423 million in 1992.

Lipton Company, a pioneer in the development of naturally decaffeinated teas, was founded in 1915 by Sir Thomas Lipton, who had been selling his teas in the United States since 1890. In 1992 Lipton reported that its Suffolk, Virginia, production facility blended more than 36 million pounds of tea. Lipton's tea products include tea bags, instant iced tea, and ready-to-drink iced tea. In 1991 the company established the Pepsi Lipton Tea Partnership, a venture undertaken to bring together expertise from Lipton's tea producers and Pepsi's bottling and distribution system. In addition to tea products, Lipton also marketed Lipton Soup Mixes, Recipe Secrets, Lipton Side Dishes, and Cup-a-Soup. The company's Lawry's division offered spice and seasoning blends, sauces, and Mexican food products.

Another major participant in the tea segment of the industry was Nestlé USA, Inc., which is comprised of 15 food and beverage companies. Products of the Nestlé Beverage Company include Nestea, Carnation hot cocoa, and Nestlé Quick, while the Nestlé Refrigerated Food Company produces Contadina refrigerated pizza kits and sauces. Other major Nestlé divisions include Nestlé Food Company, Nestlé Frozen Food Company, and Nestlé Brands Foodservice. In 1992 the Nestlé organization reported net sales of $7 billion and a staff of 43,000.

At the helm of the spice segment of SIC 2099, McCormick & Company, Inc. was founded in 1889 and, according to company literature, is the largest spice company in the world. Its product line, sold in the United States on the East Coast under the McCormick label and on the West Coast under the Schilling label, features a wide variety of spices from 18 areas around the world.

In 1992 McCormick reported sales of $1.5 billion and a work force of 8,000. McCormick's industrial and food service divisions provide flavors, seasonings, and specialty food products to more than 80 of the top 100 food manufacturers in the United States as well as to many major restaurant chains. In addition to the United States, McCormick sold products in Mexico, the United Kingdom, Canada, Europe, South America, Japan, and Australia. In 1993 the company announced its intention to pursue the development of markets in China and the Pacific Rim nations.

Universal Foods Corporation, a major producer of several items classified under SIC 2099, is an international company involved in manufacturing and marketing a wide variety of food products, including flavors and colors, dehydrated vegetables, frozen french fried potatoes, and yeast products. The company's yeast products are marketed under the Red Star label.

Red Star yeast production began during the latter part of the 1800s. In the 1920s the company perfected an aeration process that enabled it to make an improved compressed yeast product. Further work led to the development of a less perishable yeast. In the early 1990s Universal Foods claimed it was the largest and most diversified manufacturer and distributor of yeast products within the United States.

In 1993 Universal Foods reported a seven percent increase in yeast revenue. A significant portion of the gain was attributed to trends within the pizza industry toward producing extra large pizzas. Within the consumer baking market, a rise in yeast sales was attributed to the growing popularity of bread machines. According to company statistics, U.S. households owned an estimated three million bread machines in 1993, up from 18,000 in 1988.

WORK FORCE

According to figures released by the U.S. Department of Commerce, employment within SIC 2099 totaled 57,900 in 1987. The industry's combined payroll topped $1.1 billion. The leading states in employment were California, Illinois, New York, and Texas.

INDUSTRY INFORMATION SOURCES

Applebaum, Cara. "Tetly Heats Up Iced Tea." *Adweek's Marketing Week* (April 6, 1992).

"Background on Thomas J. Lipton Company." Englewood Cliffs, NY: Lipton.

Bittman, Mark. "Vinegar." *Restaurant Business Magazine* (March 1, 1992).

Branch, William D. "Peanut." *Information Finder*. World Book, Inc. 1993.

"Brand Scorecard." *Advertising Age* (October 5, 1992).

Carlsen, Clifford. "Utilitarian Soybean Curd Goes Exotic." *San Francisco Business Journal* (June 28, 1991).

Deveny, Kathleen. "Peanut Butter Makers Feel Crunch With Sales Decline in 2nd Quarter." *Wall Street Journal* (September 16, 1993).

Friedman, Martin. "Food Kits Foster One-Stop Shopping." *Prepared Foods* (August 1992).

Hartley, Tom. "Vinegar Firm Finds Success is Sweet in a Sour Industry." *Business First of Buffalo* (March 4, 1991).

Lipton: 1992 President's Progress Report. Englewood Cliffs, NJ: Thomas J. Lipton Co., 1993.

McCormick & Company, Inc.: 1992 Annual Report. Sparks, MD: McCormick, 1993.

McMath, Robert. "Whether Regular or Herbal, It's Increasingly Time for Tea." *Brandweek* (May 31, 1993).

Meeting the Growing Demand for Diversified Yeast Products. Milwaukee, WI: Universal Foods.

Miller, Cyndee. "Seeking an Image: Tofu Tired of Being 'Yucky,' Car Agency has 'Smart' Idea." *Marketing News* (October 29, 1990).

Nestlé USA, Inc. Glendale, CA: Nestlé USA, 1992.

"The Nuttiest Peanut Butter." *Consumer Reports* (September 1990).

Prince, Greg W. "Together Forever." *Beverage World* (April 1993).

"Terre Haute Turns Out Tofu." *Indiana Business Magazine* (January 1991).

U.S. Department of Commerce. *1987 Census of Manufactures*. Washington, DC: Bureau of the Census, 1990.

Universal Foods Corporation: 1993 Annual Report. Milwaukee, WI: UFC, 1993.

—Karen Bellenir

TOBACCO PRODUCTS

SIC 2111

CIGARETTES

This category covers establishments primarily engaged in manufacturing cigarettes from tobacco or other materials.

INDUSTRY SNAPSHOT

The cigarette manufacturing industry in America is among the most powerful and controversial in the country's history. Spearheaded by highly diversified international conglomerates Philip Morris Companies Inc. and RJR Nabisco Holdings Corp., who continue to champion their cigarette interests along with their other myriad businesses, the cigarette industry is a formidable economic force. According to *Business Week,* the leading tobacco companies posted total sales in 1993 of more than $80 billion. Moreover, the long-time slide in American consumption of cigarettes appears to have halted in the mid-1990s; the percentage of smokers in the American population has remained stable since 1991 at about 26 percent. Finally, American cigarette companies are optimistic about opportunities in international markets, where demand for their product is high and rules and legislation regarding usage are largely absent.

Nonetheless, the cigarette industry is a beleaguered one in many ways, all ultimately traceable to the health risks associated with consumption of their product. As *Time* noted in April 1994, "in the past few months, a rash of new restrictions, legislation and government tough talk has elevated the antismoking campaign to new heights. Before, it was a matter of health warnings, moral persuasion and segregation of the warring parties. Now smoking [in the United States] is in danger of being legislated virtually out of existence."

ORGANIZATION AND STRUCTURE

The group of manufacturers leading the industry in the 1990s was a small, entrenched collection of competitors. From the industry's nascence in the mid-nineteenth century, when many cigarette manufacturers began as tobacco farmers, to the 1990s, the number of participants generally has been limited to slightly more than a handful. Early cigarette producers were located in proximity to the tobacco fields of the southern United States, typically operating in the same region as their competition. It was an industry in which everyone knew each other's names.

Nearly a century and a half later, the cigarette industry still consisted of a small, almost fraternal group of manufacturers, several of whom had been in competition with one another since the nineteenth century. In 1992 there were 15 cigarette manufacturers in the United States generating at least three million dollars in revenue each. Roughly a quarter of these companies were subsidiary operations of the industry's two largest participants, Philip Morris Companies Inc. and RJR Nabisco Holdings Corp. Moreover, the disparity in revenue volumes among these manufacturers was vast, as great as the nearly $50 billion dollar gulf separating Philip Morris, the tenth largest publicly held corporation in the United States, and Eagle Tobacco Corp., with annual sales of roughly three million dollars.

While the number of companies involved in the industry in the early 1990s was relatively small, its revenue volume was not; it totaled over $25.52 billion in 1990. This amount, particularly large considering the limited number of manufacturers in the industry, more than doubled during the 1980s, climbing from $12.12 billion in 1982. The enormous amount of capital required to operate in the industry limited new entrants from establishing manufacturing facilities. In 1989 the average amount paid for raw manufacturing materials was $352.5 million, nearly 80 times more than the average cost per establishment for all other manufacturing industries.

Geographically, the representation of cigarette manufacturing establishments in the United States is as narrow in scope as the limited number of companies involved in the industry. In the early 1990s the production of cigarettes was confined to the four-state region comprising North Carolina, Virginia, Georgia, and Kentucky. The bulk of these manufacturing facilities were located in North Carolina.

BACKGROUND AND DEVELOPMENT

The origins of tobacco in the United States date back to before the formation of the nation itself, and the growth and sale of this product represented one of the key agricultural crops that spurred the country's growth in the eighteenth and nineteenth centuries. The use of tobacco to produce cigarettes in any widespread fashion did not occur, however, until the dawn of the 20th century. Other uses for tobacco precluded the popularity of cigarettes, as Americans in the early nineteenth century enjoyed plug and twist tobacco, then smoking tobacco, and finally cigars, all of which overshadowed cigarette production in terms of volume for most of the century. Even in the mid-1800s, the use of tobacco had its detractors, and cigarette smokers, many of whom were women, suffered from a somewhat ignoble image. As a social commentator in 1854 wrote in reference to New York: "Some of the *ladies* of this refined and fashion-forming metropolis are aping the silly ways of some pseudo-accomplished foreigners in smoking Tobacco through a weaker and more *feminine* article which has been most delicately denominated *cigarette.*"

A decade later, however, the production volume of cigarettes had increased enough to become the object of special federal taxation, which, according to the Internal Revenue Law promulgated in June of 1864, levied one dollar per one hundred packages not exceeding five dollars in aggregate value. The following year, 19.7 million cigarettes were produced, and manufacturers were buffeted by a series of tax hikes, first to two dollars per thousand and then to five dollars per thousand. This arrested the growth of the industry just as sales were beginning to elevate cigarette manufac-

turers' importance in the tobacco industry. In 1868 tax rates were cut back to $1.50 per thousand and growth resumed, marking the beginning of a 20-year period that would witness the most rapid percentage growth rate in the production of cigarettes in the history of the industry.

Cigarette production reached 500 million in 1880 and eclipsed the one billion mark five years later. By the 1880s, there were five principal manufacturers of cigarettes: Washington Duke Sons & Co., Allen & Ginter, Kinney Tobacco Co., William S. Kimball & Co., and Goodwin & Co. Together these companies produced 2.18 billion cigarettes annually by the end of the decade, 91.7 percent of the national output of 2.41 billion. These companies, referred to as the "Tobacco Trust," essentially controlled the cigarette market, enjoying a virtually unassailable lead over other, smaller manufacturers. This monopolistic trait would characterize the industry throughout much of its existence.

The ability of these companies to secure such a wide advantage over their competition was partly due to significant technological innovations achieved during the 1880s that ended the time-consuming chore of rolling cigarettes by hand. On a good day, a skilled laborer could roll 3,000 cigarettes during a ten-hour workday—a production rate that threatened to place a ceiling on the industry's growth. But beginning in 1872, the age of mechanization in the cigarette industry was initiated. The first cigarette manufacturing machine, patented by Albert H. Hook, earned a modicum of success, but did not prove to be commercially viable. By 1881, however, significant improvements had been made in a design patented by James A. Bonsack. This machine could churn out 200 to 220 cigarettes per minute, accomplishing in 15 minutes what it took an experienced production worker ten hours to complete.

Bolstered by the ability to produce more cigarettes with lower labor costs, the five companies that occupied the industry's leading positions grew quickly by moving into untapped markets and securing their overwhelming lead in the U.S. market. In 1890 the composition of the industry's manufacturers became more homogeneous when the five leading companies, at the urging of James Duke of Washington Duke & Sons Co., merged to form the American Tobacco Co., which initially focused primarily on the production of cigarettes. Over the next 20 years, the American Tobacco Co. acquired an interest in roughly 250 companies. This cigarette giant developed into a tobacco giant, securing commanding leads in every product branch of the tobacco industry with the exception of cigars. In the manufacture of cigarettes, plug, smoking tobacco, fine cut tobacco, snuff, and little cigars, the conglomerate's production output in the first decade of the twentieth century represented no less than 76 percent of the country's total volume, giving smaller manufacturers little hope of wresting market share away from the industry's predominant leader.

If the five manufacturers leading manufacturers in the 1880s justly earned the moniker "Tobacco Trust" when operating as separate companies, then their union certainly deserved the same label. The U.S. Supreme Court came to this realization in May of 1911, when it found the American Tobacco Co. in violation of the Sherman Act. Six months after the ruling, the court issued a decree stipulating that the enormously powerful tobacco company be divided into 16 independent corporations, none which could wield monopolistic control over any one product branch within the tobacco industry.

Although certainly a significant chapter in the history of the cigarette industry, the parceling of the American Tobacco Co.'s sundry divisions and subsidiaries did not affect the cigarette industry as greatly as the cigar industry, primarily because cigarettes still did not represent a major branch of the tobacco industry. The cigarette industry was burgeoning, however, and stood on the brink of catapulting past all other branches of the tobacco industry. The first step toward this end came six years after the restructuring of the industry, when the United States entered World War I and cigarettes were issued to soldiers in the U.S. Army and Navy.

Once the habit of smoking cigarettes had extended to men, thereby doubling the potential customer base of the industry, sales began to mushroom and the cigarette branch of the industry at last overtook all other branches. Over the ensuing 20 years, during which time many of the widely popular brands—Chesterfield, Lucky Strike, Old Gold, Camel, Raleigh, and Marlboro—emerged, the consumption of cigarettes grew rapidly. Domestic tobacco leaf consumption increased 42.5 percent between 1910 and 1930, while the production of cigarettes increased from 8.64 billion to 125.2 billion, a 1,339 percent increase during the 20-year period. In these first two decades following the dissolution decree, there were approximately 15 to 20 manufacturers deriving the bulk of their revenue from the production of cigarettes. Only four of these manufacturers, commonly referred to as the "Big Four," held any appreciable share of the market. Indeed, these manufacturers—the restructured American Tobacco Co., R.J. Reynolds Tobacco Co., P. Lorillard Co., and Liggett & Meyers Tobacco Co.—held as firm a grip on the U.S. cigarette market as American

Tobacco had before the U.S. Supreme Court's ruling; they controlled more than 95 percent of the market.

Clearly, the dissolution of American Tobacco had not produced the U.S. Supreme Court's intended effects; a monarchy had merely been replaced with an oligarchy. Smaller, independent cigarette manufacturers were able to record enviable profits during this period, largely because of the bountiful market itself, but none could challenge the "Big Four" in magnitude. Accordingly, as the cigarette industry continued to grow, these powerful manufacturers became more formidable, further widening the gulf separating the industry's upper echelon and the rest of the competition.

The next two decades of business brought continued success to the industry's four largest manufacturers and witnessed the rise of an additional member to the industry's elite, Philip Morris & Company Ltd., Inc. Philip Morris introduced its mainstay Marlboro brand in 1925, which reached an annual production total of approximately 500 million cigarettes. But the industry's leading brands during these years, Camel and Lucky Strike, each sold 25 billion cigarettes a year, by far outpacing Philip Morris' production volume and providing little room for the future ascension of the smaller, formerly British-based manufacturer. Instead, Philip Morris was able to climb the industry's ranking list thanks to a strong relationship with cigarette jobbers throughout its distribution network and by virtue of prudent management. By the end of the 1940s, after Philip Morris had already unseated Lorillard to occupy the industry's fourth place position, the "Tobacco Trust" now included five members, generating an aggregate sales total of $357.3 million.

The 1950s heralded a new era for cigarette manufacturers, one in which it became necessary to defend growing criticism of the product being sold. Since the industry's emergence, anti-cigarette and anti-tobacco factions from both the federal and consumer sector had railed against the sale and use of tobacco. Manufacturers had fared fairly well, effectively beating back the rising tide of protest against their business. While industry manufacturers had suffered run-ins with the Federal Trade Commission concerning misleading advertising, the federal government had subsidized a large portion of the industry before World War II, which helped to allayed the fears of manufacturers.

During the 1950s, however, medical reports linking health problems to smoking began to surface. In 1953 the Sloan-Kettering Cancer Institute's report showed a relationship between cancer and tobacco, and manufacturers consequently found themselves fighting against an entirely new and much more formidable foe—scientific fact.

In 1964 the U.S. Surgeon General issued a landmark report linking smoking with lung cancer and heart disease. A year later, the U.S. Congress promulgated the Cigarette Advertising and Labeling Act, which stipulated that health warnings be placed on each cigarette package. In 1971 cigarette advertisements on radio and television were banned. Although these announcements and restrictions did not cause the industry to collapse, the rate of smoking in the United States began to spiral downward.

The ranks of smokers in the United States diminished from 42.6 percent in 1966 to 25.5 percent by 1990, a level at which it hovered through 1994. Cigarette manufacturers began manufacturing different types of cigarettes—filter tips during the 1950s, then low-tar cigarettes during the 1960s and 1970s—and marketed these products not to create more customers, but to capture their competitor's customers. By the 1970s, however, Philip Morris and R.J. Reynolds had gained considerable ground on their competition, making the industry essentially a battle between these two behemoth corporations. Philip Morris won the battle, albeit temporarily, when the manufacturer's Marlboro brand passed R.J. Reynolds' Winston brand in 1976.

During the 1980s, lower-priced, discount cigarettes began to enter the market with increasing frequency. This enabled smaller cigarette manufacturers to thrive for a short time, until the industry's preeminent leaders dropped their own prices and set about capturing the low-end market. By this time, the reams of medical reports delineating the hazardous effects of smoking had firmly grabbed the attention of the American populace, transforming anti-tobacco factions into a powerful nationwide movement. Cigarette taxation doubled in 1983 and continued to rise, particularly during the late 1980s, increasing the popularity of lower-priced cigarettes. Consequently, cigarette manufacturers diversified their operations with unprecedented fervor, while casting an eye to international business opportunities.

CURRENT CONDITIONS

As the national economy began to recover from the recessive economic conditions of the early 1990s, manufacturers in the cigarette industry were saddled with problems much larger and more threatening than the vagaries of the economic climate. For the most part these difficulties had been nagging at the industry for the bulk of its existence, but the intensity of the groups fighting against the industry in the mid-1990s was increasingly vehement. In June 1992 the U.S. Supreme

Court reversed an appeals court ruling concerning the product liability of cigarette manufacturers. Earlier, two lower courts in Minnesota and New Jersey had ruled that the family of a woman who had died of lung cancer in 1984 could not sue Philip Morris, Loews Corporation, and the Liggett Group on grounds that these cigarette manufacturers had withheld information concerning potential health dangers. The Court's reversal sent cigarette manufacturers' stock prices cascading downward, as industry participants braced themselves for a rash of lawsuits.

Perhaps a more disheartening development for cigarette manufacturers in the early 1990s was their diminishing influence over federal lawmakers. In the past, through the combined efforts of the tobacco lobby and elected representatives from tobacco-growing states in the Southeast, manufacturers had been able to slow the rate of federally imposed cigarette taxes and mitigate to a certain extent federal legislation aimed at curbing cigarette use. But in the early 1990s, cigarette makers were assailed on several fronts with renewed energy. As *Business Week* noted, "smokers are confronting an unprecedented rush to tax their cigs. Tobacco levies passed during the 1993 legislative sessions will provide 15 percent of new state tax revenue in fiscal 1994—even though cigarette taxes are less than two percent of state tax collections nationwide, according to the National Conference of State Legislatures. Several states, including Washington and New York, levy a tax above 50 cents a pack. Michigan voters recently approved raising the state's tax to 75 cents a pack to finance public education." In addition, a hefty federal tax on tobacco is regarded as a centerpiece of the Clinton Admninistration's plan for health reform.

Additional restrictions on smoking in public areas are increasingly common as well, in part as a result of a 1993 Environmental Protection Agency report that classified environmental tobacco smoke as a class-A carcinogen and charged that 3,000 nonsmokers die annually from second-hand smoke. *Time* reported in 1994 that "in May, Maryland will institute the tightest state-wide restrictions in the nation, banning smoking in virtually all work places, except in sealed, separately ventilated rooms." Many communities across the country are instituting strict rules regarding cigarette use, and even the U.S. Department of Defense issued restrictions that ban smoking in all military work spaces, including military bases. Businesses, too, (including fast-food giant McDonald's) are banning smoking in their establishments. The poor publicity associated with such legislation, coupled with scathing reports in the news media that charge cigarette manu-

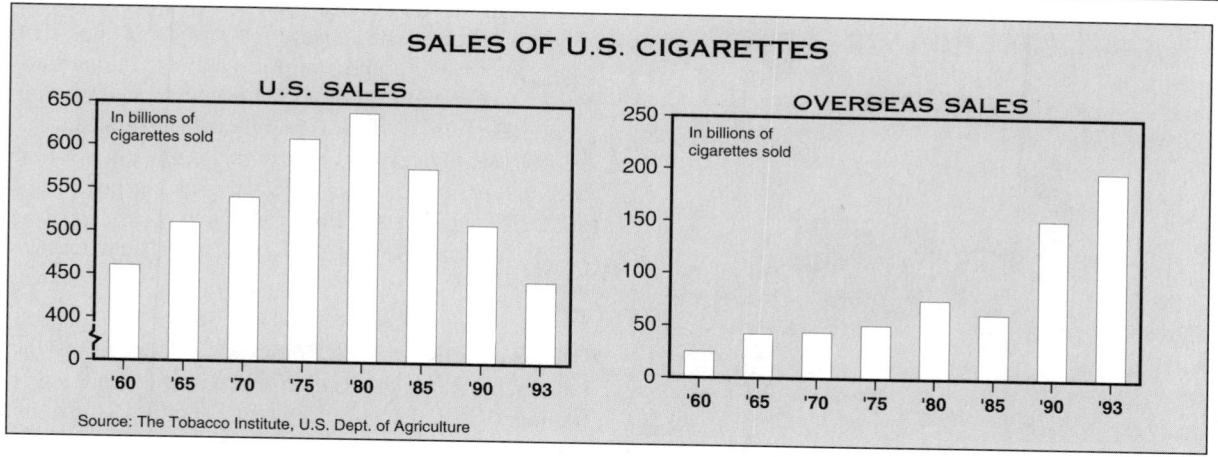

facturers with duplicity and disregard for public health, have further damaged the industry's reputation. Controversy over the "Joe Camel" advertising campaign launched by R.J. Reynolds Tobacco Co. has also been heated. Critics charge that the campaign snares a large number of under-age smokers, while the company insists that such charges are baseless. Another ominous threat to the cigarette industry, according to *Time,* is "the activist Food and Drug Administration, [which] is taking a look at whether to classify nicotine as a drug—a move that could effectively remove cigarettes from the over-the-counter market. FDA Commissioner David Kessler told Congress [in 1994] he believes that nicotine is a 'highly addictive agent' and that cigarette producers control the level of nicotine 'that creates and sustains this addiction.'" The FDA further charged in June 1994 that the Brown & Williamson Tobacco Corp. cultivated a strain of high-nicotine tobacco in Brazil expressly for use in producing its cigarettes, a charge the company heatedly denied.

Beyond these developments, the nature of the industry itself was transforming, creating further anxiety for cigarette manufacturers and particularly the industry's large, leading manufacturers. The popularity of discount cigarettes continued to climb, and by 1993, discount cigarettes accounted for nearly one-third of the volume retail sales of cigarettes in the United States. Several of the larger manufacturers were slow to acknowledge this consumer trend. Philip Morris and R.J. Reynolds Tobacco Co., however, had aggressively entered into the production of discount cigarettes, realizing that cheaper cigarettes did not represent a fleeting consumer trend, but an economic choice driven by the 12 cent annual increases in cigarette prices for the previous five years. Controlling 60 percent of the discount market by 1993, Philip Morris and

R.J. Reynolds regained the market share they had been ceding to smaller manufacturers. Yet the production of discount cigarettes generated far less profit—as much as ten times less—than traditional, higher-priced brands, further clouding the industry's financial future.

Faced with these formidable challenges, cigarette manufacturers quickly sought to ameliorate their position, as they had frequently done in the past. With the hope of alleviating some of the pressure from the legislative sector, manufacturers compiled databases of "confirmed" smokers, registering names and addresses of consumers responding to direct mail advertising and promotional offers. The marshalling of forces to combat the growing movement against the tobacco industry represented, at best, a long-term solution to manufacturers' problems. For more immediate relief, the industry increasingly looked toward foreign markets to sell their traditional, higher-priced line of cigarettes. Toward this end, U.S. manufacturers were recording considerable success, tapping into a market in which sales tripled between 1985 and 1993.

INDUSTRY LEADERS

Ranked according to sales volume, the two largest cigarette manufacturers in the United States during the early 1990s were Philip Morris Companies Inc. and R.J. Reynolds Tobacco Co., both perennial leaders in the industry. Together, the two manufacturers controlled 71 percent of the U.S. cigarette market in 1993.

Philip Morris' ascension to the number one position in the cigarette industry began shortly after the 1911 decree intended to dilute the staggering power of the American Tobacco Co. Although Philip Morris' initial magnitude paled in comparison to the industry's "Big Four"—the American Tobacco Co., R.J. Reynolds, Lorillard, and Liggett & Meyers—, its rise stands as a remarkable achievement. Beginning as the U.S.

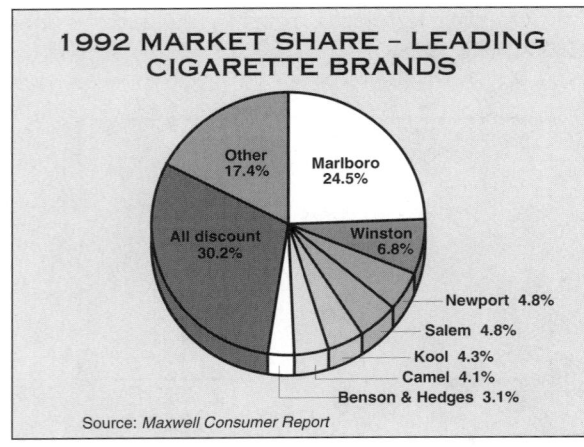

1992 MARKET SHARE – LEADING CIGARETTE BRANDS

Other 17.4%
Marlboro 24.5%
All discount 30.2%
Winston 6.8%
Newport 4.8%
Salem 4.8%
Kool 4.3%
Camel 4.1%
Benson & Hedges 3.1%

Source: *Maxwell Consumer Report*

operations of a British manufacturing company named Philip Morris Company, the manufacturing facilities were purchased by a U.S. financier George J. Whelan, who acquired several of the small manufacturing concerns left for sale after the break up of American Tobacco. Formed as a U.S. company in 1919 and renamed Philip Morris & Company Ltd., Inc., the company introduced the brand of cigarette that would eventually catapult the fledgling manufacturing concern toward the top of its market in 1925. That brand, Marlboro, did not begin its meteoric rise until the ubiquitous Marlboro Man, the rough-hewn American cowboy, first appeared on cigarette packages in 1955. In the interim, Philip Morris slowly climbed the industry's ladder through effective marketing and a strong relationship with cigarette jobbers on the East Coast, ensuring that the company's products received preferential treatment during the all-important journey from manufacturing site to retail stores.

By 1936, Philip Morris maintained a firm grip on the industry's fourth position through its widely popular English Blend cigarettes introduced three years earlier. Following World War II, several poor management decisions, including an overestimation of the nation's consumption capacity and a belated entry into the filter segment of the industry (which caught fire during the 1950s) sent the company's sales spiraling downward. By 1960, Philip Morris had fallen to sixth place in the U.S. cigarette market—last place among the major U.S. manufacturers.

The introduction of the Marlboro Man in 1955, however, strengthened Philip Morris' domestic sales, while an early move into foreign markets underpinned the company's domestic resurgence. By 1973, Marlboro cigarettes were the second most popular brand in the United States, ranking only behind RJR's Winston brand. Three years later, Marlboro eclipsed Winston,

and Philip Morris became the second-largest seller of tobacco in the world. At roughly the same time that Marlboro became the nation's preferred cigarette, Philip Morris branched into the production of low-tar cigarettes with its Merit brand, then intensified its efforts toward overseas expansion. As a result of these two marketing strategies, plus the growing popularity of Marlboro cigarettes, Philip Morris surpassed RJR in 1983 to become the world's largest cigarette manufacturer.

Incorporated in 1879 as R.J. Reynolds Tobacco Company, RJR Nabisco Holdings Corp. garnered initial success through the efforts of the company's founder, Richard Joshua Reynolds, and by virtue of its association with the American Tobacco Co. during the lucrative "trust years" in the tobacco industry. Operating as a subsidiary of American Tobacco from 1899 until the dissolution decree of 1911, Reynolds' company thrived, earning a majority of its profits through the sale of chewing and smoking tobacco under the respective Schnapps and Prince Albert brands. The company did not manufacture cigarettes until 1913—shortly after Reynolds had resumed control of the company following the U.S. Supreme Court's ruling—but once it did, the company's success came quickly with its widely popular Camel brand of cigarettes.

For the next 20 years, the company's success was primarily predicated on the popularity of Camel cigarettes, but by the late 1930s and throughout the 1940s, the company's exponential growth began to slow due to labor problems, antitrust suits, and one particular product flop—Cavalier cigarettes. By the 1950s, however, R.J. Reynolds began to effect a turnaround by selling its new filter tip brand of cigarettes, Winston, which first appeared in 1954. Two years later, the company introduced its Salem brand, the industry's first king-size filter-tipped menthol cigarette. This, combined with the continuing success of the Camel and Winston brands, elevated the company's standing in the market above all others.

When Philip Morris' Marlboro surpassed R.J. Reynolds' Winston in domestic sales in 1976, the company countered with the introduction of a "back-to-nature" brand of cigarettes called Real, but the effort failed miserably and the product was discontinued in 1980. In that same year, the company's management sought to ameliorate its position by expanding overseas, leading to an agreement with the People's Republic of China to manufacture and sell cigarettes there, the first U.S. company to reach an accord with China.

But this historic move abroad was not enough to stop the company's slide to the industry's number two position three years later, when Philip Morris ascended to the industry's number one position. In 1985, to stave off further losses, R.J. Reynolds purchased Nabisco Brands, Inc. for $4.9 billion (the same year in which Philip Morris acquired General Foods Corporation). Three years after the Nabisco purchase, the biggest leveraged buyout in U.S. history occurred when Kohlberg Kravis Roberts & Co., an investment firm specializing in leveraged buyouts, purchased RJR Nabisco for $24.88 billion. Once the company became privately held, several subsidiaries were sold to streamline the company's operations, then it once again went public in 1991 with a new issue of stock.

WORK FORCE

Moving in inverse proportion to the industry's sales during the 1980s, the number of people employed by cigarette manufacturers declined over the course of the decade. In 1980 the industry's total work force, including both hourly and salaried workers, amounted to 46,000. By the end of the decade, the industry's employment base had dropped by more than 10,000 workers, descending to 35,000 by 1990, then dropping again to 34,000 in 1992.

Throughout its history, the bulk of the industry's work force has been comprised of production workers, or those employees paid on an hourly basis to operate manufacturing machinery and perform manual tasks in the production of cigarettes. This preponderance of production workers, whose proportional representation in the cigarette industry's work force dropped by roughly four percent during the 1980s, continued to characterize the industry in the early 1990s. Of the 34,000 total employees in 1992, 26,000 were employed as production workers. These workers, generally employed on a full-time basis, but averaging 11 percent fewer hours than production workers employed by all other manufacturing industries, earned $20.68 per hour in 1992, up from $9.23 per hour in 1980. Salaried employees, or those workers paid an annual salary for performing administrative, technical, or managerial duties, composed the balance of the industry's work force, earning an average of $47,915 per year in 1991.

The average size of a cigarette manufacturing establishment, in terms of the number of employees per facility, was enormous when compared to the average size of manufacturing establishments in all other manufacturing industries. In 1989, the typical manufacturing establishment comprised 54 employees, 37 of whom were employed as production workers, while the cigarette industry averaged 2,277 employees per establishment, more than 42 times the size of all other manufacturing industries. Of these 2,277 employees per establishment in 1989, 1,700 were employed as production workers.

AMERICA AND THE WORLD

As legislation and taxation affecting the cigarette industry in the United States has become more commonplace, leading companies have increasingly turned to global opportunities. As *Newsweek* pointed out in 1994, "sixty percent of Philip Morris's sales already come from outside the United States; in the next decade it hopes to push its overseas profits closer to that 60 percent mark." This move to international markets is expected to be an expensive one, for although American cigarette exports are growing six to eight percent annually, cigarette companies recognize that establishing facilities in targeted countries is a priority. Plant construction or acquisition is expected to impact industry players for the next several years as a result.

The cigarette industry, however, views the potential profitability in those regions as too lucrative to ignore. *Forbes* pointed out in 1994 that "the tobacco companies have been buying every major Russian and Eastern European tobacco plant in sight. Over the past two years, Philip Morris has invested in tobacco companies in Hungary, the Czech Republic, Lithuania, Russia and Kazakhstan. RJR has invested in plants in Hungary, Poland, Ukraine, and Russia. . . . In two to five years, company executives say, these new and recently acquired plants could gross up to $1 billion in sales for Philip Morris and $500 million for RJR. Both companies claim their Russian operations are already profitable." Smoking is on the rise in heavily-populated regions of the world such as Asia as well, and while "American companies must sell cheaper, less profitable smokes in the Third World, but margins will improve as those economies develop and prices rise."

INDUSTRY INFORMATION SOURCES

"Anti-Tobacco Groups Push Efforts to Cut Down Number of Smokers," *Wall Street Journal,* March 9, 1962, 6.

Bart, Peter, "Advertising: Cigarette Men Eye New Threat," *New York Times,* March 18, 1962, F12.

Cox, Reavis, *Competition in the American Tobacco Industry: 1911-1932,* New York: Columbia University Press, 1933.

Faison, Seth Jr., "Cigarette Ruling: Hour of Confusion," *New York Times,* June 26, 1992, D1.

Farley, Christopher John, "The Butt Stops Here," *Time,* April 18, 1994.

Farrell, Christopher, "This Sin Tax is Win-Win," *Business Week,* April 11, 1994.

"FTC Requires Cigarette Labels, Ads to Warn Smoking May Cause Death, *Wall Street Journal,* June 25, 1964, 3.

Hammer, Alexander R., "Financing Vital to Tobacco Men," *New York Times,* December 31, 1961, F8.

Hass, Nancy, "Fighting and Switching," *Newsweek,* March 21, 1994.

"Italy Outlaws Cigaret Ads; British Firms Plan Curbs," *Wall Street Journal,* April 9, 1962, 7.

Klebnikov, Paul, "Opiate of the Masses," *Forbes,* April 11, 1994.

Lelyveld, Joseph, "Cigarette Producers Keeping Quiet, *New York Times,* January 26, 1964.

Mallory, Maria, "Is the Smoking Lamp Going Out for Good?" *Business Week,* April 11, 1994.

——,"That's One Angry Camel," *Business Week,* March 7, 1994.

Maxwell, John C., "Cigaret Scoreboard," *Barron's,* November 2, 1970, 11.

"Most Cigaret Marketers to List Tar, Nicotine in Ads," *Advertising Age,* November 2, 1970, 6.

O'Conner, John J., "New-Cigaret Brand Battle Heats Up; 14 Enter Fray," *Advertising Age,* October 20, 1975, 23.

O'Conner, John J., "PM, Russ Offer Apollo-Soyuz Smoke, *Advertising Age,* July 14, 1975, 1.

"Pall Mall Became Top Selling Cigaret in '60, Report Says," *Wall Street Journal,* December 23, 1960, 4.

"The Profits in Bootleg Cigarettes," *Business Week,* April 7, 1975, 69.

Reynolds, Patrick, and Tom Shachtman, *The Gilded Leaf: Triumph, Tragedy, and Tobacco,* Boston: Little, Brown and Company, 1989.

"R.J. Reynolds Says It Has New Cigaret Low in Tar, Nicotine," *Wall Street Journal,* April 8, 1970, 10.

Schaeffer, Lyle, "Brisk Business for the Cigarette Companies," *Magazine of Wall Street,* October 7, 1961, 79.

Shanahan, Eileen, "U.S. Plans Curbs in Cigarette Ads," *New York Times*, January 14, 1964, 1.

Shapiro, Eben, "Marlboro Smokers Defect to Discounters," *Wall Street Journal,* January 13, 1993, B1.

"Smoking More, Despite the Scare," *Business Week,* December 22, 1962, 78-80.

"Smoking Rate in U.S. Rises for First Time in 25 Years," *Wall Street Journal,* April 2, 1993, B6.

Smothers, Ronald, "Tobacco Country Is Quaking Over Cigarette Tax Proposal," *New York Times,* March 22, 1993, A1.

Statistical Abstract of the United States: 1993 (113th edition), Washington, DC: U.S. Bureau of the Census,, 1993.

Tennant, Richard B., *The American Cigarette Industry,* New Haven: Yale University Press, 1950.

"Tobacco: Britain's TV Ban," *Newsweek,* February, 22, 1965, 88.

"Tobacco: Embattled, Embittered and Uneasy," *Forbes,* July 15, 1963, 13.

"Tobacco Firm Can Be Held Liable for Death Caused by Smoking, Florida High Court Says," *Wall Street Journal,* June 6, 1963, 11.

"When Smoke Got in their Eyes," *The Economist,* April 10, 1993, 65.

"Where the Cigarette Men Go after the TV Ban," *Business Week,* November 21, 1970, 64.

"World Trade: Tobacco's Taxing Dilemma," *Time,* May 7, 1965, 98.

"The U.S. Sums It Up: Quit Smoking," *Business Week,* January 18, 1964, 43.

—Jeffrey L. Covell

SIC 2121

CIGARS

This industry consists of establishments that primarily are engaged in the manufacture of cigars. Manufacturers of other tobacco items are treated in **SIC 2111: Cigarettes**; **SIC 2131: Chewing and Smoking Tobacco and Snuff**; and **SIC 2141: Tobacco Stemming and Redrying**.

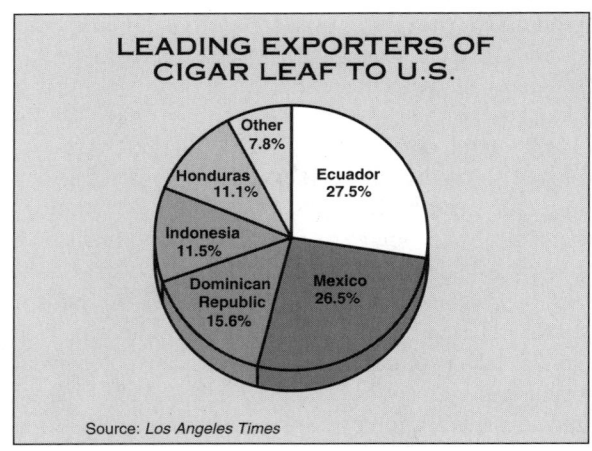

LEADING EXPORTERS OF CIGAR LEAF TO U.S.

Other 7.8%
Ecuador 27.5%
Honduras 11.1%
Indonesia 11.5%
Dominican Republic 15.6%
Mexico 26.5%

Source: *Los Angeles Times*

Like other tobacco products, the sale of cigars has dropped as Americans have become increasingly concerned about the effects of tobacco smoking on health and fitness. The volume of cigar sales has fallen about five percent a year during a 15-year period, dropping to 2.2 billion units sold in 1991. In the mid-1970s, volume was more than 5.5 billion, and at the industry's peak in 1964, unit sales reached 9 billion cigars.

Cigar smokers have traded quantity for quality, however. They smoke fewer cigars, but when they do smoke, they often smoke cigars of a high quality. Declines in volume have been offset by increases in prices and a growing market for premium cigars. Sales in dollars have risen slowly as a result, despite the volume decline, and reached about $700 million in the early 1990s. Changes in distribution systems also helped the industry, as more discount stores and supermarkets began carrying a wider variety of cigars, especially the higher-priced cigars.

Laws prohibiting smoking in public places, increased taxes on tobacco products, and medical findings that cigars cause mouth, throat, and pancreatic cancer have hurt the U.S. cigar industry. Cigar manufacturers have been combating these obstacles by increasing promotional activities with wholesalers and by introducing new products in various sizes.

The cigar industry also has been hurt by the sale of both authentic and counterfeit Cuban cigars in the U.S. The Cigar Association of America has been trying to halt the sale of these illegal products, estimating that they cost U.S. cigar makers $28 million a year. The sale of Cuban cigars has been illegal in the U.S. since 1962, when President Kennedy signed the Cuban trade embargo.

The Cigar Association of America, established over 50 years ago, consists of regular members (the cigar makers headquartered in the United States) and associate members (including foreign cigar manufacturers, importers, leaf dealers, and other suppliers.) The organization's principle activities involve maintaining cigar industry statistics, public relations efforts, and lobbying federal and state governments on issues of import to the industry, especially taxation of their products.

The number of cigar manufacturers in the U.S. has steadily shrunk during the last part of this century. Cigars were once handmade products, but technology has taken over in most companies. In Miami, however, Cuban and Central American immigrants in a half dozen small cigar factories have continued to make hand-rolled cigars. With the pool of qualified cigar rollers drying up, cigar-rolling is becoming a lost craft.

The anti-smoking trend among consumers and the government will probably continue to cut into cigar sales. Unlike the cigarette industry, however, the U.S. cigar industry has little money to spend on advertising and other activities to combat negative publicity.

INDUSTRY INFORMATION SOURCES

"Cigar industry campaigns against Cuban imports, fakes." *U.S. Distribution Journal.* August 1989.

Fucini, Suzi, "Taking a new look at an old mainstay." *U.S. Distribution Journal.* January 1990.

Maldonado, Patricia, "Keeping tradition alive." *South Florida Business Journal.* March 13, 1990.

"Puffery." *Forbes.* June 22, 1992.

"Split in cigar sales continues." *U.S. Distribution Journal.* January, 1991.

—Wendy Stein

SIC 2131

CHEWING AND SMOKING TOBACCO AND SNUFF

This industry consists of establishments primarily engaged in manufacturing chewing and smoking tobacco and snuff. Other tobacco product industries are discussed in **SIC 2111: Cigarettes; SIC 2121: Cigars;** and **SIC 2141: Tobacco and Redrying.**

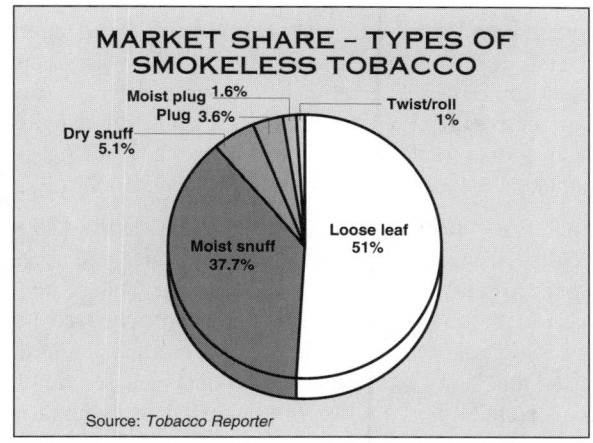

MARKET SHARE – TYPES OF SMOKELESS TOBACCO

Moist plug 1.6%
Plug 3.6%
Dry snuff 5.1%
Twist/roll 1%
Moist snuff 37.7%
Loose leaf 51%

Source: *Tobacco Reporter*

In the early 1990s, as cigarette and cigar volume dropped, smokeless tobacco products grew in volume of sales by three to five percent annually. Among smokeless products, moist snuff was the leading product. The increase in use of moist snuff was due to a number of factors: increased smoking restrictions in many places; promotions and advertising; and the waning impact of tax hikes, negative publicity, and health warnings. Manufacturers of loose leaf, plug, and dry snuff experienced a slow slide in volume sales but kept profits up through price increases. In addition, use of smoking tobacco, including pipe tobacco and roll-your-own cigarettes, showed a slight increase in the early 1990s.

U.S. Tobacco Co. has been the overwhelming leader in moist snuff sales, controlling more than 85 percent of the market with its Copenhagen and Skoal brands. In the looseleaf category, Pinkerton Tobacco Co. has established itself as a consistent leader with at least 45 percent of the market controlled by its Red Man and Granger brand lines. Conwood Tobacco Co. ranks second in sales of loose leaf tobacco products.

Pinkerton introduced a Red Man moist snuff line in 1990 to capitalize on snuff's rising share of the approximately $1.4 billion smokeless tobacco industry. Snuff accounted for well over $800 million in sales in 1988, probably because it was easier to use than other forms of smokeless tobacco.

Industry fortunes in the twentieth century. The snuff business enjoyed an upsurge in use in the mid-1970s after nearly half a century of lackluster sales, due in large part to a health-related scare about smokeless tobacco at the beginning of the twentieth century. People had just become aware of the danger of contracting tuberculosis from sputum, and spitting was considered the greatest hazard of tobacco. The hardcore market remained in the South among the older population. However in the mid-1970s, snuff began to regain some popularity, especially as young men turned to it because they thought it was a safe alternative to cigarettes. Labels warning of dangers and a ban on television and radio advertising of smokeless tobacco were not required until 1986.

The industry faced many challenges in the 1980s and 1990s, as the public became more concerned about tobacco-related health issues. Like other tobacco concerns, the smokeless tobacco industry may face increasing court challenges because of studies that indicate that smokeless tobacco products cause mouth cancer and other oral diseases. Moist snuff, which has captured a majority share of the market, is believed to be more likely to cause mouth disease because of the way it is held in the mouth.

The industry strategy for maintaining profits included value-added promotions and competitive pricing, although, like other tobacco products, price increases of smokeless products marched well ahead of the rate of inflation.

INDUSTRY INFORMATION SOURCES

Margulis, Ronald. ''Pricing, Promotion Lead Smokeless Issues.'' *U.S. Distribution Journal.* December 1991.

''Moist Snuff Lifts Smokeless Market.'' *U.S. Distribution Journal.* May 1990.

''Pinkerton Introduces Moist Snuff.'' *U.S. Distribution Journal.* April 1990.

''Smokeless Sales Show Effects of Recent Pressures.'' *U.S. Tobacco and Candy Journal.* October 5-25, 1987.

''U.S. Volumes Decline Again.'' *Standard and Poor's Industry Survey.* August 6, 1992.

White, Larry C. *Merchants of Death: The American Tobacco Industry.* New York: William Morrow, 1988.

—Wendy J. Stein

SIC 2141

TOBACCO STEMMING AND REDRYING

Establishments in this industry classification are primarily engaged in the stemming and redrying of tobacco or in manufacturing reconstituted tobacco. Establishments which sell leaf tobacco as merchants, wholesalers, agents, or brokers, and which may also be engaged in stemming tobacco, are classified in **Industry 5159: Farm Product Raw Materials, Not Elsewhere Classified**. Leaf tobacco warehouses which also may be engaged in stemming tobacco are classified in **Industry 4221: Farm Product Warehousing and Storage**.

INDUSTRY SNAPSHOT

In early 1994, the tobacco processors, like the tobacco industry as a whole, faced an uncertain outlook in the United States. The long-term trend of domestic cigarette consumption was down, owing to higher prices, tougher restrictions on smoking in public places, greater awareness of the health risks of tobacco use, and declining social acceptance. Congress debated whether to raise the Federal cigarette tax to as much as $1.25 per pack, and there were calls for regulating tobacco as a drug. Thousands of tobacco farmers, whose families had often been in the business for generations, were shifting out of the product and into other crops—cotton, in many cases.

Tobacco processing is truly an international business, however, and all of the major companies in the segment have extensive growing, processing, and sales operations overseas. These markets presented a brighter picture. While U.S. usage was on a downward trend, consumption overseas (about ten times the size of the domestic market) was expanding at 2% to 3% a year. Demand in some countries had grown enormously—cigarette consumption in China, for example, was five times greater than in 1965. U.S. cigarette exports tripled between 1985 and 1992, owing to the popularity of American tobacco products and reduced trade barriers in countries such as Japan. Consequently, the proportion of domestic cigarette production that is exported has risen sharply, from 9% in 1987 to 30% in 1993.

ORGANIZATION AND STRUCTURE

The processing of tobacco in the United States is dominated by four major companies (Universal, Standard Commercial, Dibrell, and Monk-Austin) that have large operations in the important tobacco-growing regions of the world. These companies will purchase the farmer's tobacco at auction (common in the United States) or contract to purchase tobacco directly from the farmer. In certain overseas markets where the firms have contracted to buy the farmer's entire crop, they will often provide financial and technical assistance as well to ensure the tobacco's quality. In the United States, most of the processors' tobacco purchases at auction are made to fill specific orders from the major domestic and overseas cigarette producers, with whom they often have relationships extending over many years.

After purchase, the tobacco is processed to meet the specific needs of the cigarette manufacturer, whose representatives are frequently at the processor's facilities to monitor the work on their particular orders. At the factory, the tobacco is reclassified according to grade; blended to meet customer requirements regarding color, body, and chemistry; and threshed to remove the stem from the leaf (although some tobacco is processed in whole leaf form). The processed tobacco is redried to remove excess moisture so it can be held in storage for long periods of time. The companies also perform most of the processing of tobacco that is not purchased at auction and thus enters the U.S. stabilization pool, under the auspices of the Department of Agriculture. The companies generally do not manufacture cigarettes or other consumer tobacco products.

In the United States, primarily two major types of tobacco are grown: flue-cured and burley. Flue-cured is one of the most widely grown tobaccos in the world. It is cured by the grower, usually with gas- or oil-generated heat, and it serves as the basic ingredient in light blended or "American type" cigarettes. In the United States, flue-cured tobacco is grown on the east coast, from Virginia to Florida, and especially in North Carolina. Burley tobacco, on the other hand, is air cured and is grown primarily in Kentucky and Tennessee. Mature tobacco is a perishable commodity that must be processed relatively quickly to prevent fermentation or deterioration. Tobacco processors thus locate their facilities near the principal sources of the crop.

CURRENT CONDITIONS

While the domestic consumption of tobacco products continued to trend downward in the early 1990s, the major processors remained relatively unscathed. One reason was that value-conscious consumers were switching from premium to low-cost cigarette brands, which were taking 30% of the market by 1993 versus 11% in 1988. Profits on lower-price brands might be as low as a nickel a pack, far below that for premium brands. To increase or maintain margins on cheaper cigarettes, the manufacturers imported more foreign tobacco, which was relatively inexpensive—but significantly more profitable for the processors to supply.

Moreover, primarily because of increased smoking in Asia, worldwide tobacco consumption had jumped 75% in the 1970s and 1980s and was continuing to grow 2%-3% a year. Demand for so-called American-blend cigarettes, which tasted milder compared with the stronger and harsher cigarettes smoked in most of the world, was increasing 6% per annum. Overseas demand for milder cigarettes, coupled with reduced trade barriers in important markets like Japan, helped U.S. cigarette exports to surge to 171 billion cigarettes in 1991, versus 100 billion in 1987 and 59 billion in 1985. U.S. processors were well positioned to supply the flue-cured and burley tobaccos that are used to make the relatively low-tar, low-nicotine American-blend cigarette.

By 1994, however, conditions in the tobacco processing industry had become more volatile and uncertain, and the market environment in the United States was deteriorating quickly. Good harvests in many producing countries and weaker demand in some—most notably the United States—combined to create a worldwide surplus of tobacco, in contrast to the shortages that had existed just two years earlier. Thus, cigarette manufacturers like Philip Morris continued to maintain low inventories, since they believed they could get additional supplies whenever they needed them. Under the commodity price support system that governs tobacco production in the United States, the national marketing quota—which is divided among tobacco farmers, who agree to restrict production and sales—was reduced 10% in 1994. Some industry observers anticipated an even steeper cut for 1995. While tobacco output on a per-acre basis remained quite profitable, low demand forced some growers to switch to alternative crops like cotton. The number of tobacco farms in North Carolina, which grows about two-thirds of the country's flue-cured tobacco, dropped from about 100,000 in the mid-1980s to 42,000 in 1991.

Like other industry participants, the processors were concerned about the increasingly strong steps being taken to limit tobacco use. Dozens of localities around the country had passed measures that curtailed smoking in offices, restaurants, and other public places, and nationwide restrictions were being suggested by some in Congress. Proponents of prohibiting smoking in public places were given a boost in January 1993 by the release of a report by the Environmental Protection Agency that determined passive cigarette smoke could cause lung cancer. (The report was soon challenged in court by a coalition of tobacco-related companies, including Universal, who argued that the EPA had resorted to "manipulation and cherry picking" of data to reach its findings.)

Congress was also considering a national healthcare plan, and substantially higher excise taxes on cigarettes was considered a primary means of financing it. Anti-smoking forces said that higher cigarette taxes were especially desirable since they have the dual benefit of both raising funds and curtailing smoking. Industry participants, however, argued that a tax of as much as $1.25 per pack was unduly regressive, hitting lower-income people especially hard, and that smokers were already paying $13 billion a year in cigarette taxes.

In 1993, Congress enacted legislation designed to stem the growing use of imported tobacco in domestically produced cigarettes. As noted earlier, cigarette makers had come under margin pressure because of price-cutting and growing sales of discount brands, and they had turned to overseas tobacco, which cost as much as 40% less, for their raw material needs. The increase in imports benefitted the processors, since supplying foreign tobacco was quite profitable for them. Between 1989 and 1992, U.S. tobacco imports—the bulk of which were from Brazil, Zimbabwe, Argentina, Thailand, and Malawi—had more than doubled, while domestic output had risen only 26%. The sharp rise in imports led to calls from some industry participants for stronger barriers to overseas tobacco. The measure that Congress passed as part of the Omnibus Reconciliation Act of 1993 set the minimum content of U.S.-grown tobacco in cigarettes at 75%, significantly above the proportion of domestic product in some brands. Notably, the regulation also applied to the 30% of cigarette production that is shipped overseas.

INDUSTRY LEADERS

Universal Corporation is the largest tobacco processor in the United States. In the fiscal year ended June 1993, sales were about flat at $3 billion, but net income was up 14% to $80 million. More than two-thirds of Universal's revenues came from the tobacco business, with the balance generated by lumber and agricultural products. The company has extensive overseas operations and has a major presence in leading flue-cured and burley tobacco countries, including Brazil, Malawi, and Zimbabwe. It also is an important participant in dark tobacco (used in cigars and smokeless tobacco) markets, such as the U.S., the Dominican Republic, and Indonesia. In the 1990 to 1993 period, the company spent more than $100 million to upgrade its worldwide operations. During 1993, Universal added to its international holdings with the acquisition of Britain's Casalee, the world's fifth-largest processor. While the company has benefited from its growing international exposure, it was hurt in the first half of fiscal 1994 by a decline in demand for flue-cured tobacco and the global oversupply.

Standard Commercial has expanded since its founding in 1910 as a small marketer of oriental tobaccos to become one of the largest tobacco processors in the world. Sales in fiscal 1993 (ended March 31) rose 5% to $1.2 billion, but net income fell an equal percentage to $22 million. The decline was due to sharply lower earnings in nontobacco operations, however; operating profits for tobacco were actually up. (About 70% of the company's sales are in tobacco, the rest mostly in wool.) For many years prior to 1978, almost all of the company's tobacco business was outside the United States. In 1993, approximately 36% of tobacco revenues came from sales of U.S. subsidiaries. In March 1993, the company completed an agreement in principle to merge with Dibrell Brothers, but the Board of Directors ultimately decided to remain independent.

In 1989, A.C. Monk, founded in the nineteenth century, bought the Austin Company and became Monk-Austin; the firm became a public corporation in November 1992. The company is the only major processor whose operations are solely in tobacco; in an average year it processes 200,000 tons of leaf. Like the other processors, Monk-Austin has extensive international operations; in 1993, it expanded its presence in Brazil, Malawi, Zimbabwe, and China. In fiscal 1993, sales were flat at $611 million, while net income was up about 3% to $28 million. The company's five top customers, which include Japan Tobacco and Philip Morris, accounted for 57% of the company's revenues.

Dibrell Brothers started as a partnership in 1873 and was incorporated in 1904. Tobacco accounted for 65% of fiscal 1993 sales (ended June 30) of $1.1 billion, but it generated 92% of operating profit before corporate expense; the company's other business is distributing fresh cut flowers. About 40% of the dollar value of tobacco sold by the company was from tobacco purchased in the United States, and a third was from Brazil. Two-thirds of all Dibrell Brothers tobacco sales are to non-U.S. customers. About 53% of the company's sales are to subsidiaries or affiliates of three major producers—Philip Morris, Japan Tobacco, and RJR Nabisco Holdings.

WORK FORCE

In the United States, the tobacco processors purchase flue-cured tobacco during the five-month period from July to November; for burley tobacco, the season runs from late November until January or February. Processing takes place throughout the buying season and is usually finished within two to three months following purchase. During these periods, the industry's work force swells. For example, at June 30, 1993, Monk-Austin employed 740 regular full-time employees in the United States, but during peak processing periods it may hire as many as 990 additional employees. Some of the processors' seasonal employees are covered by collective bargaining agreements with unions. Seasonal labor is also used extensively in overseas operations.

AMERICA AND THE WORLD

Both in terms of supply and demand, in the early 1990s the U.S. tobacco processing industry was increasingly looking abroad. The elimination of trade barriers and the rising popularity of lighter, American-blend cigarettes were expanding overseas markets. Between 1989 and 1992, shipments of cigarettes to Japan, the number-one destination, increased by 27%, while exports to Europe increased by 60%. Following the fall of the Berlin Wall in 1989, new markets for U.S. exports sprung up in the former Soviet republics and in Eastern Europe. And, as international suppliers of tobacco, the processors were also selling tobacco grown overseas for cigarette manufacture in non-U.S. factories.

In terms of supply, the large processors had major operations in Brazil, Zimbabwe, Malawi and other leading tobacco-growing countries. In several countries, the processor will contract directly with tobacco farmers, in some cases before harvest, and thus take the risk that the delivered product will meet the market's quality requirements. In some countries, the major processors also provide agronomy services and advances for fertilizers and supplies. Tobacco in Zimbabwe, Malawi, Canada, and to a certain extent in India, however, is purchased under a public auction system, as in the United States.

INDUSTRY INFORMATION SOURCES

Abrams, Alan, "Tobacco Shipments Fire Up US Ports," *Journal of Commerce and Commercial*, May 26, 1992.

Anderson, Lisa, "Tobacco Farmers Hit Hard," *San Francisco Examiner*, May 1, 1994.

Dibrell Brothers 1993 Annual Report and 10K, Danville, VA: Dibrell Brothers, 1993.

Greising, David, "A Cotton-Picking Land Rush," *Business Week*, May 9, 1994.

Harper, Douglas, "Subsidy: Dirty Word for Growers?" *Journal of Commerce & Commercial*, May 26, 1992.

Janofsky, Michael, "A Curb on Imported Tobacco Aids Farms and Philip Morris," *New York Times*, September 29, 1993.

Monk-Austin 1993 Annual Report and 10-K, Farmville, NC: Monk-Austin, 1993.

Morris, Kathleen, "Universal: The Only Tobacco High," *Financial World*, April 13, 1993.

Shulman, Seth, "Global Smoke Out," *Technology Review*, May/June 1991.

Standard Commercial 1993 Annual Report and 10K, Wilson, NC: Standard Commercial, 1993.

"The Weed That Rules No Longer," *Economist*, September 28, 1991.

"Tobacco: Industry Confronts Legal and Social Challenges," *Standard & Poor's Industry Surveys*, August 26, 1993.

Universal Corporation 1993 Annual Report and 10K, Richmond, VA: Universal, 1993.

—Bob Schneider

TEXTILE MILL PRODUCTS

BROADWOVEN FABRIC MILLS, COTTON

This category covers establishments primarily engaged in the production of woven fabrics more than 12 inches (30.48 centimeters) in width, wholly or chiefly by weight of cotton. Broadwoven fabrics primarily of cotton are utilized in three general end-product categories: apparel, homefurnishings, and industrial products. Most of the broadwoven cotton apparel fabrics serve the outerwear market—men's, ladies' and children's shirts, blouses, pants, and dresses. Some lightweight jackets and boxer shorts are also produced from broadwoven cotton fabric. The homefurnishings market includes terry towels; sheets, pillowcases, blankets, bedspreads, and other bedding accessories; table linens, dish towels and dish rags; draperies; and upholstery fabrics and wall coverings. Carpet and rug manufacturers are classified in **SIC 2273: Carpets and Rugs.** Establishments involved in tire cord and fabric production are classified in **SIC 2296: Tire Cords and Fabrics.** Those establishments engaged in finishing cotton broadwoven fabrics are classified in **SIC 2261: Finishers of Broadwoven Fabrics of Cotton.**

INDUSTRY SNAPSHOT

Manufacturing of cotton broadwovens—like most segments of textiles—is a mature industry. Although mature in terms of growth, there have been a number of organizational and structural changes since 1985 among the broadwoven manufacturers of cotton fabrics. A number of broadwoven manufacturers of cotton have merged, been acquired, or have sold manufacturing divisions to other companies. There were 246 companies engaged in the manufacture of

COTTON USE IN U.S. MILLS
(MILLIONS OF BALES)

Source: National Cotton Council Agriculture Dept.
1994* *Estimate

broadwoven cotton fabrics in 1993, according to the U.S. Department of Commerce's Bureau of the Census.

M. Lowenstein, one of the largest apparel and homefurnishings manufacturers in the United States, was acquired by Springs Industries in 1985. Although it kept the apparel manufacturing facilities and most of the homefurnishings manufacturing facilities, Springs Industries subsequently sold the Lowenstein upholstery division to Collins & Aikman in 1991. Fieldcrest and Cannon merged in 1987, forming Fieldcrest Cannon Co.

J.P. Stevens was the second largest textile company in the United States until its breakup and purchase by three companies in 1987. WestPoint Pepperell purchased approximately one-third of the former giant, acquiring its branded homefurnishings products. The Bibb Co. purchased approximately one-third of the former company as well, obtaining the institutional homefurnishings products. The remaining third, the industrial sector, was purchased by a management group that formed JPS Textiles.

This breakup of J.P. Stevens was followed in 1989 by a leveraged buyout of WestPoint Pepperell by William Farley, chairman of Fruit of the Loom Inc. When Farley was unable to meet the resulting gigantic debt, creditors took the company over, forming Valley Fashions Holdings, a holding company that now owns WestPoint Pepperell. Valley Fashions changed the name of the textile giant to WestPoint Stevens in 1993.

Burlington Industries, the largest publicly held textile company in the United States, was taken private by a management group in 1987, as was Cone Mills, the world's largest denim manufacturer. Both returned to the public sector in 1992.

ORGANIZATION AND STRUCTURE

Fabric weavers generally are vertically integrated companies, producing their own yarn. Fabric knitters, generally one-process operations, tend to purchase yarn from sales yarn companies. The primary reason for integrated weaving plants is that even with fashion changes that occur in the woven segment, yarn counts—the size of the yarn—as well as fabric constructions remain fairly stable. Fabric knitters, on the other hand, are faced with constant changes in yarn size and construction. Therefore, most knitters find it more economical to purchase yarn from sales yarn companies.

Textile weaving is a process that utilizes two yarn systems. The first, called warp (sometimes referred to as woof, especially in the United Kingdom), is fed into the weaving machine (or loom) from a beam and consists of several thousand individual pieces of yarn called ends. The number of ends in a warp depends on the type of fabric being woven and the width. For example, combed cotton percale sheeting is woven with 90 ends per inch (epi); muslin sheeting is woven with 60 epi; indigo dyed denim is woven with 54 epi. The yarn size also differs in each of those three fabrics, ranging from very fine yarn in percale sheeting to very coarse yarn in denim.

The second yarn system in weaving, called filling (referred to as weft in Europe), is inserted into the loom one piece of yarn at a time. Each yarn piece is called a pick. Depending on the type of fabric, looms are set up to insert a different number of picks per inch (ppi). For example, percale sheeting, muslin sheeting, and denim have 90, 60 and 38 ppi, respectively. Speed, and subsequently productivity, of looms is measured by the number of picks inserted per minute (ppm).

Warp ends run lengthwise in the fabric; filling picks run widthwise in the fabric. According to the prescribed weave pattern, the picks go over and under the ends to form the weave. A plain weave is simply one where the pick goes over every other end and under the others, alternating with each pick. Other weave patterns, i.e., twills, basket weaves, oxfords, etc., are made by the number of ends each pick goes over or under in the prescribed pattern. Fabric constructions for the purpose of manufacturing are stated by epi and ppi. For example, fabric constructions for percale sheeting, muslin sheeting and denim are 90x90, 60x60 and 54x38, respectively.

BACKGROUND AND DEVELOPMENT

Technology in the broadwoven segment of the textile industry has advanced at a rapid rate over the last 25 years. Two factors are responsible: (1) The invention of shuttleless weaving systems has increased speed and productivity while improving quality at the same time. (2) The introduction of electronics into the textile weaving area has permitted further advances in speed, increased automation and, more significantly, increased process control.

For over 100 years, textile plants have been using power looms. Until 1960, all power looms inserted each pick of filling using a shuttle. Before the invention of power looms, hand looms also inserted filling by shuttle. The shuttle, measuring approximately 16-20 inches in length, travels from the left-hand side of the loom to the right, carrying with it a bobbin of yarn. The filling yarn on the bobbin unwinds as the shuttle travels across the loom, leaving a pick of yarn as it travels. When the shuttle reaches the right-hand side of the loom, it immediately travels back to the left-hand side, also leaving a pick of yarn in the fabric.

In 1960, the first of five shuttleless filling insertion systems was introduced to the broadwoven textile industry. These five systems insert filling into the fabric without use of a shuttle. Shuttleless weaving systems offer two primary advantages over shuttle weaving systems. The first advantage is the ability to dramatically increase the speed of the weaving machine. The second advantage is that the small bobbin of yarn carried by the shuttle is eliminated. Instead, a large (10-pound) cone of yarn is attached to the loom. Each shuttleless system pulls yarn from the cone, one pick at a time, and inserts it into the fabric. Bobbins used on shuttle systems contain approximately 2.5 ounces of yarn each and must be replaced each time they are emptied. The mechanism that replaces empty shuttle bobbins with full ones is the most frequent cause of quality defects in fabrics produced by shuttle systems.

That mechanism is also the number one cause of efficiency loss on shuttle systems. Since the cone containing filling yarn on shuttleless looms is not part of the operating mechanism itself, this system does not cause defects or efficiency loss, even when it empties after the 10 pounds are used up.

The first shuttleless system to be introduced to broadwoven manufacturing operations was the projectile system. It was developed in 1960 by Sulzer Brothers Ltd., of Zurich, Switzerland. The system uses a small, three-inch projectile to carry the filling yarn across the weaving machine. Since the supply cone is stationary, the filling is always inserted from the left-hand side of the loom to the right-hand side. As the projectile reaches the right-hand side of the loom, the yarn is cut at the fabric edge. Another projectile on the left-hand side takes the next pick from the cone and begins the process of filling insertion again while the first projectile is traveling under the loom back to the starting position. Sulzer Brothers Ltd. is still the leading manufacturer of projectile weaving machines. One other company, Textilmash of Cheboksary, Russia, also manufactures projectile looms.

The second shuttleless weaving system, rigid rapier, was developed by Lindauer Dornier GmbH of Lindau/Bodensee, Germany, in the mid-1960s. A rigid shaft carries the filling across the width of the loom. This type of shuttleless weaving system requires the most floor space per machine since there must be enough space allowed beside each loom to permit the rigid shaft to come out of the loom to obtain the next pick. Lindauer Dornier continues to be a leading manufacturer of rigid rapier weaving machines and is joined by Gunne GmbH of Moehnesse-Gunne, Germany, SAMT of Mulhouse, France, Tsudakoma Corp. of Kanazawa, Japan, Michel Van de Wiele NV of Kortrijk, Belgium, and Wilson & Longbottom of Barnsley, England.

The third type of shuttleless weaving system, flexible rapier, is based on technology developed on the rigid rapier system. In this case, however, the shaft (or rapier) is flexible. The flexible rapier bends around underneath the loom instead of protruding to the side. This system also uses two rapiers. The first carries the pick from the left-hand side half way across the loom. At the midpoint in the fabric, the second rapier picks up the pick, carrying it on across to the right-hand side while the first rapier goes back to pick up the next pick. This system was developed by Ruti Ltd. of Zurich, Switzerland. Ruti was acquired by Sulzer Brothers Ltd. in 1980. The company still manufactures flexible rapier weaving machines under the name Sulzer Ruti Ltd. Flexible rapier looms are also produced by

Picanol NV of Ieper, Belgium, Nuovo Pignone Smit of Schio, Italy, Somet SpA of Colzate, Italy, Tsudakoma Corp., Nuova Vamatex SpA of Villa di Serio, Italy and Michel Van de Wiele NV.

Both air-jet and water-jet weaving systems were developed by Investa of Vsetin, Czechoslovakia. These two filling insertion systems are based on similar technological principles. The air-jet system uses a stream of air to insert the pick; the water-jet system uses a stream of water. Water-jets cannot be used to produce broadwoven cotton fabrics since cotton is a hydrophilic fiber—one that has a high water absorption. Only yarns produced from hydrophobic fiber—those that do not absorb water—may be used on water jets. Air jets operate by blowing the pick across the loom using a series of air nozzles placed strategically in the filling path.

Of special note is the fact that there are no U.S. weaving machine manufacturers on any of the above lists. However, U.S manufacturers of broadwoven cotton fabrics constitute the largest users of shuttleless weaving machines. Draper Corp., of Spartanburg, South Carolina, was the largest manufacturer of shuttle weaving systems in the world. Of those shuttle weaving machines still in operation worldwide, approximately three-fourths were manufactured by Draper Corp. Today, Draper's contribution to shuttleless weaving is in the manufacture of air-jet weaving machines to manufacture tire cord. Tire cord production is covered under **SIC 2296: Tire Cord and Fabrics.**

CURRENT CONDITIONS

In 1992 U.S. manufacturers produced 4.6 billion square yards of broadwoven cotton fabrics according to the U.S. Department of Commerce. This was the third highest annual output since 1980. For the first half of 1993, U.S. manufacturers produced 2.291 billion square yards, down slightly from 2.326 billion square yards produced during the same period in 1992.

A number of factors influence the success of companies engaged in the manufacturing of broadwoven cotton fabrics, but none has the impact to equal that of international trade. For a number of years, imports—particularly in the apparel fabrics sector—have steadily risen, severely affecting operation of U.S. manufacturers of broadwoven cotton fabrics. Manufacturers of broadwoven cotton fabrics are impacted by imported garments—which are usually cut and sewn from fabrics manufactured in the same country as the garments—as well as fabrics.

The summer of 1993 was a watershed in the history of textile and apparel imports. The months of

June, July, August, and September represented the four largest importing months in history in this area for America. Each month set a new all-time record for that particular period. Total imports during the trimester were 5.85 billion square meters, more than was imported during the entire year of 1982.

During the first nine months of 1993, total textile and apparel imports were 11.9 billion square-meter equivalents, 8.9 percent ahead of the same period in 1992. China continued to ride the crest of the import tidal wave. Imports from China were seven percent ahead of 1992 and represented one-seventh of the global total. Notable gains were also achieved by Pakistan, 11.8 percent ahead of 1992's pace, and India, up 7.8 percent. These three countries, which collectively account for 22 percent of total U.S. textile and apparel imports, have historically kept their markets closed to foreign competition.

Two historical trade agreements were enacted at the end of 1993. One, the North American Free Trade Agreement (NAFTA), should benefit U.S. manufacturers of broadwoven cotton fabrics in the long run, according to the American Textile Manufacturers Institute (ATMI). The other, the General Agreement on Tariffs and Trade (GATT), could be detrimental to the long-range success of U.S. broadwoven cotton manufacturers, according to ATMI.

The NAFTA, which became official January 1, 1994, effectively eliminates trade barriers among American, Canadian, and Mexican businesses. Gradual elimination of tariffs on U.S. textile exports to Mexico is seen as a major motivator for sales. Some U.S. companies, are in fact, spending millions of dollars to increase capacity as a result of the passage of the NAFTA.

The NAFTA eliminates tariffs on 89 percent of U.S.-made fabric exports to Mexico over a five-year period beginning January 1, 1994. Mexico eliminated tariffs immediately on January 1, 1994, on U.S. products such as denim, twills, cotton terry towels, curtains, and drapes.

Many industry analysts expect an immediate growth in apparel manufacturing plants in Mexico— generally regarded as a low-wage country. These would replace many of the apparel plants that have come about in developing countries in Africa and the Far East who have been exporting finished garments into U.S. retail operations. In a statement published in the December 1993 issue of *Textile World,* immediately after the passage of the NAFTA, U.S. Representative John Pratt, chairman of the Congressional Textile Caucus, said, ''NAFTA gives the apparel industry

an opportunity to 're-source' production from China, Hong Kong, Taiwan and Pakistan to Mexico, enabling U.S. textile companies to supply fabric and do the printing and finishing.''

While the signing of the NAFTA raises the hopes of manufacturers of broadwoven cotton fabrics, signing of GATT had just the opposite effect. Known as the Uruguay Round of GATT, the agreement was signed on December 15, 1993, by 117 nations following seven years of negotiations. This agreement completely phases out tariffs on textiles over the next ten years. U.S. textile companies had sought a 15-year phase-out to provide more time to make adjustments due to the expected rise in imports.

Another important agreement was signed in 1993 by the textile industry and the U.S. government which should benefit the broadwoven fabrics industry. The signing of the American Textile Partnership Agreement (AMTEX) may be the biggest stimulus to the industry had in years, according to many industry executives who attended the 44th annual convention of the ATMI in the spring of 1993. AMTEX links eight Department of Energy laboratories with the textile and apparel industries and supporting research groups. The agreement's goal is to create programs and develop technologies for the U.S. textile and apparel industries.

Factors other than trade matters also have an effect on the success of companies engaged in the manufacture of broadwoven cotton fabrics. Outside of trade matters, the general state of the economy, coupled with the level of consumer confidence, has the greatest impact on operations engaged in the manufacture of broadwoven cotton fabrics for apparel products. This has obviously been the case over the last several years, with companies producing fabrics for apparel enjoying success or decline in direct relationship to the state of the economy.

New housing starts, which in itself has a direct relationship with the state of the economy, is the chief factor outside of trade matters affecting those manufacturers of broadwoven cotton fabrics for homefurnishings. Although a large market exists for replacement sheets, pillow cases, towels, etc., nothing spurs this segment of the industry as much as new housing starts.

Several factors affect the demand for broadwoven cotton fabrics for industrial use. These include the success of the automotive industry, the activity in new highways, bridges, etc., and the nature of the agriculture industry. A significant section of the agriculture industry—cotton farming—also has a tremendous in-

RESEARCH AND TECHNOLOGY

Manufacturers of broadwoven cotton fabrics are replacing shuttle looms with shuttleless weaving machines as rapidly as economically feasible. In 1993 approximately half of the approximate 100,000 weaving machines in the United States were of the shuttleless variety. Shuttleless weaving speeds are geometrically higher than those of shuttle systems. Shuttleless speeds have been higher than shuttle speeds since inception of each shuttleless system. Use of electronics in the broadwoven manufacturing process has permitted even higher increases in speeds. Speeds on any filling insertion system vary depending on type and width of fabric being woven. There are, however, definite ranges within each system which permit making relative comparisons. According to *Textile World,* speeds on the different filling insertion systems used in broadwoven cotton manufacturing are as follows: projectile—320-470 ppm; rigid rapier—330-505 ppm; flexible rapier—350-600 ppm; air-jet—600-1,200 ppm. Shuttle weaving systems typically operate at 140-190 ppm.

When first developed, each shuttleless filling insertion system was designed specifically for a somewhat narrow fabric application range. As systems have been improved, modified, and computerized, the application ranges have broadened considerably. Projectile, flexible rapier, and rigid rapier systems are more versatile and can handle heavier, more complicated styles such as plaid upholstery. However, modifications to air-jet systems have broadened the application range to include more than just simple, lightweight styles such as printcloth and sheeting. Burlington Industries and Swift Textiles now both produce heavyweight denim on air-jet machines, and a few companies have begun experimenting with heavyweight upholstery fabrics on air jets as well.

Electronic technology has contributed greatly to the operation of shuttleless weaving machines in the broadwoven cotton sector. Systems have provided more control in the air bursts from the series of nozzles on air-jet machines, permitting greater manufacturing speeds and production of a broader range of fabric weights. Jacquard machines—which control multicolored, extremely complicated patterns—have incorporated electronics that permit higher speeds in the production of fancy upholstery fabrics on flexible and rigid rapiers. Electronic advances also paved the way the installation of automation features on shuttleless weaving machines such as automatic filling break re-pair, automatic cloth removal at specified lengths and automatic filling supply cone replenishment.

The biggest contribution made by electronic technology to broadwoven cotton manufacturing is in monitoring and control of the operation. Microprocessor-driven systems monitor and provide real-time data on efficiency, production, and quality. The data can be provided for any time period the manufacturer wishes to designate. This data can also be supplied for an individual machine or several machines grouped by style, job assignment, etc. Such information permits the evaluation of styles, fabrics, etc. and gives the broadwoven fabrics manufacturer the ability to select those materials most suited for the production machinery available.

As electronic systems become more advanced, they not only permit monitoring of the operation, but control of many of the functions as well. Modern systems can detect many mechanical and electrical problems. Depending on the sophistication of the system and the severity of the problem, the system can correct the problem, signal technicians as to the nature of the problem, or stop the machine until the problem is corrected.

Principle manufacturers of broadwoven monitoring and control systems include Zellweger Uster Ltd. of Uster, Switzerland, and Knoxville, Tennessee; Barco NV of Brussels, Belgium, and A.B. Carter of Charlotte, North Carolina.

INDUSTRY INFORMATION SOURCES

"ATME-I '93 Quickens Textiles' Time to Market," Textile World, June 1992, 74-75.

"At 150 Years, Collins & Aikman is Dedicated to its Markets," Textile World, June 1993, 38-72.

"Broadwoven Goods Production, 1993," Washington, DC: Bureau of the Census, United States Department of Commerce, 1993.

"Dundee Puts on the Ritz with Hot New Product Mix," Textile World, June 1988, 44-70.

"GATT Disappoints U.S. Textile Leaders," Textile World, January 1994, 23-24.

Isaacs III, McAllister. "Machinery Makers Are Responding to the Needs of Weaving Plants," Textile World, December 1993, 42-43.

———, "Textile World's Weaving Machinery Chart for 1993," Textile World, December 1993, 44-60.

Linton, George C. The Modern Textile and Apparel Dictionary, Plainfield, NJ: Textile Book Service, 1973.

"Springs Psyched for a Second Century of Success," Textile World, June 1987, 44-85.

Standard & Poor's Industry Surveys. New York: Standard & Poor's Corporation, 1993.

"Stevens Breakup Realigns Industry," *Textile World,* June 1988, 26.

Textile Highlights. Washington, DC: American Textile Manufacturers Institute, 1993.

"Textiles Ready to Reap NAFTA Rewards," *Textile World,* December 1993, 23-24.

"Weaving Speeds are not all in Machines," *Textile World,* June 1993, 78-87.

"Who's the Real Winner in Burlington Match?", *Textile World,* June 1987.

—McAllister Isaacs III

SIC 2221

BROADWOVEN FABRIC MILLS, MANMADE FIBER AND SILK

This category covers establishments primarily engaged in the production of woven fabrics more than 12 inches (30.48 centimeters) in width, wholly or chiefly by weight of manmade fiber and/or silk. Broadwoven fabrics primarily of manmade fiber are utilized in three general end-product categories: apparel, home furnishings, and industrials. Broadwoven fabrics primarily of silk are for the most part utilized in apparel products. Occasionally, broadwoven silk fabrics serve the home furnishings market.

Production of broadwoven fabrics with content wholly or primarily by weight of cotton is included in **SIC 2211: Broadwoven Fabric Mills, Cotton.** Production of broadwoven fabrics with content wholly or chiefly by weight of wool, mohair, or other similar animal fiber is included in **SIC 2231: Broadwoven Fabric Mills, Wool (Including Dyeing and Finishing).** Production of narrow fabric, generally 12 inches or less in width, of cotton, wool, silk, and manmade fiber is included in **SIC 2241: Narrow Fabric and Other Smallwares Mills: Cotton, Wool, Silk, and Manmade Fiber.**

INDUSTRY SNAPSHOT

There are 316 companies with 436 establishments engaged in the production of manmade fiber or silk broadwoven fabrics in the United States. In 1992, these establishments produced 11,326,000,000 square yards, the fourth highest annual total since 1980, according to the U.S. Department of Commerce, Bureau of the Census. During the first nine months of 1993, production of manmade fiber and silk broadwoven fabrics totaled 8,657,000,000 square yards, 224,000,000 more than for the same period in 1992. While manmade and silk broadwoven fabric production totaled more than twice that of broadwoven cotton fabrics—over 11 billion square yards vs. 4.6 billion square yards, no single manmade fiber or silk accounted for as much production as cotton by itself.

Principal fibers used in broadwoven manmade fiber fabrics for apparel are polyester, rayon, and nylon with occasional use of polypropylene or olefin fiber. These fabrics are generally used for men's, ladies' and children's outerwear including shirts, blouses, pants and dresses; leisure and activewear; heavy and lightweight jackets and coats; suits; sleepwear and lingerie; etc.

The home furnishings market for manmade broadwoven fabrics includes sheets, pillowcases, blankets, bedspreads and other bedding accessories; table linens or napery products; draperies; upholstery fabrics and wall coverings. The principal manmade fibers used in home furnishings are polyester, rayon, polypropylene, acrylic and occasionally nylon. Carpet and rug manufacturers are included in **SIC 2273: Carpets and Rugs.**

Industrial applications for broadwoven manmade fibers include materials used in the automotive, agricultural, geotextile, medical, recreational, and transportation industries. Broadwoven manmade fiber fabrics also find use in conveyor and other industrial belting products as well as in specialized applications such as soft-sided luggage and protective clothing. Tire cord and fabric production is included in **SIC 2296: Tire Cord and Fabrics.**

Broadwoven fabrics of manmade fiber for industrial applications are made from the widest variety of fiber types. Traditional manmade fibers such as nylon, polyester, acrylic, polypropylene or olefin, and rayon find numerous uses in the area of industrial fabrics. A number of industrial applications products, however, require the characteristics of some specialized manmade fibers. Some of these fibers include the aramid family with such fibers as Nomex and Kevlar, both manufactured by Du Pont. Nomex is highly flame resistant, and fabrics manufactured from this fiber are used in such products as protective clothing for firefighters, space suits, and race-car-driver clothing. Kevlar, with strength characteristics superior to steel, can be found in fabrics manufactured for bullet-proof vests and other protective devices.

Other manmade fibers with high-performance characteristics for use in specialized applications and their major producers include carbon fiber, BASF and Courtaulds; glass fiber, Owens-Corning Fiberglass Corp. and PPG Industries Inc.; polybenzimidazole, Hoechst Celanese; polyetheretherketone, Albany International and Shakespeare Monofilament; and sulfur, Albany International and Phillips Fibers Corp.

Of the numerous producers of traditional manmade fibers that are used in broadwoven fabrics, some of the principal U.S. producers are Eastman Chemical Products Inc. (Acetate); Mann Industries and Monsanto (Acrylic); Albany International, Allied Fibers, BASF Corp., and Du Pont (Nylon and Polyester); Hercules Inc. and Phillips Fibers Corp. (Olefin [polypropylene]); Courtaulds Fibers Inc. and North American Rayon Corp. (Rayon); and Globe Mfg. Co. (Spandex).

ORGANIZATION AND STRUCTURE

Producers of broadwoven fabrics of manmade fiber and silk, like the producers of other broadwoven fabrics, are for the most part vertically integrated textile manufacturing companies. That is, most broadwoven companies manufacture their own yarn requirements; many of them dye and finish their own fabrics.

Aside from the many different generic types of manmade fiber—i.e., polyester, nylon, rayon, etc.—and the different brands within each generic type—i.e., Du Pont's Dacron, Eastman's Kodel, Hoechst Celanese's Trevira, and other polyesters—fabrics may be woven from two forms of manmade fiber yarn: filament or staple. Filament yarn is a continuous strand of manmade fiber. Staple manmade fiber yarn consists of many individual fibers cut to a specific length. These fibers measure approximately one to one-and-a-half inches in length if they are to be spun into yarn on a cotton system spinning process. If they are to be spun on a woolen or worsted system spinning process, the fibers are cut up to six or eight inches in length. The form of manmade fiber yarn to be woven depends on the end-use application of the fabric. Staple fiber arrives at the textile plant in bales, just like cotton or wool. It is processed just like cotton or wool on the same machinery.

Of the more than 11 billion square yards of manmade fiber and silk broadwoven fabric woven in 1992, more than half was produced from continuous filament yarn. The percentage of manmade fiber broadwoven fabrics produced from continuous filament yarn has trended upward since 1980 when this type represented 37 percent of the 10.7 billion square yards produced. In 1988, the amount of the manmade fiber broadwoven fabric produced from continuous filament yarn reached 50 percent for the first time. Consumption of

filament fiber by broadwoven manmade fabric producers has remained at or above this level since that time.

BACKGROUND AND DEVELOPMENT

A discussion of weaving systems types and the emergence of shuttleless weaving as the most efficient, productive and quality producing system can be found in **SIC 2211: Broadwoven Fabric Mills, Cotton.** All of the shuttleless weaving systems—projectile, rigid and flexible rapier and air-jet—described in the broadwoven cotton fabrics section are in use in weaving broadwoven fabrics from manmade fiber and silk. Producers of many of the styles of broadwoven manmade fiber fabrics can also use the water-jet system of weaving as well. This requires the yarn to be hydrophobic—the fiber must not absorb moisture, the styles must be relatively simple in construction, and the material must be relatively light in weight so that a stream of water can carry the yarn across the weaving machine. Most manmade fibers are hydrophobic, rayon and its variants being the notable exceptions.

Water-jet weaving machines are manufactured by Nissan Motor Co. Ltd. and Tsudakoma Corp. of Japan and Zbrojovka-Vsetin of the Czech Republic. Water-jet weaving machines operate at a production rate of over 1,000 ppm, which is more than 500 percent faster than conventional shuttle weaving systems, approximately 200 percent faster than projectile and both rapier systems, and at least 25 percent faster than the average air-jet weaving machine.

CURRENT CONDITIONS

As a group—and aside from competition within the group—producers of broadwoven fabrics of manmade fiber and silk face two types of competition for market share, especially in the apparel sector and, to a lesser extent, in the homefurnishings market. Those two types of competition are (1) fabrics and garments imported from developing countries and (2) a trend toward increasing consumer preference for products made from natural fibers.

Increasing consumer preference for products made from natural fibers—cotton, wool, etc.—stems from several factors. The first of these is marketing and promotional campaigns conducted by Cotton Incorporated, an organization sponsored and paid for by the cotton growers of the United States. Formed in 1971 in an attempt to offset the huge gains in market share being made by polyester, the organization's purpose is to promote the use of cotton in fabrics. Since, its formation, cotton has increased in market share in the United States at the expense of manmade fiber in production of broadwoven fabrics every year. With headquarters and marketing offices in New York and research facilities in Raleigh, North Carolina, Cotton Incorporated's principal means of promotion of cotton as a fiber of choice in broadwoven fabrics are (1) massive television commercials: ''The Fabric of Our Lives;'' and (2) use of the cotton bowl logo in products made of 100 percent cotton or the cotton-blend logo in products made of at least 60 percent cotton. In a recognition survey of 12 leading product logos among consumers in 1993, the cotton logo was deemed the second most recognizable logo, behind only the Shell Oil Co. logo. The survey found that the cotton logo was more recognizable than such logos as those of CBS, Chrysler, Dutch Boy, Merrill Lynch, Prudential, Maxwell House, Kodak, Travelers and Wrigley's.

The second factor playing a part in decreasing market share among manmade fiber broadwovens compared to natural fiber broadwovens has to do with increasing environmental concerns among consumers. Most manmade fibers are produced in chemical plants from a variety of chemicals with inherent potential for environmental problems. Few, if any, fiber producers violated any environmental regulations in 1993, but the perception of potential problems is a factor producers of manmade fiber fabrics must overcome.

The third factor playing a part in decreasing market share among manmade fiber broadwovens is the minimization, if not elimination, of what has historically been the major objection to broadwoven fabrics of cotton. With current capabilities that reduce wrinkles in cotton fabrics and that make the products more in the line of ''easy care'' or ''wash-and-wear'' polyester products, cotton fabric producers have taken a giant step toward attracting additional consumers.

Three agreements enacted during 1993 could have a significant effect on producers of manmade fiber and silk broadwoven fabrics: NAFTA, GATT, and AMTEX. The first two are agreements between the United States government and governments of other countries, while the third is an agreement between the United States government and the United States textile/apparel complex.

The North American Free Trade Agreement (NAFTA) went into effect January 1, 1994. It eliminates tariffs on most products traded among Canadian, United States and Mexican businesses over a five-year period. Some of those involving textile and apparel products were eliminated on the day the NAFTA took effect.

Industry leaders from the American Textile Manufacturers Institute (ATMI) expect NAFTA to benefit the U.S. textile industry, including producers of man-

made and silk broadwoven fabrics from two standpoints. First, it will remove barriers and eliminate tariffs from the United States' trading partners. Second, over the long run, many feel that due to NAFTA, the standard of living will rise in Mexico, creating a larger market for U.S. textile and apparel products.

Evidence of those expectations can be found in the December 1993 issue of *Textile World,* which reported that several U.S. textile companies were increasing their capacities strictly because of the passage of NAFTA. Guilford Mills spent $280 million in 1993 on capital improvements to increase productivity for expected increased demand for apparel fabric. Swift Textiles expanded its denim capacity. John A. Boland III, Swift's president and CEO, said that the $20-million expansion was due to growing interest in denim in Mexico. ''There's a great appeal in Mexico for denim and that will continue to grow,'' he said.

Other companies envisioning increased business include Springs Industries, whose chairman, Walter Elisha, predicts the creation of 900 new jobs at Springs. Delta Woodside announced a $130-million investment in three South Carolina plants. Erwin Maddrey, Delta Woodside's CEO, cited the investment as an indication of how he thought his firm would be postured to compete with Mexico. Delta Woodside owns the DuckHead Apparel Co. Reflecting on the impact of NAFTA, American Textile Manufacturers Institute president Henry A. Truslow III said, ''NAFTA is a defining moment in our history whereby we will establish new trading relationships that will benefit our industry and the entire nation.''

U.S. producers of broadwoven fabrics of manmade fiber and silk were not so enthusiastic about the completion of the Uruguay Round of the General Agreement of Tariffs & Trade (GATT). After a seven-year marathon of negotiations, this agreement was concluded on December 15, 1993, and signed on April 15, 1994. The pact, approved by 117 nations, phases out tariffs on textiles over the next ten years. Some predict the expected rise in textile and apparel imports could mean elimination of one million textile and apparel jobs over that period of time.

Imports of textile and apparel products have been increasing steadily over the last several years. Following a record-breaking surge in 1992, imports of textiles and apparel jumped again in 1993, rising 9.1 percent and setting a new record of 15.8 billion square-meter equivalents (sme). Textiles bore the brunt of the increase, rising 11.5 percent to reach 8.3 billion sme. Manmade fiber broadwoven fabric imports grew ten percent in 1993. The top five exporters of textiles and apparel to the U.S. in 1993 were: China at 2.1 billion sme, Taiwan at 1.2 billion sme, Canada at 1.1 billion sme, Hong Kong at 936 million sme, and South Korea at 872 million sme.

While U.S. textile and apparel imports reached all-time highs in 1993, exports of U.S. textiles and apparel also continued to rise. Exports of U.S. textiles and apparel to Canada, Mexico, and the Caribbean surged 17 percent to reach $5.7 billion. In 1992 and 1993, the U.S. textile and apparel trade deficit with its North American neighbors has been halved, from $1.5 billion to $620 million in 1993. At the same time, the U.S. surplus in textile trade with Canada, Mexico, and the Caribbean reached $1.9 billion in 1993, up from $1.5 billion in 1991.

The top five export markets for textiles and apparel were Canada, $1.9 billion; Mexico, $1.6 billion; Japan, $871 million; the Dominican Republic, $774 million and Costa Rica, $404 million. The top five export markets for only textiles were: Canada, $1.5 billion; Mexico, $814 million; United Kingdom, $267 million; Japan, $201 million and Hong Kong, $189 million.

Strong exports were not, however, able to keep the trade deficit from increasing in the face of even larger increases for imports. As a result, the trade deficit for 1993 increased to $31.5 billion, up eight percent from 1992 and a new record. Apparel continues to account for the lion's share of the deficit (92 percent), but the textiles portion continues to grow as textile imports continue to surge into the U.S. In 1993, the textile portion of the deficit grew 24 percent to reach $2.5 billion.

The third agreement—the American Textile Partnership (AMTEX) is between the United States Dept. of Energy (DOE) and the U.S. textile/apparel complex to provide research and existing government technologies to boost U.S. competitiveness. Five projects will comprise initial joint industry-DOE efforts:

(1) Computer-Aided Fabric Evaluation (CAFE) Project: Currently, this technology is used for computer vision target recognition systems that can tell the difference between military and civilian aircraft or vehicles. It is also used for high-speed inspection systems that detect pattern and color defects in U.S. currency and postage stamps. Through AMTEX, this technology will be used to detect and classify defects as hundreds of square yards of fabric per minute "fly by" an inspection system.

(2) Electronic Embedded Fingerprints: Tiny electronic microchips and radio transponders were developed by DOE to permanently identify or tag missiles or items that were to be controlled under international treaties. While current devices are about the size of a penny, AMTEX proposes to develop a smaller version about the size of a grain of rice. It will include a small radio transmitter and will be packaged for permanent encasement in apparel or other products counterfeited in foreign markets.

(3) Environmental Quality and Waste Minimization: DOE developed environmental cleanup and waste minimization methods to separate nuclear materials and other heavy metals from waste streams and to destroy organic cleaners and solvents. Methods were also developed for reducing and recycling wastes. AMTEX proposes to use these technologies to recover dyes and process chemicals from waste streams, reducing potential pollution and recovering valuable raw materials for reuse.

(4) High-Speed Cutting of Textiles: The government invested in developing high-power lasers for the Strategic Defense Initiative program, isotope separation, and scientific investigations. The new use of these technologies will be to create a new generation of high-speed cutting machines ten to twenty times faster than current machines. This will allow both small and large companies to enter the era of demand-activated-manufacturing and custom apparel manufacturing.

(5) Demand-Activated Manufacturing Architecture (DAMA): The government has invested extensively in advanced computing, in analysis of large and complex data sets, and in simulation of complex systems. From high-speed supercomputers to geographically distributed information networks, DOE has long been a pioneer in computing and communications. For military uses, DOE laboratories have developed battlefield planning and simulation software systems to analyze and optimize movement of troops and supplies. AMTEX proposes an industry-wide computer system linking fiber producers, textile and apparel manufacturers and retailers in an electronic marketplace. U.S. companies will optimize business relationships and production practices to be more responsive to customer needs and reduce costs of shipping, handling, over-production and inventory time.

INDUSTRY INFORMATION SOURCES

"ATME-I '93 Quickens Textiles' Time to Market," *Textile World,* June 1992, 74-75.

"Broadwoven Goods Production, 1993," Washington, D.C.: Bureau of the Census, United States Department of Commerce.

"The Business Week 1000 Tables," *Business Week,* 1993 Bonus Issue, 118-63.

"Cotton Incorporated Is 'Textiles' Partner'," *Textile World,* August 1993, 47-48.

"GATT Disappoints U.S. Textile Leaders," *Textile World News*, *Textile World*, January 1994, 23-24.

Isaacs III, McAllister, "Machinery Makers Are Responding to the Needs of Weaving Plants," *Textile World*, December 1993, 42-43.

Isaacs III, McAllister, "Textile World's Weaving Machinery Chart for 1993," *Textile World*, December 1993, 44-60.

Linton, George C., *The Modern Textile and Apparel Dictionary*, Plainfield, New Jersey: Textile Book Service, Division of Bonn Industries Inc., 1973.

"Microfibers: All Dressed Up and Everywhere to Go," *Textile World*, August 1992, 37-48.

"Springs Psyched for a Second Century of Success," *Textile World*, June 1987, 44-85.

Standard & Poor's Industry Surveys. New York: Standard & Poor's Corporation, 1992 and 1993.

Textile Highlights, Washington, D.C.: American Textile Manufacturers Institute, December 1993 and March 1994.

"Textiles Ready to Reap NAFTA Rewards," *Textile World News*, *Textile World*, December 1993, 23-24.

"Textile World 1992 Manmade Fiber Chart," *Textile World*, August 1992, 49-73.

"Weaving Speeds Are Not All in Machines," *Textile World*, June 1993, 78-87.

—McAllister Isaacs III

SIC 2231

BROADWOVEN FABRIC MILLS, WOOL (INCLUDING DYEING AND FINISHING)

This category covers establishments primarily engaged in the production of woven fabrics more than 12 inches (30.48 centimeters) in width, wholly or chiefly by weight of wool, mohair or similar animal fibers; dyeing and finishing of woven wool fabrics; and those shrinking and sponging wool goods for the trade. These fabrics are used primarily for production of apparel (especially outerwear), home furnishings (especially blankets), and specialty items, such as billiard table cloth.

Establishments primarily engaged in weaving or tufting wool carpets and rugs are classified in **SIC 2273: Carpets and Rugs**. Production of broadwoven fabrics with content wholly or primarily by weight of cotton is included in **SIC 2211: Broadwoven Fabric Mills, Cotton**. Production of broadwoven fabrics with content wholly or chiefly by weight of manmade fiber and silk is included in **SIC 2221: Broadwoven Fabric Mills, Manmade Fiber and Silk**. Production of narrow fabric, generally 12 inches or less in width, of cotton, wool, silk and manmade fiber is included in **SIC 2241: Narrow Fabric and Other Smallwares Mills: Cotton, Wool, Silk, and Manmade Fiber**.

There were 106 companies that operated 118 establishments engaged in the production of broadwoven fabrics of wool, mohair or of similar animal fiber, according to the U.S. Department of Commerce, Bureau of the Census. By far, the greatest amount of production was from wool fiber. According to the Department of Commerce, the value of production shipments in 1991 for these fabrics totaled nearly $1.5 billion. The preponderance of these fabrics, nearly $1.3 billion were produced for the apparel industry. Blankets accounted for $27.9 million in shipments.

Many of the companies and establishments engaged in the production of wool and other animal fiber fabrics were located in the northeastern United States, especially New England. The two largest producers of wool fabrics, however, were located in southeastern United States. Burlington Industries, headquartered in Greensboro, North Carolina, operated most of its establishments engaged in the production of wool fabrics in North and South Carolina. Forstmann & Co., formerly the wool division of J.P. Stevens, had manufacturing headquarters in Dublin, Georgia, and its manufacturing facilities located in Georgia, although the company's corporate headquarters were in New York City.

Producers of woolen broadwoven fabrics are for the most part engaged in processes that are similar in principle to those who produce broadwoven fabrics in the cotton and manmade sectors. But wool and other animal fibers must first be scoured before they can be processed into yarn. This is necessary to remove animal greases and other debris that naturally become entangled in the wool prior to shearing.

In the processes involved in the manufacture of yarns—opening, carding, drafting, roving and spinning—machines are larger and designed to process long-staple fibers. These fibers measure four to eight inches in length, as opposed to cotton, which measures from seven-eighths to one and three-eighths inches. Most manmade fiber is cut to process on the cotton system of yarn manufacturing and is thus approximately the same length as the cotton fibers. There are some manmade fibers that are designed to go into products that replace woolen fabrics—suitings, blankets, etc.—or that will be blended with wool fibers, i.e., polyester-wool blends, which are cut to process on woolen machinery.

Like the producers of broadwoven cotton and manmade fabrics, producers of woolen fabrics are generally fully integrated; they produce, weave, then dye the yarn, and finish the woven fabric. Some companies, such as Forstmann & Co., maintain yarn manufacturing and weaving operations in one manufacturing plant and dyeing and finishing in another. Frequently, however, producers of woolen yarn and fabrics buy wool that has already been scoured. The scoured wool purchased by producers of woolen fabrics is generally known as "woolen tops".

There are three categories of manufacturing machinery for production of wool yarns. The category used is determined by the intended fabric's end use. These three are woolen, worsted, and semiworsted. The largest manufacturer of woolen and worsted yarn manufacturing equipment in N. Schlumberger & Cie, of France. Other producers of this type of equipment included Savio, of Italy, and Octir and Ommi, of Germany. Those companies also produced semiworsted yarn manufacturing machines along with James Mackie & Sons Ltd., of Ireland, Walker Technical Inc., of the United States, and Bigagli, of Italy. Mohair and other animal fibers were processed on standard woolen, worsted, and semiworsted yarn manufacturing machines with occasional modifications to adjust for variations in fiber length.

Most woolen and other animal fiber broadwoven fabrics are produced on projectile, rigid, and flexible rapier weaving machines. Air-jet weaving machines are not suitable for production of heavyweight woolen fabrics but are used occasionally if the woolen fabric is a very lightweight worsted product. Water jet weaving machines can not be used to produce broadwoven fabrics of wool and similar animal fibers.

In 1993, two companies manufactured air-jet weaving machines that could be used for production of worsted fabrics: Tsudakoma Corp., of Kanazawa, Japan, and Toyoda Automatic Loom Works Ltd., of Kariya Aichi, Japan. Sulzer Ruti Ltd., of Ruti, Switzerland, manufactured projectile machines that were widely used in the production of broadwoven fabrics of wool and similar animal fibers. There were a number of weaving machine manufacturers that produced flexible and rigid rapier looms that were used for weaving broadwoven fabrics from woolen and other animal fiber yarns. Flexible rapier weaving machines were available from Picanol N.V., of Ieper, Belgium; Nuovo Pignone Smit, of Schio, Italy; Somet SpA, of Colzate, Italy; and Nuova Vamatex SpA, of Villa di Serio, Italy. Rigid rapier weaving machines were available through woolen and other animal fiber broadwoven fabric makers such as Lindauer Dornier

GmbH, of Lindau/Bodensee, Germany; Gunne GmbH, of Moechnesse-Gunne, Germany; and Michel Van de Wiele NV, of Kortrijk, Belgium.

Dyeing and finishing of woolen fabrics was performed on machinery similar to that found in the processing of cotton and manmade fibers. However, chemicals designed specifically for woolen and other animal fibers were used. Frequently—and more often in woolen fabrics than in other types—dyeing was done prior to the manufacture of the fabric. This was done by dyeing the raw wool after scouring or by dyeing the wool yarn. Dyeing of the wool before it was made into fabric was absolutely necessary if the finished product was going to contain a plaid, stripe, or any multicolored pattern (unless the fabric was going to be printed with the design). Since many of the wool fabrics that were woven with multicolored patterns, stripes, or plaids, predyeing of the raw material or yarn was more common in woolen operations than in those processing cotton and/or manmade fiber.

Wool, mohair and similar animal fibers used to produce broadwoven fabrics were more expensive (as raw materials) than cotton and most manmade fibers. Manmade fibers with special applications for high strength, resistance to heat, etc., were the most expensive fibers used in textile applications. For this reason, apparel, blankets, and other common applications for wool and animal fibers were more expensive than those types of products produced from cotton or manmade fibers.

Moreover, most wool is raised in Australia, New Zealand, and the United Kingdom, further increasing the cost to textile plants in the United States. Many considered products made from wool to be luxury items when compared to products made from other less expensive fibers. The added cost of scouring plus the increased cost of wool processing machinery further increased the price of woolen products. The cost of mohair was even more expensive than that of wool.

As more and more products were developed using manmade fibers, the use of wool in textile products continued to decline. While products made of wool had enjoyed more success in European countries, its use in the United States had shown little if any growth during the early 1990s.

Mohair was another product that seemingly enjoyed more success in European countries than in the United States. With the end of the U.S. government's mohair price support program set for 1996, many industry observers expected U.S. production of mohair raw material to decline by 50 percent throughout the mid-1990s. The incentive program, part of the National Wool Act of 1954, paid $58.2 million to producers based on 1992 production. Payments dropped to 75 percent of the incentive for 1993, then to 50 percent in 1995, phasing out completely in 1996.

Mohair was produced in 33 states in the United States in the early 1990s, but 86 percent of total production came from about 4,000 ranchers in the Edwards Plateau region of Southwestern Texas. Other states with significant production were New Mexico, Oklahoma, Missouri and North Dakota.

Most users of mohair in the United States process this animal fiber by blending it with other fibers such as wool. Forstmann, for example, used about 150,000 pounds of mohair a year, making a 30 to 70 percent mohair-wool blend for women's coat fabrics.

Mohair production was rapidly declining worldwide. U.S. mohair production hit an all-time high in 1965 with 32.4 million pounds. In 1992, production was 15.7 million pounds. Production was expected to fall to 14.3 million pounds in 1993 and to 12 million pounds in 1994. Worldwide mohair production fell from 57 million pounds in 1988 to 36 million pounds in 1992. Production was estimated at 33 million pounds in 1993 and expected to plunge to 26 million pounds in 1994.

INDUSTRY INFORMATION SOURCES

"ATME-I '93 Quickens Textiles' Time to Market," *Textile World*, June 1992, pp. 74-75.

"Broadwoven Goods Production, 1993," Washington, DC: Bureau of the Census, U.S. Department of Commerce, 1993.

"GATT Disappoints U.S. Textile Leaders," *Textile World*, January 1994, pp. 23-24.

Isaacs III, McAllister, "Machinery Makers Are Responding to the Needs of Weaving Plants," *Textile World*, December 1993, pp. 42-43.

McCurry, John W., "Is Mohair In For More Woes?" *Textile World*, December 1993, pp. 67-73.

Standard & Poor's Industry Surveys, New York: Standard & Poor's Corporation, 1992.

Standard & Poor's Industry Surveys, New York: Standard & Poor's Corporation, 1993.

Textile Highlights, Washington, DC: American Textile Manufacturers Institute, December 1993.

Textile Highlights, Washington, DC: American Textile Manufacturers Institute, March 1994.

—McAllister Isaacs III

NARROW FABRIC AND OTHER SMALLWARES MILLS: COTTON, WOOL, SILK AND MANMADE FIBER

This category covers establishments primarily engaged in weaving or braiding narrow fabrics of cotton, wool, silk, and man-made fibers, including glass fibers. These fabrics are generally 12 inches or less in width in their final form but may be made initially in wider widths that are specially constructed for cutting to narrower widths. Also included in this industry are establishments primarily engaged in producing fabric-covered elastic yarn or thread.

Weavers of broadwoven fabrics, those that are generally greater than 12 inches in width, are covered in **Industry 2211: Broadwoven Fabric Mills, Cotton**; **Industry No. 2221: Broadwoven Fabric Mills, Manmade Fiber and Silk**; and **Industry No. 2231: Broadwoven Fabric Mills, Wool (Including Dyeing and Finishing)**.

INDUSTRY SNAPSHOT

There are 247 U.S. companies operating 272 establishments engaged in the production of narrow fabrics, according to the U.S. Department of Commerce, Bureau of the Census. In 1991, these companies shipped $1.16 billion worth of narrow fabric products. In addition, underwear makers manufacture narrow fabrics for their own use. Other waistband products manufactured by producers of apparel products that consume the waistband are also considered narrow fabrics manufacturers.

Products that fall into the narrow fabrics category include webbing for military use, industrial belting, automotive seat belts, etc.; narrow apparel products such as waistbands, straps, etc.; tapes for venetian blinds, insulating, zippers, fasteners, etc.; ribbons, laces, fringe and other trimmings; and labels, strapping, shoe laces, etc.

ORGANIZATION AND STRUCTURE

Narrow fabrics are usually divided into two categories: elastic and rigid (or nonelastic). Narrow fabrics that, when stretched, will then return to the original shape and size fall into the elastic group. Elastic narrow fabrics include waistbands, some straps, etc.

Narrow fabrics weaving machines differ from broadwovens weaving machines in more ways than the width of fabrics produced. Narrow fabrics weaving machines produce more than one fabric at a time.

Generally speaking, the wider the fabric, the fewer multiples of fabric pieces are woven. Narrow fabrics weaving machine speed is measured in the same manner as broadwoven fabrics weaving machine speed, i.e. picks per minute (ppm), as described in **Industry 2211: Broadwoven Fabrics Mills, Cotton**.

Most narrow fabrics weaving machines operate by the needle-loom principle. There are rapier narrow fabrics weaving machines as well. Some narrow fabrics are produced on broadwoven weaving machines with the fabric being slit into the narrow widths following weaving. Fabrics requiring woven selvages (edges), however, must be produced on standard narrow fabrics weaving machines. For some end uses, such as ribbons, fabrics made of man-made fibers such as polyester and nylon may be slit with a hot slitting system. This action causes the selvages to fuse, thus preventing ravelling of the fabric edges.

The top five narrow fabrics producers in the United States in 1994 were Spartan Mills of Spartanburg, South Carolina ($400 million in sales); Worldtex Inc. of Hickory, North Carolina ($175 million); BGF Industries Inc. of Greensboro, North Carolina ($120 million); JPS Converter and Industrial Corporation/JPS Glass Fabrics of Slater, South Carolina ($80 million); and CM Offray and Son Inc. of Chester, New Jersey ($51 million).

BACKGROUND AND DEVELOPMENT

Business remains fairly stable for the narrow fabrics producer. Many items do not reflect economic conditions—as do some other textile products. This is especially true for webbings for industrial and military use and tapes, bandages, gauze, etc., for the medical trade. Automotive seat belt fabrics and decorative trimmings are, however, affected by the general economic conditions.

CURRENT CONDITIONS

In the early 1990s, business was generally good for the narrow fabrics producer. New demands for quality and versatility were placed on these companies, as was the case for most other textile products manufacturers at the end of the century. Quick Response has not only had an effect on apparel producers, but the label makers for those garments as well.

Like other textile producers, narrow fabrics firms in the middle 1990s were controlling inventory at all-time low levels. When the garment manufacturers need a change in a hurry, the label supplier has to be able to respond quickly. This need for versatility

places increased emphasis on electronics machinery and, in particular, computer-controlled design stations.

INDUSTRY INFORMATION SOURCES

Isaacs, McAllister III, ''Textile World 1992 Guide To Narrow Fabrics Looms,'' *Textile World*, January 1992, pp.49-66.

Linton, George C., *The Modern Textile and Apparel Dictionary*, Plainfield, NJ: Textile Book Service, Div. of Bonn Industries Inc., 1973.

''Outlook Is Good For Narrow Fabrics Weavers, *Textile World*, January 1992, p. 48.

Standard & Poor's Industry Surveys, New York: Standard & Poor's Corporation, 1993.

Textile Highlights, Washington, D.C.: American Textile Manufacturers Institute, March 1994.

—McAllister Isaacs III

SIC 2251

WOMEN'S FULL-LENGTH AND KNEE-LENGTH HOSIERY, EXCEPT SOCKS

This industry category includes establishments primarily engaged in knitting, dyeing or finishing women's and misses' full-length and knee-length hosiery (except socks), both seamless and full-fashion, and panty hose. Those establishments primarily engaged in knitting, dyeing or finishing women's and misses' knee-length socks and anklets can be found in **SIC 2252: Hosiery, Not Elsewhere Classified**. Establishments primarily engaged in manufacturing elastic (orthopedic) hosiery are classified in **SIC 3842: Orthopedic, Prosthetic, and Surgical Appliances and Supplies**.

According to the U.S. Dept. of Commerce, Bureau of the Census, there were 109 companies operating 161 establishments engaged in the production of women's full-length and knee-length hosiery in 1991, a decrease from the 179 companies with 206 establishments registered a decade earlier. These establishments shipped approximately $1.6115 billion worth of products.

In 1987, North Carolina was the state with the most establishments registered in this category, with 93, representing almost 60 percent of the market share and home to the three largest companies producing women's hosiery (excepts socks). Other states where these industries were doing business included Pennsylvania, South Carolina, Tennessee, Florida, Georgia, Mississippi, New Mexico, and Kentucky.

Most women's hosiery products are made of textured nylon and produced on small-diameter knitting machines. The processes involved in production of the goods covered by this category include: production of POY (partially oriented yarn) nylon filament by fiber producers; texturizing (or texturing) the nylon filament; knitting the filament nylon into the hosiery product; boarding the hosiery to obtain proper size and shape; and finishing the hosiery products and packaging them. Texturing of the nylon hosiery yarn is covered in **SIC 2282: Yarn Texturizing, Throwing, Twisting, and Winding Mills**.

The biggest single event in the evolution of hosiery manufacturing was Du Pont's invention of nylon, which was introduced to the public in 1938, replacing the baggier cotton or more expensive silk stockings. Finding a commercially palatable name for what was officially polyhexamethyleneadipamide took more than two years. "Delawear" was one suggestion submitted by Lammot du Pont, then president of the company. Others were "Duparooh," an unwieldy acronym for "Du Pont pulls a rabbit out of a hat," "Neosheen," "Duponese," and "klis" (silk spelled backwards). Nylon, the word, is in fact a derivative of nylon stockings' wide rumored "no-run" feature.

Sales growth in the women's hosiery industry appeared to have slowed in 1993 and 1994. Sara Lee Corp's L'eggs Products Division, the largest U.S. producer of hosiery within this industry, announced in June of 1994 that it was closing several hosiery plants that would result in layoffs of over 850 people. Industry analysts said that the company failed to recognize a trend away from hosiery and toward a more casual manner of dress among women. Sara Lee, located in Winston-Salem, North Carolina, posted sales $668 million in 1994 and employed 6,000.

Other industry leaders included Ithaca Industries Inc., of Wilkesboro, North Carolina; Hanes Hosiery Inc., of Winston-Salem, North Carolina; Hampshire Group Ltd., of Anderson, South Carolina; and Americal Corp., of Henderson, North Carolina.

Hanes employed approximately 8,000 people in 1994, the largest employer in this category, and six companies employed more than 1,000 people. Trade negotiations during the 1990s opened up opportunities for a potential export market. However, U.S. manufacturers will be vying with overseas producers for shares of the market. More U.S. producers are shipping assembly operations to other countries to lower production costs, thereby potentially reducing employment opportunities in this category. But overall, improved technology and production techniques may provide a competitive edge for U.S. manufacturers in the in-

creasingly competitive global market. Exports may provide the most significant share of growth in sales throughout the 1990s and beyond, especially in Japan, Canada, and Mexico where trade barriers were reduced as a result of the North American Free Trade Agreement negotiated in 1994.

INDUSTRY INFORMATION SOURCES

Gibson, Richard, "Sara Lee Plans To Take Charge of $495 Million," *Wall Street Journal*, June 7, 1994.

Linton, George C., *The Modern Textile and Apparel Dictionary*, Plainfield, NJ: Textile Book Service, Div. of Bonn Industries Inc., 1973.

Standard & Poor's Industry Surveys, New York: Standard & Poor's Corporation, 1993.

Textile Highlights, Washington, DC: American Textile Manufacturers Institute, March 1994.

Thomas, Marita, and Richard G. Mansfield, "Happy Birthday, Nylon!" *Textile World*, March 1988.

—McAllister Isaacs III

SIC 2252

HOSIERY, NOT ELSEWHERE CLASSIFIED

This category covers establishments prmiarily engaged in knitting, dyeing, or finishing hosiery, not elsewhere classified. Establishments engaged in the knitting, dyeing, or finishing of anklets, boys' hosiery, children's hosiery, leg warmers, men's hosiery, socks, slipper socks, and men's and children's tights are included in this category. Establishments engaged in the production of women's full-length and knee-length hosiery and panty hose are classified in **SIC 2251: Women's Full-Length and Knee-Length Hosiery, Except Socks**. Establishments engaged in manufacturing elastic (orthopedic) hosiery are classified in **SIC 3842: Orthopedic, Prosthetic, and Surgical Appliances and Supplies**.

According to the U.S. Department of Commerce, Bureau of the Census, there were 375 companies operating 428 establishments engaged in the production of hosiery, not elsewhere classified, in 1991. Many of these were small, family-owned operations. Approximately 150 of these establishments had less than 20 employees. In 1991, establishments in this category shipped approximately $2.25 billion worth of products. Men's finished hosiery (size 10 and larger) accounted for $765 million in sales, and all other finished hosiery in this category accounted for just over $1 billion worth of shipments.

Hosiery manufactured in this category is produced on small-diameter knitting machines. These establishments, unlike most companies engaged in the weaving process of fabric formation, usually have no yarn manufacturing facilities on site, necessitating the purchase of all yarn requirements. The primary reason for this is that socks and other miscellaneous hosiery products can be made from many different yarn types, making it costly and ineffective for one establishment to produce all the different yarn types required by one knitting establishment.

Most companies classified in this category do, however, operate their own dyeing, finishing, and packaging processes. Thus, after buying the necessary yarn requirements, these establishments can produce finished products that are packaged and ready for sale at the retail level.

Products in this category are made from lightweight to heavyweight yarns, depending on the end-use requirements. They range from heavy woolen socks used by hunters to lightweight anklets worn by small children. Products in this category can be made from cotton, wool, nylon, polyester, polypropylene, rayon, mohair, and other fibers, as well as blends of two or more fibers to reach the desired properties.

Sales indicated growth in this category during the early 1990s. A turn toward more casual styles of dress and a strong movement toward active wear by most regions in the United States were encouraging indicators of continued prosperity in this industry. Men's finished seamless hosiery and anklets made of natural fibers made up slightly over 60 percent of sales within this category.

The leading producer was Kayser-Roth Corp., of Greensboro, North Carolina, with sales estimated at $400 million in 1994 and approximately 7,000 employees. Other leaders in this industry were Sara Lee Corp., Adams-Millis Division, of High Point, North Carolina; Renfro Corp., of Mount Airy, North Carolina; and Clayson Knitting Company Inc., of Star, North Carolina.

There was an average of 39,700 workers employed in this industry in 1992, representing an increase of almost 7,000 people from a decade earlier. Over 72 percent of the work force was women, reflecting relatively little change from 1982, when it was 71 percent.

INDUSTRY INFORMATION SOURCES

Gibson, Richard, "Sara Lee Plans To Take Charge of $495 Million," *Wall Street Journal*, June 1994.

Linton, George C., *The Modern Textile and Apparel Dictionary*, Plainfield, NJ: Textile Book Service, Div. of Bonn Industries Inc., 1973.

Standard & Poor's Industry Surveys, New York: Standard & Poor's Corporation, 1993.

Textile Highlights, Washington, DC: American Textile Manufacturers Institute, March 1994.

"The Business Week 1000 Tables," *Business Week*, 1993 Bonus Issue, pp. 118-163.

—McAllister Isaacs III

SIC 2253

KNIT OUTERWEAR MILLS

Manufacturers in this category are primarily engaged in knitting outerwear from yarn or in the production of outerwear from knit fabrics produced in the same establishment. Establishments that are primarily engaged in hand knitting outerwear for the trade are included in this industry. Establishments primarily engaged in knitting gloves and mittens are classified in **SIC 2259: Knitting Mills, Not Elsewhere Classified**. Those manufacturing outerwear from purchased knit fabrics are classified in the major group for apparel and other finished products made from fabrics and similar materials.

Products manufactured under this category include such diverse products as bathing suits, bathrobes, beachwear, blouses, body stockings, caps, collar and cuff sets, dresses, hats, headwear, housecoats, jackets, jerseys and sweaters, jogging suits, leotards, lounging robes, mufflers, neckties, pants, scarfs, shawls, shirts, outerwear, shoulderettes, ski suits, skirts, slacks, suits, sweat bands, sweat pants, sweat shirts, sweaters and sweater coats, T-shirts, tank tops, ties, trousers, warmup suits and wristlets.

INDUSTRY SNAPSHOT

This category contained more companies, 808, and more establishments than any other category classified in Industry Group 225 (knitting mills). In 1991, according to the U.S. Dept. of Commerce, Bureau of the Census, shipments from this industry were valued at $3.545 billion. Of this, men's and boys' shirts accounted for $1.7 billion.

One of the largest companies in this sector was Sara Lee Corp., Sara Lee Knit Products Div. (SLKP), headquartered in Winston-Salem, North Carolina. The next two companies in order of size were Fruit Of The Loom, headquartered in Bowling Green, Kentucky, and Russell Corp., headquartered in Alexander City, Alabama.

These three companies—the largest in this sector—made similar products, capitalizing on one of the fastest growing product areas in the textile industry, and the fastest growing section of apparel textile products: leisure and active wear. All three companies produced sweat suits, jogging suits, athletic uniforms, and other forms of active wear. Products manufactured by Russell and Fruit Of The Loom carried the company name as part of the brand. Champion, Pannel, and Hanes brand sweat suits were all manufactured by SLKP. Pannel and Hanes products were usually distributed in large discount chains, while Champion products were found in department stores.

Other products common among the three companies included T-shirts and golf shirts (knit shirts with collars) for men, women, and children. The T-shirt business has been one of the fastest growing businesses in the textile industry, especially with the trend toward putting messages and company names on them.

While it is a generally accepted practice that companies engaged in the weaving business are fully integrated, i.e., produce their own yarn requirements, it is also a general rule that companies engaged in knitting are not fully integrated, that is they buy their yarn requirements. The reason for this is that most manufacturers of knit products require so many different types of yarn that it is not economically feasible for them to produce their own yarn requirements.

The notable exceptions to this practice in the knitting sector were the three largest companies: SLKP, Fruit Of The Loom, and Russell Corp., for several reasons. To begin with, the three companies were all so large that they could confine specific products to certain plants. Size and volume from each of the three companies also made the investment in modern, sophisticated yarn manufacturing machinery and equipment more feasible. Moreover, even though SLKP, Fruit of the Loom, and Russell produced a larger volume than most other knitting companies, they did not produce as many types of products. Sweat suits, jogging suits and T-shirts became almost commodity items in the knitting business. While the three companies required a large volume of yarn to meet the knitting requirements, they only required a few types and sizes of yarn. For the most part, all three companies made products from either 100 percent cotton or cotton and polyester blends.

One thing similar about the operations of SLKP, Russell, and Fruit Of The Loom knitting operations to the other knitting companies that are not integrated is that knitting operations are not located in the same facilities as the yarn manufacturing operations. Dyeing and finishing of the knit fabrics is, however, usually located in the same plant building with the knitting operation.

Most of Russell Corp.'s knitting and yarn manufacturing operations were located in Alabama with a few yarn manufacturing operations in Georgia, South Carolina, and North Carolina. Most of Fruit of the Loom's knitting plants were located in North Carolina with the preponderance of its yarn making facilities in Alabama. SLKP's knitting plants were, for the most part, in North Carolina and Virginia with yarn manufacturing plants in Georgia, North Carolina, and South Carolina. One of SLKP's yarn manufacturing plants, in Mountain City, Tennessee, had been termed by many industry analysts as the most modern textile operation in the world, recognized as the model upon which future textile plants will be built.

SLKP's Mountain City Plant produced over one million pounds each week of 100 percent cotton yarn for the company's Hanes Beefy-T T-shirt products. The plant was not only modern from a machinery and equipment standpoint, it contained state-of-the-art electronic information system technology and the latest in management techniques as well. A fully automated plant, bales of cotton had to be manually unloaded from the delivery trucks, but no one touched any part of the product after that until palletized cartons of yarn were readied to be put back on the same trucks for shipment to SLKP knitting plants.

The SLKP Mountain City Plant was also a fully computer-integrated manufacturing facility. A computerized network system monitored each machine for quality, production, and efficiency. A series of alarms and shut-down capabilities alerted teams if problems occurred.

An important management technique at Mountain City was implemented that had broken industry norms. No supervisors were employed, with the exception of the plant manager. It operated 24 hours each day, seven days per week, with two pairs of 12-hour shifts. Each shift had two 20-person teams that were responsible for each half of the plant. These teams patroled operations, monitored electronic information systems, and together controlled the manufacturing facility. Teams hired and fired team members and participated in extensive training in such subjects areas as problem solving, consensus decision making, etc. All employees were salaried and had business cards. As a symbol of ownership, each employee had a tree planted on the plant's property with his or her name on a plaque by the tree. All employees were paid an incentive bonus based on plant production and quality evaluated at the knitting plant.

ORGANIZATION AND STRUCTURE

Two broad categories of knitting machines produced the products in this classification: circular and flat. Circular machines are much more prominent in this category because flat machines generally are used in the production of sweaters. Major producers of circular knitting machines were Camber International, of Leicester, England; Fukuhara Ltd., of Osaka, Japan; Mayer & Cie, of Albstadt, Germany; Monarch Knitting Machine Corp., of St. Glendale, New York; Terrot Strickmaschen GmbH, of Stuttgart, Germany; Tritex International Ltd., of Leicester, England; and Vanguard-Supreme, of Monroe, North Carolina.

Monarch and Mayer were among the major producers of flat knitting machines as well as Liba Maschinenfabrik GmbH, of Naila/Bavaria, Germany, and Karl Mayer, of Obertshauesen, Germany.

BACKGROUND AND DEVELOPMENT

While the basic principles of knitting have not changed over the years, the use of electronic technology in recent years has enhanced the process tremendously. The use of CAD/CAM (computer-aided design/compuer-aided manufacturing) systems had been the most prominent infusion of electronics into knitting. The best known system was manufactured by Monarch Design Systems. This company produced a system that increased creativity, productivity, and versatility. Products designed to be knitted on an electronic knitting machine were transferred onto a 3.5 inch disk, which would then be loaded on a Macintosh computer. The disk was then subsequently transferred to the knitting machine by a loading device on the knitting floor. This process, like new electronic processes in weaving, reduced to hours (in some cases minutes) processes that at one time took weeks.

Another form of electronics used in the knitting process was a program for monitoring performance of the process as well as production of the product. One such system was STARFISH (start as you intend to finish), developed by Cotton Technology International, of Manchester, England. STARFISH was a set of computer programs that related the properties and dimensions of a knitted cotton fabric to the knitting parameters and the finishing route. By the use of such programs, manufacturers and buyers were able to calculate quickly the performance of the most popular fabric constructions after dyeing and finishing. Thus, major savings in development time and money were achieved and decision making enhanced.

CURRENT CONDITIONS

With the increased use of leisure and active wear, business in this industry has continued to improve over the past several years. The passage of the North American Free Trade Agreement (NAFTA) also portends well for manufacturers of products in this classification. Anticipated demand for U.S. made products and U.S. style products in Mexico is expected to increase, especially for affordable T-shirts, sweat suits, and jogging suits, making international markets for U.S. products a promising trend.

INDUSTRY INFORMATION SOURCES

Gibson, Richard, "Sara Lee Plans To Take Charge of $495 Million," *Wall Street Journal*, June 7, 1994.

Isaacs III, McAllister, "Mountain City's Whiz Bang Is On The Move," *Textile World*, October 1993, pp. 61-66.

"Mountain City: Oh What A Yarn Mill!" *Textile World*, June 1991, pp. 38-40.

Standard & Poor's Industry Surveys, New York: Standard & Poor's Corporation, 1993.

Textile Highlights, Washington, DC: American Textile Manufacturers Institute, March 1994.

"Textile World 1993-94 Buyer's Guide For Machinery, Equipment & Supplies," *Textile World*, July 1993.

—McAllister Isaacs III

SIC 2254

KNIT UNDERWEAR AND NIGHTWEAR MILLS

This category covers those establishments primarily engaged in knitting underwear and nightwear from yarn or in manufacturing underwear and nightwear from knit fabrics produced in the same establishment. Companies primarily engaged in manufacturing underwear and nightwear from purchased knit fabrics are classified in the Major Industry Group 23 (apparel and other finished products made from fabrics and similar materials). Those establishments that produce knitted robes are classified in **SIC 2253: Knit Outerwear Mills**.

Products manufactured by companies in this classification include underwear briefs and knitted underwear drawers, night gowns, negligees, knit pajamas, ladies' and girls' panties, undershirts, T-shirts used as undershirts (both V-neck and regular neck), slips, and union suits or long (winter) underwear.

There were 58 companies that operated 63 establishments engaged in the production of underwear and nightwear in 1991, according to the U.S. Department of Commerce, Bureau of the Census. These establishments shipped over $1 billion worth of products, with men's and boy's underwear accounting for the biggest portion at $790 million. Ladies' and girls' underwear accounted for over $200 million. In addition, companies exported $464 million worth of women's and girl's undergarments in 1993, a 14 percent increase from 1989, and $326 million in men's and boys' underwear and nightwear, a dramatic increase over the $52 million exported in 1989. The export trend likely to continue in this industry, as well as most other industries, with the reduction of trade restrictions resulting from the 1994 passage of the North American Free Trade Agreement.

Almost all products in this category are made on circular knitting machines. Most men's and boys' underwear is made from 100 percent cotton or cotton-polyester blends. Until recently, most women's and girls' underwear was produced from nylon, with silk being used as somewhat of a luxury item.

Recently, however, the trend in women's underwear has been toward the use of cotton. During the late 1980s and early 1990s, companies, such as Jockey and Fruit Of The Loom, began modeling women's lines after men's cotton briefs. Results were successful for these companies that had traditionally strongest sales in the men's and boys' markets.

Jockey International Inc., of Kenosha, Wisconsin, showed strongest sales in the knit underwear industry, with revenues of $340 million and approximately 5,000 employees. Fruit Of The Loom Inc., of Lexington, South Carolina, was the largest manufacturer of men's briefs. The 1975 advertising campaign that introduced the ''Fruit of the Loom Guys'' to viewing audiences brought the company a 98 percent brand recognition rate and doubled its market share in men's and boy's underwear. Fruit of the Loom was also planning to invest $125 million in new equipment throughout the 1990s and increase the work force by 3,000 at plants in the United States, Canada, and Europe.

Other industry leaders included Spring City Knitting Company Inc., of Cartersville, Georgia; Martin Mills Inc., of Martinville, Louisiana; and Spring Ford Knitting Company Inc., of Spring City, Pennsylvania.

INDUSTRY INFORMATION SOURCES

Linton, George C., *The Modern Textile and Apparel Dictionary*, Plainfield, NJ: Textile Book Service, Div. of Bonn Industries Inc., 1973.

Standard & Poor's Industry Surveys, New York: Standard & Poor's Corporation, 1993.

Textile Highlights, Washington, DC: American Textile Manufacturers Institute, December 1993.

''Textiles Ready to Reap NAFTA Rewards,'' *Textile World*, December 1993, pp. 23-24.

—McAllister Isaacs III

SIC 2257

WEFT KNIT FABRIC MILLS

Establishments in this classification are primarily engaged in knitting weft, or circular, fabrics or in the dyeing or finishing of weft, or circular, fabrics. These companies may sell their fabrics to manufacturers of outerwear, underwear, or other products in the apparel or home furnishings industries. Companies engaged in knitting weft outerwear fabrics and subsequently producing outerwear in the same establishment are discussed in **SIC 2253: Knit Outerwear Mills**. Also, establishments engaged in knitting circular underwear and nightwear products and which manufacture the end-product at the same site are discussed in **SIC 2254: Knit Underwear and Nightwear Mills**. Overall, those companies who buy knit fabrics for the production of outerwear and underwear are described in the major group for apparel and other finished products made from fabrics and similar materials.

The U.S. Department of Commerce, Bureau of the Census, reported that there were 304 companies operating 334 establishments engaged in the production of weft knit fabrics in 1991. These companies shipped $3.8 billion worth of fabric, with almost $2.5 billion in shipments consisting of finished weft knit fabrics. Another $500 million in shipments consisted of greige (undyed and unfinished) weft knit fabrics. Revenue of approximately $400 million was in the form of commission and contract receipts.

The handling of circular knit fabrics is a more delicate process than handling of woven goods because the fabrics are not as stable in the finished state. Extreme care must be taken and special shipping containers must be used when shipping circular knit fabrics. Fabrics produced in this category are used across the spectrum of finished goods, from leisure and activewear, to more expensive evening wear.

Stevcoknit Fabrics Co., of Greer, South Carolina, posted 1993 sales of $130 million, the largest manufacturer in this category, and employed approximately 1,500 people. Stevcoknit, a subsidiary of Delta Woodside Industries, Inc., primarily served the apparel market with singleknit and doubleknit fabrics, mainly producing terrycloth and rib fabrics for athletic wear. Other leaders within this industry were Stony Creek Knitting Mill, of Rocky Mount, North Carolina; Cleveland Mills Co., of Lawndale, North Carolina; and Guilford Mills Inc., Fashion Apparel Division, of Lumberton, North Carolina.

INDUSTRY INFORMATION SOURCES

Standard & Poor's Industry Surveys, New York: Standard & Poor's Corporation, 1993.

''Starfish Technology For Upgrading the Performance of Circular Knitted Cotton Fabrics,'' Manchester, England: Cotton Technology International.

Textile Highlights, Washington, DC: American Textile Manufacturers Institute, March 1994.

''The Business Week 1000 Tables,'' *Business Week*, 1993 Bonus Issue, pp. 118-163.

—McAllister Isaacs III

SIC 2258

LACE AND WARP KNIT FABRIC MILLS

Establishments in this category are those that are primarily engaged in knitting, dyeing, or finishing warp (flat) knit fabrics, or in manufacturing, dyeing, or finishing lace goods. Products produced under this category include lace bed sets; lace covers for chairs, dressers, pianos, and tables; curtains and lace curtain fabrics; lace edgings; knit netting; warp knit pile fabrics; and tricot fabrics.

There were 232 companies engaged in the production of warp, or flat, knit goods, or lace products, in 1987. Of these, 155 employed 20 or more people, a decrease of eight percent from the previous year. Overall, employment slightly slipped from a high in 1982 of 21,100 employees working within this classification to 20,500 in 1988, a trend that continued into the early 1990s. New Jersey had the most mills in this category, with 59 in 1987. Other states with high concentrations of companies in this industry included North Carolina, New York, Pennsylvania, Rhode Island, Florida, Connecticut, Georgia, California, New Hampshire, and Massachusetts.

Employees worked as sewing machine operators, textile draw-out and winding machine workers, hand packers and packagers, inspectors, laborers, industrial machinery mechanics, textile bleaching and dyeing machine workers, hand workers, textile machine setters and set-up operators, blue collar worker super-

visors, general managers, top executives, and freight and stock handlers.

Warp, or flat, knitting machines resemble weaving machines in appearance, but produce fabrics more nearly like those produced on circular knitting machines. Warp knit is a specialized fabric made by a machine knit process consisting of running nylon, acetate, and polyester yarns in a lengthwise direction in the fabric, forming interlocking loops. The cost, compared to circular knit techniques, is relatively low. Producers of these types of machines include Liba Maschinenfabrik GmH, of Naila/Bavaria, Germany; Chima Inc., of Reading, Pennsylvania; Comez SpA, of Calenzano, Italy; Mayer Textile Machine Corp., of Clifton, New Jersey; Karl Mayer GmbH, of Obertshausen, Germany; and Edouard Dubied & Cie SA, of Couvet, Switzerland.

During the 1980s, sales took a slight downturn in this industry. A slump in clothing sales and a growing flood of inexpensive imports slowed growth considerably. Throughout the late 1990s, however, sales were expected to increase significantly due to the anticipated increase in shipments to Mexico as a result of the North American Free Trade Agreement.

In 1994, the largest company in this category was Guilford Mills Inc., of Greensboro, North Carolina, a public company with sales of $615 million and 3,700 employees. Guilford represented the only U.S. automotive textile company with manufacturing facilities abroad, with production plants in the United Kingdom and part-ownership in the largest warp knitting company in Mexico. In 1990, the company also became the first U.S. mill to introduce microdenier specialty fabrics, which has a high-filament count that gives a silk-like feel to stretchy fabrics. In 1991, the production of fine denier specialty yarns allowed Guilford a niche market and sales topped $5.28.8 million.

Other leaders included Liberty Fabrics Inc., of New York, New York; FAB Industries Inc., of New York, New York; Lida Inc., of Charlotte, North Carolina; Mohican Mills Inc., of Lincolnton, North Carolina; and Carisbrook Industries Inc. Native Textiles, of New York, New York.

INDUSTRY INFORMATION SOURCES

Linton, George C., *The Modern Textile and Apparel Dictionary*, Plainfield, NJ: Textile Book Service, Div. of Bonn Industries Inc., 1973.

Standard & Poor's Industry Surveys, New York: Standard & Poor's Corporation, 1993.

Textile Highlights, Washington, DC: American Textile Manufacturers Institute, March 1994.

"The Business Week 1000 Tables," *Business Week*, 1993 Bonus Issue, pp. 118-163.

                                        —McAllister Isaacs III

SIC 2259

KNITTING MILLS, NOT ELSEWHERE CLASSIFIED

Companies found in this classification are those that are primarily engaged in knitting gloves and other articles, not elsewhere classified. Establishments primarily engaged in manufacturing woven or knit fabric gloves and mittens from purchased fabrics are classified in **SIC 2381: Yarn Spinning Mills**.

Products manufactured by establishments in this category include bags and bagging, bedspreads, curtains, dishcloths, elastic girdle blanks, girdles and other foundation garments, gloves, shoe linings, mittens, stockinettes, towels, and washcloths.

Many companies in this category were small, family-owned businesses that served niche markets. In 1988, there were 77 establishments classified as operating within this industry category. Slightly more than half of them had less than 20 employees. In the same year, these companies shipped approximately $222.9 million worth of products, primarily to U.S. markets. The state with the highest number of establishments within this category was New York. North Carolina, Pennsylvania, New Jersey, Ohio, Connecticut, Massachussetts, Minnesota, Illinois, and Wisconsin also had knitting mill manufacturers, not elsewhere classified, operating.

Employees of this industry worked as sewing machine operators, textile draw-out and winding machine workers, hand packers and packagers, inspectors, industrial machinery mechanics, textile bleaching and dyeing machine workers, testers, hand workers, textile machine setters and set-up operators, blue collar worker supervisors, general managers, and material movers and handlers.

As is the case with most companies engaged in the knitting business, establishments in this category tend to purchase their own yarn requirements. Companies in this category rarely have their own dyeing and finishing operations. When dyeing and finishing is required, the companies either have these tasks performed on a commission basis or, in some cases, goods are sold to dyers and finishers who in turn deliver the finished fabric. In the case of some types of knit work

gloves, dyeing and finishing is not necessary—the gloves are manufactured from greige fabric and left the natural color.

Technological advances during the 1990s occurred in three major areas within the overall textile industry: computer-aided design (CAD), production, and communications; new modular manufacturing systems; and, ergonomics (work place instruments designed to improve the safety, health, and efficiency of workers). Only about 60 percent of the establishments within the textile industry were using any of the new technology offered. Smaller firms were found to be the least efficient. Establishments in the miscellaneous knitting mills category usually maintained only a few knitting machines, which were either circular or flat machines depending on the product being manufactured.

New technology had also produced machines that were quieter, easier-to-operate, and designed to reduce stress and injury in the workplace. Particular emphasis was placed on reducing the repetitive motions typical within the sewn products industry in light of increased government regulations, high workers' compensation costs, and increasing health care costs. Between 1987 and 1988, a 48 percent increase in establishments with 20 or more employees occurred in this industry, in spite of the fact that the total number of people employed remained the same, indicating a shift away from smaller, inefficient, and costly manufacturing sites to larger companies with greater capital, which will be needed to replace outdated equipment and compete in an expanding international market.

In 1994 the largest U.S. company within this classification was H. Warshow and Sons, Inc., of New York, New York, with sales of $41 million and 600 employees. Other industry leaders included El & El Novelty Company Inc., of New York, New York; Kleinert's Incorporated, of Alabama; Scott Mills Div., of Gastonia, North Carolina; Leading Lady Companies Inc., of Beachwood, Ohio; Novelty Textile Mills Inc., of Wauregan, Connecticut; and Cushman and Marden Inc., of Peabody, Massachussetts.

INDUSTRY INFORMATION SOURCES

Linton, George C., *The Modern Textile and Apparel Dictionary*, Plainfield, NJ: Textile Book Service, Div. of Bonn Industries Inc., 1973.

Standard & Poor's Industry Surveys, New York: Standard & Poor's Corporation, 1993.

Textile Highlights, Washington, DC: American Textile Manufacturers Institute, March 1994.

"The Business Week 1000 Tables," *Business Week*, 1993 Bonus Issue, pp. 118-163.

—McAllister Isaacs III

SIC 2261

FINISHERS OF BROADWOVEN FABRICS OF COTTON

This category covers establishments primarily engaged in finishing purchased broadwoven cotton fabrics or finishing such fabrics on a commission basis. These finishing operations include bleaching, dyeing, printing (roller, screen, flock, plisse), and other mechanical finishing, such as preshrinking, calendering, and napping. Also included in this industry are establishments primarily engaged in shrinking and sponging of cotton broadwoven fabrics for the trade and chemical finishing for water repellency, fire resistance, and mildew proofing. Establishments primarily engaged in finishing wool broadwoven fabrics are classified in **SIC 2231: Broadwoven Fabric Mills, Wool (Including Dyeing and Finishing)**; those finishing knit goods are classified in knitting mill industries; and those coating or impregnating fabrics are classified in **SIC 2295: Coated Fabrics, Not Rubberized.**

INDUSTRY SNAPSHOT

According to 1993 U.S. Bureau of the Census statistics, there are 204 establishments in the United States engaged in dyeing and/or finishing of broadwoven cotton fabrics. The vast majority of these are located in the southeastern United States, particularly in North and South Carolina. Some establishments, such as Burlington Industries Inc., Cone Mills Corp., and Thomaston Mills Inc. are engaged in both the manufacture and dyeing and finishing of broadwoven cotton fabrics. Some companies, such as Cranston Print Works, are engaged only in the dyeing and finishing of broadwoven cotton fabrics.

Over 95 percent of the broadwoven cotton fabrics that are manufactured receive some form of dyeing and/or finishing treatment. Even the industrial products that require no coloration still require some type of finishing process to render the fabric useful in its intended application. In the early 1990s, environmentally conscious products began attracting consumer attention. Sheets and pillowcases that were produced without dyeing or chemical processing became popular in department stores. But even these products necessitate a finishing process, albeit one without chemicals, to become useful bedding products.

ORGANIZATION AND STRUCTURE

Finishing of broadwoven fabrics is subdivided into three general processing categories: fabric preparation, fabric coloration, and fabric finishing. Fabric preparation consists primarily of bleaching and preparing fabrics with chemical agents to aid in subsequent processing. Such processes, depending on the end result desired, may be performed in open-width fabric form or in fabric rope form.

Coloration of fabrics consists of a variety of dyeing methods executed via batch or continuous process procedures and printing. Printing of broadwovens may be performed by screen printing machines, roller printing machines, roller-screen printing machines, or by a process known as transfer printing.

Fabric finishing is accomplished either through surface (dry) finishing or wet finishing. Surface or dry finishing consists of such processes as sueding, sanding, and napping and imparts a certain texture, hand, or feel to the fabric. Wet finishing consists of preshrinking or sanforizing, mercerization or heat-setting. Chemical finishes for water repellency, flame retardancy, mildew proofing, wash-and-wear characteristics, etc., are applied during finishing processes. Fabric straightening (elimination of bow and bias) and width setting is also performed during finishing.

Virtually all establishments engaged in dyeing and finishing of broadwoven cotton fabrics have at least part of their operations involved in commission work—dyeing and finishing services performed on fabrics owned by other companies. Dyeing and finishing facilities generally utilize much more complicated production processes than do facilities designed for other textile processes. This is due both to the volume of water used in dyeing and finishing operations and the amount of chemicals used in each dyeing and finishing process. Dyeing and finishing machines and equipment are generally custom-designed to meet specific applications and needs. Piping requirements for water, steam, and chemicals will vary from one installation to another as well. Therefore, building facilities used for dyeing and finishing operations are usually custom-designed as well. While buildings for other textile processes, such as yarn manufacturing, knitting and weaving, carry structural specifications due to the weight and vibration potential of the machines, dyeing and finishing building specifications must consider machine weight plus machine and piping design and configuration.

Primary Market Categories. Establishments engaged in dyeing and finishing of broadwoven cotton fabrics generally serve three market categories: apparel, homefurnishings, and industrials. In the United States, apparel and homefurnishings account for 75-80 percent of the broadwoven cotton fabric production. Imports are eroding those markets, however, at a time when industrial fabrics are growing in end uses. Some industry observers expect industrial fabrics to account for approximately 35 percent of production by the end of the 1990s.

In the apparel area, companies dye and finish broadwoven cotton fabrics for men's and ladies' shirts and blouses, children's wear, men's trousers and ladies' pants, leisure and sports wear, and other clothing. Because of some advances developed by Cotton Incorporated, the research arm of the cotton growers' association, companies can now produce water repellent broadwoven cotton rain wear. Cotton Incorporated has also developed some finishes that allow production of wash-and-wear (easy care, no-iron) cotton fabrics.

In homefurnishings, dyers and finishers of broadwoven cotton fabrics supply bedding products—sheets, pillowcases and shams, light comforters and blankets, and dust ruffles; bath products—bath towels, hand towels, and wash cloths; and other household items such as draperies and curtains, napery products (napkins and tablecloths), kitchen towels, upholstery fabrics, and cushion covers. In the industrial area, broadwoven cotton fabrics are dyed and/or finished towards production of medical and hospital goods, abrasive fabrics such as sanding belt fabrics, conveyor belts, tents, awnings, luggage, and other products.

CURRENT CONDITIONS

According to the U.S. Department of Commerce, more than 4.4 million square yards of broadwoven cotton fabrics were dyed and finished in 1992, compared to approximately 4.2 million square yards dyed and finished in 1991.

Two trade agreements enacted at the end of 1993 are expected to have a significant impact on this industry. It is anticipated that the North American Trade Agreement (NAFTA), which essentially removes all trade restrictions among Canadian, American, and Mexican businesses, will have a long-range positive economic effect for U.S. dyers and finishers of broadwoven cotton fabrics, according to officials at the American Textile Manufacturers Institute (ATMI). The General Agreement on Tariffs and Trade (GATT), which reduces or eliminates tariffs among 117 nations over the next 10 years will not, according to ATMI officials, have a positive impact on U.S. producers of

dyed and finished broadwoven cotton fabrics. How much of a negative impact this agreement will have on U.S. dyers and finishers remains to be seen.

INDUSTRY LEADERS

Leading companies involved in cotton finishing manufacturing include Logo 7 Inc., Duro Industries Inc., Cranston Print Works Co., Old Deerfield Fabrics Inc., and Covington Fabrics Corporation. Other private companies with annual sales of more than $35 million include Texprint Georgia, Lorber Industries of California, Santee Print Works, American Fast Print, and Facemate Corporation.

RESEARCH AND TECHNOLOGY

As a part of industry-wide efforts to remain competitive in the international arena, cotton broadwoven fabric finishers have explored several new operating systems. One such system, called Quick Response, had by 1993 already shown promise as a process that could boost production of U.S.-made broadwoven cotton products. Essentially it is a system that requires partnerships up and down the softgoods pipeline—fiber producers, textile manufacturers, apparel manufacturers, and retail establishments. The process makes use of electronic technology, especially bar coding and electronic data interchange (EDI), to enable every member of the pipeline to reduce inventories, to shorten delivery times between each pipeline partner, and to eliminate processing steps at some partner members' operations without adding them at others.

The system also permits orders from retail establishments that are smaller than season requirements and enables these retail establishments to reorder in mid-season after buying trends and patterns have been established. This process, when all elements are in place, reduces costs at all pipeline partner establishments and reduces the number of necessary markdowns at the end of the season in the retail establishments.

The other development which should aid U.S. producers of dyed and finished broadwoven cotton fabrics is the AMTEX Pact, enacted during 1993. It is a pact wherein national laboratories, in conjunction with the United States Department of Energy (DOE), will work on selected projects with the United States textile industry and its research facilities to develop systems to make the U.S. textile industry more competitive. Funding will be provided equally between the DOE and the U.S. textile industry.

The first project scheduled to be undertaken under the Pact is the Demand Activated Manufacturing Architecture (DAMA), which expands on the Quick Response system. Under the envisioned DAMA system, electronics will inform each pipeline partner of each garment sold by making use of point-of-sale data generated during scanning of bar-coded hang tags.

INDUSTRY INFORMATION SOURCES

Brassil, Robert D. "Practical Aspects of Fabric Preparation." Paper presented at the conference *Theory and Practice of Fabric Preparation,* Clemson University, 1982.

"Broadwoven Goods Production, 1993," Washington, DC: Bureau of the Census, United States Department of Commerce, 1993.

"1993 Industry Outlook: What's Ahead for America's 24 Key Industries." *Business Week,* January 11, 1993.

"GATT Disappoints U.S. Textile Leaders," *Textile World,* January 1994, 23-24.

Goldstein, Herman B. "Basics of Textile Finishing: Chemical and Mechanical." Consultation research paper, 1987.

Linton, George C. *The Modern Textile and Apparel Dictionary.* Plainfield, NJ: Textile Book Service, 1973.

Melton, Max. "Continuous Dyeing of Woven Cotton and Cotton Blend Fabrics: Reactive Dyes—Continuous Application." Research paper, Charlotte, NC: American Hoechst Corp., 1982.

"Springs Psyched for a Second Century of Success," *Textile World,* June 1987, 44-85.

Standard & Poor's Industry Surveys. New York: Standard & Poor's Corporation, 1993.

Textile Highlights. Washington, DC: American Textile Manufacturers Institute, December 1993.

"Textiles Ready to Reap NAFTA Rewards." *Textile World.* December 1993, 23-24.

"Who's the Real Winner in Burlington Match?" *Textile World.* June 1987, 23.

—McAllister Isaacs III

SIC 2262

FINISHERS OF BROADWOVEN FABRICS OF MANMADE FIBER AND SILK

Establishments in this category are primarily engaged in finishing purchased manmade fiber and silk broadwoven fabrics or finishing such fabrics on a commission basis. Those companies engaged in the dyeing and finishing of broadwoven cotton fabrics are discussed in **SIC 2261: Finishers of Broadwoven Fabrics of Cotton.** Establishments primarily engaged in finishing wool broadwoven fabrics are classified in **SIC 2231: Broadwoven Fabric Mills, Wool (Including Dyeing and Finishing)**; those finishing knit goods are classified in knitting mills industry group; and those coating or impregnating fabrics are classified in **SIC 2295: Coated Fabrics, Not Rubberized.** Finishing operations found in **2262** include bleaching, dyeing, printing, preshrinking, calendering and napping.

INDUSTRY SNAPSHOT

There are 248 companies, 288 establishments, engaged in the finishing of broadwoven manmade and silk fabrics, according to the United States Department of Commerce, Bureau of the Census. By far, the great majority of those are engaged in finishing polyester fabrics. In 1991, these companies finished and shipped $3.2 billion worth of fabrics.

ORGANIZATION AND STRUCTURE

Finishing of broadwoven fabrics is subdivided into three general processing categories: fabric preparation, fabric coloration, and fabric finishing. Fabric preparation consists primarily of bleaching and preparing fabrics with chemical agents to aid in subsequent processing. Such processes, depending on the end result desired, may be performed in open-width fabric form or in fabric-rope form. Severe bleaching of fabrics of manmade fibers isn't necessary to the extent broadwoven cotton fabric bleaching is required, because impurities from the cotton plant are found in broadwoven cotton fabrics.

Coloration of fabrics consists of a variety of dyeing methods, either in batch or continuous process procedures and printing. Printing of broadwovens may be performed by screen printing machines, roller printing machines, roller-screen printing machines, or by a process known as transfer printing.

The subcategory of finishing divides again into surface or dry finishing and wet finishing. Surface or dry finishing consists of such processes as sueding, sanding, and napping and imparts a certain texture or feel to the fabric. Wet finishing consists of preshrinking or sanforizing, mercerization or heat-setting. Chemical finishes for water repellency, flame retardancy, mildew proofing, wash-and-wear characteristics, etc., are applied during finishing processes. Fabric straightening (elimination of bow and bias) and width setting is performed during finishing.

Establishments engaged in dyeing and finishing of broadwoven manmade fiber and silk fabrics generally serve three market categories: apparel, homefurnishings, and industrials. In the United States, apparel and homefurnishings account for 75-80 percent of broadwoven fabric production. But because imports are eroding those markets and industrial fabrics are growing in end uses, industrials are expected to account for approximately 35 percent of production by 2000.

BACKGROUND AND DEVELOPMENT

The dyeing and finishing processes for broadwoven manmade fiber and silk fabrics begins with preparatory steps. In these processes, fabrics are prepared for subsequent dyeing and finishing. Primarily, preparation of manmade fiber and silk fabrics consists of bleaching, scouring, and cleaning the fabrics to remove sizing chemicals and materials used in weaving and to clean and whiten the fabric, making it easier to dye and finish. Machines most commonly used in the preparation process include kiers, J-boxes, roller steamers, conveyor steamers, semi J-box steamers, and high-temperature pressure steamers. The most common chemical agent used is hydrogen peroxide.

Dyeing is typically done through one of two types of dyeing operations for broadwoven fabrics: Batch and continuous. The continuous process is by far the most popular in the United States as it is based on high-volume, low-cost-per-unit operations. However, as more and more companies begin participating in Quick Response partnerships, it may become necessary to increase the number of batch operations, which are generally geared toward shorter-run, lower-volume products.

A number of finishing possibilities exist for broadwoven fabrics. The practice of treating fabrics with resins or other agents to impart shrinkage stabilization, creaseproofing, and shape retention has grown to tremendous importance. Collectively, these properties are now known as durable press. Fabrics can receive other finishes such as water repellency, flame retardancy, germ repellency, and insect repellency. Compressive shrinking, generally known as sanforizing, takes place during finishing and prevents shrinking of finished garments. In finishing, widths are set, while fabrics are straightened and given particular feels or hands. It is the final process in textile manufacturing of broadwoven fabrics.

CURRENT CONDITIONS

As discussed in **Industry No. 2211: Broadwoven Fabric Mills, Cotton,** two trade agreements enacted at the end of 1993 will have an effect on the future of this segment. The North American Trade Agreement (NAFTA), which essentially removes all trade restrictions among Canadian, U.S., and Mexican businesses, should have a long-range positive effect on U.S. dyers

and finishers of broadwoven manmade fiber and silk fabrics, according to officials at the American Textile Manufacturers Institute (ATMI). The General Agreement on Tariffs and Trade (GATT), which reduces or eliminates tariffs among 117 nations over the next 10 years will not, according to ATMI officials, have a positive impact on U.S. producers of dyed and finished broadwoven manmade fiber and silk fabrics. How much of a negative impact this agreement will have on U.S. dyers and finishers remains to be seen. In part, it will depend on a number of systems under development in the 1990s.

One such system is called Quick Response, and by 1993 it had already shown promise as a process that could boost U.S.-made broadwoven manmade fiber and silk products. Essentially it is a system that requires partnerships up and down the softgoods pipeline—fiber producers, textile manufacturers, apparel manufacturers, and retail establishments. The process makes use of electronic technology, especially bar coding and electronic data interchange (EDI) to enable every member of the pipeline to reduce inventories, to shorten delivery times between each pipeline partner, and to eliminate processing steps at some partner members' operations without adding them at others.

The system also permits orders from retail establishments that are smaller than season requirements and enables these retail establishments to reorder in mid-season after buying trends and patterns have been established in regard to style, size, and color. This process, when all elements are in place, reduces costs at all pipeline partner establishments and reduces the number of necessary markdowns at the end of the season in the retail establishments. When all the elements are in place and the process works as it should, the system overcomes some of the advantages held by establishments exporting products from low-wage, developing countries into the United States.

The other development which should aid U.S. producers of dyed and finished broadwoven manmade fiber and silk fabrics is the AMTEX Pact, enacted during 1993. It is a pact whereby the national labs, in conjunction with the United States Department of Energy (DOE), will work on selected projects with the United States textile industry and its research facilities to develop systems to make the U.S. textile industry more competitive. Funding will be provided equally between the DOE and the U.S. textile industry. The first project will be Demand Activated Manufacturing Architecture (DAMA), which expands on the Quick Response system. Electronics will inform each pipeline partner of each garment sold by making use of point-of-sale data generated during scanning of barcoded hang tags.

INDUSTRY INFORMATION SOURCES

Brassil, Robert D., "Practical Aspects of Fabric Preparation," presented at the conference: *Theory and Practice of Fabric Preparation,* Clemson University, Clemson, South Carolina, FMC Corp., 1982.

"Broadwoven Goods Production, 1993," Washington, D.C.: Bureau of the Census, United States Department of Commerce.

"GATT Disappoints U.S. Textile Leaders," Textile World News, *Textile World,* January 1994, 23-24.

Goldstein, Herman B., "Basics of Textile Finishing: Chemical and Mechanical," a research paper, Consultant, Chester, South Carolina, 1987.

Linton, George C., *The Modern Textile and Apparel Dictionary,* Plainfield, New Jersey: Textile Book Service, Division of Bonn Industries Inc., 1973.

Melton, Max, "Continuous Dyeing of Woven Fabrics: Reactive Dyes—Continuous Application," a research paper, American Hoechst Corp., Charlotte, North Carolina, 1982.

"1993 Industry Outlook: What's Ahead for America's 24 Key Industries," *Business Week,* January 11, 1993.

"Springs Psyched for a Second Century of Success," *Textile World,* June 1987, 44-85.

Standard & Poor's Industry Surveys, New York: Standard & Poor's Corporation, 1992 and 1993.

Textile Highlights, Washington, D.C.: American Textile Manufacturers Institute, December 1993.

"Textiles Ready to Reap NAFTA Rewards," Textile World News, *Textile World,* December 1993, 23-24.

"Who's the Real Winner in Burlington Match?" Textile World News, *Textile World,* June 1987, 23.

—McAllister Isaacs III

SIC 2269

FINISHERS OF TEXTILES, NOT ELSEWHERE CLASSIFIED

Companies included in this category are those that are primarily engaged in dyeing and finishing textiles, not elsewhere classified, such as bleaching, dyeing, printing, and finishing of raw stock, yarn, braided goods, and narrow fabrics, except wool and knit fabrics. These establishments perform finishing operations on purchased textiles or on a commission basis.

There are 178 companies with 192 establishments engaged in finishing textiles, not elsewhere classified, according to the United States Department of Commerce, Bureau of the Census. In 1991, these establishments had a shipment volume of approximately $1.2 billion.

Most of the establishments in this category are engaged in raw stock or yarn dyeing. All fibers can be dyed in the raw stock or yarn form. The top dyeing and finishing companies in the United States in 1994 were Meridian Industries Inc. of Milwaukee, Wisconsin ($130 million in revenues); Hanes Companies Inc. of Winston-Salem, North Carolina ($88 million); Mastex Industries Inc. of Holyoke, Massachusetts ($37 million); Spectrum Dyed Yarn Inc. of New York, New York ($33 million); and Valdese Manufacturing Co. of Valdese, North Carolina ($30 million).

Business has been good in recent years for companies engaged in raw stock or package dyeing. Indications are that business will continue to be good and get even better. This is because "fancy" fabrics, i.e., plaids, stripes, and various patterns, require that the yarn be colored prior to weaving or knitting. This may be done in either the raw stock form or the yarn form. This type of business also lends itself to export into Mexico. Thus the long-range effect of the North American Free Trade Agreement should further benefit this classification of companies.

INDUSTRY INFORMATION SOURCES

"ATME-I '93 Quickens Textiles' Time to Market," *Textile World,* June 1992, pp. 74-75.

"GATT Disappoints U.S. Textile Leaders," *Textile World,* January 1994, pp. 23-24.

Linton, George C., *The Modern Textile and Apparel Dictionary,* Plainfield, NJ: Textile Book Service, Div. of Bonn Industries Inc., 1973.

"Microfibers: All Dressed Up and Everywhere to Go," *Textile World,* August 1992, pp. 37-48.

Standard & Poor's Industry Surveys, New York: Standard & Poor's Corporation, 1993.

Textile Highlights, Washington, D.C.: American Textile Manufacturers Institute, December 1993.

Textile Highlights, Washington, D.C.: American Textile Manufacturers Institute, March 1994.

"Textiles Ready to Reap NAFTA Rewards," *Textile World,* December 1993, pp. 23-24.

"Textile World 1992 Manmade Fiber Chart," *Textile World,* August 1992, pp. 49-73.

"Textile World 1993-94 Buyer's Guide for Machinery, Equipment & Supplies." *Textile World,* July 1993.

"The Business Week 1000 Tables," *Business Week,* 1993 Bonus Issue, pp. 118-163.

—McAllister Isaacs III

SIC 2273

CARPETS AND RUGS

This industry includes establishments primarily engaged in manufacturing woven, tufted, and other carpets and rugs such as art squares, floor mattings, needle punch carpeting, and door mats and mattings from textile materials or from twisted paper, grasses, reeds, coir, sisal, jute, or rags. Coverage includes aircraft and automobile floor coverings, except rubber or plastics; bath mats and sets, textile; dyeing and finishing of rugs and carpets, and wilton carpets.

INDUSTRY SNAPSHOT

The honeymoon between the carpet industry and the American consumer began in the 1980s and ended during the recession of the early 1990s. After a ten-year span of steady sales, the carpet industry's primary residential and commercial clients were faced with decreased buying power and constrained budgets and thereby placed carpet buying as a low priority. Higher interest rates, slower starts in new home construction, and sluggish real estate further reduced residential interest in new carpet.

While the bottom line was not plummeting in the early 1990s, manufacturers recognized that it had certainly fallen over the last decade. In terms of production, the United States produced 54 percent of the world's carpeting during the early 1980s while 1990 figures show U.S. production at 42 percent. Profits in early 1992 were lower than those in the same period in 1991. The South Atlantic region experienced the largest drop, with a profit decrease of 11.6 percent. Gross sales for all rug and carpet manufacturers in 1989 totaled $8.7 billion, but figures produced by the *Carpet & Rug Industry Magazine* show gross sales for the top ten U.S. carpet and rug manufacturers dropped $440 million between 1990 and 1991.

ORGANIZATION AND STRUCTURE

The first carpet mill opened in Philadelphia in the 1791. Today, 198 of the 292 manufacturing plants located in 24 states are located in the state of Georgia. Carpet mills specialize in producing carpet backing as well as carpets and rugs. Cost saving measures have led several mills to acquire specialized facilities for dyeing or yarn spinning. However, integration of in-house yarn mills has not produced significant cost savings primarily because filament and some other yarns require no spinning. Following the lead of Shaw Industries' 1992 merger with Salem Carpet Mills and a later, more surprising acquisition of a polypropylene carpet fiber plant, other mills may begin to develop similar cost control strategies.

Tradition, profits, and consumer preferences, more than a specific management approach, have historically dictated the organization of the carpet industry. The product flows to residential and contract clients primarily via the following two methods: (1) directly from mill to client or (2) from mill to dealer or wholesale distributor, then to a retailer who sells to a client. If manufacturers in the industry continue to follow the lead of Shaw Industries, the contemporary industry leader, the industry's organizational mode may be revamped. According to analysts, Shaw's growth coincides with the company's novel management approach. First the company hired aggressive, no commission, straight salary sales representatives. Next, in another cost savings move, Shaw signed shorter, more flexible agreements with retailers and in the process eliminated distributors, a long standing entity in carpet promotion. Whether this strategy is adaptable industry wide remains to be seen; however, carpet manufacturers foresee several outcomes. For example, retailers are expected to begin buying most carpet directly from the mills. Secondly, total industry recovery will require the development of strategies to create more unified partnerships between manufacturers, retailers, and cleaners that would allow them to serve and sustain customer confidence.

BACKGROUND AND DEVELOPMENT

Until the mid-1800s, carpet manufacturing in the United States entailed a tedious process using hand operated machines. High quality, artful appeal, and high cost described the carpets of this period. However, during this period and continuing over the next century, several events changed the manufacturing and utility of rugs and carpets. Much of the impetus for industrialization of the carpet industry began when Erastus B. Bigelow, known as the ''Father of the Modern Carpet Industry,'' obtained a patent for his invention of a power driven loom. As power looms became more refined and functional, carpet manufacturing became a profitable venture.

The next milestone in the carpet industry came with changes in the composition of carpet. Originally all carpets were made entirely of wool because it insulated against cold and repelled water. Because of these characteristics, wool was declared an essential commodity during World War II, and consequently carpet production was severely curtailed in favor of war goods production. This setback served as an incentive for researching wool substitutes, which in turn led to the development and upgrade of new natural and synthetic carpet fabrics. By the 1960s, DuPont's man-made continuous filament carpet nylon and Chemstrand's acrylic fibers were supplying most of the fibers for broadloom carpets in the industry. Today, nylon accounts for 67.8 percent of the fibers used in carpet manufacturing, followed by 22.2 percent polypropylene, 9.4 percent polyester, and wool constitutes a little over 0.6 percent.

Weaving, needle-punch, and bonding and tufting are the principle carpet manufacturing processes, with the tufting method accounting for 95 percent of all carpets currently produced and sold in the United States. Tufting differs from weaving and other processes in that yarn is pushed through a previously manufactured backing material, while weaving produces the carpet backing simultaneously as the carpet is being manufactured. As tufting became popularized as a faster and more economical alternative to the traditional weaving process, carpet manufacturers discovered several other cost and labor advantages. Utilization of the tufting process produced broadloom eight to ten times faster, required less fined-tuned weaving skills, and ultimately lowered prices sufficiently to attract lower and middle income groups. Nearly 63 percent of the industry's tufting mills were located in the South due the area's abundance of low-cost labor and excellent water supply.

The impact of these milestones solidified the "homing" of the carpet industry. Between 1950 and 1968, U.S. production of residential and commercial broadloom carpet and rugs rose from 85.7 to 435.0 million square yards with tufted carpet shipments topping woven Axminster, Wilton, velvet, chenille, and knitted carpets by more than 81 percent in 1968. Price, esthetics, and utility changed the image of carpet from a luxury item to an essential accessory for every home. By the 1980s, consumer carpet selections included an enormous variety of colors and patterns suitable as indoor/outdoor floor or wall coverings. Moisture repellents and stain resistant treatments increased the life spans of some carpets by as much as ten years and allowed manufacturers to extend carpet warranties. Residential or "home use" carpet, one of the industry's major markets, comprised 76 percent of all residential floor coverings, 55 percent of which was used for remodeling and replacement purposes and 45 percent was used in new home construction in the early 1990s. Carpets for commercial or contract use formed the next primary market and represented the preferred floor covering for 73 percent of all commercial space in offices, schools, hotels, hospitals, airplanes, and other heavy trafficked public areas.

Ironically, just as the "homing phase" of the carpet appeal became immured in American living, both residential and commercial users began voicing concerns regarding health and environmental hazards attributed to carpet. In 1987, the Consumer Product Safety Commission received more than 130 complaints about carpeting, mostly focusing on eye and throat irritation beginning after installation of new carpet. One such incident occurred at the Environmental Protection Agency where employees complained of flu-like symptoms within days after a new carpet installation. Specific causes of the illnesses were never identified, but several areas were investigated. No toxic chemicals were found in the carpet, but questions remained regarding toxic ingredients in the carpet adhesives. Another theory postulated that noxious fumes resulted from carpet deterioration. Later tests, so named the Anderson tests after the testing company, introduced the possibility that carpet emissions capable of killing mice could also produce adverse effects on human life.

Despite disclaiming some of the hazards, the carpet industry vowed to reassess its overall manufacturing process, including the type and quality of raw materials used, the use of pesticides, microbiological contamination, and carpet installation and maintenance processes. Consistent with the industry's objectives to improve consumer confidence, The Carpet and Rug Institute, the industry's trade association, launched a labeling program listing various characteristics of carpet. The Institute is also collaborating with Environmental Protection Agency (EPA) in the development of indoor air quality guidelines for carpet.

Another, and perhaps the most significant issue confronting the carpet industry, concerns waste recycling. Several solutions have been suggested to address the problem of waste: (1) recycling or converting packaging materials and used carpet into like-new fiber or other uses (2) reducing pollutants in waste water or volatile organic compounds (VOCs) of new materials, and (3) identifying ways to keep waste out of landfills. While these solutions required a concerted industry-wide effort, a few company initiatives showed some merit. DuPont maintained a joint program with Sonoco which involved reclaiming cardboard drums used to deliver its fluorochemical products. Hoechst Celanese's introduction of a new environmental friendly carpet not only eliminated latex and the usual odor connected with indoor air quality problems, but also totally eliminated carpet waste because it was made of 100 percent recyclable polyester.

Because consumers remained unconvinced of the carpet industry's intent to alleviate the health hazards of carpet, a consumer lawsuit was filed in 1993 against several carpet manufacturers. Consumers involved in the suit were seeking monetary compensation and other rewards from manufacturers accused of promoting misleading claims regarding carpet air emissions hazards and so-called environmentally friendly carpets.

CURRENT CONDITIONS

According to one carpet manufacturer, future security appears likely because the lessons of the 1990s have sensitized the industry to prolonged hardships. The assurances of the future however do not obliterate the prevailing fiscal instabilities of the 1990s. Consequently, predicting future trends of the carpet industry may take several false starts. However, over the last twenty years, one consistently indisputable indicator has come from tracking real disposable income—as it rose or decreased, so did carpet and rug sales. Following this rationale, the industry predictions among carpet manufacturers were cautiously optimistic. Disposable income was slowly rising in 1993, and analysts predicted a 3 percent to 5 percent increase over 1992 carpet sales.

In the early 1990s, many homeowners took advantage of falling interest rates and refinanced their mortgages. This allowed homeowners to spend more money on remodeling expenditures and new carpeting. A stabilized real estate market with increased new housing starts and greater turnover in home sales would also have a positive impact on carpet sales. As businesses recovered from the recession, contract carpet dealers anticipated a gradual sales boost of about 1 percent to 2 percent, mostly for renovations of hospital, health care, and retail facilities. Some analysts warned that the commercial market may continue to be haunted by over-capacity, thus placing an extended damper on sales. Schools were also seen by many in the industry as a potential growth market.

In the U.S. Department of Commerce forecasts, total U.S. carpet and rug production for 1993 was projected at 1.38 billion square yards. Nylon face fibers were expected to continue to dominate a 67 percent share of the market with a project annual growth of 2.6 percent. Polyester was expected to increase 1.8 percent and polypropylene was projected to remain constant. Growth was expected to be at 2 percent in domestic shipments for fibers and carpets. If prior leadership patterns hold, the United States will remain the world's leader in tufted carpet and rug consumption and production.

INDUSTRY LEADERS

Certainly bigger is not always better, yet it appeared to be very helpful for several manufacturers in the carpet industry. Companies undergoing a consolidation or merger find that infusion of capital frequently means new equipment and expansion of research and development. Such organizational changes represented the norm for the carpet and rug industry in the early 1990s. Acquisitions within the industry created a new crop of mega-mills with Shaw Industries topping the list. In an unprecedented 1992 coup, Shaw Industries moved to the number one world spot by acquiring Salem Carpets, formerly the fourth-ranked carpet mill, and later buying the Amoco fiber plant. Subsequently, with $2.5 billion sales projection for 1993 along with production of 450 million square yards of carpet and rugs, Shaw captured roughly 29 percent of the domestic carpet market. In 1993 Shaw had nearly achieved its goal of establishing a worldwide niche in each important aspect of carpet manufacturing. On a similar but lesser scale, Mohawk's 1992 acquisition of Horizon positioned the new company in a third place ranking with a 7.5 percent hold of the U.S. carpet market. News of the 1993 merger between two mid-size manufacturers, K-C Steson and Specialty Carpet added another company to the top 50 mills with combined sales exceeding $30 million. Analysts expected that the acquisition and merger trend would continue and would likely produce an additional two to three mega-mills with annual carpet sales in excess of $1 billion. As of 1993, the most serious contender to Shaw's mega-mill status was the Belgium-owned, Georgia-based Beaulieu Group, which had sales of $600 million in 1991.

While such mergers raised eyebrows regarding anti-trust issues, many analysts noted the negative impact of these mergers on smaller companies. Smaller companies have more limited pricing options. Therefore, attempts by small manufacturers to duplicate the cost cutting strategies of the mega-mills generally threaten their profitability and ultimately their survival.

WORK FORCE

Between 1980 and 1991, the total number of carpet and rug employees rose from 54,000 to 59,000. Production workers made up approximately 82 percent of the work force, according to the *1991 Statistical Abstract*. Computerization of carpet manufacturing, however, was changing job functions and requirements. Machines for tufting, shearing, and many other functions connected to computers were expected to eliminate many low-skilled jobs. The industry was expected to require higher skilled laborers to operate the sophisticated machinery.

By and large, the majority of the industry's production employees had low literacy levels and were unable to interpret computer feedback. Without upgrading literacy skills of their production workers, manufacturers unfortunately stand to lose the high returns from high tech environment. In responding to the fact that more than a third of their 560 employees were deficient in literacy skills, Collins & Aikman, a Georgia-based carpet mill, developed programs combining remedial education and computer training on company time.

AMERICA AND THE WORLD

In 1993 the United States supplied about 41 percent of world carpet exports, or 127 million square yards of product that had a dollar value of $745 million. In the early 1990s, U.S. carpet sales to Canada amounted to $425 million, enough to replace Saudi Arabia as the number one export market for U.S. carpet manufacturers. While Americans attributed their spectacular performance to Canada's lack of competitiveness, Canadians viewed the growth as unfair competition. American carpet companies were accused of ''dumping'' their goods in Canada at unfairly low prices. The resulting closings of scores of Canadian carpet businesses prompted the Canadian government to institute recovery measures by imposing a permanent duty averaging 12 percent on all American carpets.

In the future, outcomes of other trade issues may well expand or reduce opportunities for U.S. manufacturers to create a global presence. In 1993, carpet mills and other textile companies awaited the impact of the North American Free Trade Agreement (NAFTA) which will merge Canada, Mexico, and the United States into one market composed of 380 million potential clients. Although the ''dumping'' issue had strained relations between the Canada and the United States, Canada was expected to remain an important market. The European Community Agreement (EC), another international trade agreement affecting the textile industry, was also expected to enhance international opportunities in textile production.

In the early 1990s industry leaders were aggressively pursuing international trade. In 1992, Shaw Industries entered the Australian market via joint ventures and had plans to acquire two more Australian carpet manufacturers. If successful, these plans will possibly lead to Shaw's owning 50 percent of more than half of Australia's $420-million carpet market. If finding an international niche means physically relocating to a lucrative market, more companies may also follow the example of Belgium's Beaulieu Group which established a facility in Georgia as part of its objective to diversify and penetrate the American market.

RESEARCH AND TECHNOLOGY

Research and technology for the carpet industry has focused on producing high quality and environmentally-friendly products, and responding to contemporary customer needs. To these ends, several innovations were in progress in 1993. New backing materials were being developed to replace the environmentally unfriendly latex. As a secondary backing bond to tufted and needle punched carpets, hot melt adhesive films produced no fumes inside or outside the mills, offered between 70 percent and 80 percent energy savings, and resulted in a 50 percent reduction in backing application time. Other ideas being studied for waste reduction included reducing widths of backings and developing pure synthetic backings to match face fibers which would allow burning or recycling of the whole carpet.

Another area of research addressed utilization of carpet to reduce physical stress, injuries, and fatigue in a variety of environments. While carpet's non-slip, pliant properties remain favorable, biomechanics studies could lift the carpet industry's sales by measuring how the human body reacts to subtle differences in floor surface properties. Research at the University of Pittsburgh's Medical and Engineering Schools is currently studying body reactions to different carpet and cushion combinations in different facilities, such as high and low impact aerobic exercise settings.

INDUSTRY INFORMATION SOURCES

''Allied Signal Fibers Offers 1993 Carpet Forecast.'' *Carpet & Rug Industry* (March 1993).

''Another Merger Creates New Member of Top 50.'' *Carpet & Rug Industry* (February 1993).

''BASF Takes Concepts '93 on the Road.'' *Carpet & Rug Industry* (March 1993).

''BASF'' Unveils New Carpet-recycling Program.'' *Hotel & Motel Management* (November 2, 1992).

''The Carpet Industry Answers Environmental Challenges.'' *Carpet & Rug Industry* (March 1993).

''The Carpet Manufacturing Process.'' *On Carpet* (September 1991).

''Carpet Sales Down 2.4 Percent for First Half of Year.'' *Carpet & Rug Industry* (December 1992).

''Changing Times.'' *Carpet & Rug Industry* (October 1992).

Cooper, Helene. "The New Educators: Carpet Firm Sets Up an In-house School to Stay Competitive. . . ." *The Wall Street Journal* (October 1992).

"CRI Responds to New Adverse Health Allegations Concerning Carpet Emissions." *Carpet & Rug Industry* (September 1992).

Elliott, Michelle. "1993 Annual Backings Report." *Carpet & Rug Industry* (February 1993).

Farnsworth, Clyde H. "Called on the Carpet." *The New York Times* (April 26, 1992).

"1993 Forum & Forecast." *Carpet & Rug Industry* (January 1993).

Herlihy, Janet. "'92 Tufting." *Carpet & Rug Industry* (December 1992).

Herlihy, Janet, and Janice Kirby. "The World's Top Carpet & Rug Manufacturers." *Carpet & Rug Industry* (November 1992).

"Hoechst Celanese Plans Shift to Recyclable Carpets." *The Wall Street Journal* (January 4, 1993).

Kirk, Robert W. *The Carpet Industry: Present Status and Future Prospects.* Philadelphia: University of Pennsylvania, 1970.

Kurtz, Josh. "After a Decade of Consolidation, Hard Times Await Carpet Makers." *The New York Times* (May 27, 1990).

"Mohawk Industries Agrees to Purchase Horizon Industries." *The Wall Street Journal* (July 28, 1992).

"Shaw Updates Global Strategy at Domotex." *Carpet & Rug Industry* (February 1993).

Smith, G. Wentworth. "Ergonomic Floor Covering Studies." *Carpet & Rug Industry* (January 1993).

"Space Dyeing." *On Carpet* (August 1991).

"The Top Fifty Carpet & Rug Manufacturers' Sales Totals - 1991." *Carpet & Rug Industry* (June 1992).

Walton, Frank L. *Tomahawks to Textiles.* New York: Appleton-Century-Crofts, Inc., 1953.

—Attrices Dean Griffin

SIC 2281

YARN SPINNING MILLS

This industry is made up of establishments primarily engaged in spinning yarn wholly or chiefly by weight of cotton, manmade fibers, silk, wool, mohair, or similar animal fibers. Products include acetate and acrylic yarn, made from purchased staple, spun; carded yarn, carpet yarn, combed yarn, cordage yarn (all of cotton); crochet yarn, cotton, silk, wood, and manmade staple, to name a few.

An average two-piece suit currently includes about 67,000 yards of yarn composed of roughly 350 million manmade fibers, textured and colored to produce a natural look. These characteristics basically describe the product flow of yarn spinning mills—from fiber, to yarn, and then to apparel and home accessories. The actual yarn spinning process entails first cleaning of cotton, wool, silk, or other fibers and then a combing or carding process which turns tangled fibers into straight, even rolls that resemble loose ropes of soft cotton yarn. Depending on the specifications, machines are set to spin yarn of multiple lengths and textures.

Yarn specifications reflect contemporary life and work styles. In today's market, yarns must satisfy consumers' demands for style, durability, flexibility, and more recently, ecological considerations. As a result of these growing concerns, many formerly popular fibers have been become obsolete because of their restricted origin or the economic impracticality of production. Consumer preferences for such fibers as natural wool, silk, cotton, and camel, have begun to shift toward manmade acrylics and other synthetics. Consumers with active lifestyles have called for more livable fabrics combining fashion with rough-ready, easy care qualities, and stretchable wear.

During the early establishment of the industry in the eighteenth century, most spinning mills operated as independent entities. Later, mergers and consolidations in the yarn spinning industry opened diversification opportunities, and many spinning mills became subsidiaries or integrated components of larger carpet or textile mills, or combined with specialized dyeing facilities.

At best, recent market conditions may be described as spotty with intermittent sales. Despite a slowdown in the early 1990s, most were holding firm on prices, unless pushed into a non-negotiable mode. According to an industry trade publication, *Textile World,* price-wise and supply-wise, fibers seemed headed for an uneventful year in 1994. Specific trends showed a softening of the cotton market, possibly in response to lower T-shirt sales and overproduction. However, consumer preferences for acrylics should reward the industry with a sales boost based on sweater and sock demand, although fleece and cotton may be noteworthy as hosiery preferences.

The top five ranking yarn spinning mills, based on sales, are as follows: Hoechst Celanese Corporation Fiber and Film ($2,600 million); Burlington Holdings, Inc. ($2,450 million); Milliken and Company ($1,800 million); Standard Commercial Corporation ($1,178.1

million); and Allied-Signal Inc. Fibers Division ($1,000 million).

One of the first objectives of the Occupational Safety and Health Administration (OSHA), formed in 1970, was to minimize illness and death resulting from cotton dust in textile mills. Referred to as "brown lung" disease, 1988 statistics estimated that 35,000 current and former textile employees had severe cases of "brown lung" and another 100,000 workers had symptoms that indicated early stages of the disease. As unions worked to improve hazardous mill conditions, textile manufacturers often opposed strict sanitation measures imposed by OSHA. In the early 1990s, questions remained as to the legality of some of the restrictions and how best to provide safer factory conditions.

Yarn spinning mills shared the textile industry's apprehension regarding the impact of the North American Free Trade Agreement (NAFTA). Some yarn spinners foresaw a negative impact based on claims that NAFTA would benefit Canada and Mexico more than the United States. Other spinners envisioned more positive results for the United States, particularly if NAFTA requires Canada and Mexico to use yarns produced in North America. The threat of mills closing or a possible mass exodus of plants to Mexico was not perceived as an immediate threat; however, the president of the American Yarn Spinners Association did envision possible long term drawbacks resulting from NAFTA. In his opinion, the more imminent threat on American yarn spinning mills was posed by GATT, another trade agreement, which in draft form, proposed to cut U.S. textile apparel import duties.

In contrast to other industries, the current growth in technological advances allows a clear vision of twenty-first-century yarn spinning mills. Already industry literature refers to spinning systems rather than spinning mills. By the year 2000, *Textile World* predicts daytime operations of spinning departments will be staffed with maintenance technicians, monitoring personnel, and a single supervisor. Night operations are expected to be staffless and monitored by sophisticated computers.

Changes in yarn, speed, styles, and other functions will become increasingly programmable or electronic functions. One certain outcome of computerization will be severely reduced manpower needs. In preparing for the coming high-tech environment, current industry research and development was focusing on refining and developing new equipment in the mid-1990s. Air-jet spinning machines, long recognized for good evenness and less defects, will achieve increased acceptance because of their ability to spin cotton-polyester blend yarn. If slippage problems can be over-come, the friction spinning machine, considered excellent in producing evenness and less defects, will be introduced for medium and fine yarn count range, especially for cotton.

Yarn spinners continued to develop new more colorful and functional yarns. In the early 1990s, three variations on DuPont's Cordura nylon went on the market. Originally introduced as a tire cord fiber, Cordura has been introduced as a fabric for outdoor recreational apparel. In addition to its light weight qualities, the Cordura/acrylic blend offered twice the abrasion resistance of ballistic nylon, three times that of vinyl or standard nylon, and four times that of cotton. Previous applications included luggage, backpacks, boots, and rugged ski apparel.

INDUSTRY INFORMATION SOURCES

Black, Jeff. "Yarn Spinning Get New Spin." *Daily News Record* (August 11, 1992).

"Candlewick: Yarns That Fit a Niche." *Carpet & Rug Industry* (March 1993).

Clune, Ray. "Yarn Spinners Optimistic for '93." *Daily News Record* (January 1993).

————. "Prices of Cotton Yarns Stable in Spotty Market." *Daily News Record* (August 26, 1992).

"Conner Plays Down NAFTA Effect." *Daily News Record* (January 1993).

Copeland, Melvin Thomas. *The Cotton Manufacturing Industry of the United States.* New York: Augustus M. Kelley Publishers, 1966.

"Dura-fleece, Spandura, New Blend Move Outdoors." *Textile World* (December 1992).

Isaacs, McAllister III. "Automation and Quality Key Spinning in the '90s." *Textile World* (January 1990).

"Late News Report." *Textile World* (February 1993).

"'Lights Out' for Yarn Making Is Here - Now." *Textile World* (December 1992).

Sawhney, A. P. S. "Air-jet Weaving Requires Special Attention to Yarn." *Textile World* (December 1992).

Stuart, Frank. "Yarn Fair Rolls a Natural." *Daily News Record* (August 19, 1992).

"U.S. Textiles Averts Bush's Tariff Cut." *Textile World* (February 1993).

Welch, Susan, John Gruhl, Michael Steinman, and John Comer. *American Government,* 2nd ed. St. Paul: West Publishing Company, 1988.

—Attrices Dean Griffin

SIC 2282

YARN TEXTURIZING, THROWING, TWISTING, AND WINDING MILLS

Establishments included in this classification are those that are primarily engaged in texturizing (or texturing), throwing (another name for texturizing), twisting, winding, or spooling purchased yarns or manmade fiber filaments wholly or chiefly by weight of cotton, manmade fibers, silk, or wool, mohair, or similar animal fibers, or in performing such activities on a commission basis. Establishments primarily engaged in dyeing or finishing purchased yarns or finishing yarns on a commission basis are classified in **SIC 2231: Broadwoven Fabric Mills, Wool (Including Dyeing and Finishing)** if the yarns are of wool and in **SIC 2269: Finishers of Textiles, Not Elsewhere Classified** if they are of other fibers. Establishments primarily engaged in producing and texturizing manmade fiber filaments and yarns in the same plant are classified in **SIC 2823: Cellulosic Manmade Fibers** or **2824: Manmade Organic Fibers, Except Cellulosic.**

INDUSTRY SNAPSHOT

According to the United States Department of Commerce, Bureau of the Census, there are 121 companies with 139 establishments in this classification. In 1991, these establishments shipped $2.762 billion worth of products. While texturizing establishments are just a small part of the total number of companies and establishments in this classification, the texturizing plants account for the largest portion of sales, shipping $1.980 billion worth of products in 1991. Unifi Corp. of Greensboro, North Carolina, is the world's largest texturizing company and accounts for well over half of the total texturizing sales.

Texturizing is a process whereby partially oriented filament yarn (POY) is stabilized through heating and drawing, providing a crimped continuous filament yarn. Generally speaking, two types of manmade POY is texturized: nylon and polyester. Ladies' hosiery is the primary end-use application for texturized nylon, while texturized polyester is used in a wide variety of apparel and homefurnishings products and, to a lesser extent, in some industrial fabric applications. There are two different types of texturizing machines. The majority of POY products are texturized on false-twist texturizing machines, but some applications require the use of air-jet texturizing machines.

ORGANIZATION AND STRUCTURE

POY comes to the texturizing plant wound on tubes, which serve as the supply packages for the texturizing machines. These are purchased from manmade fiber producers such as Du Pont, Eastman Chemical Co., Hoechst Celanese, Tollaram Fibers, American Micrell and Wellman. These packages contain anywhere from ten to one hundred pounds of POY. If a texturizing plant is to receive the more economical larger packages, it must be equipped with automated package-handling equipment, which has been available since 1990. Some older plants, especially those involved in small niche markets, have opted not to purchase the automated equipment and must order the smaller package size.

Most texturized yarn is produced by companies such as Unifi for sale to weaving and knitting establishments. Some weaving plants, such as Burlington Industries and Milliken & Co., produce yarn for their own consumption. Texturizing machines are not manufactured in the United States; instead, false-twist and air-jet texturizing machines are made by companies in Europe and Japan.

BACKGROUND AND DEVELOPMENT

Texturizing as an industry is relatively new compared to other segments of the textile industry, most of which have been around for centuries. The beginnings of texturizing go back to the invention of nylon just over 50 years ago when texturizing was used to process nylon yarn for hosiery. But it really blossomed in the 1970s as the system to produce polyester filament yarns for use during the doubleknit polyester craze. As rapidly as doubleknit polyester leisure suits grew in popularity, texturizing grew as a necessary process. And, unfortunately for the more than one hundred polyester texturizing plants that sprang up overnight, polyester texturizing died with doubleknit polyester leisure suits.

Despite its relatively young age, texturizing has enjoyed more technological advances over the last two decades than any other textile process. The Textured Yarn Association of America (TYAA) was formed in 1972 with the original purpose of establishing quality standards for what was then still considered a fledgling process. TYAA members learned at the association's 20th anniversary meeting in July of 1992 that since the association's first meeting, texturizing speeds had more than quadrupled to a one-thousand-meters-per-minute delivery speed of finished texturized yarn. Package sizes tripled during that time period. Electronics now controlled operations, temperatures, speeds, and twists and monitored quality, temperature, and efficiency. Nearly every machine maker offers at least one model loaded with automation: doffing, package handling, and creeling.

CURRENT CONDITIONS

At the first organizational meeting TYAA hosted over one hundred texturizing companies. Most of these were supplying yarn for the doubleknit polyester trade. At TYAA's 1993 annual meeting, there were ten texturizing companies represented. Membership in TYAA today, however, includes suppliers to the industry, end users of texturized yarn, and companies who actually perform the texturizing process. Annual poundage for texturizing at TYAA's beginning was in the neighborhood of 1.6 billion. Today the figure is something less than 1 billion. But the dollar value is way up, even with inflation. Those companies who divorced themselves from the doubleknit disaster are today producing products requiring high-tech specifications and much higher quality. And those companies are reportedly running flat out.

Unifi Corp. represents more than a microcosm of today's texturizing industry. In just over 20 years since it was founded in 1971 the company rang up record sales of over one billion dollars for fiscal year ending June 28, 1992. In Kurt Salmon Associate's annual profile of publicly held textile companies for 1992, Unifi ranked sixth in total sales, behind such industry giants as Burlington Industries, Springs Industries, Shaw Industries, Dominion Textiles, and Fieldcrest Cannon. But, amazingly, its net income of $62 million led all publicly held textile companies, $4.5 million ahead of second-ranked Shaw Industries. Until 1991, Unifi's largest texturizing competitor was Macfield, a company also born during the doubleknit polyester craze. In that year, Unifi acquired Macfield, thus obtaining capacity to produce over half of the texturized yarn in the United States.

One thing that Unifi has always done that other textile companies are just now trying to learn to do is export. Since the company was founded, it has had a commitment to export a minimum of 20 percent of its capacity. The company has done this, even in years when, because of circumstances, it might have been more profitable to utilize its entire capacity for production of products ticketed for the domestic market. Such a philosophy and experience insofar as exporting products are concerned portends well for Unifi over the next several years following the passage of the General Agreement on Tariffs and Trade (GATT) and the North American Free Trade Agreement (NAFTA).

INDUSTRY INFORMATION SOURCES

"ATME-I '93 Quickens Textiles' Time to Market," *Textile World,* June 1992, 74-75.

"The Business Week 1000 Tables," *Business Week,* 1993 Bonus Issue, 118-163.

"GATT Disappoints U.S. Textile Leaders," Textile World News, *Textile World,* January 1994, 23-24.

Isaacs III, McAllister, "Aaair-Jet Texturing Machine Chart 1992," *Textile World,* May 1992, 64-66.

————, "False-Twist Texturing Machine Chart 1992," *Textile World,* May 1992, 56-62.

————, "Texturing Gets Automation as TYAA Turns 20," *Textile World,* May 1992, 54-55.

————, "Unifi Tops the Sales Yarn Market and Is Still Moving." *Textile World,* August 1993, 33-37.

Linton, George C., *The Modern Textile and Apparel Dictionary,* Plainfield, New Jersey: Textile Book Service, Division of Bonn Industries Inc., 1973.

"Microfibers: All Dressed Up and Everywhere to Go," *Textile World,* August 1992, 37-48.

Standard & Poor's Industry Surveys, New York: Standard & Poor's Corporation, 1992 and 1993.

Textile Highlights, Washington, D.C.: American Textile Manufacturers Institute, December 1993 and March 1994.

"Textiles Ready to Reap NAFTA Rewards," Textile World News, *Textile World,* December 1993, 23-24.

"Textile World 1992 Manmade Fiber Chart," *Textile World,* August 1992, 49-73.

—McAllister Isaacs III

SIC 2284

THREAD MILLS

Establishments in this classification are those that are primarily engaged in manufacturing thread from cotton, silk, manmade fibers, wool, or similar animal fibers. Important products in this category include sewing, crochet, darning, embroidery, tatting, handknitting and other handicraft threads. Establishments primarily engaged in manufacturing thread from flax, hemp, and ramie are included in **SIC 2299: Textile Goods, Not Elsewhere Classified.**

There are 49 companies with 59 establishments primarily engaged in the production of thread, according to the United States Department of Commerce, Bureau of the Census. In 1991, these establishments shipped $788.1 million worth of products. By far, the largest component of this category is sewing thread. Sewing thread is a term obviously applied to the thread used in sewing garments. But the term, sewing thread, is also applied to the thread used for closing bags used for animal feed, charcoal, etc. In the traditional type of sewing thread, i.e., that used in sewing garments, Dixie Yarn Mills and Coats & Clarke are the largest manufacturers in this category.

There are three types of spinning machines used in the manufacture of sewing thread: ring-, rotor-, and air-jet spinning machines. Fine sewing thread is usually manufactured on ring-spinning machines. Coarse sewing thread is produced on either rotor- or air-jet spinning machines. Sewing thread size is measured by a system called the English yarn numbering system (Ne), which is based on yards per pound of the thread. For Ne 1, 840 yards weighs one pound. For Ne 2, it takes two times 840 yards, or 1,680 yards, to weigh one pound, and so on. Thus, the higher the Ne number, the finer the thread. As a general rule, threads that are Ne 30 or finer are produced on ring-spinning machines. Those that are coarser than Ne 30 are usually spun or rotor- or air-jet machines. Thread used in the sewing of garment ranges from Ne 60 to Ne 100. The threads used as bag closures for feed and charcoal bags will size in the range of Ne 10-20.

The future for the sewing thread business appears to be excellent. Most feel that with the enactment of the North American Free Trade Agreement, much of the apparel-making operations that have moved to the developing countries in Africa and the Far East will move to the relatively low-labor-cost country of Mexico. This should enable U.S. sewing thread plants to increase their shipments, especially to Mexico.

INDUSTRY INFORMATION SOURCES

"The Business Week 1000 Tables," *Business Week,* 1993 Bonus Issue, 118-163.

"GATT Disappoints U.S. Textile Leaders," Textile World News, *Textile World,* January 1994, 23-24.

Linton, George C., *The Modern Textile and Apparel Dictionary,* Plainfield, New Jersey: Textile Book Service, Division of Bonn Industries Inc., 1973.

"Microfibers: All Dressed Up and Everywhere to Go," *Textile World,* August 1992, 37-48.

Standard & Poor's Industry Surveys, New York: Standard & Poor's Corporation, 1992 and 1993.

Textile Highlights, Washington, D.C.: American Textile Manufacturers Institute, December 1993 and March 1994.

"Textiles Ready to Reap NAFTA Rewards," Textile World News, *Textile World,* December 1993, 23-24.

—McAllister Isaacs III

SIC 2295

COATED FABRICS, NOT RUBBERIZED

This industry includes establishments primarily engaged in manufacturing coated, impregnated, or laminated textiles, and in the special finishing of textiles, such as varnishing and waxing. Establishments primarily engaged in rubberizing purchase fabrics are classified in **SIC 3069: Fabricated Rubber Products, Not Elsewhere Classified,** and those establishments engaged in dyeing and finishing textiles are classified in various textile industries or **SIC 2231: Broadwoven Fabric Mills, Wool (Including Dyeing and Finishing).**

The coated fabrics (not rubberized) manufacturing industry is regarded as a part of the larger miscellaneous textile goods business segment. The larger miscellaneous textile goods industry has seen its employment figures gradually drop over the past decade, a common sight in most realms of manufacturing in America. In 1982 the total miscellaneous textile goods industries employed approximately 62,000 workers; by 1992 that number had dropped to about 51,000 employees. The work force is composed primarily of hourly production workers. About 80 percent of employment in the entire miscellaneous textile goods manufacturing sector is in this area.

A significant number of companies engaged in coated fabrics manufacturing post annual sales in excess of $20 million. Industry leaders include Ludlow Corp. of Exeter, New Hampshire, with annual sales of about $130 million; Columbus Coated Fabrics, a Borden, Inc. company based in Columbus, Ohio, with annual sales of more than $70 million; Industrial Coatings Group Inc., a privately-owned company headquartered in Chicago, Illinois, with annual sales of about $60 million; Spanco Industries Inc., a private company based in Sanford, North Carolina, that posts annual sales of $50 million; and Seaman Corp., a privately-owned company based in Wooster, Ohio, that enjoys annual sales of about $50 million. Other significant industry companies include Bradford Industries Inc., Neptco Inc., Health-Chem Corp., Cooley Inc., and Great Lakes Paper Co.

INDUSTRY INFORMATION SOURCES

Isaacs, McAllister, III, "Machinery Makers Are Responding to the Needs of Weaving Plants, *Textile World,* December 1993, 42-43.

Textile Highlights, Washington, DC: American Textile Manufacturers Institute, December 1993.

U.S. Industrial Outlook 1994, Washington, DC: U.S. Department of Commerce, 1994.

SIC 2296

TIRE CORD AND FABRICS

This category covers establishments primarily engaged in the production of cord and fabric of manmade fibers, cotton, glass, steel, or other materials for use in reinforcing rubber tires, industrial belting, fuel cells, and similar applications. Manufacturers of coated fabrics that are not rubberized are covered under **SIC 2296: Coated Fabrics, Not Rubberized.** For discussion of weaving systems, refer to **SIC 2211: Broadwoven Fabric Mills, Cotton.**

The U.S. Department of Commerce 1993 Census reported nine companies in the United States engaged in the production of tire cord and fabrics for the rubber tire industry. The largest of these was Goodyear Tire and Rubber Co., with principal plants in Decatur, Alabama, and Cartersville, Georgia. The next two largest manufacturers of tire cord and tire cord fabrics were Firestone Tire and Rubber Co. and Uniroyal. Other manufacturers included Utica Weavers of Utica, New York; Martha Mills Division of Dominion Textiles of Thomaston, Georgia; General Tire Plant in Barnesville, Georgia; and Richmond Converters in Richmond, Virginia.

While some tire cord was produced from steel in the early 1990s, the vast majority of tire reinforcement came from such synthetic materials as nylon, polyester, and rayon fiber. Of the 744 million tons of manmade fiber used as tire reinforcement worldwide in 1993, 57 percent was nylon, nearly 24 percent was polyester, and approximately 19 percent was rayon. Worldwide projections called for 811 million tons of tire cord to be produced in 1998, of which 57 percent was expected to be nylon, nearly 15 percent rayon, and nearly 27 percent polyester.

In North America, specifically, the 165 million tons of manmade fiber used in 1993 consisted of 55 percent polyester, nearly 43 percent nylon, and nearly two percent rayon. For 1998, projections called for 161 million tons to be produced in North America: 64 percent polyester, nearly 36 percent nylon, and less than one percent rayon.

Specifications for tire cord were generally dictated by the type of tire manufactured. The three most common types of tires manufactured in the early 1990s were radial, bias, and high performance. In the United States, radial tires were the most popular, holding about 90 percent of the market in the early 1990s. This, however, was expected to change as high-performance tires increased in popularity, potentially comprising between 20 and 25 percent of the market by the year 2000. Production demands for tire cord fabric were directly related to the number of new cars and trucks sold as well as the need for replacement tires on existing automobiles and trucks.

The manufacture of tire cord fabrics involves two general processing steps: twisting and weaving. In the twisting process, two or three ends of the tire cord material are twisted together to form a two- or three-ply yarn. The plied yarn is then taken through a second twisting operation called cabling, in which two or three strands of the plied yarn are twisted together to form 2/2, 2/3, 3/2 or 3/3 cabled yarn. In the weaving process, the cabled tire cord serves as the warp or lengthwise yarn in the tire cord fabric. Tire cord manufacturers use a light cotton thread to form the filling or crosswise yarn in the fabric. This lightweight yarn, used solely for holding the cabled tire cord in place, is dissolved during the rubberizing process, leaving only the lengthwise strands of tire cord in the fabric.

Traditionally, all tire cord fabrics were produced on shuttle system weaving machines. By the end of the 1980s, however, two companies—Draper Corp. of Spartanburg, South Carolina, and Gunne GmbH of Moehnesse-Gunne, Germany—began manufacturing air-jet weaving machines for production of tire cord fabrics. Air-jet weaving machines produced tire cord fabric about 3.5 times faster than shuttle system weaving machines, increasing the production of tire cord fabrics tremendously. However, few companies produced the air-jet weaving machine for tire cord in the early 1990s, as few companies were engaged in that business.

INDUSTRY INFORMATION SOURCES

"1993 Industry Outlook: What's Ahead for America's 24 Key Industries," *Business Week,* January 11, 1993.

Isaacs, McAllister, III, "Machinery Makers Are Responding to the Needs of Weaving Plants," *Textile World,* December 1993, 42-43.

Isaacs, McAllister, III, "Textile World's Weaving Machinery Chart for 1993," *Textile World,* December 1993, 44-60.

Linton, George C., *The Modern Textile and Apparel Dictionary,* Plainfield, NJ: Bonn Industries Inc., 1973

Textile Highlights, Washington, D.C.: American Textile Manufacturers Institute, December 1993.

"Weaving Speeds Are Not All in Machines," *Textile World,*
June 1993, 78-87.

—McAllister Isaacs III

SIC 2297

NONWOVEN FABRICS

Included in this category are establishments that
are primarily engaged in manufacturing nonwoven
fabrics by mechanical, chemical, thermal, or solvent
means, or by combinations thereof. Establishments
that are primarily engaged in producing woven felts
are classified in **SIC 2231: Broadwoven Fabric
Mills, Wool (Including Dyeing and Finishing).**
Those producing other felts are classified in **SIC 2299:
Textile Goods, Not Elsewhere Classified.**

Products made using the nonwovens process run
the gamut. They are generated by textile-, paper-, and/
or extrusion-type processes. Nonwovens produced
from textile-type processes include filtration fabrics,
shoe furnishings, insulation padding, apparel components, wipes, medical dressing, medical apparel,
coverstock, foodservice wipes, and automotive head-
liner. Nonwovens from paper-type processes include
tea bags, surgical drape, apparel components, air filtration, premoistened towelettes, and wet wipes. Those
nonwovens fabrics that are produced from extrusion-
type processes include geotextiles (fabrics used as road
beds and erosion prevention systems), protective
clothing, reinforcement fabrics, coverstock, filtration
fabrics, roofing, automobile carpet backing, laundry
aids, homefurnishings, and regular carpet backing.
Some nonwovens products are produced from a combination or hybrid of processes; these include surgical
drape, wound dressing, sorbent media, medical apparel, and disposable components.

INDUSTRY SNAPSHOT

Nonwovens is probably the fastest growing sector
of the textile business. New end uses, replacing those
in the woven and knitted sector, are being developed
every day. It is generally immune from import competition. Nonwovens as an operation is highly capital
intensive and relatively low in labor intensity. It is
therefore not an attractive process for developing
countries where putting a lot of people into the
workplace is one of the prime objectives.

Like **SIC 2295: Coated Fabrics, Not Rubberized**, this category requires sophisticated, electronically controlled machinery, and sophisticated, highly

trained fabric engineers. In almost all cases where
nonwovens fabrics can be substituted for woven and
knitted fabrics, the result is a less expensive product.
The United States Department of Commerce, Bureau
of the Census, reports that there are 111 companies
with 150 establishments engaged in primary production of nonwovens fabrics. In 1991, these establishments shipped $3.375 billion worth of products.
Freudenburg and Kimberly Clark are two of the largest
companies engaged in nonwovens processing.

ORGANIZATION AND STRUCTURE

Nonwoven is a generic term used to describe a
fabric that is produced differently from a fabric made
by weaving or, more broadly, a fabric that is different
from traditional woven or knitted fabrics. Like all fabrics, nonwovens are planar structures that are relatively flat, flexible, and porous. Unlike traditional fabrics that are made by mechanically interlacing
(weaving) or interlooping (knitting) yarns composed
of fibers or filaments, nonwovens are fabrics that are
made by (a) mechanically, chemically, or thermally
interlocking layers or networks of fibers or filaments or
yarns; (b) interlocking fibers or filaments concurrent
with their extrusion; (c) perforating films; or (d) forming porous films concurrent with their extrusion.

Terminology used in the trade to describe
nonwoven fabrics has been coined from the method
used to form the web, the technology used to bond the
web into a fabric, the forming/bonding combination,
and the end-use application. Web formation jargon
includes dry laid, carded, crosslapped, garnetted, air
laid, wet laid, cylinder formed, extruded, meltblown,
cast film, coformed, and flashspun. Terms associated
with bonding include mechanically bonded,
stitchbonded, needlefelted, needlepunched, spunlaced,
jetlaced hydroentangled, apertured, chemically
bonded, resin bonded, latex bonded, powder bonded,
print bonded, saturated, spray bonded, foam bonded,
frothed, thermal bonded, point bonded, and ultrasonically welded. Examples of forming/bonding terms
for nonwovens are card/bond and spunbond. Examples
of end-use application terminology are disposables,
durables, semidurables, coverstock, geotextiles, filter
fabric, sorbers, medical dressing, premoistened towel-
lete, and wipe. Also, nonwovens are often described
according to their fiber content such as polyester
nonwoven, rayon nonwoven, polypropylene
nonwoven, cotton/polyester nonwoven, pulp/polyester
nonwoven or polypropylene/pulp nonwoven. Other
nonwoven terms frequently encountered include film
laminate, composite, SMS, and hybrid.

BACKGROUND AND DEVELOPMENT

The nonwoven fabrics industry is international in scope. The concept of making fabrics directly from fibers on needlepunch machinery achieved commercial viability in North America and Europe over 75 years ago. Facilities for producing commercial quantities of technical fabrics using wet-laid technology were established in the United States during the 1930s. Large-scale commercial production facilities for chemically bonded nonwovens were placed in operation in the United States during the early 1940s and in Europe and Japan following World War II.

The first extrusion operations dedicated to making fabrics directly from polymer melts were opened in the United States and Europe during the mid to late 1960s. Currently, about half of the worldwide nonwoven fabric production capacity is located in North America, a third in Europe, and an eighth in Japan. Capacities in these areas are expanding at annual growth rates ranging six to ten percent through both productivity improvements and the installation of new facilities. In addition, new nonwoven enterprises are currently starting up throughout Asia and South America. About two-thirds of all nonwovens are directly from fibers, and one-third are made directly from polymers.

An interesting history of technical, market, and product emphasis has occurred during the relatively short period of nonwoven industrialization. The early thrust in nonwoven usage emphasized replacing traditional woven and knitted fabrics. During this initial phase, proprietary technology was used not only to produce fabric structures that performed better than the items they were designed to replace, but it also was used when traditional fabrics could not be used. As a result, new applications and markets were established and the industry expanded.

As the industry has matured and technology has become publicly available, emphasis in the various sectors of the industry has changed. Currently, some portions of the nonwovens industry are technology-driven while others are market-driven. A number of firms are proprietary-technology-based while others are turn-key plant operations. Some are commodity roll-goods producers while others are more oriented to niche markets with high value-added products. Many nonwovens producers continue the quest for new markets and more opportunities to compete with traditional textiles, papers, and plastics.

CURRENT CONDITIONS

Production of nonwoven roll goods in the United States climbed over the 2.5-billion pound level for the first time in 1992. By nonwoven type, application distribution is as follows: The majority of card/resinbond and card/thermalbond fabrics go into coverstock, while interlinings, wipes, and carrier sheets account for most of the remainder.

More than half of the highloft volume is used in furniture and sleeping applications. Filtration, apparel, insulation, healthcare, and geotextile products account for most of the remainder. Stitchbond fabrics are used in bedding, shoes, and a variety of coated products. Automotive trim and geotextiles account for 50-60 percent of all needlepunch fabrics. Other major applications are filtration, bedding, homefurnishings, and coating.

As much as two-thirds of all spunlace fabrics are used in medical products. Other applications are wipes, industrial apparel, interlinings, absorbent components, filtration, and coating. Medical product applications also account for about one-third of all wet laid nonwovens. Other applications include tea bags, meat casings, filter media, battery separators, and wipes.

Most bonded pulp fabrics are used as wipes or absorbent components. The largest yardage applications for spunbonds is coverstock. Other major uses are geotextiles, roofing, carpet backing, medical, filtration, furniture, and packaging. About one-half of all meltblown nonwoven roll goods are used in filtration and medical applications. Other applications include sorbents, wipes and sanitary products. Porous film applications include coverstock, medical products and laminating media. Nonwoven hybrids are used in absorbent products, wipes, filtration, and barrier applications.

The effect of the North American Free Trade Agreement (NAFTA) on the nonwovens sector is expected to be more long-range than near-term. Removing the trade barriers on textile products shouldn't have much of an impact immediately in this area because of the typical end-use applications for nonwovens products. However, as the standard of living in Mexico rises, and as such industries as automotives increase their presence in Mexico, and areas such as Mexico's highway systems undergo extensive improvements, NAFTA's effect on the nonwovens sector will be a positive one.

INDUSTRY INFORMATION SOURCES

"ATME-I '93 Quickens Textiles' Time to Market," *Textile World,* June 1992, 74-75.

"The Business Week 1000 Tables," *Business Week,* 1993 Bonus Issue, 118-63.

"Cotton Incorporated Is 'Textiles' Partner'," *Textile World,* August 1993, 47-48.

"GATT Disappoints U.S. Textile Leaders," Textile World News, *Textile World,* January 1994, 23-24.

Linton, George C., *The Modern Textile and Apparel Dictionary,* Plainfield, New Jersey: Textile Book Service, Division of Bonn Industries Inc., 1973.

"Microfibers: All Dressed Up and Everywhere to Go," *Textile World,* August 1992, 37-48.

Standard & Poor's Industry Surveys. New York: Standard & Poor's Corporation, 1992 and 1993.

Textile Highlights, Washington, D.C.: American Textile Manufacturers Institute, December 1993 and March 1994.

"Textiles Ready to Reap NAFTA Rewards," Textile World News, *Textile World,* December 1993, 23-24.

"Textile World 1992 Manmade Fiber Chart," *Textile World,* August 1992, 49-73.

Vaughn, E.A., *Nonwoven Fabric Primer and Reference Sampler,* Association of the Nonwovens Fabrics Industry, 1992.

—McAllister Isaacs III

SIC 2298

CORDAGE AND TWINE

This classification covers establishments primarily engaged in manufacturing rope, cable, cordage, twine and related products from abaca (Manila) sisal, henquen, hemp, cotton, paper, jute, flax, manmade fibers including glass, and other fibers. Products include binder and baler twine, blasting mats and rope, fiber cable, camouflage nets not made in weaving mills, cargo nets, braided cord, fish nets and seines, fishing lines, insulator pads, rope nets, rope, rope slings, and wire ropes.

There are 181 companies with 187 establishments engaged in the production of cordage and twine products, according to the United States Department of Commerce, Bureau of the Census. In 1991, these establishments shipped $880 million worth of products.

Most establishments in this industry are small. More than 100 of the 187 establishments have fewer than 20 employees. Cordage and twine plants, as a general rule, are not as modern as other textile industry establishments. Most serve specific niche markets with closely controlled product specifications.

The largest company engaged in this industry is Wellington Puritan Cordage Mills, headquartered in Madison, Georgia. Wellington has several plants engaged in the cordage and twine business with its largest market being the marine industry. Wellington produces ski ropes, life preserver ropes and ropes used in various applications on boats and ships. Some of its anchor ropes for large sea-going vessels are as much as 8-10 inches in diameter.

Almost all establishments engaged in the cordage and twine business purchase their yarn requirements from sales yarn mills. This yarn is then twisted (plied) by taking two or more strands of yarn and twisting them together to a prescribed number of turns per inch. Depending on the end-use application, cabling follows the twisting process. Cabling is a similar process to twisting except that where the twisting process involves twisting several single strands of single yarn together, cabling involves twisting several strands of plied yarns together. The cabling process can continue until the proper size twine, cord or rope is built.

As of the mid-1990s, forecasters predicted that sales in this industry would remain fairly stable for several years. Increases in demand for certain products have been offset by the decline in boat sales following the institution of the luxury tax in this area. The marine industry constitutes one of the largest markets for this industry. The North American Free Trade Agreement is expected to have little, if any, effect on this industry segment.

INDUSTRY INFORMATION SOURCES

"ATME-I '93 Quickens Textiles' Time to Market," *Textile World*, June 1992, pp. 74-75.

"Cotton Incorporated Is 'Textiles' Partner'," *Textile World*, August 1993, pp. 47-48.

"GATT Disappoints U.S. Textile Leaders," *Textile World*, January 1994, pp. 23-24.

Linton, George C., *The Modern Textile and Apparel Dictionary*, Plainfield, NJ: Textile Book Service, Div. of Bonn Industries Inc., 1973.

"Microfibers: All Dressed Up and Everywhere to Go," *Textile World*, August 1992, pp. 37-48.

Standard & Poor's Industry Surveys, New York: Standard & Poor's Corporation, 1992.

Standard & Poor's Industry Surveys, New York: Standard & Poor's Corporation, 1993.

Textile Highlights, Washington, D.C.: American Textile Manufacturers Institute, December 1993.

Textile Highlights, Washington, D.C.: American Textile Manufacturers Institute, March 1994.

"Textiles Ready to Reap NAFTA Rewards," *Textile World*, December 1993, pp. 23-24.

"Textile World 1992 Manmade Fiber Chart," *Textile World*, August 1992, pp. 49-73.

"The Business Week 1000 Tables," *Business Week*, 1993 Bonus Issue, pp. 118-163.

—McAllister Isaacs III

SIC 2299

TEXTILE GOODS, NOT ELSEWHERE CLASSIFIED

This category covers establishments primarily engaged in manufacturing textile goods that were not included in other industry codes. These include production of linen goods, jute goods, felt goods, padding and upholstery filling, and processed waste and recovered fibers and flock. Establishments primarily engaged in processing textile fibers to prepare them for spinning such as wool scouring and carbonizing and combing and converting tow to top, are also classified here.

Establishments primarily engaged in manufacturing woven wool felts and wool haircloth are classified in **SIC 2231: Broadwoven Fabric Mills, Wool (Including Dyeing and Finishing)**. Those primarily engaged in manufacturing of needle punch carpeting are classified in **SIC 2273: Carpets and Rugs**. Establishments primarily engaged in manufacturing lace goods are classified in **SIC 2258: Lace and Warp Knit Fabric Mills**. Establishments primarily engaged in sorting wiping rags or waste are classified in **SIC 5093: Wholesale Trade**.

According to the United States Department of Commerce, Bureau of the Census, there are 519 companies with 591 establishments covered in this classification. In 1991, these establishment shipped $161 million worth of products.

Of all the varied products generated under this classification, by far the bulk—in poundage, if not in establishments involved—falls under the category of textile by-products or waste. Leigh Fibers of Spartanburg, South Carolina, is the largest processor of such products. The Utilization Plant of Johnston Industries Wellington Sears Div., located in Valley, Alabama, is the largest single establishment processing such products. Normal practice for both of these operations is to purchase the by-products or waste from other textile plants and process it into a useable product. This would include such products as cotton balls, upholstery filling, etc.

The reason the relatively high number of establishments covered under this classification generate a relatively low sales dollar volume lies in the inherent nature of the products themselves. Quite simply, 50 pounds of mattress stuffing isn't worth one pound of woven silk.

In the middle 1990s, environmental concerns had made an enormous impact on the textiles by-products business. Taking by-products to the landfill was a common practice among all textile plants. Now that this isn't either economically feasible nor environmentally acceptable, plants must find other outlets for its by-products. This has opened up a world of new opportunities for companies in this classification. It isn't expected that the North American Free Trade Agreement will have any significant effect on this industry segment.

INDUSTRY INFORMATION SOURCES

"ATME-I '93 Quickens Textiles' Time to Market," *Textile World*, June 1992, pp. 74-75.

"GATT Disappoints U.S. Textile Leaders," *Textile World*, January 1994, pp. 23-24.

Linton, George C., *The Modern Textile and Apparel Dictionary*, Plainfield, NJ: Textile Book Service, Div. of Bonn Industries Inc., 1973.

"Microfibers: All Dressed Up and Everywhere to Go," *Textile World*, August 1992, pp. 37-48.

Standard & Poor's Industry Surveys, New York: Standard & Poor's Corporation, 1992.

Standard & Poor's Industry Surveys, New York: Standard & Poor's Corporation, 1993.

Textile Highlights, Washington, D.C.: American Textile Manufacturers Institute, December 1993; March 1994.

"Textiles Ready to Reap NAFTA Rewards," *Textile World*, December 1993, pp. 23-24.

"The Business Week 1000 Tables," *Business Week*, 1993 Bonus Issue, pp. 118-163.

—McAllister Isaacs III

APPAREL & OTHER FINISHED FABRIC PRODUCTS

MEN'S AND BOY'S SUITS, COATS, AND OVERCOATS

This category covers establishments primarily engaged in manufacturing men's and boy's tailored suits, coats, and overcoats from purchased woven or knit fabrics. Establishments primarily engaged in manufacturing uniforms (except athletic and work uniforms) are also included in this industry. Establishments primarily engaged in manufacturing men's work uniforms and clothing are classified in **SIC 2326: Men's and Boys' Work Clothing,** and those manufacturing men's and boys' athletic uniforms are classified in **SIC 2329: Men's and Boys' Clothing, Not Elsewhere Classified.** Knitting mills primarily engaged in manufacturing suits and coats are classified in **SIC 2253: Knit Outerwear Mills.**

INDUSTRY SNAPSHOT

There were approximately 300 companies in the United States producing men's and boy's suits and coats in the early 1990s, although the four largest companies accounted for about 25 percent of the industry's output. In 1992, U.S. companies manufactured more than ten million suits and 53 million sports coats with a value of $2.8 billion. Two-piece suits and sports coats accounted for about 80 percent of the industry. The industry employed approximately 38,000 people, about half of whom were sewing machine operators. The production of men's and boy's suits was a batch process. Garments are moved from one sewing machine operator to another until are finished. According to the U.S. Department of Commerce, production workers in **SIC 2311: Men's and Boy's Suits, Coats, and Overcoats** earned an average of seven dollars per hour.

ORGANIZATION AND STRUCTURE

The men's and boy's suits and coats industry consisted of three major types of companies: manufacturers, contractors, and jobbers. Manufacturers cut and sewed finished products entirely within their own facilities. Jobbers, however, specialized in cutting the fabric, which they then supplied to contractors for sewing. The industry was dominated by the Hartmarx Corporation, with about 11 percent of the market, along with Crystal Brand Inc., Oxford Industries, Inc., and the Polo Ralph Lauren Corporation. Among the Hartmarx brands were Hickey-Freeman, Kuppenheimer, and Hart Schaffner & Marx.

BACKGROUND AND DEVELOPMENT

The clothing industry in the United States began to develop in the 18th century, but most clothing was still made in the home until the Civil War. Quality men's wear was long the province of skilled tailors. Most ready-to-wear clothing was imported, and poorly made, ready-made coats sold to sailors in seaports were often referred to as "slops." However, urban migration, the sewing machine, and a demand for uniforms during the Civil War, forever changed the industry.

Urban Migration. The United States began to change from an agrarian to an urban society about 1820 with the development of the textile industry and other manufacturing. As people began moving to cities, they also became more concerned with their clothing. As Claudia B. Kidwell and Margaret C. Christman pointed out in *Suiting Everyone: The Democratization of Clothing in America,* "For the most part [factory workers] could not afford the services of a good tailor, but they still wanted clothing which looked in no way appreciably different from the mainstream fashion. Consequently, the demand was there—not for the inferior or specialized clothing that had previously distinguished 'ready-made,' but rather for 'equal clothing' for anyone, which anyone could afford to buy."

Tailors began to develop "scientific principles" and "proportional systems" for making clothing that would fit almost anyone. In 1848, Oliver Hudson, a men's clothier in Boston, advertised that "sizes are indicated by number and a printed tag is attached to each article, so that anyone after becoming familiar with the size will seldom find it necessary to try a second garment." Tailors also began hiring workers, usually women who worked in the home, for many of the less skilled tasks, such as sewing straight seams. *Documents Relative to the Manufactures of the United States,* published in 1832, noted that Boston tailors employed 300 men, 100 boys, and 1,300 women.

Brooks Brothers, the famous New York clothier, is believed to have introduced the first ready-to-wear men's suits in the United States in 1845. Brooks Brothers would later introduce the "sack suit" around the turn of the century. The comfortable, boxy-looking sack suit was a stark departure from the tight-fitting suits with padded shoulders and pleated trousers that were then popular in Europe, and was considered the first genuinely American business attire. The sack suit evolved into the Ivy League look of the 1950s and the celebrated gray flannel suit of the 1960s.

Sewing Machine. Although many people contributed to the invention of the sewing machine, Elias Howe Jr., an American machinist, demonstrated a working model in 1845 and received a patent the following year. Isaac Merritt Singer, another American, made improvements to Howe's machine, and introduced "The Perpetual Action Belay Stitch Machine" in 1850. Singer's was considered the first practical sewing machine. Although the two inventors would squabble over patent rights for years, I.M. Singer & Co. was formed in 1851 and garment manufacturers began placing their orders.

By some estimates, sewing machines reduced the cost of manufacturing simple ready-to-wear clothes by as much as 80 percent. In the mid-1860s, Brooks Brothers noted that a top-quality overcoat that took six days to sew by hand could be made in three using a sewing machine. A foot treadle was added in 1871, which increased productivity even more, and the Singer Sewing Machine Co., renamed after Singer's

death in 1875, introduced the first electric sewing machine in 1889. By 1900, the Singer employed more than 60,000 sales agents worldwide; in many languages "Singer" became the word for sewing machine.

Civil War. Although most clothing in the United States was made in the home before the Civil War, military uniforms were an exception. At first, the U.S. government hired outside contractors to produce uniforms that were somewhat consistent in color and style. In 1812, however, the United States Army Clothing Establishment—perhaps the first true clothing factory in the United States—was created in Philadelphia. Fabric was cut to a standard pattern and then packaged along with padding, facing cloth, thread, and buttons. The materials were then delivered to "widows and other meritorious females" working at home to be sewn into uniforms. As private clothing factories appeared, they copied the same structure.

The demand for uniforms during the Civil War had several repercussions. Since the establishment could not supply enough uniforms alone, the government awarded contracts to other clothiers, many of whom received their first exposure to mass production. Secondly, the demand led to many improvements in technology, including the development of better cutting machines, pressers, and buttonholers. The establishment also kept the first detailed records on measurements that helped manufacturers develop regular ready-to-wear sizes after the war. In 1879, Albert S. Bolles wrote in the *Industrial History of the United States* that "the home manufacture of men's garments has virtually ceased, and every one, from ploughman to railroad president, goes to the store for his goods, and can be suited, if he chooses, from the shelves of the store at once."

The E.R. Hull Mammoth Clothing House was one of the first companies to offer suits for big men. In its 1880-81 mail-order catalog, the company noted, "A large number of Gentlemen weighing from Two to Three Hundred Pounds never go to a Ready Made Clothing Store because they labor under the impression that they cannot be fitted; an idea no doubt true, when applied to the small concerns of the country, but such is not the case at Our Mammoth Clothing House. The company offered "Suits, Overcoats, Business Coats and Vest, as large as 50 inches Breast Measure, and Pantaloons big enough for anybody."

Immigration. Many of the people who worked in the early clothing industry, both as inside cutters and contract seamstresses, were immigrants, primarily Irish in the 1840s and Germans in the 1850s. Many of the Jews who emigrated from Germany after 1860 also entered the clothing trade (although more often as retailers). The industry continued to provide thousands of low-paying jobs to later immigrants, including thousands of Italians and Russian Jews, who arrived between 1880 and 1910. Many of these immigrants worked long hours in overcrowded, poorly ventilated buildings that came to be known as sweatshops.

The influx of immigrants also fueled the men's wear industry. One of the first purchases a new arrival made was a new American-made suit to replace the European. In *Suiting Everyone,* Kidwell and Christman note that a ready-made suit could instantly transform the immigrant "from 'greenhorn' to 'someone who belonged.'" In the cities, men began wearing suits to work no matter what their occupations, even if they wore aprons or other work garments to keep them clean.

Unions. In 1869, garment workers in Philadelphia, led by Uriah Stephens, formed the Noble Order of the Knights of Labor, one of the first labor unions in the United States. Among its goals were an eight-hour workday and the abolition of child labor. The Knights of Labor remained a secretive, fraternal organization until 1879, when members elected Terence V. Powderly as Grand Master Workman. Powderly called for "one big union" and welcomed workers from other industries, including Catholics, who had been excluded under Stephens. Membership in the Knights of Labor rose from about 10,000 in 1879 to more than 100,000 in 1885. In 1885, the Knights of Labor led an unsuccessful strike against the Texas and Pacific Railroad, and its influence waned. Eventually, it was supplanted by the American Federation of Labor (AFL) as the most powerful union in the United States. In the early 1900s, the United States passed laws outlawing sweatshops and regulating child labor.

Hart, Schaffner & Marx. The first men's clothing manufacturer to eliminate outside contract labor was Hart, Schaffner & Marx in 1911. Originally known as Harry Hart & Brother, the company was started as a retail outlet in Chicago in 1871 by brothers Harry and Max Hart. The company began making its own clothes in 1874. Brother-in-law Marcus Marx joined the firm in 1878, and cousin Joseph Schaffner followed suit in 1887. Hart, Schaffner & Marx eventually became the leading brand name in men's suits, and possibly the most influential men's wear manufacturer in the industry.

Toward the end of the 19th century, most clothing salesmen traveled the country with a dozen or more wardrobe trunks stuffed with samples. However, Hart Schaffner & Marx sent out its salesmen with swatches of fabric instead. Most of the industry soon copied this practice. In the early 1890s, Hart Schaffner & Marx also abandoned the traditional practice of offering discounts to large customers. The company's slogan became "One just price . . . and just one price."

In 1897, Hart Schaffner & Marx became the first clothing manufacturer to advertise nationally. According to David Powers Cleary in *Great American Brands,* the industry was not impressed. However, the company persisted, increasing its advertising budget annually. Within a few years, Hart Schaffner & Marx was the leading men's clothing label in the United States. In the early 1900s, the company also began publishing the Hart Schaffner & Marx Style Book, "the acknowledged authority on what clothes to wear." The stylebook cost six cents plus postage and contained illustrations of the company's latest fashions. Hart Schaffner & Marx also opened stores in Boston and New York.

Hart Schaffner & Marx also promoted standards for the clothing industry, such as insisting that an "all-wool" suit should be made of 100 percent wool (although the federal Wool Products Labeling Act was not passed until 1939). In 1906, Hart Schaffner & Marx announced that its ready-to-wear men's clothing came in 14 basic body types so customers could get a more tailored look. The company boasted: "We design models especially for men who call themselves hard to fit. Stouts, slims, short stout men, big and little men, men who are built 'close to the ground,' long bodies and short legs, men with slightly stooping shoulders; all the odd sizes have their special models, made to fit."

Fashion. The men's suit industry was never as volatile as women's fashions, except perhaps during the leisure-suit phenomenon of the 1970s. According to Charles Panati in *Extraordinary Origins of Everyday Things,* the concept of the suit originated in the 18th century among the wealthy class in France as informal country wear. "Lounge suits"—coat, waistcoat, vest, and trousers— were cut baggy and often made of different fabrics, patterns, and colors. It wasn't until the 1860s that the coats and trousers were generally made from the same cloth. Lounge suits were also used for riding and the back of the coat was split for comfort, a feature that still existed in the mid-1990s. Likewise, the lapel hole originally served a utilitarian function: collars were turned up and lapels buttoned across the neck for warmth.

While fashion may have been dull, there was a wide variety of prices. In 1897, the Sears, Roebuck & Co. catalog listed suits available from 98 cents to $20, although the catalog advised customers to pick a suit that cost at least $4.75. Most wealthy men still had their suits professionally tailored. According to *Suiting Everyone,* by the 1920s the men's suit industry was refined enough that ''from across the room a man's $50 suit looked much like a $250 suit.''

Men's fashions—including the leisure suit—became more colorful in the 1970s and took advantage of newer fabrics. Leisure suits were an urban adaptation of the safari jacket, and accounted for more half of all men's and boy's suits produced in the United States in 1975 when more than 12 million were sold. But sales of leisure suits were less than half that in 1976, and by 1983 the leisure suit had disappeared altogether. Similarly, knit fabrics were used in nearly 75 percent of the suits and coats made in the 1970s, but also virtually disappeared by the mid-1980s. (The Textile Fiber Products Identification Act of 1958 required clothing manufacturers to include fiber content by percentage on the labels). The early 1980s also saw a revival of the European look in men's suits, especially tight-fitting Italian styles popularized by television programs such as *Miami Vice.* However, by the late 1980s, men's fashions had returned to the classic British-tailored look.

CURRENT CONDITIONS

Sales of men's and boy's suits in the United States leveled off in the early 1990s, after several years of modest but steady growth. Analysts blamed the weak market on the continuing recession, and more significantly, on an acceptance of more casual dress in settings where suits were once *de rigueur.* U.S. companies were also updating their lines in the early 1990s to reflect renewed interest in European styles. Another trend that clothing manufacturers were watching carefully was the growing percentage of men's clothing that was actually purchased by men. In 1989, only about half of all men's clothing was purchased by men, but in 1993, men made nearly 70 percent of the purchase decisions.

RESEARCH AND TECHNOLOGY

Following World War II, improvements in the sewing machine eliminated the need to stitch button holes, pockets, belt loops, and lapels by hand. New technology introduced since the 1960s has also increased productivity, although some promising technologies were later abandoned. In the 1960s, some manufacturers replaced reciprocating blade cutting machinery with lasers. However, the lasers tended to fuse layers synthetic fabrics. Computer-controlled spreading, marking, and cutting systems were introduced in the late 1970s and early 1980s. Sewing machines also became more sophisticated beginning in

the late 1960s, eliminating much of the manual labor involved in handling and positioning garments as they moved from one sewing-machine operator to another. These advances led to significant increases in productivity, while employment fell from 128,000 workers in 1967 to 38,000 in 1992.

INDUSTRY INFORMATION SOURCES

''1993 Focus: An Economic Profile of the Apparel Industry,'' *American Apparel Manufacturers Association,* Arlington, VA, 1993.

Cleary, David Powers, *Great American Brands,* New York: Fairchild Publications, 1981.

Cocks, Jay, ''Bonfire of the Business Suits,'' *Time,* November 19, 1990, 83.

Darnton, Nina, ''Good Taste for Tough Times,'' *Newsweek,* May 28, 1990, 76.

Gross, Michael, ''Suit Wars,'' *New York,* October 3, 1988, 51.

Kidwell, Claudia B., and Margaret C. Christman, *Suiting Everyone: The Democratization of Clothing in America,* Washington, D.C.: Smithsonian Institution Press, 1974.

Landler, Mark, ''Suddenly, the Stylish Male Gets Discovered,'' *Business Week,* October 1, 1990, 72.

Panati, Charles, *Extraordinary Origins of Everyday Things,* New York: Harper & Row, 1987.

Sieling, Mark Scott, and Daniel Curtin, ''Patterns of Productivity Change in Men's and Boys' Suits and Coats,'' *Monthly Labor Review,* November 1988, 25.

Zinn, Laura, ''The Suit Market is Coming Apart at the Seams,'' *Business Week,* August 12, 1991, 42.

—Dean Boyer

SIC 2321

MEN'S AND BOYS' SHIRTS

This category includes establishments primarily engaged in manufacturing men's and boys' shirts (including polo and sport shirts) from purchased woven or knit fabrics. Establishments primarily engaged in manufacturing work shirts are classified in **SIC 2326.** Knitting mills primarily engaged in manufacturing outerwear are classified in **SIC 2253.**

INDUSTRY SNAPSHOT

In 1992, there were approximately 490 manufacturers of men's and boys' shirts in the United States. All told, these establishments constituted a $3.2 billion industry. This figure was consistent with an overall declining trend in the industry, which had peaked in

1987 and fallen every year since. Over the course of the five-year period between 1987 and 1992, the annual percentage change in the value of total product shipments averaged a negative 4.5 percent.

In 1988, woven shirts accounted for about 18 percent of total industry product, while knit shirts made up the 82-percent balance. The woven shirt, classified as a major product, includes dress and business shirts as well as sport shirts. The classification of knit shirts includes outerwear shirts, T-shirts, tank tops, sweatshirts, and others. From the years 1970 through 1982, annual U.S. production of woven shirts declined, remaining more or less flat since that time. On the other hand, domestic production of knit shirts maintained a steady upward climb during the same period. The principal economic sectors responsible for the purchase of all categories of men's and boys' shirts were personal consumption expenditures with 83 percent, and other apparel manufacturers with 12 percent.

The declining fortunes experienced by the men's and boys' shirt industry since the late 1980s was a result of several growth-retarding economic forces. Chief among these was the long-term erosion of middle-class income, which has been responsible for the majority of apparel-related expenditures. Second, firm downsizing, bankruptcies, and pervasive structural changes at both the retail and wholesale levels wreaked havoc upon the traditional, established lines of apparel distribution. For example, many of the larger retail chains flirted intermittently with carrying their own chain-identified brands of clothing. Third, there was a lack of pronounced, sustainable upward price movements which would have resulted from a business-cycle upswing. Historically, such price movements regularly occurred and were thought to instill investor confidence. But in the early to mid-1990s such a rebound was held in check by competitive price pressures exerted by producers—both domestic and foreign—who found themselves strapped with abnormally high levels of excess capacity. A fourth economic force which hampered industry growth was the amount of lingering debt payments, previously incurred to defend against hostile takeover attempts, which continued to eat away at company profits. Fifth, in a strategic response to the growth of imports, a number of U.S. manufacturers shifted parts of their shirtmaking operations abroad. Citing the lower-cost competitive advantages to be gained from foreign investment, U.S. shirt manufacturers expected this move to reverse their eroding share of the U.S. market.

There were some positive economic factors at work in the industry as well. The progressive weakness of the dollar led to a surge in the demand for exports of American-made men's and boys' shirts. In 1989, export sales accounted for nearly 6.6 percent of total sales. The current dollar estimates for the three years following were 8.6 percent; 11.8 percent; and 15.8 percent, respectively.

In another development, while sales of the shirt industry plummeted downward, the industry's larger firms were busy exploiting the competitive advantages offered by their size. In an effort to preserve or extend their dominance in the market, better-positioned firms used internally generated funds to invest in the latest apparel-related technology. At the same time, the future looked less than rosy for prospective firms who found themselves either too late in implementing new investments or unable to arrange financial backing to undertake such improvements in plant and equipment. The forward momentum of both industry downsizing and shifting market-share concentration were forecasted to propel the industry well into the 1990s.

Between 1981 and 1990, the consumption of men's dress shirts and woven sport shirts was relatively flat, ranging from 314 million units in 1981 to 302.8 million in 1990. During the same period, consumption of knit sport shirts grew steadily from 231.2 million units in 1980 to 330.5 million units in 1990. The average retail price for men's dress shirts was $10.57 per shirt in 1980; by 1990 it had risen to $14.50, resulting in a compound annual growth rate of 3.6 percent. In the category of woven sport shirts, the average retail price was $10.58 in 1980 and $13.39 in 1990. Its compound annual growth rate over this period was 2.6 percent. The average retail price for the more popular knit sport shirts was $8.40 in 1980 and $10.15 in 1990. Throughout the period its compound annual growth rate was about 2.1 percent. The fact that these increases were slight compared to earlier periods was considered indicative of the industry's highly competitive conditions.

ORGANIZATION AND STRUCTURE

Using modern production methods, the average shirt-making process requires 40 distinct operations, of which 20 are performed along a "critical path," a term denoting the number of sequential operations needed to finish a garment. For non-critical-path operations, most firms utilize a progressive "bundle" system where various parts of the entire shirtmaking operations are performed simultaneously. Batches usually consist of 1500 pieces. The unit/time per operation is specified in minutes, formally called standard allowed minutes and referred to by its acronym SAM. All told, the total time necessary for a garment to cycle through the manufacturing process is dependent on the number of operations performed along the critical and non-critical paths; the SAM of these operations; and the lot size.

A shirt's production flow is divided into three major sequential operational phases. These comprise various small-parts detail operations, assembly, and packaging. Shirt production begins with the small-parts detail operations phase being subdivided into five basic shirt component flows: collar, back, front, cuffs, and sleeves. Collar operations account for the majority of small-parts detail time, requiring 12 operations, nine of which are located in the critical path. All told, a typical shirt requires 40 critical-path and non-critical-path operations and involves 12 SAM. Assembly operations, due to their complex nature, have been generally difficult but not impossible to automate.

The primary materials consumed by the men's and boys' shirt industry, ranked in terms of cost, were: miscellaneous materials, parts, and containers; broadloom fabrics; and knit fabrics. The major supplies came from importers, manufacturers of broadloom fabrics, apparel made from purchased materials, and knit fabric mills.

The primary distribution channels for men's dress shirts changed very little during the 1980s, although conditions entered a state of flux by the 1990s. The largest percentage share was sold through department stores and averaged about 30 percent. Of this amount, the top 100 department stores were responsible for 60 percent of sales. Mass merchants accounted for the second largest share of men's dress shirt sales with about 20 percent. Specialty stores were third with 13.6 percent and in fourth place, but experiencing rapid growth during the 1980s, were wholesale/factory outlets which accounted for ten percent in 1989.

A household survey of men aged 16 and older conducted by Market Research Corporation of America indicated that the major fiber categories popular with consumers of men's and boys' shirts throughout the 1980s consisted, in order of preference, of 100 percent cotton, a 60/40 cotton-polyester blend, other cotton blends, 100 percent polyester, 80 poly/20 cotton, 65 poly/35 cotton, and other poly blends. Toward the end of the 1980s, the consumption of all-cotton and 60/40 poly-cotton blends rose sharply. By 1989 these shares had climbed to 14 percent and 23 percent, respectively. The annual average share of the 65 poly/35 cotton fiber far exceeded all fiber categories, accounting for nearly 38 percent of total fabric consumption—despite undergoing annual declines during the last half of the decade. The consumption of other cotton blends experienced the sharpest decline, falling

from 15 percent in 1986 to 9 percent in 1989. The remaining fiber categories remained stable with no category exceeding 8 percent nor falling below 2 percent.

BACKGROUND AND DEVELOPMENT

The historical development of the men's and boys' shirts industry can be divided into two basic periods: the eras before and after the 1918 introduction of the soft-collar-attached shirt. The waxing and waning influences of wars; political, industrial, and technological revolutions; government policies; apparel construction and design changes; introductions of new natural and synthetic fibers and/or improvements in their resiliency; the fleeting, even fickle, nature of fashion preferences have contributed to the current state of the men's and boys' shirt industry.

The event that gave birth to the U.S. apparel industry was the American Revolution of 1776. It created a climate in which the activities of urban-based industrialists, bankers, merchants, and various other professions and crafts could flourish. Progressing in step with this newly emergent and triumphant political/economic class of white males were styles of dress reflective of their own particular preferences. For the most part, these tastes were uniformly utilitarian in design and style. They were notable for having abandoned the frivolous pomp and highly ornamental embellishments that had characterized the clothing of the defeated nobility.

From the standpoint of economics, the uniformity of the new fashion tastes was striking, making it possible to conceive of, and eventually mass produce ready-made shirts on a scale never before seen. This flurry of economic activity initially began in the rapidly urbanizing coastal towns located throughout the Northeast. The end of the War of 1812 coincided with the emergence of a canal-based national transportation system that provided barrier-free interstate commerce. New markets for mass-produced shirts developed in the more remote, interior regions of the United States where growing urban populations began to thrive along major river routes.

It is interesting to note that the U.S. apparel industry, from its infancy at the end of the American Revolution and progressing well into its more formative years at the outbreak of the Civil War, was nurtured by a highly protectionist trade policy. Until 1816 the tariff on any type of imported clothing stood at 25 percent, rising to 30 percent from 1816 to 1828. By 1829 it was up to 50 percent, where it remained until 1860. If the same imported clothing arrived in the United States on board a ship of foreign origin, additional penalties were imposed.

The decision to finally lift the tariff and compete in an open world marketplace was motivated by the introduction of sewing-machine technology in the 1850s. Due to the increased productivity generated by the sewing machine, the U.S. apparel industry was propelled to world-class status second to none. The industry's main advantage lay in the ability to reduce the cost of labor per shirt, which led, in turn, to a sharp decrease in the selling price for its product.

In addition to its effect upon the economic marketplace, the sewing machine had a profound structural impact on the organization of the workplace. It ultimately led to greater divisions of labor based on routinization and job specialization. It also had a profound effect on the livelihood of highly paid, skilled tailors who were replaced by the low-wage semi-skilled or unskilled laborers who arrived from Europe to work in U.S. factories.

Another milestone in the shirt industry occurred with the outbreak of the Civil War. Prior to the war, manufacturers and retailers of ready-made apparel had been hampered by the absence of standard clothing sizes. In order to facilitate its clothing orders for private manufacturers, the Union Army's Philadelphia Quartermaster collected body-measurement data on over one million recruits and conscripts. These measurements were organized into tables of standardized body proportions which could be easily applied to the manufacture of civilian garments.

Toward the end of the pre-collar fashion era and extending well into the attached-collar era, changes in fashion, fabric, and design exerted a more commanding influence on the direction of the men's and boys' shirt industry. During the first decade of the 20th century, the surest sign of being in the presence of a well-dressed gentleman of property—thought to be more talented at exercising his brain than his muscle—was a stiff-bosom, detached-collar shirt. Cluett Peabody's "Arrow" line of stiff-bosom shirts, for instance, came in 20 starch collar styles of the "poke" type: a plain standing collar without tabs. By 1906, fashion tastes had shifted from the poke-type detached collar to embrace the fold or turned-down collar style. Arrow promoted this new collar through the creation of the "Arrow collar man," whose sex appeal over the next dozen or so years managed to drive the sales of Arrow's 400-plus detached-collar styles to the $32 million mark.

In 1911, the notched detached-collar shirt was all the rage. Accompanying advertisements pointed to the shirt's numerous advantages, allowing the wearer to save time, money, and temper since it prevented buttonholes from ripping, didn't tear fingernails, and bypassed the use of metal collar boutonnieres. By 1914, the detached-collar Henley shirt, with reversible double cuffs, came into vogue.

In 1918, the largest fashion wave sweeping across the United States was the splash created by the soft-collar-attached shirt. Credit for its popularity originated with World War I. During their tour of duty, many American men were impressed with the relative comfort of the soft-collar-attached khaki army shirt, especially when compared to its more irritating starched, collar-detached civilian counterpart. In fact, just prior to the widespread circulation of the collar-attached shirt in it various civilian guises, sales of military shirt, replete with regulation army cuffs, and pocket, collar, and sleeve insignias, were booming.

In 1920, John M. Van Huesen was credited with the introduction of a three-ply collar constructed in a one-piece arc. The collar incorporated the advantage of the starch collar's crisp appearance with the comfort of the soft collar. It also had the advantage of retaining its shape longer than other collars due to its construction. By 1925, the Van Huesen Shirt Company ran advertisements declaring it the "collar of the century," while incorporating the new collar into the design of their entire line of shirts.

Van Huesen also pioneered the development of a patented weaving process that introduced the industry to the one-piece collar that would become an industry standard. The collar's novel quality lay in its uniform thickness, designed and constructed without any lining so that, even after repeated wearings, it proved to be wrinkle-, blister-, and buckle-resistant.

By 1928 the popularity of colored shirts—in stripes or solids—skyrocketed. The same year also witnessed the rise of pinned, collared shirts and snap-on collar bars. Despite being the decade of the Depression, during the 1930s style changes were influenced by an affluent few, who seemed keen on embracing the latest aristocratically inspired style changes on the British fashion scene. The eyes of the fashion world seemed to be fixated on the apparel adorning such royal personalities as the Prince of Wales and his younger brother the Duke of Kent. In fact, a new collar style known as "the Prince" soon struck a popular chord among the affluent. The collar's design proved to an exact copy of what the two royal personages wore while attending a social event one evening.

The wide range of materials necessary for the apparel industry during the war effort left little room for design innovation in the early 1940s. However, government control of an economy organized for military production had a far-reaching effect—it gave rise to the economic integration of the southern- and northern-based apparel industries whose prior operations had been largely conducted on a regional basis.

Interestingly, as had happened in earlier times, the arrival of synthetic or man-made fibers—and later, their apparel spin-offs—were traceable to events surrounding the circumstances of war. Immediately following World War II, some shirt manufacturers began using nylon and other synthetic fibers. Though receiving enthusiastic support from the public, not all major shirt producers were willing to plunge headfirst into the nylon shirt fad. Cluett Peabody announced that no Arrow-label shirts would be produced from nylon. They, along with other traditional shirt producers, questioned whether synthetic fibers were an authentic ''shirting fabric.'' In their opinion, it would come as no surprise if, sooner or later, the consuming public recoiled with horror from purchasing ''parachute shirts'' made from inferior fabrics.

During the 1950s, three major technological changes occurred that had a great impact on the shirt industry. Concerns about the longevity of synthetic fibers were silenced when Du Pont became the first U.S. commercial producer of the man-made fiber polyester, which they marketed under the brand name Dacron. To the consumer, polyester was prized for its wrinkle resistance; its ability to maintain its shape after repeated washing; for requiring little, if any, ironing; and for its ability to be treated with a permanent heat-setting process which helped to maintain pleats and guard against shrinkage and sagging. For manufacturers, polyester was particularly redeeming since it could be readily blended with other fibers. Since its first appearance, polyester has undergone many significant product-enhancing modifications. Monsanto, for example, developed and commercially produced ''Spectran'' polyester, a brand which, among other things, is highly regarded for its superior stain release properties.

The year 1956 witnessed the introduction of wash-and-wear, all-cotton shirts. Thanks to a special resin treatment, apparel made of natural fibers was now able to withstand repeated laundering without losing its original shape or appearance. Finally, in 1959, the longstanding problem of a garment's susceptivity to stains received a solution when apparel products began to be treated with numerous special finishing processes that allowed stains to be washed out with plain cold water. The ''Scotchgard'' process emerged during this period.

CURRENT CONDITIONS

Downsizing and restructuring within the men's and boys' shirt industry were recognized as an established trend by the late 1980s. In the mid-1990s, it had yet to be seen whether this trend was entirely played out. Additional long-term uncertainties were thrown into the mix with the 1993 passage of the North American Free Trade Act, which was immediately followed by the General Agreement on Tariffs and Trade.

By the late 1980s, the entire U.S. apparel industry had been hit hard by the erosion of the middle class income that had previously accounted for the majority of apparel purchases. In addition, the growing trend toward relocation of apparel establishments to foreign countries as well as foreign outsourcing of apparel-related work formerly performed within U.S. borders further eroded jobs in the industry. The effect of competition from imports that led to the market-share deterioration of domestic apparel manufacturers also contributed to the industry's shakeout.

The most far reaching domestic response to the deteriorating industry conditions was the investment in state-of-the-art communications systems that could determine, and react to, consumer preferences. This consumer-driven process, known as ''quick response,'' integrates numerous dimensions of the production cycle with an eye toward shortening the cycle's duration, implementing productivity improvements, and shrinking inventory levels through the immediate transmission of consumer taste information back to manufacturers. Beginning at the retail level, quick response tracks computer-recorded sales information which is directed to manufacturers, analyzed, and used to hasten response to trends by determining what materials and styles will most likely result in a sale.

In addition to the quick response system, shirt producers directed major investments at computer-controlled automated machinery in order to effect increases in productivity. These investments targeted the areas of design, cutting, embroidery, sewing, finishing, ticketing, and various distribution operations. Independent of the particular area of operation, most apparel-industry investment projects were undertaken with the aim of reducing the labor-time component per unit of output.

When compared against the standards of other industries, the measure of labor intensity in apparel manufacturing remained excessively high and acted to inhibit productivity. In order to compete among themselves, as well as against other industries, the leading apparel firms took notice. For reasons related to their economies of scale and access to internally-generated funds, the larger shirt firms were better positioned to implement many high start-up-cost technological advances. With the passage of time, this was expected to result in an uneven pattern of technological change across the entire industry, further exacerbating the downsizing trend present throughout the industry.

INDUSTRY LEADERS

During the mid-to-late 1980s, the top brand names in the high priced category of men's dress shirts were Cluett, Peabody & Company's Arrow brand; Phillips-Van Huesen; and J. C. Penny. Brand names occupying the middle tier and experiencing very little change in relative market-share position included Salant Corporation's Manhattan and John Henry brands and K Mart. Still within the middle tier, but undergoing a relatively up-and-down performance was the Sears brand. Brand names situated on the lower tier and experiencing little volatility were Mervyn's, Warnaco's Christian Dior brand, and Bradstreet.

When grouped according to regional concentration, the largest clusters of shirt establishments were located in the South Atlantic, East South Central, and Middle Atlantic regions. Alternatively, when ranked by the number of establishments per state, the largest states (those with more than 40 establishments) were California, 75; North Carolina, 74; New York, 59; Florida, 46; Georgia, 43; and Alabama, 43.

Drawn from a 1992 list of the top 75 companies active in the men's and boys' shirt industry, the five leading companies ranked according to their estimated market share were Phillips-Van Heusen Corp., 14.4 percent; Cluett, Peabody and Co., Inc., 9.1 percent; Bugle Boy Industries Inc., 8.9 percent; Salant Corp., 7.3 percent; and Manhattan Industries, 6.2 percent. Of these five companies, only Bugle Boy was privately held.

WORK FORCE

In 1989, approximately 550 establishments engaged in the manufacture of men's and boys' shirts. Of these, about 426 operated with 20 or more employees, while the average number of employees per establishment stood at 134. The average value added per production worker amounted to $31,123—well below the average of $105,881 calculated for 459 U.S. manufacturing industries in the same year.

Total employment in the men's and boys' shirt industry stood at approximately 91,700 in 1981—by 1992 it had fallen to 67,200. Over the entire period, the annual growth in employment declined by 2.6 percent.

This less-than-optimistic figure rather accurately reflected the turbulent economic conditions of the apparel industry.

Beginning in 1981, total employment experienced a steady downward drift that culminated in a steep decline between 1984 and 1985. During this time, total employment fell from 88,900 to 79,000—a dramatic plunge of 11.1 percent. Since 1985, the industry's total employment figures have continued to drop, though at a somewhat slower pace.

While total employment was declining, the average hours worked by production workers exhibited a modest but steady rise, going from 36 hours per week in 1981 to 37.1 hours per week in 1992. For the same period, these workers' average wage rose from $4.55 to $6.56 per hour. These indicators, along with the fact that during the same period the value added per production worker increased, suggested that productivity increases were not matched by rising real wages.

Measured as a percentage of the total work force, women accounted for 85.5 percent of the overall employment in the industry. This percentage has remained fairly consistent since at least 1981. Nevertheless, the predominance of women in the industry was not translated into wage parity with men. According to data provided by the Bureau of Labor Statistics, the average hourly earnings of male production workers in 1987 stood at $5.50 while women within the same category received $4.86. Also significant in terms of the social composition of the industry's work force was a 1988 survey conducted by the Amalgamated Clothing and Textile Workers Union. The survey concluded that African-American workers comprised 21.2 percent of the overall work force, with the percentage of all minority workers falling in the neighborhood of 36 percent.

Occupational categories in the men's and boys' shirt industry fall within four production-related classifications: cutting, sewing, finishing, and miscellaneous departments. In 1987, occupational activities pertaining to the sewing function accounted for 72.7 percent of all production workers. Sewing machine operators, with 92.2 percent, were the most dominant employment category represented within this department. They were followed by loaders, with 4.4 percent.

The finishing area accounted for 15.7 percent of all production workers. Final and thread-trimmer inspectors with 27.9 percent; garment-folder inspectors, 25.8 percent; finish pressers, 17.3 percent; and baggers and boxers, 16.2 percent represented the major occupational categories within this department.

Workers performing miscellaneous functions represented 6.4 percent of total production employees, while those working in the cutting room made up the remaining 5.2 percent. Of those, 30 percent were assemblers, 29.3 percent were spreaders, and 25.3 percent were cutters.

The Bureau of Labor Statistics forecasted that most of these occupational categories would undergo a continuous state of decline through the year 2005. Assuming a continuation of the more-or-less forward momentum of the industry's productivity, in conjunction with the great number of workers in the category, employment of sewing machines operators was projected to experience the steepest decrease.

AMERICA AND THE WORLD

Since the end of World War II, the apparel industry has proven to be extremely susceptible to import competition and thus has frequently lobbied the U.S. government to impose tariffs and quotas. For shirts made from woven material, including dress/business and sport shirts, imports remained fairly flat throughout the 1970s. During the first eight years of the 1980s, however, they began to climb rapidly in response to rising demand, going from 16,316 in 1980 to 27,023 units in 1987. The pace of growth slowed and attained a more modest level in the late 1980s and into the 1990s, however. When viewed over the period from 1970 to 1990, the increase in the extent of woven shirt consumption was striking. In 1970, it stood at 28 percent, only to climb throughout the decade to 46.9 percent by 1980. The decade of the eighties was another period of steady import growth; by 1990, imports accounted for 63.9 percent of the U.S. market.

Imports of shirts made from knit fabrics rose modestly in the 1970s, from 15.9 percent in 1970 to 18.7 in 1979. During the mid-1980s the trend picked up, going from 17.8 percent in 1980 to 28.6 percent in 1984, before dipping back down in the latter part of the decade to stand at 22.4 percent in 1990.

In 1988, approximately 42 percent of all U.S. imports came from three countries: South Korea, 19 percent; Hong Kong, 12 percent; and Taiwan, 11 percent. In the same year, close to 87 percent of total imports came from countries designated by the United Nations as Less Developed Countries, consistent with the steady growth in this area since the end of World War II.

RESEARCH AND TECHNOLOGY

Reducing the large number of sewing machine, assembly, and packaging operations necessary in the manufacture of a single dress shirt has been a hurdle the industry has been struggling to clear. Measurement deficiencies contained in traditional finance formulas in wide use throughout the industry served as barriers to technological advances.

According to Ernest Schramyr, president of Jet Sew, one key variable that factored into the total time it took to process a typical lot or shirt batch, generally 1,500 shirts, was the length of time it took to move from one operation to the next. In an article in *Bobbin,* Schramyr put forward an alternative shirt production system, which called for the installation of already available robotic units as a means of rationalizing many of the critical-path and, to a lesser extent, non-critical-path, operations. If implemented, Schramyr estimated that a typical shirt would require only 27 instead of 40 total operations, thereby reducing the overall SAM to 9.

The largest impact of the introduction of advanced technology, though, would come in the total number of critical path operations, which could be reduced from 20 to 14 with the use of robotics. While such advances in machinery were being made, attempts to automate segments of production were often considered unsuccessful because they failed to meet their expected rate of return on investment. The fact remained, however, that assembly operations, which accounted for nearly half of a firm's total stitching costs, still offered the greatest opportunity for potential cost savings.

As a second feasible alternative to the existing assembly operations method, Schramyr suggested the implementation of equipment used with the unit production system (UPS). Outside the shirt industry, performance results from the UPS reported productivity gains as high as 25 percent and also reductions in material "throughput time" equal to an eye-opening 80 percent. The most notable drawbacks associated with the UPS were its relatively high start-up expenditure and, according to traditional investment criteria, its tendency to generate a marginal return on investment. Schramyr remained critical of the conservative investment philosophy espoused by corporate financial officers to weight potential investment projects. According to Schramyr such an approach neglected to factor in a host of cost savings which included: reduced work-in-process-carrying costs; reduced inventory-carrying costs; significant direct labor savings through a downsizing of the labor force; and heightened capabilities to complement such concepts such as immediate product delivery based on customer preference, production based on orders and not speculation, and the avoidance of unwanted discount markdowns. With these in mind, Schramyr advocated the development of a new, "non-traditional investment criterion." Failing that, he feared that many technological advances applicable to the industry would go ignored.

INDUSTRY INFORMATION SOURCES

Arpan, Jeffery S., Jose de la Torres, and Brian Toyne, *The U.S. Apparel Industry: International Challenge, Domestic Response,* Atlanta: College of Business Administration, Georgia State University, 1982.

Corbin, Harry A., *The Men's Clothing Industry: Colonial through Modern Times,* New York: Fairchild Publications, 1970.

Economic and Demographic Indicators of 42 ACTWU Industries, New York: Research Department, Amalgamated Clothing and Textile Workers Union, 1988.

1993 Focus: An Economic Profile of the Apparel Industry, Arlington, VA: American Apparel Manufacturers Association, 1993.

Manufacturing USA: Industry Analyses, Statistics, and Leading Companies, 3rd edition, Detroit: Gale, 1993.

Popkin, Martin, E., *Manufacture of Men's Clothing,* New York: Isaac Pittman, 1929.

Report of the General Executive Board, ACTWU and AFL-CIO Sixth Constitutional Convention, June 1993.

Schoeffler, O. E., and William Gale, *Esquire's Encyclopedia of 20th-Century Men's Fashions,* New York: McGraw-Hill, 1973.

U.S. Industrial Outlook 1993, Washington, DC: U.S. Department of Commerce, 1993.

Schramyr, Ernst, "Jets-In-Time: 13 Operation Can Go," *Bobbin,* May 1987.

Wingate, Isabel B., *Textile Fabrics and Their Selection,* Englewood Cliffs, NJ: Prentice-Hall, 1976.

—Dan King

SIC 2322

MEN'S AND BOYS' UNDERWEAR AND NIGHTWEAR

This category includes establishments primarily engaged in manufacturing men's and boys' underwear and nightwear from purchased woven or knit fabrics. Knitting mills primarily engaged in manufacturing underwear and nightwear are classified in **SIC 2254: Knit Underwear and Nightwear Mills;** and those manufacturing men's and boys' robes are classified in **SIC 2384: Robes and Dressing Gowns.**

INDUSTRY SNAPSHOT

About 85 establishments were engaged in the manufacture of men's and boys' underwear and nightwear in the United States in 1992. All told, these establishments were responsible for an inflation adjusted total product estimated at $734 million. This figure was up slightly from the previous two years yet remained consistent with an overall declining trend going back to 1987. When viewed over the period covering 1987-1992, the average annual percent change in the value of the total product declined by 5.3 percent.

Starting in the early to mid-1980s the economic fortunes of the men's and boys' underwear and nightwear industry entered a period of sharp decline. The untimely convergence of several growth-retarding protracted economic factors serve to account for a large part of the industry's demise. First, the steady decline in the level of middle class incomes, who as a group in times past were responsible for a disproportionate share of personal consumption expenditures directed at all types of apparel clothing. Second, by the late 1980s and then extending well into the 1990s, both the retail and wholesale levels of distribution had undergone a period of widespread shakeout and structural change. This led to the break-up of many established lines of distribution and sent many producers scrambling in search of new outlet sources. Even in instances where these links were not severed, traditional supplier-distributor relationships were in the process of undergoing profound structural change which typically led to the implementation of "quick response" systems. Third, as the U.S. economy began to experience a period of economic recovery in the mid-1990s, the upward movement of apparel prices historically associated with upturns in economic activity failed to materialize. The expected price rises were held in check due to stiff price competition from both U.S. and foreign producers. As a result, many in the industry found themselves burdened with levels of excess capacity that were never before encountered during previous periods of economic recovery. Finally, the lingering overhang of takeover debt piled up to defend against hostile takeover threats, a frenzy which peaked in the late 1980s and subsided in the early 1990s, continued to exert a dampening effect on company profits and growth.

On a more upbeat note, the influence imparted by the trend of a declining U.S. dollar had played a positive role in boosting export sales in the men's and boys' underwear and nightwear industry. For the period covering 1989-1992, estimates of the nominal value of exports figured at $30.5 million in 1989, climbed from $52.4 million in 1990 to $73.2 million by 1991, and by 1992 had reached the $105 million mark. In addition, while the industry itself was staggering under economic difficulties, its larger firms continued to gain market share and were well positioned to invest internally generated funds in state-of-art technologies. These new technology investments should result in a boost in productivity, which should in turn lower unit costs of production. Under the prevailing economic circumstances, if the middle and lower tier firms in the industry do not keep pace, some industry observers expect the gap related to productivity and unit cost differentials to widen, placing the continued existence of the less competitive firms in serious jeopardy.

ORGANIZATION AND STRUCTURE

Entering the 1990s, approximately 90 U.S. establishments were involved in the manufacture of men's and boys underwear and nightwear. Of these, about 70 establishments operated with twenty or more employees. For the same year the average value added per production worker was $28,242, a figure noticeably below the manufacturing average of $105,881. When ranked by order of their concentration within Census regions, the largest number of establishments were to be found in the South Atlantic, Middle Atlantic, and East South Central regions.

Data available from 1987 indicated that the primary materials consumed by the men's and boys underwear and nightwear industry ranked in terms of cost were: materials, parts, containers and supplies, $378.6 million; knit fabrics, $290.7 million; and broadwoven fabrics, $48.2 million. The major sectors of input supply came from imports, broadwoven fabric mills, knit fabric mills, and other apparel manufacturers. The major sectors responsible for the purchase of the men's and boys' underwear and nightwear outputs were private personal expenditures, about 83 percent of total sales, followed by other apparel manufacturers with 12.0 percent.

BACKGROUND AND DEVELOPMENT

Underwear. At the turn of the twentieth century underwear was designed with one purpose in mind: as apparel to be worn underneath more stylistic outer garments for the simple task of protecting the wearer against seasonal elements. During severe weather, a man could choose from several different styles and weights of either one or two-piece long-sleeved and long-legged knitted wool underwear. For the summer months, the wearer changed to underwear that was light in weight and designed to be cooler, though it was

also designed in a long-sleeved and long-legged style. A popular two-piece outfit was made of French knitted balbriggan. It featured an undershirt complete with a fancy collarette neck, pearl buttons, ribbed close fitting cuffs and a fine silky like finish. The matching drawers came with a sateen band and pearl buttons. It was available in the colors of either ecru or camel's hair. Though interest in silk underwear was growing on the margin, due not so much to its aesthetic or status symbol value but because of its superior drying quality, underwear made of knitted wool mostly dominated the fashion scene throughout the first two decades of the twentieth century.

The early twenties witnessed the arrival of the one-piece union suit. The union suit featured a more athletically tapered look and came with long or short sleeves. Made from knit of long staple combed cotton yarn and sewn with smooth flat locked seams, the union suit was specially designed to eliminate the feeling of tightness around the crotch area. The union suit was also tailored to fit different body lengths and was available in long, medium and short sizes. A modified version of the union suit soon followed. This was followed by ''athletic underwear,'' which was cut very brief and was available in a variety of staple and fancy woven cloths. It came with a ''trouser seat'' designed so that when opened it made no contact with the body.

The sleeveless athletic shirt, popular throughout the 1930s, was adapted from the top half of the tank swimsuit worn by U.S. men during the early years of the twentieth century. It was supplanted in the 1940s by the short sleeve designed T-shirt worn by World War II servicemen. These soldiers found these garments so comfortable, they continued to wear them upon re-entering civilian life. By the 1950s, the T-shirt had been transformed into a popular outerwear garment. It was propelled into the national consciousness when rebellious movie idols such as James Dean and Marlon Brando appeared sporting T-shirts, as opposed to the more traditional sportshirt, with their blue jeans.

Perhaps the biggest sensation hitting the men's underwear scene occurred in 1934 with the arrival of ''jock-type'' underwear shorts. Advertisements proclaimed its virtues and variously noted that jock-type shorts, specially designed with the male figure in mind, featured a ''No gap opening with gentle support, elastic fabric, no buttons, no bulk, and no binding.'' By 1936 lightweight jock-type underwear were available in open weave and netlike fabric, while the quality of their porosity was developed to an unprecedented degree. During the early 1940s, boxer shorts, some of them made with grippers, continued to gain in popularity but never supplanted jock-type knitted underwear, which by 1946 was available with an inverted Y-front construction accompanied by advertisements which proclaimed them as ''scientifically perfected for correct male support.''

Synthetic fabrics appeared in the 1950s. Nylon underwear took the spotlight and was soon followed by polyester and cotton blends in a variety of colors. Men's fashion critics dubbed the period of the 1960s and early 1970s the ''Peacock Revolution.'' During this period men's underwear fashions took up a regard for style and color that had been historically reserved for outerwear apparel. Undershirts and shorts, for instance, were color coordinated and could be found in a broad assortment of colors, patterns, and fabrics.

Sleepwear. Until the 1920s, when central heating became a more widespread practice, the standard boys' sleep apparel consisted of a one-piece body suit with attached feet. As for men, a muslin nightshirt designed as a collarless pullover with long sleeves and side vents passed for the standard apparel. It usually extended below the calf, had three buttons in the front and a chest pocket. In either case, the standard men's and boys' nightwear was highly regarded for their properties of warmth.

By 1925, as central heat became increasingly commonplace, the switch from men's nightshirts to pajamas gathered full force as the warmth factor obtained from the wearing of nightshirts and body suits was no longer uppermost in mind. Compared with its uneventful past, sleepwear fashion changes, especially with regard to men, soared to dizzying heights. *Men's Wear* magazine noted that the tendency to discard nightshirts in order to take up the wearing of pajamas was everywhere in evidence. Pajama manufacturers sought to portray the new product as a vastly preferable alternative to the staid old nightshirt.

At the close of the 1920s and into the early 1930s, broadcloth competed with sateen for the number one position among sleepwear fabrics. Large bold striped pajamas were the preferred fashion of choice, with the more popular selections made available in a variety of striped patterns. By 1936 pajamas designed with extended waistbands and pleats for added comfort were, for the first time, promoted not just for the sleepwear but also for at-home leisure activities.

In the early 1960s the distinction between sleepwear and other men's leisure-wear related apparel grew even more blurred. Men's pajamas regularly incorporated fashions and designs from sportswear and dress shirts. By the 1970s the transformation of sleepwear into sporty leisure or lounge wear was complete. The leading sleepwear manufacturers were busy putting together mix-match coordinate packages of either similar or contrasting fabrics. Even the once-maligned nightshirt made a comeback as Pierre Cardin marketed a lightweight floral-striped version design especially for the holiday season. Marketing buzzwords such as ''Unjamas'' and ''Kimojamas'' were created to emphasis a pajamas' dual loungewear and sleepwear characteristics. During this time the prevailing wisdom appeared to be that whatever proved popular in sportswear was to be immediately adapted to sleepwear.

CURRENT CONDITIONS

Compared to other industries within the apparel group, the downsizing and elimination of establishments with the men's and boys' underwear and sleepwear industry was less severe, though by the mid-1990s it still was not clear whether the dust had finally settled. Further long term uncertainties were introduced in 1993 with the passage of the North American Free Trade Agreement and the international meetings for the General Agreement on Tariffs and Trade.

The leading firms ranked in descending order based on the percentage estimates of their 1992 market share were as follows: Fruit of the Loom Inc., (54.4 percent); Dawson Consolidation Products Inc., (17.2 percent); Salant Corp., (3.8 percent); Delta Apparel Inc., (2.9 percent); and Host Apparel Inc., (2.7 percent).

WORK FORCE

Industry employment data for the period of 1987-1992 reflected a trend of steady job losses and were consistent with the industry's trend of declining growth. In 1987 the number of employed production workers stood at 16,200 and by 1992 had fallen to 14,900. Several structural economic factors underscored this decline, especially the drop in middle-class spending on products manufactured by this industry. Further job eroding complications arose with the growing trend of U.S. producers to relocate apparel establishments abroad or to outsource to foreign locations work formerly performed within U.S. borders.

In 1990 the leading occupational categories for the men's and boys' sleepwear and nightwear industry were sewing machine operators; precision inspectors, testers and graders; pressing machine operators; and blue collar supervisors. The overall percentage of workers engaged in sewing machine operation was 56.0 percent, a number which dwarfed all other occupational categories. The Bureau of Labor Statistics has forecasted that most of these categories are expected to decline by the year 2005.

When compared against the measures of employment by gender and race for the U.S. manufacturing sector as a whole, women, Black and Hispanic workers were a greater presence in the apparel work force than most other manufacturing industries. In 1988 demographic data gathered from a survey taken by the Amalgamated Clothing and Textile Workers Union indicated that women workers made up 84.4 percent of the men's and boys' sleepwear and nightwear work force. Black workers accounted for 21.2 percent of the work force total, while minority workers accounted for a total of 36 percent of the employee count in the industry.

RESEARCH AND TECHNOLOGY

To date, the most aggressive industry response to its economic condition has been to step up its investment in state-of-the-art communication systems that facilitate the rapid transmission of sales information back to the producer level so as to immediately adjust production to consumer preferences. Referred to as the "quick response" system, this consumer driven process more finely integrates various phases of the production cycle, shortening the duration of various production steps and reducing inventory levels to a bare minimum.

In addition to the quick response system, firms active in this industry have directed major investments at computer controlled machinery. Such purchases are undertaken in an effort to increase productivity, to minimize waste, and to secure efficiencies in traditional apparel areas such as design, cutting, embroidery, sewing, finishing, ticketing and distribution operations. Independent of the particular area of operation, the overall investment goal was intended to reduce the amount of labor-time per task, which remained high when compared to other non-apparel group industry standards.

INDUSTRY INFORMATION SOURCES

Arpan, Jeffery S., de la Torres, Jose, and Brian Toyne, *The U.S. Apparel Industry: International Challenge, Domestic Response,* Atlanta, GA: Georgia State University, 1982.

Corbin, Harry A., *The Men's Clothing Industry: Colonial Through Modern Times,* New York: Fairchild Publications Inc., 1970.

Economic and Demographic Indicators of 42 ACTWU Industries, New York: Research Department Amalgamated Clothing and Textile Workers Union, 1988.

1993 Focus: An Economic Profile of the Apparel Industry, American Apparel Manufacturers Association, Arlington, VA., 1993.

Popkin, Martin, E., *Manufacture of Men's Clothing,* New York: Isaac Pittman & Sons, 1929.

Report of the General Executive Board, ACTWU and AFL-CIO Sixth Constitutional Convention, June 1993.

Schoeffler, O.E., and Gale, William, *Esquire's Encyclopedia of 20th Century Men's Fashions,* New York: McGraw-Hill, Inc., 1973.

U.S. Industrial Outlook 1994, Washington DC U.S. Department of Commerce, 1994.

Wingate, Isabel B., *Textile Fabrics and Their Selection,* Englewood Cliffs, NJ: Prentice-Hall, Inc., 1976.

—Dan King

SIC 2323

MEN'S AND BOYS' NECKWEAR

This category includes establishments primarily engaged in manufacturing men's and boys' neckties, scarves, and mufflers from purchased woven or knit fabrics. Knitting mills primarily engaged in manufacturing neckties, scarves, and mufflers are classified under **SIC 2253: Knit Outerwear Mills**.

INDUSTRY SNAPSHOT

Approximately 125 establishments were involved in the manufacture of men's and boys' neckwear in the United States in 1992. Since peaking in 1989, however, annual total industry sales have experienced a marked decline. For the three-year period from 1990 to 1992, the annual decline in industry sales averaged just over nine percent in real terms. The major economic pressures underlying this trend were attributed to a tapering off of personal consumption expenditures on clothes, rising inventories, ongoing structural change at the retail and wholesale level, deflationary price pressures, and a climate of pervasive uncertainty surrounding the implementation and negotiated renewal of several major international trade arrangements.

The status of international trade treaties are of central importance. To a large extent, they influence business decisions in a domestic industry that has historically remained highly vulnerable to foreign import competition. The progressive growth of the import share of the U.S. neckwear market during the 1980s and early 1990s has generated considerable alarm and prompted calls for protectionism among members of the Neckwear Association of America

(NAA), the principal trade association representing U.S. domestic neckwear manufacturers. In the NAA's opinion, any further reduction in current import duties would only exacerbate a trend that has already wreaked havoc upon U.S. domestic producers.

BACKGROUND AND DEVELOPMENT

To a large extent, even before the advent of the "quick response" system, the emergence and eventual growth of the twentieth-century neckwear industry was predicated on consumer trends. An antenna-like ability to stay abreast of fashion style and design construction changes proved to be a critical factor in determining whether or not a company survived as an industry leader. Other growth-related influences of comparable importance were: the parallel twentieth-century rise in the mass popularity of the collar-attached shirt and its changing fashion style and design construction changes, for which neckwear apparel served as a complementary article of clothing; utilization of breakthrough technological processes, usually occurring in non-neckwear-related apparel industries, which led to the progressive marginalization of hand-made tailored neckwear garments in favor of machine-made methods; and the socioeconomic phenomenon rising from the development of a professional/managerial strata in the U.S. work force.

Fashion-Related Growth. Although it is impossible to account for every significant change in neckwear and shirt designs occurring over the course of the twentieth century, it is possible to note the influence exercised by a few dominant styles that, on a decade-by-decade basis, account for expansion of the neckwear industry.

At the turn of the century, the two most prominent styles worn with the popular wing collar shirt were the sailor's knot Teck and Joinville ready-tied neckwear. The Teck was available with both straight and pointed ends, while Joinville was a straight-end only model. According to a 1900 Sears, Roebuck & Co. catalog, Teck and Joinville ties 6 inches wide and 34 inches long were "the most popular and swellest gentleman's scarf ever produced" and were made from the purest of specially imported woven silk. Such ties were available in an assortment of more than 300 designs and in almost every color and shade.

During the 1910s, the last decade before the appearance of the collar-attached shirt, the white, starched-collar, high-band Belmont shirt was an instant hit. It was worn with a narrow tie whose small knot was conspicuously located at the bottom of the shirt's collar. Also meeting with wide acceptance was the Henley detached collar shirt worn with a wide-body necktie covering much of the shirt's front. Two other new forms of ties were introduced during this period: the butterfly bow and the long tie formed in a sailor's knot.

Around 1920, the civilian collar-attached shirt hit the scene and became an instant success largely due to demobilized World War I veterans who wore a military version of the shirt and found it noticeably more comfortable than its collar-detached alternative. At about the same time, a highly significant design breakthrough also occurred in the neckwear industry. The invention of a tie with a relatively higher degree of resiliency owed its instant success to a technique that incorporated a loose stitch method to sew a bias-cut wool interlining (a line cutting diagonally across a fabric's grain) that retained the tie's original shape after being knotted and unknotted and went on to become an industry standard.

In the mid-1920s, marked changes in neckwear colors and fabrics were implemented. The ties were designed to capture the attention of women shoppers, who made up the largest component of consumers responsible for the purchase of men's neckwear items. By the late 1920s, the silk-and-wool tie rose to prominence thanks to its ripple weave design, which imparted a three dimensional effect. Among the growing number of college students, the wearing of ties had taken hold and become an everyday part of dress, even though preferred styles and fashions differed across geographic regions.

The Great Depression of the 1930s ushered in the first appearance of woolen ties, whose growing popularity threatened the then undisputed reign of silk fabric ties. During this time, the influence of British fashions was at its greatest in the U.S fashion mind as witnessed by the rise in popularity of two British formal evening wear bow ties: the straight club bow and the satin butterfly bow tied in a narrow knot.

In 1936 improvements in the design and construction of the wash tie led to its gaining widespread acceptance. Wash neckwear worn in a sailor's knot tie or bow tie was now available in a twin-ply design that fortified fabric strength and wrinkle resistance. Other significant advances in the design and construction of wash ties emanated from the introduction of spiral seams, which increased durability; improvements in bias cut shapes, which permitted a more perfect-looking knot; and hand bar tacking, which eliminated the unraveling of loose stitching during laundering. Due to the popularity of the widespread collar shirt, the wash bow tie and the large knot tie, known as the Windsor knot, rose to prominence.

World War II diverted silk fabric into the manufacture of parachutes, and rayon quickly became the number one tie fabric while wool maintained its solid hold on second. Wool's persistence in the marketplace was a result of its relatively wrinkle-resistant qualities along with the fact that a person was considered extremely fashionable to sport a wool tie to go along with the ever-popular button-down shirt and single-breasted three-button suit. During the same period of the silkless tie, the highly idiosyncratic hand-painted tie, usually appearing with sporting motifs, was introduced and proceeded to become a decade mainstay.

For the period from 1950 to 1960, three significant design and construction breakthroughs reverberated through the neckwear industry. Washable, nonwrinkle, and no-stretch Dacron knit ties hit the scene in the early 1950s. Next came wash-and-wear all-cotton ties, which, due to a special resin treatment process, retained their original shape and appearance after washing. Around 1957, a more opulent line of what fashion critics referred to as ''elegant air'' ties became popular. The trouble with these rather expensive ties was an inability to withstand stains. The solution arrived in 1959, when ties were treated with a special finish, namely Scotchgard, that permitted stains to be washed out with plain cold water.

Major Technological Manufacturing Changes. While the neckwear industry has probably never been in the forefront of introducing major technological innovations, it has proven readily adept at integrating other non-neckwear apparel industry technologies to its production processes.

Beyond a doubt, the appearance of the sewing machine in 1846 prompted a reorganization of the apparel industry in general, and neckwear in particular, whose impact was still being felt some 125 years after its introduction. In fact, the era of the sewing machine served as a bridge between the transformation of the neckwear industry from a handicraft to a machine-based mass production mode of automated industrial production. The sewing machine's introduction tended to quicken the pace of the nascent division of labor and job specialization trends spreading through the apparel industry. With the sewing machine serving as the critical operation point in the overall production process, work related to the handling of material prior to and after being sewn was radically overhauled in accordance with a division of labor based on job specialization. At that time, the productivity gains made from these changes were staggering.

Before long, technological progress in apparel manufacturing equipment began to take hold of the entire industry, leading to improvements in not only sewing machine technology but also in cutting and finishing operations. Electric powered portable cutting knives, motor-driven cloth spreading machines, and gas powered pressing machines displaced such devices as smaller hand-held irons.

Later manufacturing developments included a laser beam-directed cloth cutting process and the integration of computers used for pattern making, grading, and fabric utilization. In addition, the application of computers to other areas of manufacturing operations continued. To gain an appreciation of the impact technological change has had on productivity, a comparison of value added per production worker for the year of 1940 and 1989 stood at $10,000 and $44,857, respectively.

The Managerial/Professional Strata. One of the socioeconomic consequences of the rise of modern industry was the emergence and eventual growth of a managerial and professional strata. The same phenomenon is captured in the twentieth-century sociological term ''white collar worker.'' The customary white collar style of dress has consistently emphasized the shirt and tie as standard wear, which has given a major and lasting boost to the neckwear industry.

CURRENT CONDITIONS

Beginning in the late 1980s and extending well into the 1990s, neckwear establishments, like all segments of the apparel industry group, had been investing largely in state-of-the-art communications systems that rapidly transmit information that determines and reacts to consumer preferences in the marketplace. The consumer-driven process, coined ''quick response,'' integrates aspects of shortening the production cycle with productivity improvements and inventory reductions via the immediate relay of information concerning consumer tastes to manufacturing establishments.

Beginning at the retail level, quick response operates by tracking computer-recorded sales information, which is passed on to manufacturers, analyzed, and then acted upon to determine the appropriate supply level of material destined to be transformed and most likely sold in the immediate future. At the same time, in order to determine what neckwear consumers will want to purchase in the near future, quick response compiles the results of consumer surveys measuring preferences.

Most major distribution outlets, at both the wholesale and retail level, have implemented the quick response system. Their incentive to do so translates into an acceleration of ''hot selling'' items appearing on store shelves and a significant reduction in order turn-around time.

In addition to quick response systems, neckwear firms have directed major investments at computer-controlled automated machines. Such efforts are undertaken in order to increase productivity and secure production efficiencies in the areas of design, cutting, embroidery, sewing, finishing, ticketing, and various distribution operations. Independent of the particular area of operation, most investment projects are undertaken with the intention of reducing the labor-time component per task, which remains excessively high compared to other nonapparel industry group standards.

Typically, larger neckwear firms, because of their economies of scale and access to internal finance, are better positioned to implement high-cost technological advances. As a result, the pattern of technological change has been anything but uniform across all neckwear establishments. Nevertheless, all firms, whether large or small, recognize that failure to adopt technological advances jeopardizes their future survival.

INDUSTRY LEADERS

In 1989 approximately 127 establishments, each with an average staff of 63, were engaged in the production of men's and boys' neckwear. When ranked by major area of regional concentration, the largest number of establishments were found in the Middle Atlantic, Pacific, and South Atlantic regions. If ranked by state, New York led the way with 60, followed by California with 17, and New Jersey with 10.

It was estimated in 1992 that the leading 35 men's and boys' neckwear companies accounted for approximately $375 million of industry sales. In descending order based on market share, the dominant companies in the men's and boys' neckwear industry were: Wemco Inc. (15.2 percent); Echo Design Group Inc. (12.3 percent); Mallory and Church Corp. (8 percent); Superba Inc. (6 percent); and M. Aron Corp. (5.6 percent). In every case but one, the top 35 companies were privately held corporations.

WORK FORCE

After making adjustments for business cycle fluctuations, total employment in the men's and boys' neckwear industry remained flat for the period from 1982 to 1992. Total employment in the neckwear industry in 1992 was estimated at about 8,000 workers, approximately 7,000 of which were classified as production workers. Compared to the previous year, total

employment and production employment rose by 14.3 and 16.7 percent, respectively. When looking at the five-year period covering 1987 to 1992, however, there has been only modest growth in the employment categories. For instance, the average annual percent change in neckwear total employment was approximately 1.9 percent. A similar measure specified for production workers averaged 2.8 percent. Over the same period, the average annual change in hourly earnings rose by a meager 0.5 percent in nominal terms.

In 1990 the major occupational categories for the neckwear industry included: sewing machine operators; precision inspectors, testers, and graders; pressing machine operators; and blue collar worker supervisors. About 56 percent of the work force was engaged in sewing machine operations, while the remaining categories each accounted for about 3.1 percent of the work force.

AMERICA AND THE WORLD

The subject of trade and the U.S. neckwear industry has always been a highly contentious issue. Since 1973, world trade in textiles and apparel has been regulated under the international agreement known as the Multifiber Arrangement (MFA). Yet only a portion of neckwear category types—not including most silk neckwear categories—are covered by this agreement, and no specific quota structures have been put into effect. For this reason, protectionist-minded U.S. neckwear producers have historically turned to and been successful at lobbying the U.S. government to impose tariff or import duties.

A trade agreement put into effect from 1981 through 1987, which specified a staged reduction in the level of neckwear tariff duties, highlights the industry's import vulnerability. The overall results of a report prepared for the NAA by Economic Consulting Services Inc. were less than favorable. The U.S. neckwear industry experienced a sustained decline in the level of domestic profits, production employment fell from 5,300 to 4,800 workers, and most strikingly these negative trends occurred over a period when U.S. consumption of neckwear was on the increase. During the same period, the amount of neckwear imported increased by 356 percent, going from approximately 373 thousand dozen to 1,698 thousand dozen. The report indicated that Korean and Chinese neckwear manufacturers gained the most market share throughout the period.

With the 1993 passage of the Uruguay Round of the General Agreement on Tariffs and Trade (GATT), the provisions contained in the MFA were to be supplanted and phased out gradually over the course of ten years. Much to the displeasure of the NAA, the terms of the GATT called for a significant reduction in worldwide tariff duties. Difficult as it is to separate fact from speculation, in light of the less than positive results experienced by the industry during the previous period of falling import tariffs, the implementation of the provisions called for by GATT was not expected to promote optimism among most of the industry's U.S. producers.

One important response undertaken by U.S. neckwear manufacturers to counter the gains made by lower priced import competition was to take advantage of tariff provision 9802 (formerly 807), as set forth by the Harmonized Tariff Schedule of the United States (HTSUS). The provision allows foreign factories to assemble finished neckwear from U.S. components, which are then reimported into the U.S domestic market with duty charged only on the foreign value added. In the past, Mexico and the Caribbean Basin countries were the largest recipients of HTSUS 9802 trade. With the passage of the North America Free Trade Agreement (NAFTA), Caribbean Basin countries expressed concern that 9802 economic activity in their region would shift eventually to Mexico's advantage.

INDUSTRY INFORMATION SOURCES

Arpan, Jeffery S., Jose de la Torres, and Brian Toyne. *The U.S. Apparel Industry: International Challenge, Domestic Response.* Atlanta, GA: Business Publishing Division, Georgia State University, 1982.

Corbin, Harry A. *The Men's Clothing Industry: Colonial Through Modern Times.* New York: Fairchild Publications Inc., 1970.

Economic and Demographic Indicators of 42 ACTWU Industries. New York: Research Department Amalgamated Clothing and Textile Workers Union, 1988.

Focus: An Economic Profile of the Apparel Industry. Arlington, VA: American Apparel Manufacturers Association, 1992.

Manufacturing USA: Industry Analyses, Statistics and Leading Companies, 3rd ed. Detroit: Gale, 1993.

Popkin, Martin E. *Manufacture of Men's Clothing.* New York: Isaac Pittman & Sons, 1929.

Report of the General Executive Board. ACTWU and AFL-CIO Sixth Constitutional Convention, June 1993.

Schoeffler, O. E., and William Gale. *Esquire's Encyclopedia of 20th Century Men's Fashions.* New York: Mc Graw-Hill, Inc., 1973.

Statement of the Neckwear Association of America, Inc., in Connection With the Uruguay Round Market Access Negotiations. Economic Consulting Services Inc., 1989.

U.S. Industrial Outlook 1993. Washington, DC: U.S. Department Commerce, 1993.

—Daniel King

SIC 2325

MEN'S AND BOYS' SEPARATE TROUSERS AND SLACKS

This category includes establishments primarily engaged in manufacturing men's and boys' separate trousers and slacks from purchased woven or knit fabrics, including jeans, dungarees, and jean-cut casual slacks. Establishments primarily engaged in manufacturing complete suits are classified in **SIC 2311: Men's and Boys' Suits, Coats, and Overcoats**; those manufacturing workpants (excluding jeans and dungarees) are classified in **SIC 2326: Men's and Boys' Work Clothing.** Knitting mills primarily engaged in manufacturing men's and boys' separate trousers and slacks are classified in **SIC 2253: Knit Outerwear Mills.**

INDUSTRY SNAPSHOT

Approximately 430 establishments were engaged in the manufacture of men's and boys' separate trousers and slacks in 1992. Altogether, these establishments were responsible for an inflation-adjusted total product estimated at $5.3 billion. This figure remained in line with an overall declining trend in the industry that peaked in 1987 and has fallen every year since. If viewed over the five-year period covering 1987 to 1992, the annual percentage change in the value of total product shipments averaged a negative .35 percent.

The lackluster performance of the men's and boys' separate trousers and slacks industry has been attributed to several concurrent economic pressures. A long-term decline has occurred in overall income levels of the middle class, who were previously responsible for a disproportionate share of personal consumption expenditures spent on all types of clothing. Second, a shakeout and ongoing structural change at both the retail and wholesale levels has disrupted established lines of distribution. Third, price competition from both domestic and foreign producers has held positive price movements, usually associated with upturns in economic activity, in check; as a result, capacity utilization rates have not improved in a manner experienced in previous periods of economic recovery. Finally, the lingering overhang of takeover debt piled up from the late 1980s has exerted a dampening effect on company profits and growth.

On the positive side, the weakness in the U.S dollar has spurred the export sales of men's and boys' trousers and slacks. In 1989 export sales, measured in current terms, accounted for 6.7 percent of total product sales. They rose to 8.7 percent in 1990, to 10.7 percent in 1991, and to 14.0 percent in 1992. Furthermore, while the industry itself continued to experience annual declines, the larger firms had managed to gain market share. Able to take advantage of their economies of scale, the larger firms were well positioned to invest internally generated funds to obtain apparel-related state-of-art technological operations.

ORGANIZATION AND STRUCTURE

In 1989 approximately 449 establishments were engaged in the production of men's and boys' trousers and slacks. These establishments employed approximately 165 employees per establishment. For the same year, the average value added per production worker was $44,857, a figure that was significantly below the overall average of $105,881 calculated for 459 U.S. manufacturing industries. If grouped in order of their major area of census region concentration, the largest number of establishments were located in the East South Central, West South Central and South Atlantic regions. Alternatively, when ranked by the number of establishments per state, Georgia was first with 61, followed by California with 49, Texas and Alabama with 40 each, New York with 38, and Pennsylvania with 33.

In 1992 it was estimated that top 75 companies accounted for approximately $1.6 billion worth of industry sales. In descending order based on market share, the dominant companies in the men's and boys' trousers and slacks industry were: Levi Strauss Associates Inc. (27.8 percent); its subsidiary, Levi Strauss and Co. (26.6 percent); Levi Strauss and Co. Jeans Co. (8.9 percent); Jordache Enterprises Inc. (5.1 percent); Lee Apparel Company Inc. (3.9 percent); VF Corp. Wrangler Division, (3.3 percent); and Haggar Apparel Co. (2.8 percent). In every case none of the companies were traded in public stock exchanges.

Data available from 1982 and 1987 indicated that the primary materials consumed by the men's and boys' trousers and slack industry when ranked by cost came in the form of: various materials, parts, and containers; broadwoven fabrics; and knit fabrics. The major sources of sector input supply were from imports, manufacturers of broadwoven fabrics, apparel made from purchased materials, and knit fabric mills. If disaggregated, the approximate total product share broken down by the category of its major product class was: men's and boys' jeans (54.8 percent), men's and boys' separate trousers and slacks (29.7 percent), contract and commission work of the various product categories (nearly 14.5 percent). The principal economic sectors or industries responsible for the purchase of men's and boys' trousers and slacks were private personal consumption expenditures equal to 83 percent, followed by other apparel manufacturers with 12 percent.

BACKGROUND AND DEVELOPMENT

The present configuration of companies active in the U.S. men's and boys' trousers and slacks industry typically prosper or decline according to their ability to satisfy consumer tastes. However, a historic amalgamation of several dominant political, social, and economic forces have given rise to the formation of the industry in late twentieth-century form. Several early mutually reinforcing influences have combined to propel the industry into its current state. Chief among these influences were eighteenth- and nineteenth-century wars and their attendant political events, fashion and design construction changes, technological advances leading to mass production methods, and the twentieth-century appearance of the professional/managerial occupational strata.

Prior to the successful conclusion of the American Revolution, trousers were worn by the ruling class nobility and the upper middle class for the purpose of denoting social status and wealth. Typically, these trousers, or breeches, as they were then called, were considered works of art produced by highly skilled craftsmen. Although they had some utilitarian function, no effort was spared in trying to embellish these slacks, which were made from the finest of fabrics and embellished with ornaments of distinction.

The outcome of the American Revolution thrust an emergent and growing middle class—composed of industrialists, merchants, storekeepers, and their various assistants or professionals—to the forefront of political and economic activity and had a profound impact on men's fashion. The fashion influences of the European nobility were quickly discarded, having been deemed the garb of counter-revolutionaries. Gone from the fashion scene were ornately designed trousers. Instead, pants manufactured by U.S. producers gained prominence, while those woven from imported fabrics were looked upon with political disfavor.

Indeed, the day George Washington was inaugurated as the first president of the United States, he sported a suit coat and pants of fine dark brown broadcloth woven in one of the regional hotbeds of the American Revolution, Worcester, Massachusetts. At this time an emphasis on simplicity and utility served as an underlying principle of what was then regarded as ''good taste'' in dress. To a large extent, no doubt, this reflected the equivalent of a patriotic fashion statement meant to repudiate the cultural values and tastes of the recently vanquished ruling class nobility.

Modifications in men's slacks reflected changing living conditions, and this was especially true with the rapid growth of industrialization and the consequent rise of urban development. The penchant for utilitarian designed apparel also contributed to making the possibility of producing a large volume of ready-made pants a practical reality. Tailors could now cut pants in batches and, after sewing them, store them as inventory on demand or display them on retailers' shelves.

Early advertising innovations at the retail level also played a significant role in expanding the trousers market. In Boston, George W. Simmons made extensive use of newspaper advertising when in 1842 he began to promote slacks using enclosed window displays rather than simply hanging or stacking trousers outside his shop. Simmons was also reported to have launched balloons announcing sales and to have established a successful mail order department. Similar efforts, using various novel forms of advertising meant to enhance brand recognition, were undertaken by Jacob Reed and Brooks Bros.

Almost from the end of the American Revolution until 1860, the embryonic U.S. apparel industry, including the budding trouser business, was nurtured by a highly protectionist government policy. Up until 1816, the duty for imported slacks stood at 25 percent. In 1816 the tariff increased to 30 percent and in 1828 it was raised again to 50 percent, where it remained until lifted in 1860. And during the same period, should the imported trousers happen to have arrived by foreign vessels, an additional tariff was applied.

After 1860 it was thought that U.S. producers could hold their own against foreign competitors. More than half a century of protectionist tariffs had served the infant industry well. It provided the industry with the necessary breathing space to mature and eventually enter the arena of the global marketplace with a world class level of productivity. Confidence in the industry's second-to-none productivity level was warranted, due primarily to the introduction and diffusion of sewing machine technology by the late 1850s. When compared to high quality hand-sewn articles, sewing machine-assisted labor effectively reduced the amount of labor time needed per garment, which in turn translated into a significant decrease in its selling costs.

From the standpoint of the workers, however, the sewing machine's productivity-enhancing virtues were anything but confidence instilling. The widespread diffusion of the sewing machine quickly eliminated the need for highly paid skilled laborers performing hand sewing operations. At the same time it permitted the employment of semiskilled employees, whose downward spiralling wages were to gravitate at a bare minimum subsistence level for many years to come. Whether employed in domestic tenement quarters or in the factory sweat shops, working conditions were abysmal, health hazards went unchecked, and child labor was not uncommon. For the next couple of decades, the ranks of semiskilled workers grew, and working conditions became more miserable with each successive wave of immigration. It was not until the formation of apparel-based trade unions that such conditions were put to an end.

The erection of a protectionist tariff wall also played an important role in the development of a domestic mill industry from which trouser manufacturers were able to obtain reliable supplies in a prompt and reliable manner. Trousers manufacturers had previously been dependent on import supply sources; deliveries were erratic at best and prohibitively large sums of money were required in advance of supplies. The development of the trouser industry also received an additional impetus from the rise of a national transportation network.

Up until the outbreak of the Civil War, manufacturers and retailers of ready-made pants confronted a persistent problem—the absence of any reliable sizing standards to assure that mass-produced clothing would fit properly. The solution arrived from a study performed by the U.S. Army's Philadelphia Quartermaster Depot, which had collected body size measurement data on over a million recruits and conscripts. The depot organized these measurements into tables of standard body proportions and thus created a set of data that could be readily applied to the standardization of manufactured civilian garments.

Body sizing standards, coupled with the diffusion of sewing machine technology, radically transformed the clothing industry in terms of heightening the division of labor in the tasks leading up to and following the performance of sewing operations. By 1895 these changes resulted in what came to be known as the ''bundle system'' of production, where one or more workers performed a single operation on a repetitive basis. Once the bundle limit was reached, the work in process was passed on to the next station of workers performing another distinct operation. Such a process would then continue until work on the entire trouser garment was completed. Interestingly, over the course of the last 100 years, the continual refinement, modification, and ability to integrate new technologies has rendered the bundle system one of the more flexible and enduring methods of production still in widespread use throughout the apparel industry.

Except for the introduction, diffusion, and subsequent refinements in sewing machine technology, few real improvements in non-sewing machine technology or machinery transpired. Things changed in 1880, when machinery and methods performed in cutting room stations witnessed the introduction of the sword knife and slotted table. Later came the electrically operated knife, which though immobile, proved to be the forerunner of the more modern portable, electrically driven assortment of cutting tools. In turn, the widespread application of portable rotary and reciprocating electric knives would not have been possible without earlier advances in the construction of electric motors. In the late 1890s pressing operations were transformed. Operations reliant upon gas- and coal-heated irons were replaced first by the steam pressing iron and later the steam pressing machine.

Other technological developments late in the twentieth century featured a laser beam-directed cloth-cutting process along with the integration of computers utilized for pattern making, grading, and fabric selection. The extension of computer-aided job processes to most areas of trouser production was expected to continue. Such efforts are in step with the industry's drive to raise the level of productivity, a measure usually captured by changes in the value added per production worker.

CURRENT CONDITIONS

The downsizing and elimination of establishments within the men's and boys' trousers and slacks industry was recognized as an established trend by the late 1980s. In the mid 1990s, it remained to be seen whether this trend had been entirely played out. Further long term uncertainties were thrown into this mix with the 1993 passage of the North American Free Trade Agreement (NAFTA) and the General Agreement on Tariffs and Trade (GATT).

By the late 1980s, the entire apparel U.S. industry group had been hit hard by the erosion of middle-class income earners, who generally accounted for a majority of apparel purchases. To a large extent, this was the outcome of the upward redistribution of national income consistent with the supply-side economic policies pursued during the era of the administrations of

presidents Ronald Reagan and George Bush. The growing trend toward the foreign relocation of apparel establishments and foreign outsourcing of apparel-related work formerly performed within U.S. borders no doubt added further job-eroding complications. Apparel import competition leading to the progressive market share deterioration of U.S. apparel manufacturers also contributed to the industry's shakeout.

The most far-reaching domestic response to the trouser and slack industry's deteriorating economic conditions has been to invest in state-of-the-art communications systems facilitating the rapid flow of information used to immediately react to and determine consumer preferences formed in the marketplace. This consumer-driven process, known as "quick response," integrates numerous dimensions of the production cycle with an eye toward shortening the cycle's duration. Productivity improvements can be made and inventory levels can be adjusted through the immediate transmission of consumer taste information to manufacturing establishments.

Starting at the retail level, quick response tracks computer-recorded sales information, which is relayed to manufacturers, analyzed, and then used to determine an appropriate supply of material inputs destined to be transformed and most likely to be sold in near future. At the same time, to determine what trousers will be demanded in the immediate future, quick response compiles the results of consumer surveys in order to target what slacks are most likely to be sold.

Most of the major distribution outlets, at both the retail and wholesale level, have implemented the quick response system. Their incentive to do so translates into acceleration of "hot selling" slacks and a marked reduction in order turnaround time.

In addition to the quick response system, men's and boys' trousers and slacks firms have directed major investments at computer-controlled automated machinery in an effort to increase productivity and secure production efficiencies in the areas of design, cutting, embroidery, sewing, finishing, ticketing, and various distribution operations. Independent of the particular area of operation, most investment projects were undertaken with the intention of reducing the labor-time component per task, which remains excessively high relative to other nonapparel industry group standards.

Because of their economies of scale and access to internally generated funds, the larger trousers and slacks firms have been better positioned to implement technological advances. This has resulted in a pattern of technological change that is anything but uniform across the entire men's and boys' slacks industry. Just the same, across the industry it was recognized that if these changes were not forthcoming, many firms would probably not see the dawn of the twenty-first century.

WORK FORCE

For the period from 1987 to 1991, total employment in the men's and boys' trousers and slacks industry has experienced a sharp decline. In 1987 total employment was about 93,300, 82,300 of which were classified as production workers. By 1991 there were 84,200 employed in the industry, and 72,800 of them were classified as production workers. Relevant comparisons between the two years indicate that the level of total employment fell by almost 10 percent, while the level of production workers declined by 11.5 percent. Over the same four-year period, the average annual change in nominal wages was slightly above 4.3 percent.

In 1988 demographic data gathered from an apparel industry survey undertaken by the Amalgamated Clothing and Textile Workers Union indicated that women workers made up 84.2 percent of the workforce, black workers 21.2 percent, while the percentage of minority workers was just shy of 36 percent.

In 1990 the major occupational categories for the men's and boys' trousers and slacks industry were sewing machine operators; precision inspectors, testers and graders; pressing machine operators; and blue-collar worker supervisors. Nearly 56 percent of the workforce was engaged in sewing machine operations. The remaining occupational categories each accounted for about 3.1 percent of the workforce. The Bureau of Labor Statistics forecasted that most of these occupational categories would decline by the year 2005. Assuming the forward path of the industry's productivity trend, sewing machine operators are projected to experience the steepest decrease of all the major occupational categories.

INDUSTRY INFORMATION SOURCES

Arpan, Jeffery S., Jose de la Torres, and Brian Toyne. *The U.S. Apparel Industry: International Challenge, Domestic Response*. Atlanta: Business Publishing Division, College of Business Administration Georgia State University, 1982.

Corbin, Harry A. *The Men's Clothing Industry: Colonial Through Modern Times*. New York: Fairchild Publications Inc., 1970.

Economic and Demographic Indicators of 42 ACTWU Industries. New York: Research Department Amalgamated Clothing and Textile Workers Union, 1988.

Focus: An Economic Profile of the Apparel Industry. Arlington, VA: American Apparel Manufacturers Association, 1992.

Manufacturing USA: Industry Analyses, Statistics and Leading Companies 3rd edition. Detroit: Gale, 1993.

Popkin, Martin, E. *Manufacture of Men's Clothing*. New York: Isaac Pittman & Sons, 1929.

Report of the General Executive Board. ACTWU and AFL-CIO Sixth Constitutional Convention, June 1993.

Schoeffler, O. E., and William Gale. *Esquire's Encyclopedia of 20th Century Men's Fashions*. New York: McGraw-Hill, Inc., 1973.

U.S. Industrial Outlook 1993. Washington DC: U.S. Department Commerce, 1993.

—Daniel King

SIC 2326

MEN'S AND BOYS' WORK CLOTHING

This category includes establishments primarily engaged in manufacturing men's and boys' work shirts, workpants (excluding jeans and dungarees), other work clothing, and washable service apparel. Establishments primarily engaged in manufacturing separate trousers and slacks (including jeans and dungarees) are classified in **SIC 2325: Men's and Boys' Separate Trousers and Slacks**.

INDUSTRY SNAPSHOT

About 225 establishments active in the manufacture of men's and boys' work clothing accounted for an inflation adjusted value of total product shipments of $1.2 billion in 1992. This figure, though up by 6.1 percent from the previous year, remained in line with the five year declining trend, which peaked during 1987 and 1988 and was some 13.2 percent below the peak period's level of performance. When viewed over a five year period covering 1987-1992, the annual percentage change in the inflation adjusted value of total product shipments fell by an average of 2.2 percent.

In certain cases, attempts to note statistical trends past 1987 meet with difficulties as this was the year that the U.S. Department of Commerce's Bureau of Census rearranged some of the apparel industries' categories. Prior to 1987, the men's and boys' work clothing was classified as SIC 2328 and included jeans and dungarees among its product classifications. In 1987 jeans and dungarees were excluded from men's and boys' work clothes and assigned to **SIC 2325: Men's and Boys' Separate Trousers and Slacks**.

Unlike other apparel industries, which are variously categorized within the apparel industry group according to gender, age, and body part specific garments, the men's and boys' work clothes industry produced apparel garments extending from the neck down to the feet. These included: work aprons, coveralls, work jackets and laboratory coats, institutionalized medical uniforms, work overalls and overall jackets, work pants, washable service industry apparel, work shirts, and non-tailored uniforms.

Following years of consecutive growth, the men's and boys' work clothing industry garnered a reputation for being the only recession-proof industry. This was in stark contrast to other industries within the apparel group who were highly susceptible to business cycle swings. Things changed when the work wear industry entered a protracted period of stagnant to falling growth beginning with the recession of 1981-1982. Well into the 1990s the industry had yet to regain the level of its former years of prosperity.

To a great extent the industry's woes were precipitated from its demand side. A steady and prolonged fall-off of its once core industrial and agricultural customer base left the industry in shambles. This resulted in considerable intra-industry price competition and a run-up in unused manufacturing capacity. These same economic forces were also responsible for the industry's downsizing and served to explain why the total number of establishments went from 255 in 1987 to about 225 in 1992, a decline of 11.8 percent.

A glance at the movement of some of the industry's more dominant product categories for the period of 1981-1990 provided further evidence of stagnation and decline. In terms of consumer purchases of men's work pants, for 1981-1985 the annual volume averaged around 19.0 million units. During the next five years the average annual volume fell to 16.4 million units, declining by about 13.5 percent. For the category of men's overalls, during 1981-1985 the annual volume of consumer purchases averaged 8.2 million units. Over the next five years its average annual volume fell to 6.7 million units, registering a decline of 18.3 percent. Finally, for the category of men's work shirts, for 1981-1985 the average annual volume of consumer purchases was 35.7 million units, while for the period of 1986-1990 the average annual volume dropped to 31.6 million units, a decline of 11.5 percent.

Unlike what was happening in other apparel industries, the men's and boys' work clothing industry had remained relatively immune from the deluge of imports wreaking havoc on the domestic markets of their apparel counterparts. On the work wear industry's input side however, imports were playing an important role as more companies were turning to inputs to lower labor and material costs so as to reverse the long term slide in profit margins. To this end the "outsourcing" of work formerly performed within establishments to contractors outside U.S. borders had become an established trend.

One major demand-side development, which was expected to fill the void left by the fall-off in industrial/agricultural markets, was the ongoing structural shift toward a service based economy. Such a movement carried with it the potential for opening up a vast areas of untapped demand for washable non-tailored uniforms in health care facilities, personal care services, fast food chains and other food preparation and service institutions. In addition, a trend towards the wearing of uniforms by corporations seeking to enhance their employees and company image was afoot. Viewed as a strategy to build customer recognition and loyalty, the wearing of corporate uniforms had already become an established trend among some airlines, banks, fitness centers, retail chain stores, and major hotels.

BACKGROUND AND DEVELOPMENT

In a less spectacular manner, the origins of the ready-to-wear work clothes industry followed the historical trajectory of the more colorful mens' apparel industry. With the onset of the industrial era in the early nineteenth century spurring the transformation from rural to urban life, the social demand for working apparel soon surpassed the efforts of custom tailors and housewives. In their place developed the early manufacture of mass produced work clothes which, if possible, were typically shunned due to their inferior quality and wearing discomfort. As improvements in fabrics began to seize hold of the men's apparel industry, any notion of their reputed inferiority went to the wayside. During the same period, the widespread diffusion of sewing machine technology provided added impetus to the industry's emergence and boosted its output to unprecedented levels. During the Civil War, an extensive survey compiled on the height and chest measurements of more than one million soldiers provided the first mass of statistical data on the form and build of U.S. men. Immediately after the war these results were made available to producers of men's ready-made work clothes, providing a more scientific basis on which to improve their fit.

A milestone episode that dramatically accelerated the need for ready-made work clothes occurred with the Gold Rush of 1848. The prospect of getting rich drew thousands of men westward to pan or mine for gold. Figuring that these adventurers would need tents for shelter, Levi Strauss journeyed to California with a supply of heavy fabrics for tent making. Among these fabrics was a French material referred to as "de Nime," which U.S. tongues later pronounced as "denim." Aware that a need for durable work clothes was not being met, Strauss began to make workpants from denim that featured large back pockets to hold mining tools. By adding metal rivets to strengthen the durability of the pockets, Strauss hit on an idea that brought him almost instant success—and the men's work clothes industry started booming. The continued westward migration, not just in California but in the prairie and mountain states, developed into a steady market for ready-made work clothes for decades to come. To meet the growing demand, large work clothes manufacturing centers sprung up in Chicago and St. Louis.

Beginning near the early twentieth century, the steady growth of a work force comprised of semi-skilled and unskilled laborers engaged in various mass production-related occupations—across the entire range of manufacturing and agricultural industries—proved a boon to work clothes producers. After World War II, an unprecedented rise in the consumption of consumer durables was matched by the growth of a repair industry whose workers, more often than not, were outfitted with non-tailored work uniforms. To the envy of the non-work clothes apparel industries who regularly incurred the economic vicissitudes of the traditional business cycle, the work clothes industry proceeded along its expansionary path in a steady manner until the onset of its stagnation period commencing in the early 1980s.

ORGANIZATION AND STRUCTURE

In 1989 approximately 237 establishments were active in the production of men's and boys' work clothing. The average establishment employed approximately 143 employees per establishment. For the same year the average value added per production worker was $28,540, a figure that fell significantly below an overall average of $105,881 calculated for 459 U.S. manufacturing establishments. Grouped by their order of density within the regions surveyed by the 1987 Census of Manufacturers, the largest concentrations of the industry's establishments were respectively located in the East South Central, West South Central, and South Atlantic regions of the United States. When ranked by the number of establishments per state, Tennessee was first with 29, closely followed by Alabama with 28, Mississippi with 25, and California with 22.

In 1992, from among the top 75 companies active in the men's and boys' work clothing industry, the dominant companies ranked by their estimated market share were: VF Corp.'s Red Kap Industries, (11.9 percent); Angelica Corp., (7.7 percent); Riverside Manufacturing Co., (5.8 percent); Unitog Co., (5.3 percent); Superior Surgical Mfg. Co. Inc., (4.7 percent); and Work Wear Corporation Inc., (1.9 percent). Both Red Kap and Angelica were divisions, Riverside and Work Wear were privately held, while Unitog and Superior were traded in public stock exchanges.

Input data available from 1982 and 1987 indicated that the primary materials consumed by the men's and boys' work clothing industry when ranked by cost were: materials, parts, containers, and supplies; broadwoven fabrics; and knit fabrics. The primary sources of input supply were from imports, broadwoven fabric mills, apparel made from purchased materials, and knit fabric mills. For the same two years, the share of the industry's total output disaggregated by its major product category indicated that men's and boys' work shirts accounted for 23.5 percent; men's and boys' work clothing and washable service apparel registered 58.3 percent; contract and commission work on men's and boys' work clothing in general was 9.5 percent; and men's and boys' work clothing not specified by any kind accounted for 8.7 percent.

During the late 1980s and into the 1990s, the distribution network servicing the men's and boys' work clothing industry was undergoing a fundamental transformation. For articles like washable uniforms and service related apparel, laundry rental companies had historically been the major source of distribution to large companies. But when corporate demand for a more customized look requiring a greater assortment of new fabrics, styles and colors started to reverberate through the industry, many of the industry's larger firms bypassed the traditional laundry rental channel and opened their own corporate accounts, through which they sold directly to the wearing customer. As a result, domestic fabric mills, who supplied materials to the work clothing industry, also began a closer working relationship with work wear manufacturers in a joint effort meant to better serve the industry's developing corporate accounts.

For individual purchases of work clothes, mass merchandisers and discount outlets accounted for the largest share of sales, followed by smaller specialty stores located outside of major urban areas. Catalog sales picked up noticeably during the late 1980s and

1990s and were expected to show continued strength into the future. A development of a more recent kind featured the appearance of farm/fleet stores. These were large stores located in rural areas which carried a wide assortment of work related items ranging from work clothes to farm equipment. The stores' core customer base consisted of farmers and truckers who wore functional work clothes for occupational reasons. Two major operators active throughout the Midwest were Blain Farm & Fleet and Mills Farm & Fleet.

WORK FORCE

Total employment in the men's and boys' work clothing industry was 33,000 in 1987, of which 29,000 were classified as production workers. By 1992, total employment had fallen to 31,100, of which 27,300 were production workers. For the entire period total employment fell by 5.8 percent while production employment declined slightly more by 5.9 percent. From 1987-1992 industry real wages had fallen without interruption, while value added per production worker rose, though not in a dramatic manner, suggesting that productivity improvements and real wages were moving in opposite directions.

In 1990, the dominant occupational categories for the work clothes industry were: sewing machine operators; inspectors, precision inspectors, and testers; blue collar work supervisors; pressing machine operators; hand packers and packagers; and hand cutters and trimmers. Close to 56.0 percent of the work force was engaged in sewing operations, while the remaining categories individually fell within the 3.1 to 2.0 range. According to an occupational survey undertaken by the Bureau of Labor Statistics (BLS), all of the major occupational categories within the work clothes industry were forecasted to experience significant declines by the year 2005. Given the more or less forward trajectory of the industry's productivity trend, the decline in sewing machine operators was expected to encounter the steepest decline.

Compared to their employment rates in the overall manufacturing sector, women, minority, black, and Hispanic participation rates within the industry far exceed their national counterparts. A 1987 survey conducted by the Amalgamated Clothing and Textile Workers Union indicated that women comprised 83.3 percent of the industry's work force, against a national average of 32.9 percent of women in the total work force. The percentage of black workers was 21.2 percent against a national figure of 10.4 percent. Hispanic workers accounted for 20.7 percent of the industry's work force compared to a national average of 8.7 percent. Taken collectively, in 1987 the total number of minority workers active in this industry's work force was 35.9 percent.

CURRENT CONDITIONS

The highly anticipated salvation of the men's and boys' work clothing industry was expected to come in the form of the U.S. economy's structural shift to service producing industries and occupations where career/work apparel tended to be the norm. According to BLS employment projections, approximately nine out of every 10 new jobs were to be added in service providing industries such as transportation, communications, public utilities, trade, health care, finance, insurance, real estate, food handling and production, janitors, and government. At the same time, the increasing trend towards a cultural climate of corporate uniformed-employees—as a means to foster brand recognition and customer loyalty—was already breathing new life into the industry as well as holding out the promise of future growth.

A question remained as to whether the service economy rescue scenario would arrive in time to stem the industry's downsizing. Being the first to invest in the latest apparel technologies, the larger firms were better positioned to seize the day and offer a greater volume of high quality garments at lower cost than their lesser endowed rivals. No doubt the industry's future looked bright, but whether the larger firms would cast an obliterating shadow over their smaller competitors remained uncertain.

INDUSTRY INFORMATION SOURCES

Arnold, Pauline, and Percival White, *Clothes and Cloth: America's Apparel Business*, New York: Holiday House Publishers, 1961.

de Marly, Diana, *Working Dress: A History of Occupational Clothing*, New York: Holmes and Meier Publishers, Inc., 1986.

Economic and Demographic Indicators of 42 ACTWU Industries, New York: Research Department, Amalgamated Clothing and Textile Workers Union, 1988.

Fairchild Fact File: Men's Career/Work Wear, New York: Market Research Division, Fairchild Publications, 1987.

Focus: An Economic Profile of the Apparel Industry, Arlington, VA: American Apparel Manufacturers Association, 1993.

Jarnow, Jeannette, and Miriam Guerreiro, *Inside the Fashion Business*, New York: Macmillan Publishing Company, 1991.

Lehman Brothers, *The Clothes Line*, December, 1993

Manufacturing USA: Industry Analyses, Statistics and Leading Companies, 3rd Edition, Detroit: Gale Research Inc., 1993.

Schoeffler, O.E. and William Gale, *Esquire's Encyclopedia of 20th Century Men's Fashions*, New York: McGraw-Hill Inc., 1973.

U.S. Industrial Outlook 1993, Washington D.C.: U.S. Department of Commerce, 1993.

Williams-Mitchell, Christobel, *Dressed for the Job: The Story of Occupational Costume*, Poole, United Kingdom: Blandford Press, 1982.

—Daniel E. King

SIC 2329

MEN'S AND BOY'S CLOTHING, NOT ELSEWHERE CLASSIFIED

This category includes establishments primarily engaged in manufacturing men's and boy's clothing, not elsewhere classified, from purchased or woven fabrics. These items include, but are not limited to, athletic clothing, bathing suits, down-filled clothing, shorts, nontailored sports clothing, sweaters, athletic uniforms, and windbreakers. Establishments primarily engaged in manufacturing leather and sheep-lined garments are classified in **SIC 2386: Leather and Sheep-Lined Clothing.** Knitting mills primarily engaged in manufacturing outerwear are classified under **SIC 2253: Knit Outwear Mills.**

INDUSTRY SNAPSHOT

Approximately 575 establishments were engaged in the manufacture of men's and boys' clothing, not elsewhere classified, in the early 1990s. As was true for much of the U.S. apparel industry, these establishments were generally small, family-run businesses that faced stiff competition from low-cost imports.

ORGANIZATION AND STRUCTURE

The industry was comprised of manufacturers, contractors, and jobbers. Contractors were independent manufacturers, hired by various, and often competing, manufacturers. Contractors specialized in sewing the garment from pieces provided them, and they were hired by producers that either did not have their own sewing facilities or whose own capacity had been superseded.

Jobbers were design and marketing businesses which were hired to perform specific functions, including purchasing materials, designing patterns, creating samples, cutting material, and hiring contractors to manufacture the product. After purchasing materials needed to produce the pieces, jobbers then sent the cut material to contractors for assembly.

In creating apparel from the purchased materials, manufacturers retained staffs either to produce designs or buy them from freelancers, as well as to purchase the fabric and trimmings. While cutting and sewing the garment was generally performed in the manufacturer's factories, outside contractors were hired when demand for an item exceeded the manufacturer's capacity or shipping deadlines could not be met. For the purposes of this entry, the term ''manufacturers'' will refer cumulatively to contractors, jobbers, and manufacturers.

BACKGROUND AND DEVELOPMENT

During the 1980s interest in men's fashions increased, augmented by the introduction of several new men's fashion magazines, which featured articles and advertisements centering on stylishly dressed men. During this time, office wear became more comfortable and less formal. Sales of the traditional tailored suit declined slightly as sweaters and sports coats became acceptable in some work environments. As the men's apparel industry grew and diversified, manufacturers and retailers began to target specific markets according to income, age, and education, a strategy already common in the women's fashion industry. Many retailers, from departments stores to mass merchandisers, expanded their men's wear departments, and the industry grew at a faster pace than women's wear throughout the 1980s. This trend was expected to continue throughout the 1990s.

CURRENT CONDITIONS

As in other sectors of the apparel industry, increased consolidation and the strength of imported clothing were the industry's primary concerns in the early 1990s. Despite the increased competition, however, the value of shipments for men's and boy's clothing had increased from $1.6 billion in 1982 to an estimated $2.3 billion in 1992. Furthermore, employment in the industry had expanded from approximately 44,600 in 1982 to 53,300 in 1990. The economic recession of the early 1990s prompted manufacturers to step up production of moderately priced clothing lines. Many of these lines featured fleece in the form of sweat shirts, jackets, and pants, which offered consumers a particularly comfortable and inexpensive alternative in casual wear.

INDUSTRY LEADERS

Russell Corporation, founded in Alabama in 1902, benefited from the trend toward leisure wear, and, in particular, the growing popularity of licensed sportswear. The largest U.S. manufacturer of athletic uniforms in the early 1990s, Russell Corporation was awarded the title of official supplier to major league baseball in 1991. As part of that agreement, Russell Corporation was given the exclusive rights to make and market a line of jerseys and pants—the Authentic Diamond Collection—for the general public. In 1991, Russell reported $805 million in sales and employed approximately 15,000.

Another important presence in the industry was Nike, Inc. Although known primarily as a shoe manufacturer, Nike also began producing a line of sports wear in the late 1980s, which was bolstered by it's reputation as a trend setter in the athletic shoe industry. Spending a reported $233.3 million on advertising in 1991-92, Nike showed revenues of $3.93 billion in 1993. That year, approximately 14 percent of the company's domestic sales, and 25 percent of its international sales, were generated from its apparel lines. Roughly 57 percent of Nike's clothing was manufactured in the United States in the early 1990s, while the remainder was produced in Asia and South America. With headquarters in Oregon, Nike employed around 9,600 in 1993.

WORK FORCE

Most of those employed in this category (an estimated 46,600 in 1990) were production workers, approximately half of which were union members. The production work position consisted largely of sewing-machine operators, whose average wage in 1993 was $5.85 an hour. While many manufacturers in this sector of the apparel industry, as with the industry as a whole, were small, family-owned businesses, several large and growing establishments dominated the industry. The average number of employees per establishment in the early 1990s was 91.

A long-time center of the apparel business in the United States, New York was home to the majority of men's and boys' wear manufacturers in the early 1990s. During this time, approximately 90 establishments, employing about 4,300 workers, were headquartered in New York. California, however, with its 88 establishments, reported the greatest value of shipments—about $308.6 million—and approximately 5,300 employees. Tennessee reported having the highest number of employees in the industry at about 5,700. Alabama and Pennsylvania also had significant concentrations of workers in this category.

AMERICA AND THE WORLD

In the 1960s, the U.S. men's and boys' apparel industry began to lose significant market share to imports, which offered consumers lower prices and acceptable quality. This trend accelerated in the 1970s, and, by the 1990s, imports had reached all-time highs. Moreover, with U.S. manufacturers relying more heavily on off-shore assembly plants, the industry experienced further losses.

Manufacturers in the Far East represented a significant source of men's apparel. In the 1960s, U.S. apparel makers began moving their manufacturing operations abroad, focusing on Hong Kong, Taiwan, and South Korea, where labor was cheap. By the 1980s, however, labor costs in these countries had increased and operations were moved to Bangladesh, Thailand, Pakistan, Indonesia, Malaysia, Sri Lanka, and India. By the early 1990s China had replaced Hong Kong as the greatest supplier of imports to the United States.

The North American Free Trade Agreement (NAFTA)—ratified in 1993 to create a free-trade zone between the United States, Mexico, and Canada by gradually eliminating tariffs over 15 years—was generally supported by executives in the men's apparel industry. While workers' unions sought to stem the loss of jobs among Americans in the industry by limiting the imports allowed in the country, the free-market philosophy ultimately triumphed in the passage of NAFTA.

During the early 1990s, increasingly more imports entered the United States under provision 9802 (formerly known as Section 807) of the Harmonized Tariffs Schedule of the United States. This provision allowed clothing assembled abroad—from pieces cut in the United States and then exported—to be reimported with duty paid for the value added abroad. This meant that the most labor-intensive part of the assembly process could be accomplished for lower wages. Many U.S. manufacturers took advantage of provision 9802, moving assembly operations to the Caribbean where they expected to reduce costs and more successfully compete against imports from Asia. While the process greatly decreased the turnaround time assembling more complex clothing items, its logistics sometimes proved cumbersome and time-consuming, as contractors in other countries managed the transportation, paperwork, and assembly required. Furthermore, the passage of NAFTA led some to expect that the Caribbean would largely be replaced by Mexico as a more desirable manufacturing location.

RESEARCH AND TECHNOLOGY

In the battle against imports, U.S. apparel makers tried a several strategies, including increased use of automation, delivering higher quality goods, and trying to more closely keep track of the consumer's needs and desires. Although the intrinsic "soft" quality of material made the extensive use of automated equipment difficult, most of the larger manufacturers continually sought to invest in newer machinery to improve efficiency. Nevertheless, apparel manufacture remained a highly labor-intensive industry.

Another new strategy involved "quick response," the idea that bringing apparel to the retailer more rapidly would shorten the production cycle, reduce inventories, improve productivity, and help manufacturers to avoid overstocking by providing them with more timely information regarding consumers' preferences. Using computers to track inventory, sales, and consumer response, domestic manufacturers hoped to compete more effectively with importers. Department stores and manufacturers worked together to find ways to speed deliveries and increase efficiency.

INDUSTRY INFORMATION SOURCES

Fairchild Fact File: Men's Clothing and Furnishings, New York: Fairchild Publications.

—C. Collins

SIC 2331

WOMEN'S, MISSES', AND JUNIORS' BLOUSES AND SHIRTS

This category includes establishments primarily engaged in manufacturing women's, misses', and juniors' blouses and shirts from purchased woven or knit fabrics. Knitting mills primarily engaged in manufacturing outerwear are classified in **SIC 2253: Knit Outerwear Mills.** Establishments primarily engaged in manufacturing girls', children's, and infants blouses and shirts are classified in **SIC 2361: Girls', Children's, and Infants' Dresses, Blouses, and Shirts.**

INDUSTRY SNAPSHOT

More than 900 companies were engaged in the manufacture of women's and misses' blouses and shirts in 1992. This figure marks a considerable drop in the industry, for ten years earlier there were more than 1,800 companies engaged in this area of manufacturing. Much of the drop can be attributed to anemic product demand and the increased market share en-

joyed by international competitors. In 1992 establishments in the industry accounted for an inflation-adjusted value of total product shipments estimated at $3.7 billion. This figure was consistent with an overall declining industry trend which began in 1982 and has, with only minor aberrations, continued to the early 1990s.

In addition to the loss of market share to foreign companies, the domestic industry had also felt the sting of a declining trend in middle class discretionary incomes. The decline was particularly important since in former times the personal consumption expenditures of this income strata were a cornerstone of the industry target market, responsible for a major portion of apparel purchases of all types. The lingering overhang of takeover debt accumulated from the takeover frenzy of the late 1980s also imparted a growth inhibiting effect on company profits. To a lesser extent, other significant factors contributing to the industry's decline included a stabilization in the number of women entering the work force, as well as a change in consumer buying habits to discounters and off-price stores.

One positive business trend in recent years for blouse and shirt manufacturers has been an increased ability to take advantage of overseas opportunities. The long term decline in the value of the dollar spurred the export sales of women's and misses' blouses and shirts. In the early 1990s industry watchers remained enthusiastic about the prospects for export growth as a cure for the industry's economic woes. Their optimism was further buoyed with the 1993 passage of the North American Free Trade Agreement (NAFTA) and the elimination of significant world trade barriers as specified under the General Agreement on Tariffs and Trade (GATT).

On another front, while the industry itself was continuing to reel from the downsizing trend, the industry's larger firms had managed to increase their market shares and were using internally generated funds to invest in state-of-art apparel-related technologies and industry-related acquisitions.

In 1992 the women's and misses' blouses and shirts manufacturing industry was led by the Gitano Group Inc., with 20.2 percent of the industry market share. Other notable companies included Marcade Group Inc., (12 percent); Brooks Inc., (7.5 percent); Bernaud Chaus Inc., (7.3 percent); and Koret Inc., (3.3 percent). Gitano, Marcade, and Chaus were all publicly owned, while Brooks and Koret were privately held.

ORGANIZATION AND STRUCTURE

Because many establishments within the apparel industry group (including manufacturers of women's and misses' blouses and shirts) do not always manufacture the entire garment within the establishment's premises or across the company's factories, the U.S. Census of Manufacturers separates the industry into three broad producer classifications. Just where a company or establishment falls within the classifications depends on the degree of comprehensiveness of its production activities. Producers are classified as manufacturers if they buy fabric and undertake the design, patternmaking, grading, cutting, sewing, and assembling of their garments from within their own establishment or firm. Because of their integrated structure, wholly owned manufacturers operate in a manner that allows them to exercise a considerable measure of control over the production quality of their garments. Since they require relatively large investment expenditures, such operations fall outside the financial reach of the majority of the establishments active in the industry.

A firm or establishment that carries out all garment making processes minus its sewing and (sometimes) its cutting operations, deciding instead to contract out these operations to independently owned outside firms, is defined as an apparel jobber. Many apparel firms, independent of their size, contract out their sewing and cutting needs, along with other highly skilled production functions such as embroidery, quilting, and pleating, which are performed using specialized machinery.

A firm or establishment that is independently owned and uses its own machinery and employees to sew and cut garments from the designs, materials, and specifications supplied by the apparel jobbers is classified as a contractor. The contracting system actually began in the 1880s and was then referred to as the "cottage industry" where women sewed at home doing piece work. Eventually the system was transferred to privately owned factories. The contractor system's continued existence is due to the system's ability to accommodate seasonal production peaks without the apparel jobbers having to undertake investments that are subject to periods of intense activity and idleness.

In 1987, when ranked according to their density within census regions, the largest number of establishments engaged in this industry were located in the Pacific, Middle Atlantic, and South Atlantic regions. Alternatively, when ranked by the number of establishments per state, California was first with 485 and New York was second with 294, followed by Pennsylvania with 173 and Georgia with 76.

Input data compiled from the 1980s indicated that the primary materials consumed by the industry when ranked by cost arrived in the form of materials, containers, and supplies; broadwoven fabrics; and knit fabrics. The major economic sectors responsible for the share of the industry's input supply flowed from imports (29.1 percent); broadwoven fabric mills (20.2 percent); apparel made from purchased materials, (18.3 percent); and knit fabric mills, (8.6 percent).

The disaggregated share of the total output identified according to the category of its major product class indicated that women's and misses' knit shirts and blouses accounted for 30.1 percent of total sales, women's and misses' woven shirts and blouses represented 46.7 percent, contract work performed on women's and misses' blouses and shirts accounted for 16.5 percent, and about 6.7 percent went unspecified by kind.

BACKGROUND AND DEVELOPMENT

Up until the mid-nineteenth century, women's and misses' ready-made or ready-to-wear blouses and shirts were practically nonexistent. Dating back to early colonial times, U.S. women typically wore clothes that were made in the household. Popular women's magazines carried sewing instructions for making new patterns or styles. From the 1860s until the turn of the century efforts to manufacture women's ready-wear garments met with little success. What was available was usually of inferior quality and questionable design, despite the invention and diffusion of sewing machine technology. For the most part, domestically produced garments continued to dominate the scene; mass produced ready-wear women's clothes were spoken about in derogatory terms.

Things changed slowly during the first two decades of the twentieth century, but change they did as women's ready-to-wear clothes encountered wider social acceptance. The combined influence of several concurrent social and economic forces explained this shift. For instance, ongoing improvements in European and U.S. textile technologies transformed both the quality and availability of fabrics, enabling manufacturers to produce a more comfortable and style-conscious fit. Continuous upgrades in sewing machine technologies, cutting instruments, and pressing processes permitted the output of women's clothes to increase dramatically while their prices fell. Spurred on by the burgeoning women's movement, women were able to move beyond their traditional confines of home and family and participate more fully in social life. Women increasingly entered the work force, attended college, and became more active in sports and politics. World War I found many women taking over jobs once performed by men. In sum, given their fuller participation in social affairs outside the home, women found the ready-to-wear clothes for themselves and their families a necessary convenience.

From the 1920s onwards, the women's apparel industry developed along the lines of small, privately-owned, single-product firms. By the late 1950s things began to change as larger publicly held multi-product firms started to move into the women's apparel industry. In most instances, their methods of gaining entry into the industry took the form of mergers with or acquisitions of existing firms. This growth in the industry continued unabated into the 1960s: there were only 22 publicly owned firms in women's apparel industry in 1959; by the close of the 1960s their number exceeded 100. The forward march of large, publicly-owned firms continued more or less without interruption until the mid-1980s when the trend reversed itself and large manufacturing firms began to ''go private'' again during the era of leveraged buyouts.

The progressive growth of import penetration into the domestic market for women's and misses' blouses and shirts was a significant factor in the domestic industry's protracted tailspin. As part of industry-wide efforts to lower production costs, U.S. producers participated in this import deluge through the processes of ''outsourcing'' and relocation by foreign investment. Beginning around 1982 and still in force by the 1990s, price competition from both foreign and domestic producers resulted in strong disinflationary pressures which in turn triggered a steep decline in the domestic industry's rate of capacity utilization. During the recession of 1981-1982, the percentage change in producer prices for women's apparel collapsed and then remained more or less flat for most the period covering 1983-1990. Though not as dramatic as the previous recession, disinflationary forces hit once again during the 1990-1991 recession, and then, most uncharacteristically, set out along the path of another steep decline despite being some two years into a recovery. During the past decade capacity utilization fluctuated erratically, moving up and down between the 83 to 79 percent range during the 1981-1982 recession. During the early years of the recovery it climbed upwards, peaking at the 89 percent mark in 1984. It then plummeted to settle at 76 percent in 1993, marking a drop of almost 15 percent in capacity utilization in the industry. As a direct consequence of the shakeout working through the industry's manufacturing sector, many traditional wholesale and retail linkages were sent into disarray or ruptured entirely,

spawning a number of mergers and bankruptcy declarations.

During the 1980s another new trend arose in the form of manufacturer-owned retail stores that were usually located in prime retail areas and carried a large and complete stock of the firm's product lines sold at regular prices. Such outlets provided manufacturers with a wealth of consumer information that was used to determine whether the prospect of future sales warranted future production runs.

WORK FORCE

In 1982 total employment in the women's and misses' shirts and blouses industry stood at 92,300, of which 79,400 were classified as production workers. By 1991 total employment had fallen to 55,900, of which 46,900 were production workers. During those ten years total employment fell by 39.5 percent and production worker employment dropped by 41 percent. Over the same period the annual total value added by production workers either stayed about the same or increased as their average weekly hours steadily increased from 34.0 hours in 1982 to 36.4 hours in 1991. From 1982 to 1990 the industry's value added per production worker climbed almost continuously from $23,200 to $36,000. For the same period movements in the real wage indicated a mostly downward trend, suggesting that productivity gains were not being matched by increases in the real wage.

Compared against the measures of employment by gender, race and Hispanic origin for the U.S. manufacturing sector as a whole, women, black and Hispanic workers active in the apparel work force far exceeded their national counterparts. According to Bureau of Labor Statistics estimates for 1992, women accounted for 74.7 percent of the apparel work force, a figure considerably higher than the overall manufacturing average of 32.9 percent. Black apparel workers accounted for 16.4 percent of the work force total—the total manufacturing average is 10 percent—and Hispanic workers accounted for 20.7 percent of the employee work force, compared to the national average of 8.7 percent.

AMERICA AND THE WORLD

Ever since the end of World War II, the domestic producers of women's and misses' blouses and shirts have been vulnerable to import penetration. As mentioned earlier, a particularly acute phase occurred during the period of 1983-1992. Although they still account for the largest share of U.S. imports, the market share of the ''Big Four'' countries, the People's Republic of China, Taiwan, Hong Kong, and Korea, actually declined during this period, dropping from 63 percent in 1984 to 41 percent in 1992. Shipments from all of these countries declined with the exception of China, which recorded an increase of more than 100 percent. By far the largest gains in import market share occurred were enjoyed by the Caribbean countries and Mexico. These countries increased their market share from 1983 to 1992 from seven percent to approximately 20 percent.

To an increasing degree, many U.S. garment makers actively participated in this import binge and contributed to the erosion of domestic employment in the industry through their emphasis on foreign outsourcing. With respect to the Caribbean countries, this was true as a matter of policy ever since 1983 when Congress, fearful that the spread of poverty in the Caribbean would attract large portions of its citizens to communist politics, passed the Caribbean Basin Initiative (CBI) program. The CBI permitted almost all apparel items which had been cut within the U.S. to be shipped abroad for further processing and then reenter the U.S. as manufactured or semi-manufactured goods. According to section 807 of the U.S. Tariff Code, the percentage of duty paid on the goods was equated to the value added abroad. And, as was often the case, this was set equal to the cost of foreign sewing labor, which was notoriously low when compared to the cost of U.S. workers. Among the countries participating in the program were Jamaica, the Dominican Republic, Haiti, Costa Rica, and, even though it was not a Caribbean country, Mexico. With the passage of NAFTA and GATT, trade relations between the U.S. and the rest of the world were supposed to be put on a more level playing field. Additional job losses in America, however, may well be one result. In discussing GATT's impact on the textiles and clothing industries, the *Christian Science Monitor* commented that "the accord puts the textiles sector back under multi-lateral trade rules, after a 20-year hiatus during which bilateral accords reigned under the Multi-Fiber Agreement regime. Most tariffs and quotas in developed countries will be eliminated over the decade. Developing countries will take a growing share of textiles and clothing trade, worth $250 billion in 1992. Consumers should enjoy lower prices, while developed-word manufacturers [such as those in the United States] will continue to feel the heat."

RESEARCH AND TECHNOLOGY

Despite being caught up in ongoing grip of establishment downsizing, major technological changes began to impact on the industry in the late 1980s that led to a closer integration between retailers and manufac-

turers. New labor saving and lower cost technologies were introduced at larger companies, which only served to widen the competitive cost differentials between themselves and the middle and lower tier firms in the industry. Unless rectified, this situation could also stoke the industry's downsizing trend.

A significant development in recent years between retailers and the industry's manufacturers has been the implementation of the quick response system, a computerized strategy that provides for the quick and precise replenishment of "hot-selling" garments. By means of electronic data interchange, participating apparel producers are privy to an instant and continuous flow of information concerning retail sales by styles, sizes and colors, along with the level of retail inventory. With this information in their possession, manufacturers plan further production rounds on a more precise basis by discarding slow-moving styles and devoting their efforts towards fast selling items. As a result, they avoid costly markdowns and increase turnover. In most instances quick response systems have been formed between large volume manufacturers and retailers with the high level of funds necessary to purchase these costly systems.

Internal to the establishments, new automated technologies were being installed to speed up the manufacturing process and reduce the labor time required per garment. Examples included automated marker and patternmakers, computer inspection of fabrics, scanning and measurement of fabric width variance, and shade recognition apparatus, which have all become automated parts of a fully integrated quality enhancing system. New programmable sewing units that utilize microprocessors were also instrumental in reducing sewing labor costs. Prior to their introduction the sewing of a garment accounted for the largest portion of an article's labor cost, while anywhere from 70 to 80 percent of its in-process production time was spent handling and positioning a garment. To reduce in-process handling new automatic conveyor systems are being developed, along with robotics systems and automated warehouse facilities.

INDUSTRY INFORMATION SOURCES

Arpan, Jeffery S., de la Torres, Jose, and Toyne, Brian, *The U.S. Apparel Industry: International Challenge, Domestic Response*, Atlanta, GA: Georgia State University, 1982.

Focus: An Economic Profile of the Apparel Industry, American Apparel Manufacturers Association, Arlington, VA: 1993.

Jarnow, Jeannette, and Guerreiro, Miriam, *Inside the Fashion Business*, New York: Macmillan Publishing Company, 1991.

LaFranchi, Howard, "Looking Back: Accomplishments of the Uruguay Round," *Christian Science Monitor*, December 23, 1993.

Rose, Clare, *Children's Clothes Since 1750*, New York: Drama Book Publishers, 1989.

U.S. Industrial Outlook 1993, Washington DC: U.S. Department of Commerce, 1993.

                                                        —Daniel King

SIC 2335

WOMEN'S, JUNIORS', AND MISSES' DRESSES

This entry describes establishments primarily engaged in manufacturing women's, misses', and juniors' dresses (including ensemble dresses), from purchased woven or knit fabrics, including woven or knit fabrics of paper, whether sold by the piece or by the dozen. Establishments primarily engaged in manufacturing girls', children's, and infants' dresses are classified in **SIC 2361: Girls', Children's, and Infants' Dresses, Blouses, and Shirts.** Knitting mills primarily engaged in manufacturing knit dresses are classified in **SIC 2258: Lace and Warp Knit Fabric Mills.**

INDUSTRY SNAPSHOT

There were more than 5,000 manufacturers of women's, juniors', and misses' dresses in the United States in 1993. This industry generated over $6 billion dollars in wholesale shipments, representing more than 30 percent of the $19.5 billion dollar women's and misses' outerwear category.

Centered in New York and California, the industry has more than 3,600 manufacturers in those two states; however, manufacturers can be found in 27 other states stretching from Rhode Island and Pennsylvania to Texas and Hawaii. The size and scope of these dress manufacturers varied greatly from small manufacturers operating out of their home or a single showroom to the giant VF Corporation which employed over 43,000 individuals and serviced multiple product lines and companies.

The clothing industry, particularly women's apparel, is sensitive to changes in economic conditions. In the high rolling days of the 1980s consumers were wearing designer labels and $100 jeans. The economic downturn in the early 1990s, however, caused consumers to look for value and savings. Consumer preferences shifted from fancy dressing to basic apparel at home as well as at work. As a result of this shift,

manufacturers moved to the extremes of the industry: discounters and high fashion designers. Consequently, the number of women's apparel manufacturers declined. An increase in imports further increased the competition in this already volatile and difficult industry. Although imports increased by only 5 percent per year between 1988 and 1991, they jumped 15 percent in 1992.

These events created increased competition and a reluctance on behalf of manufacturers and retailers to raise prices on apparel. Many small players were forced to close their doors and the strength of the remaining manufacturers during the mid-1990s depended on an end to worldwide recessionary conditions.

ORGANIZATION AND STRUCTURE

The American Apparel Manufacturers Association (AAMA) is the central trade association for the U.S. apparel industry. In the early 1990s, the AAMA represented three-fourths of the industry and provided its members with guidance and support through publications, statistical reports, and trade negotiations. In addition to the AAMA there are regional associations that focus on local issues and policies.

Business Centers. The industry's central business locations are New York City, Los Angeles, and Atlanta; each of these is supported by an apparel mart. These marts house showrooms in which manufacturers display their line, and buyers and sellers converge at these marts to conduct the business of selling clothes. The selling periods for women's, misses' and juniors' dresses are typically condensed into monthly "market weeks". Retail buyers visit manufacturer showrooms buying product for the coming season. In 1992, the women's apparel industry garnered retail sales of $64.5 billion.

The apparel industry operates under the principles of clustering. Clustering requires makers of similar products to congregate their operations in a small geographical location. This facilitates communication between buyers and sellers, increases the speed of innovation, and promotes a business culture that nourishes and supports an industry. Clustering is well-established in New York City and Los Angeles, thus ensuring their prominence as fashion centers for the United States.

Manufacturing Process. The manufacturing process requires an average of six to eight months to move a particular line from design to sale. The process typically begins with a designer's sketch that is turned into a pattern. Fabric is selected and a cost sheet is established to detail expenses. A wholesale price is determined by using the cost sheet as the base. The production department grades a pattern to accommodate the required size range and then cuts the fabric according to the patterns. The materials are then sewn and finished, and finally, the garments are pressed, then packed or hung on racks for shipment to the retail customer. Across all manufacturers, only the first step, that of design, was uniformly handled in-house. The ability of a manufacturer to maintain control of the remaining processes was a function of its size and capital equipment. The most frequently out-sourced process was sewing and finishing. This process was given to small contractors, typically employing immigrant labor in sweatshop-like factories. The nature of the contracting business has made the tracking of operating businesses and gross sales nearly impossible.

Financial Structure. According to *Bobbin* magazine, two-thirds of apparel manufacturers factored their receivables in the early 1990s. This accounting method entails a contract between manufacturer and factor regarding credit approval for retailers. The factor, essentially a lender, buys the manufacturer's receivables for 80 percent to 85 percent of value, and in turn sells them to a retailer. This allows manufacturers to decrease risk and increase capital turnover.

BACKGROUND AND DEVELOPMENT

The 1830s marked the emergence of the women's ready-to-wear dress industry in America. Manufacturers were able to keep pattern making and fabric cutting on their premises, typically in the tailor shop, with the pieces then contracted to workers who would sew and finish the product in the home. By mid-century, several variables emerged that pushed this nascent business towards an industry of mass production: (1) strengthening of domestic textile manufacturing techniques (2) invention of a treadle-powered sewing machine by Isaac Singer (3) influx of large numbers of immigrants, and (4) methods developed during the Civil War for the mass production of garments.

The easy availability of cheap, immigrant labor encouraged the development of large sweat shops typically housed in lofts. Not until the turn of the century did the workers begin to mobilize and organize to promote better working conditions. Their actions resulted in the 1910 Protocol of Peace which abolished home work, ended inside subcontracting, limited the workweek to 54 hours, and created an arbitration process for complaints. These benefits were granted at the expense of the workers' right to strike. The terrible images of 146 young women who died behind locked

factory doors in the Triangle Shirt Waist fire of 1911 resulted in further reforms. By World War I, the International Ladies Garment Workers Union was one of the most powerful labor organizations in America.

New York City was the undisputed center of the women's ready-to-wear apparel industry. The city's dominance was secured during the 1920s when a group of New York developers consolidated the industry around a group of buildings along Seventh Avenue that were designed to house workrooms and showrooms for apparel manufacturers.

The apparel industry was not immune to the effects of the Great Depression of the 1930s. Many manufacturers ceased operations as a result of bankruptcy; however, the manufacturing boom during World War II quickly reversed the fortunes of the industry. There were tremendous profits to be earned in servicing the needs of a fully employed population.

The labor intensive aspect of garment manufacturing requires an ongoing search for cheap sources of labor. It was this requirement, in addition to the increasing congestion and expense of doing business in New York City, that began the movement of manufacturers away from New York towards the South and West. This period also saw the rise of large scale manufacturing operations that could benefit from economies of scale not possible in the small spaces typically found in New York. This led to the wholesale manufacture of staple garments such as jeans.

The unending search for cheap labor eventually led to an increase in imported goods. Under the terms of Tariff Item 807, now called 9802, a U.S. company can send semi-finished garments overseas for incidental work, such as sewing and finishing. The company can then import the items back to the United States and pay duty only on the value-added portions of the garments. By the 1980s, the rise in imports was dramatic; 1985 imports were $15 billion, seven times that of 1972. By 1989, that number had jumped to almost $24 billion. Manufacturers were pitted against retailers in their attempts to get protectionist legislation passed through Congress. The retailers argued that such legislation would result in an increase in domestic clothing prices. As a result, textile and apparel manufacturers established the Crafted with Pride in the USA Council, designed to encourage consumers to buy American products.

CURRENT CONDITIONS

Consolidation. The apparel industry today is reacting to changing consumer buying patterns, the weak economy of the early 1990s, and the continuing increase in imported goods. These variables contributed to a decrease of 800,000 apparel and textile jobs during the 1980s. They also forced the industry to consider the increased usage of automated manufacturing processes. Although the industry is still labor intensive, computer integrated manufacturing principles and the use of electronic data interchanges for "quick response" in inventory and ordering have become increasingly popular among manufacturers. However, the capital outlays required for the transition to a more automated environment and increased economies of scale are often too costly for smaller manufacturers.

This has led to an atmosphere of consolidation wherein heavily capitalized companies that have introduced automation, expanded their operations, and increased their access to a wider strata of retailers through the acquisition of other labels. Consequently, small, independent companies were squeezed by the ever increasing import market and these large, domestic apparel corporations. The VF Corporation, one of the largest manufacturers in this category, typifies this philosophy in its control of several brands of jeans such as Wrangler, Lee, and Girbaud. Each of these product lines is produced for a different market. Liz Claiborne has also diversified its holdings, recently purchasing several brands from Russ Togs. Liz Claiborne will continue to sell its garments to department stores while these new brands allow it to do business with such high growth mass merchandisers as Sears and J.C. Penny.

Licensing. Brand licensing was a strategy employed throughout the industry to increase market share or avoid the necessity of automating a manufacturing process. Through licensing, the brand owner can reap the benefits of its name without the attendant problems of manufacturing or contracting out the goods themselves. Likewise, the licensee views a licensed brand as an opportunity to expand its line of offerings without the risk of financing a product launch. In a December 1992 *Bobbin* article, Craig Kalter, vice president of marketing and licensing for French Toast, noted that, "the advantage to the licensee is that it is able to benefit from a name that has a high degree of awareness and penetration in the marketplace."

NAFTA. The North America Free Trade Agreement (NAFTA) presented new challenges to the apparel industry. The agreement carried the possible threat of U.S. workers losing jobs to Mexico's cheaper labor source. However, the contrary argument asserted that businesses only moved production that was no longer viable in the United States to Mexico. In its study of NAFTA, the Office of Technology Assess-

ment commented that "Mexico has so far been a minor supplier of garments to the United States and will have difficulty dislodging established Asian producers. The threat to U.S. apparel jobs is global, not regional." Further, the American Apparel Manufacturers Association (AAMA), which supports NAFTA, argues that without NAFTA, such production would have moved to the Far East, thus completely eliminating U.S involvement in the manufacturing process. A 1993 survey of AAMA membership indicated that despite NAFTA, only 3 percent of respondents expected an employment decline in the coming year. A full 50 percent expected no changes in their work force, while 46 percent of the manufacturers anticipated increasing their domestic employment.

The apparel industry in general and Women's and Misses' dresses in particular are very sensitive to economic and demographic changes. The economic conditions in the 1980s, boosted by the increase of women in the work place, led to an average yearly business growth of 10 percent in terms of value of shipments for this category. During the recessionary climate of the early 1990s, however, the industry averaged only 2 percent growth. This sensitivity was further noted in the growth in sales for discount mass merchandisers at the expense of specialty boutiques and department stores. Manufacturers had to hold down costs and provide high quality garments to increasingly demanding and careful customers.

Future Expectations. A report issued by the U.S. Department of Commerce projected moderate growth for the U.S. apparel industry through the mid-1990s. This forecast, based on a favorable long-term outlook for consumer spending, housing starts, and new car purchases, also noted the increasingly competitive nature of the industry as foreign producers work to increase their share of the U.S. market.

Overseas markets have become increasingly important to U.S. apparel manufacturers particularly in the developing markets of the former Soviet Union and Eastern Europe. An economic newsletter published by the American Apparel Manufacturers Association paid particular attention to trends in the Far East that suggested opportunities for domestic apparel manufacturers. Japan, for example, has huge stores of foreign exchange but the public's living standard is below that of U.S. citizens. The cultural climate in Japan was changing in the early 1990s and Japan's citizens were beginning to enjoy more leisure time. It is anticipated that such time will lead to an increase in the consumption of personal goods and services. Likewise, the opening of trade doors to China and the increasing interest in Western goods offers tremendous growth opportunities for U.S. apparel manufacturers.

Industry Leaders

Founded in 1976 and based in New York City, Liz Claiborne Inc. has grown into one of the leading manufacturers in this industry. From 1982 to 1990, the company's sales grew from $166 million to $1.7 billion. In the early 1990s, Liz Claiborne Inc. had over 5,000 employees. Its recent acquisition of Russ Togs, which included the Russ Togs, Villager, and Crazy Horse lines, has since increased sales to over $2 billion. This acquisition strategy has allowed Liz Claiborne to gain access to lower priced, mass merchandise retailers while retaining its Liz Claiborne line exclusively for department and specialty stores. Liz Claiborne Inc. is also an aggressive player in the outlet mall market, with over 31 stores across the country. In a Standard & Poor's Industry Survey, Jerome A. Chazen, chairman of Liz Claiborne Inc., called the outlet business excellent and projected that future stores would handle all surplus inventory.

Leslie Fay Companies Inc., which include the Leslie Fay Classic, Leslie Fay Collection, Albert Nipon, and Nipon Boutique lines, was founded in 1946 and had sales of over $800 million in 1992.

Leslie Fay Companies responded aggressively to consumer demands for moderately priced, value-oriented fashion by cutting prices in several of its dress lines. This "everyday value" pricing strategy resulted in the company gaining the leading market share in the moderate-price dress category. Leslie Fay Companies Inc. is a New York-based publicly traded company, and had approximately 6,000 employees in the early 1990s.

Work Force

The apparel and textile manufacturing industries employed approximately 9 percent of the entire U.S. work force. More than one million workers were engaged in apparel manufacturing. The number of workers involved specifically in the manufacture of women's, juniors' and misses' dresses fell from a high of 122,000 in 1983 to less than 100,000 by 1993. In that same time period, average wages rose from $5.18 per hour to close to $7.00 per hour.

In the early 1990s New York and California each employed approximately 33,000 people in this industry, representing almost 30 percent of the industry's total work force. Pennsylvania employed 13,000 workers in this sector of the industry. There were also strong manufacturing centers in New Jersey, Florida, North Carolina, and South Carolina, each supporting between 1,500 and 5,500 workers. The largest percentage of workers were employed as sewing machine operators, followed by pressing machine operators and inspectors. With the exception of sales and machine mechanics, all other employment categories in the industry were anticipating work force reductions through the turn of the century.

Despite inroads into automation, the bulk of apparel manufacturing in the United States was still labor intensive in the early 1990s. Production workers in this industry made up 85 percent of the work force compared to only 68 percent for all other U.S. manufacturing. Wages in this sector were typically lower than in other manufacturing industries, resulting in an ongoing reliance on immigrant labor.

America and the World

Exports of apparel grew from 2 percent of total U.S. product shipments in 1987 to more than 7 percent in 1992. Total U.S. exports in 1992 year were nearly $4 billion. Although much of this growth represented expansion of existing or new markets, a large portion of this gain was due to semi-finished garments sent abroad for finishing and then returned to the United States under the provision of Harmonized Tariff Schedule of the United States (HTSUS) code 9802, formerly 807. Although section 807 has existed since the Tariff Act of 1790, it only gained importance during the 1980s as apparel imports dramatically increased. In the decade from 1980 to 1990, apparel imports increased 202 percent.

The 9802 program allows a manufacturer to pay duty only on the value added to the garment abroad, not the total value of the product. In 1992, HTSUS 9802 trade was slightly more than 14 percent of total imports, and nearly $900 million worth of HTSUS 9802 imports were produced in the Dominican Republic. Mexico produced approximately $700 million, followed by Costa Rica with $400 million in apparel production.

Apparel trade is governed by the Arrangement Regarding International Trade in Textiles, also known as the Multifiber Arrangement (MFA). This agreement provides guidelines for member nations regarding international trade in textiles and apparel. Apparel is further controlled under the auspices of the General Agreement on Tariffs and Trade (GATT). The Uruguay Round of talks regarding GATT, begun in the late 1980s, were also expected to have an impact on the industry.

The largest suppliers of apparel to the United States were China, Taiwan, Korea, and Hong Kong with almost $12 billion in sales for 1992. This represented nearly half of the $26 billion of all garments imported into the United States in 1992. Passage of NAFTA could give U.S. manufacturers a competitive advantage and allow them to begin to regain some of the production that relocated to Asia. Although labor costs in Indonesia, China, Pakistan and India average only $.23 per hour, wages in Singapore, Hong Kong, and Taiwan were $3.25 per hour, significantly higher than the $1.17 average hourly wage paid in Mexico. The countries of Eastern Europe and the republics of the former Soviet Union were also expected to provide significant opportunities for U.S. apparel manufacturers.

INDUSTRY INFORMATION SOURCES

Abend, Jules. "The Increasingly Common Denominator." *Bobbin* (December 1992).

American Apparel Manufacturers Association. "Apparel Industry Trends." *Economic Newsletter* (June 1993).

Barcomb, Amy. "License to Manufacture." *Bobbin* (December 1992).

Feldman, Amy. "Consumer Nondurables." *Forbes* (January 4, 1993).

Mattera, Philip. *Inside U.S. Business*. Homewood, IL: Irwin, 1991.

O'Rourke, Mary T. "Labor Costs - From Pakistan to Portugal." *Bobbin* (September 1992).

Pouschine, Tatiana. "Ridin' High." *Forbes* (November 9, 1992).

Standard & Poor's Industry Surveys. New York: Standard & Poor's Corporation, 1993.

Struensee, Chuck. "Leslie Fay Cuts Moderate Dress Prices." *Women's Wear Daily* (September 22, 1992).

———. "Revamping at Leslie Fay." *Women's Wear Daily* (September 1, 1992).

U.S. Industrial Outlook 1993. Washington, DC: U.S. Department of Commerce, 1993.

—Shula Malkin

SIC 2337

WOMEN'S, MISSES', AND JUNIORS' SUITS, SKIRTS, AND COATS

This category covers establishments primarily engaged in manufacturing women's, misses', and junior's suits, pantsuits, skirts, coats (except fur coats and raincoats), and tailored jackets and vests, from purchased woven or knit fabrics. These garments are generally tailored and usually lined. Establishments primarily engaged in manufacturing fur clothing are classified in **SIC 2371: Fur Goods;** and those manufacturing raincoats are classified in **SIC 2385: Waterproof Outerwear.** Knitting mills primarily engaged in manufacturing knit outerwear are classified in **SIC 2253: Knit Outerwear Mills.**

INDUSTRY SNAPSHOT

The U.S. apparel industry, especially the women's apparel industry, underwent dramatic change beginning in the 1960s. The increased automation of the industry, the profound surge in imports, and fundamental shifts in the retail industry all affected the manufacture of women's clothing in the United States.

Over 1,000 companies produced women's suits, coats, skirts, and jackets in the early 1990s, and they employed over 48,000 workers. Many industry establishments were small, family-owned and operated businesses, although there was a trend toward consolidation. The value of shipments of women's apparel in 1992 was less than in 1982, signaling a decade-long downward trend. Factors such as the increase in imports and a general shift toward more casual office wear had a negative impact on this segment of the U.S. market.

ORGANIZATION AND STRUCTURE

The apparel industry was composed of three types of producers: manufacturers, jobbers, and contractors. Contractors were independent firms that performed specialized work, such as sewing a garment, for a number of competing firms. Contractors were hired by producers who either did not have their own sewing apparatus or whose own capacity had been exceeded. Contractors were not involved in the retail sale of merchandise.

Sewing-machine operators completed specific parts of the garment, which were provided by the manufacturer. Through this system of piece work, operators could work more quickly and efficiently because they did not have to switch or adjust their machines. Over half of the plants making women's coats and suits were run by contractors.

Jobbers were design and marketing businesses that were hired to perform specific functions. For example, jobbers might purchase materials, design patterns, create samples, cut material, and hire contractors to manufacture the product. Most jobbers, however, did not sew garments, but instead hired contractors to sew and finish the products.

Jobbers often had their own design staffs to create seasonal lines, or they might hire free-lancers to do design work. A jobber bought the materials needed to produce the pieces, and then created the patterns for different sizes. The cut material was then sent to contractors to be sewn and finished. Orders were taken for the garments, and the finished garments were then shipped to retailers.

Manufacturers were those establishments that performed all functions involved in creating apparel from purchased materials. The manufacturer had a staff that produced designs, or it bought work from free-lancers. It then purchased the materials (fabric and trimmings) needed. Generally the cutting and sewing of the garment was done in the manufacturer's factories. However, when demand for an item exceeded the manufacturer's ability to supply it within shipping deadlines, outside contractors might be hired. The manufacturer's own sales and shipping staff took orders and sent them out.

When a manufacturer handled all stages of a garment's assembly, it clearly had greater control over the quality of the product. Nevertheless, the advantages to using contractors were numerous. For example, those companies without the capital to update machinery would find the system advantageous. Manufacturers who relied upon contractors also avoided the responsibility of hiring and training workers. And the contractor system was flexible—providing manufacturing capacity when needed at busy periods without having to meet payroll obligations at off-peak periods.

BACKGROUND AND DEVELOPMENT

The growth of the women's apparel business in the United States began in the mid-nineteenth century, when certain garments that did not need to be fitted, such as cloaks and mantles, started to be mass-produced. Small quantities of women's suits and skirts were turned out in a limited number of factories, but most women still made their own clothing at home.

The number of apparel manufacturers grew as more women chose to buy their clothing early in the twentieth century. New York City became the center of the women's apparel business for a variety of reasons. For example, manufacturers were able to take advantage of the inexpensive labor found in newly arrived immigrants—most of those working in the industry were young Jewish and Italian women. New York City also formed an ideal location for the industry due to its position as a port city and its proximity to the textile mills in New England and the South.

Soon, many manufacturers began to outgrow their quarters in an industry that was expanding rapidly. A consortium of apparel makers, investors, and a real estate developer came up with the idea of moving to an undeveloped area of New York City. Between 1918 and 1921, approximately 50 clothing makers moved to the area along Seventh Avenue that came to be known as the garment district.

Since the garment industry was unregulated, the employees in these days often worked in crowded, unsafe, and poorly lit ''sweat shops'' for low pay. Early efforts to organize the workers into unions were met with industry-wide resistance—as one shop became organized, business would then simply shift to an unorganized one.

The Triangle Shirtwaist Factory fire in 1911, in which 146 employees were killed, was a tragedy that galvanized the industry. After much resistance from business owners, industry-wide minimum standards for worker safety were put into place. In the 1930s and 1940s federal legislation made it easier for the unions to organize and more labor standards were established. Two unions largely represented U.S. apparel workers, the International Ladies' Garment Workers' Union (ILGWU) and what eventually came to be known as the Amalgamated Clothing and Textile Workers Union (ACTWU). For many years they were able to negotiate contracts with yearly pay increases and benefits.

By the 1960s apparel manufacturers started to move their production facilities out of the United States to markets where the labor was plentiful and cheap. Apparel manufacture became a global industry. Manufacturers from the United States first looked largely to Hong Kong and Taiwan, but as labor costs grew there, manufacturers moved to other Asian nations and the Caribbean. Apparel imports into the United States increased from 9 percent in 1967 to 62 percent in 1992.

Another important development came in the 1960s, when many textile companies (which produced the materials) and retailers (which bought the finished products) grew into huge companies. The apparel manufacturers responded in kind, as many merged to create large, publicly owned corporations. Historically, women's apparel companies were small businesses, often family-run. Although the new corporations were large, they sometimes lacked the flexibility needed in the ever-changing fashion industry. However, the larger companies were armed with the capital needed to upgrade machinery and modernize equipment to compete more effectively with imports.

Another trend which led to profound change in the industry was the dramatic increase in the number of women in the work force, beginning in the 1970s. As a result, the demand for professional women's wear skyrocketed.

CURRENT CONDITIONS

Personal-consumption expenditures on clothing nearly doubled during the 1980s, and women's apparel was an important part of that increase. As recession hit the industry in 1989, however, the spending splurge ended. Manufacturers responded by cutting costs. While the women's apparel industry adjusted to the recession, the larger manufacturers got even stronger as the industry continued to consolidate. Some big manufacturers were able to take advantage of the weakened position of many smaller firms and strengthen their already-dominant positions.

Retailers themselves sought to cut costs and become more efficient, as the market became more competitive. Retailers looked often to the larger apparel manufacturers that were providing merchandise that consumers recognized and respected. By limiting the number of manufacturers supplying them, retailers could reduce overhead expenses—thus favoring the larger manufacturers over the smaller ones.

The value of women's wear shipments declined gradually through the 1990s. One of the many reasons included a leveling-off of the number of women entering the work force. Historically, women's apparel accounted for half of all clothing sold, and it was sold primarily to working women, who by 1990 comprised 45 percent of the U.S. work force. In addition, office wear became more casual, and this particularly affected the sales of women's suits. And as the U.S. population aged, people often became less concerned with up-to-the-minute fashions than with saving for mortgage payments and children's educations.

Other factors changed the women's apparel industry as well. For example, manufacturers began to sell their own products, as the line between manufacturer and retailer blurred. Manufacturers were often unhappy with the way the retailers displayed their products or with the performance of sales staff. By opening their own retail spaces—either complete stores or freestanding ''shops'' within department stores—manufacturers could exert direct control of the sales, service, and environment. Another popular tactic was for manufacturers to sell through catalogs, again jumping over the middleman and appealing directly to the consumer. By marketing their own goods, manufacturers could avoid retailers who were looking to increase their profit margin at the manufacturers' expense.

Manufacturers responded to the surge in imports in a variety of ways. Some sold off their manufacturing facilities, hiring contractors to make products to their specifications; others contracted for their apparel to be produced almost exclusively offshore and then reimported. By contracting out, manufacturers could reduce their overhead, and their inventories would be more flexible. Those who kept their facilities in the United States often stressed their reliability, on-time delivery, and quality.

INDUSTRY LEADERS

Hartmarx Corporation designed, produced, and marketed both men's and women's apparel, and it was one of the largest manufacturers of women's suits. Hartmarx produced moderately priced women's clothing through its Women's International Division. It also sold clothing through the Barrie Pace Catalog division. Hartmarx grew considerably throughout the 1980s, mainly due to an aggressive acquisition strategy. Incorporated in 1911 and headquartered in Chicago, it employed 13,000 workers in the early 1990s. In 1992 it reported $1.05 billion in revenues.

The Leslie Fay Companies, Inc., designed and manufactured women's sportswear, suits, and separates at a diverse range of style and price points. Leslie Fay grew during the 1980s into one of the dominant forces of the industry through strong sales of apparel aimed at working women and a string of acquisitions. In 1988 it bought Albert Nipon, Inc., and Mary Ann Restivo, Inc., and in 1989 it purchased Non-Stop Fashions, Inc., and NS Petites, Inc. Leslie Fay also adopted the retailing approach of Calvin Klein and Liz Claiborne by opening ''shops'' within department stores.

In April 1993 the Leslie Fay Companies, Inc., declared bankruptcy after accounting irregularities were discovered and the company was found to be losing money. The company had difficulty moving its merchandise, as its apparel was criticized as overpriced and old-fashioned. Leslie Fay always relied on department stores to distribute its clothing, but the larger retailers faced stiff competition from discount and outlet stores, especially when the recession took hold in 1989.

Leslie Fay, based in New York City, employed approximately 4,600 workers in 1993 and posted 1991 revenues of $837 million. It sold suits through four divisions: the Leslie Fay division, which sold moderately priced apparel; the Albert Nipon division, which produced designer pieces; and the Castlebury Knits and the Sassco divisions, which offered better priced suits. Approximately 90 percent of the clothing Leslie Fay sold in 1991 was manufactured by contractors located in the United States and abroad. About 63 percent was manufactured abroad and then imported.

Oxford Industries Inc., based in Atlanta, Georgia, was one of the leading apparel manufacturers in the United States. It produced and distributed men's and women's apparel, including suits, skirts, and jackets, in a range of prices and styles. Oxford, like many other manufacturers, took advantage of the increased profits that came from the extended consumer spending spree of the 1980s to acquire a variety of labels and gain lucrative licensing agreements. With the recession in 1989, Oxford moved to shed its unprofitable lines and lower operating expenses.

Oxford reported sales of $573 million in 1993 and employed 9,300 workers. It sold its apparel to a variety of customers, including Eddie Bauer, L.L. Bean, Land's End, Target, and Wal-Mart. Two of its biggest customers were J.C. Penney and Sears, from which Oxford gained approximately a third of its sales in the fiscal year 1992-93. Oxford manufactured its clothing at its own factories in the United States and abroad, and it also used independent contractors. In 1991 approximately 50 percent of its apparel was manufactured domestically, while the other half was produced in 22 countries. The company was expected to shift more of its production overseas.

WORK FORCE

As imports increasingly replaced American-made clothing, the number of employees in the industry predictably declined. The International Ladies' Garment Workers' Union reported that from a peak in 1973, 34 percent of production worker jobs (nearly 25,000) were lost in 20 years in the women's and children's apparel industry, a process which accelerated in the 1980s.

There were approximately 44,600 workers involved in the manufacture of women's apparel in 1992, down from 55,200 five years earlier. The majority (approximately 36,400) were production workers, about half of whom were union members. In the apparel industry as a whole, wages averaged $7.02 an hour. Although these wages were low, wages in countries that exported apparel to the United States were often as low as 20 cents an hour. Many of those employed in the industry in the United States were recent immigrants who were willing to work for low wages.

New York was the state with the largest number of employees in the women's apparel industry, while Pennsylvania, New Jersey, California, and Massachusetts also had important concentrations of workers.

AMERICA AND THE WORLD

The U.S. women's apparel industry was dominated by imports by the early 1990s. Imports were attractive to consumers because they were often less expensive than domestically produced clothing, and they had increased in quality over time. The industry began to lose market share to imports in the 1960s. The process began to accelerate in the 1970s, and by the early 1990s imports reached all-time highs. From 1980 through the early 1990s apparel imports tripled when measured in square meters. Also contributing to the industry's decline in the United States was the reliance of manufacturers on off-shore assembly of pieces cut domestically.

Manufacturers in the Far East represented a significant source of women's apparel. When apparel makers started to move their manufacturing bases out of the United States in the 1960s, they first went to Hong Kong, Taiwan, and South Korea to take advantage of the cheap labor there. By the 1980s, however, labor costs had increased, and capital and experience from those traditional low-wage markets moved to lower wage countries such as Bangladesh, Thailand, Pakistan, Indonesia, Malaysia, Sri Lanka, and India, which became the sources for more of the imports entering the U.S. market. By the early 1990s, China replaced Hong Kong as the greatest supplier of imported clothing to the United States.

The North American Free Trade Agreement (NAFTA), which created a free-trade zone between the United States, Mexico, and Canada by gradually eliminating tariffs over 15 years, took effect January 1, 1994. Since a similar agreement was already in effect between the United States and Canada, analysts expected NAFTA to increase trade with Mexico. Apparel-industry executives supported NAFTA. The ILGWU and the ACTWU, by contrast, sought to stem the loss of jobs in the apparel industry by limiting the imports allowed into the country. However, their arguments did not succeed in challenging the free-market philosophy that ultimately triumphed in the passage of NAFTA.

Any agreement to come from the negotiations of the General Agreement on Tariffs and Trade (GATT), started in 1986, would possibly have wide-ranging impact on the U.S. apparel industry. GATT was first established in the 1960s, and it created the Arrangement Regarding International Trade in Textiles, known as the Multifiber Arrangement (MFA). The MFA regulated apparel that was imported into the United States and other member nations, and it was renewed every three years. Proposals involved in the GATT negotiations would reduce the tariffs on imports into the United States by half over time, without guaranteeing U.S. products access to markets in other countries. Some countries that exported heavily into the United States—for example, China—did not allow corresponding access to their home markets. The MFA would be superseded by any agreement reached in the GATT talks, but if no agreement was reached the MFA would be extended. The textile industry estimated that one million U.S. textile and apparel jobs would be lost under the provisions of GATT.

More and more imports entered the United States under provision 9802 (formerly known as Section 807) of the Harmonized Tariffs Schedule of the United States. This provision allowed clothing assembled abroad—from pieces cut in the United States—to be reimported with duty paid for the value added abroad. Thus, the most labor-intensive part of the assembly process could be done at lower-wage rates. Many U.S. manufacturers took advantage of the provision and moved assembly operations to the Caribbean. They noted that they could reduce costs and more successfully compete against imports from Asia. More complex items could be assembled and turned around more quickly than if created in Asia. Disadvantages included sometimes cumbersome and time-consuming logistics considerations. By 1992, apparel assembled in the Caribbean comprised 14 percent of imports. The passage of NAFTA, however, led some observers to expect that the Caribbean would become less desirable as a manufacturing destination than Mexico.

U.S. women's apparel exports grew rapidly starting in the late 1980s, from $235 million in 1989 to an estimated $568 million in 1992. U.S. clothing seemed to grow in popularity in Europe, perhaps due to the adoption by European women of a lifestyle more in line with the easy-care, comfortable clothing that women in the United States purchased. The weak U.S. dollar helped increase shipments to Japan and Canada, as well as Europe and the Middle East.

RESEARCH AND TECHNOLOGY

The large firms in the women's apparel industry had the capital to invest in new technology, but many of the smaller firms, struggling against the tide of imports, were not in a position to do so. Nevertheless, the intrinsic "soft" quality of material made it difficult to use automated equipment widely, and apparel manufacture remained a highly labor-intensive industry.

One tool that was advocated to better meet the market's demands was "quick response"—the idea of bringing apparel to the retailer rapidly by shortening production cycles, reducing inventories, improving productivity, and relaying information regarding consumers' preferences quickly back to manufacturers. By using computers to track inventory and sales as well as consumers' responses to particular items, U.S. manufacturers could respond quickly to market demand—and thus get a jump on foreign producers. Department stores and manufacturers worked together to find ways to speed deliveries and increase efficiency. Mass merchandisers were among the first to implement the quick response concept.

INDUSTRY INFORMATION SOURCES

"Apparel and Footwear Profiles for 1991," *KSA Perspective,* June 1992.

Conditions in the Women's Garment Industry, International Ladies' Garment Workers' Union, January 27, 1993.

"Women's Coats, Suits, Tailored Career Wear (Uniforms), Rainwear," *Fairchild Fact File,* 1987.

—C. Collins

SIC 2339

WOMEN'S, MISSES', AND JUNIORS' OUTERWEAR

This industry includes establishments primarily engaged in manufacturing women's, misses', and juniors' outerwear, not elsewhere classified, from purchased woven or knit fabrics. Knitting mills primarily engaged in manufacturing outerwear are classified in **SIC 2253: Knit Outerwear Mills.**

There were more than 1,700 manufacturers of women's, misses, and junior's outerwear in the United States in 1993. In 1991, wholesale shipments of $19.5 billion generated retail sales of $33 billion.

The industry is centered in California and New York. There were more than 1,100 manufacturers in those two states; however, manufacturers can be found in 35 other states stretching from New Jersey and Pennsylvania to Texas and Hawaii. The size and scope of these dress manufacturers vary greatly from small manufacturers operating out of their home or a single showroom to the giant Kayser-Roth Corporation which employed over 27,000 individuals and serviced multiple product lines and companies.

The women's apparel industry is particularly sensitive to changes in economic conditions. Consumer tastes shifted from a preference for designer labels during the 1980s to an increased interest in more casual, and inexpensive, apparel as the economic downturn of the early 1990s caused consumers to look for value and savings. This shift in consumer behavior resulted in a decrease in the number of women's apparel manufacturers. An increase in imports further increased competition in this already volatile and difficult industry. While imports increased by only 5 percent per year between 1988 and 1991, they took a jump of 15 percent in 1992.

These events created increased competition and fostered a reluctance on behalf of manufacturers and retailers to raise prices on apparel. Many small manufacturers were forced to close their doors and the strength of the remaining manufacturers during the mid-1990s depended upon an end to the worldwide recessionary conditions.

Women's, juniors', and misses' outerwear has been very sensitive to economic and demographic changes. This sensitivity was noted in the growth in sales for discount mass merchandisers at the expense of specialty boutiques and department stores. In the early 1990s, manufacturers attempted to hold down costs and provide high quality garments for increasingly demanding and careful customers.

The apparel and textile manufacturing industries employed approximately nine percent of the entire U.S. work force in the early 1990s. More than one million workers were engaged in apparel manufacturing. The number of workers involved specifically in the manufacture of women's, misses', and juniors' outerwear fell from a high of 93,500 in 1982 to less than 87,000 in 1993. In that same time period, average wages rose from $4.69 per hour to close to $7.00 per hour.

More than 22,000 people, or over 20 percent of this industry's work force, were employed in California's 670 establishments engaged in women's, juniors', and misses' outerwear manufacturing. New York employed 12,800 people in this industry. Strong manufacturing centers were also located in Georgia, Tennessee and Texas; each of these states supported between 6,000 and 9,000 workers in this industry. The largest percentage of workers were employed as sewing machine operators, followed by pressing machine operators and inspectors. With the exception of sales and machine mechanics, all other employment categories in the industry were anticipating work force reductions through the turn of the century.

Despite inroads into automation, the bulk of apparel manufacturing in the United States was still labor intensive in the early 1990s. Production workers in this industry made up 85 percent of the work force compared to only 68 percent for all other U.S. manufacturing. Wages in this sector were typically lower than in other manufacturing industries, resulting in an ongoing reliance on immigrant labor.

INDUSTRY INFORMATION SOURCES

American Apparel Manufacturers Association. ''Apparel Industry Trends.'' *Economic Newsletter* (June 1993).

Feldman, Amy. ''Consumer Nondurables.'' *Forbes* (January 4, 1993).

O'Rourke, Mary T. ''Labor Costs - From Pakistan to Portugal.'' *Bobbin* (September 1992).

Pouschine, Tatiana. ''Ridin' High.'' *Forbes* (November 9, 1992).

Standard & Poor's Industry Surveys. New York: Standard & Poor's Corporation, 1993.

U.S. Industrial Outlook 1993. Washington, D.C: U.S. Department of Commerce, 1993.

—Shula Malkin

SIC 2341

WOMEN'S, MISSES', CHILDREN'S, AND INFANTS' UNDERWEAR AND NIGHTWEAR

This category includes establishments primarily engaged in manufacturing women's, misses', children's and infants' underwear and nightwear from purchased woven or knit fabrics. Knitting mills primarily engaged in manufacturing underwear and nightwear are classified in **Industry 2254: Knit Underwear and Nightwear Mills**. Establishments primarily engaged in manufacturing women's and misses robes and dressing gowns are classified in **Industry 2384: Robes and Dressing Gowns**, and those manufacturing children's and infants' robes are classified in **Industry 2369: Girls', Children's, and Infants' Outerwear, Not Elsewhere Classified**. Establishments primarily engaged in manufacturing brassieres, girdles, and allied garments are classified in **Industry 2342: Brassiers, Girdles, and Allied Garments**.

INDUSTRY SNAPSHOT

About 350 establishments were engaged in the manufacture of women's, misses', children's and infants' underwear in 1992. These establishments were collectively responsible for an inflation adjusted value of total product shipments estimated at $18.7 billion. This figure was in line with a long term declining trend which, beginning in 1984, had fallen without interruption. When tracked over the five year period covering 1987-1992, the annual percentage change in the value of the total product shipments averaged a negative 6.1 percent.

Beginning from the early to mid 1980s, economic conditions in the women's apparel industry group turned from bad to worse, with the women's and children's underwear and nightwear being no exception. In 1982, for instance, there were approximately 604 establishments involved in manufacturing activities and by 1989 their number had dropped to 383. During the same period total employment declined from 67,800 to 49,400.

The ongoing concurrence of several major economic trends sufficed to explain the industry's sagging fortunes. First, the decline in middle class income levels, a trend which began in the mid-to-late 1970s and picked up a full head of steam during the 1980s, led to the withdrawal of a considerable amount of consumer purchasing power formerly directed at the purchase of apparel products in general.

Second, and partly as a consequence of the above, established lines of distribution at both the retail and wholesale levels were in the throes of a bankruptcy-induced crisis. Around the same period, these sectors were also undergoing widespread structural change, owing to the introduction of advanced communication systems which greatly enhanced the flow of integrated information across retail, wholesale and manufacturing levels.

Third, the change in women's apparel producer prices plunged during the recession of 1981-82. Then, to the further detriment of the industry, as the recession ended prices never climbed back to their previous levels but were to remain more or less flat instead for the period covering 1983 into the first half of 1990s. With the onset of the 1990-92 recession, women's apparel prices took another nosedive. Intense intra-industry competition from both domestic and foreign producers had played an important part in generating the unfavorable price climate and contributed to a significant ten year decline in capacity utilization. After peaking in 1984 at 88 percent, capacity utilization began to plummet on an annual basis and stood at 78 percent in 1994. Finally, the lingering overhang of takeover debt, piled up from the late 1980s period of speculative merger-mania, had exerted a retarding effect on company profits and growth.

On the positive side, however, the steady decline in the value of the U.S. dollar had proved advantageous to export sales of women's and children's underwear and nightwear, although it needs to be mentioned that export sales have traditionally figured as a rather insignificant component of the industry's overall U.S. sales. For the period covering 1989-1992, the annual change in nominal exports averaged 27.1 percent. Many in the industry were encouraged by the export surge and hopeful that the boom proved to be long- term in order to reverse the industry's fortunes.

Another important development taking shape during the 1985-1994 period was the gain in market shares posted by most of the industry's leading firms, despite the troubles experienced by the industry as a whole. The fruits of these gains placed the leading firms in a position to invest internally generated funds towards apparel-related, state-of-the-art technological operations and further solidify their commanding status. [Industry Structure]

In 1989 close to 383 establishments were involved in the manufacture of women's and children's underwear and nightwear. The average number of employees per establishment was 54. For the same year the average value added per production worker was $29,095, a figure considerably below an overall average of $105,881 calculated for 459 U.S. manufacturing industries. Efforts to redress this productivity gap have been consistently, though not uniformly, percolating throughout the industry for some time. These have variously taken the form of labor-management cooperation schemes, technology diffusion, mergers, periods of protectionism meant to provide the time necessary to restructure the workplace, and the "outsourcing" to other domestic or foreign firms of work formerly performed within a company's premises.

When tracking the density of establishments by their census region of concentration, the highest number of establishments were respectively located in the Middle Atlantic, South Atlantic, and Pacific regions. When ranked by the number of establishments per state, New York led the way with 104, followed by Pennsylvania and North Carolina with 56 each, California had 38 and New Jersey 24. In terms of industry's total employment level per state, Pennsylvania was first with 7,700, followed by New York with 4,100, California with 2,100, and New Jersey 1,800.

In 1992, market shares estimated from the top seventy-five companies indicated that the dominant firms in the women's, misses', children's, and infants' underwear and nightwear were: Vanity Fair Mills Inc., (16.2 percent); Maidenform Inc., (9.4 percent); William Carter Co., (6.8); Munsingwear Inc., (3.7); AJ

Schneierson, (3.2 percent); and Heckler Mfg. and Investment, (3.2 percent). Both Vanity Fair Mills and AJ Schneierson were registered as subsidiaries, while Maidenform, William Carter, and Heckler were privately owned companies, and Munsingwear was public. Other companies that fell below these companies in terms of market share but with some degree of industry name recognition where Sara Lee Corp., Wior Corp., and Sanmark-Stardust Inc.

An article appearing in *Sales and Marketing Management* estimated that in 1987 large plants with 100 or more employees accounted for only 41 percent of the total number of establishments but were responsible for close to 87 percent of the industry's shipments. It noted that many of the smaller establishments survived by making specialized products to supply market niches.

Data available from the U.S. Bureau of Census for the years 1982 and 1987 indicated the following input and output flow information. The primary materials consumed by the women's, misses', children's and infant's underwear and nightwear industry ranked on a cost basis were: materials, containers and supplies; knit fabrics; miscellaneous materials and parts; and broadwoven fabrics. And the major economic sectors responsible for input supply came from: imports; broadwoven fabric mills; apparel made from purchased materials; and knit fabric mills. When disaggregated, the total product share broken down by its major product classifications were: women's and children's underwear with 38.3 percent; women's and childrens' nightwear with 46.4 percent; and contract and commission work on the two combined categories was 12.2 percent. The principal economic sectors responsible for the purchase of the industry's output were: private personal expenditures with 82.7 percent; other manufacturers with 12.0 percent; exports with 1.5 percent; followed by the Federal Government with 1.0 percent.

BACKGROUND AND DEVELOPMENT

Women's underwear. The modern history of women's underwear produced for mass consumption more or less began in the 1830s to 1840s with the manufacture of ready-made undergarments. Stay stitchers and gorers using hand techniques were employed in factories or worked from home as "outworkers." Around the early 1860s, the widespread use of sewing machines pushed underwear output to unprecedented levels. Other complementary technologies, like the band knife, which enabled garment workers to slice through several layers of material at once, proved instrumental in re-organizing the factory floor along the lines of the "batch" system.

During the 1870s, underwear was available in attractively packaged boxes with decorative and typically colored labels. Large-scale advertising campaigns trumpeting the virtues of underwear became commonplace by the end of the 1870s. Well into the 1880s, the marketing themes became more explicit in an attempt to match the luxury and erotic appeal of the undergarments. Underwear could be purchased from large department stores or by mail order from companies like Sears & Roebuck of Chicago or the Great Universal Stores located across the United States.

Fashion historians refer to the period of 1890-1913 as the "Belle Epoque." It was characterized as a period of extravagance and conspicuous consumption in women's dress in general, and in women's underwear in particular. Underwear was much lighter in appearance, feel, and weight and, compared to its lackluster Mid-Victorian antecedents, more luxurious and glamorous in conception. New luxury underwear first became available in sets which included nightwear and were christened with the group name "lingerie," a term derived from the French word "linge," meaning linen. Earlier material mainstays such as cotton longcloth and flannel were replaced by cambrics, merino and silks. The extravagance in tastes and materials continued to lead the underwear fashion charge until the economic slump of the 1930s, which ushered in the era of mass-produced machine made rayon lingerie.

The introduction in the nineteenth century, and the 1930s full-scale development of, elastene stretch fabrics exerted a tremendous influence on underwear production. And it was during the 1930s period, more than ever before, that the popularity of ready-made underwear began to seize the day. It supplanted the more upscale fabrics associated with the Belle Epoque period.

During the 1940s, events surrounding the Second World War and its lingering aftereffects, put changes in the underwear industry on a ten year hold as resources used throughout the apparel industry were diverted to wartime production. For instance, foundation wear finishing tape was used for cartridge belts, brass armaments manufacture took over the production of hooks, eyes, and stocking supporters, while lace machines were used for making camouflaged nets. Nylon, invented in 1938, was used for glider tow ropes and parachutes and not until 1947 did it re-enter into the production of underwear.

During the 1950s nylon and other man-made fibers entered into the production of underwear and dominated the scene. At the time, nylon's chief drawback was its non-absorbent property but later the fabric was somewhat modified and woven to obtain a more comfortable porous state. Another man-made material achieving popularity was rayon, which when mixed with cotton created a shiny and always "new" appearance. Other man-made 1950 notables were polyester and acrylic undergarments. In 1959 Lycra, arguably one of the most important and versatile of man-made fibers, was introduced and was originally referred to as Spandex or elatomerics, only to be renamed elastene by the EEC in 1976. Containing no natural fiber at all, Lycra was lighter, proved far more durable than rubber elastic, and remained a foundation wear mainstay well into the 1990s.

The decade of the 1960s and early 1970s ushered in a tumultuous period of great social and political upheaval. Television exerted a powerful influence and Maidenform became the first U.S. company to advertise underwear on a national level. Magazines such as *Vogue* and other glossy women's magazines were highly attuned to promoting a version of what the beautiful woman looked like in terms of both her outer and innerwear garments. During this period, attitudes toward sex and the traditional woman's lifestyle, both outside and inside the house, were under assault, opening up new avenues for self-expression and lifestyle changes. Drowning in its wake were the more restrictive type of underwear previously equated with outdated notions of decency—and in their place came bikini-style briefs. The popularity of the briefs, which were available for men and women alike, rested on their comfort and accessibility for those pursuing more active lifestyles.

The teenage apparel market first became a distinct entity during the 1950s and went on to become an institutional mainstay in the 1960s. The needs of younger girls (misses) for suitable and acceptable underwear reflecting their own stage of development and active involvement in various social activities was readily acknowledged. As a result, the U.S. company Lilies of France introduced a special "Lilies" line of underwear for college-age girls along with a preteen collection called "Teenform," which was later imported into Britain by Berlei.

By the 1990s, the 30-year transformation of children's and infants underwear had achieved significant results. Unlike the underwear that was worn up to the late sixties, undergarments in the 1990s washed easier, were more attractive, lightweight, and durable, and were less prone to induce irritation. The comfort provided from t-shirts made from cotton and simple crop tops left a favorable impression on the mother or child able to recall the discomfort related to the wearing of undergarments made from knitted wool, liberty bodices, and burdensome knickers lined with breakable elastic during the 1940s, 1950s and early 1960s.

WORK FORCE

The industry's employment picture had indicated a sharp decline going back as far as 1982. For the period covering 1987-1991, the industry's total employment fell from 53,700, of which 46,700 were classified as production workers, to 45,800 with 39,200 classified as production workers. Comparison between the two years indicated that the level of total employment declined by 14.7 percent while the level of production workers fell 16.1 percent. Over the same period the real wage fell while value added per production worker either stayed the same or rose, suggesting that productivity gains were not being matched with rising wages.

In 1990, the industry's major occupational categories were: sewing machine operators; precision inspectors, testers, and graders; pressing machine operators; and blue collar supervisors. Close to 56.0 percent of the work force was active in sewing machine operations. The remaining occupational categories accounted for approximately 3.1 percent of the total work force each. The Bureau of Labor Statistics had forecasted that many of these occupational categories were expected to decline by the year 2005. Assuming no great deviations from the forward path of the industry's productivity trend, sewing machine operators were projected to experience the largest decline.

When compared to the measures of employment by gender and race for the U.S. manufacturing sector as a whole, women, black, and Hispanic workers were disproportionately represented in the industry's work force to such a large degree that they dramatically exceeded their national average counterparts. In 1988, demographic data gathered from a survey performed by the Amalgamated Clothing and Textile Workers Union concluded that women workers comprised 84.4 percent of the industry's work force and black workers 21.2 percent, while the category of overall minority workers represented in the industry measured 35.9 percent.

CURRENT CONDITIONS

In retrospect, the downsizing through elimination and mergers of the number of establishment comprising the women's, misses', children's and infants' underwear and nightwear industry became a recognized trend by the late 1980s. By the mid 1990s things began to stabilize somewhat, yet it was not clear whether the trend had been entirely played out. The opening up of the countries of the former Soviet Union and Eastern Europe, where there resided a well trained apparel work force ripe for capitalist investment, also presented the industry with untapped opportunities that looked promising even if they had not yet been fully explored. Further long term uncertainties were thrown into this mix with the 1993 passage of the North American Free Trade Agreement and, later that year, the General Agreement on Tariffs and Trade.

Well into the 1980s, the entire U.S. apparel industry group was negatively impacted by the erosion of middle-class income earners who generally accounted for the overwhelming percentage of apparel purchases. At the same time, the industry's growing trend toward the foreign relocation of apparel establishments, or else the foreign outsourcing and re-entry into the United States of intermediate apparel-related work formerly performed within U.S. borders (under the auspices of the 9802 provision of the Harmonized Tariff Schedule of the United States), did not bode well for the industry's U.S. job growth prospects. The effect of apparel import competition leading to the progressive domestic market share deterioration of U.S. apparel manufacturers also indicated no sign of abating.

To date, the most far-reaching domestic response to the deteriorating conditions impacting the industry was to invest in state-of-the-art communication systems which facilitate the rapid flow of information used to immediately react to, and determine, consumer preferences formed in the marketplace. This consumer driven process, which the industry refers to as the "quick response" system, integrates several dimensions of the production cycle with the intent of shortening the cycle's duration. Via the immediate feedback of consumer sales information from the retail to manufacturing level, producers are able to implement productivity improvements and shrink inventory levels and their associated costs to a bare minimum. To determine the changing direction of consumer tastes, the quick response system compiles the results of consumer surveys which express what consumers most likely will and will not purchase in the immediate future.

In addition to the quick response system, the industry had also directed sizable investments at computer controlled automated machinery. With the intention of increasing productivity foremost in mind, these investments targeted the areas of design, cutting, embroidery, sewing, finishing, ticketing, and several distribution operations. In order to compete within their own industry as well as against other non-apparel industries, the industry's leading firms were the first to implement these investments to any significant degree. Their ability to finance high start-up cost technological advances was related to their economies of scale and access to internally generated funds. With the passage of time, if the middle and lower tier firms failed to respond by adapting these new technologies, then across the entire industry an uneven pattern of technological change would result and most likely exacerbate the downsizing trend active throughout the industry.

INDUSTRY INFORMATION SOURCES

Arpan, Jeffery S., de la Torres, Jose, and Toyne, Brian, *The U.S. Apparel Industry: International Challenge, Domestic Response*, Atlanta, Georgia: Business Publishing Division, College of Business Administration Georgia State University, 1982.

Carter, Alison, *Underwear: The Fashion History*, London: B.T. Batsford LTD, 1992.

Ewing, Elizabeth, *Dress and Undress: A History of Women's Underwear*, New York: Drama Book Specialists, 1978.

Fairchild Fact File: Women's Inner Fashions: Nightwear, Daywear, Loungewear, New York: Fairchild Publications, Market Research Division, 1989.

Focus: An Economic Profile of the Apparel Industry, Arlington, VA: American Apparel Manufacturers Association, 1993.

Jarnow, Jeannette, and Guerreiro, Miriam, *Inside the Fashion Business*, New York: Macmillan Publishing Company, 1991.

Lehman Brothers, *The Clothes Line*, December, 1993

Manufacturing USA: Industry Analyses, Statistics and Leading Companies, 3rd Edition, Detroit, MI: Gale Research Inc., 1993.

Rose, Clare, *Children's Clothes Since 1750*, New York: Drama Book Publishers, 1989.

U.S. Industrial Outlook 1993, Washington D.C.: U.S. Department of Commerce, 1993.

—Daniel E. King

SIC 2342

BRASSIERES, GIRDLES, AND ALLIED GARMENTS

Establishments primarily engaged in manufacturing brassieres, girdles, corsets, corset accessories, and allied garments are included in this industry.

INDUSTRY SNAPSHOT

The American bra and girdle industry posted sales of over $1 billion in 1992. During its century of existence, the industry saw a number of ups and downs, influenced by a variety of factors—only some of them style-based. During World War II, for example, the cotton, rubber, silk, and steel used to make women's undergarments were needed instead for the war effort. The bra and girdle industry was forced to develop new products that made use of synthetic fabrics.

Although the braless look of the 1960s caused concern among manufacturers, who saw their profits literally going up in smoke during the "burn the bra" movement, bras and girdles did reappear—in different fabrics, shapes, and colors—and the industry remained strong. Fashion trends changed the shape of the bra and technology altered its fabric content, but the garment remained a big seller. In a 1989 tribute to the centennial of the bra, *Life* magazine estimated that more than half a million undergarments of this type were sold daily in the United States. With music stars like Madonna popularizing the look of underwear as outerwear, the numbers might surge even higher.

BACKGROUND AND DEVELOPMENT

The first bra was developed in France in 1889 by the corsetmaker Herminie Cadolle. Designed to replace the restrictive whale-bone corsets that stylish women of the time were forced to wear, the bra supported a woman's breasts without constricting her diaphragm. Americans were introduced to the bra during the 1910s—the Flapper Era—when the ideal woman's silhouette was slim and boyish. An undergarment that would flatten a woman's breasts was an ideal accompaniment to the straight-cut, form-fitting flapper dress preferred by suffragettes and stylish debutantes in Europe.

The style was brought back to America, and in 1913 New York socialite Caresse Crosby designed a brassiere out of two handkerchiefs and silk ribbons. The patent for her design was registered in 1914. Shortly thereafter, it was purchased by the Connecticut-based Warner's Company for $1,500. Warner's, previously a corset company, became one of the first American manufacturers of the bra. Other companies followed, including the now-defunct Boyshform.

Until the 1930s, the bra was more or less a "one size fits all" product. Because of the manly styles of the 1920s, women did not want to emphasize the size or shape of their breasts; rather, they tried to conceal them. In the Depression era, however, fashion designers began to emphasize women's feminine form once

again. Warner's introduced bras with fitted cups, ranging from A (small) to D (large) size, in 1935; other manufacturers quickly followed suit.

The rages of fashion shifted all the way from the World War I boyish look epitomized by the flappers to the very womanly figure of such pin-up girls as Betty Grable and Jane Russell during World War II. Even though the fabrics used to make bras and girdles—silk, cotton, and rubber—were reserved for the war effort, designers still found ways to manufacture bras and girdles that emphasized the curvaceous look favored by sweater girls and soldier boys.

Anecdotal evidence claimed that Howard Hughes's aeronautics firm once designed a bra for Jane Russell, star of the 1943 movie classic *The Outlaw*. Made of metal, the bra was heavy and uncomfortable, according to Russell, who claimed that she never wore it. But the use of metal did play an important role in the next phase of bra silhouettes. In 1946, under-cup wiring was introduced. This engineering feat allowed bra designers to uplift the bust even more, since the underwiring added extra support.

During the 1940s, bras were being manufactured by Maidenform, founded in 1922; Playtex, founded in 1932; Vanity Fair, founded in 1899; and other smaller companies including Bestform, founded in 1923; and Bali, founded in 1927.

Women's fashion took on a retro look in the postwar 1940s and 1950s, when returning soldiers reclaimed the workplace and many women returned to the role of homemaker. With sheath dresses that emphasized every curve of a woman's figure being shown in every fashion house in Europe and America, undergarment manufacturers introduced one-piece, constructed undergarments to hold in stomachs, nip in waists, and push up busts. Another fashion favorite, the tight-bodiced, full-skirted dress, also required undergarments to pull in the waist and emphasize the bust.

During the 1950s, bra manufacturers experimented with a new look, the push-up bra, in which the cup section was cut in half, leaving the cleavage exposed. Usually strapless, to be worn under the strapless formal dresses so popular in the 1950s, the push-up bra gave every woman who wore it an ample-looking, high-bosomed silhouette. Cone-shaped bras, which emphasized a pointy-busted look, were also popular in the 1950s, and were returned to popularity briefly by singer Madonna in the late 1980s.

While bras changed in shape throughout the forty-odd years they were manufactured by American companies, other undergarments also changed to keep up with the current styles. The Edwardian look of the last years of the 19th century and the first decade of the 20th century involved the wearing of a firm foundation garment that pulled in the waist and supported the bust. Corsets of the 1920s flattened the figure, but they were often too long for the short dresses being worn by young women. In response, manufacturers developed corselettes—shorter corsets—as well as slide-on garter belts and other, even briefer, undergarments.

The technological innovations of the 1930s turned up in undergarments. "Living Lastex," one of the earliest of the stretchy, shape-holding textiles, along with narrow, dependable zippers, allowed manufacturers to sell undergarments that not only helped a woman maintain a womanly shape, but also let her move and breathe with at least a bit more comfort. Panty girdles—girdles that were shaped like underpants—were invented in the 1930s, to be worn under then more acceptable slacks and shorts.

Dior's "New Look" of the late 1940s and 1950s needed new-looking undergarments. To go with the cantilevered bras required by the new silhouette, women laced themselves into guepieres, or waist cinchers—a new back-laced corset. Also at this time the Merry Widow corset, an all-in-one bra and girdle combination that was popular at the end of the 19th century, was reintroduced. The industry giant Warner's was among the first manufacturers to make the new Merry Widow available to the masses by introducing a line of them in retail stores in 1952.

The pulled-in, pushed-up look of the 1950s became the pulled-apart look of the 1960s, as women's liberation swept across America. Bras were suddenly seen as harnesses rather than supports, which held women back rather than up. Women's libbers burned bras in city streets. At the Miss America pageant of 1968—the height of the women's movement—protesters threw bras, girdles, and other symbols, such as curlers and *Cosmopolitan* magazine, into a garbage can. Bras were out, and many women appeared in public without anything under their clothes.

Bra and girdle manufacturers were undoubtedly concerned about their profits shrinking in the tide of the braless revolution. They worked hard at developing "natural-looking undergarments"—bras that held a woman's breasts without changing their natural shape, and "barely there" girdles. But it was not the revolutionary bra style that forced women back into underwear. Rather, it was the concern voiced by the medical community that women who went braless for a long period of time ran the risk of stretching their breast ligaments to a point where the breast would look elongated and feel uncomfortable.

While bra manufacturers struggled, girdle manufacturers faced a revolution even more harmful than bra burning. It was the invention of pantyhose—all-in-one stockings and panties—that struck a blow from which some manufacturers took years to recover. Pantyhose did not require garters, garter belts, or girdles. Women's libbers—and in fact almost every woman in the country—adopted pantyhose faster than anyone could possibly have foreseen.

As women became more confident about appearing in public without the entrapments of constricting undergarments, bra and girdle manufacturers had to scramble to keep up. Luckily, however, another movement—the exercise and fitness phenomenon of the 1970s and 1980s—provided a new market for their wares.

Women and men throughout the United States became exercise fanatics, spurred on by such fitness gurus as Jane Fonda. Workout attire, such as sports bras, became popular. But for many women, especially those who suddenly found themselves part of the 24-hours-a-day corporate world, an exercise regimen was difficult to maintain on a regular basis. They needed help—and the bra and girdle manufacturers of America were prepared to support them with body suits, bras, body shapers (a synonym for "girdle"), and control-top underpants, all made of lycra, spandex, and other miracle synthetics, to pull in, push up, and smooth out a myriad of lumps, bumps, and ridges.

By the late 1980s, the bra and girdle industry came almost full-circle as tastes and styles changed once again. Bras, girdles, and even corsets were popularized by performers such as Madonna, who almost single-handedly revived the bustiere industry; movies such as *Dangerous Liaisons,* in which the female characters were laced up in tight corsets; and couturiers who put their bras on the outside of dresses, rather than the inside.

CURRENT CONDITIONS

According to *U.S. Industrial Outlook 1993,* women's wear shipments, including bras and allied garments, were much lower than the industry average in 1992. Among the factors affecting the growth of the industry were demographic trends—apparel expenses became a lower proportion of total personal expenditures for the baby-boom generation. These consumers reached the point in their lives when other expenses—mortgages and their children's college tuition, for example—began to take precedence over clothing purchases.

As well, there was a shift in consumer buying habits. Instead of patronizing retail stores, a majority of shoppers began making regular visits to discounters and off-price emporiums, where they could find bargains. Bra and girdle manufacturers began offering discount lines; although there might still be a small market for luxury underclothes, most women wanted to spend less on a bra than on an evening meal.

The fashion splurge of the 1980s, when expenditures on clothes practically doubled, was replaced with frugal shopping by recession-stressed consumers who frequented Kmart and Wal-Mart more often than designer boutiques and department stores. According to Standard and Poor's *Industry Surveys* (1992), not only did the spending patterns of consumers change, but their buying patterns also took a new direction.

Basic apparel—T-shirts, sweatshirts, denims, and fleecewear—were in, as were moderately priced name brands like Fruit-of-the-Loom and Van Heusen. The major manufacturers of bras and girdles began producing basic styles at popular prices, and in that way they were able to keep abreast of this latest trend.

But manufacturers of bras and girdles also realized that undergarments were something that women—and men—would occasionally splurge on. Companies such as Victoria's Secret and Gossard, manufacturer of the new super-uplift bra launched in 1994, continued to have success selling pure silk and lace undergarments for romantic occasions like Valentine's Day and honeymoons. They also served a number of women who desired a "little bit of femininity" under their business clothes.

Although the value of shipments of bras and allied garments increased 13 percent between 1987 and 1988, the industry has declined or been stagnant since then. The worst year was 1988-1989, when the industry saw an almost 16 percent decline in the value of its shipments. In 1989 to 1990, there was a modest 2 percent gain, offset by a 1 percent decline in 1990-1991. The *1993 Industrial Outlook* forecasted a 1.7 percent increase in the value of shipments in 1991-1992.

INDUSTRY LEADERS

The largest manufacturer of bras and related intimate apparel in the United States was New York City-based Warnaco Group Inc., which posted sales of $562.5 million in 1992. Warnaco Inc., a subsidiary of the Warnaco Group, was the second-largest manufacturer of these personal items.

Playtex Apparel Inc. of Stamford, Connecticut, a subsidiary of the Sara Lee Corporation, ranked in third

position, with 1992 sales of $400 million. Vanity Fair Mills Inc. (of Monroeville, Alabama), a subsidiary of VF Corp., placed fourth, with 1992 sales of $390 million. Fifth was Maidenform, Inc., a privately owned company in Bayonne, New Jersey, with sales of $320 million in 1992. Sara Lee Corporation's Bali Company, of Winston-Salem, North Carolina, had 1992 sales of $210 million, making it the sixth-largest manufacturer of bras and girdles in the country.

Bestform Foundations Inc., a privately held company based in Long Island, New York, ranked as the seventh-largest manufacturer, with sales of $110 million in 1992. Tied with Bestform in sales was the New York City-based I. Appel Corporation, primarily a manufacturer of women's robes and dressing gowns. Warnaco's Warner's was ninth among brassiere and girdle manufacturers, with sales of $100 million in 1992. The company's Olga division ranked at number ten, with sales of $70 million.

WORK FORCE

Manufacturers of bras and allied garments employed approximately 11,200 workers in 1992, 76 percent of whom were involved in production activities. Employment within this industry declined steadily, from 13,800 in 1987 to 11,000 in 1991, but was expected to recover slightly as the U.S. economy emerged from its recession. Average hourly earnings within the industry were projected at $7.01 in 1992, an increase of 6.4 percent over the previous year.

AMERICA AND THE WORLD

The value of exports of bras and allied garments has increased rapidly since 1988, as women in Europe and other markets faced busier lifestyles and responded by adopting some U.S. fashions. The value of industry exports was projected to increase 20 percent to $264 million in 1992. At the same time, U.S. imports within the bra and girdle industry increased 14 percent as well, to an estimated $488 in 1992. Some manufacturers of basic apparel planned to open plants overseas, particularly in Europe.

RESEARCH AND TECHNOLOGY

Manufacturers of basic apparel, such as bras and girdles, were strong candidates for implementation of electronic data interchange (EDI) systems, which linked manufacturers with retailers via computer networks. Through these systems, retailers electronically scanned the bar codes on all merchandise as it was sold. Then product data—such as number, color, and size—was transmitted automatically to manufacturers. EDI allowed manufacturers to plan production more efficiently and respond more quickly to consumer demand. Many such systems also provided for "automatic replenishment," where manufacturers shipped replacement merchandise directly to retailers without the delay of processing paperwork. Manufacturers of basic apparel stood to gain most from EDI systems since their operations were more highly automated and less dependent upon fashion trends than other apparel manufacturers.

Environmental issues were another area of research that occupied bra and girdle manufacturers in the mid-1990s. The industry came under pressure to reduce the inks and dyes, fabric scrap, and packaging it used, which often ended up in landfills or water supplies. The industry responded by developing new production processes that reduced ink use and scrap, as well as reevaluating its packaging choices. Consumer preferences also shifted toward natural, organically grown fabrics, so bra and girdle manufacturers increasingly tried to incorporate these materials into their garments.

INDUSTRY INFORMATION SOURCES

Bond, David, *The Guinness Guide to 20th Century Fashion,* Enfield, England: Guinness Superlatives Limited, 1981.

Dowling, Claudia Glenn, "Ooh-La-La! The Bra," *Life,* June 1989.

Garland, Madge, *The Changing Form of Fashion,* New York: Praeger Publishers, Inc., 1970.

Glynn, Prudence, *In Fashion: Dress in the Twentieth Century,* New York: Oxford University Press, 1978.

Gray, Mitchel, and Mary Kennedy, *The Lingerie Book,* New York: St. Martin's Press, 1980.

Lurie, Alison, *The Language of Clothes,* New York: Random House, 1981.

Reda, Susan, "Sweet Dreams (Brassiere Marketing)," *Discount Store News,* May 3, 1993.

Standard and Poor's, *Industry Surveys,* November 1992.

U.S. Industrial Outlook 1993.

—Marcia K. Mogelonsky

SIC 2353

HATS, CAPS, AND MILLINERY

This category includes establishments primarily engaged in the manufacture of hats, caps, millinery, and hat bodies. Establishments primarily engaged in manufacturing millinery trimmings are classified in **SIC 2396: Automotive Trimmings, Apparel Find-ings, and Related Products**. Establishments primarily engaged in manufacturing hats and caps of paper are classified in **SIC 2679: Converted Paper and Paperboard Products, Not Elsewhere Classified**; those manufacturing caps of rubber are classified in **SIC 3069: Fabricated Rubber Products, Not Elsewhere Classified**; those manufacturing caps of plastics are classified in **SIC 3089: Plastic Products, Not Elsewhere Classified**; and those manufacturing fur hats are classified in **SIC 2371: Fur Goods**.

INDUSTRY SNAPSHOT

Approximately 355 establishments were engaged in the manufacture of hats, caps, and millinery (the design, production, and sales of women's hats) in 1990. Altogether, these establishments were responsible for an inflation-adjusted total product estimated at $736.6 million. Between the years of 1987 and 1991, total industry sales rose from $662.7 million to $801 million. Since 1987, the industry had been experiencing a modest recovery, due in large part to the fad-driven popularity of team logo sports headwear. This came as a welcomed sign of relief to an industry whose fortunes had been steadily drifting downward since the early 1960s when there was a national trend toward hatlessness. For the 10-year period covering 1982-1992 alone, the number of establishments active in the industry fell from 420 to about 330, a 21.4 percent decline.

In addition to team logo sports headwear, the industry's output included straw harvest hats; jungle-cloth helmets; opera hats; Panama hats; and hat bodies made from fur-felt, straw, and wool-felt. To professional uniform services, the industry supplied chauffeur caps, police hats and caps (excluding protective headwear), and various other uniform hats and caps. In 1989, millinery establishments contributed an estimated $180 million to the industry's overall total product sales, a rather significant turnaround when compared to the $58 million mark achieved during the late 1970s.

BACKGROUND AND DEVELOPMENT

Prior to the more recent era of hatlessness, which took root during the suburbanization wave of the 1950s and 1960s, no respectable man or woman would have thought of leaving the house without a hat. The question of whether the hat industry would survive or not was unheard of during this time. Instead, of vital concern to the successful firms competing in the industry was their ability to produce and market an unending procession of new styles or modified variations of current popular styles. Since the life of a hat as a fashion accessory was typically short, the faster a firm was able to get in and out of a hot-selling style proved the key to its success.

Although not totally isolated from historical forces of technological change sweeping through other apparel industries, up until the 1990s, opportunities to mechanize and automate the industry had proven difficult. As a result, production methods frequently required a great deal of handwork, therefore, labor-intensive manufacture has long remained the industry's norm.

Men's Hats. As the twentieth century began, most men living in urban areas of the United States wore of hats. During the first decade, men could choose from a large variety of hats with each style purported to reflect the wearer's personality. One of the most prominent was the "princely" brown or black derby hat, which was available in three basic styles. At the time, most successful or aspiring businessmen sported the derby look. One of the more notables was the financier J.P. Morgan, who popularized a flat-topped version of the derby.

The manufacture of the derby was a time-consuming and labor-intensive process. Made from felt treated with repeated applications of a shellac solution, the material was heated and then allowed to cool. As it cooled, it took on it's stiffened state. Next came an oven process, which softened it to the touch, followed by an iron mold process. To press the hat into its distinctive derby shape, a rubber bag was inserted inside the hat into which cold water was forced. Finally, the hat's brim was curled through a highly skilled operation that required a set of specialized tools referred to as "shackles."

Almost as popular as the derby was the fedora, which was made from soft felt. Except for its shaping process, the fedora's manufacturing process mimicked many of the steps involved in producing a derby. The hat was available in black, brown, and gray and received its named from the popular drama *Fedora*, penned by Victorien Sardou.

Though derby and fedora hats were to remain popular U.S. favorites for decades to come, a challenge to their popularity arrived in the form of the Homburg hat. Made popular by King Edward's recreational visits to the town of Homburg in southern Germany, the Homburg hat was of Tyrolean origin and featured a small brightly colored feather in its side band's bow. By the time the hat achieved mass appeal, it was mostly available in black and was worn with an informal evening jacket.

During the 1920s, the U.S. men's fashion scene was heavily influenced by the British, particularly items connected to the pastimes of the Prince of Wales or associated with displays of wealth. For instance, in 1925, the English international tennis team showed up to play in Newport, Rhode Island, wearing brown snap-brim soft felt hats that the Prince, just a short time earlier, had been seen vacationing in. These hats became the rage with wealthy crowds frequenting tennis matches and then proceeded to gain mass U.S. appeal. As an emphasis on dressing in style for leisure events and travel to warmer climates of the U.S. became more popular, Panama hats, which were woven from such lightweight materials as oatmeal, coconut, and rice straws, increased in popularity. Bangkoks and Ballibuntals made from bamboo grasses or bamboo saplings growing wild in the Philippines also became popular. Another lightweight favorite were Milan hats, made from Tuscan straw grown in Italy. Woven loosely, these hats offered protection from the sun and allowed for good ventilation.

Except for the affluent few, the era of the Great Depression knocked the demand out of the market for hats. Just the same, British fashion influences continued, as was evidenced by the sensation created by the "porkpie" hat's arrival in 1934. A low-crowned hat of the telescope type and made from felt, the porkpie was first worn by well-to-do men who frequented polo games and horse races. Within a short time, the porkpie hat was accepted as appropriate attire for either business or casual settings. After it's initial introduction in felt, the porkpie later became available in a variety of straws, including panamas, leghorns, and bangkoks.

Caps worn for purposes other than work also became popular during this decade. The checkered cap was deemed appropriate for golf and weekend motoring. For hunters, fishing enthusiasts, and country sports spectators, rough tweed caps were fashionable. Irrespective of whether it was worn for work or leisure purposes, the production process for cloth cap manufacture was practically the same. Cloth was cut by hand, usually with a manually operated knife, to ensure a precision pattern. The pieces were then sewn carefully to ensure that the cloth's design matched, with special attention paid to where the crown joined the visor. The cap was then steamed and ironed. Additional leather and linings were sewn in during the finishing stages. Should the cap be unlined, the crown seams were filled with tape so the threads did not appear on the outside of the cap.

With economic production geared toward military purposes, the war years of the 1940s witnessed little change in terms of style or material in men's hats. For the remainder of the decade, the war's aftershocks continued a dulling effect on the industry. By the early 1950s, the advent of man-made fabrics—many of which were washable and lightweight—dramatically transformed the material base from which most apparel garments were constructed. In turn, the reigning emphasis on lightweight materials translated into a boon for straw hats. Around the same time, the popularity of the low-crown porkpie hat increased and the wearing of the small-shape strip tweed cap outside of its more narrowly defined traditional sporting events boundaries was common. By the decade's end, hats made from man-made material, such as nylon, displaced straw hats as they proved lighter in weight and came with more ventilation and durability.

ORGANIZATION AND STRUCTURE

In 1989, about 380 establishments were engaged in the production of hats, caps, and millinery. The average establishment employed approximately 42 employees. In the same year, the average value added per production worker was $30,355, a figure that was considerably below an overall national average of $105,881 for 459 U.S. manufacturing industries. In terms of investment per production worker—usually a reliable indicator of inter-industry levels of productivity—the hats, caps, and millinery industry averaged $471, which paled significantly against the national average of $7,959.

According to the 1987 Census of Manufacturers, the largest concentration of the industry's establishments was located in the Middle Atlantic region, followed by the South Atlantic and West North Central regions, respectively. In terms of the number of establishments per state, New York topped the others with 152, followed by California with 40 and Missouri with 39.

Estimates from 1992 indicated that the leading 43 companies accounted for roughly $612 million of industry sales. In descending order based on their percentage market share, the dominant companies in the industry were: Vatex Headwear Inc. (21.2 percent), K-Products Inc. (13.1 percent), Resistol Hats (8.2 percent), Paramount Cap Mfg. Co. (5.7 percent), and Bollman Hat Co. (5.7 percent). Although not among the top five companies, AJD Cap Corp. was a rising star in the segment of men's and boys' sports headwear. Except for Resistol, a subsidiary, four of the five leading companies were privately held, as was also true for nearly all of the remaining top 43 companies.

Input data from 1982 and 1987 indicated that the major sources or sector of input supply entering into the production of felt-related headwear were from processed textile wastes, textile goods, motor freight transportation and warehousing, cyclic crudes and organics, petroleum refining, fabricated rubber products, plastic materials and resins, and electric services. On the other hand, the principal industrial recipients or sectors purchasing felt-related headwear were manufacturers of electrical machinery and general industrial machinery, exports, blowers and fans, surgical appliances and supplies, and photographic equipment and supplies.

In 1987, disaggregation of the industry's total output by its major product category indicated that cloth hats and caps, excluding millinery, accounted for 50.8 percent share. Within this category, men's and boys' hats and caps dominated with 46.6 percent, followed by all other hats and caps with 3.8 percent. It is important to note that the fad-driven growth in the sales of sports headwear bearing the team logos from the National Basketball Association (NBA), the National Football League (NFL), Major League Baseball (MLB), and the National College Athletic Association (NCAA) also fell within this major product category and that midway into the 1990s their sales continued at a record pace.

The second major product category, accounting for 18.2 percent of the total output, was hats, caps, and millinery not specified by kind. Close behind followed the classification of millinery products that accounted for 17.7 percent of the industry's total output. Shares accounted for within this classification were fur-felt and wool-felt millinery with 3.6 percent, millinery fabrics 4.9 percent, all other millinery and hat frames 3.5 percent, and millinery not specified by kind with 5.7 percent. The last major product category, responsible for 13.2 of the industry's total output, was hats and hat bodies, excluding cloth and millinery. Within this major category, the share accounted for by men's and boys' finished straw hats was 4.7 percent, by men's and boys' wool-felt hats 3.9 percent, fur-felt finished hats 2.3 percent, and hat bodies for 2.2 percent.

WORK FORCE

In 1987, the industry's total employment was 17,200, of which 14,600 were classified as production workers. In 1991, total employment was estimated at 16,300, of which 14,400 were classified as production workers. Between these years, and despite the fact that total employment had fallen by 5.2 percent, there was little change in the level of production workers, which suggests that most of the job loss was confined to management personnel. During the same period, when compared to other apparel industries—most of which experienced higher levels of decline for the categories of total employment and production workers—the hats, caps, and millinery industry had fared rather well. To a large extent, the reversal of the industry's fortunes after several decades of decline can be attributed to the growing influence of team logo sports headwear sales.

For the period of 1987-1991, the value added per production worker had risen considerably. It climbed from $368 in 1987 to $459 in 1991, an increase of 24.7 percent. At the same time, the level of hourly real wages—which were only half the national average to begin with—either stagnated or slightly declined, indicating that the industry's productivity improvements and wages were moving in opposite directions.

According to the Bureau of Labor Statistics, sewing machine operators by far constituted the industry's largest occupational category accounting for 56 percent of all occupations. Several other occupational categories falling just slightly above or below the 3 percent level were: precision inspectors, testers, and graders; blue collar work supervisors; and pressing machine operators. Traffic, shipping, and receiving clerks accounted for 2 percent of all occupational categories. Based on the expectation that the industry continued along a moderate path of productivity growth, a BLS survey forecasting the growth of the industry's occupational categories until the year 2005 indicated negative growth for all categories, with sales-related occupations being the lone exception. Sewing machine operators were projected to be the hardest hit as improvements in sewing technologies and new stitch-free techniques would exercise a displacing effect.

The industry's work force demographics, especially in terms of its race and gender components, bore little relationship to its national average counterparts for the manufacturing sector taken as a whole. According to research conducted by the Amalgamated Clothing and Textile Workers Union, women made up 78.9 percent of the industry's work force against a national manufacturing average of 32.9 percent. Workers of Hispanic origin accounted for 20.7 percent of the industry's employment compared to a national manufacturing average of 8.7 percent. Blacks surprisingly comprised only 8.9 percent of the industry's work force. This figure stood in contrast to a black participation rate of 16.4 percent for the apparel industry group, and was also noticeably below the national manufacturing average of 10.4 percent.

CURRENT CONDITIONS

As already indicated, the decline in the hats, caps, and millinery industry reaches back to at least the early 1960s, if not before, when a massive structural shift away from the wearing of hats took hold. The reversals in the industry's millinery branch appeared to be the most permanent. Although several short-lived, fad-driven waves have hit, these were hardly sufficient to restore millinery back to the level of its formative years in the 1950s, when over 400 companies supplied hats worn by the majority of U.S. women. By 1989, fewer than 80 companies produced millinery articles.

Men's and boys' team logo sports headwear was the only area breathing life into an otherwise moribund industry. This may have been sufficient enough to warrant a more optimistic outlook for the industry as a whole since data tracking the value of the industry's shipments for the period of 1987-1991 had risen significantly. In 1994 some of the top U.S. firms with leading market shares in the sports headwear market were: American Needle, Starter, Logo 7, A.J.D Cap, Drew Pearson, and Apex. In an effort to eliminate the high cost of sewing labor, some firms were experimenting with heat applied techniques to join sports headwear fabrics. The result of these undertakings were mixed as some products proved to be of inferior quality.

What impact the demand in team logo sports headwear would have on the industry's domestic work force was uncertain. For the most part, the leading firms in the sports headwear market were becoming increasingly involved in foreign outsourcing, so that while the industry's U.S.-based firms might prosper, the same could not be said for its U.S. work force. Add to the mix the passage of the North American Free Trade Agreement and the trade stimulating accord reached in the 1993 round of the General Agreements on Tariffs and Trade and the near future domestic employment picture looked less than promising.

One pathbreaking technology figuring largely in all sports headwear firms' success came from the introduction of Quick Response (QR) systems. Seldom has a system been devised that was so in line with the apparel industry's business climate where rapid change, high stakes risk, and often fickle consumer behavior play so important a role. By design, Quick Response programs electronically link textile manufacturers, apparel producers, and retailers into a computerized information network analyzing consumer sales information. Its ultimate purpose was intended to considerably shorten the turnaround time it takes for hot-selling items to arrive in retail stores, minimize systemwide inventory levels, and reduce or eliminate slow-moving articles to prevent unwanted markdown. Other technological inroads were being forged through the application of computer aid design and manufacture and laser beams used to cut cloth.

INDUSTRY INFORMATION SOURCES

Arnold, Pauline, and White, Percival, *Clothes and Cloth: America's Apparel Business*, New York, N.Y.: Holiday House Publishers, 1961.

Arpan, Jeffery S., de la Torres, Jose, and Toyne, Brian, *The U.S. Apparel Industry: International Challenge, Domestic Response*, Atlanta, Georgia: Business Publishing Division, College of Business Administration Georgia State University, 1982.

Economic and Demographic Indicators of 42 ACTWU Industries, New York, N.Y.: Research Department, Amalgamated Clothing and Textile Workers Union, 1988.

Focus: An Economic Profile of the Apparel Industry, American Apparel Manufacturers Association, Arlington, VA., 1993.

Jarnow, Jeannette, and Guerreiro, Miriam, *Inside the Fashion Business*, New York: Macmillan Publishing Company, 1991.

Lehman Brothers, *The Clothes Line*, December, 1993.

Manufacturing USA: Industry Analyses, Statistics and Leading Companies, 3rd Edition, Detroit, MI: Gale Publications, 1993.

Schoeffler, O.E. and Gale, William, *Esquire's Encyclopedia of 20th Century Men's Fashions*, New York: McGraw-Hill Inc., 1973.

U.S. Industrial Outlook 1993, Washington D.C.: U.S. Department of Commerce, 1993.

—Daniel E. King

SIC 2361

GIRLS', CHILDREN'S, AND INFANTS' DRESSES, BLOUSES, AND SHIRTS

This category covers establishments which are primarily engaged in manufacturing girls', children's, and infants' dresses, blouses, and shirts from purchased woven or knit materials. Knitting mills primarily engaged in manufacturing outerwear are classified in **SIC 2253: Knit Outerwear Mills.**

INDUSTRY SNAPSHOT

There are approximately 350 establishments which manufactured the items covered in this category, and the number declined throughout the 1980s. As was true throughout much of the U.S. apparel industry, these establishments tended to be small, often family-run businesses, and they faced stiff competition from low-cost imports. Against this backdrop, the baby boomer generation was having children which led to its own mini-boom, and these parents were better educated and had more disposable income than their parents. Also, children's clothing had become more fashionable and trendy than ever before.

ORGANIZATION AND STRUCTURE

The establishments producing children's clothing were organized as the rest of the apparel industry—that is, comprised of manufacturers, contractors, and jobbers. Contractors were independent manufacturers, hired by various, and often competing, manufacturers. Contractors specialize in sewing the garment from pieces provided to them, and they were hired by producers which either do not have their own sewing facilities or producers whose own capacity has been superceded.

Jobbers were design and marketing businesses which were hired to perform specific functions; for example, to purchase materials, design patterns, create samples, cut material, or hire contractors to manufacture the product. Jobbers buy the materials needed to produce the pieces. The cut materials are then sent to contractors to be assembled.

Manufacturers were those establishments that performed all functions, that is, creating apparel from purchased materials. Manufacturers had staffs which produced designs, or bought them from freelancers, and then purchased the materials (fabric and trimmings) needed. Generally the cutting and sewing of the garment was done in the manufacturer's factories. However, when demand for an item exceeds the manufacturers capacity or if shipping deadlines could not be met, outside contractors might be hired. The manufacturers own sales and shipping staff takes orders and then sends them out.

For the purposes of this entry, when referred to in text ''manufacturers'' will mean the three types of producers mentioned (that is, contractors, jobbers, and manufacturers), unless otherwise noted.

Children's clothing sizes are divided into separate categories. ''Infants'' covers babies up to a year in age. ''Toddlers'' includes children from ages two to three. ''Children's'' covers the ages between the ages of three and six. ''Girls''' includes girls between the ages of seven and fourteen.

Children's apparel manufacturers generally produced one line per season, typically creating four lines a year (winter, spring, summer, and fall).

BACKGROUND AND DEVELOPMENT

Children's wear production developed early in the 20th century, at about the same time as the women's apparel industry. Women turned away from making their own clothes, and they stopped making their children's clothing as well. Over time, children's clothing became more durable and the sizes became standardized.

An especially important development in children's wear was the growing importance of television in children's lives after World War II. Children could emulate what other children wore on television, and they could be appealed to directly through advertising. Children demanded a greater influence over the clothing their parents purchased for them, and often asked for stylish and fashionable clothing. They became independent consumers themselves—often with money received as gifts or allowances—and were often very fashion conscious and brand-name aware.

CURRENT CONDITIONS

The number of employees employed in this industry dropped throughout the 1980s even as the value of shipments rose. As in other sectors of the apparel industry, increased consolidation and the strength of imported clothing contributed to this trend. The value of shipments grew from $1.4 billion in 1982 to an estimated $1.8 billion in 1992. Employment fell from about 38,000 in 1982 to approximately 29,500 in 1992.

The recession that began in the apparel industry in 1989 particularly affected children's apparel producers. Domestic manufacturers were hard hit while imports slowed only moderately. Nevertheless, it was expected that children's apparel sales would continue to increase as parents, grandparents, and children themselves purchase clothing for the offspring of babyboomers.

INDUSTRY LEADERS

Gerber Products Company, well known throughout the world as a baby-food manufacturer, was also a dominant force in the children's apparel industry, and it was the largest manufacturer in SIC 2361. Gerber Products reported revenues of $1.3 billion in 1993, of which 22 percent was earned from its apparel sales. Following the sale of Buster Brown Apparel, Inc., in 1993, its apparel group consisted of Gerber Childrenswear, Inc., which earned approximately $220 million in 1993. Besides infantwear, Gerber Childrenswear manufactured sleepers, cloth diapers, bedding, underwear garments, knitwear, and vinyl baby pants.

Another important manufacturer in this category was William Carter Co., a private company founded in 1864. Its estimated revenues in 1992 were $210 million.

WORK FORCE

As stated earlier, the number of employees in this category had declined in a process that accelerated in the 1980s. From 1982 to 1992, employment in this category fell from 38,000 to an estimated 29,500 in 1992, and most of the positions lost were production jobs. Most of those employed in this category (an estimated 24,700 in 1992) were production workers, approximately half of which were union members. Most production workers were sewing-machine operators. The average wage was $6.16 an hour. Many of the manufacturers in this sector of the apparel industry, as with the industry as a whole, were small, family-owned businesses—the average number of employees per establishment was 81.

New York had the most establishments that produced the apparel in this category, indicating the state's long history as the center of the apparel business in the United States. Approximately 100 such establishments, employing about 3,400 workers, were headquartered in the state in the early 1990s. Pennsylvania was home to fewer manufacturers (approximately 65) but a greater number of employees (about 4,800). Other states with important concentrations of workers in this category were South Carolina, Florida, and California.

AMERICA AND THE WORLD

The U.S. children's apparel industry began to lose significant market share to imports in the 1960s as did other sectors of the apparel industry; imports were attractive to consumers because of their lower prices and acceptable quality. The process began to accelerate in the 1970s and by the 1990s imports had reached all-time highs. Also contributing to the industry's decline in the United States was the reliance of manufacturers on off-shore assembly of pieces cut in the United States.

Manufacturers in the Far East represented a significant source of children's apparel. When apparel makers started to move their manufacturing bases out of the United States in the 1960s, they first went to Hong Kong, Taiwan, and South Korea to take advantage of the cheap labor there. By the 1980s, however, labor costs had increased, and capital and experience from those traditional low-wage markets moved to lower wage countries such as Bangladesh, Thailand, Pakistan, Indonesia, Malaysia, Sri Lanka, and India, which became the sources for more of the imports entering the United States. By the early 1990s China replaced Hong Kong as the greatest supplier of imports to the United States.

The ratification of the North American Free Trade Agreement (NAFTA) in 1994 created a free-trade zone between the United States, Mexico, and Canada by gradually eliminating tariffs over 15 years. There had already been a free-trade agreement set into motion between Canada and the United States—the United States and Canada Free Trade Agreement, which went into effect January 1, 1989 and would phase out import duties between the two countries over ten years on virtually all products—and so the passage of NAFTA was expected to increase imports from Mexico. Apparel-industry executives supported NAFTA.

The Arrangement Regarding International Trade in Textiles, known as the Multifiber Arrangement (MFA), regulated apparel imported into the U.S. and other member nations since the 1960s, and it had been renewed every three years. In 1986, in an effort to update the provisions of the General Agreement on Tariffs and Trade (GATT), new negotiations (known as the Uruguay Round) commenced in an effort to further liberalize world trade. GATT would reduce over time the tariffs on imports into the United States by half, without guaranteeing U.S. product access into other countries. Some countries which exported heavily into the United States did not allow corresponding access to their markets—for example, China, the biggest clothing importer into the United States. The MFA would be superceded by any agreement reached in the GATT talks, but its outcome was uncertain; if no agreement was reached in the negotiations, the MFA would be extended. The textile industry estimated that one million U.S. textile and apparel jobs would be lost under the provisions of GATT. The administration of U.S. President Bill Clinton advocated fair access to the domestic markets of all the countries covered under the agreement.

More and more imports had entered the United States under provision 9802 (formerly known as Section 807) of the Harmonized Tariffs Schedule of the United States. This provision allowed clothing assembled abroad—from pieces cut in the U.S. and then exported—to be reimported with duty paid for the value added abroad; import and export data were skewed as a result. Thus, the most labor-intensive part of the assembly process could be done at lower-wage rates. Many U.S. manufacturers were taking advantage of provision 9802 and moving assembly operations to the Caribbean. They noted that they could reduce costs and more successfully compete against imports from

Asia. More complex items could be assembled and turned around more quickly than if created in Asia. Disadvantages included sometimes cumbersome and time-consuming logistics considerations; contractors in other countries took care of the transportation, paperwork, and assembly altogether. By 1992 they comprised 14 percent of apparel imports. Much of the increase appeared to be due to products that were cut in the United States and then sent abroad for assembly. The passage of NAFTA, however, led some to expect that the Caribbean would be less desirable a manufacturing destination than Mexico.

The International Ladies' Garment Workers Union and other unions supported measures to stem the loss of jobs in the industry by limiting the imports allowed in the country. Their arguments had not succeeded in challenging the free-market philosophy which ultimately triumphed in the passage of NAFTA.

RESEARCH AND TECHNOLOGY

In the battle against imports, U.S. apparel makers tried a variety of stratagems, including increased use of automation, delivering higher quality goods, and trying to more closely keep track of the consumer's needs and desires. Although the intrinsic "soft" quality of material made the extensive use of automated equipment difficult, most of the larger manufacturers had tried to invest in newer machinery to improve efficiency. Nevertheless, apparel manufacture remained a highly labor-intensive industry.

One tool that was advocated to better meet the market's demands was "quick response": the idea of bringing apparel to the retailer rapidly by shortening the production cycle, reducing inventories, improving productivity, and sending information regarding consumers' preferences quickly back to the manufacturers, thus avoiding overstocking. By using computers to track inventory and sales as well as consumers' responses to particular items, the ability to respond quickly to market demand—and thus get a jump on foreign producers often half a world away—domestic manufacturers could stave off the often inevitable-seeming stream of imports. Department stores and manufacturers worked together to find ways to speed deliveries and increase efficiency. Mass merchandisers were among the first to implement the quick response.

INDUSTRY INFORMATION SOURCES

Baby and Junior: International Trade Magazine for Children's Fashions. Meisenbach GMBH Hainstrasse 18, Bamberg, Germany 8600.

Conditions in the Women's Garment Industry. The International Ladies' Garment Workers' Union.

Earnshaw's Infants, Girls and Boys Wear Review. Earnshaw Publications, Inc., 225 W. 34th St., Rm. 212, New York, NY 10122.

Fairchild Fact File: Children's Market, Infants', Toddlers', Girls', and Boys'—Apparel, Juvenile Products, Toys/Dolls. Fairchild Publications, Inc., 7 W. 34th St., New York, NY 10001.

—C. Collins

SIC 2369

GIRLS', CHILDREN'S, AND INFANTS' OUTERWEAR, NOT ELSEWHERE CLASSIFIED

This category includes establishments primarily engaged in manufacturing girls', children's, and infants' outerwear, not elsewhere classified, from purchased woven or knit fabrics. This includes, but is not limited to, bathing suits, jeans, jogging suits, playsuits, shorts, skirts, slacks, and sweatsuits. Knitting mills primarily engaged in manufacturing outerwear are classified under **SIC 2253: Knit Outwear Mills.**

INDUSTRY SNAPSHOT

In 1993, approximately 300 establishments manufactured the clothing covered in this category. This number had steadily declined throughout the 1980s, because, as with much of the U.S. apparel industry, manufacturers faced stiff competition from low-cost imports. Nevertheless, during this time a well-educated baby boomer generation, with more disposable income than their parents had, were themselves having children and spending increasing amounts on children's clothing. Consequently, children's clothing became more fashion-oriented and expensive.

ORGANIZATION AND STRUCTURE

Clothing lines in this industry include "infant wear," for babies up to a year in age, "toddlers wear" for children from ages two to three, "children's wear" for ages three to six, and "girls' wear" for girls between the ages of seven and fourteen. Children's apparel manufacturers generally produce one new line of clothing per season, or four lines a year.

Establishments producing children's clothing were comprised of manufacturers, contractors, and jobbers. Contractors were independent manufacturers, hired by various, and often competing, manufacturers. Contractors specialized in sewing the garment from pieces provided them, and they were hired by producers which either did not have their own sewing facilities or producers whose own capacity had been superseded.

Jobbers were design and marketing businesses hired to perform specific functions, including purchasing materials, designing patterns, creating samples, cutting material, and hiring contractors to manufacture the product. After purchasing materials needed to produce the pieces, jobbers then sent the cut material to contractors for assembly.

In creating apparel from the purchased materials, manufacturers retained staffs either to produce designs or buy them from freelancers, as well as to purchase the fabric and trimmings. While cutting and sewing the garment was generally performed in the manufacturer's factories, outside contractors were hired when demand for an item exceeded the manufacturer's capacity or shipping deadlines could not be met. For the purposes of this entry, the term "manufacturers" will refer cumulatively to contractors, jobbers, and manufacturers.

BACKGROUND AND DEVELOPMENT

Children's apparel production developed early in the twentieth century, concurrent with the emergence of the women's apparel industry. During this time, as they joined the professional work force in increasing numbers, women had less time for sewing their own or their children's clothing. Advances in the industry eventually lead to the production of more durable children's clothing available in standardized sizes.

The growing popularity of television during the 1950s, particularly among children, provided a boost to the children's apparel industry. Not only did young people begin to emulate fashions worn by their peers on television, but they were especially responsive to advertising. During this time, children assumed a greater role in choosing the clothing purchased for them by their parents. Moreover, they increasingly came to represent an independent consumer market, purchasing clothing themselves with the money they received as gifts or for allowances.

CURRENT CONDITIONS

The number of employees in the industry dropped throughout the 1980s as the value of shipments rose. As in other sectors of the apparel industry, increased consolidation and the popularity of imported clothing contributed to downsizing in the industry. While the value of shipments grew from $1.3 billion in 1982 to an estimated $2.1 billion in 1992, employment fell from about 33,700 in 1982 to approximately 32,000 in 1992.

The economic recession of the early 1990s particularly affected children's apparel producers; domestic manufacturers were hard hit while imports only slowed moderately. Nevertheless, analysts expected sales of children's apparel to continue to increase as parents, grandparents, and children themselves purchased more clothing for the offspring of the babyboom.

INDUSTRY LEADERS

Oshkosh B'Gosh, Inc., which designed, manufactured, and marketed children's apparel, dominated the industry in the early 1990s. Founded in 1895 and based in Wisconsin, the company employed approximately 7,700 and saw revenues of approximately $335 million in 1993. Oshkosh B'Gosh used its own manufacturing facilities in the United States and abroad. The company also began exporting merchandise to Europe, a strategy that initially met with a disappointing response in the early 1990s.

Another industry leader, Buster Brown Apparel, Inc., became a private company in 1993 when it was sold by Gerber Products Company. Originally founded in 1903, Buster Brown had once been a highly profitable company, but leaner times necessitated Gerber's sale in an effort to cut costs. Its revenues in 1993 were estimated at $150 million, and it employed approximately 3,200.

WORK FORCE

Most of those employed in this category (an estimated 27,000 in 1992) were production workers, approximately half of which were union members. The production work position consisted largely of sewing-machine operators, whose average wage in 1993 was $5.64 an hour. While many manufacturers in this sector of the apparel industry, as with the industry as a whole, were small, family-owned businesses, there were a number of large and growing establishments dominating the industry. The average number of employees per establishment in the early 1990s was 113.

A long-time center of the apparel business in the United States, New York was home to the majority of childrens' wear manufacturers in the early 1990s. During this time, approximately 60 establishments, employing about 2,900 workers, were headquartered in New York. North Carolina and South Carolina retained fewer manufacturers (approximately 40 and 16, respectively) and more employees (about 5,500 and 5,400, respectively). Tennessee and Pennsylvania also had significant concentrations of workers in this category.

AMERICA AND THE WORLD

In the 1960s, the U.S. children's apparel industry began to lose significant market share to imports, which offered consumers lower prices and acceptable quality. This trend accelerated in the 1970s, and, by the 1990s, imports had reached all-time highs. Moreover, with U.S. manufacturers relying more heavily on off-shore assembly plants, the industry experienced further losses.

Manufacturers in the Far East represented a significant source of children's apparel. In the 1960s, U.S. apparel makers began moving their manufacturing operations abroad, focusing on Hong Kong, Taiwan, and South Korea, where labor was cheap. By the 1980s, however, labor costs in these countries had increased and operations were moved to Bangladesh, Thailand, Pakistan, Indonesia, Malaysia, Sri Lanka, and India. By the early 1990s China had replaced Hong Kong as the greatest supplier of imports to the United States.

The North American Free Trade Agreement (NAFTA)—ratified in 1993 to create a free-trade zone between the United States, Mexico, and Canada by gradually eliminating tariffs over 15 years—was generally supported by executives in the apparel industry. While the International Ladies' Garment Workers Union and other unions sought to stem the loss of jobs among Americans in the industry by limiting the imports allowed in the country, the free-market philosophy ultimately triumphed in the passage of NAFTA.

During the early 1990s, increasingly more imports entered the United States under provision 9802 (formerly known as Section 807) of the U.S. Harmonized Tariffs Schedule. This provision allowed clothing assembled abroad—from pieces cut in the United States and then exported—to be reimported with duty paid for the value added abroad. This meant that the most labor-intensive part of the assembly process could be accomplished for lower wages. Many U.S. manufacturers took advantage of provision 9802, moving assembly operations to the Caribbean, where they expected to reduce costs and more successfully compete against imports from Asia. While the process greatly decreased the turnaround time for assembling more complex clothing items, its logistics sometimes proved cumbersome and time-consuming as contractors in other countries managed the transportation, paperwork, and assembly required. Furthermore, the passage of NAFTA led some to expect that the Caribbean would largely be replaced by Mexico as a more desirable manufacturing destination.

RESEARCH AND TECHNOLOGY

In the battle against imports, U.S. apparel makers tried several strategies, including increased use of automation, delivering higher quality goods, and trying to more closely keep track of the consumer's needs and desires. Although the intrinsic "soft" quality of material made the extensive use of automated equipment difficult, most of the larger manufacturers continually sought to invest in newer machinery to improve efficiency. Nevertheless, apparel manufacture remained a highly labor-intensive industry.

Another new strategy involved "quick response," the idea that bringing apparel to the retailer more rapidly would shorten the production cycle, reduce inventories, improve productivity, and help manufacturers to avoid overstocking by providing them with more timely information regarding consumers' preferences. Using computers to track inventory, sales, and consumer response, domestic manufacturers hoped to compete more effectively with importers. Department stores and manufacturers worked together to find ways to speed deliveries and increase efficiency.

INDUSTRY INFORMATION SOURCES

Baby and Junior: International Trade Magazine for Children's Fashions, Bamberg, Germany: Meisenbach GMBH.

"Conditions in the Women's Garment Industry," The International Ladies' Garment Workers' Union.

Earnshaw's Infants, Girls and Boys Wear Review, Earnshaw Publications, Inc.

Fairchild Fact File: Children's Market, Infants', Toddlers', Girls', and Boys' Apparel, Juvenile Products, Toys/Dolls, New York: Fairchild Publications, Inc.

—C. Collins

SIC 2371

FUR GOODS

This category covers establishments primarily engaged in manufacturing fur coats, and other clothing, accessories, and trimmings made of fur. Those establishments that are primarily engaged in manufacturing sheep-lined clothing are classified in **SIC 2386: Leather and Sheep-Lined Clothing**, and those that are engaged in dyeing and dressing of furs are classified in **SIC 3999: Manufacturing Industries, Not Elsewhere Classified.**

Furs were once considered a luxury that only a few could afford. The huge influx of women entering the work force in the 1970s, though, changed that perception forever. Their increased disposable income allowed many women to buy for themselves an item that historically had been purchased by men as gifts to their wives. From 1971 the U.S. fur market grew steadily, and by the 1980s furs had surged in popularity. In 1965 the average age of the first-time fur buyer was 50; by 1985 it was 26.

The popularity of fur goods exploded in the 1980s—fur sales increased an average of ten percent a year between 1979 and 1986. However, the majority of those furs were mass-market priced (under $5,000) and of lesser quality, and most of those furs were imported from such places as South Korea and Hong Kong, where labor costs were low. By the mid-1980s, more than 50 percent of the furs sold in the United States were imported.

As the popularity of furs grew among working women, more furs were sold at prices lower than ever before; thus, although sales increased throughout the 1980s, the U.S. fur goods industry saw that increased competition from imports kept the value of the goods shipped relatively constant, and the total work force in the United States declined. The increase of imports led to a reduction in the number of small manufacturing establishments, and so a further concentration of the share was held by the largest establishments.

A surplus of pelts on the international market and price battles among retailers led to lower profits. By 1992, however, pelt prices had begun to turn around. By 1993 they had increased 13 percent over 1992, and prices were thus set to increase. Over-production saw retail prices fall 40 percent below their peak in 1986.

By the early 1990s, there were approximately 320 companies that manufactured fur goods in the United States, down from 503 in 1982. The number of workers employed by the industry fell from 2,500 in 1982 to 1,500 in 1990. Over half of those employed were sewing-machine operators. The industry was concentrated in the state of New York, with almost 90 percent of manufacturers based there in 1987. The biggest fur manufacturers were privately held companies. Flemington Fur Company, based in Flemington, New Jersey, and Revillon, Inc., headquartered in New York City, were the two largest companies in the fur industry.

In the 1980s animal-rights activists targeted the fur industry with an advertising and public relations campaign that attempted to reduce the demand for fur, and they won much publicity. The fur industry responded by creating its own trade association, the Fur Information Council, in 1986, and it mounted its own public relations offensive. Animal-rights groups pointed to the declining numbers in the industry and claimed their campaign had been successful. Other analysts saw other factors—a series of mild winters, the economic downturn of the early 1990s, and a glut of pelts on the market—as much more important. In the early 1990s lower prices helped increase the unit sales of furs, but dollar sales remained constant.

INDUSTRY INFORMATION SOURCES

Agins, Teri, "Holiday Season Is Bringing Little Cheer to Furriers," *Wall Street Journal,* December 19, 1991.

Hinge John B., "Fur Industry, Under Fire, Shows Its Claws," *Wall Street Journal,* January 3, 1991.

Reilly, Patrick M., "Furriers Hustle to Keep Sales Warm," *Wall Street Journal,* September 21, 1993.

Women's Coats, Suits, Tailored Career Wear (Uniforms), Rainwear, Fairchild Fact File, Fairchild Books.

—Cheryl L. Collins

SIC 2381

DRESS AND WORK GLOVES, EXCEPT KNIT AND ALL-LEATHER

This industry includes establishments primarily engaged in manufacturing dress, semidress, and work gloves and mittens from purchased woven or knit fabrics, or from these materials combined with leather or plastics. Knitting mills primarily engaged in manufacturing gloves and mittens are classified in **SIC 2259: Knitting Mills, Not Elsewhere Classified**; establishments primarily engaged in manufacturing leather gloves are classified in **SIC 3151: Leather Gloves and Mittens**; those manufacturing sporting and athletic gloves are classified in **SIC 3949: Sporting and Athletic Goods, Not Elsewhere Classified**; and those manufacturing safety gloves are classified in **SIC 3842: Orthopedic, Prosthetic, and Surgical Appliances and Supplies**.

Glove manufacturers produce gloves for a variety of purposes that range from the functional to the purely ornamental. Because of their ability to serve work, industrial, casual, and fashion needs, gloves have long been a popular accessory for men, women, and children. Glove manufacturers are part of the larger apparel and accessories industry. In 1991 this particular segment of the industry employed approximately 37,000 people, 30,000 of whom were in production work. All tolled, the industry shipped more than $2 billion worth of goods.

The two major types of gloves are work or industrial gloves and casual or dress gloves. Since industrial gloves are designed to provide protection, they are necessarily constructed of more durable materials such as cotton or wool, and some are made out of leather. Some of the leading manufacturers of such gloves are Best Manufacturing, Wells Lamont, Pioneer, and Premier. These manufacturers ship products directly to industries and retailers throughout the year. In 1993 Wells Lamont, an Illinois-based company, posted sales of $110 million and employed 2000 workers.

Nurseries, gardening stores, and hardware stores stock gloves made from synthetics, heavier cottons, leather, cowhide, deerskin, goatskin, and sheepskin. These serve a purely functional purpose for gardeners and shade-tree mechanics. While the natural skin gloves are very popular, the heavy cotton gloves are soft, cool, and absorbent, and protect hands against blisters, dirt, and grease; the cotton gloves are also relatively inexpensive, selling for $5 per pair or less.

Casual and dress gloves are different from work gloves in many ways. They, like their more durable counterparts, are manufactured in a wide array of materials; these materials, though, include finer fabrics such as linen and silk, and can include finer weaves of cotton and wool. Because of the dictates of fashion, their popularity as an accessory rises and falls accordingly. For example, when First Lady Jacqueline Kennedy wore short, white, kid gloves, they suddenly became a fashion must, and women all over the country scrambled to buy them. Since then, their popularity has for the most part declined, and many retailers do not even bother to stock them during the warmer months. One of the leading manufacturers of dress and casual gloves is Isotoner, Inc., a division of Sara Lee Corporation. In 1993 Isotoner employed approximately 200 workers and posted sales of $250 million.

Gloves have existed at least since the 14th century BC—linen gloves were found in the tomb of King Tutankhamen. The popular accessories have served a variety of purposes for both men and women throughout history and were among the costliest items of clothing. In 1834 Xavier Jouvin, a French glove maker, invented a press that could cut six gloves simultaneously, thus bringing down the cost and increasing their popularity and availability.

INDUSTRY INFORMATION SOURCES

"Glove Story," *Connoisseur,* February 1988, 65.

Kimber, Robert, "Tough, Supple Work Gloves," *Country Journal,* July-August 1992, 59.

McCauseland, Jim, "Matching Gloves to Garden Chores," *Sunset,* November 1993, 64.

Statistical Abstract of the United States 1993, U.S. Department of Commerce.

U.S. Industrial Outlook 1994, Niles, IL: Wells Lamont Company.

—Joan R. Neubauer

SIC 2384

ROBES AND DRESSING GOWNS

Establishments in this industry are primarily engaged in manufacturing men's, boy's, and women's robes and dressing gowns from purchased materials and fabrics. This classification includes the manufacturing of bathrobes, caftans, housecoats, lounging robes, and men's smoking jackets. Companies primarily engaged in manufacturing girls', children's and infants' robes are classified in **SIC 2369: Girls', Children's, and Infants' Outerwear, Not Elsewhere Classified**. Knitting mills which manufacture robes and dressing gowns are classified in **SIC 2253: Knit Outerwear Mills**.

In 1993, there were 21 companies in this industry. Together, these companies reported $484 million in gross sales and employed more than 9,000 workers that year. The three industry leaders were Sanmark-Stardust, Inc., with $121 million in sales; I Apparel Corp., with $110 million; and Miss Elaine, Inc., reporting $40 million in sales. The remaining companies in this industry each had less than $30 million in sales in 1993.

Establishments in this industry have traditionally sold their products mostly to large department store chains. During the late 1980s this started to change with a growth in both specialty stores for women's lingerie and in mail order catalogs (which in 1990 accounted for nearly 50 percent of robes sold in America). For manufacturers this has meant the increased distribution of these items to smaller businesses. Another significant change in robe and dressing gown retail sales to affect this industry has been a lesser interest in designer products; this has been attributed to the economic recession of the late 1980s and early 1990s.

Upon entering the 1990s, companies in this industry, along with others in apparel manufacturing, witnessed a slight increase in sales due to an overall increase in consumer spending on apparel items. At the same time, the number of establishments in this industry have gradually decreased as sales have gone to larger apparel manufacturers who have diversified into this sector of apparel production.

While exact figures are not available, employment in this industry has been on the decline since the late 1970s. In 1993, roughly 80 percent of this industry's work force was comprised of production workers.

American companies manufacturing robes and dressing gowns have long been in competition with overseas manufacturing, mostly from China and Taiwan. In 1993, over half of the robes and gowns sold in America were imported. American exports of these products have traditionally been small; however, their numbers increased to nine percent of United States products in this apparel sector. American exports are expected to be one of the main factors in increased production in this industry by the end of the twentieth century.

Technological advances have helped manufacturers of robes and dressing gowns to improve efficiency in production and distribution of their goods. Three areas in particular have been improved in this industry with technological developments: computer-aided design, production, and communications; modular manufacturing systems; and ergonomics (work place equipment designed with respect to worker health and safety).

Like other areas of apparel manufacturing, the robes and dressing gowns industry witnessed a slight increase in sales due to an overall increase in consumer spending on apparel items. At the same time, the number of establishments in this industry have gradually decreased as sales have gone to larger apparel manufacturers who have diversified into this sector of apparel production.

While exact figures are not available, employment in this industry has been on the decline since the late 1970s. In 1993, roughly 80 percent of this industry's work force was comprised of production workers.

American companies manufacturing robes and dressing gowns have long been in competition with overseas manufacturing, mostly from China and Taiwan. In 1993, over half of the robes and gowns sold in America were imported. American exports of these products have traditionally been small; however, their numbers increased to nine percent of United States products in this apparel sector. American exports are expected to be one of the main factors in increased production in this industry by the end of the twentieth century.

Technological advances have helped manufacturers of robes and dressing gowns to improve efficiency in production and distribution of their goods. Three areas in particular have improved in this industry with technological developments: computer-aided design, production, and communications; modular manufacturing systems; and ergonomics (work place equipment designed with respect to worker health and safety).

INDUSTRY INFORMATION SOURCES

"Consumer Watch: Women's Robes," *Chain Store Age General Merchandise*, November 1982.

Joyce, Katherine, "Relax in Style," *Stores*, November 1985.

Reda, Susan, "Robes: Tough Sell for Spring," *Stores*, November 1992.

—Paola Trimarco

SIC 2385

WATERPROOF OUTERWEAR

This category includes establishments primarily engaged in manufacturing raincoats and other waterproof outerwear from purchased rubberized fabrics, plastics, and similar materials. Included in this industry are establishments primarily engaged in manufacturing waterproof or water-repellant outerwear from purchased woven or knit fabrics other than wool. Establishments primarily engaged in manufacturing men's and boys' oiled-fabric work clothing are classified in **SIC 2326: Men's and Boys' Work Clothing;** those manufacturing vulcanized rubber clothing and clothing made from rubberized fabrics produced in the same establishment are classified in **SIC 3069: Fabricated Rubber Products, Not Elsewhere Classified.**

Raincoats make up by far the largest share of products produced by establishments classified in this industry. In 1987, these companies shipped goods with a total value of $333 million. That year, raincoats and raincapes accounted for $256 million in shipments made by companies in this and other industry classifications.

By August of 1993, with over half of the industry's orders for the spring season already received, a 15 percent increase in bookings was reported over the previous year. Rainwear is an item that seems to be particularly resistant to recessions. As waterproofing technology continues to advance, consumers are likely to continue buying whatever new outerwear the manufacturers in this industry have to offer.

The 1990s brought a return of polyurethane-coated fabrics to the forefront of raincoat fashion. Polyurethane gives fabrics the shiny look associated with rain slickers of the 1960s. The newer versions of the shiny raincoat have benefitted from improvements in the technology used to coat the fabrics. Softer fabrics, such as rayon, cotton, and polyester, can now be used to back a very thin layer of polyurethane, creating a much more comfortable garment than was previously possible. Technological improvements have also expanded the number of softer styles available, some of which use new microfibers, as well as sueded cotton and velvet, treated with water-repellant chemicals. These improvements in waterproofing techniques have given linens an important role in outerwear for the first time.

Like many industries involving the manufacture of apparel, a large percentage of production jobs in the waterproof apparel industry have left the United States in recent years. The 6,400 industry workers in the United States in 1987 were 31 percent less than the number employed five years earlier. Employment in this industry is concentrated on the East Coast, particularly Maryland, Massachusetts, and New Jersey, which together account for about half of the industry's jobs. Nearly half the establishments in the waterproof outerwear industry have less than 20 employees. 21 companies have between 20 and 99 employees, and 18 companies employ at least 100 workers. In 1987, workers in this industry earned $60.9 million in wages.

The waterproof outerwear industry is dominated by Londontown Corp., which produces the well-known London Fog line of outerwear. The company also licenses the London Fog name to a wide range of products. The London Fog brand name is recognized by an amazing 98 percent of consumers. Londontown has estimated sales of $110 million, more than four times its nearest competitor. Londontown is based in Eldersburg, Maryland and has about 2,000 employees. The company was founded in 1928.

INDUSTRY INFORMATION SOURCES

Pogoda, Dianne M. "Londontown: Refinanced and Ready to Grow." *Women's Wear Daily*, August 21, 1990: 6.

———. "Rainwear: Short and Slicker." *Women's Wear Daily*, March 15, 1991: 8.

Salfino, Catherine. "Outerwear Orders Rolling In." *Daily News Record*, August 10, 1993: 1.

—Robert R. Jacobson

SIC 2386

LEATHER AND SHEEP-LINED CLOTHING

This category consists of manufacturers of many types of leather and sheep-lined clothing, including coats, jackets, hats, pants, skirts, vests, and other garments. Companies that make leather gloves and mittens are included in **SIC 3151: Leather Gloves and Mittens.** Fur clothing is classified separately in **SIC 2371: Fur Goods.**

In 1992, the leather wearing apparel industry shipped about $143 million in products. This figure represented a 14 percent increase over the previous year's shipments. Employment in this industry grew at a comparable rate as well. Retail sales of leather sportswear and outerwear increased by about ten percent for the year, reaching $3.3 billion. Overall, retail sales of leather apparel have quadrupled since 1985. These increases reflected the end of a rising trend in the price of leather. The cost of leather relative to other clothing materials has proven to be a reliable indicator of the leather apparel industry's performance from year to year. As is the case in the apparel industry in general, patterns of consumption can change rapidly as customer demand is influenced by fashion developments. Leather clothing, which is both high-fashion and high-cost in the world of apparel, is particularly susceptible to both of these kinds of fluctuations in demand.

Leather coats and jackets are by far the most important segment of the leather and sheep-lined clothing industry. According to the 1987 *Census of Manufacturers,* men's and boy's leather coats and jackets accounted for nearly 40 percent of the $175 million in products shipped in the industry that year. Women's and girls' coats and jackets contributed another $63 million of the total. Leather coats and jackets have enjoyed a surge in popularity since the early 1990s, resulting in the entry of several well-known designer brands, such as Bill Blass and Guess, into the retail market. The longer, more expensive three-quarter length coats have led the swell in consumer interest.

Employment in SIC 2386 is concentrated along the U.S. coasts. California, New Jersey, and New York together employed about 70 percent of the industry's United States work force in 1987. That year, the industry employed 2,100 workers, a startling 51 percent decrease from the 4,300 employees reported five years earlier. One reason for the disappearance of jobs in leather clothing manufacturing is the prevalence of imports. Imports of leather apparel in 1992 were valued at $1.5 billion, a jump of 39 percent, with South Korea and China contributing the most. By contrast,

the United States exported about $53 million in leather apparel, a drop of eight percent from the previous year.

The leading U.S. company in the leather apparel industry is Sawyer of Napa Inc., a privately-owned California firm. Sawyer has been in business since 1869. The company has about 50 employees and yearly sales of about $27 million. Another important company is the Detroit-based Reed Sportswear Manufacturing Company. Reed is also privately owned. It has annual sales of $15 million and employs 80 workers. The company was founded in 1950.

Although demand for leather apparel is expected to rise slightly as the American economy improves, the market share lost to imports is expected to increase as well. In addition, American companies are moving more of their manufacturing abroad to reduce labor costs. These are the most severe challenges facing the industry in the 1990s.

INDUSTRY INFORMATION SOURCES

Friedman, Arthur, "Primed for a Revival," *Women's Wear Daily,* March 23, 1993, 12.

Pogoda, Dianne M., "New Plans for Leather," *Women's Wear Daily,* June 25, 1991, 8.

—Robert R. Jacobson

SIC 2387

APPAREL BELTS

This category includes establishments primarily engaged in manufacturing apparel belts. Companies that produce all types of belts for clothing are grouped in this industry, regardless of the material from which the belts are made.

In 1987, the value of shipments made by companies in SIC 2387 was $627.8 million. A surge in the popularity of leggings and stretch pants for women that took place at the end of the 1980s created a slump in sales for makers of belts. Since the beginning of the 1990s, however, the industry has been quite strong in spite of a sluggish overall economy.

The apparel belt industry lost about ten percent of its U.S. jobs between 1982 and 1987. At the end of that period, 10,500 U.S. workers were employed in the industry. Four states provided 70 percent of those jobs: New York, California, Texas, and Connecticut. Of the 265 companies classified in SIC 2387 in 1987, nearly half had less than 20 employees. Only 27 companies employed more than 100 people. The industry's employees earned a total of $85.6 million in wages that year.

Leather is by far the most important material for apparel belts. The value of leather belts shipped in 1987 was $329 million. Since the beginning of the 1990s, Nubuck suede has become an important material in the manufacture of apparel belts. Nubuck is a softened leather that is available in a variety of colors and textures. Nubuck first appeared as a footwear material, and soon began to show up in women's accessories. Men's belts, which have traditionally been closely linked to footwear in terms of leather trends, followed soon thereafter.

An important factor in the belt industry's success in the early 1990s has been an increasing emphasis on casual styles. The glossy look of 1980s accessories has given way to a more down-to-earth flavor in belts. With the comeback of jeans, denim has emerged as a popular belt material, both as a Western theme and a 1960s nostalgia item. Braided leather belts have also been an important part of this trend, as have belts with fringe or an attached chain. Furthermore, belt manufacturers have attempted to capitalize on a new crossover market in men's belts, which includes leather belts with a matte finish that can be worn in both dressy and casual combinations. A renewed interest in buckles has emerged as well. On the women's side, the reappearance of long skirts and pants has contributed to the health of the belt industry in the 1990s.

Tandy Brands Accessories Inc. of Arlington, Texas is the leader among companies primarily engaged in manufacturing apparel belts. Tandy is a public company, founded in 1919. The company has 365 employees and annual sales of about $36 million. Another important belt manufacturer is the San Francisco-based Circa Corporation. A privately-owned company, Circa has 275 employees. The company has annual sales of $23 million and was founded in 1967.

INDUSTRY INFORMATION SOURCES

"Belts Keep a Wrap on Fashion," *Women's Wear Daily*, March 26, 1993, A10.

Hart, Elena, "Jeans Belts Are Hot in Early Bookings," *Daily News Record*, May 8, 1992, 2.

———, "Leather Belts Being Shorn of Their Sheen," *Daily News Record*, October 22, 1990, 118.

———, "Nubuck Spells New Bucks for Belts," *Daily News Record*, June 3, 1992, 22.

Lloyd, Brenda, "Belt Business Wants It Both Ways," *Daily News Record*, January 3, 1992, S21.

Meadus, Amanda, "Buckling Up Gains," *Women's Wear Daily*, October 23, 1992, A1.

—Robert R. Jacobson

SIC 2389

APPAREL AND ACCESSORIES, NOT ELSEWHERE CLASSIFIED

This industry consists of establishments primarily engaged in manufacturing suspenders, gaffers, handkerchiefs, and other apparel not elsewhere classified, such as academic caps and gowns, vestments, and theatrical costumes. Also included are establishments primarily engaged in manufacturing clothing by cutting and joining (for example by adhesives) materials such as paper and nonwoven textiles.

The apparel and accessories industry is made up of a wide variety of products. Ecclesiastical vestments and other clothing make up 35.03 percent; academic caps and gowns, costumes, and theatrical makeup constitute 29.67 percent; and apparel and accessories, not elsewhere classified, make up 11.26 percent. Other items in this category are, in descending order, as follows: garters, hose supporters, arm bands, and suspenders, all at 7.03 percent; men's and boys' handkerchiefs, at 6.88 percent; women's and children's handkerchiefs, at 5.87 percent; burial garments, at 2.24 percent; and garter belts, at 2.01 percent.

Industry output is concentrated in the northeastern portion of the United States. The top three states that produce these products are Pennsylvania, New York, and New Jersey. Pennsylvania is responsible for $94.5 million, or 24.6 percent of outputs; New York registers $53.1 million, or 13.8 percent; and New Jersey outputs $14.4 million, or 3.8 percent. California and Texas also have high concentrations of apparel and accessory manufacture, as does the southeastern region of the country, including Florida, Tennessee, Virginia, Georgia, and South Carolina.

The modern manufacture of apparel and accessories within this listing is characterized by a high level of specialization, with some cross-item production. For example, industry leaders include specialty and product-specific manufacturers such as Art Stone Theatrical Inc., Oak Hall Cap and Gown Co., and Eaves and Brooks Costume Co. Multi-product manufacturers include I. Shalom and Company, Inc., which manufacturers both women's accessories and men's handkerchiefs, and White Knights, which manufactures disposable medical products, including hospital gowns.

Labor and occupations are specialized within this category. Sewing machine operators constitute 56 percent of occupations; garment inspectors, testers, and graders constitute 3.2 percent; and precision blue collar worker supervisors constitute 3 percent. Other occupations include pressing machine operators, shipping and receiving clerks, hand packers and packagers, helpers, laborers, and materials movers.

In relation to the manufacturing industry as a whole, this industry subset is characterized by relatively low wages and low value added per employee. For example, annual payroll expenditure per establishment in this industry is $363,402 versus $1,398,674 in manufacturing as a whole. Annual payroll per employee in the apparel and accessories industry is $13,302 versus $26,028 in manufacturing as a whole; industry wage per hour is $6.10 versus $10.49 in manufacturing as a whole; and value added per employee is $27,660 versus $73,491 in manufacturing as a whole.

The majority of goods manufactured within this industry are made for personal consumption. For example, 82.7 percent of the economic sector buying the outputs of this industry is personal consumption expenditures, followed at 12 percent by apparel made from purchased materials and 1.5 percent by exports. Others buying fractional amounts of the outputs of this industry include, in descending order: Federal Government purchases; pleating and stitching; knit outerwear mills; hospitals; laundry, dry cleaning, and shoe repair; government purchases for hospital and health; portrait and photographic studios; and government purchases for public assistance and relief.

INDUSTRY INFORMATION SOURCES

Apparel Merchandising, May 3, 1993, A10.

Apparel Merchandising, June 21, 1993, A10.

Darnay, Arsen J., editor, *Manufacturing USA,* Detroit, MI: Gale Research Inc., 1993, 425-428.

—Karyn Bober Kuhn

SIC 2391

CURTAINS AND DRAPERIES

The establishments covered in this category are primarily engaged in manufacturing curtains and draperies from purchased materials. Those establishments that are primarily engaged in manufacturing lace curtains on lace machines are classified in **SIC 2258: Lace and Warp Knit Fabric Mills,** and those manufacturing shower curtains are classified in **SIC 2392: Housefurnishings, Except Curtains and Draperies.**

Curtains and draperies were once considered the only options for dressing windows, especially in the home. Attitudes shifted over time, however, and by the 1980s consumers wanted their homes to feel more comfortable and less formal. Curtains and draperies, with their often complicated hardware, declined in popularity, while alternative window treatments such as blinds, mini-blinds, pleated shades, and vertical louvers surged in popularity.

Although spending on home textiles grew throughout the 1980s and imports did not have much of an impact on this segment of the market, the value of U.S. manufacturers' shipments flattened, starting approximately in 1986. Shipments increased in the years from 1982 to 1987 by 43.5 percent to $1.5 billion, as consumers' disposable income rose, but by the early 1990s curtain and drapery sales fell annually. The traditional tiered curtain plunged in popularity. The decline in lined, pinched, and pleated draperies was tied to the increased popularity of one-inch mini-blinds, which was thought to have peaked in 1987.

Most curtains are sold ready-made and are available in standard sizes. Draperies include ready-made items as well as made-to-measure and custom-made versions. The made-to-measure drapery market was dominated by retailers Sears, Roebuck & Co. and J.C. Penney Company, Inc. (which by the late 1980s held approximately 50 percent of the market); these made-to-measure draperies were based on showroom or catalog models and then produced in a manufacturing plant. Custom-made items were those with color, fabric, and size specifications for commercial or residential customers, often chosen by an interior decorator, and then produced in a local shop.

Many of the manufacturers of traditional window treatments had expanded into alternative treatments by the early 1990s, as many analysts saw the industry as a dying one. The industry leader was Arly Merchandise Corporation, a private company based in Massachusetts and founded in 1947. The CHF Corporation, which was compromised of such names as Aberdeen, Cameo Interiors, and Joanna, was also a dominant force.

Most of the employees in this category worked in Massachusetts, North Carolina, and California. By the late 1980s, there were approximately 1,100 curtain and drapery manufacturing establishments, which employed around 23,000 workers; employment levels had flattened during the 1980s. Most of these establishments were small (with less than 20 employees) and produced custom-made draperies, yet the majority of the business in this category went to the larger firms.

INDUSTRY INFORMATION SOURCES

Home Textiles and Related Products, Fairchild Fact File, Fairchild Books.

Information from *Home Furnishings Daily* was also used to compile this article.

—Cheryl L. Collins

SIC 2392

HOUSEFURNISHINGS, EXCEPT CURTAINS AND DRAPERIES

This category covers those establishments primarily engaged in manufacturing housefurnishings (such as blankets, bedspreads, sheets, tablecloths, towels, and shower curtains) from purchased materials. Those establishments that produce housefurnishings primarily of fabric woven at the same establishment are classified, according to fiber, in **SIC 2211: Broadwoven Fabric Mills, Cotton; 2221: Broadwoven Fabric Mills, Manmade Fiber and Silk; 2231: Broadwoven Fabric Mills, Wool (Including Dyeing and Finishing);** or **2299: Textile Goods, Not Elsewhere Classified.**

Home textile products such as sheets, towels, and blankets were once seen as ''commodity'' items—products that were basic household necessities. In the growing economy after World War II, however, these products could be manufactured with new technology in an expanding palette of colors, prints, and styles and could thus become more of an expression of personal taste. By the 1990s, redecorating could be done affordably simply by changing a room's curtains, sheets, comforter, or pillows. Marketing concepts like ''bedroom-in-a-bag'' were introduced to increase sales to busy consumers who did not have time to shop for items separately.

The home textile market grew throughout the 1980s, and its rate of growth was greater than other textile markets; sales flattened only as the economy on a whole slowed late in the decade. From 1982 to 1987 the value of shipments in this category rose from $3.3 billion to $4.5 billion, or 37 percent. By 1990, the value of shipments had grown to $4.9 billion. Several factors contributed to the industry's relative strength.

The home textile market was less penetrated by imports than other sectors of the textile industry. Also, home textiles were manufactured in a more automated process with longer runs than, for example, the apparel industry, and much of the capital spending by home-textile firms was used to upgrade their technology.

Although the manufacture of sheets and towels was dominated by several large manufacturers, the other products covered in this category—tablecloths, pillows, garment bags, chair covers, boat cushions, mops, place mats, shoe bags, wardrobe bags, bath mitts, laundry bags, ironing board pads, shower curtains, carpet linings, polishing cloths, slipcovers, mattress pads, hassocks, dust cloths, and table scarves and mats—were produced by a variety of small manufacturers, thus creating a very fragmented sector of the market. Much of this industry was located in North Carolina and New York state, as well as California and Massachusetts.

There were approximately 45,000 employees in this category in the early 1990s, and the majority (38,000) were production workers. The average number of employees per establishment was 52, and the average wage was $6.43 per hour. This category was dominated by the giant textile manufacturer Fieldcrest Cannon, Inc. This company was created in 1986 after Fieldcrest Mills purchased its competitor, Cannon Mills, thus merging the two largest U.S. manufacturers of sheets and towels. The company produced a wide variety of home textile products at a range of price points. Its sales in 1992 reached $1.2 billion, and it employed 17,000. In 1994 Fieldcrest Cannon was ordered by the National Labor Relations Board to pay back wages of $3.5 million (and interest) and rehire a number of fired workers following a protracted labor dispute. *Business Week* noted that the Amalgamated Clothing and Textile Workers Union ''had accused the nation's largest towel manufacturer of some 183 labor law infractions during a 1991 organization drive, including threatening to deport or imprison Spanish-speaking workers who voted in favor of the union.'' Fieldcrest Cannon indicated that it would appeal the ruling.

INDUSTRY INFORMATION SOURCES

Fairchild Fact File: Home Textiles and Related Products, New York, NY: Fairchild Publications.

''Labor Snaps a Wet Towel at Fieldcrest,'' *Business Week,* March 21, 1994.

Information from *Home Furnishings Daily* also was used to compile this article.

—Cheryl L. Collins

SIC 2393

TEXTILE BAGS

This category includes establishments primarily engaged in manufacturing shipping and other industrial bags from purchased fabrics. Establishments primarily engaged in manufacturing plastic bags are classified under **SIC 2673: Plastics, Foil, and Coated Paper Bags;** those manufacturing laundry, wardrobe, shoe, and other textile housefurnishing bags are classified under **SIC 2392: Housefurnishings, Except Curtains and Draperies;** and those manufacturing luggage are classified under **SIC 3161: Luggage.**

The value of shipments in the textile bag industry in 1991 was $538 million, up from $422 million in 1982. 1988 was a peak year with $626 million in shipments. One of the rapidly growing substitutes for textile shipping bags is low-density polyethylene bags. There are about 250 establishments in the industry. Forty-five percent of these establishments have 20 or more employees. Average firm size as measured by the number of production workers per establishment is 45 percent smaller than that for the manufacturing sector as a whole. Annual capital investments ranged between $4.2 million and $6.2 million from 1982 to 1991.

The textile bag industry employed 4,700 production workers in 1991, down from 7,700 in 1982 and a peak of 9,200 in 1988. The industry is highly labor-intensive, having only 12 percent as much investment per production worker as that for the manufacturing sector as a whole. Annual hours worked by production workers in the industry are ten percent lower on average than those worked in the manufacturing sector at large, and hourly wages were 31 percent lower.

Of the top 43 firms by sales in the industry, fully 84 percent are private independents. The capital requirements for the industry are very low, with average investment per establishment only seven percent of that for the manufacturing sector as a whole. The top three firms in the textile bag industry are the BHA Group Inc. of Kansas City, Missouri, Mid-America Packaging of Pine Bluff, Arkansas, and Menardi-Criswell of Augusta, Georgia. Together these firms account for 27 percent of total sales for the industry. The BHA Group had $70 million in sales and 550 employees in 1992. BHA is a publicly held firm founded in 1975. Mid-America Packaging had $44 million in sales and 210 employees in 1992. Founded in 1962, Mid-America is a subsidiary of the publicly held Gaylord Container Corp. of Deerfield, Illinois. Menardi-Criswell had $30 million in sales and 250

employees in 1992. Founded in 1957, the firm is a subsidiary of Hosokawa Micron International Inc. of New York City.

The states ranking in the top ten by number of establishments in the industry are California (with 35), New York (with 23), Pennsylvania and Massachusetts (with 12 each), New Jersey, Florida, and Texas (with 11 each), North Carolina (with 10), Georgia (with 9), and Utah (with 8). Together these ten states account for two-thirds of total employment in the industry. California is by far the most important state for textile bag production, by itself accounting for 19 percent of total employment for the industry. The top four industries and sectors buying the outputs of the textile bag industry are: personal consumption expenditures, with a 22.5 percent share; banking, with a 19.9 percent share; agricultural, forestry, and fishery services, with a 13.1 percent share; and wholesale trade, with a 12.1 percent share.

INDUSTRY INFORMATION SOURCES

Annual Survey of Manufactures, Washington, DC: U.S. Census Bureau, 1991.

Darnay, Arsen J., editor, *Manufacturing USA: Industry Analysis, Statistics, and Leading Companies* (3rd edition), Detroit, MI: Gale Research Inc., 1993.

"LLDPE Fills Product Niches in Film Shipping Sacks," *Modern Plastics,* December 1991.

U.S. Industrial Outlook, Washington, DC: U.S. Department of Commerce, 1994.

Ward's Business Directory of U.S. Private and Public Companies, Detroit, MI: Gale Research Inc., 1993.

—David Kucera

SIC 2394

CANVAS AND RELATED PRODUCTS

This category covers establishments primarily engaged in manufacturing awnings, tents, and related products from purchased fabrics. Establishments primarily engaged in manufacturing canvas bags are classified under **SIC 2393: Textile Bags.**

The value of shipments in the canvas products industry in 1991 was $1.06 billion, up from $752 million in 1982. 1990 was a peak year with $1.13 billion in shipments. There are about 1,200 establishments in the industry, only 16 percent of which had 20 or more employees. Average firm size as measured by the number of production workers per establishment is 69 percent smaller than that for the manufacturing sector as a whole. Annual capital investments hovered around $20 million from 1984 to 1991.

The canvas products industry employed 13,300 production workers in 1991, up from 11,300 in 1982, but down from a peak of 13,900 in 1989. The industry is highly labor-intensive, having only 20 percent as much investment per production worker as that for the manufacturing sector as a whole. Annual hours worked by production workers in the industry is 12 percent lower on average than those worked in the manufacturing sector at large, and hourly wages are 29 percent lower. Of the top 43 firms by sales in the industry, fully 83 percent are private independents. The capital requirements for the industry are very low, with average investment per establishment only 6 percent of that for the manufacturing sector as a whole.

The top three firms in the canvas products industry are American Recreation Products Inc. of St. Louis, Missouri, North Sails Group Inc. of Milford, Connecticut, and the Astrup Co. of Cleveland, Ohio. Together these firms account for 12 percent of total sales for the industry. American Recreation Products had $65 million in sales and 600 employees in 1992. The firm is a subsidiary of the publicly held Kellwood Co., also of St. Louis. The North Sails Group had $39 million in sales and 500 employees in 1992. Founded in 1964, the firm is a subsidiary of the private Windway Capital Corp. of Sheboygan, Wisconsin. North Sails announced in 1991 that it had formed a new division called Fabritech in order to facilitate its marketing of non-boating products. The Astrup Co. had $25 million in sales and 375 employees in 1992. The privately held firm was founded in 1876.

The top canvas products by share are awnings (14 percent), non-camping tents (9 percent), fitted tarpaulins (7 percent), camping tents (7 percent), flat tarpaulins (6 percent), and sails (5 percent). One of the important new markets for the industry is the use of truck trailers with flexible fabric sides, called curtainsiders. The states ranking in the top ten by number of establishments in the industry are California (with 151), Florida (with 129), New York (with 102), Texas (with 62), Ohio (with 56), Michigan (with 55), Pennsylvania (with 52), New Jersey (with 49), Washington (with 45), and Massachusetts (with 44). Together these ten states accounted for 50 percent of total employment in the industry. The top five industries and sectors buying the outputs of the canvas products industry are: personal consumption expenditures, with a 27.2 percent share; pipelines, except natural gas, with a 9.2 percent share; water transportation, with a 6.5 percent share; vegetables, with a 5.3 percent share; and retail trade, except eating & drinking, with a 4.0 percent share.

INDUSTRY INFORMATION SOURCES

Annual Survey of Manufactures, Washington, DC: U.S. Census Bureau, 1991.

Darnay, Arsen J., editor, *Manufacturing USA: Industry Analysis, Statistics, and Leading Companies* (3rd edition), Detroit, MI: Gale Research Inc., 1993.

"Fabric Sides Are Opening Up Trucking," *New York Times,* November 4, 1992.

"North Woos Non-Marine Market," *Soundings Trade Only,* November 1991.

U.S. Industrial Outlook, Washington, DC: U.S. Department of Commerce, 1994.

Ward's Business Directory of U.S. Private and Public Companies, Detroit, MI: Gale Research Inc., 1993.

—David Kucera

SIC 2395

PLEATING, DECORATIVE AND NOVELTY STITCHING, AND TUCKING FOR THE TRADE

The establishments covered in this category are those engaged in pleating, decorative and novelty stitching, and tucking for the trade. Establishments primarily engaged in performing similar services for individuals are classified in service industries. Establishments primarily engaged in manufacturing trimmings are classified in **SIC 2396: Automotive Trimmings, Apparel Findings, and Related Products**. Establishments primarily engaged in manufacturing Schiffli machine embroideries are classified in **SIC 2397: Schiffli Machine Embroideries**.

The products which are covered in this category include art needlework, quilted fabrics or cloth, Swiss loom embroideries, machine-made crochet ware, burnt-out lace, embroidered emblems, and metallic, beaded, and sequined embroideries. Also covered are various products for the trade, including appliqueing, buttonhole making, eyelet making, hemstitching, looping, permanent pleating and pressing, pleating, quilting, ruffling, scalloping, decorative and novelty stitching, and tucking.

There were approximately 630 establishments, with roughly 14,000 employees, which manufactured products in this category in the early 1990s. Throughout the 1980s the number of establishments in this SIC dropped from 912 in 1982 to 631 in 1989; during the same period the value of shipments fell from $673 million to $691 million. However, the industry rebounded in the early 1990s as apparel manufacturers made greater use of embroideries, trimmings, and appliques to enhance the uniqueness, and thus the value, of garments. Popular themes in appliques were baseball nostalgia, motorcycle motifs, and western themes. Trims and embroideries that proved popular were fringe for western style apparel, chenille, geometric shapes, and lace and ruffles.

The leading companies in this category were Unitog Company, whose St. Louis Embroidery division, founded in 1667, concentrated on manufacturing embroidery products and was headquartered in St. Charles, Missouri; and Southern Quilters-Carolina Comforters Inc., a home furnishings manufacturer which was based in Henderson, North Carolina.

INDUSTRY INFORMATION SOURCES

Darnay, Arsen J., ed., *Finance, Insurance, and Real Estate, U.S.A.*, Detroit: Gale Research Inc., 1993.

Occupational Outlook Handbook 1992-1993, Washington: U.S. Department of Labor, 1992.

—Cheryl L. Collins

SIC 2396

AUTOMOTIVE TRIMMINGS, APPAREL FINDINGS, AND RELATED PRODUCTS

This category covers establishments primarily engaged in manufacturing automotive trimming, apparel findings, and related products. Included are establishments primarily engaged in printing and stamping on fabric articles.

Manufacturers classified under this industry make trimming and bindings for hats, suits, and coats, as well as linings for purses, hats, luggage, and men's and women's clothing. Also included are companies that provide printing and embossing on fabric, silk screening fabrics, and stamping fabric for embroidering. Others supply fabric for automobiles and furniture. Companies within this industry belong to one of eight industries that make up Industry Group 239 (miscellaneous fabricated textile products). These industries accounted for 26 percent of all 1993 shipments in the major group for Apparel and Other Finished Products Made from Fabrics and Similar Materials.

According to the Bureau of Labor Statistics, 7,816 establishments manufactured fabricated textile prod-

ucts and employed 204,700 workers. As with all textile industries, production workers have accounted for more than 80 percent of the total employment within this industry from 1988 to 1993. Earnings for production workers has continued to be nearly 40 percent below the average for all manufacturing employees in the United States. Approximately 80 percent of all fabricated textile production workers have been women.

Following an almost continuous decline since 1988, employment in all fabricated textile industries, including this category, increased in 1993. Employment for machinery operators, however, is expected to decline through the year 2005. Increased productivity created by more efficient machinery and relaxed trade restrictions could be two main reasons for the projected reduction in machinery operators. Depending upon the product being made and the nature of the raw materials, textile machinery operators can work with a variety of machines. Operators and tenders run machinery that cleans, cards, combs, and draws the fiber; spins the fiber into yarn; and weaves, knits, or tufts the yarn into textile products.

Some workers oversee machinery that manufactures man-made fibers. These machines take melted wood pulp or chemical compounds and force (or extrude) the liquid into metal plates with small holes. Workers operating these machines are called extruders, and forming machine operators and tenders. Once the yarn has been made, it is taken to be woven, knitted, or tufted. The type of textile product to be made determines the type of machinery used. Textile machine setters and setup operators work with these machines. Because of the complexity of textile machinery, these workers usually specialize in one type of equipment. Once produced, the fabric is ready to be finished and dyed. Workers who operate these machines are known as bleaching and dyeing machine operators and tenders.

Research and technology in fabricated textile manufacturing has focused on quality control. Recent achievements include computer-aided design (CAD), new modular manufacturing systems, and ergonomics. Only about 60 percent of the industry uses this new technology, with the larger firms being the most advanced and the smaller firms lagging in technology and efficiency.

Exports of fabricated textile products, including automotive and apparel trimmings, continued to expand in 1993. Canada and Mexico have been the largest export markets, buying more than 50 percent of total exports of this industry since 1989. Imports of fabricated textile products, which accounted for only nine percent of the industry's total imports, rose 15 percent in 1993. The major supplying countries have been Canada, China, India, and Mexico.

Future trade regulations could significantly impact the fabricated textile products industry, including the automotive trimmings and apparel findings industry. Relaxed trade restrictions could increase competition and imports from countries with lower paid workers. Although exports also are expected to increase, a trade deficit for fabricated textile products, which reached $2.1 billion in 1993, should remain.

INDUSTRY INFORMATION SOURCES

Career Guide to Industries, Washington, DC: U.S. Department of Labor, September 1992.

Occupational Outlook Handbook (1992-93 edition), Washington, DC: U.S. Department of Labor, 1991.

U.S. Industrial Outlook—1994, Washington, DC: Department of Commerce, 1993.

Ward's Business Directory of U.S. Private and Public Companies, Detroit, MI: Gale Research Inc., 1994.

—Catherine A. Quagliana

SIC 2397

SCHIFFLI MACHINE EMBROIDERIES

Establishments primarily engaged in manufacturing Schiffli machine embroideries.

Schiffli lace is a type of embroidery that once was made by hand using needles that were pointed at both ends. Today, schiffli lace is produced by a machine with several hundred needles placed horizontally one above the other. With fabric held in a frame covering the full width of the machine, the needles move back and forth through the material. The yarn used to embroider the fabric is supplied from individual spools.

The lasting popularity of hand-made lace led to the invention of lace-making equipment like schiffli machines. Many types of laces now are machine-made, frequently with geometrically shaped netting used as backgrounds. Once made only from cotton, schiffli lace, like other laces, can be manufactured from man-made fibers.

The manufacturing of schiffli lace is one of eight industries that make up Industry Group 239, the fabricated textile products industry. The others include curtains and draperies (SIC 2391), house furnishings (SIC 2392), textile bags (SIC 2393), canvas and related products (SIC 2394), pleating and stitching (SIC 2395)

automotive and apparel trimmings (SIC 2396), and fabricated textile products, not elsewhere classified (SIC 2399). All of these industries, including SIC 2397, accounted for 26 percent of all 1993 shipments in the apparel and fabricated textile products industry, Major Classification 23.

According to the Bureau of Labor Statistics, 7,816 establishments manufactured fabricated textile products and employed 204,700 workers in 1990. However, *Ward's Business Directory of U.S. Private and Public Companies 1994* lists only eight firms with schiffli lace production as their primary SIC classification. These companies employed approximately 800 workers in 1993.

Similar to all labor-intensive textile industries, production workers have accounted for more than 80 percent of the total employment for SIC 2397 from 1988 to 1993. Machine operators, the most common kind of production worker, operate equipment that manufactures schiffli lace. Earnings for all textile production workers, including machine operators, have been nearly 40 percent below average for manufacturing employees in the United States. Nearly 80 percent of all fabricated textile production workers have been women.

Following an almost continuous decline since 1988, employment in all of the fabricated textile industries, including SIC 2397, increased in 1993. However, employment for machinery operators is expected to decline through 2005. Increased productivity created by more efficient machinery and relaxed trade restrictions could be two main reasons for the projected reduction in machinery operators. Manufacturers have been investing in high-technology machinery, such as computerized embroidery machines. As the textile industry continues to become increasingly automated, operators and setters will need to understand complex machinery and have sufficient computer skills.

Exports of fabricated textile products, including schiffli lace, continued to expand in 1993. Canada and Mexico have been the largest export markets, buying more than 50 percent of all SIC 239 exports since 1989. Imports of fabricated textile products, which accounted for only nine percent of total SIC 23 imports, rose 15 percent in 1993. The major supplying countries have been Canada, China, India, and Mexico.

Future trade regulations could significantly impact the fabricated textile products industry, including SIC 2397. Relaxed trade restrictions could increase competition and imports from countries with lower paid workers. Although exports also have been expected to increase, a trade deficit for fabricated textile products, which reached $2.1 billion in 1993, should remain.

INDUSTRY INFORMATION SOURCES

Career Guide to Industries, Washington, D.C.: U.S. Department of Labor, September 1992.

Occupational Outlook Handbook 1992-93, Washington, D.C.: U.S. Department of Labor, 1991.

The New Encyclopedia Britannica 1993, Chicago: Encyclopedia Britannica Inc., 1992.

U.S. Industrial Outlook 1994, Washington, D.C.: U.S. Department of Commerce, 1993.

Ward's Business Directory of U.S. Private and Public Companies 1994, Detroit: Gale Research Inc., 1993.

—Catherine A. Quagliana

SIC 2399

FABRICATED TEXTILE PRODUCTS, NOT ELSEWHERE CLASSIFIED

This category covers establishments primarily engaged in manufacturing fabricated textile products, not elsewhere classified.

Companies classified here include manufacturers of banners, flags, sleeping bags, nondisposable diapers, fishing nets, parachutes, and seat belts. Others produce aprons, horse blankets, seat covers, hammocks, pennants, and nonleather straps. Companies within this industry belong to one of eight industries that make up Industry Group (miscellaneous fabricated textile products). These industries, including fabricated textile products, not elsewhere classified, accounted for 26 percent of all 1993 shipments in the major group for apparel and other finished products made from fabrics and similar materials.

According to the Bureau of Labor Statistics, 7,816 establishments manufactured fabricated textile products and employed 204,700 workers. As with all labor-intensive textile industries, production workers have accounted for more than 80 percent of the total employment for this category from 1988 to 1993. Machinery operators, the most common type of production worker, use equipment that manufactures textile

goods. Earnings for textile production workers, including machine operators, has continued to be nearly 40 percent below the average for all manufacturing employees in the U.S. Nearly 80 percent of all fabricated textile production workers are women.

Following an almost continuous decline since 1988, employment in all fabricated textile industries increased in 1993. However, employment for machinery operators is expected to decline through the year 2005. Increased productivity created by more efficient machinery and relaxed trade restrictions could be two main reasons for the projected reduction in machinery operators.

Although the apparel and textile products industry historically has not been export-oriented, manufacturers have become increasingly interested in overseas markets. Exports of miscellaneous fabricated textile products have grown at an average annual rate of more than 25 percent since 1989 and have accounted for more than 50 percent of the total miscellaneous fabricated textile product exports. Canada and Mexico have been the largest export markets, buying more than 50 percent of total exports within this industry since 1989. Imports of fabricated textile products, which accounted for only nine percent of total cutting-up and needle trades group, rose 15 percent in 1993. The major supplying countries are Canada, China, India, and Mexico.

Future trade regulations could significantly impact the fabricated textile products industry. Relaxed trade restrictions could increase competition and imports from countries with lower paid workers. Although exports also are expected to increase, a trade deficit for fabricated textile products, which reached $2.1 billion in 1993, should remain.

INDUSTRY INFORMATION SOURCES

Career Guide to Industries, Washington, DC: U.S. Department of Labor, September 1992.

Occupational Outlook Handbook (1992-93 edition), Washington, DC: U.S. Department of Labor, 1991.

U.S. Industrial Outlook—1994, Washington, DC: U.S. Department of Commerce, 1993.

Ward's Business Directory of U.S. Private and Public Companies, Detroit, MI: Gale Research Inc., 1994.

—Catherine A. Quagliana

LUMBER & WOOD PRODUCTS, EXCEPT FURNITURE

LOGGING

This category covers establishments primarily engaged in cutting timber and in producing rough, round, hewn, or riven primary forest or wood raw materials, or in producing wood chips in the field. Independent contractors engaged in estimating or trucking lumber, but who perform no cutting operations, are classified in non-manufacturing industries. Establishments primarily engaged in the collection of bark, sap, gum, and other forest products are classified in **SIC 0811: Timber Tracts; SIC 0831: Forest Nurseries and Gathering of Forest Products; and SIC 0851: Forestry Services.**

INDUSTRY SNAPSHOT

Logging, among the oldest of American industries, has become one of the most controversial. Environmentalists have severely attacked harvesting practices, and they have scored significant victories. Much of the dispute thus far has centered on protecting government forests in the Pacific Northwest to ensure the survival of the northern spotted owl. The strife between the industry and its opponents extends far beyond the well-being of a single species, however, and prolonged hostilities on several fronts appear likely. While most observers believe the industry itself is not endangered, it will probably be transformed by the battles it faces.

The conflicts have already had a major impact on the geographic distribution of logging within the United States. The South and, especially, the Pacific Northwest have been the two traditional centers of logging in the industry. In the South, loggers have relied on private holdings, which account for some 90 percent of all timberland in the region. In the Pacific Northwest, however, much of the supply has come from federal forests. With harvesting of government-owned land down sharply, the Pacific Northwest has accounted for a shrinking portion of the nation's production. Leadership in the industry thus continues to shift to the South.

The curtailment of harvesting on federal lands has had a disparate impact on firms in the wood products industry. In general, the major forest products companies performed poorly during 1991 and had mixed results in 1992, as the recession took its toll. In the first half of 1993, however, large firms that had extensive land holdings of their own recorded sharply higher earnings, as they benefited from the price increases that accompanied shrinking supply. Other companies, however, including many small sawmills without timber assets, faced increasing margin pressure as their raw material costs rose.

ORGANIZATION AND STRUCTURE

A diverse group of economic entities and individuals are involved in logging. Among the participants are the giant, integrated forest products firms, like Weyerhaeuser and Georgia-Pacific, which may own millions of acres of private timberlands; small sawmills that may harvest relatively few trees on federal lands for their own use; and independent cutters, who are compensated according to the number of trees they are able to distribute to mills. Logging activities are thus distributed among different types of firms and individuals, but they can also be integrated with other operations within a single, large company.

According to the government, products and services sold by the logging industry in 1992 had an estimated value of $12.7 billion. Broad estimates of the total size of the forest products, and related industries, of which logging is but a small segment, run to about 4 percent of gross national product, or $200 billion.

BACKGROUND AND DEVELOPMENT

Wood was a commodity of great value in ancient Rome, and in Athens its export was banned—a harbinger of the recent controversy over sending U.S. logs abroad to Asia. In the United States, of course, logging is older than the country itself, and wood products have played a central role in the economy's development.

The clearing and revival of the U.S. forest has been extraordinary. The land area of the coterminous United States is 1,903 million acres. Between 822 and 850 million acres, or about 45 percent of the country's land area, was originally covered by commercial forest. By 1920, owing to agricultural clearing, lumbering, and other activities, the original cover had fallen to about 470 million acres, of which only 138 million acres were original forest (some 250 million acres were significantly disturbed through grazing, cutting, and burning and could not sustain second growth, while 81 million acres were both nonrenewable and non-restoring). By 1977, however, because of better management, the suppression of fire, replanting, and other factors, the trend had reversed itself: the commercial forest had grown to 483 million acres. The Forest Service estimates that there were 490 million acres of timberland in 1992.

Logging in the great forests of the Pacific Northwest was begun by the Hudson Bay Company at its Fort Vancouver trading post on the Columbia River in 1820. In 1825, the Royal Horticultural Society of London sent out a Scottish botanist, David Douglas, to the area; he returned to England with a sprig of what is now the most important commercial tree of these forests, the eponymous Douglas fir. Logging as an industry began in the region at the time of the Gold Rush, which produced a new market for timber in California. It was the timber barons from the East who saw the potential of the Pacific Northwest forests. Most famous among them was George Weyerhaeuser, who incorporated his company in 1900 in Tacoma, Washington; often a pioneer in the industry, Weyerhaeuser began the practice of hand-planting new trees on clearcuts in 1938. In the early 1990s, the firm had average annual sales in excess of $9 billion.

CURRENT CONDITIONS

The national recession during the early 1990s hurt the wood products sector badly, but as the recession waned the industry began to recover. Due largely to the strength of higher housing starts and firmer timber prices, the wood products operations of the major forest products companies did better in 1992 and 1993 than in 1991. In the first-half of 1993, profits at those companies that rely most heavily on wood products were up 179 percent from the same period in 1992, according to *Business Week*. Nevertheless, the prospect of sustained cutbacks in the timber supply raised significant questions about the long-term health of the industry.

Environmental constraints on logging have not had a major impact in most of the South, the Northeast, and North Central regions of the country. It is important to remember, however, that about half of the country's timber for wood products has come from the Pacific Northwest. The deterioration of the climate for timber harvesting in that region has been so dramatic that it has already had a significant impact on the nation's overall supply. More importantly, the political and social forces that have caused the industry such problems in the Northwest are expected to continue in the future.

Most of the nation's timber supply has come from softwoods, which are used predominately in housing construction; hardwoods, which have a variety of uses, are harvested primarily in the South. In 1987, approximately 35 percent of the nation's softwood lumber came from sales of timber on federal lands in the Pacific Northwest. By 1992, that contribution had dropped to 25 percent. Sales of timber from federal forests in the region have fallen from 6.0 billion board feet in 1987 to 1.5 billion in 1992.

It has been estimated that once the environmental controversies in the Northwest are settled, government timber sales in the West will be at about 40 percent of historical levels. Given that 35 percent to 40 percent of the U.S. timber supply has historically come from federal lands in the area, these curtailments would represent a 22 percent decline in the national timber harvest. A drop in the timber supply of that magnitude portends higher log prices, as well as narrower margins for wood products firms that do not own timber acreage.

The Spotted Owl Controversy. On June 26, 1990, the government listed the northern spotted owl as a threatened species under the Endangered Species Act. Unlike most other species protected by the Act, the spotted owl's habitat covers a much larger area: it ranges from southern British Columbia, Canada, to Marin County, California. Under the terms of the act, more than five million acres of forests were designated as conservation areas; these generally contained conifers of mixed varieties that were over 200 years old, i.e., old-growth forests.

Technically, logging was still allowed within the conservation areas as long as it did not threaten the spotted owl, but as a practical matter much of the owl's habitat was off-limits to loggers. The U.S. Forest Service reported that in total it sold 4.45 billion board feet of timber in fiscal 1992—less than half of its sales in 1990. The agency managed to sell only 20 percent of the Congressionally-approved volume in the Pacific Northwest and 40 percent in California. Most if not all of this shortfall stemmed from measures taken to protect the spotted owl and other species. Loggers cut 61 percent more national forest timber in 1992 than was sold during the year.

Some observers believed that the timber industry had only itself to blame for its problems with the owl. They argued that the industry ignored the bird, and attempted to discredit research that showed the owl was truly endangered. They also said that the timber on the federal lands which the spotted owls inhabit represent public assets—assets that, in their view, have often been sold at below cost by the Forest Service and the Bureau of Land Management for the industry's benefit.

Many industry supporters, however, said there is much evidence that spotted owls of one subspecies or another are thriving on millions of acres of privately and publicly managed second-growth forests. They also noted that counts of the northern spotted owl have risen substantially over the past several years. They argued, additionally, that even if the spotted owl was indeed endangered, it did not provide sufficient reason to throw thousands of workers out of their jobs and destroy dozens of timber communities.

While the clash between the timber industry and environmentalists (or preservationists, the term the industry prefers) has centered on the survival of the northern spotted owl, campaigns to protect other species may affect the industry in the future. Timber executives are also worried about the impact of logging on salmon. Because logging often damages the streams in which salmon spawn, the species could eventually become federally protected and thus further limit the industry in the Northwest.

Some observers, both within the industry and the environmental movement, believe that efforts to save individual species are merely tactical devices in the battle to curtail logging. The environmental movement needed a weapon to shut down logging on federal lands, they say, and the Endangered Species Act merely happened to be conveniently at hand. Andy Stahl, an environmentalist, is quoted in the book *The Final Forest* as saying "I've often thought that thank goodness the spotted owl evolved in the Northwest, for if it hadn't, we'd have to genetically engineer it."

Environmentalists recognize that the total amount of woodland in the United States is not contracting— new plantings more than offset cuttings. Still, many are concerned that the way the nation's forests have been managed reduces biodiversity. When loggers cut down mixed forests with trees of different ages, they often replant with a single species (such as the Douglas fir, which reaches maturity in a relatively fast 50 years) of the same age. Some environmentalists argue that in a naturally regenerating forest, there are dead trees, clearings, old trees, and young trees, and each attracts its own group of plant and animal species. But when a forest consists solely of one tree type, all of the same age, only one set of species is attracted. Ecologists believe that this hurts the forest's ecosystem, and leaves it prone to pest infestations.

In rebuttal, the industry's supporters pointed to the expansion in total timberland over the last fifty years, and the millions of acres, including much old-growth (trees over 200 years old), in national and state forests that are protected from logging. They also called attention to the significant advances in forestry management over several decades. For example, after the volcanic eruption of Mount St. Helens on May 18, 1980, Congress, in 1982, established a 110,000 acre National Volcanic Monument. In this area nature would be allowed to take its course, and the land would be left undisturbed. On the acreage adjacent to it, Weyerhaeuser and other companies salvaged the downed trees and planted new seedlings. According to some observers, the result of this effort is a forest not significantly different from the original (pre-1980) cover below the slopes of the volcano. By 1992, many of the trees Weyerhaeuser had planted were already 25 or 30 feet high. Next door, the National Volcanic Monument was recovering much more slowly—but, some would argue, more completely.

Others in the industry said that the uncertainty that surrounded harvesting in 1993 would have long-term repercussions for the industry. In this regard, *The Economist* cited the words of a Weyerhaeuser economist: "Planting trees is an act of faith." It takes some 80 or 90 years for a forest to regrow on its own after cutting, versus 50 to 60 years in a managed forest. So if timber firms lose confidence that they will be able to harvest the tree they have sown, they are unlikely to put much effort in expensive forest-management techniques.

In February 1993, news reports indicated that the Clinton Administration was trying to modify the policies of the Department of Interior (DOI) so that ''national train wrecks'' (in the words of DOI Secretary Bruce Babbitt), like the one over the spotted owl in the Pacific Northwest, could be averted in the future. Instead of protecting single species, the DOI would seek preventive measures to insure long-term protection of whole ecosystems and all of their species. The theory behind such an approach is that both conservation and business interests are better served by pre-planning the fate of entire ecosystems, before any single species is threatened.

Winners and Losers. Cutbacks of harvesting on federal lands has had a diverse impact on industry participants. Some believe that the largest companies—at least those with substantial timber holdings of their own—have been less than vigorous in fighting curtailments of logging on federal land. These firms have huge plantations of genetically improved trees, which afford them ample supply. Their reliance on federal sales of old-growth trees is relatively small, and the spotted owl doesn't appear to thrive on their own second- and third-growth forests. It has been argued, therefore, that these companies have been willing, and even happy, to accept restrictions on logging of federal lands.

Small, independent sawmill owners, on the other hand, have since World War II relied on public lands to supply the old-growth logs that can be turned into specialty products. The trees they used were often as much as five centuries old; consequently, they were often inhabited by the spotted owl. The trees that have been engineered by big corporations are but a tenth the age and only half the height of the old-growth trees. Often they are too small for the saws and conveyor belts of the old-time sawmills.

Lumber prices rose sharply in the first-quarter of 1993, and while they fell back in the spring, they were still significantly above 1992 levels. Meanwhile, however, smaller sawmill companies in the Pacific Northwest were hurt by contracting supply and continued to decline in number. Some observers argued that these companies have only themselves to blame, since they tended to disregard forecasts, dating back to the 1970s, of a looming timber shortage during the 1990s. They also suggested that at the rate the loggers were cutting, the Pacific Northwest would have had severe supply problems by the year 2000, regardless of the spotted owl endangerment controversy.

The South. Level terrain, frost-free winters, and numerous highways made logging much easier in the South than it was in the Northwest. Trees in the region grew faster because of the relatively warm winters. Since most of the South's acreage was logged years ago, there is little of the old-growth forest that has aroused such strong environmental opposition in the Northwest. Most notably, some 90 percent of Southern timberland is privately owned.

The conflicts between the environmentalists and timber interests that halted logging in much of the Northwest has been comparatively rare in the South. The two sides have actually worked together to balance environmental and economic concerns. Georgia-Pacific, which moved its headquarters from Portland, Oregon, to Atlanta in 1982 and has an important presence in the region, believes that it is successfully dealing with the red-cockaded woodpecker, which some see as a potential ''spotted owl'' of the South. Others, however, believe it is only a matter of time before the environmental movement begins to become more aggressive in opposing logging in the South.

In July of 1993 the Clinton Administration issued a plan that would reduce timber harvests on national forests in the Pacific Northwest to 1.2 billion board feet per year, down 75 percent from peak levels in the mid-1980s. At the same time, the proposal made available $1 billion to $2 billion in funds to help retrain loggers and aid lumber communities. Both environmentalists and industry officials attacked the plan, and it was unclear whether it would offer a long-term solution to the controversy.

INDUSTRY LEADERS

The business operations of the large, integrated forest product companies were usually divided into three areas: paper, pulp, and packaging; wood and building products; and other miscellaneous activities. The three largest forest products companies—International Paper, Georgia-Pacific, and Weyerhaeuser—were notably larger than other firms, and each had more than $8 billion in sales in 1991. However, only about 10 percent of International Paper's sales came from wood products. Consequently, the industry leaders in this segment are Georgia-Pacific, where wood products accounted for 47 percent of sales, and Weyerhaeuser, where they represented 33 percent of sales. Among the smaller of the top ten companies, Louisiana-Pacific derived some 90 percent of its $1.7 billion in sales from wood products, the highest percentage among industry leaders.

Weyerhaeuser is a company that stands to benefit from any shortages in the timber supply. In 1991 the company had more than 5,500,000 acres in timber holdings, so it had much to gain from any run-up in prices resulting from curtailed supplies. In fact, during the first six months of 1993, when lumber prices surged, the company's profits rose 100 percent. Still, the environmental movement has not been an unmixed blessing: logging on some 320,000 acres of its land is restricted because of federal and state rules protecting the spotted owl, and the company was worried about further restrictions on its supply. Further, the movement to restrict log exports to Japan and other countries could also hurt the company in the longer term.

In the 1980s Weyerhaeuser had embarked on a diversification program that was generally considered to have been ill-conceived. Among the failed operations were garden supplies, lettuce factories, mortgage banking, and dog food. As a result, while the timber industry as a whole posted a combined 18.5 percent return on equity in the 1980s, Weyerhaeuser posted just 10 percent. Although the proportion of ''other activities'' among all of its businesses was still higher than most of its competitors in 1992, it had slimmed down considerably and shed many of its extraneous operations.

As logging on public lands in the Northwest came under increasing attack from environmental groups in the 1980s, Georgia-Pacific began to increase its holdings of fast-growing pine forests in the Southeast where it had logged extensively earlier in the century. Losses from the paper side of the business, which had been expanded significantly with the purchase of Great Northern Nekoosa in 1990, more than offset gains from logging in the early 1990s. The acquisition also saddled the company with debt. In 1992, however, operating profits from the building products division reached a record level of $691 million, more than double the 1991 total of $344 million.

Among the ten largest forest product companies, Willamette has turned in the strongest consistent performance. Return on equity averaged 21 percent between 1987 and 1991, compared with the industry median of 15 percent. Debt in early 1992 was a modest 39 percent of the company's total capital. Willamette began to expand eastward in the early 1980s when it realized that opportunities for growth were drying up in the West. In 1992, the company generated more than 60 percent of its sales on products made east of the Rockies.

WORK FORCE

In May of 1993, total employment in the lumber and wood products industries was estimated to exceed 670,000 people. According to government statistics,

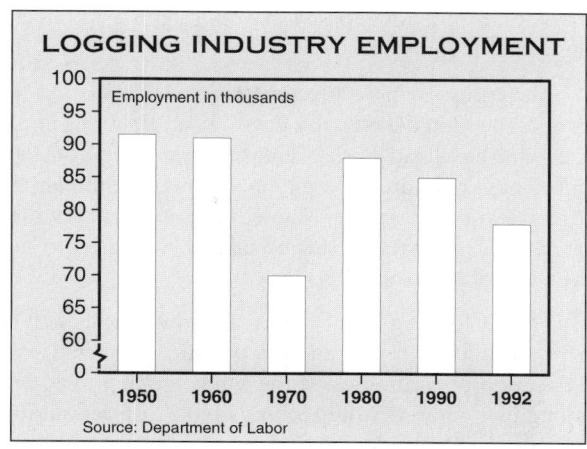

LOGGING INDUSTRY EMPLOYMENT

Employment in thousands

Source: Department of Labor

about 65,000 people worked in the logging segment alone, down from 72,000 in 1987.

Estimates of the number of jobs that would be lost due to federal protection of the spotted owl habitats varied widely. In early 1993, the U.S. Fish and Wildlife Service attempted to estimate cuts in timber-related employment if the level of owl protection remained at existing levels. They forecast that by 1995 about 32,000 jobs would be lost, including 6,500 in Washington, 21,600 in Oregon, and 4,300 in California. The Clinton Administration estimated that under its plan introduced in July of 1993, 6,000 jobs would be lost. Still, some in the timber industry said that the number of lost jobs would be ten times that level.

Even without the threat of continuing job losses due to environmental concerns, employment in the industry was likely to decline because of increasing automation. Between 1979 and 1989, timber employment fell from 160,000 to 130,000 in Oregon and Washington, though the wood harvest in both years was roughly the same. Most of the decline had little to do with protecting rare species or setting aside old-growth, but rather was the result of increasing mechanization in the industry. In 1991, for the first time in decades, more people worked in the food industry in Washington state than in forest products. The number of forest workers had fallen to 36,500 from 41,000 in 1988, while food industry workers climbed from 33,100 to 37,400 during that period.

Some loggers have been successful in finding alternative sources of revenue within the industry itself or in related businesses. For example, loggers have sold pine cones and moss-covered sticks to floral designers, and they have found work harvesting herbs for use in the decorative, culinary, and medicinal markets. These activities, however, tend to pay less than cutting trees, and some loggers say they enjoy the work much less than logging.

Logging is in fact very dangerous work. Many workers within the industry have suffered serious injuries and have had friends and relatives killed on the job. These risks are apparent in workmen's compensation rates for loggers. In Maine, for example, they run about $37 for every $100 in salary, compared to an average of $12 for carpenters.

Some logging communities are now looking to the Clinton plan to revive their economic bases and enhance job opportunities. If the funds are approved by Congress, money would be available for retraining programs. Some ideas for economic regeneration on the Olympic Peninsula in Washington state, an area that has been hurt by logging restrictions, included docks for cruise ships, Indian cultural centers, and industrial parks.

AMERICA AND THE WORLD

Exports. Total log exports from Pacific Coast ports in 1992 were 2.73 billion board feet, down from approximately 3.15 billion feet in 1991. The drop continued the decline in log shipments since 1988, when exports peaked at 4,331 million feet. Log exports to Japan totaled 2.03 billion feet, or over 70 percent of total shipments. It is estimated that U.S. log exports in the first three quarters of 1992 represented 57 percent of all softwood imports in Japan. Other important destinations were China and South Korea, although exporters faced increasing competition from New Zealand for those markets.

The issue of log exports, especially to Japan, has become a source of controversy. It was estimated that about 40 percent of all logs felled in Washington state were being shipped overseas in the early 1990s, and sawmill operators complained that they were unable to get wood because of the large number of logs being sent abroad. While the export of logs from federal lands is prohibited, some mill operators said that companies substituted logs from private holdings for export and sawed the government logs for domestic use. Indeed, the issue has become embroiled with the spotted owl controversy, with environmentalists suggesting that overseas shipments were the reason for any lumber shortages, while major exporters attributed supply shortages to the impact of the Endangered Species Act.

Imports. Despite potential problems in the domestic timber supply, imported logs were not expected to gain a significant market share in the United States. The U.S. market is huge, and far beyond the capability

of most overseas timber producers to supply in quantity. Almost all U.S. imports currently come from Canada, particularly the province of British Columbia. But the province's forests have been more aggressively cut than U.S. acreage, and Canada's environmentalists are trying to reduce harvests.

The former Soviet Union still had bountiful forests in the early 1990s, but it lacked the infrastructure to make harvesting worthwhile. It would take billions of dollars in roads as well as a stable government for Russia to become a major producer. Moreover, some Russian acreage is believed to be infested with pests that could harm Northwest trees. Earlier attempts to process Russian logs in California were stymied by costly pesticidal treatments that had to be performed before the logs were allowed into the country.

Ironically, the first logs to be imported in quantity may be transplanted Californian natives. New Zealand and Chile have large plantations of radiata pine, and both countries already export large volumes of logs. The radiata is known as Monterey pine in its native California, where it is not grown commercially.

RESEARCH AND TECHNOLOGY

As a result of mechanization and automation, timber companies can now log more efficiently while doing less harm to the environment. Huge ''feller-bunches'' now often replace individual loggers in second-growth forests. These vehicles are built like tanks and have enormous ''scissors'' mounted in front; they are able to snip mature trees and lay them down carefully to avoid smashing small, still-growing ones. Additionally, mechanized skidders that are used to haul logs out of the forest are being fitted with extra-wide tracks or oversized tires to spread their weight and reduce damage to the forest floor.

Timber companies are also experimenting with different forestry techniques. After harvesting, some loggers are leaving behind the odd mature tree, dead-sun-silvered trunks, and the usual litter of the woods. The hope is that, as new trees grow, their surroundings mimic what would follow a natural fire or windstorm, which a forest can survive.

Timber shortages and the possibility of higher lumber prices over the long-term are encouraging the creation of new offerings and the promotion of relatively inexpensive existing products. Forest products producers face a threat from the steel industry, which is promoting steel studs as replacements for wood in residential construction. To fend off this and other challenges to its products, the industry is focusing on promoting such engineered wood products as oriented strand board and particle board.

INDUSTRY INFORMATION SOURCES

Burrow, Clive. ''Tech Notes: With Tall Trees in Short Supply. . . .'' *The New York Times* (December 13, 1992).

Chipello, Christopher. ''Paper, Lumber Are Diverging in Their Results.'' *The Wall Street Journal* (April 12, 1993).

Clark, Earl. ''When the Bullwhacker Reigned Supreme.'' *American Forests* (September/October 1991).

Conway, Richard S., et. al. *The Forest Products Economic Study.* Olympia, Wash.: Washington Forest Protection Association, 1991.

''Corporate Scoreboard.'' *Business Week* (August 16, 1993).

Dietrich, William. *The Final Forest.* New York: Simon & Schuster, 1992.

Egan, Timothy. ''Thunder of Debate on Owls and Jobs Rings in Forests as Opponents Face Off.'' *The New York Times* (April 2, 1993).

———. ''The Things That Get Left Out in the Fight for the Wild Northwest.'' *The New York Times* (May 30, 1993).

Forest Industries 1992-93 North American Factbook. San Francisco: Miller Freeman, 1992.

Forest Resource Fact Book. Memphis: National Hardwood Lumber Association, 1993.

''Forest Service Issues Logging Restrictions to Aid Owl Species.'' *The New York Times* (January 15, 1993).

''The Future of Forests.'' *The Economist* (June 22, 1991).

Ifill, Gwen. ''Clinton Backs a $1 Billion Plan to Spare Trees and Aid Loggers.'' *The New York Times* (July 1, 1993).

Killian, Linda. ''Forest Products & Packaging'' *Forbes* (January 4, 1993).

Knize, Perri. ''The Mismanagement of the National Forests.'' *Atlantic Monthly* (October 1991).

McCoy, Charles. ''Even a Logger Praised as Sensitive to Ecology Faces Bitter Opposition.'' *The Wall Street Journal* (April 1, 1993).

Norvell, Scott. ''Southern Comfort for a Timber Giant: Georgia-Pacific Is Sitting Pretty Far from the Troubled Northwest.'' *The New York Times* (March 28, 1993).

''Owlmageddon.'' *The Economist* (May 4, 1991).

Pacelle, Mitchell. ''It Takes Guts Telling Paul Bunyan to Get Herbs, Spare Timber.'' *The Wall Street Journal* (November 27, 1992).

Passell, Peter. ''Economic Scene: The Pacific Timber Industry Isn't Really on the Endangered List.'' *The New York Times* (April 1, 1993).

Pease, David. ''Timber Shortages Will Encourage New Products.'' *Forest Industries* (July/August 1992).

Ray, Dixy Lee. ''A Forest Rises From the Ashes, Privately.'' *The Wall Street Journal* (April 1, 1993).

Rice, James Owen. ''Where Many An Owl Is Spotted.'' *National Review* (March 2, 1992).

Richards, Bill. ''Owls, of All Things, Help Weyerhaeuser Cash In on Timber.'' *The Wall Street Journal* (June 24, 1993).

Standard & Poor's Industry Surveys. New York: Standard & Poor's Corporation, 1993.

Statistical Yearbook of the Western Lumber Industry, 1992. Portland, Ore.: Western Wood Products Association, 1993.

Stevens, William. ''Interior Secretary Is Pushing A New Way to Save Species.'' *The New York Times* (February 17, 1993).

Suskind, Ron. ''Guys Holding Axes and Chainsaws Get to Use Any Name They Like.'' *The Wall Street Journal* (February 26, 1993).

Taylor, John A. ''The Ducks Are Flying.'' *Forbes* (July 20, 1992).

''The Timber Industry: Log On.'' *The Economist* (November 9, 1991).

''To the Dinosaurs.'' *The Economist* (July 10, 1993).

U.S. Industrial Outlook 1993. Washington, DC: U.S. Department of Commerce, 1993.

Waker Jr., Donald. ''A Logger's Story.'' *The Wall Street Journal* (May 15, 1992).

Weaver, Jim. ''Troubles for Timber.'' *The New York Times* (April 2, 1993).

Wilhelm, Steve. ''Food Firms Overtake Timber in Employment.'' *Puget Sound Business Journal* (October 30-November 5, 1992).

Williams, Michael. *Americans & Their Forests: A Historical Geography.* Oxford: Cambridge University Press, 1989.

—Bob Schneider

SIC 2421

SAWMILLS AND PLANING MILLS, GENERAL

This industry includes establishments primarily engaged in sawing rough lumber and timber from logs and bolts, or resawing cants and flitches into lumber, including box lumber and softwood cut stock; planing mills combined with sawmills; and separately operated planing mills which are engaged primarily in producing surfaced lumber and standard workings or patterns of lumber. The industry also includes establishments primarily engaged in sawing lath and railroad ties and in producing tobacco hogshead stock, wood chips, and snow fence lath. Establishments primarily engaged in manufacturing box shook or boxes are classified in wood container manufacturing industries; those manufacturing sash, doors, wood molding, window and door frames, and other fabricated millwork are classified in millwork, veneer, plywood, and structural wood industries; and those manufacturing hardwood dimension and flooring are classified in **SIC 2426: Hardwood Dimension and Flooring Mills.**

INDUSTRY SNAPSHOT

Lumber, primarily made from softwood logs, represents approximately 70 percent of the output of the sawmill and planing sector. In 1992, production in the western United States accounted for over half of global softwood lumber output, and more than two-thirds of this output was concentrated in the Pacific Northwest. Thus, the efforts by environmentalists to curtail logging on government lands in the Northwest have had a major impact on the sawmill and planing mill sector.

Relatively small mills without their own timber holdings have come under increasing pressure as logging on federal lands has declined: between 1991 and 1992, more than 100 lumber and panel products mills closed in the Pacific Northwest. The major, integrated forest products companies that have large timber holdings of their own, however, have remained competitive. While the big firms are not insulated from losses related to environmental legislation—industry leader Willamette, for example, closed three mills during the period—they are generally in a stronger position to benefit from the higher prices that follow restricted supplies.

There has also been a notable shift in lumber production away from the Northwest and toward the South, where most timberlands are privately owned. During the 1980s the seven largest forest products companies cut their mill capacity in the Pacific Northwest by 35 percent, while they increased it in the South by 121 percent.

ORGANIZATION AND STRUCTURE

According to an annual survey of North American producers in the trade publication *Forest Industries*, the 10 largest lumber producers in the United States cut a total of 12.5 billion board feet in 1991, or some 28 percent of total domestic production. Although only 3 percent of their production was hardwoods, they accounted for about 36 percent of all softwood output. For all of North America, the 20 largest producers cut 20.9 billion feet, or 32 percent of total output. These 20 firms operated 283 mills —205 in the United States and 78 in Canada. The 100 largest companies in North America generated about 61 percent of the industry's total production.

Even without any impact from curtailments of logging due to the spotted owl controversy, there has been a general trend toward consolidation in this industry. One study completed on the lumber industry in Idaho noted that in 1956, the state had 311 sawmills, with 37 producing more than 10 million board feet. By 1990 the number of sawmills had fallen to 80, with 40 producing more than 10 million feet. In 1956, 73 percent of lumber production came from mills producing more than 10 million feet annually. In 1979, mills with yearly output of 10 million feet represented 93 percent of the state's lumber supply. In 1990, the forty mills in this category produced 98 percent of Idaho's 2.06 billion feet of lumber.

BACKGROUND AND DEVELOPMENT

The first sawmill in the United States is said to have been built York, Maine in 1623. Sawmills quickly became a common sight in frontier settlements. Most were small enterprises with just one or two workers, and nearly all of these mills were located on rivers, using running water as their power source. As railroads spread across the country in the nineteenth century, the best spot to put a sawmill became the bank of a log-driving stream where a railway crossed it. With the shift from water to steam power, mills became larger and more complex. One mill on the Saginaw River produced 14 million board feet during the first half of 1874 and employed 150 men. Circular saws replaced the old-fashioned up and down saws in the 1860s, and the contemporary invention of a method for repairing worn or broken teeth greatly extended their useful lives. Electric power began to replace steam power in the early twentieth century, and by 1929 it accounted for 45 percent of all energy sources.

CURRENT CONDITIONS

According to statistics of the Western Wood Products Association (WWPA), lumber production increased more than 5 percent during 1992, to a level of 45.7 billion board feet compared to the 43.4 billion feet produced the year before. The total value of these shipments was approximately $18 to $19 billion. The residential construction industry, which is softwood lumber's primary market, began recovering from the recession in 1992, increasing the demand for and stabilizing the price of lumber. Housing starts increased by 20 percent, to 1.2 million units, and starts of single-family homes rose 25 percent, from 0.8 million in 1991 to 1.0 million in 1992. While this rebound benefited the sawmills and planing mills, total housing starts were still substantially below the 1986 peak level of

1.8 million units. Total sales of the home improvement industry, another major market for the sector, rose approximately 10 percent that year to reach $46.5 billion.

Because of the rise in single-family home construction and the increasing restrictions on the lumber supply, lumber prices rose dramatically in 1993. For example, the price of lumber for March delivery jumped nearly 150 percent from $180 in November of 1992 to a closing price of $445 on February 24, 1993. While some observers worried that surging lumber prices would stall housing starts, others noted that lumber represents just 10 percent to 15 percent of the expense of constructing a house, which in turn is just half of a house's retail cost.

The efforts by environmentalists to limit cutting of old-growth trees on federal lands, and thus significantly reduce total supply, was of immediate concern to owners of small sawmills. Some observers, however, wondered whether adequate supply would be a major problem for the lumber industry as a whole. New technologies like Parallam, a parallel strand lumber that can be made from trees that are too small to yield much traditional lumber, are producing a larger amount of wood products from the same amount of harvested wood. The recycling of paper similarly reduces demands for logs: the American Forest & Paper Association says that the recovery rate for U.S. paper and paperboard in 1992 rose to 38 percent from 28 percent five years earlier. Finally, much replanted wood in the western United States is due to be harvested in 20 to 30 years.

Move to the South. The wood products industry began to shift from the Pacific Northwest to the South in the late 1980s and early 1990s, due largely to environmental legislation passed in the Pacific Northwest. Lumber production in the 12 states tracked by the WWPA accounted for 54.4 percent of all U.S. softwood output in 1992 versus 62.6 percent in 1987. Total production of lumber from softwoods, which predominate in the Northwest, fell from 38.2 billion board feet to 34.5 billion board feet over the five-year period. Meanwhile, production of lumber from southern pine rose from 12.6 billion feet to 14.1 billion feet over the same period, just slightly below the record of 14.8 billion feet set in 1913.

Many sawmills in the Pacific Northwest, particularly those that had relied on old-growth trees from federal lands for their logs, experienced dramatically reduced profit margins and were struggling to survive. In 1991, 46 sawmills and panel plants shut down permanently in Washington, Oregon, California, and Idaho, and 4,100 workers lost their jobs. In 1990, 51

mills were closed, costing 4,076 jobs. In the first half of 1992 only 14 mills were shut, but 2,500 jobs were lost. It is estimated that between 1988 and 1992 the number of pine sawmills in the West fell 26 percent from 119 to 88.

In April of 1993 President Clinton held a major conference with timber industry officials and environmentalists in Portland, Oregon. In July he issued a plan that would reduce logging in federal forests in the Pacific Northwest by about 75 percent from the levels of the mid-1980s, but the plan would also provide over $1 billion in aid for the retraining of timber workers and their communities. Both industry officials and environmentalists immediately attacked the plan, and how much of its objectives would eventually be realized remained uncertain.

INDUSTRY LEADERS

The dependence of the large, integrated forest products companies on wood and building product sales varied widely in the early 1990s, since most had large paper operations and a few were significantly diversified. In 1991, wood and building products represented nearly 90 percent of Louisiana-Pacific's revenue, but they accounted for only 6 percent Union Camp's sales. The industry's leading companies were concentrated primarily in forest products. Weyerhaeuser held the top spot; its 36 sawmills cut 2.9 billion board feet of lumber. Georgia-Pacific's 45 mills cut 2.6 billion feet, and Louisiana-Pacific operated 53 mills and produced almost 1.8 billion feet. With their large timber holdings, these companies were well positioned to take advantage of the higher lumber prices that stemmed from tighter supply. Indeed, in the first half of 1993, each firm recorded substantially higher profit margins.

WORK FORCE

Employment at sawmills in 1992 was estimated at 143,000 by the U.S. Department of Labor, reflecting the continued drop in employment in this industry, from 152,000 in 1988. The decline reflects the closure of over 100 sawmills in the Pacific Northwest during that period. The decline was also attributable, however, to technological change that allowed sawmill owners to run their operations with fewer employees.

AMERICA AND THE WORLD

Total U.S. lumber exports in 1992 in volume terms fell about 3 percent to 3.7 billion board feet, of which 72 percent were softwoods and 28 percent were hardwoods. Softwood lumber exports in 1992 declined from 2.9 billion feet to 2.7 billion feet. Japan pur-

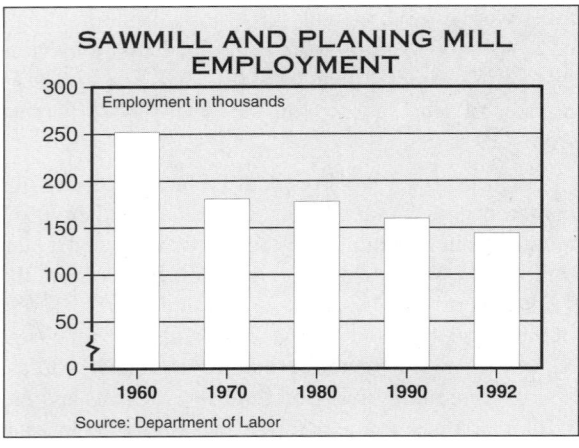

SAWMILL AND PLANING MILL EMPLOYMENT

Employment in thousands

Source: Department of Labor

chased about 38 percent of that total, or 1.1 billion feet. Mexico, the next largest importer of U.S. softwood lumber in volume terms, purchased 409 million feet. Hardwood lumber exports increased about 11 percent in 1991 to 977 million feet. The major export markets for U.S. hardwood lumber were Canada, Japan, and Italy.

Small sawmill owners expressed their anger at the large number of logs exported to Japan in the early 1990s. Some believed that exporting unfairly drove up the cost of logs for small firms and hurt their profitability. Congress had banned the export of logs from federal forests in the 1970s, but it wasn't until 1990 that the export ban was extended to include logs from state forests. All the state-owned trees cut in Oregon and 75 percent of those cut in Washington are required to be milled domestically.

Some companies in Japan were also disturbed by the high level of wood imports from the U.S. and other nations in the early 1990s. Japanese firms were facing high production costs and shortages of domestic logs, as well as the relative abundance of cheap imports. The number of small sawmills in Japan fell from 24,230 in 1960 to 18,260 in 1985, and during the same period the number of forestry workers fell by nearly half.

RESEARCH AND TECHNOLOGY

New technology has greatly improved productivity in the industry. In the early 1990s, mills were using computer-guided saws to maximize the amount of lumber obtained from a log. Waste materials were being used to fire boilers that provided the mills with electricity.

Automation greatly improved the output of many companies. An industry trade magazine, *Wood Technology,* discussed the experience of one mill in Geor-

gia that increased its productivity by upgrading its plant. Since logs accounted for 75 percent of its costs, the sawmill owners invested their money in developing techniques to get more lumber from the logs. Beginning in 1986 the company began an extended program to improve its facilities, which included adding sophisticated scanning systems and more efficient machine centers. The owners noted that over the five-year period they hadn't used any more logs, but their production had increased from between 10,000 and 12,000 board feet per hour to 18,000 to 20,000 board feet.

INDUSTRY INFORMATION SOURCES

Burrow, Clive. "Tech Notes: With Tall Trees in Short Supply. . . ." *The New York Times* (December 13, 1992).

Conway, Richard S., et. al. *The Forest Products Economic Study.* Olympia, Wash.: Washington Forest Protection Association, 1991.

Dietrich, William. *The Final Forest.* New York: Simon & Schuster, 1992.

Egan, Timothy. "Thunder of Debate on Owls and Jobs Rings in Forests as Opponents Face Off." *The New York Times* (April 2, 1993).

Forest Industries 1992-93 North American Factbook. San Francisco: Miller Freeman, 1992.

Forest Resource Fact Book. Memphis, Tennessee: National Hardwood Lumber Association, 1993.

Keegan III, Charles A., et al. *Idaho's Forest Products Industry: A Descriptive Analysis, 1990.* Missoula, Mont.: The University of Montana, 1992.

Killian, Linda. "Forest Products & Packaging" *Forbes* (January 4, 1993).

Little, Jane. "Land of the Pampered Plantation." *American Forests* (January/February 1991).

Passell, Peter. "Economic Scene: The Pacific Timber Industry Isn't Really on the Endangered List." *The New York Times* (April 1, 1993).

Pease, David. "Millwork Producers Seek 'Other' Raw Material Resources." Wood Technology, July/August 1993.

———. "Timber Shortages Will Encourage New Products." *Forest Industries* (July/August 1992).

Recovered Paper Statistical Highlights 1992. Washington D.C.: American Forest and Paper Association, 1993.

Standard & Poor's Industry Surveys. New York: Standard & Poor's Corporation, 1993.

Statistical Yearbook of the Western Lumber Industry, 1992. Portland, Ore.: Western Wood Products Association, 1993.

Taylor, Jeffrey. "Lumber Futures Continue to Rise, but Cash Price May Be High Enough to Cut Demand for Wood." *The Wall Street Journal* (February 25, 1993).

Taylor, Jeffrey. "Bull Market in Lumber May Be Over." *The Wall Street Journal* (April 2, 1993).

Taylor, John A. "The Ducks Are Flying." *Forbes* (July 20, 1992).

"The Future of Forests." *The Economist* (June 22, 1991).

"The Timber Industry: Log On." *The Economist* (November 9, 1991).

U.S. Industrial Outlook 1993. Washington, DC: U.S. Department of Commerce, 1993.

U.S. Department of Commerce. "Housing Starts - Current Construction Reports" (June 1993).

Williams, Michael. *Americans & Their Forests: A Historical Geography.* Oxford: Cambridge University Press, 1989.

—Bob Schneider

SIC 2426

HARDWOOD DIMENSION AND FLOORING MILLS

This classification consists of establishments primarily engaged in manufacturing hardwood dimension lumber and workings therefrom; and other hardwood dimension, semifabricated or ready for assembly; hardwood flooring; and wood frames for household furniture. Establishments primarily engaged in manufacturing stairwork, molding, and trim are classified in **SIC 2431: Millwork;** and those manufacturing textile machinery bobbins, picker sticks, and shuttles are classified in **SIC 3552: Textile Machinery.**

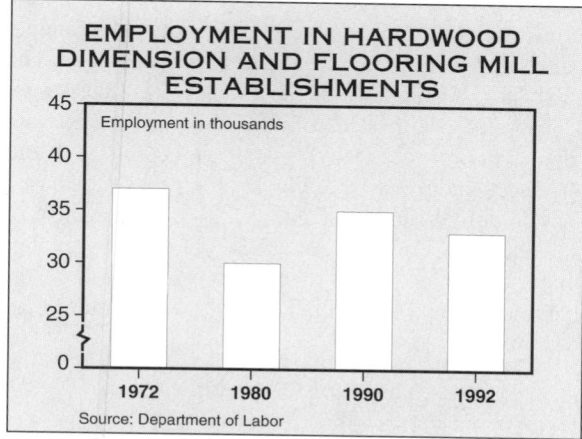

EMPLOYMENT IN HARDWOOD DIMENSION AND FLOORING MILL ESTABLISHMENTS

Employment in thousands

Source: Department of Labor

Hardwood flooring and parts used in furniture production make up the largest shares of output in this industry segment. These two segments account for 44

percent and 36 percent of the industry's volume respectively. The remaining output includes a huge variety of items, including such specialties as skis, golf clubs, and tool handles. Wood blocks for bowling pins and textile machinery accessories, rounds or rungs for ladders, and spool blocks and blanks are also on the list of items produced by this industry.

The total value of all products and services sold by establishments in the hardwood dimension and flooring mills industry was $1.74 billion in 1990. This figure represented a slight decrease from the previous year. Since the health of this industry is closely tied to housing starts in the United States, the sluggish economy of the early 1990s has contributed to recent declines in revenue, despite increases in home repair and remodeling, another major market for hardwood dimension.

Oak and maple are the species most commonly used in furniture and flooring manufacture in the United States. Ash, birch, cherry, poplar, and walnut are also frequently used. Four major types of flooring are regularly produced. They are strip, parquet, plank, and laminated. Strip and plank flooring combined to account for nearly two-thirds of the lumber used in flooring in 1989.

Hardwood dimension and flooring generally account for eight to ten percent of hardwood lumber exports by value. Canada, Japan, and Taiwan are the most frequent destinations of dimension and flooring exported from the United States. About 12 percent of the dimension and flooring consumed in the United States is imported, with the biggest suppliers being Canada, Taiwan, and, prior to its breakup and subsequent regional hostilities, Yugoslavia.

Triangle Pacific Corporation, with annual sales of about $293 million, is the biggest company with **SIC 2426: Hardwood Dimension and Flooring Mills** as its primary industry. Founded in 1943, Triangle Pacific manufactures hardwood floors, as well as kitchen and bathroom cabinets. Coastal Lumber Company of Weldon, North Carolina, a manufacturer of hardwood dimension lumber, is another important establishment in the industry. Coastal Lumber is a privately owned company with sales of about $154 million annually.

For 1990, the industry's 24.6 million production workers earned an average hourly wage of $7.53. Four states, North Carolina, Tennessee, Mississippi, and Arkansas, account for nearly half of the 29,000 total jobs in this classification. Nationwide, there were 729 companies in this industry in 1990. Of those, only three companies had more than 500 employees; 79 employed between 100 and 500 workers, 162 companies had 20 to 49 employees, and 178 companies had fewer than five employees.

Several issues will affect the hardwood dimension and flooring industry in the coming years. Changes in logging and land management regulations could have a major impact. Those changes, coupled with stricter air pollution laws, could potentially drive up the cost of lumber. A resurgence in home construction that would accompany an upturn in the American economy as a whole represents the best possible trend for the hardwood dimension and flooring mills industry.

INDUSTRY INFORMATION SOURCES

1987 Census of Manufacturers, Washington, D.C.: U.S. Department of Commerce, 1987.

U.S. Industrial Outlook, Washington, D.C.: U.S. Department of Commerce, 1991.

—Robert R. Jacobson

SIC 2429

SPECIAL PRODUCT SAWMILLS, NOT ELSEWHERE CLASSIFIED

This industry classification includes mills primarily engaged in manufacturing excelsior (wood shavings used for packing or stuffing), wood shingles, and cooperage stock; and in sawing special products, not elsewhere classified. The production of pads and wrappers made from wood excelsior is included in this industry. This industry also includes the manufacture of all types of wood shingles and shakes, which are hand-split shingles. Cooperage stock refers to staves, headings, and hoops used for making barrels, although the construction of the barrels themselves are classified in **SIC 2449: Wood Containers, Not Elsewhere Classified.**

Special product sawmills saw the total value of their shipments reach a high of $211.3 million in 1990 after a decade—the 1980s—in which industry performance varied considerably. From $154.6 million in 1982, shipment value bottomed out at $97 million in 1986 before rebounding throughout the second half of the decade. The number of companies primarily classified in this industry has been gradually shrinking since the early 1980s, and is now at about 200.

Shingles and shakes make up the largest share of the industry's products, accounting for nearly half of its output. The overwhelming majority of shakes and shingles produced are made of red cedar, which is grown mainly in the northwestern part of the United States. Red cedar shakes and shingles alone accounted for over 47 percent of the industry's production in 1987. Other woods sometimes used for shakes and shingles are northern white cedar, bald cypress, and redwood. In the last few years, the use of wood shingles has come under attack in areas that are prone to fires. In California, several local governments have enacted outright bans on new roofs made of wood products. Movements for such legislation have arisen throughout the state in the wake of a number of disastrous fires that have claimed hundreds of homes since 1990.

Cooperage stock makes up about 16 percent of the industry's output. This includes stock for both tight (used to hold liquids) and slack (for non-liquid use) cooperage, including buckets, hot tubs, and storage vats in addition to barrels. Excelsior, also known as wood wool, accounts for another 7.5 percent of production.

The majority of special product sawmills are small operations. Nearly half of them employ fewer than five workers. The total annual payroll for the industry's 2,300 workers is about $40 million. Workers earn approximately nine dollars an hour on the average. A huge share of the industry's activity takes place in the state of Washington, which accounted for 59 percent of industry employment in 1987, up from 43 percent five years earlier.

American Excelsior Co., based in Arlington, Texas, is the leading specialty product sawmill operation. As its name suggests, the company specializes in manufacturing cushioning made from wood fibers. American Excelsior is privately-owned and has annual sales of about $75 million. It was founded in 1888. The next largest company in the industry is Shakertown Corporation, with sales of $60 million. Shakertown, also a private company, was founded in 1923 and produces mainly cedar siding for buildings. It is based in Winlock, Washington. Blue Grass Cooperage Co., a subsidiary of Brown-Forman Corporation, is another major company. It is primarily a producer of stock for oak barrels, and has posted annual sales of more than $25 million.

INDUSTRY INFORMATION SOURCES

Groves, Martha, "Wood Shingle Firms Halt Fire Safety Standard Fight," *Los Angeles Times,* October 26, 1991.

Spencer, Albert G., and Jack A. Luy, *Wood and Wood Products,* Columbus, OH: Charles E. Merrill Publishing Co., 1975.

U.S. Industrial Outlook 1994, Washington, DC: Department of Commerce, 1994.

—Robert R. Jacobson

SIC 2431

MILLWORK

Establishments primarily engaged in manufacturing fabricated wood millwork, including wood millwork covered with materials such as metal and plastics. Planing mills primarily engaged in producing millwork are included in this industry, but planning mills primarily producing standard workings or patterns of lumber are classified in **SIC 2421: Sawmills and Planing Mills, General.** Establishments primarily engaged in manufacturing wood kitchen cabinets and bathroom vanities for permanent installation are classified in **SIC 2434: Wood Kitchen Cabinets.**

INDUSTRY SNAPSHOT

According to the U.S. Labor Department and the Bureau of the Census, 2,000 mills in America employ nearly 85,000 workers to manufacture products almost entirely for the construction industry. The 1993 Bureau of the Census reported the value of output for the industry at $9 billion in 1991. The composition of output shifted in the late 1980s as renovation and repair increased faster than new construction; new construction starts have increased significantly, however, in the early 1990s. According to the Department of Commerce, mill output is primarily used in construction, specifically residential construction. Residential construction utilizes more than 60 percent of mill output, while non-residential construction accounts for approximately 15 percent.

Recent environmental legislation has put the industry under tremendous supply pressures, although the effect on employment has been minimal compared to the logging, sawmill, and plywood industries. Nevertheless, the pressures are shifting the direction of technological change and marketing techniques in the industry. Most establishments specialize in one product class, such as wood door units, stairs, or railings, and are concentrated primarily in the Pacific Northwest, the Midwest, and Texas.

ORGANIZATION AND STRUCTURE

Mills in this industry cut down raw logs or stock lumber to produce wood shapes for window and door trim, baseboards, railings, window sashes, and other items. Wood pieces are also assembled with glass, vinyl, and aluminum cladding to make window sashes and frames. Often an inert gas such as argon fills the space between the glass panes to enhance insulation. Doors may be constructed out of solid pieces for high-end uses or, more commonly, consist of a frame, two-panels and filling. Exterior doors and interior apartment entrance doors often use steel to enhance security.

Over time the breakdown in the industry's dependence on new construction and repair, remodeling, maintenance, and home improvements has been shifting. During economic downturns, new construction subsides and repair work increases its share of construction activity. During the real estate boom of the 1980s, new construction outpaced repair work, especially in non-residential construction. However, through the 1990-1991 recession, repair work held steady while new construction plummeted.

According to 1993 reports of the Department of Commerce, the primary products produced by the millwork industry are doors (30 percent of total industry output), wooden windows and sashes (26 percent), and moldings (12 percent). Increasingly, doors and especially windows are clad with vinyl, aluminum or other metals. Energy concerns over the last two decades have led to the development of vinyl and aluminum windows. However, wood windows are regaining popularity because of their strength, beauty and natural insulating properties. Recent industry developments allow aluminum and vinyl clad wood windows to be produced in unlimited shapes and sizes. Solid wood doors, though, have lost market share in recent years to non-solid wood doors, steel, and steel-covered exterior doors.

CURRENT CONDITIONS

Forest product mills in the Pacific Northwest have taken a double beating in recent years. On the demand side, the 1990 economic recession resulted in a downturn in housing starts. On the supply side, recent legislation over the spotted-owl has led to a reduction in timber harvests on federal lands. According to Tom Kenworthy of the *Washington Post,* the blow resulted in the closing of 132 mills and the loss of approximately 13,000 jobs between 1990 and April of 1993 in the larger logging industry. The impact on the profits for mill owners was mixed. Companies that had private sources of timber or were located away from spotted owl habitats such as those in southern locales benefited from the increased price of lumber.

For the millwork industry itself, the job impact has been minimal. Employment lost in the downturn and since the logging ban has been restored somewhat by the economic upturn of 1992 and 1993. The mill industry is dependent, however, on the supply of wood. Some observers argue that the recent increase in construction doesn't guarantee the millwork industry unlimited success, however. Environmental and regulatory concerns regarding the industry's staple materials—Douglas fir and western pines—remain.

Wood Technology magazine noted in 1993 that some millwork plants have sought alternatives to western pines and Douglas fir, which are in short-supply and dwindling fast. Some of these alternatives are radiata pine imported from Chile and New Zealand, southern pine, hem-fir, sitka spruce, eastern white pine, and hardwoods. These new alternatives require mills to be flexible in their handling of woods. Each species requires its own methodologies of treatment, drying, and handling of imperfections. This is not only because of the unique characteristics of each kind of wood, but also because of the harvesting and storage practices of distant vendors, both in the U.S. and abroad.

Environmental Issues. The millwork industry is impacted by a variety of environmental issues. Logging restrictions on federal lands, due to concern for the future of the spotted owl and a general desire to leave remaining forestlands untouched, is a major environmental issue in the wood products industries. Boycotts and export restrictions on tropical wood affect imports and export markets. Concern over the health effects on workers and consumers of volatile chemicals have resulted in advances in wood treatment. Energy-loss concerns have led to major innovations in window and door production over the last fifteen years.

Logging restrictions are a source of particular concern to the industry, as they directly influence the price and availability of millwork establishments' primary production materials. In 1989 environmental groups invoked the Endangered Species Act of 1973 to halt logging in many forests to protect the spotted owl. In 1993 the ban was extended to parts of California to protect the California spotted owl, which is listed only as a sensitive species, not endangered. The move has sparked debate about trading jobs for the environment. The effect of the logging restrictions on jobs has been devastating in the northwestern logging and wood products industries.

On April 2, 1993, President Clinton held a timber conference in an attempt to find common ground and compromise between environmentalists and forest product workers. The compromise plan allowed 1.2 billion board feet a year to be cut from federal forests. This was approximately one-quarter of the amount permitted at the height of the 1980s. The proposal also established spotted owl reserves and water system buffer zones to protect the owl from extinction and streams from erosion. The President also proposed the development of ten intermediary zones. Loggers can experiment with new harvesting techniques in these zones, while forest management and environmental effects are monitored.

Greater flexibility in applying the restrictions could also allow logging on land that is less important to the spotted owl and to allow the clearing of dead and dying trees. Partially to compensate for lost jobs, another proposal was to provide retraining and to employ forest product workers in environmental projects to rebuild the forests and protect watersheds.

INDUSTRY LEADERS

The privately-owned Anderson Corp., based in Bayport, Minnesota, is the leading window and door manufacturer in the industry. It utilizes high-profile marketing to promote its product to the end user and keeps cost down by producing a large variety of standard sizes. Anderson boasted sales of approximately $900 million in 1993.

Marvin Lumber and Cedar Co., with headquarters in Warroad, Minnesota, specializes in high-value custom production for replacement windows and doors and for unusual architectural arrangements on new construction. Marvin, a privately-owned company, has sales of $280 million in 1992.

Trus Joist International has developed a long-term market strategy of focusing on engineered woods to improve strength and conserve old growth timber. TJ International markets most of these products for structural uses such as beams and framing materials. However, 28 percent of its business is in windows and doors, which it produces and markets through its subsidiaries, Dashwood Industries, Laffamme & Frere, and Norco Windows. It has, however, begun marketing windows constructed with laminated strand lumber through these subsidiaries.

Other leading companies in the millwork industry include Jeld-Wen Inc., of Klamath Falls, Oregon; Clopay Corp., based in Cincinnati, Ohio; Huttig Sash and Door Co., of Chesterfield, Missouri; and Pella Corporation of Pella, Iowa.

WORK FORCE

Safety issues. According to the United States Department of Commerce, the accident rate for millwork was higher than for related industries of wood kitchen cabinets, hardwood veneer and plywood, softwood veneer, and plywood, but lower than industries categorized in **SIC 2439: Structural Wood Members, Not Elsewhere Classified.** The rate of injuries sustained per 100 full-time workers was greater in large mills (defined as twenty or more workers) than in small mills.

The Labor Department's Bureau of Labor Statistics lists back strain and hand and finger injuries as the two highest types of injuries in the millwork industry. Back strain injuries were primarily the result of lifting heavy objects. Serious hand and finger injuries were received while operating stationary saws and other machinery. Other safety issues that have received attention in recent years include the respiratory effects on workers involved in sanding and the application of volatile materials such as polyurethane and formaldehyde. The Labor Department believes that many accidents are preventable through education and training and minor machinery enhancements.

Employment. The Bureau of the Census reported in 1993 that 84,900 people were employed in the industry in 1991, with an average hourly wage of $9.75. According to the Labor Department, despite the large number and variety of machines employed in the industry, it is quite labor intensive. For each dollar of value that mills add to raw materials, it uses 72 percent more production-worker hours than in manufacturing as a whole. According to Brad Knickerbocker, writing in the *Christian Science Monitor,* recent technical innovation has enabled the membership of the timber industry to record gains in productivity of as much as 40 percent; this has created a corresponding decline in timber industry employment. More recently, especially with the shortages of raw materials, technological innovation has taken a shift toward the maximization of materials savings, rather than labor savings.

A 1992 article in the *Christian Science Monitor* estimated that Oregon lost 12 percent of its work force employed in the timber industry because of logging restrictions and a weak market for construction. Employment in wood products fell from 70,000 in 1988 to 52,000 in the last quarter of 1992 in the region. According to the Commerce Department, employment in the millwork industry in particular was affected more by the recession than by the spotted owl crisis. The Bureau of the Census reported that employment began slipping in 1990. It plummeted nearly seven percent (6,200 jobs) between 1989 and 1991. However, employment climbed more than eight percent (6,900 jobs) between 1991 and 1992. Between 1992 and 1993 another 600 jobs were created in the industry.

AMERICA AND THE WORLD

Trade patterns in millwork and other wood products have undergone considerable change recently due to environmental pressures, the reduction of trade barriers, and the end of the cold war.

According to Robert Shaw of *Construction Review,* international trade in construction materials, including wood products, nearly doubled between the mid-1980s and 1990. According to 1993 reports by the Commerce Department, trade liberalization in Canada and Mexico and a weak dollar led to the first trade surplus for millwork in the last 20 years. Millwork exports doubled between 1989 and 1991, from $102 million to $207 million. Then they jumped 40 percent from 1991 to 1992 and 25 percent from 1992 to 1993. Meanwhile, imports rose less than an estimated 10 percent between 1989 and 1993.

Developing countries have advantages in low-cost labor and raw materials when competing in international trade. They have utilized these advantages to develop wood-working industries and increase their exports of furniture and millwork products to America. Many industry observers expect American imports of such products to increase as a result of the North American Free Trade Agreement and the General Agreement on Tariffs and Trade.

Environmental concerns have reduced the international supply of millwork's principal raw material—logs, although the U.S. Supreme Court reversal of a federal law restricting log exports has somewhat eased international supply. Indonesia banned the export of logs in the early 1980s to slow the consumption of its own forests while expanding employment in wood products industries. By doing so, the Indonesian government stimulated the development of wood processing industries such as milling and plywood. The exportation of processed woods is encouraged. Malaysia also recently restricted its exports of raw logs to preserve its forests and develop its wood-working industries.

According to Jonathan Friedland, writing in the *Far Eastern Economic Review,* the reduction in the supply raw logs, especially in East Asia, caused a crisis in the Japanese millwork, plywood, and construction industries. Prices of East Asian hardwood jumped 110 percent and prices of North America Douglas Fir climbed 60 percent. If these high prices are sustained, Japan may look to Russia for a greater proportion of its wood materials.

In January 1993 Canada and the United States signed a free-trade agreement that will phase in 50- to 100-percent tariff reductions over five years. Mexico has also been reducing its tariffs since the mid- to late-1980s and will continue to do so under the North American Free Trade Agreement. In recent years Mexico has attracted large amounts of foreign investment and lowered its tariff barriers. This inflow of capital raised foreign exchange income, which in turn allowed it to raise imports. As a result, Mexico has increased its importation of wood and wood products from the United states. According to 1993 Department of Commerce statistics, Mexico bought 26 percent of U.S. window exports and 48 percent of door exports in 1992. The passage of the North American Free Trade Agreement in the United States Congress is expected to quicken this flow of capital to Mexico and further reduce tariffs.

According to David A. Pease, writing in *Wood Technology* in 1992, extensive development of Russia's forestry industries may drive down bloated prices on the international market, but this will not happen soon. Russia's political turmoil and poor infrastructure in the areas with the largest forests will require large capital investments in a risky policy environment. Nevertheless, Korean and Finnish firms have already developed joint ventures with Russians to develop forestry products. The Korean industrial giant Hyundai ships logs from Russia's Pacific coast. The United States' largest forest products company, Weyerhaeuser, is also attempting to purchase logs from the same region. On the Atlantic side, Finnish concerns have established a joint effort with Russian concerns to produce wood products such as plywood.

RESEARCH AND TECHNOLOGY

Concerns about energy costs, maintenance requirements, and personal security have led to significant technological change over the last two decades in the millwork industry. Environmental restrictions on raw materials and worker safety are beginning to lead another wave of technical change in the present decade.

For both doors and window frames, the newest technological advances are coming in the area of materials conservation. Sustained high costs for woods such as Douglas fir, Ponderosa, and other western pines have spurred innovation in window frame and door production. Increasingly, composite materials are used as substitutes for solid wood parts, while window frames are increasingly produced from engineered woods. Trus Joist International, for example, produces window frames made from laminated strand lumber. This technology is still in its infancy. As the industry continues to substitute engineered woods such as laminated strand lumber for sawn wood, it will have to

focus technological attention on worker safety issues such as exposure to dust, formaldehyde, and other volatile organic compounds. Currently the industry is developing a voluntary standard for formaldehyde levels.

INDUSTRY INFORMATION SOURCES

Council of Economic Advisers. "Economic Indicators." *Economic Indicators,* June 1993.

"Eastern German Housing to Boom." *Wall Street Journal,* June 22, 1993: A11.

Freeman, Emily N. "WWPA spring meeting explains how to go Green." *Wood Technology,* 120, No. 3, May/June 1993: 12.

Friedland, Jonathan. "Meany greenies: Japan faces soaring cost of imported timber." *Far Eastern Economic Review,* March 4, 1993: 43-44.

Grogan, Tim, et. al. "Third Quarterly Cost Report." *ENR,* 13, September 28, 1992: 25-40.

Irland, Lloyd C. "Wood producers face Green marketing era." *Wood Technology,* March/April 1993: 34-36.

Kenworthy, Tom. "The Owl and the Lumberjack: Can Clinton Break the Logjam?" *The Washington Post,* April 2, 1993: A4.

Knickerbocker, Brad. "Saving Endangered Jobs as Well as Owls." *Christian Science Monitor,* March 5, 1992: 17.

The 1982 Benchmark Input-Output Accounts of the United States. Washington, DC: U.S. Department of Commerce, Bureau of Economic Analysis. 1991.

Pease, David A. "Joint-venture mill taps Russian forest resource." *Wood Technology,* 6, November/December 1992: 13-15.

———, "Millwork producers seek 'other' raw material sources." *Wood Technology,* 4, July/August 1993: 6.

Personick, Martin E., and Biddle, Elyce A. "Job Hazards Underscored in Woodworking Study." *Monthly Labor Review,* 9, September 1989: 18-23.

Shaw, Robert M. "World trade in building projects." *Construction Review,* Winter 1993: vii-xvii.

Stanley, J. "TJ International - Company Report." A.G. Edwards and Sons, Inc., 1992.

Statistical Abstract of the United States. Washington, DC: U.S. Bureau of the Census, 1993.

Trumbull, Mark. "Northwest Growth Leads Nation." *Christian Science Monitor,* December 10, 1992: A8.

U.S. Industrial Outlook 1993. Washington, DC: U.S. Department of Commerce, 1993.

Warren, Debra D. *Production, Prices, Employment, and Trade in Northwest Forest Industries, Fourth Quarter 1985,* Washington, DC: U.S. Forest Service, 1986.

—Joseph Kirchner

SIC 2434

WOOD KITCHEN CABINETS

This industry includes establishments primarily engaged in manufacturing wood kitchen cabinets and wood bathroom vanities, generally for permanent installation. Establishments primarily engaged in manufacturing free-standing cabinets and vanities are classified in various furniture-manufacturing industries. Establishments primarily engaged in building custom cabinets for individuals are classified in **SIC 5712: Furniture Stores.**

WOOD KITCHEN CABINET MANUFACTURING EMPLOYMENT

Employment in thousands

Source: Department of Labor

In 1993 the Bureau of the Census reported the value of output for the wood kitchen cabinet manufacturing industry as $4.2 billion for 1991. The demand for wood kitchen cabinets is heavily dependant upon new construction, for more than 90 percent of the industry's output goes toward new construction. Of that total, the Commerce Department noted in 1991 that more than 85 percent went to residential new construction.

Wood kitchen cabinets have been facing pressures from both the supply and demand side. On the supply side, plywood and composite board prices have been soaring in response to timber shortages in the Pacific northwest. On the demand side, the industry's dependance on the health of the larger construction industry resulted in a loss of output during the course of the 1990-1991 recession; this downward trend was alleviated, however, by the economic recovery of the mid-1990s, which saw a dramatic rise in housing starts.

According to 1993 Bureau of the Census statistics, more than 57,000 people were employed in the industry in 1991. According to the United States Depart-

ment of Labor, the wood kitchen cabinet industry had an injury and illness rate 32 percent higher than for general manufacturing in 1987.

Leading establishments in the wood kitchen cabinet manufacturing industry include Triangle Pacific Corp. of Dallas, Texas, a privately-owned company that posted estimated sales of $280 million in 1992, and Merillat Industries Inc. of Adrian, Michigan, which garnered $400 million in sales in 1992. Other major establishments include Aristokraft Inc., Distributors USA Inc., American Woodmark Corp., and HomeCrest Corp.

While the industry has seen few dramatic technological breakthroughs, several changes in the appearance of the industry have taken place in recent years. Raw material shortages are forcing some manufacturers to use more composite and engineered woods. Frameless cabinetry design, in which shelf space can be utilized right up to the cabinet wall rather than sacrificing one inch around to the frame, is also increasing. Finally, manufacturers are offering a greater variety of easy access storage designs.

INDUSTRY INFORMATION SOURCES

The 1982 Benchmark Input-Output Accounts of the United States. Washington, DC: U.S. Department of Commerce, Bureau of Economic Analysis, 1991.

U.S. Industrial Outlook 1993. Washington, DC: U.S. Department of Commerce, 1993.

Statistical Abstract of the United States. Washington, DC: U.S. Bureau of the Census, 1993.

Personick, Martin E., and Biddle, Elyce A. "Job Hazards Underscored in Woodworking Study." *Monthly Labor Review,* 9, September 1989: 18-23.

—Joseph Kirchner

SIC 2435

HARDWOOD VENEER AND PLYWOOD

This classification covers establishments primarily engaged in producing commercial hardwood veneer and those primarily engaged in manufacturing commercial plywood or prefinished hardwood plywood. This includes nonwood backed or faced veneer and nonwood faced plywood, from veneer produced in the same establishment or from purchased veneer. Establishments primarily engaged in the production of veneer which is used in the same establishment for the manufacture of wood containers, such as fruit and vegetable baskets and wood boxes, are classified in various wood container manufacturing industries.

INDUSTRY SNAPSHOT

Plywood manufacturing and related industries have been passing through hard times as the result of several challenges to the industry. Industry obstacles in recent years have included a shortage of available lumber, resulting in higher operating costs, and the general economic recession of 1989-1991, which resulted in numerous plant closings and lost jobs. Many small firms in the Pacific Northwest, dependent on timber from federal lands, have been particularly affected. Industry critic Paul Ehinger claimed in a 1992 issue of *Forest Industries* that an estimated 133 sawmills, plywood, and veneer plants—20 percent of the mills in the Pacific Northwest—closed in the region between January 1990 and May 1992. This is an acceleration of a trend that saw 145 mills close in the 1980s. On the other hand, plywood firms with access to timber unaffected by legislation designed to protect the spotted owl, such as those in the south or large firms with private sources of timber, have benefited from the soaring prices of plywood. According to a report of S.G. Warburg & Co. Inc., plywood prices rose 67 percent between 1991 and March 1993.

To cope with supply pressures, firms have developed new products such as engineered woods. Some observers expect this trend will continue to shift the composition of output in the industry. As a result, the plywood and veneer hardwood industry is losing market share to establishments involved in the manufacture of reconstituted panel products, which includes particleboard, medium density fiberboard, and oriented strand board, among other products.

Another challenge on the horizon for the industry membership is the cost of complying with growing environmental regulation of indoor pollutants. This regulation affects the production of composite boards and plywood itself. The industry has set voluntary formaldehyde emission standards; in the meantime, the U.S. Environmental Protection Agency is collecting information on other forms of indoor pollutants.

The Bureau of the Census reported the value of output for the industry as $1.9 billion for 1991. According to 1991 Department of Commerce reports, the demand for veneer and plywood is heavily dependent upon construction, but not quite as dependent as is the millwork industry. Nearly one-half (48 percent) of veneer and plywood output goes to construction, mainly residential. Roughly a quarter of the output is used in other lumber and wood products industries,

with another 11 percent used in furniture and fixtures. According to 1993 Department of Commerce statistics, plywood sales constituted 45 percent of the industry's total output for 1992, while hardwood veneer products constituted an additional 25 percent of output.

Veneer production peels layers of wood from logs. Plywood production glues these veneer sheets together, alternating the direction of the grain for each sheet. Typically, plywood sheets are four feet by eight feet. Veneer is also glued to lumber, fiberboard and medium density fiberboard. It is also used in the production of oriented strand lumber and other engineered woods.

CURRENT CONDITIONS

The Department of Commerce notes that plywood is dependant on construction for nearly 50 percent of its sales. Construction was hard hit in the 1990 recession and did not rebound as quickly as in past recoveries despite low interest rates. Residential construction did not recoup its 1989 levels until late 1993, while the overall economy surpassed 1989 levels by mid-1992. Non-residential construction continued its recession well into 1993.

Environmental issues. Logging restrictions on federal lands coupled with export restrictions of tropical hardwoods are the major environmental issues affecting the supply of raw materials for the industry. Environmental concerns regarding levels of dust, formaldehyde, and noise in plywood and hardwood veneer production have also grown in recent years.

According to David A. Pease, writing in *Wood Technology* in 1993, this concern is not limited to American manufacturers. The Dutch have adopted strict dust level restrictions of 1.7 parts dust per million parts air (by weight). They set formaldehyde at .3 parts per million of air and noise exposure to 90-dbA with hearing protection. The Germans have implemented similar limits as well. As a result of these issues, the EPA is drafting a catalogue of indoor air pollutants such as formaldehyde and other volatile organic compounds that result from the production of plywood, particleboard, medium density fiberboard, oriented strand board, and other engineered wood products.

The plywood industry is experimenting with several means of reducing these emissions. One is to use other chemicals to bond particleboard, plywood, and other products. Another possible solution is to treat the product with ammonia after it has been glued with traditional compounds. Further complicating these efforts to address these environmental concerns, however, is the increasing emphasis on engineered wood production; production of these goods require the use of volatile organic compounds.

INDUSTRY LEADERS

Leading companies in the industry include Ply Gem Industries, Inc., based in New York City, which posted sales in 1992 of more than $600 million; Plywood Panels Inc., headquartered in New Orleans, Louisiana; Darlington Veneer Company, Inc., based in Darlington, South Carolina, which garnered sales of $140 million; and Columbia Forest Products Inc., of Portland, Oregon, with $200 million in sales in 1992.

WORK FORCE

Worker-participation in management and ownership is prevalent in the plywood manufacturing industry. For nearly three-quarters of a century a large number of plywood mills in the Pacific Northwest have been operated by worker cooperatives. These firms are owned and controlled by worker-owners. Major decisions are made, policy is developed, and a board of directors is chosen democratically at the quarterly or semiannual meeting of the general membership. The board elects officers from its own ranks subject to approval from the membership.

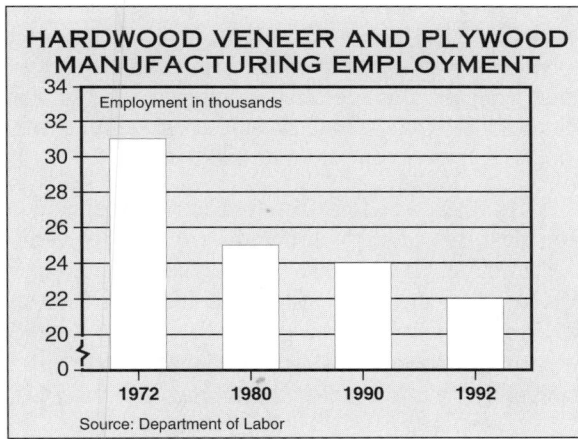

HARDWOOD VENEER AND PLYWOOD MANUFACTURING EMPLOYMENT

Employment in thousands

Source: Department of Labor

Christopher E. Gunn notes in a study of Pacific Northwest plywood cooperatives published in *Economic Analysis and Workers' Management* that proceeds of the worker-enterprises are generally distributed according to work performed rather than on an equal basis or by capital stake. Members tend to prefer to forgo earnings rather than suffer unemployment. The enterprises tend to be efficient users of raw materials and are less capital intensive then conventional mills.

Worker-participation is not limited to worker-owned mills. Some of the conventionally owned mills are attempting to incorporate some of the ideas of worker participation in management. For example, as a 1991 *Forest Industries* article by Ted Blackman notes, Potlatch has introduced a new management style in which workers at the team level have decision making influence and responsibility in production, investment, and hiring new workers.

According to U.S. Department of Labor statistics, the hardwood veneer and plywood manufacturing industry has a high injury and illness rate—approximately 50 percent higher than for general manufacturing.

Employment varies considerably over time in hardwood plywood and veneer manufacturing establishments because of its dependence on the larger construction industry. The hardwood plywood and veneer industry in particular was affected more by the spotted owl crisis than by the recent recession. Department of Commerce statistics indicate that employment in the industry began slipping in 1989. Between 1989 and 1991 it plummeted 17 percent and only regained 4.2 percent in 1992, when most construction related industries saw a much greater surge in employment. In 1991 approximately 17,300 people were employed in the industry, at an average hourly wage of almost $8.

AMERICA AND THE WORLD

International trade has been favorable for the United States plywood industry in recent years. According to the Commerce Department, between 1989 and 1993 imports grew only 1.5 percent while exports shot up 62 percent. The reduction of trade barriers between Canada, Mexico, and the United States as a result of the North American Free Trade Agreement (NAFTA) will continue to shift international trade patterns.

The free trade agreement between Canada and the United States scheduled gradual reductions in plywood tariffs. According to a 1993 *Wood Technology* article, U.S. import duties on Canadian plywood were reduced from 20 percent to 15 percent in 1993 and Canadian duties were reduced from 15 to 7.5 percent. By 1998, duties should be eliminated altogether. Tariffs on newer products such as oriented strand board and particleboard have already been eliminated. Similar tariff reduction schedules are taking effect with Mexico as a part of the NAFTA.

RESEARCH AND TECHNOLOGY

Technological change is shifting in emphasis from labor-saving innovation to material-saving innovation. In order to get more lumber out of a given amount of wood pulp, producers are developing engineered wood products such as laminated veneer lumber, particleboard, medium density fiberboard, and oriented strand board.

Laminated veneer lumber has the added advantage that it can be made wider, longer, stiffer, and stronger than traditional lumber products. Defects in the wood such as knots are reduced in size and redistributed through lamination. For lengths longer than eight feet, short lengths can be joined with finger joints. Laminated veneer lumber is produced in a manner similar to plywood except it is two inches thick and the grain is all in the same direction. Thick planks as wide and long as plywood are then cut down to standard lumber sizes.

The shift to particleboard, medium-density fiberboard and oriented strand board represents a shift out of this industry and into reconstituted panel products (see **SIC 2493: Reconstituted Wood Products**).

INDUSTRY INFORMATION SOURCES

Blackman, Ted. "'Team Concept' Involves Crews in All Aspects of Mills." *Forest Industries,* 9, November 1991: 14-15.

"Computer Model Showed Way to Run Plant More Profitably." *Forest Industries,* September/October 1992: 28-29.

Gunn, Christopher E. "Plywood Co-operatives of the Pacific Northwest: Lessons for Workers' Self-Management in the United States." *Economic Analysis and Workers' Management,* XIV, 3 (1980): 393-416.

Kirk, B. "Weyerhaeuser/Georgia-Pacific/Louisiana-Pacific-Company Report." S.G. Warburg & Co. Inc., 1993.

1982 Benchmark Input-Output Accounts of the United States. Washington, DC: U.S. Department of Commerce, Bureau of Economic Analysis, 1991.

Pease, David A. "Board plant designers set environmental pace." *Wood Technology,* 3, May/June 1993: 26-28.

———, "Timber Shortages Will Encourage New Products." *Forest Industries,* 4, July/August 1992: 21-22.

Personick, Martin E., and Biddle, Elyce A. "Job Hazards Underscored in Woodworking Study." *Monthly Labor Review,* September 1989: 18-23.

"Plywood pact paves way to U.S.-Canada duty cuts." *Wood Technology,* January/February 1993: 25.

Statistical Abstract of the United States. Washington, DC: U.S. Bureau of the Census, 1993.

U.S. Industrial Outlook 1993. Washington, DC: U.S. Department of Commerce, 1993.

Wigder, W. M. "Potlatch - Company Report." The First Boston Corporation, 1993.

Zaret, J.L. "Louisiana-Pacific - Company Report." Nomura Research Institute America, Inc., 1993.

—Joseph Kirchner

SIC 2436

SOFTWOOD VENEER AND PLYWOOD

Establishments primarily engaged in producing commercial softwood veneer and plywood, from veneer produced in the same establishment or from purchased veneer. Establishments primarily engaged in producing commercial hardwood veneer and plywood are classified in **SIC 2435: Hardwood Veneer and Plywood.** Establishments primarily engaged in the production of veneer used in the same establishment for the manufacture of wood containers such as fruit and vegetable baskets and wood boxes are classified in various wood container manufacturing industries.

The Bureau of the Census reported the value of output for the plywood and veneer (softwood) manufacturing industry as $4.6 billion for 1991. The demand for veneer and plywood is dependant upon construction. Nearly one-half (48 percent) of veneer and plywood output goes to construction, mainly residential. Roughly a quarter of the output is used in other lumber and wood products industries, with an additional 11 percent in furniture and fixtures.

As with other construction material producing industries, this industry suffered during the economic recession of 1990-1991, but has benefited tremendously from the surge in housing construction at the end of 1993. Despite the positive economic situation entering the mid-1990s, however, the industry still is grappling with a troublesome shortage of materials.

Another challenge on the horizon is the cost of complying with growing environmental regulation of indoor pollutants. The industry has set voluntary formaldehyde emission standards and the United States Environmental Protection Agency is collecting information on other forms of indoor pollutants.

Leading companies in the industry include Georgia-Pacific Corp., based in Atlanta, Georgia; Champion International Corp.'s Forest Products Group, headquartered in Stamford, Connecticut; and Roseburg Forest Products Co., based in Roseburg, Oregon.

Worker-participation in management and ownership is prevalent in the plywood industry. For nearly three-quarters of a century a significant number of plywood mills in the Pacific Northwest have been operated by worker cooperatives. These firms are owned and run by worker-owners. According to the Labor Department, the softwood plywood and veneer industry's injury and illness rate is closer to the average for manufacturing than is that of other woodworking industries. In 1987, the softwood plywood and veneer industry's 13.2 injury and illness rate per 100 full-time workers was significantly closer to the overall manufacturing 11.9 rate per 100 than the 18.0 average rate posted by establishments engaged in millwork, wood kitchen cabinets, hardwood plywood and veneer, and miscellaneous structural wood product manufacturing.

According to the Commerce Department, total employment for the industry dropped 15 percent from 35,200 in 1987 to 30,000 in 1992. Average earnings for workers in the industry rose during that time span from just under $10 an hour to approximately $10.50 an hour. In the Pacific northwest and amongst smaller mills without access to private sources of timber, the employment situation is generally worse.

International trade has been favorable but volatile for the United States softwood plywood and veneer industry in recent years. The economic recession led to sharp declines in imports by 32 percent between 1989 and 1991. The gradual economic recovery, coupled with timber-cutting restrictions that arose out of environmental concerns and the liberalization of trade, resulted in a sharp reversal of this decline in imports. Between 1991 and 1993 imports soared 55 percent. Meanwhile exports surged as a result of trade liberalization, increasing 27 percent between 1989 and 1993, despite a drop of 16 percent between 1990 and 1991.

INDUSTRY INFORMATION SOURCES

1982 Benchmark Input-Output Accounts of the United States. Washington, DC: U.S. Department of Commerce, Bureau of Economic Analysis, 1991.

U.S. Industrial Outlook 1993. Washington, DC: U.S. Department of Commerce, 1993.

Statistical Abstract of the United States. Washington, DC: U.S. Bureau of the Census, 1993.

Personick, Martin E., and Biddle, Elyce A. ''Job Hazards Underscored in Woodworking Study.'' *Monthly Labor Review,* 9, September 1989: 18-23.

—Joseph Kirchner

SIC 2439

STRUCTURAL MEMBERS, NOT ELSEWHERE CLASSIFIED

This classification covers establishments primarily engaged in producing laminated or fabricated trusses, arches, and other structural members of lumber. Establishments primarily engaged in fabrication on the site of construction are classified in Division C, Construction. Establishments primarily engaged in producing prefabricated wood buildings, sections, and panels are classified in **SIC 2452: Prefabricated Wood Buildings and Components.**

The Bureau of the Census reported the value of output for this industry as $1.8 billion for 1991. According to 1991 Commerce Department data, output is almost entirely used in new construction, with a fairly even distribution between residential and non-residential markets. Consequently, the industry is highly sensitive to the business cycle. While residential construction picked up in 1992 and surged in the latter part of 1993, non-residential construction grew at a sluggish rate due to the excessive building of the 1980s. The industry faces the same supply constraints as do the other wood working industries. This is the result of environmental pressures to save the endangered spotted owl in the Pacific northwest and to save tropical rain forests abroad.

Traditionally, mills in this industry cut joists, beams, and other structural members from logs of large dimensions. Recently the industry has developed several engineered wood products to save on raw materials and to strengthen structural members such as beams, trusses and joists. These engineered products are constructed by gluing veneer sheets or strands of wood with a compound, pressure, and heat.

TJ International Inc. is the leader in engineered woods for structural members and framing materials. It has positioned itself on this cutting edge to take advantage of the current timber shortage and consequent price hikes. The company has two main product lines. Its Trus Joist MacMillan subsidiary makes engineered wood structural members and framing boards. Its other primary subsidiary in this area, its Western Division, produces windows and doors. Other notable industry establishments include Elk River Enterprises Inc., Shelter Systems Corp., and Trussway, Inc.

In order to capture the opportunities created by supply constraints, TJ International formed a joint venture with the Canadian-based MacMillan Bloedel Inc. The new company, formed in September 1991, dominates the high tech and environmentally friendly end of structural and framing lumber. The venture, which is 51 percent owned by TJ International, has developed several new products that are as good or superior in quality to established lumber equivalents using fast-growing timber produced on tree farms. A 1993 article in *Wood Technology* notes that Boise Cascade is also venturing into the production of these new technologies. It installed capacity to produce laminated veneer lumber for beams and joists.

According to the Bureau of the Census (1993), 18,900 people were employed in the industry in 1991. Labor Department statistics indicate that the industry has one of the highest accident rates of any manufacturing industry, and suffers from a higher accident/illness rate than that posted by any of the other woodworking industries.

Like other woodworking industries, the structural members industry is responding to the crisis in timber supply through innovative technology. The industry is developing engineered products that have the advantage of using fast-growing small dimension timber to produce products that are often superior to those created using sawn woods. Among the new products being developed are wooden I-joists, series joists, laminated veneer lumber, parallel strand lumber, and laminated strand lumber. Wooden I-Joists are so strong that they compete with steel I-beams in small buildings where building codes don't prohibit the use of wood. Series joists, marketed under the trademark ''Silent Floor'' joists by Trus Joist Macmillan, are used to support floors or ceilings. They help to reduce squeaky floors because they are less prone to warping. Laminated veneer lumber is made from numerous layers of high grade thin veneer which are glued using an adhesive, heat, and pressure. Laminated veneer lumber is used for the flanges of I-joists and as beams.

INDUSTRY INFORMATION SOURCES

Bland, John D. ''Quality Assurance Tops List at Parallel Strand Lumber Mill,'' *Forest Industries,* 2, March 1991: 15-18.

Moran, D. S., et. al. ''TJ International, Inc. Company Report,'' Dillon & Read & Co., 1993.

1982 Benchmark Input-Output Accounts of the United States, Washington, DC: U.S. Department of Commerce, Bureau of Economic Analysis, 1991.

Personick, Martin E., and Biddle, Elyce A. ''Job Hazards Underscored in Woodworking Study,'' *Monthly Labor Review,* 9, September 1989: 18-23.

Statistical Abstract of the United States, Washington, DC: U.S. Bureau of the Census, 1993.

U.S. Industrial Outlook 1993. Washington, DC: U.S. Department of Commerce, 1993.

—Joseph Kirchner

SIC 2441

NAILED AND LOCK CORNER WOOD BOXES AND SHOOK

This industry classification includes establishments primarily engaged in manufacturing nailed and lock corner wood boxes (lumber or plywood), and shook for nailed and lock corner boxes.

The nailed and lock corner boxes and shook classification covers the production of a wide range of containers made wholly or partly of wood. Containers in this category that are built for specific uses include ammunition boxes, tool chests, wooden cigar boxes, and cases for packing produce. Shook refers to sets of box parts, including sides, tops, bottoms, and ends, ready to be put together.

Unlike pallets and skids, the largest segment of the wood container industry, wooden boxes have not experienced much growth in market demand in recent years. Fierce competition has arisen from containers made of other materials. Most notable among these box alternatives are those made from corrugated paperboard. Another area in which nailed and lock corner wood boxes are lagging in comparison to the pallets and skids industry is in the use of advanced technology to improve production efficiency. Because the variety of boxes being manufactured is so diverse, production runs large enough to take advantage of a high degree of automation are not the norm. Improved conveyors and material handling equipment have enhanced productivity for manufacturers whose markets require large numbers of a specific type of box. Elsewhere, however, the highest level of technology used in box assembly is a nail gun. Therefore, of the 2.8 percent average annual growth in output and 2.2 percent average growth in productivity in the wood container industry (which includes **SIC 2448: Pallets and Skids** and **SIC 2449: Wood Containers Not Elsewhere Classified**) between 1977 and 1989, only a minor share is attributable to nailed and lock corner wood boxes.

The nailed and lock corner wood box and shook industry is composed mainly of smaller companies. In 1987 only two percent of the establishments in this area employed 100 or more workers, while 50 percent of the companies in this industry had less than ten employees. Industry leaders include Love Box Company of Wichita, Kansas ($70 million in sales, 800 employees), A. Klein and Co. in Claremont, North Carolina ($20 million, 300 employees), and Seattle Box Co. of Kent, Washington ($20 million, 100 employees).

During the industry's peak in the 1970s, approximately one billion nailed wood boxes were manufactured each year. The 1977 Census of Manufacturers estimated the value of nailed wooden boxes and box components shipped that year at $261 million. Since then, a shift has taken place in the industry largely due to the loss of some markets to improved plastic and corrugated container technology. Boxes made of these materials cost far less to produce. Wood boxes began to appear increasingly as a specialty packaging item that, it was hoped by marketers, lent a product an air of high quality. Wooden boxes continue to be attractive to consumers for their durability and reusability.

Like the wood containers industry as a whole, wood boxes have not historically faced any significant competition from manufacturers in other countries. This industry's primary concerns will most likely continue to involve the relative expense of producing wooden boxes compared to that of producing containers of other materials.

INDUSTRY INFORMATION SOURCES

"The New Growth of Wooden Boxes," *Modern Packaging* (Nov. 1979).

Spencer, Albert G., and Jack A. Luy. *Wood and Wood Products*, Columbus, OH: Charles E. Merrill Publishing Company, 1975.

York, James. "Productivity in Wood Containers," *Monthly Labor Review* (Oct. 1992).

—Robert R. Jacobson

SIC 2448

WOOD PALLETS AND SKIDS

This classification covers establishments primarily engaged in manufacturing wood or wood and metal combination pallets and skids.

The manufacture of wood pallets and skids is the largest segment of the wood container industry. Pallets are platforms that are specially designed to allow heavy crates and boxes to be easily moved by forklift. Pallets play an important role in the shipping, handling, and storage of a huge variety of materials in an equally vast array of industries. In the United States,

approximately 2,200 companies produce pallets. The industry is dominated by small firms, which on the average have about 18 employees per operation. The largest concentration of these companies is in Michigan, where approximately 300 such firms are located. Of all the pallets and skids produced in the United States in 1991, 90 to 95 percent were made of wood, although this percentage is likely to decrease as advances are made in the construction of pallets using alternative materials.

The total value of the wood pallets shipped in 1991 was $1.7 billion. This represented a slight decline from the previous year, largely attributable to the sluggishness of the economy in general. The production of pallets in the United States had actually grown by over 60 percent in the preceding decade. In 1990 about 460 million wood pallets and skids were manufactured in the United States.

The most commonly used wood for producing pallets is oak, which accounted for about one-third of the 5.1 billion board-feet of hardwood lumber, logs, and cants used by the industry in 1991. Smaller amounts of softwood lumber (1.7 billion board-feet), plywood (2.3 billion square feet), and other types of board were also used.

The biggest users of pallets are the grocery, agricultural, paper and printing, steel, and chemical industries. The pallet most commonly produced is the non-reversible 48 by 40 inch double-faced version popular in the grocery business. Since the 1980s, technology has played an increasingly important role in the pallet and skid industry, contributing to both production and design improvements. Most pallet manufacturers were still making use of hand-held nailers and semi-automated equipment as recently as 1980. By the early 1990s, however, the implementation of fully automated assembly systems enable two laborers to put together 1,200 pallets in a day, at least four times the rate of production that hand nailers would allow.

In the area of engineering, computers have had a major impact on pallet design since about 1980. Recent technology has enabled manufacturers to more completely analyze the pallet needs of a particular material to be shipped or stored, providing for the production of pallets that are specifically tailored for that material. For example, a company dealing in a fairly light commodity could save money by using pallets made from a softer, less expensive wood.

In recent years, the pallet industry has also become more interested in recycling. About 90,000 used pallets were recycled in 1991. Recycling will probably become a more common low-cost option for wood pallet companies in years to come, as competition from non-wood pallet producers increases. Production of pallets made of paperboard (over five million units in 1991) and plastic (nearly one million) is growing rapidly. The wood pallet industry has responded to this challenge with the development of "enhanced pallets," which are more resistant to fire and rot than conventional pallets.

INDUSTRY INFORMATION SOURCES

"Alternatives to Wood Pallets Sparking Market Demand," *Chemical Marketing Reporter* (Sept. 28, 1992).

Schwind, Gene. "Engineering Your Wooden Pallet Can Reduce Handling Costs," *Material Handling Engineer* (Oct. 1981).

Spencer, Albert G., and Jack A. Luy. *Wood and Wood Products.* Columbus, OH: Charles E. Merrill Publishing Company, 1975.

York, James. "Productivity in Wood Containers," *Monthly Labor Review* (Oct. 1992).

—Robert R. Jacobson

SIC 2449

WOOD CONTAINERS, NOT ELSEWHERE CLASSIFIED

This industry classification includes establishments primarily engaged in manufacturing wood containers, not elsewhere classified, such as cooperage, wirebound boxes and crates, and other veneer and plywood containers. Establishments primarily engaged in manufacturing tobacco hogshead stock are classified in **SIC 2421: Sawmills and Planing Mills, General** and those manufacturing cooperage stock are classified in **SIC 2429: Special Product Sawmills, Not Elsewhere Classified**.

This classification covers the manufacture of just about any wooden container that is not a pallet and is not a nailed or lock corner box. Many of the types of containers in this classification are those made from staves. This group of products is generally called cooperage. Containers made in this way include barrels, storage vats, and buckets. Tight cooperage refers to containers of this type that are used to store liquids, such as wine casks and beer barrels, and hot tubs. Containers that are built to hold solid materials are called slack cooperage. Cooperage is usually built in one facility from pieces that have been constructed in another. The components from which cooperage is assembled are staves, heads, and hoops. The wood

used for the staves can vary depending on the material to be shipped or stored. For instance, high quality white oak is used for bourbon whiskey production, while seafood is often shipped in smaller kegs made of southern yellow pine. Hoops can be made from steel, wire, or wood.

Another significant portion of this industry classification is wirebound boxes. About 60 percent of the market for wirebound boxes comes from agriculture, with fruit and vegetable growers accounting for a growing share. The military is another important user of wirebound boxes. Unlike producers of coopered containers, wirebound box manufacturers often process their own lumber or veneer. The technology for making wirebound boxes is relatively simple. Box parts are carried along a conveyor belt, where wire is stapled to the box. A fastening machine then binds the wire ends together.

Like the other segments of the wood container industry, establishments involved in this area of manufacturing are mostly small companies. Sixty-one percent of the establishments in this industry had less than ten employees in 1987. Compared to the other segments, however, a far greater portion employed at least 100 workers (nine percent of the total, versus one percent of wood pallet producers). Among the largest companies whose primary business is the production of wood containers, not elsewhere classified are: Calpine Containers Inc., a privately-owned company based in Walnut Creek, California ($95 million in sales); and Elberta Crate and Box Co. of Bainbridge, Georgia, also privately owned ($35 million in sales).

Although the wood container industry as a whole has seen considerable growth in productivity in recent years, little of this growth can be contributed to miscellaneous wood containers. This is partly due to the dramatic rise in competition from containers made of other materials, particularly corrugated paperboard and plastic. In addition, because of the tremendous variety in the size and shape of containers in demand, technology that makes high-volume production cheaper and faster has not been as useful in this industry as it is in the manufacture of more homogenous products, such as pallets. Nevertheless, the demand for quality containers made of wood is not likely to vanish overnight, regardless of the new products that become available. This, coupled with the lack of significant competition from foreign companies, seems to indicate a reasonably positive outlook for the U.S. wood container industry.

INDUSTRY INFORMATION SOURCES

Spencer, Albert G., and Jack A. Luy. *Wood and Wood Products.* Columbus, OH: Charles E. Merrill Publishing Company, 1975.

York, James. "Productivity in Wood Containers," *Monthly Labor Review* (Oct. 1992).

—Robert R. Jacobson

SIC 2451

MOBILE HOMES

This category covers establishments primarily engaged in manufacturing mobile homes and nonresidential mobile buildings. These units are generally more than 35 feet long, at least eight feet wide, do not have facilities for storage of water or waste, and are equipped with wheels. Trailers that are generally 35 feet long or less, eight feet wide or less, and with self-contained facilities are classified in **SIC 3792: Travel Trailers and Campers.** Portable wood buildings not equipped with wheels are classified in **SIC 2452: Prefabricated Wood Buildings and Components.**

INDUSTRY SNAPSHOT

Approximately 200 companies in the United States were involved in manufacturing mobile homes in 1990. The industry suffered a precipitous decline in manufacturers during the 1980s, dropping from 261 companies in 1982 to 207 in 1989, then falling to the rough estimate of 200 by 1990. Total sales recorded by the industry during this period remained relatively flat. The industry's aggregate value of shipments in 1982 stood at $3.60 billion, rising to $4.78 billion the following year, but slipping to an average of $4.25 billion for the rest of the decade. Still affected by recessive economic condition in the early 1990s, the industry posted $3.90 billion in sales in 1992, only $300 million more than it had recorded ten years earlier.

Of the two primary products manufactured by the industry, residential mobile homes measuring 35 feet or more in length are by far the most abundantly produced product, accounting for 86 percent of the industry's total shipments. Nonresidential manufactured buildings equipped with wheels, such as mobile buildings intended for commercial or industrial use, composed the balance of the industry's shipments.

Due to the expensive costs associated with shipping mobile homes, which generally measure 14 by 70 feet in length or larger, the number of mobile homes shipped abroad represents only a negligible portion of the industry's business. (The same holds true for mobile home imports entering the U.S. market.) In fact, manufacturers typically are limited to markets located relatively close to their plants, since transporting mobile units to distant markets—or even from state to state—results in prohibitively expensive shipping costs. Consequently, the industry's facilities dot the nation's landscape, with each manufacturing plant wedded, to a certain degree, to its surrounding market.

ORGANIZATION AND STRUCTURE

The mobile home industry is predominantly populated by manufacturing facilities employing more than 20 people. Of the 341 establishments operating in the industry in 1989, 290 employed more than 20 workers. In 1989 mobile home establishments employed an average of 117 people. Geographically, the majority of facilities engaged in mobile home manufacturing were located in the South Atlantic region of the United States, although more than half of the nation's states contained mobile home manufacturing establishments. Wisconsin, Ohio, and Indiana formed the second largest regional concentration of facilities, while California, Oregon, and Washington composed the third largest regional concentration. California contained the greatest number of manufacturing facilities, with 45, followed by the 39 facilities located in Texas. In descending order after Texas, Florida ranked third, with 38 establishments, Georgia fourth, with 36, and Indiana fifth, with 32.

BACKGROUND AND DEVELOPMENT

During the mobile home industry's nascence, its products answered the need of a small percentage of the American populace: temporary shelter primarily used by migrant farm workers and equally nomadic construction workers. Although these were not the only purchasers of mobile homes, they did account for the bulk of the industry's sales and, consequently, limited the potential of the industry's future expansion. Since both of these market niches composed a negligible portion of the nation's consumer base and any significant increase in their size—at least in proportion to the rate of population growth—appeared unlikely, the mobile home industry seemed destined to remain a relatively small industry, catering to customers without the aggregate purchasing power to launch manufacturers toward exponentially higher sales volumes.

This restrictive quality inherent in the industry's market would not inhibit mobile home manufacturers for long, however; once a product was manufactured and marketed that could attract a more diverse clientele and fulfill a need overlooked by the traditional construction industry, sales would increase. But during the 1920s, when mobile homes were first emerging, and into the 1930s, as the industry began to take shape, sales figures remained unsubstantial.

The onset of World War II provided an unexpected boost for mobile home manufacturers, infusing the industry with production orders for military personnel shelters (essentially miniature barracks on wheels) and mobile housing for defense workers. By the conclusion of the war, mobile home manufacturers had enjoyed several years of comparatively prodigious production levels, thanks primarily to defense contracts. Mobile homes had become, as a consequence of this war-related work, familiar fixtures in many encampments across the country. Moreover, once the war ended, America had, in effect, a standing army: a new social class of military personnel subject to the sometimes itinerant demands of military life. Mobile homes afforded members of the armed forces—especially those with families—the housing flexibility that their frequent relocation orders required, supplying mobile home manufacturers with a new market niche for their products. Two years after the war, in 1947, the mobile home retail market neared $150 million in sales, garnered from the sale of 60,000 units.

The following year sales eclipsed $200 million and unit sales leapt to 85,000, as the mobile home industry began to show signs of dramatic growth. In 1949, however, optimism regarding the industry's growth potential faded. Retail sales for the year were a disappointing $122 million and unit sales plunged to 46,200.

As the industry entered the 1950s, it effected a recovery from the dismal showings of 1949, posting successive gains in annual sales until 1956, a year that would mark the beginning of a new era in the mobile home industry. Originally, the size of mobile homes varied in length, but always measured eight feet in width to conform to the maximum width permissible by law for vehicles on highways. These homes, after all, were intended to be mobile. But in 1956, manufacturers first introduced 10-foot-wide models, or "ten wides," which quickly became the industry standard. By 1958, ten wides accounted for 65 percent of the industry's shipments and two years later, represented over 85 percent.

It rapidly became apparent to manufacturers that mobility was not the primary asset mobile homes offered consumers. Instead, consumers were attracted by their affordability. To be sure, mobility was still an important feature, but mobile home owners moved their units on average only once every two and a half years, becoming for many a semi-permanent dwelling, and for some a house on wheels that never moved. Further, mobile homes came from the factory equipped with all the basic domestic appurtenances homeowners or renters of conventional houses ordinarily would have to purchase separately, a total package for the mobile home customer that came with a significantly lower price tag than a bare conventional home.

This need for a cheaper alternative to traditional housing prices was tapped with the emergence of ten-foot-wide models, which approximated the size of conventional homes more closely than the eight-foot-wide models. Accordingly, mobile home manufacturers now found themselves making units for market segments, rather than market niches, as the popularity of ten wides taught industry participants that their business had less to do with the automotive industry and more to do with the construction industry.

The magnitude of the mobile home industry had reached respectable proportions by relying solely on the production of eight-foot-wide models, reaching $462 million in retail sales from the sale of 111,900 units in 1955, the last year in which eight-foot-wide models represented 100 percent of the mobile home market. Although ten wides quickly dominated the market, their introduction did not initially spark an exponential increase in either unit production or in the industry's overall revenues. They did, however, provide the industry with a more stable and potentially rewarding foundation from which to build on in the future. Newly married couples and those over 50 years of age became two of the industry's largest market segments, attracted by the affordability and flexibility mobile home housing offered at a time when both these components of the American populace were growing faster than the rate of population growth as a whole.

Along with these favorable developments came the ills suffered by any industry whose target market has transformed into a more lucrative audience. For the mobile home industry these growing pains came in the form of increased competition during the late 1950s, as the low initial investment required to establish a mobile home manufacturing facility enabled hopeful entrepreneurs to enter the industry, causing the market to become quickly saturated. This influx of small, single plant manufacturers created considerable turmoil in the mobile home market between 1960 and 1961, when a number of small manufacturers failed and their inventories entered the market at panic prices. Units shipments for the industry fell from 120,500 in 1959 to 90,200 in 1961, while industry revenues dropped by roughly $100 million to $505 million.

The anxiety caused by this decline led to a period of consolidation in the mobile home industry during the early 1960s, as a handful of publicly owned conglomerates wrested control of the market from a scattered group of small, privately owned manufacturers through mergers and acquisitions. On the whole, however, the industry continued to be populated primarily by small, independent companies (the high cost of shipping mobile homes made large, centralized manufacturing consortiums impractical), but for the first time the industry's leaders were primarily comparatively larger, publicly held companies, such as Elkhart, Indiana's Skyline Homes, Dryden, Michigan's Champion Home Builders, New York's Divco-Wayne Corp., and Redman Industries located in Dallas, Texas.

By 1963 the mobile home industry had fully recovered from the losses suffered during the decade's first two years. Retail revenues stood at $862 million and unit sales topped 150,000, surpassing for the first time the figures recorded in 1959. By the following year, mobile homes accounted for one of every nine housing starts, with approximately 220 companies competing for the burgeoning business occasioned by the advent of ten wides, which was finally coming to fruition six years later. Twelve-foot-wide mobile homes had been introduced two years earlier, in 1962, as the inevitable offshoot of ten wides, garnering an encouraging ten percent share of the industry's 1964 sales. "Double wides," the joining of two ten wides to form a single unit, were also widely popular as the industry entered the mid-1960s, giving owners up to 1,000 square feet of living space.

The consolidation of the previous years now left the five largest companies controlling 30 percent of the market, the demographics of which had changed considerably in the previous 20 years. Families in which the head of the household was older than 51 years of age represented 35 percent of all mobile home residents, but only eight percent of these owners were retired. Nomadic construction and factory workers, once the mainstays of the mobile home market, accounted for 19 percent of mobile home ownership, yet were surprisingly outnumbered by professional and business people, who represented 25 percent of all owners.

Added to these changes in the composition of the mobile home market was the emergence of an entirely new market segment in the early 1960s—commercial and industrial customers. Businesses such as banks used mobile "offices" as temporary branch outlets, manufacturing companies requiring temporary additional space to execute contract work used mobile home structures, and school systems used mobile homes as portable classrooms. These mobile "home" structures were custom built, or converted from existing mobile home units, requiring the retooling of production machinery that many of the larger mobile home manufacturers found disruptive to their assembly lines. Consequently, the smaller manufacturers in the industry benefited from the majority of the commercial and industrial business, building each structure according to the specifications required for its particular application. Although industrial and commercial business accounted for only five percent of the industry's total sales during the early and mid-1960s, the market was just opening up and promised to develop into a lucrative component of the mobile home industry.

By 1965 mobile homes accounted for one out of every six and a half housing starts, representing 324,050 unit sales for the year, while total revenues for the industry exceeded $1.2 billion. The industry also demonstrated encouraging independence from the traditional housing market in the mid-1960s, as it rapidly matured and began to stand on its own, rather than merely existing as an adjunct to the construction industry. When mobile home manufacturers suffered losses in the early 1960s, some of the difficulties stemmed from the proliferation of imprudent manufacturers, but the drop in unit sales and revenues also mirrored the curtailment of conventional housing construction. Once conventional housing construction resumed normal activity in 1962, mobile home unit sales tagged along, showing a rise as well. But in the mid-1960s, when decreased spending once again negatively affected housing construction, mobile home sales remained robust. Released, to a large extent, from its dependence on the cyclical housing market, the mobile home industry was instead buoyed by the deleterious economic conditions. Mobile home manufacturers reaped business from prospective home-buyers unwilling to spend the amount of money required to construct new homes.

Toward the close of the 1960s, the optimism pervading the industry grabbed the attention of those outside the industry, leading to some fantastic and, in retrospect, starry-eyed predictions for the industry's future. Some of these futuristic visions were extrapolations of the diverse applications for which mobile homes were used during the late 1960s. One such use was as an alternative to low-cost housing, a housing need particularly well-suited for mobile homes, considering their affordability and mobility. In 1968 alone, three cities, Atlanta, Chicago, and Washington D.C., began employing mobile homes as temporary housing for individuals forced from their homes as a result of rehabilitation or redevelopment projects. Mobile homes, with their wheels removed, were also stacked on top of each other to form low-rise apartment complexes in Baltimore, Amherst, Massachusetts, and Michigan City, Indiana. From these utilizations, plans for mobile home "skyscraper" structures were born. Architects were swept up by the enthusiasm surrounding the industry, envisioning the creation of mobile modular homes that could removed and reinserted into high-rise structures, trailing the migratory travels of the owner. Although such structures never materialized, their creation, at least on paper, was indicative of the promising conditions characterizing the mobile home industry in the late 1960s.

Entering the 1970s, the industry had enjoyed a decade of prodigious growth, expanding at an annual rate of 20 percent throughout the 1960s and at 30 percent in the last two years of the decade. Unit shipments in 1970 topped 400,000, representing one mobile home for every four and a half conventional housing starts, and revenues for the industry approached $3 billion. Twelve-foot-wide models had eclipsed ten-foot-wide models in popularity by 1965, continuing the trend toward larger mobile homes. These dominated the mobile home market by the early 1970s, followed, in terms of production volume, by even larger models.

At this point in the industry's history, several characteristics demonstrated by the industry augured increased growth for mobile home manufacturers, while some potentially hazardous market conditions loomed in the near future. On the favorable side, the average price for a mobile home had increased only negligibly, from $5,600 to $6,000, throughout the 1960s, while single family housing construction costs had risen sharply. This disparity was primarily due to the cheaper labor costs incurred by mobile home manufacturers than the wages construction contractors were obliged to pay, increasing the industry's grip on the under $20,000 housing market. In fact, considering that mobile home units had increased in size since the introduction of ten wides in 1956, yet had increased only marginally in price during the intervening years, the price per square foot had actually declined. Additionally, financing a mobile home, a process resembling the financing of an automobile, was made easier through the enactment of the Housing and Urban Development Act of 1968, which permitted saving and loan associations to finance mobile home purchases.

The negative factors affecting the industry's future, however, were numerous, the most pressing of which was the decreasing space available for mobile homes. For the 400,000 units that entered the market in 1969, there were only an estimated 118,000 new mo-

bile home park sites available, and the number sites for future mobile home parks were scarce. Almost entirely relegated to rural areas, mobile home parks, in which roughly 80 percent of all mobile homes were parked, were generally not well respected by urban residential neighborhoods and were often banned from existing alongside conventional houses through zoning restrictions. This left mobile home manufacturers unable to respond to the urgent need for low-income housing—a large segment of the under $20,000 housing market from which manufacturers derived almost all of their earnings—during the early 1970s. This additional business could have offset, in part, the mounting competition that continued to plague the industry, making market saturation an imminent reality. In 1969 alone, 110 new manufacturers joined the fray, attracted by the robust growth demonstrated by the industry and the low capital investment required to establish a mobile home manufacturing facility.

Despite the development of these conditions, the industry posted the most successful year in its history in 1972, recording remarkable production and sales volumes that would stand as benchmark figures for the rest of the decade. Unit shipments totaled 575,940 for the year and sales reached the $4 billion plateau, quelling observations that the industry was headed for less prosperous years. These voices were not silenced long, however. Two years later, after the industry enjoyed a successful 1973, the two decades of solid growth that had been marred only by several minor economic downturns shuddered to a stop.

Unit shipments in 1974 plunged 42 percent from the previous year's level to 329,300. Sales plummeted to $2.5 billion, as the industry quickly joined the nation in a recessive slide. The results from the next year's efforts were equally as dismal. Unit shipments dropped by an additional 35 percent from 1974's poor showing to 212,690, while revenues dropped only slightly to $2.4 billion. The less dramatic spiral of these dollar values, however, did not reflect the actual extent of the losses incurred by the industry during these two years; artificially buoyed by soaring inflation, revenues in reality were lower than they appeared.

Indeed, the losses suffered by the industry were severe and the reasons for the decline were manifold. Perhaps the single greatest contributing factor to the industry's demise was the economic downturn affecting the entire nation during this time. Unemployment rose and consumer income dropped, which threw a surfeit of repossessed mobile homes, over 100,000, on the market. This, in turn, made financing a mobile home purchase more difficult, as the tight money conditions combined with the increasing size and price of mobile homes extended loan payback terms from five to ten years, to 10 to 20 years. Since mobile homes depreciated in value, rather than appreciating like conventional houses, lenders were reluctant to provide loans, rejecting 60 percent of all mobile home loan applications during the two-year slump. Compounding these difficulties was the growing popularity of condominiums, which impinged on the mobile home market, eroding manufacturers' customer base further.

As a result of the losses sustained during this period, the proliferation of manufacturing facilities that preceded the recession (a net total of 295 plants had sprouted up between 1969 and 1973) was halted, then reversed, when over 40 percent of the 550 firms involved in the market went bankrupt. Production capacity dropped by 43 percent from 1973 levels, nearly matching the increase in capacity during the four years leading up to the downturn.

To effect a recovery, several measures were taken—some which were initiated by the mobile home industry itself, while others came through federal intervention. Internally, mobile home manufacturers increased their output of larger mobile homes, concentrating on 14-foot-wide models and double-wides. Quality control was also a problem, engendered, in part, by unscrupulous manufacturers entering the field in the late 1960s and early 1970s. Many of these companies failed during the recession, solving part of the problem, but the more reputable companies also intensified their efforts toward producing higher quality mobile units. To increase consumer confidence further, the federal government established uniform building codes and warranty standards, mandates that made entry into the industry by unethical manufacturers somewhat more difficult.

In addition to these changes, the federal government eased mobile home financing by permitting federally chartered credit unions, which historically were short-term lenders, to provide longer-term credit to mobile home buyers. Also, the Veterans Administration increased the loan guarantee limits for mobile homes from 30 percent to 50 percent.

These ameliorations led to a slow recovery of the mobile home industry. Because of their expanded size and better workmanship, mobile homes began to appreciate in value after the mid-1970s, and began to increase their presence in conventional housing neighborhoods, as zoning restrictions eased. In 1976 unit shipments increased 16 percent to 246,120, still far below the level recorded in 1972, but, nevertheless, an improvement from the successive, precipitous drops suffered during the previous two years.

Also aiding the industry's recovery was the escalating price of conventional housing. Between 1974 and 1978, the average price of a new house rose 61 percent from $38,900 to $62,500, while the average price of a mobile home in 1978 was $15,900. Mobile homes had actually increased at greater rate than conventional houses during this period, leaping 71 percent from 1974's average price of $9,300, but the price disparity between the two housing choices was great enough to invigorate sales for mobile home manufacturers. In fact, the soaring costs of conventional houses attracted a new breed of mobile home customers by the end of the decade—middle class consumers.

Although these development provided enough of an impetus to pull the industry out of its doldrums, a complete turnaround was not achieved, and growth of the industry remained stunted as it entered the 1980s. Unit shipments in 1980 were still well below half the total recorded in 1972 and even below the number of units shipped in 1976, the first year of the industry's recovery. After a 23 percent increase in 1983, unit shipments rose to 295,000, and topped 300,000 by the following year. Revenues during this period eclipsed the record year of 1972, peaking at $4.78 billion in 1983, and then dwindling down to just over $4 billion a year for the rest of the decade.

According to the Census Bureau, mobile homes were the fastest-growing type of housing during the 1980s, a distinction earned primarily from robust sales in the fist half of the decade. The late 1980s brought recessive conditions to the fore once again, causing unit shipments to decline, but mobile home manufacturers avoided significant losses, as mobile homes continued to be the only housing alternative for many consumers.

CURRENT CONDITIONS

Emerging from a recession in the early 1990s, the mobile industry was showing signs of revitalization as it entered the mid-1990s. Unit shipments increased 15 percent toward the end of the recession in 1992 totaling approximately 197,000 units, a production output below the industry's most recent boom era in the early 1980s, but encouraging, nonetheless, considering the deleterious financial conditions of the early 1990s.

By 1992, nearly 16 million people were living in mobile homes, some because they simply could not afford any other type of housing, others because they preferred to own their living space, rather than renting it, while some opted for mobile homes because they were attracted by the potential mobility a house on wheels offered. This latter group, however, enjoyed the possibility of mobility more often than actually moving their homes. Indeed, by the 1990s, the label "mobile home" had become a misnomer since 98 percent of mobile homes never moved once located on their original site. Locating a suitable site for permanent residence, however, proved difficult for many mobile home owners due to zoning codes that excluded mobile home units, which, in turn, negatively affected mobile home manufacturers.

A large part of the industry's future growth depends on opening up additional areas for mobile home placement, a formidable challenge for the industry that requires shedding some of the stigma associated with mobile homes both in the eyes of potential customers and, more important, in the perceptions held by American society as a whole. While this may prove impossible, some headway has been made through legislation. By 1992, 22 states had outlawed "anti-mobile home" zoning restrictions, declaring them discriminatory. Further progress achieved in this direction should provide additional business to mobile home manufacturers as they look ahead to the mid-1990s.

INDUSTRY LEADERS

Ranked according to sales volume, the two largest manufacturers of mobile home are Redman Industries Inc., located in Dallas, Texas, and Champion Enterprises Inc., headquartered in Auburn Hills, Michigan. Both of these companies have figured prominently in the industry's history, consistently ranking at least among the industry's top ten manufacturers.

Redman Industries ascension to the top of the mobile home market essentially began in the early 1960s, when the industry was beginning to experience a dramatic surge in business. Jumping from four cents a share in 1962 to $1.43 the following year, Redman's stock soared between 1962 and 1963, while revenues increased from $28 million to $44 million. By the middle of the decade, sales exceeded $50 million and, despite a temporary drop in earnings in 1966, the company barreled forward, shipping more than 20,000 mobile home units by the close of the decade.

As Redman entered the 1970s, braced for continued success, the industry's disastrous 1974-1975 years loomed on the horizon. Fortunately for Redman, management had decided to exit the recreational vehicle business in 1973, avoiding losses the company would have otherwise suffered when the energy crisis crippled the industry a short time later, but the damage suffered from the cascading mobile home market in 1974 and 1975, unfortunately, could not be avoided.

Redman recorded a $25 million loss in 1974 and did not begin to recover from the affects of the recession until 1978. Once conditions did turn around, the company relied on an increasingly larger proportion of 14-foot-wide and double-wide models than in the late 1960s to lift itself out its slump. In the 1980s, this product mix in addition to the company's involvement in manufacturing aluminum building parts, enabled Redman to successfully rebound from the debilitating 1970s and assume its leadership role in the industry. Redman, with approximately 4,000 employees, recorded $375 million in revenues in 1992.

Champion Enterprises Inc., incorporated in 1953, was as severely affected by the tumultuous early 1970s as was Redman, if not more, but unlike Redman, Champion continued to manufacture recreational vehicles throughout the 1970s and into the 1990s. Before the early 1970s, Champion had recorded considerable success, posting over $30 million in revenues by the mid-1960s, and had earned the reputation as one of the industry's most efficient and self-sufficient manufacturers.

By the beginning of the 1970s, Champion's revenues hovered near $100 million a period during which the company, unlike many of its competitors, manufactured and assembled every component and fixture included in a finished mobile home. This wide spectrum of manufacturing tasks included plumbing and roofing material, furniture, drapes, and even bedsprings. This level of vertical integration enabled the company to produce one mobile home unit per week with the labor of only two workers, a productivity ratio that was twice that of nearly all of its competitors.

Despite these enviable capabilities, Champion was severely shook by the recessive early 1970s, causing the company to operate at a loss until the end of the decade. Although Champion relied on a product mix largely comprised of double-wide units as did Redman, Champion's primary markets did not recover their demand for mobile homes as quickly as Redman's markets did. Champion's turnaround, instead, came from the strong sales recorded by products other than mobile homes, particularly its line of recreational vehicles and low-priced mini-motor homes.

Building from earnings provided by the sales garnered from these products, Champion was able to resuscitate its mobile home product line during the 1980s to stand as the second largest manufacturer of mobile homes by the 1990s. Employing 2,200 workers, Champion posted roughly $290 million in sales in 1992.

WORK FORCE

Total employment in the mobile home industry gradually declined during the 1980s, falling from a peak of 80,000 in the early 1970s to a low of 38,800 in 1992. The sharpest reduction of the industry's employment base occurred during the mid-1970s.

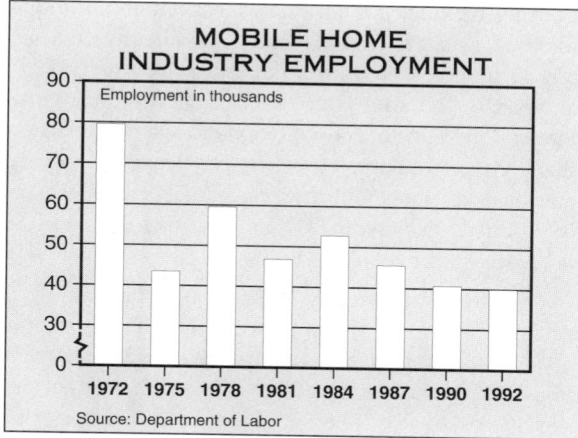

MOBILE HOME INDUSTRY EMPLOYMENT

Employment in thousands

Source: Department of Labor

Of the 38,800 people employed in the mobile home industry in 1992, 7,800 were salaried employees, or those performing managerial, administrative, or technical duties, while the remainder of the work force comprised 31,000 production workers. A typical mobile home manufacturing facility in 1989 employed 96 production workers and 21 salaried employees.

Generally, production workers in the industry were employed on a full-time basis, but averaged four percent fewer hours per year than their counterparts in all other manufacturing industries. Production workers in the mobile home industry earned 18 percent less per hour than other production workers in 1989, averaging $8.61 an hour compared to the $10.49 per hour earned by production workers employed by all other manufacturing industries. Mobile home production workers' hourly wage increased in the subsequent years to $9.10 in 1992. Salaried employees in 1990 earned an average of $33,656 a year.

INDUSTRY INFORMATION SOURCES

Darnay, Arsen J., ed., *Manufacturing USA,* Detroit: Gale Research Inc., 1993.

Elliot, Richard J. Jr., "Long, Long Trailer: Mobile-Home Producers, Old and New Alike, Have Over-Expanded," *Barron's,* February 23, 1970, 3.

Jaffe, Thomas, "Mobile No More," *Forbes,* September 14, 1981, 140-144.

Johnson, Dirk, "Life in a Trailer Park: On the Edge, but Hoping," *New York Times,* July 4, 1992, 1.

King, Michael L., "Trailer Turnabout," *Wall Street Journal,* August 1, 1979, 1.

von Koschembahr, John C., "Mobile Homes: The Comeback That Died," *Financial World,* December 1, 1978, 37-39, 46.

Mayer, Lawrence A., "Move into the Breach," *Fortune,* March 1970, 127-130, 144-146.

"The Mobile Home Builders," *Financial World,* August 5, 1964, 7.

"Mobile Home Comeback Expected as New Models Begin Lifting Sales," *Advertising Age,* July 19, 1976, 22, 24.

"Mobile Homes Take on New Forms for Low-Cost Housing," *Engineering News-Record,* April 25, 1968, 38-40.

"No Detour: Tight Money Has Not Slowed Down the Mobile-Home Builders," *Barron's,* June 6, 1966, 11-18.

"Offices That Can Hit the Road," *Business Week,* September 22, 1962, 68-70.

"On the Move," *Financial World,* November 27, 1963, 13, 26.

Simonson, Robert, "The Mobile Home Industry," *Wall Street Transcript,* March 16, 1970, 19, 931-32.

Thomas, Dana L., "Road to Recovery: Makers of Mobile Homes Are Emerging from Their Slump," *Barron's,* January 2, 1978, 11, 27-28.

U.S. Industrial Outlook, Washington, DC: U.S. Department of Commerce, 1960-1993.

Willatt, Norris, "Trail Blazers: The Mobile Home Business Is Venturing into New Areas," *Barron's,* May 14, 1962, 11-12.

—Jeffrey L. Covell

SIC 2452

PREFABRICATED WOOD BUILDINGS AND COMPONENTS

Companies primarily engaged in manufacturing prefabricated wood buildings, sections, and panels comprise the prefabricated wood buildings and components industry. Manufactured and mobile homes that are delivered to a site are not part of this industry. Companies that assemble panels and components on-site are classified in various construction sectors.

INDUSTRY SNAPSHOT

Modern techniques of prefabrication date back to about 1905. The popularization of gasoline-powered trucks and the post-World War II U.S. housing boom helped build an identifiable prefabrication industry by the mid-1900s. By the early 1980s, industry participants were shipping over $1 billion worth of goods and employing over 16,000 workers.

Healthy construction markets and a greater demand for labor-saving prefabricated wood building products more than doubled the size of the industry during the 1980s. When housing starts recessed during the late 1980s and early 1990s, prefab sales slipped. However, advantages related to productivity and quality assured a bright future for pre-made wood units.

Going into 1994, producers were benefitting from a recovery in housing starts and renewed demand for prefabricated products. Low interest rates and economic growth were expected to boost sales throughout the year. Furthermore, some industry niches, such as log homes, were providing sound growth opportunities.

ORGANIZATION AND STRUCTURE

The prefabricated wood components industry encompasses numerous products, including pre-made panels and sections for chicken coops, farm buildings, geodesic domes, marinas, sauna rooms, hotel rooms, and decks. The industry is highly fragmented and entrepreneurial, and is represented by a wide range of enterprises, many of which are extremely unique.

The primary advantage of prefabricated wood building products is that they save money for builders. Because large pieces of the structure are built in a factory and designed for quick and easy assembly on-site, builders eliminate costly on-site labor expenses and workers' compensation insurance costs. Assembly-line production techniques also allow many prefab manufacturers to achieve greater quality control.

The cost advantage of prefabricated buildings is reflected in the price disparity between site-built and manufactured homes, which are delivered to the site completely built. The average site-built, single-family dwelling cost about $70 per square foot in 1992. In contrast, manufactured homes were priced at an average of approximately $23 per square foot. Most prefabricated homes fell somewhere within this price range.

The largest segment of the prefab wood products industry is single-family homes, which accounted for approximately 65 percent of sales in 1991. Homes built using prefab units are referred to as component or prefabricated housing. Examples of traditional prefab housing products are roof trusses, wall frames, and floors. In addition, many builders use pre-made wall units complete with insulation, plumbing, electrical wiring, ventilation systems, and doors. Such builders utilize standard home plans with wall dimensions of

eight feet by four, eight, 16, or 24 feet long. They are then able to order standard prefab units with a range of different window, door, and amenity configurations.

Builders of both detached and attached homes that use prefab products employ a systems approach to building, which represents a hybrid of site-built and manufactured housing. The four types of systems-built housing include: pre-cut homes, for which all lumber and materials are shipped to the site already cut; panelized homes, for which the main wall panels are shipped to the site, often with plumbing and wiring already installed; sectional homes, which are more than 90 percent complete when they leave the factory, and have cabinets and flooring already installed; and log homes, which are essentially factory-made kit homes.

Markets. In the early 1990s, about one-third of all prefabricated units produced were classified as stationary buildings, with floors and walls, and usually ceilings and roofs, attached in three-dimensional assemblies. About 17 percent of sales were of stationary buildings sold as complete units but shipped as flat panels for assembly on-site. Sixteen percent of revenues were derived from precut packages, such as log homes, that were sold as complete units but shipped in pieces to be put together on-site. Seventeen percent of prefab products were individual components that were not sold as a complete unit. Miscellaneous parts and attachments accounted for the remaining 16 percent of sales.

Prefab units for single-family, detached-home construction, including remodeling, accounted for 50 percent of industry sales in the early 1990s. Products used for apartment buildings represented about 10 percent of revenues, and prefab office building units made up 19 percent of shipments. The remainder of the market was fragmented. Units used to build warehouses, for example, accounted for just more than three percent of sales, as did farm construction. Other markets for wood prefab products included hotels, service stations, schools, and the armed forces. The remaining 3.2 percent of production was exported.

BACKGROUND AND DEVELOPMENT

Assemblage of wooden building components at a location other than the construction site has been practiced for centuries. The modern concept of prefabrication, which entails mass production of uniform panels and components, dates back to the early 1900s. Builders of that period, which were often the homeowners as well, began purchasing light-weight, pre-made frames and trusses to simplify the construction process. The popularization of the gasoline-powered truck early in the decade boosted sales of prefab products, and allowed manufacturers to build larger, heavier components.

The fledgling prefab industry blossomed during the post-World War II U.S. economic expansion. As the economy and population flourished, housing starts soared. In addition, government housing programs, such as the Veteran's Administration Home Loan Guarantee Program of 1944, prodded demand for new construction. Single-family housing starts rocketed from 139,000 per year in 1944 to 1.9 million in 1950.

Throughout the 1950s and 1960s, as the post-war economy thrived, families flocked to the housing market in a buying frenzy. Thousands of tract subdivisions were built on the perimeter of urban America— typically offering quality detached homes for less than $10,000 in the 1950s, with mortgage payments of under $100 per month. To keep up with demand, both residential and commercial builders began seeking more efficient production methods, including prefabrication.

New construction techniques and standards augmented the viability of component construction during the 1950s, 1960s, and 1970s. New federal and state regulations were enacted, for example, that mandated structural integrity and uniform building practices. Plywood, plastics, and aluminum, all of which were eventually integrated into various wood prefab units, also increased sales. While wood components still represented a minor element of U.S. construction, industry sales surpassed $1 billion in the early 1980s, and employment topped 16,500.

The 1980s and Early 1990s. Although the demand for new construction remained strong during the 1980s, several economic factors, including increased construction costs, dampened demand in comparison to past decades. As housing affordability and home ownership rates dropped, many builders began looking to component construction to cut costs. At the same time, higher quality components helped the industry gain a foothold in upscale markets. In addition, the demand for heavy-duty units for commercial and industrial units expanded.

Industry sales surged to nearly $2.5 billion by 1987, reflecting average annual growth of more than 12 percent between 1981 and 1987. Although commercial and residential construction markets stalled in the late 1980s and early 1990s, prefab industry revenues declined only marginally as the search for less-expensive production methods escalated. Sales slipped to about $2.3 billion in the early 1990s, but demand was revived by strengthening construction markets going into the mid-1990s.

CURRENT CONDITIONS

Sales of prefabricated wood products rose in 1992 and 1993. Shipments for single-family units, alone, approached $3 billion. A 20 percent jump in 1992 housing starts, greater public acceptance of component construction, and low interest rates spurred sales in almost all prefab industry segments. Even profit-gouging lumber inflation, which stung producers in the early 1990s, was receding in 1993.

A trend toward component construction boded well for industry participants in the long run. Export opportunities seemed especially plentiful, as burgeoning Third World nations were increasingly seeking low-cost prefabricated homes for swelling populations. Several savvy U.S. firms were already participating in overseas markets, often through joint ventures and foreign manufacturing subsidiaries.

Future profitability will continue to be influenced by lumber supplies from the Northwest and other regions where environmental regulations were limiting logging in the mid-1990s. The increased use of wood substitutes, particularly new high-performance synthetic resins, could also affect long term wood component demand. Nevertheless, the industry outlook was positive through the 1990s.

Log Homes. Aside from steadily growing demand for prefabricated traditional homes, one of the largest and fastest-growing segments of the industry was log homes. At least one estimate placed log home sales at about 12 percent of the total industry revenues, though sales and growth statistics are scant for this private-company-dominated sector. Following a severe reduction in demand in the late 1980s, U.S. log home sales were surging. At an average 1993 price of just $67,000, ready-to-assemble log homes provided low-cost, comfortable living.

Log home exports, particularly, were on the rise. For example, New England Log Homes, Inc. of Connecticut was shipping components to regions such as Israel, Europe, and Japan. Precision Craft, Inc. of Idaho, which began building log homes in 1992, had revenues of more than $4 million within six months, $1 million of which were from sales to Japan. Demand for U.S. log homes was also strong in Mexico, Jamaica, and South Korea.

Industry Niches. Besides prefab growth in single-family and log homes, which accounted for over 60 percent of industry revenues, numerous sectors of the wood component industry were offering solid growth opportunities in the early 1990s, and completely new product introductions were rapidly expanding the breadth of the wood prefabrication business. Many utilities, for example, were experimenting with prefabricated power-control centers (PCCs) that came pre-wired and tested. The pre-made units offered reduced construction and maintenance costs, greater durability, and improved aesthetics.

One of the fastest growth niches in the mid-1990s was prefabricated units that were used to construct restaurant carts, kiosks, and drive-thrus. The units are designed for fast, inexpensive assembly. Rally's, a hamburger drive-thru chain, was building its modular units for thousands of dollars less than the cost of traditional brick and mortar buildings. Similarly, about 1,000 Checkers restaurants, which were also built with prefab components, were scheduled for completion by 1995.

Interestingly, inventor Al Rice launched a chain of ultra-economy minimotels in 1993. The prefabricated 140-square-foot hotel rooms feature a double bed, bathroom, television, and telephone for less than $20 per night. The units are designed to be assembled in groups of ten to 30 and are operated using a patented Autoclerk system. Guests check into the rooms electronically using their credit card. The Autoclerk provides wake-up calls and security, and allows the travelers to communicate with a manager at a remote site.

INDUSTRY LEADERS

About 650 companies participated in the prefabricated wood component industry in the early 1990s. Because it is a localized industry by logistic necessity, most companies are extremely small. Even the majority of the top 50 competitors had sales of less than $25 million per year in the early 1990s and employed fewer than 150 workers.

The largest U.S. supplier of wood building components in the early 1990s was Gelco Space of Pennsylvania. Gelco generated 1991 sales of $160 million and employed about 500 workers. Wausau Homes, Inc. of Wisconsin, the second largest manufacturer, shipped $76 million worth of product in 1991 and employed a work force of 400. Ritz-Craft Corporation of Pennsylvania had sales of $62 million, and Patriot Homes, Inc. of Indiana boasted $58 million in revenues. Other industry leaders included DKM Building Enterprises L.P. of New Jersey and Guerdon Industries, Inc. of Oregon.

Alpine Log Homes, Inc. is representative of many firms in the prefab industry because it is small, entrepreneurial, and niche-oriented. The company was started by Ken Thuerbach, who left his job as a financier to build log cabins in Montana. Alpine builds each log home in Montana, dissects the home, and transports it to a site where it is reassembled. It also builds multimillion-dollar structures, such as the University of Montana's Entrepreneurial Center. Thuerbach reported annual revenues in the early 1990s of between $9 million and $14 million per year.

One of the more successful foreign prefab producers in the early 1990s was French constructor Dragages et Travaux, whose work was purchased in 1990 by the Bouygues Group. Dragages' use of high-tech prefabrication techniques helped it to become the biggest player in the Hong Kong construction market.

WORK FORCE

While employment expanded rapidly during the 1980s (in contrast to most other U.S. manufacturing industries) to more than 22,500, wages in the prefab industry lagged. The average hourly production worker's wage in 1991, for example, was $8.82 per hour, compared with $10.49 for all other U.S. manufacturing laborers. The average annual 1991 payroll per industry employee, moreover, was only $19,297, compared to $26,028 for other manufacturers. The industry employs large numbers of assemblers, fabricators, and woodworkers.

RESEARCH AND TECHNOLOGY

Most technological innovations going into the mid-1990s centered around prefab housing's advantages of low-cost, ease of construction, and uniform quality. Prefab manufacturers were also developing products that could infringe on traditional construction markets, such as high-rise buildings. For instance, component makers in Japan began marketing sections and panels for medium-rise apartment buildings as high as five stories.

Japanese companies were leading technological advances in other areas of the industry, as well. Shimizu Corporation's Smart System, introduced in 1993, was designed to cut the number of man-hours required to complete a 20-story office building by 30 percent. The Smart System uses a network of nine computer-controlled cranes that scale the frame of the building and attach components automatically.

U.S. home builder Land & Houses was using direct mail to market its high-tech prefabricated units to consumers in Thailand. In 1993, it was building an assembly line factory in that country that would produce prefabricated floors and walls that could be used to construct low-cost residential units on a massive scale.

Technological developments that detracted from wood component industry strength in the early 1990s included advancements related to wood substitutes. Producers in Saudi Arabia, for example, were mass-producing prefabricated aluminum homes and buildings. Similarly, manufacturers in Poland were shipping prefabricated metal and reinforced plastic components. The panels and sections were being assembled into retail kiosks to support the burgeoning entrepreneurial population.

INDUSTRY INFORMATION SOURCES

Al-Dohaim, Yasser A. and Syed Abid Ali, ''Using Work Design Techniques and Method Engineering to Enhance Productivity,'' *Industrial Engineering,* July 1993.

Bond, Helen, ''Investor Eyes New Niche,'' *Hotel & Motel Management,* June 7, 1993.

Bretz, Elizabeth, ''Busy Utilities Turn to Pre-Fab Control Buildings,'' December 1992.

''Exporting Pays Off,'' *Business America,* August 24, 1992.

Friedland, Jonathan, ''Home Run: Thai Builder Pioneers Mass-Produced Housing,'' *Far Eastern Economic Review,* November 8, 1990.

Goldstein, Carl, ''Tall Storey: Hong Kong's Top Contractor Is Dragages of France,'' *Far Eastern Economic Review,* April 19, 1990.

Harper, Doug, ''Export Boom Gives Log Home Industry Badly Needed Boost,'' *Journal of Commerce and Commercial,* November 9, 1992.

Hooser, Dwane D., ''Montana's Log Home Industry,'' *Montana's Business Quarterly,* Autumn 1990.

Joint Center for Housing Studies, *The State of the Nations Housing 1993,* Boston: Joint Center for Housing Studies, 1993.

Menzel, Thomas R., ''Going Global From Scratch,'' *World Trade,* January 1993.

National Association of Home Builders, *50 Years of Housing—50 Years of NAHB,* Washington, D.C.: National Association of Home Builders, 1992.

National Association of Home Builders, Public Affairs Division, *Housing Backgrounder,* Washington, D.C.: National Association of Home Builders, 1993.

Normile, Dennis, ''Building-By-Numbers in Japan,'' *Engineering News Record,* March 1, 1993.

Paliwoda, Stan, ''Optimistic Report From Poland: Veteran Analyst Describes Changes, Investment Opportunities,'' *Marketing News,* September 13, 1993.

''Prefabricated Modular Buildings,'' *Communications News,* June 1991.

Standard & Poor's Industry Surveys, New York: Standard & Poor's Corporation, August 5, 1993.

Taras, Susan, ''Easy to Log Quality Time in Homes of Good Timber,'' *Advertising Age,* January 11, 1993.

''Trade and Industry Briefs: Synthetic Fibers; Housing,'' *Mitsubishi Bank Review,* January 1992.

U.S. Industrial Outlook 1993, Washington, D.C.: U.S. Department of Commerce, January 1993.

Wallace, Don, ''Leisure Class: The Creative Adventurer,'' *Success,* September 1991.

Walter, Kate, ''Breaking With Brick,'' *Restaurant Business,* September 1, 1993.

—Dave Mote

SIC 2491

WOOD PRESERVING

The wood preserving industry is comprised of establishments primarily engaged in treating wood, sawed or planed in other establishments, with creosote or other preservatives to prevent decay and protect against fire and insects. This industry also includes the cutting, treating, and selling of poles, posts, and piling, but other establishments primarily engaged in manufacturing other wood products, which they may also treat with preservatives, are classified elsewhere.

People have been coating wood with crude preservatives, such as tar and pitch, for ages. Chemicals and processes developed during the 19th and 20th centuries, however, have resulted in preservation techniques that allow wood to last 35 years or more. Untreated wood that is exposed to the elements typically lasts about three years. Perhaps the greatest industry innovation during the 1900s was the high-pressure chemical treatment process, which accelerated wood's absorption of preservatives and increased the treatment's depth. Ninety-five percent of all preserved wood was treated using this process in the early 1990s.

Utility poles, which make up the single largest market segment for wood preservers, accounted for roughly 25 percent of sales in the early 1990s. Various residential, commercial, and institutional construction industries consume the bulk of industry output. Three-quarters of all wood products are treated with chromated-copper-arsenate. Pentachlorophenol and creosote account for the remaining one quarter. Besides utility poles, the most commonly treated wood products are lumber, plywood, timbers, posts, and railway ties. Southern yellow pine accounted for 75 percent of all treated wood in 1991. Demand for treated hard-woods is meager.

In the early 1990s, wood preservers were treating about 550 million cubic feet of wood products per year. Combined revenues were about $2.5 billion, $50.5 million of which were attributable to exports. 1990 sales of $2.6 billion reflected a healthy average revenue growth rate of over seven percent per year since 1982. Despite manufacturing productivity gains, employment climbed from around 11,000 in 1980 to about 12,000 by the early 1990s. The industry contin-ued to increase its trade surplus in the early 1990s, from about $19 million in 1989 to $28 million by 1992.

Notwithstanding export gains, revenues fell from their 1990 high to $2.5 billion in 1991 as construction markets collapsed. Sales growth remained stagnant in 1992 and 1993, but was expected to recover slightly in 1994. Besides a general U.S. economic malaise, wood preservers were also battling new environmental re-strictions. In 1990 the Environmental Protection Agency identified the by-products of wood preserving processes as hazardous waste, and chose to begin regu-lating the industry in 1991. However, industry spokespeople considered this costly development survivable.

Approximately 500 companies participated in the wood preserving industry in the early 1990s. Fireboard Corp., of California, was the largest with 1991 reve-nues of about $245 million and 2,200 employees. Koppers Industries, the second largest industry mem-ber, had sales of $170 million and 1,900 workers. Other industry leaders included Osmose Wood Pre-serving Inc. and Tolleson Lumber Company Inc., both located in Georgia, and Cox Wood Preserving Co., of South Carolina. The majority of the top 50 firms had under $10 million in sales and fewer than 50 workers.

Industry growth should recover in the long run, boosted by a U.S. economic recovery and increased exports to the Caribbean Basin, Mexico, and Canada. Naphthenate and other substitutes will increasingly of-fer viable alternatives to preservatives that spawn high-cost toxins. Higher yellow pine costs will spur a transition to more spruce, pine, and fir, as well as some nontraditional hardwoods. Despite growth in the 1980s, industry employment will decline in the wake of productivity gains. Most occupations, in fact, will realize a work force reduction of 5 to 25 percent between 1990 and 2005, according to the Bureau of Labor Statistics.

INDUSTRY INFORMATION SOURCES

Darnay, Arsen J., ed., *Manufacturing USA; Industry Analy-ses, Statistics, and Leading Companies,* Detroit: Gale Re-search Inc., 1993.

Hein, Richard W., ''Are Treated Poles an Asset, or a Liabil-ity?'' *Telephone Engineer & Management,* April 15, 1989.

Standard & Poor's Industry Surveys, New York: Standard & Poor's Corporation, August 5, 1993.

U.S. Industrial Outlook 1993, Washington, D.C.: U.S. De-partment of Commerce, January 1993.

—Dave Mote

SIC 2493

RECONSTITUTED WOOD PRODUCTS

The reconstituted wood products industry is com-prised of establishments primarily engaged in manu-facturing hardboard, particleboard, insulation board, medium-density fiberboard, waferboard, and other panelized products made from wood chips and parti-cles.

Particleboard accounted for about 28 percent of industry revenues in the early 1990s, and 6.9 million cubic meters of product. It is created from wood flakes, shavings, or splinters that are discharged when wood products are processed. The particles are bonded to-gether under pressure and heat with resin and adhe-sives to make an expensive, durable wooden panel. Approximately 80 percent of all particleboard is used to make furniture, cabinets, and doors.

Hardboard, or fiberboard, represented about 25 percent of industry revenues in the early 1990s. A hardboard panel is made from wood fibers that are steamed, rubbed apart, and then compacted under heat and pressure. Unlike particleboard, only a small amount of resin or adhesive is used to bond the fibers. Hardboard has a smooth finish, and is used primarily for exterior house siding, indoor cabinets, and fixtures.

Waferboard and oriented strandboard (OSB) made up about 20 percent of industry sales in the early 1990s. Waferboard is similar to particleboard, but only three-inch, square wood flakes are used. OSB is a type of waferboard, but its flakes are layered and oriented in a way that makes it much stronger than waferboard, yet still less expensive than plywood.

Commercially useful wood particle panels re-sulted from the chemical industry's development of high-tech synthetic resins and adhesives, particularly during the 1960s, 1970s, and 1980s. Reconstituted panel sales grew steadily during the 1980s to nearly $3.2 billion per year by 1989. U.S. economic recess in the early 1990s, however, caused revenues, adjusted for inflation, to fall by 2.1 percent in 1990 and 3.7 percent in 1991.

A tepid recovery boosted industry sales about four percent in both 1992 and 1993 to about $3.3 billion. Recovering demand in housing and furniture markets was expected to result in similar growth throughout the mid-1990s. Increased demand will also be driven by improved panel products and exports. Exports had already doubled between 1987 and 1992 to more than $240 million, and were expected to benefit from the 1994 North American Free Trade Agreement (NAFTA). Strong growth in imports, however, could overshadow any cross-border gains.

Despite overall growth, opportunities in most occupations in the industry will likely decline significantly between 1990 and 2005, according to the Bureau of Labor Statistics. Jobs for assemblers and fabricators, which account for 14 percent of the work force, will fall by more than 25 percent. Most positions, in fact, will decline five to 20 percent by 2005. About 22,500 workers served the industry in 1993—most were blue-collar laborers.

The largest U.S. producer of reconstituted wood products in the early 1990s was Celotex Corp. of Florida. Celotex had 1991 sales of $609 million, and about 3,000 employees. Louisiana-Pacific Corp. of Idaho was the second biggest competitor, with revenues of $350 million. Georgia-Pacific Corp. of Georgia had $325 million in sales, and Masonite Corp. of Illinois had $250 million.

INDUSTRY INFORMATION SOURCES

Darnay, Arsen J., ed., *Manufacturing USA; Industry Analyses, Statistics, and Leading Companies,* Detroit: Gale Research Inc., 1993.

Standard & Poor's Industry Surveys, New York: Standard & Poor's Corporation, August 5, 1993.

U.S. Industrial Outlook 1992, Washington, D.C.: U.S. Department of Commerce, January 1992.

U.S. Industrial Outlook 1993, Washington, D.C.: U.S. Department of Commerce, January 1993.

—Dave Mote

WOOD PRODUCTS, NOT ELSEWHERE CLASSIFIED

This category covers establishments primarily engaged in manufacturing miscellaneous wood products, not elsewhere classified, and products from rattan, reed, splint, straw, veneer, veneer strips, wicker, and willow.

This industry covers a plethora of wood products not categorized under other classifications, such as ship masts, dowels, rowboat oars, clipboards, rattan seat covers, shoe trees, tool handles, toothpicks, washboards, paint stirring sticks, and wooden ladders. While the breadth of this industry is enormous, some categories account for a significant portion of overall sales. For example, picture and mirror frames were by far the largest category and supplied about 18 percent of industry revenues in the early 1990s. Wooden reels for wire and cable represented almost 4 percent of production. Ice cream sticks and tongue depressors accounted for about 1.8 percent of industry output. Dowels made up 1.7 percent of sales, and stepladders garnered 1.5 percent of receipts.

Individuals, the largest consumers of miscellaneous wooden goods, accounted for about 22 percent of industry sales in the early 1990s. Office building owners and managers were the second-largest sector, representing about 4 percent of the market. Other major consumers of industry output were furniture manufacturers, makers of glass products, and paperboard mills. 3.5 percent of production was exported.

The industry is intangible and unstructured in comparison to most other industrial categories. In the early 1980s, it comprised approximately 3,400 firms that sold about $3.4 billion worth of miscellaneous wooden items. The industry experienced wide swings in revenues during the 1980s, according to the U.S. Census of Manufacturers. By the early 1990s, however, the Census estimated that about 2,700 firms had combined sales of approximately $3.9 billion.

An estimated 61,000 workers served the industry in 1990. About 15 percent of those workers were thought to be assemblers and fabricators. Other significant occupations in this industry include machine operators, sawers, blue-collar work supervisors, and truck drivers. The average wage for laborers in this classification was estimated at $6.85 in 1989—well below the national manufacturing average of $10.49. Likewise, the average annual salary in the industry was about 60 percent of the national average.

Industry sales and profit growth in the long term will depend on individual product segments. Overall employment, however, was expected to decline significantly between 1990 and 2005, according to the Bureau of Labor Statistics. Assembler and fabricator jobs, for example, would plummet by more than 26 percent, as well as positions for machine operators and book-keepers. Most occupations, it was anticipated, would realize a work force reduction of 5 to 20 percent as companies sought to automate and increase productivity. Sales and marketing professionals, in contrast, will see positions in this industry grow by nearly 20 percent.

The largest producer of miscellaneous wood products in the early 1990s was Masonite Corp. of Illinois. Masonite generated revenues of $535 million in 1991 from its diversified operations and employed about 5,000 workers. Intercraft Industries, a limited partnership in Texas, boasted sales of about $160 million with 1,800 employees. Other industry leaders included Greif Brothers Corporation's Norco Division, of Minnesota, and Longaberger Company, of Ohio. The majority of the top 75 companies in the industry attracted revenues of less than $20 million and had fewer than 200 people on their payroll.

INDUSTRY INFORMATION SOURCES

Darnay, Arsen J., ed., *Manufacturing USA; Industry Analyses, Statistics, and Leading Companies,* Detroit: Gale Research Inc., 1993.

Standard & Poor's Industry Surveys, New York: Standard & Poor's Corporation, August 5, 1993.

U.S. Industrial Outlook 1992, Washington, D.C.: U.S. Department of Commerce, January 1992.

U.S. Industrial Outlook 1993, Washington, D.C.: U.S. Department of Commerce, January 1993.

—Dave Mote

FURNITURE & FIXTURES

SIC 2511

WOOD HOUSEHOLD FURNITURE

This classification consists of establishments engaged in manufacturing wood furniture commonly used in dwellings, with the exception of television, radio, phonograph, and sewing machine cabinets; also, millwork production is classified in **SIC 2431: Millwork**; wood kitchen cabinets are classified in **SIC 2434: Wood Kitchen Cabinets**. Cut stone and concrete furniture are classified in the major group for stone, clay, glass, and concrete products; laboratory and hospital furniture, except hospital beds, are in the major group for measuring, analyzing, and controlling instruments; photographic, medical and optical goods; watches and clocks; beauty and barber shop furniture are classified in the major group for miscellaneous manufacturing industries; and those engaged in woodworking to individual order or in the nature of reconditioning and repair are classified in nonmanufacturing industries.

Since the average consumer spends more on furniture within two years of moving into a new house than at any other time, slow growth in housing in the early 1990s undoubtedly depressed household furniture sales. However, housing starts rebounded in 1993 and 1994. Total wood household furniture sales—comprising about 42 percent of household furniture shipments—were $9.3 billion in 1993 out of a total of $22.2 billion for wood, upholstered, and metal household furniture.

An increase in consumer confidence seemed to benefit wood furniture makers such as Bassett Furniture Industries, which earned $27.5 million on sales of

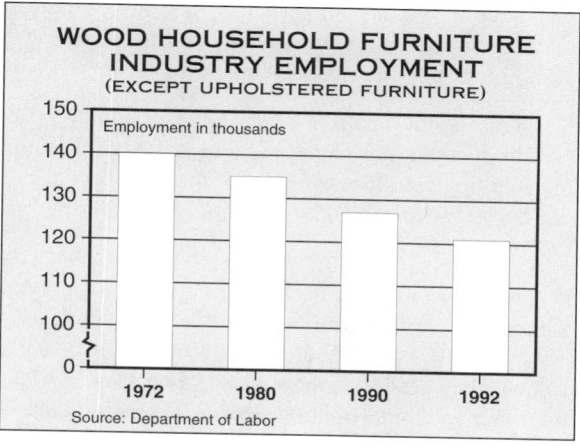

WOOD HOUSEHOLD FURNITURE INDUSTRY EMPLOYMENT (EXCEPT UPHOLSTERED FURNITURE)

Employment in thousands

Source: Department of Labor

$473.4 million in the fiscal year ending November 30, 1992. Chairman and chief executive officer Robert H. Spilman commented in the *Wall Street Journal* that his company had had no backlogs of wood furniture since the stock market crash of 1987. "The opportunity has been much easier in upholstery," Spilman said. Bassett's largest customer was J.C. Penney and most of its efforts concentrated on mid-priced furniture. The company has 44 factories in the United States. The bedroom and dining room furniture segment has been hardest hit, according to Spilman. In 1992, Acton Corp. closed a wood furniture factory employing 200 people in Mebane, North Carolina, citing decrease demand for high-end bedroom and dining room furniture. In the same year, Stanley Furniture Co., a $160 million a year wood furniture company, closed a plant in Waynesboro, Virginia.

Ready-to-assemble (RTA) furniture was the fastest-growing segment of the wood furniture market in the early 1990s, accounting for 13%, or $1.3 billion, of the market in 1991, up from 8.9% in 1987, according to industry estimates. Ladd Furniture acquired Fournier Furniture Corp., a firm specializing in this type of furniture, in an attempt to capitalize on this trend.

The increase in sales of RTA furniture was due partly to an improvement in quality—the products were no longer merely the stuff of college dorms, with imitation wood finishes. Typical products included wood veneer finishes, and details such as rounded corners and beveled glass doors. A piece of RTA furniture can be assembled quickly, usually in less than an hour. O'Sullivan Industries has even utilized Velcro fasteners instead of screws to help speed up assembly. An average price for a ready-to-assemble desk was $225, 65% less than a factory-finished product. The low cost of RTA furniture and the ease of stocking it has made it popular among large mass merchandisers and warehouse-type stores, which had themselves become more popular among consumers.

Traditional furniture stores worked with vendors to introduce vendor-ship programs, with manufacturers shipping furniture directly to the customer, allowing the stores to carry less inventory and insuring safe delivery of the products.

International Trade. Most exports of American wood household furniture went to Canada (39%), Mexico (12%), and Saudi Arabia (9%). Imports came from Taiwan (29%), Canada (14%), and Mexico (7%). International trade liberalization agreements such as GATT and NAFTA seemed poised to benefit U.S. exports of wood household furniture, though developing nations seemed poised to pursue aggressive forest management and export policies.

EPA regulations mandated in the Clean Air Act Amendments of 1990 could eventually cost the industry anywhere between $53 million and $624 million by forcing it to reduce volatile organic compound (VOC) emissions.

INDUSTRY INFORMATION SOURCES

"Textiles, Apparel, and Home Furnishings," *Industry Surveys*, November 26, 1992, p. T90 - T93.

Agins, Teri, "Marketing—Home Furnishings," *The Wall Street Journal*, November 22, 1993, p. B1.

"Stanley Furniture Co.: Restructuring Plan Gives Stake to Preferred Holders," *The Wall Street Journal*, November 10, 1992, p. A13.

Blumenthal, Robin Goldwyn, "Bassett Furniture Expects Increases in Fiscal '93 Results," *The Wall Street Journal*, January 18, 1993.

"Acton Unit to Close Factory," *The Wall Street Journal*, November 12, 1992, p. A6.

Frederick C. Ingram

SIC 2512

WOOD HOUSEHOLD FURNITURE, UPHOLSTERED

This category covers those establishments primarily engaged in manufacturing upholstered furniture on wood frames. Shops primarily engaged in reupholstering furniture, or upholstering frames to individual order are classified in Services, **SIC 7641: Reupholstery and Furniture Repair,** or Retail Trade, **SIC 5712: Furniture Stores.** Establishments primarily engaged in manufacturing dual purpose sleep furniture, such as convertible sofas and chair beds, are classified in **SIC 2515: Mattresses, Foundations, and Convertible Beds,** regardless of the material used in the frame. Establishments primarily engaged in manufacturing wood frames for upholstered furniture are classified in **SIC 2426: Hardware Dimension and Flooring Mills.**

This industry is defined primarily by the materials with which the products are constructed, rather than the end product itself. All products feature wood frames and fabric or leather upholstery. Establishments within this industry produce a wide range of upholstered furniture for the home, including such upholstered living room furniture as chairs, rockers, couches, sofas, and recliners. Products manufactured in this industry include other household furniture as well as juvenile furniture.

Establishments in this industry produce goods that are sold to distributors or directly to retailers. Manufacturers produce goods for sale at a variety of price points and under a variety of brand names. *Standard and Poor's Industry Survey* estimated that approximately 44 percent of upholstered furniture is sold through furniture stores, 10 percent through department stores, and 44 percent through mass merchandisers. New retailing techniques are affecting the industry. Standard and Poor's noted a growing tendency among manufacturers to enter into agreement with a retailer to open a gallery devoted to the manufacturer's goods, a concept that has been "very successful in attracting customers and generating sales." The arrangement is mutually advantageous because the retailer has proprietary rights on the goods while the manufacturer gets a dedicated retail outlet for its merchandise.

According to *U.S. Industrial Outlook 1994,* establishments in this industry sold an estimated $6.69 billion worth of products in 1993. This amount equaled approximately 30 percent of the total sales recorded by the household furniture manufacturing industry as a whole. Furthermore, the industry is an important source of jobs. According to the *1991 Annual Survey of Manufacturers,* the industry employs approximately 80,000 people and maintains a payroll of approximately $1.09 billion.

Manufacturers of upholstered wood furniture benefited from an expanding market in the early 1990s, leading to approximately five to six percent growth between 1992 and 1993 alone. The industry is influenced by the rate of new home construction and the number of existing homes being remodeled. Standard and Poor's estimated that the upholstered wood household furniture industry will continue to expand through the mid-1990s due to changing demographics. Baby Boomers are "getting older and richer and will soon want nicer things to suit their more upscale lifestyles." According to *Ward's Business Directory of U.S. Private and Public Companies,* the largest manufacturers in the industry were Masco Corp., the La-Z Boy Chair Company, Mohasco Corporation, and Klaussner Furniture Industries, Incorporated.

INDUSTRY INFORMATION SOURCES

American Furniture Manufacturers Association materials, High Point, NC.

Annual Survey of Manufactures, Washington, DC: U.S. Department of Commerce, 1991.

1987 Census of Manufactures, Washington, DC: U.S. Department of Commerce, 1987.

Standard and Poor's Industry Surveys, New York: Standard and Poor's Corporation, 1994.

U.S. Industrial Outlook 1994, Washington, DC: U.S. Department of Commerce, 1994.

Ward's Business Directory of U.S. Private and Public Companies, Detroit: Gale Research Inc., 1993.

—Jim Cuene

SIC 2514

METAL HOUSEHOLD FURNITURE

Establishments primarily engaged in manufacturing metal furniture of a type commonly used in dwellings.

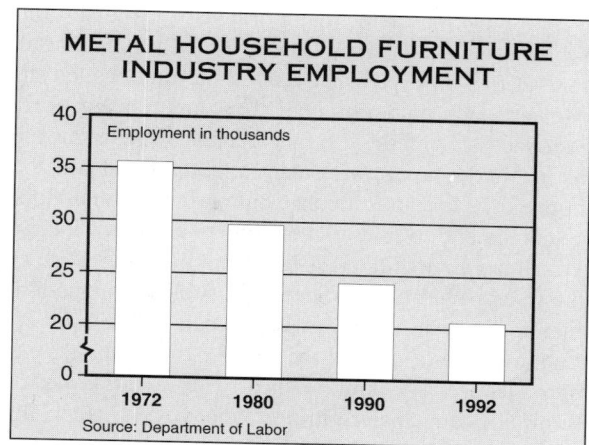

Metal furniture dates back almost as far as the use of wrought iron, with society witnessing an extraordinary increase in the use of metal furniture by the end of the 18th century. By the beginning of the 19th century, both English and American craftsmen began constructing Windsor-style chairs in wrought iron. In 1851 at the Great Exhibition in London, England, the American Chair Company of New York exhibited a metal-framed, sprung, revolving chair, one of several styles with frames made largely of cast-iron, steel, or a combination of the two. And by the 1890s, metal beds had become one of the most popular selling furniture items in America.

But it was not until the development of steel and other innovations in metal production by American manufacturing companies, during the 1920s and early 1930s, that major impacts on furniture design were felt. The abundance of ready steel made it a popular and reasonably cheap material for furniture. One of the most dramatic new processes, discovered in the early 1920s by an American inventor named Mannesman, produced seamless tubular steel. This new material had the combined advantages of being light, strong, and modern.

The role that bent metal furniture played in the design culture of the 1920s and 1930s has never been equalled by any other material or at any other time in design history. The development of modern tubular steel furniture can be seen in terms of the technical accomplishments of modern industrialization, with its improved methods of steel production, metal plating and welding—all of which helped to disseminate the new furniture to a wider market. But above all of this is the fact that steel furniture came from the world of modern art and architecture and its preoccupation with the idea and image of the machine.

For that reason the major drawback to metal furniture was that its look appealed to a small, sophisticated market that enjoyed what was, at the time, called the Modern style of design. For that same reason, there remained for several years a great deal of resistance to its use in the home, with many feeling that it was too impersonal for domestic use, but perfectly suitable for hospitals and offices. Then, in 1933, the Chicago World's Fair exhibited a large number of pieces of tubular steel furniture. Seen as a symbol for modern life, the use of steel was advertised at the Fair as, "natural, therefore that the modern spirit should express itself in striking, radically different kinds of furniture—and that furniture should be of steel, for this is the age of steel, and steel sounds the keynote of practicability, energy, and strength which dominates our modern life." By the mid-1930s tubular steel furnishing was being more easily accepted into domestic use, with steel items coming out of American factories in ever-increasing, large numbers.

Companies, such as the Chicago and Grand Rapids Company of Michigan, immediately began producing large quantities of tubular steel furniture. The American industrial designer, Donald Deskey, designed a line of metal furniture that was mass-produced around 1930 by the Ypsilanti Reed Furniture Company. A 1930 ad for the company pointed out that Ypsilanti Reed had pioneered steel furniture in America, "and in less than two years has assumed outstanding leadership in style and quality in this singular furniture."

By 1933 the Howell Company of Geneva, Illinois, began mass-producing tubular steel furniture, including the best-selling "Beta," a chrome-plated, tubular steel and upholstered chair, as well as other innovative chair forms, such as the "S" chairs, with their bent metal frames, that were produced and sold in high volume throughout the 1930s.

The famous industrial designer, Gilbert Rohde, was among the first American innovators who worked with bent metal to create innovative furniture designs. His earliest tubular steel design was manufactured by the Troy Sunshade Company of Troy, Ohio in 1931. Because the company had additional offices in Amsterdam and Rotterdam in the Netherlands, Rohde's designs were sold in Europe as well.

The Kroehler Manufacturing Company of Chicago, Illinois also employed Rohde, who designed furniture not only from tubular steel, but from stainless steel, aluminum, and chrome. Rhode's pieces were advertised by the company as "functional and modern" with "a hygienic quality (no nooks and crannies to conceal dirt) that reduced dusting to a minimum while retaining their luster without the drudgery of polishing."

By 1930 Gilbert Rohde moved on to take over the design leadership for the Herman Miller Furniture Company of Grand Rapids, Michigan. With Rohde at its helm, the company began an extensive program to produce modern furnishings, most of which incorporated the use of bent metal elements in many of their designs. In fact, throughout the decade leading up to World War II, the Herman Miller Company continued to increasingly produce bent metal furnishings designed by Gilbert Rohde.

Although metal furniture was seen as innovative to the American public, many American designers, like Gilbert Rohde, owed a great debt to their European counterparts during the decades between the two world wars. Many progressive European publications published designs for tubular steel furniture. In fact, some of the most copied modern tubular steel furniture designs belonged to Marcel Breuer, the avant garde designer, and were originally created while he was at the Bauhaus, the German experimental design school, as early as 1925.

With the dissemination of European tubular steel designs to a wider, world market and manufacturers producing their own interpretations of bent metal furniture, the originality and inventiveness of design had largely ended by the early years of the 1940s.

After World War II, the profound changes in design and manufacturing moved the center of progressive development of metal furniture from Europe to the United States. Charles and Ray Eames, a husband and wife team of industrial designers, helped to develop new, and even more innovative, metal furniture designs for the Herman Miller Company in the 1940s and 1950s.

Research into new materials such as molded plywood, and the use of light metal alloys (especially aluminum and magnesium, which were developed during the War) provided an entire new range of possibilities for post-war furniture.

The American furniture manufacturer, Knoll International, produced such innovative designs as the 1952 metal "Grid" chair by the artist/designer, Harry Bertoia, as well as several other metal pieces. And, in the 1960s, Knoll produced the internationally acclaimed architect/designer Mies van der Rohe's last body of furniture designs of tubular and flat steel.

But by the end of the 1950s, metal was being used less and less frequently for innovative furniture designs. The Herman Miller Company and Knoll International continued to manufacture steel bent and tubular steel "design classics" from the 1930s, but with new and even more innovative materials, such as plastics, arriving on the scene, metal furniture was relegated to experimental, one-of-a-kind and limited edition pieces by artist/designers who did not look for mass production or wide audience acceptance.

Because metal was the symbol of the machine age, it was quite natural for metal furniture's high point to coincide with the era of the "machine age," that of the 1930s. The bent metal furniture designed and manufactured during that period was never equalled again.

INDUSTRY INFORMATION SOURCES

Wilson, Richard Guy, Pilgram, Dianne H., and Dickran Tashjian, *The Machine Age in America, 1918-1941*, New York: Harry N. Abrams, Inc., Publishers, 1986.

Sparke, Penny, *Design in Context*, London: Quarto Publishing, 1987.

Alvera, Allessandro, Dry, Graham, and Robert Keil et.al., *Bent Wood and Metal Furniture: 1850-1946*, New York: The American Federation of the Arts, 1987.

Lucie-Smith, Edward, *A History of Industrial Design*, Oxford: Phaidon Press Ltd., 1983.

Garner, Philippe, *Twentieth Century Furniture*, London: Adkinson Parrish Ltd., 1980.

—Dorothy Spencer

SIC 2515

MATTRESSES, FOUNDATIONS, AND CONVERTIBLE BEDS

This category covers establishments primarily engaged in manufacturing innerspring mattresses, box spring mattresses, and non-innerspring mattresses containing felt, foam rubber, urethane, hair, or any other filling material; and assembled wire springs (fabric, coil, or box) for use on beds, couches, and cots. This industry also includes establishments primarily engaged in manufacturing dual purpose sleep furniture, such as convertible sofas and chair beds, regardless of the material used in the frame. Establishments primarily engaged in manufacturing automobile seats and backs are classified under **SIC 2531: Public Building and Related Furniture;** those manufacturing individual wire springs are classified under **SIC 3495: Wire Springs;** and those manufacturing paddings and upholstery filling are classified under **SIC 2299: Textile Goods, Not Elsewhere Classified.**

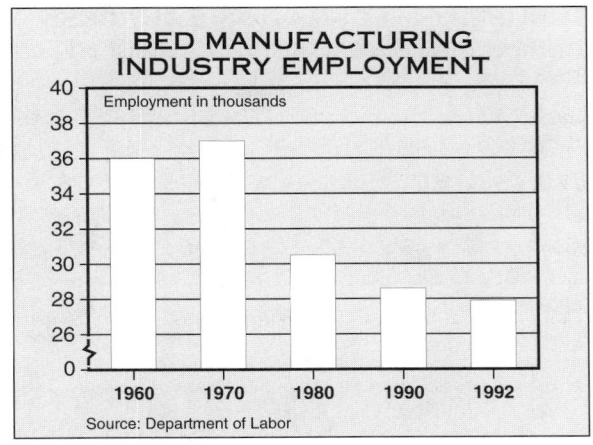

BED MANUFACTURING INDUSTRY EMPLOYMENT

Employment in thousands

Source: Department of Labor

Establishments that manufacture mattresses, foundations, and convertible beds are part of the $22.2 billion household furniture manufacturing industry. According to *U.S. Industrial Outlook 1994,* manufacturers within this classification sold approximately $3.2 billion dollars worth of products in 1993. As of 1987, the most recent year for which there was a census, the industry consisted of approximately 840 manufacturing establishments operated by 721 companies. This number was down from 902 establishments being run by 786 companies documented in the 1982 Census of Manufacturers.

The industry seems to be populated by smaller manufacturing facilities. Of the approximately 840 establishments in operation, about 500 had less than 20 employees. The industry employs approximately 24,000 people (including almost 18,000 as production workers) with a $508 million payroll. The states with the most people employed in the industry are California, Texas, New Jersey, and Florida.

Manufacturers create products to be sold under different brand names at a variety of price points. A high quality mattress can cost the retail consumer as much as $899 or more. Establishments in this industry distribute their goods to specialty stores that deal only in mattresses and foundations. According to *Standard and Poor's Industry Survey 1994,* 45 percent of bedding is sold through such stores, followed by discount stores and department stores, which sell 13 percent and 12 percent of manufacturer's goods, respectively.

According to *Ward's Business Directory of U.S. Private and Public Companies,* the largest manufacturer of mattresses and bedsprings is Legget and Platt, Inc., of Carthage, Missouri. Behind them is Sealy, Inc., of Cleveland, Ohio, and the Simmons Company. Serta, Inc., and Restonic, Inc., are also among the industry leaders in sales and numbers of employees.

INDUSTRY INFORMATION SOURCES

American Furniture Manufacturers Association materials, High Point, NC.

Annual Survey of Manufactures, Washington, DC: U.S. Department of Commerce, 1991.

1987 Census of Manufactures, Washington, DC: U.S. Department of Commerce, 1987.

Standard and Poor's Industry Surveys, New York: Standard and Poor's Corporation, 1994.

U.S. Industrial Outlook 1994, Washington, DC: U.S. Department of Commerce, 1994.

Ward's Business Directory of U.S. Private and Public Companies, Detroit, MI: Gale Research Inc., 1993.

—Jim Cuene

SIC 2517

WOOD TELEVISION, RADIO, PHONOGRAPH, AND SEWING MACHINE CABINETS

This category covers establishments primarily engaged in manufacturing wood cabinets for radios, television sets, phonographs, and sewing machines.

Comprised of companies principally employed in manufacturing wood cases for audio and visual equipment, this industry produces such products as wooden speaker boxes, stereo cabinets, sewing machine cases, and television cabinets. It is part of the larger household furniture industry. About 60 percent of industry output in the early 1990s consisted of TV cabinets, or cases for combinations of TV, stereo, or radio. Stereo and radio cabinets constituted 20 percent of the market. Wooden sewing machine cases accounted for only 3 percent of industry sales, and miscellaneous items comprised the remainder of revenues. Radio and television manufacturers consumed nearly 85 percent of industry production in the early 1990s. Personal consumption expenditures represented less than 8 percent of sales.

A limited market existed for sewing machine cases and radio cabinets early in the 20th century. Not until after World War II, however, did the U.S. wooden cabinet business emerge as a small industry. A consumer spending boom, boosted by a surging demand for television cabinets beginning in the 1950s, resulted in healthy industry growth throughout the 1950s, 1960s, and much of the 1970s. Indeed, by the early 1980s, television and radio cabinet producers were shipping more than $300 million worth of products per year and employing about 7,000 workers.

Although industry sales swelled to nearly $400 million in 1984, the industry was destined for failure. The two primary culprits of imminent demise were foreign competition and plastic. As imports of consumer electronics into the United States, particularly from Japan, ballooned throughout the 1980s, domestic demand for TV and radio cabinets plummeted. Even producers that kept factories in the United States were increasingly replacing wood with cheaper, more versatile plastic cabinets.

Wood cabinet sales tumbled at a rate of nearly 9 percent per year between 1984 and 1990, depressing industry revenues below a discouraging $250 million per year. As competitors scrambled to cut costs and increase productivity, the work force was mercilessly slashed to about 3,000 workers by the early 1990s—less than half its size just eight years earlier. To make matters worse, a U.S. economic recession battered the business in the early 1990s, causing some competitors to exit.

Overall furniture industry sales were expected to rise at a rate of 2.5 percent to 3 percent throughout the mid-1990s, and employment will likely grow by more than 20 percent between 1990 and 2005, according to the Bureau of Labor Statistics. Wooden cabinet producers, however, will be exempt from such gains. Wood substitutes and foreign consumer electronics producers will continue to crush domestic manufacturer profits. Many savvy cabinet makers will simply exit the industry and try to compete in related furniture segments.

Only about 30 producers competed in this industry in the early 1990s. The largest U.S. maker of TV and radio cabinets was Fournier Accessory Furniture, of Minnesota. Fournier earned $100 million in 1991 revenues and employed a work force of approximately 400. Rospatch Corp., of Michigan, was the second-largest rival, with 1991 sales of $68 million and about 500 workers. Other industry leaders included a division of Philips Consumer Electronics Co. in Tennessee and Crown Wood Products Co. in North Carolina.

INDUSTRY INFORMATION SOURCES

Darnay, Arsen J., editor, *Manufacturing USA; Industry Analyses, Statistics, and Leading Companies,* Detroit: Gale Research Inc., 1993.

Standard & Poor's Industry Surveys, New York: Standard & Poor's Corporation, August 5, 1993.

U.S. Industrial Outlook 1993, Washington, D.C.: U.S. Department of Commerce, January 1993.

—Dave Mote

SIC 2519

HOUSEHOLD FURNITURE, NOT ELSEWHERE CLASSIFIED

Establishments primarily engaged in manufacturing reed, rattan, and other wicker furniture, plastics and fiberglass household furniture and cabinets, and household furniture not elsewhere classified.

Wicker, Rattan and Reed Furniture. Wicker furnishings have been used in American households since the seventeenth century. The first known craftsmen to advertise wicker furniture were early nineteenth-century basket weavers. It was during that period that straw and willow were replaced by rattan, which was imported by the East India Company.

In the mid-nineteenth century wicker furniture, customarily styled with closely woven can seats and looped reed backs and arms, became increasingly popular. Furniture frames were constructed from hickory and oak pieces that were steamed and bent into shape, then wrapped with split cane. It was during this period that the building of wicker furniture went from craft to industry.

Between 1875 and 1910, wicker furniture reached the height of its popularity, at least in part because of its association with exotic, foreign countries. In 1917 the Lloyd loom, a wicker-weaving machine that used fiber material, was invented by Marshall B. Lloyd. During this period many wicker manufacturers began to experiment with materials such as prairie grass and fiber. The wire grass used was from the prairie marshes of northwest America which was converted into a pliable twine and woven into furniture.

By the end of World War I, the skilled labor needed to weave wicker became scarce in the United States, and imports began replacing domestic manufacturing. By the close of the second world war virtually all wicker furniture sold in America was imported, a state of affairs that continues in the same vein today.

Plastics and Fiberglass Furniture. Although plastics had been developed in the late nineteenth century, it wasn't until 1909, when the American chemist Leo Baekeland developed Bakelite, that plastics began to gradually replace metal for body-shells in industrial applications. Baekeland, along with two Westinghouse Corporation engineers, Harold Faber and Daniel O'Connor, developed a laminate, originally intended for electrical insulation. The development of this formula in 1913, however, eventually resulted in the establishment of the Formica Corporation. By the mid-

1920s Formica's laminate was used to produce furniture.

With the demands for light weight seat furniture brought on by the aircraft industry during World War II, the development of plastics for constructing furniture took on new meaning. Two early pioneers of American furniture design, Eero Saarinen and Charles Eames, began experimenting with molded polyester in 1941.

Saarinen's "Womb" chair, the first fiberglass design to be mass-produced in America, was manufactured by Knoll Associates in 1946. The chair has remained in continuous production for over four decades. In 1950 New York's Museum of Modern Art held an exhibition entitled "Organic Design in Home Furnishings." The prizewinning fiberglass armchair designed by Charles Eames was manufactured by the Herman Miller Furniture Company. Eames' molded plastic chair series—which also included a stacking chair—became one of the most basic and popular lines of American seating furniture.

Entering the mid-1990s, leading companies in this manufacturing industry included Rubbermaid Inc. (under its Rubbermaid Specialty Products Inc. division), Syroco Inc., AB Plastics Corporation, Emerson Leather Inc., Tropitone Furniture Company Inc., Lamont Ltd., and the Ello Furniture Manufacturing Co. While establishments such as Rubbermaid Specialty Products are part of larger companies, the majority of the manufacturers in this industry remain privately owned.

INDUSTRY INFORMATION SOURCES

Sparke, Penny, *Design in Context*, London, England: Quarto Publishing, 1987.

Lucie-Smith, Edward, *A History of Industrial Design*, Oxford, England: Phaidon Press Ltd., 1983.

Garner, Philippe, *Twentieth Century Furniture*, London, England: Adkonson Parrish Ltd., 1980.

Menz, Katherine, *Nineteenth Century Furniture*, New York: Art & Antiques Books, 1982.

—Dorothy Spencer

SIC 2521

WOOD OFFICE FURNITURE

This classification covers establishments primary engaged in manufacturing office furniture, chiefly of wood, including benches, bookcases, cabinets, chairs, desks, filing boxes and cabinets of wood, panel furniture systems, stools, tables, partitions, and modular furniture systems.

INDUSTRY SNAPSHOT

Approximately 2,500 wood office furniture manufacturers operated in this industry during 1993. This represented an increase of 54 over the previous year. Another 831 businesses classified in other industries participated in some capacity, compared with 782 in 1992. Shipments for the industry were worth $1.7 billion in 1991, the last year for which complete figures were available. This was down from $2.1 billion in 1989 and $2 billion in 1990.

CURRENT CONDITIONS

At the end of 1993 the wood office furniture industry was experiencing slight growth. The Business and Institutional Furniture Manufacturers Association predicted that shipments of wood office furniture would grow in 1993. However, shipments increased only slightly. The industry was still shaken by recession, and a return to the strong growth of the 1980s was not expected. From the late 1980s until the early 1990s, the industry was affected by rash downsizing. Lost sales were reflected in the dive in the volume of shipments of desks and chairs. In 1988 shipments of seats amounted to 2.8 million units. This dipped to 2.7 million units in 1989, 2.5 million in 1990, and 2.3 million units in 1991. Similarly, shipments of desks fell from 1.4 million units in 1988 to 1.2 million in 1990, and one million units in 1991.

Even with the upturn in the economy in 1993, many industry executives were concerned about the prevailing economic climate, and they expected more job cuts in that year. The continuing woes of the industry were reflected in the oversupply of U.S. office space. Oncor's *Office Market Data Book* reported that at year-end 1992 office vacancy rates of more than 20 percent existed in 18 major U.S. central business districts, including Los Angeles, Chicago, Denver, and Dallas.

Many wood office furniture manufacturers were having to reassess their markets going into 1994. Most of the growth in demand for office furniture was coming from small companies with limited budgets and a desire to stretch them as far as possible. High end products were out of their reach. Manufacturers were increasingly realizing that the strongest demand existed for mid-range products, and few industry analysts predicted a return to the deep-pocket corporate spending of the early 1980s.

Wood office furniture manufacturers are exploring new niche markets such as home offices that can replace diminished demand from their traditional customer base. Another growth market is ergonomically designed furniture, which client companies hope will increase productivity and reduce occupational injuries such as repetitive strain injuries and backache, thus diminishing their health care costs.

Industry observers also expressed concern about the common practice of price discounting in the industry. Because it drains a manufacturer of financial resources, discounting is blamed for increasing the likelihood of smaller manufacturers being bought out by larger competitors. During the early 1990s many small companies were acquired by larger ones, especially those wishing to enter a particular niche market where the smaller company may already have a foothold. In 1992, major acquisitions were made by HON Industries Inc. and Kimball. Many companies called for an end to discounting and damaging price wars.

New Regulations. Wood office furniture manufacturers are apprehensive about the effect environmental ordinances might have on their bottom lines. Under the Clean Air Act Amendment of 1990, wood furniture finishing products may be regulated. Such rules were being drawn up in 1993 to form the basis for a draft national emission standard for hazardous air pollutants. Chiefly affected will be substances known as volatile organic compounds which are used in finishes. Also targeted are two types of adhesives, urea-formaldehyde resins and contact adhesives. Some U.S. wood office furniture companies have already adopted water-based finishes in anticipation of possible legislation.

INDUSTRY LEADERS

A leading company in the wood office furniture industry is Boise Cascade Corp., a highly diversified company with $3.7 billion in revenues in 1993. Another top general office furniture manufacturer is Steelcase Inc. with $2.4 billion in sales in 1993. Herman Miller Inc., with $920 million in sales in 1993, was third. Other notable companies include HON Industries Inc., with gross earnings in 1993 of $707 million; Knoll Group Inc., with gross earnings of $578 million; Hunt Manufacturing Company, which earned $235 million in 1993; and Carolina Mills Inc., with gross revenues in 1993 of $179 million.

Boise Cascade Corp., a major producer of paper, paper products, wood building supplies, and office furniture, was formed in 1957 when two small lumber companies merged. The company moved into the office products market in 1964. During the late 1960s and early 1970s the company diversified, moving into building materials, publishing, real estate, paper products, and recreational vehicles. By 1972, however, Boise Cascade was $1 billion in debt, having fallen victim to a timber shortage and disruption of some of its business plans. Later in the 1970s it streamlined its business. This was not sufficient, however, to spare it a rough ride through the recession. The company's income decreased from $4.4 billion in 1989 to $4.2 billion in 1990. In 1991, it fell again to $4 billion. Sales were $3.7 billion in 1993. Boise Cascade gets almost half its timber from its own forests.

Steelcase, Inc. is the foremost office furniture manufacturer in the world. In addition to manufacturing wood office furniture, Steelcase makes non-wood office furniture, systems furniture, lighting systems, computer software that aids in designing office environments, and customized millwork. The company has six divisions—Steelcase North America, Steelcase Design Partnership, Steelcase Export, Steelcase Japan, and the Atwood Corporation. The Michigan-based company was founded in 1912 and maintains wood products manufacturing divisions in Grand Rapids, Michigan, and Fletcher, North Carolina. Like many companies in the market, Steelcase suffered a downturn during the early 1990s, particularly in its dominant North American market. During the 1993 fiscal year, the firm underwent downsizing and refocused its operations to survive an increasingly competitive market. The company's strategy paid off and in 1993 it reported an increase of 4.6 percent in revenues.

The third largest wood office furniture manufacturer is the nation's second largest general office furniture manufacturer. Herman Miller Inc. had sales of $920 million in 1993, of which office furniture sales accounted for $800 million. Exports accounted for about 16 percent of the company's sales. Herman Miller restructured in 1992 in an effort to combat the negative impact of the recession and decreased demands for its high end products.

HON Industries, Inc. is a diversified company that markets its wood office furniture lines under the Gunlocke Company brand name. It had total sales of $850 million in 1993 and sales from office furniture of $700 million. It owns seven office furniture and office products companies.

WORK FORCE

While level of employment in the total office furniture industry has held steady in recent years, the wood office furniture industry segment suffered job losses during the recession. After climbing steadily through the early and mid-1980s, jobs were lost in

TOTAL OFFICE FURNITURE INDUSTRY EMPLOYMENT
(INCL. WOOD, PLASTICS, METAL & OTHER MATERIALS)

Source: Department of Labor

modest numbers beginning in 1988. The work force fell from 31,000 in 1987 to 30,800 in 1988. It rose slightly in 1989 to 31,000, before falling to 28,200 in 1990, and plunging to 22,500 in 1991. Amongst production workers, jobs fell from 24,600 in 1988 to 24,300 in 1989, 22,100 in 1990, and to 17,000 in 1991. Although the decline was reversed in 1992 and 1993, it is unlikely that all of the jobs lost will be replaced. Instead, manufacturers are seeking to increase the productivity of existing employees. The result has been a reduction in the total number of hours worked from 49 million in 1989 to 34.1 million in 1991. Reductions in the work force kept payrolls from rising.

AMERICA AND THE WORLD

With no imminent surge in demand expected in the U.S. market, wood office furniture manufacturers were looking to oversees markets for increased sales. According to the United States Department of Agriculture Forest Service Report, at the end of the 1992 third fiscal quarter, U.S. wooden office furniture exports exceeded $54 million, more than $6.8 million above the 1991 level. Between 1989 and 1993, exports of wood office furniture have increased by over $32 million.

INDUSTRY INFORMATION SOURCES

Adams, Larry, "Overall, Wood Industry Stronger in '93 Than '92: Industry Overview," *Wood and Wood Products*, November 1993.

"Adhesives are 'Last Minute' Inclusion in Reg-Neg," *BIFMA*, October 1993.

"Clean Air Negotiations Status Update: Reg-Neg Reaches Tentative Agreements," *BIFMA News*, December 1993.

Derning, Sean, "Economy Still Top Concern of Contract Furniture Manufacturers," *Wood and Wood Products*, February 1993, 43.

Dun's Census of American Business 1993, New Jersey: Dun & Bradstreet, 1993.

Parker, Marcia, ''Ergonomic Chairs Won't Cost Arm, Leg Now,'' *Crain's New York Business,* December 14, 1993, 20.

—Avril McDonald

SIC 2522

OFFICE FURNITURE, EXCEPT WOOD

This category describes establishments primarily engaged in the manufacturing of office furniture, except furniture chiefly made of wood. Establishments primarily engaged in manufacturing safes and vaults are classified in **SIC 3499: Fabricated Metal Products, Not Elsewhere Classified.** The products manufactured by the industry include: office benches, bookcases, chairs, cabinets, desks, filing cabinets, modular furniture systems, panel furniture systems, office partitions, stools, tables, and wall cases.

INDUSTRY SNAPSHOT

The office furniture industry (except wood) included about 900 operators in 1993. The majority of businesses were large-scale enterprises with over $5 million in annual sales. The industry leaders earned substantially more. The industry as a whole was worth approximately $7.9 billion in 1993, up from $7.6 billion in 1992 and $7.2 billion in 1991. This modest increase reflected a slight improvement in the economy, both domestically and overseas.

BACKGROUND AND DEVELOPMENT

As recently as the 1950s, American offices and furniture were usually drab, stark, and purely functional. Beginning in the late 1960s and early 1970s, however, office design, layout, and furniture began to be influenced by modern ideas of worker productivity and the realization that a link exists between employee performance and the quality of an office environment. From the late 1970s through the mid-1980s, the office furniture manufacturing industry grew by an average of 19 percent annually, according to the Business and Institutional Furniture Manufacturers Association (BIFMA), a major trade organization. The boom was fueled by the rapid growth of white-collar workers needed to staff the developing service economy.

The office furniture manufacturing industry had its heyday during the 1980s as corporations rapidly expanded their office staffs and the computer and other information industries exploded. Sales of office furni-

ture boomed for most of the decade—between 1980 and 1987 they grew at an annual rate of 12 percent. These sales were largely driven by systems furniture, or mix-and-match cabinets, desks, and partitions. In recent years, however, sales of freestanding seating and tables have grown at the expense of system furniture products. According to an article in *Buildings Magazine,* as recently as 1986 the office environment was ruled by a drive for efficient use of space and cost reductions. By the early 1990s, however, ''both the office furnishings industry and facilities managers were replacing their efficiency fervor with a more harmonious decision-making process in which comfort and personalization of the physical workplace take precedence.''

Changing working habits and patterns propelled the need for new products. The rise of the computer and related hardware helped to spawn new types of workstations, printer tables, and movable walls and partitions that allow facilities managers to easily reconfigure office space as needs change. Modern partitions are also designed to facilitate wiring and networking of computers. The trend toward more communicative, less territorial, and less isolated workspaces has called for new types of furnishings.

Keeping its members on top of new trends and aware of the state of their industry is the job of BIFMA. At the organization's inception in 1973 it was made up exclusively of office furniture manufacturers. But as the industry's complexion changed in the ensuing years, BIFMA's roll expanded to include institutional furniture manufacturers. Today, companies serving this market, such as Kewaunee Scientific and Falcon Products, make up five percent of BIFMA's members, while 95 percent of the organization's 126 regular members are office furniture manufacturers like Steelcase, Herman Miller, HON, and Haworth. In 1993, BIFMA had 148 regular manufacturing members, 63 associate members, and 24 international members.

CURRENT CONDITIONS

The entire office furniture industry was hit extremely hard by the recession. From 1986 until 1992, industry growth fell precipitously from previous heights to just three percent per year. Shipments for the metal office furniture manufacturing industry fell from $6.2 billion in 1989 to $5.6 billion in 1991. Exports, which doubled between 1988 and 1989 from $86.7 million to $170.8 million, fell during this period as well.

The recession resulted in layoffs of hundreds of thousands of office workers as one company after another downsized their staffs. Office space, which had mushroomed during the boom years of the 1980s when demand was high, was left vacant. Few new offices were built during the late 1980s and early 1990s, which meant a fall in demand for new office furniture. Struggling corporations desperate to save money every which way began to regard new office furniture as a luxury item. The wheezing economy forced some office furniture manufacturing companies out of business, especially those that specialized in high-end products. To remain competitive, manufacturers were forced to reduce staff and increase productivity.

Heading into the mid-1990s, the industry seemed to be on course for a sustained recovery from the bruising it suffered during the recession. Although it had not recovered the momentum it enjoyed during the 1970s and for most of the 1980s, it was at least growing and not shrinking as the mid-1990s approached. According to the Business and Institutional Manufacturers Association (BIFMA), real growth in 1994 was expected to be two percent.

The improved fortunes of office furniture manufacturers toward the mid-1990s reflected an overall upswing in the economy. Non-residential building construction starts were up in 1993 by five percent, indicating that demand for office furniture would increase. Areas reporting an increase included the North Central (three percent), the South Atlantic (nine percent), and South Central (11 percent). Employment was also up slightly in the country as a whole, stimulating demand for new office furniture. Exports were again growing, and a number of niche markets were showing considerable promise. All of these indicators left room for guarded optimism in the industry going into the mid-1990s. Despite its improved prospects and performance, the office furniture manufacturing industry continued to suffer from too many suppliers competing for increasingly few customers in the mid-1990s. This made for cut-throat competition. Manufacturers are routinely forced to cut their prices by as much as 50 percent on high volume purchases in order to win lucrative contracts.

Manufacturers are realizing that they cannot necessarily compete on product alone and are looking to provide more services. Terms such as ''value added partnering'' are becoming part of the industry lingo. Other changes in the industry since the early 1990s include a refocus on distribution. Many of the industry leaders, including Steelcase, Herman Miller, Haworth, and Knoll have moved to dedicated dealers. Others, such as HON Industries, have moved in the opposite direction and are distributing their products through discount outlets like office supply superstores.

Another strategy, adopted particularly by the high-end manufacturers in order to increase their competitiveness and reorient themselves in a changing market, has been to acquire smaller companies with a foothold in growth niche markets, such as the ready-to-assemble (RTA) market. In late 1993, for example, Haworth purchased Hendersonville, Tennessee-based Globe Business Furniture, an RTA supplier specializing in partially assembled chairs. Globe's sales grew an average of 25 percent between 1981 and 1992, in contrast to Haworth, which slowed from a high of 20 percent annual growth during the 1980s to lower double digits in the early 1990s. Other takeovers of RTA manufacturers by traditional office furniture suppliers include LADD's takeover of Fournier. Industry experts expected the trend to continue, but warned producers against moving to RTA as a quick-fix method for regaining market share. For one thing, RTA requires an entirely different cost structure than that employed by traditional office furniture manufacturers.

Another booming niche market is that for home office furniture. The number of people who work from home was estimated at 35 million in 1992 and was expected to grow to 45 million by the year 2,000. By 1996 as many as 80 million computers are expected to be in American homes, representing a dynamic new market for workstations, office chairs, shelving units, file cabinets, and accessories. Sales of home office and computer furniture comprised 25 percent of all household furniture sales in 1991, ahead of all categories except home theater/entertainment furniture (35 percent).

Also lucrative is the market for ergonomically designed office furniture. In fact, it is the fastest growing segment of the market. As awareness about the causes of computer-related, white-collar occupational hazards such as repetitive strain injury, carpal tunnel syndrome, backache, repeat performance syndrome, and countless other ailments has grown, the demand for furniture that will ameliorate the injuries has mushroomed. Office furniture manufacturers have been at the forefront of the development of ergonomically designed office furniture that is believed to increase productivity and reduce occupational stresses and strains. Sales of high-end products, such as workstations that afford workers' maximum comfort and flexibility and cost as much as $3,000 each, are helping to propel growth in the industry. One company, Tiffany Office Furniture, designed a workstation, for example, which lets the user sit or stand while they work. It also features a monitor shelf that can be tilted to suit the user, and an adjustable keyboard shelf. Demand for less expensive ergonomic furniture is also strong. Small companies concerned about liability for their employees' work-related injuries are often unable to afford traditional high-priced ergonomic furniture. Companies are responding to this dilemma by coming out with new lines of discount ergonomic furniture. The "Accolade," chair, for example, retails for about $650, yet offers ergonomic adjustability.

The major players are diversifying their operations in ways other than by developing new products. In March 1994, Steelcase announced that it would establish a consulting and service management subsidiary called Tangerine. The company will be charged with helping companies identify their workplace needs, both on- and off-site, and catering to those needs. This move by the industry leader is a clear recognition of the changing nature of the workplace and of working patterns.

INDUSTRY LEADERS

The top manufacturer of office furniture in the USA was Steelcase, Inc., with total revenues in 1992 of $2.4 billion. Second was Herman Miller Inc., with $855 million in revenues. The third-placed company was HON Industries. It grossed $706 million in 1993. The country's fourth largest office furniture manufacturer was Haworth, a private company based in Holland, Michigan. Other notable companies in the industry include HMK Enterprises Inc. and Knoll Group Inc.

With sales of approximately $1.7 billion in office furniture in 1993, Steelcase, Inc., a diversified company with total revenues of $2 billion, controlled 19 percent of the domestic office furniture manufacturing market in 1993, down from 20.5 in 1991. As well as making office furniture, Steelcase produces wooden office furniture, systems furniture, lighting systems, computer software that aids in designing office environments, and customized millwork. The company is divided into six subunits: Steelcase North America, Steelcase Design Partnership, Steelcase Export, Steelcase Japan, and the Atwood Corporation.

Established in 1912, Steelcase Inc. is based in Grand Rapids, Michigan, also home to some of its office furniture production plants. Its two lines of filing cabinets, seven lines of desks, tables, credenzas, bookshelves, and some chair lines are produced here, while other lines of office chairs are made in Tustin, California, and Toronto, Canada. During the 1993 fiscal year, Steelcase underwent downsizing and refocused its operations to compete in an increasingly competitive market. These changes took place against a backdrop

of continued losses in the late 1980s and early 1990s. The company's strategy paid off in 1993 when it reported an increase of 4.6 percent in revenues compared with the previous year.

Herman Miller, Inc., the industry's number two player, is primarily an office furniture manufacturer, catering mainly to the higher end of the office furniture market. Its revenues in 1993 were $920 million, while its revenues from office furniture sales amounted to $800 million. For the three months ending February 26, 1994, its net sales were $242 million and its net income was $11.2 million. This compares with net sales of $218 million and net income of $7.2 million for the three months ending February 27, 1993. The bulk of the company's sales are generated through corporate bids and interior designers. In response to a decline in sales, it underwent a major restructuring in the early 1990s. The company also manufactures furniture for use in hospitals and other institutions. Foreign sales account for about 16 percent of the company's sales.

Haworth Inc., with revenues of $570 million, is a privately owned firm. Haworth made its initial impact on the industry with its introduction of a prewired workstation panel that allowed office cubicles to be constructed simply by snapping panels together, thus eliminating the need to bring in electricians to rewire the spaces. In recent years, this success has been cemented by savvy business decisions, including Haworth's acquisition, either outright or partial, of nine other companies. Approximately 22 percent of Haworth's revenue in the early 1990s came from overseas, a market the company hopes to further explore in the future.

WORK FORCE

Jobs have been steadily lost in all sectors of the office furniture manufacturing industry since 1988. When the recession struck, forcing the industry's corporate customers to rethink their priorities and postpone buying new furniture, office furniture manufacturers responded by targeting their payrolls for cutbacks. This trend is expected to continue into the mid-1990s. Increased automation and efficiency have squeezed the work force as well, and may ensure that lost production jobs will never be replaced.

At its peak in 1989, the office furniture industry as a whole employed 71,300 people. In the following years this fell steadily to 68,000 in 1990, 62,600 in 1991, and 61,900 people in 1992. Production workers comprised 45,800 of the total in 1992, a drop from 46,100 in 1991, 50,600 in 1990, and 52,900 in 1989. With fewer workers, production employees labored longer, putting in 40 hours a week on average in 1992, compared with 37.9 in 1991. Production payroll costs were $1.1 billion in 1991, substantially less than just two years earlier, when the figure was $1.3 billion.

AMERICA AND THE WORLD

All of the United States' biggest manufacturers have stakes in overseas markets. Steelcase, the leading domestic manufacturer, is also number one in the world office furniture market, with offices in Europe, Asia, and Japan. Almost 20 percent of Herman Miller's business is in the export area, a segment that it has explored over the past few years in order to increase its competitiveness. Herman Miller was also vying for a slice of the lucrative Japanese market. In 1991 it opened its first Japanese office furniture showroom. Both the Japanese market, worth an estimated $4 billion, and Eastern Europe have been identified as potential growth areas. The passage of the North American Free Trade Agreement in 1993 and the completion of the Uruguay Round of the General Agreement on Tariffs and Trade will open the doors to a heavier volume of office furniture exports in the late 1990s.

INDUSTRY INFORMATION SOURCES

Becker, Franklin, "The Ecology of New Ways of Working: Non-territorial Offices," *Site Selection,* February 1993.

"Competition Hits Office Furniture: Office Products and Business Systems," *Purchasing,* November 21, 1991, 105.

Derning, Sean, "Economy Concerns Top Contract Furniture Makers," *Wood and Wood Products,* February 1992, 50.

Derning, Sean, "Economy Still Top Concern of Contract Furniture Manufacturers," *Wood and Wood Products,* February 1993, 43.

"Economic Use of Space, Equipment, and Energy Still Considerations," *Modern Office Technology,* January 1983, 42.

Garet, Barbara, "Offices To Go," *Wood & Wood Products Magazine,* August 1992, 44.

"High Point Furniture Industries: Nineties Point Furniture in a New Direction," *Managing Office Technology,* July 1993, 57.

Marks, Robert, "Accent on Home Office: Furniture Manufacturers Targeting Market," *The Weekly Home Furnishings Newspaper,* November 18, 1991, 19.

Marks, Robert "More Demand for RTA Office Products Seen; Ready-to-assemble Office Furniture," *The Weekly Home Furnishings Newspaper,* January 7, 1991, 172.

Monroe, Linda, "Facilities Challenges in the Information Age," *Buildings,* May 1991, 70.

Mumfor, Steve, "The Straight Facts About Human Factors," *Buildings,* March 1993, 38.

Parker, Marcia, "Ergonomic Chairs Don't Cost Arm, Leg Now," *Crain's New York Business,* December 14, 1993, 20.

Stepanek, Steven, "Dividing and Conquering with Walls and Partitions: Office Interiors Management," *Buildings,* July 1991, 60.

"Traditional Furniture Manufacturers Buying RTA Vendors to Share in Sales Boom: Ready-to-assemble Office Furniture," *Discount Store News,* October 18, 1993.

—Avril McDonald

SIC 2531

PUBLIC BUILDING AND RELATED FURNITURE

This category primarily encompasses establishments engaged in manufacturing furniture for public use found in schools, theaters, assembly halls, churches, and libraries. Examples of such furniture include bleacher and stadium seating, church pews, library chairs and tables, and blackboards. The public building and related furniture category also includes seating for public conveyances such as automobiles, aircraft, and passenger trains. This category does not include manufacturers of stone furniture, which are classified under **SIC 3281: Cut Stone and Stone Products,** nor does it include those that manufacture concrete furniture, which can be found under **SIC 3272: Precast Concrete Products.**

INDUSTRY SNAPSHOT

More than 491 companies manufactured goods that fell under the category of public building and related furniture in the United States in 1987. The total value of shipments generated by the industry amounted to over $3.1 billion in 1991. The companies that comprised this category differed greatly in structure, marketing strategy, and fiscal health, due to the variegated nature of the classification. Nearly half were smaller firms with less than 20 employees on the payroll, while roughly ten percent were corporate subsidiaries. The majority of companies in the industry were "single establishment companies," which were not part of a larger parent corporation.

The variety of products manufactured by the public building and related furniture industry defies a general description of industry outlook. A smaller and less profitable segment of the industry involved the manufacture of church furniture, while providers of car seats to automobile manufacturers were more visible and fiscally sound. While earlier in the twentieth century much of the public seating furniture was made of wood, the incorporation of new technologies such as plastic have radically altered manufacturing processes in this category. Entering the 1990s, many companies were compelled to re-market their products to meet changing demands and a tougher economic situation. Increasingly stringent government regulations in regard to consumer safety and access for the disabled have also forced period changes in the industry.

ORGANIZATION AND STRUCTURE

Most companies in the public building and related furniture industry were comprised of divisions responsible for different steps of the manufacturing process, including research and development, executive decision-making, manufacturing, marketing strategy, and customer support. Many of the products manufactured in the industry were marketed to other companies or institutions, rather than the general public. Automobile seats, for example, were sold to firms specializing in seat frames and exteriors, which, in turn, sold the completed seating unit to automobile manufacturers. Manufacturers commonly advertised in trade journals, such as *Automotive News, Library Journal,* and other publications aimed at executives, buyers, and other upper-level personnel.

During the economic recession of the early 1990s, many public building and related furniture manufacturers focused on customer satisfaction and product reliability as part of their plan to survive in the industry. This represented a particular challenge, as many public building and related furniture manufactures marketed their products to other companies, rather than the ultimate consumer, making it difficult to gauge product satisfaction.

BACKGROUND AND DEVELOPMENT

Many of the firms engaged in manufacturing public building and related furniture date back to the late nineteenth century. During this period, the Industrial Revolution and the urbanization of America played a key role in the development and growth of the industry, as a variety of new demands for public-use furniture developed. For example, when educational reform in the United States led to the replacement of the one-room schoolhouse with large school buildings in consolidated districts, the subsequent demand for school desks and blackboards was filled by newly formed firms in the industry. Furthermore, newly-prosperous industrial magnates founded and endowed hundreds of colleges and universities, necessitating the development of firms that could manufacture and ship seats and desks all over the country. U. S. Steel founder Andrew Carnegie funded the construction of over 2,800 public libraries across the country, and a new

niche in the market arose to meet the demand for librarians' desks as well as patron tables and chairs.

The Industrial Revolution was also responsible for major shifts in population from rural regions to larger urban centers and, later, suburban communities. The shift in demographics was compounded by waves of immigrants from Europe, necessitating the construction of new and larger churches to serve the needs of evolving communities. A demand for more interior furniture, such as church pews, accompanied the exponential growth of churches.

The increased popularity of leisure and entertainment activities in the United States also played a key role in the genesis of the public building and related furniture industry. The development of organized community and collegiate sports, such as baseball and football, necessitated the construction of stadiums and arenas able to seat spectators. Moreover, as plays and motion pictures gained popularity, theaters were built in all but the most rural of American cities, and many competed to provide patrons with the most luxurious interiors, including plush seating.

Perhaps most importantly, the development of new technology in the transportation industry augmented the public building and related furniture industry. The growth of a network of railroads in America gave rise to the popularity of passenger rail travel, and companies evolved to provide comfortable seating for the new long-distance traveler. The invention of the automobile and its rapid rise as a major form of transportation necessitated the evolution of a parallel supplier industry for interior automotive equipment, including seats. During the 1950s and 1960s, the increasing affordability of passenger air travel fueled a great demand for new aircraft, with cabin accoutrements and furnishings.

CURRENT CONDITIONS

The 1980s was a period of growth for the public building and related furniture industry. The value of shipments nearly doubled from $1.1 billion in 1982 to $2 billion in 1987; by 1991 this figure had reached $3.1 billion but showed a small decline from the previous year. The number of employees in this field jumped from 18,800 in 1982 to 21,800 in 1987, and by 1991 this figure had reached 25,900. The largest and most competitive companies in this industry were automobile and airline seat manufacturers, which had to possess the working capital and financial solvency to meet the high costs of developing specialty seats built to withstand accidents. Such companies had to invest large sums in research and development, attract well-qualified engineers for product design, and have the promotional budgets to capture greater market share.

INDUSTRY LEADERS

The companies that manufactured public building and related furniture were as diversified as their products. In the automotive industry, the main suppliers of car seats were Johnson Controls, Inc. and Douglas and Lomason Co. Johnson Controls, founded in 1900 and headquartered in Milwaukee, was a major manufacturer of automobile seats, but was best known as a provider of electronic control systems that regulate heating, cooling and security for commercial buildings. Total sales for the firm were $5,157 million in 1992, and the international company employed 46,800. In 1991 Johnson Controls purchased Lahnwerk GmbH, a German company that supplied seat components and metal seat frames to the European auto industry. Two years later it acquired a similar Mexican firm, Grupo Summa. The company's 50 manufacturing plants involved in automotive seating were located in Michigan, Tennessee, and California, as well as in Portugal and Austria. The other large supplier of seats to the American automotive industry was Douglas and Lomason Co., a suburban Detroit firm founded in 1902. Douglas and Lomason primarily manufactured stamping and conveyer equipment for the industry. The company's total sales for 1992 were $391.2 million, and it had 5,817 employees on its payroll.

In aircraft cabin seating, the largest segment of the market was held by BE Aerospace, Weber Aircraft, Inc., and Burns Aerospace Corp. BE Aerospace was the largest integrated supplier of aircraft cabin accessories, selling approximately 25 percent of the seat market according to 1992 figures. Headquartered in Florida, the company was founded in 1987 and expanded in 1992 when it acquired the Connecticut-based aircraft cabin seat company PTC Aerospace. With other acquisitions of cabin supplier firms that produced such components as galley appliances and video monitors, BE Aerospace's sales went from $24 million in 1991 to nearly $200 million by 1992, providing the airline industry with all cabin products except for lighting fixtures and lavatories. Although the demand for new aircraft has declined in the early 1990s, BE Aerospace remained a strong leader in the field. Second in sales of aircraft cabin seats was the California-based firm of Weber Aircraft, Inc., which reported 1992-93 sales of $80 million, controlling 19 percent of the market and employing 800. Burns Aerospace Corp., a subsidiary of Eagle Industries, Inc.,

employed 700 and posted sales of $80 million, representing 16 percent of the market.

The largest supplier of library furniture in the early 1990s was Gaylord Brothers, a Syracuse, New York, firm dating back to the end of the nineteenth century. Gaylord was started by two brothers, bank clerks who developed a gummed parchment that they marketed to libraries for use in repairing books. When the business turned a profit in 1909, the Gaylord brothers quit the bank and developed their company into a full-service provider for the American libraries. Their products included book shelving systems, magazine display units, storage facilities, librarians' desks, and patron chairs and tables. Gaylord Brothers, which became a subsidiary of the Croydon Company, marketed its products by catalog.

WORK FORCE

In the public building and related furniture industry, the majority of jobs were concentrated in the actual manufacturing process. In 1991 the total number of jobs was 25,900 for the industry, with production workers accounting for 19,800 positions in that figure. Payroll totals for the same year were $558.8 million.

AMERICA AND THE WORLD

In the public building and related furniture industry, seating for public conveyances such as automobiles and airline cabins represents the most common export. The costs for importing other types of furniture, such as classroom or stadium seating, proved prohibitive for many foreign countries that already had successful furniture industries. American automotive seat suppliers such as Johnson Controls faced domestic competition from Japanese firms such as Atoma and Toyo Seat USA, and have made acquisitions to expand into a lucrative foreign automobile market.

RESEARCH AND TECHNOLOGY

Government regulations have prompted the development of new technologies in the public building and related furniture industry, particularly in automotive and airline seat manufacturing. Minimum criteria for car seats, set by The National Highway Traffic Safety Administration (NHTSA), stipulated that seats have no parts that might injure drivers or passengers on impact and that the seat withstand the force of a crash up to a specified gravitational force, requiring seat frames made of especially resilient material firmly attached to car floor.

Auto seat manufacturers were also concerned with the seat's overall performance in terms of comfort, durability, and appearance. As changing demographic patterns engendered longer commuting times for many consumers, the average amount of time they spent sitting in a car seat increased. In response, researchers measured the amount of lumbar support various types of seat cushions provided, developing two methods used in the suspension of automotive seats. The most common type of seat consisted of foam block, a combination of a polyurethane cushion and springs, while another featured a light platform supported by a system of springs.

Governmental regulations, issued by the Federal Aviation Administration (FAA) and the National Transportation Safety Board (NTSB), also affected the industry. Due to the potential for extremely high impact crashes in air travel, regulations on aircraft cabin seat construction was more stringent than for any other area of the public building and related furniture industry. Initially, the industry resisted modifications of cabin seating, complaining that heavier anchoring components used to bolt seats to the floor added too much weight to the aircraft. However, the development of new technology and materials in the 1980s allowed for seats that could withstand up to 9g in gravitational force. In 1988 the FAA ruled that all newly-certified aircraft be outfitted with such seats, and proposed that all seats aboard U.S. aircraft meet a 16g requirement by 1995. In accordance, most seat manufacturers, including Weber, had switched production to the 16g seats by 1990. During this time, manufacturers marketed a two-seat row of first-class seats for around $10,000, while a three-seat row for the coach compartment sold around $5,000.

The fabric used in aircraft cabin seats was also regulated, ensuring cushions that were fire retardant and able to serve as floatation devices. Furthermore, regulatory officials continued to monitor the number and placement of seats on a given aircraft, a procedure that directly affected the profits of both the airline industry and the public building and related furniture industry. Some innovations in airline seating expected to be developed toward the end of the century included seats featuring attached shoulder harnesses, as well as seats that could rotate the legs of their inhabitants upward and out of danger in the event of an impending crash.

INDUSTRY INFORMATION SOURCES

Berry, John, ''The Past Defines the Present at Gaylord,'' *Library Journal,* April 15, 1991.

Edwards, Mary, and Elwyn Edwards, *The Aircraft Cabin: Managing the Human Factors,* Brookfield, VT: Gower Publishing, 1990.

Flint, Perry, ''BE Aerospace Breaks the Mold,'' *Air Transport World,* September 1993.

''Measuring Seat Comfort,'' *Automotive Engineering,* July 1993.

Meier, Barry, ''Airlines Phasing in Safer Plane Seats,'' *New York Times,* June 2, 1990.

Ott, James, ''Seat Manufacturers Seek Ways to Meet New Criteria,'' *Aviation Week and Space Technology,* November 23, 1992.

—Carol Brennan

SIC 2541°

WOOD OFFICE AND STORE FIXTURES, PARTITIONS, SHELVING, AND LOCKERS

This category covers establishments primarily engaged in manufacturing shelving, lockers, and office and store fixtures, plastics laminated fixture tops, and related fabricated products, chiefly of wood. It also includes prefabricated partitions made of wood if they are designed to be attached to floor; if they are designed to be free-standing or part of an office furniture panel system, they are classified under **SIC 2521: Wood Office Furniture.** This category excludes wooden refrigerated cabinets, showcases, or display cases, which are found under **SIC 3585: Refrigeration and Heating Equipment.**

More than 1,867 companies were engaged in the manufacture of wood partitions and fixtures for commercial use in the United States in 1987. In 1991, the combined value of shipments for these firms was over $2.8 billion, representing a decrease from the previous year's figure of $3.1 billion. The industry encompassed many types of products which are now either obsolete or rarely manufactured, such as butcher shop display cases and telephone booths. Other products have become prohibitively expensive both to manufacture and purchase, due to the high cost of materials and labor. However, many of the firms that supply wood partitions and fixtures are thriving due to the increased demand for retail shelving and display units made of wood. In a flooded retail market in which a product must be attractively displayed to catch the eye of the prospective buyer, wooden display cases are regarded as lending appeal to their contents. The industry has also benefited from the development of laminated-plastics coatings to provide a much-used wood surface with increased durability.

Over 12 percent of the firms in wood partitions and fixtures industry were single-establishment businesses, according to 1987 data. Of the 1,867 firms, 135 were part of a larger parent company, while 310 were individual proprietorships or partnerships acting as product suppliers to other companies or institutions, which might require additional shelving units or other structures used for storage space.

Most companies in the wood partitions and fixtures industry were organized into divisions reflecting those of potential customers. However, a company in this industry generally placed less emphasis on research and development, concentrating instead on keeping highly skilled woodworkers in production areas. Large companies might also have an executive decision-making body, marketing strategists, and finally, a team to provide customer support. Manufacturers of wood partitions and fixtures commonly advertised in trade journals, such as *Restaurant Hospitality, Chain Store Age Executive,* and other publications aimed at store and restaurant owners and personnel.

The growth of the wood partitions and fixtures industry arose out of the expansion of the U.S. economy in the late nineteenth century. Increasing industrialization brought large numbers of people to cities, leading to the development of expansive urban commercial districts. The proliferation of smaller specialty shops along with larger department stores necessitated a prodigious supply of fixtures for merchandise display. Wooden telephone booths, a small segment of the industry that is now defunct, were invented by William Gray and first appeared in 1889 outside a bank in Hartford, Connecticut. Western Electric manufactured wooden telephone booths until the late 1940s, when a California firm, Benner-Nawman, invented the more durable glass and steel booth. By the 1990s, wooden phone booths were considered collectible and sold for as much as $3,000.

The wood partitions and fixtures industry showed a marked decline in value of shipments from a 1990 peak of $3.1 billion to $2.8 billion in 1991. This decline was attributed in part to the fact that many products became obsolete. Furthermore, the costs involved in producing manufactured wood items for a market saturated with plastic imitations has had a severe impact on the overall health of the industry.

In the early 1990s, one of the largest suppliers of wood partitions and fixtures was Knape & Vogt Manufacturing of Grand Rapids, Michigan, founded in 1906. This company reported annual sales of $123.4 million in 1992, a figure that included sales of wooden store fixtures and shelving as well as those made from materials other than wood. Another leading manufacturer of wood partitions and fixtures during this time

was Lee/Rowan Co., a St. Louis, Missouri, firm that employed 900. The company, whose 1992 sales were in the $70 million range, was purchased in 1993 by housewares giant Newell, a major conglomerate that also owned Mirro cookware and Anchor Hocking glassware. Smaller firms in the wood partitions and fixtures industry included Bernhard Woodwork Ltd., of Northbrook, Illinois, with 65 employees providing custom-made products and 1992 sales of $8 million, and Precision Manufacturers, Inc. of Bentonville, Arkansas, a privately held company employing 60 and reporting 1992 sales of $6 million.

In 1991 the industry's total work force numbered 35,900, representing a slight decrease from the previous year's figure of 40,100. In the wood partitions and fixtures industry, the majority of jobs were concentrated in the actual manufacturing process. Production workers accounted for 26,800 jobs in the industry in 1991, and payroll totals for the same year were $841.8 million.

INDUSTRY INFORMATION SOURCES

Hillinger, Charles, ''Welcome to the Phone Booth Capital of America,'' *Los Angeles Times,* September 30, 1990.

United States Census of Manufactures, Washington, DC: U.S. Department of Commerce, 1977, 1992.

—Carol Brennan

SIC 2542

OFFICE AND STORE FIXTURES, PARTITIONS, SHELVING, AND LOCKERS, EXCEPT WOOD

This category covers establishments primarily engaged in manufacturing office and store fixtures, shelving, storage racks, lockers, and related fabricated products, chiefly of materials other than wood. This industry also includes prefabricated partitions if they are designed to be attached to the floor; those designed to be free-standing or part of an office furniture panel system are instead classified in **SIC 2522: Office Furniture, Except Wood.** Establishments primarily engaged in manufacturing refrigerated cabinets, showcases, or display cases, are classified in **SIC 3585: Air-Conditioning and Warm Air Heating Equipment and Commercial and Industrial Refrigeration Equipment.** Companies engaged in manufacturing safes and vaults are classified in **SIC 3499: Fabricated Metal Products, Not Elsewhere Classified.**

Nearly 600 companies in the United States were engaged in the manufacture of metal office and store fixtures, partitions, shelving, and lockers in the latter part of the 1980s. The value of shipments generated by these companies was $3.1 billion in 1991, and the industry provided approximately 31,000 jobs that year.

This is a thriving industry, due in part to an increased demand for unique store fixtures to showcase products for the burgeoning retail sector of the U.S. economy. Larger specialty "superstores" such as Office Depot and Builders' Square rely heavily on massive product displays in myriad store areas. This emphasis on merchandising display is also crucial in smaller yet highly-competitive retail outlets such as grocery stores. Custom-fabricated displays showcase specific products and serve to differentiate them from those of competitors.

Historical Growth. The growth of the metal partitions and fixtures industry in the United States is directly related to both the growth of the retail industry and the development of new technology. After World War II the growth of suburban communities fueled the construction of large retail outlets such as supermarkets; demand rose correspondingly for fixtures to provide miles of shelf space. Concurrently, new manufacturing processes were able to craft store fixtures and partitions fabricated from lightweight blends of metal alloys, and these began to replace the standard wood fixtures. These affordable products, such as shelves and garment racks, were more mobile and appealed to executives and managers of the burgeoning retail sector of the U.S. economy.

Industry leaders include the various divisions of LA Darling Co., headquartered in Paragould, Arizona, which combined to post annual sales in the early 1990s of more than $285 million; American Seating Co., a privately-owned company based in Grand Rapids, Michigan, that posted sales of about $130 million; and the privately-owned Edsal Manufacturing Co. of Chicago, Illinois, which posted annual sales of $110 million in the early 1990s.

Other leading manufacturers of non-wood partitions, fixtures, and shelving units include Lee/Rowan Co., a St. Louis, Missouri, firm that employs 900. The company, whose 1992 sales were in the $70 million range, was purchased in 1993 by housewares giant Newell. Another leading company engaged in manufacturing metal partitions and fixtures is Knape & Vogt Manufacturing of Grand Rapids, Michigan. It is a publicly-traded company with annual sales of $123.4 million, but only part of that figure is from its metal shelving division; it also manufactures wood shelves and drawer slides. Schulte Corp. of Cincinnati, Ohio,

is best known as a primary supplier of epoxy-coated shelving units.

Employment in the metal partitions and fixtures industry remained steady over the 1970s. Data for 1977 showed 28,000 workers engaged in the industry, a number that remained unchanged in 1982. By 1987 the industry employed 33,500 people, but the recession and economic restructuring of the early 1990s accounted for a decrease in the industry's labor force to 31,000 in 1991. For the same year, companies in this category spent nearly $780 million in payroll costs. Almost two-thirds of workers in this industry were engaged in the production sector.

INDUSTRY INFORMATION SOURCES

Dykema, William N., "Successful Retailers Display High Shelf Respect," *Chain Store Age Executive,* October 1991.

Palmer, Jay, "On the Shelf No More? The Outlook Improves for Knape & Vogt," *Barron's,* January 13, 1992.

"Schulte Snares Spur Shelving Line Distribution," *HFD: The Home Furnishings Daily,* March 29, 1993.

"Shelf Makers Look to the '90s," *HFD: The Home Furnishings Daily,* December 12, 1988.

Stankevich, Debby Garbato. "Lee/Rowan Sees New Growth," *HFD: The Home Furnishings Daily,* September 20, 1993.

United States Census of Manufactures, 1992 Supplement. Washington, DC: U.S. Department of Commerce, 1992.

—Carol Brennan

SIC 2591

DRAPERY HARDWARE, WINDOW BLINDS AND SHADES

This category covers establishments primarily engaged in the manufacture of curtain and drapery rods, poles, and fixtures, venetian blinds, horizontal miniblinds, and vertical blinds in all materials except canvas. Establishments primarily engaged in manufacturing canvas window shades and awnings are classified in **SIC 2394: Canvas and Related Products.**

INDUSTRY SNAPSHOT

Companies engaged in the manufacture of drapery hardware and window coverings have witnessed an astounding demand for their wares since the 1980s, and have introduced many new types of products to satisfy consumer needs. However, U.S. manufacturers in this category face stiff competition from overseas companies that produce cheaper imitations for the consumer market.

According to 1992 sales figures, mini-blinds comprise 38 percent of window-covering sales in the United States, followed by vertical blinds at 24 percent. Drapery hardware sales comprise 17.7 percent of the market, with pleated shades making up an additional 17 percent of sales figures. Wood blinds round out the total at nearly two percent of sales. The value of shipments generated by this industry was $1.7 billion in 1991, a clear indication of the growth of the industry since value of shipments posted in 1977 was only $675 million. Correspondingly, the drapery hardware and window blinds industry employed 13,600 in 1977, but by 1991 the number of workers employed in the industry had increased over 27 percent to 17,300.

ORGANIZATION AND STRUCTURE

Many of the U.S. firms that manufacture and sell drapery hardware and window blinds are private companies, but some are subsidiaries of much larger home-furnishings conglomerates that are publicly-traded enterprises. Like other manufacturers, they are comprised of many specific divisions, but one of the largest concerns is in providing consumers with up-to-date and contemporary styles. For this reason research and development departments play an important role in companies engaged in manufacturing drapery hardware and window blinds. This division keeps an eye on general trends in consumer lifestyle patterns, home-furnishing expenditures, and overall color and pattern changes in the interior design industry. Design analysts in the research and development departments look for certain color groups and textures that they believe will appeal to the broadest range of consumers. For instance, in the 1980s dramatic changes in the American lifestyle and consumer spending patterns, with the burgeoning emphasis on high-tech products, refashioned the home environment. A new edginess to interior design was manifested in sharp angles and artificial colors such as mauve. A downturn in the economy in the late 1980s, combined with a growing awareness of the concept of the global village, brought a new palette of colors to the window coverings industry and encouraged the introduction of the wood mini-blind.

In the interior furnishings industry, window blinds fall under the category of home textiles, although they are not specifically textiles. Previously, curtains and drapes, geared to match furniture and bedspreads, were the dominant force in the category, but were replaced by the popularity of mini-blinds in the 1980s. Consumers switched from buying pinch-pleated draperies and curtains to mini-blinds accessorized with a "top treatment"—a swath of fabric that matches the bedspread or some other component of the interior. In the industry, mini-blinds, vertical blinds, and pleated shades were first known as "alternative window treatments," to differentiate them from fabric-based draperies and curtains. Yet by 1991 this "alternative" category achieved retail sales figures of $2.78 billion dollars.

Manufacturers of mini-blind products are divided over the two segments of the market, aluminum and vinyl. Vinyl blinds cost less to manufacture, do not rattle in the wind, and won't develop bend marks. Yet they are susceptible to flapping on windy days, let a good deal of light through even when completely closed, can become discolored, and have a tendency to lose shape over time. They are popular with consumers, however, because of low cost, range of standard sizes, relative ease of installation, and ultimate disposability. On the other hand, aluminum blinds are perceived as a much more durable investment. Heavier than vinyl, aluminum does not flap in the breeze, keeps out light more effectively, and its colors and finishes will last longer than plastic. Aluminum blinds may scratch a window, however, and can fall victim to dents and creases in its surface. Major manufacturers such as Hunter-Douglas and Levolor concentrate primarily on the custom-made aluminum blind market, and have left the vinyl blind market primarily to the cheap imports. However, some companies offer stock aluminum blinds available in retail outlets, and may also sell custom-made vinyl blinds.

Another large segment of the window coverings industry is newly geared to marketing pleated shades to replace standard mini-blinds and curtains. The pleated shades owe their development in part to new manufacturing processes that combine versatile fabrics in lightweight weaves to allow a great deal of light through, yet also possess insulating properties. The new processes have also allowed a variety of textures to be introduced. A leading brand in this new segment of the industry is Duette, a brand line manufactured by Hunter-Douglas. The product was introduced in 1985 and proved popular with consumers, in part because the pull cord could be hidden. The company has also introduced another version of the pleated shade under the brand name Silhouette. Wood blinds, with their natural appearance, also occupy a growing segment of the window covering market.

In the field of drapery hardware and window coverings, department stores are the primary retail outlets to consumers, led by the entrenched home-decorating departments at national chains such as J.C. Penney and

Sears. However, the larger stores are being jostled in the home-furnishings market by such specialty retailers as Bed Bath and Beyond. These smaller national outlets provide consumers with either in-stock or custom-made window coverings in a large variety of styles, along with accompanying hardware.

BACKGROUND AND DEVELOPMENT

Prior to the mini-blind-dominated era in interior window coverings, there was a relatively limited range of styles and options for consumers. Drapery hardware was relatively standardized and available in a narrow range of styles. Venetian blinds were originally made of wood, but later an aluminum version became ubiquitous. The companies that produced venetian blinds primarily sold them to institutions such as schools and offices. Most interior window treatments in kitchens, bathrooms, and bedrooms consisted of curtains made of a lightweight fabric with a pull-down vinyl shade spanning the window. In living rooms, heavy pinch-pleated draperies were the primary window coverings.

The popularity of the aluminum mini-blind helped fuel the tremendous growth of this sector of the consumer home-furnishings market. Later, vertical blinds and window shades newly developed from stronger, light-emitting materials were also introduced onto the market. However, in the late 1970s, Taiwan restructured its polyvinylchloride (PVC) manufacturing industry to mass-produce and import mini-blinds. This resulted in the flooding of the U.S. market with cheaper plastic imitations of aluminum blinds. Manufacturers responded by diversifying their aluminum lines into a greater selection of colors and finishes, producing a competing stock line of more affordable vinyl blinds, and keeping a strong foothold in the custom-made aluminum mini-blind market. This has proved to be a popular segment of the window coverings industry—consumers can take their window measurements to a retail outlet, sift through catalogs of styles, and in a few weeks have their custom-crafted aluminum blinds installed throughout their home. These custom-made products accounted for 80 percent of the domestic mini-blind market in the early 1990s.

The drapery hardware segment of the industry has made a concerted effort to come out from behind-the-scenes. When long, heavy, pinch-pleated draperies were in vogue for many years, the accompanying hardware was designed to stay hidden. The poles, rods, and tieback elements served a basic functional need and were correspondingly utilitarian in design. However, the emerging popularity of top treatments for windows—swaths of fabric that added a decorative element to the mini-blinded or pleated-shade window

below—paved the way for a new emphasis on drapery hardware. Sales figures for 1989 for drapery hardware reached $527 million and increased the next year, despite recessionary conditions, to $538 million. These products are generally manufactured from a variety of metals, including steel, bronze, and brass, but some companies offer poles and rods in numerous wood finishes. Consumers may purchase drapery hardware in a variety of novelty styles. Drapery hardware products are made available in both traditional and contemporary styles, and many now have removable elements that give them a greater versatility.

CURRENT CONDITIONS

The economic restructuring and recession of the late 1980s and early 1990s had a negative impact on the drapery hardware and window coverings industry. Sales dropped during these years and, as with other manufacturing industries, some budgetary restructuring and across-the-board layoffs took place.

The industry was also witness to changes in its overall corporate structure through acquisitions and mergers that took place during this period. Companies struggled to hold on to their segment of the consumer-durables market while also introducing products to fill new niches. Consumers became increasingly price-conscious and firms competed to offer the best dollar value among a range of similar products. Industry leaders began to introduce more upscale products, such as aluminum blinds with elegant finishes, that appealed to consumers yet were inexpensively priced.

INDUSTRY LEADERS

Many of the top U.S. companies engaged in the manufacture of drapery hardware and window coverings are major corporations. One of the largest is Hunter-Douglas, Inc. of Upper Saddle River, New Jersey. It is a private company founded in 1963 that employs 4500. Sales figures for 1992 were $600 million. Another corporate giant is the Newell Co., a major housewares conglomerate that sells window shades and drapery hardware under the brand name Window Furnishings. Based in Freeport, Illinois, the company traces its roots back to 1903 and reported annual sales of $1.451 billion in 1992 (a figure that represents the total for all of its corporate holdings, which include glassware, cookware, and hardware companies). In 1993 Newell acquired the Levolor Corp. of San Jose, California. Levolor was founded by the Lorentzen family in 1911, but in recent years its brand name became nearly synonymous with the mini-blind. At its peak, sales neared $300 million, and Levolor held onto a 40 percent share of the market. But during the 1980s, the company was beset by internal squabbling and the company suffered from this diversion. Instead of cultivating and maintaining valuable accounts with industry distributors, it instead concentrated on selling directly to the consumer and subsequently lost some major distributor accounts to more aggressive competitors. Sales declined, and in 1988 the company was sold to an investment firm for only $135 million.

Other leading companies in the window coverings manufacturing industry include Springs Industries, a Middleton, Wisconsin-based company, that reported sales of $250 million for 1992. Founded in 1938, it also exports its products overseas and provides jobs for 2400. Home Fashions, Inc. of Westminster, California, sells its products under the Del Mar brand name. The company employs 775 and sales figures for 1992 were $90 million for the privately-held firm. The leading manufacturer of drapery hardware is Kirsch, a company based in Sturgis, Michigan, followed by Graber Industries and Kenney Manufacturing.

WORK FORCE

The work force engaged in manufacturing drapery hardware and window coverings numbered 17,300 in 1991. The recession of the early 1990s had a negative impact on the drapery hardware and window coverings industry, as employment figures dropped precipitously from 19,000 in 1990, a decline of nearly ten percent. Among the 17,300 workers employed in 1991, 12,200 of the jobs were in the production sectors. Payroll figures for this industry were $341.6 million for the same year.

AMERICA AND THE WORLD

The relative ease with which cheap window coverings can be manufactured by overseas companies, primarily in Taiwan, and exported into the U.S. market has negatively impacted the window coverings segment of this industry. The domestic drapery hardware business, meanwhile, has been invaded by a leading European manufacturer, Blome. The German company launched some of its products on the U.S. market in 1991. The company has mainly distributed its products through intermediary outlets, but has plans to also market its wares in upscale department stores.

RESEARCH AND TECHNOLOGY

Industry critics of vinyl blinds, which are primarily exported from Taiwan, have decried their saturation in the U.S. market and charge that the imported products are not subject to the same lead-content restrictions as U.S. manufacturers. Critics charge that the

Taiwanese vinyl blinds are ecologically unsound, since they will eventually wind up in American landfills and take decades to disintegrate. Another problematic area for the window coverings industry has been the danger of the pull cords that raise and lower the blinds. Their looped construction has proven hazardous to both small pets and children over the years since the product's introduction on the market. A 1981 Consumer Product Safety Commission report found that the cords were the leading cause of accidental child-strangulation deaths. However, there was little reaction from the industry to modify the cords. Between the year of the report and 1993, 69 children died as a result of accidents involving mini-blind pulls. However, in 1993 one of the largest manufacturers of mini-blinds, Hunter-Douglas, entered into a venture with the baby-product giant Gerber. Hunter-Douglas began manufacturing a patented "Break-Thru Safety Tassel," which is a two-piece cord attachment designed to come apart at the slightest touch. Gerber began marketing the device under its own name along with its other child-safety items, but Hunter-Douglas also made it a standard feature of one of its major product lines.

INDUSTRY INFORMATION SOURCES

Bermingham, Geoffrey B., "Aluminum vs. Vinyl: Mini Blind Battle Rages On," *HFD: The Home Furnishings Daily,* August 24, 1992.

———, "Child-Safe Mini-Blind Cords," *HFD: The Home Furnishings Daily,* May 31, 1993.

———, "Drapery Hardware: Out of Hiding, Into the Light," *HFD: The Home Furnishings Daily,* December 16, 1991.

———, "Hard-Side Guys: Leading Suppliers of Alternative Window Fashions Cite the Challenges Facing Their Changing Industry," *HFD: The Home Furnishings Daily,* August 24, 1992.

———, "The Nature of the '90s'," *HFD: The Home Furnishings Daily,* March 16, 1992.

———, "Window Situation Cloudy: Industry Sectors Differ on the Role of Curtains and Draperies in the Market," *HFD: The Home Furnishings Daily,* September 27, 1993.

Byrne, Harlan S., "Newell Co.: It Is Adding Products, Slashing Costs," *Barron's,* April 12, 1993.

McNamara, Michael D., "Makers Set to Fuel Growth in 1990s," *HFD: The Home Furnishings Daily,* February 5, 1990.

Moody's Industrial Manual 1993, New York: Moody's Investors Service.

United States Census of Manufactures, 1992 Supplement, Washington, DC: U.S. Department of Commerce, 1992.

Wendlinger, Lisa D. "Curtain and Drapery Business: A Tough Sell," *HFD: The Home Furnishings Daily,* June 17, 1991.

—Carol Brennan

SIC 2599

FURNITURE AND FIXTURES, NOT ELSEWHERE CLASSIFIED

This classification covers establishments primarily engaged in manufacturing furniture and fixtures, not elsewhere classified, including hospital beds and furniture specially designed for use in restaurants, bars, cafeterias, bowling centers, and ships.

Unlike other segments of U.S. manufacturing, this miscellaneous furniture and fixtures industry remained relatively healthy throughout the economic downturns of the 1980s and 1990s. The flourishing service industries of eating establishments and medical facilities played an important role in its staying power. In the late 1980s nearly 1,600 companies were engaged in manufacturing furniture in this category. The industry employed 29,300 workers, with almost 75 percent of those jobs concentrated in the production sector. The value of shipments for the industry in 1991 totaled more than $2.4 billion, an increase of 30 percent over a five-year period.

Data from 1987 showed a large proportion of single-establishment types of ownership in the furniture and fixtures category. Only 101 of the 1,597 companies in this industry were part of a larger corporate parent. Interestingly, 254 of the companies were either individual proprietorships or partnerships, pointing to an industry concentration of small specialty firms. Only 352 of the firms involved in this niche industry employed 20 or more people. The firms in this category are products suppliers, which means they market their wares not to the public but rather to other companies or institutions. A company may produce only hospital beds, and sell its product to medical facilities across the country, or it may be the major regional supplier of bowling alley furniture.

The manufacturing of furniture and fixtures in this category primarily arose to fill specific needs within the service industry market. For instance, the rise of bowling as a recreational sport across the United States after World War II necessitated the construction of a plethora of alleys to satisfy a growing demand. This industry also filled the needs of the growing industrial economy of the United States. The factories and manufacturing plants that sprouted up all across the country needed specific interior furniture for a wide variety of purposes. Later, as orders for factory furniture declined due to the drop in overall manufacturing, the furniture and fixtures industry accommodated other segments of the economy. Hospital furniture manufacturing firms met the increased demand for new beds as medical facilities were built to serve more populous suburban communities. The growing consumer willingness to spend more entertainment dollars on dining out during the 1970s and 1980s fueled the construction of restaurants and the corresponding need for sturdy yet attractive furniture to fill the interiors.

Current Industry Status. The number of people employed in the furniture and fixtures industry has declined slightly in recent years. In 1990 the segment provided jobs for 31,900, but that number dropped marginally to 31,000 the following year. The value of shipments for the same period also decreased from $2.547 billion to $2.487 billion, but these diminutions were barometers of the recession of the early 1990s; many other segments of U.S. manufacturing showed a much more precipitous drop in both employment and sales. Industry leaders entering the mid-1990s included Kinetic Concepts Inc., Corber Corp., Kewaunee Scientific Corp., and Support System International Inc.

INDUSTRY INFORMATION SOURCES

United States Census of Manufactures, 1992 Supplement, Washington, DC: U.S. Department of Commerce, 1992.

—Carol Brennan

PAPER & ALLIED PRODUCTS

PULP MILLS

This category covers establishments primarily engaged in manufacturing pulp from wood or from other materials, such as rags, linters, wastepaper, and straw. Establishments engaged in integrating logging and pulp mill operations are classified according to the primary products shipped. Establishments engaged in integrated operations of producing pulp and manufacturing paper, paperboard, or products thereof are classified in **SIC 2621: Paper Mills** if primarily shipping paper or paper products; in **SIC 2631: Paperboard Mills** if primarily shipping paperboard or paperboard products; and in **SIC 2611: Pulp Mills** if primarily shipping pulp. Establishments primarily engaged in cutting pulpwood are classified in **SIC 2411: Logging.**

INDUSTRY SNAPSHOT

Pulp mills in the United States produce a wide variety of pulps for making paper and paperboard. Most of the pulp produced in the United States is chemical pulp, which is produced by a chemical digesting process that converts wood chips into pulp by chemically liberating the cellulose fibers from the lignin that hold them together in the wood. Mechanical pulps are made with large "grinders" which physically shred the wood pulp into individual fibers. Some processes combine elements of mechanical and chemical pulping.

After the wood chips are digested or ground, they are called wood pulp. This wood pulp is cleaned, screened and refined. If the pulp will be used for white

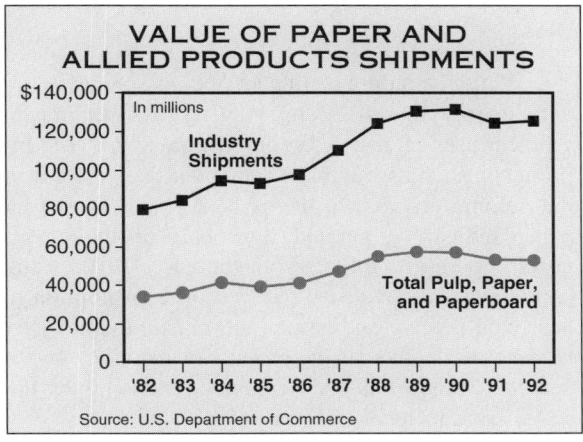

VALUE OF PAPER AND ALLIED PRODUCTS SHIPMENTS

Source: U.S. Department of Commerce

paper, it is bleached (otherwise the pulp retains its natural brown color). At this point, the pulp is ready to be used in papermaking. Various grades of pulp can be made from softwood trees such as southern pine, hardwood trees such as oak, or from other sources that include recovered paper, rags, or agricultural products such as cotton linters, kenaf, bagasse, or straw.

In 1993, there were approximately 203 wood pulp mills producing a variety of pulps for 547 U.S. paper mills. Most of this pulp was used in "integrated" pulp and paper mills, which means that the pulp mill and the paper mill were owned by the same company and operated in many cases at the same location. There were numerous smaller paper mills, however, that were not connected with a pulp mill; they purchased "market pulp" on the open market from other pulp producers. Some companies produced only market pulp; other companies sold the excess pulp that could not be used by their paper machines.

ORGANIZATION AND STRUCTURE

U.S. pulp mills maintain a dominant share of the U.S. market for pulp—over 90 percent—and are also very strong competitors in global markets. One reason for this market strength is good economic fundamentals: U.S. pulp mills have access to low cost and abundant raw materials, a highly trained work force, and they operate with world-class plants and equipment.

In most cases, pulp mills need to be located near their raw materials—trees or wastepaper—to minimize transportation costs. The United States has a very large growing stock of pulpwood in several areas: the Pacific Northwest, the upper Midwest, the northeast, and the southeast. This, combined with an efficient manufacturing base, makes the United States the low cost producer of many grades of pulp throughout the world.

While the pulping and papermaking processes are very energy intensive, the industry has become an efficient user of energy by burning its own waste by-products, such as tree bark and spent chemicals from the pulping process. In the early 1990s, the pulp and paper industry generated over half of the energy needed to run its mills. From the early 1970s to the early 1990s, the industry reduced oil consumption by nearly 66 percent and natural gas consumption by ten percent while increasing production capacity by 60 percent. Some mills even generate excess power and sell it back to local utilities.

Pulp mills and paper mills use a large amount of water from lakes, rivers, and in some cases oceans. They must reuse and/or clean all of this water before it is returned to the body of water from which it came. In the early years of the industry, pulp mills would discharge untreated waste (effluent) back into the receiving body of water. By the 1990s, however, the industry operated under strict water use regulations which required primary, secondary, and in some cases tertiary treatment of wastewater. Also, to cut down on treatment costs, mills are re-using a large portion of the water they use elsewhere in the pulping and papermaking process.

In the early 1990s, it took 60 percent less water to make a ton of paper than it did about two decades ago. The water that cannot be reused goes to large outdoor water treatment plants. The biochemical oxygen demand (BOD) of the treated water—a measure of environmental impact—has been reduced by 70 percent in 25 years, even though total paper production has gone up 50 percent.

Captive Pulp. The vast majority of pulp produced in the United States—about 85 percent—is "captive," in that it is used in an integrated pulp and paper operation and is not sold on the open market. Market pulp sold on domestic and foreign markets accounts for the remaining 15 percent of total U.S. pulp production. While captive pulp accounts for the majority of pulp used in the United States, much more information and documentation is available for market pulp since it is bought and sold publicly.

While wood pulp production has been expanding in recent years, the percentage of virgin wood fiber used in paper and board production in the United States and other countries has been steadily declining. Wood fiber, as a percentage of total global paper and board production, has dropped from about 75 percent in 1970 to less than 62 percent in 1992. It is projected to decline further to barely 60 percent by 1997.

This decline is explained by several trends. While virgin wood fiber has long been the fiber of choice in most advanced papermaking operations, it is coming under sustained challenge from other fiber sources. For example, the use of recovered (recycled) paper is increasing dramatically and is already displacing large amounts of virgin wood fiber in the pulping marketplace. The increased use of recovered paper is being driven by society's desire to reduce the amount of paper going to landfills. Cost has been cited as a factor in the move toward recycling, but in most grades the total cost of processing recycled fiber is no less than or is more expensive than virgin fiber.

North American paper producers have dramatically increased their use of recovered paper in recent years. The percentage of paper recycled in the United States has risen from about 30 percent in 1990 to 40 percent in 1993. The American Forest and Paper Association, the trade association that represents the paper industry, has announced a goal of recycling 50 percent of all paper produced by the year 2000.

Virgin wood fiber also faces a challenge from the growing use of mineral coatings and inert "fillers," mainly in printing and writing papers. Producers of these grades have nearly completed a long-term shift from acid pulp to alkaline pulp. One reason for this shift is that paper produced from acid pulp becomes brittle and breaks up over time, while alkaline papers tend to last for years. The main reason, however, is that alkaline papermaking tends to be less expensive since it permits greater use of fillers, such as calcium carbonate, that replace a percentage of the wood fiber in the finished paper. In U.S. printing and writing papers, such as copy paper, the amount of filler can be ten to 20 percent of the finished paper or higher. The cost of fillers is about one third that of wood pulp, so paper mills have a financial incentive to increase their use of fillers. Papermakers use filler not only to reduce the amount of wood fiber used, but also to increase the smoothness and opacity of their finished products. As techniques to use more filler are developed, wood pulp will be displaced.

While wood pulp's percentage of finished paper products will continue to decline, its use will still grow—at least slightly— as the entire market for paper expands. The United States production of wood pulp should rise a little over two percent per year for the next two decades worldwide. In the United States, wood pulp will probably grow more slowly since growth in recycled fiber will be strong. However, foreign markets will likely absorb an increasing amount of U.S. market pulp.

Chemical Pulp. Within the overall market for wood pulp, the use of chemical pulp—mostly kraft pulp, which is produced using the sulfate process—is increasing. In 1992, chemical pulp accounted for 69 percent of all market pulp produced throughout the world, up from 66 percent in 1970. This figure should reach 70 percent by 1997. In the United States, chemical pulp accounts for an even higher percentage of wood pulp capacity—80 percent. Semi-chemical pulp accounts for about 6.6 percent and mechanical pulp for about 10.3 percent, with other grades accounting for the remaining three percent. The trend toward greater use of chemical pulp is driven by the desire of papermakers for its higher strength characteristics, which are needed as papermakers begin to blend less costly and weaker mechanical pulps and recycled paper fibers into the "furnish" they use to make paper.

Kraft pulp was the primary product of the U.S. market wood pulp industry in the early 1990s. Kraft pulp includes bleached, partially bleached and unbleached softwood and hardwood pulp, and accounted for about 84 percent of total domestic market wood pulp capacity. As of 1993, bleached softwood kraft pulp was the largest market wood pulp grade, consisting of 49 percent of all U.S. capacity. Bleached hardwood kraft pulp was the second biggest category (33 percent). Dissolving pulp accounted for 14 percent of capacity, while unbleached kraft pulp and sulfite pulp accounted for about two percent each.

Overall, U.S. market wood pulp capacity is expected to fall about two percent between 1992 and 1996, from 10.74 million short tons to 10.56 million short tons. The main reason for this fall will be the explosive growth of recovered paper market pulp capacity. It is expected to quadruple during the same period, from 424,000 short tons in 1992 to 1.65 million short tons in 1996.

The United States has almost 30 percent of the world's capacity to produce paper and paperboard and more than one third of the world's capacity to produce wood pulp. As mentioned earlier, the majority of U.S. paper mills are integrated with "captive" pulp mills that do not sell pulp on the open market. Despite this fact, the United States is still the world's largest importer of wood pulp. In 1992, when world demand for market pulp reached 30.4 metric tons, the United States accounted for 17 percent of that year's deliveries.

BACKGROUND AND DEVELOPMENT

Before the U.S. Civil War, paper was made exclusively from rags in the United States and around the world. Rag collection for papermaking was a major part of the U.S. economy. However, as the demand for paper continued to increase, the demand for rags began to outstrip supply.

This changed between 1851 and 1918, when wood pulp was invented, developed, and industrialized. The Civil War created a huge demand for both paper and rags; this helped spur research into using the fiber from trees for papermaking. This time period saw the development and commercialization of all the major wood pulping processes, including groundwood, soda, sulphite and kraft (sulphate). Wood pulp quickly reduced the cost of papermaking, allowing the use of paper in new applications and new products.

Soda pulping was invented by Burgess and Watt in England and was patented in 1854 in the United States. Groundwood became established later, in the 1860s. The first chemical wood pulp was manufactured in 1864 in Manyunk, Pennsylvania, and the first kraft pulp mill came on line in 1909. Kraft pulping had been invented in 1884 by German chemist Carl Dahl using sodium sulfate as the pulping agent. The pulp produced a strong brown paper, which was then described with the German word for strong: kraft.

While other materials were used for pulping— including bagasse cactus, cudweed, straw, cornstalks and even cow dung—wood pulp quickly became the preferred source of pulp. By the 1870s, pulp mills were springing up in heavily forested areas such as New York, Massachusetts, Michigan, Ohio, and Wisconsin. These areas continued to develop as key pulp and paper regions throughout the early 20th century and most remained so in the early 1990s.

The science of pulping continued to develop along with the growth of papermaking. Major pulping milestones included the invention of the recovery boiler, in which spent pulping chemicals are burned. This process recovers the energy in the chemicals and the chemicals themselves, which can then be reused. Another milestone was the development of the continuous digester, which replaced the slower batch digesting process.

More recently, in the 1980s, entire pulp mills were rebuilt to increase capacity and quality. Popular additions included new chip screening, handling and storage systems, new digester cooking controls, new washing systems, more screening and cleaning, new bleaching systems emphasizing oxygen, and better mixing. Pulp and paper mills also took advantage of process control to more closely control the process and produce better quality products.

CURRENT CONDITIONS

There were two major conditions that characterized the pulp industry in the early to mid-1990s—low pulp prices and high environmental demands. After factoring out inflation, the price of pulp in 1993 was the lowest it had been in many decades. At the same time, many pulping operations were anticipating heavy spending on new equipment and technology throughout the 1990s to meet increasingly stringent environmental regulations.

Water Regulations. The environmental pressure on pulp mills is in three areas: water regulations, recycling, and timber harvesting. The first area centers on the toxic chemical dioxin, which was discovered in extremely small amounts in pulp mill water-borne effluent in the mid-1980s. Despite the lack of hard evidence that dioxin in extremely minute quantities poses a human health risk, the paper industry voluntarily spent over one billion dollars to reduce dioxin discharges by over 75 percent by the early 1990s.

In November of 1993 the Environmental Protection Agency (EPA) proposed new regulations further restricting dioxin emissions by pulp mills, among other toxic chemicals. These new regulations had their beginning in the late 1980s, when the EPA formed a "pulp and paper cluster group" to coordinate regulatory actions involving the pulp and paper industry. The EPA wanted to use the cluster group to bring a more rational, integrated approach to rule making in the paper industry and other regulated industries.

The EPA's pulp and paper cluster group focused on two major rule making efforts. The first involved issuing revised effluent guidelines mandated by the Clean Water Act and required by a consent decree signed by the EPA after being sued by environmental groups over dioxin discharges from pulp mills. The second area involved defining maximum achievable control technology (MACT) emissions standards for pulp and paper mills, which was required under the Clean Air Act Amendments of 1990.

The Clean Air Act Amendments dramatically changed the type and amount of permitted emissions by existing sources and new sources. Based on emissions such as ozone, carbon monoxide, and particulates, areas of the country can be classified as "nonattainment areas." If pulp and paper mills happen to be in one of these areas they, like other industries, can be subject to severe restrictions.

The costs for pulp mills to comply with the Clean Air Act, while extensive, pale in comparison with the new water rules, which were issued in November, 1993. The EPA is required to put the final regulations into effect by April of 1995. The paper industry then has up to three years to comply with the new regulations.

The Clean Water Act also requires the EPA to periodically revise and update effluent limitation guidelines for various industry groups. These guidelines impose limitations on the types and volume of pollutants that may be discharged by industrial sources either into receiving waters in the United States or into municipal wastewater treatment systems.

The statute provides different standards depending on how a pollutant is categorized. Toxic pollutants (such as dioxin) and non-conventional pollutants (such as color) require treatment with the "best available technology" (BAT), while conventional pollutants such as BOD require the use of best conventional technology (BCT).

The new BAT standards for the relatively few toxic and non-conventional pollutants found in pulp and paper industry wastewater were contained in the November, 1993 proposal. As issued, the proposed limits would effectively require bleached kraft paper grade pulp mills to install oxygen delignification systems and fully substitute chlorine dioxide for chlorine in the bleaching process to reduce dioxin, furans, and 12 specified chlorinated organic compounds below measurable levels. Adsorbable organic halides (AOX) would be limited to 0.16 kg per ton of pulp produced. (AOX is a measure of pollutants, not a pollutant itself.) The median discharge of AOX in U.S. bleach kraft mills in 1993 was about 1.1 kg per ton. The proposed limit of AOX is so low that even the installation of oxygen delignification may not enable all mills to reach the limit.

According to the EPA, implementation of the proposed water regulations would cost the paper industry four billion dollars in capital expenditures and $407 million in increased operating and maintenance costs. The total annualized cost of implementing the regulation would then be $890 million. The EPA maintains that the new plan would result in the closure of 11 to 14 pulp mills and would cost 2,800 to 11,000 workers their jobs.

According to the American Forest and Paper Association (AFPA), the new limits would cost the industry far more in capital expenditures—ten billion dollars—and about $300 million in increased operating and maintenance costs. The total annualized cost of these regulations would then be $1.2 billion. The AFPA says the new regulations would cause the closure of 30 to 33 pulp mills and the loss of 22,000 jobs. These expenditures will be an enormous burden for an industry that, in the mid-1990s, was still struggling with low pulp prices and attempting to return to profitability. The long term effect of these regulations on the global competitiveness of U.S. pulp mills remains to be seen.

Recycling. The second major environmental trend affecting the pulping industry is recycling. Public interest in paper recycling began to build in the late 1980s and hit a crescendo in the early 1990s, when many major media outlets discussed the "landfill crisis." The common element in much of this coverage was that the United States was running out of landfill space and had to reduce its production of household and industrial waste. Some recent studies have shown the landfill crisis to be highly overstated, and several large, technologically advanced landfills should be able to accommodate the nation's trash for many years.

Nonetheless, the push for recycling—primarily through federal and state legislation—continues and paper companies are responding with a wide variety of new recycled grades. Much of the new pulping capacity being built or planned uses wastepaper instead of virgin fiber as its raw material. This change will have a major impact on traditional pulping of wood fiber.

Much of the impetus for recycling comes from government. There are probably thousands of local, state and federal laws that either establish voluntary targets for paper recycling or mandate specific amounts of recycled paper to be used or produced by certain dates. Many of these laws specify precise levels of "postconsumer" content (paper that has been used and discarded by a consumer) and restrict the amount of "preconsumer" wastepaper that can be used. Examples of preconsumer wastepaper might include trimmings from the printing or papermaking process,

unsalable newspapers, or overprints of magazines. There is, however, considerable disagreement over where the line should be drawn between postconsumer and preconsumer.

Paper companies also face other recycling hurdles, including: regulations on companies that use "green labeling" product claims; limits on permissible types of packaging; guidelines and strict requirements on secondary fiber content; procurement preferences for certain kinds of recycled paper; and surcharges on paper products not meeting certain recycled standards. Consumers also face legal requirements for collection and separation of waste paper. In many areas, both consumers and businesses are subject to outright bans on disposal of paper products.

Much of the legislative activity on recycling started in 1988, when the EPA established guidelines for federal purchases of recycled paper. The EPA's guidelines required federal agencies to give purchasing preference to recycled paper whenever possible and established specific content rules defining recycled paper.

These guidelines were criticized by environmental groups and other parties for not requiring more recycled content. Many states passed laws requiring higher levels of paper recycling. In 1993, President Clinton signed an executive order toughening the federal recycling preference policy. The executive order specified that federal agencies must purchase uncoated printing and writing papers with at least 20 percent postconsumer content beginning December 31, 1994. The percentage increases to 30 percent on December 31, 1998.

These regulations are significant for pulp producers because they must manufacture the recycled pulp to be used in making the paper that meets the specifications. For uncoated specialty papers, the content requirement is 50 percent recovered materials, including 20 percent postconsumer materials by the end of 1994, increasing to 30 percent by the end of 1998. As used here, the term recycled material is synonymous with the term wastepaper used in the EPA's paper procurement guidelines; it includes postconsumer and certain preconsumer materials. The order applies only to uncoated papers, except for carbonless paper, and agencies are instructed to begin buying paper with some level of postconsumer content immediately. The executive order also requires the EPA to propose comprehensive procurement guidelines by April 18, 1994.

The executive order applies only to uncoated paper purchased by the executive branch and federal agencies. In the early 1990s, federal government purchases of printing and writing paper accounted for less than two percent of the total market for this segment. However, many state and local governments and private businesses are expected to follow the executive order. New York City issued a nearly identical edict a week after President Clinton signed the federal order.

While paper recycling is an important part of waste minimization, it is only part of what is needed to reduce the generation of solid waste. It should also be noted that recycling itself generates a considerable waste stream. In recycled newsprint pulp mills, for example, only 85 percent of incoming newsprint is usable as fiber. The rest is unusable sludge that must be cleaned out of the process and then burned or placed in landfills. In some recycled grades, sludge can be up to 50 percent of the incoming waste paper. Some large paper mills make up to 2,500 tons per day of paper, and when they use recycled fiber they will generate enormous amounts of sludge.

Timber Harvesting. The third major environmental challenge facing pulp mills in the 1990s is timber harvesting, which is used to create lumber products as well as pulpwood. Access to pulpwood is vital for all virgin wood pulp mills, but that access has been severely restricted in some areas—most notably the Pacific Northwest. Court decisions in the early 1990s reduced harvesting drastically in many national forests and other federal areas in the northwest. Through the Endangered Species Act, environmental groups filed successful lawsuits restricting harvesting in order to protect the Northern Spotted Owl, among other species. While the Clinton administration attempted to broker a compromise between timber interests and environmentalists in 1993, harvests in 1993 were at one sixth of those in the 1980s.

This situation has led some pulp mills to close and others to seek raw materials from different sources, such as recycled paper and foreign wood chips. The long term effects are likely to permanently reduce tree harvesting and pulping in the Pacific Northwest, and pulp producers in foreign countries and the Southern United States are likely to take up the lost volume.

Forest products companies and pulp and paper companies around the country still face pressure from environmental groups and government bodies to change their harvesting practices. Many groups want to eliminate clear cutting, which the industry argues is the most efficient harvesting method and environmentally sustainable, provided that the clear cut is replanted. In the early 1990s, the industry planted more trees than it cuts down. In 1992, over three million acres of forestland were planted with nearly three billion seedlings. The net effect of tree planting on

government, corporate and private land is that the net amount of forested land in the United States is actually increasing. From the early 1980s to the early 1990s, forest growth has exceeded the volume of trees cut or burned in forest fires. From the early 1970s to the early 1990s, the number of trees growing in the United States increased by 20 percent.

Low Profits. Aside from environmental challenges, in the early to mid-1990s pulp mills faced the prospect of low profits or losses due to a major collapse in prices. This collapse was caused by stagnating demand and a huge oversupply of pulp. In the late 1980s, pulp prices reached record highs and pulp producers were reaping record profits. A large share of these profits were reinvested in new capacity. When the U.S. economy went into recession from 1989 to 1990, much of this new pulp capacity was coming on line. By 1992, the average price for pulp in real dollars had reached the lowest point in decades. The increased use of recovered paper, a large excess of global pulping capacity, higher manufacturer inventory levels, and a "no-growth" global market for paper and board conspired to drive prices for Northern bleached softwood kraft (NBSK), a benchmark wood pulp grade, from $830 per metric ton in the first quarter of 1990 to $500 per metric ton by the end of 1991. In spot markets for pulp—sales not tied to long term contracts—some pulp prices plunged below $400 per ton and even below $300 a ton in some areas.

Despite the low prices, U.S. market pulp mills operated at 94 percent of capacity during the first six months of 1992, up from 89 percent for the same period in 1991. As a result of overcapacity and low prices, U.S. wood pulp capacity is expected to grow only 0.6 percent between 1994 and 1996, compared to annual growth of 1.7 percent between 1982 and 1992.

INDUSTRY LEADERS

In 1992, Atlanta-based Georgia-Pacific Corp. was the world's second largest paper company and the leader in the production of market pulp. It was the U.S. leader in the manufacturing of building products as well. Georgia-Pacific Corp. also produced the most printing and writing papers, was number two in the production of containerboard, and was the fifth largest U.S. tissue maker.

Primarily known as a producer of food and health and beauty aid products, Procter & Gamble Company (P&G), Cincinnati, was also the inventor of the disposable diaper market and a major producer of such paper products as towels and tissues. In 1992, P&G's pulp, paper and diaper product sales were an estimated $6.7 billion. While the company was formerly a major pulp producer, it sold these operations in 1992 to Weyerhaeuser Company. The company, however, maintained a strong global presence in paper products, including the market for disposable diapers.

A major manufacturer of white paper for business communications, printing, publication and newspaper applications, Stamford, Connecticut-based Champion International Corp. owned 6.1 million acres of U.S. timberland in 1992, making it one of America's largest private landowners. It was also the largest U.S. producer of lightweight publication papers and a leading producer of paperboard beverage containers, such as milk cartons. Champion's total sales of pulp and paper were up five percent in 1992.

Like other paper producers, Champion faced worldwide overcapacity and low prices for pulp and paper grades in the early 1990s. In 1992, selected grades of white paper hit their lowest price levels in more than a decade. Despite the recession, Champion embarked on a $5.5 billion capital spending program in the early 1990s, which was mostly completed at the end of 1993. Champion had 1992 sales of $4.93 billion.

Philadelphia-based Scott Paper Company was the first U.S. company to market toilet paper. In 1992, it was the world's leading producer of paper towel and tissue products, and had sales of $4.89 billion. Scott Paper produced 80 percent of its own pulp from virgin fiber and recycled paper. Like other producers, Scott began the 1990s facing weak markets for consumer tissue and paper markets. The coated paper market declined and strong competition from foreign producers, primarily in Scandinavia and Europe, helped reduce profits. In the early 1990s, Scott adopted a major cost cutting program, laying off close to 5,000 workers and selling non-core businesses such as its foodservice container and bulk nonwovens businesses.

WORK FORCE

Total employment in the pulp, paper and converting industries was about 627,000 in 1992. The level of employment remained steady during the past five years despite large capacity increases. Employee wage increases remained at or below the inflation rate in the early 1990s, averaging about 2.5 percent. These increases were far below the average 7.5 percent annual increases recorded during the period from 1975 to 1985.

Like other manufacturing industries, the paper industry employs many unionized workers. However, the heaviest concentrations of union employees are in older mills which were organized years ago. Almost all

new pulp and paper mills are non-union operations, including mills constructed by companies with unionized mills in other locations. In general, the wages and benefits provided by non-union mills are comparable to unionized mills.

There has been relative labor peace in the paper industry during the 1980s and early 1990s. In exchange for salary increases, management was able to obtain work rules changes that allowed workers to perform more jobs in the mill and eliminate pay differentials for Sunday and holiday pay. One dramatic strike in the 1980s ended in failure when unionized workers at International Paper's mill in Jay, Maine, were permanently replaced by new workers. Only a handful of the original workers regained their jobs. Since that strike, there have been no major work stoppages in the paper industry.

AMERICA AND THE WORLD

Market pulp is a truly global commodity, with prices changing quickly in response to capacity changes, inventory levels, and purchase levels. While market pulp is produced in about 25 countries, more than two thirds of world output comes from five northern countries: the United States, Canada, Sweden, Finland, and Norway.

Southern producers, however, are growing fast. New, technologically advanced market pulp mills have been built in Brazil, Chile, Argentina, Portugal, and Spain. Many of these mills include North American pulp and paper companies as investors. One major advantage of mills in South America is access to incredibly fast-growing pulpwood trees, such as eucalyptus and radiata pine species. These trees reach pulping maturity in about seven years or less, compared to 30 years in some northern countries. Other advantages of these new market pulp mills include lower operating costs, lower labor costs, and less costly environmental regulation. Established pulp producers will have to carefully control costs and increase productivity in order to compete with these new market factors.

Increased Foreign Demand. In the early 1990s, the U.S. market pulp industry grew in volume despite a lingering recession, flat or declining domestic markets, growing use of secondary fiber, and sluggish growth in domestic paper and board production. Increased foreign demand was the main reason. Market pulp shipments by the U.S. market pulp industry increased about eight percent, from 8.1 million metric tons in 1991 to almost 8.8 million metric tons in 1992. Cost advantages, the low value of the U.S. dollar compared to other currencies, and the high quality of U.S. pulp spurred strong foreign demand in Europe, Asia, and

Latin America. However, U.S. producers still struggled to make even minimal profits from their operations due to the price collapse of the early 1990s.

Despite sluggish markets throughout the world in the early to mid-1990s, the United States is expected to remain a strong global market pulp competitor throughout the decade. The U.S. market pulp industry should increase the volume of its pulp shipments about three percent per year through 1997, when the value of foreign pulp shipments is expected to be nearly 75 percent of all market pulp produced in the United States.

The exchange rate was and is one of the main reasons U.S. market pulp producers are so competitive worldwide. Finland and Sweden sought to counter this advantage by devaluing their currencies. In 1992, for example, the Finnish mark was devalued nearly 30 percent. Nonetheless, U.S. market pulp producers increased foreign sales dramatically in the early 1990s. Other factors favoring U.S. producers in the world market included lower pulp prices, abundant domestic raw material, and a small increase in global pulp demand.

The main market pulp grade traded by U.S. manufacturers is bleached and semi-bleached kraft pulp, accounting for over 78 percent of all U.S. pulp exports and 84 percent of U.S. pulp imports in 1992. U.S. market pulp exports grew to 6.2 million metric tons in 1992, up eight percent from 5.75 million metric tons the year earlier. Lower prices depressed the value of shipments, though, which increased just six percent. Japan, Italy, and South Korea were the three largest U.S market pulp customers.

Despite producing and exporting large volumes of market pulp, the U.S. pulp and paper industry still imports a large amount of the commodity. In 1992, U.S. market pulp imports increased to 4.7 million metric tons, a three percent increase from the 1991 total of 4.5 million metric tons. These imports accounted for 7.5 percent of total U.S. wood pulp consumption. Prices of imported pulp continued to decline sharply in the first six months of 1992, depressing the value of pulp imports by nearly ten percent, from $2.1 billion to $1.9 billion. Canada was by far the leading U.S. supplier, accounting for 84.5 percent of the total.

While domestic producers' share of the U.S. market slipped from 45 percent in 1991 to 43 percent in 1992, the Canadian share picked up one percentage point—from 45 percent in 1991 to 46 percent in 1992—making it the largest supplier to the U.S. pulp market. Meanwhile, Brazil also increased its share by one percentage point—from eight percent in 1991 to

nine percent the following year—reflecting the increasing proportion of bleached hardwood market pulp imported by U.S. companies. Chile, the Nordic countries, Spain, and Portugal each held about a one percent share of the U.S. market in both years.

Reasons To Import. In 1992, U.S. pulp mills had the capacity to produce 8.4 million metric tons of chemical paper grade market pulp, but domestic market pulp customers only used about 4.4 million metric tons. Even though the United States has far more market pulp capacity than it uses, U.S. paper producers still import market pulp in order to exploit the different properties of foreign market pulp. The domestic market pulp industry is largely based on southern pine and hardwood, and many U.S. mills prefer the special properties of other grades, such as NBSK, produced in Canada, and eucalyptus pulp produced in countries like Brazil. At the same time, a large number of foreign paper mills desire the southern pine and hardwood market pulp produced by U.S. market pulp mills. Between 1988 and 1992, over 80 percent of the new pulp brought on line by U.S. market pulp mills was exported.

RESEARCH AND TECHNOLOGY

Pulping processes, both chemical and mechanical, will see continued improvement in research and technology. Pulp mills will focus on greater recovery of energy, which can then be used in other mill processes. This will be essential to the future profitability of many mills facing competition from mills with lower cost structures. Energy is already a major cost for the pulp and paper industry, which is one of the largest industrial users of electricity. Other areas of improvement include: the use of additives to speed up the chemical digesting process to increase fiber yields; new technical and environmental processes to reduce air and water pollution; and increased process control, monitoring and automation. Similar measures to keep costs down and productivity high will be needed for the industry to remain competitive and expand its market share in world pulp consuming markets.

With more and more regulatory attention focused on pulp mill emissions, there has been more research devoted to the "effluent free" mill, also called the "closed mill." In theory, the closed mill perfectly balances all the "inputs and outputs" to the pulping and papermaking process, so that the mill reuses, recycles, or cleans all waste materials. This would mean that the mill produces no air or water pollution.

Widely regarded as impossible just a decade ago, this prospect appears to be feasible provided that current technology continues to develop and the cost of implementation decreases. For example, the Institute of Paper Science and Technology has been directed by its member companies to increase its research efforts on how heat and contaminants build up in closed pulping and papermaking systems; where the optimum ''purge'' points are in the process; and how to deal with the increased metal corrosion in closed systems. Many industry experts consider the truly closed mill to be a decade or two away, but it may be much closer than once thought.

Sweeping Changes. Other areas of interest include the bleaching of chemical pulping, which is in turmoil as pulp mills race to meet new EPA regulations. In a very short time—before the turn of the century—virgin pulp mills will have to implement sweeping changes in order to comply with new government regulations. This will require more research in using relatively new techniques such as oxygen delignification and ozone bleaching. Much of the research in ozone bleaching will focus on which of two processes—high consistency ozone or medium consistency ozone—produces optimum results.

Research will also focus on the use of ozone for bleaching recycled pulp. Much of the research will focus on the ability of ozone to destroy dyes—particularly fluorescent dyes—present in recycled paper and brighten the pulp so that the recycled fiber can be used to make food grade packaging, which must meet strict Food and Drug Administration rules.

One other major research area affecting pulp mills is in high yield forestry. The industry needs to reduce the time it takes to produce a mature pulpwood tree from 28 years to about seven or eight years. There are two reasons for this. One is to compete with pulpwood from countries such as Brazil, which today can produce a mature pulpwood tree in seven years. The other is to reduce the amount of forestland used for harvesting trees. There is a great deal of pressure on the pulp industry to minimize its harvesting operations, and if it can produce the same amount of pulpwood from a smaller amount of land, it may mollify some of its critics. However, this will require major investment in plant biology and other high-tech genetic research. This area in particular will require more extensive networking between the pulp and paper companies, research institutions and government agencies.

INDUSTRY INFORMATION SOURCES

Biermann, Christopher J., *Essentials of Pulping and Papermaking,* San Diego: Academic Press, 1993.

Hoover's Handbook of American Business 1993, Austin, TX: Reference Press, 1992.

Kirk, Bruce, *Paper & Forest Products,* New York: S.G. Warburg, October 1993.

Paper: Linking People and Nature, Washington, D.C.: American Forest & Paper Association, 1992.

Paper, Paperboard, Pulp Capacity and Fiber Consumption, Washington: American Forest & Paper Association, 1993.

Smook, Gary A., *Handbook of Pulp & Paper Terminology: A Guide to Industrial and Technological Usage,* Bellingham, Washington: Angus Wilde Publications, 1990.

Thesaurus of Pulp and Paper Terminology, Atlanta, Georgia: Institute of Paper Science and Technology, 1991.

U.S. Industrial Outlook 1993, Washington: U.S. Department of Commerce, 1993.

''Vision 300: A Celebration of American Papermaking,'' *pima,* January 1991.

Wright, Helena, *300 Years of American Papermaking,* Washington: Smithsonian Institution, 1991.

—Alan Rooks

SIC 2621

PAPER MILLS

This category covers establishments primarily engaged in manufacturing paper from wood pulp, wastepaper, and other fiber pulp, and which may also manufacture converted paper products. Establishments primarily engaged in integrated pulping and papermaking are included in this industry if primarily shipping paper or paper products.

INDUSTRY SNAPSHOT

The U.S. paper industry is one of the few ''smokestack'' industries that remains prosperous and relatively unscathed by foreign competition. Nearly 550 U.S. paper and paperboard mills produce the vast majority of paper consumed in the United States. In 1993, a total of 1,216 paper machines were used to produce all U.S.-made paper, while just 75 paperboard machines produced all U.S. paperboard. Taken as a whole, the U.S. pulp, paper and converted paper products industry is the eighth largest U.S. manufacturing industry in dollar sales. While imports—mostly from Canada—account for about ten percent of the paper consumed each year in the United States, domestic manufacturers dominate most segments of the industry.

While paper mills are separate from pulp mills in the Standard Industrial Codes, the two are, in reality, directly connected. About 70 percent of all paper is produced at mills that are ''integrated'' with a pulp mill at the same site, both of which are typically owned by the same company. Almost all high volume ''commodity'' paper and paperboard grades—such as newsprint, uncoated freesheet, and linerboard—are produced in this fashion. Some smaller paper mills producing specialty grades may not be connected with a pulp mill. They procure pulp from other mills owned by the same company or buy ''market pulp'' produced by other companies.

The U.S. pulp and paper industry employs about 240,000 people, and is by far the world's largest manufacturer of pulp, paper and paperboard. The United States produced 83 million tons of paper and paperboard in 1993, about a third of all the paper made in the world.

While papermaking is a very energy intensive industry—being the third largest U.S. industrial consumer of energy—the pulp and paper industry itself produces 56 percent of the energy it uses through cogeneration and burning of waste fuels, such as bark and spent pulping chemicals.

Converters of paper products, which are often owned by paper companies, add value to paper and distribute their products to consumers and industrial users. This sector is more widely distributed and includes firms that are directly integrated with paper manufacturers as well as firms that purchase paper, paperboard, and plastic film from manufacturers. Converters transform these materials into thousands of different finished products. The largest number of converters are fully independent operations. However, the converters that are directly owned by or connected to paper and board manufacturers tend to be very large and account for a disproportionate percentage of total industry sales.

ORGANIZATION AND STRUCTURE

Papermaking starts where the pulping process leaves off. The first step in papermaking is when the pulp is piped to the headbox of the paper machine. At this point the pulp—now called the furnish—is 99 percent water and one percent fiber. At the headbox, the pulp is laid onto an endless mesh belt made of plastic, which is called a wire or a forming fabric. This wire can be as wide as 33 feet. As the water drains out, the fibers bond to each other and form a strong web. This web is taken off the wire by a series of rolls and put into a press section, where more water is squeezed or vacuumed out of the web. Then the web enters a long series of dryer rolls which are heated by steam. As the web comes in contact with these rolls, the water flashes off. By the time it leaves the dryers, the web is

three to four percent water. After the paper is wound on a reel at the end of the paper machine, many things can happen, depending on the grade. It can be slitted and shipped as a large roll, or converted into paper products at the same location.

Paper mills are organized by the type of paper they produce. For example, some paper mills produce only printing and writing paper, while others produce newsprint. Many paper mills produce ''white'' paper, in which brown wood pulp is bleached to remove color and other impurities. Many paperboard mills, which are discussed in **SIC 2631: Paperboard Mills,** manufacture unbleached ''brown grades'' of paperboard, some of which are used for making corrugated shipping containers. However, some paperboard mills produce ''white'' products, such as the bleached paperboard used to make folding cartons for products such as breakfast cereal boxes. And some paper mills produce unbleached brown paper for products such as grocery sacks.

Financial Structure. The paper industry is the most capital intensive of all basic U.S. manufacturing industries, requiring nearly continuous major investments for plant and equipment. It ranks first or second among all industries in capital expenditures, depending on what calculations are used. This has led major paper companies to invest in enormous, high speed machines that can use economies of scale to produce paper at the lowest possible cost.

After paper companies enjoyed record profits in the late 1980s, the early 1990s saw a dramatic drop in paper prices and very difficult financial circumstances for many paper companies. Prices for most paper products started to drop in mid-1989 and remained low well into the 1990s. Despite low prices being paid for paper, many paper companies had embarked on major capital projects to build new paper machines and expand existing units. The twin conditions of new capacity coming on line and soft demand conspired to keep prices low even when demand began to recover in the mid-1990s.

This business cycle has plagued the paper industry for years. Plans for big greenfield (new) mills and machine additions are usually made in the middle of an economic recovery, when paper company profits are rising. These projects involve complicated engineering and take about three to four years to complete. This means new or expanded mills tend to come on line in the middle of a recession, which is what happened in the early 1990s.

After a burst of new mills and paper machines in the early 1990s, the mid-1990s saw very low growth in papermaking capacity. Capacity additions from 1994 to 1996 were expected to average 1.9 percent a year, well under the 1982 to 1992 annual rate of 2.3 percent. The economic recovery of the early 1990s was anemic, which hurt paper companies further. The slow growth environment barely covered the incremental capacity increases that come from routine efficiency improvements made on paper machines. The faster speeds and reduced downtime that result from these projects typically increase capacity by one or two percent each year.

Paper companies also faced an added problem in the early 1990s: low inflation. While there was a gradual upturn in orders in the early to mid-1990s, it was much harder for paper companies to raise prices than in past upturns. Since they were aware of the unusually low U.S. inflation rate, customers tended to resist price increases. For example, during the recession of 1981 and 1982, inflation was over nine percent. Even in 1989 and 1990, inflation was as high as five percent. By 1992, however, inflation had dropped to about three percent. Paper companies had to be very cautious with price increases in this relatively non-inflationary climate.

The financial structure of the paper industry in the 1990s was also undergoing a major structural change that will affect the industry for years to come. In the 1982 recession, the paper industry's main problem was soft demand. In the early to mid-1990s, demand recovered but supply was too high. This was the result of several factors.

In 1992, pulp and paper companies produced about 40 percent more tonnage with four percent *fewer* employees than in 1982. This was caused directly by paper companies' huge investment in high capacity, heavily automated machines. For example, in 1980 there were three uncoated free sheet machines producing more than 150,000 tons per year. In 1992, there were 15. These large investments, however, created high fixed costs for paper companies. The expense of building and maintaining plants and equipment have become a much greater percentage of a paper company's total costs, while labor has become a lower percentage of costs. Because huge, automated mills need fewer people to run them, paper companies cannot adjust to lower demand by laying people off and taking capacity out for short periods.

Most paper companies now run their operations at full capacity no matter what the market is doing—not only their paper machines, but even their finishing and converting operations. At one time, finishing was labor intensive and paper companies could control costs with a reduced work force. Today, even if demand is slack, operating rates stay high—which means pricing becomes more volatile. A growing market can solve some of these problems, but this underlying change will mean that pricing may remain volatile and that smaller mills will simply be unable to compete.

BACKGROUND AND DEVELOPMENT

American papermaking began just over 300 years ago in Philadelphia. In September of 1690, an entrepreneur named William Bradford—a recent English immigrant—built the first American paper mill on the shore of Wissahickon Creek in Philadelphia. At the time, paper manufacturing had not yet become an important part of the colonial economy. The small amount of paper consumed in the Colonies was produced in Holland and France.

However, economic growth in the Colonies would soon create a booming market for paper. Bradford and other papermakers were soon ready to produce products for this market. Bradford built his mill with the assistance of William Rittenhouse, an immigrant from Holland, and other financial backers. The mill produced about 20 pounds of pulp, paper and board a day. While at the time there was some mechanization of papermaking, it was largely a "handmade" process.

After 1690, the population of the American colonies grew quickly and so did the number of U.S. paper mills. By the time of the American Revolution—in which printed materials played a key role—there were more than 45 mills producing about 300 tons of paper per year. This production was used by more than 50 printers throughout the new nation.

At the beginning of the 1800s, an event occurred that would revolutionize the paper industry throughout the world. A Frenchman, Louis-Nicolas Robert, invented a machine to produce paper. Eventually, the machine patents were purchased by two English papermakers, the brothers Henry and Sealy Fourdrinier. After modification, the fourdrinier machine began to catch on in England, and it later was produced in the United States as well. The name "fourdrinier" is still used today to describe certain paper machines. The development of the paper machine changed what had been a lengthy and time consuming handmade "art" into a manufacturing process.

The other event that forever changed papermaking occurred in the middle of the century. After 1851, the preferred fiber source for papermaking began to change from old rags to wood pulp. This event, along with the invention of the paper machine, in effect created the modern paper industry (see "Background and Development," **SIC 2611: Pulp Mills**). The size and speed of paper machines increased rapidly between 1850 and 1916. Paper use was booming by 1889, when the annual U.S. production of paper reached one million tons. This figure doubled in the next ten years.

At the end of World War I, the United States began a period of rapid economic growth and the paper industry grew along with the general economy. Several new associations, including the Paper Industry Management Association and the Technical Association of the Pulp and Paper Industry were founded and developed during this time. Paper containers and packaging, a growing use of corrugated medium and linerboard to make shipping boxes, and a host of new products—such as tissues and sanitary napkins—all emerged as major trends in the post-war era. It was during this time that Canadian mills became dominant in newsprint manufacture, producing the majority of American newsprint. It is only recently that U.S. manufacturers have produced the majority of newsprint consumed in the United States.

Southern Growth. It was also during this period that the Pacific Northwest became a major pulp producer. The southern United States, however, saw the greatest growth. Prior to this time, it was difficult to use southern pine to make paper because of its high resin content. However, new processes were developed that allowed the use of southern pine to make bleached and unbleached kraft paper. Southern pine was ideal for this type of paper because its long fibers produced very strong paper and board. Kraft production in the South shot up from just 258 tons per day (tpd) in 1919 to 9,128 tons a day in 1940. By the end of World War II, this total was up to about 13,000 tpd.

The growth of southern paperboard mills—and other board mills around the country—was greatly enhanced by a 1914 Federal Trade Commission decision that legalized the use of corrugated medium packaging in shipping. Prior to that, wooden boxes were used for shipping goods around the country. Military development of paper packaging materials during World War I helped provide new technology and methods for producing superior paper packaging. Southern newsprint production also began during this time, due in large part to the talents of Charles H. Herty. Methods developed by Herty and his relentless promotion of southern papermaking helped create today's paper industry in the South.

While the Great Depression of the 1930s severely hurt other industries, it did not affect the pulp and paper industry as much since paper was being used in new ways throughout the economy. It was around 1930 that machine coated paper was first manufactured in the United States.

During World War II, the paper industry worked closely with the federal government to make sure that adequate supplies of paper were available for both domestic use and for the armed forces. Paper was one of the main materials used for shipping and storing military supplies. Recycling of paper reached a peak during the war years as well, with paper drives being common in many big cities.

Post-War Growth. After World War II, the paper industry continued growing. New pulping strategies and tree planting allowed the paper industry to develop the fiber sources it needed to meet the expanding demand. Prior to this time, paper companies tended to cut down trees and not replant. It was during this time that southern pine first began to be used to make white printing paper.

During the late 1940s, all areas of the paper industry were growing fast, but some new areas—such as milk cartons and drinking cups—saw exponential growth. Many of the growth trends were centered around the use of disposable paper products, a trend that had started in World War II.

In the 1950s and 1960s, paper machines grew wider and faster, which helped multiply the supply of paper and board. By 1970, however, the paper industry faced sustained challenges to its environmental practices. New clean air and water rules from federal and state governments in the early 1970s forced the industry to install expensive new treatment systems. Many other capital projects were put on hold and then frozen when the economy entered a severe recession in the early 1980s. However, in the mid- to late-1980s the paper industry initiated what has been called its greatest modernization ever. These capital intensive projects included mill-wide automation, technological innovations, mill modernization, environmental upgrades, and a push for total quality. The U.S. paper industry began competing more effectively in global markets during this time as well.

CURRENT CONDITIONS

The paper industry of the 1990s is highly competitive, both in domestic and foreign markets. It has a modern, efficient manufacturing base, labor peace, and strong markets. However, the industry faces several major challenges, including environmental compliance, recycling, and alternative media.

Environment. Environmental compliance is the most daunting—and expensive—challenge the paper industry faces in the 1990s. There is sustained opposi-

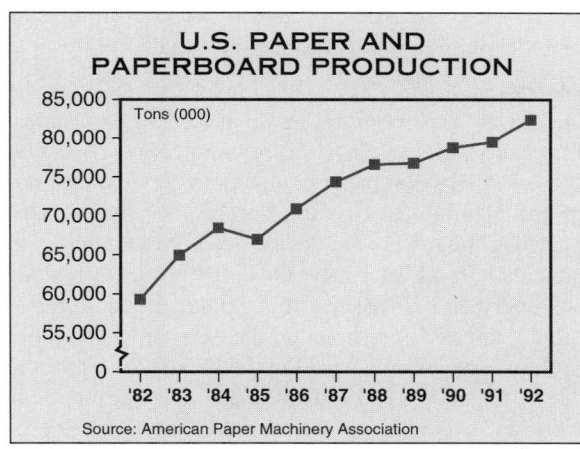

U.S. PAPER AND PAPERBOARD PRODUCTION

Tons (000)

Source: American Paper Machinery Association

tion from environmental groups and increased government regulation in nearly all steps of production, and harvesting of trees is under legal challenge in federal forests. For example, the lumber industry in the Pacific Northwest has been drastically reduced in scale. Due to successful court challenges by environmental groups under the Endangered Species Act, tree harvests in the early to mid-1990s dropped to one sixth of harvesting levels in the mid-1980s. Pulp and paper mills dependent on the residue of lumber operations for raw material had to look elsewhere—even overseas—for sources of wood chips. Also, the pulping and bleaching wood fiber came under stringent and costly new federal regulation in the mid-1990s (see Current Conditions, **SIC 2611: Pulp Mills**).

The intensity of environmental regulation is likely to have a major financial impact on the paper industry. In the mid-1990s, the cost of complying with environmental regulations began to grow toward levels last experienced in the 1970s, when nearly 25 percent of all paper industry capital expenditures were devoted to environmental projects.

Recycling. Paper recycling has become another major environmental challenge. Despite having reached an overall recycling rate of 40 percent in 1993, the industry is under pressure to increase that rate even more—particularly in printing and writing papers. While paper and paperboard are the largest individual components of the waste stream in the United States— about 40 percent of the total—they also account for more than 60 percent of the materials recovered for recycling and composting in the United States. In 1992, for the first time, there was more paper recovered for recycling than paper that went to landfills. In 1993, the paper industry announced a goal of recycling 50 percent of all paper produced by the year 2000.

Recycling of certain grades, such as newsprint and old corrugated containers, has always been high while other areas, such as printing and writing papers, has been fairly low. For example, over 50 percent of all newsprint used in the United States was recovered in 1991, up from just 29 percent in 1980. In linerboard, almost all capacity increases in the early 1990s came from new recycled linerboard mills, and about 57 percent of old corrugated containers—known as OCC in the business—were recycled.

Recycling of printing and writing paper, however, amounted to just seven percent of production in 1992. Aggressive state and federal legislation in the early 1990s sought to increase recycling rates in all grades. In 1993, President Clinton signed an executive order mandating higher levels of recycled fiber in paper purchased by the federal government (see Current Conditions, **SIC 2611: Pulp Mills**).

While highly touted as an environmental "silver bullet," recycling itself has some environmental liabilities. Most recycling mills generate a major waste stream and consume large amounts of purchased energy. With recycled newsprint, for example, only 85 percent of incoming newsprint is usable as fiber. The rest is unusable sludge that must be cleaned out of the process and then burned or placed in landfills. In some recycled grades, sludge can be up to 50 percent of the incoming waste paper. Considering that some mills make up to 2,500 tons per day of paper, sludge can become a major waste problem.

Also, since recycling mills cannot burn bark or spent pulping chemicals to generate electricity on their own, they must purchase large amounts of power from local utilities. For example, FSC Paper, a major producer of recycled newsprint and tissue paper in Alsip, Illinois, spends $800,000 per month to purchase electricity and natural gas to run its processes.

In the mid-1990s, recycling began to change the geographic distribution of paper mills. So called "mini mills" begin to crop up near major U.S. cities. These mini mills remove ink and recycle old newsprint and other grades of wastepaper and make new newsprint and linerboard on relatively small paper machines. Since they are close to where much of the country's wastepaper is collected—major cities—they are able to greatly reduce shipping costs.

Alternative Media. A third major challenge to the paper industry comes from the electronic display and storage of information. In the 1970s and early 1980s, some people predicted that computers would soon replace paper in the so called "paperless office." In reality, computers encouraged users to print out even more paper than ever before, fueling a boom in printing and writing papers.

Today, however, computers are being used more often to replace paper for the storage and transfer of information previously accomplished only on paper, such as the filing of legal papers with the Securities and Exchange Commission. Some observers feel that this may curtail the growth of paper. However, other observers point out that computers have vastly expanded the amount of information that can be stored. Even if a smaller percentage of this information is printed out, it is predicted that the use of paper should still grow.

Financial Conditions. In the early 1990s, the paper industry produced more paper than ever before but was unable to maintain effective pricing. In fact, paper prices fell in 1991 and 1992. Increases in production offset the falling value of paper products, so the value of all pulp, paper, paperboard and converted products was up 1.5 percent in 1992 over 1991 and was estimated at just over $126 billion. The two main reasons for the price decline were lackluster growth of the U.S. economy and oversupply of papermaking capacity. Deep discounts off list prices were common in many paper grades in the early 1990s.

Operating rates are another key to profits in the paper industry. In general, operating rates—the percentage of time that mills are in operation—need to be over 90 percent for the mill to be profitable. This means most large mills operate 24 hours a day, seven days a week. Operating rates dropped in 1990 and 1991, but rebounded to about 90 percent for paper producers and 95 percent for paperboard manufacturers in 1992.

Another measure of paper industry economic health is capital expenditures for new plants and equipment. When paper companies are profitable, they tend to reinvest a large share of their profits into capital expenditures. However, the early 1990s saw sharp declines in capital expenditures as the economy deteriorated. In 1991, for example, capital expenditures plunged 42 percent from 1990, and in 1992 were down three percent from 1991. Total 1992 expenditures were about $11.3 billion, or about one third less than the record 1990 level of spending. Environmental protection accounted for between 11 and 12 percent of total capital outlays in 1992.

INDUSTRY LEADERS

The following profiles cover the top ten pulp and paper companies in the United States, based on total 1992 sales. The sales volume of several companies includes lumber and forest product sales.

International Paper Co. Founded in 1898 by the merger of 18 Northeastern pulp and paper companies, International Paper Co. (IP), Purchase, New York, was the world's largest paper company in 1992. With sales of $13.6 billion, it was the number one producer of bleached board for milk and food packaging and uncoated freesheet paper. Other IP products include stationery and art papers. IP's capital expenditures in 1992 totaled $1.4 billion and the company owned 6.3 million acres of timberland in the United States. In the late 1980s and early 1990s, IP made many acquisitions worldwide, expanding its presence as a global producer of paper and paper products.

Georgia-Pacific Corp. In 1992, Atlanta-based Georgia-Pacific Corp. (G-P) was the world's second largest paper company and the leader in the production of market pulp. It was the U.S. leader in the manufacturing of building products as well. G-P also produced the most printing and writing papers, was number two in the production of containerboard, and was the fifth largest U.S. tissue maker.

Weak prices and overcapacity hit many of G-P's product lines hard in the early 1990s at the same time that the company was trying to digest its acquisition of Great Northern Nekoosa Corp. (GNN). G-P acquired Great Northern in a 1990 hostile takeover, an unusual event in the typically collegial paper industry. By 1992, G-P had sold off $1.6 billion of assets in order to pay down the huge debt it accumulated in the purchase of GNN. G-P had 1992 sales of $11.85 billion. Like other integrated forest products companies, G-P reported operating profits for its building products business, profits that were offset by a decline in pulp and paper results.

Weyerhaeuser Company. As the world's largest private owner of softwood timber, Tacoma, Washington-based Weyerhaeuser Company owned 5.5 million acres of U.S. timberland in 1992 and had cutting rights to more than 134 million acres in Canada. The company was reputed to be a leader in U.S. forest management. For example, it was one of the first paper companies to replant timberlands after cutting. While Weyerhaeuser was primarily known as a forest products company, it was also a major producer of paper products, was the number three producer of containerboard, and was a major exporter of newsprint to the Far East.

The company struggled with very low return on investment (ROI) in the mid-1980s to the early 1990s. To improve financial results, Weyerhaeuser sold off unprofitable business in nonforest and paper areas. It had 1992 sales of $9.22 billion. Weyerhaeuser also made several acquisitions in 1992, including two large pulp mills from Proctor & Gamble.

Kimberly-Clark Corp. Dallas-based Kimberly-Clark Corp. (K-C), best known for its Kleenex, Huggies, and Kotex brand consumer products, makes paper and fiber products for personal care, health care, and industrial uses. Total 1992 sales were up 4.6 percent to $7.09 billion. In the early 1990s, K-C controlled 45 percent of the U.S. facial tissue market and 35 percent of the feminine pad market. The company's commercial products included Neenah business paper, cigarette paper, and newsprint. Like other consumer paper product producers, K-C operated many production plants in foreign countries since most of these markets are growing faster than U.S. markets.

Procter & Gamble Company. Primarily known as a producer of food and health and beauty aid products, Procter & Gamble Company (P&G), Cincinnati, was also the inventor of the disposable diaper market and a major producer of such paper products as towels and tissues. In 1992, P&G's pulp, paper and diaper product sales were an estimated $6.7 billion. While the company was formerly a major pulp producer, it sold these operations in 1992 to Weyerhaeuser Co. The company, however, maintained a strong global presence in paper products, including the market for disposable diapers.

Stone Container Corp. Chicago-based Stone Container Corp., with 1992 sales of $5.52 billion, was the world's leading manufacturer of unbleached containerboard and kraft paper. In the early to mid-1980s, Stone made several major acquisitions at very low prices when the paper industry was at the bottom of its business cycle. However, Stone acquired Canadian paper company Consolidated-Bathurst in 1989 at the peak of the business cycle. After that, both the U.S. and Canadian paper markets turned sharply downward, leaving Stone Container with a very high level of debt. Since it competed in many commodity markets, Stone Container relied on a ''value-added'' approach to maintain its share of those markets.

Champion International Corp. A major manufacturer of white paper for business communications, printing, publication and newspaper applications, Stamford, Connecticut-based Champion International Corp. owned 6.1 million acres of U.S. timberland in 1992, making it one of America's largest private landowners. It was also the largest U.S. producer of lightweight publication papers and a leading producer of paperboard beverage containers, such as milk cartons. Champion's total sales of pulp and paper were up five percent in 1992.

Like other paper producers, Champion faced worldwide overcapacity and low prices for pulp and paper grades in the early 1990s. In 1992, selected grades of white paper hit their lowest price levels in more than a decade. Despite the recession, Champion embarked on a $5.5 billion capital spending program in the early 1990s, which was mostly completed at the end of 1993. Champion had 1992 sales of $4.93 billion.

Scott Paper Company. Philadelphia-based Scott Paper Company was the first U.S. company to market toilet paper. In 1992, it was the world's leading producer of paper towel and tissue products, and had sales of $4.89 billion. It was also one of the leading domestic producers of coated publication-quality papers, made by the company's S.D. Warren division. Scott also marketed commercial products, such as paper towels and soap dispensers for public restrooms.

Scott Paper produced 80 percent of its own pulp from virgin fiber and recycled paper. Like other producers, Scott began the 1990s facing weak markets for consumer tissue and paper markets. The coated paper market declined and strong competition from foreign producers, primarily in Scandinavia and Europe, helped reduce profits. In the early 1990s, Scott adopted a major cost cutting program, laying off close to 5,000 workers and selling non-core businesses such as its foodservice container and bulk nonwovens businesses.

James River Corp. Since its founding in 1969, James River Corp. in Richmond, Virginia, has quickly become one of the leading companies in the paper industry. James River used acquisitions and join ventures to expand operations rather than build its own pulp and paper mills. Using this strategy, James River has grown from assets of $2.7 million in 1970 to $5.6 billion in 1991. Total James River sales in 1992 were $4.73 billion, and the company had interests in consumer products, food and consumer packaging and communications papers.

In 1992, James River was a leading producer of towel and tissue products. A European joint venture, JA/MONT, gave the company a strong position in the European towel and tissue market. In addition, James River was also a major producer of paperboard and plastic beverage and food service products, including Dixie brand plates and cups.

The Mead Corp. Dayton, Ohio-based Mead Corp. was a leading manufacturer of paper-based school and office supplies, with sales of $4.7 billion in 1992. It was also the world's leading supplier of multiple beverage packaging (such as 12 and 24-packs for aluminum beverage containers). The company's 1.37 million acres of U.S. timberland supply 17 percent of its fiber needs.

Mead's Zellerbach division was a major wholesaler and retail distributor of printing and industrial papers, plastic products, and packaging equipment and supplies in the early 1990s. Another division—Mead Data Central—developed the LEXIS and NEXIS database research services. This unit accounted for ten percent of Mead's sales in 1991. Mead's packaging operations reported strong results and containerboard profits were also up, with improved results at Mead's eight corrugated box plants.

WORK FORCE

Total employment in the pulp, paper and converting industries was about 627,000 in 1992. The level of employment remained steady during the past five years despite large capacity increases. Employee wage increases remained at or below the inflation rate in the early 1990s, averaging about 2.5 percent. These increases were far below the average 7.5 percent annual increases recorded during the period from 1975 to 1985.

Like other manufacturing industries, the paper industry employs many unionized workers. However, the heaviest concentrations of union employees are in older mills which were organized years ago. Almost all new pulp and paper mills are non-union operations, including mills constructed by companies with unionized mills in other locations. In general, the wages and benefits provided by non-union mills are comparable to unionized mills.

There has been relative labor peace in the paper industry during the 1980s and early 1990s. In exchange for salary increases, management was able to obtain work rules changes that allowed workers to perform more jobs in the mill and eliminate pay differentials for Sunday and holiday pay. One dramatic strike in the 1980s ended in failure when unionized workers at International Paper's mill in Jay, Maine, were permanently replaced by new workers. Only a handful of the original workers regained their jobs. Since that strike, there have been no major work stoppages in the paper industry.

AMERICA AND THE WORLD

In 1992, the U.S. paper industry exported about nine million tons of paper and paperboard, which amounts to a little over 11 percent of total industry production. During this same year, it imported 12.5 million tons of paper and board, mostly from Canada.

Newsprint accounted for about 60 percent of these imports.

Because of the large amount of market pulp and newsprint imported from Canada, the U.S. paper industry has usually run a small trade deficit. However, this deficit narrowed to just $330 million in 1992, compared with $1.1 billion in 1991. This figure does not include about $615 million for wastepaper exports, an area where the United States leads the world. In fact, the United States has been called the "Saudi Arabia" of wastepaper, with a large share of wastepaper exports going to the fiber-starved Asian countries. Japan and Korea are two of the leading Asian wastepaper importers.

Exports played a key role in stabilizing the paper industry during the recession and sluggish growth of the early 1990s. In fact, the value of industry exports increased about five percent in 1992, following a seven percent rise in 1991. These increases helped offset the very low growth in the value of domestic shipments.

Overall, U.S. exports of paper and allied products—including wastepaper—were aided by the declining value of the U.S. dollar in the early 1990s and competitive pricing. Exports totaled an estimated $10.4 billion in 1992. Market pulp was the biggest export category, accounting for 31 percent of the total value of exports. Sanitary and all other converted products were a close second, accounting for almost 30 percent. Printing/writing papers and newsprint were the next largest category, accounting for 15 percent; linerboard checked in at 11 percent; wastepaper at six percent; and boxboard at eight percent.

Newsprint Growth. Newsprint is one of the major areas where U.S. producers have become more competitive in the global economy. Canadian newsprint, which until the early 1980s held a dominant 60 percent share of total U.S. consumption, has fallen on hard times. In the late 1980s, Canadian newsprint became significantly less competitive with U.S. newsprint because of higher production costs, new state government requirements for recycled newsprint, and growing U.S. newsprint capacity. In 1993, Canadian newsprint accounted for only slightly more than 40 percent of U.S. newsprint consumption, compared with about 52 percent in 1991. Many Canadian newsprint mills are located in rural Quebec, far from recycled fiber sources, and are old and have high production costs. As a result, many market observers expect the Canadian market share to decrease. However, some Canadian producers have made aggressive moves to obtain recycled fiber and build mills closer to urban areas in order to compete in the market for recycled newsprint.

The Japanese market remains a major challenge for U.S. producers. Despite major cost advantages, U.S. producers have a very small market share in Japanese markets. In fact, imports of pulp and paper accounted for a mere 2.5 percent of Japan's $27 billion total annual consumption. This low market share has been attributed to structural impediments in the Japanese market and a general reluctance to use imported products.

However, the U.S. industry achieved a major breakthrough in the early 1990s, at least in theory. After lengthy negotiations, a formal five year agreement was concluded in 1992 between the governments of the United States and Japan on measures that open Japan's paper market to foreign suppliers. The agreement requires the Japanese government to encourage Japanese paper distributors, converters, printers and other major consumers of paper products to use more imported paper and develop long-term buying relationships with foreign producers. Paper users in Japan are also expected to establish nondiscriminatory purchasing practices and develop purchasing guidelines that can be followed by both domestic and foreign suppliers of paper and paper products. The agreement calls on the Japanese government to work with local users of paper products, including 164 major companies that participate in the import expansion program sponsored by the Japanese Ministry of International Trade and Industry (MITI). Under the agreement, the two governments will periodically review the implementation of the pact.

Prospects. While the global economy slowed considerably in the early 1990s and went into recession in some areas, most U.S. producers remained very competitive worldwide. The U.S. industry still maintained substantial raw material and energy advantages over many of its foreign competitors. The U.S. also employed a large, well trained work force that had access to the latest process control technology. All told, the U.S. industry should have a long-term competitive edge over other paper producers in Japan, Europe, and Scandinavia.

While the paper industry's global position appears strong, questions remain about the overall financial impact of major environmental expenditures required under new EPA water and air rules. Some observers say that the ten billion dollars in capital required to meet new EPA water regulations will hurt the competitive position of the U.S. industry. These investments are not likely to improve productivity or increase capacity. If foreign producers are not held to the same standards, they may be able to reduce the cost advantages now held by U.S. producers.

RESEARCH AND TECHNOLOGY

Traditionally, papermaking research has focused on making faster, wider machines that experience fewer paper breaks. To support these goals, research is continuing in every area of the paper machine: the forming section, the press section, the drying section, and the finishing and converting areas. Much of this research is being performed by supplier companies to the paper industry, which have traditionally assumed a much larger research role than the paper companies. However, paper companies—as well as suppliers—are expanding their support of cooperative research at the nation's pulp and paper schools, such as North Carolina State University, the University of Maine, and the University of Wisconsin-Stevens Point. They also support non-profit research groups such as the Institute of Paper Science and Technology, the Pulp and Paper Research Institute of Canada (PAPRICAN) and the Herty Foundation.

Recycled Research. Much of the research in the paper industry is focusing on how to effectively use more recycled fiber. This is particularly important as the paper industry works to meet its own challenge of recycling 50 percent of all paper produced by the year 2000 and government mandates such as President Clinton's 1993 executive order on recycled paper.

Much of this research will focus on improving the physical chemistry of the ''flotation cells'' of the deinking process. This technology uses air bubbles to literally ''float'' detached ink particles to the top of a mixture of ground up paper and water, where the inky froth is skimmed off. Improving the efficiency of this system would speed up production and lower costs.

Research will also focus on using new chemical processes to help produce recycled paper that matches virgin uncoated freesheet in quality. Uncoated freesheet, used in products such as copy paper, is one of the biggest grades of paper, and one of the most demanding in terms of quality.

Impulse drying of paper on the paper machine is another important research area. At the beginning of 1994, Beloit Corp., Union Camp Corp., and the Institute of Paper Science and Technology were working on a pilot impulse drying system in which a heated press roll displaces a large amount of the water in the sheet. Traditionally, drying takes place only in the drying section of the paper machine, where a long series of heated rolls removes most of the water from the sheet. By using impulse drying in the press section, where water was traditionally squeezed—but not dried—out of the sheet, the group hopes to increase production speeds and produce a denser, higher strength sheet that can use a higher percentage of weaker recycled fiber. The U.S. Department of Energy is providing some of the research funds for this project.

There are hundreds of other ongoing research projects in the paper industry. The industry is seeking closer cooperation among all players—paper companies, suppliers, research institutions and government agencies, as it tries to improve on the complex art of making paper.

INDUSTRY INFORMATION SOURCES

Biermann, Christopher J., *Essentials of Pulping and Papermaking,* San Diego: Academic Press, 1993.

Hoover's Handbook of American Business 1993, Austin, TX: Reference Press, 1992.

Kirk, Bruce, *Paper & Forest Products,* New York: S.G. Warburg, October 1993.

Kline, James E., *Paper and Paperboard: Manufacturing and Converting Fundamentals,* San Francisco: Miller Freeman Publications, 1982.

Paper: Linking People and Nature, Washington, D.C.: American Forest & Paper Association, 1992.

Paper, Paperboard, Pulp Capacity and Fiber Consumption, Washington: American Forest & Paper Association, 1993.

''Pima's Top 50 North American Paper Companies,'' *pima,* June 1993, 34.

Smook, Gary A., *Handbook of Pulp & Paper Terminology: A Guide to Industrial and Technological Usage,* Bellingham, WA: Angus Wilde Publications, 1990.

Thesaurus of Pulp and Paper Terminology, Atlanta, GA: Institute of Paper Science and Technology, 1991.

U.S. Industrial Outlook 1993, Washington: U.S. Department of Commerce, 1993.

''Vision 300: A Celebration of American Papermaking,'' *pima,* January 1991.

Wright, Helena, *300 Years of American Papermaking,* Washington: Smithsonian Institution, 1991.

—Alan Rooks

SIC 2631

PAPERBOARD MILLS

This industry consists of establishments primarily engaged in manufacturing paperboard from wood pulp and other fiber pulp. Paperboard mills may also manufacture converted paperboard products. Establishments primarily engaged in integrated pulp production and paperboard manufacturing are included in this industry if they ship mostly paperboard or paperboard products. Establishments primarily engaged in manufacturing converted paperboard products from purchased paperboard are classified in Industry Group 265 or 267. Establishments primarily engaged in manufacturing insulation board and other reconstituted wood fiberboard are classified in **SIC 2493: Reconstituted Wood Products.**

INDUSTRY SNAPSHOT

The total value of U.S. paperboard mill shipments reached $15 billion in 1991, and production capacity reached 45.6 million tons in 1993, slightly more than paper production capacity, which was 45.5 million tons. Paperboard capacity is projected to grow by a total of 3.3 million tons between 1994 and 1996—an annual rate of 2.4 percent. The most extensive use of paperboard is to make shipping containers, cartons and packaging. Recycled containerboard will be the fastest growing paperboard segment from 1994 to 1996, averaging 10.1 percent annual growth.

U.S paperboard producers manufacture the vast majority of paperboard consumed in the United States. In addition to dominating the domestic market, U.S. paperboard producers hold a strong position in the international market, with exports accounting for just over ten percent of total U.S. production in 1992.

Two grades of paperboard—corrugating medium and linerboard—are used to make corrugated shipping containers. These two grades account for the majority of paperboard produced in the United States. A third grade—solid bleached sulfate (SBS), used for folding cartons in retail stores—accounts for a large share of the remaining production. One major distinction among paperboard grades is if they are folding or nonfolding grades. Folding grades have to be flexible enough so that when the board is folded to make a box—such as a cereal box—the surface will not split or crack.

ORGANIZATION AND STRUCTURE

More paper and paperboard is used to make packaging than in any other single application. While most paperboard is still made from virgin fiber (trees), paperboard mills have traditionally used a large percentage of recycled fiber because of favorable economics. The use of recycled fiber in paperboard production is growing quickly. The major use of recycled fibers has been in products where the reclaimed pulp does not need to be cleaned. Combination boxboard, for example, is used in cereal cartons where two white outside layers mask a recycled, gray inner layer.

Paperboard produced on "cylinder" board machines has commonly been made from secondary or recycled fibers. This is because cylinder machines form the paperboard "web" in separate layers, which are then pressed together. This makes it possible to hide a layer of recycled board, which can have poor appearance and lower strength, in between two outside layers of virgin material.

Fourdrinier paperboard machines, which traditionally have made paperboard in a single web, are generally used to make virgin paperboard since it makes a superior web from one fiber source. Newer paperboard machines, however, include machinery that allow the formation of a single web from different fiber sources.

Kraft softwood has been the preferred pulp for making paperboard because of its superior strength characteristics. While most paperboard is unbleached, retaining the characteristic brown color of the pulp, bleached grades are often used where the consumer is likely to see the box—such as gift boxes and food and beverage packages. Besides food applications, cosmetics and other high-profit products use the more expensive bleached board because they can afford its higher cost.

Paperboard comes in a wide variety of styles and qualities, but is basically divided into two categories: containerboard, which includes all the materials used for making corrugated boxes; and boxboard, which includes all the materials used for making non-corrugated packaging such as food containers and department store boxes. Containerboard is divided further into two subcategories, corrugating medium, the inner "fluted" part of the box, and linerboard, which makes up the outer "faces," or layers of the box. Corrugating medium—or just "medium," as it is often called in the trade—is made from both semichemical pulp and recycled fiber. According to industry standards, semichemical medium may contain no less then 75 percent virgin wood pulp.

Boxboard is divided into three subcategories: folding boxboard, set-up boxboard and milk carton/food service boxboard. Most paperboard can be coated with a pigment such as clay to improve printing properties. Most grades of paperboard can also be made impermeable to air and liquids by using plastic coating and laminating. This is essential for products such as milk carton stock.

Corrugated Boxes. The universal use of corrugated containers for shipping manufactured goods by truck, train or ship makes this grade one of the largest in the paper and board industry. There are a large number of converting plants located throughout the country that use corrugating medium and linerboard to make boxes. These converting plants are located close to users of the containers and are often owned by the same company that manufactures the linerboard and medium.

The main raw material used to make corrugating medium is semichemical hardwood pulp. Hardwood pulp, which is made from deciduous trees such as oak and maple, is used rather than softwood pulp, made from conifers such as southern pine. Hardwoods are used because they are less costly and help make the corrugating medium stiff since they are less flexible than softwood fibers.

Unlike the pulp used in other types of paper and paperboard, the pulp used for making medium still contains some lignin, the chemical "glue" that holds fibers together in the tree. This is because medium pulp is not washed as intensively as pulps used in making other grades. In this way, the lignin and other wood byproducts are left in the pulp and formed into the web of paperboard. When the paperboard web goes through the corrugator, the remaining wood byproducts help form the rigid fluted shape.

Growth Of Recycling. Like other predominantly virgin paper and paperboard grades, semichemical medium has seen its share of total capacity decline as a result of increased production of recycled products. Semichemical medium's share of total medium production declined to about 72 percent in 1992 from 79 percent in 1980, while recycled's share grew to 28 percent. While there are many basis weights for both semi-chemical and recycled medium, including 22, 26, 33, 36 and 40 pound, the standard weight is 26 pound. It accounts for about 77 percent of all production.

Medium production is directly related to U.S. corrugated box shipments, which grew less than three percent in 1993. In the late 1980s and early 1990s, box shipments grew faster than the general economy. Through the rest of the 1990s, growth in box shipments is expected to track more closely with growth in the general economy.

Linerboard. Unlike medium, linerboard is made mostly from softwood fibers. However, linerboard may contain up to 20 percent hardwood pulp or recycled fiber. The recycled fiber may be made from cuttings from corrugating plants or other recovered corrugated material. Softwood is needed to give linerboard adequate strength properties. Most softwood pulp for linerboard is produced using the kraft pulping process. To suit the varied packaging needs of box consumers, bleached kraft linerboard is made in many different basis weights. The standard variety is 42 pound, but other major grades include 26 pound, 33 pound and 69 pound. While production of recycled linerboard is significantly less than virgin linerboard, 100 percent recycled linerboard has been growing very fast in the United States since the late 1980s and is projected to grow even faster during the mid to late 1990s.

SBS. Solid bleached sulfate (SBS) is a top-quality paperboard made from pulp that includes at least 80 percent bleached virgin fiber. Most U.S.-produced SBS is coated with a clay solution to improve its surface for printing. SBS used for food packaging—such as milk carton stock—is often coated with polyethylene. Basis weights for SBS range from 40 to 100 pounds. SBS is also used for products such as disposable cups and plates and as linerboard for corrugated boxes and displays that need an outside surface for high quality, four-color printing.

Another product made by some mills that produce SBS is bleached bristol. This product, usually a lightweight grade, is used for greeting cards, paperback book covers and telephone directories, among other products. Bristol is usually classified under paper production, rather than paperboard.

In 1993, the capacity of U.S. mills to produce SBS reached 4.96 million tons. Bristols accounted for an additional 1.41 million tons. By 1996, these totals are expected to grow to 5.59 and 1.42 million tons. In 1992, SBS output declined by 1.5 percent to 4.5 million short tons. This was caused by continued lower demand in the domestic folding carton segment and lower export growth. At the same time, bleached bristol production remained flat at 1.14 million tons. Mill operating rates fell to 89.4 percent in 1992, down from 91.9 percent in 1991.

BACKGROUND AND DEVELOPMENT

Since the majority of paperboard capacity is used to make materials for corrugated boxes, the background and development of paperboard mills tends to mirror growth in the use of these boxes. Before corrugated containers became the accepted standard for domestic and international shipping, wooden crates and boxes were the preferred method.

However, this began to change dramatically after the U.S. Federal Trade Commission, in the 1914 Pridham decision, legalized the use of corrugated packaging in shipping. Also, during World War I, the U.S. military spurred research and development of corrugated packaging to ship military supplies.

As new methods helped improve the strength and durability of corrugated containers, their use in the general economy increased dramatically. For example, between 1935 and 1942, 29 new paperboard machines came on line. Collectively, these machines produced 15,545 tons per day. During World War II, military needs fostered improvements in corrugated shipping containers, including water and temperature resistance. In the post-war years, the growth of corrugated containers more than kept pace with the general economy, which itself was growing rapidly. Also, the development of more disposable containers for products such as foods and beverages fueled solid increases in the production of SBS board. Paperboard is now so entrenched in the general economy that it has become an indicator of overall economic activity. Paperboard accounted for slightly more than half of the overall production of paper and paperboard in the United States in the early 1990s.

CURRENT CONDITIONS

In the late 1980s and early 1990s, the domestic market for paperboard was relatively flat and most growth occurred as the result of increased exports. However, by 1992 this trend was reversing as the export market for paperboard was essentially flat while production of containerboard (the combined total of linerboard and corrugated medium) for domestic use increased about eight percent to 29.4 million tons. This represented 69.5 percent of all U.S. paperboard production in 1992. Overall, U.S. production of paperboard for domestic and export markets increased more than six percent in 1992.

Linerboard Conditions. U.S. linerboard production in 1992 reached a total of 17.8 million tons. This accounted for 61 percent of total containerboard production and about 42 percent of all U.S. paperboard production. Unbleached kraft linerboard accounted for most U.S. linerboard production. Unbleached linerboard is brown in color. However, in recent years, white-surface, high performance and recycled linerboard grades have shown the strongest growth, albeit from smaller bases.

U.S. linerboard is recognized worldwide as being the highest quality and best performing linerboard for most packaging applications. One of the major changes in linerboard occurred in the early 1990s when "Rule 41, Item 22" of the freight classifications was changed to emphasize "ring crush," which measures resistance to compression, instead of bursting strength. This change allowed U.S. manufacturers to begin making more "high performance," linerboard, which is lighter in weight than traditional liner but still useful for shipping. As a result, U.S. producers have developed a number of high performance bleached and unbleached linerboard grades.

Linerboard price behavior since the recession during the late 1980s and early 1990s can be compared to that in the post-1975 recession period, when pricing also stalled and even declined after the economy began to recover. The main reason for poor pricing in the early to mid-1990s was excess linerboard production capacity.

Total linerboard capacity is expected to increase 1.7 percent per year between 1993 and 1995. Most of this capacity expansion will be in recycled linerboard, which is expected to increase by over one million tons, from about 700,000 tons in 1991 to 1.76 million tons by 1995. By comparison, kraft linerboard capacity growth will be less than half of that, increasing only 479,000 tons during the same period.

Corrugating Medium Conditions. One of the biggest changes in corrugating medium in recent years has been an increase in the amount of recycled fiber used to make the grade. In 1992, about 75 percent of U.S. corrugating medium was semi-chemical (virgin fiber) and one quarter was recycled medium. However, some chemical medium may contain as much as 20 to 25 percent recycled fiber, and many manufacturers have been moving upward toward that amount.

In 1992, total domestic production of medium showed significant gains of more than six percent, reaching about 7.96 million tons. Medium accounted for slightly more than 27 percent of U.S. containerboard production (the combination of corrugating medium and linerboard) and 19 percent of total U.S. paperboard production in 1992. As was the case for linerboard, higher production for medium in 1992 was spurred by increased demand from domestic corrugated box plants. Capacity for semichemical medium is expected to rise only about 0.5 percent in 1994 and again in 1995, while recycled medium will be up 1.4 percent in 1994 and 0.5 percent in 1995.

INDUSTRY LEADERS

Many paper companies produce large quantities of both paper and paperboard, so the industry leaders tend to be the same companies that are listed in **SIC 2621: Paper Mills.** However, some large companies such as Stone Container Corp., Packaging Corporation of America, Temple-Inland Inc. and Federal Paper Board Company Inc. tend to specialize in paperboard.

Different companies are leaders in individual grades of paperboard. For example, in corrugating medium, Stone Container is the leading producer with about 11 percent of total capacity, followed closely by

Georgia-Pacific and Packaging Corporation of America, each with about ten percent. Other significant factors in this grade include Weyerhaeuser, Temple-Inland and Jefferson Smurfit Corp.

In bleached paperboard, International Paper Company is the clear leader, with about 22 percent of capacity, followed by Federal Paper Board with 15 percent and Westvaco with ten percent. Other leading companies include Potlatch, Georgia-Pacific, Temple-Inland and Champion International. This category is dominated by a few large players, with the top five companies accounting for about 62 percent of total capacity and the top ten companies holding nearly 83 percent.

The two top linerboard manufacturers together control over 24 percent of U.S. capacity, with Stone Container holding about 13 percent and Georgia-Pacific 11.2 percent. Other significant players include International Paper (9.1 percent), Union Camp (nine percent), Jefferson Smurfit (8.4 percent), Temple-Inland (eight percent), and Weyerhaeuser (7.6 percent). Gaylord Container, Willamette and Westvaco are also significant factors.

Recycled paperboard is a fast growing segment of the market, with capacity set to grow from 11.2 million tons in 1992 to 13.7 million tons in 1996. Within this category, recycled containerboard will grow the fastest, jumping from 3.5 million tons in 1992 to 5.7 million tons in 1996. The leading recycled paperboard producer is Jefferson Smurfit Corp., with capacity of 1.4 million tons in 1992, which represents about 12 percent of the market. It is followed by Newark Group Inc. and Sonoco Products Co., each with about eight percent of capacity. Other major market factors are Inland Container, Stone Container, Caraustar Industries and Rock-Tenn Co.

WORK FORCE

In 1991, paperboard mills employed a work force of 51,000 with an annual payroll of 2.03 billion. Production workers numbered 39,000 and worked 87 million man hours for wages of $1.46 billion.

AMERICA AND THE WORLD

Paperboard—particularly linerboard—is one of the strongest export products for the pulp and paper industry. U.S. linerboard mills, mostly in the Southern United States, are the low-cost producers throughout the world. In 1992, U.S. paperboard mills produced 3.3 million tons of containerboard for export—11.1 percent of all U.S. production of containerboard. U.S. mills also produced 1.1 million tons of boxboard for export in 1992—about 8.4 percent of all U.S. production of boxboard.

In the early 1990s, the lower-valued U.S. dollar, increased foreign demand and lower unit costs for high quality U.S. paperboard helped the U.S. paperboard industry grow its exports significantly. Linerboard exports, for example, averaged growth of 17 percent a year in 1990 and 1991. In 1992, however, poor economic conditions in many overseas markets caused paperboard exports to flatten, growing just 0.5 percent. By 1993, export tonnage actually fell back slightly, hurt by decreases in European corrugated container production. Decreases in Europe make a major impact on U.S. producers since 27 percent of total U.S. linerboard exports are shipped there. Also, price reductions caused mainly by overcapacity in many grades in the early to mid-1990s reduced the overall unit value of some export products.

RESEARCH AND TECHNOLOGY

Many of the same research trends affecting paperboard mills are the same as those affecting paper mills (see **SIC 2621: Paper Mills**). However, there is some interest in using new concepts such as stratification in making paperboard. Stratification involves using a special headbox that can produce three or more layers simultaneously from different fiber sources. In this way, a layer of recycled fiber or some other lesser quality fiber source could be sandwiched between layers of better quality fiber. With newer model headboxes, these layers can be extremely thin.

Like other grades, much of the effort in research and technology in paperboard is to create machines that will produce a wider web of paperboard at higher speeds. In this way, paperboard mills can run their mills more productively. Also, as in other grades, mill processes are becoming more automated and less subject to product variation. This, and continual improvements in paperboard quality, are the main reasons that U.S. paperboard mills can continue to lead the world both in price and product quality.

INDUSTRY INFORMATION SOURCES

Biermann, Christopher J., *Essentials of Pulping and Papermaking,* San Diego: Academic Press, 1993.

Kirk, Bruce, *Paper & Forest Products,* New York: S.G. Warburg, October 1993.

Kline, James E., *Paper and Paperboard: Manufacturing and Converting Fundamentals,* San Francisco: Miller Freeman Publications, 1982.

Paper, Paperboard, Pulp Capacity and Fiber Consumption, Washington, D.C.: American Forest & Paper Association, 1993.

Smook, Gary A., *Handbook of Pulp & Paper Terminology: A Guide to Industrial and Technological Usage,* Bellingham, WA: Angus Wilde Publications, 1990.

Thesaurus of Pulp and Paper Terminology, Atlanta, GA: Institute of Paper Science and Technology, 1991.

U.S. Industrial Outlook 1993, Washington: U.S. Department of Commerce, 1993.

"Vision 300: A Celebration of American Papermaking," *pima,* January 1991.

—Alan Rooks

SIC 2652

SETUP PAPERBOARD BOXES

Establishments in this industry manufacture setup (rigid) paperboard boxes from purchased paperboard. This classification includes setup paperboard boxes, paperboard filing boxes and metal-edged newsboard boxes. These products differ from other paperboard boxes in that they are not folded down, like corrugated boxes, and are shipped to customers in their final form.

Setup paperboard box manufacturers comprise one of the smaller paper and board products industries. The value of setup paperboard box product shipments grew 29.7 percent over the ten years from 1982 to 1991, from $433.2 million to $562 million. While the average annual growth rate over this period was 3.3 percent, the setup paperboard box industry's sales performance was uneven. Sales tended to spike up and down throughout the 1980s. For example, after rising to $569 million in 1983, sales dropped to $466 million in 1984, before rising to $479 million in 1985 and $552 million in 1986.

By the late 1980s and early 1990s, sales had stabilized somewhat. The value of shipments in 1989 was $531 million, rising to $565 million in 1990 before dropping slightly to $562 million in 1991. Since this is a small industry, some of the spikes in shipment values may be explained by changes in customers' inventory levels. If customers hold more product in inventory one year, they tend to purchase less the next year, even if their consumption rate is steady.

The production of setup paperboard boxes is concentrated in the Eastern half of the country, with the three largest production areas being New York/New Jersey/Pennsylvania; the Northeast; and the North Central states, including Wisconsin, Illinois, Ohio, Michigan, and Indiana.

Customers of the setup paperboard box industry are divided among several different product groups. Setup boxes used by department stores and other retailers accounted for 21.2 percent of the market in 1987, while candy products manufacturers used another 12.3 percent and clothing manufacturers 10.6 percent. Makers of cosmetics accounted for another 6.3 percent; stationery and office supply manufacturers another 5.9 percent; and hardware and household supplies another 2.48 percent. Setup paperboard boxes are used for a wide variety of other products as well: the ''all other'' category in this industry accounted for 41.3 percent of the market in 1987.

The setup paperboard box industry is expected to grow with the general economy throughout much of the 1990s. While this is a ''mature'' industry with little chance for exponential growth, it appears to be a stable one. Since setup paperboard boxes are, by definition, rigid packaging, they face little competition from alternative materials such as plastic that cannot provide rigidity without undue cost. Also, the recyclability of setup paperboard boxes is seen as an environmental plus and they can be easily made from recycled materials.

Most of the companies in this industry are smaller, ''niche'' manufacturers. All but one had annual sales under $100 million in the early 1990s. Caraustar Industries is the largest manufacturer in this industry, but it makes products in other industries as well. Other leaders in the setup paperboard box industry include Old Dominion Box Co.; Russell Stover Candies Inc. (which makes boxes for its own products); C.W. Zumbiel Co.; and Illinois Tool Works Inc.

In 1991 setup paperboard box plants employed about 9,000 people nationwide with an annual payroll of about $150 million. Production workers accounted for about 7,000 of that total and put in 14 million man hours, earning wages of $102 million.

INDUSTRY INFORMATION SOURCES

Darnay, Arsen J., *Manufacturing USA,* Detroit: Gale, 1993.

Paper, Paperboard, Pulp Capacity and Fiber Consumption. Washington, DC: American Forest & Paper Association, 1993.

Smook, Gary A., *Handbook of Pulp & Paper Terminology: A Guide to Industrial and Technological Usage.* Bellingham, WA: Angus Wilde Publications, 1990.

U.S. Industrial Outlook 1993. Washington, DC: U.S. Department of Commerce, 1993.

—Alan Rooks

SIC 2653

CORRUGATED AND SOLID FIBER BOXES

This category covers establishments primarily engaged in manufacturing corrugated and solid fiber boxes and related products from paperboard or fiber stock. Important products of this industry include corrugated and solid fiberboard boxes, pads, partitions, display items, pallets, single face products, and corrugated sheets.

INDUSTRY SNAPSHOT

Corrugated paperboard products are used to ship almost all of the nondurable goods manufactured in the United States and a majority of the nondurable ones as well. They face relatively little competition from alternative shipping methods. The total value of corrugated paperboard product shipments in 1991 reached $18.03 billion.

Corrugated paperboard products have long accounted for the majority of American paperboard container shipments. In 1992 such products accounted for 61 percent of the total market of $31 billion. Corrugated product shipments also hold a major share of the $74 billion overall domestic packaging market—which includes packaging made from wood, paper/paperboard, plastic, metal, glass, composites, and other materials.

As the statistics above indicate, the United States is a major consumer as well as a major producer of corrugated products. In 1992, per capita U.S. consumption of corrugated products was the highest in the world—82 kilograms (kg). Japan was the second leading consumer, at 67 kg. European nations make up the remaining leaders, with Germany at 48 kg, Italy at 44 kg, Spain at 40 kg and the United Kingdom at 31 kg.

Variations in end-use markets. The vast majority of corrugated products are used to package nondurable goods, such as food products. In 1991 over 77 percent of corrugated products were used to package nondurable goods. The percentage of corrugated products directed toward nondurable goods tends to rise during recessions since the number of high-ticket durable goods shipped—such as stoves and refrigerators—decreases. For example, by 1991 the extended national economic slowdown had reduced the proportion of the corrugated product sales used for durable goods to 22 percent from about 25 percent in 1989.

One of the key trends in corrugated boxes is recycling. This affects both the material used to make the boxes and how they are disposed of after use. Corrugated boxes are easily recycled and are biodegradable, which tends to help them compete well against plastic products among "green" consumers. Most corrugated products are unbleached, which exempts them from the recent controversy surrounding bleaching processes in the paper industry. Nearly 60 percent of corrugated products are recovered for recycling into new boxes or other paperboard products. That represents the second highest recovery level of any major consumable material (aluminum cans are first). Increased collection of corrugated boxes—including those coming from the homes of consumers—is expected to increase gradually each year through the 1990s until it nears 70 percent by the year 2000.

ORGANIZATION AND STRUCTURE

The corrugated box market is about 80 percent integrated. This means that 80 percent of all containerboard (the linerboard facing and corrugated fluting that together make a corrugated box) is not sold on the open market. Instead, it is delivered from containerboard mills to corrugated box plants owned by or affiliated with the same organization. The remaining 20 percent is sold by containerboard producers to independent box plants.

Corrugated and solid fiber box deliveries mirror the economic activity of the products shipped in them. When industrial activity picks up so do box shipments. For example, corrugated box shipments were up about four percent in 1992 to $19.3 billion, reflecting the recovery in the general economy. The recovery fueled demand for various corrugated packaging, such as paperboard containers, partitions and pallets. These and other corrugated products are used to package and transport all but ten percent of industrial and consumer goods made in the United States.

Corrugated products shipments in 1992 rose to their highest level ever—332 billion square feet—making the United States by far the world's leading producer of this product. U.S. production is 100 percent higher than that of Japan and almost 40 percent higher than the combined corrugated box shipments of the European Union.

Making corrugated board. Corrugated medium and linerboard are made into corrugated board at box plants. In 1993 the value of the corrugated board market in the United States was more than $7.5 billion. Many weights, thicknesses, and combinations of liners and corrugated medium are used to make different types of corrugated board. In this process, flat corrugated medium board is softened with heat and moisture and passed between a set of corrugating rolls to form it into flutes. Adhesive is applied to the flute tip

on one side of the medium. A separate, single face linerboard is then brought into contact with the fluted medium under heat and pressure to produce a single facer web.

This web is conveyed to the double backer station, where adhesive is applied to the exposed flute tips and the double back liner is applied. The combined corrugated board in then passed over a series of hot plates to set the adhesive. Modern corrugating machines run at a variety of speeds, ranging from as low as 100 feet per minute (fpm) to as high as 1,000 fpm, depending on the type of corrugated board under production.

After this, the corrugating board is cut into individual sheets, or blanks, on a trimmer-cutter. The blanks are then fed to a printer-scorer-slotter or some other device, which turns the blank into a flat box that can then be opened and glued by the end user.

Recycled Corrugated. Corrugated boxes have the image of being "environmentally correct" because they can be recycled into new boxes and other products. That image is to a large extent justified, since the recycled fiber content of corrugated is generally the highest of any paper product: it is around 60 percent on average and still climbing. While corrugated products are often re-used and the majority are recycled, some corrugated boxes do end up as waste in landfills. Some states, such as Minnesota, are considering banning corrugated boxes from landfills because they are one of the heaviest components of solid waste.

To produce recycled linerboard and recycled corrugating medium, many paperboard mills use both preconsumer and postconsumer old corrugated (OCC). Preconsumer waste is corrugated materials such as off-rolls and trimmings from box plants. Postconsumer waste includes boxes that have been used for shipping and subsequently discarded.

Standard corrugated boxes are fairly easy to recycle since they are printed lightly and require little or no de-inking. The pulp made from OCC needs little cleaning and does not have to be bleached. Unlike many grades of recycled paper, OCC suffers a minimal loss in fiber strength and other physical properties. However, there is a limit to how many times fibers can be recycled. For example, Asian corrugated boxes, which have been recycled many times due to chronic virgin fiber shortages in those countries, tend to be weaker and less resistant to water than U.S. corrugated boxes. The fiber quality of Asian OCC is so low that many American recycling mills exclude it from their processes.

CURRENT CONDITIONS

In 1992 the domestic corrugating industry consisted of more than 1,500 plants. This total included about 650 corrugator or converting establishments—integrated plants that both produce containerboard and manufacture packaging products—and 930 sheeting plants, which manufacture boxes from board purchased from the converters. The Southeast and West Central regions of the United States demonstrated rapid growth rates during the early 1990s. By 1992, they accounted for more than 40 percent of total U.S. corrugated shipments. The Southwest has also been an area of significant growth.

The leading use of corrugated packaging is for food and other grocery products being shipped to the nation's supermarkets and other retail outlets. In 1991 the food and kindred products category increased its share among nondurable goods users of corrugated boxes to 40 percent of box deliveries, up from 38 percent the previous year. In this same nondurable category, the paper industry is its own second-best customer, with paper and allied products using about 21 percent of the total. Other significant nondurable product markets include the chemicals and allied products, which accounted for six percent of shipments, and rubber and plastics products (five percent)

The durable goods market for corrugated products is considerably more fragmented, with toys and sporting goods leading the corrugated box users market in this category with just five percent of 1991 shipments. Other leading users include stone, clay and glass producers (four percent) and electrical machinery and equipment (three percent).

One recent change for boxmakers has been the modification of Rule 41 and Item 22 of the freight classifications. These standards specify corrugated box design criteria, and after the modification they now stress performance-based edge compression tests rather than the old mullen/burst strength-based test. This allows boxmakers to design lighter weight containment packaging. The revised classifications also create wider opportunities for the use of other types of corrugated boxes that use high performance linerboard (often with a predominantly virgin fiber furnish) and standard liners (usually having a fairly high recycled fiber furnish).

Industry Growth Predicated on Other Industries. The fortunes of the corrugated and solid fiber box manufacturing industry have historically risen and fallen with the shipping needs of other industries. Corrugated container shipments are expected to continue to track with growth in the general economy throughout the 1990s. For example, in 1991, while the United States was struggling to emerge from recession, corrugated container shipments grew just 0.6 percent to a total of 320.1 billion square feet (bsf). In 1992, however, as the economic recovery picked up steam, shipments were up 4.8 percent to 335.7 bsf. From 1992 to 1995, shipments are expected to rise at an annual rate of 2.6 percent, reaching 361.4 bsf in 1995.

While U.S. box production was at record highs in the early to mid-1990s, domestic prices of corrugated boxes and the materials they are made from—linerboard and corrugated medium—were headed in the other direction. The price decline in corrugated boxes was caused by the unusually long U.S. economic slowdown in the late 1980s and early 1990s, too much box making capacity, and lower demand for boxes. The average price for corrugated boxes dropped from a 1989 high of $47.72 per thousand square feet (msf) in 1989 to $46 per msf in 1990 and $44.08 in 1991, before recovering to $45.03 per msf in 1992. Full price recovery is not expected until the late 1990s.

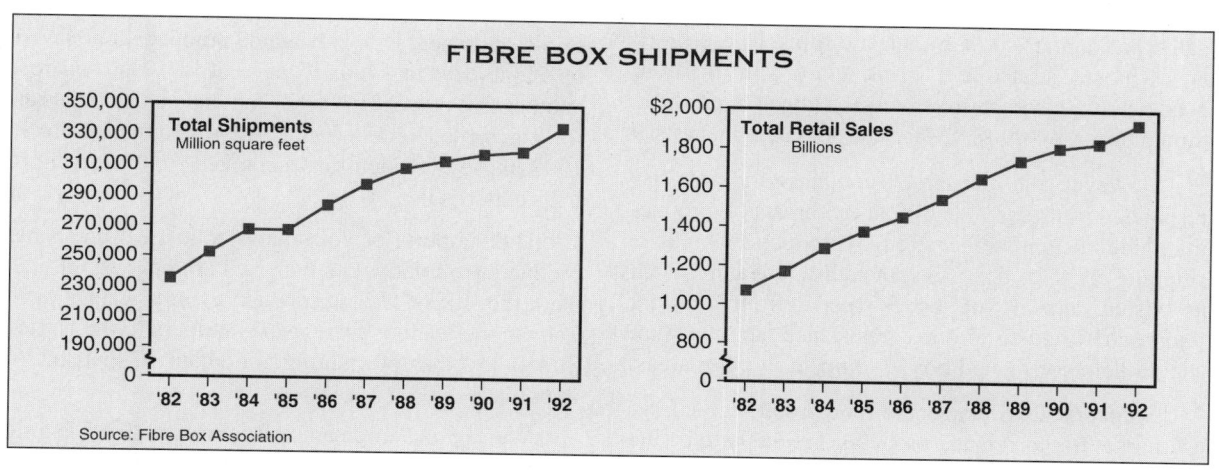

FIBRE BOX SHIPMENTS

Source: Fibre Box Association

However, the price situation could have been even worse for U.S. box producers if not for very strong export demand for American corrugated products in the late 1980s and early 1990s. Overseas shipments helped keep domestic prices from going even lower. Sluggish demand and a relatively non-inflationary climate hurt several attempts by major U.S. containerboard producers to raise prices, keeping raw materials costs for boxmakers low. While those conditions were expected to improve with the economy, several conditions conspired to hurt profit levels at containerboard and box producers. The economies of Japan and Europe—major customers for U.S. producers—went into recession in 1992-93, just as the U.S. economy was coming out of its sluggishness.

Preprinted Linerboard. One of the major recent changes in the corrugated box industry has been the fast-growing use of preprinted linerboard. This product is used to make boxes with a white enamel surface that can be printed on with four-color graphics, while the rest of the box remains the same unbleached brown color. In 1992 corrugated box manufacturing facilities used more preprint than ever before, as several large containerboard producers added preprint capacity to their mills.

The main reason for the growth of preprint has been the growing belief by manufacturers that an attractive box can influence consumer buying decisions at the "point of purchase" in the store. Simply put, an attractively packaged product is more likely to be purchased than one in a brown box. Some studies have shown that up to 80 percent of buying decisions are made at the point of purchase, so the additional "advertising" from a colorful box can help influence that decision. In 1993 total annual North American preprint linerboard capacity was estimated to be about 540 million square feet annually.

Competitors. One of the market threats to corrugated packaging is flexible plastic films. These products—mostly stretch and shrink wraps—are likely to become more competitive with corrugated products throughout the 1990s, at least in domestic markets.

However, the corrugated container industry has responded to these kinds of market threats by producing lighter weight, higher strength products that reduce shipping costs for box users. In addition, features such as visual appeal (of boxes made from preprint linerboard) and improved resistance to moisture should help corrugated boxes compete in other areas.

Shippers and packagers of food products, the largest market for corrugated products, are likely to be the highest growth market for the corrugated industry in

the 1990s. Also, shippers are using more corrugated pallets to replace wooden ones because of concerns over costs and recycling.

INDUSTRY LEADERS

The industry leaders in this category tend to be the same as the leaders in the production of containerboard since so much of box production is fully integrated. Some of the leading corrugated and solid fiber box producers include: Boise Cascade, Container Corporation of America, Jefferson Smurfit Corp., Weyerhaeuser Co. and Temple-Inland Inc. Other significant players include Union Camp Corp., Wilamette Corp., Packaging Corporation of America, Sonoco Products Co., and Stone Container Corp.

WORK FORCE

The corrugated and solid fiber box industry employed 109,000 people in 1991 with an annual payroll of $3.05 billion. Of that total, 79,000 were production workers putting in 166 million man hours for wages of $6.06 billion.

AMERICA AND THE WORLD

The operations in the nations of the European Union are significant competitors in this industry. The EU had nearly 550 corrugator plants operating in 1992. These plants shipped a total of about 240 billion square feet of corrugated products. Japan, another large producer of corrugated products, shipped almost 140 billion square feet from 335 converting plants.

International competitiveness. Since U.S. containerboard producers are often the low-cost producer in world markets, U.S. corrugated products tend to be very competitive in global markets. When the U.S. dollar is low against foreign currencies, U.S. corrugated products are even more competitive. This was the case in the early 1990s, when U.S. corrugated exports boomed. U.S. corrugated product exports were up 25 percent in 1990, 15 percent in 1991, and rose another five percent in 1992. The main export markets for corrugated products are Mexico and Canada. In 1992, those two countries accounted for 85 percent of U.S. export sales.

U.S. imports of corrugated containers and other products are relatively small, and are only about one-tenth the size of U.S. corrugated exports. Canada and Taiwan are leading corrugated suppliers to the United States, together accounting for about 33 percent of imports.

Worldwide shipments of corrugated packaging reached $45 billion in 1992 and are expected grow as fast as four percent annually between 1993 and 1997. As the global low-cost producer, the U.S. is likely to maintain its 35 percent share of the total number of boxes produced during the next five years. That share amounts to over 24 million metric tons. If the economies of Eastern Europe are able to shake off their lethargy, and nations such as China and India continue their strong growth trends, it is likely that their domestic industries will be unable to satisfy the growing need for packaging and shipping containers. If so, U.S corrugated manufacturers may be able to expand in these markets.

U.S. exports of corrugated products are forecast to climb an average of ten percent in dollar value annually during the 1993-1997 period, buoyed by increasing sales to the two major markets: Canada and Mexico. The lower duties on paper products due to be phased in as part of the North American Free Trade Agreement (NAFTA) should help improve growth prospects for U.S. box producers.

Expanded shipments will also go to Latin America, the Pacific Rim, and Eastern Europe. U.S. corrugated products are expected to remain highly competitive in foreign markets as continuing technological advances produce boxes that should meet the most stringent overseas quality and environmental requirements.

RESEARCH AND TECHNOLOGY

Much of the research and technology in corrugated box production in the 1990s will focus on improved process control and computerized order entry and production scheduling.

One area of concern to researchers is twist warp—the loss of flatness—in linerboard when it is converted into corrugated board. This problem was relatively unknown until the past few years, when corrugating machines began to run at faster speeds—around 1,000 feet per minute. At these speeds, linerboard with twist warp can cause malfunctions on the corrugator. While paperboard producers are currently focusing on making operating changes to minimize the problem, more research is needed into the fundamental reason for twist warp in order to help solve the problem.

Other research efforts will focus on how to maximize quality and minimize cost as the U.S. corrugated box industry attempts to preserve its strong market advantages into the next century.

INDUSTRY INFORMATION SOURCES

Biermann, Christopher J., *Essentials of Pulping and Paper-making*. San Diego: Academic Press, Inc., 1993.

Hoover, Gary, *Hoover's Handbook of American Business 1993*. Austin, TX: Reference Press, 1992.

Lynn, E.S., ''Paper Industry/Linerboard Outlook,'' Dean Witter Reynolds, August 16, 1993.

Paper: Linking People and Nature. Washington, DC: American Forest & Paper Association, 1992.

Paper, Paperboard, Pulp Capacity and Fiber Consumption. Washington, DC: American Forest & Paper Association, 1993.

Smook, Gary A., *Handbook of Pulp & Paper Terminology: A Guide to Industrial and Technological Usage*. Bellingham, WA: Angus Wilde Publications, 1990.

Thesaurus of Pulp and Paper Terminology. Atlanta: Institute of Paper Science and Technology, 1991.

U.S. Industrial Outlook 1993. Washington, DC: U.S. Department of Commerce, 1993.

—Alan Rooks

SIC 2655

FIBER CANS, TUBES, DRUMS AND SIMILAR PRODUCTS

Establishments in this industry are primarily engaged in manufacturing fiber cans, tubes, drums, cones and similar products from purchased paperboard. These products can be made with or without metal ends. This industry segment produces a wide variety of products, including paper fiber bottles, fiber bobbins, composite cans, 100 percent fiber cans, fiber drums (metal-end or 100 percent fiber), fiber cores, mailing cases and tubes, and tubes for chemical and electrical use, among other products.

In the ten years from 1982 to 1991, the value of this industry's product shipments increased 32 percent, from $1.46 billion in 1982 to $1.93 billion in 1991. Despite an annualized growth rate of 3.5 percent, though, this industry had its ups and downs in the 1980s. After increasing to a peak of $1.7 billion in 1985, the value of product shipments dropped to $1.57 billion in 1986 and $1.54 billion in 1987. Then, when the rest of the paper and paperboard products industry was going into recession, the fiber can, tube and drum industry increased its sales for four straight years, moving from $1.63 billion in 1988 to $1.93 billion in 1991.

The manufacture of fiber cans, tubes and drums is concentrated east of the Mississippi River. The top three producing regions, in terms of total shipments, are the North Central, Southeast/Mid-Atlantic, and Northeast United States.

Fiber cans and tubes are by far the largest category of products produced by this industry, accounting for 72.5 percent of all product shipments in 1987. Within this category, fiber cans (including composites) accounted for 30 percent of the entire fiber can, tube and drum market, while cores and tubes accounted for 36 percent. Paperboard fiber drums, a larger sized product, accounted for 21 percent of total shipments in 1987.

Paperboard mills are the biggest raw material supplier to the fiber can, tube and drum industry, accounting for 58 percent of all inputs in 1982. Paperboard containers and boxes (used to ship finished products) accounted for six percent of supplies, followed by a wide range of other materials and services.

Like other paper product producers, the makers of fiber cans, tubes and drums are using more recycled paperboard and less virgin paperboard in order to satisfy end user demands. In the late 1980s and early 1990s, this industry appeared to benefit from the desire by consumers and the government to use more products that were made from recycled materials or were more recyclable than competing products. This environmental factor was a distinct advantage for industry manufacturers since many competing products are made from plastic, which is perceived to be a less recyclable product.

The paper industry is a good customer as well as a supplier for the fiber can, tube and drum industry. Many mills use heavy duty fiber cores to wind their paper and paperboard rolls. These cores are either shipped in long lengths and cut at the mill or pre-cut by the core manufacturer. This market shows little sign of moving toward alternative products, such as steel cores.

Drum Declines. The fiber drum has seen its market share decline since many industrial users are trying to eliminate the use of disposable containers. For example, for regulatory reasons the chemical industry is moving away from using drums of any kind—including fiber or metal drums. Instead, they are using more portable chemical feed containers that are dropped off by the chemical manufacturer and then picked up to be reused when empty. In 1993, two specialty chemical producers—Nalco Chemical Co. and Betz Industrial—announced they had entirely eliminated the use of drums to ship their products.

Some of the industry leaders in this category are integrated manufacturers, in that they produce fiber cans, drums, and tubes, as well as the paperboard they

are made from. Other fiber can, tube, and drum manufacturers are independent converters of purchased paperboard. One of the leading companies in this industry, Sonoco Products Co., is an integrated producer, as is Caraustar Industries and U.S. Paper Mills Corp. Other leaders in this industry include Greif Bros. Corp.; Star Paper Tube Inc., Hayes Manufacturing; and South Texas Can Co.

In 1991 this industry segment employed 13,000 people with an annual payroll of $341 million. Of that total, 11,000 were production workers who put in 23 million hours for wages of $247 million.

INDUSTRY INFORMATION SOURCES

Paper, Paperboard, Pulp Capacity and Fiber Consumption. Washington, DC: American Forest & Paper Association, 1993.

Smook, Gary A., *Handbook of Pulp & Paper Terminology: A Guide to Industrial and Technological Usage.* Bellingham, WA: Angus Wilde Publications, 1990.

U.S. Industrial Outlook 1993. Washington, DC: U.S. Department of Commerce, 1993.

—Alan Rooks

SIC 2656

SANITARY FOOD CONTAINERS, EXCEPT FOLDING

This category includes establishments primarily engaged in manufacturing non-folding food containers from special foodboard. Industry products include paperboard beverage cartons, round, nested food containers, paper cups for hot or cold drinks, and stamped plates, dishes, spoons and similar products. Establishments primarily engaged in manufacturing folding sanitary cartons are classified in **SIC 2657.**

Sanitary food containers have been a strong growth market for the paper industry. Despite increasing consumer interest in reducing usage of disposable products, the convenience of disposable paper products has continued to appeal to growing numbers of consumers. Also, the use of paperboard milk cartons in alternative, non-food markets has given that part of the industry a healthy boost.

In the late 1980s and early 1990s, the value of sanitary-food-container product shipments increased steadily. From 1987 to 1991, that value increased 31 percent, far outpacing many other paper product categories. In 1987, the value of sanitary-food-container shipments was $2.08 billion. That increased to $2.19

billion in 1988 and $2.54 billion in 1989, before falling back slightly in 1990—a recession year—to $2.51 billion. In 1991, the growth in the production of sanitary food containers resumed again as the value of shipments reached a record $2.73 billion.

Personal consumption expenditures account for the vast majority of sanitary-food-container purchases, reaching 79.1 percent of total sanitary-food-container purchases by 1982. Eating and drinking establishments purchased another 6.1 percent and 2.9 percent of the products were exported in that year. A variety of other businesses and government agencies accounted for the remaining 11.9 percent of market purchases.

Drinking cups and portion serving cups account for the largest share of products produced by this industry with 40.5 percent of the market in 1987. Milk and milk-type paperboard cartons were the next biggest category, holding 28.7 percent of the market in 1987. Pressed plates, dishes, spoons, and similar products accounted for another 14.1 percent while other sanitary paper and paperboard food containers, boards and trays accounted for 23.6 percent.

The market for paper cups, plates, and other disposable paper products appeared healthy going into the 1990s. Increased strength and grease resistance allowed paper plates, in particular, to be used in an increasing number of applications, while household use of paper cups showed no signs of abating.

Paperboard milk cartons had a rougher road but, after some downturns, they too picked up speed once again. Plastic milk cartons captured a growing share of the milk market in the 1970s and 1980s, most particularly in the gallon size. However, an extended decline in sales of paperboard milk cartons began to slow and even stop in the 1990s when it became widely known that paperboard milk cartons retain vitamins better than their plastic counterparts (fluorescent lights in dairy cases leach vitamins from milk in translucent plastic jugs). This knowledge led some dairies and consumers to once again favor paperboard.

Also, because of their ease of storage and ability to withstand repeated access, many additional domestic uses for paperboard milk-style carton were developed. These included uses as packaging for non-dairy flavored drinks, fruit juices, dry pet foods, laundry detergents, candy, and hardware. Such alternative uses helped increase the sale of milk cartons: In 1980, non-dairy carton tonnage accounted for only 13 percent of all milk-carton sales. By 1990, that percentage had more than doubled to 28 percent.

Leaders in this industry have included a mixture of major paper companies and independent converting

companies. One of the leading companies is James River Corp., manufacturer of "Dixie Cups" and other sanitary paper products. Other key market factors include Champion International, which manufactures milk carton stock, Solo Cup Co., Sealright Co., and Imperial Bondware Inc. Westvaco Corp., another major paper company, is also a major producer of milk-carton stock.

Sanitary-food-container manufacturers employed 18,000 people in 1991 with a payroll of $411 million. Production workers accounted for 14,000 of the total, working 29 million man-hours for wages of $296 million.

INDUSTRY INFORMATION SOURCES

Darnay, Arsen J., ed. *Manufacturing USA: Third Edition,* Detroit, Gale, 1993.

Darnay, Arsen J., ed. *Market Share Reporter 1992,* Detroit, Gale, 1992.

Paper, Paperboard, Pulp Capacity and Fiber Consumption, Washington, DC: American Forest & Paper Association, 1993.

Smook, Gary A. *Handbook of Pulp & Paper Terminology: A Guide to Industrial and Technological Usage,* Bellingham, WA: Angus Wilde Publications, 1990.

U.S. Industrial Outlook 1993, Washington, DC: U.S. Department of Commerce, 1993.

—Alan Rooks

SIC 2657

FOLDING PAPERBOARD BOXES, INCLUDING SANITARY

Establishments in this industry are primarily engaged in manufacturing folding paperboard boxes from purchased paperboard, including folding sanitary food boxes or cartons (except milk cartons). Products include folding paperboard boxes such as cereal boxes; folding cartons; frozen food containers; ice cream containers; folding sanitary food pails such as those used for takeout food from restaurants; and paperboard backs for blister packages.

INDUSTRY SNAPSHOT

The folding-paperboard-box industry demonstrated strong growth each year in the late 1980s and early 1990s. The value of shipments grew from $5.7 billion in 1987 to $7.3 billion in 1991, an average annual increase of seven percent a year. The industry achieved this despite a recession that reduced the value of shipments in other paper and paperboard product industries. However, the industry appeared to peak in 1991; since 1992, tonnage was down slightly to 3.2 million short tons.

Food products represent some of the best markets for the folding-paperboard-box industry, with strong growth reported in packaging materials for beverages, dry bakery goods, and cereals during the early to mid-1990s. Other non-food markets reporting good growth rates included toys, sporting goods and textiles.

The production of folding paperboard boxes is divided fairly evenly across a wide range of food- and non-food consumer products. Manufacturers of bottled and canned beverages (such as 24-packs of canned soft drinks) are the single biggest user folding paperboard packaging, consuming ten percent of production in 1987. Other significant users include manufacturers of cosmetics and medicinal products (9.29 percent); dry food and produce (8.76 percent); frozen foods (6.54 percent); paper goods or products (5.76 percent); hardware or household supplies (4.71 percent); and butter and ice cream packages (4.69 percent).

While shipments of folding boxes were growing in the early 1990s, box prices were not keeping pace. An anemic national economy, low inflation, and weak pricing for paperboard conspired to keep price increases moderate, at best. The average U.S. price for solid bleached sulfate board (SBS), the principal virgin-fiber grade used by the industry, was $870 per short ton in mid-1992. Clay-coated paperboard, the industry's largest recycled grade, was averaging $550 per ton during the same time frame.

Folding-paperboard-box manufacturers, on average, enjoyed a 3.2 percent sales increase in total sales in 1992 (not adjusted for inflation). Still, folding box makers, in general, must produce a lot of boxes to make a meager profit: In 1991, after-tax profit margins for the industry were just 3.1 percent.

In the recession-plagued years of the early 1990s, this financial performance was considered a good one. The folding paperboard box industry continued to benefit, to some extent, from the fact that it is a very consumer-oriented business. Folding paperboard boxes are used extensively to package consumer products. Many of these products, such as food, are purchased in spite of poor economic conditions. That means that folding paperboard boxes tend to be less prone to the ups and downs of the economy than other parts of the paper and paperboard packaging industry. It also helps to explain the strong sales performance of the industry in the late 1980s and early 1990s, when other sectors were struggling.

ORGANIZATION AND STRUCTURE

In the early 1990s, the U.S. folding-paperboard-box industry was made up of just under 500 plants. These plants are mainly located in major urban areas in the Mid-Atlantic, Southern, Midwest and Northeast regions.

In the 1980s, the Southern United States emerged as the fastest-growing folding-paperboard-box-producing region in the country, averaging three percent growth annually. By 1992, Southern plants accounted for 25 percent of U.S. folding paperboard box sales. In 1992, growth in shipments by Southern plants—nearly ten percent—was almost double that of other regions. The North Central region actually lost tonnage in 1992, as much as four to five percent, but still accounted for about 45 percent of total industry sales.

The Pacific Northwest, not a major player in the folding paperboard box market, was predicted to become even less of one by the close of the 1990s. That region was expected to lose about three percent of capacity annually in the mid-1990s, with 1997 predicted to hold at just 7.5 percent of folding-paperboard-box capacity. One reason for this was the anticipated high cost of raw materials for pulp in the Pacific Northwest region. Severe restrictions on logging in Federal lands, brought about by environmental legislation designed to protect the Northern Spotted Owl, reduced timber harvesting and raised the cost of wood. Since pulp mills in the Northwest continue to depend on the waste from saw mills for their raw materials, the availability and cost of pulp were also expected to rise.

The growth of food-related packaging and other retail applications has helped expand the retail market for folding paperboard boxes. The growing use of folding boxes as beverage carriers has also helped fuel growth in folding-paperboard-box sales. Both beer and soda bottlers were using 24-can "cases" as promotional vehicles in the mid-1990s. As a result, more of those products were being sold in folding paperboard boxes and fewer in the traditional six-packs held together by plastic carriers.

Folding box manufacturers began producing a higher quality, high-whiteness box suitable for four-color-process printing. Better visual appeal of such packaging often translated into higher "impulse" purchases by consumers, and folding boxboard customers were often willing to pay a premium price for goods so boxed.

However, unlike its corrugated container cousins, the folding paperboard box has faced direct competition from alternative materials, principally the bewildering array of plastics. The growth of flexible bags, pouches, and wraps, as well as rigid carriers and containers made from plastics, has created a serious challenge to the dominance of the folding paperboard box in the packaging marketplace. For example, some detergent and fabric-softener manufacturers began selling their concentrates packaged in flexible composite ''pouches.'' However, while this type of packaging gained in popularity in Europe, it had yet to catch on in the United States. Early reports from U.S. manufacturers using pouches were not promising.

Folding paperboard boxes have also faced competition from some other paperboard products. In some retail applications, corrugated products and carded ''blister packs'' (paperboard backings that hold a molded plastic insert) have been used as a substitute for paperboard boxes.

CURRENT CONDITIONS

While still facing formidable competition from alternative packaging such as flexible pouches, the folding paperboard box industry was expected to grow throughout the 1990s. Improved strength and lighter-weight folding boxboard helped to improve the competitive position of folding paperboard boxes in the packaging marketplace. Folding paperboard boxes also benefited from the fact that they are recyclable and contain recycled fiber. Both of these attributes were actively promoted on retail packages.

Paperboard's recyclability is significant since packaging in general has garnered a reputation for contributing to the solid waste crisis in the United States. Manufacturers were encouraged to reduce or eliminate packaging for their products, and some state legislatures went so far as to ban specific types of packaging. However, folding paperboard boxes have avoided product bans, in part because they are recyclable and have been composed an ever-increasing percentage of recycled fiber with each passing year. The growing use of recycled fiber in folding paperboard boxes helped the U.S. paper and paperboard industry meet its self-imposed goal of recycling 40 percent of the paper and board it produces in 1993, two years ahead of schedule. The paper industry hopes to recycle 50 percent of production by the end of the century.

The majority of folding boxboard produced in the United States is used by the folding paperboard box industry. Of the 4.5 million tons of boxboard used by the folding box industry in 1992, SBS accounted for close to 30 percent of the total. SBS is favored by manufacturers of folding paperboard boxes for the packaging of cigarettes, frozen and wet foods, meats, non-prescription drugs, bakery foods, and cosmetics. These manufacturers appreciate its superior visual and

performance characteristics. Throughout the 1980s and early 1990s, SBS accounted for about 35 percent of the folding boxboard used by the domestic folding paperboard box industry.

However, in the early 1990s, SBS was challenged by two market forces that helped to erode its market share—competition from lower cost alternatives and the growth of recycling. As the quality of lower-cost kraft- and recycled-board grades increased, some boxmakers opted for the cost savings those grades could provide.

Also, many companies purchasing folding paperboard boxes wanted to demonstrate environmental awareness to their retail customers by providing the ultimate end-user with products encased in recycled packaging. For example, in the early 1990s, Marshall Field's, a major Chicago-based department store chain, replaced its trademark green retail folding paperboard box with a brown box that would be easier to recycle—even though the newer box lacked the prestige and status-appeal of the older box.

During the late 1980s and early 1990s, virgin SBS capacity grew at just 0.8 percent per year. This growth rate was expected to increase to an average rate of about three percent each year between 1992 and 1996.

The losses of SBS in the folding box market have been made up by other grades, most notably recycled paperboard. By 1992, clay-coated recycled paperboard accounted for over 40 percent of the folding paperboard box industry's board consumption.

Almost 80 percent of recycled paperboard produced each year in the United States goes into folding paperboard boxes. Capacity to produce recycled paperboard for folding paperboard boxes was expected to increase from 285,000 tons in 1993 to 3.2 million tons in 1996, a huge gain of 179,000 annual tons.

The success of this grade is due to several reasons. Obviously, the tremendous interest in recycling has helped. But most industrial users would be unwilling to accept an inferior product simply because it was more environmentally friendly. Better recycling procedures and improvements in strength, formation, and surface coating have allowed quality recycled clay-coated board to compete in several market areas it was previously shut out of. In 1992, recycled boxboard grades accounted for a record 56 percent of the industry's total board consumption.

In the early to mid-1990s, folding-paperboard-box volume shipments tended to mirror the general economy, growing only as fast as GNP. However, since these figures are based on tonnage, it must be taken into account that today's folding-paperboard-box manufacturers are producing lighter-weight boxes that still meet existing strength tests and other industry standards. As a result, lighter boxes—which reduce industry tonnage—are replacing heavier products.

This fact, combined with expectations of only moderate market growth, means that shipments of folding paperboard boxes are likely to grow only about one percent annually during the mid- to late 1990s. By 1997, folding paperboard box volume should grow to 3.3 million tons.

INDUSTRY LEADERS

The folding paperboard box industry is highly integrated. This means that the leading producers of folding paperboard boxes also produce the folding boxboard used to make the product. Leading producers of folding paperboard boxes include Georgia-Pacific Corp.; James River Corp.; Jefferson Smurfit Corp.; Westvaco Corp., Packaging Corporation of America; and Rock-Tenn Co. Other leading companies include Field Container Corp.; Green Bay Packaging Inc.; Waldorf Corp. and Gulf States Paper Corp.

WORK FORCE

Folding paperboard box plants employed 51,000 people in 1991, with a total payroll of $1.44 billion. 39,000 of those were production workers with annual wages of $998 million.

AMERICA AND THE WORLD

The folding-paperboard-box industry has traditionally imported more than it has exported, even though the difference is relatively small. In the early 1990s, however, that trade imbalance widened. For example, while exports rose a healthy 22 percent in value during 1992, imports were up even more—48 percent in value. About 65 percent of those folding paperboard boxes came from Canada, which greatly benefitted from lower duties on folding paperboard boxes under the U.S.-Canada Free Trade Agreement. Lower duties and competitive Canadian prices have combined in a major surge in imports from Canada into the United States. In 1992 alone, Canada increased its shipments by about almost 75 percent.

While imports grew in the early to mid-1990s, it should be kept in mind that they did so from a small base. In 1992, for example, imports accounted for less than two percent of domestic folding-paperboard-box consumption.

One aspect of foreign trade in this category goes essentially unreported. When U.S. products are packed in boxes and shipped overseas, the box is not counted as an export, even though it is shipped overseas. Likewise, foreign-made consumer goods coming into the U.S. often come pre-packaged without the need for further packaging in U.S.-produced folding paperboard boxes.

U.S. exports of folding paperboard boxes maintained a healthy profile in the early 1990s. By 1992, exports achieved record levels, exceeding $100 million for the year. Most of these exports went to the neighboring countries of Mexico and Canada. Together, these two countries accounted for 75 percent of all folding paperboard box exports, in terms of value. With congressional passage of the North American Free Trade Agreement (NAFTA) in 1994, cross-border shipments were expected to rise as duties fell. This was expected to lead to both increased export and import opportunities for U.S. folding-paperboard-box manufacturers.

While exports continued to grow, they have by no means been considered a major market by industry manufacturers. It usually makes the most economic sense to export folding boxboard in sheets or rolls and then convert them into boxes locally. Many U.S. folding-paperboard-box manufacturers possess sites for foreign conversion for this reason. As a result, exports of unconverted folding boxboard were roughly three-and-a-half times the size of finished folding-paperboard-box exports in the early 1990s. For example, U.S. exports of folding boxboard were about $360 million in 1992.

Foreign trade is expected to continue to play a minor role in total industry shipments through the end of the 1990s, even though exports to Mexico, other Latin American countries, and Pacific Rim countries may increase. The domestic market will remain the central focus of folding-paperboard-box manufacturers. The historically high U.S. per-capita consumption of folding paperboard boxes—now over 37 pounds per year—will help maintain that focus. By comparison, Western European per-capita consumption has been documented as only about half that of the United States.

INDUSTRY INFORMATION SOURCES

Darnay, Arsen J., ed. *Manufacturing USA: Third Edition,* Detroit, Gale, 1993.

Darnay, Arsen J., ed. *Market Share Reporter 1992,* Detroit, Gale, 1992.

Paper, Paperboard, Pulp Capacity and Fiber Consumption, Washington, DC: American Forest & Paper Association, 1993.

Smook, Gary A. *Handbook of Pulp & Paper Terminology: A Guide to Industrial and Technological Usage,* Bellingham, WA: Angus Wilde, 1990.

U.S. Industrial Outlook 1993. Washington, DC: U.S. Department of Commerce, 1993.

—Alan Rooks

SIC 2671

PAPER, COATED AND LAMINATED PACKAGING

This classification covers establishments primarily engaged in manufacturing coated or laminated flexible materials made of combinations of paper, plastics film, metal foil, and similar materials (excluding textiles) for packaging purposes. These are made from purchased sheet materials or plastics resins and may be printed in the same establishment. Establishments primarily engaged in manufacturing coated or laminated paper for other purposes are classified in **SIC 2672: Coated and Laminated Paper, Not Elsewhere Classified,** including establishments manufacturing all gummed or pressure sensitive tape. Those establishments that manufacture unsupported plastics film are classified in **SIC 3081: Unsupported Plastics Film and Sheet.** Establishments manufacturing aluminum foil are classified in **SIC 3497: Metal Foil and Leaf,** while those manufacturing paper from pulp are classified in **SIC 2621: Paper Mills.**

The packaging industry represents one of the smallest and most fragmented industries within the paper industry group. Shipments total close to $3 billion a year, less than three percent of the paper and allied products group. While the industry has historically tended to follow fluctuations in the U.S. economy, increasing segmentation and specialization has caused a minor reconfiguration of the industry landscape. Environmental concerns have resulted in the industry paying considerably more attention to issues such as recycled content and biodegradability.

The industry is considerably more fragmented than most other paper industries, with a number of small players competing either in highly specialized product niches or regions. A company might, for example, have a leading position in one segment but have no products in any of the other segments. A distinguishing feature of the industry is the fact that an inordinately high percentage (approximately 20 percent) of potential clients such as manufacturers package their own goods. This means that firms within the industry are often competing with potential clients.

Because the modern packaging market requires specialized skills to compete effectively, a large, vertically integrated firm cannot dominate the industry or a segment within the industry as it can in other industries within the paper group. The packaging industry is one of the least concentrated in the paper group. Geographically, establishments are located primarily in the East, with a concentration centered around the Midwest. This is not surprising given the fact that some of the main users of products in this industry are food processors, many of which are located in the Midwest.

Since the 1960s, the industry has generally followed the cycles of the U.S. economy. The industry slowdown experienced in the early 1990s, therefore, could be attributable to the slowdown in the U.S. economy as a whole. At the same time, however, the most successful companies have demonstrated an ability to adapt to the changing requirements of the marketplace.

Some of the more notable changes the industry has experienced include: new materials, environmentally conscious products, and specialization and technological innovation. The industry has experimented with new materials as customers have demanded lighter weight, stronger materials for packaging. Some of the new materials include lighter-weight, high-tech plastics and reinforced paper. The increased popularity of the microwave, for example, has caused a greater need for a wider range of uses for existing and new materials.

Biodegradable, recyclable, and recycled materials have become essential in the packaging industry. Packaging accounted for about 30 percent of U.S. solid waste in the early 1990s. In response to environmental pressures as well as to higher prices for landfill usage and subsequent higher costs for non-recyclable materials, producers have incorporated "green" products and raw materials into their packaging.

With manufacturers demanding more from packaging, producers have had to incorporate new skills and materials into producing packages. This has lead to specialization and technological innovation. An example of such innovation is razor packaging, which has been made to simulate the look of a mirror.

Three firms maintain enough flexibility to adapt to the changing needs in the packaging industry. Bemis Corp. of Minneapolis is primarily active in flexible film packaging. Bemis boasts sales of approximately $1.2 billion per year. James River Paper Corporation and Minnesota Mining & Manufacturing also maintain a strong presence in the industry.

INDUSTRY INFORMATION SOURCES

Darnay, Arsen J., ed. *Manufacturing USA*, 2d ed. Detroit: Gale Research, 1992.

Mariner, Judi, et al., eds. *Dun's Business Rankings*. Bethlehem, PA: Dun & Bradstreet Information Services, 1993.

Packaging Industry Outlook Conference: Annual Review and Outlook. Cleveland, OH: Prescott, Ball & Turben, Inc., 18-19 April 1990.

Staphos, George L. *Packaging Wrap-up: February Survey.* New York: Paine Webber Research, 23 February 1993.

Weeks, Lyman Horace. *A History of Paper-Manufacturing in the United States, 1690-1916.* New York: Burt Franklin, 1916, reprinted 1969.

—Andrew Ballard

SIC 2672

COATED AND LAMINATED PAPER, NOT ELSEWHERE CLASSIFIED

This industry covers establishments primarily engaged in manufacturing coated, laminated, or processed paper and film from purchased paper, except for packaging. Also included are establishments primarily manufacturing gummed paper products and pressure sensitive tape with backing of any material other than rubber, for any application. Establishments primarily engaged in manufacturing coated and laminated paper for packaging are classified in **SIC 2671: Packaging Paper and Plastics Film, Coated and Laminated**; those manufacturing carbon paper are classified in **SIC 3955: Carbon Paper and Inked Ribbons**; and those manufacturing photographic and blueprint paper are classified in **SIC 3861: Photographic Equipment and Supplies.**

INDUSTRY SNAPSHOT

This classification incorporates a wide variety of products and companies. Industry shipments in 1990 totalled approximately $8 billion, or roughly 6.7 percent of the paper industry group as a whole. Establishments employed approximately 23,000 workers in 1991. The compound annual growth rate for the classification has been approximately ten percent since its creation in 1987; growth has slowed in recent years, however, to around five percent.

ORGANIZATION AND STRUCTURE

Most companies in this industry limit their activities to the coating of paper or other materials, but produce diverse products from this process. Of the many products in the industry, the vast majority of industry shipments come from one of two sectors: pressure-sensitive products and coated and laminated paper. The pressure-sensitive products group includes cellophane tape, almost all labels, and a variety of other pressure-sensitive adhesives (PSAs), but does not include gummed tape. Coated and laminated paper products include paper which is treated or coated to enhance the paper's utility. These two sectors account for 58 percent and 20 percent of the aggregate industry shipments, respectively.

Pressure-Sensitive Products. Even within this subsegment of the industry, there is a great deal of diversity. Pressure-sensitive products range from cellophane tape to shrinkable labels to sealing tapes. Advances in adhesive technology and continuing development work by manufacturers of pressure-sensitive adhesives (PSAs) have led to increases in the applicability and quality of PSAs. Greater flexibility, lighter weight and reduced cost have caused producers to use some types of adhesives in place of rivets, bolts, and chemical compounds in assembly processes. Even heavy industrial processes such as engine manufacture and truck frame assembly have found applications for PSAs.

To produce PSAs, manufacturers use paper, plastic films, nonwoven cloth, or polyethylene as a base. A chemical solvent or waterborne acrylic, which provides the adhesive necessary for the PSA to stick, is applied to the base, usually to one side. PSAs can be measured on three different criteria: tack, or how well the PSA bonds with a given surface; peel, or how difficult it is to remove the tape from the surface; and shear resistance, or how well the PSA responds to ''creep'' over time. The type of adhesive which coats the film depends on the PSA's desired application.

Another common application of PSAs is found in the $3 billion label industry. The label market has seen growth of eight to ten percent in recent years and is considered one of the most promising areas of the industry. Labels can be made of paper, polystyrene, film, or new space-age materials, but the defining feature of a label is its mode of application. There are three common application forms: wet glue, pressure-sensitive, and shrink sleeve. Wet glue applications affix a paper or plastic label via a pre-applied adhesive. Beverages and foods in glass containers often use this form of label. Pressure-sensitive applications involve a process in which the label is applied by a small amount of pressure. Aside from standard office use, pressure-sensitive labels can be found on many drug containers and have been increasing in applications. Shrink sleeve applications, wherein the label is first wrapped around the product and then shrunk directly on to it to form a bond, are most common on batteries and film products. The wet glue and pressure-sensitive methods account for the vast majority of labels and are anticipated to hold a near 90 percent share of the market in the 1990s.

Coated and Laminated Papers. The products produced through the coating and laminating process range from simple printing and writing stock to carbonless and thermographic business papers. The vast majority of coated paper is produced at the site; most paper manufacturers have off- or on-roller coaters which can be set to coat the paper (or be left off to produce uncoated paper) as it leaves the production line. Companies included within this classification generally are not involved with the papermaking process, but instead limit themselves only to the coating and laminating process.

Some of the factors involved in coating papers include the printing process (offset, rotogravure, non-impact, etc.), the type of ink used (colored, black and white, thickness), and environmental considerations. Coating must take into account the uniformity of the coating application, the evenness of the coat weight, and the smoothness and uniformity of the coat. Coated papers are broken down into five grades, with number one being the heaviest and generally the highest quality.

Paper is coated with pigments, which can consist of either chemical solutions or clay compounds. Titanium dioxide has long been a favorite coating material because of its opacity. Other popular coatings have included calcium carbonate and kaolin, a naturally-occurring mineral. Recently, more attention has been paid to the environmental impact of coating materials. Because of its easy biodegradability, kaolin has grown in popularity.

Within the coated and laminated paper sector, converters might apply any number of coatings to change the function or quality of paper. Gummed resins might be applied to make flypaper or gummed adhesive tape; cloth or fluids might be incorporated into the papermaking process to produce cloth-lined or porous impregnated papers. One segment which saw particularly strong growth through the 1980s was the carbonless paper segment. This type of paper is manufactured by weaving small beads of ink into the paper fiber itself. When pressure is applied, the beads are broken and ink darkens the paper to emulate the pen strokes of the writer.

BACKGROUND AND DEVELOPMENT

As long as manufacturers have been producing paper, the companies have been developing coatings for increased applications. Advances in coatings, paper manufacturing processes, and application technologies have all impacted the industry substantially although events have tended to move in evolutionary rather than revolutionary stages.

One clear event which prodded the growth of the label industry was the development of the self-adhesive label by Stanton Avery in 1935. From this initial product line came a whole range of self-adhesive (now called pressure-sensitive) products, including thermal films, airline bag tags, computer imprintable films, and thermal transfer self-adhesives.

As one of the more diverse industry classifications, the companies in the laminated paper sector are not specific to any one part of the country. The geographic locations of the companies tends to be roughly correlated with the population of the United States as a whole. The relatively low barriers to entry into the industry have meant that many firms concentrate their business on a local or regional basis. None of the firms in this industry have sales of over $1 billion.

CURRENT CONDITIONS

Since its classification as an independent industry in 1987, the industry has been characterized by small firms that have sought to stake out dominant shares in niche markets. Product differentiation and continuous improvement are the most influential factors of market share; however, players are only able to succeed insofar as they are able to stay ahead of customers' demands through innovation. Because of the degree of specialization in this industry, larger trends within the paper group as a whole have tended to have a smaller impact on producers than in more commodity-oriented industries.

Coated Paper Markets. Along with much of the rest of the paper industry, the coated market experienced slow growth through the downward business cycle of the early 1990s. While coated paper tends to remain more resilient in times of economic downturns than lower value-added products, the coated market experienced particular troubles in the 1990s because a number of international players moved into the higher-end coated markets in response to higher raw materials profits.

Some demographic trends impacted the demand for coated paper. Pressure on producers came from two directions and led to different conclusions. On the one hand, demand for lower-grade product lines slackened. Lower-grade coated paper is primarily used for general interest magazines and Sunday supplements; end-user demand in these segments trailed off with declines in consumer interest in reading and the rise of electronic media. Higher-grade lines, using heavier grade papers and better quality coatings, witnessed strong demand in recent years. Retailers have increasingly adopted "life-style retailing" techniques and often utilize mail-order catalogues as a vehicle for communicating with customers. The printing and processing of catalogues generally requires a higher grade of coated paper.

The opposing factor to the new growth sector of higher-grade papers in the coating market is environmental regulation. Environmental pressures within the industry oppose many of the processes used to coat high quality paper. Some of the chemical compounds used in coated paper have come under attack as being detrimental to the environment. Furthermore, regulations stipulating certain amounts of recycled content have forced producers to use wastepaper, generally a lower-quality raw material. The industry is thus in a quandary: just as end-user demand has forced manufacturers to shift to higher-quality product, environmental considerations have forced them to change many of their basic manufacturing processes. The result of these opposing forces has been to force changes in raw material sourcing, production, and quantity of grade manufacture.

Growth in Pressure-Sensitive Products. Growth within the pressure-sensitive areas has come from increased industrial sector adoption, improved quality (due in part to advances in materials technology), and new products targeted toward the consumer sector. With some growth areas maturing—such as the adhesive-coated notepads sold under the brand name Post-it Notes—producers have looked for new product niches and ways of expanding product applications.

The label markets, however, have continued to grow at a significantly faster pace than the rest of the economy over the past few years and this segment has become one of the fastest-growing within this classification. Some of the factors contributing to the growth of this sector include: increased use of bar codes at end point-of-sale processors; legislation which requires food manufacturers to disclose an increased amount of information on food labels; and advances in application and material technologies which have allowed manufacturers to increase the use of labels.

Wet-glued, adhesive-applied labels account for roughly 55 to 60 percent of the developed markets. This method is generally the least expensive on an ongoing basis; however, in order to effectually practice it requires substantial investment in equipment and machinery. Market share for this group is expected to decline over time, because of increased competition from pressure-sensitive labels. Growth in the wet-glue sector is expected to average no more than one to three percent through the 1990s.

The best prospects for growth in the label markets are considered to be found in the shrink sleeve and in-mold sectors. Shrink sleeve achieved growth rates as high as 30 percent in the 1980s, albeit from a very small base. While pressure-sensitive labels are also expected to maintain their historical growth rates, increasing competition from alternative labeling methods and direct decoration have come into play as never before. In addition, growing environmental pressures have forced label manufacturers to pay attention to recoverability, recycled content, and environmental friendliness of adhesives.

INDUSTRY LEADERS

The fragmented and specialized nature of the industry makes true dominance across all sectors a virtual impossibility. Certain firms, however, have managed to carve out strongly defensible niches and have consistently maintained innovation and expertise to keep a strong position in their particular sector. The largest firm by revenues in the industry is Appleton Papers, Inc., a division of the United Kingdom firm Arjo Wiggins Appleton (AWA). Appleton had an estimated revenue of $700 million in 1990 from more than a dozen sites across the United States. Appleton is a market leader in carbonless and thermographic papers.

Among the notables in the pressure-sensitive products area is the Minnesota Mining & Manufacturing Company (3M). 3M pioneered cellophane tape and manufactures some of the best-known brand names in the industry with its Scotch tape and Post-it notes. 3M manufactures only part of its products within this industry, but still has a sizeable representation within the industry leaders. 3M had 1990 revenues of approximately $13 billion and employs 19,000 people.

WORK FORCE

Because of the extremely specialized nature of the industry, workers who work with coated and laminated papers tend to be more specialized than workers within the rest of the paper industry group. At the same time, the wide array of activities within the classification tends to minimize variance of wages; wages within the industry average approximately $11 per hour, roughly on par with the rest of the paper industry. Because of the dispersion and fragmentation of the industry, organized labor tends to be less represented.

AMERICA AND THE WORLD

A high value-to-weight ratio along with the unique nature of many of the products within the industry have contributed to a globalization of the industry. Since technologies are often proprietary, few barriers exist to stop products from migrating from one market to another. A list of the world's leading thermal coaters, for example, would list few U.S. firms. Another factor hindering the United States' growth in the sector is the fact that many of the advances in coating equipment technology have come from overseas. This has meant a delay in the diffusion of technology to the United States and a subsequent lag in U.S. competitiveness in certain sectors. Continuing advances in specialty coatings, material technology, and environmental friendliness will dictate the success of firms in the United States throughout the 1990s.

INDUSTRY INFORMATION SOURCES

Darnay, Arsen J., ed. *Manufacturing USA*, 2d ed. Detroit: Gale Research, 1992.

Klein, James E. *Paper & Paperboard Manufacturing and Converting Fundamentals*, 2d ed. San Francisco: Miller-Freeman, Inc., 1991.

Mariner, Judi, et al., eds. *Dun's Business Rankings*. Bethlehem, PA: Dun & Bradstreet Information Services, 1993.

1993 North American Pulp & Paper Factbook. San Francisco: Miller-Freeman, Inc., 1992.

1992 Labelexpo USA Conference Proceedings: Trends and Opportunities. Chicago: Tag & Label Manufacturers Institute, Inc., 1992.

Rothwell, Tim. *Bowater plc*. London: Barclays de Zoete Wedd Research, Ltd., June 1992.

Stratton, William M., and Richard T. Glackin. "Getting Acquainted with Pressure-Sensitive Adhesive Tapes." *Machine Design*, 21 May 1992.

Veverka, Arthur C. "Coated Paper Outlook." *FOLIO: Sourcebook 1991*, 1991.

Weeks, Lyman Horace. *A History of Paper-Manufacturing in the United States, 1690-1916*. New York: Burt Franklin, 1916, reprinted 1969.

SIC 2673

PLASTICS, FOIL AND COATED PAPER BAGS

This category covers establishments primarily engaged in manufacturing bags of unsupported plastic film, coated paper, metal foil, or laminated combinations of these materials. These bags can be printed or unprinted. Establishments primarily engaged in manufacturing uncoated paper bags and multiwall bags and sacks are classified in **SIC 2674: Uncoated Paper and Multiwall Bags;** those manufacturing textile bags are classified in **SIC 2393: Textile Bags;** and those manufacturing garment storage bags, except of plastics film and paper, are classified in **SIC 2392: Housefurnishings, Except Curtains and Draperies.**

Products included in **SIC 2673: Plastics, Foil and Coated Paper Bags** include merchandise bags, trash bags, waste bags, frozen food bags, garment storage bags, and wardrobe bags. The majority of products produced in this sector are specialty bags and liners made from polyethylene single-web film. This segment accounted for nearly 58 percent of all product shipments in this category in 1987. Within the polyethylene single-web segment, refuse bags are by far the largest component, accounting for nearly 22 percent of total shipments in this industry, while grocery and variety bags account for another 12 percent. Other significant products in this classification include specialty bags and liners made from coated single-web paper, which accounted for ten percent of industry shipments in 1987. Specialty bags and liners made from multiweb laminations and foil accounted for another ten percent that same year.

The biggest purchaser of plastic, laminated and coated paper bags continues to be retail trade outlets (not including eating and drinking establishments). These retail outlets purchased nearly 60 percent of all bags produced in this category in 1987. Personal consumption accounted for another 8.5 percent of the output and wholesale trade another 6.7 percent. The remainder of product shipments were purchased by a wide variety of other sectors of the economy, mostly in manufacturing.

While paper is a major raw material for bags, the vast majority of products produced in this classification are made from plastic resins or sheets. Plastic resins used in granule, pellet, powder or liquid form accounted for $1.04 billion of the $2.2 billion worth of materials consumed by this sector in 1987. Plastic products used in the form of sheets, rods, tubes, and other shapes accounted for another $149 million. By contrast, paper accounted for just $141 million. Other significant raw materials for this category include printing ink ($51.7 million), paperboard containers, boxes and corrugated paperboard used to ship finished products ($116 million), and glues and adhesives ($27 million).

Despite grappling with a difficult recessionary environment in the late 1980s and early 1990s, manufacturers of plastic, laminated, and coated bags maintained a relatively steady business during this time frame. Between 1987 and 1989, the value of product shipments in this category shot up 11.7 percent annually, from $4.58 billion in 1987 to $5.65 billion in 1989. The value of shipments dropped slightly in 1990, to $5.50 billion before rebounding to $5.95 billion in 1991. The outlook for this industry is generally thought to be quite positive, as more retail outlets convert to plastic merchandise bags and other applications are developed.

Several different types of companies are leaders in this industry. Mobil Chemical Co., a division of Mobil Oil Corp., is one of the leading companies as is First Brands Corporation, which manufactures a wide variety of trash bags, among other consumer products. Other leaders include W.R. Grace & Company, Presto, Duro Bag and Sonoco Products Company. This industry segment employed 35,000 people with a payroll of $875 million in 1991. The average annual salary was $25,000. Of that total, 29,000 were production workers who worked 61 million man hours for wages of $621 million, or $21,400 per worker.

Development in high-tech plastic materials are likely to change the raw material mix in this industry. For example, new polyolefin/polystyrene materials are likely to be used to manufacture carryout bags, among other products. While demand for these materials will not fully develop until late in the 1990s, the availability of polyolefin/polystyrene metallocene based materials and metallocene based materials are expected to fundamentally alter the manufacture of liners, films and bags. By 1998, consumption of new polyolefin/ polystyrene materials for carryout bags is expected to reach 90 million pounds by 1998. That compares with the 2.7 billion pounds of plastics resins consumed by manufacturers in this industry in 1987 for all types of plastic bags.

INDUSTRY INFORMATION SOURCES

New Technologies and Trends for Upgrade Commodities, Norwalk, CT: Business Communications Co., Inc.

"1994 Converting Business Forecast," *Paper, Film & Foil Converter,* February 1994.

U.S. Industrial Outlook 1993, Washington, DC: U.S. Department of Commerce, 1993.

—Alan Rooks

SIC 2674

UNCOATED PAPER AND MULTIWALL BAGS

This classification includes establishments primarily engaged in manufacturing uncoated paper bags or multiwall bags and sacks, whether or not coated or containing plastics film or metal foil. Establishments primarily engaged in manufacturing bags from plastics, unsupported film, foil, coated paper, or laminated or coated combinations of these materials, are classified in **SIC 2673: Plastics, Foil, and Coated Paper Bags.** Those establishments manufacturing textile bags are classified in **SIC 2393: Textile Bags.**

INDUSTRY SNAPSHOT

The uncoated paper and multiwall bag industry is not a growing industry, but it has stabilized at a fairly high level of total sales. The value of shipments in this industry remained almost unchanged in the late 1980s and early 1990s. In 1988 the value of shipments was $2.73 billion. That figure rose slightly in 1989, to $2.79 billion, before falling in 1991 ($2.75 billion) and 1992 ($2.65 billion).

In all uncoated paper and multiwall bag applications, the package must contain and protect the product or contents. Paper is used because of its ability to contribute strength and stiffness or rigidity to the container. Plastics may also offer strength, but paper is more resilient than plastics over a wider temperature range. Paper is more easily printed on than other materials. However, in many applications paper bags must be coated with waxes or plastics or laminated to plastic films or foil to develop effective barriers to water, vapor, gases or odors.

Market shares. The uncoated paper and multiwall bag industry is almost evenly split between two categories: grocers' bags, sacks, variety and shopping bags, which held 48.34 percent of the market in 1987; and shipping sacks and multiwall bags, which held 50.71 percent of the market in the same year. Those figures are likely to change in the 1990s, with the continued decline of the grocers' bag market. Plastic bags have assumed a dominant share of this particular market.

Nonetheless, grocers' bags and sacks still had the biggest share of any bag category in this industry in

1987, with 39.1 percent of total production. The next biggest category was multiwall shipping sacks, with 33 percent of production. Single and double wall shipping sacks was the third-largest category, with 16 percent of production.

In the industry's terminology, paper sacks refer to the large bags used to hold customers supermarket purchases. The 1/6th barrel sack is the standard paper sack used in supermarkets. It is called that because in the early 1900s, when paper bags were gaining in popularity, they were used to hold 1/6th of a barrel of flour. Another popular size is the 1/8th barrel sack.

Paper sacks come in a variety of basis weights. Single-ply bags range in basis weight from 60 pound to 80 pound. Some stores prefer a double-ply bag, made of two 40-pound basis weight bags, since it can hold heavier items. Stores using this double-ply bag can avoid the "double bagging" common at checkouts of supermarkets using single-ply bags.

The bag industry refers to smaller, lighter weight bags as "grocery bags." These bags are used in outlets such as convenience stores and fast food restaurants. They come in a variety of sizes, from 1/2-pound bags to 25-pound bags. These weights are based on early 1900s terminology, when paper bags were graded by how much sugar they could hold. For example, a 1/2-pound bag could hold 1/2 pound of sugar. Retail trade establishments remain this manufacturing industry's primary customer.

ORGANIZATION AND STRUCTURE

The uncoated paper and multiwall bag market was a steadily growing and relatively stable industry into the 1970s. Paper accounted for the vast majority of bags produced for retail outlets, such as supermarkets. However, in the 1970s, plastics manufacturers began to perfect the single ply polyethylene shopping bag, which could compete effectively with the traditional paper sack. While lacking some of the characteristics of the paper sack, such as stiffness, the plastic sack had one big advantage—lower cost. Today, individual plastic bags cost about one-third as much as the average paper sack. With supermarket net profits averaging about one penny for every dollar of sales, these retailers have been quick to convert to plastic bags.

Prices prevalent in the mid-1990s clearly demonstrate the cost differential. For example, the average paper grocery sack cost $32 to $34 per 1,000, or 3.2 to 3.4 cents each, while the typical high density, 1/2 mil polyethylene sack cost $13 to $15 per 1,000, or 1.3 cents to 1.5 cents each. While plastic bags do not hold as much as comparable paper bags, supermarket

chains still see substantial cost savings in using plastic bags. While some supermarket chains still use paper sacks exclusively, and others offer customers a choice of paper or plastic, that has not stopped the steady erosion of paper's market share. Also, other retail outlets, such as mass merchandisers, use plastic bags exclusively. K mart converted from paper in the 1980s. This led Union Camp Corp., formerly a major supplier of paper sacks to K Mart, to invest in plastic bag manufacturing in order to continue supplying K Mart. In the early 1990s, Wal-Mart, the nation's largest retailer, converted to using plastic bags exclusively.

Multiwall market stronger. Multiwall paper bags, which use three or more plies of paper, are used heavily in industrial applications for the transport and sales of products such as seed and fertilizers. They have fared better recently than their paper sack cousins. Multiwall bags are used for many business-to-business transactions, such as the sale of fertilizer to farmers, and also for consumer transactions, such as pet food. As a result, multiwall bags are sold in a bewildering variety of shapes, sizes, and constructions, from the plain brown bags used for cement mix to the high quality, four-color packages used to merchandise pet food or lawn fertilizer.

Multiwall bag producers divide their market into two categories: paper multiwall packaging, designed for products weighing 20 pounds and over; and consumer packaging, designed for products weighing five to 10 pounds, such as pet food and charcoal.

The number of packaging layers depends on the application. For example, multiwall bags for products being shipped overseas may have as many as five or six layers to withstand severe handling and extreme temperature conditions. Pet food bags, on the other hand, may have just three layers, with one being a grease-resistant paper. Cement bags usually include a polyethylene liner to keep the moisture from the product out of the outer paper layers. However, some bag manufacturers, in order to make their bags more "environmentally friendly" and recyclable, are looking for ways to eliminate the plastic film inner layer by using specially-treated paper instead.

BACKGROUND AND DEVELOPMENT

Paper bags have been a major product for the paper industry for well over 100 years. One of the earliest bag makers, Union Paper Bag Machine Co. (now Union Camp), was founded in 1861 in Bethlehem, Pennsylvania, to make and sell machines for making paper bags. In the late 1800s and early 1900s, the use of paper bags continued to grow along with the economy. The bag market received a major boost from the invention and development of self-serve grocery stores in the early 1900s. As self-serve stores continued to expand in other retail environments, the use of paper bags boomed.

CURRENT CONDITIONS

The big issue for the uncoated paper and multiwall bag industry continues to be the penetration of plastic bags into markets previously dominated by paper. The degree of penetration varies greatly by category.

In the paper sack market, plastics had taken over 68 to 75 percent of the market in the early to mid-1990s. That was a dramatic reversal from the early 1980s, when paper sacks accounted for the majority of the market. In 1993, paper sack shipments were forecast to drop as much as 20 percent. However, paper is expected to "bottom out" and hold on to the 25 percent market share it held in the mid-1990s since many customers still prefer the paper sack in supermarkets.

In the grocery bag market, plastics penetration has been far less pervasive. In the mid-1990s, paper still accounted for about 70 percent of the market. Much of the strength in this market is accounted for by the growth of the fast food marketplace. Fast food chains such as McDonalds and Burger King use a very high volume of grocery bags to package customers' orders. Plastics have almost no penetration in this particular market segment. The main reason is that plastics have no rigidity, a real problem when food, drinks, and other items are combined in one bag.

The product mix in the fast food bag segment changed radically in the early 1990s as demand for recycled products grew. For example, the McDonald's chain converted from a bright white bleached bag made from virgin fiber to a 100 percent recycled, unbleached brown bag for the majority of its carryout orders. Other chains, such as Burger King, soon followed with other types of bags made from recycled paper.

The "notions and millinery" sector includes the flat bags (without folded bottoms) used to hold customer purchases in variety stores and department stores. Plastic has made heavy inroads into paper's market share in this category, accounting for about 70 percent of this market. However, paper seems to be holding steady at about 30 percent of the market.

The only paper bag product line seeing any real growth in the mid-1990s was heavy duty, cord-handled shopping bags used by many department store chains. Many retail outlets use these bags for marketing purposes, since they can be made from high-

quality bleached, clay-coated paper for four-color printing. Many stores use these bags as a customer service—often charging for them—so that customers can consolidate their purchases from different areas of the store.

Slow growth in multiwall. The multiwall bag market grew at an annual rate of 1.5 percent a year in the early to mid-1990s, but the market would have grown faster had it not lost some market share to low-density plastic bags and wraps. One of the fastest growing bag applications, for example, is multilayer industrial plastic film bags, which are replacing multiwall paper bags for products such as herbicides, pesticides and fertilizers.

By the early to mid-1990s, plastics had taken about 18 to 22 percent of the market previously held exclusively by multiwall paper bags. For example, plastic bags are often used for high-moisture products, such as bark chips.

However, manufacturers are also producing combination bags, which include several outer layers of paper and inner liners made of plastic. This hybrid bag combines the barrier properties of plastic with the rigidity and strength of paper. Also, manufacturers have found that layers of different materials, such as paper and plastic, can provide a better odor barrier in some instances than either material can by itself.

However, some multiwall bag applications are moving toward 100 percent plastic. Bags of plastic resin for industrial applications, for example, are packaged more frequently in packages made from that resin so that when the product is used it can be tossed into the process, bag and all. Also, some 100 percent plastic bags are being made with three or more layers of different plastics to accommodate specialized packaging processes. For example, some products are packaged with a "hot fill" process, where the product is put into the package while still hot. The inner plastic layer can handle the hot product while the outer layers are designed to protect the product in transit.

INDUSTRY LEADERS

Major manufacturers of uncoated paper and multiwall bags include Stone Container Corp., Duro Bag Manufacturing Co., International Paper Co., Gaylord Container Corp., and Union Camp Corp. The top three manufacturers, Stone, Duro and Gaylord, held about 80 percent of the paper sack market in the mid-1990s. Of the five manufacturers listed above, both Duro and Union Camp are heavily integrated, in that they produce both plastic and paper bags. These same companies are also leaders in the production of multiwall bags. Other significant manufacturers of uncoated paper and multiwall bags include Shurfine-Central Corp. (a wholesale food company); Equitable Bag Co. Inc.; Hargro Packaging Corp.; and Port Townsend Paper Corp.

The uncoated paper and multiwall bag industry employed 18,000 people with a payroll of $398 million in 1991. Average wages for employees in this segment amounted to $22,111. The industry employment total includes 15,000 production workers who put in 30 million total hours for $299 million, or an average annual wage of $19,933.

INDUSTRY INFORMATION SOURCES

Biermann, Christopher J., *Essentials of Pulping and Paper-making.* San Diego: Academic Press, Inc., 1993.

Darnay, Arsen J., *Manufacturing USA,* 3d ed., Detroit, Gale, 1993.

Paper, Paperboard, Pulp Capacity and Fiber Consumption. Washington, DC: American Forest & Paper Association, 1993.

Thesaurus of Pulp and Paper Terminology. Atlanta: Institute of Paper Science and Technology, 1991.

U.S. Industrial Outlook 1993. Washington, DC: U.S. Department of Commerce, 1993.

—Alan Rooks

SIC 2675

DIE-CUT PAPER AND PAPERBOARD AND CARDBOARD

Establishments in this industry are primarily engaged in die-cutting purchased paper and paperboard and in manufacturing cardboard by laminating, lining or surface coating paperboard. Establishments primarily engaged in laminating building paper from purchased paper are classified in **SIC 2679: Converted Paper and Paperboard Products, Not Elsewhere Classified.**

Products produced by manufacturers in this industry classification include pasted chip board; bottle caps and tops; cardboard foundations and cutouts; pasted, laminated line and surface coated paperboard; plain paper cards; tabulating cards; die-cut paper and paperboard; egg cartons and egg case fillers and flats; and filing folders, index cards, and paperboard library cards.

In the late 1980s and early 1990s, manufacturers in the die-cut paper and board industry performed better than many other paper and paperboard companies. The value of product shipments in this industry increased steadily from 1987 to 1991, despite a major recession and generally lower selling prices for paper and paperboard products. In 1987 the value of shipments in the die-cut paper and board industry was $1.75 billion. That increased to $1.85 billion in 1988, $1.98 billion in 1989 and $2.12 billion in 1990. By 1991, the value of shipments had reached a record $2.16 billion. From 1987 to 1991, the value of shipments increased 23 percent.

Most of the products produced by this industry are office supplies. Die-cut paper and board office supplies accounted for 53 percent of all industry products in 1987. Pasted, lined, laminated or surface coated paperboard was the next largest category, with 27.6 percent of the total. All other die-cut products accounted for the remaining 19.4 percent of the products produced by this industry. Die-cut paper and board manufacturers tend to be located in areas where business activity is highest. Industry players are thus concentrated in states such as California, New York, and Illinois.

This industry produces a wide variety of products and appears to have benefitted from the general increase in boxmaking capacity in the early 1990s, since many of its products are used as inserts in boxes. Also, many of the products produced by the die-cut paper and board industry are made from recycled fiber— often 100 percent recycled fiber. The desire by consumers and businesses to buy products made from recycled materials appears to have spurred demand for products from the die-cut paper and board industry.

Die-cut paper and board industry leaders tend to be independent converters; there are few major paper companies with holdings in die-cut paper and paperboard. Some of the leading companies include ACX Technologies Inc., Ivex Packaging Corp., American Trading and Production Corp., and Fleer Corp. Simpson Paper Co. is one of the few paper companies with a large market share in this industry. Other players include Rostra Holdings Inc., Chesapeake Display, Anthony Industries, and Avery Dennison Corp.

The die-cut paper and board industry employed 17,000 employees in 1991 with an annual payroll of $408 million. The average annual wage was $24,000. Of that total, 14,000 were production workers who worked 28 million hours for wages of $279 million.

INDUSTRY INFORMATION SOURCES

Paper, Paperboard, Pulp Capacity and Fiber Consumption, Washington, DC: American Forest & Paper Association, 1993.

Smook, Gary A., *Handbook of Pulp & Paper Terminology: A Guide to Industrial and Technological Usage,* Bellingham, WA: Angus Wilde Publications, 1990.

U.S. Industrial Outlook 1993, Washington, DC: U.S. Department of Commerce, 1993.

—Alan Rooks

SIC 2676

SANITARY PAPER PRODUCTS

Covers establishments primarily engaged in manufacturing sanitary paper products from purchased paper, such as facial tissues and handkerchiefs, table napkins, toilet paper and paper towels, disposable diapers, and sanitary napkins and tampons.

INDUSTRY SNAPSHOT

The sanitary paper products industry is composed of industries engaged in converting paper into finished products with sanitary applications. Shipments in the sanitary paper industry were estimated at approximately $15.6 billion in 1992, accounting for some 12.7 percent of the paper and allied products industry group as a whole. Products contained in this classification most closely define the point where the paper industry meets the consumer products industry and therefore the industry spends more on advertising than any other part of the paper industry. Many of the products contained within this classification are considered nondiscretionary and as a result sales within this classification have tended to follow different business cycles than those of more commodity-oriented paper lines. On the other hand, as of the early 1990s, sanitary paper producers have found themselves in a much more competitive environment characterized by high penetration rates, slowing growth, and increasing price pressure. All of these trends are expected to continue or intensify into the latter half of the decade. In order to maintain growth, firms have begun to focus on expansion abroad while at the same time continuing to segment the market and introduce new products domestically.

ORGANIZATION AND STRUCTURE

The sanitary paper industry can be broken down into two broad segments: woven sanitary products (sanitary tissue), or products woven into paper strictly from wood fiber; and nonwoven (absorbent) sanitary products, or products which use either natural or synthetic fibers bonded together by cohesion, friction, and/or adhesion. While some of the more general attributes of the industry apply to both sectors (work force, business cycles, etc.), the industry leaders, key success factors, and necessary technological skills differ substantially between the two segments. Each segment can be further subdivided into the consumer and commercial and industrial (C&I) sector. Customers in the C&I category of sanitary paper might be schools, hospitals, offices, or anyone who needs large amounts of sanitary paper products. C&I shipments comprise about one-third of sanitary tissue sales and a much smaller percentage of nonwoven sales.

Woven Sanitary Products. Most commonly used household paper products, including bathroom tissue, napkins, paper towels, and facial tissues, fall within this category. Sanitary tissue accounted for approximately 60 percent of all sanitary paper shipments in 1992. Bathroom tissue comprised the largest group with estimated 1992 shipments of 10.8 million rolls worth $2.5 billion. Household towels, with 3.1 billion rolls valued at $1.9 billion, were the segment's second-largest group.

The processes used to make woven sanitary products are in many ways similar to those used to create other types of paper. In the standard papermaking process, wood fibers are stripped from wood chips in either a chemical or mechanical process to produce wood pulp. This pulp, a combination of wood fibers and water, is then spread on a continuous fine screen. The resulting mat is then passed over vacuum boxes (to remove some water) and run through successive drying and pressing processes until the finished paper product is achieved.

The major differences between general paper manufacture and tissue manufacture lie in the type of raw material used and the converting processes. Because of the relationship between the softness of the raw material and the softness of the final product, lightly refined softwood fibers are generally preferred for consumer-oriented products. Products for the C&I market will place a higher premium on strength as opposed to softness and will usually be made from a coarser grade of wood. Sulfite pulping processes tend to produce a softer pulp, although pollution concerns arising from the sulfite process have caused some producers to shift to recycled or kraft inputs.

Once the tissue paper is formed, producers usually convert it into consumer products on site. Depending on the type of product, dyes and perfumes might be added and the paper might be embossed. The tissue is then prepared for market: facial tissues are folded and boxed; bathroom tissue is rolled and prepared for shipment. From this point on, the fate of the sanitary tissue lies in the hands of the producers' marketing departments.

Nonwoven Sanitary Products. A second segment of the sanitary paper market consists of products which incorporate nonwoven fabrics in their manufacture. Nonwoven products include: disposable diapers/training pants, feminine hygiene products, adult incontinence products (including consumer adult pads and institutional adult pads and bed pads), and pre-moistened tissues (including baby wipes). Advances in nonwoven technology have increased the number of nonwoven applications and enhanced the use of nonwovens in existing applications.

Although many of the processes in making nonwovens are similar to those of wovens, nonwovens are so called because fibers (either synthetic or wood pulp) used in their fabrication are bonded together instead of woven. This bonding can take the form of an adhesive applied prior to the fiber mat before or after forming or can be the result of a chemical reaction.

The typical nonwoven product, however, will incorporate many steps into its fabrication. A diaper, for example, will begin with a polyethylene outer shell. Bonded to the shell will be dry formed wood pulp (fluff pulp) within layers of impervious nonwoven fabric. Glues, resins, and adhesives will be used to bind the various components to one another. The typical adult incontinence pad, sanitary napkin, and tampon will incorporate many of the same steps into its manufacture.

In the manufacturing process, nonwovens are often treated with super-absorbent polymers (SAPs) which can absorb as much as 70 to 80 times their weight in liquid. A further distinguishing feature of SAPs is that, unlike a sponge or other woven absorbent products, SAPs retain water even when squeezed. A sponge, for example, retains water in channels or pores. SAPs chemically bind with the fluid to form a gel. Under extremely heavy pressure, SAPs might release a type of gel, but most liquids remain in their chemical compound.

Aside from sanitary applications, nonwovens can also be found in other applications either as a substitute for cloth or in applications requiring a high degree of absorbency (filters, car covers, durable shop towels). Since most producers of nonwoven sanitary products are also producers of nonwoven fabrics, the strength of these related industries can also have an impact on these companies' results.

Marketing. After the final product is ready, the process moves from manufacturing to marketing. The need to market effectively drives two additional defining features of the industry. First, there is the need for extensive promotion: companies within the sanitary paper industry spend the highest percentage on advertising of any paper-producing industry. Secondly, companies have also recognized the need for sophisticated marketing techniques. Increased segmentation and "database marketing"—using elaborate information banks to determine lifestyle predictors for a target segment—have become important success factors in the industry. Marketers comprise only a small percentage of employment (less than one percent), but the importance of marketing has increased tremendously through the early 1990s and continues to occupy a central position in the strategy of most firms.

Establishment Size and Distribution. The manufacture of sanitary products requires a number of raw materials; it therefore behooves sanitary product converters to locate near raw material sources. Success in the industry, however, can also be determined by a company's ability to bring its product to market. For a company to expand in a region, for example, it is often necessary for it to service the region from a relatively close plant. This is especially true for more commodity-oriented product lines like bathroom tissue and household towels. For products with a lower weight-to-value ratio (tampons, ultrathin pads) or niche products (pre-moistened tissues, baby wipes), companies will supply markets from only one or two manufacturing facilities. Company headquarters are almost all located east of the Rocky Mountains although this probably has more to do with U.S. population distribution and historical accident than with factors such as proximity to facilities.

The twin requirements of converting massive amounts of raw materials and bringing products to market also defines another aspect of the industry: its concentration. The leading five firms in the industry—Scott Paper, James River, Kimberly-Clark, Procter & Gamble, and Fort Howard—hold more than three-quarters of total sales. In the disposable diaper segment, the leading two firms share more than 70 percent of the total market. While private label manufacturers have been gaining market share in the sanitary tissue sector, the entrance of a major player into that market in 1992 foretold increasing competition among the largest producers.

BACKGROUND AND DEVELOPMENT

The development of the sanitary paper market in the United States has parallelled the development of the two broader categories the market represents, the paper and consumer products industry groups. The advances made in paper production technology from the latter half of the nineteenth century to the early part of the twentieth century which had an impact on the paper industry as a whole also had an impact on the sanitary paper industry.

Woven Sanitary Products. As with most of the paper industry, the sanitary tissue sector owes much of its growth to advances in automation and wood processing made in the last century. The development of the Fourdrinier process in the first half of the nineteenth century allowed greater volumes of paper to be produced at a lower price. This process is particularly relevant for sanitary tissue since it is still the ideal process for lighter weight grades in general and tissue manufacture in particular.

Developments in wood processing from 1850 until the beginning of the twentieth century provided paper manufacturers with a cheap, reliable source of raw materials. Prior to these discoveries, the main raw materials for paper production were rags, cloth, and straw. By the 1850s, automation had already substantially reduced the costs of producing paper, but constraints on the supplies of raw materials limited paper production to specific applications. Once a process was developed for wood fiber to be converted into pulp, greater applications for paper became possible and the sanitary paper industry was born. Paper began to find its way into more and more households and assumed the roles held by towels, leaves, and rags.

The marketing of the sanitary paper products did not assume its current importance until the early part of the twentieth century. Prior to that, competition in the industry seemed to be oriented toward consolidation and acquisition. The United Paper Company made a series of acquisitions in the 1890s in an attempt to form a "tissue trust," but the trust was broken and the company forced into bankruptcy when other paper producers switched to tissue production and undercut the trust's position.

From the early part of the twentieth century, developments in the sanitary sector were not so much technology- as consumer-driven and the role of the sanitary paper producer switched from being a provider of specific products to responding to consumer needs as they developed. The development of one company, Scott Paper Company, reflects many of these changes. In 1902, the company introduced Waldorf, one of the first branded bathroom tissues, and moved quickly into a position of dominance in this product line. Scott's invention of paper towels in 1907 further consolidated the company's position. By the 1950s, Scott held more than 50 percent of the sanitary tissue market. Over time, however, new product intro-

ductions and sustained marketing efforts by competitors ate into Scott's dominance.

Perhaps it was Kimberly-Clark's long experience with marketing that allowed them to gain at least some of Scott's market share with their own offerings. In 1915, Kimberly-Clark developed Cellu-cotton, an absorbent wadding which was later to be used in feminine hygiene products. In 1924, Kimberly-Clark introduced one of the most ubiquitous brand names in America: Kleenex. Originally developed as a tissue for removing cold cream, the company found that it sold better as a disposable handkerchief and, thanks to technological innovations in folding and packaging, Kimberly-Clark was able to market it as such.

Since these developments, the sanitary tissue sector has been marked more by evolutionary realignments than revolutionary innovations. The basic product offerings of the major producers in the sector have remained essentially the same, but improvements in quality, strength, packaging, and (in the C&I sector) service, have been the driving forces in the market. Since the 1960s, the sanitary paper market has witnessed intensified competition among a number of strong competitors. Low-cost producers have captured large segments of the low-end market while marketing and consumer products powerhouses have gained substantial market share in the premium branded segments. James River Corporation, founded in 1969, used acquisitions and joint ventures to expand its activities rapidly. James River moved from a start-up operation in the early 1970s to become the second-largest tissue producer (in terms of capacity) in 1992.

Nonwoven Sanitary Products. The nonwoven sector, with its emphasis on consumer goods, reflects the development of the power of marketing on American lifestyles. At the same time, the technological innovations in superabsorbent polymers and nonwoven fabrics have marked advances in the sector technologically.

Disposable diapers comprise the largest sub-segment in the nonwoven product group. Procter & Gamble first introduced disposable diapers with the Pampers brand in 1961. Since that time, the market has exhibited steady growth based mainly on increasing penetration rates. Continuous product enhancements and forceful marketing by the two main players in the disposable diapers field—Procter & Gamble and Kimberly-Clark—led to high adoption rates among parents. Nearly annual new product introductions have kept competition high and continuously improved the attractiveness of disposable diapers to parents. Advances in nonwoven technology have led to improvements in absorbency and reductions in size, therefore enabling producers to achieve savings in transportation and packaging. The next generation of diapers is expected to allow for even greater absorbency so as to stay dry even through multiple wettings.

Sanitary napkins are the second-largest component within the nonwoven product group, with 11.9 billion units accounting for $1.1 billion in sales or approximately 17 percent of the nonwoven market in 1992. Kimberly-Clark first entered the consumer products segment in the 1920s with a feminine pad under the brand name Kotex. During World War I, Army nurses had found creped tissue wadding in surgical dressings suitable for feminine care. At first, societal norms prevented feminine care products from receiving necessary exposure and display space, as many magazines refused to carry advertising for feminine care products and stores were reluctant to stock the product. Despite societal norms and relatively high prices, consumer acceptance of the products was high.

Improvements in nonwoven technology have also allowed for improvements in feminine care products. Beginning in the 1990s, the market has seen the introduction of winged napkins, improved pantiliners, and ultrathin pads. The added convenience of ultrathin pads, offering higher absorbency in a thinner pad, has caused their share of the feminine care products markets to increase from 25 percent in 1988 to 33 percent in 1990.

CURRENT CONDITIONS

The sanitary paper market has experienced slow but steady growth into the early 1990s. The non-discretionary nature of many of its product lines ensures there will be at least a base of demand into the near future. At the same time, many producers see limited growth opportunities in the domestic market. The aging of the American population, the static domestic birth rate, and increasing competition from well-heeled competitors does not bode well for the industry's major players.

Woven Sanitary Markets. Growth within the domestic woven sanitary sector showed signs of stagnating through the early 1990s. Increasing price pressure in the tissues and towels segment caused the total value of shipments to decline by approximately three percent in 1992, with even greater declines in paper napkins and facial tissues. Despite the non-discretionary nature of many of the segment's product lines, the effects of the 1990-92 recession were felt in this sector, as volume remained relatively steady. One of the main reasons cited for this decline in values was the emergence of another major player into the premium bathroom tissue segment in mid-1990. The in-

creased competition sparked a round of price reductions (and subsequent reductions in sheet counts) and heated up promotional activity in this segment. Activity in the C&I segment was hurt by the recession as reductions in time away from home (employment, travel, etc.) had their impact.

Continuing product innovations in pre-moistened towels are expected to eat into the woven products' market share over time. The development of virucidal tissues should impact the more traditional products' market share although tissue's lower cost should keep demand reasonable into the foreseeable future. Within the C&I sector, improved economies of scale and packaging advances have made productivity increases possible among most major producers. Larger rolls have required less packaging and thus allowed for improvements in transportation costs. Within the C&I sector, increased specialization has also led to advances in dispensing equipment with producers finding and distributing more efficient means of dispensing their products.

Nonwoven Sanitary Products. Improvements in nonwoven fabrics and advances in polymer technology have enabled producers to continuously upgrade product in the nonwoven sector. While competition in the nonwoven sector is not as intense as in the sanitary tissue sector, larger demographic trends point toward slowing growth in nonwoven product lines.

Producers have seen slow but steady growth in the disposable diaper market since the product's introduction. Total manufacturers' sales were estimated at $3.9 billion in 1992, approximately 58 percent of the "absorbent" sector and greater than 50 percent of the nonwoven sector generally. Growth in the domestic diaper industry reached a plateau in the late 1980s and early 1990s with a decline in net births and stabilization of market penetration. Much of the growth can be accounted for by increased market penetration by the sector's major players and high adoption rates by parents as the product has improved, but marketers view opportunities for domestic growth as limited.

As diaper penetration rates have stabilized, makers of disposable diapers have tried to use their capabilities to introduce products for market segments exhibiting increasing growth. Some of these products include training pants (for children making the transition from diapers) and adult incontinence products. The adult incontinence segment is considered one of the fastest-growing in the country despite the relatively low level of sales in this segment ($303 million).

Sanitary napkin usage as a percentage of the feminine care sector has continued to decline in favor of tampon usage. The total tampon market is estimated at $700 million and is expected to grow more rapidly than the feminine pad sector through the end of the 1990s. Overall, feminine pads currently hold about 62 percent of the feminine care market, with tampons accounting for the rest. This level is down from the late 1980s, reflecting increasing strength in the tampon market. The share of tampons peaked at around 50 percent in the late 1970s, but declined with the adverse publicity associated with toxic shock syndrome. Since then, the passage of time and medical improvements in tampon manufacture have caused increased acceptance of these products and the tampon market rebounded in the early 1990s.

Environmental Concerns. In the late 1980s and early 1990s, environmental concerns ranked near the top of issues facing the paper industry group. Restrictions on timber-cutting, landfill constraints, and limitations on some production processes have all dogged many sectors of the industry. However, many of the Northwest timber-cutting restrictions which have dogged other industries have not had the same impact on the more eastern-focused sanitary products producers. Indeed, most producers have seen prices of tissue stock remain flat or decline through the late 1980s and early 1990s.

In the production processes, many manufacturers face emerging regulations which may further limit discharges and emissions from their facilities. The Federal Clean Water and Clean Air Acts are scheduled to be promulgated by 1995 and will probably further limit discharges, particularly of dioxin, chloroforms and other chlorinated organics arising from the pulp manufacturing process. Many tissue producers have increased recycled content; all new domestic tissue production capacity planned for 1993 will use recycled fiber in part or as the total fiber mix. One major tissue manufacturer estimates that 25 percent of its total tissue stock comes from recycled paper.

Producers of nonwovens have had other concerns to deal with. Continuing environmental pressure about disposable diapers in landfills has caused some concern among producers. Since diapers only account for two percent of solid waste in the average municipal landfill, it is expected that these concerns will not be a long-term problem. Nonetheless, the publicity generated by the problem has proven to be a thorn in the side of manufacturers. To allay fears about diapers' biodegradability, further technological work has been done on achieving more eco-friendly products.

One strategy for maintaining competitiveness in the current environment is continued cost reduction. Modernization of paper lines, improvements in manufacturing efficiency, and longer-term contracts with labor have all played a significant role in attempting to reduce costs and enhance profits. In particular, sanitary tissue producers have utilized capital improvement to squeeze the greatest productivity out of their plants. For the first time, in 1992 more capacity was added through facility enhancements than through additional facilities. Most producers, however, view the greatest opportunities for growth in the sanitary paper markets in overseas expansion. The relatively large size of U.S. producers compared to their foreign counterparts, the marketing strength of U.S. companies, and relatively low levels of penetration of sanitary products in foreign markets all point toward continued globalization efforts on the part of the major U.S. players.

INDUSTRY LEADERS

The largest companies within the sanitary paper segment are Scott Paper Company, Kimberly-Clark Corporation, Procter & Gamble Co., James River Corporation, and Fort Howard Paper Company. Scott Paper is one of the oldest paper producers in the country. Some of Scott's brand names include ScotTowels, ScotTissue, Viva, Cottonelle, Baby Fresh, and Washa-bye Baby. The company had 1991 sales of approximately $5 billion and 30,800 employees. Scott has historically had a strong presence abroad, with brands such as Andrex and Scottex holding leading market positions in their respective categories in Europe.

Dallas-based Kimberly-Clark Corporation has experienced tremendous growth over the past twenty years and has blossomed into one of the country's strongest consumer-products marketers. Sales at Kimberly in 1991 were $6.8 billion and market share in many strategic lines remained high. Some of the best-known brand names in the United States— Kleenex facial tissues, Kotex feminine hygiene products, and Huggies disposable diapers—are Kimberly-Clark products.

Procter & Gamble is one of the world's largest consumer products companies with revenues of $30 billion and 106,000 employees. Its Bounty household towels, Charmin bathroom tissue, and Pampers disposable diapers brands are leaders in their respective categories.

Founded in 1969, James River is the youngest of the industry's stronger competitors. James River expanded rapidly in the 1970s and 1980s by acquiring mills considered obsolete and re-tooling them for efficient use. Its purchase of Dixie-Northern in 1982 thrust it into the forefront of bathroom tissue competitors. James River's 1991 sales were $4.6 billion; the company employs 38,000 workers.

Milwaukee-based Fort Howard competes mostly in the commercial sector of the market, holding about 25 percent of this market. The company went private in a 1988 leveraged buyout and has since struggled to maintain competitiveness in the capital-intensive sanitary paper environment.

The feminine hygiene market contains a number of other players: Johnson & Johnson's Personal Products Care division holds the lead in this segment with a 27 percent market share. Tambrands and Playtex, two firms which manufacture feminine hygiene products almost exclusively, also have a strong presence in this market.

WORK FORCE

Labor requirements for the sanitary paper producers tend to be similar to those of other paper goods manufacturers. The capital-intensive nature of paper manufacture generally relegates work force-related issues to a lower priority than equipment and capital expenditure. At the same time, labor unrest has been a point of concern for many producers and therefore has been receiving increased attention.

A typical plant will employ machinists, millwrights, mechanics, paper-machine tenders, hands (who assist in removing finished paper rolls from paper machines), guards, and janitors. According to a 1989 survey, wages for these workers averaged between $10 and $16 per hour. Sanitary paper producers also have a slightly stronger bias toward marketers and will have more ''brand managers'' than similar paper industries.

Organized Labor. As one of the oldest and most mature industries in the United States, the papermaking industry generally retains a high degree of unionization. The sanitary paper industry is consistent in this regard, although the wider variety of positions and greater representation within the industry tend to reduce the unions' effects. The United Paperworkers International Union is the single largest union and was represented in all but four of the contracts up for renegotiation in 1992. The Association of Western Pulp and Paperworkers is another large union, although its membership is largely confined to the West Coast.

AMERICA AND THE WORLD

The capital-intensive nature of paper manufacture has also meant that cheaper labor abroad has no real impact. U.S. manufacturers face little threat from abroad; only one foreign paper manufacturer, Finland-based Molnlycke, has established a significant presence in U.S. sanitary markets. For the most part, the internationalization of the sanitary paper industry has meant U.S. firms going abroad. Superior product quality and marketing ability has given the United States a competitive advantage in a number of foreign markets.

For most sanitary paper producers, Europe is viewed as particularly promising: the European Community contains five percent of the world's population, but consumes only 25 percent of the world's sanitary tissue. This compares with three percent and 40 percent for the United States. One major tissue manufacturer experienced sales growth in Europe of approximately eight percent from 1989 to 1992 despite stagnant growth elsewhere. Through the early 1990s, almost all large U.S. producers had made efforts to secure footholds in the European Community.

Sanitary paper producers' attempts to expand in Asia have met with similar frustrations and opportunities that have greeted other companies in this region. While the Japanese market is highly fragmented and thus viewed as vulnerable to the sophisticated marketers of U.S. products, intricate supplier-retailer relationships have thus far prevented any U.S. producer from establishing a significant presence. Further consolidation in the industry has also meant falling margins and more severe price wars. A number of U.S. companies have begun focusing on newly-industrialized countries and view significant opportunities in the rest of the Pacific Region.

RESEARCH AND TECHNOLOGY

Changes in the manufacture of paper have historically been evolutionary rather than revolutionary. The same processes used to manufacture paper from rags in the middle of the nineteenth century are in many forms still used late in the twentieth century. In a 1979 study, it was found that 71.6 percent of the paper industry's productivity between 1958 and 1976 could be accounted for by increased capital, while technological change accounted for only 28.4 percent. The importance of capital to the process, then, should be clear. Capital expenditures in 1990 as a percentage of product shipments were 3.75 percent. This is even greater than the **SIC 3711: Motor Vehicles and Car Bodies Industry** and **SIC 3523: Farm Machinery and Equipment** (2.2 percent and 1.9 percent, respectively), two industries usually considered among the most capital-intensive in the United States.

INDUSTRY INFORMATION SOURCES

Arpan, Jeffrey, et al. *The U.S. Pulp & Paper Industry: Global Challenges and Strategies.* Columbia, SC: University of South Carolina Press, 1984.

Chrysikopoulos, John C. *Kimberly-Clark II: Trends in Absorbent Sanitary Markets*. New York: Goldman Sachs Research, November 1992.

————. *Scott Paper Company*. New York: Goldman Sachs Research, March 1992.

Darnay, Arsen J., ed. *Manufacturing U.S.A.*, 2d ed. Detroit, MI: Gale Research, 1992.

Four Men and a Machine: Commemoration of the 75th Anniversary of the Kimberly-Clark Corporation. Neenah, WI: Kimberly-Clark Corporation, 1947.

Klein, James E. *Paper & Paperboard Manufacturing and Converting Fundamentals*, 2d ed. San Francisco: Miller-Freeman, Inc., 1991.

Mariner, Judi, et al., eds. *Dun's Business Rankings*. Bethlehem, PA: Dun & Bradstreet Information Services, 1993.

1993 North American Pulp & Paper Factbook. San Francisco: Miller-Freeman, Inc., 1992.

United States Industrial Outlook 1993. Washington, DC: U.S. Department of Commerce, 1993.

Weeks, Lyman Horace. *A History of Paper-Manufacturing in the United States, 1690-1916*. New York: Burt Franklin, 1916, reprinted 1969.

—Andrew Ballard

SIC 2677

ENVELOPES

This category includes establishments primarily engaged in manufacturing envelopes of any description from purchased paper and paperboard. Establishments primarily engaged in manufacturing stationery are classified in **SIC 2678: Stationery, Tablets, and Related Products.**

INDUSTRY SNAPSHOT

In 1992 U.S. envelope manufacturers shipped $2.7 billion worth of products. Of that total, 70 percent consisted of standard business and commercial stationery envelopes. The envelope category is classified as a converting operation, since it transforms a finished product—rolls and sheets of paper and paperboard or synthetic materials—into envelopes. In 1987 envelope converters consumed $845 million worth of paper and another $8.5 million worth of paperboard. Converters also used $290 million worth of other materials, parts, containers, and supplies, which include the plastics, olefin, and other nontraditional materials that are used to manufacture envelopes.

To some observers, the continued growth in envelope shipments is surprising considering increasing competition from communications mediums such as fax machines, voice mail message systems, electronic mail, and other electronic communications systems. However, other observers point out that new technologies rarely eliminate "old" technologies—they simply move them into new applications. Just as television did not eliminate radio broadcasts, electronic communications are not likely to eliminate or even diminish the use of "old-fashioned" mail. While fewer envelopes may be used for personal communication, for example, more will probably be used for marketing purposes.

ORGANIZATION AND STRUCTURE

Envelope manufacturing is widely thought of as a mature industry, meaning that future growth is likely to occur only with boosts in the general economy. Some segments of the envelope industry, however, are growing faster than others and are well ahead of the general economy.

Envelope manufacturing is widely distributed throughout the United States and basically involves folding, gluing, and printing on high-speed converting equipment. There are many companies involved in envelope manufacturing, including numerous small producers. As in other industries, though, the envelope industry is consolidating as larger, more efficient producers buy up smaller entities or force them out of business.

Envelope consumption is sensitive to overall economic conditions, and like the rest of the paper and allied products industry, envelope manufacturers suffered from sluggish demand and overcapacity in the early 1990s. In 1992 a recovering economy combined with the strong growth in third class advertising, better known as "junk mail," and new applications for specialty envelopes helped fuel a 2.5 percent rise in product shipments by U.S. envelope converters.

Despite good long-term prospects, the domestic envelope sector continued to suffer from overcapacity, low capacity utilization rates, and depressed prices in the early to mid-1990s. In simple terms, there was far too much envelope-folding machine capacity compared to total envelope demand. Many converters reacted by scrapping older, less efficient equipment or even closing some plants. It is expected that few new plants will be built in the 1990s, as converters instead pursue a strategy of rebuilding or refurbishing older machines so that they can compete more effectively with new equipment.

While standard business and commercial stationery envelopes still account for the majority of envelopes produced in the United States, the specialty envelopes sector has been the fastest growing in recent years. This growth has been spurred by several factors, including the proliferation of specialty "quick print" shops and home-based envelope printing. Many quick print shops use personal computers and laser printers to create custom-printed business forms, stationery, and envelopes.

Envelopes for the specialty envelope market must be able to accept the output of laser printers, which use dry plastic "toner" ink that is fused to the paper in a heating process similar to that of copier machines. Specialty envelopes also require special adhesives and cannot use windows, snaps, buttons, or clasps. They must also be made of paper, since nylon, plastics, and olefin cannot accept the dry ink process.

Another growing market for specialty envelope converters is the overnight parcel delivery industry. Providers of these services—such as Express Mail, Federal Express, and United Parcel Service—offer shipping envelopes free to their customers. These envelopes are made from several materials, including paper, paperboard, spunbonded olefin, and plastic. The overnight package delivery industry, begun in the 1970s, was delivering more than 3.5 million packages each day in the early to mid-1990s.

Mailing and in-house envelopes, which use adhesive seals, metal clasps or string-and-button closures make up another segment of the envelope industry. This sector racked up total sales of $374 million in 1992, which accounted for 15 percent of total envelope sales.

Heavy-duty padded shipping envelopes and mailers also comprise a major sector of the envelope industry, enjoying 1992 sales of $373 million—nearly 15 percent of total envelope sales. Catalog services, which proliferated in the 1980s and early 1990s, are a major market for shipping envelopes. Aided by the vast expansion of credit cards and toll-free telephone numbers, catalogs exist for every imaginable consumer need. Each catalog order must be shipped in envelopes or paperboard boxes.

In addition to catalogs, telemarketing and television shopping networks, such as the Home Shopping Network, are major users of shipping envelopes and mailers. Also, consumers responding to direct mail solicitations often trigger an avalanche of paper use, including the paper and envelope for the solicitation, the paper and return envelope containing the order, and the envelope or box in which the product is shipped to the consumer. Envelopes and mailers for catalog and direct mail orders must meet strict shipping require-

ments and thus are heavier and more expensive than other envelopes. They come in a staggeringly wide range of shapes, sizes, and combinations of base construction materials.

While paper envelopes have traditionally been made from 100 percent virgin fiber, many converters have reacted to public demand for more environmentally friendly products by introducing standard business and specialty envelope products that contain varying amounts of recycled materials. Since the products themselves can be recycled, they hold an advantage over newer plastic and olefin envelopes. In fact, some municipal collection programs have begun collecting "junk mail," giving paper-based envelopes an environmental plus.

Postal Service Is Key. While overnight parcel services are a growing market, the U.S. Postal Service (USPS) remains the dominant carrier of envelopes. Each year, the USPS handles about 80 billion pieces of first-class mail, which translates into an enormous demand for a wide variety of envelopes, particularly plain, unprinted envelopes. A major portion of these envelopes are sold directly to individual consumers and the business community. Another large portion of the plain envelope market is consumed by printing and publishing operations for customized business and personal envelopes. As discussed earlier, the personal computer and high quality printers have enabled many users to print their own stationery and envelopes, bypassing traditional offset printers.

Third-class, direct mail advertisers are another major market for envelope converters. Direct mail experienced an enormous boom in the 1980s and continued to grow in the late 1980s and early 1990s despite negative economic conditions. In fact, in 1992, when U.S. advertisers reduced spending in all but a handful of media outlets, direct mail advertising spending grew nearly four percent over 1991. While many consumers profess to dislike direct mail advertising, they continue to respond to it in record numbers. While costly, direct mail allows manufacturers to target their marketing efforts directly to consumers most likely to purchase their products, avoiding the "waste" of traditional mass media, where many consumers reached by an ad are unlikely to buy the product or service it promotes.

One of the major costs of direct mail advertising is postage. Postal rates have been rising far faster than inflation as the USPS attempts to come closer to recouping its actual costs for each class of mail. Direct mail advertisers were aware that the major postal rate hike in 1991 would be followed by others, so they were looking for ways to reduce the cost of each mailing.

One way of reducing costs is by "lightweighting" envelopes, using envelopes made with either lighter paper or with lightweight plastics or composites. Envelopes made from nontraditional materials are more resistant to tearing and puncturing and are more resistant to water. However, traditional paper envelopes still dominate both the standard and specialty envelope sectors because of their low cost and other properties, such as high strength, rigidity, and resistance to curl and fold.

CURRENT CONDITIONS

The value of U.S. envelope industry shipments increased every year in the late 1980s to a high of $2.8 billion in 1990. The economy soon stalled, though, and the value of shipments dropped to $2.7 billion in 1991 and $2.69 billion in 1992. That decrease was largely caused by lower envelope prices. Actual product shipments were up 2.5 percent in 1992.

In the late 1980s and early 1990s, the specialty envelopes emerged as the fastest-growing segment of the envelope industry. Its existing markets expanded rapidly and new markets were opened. The standard business envelope market is considered to be "mature" and is expected to grow at the same level as the Gross National Product (GNP). As a result, many envelope converters are concentrating their development efforts on the specialty envelope sector. Some of these envelopes are made from paper, but many others are made from unconventional materials such as nylon, plastic and plastic resin, and combinations of different materials.

Short-Term Outlook. As the recovery of the U.S. economy picked up speed in the mid-1990s, the envelope industry also increased its growth rates. For example, in 1993 product shipments increased three percent in inflation-adjusted dollars as business activity and direct-mail marketing efforts increased. While standard business envelopes are expected to grow relatively slowly throughout the 1990s, the specialty envelope sector should continue its rapid rise. In January of 1993 the final stage of tariff elimination under the United States-Canada trade agreement takes place, and there will be a positive impact on U.S. shipments to Canada.

In the 1990s the U.S. envelope industry is expected to continue its drive to increase operating efficiency and reduce heavy overcapacity in converting equipment. This strategy should boost the relatively low operating rate—the percentage of time equipment is operating—that plagued the industry in the early 1990s. As less efficient converters with aging plants become uncompetitive, more plant closures and lay-offs are expected in the envelope industry. U.S. envelope manufacturers will also keep a close eye a major USPS reorganization, which is expected to increase productivity and reduce operating costs.

Long-Term Outlook. The value of domestic envelopes shipments is expected to grow at an annual rate of 2.5 percent between 1993 and 1997 in inflation-adjusted dollars. All major envelope sectors—including standard business, specialty, and direct-mail—-are also expected to grow, though at different rates. A stable U.S. dollar and falling trade barriers should contribute to stronger foreign demand for U.S. envelopes.

The continued growth of recycling in order to reduce the amount of solid waste going to U.S. landfills will require envelope manufacturers to make changes to their operations throughout the 1990s. Customers continue to demand envelopes with higher recycled content. (Paper used to make "recycled" envelopes typically contains a mix a recycled fiber and virgin fiber.) Federal agencies and state government are required by law to choose recycled paper products, including envelopes, if they are available. As a result, converters are developing and aggressively marketing new recycled/recyclable envelopes and mailers. As the paper mills that produce the paper used to make envelopes learn how to incorporate more recycled fiber into their products, envelope converters will be able to produce envelopes with a higher level of recycled fiber.

INDUSTRY LEADERS

Unlike other paper categories, where paper manufacturers also control most of the converting operations through integrated subsidiaries, most of the leading envelope converters are independent of paper producers. Leading companies in this category include Henry Crown and Co., CC Industries Inc., American Business Products Inc., Mead Corp. school and office products division, and Westvaco Corp. envelope division. The last two are among the few paper companies with envelope-converting holdings. Other leaders include Mail-Well Envelope Co., Curtis 1000 Inc., Tension Envelope Corp., and American Envelope Corp.

WORK FORCE

The envelope segment employed 25,000 people in 1991 with a payroll of $616 million, making the average annual salary $24,640. Production workers accounted for 19,000 of that total and worked 39 million hours to earn $410 million for an average yearly income of $21,578. The number of people employed by envelope converters has been dropping as the industry decreases the total number of plants producing envelopes and invests in more heavily automated operations. Total employment dropped from 28,000 in 1987 to 25,000 in 1991, while the total number of establishments decreased from 100 to 92 during the same time period.

AMERICA AND THE WORLD

International trade in envelopes is relatively small, since envelopes tend to be manufactured close to where they are ultimately used. Nonetheless, U.S. converters have expanded their exports, mostly to nearby trading partners such as Canada and Mexico. The North American Free Trade Agreement (NAFTA) with Mexico and Canada, ratified by the U.S. in 1993, is expected to help expand the exports of efficient U.S. converters.

The Free Trade Agreement (FTA), signed earlier with Canada alone, has had a dramatic impact on U.S. envelope exports. From 1988 to 1992, U.S. envelope shipments to Canada rose more than 380 percent, from $3.6 million to $17.6 million. The United States has thus seen a dramatic increase in its the total export market, since Canada accounted for 77 percent of the $23 million U.S. envelope export market in 1992. Other significant customers include Mexico at eight percent and the United Kingdom at 6.5 percent. Forty-three other countries accounted for the remaining 8.5 percent.

By comparison, U.S. imports of envelopes have seen a downward trend. For example, in 1992 imports dropped nearly 20 percent in large part due to decreased imports from Canada. While the United States imported envelopes from 28 countries in 1992, three countries accounted for almost 70 percent of the total: Canada (51 percent), Denmark (11 percent), and Italy (7.5 percent). In 1993, total U.S. envelope exports to all markets increased nearly five percent, while imports climbed more slowly, at three percent.

RESEARCH AND TECHNOLOGY

Much of the research and technology in envelope manufacturing has focused on improving converting equipment, which allows envelopes to be produced faster and with better quality. When the speed of the equipment increases, however, new problems emerge. Previously, for example, most paper was produced using an acid process. However, due to the desire to reduce costs and improve the life of paper products, the majority of mills producing fine paper—which is used in many envelopes—have converted to the alkaline process.

Alkaline paper is usually produced with a synthetic "sizing" product, such as alkylketene dimer (AKD), to improve the surface of the paper. AKD is used to produce many fine paper grades, including envelope paper. On newer, high-speed precision converting equipment, AKD paper has been known to "slip," causing runnability problems. Recent research, though, has prompted the development of new sizing products that allow envelope manufacturers to use alkaline paper without concerns about runnability. Such innovations will help improve efficiency and keep the industry competitive.

While it is true that envelope converters face competition from electronic personal communications and electronic data interchange, the industry was not expected to experience undue harm. While envelopes may be the carriers of a smaller percentage of the total market for "communications," their use will grow as the entire market grows even faster. In addition, the fact that envelopes are still a very low-cost, attractive way to send information means that the envelope market will remain healthy for the foreseeable future.

INDUSTRY INFORMATION SOURCES

Biermann, Christopher J. *Essentials of Pulping and Papermaking.* San Diego: Academic Press, Inc., 1993.

Darnay, Arsen J., ed. *Manufacturing USA: Third Edition.* Detroit: Gale Research Inc., 1993.

———. *Market Share Reporter 1992.* Detroit: Gale Research Inc., 1992.

Hoover, Gary. *Hoover's Handbook of American Business 1993.* Austin, TX: The Reference Press, Inc., 1992.

Paper, Paperboard, Pulp Capacity and Fiber Consumption. Washington, DC: American Forest & Paper Association, 1993.

Smook, Gary A. *Handbook of Pulp & Paper Terminology: A Guide to Industrial and Technological Usage.* Bellingham, WA: Angus Wilde Publications, 1990.

Thesaurus of Pulp and Paper Terminology. Atlanta: Institute of Paper Science and Technology, 1991.

U.S. Industrial Outlook 1993. Washington, DC: U.S. Department of Commerce, 1993.

—Alan Rooks

SIC 2678

STATIONERY, TABLETS AND RELATED PRODUCTS

Establishments in this industry are primarily engaged in manufacturing stationery, tablets, loose-leaf fillers, and related items from purchased paper. Products include correspondence-type tablets, paper desk pads, loose-leaf filler paper, memo books, newsprint tablets and pads, notebooks, stationery, and various other padded paper products.

Sales volume in the stationery products industry remained stagnant throughout the 1980s and '90s. Beginning in the late '80s and carrying through to the next decade, the value of industry product shipments averaged between $1.2 and $1.3 billion. In 1988, the value of shipments was $1.28 billion. The value of shipments increased slightly in the next two years, rising to $1.32 billion in 1989 and $1.33 billion by 1990. However, a recession in the United States pushed the value of shipments down to $1.24 billion in 1991. Some of this decline was due to an overall decrease in paper prices, so volume shipments remained steady through 1991 into the following year.

The stationery products industry consists of three categories: stationary items, loose sheets of filler paper, and the tablets, pads and related products that account for the majority of products produced by this industry. Tablets and padded paper products accounted for 62.3 percent of industry sales in 1987, stationery accounted for 26.4 percent of shipments, and unspecified stationery products accounted from the remaining 11.3 percent.

Stationery products are produced by a wide range of companies. Some of the larger paper manufacturing companies have divisions that convert and distribute their own brand of stationery products. Smaller independent stationery converters have also managed to survive and thrive in this market.

In addition to being a participant as a manufacturer of stationery-related products, paper mills were the largest supplier to the stationery products industry in 1982, providing 56.8 percent of its raw materials. Wholesale trade accounted for another 9.1 percent while paperboard mills supplied 5.8 percent. The paperboard containers and boxes used to ship stationery products accounted for another 4.3 percent.

Personal consumption expenditures accounted for the largest share of purchases in this classification in 1982, at 51.4 percent. Retail trade was the next largest customer, at 5.4 percent. A wide variety of other sectors—including manufacturing firms, service firms and government agencies—accounted for the remaining 43.2 percent.

The stationery products industry is considered a mature industry, meaning that sales increases are likely to come only from general growth in the economy. The industry has been negatively impacted by the increased use of personal computers for home and office use, which has reduced the demand for a wide variety of stationery products. While computer printers have increased the use of paper in general, such increases have come in the use of continuous-form computer paper, which is not included in this classification. Also, major restructuring and layoffs in the middle management of hundreds of U.S. companies, as well as related efforts to reduce corporate overhead in the early 1990s, have negatively affected the use of all office paper products, including stationery.

One major change in the stationery products industry was the manner in which its products have been marketed to consumers. While stationery products were once sold primarily by small, independent stationery stores, much of that sales volume has been captured by office product ''superstores'' such as Office Max and Office Depot which, because of their size, were able to force smaller retailers out of the marketplace and drive wholesale prices down.

Several large paper companies have led this industry, including International Paper Co., Georgia-Pacific Corp. and Mead Corp. However, there has remained room for some mid-sized independent converters such as Herff Jones Inc., Duplex Products Inc., Smead Manufacturing Co., Avery Dennison Corp. and Stuart Hall Co. to maintain profitability.

The stationery products industry employed 10,000 people in 1991. The industry payroll of $209 million translated into an average annual wage of $20,900 per employee. Production workers accounted for 8,000 of that total, putting in 15,000 man-hours for an average annual wage of $17,250.

INDUSTRY INFORMATION SOURCES

Darnay, Arsen J., ed. *Manufacturing USA: Third Edition,* Detroit, Gale, 1993.

Darnay, Arsen J., ed. *Market Share Reporter 1992,* Detroit, Gale, 1992.

Paper, Paperboard, Pulp Capacity and Fiber Consumption, Washington, DC: American Forest & Paper Association, 1993.

Smook, Gary A. *Handbook of Pulp & Paper Terminology: A Guide to Industrial and Technological Usage,* Bellingham, WA: Angus Wilde Publications, 1990.

U.S. Industrial Outlook 1993, Washington, DC: U.S. Department of Commerce, 1993.

—Alan Rooks

SIC 2679

CONVERTED PAPER AND PAPERBOARD PRODUCTS, NOT ELSEWHERE CLASSIFIED

Establishments in this category are primarily engaged in manufacturing miscellaneous converted paper or paperboard products, not elsewhere classified, from purchased paper or paperboard. Products in this classification include gift wrap, pressed and molded pulp goods, laminated building papers, cigarette paper, fiber conduits, crepe paper, pressed and molded pulp cups, pressed and molded dishes, molded pulp egg cartons, and converted filter paper.

Sales volume in this industry exhibited a series of sharp upward and downward movements in the late 1980s and the early 1990s, but annual sales held steady at an average of $4 billion. In 1988, for example, the value of industry product shipments jumped nearly 12 percent to $4 billion, before dropping back to $3.8 billion the following year. In 1990, sales shot up to $4.1 billion before dropping back again to $4 billion in 1991.

The paper products in this classification are best described as specialty products since their diversity makes it hard to generalize about them. The largest product in this industry, by share of total production, is gift-wrap paper at 34 percent of the total, followed by wallcoverings at 15 percent, molded pulp goods such as egg cartons at 8.4 percent, and novelties, games, displays and similar products carrying 5.3 percent of total production. A large group of miscellaneous paper products account for 27 percent share of production.

Materials, parts, containers, and supplies—the biggest category of raw materials used by this industry—carried a market value of $1.6 billion in 1987. Paper was the next largest raw material, at $569 million, followed by paperboard with a value of $99 million. Paperboard containers, boxes, and the corrugated paperboard used to ship their products cost manufacturers in this industry $53 million.

Paper mills have been the largest supplier to this industry, providing 28.3 percent of its raw materials in 1982. Imports accounted for the next-largest volume, at 21 percent, followed by wholesale trade with 9.2 percent; paperboard mills with 6.6 percent; and plastics materials and resins with 2.5 percent.

Personal consumption expenditures accounted for the largest share of purchases from the miscellaneous-converted-paper-products industry in 1982, at 28.5 percent. The wholesale trades were the next-largest customer, with 11 percent of total purchases.

Trends for this industry are highly product-specific. As the largest component in the miscellaneous-converted-paper-products industry, gift wrap continues to grow with the general economy. Sales of gift paper are directly related to the level of gift purchasing in the U.S. After several mediocre years during the recession in the late 1980s and early 1990s, gift paper enjoyed an upward sales trend in the mid-1990s as gift buying—particularly during the key Christmas period—accelerated along with the general economy. Some environmental groups discouraged the use of gift paper, deeming it wasteful, but their disapproval did not appear to negatively impact gift-wrap sales.

Wallcoverings enjoyed a boost in the mid-1990s as a result of the acceleration in new home construction. Molded pulp products—primarily egg cartons—enjoyed a resurgence in the early 1990s due to public interest in recycling. These gray cartons, often made of recycled newsprint, lost share in the 1980s to molded plastic products. But as consumers began to express some displeasure with hard-to-recycle plastic cartons, some egg producers responded by moving back to molded pulp products.

Another significant product in this category, cigarette paper suffered as a result of the general downturn in cigarette consumption that began in the mid-'80s. The combination of high excise taxes on cigarettes and increased restrictions on public smoking contributed to large-volume decreases in domestic cigarette consumption. Losses in the U.S. market were at least partially offset by increases in the export market for cigarettes, but cigarette paper sales remained at best stagnant in the early 1990s. Excess cigarette paper capacity also contributed to demands for price concessions from cigarette manufacturers.

This industry segment employed 31,000 people in 1991 with a payroll of $711 million which translated into an average annual wage of $22,935. Of that total, 23,000 were production workers putting in 49 million man-hours to earn $475 million in wages, or an average annual wage of $20,652.

INDUSTRY INFORMATION SOURCES

Darnay, Arsen J., ed. *Manufacturing USA: Third Edition,* Detroit, Gale, 1993.

Darnay, Arsen J., ed. *Market Share Reporter 1992,* Detroit, Gale, 1992.

Smook, Gary A. *Handbook of Pulp & Paper Terminology: A Guide to Industrial and Technological Usage,* Bellingham, WA: Angus Wilde Publications, 1990.

U.S. Industrial Outlook 1993, Washington, DC: U.S. Department of Commerce, 1993.

—Alan Rooks

Printing & Publishing Industries

NEWSPAPERS: PUBLISHING, OR PUBLISHING AND PRINTING

This category includes establishments primarily engaged in publishing newspapers, or in publishing and printing newspapers. These establishments carry on the various operations necessary for issuing newspapers, including the gathering of news and the preparation of editorials and advertisements, but may or may not perform their own printing. Commercial printing is frequently carried on by establishments engaged in publishing and printing newspapers, but, even though the commercial printing may be of major importance, such establishments are included in this industry. Establishments not engaged in publishing newspapers, but which print newspapers for publishers, are classified in the Commercial Printing industries. News syndicates are classified in **SIC 7383: News Syndicates.**

INDUSTRY SNAPSHOT

More than 1,500 daily and 7,400 weekly newspapers operated in the United States in 1991. Together, these publications generated $39.3 billion in revenues, a figure combining $30.4 billion from advertising with $8.9 billion from circulation.

Newspaper publishing was an industry especially hard-hit by the economic recession of the late 1980s and early 1990s. Many papers with long histories were forced to shut down, and many more reported losses. To counteract this crisis, publishers reduced editorial and productions staffs through layoffs and hiring freezes, raised the prices that they charged to advertisers and readers, and experimented with the format of their papers in order to boost circulation and stay current. While they debated whether the slump was merely a temporary phenomenon or an indication that the entire industry was moving toward extinction, they kept a watchful eye on their competitors. Along with long-standing rivals television and radio, recently developed electronic media were often mentioned as threats to the existence of newspapers.

From the 1960s until the 1990s, newspaper management underwent a transformation from essentially family-run companies to the concerns of multimedia corporations. By 1989, Washington Post, Times Mirror, New York Times, Gannett, and Knight-Ridder combined were responsible for approximately one-fourth of the newspapers read each day in the United States. By linking newspapers in distant cities, these corporations produced a standardization of the style and content of the newspaper. Gannett's national daily USA Today, with its color photographs and emphasis on short, easily understood stories, was the most influential—and controversial—example for publishers considering the way their newspapers looked and read. In keeping with the overall transformations in the industry, the corporations that controlled newspapers began to branch out into other related ventures such as book publishing and marketing, and as a result the newspapers became parts of entire communications systems, rather than self-contained enterprises.

ORGANIZATION AND STRUCTURE

A variety of types of publications could be called newspapers. The most common format was the gatefold, which described a paper divided into sections that had to be opened individually to be read. Pagination in a gatefold newspaper restarted in every section. The other major format, the tabloid, was read like a book or a magazine. Tabloids were usually smaller, contained fewer articles, and were paginated without interruption from beginning to end. Traditionally, tabloids were considered less serious and comprehensive than gatefolds.

Frequency of publication was another variable among newspapers. The papers with the greatest circulation were dailies; these usually issued an edition with more content and a higher price on Sundays. There were far more weeklies in operation, though their circulation was smaller. The two most common types of weeklies were the community newspaper and the alternative newspaper. The community newspaper highlighted current events related to the community in such areas as education, high school sports, and local politics. The alternative newspaper provided coverage of news items and arts-related activities that were overlooked by the mainstream press. Because of the way advertising was built into the financial structures of weeklies, these newspapers could often be distributed without charge to readers.

Most newspapers relied on circulation and advertising to finance their operations, though some were distributed without charge and a small number published without advertiser support. Measured in linage, advertising amounted to about 80 percent of an average newspaper's income. Publishers tried to strike a balance between advertisements and news. This process involved insuring that no conflicts of interest arose between the content of the news and the message of advertisements. Placement of advertisements was also a significant factor; the section and page of an ad, as well as its size, determined its price. Department stores were traditionally a major source of advertising dollars, taking up page after page with drawings or photographs of their merchandise. Classified advertising, frequently overlooked, was a reliable and profitable endeavor for newspapers, adding up to 35 percent of newspapers' advertising income. This type of advertising was sold by the word.

One recent development in the newspaper advertising field was the ''advertorial,'' or paid announcement on the opinion page—which was normally reserved for the comments of the editors or independent writers—or in some other section of the paper where the advertiser expected to gain from its context. Other advertisements of this type consisted of multipage inserts or theme magazines distributed with papers. Paid announcements were labeled as such to avoid confusion, but this measure did not address all of the objections that these advertisements generated, especially among editors who felt the ads jeopardized the integrity of their contributions to the publications.

Newspapers were sold individually in vending machines and by privately owned newsstands, or by subscription, which allowed customers to pay a reduced rate per issue and to have the paper delivered to their home or business. Newspapers profited from subscribers because they meant guaranteed, consistent sales. In determining a price for newspapers sold on the street or by subscription, publishers had to weigh the potential earnings from sales against the amount the reader was willing to pay. If the price was set too low, circulation might be healthy, but profits could decline. If the price was too high, circulation could drop.

Because circulation figures were examined by advertisers to determine which medium would reach the most people—or the most people of a certain demographic group—every effort was made to keep newspapers affordable. Traditionally, men were most inclined to buy newspapers, so some publishers created special sections for women, children, and senior citizens, whose attention was important for certain advertisers. Even when their newspapers had little or no competition from other newspapers in the market, publishers normally mounted promotional campaigns to boost circulation. This type of advertising might target those demographic groups that were considered to be ''at risk,'' or sporadic readers of newspapers who tended to choose other ways of staying informed.

Averaging 42 percent of total costs, personnel represented the largest expenditure for newspapers. Among the types of employees at newspapers were management, editorial, advertising, circulation, and production. Within the editorial department, the staff was divided according to section of the paper. Newspapers had sections for local and national news, sports, entertainment and the arts, business, opinion, and others, depending on the paper's size and focus. Production workers, including printers, often belonged to labor unions, which were known to resist wage and hiring freezes, even in the most difficult economic times.

Newsprint was the second most expensive necessity in the newspaper industry, amounting to between 19 percent and 26 percent of total costs. The United States consumed over one-third of the world's newsprint, most of that going for the nation's newspapers. A dip in newsprint costs could save a newspaper during hard times, and since a failed newspaper meant loss of business for the newsprint manufacturer, most offered substantial discounts from list prices. In 1992, for instance, a metric ton of newsprint listed at $719, while the actual price paid was closer to $400. However, publishers such as the New York Times Company and the Tribune Company themselves owned paper mills, and consequently suffered when newsprint sold for too little. Equipment such as printing presses and cameras represented the third greatest cost to newspapers.

BACKGROUND AND DEVELOPMENT

Newspapers served to inform the public of events and circumstances pertaining to society, government, and commerce. The providers of information were normally trusted to be reliable and current, without neglecting their function of entertaining the literate population. The *Acta Diurna* of the Roman empire and the Chinese gazettes of the first century A.D. were newspapers' distant ancestors. The first modern newspapers began appearing in Europe in the sixteenth century.

The first great moment in American journalism came in 1735 with the court case deciding the issue of freedom of the press. The editor John Peter Zenger was brought to trial on charges of seditious libel for printing articles that were critical of the colonial governor Sir William Cosby. In his successful defense of Zenger, Alexander Hamilton invoked the Magna Carta and stressed that opposition to the establishment was a basic civil liberty, thus creating the foundation on which the American press was built. Newspaper reporters traditionally regarded their responsibility to function as watchdogs against injustice, corruption, and impropriety as sacred, and the right to expose these qualities in public figures was protected in the First Amendment to the Constitution of the United States, which guaranteed a free press.

An overriding objective for American newspapers was traditionally to reach as many readers as possible. One early manifestation of this aim could be seen in the *New York Tribune*, founded by Horace Greeley in 1841. Priced at one penny, the paper was written by Greeley and other advocates of social change in a style that was described as simple but not condescending. It boasted a tremendous readership throughout the country as well as in New York, and this led to enthusiastic support from its advertisers. The populist instincts that Greeley embodied eventually evolved into Yellow Journalism, a term originally referring to the practices of many of the New York daily newspapers published during the 1880s and 1890s. Joseph Pulitzer, editor of the *New York World*, and William Randolph Hearst, editor of the *New York Journal*—the dominant figures of the age—strove to increase circulation through a variety of aggressive tactics, such as reporting sensational stories, setting headlines in extremely large type, making extensive use of pictures, and issuing Sunday supplements containing color comics. The events of

the Spanish-American War in 1898 were closely linked to, and some said caused by, the reporting style of the Hearst and Pulitzer papers.

Telegraph lines, which by the turn of the century reached points all over the United States as well as crossing the Atlantic Ocean, were essential to the dissemination of news, and they facilitated the rise of cooperative news gathering. The Associated Press, formed by the morning newspapers of New York City and spread around the country, allowed member newspapers to run each other's stories. England's Reuters news service and other similar European agencies established reciprocal agreements with the Associated Press, fostering the potential for newspapers to run stories from around the world. The United Press and the International News Service were established to compete with Associated Press during the 1920s and 1930s. In 1958, these two services merged to form United Press International.

In the first half of the twentieth century, newspapers began to contend with the rise of new media capable of bringing more and different kinds of information and entertainment into people's homes faster. The formation of the Radio Corporation of America (RCA) in 1919 represented the first of these challenges. In 1929, advertising revenues at newspapers reached $800 million and were still far ahead of those of radio, but the newer medium was on the move, up to $40 million in 1929 from just $4 million in 1927. The Depression, which left the newspaper industry with just over half of its advertising income, hardly slowed the progress of radio advertising, which doubled in the years from 1929 to 1933. A second new forum for receiving the news arose in the 1930s and 1940s: the newsreel, which was shown between features at the movie theater.

Following on its heels was television, which by capturing the imagination and leisure time of America in the 1950s siphoned advertising dollars away from newspapers. Network television news became more readily identified with major events, such as the assassination of President John F. Kennedy. As one indication of their flagging relevance, the number of daily newspapers in American declined from 1,772 in 1950 to 1,586 in 1991, even as the population soared with the baby boom. The 24-hour Cable News Network (CNN) debuted in 1980, and its phenomenal growth contributed still more to the sense that newspapers were becoming an outmoded form of transmitting breaking stories. The Persian Gulf War of 1990 was as inextricably bound with CNN as the Spanish-American War had been with the newspapers that practiced Yellow Journalism.

Newspaper publishers during most of the twenti-eth century were powerful and often single-minded individuals who left a personal stamp on the editorial content and style of their papers. There were many prominent figures besides Pulitzer and Hearst. In small papers throughout the midwest, Edward Wyllis Scripps pushed for labor unions and collective bar-gaining. Adolph Ochs ran the *New York Times* from 1896 to 1935, catering to the reading interests of business people and intellectuals. Robert McCormick brought sensationalism and ultraconservative politics to the *Chicago Tribune*. When it came time for such strong personalities to step down, they usually named a family member to take charge, resulting in long-lasting dynasties in the newspaper business.

According to Ellis Cose, president of the Institute for Journalism Education at the University of Califor-nia-Berkeley and author of *The Press* (1989), 1963 brought the first sign that the newspaper industry was in for a change. That year, the Chandler family, owner of Times Mirror, the chief holding of which was the *Los Angeles Times*, listed the company on the New York Stock Exchange. Soon other newspapers went public, making their actions accountable to share-holders and not just the families that ran them. This situation led to chains of newspapers and the prolifera-tion of corporate culture, which stressed profits and growth over conventions of journalism—a system of values of which publishers had long been wary.

This fundamental shift in the objectives of news-papers did not result in an immediate change from their traditionally antiestablishment character, but rather a gradual softening of resistance to the advice of market-ing experts pushing for a more appealing product. The trend was welcomed by some as an indication that newspapers were willing to stay competitive in an age where television dominated. In the eyes of some ex-perts, however, personality-driven, ideologically fuzzy journalism came at the price of in-depth investigative reporting. Another traditional aspect of the newspa-per—the predominantly male, predominantly white composition of its work force—eroded with the social changes of the 1960s and 1970s, and African-Ameri-can and female journalists began to exert an influence.

CURRENT CONDITIONS

The economic recession at the end of the 1980s brought crippling losses in advertising and circulation to American newspapers. The effects were felt in such recently founded publications as the *St. Louis Sun*, a tabloid created in September 1989 by Ralph Ingersoll

II with money from junk bonds and closed the follow-ing August. Another new publication, the *National*, a nationwide sports daily, ran only eighteen months be-fore folding in June 1991. By 1991, papers with long histories, many that had survived the Great Depres-sion, were beginning to shut down as well. These included the *State-Times* of Baton Rouge, Louisiana, and the *Dallas Times Herald*, a closing that meant 900 people lost their jobs and made that city the largest in the country with only one daily. In 1991, United Press International filed for bankruptcy for the second time in six years.

With regards to advertising, 1990 and 1991 were two of the worst years ever for the newspaper industry. For the first time since the Depression, there were back-to-back losses in annual advertising revenues as national, retail, and classified linage all shrunk. Ad revenues saw a slight turnaround in 1992, with less than 1 percent increase, but this was due to higher prices rather than greater linage. Losses were also cushioned in 1992 by drastically reduced newsprint prices.

One solution to the dire conditions in which news-papers found themselves was the Joint Operating Agreement (JOA). Under the Newspaper Preservation Act of 1970, newspapers were largely exempt from antitrust suits, opening the door for JOAs allowing two or more newspapers to continue executing their edito-rial matters independently while sharing advertising, business, circulation personnel, or other resources. Af-ter a lengthy court battle in which representatives from both newspapers testified that they were on the brink of failure, the most substantial agreement, between Knight-Ridder's *Detroit Free Press* and Gannett's *Detroit News*, was finalized in November 1989. While similar agreements saved newspapers in other cities, both papers continued to lose money into the 1990s, and their shared entity, the Detroit Newspaper Agency, continued to reduce its staff through retirement incen-tives.

In the 1990s, advertising departments began to experiment with nontraditional approaches to their field. Where they once aimed at reaching the greatest number of readers, they refined their methods to reach geographically and demographically desirable readers with special sections and zoned editions. They also adapted classified advertising, such as automobile an-nouncements and personal ads, for telephone use. Other ventures into non-print areas of communication included voice information lines for late-breaking news, sending news updates by facsimile, and vid-eotex, which allowed subscribers to receive the news by modem and read it on the screen of their personal computers.

One major concern of the newspaper industry during and after the recession was that of readership. Through academic studies and marketing surveys, publishers attempted to discover who was reading the newspaper with regards to such factors as age, sex, and financial status; frequency and duration of an average read; the instances where one newspaper was shared by two or more readers; and the sections of the newspaper that were read or ignored. In most cases these inquiries yielded discouraging results. A study by the Memphis State University journalism professor Gerald Stone, for instance, determined that between 1967 and 1989, the number of people aged 18 to 29 who read a daily paper declined 35 percent. According to Stone, this condition arose from parents passing on to their children their disinclination to reading the paper, resulting in an ever-deepening alienation from the publications. The trend was linked to a pervasive apathy towards current events. A study by the Times Mirror Center for the People and Press, for example, found that merely 42 percent of those under 30 years old showed an interest in the fall of the Berlin Wall, an event given terrific attention by newspapers.

Publishers began trying to make newspapers more relevant to the younger generation, to whom they looked for sustaining the industry in the years to come, by incorporating information on such topics as child care, commuter traffic, and health. These and more radical alterations to the traditional newspaper format incited an ongoing debate among journalists and other industry professionals regarding the scope and purpose of the newspaper on the threshold of the twenty-first century.

USA Today was the industry's most revolutionary gesture towards appealing to a mass readership. Pioneered by Gannett's Allen Neuharth in 1982, *USA Today* modified the approach of other newspapers aiming at the entire nation—the *New York Times*, the *Wall Street Journal*, and the *Christian Science Monitor*. The paper was printed in regional plants via satellite transmissions from its editorial centers. Aware that advertisers and readers tended to regard the average daily newspaper as visually bland and difficult to navigate, designers of *USA Today* incorporated such features as an easily read index on the front page, bold graphics featuring statistical information related to the day's events, and a large color weather map. The newspaper was even distributed in vending machines designed to resemble television sets. Neuharth limited the number of sections in his paper to four: a news section emphasizing the positive side of current events; a "Money"

section devoted to business coverage with a strong consumer orientation; an extensive sports section providing a large number of pictures and ample statistical data; and a "Life" section encompassing health and education as well as entertainment.

By 1993, after eleven years of operation, *USA Today* had become the most widely circulated newspaper with nearly two million readers every day, though it had yet to turn a profit. Newspaper editors around the country looked to *USA Today* with a combination of distaste for what they considered its superficial style and respect for its impressive figures. Consequently, the steps other papers took in adopting aspects of its style were sometimes tentative.

INDUSTRY LEADERS

The Gannett Company, ranked number one by daily circulation in 1992, reached six million readers every day with its 81 dailies and 65 Sunday editions. Begun by Frank Gannett in 1906, the company first began acquiring newspapers throughout New York State. It owned 22 dailies by 1947, the year he died. Allen Neuharth joined the company in 1963, and he was credited for building it into a major force in the industry. After going public in 1967, Gannett absorbed small newspapers all over the country, bringing to them exacting management requirements and transforming them into profitable enterprises. Additionally, Gannett augmented its holdings with radio and television stations, as well as entered the field of billboard advertising. The birth of *USA Today* in 1982 was facilitated by the fact that Gannett's reporters, editors, and technology were established in every region of the nation. Gannett's News 2000 program was launched in 1991 to discover newspaper readers' expectations and wants from Gannett papers, with the objective of tailoring future modifications to the survey's results.

Knight-Ridder, with the second largest daily circulation at 3.8 million, resulted from the 1974 merger of the Knight and Ridder newspaper chains. In addition to owning such respected and widely read newspapers as the *Philadelphia Inquirer*, *Miami Herald*, and *Detroit Free Press*, Knight-Ridder became a leader in the related field of information services, acquiring Dialog Information Services in 1988. A database project at the *San Jose Mercury News*, which would include audio, video, and facsimile elements and be available on the America Online personal computer service, was announced in 1992.

In 1992, Times Mirror boasted the fourth largest daily circulation at 2.8 million. Unlike Gannett and Knight-Ridder, which owned a great number of small newspapers, Times Mirror's holdings were concentrated on large big-city dailies, including the *Los Angeles Times* and *New York Newsday*. As the recession hit this category of newspaper with particularly brutal force, Times Mirror went down from an estimated $200 million in operating profits in 1985 to $184 million (before one-time accounting charges) in 1992.

The New York Times Company, which in 1992 was in seventh place in terms of daily circulation at 2.1 million, was a longtime stronghold of journalistic standards, beginning when Adolph Ochs and his son-in-law Arthur Hays Sulzburger emphasized comprehensive coverage and news writing of the highest order in the *New York Times*. In 1992, the New York Times Company owned 24 other newspapers, and in 1993 it announced the purchase of Affiliated Publications, owners of the *Boston Globe*, for $1.1 billion.

WORK FORCE

USA Today was an industry leader when it came to progressive hiring policies, placing relatively more women and minorities in leadership positions. Other newspapers were more gradual in attempting to make their newsrooms reflect the sexual and racial make-up of the communities they served. In 1991, 8.72 percent of newsroom professionals were from minority groups, compared with 21 percent in the general work force of the United States. Some newspapers began affirmative action policies in response.

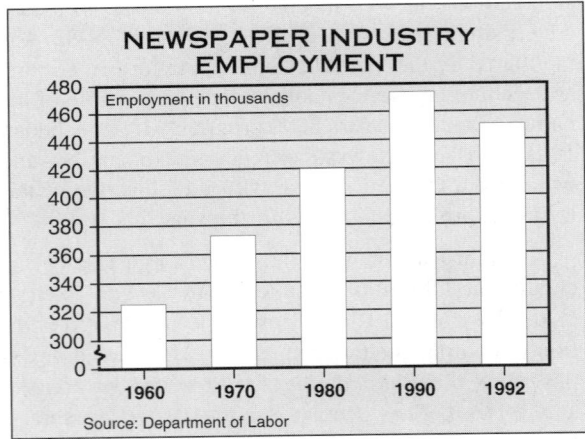

NEWSPAPER INDUSTRY EMPLOYMENT

Employment in thousands

Source: Department of Labor

In 1990, there were nearly 50,000 reporters and correspondents working for newspapers in America, averaging just over $34,000 in annual wages. In light of the changes that took place in the way newspapers were managed and produced during the 1980s and early 1990s, those working in the industry were obligated to learn new skills and take on new duties. Foremost among these were related to the computer revolu-

tion, as word processing programs and developments in page design proliferated in newsrooms. Some of the tasks that previously belonged to production departments, such as typesetting, were made obsolete or were dramatically altered with technological developments.

Throughout the newspaper industry, the lines between different departments began to disappear, meaning positions that were previously specialized and isolated gave way to positions that required proficiency in a number of areas and an awareness of how the entirety of a newspaper operated. One manifestation of this shift in consciousness was the 1992 merger of the American Newspaper Publishers Association (ANPA) with the Newspaper Advertising Bureau (NAB) into the Newspaper Association of America (NAA). In her 1992 address to the American Society of Newspaper Editors, Cathleen Black, the first president and chief executive officer of NAA, urged editors to consider advertisers as well as readers when making editorial decisions, an idea that might have been regarded as treasonous to journalism ideals in a previous era. Similarly, she stressed the need for editors to communicate with circulation departments in order to comprehend the needs and wants of their readerships.

RESEARCH AND TECHNOLOGY

Cathleen Black said the merger of ANPA and NAA would also enable the newspaper industry "to speak with a unified voice—on Capitol Hill and also to the advertising community." Black underscored the need for unity in the face of the growing consensus that newspapers were competing not so much with one another but with other providers of information services. The seven regional Bell Telephone companies, known as Baby Bells, were identified as the most potentially damaging force in this new industry. If the Baby Bells were allowed to act as suppliers of data and not just as conduits of information, Black feared, they could soon usurp advertising dollars and readership away from newspapers. In turn, the newspapers would inevitably suffer, since they had to rely on Bell phone lines to transmit their own data. In 1984, the year antitrust regulation forced the breakup of AT&T, the Baby Bells were forbidden from initiating business in the emerging field of information services. In 1991, this measure was qualified to allow the companies to provide information on their own services over their own lines, a prospect that alarmed Black and others. The change, coupled with other developments, raised new questions about the place of newspapers on what became known as the "electronic information superhighway"—a vision of interactive technologies utilizing phone lines for the exchange of video, audio, and textual information.

In the beginning of the 1990s, some newspapers began to move toward becoming electronic information suppliers, without yet eschewing the print medium altogether. They accomplished this by making their databases available to subscribers, enhancing their classified advertising to allow for hi-tech, shop-at-home possibilities, and creating special electronic editions. As Cathleen Black told the American Society of Newspaper Editors in 1992, ''Reader involvement through audio and video technology is a natural extension of newspapers' great strengths.''

INDUSTRY INFORMATION SOURCES

ASNE—1990, Washington, D.C.: American Society of Newspaper Editors, 1990.

ASNE—1991, Washington, D.C.: American Society of Newspaper Editors, 1991.

ASNE—1992, Washington, D.C.: American Society of Newspaper Editors, 1992.

Cose, Ellis, *The Press,* New York: Morrow, 1989.

Emery, Edwin and Michael, *The Press and America: An Interpretive History of the Mass Media,* Englewood Cliffs, N.J.: Prentice-Hall, 1984.

Fost, Dan, ''Newspapers Enter the Age of Information,'' *American Demographics,* September 1990.

Garneau, George, ''Small Gains Forecast for Newspapers in '93,'' *Editor & Publisher,* January 2, 1993.

''1990-in-Review,'' *Editor & Publisher,* January 5, 1991.

''1991-in-Review,'' *Editor & Publisher,* January 4, 1992.

Standard & Poor's Industry Surveys, New York: Standard & Poor's, 1993.

Taylor, John H., ''Betting on the Wrong Horses,'' *Forbes,* April 12, 1993.

—Mark Swartz

SIC 2721

PERIODICALS: PUBLISHING, OR PUBLISHING AND PRINTING

This category covers establishments primarily engaged in publishing periodicals, or in publishing and printing periodicals. These establishments carry on the various operations necessary for issuing periodicals, but may or may not perform their own printing. Establishments not engaged in publishing periodicals, but which print periodicals for publishers, are classified in commercial printing industries.

INDUSTRY SNAPSHOT

The first American magazines were published in 1741. From the start, the business was plagued with an exorbitant failure rate. Nevertheless, by 1994 the periodicals industry was distributing more than 11,000 different publications, generating revenues of over $23 billion per year, and employing more than 110,000 Americans. Besides providing important economic benefits for the nation, the U.S. periodicals industry is also a major source of information and entertainment for most Americans and serves as a vital advertising medium for other industries.

Although the demand for periodicals advanced steadily through the early and mid-1900s, spectacular growth during the 1980s more than doubled industry revenues. New production technologies, positive demographic trends, and a general increase in the need for information all served to vault the industry to unprecedented prominence. Growth slowed in the late 1980s and early 1990s, however, as key markets became saturated and a recession diminished revenues and profits.

To overcome the effects of maturing markets, publishers in the mid-1990s were striving to reduce costs and retain their share of U.S. advertising expenditures. A primary tactic was the introduction of niche periodicals for small target audiences. Many firms were also finding growth overseas. Industry receipts will likely rise at an annual rate of one to two percent above inflation through the turn of the century.

ORGANIZATION AND STRUCTURE

Periodical publishers earn money by charging companies to place ads in their publications, or by charging readers for subscriptions or individual issues. The periodical's content is essentially a tool which the publisher uses to boost sales and ad revenues. By adjusting or improving the content of a publication, successful periodical companies can develop a medium that maximizes sales and ad revenues derived from a target market. Many publishers also generate income thorough database marketing techniques, such as selling subscriber lists or marketing ''back-end'' products and services to their customers.

Periodicals sales and ad revenues each account for about 50 percent of the average publisher's receipts. Although 80 percent of all periodicals are purchased through mail-order subscriptions, 30 percent of sales dollar volume is garnered through newsstand sales. The average annual subscription price of a U.S. periodical in 1992 was about $27. The typical newsstand price per individual issue was roughly $2.85. Forty-five percent of all newsstand sales occurred at supermarkets in 1993. Convenience and specialty stores accounted for 15 percent and 12 percent, respectively. The remainder of individual magazine revenues were derived from drugstores, newspaper stands, bookstores, and discount centers.

Markets. The largest periodical target market, by ad revenue, is women. In early 1994, about 19 percent of all advertising dollars in the industry were captured by publisher's of women's periodicals, such as *Woman's Day, Better Homes and Gardens,* and *Working Woman.* Journals in this market are aimed at multiple niches, like new mothers, soon-to-be brides, and homemakers. The second largest sector of the industry was newsweeklies, such as *Time* and *Newsweek,* which represented about 11 percent of ad revenues in early 1994. Business magazines, particularly *Business Week,* accounted for slightly less than 11 percent of periodical ad expenditures. Periodicals aimed at large, general audiences, such as *Reader's Digest* and *National Geographic,* made up the fourth largest industry category. Other popular segments, in order of ad sales, include sports, Sunday feature magazines (that are usually inserted into newspapers), entertainment, home and house improvement, travel, and parenting.

Aside from general merchandise, the industrial sectors that purchase the greatest amount of advertising from periodical publishers are transportation and agricultural, which contributed about 20 percent of all ad dollars in early 1994. Specifically, the auto and truck industry was spending about $70 million per month for ad space. Business and financial products and services represented about 18 percent of magazine ad sales, and drug and toiletry industries purchased about 14 percent of advertising space. Food and beverage products represented 11 percent of ad receipts. Cigarette ads alone accounted for over $20 million per month of sales in that category.

About 66 percent of all periodicals in the early 1990s were sold to individual consumers. State and local governments, including schools, purchased three percent of industry output. Retail establishments bought two percent of production, and libraries consumed 1.7 percent of all periodicals. Other markets include hospitals, social services, and colleges and universities.

Competition. The periodicals industry, which sustained over 4,000 competitors in 1994, is highly fragmented. Although the top four companies had sales of more than $1 billion in 1991, the majority of the top 75 firms gleaned revenues of less than $150 million and employed fewer than 1,000 workers. The average number of employees per establishment was only 28—about half the average for all other U.S. manufacturers.

Publishers yielded approximately 11,240 different titles in 1991. Because competition for ad and circulation dollars is intense, the turnover rate of publications is enormous—particularly for start-up periodicals. Between 1988 and 1993, for example, 900 new magazines were introduced as 760 were terminated. Furthermore, well over 50 percent of all new periodicals fail within one year of start-up. Low barriers to entry—in comparison to most other industries—contribute to the high failure rate, because anyone with several thousand dollars and an idea can start a new periodical. Poor business planning and inadequate market research, however, usually accompany such endeavors.

BACKGROUND AND DEVELOPMENT

Periodicals emanated from book notices that were inserted in European newsbooks published during the early 1600s. In the 1640s publishers began to include critical commentary in the memos. And by the 1650s, the notices began appearing as regular features of newsbooks and papers. About the same time that book notices were evolving, digests and abstract journals began appearing. These periodicals provided such information as summaries of published books, author biographies, and reports on important philosophical, literary, and scientific matters. The *Journal des scavans,* first issued in Paris on January 5, 1665, is recognized as the parent of the modern periodical industry.

Throughout the remainder of the 17th century, several publishers, mostly in Great Britain, began delivering periodicals offering opinion, news, and entertainment. Early in the 1700s, journals of political opinion became particularly popular. Great Britain's *Spectator,* for example, achieved a circulation of 4,000. Other British journals of notoriety during the 1700s included *Farmer's Magazine, Gentlemen's Magazine,* and *London Review.* Likewise, as the European industry evolved during the 19th century, journals appealing to a broad range of interests emerged. Great Britain's *Westminster Review,* Italy's *Scena Illustrata,* and Russia's *Russky Vestnik* were a few examples. Indeed, the industry broadened during the 1800s to include periodicals for children, physicians, women, and other societal niches.

The first American periodicals were Andrew Bradford's *American Magazine* and Benjamin Franklin's *General Magazine,* both of which started and failed in 1741. Other early efforts included *The Columbian* and Thomas Paine's *Pennsylvania Magazine.* In all, about 100 magazines were eventually started in the colonies; most of them failed within a few years. After numerous duds and over 500 new periodical start-ups during the early 1800s, by 1825 about 100 magazines and journals were circulating on U.S. soil. Spurred by a demand for weekly literary journals, as well as children's, women's, religious, and political periodicals, the total number of magazines in circulation rose to 600 by 1850. Two famous titles of that time were *North American Review* and *Southern Literary Messenger*.

The 1850s ushered in a new era for the periodicals industry. *Harper's New Monthly Magazine,* started in 1850, was a richly illustrated periodical that sprouted a horde of highly successful imitators. *The Nation, Outlook, Scribner's Magazine,* and *Christian Union* were of few of the titles that rocketed the number of U.S. periodicals to 1,200 in 1870, 2,400 in 1880, and nearly 3,000 by 1890. In the 1890s, moreover, low-priced illustrated monthlies were introduced that cost only 15 cents per copy, compared to the 35 cents charged by their predecessors. Many of these magazines were "muckrakers" that exposed government corruption.

The number and circulation of periodicals continued to proliferate rapidly during the early 1900s. *Reader's Digest* (founded in 1922), *Life* (1923), and *Newsweek* (1933) were three of the most popular publications started during the first half of the century. *Reader's Digest* became a classic American success story, as its circulation lurched to a stunning 21 million during the 1950s. *Life* and a similar picture magazine, *Look,* reached combined sales of seven million during the 1960s. Among the most popular publications during the early and mid-1900s were women's periodicals, such as *Good Housekeeping* and *Ladies' Home Journal.*

The periodical publishing industry encountered new challenges in the 1950s and 1960s. Most important was the advent and successive popularization of television. This medium, combined with radio, altered American reading habits and allowed periodical publishers an increasingly smaller proportion of overall advertising expenditures. Augmenting this trend were diminished profit margins caused by growing production expenses and higher postal rates. Media competition and rising costs could not suppress strong circulation growth throughout the mid-1900s, however. Publications like *Playboy* and *Seventeen* opened up entirely new, and massive, market segments. Likewise, a plethora of trade and business journals boosted industry breadth and earnings. In addition, entire sub-industries sprang up during the 1970s to serve automo-

tive enthusiasts, fashion fans, pornographers, and other niche readers. New marketing channels, such as the Publisher's Clearinghouse Sweepstakes, also spurred growth. By the end of the 1970s, in fact, the periodicals industry was grossing more than $10 billion in sales and employing a work force of over 90,000.

The periodicals industry continued to expand steadily during the 1980s. A general increase in the demand for all types of current information, combined with escalating advertising expenditures, helped boost circulation. In addition, an aging population spent more of its income on periodicals. Finally, major new markets appeared. For example, computer and office equipment magazines, which were practically non-existent prior to 1980s, were attracting over $200 million to the industry in advertising revenues alone. That figure bolted past $275 million by 1989. Other industries which significantly increased their magazine ad expenditures included apparel and travel.

As periodical demand rose and ad revenues climbed, the number of periodical titles increased from 10,700 in 1982 to about 11,000 by 1990. During the same period, total industry sales jumped from $11.5 billion to $23.1 billion, representing an impressive average annual growth rate of more than seven percent. Despite striking productivity gains in printing and publishing manufacturing operations, moreover, industry employment surged from 94,000 in 1982 to approximately 115,000 by 1992. Some of the readership niches that offered the best opportunities were computers, medical and surgical, women's, newsweeklies, and senior citizens.

Periodical prosperity waned in 1989 and the early 1990s. A U.S. and global economic recession blasted ad revenues, stalled subscription growth, and slashed newsstand sales. In addition, some analysts believed that the market was becoming saturated and mature, thus offering fewer profit opportunities. Finally, periodical producers were slowly losing their share of U.S. ad dollars to other media, such as direct mail and catalogs.

Total magazine advertising revenues rose less than 2.5 percent in 1990 before plummeting almost five percent in 1991. Factoring in discounts and incentives that publishers offered to advertisers, however, those figures are likely optimistic. Total industry receipts, adjusted for inflation, actually fell .4 percent in 1989, 3.6 percent in 1990, and 4.7 percent in 1991. As publishers scrambled to compete for scarce ad and sales dollars, the number of periodical titles slipped from 11,556 in 1989 to only 11,092 in 1990.

Interestingly, start-up magazine publishers seemed undaunted by the industry slump. 599 and 553 new periodicals were launched in 1989 and 1990, respectively, and 541 new titles crowded the business in 1991. New title growth was largely attributable to a trend toward highly targeted publications that could maximize the impact of advertiser's dollars.

CURRENT CONDITIONS

After losing ground in 1990 and 1991, periodical publishers realized a modest recovery in 1992 and 1993 that seemed to be accelerating as they entered 1994. Gross receipts climbed an encouraging eight percent in 1992 as inflation remained low. Furthermore, employment jumped about 2,000 after dipping to 110,000 in 1991. A slow U.S. economic recovery and an upsurge in new product introductions helped to revive sales and profit growth.

Ad revenues climbed 7.1 percent in 1992 based on published advertising rates; real ad revenue growth was estimated at a tepid 2 percent. Leading ad sales were increases in advertising spending on drugs and remedies, which swelled 66 percent in 1992, and computers and office equipment, which leapt over 20 percent. Toiletries and cosmetics expenditures also grew, by about 12 percent, as automotive ad sales climbed ten percent. Sales of tobacco ads plunged 15 percent, however. Magazine categories that realized the strongest ad growth were women's, fashion, national business news, outdoor, sport, and automotive.

The growth in revenues resulted from a combination of higher rates and greater volume. Indeed, published magazine ad rates grew about six percent in 1993, as total ad volume jumped five percent. Overall, magazines' share of total U.S. media ad spending remained at 5.2 percent. To retain this share, publishers in 1992 and 1993 offered increased incentives and multi-media packages. Many also redesigned their publications and tried to eliminate marginal readership that diluted advertisement impact.

Besides ad revenues, publishers were also enjoying a slight reprieve from lackluster circulation sales. Receipts grew by about one percent in 1992 and rose at a slightly faster rate in 1993. Subscription sales rose about 1.2 percent in 1992. The average yearly cost of a U.S. magazine subscription increased as well, by about one percent, following a decline in 1991. The rise in subscription price, moreover, was accompanied by a reduction in the average number of annual issues, which had fallen from 12.2 in 1988 to 11.8 in 1993. Overall gains in circulation revenues, however, continued to be partially offset by sharp postal rate increases that were implemented in 1991.

Besides subtly reducing the number of annual issues, publishers were also trying to reduce costs through other strategies. For instance, by pre-sorting mail and including four-digit zip code suffixes to address labels, some producers were able to cut second-class postage costs by as much as five percent. Other publishers were switching to lightweight paper, and trucking magazines to regional distribution centers. Many producers were also increasing their database marketing efforts and striving to garner follow-up retail sales from their subscribers. The largest gains, though, were being accomplished through layoffs, salary freezes, and benefit cutbacks.

Newsstands Drag Down Profits. While both subscription and ad revenues realized slow but steady gains in 1992 and 1993, newsstand sales were dragging down industry gains. In fact, individual magazine sales had been declining for the past decade. Fewer trips to the supermarket by most Americans and an increase in more convenient subscriptions were the primary factors driving the decay of this important distribution channel. Because most periodical sales are impulse purchases, moreover, the recession in the late 1980s and early 1990s especially devastated the newsstand. Also hurting issue sales going into the mid-1990s was pressure by retail outlets, some of which were demanding greater compensation in return for valuable shelf space.

Sales of the top 150 newsstand magazines increased only 3.5 percent between 1988 and 1992 to $1.15 billion. And the average magazine's unit sales plummeted from 67.19 million to 59.35 million, a fall of nearly 12 percent. In an effort to revive ailing newsstand traffic, which accounted for roughly 15 percent of industry revenues, publishers were resorting to a variety of tactics. Many were offering discount coupons, for instance, or lowering cover prices in various regions or during certain seasons of the year. Combining issues with special inserts was also an increasingly popular marketing gimmick.

In 1993 a data-gathering service was started called Periodical Retail Information Management (PRIM). The system was designed to provide timely and accurate data to retailers, wholesalers, and publishers. The system was expected to eventually assist with the distribution of more than 3,000 titles to more than 189,000 retailers each month, and would keep close track of title data related to each retailer's sales, including promotion and discount information.

Winners and Losers. In the face of slow overall growth, publishers were jockeying to take advantage of a few healthy industry niches. Regional magazines, for example, realized an increase in successful titles of

38 percent between 1988 and 1993. The number of not-for-profit periodicals, which make up about 18 percent of total consumer magazine circulation, jumped as well, by 22 percent. Two American Association of Retired Persons (AARP) periodicals with combined circulation of over 22 million lead not-for-profit growth. Rapid sales growth also occurred in travel, golf, camping, and pet publications.

Erotic and pornographic titles continued to lead new magazine start-ups—66 such periodicals entered the market in 1991. Gay and lesbian publications were also showing strong growth, as 22 new titles appeared in 1992, compared to only ten in 1990. Other growing niches related to crafts and games, fishing and hunting, comics, military, and computers. Examples of successful start-ups in the early and mid-1990s included *Story, PC Lap Top, Celebrate Midwest, Doll Collector's Price Guide, Where to Retire, Card Monthly, Comic Book Collector,* and *Turkey & Turkey Hunting.*

The most rapid declines in 1993 were taking place in periodicals related to airline flight, television and radio, and business computers, all of which had previously offered solid gains. Boating, dancing, gardening, and dressmaking segment revenues were declining more slowly, as were magazines about horses. Declining numbers of titles in the early 1990s were occurring in subjects related to health, men, motorcycles, and lifestyle. Some well-known periodicals that ceased circulation in the early 1990s were *Ovation, Christian Herald, HG, NY Woman, Motorboat, Trumps Business Month,* and *Fame.*

The Future. Although U.S. media advertising expenditures are expected to grow by about six percent (in inflation adjusted dollars) annually during the mid-1990s, total periodical industry receipts will rise by only one to two percent above inflation each year. As a result, publishers will concentrate on growing revenues and profit margins associated with circulation sales. As markets mature, moreover, periodical manufacturers will increasingly seek additional revenues from back-end sales to their subscriber database. Many publishers had already initiated aggressive campaigns to sell products and materials that complement their publications.

Maturing market segments will push publishers toward more targeted editorial products, though magazines aimed at general audiences were holding their own in 1993. Magazines that zero in on specific readers and their interests will be able to lure advertisers away from less ad-efficient general publications. Similarly, more magazines will begin offering different ads and editorial sections for the same publication, so that different customer segments will receive issues tailored to their demographic profile.

Environmental considerations will receive growing industry attention in the 1990s and 2000s. (Competitors were already viewed as major contributors to toxin and landfill problems.) Government and special interests, alike, were prodding publishers to reduce their use of hazardous inks and to utilize more recycled materials in their production processes. However, problems associated with quality, price, and availability of recycled stock plagued recycling efforts. As Congress threatened to legislate the mandatory use of recycled paper, the number of publishers that were using at least some recycled materials rose from 24 percent in 1991 to 35 percent in 1992.

In the short term, industry participants will be forced to deal with higher production costs. Paper prices rose about five percent in 1992 and were expected to rise through 1994. Worse yet, postal costs were expected to jump by as much as 20 percent in January of 1995, a result of higher postal rates and increasingly complex regulations.

INDUSTRY LEADERS

The largest U.S. publisher of periodicals in the early 1990s was R. R. Donnelley and Sons Co., of Illinois. This publishing behemoth generated revenues of $3.5 billion in 1991 and employed 30,000 workers. Besides providing printing, publishing, and allied services, Donnelley is also engaged in various book, catalog, and telecommunications businesses. Going into the mid-1990s, the conglomerate operated more than 100 offices in the United States and several subsidiaries in Japan and the United Kingdom.

Canadian Richard Robert Donnelley founded the company in 1870 in Chicago, under the name The Lakeside Publishing and Printing Company. The company built a massive enterprise during the late 1800s and 1900s by printing directories and books. Its first major magazine printing contracts were signed in 1927, when the company contracted to publish both *Time* and *Life.* Important production technology introductions shortly thereafter included Deeptone processing and sheet-fed gravure presses, both of which increased the quality and productivity of magazine manufacturing.

The second largest U.S. periodical publisher in mid-1990s was McGraw-Hill Inc., of New York. This diversified publisher generated 1991 sales of nearly $2 billion with about 14,000 employees. It was followed closely by New York's Reader's Digest Association Inc., the third largest competitor by revenues, which

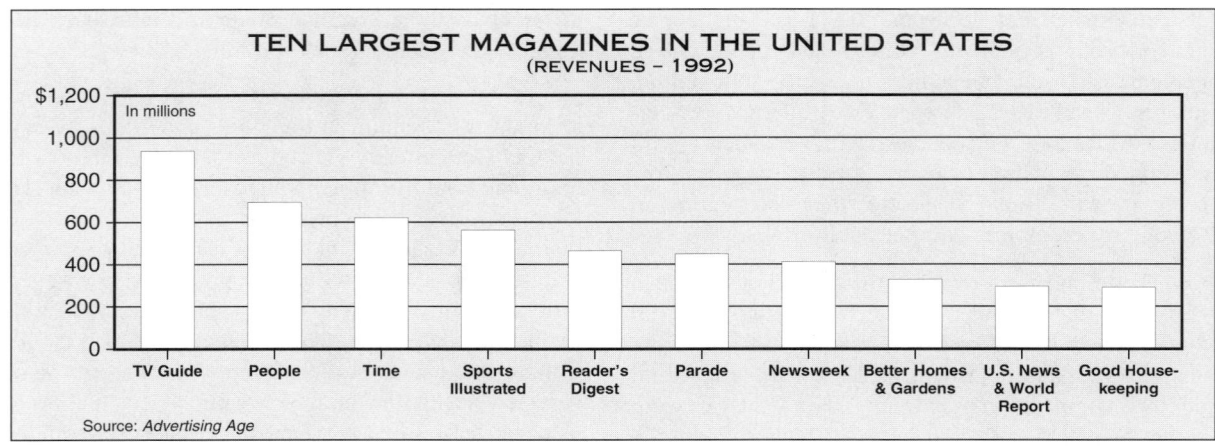

TEN LARGEST MAGAZINES IN THE UNITED STATES
(REVENUES – 1992)

Source: *Advertising Age*

grossed about $1.8 billion in 1991 receipts and employed over 7,000. Other sales leaders in 1991 included Meredith Corp, of Iowa (which generated $735 million in sales), Time Incorporated (with $580 million in 1991 sales), and Hachette Magazines Inc. ($517 million).

The company that garnered the most magazine advertising revenues in 1992 was Time Warner Inc. (Formerly Time Inc.). This enterprise capture over 19 percent of all industry ad revenues in 1992. Hearst Magazines placed second in order of ad revenues, with about eight percent of the market. Conde Nast Publications, Inc., a major supplier of travel magazines, captured over seven percent of industry ad dollars. Parade Publications, The New York Times Company, and Hachette were other top ad sellers.

The top ad revenue generating periodical in the United States in 1992 was *TV Guide,* which sold over $822 million worth of ad space and circulated 15 million copies weekly. *People,* the second greatest ad earner, had advertising revenues of $562 million in 1992. Other ad leaders included *Time* ($446 million in 1992 ad sales), *Sports Illustrated* ($437 million), *Reader's Digest* ($428 million), *Parade* ($328 million), and *Newsweek* ($310 million).

The largest magazine by total number of issues circulated was *Parade,* a weekly newspaper insert. It boasted a weekly circulation of over 36 million in 1992. Other major periodicals, by circulation totals, were *Modern Maturity* (with 22.6 million subscribers in 1992), *Reader's Digest* (17 million), *USA Weekend* (15.8 million), and *National Geographic* (9.9 million).

Of the top 100 U.S. magazines, the fastest growing periodical, by circulation, was *Parenting,* which boosted its circulation 31 percent in 1992 to 921,000 per month. *Vanity Fair* unit sales jumped 23 percent,

past one million per month, and *Conde Nast Traveler* circulation rose 21 percent, to 870,000. The largest declines were experienced by *Barron's* (with a circulation drop of 23 percent in 1992), *Computerworld* (20 percent), and *The Cable Guide* (17 percent).

WORK FORCE

The periodical industry employed roughly 115,000 workers as it entered the mid-1990s. Workers in the industry are relatively well paid and work fewer hours than the average manufacturing industry employee. The average payroll per employee in 1991, for example, was $29,532, compared to $26,028 for all other manufacturers. Production workers earned an average of $12.49 per hour, compared with $10.49 for the U.S. average. Furthermore, the average work week in this industry was only 30 hours in 1991, compared with 38 hours for all other manufacturing sectors.

The industry is a major employer of writers, editors, and technical writers, which together constitute 13 percent of this industry's work force. Many employees begin as copywriters, copyeditors, or production editors, and work their way up to various editorial management positions. Senior editors, for example, write copy and may also manage other editorial employees or free-lancers. The average senior editor's salary in 1993 was $43,400, though the top third averaged $62,600, according to a survey with 404 respondents in the August 1, 1993 issue of *Folio.*

Managing editors coordinate the editorial, art, and production departments of a publication and oversee proofreading and copywriting functions. Salaries for this job averaged $41,000 in 1993. Editors, who are responsible for directing the content of a publication, averaged $47,000 in 1993, though the top one-third of survey respondents earned over $70,000. Editorial managers may have various titles, such as publisher,

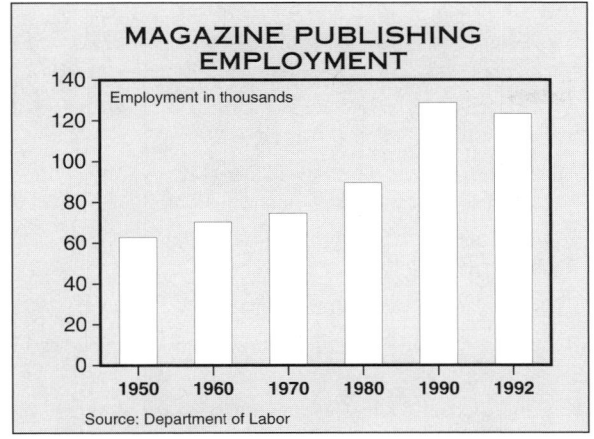

MAGAZINE PUBLISHING EMPLOYMENT

Employment in thousands

Source: Department of Labor

but are responsible for setting editorial policy and managing operations. The average salary for this function was $66,400, although the average for the top one-third of this group topped $100,000 and went as high as $250,000. Salaries for all positions vary primarily according to the circulation volume of the periodical.

Periodical producers also employ a large number of ad salespeople, which make up 12 percent of industry employment. According to a survey with 441 respondents in the September 15, 1993 issue of *Folio,* the average director of ad sales earned $90,208 in 1993. The top one-third of the directors, however, averaged $137,310. Even branch and regional ad sales managers averaged over $70,000, and the top one-third earned $108,722. The latter group also included category managers that specialize in selling ads for just one product or service.

Although overall compensation slumped in the early 1990s, the long-term employment outlook for the periodicals industry was very positive going into the mid-1990s. Jobs for writers and editors should balloon over 50 percent between 1990 and 2005, according to the Bureau of Labor Statistics. Sales and related positions, moreover, will leap over 65 percent. Indeed, almost every occupation in the industry was forecast to jump by over 30 percent. Jobs for executives, for example, should rise 28 percent, and administration and support staff will likely grow by over 30 percent. Opportunities for computer programmers should bound nearly 80 percent by 2005.

AMERICA AND THE WORLD

In an effort to boost earnings in slow domestic markets, many periodical publishers in the early 1990s were seeking growth overseas. Although total industry exports amounted to only 3.5 percent of receipts in 1993, cross-border shipments had grown almost 100

percent since 1989 and were expected to increase at a rate of five to ten percent annually through the turn of the century. Furthermore, U.S. publishers had a stranglehold on domestic markets, as imports amounted to less than $170 million in 1993 and the industry's trade surplus topped $600 million.

Canada consumed about 78 percent of all periodical exports in the early 1990s, but other countries were exhibiting solid market growth. The United Kingdom, for example, purchased six percent of periodical exports, and Mexico and the Netherlands each purchased three to four percent. Consumer and farm magazines were the greatest sellers. Helping to increase foreign sales in the early 1990s were U.S. joint ventures with overseas publishers that were directing local marketing and publishing efforts. For example, IDG, a global computer-related publisher, entered a joint venture in China to publish *Electronics International.*

While the majority of magazine exports have traditionally gone to English speaking foreigners, U.S. publishers began significant efforts during the 1980s and early 1990s to establish foreign editions of their publications. Some of these efforts were quashed by the global recession of the early 1990s. An example of a successful project launched in 1992, however, was the British edition of *Esquire.*

Other companies that had successfully invaded foreign periodical markets in the early 1990s included Miller Freeman, Inc., of California, PennWell Publishing, of Texas, Advanstar Communications, of Ohio, and several others. Cahners Publishing, of Illinois, for example, was selling 38 percent of its 58,000 monthly circulation of *Hotels* to overseas readers in 1993. Likewise, Paisana Publications was shipping over 68,000 issues of the semi-monthly *Easyriders,* a Harley Davidson motorcycle enthusiasts magazine, to foreign customers. *Surfing,* published monthly by California's Western Empire Publishing, had about 13,744 overseas subscribers in 1993.

Despite some overseas success, the export potential for U.S. periodicals remained limited by multiple factors going into the mid-1990s. Most important, postal rates in most European and Asian countries are much higher than U.S. rates, severely restricting subscription sales. U.S. publishers also often incur great difficulty obtaining effective mailing lists which they can use to market their publications. The U.S. list industry is highly advanced by comparison. Furthermore, some important markets like Germany have strict environmental and privacy regulations that limit periodical sales through the mail.

U.S. exporters will likely experience little relief from foreign regulations in the near future. Pending revisions to the European's Community's law on privacy and data protection, in fact, threatened to make it very costly for U.S. publishers to acquire customer lists. Nevertheless, Europe, as well as the Far East and Latin America, will remain the focus of joint ventures and licensing arrangements aimed at boosting overseas sales. The North American Free Trade Agreement (NAFTA), signed in 1994, was expected to have a negligible impact on industry participants.

RESEARCH AND TECHNOLOGY

In the long term, periodical publishers will start to view their role as providers of information services, rather than just product publishers. This will occur as electronic and digital publishing proliferates, and as publishers seek to enhance revenue streams through advanced media options. Many publishers were already experimenting with multi-media markets in the early 1990s, and several publishers had been offering their periodicals on CD-ROM or on-line since the 1980s. Some analysts believed that electronic publishing, in some form, would dominate the industry by the 2010s, with paper publishing used only as a side or specialty media.

Indeed, as the number of American households with a modem-equipped personal computer rose from 13 percent in 1993 to an estimated 25 percent by 1995, publishers were increasingly striving to take advantage of this media. The number of subscribers to on-line services, in fact, jumped 10.6 percent in 1993 to nearly 7 million users. Publishers of *Consumer Reports* pioneered the on-line environment in the mid-1980s and were offering that publication on at least three popular services going into the mid-1990s. Other major publishers going on line in the mid-1990s included Time Warner and Disney.

Evidencing the trend toward electronic media was a partnership formed in 1993 by Jeffrey Dearth, president of the *New Republic,* and Rob Raisch, president and founder of The Internet Co. Their on-line partnership, The Electronic Newsstand Inc., is designed to give print publishers a "point of presence" on the Internet, a global computer network. More than 50 magazines were represented on The Electronic Newsstand by 1994, including such titles as *Arthritis Today* and *New Yorker.* "Ultimately, I believe we're looking at more and more magazines coming online and providing full content, along with graphics, sounds, and interactivity," predicted Raisch, in a December 1993 issue of *Folio.*

INDUSTRY INFORMATION SOURCES

Alexander, Bob, "The State of the Newsstand," *Folio: Special Sourcebook Issue 1994,* January 1994.

Angelo, Jean Marie, and Rachel Drucker, "Editors Report Stalled Earnings," *Folio,* August 1, 1993.

Angelo, Jean Marie, "Ad Sales Salary Survey," *Folio: Special Sourcebook Issue 1994,* January 1994.

Forbes, Thomas, "Testing the Waters Online," *Folio,* December 1, 1993.

Hovey, Susan, "Away From Home," *Folio,* June 15, 1993.

Huhn, Mary, "In a Tight Spot," *Brandweek,* September 13, 1993.

Kaplan, Michael, "The Resurrection of Larry Flint," *Folio,* June 15, 1993.

Kobak, James B., "Magazine Trends," *Folio: Special Sourcebook Issue 1994,* January 1994.

"Market Trends: Magazines," *MEDIAWEEK,* January 10, 1994.

McDougall, Paul, "The Best and the Biggest," *Folio,* September 15, 1993.

Pace, Charles L., "New Directions for the U.S. Postal Service," *Folio: Special Sourcebook Issue 1994,* January 1994.

Saffo, Paul, John Warnock, Brenda Laurel, and Perry Barlow, "It's 2013: Do You Know What Your Magazine Looks Like?" *Computer Pictures,* May/June 1993.

Standard & Poor's Industry Surveys, New York: Standard & Poor's Corporation, January 20, 1994.

U.S. Industrial Outlook 1993, Washington, D.C.: U.S. Department of Commerce, January 1993.

—Dave Mote

SIC 2731

BOOK PUBLISHING

This category includes establishments primarily engaged in publishing, or in publishing and printing, books and pamphlets. Establishments primarily engaged in printing or in printing and binding (but not publishing) books and pamphlets are classified in **SIC 2732: Book Printing.**

INDUSTRY SNAPSHOT

The book publishing industry experienced extraordinary growth over the past 30 years. From $1.68 billion in 1963, annual book sales doubled by 1973, tripled to reach $8.6 billion in 1983, and nearly doubled again to $17.17 billion in 1993. The total value of shipments for 1993 reflected a 7.5 percent increase over 1992, and was projected to increase again by 8.5

percent for 1994. The industry published just under 50,000 new titles in 1992, and at least 800,000 books were in print. About 70 million adults in the United States reported buying books regularly.

Part of the increase in the early 1990s was attributed to the proliferation of large, retail bookstore chains. By offering conveniences such as comfortable browsing areas, coffee bars, and live piano music, many of these chains created an enjoyable atmosphere for consumers and expanded the overall market for books. At the same time, however, many publishers moved toward creating "book" products in electronic formats and introduced more general entertainment products for home computers. Electronic publishing exposed book publishers to unprecedented competition from software and communications companies, which resulted in significant new pressure upon the bottom line.

ORGANIZATION AND STRUCTURE

In some respects, book publishing appeared to be a fragmented industry, with over 20,000 companies participating in the United States in 1992. In reality, however, the industry was dominated by seven giant publishing houses that accounted for 80 percent of all best-sellers. These large publishers consolidated many of their smaller imprints in the early 1990s in order to cut costs and reposition themselves for the onset of electronic publishing. According to Malcolm Jones of *Publishers Weekly,* most of these companies considered themselves to operate within "the publishing aspect of the communications industry." However, this concentration of power among relatively few publishers led to criticism regarding the quality and diversity of materials published. Many industry observers saw an increasing role for small presses to publish works of literary quality that did not necessarily have enormous sales potential.

Products within the book publishing industry could be divided into five major categories: trade books; textbooks; technical, scientific, and professional books; mass-market paperback books; and all others. Trade books encompassed all general-interest publications, such as adult and juvenile fiction, nonfiction, advice, and how-to books. The trade category maintained the largest share of the book market at 27 percent, or $4.3 billion in shipments, in 1992. The proliferation of large, chain bookstores and the population growth among school-age children and high-income adults contributed to the growth of trade sales.

Elementary and high school (el-hi) and college textbooks accounted for the second-largest share of the market at 26 percent, or $4.1 billion in shipments, in

1992. The weak U.S. economy led to lower government funding for education, which resulted in sluggish sales in the el-hi market. In addition, high prices for new college texts led to a stronger market for used textbooks on college campuses, where they accounted for one-third of sales.

Technical, scientific, and professional books showed a strong increase to 17 percent market share, or $2.7 billion in shipments, in 1992. A full 20 percent of sales in this category went to overseas markets, due in part to the adoption of English as the language of business. Sales of mass-market paperbacks remained virtually unchanged at 7 percent, or $1.1 billion, partly due to an overall increase in prices.

The "other" category of books accounted for a total of 23 percent of the market, or $3.7 billion in shipments, in 1992. Included within this category were book-club and mail-order sales, which declined slightly to $1.48 billion as a result of strong competition from discount bookstore chains; reference books, which increased to $775 million on the strength of electronic product introductions; religious books, which grew to $900 million; and university press publications, which remained stable at $275 million.

The book publishing process was fairly similar across these product categories. Most books originated as a concept or idea, which was either submitted by an outside author or generated internally by the publisher. The concept was usually refined using market analysis, and the final decision to proceed resulted from a comparison of the product's expected costs and potential revenues. Next came the actual compilation of the book's content, followed by editorial work to ensure its quality and tailor it specifically to a target market. Meanwhile, the marketing and art departments designed the finished product, including type style, page size and layout, presentation of graphics, and appearance of the cover. Then the book was typeset (set in final, camera-ready form for printing), either by an outside vendor or with an in-house desktop publishing system. Finally, the book was transformed into plates, printed, and bound, usually by an outside vendor or affiliated company rather than the publishing house.

Book publishers sold their products to five primary markets: independent and chain retail bookstores, which accounted for 35 percent of book sales in 1991; consumers, who purchased 21 percent of books directly; college bookstores, which claimed 17 percent of publishers' output; elementary and high schools, which accounted for 16 percent; and libraries and other institutions, which made up an additional 9 percent. Among these markets, large chain bookstores proliferated and gained importance in the early 1990s—

making book-buying into a form of entertainment and siphoning sales away from mail order and book clubs. In addition, the library market, though small, was considered crucial in that it guaranteed publishers a minimum number of sales and required little in terms of marketing attention.

BACKGROUND AND DEVELOPMENT

The U.S. book publishing industry grew after the Civil War, as the country moved from an agrarian to an industrial society and people increasingly sought information about emerging technology. World War I increased demand for engineering manuals, especially with regard to radio communication, aviation, construction, and aerial photography. During World War II, training manuals gained importance as factories had to hire untrained people to replace soldiers. Publishers who could provide this information quickly received special allocations of paper, which was scarce during wartime.

Beginning in the mid-1800s, publishing houses provided gathering places for literary talent of the time, especially in London and New York City. Most writers formed relationships with particular editors—who often became well-known public figures in their own right—and followed them from one publishing house to another. Several publishing houses became prominent in the fight against censorship in the early twentieth century. One celebrated case occurred in the 1930s when Bennett Cerf, one of the founders of Random House, intentionally notified U.S. Customs about the arrival of James Joyce's allegedly obscene novel *Ulysses* from Paris. Cerf wanted Customs to confiscate the book so that he could fight the censorship in court. Publishing houses that supported freedom of speech often attracted the top literary and editorial talent.

Paperback books first appeared in the United States in the 1770s, but they did not gain a wide audience until Simon & Schuster introduced its line of Pocket Books in 1939. These early softcover editions sold for 25 cents each and met with great success—over 25 million copies were shipped overseas during World War II. Public acceptance of paperbacks increased the overall market for books and made it necessary for publishers to adopt high-volume, low-cost production methods.

In *Publishers Weekly*, John F. Baker called the 1940s and 1950s "the golden age of publishing," when the industry was a "comparatively small business producing a comparatively limited number of books for a cozily elite readership whose access to bookstores was limited by geography." As the U.S.

population grew and became more educated, however, book publishing boomed. This rapid growth culminated in what Baker described as "the decade of the Great Communications Conglomerate Takeover" in the 1960s. Many publishing houses either acquired one another or joined forces with communications conglomerates that held interests in newspapers, magazines, television, and motion pictures. By the early 1970s, the industry was dominated by about 15 giant companies. The consolidation of power continued into the 1990s, when about seven publishers controlled the industry.

CURRENT CONDITIONS

The book publishing industry faced a transformation entering the mid-1990s. Many observers noted that the industry, which once could be characterized as gentlemanly and literary, had quickly become more cutthroat and businesslike. *National Review* cited as evidence the trend for large publishing houses to replace long-time chief executives, best known for their "literary sensibilities," with industry outsiders steeped in "modern management techniques." As a result, many employees within the publishing industry shifted their focus from building relationships with authors and carefully tailoring manuscripts to cutting costs and analyzing profit and loss statements.

Some analysts felt that this shift was overdue, since book publishing faced challenges on a number of fronts yet lagged behind other industries in seeking efficiencies in production, distribution, and marketing. One problem addressed by many large houses was their overproduction of titles, which resulted in an average of 30 percent of trade books (and up to 48 percent of paperbacks) being returned unsold for credit. Large production runs were less costly for publishers, and retailers tended to over-order some titles to attain volume discounts and hopefully predict the next best-seller. In response, some publishing houses utilized new technology to make shorter production runs more profitable, and the average first-run dropped to 2,000-5,000 books, down from 7,000-10,000 in the late 1980s. In addition, several publishers began experimenting with "no-return" policies in hopes of forcing booksellers to make more realistic orders.

Another factor affecting the book publishing industry was the proliferation of large, influential retail bookstore chains. While these chains expanded the overall market for books, they also had the power to limit pricing and affect the selection of books that publishers could offer profitably. Some critics argued that by catering to a mass market, chains caused publishers to create books of broad appeal, but low quality.

For example, the early 1990s saw many publishers adopt genre publishing—focusing on books with similar themes in order to limit their risk. One highly criticized result of this trend was the battle to attain publishing rights for headline-grabbing, ''true-life'' stories of questionable literary value, such as plane crashes and serial murders. Some analysts also worried that chains would disrupt the business of independent booksellers, who were often closely linked to tastes within their communities and provided a market for more eclectic books.

Book publishers also faced a challenge to their continued profitability due to the 1980s legacy of offering huge cash advances to prominent authors. Some industry executives likened the impact of this trend to mass suicide by publishers, since it meant that only one in five products were successful enough to turn a profit. In addition, large advances were criticized within the industry for preventing publishers from nurturing talented, yet less well-known, authors. However, other industry observers argued that the proceeds from one best-seller could often support a number of ''more literary'' releases. Overall, many publishers expressed their intention to limit future advances.

Book publishers also faced keen competition for the leisure time of their traditional customers from cable television, VCRs, video games, and multimedia products. In addition, the recession of the early 1990s led to cutbacks in education and library funding, with subsequent reductions in book purchases by these markets. These trends reinforced industry concerns about declining literacy rates in the United States, and led several houses to participate in programs to encourage a more book-oriented culture. Many publishers also faced shrinking profit margins in key areas. For example, author royalties generally accounted for 10 to 15 percent of the cover price of trade books, which left publishers with an average margin of 9.5 percent. For textbooks and professional books, however—which were less expensive to produce and usually sold in larger quantities—houses obtained an average margin of 20 percent.

Many book publishers responded to these challenges by cutting costs, streamlining operations, and adopting new technologies. Annual capital expenditures within the industry doubled during the past decade, to reach $350 million in 1992, with much of the increase attributable to computerization. In addition, many publishing houses released fewer titles and concentrated their efforts more closely on selected target markets. As a result, overall industry output of new titles fell below 50,000 in 1992, compared to its peak of over 56,000 in 1987. The average price for a hardcover book was just under $40 in 1990, while paperbacks sold for nearly $4.50 apiece. However, some trade publishers saw $20 as the informal, upper price limit for hardcover fiction. Many publishers also reacted to industry challenges by moving toward electronic books, which were envisioned to be portable, interactive devices in CD-ROM format. There was little market for such products in the early 1990s due to their high price, but many houses saw them replacing audio books as the wave of the future.

As John F. Baker explained in *Publishers Weekly*, ''Publishing is changing quite markedly, to the extent that there's more caution, a much greater sense of the potentials, up and down, of the market, and a determination to focus more sharply, among the big houses; new skills, better distribution, and a real sense of a significant role to play, among the smaller ones.'' As the U.S. economy began to recover in the mid-1990s, the outlook for the book publishing industry also began to improve. Shifting demographics pointed toward higher enrollment levels in schools and colleges, while the Clinton administration appeared likely to increase funding for libraries and the arts. Many publishers expected growth among medical and health care-related titles to correspond with concerns of the aging U.S. population, as well as growth in professional and technical products to support rapid changes in office technology.

Many of the challenges facing the book publishing industry were reflected in the children's literature boom of the late 1980s. Children's books traditionally represented a quiet, consistent segment of the market, and were virtually ignored by most large houses except for the revenue generated by the classics year after year. However, sales of children's books exploded during the ''baby boomlet''—a result of the financially secure baby-boom generation reaching child-bearing age—from $336 million in 1985 to $1.1 billion in 1992. As more publishers jumped on the bandwagon and expanded their children's divisions, annual output grew from 3,800 titles in 1985 to over 5,000 in 1991 and the number of children's-only bookstores doubled. However, such rapid expansion led to an oversaturation of the market with books of mediocre quality, which was compounded by the recession and decreases in library budgets. As a result, sales growth suddenly dropped by half, retailers returned unprecedented numbers of unsold books, and many publishers were forced to reevaluate their approaches in the face of fierce competition. According to M. P. Dunleavy in *Publishers Weekly*, ''the publishing of children's books has not only grown up but completed an odyssey,'' and the industry learned in the process that it must adopt a longer-term outlook in order to survive.

INDUSTRY LEADERS

The largest publicly held book publishers, ranked in order of 1992 revenues, were: Paramount Publishing, with $1.6 billion; Times Mirror, with $1.2 billion (including newspaper revenues); HarperCollins, with $1.1 billion; Harcourt General, with $987 million; and McGraw-Hill, with $567 million. Operating margins ranged from 9.1 percent at Times Mirror (down from 16.2 percent in 1991) to 15 percent at Harcourt General (rebounding from an operating loss in 1991). Rounding out the ten largest publishers were Western Publishing, Scholastic, Houghton Mifflin, Torstar, and Addison-Wesley.

The largest publishers of trade books, ranked in order of 1992 sales, were: Random House, with $1.1 billion (an increase of 8.4 percent over 1991); Bantam Doubleday Dell, with $650 million; HarperCollins and Paramount Consumer, with $387 million each; and Penguin USA, with $325 million (an increase of 16 percent over 1991). The top eleven trade publishers—which also included Time Warner, Putnam Berkley, Macmillan, Hearst, St. Martin's, and Houghton Mifflin—controlled 66 percent of the market.

Paramount Publishing, the leader in the book publishing industry, obtained its position by acquiring prominent publishing houses such as Simon & Schuster, Macmillan, Prentice Hall, and St. Martin's. Once known as Gulf + Western, the conglomerate changed its name to Paramount Communications in 1989. Paramount published trade books under its own name as well as through its major subsidiaries.

Paramount subsidiary Simon & Schuster, Inc. was founded in New York City in 1924 by Richard L. Simon and M. Lincoln Schuster, who began their careers by publishing highly popular books of crossword puzzles. Some of the company's most famous publications over the years included Leon Trotsky's *History of the Russian Revolution,* Felix Salten's *Bambi,* Dale Carnegie's *How to Win Friends and Influence People,* Dr. Benjamin Spock's *Baby and Child Care,* and Bob Woodward and Carl Bernstein's *All the President's Men.* In 1939 the company introduced Pocket Books, which created the market for inexpensive, paperback books. In 1942 Simon & Schuster followed this effort with the equally successful introduction of Little Golden Books, aimed at the children's market. The company went public in 1966 and was acquired by Gulf + Western in 1975. Simon & Schuster expanded aggressively during the 1980s by launching a dozen

new imprints and acquiring interests in textbooks and software.

Fellow Paramount subsidiary Macmillan, Inc. was originally formed in England by two brothers in 1843. In the early days, its impressive stable of writers included Lewis Carroll, Lord Tennyson, William Butler Yeats, and Rudyard Kipling. Prominent U.S. first editions included Margaret Mitchell's *Gone with the Wind* and Jack London's *The Call of the Wild.* Macmillan's U.S. subsidiary was established in 1869 and became a separate entity in 1896. The company acquired and sold off interests in other areas, such as information services, retail sales, and printing, over the years. Macmillan merged with Crowell-Collier Publishing Company in 1960, but the two operated separately. After several takeover attempts, Macmillan finally was acquired in 1988 by controversial British media mogul Robert Maxwell. Following Maxwell's death in 1991, however, his empire was dismantled to pay off creditors, and Macmillan was sold to Paramount.

The Times Mirror Company, the second-largest publisher in 1992, obtained 33 percent of its revenues from book and magazine publishing, while 52 percent came from newspaper publishing (most notably the *Los Angeles Times)* and 15 percent from cable and broadcast television interests. It maintained over 28,000 employees worldwide.

HarperCollins, the third-largest publisher, was a subsidiary of Rupert Murdoch's News Corporation Limited. Murdoch was born in Australia in 1931 and spent several decades building a newspaper empire in the United Kingdom. He purchased controlling interest in British publisher William Collins and Sons in 1981, then added American house Harper & Row in 1987, and combined the two along with other publishing companies (including Basic Books, T.Y. Crowell, and Scott Foresman) to form HarperCollins in 1989. Besides one of the largest English-language publishers in the world, News Corporation also owned Twentieth Century-Fox studios and the Fox Broadcasting network.

Harcourt General, the fourth-largest U.S. publisher, was formed through a 1991 merger of Harcourt Brace Jovanovich, Inc. (HBJ) with General Cinema. HBJ published about 5,000 titles per year, mostly for the trade and textbook markets, and accounted for about 27 percent of Harcourt General's revenues. The house was founded by Alfred Harcourt and Donald Brace in New York City in 1919. Over the years it published many well-known authors, including T. S. Eliot, Flannery O'Connor, and Sinclair Lewis. HBJ was one of first companies to offer equal opportunities to women in the 1920s, and also formed one of the earliest children's book departments, headed by famous editor Margaret K. McElderry. In 1960, the company went public and then merged with World Book. William Jovanovich, who served as president or chairman from 1961 until 1990, moved HBJ's headquarters from the publishing mecca of New York City to Orlando, Florida, in 1982. In 1986 the company acquired Holt, Rinehart and Winston and W.B. Saunders to become the world's largest publisher of el-hi textbooks. HBJ took extreme measures to defend itself against a takeover attempt by Robert Maxwell in 1987, which left it in poor financial shape and led to the merger with General Cinema.

McGraw-Hill, Inc., the fifth-largest book publisher, produced multimedia products for the business, industry, professional, education, and government markets. The company was formed in 1909 through the combination of two competing publishers of railroad and technical magazines. It benefitted from the increased interest in technical and engineering manuals and expanded rapidly during wartime. In the late 1970s, McGraw-Hill became one of the first companies to enter electronic publishing. By the 1990s it implemented an electronic textbook publishing service, which allowed teachers to custom design books and see the results within 48 hours.

Random House, the largest American trade book publisher, became a subsidiary of Advance Publications (formerly Newhouse Publications) in 1980, when it was acquired for $70 million. Random House was founded when Bennett Cerf and Donald Klopfer purchased the Modern Library series—popular books in an inexpensive format—in 1925. The founders decided to publish luxury editions "at random" in 1928, and named their company Random House. Over the years, the company retained such prominent authors as Eugene O'Neill, Robinson Jeffers, Dr. Seuss (Theodore Geiser), Willa Cather, John Updike, and James Joyce (whose books were the cause of celebrated legal battles). Random House merged with Knopf in 1960 and Pantheon in 1961, became an independent subsidiary of RCA in 1966, and acquired Ballantine paperbacks in 1973 to become a full-line book publisher.

Bantam Doubleday Dell, the second-largest trade publisher, was a subsidiary of German conglomerate Bertelsmann A.G. Bertelsmann was founded in 1835 as a family publisher of evangelical materials, and grew to become the largest media group in Europe. The parent acquired Bantam Books in 1980, then combined it with Doublday in 1986.

Penguin USA, the fifth-largest trade house, was a subsidiary of London-based holding company Pearson PLC, which also owned controlling interest in Addison-Wesley and Longman. The Pearson conglomerate originated with holdings in construction and oil, began acquiring banks and newspapers in the 1920s, and expanded into book publishing throughout the 1980s. Under the Pearson umbrella, Longman (acquired in 1982) became a major publisher of professional, educational, and general reference books; Penguin (acquired in 1985) became prominent in both hard and softcover fiction; and Addison-Wesley (acquired in 1987) contributed a strength in textbooks. Books accounted for 44 percent of Pearson's revenues in 1992. The parent had 28,000 employees and operated in every country of the world.

Some critics argued that the consolidation of book publishing among these few large corporate groups meant that the materials published would become less diverse and have a bland influence on American culture. However, other analysts viewed the situation as an ideal opportunity for small publishers to fill the gap. "Small presses do constitute one of the bright spots in American publishing," Malcolm Jones claimed in *Publishers Weekly*. "These diverse grass-roots efforts act as a natural corrective to the concentration at the top."

WORK FORCE

In an assessment for *Black Enterprise,* Lolis Eric Elie called book publishing "an industry that rewards creativity, treasures personal taste, and provides opportunities to combine work with a socially responsible endeavor." In addition to editorial work, publishing offered career potential for individuals with backgrounds in business, marketing, sales, graphic design, and computer applications. Traditionally, however, "low entry-level salaries, long hours, and slow advancement have deterred those who tried their hand in the field," Elie continued.

Total employment in the book publishing industry increased slightly to reach 73,000 in 1992, after declining for the previous two years. Most of this increase took place in production jobs, which accounted for almost 25 percent of industry employment. The average hourly earnings of production workers in 1992 was $12.30. According to a 1992 *Publishers Weekly* survey, the average publishing company showed annual revenues of $9 million and had 63 employees. Almost half of the companies in the book publishing industry reported no change in their level of employment from 1990 to 1991, while 36 percent increased and 15 percent decreased their staffing levels. Most publishers expected these figures to continue to hold true for 1992. The average salary increase respondents predicted for 1992 was 5.64 percent, down slightly from 1991.

The survey indicated that publishing company presidents earned the highest average annual salaries in the industry at $94,634, which ranged from an average of $31,102 at small publishing firms (those with 1990 revenues less than $250,000) to an average of $165,800 at large houses (with revenues greater than $10 million). The average head of an editorial department made just under $50,000, while an entry-level editorial assistant's salary was less than $19,000. The heads of marketing and sales departments earned an average salary between $65,000 and $70,000, while entry-level employees in these areas made about $20,000 annually. Other areas commonly found within publishing companies included production departments, where salaries ranged from $52,000 for a vice president to $19,000 for an entry-level employee; art departments, which paid over $43,000 for a vice president and over $19,000 at the entry level; and rights and permissions departments, which offered over $40,000 for a vice president and $21,000 for an entry-level employee.

Some industry observers predicted that technology would redefine the roles of everyone in the publishing industry in the late 1990s. As Susan Trowbridge, vice president of publishing technology at Addison-Wesley, explained in *Publishers Weekly*, "the new technological capabilities are causing us to re-examine the roles and procedures of all the publishing participants, from author to editor to designer to manufacturer." Trowbridge foresaw desktop publishing technology moving upstream into editorial functions as well as downstream to manufacturers; a more coordinated focus on the development of multimedia products, involving teamwork between editorial, marketing, and technical experts; and increased automation of administrative processes, such as scheduling and cost-tracking. Employees in all sectors of the publishing industry increasingly required some knowledge of computers in order to be successful in their careers.

AMERICA AND THE WORLD

The U.S. publishing industry was by far the world's leading exporter of books. Exports accounted for nearly 10 percent of U.S. publishers' shipments in 1993, or about $1.7 billion. Half of U.S. exports were textbooks or professional and technical products. The major markets for U.S. book exports were Canada (42 percent), the United Kingdom (14 percent), Europe (13 percent), Asia (10 percent), and Australia (8 percent). The predominance of U.S. exports was explained in part by the increasing numbers of people worldwide

who used the English language to conduct business. In the meantime, total U.S. imports of books reached $1 billion in 1992, an increase of 13 percent over the previous year. The United Kingdom, Hong Kong, Japan, and Canada were the sources for most imported books, although the figures also included shipments of books manufactured abroad for U.S. publishers.

Industry analysts expected international sales of U.S. books to continue to improve, particularly in emerging markets such as the former Soviet Union, Mexico and Latin America, and the Far East. U.S. publishers faced some challenges in international sales, however, due to inconsistent application of copyright, or "intellectual property right," laws overseas. Publishers of audio books and electronic products, in particular, were displeased with the lack of specific protection afforded by the General Agreement on Tariffs and Trade (GATT) when it concluded in late 1993.

Another area of some concern within the industry was that several of the most respected U.S. publishing houses were acquired by foreign owners in the 1980s. For example, German media conglomerate Bertelsmann A.G. acquired Bantam Books in 1980 and Doubleday in 1986 to form Bantam Doubleday Dell, the second-largest trade publisher in the United States. Similarly, Australian mogul Rupert Murdoch's News Corporation Limited purchased Harper & Row in 1987, then merged it with William Collins and Sons in 1989 to form HarperCollins, the third-largest book publisher in the United States. Finally, Japanese giant Matsushita Electric Industrial Corp. acquired MCA in 1990, through which it also gained ownership of Putnam Berkley, the seventh-largest U.S. trade book publisher.

RESEARCH AND TECHNOLOGY

The traditional, printed book might never disappear completely, but new technology revolutionized production, distribution, and nearly every other aspect of operations in the publishing industry in the 1990s. As *Publishers Weekly* predicted, "The definition of 'publisher' will change. It won't just refer to a person who makes books, but a person who holds information or intellectual property, and disseminates that information in any way he or she can benefit from it." Most publishers began to store information in digital form on computer systems so that it could be readily translated into a variety of electronic product formats. While the conversion to the new technology was often difficult and costly for publishers, most electronic products essentially repackaged information the publishers already owned and thus offered higher margins than print products.

The advent of new technology raised a number of interesting issues within the publishing industry. First, publishers faced unprecedented competition from software and communications companies entering the electronic publishing market. These industries began to converge—through partnerships and acquisitions—into something analysts called "the new media." Second, authors and publishers disagreed about who owned electronic publication rights, and significantly more complex contract negotiations became the norm. Third, some confusion arose about which channels of distribution would be most appropriate for electronic products, since bookstores, software stores, and direct mail all formed possible outlets. Fourth, many publishers were concerned about what would emerge as the dominant technological platform for electronic publishing. Libraries initiated the movement toward electronic publishing by purchasing reference products in on-line and CD-ROM formats. However, since 100 million American homes, or 26 percent, were equipped with personal computers, this presented a formidable market for entertainment and educational products on CD-ROM or diskette. In addition, small, hand-held electronic books such as the Sony Data Discman and the Philips CD-Interactive, which sold for $400-600 each, gained acceptance as their prices fell. Some observers predicted that CD-ROM drives might become standard accessories on television sets in the near future, while others claimed that telecommunications would provide the next mass-distribution medium for electronic publishing. Finally, all of these issues had strong implications for the current organization and future staffing of book publishers. They had to become more flexible and technologically adept in order to compete.

Accessing information electronically offered a number of advantages for consumers. For example, CD-ROM products allowed easy sorting of information from a wide variety of databases, as well as made it possible to combine text, graphics, sound, and animation. Some examples of innovative CD-ROM products included a dictionary that could pronounce words, an encyclopedia that could show video clips about entries, and a book that could help a child learn to read. Another common format for electronic information was on-line through computer subscription services. On-line materials were less expensive for publishers to distribute than paper, easier for users to search, and also provided quick publication for time-sensitive information such as medical advances.

Computers also had a significant impact on book production technology. Desktop publishing systems—which featured sophisticated yet simple graphic design software to manipulate digitized text and images into publishable form—made many operations quicker and less expensive for publishers. For example, desktop publishing made it possible for houses to reprint fewer copies of books more often, and thus avoid inventory costs. In addition, the technology allowed publishers to save up to 70 percent in typesetting and other production costs. However, since publishers performed more operations themselves, desktop publishing led to significant changes in the roles of suppliers. In response, many typesetters and printers offered creative services—such as 24-hour turnaround, consulting and training in the use of electronic systems, and management of huge amounts of data—in order to continue to add value.

Technology also began to impact distribution and marketing within the book publishing industry. One new system was PUBNET, an electronic book-ordering system that linked 65 publishers with 2,400 bookstores. PUBNET had the capacity to provide publishers with timely, in-depth sales information, which they hoped to better incorporate into upstream decisions. The system was scheduled to be expanded to include marketing as well as distribution information.

Several industry analysts predicted that environmental issues would gain importance within the publishing industry. For example, some consumer groups demanded that books, especially paperbacks, be made recyclable. Publishers cooperated with printing and binding companies to make book-binding processes and cover materials more environmentally sound, and some products were developed that could be un-bound easily.

INDUSTRY INFORMATION SOURCES

Baker, John F., "Anxieties and Openings," *Publishers Weekly,* January 4, 1993.

———, "Hard Times, Hard Choices," *Publishers Weekly,* January 4, 1993.

———, "Rates of Pay in Publishing," *Publishers Weekly,* January 6, 1992.

———, "Reinventing the Book Business," *Publishers Weekly,* March 14, 1994.

The Business of Publishing: A Publishers Weekly Anthology, New York: Bowker, 1976.

"The Changing Role of Suppliers," *Publishers Weekly,* September 14, 1992.

"Do Not Panic: How Emphasis on Business Has Changed Book Publishing," *National Review,* February 5, 1990.

Dunleavy, M.P., "The Crest of the Wave?," *Publishers Weekly,* July 19, 1993.

Elie, Lolis Eric, "Industry Overview: A Career You Can Make Book On," *Black Enterprise,* February 1991.

Hilts, Paul, "The American Revolution in Book Publishing," *Publishers Weekly,* September 14, 1992.

Industry Surveys, Standard and Poor's, 1993.

"Innovations in Binding," *Publishers Weekly,* September 14, 1992.

International Directory of Company Histories, London: St. James, 1991.

Jones, Malcolm, "The New Publishers' Row," *Newsweek,* February 21, 1994.

Langstaff, Margaret, "Selling the New Media," *Publishers Weekly,* May 10, 1993.

"Lean, Green, and on the Screen: Book Publishers Look to the Advantages of CD-ROM Publishing," *Economist,* July 13, 1991.

Mutter, John, "Heated Competition Gets Hotter," *Publishers Weekly,* January 4, 1993.

"New Roles for Publishers in an Electronic World," *Publishers Weekly,* September 14, 1992.

"Reshaping the Flow of Production," *Publishers Weekly,* September 14, 1992.

Reuter, Madalynne, and Calvin Reid, "State of the Business," *Publishers Weekly,* September 29, 1989.

Robinson, Carol, "Publishing's Electronic Future," *Publishers Weekly,* September 6, 1993.

U.S. Industrial Outlook 1993, Washington, D.C.: U.S. Department of Commerce, 1993.

—Laurie Collier Hillstrom

SIC 2732

BOOK PRINTING

This category includes establishments primarily engaged in printing, or in printing and binding, books and pamphlets, but not engaged in publishing. Establishments primarily engaged in publishing, or in publishing and printing, books and pamphlets are classified in **SIC 2731: Books: Publishing, or Publishing and Printing.** Establishments engaged in both printing and binding books, but primarily binding books printed elsewhere, are classified in **SIC 2789: Bookbinding and Related Work.**

INDUSTRY SNAPSHOT

While the earliest printing techniques were developed in China in the second century A.D., the printing industry in the Western world started when Johannes Gutenberg, Johann Fust, and Peter Schöffer invented moveable type and the printing press, producing the first printed books in the middle of the fifteenth century. Printing came to the United States with some of the earliest English immigrants; the first book printed in the new world was the *Bay Psalm Book,* printed by Steven Day in 1640. Since that time, design improvements and new inventions have made the process quicker and less costly. Almost from the beginning, printing and publishing were separate enterprises. Today, publishers decide what to print and how it will look, and printers put the words on the page to the publisher's specifications.

ORGANIZATION AND STRUCTURE

The publication of books in the United States is characterized by a clear division of labor between book printer and book publisher. The publisher selects the books to be printed, makes all of the decisions regarding the appearance of the final product, from page layout and illustrations to type font and paper quality, and finances the production. The printer takes the camera-ready copy or the film negative and reproduces them in the quantities required by the publisher, on the paper specified and often already purchased by the publisher. The printer's role in the publishing process is one of reproduction rather than production.

Depending on whether the publisher supplies the camera-ready copy, a phototypeset film negative, or a computer text file, the printer's job begins either with making film negatives of each page or printing plates. In some cases, graphic artists working for the publisher take the corrected typeset hard copy of the text and lay out each page with any necessary graphics. These camera-ready pages, called mechanicals, are then sent on to the printer. The printer then photographs these mechanicals to produce the film copy necessary in the plate-making process.

With recent advances in computer graphics capabilities, many computer systems can bypass both the lay-out process and the photographing process. Computer programs can combine text and graphics, so page layout can be done on computer rather than the drafting table. Hardware peripherals can generate output in the form of a film, ready for platemaking.

Metal, paper, or plastic plates are what actually put the images of the text onto the paper. Using photochemical processes, the image to be printed is transferred from the film negative onto the plate. The prepared plate has image areas that chemically accept ink and can therefore pass the ink onto a piece of paper, and non-image areas that chemically repel ink and therefore pass nothing onto the paper, leaving spaces between the letters, images, and lines.

Having made the plates, the printer can begin the reproduction process. Most printing is offset. The inked plates pass a reverse image onto a rubber sheet, which then passes a positive image onto the paper; offset tends to produce a clearer image than direct printing. Black and white graphics, and text only pages, need only pass through the machine once to produce the complete image. Color pictures complicate the process, however, and are usually sent through several times for different colored inks. After the actual printing, some print shops also bind the books while others ship the product back to the publisher or on to the bindery unbound.

BACKGROUND AND DEVELOPMENT

It is thought that the Chinese invented the earliest printing. During the second century A.D., they carved religious texts and images into marble columns around their temples; devotees and pilgrims would ink the columns and press paper to it to make their own copies of the text. Small seals were carved for similar purposes, and by the sixth century, artisans carved wood blocks with which to make prints as well. The oldest known printed works were made with wood blocks in Japan in the eighth century. In the eleventh century, moveable type was invented in China, but the enormous number of characters needed to print any one book inhibited the growth of a large industry.

Paper making, a necessary predecessor to printing, came to Europe via the Arabian presence in Spain between the twelfth and the thirteenth centuries. Wood-carving prints survive from the fourteenth century, but the printing industry really started in Germany in 1455 with the invention of metal moveable type and a printing press by Johannes Gutenberg. Gutenberg made molds of individual letters which then could produce many type pieces of the same letter, all identical. The printer then arranged the pieces in a composing stick in the proper order, and fastened each stick onto the press, which could print many copies of each page. Type pieces could then be removed from the composing stick and revised for the next page.

In the first century of printing, printers were publishers and publishers were printers: the printer decided what to print and provided the initial financial investment. In the sixteenth century, as the church and different governments gained control over the trade and determined what would and would not be printed, they granted licensing rights to only a small number of men to produce a small number of politically acceptable books. In England, booksellers were granted these rights rather than the printers, so the printers lost the power to decide what to print, and the publishing industry was born. The English booksellers' guild, called the Stationers' Company, had the authority to inspect any printing office and destroy unauthorized publications, so the members of the company became the sole (legal) publishers in the country, and law-abiding printers worked on commissioned jobs.

Printing and publishing have always been separate ventures in the United States. The Reverend Jose Glover brought the first printing press from England to America in 1638, and hired Stephen Day to do the printing. Glover died during the voyage; the press passed to his wife, who brought the press to the newly-established Harvard College. The first president of Harvard, Henry Dunster, oversaw the printing in 1641 of the first book in this country, *The Whole Booke of Psalmes Faithfully Translated into English Meter,* by Stephen Day and his son, Matthew.

The history of the U.S. printing industry is essentially the history of the technology. Minor improvements have driven continuous improvements in the speed and efficiency of the presses, and major new inventions have periodically altered production. In the process of stereotypy, molds were made for each page before printing to free the type pieces before the printing process and allow more than one press to be used simultaneously. By the end of the next century, photography was applied to the process, and photoengraving was invented. This process used film, light, and chemical reactions to engrave the text on a thin plate which was then used for printing.

Composition, the process of setting the type, also underwent several changes. By the late nineteenth century, the invention of the linotype and monotype machines improved typesetting speeds over hand composition. In the middle of the twentieth century, the invention of computers revolutionized typesetting once again. Today, the computer is used to set the type, and can either produce a hard copy on paper that is then photographed to make the plates, or can generate the image on film rather than paper to be used immediately to produce a plate; some of the newest machines can even make plates directly from the computer file, sidestepping the film stage completely.

CURRENT CONDITIONS

The printing industry has been effected predictably by general economic trends. In the economic growth years of the early 1980s the industry grew tremendously. But the recession of the late 1980s and early 1990s slowed business dramatically. School and library budgets were cut, affecting a large part of the market. Like other manufacturers, printers became cautious about adding new equipment and employees, and concentrated on cutting waste and becoming more efficient.

In 1992, the industry witnessed the beginning of a recovery. The publishing industry saw an increase of 2.9 percent in sales, which reached $17.1 billion. In January of 1993, the Printing Industries of America estimated that growth for that year for the printing industry would be 7.5 percent. The three largest American printing companies began to see healthy sales at the beginning of the economic recovery. Sales for R. R. Donnelly and Sons, which prints books, magazines, catalogs, directories, and newspapers, reached $3.9 billion. Quebecor Printing, a Canadian firm with American subsidiaries that prints books, directories, magazines, and catalogues, had $1.39 billion in sales in 1991. Arcata Graphics recorded $565 million in sales, and Western Publishing of Racine Wisconsin had $466 million.

INDUSTRY LEADERS

A few large corporations dominate the book printing industry. Some are part of large conglomerates that also own publishing houses. Bertelsmann USA, the American branch of a German conglomerate, includes Bertelsmann Printing and Manufacturing Corporation, but also the Bantam, Doubleday, and Dell publishing group. They also own RCA Records and Brown Printing, which produces magazines. The largest printing companies have subsidiaries all over the country and the world. R. R. Donnelly and Sons, headquartered in Chicago and considered by *American Printer* to be the largest printer in the United States, operates 47 plants around the world, with facilities in Iowa, Virginia, North Carolina, and Arizona, as well as London, Tokyo, Barbados, and Ireland. They had $3.9 billion in sales in 1991.

Arcata Graphics Company is the third largest book printing firm in the country, behind Quebecor Printing, and the fourteenth largest commercial printer. The company began as a lumber business, Arcata Redwood, located in California. In 1969, they entered into printing with their acquisition of plants in Tennessee and Massachusetts. By 1992, they owned ten plants and employed 6200 people. Their clients have included Random House, Crown Publishers, Harper and Row, and Farrar, Strauss, and Giroux.

Arcata's book plants offer full service facilities: they have composition computers for the initial steps and bindery operations for the final ones. They print medium to large size runs, producing anywhere between 10,000 and 1,100,000 books in a single run. In December of 1992, the company sold three of their non-book printing plants to Quebecor of Montreal. They decided to concentrate on book printing in part, at least, because of their belief that, as Ed Owens of Arcata Graphics Company told *Publisher's Weekly,* "I can not see any reason the American Public is going to quit buying books."

The Thomas-Shore company of Dexter, Michigan is a small company, but a leader among short run printers. Both the 1990 *Directory of Short Run Book and Catalog Printers,* as well as the 1990 *Small Press Review,* ranked the company number one in quality and service. In 1972, Ned Thomson and Harry Shore, both of whom worked for another Ann Arbor, Michigan small press, left their jobs and started their own company with their own business philosophy. Decisions are made by committees of employees, who own one third of the company. They employ no sales force. "We don't make sales calls," Thomson told *American Printer* in 1990. "Customers come to us, and we've made our entire effort based on the idea that quality would sell for us if we did better than our competition."

After almost twenty years of just printing books, Thomson-Shore began to branch out into pre- and post-press activities. In 1990, they started a bindery operation. The following year, they bought a page-making program for their computers with an eye towards eventual composition work. They specialize in short runs. "Publishers are demanding even shorter runs," Shore told *American Printer* in 1990. "Many publishers believe reprint costs are cheaper than carrying long-term inventories." Thomson-Shore's average runs are between 300 and 5000 copies, but they can print 25 copies just as easily.

WORK FORCE

Printing companies employ skilled technicians, mid-level management, and high-level management. The actual production is carried out by skilled workers using highly complex machines. Vocational and technical colleges offer training, as do some high schools and two year colleges. Workers can often rise to mid-level management jobs, such as foreman or production control. A college education is frequently required for the higher-level management positions. A few schools offer degrees in printing technology, but science, art, or business degrees can also be helpful.

AMERICA AND THE WORLD

Historically, printing has been a national business. American copyright laws have kept foreign printers from American publishers, and American printers have been kept busy with the domestic market. In the late 1980s and early 1990s, however, American printers began to take on more international business. Long-standing disadvantages to overseas work include language barriers, shipping costs, and cultural differences. As the Eastern Block countries began to open up, however, American technology and supplies, far superior to those available in many other countries, became increasingly in demand. Ten to fifteen percent of the business of W. L. Litho International, for example, is foreign. The company has clients in England, Australia, Japan, the Bahamas, the Grand Caymans, Central and South America, and the former Communist-bloc countries. Some companies, like R. R. Donnelly, have subsidiaries overseas as well. Exports in the printing and publishing industries grew steadily over the 1980s and into the 1990s; in 1990, they reached $3.8 billion, with books and magazines comprising between 70 and 80 percent of the material.

RESEARCH AND TECHNOLOGY

Book printers are becoming increasingly responsive to the needs of their different customers. Large publishing firms that need large quantities of best sellers are only one segment of their market. More and more, shorter runs are required, as are copies on demand. The printing industry has sought new technology to meet these needs.

Small publishers, and publishers producing books with limited appeal, such as university presses and the scholarship they support, frequently do not want large runs of books. Usually, the fewer the books printed at one time, the more each book costs to make, primarily because of the time needed for composition. Because more and more publishers are gravitating toward shorter runs, to cut down on storage costs and to realistically reflect the market, book printers are beginning to specialize in smaller runs, with new computer composition techniques. Computer graphics produce illustrations more efficiently than draftsmen. New machinery has introduced new methods of plate production directly from a computer file without the middle step of a film. Each reduction in the time and cost of composing reduces the cost and increases the efficiency of shorter book runs. Some companies can produce any number of books—from 25 to 5000—cost effectively.

Printing on demand is also becoming popular and necessary. Many large industrial or technological firms need to produce manuals for their employees and consumers, but do not want to get into the printing business. New companies, such as Corporate Publishing Services of Freemont, California, have been established to fill their needs. "Our mandate is to become 'information services specialists' who can process information in all forms for all methods of distribution," Leslie Spencer, the president of Corporate Publishing, told *Publisher's Weekly* in 1991. Their goal is take data from their clients, usually in the form of computer files, and with their high-quality computer printers, xerographic copying machines, and in-house bindery presses, provide custom quantities of publications within hours. Recent advances in computer laser printing and computer composition have made this realistic and economically feasible.

INDUSTRY INFORMATION SOURCES

Adams, J. Michael, David D. Faux, and Lloyd J. Rieber, *Printing Technology,* 3d ed., Albany, NY: Delmar Publishers, 1988.

Baker, John F., "Big Changes Seen for Arcata, Quebecor," *Publishers Weekly,* December 7, 1992, 9.

Ferris, Fren, "Book Smart," *American Printer,* September 1992, 30.

"Foreign Trade," *American Printer,* November 1991, 42.

"The Foremost Ranking of Top Printing Companies," *American Printer,* July 1992, 56.

Goddard, Connie, "Working Smarter, Not Harder," *Publishers Weekly,* May 31, 1991, 50.

Greenfeld, Howard, *Books: From Writer to Reader,* New York: Crown, 1976.

Hilts, Paul, "Arcata/Kingsport Turns 70 Years Young," *Publishers Weekly,* July 13, 1992, 27.

Peterson, Debbie, "Be a Best Seller," *American Printer,* September 1992, 26.

———, "The State of Plates," *American Printer,* February 1992, 26.

Piechowski, Rod, "From Cover to Cover," *American Printer,* June 1990, 100.

"Print Markets and the Recession," *American Printer,* January 1993, 11.

Rosen, Robert H., "Coping with a Changing Industry," *American Printer,* August 1991, 92.

Taylor, Sally, "Bertelsmann Targets a New World in Publishing," *Publishers Weekly,* July 12, 1991, 41.

—Robin Armstrong

SIC 2741

MISCELLANEOUS PUBLISHING

This classification includes establishments primarily engaged in miscellaneous publishing activities, not elsewhere classified, whether or not engaged in printing. This includes the publishing of atlases, business service newsletters, calendars, catalogs, directories, guides, maps and map globe covers, paper patterns, race track programs, racing forms, sheet music, shopping news, technical manuals and papers, telephone directories, and yearbooks, as well as the activity of micropublishing.

INDUSTRY SNAPSHOT

Miscellaneous publishers tend to be specialized within their own narrow category of publishing. However, in addition to independent publishing companies, some book and periodical publishers also have divisions or departments engaged in miscellaneous publishing. The industry spans a range of some of the largest companies in publishing down to sole-proprietorship enterprises. The activities of some miscellaneous publishers more closely resemble book publishers, while others more closely resemble periodical publishers.

ORGANIZATION AND STRUCTURE

Telephone Directories. The largest category within miscellaneous publishing, comprising about a third of the industry's revenues, is telephone directory publishing. There are over 6,000 telephone directories published in the United States annually by approximately 200 publishers. This includes both telephone companies or their subsidiaries and independent publishing companies. Telephone directories come in several kinds. The utility or core directory is the standard directory provided by telephone companies for their service areas, with an edition distributed free to the owner of each phone line. Directories for smaller regional areas, such as a specific town or neighborhood, or larger regions than the core directories cover may be published by either a telephone company or an independent publisher. Telephone company publishers also publish business-to-business directories whose listings include establishments that would be of interest to other businesses. Finally, there are independent companies which publish special interest directories, such as those targeted at specific ethnic groups.

The telephone directory publishing industry is often synonymous with the term yellow pages publishing, because the same companies publish both comprehensive alphabetical telephone listings and categorized paid advertising listings known generically as yellow pages. Even if certain directory editions do not contain classified business listings, their publishers earn their revenues from the yellow pages that they publish, whether as part of a directory or in a separate volume. Telephone directory publishing is thus an unusual in-

dustry, because the bulk of its revenues are earned through advertising services and not the selling of the publications. Nevertheless, the yellow pages publishing companies are traditionally categorized under Miscellaneous Publishing, rather than under the advertising industry.

Directories. Directories that do not base their revenues on selling advertising space usually provide more comprehensive information on their entries than merely the telephone number and street address—and list individuals or organizations based on a common specialization. These directories are published by a different category of publishers than the telephone directory publishers. Publishers of specialized directories typically create and own their own databases of information to be published. Directory publishers may be primarily publishers of periodicals, such as trade journals, and publish directories focused on their journals' specialization. Other comprehensive directories, which provide substantive additional information, are published by reference book publishers. Directories are also published by nonprofit organizations, such as professional or trade associations.

Catalogs. The catalog industry is primarily a printing industry, rather than publishing, because catalogs are usually produced on contract for manufacturing, wholesale, or retail companies for the marketing of their products. In some cases, however, publisher-printers create catalogs on their own as a business initiative. The same is true for shopping news publications.

Business Service Newsletters. The distinction between business service newsletters and regular periodical publishing is often blurred. In general, though, business service newsletters contain no advertisements, charge high subscription rates, are narrowly focused, and contain articles, tables or graphs oriented towards data rather than commentary. Such newsletters are often available in electronic form in addition to, or instead of, print. Companies in this industry may be independent firms, but the largest publishers are often divisions or subsidiaries of market research or financial information services firms. Other business service publications, not necessary newsletters, are sometimes grouped with this category; these would include such publications as bibliographic databases.

Sheet Music. Like trade book publishers, publishers of sheet music publish, market, and hold existing copyrights to creative works of independent composers and lyric authors, not their own employees. Many music publishers, however, derive the majority of their revenues from sources other than sheet music, namely from performance royalties or recorded music royalties for the music to which they own the copyrights. Thus, these publishers are categorized instead under the financial industry for patent and trademark owners and lessors. Publishers which gain most of their business from printed sheet music publishing, and thus are part of the miscellaneous publishing industry, tend to be publishers of classical music, in which most of the written music is in the public domain and no royalties are paid. Sheet music publishers may also publish collections of their music as books.

Maps and Atlases. Map and atlas publishers create maps with their own copyright, although based on public domain geographic surveys. The publishers' cartographers draw up their own maps according to standard geographic surveys of the federal government, altering the map sizes and adding or deleting data to the maps. Major publishers publish their maps both in book form as atlases and as free-standing poster-style maps. Smaller map publishers create local and regional maps for their local market. There also exist small cartographic companies which draw up maps on request for clients, typically book publishers and advertising agencies. Other book or periodical publishers may also publish atlases as a secondary activity. Roadmaps in the United States were first published by gasoline station companies—a practice which in some part continues.

Trading Cards. Cards for trading or collecting are dominated by baseball cards, but also include the publishing of other sports cards and entertainment cards depicting personalities or scenes from films, television shows, and music. Companies may publish a full range of cards or they may specialize. In 1991, 60 percent of the trading card publishing business was in baseball cards, with about 81 billion cards produced annually; 11 percent of the cards were for football, 8 percent basketball, 3 percent hockey, 3 percent other sports, and 15 percent were entertainment cards. Sport trading card publishers have licenses from the professional sports leagues, and pay royalties to the players or teams pictured. There are approximately 100 companies in the sports and entertainment trading card business. Sport cards were originally sold with bubble gum, but are increasingly sold separately and marketed toward adult collectors. Trading card publishers are often categorized under the printing industry instead of publishing.

Calendars. Approximately 200 companies publish calendars in the United States. These comprise both specialized calendar publishers and those with other publishing or nonpublishing activities. The industry does not include the multitude of companies that have calendars produced in their name as marketing devices.

Micropublishing. Micropublishing comprises microfilm and microfiche publishing, known collectively as microform. Publishing on microform typically involves the reproduction of printed material, especially periodicals, for distribution primarily to libraries. Microform publishers usually are not the original copyright holders of documents, but must obtain licenses from the original print publishers to publish microform editions. Newspapers and magazines are usually reproduced on reels of microfilm, whereas government documents and telephone directories are the texts most commonly published on microfiche. Some print publishers, such as The New York Times Company, publish there own microform versions.

BACKGROUND AND DEVELOPMENT

Telephone Directories. The first telephone directory, which listed 50 names, was published in New Haven, Connecticut, in 1878, just two years after Alexander Graham Bell invented the telephone. The first directory with classified business headings was published in 1883. It is said that the first yellow pages were printed in 1883 when a printer in Cheyenne, Wyoming, ran out of white paper and had to use yellow sheets instead. Telephone directories were originally produced as a service for telephone users, and the business of taking in revenues from advertising developed later.

The telephone company American Telephone and Telegraph (AT&T), the major phone company in the United States, became the largest directory publisher, earning over $1.5 million from its yellow pages business in the late 1970s. AT&T had introduced the name Yellow Pages and the famous walking fingers logo, but chose not to trademark either name or logo, which have since been adopted by numerous publishers. When AT&T divested its Bell companies in 1984, the directory publishing business was also divided among the seven new regional holding companies, resulting in a publishing subsidiary or division for each company. This led to greater competition for advertisers, as the regional Bell companies introduced directories for regions beyond their own service areas. Meanwhile, independent yellow pages publishers had existed for decades.

The yellow pages industry grew rapidly in the 1980s from revenues of $2.9 billion in 1980 to that of $8.9 billion in 1990, including non-publishing marketing and advertising service sales. The number of directory editions published increased steadily to a peak of 6,500 in 1986, when the number began to decline somewhat. The regional Bell companies withdrew to publishing for only their own territories in response to consumer confusion and advertiser complaints over multiple yellow pages for the same region. Also, some niche publications, such as one by Southwestern Bell that targeted the elderly, were unsuccessful. Although traditionally considered a recession-proof industry, yellow pages advertising sales slowed, but did not decline during the recession of 1990-92.

Several trends affected yellow pages publishing in the early 1990s. Publishers are increasingly relying on third-party marketing agencies. The industry was working toward a standardized advertising menu in 1993. Targeted niche marketing is being further developed. The growth of 800-numbers has led to an increase in national advertising whereby a company chooses to advertise in various yellow pages throughout the country. Most recently, audiotex services are being introduced in some areas. Sometimes referred to as ''talking yellow pages,'' voice information services permit callers to enter in codes for information on the advertised product or service. Yellow pages publishers, both independent and utility, are teaming up with newspaper publishers to offer these information services. Another trend among telephone directory publishers is a greater dedication to community service with the publishing of community-oriented information pages.

CURRENT CONDITIONS

The industry as a whole had sales of $9.7620 billion in 1991, according to the *Census of Manufacturers*. With the inclusion of sales figures for companies for whom miscellaneous publishing is a secondary activity, the industry total came to $10.1375 billion, with a strong growth rate of 14.1 percent. In that year industry was capitalized at $165.5 million, and its inventories were $721.1 million.

Revenues for telephone directories in 1991 were $3.8227 billion. The yellow pages industry as a whole, which comprises advertising-related services, has much higher revenues, totaling $9.2 billion in 1991.

Sheet music publishing generated sales of $153.8 million in 1991. This compares with revenues of $1.1 billion, made up largely of royalty payments, for the entire music publishing industry. Growth in sheet music publishing revenues is limited by the tendency toward copyright violations. Since sheet music usually takes up only a couple of pages, it is easily photocopied illegally.

Trading cards had sales of $1.4 billion in 1992, up from $1.1 billion in 1991. Sports cards in 1991 ac-

counted for more than $600 million, up from $425 million in 1986. There appears to be more opportunity for growth in the non-sports card categories. Sales of non-sports cards totaled $55-60 million in 1992. Meanwhile the secondary market of dealers and collectors is several times bigger. The industry has been growing recently due to increases in sales to adults, sophistication in marketing, and the use of nonexclusive licensing contracts by professional sport leagues as a means of improving their images and marketing their players and teams.

Map and atlas publishing was estimated to be a $200 million industry in 1990 and was expanding at 10-12 percent annually. Increased international travel by Americans as well as changing borders and city names in Eastern Europe and the former Soviet Union contributed to increased sales.

Other categories' sales figures for 1991 include business service publications (not just newsletters) with $927.4 million in revenues, shopping news sales of $838.9 million, directories (other than telephone directories) and catalogs with combined revenues of $634.2, and paper clothing patterns with sales of $186.8 million.

INDUSTRY LEADERS

The major telephone directory publishers are the seven regional Bell companies —Bell Atlantic Corporation, Bell South Corporation, Pacific Telesis Group's Pacific Bell Directory subsidiary, Nynex Corporation, U.S. West Incorporated, Southwestern Bell Corporation, and Ameritech Corporation—as well as GTE Corporation, United Telecom, Sprint, Reuben H. Donnelley Corporation, and DonTech (a joint venture of Ameritech and Reuben H. Donnelley). In 1992 the leading telephone directory publisher was BellSouth with $1.46 billion in yellow pages revenues, followed by GTE with $1.22 billion.

Of other companies operating in other sectors of this SIC, the leading business service publishers include Dow Jones and Company Incorporated, Dun & Bradstreet Corporation and its Moody's Investors Service subsidiary, Thomson Information Publishing Group, Value Line Incorporated, and Disclosure Incorporated. The largest music publishers include Hal Leonard Publishing Corporation, EMI Music Publishing Worldwide, and CPP/Belwin Incorporated. The biggest catalog publisher-printer is R.R. Donnelley and Sons Company. Another leader is World Color Press Incorporated.

The leading publishers of sports cards, based on 1993 market share, were Upper Deck, with 24 percent of the market, Topps Company Incorporated—historically the market leader—with 22 percent, Marvel Entertainments Group Incorporated's Fleer with 22 percent, Score Group Incorporated with 10%, and Leaf Incorporated's Donruss division with 8 percent.

The top map publisher is Rand McNally Company. The U.S. subsidiaries of Munich-based Langenscheidt are second in sales combined. Third is Simon & Schuster, which owns Mobil Road Atlas and H.M. Gousha, and fourth is Hammond Incorporated. The nonprofit National Geographic Society is also a major publisher of maps and atlases.

The leading school yearbook publishing and printing companies are Taylor Publishing Company and Jostens Incorporated. The largest clothing patterns manufacturer is Butterick Company Incorporated with sales of $130 million. The other major companies are McCall Pattern Company and Simplicity Pattern Company Incorporated. The foremost publisher of microfilm for other newspapers, magazines, and academic dissertations is University Microfilms International.

WORK FORCE

The miscellaneous publishing industry was one of the top 20 industries by three-digit S.I.C. code for rate of employee growth during the 1980s. Its work force increased 79.6% between 1979 and 1989. The work force in all categories of miscellaneous publishing was approximately 798,000 workers in 1992, of which 476,000 were female workers, and 392,000 were production workers. In 1992 the production worker's wage rate average $11.09/hour. While the industry's work force is not expected to maintain the high growth of the 1980s, it is predicted to be the fastest growing category of the publishing and printing industries, to reach around 1.13 million workers in the year 2000.

AMERICA AND THE WORLD

Had it not been for the breakup of AT&T, the United States might have had the largest yellow pages publisher in the world, but that honor goes to Bell Canada's subsidiary Tele-Direct Publications. Tele-Direct and U.S. publishers both have expanded their operations overseas in countries where no large-scale yellow pages had existed. While local and national telephone utilities continue to publish the alphabetical directories, the commercial market has been left wide open for experienced North American publishers. Tele-Direct has been active publishing yellow pages through joint ventures, especially in the Middle East. More recently, U.S. publishers have won contracts to publish directories in Eastern Europe and Russia as those countries move to a free-market economy. In

1992 Nynex Information Resources Company won the contract for publishing the Prague yellow pages in the Czech Republic. An international yellow pages publisher can also offer international advertising exposure to its advertising clients within a common commercial region of more than one country.

Sheet music publishing is a very international business, along with music publishing as a whole. Publishers contract with licensed distribution agents in each country or region in which they distribute their music. In printed music, the United States is the world leader, holding 38.6 percent of the world's business in 1990. The revenues of U.S. music publishers have been growing faster internationally than domestically. The United States is followed by Germany with 21.4 percent of the world market share, while companies located in the United Kingdom command 12 percent of the market.

Business service publishers are increasingly marketing their publications internationally to serve business people interested in market conditions in different countries. Newsletters are much lighter than business magazines and therefore ship well by airmail. Whether companies are sending articles, bibliographic or directory databases, or numeric tables, business service publications in electronic formats are by far the easiest to "export."

RESEARCH AND TECHNOLOGY

More so than the other publishing industries, miscellaneous publishing is rapidly being transformed by the adoption of electronic media, such as CD-ROM and online services. Many publishers of printed material have begun publishing versions of their books or periodicals on CD-ROM, while others license their data to specialized CD-ROM publishers and online vendors. A wide range of miscellaneous publishing exists on CD-ROM: telephone directories, other directories, maps, business service publications, business newsletters, guides, and even forms of catalogs and yearbooks. Some business service publishers now publish more information in electronic form than either print or microform. Fax and online information services are being utilized especially by business newsletter publishers, who need to provide speedy delivery of information.

Some may consider CD-ROM (compact disc read-only memory) the newest category of miscellaneous publishing, categorized under micropublishing. Indeed, a whole industry has emerged since the last revision of the Standard Industrial Classification system. Since CD-ROM is merely a medium for data, it is the type of data written on it that probably best determines the classification of its producers. If the data is principally text, then the CD-ROM producer is classified under the appropriate publishing industry. Although all CD-ROMs contain some computer software, if the software is the primary feature of the CD-ROM product, such as in an interactive game, then the producer would be classified under the computer software industry.

INDUSTRY INFORMATION SOURCES

1990-91 International Survey of Music Publishing Revenues, New York: National Music Publishers' Association, 1992.

Andrews, Edmund L., "Changing Shopping Habits Keep Those Fingers Walking," *New York Times*, July 1, 1990.

Belsky, Gary, "Trading Up," *Money*, May 1991.

Bowles, Elena, "East Europe Entices Publishers," *Advertising Age*, March 16, 1992.

Hilts, Len, "Maps that Fill a Gap," *Publishers Weekly*, January 27, 1992.

Levy, Clifford J., "So Long, Grim Slugger: It's a New Card Game," *New York Times*, March 18, 1992.

Steinhauer, Jennifer, "With Computers, Mapmakers are Redrawing the World," *New York Times*, December 2, 1990.

Strand, Patricia. "Yellow Pages: Industry Bumps Ante and Rolls the Dice in Bid for National Ads," *Advertising Age*, September 27,1993.

Yellow Pages: Meet the Industry Behind the Books, Troy, Michigan: Yellow Pages Publishers Association.

Yellow Pages: Industry Facts Booklet 1992-93 Edition, Troy, Michigan: Yellow Pages Publishers Association, 1992.

— Heather Behn Hedden

SIC 2752

COMMERCIAL PRINTING, LITHOGRAPHIC

This category includes establishments involved primarily in printing by various processes involving lithography. It includes printers using both web and flat sheet technologies. Terms describing the processes include offset printing, photo-offset printing, photolithography, and planography.

Most of this industry's work is done on a custom-job basis. Typical products include advertising posters, circulars, coupons, and labels. In addition, some products such as calendars, maps, posters, and decalcomanias are bulk manufactured and offered for sale. Greeting card printers, however, are classified in **SIC 2771**.

Lithographed newspapers and periodicals manufactured by printing companies who are not publishers are also included in this industry. Establishments primarily involved in printing books are classified in **SIC 2732**. Newspaper, periodical, and book publishers are classified in **SICs 2711, 2721,** and **2731,** respectively.

Establishments primarily involved in preparing plates and related pre-press services are classified in **SIC 2796.** Establishments offering photocopying services are classified in **SIC 7334.**

INDUSTRY SNAPSHOT

"Lithography" is a term describing a specific type of printing process where ink is transferred from a plate with a level surface that has been chemically treated to make some areas ink-receptive and others ink-repellant. The term "offset lithography" was coined to describe the process by which an image is transferred from a lithographic plate onto a rubber blanket cylinder and then pressed from the cylinder onto paper or other substrates. About half of all the printing done in the United States is accomplished by lithography.

According to figures published by the U.S. Department of Commerce, commercial printing by lithography drew in receipts totalling $32.7 billion in 1987. Of this amount, $30.0 billion represented products considered primary to the industry. These statistics yielded a specialization ratio of 94 percent for 1987, an increase over the 91 percent reported in 1982. The combined value of commercial printing by all methods in 1987 was estimated at $44.7 billion.

By 1991, the commercial printing industry had grown to $55.7 billion, however, profit margins for many establishments were down as a result of intensified price competition during the national recession. Advertising and related materials represented the largest category of printed products. These included posters, catalogs, magazines, shopping news, direct mail, inserts, and display items. Combined they accounted for 65 percent of commercial printing shipments in 1991. Although advertising was the fastest growing market segment for commercial lithographers, analysts blamed a 1991 postal rate increase with suppressing additional potential growth. Magazine printers faced slackened growth as the total number of advertising pages fell and limited funds were made available for new publications.

Label and wrapper printers accounted for eight percent of commercial printing shipments in 1991. Their products were valued at $4.4 billion. Environmental awareness brought increased demand for labels as manufacturers sought ways to reduce packaging.

According to figures published by the National Association of Printers and Lithographers, commercial printing represented the fifth largest manufacturing industry in the United States. During the early 1990s, government statistics indicated that commercial printing was growing faster than general manufacturing in all 50 states. Forecasters anticipated annual growth rates of 3.5 percent through 1996.

One challenge facing the commercial printing industry was the advancement of electronic communication. Information providers increasingly turned to computer technology to produce disk versions of previously printed products such as directories and manuals. In response, some printing companies began expanding their product lines to offer supplemental computerized versions of printed documents. Typically, printed versions were produced less frequently and updated information was provided by computer disk.

Compliance with national, regional, and local environmental regulations posed another challenge to the industry. Commercial lithography depended on the use of solvents, volatile organic compounds (VOCs), and other substances classified as toxic. The printing process also generated waste materials which were considered hazardous. In addition, some environmental groups criticized the industry for its mass production of newspapers, periodicals, catalogs, and direct mail items which used paper resources and congested the nation's landfills.

BACKGROUND AND DEVELOPMENT

The term ''lithography'' comes from two Greek words: lithos, meaning ''stone,'' and graphien, meaning ''to write.'' The process was developed by the German inventor Aloys Senefelder. Senefelder discovered that by treating limestone with gum arabic, nitric acid, and a mixture of soap and tallow he could make parts of the stone repel printing ink and parts of it repel water. In 1798, he perfected his process for use in printing.

Early lithographic plates were made from limestone, and presses were made of wood. During the first two decades of the 1800s, technical advances were made. Cast iron platens helped improve impression quality, and steam-driven cylinder presses increased operating efficiency. The ability to print in color was developed in 1837. Publishers of popular travel books were among the first to replace the more expensive methods of etching and engraving with lithography. A

typical nineteenth century press could print approximately 600 impressions per hour.

The twentieth century brought innovations to increase press speeds and improve image resolution. Ira W. Rubel and Caspar Hermann, both of New Jersey, developed thin metal plates in 1904. Their success enabled the development of rotary lithography, a procedure in which the plate was mounted on a cylinder. By the late 1980s, advances in offset rotary press technology had produced presses capable of making 30,000 impressions per hour, printing on both sides of the paper, and receiving paper in sheets or from large rolls called ''webs.''

Despite its widespread use, many people find lithography more difficult to understand than other printing processes. Unlike methods in which printing plates contain raised or etched images, lithographic plates are flat. To create a lithographic plate, a plate maker begins with a thin piece of metal coated with an oil-based emulsion. A photographic negative of the image to be printed is placed over the plate, which is then exposed to a bright light. The light reacts with the uncovered emulsion so that when the plate is chemically washed the emulsion remains only in the image area. During the printing process, water is used to wet the bare metal, non-image areas of the plate. Printing ink, an oil-based product, is able to adhere only to the emulsion in the image area.

CURRENT CONDITIONS

As commercial lithography entered the 1990s, the industry continued striving toward faster presses, quicker set-up, improved color reproduction, and better material handling procedures. One noted trend was toward shorter but more numerous press runs. Industry analysts attributed this to ''just in time'' inventory systems and to advertisers' ability to target markets with greater precision.

Another observed trend was increased use of color. Previously, four color presses were considered the industry standard for reproducing photographic images. Four-color process printing created shades and tones of color by employing a technique called color separation, which involved filtering an image through a screen to produce a series of single-color plates, each containing an image comprised of tiny dots. In four-color process printing, three of the plates were made for specific individual colors chosen for their ability to render a full palette of all the visible colors by precisely overlaying their printed dots. The fourth was a black plate used to create contrast and enhance shadows. Although in theory, four color process printing should have been able to exactly duplicate a photograph, in practice limitations based on ink capabilities and screen size prevented flawless reproductions. Improvements made during the early 1990s included the use of smaller screens and the addition of more ink colors. Six- and eight-color presses enabled printers to exactly match distinctive colors, take advantage of special effects such as the application of metallic inks, and apply coatings or other finishes.

Another important development within commercial lithography was the increasing impact of environmental regulations. Systems used to produce proofs (samples made before printing to exactly depict the finished product) were criticized because of their reliance on solvents associated with air and water pollution. Many local ordinances controlled waste water discharges from printing establishments by defining acceptable pH levels, restricting the discharge of ignitable substances, and banning the presence of heavy metals. Worker safety regulations mandated chemical exposure limits, and the storage and handling of hazardous substances were controlled by legislation. The Clean Air Act Amendments of 1990 required companies to obtain permits for press equipment, and some states also ordered permits for vented pre-press equipment. In some places, local governing authorities restricted the number of hours a day certain types of presses were allowed to run and limited the acquisition of additional printing capacity.

INDUSTRY LEADERS

One of the largest commercial printers operating in the United States during the early 1990s was Quebecor Printing (USA) Corporation. Quebecor USA maintained its headquarters in Boston, Massachusetts. The company's parent organization, Quebecor Inc., was founded in 1965, and its corporate headquarters are located in Montreal, Canada. In 1992, Quebecor operated 61 printing and related service plants in North America with locations in 17 states, six Canadian provinces, and in Mexico. The company reported annual sales of $1.4 billion and employed 13,504 workers, 8,990 in the United States.

Quebecor's principal products included advertising inserts, circulars, flyers, magazines, catalogs, and books. Divisions producing these items provided more than 77 percent of the company's revenue in 1992. Other divisions included specialty printing, directory printing, securities printing, newspaper printing, and other printing services such as pre-press support, circulation fulfillment, and list management.

Another leader in the commercial printing industry was Valassis Communications, Inc. Valassis, located in Livonia, Michigan, was founded by George Valassis in 1969. The company's growth followed its pioneering work with Free Standing Inserts, coupon compilations distributed with newspapers. In 1986, Valassis was purchased by an Australian firm, Consolidated Press Holdings (CPH). In 1992, however, CPH sold 51 percent of its interest in Valassis through a public stock offering.

Following its shifts in ownership, Free Standing Inserts (FSIs) continued to be the company's major product, representing 86 percent of its revenues in fiscal 1992. Industry analysts estimated that Valassis held fifty percent of a national FSI market estimated at $1 billion. Valassis's customers included many large, well-known national organizations including Procter & Gamble, Lever Brothers, McDonald's, and General Mills. Its distribution network included 340 major market newspapers. According to company statements, 77 percent of U.S. households used coupons in 1991, and shoppers saved $4 billion by redeeming 7.5 billion coupons.

Other Valassis products included single inserts, specialty print promotions, brochures, catalogs, posters, magazine inserts, and customized projects using fragrances, rub-offs, die cuts, and special folding. For the fiscal year ending June 30, 1992, Valassis reported revenues of $684 million and a net income of $70.0 million.

WORK FORCE

The commercial printing industry was one of only five manufacturing industries to post a net gain in employment during the 1980s. In 1987, the U.S. Department of Commerce reported that commercial lithography employed 403,000 people, a 29 percent increase over employment figures of 311,900 reported in 1982. The four top states in employment were California, New York, Illinois, and Pennsylvania. Combined they accounted for about one-third of the industry's total employment. Among commercial printers by all processes total employment was expected to climb to 575,000 in 1992. The National Association of Printers and Lithographers anticipated further increases in employment to add 100,000 to 153,000 workers between 1993 and 1997.

Workers within the commercial printing industry were facing rapid changes as new production methods and materials were adopted. Some, critical of the innovations, claimed that craftsmanship was being replaced with technology; others claimed that technological improvements enhanced traditional craftsmanship. Changes resulted in the elimination of some job classifications but created shortages of experienced labor in others. The pre-press and post-press areas were expected to yield the greatest gains in employment opportunity.

According to U.S. Government statistics, approximately 37,000 establishments were involved in commercial printing during 1991. These businesses were located in virtually every U.S. town and county. The National Association of Printers and Lithographers stated that ''Though commercial printing is a huge industry, it is an industry of numerous small businesses, embodying the U.S. entrepreneurial spirit.'' Forty-three percent of commercial printing establishments employed fewer than four employees; 66.2 percent employed fewer than ten; 85 percent fewer than 20; and 93.4 percent of the nation's commercial printers employed fewer than 50 employees.

During 1991 and 1992, average production wages reported for the commercial printing industry were between $10.85 and $11.94 per hour. The recession of the early 1990s was blamed for job losses in the Northeast and Midwest regions of the nation and slower than anticipated wage increases.

RESEARCH AND TECHNOLOGY

Evolving technology played a vital role in the development of the commercial printing industry. Analysts estimated that printers invested more than $2 billion in new technology during 1991 to maintain their competitiveness. The development of high-quality copying machines drove printers to adopt presses capable of offering more benefits. Innovations brought improvements in color capacity, press speeds, and automation.

As press speeds approached 2,500 feet per minute, automated equipment became increasingly important because of human physical limitations. New methods of feeding paper into the press and taking printed matter away from the press were developed. Researchers designed computers to help achieve optimal results by automatically monitoring press temperatures, plate register (how images fit together), and web tension. One device that facilitated the development of higher speed presses was a densitometer. A densitometer was a device used to insure color integrity throughout an entire press run by automatically making adjustments to the ink fountains. Prior to the development of densitometers, ink fountain adjustments were made by an experienced pressman based on visual perception.

Other technological changes were aimed at improving the ability to quickly set up a press and to reduce paper waste. One area under study was the automatic setting of press variables from pre-press operations. For example, if computerized color separations could be used to directly set press ink keys, exact color reproductions could be made without wasting time and paper in experimental attempts to duplicate the required visual results. Other evolving technologies included faster plate changes, reductions in the amount of blank space required to lock plates onto press cylinders, additional in-line finishing capabilities, optimized material handling at the end of the press run, and better photographic reproductions.

One system gaining acceptance was called dry lithography. Dry lithography used waterless ink systems. In traditional lithography, water was necessary to dampen the plate. A precise ink/water balance was essential for superior quality. Systems printing without water achieved higher-quality results and operated more efficiently. Waterless printing also enabled printers to work with higher resolutions. For example, commercial printers traditionally reproduced photographs using screens of 150 lines per inch. Using waterless technology, printers could employ screens of 300 to 500 lines per inch.

Despite its promise, waterless lithography presented printers with a unique set of problems. The technology required special inks and special plate materials able to repel the inks from non-image areas. In addition, press temperatures were more difficult to control. Using traditional water systems, the water served not only to keep ink away from non-image areas, but also to cool the press. Waterless systems required chilling rolls to carry off excess heat or ink adjustments to compensate for higher temperatures.

INDUSTRY INFORMATION SOURCES

''A Colorful Explanation.'' *Indiana Business Magazine*, April 1991.

Borowsky, Irvin J. *Opportunities in Printing Careers*. Lincolnwood, IL: NTC Publishing Group, 1992.

Borowsky, Mark. ''Skill Hard to Find in New Technology.'' *Memphis Business Journal*, 15 January 1990.

Cross, Lisa. ''Eco Impact on Proof Systems.'' *Graphic Arts Monthly*, March 1993.

Cross, Lisa. ''Waterless Ignites Renewed Interest.'' *Graphic Arts Monthly*, April 1992.

Koeslka, Rita. ''How to Print Money.'' *Forbes*, 24 December 1990.

Koren, Michael. ''Keep Your Balance.'' *American Printer*, September 1992.

Lorenzi, Neal. ''Web Offset Moves into the 1990s.'' *American Printer*, May 1989.

Merkli, Werner. ''Landmarks in Printing.'' *UNESCO Courier*, July 1988.

Petersen, Debbie. "In Search of Excellence." *American Printer*, October 1989.

Quebecor Printing, Inc. *Corporate Review*. Montreal, Quebec: Quebecor, March 1992.

———. *Fact Sheet*. Montreal, Quebec: Quebecor.

Toth, Debbi. "Multicolor Sheetfeds: In a Quick Tournabout, Six-Colors Rule the Market." *Graphic Arts Monthly*, March 1989.

U.S. Department of Commerce. *1987 Census of Manufactures*, Washington, DC: Bureau of the Census, March 1990.

U.S. Department of Commerce. *U.S. Industrial Outlook 1992*, Washington, DC: U.S. Department of Commerce, 1992.

Valassis Communications, Inc. *1992 Annual Report*. Livonia, MI: Valassis, 1992.

Vicary, Richard. *Manual of Lithography*. New York: Scribner's, 1976.

—Karen Bellenir

SIC 2754

COMMERCIAL PRINTING, GRAVURE

This category includes establishments primarily engaged in commercial printing using the gravure process. Other terms often used to describe current methods of gravure production are "photogravure," "rotogravure," and "intaglio." Examples of products in this industry include calendars, catalogs, coupons, directories, menus, playing cards, postcards, trading stamps, and wrappers.

INDUSTRY SNAPSHOT

Gravure is a form of intaglio printing. The word "intaglio" comes from an Italian word meaning "to engrave;" the word "gravure" is taken from the French and has the same meaning. Intaglio printing methods were developed by carving or engraving an image in stone or metal. In contemporary commercial gravure printing, a reversed image is cut into a thick metal plate. Ink, applied to the plate and wiped off the surface, remains in the incised image area so that when paper is placed against the plate it absorbs the ink and produces a copy of the image. The gravure printing process is typically used for very long press runs or for projects requiring better than average color accuracy and clarity. Gravure's primary advantage over other forms of printing is its ability to produce millions of impressions without suffering any image deterioration. Its disadvantages include higher plate costs and increased press set-up time.

According to figures released by the U.S. Department of Commerce, commercial gravure printers received $3.1 billion in revenues in 1987. Of this amount, $2.6 billion represented products considered primary to the industry and $458.8 million represented products considered secondary. These statistics yielded a specialization ratio of 85 percent, a figure lower than that reported for commercial printing by other processes.

Magazine printers made up one of the biggest segments within the commercial gravure industry. In 1991, magazine printing shipments equaled $8.3 billion. Although not all magazines produced were printed by the gravure method, gravure printers were adversely affected as declining numbers of new magazines entered the marketplace.

Catalog and directory printers represented another substantial segment of the gravure market. Within the United States, catalog and directory output represented 13 percent of all printing shipments and had a combined value of $7.2 billion. Trends within the industry toward shorter print runs aimed at more focused markets lessened gravure's advantages and brought increased competition from other print technologies.

BACKGROUND AND DEVELOPMENT

The gravure printing process developed from copperplate engraving techniques employed during the fifteenth century. Early plates were flat and had to be hand engraved. The development of engraved cylinders to replace flat plates led to rotary gravure, called "rotogravure." Rotary gravure presses operated by squeezing paper between the image cylinder and a second cylinder called an impression cylinder. Rotary technology enabled the development of presses with increased printing speeds. A process by which rotary gravure presses were able to print on both sides of the paper was patented in 1860 by Auguste Godchaux, a publisher located in Paris. A photographic etching technique developed in 1878 by a Czech painter helped simplify plate-making procedures.

Gravure printing was further refined in 1908 when two German textile printers, Ernst Rolffs and Eduard Mertens, developed the "doctor blade." Gravure printing techniques relied on creating height differences between the image and non-image areas of the plate. An image was formed by making small recessed ink cells. The doctor blade assured the removal of excess ink from the surface level and enhanced the quality of reproductions.

One of the most popular items reliant on gravure technology was the Sunday newspaper magazine section. Many magazine sections even used the term "rotogravure" as part of their name. Although gravure newspaper supplements were not suited for up-to-the-minute reporting because of their lengthy preparation requirements, they made color advertising possible.

Despite advances made in gravure technology during the early twentieth century, plate-making expenses and the length of time required to set up press runs remained problematic. The industry responded with efforts aimed at increasing gravure's efficiency. According to a study conducted by the Gravure Research Institute in 1969, 38.5 man-hours were required to complete the necessary pre-press work for each color page printed using available gravure technology. By 1986, improvements including computer assisted pagination and innovative photographic techniques had cut the pre-press time to less than 15 man-hours.

By the mid-1980s, most gravure printing was done using engraved chromium-coated copper cylinders. Typical cylinders measured eight feet long and two feet in diameter, although larger and smaller cylinders were also used. In some cases, cylinders were engraved with laser technology. Because of their large size and complexity, gravure cylinders remained expensive to create and handle. Standard paper rolls, called "webs," for gravure presses measured up to 100 inches wide and up to 50 inches in diameter. Although most gravure output was cut into sheets, sometimes it was rewound.

In magazine printing, the press output was discussed in terms of "signatures." A signature was defined as a large, single printed sheet folded to yield a specified number of magazine pages. Based on a standard 8.5 x 11 inch page size, the most popular signature of 16 pages was achieved by printing four pages across the cylinder and two pages around the circumference of the cylinder. When the paper was printed on both sides, it yielded 16 printed pages. A 32-page signature was achieved by adding a second print unit and a second roll of paper. Other signature sizes were possible by varying the length of the cylinder to yield a different number of pages across the width of the web or by varying the cylinder circumference to produce a different number of pages around the cylinder.

In comparison with offset lithographic presses, gravure presses tended to be larger, faster, and more expensive. A gravure press during the late 1980s could cost as much as $10 million, not counting the costs associated with other equipment such as engraving devices, cylinder handling systems, ink, and paper rolls. A report published by the Gravure Research Institute, prior to its merger with the Gravure Technical Association to form the Gravure Association of America (GAA), analyzed the annual costs associated with running a typical gravure press 24 hours a day, six days a week, with five holidays per year. The total annual operating cost of one press was $37.4 million dollars.

The high cost of gravure production was blamed as a contributing factor in the decline of many Sunday newspaper magazines, although some analysts also attributed the decline to improvements in print processes making color available in other newspaper sections. According to statistics gathered by the Gravure Association of America, gravure Sunday magazine production was 12 percent higher in 1988 than in 1987 but the total number of individual magazines produced had dropped. By the end of the decade, they numbered less than 50, and the 1990s reduced their numbers further. Discontinued magazines included publications offered by the Des Moines *Register, Denver Post, Oakland Press, Sacramento Union,* New York *Daily News,* and *Newsday.*

The fact that total production had not also fallen was attributed to two growing national Sunday supplements, *Parade* and *USA Weekend,* both gravure products. By 1991, *Parade* was distributed in 340 newspapers, and its circulation totaled 35 million; *USA Weekend* was distributed in 333 newspapers, and it had a circulation of 16 million.

CURRENT CONDITIONS

During the early 1990s, analysts noted uncertain conditions within the commercial gravure industry. Among catalog and directory printers, gravure held approximately one fourth of the market share and growth in gravure print orders for catalogs was growing at a faster rate than the overall growth rate for catalog printing. One example was the Lands' End catalog. Lands' End of Dodgeville, Wisconsin ordered 60 million catalogs in fiscal year 1989 and planned to print 65 to 70 million in fiscal 1990. The company's catalogs were printed by two gravure printers in lots of two to seven million copies. Lands' End preferred gravure because of its cost advantages during long press runs and its superior color consistency.

In other areas, however, gravure printers were experiencing decreasing demand as publishers and advertisers turned to other print processes. According to figures released in 1989 by the Gravure Association of America, annual increases in gravure advertising totaled only six percent during the 1980s while offset advertising print orders had increased at an annual rate of 13.6 percent. In addition, gravure's market share for inserts had dropped to 8.5 percent from 19 percent recorded in 1982. Among magazine printers, annual increases in page production fell short of increases in print capacity and productivity. This led to increased competition and reduced profit margins.

In addition to competition among gravure printers, the commercial gravure industry as a whole faced competition for advertising dollars from television and other printing processes. Trends toward shorter press runs to produce demographic editions of large-circulation magazines and similar trends among catalog publishers toward smaller specialty catalogs lessened the economic advantages offered by gravure's long run capability. At the same time, improvements in the ability of competing print processes to achieve high-quality photographic reproductions further eroded gravure's traditional advantages.

Industry analysts expected that the gravure print method would continue to face challenges from other print processes and that its long term success hinged on the development of innovative technology aimed at reducing cylinder costs and shortening press set-up times. Some industry watchers, however, expected gravure to benefit from increasing concern surrounding the environmental impact of commercial printing. Lithographic processes generally employed solvent-dependant ink systems, and some analysts felt gravure could achieve superior results following an industry-wide switch to water-based technology.

INDUSTRY LEADERS

One of the largest gravure printers operating in the United States was Quebecor Printing, Inc., a Canadian firm whose U.S. headquarters were located in Boston, Massachusetts. Quebecor operated 41 gravure presses and produced Sunday newspaper magazines, including *Parade* and *USA Weekend,* and retail inserts. The company's major advertising clients included Sears, Target Stores, Montgomery Ward, Radio Shack, and Woolco-Woolworth. Quebecor also printed magazines including *Time, Reader's Digest,* and *People.* In a corporate review booklet printed in 1992, Quebecor stated that its "products touch the lives of millions of North Americans each day. From books, magazines, directories and newspapers to currency, stamps, training manuals and cheques, our printed products can be found in virtually every North American home and business." Despite its heavy involvement in gravure printing, however, Quebecor's primary SIC classification was commercial lithography.

One of the largest organizations with a primary SIC classification of commercial gravure was Arcata Graphics. In 1992, Arcata posted annual sales of $330 million and employed 3,500 workers. The company operated six plants and printed materials for more than 1,000 U.S. publishing firms. Arcata's services included pre-press operations, one- to six-color printing capabilities, a full range of binding options, distribution assistance, and subscription fulfillment.

In addition to its service to periodical publishers, Arcata Graphics served book publishers and was the second largest book manufacturer in the United States, producing 270 million bound books annually. During 1992, Arcata announced its intention to concentrate on its book printing operations. As a result, the company signed a letter of intent with Quebecor Printing to sell three of its publication and commercial printing plants to Quebecor. The three plants, two in Tennessee and one in Buffalo, New York, produced approximately $200 million in gross sales and employed 2400 workers.

AMERICA AND THE WORLD

Gravure's popularity was increasing faster in Europe during the late 1980s than in the United States. Large gravure presses capable of "all-at-once" production were used to print entire magazines in a single print pass. Popular weekly news magazines featuring topical issues, televisions listings, and celebrity news required regular press runs of several million copies.

According to industry analysts, the European market trends differed from trends within the U.S. market. U.S. production was shifting to shorter runs with smaller signatures and heavier reliance on bindery technology to produce customized publications for narrowly targeted markets. In Europe, however, printers favored all-at-once printing to save time and labor, and virtually eliminate the need for special bindery operations.

Some industry watchers, however, predicted that the popularity of all-at-once magazine production would diminish as political systems changed and free market conditions expanded. In 1988, Roger Ynostroza, editor of *Graphic Arts Monthly*, wrote "the concept [of all-at-once production] just might be ill-timed for emerging changes in the European marketplace, an economic community scheduled for free market status by 1992." According to Ynostroza, "If consumers there begin demanding more customized products and magazine publishers embrace targeted marketing techniques, a chilling scenario could emerge: a perfectly engineered manufacturing system, totally unsuited for the new needs of a changing market."

RESEARCH AND TECHNOLOGY

The biggest challenge facing the gravure industry was shortening its pre-press work and press set-up time requirements. One method under study was called direct digital engraving. Direct digital engraving methods used laser technology to etch cylinders without making an intermediate film copy of an image. A technique capable of engraving a 99-inch plastic-coated cylinder at 300 lines per inch in approximately 20 minutes compared favorably with other engraving methods which took about two hours. The procedure's developers abandoned the project, however, because of problems encountered with cylinder scratching. Cylinders developed scratches after less than 7,000 revolutions, much less than the 6.5 million revolutions produced by a traditional chromium-plated cylinder.

Another obstacle faced by printers seeking to adopt direct digital engraving methods was the lack of a system to provide proofs. A proof was a sample created to replicate the anticipated final results of printing. Because direct digital engraving saved time and expense by etching cylinders without making a film copy of the image, it failed to provide a medium from which a proof could be fabricated. Two prototypes of digital color proofing systems were disclosed by Minnesota Manufacturing and Mining Company (3M) and Eastman Kodak in 1990. Many analysts, however, did not expect them to be commercially viable until the middle of the decade.

INDUSTRY INFORMATION SOURCES

"Arcata Graphics Company Fact Sheet." Baltimore, MD: Arcata.

Borowsky, Irvin J. *Opportunities in Printing Careers*. Lincolnwood, IL: NTC Publishing Group, 1992.

Fitzgerald, Mark. "Ironic Victims of Newspaper Color." *Editor and Publisher*, 28 September 1991.

Hilts, Paul. "Big Changes Seen for Arcata, Quebecor." *Publishers Weekly*, 7 December 1992.

Hunter, Margaret. "Direct Digital Color Proofing (DDCP)." *Folio*, July 1990.

Johnston, Peter. "The Gravure Forecast: Partly Cloudy." *Graphic Arts Monthly*, June 1989.

———. "Gravure Revisited." *Graphic Arts Monthly*, April 1987.

Lessner, Ivy. "Gravure Update." *American Printer*, March 1989.

Merkli, Werner. "Landmarks in Printing." *UNESCO Courier*, July 1988.

Quebecor Printing Inc. *Quebecor Printing Inc. Corporate Review*. Montreal, Quebec: Quebecor, 1992.

Toth, Debbi, and Roger Ynostroza. "The Issue of Page Configuration." *Graphic Arts Monthly*, May 1992.

U.S. Department of Commerce. *1987 Census of Manufactures*. Washington, DC: Bureau of the Census, March 1990.

U.S. Department of Commerce. *U.S. Industrial Outlook 1992*. Washington, DC: U.S. Department of Commerce, 1992.

Ynostraza, Roger. "Gravure's Jumbo Generation." *Graphic Arts Monthly*, July 1988.

—Karen Bellenir

SIC 2759

COMMERCIAL PRINTING, NOT ELSEWHERE CLASSIFIED

This industry classification is comprised of establishments involved in commercial or custom-job printing not categorized elsewhere. Example products include newspapers and periodicals printed on behalf of publishers, engraved announcements, circulars, maps, tags and labels, directories, stock certificates, and currency. Establishments primarily involved in platemaking and related services are classified in **SIC 2796: Platemaking and Related Services.**

INDUSTRY SNAPSHOT

Although many items made by commercial printers not elsewhere classified are similar to those offered by commercial lithographers and commercial gravure press operators, the industry's participants primarily use varying combinations of print technologies including embossing, engraving, flexography, letterpress, non-impact printing, thermography, and screen printing (other than on textiles). In 1987, receipts for SIC 2759 totaled $9 billion. Of this amount, $8 billion represented receipts for products considered primary to the industry, $642.3 million represented products considered secondary, and $338.6 million represented miscellaneous transactions. The industry's specialization ratio was 93 percent. During the early 1990s, non-impact print methods were still evolving. Computer and laser technology helped bring about advances in electrostatic printing and ink jet systems enabling printers to achieve high quality results without traditional printing plates.

ORGANIZATION AND STRUCTURE

Letterpress and flexography are two common "relief printing" methods. In relief printing, plates are cast or engraved in a manner to produce a raised image. The image is transferred by applying ink to the plate's surface and pressing it against paper or other substrates. Letterpress and flexographic technologies are similar except that letterpress plates are made from metal and flexographic plates are made from rubber or photopolymer materials. As a result of its different plate composition, flexographic processes require special inks to avoid plate damage.

Screen printing (sometimes called porous printing or silk screening) employs a screen stencil. The image area is left open and non-image areas are sealed using a substance called ''resist.'' Ink is applied to the screen and forced through its mesh onto paper or other substrates such as glass, plastics, and metal (including highway signs). Screen printing is commonly used for limited quantity outdoor posters such as billboards and point-of-purchase advertising displays.

Thermography, also called raised printing, is used primarily for business cards and stationery. The raised effect is achieved by applying a colorless resin powder to the wet ink. The powder then assumes the color of the underlying ink and, when heated, bubbles and bonds to the paper. Some printers use pearlescent and glitter powders to create special affects.

BACKGROUND AND DEVELOPMENT

Humankind's interest in making multiple copies of art and documents dates back many centuries. The Chinese, credited with the invention of paper, designed a kind of wooden movable type based on Chinese characters. Modern print methods, however, trace their beginnings back to the early 1400s when Johannes Gutenberg, a German publisher, developed movable metal type based on alphabetic characters. Gutenberg created molds for individual letters and cast them using a metal alloy made of lead, antimony, and tin. He hand assembled text, letter by letter, from pieces of type which were kept in a special ''type case'' with compartments for each letter, accent mark, and punctuation mark. To print, Gutenberg locked the type in a frame and placed the frame in a fixed position on a hand-operated wooden press. He spread ink made of soot and linseed oil on the surface of the type and pressed paper against it with a movable flat platen.

Wilhelm Haas, a Swiss type maker, developed an all metal hand press in 1787. Haas's press produced higher quality impressions than previously existing wooden presses. Further print improvements came during the early 1800s, when flat platens were replaced with steam-driven ''impression cylinders.'' Because an impression cylinder rolled over a plate, it created even pressure across the entire surface and required less energy to operate. The first press to replace its flat plate with a metal cylinder was constructed in the United States by Richard Hoe in 1844.

A major innovation in typesetting technology occurred in 1884 when Ottmar Mergenthaler, a German immigrant to the United States, invented the Linotype machine. It operated by casting lines of type rather than individual letters. A Linotype machine stocked engraved letter dies in a storage area. The letters were released by typing on a keyboard. The machine ordered them, along with punctuation marks and spaces, into entire lines which could then be cast into metal bars. After lines were cast, the individual letters were routed back into storage for future use. The metal bars of type were used to make printing plates. Prior to the invention of the Linotype machine, typesetters could set approximately 1,400 characters per hour. A Linotype machine could set 6,000 characters per hour.

Other typesetting refinements included the Monotype machine, which was invented in 1897. The Monotype machine produced a perforated paper tape to control typecasting equipment. Photographic typesetting techniques were developed by René Higonnet and Louis Moyroud during the 1940s. During the 1950s, computer technology began to be employed. Further progress over the next several decades brought additional improvements in typesetting capabilities through the advancement of Optical Character Recognition and digital scanning. Prior to the development of offset lithography during the early twentieth century, letterpress was the most common form of printing in the United States and other developed nations. Even during the latter twentieth century it remained the most popular printing method in economically developing nations.

CURRENT CONDITIONS

Because of advances in offset lithography, some prognosticators predicted that letterpress and flexography would fall into disuse. Enhancing technologies emerged, however, and brought increased interest to these print processes. For example, during the early 1990s industry watchers reported a resurgence in the popularity of flexographic methods for printing newspapers and directories. An article published in 1992 by *Graphic Arts Monthly* claimed that nearly all telephone directories and full-color newspaper comics were being printed by flexography and that the volume of regular newspaper sections printed by flexography had doubled within the previous few years. The report anticipated that the future availability of better paper grades and improved inks would also bring increased use among magazine printers.

In 1991, the National Four-Color Newspaper Network began accepting membership applications from newspapers printed with flexographic and letterpress technology. The organization, which had begun in 1985 with 95 offset-only members, was formed to enforce print standards among its members and assure advertisers of uniform quality. Its willingness to receive members using letterpress and flexography was seen as an acknowledgement of their color capabilities and a recognition of the need to expand the network. When it began testing potential letterpress and flexographic members, the Network consisted of more than 300 members and distributed papers to more than 34 million households.

Another print process involved in adopting industry standards was screen printing. According to *American Printer,* the screen printing industry was previously a secretive and ''unwieldy group of individualistic entrepreneurs.'' To meet future challenges the Screen Printing Association International, headquartered in Fairfax, Virginia, established the Screen Printing Technical Foundation in 1985. The non-profit foundation was charged with the responsibility of developing guidelines, testing methods, and uniform practices. Specific areas under study included ink opacity, weather exposure, process colors, ink drying techniques, and ways to eliminate ''moire,'' a problem pattern caused by improper screen placement. Screen printers hoped that standardization would help the process become more conventional and result in increased sales.

Screen printers also benefitted from four-color-process work refinements, increased press speeds, and environmentally responsive improvements. In anticipation of governmental regulations mandating cuts in solvent use, screen printers began turning to water-based inks cured with ultraviolet (UV) light. Traditional inks contained solvents to aid in drying; UV inks were dried with UV light. According to the Screen Printing Association International, the number of screen printers printing on paper using UV inks increased from seven percent in 1982 to 13 percent in 1987. In addition to their environmental advantages, UV inks enabled printers to use a finer mesh screen and to overlay halftone dots to create more colors with fewer plates. The Screen Printing Association International also reported that its members were adopting other efforts aimed at preserving the environment and maintaining a healthy work place. According to the organization's statistics for 1987, 33 percent of the screen printers surveyed employed air-filtration equipment; 29 percent recycled solvents; 14.6 percent used silver recovery equipment; 13.5 percent filtered or

treated their water; and 7.5 percent had solid waste treatment systems.

INDUSTRY LEADERS

One of the largest organizations classified in SIC 2759 is the Deluxe Corporation. Deluxe was established in 1915 and maintains its corporate headquarters in St. Paul, Minnesota. In 1992, the company reported total sales of $1.53 billion. Checks accounted for 61.5 percent of the company's revenues, placing Deluxe at the top of the $1.8 billion U.S. check printing market. Deluxe also offered other services related to payment systems including electronic funds transfer (EFT) processing, ATM card services, and account verification support. In addition, Deluxe pioneered Electronic Benefit Transfers, which enables governmental units to reduce costs associated with providing foods stamps and general assistance. Through some of its other divisions, Deluxe provides short-run computer forms, business forms, and electronic tax filing services. Deluxe's subsidiary, Current, Inc., is the nation's largest direct-mail marketer of specialty products, offering a variety of items including gift wrap and stationery.

The nation's second largest check printer, the John H. Harland Company of Atlanta, Georgia, was founded in 1923 and reported total 1992 sales of $445 million. In addition to checks, the company provides systems for optical mark reading, optical character recognition, and bar coding. These products help users collect data automatically. The company's Scantron subsidiary provides forms and services to organizations such as schools and survey conductors. Scantron capabilities enable users to read data, tabulate results, and create reports.

Another leading printer is Quad/Graphics, a privately-held company founded in 1971 by Harry V. Quadracci. Quad/Graphics headquarters are located in Pewaukee, Wisconsin. In 1992, Quad/Graphics operated six printing plants and nine sales offices. The company prints magazines and catalogs for clients such as *Time, Newsweek,* and J. Crew. It uses a variety of print methods including gravure and offset. In 1992, Quad/Graphics announced its intentions to spend $50 million in plant expansions and new construction. In 1993, the company encountered difficulty obtaining the air pollution rights necessary to open a plant in southeastern Wisconsin because the region was designated as an ozone non-attainment area by the federal government. In order to construct a plant that would emit 200 tons of air pollution, existing regulations required that the company secure the removal of 260 tons from other sources in the area. Some analysts questioned whether such a reduction in air pollution would be possible.

The United States Banknote Company, another large printer with headquarters in New York and production facilities in Philadelphia, Chicago, and Los Angeles, is primarily a security printer. In 1992, the company reported sales of $171.9 million. U.S. Banknote produces a wide variety of security items for corporate and commercial customers. These include products such as stock and bond certificates, travelers checks, gift certificates, promotional coupons, dividend checks, union benefit stamps, certificates of deposit, and motor vehicle certificates of origin. U.S. Banknote also supplies certificates for the emerging stock and bond exchanges in Eastern Europe and some of the former Soviet Republics. In 1992, corporate and commercial products made up 38 percent of U.S. Banknote's revenue.

The largest segment of the company's business, however, involves products printed on behalf of governmental agencies. These sales accounted for 48.5 percent of the company's 1992 revenues. U.S. Banknote boasts a long history of providing products to foreign, federal, state, and local governments. The company printed stamps for the Postal Service's inaugural stamp offering in 1847. It also printed the nation's first commemorative stamp in 1893 and the first multicolored stamp in 1943. In addition to postage stamps, other products printed for governments included birth certificates, vehicle titles, and food stamps.

One of U.S. Banknote's fastest growing products was currency printed for foreign governments. The company's customers include Lithuania, Estonia, Malaysia, Haiti, and Venezuela. Although under normal usage, paper currency is generally replaced after approximately 15 months in circulation, the political turmoil experienced around the globe during the early 1990s resulted in more frequent changes. Changing political regimes caused some nations to redesign their money; countries achieving independence following the break-up of the Soviet Union sought to establish their own national currency; and countries experiencing rapid inflation required increased amounts of currency and changes in its denominational units. According to a report published in the *New York Times,* a U.S. Banknote spokesperson estimated the cost of money was between $26 and $45 per thousand bills regardless of the denomination. Price variables depended on features employed against potential counterfeiting and other options.

To guard against counterfeiting, U.S. Banknote and other currency printers have used a variety of techniques. Plates containing elaborately engraved swirls are difficult to duplicate and watermarks in the paper hard to reproduce. As early as the 1920s, U.S. Banknote developed a special intaglio printing method to give documents a special raised-ink feeling. Some of the biggest threats to currency security during the 1990s were advances in color copy machines, computer scanners, and laser print technologies. To guard against copying currency and other negotiable documents, security printers used special inks that were not available for copier use. One type of ink, called "optically variable ink," changed color based on the way light struck it. Other anti-counterfeiting measures include the use of special papers with distinctive threads and microprinting, a process that inscribes a legend in letters too small for copiers to reproduce legibly.

Holograms are another method sometimes used to protect money and other products. Some Middle Eastern countries use holograms to protect currency. Corporate and commercial customers have used hologram products to provide security labels for credit cards, videotapes, and computer software. Holographic laminates covered driver's licenses and other identification cards. Holographic stripes protected checks, transportation passes, and gift certificates. U.S. Banknote is a leading producer of holograms. Its American Bank Note Holographics subsidiary earned 13.5 percent of the company's revenues in 1992.

RESEARCH AND TECHNOLOGY

The commercial printing industry has relied on continuously improving technology to remain competitive. One area under study during the late 1980s and early 1990s was the development of better flexographic inks containing higher levels of pigment solids to improve drying and color density. Letterpress operators investigated keyless inking systems. One such system, the Civilox system, employed an ink-carrying drum to provide a continuous, evenly distributed and automatically monitored ink supply. Advocates of Civilox technology noted that converting letterpress equipment costs an estimated $100,000, much less than the $1 million price tag associated with switching to an offset press.

Another innovation developed during the early 1990s was a hybrid of web-fed technology and plateless printing, in which a special light-sensitive drum was used to print variable information for each impression made during a press run. This computer enhanced system enabled its operators to offer personalized, mass-printed output. One industry analyst predicted that as computer and printing technologies advanced, future recipients of documents would be unable to tell the difference between an item printed on a printing press and one individually generated with a computer.

INDUSTRY INFORMATION SOURCES

Berreby, David. "The Companies that Make Money from Making Money." *The New York Times*, 23 August 1992.

Borowsky, Irvin J. *Opportunities in Printing Careers*. Lincolnwood, IL: NTC Publishing Group, 1992.

"Delving into Digital Proofing." *Graphic Arts Monthly*, July 1992.

The Deluxe Corporation. *Deluxe Corporation 1992 Annual Report*. St. Paul, MN: Deluxe, 1993.

The John H. Harland Company. *John H. Harland Company 1992 Annual Report*. Atlanta, GA: Harland, 1993.

Karol, Michael. "UV Inks Put Bally in the Game." *Graphic Arts Monthly*, April 1993.

Keuny, Barbara. "Presses at Milwaukee-area Printers Ready to Roll Out of Recession." *The Business Journal Serving Greater Milwaukee*, 27 May 1991.

Kirchen, Rich. "Pollution Credits Could Choke QuadGraphics' Plans." *The Business Journal Serving Greater Milwaukee*, 27 February 1993.

————. "The Quad/Plan: Money from Within." *The Business Journal Serving Greater Milwaukee*, 17 October 1992.

Lessner, Ivy. "Specially Yours: Big Buck Profits From Specialty Printing." *American Printer*, October 1987.

Lorenzi, Neal. "Letterpress Dead? Don't Be Too Sure." *American Printer*, April 1988.

Lustig, Theodore. "Flexography: Growing and Changing." *Graphic Arts Monthly*, July 1992.

Merkli, Werner. "Landmarks in Printing." *UNESCO Courier*, July 1988.

Morris-Lee, James. "New Technology Helps Marketers Get Personal." *Direct Marketing*, February 1992.

Rosenberg, Jim. "Not Just for Offset Anymore." *Editor & Publisher*, 28 September 1991.

Topkis, Maggie. "U.S. Banknote: Misunderstood Money Machine." *Financial World*, 13 October 1992.

The United States Banknote Corporation. *United States Banknote Corporation 1992 Annual Report to Shareholders*. New York: U.S. Banknote, 1993.

U.S. Department of Commerce. *1987 Census of Manufactures*, Washington, DC: Bureau of the Census, March 1990.

—Karen Bellenir

MANIFOLD BUSINESS FORMS

This category covers establishments primarily engaged in designing and printing, by any process, special forms for use in the operation of a business, in single and multiple sets, including carbonized or interleaved with carbon or otherwise processed for multiple reproduction.

The status of the manifold business form industry is directly tied to the overall health of the business sector in the United States. A bustling economy, with established businesses reporting growth and new enterprises entering the field and surviving during their first years of operation, breeds a demand for business products. The establishments engaged in printing and manufacturing manifold business forms generally limit their product lines to such forms. The number of these establishments grew steadily during the 1970s and 1980s. According to 1972 data from the U.S. Department of Commerce, 667 establishments fell within this industry classification; by 1987 the number had grown to 847. The value of shipments for 1987 was $7.3 billion, up from $1.4 billion in 1972.

The number of people employed in the industry also grew, from 38,600 in 1972 to 53,000 fifteen years later. According to the 1987 employment data, production workers accounted for 37,100 of all industry jobholders. Payroll costs for the industry were $1.273 billion for the same year.

Manifold business forms are printed by commercial printing establishments and then sold to other businesses for use in all manner of transactions. Many of the establishments in this industry are regional in scope, gearing their sales and distribution efforts to a limited area. Such companies may market their products through an in-house sales team that targets area businesses, or they may sell their wares through retail office supply outlets or local printing shops. The products can be classified into two sub-categories: custom and stock. Custom forms are printed to a specific enterprise's particular needs, while stock forms can be sold to and used by a wide range of establishments. Stock manifold business forms include sequentially-numbered tickets, cash receipt journals, message memo pads, invoice books, and spreadsheet books. Blank standard legal documents, such as lease agreements for landlords and incorporation forms, are also a vital component of the manifold business form industry. Most Americans encounter manifold business forms in a variety of daily public transactions, but their use is often vital to behind-the-scenes business operations as well.

Partly due to a downturn in the American economy, the manifold business form industry began posting negative annual growth rates in the late 1980s, a trend expected to continue during the 1990s. Department of Commerce statistics forecasted a five percent decline in the industry's value of shipments between 1993 and 1994. Another cause of the overall decline of the industry is the growing use of computers in businesses of all sizes. Affordable laser printers can easily produce mass-volume custom business forms of all types, rendering unnecessary the need to purchase standard manifold forms. The proliferation of electronic financial transactions has also hurt the industry, resulting in a reduced demand for standard commercial checkbooks. On the other hand, another technological innovation, the fax machine, has bred a demand for custom manifold forms tailored to work with that transmission device. An important factor in the financial health of the manifold business form industry is the price of its chief component, paper. Paper price increases in the late 1980s severely impacted the manufacturers' profit margins. Paper costs, combined with the threat posed by computerization and laser printing, suggests a challenged industry in the years ahead.

INDUSTRY INFORMATION SOURCES

1987 Census of Manufactures, Washington, DC: United States Department of Commerce, 1989.

''American Business Products,'' *Wall Street Transcript,* January 2, 1989.

Current Industrial Reports: Business Forms, Binders, Carbon Paper, and Inked Ribbons 1986, Washington, DC: United States Department of Commerce, September, 1987.

''Legal Kit Sales Hold Steady,'' *Discount Store News,* January 6, 1992.

''Paying Taxes Gets Cleaner Due to ADP Form Change,'' *Wall Street Journal,* December 4, 1989.

United States Industrial Outlook 1992, Washington, DC: United States Department of Commerce, January, 1992.

United States Industrial Outlook 1994, Washington, DC: United States Department of Commerce, January, 1994.

Wandyez, Katarzyna. ''Limited Options,'' *Forbes,* November 27, 1989.

—Carol Brennan

SIC 2771

GREETING CARDS

This category includes establishments which publish and/or print greeting cards for all occasions. Producers of hand-painted greeting cards are classified in **SIC 8999: Services, Not Elsewhere Classified**.

INDUSTRY SNAPSHOT

In 1993 just over 1,000 establishments made up the U.S. greeting card industry. Two manufacturers dominate the industry: American Greetings Corp., the largest publicly owned greeting card manufacturer in the world, and Hallmark Cards, Inc., the largest privately owned manufacturer. Together, these two companies entered the 1990s controlling 75 percent of the $5.6 billion in annual U.S. greeting card sales. Gibson Greetings held ten percent of the sales in this industry with the remaining 15 percent spread across more than nine hundred establishments.

Throughout the latter part of the twentieth century, this industry has grown annually by roughly one percent, based on sales revenues. However, the Greeting Card Association has predicted an annual growth rate of five percent by the start of the twenty-first century due to developments in marketing and technology.

ORGANIZATION AND STRUCTURE

This industry operates on two types of structures. The large establishments have in-house creative staff, including graphic artists, designers, creative consultants/directors, and writers. The small establishments typically use free-lancers to provide these services. Generally, printing is done in-house by both large and small establishments; the notable exception to this, however, is Hallmark Cards, Inc., which has used an outside printer since the late 1940s. Common to both types of establishments is the emphasis on marketing. Leaders in this industry have highly developed distribution and marketing research and promotion systems.

Distribution. Since greeting cards appear mainly in drug and grocery stores in relatively small quantities, manufacturers rely heavily on small-package delivery services. Hallmark Cards, Inc. uses long-haul trucks and trains to ship cards from their distribution centers in Liberty, Missouri and Enfield, Connecticut to distribution points throughout the country. From there, smaller courier services handle regional distribution.

The importance of the greeting card industry and courier relationship lies in the special needs of greeting card manufacturers, according to *Distribution*. Because of the seasonal nature of most greeting cards, these manufacturers require timeliness of shipments and a courier that is able to handle the returned unsold cards at the end of a season. Moreover, throughout the year unsold cards need to be returned and replaced speedily as part of this industry's marketing strategy.

Marketing Research and Promotion. Greeting card manufacturers have structured their marketing divisions to engage in marketing research and promotion at two levels. One level addresses retailers and works with each store or regional chain to create a product mix and display specific to each retailer's sales record. The other level addresses customers directly by using consumer-specific research. The industry uses demographic studies and surveys of consumer tastes and purchasing behaviors extensively.

BACKGROUND AND DEVELOPMENT

Louis Prang, a German-born immigrant who founded a lithography business in Boston, made the first commercially printed greeting cards in America during the Christmas season of 1874. His folded cards contained messages inside, copying the newly formed tradition of Victorian English Christmas cards. Since Americans were not accustomed to purchasing greeting cards, Prang's first year of business went exclusively to England. He put his cards on the American market the following year and soon added birthday and Easter cards to his product line. But sales were slow, and by 1890 he had stopped producing cards. In *The Romance of Greeting Cards,* Ernest Dudley Chase suggests that Prang's lack of success with the American market was due in large part to the popularity of less expensive German-made greeting cards, which were closer in appearance to postcards than greeting cards. Prang's cards were also more costly to produce due to their use of colors.

Joyce C. Hall, founder of Hallmark Cards, entered the greeting card industry in the early 1900s by producing postcards similar to the German-made cards. Hall had predicted that the postcard craze would not last because he felt that postcards were an inadequate means of personal communications. Hall's prediction was realized at the onset of World War I. At this time greeting cards, as known from the Victorian era, were reintroduced to the American consumer because the war curtailed postcard shipments from European manufacturers and because greeting cards filled a niche by providing sentiments and "morale boosters" to send to soldiers.

World War II saw another increase in card sales, as greetings were again sent to soldiers overseas. But this time, card sales continued to grow in post-war America as more people moved across the country and corresponded more by mail. Also, the industry grew with increased competition; at the end of the war, American Greeting Publishers (later American Greetings Corp.) entered the market and by the mid-1950s proved to be a major competitor for Hallmark. The competition between these two industry leaders and the increase in television advertising evolved into the marketing-oriented greeting card industry of the late twentieth century.

Sales Trends. From the 1970s to the early 1990s marketing underwent major changes within this industry. At the retail level, sales to chain variety stores and drug and grocery stores increased while sales to card shops decreased. This shift from card shops to departments of other retail stores resulted in large part from changes in consumer habits, for people wished to purchase cards at the same store where they made their other purchases. In the mid-1980s, this shift was fueled by a price war among industry leaders which dramatically reduced prices for retailers while retaining the same pre-printed prices for consumers.

Marketing directed at consumers has been historically difficult for this industry. According to *Drug Topics,* studies have revealed that card shoppers (90 percent of whom are female) do not tend to purchase cards on the basis of brand names. One approach to this marketing problem has been to attract customers through messages available in greeting cards, which reflect trends in consumer interests and lifestyles. In *Discount Merchandiser,* Ela Schwartz observes that "when it comes to responding to shifts in consumer behavior or picking up on the latest trends, greeting-card vendors are in the forefront."

The 1980s marked a departure from tradition for card manufacturers as they responded to changes in consumer behavior with "alternative" or "non-occasion" cards. The demand for such cards emerged from changes in letter-writing habits and in personal relationships. As Karen Durand, product manager at Gibson Greetings, explained to *Discount Merchandiser,* "The customer doesn't want to spend 20 minutes writing a letter, but they will spend ten to 20 minutes finding the right card." The alternative cards assist personal communications by dealing with such topics as drug and alcohol addiction. These cards have also responded to changes in personal relationships with messages addressing topics such as coping with a divorce or living with a step-parent. Alternative cards grew in sales by nearly ten percent per year in their first few years of production.

Another notable shift in the types of messages in greeting cards has been movement away from the more traditional poetry to conversational verse and prose. Marketing research for alternative cards showed consumers wanted straightforward messages written in a straightforward style. An exception to this trend for prose messages has been in religious cards. All of the industry leaders produce a religious or inspirational line of cards, which experienced an increase in sales at the beginning of the 1990s.

Innovations and Developments. The mid-1980s and early 1990s brought on significant developments in the greeting card industry in the areas of production and distribution. In the mid-1980s an innovation in printing added to the many printing processes used by greeting card manufacturers. A process called Prismatic Imaging stamps a card with a silver dye and then prints on top of the stamping. By 1991, the House of Gold, New Jersey, which has exclusive license on the process, stamped 40 million cards annually for the greeting card industry.

In 1991, Gibson Greetings introduced a line of recyclable cards. At that time, Hallmark Cards and American Greetings had started using recyclable paper to a lesser extent in some of their products. Gibson Greetings also began using other environmentally-sensitive materials in production, such as organic dyes, inks, and cleaning solutions.

A significant development in the distribution of greeting cards emerged with the use of electronic ordering and inventory control systems, known as electronic data interchange (EDI). Replacing the use of the postal service, EDI systems allow retailers to order cards through a computer directly linked with manufacturers and independent distributors. This has facilitated speedier ordering and more accurate inventory controls.

In 1992, Hallmark Cards, Inc. and American Greetings Corp. introduced self-access personalized greeting cards. The cards are produced at a computer kiosk from which customers choose the design, colors, and typeface for their cards and then supply their own message. The near simultaneous introduction of these computer kiosks resulted in controversy over patent rights. In 1992, Hallmard Cards, Inc. filed a claim against American Greetings Corp., claiming that Hallmark marketed the concept first with its Touch-Screen Greetings, patented in July 1991. American Greetings patented CreataCard in October 1991. At the center of

this dispute has been Custom Expressions, Inc., who invented the technology behind these kiosks.

Morry Weiss of American Greetings Corp. has predicted that his company's CreataCard kiosks will generate nearly $500 million in annual sales by the end of the century, according to *Industry Week.* This innovation is expected to give the greeting card industry a boost by widening its target market to include young people and men and by facilitating consumer-oriented marketing research as customers' tastes are specified by their own choices.

INDUSTRY LEADERS

Founded in 1910 as Hall Brothers, Hallmark Cards, Inc. has become the leading producer of greeting cards sold in the United States, with 1993 sales of $3.4 billion. Along with the other industry leaders, American Greetings Corp. ($1.7 billion in 1993 sales) and Gibson Greetings, Hallmark also manufactures wrapping paper and other gift and holiday paper products. By the early 1990s, only 52 percent of Hallmark's sales came from greeting cards.

In 1992, this company employed 22,900 workers, with roughly 5,500 working in production (printing, lettering, die-cutting and related jobs) and 700 in writing and designing. Up until the early 1990s, staff developing new cards worked independently within their own department. Hallmark re-engineered this process so that a team of mixed-occupation personnel (artists, writers, lithographers, merchandisers and administrators) worked on a single holiday. This system is not expected to completely replace departments, but "should cut cycle time in half, which will not only save money, but will also make the company more responsive to changing tastes," according to *Fortune.*

Due to the slow growth of this industry, Hallmark and other industry leaders have diversified into new markets. By 1992, Hallmark owned over nine Spanish language television stations, a cable television company and Binney and Smith, which produces Crayola crayons. At this time Hallmark also investigated selling the remaining 170 Hallmark Card Shops that they still owned. Of the more than 10,000 shops which exclusively sell Hallmark products, the majority are now privately owned.

Upon entering the 1990s, Hallmark, like other commercial publishers and printers, was concerned about regulations on the use of solvents, which are primarily employed for cleaning printing presses. According to Jennifer Hicks of *American Printer,* Hallmark might have to change its use of solvent-laden cleaning cloths as a result of legislation in Kansas against such solvents. This legislation could reverse the use of time-saving cleaning techniques, which have taken years to develop.

WORK FORCE

In America, greeting card manufacturers employ an estimated 60,000 workers. Administrative and marketing staff make up 50 percent of the workers; additional marketing and public relations agencies frequently provide temporary personnel. Printers and production specialists make up nearly 40 percent of this work force. Graphic artists and writers account for only ten percent, but their numbers are expected to increase with increased production of alternative cards.

AMERICA AND THE WORLD

According to the Greeting Card Association, this industry has virtually no competition from foreign manufacturers selling in the United States. As exporters of greeting cards, the American industry has limited its business due to the high cost of small shipments. American exporters primarily license foreign printers to print their cards. Canada and the United Kingdom are the largest importers of American-made greeting cards.

INDUSTRY INFORMATION SOURCES

"American Greetings Corp." *Wall Street Journal,* August 12, 1992.

"Among Greeting Cards Shoppers, Brand Switching Is Commonplace." *Discount Store News,* October 15, 1990.

Appelbaum, Cara. "Gibson Greetings Goes Green." *AdWeek's Marketing Week,* February 11, 1991.

Bowman, Robert. "Casebook: Hallmark Cards." *Distribution,* May 1990.

————. "Casebook: Hallmark Cards." *Distribution,* June 1992.

Butcher, Lola. "Log On, Type: Zap! Greet 'Em Yourself." *Kansas City Business Journal,* May 15, 1992.

Chase, Ernest Dudley. *The Romance of Greeting Cards.* Detroit: Tower Books, 1971.

Gordon, Jay. "Managing Small Shipments Is Big Business at Hallmark." *Distribution,* September 1989.

"Greeting Cards." *Progressive Grocer,* August 1992.

Hicks, Jennifer. "A Clean Sweep." *American Printer,* August 1991.

Johnson, Gregory S. "Data Link Keeps It All in Order." *Journal of Commerce,* November 18, 1991.

Kiley, David. "Hallmark's Cards Address Modern Family Problems." *AdWeek's Marketing Week,* March 27, 1989.

McKenna, Joseph F. "From JIT, with Love: American Greetings Sends a Trump Card to Competitors by Way of Do-It-Yourself Retailer." *Industry Week,* August 17, 1992.

"Mix-and-Match Sentiments." *New York Times,* July 29, 1992.

Mooney, Barbara. "American Greetings Shopping for CreataCard PR Aid." *Crain's Cleveland Business,* August 10, 1992.

Much, Marilyn. "Hallmark Pursues Best Customers." *Direct,* August 1992.

Oliver, Suzanne. "Christmas Card Blues." *Forbes,* December 24, 1990.

Pyle, Diane L. "How to Interview Your Customers." *American Demographics,* December 1990.

Rouland, Renee Covino. "Micromarketing and Best Wishes." *Discount Merchandiser,* July 1992.

Schwartz, Ela. "The Next Cycle in Greeting Cards." *Discount Merchandiser,* July 1990.

"Slow Economy Helps Boost Sales of Greeting Cards." *Drug Topics,* July 20, 1992.

Stern, Ellen Stock. *The Very Best From Hallmark: Greeting Cards Through the Years.* New York: Abrams, 1988.

Stern, William M., "Loyal to a Fault," *Forbes,* March 14, 1994.

Stewart, Thomas A. "The Search for the Organization of Tomorrow." *Fortune,* May 18, 1992.

Toth, Debra. "Cards Compete in New Outlets." *Graphic Arts Monthly,* December 1991.

Touby, Laurel. "Congratulations on Your Big Earnings Increase!" *Business Week,* August 17, 1992.

Wandycz, Katarzyna. "Love Means Never Having to Say Anything." *Forbes,* April 1, 1991.

—Paola Trimarco

SIC 2782

BLANKBOOKS, LOOSELEAF BINDERS AND DEVICES

This industry consists of establishments primarily engaged in manufacturing blankbooks, including checkbooks and books with ruling paper, and looseleaf binders. Other items included in this industry are albums, ruled chart and graph paper, and record albums.

In 1992 the three largest U.S. companies in terms of sales for blankbooks and looseleaf binders were Safeguard, Inc., Clarke American Checks, Inc., and Acco USA, Inc., totalling nearly $600 million in sales for that year. According to Binding Industries of

America, there were 600 manufacturers of looseleaf binders alone in 1993.

While blankbooks have been produced since the advent of the first printing presses, the modern-day concept of the looseleaf binder is only 40 years old in the United States. The production of blankbooks, which includes checkbooks, ledgersheets, accounting books, and diaries, has changed little in its U.S. history.

Modernization has replaced letterpress with offset printing (which uses large rubber rollers to make impressions of full pages) for the small amount of actual printing involved in blankbook manufacturing. Consequently, producers of blankbooks have seen more substantial growth through diversification. Deluxe Corp., which controlled 50 percent of the checkbook manufacturing market by 1991, also entered the software market for automatic teller machines and electronic fund transfers. In a similar move, John H. Harland Co., which held 25 percent of the checkbook market by 1991, diversified by making standardized test forms and the scanning machines used to read them.

The looseleaf binder manufacturers have seen growth through innovation and diversification within their product lines. According to Fred Ferris of *American Printer*, the ''most exciting development'' in this sector of the industry in recent years has been the use of 4-color lithograph on vinyl. This has greatly eased the majority of the industry's manufacturing, which entails the production of custom-designed binders with company logos and other artwork.

Another major development for looseleaf binder manufacturers has been the introduction of new flexible vinyls for binder covers; these vinyls are more durable and tighter fitting than their predecessors. However, these new vinyls have posed problems for the industry because they are harmful to the environment; the vinyl does not decompose in landfills and releases a hazardous chemical when incinerated. Whereas European looseleaf binder manufacturers opted for alternative recyclable vinyl, according to *American Printer*, American manufacturers have been reluctant to change vinyls due to the lesser quality of recyclable types.

Given that most producers of looseleaf binders used similar materials and methods of production, competition among manufacturers in the 1980s and early 1990s was concentrated in the area of accessories such as supplementary pockets and slots designed to carry additional awkward items. In the mid-1980s binders with accessories were in strong demand with the advent of organizers—looseleaf datebooks with

inserts, such as foldout maps and charts. These were, in effect, more affordable versions of the British Filofax. For looseleaf binder manufacturers involved in the production of organizers, diversification has also been realized with profits derived from the sale of a large variety of insert refills.

Despite recurring predictions that blankbooks and looseleaf binder manufacturers would suffer as a result of the emergence of the computer industry, the industry has experienced considerable growth during the 1980s and the early 1990s. In fact, with the increase of computer use, this industry has increased its production for computer-related products.

INDUSTRY INFORMATION SOURCES

Chithelen, Ignatius. ''Printing Money,'' *Forbes*, March 18, 1991.

''Custom Binders Do More Than Capture Paper,'' *American Printer*, February 1989.

Ferris, Fred. ''Loose Talk,'' *American Printer*, March 1991.

Slovak, Julianne. ''Companies to Watch: John H. Harland,'' *Fortune*, March 27, 1989.

Tenner, Edward. ''The Right Organizer Can Make Your Day,'' *Money*, December 1985.

—Paola Trimarco

SIC 2789

BOOKBINDING AND RELATED WORK

This industry covers establishments providing edition, trade, job, and library bookbinding and related services, such as paper bronzing, gilding and edging, and mounting of maps and samples. The classification covers only establishments primarily binding books printed elsewhere; establishments binding books printed at the same establishment are classified in **SIC 2731: Books: Publishing, or Publishing and Printing** and **SIC 2732: Book Printing**.

In 1993 Binding Industries of America reported 1200 binderies in operation in the United States. In the early 1990s the two leading binders in America were Hart Graphics, Inc. and Nicohstone, Inc. The majority of small to medium binderies are subsidiaries of the commercial printing industry.

Until the 1980s few developments were made in the binding process, although more establishments were set up in response to demand for more magazines and books. In 1988 Otava Publishing in Finland introduced to America a binding process called Otabind, which enables books to stay open and lie flat without damaging the spine of the book. The process was developed in 1980 and has since been used increasingly throughout Europe. Otabind has proven highly valuable to trade printers who produce computer manuals, previously made with costly spinal binders. The predecessors to Otabind were the centuries-old casebinding, wherein cases (folded sheets of paper) were stitched together, and perfect-binding, a modern innovation that applied durable adhesives directly to the edge of unfolded paper, replacing the time-consuming folding and stitching process.

Given the expense of new machines and adhesives need to implement the Otabind process, it was slow to gain popularity with binders. In order to justify costs, binders would have to take on large runs using Otabind. This problem was reduced with the introduction of RepKover (meaning reinforced paperback cover), which uses cloth strips for pre-assembly of covers, allowing printers to send partially bound books to a binder for Otabinding. This has enabled binders to accept numerous small orders that add up to a large run.

By 1992 the inventors of Otabind had issued 29 licenses to binders in the United States to use their process. However, American versions of this process were beginning to emerge in the early 1990s, and more versions are expected to be developed by the end of the century.

Other significant innovations in this industry have come from the use of new adhesives and less labor-intensive machines. PUR (polyurethane resin) has added durability to bindings and PVA (polyvinyl acetate) has added flexibility and has proven valuable in manufacturing because it can be applied cold. Less labor-intensive machines have also appeared in binderies in response to employee health problems such as carpal tunnel syndrome, a result of hand gathering and feeding.

As the industry entered the 1990s, new concerns arose over the education and safety of employees. The rapid technological changes in the industry required employee training and specialized education. Employee safety became increasingly important with discoveries that the new adhesives were hazardous to air quality; this factor also gained the attention of customers, concerned about the contents of the chemicals used in the binding process and the environmental consequences of getting rid of bound materials.

INDUSTRY INFORMATION SOURCES

"Bound For Change," *Graphic Arts Monthly*, May 1990.

Ferris, Fred. "The State of the Bindery," *American Printer*, June 1991.

Hilts, Paul. "New Developments in Otabind: A Better Mousetrap Gets Better," *Publishers Weekly*, June 28, 1991.

Toth, Debora. "Adhesive Binding Widens Its Reach," *Graphic Arts Monthly*, October 1992.

—Paola Trimarco

SIC 2791

TYPESETTING

This classification includes establishments primarily engaged in typesetting for the trade, including advertising typesetting, hand or machine composition, photocomposition, phototypesetting, computer-controlled typesetting and typographic composition.

INDUSTRY SNAPSHOT

The typesetting industry has been revolutionized by electronic technology, resulting in frequently upgraded equipment, redefined job functions, retraining of workers, and expansion of services provided to clients. New technology has allowed faster turnaround on jobs, and typesetting companies are under pressure to continue to improve their equipment for even faster results.

The growing popularity of desktop publishing has allowed many of typesetting's traditional clients to produce their own newsletters, advertising, and other print materials instead of contracting with typesetters for the work. Many organizations and businesses, however, have elected not to become their own publishers and continue to contract with typesetters and other preprint services. With the burst of personal computers at home and in businesses, many producers of printed materials use a combination of their own computer-based technology and outside typesetting services. Typesetting remains in the 1990s a vital service industry for book publishers, magazine publishers, advertising agencies, catalog companies, and other large and small businesses.

ORGANIZATION AND STRUCTURE

The typesetting industry includes large, multi-million dollar shops with several hundred employees as well as small shops with only a few employees. Many of the larger companies offer related services, including printing, bookbinding, development, and sales of custom computer systems for desktop publishing or typesetting to client companies. Many large typesetting companies have areas of specialization as well, producing catalogs for car parts companies, textbooks, trade paperbacks, and so on.

Typesetting companies have realigned their services and often work in partnership with client companies to help them with the technical aspects of desktop publishing and with the technology necessary for interfacing of desktop and typesetting capabilities.

Jobs that come into typesetting establishments must be compatible with the typesetting system. Creating this compatibility can be complex. Copy input on word processors or personal computer disks must be converted for typesetting or for use with another computer program. Typesetting companies accept word processing disks from clients and convert them to use on their own systems and software so that the manuscript does not have to be re-keyed for typesetting. With the new flexibility—but potential incompatibility—of increasingly sophisticated systems, software, and hardware, the typesetting shop may enter the publishing process sooner than it has in the past. With electronic capabilities, the client and typesetting shop may test various formats and styles before actually doing the typesetting job to make sure that the two systems will work together without glitches and to be sure that the client's word processing control codes can automatically be converted to phototypesetting control codes. Most of the code conversion can be done automatically, with the typesetting operator making few decisions other than those concerning hyphenation, justification, and final output.

Desktop systems offer "what you see is what you get" technology. That is, the screen displays the text and layout exactly as it will appear on the finished page. Commercial digitized typesetting equipment also offers this electronic pagination. Once material is input, the page can be automatically arranged according to batch page processing, or an operator can manipulate the elements on the page. Because the material can be altered on screen before any hard version has been produced, changes are less expensive and time consuming.

Large companies, such as Black Dot Graphics in Crystal Lake, Illinois, have expanded their services to a point where they are considered "electronic prepress service bureaus." They provide technical assistance as well as typesetting to their clients. According to *Publishers Weekly*, these companies "are at the forefront of technical innovation in a field where technology is advancing at a breathless rate." When Black Dot began in the 1960s, it provided photocomposition services to book publishers. By the 1990s, Black Dot and other typesetters were providing a broad range of services for both color and black-and-white jobs, from initial input of data to output of printing plates or final page proofs, or any services in between, including illustration, pagination, and integration of words and graphics.

BACKGROUND AND DEVELOPMENT

Typesetting has changed drastically during the last 40 years of the twentieth century. For hundreds of years, type was set with metal printing elements; this was called "hot type" because molten lead was used to manufacture individual letters which were then set into complete words, sentences, and paragraphs. At first, the molten lead letters were set by hand, one letter or space at a time. The letters were mirror images of actual letters so that, when printed, they would read correctly. The set type was locked into a frame and ink applied to it, and the paper was printed directly from the type.

In 1886 Ottmar Mergenthaler invented a typesetting machine, which became known as a Linotype machine. This was also a hot type method, but it speeded up typesetting considerably. Typesetting machines became faster and more sophisticated for the next 80 to 90 years, but operated on the same principle as the one Johann Gutenberg had used in the 1400s when he invented movable type.

Unlike hot type, which is three-dimensional, "cold type" is two-dimensional. Cold type is generally regarded as any of a variety of methods in which photographic principles are used to create an image on specially treated paper. It came into widespread use in the 1970s. As a typesetter keyed in the letters, the machine made photographic images of them and reproduced those images on photosensitive paper or film. The images were arranged on a layout sheet and the printer photographed it to make a film negative from which a printing plate was then made. The creation of text photographically is called photocomposition.

Cold type has undergone several generations of change in both data storage and output. They all begin with keying in the text on a keyboard like that of a typewriter. That data input may be done by a typesetter, but more and more that is being done by the author as he or she composes on a personal computer.

The first phototypesetting equipment stored the text on paper tape. The tape was punched using a special keyboard, and this specially-punched encoded tape drove the typesetting equipment, sending instructions about typeface, size, and appearance of the set type.

The next development in phototypesetting brought equipment with powerful software, photo fonts, and magnetic data storage. This was actually the first true phototypesetting machinery, and in the 1990s, was still in use in many typesetting operations.

The next generation of cold type created characters from digital information instead of a photo negative. Output is produced on photosensitive paper or film. This equipment became the standard in the 1980s. Subsequent generations of equipment employ various laser technologies for output. This is not phototypesetting since it does not employ photographic technology and output is on regular paper rather than photosensitive paper.

CURRENT CONDITIONS

The application of electronics and computers has moved the industry to digitized imaging in which material is printed directly from the computer to paper or a printing plate. More typesetting companies are offering extensive preprinting services, including digital color scanning with electronic dot generation, electronic color page composition, electronic page layout, and off-press color proofing. Although many typesetting shops were still using traditional phototypesetting equipment in the early 1990s, digital typesetting is likely to make such methodologies obsolete in years to come.

Digitized typesetting opened up a world of possibilities for interface technology, the ability of two computers to communicate with one another. Some experts in the typesetting industry were predicting that by the year 2000, 50 to 75 percent of typesetting would be accomplished via interface technology.

Data may be transferred through direct or remote interfacing. Direct interface includes a cable connection with other computers such as word processors or personal computers; optical character recognition by means of scanners; media conversion (conversion of word processing program on disk to typesetting software), or reading magnetic or paper tape. Remote interfacing refers to telecommunication through a modem.

Interfacing, regardless of the method, however, requires appropriate software for conversion from word processing to typesetting equipment. Not all word processing programs and typesetting equipment, however, are compatible, requiring client and typesetter to coordinate their work in advance of transmission. Typesetters do not ordinarily have the capability to convert all of the hundreds of wordprocessing programs to their typesetting programs; however, a third-party service bureau can handle most conversions.

Such varied technology advances, however, has also allowed publishers to transmit manuscripts to keyboarders or typesetters in other countries with lower wages, thereby cutting publishing costs. Use of satellite and other technology is expected to further expand publishers' options.

The role of typesetting is expected to expand to include some layout or "paste-up" work as well. Desktop publishing systems offer this capability, and its use in commercial typesetting is growing. While in the past, typeset copy was passed on to an artist who arranged the various graphic and textual components on the page and then pasted them up on a layout sheet, components can now be arranged on the computer screen and corrections made before anything is printed out on paper or film. Even photographs or illustrations can be inserted on screen by use of sophisticated digital scanners. Once the layout is complete, it is transmitted for reproduction onto paper, film, or even directly onto a plate for printing.

INDUSTRY LEADERS

The typesetting industry was led in the early 1990s by Merrill Corp., a public company based in St. Paul, Minnesota, that boasted annual sales during that period of around $150 million. Other typesetters of note included Black Dot Graphics Inc., headquartered in Crystal Lake, Illinois; York Graphic Services Inc., based in York, Pennsylvania; and International Computaprint Corp. of Fort Washington, Pennsylvania.

WORK FORCE

In 1990 14,000 people were employed as compositors and typesetters. That number, however, reflected people employed in in-house or in-plant composition departments, newspapers, printing companies, as well as typesetting companies.

Electronic technology has changed the nature of work that typesetters do, requiring knowledge and familiarity with computers and a multitude of software programs. In typesetting, as in other prepress functions, technology has called for constant upgrading of skills and retraining of the work force as more and more functions become computerized.

INDUSTRY INFORMATION SOURCES

"Disk-to-Disk Conversion System to Expand In-House Services," *Graphic Arts Monthly,* March 1988, 60-3.

"Expertise Pays Off," *Graphic Arts Monthly,* March 1987, 98-100.

Frank, Jerome P., "Changes in Typesetting Create Faster Turnaround," *Publishers Weekly,* February 5, 1988, 67-69.

Hilts, Len, "Avoiding Potholes in the Desktop Publishing Road," *Publishers Weekly,* October 18, 1991, 34-36.

Negru, John, *Computer Typesetting,* New York: Van nostrand Reinhold Company, 1988.

Parnau, Jeff, "The Short Life of Typesetting Equipment," *Folio,* March, 1986.

—Wendy J. Stein

SIC 2796

PLATEMAKING AND RELATED SERVICES

This category covers establishments primarily engaged in making plates for printing purposes and in related services. Also included are establishments primarily engaged in making positives or negatives from which offset lithographic plates are made. These establishments do not print from the plates they make, but prepare them for use by others. Engraving for purposes other than printing is classified in **SIC 3479: Coating, Engraving, and Allied Services, Not Elsewhere Classified.**

INDUSTRY SNAPSHOT

The platemaking and related services industry was comprised primarily of companies that made printing plates used in offset lithographic printing processes. It also encompassed platemaking for numerous miscellaneous printing processes, such as gravure and letterpress. Lithography was introduced in 1796 and became popular during the 1900s. Offset printing, first applied in 1902, came to represent about 40 percent of all U.S. printing.

Steady demand growth for lithographic and related printing boosted platemaking service industry revenues to about $2.4 billion in 1987, the first year in which this industry was separately classified. Steady growth in printing markets pushed platemaking industry sales steadily upward to about $3.2 billion by 1992. Likewise, sales and employment were forecast to continue growing throughout the 1990s and early 2000s, bolstered by new printing technologies and greater demand.

ORGANIZATION AND STRUCTURE

Most companies in the platemaking industry served lithographic printers. Lithography was a printing process whereby ink was applied to a flat printing surface (plate) that was treated with grease. Blank, or nonimage, areas of the surface repelled the ink, while the greased areas held it. The inked surface could then be transferred directly to paper by means of a press. In the popular offset (planographic or litho-offset) process, the inked image was first printed on a rubber cylinder and then transferred to other materials.

Platemaking companies created the templates that printers used to transfer images to the rubber cylinder or other printing media. The plate cylinder was usually zinc, aluminum, or a special alloy. Its porous surface was coated with a photosensitive material. When exposed to an image, the coated area hardened and the coating on the nonimage areas was washed away. Ink, which was continually deposited on the plate cylinder by inking rollers, was accepted by the greasy image on the plate. Modern offset printing plates were usually cylindrical, allowing them to provide a continuous transfer of ink to a rubber-covered, or blanket, cylinder.

A variety of plates were used for different offset printing processes and print jobs. Basic monometal plates were made of zinc or aluminum and functioned as described above. The plate was usually exposed to an image by covering it with a negative of text or illustrations and exposing it to intense light, after which the coating on the unexposed areas was washed away. A slight variation was the presensitized plate, which had a coating with a longer life span and could be made of paper or plastic for short print jobs.

Deep-etch plates, in contrast to monometal, exposed the plate to a positive of the text or illustration. The nonprinting areas were hardened and the printing areas were washed away. A mild acid bath etched the metal of the printing areas. The plate was then treated with an ink-receptive lacquer. Deep-etch plates were used for longer print runs of 250,000 or more copies. Bi-metal and tri-metal plates were more durable, and could dependably endure runs of 500,000 copies or more. They were created using two or three metal plates, one or two of which covered the primary plate as a microscopic film. A photoengraving process partly removed the thin metal layers.

In addition to conventional offset plates were several other platemaking processes. Electrostatic (xerographic) plates, for example, were electrically charged plates that absorbed images. A negatively charged powder stuck to the positively charged image, was heated and hardened, and acted as the ink-receptive printing surface. Similarly, immediate offset plates incorporated a polymer layer that responded to heat, as opposed to light.

In addition to lithography, other types of printing processes used plates. Rotogravure, for example, transferred fluid ink contained in the cells of the printing cylinder, or plate. Nonprint areas of the plate were kept ink-free through constant wiping. Rotogravure plates were made in a process that utilized carbon tissue paper soaked in an emulsion and exposed to an image. The carbon-imprint was then transferred to a (usually copper) cylindrical plate. Rotogravure was often used to produce high-quality color illustrations. In addition to plates for rotogravure printing were plates for collotype printing, which generated high-quality color photo reproductions; flexographic printing, used for large-scale commercial printing (e.g., newspapers and magazines); and other miscellaneous processes.

BACKGROUND AND DEVELOPMENT

During the second century A.D., the Chinese were capable of printing on paper using ink on stone surfaces with carved impressions, precursors to modern day printing plates. In about 1040, Chinese alchemist Pi Sheng designed a crude printing plate consisting of an iron plate coated with a mixture of resin, wax, and paper ash. Other rough printing plate forms were used in subsequent print processes, such as xylography (fourteenth century), metallographic printing (1430), typography (fifteenth century), and stereotypy (eighteenth century).

Czechoslovakian Aloys Senefelder envisioned the lithographic printing process in 1796. The first mechanized lithographic printer, complete with a plate cylinder, was constructed in 1850. Importantly, technological advancements during the early 1800s related to etching and photosensitivity made Senefelder's design possible. Gravure and rotogravure platemaking processes were first used in the 1890s.

It was not until the early 1900s that lithographic platemaking became widespread. The popularity of lithography, and even of modern day printing techniques, was largely a result of American Ira W. Rubel's discovery of offset printing in 1902. Rubel accidentally transferred an image from a plate cylinder to a rubber blanket, discovering that the rubber offset produced a superior image to that of the metal plate. The popularity of offset lithography spawned a flurry of advancements during the middle 1900s in the area of chemical etching, electroplating, and other technolo-

gies that were integrated into the printing and plate-making process.

Besides general economic expansion during the 1960s, 1970s, and 1980s, new inks and printing processes bolstered platemaking industry revenues. By 1987, the first year in which this industry was separately classified, platemaking companies garnered about $2.4 billion annually and employed a work force of more than 30,000. Despite a lengthy U.S. and global recession during the late 1980s and early 1990s, moreover, industry sales continued to expand to more than $3 billion annually in the early 1990s.

CURRENT CONDITIONS

Platemaking service industry revenues approached $3.2 billion in 1992, stimulated by a general increase in demand for printed materials as well as technological advancements that increased the use of plate printing processes. For example, markets for several types of printed packaging ballooned, as did demand for direct mail and catalog printing. And higher quality, faster, and less expensive printing processes, such as waterless sheetfed printing, boosted demand. Likewise, new computer technologies improved the platemaking process. Advanced desktop publishing software, for example, was integrated into digital platemaking processes to quickly produce relatively inexpensive, high-quality plates.

Going into the 1990s, lithographic platemaking services accounted for about 57 percent of industry sales. Color film platemaking represented the large majority of the lithographic segment, followed by various noncolor plate services. Deep-etch metal plates accounted for less than .5 percent of industry receipts, as did multi-metal plate processes. Aside from lithography, gravure cylinders made up almost 6 percent of industry revenues, and flexographic plates represented about 3 percent. Miscellaneous services, such as letterpress and electrostatic platemaking, comprised the remainder of sales.

Commercial printers of consumer packaging, marketing materials, and a plethora of other media accounted for roughly 75 percent of the demand for platemaking services in the early 1990s. The balance of the market was comprised of newspaper publishers (which contributed 8 percent of revenues), book printers and publishers (7 percent), magazines (1 percent), and numerous smaller markets. About 1.5 percent of platemaking industry revenues were garnered overseas.

INDUSTRY LEADERS

More than 1,300 U.S. companies provided plate-making services going into the 1990s. The industry was highly fragmented, consisting mostly of small, localized manufacturers with just a few employees. Polychrome Corp. of New York was the largest industry participant, with $300 million in sales and about 2,000 workers in 1991. Eastman Kodak followed with 1991 sales of $160 million from platemaking services. Other industry leaders included Matthews International Corp. of Pennsylvania, and Techtron Graphic Arts Inc. of Illinois, both of which had revenues of $100 million in 1991.

WORK FORCE

Contrary to employment prospects for most U.S. manufacturing industries, job growth in printing trade services was expected to be robust between 1990 and 2005, according to the Bureau of Labor Statistics. Overall employment for platemaking laborers was forecast to rise 30 percent by 2005, despite anticipated productivity gains resulting from automation. Even positions for general managers and executives should rise an estimated 20 percent. Furthermore, employees in this industry were well compensated. The average laborer earned about $14.71 per hour in the late 1980s, almost 30 percent more than the average U.S. manufacturing laborer. And the average payroll for all employees was $32,713 annually, compared to $26,028 for the U.S. manufacturing average.

INDUSTRY INFORMATION SOURCES

Cross, Lisa, "Litho Plate Technology Meets Productivity, Eco-Challenges," *Graphic Arts Monthly,* June 1993.

Darnay, Arsen J., editor, *Manufacturing USA; Industry Analyses, Statistics, and Leading Companies,* Detroit: Gale Research, 1993.

"Redesigned Lith-Laminator Ideal for Specialty Packaging," *Paperboard Packaging,* February 1994.

Wong, Michael, "Adobe Systems Announces Adobe Brilliant Screens Technology for High-End Color Printing," *Business Wire,* March 22, 1994.

—Dave Mote

CHEMICALS & ALLIED PRODUCTS

SIC 2812

ALKALIES AND CHLORINE

This industry classification includes establishments engaged in manufacturing alkalies and chlorine. Examples of products include compressed or liquefied chlorine, sodium or potassium hydroxide, sodium bicarbonate, and soda ash (not produced at mines). Alkalies produced by mining are classified in **SIC 1474: Potash, Soda, and Borate Minerals.**

INDUSTRY SNAPSHOT

The two primary commodities offered by the alkalies and chlorine industry are chlorine and sodium hydroxide (caustic soda). Together they represent about 82 percent of all shipments. The third largest commodity, soda ash, which is an alkali product used in glass making, water treatment, pulp bleaching, and detergent manufacturing, accounts for only 14 percent of shipments. Other remaining products account for 4 percent.

Chlorine and caustic soda have consistently appeared on lists of the top ten U.S. chemicals according to production weight. They are both co-products of the same chemical process. This means they are created at the same time and that the production of one results in the production of the other. Although there are several modern procedures used to produce chlorine and caustic soda, most rely on a technique called electrolysis. As electricity is passed through brine (a salt water solution), the brine's components, salt (sodium chloride) and water (made up of hydrogen and oxygen), recombine to form chlorine and sodium hydroxide (caustic soda) in approximately equal amounts. Some

"left-over" hydrogen gas also results from the process.

Organic chemical manufacturers are the primary chlorine users in the United States. Some examples of chemicals produced with chlorine are ethylene dichloride, carbon tetrachloride, and methylene chloride. These and other chlorinated organic chemicals are used to make many products including flame retardants, herbicides, solvents, refrigerants, PVC pipe, and pigments. The second largest chlorine user is the pulp and paper industry, which uses chlorine as a bleaching agent. Chlorine products are also used as raw ingredients in household and commercial bleaches, scouring powders, and automatic dishwashing compounds. Other chlorine uses include water treatment, sewage treatment, sanitizing, and metal extracting.

Caustic soda has a wide range of industrial applications. It is used in petroleum exploration and by water treatment facilities, tanneries, and the textile industry. It also plays a role in food processing, metal fabrication, and chemical manufacturing. Caustic soda is also used in industrial complexes to remove boiler scale.

According to U.S. Department of Commerce statistics, shipments within the alkalies and chlorine industry totaled $1.5 billion in 1987. Of this figure, $1.3 billion represented products considered primary to the industry. Growth patterns of the various industry segments varied. Although overall growth within the chlorine and alkalies industry was expected to increase at a rate of 2 percent to 3 percent through the mid-1990s, some industry forecasters predicted the slowest growth would occur within the chlorine segment.

During the late 1980s, chlorine production increased, but demand and productions declined in the early 1990s. The shift was attributed to economic and environmental conditions. As the national economy suffered during the recession of the late 1980s and early 1990s, construction slowed and demand for polyvinylchloride (PVC) products fell sharply. At the same time, pulp and paper manufacturers were turning away from chlorine-based processes because of concerns about the toxicity of dioxins, which were formed from the combination of chlorine and residue organic compounds. Other major chlorine products such as chlorofluorocarbons (CFCs) and chlorinated solvents were also under increasing criticism because of their damaging effects on the environment.

Dropping demand led to an oversupply, which consequently reduced chlorine prices. Chlorine sold at $145 per ton in 1986 and fell to about $50 per ton in 1991. Conditions within the chlorine segment of the industry affected other products. Because chlorine and caustic soda were co-products of the same chemical process, cuts in chlorine production led to shortages and higher prices within the caustic soda market. The price of caustic soda rose from approximately $120 per ton in 1986 to $300 per ton in 1991. High caustic soda prices led to increased demand for alternative products such as hydrogen peroxide and soda ash.

Although historically soda ash has been manufactured synthetically from the evaporation of brines, it is primarily produced from trona, a mined product. The last synthetic soda ash facility in the United States closed in 1986, idling 700,000 tons of capacity. Operators closed the plant because it could not produce soda ash at prices low enough to compete with the trona-reliant process. Almost half of the domestic production of soda ash is used by glass makers.

ORGANIZATION AND STRUCTURE

Approximately 99 percent of the chlorine and alkali chemical manufacturers in the United States and Canada belong to the Chlorine Institute. The Chlorine Institute was founded by ten industry leaders in 1924. Although their original purpose was to further the demand for chlorine, their focus shifted to providing the industry with supervision and direction following a destructive hurricane in 1926. The hurricane wrought havoc on Florida's water treatment facilities. Thousands of chlorine cylinders were shipped to the state to aid in restoring safe water supplies, but many could not be used because the industry had not previously adopted standardized fittings. The emergency chlorine supply sat idle until adaptors and valves could be obtained.

As a result of the experience, the Chlorine Institute initiated a study of valve and fitting designs. Fol-

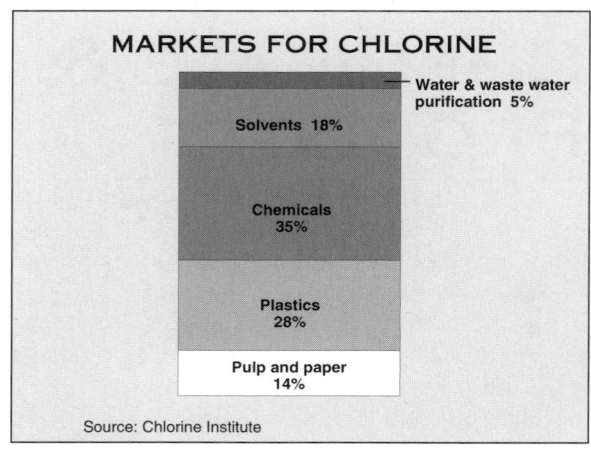

MARKETS FOR CHLORINE

Water & waste water purification 5%

Solvents 18%

Chemicals 35%

Plastics 28%

Pulp and paper 14%

Source: Chlorine Institute

lowing its recommendation, producers voluntarily adopted one single standard. Federal officials later relied on information from the Chlorine Institute in establishing standards for all compressed gases.

The Chlorine Institute also began working on programs to improve the safety record of the industry. In the 1930s, an informal policy was established for responding to emergencies. Later the institute developed a formal program called CHLOREP (*CHLOR*ine *E*mergency *P*lan). CHLOREP consisted of volunteer teams who were available to respond to chlorine emergencies 24 hours a day, seven days a week. By 1991, the Chlorine Institute had trained 250 CHLOREP teams comprised of members from more than 40 companies, and they were placed at more than 100 locations throughout the United States and Canada.

In addition to establishing standards and emergency response programs, the Chlorine Institute published a wide range of manuals, pamphlets, and audio/visual materials to provide technical and safety information. The institute also worked on behalf of its members with the government agencies responsible for regulating various aspects of chemical production and shipment such as the Department of Transportation (DOT), the Interstate Commerce Commission (ICC), the Coast Guard, and the Occupational Safety and Health Administration (OSHA).

BACKGROUND AND DEVELOPMENT

The use of chlorine compounds in chemical processes dates back to at least 77 A.D., but the isolated element itself was not produced until 1774. Although chlorine is a common element, in nature it exists only in compounds because it reacts readily with other substances, both organic and inorganic. For example, salt, or sodium chloride, is made from chlorine and sodium.

A Swedish chemist, Karl Scheele, is acknowledged as the first person to create and identify chlorine. Scheele (who also discovered oxygen) generated a greenish-yellow gas during experiments with sea water. He called it "dephlogisticated marine acid air." The word "dephlogisticated" referred to the fact that it was not susceptible to combustion. The phrase "marine acid air" identified the new gaseous material produced from the acid obtained from marine brine. The name chlorine was not bestowed until the early 1800s when Sir Humphry Davy, used electricity to demonstrate that the gas was an element. Davy borrowed a word from the Greek language referring to the gas's greenish-yellow hue and renamed it "chlorine."

The bleaching effects of chlorine were first put to commercial use by textile makers in France during the end of the eighteenth century. Natural cottons and linens were light brown and had to be bleached before they could be dyed with light or bright colors. Under traditional practices, bleaching was accomplished by spreading the fabrics out and exposing them to the sun. Bleaching cotton had taken up to three months and linen as long as six months. Chlorine bleaching compounds enabled textile manufacturers to keep up with fast-paced increases in production following improvements in spinning and weaving methods.

Chlorine products were greatly improved by technology during the early nineteenth century. In 1792, a process for bleaching rags used in paper making was developed. Bleaching powder, or calcium hypochlorite, was first introduced in 1799. The ability to transport chlorine to markets distant from manufacturing plants was achieved through the formation of potassium hypochlorite, a liquid product created with chlorine and caustic potash.

The development of chlorine production based on electrolysis lowered chlorine prices and increased the chemical's popularity. Electrolysis methods evolved through the mid-nineteenth century and by the century's close had become commercially viable in areas with low cost electricity. The first commercial plant in the United States opened in Rumford, Maine in 1893.

As the twentieth century began, chlorine was being used for an increasing number of purposes. Jersey City, New Jersey, was the first city to use chlorine to disinfect drinking water supplies. Its chlorination efforts began in 1908 and were soon followed by other major cities, including New York. Sewage treatment methods based on liquid chlorine were first adopted in Altoona, Pennsylvania in 1913. The use of chlorine by water and sewage treatment facilities helped virtually eliminate diseases such as cholera, typhoid, and dysentery.

Not all chlorine's uses, however, were benevolent. During World War I chlorine gas, an extremely poisonous substance, was used as a weapon against the Allies. Despite the horrors associated with chlorine gas, the U.S. chlorine production industry benefited from the war. Imports of chemicals from Europe were sharply curtailed because of submarine warfare. As a result, domestic production tripled and continued to grow after the war. Chlorine has also played a role in the development of insecticides, anesthetics, dry cleaning fluids, and fire fighting compounds. The fledgling plastics industry relied on chlorine to make its vital vinyl chloride products. Between 1955 and 1970, chlorine usage grew approximately 5.8 percent per year.

The 1970s ushered in an era of changes. Although the decade closed with chlorine production at its historic high, growth stagnated. Environmental questions hampered producers and economic woes diminished demand by users. By the early 1990s, chlorine production and demand were still less than they had been in 1979.

CURRENT CONDITIONS

Modern methods of chlorine production were developed around electrolysis. The three most often used technologies, diaphragm cells, mercury cells, and membrane cells, all produced chlorine and caustic soda by decomposing brine (salt water). Combined, they accounted for 98 percent of U.S. chlorine production in 1988. The brine used as a raw material was obtained from natural deposits under the earth's surface or was made from salt and water.

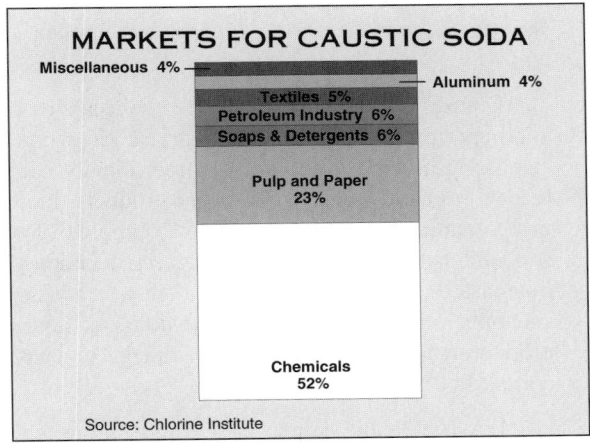

MARKETS FOR CAUSTIC SODA

Miscellaneous 4% — Aluminum 4%
Textiles 5%
Petroleum Industry 6%
Soaps & Detergents 6%
Pulp and Paper 23%
Chemicals 52%

Source: Chlorine Institute

Diaphragm cells, the oldest and most widely used of the modern methods, produced more than three quarters of the nation's chlorine. They used direct current to separate salt and water into chlorine, hydrogen, and sodium hydroxide (caustic soda). An internal asbestos fiber-coated device called a ''diaphragm'' helped keep the chlorine and caustic soda separate. Manufacturers relied on additional evaporation and drying procedures to create products in marketable concentrations.

Mercury cells accounted for 17 percent of the U.S. chlorine production in 1988. Mercury cells employed a different technique for keeping manufactured chlorine and caustic soda separate. Because of the presence of mercury during the application of the cell's electric current, the sodium could be isolated and dissolved into the mercury. A secondary process recaptured the mercury and released the sodium to form sodium hydroxide (caustic soda). During the early 1990s, producers were moving away from mercury cells because of environmental concerns surrounding the mercury content of plant waste water.

Membrane cells, the most rapidly growing form of production, accounted for only five percent of U.S. chlorine production in 1988. Membrane cells employed an ion exchange membrane to separate the chlorine and caustic soda. Membrane technology required less electricity and produced grades of chlorine and caustic soda with higher purity than other methods.

Despite improvements ameliorating the environmental impact of chlorine and caustic soda production, the industry continued to suffer from adverse publicity concerning chlorine use. Chlorine compounds reacted with organic substances to form dioxins. Dioxins were suspected carcinogens and posed potential health hazards including birth defects and damage to the body's skin, liver, neuroendocrine system, and immune system.

Controversy about dioxins affected usage by pulp and paper producers, one of the largest chlorine-consuming industries. Chlorine was traditionally used to bleach pulp and create white paper products. Increasingly, manufacturers were turning to innovative oxygen and hydrogen peroxide bleaching technologies. Forecasters expected the pulp and paper industry to use only about 9 percent of the domestic chlorine production in 1994, a drop from the 15 percent recorded in 1990.

Environmental groups increasingly protested the use of chlorine in other areas as well. Chlorofluorocarbons (CFCs) were suspected of damaging the ozone layer of the earth's upper atmosphere. Chlorinated solvents were considered a source of air pollution because of their emissions. In addition, some water treatment

facilities began turning away from chlorine to other methods of water purification. According to the Chlorine Institute, however, calls to eliminate chlorine were unreasonable, citing the heavy financial burden of meeting such restrictions.

Despite the problems associated with chlorine and its declines in traditional markets, industry analysts anticipated overall demand to grow and prices to increase as much as 15 percent by 2002. Vinyl exports and PVC use in new construction and in remodeling were expected to make up for the declines in other areas.

EPA Limits on Toxic Pollution. In 1994 the Environmental Protection Agency announced that chemical companies in the United States will have to cut their manufacturing plants' toxic air pollution by almost 90 percent from 1990 levels. The rule, noted the *Detroit Free Press,* ''requires the companies . . . to install equipment to better prevent evaporation and leaks of 112 toxic chemicals. . . . About 370 chemical plants in 38 states will be forced to cut toxic air pollution by a total of 506,000 tons, an EPA statement said.'' While the new rules, instituted as a part of the 1990 Clean Air Act, will involve significant expenditures on capital improvements for the affected companies, regulators note that chemical companies have already taken significant steps to address the new requirements in anticipation of the announcement.

INDUSTRY LEADERS

According to industry statistics for 1989, 25 U.S. companies were involved in chlorine production. Two, Dow Chemical USA and Occidental Chemical Corporation, accounted for more than half of the total production capacity.

PPG Industries Chemicals Group was one of the nation's largest merchant producers of chlorine. PPG, a pioneer in barge shipment techniques, supplied chlorine as a compressed, liquefied gas and produced varying grades of caustic soda in liquid and dry forms.

WORK FORCE

The U.S. Department of Commerce reported that the chlorine and alkalies industry employed 5,000 workers in 1987. The figure represented a drop of 25 percent from 1986 and was 34 percent less than figures for 1982. Four states, West Virginia, Louisiana, Texas, and Alabama, accounted for more than half of the industry's employment.

AMERICA AND THE WORLD

Chlorine production in the United States accounts for almost 30 percent of the world's capacity, but there is little international movement of chlorine because of difficulties related to its transportation and storage. Producers generally prefer to erect production facilities in regions where demand exists.

In 1992, analysts predicted that worldwide chlorine demand would grow at a rate of less than one percent per year, but they forecasted wide regional fluctuations. Japan, Europe, and Canada were expected to experience declining demand for chlorine. High demand growth rates, however, were predicted for the Middle East, where annual increases of about 9 percent were expected. Other regions with potentially rapid growth rates were the Asian Pacific, Latin America, and Africa.

The overall slow growth experienced with chlorine demand resulted in an increased demand for soda ash. Pulp and paper manufacturers and water treatment facilities were among those using soda ash as a chlorine substitute. The global soda ash industry included many non-U.S. companies. For example Solvay, the world's largest soda ash producer (headquartered in Brussels), purchased Tenneco's soda ash division in 1992. As a result of the acquisition, Solvay controlled almost half of the U.S. soda ash production and was positioned to expand in the Asian Pacific and Latin American markets.

INDUSTRY INFORMATION SOURCES

"Chemicals," *Standard & Poor's Industry Surveys.* New York: Standard & Poor's Corporation, 1993.

"Chloralkali Industry Sees Changes," *Chemical Marketing Reporter,* September 21, 1992.

Chlor-Alkali Chemicals and the Chlorine Institute, Washington, DC: Chlorine Institute, 1991.

"Chlorine Surge to Taper Off, But Long-Term Growth is Seen," *Chemical Marketing Reporter,* January 11, 1993.

"Dioxin Battle Flares Anew in Capital," *Chemical Marketing Reporter,* June 15, 1992.

Flaschen, Steward S., *Search and Research: The Story of the Chemical Elements,* Boston: Allyn and Bacon, 1965.

Kirschner, Elisabeth, "Total Chlorine Phaseout Would Cost $102 Billion/Year, Says CI," *Chemical Week,* April 28, 1993.

Martorella, Maurice, and Ian Young, "Soda Ash: Still a Steady Player," *Chemical Week,* July 29, 1992.

Mullin, Rick and Emily Pilsher, "Bit Ticket Changes in Store for North American Pulp and Paper," *Chemical Week,* April 21, 1993.

Roberts, Michael, "Structural Changes in Chlor-Alkali," *Chemical Week,* November 4, 1992.

Williams, Mike, "EPA Sets New Limits on Toxic Pollution," *Detroit Free Press,* March 2, 1994.

U.S. Industrial Outlook 1994, Washington, DC: Department of Commerce, 1994.

—Karen Bellenir

SIC 2813

INDUSTRIAL GASES

This industry classification contains establishments primarily involved in manufacturing industrial gases (organic as well as inorganic) which may be sold in compressed, liquid, or solid forms. Industrial gases include acetylene, argon, carbon dioxide, helium, hydrogen, neon, nitrogen, nitrous oxide, and oxygen. Products excluded from this classification are fluorine, sulfur dioxide, and sulfur hexafluoride (**SIC 2819: Industrial Inorganic Chemicals, Not Elsewhere Classified**), industrial ammonia (**SIC 2873: Nitrogenous Fertilizers**), household ammonia (**SIC 2842: Specialty Cleaning, Polishing, and Sanitation Preparations**), chlorine (**SIC 2812: Alkalies and Chlorine**) and fluorocarbon gases (**SIC 2869: Industrial Organic Chemicals, Not Elsewhere Classified**). Industrial gas distributors, including liquid oxygen shippers, are classified in **SIC 5169: Chemicals and Allied Products, Not Elsewhere Classified**.

INDUSTRY SNAPSHOT

In the United States, industrial gases touch virtually every facet of twentieth-century life. The three major atmospheric gases, oxygen, nitrogen, and argon are used in steel production. Oxygen enhances kiln firing to reduce brick making costs. Liquid oxygen and liquid hydrogen fuel rockets. Nitrogen is used in brewing beer, recycling tires, and applying metallic finishes on toys. Liquid nitrogen and liquid carbon dioxide are used to make plastic fittings for moldings, enhance oil recovery from wells, and enable solvent recycling. Argon contributes to stainless steel manufacturing and serves as a component in fluorescent tube lighting.

The industrial gas industry differs from many other types of manufacturing because its raw materials are primarily extracted from the atmosphere. The two principal gases produced by the industry are nitrogen and oxygen. Dry air is composed of 78.1 percent nitrogen, 20.9 percent oxygen, and just under 1 percent argon. All other atmospheric gases, often called rare gases, make up the remaining one-tenth of a percent. Additional industrial gases such as hydrogen, acetylene, and carbon dioxide are obtained as co-products or by-products from other operations. Production costs within the industry are divided fairly evenly among labor, energy, and distribution.

The industry uses three different techniques to separate gases from the atmosphere. Cryogenic methods are the oldest and most widely used. Cryogenic separation relies on cooling and pressurizing the air until it becomes liquid. Oxygen, when held at a pressure of 80 pounds per square inch, liquefies at minus 274 degrees Fahrenheit; nitrogen liquefies at a colder temperature. As the atmospheric gases liquefy, they are extracted by means of a distillation process. Additional distillation steps are necessary to produce argon and other rare gases such as krypton and xenon. Helium liquefies only at temperatures approaching absolute zero. As a result, cryogenic production is not economically feasible for helium. Most commercially available helium is derived from natural gas rather than from the atmosphere.

Two non-cryogenic gas production methods are membrane separation and pressure swing absorption (PSA). Membrane separation uses hollow fibers, most frequently made of organic polymers, to recover gases such as hydrogen from oil refineries or carbon dioxide from natural gas supplies. Pressure swing absorption (PSA) relies on a molecular sieve material that selectively absorbs atmospheric components at specific temperatures and pressures.

According to U.S. Department of Commerce statistics, the industrial gases industry shipped products valued at $2.6 billion in 1987. Of this total $2.5 billion represented products considered primary to the industry. Although industry sales declined in the late 1980s, growth was reported during the early 1990s. In 1991, oxygen production was estimated at 465 billion cubic feet and nitrogen production at 770 billion cubic feet. Argon production was approximately 13 billion cubic feet.

In addition to its major products, the industry produced almost 100 different specialty gases such as krypton, xenon, and neon. Many specialty gases were used for medical, communications, electronics, aerospace, laser, and special lighting applications. Although specialty gases accounted for only about 8 percent of the industry's total production in 1992, they accounted for 29 percent of its revenues.

ORGANIZATION AND STRUCTURE

The industrial gas industry is divided into two major segments. The first, called the "tonnage" or "supply scheme" market, is comprised of large volume users who usually receive gas directly from an on-site production facility via pipeline. Under typical on-site contracts, a gas supplier constructs a production plant at or adjacent to a gas user's facility. The gas supplier owns and operates the plant for the benefit of the gas customer. Long-term contracts dictate that the customer take a specified volume of gas, often the entire amount produced. Many contracts contain adjustment clauses to account for increasing energy prices, variances in productivity, or changes in labor costs. Within this market segment, gas sold is measured in terms of tons per day. Examples of customers who routinely purchase industrial gases on the tonnage market include chemical, petroleum, electronics, and steel manufacturers.

The other major market segment is known as the "merchant" or "bulk liquid" market. Customers within this market generally have fluctuating demand rates or operate multiple facilities in scattered locations. They often purchase gas products under short term contracts of less than five years in duration. Suppliers deliver liquid gas in cryogenic tanker trucks or by rail. Gases are shipped and stored in liquid form because of volume constraints. For example, liquid oxygen takes up less than one percent of the space required to contain the same amount in a gaseous state. Examples of customers in this category include the metal, food processing, electronics, chemical, aerospace, plastics, medical, glass, and paper industries.

A third, but much smaller market segment, consists of cylinder gas deliveries. Cylinder gas shipments are generally limited to expensive specialty gases and mixtures. A typical tanker truck carries the equivalent of 1,600 large cylinders. A train of ten cars, carries the equivalent of 57,000 cylinders.

BACKGROUND AND DEVELOPMENT

The gases that make up the multi-billion dollar industrial gas industry were discovered by various researchers living in several different countries beginning in the later half of the eighteenth century. One year before the United States declared its independence from England, oxygen was discovered by two chemists working independently in Europe. During the later part of the 1800s, it was used for medical purposes and put to use commercially in welding. Oxygen was also used to generate limelight for theaters and music halls.

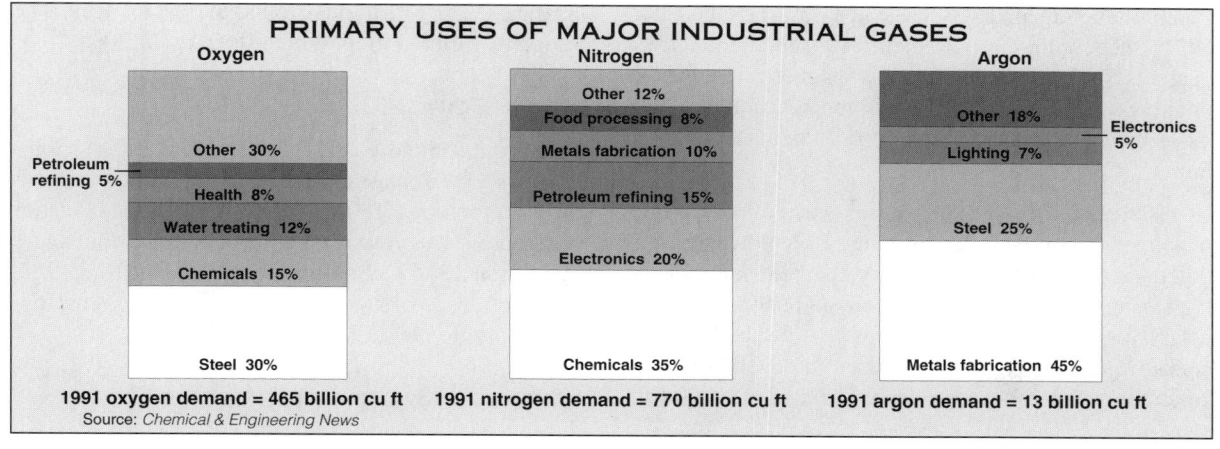

PRIMARY USES OF MAJOR INDUSTRIAL GASES

Oxygen

Other 30%
Petroleum refining 5%
Health 8%
Water treating 12%
Chemicals 15%
Steel 30%

1991 oxygen demand = 465 billion cu ft

Nitrogen

Other 12%
Food processing 8%
Metals fabrication 10%
Petroleum refining 15%
Electronics 20%
Chemicals 35%

1991 nitrogen demand = 770 billion cu ft

Argon

Other 18%
Electronics 5%
Lighting 7%
Steel 25%
Metals fabrication 45%

1991 argon demand = 13 billion cu ft

Source: *Chemical & Engineering News*

Acetylene was discovered in 1863 and first produced commercially in 1892. In 1897, Georges Claude, a French researcher, developed a method of dissolving acetylene in acetone at low pressures. Claude's process enabled the development of methods which allowed the movement of the gas via transportation cylinders. The first acetylene-burning torches were developed around the turn of the century.

In 1902, two researchers, one in France and one in Germany, developed similar processes for the fractional distillation of liquid air. This procedure made it possible to produce large volumes of oxygen economically. In 1903, the Linde Air Products Company constructed the first commercial oxygen plant in the United States.

Events of the early twentieth century demanded increasing amounts of industrial gases. World War I required large amounts of oxygen and acetylene for welding; pilots of high-altitude aircraft during World War II needed oxygen for their flights. Following the wars, researchers put inert gases such as argon and helium to use in electric arc welding.

Growing industrialization in the Western World brought rapid expansion to the gas industry. Oxygen demand continued growing through the 1950s as steel manufacturers turned to the gas to improve production methods. Maturing uses for nitrogen, previously considered a waste material, developed during the 1960s along with advances in the uses of helium and argon. The 1970s brought large scale expansions in the nation's capacity to produce industrial gases. The decade also saw growth in the use of specialty gases by the electronics industry. By the mid-1980s, the electronics industry used an estimated 15 percent of the nation's nitrogen output.

CURRENT CONDITIONS

Although demand for nitrogen in 1960 had been practically non-existent, by the early 1990s nitrogen sales surpassed the sales of all other industrial gases. Because nitrogen did not readily react with other materials, several industries used it as a "blanketing agent," which is a compound able to prevent unwanted reactions. For example, when nitrogen was used as a blanketing agent with embers, it prevented them from igniting. Nitrogen was therefore used to ensure product quality and improve plant safety. Oil producers used nitrogen to stimulate and pressurize wells. The gas also found use in steel processing, food production, cooling, refrigeration and freezing systems, solvent recovery, chemical and glass production, and in the electronics and aerospace industries.

Measured in terms of sales volume, the second most significant industrial gas of the early 1990s was oxygen. Oxygen was used to intensify or control combustion in a variety of industries. Its other uses included speeding fermentation, providing life support, and controlling odors. Chemical manufacturers, brick makers, and metal fabricators all relied on oxygen. Innovative uses included processes aimed at restoring or maintaining environmental integrity. Oxygen was used in hazardous waste cleanup efforts, waste water treatment facilities, and coal gasification systems (a process designed to reduce the hazardous emissions associated with burning coal). One of the fastest growing areas of oxygen use, however, was as a replacement for chlorine in bleaching, especially by pulp and paper manufacturers.

Another gas with a rapidly growing demand in the early 1990s was helium. Helium, traditionally used in welding, balloons, and leak detection, was finding new applications in cryogenic cooling. Liquid helium was the only gas known to get cold enough for use in the superconducting magnets used in body scanners. By 1991, the cooling requirements of superconductive magnets such as those used by magnetic resonance imaging (MRI) diagnostic equipment accounted for more than one fourth of the world's demand for helium.

Demand for specialty gases such as krypton, xenon, and neon was also growing. Low power lamps relied on krypton, high-intensity filament lamps and CAT scanners depended on xenon, and neon was necessary for lasers, display lighting, and bar code scanners. All three rare gases were used to develop radial-keratotomy, an innovative form of laser surgery for eyes.

INDUSTRY LEADERS

In the mid-1980s Union Carbide was the largest industrial gas supplier in the United States. It provided approximately one third of the nation's merchant gas. In 1985, the company opened six new nitrogen plants with most of its production capacity aimed at the fast-growing high-tech market. In 1992, Union Carbide's industrial gas unit was spun-off to become an independent entity, Praxair Corporation.

Another major producer was Air Products and Chemicals. Air Products, founded in 1940, pioneered on-site industrial gas manufacturing. In 1991, the company introduced small volume, low cost, non-cryogenic nitrogen for use by metal heat-treating firms. In 1992, Air Products served more than 100,000 customers in 29 countries and its global sales exceeded $3 billion.

Liquid Air Corporation, a subsidiary of the French company L'Air Liquide, entered the U.S. market in 1968. By the mid-1980s, L'Air Liquide operated in 66 countries. Liquid Air served as the company's headquarters for its operations in North and South America. It supplied products including oxygen, nitrous oxide, hydrogen, nitrogen, specialty gases, chemical gases and rare gases to a wide variety of industrial users. Big Three Industries, another L'Air Liquide unit, sold most of its production to chemical and petroleum producers via a pipeline system located in the Gulf Coast region.

Another international gas producer with a strong presence in the U.S. market was the BOC Group. The BOC Group originated in England with the incorporation of the Brins Oxygen Company Limited in 1886. BOC acquired the American company Airco in 1978. By the mid 1980s Airco provided 20 percent of the U.S. domestic merchant gas. BOC's expansion continued and by the early 1990s the company operated units in North and South America, Europe, India, Australia,

Japan, and other locations around the Pacific Rim. The company's global employment totaled 40,000.

WORK FORCE

In the United States, the Department of Commerce reported that the industrial gases industry employed a total of 8,100 workers in 1987. The statistics represented a decrease of 6 percent from the figure reported in 1986 and a drop of 11 percent from 1982. The three leading states in terms of industry employment were Texas, California, and Ohio.

AMERICA AND THE WORLD

The global market for industrial gases was estimated at $20 billion in 1992. Because of problems related to the transportation and storage of gas products, most production occurred close to its point of use. There was, therefore, very little international trade in industrial gases. Instead of transporting products, large international corporations functioned by operating production facilities in many countries.

The types and volumes of gases provided in an area depended on the development of the region's economy. Regions with emerging economies typically required high volumes of oxygen, whereas countries with economies based on high-technology and service, needed greater amounts of nitrogen. According to the BOC Group, the ratio of nitrogen sales to oxygen sales could be used as a measurement of a nation's industrial development.

RESEARCH AND TECHNOLOGY

During the early 1990s, pollution abatement was one of the most rapidly developing areas of study within the industrial gases industry. Researchers were examining methods of improving waste water treatment by oxygen injection. Recovery systems using nitrogen to condense and recapture solvents and chemical vapors helped manufacturers come into compliance with the Clean Air Act Amendments of 1990. An innovative technology based on carbon dioxide offered promise for reducing the environmental impact of solvent use within the paint and coatings industry. Additionally, carbon dioxide-based refrigeration systems were introduced to replace systems that relied on chlorofluorocarbons (CFCs).

Research into new or refined uses for industrial gases also continued. Liquid nitrogen was being considered as a possible aid in reducing problems associated with cracking in structural concrete. Xenon provided sun-like brightness to meet the special lighting needs of airports, stadiums, the motion picture industry, and copying machine manufacturers. Other rare gases were also being developed for use in diagnostic technologies and pharmaceutical applications.

INDUSTRY INFORMATION SOURCES

Agoos, Alice. "Industrial Gases Travel an Upward Road." *Chemical Week* (January 1, 1986).

Air Products and Chemicals, Inc. 1992 Annual Report. Allentown, Penn.: Air Products, 1993.

Banov, Abel. "Revolutionary Technology Unveiled: Union Carbide Process may Reduce Solvent Content 30 - 70%." *American Paint & Coatings Journal* (July 24, 1989).

"Chemicals." *Standard & Poor's Industry Surveys*, New York: Standard & Poor's Corporation, 1993.

Deal, Richard, Richard Hendrickson, and William Lewis. "Onsite Oxygen Plants Can Reduce Pulp Mill Costs for Volume Users." *Pulp and Paper* (September 1991).

Greek, Bruce F. "Rising Demand for Industrial Gases Paves Way for Price Increases." *Chemical & Engineering News* (December 2, 1991).

Industrial Gases: The Invisible Fabric of the Modern World. London: The BOC Group, 1984.

"Liquid CO2 — An Alternative to Freon (CFCs) for the Frozen Food Shipping Industry." *Frozen Food Digest* (October 1992).

Loesel, Andrew. "Inert but Growing." *Chemical Marketing Reporter* (December 9, 1991).

Taub, J. S. "Liquid Air Finding New Markets for Its Industrial Gases." *San Francisco Business Journal* (March 3, 1986.)

This is Air Products. Allentown, Penn.: Air Products, 1993.

Union Carbide Corporation Annual Report 1992. Danbury, Conn.: Union Carbide, 1993.

U.S. Department of Commerce. *1987 Census of Manufactures.* Washington, DC: Bureau of the Census, 1990.

U.S. Department of Commerce. *U.S. Industrial Outlook '92.* Washington, DC: Department of Commerce, 1992.

We're Out to Win Your Business. Murray Hill, N.J.: Airco, (December 1991).

Wood, Andrew. "Making Acetylene Competitive." *Chemical Week* (February 21, 1990).

—Karen Bellenir

SIC 2816

INORGANIC PIGMENTS

This industry classification is comprised of establishments engaged in manufacturing inorganic color pigments, white pigments, and black pigments, including animal black and bone black. Carbon black is classified in **SIC 2895: Carbon Black.** Organic color pigments are classified in **SIC 2865: Cyclic Organic Crudes and Intermediates, and Organic Dyes and Pigments.**

INDUSTRY SNAPSHOT

Pigments are insoluble substances that can be incorporated into a material to selectively absorb or scatter light. Depending on the specific pigment used, different visual effects can be produced. Inorganic pigments may be obtained from a variety of naturally occurring or synthetically produced mineral sources. Organic pigments are carbon compounds derived from petroleum sources. Although pigments are best known for their ability to impart color to materials, they are also used to add rust inhibition, rigidity, and abrasion resistance.

In comparison with organic pigments, inorganic pigments are generally better able to withstand the affects of sunlight and chemical exposure. They provide superior opacity, which means they can render a substance or object opaque by prohibiting light from passing through it. Inorganic colors, however, tend to be less bright, pure, and rich than their organic counterparts. Because inorganic pigments possess less tinting strength, more pigment is needed to produce the desired effect. This generally makes them more durable. Almost all inorganic pigments are completely insoluble; consequently, they do not bleed or leach out of coatings, inks, or plastics. In addition, inorganic pigments are usually less expensive than similar organic colors.

Pigments differ from dyes as a result of their distinctive chemical natures. Dyes are soluble, and to impart color they are dissolved in a carrier and applied by a process that involves chemical changes. Pigments, however, remain unchanged physically and chemically. They function without altering their crystalline or particulate structure.

Some inorganic pigment classifications are single-metal oxides, mixed-metal oxides, and earth colors. Single-metal oxides include pigments made from titanium, zinc, cobalt, and chromium. Mixed-metal oxides include pigments such as cobalt aluminate blue, which is used in ceramic glazes, and nickel antimony titanate, manganese antimony titanate, and chromium antimony titanate, which are used for outdoor coatings and plastic siding. Earth colors, including siennas, ochers, and umbers, are generally made from iron oxides and lead chromates. A method of high-temperature firing called calcination is used to produce pigments with improved heat resistance.

Pigment manufacturers supply inorganic colors in a variety of forms such as powders, pastes, granules, slurries, and suspensions. Pigment users include manufacturers of paints and stains, printing inks, plastics, synthetic textiles, paper, cosmetics, contact lenses, soaps and detergents, wax, modeling clay, chalks, crayons, artists' colors, concrete and masonry products, and ceramics.

According to figures released by the U.S. Department of Commerce, shipments of inorganic pigments were valued at $2.4 billion in 1987. Of this amount, $2.2 billion represented products considered primary to the industry. The largest end user was the paint and coatings industry.

Within the inorganic pigments classification, the largest selling individual pigment was titanium dioxide, a white pigment with opacifying characteristics. Growth in production and demand for titanium dioxide increased rapidly through the 1980s. By 1989 production was 67 percent above the 1982 level. Although demand declined in 1990, industry analysts predicted annual domestic growth within the titanium dioxide market of about 2 percent during the mid-1990s. Globally, demand was expected to increase about 3 percent per year. Almost half of the titanium dioxide produced in the United States was used by paint and coatings manufacturers. Other users included the plastics, rubber, printing inks, floor coverings, ceramics, textiles, cosmetics, and paper industries.

BACKGROUND AND DEVELOPMENT

Man's exploitation of color dates back to the prehistoric era. Pigments were made by grinding naturally colored materials into minute particles and then mixing them into a binder material. Some of the substances used to produce paintings on cave walls were still used during the twentieth century. For example, the reds used to produce the drawings in the Lascaux caves of southern France were made from red iron oxide.

During the early part of the twentieth century, the pigments industry relied heavily on lead-based ingredients. One ingredient, lead carbonate (white lead) was known to be toxic as early as the late nineteenth century, and although some countries began imposing restrictions on its use in the 1920s, the United States was not among them. The toxicity of lead carbonate, especially to children who ate paint chips, received increasing publicity. By the mid-1960s paint manufacturers were required to begin phasing out its use.

According to industry researchers, lead carbonate caused lead poisoning because of its solubility. The solubility enabled it to interfere with the human body's biochemical system. Investigators claimed that other lead pigments suffered from non-specific adverse publicity resulting in regulations that failed to differentiate between soluble and insoluble lead compounds. One researcher claimed that a reduction in the use of lead chromate pigments during the 1970s resulted in increased costs of more than $1 billion because available replacements were inferior.

To address issues such as environmental matters, tariffs, toxicity, and worker health, the Dry Color Manufacturers Association (DCMA) was formed. Originally organized in 1925 and headquartered in New York City, the trade association moved to New Jersey and then to Washington DC. In 1993, the organization changed its name to the Color Pigments Manufacturers Association, Inc. (CPMA).

CURRENT CONDITIONS

As the inorganic pigments industry entered the 1990s, the largest single product produced was titanium dioxide. Titanium dioxide production relied on two different raw materials containing titanium: ilmenite and natural rutile. Both minerals were primarily mined in Australia and South Africa. Ilmenite contained less titanium than rutile, but it was more plentiful and less expensive.

Manufacturers used two basic processes to make titanium dioxide. The sulfate process, which produced slightly less than half of the world's supply of titanium dioxide, was the older method. It used sulfuric acid to dissolve the titanium dioxide. Further refinement was required to produce different grades of the finished product.

The newer method, called the chloride process, centered around the use of chlorine and accounted for 51 percent of the world's titanium dioxide capacity. By this method, chlorine was reacted with titanium-containing minerals to produce titanium tetrachloride. The titanium tetrachloride was reacted with oxygen to form titanium dioxide and recyclable chlorine. Advantages of the chloride process included its ability to create higher grades of titanium dioxide without additional handling, its use of less labor and equipment, and its ability to produce in a continuous, as opposed to a batch, process.

The chloride process also produced a smaller volume of waste by-products. Up to 12 tons of waste material were generated when the sulfate process was used in making one ton of titanium dioxide from ilmenite. The chloride process generated four to five tons of waste in producing the same amount of titanium dioxide. A large part of the wastes generated by the chloride process, however, consisted of iron chloride. Disposal of iron chloride created controversy because of its acidic properties and hazardous nature. To reduce the amount of iron chloride waste, manufacturers were forced to rely on higher priced rutile or other purified forms of titanium-containing raw materials. High grade rutile generated only about 70 pounds of iron chloride to yield one ton of titanium dioxide.

Titanium dioxide was also being used to create synthetic pearlescent pigments. Pearlescent pigments, a twentieth century innovation, were developed in an attempt to create the visual sense of depth associated with natural pearls. Initial pearlescent pigments were made from crystals obtained from fish scales. Rosary bead manufacturers were among the first users of these products.

Researchers identified two chemical compounds with similar light reflective properties. One of these, carbonate white lead, was withdrawn because of its toxicity. The other, bismuth oxychloride, found wide use in applications such as cast polyester buttons, automotive paints, fingernail enamels, cosmetics, wall papers and plastics.

Synthetic pearlescent pigments, however, failed to exactly duplicate those of fish scales. The search for other synthetic pearlescent pigment compounds led to the use of such minerals as mica. Mica, when coated with titanium dioxide, was judged to reflect light in a manner suitable for use in pearlescent pigments.

The second largest family of pigments was iron oxides. Although iron oxides produced pigments in a wide range of colors, reds accounted for almost half the consumption. By the early 1990s, synthetic iron oxides had captured two-thirds of the market. Industry forecasters expected increased interest in synthetic iron oxide pigments because they offered improved color strength over naturally occurring ores. The primary users of iron oxide pigments were paint and coatings manufacturers.

Lead chromates represented the third largest family of pigments. By the early 1990s, approximately 42 million pounds of these pigments were being sold annually. Nearly 18 million pounds of these pigments were used by traffic paint manufacturers. Despite their popularity, lead chromates were being subjected to increasing Congressional scrutiny because of concerns about lead toxicity and environmental integrity.

Questions about environmental degradation and the toxicity of heavy metals challenged the inorganic pigment industry throughout the 1980s and early

1990s. Heavy metals such as lead, cadmium, chromium, and mercury were associated with ailments including cancer and liver disease. Both the Congress and the Environmental Protection Agency (EPA) considered legislative and regulatory initiatives to control, limit, and in some cases ban, the use of several of the industry's essential raw materials. Some manufacturers responded by backing away from heavy-metal pigments. Others defended their formulations and offered evidence that if raw materials were banned, certain colors would become unavailable.

In addition to struggling with direct toxicity problems, pigment manufacturers faced charges claiming that their disposal of heavy-metals used in pigments were threatening the nation's water supplies. Products undergoing incineration or degradation in landfill sites created a potential hazard as heavy metals were released into the environment. As a result of this growing environmental concern, the Conference of North East Governors (representing nine northern states) and the legislatures in several other states, began working toward bans on heavy metals in packaging materials. During the early 1990s, industry watchers expected the number of environmental regulations regarding the use of heavy metals in pigments to increase.

Many inorganic pigment formulas relied on heavy metals. Some colors were not achievable without their traditional raw materials. In other cases, colors could be matched using organic ingredients but the resulting pigment suffered from decreased light stability, poor opacity, and an inability to withstand high-temperature processing. Acceptable organic pigment substitutes were often more expensive than the inorganic pigments. Analysts suggested that switching to organic pigments could increase the price of a color concentrate by as much as 300 percent.

An often cited example of the difficulties faced by industries forced to switch away from heavy metal inorganic pigments was the problem of the Pennzoil oil bottle. The Pennzoil oil bottle, fabricated from an identifying bright yellow plastic, depended on yellow lead chromate. During the early 1990s yellow lead chromate cost between $1.00 and $1.50 per pound, but as legislation was likely to continue to limit the use of lead chromate, the company was forced to look for substitutes for the ingredient. One commonly used substitute cost between $6.00 and $7.00 per pound and other organic yellows cost up to $30.00 per pound. Facing a similar situation, Caterpillar (a manufacturer of heavy equipment) switched from its traditional color to a less bright yellow.

INDUSTRY LEADERS

One of the nation's largest corporations producing inorganic pigments was Ferro. Ferro began operating in 1919 as a frit manufacturer. Frit is a special glass material used to produce porcelain enamel and ceramic glaze. Color pigments for the ceramics and coatings industries were added to the company's product line in 1939. The company began supplying pigments to the plastics industry in 1947. By 1993, Ferro operated 12 color production facilities and sold its products in more than 100 countries.

Ferro's line of inorganic mixed metal oxide pigments are used primarily to color vinyl siding, window profiles, appliance housings, garden tools and automotive components. The company's ultramarine blue and violet pigments are manufactured in Spain from sodium aluminum sulfosilicate complexes. They find use in thermoplastic resins, rubber compounds, paints, printing inks, artists' colors, and roofing granules. A third line of colors, called complex inorganic color pigments, are man-made minerals that are heat-stable, light-stable and weather resistant. According to the manufacturer they are the most chemically resistant pigments known to exist. They are recommended for use in exterior building applications and engineering plastics.

One of the nation's largest titanium dioxide manufacturers was SCM Chemicals, a Hanson PLC company. By 1992, the company, which began its involvement in titanium production in 1933, was the third largest producer of titanium dioxide in the world. SCM operated eight plants in the United States, England, and Australia and reported an annual production of 446,000 metric tons.

AMERICA AND THE WORLD

In 1990, estimates suggested that titanium dioxide accounted for about 30 percent of global pigment sales, and demand for the white pigment was expected to grow at approximately 3 percent per year. Industry forecasters expected new global production capacity, estimated to add 850 thousand tons between 1990 and 1995, to result in a slight over-supply and keep prices down.

Western Europe, however, was expected to see reduced production. Approximately 73 percent of the region's existing capacity was based on the sulfate process, which was subject to increasing criticism from environmental groups. A European Community directive to stop ocean dumping of wastes, slated to take effect at the end of 1993, was expected to increase operating expenses by about 15 percent and force older plants out of the global market.

Heavy metal pigment manufacturers were also facing difficulty in some parts of the world. In Japan, cadmium was replaced in 1980 and European manufacturers began phasing it out several years later. By 1990, an estimated 50 to 60 percent of European cadmium production had been eliminated. Some industry observers suggested that the banning of heavy metal pigments resulted in an increased reliance on duller colors in some regions.

RESEARCH AND TECHNOLOGY

Much of the developing technology within the inorganic pigments industry focused on attempts to lessen the risks such pigments presented to humans and the environment. One innovation, called silica encapsulation, involved encasing pigment particles or crystals within a shell of silica (a glass like substance). Researchers claimed that encapsulated lead chromate pigments were protected from chemical, photochemical, and thermal degradation. The encapsulation process also reduced their toxicity by making them less able to be absorbed by the body. Researchers also claimed that silica encapsulation improved the brightness and intensity of the pigments, making them better suited for use in high-temperature applications such as plastic manufacturing.

Other researchers were examining methods of producing low dust, low soluble cadmium pigments. One newly developed product line contained less than one part per million of soluble cadmium, falling under the threshold defined by the EPA to identify a hazardous waste material. Low dust products also helped industry manufacturers to meet the standards set by the Occupational Safety and Health Administration (OSHA).

INDUSTRY INFORMATION SOURCES

Armanini, Louis. "Ah, the Beauty of a Pearl." *Industrial Finishing* (April 1992).

"Chemicals." *Standard & Poor's Industry Surveys*. New York: Standard & Poor's Corporation, 1993.

"Colorants and Pigments." *American Paint and Coatings Journal* (June 8, 1992).

Dry Color Manufacturers' Association. "Pigments — A Primer." *American Ink Maker* (June 1989). Reprinted by Color Pigments Manufacturers Association, Inc. (formerly DCMA).

Ferro 1992 Profile. Cleveland, Oh.: Ferro, 1992.

Ferro. "Geode: Complex Inorganic Color Pigments." Cleveland, Oh.: Ferro, nd.

————. "Inorganic Mixed Metal Oxide Pigments." Cleveland, Oh.: Ferro, nd.

————. "Ultramarine Pigments." Cleveland, Oh.: Ferro, nd.

Gray, Donald. "Putting Risk Into Perspective." *American Paint and Coatings Journal* (September 24, 1990).

Kiesche, Elizabeth S. "Pigments and Dyes Adapting to New Environments." *Chemical Week* (October 3, 1990).

Loesel, Andrew. "Color Concentrate Makers Will Phase Out Heavy Metals." *Chemical Marketing Reporter* (June 11, 1990).

Loesel, Andrew. "Color Me Bleak." *Chemical Marketing Reporter* (October 19, 1992).

Loesel, Andrew. "Lead Chromate Makers Worry About Lead Ban." *Chemical Marketing Reporter* (June 18, 1990).

Loffredo, Douglas. "Pigment Producers Face Tougher Times." *Chemical Marketing Reporter* (October 29, 1990).

Maty, Joe. "Suit Seeks Lead Cleanup Help: Companies Face Specter of Millions in Abatement Costs." *American Paint and Coatings Journal* (November 26, 1990).

"Pigment Makers Seek Stay of OSHA Cadmium Rule." *American Paint and Coatings Journal* (January 11, 1993).

SCM Chemicals. *Titanium Dioxide in Today's Environment: A Responsive and Responsible Industry.* Baltimore, Md.: SCM, nd.

————. *World View.* Baltimore, Md.: SCM, 1993.

Singletary, Lynda. "Black and White." *Chemical Marketing Reporter* (November 4, 1991).

U.S. Department of Commerce. *1987 Census of Manufactures.* Washington, DC: Bureau of the Census, 1990.

U.S. Department of Commerce. *U.S. Industrial Outlook '92.* Washington, DC: Department of Commerce, 1992.

Wallace, David. "Paint Suit May Yield Thousands of Plaintiffs." *Philadelphia Business Journal* (July 8, 1991).

Wriede, Peter A., and Donald Gray. "Heavy-Metal Based Pigments: Putting use Risks in Perspective." *American Paint and Coatings Journal* (January 6, 1986).

—Karen Bellenir

SIC 2819

INDUSTRIAL INORGANIC CHEMICALS, NOT ELSEWHERE CLASSIFIED

This category includes establishments primarily involved in manufacturing industrial inorganic chemicals not elsewhere classified. A few examples are alum, ammonium compounds (except for fertilizer), industrial bleaches (sodium or calcium hypochlorite), chemical catalysts, hydrazine, hydrochloric acid, hydrogen peroxide, inorganic sodium compounds, and sulfuric acid.

Establishments primarily engaged in mining, milling or otherwise preparing natural potassium, sodium, or boron compounds (other than common salt) are classified in **SIC 1474: Potash, Soda, and Borate Minerals;** establishments primarily engaged in manufacturing household bleaches are classified in **SIC 2842: Specialty Cleaning, Polishing, and Sanitation Preparations;** those manufacturing phosphoric acid are classified in **SIC 2874: Phosphatic Fertilizers;** and those manufacturing nitric acid, anhydrous ammonia, and other nitrogenous fertilizer materials are classified in **SIC 2873: Nitrogenous Fertilizers**.

INDUSTRY SNAPSHOT

In 1992 this category of industrial inorganic chemical production, which includes a wide array of products, accounted for almost two-thirds of the nation's production of inorganic chemicals. Inorganic chemicals are those derived from inanimate earth materials such as minerals and the atmosphere. They are differentiated from organic chemicals, which are derived from plant and animal sources. Organic chemicals are based on carbon; inorganic chemicals are based on all the other naturally occurring and synthetically produced elements.

The major chemicals within this classification are known as "basic" chemicals. They are also sometimes referred to as "heavy," "bulk," or "commodity" chemicals. Manufacturers typically produce them from ores or brines, or as co-products or by-products of other processes. They serve industrial users who put them to work in the creation of other products. Some common applications include their use as processing aids and chemical catalysts. Inorganic chemicals are also sometimes used as ingredients in non-chemical products. The primary markets for chemical products are paper, housing, automobiles, water treatment, fertilizer, petroleum refining, steel production, manufacturing, and soap and detergent production.

In 1987, the U.S. Department of Commerce reported that the value of shipments within this industry totaled $13.2 billion. Products were provided by approximately 700 establishments. About half of these firms were small companies that produced small volumes of specialty chemicals. These types of establishments accounted for only 4 percent of the industry's total shipments, but according to government projections, demand for specialty chemicals was expected to grow faster than demand for commodity chemicals.

During the early 1990s, the largest single chemical produced within the industry was sulfuric acid. In 1991, producers generated 43 million tons of the chemical. Although some sulfuric acid was manufactured as a by-product of smelting operations and some was regenerated from previously used acid, most was created through the oxidation of sulfur.

Another prominent chemical produced by the industry was hydrogen peroxide. Although production volumes of hydrogen peroxide fell far short of other products, its growth rate and anticipated potential were notable. Pulp and paper manufacturers, chemical manufacturers, and water treatment facilities were among the industries turning to technologies based on hydrogen peroxide and away from production methods that relied on chemicals that possessed greater environmental risks. Other users included the textile industry, suppliers of laundry products, electronics manufacturers, and food processors. Industry analysts expected demand for hydrogen peroxide to have an annual growth rate of approximately 10 percent through the mid-1990s.

According to the 1993 edition of *Standard and Poor's Industry Surveys* the chemical industry as a whole was experiencing a slow recovery after a national economic slowdown during the early 1990s. Forecasters expected the overall industrial inorganic chemicals industry to grow at a rate comparable to the nation's economic growth rate. Government projections predicted a three percent growth rate for 1992 and expected similar rates to be achieved through the middle of the decade.

ORGANIZATION AND STRUCTURE

Chemical producing companies range in size from small establishments providing a single chemical to multi-national corporations offering an array of a thousand or more different chemical products. The Chemical Manufacturers Association (CMA) was established to represent the industry's interests in local, state, and national affairs. In 1978, the CMA (formerly the Manufacturing Chemists Association), adopted an Advocacy Charter to define its lobbying role. According to the CMA's 120th Annual Report covering the fiscal year 1991-1992, one of the organization's goals was to become "a positive and proactive force for the industry." The CMA's stated challenge was "to balance industry's interests with those of its many publics— legislators, regulators, the courts and, especially, employees and neighbors."

To help it achieve these goals, the CMA adopted a program called Responsible Care®. Responsible Care® established standardized practices and implemented codes for community awareness and emergency response, process safety, distribution, pollution prevention, employee health and safety, and product stewardship. CMA reported that by 1992, its members were making progress fulfilling the program's practices despite the economic difficulties facing the industry. The organization was also in the process of adopting ways to measure the program's success.

Historically, efforts made by chemical producers to address hazards included plant safety considerations and voluntarily withdrawing dangerous products from the market. In addition, several governmental agencies existed to regulate specific facets of the industry. For example, regulations covering railroad shipments of hazardous materials were instituted following the Civil War; and during the closing years of the 1800s, the Bureau of Chemistry (within the U.S. Department of Agriculture) was responsible for overseeing the safety of chemicals used in foods and drugs.

Governmental efforts to insure product safety, establish worker safety laws, and protect the environment intensified during the 1970s, beginning with the establishment of the Environmental Protection Agency (EPA) in 1970. The decade brought along the following host of new regulations: revisions of the Clean Air Act (1970 and subsequent amendments); the Occupational Safety and Health Act (1970); the Resource Recovery Act (1970); the Federal Water Pollution Control Act (1972); the Safe Drinking Water Act (1974); amendments to the Federal Insecticide, Fungicide, and Rodenticide Act (1972); the Resource Conservation and Recovery Act (1976); and the Toxic Substances Control Act (1976). The 1980s opened with the passage of the Comprehensive Environmental Response, Compensation, and Liability Act (also known as the "Superfund" Act.)

Federal regulations mandated that new chemicals be evaluated for safety before use, that new uses of existing chemicals be evaluated, and that all chemicals meet specific safety and health standards. In addition, governmental bodies regulated by-products and co-products, controlled transportation, and monitored waste disposal. In her 1984 work *Toxic Substances Controls Primer* Mary Devine Worobec noted, "virtually every chemical and substance used in the United States is subject to some type of control. During manufacture, workers who are exposed must be monitored. During use, by-products are created that must be treated in specified ways and when use of a substance is completed, the wastes that remain must be disposed of in approved ways. And at each juncture, the chemical must be transported to the site of the next stage in a proper manner."

BACKGROUND AND DEVELOPMENT

The first attempt to identify the "elements," basic indivisible materials, resulted in a list of four substances: earth, air, water, and fire. The ancient Greeks identified nine modernly recognizable elements: gold, silver, mercury, copper, lead, tin, iron, sulfur, and carbon. As elements and compounds were identified and understood, they were put to work. Early uses for chemicals included dyeing, bleaching, tanning, brewing, embalming, baking, mining, and cleaning. Chemicals were also important to the development of art and medicine.

One of the first products of the chemical industry was borax. Borax, a naturally occurring compound containing sodium, boron, and oxygen, was known to the Babylonians and Egyptians. Marco Polo inaugurated trade in borax between the Far East and Europe. Another early product still traded in modern times was alum. Alum was used during the fifteenth century to stop bleeding. It also served as an additive to dyes to improve their ability to adhere to fabrics.

The modern inorganic chemicals industry has its roots in the discovery of the elements. The first element discovered since the time of the ancient Greeks was phosphorous. A German alchemist, Henning Brand, discovered it in 1669 during his attempts to make gold. Modern applications of phosphorous included matches (invented in 1831) and tracer bullets.

During the 1700s, a Dutch chemist decomposed borax to make boric acid. French chemists further decomposed the boric acid and discovered the element boron. Uses of boron compounds in the twentieth century have included water softeners, cleansers, fiber glass, gasoline additives, rocket fuel, fire proofing and fire fighting compounds, cosmetics, pharmaceuticals, and soldering flux. One of the most well known products was Pyrex glass. Pyrex glass was made with boron oxide to reduce the amount of expansion that occurred upon heating. As a result, unlike regular glass, Pyrex was not susceptible to cracking during heat changes. Boron was also used as a neutron-absorbent material to help control nuclear energy during power production.

In 1730, innovative procedures led to the production of sulfuric acid on a commercial scale. The corrosive substance had been used since the eighth century for a variety of purposes including tanning, tin-plating, brass-founding, and hat and button making, but the time-consuming methods employed created only weak acid. Changes introduced by Joshua Ward and improved upon by John Roebuck during the eighteenth century led to the industry's ability to produce stronger acid in greater volumes. By the end of the twentieth century, sulfuric acid topped the list of the most widely sold inorganic chemicals.

Other eighteenth-century discoveries included Georg Brandt's identification of cobalt, Axel Cronstedt's discovery of nickel, and Nicolas Vauquelin's identification of chromium. Cobalt chloride achieved popularity as an invisible ink, and in 1948 cobalt-60, a radioactive isotope, was found to be helpful in treating cancer, preserving foods, and sterilizing medical supplies. Nickel, previously thought to be a form of copper, was used to strengthen gold, silver, and copper. Twentieth-century applications included use in high-strength magnets and household appliances. A chromium compound developed in 1913 by Harold Brearely, an English metallurgist, became widely known as "stainless steel." By the late eighteenth century, 30 elements were known.

During the early nineteenth century, researchers learned more about separating the components of naturally occurring compounds. It was a time of rapid discovery and many more ingredients used by the modern inorganic chemicals industry were identified. For example, Sir Humphry Davy, an English scientist, discovered sodium, potassium, magnesium, calcium, barium, and strontium. A French chemist, Bernard Courtois, accidentally discovered iodine during experiments with seaweed in which he was trying to produce sodium nitrate to make gunpowder for Napoleon's army. Antoine Balard, another French chemist, discovered elemental bromine. Although pure bromine was poisonous, compounds were used as sedatives and in synthetic dyes. Silver bromide, a light-sensitive compound, was a critical component used to produce photographic film. In gasoline, bromine served as an antiknock additive. Johann Afrwedson, a Swedish chemist, discovered lithium. Lithium, a light alkali metal, weighed only one fifth as much as aluminum and burned when exposed to air. Copper and steel manufacturers exploited this tendency and used lithium to eliminate gas pockets that occurred during metal fabrication. Lithium compounds were also used during World War II to lift emergency radio antennas. They have also served as solid rocket fuels.

In 1860 German chemists Robert Bunsen and Gustav Kirchhoff discovered cesium. Cesium was the first element to be discovered using a light spectroscope, a device used to measure the light given off from a heated material. According to spectroscopic theory, no two materials emitted the same light pattern, each element had its own "fingerprint." Cesium, an element that easily released its electrons when exposed to light, was later used in the development of television and space technologies.

Another discovery made during the 1860s was the creation of elemental fluorine by the English chemist George Gore. Gore succeeded in creating only a small amount of fluorine, however, and it spontaneously exploded. In 1886 Henri Moissan, a French chemist, developed a process to produce fluorine in platinum vessels without explosive results. In the twentieth century, fluorine was used in the separation of uranium for atomic weapons, as a component in liquid rocket fuel, and in combination with carbon to make fluorocarbons. Fluorocarbons were used to replace ammonia in refrigeration systems and as propellants in aerosol cans before they were banned due to their damaging environmental impact. Fluorine was also used as a water additive to prevent tooth decay.

The 1860s also brought the development of synthetic dye manufacturing in Germany. The German synthetic dye producers evolved into world chemical production leaders. BASF (Badische Anilin und Soda Fabrik), for example, was established in 1861 originally as a manufacturer of alkali and related products. A BASF chemist enabled the company to expand by developing a method to produce alizarin (a yellowish-red compound) on a commercial scale. Other large German dye companies included Hoechst and Bayer. By the early twentieth century, the German companies held almost 90 percent of the world's dye production ability.

The Dow Chemical Company, founded in 1897, originally sold bromine and chlorine. The first additions to its product line included chloroform, sodium, magnesium, and calcium. Soon after, other corporations joined the roster of chemical manufacturers. They included the Hooker Electrochemical Company (1905), American Cyanamid (1907), Shell Chemical (1912), and Occidental Chemical (1920).

One of the biggest influences on the early twentieth century chemical industry was World War I. During this period, governments sponsored research and guaranteed purchase contracts for finished products. As a result, chemical companies developed new products more quickly than would have been economically possible during times of peace. Following World War I, the German chemical companies regrouped and formed IG Farben, the largest chemical group outside the United States. According to one estimate, IG Farben employed one out of three chemical workers in Germany by 1928. Following World War II, however, IG Farben was divided into three companies, BASF, Bayer, and Hoechst, its principal founders.

In the United States, DuPont invested its war profits by expanding into production areas such as rayon, plastics, ammonia, heavy chemicals, insecti-

cides, electrochemicals, paints, pigments, and varnishes. American Cyanamid, originally a producer of fertilizers, also expanded. New areas included chemicals and chemical catalysts.

During the 1920s, mergers and acquisitions expanded the political influence held by U.S. chemical companies. Allied Chemicals was formed in 1920 through the merger of five previously existing chemical companies. Allied specialized in heavy inorganic chemicals and dyes. Union Carbide was founded in 1920 from three previously existing firms. Domestic chemical producers benefited from reduced foreign competition in the years between World War I and World War II. The Fordney-McCumber Act of 1922, for example, required that imported chemical products be sold at the same price as domestically produced chemicals. As a result, the chemical industry was one of the fastest growing industries in the country. By 1935, the combined value of the nation's 26 chemical companies was estimated at $1.7 billion.

World War II brought increased demand for chemical products. These included chemical weapons, bombs, and incendiary devices, as well as a host of new products designed to meet the demands of developing technologies such as aviation. Other products developed by the industry included flameproofing and waterproofing materials. From 1947 to 1978 U.S. chemical production increased 900 percent. During the 1970s, however, environmental issues came to the forefront of the nation's conscience and challenged the safety of many products produced by the inorganic chemicals industry. The Environmental Protection Policy Act of 1970 established the Environmental Protection Agency (EPA) and subsequent legislative and regulatory efforts had far reaching effects on the industry. For example, the Toxic Substances Control Act of 1976 gave the EPA authority to regulate chemicals posing a risk to the environment or to human health.

Nevertheless, expansion continued. By the mid-1980s approximately 60,000 chemicals were being used in the United States, and new industrial chemicals were being developed at a rate of about 1,000 per year. Concerns about safety also escalated, and waste disposal methods were criticized. In 1984, Lee Niedringhaus Davis, a writer specializing in the social impact of high technologies, wrote, ''each person now contains within his or her body a mixture of poisonous chemicals that no generation throughout humankind's entire history ever accumulated. Their long-term consequences we can only guess at.''

Chemical-producing companies employed the following methods to reduce the amounts of waste generated: recapturing and reusing materials previously discharged; using wastes as raw materials for other products; increasing the efficiency of chemical reactions; using waste materials as energy sources; and processing wastes into products by finding innovative uses for them. As companies began to change their views about waste materials, terminology changed. According to Davis, the increasing popularity of the term "co-product" reflected a changing attitude where substances previously discharged as polluting wastes were instead viewed as potential products.

CURRENT CONDITIONS

As the inorganic chemicals industry entered the 1990s, questions about pollution and other environmental and health issues remained major concerns. One chemical under increasing criticism is hydrofluoric acid (HF). Overall demand for HF, an ingredient in the manufacture of chlorinated fluorocarbons (CFCs), was falling during the early 1990s as a result of CFC phaseouts. Some industry analysts expected demand for the chemical to continue declining, but others anticipated a rebound as CFCs were replaced with chemicals containing greater percentages of HF.

HF, however, had many other uses. It was commonly used for the manufacture of other chemicals, aluminum production, stainless steel pickling, and as an octane booster in the petroleum industry. Some well-known end products created with HF technology included computer screens, fluorescent light bulbs, semiconductors, and fluoride toothpaste. Despite its wide-spread use, *Audubon* magazine called HF "the most dangerous chemical in town." HF, a hazardous material, boils at 68 degrees Fahrenheit. As a result, spills of the chemical form dense, low-lying toxic clouds. One accident in 1987 sent more than 1,000 people to the hospital.

A legal action against Mobil in California led to the issuance of a consent decree in 1990 requiring all refineries in the state to stop using HF by the end of 1997. Industry watchers estimated that nationwide consumption of HF by gasoline refineries totaled 40 million pounds per year. Nevertheless, only half the gasoline refineries in the country depended on HF; the rest relied on sulfuric acid. According to Mobil, expenses related to switching from HF to sulfuric acid were expected to approach $100 million. Sulfuric acid, although still considered a hazardous chemical, posed less danger than HF. Sulfuric acid had a much higher boiling point, 625 degrees Fahrenheit, and as a result, remained in a liquid state if spilled. Because sulfuric acid does not boil at naturally occurring ambient temperatures, it poses no threat of hard-to-control toxic cloud formation.

During the early 1990s, sulfuric acid was one of the most widely used industrial chemicals. Annual demand exceeded 40 million tons and was expected to top 45 million tons by 1995. As the petroleum refining industry turned away from HF, some industry watchers predicted increased domestic demand for sulfuric acid. Others, however, expected no overall demand increase because of its reduced use in historically important markets, such as rayon production. Sulfuric acid was also used in phosphate and nitrogen fertilizers, ore processing, inorganic pigments, inorganic and organic chemicals, pulp and paper manufacturing, synthetic rubber production, plastics, water treatment, and soaps and detergents.

Another product of the inorganic chemicals industry facing environmental and safety challenges was hydrazine. Approximately 40 percent of the hydrazine produced in the United States was used as an anti-corrosion agent in boilers; however, users began turning to alternative products after hydrazine was identified as a carcinogen. Some hydrazine producers began promoting closed handling systems to permit customers to continue using hydrazine without exposing their workers to dangerous concentrations of the chemical.

One chemical product benefiting from the increasing emphasis on environmental safety was hydrogen peroxide. A report published in 1993 suggested that the North American hydrogen peroxide market was expanding at a rate of about 10 to 12 percent annually. One of its primary uses was as a substitute for chlorine in the pulp and paper industry. Other areas of anticipated growth included the detoxification of cyanide used in gold mining, laundry and cleaning products, water treatment, and pollution control.

New EPA Limits on Toxic Pollution. In March 1994 the Environmental Protection Agency announced long-expected regulations regarding toxic air pollution as part of the 1990 Clean Air Act. Under the new rule, "the nation's chemical companies will have to cut their plants' toxic air pollution by almost 90 percent from 1990 levels," according to the *Detroit Free Press.* "The rule requires the companies . . . to install equipment to better prevent evaporation and leaks of 112 toxic chemicals." Environmental Protection Agency Administrator Carol Browner called the rule the most far-reaching effort ever taken to reduce air toxics. Prior to the new regulations, only 13 air toxics were federally regulated, with others regulated in varying fashions at the state level. To meet the requirements of the new rule, the EPA estimates that approximately 370 chemical plants across the nation will be forced to cut toxic air pollution by a total of 506,000 tons. David Driesen of the Natural Resources Defense Council commented that "it's the first time that the agency has really addressed the wide variety of toxic emissions from these plants." The *Detroit Free Press* pointed out, however, "the chemical industry will have to spend $450 million on capital improvements and another $230 million a year in ongoing costs to satisfy the requirements, which will go into effect in most cases within three years." The *Free Press* noted that chemical companies have in many cases already initiated efforts to improve their pollution emissions in anticipation of the EPA ruling. Company spokespersons for Dow Chemical and Upjohn, for instance, say that both companies have reduced air pollution levels at their plants by more than 50 percent in recent years.

INDUSTRY LEADERS

One of the largest companies in the industrial inorganic chemicals category was Dow Chemical Company. The organization was founded in 1897 by Herbert Henry Dow, and its first two products were bromine and chlorine. Other products added during the company's early years included sodium, magnesium, calcium, synthetic dyes, chemical fertilizers, food preservatives, solvents, and caustic soda. Throughout the twentieth century, Dow acquired other companies and diversified into many areas including chemicals, plastics, hydrocarbons, energy, pharmaceuticals, and consumer products.

Dow was an early pioneer in toxicology work. The company established its first toxicology laboratory in 1933 following the deaths of workers from chemical exposure. Dow was also working to reduce the environmental impact of its products and manage solid wastes in a more responsible manner. In 1991 Dow created a Corporate Environmental Advisory Council, the first of its kind in the industry. The Council was comprised of professionals from the government, education, environmental protection, and scientific communities who met together to discuss issues concerning environment, health, and safety.

By 1992, Dow was the sixth largest chemical company in the world, measured in terms of sales. Dow's sales totaled $19 billion, a slight increase over 1991; however, because of falling prices due to recession of the global economy, the increased sales brought reduced profits. Dow manufactured its products at 178 facilities in 33 countries and offered a product line of more than 2,000 goods and services. Global employment reached 61,000. The company

boasted that in 1992 its researchers received 335 U.S. patents and 1,385 international patents.

Another leading company involved in the production of industrial inorganic chemicals was W. R. Grace and Company. In 1992 Grace reported annual sales in excess of $5 billion. The company was active in 48 states and 50 countries. Grace, the world's largest specialty chemicals company and largest manufacturer of catalysts, also supplied products to the construction and water treatment industries. Grace additives provided fireproofing, waterproofing, insulation, and anticorrosive benefits.

The company's Grace Dearborn Division provided products for wastewater treatment and industrial cooling and boiler water systems. The division also supplied chemicals to the paper, oil, and petrochemical industries. In 1992, Grace Dearborn finished a $1.7 million expansion of its research facility in Antwerp, Belgium in order to better serve increasing global demand for water treatment products.

In 1992, Grace introduced Grace Emission Control Products, a new line aimed at the environmental market. One example in this innovative category, was a system designed for use by industrial customers attempting to reduce their emissions of volatile organic compounds. Grace reported its own annual expenditures to meet and surpass environmental, health, and safety standards totaled $150 million.

A third leader within the industry was the FMC Corporation. FMC reported sales of $4 billion in 1992. Approximately 45 percent of the company's total sales represented foreign trade. FMC divisions held top positions in several segments of the inorganic chemicals market. Its Lithium Division, the world's largest producer of lithium chemicals, served a wide range of customers including manufacturers of aluminum, ceramics and glass, lubricating greases, textiles, air conditioning, and pharmaceuticals. The company's Peroxygen Chemicals Division was one of the world's largest producers of hydrogen peroxide and served such customers as the pulp and paper, textile, detergent, electronics, and environmental industries. FMC Foret, S.A., the company's European division, supplied products to a variety of users including other chemical manufacturers and the detergent industry.

Like many of its competitors, FMC was heavily affected by environmental legislation. The company reported that its waste releases were decreased by 30 percent between 1987 and 1992. In addition, FMC voluntarily participated in an Environmental Protection Agency (EPA) program to reduce its emissions of specific hazardous chemicals.

WORK FORCE

According to government statistics for 1992, this industry employed 88,000 workers. This figure reflects a continued steady level in the employment picture for this industry. In 1981 Department of Labor statistics indicated a total work force in the industry of more than 107,000 employees; by 1987 the number of workers had fallen to 87,000, but the industry has held steady at about that figure since that time. Four states, South Carolina, Tennessee, Washington, and Ohio, accounted for over half the employment within the industry. Of the almost 700 companies classified in the industry, about 50 percent employed fewer than 20 people.

One of the major issues confronting the industry's labor force was worker health and safety. The chemical industry had a long history of exposing its workers to hazardous situations. For example, in the latter half of the 1800s, the Leblanc method of reacting sulfuric acid on salt to produce alkali created hydrochloric acid gas as a by-product. The hydrochloric acid gas rotted workers' teeth, led to chronic bronchitis, and caused skin ailments. Moreover, industrial accidents involving chemicals often resulted in greater harm to workers and the environment than accidents in other industries.

To address the needs of workers, Congress passed the Occupational Safety and Health Act of 1970. The Act created the Occupational Safety and Health Administration (OSHA) within the U.S. Department of Labor. OSHA's responsibilities included establishing safe standards for chemical exposure and keeping workers informed of potential risks. Chemical companies also began to address safety needs with greater vigor and introduced increasing numbers of voluntary measures to help ensure employee and public safety.

RESEARCH AND TECHNOLOGY

As the chemicals industry evolved during the twentieth century, the cost of investigating and developing new products was very high. Many new compounds studied by researchers were rejected because they failed to meet expectations, were too expensive to produce, or posed safety problems. Another related problem was rapid obsolescence of products and related manufacturing methods. Because technologies changed so quickly, new products were sometimes outdated before their developing companies could recapture costs associated with research and development. Additionally, as technologies changed many manufacturing methods were also becoming obsolete.

By the 1990s, however, many products within this industrial classification were considered basic commodities. As a result, research activities to develop new products were conducted with less vigor than in other segments of the chemical industry. Instead of focusing on new product development, most research looked at ways to reduce production costs by reducing labor costs, cutting energy needs, improving process efficiencies, and finding new applications for existing products. Researchers also investigated ways to meet environmental mandates by curtailing emissions, putting waste products to work, recapturing materials, and rendering hazardous substances inert.

INDUSTRY INFORMATION SOURCES

Busch, Gretchen, "HF Future Tied to CFC Phaseout," *Chemical Marketing Reporter*, July 13, 1992.

Chemical Manufacturers Association 1991 - 1992 Annual Report. Washington, DC: CMA, 1992.

"Chemicals," *Standard & Poor's Industry Surveys*, New York: Standard & Poor's Corporation, 1993.

Coeyman, Marjorie, and Natasha Alperowicz. "Future Stays Bright for H2O2 Despite Slower Growth, Overcapacity in 1992," *Chemical Week*, February 17, 1993.

Davis, Lee Niedringhaus, *The Corporate Alchemists: Profit Takers and Problem Makers in the Chemical Industry*, New York: William Morrow and Company, 1984.

Dow at a Glance, Midland, MI: Dow, nd.

Dow 1992 Annual Report. Midland, MI: Dow, 1993.

Flaschen, Steward S. *Search and Research: The Story of the Chemical Elements*. Boston: Allyn and Bacon, 1965.

FMC 1992 Annual Report. Chicago: FMC, 1993.

"Grace Fact Sheet," Boca Raton, FL: W. R. Grace, 1993.

Grace, W. R. & Company Annual Report 1992. Boca Raton, FL: W. R. Grace, 1993.

Hunter, David. "Hydrazine: An Uproar Over New Projects." *Chemical Week*, February 8, 1989.

"Hydrofluoric Acid," *Chemical Marketing Reporter*, July 29, 1991.

Peterkofsky, David, "Running Hot and Cold," *Chemical Marketing Reporter*, April 13, 1992.

Santos, William, "Sulfuric Acid Oversupply Keeps Prices in Abeyance," *Chemical Marketing Reporter*, April 19, 1993.

Selcraig, Bruce, "The Most Dangerous Chemical in Town," *Audubon*, November-December 1992.

Sternberg, Ken, "Use of Hydrofluoric Acid Comes Under the Gun in California," *Chemical Week*, October 31, 1990.

"Sulfuric Acid," *Chemical Marketing Reporter*, September 16, 1991.

Trost, Cathy, *Elements of Risk: The Chemical Industry and Its Threat to America*, New York: Times Books, 1984.

"U.S. Chemicals Challenged in Global Marketplace," *Chemical Marketing Reporter*, April 5, 1993.

U.S. Industrial Outlook 1994, Washington DC: Department of Commerce, 1994.

Williams, Mike, "EPA Sets New Limits on Toxic Pollution," *Detroit Free Press*, March 2, 1994.

Woodburn, John H., *Opportunities in Chemistry Careers*, Chicago: National Textbook Company, 1987.

Worobec, Mary Devine, *Toxic Substances Controls Primer*, Washington, DC: Bureau of National Affairs, Inc., 1984.

—Karen Bellenir

SIC 2821

PLASTICS MATERIALS AND RESINS

The plastics materials and resins industry is comprised of companies primarily engaged in manufacturing various resins and plastics for sale to other industries that create plastic sheets, rods, films, and other products. Information on related products can be found under **SIC 2822: Synthetic Rubber, SIC 2823: Cellulose Manmade Fibers,** and **SIC 2824: Organic Fibers—Noncellulosic.**

INDUSTRY SNAPSHOT

Synthetic plastic was invented late in the eighteenth century, and did not reach widespread use in the United States until the 1900s. Swift advances in chemical and manufacturing technologies during the twentieth century, however, made plastic one of America's most important manufacturing materials. Massive demand for plastic had propelled the industry past $30 billion in annual sales by the early 1990s—a figure approximately equal to personal computer industry revenues. Plastic manufacturers employed over 60,000 workers in 1993 and exported more than $4 billion worth of material.

The industry realized a healthy average growth rate of about six percent during the 1980s, as plastics increasingly invaded markets formerly dominated by wood, metal, glass, and paper products. Moreover, growth was spurred by the development of new and better plastics that spawned new uses for industry output. Although an economic recession caused growth to lag and profit margins to suffer in the early 1990s, the long-term outlook for plastics was optimistic in the mid-1990s. New technology and increased demand were expected to boost production and profits throughout the decade and into the twenty-first century.

ORGANIZATION AND STRUCTURE

Plastics provide an important alternative to natural materials for a plethora of applications. One of the most important distinguishing factors between plastic and other materials, such as metals or ceramics, is plastic's ability to "creep" under load, or gradually stretch or flow when subjected to stress. While metals and ceramics exhibit this property as well, they do so only at much higher temperatures. Plastics also resist erosion and do not require a coating to protect them against inorganic acids, bases, and water or salt solutions. Perhaps the greatest advantage that plastics offer, however, is their ability to be molded into any shape and to be processed to exhibit any of a massive number of physical characteristics.

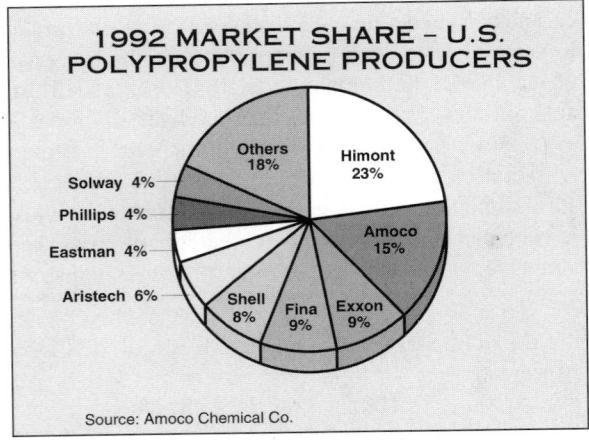

Source: Amoco Chemical Co.

Competition and Market Structure. The synthetic materials industry is considered a segment of the overall chemical industry, of which synthetic manufacturers represent about 20 percent. The plastics industry comprises about 70 percent of the entire synthetic materials industry, which also encompasses rubber and manmade fibers. Manufacturers produce about 500 different types of resins and compounds. Each of these products is available from various suppliers in multiple grades. Furthermore, each grade may offer varying physical properties and prices.

About 500 manufacturers competed in the plastics industry in the early 1990s, making it highly concentrated in comparison to most other U.S. manufacturing businesses. The average revenue per plastics establishment during this time was over $65 million—about eight times greater than the average for all other U.S. industries. The top eight producers controlled 40 percent of the market in 1987, while the top 20 firms accounted for 66 percent of production. Like many other capital intensive and concentrated industries, high barriers to entry, such as large start-up costs and technical competency, discourage potential entrants from vying for market share.

The largest consumer of plastics in the early 1990s was the packaging industry, which creates bags, bottles, food containers, and related items. That sector purchased about 30 percent of all plastics shipped. Building and construction supply manufacturers, which make plastic pipe, conduit, geotextiles, and other materials, represented about 20 percent of the plastics market. Exports accounted for an impressive 20 percent of industry output, while the remaining 30 percent of shipments were consumed by various commercial, institutional, and consumer markets. Electrical appliance and electronic component manufacturers, for instance, bought about five percent of all plastics in 1991.

Production. Plastics are giant polymers, or long-chain molecules that contain thousands of repeating molecular units. When combined with other ingredients called additives, the polymers can be shaped and molded under heat and pressure into a resin. Resin usually takes the form of pellets, flakes, granules, powder, or liquid. Most resins are not used in their natural state, but are instead combined with other materials by mixing or melt-state blending. The end result is a plastic compound, still in the form of pellets, granules, or powder, that is ready to be delivered to a processor.

The physical properties of the final plastic product can be altered at various stages of the polymerization and production process. The most versatile method of varying properties is by compounding. With this method, additives—such as colorants, flame retardants, heat or light stabilizers, or lubricants—may be added to the resin to achieve a desired result. Fillers or reinforcement—such as glass fibers, particulate materials, or hollow glass spheres—may instead be added to the resin, as may other polymers, which form a polymer blend or alloy.

Plasticizers are the most common additives used to alter plastic resins. Plasticizers increase a resin's flexibility and are often used to make polyvinyl chloride resins used in construction products. Impact modifiers are an additive used to boost a plastic's resistance to stress. Similarly, antidixodiants retard the oxidation and breakdown of plastics, and heat stabilizing additives help resins to maintain their physical structure during processing. Light stabilizers filter out radiation that can cause a plastic to deteriorate as a result of exposure to sunlight, and flame retardants enable resins to resist combustion. Colorants are another major additive used in the compounding process.

Four major commercial divisions of plastic resins are manufactured. Commodity resins, which represent the bulk of industry production, are low-tech plastics available in standardized formulas from many companies throughout the world. Intermediate resins are generally considered more advanced and somewhat specialized in comparison to commodity resins. Similarly, engineering resins generally exhibit more advanced performance characteristics and are produced on a smaller scale than other types of resin. Finally, advanced resins are generally those most capable of withstanding impact and high heat, carrying loads, and resisting attacks by chemicals and solvents.

Thermoplastics. The two main classes of plastic are thermosets and thermoplastics. Thermoplastics account for about 90 percent of industry output. They solidify by cooling and may be remelted repeatedly to form new shapes. Examples of thermoplastic resins are polyethylene, polypropylene, and polystyrene. Polyethylene is the highest volume plastic, accounting for about 40 percent of thermoplastic production, and is used primarily to create packaging, though many consumer and institutional products are made as well. About 20 billion pounds of polyethylene were produced in 1991. Major manufacturers of this resin include Quantum Chemical, Union Carbide, and Dow Chemical Co.

Polyvinyl chloride (PVC) makes up the second largest share of the thermoplastics segment. It is used primarily to make gutters, pipes, siding, windows, and other products used by construction and building industries. About 11.2 billion pounds of PVC were shipped in 1991. Major producers include Occidental Petroleum, Shintech, and Formosa Plastics. Polypropylene, another thermoplastic, accounted for about 8.3 billion pounds of production in 1991. This resin is used mainly in the creation of fiber and filaments, as well as in the production of packaging and molded consumer products. Leading U.S. producers include Amoco, Exxon, and Fina.

Polystyrene, a fourth major thermoplastic product, represented about five billion pounds of production in the early 1990s. This resin is used to make disposable packaging, furniture finishings, and miscellaneous consumer products. Other thermoplastics segments include polyamide resins, styrene-butadiene, and some polyesters.

Thermosets. Thermosets, the other division of the plastics industry, account for about ten percent of output. Unlike thermoplastics, thermosets harden by chemical reaction and cannot be melted and shaped after they are created. Thermosets are also considered the more mature and less dynamic segment of the industry. Total 1991 thermoset output was less than six billion pounds.

Typical thermosets are phenolics, urea-formaldehyde resins, epoxies, and polyester. Phenolics, which account for over 50 percent of all thermoset production, are used principally for construction products. Such materials include plywood adhesives, insulation, laminates, moldings, and abrasives. Urea, the second largest segment of the thermoset division, is also used as an adhesive for plywood and particle board. Other uses of this resin include protective coatings and textile and paper treating and coating.

Thermoset polyesters, of which just more than one billion pounds were produced in 1991, are used to create plastics that are reinforced with glass fiber and other materials. They are also used to make various construction supplies, boat and marine equipment, transportation products, and electronics. Epoxy is used mostly as a protective coating for metal goods, such as beverage cans and automobiles, but is also used in multiple construction applications. In 1991, 530 million pounds of epoxy were produced.

BACKGROUND AND DEVELOPMENT

The first plastic used in the United States was a natural material known as Keratin, which was made from animal hooves, horns, feathers, and hair. Keratin was used as a fabricating material to make lantern windows and other items as early as 1740. In the late 1800s, Americans copied a technique observed among Malayan natives, who molded a plastic made from gutta percha, or gum elastic, into knife handles and other articles. This technique had a variety of applications in the United States, from ocean cable insulation to billiard balls. Samuel Speck, regarded as the first American to mold plastics, helped to introduced shellac plastics in the 1850s. By then, in fact, different types of natural plastics were being used to produce such items as checkers, buttons, picture frames, and insulators.

"Parkesine," the first synthetic plastic, was invented in 1862 by Alexander Parkes, an Englishman. Recognizing the important plasticizing effect in the Parkesine production process, American John Wyatt renamed the substance celluloid in 1870, and was credited with originating the production of synthetic plastics in the United States. Celluloid, despite its inflammability, was used to make carriage and automobile windshields and motion picture film.

Dr. Baekland, also an American, invented the world's first moldable plastic material in 1909. Baekland's thermosetting phenolformaldehyde resin

provided a tremendous impetus for other inventors, who began developing molding techniques and adding resins to paints and varnishes. Baekland's resin, later called "bakelite," was also used in the electrical industry to make some of the first molded synthetic plastic components. The first colorless resin, urea-formaldehyde, was invented in 1918 and sold commercially in 1928.

Plastics research and development began to proliferate in the 1920s and 1930s. The Germans pioneered the creation of many new thermosetting resins, while Americans and several Europeans made significant contributions in the area of plastic molding and extrusion machines, and later in the advancement of thermoplastics. During World War II, the plastics industry realized significant advances, as warring nations hurried to develop new and better materials for their war machines.

Postwar economic expansion augmented the development of the plastics industry. As demand for all types of consumer, commercial, and institutional products soared, plastics producers scrambled to keep pace with expanding markets. Successive breakthroughs in chemical technology and production techniques opened up vast new markets for manufacturers. Most importantly, however, producers in other industries began to realize the advantages of substituting plastics for more expensive, less flexible, natural materials. By the 1970s the plastics industry was shipping more than $10 billion worth of resins per year. U.S. producers also controlled a major share of aggregate world exports.

Sales of all types of plastic resins continued to multiply throughout much of the 1980s. A variety of factors, such as excess capacity and high petroleum costs, contributed to brief periods of slow production or decreased profits. In general, however, industry participants benefitted from several factors. Growth in exports, for example, contributed to the industry's success; although U.S. chemical firms lost world market share, exports more than doubled from $2.7 billion in 1980 to $6.3 billion by 1990.

New additives and plastic alloys also increased in demand, opening entirely new markets for resins and prompting other industries to substitute plastic for more expensive, less flexible organic products. Furthermore, as many segments of the industry matured and became more competitive, falling prices allowed plastics to penetrate a number of metal, glass, and wood markets. Reinforcing downward pricing pressures were massive industry investments in research, development, and more efficient production facilities, allowing producers to remain extremely competitive domestically.

Automobile and truck makers, for example, became a vital market for resins during the 1980s as those manufacturers increasingly sought advantages related to cost and the physical properties of plastics. Similarly, electronic equipment makers, appliance producers, and other consumer products industries significantly increased their use of various resins. Packaging markets grew as well during the 1980s as disposable items, microwave foods, beverage containers, and other products that were suited to plastic gained in popularity. Importantly, a boom in U.S. construction inflated demand for resins in that important segment.

Between 1982 and 1989, plastic industry shipments rocketed from $15.8 billion per year to over $33 billion—representing average annual growth of about 8.8 percent per year. Despite massive productivity gains, moreover, employment crept upward from 54,000 in 1982 to about 62,000 by 1989. Profits surged in the late 1980s as shipments rose and manufacturers began reaping the rewards of earlier capital investments.

An economic recession in 1989, which lingered through 1993, stabilized the demand for plastics. Transportation, consumer and industrial, and packaging sectors all temporarily scaled back their consumption of resins. The construction industry, which had plunged into a virtual depression by 1990, proved a major detriment to sales growth for all types of plastics. Revenues slipped nearly $2 billion in 1990, to $31.3 billion. Correspondingly, employment shrank nearly three percent the following year, to about 61,000. Buoying earnings, however, was a 30 percent growth in 1991 exports—largely a result of a weak U.S. dollar.

Despite a lull in prices, profits, and revenues throughout 1991 and much of 1992, the industry showed signs of renewed growth. Prices and production picked up, and the U.S. economy as a whole began to improve. Although employment continued to decline, analysts remained optimistic, citing newly developed additives and compounds as boding well for the industry's continued success.

CURRENT CONDITIONS

Although 1992 profits were disappointing for most competitors, they represented an improvement over figures for 1991, prompting optimism among participants in the synthetic plastic and resin industry. Sales topped $32.7 billion in 1992, and were forecast to rise three percent in 1993. Demand also seemed to

be growing in 1993, particularly in awakening automobile and construction sectors. Prices remained relatively weak, however, following a four-year slide that ended in 1992. Although profits for the largest competitors slipped as well in 1992, smaller and mid-sized firms had stable earnings.

In the mid-1990s, many producers began to realize the benefits of cost reduction efforts implemented over the past several years. Such efforts included reducing employment, restructuring management, and closing some production facilities. Growth in emerging foreign markets, as well as solid expansion of various niches of the resin market, also encouraged competitors. Continuing development of new compounds, spurred by ever-increasing expenditures on research and development, were boosting the industry's overall share of the U.S. economy.

Industry Segment Performance. Thermoplastic resins, which led industry gains throughout the 1980s, continued to experience demand growth in the mid-1990s, particularly in the area of high-grade, low-volume resins that could serve niche markets. High-tech applications in the auto and aerospace industries for engineering and advanced resins, for example, were proliferating. Intermediate and commodity products were showing gains too. After posting an average annual production growth rate of seven percent between 1982 and 1991, thermoplastics advanced six percent in 1992 and were forecast to rise by seven percent or more in 1993.

The important polyethylene segment, which accounted for over 40 percent (22 billion pounds) of total thermoplastic output, grew slightly less than six percent in 1992. Demand for high-density polyethylene, which made up 50 percent of that segment, increased at a rate of seven percent in 1993. Prices in this category had stabilized by 1993. New technology promised several advances in polyethylene resins in the late 1990s. New compounds were being marketed in 1993, for instance, that allowed producers of shrink-wrap, carpet wrap, liner, and other film products to reduce the thickness of their material by 30 percent without compromising strength.

PVC resin production grew seven percent in 1992 to about ten billion pounds—a disappointing figure compared to the nine percent increases between 1982 and 1991. Recessed growth was largely a result of environmental restrictions implemented by both domestic and international governments. Switzerland, for example, instituted a ban on PVC water bottles in 1992 while the Netherlands contemplated similar actions. In Austria, European producers were embroiled in a lawsuit against the environmental activist group

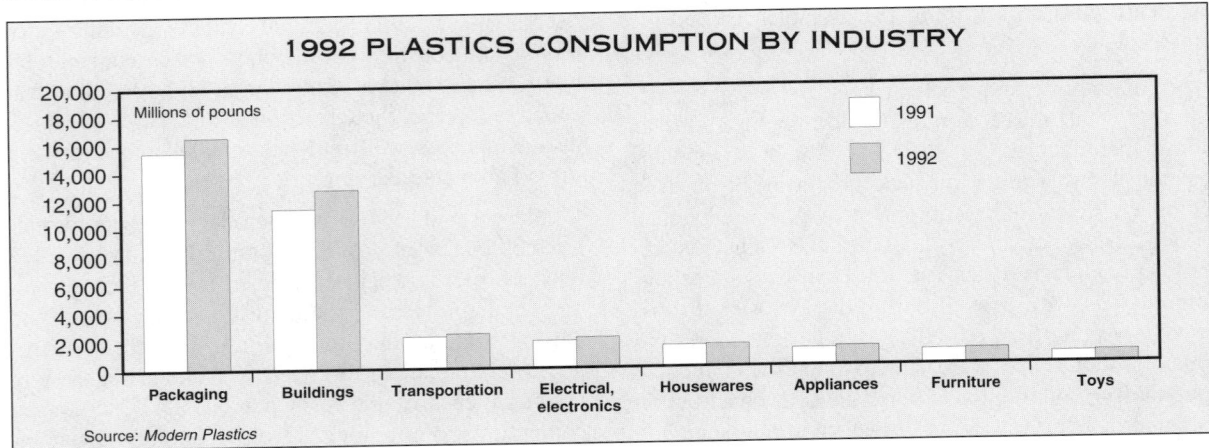

1992 PLASTICS CONSUMPTION BY INDUSTRY

Millions of pounds

☐ 1991
■ 1992

Packaging | Buildings | Transportation | Electrical, electronics | Housewares | Appliances | Furniture | Toys

Source: *Modern Plastics*

Greenpeace, which ran an advertising campaign equating PVC with poison in 1991.

Polypropylene, the third major thermoplastic, grew an encouraging nine percent in 1992 to 8.4 billion pounds produced, up from one percent annual growth between 1982 and 1991. Aided by new technological improvements and strong demand overseas, this resin was expected to realize solid gains. Prices remained weak in 1993, however—a result of global production overcapacity. High-tech resins used in car interiors and appliances were leading this segment.

Smaller thermoplastic segments posted the greatest advances in the mid-1990s. Production of styrene-butadiene, polyamides, and thermoplastic polyester grew about 15 percent in 1992. These three categories represented a combined output of about 5.7 billion pounds. Improved additives, particularly colorants, were boosting styrene-butadiene sales, though long-term growth of that resin was in question. While sales of polyester suffered due to environmental concerns, the material was becoming a viable substitute for telephone and light poles, steel and concrete, and other construction materials.

While thermosetting resins lagged behind thermostats during the 1980s, they were posting solid gains in the mid-1990s. Total thermoset output jumped seven percent to 6.3 billion pounds in 1992, contrasting with average annual gains of just four percent between 1982 and 1991. Phenolics, the largest thermoset segment, increased ten percent in 1992 to 2.9 billion pounds. New applications for transportation and other high-volume markets, improved additives and compounds, and low prices all contributed to the surge. Thermoset polyesters gained nine percent in 1992, while urea production swelled a less impressive five percent. Epoxy resins, which accounted for only four percent of

thermoset production by weight, realized output growth of 18 percent.

Environment. In 1993, the chemical industry as a whole was the largest polluting industry in the United States, producing more than three times as much hazardous waste as the second greatest offender. The industry also spent more on pollution control and clean-up than any other business sector. In 1992, for example, all chemical industries spent more than $4.9 billion on pollution abatement efforts. Furthermore, over 20 percent of all capital expenditures in the industry went toward pollution control projects in 1992.

Government efforts to counter the effects of dangerous pollutants were stepped up in the 1980s and began to pay off in the early 1990s. Chemical industry emission of toxic waste was down four percent in 1991 from 1990 levels, having declined 34 percent since 1988. Nevertheless, new regulations were forcing producers to further reduce pollution and clean up the environment. The 1990 Pollution Control Act, for example, expanded the reporting requirements for resin producers and required recovery and reuse of some production materials. Another major development in this area was the announcement in March 1994 of a new federal government rule devised as part of the 1990 Clean Air Act. As a result of the new rule, ''the nation's chemical companies will have to cut their plants' toxic air pollution by almost 90 percent from 1990 levels,'' observed the *Detroit Free Press*. ''The rule requires the companies . . . to install equipment to better prevent evaporation and leaks of 112 toxic chemicals. . . . Under the 1990 Clean Air Act, the EPA was supposed to issue regulations curbing industrial toxic chemical releases by November 1992, specifically requiring chemical manufacturers to install the best available technology to capture the releases. Environmentalists accused the Bush administration of delaying action because of industry pressure and filed suit.'' The new ruling by the EPA is aimed at meeting that federal judge's ruling. The Environmental Protection Agency calls the new regulations the most comprehensive effort ever taken to reduce toxic air pollution, while representatives of the chemical industry point out that many chemical companies have already drastically reduced their toxic pollution emissions in anticipation of the new rule. They argue that EPA estimates ($450 million on capital improvements and $230 million annually in ongoing costs) of the cost of satisfying the requirements are far too low.

Environmental regulations also affected the businesses of resin buyers. Packaging producers, for example, struggled to find ways of reducing their contribution to overburdened landfills. Auto and truck makers met with some success in developing recyclable vehicle components—often with the help of plastics companies. Similarly, many plastic products were being used to solve environmental problems. Advanced geotextiles, for example, were used to develop cleaner and more efficient landfills, and recycled plastic was used in the manufacture of a wide variety of consumer goods, including outdoor furniture and parking bumpers.

INDUSTRY LEADERS

The largest U.S. company actively producing synthetic resins, plastics materials, and nonvulcanizable rubber in the early 1990s was Monsanto Corp., of Missouri. This diversified company employed over 40,000 and generated $9 billion in sales in 1991, about 70 percent of which was attributable to chemical sales. Monsanto Chemical Works was established in 1901 by John Queeny, who was able to take advantage of the country's shift to domestic chemical production after years of relying on European suppliers. Queeny's son Edgar carried the company through a period of immense expansion from 1930 through the 1950s. Subsequent sporadic growth continued through the 1980s under the direction of several leaders. The company restructured its operations in the 1980s, releasing many of its middle managers and committing greater resources to capital investments. Sales from Monsanto's chemical divisions dropped 1.3 percent in 1992, to $5.3 billion, and profits fell ten percent.

Hoechst Celanese Corp., of New Jersey, was the second largest competitor in the industry in the early 1990s. This petroleum company earned revenues of about $6.4 billion in 1991, 92 percent of which represented sales of chemicals. Although revenues grew 2.3 percent in 1992, to $6.5 billion, profits slipped over nine percent. Other large competitors included General Electric Corporation, of Massachusetts, with $5 billion in 1991 sales, and Shell Chemical Co., of Texas, with $3.6 billion in sales.

WORK FORCE

In 1993, about 61,500 workers were employed in the plastics industry. This represented a slight decline since 1990, when employment hit a peak of 62,400. Despite solid increases in the bulk weight of resins produced, producers hesitated to hire more workers, echoing a trend that prevailed throughout the 1980s, during which the value of production rose over 100 percent while total employment grew only 13 percent. The reduced work force resulted from massive increases in productivity, attained through elimination of managers, automation of manufacturing facilities, and the displacement of support staff by computer and information systems. Furthermore, decreased employment figures reflected the fact that established workers were putting in more hours.

Despite stagnant job growth, the plastics industry offered opportunities for qualified individuals in the mid-1990s. Production workers, which made up about 50 percent of the industry work force, were among the highest paid industrial workers in the United States. The average 1992 production wage of $15.92 was 52 percent greater than the average for all other U.S. manufacturers. Manufacturing positions were on the decline, however, and fell five percent in 1992 alone.

The industry remained a major supplier of high-paying jobs for those specializing in science, particularly chemists. The average chemist's annual salary in 1992 was $56,000. Chemists with master's degrees averaged $58,000, while those holding doctorates earned an average of $75,000. Opportunities for such highly educated workers decreased only slightly in the early 1990s. Nevertheless, unemployment among chemists was at its highest level since 1983, and despite salary increases of more than four percent in 1992, unemployment grew to 7.2 percent.

Although industry output and profits were expected to rise steadily, jobs for production workers were likely to drop by ten to 20 percent on average between 1990 and 2005, according to the Bureau of Labor Statistics. Experts estimated that opportunities for machine operators would realize the greatest decline—over 25 percent—and that mechanic and equipment controller jobs would fall 15 percent or more. Increases in work force were expected to affect positions related to sales, marketing, and advertising as well as engineering, mathematics, and science.

AMERICA AND THE WORLD

The U.S. plastics industry, by far the largest and most advanced in the world, was heavily dependent on exports in the mid-1990s. Overseas sales consumed about $7 billion, or over 20 percent, of U.S. resin output in 1992. Plastics accounted for about 25 percent of total U.S. chemical exports, and U.S. resin producers accounted for an estimated 36 percent of total world production in 1992. Japan, the next largest producer, manufactured less than half that amount, at 16 percent of world output, and Germany placed third with a nine percent share of the market.

European and Japanese suppliers suffered setbacks even worse than those faced by U.S. manufacturers in the late 1980s. Overcapacity and relatively low productivity plagued European community producers. Moreover, after realizing chemical industry profits of over $2 billion per year in both 1988 and 1989, Japanese plastics producers were hammered in the early 1990s by weak foreign and domestic demand. Net profits plunged to just over $1 billion per year in 1992 and 1993, as exports and revenues declined, and the country remained mired in a severe recession.

Although U.S. plastics exports doubled during the 1980s and continued to grow rapidly in the early 1990s, the United States was steadily losing its share of the global market. Expanded overseas production, particularly in the Far East, was displacing U.S. sales. Nevertheless, burgeoning foreign markets offered promising prospects for growth to savvy U.S. exporters. Furthermore, U.S. technology and productivity had succeeded in protecting domestic market share. The overall U.S. chemical industry maintained a combined trade surplus of about $16 billion in 1991. Plastic imports, moreover, accounted for only $1.8 billion of the domestic market.

The largest buyer of U.S. plastics was Canada, which purchased 16 percent, or $1.2 billion, of total U.S. exports in 1991. Mexico, the second largest customer, accounted for about eight percent, or $588 million, of exports. Belgium purchased 7.1 percent of overseas shipments, while Japan and the Netherlands each consumed about 6.9 percent of resin exports. Canada was also the largest exporter of chemicals to the United States, with 33 percent of all foreign sales. Japan held a 17 percent share of the U.S. import market, while Germany followed with 14 percent. The United Kingdom and France each represented about five percent of plastic imports.

Although U.S. exports were expected to rise two percent in 1993, observers had initially hoped for a much greater increase. Weak European and Asian markets were primarily to blame; many Asian consumers were beginning to rely on new domestic sources of resins and plastics, while the European community was simply mired in a recession. Latin American markets, in contrast, were proving surprisingly vital. Shipments to Mexico, for instance, nearly doubled between 1988 and 1992, explaining the industry's strong support for the North American Free Trade Agreement (NAFTA). Industry participants in 1993 were also strongly supportive of the pending General Agreement on Tariffs and Trade, an agreement that promised to significantly boost sales in Europe.

Unable to significantly penetrate U.S. markets, foreign companies participated in U.S. plastics markets primarily through direct investment during the 1980s and early 1990s. Overseas investment in the overall chemical industry climbed from just $14.4 billion in 1982 to $45.6 billion in 1990, and to $49.1 billion by 1991. Foreign chemical companies that invested in U.S. companies sought access to U.S. technology, markets, and research and development. Such investment was expected to continue throughout the 1990s, though on a smaller scale.

RESEARCH AND TECHNOLOGY

The plastics industry invested a major portion of its resources in research and development. In the early 1990s, industry participants were making capital investments of over $2.5 billion annually, amounting to about eight percent of total revenues. The industry invested about six times more per employee than did the average U.S. manufacturer in 1992. While many investments in the 1980s were used to expand production capacity and develop new products, producers in the early 1990s emphasized investments in productivity gains rather than capacity.

Research and development related to new products focused on the creation of specialty materials for niche markets, designing high-performance resins, and upgrading the properties of commodity thermoplastics. Thermoplastic research and development also concentrated on formulating resins that could compete with lower-priced materials. New additives and alloys played an important role in such advancements. However, emerging polymerization technology also offered strong growth potential for cutting-edge manufacturers. For instance, numerous and promising breakthroughs in bimodal resins, which typically combined two polymer types, were helping to enhance the balance of properties and processability of plastics.

Technological advancements occurring in other industries also promised to boost plastics sales. Resin processors, for instance, had developed new extrusion and molding devices, allowing manufacturers to maximize the benefits of new compounds and alloys. Such compounds held promise for makers of cars and appliance manufacturers, which sought stronger, light-weight materials. Similarly, processing techniques that complemented lighter, stronger, and thinner plastics promised to boost the use of plastics in all types of packaging applications.

Environmental concerns continued to fuel major research efforts. Low-styrene emission products, which limited volatile organic compound emissions during production, were receiving much attention in the mid-1990s, as were polyester composites that could be used to enhance corrosion resistance properties. Hastening to conform with new chlorinated fluorocarbon (CFC) emissions standards, foam producers learned to use resins to create carpet padding and packaging foams, for example, that emitted little, if any, CFC.

New biodegradable plastics, including weak-link and bacterial polymers, also offered growth opportunities in the industry. Although the price of many biodegradable plastics in the mid-1990s was between two and 25 times greater than traditional resins, prices were expected to fall as the technology was refined. Biodegradable plastics were considered important for reducing the volume and longevity of waste in landfills; in the early 1990s, plastics accounted for about ten percent of all solid waste.

One of the most interesting discoveries occurred in 1993, when Maurice Ward unveiled a new polymer that withstood heat, lasers, and flames with little or no damage and let off virtually no toxic fumes in the process. "Starlite," as the new plastic was called, was intended to serve as a flame retardant material, though its uses could be widespread.

INDUSTRY INFORMATION SOURCES

Anderson, Earl V., "Foreign Trade: U.S. Chemical Trade Surplus Declines," *Chemical & Engineering News,* December 13, 1993.

Anderson, Earl V., "Japan: Once Booming Economy Struggles Through Times," *Chemical & Engineering News,* December 13, 1993.

"Chemical and Additives," *Modern Plastics,* September 1993.

Dagani, Ron, "Wonder Plastic Resists Lasers, Nuclear Heat," *Chemical & Engineering News,* April 26, 1993.

Dubois, J. Harry, *Plastics,* New York: Van Nostrand Reinhold Company, 1974.

"Facts & Figures for the Chemical Industry," *Chemical & Engineering News,* June 28, 1993.

Heylin, Michael, "Job Market for Chemists Remains Depressed, Salaries Gain 5%," *Chemical & Engineering News,* July 12, 1993.

Layman, Patricia, "Europe: Definite Though Modest Recovery Forecast for 1994," *Chemical & Engineering News,* December 13, 1993.

Loesel, Andrew, "Now You See It . . . Degradable Plastics May Be Gaining a New Life as a Second Generation of Polymers is Taking Shape," *Chemical Marketing Reporter,* July 6, 1992.

Palmisano, Anna C., and Charles H. Pettigrew, "Biodegradability of Plastics," *BioScience,* October 1992.

Rawis, Rebecca L., "Salaries," *Chemical & Engineering News,* October 25, 1993.

"Resins 1993: What's in the Pipeline?" *Modern Plastics,* January 1993.

Storck, William J., "United States: Chemical Industry Lackluster This Year," *Chemical & Engineering News,* December 13, 1993.

Tuczal, Eva, and Frank Cortolano, "Reformulating PVC to Eliminate Heavy Metals and Protect Performance," *Modern Plastics,* October 1992.

Williams, Mike, "EPA Sets New Limits on Toxic Pollution," *Detroit Free Press,* March 2, 1994.

—Dave Mote

SIC 2822

SYNTHETIC RUBBER (VULCANIZABLE ELASTOMERS)

This category covers establishments primarily engaged in manufacturing synthetic rubber by polymerization or copolymerization. An elastomer for the purpose of this classification is a rubber-like material capable of vulcanization, such as copolymers of butadiene and styrene, or butadiene and acrylonitrile, polybutadienes, chloroprene rubbers, and isobutylene-isoprene copolymers. Butadiene copolymers containing less than 50 percent butadiene are classified in **SIC 2821: Plastics Materials, Synthetic Resins, and Nonvulcanizable Elastomers.** Natural chlorinated rubbers and cyclized rubbers are considered as semi-finished products and are classified in **SIC 3069: Fabricated Rubber Products, Not Elsewhere Classified.**

INDUSTRY SNAPSHOT

Production of synthetic rubber on a commercial scale began in the United States during the 1930s, though natural rubber has been used since the early 1800s for multiple applications. The United States assumed an early lead in the development and production of vulcanizable elastomers—a position which it maintained throughout the 20th century. Indeed, by the early 1990s the more than 11,000 Americans employed in the industry were churning out about 2.7 million metric tons of synthetic rubber. Industry sales exceeded $4.2 billion in 1990, about 25 percent of which were garnered from exports.

Rubber manufacturers were limping into the mid-1990s, following a gradual industry decline during the 1980s. Product maturity, stagnant demand growth, and increasing foreign competition were the dominant factors suppressing industry profitability. Although producers tried to counter this downward momentum with increased productivity and the development of new rubbers, falling prices and a sluggish world economy in the early 1990s proffered little reason for optimism. Ironically, past industry successes contributed to the industry's malaise. Long-lasting rubbers, for instance, reduced demand in large market segments such as the tire industry. Competitors were looking to new rubbers for growth in the 2000s.

ORGANIZATION AND STRUCTURE

The synthetic rubber industry represents about eight percent of the entire U.S. synthetic materials manufacturing sector. Plastics (**SIC 2821: Plastics Materials, Synthetic Resins, and Nonvulcanizable Elastomers**) and manmade fibers (**SIC 2824: Manmade Organic Fibers, Except Cellulosic**) are the other synthetics. The synthetic materials industry is considered part of the overall U.S. chemical industry, of which synthetics account for about 25 percent. Natural rubber, which represents about 20 percent of all rubber consumed in the United States, is derived from rubber trees and other organic sources. Production and processing of natural rubber is not included in the industrial classification.

Rubber offers important advantages over natural materials. Among its most beneficial characteristics are its great resistance to corrosion caused by fluids and gases, its very poor electrical conductivity, and its ability to flex and then regain its original shape. Because of the endless variety of compounds that can be created, rubber has increasingly been used as a substitute for more expensive, lower performance natural materials. Besides displacing woods, metals, and ceramics in many traditional applications, rubber has allowed the creation of completely new products.

The synthetic rubber industry shipped $4.4 billion worth of material in 1993, which was equivalent to about one quarter of the value of sales by U.S. tire and inner tube manufacturers. Despite its relative economic insignificance, however, the industry supplies billions of pounds of material and is an integral part of the United States and global industrial machine. Rubber serves a vital role in transportation industries, but is also an important production material for medical supplies, packaging and sealing devices, construction equipment, and other goods. Furthermore, U.S. producers supply about one quarter of total world rubber consumption.

Competition and Markets. The industry is highly consolidated, with only about 75 firms competing in the early 1990s. The average number of workers per company, for example, is nearly three times greater than the average for all other U.S. manufacturers. The top five establishments in the industry enjoyed combined revenues from diversified operations of over $2 billion per year in the early 1990s—equal to about 50 percent of all rubber sales. They also employed an average of 2000 workers. In contrast, the majority of even the top 40 competitors employed fewer than 100

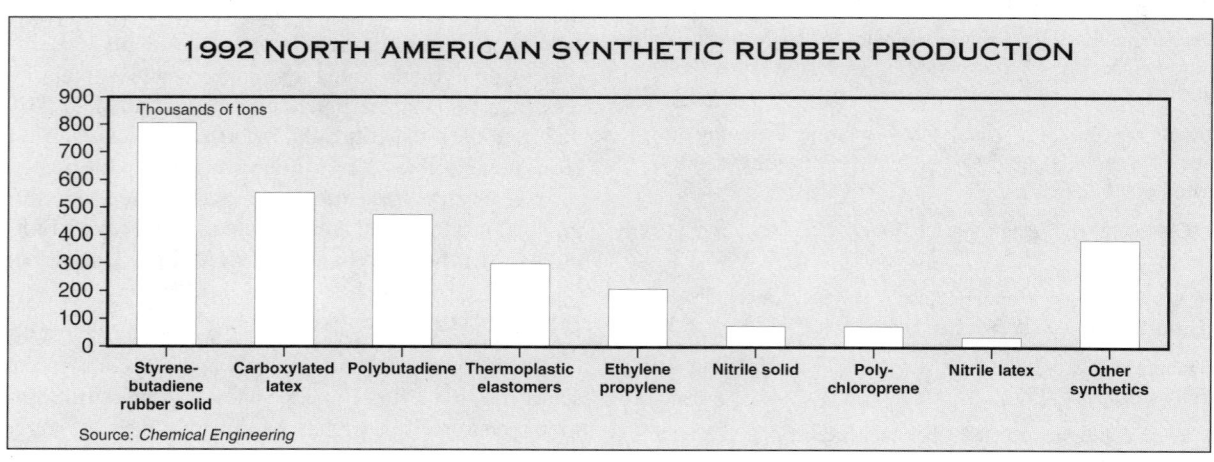

1992 NORTH AMERICAN SYNTHETIC RUBBER PRODUCTION

Source: *Chemical Engineering*

workers. Most industry participants generate less than one million dollars per year in sales. High start-up costs, low profit margins, and established market leaders discourage potential entrants to the business.

Tire and inner tube manufacturers consumed about 30 percent of industry output in the early 1990s. The remainder of the rubber market, though, is highly fragmented and is represented by a vast array of fabricated rubber products. Paper mills and floor covering producers each use about five percent of all rubber absorbed domestically, while about three percent of output is required to make hoses and belts. Adhesives, gaskets, sealants, and packing devices also consume about five percent of production. Other popular uses of rubber include the manufacture of sporting goods, medical supplies, footwear, paint, printing ink, chemical preparations, communication equipment, batteries, and cord. Outside of North America, tires and inner tubes represent about 60 percent of rubber demand.

Rubber Production. Synthetic rubber is produced by first chemically rearranging molecules in a process called polymerization, during which the molecules are made to link up in very long chains. The polymer exists as a soft, tacky thermoplastic, which can be remelted and manipulated. The thermoplastic resin is then treated with heat and chemicals to create a thermoset, a compound which cannot be remelted and formed. This process, called vulcanization, is what contributes to the resilience and elasticity of rubber compounds—physical properties that have earned rubbers the name elastomers. Most elastomers are made using petroleum, although potatoes and grains, coke (made from coal), limestone, salt, or sulfur may also be used.

Endless varieties of rubbers are produced, each of which offers different physical properties and comes in a variety of grades. Different rubbers are created during the production process, for instance, by integrating additives, adding processing chemicals, or by creating alloys with natural rubber or other thermoplastics. Numerous chemical processing agents include accelerators, activators, vulcanizing agents, antidegradants, antioxidants, flame retardants, and stabilizers. Additives include reinforcement fibers, fillers, colorants, and catalysts, such as carbon black and sulfur.

The two major elastomer divisions are commodity and specialty. Commodity elastomers, which account for the bulk of industry sales, are available at relatively low prices from several manufacturers. The most popular commodity rubber is styrene butadiene rubber (SBR), which represented about 40 percent of total output in the early 1990s. SBR is used primarily in tires and inner tubes, though it is also found in indus-

trial applications such as carpet backing, nonwoven materials, and paper coatings. Major manufacturers of this compound include Uniroyal, Goodrich Tire Co., and Goodyear.

Polybutadiene, the second largest industry segment at about 20 percent of sales, is also used mostly to create tires and treads. In addition, it is an important production material for hoses and belts. Ethylene-propylene elastomers (EP) accounted for approximately ten percent of shipments in the early 1990s. This compound is used in the construction supply industry for such products as roof membranes and foundation sealants. It is also used as an impact modifier for plastic resins. Other uses include oil viscosity additives and various auto parts, such as gaskets and seals, hoses, belts, and tubing. Other commodity thermoset elastomers include nitrile, butyl, polyisoprene, polychloroprene, and silicone.

Specialty elastomers, the second division of the synthetic rubber industry, represented about eight percent of sales in the early 1990s. Specialty elastomers offer enhanced performance characteristics, are typically more expensive, and are sold by fewer competitors than are commodity elastomers. The two main categories of specialty rubbers are silicones and fluorocarbons. Silicones are used to make vehicle mechanical parts and sealants, adhesives for construction, and electronic products. Fluorocarbons are used for O-rings, seals, and gaskets. They are also used in high-tech aerospace, automotive, electrical, and petrochemical applications.

In addition to thermosets, the specialty category also encompasses a relatively new category of rubbers called thermoplastic elastomers (TPEs). TPEs are often more economical to produce and easier to process than are thermosets. TPEs can be categorized as styrenics, polyolefins, elastomeric alloys, polyurethanes, copolyesters, and polyamides. They are often used to create high-performance adhesives, to modify plastics during the production process, and in various consumer goods applications. TPEs provide benefits associated with recycling, and typically offer greater durability, hardness, and chemical resistance.

BACKGROUND AND DEVELOPMENT

Natural rubber has been in use since at least the 15th century. Christopher Columbus, for one, witnessed Haitian natives playing games with balls "made of the gum of a tree." The first record of rubber used for purposes other than recreation was made by explorer F. Juan D. Torquemada in 1615. He saw Indians brush rubber on their cloaks as waterproofing, and also witnessed them compressing rubber in earthen molds to create footwear and bottles. Rubber was brought to Europe in the 18th century from the East Indies and used to rub out lead pencil marks—hence the term "rubber." Rubber was later transported to Europe to make raincoats and rubber thread.

A recognizable natural rubber industry evolved in the United States by the 1830s, as numerous factories sprouted along the Eastern seaboard. U.S. producers pioneered many important processing machines that furthered industry growth. For example, Mr. Edward M. Chaffe invented a rubber milling and rolling machine in 1836. Chaffe's machine, which was nicknamed "The Monster," was completed in 1937 at a cost of $30,000 and a weight of 30 tons. In another important industry breakthrough of the late 1830s, rubber's tendency to soften with heat and harden with cold was mitigated. Indeed, Charles Goodyear's discovery of vulcanization in 1839 lead to the use of rubber in many demanding mechanical applications.

Realizing the potential benefits of creating a synthetic replacement for natural rubber, scientists had been searching for a formula since the early 1800s. In 1826 Michael Faraday, an English scientist, was one of the first to successfully chemically analyze rubber. It was not until 1910, however, that S. V. Lebedev, a Russian, polymerized butadiene to produce the first synthetic rubber. This breakthrough, combined with processing and vulcanizing technologies developed during the 1800s, initiated a new era for the rubber industry.

By the 1930s, synthetic rubbers were being produced on a commercial scale only in Russia and Germany. World War I and World War II both pushed synthetic advances, as countries on all continents sought to sever their dependency on foreign natural rubber supplies. The United States, traditionally dependent on South American suppliers for natural rubber, shifted into overdrive during World War II in its quest for an inexhaustible synthetic supply. Between 1939 and 1945, in fact, U.S. production of synthetic rubber rose from a negligible experimental yield to about 820,000 tons per year.

Post World War II. World output of synthetic rubber was estimated at 10,000 tons in 1935, and 72,000 tons by 1939. Germany and Russia produced all but a small fraction. By the end of World War II, though, global production had skyrocketed to well over one million tons per year, of which the United States supplied the lion's share. Correspondingly, the share of U.S. rubber consumption served by natural rubber declined during the 1940s. In 1939, about .3 percent of all rubber used in the United States was synthetic. By 1950 that share had grown to 43 percent,

and the United States was devouring a whopping 55 percent of total global elastomer output.

Although large quantities of synthetic rubber continued to be produced after World War II, natural rubbers still dominated the market because of their superior physical characteristics. Advances in the use of recycled natural rubber boosted its popularity. In 1953, however, German chemists Karl Ziegler and Giulio Natta discovered a polymerization process that resulted in a synthetic rubber virtually identical in molecular structure to that of natural rubber. Commercial production of cis-1,4-polyisoprene was immediately undertaken in the United States, which became the dominant supplier for many war-ravaged European countries.

Augmenting the proliferation of synthetic rubber in the 1950s and 1960s was the development of new additives. New reinforcing materials allowed manufacturers to strengthen synthetics and reduce production costs, while at the same time achieving advanced performance. Asbestos, hard clay, limestone, and carbon black were among theses fillers. Similarly, plasticizers and softeners allowed producers to develop synthetics with physical properties superior to many natural rubbers. Curing and vulcanizing agents, accelerators, and age resistors all lead to the substitution of synthetics for natural rubbers and other organic materials.

Besides advances in quality and variety, synthetic rubber also benefitted from simultaneous breakthroughs in processing and molding technology used in other industries. Furthermore, the postwar U.S. economic expansion generated huge demand growth. Most importantly, the staggering growth of the automobile and truck industries during the 1950s and 1960s resulted in a vast market for tires, inner tubes, belts, and hoses. Construction and consumer markets ballooned as well. By 1960, global production of synthetic rubber stood at over two million tons per year. The United States alone produced about 1.5 million tons and devoured over 40 percent of global output. Although natural rubber still held over 50 percent of the world rubber market by 1960, synthetics supplied about 70 percent U.S. rubber demand.

While it continued to realize growth during the 1960s and 1970s, the rubber industry had clearly surpassed its stage of rapid expansion by the 1970s. Even the 1960s showed evidence of industry maturation, such as consolidation. The number of competitors manufacturing tires, for instance, plummeted from about 60 in the late 1940s to just a handful of big producers by the 1970s. Spiraling petroleum prices during the late 1970s, moreover, dampened industry profitability. Furthermore, popular synthetics that were once cutting edge materials, such as styrene-butadiene, became low-margin commodities. Foreign competition, too, began eating away at U.S. global dominance.

The 1980s. By 1980, U.S. synthetic rubber output was about 1.8 million metric tons per year. This represented a relatively slight increase over production levels of the late 1960s and early 1970s. Falling energy prices and an uptick in demand during the early 1980s, however, boosted industry output and profitability. Although the value of shipments jumped less than one percent between 1982 and 1983, the cost of production materials fell by about three percent as output jumped nearly eight percent. In 1984, moreover, output value leapt over eight percent as demand climbed steadily, causing revenues to surpass $3.4 billion.

After 1985, overall U.S. rubber output stagnated. Despite a healthy economy, U.S. synthetic rubber manufacturers were hurt by several factors, including increased imports of automobile, tire, and rubber products; the trend toward smaller cars that used smaller tires; and the increased use of long-lasting radial tires. Exports from Southeast Asia, as well as other regions of the world, were also cutting into demand from other market segments. Between 1982 and 1990 total industry output grew just 22 percent, from about 1.8 million to 2.2 million tons.

Despite sluggish demand in traditional commodity synthetic rubbers, such as SBR, the industry managed to maintain a fairly strong revenue growth rate of about five percent during the 1980s. This was accomplished through the development and sales of improved compounds and specialty rubbers. Production volumes of polybutadiene and ethylene-propylene, for instance, advanced 44 percent and 89 percent, respectively, between 1982 and 1991. Specialty TPEs, moreover, grew from a negligible share of the market in the early 1980s to account for about eight percent of domestic industry consumption by 1991.

Although their share of the world rubber market declined in the 1980s and early 1990s, industry participants enjoyed solid export growth as foreign consumption of rubber slowly, but steadily escalated. Despite sluggish domestic markets, exports grew between three percent and five percent per year in the late 1980s and early 1990s. The demand for proprietary high-tech rubbers by overseas consumers was particularly strong.

CURRENT CONDITIONS

Synthetic rubber manufacturers were able to buoy earnings throughout the early 1990s. Unfortunately,

though, a domestic and global economic recession that began in 1989 and lingered through 1993 put the squeeze on industry profitability. Shipment volume declined .03 percent in 1989, .07 percent in 1990, and over four percent in 1991, while plant utilization dipped to a depressing 68 percent. Industry revenues grew about than one percent per year in 1987 dollars during that period. Although output jumped a surprising nine percent in 1992, revenues gained only four percent, rising to about $4.4 billion, and an industry profit slump persisted.

A tepid economic recovery helped to boost industry expectations in 1992 and 1993. Analysts were discouraged, however, by fundamental weaknesses in rubber markets. Importantly, demand by the auto industry, which consumes 70 percent of SBR, was recessed. Overall production of SBR, in fact, had slipped from 876,000 tons to about 850,000 by 1992. Although shipments to tire producers rose about eight percent in 1992, long-term growth in that segment was expected to remain weak.

Boosted by surging exports, SBR consumption was expected to grow by about two percent annually between 1993 and 1996, according to the International Institute of Synthetic Rubber Producers (IISRP). This growth rate was expected to fade, however. A continuing preference for other synthetic polymers in non-tire applications was expected to contribute to slack price and demand growth. ''I see very low rates of growth long-term . . . ,'' said Vic Case, Marketing Manager for SBR at Goodyear, in the November 2, 1992 issue of *Chemical Marketing Reporter.* ''This is not where you would want to invest your money.''

Although commodity polybutadiene and ethylene-propylene elastomers generally outperformed SBR during the 1980s and early 1990s, continued expansion of these segments was in question. As it entered a phase of maturity, polybutadiene was expected to offer a tepid growth rate of only two percent through the mid-1990s. Commodity ethylene-propylene markets were already recessing in the early 1990s, following a rapid rise during the early and mid-1980s. Although sales surged slightly in 1992, weak auto and construction markets were expected to restrain demand for this thermoset.

High-Tech and Thermoplastic Opportunities. To sustain profits going into the mid-1990s, producers were looking to smaller industry segments for expansion. The greatest opportunities for profits in the mid-1990s were expected to be in TPEs. Besides their recyclability and often lower production costs, thermoplastics combined the rubber-like flexibility characteristic of thermoset rubbers with the heightened processing versatility of plastic. As a result, TPEs were expected to grow by seven percent or more per year throughout the 1990s. Furthermore, worldwide consumption of TPEs should rise from 680,000 tons in 1992 to more than 1.1 million tons by the year 2000.

Besides cannibalizing market share held by thermoset rubbers, TPEs were creating entirely new markets for the industry. Styrenic TPEs, for example, offered significant potential for use as an asphalt modifier to keep roofing and roadways from cracking. High-tech niche TPEs were making inroads into industries such as medical, construction, and food packaging. New TPEs, for example, were being used in the plumbing industry to deliver drinking water that could meet strict new federal standards. Other TPEs were being developed to make everything from ski boots and swimwear to auto body panels that could be painted without a primer coat.

Like TPEs, high-performance thermosets also promised to buoy the earnings of the most savvy producers. Growth rates for some specialty ethylene-propylene elastomers, for instance, were expected to exceed 15 percent in the mid-1990s. High-performance nitrile rubbers were finding use in applications that required heat, chemical, and abrasion resistance. Some nitrile rubbers were forecast to realize 15 percent to 35 percent growth during the mid-1990s.

Environment. One of the greatest obstacles to success for synthetic rubber producers in the mid-1990s was environmental controls. The overall chemical industry was by far the largest polluting industry in the United States, and rubber producers contributed significantly to that reputation. Besides emitting large doses of hazardous chloro-fluorocarbons (CFCs) into the air during the production process, rubber producers were also charged with creating end-user products that would not degrade. Furthermore, rubber manufacturers suffered from environmental controls that impacted their consumers, such as fuel efficiency and emissions standards that were encouraging the production of smaller cars (and tires).

New environmental mandates (see **SIC 2821: Plastics Materials, Synthetic Resins, and Nonvulcanizable Elastomers**) were forcing manufacturers to bring their production facilities into compliance with federal and state rules. Such retrofitting was costing many companies millions of dollars. "We're faced with an immense amount of cost considerations and capital investment, and a severe loss in revenue generating power for the business," said Glen Steady, vice-president of Industrial Business at Copolymer Rubber & Chemical, in the November 2, 1992, issue of

Chemical Marketing Reporter. "All this finds its way onto the balance sheet."

Partially in an effort to allay criticism of nondegradable rubber waste, The Rubber Manufacturer's Association (RMA) had taken a lead role in reclamation and recycling efforts during the 1980s and 1990s. Although thermoset elastomers cannot be truly recycled, efforts were underway to convert rubber waste to other uses in the mid-1990s, such as highway asphalt production and fuel for energy plants. Tires, which consume about 60 percent of all elastomer output, were a focal point of such endeavors. In 1990 about eight percent of the 240 million tires discarded annually were reused. By 1992 this percentage had jumped to 24 percent. By 1994, moreover, the RMA's Scrap Tire Management Council expected that figure to double to nearly 50 percent.

INDUSTRY LEADERS

The largest company competing in the synthetic rubber industry in the early 1990s was Uniroyal Chemical Co. Inc., of Connecticut. This diversified industry giant generated $832 million in 1991 sales and employed nearly 3,000 workers. Uniroyal's Ameripol-Synpol unit was a major supplier of SBR for the tire and automotive industries. Company revenues grew 2.8 percent in 1992 to $856 million, and operating profits climbed 7.1 percent to $110 million.

The second largest competitor in this highly consolidated industry was GenCorp Polymer Products, of Ohio. GenCorp, by far the largest enterprise primarily engaged in the production of rubber, generated 1991 sales of $491 million. Although revenues slipped to $482 million in 1992, operating profits climbed an impressive 9.8 percent to $45 million. GenCorp employed about 3,000 workers.

Jesup Group Inc., of Florida, was the third largest player in the industry in the early 1990s. Jesup earned revenues of $292 million in 1991 and employed 2,100 workers. Mobay Corp., of Ohio, had 1991 sales of $270 million and employed 900. Copolymer Rubber, of Louisiana, followed closely with sales of $250 million and about 700 workers. Copolymer is a major producer of ethylene-propylene. Other large synthetic rubber makers include Union Carbide Corp., of Connecticut, and Polysar, of Texas.

WORK FORCE

The economic stability of some of the larger players in the industry was largely the result of actions taken during the 1980s and early 1990s. To combat downward profit pressures, manufacturers attempted to cut costs and boost productivity. A large portion of the massive capital investments made by the industry during the 1980s, in fact, was used to automate production facilities and improve information systems. Many companies also realigned their management structure and moved production facilities to foreign countries. The end result of such efforts was stagnant employment growth. Despite production increases, the number of U.S. workers employed in the industry actually declined between 1982 and 1992, from 11,800 to 11,100.

Regardless of work force cutbacks, the synthetic rubber industry, like most chemical businesses, remained a high-paying haven for most of those fortunate enough to find jobs. The average rubber production worker, for instance, earned about $36,000 per year in the early 1990s, which compared favorably to the national production worker average of about $21,000. Workers in this industry averaged about 2.5 more hours of work per week, however. Overall, the average payroll per employee was about $40,000 in the early 1990s, or about 50 percent higher than the average for all other U.S. manufacturers.

Slight productivity gains combined with stagnant output growth forecast for the 1990s and early 21st century bode poorly for future employment in the synthetic rubber industry. Jobs for most machine operators, which account for about ten percent of the work force, should decline by over 25 percent between 1990 and 2005, according to the Bureau of Labor Statistics. Positions for chemical equipment controllers, which make up seven percent of the work force, will fall by over 15 percent. Indeed, most blue-collar jobs will dwindle by at least five percent to ten percent. On the bright side, occupations related to sales and marketing will leap by over 15 percent, and work for systems analysts and computer scientists will increase by a hearty 37 percent.

The synthetic material industries are major employers of chemists and engineers. Jobs for these professionals in the rubber industry will likely grow by ten percent to 15 percent by 2005. For more information about chemical and engineering employment in this industry, see **SIC 2821: Plastics Materials, Synthetic Resins, and Nonvulcanizable Elastomers.**

AMERICA AND THE WORLD

The United States has gradually lost the unmitigated dominance of world rubber markets that it enjoyed in the 1950s, when U.S. synthetic rubber producers supplied over 50 percent of global demand. Nevertheless, the U.S. elastomer industry remains the largest, most advanced, and most productive in the world. America produced about 23 percent of total global output in 1992—far more than any other nation. It also exported over one billion dollars worth of rubber and maintained a hefty trade surplus of about $450 million.

U.S. exports rose over five percent in 1992 and were expected to jump similarly in 1993. Capital investments made during the 1980s that helped domestic producers become more competitive globally were partially responsible for export growth. Also spurring overseas demand in 1992 was a weak U.S. dollar. Canada, the largest buyer of U.S. elastomers, accounted for about 19 percent of total U.S. exports in the early 1990s. Belgium consumed 18 percent of overseas shipments, while Brazil and Mexico each purchased about 7.5 percent of domestically produced exports. Japan, the fifth largest importer of U.S. rubber, demanded about six percent of shipments. The European Community represented 35 percent of U.S. exports in the early 1990s.

U.S. consumers purchased about $530 worth of overseas elastomers per year in the early 1990s. Canada supplied 33 percent of these imports, while Japan and France each delivered 12 percent. The European Community sold approximately 43 percent of all U.S. rubber imports. Imports grew about 8.4 percent in 1992, though they declined 8.6 percent in 1991. Imports to the United States were expected to grow at a rate slightly greater than that of U.S. exports in the mid-1990s.

Notwithstanding increased use of rubber by many emerging industrial nations, overall global demand for rubber was expected to rise by only two percent to three percent per year during the 1990s. This sluggish growth will result from depressed demand for commodity rubbers in some European and Asian markets, caused in part by longer lasting rubber products.

Going into the mid-1990s, global demand for both natural and synthetic rubber was being repressed by feeble European and Japanese markets. Central Europe, for instance, registered a decline in demand of over 15 percent in 1992, as it battled prolonged economic malaise. The Commonwealth of Independent States saw a similar decline in demand of about ten percent. Likewise, consumption in Latin America and Africa slipped by three percent and five percent, respectively. Demand in Asia sunk one percent, though much of this drop was attributable to a deep recession in Japan—consumption in China, North Korea, and Vietnam expanded six percent. These figures contrasted with a rebound in total North American consumption of 11 percent in 1992.

Despite stalled growth for the overall synthetic elastomer industry, consumption of high-tech and specialty rubbers, such as TPEs, will grow at a pace of about six percent per year through the mid-1990s. Furthermore, uses of nontire rubber should grow about 40 percent faster than tire applications. Because the United States is a leader in the production of many niche elastomers, it should benefit disproportionately from global trends.

Regions of greatest demand growth in the mid- and late-1990s will include Southeast Asia and South America. Emerging industries in these regions should buoy demand for manufacturing and automobile applications. The United States will be increasingly forced to compete with low-cost domestic producers in those regions, however. American firms will significantly benefit from the 1993 passage of the North American Free Trade Agreement (NAFTA). Likewise, U.S. producers in 1993 expected to benefit from expanded access to EC markets—pending passage of the General Agreement on Trades & Tariffs (GATT) in 1994.

RESEARCH AND TECHNOLOGY

Companies in the synthetic rubber industry are heavily dependent upon research and development to maintain competitiveness. The average rubber manufacturer in the late 1980s, for instance, invested over four times more money per employee in research and development than did the average U.S. manufacturer. This amounted to five percent to seven percent of total industry sales. In 1990, moreover, the industry funneled a full nine percent, or $380 billion, of total revenues into capital investments.

Although capital investment subsided slightly in the early 1990s, elastomer producers continued to advance on three technological fronts; new product development, compliance with environmental regulations, and increased manufacturing productivity. The latter of the three was evidenced by productivity gains achieved in the early 1990s, as well as in the 1980s. Investments in new production facilities and information systems helped boost industry productivity four percent in 1990, 2.5 percent in 1991, and an impressive 6.4 percent in 1992. By contrast, the average productivity gain for all other manufacturing industries was only 2.9 percent in 1992. Gains in the early 1990s mimicked productivity jumps achieved throughout the 1980s.

Technological advances in regulatory compliance were essentially a reaction to the 1990 Pollution Prevention Act, the Clean Air Act, and a multiplicity of other state and federal controls. Although producers were making large investments in new equipment and compounds that would allow them to produce rubber with fewer hazardous emissions, they were also focusing on the development of new recyclable rubbers that would result in less after-market waste. The most important of these was recyclable TPEs. Besides offering many advantageous physical characteristics, TPEs were increasingly being used as a substitute for many nondegradable thermoset rubbers.

Progress in the recovery of thermoset rubber waste was progressing, though at a relatively slow pace. Industry participants were still searching for economically viable uses for the nondegradable compounds. Besides asphalt modification and waste-to-energy applications, elastomer refuse was being used in several civil engineering functions. It was being utilized, for example, to create road embankments, artificial reefs, and as a replacement for gravel in water cleansing systems. Some recycled rubber was also being used as a filler for tires, and to make low-tech items like mud guards for trucks.

In addition to demands for more environmentally-friendly rubber products, elastomer manufacturers were constantly under pressure to create new high-performance, cost-efficient products. While huge breakthroughs in tire longevity had been achieved throughout the 1960s, 1970s, and 1980s, for instance, producers in the early 1990s were introducing much better products. In 1991, for example, Michelin, the French tire company, introduced a cutting edge tire called the XH4. The company guarantees the tire to last 80,000 miles—longer than most people own their car. Michelin also introduced a tire in Europe in 1993 called the MXN. It delivers four percent to five percent better gas mileage than competing tires.

Many breakthroughs were occurring in the area of specialty elastomers in the early 1990s. One such example was hydrogenated nitrile, a product for which demand was expected to grow by 15 percent to 35 percent per year in the mid-1990s. Besides allowing manufacturers to more easily meet environmental emissions requirements, the substance offered superior thermo and mechanical properties. Hydrogenated nitrile can withstand temperatures of over 300 degrees Fahrenheit, for example, while normal nitrile can only endure 212 degrees of heat.

INDUSTRY INFORMATION SOURCES

Adam, Peter S., "Slow Growth Mode," *Chemical Marketing Reporter,* November 2, 1992.

Anderson, Earl V., "Foreign Trade: U.S. Chemical Trade Surplus Declines," *Chemical & Engineering News,* December 13, 1993.

Caney, Derek J., "Battles Brewing," *Chemical Marketing Reporter,* November 2, 1992.

"Chemical and Additives," *Modern Plastics,* September 1993.

"Facts & Figures for the Chemical Industry," *Chemical & Engineering News,* June 28, 1993.

Gibson, David W., "Depth and Diversity," *Chemical Marketing Reporter,* November 2, 1992.

Heylin, Michael, "Job Market for Chemists Remains Depressed, Salaries Gain 5%," *Chemical & Engineering News,* July 12, 1993.

Loesel, Andrew, "Fuel of Filler," *Chemical Marketing Reporter,* November 2, 1992.

Naude, Alice, "Down to the Bone," *Chemical Marketing Reporter,* November 2, 1992.

Rawis, Rebecca L., "Salaries," *Chemical & Engineering News,* October 25, 1993.

Reisch, Marc S., "Rubber: Slow Growth Ahead," *Chemical & Engineering News,* May 10, 1993.

Springer, Neil, "Signs of Life," *Chemical Marketing Reporter,* November 2, 1992.

Standard & Poor's Industry Surveys, New York: Standard & Poor's Corporation, December 31, 1993.

Storck, William J., "United States: Chemical Industry Lackluster This Year," *Chemical & Engineering News,* December 13, 1993.

Topfer, Kurt, "Opening New Doors," *Chemical Marketing Reporter,* November 2, 1992.

U.S. Industrial Outlook 1993, Washington, D.C.: U.S. Department of Commerce, January 1993.

—Dave Mote

SIC 2823

CELLULOSIC MAN-MADE FIBERS

The cellulosic manmade fiber industry is comprised of establishments primarily engaged in manufacturing rayon and acetate fibers in the form of monofilament, yarn, staple, or tow. These fibers are suitable for further manufacturing in other industries on spindles, looms, knitting machines, or other textile processing equipment. Synthetic fibers, which represent about 90 percent of all U.S. manmade fiber output, are classified in **SIC 2824: Manmade Organic Fibers, Except Cellulosic.**

Cellulose fibers are made from modified wood pulp that has been dissolved in a liquid. The solution is forced through small holes called spinnerets. The extrusion dries into a hard filament. The shape and physical properties of the fiber can be modified during extrusion and processing to yield numerous fiber types and grades.

Over 90 percent of industry output is rayon. This fiber is used to make apparel, home furnishings, nonwoven products, tires, and industrial goods. Less than ten percent of production the early 1990s was acetate, which is primarily used to create apparel, home furnishings, and cigarette filters. The largest consumer of rayon and acetate is the broadwoven fabric industry, which consumes over 40 percent of total production. Knit fabric manufacturers account for 20 percent of the U.S. market. 3.5 percent of industry revenues are garnered from exports.

The first patent related to the manufacture of cellulose fibers was granted in 1855. In 1883 Sir Joseph Wilson Swan, a British scientist, created the first non-flammable cellulose fiber. Commercially viable rayon fibers were invented during the 1890s. Acetate filaments were developed in the late 1800s as well, but did not receive commercial acceptance until the 1920s. During both world wars, particularly World War II, fiber development and production ballooned as warring nations sought inexhaustible supplies of apparel and textile fibers.

Rayon increased in popularity during the post-World War II U.S. economic expansion. By 1980, in fact, U.S. companies were generating more than 580 million pounds of fiber each year. Despite past growth, however, cellulose fibers were quickly losing favor to newer and better synthetic fibers, such as polyester and nylon. Between 1970 and 1990 the percentage of U.S. fibers (including organic filaments) made from cellulose declined from 28 percent to six percent.

The industry suffered stagnation and decay during the 1980s. Besides the increasing popularity of synthetic fibers, foreign competition battered industry participants. Total cellulosic fiber production slipped to about 540 million pounds per year in 1992, as industry profit growth stalled. Revenues lagged inflation with an averaged growth rate of less than one percent per year, and industry employment fell from over 14,000 in the early 1980s to about 9,500 by 1992.

Going into the mid-1990s, the nine U.S. cellulose fiber producers were hoping that lyocell, a new fiber, might spare their gasping industry. Two of the largest competitors, Courtaulds Textiles PLC and Lenzing Fibers Corp., were vying for domination of this new market segment. Lyocell offers superior performance compared to Rayon, and can be manufactured with fewer emissions of hazardous wastes. Fiber makers were also hoping to benefit from massive capital investments made during the 1980s to improve productivity and develop better fibers.

Despite manufacturer's efforts, the long-term industry outlook remained bleak. Producers in emerging industrial nations, such as China and Malaysia, will likely devour greater global market share. More stringent environmental regulations will also take their toll on U.S. competitors (see **SIC 2824: Manmade Organic Fibers, Except Cellulosic**). Employment by cellulosic fiber production workers was forecast to fall by 15 percent to 25 percent between 1990 and 2005, according to the Bureau of Labor Statistics. Even high-paying research and engineering jobs were expected to increase only slightly during that period.

INDUSTRY INFORMATION SOURCES

"Facts & Figures for the Chemical Industry," *Chemical & Engineering News,* June 28, 1993.

Layman, Patricia, "Developing Nations Lead in Fibers Production," *Chemical & Engineering News,* April 5, 1993.

McNamara, Michael, "Courtalds, Lenzing Duke it Out Over Lyocell Turf," *WWD,* July 6, 1993.

Standard & Poor's Industry Surveys, New York: Standard & Poor's Corporation, December 31, 1993.

U.S. Industrial Outlook 1993, Washington, D.C.: U.S. Department of Commerce, January 1993.

—Dave Mote

SIC 2824

ORGANIC FIBERS—NONCELLULOSIC

Establishments primarily engaged in manufacturing noncellulosic, or synthetic, fibers comprise the manmade organic fibers industry. The fibers are created in the form of monofilament, yarn, staple, or tow suitable for further manufacturing on spindles, looms, knitting machines, or other textile processing equipment. Textile glass fibers and cellulosic manmade fibers, such as rayon and acetate, are classified elsewhere.

INDUSTRY SNAPSHOT

Although experimental organic fibers existed as early as 1913, the first commercially viable synthetics were invented during the 1930s and 1940s. Explosive industry growth occurred mid-century as new fibers, such as polyester, made synthetic materials a staple of American life. By the early 1980s industry participants were generating over seven billion pounds of fibers annually worth more than $8 billion. The fibers had a

wide variety of applications and were used in the manufacture of such diverse products as underwear and truck tires.

Rapid industry expansion subsided in the 1980s, as important sectors of the fiber business matured. Although production tonnage and revenues increased slightly throughout the decade, profit margins were confined by stagnant export growth and a rising tide of imports in the form of apparel and textiles. Environmental regulations and economic recession in the late 1980s and early 1990s suppressed profits further, as manufacturers scrambled to consolidate and reduce costs.

The industry seemed to be entering a stage of modest recovery in 1992. Production increased for the first time in four years, and prices surged. Nevertheless, producers still faced stiff foreign competition and sluggish market growth, which they sought to combat by taking advantage of new technologies that allowed productivity gains and the development of new types of fibers.

ORGANIZATION AND STRUCTURE

Manmade fibers offer a less expensive substitute for many natural fibers, such as cotton, wool, and silk. In addition, many synthetic fibers have greater durability, hold their shape better, and are more uniform than natural fibers. Products created with manmade fibers typically afford greater resistance to aging and breakdown as a result of exposure to the elements. Because they can be modified to create a great variety of filaments with different physical properties and grades, synthetics provide great flexibility for manufacturers of apparel and textiles.

The two categories of manmade fibers are cellulosic and synthetic. Cellulosic fibers include such products as rayon, acetate, and triacetate, which are derived from modified wood pulp that has been dissolved in a liquid. Synthetic fibers, manufactured under SIC 2824, are derived from molecules containing various combinations of carbon, hydrogen, nitrogen, and oxygen. Examples of products in this group are nylon, olefin, polyester, and spandex.

Synthetic fibers accounted for about 90 percent of U.S. manmade fiber output in 1993. Manmade fibers constituted approximately 25 percent of the larger U.S. synthetic materials industry, which also encompassed plastics and rubbers. Synthetic materials, in turn, represented about 25 percent of the overall $300 billion per year U.S. chemical industry.

About 70 U.S. firms competed in this highly consolidated industry during the early 1990s. Even amongst the handful of competitors, earnings were top-heavy; the combined revenues of the top five firms in the business, for example, were nearly four times greater than the aggregate sales of the next five largest companies. Moreover, the majority of the largest 20 establishments employed fewer than 200 workers— compared to between 10,000 and 20,000 employed by the top few companies. Extremely high start-up capital requirements, entrenched market leaders, and proprietary technology necessary to produce high-margin fibers discouraged potential market entrants to this exceptionally competitive business.

The largest market for synthetic fibers in the United States during the early 1990s was floor covering manufacturers. This sector consumed 32 percent of fiber output to create carpeting for commercial, institutional, and consumer applications. Apparel producers commanded about 25 percent of industry production during this time, and makers of various home textile products controlled ten percent of output. Industrial products and miscellaneous consumer goods that represented 30 percent of consumption included such items as tire reinforcements, rope, surgical and sanitary supplies, fiberfill, electrical insulation, and plastic reinforcements. About four percent of total output was shipped to other countries.

Production Process. Synthetic fibers are extremely long, threadlike molecules comprised of hundreds of thousands of atoms strung together in chains. They typically originate from petroleum-based chemicals, which must first be converted into a liquid state by either dissolving it in a solution or melting it. The free-moving molecules that form the liquid are then extruded through small holes called spinnerets. The fine strands of liquid that emerge from the spinnerets are hardened to form long, silk-like filaments.

The three most popular spinning processes are known as dry, wet, and melt. In dry spinning, the fiber-forming substance is dissolved in a solvent, extruded through a spinneret, and then exposed to hot air. The heat causes the solvent to evaporate from the fiber, leaving a solid filament. Wet spinning works in a similar manner, except that the extrusion is jettisoned into a coagulating bath, which causes the fiber to harden as a result of chemical or physical change. Melt spinning is accomplished by simply melting and extruding a substance that dries upon contact with the air.

During the spinning process the filament can be manipulated to result in various physical properties and forms. This manipulation determines such attributes as drapability, softness, elasticity, perceived coolness or warmth, stiffness, roughness, and resilience. Fibers that are formed to have a dog-bone or

lobed cross-section, for instance, result in fabrics with greater density, while flat fibers give fabrics a rough feel.

After spinning, fibers go through a stretching and orientation process. During this procedure, the long molecules that constitute the fiber are pulled into alignment along the longitudinal axis of the filament. Through various techniques, the molecules can be aligned, packed, and manipulated to result in a variety of different physical characteristics. Tensile strength, dyeing properties, stretching ability, water penetrability, and resistance to breakdown are a few of the attributes that are influenced through stretching and orientation of the molecules.

Finished fibers are usually formed into monofilament, yarn, staple, or tow that can be used by other manufacturing sectors. Monofilaments, as their name suggests, are single, long strands of fiber used to create items such as nylon stockings and toothbrush bristles. Staple consists of fibers that have been cut into short lengths, usually between one and six inches. Staple can be mixed with other natural or manmade fibers to create yarns and fabrics. Tow is a fiber that is spun with hundreds of thousands of filaments bundled together into a loose rope and wound onto a spool. Tow is used like staple, but the cutting is done at a later stage to ensure that the filaments remain parallel to one another.

Products. Polyester fibers, the largest industry segment by production tonnage, constituted about 40 percent of industry shipments in the early 1990s. Among other qualities, this fiber sports low moisture retention, good electrical insulation characteristics, and high resistance to solvents. Nearly 80 percent of polyester fibers were used to produce textiles, apparel, and home furnishings. Eight percent of this segment was purchased by the tire industry to be used as rubber reinforcements, seven percent was used for other industrial applications, and five percent went towards the production of carpeting. The majority of polyester was sold in the form of either yarn or staple. Tow represented a relatively small share of segment sales.

The second most popular synthetic fiber in the early 1990s was nylon. This fiber, which comes in a multitude of characteristics and grades, accounted for nearly 30 percent of industry output. Nylon's advantages include a high strength-to-weight ratio, excellent recovery from deformation, and high abrasion and flex resistance. Seventy percent of nylon output was used to make carpeting, while about 20 percent was integrated into apparel and non-carpet home furnishings. Manufacturers of industrial products, such as tires and rope, represented the remaining ten percent of this market. Most nylon was sold as yarn, though a substantial share of output took the form of tow.

Much of the remaining 30 percent of synthetic fiber revenues were derived from the sale of olefin and acrylic fibers. Olefins, which were the fastest growing segment of the industry in the early 1990s, are used to create durable carpeting and other textiles. Acrylic, the smallest volume synthetic fiber at about five percent of the market, is used to make clothing and home furnishings, such as blankets.

BACKGROUND AND DEVELOPMENT

Evidence suggests that hemp, presumably the oldest cultivated fiber plant, was grown in China as early as 4500 B.C. Furthermore, Egyptians were already weaving and spinning linen by 3400 B.C. The spinning of silk, which provided a major impetus for the creation of artificial fibers, dates back to 2640 B.C. Flax and wool fabrics dating back to the sixth and seventh centuries B.C. have been excavated in Switzerland.

English physicist Robert Hooke was one of the first scientists to explore the possibility of extruding artificial silk, proposing a mechanical device that mimicked the silkworm. Louis Schwabe, an English weaver during the nineteenth century, was the first to successfully produce filaments from molten glass. He forced the liquid through nozzles, which caused a strand of glass to protrude and harden into a fiber. These early experiments initiated the discovery and development of manmade cellulose filaments (see **SIC 2823: Cellulosic Manmade Fibers**).

Chemists carried out the first extensive research into possible methods of creating synthetic fibers after World War I. Finding that many polymers (long chains of molecules) could be dissolved in solvents, they began extruding different polymers in spinnerets. Their initial goal was to imitate rayon, a cellulosic fiber. Breakthrough synthetic fibers were produced by German chemists in 1913 and through the 1920s. Important advances occurred in 1928, for example, when vinyl chloride and vinyl acetate were used to produce fibers. This breakthrough lead to the development of the first commercially viable synthetic textile fibers in 1936.

The synthetic industry got its practical start in 1935, when American Wallace H. Carothers, working at E. I. Du Pont de Nemours & Company, developed the first nylon fiber. This important discovery prompted intense research during and after World War II that resulted in many new classes of commercially useful synthetic textile filaments. The first polyester fiber, for example, was invented in 1941 by British

researchers. Eastman Chemical Products Inc., of the United States, introduced a vastly improved and more marketable version of that fiber in 1958. Acrylics and other polyvinyl-based fibers were developed during the 1950s.

Rapid technological advances during and after World War II paved the way for a massive synthetic fiber industry expansion during the 1960s and 1970s. Although polyester and vinyl fibers had existed for several years prior, public acceptance of textiles and apparel created with artificial filaments lagged behind technology. During the 1960s, however, fiber producers began making a wide variety of different products. Furthermore, they became proactive in opening new markets and convincing every conceivable manufacturing sector to consider their products.

Nevertheless, the fiber industry was still dominated by cotton and other natural materials. Increased public acceptance of synthetics, combined with other influences, began to change this situation during the 1970s. For instance, pivotal synthetic fiber technology was developed for the space program, as well as for the military during the Vietnam era and the Cold War. These advances inspired new products that found favor in civilian markets. Most importantly, new production and processing techniques evolved, such as texturizing and chemical crimping, that allowed competitors to vastly improve the quality, look, and feel of their fibers.

In the early 1950s, manmade fibers accounted for about 13 percent of worldwide fiber production—synthetic fibers represented a negligible share of this total. By the late 1960s, however, manmade fibers met over 30 percent of global fiber demand, and synthetics were quickly displacing their cellulosic cousins. Boosted by postwar economic expansion, worldwide manmade fiber production rocketed from just 4.6 billion pounds in the early 1950s to over 16.2 billion pounds by 1970. Furthermore, the United States supplied a major share of global exports in this new, high-tech industry.

Continued technological advances prompted expansion of the synthetic fiber industry throughout the 1970s. While no completely new apparel and textile fibers were invented during that decade, modifications and processing advancements were numerous. Du Pont developed Antron nylon, as well as extremely light-weight, thin polypropylene fibers. Similarly, BASF introduced conductive nylon carpet fibers that reduced static. Popular anti-cling nylons were developed as well. "Pluscious" brushed nylon, created by Dow Chemical Co., became the preferred fiber for women's and children's sleepwear. Moreover, new polypropylene fibers with improved pigments and ultra-violet light inhibitors became popular in automotive and outdoor markets.

As industry revenues and output skyrocketed, the synthetic fiber industry adopted a more consolidated structure. The industry had consisted of a multitude of innovators attempting to establish themselves as leaders in this new high-tech industry. However, commercial development of synthetic fibers proved to be an extremely capital-intensive endeavor, and research and development costs, plant construction, and ongoing fiber improvement expenditures became more than many companies could bear. As a result, many fiber makers were merged to create economies of scale.

The rapidly increasing popularity of polyester and nylon fabrics drove industry gains in the 1970s. In fact, by 1979, polyester accounted for 50 percent of all shipments by weight, while nylon held a 30 percent share of the market, and olefin and acrylic fibers each comprised ten percent of output. Overall synthetic fiber output peaked at about 6.5 billion pounds in 1979.

Despite this impressive expansion, industry growth stalled in the 1980s. High petroleum prices helped to depress profits during the early part of the decade, and the industry faced more fundamental and long-term obstacles as well. Specifically, the major innovations that had propelled growth during the previous 20 years were no longer new, and the synthetic fiber industry was entering a stage of maturity.

The declining market for polyester, the industry's mainstay, was of primary concern for struggling manufacturers in the 1980s. U.S. production jumped an encouraging 11 percent in 1983, but slipped for four consecutive years to only 3.3 billion pounds by 1986. Total production in this important segment climbed only one percent annually between 1982 and 1991. The other major class of fibers, nylon, reflected a similar growth pattern. From 1.9 billion pounds of output in 1982, demand rose an average of just two percent per year through 1991, to 2.5 billion pounds.

Olefin fibers continued to realize strong demand. That segment grew an average of 11 percent per year during the 1980s, topping 1.8 billion pounds per year by 1990, when olefin fibers accounted for over 20 percent of industry shipments. Acrylic fibers, by contrast, plummeted from 624 million pounds sold in 1982 to just 454 million by 1991, exhibiting an average annual decline of four percent. Consumer preference for cottons and polyester served to reverse expansion in this sector.

During this time, stiff foreign competition in commodity fiber markets emerged. U.S. fiber makers faced a serious challenge to their global dominance from Europe, Japan, and emerging industrial nations. Taiwan and Korea became particularly aggressive competitors during the decade, and significant threats also came from low-cost producers in such countries as Indonesia, Bangladesh, and Malaysia.

U.S. synthetic fiber imports had reached over $900 million per year by 1992, approaching ten percent of domestic sales. Besides cutting into domestic profits, foreign filament producers were quickly capturing global market share. As U.S. apparel and textile manufacturers moved their production facilities overseas, they often turned to cheaper foreign fiber suppliers. By 1990, the total U.S. share of global industry output fell to 18 percent, down significantly from the over 50 percent the country had held in 1950.

In an effort to combat downward price and profit pressures exerted by foreign competitors, U.S. companies scrambled to cut costs and improve their products. Massive capital investments made during the early 1990s were used to update manufacturing facilities, increase automation, and integrate new information management systems. Investments also were used to create thinner, lighter, stronger, and more versatile fibers. Despite these efforts, however, industry sales climbed an average of only four percent per year between 1982 and 1990, to about $11.5 billion. Total output during that period remained stagnant at about 3.2 billion pounds. Only gains in productivity helped to buoy profits for many struggling competitors.

As if heightened competition and stagnant demand were not enough of a challenge for U.S. synthetic fiber manufacturers, the country experienced economic recession from 1989 through 1991. Output slipped about one percent in 1989 before plunging four percent in 1990. Revenues fell four percent as well. Sales slipped again in 1991 by less than one percent, disappointing many who had anticipated a significant recovery. Besides increased imports of apparel and textiles, fiber makers were hit particularly hard by a depression in the construction industry, a major consumer of carpet fibers.

CURRENT CONDITIONS

Bolstered by a weak U.S. dollar in overseas markets and overall improvement in the country's economy, American synthetic fiber markets began to show definite signs of recovery in 1992 and 1993. The value of shipments rose four percent (two percent in inflation adjusted dollars), and output climbed a hearty 3.6 percent. Analysts projected similar growth for 1993. Furthermore, manufacturers continued to achieve cost-saving productivity gains.

Manufacturers of polyester anticipated a relatively stable future. They were benefitting from management and production restructuring, as well as from a slowdown in the growth of apparel imports that occurred in the late 1980s. Demand for polyester was also increasing from producers of high-performance tires and nonwoven products, such as disposable medical garments. Market demand for new polyester microfibers, which give polyester the feel of silk, encouraged manufacturers as well. Nevertheless, fiber imports from the Far East remained a threat.

Nylon producers expected to benefit from an increase in carpet demand in the mid-1990s. Despite generally weak markets, nylon fiber makers were scrambling to fill surging demand in the automotive air bag market, a lucrative niche expected to grow 15-fold between 1990 and 2000. Overall nylon production grew less than one percent in 1992, to 2.5 billion pounds. While U.S. producers maintained a 28 percent share of global nylon fiber production in the mid-1990s, foreign competitors threatened to whittle away at this lead.

Olefin fibers continued to lead industry growth in the 1990s. Output jumped a hearty seven percent in 1992 to about 2 billion pounds. Encouraging producers in this segment was a growing demand by carpet makers and greater use of this fiber for nonwoven products, such as disposable garments. Amoco, for example, began marketing a new olefin fiber carpet for residential use, which was touted as being highly resistant to the matting and crushing characteristic of nylon products.

While output of acrylic fibers remained stagnant in the early 1990s, the introduction of new acrylic microfibers led producers to believe that they might regain market share from cotton and polyester producers. Acrylic output dropped to 439 million pounds in 1992.

The long-term health of the U.S. synthetic fiber industry was questionable in the mid-1990s. Opportunities for impressive productivity gains seemed limited. Most competitors were already operating at low costs compared to foreign producers, particularly those in Europe and Japan, and gains allowed by automation and information technology had been largely exhausted.

Industry analysts expected the United States to realize a continued decline in its share of the global market. Fiber producers in such newly industrialized countries as South America and Asia were likely to dominate those regions, exerting downward pressure on global fiber prices as they competed in markets around the world. Moreover, increasingly stringent environmental rules and regulations frustrated American manufacturers. To reduce toxic emissions, federal and state governments began requiring producers to meet strict manufacturing regulations (see **SIC 2821: Plastics Materials and Resins**). In order to comply, U.S. companies were spending millions of dollars retrofitting their factories and searching for cleaner production technologies. Meanwhile, foreign producers with less demanding environmental standards gained an edge.

INDUSTRY LEADERS

The largest company competing in the synthetic fibers industry in the early 1990s was E. I. du Pont de Nemours, of Delaware. This diversified conglomerate increased its revenues 1.1 percent in 1992 to more than $15.5 billion. Its operating profits, however, jumped 9.6 percent to $1.38 billion. Du Pont, the inventor of nylon, remained the world's largest producer of that fiber, controlling about 36 percent of the nylon carpet fiber market in 1992, and 21 percent of the market for polyester staple fibers.

While Du Pont had reduced its toxic emissions substantially since the late 1980s, the company released over 250 million pounds of waste in 1991 (as classified under federal toxic release inventory guidelines). Therefore, in July 1991, Du Pont announced plans to invest $300 million to modernize its polyester production facilities by 1994, and to expand filament capacity by 20 percent, a plan that would eliminate 1,000 jobs. In 1993, the company announced further plans to cut 1,600 jobs from its nylon business unit as part of an overall 4,500 company-wide work force reduction, which the company hoped would cut its fixed costs by 20 percent. In an effort to increase its competitiveness in the European community's nylon market, Du Pont announced a major acquisition in 1993 of the nylon fiber arm of ICI, a major supplier of nylon to Europe. This acquisition would result in a fiber behemoth, with nylon sales of $4.5 billion annually.

The second largest manufacturer of synthetic fibers in the early 1990s was Hoechst Celanese Corp., based in North Carolina. This competitor earned operating profits of $42 million in 1992 from revenues of $6.5 billion. Sales rose 2.4 percent over 1991, though profits slipped by more than nine percent. Hoechst Celanese was the largest producer of polyester staple fiber—with over 31 percent of the world market—and the second largest manufacturer of polyester. The company spent $300 million in the early 1990s to upgrade its production facilities and add 100 million pounds of capacity.

Two of the next largest producers in the industry, Allied Signal Inc., of New Jersey, and BASF Corp. Fibers Division, of Virginia, announced plans in 1993 to merge their nylon operations. By increasing their production capacity to 850 million pounds per year, this merger would displace Monsanto Corp., of St. Louis, as the second largest manufacturer of nylon fiber. Allied Signal reported profits of $249 million in 1992 from sales of $2.6 billion, while BASF had 1991 sales of $4 billion from its diversified operations.

WORK FORCE

About 48,000 workers were employed in the U.S. synthetic fiber industry in the early 1990s. This reflected an employment decline of over 20 percent since 1982, when over 60,000 workers served the industry. Although many jobs had moved overseas to factories in low-cost regions, workforce reductions were largely a result of huge productivity gains. Heavy investments in labor-saving automation, for instance, resulted in the elimination of many production workers. Similarly, new information systems reduced the demand for managers and support staff.

Employment increased slightly during 1992 in response to slowly recovering markets. Employment prospects for the long term, however, remained unencouraging. Most chemical equipment controllers and machine operators, which accounted for approximately 20 percent of the industry's labor force, were likely to see their positions decline in number by 15 to 25 percent between 1990 and 2005. Nevertheless, high-paying jobs for chemists, engineers, and scientists were expected to increase by five to 15 percent by 2005. Moreover, experts projected that positions related to sales and marketing would surge about 17 percent. The greatest opportunities would likely arise in the fields of systems analysis and computer science, with a potential increase of over 35 percent by 2005.

Despite unenthusiastic expectations for growth in work force, those established in the industry were relatively well paid. In 1989, for example, the average production worker earned $13.84 per hour—about 32 percent higher than the average for all other U.S. manufacturing sectors. Furthermore, the average annual payroll per employee topped $32,000, compared to $21,000 for workers in other manufacturing industries.

The highest paid workers in the business were generally scientists and engineers, particularly highly educated chemists involved with management or research and development. Salaries for these professionals averaged between $60,000 and $90,000 in 1993, depending on education level. For more information on chemical engineering jobs in the synthetic materials industries, see **SIC 2821: Plastics Materials and Resins.**

AMERICA AND THE WORLD

U.S. fiber manufacturers served 18 percent of global demand in 1992—more than all Western European producers combined. Taiwan was the second largest producing nation, with 11 percent of the world market in 1992. Japan followed closely with ten percent. Other major producers included Austria, Germany, Canada, the United Kingdom, Korea, China, and several developing countries.

Despite encroaching competition, U.S. producers managed to control over 90 percent of the domestic market. With exports of over $1.7 billion in 1992, the U.S. synthetic fiber industry produced a trade surplus of about $800 million. Canada was the largest importer of U.S. fibers, consuming over 14 percent of U.S. exports in the early 1990s. Belgium was the second largest customer at ten percent. China absorbed eight percent of U.S. exports, while Hong Kong and Japan accounted for about seven and 4.5 percent, respectively. The European community purchased about 26 percent of U.S. exports, as did East Asia (excluding China).

Importers were quickly eliminating the U.S. trade surplus in the mid-1990s. Canada supplied about 28 percent of all fiber imports into the United States, while Germany and Japan each accounted for about 12 percent of imports. The United Kingdom sold ten percent of U.S. imports, while South Korea captured about five percent. The United States bought 33 percent of its fiber imports from the European community.

Although they held a small share of the U.S. market, fiber producers in Southeast Asia were making the greatest gains in capturing worldwide and U.S. market share. Pacific Rim countries were expected to increase their portion of the world synthetic fiber market to 40 percent by 2001. Indeed, all developing nations combined produced more than 11 million metric tons of manmade fibers in 1992, or about 54 percent of total global output. These competitors were gouging U.S. profits in major overseas markets, particularly Europe.

As production in many developing nations escalated in the mid-1990s, synthetic fiber output in most leading industrialized countries stagnated. Global nylon production, for example, was forecast to grow six to eight percent per year throughout the 1990s. Asian nylon production, however, was expected to grow by nine to 12 percent. While production in the United States seemed to have stabilized in 1992 and 1993, demand for fiber in Japan and Western Europe continued to decline. Japanese producers were scrambling to overcome slack demand and increased competition from neighboring nations. Similarly, western European producers were battling an ongoing regional recession, environmental problems, and an influx of inexpensive fibers from Eastern Europe and the Commonwealth of Independent States.

Facing fierce competition and global demand growth for all manmade fibers of only two to five percent per year, U.S. producers were searching for high-tech products to bolster overseas profits in the 1990s. They were also looking forward to sales growth as a result of the North American Free Trade Agreement (NAFTA). That pact, which would remove import quotas on polyester fibers, was expected to boost demand for U.S. fibers from Mexican textile and apparel manufacturers. Pending General Agreement on Trades and Tariffs (GATT) accords in 1994 were forecast to produce similar results for U.S. fiber makers competing in the European community.

RESEARCH AND TECHNOLOGY

Significant capital investments were made during the 1980s and 1990s to increase productivity and reduce hazardous manufacturing emissions. In 1990, synthetic fiber makers invested over $800 million, or about ten percent of total revenues, back into their businesses, a figure roughly equal to three times the investment per employee of the average U.S. manufacturer and double the amount spent by the industry less than ten years earlier.

U.S. producers sought to develop cutting-edge fibers that could deliver high profit margins and displace commodity fibers increasingly supplied by emerging industrial nations. One significant product introduction during the early 1990s included Hoechst Celanese's Polarguard HV (high void continuous filament), which provided greater warmth from lightweight, outdoor polyester fiberfill products. Similarly, the company introduced a 100 percent recyclable, all-polyester carpet system in 1993.

Also that year, Du Pont was improving its Micromattique MX, intended as a substitute for cotton in sportswear. Furthermore, Du Pont revealed plans during this time to develop nylon recycling technology. Planning to begin marketing recyclable fibers by 1997, the company hoped to eventually corner 85 percent of the used nylon market. Seeking to revive the struggling

acrylic sector, American Cyanimid Corp. introduced MicroSupreme, a microfiber product that offered superior softness and strength as well as greater wicking and heat barrier characteristics.

Promising technological breakthroughs were also occurring outside of the private sector. Researchers at the University of Minnesota, for example, developed a method of growing poly fibers in a vertical glass tube. The system, which allowed the shape and diameter of the fiber to be altered, offered a potential alternative to the traditional extrusion process.

For more information about capital spending to increase productivity and to meet environmental regulations in the synthetic chemical industry in general, see **SIC 2821: Plastics Materials and Resins.**

INDUSTRY INFORMATION SOURCES

"AlliedSignal, BASF Join Their Nylon Fiber Lines," *Chemical Marketing Reporter,* October 18, 1993.

Anderson, Earl V., "Foreign Trade: U.S. Chemical Trade Surplus Declines," *Chemical & Engineering News,* December 13, 1993.

Anderson, Earl V., "Japan: Once Booming Economy Struggles Through Times," *Chemical & Engineering News,* December 13, 1993.

"Du Pont Looks at Used Nylon for Recycling," *Journal of Commerce and Commercial,* October 14, 1992.

"Facts & Figures for the Chemical Industry," *Chemical & Engineering News,* June 28, 1993.

Heathcote, Mary, "NAFTA Set to Free the Flow of Fibres," *ECN-European Chemical News,* August 9, 1993.

Hirano, Koju, "Japanese Firms Count on Microfibers to Shore Up Sagging Sales," *Daily News Record,* June 24, 1993.

Layman, Patricia, "Europe: Definite Though Modest Recovery Forecast for 1994," *Chemical & Engineering News,* December 13, 1993.

Layman, Patricia, "Developing Nations Lead in Fibers Production," *Chemical & Engineering News,* April 5, 1993.

"Market Outlook: Fiber Markets Also Stay Sluggish," *Textile World,* August 1993.

Maycumber, S. Gray, "New Du Pont Microfiber Development, Called MX, May be Rx for Market," *Daily News Record,* June 24, 1993.

Maycumber, S. Gray, "Manmade Fibers Suffer Summer '93 Shipment Chill," *Daily News Record,* September 2, 1993.

Maycumber, S. Gray, "Du Pont to Slash 4,500 Jobs; 1,600 Are in Nylon," *Daily News Record,* September 14, 1993.

"PP Stakes Claim as Asia Dominates Fibres Sector," *ECN—European Chemical News,* July 5, 1993.

Rawis, Rebecca L., "Salaries," *Chemical & Engineering News,* October 25, 1993.

Reisch, Marc, "Plastics, Synthetic Fibers Output Increases," *Chemical & Engineering News,* April 12, 1993.

Reisch, Marc S., "Many Nylon Fiber Producers Moving to Consolidate, *Chemical & Engineering News,* August 2, 1993.

Rzadzki, John, "Nylon Makers Head East in Search of High Growth," *Chemical Marketing Reporter,* July 19, 1993.

Storck, William J., "United States: Chemical Industry Lackluster This Year," *Chemical & Engineering News,* December 13, 1993.

Thomas, Marita, "Fibers: Enhanced in the Last Quarter Century," *Textile World,* September 1993.

Walker, Marjorie, "Europe Loses the Thread," *ECN Chemscope,* December 1993.

—Dave Mote

SIC 2833

MEDICINAL CHEMICALS AND BOTANICAL PRODUCTS

This classification covers establishments primarily engaged in: l) manufacturing bulk organic and inorganic medicinal chemicals and their derivatives, and 2) processing (grading, grinding, milling) bulk botanical drugs and herbs. Included in this industry are establishments primarily engaged in manufacturing agar-agar and similar products of natural origin, endocrine products, manufacturing or isolating basic vitamins, and isolating active medicinal principals from botanical drugs and herbs.

INDUSTRY SNAPSHOT

Companies in this drug industry segment furnish the active ingredients used by pharmaceutical firms to compile their finished products, called pharmaceutical preparations (**SIC 2834: Pharmaceutical Preparations**). Active ingredients are the portion of a finished drug which create the desired effect, therapeutic or preventive, for humans and animals. Extracts of crude drugs (not yet processed) derived from plant or animal sources are important examples of the components produced by this industry sector. By the 1960s, however, synthesized chemicals, either a manufactured copy of an organic or inorganic substance, or a new chemical entity (NCE), had become common active ingredients in pharmaceuticals, from vitamin pills to hormones. Meanwhile, the biotechnology revolution, beginning in earnest in the 1980s, resulted in ways of inserting genetic material into small microorganisms, making them miniature factories for the production of active drug ingredients like insulin, and in the process creating patentable new molecular entities (NME's).

ORGANIZATION AND STRUCTURE

Ward's Business Directory 1994 listed 65 companies in the medicinals and botanicals industry. Of these, fully 25, accounting for over half of production, were divisions or subsidiaries of other firms, including pharmaceutical industry giants such as Merck and Hoffmann-La Roche. Parent firms that have developed in-house active ingredient suppliers are said to be "back-integrated" and their chemical products are referred to as "captive," dedicated to the parent firm, whereas chemicals produced by firms independent of the final purchaser are called "merchant."

Many "fine" chemical companies producing for the merchant market are contracted to large pharmaceutical companies to supply custom, or specialty chemicals, while others produce and sell on the open market. The latter often manufacture well-known bulk pharmaceutical compounds, like those used in the production of aspirin. Custom and specialty chemicals are made in smaller quantities than bulks and frequently combine several different chemical compounds called intermediates—they are more expensive. Traditionally, "fine" chemicals were those whose freedom from impurities was far higher than industrial chemicals not intended for human consumption. *Chemical Marketing Reporter* noted in 1992, however, that "fine" chemicals could also be defined by their price.

Both the back-integrated firms and the independent fine chemical companies are involved in the complex process of producing extracts of natural substances, synthetic inorganic and organic chemicals, or combinations of any or all of these, that go into most modern medicines. The specific formulas for these substances can be found in academic monographs, or in the official U.S. Pharmacopeia (USP) and the National Formulary (NF). If they have not been manufactured on an industrial scale before or are entirely new compounds (NCE's or NME's), the pharmaceutical firm creates a similar document as a reference for its own in-house producers, or as a guide to firms contracted to supply active ingredients. These references provide manufacturers with the acceptable legal standards of purity and potency for their products. A new manufacturing process, as well as an NCE or NME, is patentable in the United States.

Active ingredients from natural sources start as crude drugs. According to the standard text on drug extraction from natural sources, *Pharmacognosy,* crude drugs from vegetative or animal (even insect) origins are "natural substances that have undergone only the processes of collection and drying.'' Natural substances are those ''found in nature . . . that have not had changes made in their molecular structure.'' The sources of these substances, medicinal plants or the animals from which glands and organs are needed, can either be raised commercially or collected in the wild. But environmental concerns tended to support the former in the 1980s and 1990s. Especially with plants, it is of vital importance that the correct species is identified before collection. Once a crude drug has been collected and the needed portions separated and cleaned, it must be safely stored or immediately processed, according to how quickly the active ingredient might lose its potency or spoil. Plants are often stored over long periods because storage can help decompose unwanted plant components while leaving the desired portions intact. Animal glands and organs, however, are generally processed quickly to avoid deterioration.

If the crude drug is a plant, the active constituent (the ingredient desired for the final drug product) must be extracted. The first step in this procedure is grinding and mincing the appropriate plant parts, such as the leaves or the seeds. Production facilities in this industry house hammer mills, knife mills, and teeth mills designed to reduce leaves, stems, seeds, or roots to a manageable powder composed of evenly-sized granules. Some plant products, such as herbal remedies, can be sent at this point, in either ground or whole leaf form, to be packaged for sale or combined into other preparations. For most plant-derived drugs, the powdered plant must be submitted to a series of solvent baths (a process called maceration), such as alcohol or ether, or a series of distillation procedures (in the case of volatile oils), that separate the desired ingredient from the crude material. Animal glands or organs are also minced, then mixed with a solvent which aids extraction and often preserves the substance. After centrifugation, the animal extract is filtered to separate remaining impurities. Antibiotic molds, on the other hand, are actually grown in large fermentation tanks. The molds release their medicinal yield, spores, into a fermenting medium or solution. These fluid mixtures of either mold, plant, or animal materials are submitted to ''precipitation,'' which involves the application of either heat or freezing cold, or the addition of salts or some other compound that separates or isolates the target active ingredient from the fluid. These isolates go by many names. If plant-derived, they may be alkaloids like morphine from opium poppies, or glycosides like digitoxin from foxglove. If animal-derived, the isolate could be insulin from the pancreas of a pig or a sheep. If a mold, the precipitate might be penicillin. Isolates are then sent to the customer in either powdered or fluid form to be assembled into a marketable drug.

Medicinal chemical producers start with a molecular formula for a target ingredient. They then devise or follow a known process whereby various chemicals will be combined, often under heat or pressure in large vats, to create a single pharmaceutical compound or an intermediate that will join other intermediates to form the active portion of a drug. There are several such processes, ranging from the simple addition of two compounds or pure chemicals in a flask, to acetylation, animation, carboxylation, hydrolysis, esterification, etc. Acetylsalicylic acid (aspirin), for example, is made by esterification—the addition and consequent reaction of an acid to (in this case) salicylic to an alcohol (acetic anhydride) which is then mixed with water (because aspirin does not dissolve readily in water). From this, aspirin is easily crystallized (precipitated as in natural products) by the addition of glacial acetic acid.

Manufacturers of these active ingredients ship their finished products in ''batches'' to the preparation firm awaiting them. The chemical composition of these shipments must match a parent batch (to ensure purity and strength), and must meet with the approval of the Food and Drug Administration (FDA) as well as the customer company. A sample remains as a reference for future batches. Customer firms, desiring a regular supply of high-quality materials, will often inspect manufacturing plants—even of independent companies—before assigning a production contract for active ingredients. The FDA, besides comparing active ingredients to the gold standard, is responsible for assuring that every step in the process of pharmaceutical raw material production meets specific production standards, called Good Manufacturing Practices (GMPs). In fact, the FDA inspects facilities of overseas as well as domestic producers.

BACKGROUND AND DEVELOPMENT

Raw material suppliers for pharmaceutical companies, in the form of fine chemical producers, actually predated the pharmaceutical industry. Until well into the 19th century, doctors and apothecaries (pharmacists) collected and processed their own botanical remedies and compounded their own medicinal chemicals. Drugs in the limited and non-standardized pharmacopeia were herbal remedies whose provenance dated back centuries or millennia and could be prepared simply. What chemical treatments there were, pharmacists could produce in their drugstore using unsophisticated equipment. Because of the similarity of pharmaceutical chemicals to the processes for making industrial chemicals, like dyes, small-scale producers often engaged in the manufacture of both. In fact, many modern medicinal chemical suppliers, like Dow and Hoechst, make industrial chemicals as well.

An increase in the scientific study of chemistry and botanical extracts in the 19th century yielded a whole range of new chemicals and isolates with pharmaceutical potential. Included among these were the anesthetics ether and morphine. These new drugs required a greater degree of standardization and production expertise than earlier treatments. Their efficacy also increased public demand. Pharmacists, like H.E. Merck in Germany, as well as doctors and fine chemical producers, started developing and building the manufacturing capacity to meet these needs. The new pharmaceutical firms called themselves ''ethical'' manufacturers in order to differentiate themselves from the ''patent'' medicine producers, who bottled popular concoctions with broad therapeutic claims but dubious medicinal value. The makers of ethicals clearly labeled the contents of their products, and promoted the therapeutic strength and purity of their medicines.

Many of the early active ingredient suppliers for both the American ethical and patent producers were European fine chemical companies. But wars such as the War of 1812, the Civil War, and World War I tended to disrupt European supplies and spur American companies to increase their capacity for domestic chemical manufacture. American companies like Squibb (which became Bristol Myers-Squibb), started by Edward R. Squibb, established themselves by supplying medicines for the Union armies—in Squibb's case ether of consistent purity and strength.

By the first decades of the 20th century, breakthroughs in understanding the bacteriological basis of many diseases (Louis Pasteur), and the effect of chemicals on certain parts of the body (Paul Ehrlich), had led to a new era in pharmaceutical science, where specific compounds could be screened for their effectiveness against known disease organisms. The discovery of such ''wonder drugs'' as the anti-infective sulfanilimides, and various vaccines, increased the demand for reliable new drug treatments. Most drugs, however, with the exception of injectibles, still did not reach the physician or pharmacist in finished form. Pharmaceutical firms still purchased fine chemicals from companies like Pfizer or Merck (now an American firm as well), and compounded them into pharmaceutical mixtures for distribution to hospitals and pharmacists. Pharmacists mixed these bulk ingredients into finished form in the drugstore. Furthermore, these treatments did not displace botanical products as the dominant form of drug treatment until after World War II.

The war, with its emergency demand for the new anti-infectives like the antibiotic penicillin, as well as sulfa drugs, changed the structure of the pharmaceutical industry. Bulk suppliers like Pfizer and Merck found themselves producing drugs on a massive scale, in both finished and bulk form. After the war, these companies stayed in the profitable ethicals business, making prescription-only pharmaceutical preparations. With a high public demand for new life-saving or extending medications, companies financed enlarged research and development departments to discover and develop important (and profitable) new therapies. A vast array of new drugs resulted in the 1940s, 1950s, and 1960s, including tranquilizers, steroids, vaccines, and more antibiotics. Many of these drugs derived from the laboratory screening of botanicals and animal products, like steroids from yams used to make a cortisonal treatment for arthritis, and insulin from animal pancreas extracts, used to control diabetes. The limits of natural supply, however, prompted many pharmaceutical companies to synthesize the active ingredients in these medicines.

Meanwhile, new federal regulatory requirements slapped tight new restrictions on the production of drugs after 1962, when a popular European sleeping pill, Thalidomide, was found to cause severe birth defects in some newborns. Previous restrictions had resulted from other such scares. The 1906 Food and Drug Act followed the exposure of widespread food adulteration in Upton Sinclair's *The Jungle,* while the 1938 Food, Drug, and Cosmetic Act passed in the wake of over 100 reported deaths resulting from the inadvertent and untested mixture of a sulfa drug with a sweet-tasting but deadly compound, diethylene glycol. In response to the Thalidomide crisis, Congress passed the 1962 Kefauver-Harris Amendments to the 1938 legislation. The legislation required FDA licensing and oversight of all pharmaceutical manufacturing facilities and processes, including those of bulk pharmaceutical suppliers. Similar production controls had already been instituted after 1949 for ''batches'' of bulk penicillin.

Kefauver-Harris reinforced trends in the industry towards in-house production of active ingredient supplies for pharmaceuticals. Because the pharmaceutical company was ultimately responsible for the purity of its product, even if an outside supplier provided ineffective or dangerous compounds, companies thought it safer to have internal oversight and production control. Perhaps as important for major firms was a desire to maintain command of active ingredient supply even after patents had run out on new medications. In his short history of the pharmaceutical industry, *The Structure of American Industry,* Walter S. Measday cited a situation in which "upwards of 150 companies" offered Vitamin C in dosage form while "the entire output of the vitamin itself is produced by Merck, Pfizer, and Hoffmann-La Roche." If ethical pharmaceutical companies could control bulk supplies for more advanced medications than Vitamin C, even after product patents ran out, they would effectively extend their patent period, and associated high profits, indefinitely. These and other motivations fueled the continued drive towards in-house production of active ingredients in the 1970s and 1980s.

CURRENT CONDITIONS

In the late 1980s and early 1990s, pharmaceutical firms began reversing their trend towards in-house production of active ingredients in favor of a more complex combination of captive production and long-term contracts with outside custom suppliers. Among the factors fueling this trend were the 1992 recession and excess world chemical capacity, the increasing costs in both time and money to negotiate regulatory hazards, the complexity of new drug compounds, and the desire to avoid tying up too much capital in supply factories. Pharmaceutical firms in the 1980s had found themselves spending seven to ten years of their 17-year patent period on new drugs going through clinical trials and awaiting subsequent FDA approval. By looking more to outside fine chemical suppliers, drug companies could, as the *Chemical Marketing Reporter* put it in 1992, be "spared the cost of planting steel in the ground to produce a substance that may still require government approvals and has yet to prove commercially viable." For those companies lucky enough to sign on with a major pharmaceutical manufacturer on a long-term supply contract, they could be assured of a seven to ten year market for their products. But, for the others, the competition in the open market promised to get more furious, suggesting consolidations might accelerate in the latter half of the 1990s.

Meanwhile, the highly-politicized drive for health-care reform in the late 1980s and early 1990s created downward pressure on the prices the big pharmaceutical firms could charge for their prescription drugs, even for new "breakthrough" treatment therapies that cost considerable amounts of money to develop. The immediate winners in this contest over drug prices seemed to be the smaller independent generics companies. Generics, markedly cheaper therapeutic and chemical equivalents of prescription patented medicines, went into production once the patent pro-

tection on a prescription drug expired. Generics companies could manage cheap prices because they only had to copy, not research and develop, the drugs they produced.

Because of this fact, however, the active ingredients in generics accounted for almost half of their sale price—a ratio three to four times greater than prescription versions of the same drug. This made the generic companies susceptible to changes in the supply of active ingredients worldwide. When, as *Drug Topics* reported in 1994, the European Economic Community temporarily "outlawed the exportation of bulk/fine chemicals," generics companies were faced with a cutoff of 85 percent of their supply. At the same time, the prescription pharmaceutical firms controlled the current capacity on the active ingredients in their drugs coming off-patent. Combined with a wave of takeovers or start-ups of generics firms by large pharmaceutical producers, the cutoff in supplies threatened to squeeze independent generic producers out, and effectively extend prescription patents and higher drug prices much longer than health-care reform advocates desired.

INDUSTRY LEADERS

This industry sector was dominated by the subsidiaries and divisions of larger drug companies like Merck and Hoffman-La Roche as late as 1993. As of 1990, Roche, as the Swiss company is known, was, according to *Everybody's Business,* "the world's foremost producers of vitamins," in addition to marketing "50 prescription drugs," and owning a 60 percent share of biotechnology pioneer Genentech. However, other producers, like Eastman Fine Chemicals, were profiting from the switch to custom production, according to the *Chemical Marketing Reporter* for September 7, 1992.

AMERICA AND THE WORLD

Despite the 20th century revolution in chemical pharmaceuticals, Wijesekera noted in *The Medicinal Plant Industry* that "50 percent to 80 percent of the developing world depends on traditional therapies for their health care," namely plant-derived remedies. In China and Southeast Asia, indigenous industries process and package plant-based remedies based on ancient recipes. Some processors utilize the same machinery and manufacturing expertise as American companies, while others are extremely small and use traditional methods. This system of traditional active ingredient production for drugs, except to the extent that Western-style medicines were adopted or locally produced for export to the West, remained relatively untouched by American corporate influences.

Suppliers of fine chemicals for American pharmaceuticals, however, have never been limited to the country's borders. European chemical companies, except for temporary alterations during various wars, have always had, and continued to have in the late 20th century, a large presence in the American market. The *Chemical Marketing Reporter* noted in 1992 that the U.S. share of the fine chemicals market only came to about 30 percent, while European companies controlled over 50 percent. American producers, however, more than held their own in domestic markets. In the 1990s industry leadership remained in European and American hands, which, with the addition of Japan, were estimated to control almost 90 percent of the market, according to industry analyst E. Polastro in *Chemical and Engineering News.* A growing threat to this Western fine chemical hegemony were Asian and Indian producers, who do not have the strict Western environmental codes applied to U.S. producers. Asian producers showed themselves particularly competitive in the bulk pharmaceutical and intermediates classes in the 1980s.

INDUSTRY INFORMATION SOURCES

Akerele, Olayiwoia, "Summary of WHO Guidelines for the Assessment of Herbal Medicines," *HerbalGram,* No. 28, 1993.

Begley, Ronald, and Emma Chynoweth, "Facing the Era of Post-Health Care Reform," *Chemical Week,* March 31, 1993.

De Sain, Carol, *Drug, Device and Diagnostic Manufacturing,* Buffalo Grove, IL: Interpharm Press, Inc., 1991.

"The Generic Industry '94: It's a Jungle Out There," *Drug Topics Supplement,* 1994.

Gibson, W. David, "Rising Prominence: Intermediate Chemicals '92, Custom Manufacture," *Chemical Marketing Reporter,* September 7, 1992.

Harvey, Alan L., *Drugs From Natural Products,* New York: Ellis Horwood, 1993.

International Directory of Corporate Histories, Vol. I, Chicago: St. James Press, 1990.

Liebenau, Johnathan, *Medical Science and Medical Industry,* Baltimore, MD: Johns Hopkins University Press, 1987.

Mahoney, John, *The Merchants of Life,* New York: Henry Holt and Company, 1992.

Mattera, Philip, *Inside U.S. Business,* Homewood, Illinois: Business One Irwin, 1991.

World Class Business, New York: Henry Holt and Company, 1992.

Measday, Walter S., "The Pharmaceutical Industry," *The Structure of American Industry,* New York: Macmillan, 1971.

Morris, Gregory DL, "Rx Intermediates: Business Booms," *Chemical Week,* April 8, 1992.

Moskowitz, Milton et al, eds., *Everybody's Business,* New York: Doubleday, 1990.

Mullin, Rick et al, "Manufacturers Head for Technology's High Ground," *Chemical Week,* February 2, 1994.

Nielsen, Robert, *Handbook of Federal Drug Law,* Philadelphia: Lea and Febiger, 1992.

1987 Census of Manufactures: Drugs, Washington, DC: U.S. Department of Commerce, 1990.

Plishner, Emily S. and Debbie Jackson, "Generics Set to Take Off," *Chemical Week,* August 12, 1992.

Shon, Melissa, "Growing Pains, Bulk Actives," *Chemical Marketing Reporter,* September 7, 1992.

Spilker, Bert, *Multinational Drug Companies: Issues in Drug Discovery and Development,* New York: Raven Press, 1989.

Springer, Neil, "The Big Question," *Chemical Marketing Reporter,* September 7, 1992.

Stinson, Stephen C., "Custom Chemicals," *Chemical and Engineering News,* January 31, 1994.

Tilton, Helga, "For the Nimble," *Chemical Marketing Reporter,* September 7, 1992.

Tyler, Varro et al, *Pharmacognosy,* 8th edition, Philadelphia, PA: Lea and Febiger, 1981.

Ward's Business Directory of U.S. Private and Public Companies, Detroit: Gale Research, Inc., 1994.

Wijesekera, R.O.B., *The Medicinal Plant Industry,* Boca Raton: CRC Press, 1991.

—J. Jacob Jones

SIC 2834

PHARMACEUTICAL PREPARATIONS

This industry category includes establishments primarily engaged in manufacturing, fabricating, or processing drugs in pharmaceutical preparations for human or veterinary use. The greater part of the products of these establishments are finished in the form intended for final consumption, such as ampoules, tablets, capsules, vials, ointments, medicinal powders, solutions, and suspensions. Products of this industry consist of two important lines, namely: (1) pharmaceutical preparations promoted primarily to the dental, medical, or veterinary profession; and (2) pharmaceutical preparations promoted primarily to the public.

INDUSTRY SNAPSHOT

Behind oil, auto, and electronics companies, only eight pharmaceutical firms were listed among the ranks of the top 100 world corporations by revenues in the 1992 *World Class Business.* However, no less than nine were in the top 50 by net income, including two American industry leaders, Merck and Bristol-Myers Squibb, in the top ten.

Since World War II, which established the American drug industry on a permanent footing, pharmaceutical firms had come to expect a high level of profitability. The discovery and development of dozens of life-saving medications in company research labs created enormous demand for pharmaceuticals, while patent protection and sophisticated marketing structures maintained sales and profits. The high cost of drug development and marketing, though, tended to concentrate industry earnings in several large firms. Thus, as *Standard and Poor's* reported in 1992, despite "hundreds of companies operating in this industry . . . the four largest players accounted for more than 25 percent of annual U.S. pharmaceutical sales in 1992." Even with strict regulatory oversight and periodic crises, like the Thalidomide scare of 1962, the American pharmaceutical industry, or at least its major players, managed to remain both profitable and largely beneficial to world health while avoiding the price controls commonplace in other industrialized nations.

The American health-care reform movement of the late 1980s and 1990s threatened to end the comfortable position of the large drug companies. Coming at a time when market forces had already begun to alter the internal dynamics of the industry, a political backlash against soaring health-care costs and high drug company profits included calls for government controls over drug prices. The situation remained unresolved by 1994. But regardless of the outcome of federal health care legislation, the pharmaceutical industry faced an era of continued restructuring in the latter 1990s.

ORGANIZATION AND STRUCTURE

Pharmaceutical preparations (a government euphemism for finished-form drugs) companies maintained their traditional leadership of the industry into the latter part of the century, accounting for over 75 percent of pharmaceutical sales in 1993. Industry production and employment was concentrated in the states of New Jersey, Indiana, Pennsylvania, and New York. *Business Week* reported that just in New Jersey, headquarters of industry leaders Johnson & Johnson and Merck, "25 percent of all U.S.-made drugs are produced."

Companies in the preparations sector have always shared similar manufacturing techniques. They combine active medicinal ingredients, chemicals, or natural products with excipients (i.e. buffered powders) or sterile water to produce the finished, or dosage, drug form. This is the form in which the patient ultimately takes the medication. Dosage forms are most commonly oral (tablets, liquid suspensions, etc.), parenteral (by injection), or solid (suppositories, ointments). More novel drug delivery systems appeared in the 1980s and 1990s, including polymer implants, transdermal patches, and controlled-release sponges inside tablets.

Preparations firms also share a concentration on the development, production, and marketing of therapeutic agents; drugs designed to treat, cure, or prevent specific diseases (i.e., antibiotics), suppress symptoms (analgesics), or supply deficiencies (vitamins). Meanwhile, other industry segments concentrate on making drugs to create immunities (i.e., vaccines) or aid diagnosis (i.e., radioactive iodine for X-rays-see). Within

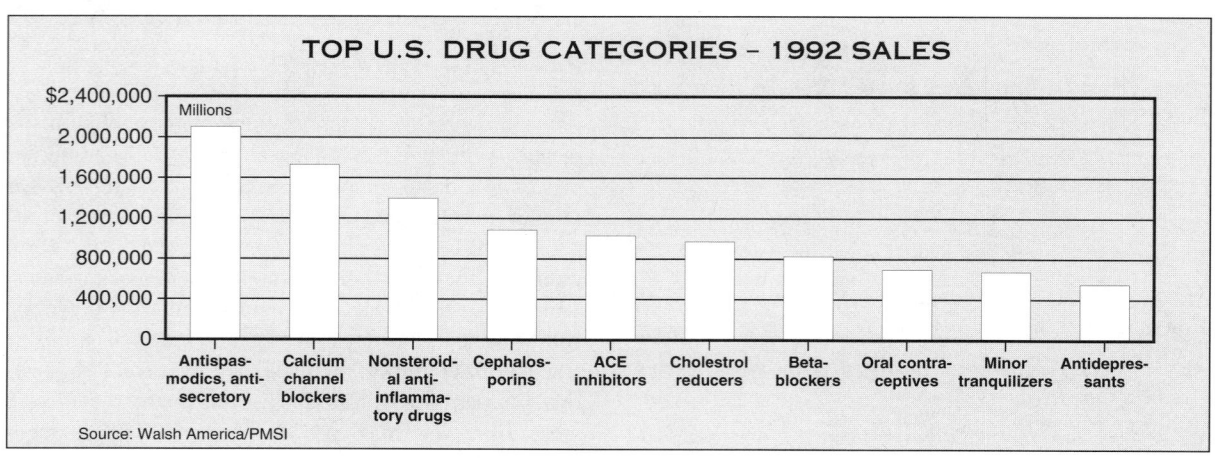

TOP U.S. DRUG CATEGORIES – 1992 SALES

Source: Walsh America/PMSI

the general area of therapeutics, pharmaceutical companies develop expertise in one or more of the eight therapeutic classes of drugs, such as cardiovasculars, or even a specific disease, such as hypertension. Smaller companies, in fact, occasionally produce only one drug. Industry leaders generally manufacture and market drugs in several therapeutic categories.

All companies in the pharmaceutical industry operate within a strict regulatory environment. Because it combines the manufacture of potentially harmful yet socially necessary products with the common business desire for profit, the pharmaceutical industry has had a complex relationship with government regulators charged with protecting the public and encouraging business growth. Major incidents of adverse or fatal reactions from drugs, evidence of collusion or corruption within the industry, and the government's desire to move the industry in a particular direction have historically prompted new regulation. From the Food and Drug Administration (FDA) to the Federal Trade Commission (FTC), pharmaceutical companies and the Federal Government are linked at all stages, including development, production, and marketing.

Despite similarities, division and segmentation also characterize the industry. Some segmentation resulted from federal regulation, while the pressures of a highly-competitive marketplace did the rest. One regulatory division has been that between "ethical" drugs and over-the-counter (OTC) drugs. Ethical drugs require a prescription from a physician before being dispensed to the patient, while the consumer can purchase OTC medications (such as aspirins and antacids) without a doctor's prescription. Ethical drugs represented 79 percent of sales among preparations companies in 1992, while OTC's accounted for the remainder.

The ethical drug segment of the industry can be further subdivided into "patented" and "generic" prescription drugs. Patented drugs are therapies developed by pharmaceutical companies whose formulas, production processes, and trade names (they have often been called branded prescription drugs) enjoy seventeen-year protection under U.S. patent laws. Patented prescription drugs were the driving force behind pharmaceutical industry sales after World War II, and continued their traditional market domination by controlling fully 60 percent of all pharmaceutical industry sales in 1992. Branded prescriptions also included almost all of the major breakthrough therapies developed in drug research labs since the 1940s, continuing the drug industry's unusual combination of health- and profit-driven research. Meanwhile, an alternative to some of the most popular OTC remedies are generics,

markedly cheaper chemical and therapeutic equivalents of patented prescription drugs that go into production once brand-name therapies have come "off-patent."

In addition to drugs for humans preparations companies produced drugs for the veterinary market. Accounting for a relatively small percentage of overall industry sales—just over $1.2 billion in 1992, according to the Animal Health Institute—many drug industry leaders either maintained specific animal health divisions or were involved in all areas of the animal health care industry.

Beginning in the early 1980s a new force entered the pharmaceutical arena—biotechnology. From the discovery of DNA structure in 1953 and new knowledge of "genetic blueprints" that direct protein growth by messenger RNA, scientists were able to clone proteins in the laboratory. Knowledge of a specific protein's function in the body, to stimulate infection-fighting cells or block a destructive internal process for example, allowed physicians to induce desired reactions in patients by injecting biotechnology-produced cloned proteins, "magic bullets" as they were called, into the body. Though biotech companies managed to create and patent many such exciting new treatments in the 1980s, they were generally inconsequential, lacked marketing structures, consumed vast amounts of research capital, and created little profit compared to those offered by the industry leaders. Nevertheless, because of their potential to continue providing "breakthrough" treatments and vaccines for some of our most stubborn diseases, biotechnology companies became the target of buyouts and mergers as well as joint ventures in the 1980s and 1990s. In one such move, industry giant Roche purchased a controlling interest in biotechnology pioneer Genentech in 1990.

BACKGROUND AND DEVELOPMENT

Before the late 19th century, the American pharmaceutical industry possessed few of its modern characteristics. Simple chemical compounds like iodine chlorate, along with plant extracts such as quinine, constituted the prime ingredients in available remedies. Some of these traditional treatments, like digitalis, remain part of the pharmacological arsenal. However, these drugs had common names and lacked specific scientific formulas, and thus a doctor's order for a medication might not yield the product intended. To offset this problem, doctors often dispensed and prescribed medicines. But they did not have a monopoly on medical advice or drug selection for patients. Given the uneven quality of medical care before the

20th century, patients often chose to dose themselves with "patent" medicines or describe their symptoms to the druggist who would obligingly offer his own remedy for purchase.

From a manufacturing standpoint, the War of 1812 and the Civil War stimulated an increase in domestic pharmaceutical manufacturing capacity. Both events temporarily disrupted the supply of fine chemicals (those with a purity level high enough for human consumption) from Europe with which pharmacists and doctors produced what few chemical medicaments they knew. Advances in the isolation and creation of new chemical substances, such as the 1840 discovery of the medicinal applications for nitrous oxide (laughing gas) by an American dentist, Horace Wells, stimulated demand for more fine chemical capacity—Wells saw the gas used as a party gag. During the Civil War, American firms like Squibb were able to establish themselves profitably by providing advanced machinery and quality products to the Union Army.

As the century progressed, other companies turned to the production of "ethical" drugs for physicians and hospitals. These drugs had clearly labeled and pharmacologically reliable contents (thus ethical). They were intended to supply medical professionals with drugs of standardized quality. Brand name ethicals were also promoted as alternatives to the wide variety of other proprietaries, mainly bottled "patent" medicines. These extremely popular elixirs claimed great therapeutic value while their contents—often only colored water, alcohol, and opiates—were generally ineffectual and occasionally dangerous. The reliability of the new ethical suppliers, on the other hand, induced doctors to begin requesting branded pharmaceuticals in their prescriptions by the end of the century.

Demand for these reliable drugs and vaccines would soon increase following scientific breakthroughs in understanding the causes and potential treatments for many of the diseases that had long been the scourge of mankind. The germ theory of disease, based upon the research of bacteriologists like Pasteur, revolutionized medicine and drug therapy in the two decades immediately before, and after, World War I. Laboratory isolation of disease organisms meant that physicians could diagnose patients by tracing their illnesses to specific sickness-inducing organisms, while drug researchers finally had a clear therapeutic target. New knowledge of the manner in which chemical treatments operated in the body, based upon the research of the German scientist Paul Ehrlich, opened up pathways of attack against these disease organisms. By World War I, "medical science," as this marriage of disease and therapeutic research came to be called, had created significant breakthroughs, especially in the development of vaccines and what Ehrlich called "chemotherapy."

Larger pharmaceutical companies like Smith-Kline expanded their clinical departments in response to the popularity and promise of medical science. They added research into new drug therapies to their quality control activities. On the eve of World War I, however, these companies lagged far behind German manufacturers like Bayer in the development and patenting of new therapies. German companies had a long history of combining basic bacteriological research with the applied science of drug development. And, unlike American firms, they had no compunction about creating exclusive markets for their therapeutic inventions by patenting their drugs in the United States and Germany. Novel treatments, such as the popular anti-syphilitic arsenical drug, Salvarsan, discovered by Ehrlich and produced by the chemical giant Hoechst, illustrated the potentially large new markets for "scientific" pharmaceuticals. When, during the War, most German companies had their American patent rights suspended, American pharmaceutical firms began manufacturing patented drugs invented in Germany (like Salvarsan and Bayer aspirin) and reaping the profits.

Between the two world wars American firms copied the research orientation and patenting habits of their German counterparts. Merck and Squib opened direct ties with academic research institutions, financing research fellowships, laboratories, and institutes in the natural sciences. Drug companies hired academic research leaders to head or staff their in-house labs. Firms developed some interest in basic research, but their major concern was using expanded research staffs and investments in development capabilities to create new drug products for the market. The major companies like Squibb, Merck, Abbott, and Upjohn, all had research staffs of about 20 with budgets of at least $100,000 by World War II. Nevertheless, the discovery of the two major drug treatments of the war years, the sulfanilimides and the antibiotics, both resulted from European research. The sulfa drugs, chemotherapeutic anti-infectives derived from coal tars, were first developed at Bayer in 1935. One of the most important drug therapies of the 20th century, mold-derived anti-infective penicillin, was first isolated and described by Alexander Fleming in England in 1928. Both the sulfa drugs and antibiotics became cornerstones of the American pharmaceutical industry from the 1930s to the 1950s.

Patent protection for the sulfas expired in the 1930s, and American companies, including Merck and American Cyanimid, began domestic manufacture of the anti-infectives. Meanwhile a grant by the Rockefeller family brought penicillin to America, where, in a Peoria, Illinois lab in 1941, scientists discovered how to mass produce penicillin mold by deep fermentation (as opposed to the slower surface culture). Several drug companies, including Pfizer, Squibb, and Merck, quickly geared up to produce marketable quantities of the "wonder drug" for use by armies and general populations. By 1945, American manufacturing capacity for drugs had expanded so quickly that penicillin prices fell from $20 to one dollar per dose, less than the labeled bottle containing it. This vastly expanded productive capacity on the part of pharmaceutical companies, an awareness of the potential market for antibiotics, and American domination of world markets after the War. Those factors resulted in the establishment of American pharmaceutical firms as potential research, manufacturing, and eventually marketing powerhouses.

Before the War, a tragedy with one of the sulfanilimides led to the passage in 1938 of landmark legislation for drug production. But the first important federal law governing drug production came in 1902 with a law requiring the inspection and licensing of biologicals (vaccines, antitoxins) by a new federal agency, the Hygienic Laboratory, precursor of the National Institute of Health (NIH). Soon thereafter, public outcry over the dangers of adulterated foods after the publication of Upton Sinclair's *The Jungle* secured passage of the second major legislation covering therapeutic drugs, the Pure Food and Drug Act of 1906. This act prohibited adulterated or misbranded food or drugs from interstate commerce and granted authority to ban dangerous drugs.

Then, in 1937, an American sulfanilimide producer, the Massengill Company of Tennessee, marketed a sore throat remedy that dissolved the sulfa drug in diethylene glycol, now the main ingredient in radiator antifreeze. Apparently, the manufacturer chose this particular solvent because of its pretty red color and sweet taste. No clinical trials for toxicity were performed. Over 100 reported deaths from kidney failure resulted from its ingestion before investigators determined the source of the fatalities. Public clamor over this incident led to the passage of the Food, Drug, and Cosmetic Act of 1938. This legislation required that all drugs must submit to tests for proof of safety by the newly-created Food and Drug Administration. Packaging was required to carry labels clearly describing the contents of the drug, how it should be administered,

and possible side effects. Attendant legislation gave the Federal Trade Commission responsibility for ensuring valid drug advertising. Experience showed, however, that most consumers did not bother to read the extensive labels on their medication. As a result, the Durham-Humphrey Amendment of 1951 exempted prescription drugs from full labeling requirements. These drugs, to be dispensed only by a licensed pharmacist under written direction of a physician, need only carry a "legend" label, "Caution: Federal law prohibits dispensing without a prescription." Legend drugs thereafter became another name for prescription or ethical drugs.

Despite regulatory hurdles, World War II and America's sustained postwar economic dominance secured the foundation for phenomenal growth in the pharmaceutical industry. The desire to find new drugs, especially antibiotics, led companies to sometimes absurd extremes. Pfizer requested that all sorts of people send them samples of dirt from all corners of the world on the chance that some might contain new molds from which to extract antibiotics. In fact, a Pfizer employee did find a profitable new treatment, terramycin, in a sample of dirt outside a company plant in Indiana. This and other "broad-spectrum" antibiotics, effective for a wide range of illnesses, provided revolutionary therapeutic regimens for physicians after the 1940s. Other breakthrough medications in the 1950s included Jonas Salk's polio vaccine, and tranquilizers and amphetamines, like Librium and Dexedrine, which promised to significantly aid patients suffering from mental illness. According to the Pharmaceutical Manufacturers Association (PMA) in its 1980 *Factbook*, new drug introductions increased from an annual average of ten to 30 in the 1940s, to an average of 30 to 50 in the 1950s.

The array of new products meant that individual physicians and pharmacists could not know all the available treatments at any one time. Pharmaceutical companies began to send out sales representatives, or "detail" men, as both educators in new therapies and promoters of company brands. Spending large sums on free physician samples and advertising in professional journals led to increased brand loyalty on the part of doctors. This marketing structure was expensive, but also supported high profits. Trained to think only of treatment regimens, doctors, often unaware of drug prices, prescribed medication where cheaper and equally efficacious therapeutic alternatives existed. Even if pharmacists wanted to substitute a cheaper generic for a doctor's prescription, doing so made little sense for a drugstore's profitability, might anger the physician, and was illegal in some states. The relationship established in the 1940s and 1950s between drug companies, pharmacists, and doctors, therefore, tended to perpetuate itself.

Fallout from another scandal, the Thalidomide crisis of 1962, however, placed more pressure on the industry. A popular European sleeping pill, Thalidomide was under investigation in 1962 by an American firm, the William S. Merrell Company, that wanted to start U.S. sales of the drug. The company's tests revealed that the drug could cause severe birth defects in babies if taken by a pregnant mother. Despite the fact the drug was never sold in the United States, its inadequate premarket testing in Europe and its near-entry into the American market revealed that a thin line of regulation was all that stood between dangerous drugs and the general public. As James Nielson wrote in *The Handbook of Federal Drug Law* in 1992, the Thalidomide disaster made it clear "that people were taking drugs" for which "neither the prescriber nor the manufacturer had a clear knowledge of their effects." The Thalidomide crisis, along with public dissatisfaction with exorbitant drug-company profits, meant "drugs never again received the universal public acceptance they had previously enjoyed."

The federal government responded to the uproar over the Thalidomide crisis by passing the Kefauver-Harris Amendments of 1962. These amendments to the Food, Drug and Cosmetic Act of 1938 required pharmaceutical companies to prove both safety and efficacy before a drug entered the marketplace. Formal procedures for new drug applications (NDA's) to the FDA and for the clinical investigation of potential therapies were established. All adverse drug reactions in clinical studies would have to be fully reported, and human clinical subjects had to be informed of the dangers of involvement in trials before giving consent. Additionally, the new act required that drugs must follow specific production guidelines, called Good Manufacturing Practices (GMP). Manufacturing plants became subject to both registration and inspection procedures. Finally, advertising for prescription drugs was placed under FDA supervision, while OTC drug advertising continued under FTC oversight. The price controls for pharmaceuticals included in Senator Kefauver's original legislative proposal were dropped along the way.

The immediate effect of the Kefauver-Harris amendments was to drastically slow the rate at which pharmaceutical manufacturers introduced new drugs to the market. According to the PMA, drug introductions fell from 45 to 24 annually between 1961 and 1962 alone. In the 1970s, they stayed below 20 in most years. Despite this slump, by the 1980s reinvigorated

research efforts using advanced techniques in "molecular biology and biochemistry were promising a new generation of highly effective drugs for specific ailments, or magic bullets." One of the magic bullets was Smith-Kline and Beecham's Tagamet, an anti-ulcer medication that quickly became "one of the most widely prescribed pharmaceuticals in the world" and prompted an increase in the research investments of pharmaceutical companies from "$1 billion in 1976 to $4 billion in 1985."

These larger research budgets yielded a whole crop of profitable new drug therapies in the 1980s, including drugs for hypertension (Merck's Vasotec), cholesterol treatment (Lopid from Warner-Lambert and Mevacor from Merck), and blood-clot dissolvers for heart-attack victims (Genentech's TPA). Meanwhile, Ortho Pharmaceutical's (owned by Johnson & Johnson) anti-acne Retin-A, and Upjohn's baldness treatment Rogaine, created new markets for cosmetic drugs. Even standbys like aspirin enjoyed increased sales as a result of studies that showed its potential to avert some heart attacks.

Despite some victories, by the end of the 1980s the prospects for the preparations industry did not look bright. Decades of expensive applied research, a wide patent umbrella, strong overseas sales, and aggressive marketing had sustained high profit and growth in the American prescription pharmaceutical industry since World War II. The system produced important new therapies that prolonged lives, banished ancient diseases, and made the aches and pains of modern existence easier to bear for those who could afford to purchase these new medications. But the highly structured corporate research, manufacturing, and marketing systems of industry leaders also required that wonderful new medications carry, what seemed to many, improperly inflated price tags. Some analysts felt that price was determining costs rather than the other way around. This trend continued into the 1980s. Thus, some industry critics claimed that the big brand pharmaceutical companies were charging unjustifiably high prices for their drugs while spending more money on advertising, brand support, and lobbying efforts than they did for research and development. The prices of drugs were less related to cost inputs, therefore, than to companies' needs to maintain their corporate structures. Meanwhile, the soaring costs of health-care in general in the 1980s and early 1990s added fuel to demands for drug price control policies similar to those in Europe. Medications sold in Europe and America were reported to have price differentials exceeding 50 percent. Meanwhile, continued reports of industry profits added fuel to reform fires. According to industry analyst Robert Helms, quoted in a 1992 *Drug Topics*, "profits for the top ten drug companies averaged 15 percent of sales, compared to four percent for all other industries."

CURRENT CONDITIONS

In 1991 legislation allowed state-funded Medicaid insurance programs to demand rebates from drug manufacturers for medications purchased by program recipients, resulting in downward price pressures. Standard and Poor's reported in its 1994 *Industry Surveys* that Medicaid accounts for about 15 percent of all U.S. pharmaceutical sales. Similar programs for the Federal Government's Medicare program were included in President Clinton's 1993 health-care reform proposals. Downward pressures on drug prices also resulted from rises in the 1980s and 1990s of private managed care organizations such as health maintenance organizations (HMOs). Standard and Poor's estimated that HMO enrollment alone may top 50 percent of the population by the year 2000. These organizations increasingly adopted restrictive drug formularies (the list of drugs that can or cannot be purchased by an organization) that stressed economical medication in therapeutic groups, often demanding discounts from manufacturers and the use of cheaper brands or generics to treat illness. Both of these movements created what one industry analyst, Paul Hanson, in an April 1994 *Chemical Week* article called a "strategic shift in power in pharmaceuticals from suppliers to consumers."

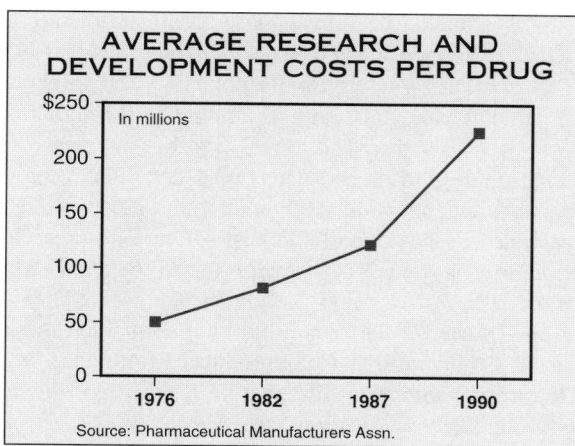

AVERAGE RESEARCH AND DEVELOPMENT COSTS PER DRUG

In millions

Source: Pharmaceutical Manufacturers Assn.

The price and consumer-oriented generics and OTC segments, in fact, were poised to benefit from the health-care reform movement. At least since the passage of the Drug Price Competition and Patent Term Restoration Act of 1984 (commonly called the

Waxman-Hatch Act), the Federal Government had attempted to increase industry competition and help supply cheaper drugs for the public by aiding the generally smaller and independent generics manufacturers. The Act allowed generics companies to present a shorter version of the standard New Drug Application (NDA) to the FDA in order to gain approval for generic substitutions of branded drugs coming "off-patent." Generic companies needed only to establish the bioequivalency of their products to the patented drugs they copied. Bioequivalence determinations, testing whether the drug matched the patent medication chemically and therapeutically, could be made fairly cheaply, requiring only laboratory assay and short clinical trials.

Despite a corruption scandal in the generics industry between 1988 and 1990, in which companies were found to have bribed FDA officials and circumvented the approval process, the generics segment returned to high growth within a few years. Because of their cheaper price tag, generics only accounted for 14 percent of drug industry sales in 1992, but they were used in over 40 percent of all prescriptions—a figure that industry analysts expected to rise steadily through the 1990s. The dozens of branded drugs coming off-patent in the 1990s were expected to accelerate sales and market share for this industry segment.

The OTC sector was expected to increase substantially in the 1990s as well, following a trend in the shifting of major medications from prescription to OTC status. OTC companies looked to profit from blockbuster drugs like Glaxo's anti-ulcer Zantac, which reached the open shelves of drugstores and groceries in the 1990s. Like generics, OTCs represented a significant price advantage over branded prescriptions. In addition, patients were more likely to diagnose and treat themselves with the drugs than to visit a doctor and receive a prescription.

Even with these changes, the pharmaceutical preparations industry continued to be dominated by the existing large branded firms. Through buyouts and in-house start-ups, as well as a continuation of the merger movement of the late 1980s, large companies adjusted to both market changes and reform movements in the 1990s. Many of the bigger companies, including industry leaders Marion Merrell Dow and Hoechst moved swiftly to buy or create generics divisions in the early 1990s. Industry sources estimated that approximately 40 percent of the generics market was already controlled by the leading branded pharmaceutical companies in 1992. Meanwhile, most major OTC companies were also prescription producers, and the majority of Rx to OTC switches might easily be carried out within these companies. As Roche did with Genentech, the majors also moved to purchase smaller competitors or start their own innovative biotechnology companies. Along with a number of new and important breakthrough drugs coming out of the majors' drug research pipelines, an aging population with greater drug demand, and what Standard and Poor's 1994 *Industry Survey* called the "recession-resistant nature of the business" boded well for at least some of the industry's large companies.

INDUSTRY LEADERS

Seven major companies produce a third of all U.S. pharmaceuticals. Over 300 companies were involved in the pharmaceutical preparations industry in 1993, according to *Ward's Business Directory,* but the top ten companies accounted for over half of American sales. Despite a lack of industry domination by any one, or even three, companies a handful of companies provide leadership in both the ethical pharmaceutical and OTC segments of the preparations industry. Buyouts and competition among the major pharmaceutical companies for control of the generics market in the 1990s, however, left the potential industry leaders in generics ill-defined.

Merck and Company, a traditional industry leader in prescription drug research, had sales of over $9 billion in 1992, up from $8.6 billion in 1991. Merck controlled five percent of the global market in 1992, while maintaining a production and research presence on three continents. In 1991 Merck's research investment of almost $1 billion dollars accounted for ten percent of U.S. and five percent of global pharmaceutical research. The company held the largest market share among pharmaceutical concerns in the United States in 1991.

Merck originated as a German apothecary shop, and the family name has been associated with pharmaceutical manufacturing for over 300 years in that country. In 1891 George Merck began American operations. In World War I, Merck avoided confiscation by giving the majority of its stock to the United States Government, which sold it after the War to start American Merck. In the 1930s and 1940s Merck created a name for itself by making breakthroughs in the discovery and synthesis of vitamins, including B12 in 1948. In a non-drug area, Merck's *Manual of Diagnosis and Therapy* became a medical standard. Merck scientists also led in the synthesis of steroids and funded the researcher who discovered streptomycin in 1943. Five Merck scientists received Nobel Prizes in the 1940s and 1950s for these and other pharmaceutical breakthroughs.

Despite its tradition for significant research and development, and its merger with Sharp & Dohme in 1953 which boosted its sales force, Merck's drug pipeline fell to a trickle and company fortunes slumped in the 1960s. But a renewed commitment to research and development (R&D), started by new Chairman John Horan (1976) and continued by his biochemist successor Roy Vagelos (1985), yielded important new therapies. Two of these, Vasotec, an anti-hypertensive, and Mevacor, which lowered cholesterol levels, reached annual sales of $1 billion apiece. One of the few large companies to take advantage of biotechnology breakthroughs, Merck began marketing the first genetically-engineered human vaccine for hepatitis B late in the decade.

Rather than join the merger and buyout trend of the late 1980s and early 1990s, Merck sought to complement its industrial leadership in ethical pharmaceuticals by moving into joint ventures with companies like chemical industry leader DuPont in 1991, and OTC leader Johnson & Johnson. However, Merck did buy the mail-order drug distributor Medco in 1993. This, and new supplier agreements with MCOs, showed that even giants like Merck were girding themselves for the changes wrought by health-care reform. Nevertheless, with older patented drugs maintaining profitability, a number of new drugs in the approval pipeline, a continuing commitment to research and development expenditures, and a potential blockbuster in its prostate drug Proscar, Merck entered the mid-1990s in a strong position.

Merck's joint venture partner, Johnson & Johnson, also one of the largest pharmaceutical firms in the world, was the industry leader in OTC sales in 1992. Rx to OTC switches for its popular yeast infection treatment, Monistat 7, and its antidiarrheal Immodium promised to improve its OTC position even further. Johnson & Johnson had also managed to build its pain-reliever Tylenol back to the point in the 1990s where it regained its position as the best-selling non-prescription drug in the country. According to the 1994 *Standard and Poor's* report, Tylenol represented about "one-quarter of the $2.8 billion dollar analgesic market." Other familiar OTC products from Johnson & Johnson include the athlete's foot medication Micatin and the sinus medication Sine-Aid.

Headquartered in New Brunswick, New Jersey, Johnson & Johnson got its start when founder Robert Wood Johnson decided to begin the production and distribution of plaster wound dressings he observed during the Civil War. High-quality sterile dressings, including the world famous Band-Aid, made the familiar Johnson & Johnson red cross logo ubiquitous in hospitals and bathroom medicine cabinets. The company also successfully promoted the placement of first-aid kits in homes, railroad cars, and businesses. Beyond Band-Aids, Johnson & Johnson became best known for its familiar line of baby-care products, like shampoos. The purchase of McNeil labs in 1959 expanded Johnson & Johnson's product line into prescription drugs like sedatives, muscle relaxants, and eventually the analgesic Tylenol which went to OTC status in the 1960s. Other successful prescription introductions for the company have included the acne treatment Retin-A and the Ortho-Novum group of oral contraceptives.

In 1982 someone began lacing Tylenol tablets in the Chicago area with cyanide, eventually killing seven people and associating the pain killer with death in the public mind. Swift product recall, a frank public relations campaign, and the reissuing of Tylenol in tamper-resistant packages reestablished the drug's market share. Along with its record of public benefaction and good employee relations, Johnson & Johnson's handling of the Tylenol affair added to its meretricious corporate image. Into the 1990s, Johnson & Johnson maintained and expanded its strong position in the OTC market while continuing as an important medical-care and consumer products supplier.

WORK FORCE

The work force in the preparations segment of the pharmaceutical industry is concentrated in the largest companies. The combined personnel of the seven largest firms in 1993 accounted for over 40 percent of the total employment among the 341 companies operating in this industry segment. Unlike other manufacturing sectors, employment in the pharmaceutical industry grew 45 percent from 1980 to 1992. Just under half of all industry employees in 1987 worked in production,

while research, marketing, and administration accounted for the remainder. For the branded prescription PMA companies, just over 30 percent of employees were in production in 1991, while another 30 percent worked in marketing, and 23 percent in research and development. The differences in this distribution likely reflected the dominant emphasis on research and marketing among PMA member firms.

Several pharmaceutical companies have had reputations as good employers. Scientists have found Merck and Squibb fulfilling places to work because of their aggressive research departments. Merck did, however, endure a 15-week strike by its unionized workers in 1985. Johnson & Johnson has also enjoyed a solid reputation as an employer, offering progressive child-care and maternity leave policies.

The health-care reform movement of the early 1990s disrupted industry employment patterns. The rise of MCO's and chain hospitals reduced the need for the large sales staffs the major companies have traditionally employed. The January 1994 issue of *Chemical and Engineering News* quoted the PMA as saying that "more than 30,000 jobs have been cut or are being cut" from the PMA member firms total of 250,000 employees. Most of the cuts were coming from "marketing and promotion personnel" rather than vital research and development employees.

AMERICA AND THE WORLD

The U.S. Department of Commerce estimated in 1994 that American pharmaceutical manufacturers produced nearly half of the major pharmaceuticals marketed worldwide, while the domestic market consumed approximately 65 percent of this output. Nevertheless, exports accounted for over 30 percent of sales for several major American drug companies in 1992, including Merck, Pfizer, and Johnson & Johnson. Eu-

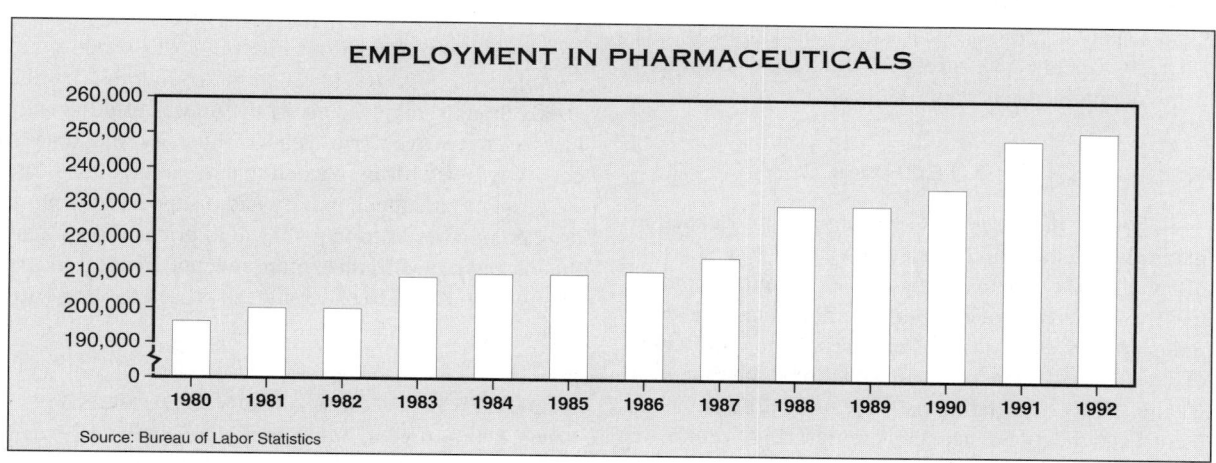

EMPLOYMENT IN PHARMACEUTICALS

Source: Bureau of Labor Statistics

rope, alone, consumed half of American pharmaceutical shipments, though sales to European Community (EC) countries and Japan slumped in 1993 because of world-wide recession and new price controls in many European nations. The finalization of the EC economic union in 1993, along with the passage of the North American Free Trade Agreement (NAFTA) in 1994 promised to improve the competitive position of American pharmaceutical companies overseas.

The completion of the formal economic unification of EC countries in 1993 did not immediately fulfill industry expectations. Before unification, American companies selling or producing in Europe navigated a mine field of conflicting national price controls (most European countries have national healthcare systems that control costs), quality standards, and approval requirements for each new drug introduction, while also worrying about adequate patent protection. Similar problems faced U.S. pharmaceutical companies in Japan, the country with the highest per capita consumption of pharmaceuticals in the world with over 20 percent of the global market.

The importance of international relationships illustrated the traditionally global character of the pharmaceutical industry. Like their European and Japanese counterparts, American companies historically produced, manufactured, and marketed in each other's backyard. Rather than directly investing in full-scale overseas operations, many formed joint licensing agreements or joint ventures with home companies overseas to manufacture and market their products in other countries. In the 1990s American OTC leader Warner-Lambert, started a joint venture with British Glaxo to develop and market an OTC version of Glaxo's blockbuster anti-ulcer drug Zantac. Many American pharmaceutical firms, including Warner-Lambert, however, continued to have overseas production and marketing networks under their own control. Giants such as Merck, American Home Products, and Eli Lilly, operated worldwide, while many European firms maintained extensive U.S. operations.

RESEARCH AND TECHNOLOGY

Though the Federal Government and academic institutions pursue both basic and applied research that often directly affects drug development, approximately 90 percent of new drugs come from the drug industry. However, analysts emphasize the importance of researchers financed by the National Institutes of Health (NIH) in initiating path-breaking drug developments, and the role of academic researchers (often with both NIH and drug-company financing) in revolutionary cell-receptor research as well as initial chemical trials cannot be denied.

The PMA estimated in 1993 that its member companies invested, as an annual average, between 11 percent and 16 percent of the value of pharmaceutical sales in the research and development of new drugs between 1970 and 1992. Meanwhile, Standard and Poor's reported in its 1994 *Survey* that the drug industry's "ratio of research-to-sales ranks as the highest of all major domestic industrial groups."

For patented prescription producers, the actual research and development of new drugs, especially after the adoption of the 1962 FDA regulatory guidelines, had always been an intricate process, sometimes referred to as "playing chess with nature." Company researchers began by screening or developing any number of New Chemical Entities (NCE's) that showed promise in a therapeutic class, on a specific disease, or with a specific cell receptor. Once one of these showed therapeutic potential, the company proceeded to move the new compound through a series of preclinical trials with animals to determine its toxicity at various doses. After the initial testing, the research company generally patented its new chemical and announced to the FDA its intention to begin human trials. The potential drug then moved through three distinct phases of human clinical trials, often taking seven years. The process was designed to expose possible adverse reactions, determine safe and effective dosages for humans, and test treatment. Once an NCE successfully survived these trials, and 19 of 20 did not because of ineffectiveness or toxicity, the company submitted a completed New Drug Application to the FDA seeking final market approval for the new therapy. Even after market approval, a fourth phase could result in a recall or new label warnings if the drug showed adverse reactions in the larger population.

By its own regulations, the FDA was supposed to complete an NDA review within six months. By the 1990s though, review time in the understaffed agency had risen to over two years. Thus, by the time a company's new drug reached market, almost ten of its 17 years of patent exclusivity had disappeared, a point drug companies used to justify high prices. To address this problem, and to raise more revenue in order to add review staff to the FDA, Congress passed the Prescription Drug User Fee Act in 1992.

INDUSTRY INFORMATION SOURCES

Ballance, Robert et al, *The World's Pharmaceutical Industries,* Brookfield, VT: Edward Elgar Publishing, 1992.

Borman, Stu, "Growth of Drug R&D Spending Slow in '94," *Chemical and Engineering News,* January 17, 1994.

Conlan, Micheal, "OTA Undermines Industry R&D Case, but PMA Cries Foul," *Drug Topics,* April 5, 1993.

The Contribution of Pharmaceutical Companies: What's at Stake for America, Boston: The Boston Consulting Group, September 1993.

Cuteia, Jane H., "Swallowing a Bitter Pill," *Business Week,* January, 11, 1993.

Flynn, Julia et al, "A Shot in the Arm for Drugmakers," *Business Week,* September 21, 1992.

Gennaro, Alfonso R., *Remington's: Pharmaceutical Sciences,* Easton, PA: Mack Publishing Co., 1990.

Higby, Gregory, and Elaine Stroud eds., *Pill Peddlers,* Madison, WI: American Institute of the History of Pharmacy, 1990.

Hoover, Gary ed., *Hoover's Handbook of American Business 1993,* Austin, TX: The Reference Press, 1992.

Inside U.S. Business, Homewood, Illinois: Business One Irwin, 1991.

"Internal Biotechnology Units Offer Growth for Pharmaceutical Firms," *Chemical and Engineering News,* December 6, 1993.

International Directory of Corporate Histories, Chicago: St. James Press, 1990.

Liebenau, Jonathan, *Medical Science and Medical Industry,* Baltimore, MD.: Johns Hopkins University Press, 1987.

Mahoney, John, *The Merchants of Life,* New York: Harper Brothers, 1959.

Mattera, Philip, *World Class Business,* New York: Henry Holt and Company, 1992.

Moskowitz, Milton, ed., *Everybody's Business,* New York: Doubleday, 1990.

Nielsen, Robert, *Handbook of Federal Drug Law,* Philadelphia: Lea and Febiger, 1992.

1994-95 Resource Book, Alexandria, VA: Animal Health Institute, 1994.

"Pharmaceuticals '93, a CMR Special Report," *Chemical Marketing Reporter,* March 8, 1993.

Prescription Drug Industry Fact Book 1980, Washington: Pharmaceutical Manufacturer's Association, 1980.

Shon, Melissa, "Industry, Heal Thyself: Pharmaceuticals '94, a CMR Special Report," *Chemical Marketing Reporter,* March 7, 1994.

Spilker, Bert, *Multinational Drug Companies: Issues in Drug Discovery and Development,* New York: Raven Press, 1989.

Standards & Poor's Industry Surveys, New York: Standard and Poor's Corporation, 1993.

Sterne, Diana, "How Come Drug Prices are So High? Conference Hears Answer," *Drug Topics,* April 20, 1992.

The Structure of American Industry, fourth edition, New York: Macmillan, 1971.

Thayer, Ann M., "Biopharmaceuticals Overcoming Market Hurdles," *Chemical and Engineering News,* February 25, 1991.

Trends in U.S, Pharmaceutical Sales and R&D, Washington: Pharmaceutical Manufacturers Association, 1993.

U.S. Industrial Outlook 1994, Washington, DC: U.S. Department of Commerce, January 1994.

1987 Census of Manufacturers: Drugs, Washington, DC: U.S. Department of Commerce, 1990.

Ward's Business Directory of U.S. Private and Public Companies, Detroit: Gale Research, Inc., 1994.

Weatherall, M., *In Search of a Cure,* Oxford, England: Oxford University Press, 1990.

—J. Jacob Jones

SIC 2835

IN VITRO AND IN VIVO DIAGNOSTIC SUBSTANCES

This category covers establishments primarily engaged in manufacturing in vitro ("in glass," such as a test tube) and in vivo ("in the body") diagnostic substances, whether or not packaged for retail sale. These materials are chemical, biological, or radioactive substances used in diagnosing or monitoring the state of human or veterinary health by identifying and measuring normal or abnormal constituents of body fluids or tissues.

According to data compiled by the U.S. Department of Commerce, shipments made by establishments classified in **SIC 2835: In Vitro and In Vivo Diagnostic Substances** during 1990 were valued at $2.46 billion, an increase of 5.9 percent over figures for 1989. In 1993 shipments were valued at $5.2 billion, a five percent increase. Also in 1993, exports reported a nine percent jump to reach $1.5 billion. The primary market for these diagnostic substances has been hospitals and laboratories, but sales to physicians and individual consumers have seen considerable growth.

Government analysts predicted that the market for medical diagnostic products would increase by approximately two percent in 1994. Projections for long-term growth were modest—again, two percent per year—in light of President Clinton's proposed health care reforms. Industry watchers expected a reduction in the number of establishments as a result of industry consolidation. Areas within the industry that are expected to see the most expansion are establishments providing diagnostics for sexually transmitted diseases, diabetes, and cellular disorders.

Many of the products produced by the in vitro and in vivo diagnostics industry were regulated by the U.S. Food and Drug Administration (FDA). In 1989 the FDA gave its approval to new non-ionic (having no electrical charge) contrast media for use with innovative X-ray technologies including computed tomography (CT) and magnetic resonance imaging (MRI). These "in vivo" (used in the body) non-ionic products were able to disperse more readily and created fewer side effects such as nausea, pain, and allergic reactions. FDA approval of other products, such as an imaging agent for use with ultrasound technology, was expected to help bolster the industry. Yet, as the industry has grown, FDA approval time has slowed and more stringent governmental regulations have been enacted.

One of the leading companies classified in **SIC 2835: In Vitro and In Vivo Diagnostic Substances** was Bio-Rad Laboratories, Inc. Based in Hercules, California, Bio-Rad supplied more than 4,500 different products for laboratory and medical research including chemicals and instruments to diagnose and monitor diseases such as anemia, diabetes, and AIDS. Established in 1957 with four employees, by 1991 Bio-Rad employed almost 2,400 workers in the United States and abroad. Sales were reported to be $310 million. The company's 25,000 customers included universities, pharmaceutical companies, biotechnology firms, medical laboratories, and government agencies. Slower than anticipated sales during the early 1990s caused Bio-Rad's sales to fall behind projections. Earnings per share during the second quarter of 1993 were reported to be $0.03 compared with $1.07 for the same period in 1992. Bio-Rad instituted a freeze on employment and initiated other programs aimed at improving its profitability.

INDUSTRY INFORMATION SOURCES

"Bio-Rad laboratories, Inc." *San Francisco Times,* August 6, 1993.

Kleinfield, N. R., "The Do-It-Yourself Armamentarium," *New York Times Magazine,* October 3, 1993.

Lipold, John, "Diagnostics Leap into the Future," *Chemical Marketing Reporter,* March 20, 1989.

Rauber, Chris, "High-Tech Outfit Tends Low Profile," *San Francisco Business Times,* December 6, 1991.

Thompson, Bradley Merril, "In Vitro Diagnostics," *Medical Device & Diagnostic Industry,* May 1993.

U.S. Industrial Outlook 1994, Washington, DC: U.S. Department of Commerce, January 1994.

—Karen Bellenir

SIC 2836

BIOLOGICAL PRODUCTS, EXCEPT DIAGNOSTIC SUBSTANCES

This category covers establishments primarily engaged in the production of bacterial and virus vaccines, toxoids, and analogous products (such as allergenic extracts), serums, plasmas, and other blood derivatives for human or veterinary use, other than in vitro and in vivo diagnostic substances. Included in this industry are establishments primarily engaged in the production of microbiological products for other uses. Establishments primarily engaged in manufacturing in vitro and in vivo diagnostic substances are classified in **SIC 2835: In Vitro and In Vivo Diagnostic Substances.**

INDUSTRY SNAPSHOT

According to statistics compiled by the U.S. Department of Commerce, establishments classified in **SIC 2836: Biological Products, Except Diagnostic Substances** shipped products valued at $2.16 billion in 1990. By 1993, shipments had reached $2.6 billion, an increase of four percent over 1992. Exports stood at $1.2 billion in 1993. The largest class of products within the industry were blood and blood derivatives. They accounted for 33.3 percent of sales. Other major product classifications were vaccines, toxoids, and antigens (24.9 percent); biological products for veterinary, industrial and other uses (21.7 percent); and antitoxins, antivenins, immune globulins, therapeutic immune serums, and allergic extracts (9.8 percent). Other biological products (except diagnostics) not specified by kind accounted for the remaining 10.3 percent.

Government forecasters anticipated that sales of products derived from biotechnology would experience annual increases of 15 to 20 percent between 1992 and 1997. The greatest growth was expected in medical products, but analysts warned that their development could be restrained as a result of changes in national health care priorities, strategies, and payment practices. Advances made in the evolution of non-medical biotech products were expected to be limited because of price constraints and uncertain public acceptance of genetically engineered foods and products.

BACKGROUND AND DEVELOPMENT

Biological products were created with biotechnology, the scientific and engineering procedures involved in manipulating organisms or biological components at the cellular, subcellular, or molecular level. These manipulations were carried out to make or modify plants and animals or other biological substances with desired traits. Although examples of primitive biotech processes dated back to ancient times (such as the use of fermentation in brewing and leavening agents in baking), their use in medical and pharmaceutical applications was an innovation of the latter decades of the 20th century. Some analysts compared the biotech industry's impact on global medical care with the computer industry's impact on communication.

Biotech researchers produced products in essentially three ways: by developing ways to achieve commercial production of naturally occurring substances; by genetically altering naturally occurring substances; and by creating entirely new substances. Some of the tools used by biotech researchers included recombinant DNA and monoclonal antibodies. Recombinant DNA involved the ability to take the deoxyribonucleic acid (DNA) from one organism and combine it into the DNA from another organism thereby creating new products and processes. By using recombinant DNA techniques researchers were able to select specific genes and introduce them into other cells or living organisms to create products with specific attributes. Monoclonal antibodies were developed from cultures of single cells using cloning techniques. They were designed for use in attacking foreign toxins, viruses, and cancer cells.

The U.S. Food and Drug Administration (FDA) required extensive scrutiny of products developed by biotech researchers before they could be offered for sale. Because the biological products presented for approval often involved new technologies or innovative therapies for diseases that had not been previously treated successfully, the approval process frequently proved to be long and costly. Many companies struggled financially through the 1980s waiting for an FDA determination.

One of the earliest biological products introduced to the U.S. marketplace was a blood protein first sold in 1966. The blood protein, called Factor VIII, was used by patients with hemophilia A to control bleeding episodes. Factor VIII, the blood factor responsible for normal clotting action, was manufactured from human blood received from donors. It was followed by the development of Factor IX for patients with hemophilia B.

During the early 1980s, problems arose as a result of AIDS contamination in the blood supply used to produce blood clotting factors. In 1984 manufacturers began using a heat treatment process to guard against future contamination, but, according to a report in the *Wall Street Journal,* approximately half of the nation's 20,000 hemophiliacs contracted AIDS.

The earliest FDA approval for a modern biotech product designed for human therapeutic use was given to human insulin in 1982. Human insulin was used for treating patients with diabetes. Other product approvals followed in subsequent years. In 1984 the FDA approved an agricultural vaccine against colibacillosis (a disease commonly called scours which causes diarrhea or dysentery in newborn animals). Approval was given in 1985 to a human growth hormone (HGH) for the treatment of dwarfism.

The first genetically engineered vaccine approved for use in the United States was a vaccine against hepatitis-B. It received approval in 1986. The vaccine had been created by inserting part of a hepatitis-B virus into yeast cells. Although the portion of the hepatitis-B virus used was not infectious, it caused an immune reaction against infection from the entire hepatitis-B virus.

Other firsts occurring in 1986 included the approval of therapeutic monoclonal antibodies (MABs) and alpha interferon. MABs were approved for use along with immunosuppressive drugs to help prevent kidney rejection in transplant patients. Alpha interferon's first approved use was in the treatment of hairy cell leukemia. Other approved uses for alpha interferon followed: for Kaposi's sarcoma in 1988, venereal warts in 1988, Non-A/Non-B hepatitis in 1991, and hepatitis-B in 1992. A product to dissolve blood clots in patients with acute myocardial infarction (heart attacks) was approved in 1987. Another agricultural vaccine, one to protect against pseudorabies, won FDA approval the same year.

Erythropoietin (EPO), which was to become the largest single biotech product, received its first approval in 1989. EPO, a protein that stimulates production of red blood cells, won initial approval for use with anemia associated with kidney disease. In the same year, the Health Care Financing Administration agreed to pay for EPO given to dialysis patients under the Medicare program. Within a few years EPO was being used by approximately 82,000 dialysis patients in the United States. In 1991 the FDA gave additional approval for its use in treating AIDS-related anemia.

Advances continued during the 1990s. As the industry matured, cooperation between product developers and government regulators improved. The steps in the approval process became more predictable, and a shift in technology was also noted. The primary products of the 1980s had involved the use of recombinant DNA proteins without further alterations. During the early 1990s, researchers turned their attention to products requiring more extensive genetic modification and to more obscure applications.

During the first few years of the decade, the FDA granted approval for several products with uses targeting human conditions. These included a treatment for chronic granulomatous disease (a genetic abnormality affecting the immune system and resulting in severe or life-threatening infections), for acute pulmonary embolism, to aid in chemotherapy and bone marrow transplants, and for kidney cancer. Products wining FDA approval for veterinary use included a vaccine against feline leukemia and a treatment for canine lymphoma.

CURRENT CONDITIONS

By the end of the 1980s, sales of products developed around recombinant DNA technology exceeded $1 billion according to a study done by Consulting Resources and reported in *Chemicalweek*. Consulting Resources expected such sales to reach $4.29 billion by 1995 and to more than double again by the end of the century.

Some industry watchers predicted that most of the pharmaceutical products developed during the 1990s would result from ongoing biotechnical research. The 1993 *U.S. Industrial Outlook* reported that recent FDA approvals for vaccines against rabies, tetanum toxoids, and pertussis had been made. According to government statements, vaccines were one of the most effective and cheapest ways to eradicate some diseases. Concern about health care costs during the early 1990s focused the national spotlight on the pharmaceutical industry and questions were raised about the high cost of biological products.

INDUSTRY LEADERS

One of the leading establishments classified in **SIC 2836: Biological Products, Except Diagnostic Substances** was Genetech, Inc. Headquartered in south San Francisco, Genetech pioneered the development of first-generation biotech products. In 1988 the FDA approved the company's application for Activase which was used to dissolve blood clots in heart attack patients. Approval, however, came only after a lengthy regulatory review and initial sales failed to meet projections. These difficulties left the company financially unstable. Roche Holdings Ltd., a Swiss pharmaceuti-

cal maker, acquired majority ownership of Genetech in 1990. Under Roche's umbrella, Genetech continued to make significant contributions to the industry.

According to a report in *Chemical and Engineering News,* five of the twelve biopharmaceuticals on the market in 1991 were products developed by Genetech. The company's human growth hormone (HGH) was used to treat patients with pituitary growth hormone deficiencies. During the 1990s other uses of HGH were under study including a treatment for Turner's syndrome (a genetic abnormality associated with the absence of a second sex chromosome often resulting in short stature and lack of some aspects of sexual development after puberty), pediatric burns, and growth retardation related to kidney disease. In 1990 sales of HGH by Genetech were reported to be $155 million.

In 1993 the FDA granted Genetech's request for approval of Pulmozyme, the first drug treatment developed for cystic fibrosis, a genetic disease associated with life-threatening mucous secretions in the lungs and lung infections. Pulmozyme was also being studied for its effectiveness in treating chronic bronchitis, a disease sometimes affecting long-term smokers. Other products in various stages of research and development included substances to treat kidney cancer, AIDS, diabetes, breast cancer, and ischemic stroke. Genetech's researchers were also working to develop a vaccine against the HIV virus and on substances to aid in immunotherapy for HIV-infected patients. The *New York Times* reported that Genetech's earnings totaled $58.9 million in 1993, more than double its income of $20.8 million in 1992. The company's revenues of $649.7 million in 1993 were also up substantially from the $544.3 million reported in 1992.

Another industry leader, Baxter Healthcare Corporation, Hyland Division, was headquartered in Glendale, California. In December of 1992, Baxter received approval from the FDA to sell Recombinate, the first genetically engineered drug to be used in the treatment of hemophilia A. Although Recombinate was expected to be more expensive than blood-derived Factor VIII, it did not carry the risk of transmitting AIDS or hepatitis and its supply was not constrained by blood shortages.

In 1994 Baxter withdrew one of its products, Gammagard, from the market because of possible contamination with hepatitis-C, a virus potentially leading to chronic hepatitis or liver disease. Gammagard, an intravenous immune-globulin product used to treat inherited immunological disorders and to aid in bone-marrow transplants, was made with concentrated human proteins derived from donated blood plasma. Although no approved diagnostic was able to directly test for the presence of hepatitis-C, the company screened all donated blood for hepatitis-C antibodies. According to a report in the *Wall Street Journal*, Baxter stated that 14 patients being treated with Gammagard had contracted hepatitis-C but it was uncertain if other risk factors may have been involved.

Genzyme Corporation, with headquarters in Cambridge, Massachusetts, is another major producer of biological products. The company's researchers produced products in niche markets, especially those targeted at genetic diseases. Genzyme's product line had an estimated potential worldwide market of about $2 billion. The *New York Times* called Genzyme "one of a handful of biotech companies that can boast of being in the black." In 1991 the company announced a decision to build a $75 million biopharmaceutical production facility in Massachusetts. Scheduled for completion during 1994, the new facility was expected to initially employ an additional 200 workers.

One of the best known Genzyme products was Ceredase, which was used to treat Gaucher's disease. Gaucher's disease, an incurable metabolic disorder most common among people of Eastern European Jewish ancestry, affected between 2,000 and 3,000 people in the United States. The *Wall Street Journal* said Ceredase sales accounted for about half of the company's revenues during the first nine months of 1993. Although successful from an economic point of view, Ceredase was considered controversial because of its cost. Costs to patients varied depending on age, weight, and severity of the disease, but averaged around $140,000 per year and were reported to run as high as $300,000.

In addition, Ceredase was made from GCR, a human placental product available only from one supplier in France, Pasteur Merieux. Following problems with contaminated blood, the French health ministry issued a ruling in 1993 ordering Pasteur Merieux to stop the production of human albumin from placentas. Although Ceredase did not contain human albumin, the cost of extracting its ingredient (GCR) had previously been shared with the costs of extracting human albumin. With extraction costs falling exclusively on GCR production, Genzyme's annual costs to make Ceredase were expected to increase up to $22 million. In August of 1993, Genzyme announced it had received a patent on a new drug to treat Gaucher disease using recombinant human glucocerebrosidase (r-GCR). Although the r-GCR was expected to alleviate supply constraints due to the controversy over human placental tissue, the new form of the drug was not expected to be significantly less expensive than Ceredase.

AMERICA AND THE WORLD

Exports by U.S. biotech companies exceeded imports. According to government statistics, exports totaled $837 million in 1989, $973 million in 1990, $1.03 billion in 1991, $1.19 billion in 1992, and $1.2 billion in 1993. Imports totaled $191 million in 1989, $271 million in 1990, $325 million in 1991, and $420 million in 1992.

Although U.S. biotech companies pioneered the development of the industry, other countries were making significant progress. For example, in Switzerland research for an AIDS vaccine led to increased understanding of therapeutic vaccines. Industry watchers also noted that Japanese scientists were making gains. Some feared that future market domination by the Japanese could parallel the earlier experience of the electronics industry.

RESEARCH AND TECHNOLOGY

In 1987 the U.S. Patent and Trademark Office announced that it would issue patents on non-naturally occurring nonhuman animals. Although some hailed the decision as a boon to biotechnical research, others objected on ethical and religious grounds. The decision also drew protests from animal rights activists and environmental groups.

Investment in research and improved technology has been a key component of the biological products industry. Although spending on research declined overall in the United States during the early 1990s, in the pharmaceutical industry it increased. Research expenditures made in 1992, for example, surpassed those made in 1991 by 13 percent and reached a total of approximately $11 billion. The industry's practice of spending more than 16 percent of its sales revenues on research and development was one of the highest proportions recorded by any U.S. industry. Products expected to be considered for FDA approval during the mid-1990s included a herpes simplex II vaccine, an insulin-like growth factor, an antitumor necrosis factor, and a product using a toxic protein to combat septic shock. In addition, biotech researchers were studying ways to combat bacterial diseases resistant to antibiotics such as drug-resistant tuberculosis.

AIDS research also received considerable attention. Recombinant DNA techniques had been used to demonstrate the life cycle of the human immunodeficiency virus (HIV) and show how the virus caused AIDS. Recombinant DNA techniques were also being used in the search for vaccines and therapeutic agents for AIDS treatment. Other areas of on-going research in ways to use DNA focused on heart disease, cancer,

Parkinson's disease, and bone marrow recovery in patients following transplantation.

INDUSTRY INFORMATION SOURCES

"Baxter Withdraws Gammagard, Citing Hepatitis C in Users," *Wall Street Journal,* February 25, 1994.

"Biotech Booms in Boston," *Barron's,* April 13, 1992.

Burton, Thomas M., "Hemophiliacs Sue Firms, Foundation Over AIDS in '80s," *Wall Street Journal,* October 1, 1993.

Fisher, Lawrence M., "Rehabilitation of a Biotech Pioneer," *New York Times,* May 8, 1994.

"Genzyme Gets Patent on Second Treatment for Gaucher Disease," *Wall Street Journal,* August 31, 1993.

Heller, Karen, "For Investors, It's More Than Just Hope Now," *Chemicalweek,* January 17, 1990.

"Hemophilia Drug Approved," *New York Times,* December 11, 1992.

Hunter, David and Gregory Morris, "Biotech Grows Up" and "New Techniques Drive Drugs to Market," *Chemicalweek,* January 17, 1990.

Rotman, David, "States Fight Inertia in Biotech Regs," *Chemicalweek,* January 17, 1990.

"Ruling May Push Up the Price of Ceredase, Genzyme's Key Drug," *Wall Street Journal,* December 3, 1993.

Schoepke, Hollis G., "Biotechnology and Biological Preparations."

Encyclopedia of Pharmaceutical Technology, Volume 2, edited by James Swarbrick and James C. Boylan, New York: Marcel Dekker, July 1989.

Thayer, Ann M., "Biopharmaceuticals Overcoming Market Hurdles," *Chemical and Engineering News,* February 25, 1991.

U.S. Industrial Outlook 1993, Washington, DC: U.S. Department of Commerce, January 1993.

Ward, Leah Beth, "Play-It-Safe Genzyme Defies the Biotech Stereotypes," *New York Times,* January 24, 1993.

—Karen Bellenir

SIC 2841

SOAP AND OTHER DETERGENTS, EXCEPT SPECIALTY CLEANERS

This category includes establishments primarily engaged in the manufacture of soap and detergents. It includes companies who make crude and refined glycerin products from fats, or synthetic detergents such as laundry detergents, dishwashing compounds, and personal cleansing bars. Establishments primarily involved in the manufacture of specialty cleaning prod-

ucts are classified in **SIC 2842: Specialty Cleaning, Polishing, and Sanitation Preparations.** Establishments primarily involved in the manufacture of shampoos and shaving products are classified in **SIC 2844: Perfumes, Cosmetics, and Other Toilet Preparations.**

INDUSTRY SNAPSHOT

In 1991, the soap and detergent industry's shipments were valued at $14.4 billion. The amount represented an increase of 3.2 percent over figures from 1990, but the rate of growth was smaller than in previous years. Officials with the U.S. Department of Commerce attributed the slowing growth to the overall national economic picture. Among the factors negatively impacting demand for cleaning products, government analysts cited industrial cost-cutting measures and reduced consumption by hotels, schools, restaurants, hospitals, and other institutional users. International demand, however, was growing. In 1991, U.S. exports of soap and detergent products increased by 25 percent, totaling $487 million. At the same time, imports dropped four percent.

The household detergent segment of the market totaled $3.2 billion, which was split between powders ($1.9 billion) and liquids ($1.3 billion). The U.S. household market also consumed approximately 500 million pounds of automatic dishwashing detergent. An additional 300 million pounds of automatic dishwashing detergents were sold to the industrial and institutional markets.

The bar soap market, which had grown at an average rate of about 4.1 percent annually in the early 1980s, entered the 1990s with a growth rate of about 4.9 percent. Industry analysts attributed the increase to the introduction of body soaps and multipurpose bar soaps. Beauty bars comprised the fastest growing segment of the bar soap market, with sales increasing at a rate of about seven percent per year.

Many of the companies in this classification also shipped secondary products. In 1987, for example, establishments in this category shipped $11.6 billion in products; $8.6 billion represented products considered primary to the industry, and $2.1 billion represented secondary products (The remaining $778.1 million represented miscellaneous transactions). These figures indicated a specialization ratio of 80 percent, a drop from 1982's ratio of 84 percent. The trend toward decreased specialization was seen in the expansion and diversification efforts of many industry leaders.

One of the most significant challenges facing the soap and detergent industry during the early 1990s was growing concern over environmental issues. Consumer demand and government regulations combined to push producers toward reformulating products with an emphasis toward "earth friendly" materials. As a result, manufacturers intensified their efforts to develop detergent formulas capable of meeting environmental concerns without sacrificing product performance or convenience.

The development of concentrated and super-concentrated formulas was an important step in these efforts. Concentrates and super-concentrates required fewer filler materials and chemicals than standard formulations. Their smaller size reduced transportation costs and decreased the volume of packaging materials required. Producers highlighted their environmental emphasis by offering many of the new formulations in recyclable packages made of recycled materials containing post-consumer waste. Despite the heavy emphasis on advertising environmental benefits, some industry watchers reported that consumers placed safety, cost, and performance ahead of environmental issues. Melinda Sweet, director of environmental affairs at Lever Brothers, told *Soap, Cosmetics, Chemical Specialties* that confusion about recycling caused some people to think that recycled products were used products. As a result, some customers thought that products in recycled packages ought to be cheaper.

BACKGROUND AND DEVELOPMENT

The soap and detergent industry's origins are obscured in antiquity. Michael C. Crossin, writing for *Soap, Cosmetics, Chemical Specialties,* stated "the caveman who fell into the river with his fur still on quickly learned that water is an excellent aid in the removal of soils and odors from garments." Crossin calls this find "The single most important discovery in laundry history."

Water alone, however, was not sufficient for all cleaning needs. The next important breakthrough was the development of soap. Different accounts place its invention between 2500 B.C. and 300 B.C. The word "soap" may have been derived from Mt. Sapo, near Rome, a place where burnt offerings were made to the gods. People discovered that the fat and ash residue from the offerings had cleaning properties.

By definition, soap is a cleansing product created through the chemical process of combining a fat or natural oil with an alkali (such as wood ashes or lye) under controlled conditions. Soap-producing factories developed in France and Italy where olive oil was plentiful and used as the main ingredient throughout the sixteenth, seventeenth, and eighteenth centuries. In the nineteenth century, palm oil began to replace olive

oil in formulations. By the turn of the twentieth century, many people still made soap by boiling fats and lye to produce solid cakes.

In the United States, the soapmaking industry marks 1837 as an important year. In that year, William Procter and James Gamble established a candle and soapmaking business. Their company, Procter and Gamble, went on to become one of the foremost soap and detergent makers in the country. Procter and Gamble's famous "Ivory" soap bar was first introduced in 1882. Lever Brothers, another major soap and detergent company, offered "Lifebouy" and "Sunlight" soap bars in 1895.

Procter and Gamble introduced Oxydol, a flaked laundry soap, in 1924. Oxydol was followed in 1933 by Dreft, the nation's first synthetic household detergent. Instead of soap, Dreft's formula was based on alcohol sulfates. Alcohol sulfates were the first type of surfactants to make a significant impact in the formulation of cleaning products.

The term "surfactant" comes from shortening the phrase "surface active agent." A surfactant is a type of chemical capable of changing the surface properties of a liquid. As a result of their chemical nature, surfactants help wash water wet the surface to be cleaned quickly and thoroughly. When water and mechanical action combine to remove soils from a surface, surfactants also help keep the soil suspended in the liquid so that it does not redeposit on the item being cleaned. Surfactants are basic ingredients in most products intended for use in washing clothes and dishes.

The first synthetic detergents based on sodium dodecylbenzene sulfonate were developed in 1939. They were followed by detergents based on alkylbenzene sulfonate (ABS), which provided better cleaning and more suds than traditional soaps at lower prices. ABS grew in popularity and its use expanded with the introduction of front-loading drum washing machines.

In addition to surfactant technology, the 1930s brought the introduction of "built" soap powders and detergents. "Builders" were materials used to enhance the efficiency of a cleaner. Although they had several purposes, such as providing alkalinity to aid cleaning, keeping removed soil from redepositing, and helping to emulsify oil and grease, one of their primary functions was to overcome problems associated with water hardness. Water hardness is a measurement of the soluble metal salts (primarily formed from calcium, magnesium, iron, or manganese) in the water supply. According to the U.S. Geological Survey, water is termed "soft" when it is relatively free of soluble metal salts. It is termed "moderately hard,"

"hard," or "very hard" based on the amount of hardness chemicals present.

When soap products were used in hard water, a substance called "soap curds" or "lime soap" formed. The lime soap precipitate, which would not dissolve, formed in the water and stuck to surfaces causing films and deposits. Builders were used to help counteract these problems. Several types of builders were developed and they worked in different ways. Sodium carbonate, a precipitating builder, caused the water hardness materials to precipitate from the wash solution. Sodium aluminosilicate, another type of builder, inactivated water hardness materials by a chemical process called ion exchange. The most commonly used builders, complex phosphates, worked by holding water hardness materials in the wash solution through a process called sequestration.

By the late 1930s, built soaps and soap in granular form had virtually replaced laundry bar soaps. A decade later, built detergents were becoming popular. The shift from soap to detergent formulations was driven primarily by efforts to overcome problems associated with water hardness.

Detergents, although similar in function to soaps, differed from them chemically. Detergents were made from other raw materials including petroleum products and fatty acids. They often contained additional ingredients such as fluorescent whitening agents, antiredeposition agents, corrosion inhibitors, suds control agents, non-chlorine bleaches, colorants, fragrances, enzymes, blueing, and processing aids.

Built detergents, like built soaps, also contained builders to help improve cleaning efficiency. The first and most widely used builder was sodium tripolyphosphate (STPP). Formulators found STPP effective and relatively easy to process in granulated detergent. Although most built detergents were designed for laundry use, some were adapted for non-laundry household chores. Typically these adapted formulas were high sudsing detergents and could be used for tasks such as hand dishwashing or floor care.

In 1946, Procter and Gamble test marketed their new phosphate built Tide. Tide was launched nationally in 1947 and gained widespread acceptance. Built detergents based on surfactants continued to increase in popularity and by 1953 the poundage of surfactant products sold exceeded that of soaps. The rapid expansion of synthetic detergents, however, led to problems. Reports of foaming in streams and waste water treatment plants were first heard in the late 1940s, and by the early 1950s scientific evidence identified synthetic detergents as the cause. ABS, the most widely used surfactant, was not biodegradable and led to water contamination.

In 1951, the Association of American Soap and Glycerine Producers, predecessor to the Soap and Detergent Association, began to study the industry's environmental concerns and search for biodegradable surfactants. The federal government also investigated the environmental impact of detergents and began to address national concerns with the Federal Water Pollution Control Act of 1956.

During the early 1960s, chemists developed a new form of ABS with a different molecular structure. The new surfactant, called linear alkylbenzene sulfonate (LAS), possessed the appropriate characteristics necessary for biodegradability. In 1965, U.S. detergent manufacturers switched from ABS to LAS in household laundry detergents. Within a few years the number of foaming incidents had dropped and the amount of surfactants in the nation's waterways had been reduced.

Foaming in waterways and treatment facilities, however, was only one problem with early synthetic detergents. Another was "eutrophication." Eutrophication refers to the process of adding nutrients to bodies of water. Excess nutrients caused excessive algae growth, and when the algae decayed, oxygen levels in the water decreased. With diminished levels of oxygen, water bodies were unable to support their fish populations.

Although eutrophication occurs in nature, it takes place over thousands of years. Accelerated eutrophication of water bodies, sometimes referred to as cultural eutrophication, occurred when wastewater carrying nutrients such as phosphorous and nitrogen was dumped into lakes and streams. The phosphate builders used in synthetic laundry detergents were one source of phosphorous in the nation's wastewater.

How much laundry detergents contributed to cultural eutrophication was a controversial question. Proponents of phosphate bans cited studies indicating that 25 to 30 percent of wastewater phosphorus came from laundry detergents. Those opposing phosphate bans claimed that detergents contributed only three percent of the phosphorus entering the nation's surface water, and that most eutrophication could be attributed to agricultural practices.

In the early 1970s, the United States faced rising concern about environmental issues and the problems associated with phosphates. Initial phosphate bans were enacted during the early 1970s. By 1992, statewide phosphate bans for household laundry products were in effect in Georgia, Indiana, Maryland, Michigan, Minnesota, New York, North Carolina, Pennsylvania, Vermont, Virginia, and Wisconsin. Additionally, the city of Washington, D.C., and parts of Idaho, Illinois (including Chicago), Montana, New Hampshire, Ohio, Oregon, and Washington had instituted similar bans. The states of Connecticut, Florida, and Maine, while not banning phosphates outright, limited their use.

Industry analysts differed in their predictions over future demand for phosphate-built products. Some predicted steady or expanded use. They noted that by the early 1990s the rate at which bans overseas were being enacted had dropped, and that in 1991 the United Kingdom refused to institute a ban. They expected domestic demand to remain stable and demand for exports, particularly to Mexico and South America, to increase. Others, however, predicted that phosphates would be completely replaced in laundry products as alternatives were developed. Citing distribution problems associated with meeting varied local regulatory requirements and prevalent consumer perceptions connecting phosphates with environmental jeopardy, they anticipated phosphates would be phased out by the end of the century.

In the United States, phosphate bans helped encourage the development of liquid laundry detergents which were formulated without phosphates. Liquids began to achieve popularity by the mid 1970s and by the close of the 1980s had captured about half the market.

CURRENT CONDITIONS

In addition to environmental and health questions, societal transformation propelled changes in the soap and detergent industry during the early 1990s. Among the numerous factors presenting challenges to detergent formulators were: the need for improved sanitation; the increasing numbers of women working outside the home; the development of time-saving appliances; the trend towards using less energy by lowering wash temperatures; the need to conserve water; and changes in textiles and other cleanable surfaces.

Detergent modifications were also spurred by technical innovation, such as bleach additives, better optical brighteners, and improved technologies to release soils. Marketers packaged products differently to meet the needs of specialized users, such as households with infants or with men performing tasks traditionally associated with women's roles. To meet the needs of various market segments, the industry saw a proliferation of brands and varieties. For example, a typical large supermarket might contain more than forty varieties of laundry detergents including both liquids and powders.

The 1990s also saw a move away from premium pricing for name brands as customers became more value conscious. Although exceptions existed, many soaps and detergents were seen as undifferentiated commodity items. In 1992, reduced value pricing was being used by approximately 40 percent of detergent manufacturers. Typically, a value-priced product cost $1 or more less than a premium-priced product.

A similar trend brought the increased popularity of "value added," multi-purpose products. These included items such as detergent with bleach or fabric softener and three-in-one personal cleansing bars. Moisturizing, deodorant, and anti-bacterial multi-benefit synthetic detergent (also called syndet) bars and soap/syndet combination bars became popular following the introduction of Lever 2000 in 1990. Analysts expected multi-benefit bars to capture 10 to 20 percent of the soap market by the mid-1990s.

The automatic dishwashing detergent (ADD) market was also undergoing transformations. Although customers had rejected first-generation ADD liquids because they separated and were difficult to get out of their bottles, gels were gaining acceptance. ADD gels, first introduced in 1991, were easier to dispense than their liquid predecessors and maintained product consistency. By the beginning of 1992, gels accounted for 35 percent of the ADD market.

While the ADD market was not as directly impacted by the growing concern over environmental issues as was the laundry detergent market, it was influenced. ADD formulas contained four basic types of ingredients: builders, bleaching agents, surfactants, and fragrances. The builder most often used was sodium tripolyphosphate (STPP). During the early 1990s, an estimated 250 million pounds of STPP were used annually in ADD products.

By 1992, phosphate use in ADD products had not been banned as it had been for laundry detergents, and no acceptable alternative for widespread use in household, institutional, and industrial applications had been discovered. In some jurisdictions, however, phosphate use had been limited, typically to 8.7 percent of the product by weight. Even in areas unaffected by such restrictions, manufacturers often reduced the phosphate content of their products from previous levels of 14 to 16 percent to 8.7 percent for the purpose of simplifying the national distribution of their merchandise.

By the end of 1992, Shaklee Corporation (Haywood, CA) was the only U.S. company having a no-phosphate ADD product on the market. Industry analysts expected consumer demand for environmentally safe products to stimulate other manufacturers in their efforts to develop additional no-phosphate ADD alternatives. Environmental concerns were also expected to move the ADD market toward concentrated formulations. The ability to produce concentrated automatic dishwashing detergents was expected to be more difficult than reformulating laundry detergents had been because ADDs do not have as many inert fillers.

Within the laundry detergent segment of the industry, environmental concerns remained primary. Along with environmental issues came an emphasis on "natural" products because they were perceived by consumers to be better for the environment. Formulations were developed for detergents without added fragrances or colors to reduce the number of chemicals used. Manufacturers also promoted "mildness" because it was seen as less harsh for the environment.

The environmental movement led to the promotion of "green" products, products said to be "earth friendly." In contrast to general trends toward value-pricing, U.S. consumers demonstrated a willingness to pay slightly higher prices for environmentally friendly products. U.S. consumers, however, were not willing to accept "green" products that were inconvenient to use or those with diminished performance capabilities.

Concern for the increasing amounts of solid waste in U.S. landfills also factored into the development of concentrated detergents. The nation produced 90 million tons of garbage annually in 1960; by the 1990s that amount had risen to 160 million tons, and some forecasters expected it to reach more than 190 million tons by the year 2000. Manufacturers discussed the nation's growing problems with solid waste management experts and developed responses. Concentrates used smaller volumes of some chemicals, required less packaging, and reduced transportation expenses. The percentage of plastic in the nation's garbage had been less than three percent in 1970, but was expected to reach nine percent by 2000. To emphasize their proactive environmental policies, manufacturers promoted the waste-reduction benefits of cartons made from recycled paper, measuring scoops made from recycled plastics, and containers which were recyclable.

The use of phosphates continued to be controversial. By 1990, phosphate usage in laundry products for household use had been banned in all the Great Lakes states and in many states draining into the Chesapeake Bay. The issue was still politically alive in the Pacific Northwest, and the industry continued its search for cost-effective, high-performance alternatives. Industry watchers expected major manufacturers to turn more heavily to non-phosphate detergents even in areas unaffected by bans because of distribution problems associated with supplying different formulas to different regions.

In addition to environmental questions, another area of concern for manufacturers involved the use of animal testing. During the 1970s and 1980s, animal testing had been widely used as a tool in investigating the safety of detergent ingredients. Animals were used to determine the likelihood of human reactions, the severity of possible injuries, and the time necessary for healing. Rabbits and monkeys were frequently used to discover if certain chemicals or combinations of chemicals would cause eye irritation. Animal rights organizations promoted bans on certain kinds of tests and favored regulations which would require labels to state if animal testing had been used in developing a product. The soap and detergent industry responded with claims that it was working on developing alternatives but some animal tests were still required. One promising alternative was the development of "in vitro" (meaning "in glass") tests.

According to Keith A. Booman, Technical Director for the Soap and Detergent Association, the use of animal testing was reduced by 64 percent between 1980 and 1988. In 1989, Booman wrote in *Soap, Cosmetics, Chemical Specialties,* "Further reductions in animal testing by the detergent industry at this time would impair its ability to evaluate the safety of new products for consumers." He predicted, however, that with further research the causes of chemical-induced injuries would be better understood. The results would thus assist researchers in their efforts to develop batteries of non-animal tests to help further reduce reliance on animal testing.

INDUSTRY LEADERS

One of the oldest and largest companies in the 2841 classification is Procter and Gamble (P&G). P&G was founded in 1837 by two brothers-in-law. The company originally made soap and candles, but throughout its history it has added many other products. By 1992, P&G provided more than 100 brands to 140 countries. Its product list included laundry and cleaning products (Tide, Mr. Clean, Downy, Spic and Span), health and beauty aids (Noxzema, Clearasil, Head & Shoulders, Secret, Ivory), paper products (Charmin), and even foods and beverages. Sales approached $30 billion. In the worldwide market, P&G's laundry detergents held the largest share and overseas trade represented P&G's fastest growing market. In Europe alone, sales topped $8 billion.

One of P&G's biggest competitors in the United States and abroad was Unilever. For example, although P&G had entered the European continental market in 1954, Unilever had already begun marketing a synthetic detergent, OMO, in Italy in 1951. In the United States, Lever Brothers (a Unilever unit) and P&G faced off in several areas. One market in which they both competed was automatic dishwashing detergents. Between them, they held the top two leading automatic dishwashing detergents. P&G's Cascade was the nation's best seller; Lever's Sunlight was number two.

Another area in which the two companies competed was the bar soap market. Industry analysts estimated Lever's market share to be 31 to 34 percent and P&G's market share to be about 32 percent. In 1990, Lever Brothers introduced a new three-in-one moisturizing, deodorant, and anti-bacterial cleansing bar called Lever 2000. Lever 2000 competed with several P&G products such as Safeguard, Coast, and Zest. Another Lever product, Dove, climbed to the top selling position, supplanting Dial, which had been the historic market leader in bar soaps. Dial continued to hold its position, however, in the liquid soap category.

Dial Corporation, another example of a diverse, global company, reported 1992 revenues of $3.4 billion from its operations in North America and Europe. Its products included bar soaps (Dial, Tone, Pure & Natural, Mountain Fresh, Spirit, Fels Naptha), Liquid Dial, Purex laundry products, and Brillo scouring pads. The company also produced specialty cleaners, personal care products, and food items, and operated divisions in transportation manufacturing and service companies.

Following Dial, holding fourth place among soap manufacturers, was Colgate-Palmolive. In an attempt to be more competitive, Colgate-Palmolive replaced its original Palmolive soap with Palmolive Gentle Skin Bar. In liquid soaps, the company's SoftSoap made gains but by 1992 was still behind Dial Liquid in market share. Colgate-Palmolive's total assets and net sales, however, exceeded those of Dial and the company held third place in automatic dishwashing detergents (followed by Benckiser's Electrasol).

In addition to providing products in the soap and detergent industry, Colgate-Palmolive manufactured oral and personal care products such as toothpastes, toothbrushes, oral rinses, and shampoos. The company also operated divisions in specialty fabric care products and in pet dietary care products. Colgate-Palmolive's domestic sales made up only 36 percent of its net sales in 1992. European sales accounted for 31 percent; sales in Latin America equaled 19 percent; and

the Asian and African markets combined to total 14 percent.

In the industrial and institutional segment of the soap and detergent industry, Ecolab held the number one position. Ecolab, founded in 1924, served customers such as hotels, restaurants, health care facilities, dairy plants, farms, and food and beverage processors. In 1992, the company operated in 26 countries, exported products to 87 additional countries, and directly employed 7,400 people.

WORK FORCE

In 1987, soap and detergent establishments employed 31,700 workers, two percent less than in 1986 and ten percent less than in 1982. By 1992 employment had risen to more than 40,000 workers. Sixty-five percent were production workers. As the industry automated, worker productivity increased. Government officials attributed the ability to keep U.S. products competitive on the overseas market to the industry's high level of automation. States with the highest employment in the industry were Michigan, California, Ohio, and Illinois.

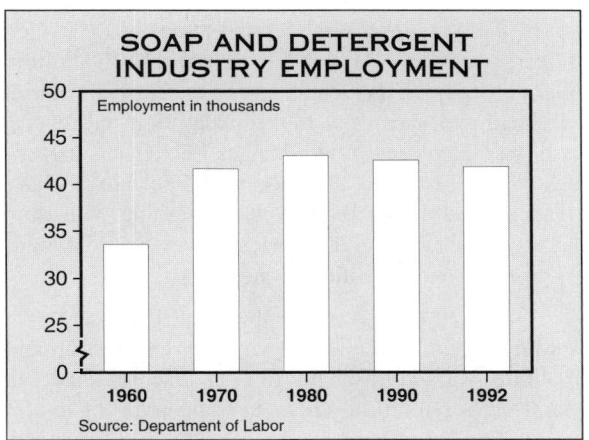

SOAP AND DETERGENT INDUSTRY EMPLOYMENT

Employment in thousands

Source: Department of Labor

AMERICA AND THE WORLD

The soap and detergent industry is an international industry, and during the early 1990s world demand for its products increased one to three percent per year. Many of its participants competed on a global basis. Analysts, noting a firm correlation between a nation's standard of living and its usage of soap and detergent products, expected the market to continue growing in both industrialized and developing nations.

U.S. companies involved in foreign trade found the markets in Western Europe, Japan, and East Asia to be about the same size as the U.S. market. In Japan and Europe, demographic shifts toward older populations and smaller households were similar to the U.S. situation. Forecasters expected the greatest future export opportunities to occur in the developing economies of Eastern Europe. Eastern Europe was also considered a good location for new manufacturing plants.

One of the world's largest non-U.S. soap and detergent manufacturers was the Kao Corporation. Kao, an industry leader in Japan, supplied a broad range of products including laundry detergents, dishwashing detergents, cleaners, toilet soaps, and personal care products. In 1988, Kao entered the U.S. market through its acquisition of the Andrew Jergens Company. By the early 1990s, its global network included several Asian and Pacific nations and the company planned to expand into Australia.

Japanese and other foreign marketers, like their U.S. counterparts, struggled with environmental issues. For example, by 1990 superconcentrates had captured 80 percent of Japan's powdered detergent market, and Kao was switching its formulations to natural-based surfactants. In Europe, environmental efforts resulted in regulations stricter than many enacted in the United States. Refillable containers, which were considered innovations in the United States in 1992, were already popular in Holland and Germany. In addition, German consumers were required to return all outside packaging. Issues of water consumption and energy use were also prompting changes in overseas markets faster than in domestic markets. Some industry analysts expected that trends toward washing with room temperature water and with less water would eventually spread to the United States.

The controversy over phosphates affected soap and detergent marketers on virtually every continent. Sodium tripolyphosphate (STPP) use increased in some areas but fell in others. In Canada during the fall of 1990, a brand war emphasizing the environmental benefits of phosphate-free detergents caused phosphate detergents to drop from 90 percent of the market to 40 percent in only six months. In 1991, however, forecasters expected phosphate sales to increase in Eastern Europe and Asia. Industry analysts also predicted continued growth in phosphate usage within the industrial and institutional segment of the market and in automatic dishwashing detergents.

RESEARCH AND TECHNOLOGY

The need to meet environmental regulations both in the United States and abroad drove many of the research efforts undertaken by the soap and detergent industry during the early 1990s. Zeolite, sodium ci-

trate, sodium carbonate, and sodium nitrilotriacetate were under investigation as possible builders to replace phosphates. Other questions being addressed included product safety, water quality, chemical disposal, the ability to wash in unheated water, and indoor air quality.

Although technological developments and an expanding understanding of chemical processes had improved the industry's ability to restore soiled garments and other objects to their pre-soiled condition, available soaps and detergents still failed to achieve perfect results. Chemical scientists, therefore, continued to work on developing innovative laundry additives such as new enzymes and oxygen bleaches.

INDUSTRY INFORMATION SOURCES

Ainsworth, Susan J. "Soaps & Detergents." *Chemical and Engineering News*, 20 January 1992.

Artzt, Edwin L. "Whither Procter & Gamble in the Cosmetic Business?" *Drug and Cosmetic Industry*, February 1992.

Booman, Keith A. "Animal Testing Alternatives." *Soap, Cosmetics, Chemical Specialties*, October 1989.

Brenner, Theodore E. "Some Current & Future Issues Facing the Detergent Industry." *Soap, Cosmetics, Chemical Specialties*, November 1989.

Caney, Derek J. "STPP Market Improving Despite Bans." *Chemical Marketing Reporter*, 13 January 1992.

Carsch, Gustav. "Making Scents of Detergents." *Soap, Cosmetics, Chemical Specialties*, January 1993.

The Colgate-Palmolive Company. *Colgate-Palmolive Company 1992 Annual Report*. New York: Colgate-Palmolive, 1993.

Crossin, Michael C. "Second Generation Detergent Protease Offered for Today's Multifunctional Laundry Detergents." *Soap, Cosmetics, Chemical Specialties*, August 1987.

The Dial Corporation. *The Dial Corp. 1992 Annual Report*. Phoenix, AZ: Dial, 1993.

Donohue, Janet. "Cleaning products." *Soap, Cosmetics, Chemical Specialties*, January 1989.

Ecolab. *Ecolab 1992 Annual Report*. St. Paul, MN: Ecolab, 1993.

Hunter, David and David Rotman. "Phosphate Use Continues to Take Its Lumps." *Chemical Week*, January 30, 1991.

Kilburn, David. "How Kao Rules Japan." *Advertising Age*, 10 April 1989.

Kilburn, David, and Laurie Freeman. "Kao Angles Its Way Onto the U.S. Stage." *Advertising Age*, 10 April 1989.

Kintish, Lisa. "Laundry Detergents: The Golden Years." *Soap Cosmetic Chemical Specialties*, January 1992.

Mullin, Rick. "Japan's Market Under Pressure: Kao Moves on Asia/Pacific." *Chemical Week*, 27 January 1993.

Naude, Alice. "Family Resemblance: The Automatic Dishwashing Detergents Market is Beginning to Look More Like Laundry Detergents." *Chemical Marketing Reporter*, 25 January 1993.

The Procter & Gamble Company. *The Procter & Gamble Company 1992 Annual Report*. Cincinnati, OH: P&G, 1992.

Singletary, Lynda. "No-Soap Soaps Up: Bar Soaps, No Longer in the Doldrums of Maturity, Are Getting a Big Boost from Syndets and Liquids." *Chemical Marketing Reporter*, 27 January 1992.

Sivak, Andrew. "LAS: A 25-Year Success Story." *Soap, Cosmetics, Chemical Specialties*, April 1988.

Soap and Detergent Association. *A Handbook of Industry Terms*. New York: SDA, 1987.

Soap and Detergent Association. "Types of Laundry Products," New York: SDA, 1991.

U.S. Department of Commerce. *1987 Census of Manufactures*. Washington, DC: Bureau of the Census, February 1990.

U.S. Department of Commerce. *U. S. Industrial Outlook 1992*. Washington, DC: Department of Commerce, 1992.

Van Raalte, John A. "Tale Ends." *Soap, Cosmetics, Chemical Specialties*, April 1988.

Zahodiakin, Phil. "Phosphate Bans Not Washed Up Yet." *Chemical Marketing Reporter*, 30 January 1989.

—Karen Bellenir

SIC 2842

SPECIALTY CLEANING, POLISHING, AND SANITATION PREPARATIONS

This category includes establishments primarily engaged in manufacturing specialty cleaning products (those designed for specific surfaces and/or soils such as bathroom, oven, drain, carpet, and upholstery cleaners), polishes and waxes (such as for furniture, metal, flooring, and glass), and other sanitation preparations including disinfectants and non-personal deodorants. This category also includes establishments making products such as household bleaches and ammonia, laundry starches, and fabric softeners. Establishments primarily involved in the manufacture of industrial bleaches are classified in **SIC 2819: Industrial Inorganic Chemicals, Not Elsewhere Classified**. Establishments primarily involved in making household pesticides are classified in **SIC 2879: Pesticides and Agricultural Chemicals, Not Elsewhere Classified**.

INDUSTRY SNAPSHOT

In 1987, the specialty cleaning, polishing, and sanitation preparation industry had shipments valued at $5.6 billion. Of this total, $3.9 billion were considered primary to the industry and $1.5 billion represented secondary products. Miscellaneous transactions accounted for the remaining $227.9 million. Based on these figures, the industry's specialization ratio was 73 percent, a one percent drop from 1982. The industry experienced modest growth in the late 1980s and by 1991 shipments totaled $6 billion, an increase of 2.7 percent over 1990. Exports, valued at $455 million, exceeded imports, which totaled $175 million. Government forecasters expected the industry's growth rate to be between 2.5 and 3 percent during the mid-1990s.

Goods sold within the industry were typically classified as commodity cleaners or specialty cleaners. Commodity cleaners were usually sold in large volumes at lower prices. Specialty cleaners were sold in smaller quantities but at higher prices. Approximately 65 percent of the products produced were sold to the industrial and institutional (I&I) market. Examples of I&I users included contract cleaning firms, office buildings, restaurants, hospitals, schools, and hotels. Analysts expected the I&I market to grow between one and three percent per year. The nursing home market, which had experienced a growth rate of 7.5 percent in 1992, held the most promise for future growth.

The fabric softener segment of the industry saw annual growth rates of two to three percent in the early 1990s. Sales of fabric softeners intended to be used in the dryer were increasing faster than sales of traditional liquid products formulated to be used during the rinse cycle of a washing machine. Detergents with added softeners were experiencing sales declines.

BACKGROUND AND DEVELOPMENT

There are hundreds of products made by the specialty cleaning, polishing, and sanitation preparation industry, each of them serving the specific cleaning needs of consumers in various market segments. Each of the industry's products was developed in response to changes in technology, consumer need, government regulation, and many other factors, making generalizations about the development of the industry as a whole difficult. The development of fabric softeners, however, demonstrates some of the types of factors affecting the industry.

Fabric softeners were first introduced during the early 1950s following the increasing popularity of synthetic laundry detergents. Because detergents stripped natural oils out of fabrics as they cleaned, materials were left scratchy and susceptible to developing negative ionic charges (static cling) in the dryer. The first fabric softeners were liquids that were designed to be added to the wash during the rinse cycle. In the 1970s, fabric softeners intended for use in the dryer were developed. These consisted of softener-impregnated sheets or porous foam. Other types of dryer-added softeners included sprays and dispensing bars. The 1980s brought the development of all-in-one detergents containing fabric softeners designed for use during the wash cycle.

Technical developments in the fabric softener segment occurred as manufacturers worked to improve the product. One negative side effect of softener usage occurred when material fibers began to appear dingy as a result of the softener's coating action. Optical brighteners, also called florescent whitening agents (FWAs), were developed to counteract this problem. FWAs were chemical compounds that made fabrics appear to be brighter by converting ultraviolet light into visible blue light.

Fabric softeners made fabrics fluffy by coating the fibers with fatty compounds. They eliminated static cling through the use of "cationic surfactants," chemicals that were added to liquids to facilitate the wetting, foaming, dispersing, emulsifying, or penetrating actions of the solution on a surface while introducing positive charges to offset the negative ionic charges associated with static electricity. In addition to cationic surfactants, which by themselves were not considered effective cleansing products, other types of surfactants were developed. These included anionic, nonionic, and amphoteric surfactants. Anionics, the most widely used surfactants in the detergent industry, carried negative charges and were typically high sudsing. Nonionics carried no functional ionic charges and were effective against oily soils. Amphoterics might be either positively or negatively charged depending on water solution conditions.

CURRENT CONDITIONS

A national trend toward mild, natural, and environmentally safe products affected fabric softener development during the early 1990s. Although historically customers had expected softeners to add fragrance, an emphasis on using fewer chemicals led to new formulations. Procter & Gamble, for example, introduced Bounce Free, which contained no perfumes, inks, or extra additives. The environmental movement's campaign to cut down on the amount of trash generated led to the development of concentrates and refills. In 1990, Procter & Gamble introduced

Downy Refill. Downy Refill, which customers mixed with water to make full strength, required 75 percent less packaging than the original 64-ounce bottle. By mid-1991, refills accounted for 40 percent of Downy's sales.

Environmental concerns also affected polishes and waxes. Many ingredients and industry by-products lacked biodegradability. Floor wax makers were challenged by the Clean Water Act to meet product disposal requirements. Regulations concerning volatile organic compounds led some manufactures to move away from solvent-based products and to increased usage of water-based systems. Zinc was found to cause problems in sewage treatment facilities, and as a result the Environmental Protection Agency regulated zinc emissions. In addition, many individual states and municipalities enacted their own zinc regulations.

During the early 1990s, the market for household polishes and waxes declined. The popularity of no-wax floors and a related move toward convenience-oriented products diminished the demand for floor wax. Within the industrial and institutional market, improvements in maintenance technology, such as the development of high-speed buffing, reduced the need for floor wax. New floor materials made of acrylic also required little maintenance.

In other areas related to floor care, however, demand was increasing. The growing popularity of mineral surfaces, such as marble, terrazzo, quarry tile, and ceramics, brought a corresponding need for new types of cleaners. In addition, old asbestos flooring required constant care to keep it polished and sealed.

Carpet cleaners saw high growth rates during 1990 as manufacturers introduced new products with deodorizing ability. Although their growth stabilized the following year, specialty products (such as those formulated for pet owners) continued to do well. The carpet care industry also responded to environmental concerns and questions about indoor air quality. Formulas that were less harsh, non-toxic, and pleasant smelling were emphasized, while some companies promoted all-natural formulas. Packaging moved away from aerosols and favored plastic bottles with trigger delivery systems. More communities were able to recycle plastic than steel, so plastic was seen as a better choice for the environment. In addition, aerosols were perceived to be dangerous to the environment even though CFC's (chlorofluorocarbons) had been previously removed following a ban in 1978.

Within the household bleach market, concerns for environmental safety made less of an impact. Although perborate bleaches (the most widely used type of non-chlorine bleach) were judged to be safer for the environment and gentler on clothes than chlorine-based bleaches, their acceptance within the United States was not as strong as forecasters had anticipated. Perborate bleaches performed poorly at the low wash temperatures preferred by many Americans. In Europe, where higher wash temperatures were popular, perborates had captured 80 percent of the bleach market. In 1992, U.S. industry analysts expected chlorine-based bleaches to remain in the forefront with combined liquid and dry formulas capturing up to 90 percent of the market. One product expected to bring increased acceptance of perborates was Tide with Bleach. Tide with Bleach contained a patented low-temperature activator called sodium nonan-oyloxbenzene sulfonate (SNOBS).

Another trend during the early 1990s was increased concern about the spread of infectious diseases. This brought a growing interest in disinfectants, especially those effective against HIV, the virus connected to Acquired Immuno-Defiency Syndrome (AIDS). Primary disinfectant users within the industrial and institutional market were hospitals and clinics, but others included schools, building service contractors, and hotels. The overseas market was also growing as developing countries demonstrated increased disinfectant use. For example, in South America disinfectants were being employed in the fight against cholera.

The disinfectant industry came under scrutiny in 1990 following a report issued by the United States General Accounting Office. The report stated that perhaps as many as 20 percent of the disinfectants on the market were ineffective and that the U.S. Environmental Protection Agency lacked the ability to ensure consumers that registered disinfectants worked in accordance with their claims. The Chemical Specialties Manufacturers Association (CSMA), responded to criticism against the disinfectant industry by developing plans to monitor the quality of test data and check the performance of disinfectants on the market. The CSMA's Laboratory Accreditation Program evaluated laboratories' ability to perform accurate testing. Its Post-Registration Product Efficiency Testing program conducted random product reviews, initially concentrating on hospital disinfectants. According to the CSMA, U.S. disinfectants were effective and were subject to the most stringent testing procedures in the world.

Disinfectant registration was a source of contention within the industry. Industry leaders complained that the registration process took too long and made the cost of creating new products prohibitive. They claimed that the process was further complicated by individual state requirements which were often different from the EPA requirements. CSMA favored standardized regulations that would apply nationwide.

Another problem involved products aimed at stopping the spread of HIV and Hepatitis. Occupational Safety and Health Association (OSHA) regulations required health care employees to work under the assumption that all body fluids were infected with HIV or Hepatitis. Disinfectant makers complained that the EPA measured the strength of disinfectants according to their ability to kill the bacteria responsible for tuberculosis. According to the industry, the efficacy tests were not comparable because tuberculoides were airborne and many of the disinfectants made for use against HIV and Hepatitis were designed for surface use.

The disinfectant industry also came under scrutiny by the environmental movement. As a result, formulators began investigating ways to make products safer for the environment by reducing the use of volatile organic compounds and making products more biodegradable. In addition, marketers turned to packaging made from recycled post-consumer waste.

Another segment of the specialty cleaning industry to feel repercussions from the environmental movement was the portion involved in manufacturing dry cleaning preparations. Chemicals which were improperly discarded or leaked from faulty equipment were found to be seeping into the ground and contaminating wells and aquifers. One of the biggest offenders was perchlorethylene (PCE, also called perc). Perc was used by more than 80 percent of U.S. dry cleaners. Approximately 500 million pounds of perc were produced in the United States every year. The Clean Air Act of 1990 listed Perc as a hazardous pollutant which could cause dizziness and headaches. Some studies linked perc to miscarriage and cancer. The Environmental Protection Agency proposed that dry cleaners reduce perc emissions by 13 to 26 percent by 1996.

INDUSTRY LEADERS

One of the largest companies in the industry is The Clorox Company. Clorox, formerly a division of Procter & Gamble, became an independent company in 1969 as a result of antitrust regulations. By 1992, the company offered 24 national retail brands in 94 countries. In addition to Clorox brand bleaches, its product line included top sellers such as Formula 409, Soft Scrub, and Liquid Plumr. The company acquired Pine-Sol, the nation's best selling dilutable cleaner, in 1990.

In 1992, Clorox held approximately 60 percent of the domestic market for hypochlorite bleaches. A company report boasted, "U.S. consumers add Clorox liquid bleach to their laundry loads at the rate of more than 130 cups per second." To meet customer demand, Clorox operated more than 40 manufacturing facilities worldwide and employed about 5,800 workers. Not all of Clorox's efforts produced positive results, however. A combination detergent with bleach offered by the company failed to capture a sufficient share of the market and was withdrawn. Other manufacturers offering combination detergents, such as Procter & Gamble's Tide with Bleach, drew sales away from Clorox's stand alone bleaches.

Another leader within the specialty cleaners classification was L&F Products. L&F, an independent operating unit of Eastman Kodak, carried brands such as Lysol disinfectants, Resolve carpet cleaners, and Thompson's Water Seal. In 1993, L&F introduced a new scent, "Country Home," to its Love My Carpet line. The manufacturer also marketed carpet cleaners to different market segments. Cleaners with aerosol foams were sold for cleaning large areas; trigger sprays and sticks were aimed at the spot removal market; and specialty cleaners were designed for specific problems such as pet stains.

Within the industrial and institutional market, Zep Manufacturing was one of the nation's top ten manufacturers. Zep, a subsidiary of National Service Industries, served almost half a million customers in the United States, Canada, and Western Europe. In 1992, the company completed a $20 million modernization and expansion project at its manufacturing and administrative facilities in Atlanta, Georgia.

WORK FORCE

Employment within SIC 2842 fell during the 1980s. In 1987, the industry employed 20,600 workers. The 1987 figures were two percent below 1986 and ten percent below 1982. According to U.S. Department of Commerce statistics, in 1991 the industry employed 21,700 people. The states with the highest number of workers were Illinois, New Jersey, Wisconsin, and Georgia.

RESEARCH AND TECHNOLOGY

In 1992, government forecasters predicted that changing regulations and environmental concerns would encourage continuing work on the development of technologies and products deemed "earth friendly." One area already in the forefront was the development of packaging using resin from recycled products. Clorox, for example, launched efforts to increase its use of post-consumer waste in containers. Some Clorox bleach bottles were slated to contain 20 percent; popular sizes of Soft Scrub products and Formula 409 were to contain 25 percent; and bottles of dilutable Pine-Sol were expected to be made from 100 percent recycled polyethylene terephtalate. Clorox claimed its efforts saved eight million pounds of virgin plastic, glass, and corrugated paper board in 1992. Other efforts to reduce the use of packaging materials included making caps and labels smaller and eliminating exterior packaging.

Product formulators also faced challenges in making cleaning products that were safe for the environment without sacrificing performance or convenience. Manufacturers were exploring ways to reduce their reliance on volatile organic compounds used in solvent-based formulas, improve the biodegradability of products, and lessen products' impact on sewage treatment plants. Some efforts toward producing products with lessened environmental consequences came as a result of evolving federal and state regulations. Other efforts were market driven. Some industry analysts predicted that many necessary innovations toward "environmental friendly" formulas would come from small suppliers.

INDUSTRY INFORMATION SOURCES

Binenstock, Alan. "Floor Care Products." *Soap Cosmetics Chemical Specialties*, June 1989.

"Cleaner Dry Cleaners." *Time*, 30 November 1992.

The Clorox Company. *The Clorox Company 1992 Annual Report*. Oakland, CA: Clorox, 1992.

"Downy Refill Reduces Waste." *U.S. Distribution Journal*, 15 November 1990.

Eastman Kodak Company. *Eastman Kodak Company 1991 Annual Report*. Rochester, NY: Eastman Kodak, 1992.

Hoffman, John. "Less Than Bright." *Chemical Marketing Reporter*, 25 January 1993.

Johnson, Bradley. "Clorox's Identity Crisis." *Advertising Age*, 6 May 1991.

Kintish, Lisa. "Disinfectants in Distress." *Soap, Cosmetics, Chemical Specialties*, November 1992.

———. "Disinfectants under Attack." *Soap, Cosmetics, Chemical Specialties*, November 1990.

———. "Polishing Up Their Act." *Soap, Cosmetics, Chemical Specialties*, September 1991.

National Service Industries, Inc. *National Service Industries, Inc. 1992 Annual Report*. Atlanta, GA: NSI, 1992

Pellicano, Mary. "Toward a Softer, Static-Free World." *Soap, Cosmetics, Chemical Specialties*, August 1991.

Perrault, Mike. "Dry Cleaning Can Be Dirty Business." *Orlando Business Journal*, 3 April 1992.

Singletary, Lynda. "Some Open Doors: Additives Producers are Responding to Emerging Opportunities in the Wake of Technology Changes." *Chemical Marketing Reporter*, 25 January 1993.

Soap and Detergent Association. *A Handbook of Industry Terms*. New York: SDA, 1987.

Springer, Neil. "No Recession Here." *Chemical Marketing Reporter*, 25 January 1993.

Strandberg, Keith W. "The Carpet Care Market." *Soap & Cosmetic Chemical Specialties*, February 1993.

Strandberg, Keith W. "Floor Waxes and Polishes Update." *Soap, Cosmetics, Chemical Specialties*, September 1992.

U.S. Department of Commerce. *1987 Census of Manufactures*. Washington, DC: Bureau of the Census, February 1990.

U.S. Department of Commerce. *U.S. Industrial Outlook 1992*. Washington, DC: Department of Commerce, 1992.

—Karen Bellenir

SIC 2843

SURFACE ACTIVE AGENTS, FINISHING AGENTS, SULFONATED OILS, AND ASSISTANTS

This industry classification includes establishments primarily involved in making compounds that, when dissolved in water, reduce the water's surface tension. Products include preparations such as wetting agents, emulsifiers, and penetrants. These ingredients are raw materials for soap and detergent manufacturers. This industry classification also includes establishments primarily involved in producing sulfonated oils and fats and related products.

Surface active agents are chemical compounds that enable solutions to more quickly saturate surfaces. The name "surface active agent" is frequently shortened to "surfactant." In 1987, the surfactant industry's shipments were valued at $3 billion. Of this total, $2.2 billion represented products primary to the industry; $714.5 million represented secondary products, and miscellaneous transactions accounted for $127.2 million. According to these figures, the industry's specialization ratio was 75 percent, a reduction in specialization from 1982 when the ratio was 81 percent.

The industry saw modest growth during the early 1990s. In 1991, shipments were valued at $3.3 billion. Exports equalled $480 million and imports totaled $140 million. Government forecasters predicted that the industry would continue to grow at a rate of approximately five percent per year through the mid-1990s.

Customer demand and legislative requirements combined to bring changes to the surfactant industry during the early 1990s. Manufacturers worldwide focused on the development of milder products, increased use of natural ingredients, and emphasized environmental safety. In 1992, *Soap, Cosmetics, Chemical Specialties* quoted Ed Tobey, vice president of national accounts for Stepan Company, as saying, "There isn't any product that hasn't changed in the past 12 months."

One of the most profound changes was the shift to concentrated and superconcentrated formulas, not only within household products but also in the industrial and institutional markets. Some industry analysts feared that the increasing demand for superconcentrated surfactants produced by large manufacturers would impede the development of small companies because the formulas were difficult for smaller manufacturers to reproduce.

Environmental regulations also called for formulation changes. Personal care product manufacturers required solutions with less alcohol, makers of specialty cleaners were shifting from solvents and volatile organic compounds to water-based systems, and some communities upgraded biodegradability standards. Environmental concerns were impacting the European surfactant industry even more profoundly. Industry watchers expected some classes of surfactants to be banned by the mid-1990s because of problems with wastewater treatment facilities.

An international phenomenon impacting the industry in the 1990s was consolidation. As large global corporations bought smaller national companies, fewer independent manufacturers remained. Although the trend toward fewer, bigger corporations was expected to continue, the rate of industry consolidation was expected to subside.

The Stepan Company, founded in 1932 and headquartered in Northfield, Illinois, is one of the nation's largest surfactant producers. In 1992, the company reported net sales of almost $436 million. Stepan's customers included detergent, shampoo, lotion, toothpaste, cosmetic, and other manufacturers. Stepan entered the foreign market in 1976 with its acquisition of a firm in France and the company continued to expand its global presence throughout the 1980s. In 1992, Stepan expected most of its future growth to take place in the overseas market.

INDUSTRY INFORMATION SOURCES

Richards, David. "Going Natural." *Chemical Marketing Reporter*, 25 January 1993.

Shaw, Anita Hipius. "Surfactants: Evolution or Revolution?" *Soap, Cosmetics, Chemical Specialties*, September 1992.

Soap and Detergent Association. *A Handbook of Industry Terms*. New York: SDA, 1987.

The Stepan Company. *Stepan 1992 Annual Report*, Northfield, IL: Stepan, 1993.

U.S. Department of Commerce. *1987 Census of Manufactures*. Washington, DC: Bureau of the Census, February 1990.

U.S. Department of Commerce. *U.S. Industrial Outlook '92*. Washington, DC: Department of Commerce, 1992.

—Karen Bellenir

SIC 2844

PERFUMES, COSMETICS, AND OTHER TOILET PREPARATIONS

This category includes establishments primarily engaged in manufacturing perfumes, cosmetics and other toilet preparations. Manufacturers of shampoos, shaving products, personal deodorants, hair preparations, suntan lotions and oils, talcum powders, toothpastes and powders, mouthwashes, and premoistened towelettes are included.

INDUSTRY SNAPSHOT

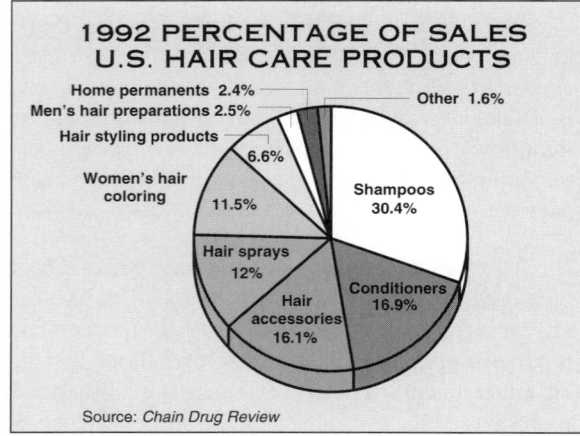

1992 PERCENTAGE OF SALES U.S. HAIR CARE PRODUCTS

Home permanents 2.4%
Men's hair preparations 2.5%
Hair styling products
Women's hair coloring 11.5%
Hair sprays 12%
Hair accessories 16.1%
6.6%
Shampoos 30.4%
Conditioners 16.9%
Other 1.6%

Source: *Chain Drug Review*

Shipments of the perfumes, cosmetics, and other toilet preparations industry were valued at $14.6 billion in 1987. Of this total, $13.1 billion represented products primary to the industry, $679.9 million represented secondary products, and $849.9 million represented miscellaneous sales. These figures resulted in a specialization ratio of 95 percent, just under the 1982 specialization ratio of 96 percent. Modest growth between 1987 and 1991 resulted in an increase in the value of shipments to an estimated $16.8 billion.

Although government forecasters considered the total U.S. market for perfumes, cosmetics, and toilet preparations to be saturated and predicted only a modest 3.1 percent overall growth during the mid-1990s, the industry's various segments reacted differently to existing economic conditions. Specific segments with the most potential for growth included specialty sun care products, functional products, and unisex items that encouraged men's use of non-traditional merchandise like bath salts and skin-care lotions.

Projections for other items varied greatly. Cosmetics used to color the face (such as lipstick, blush, and eye shadow) were referred to as the "color market." Industry forecasters projected ten percent annual growth in the color market during the 1990s. The hair care segment, however, was expected to grow at a rate of only two percent per year. Some hair care products with greater growth potential were hair colorings and dual-purpose shampoos with conditioners. Within the dental products segment of the industry, anti-plaque toothpastes offered the best potential for growth. Fragrances, with annual domestic sales estimated at $3 billion, represented one of the largest segments within the industry, and men's products accounted for about 25 percent of the U.S. fragrance market.

Ethnic markets represented another growth area within the industry. Sales of products formulated for black consumers were estimated at $600 million annually. Hair care and styling products accounted for the bulk of these sales. Approximately $100 million represented color cosmetics for blacks. Industry analysts estimated about eight million black women used color cosmetics daily. Some analysts questioned whether demand was large enough to support the infusion of product lines aimed at black women.

The nation's economic condition during the 1980s and early 1990s was also bringing about changes in the industry's distribution patterns. Traditionally, retail products had been classified as upscale, mid-level, or low-scale, depending on where they were sold and their pricing structure. Upscale product lines were typically sold in major department stores or specialty boutiques; mid-level product lines were sold in department stores at lower prices; and low-scale product lines were sold in drug stores or through catalogs. Industry analysts reported that customers were turning away from upscale products and switching to lower priced brands which were increasingly being sold in mass market outlets. Department stores had sold almost 20 percent of upscale cosmetics in 1985, but by 1991 the figure had dropped to 12 percent, according to a study conducted by Business Trend Analysts reported in *Drug and Cosmetic Industry.*

ORGANIZATION AND STRUCTURE

Many participants in the cosmetics, fragrances, and personal care products industry were members of the Cosmetic, Toiletry and Fragrance Association (CTFA). The CTFA, which was founded in 1894, represented manufacturers and distributors as well as industry suppliers. It provided scientific, legal, regulatory, and legislative services. According to a report published in *Soap, Cosmetics, Chemical Specialties* summarizing the events at CTFA's 97th Annual Meeting in Boca Raton, Florida, the organization's mission was "to provide an environment free of unnecessary government regulation."

The federal agency most often involved in regulatory encounters with the industry was the Food and Drug Administration (FDA). The FDA required that color additives be tested and approved prior to use. It banned or restricted the use of some specific ingredients including mercury compounds, chloroform, and methylene chloride. Other regulations dictated that cosmetics contain no poisonous or harmful substances, no filthy, putrid, or decomposed substances, and that they must be manufactured and held under sanitary conditions. The FDA also instituted labeling requirements which compelled manufacturers to list cosmetic ingredients in descending order according to the quantity used, with some flexibility allowed for the protection of trade secrets. The FDA also had the authority to take legal action against cosmetic companies if problems developed with the safety of products already on the market. In order to do so, the agency was required to prove in court that the product was harmful or misbranded.

The FDA, however, did not require the same type of pre-market approval for cosmetics as was required for drugs. According to a report published in *FDA Consumer,* cosmetics were legally defined as "articles other than soap which are applied to the human body for cleansing, beautifying, promoting attractiveness, or altering the appearance." The FDA recognized 13 categories of cosmetics: skin care products, fragrances, manicure products, eye makeup, makeup other than eye makeup, hair coloring preparations, shampoos and other hair products, deodorants, shaving products,

baby products, bath oils and bubble baths, mouthwashes, and sunscreens.

The distinction between cosmetics and drugs was sometimes vague. According to FDA guidelines, products claiming to offer medical benefits or physiological effects were over-the-counter (OTC) drugs. Examples of items with controversial classifications included antiperspirants, which were classified as OTC drugs in the late 1970s, sunscreen products that listed a Sun Protection Factor (SPF) number, hair care products claiming to protect or restore hair, and shampoos professing to cure or remove dandruff. If the FDA deemed a cosmetic product to be an OTC drug, it was regulated as a new drug. The manufacturer was then required to demonstrate product safety and efficacy in order to gain FDA approval.

The cosmetic industry, under the sponsorship of CTFA, developed the Cosmetic Ingredient Review (CIR) in the mid-1970s in order to gather information about ingredient safety and make the information available to manufacturers. Reviews were conducted by a panel of scientific and medical experts. One report claimed that by 1988, 85 percent of the most frequently used 700 cosmetic ingredients had been reviewed, were under review, or were being regulated or studied by other procedures such as the FDA's process of reviewing over-the-counter drugs. Another report claimed that a review performed by the National Institute of Occupational Safety and Health found that 884 of the 2,983 chemicals used as ingredients in cosmetics were toxic substances. The CTFA refuted the claim and maintained that scientific and medical studies demonstrated the safety of ingredients used within the industry.

The fragrance segment of the industry organized the Research Institute for Fragrance Materials (RIFM) in the mid-1960s to independently test and certify the safety of natural and chemical aromatics. During its first 25 years of operation, the RIFM tested approximately 1,400 different materials. The studies resulted in recommendations to restrict or prohibit about 100 of the ingredients reviewed.

In an effort to further cooperation between cosmetic and fragrance manufacturers and the FDA, the regulatory agency instituted a voluntary registration program in which manufacturers participated in monitoring adverse reactions to products. The program provided for information exchanges among participants and with the government. By 1991, more than 165 companies had registered and the FDA planned to expand the program to include a larger percentage of eligible participants and to provide more useful services.

Donald A. Davis, editor of *Drug and Cosmetic Industry*, wrote in September 1992 that government regulation of the industry could help it achieve improved quality and higher standards, noting that regulation created "an aura of confidence." According to Davis, "The mere existence of the FDA and its role in regulating the food, drug, and cosmetic industries stimulates the consumer to assume that the products of these industries are inherently safe and (to some degree) effective because they are the subject of surveillance by a prestigious government agency with what appears to be real clout." He parenthetically commented, "Never mind that some of this is illusion, especially in the case of cosmetics."

BACKGROUND AND DEVELOPMENT

The use of cosmetics, fragrances, and personal care products can be traced back to human's earliest days. Neanderthal man painted his face with reds, browns, and yellows derived from clay, mud, and arsenic. Bones were used to curl hair. Makeup, tattoos, and adornments conveyed necessary social information. The ancients also used fragrances. Some believed that a flower's aroma contained the presence of a deity, while others burned incense during religious rites. Different fragrances often had symbolic meanings and ceremonial oils were used for anointing.

During the reign of the Pharaohs, Egyptian aristocrats wore cones of solidified perfume that would melt under warm temperatures to provide cooling and mask odors. A mineral called hematite was applied as rouge and faces were painted with white lead. Black kohl encircled eyes. Egyptians curled their hair with sticks or straightened their hair with iron bands and weights. Aloe vera was known as an anti-irritant.

Greek women also painted their faces white and put red circles on their cheeks. Galen, an ancient Greek physician, invented cold cream. The Romans used oil-based perfumes on their bodies, in their baths and fountains, and applied them to their weapons. In the ninth century, Arabs developed alcohol-based perfumes. Crusaders of the thirteenth century brought fragrances back to Europe from the Far East.

The perfumes developed during the sixteenth century were powders or gelatinous pastes. They could be applied to scented fans or carried in jewelry with fragrance compartments. The ability to create new fragrances by blending ingredients was developed during the seventeenth century in France. A person who developed new perfume scents by blending ingredients was called a "nose." Some of the compounding establishments developed in France during the eighteenth and nineteenth centuries were still operating at the close of the twentieth century. America's first cologne water, Caswell-Massey's Number Six, was a blend of 27 ingredients and was said to have been a favorite of George Washington.

Natural perfumes were made from a variety of ingredients containing aroma. These included essential oils, which were found in flowers, roots, fruits, rinds, or barks depending on the type of plant, resinoids, which were gums or resins that were purified with a solvent, and absolutes, which were aromas extracted with solvents existing in viscous liquid form. Natural perfumes were expensive, primarily because of the labor involved in gathering ingredients. For example, *Smithsonian* magazine reported that a pound of jasmine flowers contained approximately 5,000 blooms, and one pound of the flowers yielded only 1/800th of a pound of jasmine absolute.

Chemical formulations developed during the nineteenth century began to replace expensive natural ingredients and make perfumes more widely available. Early synthetic fragrances included vanilla and violet. In the United States, Francis Despard Dodge developed citronellol and citronellal with various floral scents.

The nineteenth century also brought changes in facial makeup. Ceruse, a cosmetic that had been widely used in Europe since the time of the second century, was replaced by a powder made from zinc oxide. Ceruse, made from white lead, was discovered to be toxic. It was blamed for causing physical problems such as facial tremors, muscle paralysis, and even death.

Antiperspirants and deodorants were developed during the 1890s. Aluminum chloride, the original active ingredient, frequently caused skin irritation and damage to clothes. These difficulties were overcome during the 1940s when aluminum chlorohydrate was developed. Although additives were subsequently produced to improve antiperspirant activity, aluminum chlorohydrate remained the primary ingredient in antiperspirants for the remainder of the twentieth century.

Following World War II, biological ingredients began to receive attention. Human placental products were first used in cosmetics during the 1940s. Cosmetic makers claimed that they stimulated tissue growth and removed wrinkles. The FDA ruled that such claims were medical in nature, and as a result classified these products as drugs and declared them ineffective. Placental products later reappeared in cosmetics but were listed only as a source of protein. Other biological ingredients (derived primarily from cows) included amniotic liquid, collagen (a protein substance), and cerebrosides (fatty substances with carbohydrates produced at the deepest layer of skin).

Fashion trends continued to bring new innovations. Artificial skin tanning aids were developed during the late 1950s. False eyelashes became popular during the 1960s. The 1960s also saw the introduction of ''natural'' products based on botanical ingredients such as carrot juice and watermelon extract. During the 1970s, the growing environmental movement brought challenges to the cosmetic and fragrance industry. The use of some popular ingredients was banned following the enactment of endangered species protection legislation. Some examples included musk (from Himalayan deer, Ethiopian civet, and certain types of beaver) and ambergris (taken from sperm whales).

Concerns about contaminated makeup emerged during the late 1980s. An FDA report in 1989 found that over five percent of samples collected from counters in department stores were contaminated with molds, fungi, and pathogenic organisms. Such contamination was supposed to be controlled by preservatives in the cosmetics. Preservatives, however, proved ineffective against the microorganisms responsible for causing product contamination when they lacked stability or when a particular product was kept longer than the shelf life of its preservative system.

Although cosmetic products seldom caused serious injury, some problems did occur. Most common among them were eye infections (caused by scratching the eyeball with a contaminated mascara wand) and allergic reactions. Fragrance additives were often blamed as a source of allergic responses. Two fragrances, acetylethly tetramethyltetralin (AETT) and 6-methyl coumarin (6-ME), caused sufficient numbers of adverse reactions for the FDA to take action against them. AETT, a neurotoxic, caused flushing, dizziness, nausea, and other reactions. 6-ME, which was frequently used in sunscreens, was photo-toxic and interacted with UV radiation occasionally leading to irreversible skin depigmentation and/or hyperpigmentation.

Manufacturers began to offer products labeled ''hypoallergenic'' or ''natural.'' The term ''hypoallergenic'' meant a product was considered by its manufacturer to offer less potential for allergic reaction. Some makers conducted clinical tests to determine the likelihood of allergic responses. Others merely reformulated products without adding fragrances. An effort by the FDA to regulate a precise meaning for the term ''hypoallergenic'' was overturned in the courts. The industry used the word ''natural'' to refer to any ingredient that was not synthetically produced. It had no regulated meaning implying ''pure'' or ''clean.''

Controversy continued into the 1990s over cosmetic ingredients and claims. Some popular materials were Nayad, liposomes, and vitamins. Nayad (a trade name) was a yeast extract said to make the skin look and feel smoother by reducing lines and wrinkles. Liposomes were round, microscopic sacs made of fatty substances which cosmetic makers claimed could penetrate the skin's surface to deliver other ingredients into deeper skin layers. Vitamins were listed on display labels to imply that their usage would nourish the skin. The FDA, however, prohibited manufacturers from making therapeutic claims based on the vitamin content of skin care products.

CURRENT CONDITIONS

As the perfume, cosmetic, and toiletry preparations industry entered the 1990s, it faced many challenges including regulatory changes, product safety concerns, calls for scientific data to document product claims, increasing environmentalism, and pressure from the growing animal rights movement. Congress began investigating possible revisions to the traditional ''drug'' and ''cosmetic'' definitions established under the Food, Drug and Cosmetic Act. A report titled ''Classification and Regulation of Cosmetics and Drugs: A Legal Overview and Alternatives for Legislative Change'' included provisions for a third category of ''cosmeceuticals'' to include products like sunscreens which fell in the gap between ''drugs'' and ''cosmetics.'' Some industry analysts welcomed legislative changes to clarify product distinctions but doubted whether manufacturers would accept proposals that would require safety and efficacy testing to substantiate label claims.

The FDA continued compiling complaints from customers about neurological reactions to perfumes including symptoms such as burning of the eyes, nose and throat, flushing, dizziness, nausea, difficulty in breathing, memory loss, and drowsiness. Some hospitals banned the use of perfumes by operating room nurses. A group calling itself the National Foundation of the Chemically Hypersensitive wanted to ban the use of fragrances in public meeting places.

Some spokesmen within the fragrance and cosmetic industry claimed that, because no one had ever been killed or seriously injured as a result of fragrance use, the FDA's resources would be better spent on bigger health problems. They advocated individual avoidance of offending ingredients as a solution to skin irritations and allergic responses. Although the industry's safety record prior to the 1990s had been good, some seasoned industry watchers expressed concern about continued safety as many small, new companies emerged.

Growing concern about environmental issues also impacted the industry. Several surveys demonstrated increased awareness of pollution and related issues. In 1976, 64 percent of one survey's respondents favored banning products that polluted the environment; by 1988, 73 percent supported such a ban. In another survey, 82 percent of respondents claimed to have changed purchasing decisions as a result of environmental concerns; 77 percent said that the environmental reputation of a company was important to them when making brand decisions; and 56 percent had refused to buy a product during the previous year because of environmental concerns. In 1990, Find/SVP (a New York survey group) estimated that 18.8 million U.S. households were environmentally interested shoppers. These consumers, called "Green consumers," accounted for about 20 percent of the U.S. population and their number was expected to increase. In a report on Green consumers, Find/SVP cited three main concerns: animal rights and species preservation, availability of clean air and water, and waste management.

One of the most controversial environmental matters facing the fragrance industry was pressure to reduce its use of volatile organic chemicals (VOCs). The most popularly used VOC was ethyl alcohol, which functioned as a solvent. The industry claimed that water was not a good substitute for ethyl alcohol because many fragrance ingredients were not water soluble. Ingredients designed to help materials dissolve in water affected product texture and also presented possible safety concerns. Propellants and many other ingredients used within the industry were also VOCs.

VOCs were blamed for contributing to ground-level ozone. In California, VOC emissions from colognes, perfumes, toilet water, aftershaves, and body splashes were estimated at almost 1700 pounds per day. Consequently in the early 1990s, California proposed limits on VOC usage in fragrances. New York and other states were expected to follow. In California, the proposed regulations scheduled to take effect on January 1, 1995, limited VOCs to 70 percent of perfumes, colognes, and toilet waters; 60 percent of aftershaves; and 50 percent of other fragrances. Industry negotiators and the California Air Resources Board agreed to exempt colognes, perfumes and toilet waters that were on the market before the regulations took affect.

In addition to planned compliance with VOC regulations, many fragrance and cosmetic companies brought "green" products to the market place. Estee Lauder, introduced its Origins Natural Resources line of skin care, body products, aromatherapy, and makeup. The line was promoted as natural and non-animal tested. Items were sold in recyclable containers. Revlon brought out New Age Naturals, skin care products made of all degradable ingredients, and Pure Skin Care, a line of products developed without animal testing. Mary Kay Cosmetics's Countryside Colors line emphasized its use of recyclable packaging made from recycled materials. Mary Kay also eliminated most external packaging on men's skin care products. As some companies eliminated, reduced, or refrabricated outer packaging to emphasize their concern about waste disposal problems, others, particularly fragrance manufacturers, expressed concern about the trend because packaging contributed to their image.

Critics claimed that many of the environmental efforts advertised by cosmetic and fragrance manufacturers were exaggerated, false, or meaningless. For example, "biodegradable" packages were incapable of degrading under conditions present in most landfills. Some products were labeled "ozone friendly" because they did not contain chlorofluorocarbons (CFCs), but CFCs had been banned since the late 1970s. "Recyclable" notations on plastic containers were meaningless when recycling plants for particular plastics (like polystyrene) were not available.

Along with increased environmental awareness came concern for healthy products. Items seen as safe for the environment were perceived as healthy for users. This philosophy drove a trend toward increased use of natural products containing ingredients such as proteins and vitamins. It also brought expanded use of botanical ingredients such as aloe, cucumber, and berry extracts. In perfumes, the trend led to the increasing popularity of discreet scents, floral freshness, and sea smells. In makeup, consumers began turning to functional products. Cosmetics were expected to do more than add color and cover skin imperfections. Buyers wanted products to contain ingredients such as sunscreens and emollients to nourish and protect their skin. The focus on natural products also led to more realistic product claims.

The emphasis on natural ingredients, however, extended only to plant sources. Animal products were shunned and animal-testing fell into disfavor. Many companies promoted cosmetic lines that were developed without animal testing. One example was SafeBrands Inc. (California). SafeBrands prohibited the use of animal testing in the development of its products and by its raw ingredient suppliers.

The Cosmetic, Toiletries, and Fragrance Association (CTFA) remained firm in its support of some animal testing, however. According to the CTFA, even products that claimed to use non-animal test methods relied on models that were acquired as a result of animal testing. The organization believed that human health and safety were more important than animal rights. The CTFA reported that 74 percent of Californians polled opposed legislation that would prohibit animal testing to insure product safety.

The most widely used animal test, and perhaps the most controversial, was the Draize Eye Irritancy Test. The Draize test involved putting drops in the eyes of albino rabbits so investigators could note redness, swelling, cloudiness, and opacity. Also of importance was the eye's ability to recover from any injuries sustained. In 1991, the CTFA reported that acceptable alternatives to animal testing had not been perfected but that research would continue.

In addition to the social and political concerns surrounding animal testing, environmentalism, and product safety, the industry was also impacted by the nation's economic situation. The perfume, cosmetic, and personal care products industry had established a "recession proof" image when sales of inexpensive cosmetics had outsold mid-priced food items and clothing during the depression of the 1930s. Cosmetics also did well during the recessions of the 1960s and 1980s. The recession of the early 1990s, however, brought new challenges. Counterfeit products were offered at low prices. Customers resisted high prices and demanded value. The numbers of distribution channels for upscale lines decreased as traditional department stores closed. Costs associated with product promotion increased and marketers turned more often to expensive strategies such as giving free complementary products.

In an effort to move away from traditional department store cosmetic counters, upscale manufacturers turned to self-serve packaging and sold greater volumes to discounters. This enabled retailers to place items on sale. Depressed pricing, however, sometimes diminished a product's image. Bridge brands increasingly aimed at a niche between the upscale and mass markets. Mass marketers focused on increasing volumes to generate more profit.

INDUSTRY LEADERS

One of the largest companies involved in the perfume, cosmetic, and toilet preparations industry was Procter & Gamble (P&G), which posted operating sales in the early 1990s of $5.4 billion (including some noncosmetic items). In 1990, P&G's Cover Girl held 59 percent of the makeup market; Oil of Olay was the leader in mass-market skin care with a 29.7 percent share; and in men's products, Old Spice was a best seller. In order to expand Old Spice's appeal to younger men, P&G developed a new marketing campaign, which focused on sports and action. The campaign included an amateur athlete feature in *Sports Illustrated* magazine during parts of 1992 and 1993. P&G also introduced an after-shave conditioner in the Old Spice line.

In 1991, P&G increased its involvement in the global cosmetics market through the purchase of Beatrix and Max Factor. Beatrix, a German-based cosmetic manufacturer, had annual sales estimated at $200 million. Max Factor's sales were estimated at $600 million per year. Domestic sales accounted for only 25 percent of the total. Japan and the United Kingdom were the largest overseas customers.

Max Factor, the company, took its name from the Hollywood makeup artist Max Factor. In 1914, Factor began making cosmetic products according to the demands of the technologically evolving film industry. One Factor creation, Pan Cake makeup, first appeared on the screen in 1937. Max Factor continued to develop new formulas to meet the needs of Technicolor movies and color television. In 1990, the company introduced a new makeup designed to meet the demands of high density television in Japan. New Definition Perfecting Makeup used four times more pigment dots than other products. Max Factor was also a leader in cosmetic development outside the film industry. In 1988, the company introduced the "no makeup look" with a no-color mascara and "Invisible Makeup," made of light-diffusing ingredients to blur skin imperfections. The "Transparencies" line, introduced in 1991, used a new combination of color pigments to avoid heaviness or opacity.

Within the fragrance segment of the industry, Estee Lauder was one of the nation's largest companies. Estee Lauder first began marketing skin products in 1946. Lauder's earliest perfume, called Youth Dew, was introduced in 1953. Since then, other perfumes were developed including Estee, Cinnabar, and Beautiful. Lauder's marketing efforts presented American women with the idea of wearing perfume all day long, not just on special occasions. During 1991, Lauder's estimated world sales totaled $2.5 billion, most of which was in prestige markets. Industry analysts expected the company to be heavily impacted by a trend away from traditional department store cosmetic and fragrance counter sales.

Within the men's toiletries market, many companies were experiencing declining profits during the

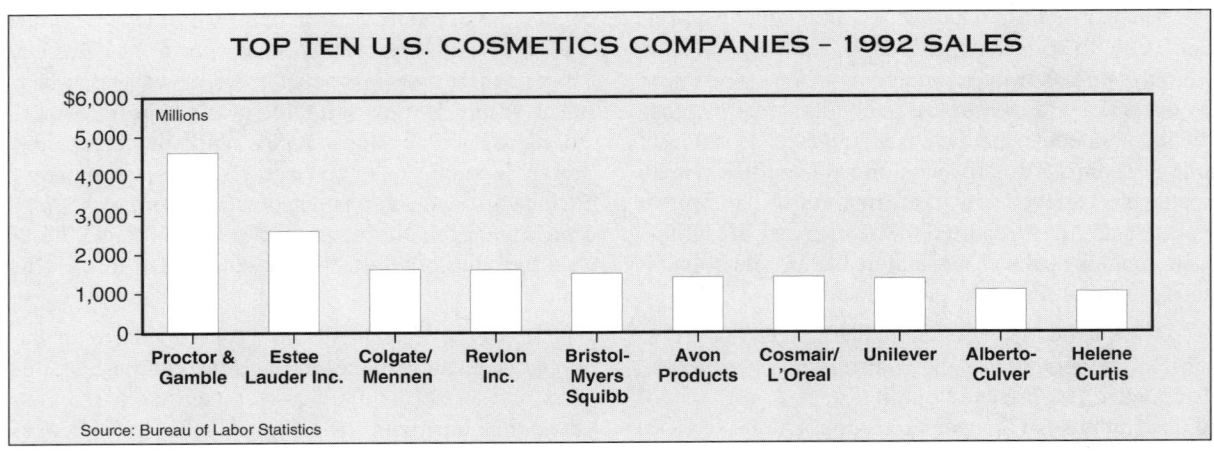

TOP TEN U.S. COSMETICS COMPANIES – 1992 SALES

Source: Bureau of Labor Statistics

early years of the 1990s. An exception was Gillette. Gillette, founded in 1901, was the world's leader in sales of razors and blades. The company's line of toiletries was one of the top sellers in the United States. The innovative Gillette Sensor razor was introduced in 1990 and sold at premium prices that helped bolster the company's bottom line. As a result of the Gillette Sensor's success, the company expanded efforts to upscale some of its lines and aim them at a market niche between mass market items and upscale products. Gillette was also working toward encouraging retailers to group men's grooming products together in a single section containing shaving supplies as well as men's fragrances. Other significant companies in the industry include L'Oreal, a European-based company that posted operating profits of $560 million and operating sales of $5.2 billion in the early 1990s, and Unilever, with $4.8 billion in operating sales (including some noncosmetics) and $468 million in operating profits.

WORK FORCE

Although industry shipment figures demonstrated overall growth during the 1980s and the early 1990s, employment figures fell. In 1987, the toilet preparation industry employed 58,500. This was one percent below 1986 employment and three percent below 1982. In 1991, several manufacturers including Colgate-Palmolive, Gillette, Revlon, Procter & Gamble, and American Cyanamid closed plants or announced future plant closings. According to a government report issued in 1992, industry employment had dropped to 55,600.

Mergers, corporate acquisitions, and takeovers restructured the industry. Major participants like Faberge, Max Factor, Almay, Halston, Germaine Monteil, Shulton, and Yardley changed owners. Con-

solidation and cost cutting measures eliminated less profitable products and resulted in the loss of many blue and white collar jobs. A few companies, such as Amway and Kao's Andrew Jergens Division, were expanding employment opportunities but not at a pace sufficient to counteract the shrinking work forces at other organizations.

AMERICA AND THE WORLD

In 1991, the United States was a net exporter of perfumes, cosmetics, and toilet preparations. Canada, the United Kingdom, Japan, and Mexico were major purchasers of U.S. goods. About 55 percent of the nation's imports were received from France. Other countries supplying products to the U.S. market included the United Kingdom, Japan, and Mexico. The world wide fragrance market was estimated at $10 billion. Within this segment, U.S. demand represented the largest national market in the world, only slightly smaller than the entire European market. Demand in Japan was estimated to be about one third the size of the U.S. market.

As the industry moved increasingly toward globalization, new markets were developing in Latin America, Eastern Europe, and the Pacific Rim. While American companies like Procter & Gamble increased their penetration in overseas markets, foreign companies increased their involvement in American markets. Globalization brought efforts to adopt common terminology, particularly in describing ingredients. The Cosmetic, Toiletries and Fragrance Association (CTFA) expected wider use of the CTFA Ingredient Dictionary.

RESEARCH AND TECHNOLOGY

During the early 1990s, research and technological improvements within the industry focused on reformulating products to move away from synthetic chemicals and to rely on natural products. Within the class of natural products, the primary emphasis was on vegetable and plant materials. Chemists also sought to meet customer demands for mildness and reduced toxicity. Within the growing sun-care segment of the industry, scientists researched products with improved protection, especially against year-round ultraviolet rays. Color market formulators worked to develop new silicon-based products which promised better color retention and improved waterproofing capabilities.

According to a report published in *Seventeen* magazine, Tony Barone, vice president of Barone Cosmetics, predicted further changes within the cosmetic industry. He guessed that as Americans shunned the sun because of health concerns, paler faces would become more fashionable. He speculated that modern habits of living in controlled environments would lead to a loss of body hair including diminished eyebrows and less head hair. Barone considered the advancement of medical cosmetics, where beauty doctors would tattoo permanent makeup in place and perform routine cosmetic surgery, a possible future development.

INDUSTRY INFORMATION SOURCES

Abrutyn, E. S., B. C. Bahr, and S. M. Fuson. "Overview of the Antiperspirant Market: Technology and Trends." *Drug and Cosmetic Industry*, August 1992.

"The Big Picture: Cosmetic Figures Strong, Despite Recession Worries." *Drug and Cosmetic Industry*, June 1992.

"Can the Queen of Cosmetics Keep Her Crown?" *Business Week,* January 17, 1994.

Carsch, Gustav. "The Safety of Fragrance Ingredients." *Soap, Cosmetics, Chemical Specialties*, July 1992.

Christiansen, Suzanne. "Regulations Cast Cloud Over CTFA." *Soap, Cosmetics, Chemical Specialties*, April 1991.

"Cosmetics (Perhaps Too Many) for Women of Color." *Drug and Cosmetic Industry*, November 1992.

"Cosmetics Use Both Praised and Criticized." *Chemical Marketing Reporter*, 19 September 1988.

"CTFA Scientific Conference: VOC Limits for Fragrances, Coming Sunscreen Monograph." *Drug and Chemical Industry*, December 1991.

Darconte, Lorraine. "New Naturals." *Soap, Cosmetics, Chemical Specialties*, May 1991.

Davidowitz, Esther. "The History of Makeup." *Seventeen*, March 1987.

Davis, Donald A. "Anticipated Problems." *Drug and Cosmetic Industry*, September 1992.

———. "Cosmeceuticals Come Into Vogue." *Drug and Cosmetic Industry*, October 1990.

———. "The 'Green' Movement Comes to Cosmetics." *Drug and Cosmetic Industry*, June 1990.

Eiermann, Heinz J. "Regulating Cosmetics Can Be Done More Uniformly Worldwide." *Soap, Cosmetics, Chemical Specialties*, February 1988.

"Even Pharaohs Had Facials." *Newsweek*, 11 December 1989.

Foulke, Judith E. "Cosmetic Ingredients: Understanding the Puffery." *FDA Consumer*, May 1992.

"Fragrance Flashback!" *Teen*, April 1986.

Garrett, Anne Wolven. "Skin Deep." *Drug and Cosmetic Industry*, October 1989.

The Gillete Company. *The Gillette Company 1992 Annual Report*. Boston: Gillette, 1993.

Goldemberg, Robert L. "Fragrance-Free Zones." *Drug and Chemical Industry*, December 1991.

Green, Timothy. "Making Scents is More Complicated Than You'd Think." *Smithsonian*, June 1991.

Kintish, Lisa. "Making Sense of Male Scents." *Soap, Cosmetics, Chemical Specialties*, December 1990.

Lord, Shirley. "Makeup—The Modern Interpretation of Face Paint—Is Still Evolving." *Vogue*, February 1990.

Roach, Virginia. "Green is Beautiful." *Drug and Cosmetic Industry*, February 1991.

Stehlin, Dori. "Cosmetic Safety More Complex Than at First Blush." *FDA Consumer*, November 1991.

Strandberg, Keith. "Men's Toiletries: An Overview." *Soap, Cosmetics, Chemical Specialties*, December 1992.

Tilton, Helga. "Global Makeup." *Chemical Marketing Reporter*, 22 July 1991.

U.S. Department of Commerce. *1987 Census of Manufactures*. Washington, DC: Bureau of the Census, February 1990.

U.S. Department of Commerce. *U.S. Industrial Outlook '92*. Washington, DC: Department of Commerce, 1992.

—Karen Bellenir

SIC 2851

PAINTS, VARNISHES, LACQUERS, ENAMELS, AND ALLIED PRODUCTS

Establishments primarily engaged in manufacturing paints (in paste and ready-mixed form); varnishes; lacquers; enamels; shellac; dry powder coatings; putties, wood fillers, and sealers; paint and varnish removers; paintbrush cleaners; and allied paint products.

Establishments primarily engaged in manufacturing carbon black are classified in **SIC 2895**; those manufacturing bone black, lamp black, and inorganic color pigments are classified in **SIC 2816**; those manufacturing organic color pigments are classified in **SIC 2865**; those manufacturing plastics materials are classified in **SIC 2821**; those manufacturing printing ink are classified in **SIC 2893**; those manufacturing caulking compounds and sealants are classified in **SIC 2891**; those manufacturing artists' paints are classified in **SIC 3952**; and those manufacturing turpentine are classified in **SIC 2861**.

INDUSTRY SNAPSHOT

Less than 900 firms produced paint in the United States in the early 1990s. Combined, these companies manufactured over one billion gallons of paint, generating $12.3 billion. The paint and coatings business was considered a mature industry, with growth projected at about 1 to 2 percent annually.

Paint remained small in relation to other businesses—the entire industry would only rank about 36th among *Fortune* magazine's list of America's top 500 companies. But in spite of its relatively small revenues, the industry's products affected virtually every aspect of modern life. From cars and homes, to containers for food and beverages, to appliances and furniture, paints and coatings protected, personalized, and beautified our surroundings.

The paint industry became essential to nine major manufacturing industries, including: automobiles, trucks and buses, metal cans, farm machinery and equipment, construction machinery and equipment, metal furniture and fixtures, wood furniture and fixtures, major appliances, and coil coating (high speed application of industrial coatings to continuous sheets, strips, and coils of aluminum or steel). These nine markets comprised 14 percent of all goods manufactured in the United States each year. Paint and coatings were also an integral contributor to the new and resale housing industry.

The paint industry underwent significant changes in the 1980s and early 1990s, including a gradual expansion of specialized end-user markets, progressively stricter environmental regulations, and an increase in foreign corporate ownership. These factors, combined with increases in raw material costs and softness in two of the industry's primary markets (automotive and housing), squeezed profits in the early 1990s.

ORGANIZATION AND STRUCTURE

The paint industry's first national professional organization, the National Paint, Oil, and Varnish Association, was founded in 1888 in Saratoga, New York. Industry associations proliferated in the early twentieth century until the Great Depression, when government officials and top paint company executives urged the creation of a single national organization. The National Paint, Varnish, and Lacquer Association was formed in 1933, and was later renamed the National Paint and Coatings Association (NPCA).

The NPCA's membership constituted over 75 percent of the entire paint industry in the early 1990s. The organization existed to represent the industry to government regulators and the general public. Its public relations and educational programs focused primarily on the technical and aesthetic qualities of architectural paint. The group's annual "Clean-Up, Paint-Up, Fix-Up" campaign, which encouraged neighborhood pride through house painting, was first undertaken in 1912 and lasted through the early 1970s. Other NPCA projects have included "Save the Surface and You Save All" (1919-1930), "Paint America Beautiful" (1970s), and "Picture It Painted" (1980—). In the 1990s, campaigns countered paint's persistently bad image as a noxious, but necessary, maintenance product. Following the lead of such successful "category marketers" as the cotton and milk industries, the NPCA promoted paint as a versatile decorating tool.

Competitive Structure. In the early 1990s, the paint industry's top four producers accounted for 29.8 percent of U.S. shipments, a proportion that remained unchanged from about 1985. The twenty largest manufacturers comprised about 62.7 percent of the market. Despite numerous mergers, the high cost of regulation, and increasingly expensive, complex manufacturing processes, a significant proportion of the paint industry—35.35 percent—was composed of companies with annual sales of less than $5 million. These regional paint companies were important suppliers to local hardware stores and smaller home repair centers. Another 21.21 percent of companies had revenues between $5 million and $20 million, and 39.39 percent of manufacturers had annual sales over $20 million.

The geographic dispersal of paint manufacturers was historically dictated by the high transportation costs associated with paint distribution. The weight of prepared paint encouraged the development of a regionalized structure of small manufacturers by the end of the nineteenth century. Paint companies gravitated toward major population and industrial centers like Cleveland, New York, St. Louis, and Chicago. This arrangement dominated the industry until the 1940s and 1950s, when the leading paint manufacturers began to consolidate paint plants and develop wider distribution networks.

By the early 1960s, however, that trend reversed again, and smaller branch plants were built to lower freight costs, avoid some state taxes, and facilitate more personalized service. In 1967, about 66 percent of paint was consumed within 500 miles of its manufacture. Decentralization persisted through the 1990s, represented by the industry segment of small- to medium-sized paint manufacturers who served limited regional markets.

Market Segments. Three basic segments existed within the industry: architectural coatings, original equipment manufacturer (OEM) product coatings, and special purpose coatings.

Architectural coatings, known in the industry as trade sales paint and commonly referred to as house paint, comprised the largest segment, contributing 42.2 percent of annual revenues in 1993. About 60 percent of the 285 million gallons of architectural coatings sold in 1992 went to the residential market. By the early 1990s, interior paints accounted for 57 percent of shipments, exterior paints contributed 40 percent, and lacquers and all others added 3 percent. Water-based, or latex, paints accounted for 73 percent of trade sales in 1990. Do-it-yourselfers purchased over two-thirds of the paint destined for this market, and professional painting contractors bought the remainder.

The bulk of architectural coatings were distributed through wholesale and retail outlets. Marketing these paints encompassed both formulation and aesthetic factors. Safety, durability, consistency, washability, and convenience were some common consumer concerns with regard to formulation. But color and appearance were also important, so paint manufacturers were often obliged to keep up with decorating trends.

Sales in this industry segment were keyed to weather (which could limit the application of exterior paints), new housing starts, sales of existing homes, and to a lesser degree, commercial and industrial construction. Architectural coatings were subject to competition from vinyl siding, wallpaper, wood paneling, and glass. Major producers for this segment included Sherwin-Williams Co., PPG Industries, Inc., Grow Group, Valspar Corp., Glidden Co., and Benjamin Moore and Co.

OEM paints constituted 34.9 percent of industry sales in 1993. These products were often custom formulated in consultation with the end-user and applied during manufacturing. These coatings were used in such durable goods markets as automobiles, appli-

ances, furniture, metal containers, sheet and coil metals, and industrial equipment. Dollar shipments for this industry segment in 1991 were a record $4.24 billion, up 3.2 percent from 1990. Unit shipments rebounded 4.3 percent in 1991, after declining for the prior two years in reaction to weak automobile and consumer durables markets.

One major challenge facing OEM producers in the early 1990s was the increased use of plastics in automobiles and appliances, which created the need to match the paint finish of metal panels with plastic panels that were painted separately. Major companies with interests in OEM markets included E. I. DuPont de Nemours, PPG Industries, Inc., Grow Group, and Glidden Co.

Special purpose or industrial coatings, which largely developed after World War II, accounted for 22.8 percent of industry volume in 1993. While similar to architectural coatings in that they could be classified as stock or shelf goods, special purpose coatings were formulated for specific applications or environmental conditions, and were often sold directly to the end user. Primary markets for these products included automotive and machinery refinishing, industrial maintenance (including factories, equipment, tanks, utilities, and railroads), bridges, traffic markings, metallic coatings, and marine coatings. Decreased industrial, state, and municipal maintenance spending in the face of an early 1990s recession forced this segment's 11 percent financial decline. But a 1992 federal highway bill was expected to increase maintenance work on roads and bridges during the decade. E. I. DuPont de Nemours, PPG Industries, Inc., Sherwin-Williams Co., RPM Inc., Courtaulds Coatings, Inc., Glidden Co., Akzo Coatings, Inc., and Valspar Corp. were all important producers of specialty coatings.

BACKGROUND AND DEVELOPMENT

Industry Origins. The first recorded paint mill in America was established in Boston in 1700 by Thomas Child, who had emigrated from England. His business manufactured the components of paint in a paste form. During most of the nineteenth century, professional painters mixed their own paints from linseed oil, white lead, turpentine, and pigments. Their formulas were inconsistent, and the paint they produced had virtually no shelf life.

In 1867, D. R. Averill, an Ohioan, patented ready-to-use paint. But early factory-made paints were notorious for their poor quality and unreliable performance. It was not until the 1880s that quality ready-mixed paints were produced. By 1888, the paint industry generated about $45 million in annual revenues.

During World War I, paint and varnish were vital to the U.S. military effort for protection and camouflage of equipment and personnel. The war exposed the industry's dependence on imported raw materials, and frequent shortages encouraged the development of domestic and synthetic replacements. By 1922, annual industry volume neared $300 million.

The prosperity of the decade between the two World Wars encouraged paint industry revenues to top $400 million by 1926, but the Great Depression reduced volume to $289 million by 1933.

Paint and coatings were vital to the Allied effort during World War II, as the products once again preserved and camouflaged virtually everything. The unique needs of the military compelled the development of specialized paints and coatings. There were acid-proof, corrosion-proof, and waterproof coatings; fire-retardant, ice-repellant, fungus-resistant, weather-resistant, and water-resistant compounds that enhanced fabrics; and phosphorescent and florescent paints that proved strategically vital. The NPCA's "Paint Protects America" slogan summed up the industry's wartime contributions.

A Maturing Industry. After more than quadrupling from 1933 to 1947, it took the paint industry 17 years to increase from $1.25 billion to $2 billion. The American market was nearing saturation, and the same high transportation costs that prevented the consolidation of paint plants impeded expansion into overseas markets.

Overcapacity, increased competition, and rising expenses also plagued the paint industry. The U.S. Department of Defense reported on overcapacity in the paint industry during World War II, noting that "only 100 of the then 1400 paint manufacturers, working only one shift, could meet any emergency needs of the entire country." By the 1960s, alternatives like aluminum siding, concrete, and stucco for exterior application, and vinyl, wood, and paper wallcoverings for the interior, entered the already-crowded market. Paint producers began to sacrifice their profit margins in an attempt to maintain market share.

At the same time, labor, packaging, and distribution costs rose dramatically. From 1965 to 1970, wage costs rose 33 percent, but the dollar value of industry-wide shipments rose only 26 percent and productivity increased only 2 percent—not enough to account for the difference. By 1970, the industry's average return fell to 6.2 percent, compared to a 10.1 percent average for all industries.

As the growth and profits of the paint industry trailed the rest of the economy, top paint manufacturers diversified into everything from fertilizer to foods to garner profits. But promotional sales exacerbated the profit squeeze during the 1970s. Many in the industry blamed mass merchandising of paint. Discounters could afford to slash margins and even take a loss to capture market share. Paint manufacturers were forced to follow suit to hang onto their share. Another factor that emerged during the 1970s was the oil crisis, which caused the price of many of the industry's raw materials to rise rapidly.

As the paint industry matured and profit margins decreased, many firms merged to consolidate their resources and achieve economies of scale. In 1960, there were about 2,000 companies in the industry. Between 1963 and 1968 alone, 71 paint companies changed hands, often merging several smaller businesses into one substantial company. The larger, more powerful companies sought increased market share and the higher sales base this afforded. The income was required to support research, development, and national advertising budgets.

Rebound. The paint industry endured a recession in the early 1980s along with the rest of America, but from 1983 to 1990 growth was buoyed by strong construction and durable goods markets. Volume increased dramatically, from less than 420 million gallons shipped in 1982 to over one billion gallons in 1990. The physical increase was accompanied by a leap in dollar sales, from about $3.1 billion in 1982 to about $9.3 billion in 1985 and over $11.7 billion in 1990. Consolidation of the paint industry continued during the 1980s. By the end of 1992, less than 900 companies remained, down from 1,100 in 1984. Manufacturers also sought to increase their profit margins through applied research and development directed at refining existing technologies.

CURRENT CONDITIONS

In the 1990s, paint manufacturers' primary concerns centered on progressively stricter environmental regulations, increasing foreign ownership, greater likelihood of mergers and acquisitions, and accelerating technological advances.

After decades of practice, paint and coatings companies had come to anticipate environmental regulation and tried to prepare for it in advance. So when the Environmental Protection Agency estimated that coatings solvents were responsible for 8 to 10 percent of all volatile organic compounds (VOCs) released in the United States, coatings formulators stepped up their efforts to produce high-performance, low-VOC paints before solvents were banned.

Government and independent analysts agreed that foreign investment in the U.S. paint industry was likely to continue in the 1990s, due to high currency values and low interest rates. And although consolidation within the industry was also expected to continue, some savvy smaller companies were able to hold their own by capitalizing on technical expertise, new products, and quick customer service.

Sales volumes in the paint and coatings industry fell 4.9 percent to about $11.39 billion in 1991, largely due to the recession's impact on the architectural and special purpose segments. From 1988 to 1991, raw materials prices increased 24 percent, but paint prices increased only 12 percent.

The financial picture brightened in 1992 and 1993, as sales of existing homes increased due to artificially low interest rates. Some analysts noted that owners of offices and light manufacturing buildings purchased more paint to maintain their properties as well. These factors kept the paint industry growing slowly at an annual rate of about 2.9 percent from 1987 to 1992.

One analyst predicted that U.S. manufacturers' sales of paints and coatings would expand at an average annual rate of 6.3 percent, reaching $21.1 billion by 1996. Real growth, accounting for inflation of approximately 4.5 percent annually, was estimated at about 1.8 percent per year.

INDUSTRY LEADERS

Sherwin-Williams Co. One of the founding firms of the American paint industry, Sherwin-Williams celebrated its 125th anniversary in 1991 with sales of $2.5 billion. The Cleveland-based company became America's largest paint manufacturer in 1905. Its vertical integration, which extended from raw materials and packaging to retail stores, helped the company become a low cost manufacturer and the broadest distributor of architectural coatings in the United States.

Sherwin-Williams always emphasized architectural coatings, offered under the company's namesake brand and its acquired Dutch-Boy label, but by the early 1990s also produced industrial finishes for the automotive after-market and painting accessories. In 1990, Sherwin Williams acquired Krylon brand aerosol paint and DeSoto, a major producer of architectural paints.

PPG Industries Inc. Formerly known as Pittsburgh Plate Glass, this company was founded in 1883. As the company name implied, paint was not its primary product: by the late 1960s, coatings constituted less than 20 percent of PPG's annual sales. PPG Industries increased its architectural paint business by more

than half, to over $250 million annually, with the 1989 purchase of Lucite brand house paint and Olympic brand wood stain from Clorox.

The Glidden Co. Another Cleveland-based paintmaker, Glidden was founded in 1875. The company was a subsidiary of ICI Americas, Inc., and a division of the world's leading paint manufacturer, Great Britain's ICI Paints. Glidden's overall sales totalled $900 million in 1991, and the company pioneered zero-VOC paints in 1992.

WORK FORCE

The paint and coatings industry employed 57,000 Americans in 1992, down from about 61,800 in 1990. Production workers comprised over 52 percent of that total. About 25 percent of the industry's employees were managers and administrators, and another 20 percent were professional chemists and sales representatives.

Production workers operated and fixed machinery, moved raw materials, and monitored the production process. High school graduates qualified for entry-level production jobs, and advancement into better-paying jobs requiring higher skills or more responsibility was possible through on-the-job experience or additional vocational training at a two-year technical college. The average weekly earnings of paint production workers was approximately 12 percent higher than the national average for manufacturing production jobs.

Most administrative and management positions required a bachelor's degree and experience in the industry. Support workers often held two-year technical degrees or some college, but these were not required.

Research and development specialists in the paint industry included chemists and chemical engineers. They typically conducted research and experimented with new products and processes. Advanced degrees were often essential for these positions. Some senior chemists were promoted to management positions.

Marketing and sales representatives promoted sales of their companies' products by helping to develop new products, creating plans to market them, and advertising them to retail and industrial customers. These positions often required a degree in marketing, chemistry, or chemical engineering.

Employment in the paint and coatings industry was projected to decline over the course of the 1990s. More efficient production processes, increased plant automation, growth of environmental awareness, health and safety concerns, and rising foreign competition were all expected to influence paint and coatings employment significantly and negatively.

AMERICA AND THE WORLD

Historically, overseas trade did not contribute significantly to the U.S. paint market. In the early 1990s, foreign sales continued to represent a small percentage of total domestic revenue. In 1991, U.S. paint manufacturers exported only $696 million worth of goods, over half of which went to Canada and Mexico.

The United States dominated the global paint trade after World War I, when Germany relinquished its top position in chemicals. But after World War II, foreign countries grew increasingly self-sufficient. In 1960, the industry's total export business constituted less than 2 percent of total production. The United States dominated the global paint industry by the mid-1900s, accounting for 40 percent of the $5.2 billion value and 50 percent of the supply. West Germany ranked a distant second with revenues of about $460 million, and Great Britain, France, and Italy followed suit.

During the 1960s, tariffs, quotas, licensing and exchange restrictions, and special import fees hamstrung U.S. coatings manufacturers' world trade. Trade barriers encouraged some paint producers to enter into joint ventures with their foreign competitors so that they could market their products overseas.

Globalization. Globalization of the paint industry occurred as U.S. companies followed their primary OEM customers from America to the Far East and other lower-cost areas. At the same time, foreign producers sought growth through acquisition of U.S. paint companies. These international movements enabled some large corporations to capitalize on their technological advantages in new markets.

Two major purchases by foreign paint companies were BASF's acquisition of Inmont Corp. from United Technologies Corp. in late 1985, and Imperial Chemicals Industries' acquisition of the Glidden paint operations of SCM Corp. in 1986. The Glidden acquisition marked ICI's entry into the U.S. paint industry and made the British conglomerate the world's largest paint company.

By 1990, ten multinational companies held an estimated one-third of total world production, compared with one-fifth in 1980. By that time, the top five companies worldwide were ICI, PPG, Akzo, Sherwin-Williams, and BASF. The Europeans and Japanese, historically the stiffest competitors of the United States, emerged in a particularly strong position internationally.

RESEARCH AND TECHNOLOGY

As of the 1990s, paints and coatings incorporated a myriad of chemical compounds uniquely formulated to fulfill the varied requirements of hundreds of thousands of applications. But the industry was not always so technically inclined.

From its inception in 1700 until the mid-1900s, paint formulation remained relatively unchanged. The switch from paste to ready-mixed paint in the 1860s and the mechanization of the manufacturing process in the mid-1880s were two significant innovations. But for the first half of the twentieth century, the manufacture of paint was a relatively simple process of mixing and grinding oils and pigments using "secret" recipes usually concocted by trial and error.

As previously mentioned, World War II inspired many innovations in paint formulation. One observer noted that there was more technological progress in the paint industry from 1947 to 1967 than in the previous 1,000 years. Product developments occurred so quickly that an estimated 90 percent of 1960's trade sales consisted of items that did not exist a decade before.

Most of the raw materials used in the contemporary paint industry were developed during the postwar era. They were derived from petroleum, then mixed in varying proportions with specific chemical agents to produce such distinct characteristics as durability, elasticity, and chemical and thermal resistance. By the mid-1960s, the major industrial paint manufacturers offered as many as 20,000 different products.

Color. During the late 1950s, some manufacturers of architectural paint offered an increased selection of colors to consumers by shipping a white base paint to retailers with separate oil or powdered pigments. The desired paint color would be concocted at the point of sale upon the customer's request. This system gave the customer a wider choice of colors (over 1,000 in some cases) and reduced the retailer's risk of overstocking an unpopular color. By 1960, these "custom" systems constituted about 5 percent of retail paint sales.

The Latex Revolution. The architectural paint market, and eventually the entire industry, was revolutionized by the introduction of waterborne, or latex, paint. Unlike its oil-based predecessors, latex paint required no ventilation, was non-flammable and scrubbable, gave a good finish, was easy to clean off brushes, newly introduced paint rollers, and skin, and dried in about 20 minutes.

Latex began its ascent to prominence in the industry in the 1950s. Before that time, solvent- or oil-based products dominated gallonage consumption, while waterborne, high-solids, and powdered coatings constituted only 10 percent of industry volume. By the early 1990s, water-based paints alone constituted over 75 percent of gallonage. Convenience was clearly a factor in the widespread commercial acceptance of water-based paints, but in the 1970s, another strong influence drove their industrial acceptance: government regulation.

Government Regulation Drives Innovation. By the beginning of the 1980s, nearly every aspect of the paint business was regulated. The Occupational Safety and Health Administration monitored the workplace. The Environmental Protection Agency regulated the introduction, generation, transportation, treatment, and disposal of hazardous materials used in or produced by the coatings industry. The Consumer Product Safety Commission protected paint customers by controlling what could be bought and sold.

Although many in the paint industry resisted government efforts to monitor the business, state and federal regulation actually encouraged several technological advances. An early example of this phenomenon occurred just after the turn of the century, when legislation was enacted in North Dakota requiring formula labels on house paints. The idea gained popularity among consumers and congressmen throughout the country. But paint manufacturers feared revealing their ''secret formulas,'' and warned that the new law would inhibit research on new formulations. In hindsight, the rules encouraged the use of quality ingredients and fostered more scientific formulations.

Regulation of the industry accelerated dramatically during the environmentally conscious 1970s, when federal clean air regulations were adopted to encourage the production of less-polluting, less-toxic paints.

Lead. Once a primary component of paint, lead ranked as the top environmental threat to children's health in the 1990s. Lead poisoning affected the nervous system, the gastrointestinal tract, and the blood-forming tissues, and was especially harmful to children. The deleterious effects of lead—which was also used in gasoline, ceramic finishes, plumbing, and many other products—were discovered in the 1930s. White lead pigments were essentially eliminated from architectural paints in the 1940s, but it was not until 1977 that the use of lead-based paints was outlawed in the United States.

Government and medical reports published in the late 1980s and early 1990s revealed evidence that lead poisoning could occur with much lower doses than was previously thought, so the lead problem was more pervasive than earlier believed. Some public health officials estimated that there could be accessible lead paint in up to 42 million homes and apartments housing 12 million children.

In the increasingly litigious American society, paint manufacturers rightly feared a wave of lawsuits. Some analysts predicted that lawsuits involving lead-paint poisoning could eventually eclipse asbestos suits. And in 1993, all paint manufacturers in California were assessed special fees under that state's Childhood Lead Poisoning Act of 1991. Paint industry spokespersons contended that the fines unfairly punished manufacturers and sellers that may not have been in business when the lead paint was sold, and that parents, contractors, and property managers should share the blame and the cost.

Superfund. Proposed in 1979, Superfund legislation mandated the accumulation of a multi-million dollar fund to pay for the cleanup of oil and hazardous waste spills and disposal sites. The fund would be amassed through fees assessed to businesses, municipalities, and individuals who were designated as Potentially Responsible Parties in the pollution of the sites. Since the Resource Conservation and Recovery Act (RCRA) had already classified paint wastes as hazardous materials, virtually all paint manufacturers found themselves subject to fee collection under Superfund. Representing the paint industry, the National Paint and Coatings Association argued that it was unfair to single out certain industries for problems created by the entire society.

Volatile Organic Compounds. Organic solvents, the oils that liquified many paints, were blamed for some air pollution. As paint dried, the liquid portion evaporated. When the liquid was an organic solvent, volatile organic compounds (VOCs) were released in the drying process. VOCs reacted with sunlight to contribute to smog. State VOC regulations started to proliferate in the wake of 1977's Clean Air Act Amendments, which required states to regulate geographic areas that failed to meet ambient air quality standards. Control of VOCs was a significant aspect of compliance. California was one of the first, and most stringent, state-level regulators.

Rather than resisting these state laws, the NPCA called for uniform federal guidelines, as opposed to the confusing array of state and local initiatives that cropped up. The NPCA supported the ''bubble concept'' of plant compliance, which allowed individual factories to develop plant-wide emission reduction plans using an average emission level of VOCs.

Four basic coatings designed to save energy and pollute less were developed. Water-soluble paint eventually reduced the use of petroleum-based solvent in paints by about 90 percent. High solids paints contained more resins and pigments than solvents. Accelerated cure coatings were dried by ultraviolet light or an electron beam. Powdered coatings, which contained virtually no organic solvents, also sidestepped the VOC problem. New application processes also helped reduce the volume of paint required to perform a particular function.

The Glidden Co. became the first paint manufacturer to introduce major architectural paint lines containing no VOCs in 1992. Although consumers in the 1990s were clearly interested in environmentally sound products, zero-VOC paints had several drawbacks, including a reduced range of colors and lower performance.

Other new technologies included high solids-based, two-stage, base coat/clear topcoat systems for the auto industry and water-based coatings for cans, prefinished wood, and flat board.

Powder and radiation-curable coatings were considered two of the more exciting new developments, with a projected growth rate of 12 to 15 percent annually. Powder coatings were sprayed on dry and electrically adhered to the surface. Major markets for powder coatings in 1992 were metal finishing (53 percent), appliances (22 percent), automobile applications (20 percent), and architectural products (5 percent). Radiation-curable coatings, intended for use on plastics, paper, wood, and metals, were hardened by ultraviolet light or electronic beam energy. Although the conversion to these new techniques was costly, factors like increased material utilization, reduced energy and lab costs, and the elimination of solvent emissions promised to more than offset the initial cost disadvantages. Powder and radiation-curable coatings were expected to replace many conventional solvent-based coatings.

INDUSTRY INFORMATION SOURCES

Avery, Susan, "The Perils of Purchasing Paint," *Purchasing,* March 21, 1991, pp. 56-69.

Babyak, Richard J., "Painting Plastics," *Appliance Manufacturer,* April 1991, pp. 32-33.

"Building Downturn Hasn't Hit the Paint Companies," *Financial World,* December 7, 1960, pp. 4, 30.

"Changing Paint Mix," *Chemical Week,* November 21, 1973, p. 17.

"Coatings Business Lively This Year after a Long Lull," *Chemical Marketing Reporter,* August 14, 1972, pp. 7, 40.

Colgan, Kevin, "Coatings Makers Enter '80s Facing U.S. Regulatory Burden, *Chemical Marketing Reporter,* October 27, 1980, pp. 36-37.

"Concentrating on the Home," *Economist,* July 9, 1960, p. 200.

Dickstein, George, "Paint Industry Is Using Spruced Up Ad Approach to Dispel Odorous Image," *Advertising Age,* June 6, 1966, pp. 4, 98.

Dill, Larry, "California Paint Makers Face $1.8 Million Fee," *Modern Paint & Coatings,* May 1993, pp. 13-16.

Gautier, Tom and Julie Larson Bricher, "Lead Paint: Old Coats Lead to New Suits," *Business & Society Review,* Fall 1991, pp. 10-21.

"'Home fever' Spurs New Paint Promotions," *Chemical Week,* November 5, 1980, pp. 14-15.

Jacobs, David E., "Abating Lead-Based Paint," *Journal of Property Management,* March/April 1991, pp. 32-34.

Kalkbrenner, Eric J., "Environment, Worker Safety Dominate Washington's Mind," *Chemical Marketing Reporter,* October 29, 1979, p. 48.

Kearney, Stephen, "Superfund Has Full Attention of Paint and Coatings Makers," *Chemical Marketing Reporter,* November 4, 1985, p. 39.

Kemizis, Paul, "Wait-and-See Stance Taken on Zero-VOC Architectural Paints," *Chemical Week,* October 14, 1992, pp. 52-53.

Krizan, William G., "Regulators Putting the Lid on Paint," *ENR,* October 5, 1989, pp. 30-33.

Major, Michael, "Spotlight on Ways to Boost the Paint Industry's Image," *Modern Paint & Coatings,* October 1992, pp. 8, 10.

McGowan, Owen P., "Deflecting Liability in Lead-Poisoning Suits," *Best's Review,* February 1993, pp. 62-63.

"More New Paints Counted On to Offset Slowing Growth," *Industry Week,* December 15, 1975, pp. 42, 44, 46.

"The New Gloss at Sherwin-Williams," *Business Week,* July 15, 1967, pp. 154-156.

"NPCA Proposes Lead Regulation for Home Paints," *Chemical Marketing Reporter,* September 20, 1976, pp. 4, 35.

"Paint: Americans Wield the World's Widest Brush," *Oil, Paint and Drug Reporter,* March 13, 1967, pp. 5, 45.

"Paint Industry Outlook for the New Year," *Modern Paint & Coatings,* January 1993, pp. 28-32.

"Paint Industry Sales This Year Will Fall Short of $2 Billion Goal," *Oil, Paint & Drug Reporter,* November 7, 1960, pp. 7, 48.

"Paint Industry's World Trade Is Seen Facing Many Obstacles," *Oil, Paint & Drug Reporter,* August 8, 1960, pp. 4, 52.

"The Paint Makers," *Financial World,* August 25, 1965, pp. 11, 23.

"Paintmakers Scrap for Sales," *Chemical Week,* November 18, 1961, pp. 25-30.

"Paintmakers View the Big Picture," *Chemical Week,* November 2, 1977, pp. 26-28.

Randel, Susan, "The Countertrend of House Paints," *Chemical Business,* October 1992, pp. 6-9.

"'Sales' Buy Trouble for Paintmakers," *Chemical Week,* April 26, 1978, pp. 23-24.

Sobrino, Frank, "Paint Firms Jockey for Share of Big $4 Billion U.S. Market," *Chemical Marketing Reporter,* October 22, 1984, p. 41.

Standard & Poor's Industry Surveys, January 1988, pp. C33-C34.

Standard & Poor's Industry Surveys, July 1993, pp. C41-C43.

Trigg, Ernest T., *Fifty-five Colorful Years; The Story of Paint in America,* Stonington, Connecticut: Pequot Press, 1954.

"U.S. Paint Industry Faces Reduced Growth," *Modern Paint & Coatings,* May 1991, pp. 10-16.

"U.S. Paint Industry Sales in 1975: Volume of $3.45 Billion Forecast," *Oil, Paint and Drug Reporter,* June 1969, pp. 7, 46.

Waggoner, Mary E., "Antique Restorations Vying with Brightly Colored Decor," *Chemical Marketing Reporter,* October 29, 1979, p. 46.

—April S. Dougal

SIC 2861

GUM AND WOOD CHEMICALS

The gum and wood chemicals industry is comprised of establishments primarily engaged in manufacturing hardwood and softwood distillation products, natural dyes, tanning materials, and related products. Companies that make synthetic organic tanning materials and synthetic organic dyes are classified in **SIC 2869: Industrial Organic Chemicals, Not Elsewhere Classified** and **SIC 2865: Cyclic Organic Crudes and Intermediates, and Organic Dyes and Pigments,** respectively. Gum and wood chemical producers are part of the larger, industrial organic chemical industry.

Like organic chemicals derived from petroleum and natural gas, thousands of different natural chemical products can be distilled from wood. Turpentine, for example, is extracted from pine gum and pine wood. Numerous oils and finishes can also be obtained from pine, or other woods, as can many dyes, fuels, and rosins. Popular industry products in the early 1990s included methanol (wood alcohol), charcoal, tar

and tar oils, tanning extracts, pitch, and dyes. About 40 percent of industry revenues came from sales of hardwood charcoal briquets. Hardwood distillates, such as oak extract, accounted for about 30 percent of industry output. Softwood distillates, like rosin and turpentine, represented 17 percent of sales in the early 1990s.

The largest buyers of gum and wood chemicals are individual consumers, who primarily purchase charcoal, turpentine, and other products for home use. Manufacturers of plastics used 11 percent of production in the early 1990s to create base resins and additives. Distillates and extracts were consumed by other industries in the manufacture of soaps and detergents, paperboard, drugs, paints, printing ink, leather tanning chemicals, rubber, adhesives, sealants, and many other goods. About 12 percent of production in the early 1990s was exported.

Humans have been using charcoal and making dyes from charcoal long before the start of recorded history. Discovery of rosins, wood alcohol, tar, and other distillates and extracts occurred at various intervals. U.S. industry shipments realized the strongest growth following World War II. Construction industries, for example, generated a demand for wood treatment chemicals, adhesives, and sealants. Growth in the popularity of outdoor barbecue grills during the 1950s and 1960s especially boosted sales. Demand for ink dyes and tanning chemicals also grew during the postwar U.S. economic expansion.

By the early 1980s, the gum and wood chemicals industry was shipping over $600 million worth of products and employing about 3,500 workers. Revenues and profits recessed during the 1980s, however, for several reasons. Most important, synthetic chemicals displaced many natural wood and gum chemicals in everything from dyes to sealants. In addition, state and local environmental laws that restricted the burning of charcoal cut into profits. Total revenues fluctuated around $600 million per year through the early 1990s, as productivity gains and cost-cutting measures reduced the work force to below 2,500.

Going into the mid-1990s, industry participants were hoping to benefit from a trend toward the use of natural chemicals, such as dyes and fuel additives, in response to environmental concerns about synthetics. Despite these hopes, the industry was expected to realize negligible growth through the turn of the century. Employment opportunities for most positions, in fact, were expected to plummet by five to 30 percent between 1990 and 2005, according to the Bureau of Labor Statistics.

The largest competitor in this business in the early 1990s was Royal Oak Enterprises Inc. of Georgia. This manufacturer of wood treatment chemicals earned $50 million in sales during 1991, and employed about 500 workers. T.S. Ragsdale Company Inc. of South Carolina was the second largest competitor, with about $43 million in revenue and 200 workers. Kingsford Products Co. of Kentucky, a maker of charcoal, was the third largest firm with sales of $33 million and about 600 employees.

INDUSTRY INFORMATION SOURCES

Darnay, Arsen J., ed., *Manufacturing USA; Industry Analyses, Statistics, and Leading Companies,* Detroit: Gale Research Inc., 1993.

Encyclopedia Britannica, Chicago: Encyclopedia Britannica, Inc., 1980.

"Facts & Figures for the Chemical Industry," *Chemical & Engineering News,* June 28, 1993.

Reisch, Marc S., "Top 50 Chemicals Production Recovered Last Year," *Chemical & Engineering News,* April 12, 1993.

Standard & Poor's Industry Surveys, New York: Standard & Poor's Corporation, January 20, 1994.

U.S. Industrial Outlook 1993, Washington, D.C.: U.S. Department of Commerce, January 1993.

—Dave Mote

SIC 2865

CYCLIC ORGANIC CRUDES AND INTERMEDIATES, AND ORGANIC DYES AND PIGMENTS

This industry covers establishments primarily engaged in manufacturing cyclic organic crudes and intermediates, and organic dyes and pigments. Important products of this industry include: (1) aromatic chemicals, such as benzene, toluene, mixed xylenes naphthalene; (2) synthetic organic dyes; and (3) synthetic organic pigments. Establishments primarily engaged in manufacturing coal tar crudes in chemical recovery ovens are classified in **SIC 3312: Steel Works, Blast Furnaces (Including Coke Ovens), and Rolling Mills,** and petroleum refineries which produce such products as byproducts of petroleum refining are classified in **SIC 2911: Petroleum Refining.**

INDUSTRY SNAPSHOT

U.S. manufacturers produced $11 billion worth of fine chemicals in 1993, or about 25 percent of global output. The 180 U.S. competitors employed 23,000 workers and exported almost $1.4 billion worth of products per year in the early 1990s. Industry output provided an important supply of base manufacturing material for pharmaceutical, dye, fuel, and agricultural sectors.

Industry sales surged throughout the 1980s, as revenues jumped from about $7 billion in the early 1980s to over $11 billion by the early 1990s. Going into the mid-1990s, however, many intermediates producers were struggling to sustain profitability. Overcapacity, a weak global economy, and downward price pressures in end-user markets were largely to blame for industry woes. In addition, burgeoning foreign competition was devouring both domestic and overseas U.S. market share.

In response to a hostile business environment, U.S. firms were striving to increase productivity, focus on the development of new compounds and production processes, and restructure their organizations to emphasize core competencies. The industry was also scrambling to comply with increasingly stringent environmental regulations that threatened to diminish their competitiveness in export markets.

ORGANIZATION AND STRUCTURE

Industrial organic chemicals are created from substances that contain carbon, such as petroleum, coal, and natural gas. Inorganic chemicals, in contrast, come from inanimate materials within the earth's crust (though they may also contain carbon). The aromatics classified in this industry are separated from other organics by their closed-ring molecular structure. This structure allows them to be combined with other chemicals, including inorganics, to make a vast array of intermediate compounds. Intermediates are consumed by other industries for the production of plastics, pharmaceuticals, fertilizers, and several other products.

In 1992, chemicals classified in this industry constituted 20 percent of the $53 billion U.S. industrial organic chemical industry, which also includes gum and wood chemicals, and industrial organics not elsewhere classified. Industrial organic chemicals, in turn, comprised 66 percent of the overall chemical industry, which includes inorganic and agricultural chemicals. The encompassing chemical and related products industry represents a $230 billion business, of which organics account for about one-third. Many products and compounds generated in the fine chemicals industry, however, are used to produce other chemicals and related goods.

Twenty percent, or about $2.2 billion, of the $11 billion worth of aromatic, intermediate, and synthetic dye output in the early 1990s was consumed by manufacturers within the industry to produce other fine chemicals. An aromatics producer, for example, might sell benzene to a company that makes the intermediate chlorobenzene. Plastics materials and resin manufacturers demanded 13 percent of U.S. production, as did the organic synthetic fiber industry. Though they each accounted for less than three percent of the fragmented market, other major customers included petroleum refiners, pharmaceutical companies, paint and coating manufacturers, and semiconductor producers. Exports made up 13 percent of industry shipments during the early 1990s.

Products. The three primary aromatic chemicals used to create intermediates are benzene, xylene, and toluene. These three chemicals represent about ten percent of U.S. industry output. Intermediates created using these base organics, however, account for an additional 70 percent of total production. Benzene, the simplest and most widely used aromatic, is combined with sulfuric acid or other chemicals to create many intermediates. U.S. manufacturers generated over 1.6 billion gallons of benzene in 1993. Major uses of benzene intermediates include plastic resins, epoxy, nylon, polyurethanes, synthetic rubber, and detergents.

The most common derivative of benzene is ethylbenzene/styrene, which accounts for 50 percent of demand for this aromatic. Nearly 21 billion pounds of ethylbenzene and styrene were produced in 1992. Styrene is a major ingredient in plastics and synthetic rubber. Cumene/phenol and cyclohexane represented 21 percent and 14 percent, respectively, of benzene derivative sales. Phenol is used to produce adhesives and high-grade plastics and epoxies. Other major intermediates in this category include nitrobenzene/aniline (six percent), alkybenzene (two percent), and chlorobenzene (two percent).

Xylene is utilized mostly as a gasoline additive and a solvent. It is separated into three commercial substances; paraxylene, orthoxylene, and metaxylene. Paraxylene derivatives are used to make polyester fiber and films, beverage bottles, and specialty engineering resins. Consumption of this chemical topped 5.6 billion pounds in 1992. In 1992, 918 million pounds of orthoxylene were generated. It is used primarily to make intermediates that are utilized in the production of plasticizers (plastic additives) and polyester resins. Metaxylene has limited uses in the manufacture of coatings and plastics.

The industry produced 833 million pounds of toluene in 1992. This aromatic is used to create benzene.

End markets also include manufacturers of adhesives, solvents, photographic film, textiles, pharmaceuticals, inks, and coatings.

Besides aromatics and their intermediate offspring, organic dyes and pigments each make up about eight percent of industry sales (tar and pitch compounds round out industry offerings with four percent of revenues). Dyes are typically obtained from petroleum through lengthy chemical processes and must conform to rigid safety standards before they can be used to color food, clothing, and other goods. About 245 million pounds of synthetic organic dyes and pigments valued at $761 million were shipped by U.S. manufacturers in 1991. Two-thirds of production was consumed by textile industries.

BACKGROUND AND DEVELOPMENT

William Henry Perkin, an Englishman and the father of the organic chemical industry, was the first chemist to synthesize an organic chemical for commercial use. In 1856 Perkin accidentally created mauve, a synthetic dye, from a piece of coal tar. Friedreich Von Kekule was the first to explain Perkin's invention when, in 1865, he proposed his breakthrough theory of the benzene ring. During the remainder of the 19th century, German chemists developed most of the dye classes and many of the individual dyes that were still being used in the early 1990s.

Until World War I, the advancement of aromatics, intermediates, and dyes in the wake of Kekule's discovery were considered relatively unimportant outside of Germany. Great Britain, France, and the United States frantically developed an organic chemical industry during the war, however. Likewise, World War II brought massive industry expansion, especially as producers learned to derive aromatics from petroleum rather than coal tar. By the end of World War II, the United States was the major global supplier of aromatics and intermediates. Industry growth was rampant during the postwar U.S. economic expansion.

The aromatic, intermediate, and synthetic dye industry grew at a healthy rate of five percent per year between 1982 and 1990. Though this reflected a decline in growth rates compared to the 1960s and 1970s, it exceeded gains in most other U.S. manufacturing sectors. Sales rose from $7.1 billion in 1982 to $10.9 billion by 1990. The demand for new high-performance intermediates, particularly by pharmaceutical and agricultural sectors, drove growth.

In addition to revenue gains, producers also benefitted from increases in productivity and the development of new processing techniques during the decade.

Productivity gains of about four percent per year in the 1980s were the result of massive capital investments in automation and information systems, which allowed manufacturers to eliminate both production workers and managers. Indeed, as production volume steadily rose throughout the 1980s, industry employment gradually shrank. The work force declined from over 27,000 in the early 1980s, to about 23,000 by the early 1990s. In addition to keeping the lid on labor costs, many manufacturers were able to reduce productions costs through advanced processing techniques.

Despite massive capital investments surpassing $43 billion during the 1980s, productivity and manufacturing gains were substantially offset by changing dynamics in the global organic chemical industry. Two primary factors stunting profit growth in the 1980s— and 1990s for that matter—were increased foreign competition and environmental regulations. In addition, regulatory intervention in important end markets, such as pharmaceuticals, were hindering competitors. Also hurting industry participants in the early 1990s was a U.S. and global economic recession. Overcapacity, a result of slower-than-expected growth in the early 1990s, was causing severe price suppression and reduced profits for most companies. Even as the United States experienced a modest recovery in 1992 and 1993, overseas markets remained flat.

CURRENT CONDITIONS

Going into the mid-1990s, aromatic, intermediate, and dye producers continued to suffer from downward price pressures. While the demand for styrene, for example, grew about 13 percent between 1990 and 1993, excess production capacity in the United States crushed price growth in that segment. Many benzene derivatives were suffering a similar scenario, as were the xylenes. Only phenol dodged the burden of oversupply. U.S. prices and demand recovered slightly in 1993, but primary global markets remained recessed.

Besides slack markets, increasingly stringent environment regulations were also taking their toll in the mid-1990s. A string of new rules implemented during the 1980s to cap hazardous waste emissions were heavily impacting manufacturers. And the Clinton administration planned to step up efforts to reduce waste from this high-polluting industry. The Clean Air Act Amendment of 1990, the EPA's Toxic Inventory Release (TRI) program, the federal Emergency Planning and Community Right-to-Know Act, and voluntary Chemical Manufacturer's Association (CMA) programs were just a few of the initiatives expected to cost the industry millions of dollars during the mid-1990s.

Perhaps the greatest challenge for most intermediate and dye producers in the mid-1990s was growing foreign competition. Although the European Community, Japan, and the United States remained the primary global suppliers for this industry, emerging industrial nations posed a real threat to their dominance. East Asian nations (excluding Japan), particularly, were capturing market share, as were producers in South America, Eastern Europe, India and other regions.

Access to cheap labor and freedom from strict environmental regulations were expected to help manufacturers in these nations advance rapidly in the mid-1990s. The average Chinese worker, for example, cost a company $1,000 per year in 1992. Conversely, the average U.S. aromatic production worker received over $35,000 in salary alone. As a result, dye imports to the United States almost doubled between 1981 and 1991 as the total value of U.S. dye production fell. Although intermediates had fared much better than dyes, U.S. global organic market share diminished from 30 percent to 25 percent between 1988 and 1992.

The Future. Demand for U.S. benzene and intermediates should grow about three percent per year throughout the 1990s, as will the market for xylenes. Demand for synthetic organic pigments and dyes will increase, but U.S. production will likely remain stagnant or decline as exports flood that market. Pharmaceutical intermediates and fuel additives will offer some of the greatest profit potential, as will environmentally safe compounds. To remain competitive in global markets, U.S. producers in the 1990s will be forced to focus their efforts on the development of high-tech, high-margin specialty intermediates and dyes. Consumers of large-volume, low-tech, commodity-like aromatics, intermediates, and dyes will increasing seek low-cost producers in emerging nations.

INDUSTRY LEADERS

The fine chemicals industry is consolidated in comparison to most other U.S. manufacturing industries. Only 180 U.S. companies competed in the early 1990s. The top five companies generated combined revenues of about $1.7 billion. The majority of the top 25 firms, moreover, had sales of over $50 million and employed more than 300 workers. By contrast, the bottom 140 competitors each generated revenues of less than $1 million and employed fewer than 100 people.

The largest company in the industry in the early 1990s was First Mississippi Corporation with 1991 sales of almost $500 million. Crompton and Knowles Corp. of Connecticut, was the second greatest competitor with $390 million in revenues. Sun Chemical Corp. of Ohio and Sandoz Ltd. of North Carolina boasted 1991 sales of $300 and $290 million, respectively. Other large companies primarily engaged in this industry included Mobay Corp., Hoeschst Celanese Corp., and Atochem North America. Major aromatics and intermediates producers principally active in other industries include Exxon, Dow Chemical, Shell, Occidental Petroleum, Amoco, and Lyondell Petrochemical.

WORK FORCE

Job prospects in the industry were terrible going into the mid-1990s. While productivity gains continued to chip away at the labor force, movement of production facilities overseas and increased competition were also depleting opportunities. Positions for chemical equipment controllers, which account for about nine percent of the work force, will likely plunge by 25 percent between 1990 and 2005. Opportunities for machine operators and laborers will decrease similarly. Even positions for general managers, top executives, and support staff will plummet by about 20 percent. Jobs in sales and marketing, on the other hand, should rise by about five percent, and engineering positions should increase by one to four percent.

AMERICA AND THE WORLD

With sales of about $11 billion per year in the early 1990s, U.S. producers accounted for roughly 25 percent of global fine chemicals output. The European Community met 40 percent of worldwide demand, and Japan represented 20 percent of production. Like the United States, which shipped $1.4 billion of its output overseas in 1992, Japan and the European Community were major suppliers of global export demand. These three regions also represented the lion's share of world consumption.

Market share held by all major producers was steadily eroding in the mid-1990s. Eastern European and South American manufacturers, for example, generated about $2 billion and $1 billion worth of product in 1993 and were striving to boost exports. East Asia, which sold $2 billion to $3 billion of aromatics and intermediates in 1992, was growing its output by eight to ten percent per year in the early 1990s.

Two of the fastest growing export nations were China and India. China exported $800 million worth of intermediates in 1992, while India shipped about $500 million. Both countries were expected to surpass U.S. exports by the turn of the century. "China is in a major, major buildup," said Joshua Pratter, manager of technical marketing and planning at ICG, a Califor-

nia-based intermediates producers, in the August 30, 1993 issue of *Chemical Marketing Reporter*. "They're buying a lot of technology."

Another trend taking place in the early 1990s was the movement of U.S. production facilities overseas. Dow Chemical Co., for example, received a license in 1992 to build a polystyrene plant at Map Ta Phut, Thailand—its fifth plant in that country. Likewise, many other producers were moving production to Mexico, Singapore, and other developing regions.

RESEARCH AND TECHNOLOGY

U.S. manufacturers were making capital investments during the early 1990s of more than $5.5 billion per year. This represented an investment per employee about five times greater than the average U.S. manufacturer. Indeed, the United States maintained the most productive and technologically advanced intermediates industry in the world. In the 1980s and early 1990s, the industry dumped billions of dollars into raising productivity through automation and information systems, growing capacity, and complying with environmental laws. In the mid-1990s, new product research and development was the primary investment focus.

To open new markets and battle foreign commodity producers, intermediate and dye manufacturers were scrambling to develop high-tech molecules and compounds. Advances in intermediates used to make pharmaceuticals, for example, allowed the most savvy producers to reap significant rewards. Also in demand were high-performance intermediates that could be used to make cleaner fuel additives, new resins and fibers, better rubber, and environmentally friendly chemicals. "Customers are needing more sophisticated molecules, which are more expensive and smaller in volume," said Jim Cornell, manager of business development at Eastman Fine Chemicals, in the August 30, 1993 issue of *Chemical Marketing Reporter*.

Numerous breakthrough were occurring throughout the industry in the early and mid-1990s. Monsanto Corp., for example, was perfecting a method in 1993 that might make it possible to produce important aromatics in an environmentally safer way. The development offered potentially major commercial consequences. An important growth area in the late 1990s will likely be peptide intermediates. Already being developed in the early 1990s, drugs made using peptides can be used to cause chemical changes in the human body that fight off diseases. Peptide-based drugs offered potential therapy for cancer, AIDS, and other major afflictions.

INDUSTRY INFORMATION SOURCES

Alperowicz, Natasha, "Thailand: Dow Plans Polystyrene, Aromatics Project Reviewed," *Chemical Week,* April 15, 1992.

Anderson, Earl V., "Developing Nation's Chemical Exports Surge," *Chemical & Engineering News,* August 2, 1993.

Anderson, Earl V., "Foreign Trade: U.S. Chemical Trade Surplus Declines," *Chemical & Engineering News,* December 13, 1993.

Anderson, Earl V., "Japan: Once Booming Economy Struggles Through Times," *Chemical & Engineering News,* December 13, 1993.

Bahner, Benedict, "Intermediates '93: Hanging in There," *Chemical Marketing Reporter,* August 30, 1993.

"Chemical Industry R&D Rose 7 percent in 1992," *Chemical & Engineering News,* August 23, 1993.

"Facts & Figures for the Chemical Industry," *Chemical & Engineering News,* June 28, 1993.

Layman, Patricia, "Europe: Definite Though Modest Recovery Forecast for 1994," *Chemical & Engineering News,* December 13, 1993.

Loesel, Andrew, "Intermediates '93: Getting Smarter," *Chemical Marketing Reporter,* August 30, 1993.

Naude, Alice, "Intermediates '93: Waiting for Harvest," *Chemical Marketing Reporter,* August 30, 1993.

Reisch, Marc S., "Top 50 Chemicals Production Recovered Last Year," *Chemical & Engineering News,* April 12, 1993.

Reisch, Marc S., "New Woes May Trigger Another Shakeout for U.S. Dye Producers," *Chemical & Engineering News,* July 5, 1993.

Rzadzki, John, "Intermediates '93: Region on the Rise," *Chemical Marketing Reporter,* August 30, 1993.

Shon, Melissa, "Intermediates '93: Shakeout Time," *Chemical Marketing Reporter,* August 30, 1993.

Springer, Neil, "Intermediates '93: Looking Outward," *Chemical Marketing Reporter,* August 30, 1993.

Standard & Poor's Industry Surveys, New York: Standard & Poor's Corporation, January 20, 1994.

Storck, William J., "United States: Chemical Industry Lackluster This Year," *Chemical & Engineering News,* December 13, 1993.

Tomasula, Dean, "Cumene Yet to Benefit From Economic Recovery," *Chemical Marketing Reporter,* January 3, 1994.

U.S. Industrial Outlook 1993, Washington, D.C.: U.S. Department of Commerce, January 1993.

—Dave Mote

SIC 2869

INDUSTRIAL ORGANIC CHEMICALS, NOT ELSEWHERE CLASSIFIED

The Industrial Organic Chemicals, Not Elsewhere Classified (NEC) Industry is comprised of companies primarily engaged in the production of organic chemicals used by other manufacturing industries. It encompasses the majority of U.S. organic chemical output, and represents the single largest segment of the overall chemical industry. Materials created using these chemicals, such as plastic and fiber, are classified in their respective industries.

INDUSTRY SNAPSHOT

Scientists began producing synthetic organic chemicals in the 1850s. Not until the 1900s, however, did production grow to surpass inorganic output. Rapid expansion during this century has made the overall chemical industry one of the largest businesses in the United States, and the biggest exporting sector of the American economy. Indeed, in 1992 U.S. organic chemical manufacturers sold $54 billion worth of materials and employed 100,000 workers. They shipped almost $11 billion worth of exports, and accounted for about 25% of global organic chemical output.

The industry realized healthy revenue and profit growth during the late 1980s. Production volume and sales continued to climb in the early 90s. However, overcapacity and a weak global economy diminished manufacturers' earnings. As they entered the mid-1990s, producers faced other roadblocks as well. Increasing foreign competition and stiff environmental regulations were two of the greatest challenges confronting the industry. To combat these negative influences, manufacturers were increasing their productivity, focusing on high-margin specialty chemicals, and restructuring their organizations.

ORGANIZATION AND STRUCTURE

The chemical industry is divided into organic and inorganic substances. Inorganic chemicals, which are derived from the inanimate material of the earth's crust, include compounds such as sulfuric acid, sulfur, phosphoric acid, and hydrogen peroxide. Organic chemicals are so named because in the industry's early days they were obtained from living organisms. Today they are derived from substances that contain carbon, such as petroleum, coal, and natural gas. Petroleum-based chemicals, or petrochemicals, account for about

80% of industry output by weight and 50% of production by value.

Organic chemicals, particularly petrochemicals, play an indispensable role in modern society. They are essential ingredients to plastics, synthetic fibers, rubber, fertilizers, and chemical intermediates, which are converted into a plethora of consumer and industrial products. They are the primary building blocks of important materials supporting health, food, transportation, and communication industries. Organic substances have also made possible many important specialty items, such as protective clothing and materials used for space exploration.

Organics constituted about 66%, or $54 billion, of the $81 billion chemical industry in 1992. Inorganic and agricultural chemicals made up the remainder of production. Likewise, the chemical industry represented about 46% of the overall chemicals and related products industry. Other segments of the general industry include synthetic materials, such as plastic and fibers, and chemical products, like paint, drugs, and soap.

Because organic chemicals are used to make so many products within the overall chemical and related products divisions, the industry eludes clear definition. Most industrial organic chemicals, in fact, are consumed by chemical-related businesses. For instance, companies that produce cyclic crudes and intermediates, such as aromatics and dyes (see **SIC 2865: Cyclic Organic Crudes and Intermediates, and Organic Dyes and Pigments**), purchased about 20% of industry output in the early 90s. Plastic resin manufacturers (see **SIC 2821: Plastics Materials, Synthetic Resins, and Nonvulcanizable Elastomers—Con.**) consumed 13% of production. Synthetic fiber producers (see **SIC 2824: Manmade Organic Fibers, Except Cellulosic**) accounted for about 6% of industry revenues, and elastomer companies (see **SIC 2822: Synthetic Rubber (Vulcanized Elastomers)**) absorbed 3% of production. 13% of organic chemical sales were garnered from exports.

The remaining 45% of organic output was used by numerous manufacturing sectors. Steel and aluminum mills, paper mills, semiconductor manufacturers, drug companies, carpet mills, and battery producers are relatively large customers. Other chemical uses include the production of items such as pipe, photographic equipment, electrical insulation, and food containers.

Production. The organic chemical industry serves one primary purpose; to take a relatively few fundamental raw chemicals that contain carbon and combine them into new substances with desirable physical properties. Using carbon as a basic building block, chemists are able to unite other elements, such as nitrogen, hydrogen, oxygen, sulfur, and chlorine, to generate a multitude of different compounds. Furthermore, each resultant compound can be manipulated, with heat or additives for example, to produce an infinite variety of characteristics and grades.

The most common category of organic chemicals are Aliphatics, or Olefins, which are straight-chain hydrocarbons. Olefins can be made using petroleum or natural gas, though most U.S. manufacturers use the latter. To produce Olefins, natural gas is separated into ethane, propane, and butane. From these gases, smaller percentages of marketable ethylene, propylene, and butadiene are extracted. These three substances are the basic building blocks for most organic chemicals and synthetic materials. Major producers of aliphatics include Dow Chemical, Union Carbide, Lyondell Petrochemical, Occidental Petroleum, and Quantum Chemical.

Ethylene is the largest-volume organic chemical produced in the United States. In 1992, domestic competitors made about 41 billion pounds of ethylene valued at over $8 billion, or more than 15% of industry revenues. Approximately 75% of all ethylene is utilized to produce plastics, such as polyethylene, polyvinyl chloride, and polystyrene. It is also widely used to make antifreeze, synthetic fibers, rubber, solvents, and detergents. Derivatives of ethylene represent a significant share of total industry output as well. Nearly 16 billion pounds of ethylene dichloride, for example, were sold in 1992.

The second largest olefin, by production volume, is propylene. The industry churned out more than 22.5 billion pounds of this organic in 1992. 40% of propylene is used to make polypropylene, which in turn is utilized to manufacture film, packaging, foams and coatings, solvents, gasoline, and fibers. In addition, propylene is used to make other popular chemicals, such as acrylonitrile, propylene oxide, isopropanol, and cumene. Over 4.5 billion pounds of cumene, as an example, were produced in 1992.

Butadiene, the third most popular olefin, is employed primarily in the manufacture of synthetic rubber. The remaining one-third of butadiene production is consumed by makers of latex, resins, and nylon fibers. In 1992, about 3.2 billion pounds of this compound were produced in the United States.

Aside from olefins and their offspring, synthetic methanol accounts for a large share of industry output—more than 8.7 billion pounds in 1992. Important derivatives include formaldehyde, acetic acid, methyl methacrylate, and various solvents. About 50% of all methanol is utilized in the production of adhesives, fibers, and plastics. In addition, it is an important ingredient in antifreeze and gasoline additives. Methyl tert-butyl ether (MBTE), a methanol derivative, is used as an oxygenate in automobile gasoline. MBTE production topped 10.5 billion pounds in the early 1990s. Major producers of methanol include Beaumont Methanol, Borden, Lyondell Petrochemical, Quantum Chemical, and Georgia Gulf.

Environmental Impact. Laws and initiatives regarding hazardous emissions generated during organic chemical production and use are important dynamics that shape the industry. Indeed, the chemical business is by far the largest polluting U.S. industry—generating at least three times more pollution than the second greatest offending industry.

In 1991, chemical producers released more than 1.5 billion pounds of toxins (as defined by the Environmental Protection Agency's (EPA) Toxics Release Inventory, or TRI). This figure represented a full 46% of all U.S. industrial toxic emissions. 40% of this waste was dumped into the air, 40% into underground wells, and the remainder was released into water and land.

To minimize the detrimental effects of chemical industry pollutants, multiple local, state, and federal laws govern producers. The federal Emergency Planning and Community Right-to-Know Act (EPCRA), for example, requires many manufacturers to submit detailed emissions data to the EPA. Similarly, the Pollution Prevention Act (1990) requires those same companies to report their waste management and pollution reduction activities.

Other federal regulations Impacting producers include the Safe Drinking Water Act, the Clean Air Act Amendments of 1990, and other laws that restrict hazardous wastes. In addition to legal restrictions, both the EPA and the Chemical Manufacturers Association (CMA) sponsor successful voluntary pollution reduction programs that encourage environmental sensitivity.

In an effort to comply with voluntary and mandated measures, chemical companies spent nearly $5 billion in 1992 on pollution abatement. Expenditures were used primarily to create cleaner production facilities and to research and develop new methods of reducing hazardous wastes.

BACKGROUND AND DEVELOPMENT

Ancient Egyptians and Chinese were the first to experiment with chemical processes in carrying out dyeing, leather tanning, and glassmaking activities. It was not until 1790, however, that Nicolas Leblanc, a Frenchman, gave birth to the chemical industry. He is credited with being the first person to successfully carry out a deliberate plan to convert one or more chemical products into one wholly different substance, keeping in mind not only the end product but also the economics of the process. Leblanc was inspired by a reward of 12,000 francs offered by the French Academy of Sciences to anyone who could devise a method for making inexpensive alkali.

While Leblanc's discovery was neglected in France, it became extremely important in England in the soap and textile industries. As British alkali producers advanced the inorganic chemical industry during the 1800s, they laid the foundation for organic chemistry. Although organic compounds had been known to man for centuries, it was not discovered until early in the 19th century that they *all* contain carbon. Once scientists realized that they could unite carbon with other common elements, they quickly began to create their own substances. Chemists at first sought to create elements that imitated natural, known substances. Later, though, they learned how to create a vast variety of unknown compounds.

The first chemist to synthesize an organic chemical for commercial use was Englishman William Henry Perkin, the father of the organic chemical industry. 18-year-old Perkin, working in his father's house in 1856, accidently created a synthetic dye using a piece of coal tar. Although he received knighthood for his efforts, it wasn't until 1865 that the chemical structure of Perkin's dye was understood. In that year, Friedreich von Kekule announced his breakthrough theory of the benzene ring. Using Kekule's theory, chemists were able to build millions of new organic chemicals during the 19th and early 20th centuries, many of which displaced natural materials and dyes.

Chemists did not begin synthesizing petroleum and natural gas to create petrochemicals on a commercial scale until the 1920s. A huge demand for gasoline, rubber products, textiles, detergents, and plastics that could be created with petrochemicals in the 1920s and early 1930s boosted industry growth. It was World War II, however, that launched the organic chemical industry to national prominence. During this period, a shortage of natural and manmade materials that had previously been supplied by other sources resulted in rapid industry expansion. Production of synthetic rubber, for example, bolted from just 72,000 tons in 1939 to more than 800,000 tons in 1945.

Organic chemical sales continued to balloon after WWII, as the post-war U.S. economy expanded. The explosion in automobile production during the '50s, '60s, and '70s, for example, created a massive demand for chemicals utilized in the production of rubber, paint, and gasoline. Importantly, commercial and residential construction booms generated a huge need for paneling, roofing, insulation, carpet, draperies, upholstery, varnishes, and other chemical-based building materials. Likewise, the call for clothing created from organic chemicals ballooned as a rising population sought viable alternatives to costly natural fibers. Defense and consumer products markets grew as well. Besides meeting demand in domestic markets, moreover, the United States became a major chemical supplier to European countries that had been devastated by war.

As organic chemical revenues blossomed throughout most of the period between the 1950s and 1970s, overall chemical industry sales, including inorganics, reached approximately $50 billion. Production volume of ethylene and propylene, combined, topped 30 billion pounds, while total organic output climbed past 120 billion pounds. Heading into the 1980s, industrial organic chemical producers were employing more than 120,000 workers and shipping more than $5 billion in exports.

In the early '80s, organic producers were battered by high petroleum prices and a deep U.S. economic recession. As sales stalled throughout the early years of the decade, inventories swelled and profit margins collapsed. Demand began recovering in 1983, however, pushed by a revival in housing starts and automobile markets. The demand for organics used to create plastics and textiles was especially strong, and consumption by paperboard and furniture markets recuperated. Sales climbed 9% in 1983, from $30.4 billion to $33.3 billion, and about 8% in 1984, to $35.8 billion.

Despite a temporary downturn in 1985 and 1986, industry expansion accelerated during the late 1980s. Sales rose to $42 billion in 1987 before jumping 16% to $49.1 billion in 1988. Prices and profits also improved, following stagnation throughout most of the decade. Overall chemical industry profits, for example, rose to $4 billion in 1987, from just more than $2 billion per year between 1982 and 1985. Profit margins climbed from 4% in 1985 to a peak of almost 10% in 1988, boosting overall earnings past an annual rate of $7 billion in early 1989.

Production volume of many organics mushroomed during the 1980s. Propylene output, for example, rocketed from 12.5 billion pounds in 1982 to 21.8 billion by 1990, representing annual growth of more than 6%. Consumption of butadiene rose similarly, to

about 3 billion pounds by 1990. Ethylene production climbed at an annual rate of more than 5%, from 24.5 billion pounds in 1982 to 36.5 by 1990. More importantly, however, many derivatives of the three major olefins realized average annual growth rates in excess of 10% throughout the decade. In anticipation of continued growth, producers responded in the late 1980s by making heavy capital investments to increase their production capacity.

Notwithstanding a surge in the latter years of the decade, chemical market growth during the 1980s was modest in comparison to the expansion enjoyed during the previous three decades. Indeed, many organic chemical producers realized that the industry was entering a new stage of maturity. The massive growth opportunities of the mid-20th century, propelled by economic expansion and uncontested global dominance, had diminished significantly even by the late 1970s.

Particularly disconcerting to producers of commodity-like organics was the steep rise of foreign competition that was already occurring in the early 1980s. Besides expanded output by Japan and the European Community (EC), U.S. producers were also being challenged by low-cost producers in such nations as Korea and Singapore. Indeed, despite overall export growth by domestic chemical manufacturers in the mid-1980s, the U.S. share of the world chemical export market plummeted from about 17% in 1984 to less than 14% in 1987. Although inorganic commodity chemicals represented much of this decline, the share of U.S. exports represented by organic chemicals slipped from more than 30% in the mid-1980s to about 25% by the early '90s. U.S. global chemical export market share recovered slightly in 1989, to about 15%.

To combat long-term downward profit pressures exerted by relatively flat market growth and increased competition, many producers in the early 1980s began cutting costs, consolidating operations, increasing research and development spending, and implementing cost-saving automation and information systems. Most producers that were slow to implement such initiatives had climbed aboard the bandwagon by the late '80s— and these efforts were evidenced by a decline in employment. Indeed, even as organic manufacturers scrambled to boost their productivity during the 1980s, employment fell from 111,000 in 1982 to about 100,000 by 1990. This occurred despite steady growth in production volume.

CURRENT CONDITIONS

After steady growth through 1989, industrial organic chemical manufacturers suffered serious setbacks in the early 1990s. A U.S. and global economic recession stumped profit growth, as the value of petrochemical and related products sales dropped 1.5% in 1990 to $54.1 billion. Sales rose just 1% in both 1991 and 1992 (using inflation adjusted dollars), and overall organic chemical output rose only slightly between 1990 and 1992. This tepid growth, moreover, was offset by stagnant prices and declining profits. Indeed, from a peak of nearly 10% in 1988, chemical industry profit margins sank to about 5% in 1992.

Compounding industry woes in the early '90s was excess production capacity, the result of expansion in the previous half-decade. Oversupply was still depressing organic prices into the mid-1990s, thus eliminating profit growth. Despite ongoing successful efforts to increase productivity and improve products, U.S. competitors were unable to overcome the effects of the latest downturn. Even a slow but steady increase in organic exports did little to alleviate the impact of sluggish domestic markets. After all, imports to the United States rose at a rate about 15 times greater than U.S. exports in 1992, augmenting downward price pressures.

In an effort to buoy earnings, domestic competitors continued restructuring in the 1990s. Companies were cutting costs out of every phase of the production process, often leading to massive lay-offs. DuPont, for example, announced a work force reduction of as many as 4,500 employees in late 1993, adding to about 5,500 lay-offs made by that company since 1991. Likewise, Dow Chemical eliminated 4,700 jobs in 1993, and Air Products reduced its work force by 1,300. Many companies were also restructuring by selling unprofitable operations and focusing on their core competencies.

While revenues improved and prices gained slightly in 1993, overcapacity and weak markets persisted into 1994. Industry shipments grew between 1% and 2% in 1993, and were expected to increase similarly in the near-term. This growth was expected to eventually reduce overcapacity, however, allowing manufacturers to raise prices slightly. The effects of a reduction in oversupply may be offset by the diminished stature of U.S. producers in the global marketplace. U.S. firms will increasingly be forced to shift production from high-volume commodity-like organics to low-volume specialty and high-tech compounds that demand higher prices.

Major Segment Status. Demand for ethylene and its derivatives was expected to grow at a rate of about 3% during the mid-1990s, pushed by increases in the need for lower-volume derivatives. Output for pure ethylene stood at 41.5 billion pounds in 1992. Al-though ethylene output had climbed steadily since 1989, overcapacity in this segment was hurting profits. Demand was expected to catch up with output potential, which approached 50 billion pounds, by the late '90s.

The large propylene and polypropylene segment realized growth of about 3% per year in the early 1990s, and was expected to climb at an average annual rate of about 3.5% through the decade. Prices remained extremely weak, however, going into 1994. Butadiene markets remained flat in 1993 as well. Although the demand for this organic rose steadily during the previous decade, reduced consumption by rubber manufacturers was expected to minimize butadiene's potential for growth in the '90s.

Methanol output stagnated during the early '90s, but derivative products, such as MBTE, were thriving. MBTE output gained 13% in 1992, according to one estimate, and was expected to surge throughout the decade as the Clean Air Act Amendments of 1990 spurred the growth of fuel oxygenators. In contrast, some of the big losers in the organic industry included methyl methacrylate, which suffered a demand reduction of 24% in 1992, and methylene chloride, which fell 8%.

Regulatory Impacts. While increasing federal and state regulations posed an ongoing challenge to chemical industry participants, positive signs indicated that the industry was successfully clearing these hurdles and was even benefitting from some laws. Indeed, the overall chemical industry reduced its emissions of TRI wastes by 34% between 1988 and 1991, and expected to display like-reductions in 1992 and 1993. Water and air emissions were down by 19% and 29%, respectively, between 1988 and 1991, while underground injections had fallen a significant 34%. During the same period, moreover, total industry production climbed 11%.

Despite industry gains, chemical pollutants remained a major concern for regulators. Some regulations, though, were expected to boost industry profits. The Clean Air Act Amendments of 1990, for example, required automobile carbon-monoxide emissions to fall below certain levels by 1995. As a result, the demand for organic gasoline additives that allow such reductions was forecast to balloon.

Besides environmental restrictions, manufacturers were also burdened with increased costs related to new safety initiatives. The EPA's proposed risk management rule, for example, was pending in 1994. This law was designed to prevent, detect, and respond to the release of extremely hazardous substances from chemical plants that affected neighboring communities. Companies would be required to develop emergency response plans and implement new prevention programs under the proposal.

A similar Occupational Health and Safety Administration (OSHA) law, which was passed by Congress in 1992, was aimed at preventing accidents in the work place. OSHA estimated that its new law would cost about $863 million per year between 1992 and 1997. The EPA rule, according to government estimates, would cost $503 million in the first year, but would save $890 million in environmental damage and response costs. Organic chemical producers also anticipated expenses starting in 1994 as a result of a CMA initiative. The CMA's Responsible Care Program would require its members to file safety incident reports for manufacturing mishaps.

RESEARCH AND TECHNOLOGY

The organic chemical industry continues to invest a major share of its revenues in research and development. Most expenditures are used to increase productivity and meet stringent environmental regulations, as discussed above. The average organic manufacturer made capital investments equivalent to $35,589 per employee in 1989, about 7 times more than the average U.S. manufacturer.

Total research and development expenditures by organic chemical manufacturers rose 7.4% in 1990 to $4.3 billion. Investments leveled off in 1991 and 1992, increasing 2% per year; nonetheless, total capital spending had increased significantly since the early 1980s, when disbursements fluctuated between $1.6 and $2.5 trillion. In 1994, the chemical and related products industries employed 12% of all U.S. industrial scientists and engineers.

INDUSTRY LEADERS

About 650 companies participated in the industrial organic chemical industry in the early 1990s. The top 15 competitors all had sales of more than $1 billion from various businesses, and most of them employed several thousand workers. Most of the top 75 firms in the industry, though, had fewer than 500 workers and generated revenues of less than $200 million per year. The industry is highly consolidated in relation to most other U.S. manufacturing sectors. High start-up costs, technical expertise, and entrenched segment leaders discourage new competition.

The largest producer of industrial organic chemicals is the Midland, Michigan-based Dow Chemical Company. Herbert Dow began Canton Chemical in 1890, which failed. He quickly rebounded, however, by starting the Dow Chemical Company, however, which achieved $4 million in sales by 1920, and $15 million by 1930. Dow's research and development strength helped it serve U.S. needs during WWII, when it took a leading role in providing butadiene for synthetic rubber production. Sales quadrupled from $200 million in 1949 to over $800 million by 1960, and grew at a rate of over 10% per year through the early 70s. The chemical giant earned 1992 chemical operating profits of $592 million from sales of $12.9 billion. Its revenues slumped 2.7% in 1992 as profits rose 4.6% over 1991 levels. Dow employed 18,000 workers in its diversified operations in 1991.

The second largest player in the organic chemical industry is Connecticut-based Exxon Corporation. Exxon earned chemical operating profits in 1992 of $660 million from sales of $10.7 billion. Chemical profits declined 1.8% in 1991, though they represented only 9% of this petroleum giant's business. Exxon employed 46,000 workers in its diversified operations.

The third largest firm in the industry is Union Carbide Corporation, also of Connecticut. 1992 sales of $4.8 billion earned this diversified producer chemical operating profits of $316 million. Union Carbide announced a major cost-cutting effort in 1993. Other leading competitors in the industry are Bayer USA Inc. of Pennsylvania, Amoco Chemical Co. of Chicago, and Chevron Chemical Co. of California.

WORK FORCE

Approximately 100,000 workers served the industrial organic chemical industry in 1992. This represented a decline of about 10% since the early 1980s. Production workers accounted for about 76,000 of this group. Their numbers declined 6% in 1992, and averaged an annual reduction rate of 1% between 1982 and 1992. Largely to blame for cutbacks in both white- and blue-collar jobs were productivity increases achieved by manufacturers. Efficiency gains in the overall chemical industry averaged about 4% per year between 1983 and 1992, which was more than enough to offset gains from increased output. Furthermore, productivity jumped an impressive 6.4% in 1992, compared to average gains of just 2.9% in all other U.S. manufacturing businesses.

Employment growth in the organic chemical industry is expected to remain weak in the short-term. Although output was rising going into 1994 and some firms were adding production workers, major producers continued to announce lay-offs, particularly of white-collar management employees. It is the blue-collar workers that will suffer most from long-term trends, however. Positions for chemical equipment controllers, which account for a full 9% of the organic chemical industry work force, will fall by 25% between 1990 and 2005, according to the Bureau of Labor statistics. In fact, jobs for most production workers, such as technicians, supervisors, and machine operators, are expected to plummet by between 5% to 35% by 2005.

Jobs for white collar workers and support staff will also fall. The demand for administrators and managers will decline 14% between 1990 and 2005, as clerical jobs plunge almost 25%. General management and top executive positions will drop by 18%. Even chemists will see opportunities erode by about 6%. On the bright side, some engineering jobs will rise 3%. Sales and marketing positions, moreover, will jump 5%. The need for systems analysts and computer scientists in this industry are expected increase by 22% by 2005.

A primary factor driving work force cutbacks in the 1980s and early '90s was high wages. Indeed, workers in the organic chemical industry are among the highest paid manufacturing employees in the United States. The average organic chemical production worker, for example, earned $17.23 per hour in 1992, compared with the average of just $10.49 for all U.S. manufacturing laborers. For the entire organic chemical industry, payroll per employee topped $40,000 per year in 1992—about $14,000 more than the average for other U.S. manufacturers. Industry wages rose 4.2% in 1992, and 3.6% in 1991.

The best paying jobs in the industry go to highly educated chemists that are involved in research or management, who earned about $90,000 per year in 1992. The average staff chemist's annual salary, in contrast, was $56,000. Chemists with masters degrees averaged $58,000, while PhDs earned an average of $75,000. However, unemployment among chemists was at its highest level since 1983. And, despite salary increases of more than 4%, joblessness among chemists' grew to 7.2% in 1992.

Chemists entering the chemical industry out of school in 1993 could expect to earn $25,000 per year at the undergraduate level, $33,000 with a graduate degree, and about $50,000 if they had a doctorate. 25% of graduating chemical engineers in 1992, however, were still seeking employment eight months after graduation. Even among chemists employed by the industry in 1993, surveys showed that one out of 25 had experienced joblessness during the past year.

AMERICA AND THE WORLD

The U.S. industrial organic chemical industry is a large part of a global industry, and was shipping over $11 billion worth of output overseas going into the mid-1990s. American manufacturers produced more than 25% of global organic output in the early 90s, and accounted for one-quarter of all U.S. chemical exports. Chemical exports, in turn, represented 10% of total U.S. merchandise exports. The U.S. organics industry remains the largest and most technologically advanced in the world. Its supremacy has waned considerably since the 1950s, however, when U.S. organic producers supplied more than 50% of global output.

The largest foreign buyer of U.S. petrochemicals in 1991 was Canada, which consumed 11.3% of overseas shipments. Japan, the second largest importer, purchased 9.6% of all petrochemical exports, while China represented 8.7% of the foreign market. Taiwan and Belgium each bought about 7% of U.S. exports. East Asia was the largest region of U.S. organic consumption, constituting 25% of overseas orders. The European Community (EC) represented a combined 23% of foreign demand.

Despite the strength of the U.S. organic industry, foreign competition continued to erode its comparative might. Although American companies managed to boost organic exports again in 1992, by about 1%, imports advanced 15% and the Industry's trade surplus slipped to about $1.6 billion—while only three years earlier the surplus had exceeded $2.3 billion. Indeed, as the percentage of U.S. chemical exports represented by organics declined from 30% in the mid-1980s, the proportion of U.S. imports made up of organics climbed to 33%.

Economic stagnation in key export markets, such as Japan and the EC, combined with recovering U.S. demand helped importers to increase their share of the U.S. market in the early '90s. However, long-term structural changes in global chemical markets were also at work. Importantly, producers in emerging economies were increasingly challenging U.S. suppliers for both domestic and export sales. In fact, overall chemical exports by developing nations rocketed nearly 400% during the 1980s, from $10.5 billion in 1980 to $38.8 billion in 1991. East Asian countries, particularly, were increasing production. Of 28 new ethylene producers preparing to begin operation in the mid-1990s, for instance, 18 were in the Far East, and only 1 was in Japan. Likewise, 46% of new global styrene capacity scheduled to be added by 1995 was in the Far East. New competitors in South America, Africa, and the Middle East also threatened to depress both global and domestic prices and reduce U.S. market share.

The largest importer of petrochemicals to the United States in 1991 was Canada, which supplied nearly 15% of imports. Germany and Japan supplied 14.3% and 12.7%, respectively, of all cross-border purchases by Americans. The United Kingdom held about 9% of the U.S. import market, and France captured 6.3%. The EC supplied 43% of U.S. petrochemical imports. Although Mexico supplied only a small share of imports in the early 1990s, that country's import activity was expected to rise substantially throughout the decade in the wake of the North American Free Trade Agreement (NAFTA) passed in 1993. NAFTA eliminated tariffs on cross-border chemical sales.

In the long term, growing foreign organic chemical production will result in fierce competition and reduced opportunities for U.S. manufacturers. The United States, Europe, and Japan will remain the key producers, but much of the market for high-volume, commodity-like organics will be surrendered to emerging powers. To sustain profitability, U.S. competitors will be forced to boost their production of high-tech compounds that will outperform existing chemicals and open new markets.

INDUSTRY INFORMATION SOURCES

Anderson, Earl V., Chemical & Engineering News, "Exports of Large-Volume Chemicals Weakened Last Year," April 19, 1993; "Chemical Industry Faces Slower Growth," November 15, 1993; "Foreign Trade: U.S. Chemical Trade Surplus Declines," December 13, 1993; "Japan: Once Booming Economy Struggles Through Times," December 13, 1993; "Developing Nation's Chemical Exports Surge," August 2, 1993.

"Chemical Industry R&D Rose 7% in 1992," Chemical & Engineering News, August 23, 1993.

Darnay, Arsen J., ed., Manufacturing USA; Industry Analyses, Statistics, and Leading Companies. Detroit: Gale Research Inc., 1993.

Encyclopedia Britannica, Chicago: Encyclopedia Britannica, Inc., 1968; 1980.

"Facts & Figures for the Chemical Industry," Chemical & Engineering News, June 28, 1993.

Hast, Adele, ed., International Directory of Company Histories, Volume III. Chicago: St. James Press, 1991.

Heylin, Michael, "Job Market for Chemists Remains Depressed, Salaries Gain 5%," Chemical & Engineering News, July 12, 1993.

Illman, Deborah L., "New Initiatives Take Aim at Safety Performance of Chemical Industry," Chemical & Engineering News, November 29, 1993.

Layman, Patricia, Chemical & Engineering News, "Europe: Definite Though Modest Recovery Forecast for 1994," De-

cember 13, 1993; "Global Industry Forum Charts Challenges, Woes," May 10, 1993.

Rawis, Rebecca L., "Salaries," Chemical & Engineering News, October 25, 1993.

Reisch, Marc S., "Top 50 Chemicals Production Recovered Last Year," Chemical & Engineering News, April 12, 1993.

Standard & Poor's Industry Surveys, New York: Standard & Poor's Corporation, January 20, 1994.

Storck, William J., "United States: Chemical Industry Lackluster This Year," Chemical & Engineering News, December 13, 1993.

Thayer, Ann M., "Growing Exchange of Information Spurs Pollution Prevention Efforts," Chemical & Engineering News, July 26, 1993.

U.S. Industrial Outlook 1993, Washington, D.C.: U.S. Department of Commerce, January 1993.

—Dave Mote

SIC 2873

NITROGENOUS FERTILIZERS

This category includes establishments primarily engaged in manufacturing nitrogenous fertilizer materials or mixed fertilizers from nitrogenous materials produced in the same establishment.

The main source of nitrogen for use in fertilizer production is atmospheric nitrogen, of which there is abundant supply; it has been estimated that there are about 35,000 tons of nitrogen over every acre of land. In order for plants to utilize this element, however, it must first be combined with either oxygen or hydrogen in a process called "fixation." The primary ingredient of most nitrogenous fertilizers is anhydrous ammonia, which the fertilizer industry typically forms by fixing atmospheric nitrogen with the hydrogen found in natural gas (methane). The resultant compound is a gas which is 82.25 percent nitrogen. This gas is stored in containers which are pressurized and usually refrigerated. It may be directly applied as a fertilizer beneath the soil surface with the use of injection equipment. It is the least expensive and one of the more common nitrogenous fertilizers used for direct application in the United States.

Anhydrous ammonia may be reacted with nitric acid to produce ammonium nitrate. While it is an excellent fertilizer, ammonium nitrate is also highly combustible. Once the world's leading directly-applied nitrogenous fertilizer, it appears to be giving way to urea. Produced by reacting anhydrous ammonia with carbon dioxide, urea has a higher nitrogen content and is easier and safer to store and handle than is ammonium nitrate.

The cost of ammonia production is closely tied to the cost of natural gas. As the cost of natural gas has risen in the United States, so has the cost of ammonia and nitrogenous fertilizers. In the last half of 1992, natural gas prices shot upwards and accounted for between 70 and 85 percent of total ammonia production costs. This has put the United States at a cost disadvantage compared to countries such as Russia, Canada, and Mexico, which have abundant and lower-priced sources of natural gas. In terms of production volume, the United States lags behind Russia and China and may be facing persistent erosion of world market share.

Two of the major producers of fertilizers in the United States, Arcadian Partners, L.P. and Terra Industries, took steps in 1993 to increase their production capacity for nitrogenous fertilizers. In March, Arcadian acquired both the Fertilizers of Trinidad and Tobago Limited and the Trinidad and Tobago Urea Company Limited. These two acquisitions both have top-notch ammonia and granular urea production facilities, as well as access to ample and low-cost natural gas. The following month, Arcadian acquired the nitrogenous fertilizer business from BP Chemicals Inc., a unit of British Petroleum Co. The deal gave Arcadian a multi-plant production facility in Lima, Ohio with capabilities for producing ammonia, urea, and nitric acid. Also in April, Terra Industries acquired a nitrogenous fertilizer manufacturing plant, regarded by many in the industry as one of the most efficient plants at converting natural gas to ammonia, from ICI Canada. The plant is located in Canada, and in 1992 its product sales were over $110 million (Canadian). Other major U.S. nitrogenous fertilizer producers are Unocal Corporation and CF Industries.

INDUSTRY INFORMATION SOURCES

"Arcadian Acquires Nitrogen Fertilizer Business of BP Chemicals Inc." *PR Newswire*, 11 May 1993.

"Arcadian to Acquire Fertrin and TTUC Caribbean Nitrogen Fertilizer Businesses," *PR Newswire*, 25 March 1993.

Farm Chemicals Handbook 1992. Willoughby, OH: Meister Publishing Company, 1992.

Follet, Roy Hunter, Larry S. Murphy, and Roy L. Donahue. *Fertilizers and Soil Amendments*. New Jersey: Prentice-Hall, 1981.

Soil Improvement Committee, California Fertilizer Association. *Western Fertilizer Handbook*. Danville, IL: The Interstate, 1985.

Standard & Poor's Industry Surveys. New York: Standard & Poor's Corporation, 1993.

"Terra Industries Completes Acquisition." *PR Newswire*, 8 April 1993.

Tinsdale, Samuel L., Werner L. Nelson, and James D. Beaton. *Soil Fertility and Fertilizers*. New York: Macmillan, 1985.

U.S. Industrial Outlook 1993. Washington, DC: U.S. Department of Commerce, 1993.

—J. T. Wingett

SIC 2874

PHOSPHATIC FERTILIZERS

This category includes establishments primarily engaged in manufacturing phosphatic fertilizer materials, or mixed fertilizers from phosphatic materials produced in the same establishment.

Although the original sources of phosphorus for plant fertilization were guano (i.e., bird and bat excrement) and ground bone, a more plentiful source came to be found in phosphate rock, which was the only commercially important source of fertilizer phosphorus in the 1990s. Chief sources of the world supply of phosphate rock are the United States (principally Florida and North Carolina), the Kola Peninsula in Russia, and Morocco. After being mined, the phosphate rock must be refined and concentrated for use as fertilizer. Sometimes, finely ground phosphate rock is applied directly to soil, but usually it is converted, using sulfuric acid, into a more water-soluble form. The United States is the world's leading producer of phosphatic fertilizers, but Morocco, which actually has four times the phosphate rock deposits of the United States, is expected to overtake the United States in fertilizer phosphates production by the end of the twentieth century.

The most widely used of the phosphatic fertilizers is diammonium phosphate (DAP). During the crop year which ended in the summer of 1991, about one-fifth of the 10.7 million tons of DAP exported by the United States went to India, and nearly one-half went to China. The forecast entering 1992 was for increased DAP demand, coupled with lower costs for sulphur, an expensive raw material. Optimism for a boom year in the industry, however, was followed by disappointment. Manufacturers, having increased their DAP inventories in anticipation of an increase in demand, faced a DAP glut as both domestic demand and the market for exports weakened. Prices for DAP fell to their lowest point in nearly 15 years.

The result of the economic difficulties was that IMC Fertilizer, Inc., one of the larger U.S. producers of phosphatic fertilizers, was forced in the first quarter of 1993 to close indefinitely a phosphate mine and DAP plant, both in central Florida. The following summer, IMC and Freeport-McMoRan Resource Partners LP formed a joint venture, called IMC-Agrico Co., through which the two companies combined their phosphatic fertilizer business. The industry consolidated further in May of 1993 when Cargill Fertilizer, Inc. bought the phosphate mining and phosphate fertilizer production assets of Seminole Fertilizer Corporation. This consolidation transformed Cargill Fertilizer into a major U.S. producer of phosphatic fertilizers.

The depressed state of the industry in mid-1993 may have just been a cyclical trough. About 45 percent of the phosphatic fertilizer produced in the United States is used on its domestic corn crop, so corn acreage is one determinant of domestic demand; other determinants are grain prices, the ability of U.S. farmers to compete globally, and the weather. Short term fluctuations in the domestic market are thus difficult to predict, but prices were expected to rebound by the mid- to late-1990s. The export market also holds some promise for the long term, given the U.S. industry's cost advantage over many foreign producers with respect to phosphate rock and sulphur, two key raw materials.

INDUSTRY INFORMATION SOURCES

"Cargill Completes Seminole Purchase." *PR Newswire*, 4 May 1993.

Farm Chemicals Handbook 1992. Willoughby, OH: Meister Publishing Company, 1992.

"IMC Fertilizer Joint Venture Formed." *Reuters News Service*, 1 July 1993.

"IMC Fertilizer to Close Fertilizer Plant Due to Deteriorating Prices." *PR Newswire*, 19 March 1993.

McMurray, Scott. "Fertilizer Firms' Hopes for Turnaround Are Frustrated." *Wall Street Journal*, 12 December 1993.

Soil Improvement Committee, California Fertilizer Association. *Western Fertilizer Handbook*. Danville, IL: The Interstate, 1985.

Standard & Poor's Industry Surveys. New York: Standard & Poor's Corporation, 1993.

Tinsdale, Samuel L., Werner L. Nelson, and James D. Beaton. *Soil Fertility and Fertilizers*. New York: Macmillan, 1985.

"Tosco Completes Sale of Subsidiary." *PR Newswire*, 4 May 1993.

U.S. Industrial Outlook 1993. Washington, DC: U.S. Department of Commerce, 1993.

—J. T. Wingett

SIC 2875

FERTILIZERS, MIXING ONLY

This category covers establishments primarily engaged in mixing fertilizers from purchased fertilizer materials. In the industry, "fertilizer materials" refers specifically to fertilizers which have no more than one of the three primary plant nutrients (nitrogen, phosphorus, and potassium). This category also includes manufacturers of compost and potting soil; these products condition the soil to promote plant growth but contain relatively small amounts of plant nutrients.

There are three major types of mixed fertilizers: homogeneous mixtures, bulk blends, and fluids. A key process performed by producers of homogeneous mixtures, as well as by producers of fertilizer materials, is granulation. Before the granulation process, nongranulated dry fertilizer powders had a tendency to form hardened cakes, which made the product difficult to handle. The hardened cakes were not always broken up easily. Explosives were sometimes utilized to break up these cakes which had formed on heaps of stored fertilizer. Another problem with fertilizer mixes before the granulation process was the propensity for the component fertilizer materials to segregate, according to particle sizes, during transport and handling. Granulation addresses the problem of caking and segregation by forming the constituent parts of the fertilizer mix into larger granules which are relatively equal in size and which each have the same nutrient analysis. The manufacture of this type of mixed fertilizer is a complex process requiring sophisticated equipment.

Bulk blending plants, by contrast, do not perform granulation or any chemical processes and their basic equipment needs are rudimentary (i.e., bins, front-end loaders, mixers, and scales). They keep an assortment of fertilizer materials on site, from which they select desired proportions for mixing together, often to suit the specific nutrient needs of the customer. The mix may be bagged, or it may be taken directly to the customer's field and applied.

Fluid mixed fertilizers have the smallest share of the mixed fertilizer market. They are generally made by either the hot-mix or cold-mix process. Hot-mix plants combine ammonia with phosphoric acid, a reaction which releases considerable heat. The cold-mix process usually does not involve heat-producing chemical reactions, and the equipment needs for cold-mix plants are simpler than those for hot-mix plants.

The commercial usage of multi-nutrient fertilizers is somewhat controversial. Some governments have argued against the practice on the grounds that optimal results are obtained when farmers tailor their fertilizer usage to their specific crop/soil combination, and that this is best done with the use of single-nutrient fertilizers applied in the proper proportions. Research results have supported that argument, and advances in soil nutrient analysis technique have made it easier to determine which specific nutrient a particular plot of land may need. The result of the arguments has been a trend away from the use of mixed fertilizers. Data for fertilizer consumption in the United States, covering the period between 1955 and 1980, indicates that beginning in 1955 the use of mixtures was roughly twice that of direct application fertilizer materials. Over the subsequent years the use of single-nutrient fertilizers grew, both in absolute terms and relative to mixtures, and in the early 1970s surpassed the use of mixtures. However, the manufacture of mixed fertilizers remains a major agricultural industry.

INDUSTRY INFORMATION SOURCES

Farm Chemicals Handbook 1992. Willoughby, OH: Meister Publishing Company, 1992.

Manufacturing USA. Detroit: Gale Research Inc., 1989.

Soil Improvement Committee, California Fertilizer Association. *Western Fertilizer Handbook*. Danville, IL: The Interstate, 1985.

Tinsdale, Samuel L., Werner L. Nelson, and James D. Beaton. *Soil Fertility and Fertilizers*. New York: Macmillan, 1985.

—J.T. Wingett

SIC 2879

PESTICIDES AND AGRICULTURAL CHEMICALS, NOT ELSEWHERE CLASSIFIED

This category includes establishments primarily engaged in the formulation and preparation of ready-to-use agricultural and household pesticides from technical chemicals or concentrates, and the production of concentrates which require further processing before use as agricultural pesticides. This industry also includes establishments primarily engaged in manufacturing or formulating agricultural chemicals, not elsewhere classified, such as minor or trace elements and soil conditioners. Establishments primarily engaged in manufacturing basic or technical agricultural pest control chemicals are classified in industries that manufacture industrial organic or inorganic chemicals.

INDUSTRY SNAPSHOT

During the 1980s, the pesticide industry faced increased economic pressures due to governmental regulations aimed at addressing environmental and food safety issues. The regulation led to a dramatic increase in research and development costs, as companies were forced to conduct exhaustive toxicology tests for pesticide effects on the environment, fish, and wildlife, as well as on human life. In 1988, the EPA began a program to re-register all agricultural pesticides, a procedure which pesticide manufacturers have claimed is both time-consuming and costly for the registrant. Faced with increased costs and a mature domestic market for their product, the industry rationalized and consolidated. The result was that the number of pesticide manufacturing firms fell from 286 companies in 1986, to about 238 in 1991.

Adjuvants are a wide range of inert additives which are designed to make pesticides more effective. Examples are attractants, defoaming agents, extenders (which prolong the active life of the pesticide by screening out ultraviolet light), stickers (which prevent pesticides from washing off the treated crop in the rain), and surfactants. The market for these products is much smaller than the market for pesticides, but it may benefit from the same regulations which plague the pesticide industry because adjuvants serve to lower pesticide dosage requirements and do not need to be registered with the EPA.

Pesticides are typically manufactured in a concentrated form, and need to be mixed with adjuvants before they are of practical use to the consumer. This mixing process is called "formulation," and some establishments, which do not manufacture the concentrated form, may formulate the pesticide for the end user, who may be a commercial farmer or just a homeowner with a lawn or garden. Manufacturers of the principal adjuvant ingredients supply their product to adjuvant formulators/distributors, who prepare the product and market it for sale to pesticide manufacturers.

About 85 percent of domestic pesticide sales are to the agriculture industry, with the remainder going to residential users. The largest of the pesticide subgroups is herbicides, which accounted for 64 percent in domestic sales in 1991, followed by insecticides at about 23 percent and fungicides at eight percent. The largest crop for pesticide application in 1991 was corn, followed by soybeans and cotton.

BACKGROUND AND DEVELOPMENT

Prior to World War I, pesticide use in the United States was limited. The Insecticide Act of 1910 imposed some regulations on pesticide manufacturers, but was mainly concerned with product effectiveness rather than public safety. After World War II, pesticides became more sophisticated, and their use more widespread. In 1947, Congress updated the Insecticide Act with the more comprehensive Federal Insecticide, Fungicide, and Rodenticide Act (FIFRA). The new legislation required pesticides which were distributed across state lines to be registered with the U.S. Department of Agriculture (USDA). However, the emphasis was on proper labeling and product efficacy.

It was not until 1954 that public health concerns were addressed by legislators. In that year, Congress amended the Federal Food, Drug, and Cosmetic Act (FDC Act) with a section (section 408) that directed the Food and Drug Administration (FDA) to set residue tolerance levels (i.e., maximum allowable pesticide residue) for pesticides used on raw produce. These tolerance levels were set using a risk/benefit analysis, whereby public health risks were weighed against benefits to the food supply. Four years later, in 1958, Congress added the controversial Delaney Clause, requiring that pesticides which may remain in processed foods in amounts which exceed their tolerance for raw produce, and which have been found to cause cancer in laboratory animals, will not be approved for any use on food crops, regardless of any countervailing benefit of those pesticides. In 1970, the newly created Environmental Protection Agency (EPA) was given responsibility for setting residue tolerances. Enforcement of the EPA pesticide tolerances remained the responsibility of the FDA.

In 1972, Congress amended FIFRA with the Federal Environmental Pesticides Control Act. The new act required all pesticides manufactured in the United States to be registered with the EPA. It also provided for civil penalties of up to $5,000 for each violation and criminal penalties of up to $25,000, plus one year in prison. In 1976, Congress enacted the Toxic Substances Control Act, which required the EPA to monitor the production of chemical substances, including pesticides, and to impose testing requirements on the manufacturers of those chemicals to determine any threat to the environment or to public health which those substances may present. In 1988, Congress amended the FIFRA to require the reregistration of all pesticides previously registered before November 1,

1984. The reregistration was supposed to have been completed in nine years, but was not yet complete in 1993.

Controversy. The EPA has struggled to find the best interpretation for administering the Delaney Clause. In 1988, it announced that it would grant exceptions to the Delaney Clause when the pesticide in question posed only a minimal risk of cancer in processed food. However, in July 1992, a decision by the U.S. Ninth Circuit Court of Appeals ruled that such exemptions were contrary to the legislation. The decision, however, was controversial. This "zero risk" criterion was considered to be unreasonable by many in the agrochemical industry, and in the spring of 1993, two members of the U.S. House of Representatives introduced the Food Quality Protection Act in an attempt to loosen the EPA's pesticide tolerance-setting criteria. Both the National Association of State Departments of Agriculture and the National Food Processors Association supported the proposed act. But any lessening of pesticide regulations would receive opposition from environmental groups, especially in light of a National Academy of Science study released in June 1993, which charged that federal regulators were not adequately protecting children from pesticide poisoning.

The argument over pesticide regulation extended further than the Delaney Clause. In 1992, the U.S. Supreme Court ruled that state and local governments have the right to enact pesticide regulations which are more stringent than those required by the federal government, as about 12 states had done. In response, Congress began considering passage of the Federal-State Pesticide Regulation Partnership Act, which would prohibit local regulation of pesticides. In a 1993 report, the Industrial Biotechnology Association anticipated that a compromise form of the act would be passed eventually.

CURRENT CONDITIONS

In general, the political climate in the early 1990s did not favor the domestic pesticide industry. The Clinton Administration announced a program to reduce the use of agricultural pesticides in the United States, and appeared to support the proposed Circle of Poison Prevention Act, which would prohibit U.S. manufacturers from exporting those pesticides which are banned in this country. The "circle of poison" refers to the U.S. export of pesticides which are banned domestically, and the subsequent use of those pesticides on crops in foreign countries, which are then imported back into the United States. The pesticide industry argued that the proposed bill will inappropriately apply U.S. risk/benefit criteria to countries where the benefits may outweigh the risks, thereby depriving those countries of needed improvements to their food supply; will fail to distinguish between pesticides which have been refused registration by the EPA for public health reasons from those pesticides which the manufacturers have decided not to register in the United States due to a poor domestic demand; and will simply allow competitors from other countries to gain global market share by selling identical pesticides to the same countries. The combination of industry-adverse regulation in the United States and the proposed export restraint on pesticides is the impetus for the trend among pesticide manufacturers to send research and development and production operations overseas.

INDUSTRY LEADERS

Leading U.S. establishments in this category are Du Pont Agricultural Products, Monsanto Company, FMC Corp., and American Cyanamid Agricultural Division. Some of the larger foreign manufacturers have U.S. subsidiaries. Some of the leading foreign companies are Ciba-Geigy AG (Switzerland), which is the world's largest agrochemicals company, Rhône-Poulec Inc. (France), Imperial Chemicals PLC (Britain, whose U.S. subsidiary is ICI Americas, Inc.), Bayer Group (Germany, whose U.S. subsidiary is Miles, Inc.), BASF Group (Germany), and Hoechst AG (Germany).

Although E.I. Du Pont de Nemours, the parent company of Du Pont Agricultural Products, reported sales of $37,386 million in 1992, it posted a loss of $3,927 million for the same year. The loss was the worst, in absolute dollars, of any of *Fortune* magazine's top 45 chemical companies. One source of trouble for the company has been its fungicide, Benlate DF. As of June 1993, the company had paid out $500 million in out-of-court settlements to 2,000 farmers who used the product and then claimed that it adversely affected their flowers and shrubs. These payments caused a 7.5 percent reduction in Du Pont's 1991 net income, and a 8.3 percent reduction for 1992. After Du Pont scientists purportedly found evidence that the Benlate DF was not at fault, the company discontinued its policy of settling the claims, and now faces 500 lawsuits, the first of which asks for $148 million in punitive and actual damages.

Another problem is Du Pont's pesticide, bromacil. In June 1993, a study was released jointly by the National Coalition Against the Misuse of Pesticides (NCAMP) and the United Mine Workers of America (UMWA), which charged that bromacil was causing widespread contamination of ground water. The

groups asked the EPA and other regulators to stop the use of this pesticide.

Monsanto Company, ranked by *Fortune* magazine as the world's 15th largest chemical company, reported 1992 sales of $8,485 million but also reported a net loss for that year. In May 1993, the company purchased the Ortho Consumer Products Division from Chevron Chemical Company for approximately $400 million. The Ortho line includes fertilizers and pesticides for residential use.

FMC Corp., whose 1992 sales were $3,992 million, agreed to a long term plan for cleaning up its 30-acre hazardous waste landfill in the state of New York. It is estimated that the plan, crafted by the EPA and the New York State Department of Environmental Conservation and finalized in 1993, will cost the pesticide manufacturer $8.4 million. FMC also faces a potential Canadian ban on its insecticide, carbofuran (trade name: Furadan). The World Wildlife Fund Canada has requested that the Canadian Minister of Agriculture ban the use of carbofuran when its registration expires December 31, 1995, because, it is alleged, the chemical poses a risk to the survival of the Burrowing Owl and also threatens other wildlife.

Originally formed to manufacture calcium cyanamide as a basis for nitrogenous fertilizer in 1907, the American Cyanamid Company has grown to comprise three business groups: Medical, Agricultural, and Chemicals. $1,206 million, or slightly less than one quarter of the total net sales, was from agricultural sales, making it a major producer of agricultural products such as herbicides and plant growth regulators, as well as animal feed supplements and health products. In addition, in 1993 the company was planning to purchase the agrochemicals division from Shell, a Dutch-UK oil and chemicals group whose pesticide products include fungicides and leaf insecticides.

WORK FORCE

Employment levels in the pesticide industry, as well as the agricultural chemical industry in general, exhibited a slight downward trend during the 1980s, a trend projected by the Bureau of Labor Statistics to continue to the year 2000. Statistics for 1986 indicate that the average number of employees per establishment was 54, 32 of whom were production workers. Occupations utilized by the industry include chemical equipment controllers, chemical plant and system operators, maintenance repairers, truck drivers, secretaries, mechanics, chemists, electricians, warehouse workers, shipping clerks, and office workers.

AMERICA AND THE WORLD

The United States is the world's largest manufacturer of pesticides, followed by Germany and Japan, and it enjoyed a favorable pesticide trade balance with the rest of the world into the 1990s, even though the ratio of exports to imports fell from 2.3 to 1.9 during the first three years of the 1990s. The largest market for U.S. exports of pesticides is Japan, which accounted for about ten percent in 1992. Although the world market for pesticides, which was $22.5 billion in 1992, had been forecasted by the U.S. Department of Commerce to grow at a rate of about 2.5 to 3 percent per year, a drop of about 12 percent in the European Community market and increased price competition in the United States pulled the world market for pesticides downward in 1992. The bioscience division of Imperial Chemicals estimated that the drop in the world market would be two to three percent. Allan Woodburn, of the market research firm Allan Woodburn Associates, expected the EC market to continue to decline through 1995 or 1996, so near term prospects for the industry, as of mid 1993, were uncertain. The U.S. adjuvant market was expected to grow 1.5 percent to 2 percent per year, but the export market could increase by as much as five to seven percent per year.

RESEARCH AND TECHNOLOGY

Research and development costs have risen to high levels and are expected to continue to rise as regulatory requirements for more environmentally safe pesticides increase. The 1990s ushered in a trend among agrochemical manufacturers to develop low-dosage pesticides as a means of reducing the amount of chemical residue left on crops. Monsanto, for example, has a policy that any new pesticides which it develops must be designed for low-dosage application, must have low toxicity, and must be have low impact on the environment. The company has developed two low-dose herbicides for use on corn and hopes to have the products approved for commercial use by the 1995 season.

Another area which holds promise for the industry is biotechnology. Biotechnology involves the genetic engineering of plants to make them resistant to diseases, insects, drought, pollution, and herbicides, in addition to the use of bacteria and viruses to create biological insecticides. One especially promising group of viruses for use as ''bioinsecticides'' is the baculoviruses. These viruses are naturally occurring and only attack specific insects; they pose no threat to humans, wildlife, or non-targeted insects. In 1992, American Cyanamid Co.'s Agricultural Research Division signed an agreement with the University of Georgia Research Foundation Inc. to develop ways to make these viruses more effective.

INDUSTRY INFORMATION SOURCES

Abrahams, Paul. ''EC Reforms Hurt Agrochemicals—Schering's Mooted Deal with Hoechst.'' *Financial Times*, 13 May 1993.

''American Cyanamid Signs Research Agreement with the University of Georgia Research Foundation.'' *Business Wire*, 24 February 1992.

Bahner, Benedict. ''The Stage Is Set for Change: Market for Agricultural Chemical Adjuvants Is Changing.'' *Chemical Marketing Reporter*, 17 May 1993.

Commins, Patricia. ''Pesticide Makers Focus on Low-Dose Chemicals.'' *Reuters*, 2 July 1993.

''Du Pont Pesticide Shown to Contaminate Ground Water, According to Study.'' *PR Newswire*, 30 June 1993.

''$8.4 Million Cleanup Selected for the FMC Dublin Road Superfund Site in Orleans County, New York.'' *PR Newswire*, 12 April 1993.

Farm Chemicals Handbook 1992. Willoughby, OH: Meister Publishing Company, 1992.

''Guide to the Global 500.'' *Fortune*, 26 July 1993.

Manufacturing USA. Detroit, MI: Gale Research Inc, 1989.

Miller, Marshall Lee. ''Pesticides and Toxic Substances.'' *Environmental Law Handbook*. Bethesda, MD: Government Institutes, Inc., 1975.

''Monsanto Co.—Acquisition Completed.'' *Regulatory News Service*, 17 May 1993.

Moody's Industrial Manual. Moody's Investor Services, Inc., 1992.

''Pesticide Bill Draws Fire from Industry; Food Threat Seen.'' *Chemical Marketing Reporter*, 23 September 1991.

Regulating Pesticides in Food: The Delaney Paradox. Washington, DC: National Academy Press, 1987.

Rhein, Reginald. ''Five Biotech Bills Signed into Law, New Congress Ponders Many More.'' *Biotechnology Newswatch*, 4 January 1993.

''Shell to Sell Agro-Chemicals Division to American Cyanamid.'' *European Report*, 30 June 1993.

Standard and Poor's Industry Surveys. New York: Standard and Poor's Corporation, 1993.

U.S. Department of Commerce. *U.S. Industrial Outlook 1993*. Washington, DC: U.S. Department of Commerce, 1993.

Weber, Joseph, Gail DeGeorge, and Mary Beth Regan. ''So Much for Making Nice.'' *Business Week*, 28 June 1993.

''World Wildlife Fund Calls for Ban on Carbofuran Pesticide Toxic to Threatened Burrowing Owl and Other Wildlife.'' *Canada News Wire*, 24 March 1993.

—J.T. Wingett

SIC 2891

ADHESIVES AND SEALANTS

The adhesives and sealants industry consists primarily of manufacturers of industrial and household adhesives, glues, caulking compounds, sealants, and linoleum, tile, and rubber cements from vegetable, animal, or synthetic plastics materials, purchased or produced in the same establishment. Establishments primarily engaged in manufacturing gelatin and sizes are classified in **SIC 2899: Chemicals and Chemical Preparations, Not Elsewhere Classified,** and those manufacturing vegetable gelatin or agar-agar are classified in **SIC 2833: Medicinal Chemicals and Botanical Products.**

INDUSTRY SNAPSHOT

The adhesives and sealants industry includes two chemically similar but functionally different groups of formulated products. Adhesive products are used to create a bond between two different or similar materials. Sealants are used to create an impenetrable barrier to gas or moisture. Adhesives and sealants are made from precise blends of petroleum-derived plastic resins, synthetic rubber elastomers, and agents or additives used to enhance certain characteristics. The final formulation ultimately depends on the end use. Industries which typically use adhesives and sealants include construction, consumer products, assembly, packaging, labeling, and transportation.

As the adhesives and sealants industry moved into the 1990s, manufacturers experienced flat markets. The commercial construction segment of the industry fared the worst and manufacturers found themselves increasingly dependent on the renovation and do-it-yourself markets.

Manufacturers contend that a resurgence in the structural markets and relatively recession-resistant packaging segment may translate into overall improvement for the $5.4 billion industry, which has typically seen growth rates exceeding the Gross National Product by two percent. Concurrent with these developments, stricter environmental regulation accelerated the development of new technologies.

Packaging holds the biggest share of the manufacturing adhesives market with $1.1 billion in annual sales and a growth rate of 1.5 percent. Construction-related sectors, including forest products and wood working, are estimated at $675 million annually. The construction original equipment market claims about $430 million in annual sales.

Overall, the growth rate of the formulated adhesives market should be four percent in the near future according to some industry analysts. The waterborne adhesives market was estimated at about 64 percent of the total adhesives market and should post a four percent increase. For hot melts, representing about 18 percent of the total market, a growth rate of five percent is projected. The solvent-based sector of the manufacturing adhesives market claimed about 12 percent of the total and was expected to have flat growth. Specialty technologies, including reactives, experienced a growth rate of less than ten percent.

Compound manufacturers are charting a new course as their customers change priorities and plastics recycling continues to emerge as a major factor in this regard. Combined with recyclability, customers have tightened quality requirements. New specifications are forcing manufacturers of compounds toward more complex processes and more advanced equipment. Indeed, compounds themselves have become more complex because they combine difficult-to-mix components, as in the case of stainless steel reinforced compounds. This type of high technology manufacturing drives capital requirements higher and makes it more difficult for small, entrepreneurial ventures to stay profitable.

ORGANIZATION AND STRUCTURE

The industry serves two broad markets: the captive market of firms that formulate products for their own use and the merchant market that formulates products to sell to final consumers. The merchant market comprises about two-thirds of total shipments. In 1990 total product shipments reached $5.4 billion. In 1991 the total value of product shipments in the industry dropped slightly to $5.381 billion.

CURRENT CONDITIONS

The adhesives and sealants industry's development can best be explained by the economy-wide transition from conventional materials (glass, stone, wood, and metal) to lighter and more economical resources, mainly petroleum-based plastics. These new materials have mandated new methods of assembly, and suitable bonding components. A generation of new products has emerged to service this rapid growth area.

Adhesive manufacturers have been hurt by the downturn in the automotive industry. Yet, concurrent with this trend, a rapidly changing business climate in Detroit is causing U.S. automakers to become more competitive. The net result is that adhesive manufacturers are being challenged and industry observers expect business in this area to improve. For structural adhesives, the greatest adjustments have been in bonding new body panel materials. Environmental and worker safety regulations are also playing an equally important hand in the evolution of systems.

The market for reactive adhesives is growing because the automotive industry is moving away from mechanical fasteners. At the same time, packaging applications for reactives are on the rise, adding buoyancy to the adhesives industry. The reactives sector of the industry is dominated by epoxy and polyurethane systems. Urethanes are commanding a significantly larger portion of the market. About 100 million pounds of urethane resin went to adhesives and sealant applications in the early 1990s, compared to 28 million pounds of epoxy resin. Stronger performance for polyurethanes is attributed to their broader range of adhesive applications. Some applications are experiencing very rapid growth. Urethanes are most often used with flexible materials in high impact applications, while epoxies are known for their hardness and are used with more rigid substances.

The development of epoxy/urethane hybrids is attracting particular interest because of the broad range of demands being placed on adhesives used in the automotive industry. Both manufacturers and users of these products are looking for the best of both worlds: combining high tensile strength and compatibility with flexible materials. The problem is that a sacrifice is usually made in shelf life, toughness, or curing flexibility.

Developments in reactive adhesives for the auto industry have brought benefits to other industrial sectors. For example, appliance manufacturing is an area that has taken cues from adhesive formulations originally developed for the automotive industry. At the same time that these developments are taking place, there are new areas of application that are seeing growth from a small base. As an example, solvent replacement in the lamination of packaging films is one that is contributing to the overall high growth rate of urethanes. Industry experts believe that two-component systems based on polyurethanes meet the performance criteria, but require costly special application equipment.

The generally improved outlook for the automotive industry, coupled with the industry's dependence on the transportation sector, bodes well for constant-dollar shipments, which are expected by some observers to grow at about a three percent clip for the next few years. Unless the construction sector regains sustained momentum, sealants use in the con-

struction industry will probably lag behind the three percent growth rate.

INDUSTRY LEADERS

The adhesives and sealants industry is comprised of more than 160 publicly and privately held companies that generate over $14.3 billion in annual sales and employ over 81,600 people.

With over $2.5 billion in annual sales, Avery Dennison is a leading manufacturer of pressure sensitive adhesives and materials. In 1990 Avery International and Dennison Manufacturing Companies were combined to form the present company. Its three operating divisions include pressure sensitive adhesives and materials, office products, and product identification and control systems.

At Avery Dennison, the pressure sensitive adhesives and materials segment of the business manufactures and markets pressure sensitive coated papers, films, and foils in roll and sheet form for conversion into labels. Customers include manufacturers of automobiles, consumer packaged goods, labels, health care products, and appliances. In 1992 this sector had operating income of $131 million on sales of $1.3 billion. As the corporation moves into the mid-1990s, sales and income are expected to continue to increase.

Other key organizations in the industry include Chicago-based Morton International, with sales in 1992 of $1.9 billion and 10,200 employees, and National Starch and Chemical, located in Bridgewater, New Jersey, which posted sales of $1.7 billion and maintained a work force of 7,400 employees. The fourth largest corporation in the industry was American Cyanamid Company Polymer Products, located in Southfield, Michigan. Their sales were $1.1 billion in 1992. Another key organization in this industry is Dexter Corporation, located in Windsor Locks, Connecticut, which tallied sales of $938 million in 1992 and employed 5,600 workers.

Sealant Manufacturers. Major sealant manufacturers supplying the automobile industry include National Starch's Thiem, HB Fuller, EMS Togo, and Essex. Essex has the dominant position in automotive windshield bonding market. This provides a boon for urethane sales and accounts for 20 percent of sealant sales to original equipment manufacturers. Several manufacturers such as BASF and Ashland have attempted to break into this $60 million market, but none has been successful. Essex controls over 90 percent of the domestic windshield bonding market and claims 60 percent of the so-called transplant market, comprised of Japanese automakers who have built plants in the

United States. The corporation was able to capture this market segment via licensing agreements garnered through exposure in Japan as a part of Sunstar/Essex. International glass bonding manufacturers, however, are looking to break into this tightly held market niche.

The aerospace industry is another important sealant market. Because this market contracted in the 1990s, manufacturers aggressively sought new markets and product applications. About 60 percent of the business is dependent on commercial aircraft. The remaining 40 percent of the market depends on military spending, a sector in decline in the early 1990s because of the end of the Cold War.

The aerospace sealant market is dominated by polysulfide, which constitutes 80 percent of the products sold. Its primary supplier is Courtaulds. Other participants in this market segment include Fiber Resins, a division of HB Fuller; Chem Seal; and Morton International, which is the world's only producer of the polysulfide raw material. This is a diverse market, with numerous varieties of polysulfide sealants and about 1500 products.

AMERICA AND THE WORLD

The 1990s began with demand for global compounds of 700,000 metric tons annually, and a relatively flat growth rate of one to 1.5 percent. Industry experts estimate that worldwide annual growth rates of six to seven percent will prevail through the middle of the decade and product demand will grow to an estimated one million tons during this time period. By the end of the century total global demand is estimated to reach 1.3 million tons annually.

Numerous mergers and acquisitions indicated higher levels of foreign participation in the domestic industry in recent years. As industry-wide restructuring drew to a close in the United States, however, consolidation of the European industry continued, with a few highly diversified multinational corporations purchasing small privately-held firms. Companies in Japan, the United Kingdom, and Germany have emerged as major competitors of U.S. firms in the world arena.

The United Kingdom. The United Kingdom's market for adhesives and sealants was valued at $1.5 billion at the beginning of the 1990s. Three main product groups split this market: sealants, prepared adhesives, and formulated adhesives. Sealants is the smallest sector and represents a market of $157 million. Prepared adhesives represent a market value of $386 million. The formulated adhesives market is the largest segment, with a value of $978.2 million. The industries

primarily using adhesives and sealants are medical supplies, general manufacturing, aerospace, electronics, transport, construction, paper, and packaging. The market for adhesive and sealant products in these areas increased steadily during the last half of the 1980s. As the industry entered the 1990s, however, the recession in U.K. manufacturing led to a decline in the market.

RESEARCH AND TECHNOLOGY

Adhesives and sealants manufacturers are counting on proactive research and development to keep them one step ahead of environmental regulators and market demands. Among the challenges faced are California regulations that hope to reduce volatile organic compound emissions by 80 percent within three years. Such legislation is indicative of growing efforts, manifest in legislation such as the Clean Air Act, to bolster pollution prevention measures. One of the most pressing factors facing the industry in this realm is a 1995 chlorofluorocarbon phaseout deadline, which will mean a quicker end to production of heavily-used 1-1-1-trichloroethane, a component of many sealant formulations.

Technological advances have contributed to the growing use of adhesives that have helped car makers build lighter and more fuel-efficient vehicles. Corporate Average Fuel Economy (CAFE) standards have driven the weight of automobiles down. Adhesives are replacing mechanical fasteners and are increasingly taking the place of spot welds. They are also reducing the corrosion problems associated with traditional bonding methods.

The biggest growth area for adhesive technology has come as a result of changes in the materials used in auto body parts. The most significant of these new materials is the sheet molded compound (SMC). Many opportunities for weight reduction with sheet molded compounds have not been fully explored yet, so this remains a developing technology.

Newer areas of technological challenge in terms of bonding are glass-reinforced polyesters. One emerging plastic technology is resin transfer molding (RTM). This is a polyester material, based on resin, that is being used in lower volume auto and truck applications such as sporty or upscale car models.

A growing number of players in the adhesives and sealants industry have expressed a desire to move away from the use of primers in adhesive systems because of their flammability and volatility. Such a change, however, presents difficulties in getting the right adhesion to certain materials. Physical and chemical changes can be made to the surface of these materials, but the focus of new development is to make adhesives and sealants that will incorporate the function of a primer. Environmental mandates on chlorofluorocarbons, volatile organic compound emission standards, and other ecological considerations are thus forcing adhesive formulators to nudge solvents out of their products and find alternatives. Research continues on meeting high-performance parameters such as water resistance, durability, and humidity resistance without using such solvents. In addition, a number of large users of solvent-borne adhesives have already installed equipment to recapture and recycle, or properly incinerate solvent, and are less likely to change to solventless products. Already, adhesive manufacturers have moved production of industrial adhesives away from solvents to 100 percent solids, epoxies, and urethanes. With respect to pressure sensitive adhesives such as duct tape and heavy duty industrial tapes, manufacturers have raised solid content to 65 percent, from as low as 35 percent.

INDUSTRY INFORMATION SOURCES

Caney, Derek. "Sticking to Their Guns," *Adhesives,* July 27, 1992, SR 14.

Loesel, Andrew. "Plugging Along," *Chemical Marketing Reporter,* March 27, 1992, SR 19.

Kirschner, Elisabeth. "Formulators Pace Environmental Laws," *Chemical Week,* March 11, 1992, 34-35.

Naude, Alice. "Renovating Growth," *Adhesives,* July 27, 1992, SR 22.

Naude, Alice. "Rolling With the Punches," *Automotive Chemicals,* February 17, 1992, SR 18.

Shon, Melissa. "A More Measured Pace," *Chemical Marketing Reporter,* February 15, 1993, SR 12-13.

"Specialty Recovery Still Coming," *Chemical Marketing Reporter,* July 26, 1993, 7, 21.

Springer, Neil. "Solvent-based Disappearing Act," *Chemical Marketing Reporter,* July 27, 1992, SR9-10.

Statistics for Industry Groups and Industries, 1991, U.S. Department of Commerce, Bureau of the Census, Economics and Statistics Administration.

Tilton, Helga. "Sticking to Basics," *Chemical Marketing Reporter,* July 27, 1992, SR 3-8.

U.S. Industrial Outlook, 1993, Chemicals and Allied Products. Washington D.C.: U.S. Department of Commerce, Bureau of the Census, In ternational Trade Administration.

Value of Product Shipments, 1991, U.S. Department of Commerce, Economics and Statistics Administration, Bureau of the Census.

—Garth K. Daniels

SIC 2892

EXPLOSIVES

This industry covers establishments primarily engaged in manufacturing explosives. Establishments primarily engaged in manufacturing ammunition for small arms are classified in **SIC 3482: Small Arms Ammunition,** and those manufacturing fireworks are classified in **SIC 2899: Chemicals and Chemical Preparations, Not Elsewhere Classified.**

Historically, the explosives industry has been closely aligned with the coal mining industry. According to Robert B. Hopler in *Mining Engineering,* the coal mining industry consumed 68 percent of domestic explosives in 1991. Explosives such as black powder were introduced in the metal industry in 1627 and these were soon utilized by coal miners. Before Alfred Nobel invented dynamite in 1866, blasting for engineering purposes was conducted with gunpowder.

In 1905, E.I. du Pont de Nemours & Company supplied 56 percent of the national production of explosives and stood as one of the United States's largest companies. Du Pont continued to strengthen its hold on the market, and, in 1907, the U.S. government began antitrust proceedings against the company. In 1912 Du Pont was forced to divest segments of its businesses. This resulted in Atlas Chemical Industries and Hercules Powder Company. Later, Atlas was purchased by Imperial Chemical Industries PLC, Du Pont's explosives division was sold to Explosives Technologies International, and Hercules explosives division was sold to Dyno Nobel, Inc.

In the early years of the industry, the volatile nature of explosives played a significant role in the organization of explosives manufacturers. Companies operated numerous small plants to ensure that their entire business would not be wiped out in the event of an explosion. In addition, plants were located near the consumer rather than the raw materials sources because of the danger in transporting the product.

Products of the explosives industry have changed dramatically over the years. ANFO, or ammonium nitrate mixed with fuel oil, was invented in 1953. Since 1959, it has become the most widely utilized explosive in surface coal mining. By the early 1990s, ANFO held 75 percent of the market. Dynamite has declined in importance from about one billion pounds in the mid-1950s to approximately 100 million pounds in 1993. Because of the drastic decline in the use of dynamite, manufacturing plants for that product have decreased from 30 in the 1950s to one in 1993, which was owned by Dyno Nobel. Emulsions have gained popularity in the 1990s because of their water resistance and low density.

In 1991 approximately 125 establishments employing 13,600 people existed in the explosives industry. Wages, on average, were nearly $12 per hour. In the United States, Ensign-Bickford Industries Inc. of Simsbury, Connecticut, and Atlas Powder Co. ranked as the largest domestic manufacturers of explosives. The international explosives industry was dominated in the early 1990s by three major corporations: Dyno Nobel Inc., Explosives Technologies International, and Imperial Chemical Industries PLC. Dyno Nobel Inc., a Norwegian-based company, stands as one of the world's top manufacturers and exporters of explosives, largely on the basis of its patents. In 1993 the company completed construction of a major new manufacturing facility at its Port Ewen, New York detonator facility.

INDUSTRY INFORMATION SOURCES

"Custom Designed Explosives for Surface and Underground Coal Mining," *Mining Engineering,* October 1993.

Ward's Business Directory of U.S. Private and Public Companies, Detroit: Gale Research. 1993.

What's New in Blasting—the Explosives Industry and Its Products in 1993, (Presented at the Associated General Contractors 1993 Midyear Meeting), Washington, D.C., October 1993.

—Garth K. Daniels

SIC 2893

PRINTING INK

This classification includes establishments primarily engaged in manufacturing printing ink, including gravure ink, screen process ink, and lithographic ink. Establishments primarily engaged in manufacturing writing ink and fluids are classified in **SIC 2899: Chemicals and Chemical Preparations, Not Elsewhere Classified.** Those establishments manufacturing drawing ink are classified in **SIC 3952: Lead Pencils, Crayons, and Artists' Materials.**

The printing ink industry is one of America's oldest, going back approximately 260 years to the pre-Revolutionary War days. As the printing ink industry entered the decade of the 1990s, there was little change in the structure of the industry. The top domestic manufacturers included Sun Chemical Corporation, Flint Ink Corporation, Inx International Ink Company, United States Printing Ink Corporation, and BASF.

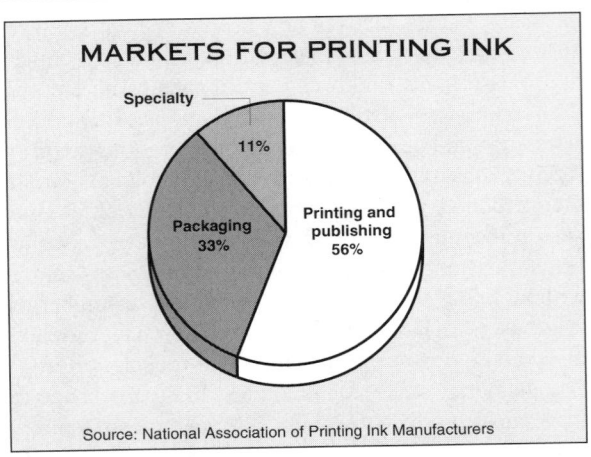

MARKETS FOR PRINTING INK

Specialty 11%

Packaging 33%

Printing and publishing 56%

Source: National Association of Printing Ink Manufacturers

The biggest ink manufacturers still remain profitable, but with reduced margins. The smaller ink companies have suffered the most in recent years, with a number of them expected to close their doors if business does not pick up decidedly in the near future. Concurrent with these developments, there are segments of the market where new ink companies are emerging.

Overall, total 1991 sales for printing inks consumed in the United States was $2.8 billion, an increase of approximately $200 million over the previous year. The 1991 total included domestic commercial and captive ink production plus imports, but excluded exports.

A current concern in the domestic printing ink industry is the high percentage of foreign ownership of American corporations, now between 40 percent and 50 percent. Very few of the larger ink companies remain independent. Many of these companies are candidates for either purchase or merger.

During the recession at the beginning of the 1990s, raw material prices stabilized considerably. Purchasing experts in the ink industry believe that there are only a few areas where upward price pressure may continue into the mid-1990s. The major factor affecting prices is the stable price of crude oil, from which more than 75 percent of the raw materials for ink is derived. The industry's membership has sought to take full advantage of the relatively low raw material costs, resisting any price increases from raw materials suppliers unless they become fully justified. In some product areas, the companies have been able to negotiate price reductions, which has helped the industry hold the line on its own prices.

The printing ink industry has anticipated efforts to reduce the environmental burden of its products. Before passage of the Clean Air Act, printing ink manufacturers were developing water-based ink systems to replace inks containing volatile organic compounds (VOCs). Many years before the first "CONNEG Law" was passed to reduce heavy metals in packaging, the printing ink industry had been reducing the use of lead-bearing pigments in packaging inks.

INDUSTRY INFORMATION SOURCES

Graphic Arts Monthly, vol. 64, no. 2, February 1992, 40.

U.S. Industrial Outlook 1993, Washington DC: U.S. Department of Commerce, 1993.

Ward's Business Directory of U.S. Private and Public Companies. Detroit: Gale Research, 1993.

—Dr. Garth K. Daniels

SIC 2895

CARBON BLACK

This category covers establishments primarily engaged in manufacturing carbon black (channel and furnace black). Establishments primarily engaged in manufacturing bone and lamp black are classified in **SIC 2816: Inorganic Pigments.**

INDUSTRY SNAPSHOT

Carbon black is essentially an oil by-product used to strengthen rubber. It is made by shooting a hot mist of oil particles into a flame, a very expensive process that has limited the number of competitors in the industry. In addition to its main use in tires, the powdery reinforcing agent was used to make inks and other everyday products.

Carbon black is a general name for a variety of trade name products such as acetylene black, attrited black, channel black, flame black, furnace black, lamp black, and thermal black. Carbon black required a commitment of over $384,000 fixed capital per production worker in 1987, as compared with about $71,000 per production worker to manufacture printing ink, and about $36,000 per production worker in explosives production. Carbon black production also requires large amounts of heat.

Carbon black producing establishments recorded $691.9 in sales in 1990. Total value of shipments increased 21 percent from 1987 to 1990. Although the leading producers in the industry were U.S. companies, fierce price competition and lagging auto sales, a prime carbon black market, compelled U.S. producers to enter overseas markets. In the early 1990s, U.S.

producers opened operations in Europe and in Japan. By far the leading U.S. producer was Cabot Corporation, which recorded negligible profits in the United States, but generated huge profits abroad.

ORGANIZATION AND STRUCTURE

In 1989 approximately 23 establishments were engaged in the production of carbon black. These establishments employed approximately 83 workers each, 57 of which were employed as production workers.

Geographically, all of the 13 establishments producing carbon black in 1987 were located in either Texas or Louisiana. Texas contained eight establishments while Louisiana contained five. Shipments from Louisiana establishments were worth $212.6 million, or 37.3 percent of the U.S. total, while Texas' eight establishments produced $197.8 million worth of shipments.

In 1992, Cabot Corporation accounted for well over half of total industry sales. Ranked according to market share, the dominant companies in the carbon black industry were: Columbian Chemicals Company with about 14 percent of the market; J.M. Huber Corporation, with 3.6 percent; Witco Corporation Concarb Division, with 3.4 percent; Sid Richardson Carbon, with 2.6 percent; Reynolds Metals Company, with two percent; Cabot Corporation Franklin Division, with 1.1 percent; and Pioneer Asphalt Corporation, with 0.7 percent. Two other companies controlled the remaining one percent. Five of the industry's largest ten manufacturers were divisions of larger companies and two were subsidiaries. Only Sid Richardson Carbon and Pioneer Asphalt Corporation were private companies.

Carbon black is largely a homogenous product with many trade names and is essentially an oil by-product used to make tires, inks, and other products. The principal economic industries responsible for the purchase of carbon black were overwhelmingly domestic manufacturing industries, which purchased nearly 95 percent of the industry's shipments. The only other sector purchasing carbon black was the export sector. When ranked by share of purchased carbon black output, the principal industries responsible for the purchase of carbon black were: tires and inner tubes, which purchased 51.8 percent of the industry's shipments; fabricated rubber products, which purchased 13.5 percent; and the chemical preparations industry, which purchased 8.2 percent.

BACKGROUND AND DEVELOPMENT

As early as 1864 carbon black was used as a printing ink, an application for carbon black still employed in the 1990s. But its most revolutionary application was in the rubber industry, which discovered that carbon black made tires tougher. In 1920 the rubber industry consumed only 40 percent of the carbon black produced, but, by the early 1990s, consumed roughly 95 percent of the industry's shipments.

The Cabot family was involved in carbon black production from the industry's outset. In 1882, Godfrey Cabot built a carbon black plant in Buffalo Mills, Pennsylvania. At the time, carbon black was made by impinging a gas flame against steel. After World War I it was discovered that carbon black had properties for reinforcing rubber products. It was this innovation that fueled the industry's growth.

By 1972, carbon black prices were deteriorating because of too much production capacity. Production was three billion pounds per year, while production capacity was about four billion pounds per year. In addition, the cutback in gasoline usage that followed the oil embargo of 1973 took a heavy toll on carbon black demand. At that time, 95 percent of carbon black use was associated with automobile applications; 70 percent went into tire production alone. Higher costs were also having a detrimental effect on the industry, pushing carbon black prices higher and further reducing demand for the industry's products. By the late 1970s and early 1980s capacity fell from an estimated 4.21 billion pounds in 1979 to 3.38 billion pounds in 1981. The decline in 1978 and 1979 mirrored the downturn in the U.S. automotive industry, but export business buoyed the industry.

By the 1980s, with four or five years of increasing prices behind it, relative stability had returned to the market. Prices generally followed oil prices and, with oil prices stabilized, carbon black prices stabilized as well.

The leading player in the carbon black industry in the early 1990s remained the Cabot Corporation, a conglomeration of specialty metals, chemical, and energy businesses. When the carbon black market staggered in the early 1980s, Cabot was in danger of failing, but then expanded into fields such as high-technology ceramics. After a series of restructuring moves, including drastic reductions in unit costs to counter the heavy fixed capital investment required for carbon black production, Cabot kept effective control over the slow growth carbon black segment of its market.

CURRENT CONDITIONS

The early 1990s witnessed the further consolidation of the industry, the development of new low cost production processes, the influence of recycling efforts in the rubber and tire industries, and the continued expansion of the industry overseas. In the competitive war to reduce costs, new methods of producing carbon black were developed. For example, a chemical engineering professor at Ohio University developed a method of producing carbon black from coal with an ash content of up to 14 percent. Although only part of this coal is convertible to carbon black, with a carbon black yield of 20 percent, the raw material cost for one kilogram of product was 14 cents, a savings of 8 cents per kilogram from the petroleum feedstock.

International markets continued to expand for the leading companies in the early 1990s, especially for Cabot Corporation. In 1992, Cabot, the world's leading producer, opened a new carbon black plant, Cabot Kashima, in Jashima, Japan which produced special grades of carbon black. Many in the industry were also expanding into the nascent capitalist societies of eastern Europe. Cabot entered into a joint venture with Deza, a tar processing company in Czechoslovakia, in a $90 million venture to produce carbon black. Cabot had a 52 percent capital stake in this project, which was created to produce carbon black for tire and plastic products. The project was given a $20 million credit by the International Finance Corporation, a World Bank subsidiary.

As it entered the mid-1990s, the industry was facing stiffer competition from traditionally import-oriented countries. U.S. producers were seeking new markets in developing economies such as China, where demand is expected to grow 6.6 percent per year to the end of the 1990s. U.S. consumption of carbon black was projected to increase an average of 2.7 percent annually to $640 million in 1997. This projection was predicated on the gradual recovery of the auto industry.

WORK FORCE

From 1987 to 1990, total employment growth in the carbon black industry was flat, remaining at approximately 1,800 workers. Production worker employment over the period actually declined, from 1,400 workers to 1,200 workers. The 1980s witnessed a 15 percent decline in industry employment and a 25 percent decline in production worker employment.

Bureau of Labor Statistics forecasted that most of the industry's occupational categories were expected to increase until 2005, reflecting the projected growth in demand for the industry's products. However, many of the occupations expected to grow most rapidly were non-production jobs such as sales workers and highly skilled professional positions, including engineering, mathematical and science managers.

INDUSTRY INFORMATION SOURCES

"A Low-Ash Carbon Black From Coal: Carbon Black has Been Produced From Coal with Ash Content of up to 14%," *Chemical Engineering,* December 1991.

"Blend Targeted at Static-Sensitive Uses," *Plastics News,* April 27, 1992.

"Cabot Opens Japanese Carbon Black Plant," *Plastics Industry Europe,* January 31, 1992.

"Carbon Black Faces Unsteady Future," *Ceramic Industry,* May 1993.

"Carbon Black Stability Is Stressed," *Journal of Commerce,* January 27, 1980.

"Carbon Black Takes Road to Recovery," *Chemical-Marketing-Reporter,* February 8, 1993.

"Consumption of Dyes, Carbon Black, Organic Pigments to be up 6.1%/year by 1997," *Chemical Week,* September 22, 1993.

"Deza Together With Cabot," *Mlada-Fronta,* April 2, 1992.

Earle, Beth Ann, "Witco Restructuring Divisions," *Rubber and Plastics News,* January 4, 1993.

Hammonds, Keith, "Can Cabot Go Home Again," *Business Week,* December 10, 1990.

Jenkins, Gilbert, *Oil Economists' Handbook 1985,* London: Elsevier Applied Science Publishers, Limited, 1985.

Kokish, Brian, "Demand Creating Carbon Black Shortage: Auto Industry Recovery Contributes to North America Carbon Black Shortage," *Rubber and Plastics News,* May 3, 1993.

Mantell, Charles L., *Carbon and Graphite Handbook,* Huntington: Robert E. Krieger Publishing Company, 1979.

Manufacturing USA: Industry Analyses, Statistics, and Leading Companies, 3rd Edition, Detroit: Gale Research Inc., 1993.

"Market Newsletter," *Chemical Week,* November 11, 1972.

"Organic Dyes and Pigments See Market Growth," *Chemical-Marketing-Reporter,* September 20, 1993.

"Rebuilding the Cabot Legacy," *Forbes,* April 14, 1980.

"Sun Chemical Develops Carbon Black for Newsprint Inks that Rub Off Less on Readers of Newspapers," *American-Ink-Maker,* August 1993.

"Top 50 Chemicals Production by Volume, part 2," *U.S. Chemical Industry Statistical Handbook,* 1992.

Tuthill, Mary, "Louis Cabot: He Made Room at the Top," *Nation's Business,* December 1980.

U.S. Department of Commerce, Bureau of the Census, *Census of Manufactures: Miscellaneous Chemical Products,* Washington: U.S. Government Printing Office, April, 1990.

U.S. Department of Commerce, International Trade Administration, *U.S. Industrial Outlook 1994,* Washington: U.S. Government Printing Office, January 1994.

—John A. Sarich

SIC 2899

CHEMICALS AND CHEMICAL PREPARATIONS, NOTE ELSEWHERE CLASSIFIED

This industry consists primarily of establishments engaged in manufacturing miscellaneous chemical preparations, not elsewhere classified, such as fatty acids, essential oils, gelatin (except vegetable), sizes, bluing, laundry sours, writing and stamp pad ink, industrial compounds, such as boiler and heat insulating compounds, metal, oil, and water treating compounds, waterproofing compounds, and chemical supplies for foundries. Establishments primarily engaged in manufacturing vegetable gelatin are classified in **SIC 2833: Medicinal Chemicals and Botanical Products;** those manufacturing dessert preparations based on gelatin are classified in **SIC 2099: Food Preparations, Not Elsewhere Classified;** those manufacturing printing ink are classified in **SIC 2893: Printing Ink;** and those manufacturing drawing ink are classified in **SIC 3952: Lead Pencils, Crayons, and Artists' Materials.**

As the specialty chemicals industry entered the decade of the 1990s, many corporations implemented organizational restructuring coupled with cost reduction measures. Based on these management decisions, the industry appears to be in the beginning of a business recovery from the cyclical downturn experienced during the last portion of the 1980s. However, the pickup has been more difficult and slower that expected, in part because of the continued sluggishness of foreign economies. This factor has reduced the export demand for chemicals and, consequently, the industry's trade surplus.

The growth of miscellaneous chemicals such as sodium chlorate posted double-digit growth since the late 1980s. This chemical is used in the form of chlorine dioxide as a substitute for traditional chlorine in pulp and paper bleaching. While the substitution of sodium chlorate has been greater in Canada than the United States, reflecting greater environmental concerns over chlorine, the use of the chemical in the United States is expected to continue increase. About two-thirds of the North American production capacity of sodium chlorate is located in Canada. In view of the dramatic growth prospects for sodium chlorate, major producers have made sizeable capacity expansions in recent years.

The biggest consumers of basic chemicals are the industrial and agricultural sectors of the economy. In the recent past, demand for basic chemicals strengthened in response to the prolonged economic expansion of the 1980s. Output in 1991, as measured by the Federal Reserve Board (FRB) Basic Chemicals Production Index, was at its highest level since the prior peak reached in the late 1970s. Production in 1991 advanced three percent over the 1990 level. Over the long run, the demand for basic chemicals is expected to pace the rise in real (inflation-adjusted) gross domestic product (GDP), with the automobile, housing, export, agricultural, and paper markets, in particular, holding sway.

Major United States corporations that produce specialty chemicals include the Nalco Chemical Co., Lubrizol Corporation, Ferro Corporation, Rachem Corporation, and Dexter Corporation. Other corporations in the specialty chemicals industry include the Fuller Company, Petrolite Corporation, Henkel Corporation, Morton International Inc., and Betz Laboratories.

INDUSTRY INFORMATION SOURCES

Standard and Poor's Industry Surveys. Standard & Poor's, July 1993.

U.S. Industrial Outlook 1994, Washington, DC: U.S. Department of Commerce, 1994.

—Dr. Garth K. Daniels

PETROLEUM REFINING & RELATED INDUSTRIES

SIC 2911

PETROLEUM REFINING

This category covers establishments engaged primarily in producing gasoline, kerosene, distillate fuel oils, residual fuel oils, and lubricants, through fractionation or straight distillation of crude oil, redistillation of unfinished petroleum derivatives, cracking, or other processes. Establishments primarily engaged in producing natural gasoline from natural gas are classified in mining industries. Those manufacturing lubricating oils and greases by blending and compounding purchased materials are classified in **SIC 2992: Lubricating Oils and Greases.** Establishments primarily engaged in manufacturing cyclic and acyclic organic chemicals are classified in various chemicals and allied product manufacturing industries.

INDUSTRY SNAPSHOT

There were more than 180 operating petroleum refineries in the United States in 1992, generating approximately $1.5 billion in products. These products included 7.24 million barrels per day (b/cd) of motor gasoline, 1.5 million b/cd of jet fuel, 3 million b/cd of distillate fuel oil, 1.12 million b/cd of residual fuel oil, and 4.03 million b/cd of other products. Output reflected a utilization rate of approximately 85 percent.

A mild recovery in demand for refined goods could not alleviate the strain refiners experienced in the early 1990s due to unimproved profit margins. Reduced operations, refinery closures, and low sales characterized a gloomy market. The 1991 recession had taken its toll, and the industry was braced in anticipation of new federal manufacturing standards.

These new standards, prompted by a growing concern for the environment, meant that depressed market conditions were compounded by rigorous, expensive mandatory upgrading. Of paramount impact, however, is the low price of oil due to the world surplus supply. *Forbes* observed in 1994 that the price of oil at that time was near 20-year lows because world oil consumption actually fell by a miniscule amount in 1993 while "while oil supply exceeded world demand by about half a million barrels a day, swelling inventories."

To succeed in the 1990s, petroleum refiners will have to continue to cut costs internally in order to meet the expense of compliance with new environmental legislation. Also, they will have to develop new production methods and products to cut solid waste, boost efficiency, and diversify their markets.

ORGANIZATION AND STRUCTURE

Downstream. The process of turning crude oil into refined products, the "downstream" side of the oil business, involves several key participants and cannot be fully understood without a rudimentary knowledge of the "upstream" side of the oil business, the process of obtaining crude oil. Upstream operations consist of exploration, geological evaluation, and the testing and drilling of potential oilfield sites, that is, all of the procedures necessary to get oil out of the ground (see **SIC 1311: Crude Petroleum and Natural Gas**). Downstream operations include pipelining crude oil to refining sites, refining crude into various products, and pipelining or otherwise transporting products to wholesalers, distributors, or retailers.

Because many downstream companies are subsidiaries of conglomerates that also maintain upstream subsidiaries, the sale of raw materials to refiners is often essentially a transfer of products between different operating units of the same corporation. Petroleum refiners, therefore, often depend on the upstream arms of their parent corporations for supplies of crude, and, in turn, supply wholesalers (who then sell to independent retailers) and retailers (company-owned gasoline stations, for example) who are also part of the same corporation. All major oil operating in this system are known as "integrated oil companies"' non-integrated companies are often referred to as "independents."

This tendency toward massive, integrated supply systems affects the oil industry in general and refiners in particular in that any shift in condition at any point in the crude-to-product chain is felt equally at all levels; economic trickle-down, as it exists in other industries, offers no stabilization.

Processes and Terms. Petroleum refineries turn crude oil into a variety of products which are used in a wide range of products from asphalt to plastics. All products begin in much the same way: with the distillation, or vaporization, of crude. Distillation begins when crude oil boils; components within crude condense at different rates, and so are extracted at progressive points along a time/temperature continuum. Lighter, high-value products—propanes, butanes, gasoline, jet fuel—condense at lower temperatures while heavier compounds require high temperatures or a special extraction method to be transformed into such products as diesel fuels, heavy fuel oil, and asphalts. The components of distillated crude vary according to the make-up of the raw crude, with some batches containing large amounts of sulfur, for example, while others may be bituminous and full of heavier compounds.

Prior to distillation, crude is stored in groups or "farms" of steel tanks. Distillation then occurs in a fractionating tower, in which the various fractions, or portions, of the crude are separated. The "straight runs" obtained in the fractionating tower are treated in secondary stages to create final products.

Some secondary processing involves simple heat and pressure manipulations, while others include complex chemical reactions. Thus not all refineries are capable of all processing techniques. Some of the most common processes include coking, which creates gasoline and gas oils from the heaviest molecules of the crude. Catalytic cracking uses heat, pressure, and a chemical catalyst to double the gasoline yield in a barrel of crude by converting heavy cuts to lighter products. Hydrocracking uses hydrogen to make 100 percent gasoline from the light gas oils which catalytic cracking and coking produce. Hydrofining removes

sulfur from the crude, making a cleaner-burning base fuel and allowing the sulfur to be sold as a byproduct. Reforming rearranges molecules in a low-octane gasoline to produce a higher octane. Alkylation enlarges propane and butane molecules, allowing them to be mixed with gasoline.

From these processes emerge products which can be sorted into three main headings. Gas and gasoline, or "white" products, which comprise the lighter end of the barrel, usually about 20 percent of the total yield, are used for automobile gas, aviation fuel, and feedstocks for petrochemicals. Middle distillates, the middle quarter of the barrel, yield kerosene and light gas-oil, heating oil, diesel oils and waxes. Fuel oil and residuals, comprising the heaviest, bottom 55 percent, make up heavy fuel oils—for use in power stations and ship furnaces—asphalt, and bitumen.

Petroleum products have a wide variety of uses. Solvents, for example, go into ink, oil-base paints, dry cleaning solutions, rubber cement, and metal cleaners. Sodium hydrosulfide improves paper pulp and tans leather, while organic chemicals serve an entire, separate spectrum of uses as petrochemicals.

Ethylene, the largest-volume organic produced in the United States, goes mostly into fabricated plastics but is also used in antifreeze, synthetic fibers and rubbers, and detergents. Propylene has several chemical offshoots which are used mainly in film, packaging, and fibers. Butadiene goes primarily into synthetic rubber, but is also used in ABS resins, latexes, and nylon fibers.

Aromatics, including benzene, toluene, and the xylenes, are primarily useful as blending agents in gasoline, as well as in increasing the octane rating of unleaded gas. Methanol is traditionally used in formaldehyde, acetic acid, solvents and polymers for adhesives, fibers, and plastics. But in years to come, methanol is likely to be in greater demand to make the oxygenate MTBE (methyl tertiary-butyl ether). MTBE, used since 1979 when lead additives began to be phased out, is slated as a component of reformulated gasolines in cities designated by the Clean Air Act of 1990. Some projections indicate that demand for MTBE may triple by 1995.

Product yields per barrel have shifted with demand. While in 1981 10.4 percent of a barrel went toward residual fuel oils, only 6.7 percent was used in such fuel oils in 1991. Moreover, while 7.6 percent of a 1981 barrel went for jet fuel, 10.3 percent of a 1991 barrel was used in jet fuel. This trend should continue, and may become more pronounced, as various emissions regulations are adopted. In particular, federal requirements for low sulfur diesel fuel and re-formulated gasoline should change the yield of a barrel of crude; at the same time, wastewater and toxic solids limitations will change the methods of obtaining yields.

Financial Structure. Once crude oil has been refined, its products may be sold as raw materials to other manufacturers, such as plastics or pharmaceutical companies. Other products may be in a final, packaged form and destined for retail sale in service stations or chemical companies.

Within an integrated oil company, a refinery's profits then are part of the total profits made on the front-end. Its ability to compete depends entirely on efficient production without excessive expenditures, so that retail prices can remain low. Like the supply side interdependency of integrated oil companies, integrated profit margins are cumulative. They must absorb the costs of every aspect of the oil business, including geological research, refining procedures, and trucking the finished product, to show real net gain.

For refiners operating independently, turning a profit traditionally rested in purchasing crude at low enough rates to allow final product levels to match those of the integrated oils. Free from the overhead of exploration and test drilling, independents were able to compete effectively for years simply by taking advantage of plentiful, cheap supplies of crude. However, the increasingly stringent environmental requirements of the 1980s and 1990s put independents at a distinct disadvantage. Even with low crude prices, facility upgrading cut deeply into revenues and forced profit margins to fall.

Competitive Structure. Integrated international oil companies, integrated domestic oil companies, and independent domestic refining/marketing companies comprise the petroleum refining industry in America. Like the oil business in general, refining was dominated in the early 1990s by integrated internationals, specifically a few large companies such as Exxon Corporation, Mobil Corporation, and Chevron Corporation—all of which ranked in the top ten of Fortune's 500 sales ranking.

Of the nonintegrated refining companies—independents that focused exclusively on refined goods production and marketing—Ashland Oil, Inc., Diamond Shamrock, Inc., and Total Petroleum of North America stood out as major players. However, no independent companies competed on the same level as any integrated international in terms of net profits or refined goods sold.

Capacity also distinguished leading refiners as arms of integrated oils. Chevron and Exxon had over a million barrels per day capacity, with Amoco, Shell, Mobil, and BP America trailing them closely. A further 26 companies had over 100,000 barrels per day capacity, and the smallest 44 had less than 100,000.

As the costs of upgrading refineries escalates, the difficulties of small refining operations will probably intensify. Only with mass infusion of capital can existing refineries remain viable through the 1990s, and only large integrated oils have cashflow to divert. Even the majors struggled. Chevron, for example, put two of its refineries on the market in 1992, and downsized several others. Analysts speculated that upgrading and compliance costs may continue to shift the competitive structure of the American refined petroleum products market toward a monopoly by integrated internationals.

BACKGROUND AND DEVELOPMENT

The use of semi-refined fossil fuels dates back several millennia B.C. Six thousand year-old inscriptions in Mesopotamia include descriptions of oil and asphalt use as waterproofing materials. Egyptians embalmed their dead in asphalt, and Romans wrote by the light of oil lamps and drove chariots with wheels lubricated by crudely refined greases.

The invention of the kerosene lamp by Dr. Abraham Gesner of Pittsburgh prompted the formation of the Pennsylvania Rock Oil Company in 1854. During this time Americans sought alternative lamp fuels in response to a shortage of whale oil. Dr. Gesner extracted his "improved illuminating oil" from coal, but his methodology proved invaluable to petroleum refining's founding father, Benjamin Silliman, Jr., who wrote a treatise on the chemistry of petroleum in 1855 and then promptly figured out how to distill it. Steam was introduced into the distillation process in 1858. In 1860, the first semi-continuous refining system, operating in a battery of stills, was patented by D.S. Stombs and Julius Brace of Virginia. Luther Atwood cracked petroleum later that year, and Jean Lenoir then produced a three horsepower motor which ran on benzene. The first full-fledged refinery began production in 1861 near Titusville, Pennsylvania, adjacent to the site where Edwin Drake and W.A. Smith had discovered the first producing oil field in the country at Oil Creek. The refinery churned out little except kerosene; contemporaneous demand for lubricating oils and greases wasn't high enough to keep anyone in business, and petroleum as a transport fuel was still several decades away.

Julius Hock's invention of the noncompression petroleum engine in Vienna in 1869 perhaps marked the beginning of the modern refining process, as engine fuel would become the primary vehicle for petroleum markets worldwide. "Horseless carriages"—powered by burning hay, steam, or electricity until Frank and Charles Duryea built the first gasoline-powered automobile in 1892—eventually became the channel through which refined petroleum captured public attention. The internal combustion engine, invented early in the twentieth century, and then Henry Ford's production of the Model T, changed the world and brought petroleum suddenly to a pinnacle of economic significance.

In the early part of the twentieth century new technology was developed in petroleum-driven locomotion: automobiles, airplanes, and military vehicles proliferated as petroleum exploration and refining outpaced itself annually. Intense demand for petroleum products during World War I led to production facilities that would continue to produce innovations even after the war; solutions to agricultural, industrial and transportation problems came with each new piece of understanding about the capabilities of a barrel of crude. Even food supply was drastically affected, as gasoline powered tractors enabled farmers to increase their productivity, and asphalt surfaces on highways allowed diesel-powered trucks to speed goods to market.

World War II also prompted an upsurge in refining capacity, yielding subsequent massive peacetime productivity. American consumers during the 1950s demanded large, stylish automobiles, warm houses, and air travel. For nearly three decades, Americans found uses for more refined petroleum. The "more is more" credo became refining's byline; a constant, steadily increasing demand for new products was met by the constant, steadily increasing supply of new crude oil supplies. Unfettered by environmental controls or financial limits, refiners expanded and enjoyed a long, golden age of prosperity.

Then, in 1973, a political crisis in the Middle East spurred a severe recession and highlighted the extent to which America had become dependent of foreign oil supplies. Furthermore, the fall of the Shah of Iran in 1979 precipitated a series of supply interruptions and price increases. Overcompensating for the shortages brought on by Iran's domestic turbulence, refiners misjudged the oil demand for the early 1980s. While worldwide refining capacity had increased tenfold between 1938 and 1981, "more is more" no longer held true, and in the 1980s refiners faced a loose market with substantial excesses in place.

Refiners entered the 1990s burdened by unpredictable supply and demand factors and the potential business consequences of the burgeoning environmental movement. Such issues as recycling, the hole in the ozone layer, and water pollution became an increasingly more important part of America's legislative agenda. Consequently, the business strategy of refiners shifted to finding cleaner-burning, more efficient fuels for smaller cars, as well as finding more environmentally friendly ways in which those fuels could be created.

CURRENT CONDITIONS

Petroleum refining, like the rest of the oil industry, saw profits dwindle to a five-year low in 1992, while spending on refining simultaneously rose 8.3 percent in an effort to meet costs of upgrading and research into alternative processing. Moreover, the 1991 economic recession had prompted shutdowns totaling 114,850 b/cd capacity and had dampened domestic refined product consumption. Though most integrated firms diversified as protection against unpredictable commodity prices, diversification was not enough to keep commodities and refined products from falling in 1991.

In 1992, due to intense gasoline price competition, profit margins at service stations dwindled. Furthermore, surplus production capacity dropped the price of petrochemicals, and the weak economy sabotaged demand. Widespread domestic downsizing, along with massive staff reductions and much asset stripping, resulted in low morale in the industry.

Added pressures in 1993, from excess fuel oil stocks at the beginning of the year, costs of regulatory compliance, and a relatively warm winter in 1992-1993, kept refined product margins and refiner profitability low. Surplus oxygenates and gasoline dragged gasoline prices down despite a 2.5 cents per gallon rise in crude oil prices.

Sales in 1992 by integrated international refineries went from a five-year average growth of 7.6 percent to a 12 month decline of 5.1 percent. The list of petroleum product casualties in the domestic arena was extensive. The meager 1.2 percent increase in demand for motor gasoline in 1992 was projected to increase by only one percent in 1993 and 1994; record import levels would be necessary even to accommodate this demand as refinery capacity dropped. Jet fuel demand was down 1.4 percent in 1992, demand for residual fuel oil hit its lowest point in decades, and distillate fuel oil demand grew only modestly. The sole increase reported in the industry was in minor petroleum products, which went up by 5.9 percent in 1992.

By 1993, *Forbes* noted, "oil supply exceeded world demand by about half a million barrels a day, swelling inventories. . . . After hovering around $18 a barrel since the end of the 1991 Gulf war, benchmark crude prices dove in November [1993] to below $15; adjusted for inflation, oil now sells for what it did in 1973. That's particularly devastating to the big oil companies because so much of the investment on their books was made based on oil prices $3 to $4 higher than reality. Falling prices have made a mockery of much of the oil industry's elaborate exploration projects."

One legislative package designed to address environmental pollution has had a significant impact on the industry. 1990's Clean Air Act requires that America's 39 smoggiest cities substitute oxygenated gasoline for winter use beginning in November 1992. By 1995, the country's nine smoggiest cities—Baltimore, Chicago, Hartford, Houston, Los Angeles, Milwaukee, New York, Philadelphia, and San Diego—were to have implemented its Phase I specifications. Phase I stipulated that oxygenates (MTBE) be substituted for aromatics (which do not burn completely) in octane enhancers, essentially prescribing complete reformulation of automotive gasoline. This new gasoline must have a minimum oxygen content of two percent by weight, a maximum of one percent benzene by volume, a maximum aromatics content of 25 percent, and no heavy metals. It must not cause an increase in nitrogen oxide emissions and must create less tailpipe emissions of volatile organic compounds and toxic air pollutants (relative to a baseline of 1990 summertime gasoline). The cost to refiners of implementing substitutions and reformulations prescribed in Phase I was estimated to run $3 billion to $5 billion.

Furthermore, the California Air Resources Board (CARB) instituted standards exceeding those of the Clean Air Act, requiring them to be met by 1996. Some analysts predicted the CARB standards would eventually replace Clean Air standards nationwide.

Costs of compliance prompted a spate of refinery closures in the early 1990s, including five smaller company sites in 1992, representing a total of 145,00 b/cd capacity lost. More streamlining was required of major companies, particularly Chevron. Chevron drastically scaled back operations at its Port Arthur, Texas, refinery (140,000 b/cd lost) and cut its Richmond, California, refinery capacity by 40,000 b/cd.

Estimates for upcoming compliance costs for U.S. refiners fall within the $20 billion range, as four more major amendments of the Clean Air Act come into play. In October 1993 ultra low-sulfur diesel fuel (.05 percent by weight) was to be required nationally. Janu-

ary 1995 marks the deadline for nationwide Stage I gasoline reformulation, and, by January 1997, Stage II should also have been met, requiring adherence to a "complex" model as opposed to Stage I's "simple" model. Finally, January 2000 will see an additional ten percent reduction in organic compounds and air toxics from the 1990 baseline fuel, with no increase in nitrogen oxides.

INDUSTRY LEADERS

Ranking by barrels per day refining capacity, the largest petroleum refiner in America in 1992 was Chevron Corporation, with a capacity of 1,503,700 b/cd. Net income was $1.569 billion, and earnings per share were $4.63. This record year of net profits for the company was due in large part to sales of assets and to drastic cost cutting measures.

Begun in the late nineteenth century as Standard Oil of California, Chevron developed international capacity early and integrated upstream and downstream with enormous success even before the advent of mass pipelining or automotive transport. The company nearly doubled its domestic holdings in 1989, when it merged with Gulf Oil Company. In 1992 Chevron operated refineries in Canada, Wales, Asia, Africa, the Middle East, Australia, and New Zealand, as well as El Segundo and Richmond, California; Port Arthur, Texas; Pascagoula, Mississippi; and Philadelphia, Pennsylvania.

Chevron described a prospected five-year investment schedule for its refineries which would total $2 billion by 1997. Stressing upgrading of facilities and compliance with both federal and CARB standards, Chevron also defended its reduced operations by pointing to costs cut.

The second largest refiner in the United States by capacity was Exxon, with 1,157,000 b/cd in 1992. That year Exxon earned a net income total of $4.8 billion, of which $1.6 billion came from combined refining and marketing ventures. This latter figure represents a reduction from 1991's $2.5 billion income, which Exxon attributed to excess capacity and cleaner-burning fuel requirements. Earnings per share in 1992 were $3.79.

Exxon was formed in 1934, with the merger of Standard Oil Company of New Jersey and Anglo-American Oil Company Ltd. In 1992, it was the giant of integrated internationals, with gross operating revenues of $117,106 million, more than twice as large as the next-largest international, Mobil, whose gross operating revenues were $64,076 million.

Exxon's vast international holdings allowed it to focus almost exclusively abroad for its refined product markets and to write off the future of its U.S. refining as "mature." While expanding refineries abroad, Exxon streamlined domestic capacity and reached a sales agreement with Tosco Corporation for its Bayway Refinery in Linden, New Jersey. Exxon expanded refinery capacity in eastern Germany as new markets became open there. Other European refineries received cash infusions to increase production of profitable lines. Exxon's Sriracha Refinery in Thailand benefitted from a $750 million expansion, and the company stressed the Asia-Pacific region as its center for future growth potential in refined product sales.

While Exxon continues to enjoy financial prosperity, it has been unable to shake the fallout resulting from the *Exxon Valdez* disaster, in which an Exxon shipping vessel ran aground and caused an 11-million-gallon oil spill in Prince William Sound in Alaska on March 24, 1989. The disaster caused significant environmental and economic harm to the region (though Exxon has pointed to the millions of dollars it has spent in clean-up efforts) and in mid-1994 a jury blamed recklessness by Exxon Corp. and *Exxon Valdez* Captain Joseph Hazelwood for the disaster, allowing victims of the nation's worst ever oil spill to seek $15 billion in damages. Plaintiffs in the federal lawsuit include more than 10,000 Alaskan natives, property owners, and commercial fishermen who claim they suffered economic harm as a result of the spill. The ultimate impact of the disaster on Exxon's reputation and wallet is yet to be determined.

While Chevron is a huge producer of oil, in terms of profits and sales, Exxon Corporation is the industry leader. In 1993 Exxon posted profits of $5.28 billion on total sales of $97 billion. Mobil Corp. ranked second, with $2.08 billion in profits from sales totaling $56.6 billion. Other industry leaders in 1993 included Texaco Inc., with profits of $1.07 billion on sales of $34 billion; Shell Oil Co., with profits of $781 million on sales of $20.8 billion; and Chevron Corp., with sales revenue in 1993 of $32 billion and $1.26 billion in profits. Other notable companies include Atlantic Richfield Co. ($269 million in profits, $17 billion in sales in 1993), Conoco Inc., Amoco Corp., and BP America Inc.

WORK FORCE

Refiners employed 120,000 people in the United States in 1991. Employees earned an average of $18.51 per hour doing a variety of tasks centering on keeping technical processes functioning smoothly.

Within refineries, operators and craftsworkers monitored products via computers. They analyzed data and made adjustments to machinery to ensure opti-

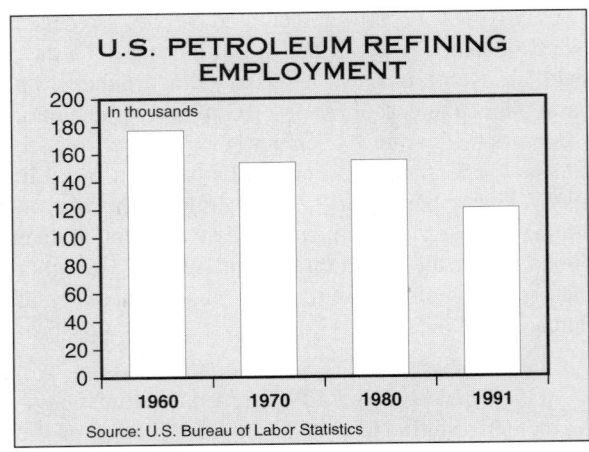

mum yields, repair faulty equipment, and make statistical reports on output. Mechanical engineers worked closely with operators, developing new machinery and making improvements whenever possible. These highly skilled technicians and scientists comprised the core of all refineries' staffs.

As refiners streamline staffs and close some operations altogether, employment prospects in petroleum refining during the 1990s weren't encouraging. Large numbers of experienced workers may be laid off as domestic refining capacities shrink and majors shift operations overseas.

Labor Negotiations. In 1993 the major oil refining outfits reached agreement with the Oil, Chemical and Atomic Workers on a new three-year contract that, according to the *Monthly Labor Review,* "struck a balance between the union's goal of improved wages and benefits, safety concerns, and a national health care program and the companies' desire to contain costs and retain operational flexibility." Labor goals in the petroleum refining industry have traditionally been articulated at the national level through the Oil, Chemical and Atomic workers, while the actual negotiations take place at the local level. As *Monthly Labor Review* observed, "the first [local] settlement serves as a pattern, with the terms of the new contract reached with the leadoff oil company being matched by most other oil companies." The trendsetting settlement in 1993 was reached with Amoco Oil Co. and covered 4,500 Amoco employees. This agreement set the tone for subsequent agreements covering another 26,000 workers in the industry.

AMERICA AND THE WORLD

America was a pioneer in petroleum refining, perfecting most technical procedures before other nations and developing synchronized upstream and downstream supply lines early. U.S. petroleum refiners are still regarded as the world leaders, with an average yield of 52 percent gasoline from every barrel of crude as opposed to 25-30 percent for foreign equivalents. The main difference between American petroleum refiners and refiners elsewhere lies in the country's free market operations. In no other country has petroleum production and refining developed with such complete autonomy from government.

This autonomy has led to minor competitive disadvantages for Americans selling in nationalized markets in that, unlike foreign refinery products, no correlative subsidies or guarantees existed for American goods. However, global economic stagnation and widespread failure of centrally planned economies catalyzed a surge in privatization in markets during the early 1990s, as nationals went private in the petroleum industry worldwide, a trend anticipated to continue throughout the decade.

Many major national systems being privatized in the early 1990s were inspired by Mexico, whose president, Carlos Salinas de Gortari, used privatization as one method to turn around his country's flagging economy. The Mexican example was held by economists as a lesson in the ills of planned economies and the virtues of market controls, a lesson particularly applicable to republics of the former Soviet Union, struggling with the absolute collapse of their national systems.

In 1993, the Italian state petroleum holding company Ente Nazionale Idrocarburi began to unfold one of the largest privatization programs ever. Most key oil producing nations in Latin America, growing economies in the Asia-Pacific region, and much of western Europe were all in various stages of privatization in the early 1990s, depending on freer markets to sustain their national economies.

Members of the European Community faced challenges in both their individual privatization efforts and their collective energy legislative programs. For example, when EC efforts to reduce excess capacities required that England streamline some operations, the English public protested, claiming that mass unemployment in already-depressed areas would follow. Government systems were thereby forced to continue supporting unprofitable operations.

The situation in England highlighted the reason that nationalized petroleum may become an industry of the past: because of the decidedly global nature of petroleum markets, national systems might not be able to compete, once a majority of producer/refiners become private industries. As more organizations adopt

efficient, profit-motivated structures, the standards for products worldwide may begin to resemble those in the United States in terms of stringent environmental standards, and, if so, the American market may become accessible to foreign competition.

There has already been a long history of joint venture and investment in the United States by refiners based overseas, and some of the integrated internationals which dominate in the United States are based in foreign countries, such as the Royal Dutch/Shell Group and British Petroleum.

The state energy companies of several OPEC countries, particularly Kuwait, Saudi Arabia, and Venezuela, invested heavily in U.S. downstream capacities in the early 1990s. Petreolos de Venezuela S.A. (PDVSA, the state petroleum company of Venezuela and Saudi Arabia) acquired the remaining 50 percent interest in Citgo Petroleum in 1991, becoming the full owner of this subsidiary. Star Enterprise, a 50/50 petroleum refining and marketing joint venture between Saudi Arabia's ARAMCO and Texaco, began operating in 1989. And Delta International, another state-owned Saudi company, began negotiating a joint venture with Fina Oil and Chemical, the U.S. subsidiary of Petrofina, a Belgian firm, for its U.S. refining and marketing operations. Furthermore, the as yet unprivatized Pemex Corporation of Mexico acquired a 50 percent interest in Shell Oil's Deer Park, Texas, refinery and began negotiations with other Gulf Coast refiners.

The increasingly complex subsidiary networks of integrated internationals should link many refineries in the United States in the next decade. As the global economy shrinks and ties between nations become stronger, the already cosmopolitan arena of petroleum refining will know increasingly fewer political borders. Consequently, American refiners may compete more directly with foreign firms for markets both at home and abroad.

RESEARCH AND TECHNOLOGY

Although new advances in reformulating gasoline, substituting cleaner fuel bases, and eliminating production waste represent significant innovations in the industry, perhaps the most important revolution in petroleum refining technology involves the implementation of computers. In the early 1990s, distilling and manufacturing industries relied on mainframes that could record, compile, and recall data on all elements, from viscosity to sulfur levels, in any given barrel of crude. Everything from measuring proportions of ingredients to monitoring chemical reactions could be performed with computers, and engineers relied as much on three-dimensional graphic and diagramming software as on actual valves and gages to determine improvements in processes.

With upstream technology breakthroughs such as 3-D seismography, horizontal and directional drilling, and enhanced oil recovery (EOR) helping to ensure that every drop of oil was pumped from the ground, the impetus to utilize every drop of oil at maximum efficiency had never been stronger. Computers allowed such efficiency not only by storing and retrieving data in a central, accessible medium, but also by cutting the time required for compilation and computation. Moreover, by implementing self-cleaning machines monitored by more sophisticated computers, petroleum refiners should be able to produce the low-toxicity fuels in demand, and, eventually, find new areas for growth.

Nevertheless, patience, thrift, and ingenuity will be paramount to survival in the refining industry. Demand for petroleum products is forecast to grow at only half the rate of the U.S. economy. New regulations will limit the use of products which once had diverse applications, restricting them by season, geographical area, applications, and production costs. Federal standards requirements are likely to continue to proliferate, absorbing time and capital and man for research and experimentation. A restructuring of the industry will likely occur and continue beyond the 1990s into the next century.

INDUSTRY INFORMATION SOURCES

Anderson, Robert O. *Fundamentals of the Petroleum Industry,* Norman: University of Oklahoma Press.

Basic Petroleum Data Book. Washington DC: American Petroleum Institute.

Bremner, Brian, et al. ''Ho, Ho, Ho Chi Minh, Corporate America Rushes In,'' *Business Week,* January 11, 1993.

Chevron Corporation Annual Report 1992

Cimini, Michael H., Susan L. Behrmann, and Eric M. Johnson, ''Labor-management Bargaining in 1993,'' *Monthly Labor Review,* January 1994.

Economist Newspaper. New York: Economist & Newspaper Ltd.

Exxon Corporation Annual Report 1992

''The Fortune 500,'' *Fortune,* April 18, 1994.

Guthrie, Virgil B., ''Petroleum Products.'' In *The Petroleum Processing Handbook,* edited by William F. Bland and Robert L. Davidson. New York: Macgraw Hill, 1963.

Mack, Toni, James R. Norman, Howard Rudnitsky, and Andrew Tanzer, ''History is Full of Giants That Failed to Adapt,'' *Forbes,* February 28, 1994.

Monthly Labor Review, Washington, DC: U.S. Bureau of the Census, July 1993.

1992 U.S. Statistical Abstract, Washington, DC: U.S. Bureau of the Census.

Occupational Outlook Handbook, 1992-1993 Edition. Washington, DC: U.S. Department of Labor, 1992.

Petroleum Intelligence Weekly. New York: Intelligence Weekly, Inc.

Petroleum Outlook. Greenwich, CN: Herald, Inc.

Short Term Energy Outlook, Second Quarter 1993. Washington, DC: Energy Information Administration, 1993.

Sinclair, Stuart. *The World Petroleum Industry,* New York: MGB.

''Sixty Percent of Oil Companies show declines in Asset Values,'' *National Petroleum News,* Mid-June 1993.

Standard and Poor's Industry Surveys. New York: Standard and Poor's Corporation, 1993.

Steedley, Gilbert. ''Who's Where in the Stock Market,'' *Forbes,* January 4, 1993.

U.S. Industrial Outlook 1993. Washington, DC: U.S. Department of Commerce, 1993.

Woodburn, John H. *Opportunities in Energy Careers,* Lincolnwood, Ill.: NTC Publishing Group.

Zellner, Wendy. ''Now, They're Cooking with Gas,'' *Business Week,* January 11, 1993.

—Shannon Summers

SIC 2951

ASPHALT PAVING MIXTURES AND BLOCKS

This category describes companies principally employed in manufacturing asphalt and tar paving mixtures, and paving blocks made of asphalt mixed with other materials.

Asphalt is a blackish-brown material with a consistency ranging from a viscous liquid to a glassy solid. Most asphalt is obtained as a byproduct of the distillation of petroleum or other natural materials. Natural asphalt, rarely used by the 1990s, is formed during the early stages of the breakdown of organic marine deposits into petroleum.

Asphalt is used most often in the construction of roads, parking lots, walkways, and other paved surfaces. It is also commonly utilized in reservoir linings, dam facings, and other harbor and sea applications. Highway and street constructors purchased about 45 percent of industry output in the early 1990s, and an additional 25 percent or more was used in the construction of parking lots and walkways for commercial buildings. The remainder of the asphalt market is fragmented.

The primary advantages that asphalt has over concrete are cost and flexibility. Because it softens when heated and is comparatively elastic, asphalt offers a high degree of adaptability in construction applications. Its physical properties also make it less susceptible to cracking and weathering. Furthermore, asphalt is easier to remove and costs much less than either concrete or natural paving materials.

Historic uses of asphalt date back to 3000 B.C., when natural asphalt was used to seal a reservoir at Mohenjo-Daro, Pakistan. It was later used throughout the Middle East to pave roads and seal waterworks. Pitch Lake on the Island of Trinidad was the first large commercial source of the material. The development of petroleum-based materials such as asphalt during the 18th, 19th, and 20th centuries gradually replaced natural supplies.

The demand for asphalt that accompanied the post-World War II economic expansion in the United States drew primarily on petroleum-based supplies. By the early 1990s, asphalt paving mixture producers used over 50 million barrels of asphalt per year, selling more than $4 billion worth of mixtures and blocks annually.

Asphalt sales benefitted from a period of growth in industry revenue from about $3 billion in 1982 to more than $4.5 billion by 1988. Unfortunately, a slump in construction reduced the demand for asphalt mixtures as sales dipped 12 percent in 1989 and recuperated only slightly by 1990. Growth in demand stagnated in the early '90s, though a modest recovery buoyed earnings in 1993. Competitors looked to increased government infrastructure spending and slowly recovering commercial markets to sustain meager growth by 1994.

Over 1,000 companies competed in this highly fragmented industry in the early '90s. Beazer East Inc. of Pennsylvania was the largest with $800 million in 1991 sales generated by its 5,500 workers. New Jersey-based Huls America Inc. placed second with $500 million in sales and about 1,500 workers. CalMat Co. of California garnered revenues of $425 million with 1,700 employees. One of the most innovative competitors was Granite Rock Co., which received a Malcom Baldridge National Quality Award in 1992. The majority of the top 50 firms in the industry earned less than $40 million and maintained an average of less than 200 employees.

The asphalt paving mixture industry employed about 14,000 workers in the early 1990s—down from 15,000 a decade earlier. Most employees are blue-collar laborers, such as truck drivers and machine operators. The average hourly wage in 1989 was $12.53 per hour, compared to an average of $10.49 for all U.S. manufacturing workers. As a result of automation and increased productivity, opportunities for most occupations in the industry were expected to decline by 5 to 20 percent between 1990 and 2005, according to the U.S. Bureau of Labor Statistics.

Among the most prominent technological breakthroughs in the industry in the 1990s was stone mastic asphalt (SMA). Developed in Europe, SMA incorporates cellulose fibers that make it stronger than conventional asphalt. Efforts to use recycled rubber tires as an asphalt ingredient were encouraged by 1991's Intermodal Surface Transportation Efficiency Act (ISTEA) which mandated the use of scrap tires in federally funded state roads.

INDUSTRY INFORMATION SOURCES

Blumenthal, Michael H., and John R. Serumgard. ''Scrap Tires Find Future on the Road and in the Tank,'' *World Wastes,* August 1992.

Darnay, Arsen J., ed. *Manufacturing USA; Industry Analyses, Statistics, and Leading Companies,* Detroit: Gale, 1993.

Green, Peter. ''U.S. Road Builders Look to Europe,'' *Engineering News Record,* August 12, 1991.

Kendrick, John J. ''Granite Rock Co.,'' *Quality,* January 1993.

U.S. Industrial Outlook 1993, Washington, DC: U.S. Department of Commerce, January 1993.

—Dave Mote

SIC 2952

ASPHALT FELTS AND COATINGS

This category is comprised of establishments that manufacture asphalt in roll or shingle form, either smooth or faced with grit, and roof cements or coatings. Examples of products include asphalt brick siding, tar coating compounds, roofing fabrics, pitch, shingles, and tar paper. Manufacturers of asphalt paving mixtures and blocks are described in **SIC 2951: Asphalt Paving Mixtures**.

Asphalt is a compound made of hydrogen and carbon, with minor proportions of nitrogen, sulfur, and oxygen. It exists in forms ranging from a black liquid to a glassy solid. Most asphalt is obtained as a byproduct of the distillation of petroleum or other natural materials. Some natural asphalt, however, is extracted from organic mineral deposits in the early stages of their breakdown into petroleum.

When formed into felts and coatings, asphalt provides a reliable protectant and sealant. It is extremely water-repellent, tolerates temperature fluctuations, and resists the breakdown and decay caused by exposure to the elements. These characteristics make asphalt ideal for roofs, coatings, floor tilings, and waterproofing. Asphalt coatings and sheets are also popular soundproofing materials. Roofing shingles represented 40 percent of the total industry output in the early 1990s, and all roofing and siding fabrics combined made up 75 percent of production. Roofing cements and coatings accounted for an additional 15 percent of sales.

Although asphalt was used to line reservoirs as early as 3000 B.C., it didn't achieve widespread commercial application in the United States until the 20th century. Aided by technological advancements in petroleum-based materials during World War II, the asphalt felt and coating industry mushroomed during the post-war economic expansion. Specifically, residential and commercial construction booms launched the industry to nearly $3 billion in sales by the late 1970s.

Industry growth stalled during the 1980s. A reduction in the number of housing starts in comparison to past decades contributed to the malaise. Competition from new synthetic materials also cut into producer's profits. Sales rose from $3.3 billion to $3.6 billion between 1983 and 1990, lagging behind the rate of inflation. Likewise, industry employment declined from about 14,000 to 12,400 as manufacturers boosted productivity through automation and layoffs. Depressed construction markets in the late 1980s and early '90s further reduced earnings.

As profitability declined during the '80s and early '90s, the already consolidated industry became more concentrated. The number of industry participants declined from 273 in 1982 to about 250 over the next ten years. In 1991, the combined revenues of the top ten companies were roughly equivalent to one half of total industry sales.

Tremco Inc. of Ohio, the largest competitor, earned $330 million in 1991 with about 2,200 employees. The 180 workers of New Jersey-based GAF Building Materials Corp. generated sales of $270 million. The third-largest player was GS Roofing Products Co. of Texas, with sales of $200 million. The majority of the top 50 rivals each garnered less than $20 million and employed fewer than 100 workers.

Future employment prospects in this industry were predicted to be poor due to increased automation and a decrease in the growth of demand for asphalt-based products. Positions in the majority of occupa-

tions for this mostly blue-collar workforce were expected to decline by 10 to 20 percent between 1990 and 2005, according to the U.S. Bureau of Labor Statistics.

INDUSTRY INFORMATION SOURCES

Darnay, Arsen J., ed. *Manufacturing USA: Industry Analyses, Statistics, and Leading Companies,* Detroit: Gale, 1993.

''Journal of Housing LAB: Roofing,'' *Journal of Housing,* November/December 1993.

Sanders, Russell. ''Selecting the Best Roofing Options,'' *Journal of Property Management,* September/October 1993.

U.S. Industrial Outlook 1993, Washington, DC: U.S. Department of Commerce, January 1993.

—Dave Mote

SIC 2992

LUBRICATING OILS AND GREASES

SIC 2992 includes establishments primarily engaged in blending, compounding, and re-refining lubricating oils and greases from purchased mineral, animal, and vegetable materials. Petroleum refineries engaged in the production of lubricating oils and greases are classified in **SIC 2911: Petroleum Refining.**

Lubricants are unique among petroleum products marketed, indeed among merchandized goods and services in general, in that every advancement of quality made in their manufacture lengthens their period of use and therefore diminishes the relative volume of their sales. For this reason, this industry represented a fairly contained market in the early 1990s, which was predicted to remain relatively static for the foreseeable future.

In 1992, approximately 140 companies vied in this industry classification. Forty-seven of these companies produced brake fluid, cutting oils, lubricating greases and oils, hydraulic fluids, rust arresting compounds, and transmission fluid exclusively, while the rest produced such products in tandem with other goods not included in the SIC 2992 group. Manufacturers of lubricating oils and greases employed a total of 11,284 people and produced over 57 million barrels of finished compounds. Sales in 1991 totaled 2.18 million gallons of oils, 52,000 gallons of greases and 2.23 million gallons of lubricants.

Manufacturers falling within SIC 2992 competed directly with petroleum refiners in many instances. However, the increasing degree of specialization required within the lubricants market gave lubricant manufacturers an edge over general refiners in that specialized equipment and multiple blending agents were more difficult to maintain in an integrated refining plant than in a lubricants plant.

Several thousand different lubricant products were manufactured in the United States in the early 1990s, all of which fell into one of three categories: automotive, industrial, or industrial for non-lubricating purposes.

Within the automotive category, the three main types of lubricant included crankcase oils, transmission and axle lubricants, and fluids for hydraulic torque converters and fluid couplings used in automatic transmissions. Each category had subdivisions based on viscosity, or resistance to molecular rearrangement or flow. Automotive lubricants kept various parts of auto bodies and engines running smoothly by cushioning adjacent metal pieces, oiling moving parts, and keeping dirt out of combustion chambers.

Industrial lubricants ranged from machine oils to steam-turbine oils. These products served similar purposes as automotive lubricants, with added capabilities and endurance capacity, which allowed them, for example, to prevent rust from high-temperature steams. Again, viscosity represented the main difference between lubricant uses.

A lubricating grease is a solid or semisolid lubricant composed of a fluid lubricant with an added thickening agent. Generally the fluid base is petroleum derived, while the thickening agent usually consists of soap made from aluminum, barium, calcium, lithium, sodium, or strontium. Sometimes, if wide temperature variations will be encountered in usage, the fluid base is a synthetic, such as silicone or polyalkylene glycol. In some instances, non-soap thickeners such as modified clay or fine silica may be used. Like lubricants, greases fall into automotive or industrial classifications.

As automobile makers and industrial manufacturers continue to improve and upgrade their facilities and products, lubricating oils and greases will have to meet increasingly exacting standards and serve more precise functions. In response to such demands, for example, Exxon's Lubricants division introduced Teresso Synthetic HP, an industrial oil developed to withstand extremes of temperature while lubricating industrial equipment, and Unirex RS 300, a premium grease formulated to withstand the unique conditions and high temperatures generated by papermaking machines.

INDUSTRY INFORMATION SOURCES

Exxon Corporation Annual Report, New York: Exxon Corporation, 1992.

Guthrie, Virgil B. "Petroleum Products." In *The Petroleum Processing Handbook,* edited by William F. Bland and Robert L. Davidson. New York: McGraw Hill Book Company, 1963.

"Lubricant Statistics." *National Petroleum News.* Mid-June, 1993, pp. 54-98.

Standard and Poor's Industry Surveys, New York: Standard and Poor's Corporation, 1993.

U.S. Industrial Outlook 1993, Washington, DC: U.S. Department of Commerce, 1993.

U.S. Statistical Abstract, Washington, DC: U.S. Bureau of the Census, 1992.

—Shannon Summers

SIC 2999

PRODUCTS OF PETROLEUM AND COAL, NOT ELSEWHERE CLASSIFIED

This category includes establishments primarily engaged in manufacturing packaged fuel, powdered fuel, and other products of petroleum and coal not elsewhere classified. Products produced by members of this industry include calcined petroleum coke, regular petroleum coke, fireplace logs, fuel briquettes, or petroleum waxes, independently of petroleum refineries.

Raw materials for companies grouped in this area are procured from petroleum refineries or coal processors, while goods produced are shipped either to distributors for the retail market or other manufacturers. Solid, packaged fuels, including fireplace logs and fuel briquettes produced by companies are sold for general consumer use nationwide.

Petroleum coke, a byproduct derived from the thermal cracking of reduced crudes and residuums, is viable as domestic and industrial fuel. Used primarily in its refined form for heating, on the east coast where most of its manufacturers are based, petroleum coke is used in aluminum anodes, furnace electrodes and liners, carbonaceous pastes and cements, as well as various carbon and graphite products. Highly purified graphite derived from petroleum coke can be used for construction materials in nuclear plants.

Petroleum waxes—paraffin wax and petrolatum—are destined primarily for paper manufacturing; both the manufacture of paper and the coating and impregnating of paper and paperboard for protective wrapping of foods require petroleum wax. In the manufacture of rubber tires, petroleum waxes serve as an anti-ozonant, while in PVC manufacturing, the waxes serve as internal lubricant. Paraffin wax is used in making candles, cosmetics, and pharmaceuticals.

Entities within this industry generally compete with major petroleum refineries, holding a relatively small market share among fuel producers. However, niche markets that demand specialty wax applications require blending capacities that are regarded as too costly for major refiners to install and maintain. In such niche markets producers can excel.

Leading firms in this industry include Phillips Puerto Rico Core Inc., of Guayama, Puerto Rico; Detroit Coke Co., of Detroit, Michigan; Walnut Hill Enterprises Inc., of Bristol, Pennsylvania; and VENCO of Houston, Texas. Both Detroit Coke and Walnut Hill Enterprises are privately owned companies.

INDUSTRY INFORMATION SOURCES

Bland, William F., and Robert L. Davidson, eds. *The Petroleum Processing Handbook,* New York: McGraw-Hill, 1963.

U.S. Industrial Outlook 1993. Washington, DC: U.S. Bureau of the Census, 1993.

—Shannon Summers

RUBBER & MISCELLANEOUS PLASTICS PRODUCTS

TIRES AND INNER TUBES

This category covers establishments primarily engaged in manufacturing pneumatic casings, inner tubes, and solid and cushion tires for all types of vehicles, airplanes, farm equipment, and children's vehicles; tiring; camelback; and tire repair and retreading materials. Establishments primarily engaged in retreading tires are classified in **SIC 7534: Tire Retreading and Repair Shops.**

INDUSTRY SNAPSHOT

The tire industry has developed in the twentieth century as a major supplier to the manufacturers of automobiles and other vehicles and to vehicle users seeking replacement tires. The tire and rubber industries have traditionally been based in Akron, Ohio, where most of those industries' company headquarters were located.

Annual sales have exceeded $11 billion in 1991, and the industry then employed over 65,000 workers. About half the tires manufactured are for passenger cars, the balance for trucks and other vehicles.

Tire Types and Characteristics. Though a small number of tires sold consisted of solid rubber, practically all are pneumatic, or inflated with air. The pneumatic tire was developed in the late 1800s for use in bicycles, just prior to the onset of the automobile industry. Thousands of sizes and types of pneumatic tires were made available for passenger cars and other vehicles, including trucks, buses, tractors, motorcycles, airplanes, and construction vehicles. Tire sizes

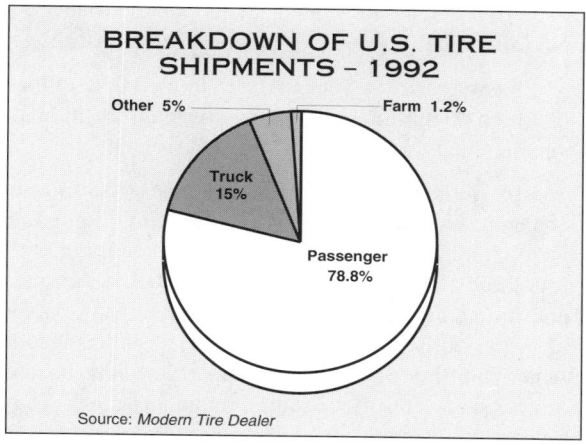

BREAKDOWN OF U.S. TIRE SHIPMENTS – 1992

Other 5%
Farm 1.2%
Truck 15%
Passenger 78.8%

Source: *Modern Tire Dealer*

range from under two pounds to over three tons for earth-moving equipment.

Tire casings are made from layers of rubber compounds and synthetic fibers or steel wire. The design and arrangement of these layers, or plies, affect qualities like cornering ability, vibration absorption, and durability.

Changes in Ownership. Like the automobile industry, tire manufacturing developed in the early part of the 1900s and was dominated by U.S. enterprises. In the later part of the century, however, foreign companies purchased several major U.S. tire producers, and most of the largest tire manufacturers became foreign-owned.

ORGANIZATION AND STRUCTURE

Most tires are manufactured by relatively large companies that produce a wide range of types and sizes; smaller tire producers tend to limit their output to specialized product groups. While a major portion of sales in the industry are to vehicle manufacturers for installation as original equipment, a larger share are sold as replacements through various distribution channels.

The tire and inner tube industry depends chiefly on rubber suppliers for raw materials and automobile manufacturers for sales. Well over half of the world's production of rubber goes into the manufacture of automobile tires. The tire and inner tube industry is the largest element of the rubber industry group as a whole, constituting over 40 percent of that group's product sales. The rubber industry group is represented by the Rubber Manufacturers Association (RMA). The RMA members make up more than three-fourths of the dollar sales of the rubber industry group as a whole. One effort of the RMA has been the establishment in 1990 of a Scrap Tire Management Council to promote environmentally proper disposition of scrap tires.

Passenger tires sold in 1992 totaled 212 million, of which 46 million were for original equipment on the vehicles and 166 million were replacements.

In the late 1980s, the tire and inner tube industry changed from one in which most leading companies were United States owned to one in which three of the four largest companies are owned by French, Japanese, and Italian nationals. British interests have attempted, unsuccessfully, to acquire control of other leading American tire producers. Competition has become more severe and more international in scope. These ownership changes have been a part of a trend toward mergers of many of the major companies, resulting in larger but fewer independent companies in the top structure of the industry. An important influence encouraging the purchases of American tire companies by foreign organizations has been the weaker dollar which eliminated the price advantage for foreign companies when the dollar was stronger.

BACKGROUND AND DEVELOPMENT

The History of Rubber. Christopher Columbus noted the existence of rubber on his second voyage to the New World when he observed Indians playing with balls they had made from a liquid obtained from a tree. Practical uses of rubber products began in the early 1800s, particularly with the use of rubber in clothing as a means for waterproofing. However, widespread applications were limited because the rubber material was somewhat sticky, odorous, and easily affected by shifts in temperature.

An American inventor, Charles Goodyear, developed the vulcanization process of rubber in 1839. By incorporating lead and sulphur with rubber and applying heat, Goodyear created qualities of durability and stability, which facilitated the use of rubber in many practical and beneficial products, particularly tires.

In 1876, Sir Henry Wickham planted some rubber trees in Kew Gardens from rubber tree seeds he brought from Brazil. These trees were transferred to Ceylon (Sri Lanka) and the Malay Peninsula where a rubber plantation industry developed that produced almost three million tons a year. Some of the larger tire producers later acquired and managed their own rubber plantations.

Tire Design Developments. The pneumatic principle was first developed in 1845 by a British engineer, Robert William Thomson, who applied it with modest success to carriage tires. However, solid rubber tires remained more popular until John Boyd Dunlop patented a more practical pneumatic tire in 1888. Dunlop's tire consisted of a vulcanized rubber and canvas tube with a valve attached to a solid wood wheel.

In 1890 further tire design refinements were developed by Charles Kingston Welsh and William Erskine Bartlett. A design featuring for a detachable pneumatic tire, created and patented by Welsh, continued to be used in the twentieth century. Bartlett developed the beaded edge for the tires so that the tire's edge could be hooked securely to the wheel's rim and remain firmly attached by compressed air in the tire.

Synthetic Rubber. The early 1900s saw the growth of the automobile and tire industries. The business increased when the steel wheels of agricultural tractors were replaced with rubber tires. All tires were made from natural rubber until the 1940s when the supply of natural rubber was cut off from Asian plantations as a result of World War II hostilities. Out of necessity, a synthetic rubber was quickly developed and remained an important raw material in the industry. In the 1960s, synthetic rubber sales equalled that of natural rubber as a raw material for tires, and synthetic rubber eventually became the preferred material.

Tire Structure and Features. Tires are manufactured by assembling plies of rubberized fabric on a cylindrical drum. Various materials may be used in the plies, including cotton, rayon, nylon, and polyester. Steel wire or glass fibre is incorporated in radial tires, perpendicular to the direction of the tire's motion, providing more stability.

Radial tires were first sold in the United States after World War II by France's Michelin. They were not produced extensively by U.S. tire manufacturers until the Lincoln Continental adopted Michelin radials as standard for its 1968 model. Radials eventually became the most popular tire, comprising over 90 percent of the passenger car tires and 65 percent of truck tires purchased in 1990.

The performance of tires has improved greatly over the years. Manufacturers have improved their durability, traction, cornering, shock absorption, and ease of mounting. Designs for tires with greater width and lower height have given vehicles greater contact with the road, lowering their center of gravity.

Changes in Facilities, Employment, and Shipments. A 1987 report issued by the Bureau of the Census showed that the number of companies in the industry decreased from 136 in 1972 to 115 in 1987, and the number of production facilities decreased from 206 to 163 in that period. Employment dipped dramatically from 107,500 to 65,400, while the dollar value of the tires and inner tubes shipped increased from $5,747.1 million $10,427.4 million. Those dollar figures reflected the substantial reduction in the value of the dollar. Also during that period, the industry's total payroll went from $1,214.1 million to $2,069.9 million, also reflecting significant inflation, as the payroll dollars per average employee increased 180 percent during that same period, 1972 to 1987.

The census report showed further that the value of tire and inner tube shipments in 1987 represented 42 percent of entire the rubber products group, which consisted of manufacturers of several rubber products such as rubber footwear, hose and belting, and other fabricated and mechanical rubber goods. Of course many of the tire and tube producer companies and establishments also manufactured products in some or all of the other rubber goods categories. However, the value of tire and inner tube shipments from the 163 tire and inner tube producing establishments in 1987 represented 95 percent of the total value of their shipments.

Relationship with Auto Industry. The tire and inner tube industry has always been heavily dependent upon the automobile industry. Competition among the tire manufacturers has been fierce, particularly competition for status as original equipment for automakers. Since car buyers tend to purchase replacement tires of the same brand originally sold on the car, it behooves a tire producer to cut prices and induce auto producers to select its brand. For each tire included as original equipment, an average of three replacement tires will be bought.

CURRENT CONDITIONS

The tire business is reasonably assured of stable sales. While the demand for vehicles can fluctuate with changing economic conditions, the purchase of re-

placement tires cannot be long deferred, giving a relative evenness to the rate of tire purchases. Unfortunately, however, the increased durability of tires, because of technical improvements, has decreased the rate of replacement purchases.

Market Share Competition. The industry's strength and stability belies an undercurrent of competition and economic issues that have changed the industry's structure and led to abandonment of plants, reductions of employees, and limited profitability.

The tire industry's vigorous competitive atmosphere has hindered opportunities to improve profits through price increases. The tire manufacturers' Producer Price Index increased only 7.6 percent between 1982 and 1992, while manufacturing prices in general increased an average of 21.1 percent during that period.

Changing Company Ownership. Except for French-owned Michelin, technically and commercially successful since the late 1800s, the tire market was dominated by well-known U.S. company brand names such as Goodyear, Goodrich, Uniroyal, Firestone, Dunlop, General, and Armstrong. However, producers of most of these brands were purchased by foreign companies between 1985 and 1993. France's Michelin purchased Uniroyal-Goodrich, achieving top position worldwide.

A major reason for the purchase of U.S. tire companies by foreign firms was the decreasing value of the dollar. Furthermore, due to the weak economy, U.S. tire companies and foreign-owned companies operating in the United States were unable to overcome the fact that more tires have been imported than were exported to the United States between 1971 and 1993. Nevertheless, three of the top tire companies planned modest price increases, and some considered plant expansion and further hiring in 1993.

INDUSTRY LEADERS

Goodyear Tire & Rubber Co. Based in Akron, Ohio, traditionally the global center of the tire and rubber industries, Goodyear has for years made more tires than any other tire producer. Since most of Goodyear's domestic tiremaking competitors were acquired by foreign firms since the mid-1980s, Goodyear became the only principal tire producer headquartered in the United States. In 1991, Goodyear had revenues of $10.9 billion, net income of $96.6 million, and 99,952 employees.

Goodyear was founded in 1898 by Frank A Sieberling, who named the company after Charles Goodyear, inventor of the vulcanization process. By

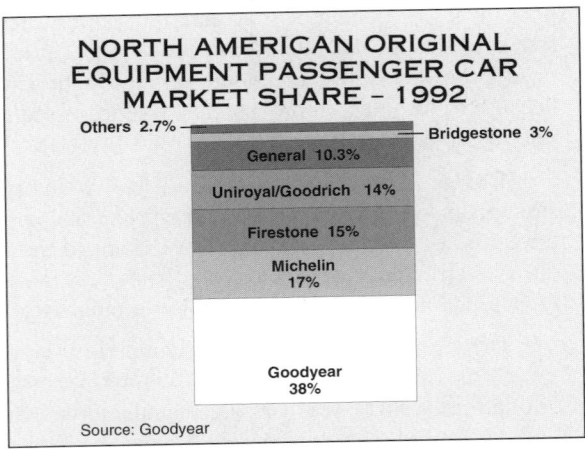

NORTH AMERICAN ORIGINAL
EQUIPMENT PASSENGER CAR
MARKET SHARE – 1992

Others 2.7% ——— ——— Bridgestone 3%

General 10.3%

Uniroyal/Goodrich 14%

Firestone 15%

Michelin 17%

Goodyear 38%

Source: Goodyear

World War I, after making a variety of technical and practical design improvements, Goodyear had the largest tire sales volume of any company. Between the two world wars, the company survived some financial difficulties, developed production operations in four other countries, owned and managed rubber plantations, and created the famous Goodyear blimp as a promotional tool. After World War II, Goodyear set up production facilities in six more countries and promoted the development of synthetic rubber. Goodyear addressed tough competition from Michelin's radial tire by developing its own design innovations, creating a new all-weather tire and expanding its interests into the field of gas and oil pipelines.

In 1986 a British financier attempted to buy Goodyear. To fend off this move, Goodyear sold its cotton-growing and aerospace businesses, including its blimp manufacturing activity. From those resources and heavy borrowing, Goodyear bought back $2.6 billion of its stock. In 1991 a new chief executive was selected from its board of directors to strengthen the company and surmount the burden of its heavy debt load. In 1991, Goodyear operated 41 factories in the United States and 43 in 25 other countries, six rubber plantations, and over 2,000 tire retail facilities worldwide.

Compagnie Générale des Éstablissements Michelin. Michelin was one of the earliest producers of tires for bicycles and carriages and has become the world's largest maker of tires for automobiles and other vehicles. In 1863, two brothers who had operated a rubber products business for some 30 years formed a new company, developing a detachable pneumatic bicycle tire in 1891, and producing similar products for carriages and then automobiles.

In the early 1900s, Michelin pioneered tire design improvements including the first tubeless tire and a low profile shape. The company soon added plants in Italy and the United States to its French production facilities. Michelin marketed the first radial tire, which significantly helped tire traction and wear, in the 1930s. U.S. tire producers did not follow Michelin's lead in radials until decades later.

Always a leader in Europe, Michelin broke into the United States market by selling its innovative radials to Ford and other automakers in the 1960s. By 1980 Michelin had four tire facilities in the United States.

In 1989 Michelin bought the Uniroyal-Goodrich Tire Company, a firm formed when two struggling tire companies merged in the mid-1980s. Absorbing these troubled organizations, along with a highly competitive tire market, resulted in heavy losses for Michelin in 1991. In 1991, Michelin had revenues of $13.1 billion, a net loss of $195.6 million, 131,976 employees.

Bridgestone. Bridgestone was a leading Japanese tire manufacturer, as well as a producer of bicycles, sporting goods, and various rubber industrial products, when it decided to purchase the third-ranking tire producer in the United States, Firestone. Bridgestone bid for Firestone against Italy's Pirelli in 1988, and ended up paying $2.6 billion for the American company. In 1991, Bridgestone had revenues of $14.1 billion, net income of $59.8 million, and 95,276 employees.

The company's name is an English translation of its founder's name. The company evolved from a family clothing business that added a rubber sole to its line of footwear. A line of tires was initiated in 1923. After the Korean War, Bridgestone established tire plants in Singapore, Thailand, and Indonesia, and also formed a collaborative effort with Spaulding in the United States for making golf balls. In the 1980s, Bridgestone began tire production at a Firestone plant it acquired in Tennessee and a few years later purchased the entire Firestone company.

Firestone was formed in Akron, Ohio, by Harvey S. Firestone in 1900, and Ford was one of its early and regular customers. Later Firestone encountered several problems, including defects in its steel-belted radial tires, as well as alleged tax violations and illegal campaign contributions. These problems led to a period of retrenchment during which plants closed, employment dropped, and several businesses were sold.

Shortly after Bridgestone purchased Firestone, General Motors dropped the company as a supplier. Such difficulties have produced a period of losses for Firestone's operations which have reduced Bridgestone's profitability significantly. Nonetheless,

Bridgestone has planned to invest an additional $1.4 billion to build up its Firestone operation.

Cooper Tire & Rubber Co. While Goodyear, Michelin, and Bridgestone earned profits of just under one percent in 1991, Cooper's reported profits of eight percent. Rather than striving for market share by cutting prices of tires sold to automobile manufacturers, it has targeted the replacement tire market and a more ample gross margin. Instead of growth, Cooper has focused on return on investment. In 1991, Cooper had revenues of $1.0 billion, net income of $79.4 million, and 6,545 employees.

Although the replacement market was dampened by increasingly longer lasting tires, cars also lasted longer and consumers were driving more miles per year than ever before, giving the total market a modest growth rate. Cooper has been distributing about half its tires via independent distributors and the other half as private brand labels through oil company retail systems.

Cooper has also saved by eliminating most research and development. Rather than develop unique designs, the company adopts the features of its competitors tires, which have proven successful in the marketplace. The company's profitability was also attributed to its dedicated work force, motivated by a variety of pay incentives and leading to an unusually low turnover. Many employees achieved substantial gains from their company stock purchases, since the stock made a remarkable rise of 6,800 percent in the 1980s. Fifteen percent of the company's shares are owned by its employees.

WORK FORCE

In 1992 the tire and inner tube industry employed more than 70,000 workers, of which 80 percent were production workers. The most plentiful jobs in the industry were in the production and maintenance areas. More technical activities are in the research and development, production planning and control, accounting and finance, and information systems functions. Career paths can proceed from production operator to supervisor, department head, and plant manager. Such lateral moves can be made as from production supervisor to production control technician.

Opportunities for careers in the industry have generally been fewer than in other industries, largely because of severe competition resulting from many mergers and acquisitions, excess capacity, and the efforts of most companies in the industry to keep prices low to gain or maintain market share. Conse-

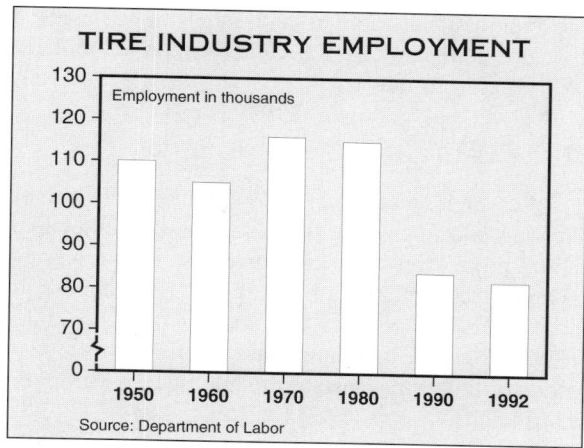

TIRE INDUSTRY EMPLOYMENT

Employment in thousands

Source: Department of Labor

quently, tire companies have sought to cut costs, eliminate plants, and resist pay increases. Nevertheless, some companies planned to increase prices and production capacity. Furthermore, at the top levels, opportunities have been created for business leaders to help organizations overcome losses or unsatisfactory profit margins.

In 1991, the average tire industry production worker earned $17.70 per hour, or an annual salary of $33,609. The average non-production worker that year earned $40,107. In addition to salaries, the companies spent an average of $3,992 per employee for government mandated plans such as Social Security and unemployment insurance, and $9,327 per employee for benefits such as medical plans, insurance, pensions, and stock plans, both for benefits provided voluntarily and for those required by union agreements.

Unions. The United Rubber Workers (URW) has represented employees at Goodyear, Firestone, and Uniroyal-Goodrich's predecessor organizations since the 1930s and 1940s. Goodyear experienced several confrontations and strikes from the URW, and achieved modest concessions in the 1980s to help meet its competitive challenges. Firestone's union workers endured long strikes in 1936 and 1976; in 1981 its URW members agreed to wage reductions. Michelin applied various tactics over the years to oppose the influence of unions, such as moving operations to areas where unions have less strength.

AMERICA AND THE WORLD

Most of the leading companies had tire plants in several countries and sold their products in international markets. Since the latter part of the 1980s, the tire industry has also become much more multinational in ownership as many of the top tire companies in the United States were bought by foreign concerns. In fact, the multinational mergers and acquisitions have left few tire companies in the United States unaffiliated with foreign firms.

RESEARCH AND TECHNOLOGY

Research and technology's emphasis has been on creating and improving the design and specifications of tire products to meet customers' needs and wishes. Though technical skills have always been applied to production methodology and cost controls, operating efficiency has been a dominant objective in the 1980s and early 1990s because of the intense competition in that period.

Tire Design and Specifications. Historically, research and technology have been used to design better tire products for the purpose of developing strong competitive positions in the marketplace. Major breakthroughs include pneumatic tires for cushioning, removable tires for convenience, synthetic rubber to overcome material shortage, and radials to enhance durability and performance.

Goodyear and Bridgestone have been developing a tire that can run safely for 200 miles after a flat, eliminating the inconvenience and dangers in changing a tire on the roadside. Goodyear also has been working on microprocessors to monitor the tire's air pressure, temperature, and wear, which might extend a tire's life by 15 percent. Other research involves creating a tire guaranteed to have a life of 80,000 miles.

Manufacturing and Cost Controls. Since the mid-1980s especially, when merger and acquisition activities have dominated the industry, the intensified competition has encouraged or required the tire producers to reduce costs so they could trim prices and survive with slimmer profit margins. To cut costs, producers have engaged in re-engineering or "downsizing," eliminating inefficient plants, and streamlining operations. These cost improvement activities have required the companies' technical staffs to design better production methods and apply computer techniques to save workers' time, speed processes, and improve quality.

INDUSTRY INFORMATION SOURCES

French, Michael J. *The U.S. Tire Industry: A History.* Boston: Twayne, 1991.

Mattera, Philip. *World Class Business.* New York: Henry Holt and Company, 1992.

1987 Census of Manufacturers, Rubber Products. Washington, DC: U.S. Bureau of the Census, 1990.

—Douglas B. Hoyt

SIC 3021

RUBBER AND PLASTICS FOOTWEAR

This category covers establishments primarily engaged in manufacturing fabric footwear having rubber or plastic soles vulcanized, injection molded, or cemented to the uppers, and rubber and plastics protective footwear. Establishments primarily engaged in manufacturing rubber, composition, and fiber heels, soles, soling strips, and related shoe making and repairing materials are classified in **SIC 3069: Fabricated Rubber Products, Not Elsewhere Classified**; those manufacturing plastic soles and soling strips are classified in **SIC 3089: Plastics Products, Not Elsewhere Classified**; and those manufacturing other footwear of rubber or plastics are classified in **SIC Group 314: Footwear, Except Rubber**.

SIC 3021 consists primarily of two product areas. One area includes the waterproof footwear worn over shoes to protect them from inclement weather. Such products are often referred to as rubbers, overshoes, galoshes, and arctics. Also included in this area are rubber boots which are not worn over shoes but protect the feet from mud and water. The second area consists of rubber soled canvas shoes, generally known as sneakers. While other athletic shoes featuring rubber soles and a fabric upper are considered in this category, those with leather uppers belong to other SIC classifications.

The rubber footwear industry is largely based on the ability of rubber to protect against water and rain. An early breakthrough was made around 1920 by a Scottish chemist, Charles Macintosh, who developed rubberized waterproof cloaks which became known as "mackintoshes." Later, Macintosh's associate, Thomas Hancock, devised ways to process rubber so that it could be used as a material for footwear. By the 1990s, the manufacture of footwear required more rubber than that of any other product except tires. The sewing of uppers to rubber soles had been superseded by the use of adhesives or vulcanizing directly.

The rubber and plastics footwear industry in 1987 was made up of 55 companies operating 65 establishments with a total of 10,900 employees. Some of the companies manufactured rubber plastic footwear exclusively, while others maintained it as a modest or minor product line. The 65 establishments in 1987 were located in 14 states, with a concentration of eight companies in California and six in New York and Pennsylvania each. The industry has maintained fairly level sales between 1989 and 1992. In 1992, total sales amounted to $797.2 million.

Companies devoted exclusively to rubber and plastic footwear in 1992 included Vans Inc. of Orange, California, which had $70.2 million in annual sales and 2,200 employees; Suave Shoe Corp. of Hileah, Florida, with $53 million annual sales and 1,250 employees; and La Crosse Footwear Inc. of La Crosse, Wisconsin, showing $60 million in annual sales and maintaining 750 employees. Converse Inc. of North Reading, Massachusetts, was primarily but not exclusively engaged in the manufacture of rubber and plastics footwear. Its rate of annual sales in 1992 was $300 million, and it had 2700 employees.

Although these companies represented the leading manufacturers of rubber and plastics footwear in the United States, the leaders in the wholesale sneaker market in 1990 produced well-known brand name products using facilities outside of the United States. Of the American sneaker market, Nike controlled 26.2 percent, Reebok held 23.49 percent, L.A. Gear held 15.36 percent, and Keds held 4.52 percent.

Much of the rubber and plastic footwear sold in the United States has been produced in other countries, largely due to lower production costs available in foreign countries. Although sneakers represented a $5.5 billion industry in the United States in 1990, the value of rubber or plastic soled footwear produced and shipped within the United States was estimated at only $561.230 for that year.

Employment in the industry decreased by 65 percent, from 31,600 to 17,600, between 1972 and 1987, caused in part by moves to lower cost suppliers overseas. Nevertheless, total employment had risen from 10,900 in 1987 to 11,700 in 1991, indicating a stabilization trend in the industry.

Support for the industry's activities and interests are provided by the Footwear Industries of America (FIA), a trade association founded in 1869 for footwear producers, marketers, and suppliers. FIA is based in Washington, D. C.

Furthermore, the Shoe and Allied Trades Research Association (SATRA) maintains a Footwear Technology Centre in England. This group of 170 scientists, technicians, and support staff assists its 1,100 members in 40 countries by helping to control manufacturing costs and improve quality. Its members are footwear manufacturers, material and machinery suppliers, repairers, and retailers.

SATRA has done a great deal of pioneering research, providing industry members with technology too costly for the modest to small companies in the footwear business to develop on their own. For example, SATRA has developed beneficial concepts in the areas of ergonomics, color durability, the environment, materials standards, quality control, and computer applications like CAD/CAM, robotics, and bar coding.

INDUSTRY INFORMATION SOURCES

Current Industrial Reports, Footwear, Fourth Quarter 1992, MQ31A(92)-4. Washington, D.C.: Bureau of the Census.

—Douglas B. Hoyt

SIC 3052

RUBBER AND PLASTICS HOSE AND BELTING

This category covers establishments primarily engaged in manufacturing rubber and plastics hose and belting, including garden hose. Establishments primarily engaged in manufacturing rubber tubing are classified in **SIC 3061: Molded, Extruded, and Lathe-Cut Mechanical Rubber Goods** and **SIC 3069: Fabricated Rubber Products, Not Elsewhere Classified.** Those companies manufacturing plastics tubing are classified in **SIC 3082: Unsupported Plastics Profile Shapes.** Those establishments manufacturing flexible metallic hose are classified in **SIC 3599: Industrial and Commercial Machinery and Equipment, Not Elsewhere Classified.**

INDUSTRY SNAPSHOT

More than 125 companies make hose and belting in the United States in a market that approached the $3-billion-a-year range entering the mid-1990s. Manufacturing companies range from a myriad of small shops filling niche markets all the way up to several firms producing broad product lines with sales approaching or exceeding $1 billion a year.

The number of companies in the industry, however, actually dropped from the late 1980s to the early 1990s because of the effects of restructuring and a move toward automation. These actions, though, helped the remaining players be more productive.

Hose and belting products find usage in a wide variety of industries. Hoses are used in such varied markets as automobiles, construction, and oil and gas. Transmission belting is used to help power cars, industrial machinery, agricultural equipment, household appliances, and construction equipment. Flat belting, commonly known as conveyor belting, finds usage from traditional markets such as mining and material handling as well as in lighter weight applications such as food handling and airline luggage conveyor systems.

Economies of scale are difficult to achieve except for some of the larger firms because a large number of products need short runs, and many of the lines have differences in chemical compounds and machinery needs. States with the greatest amount of hose and belt production include Colorado, Nebraska, North Carolina, and Ohio.

In the market, rubber remains the predominant material, accounting for between 70 and 80 percent of the products. For example, rubber is the main material for hose, except in garden hose, where plastic takes the majority of share. Other materials, though, are expected to make some inroads as higher performing products are needed.

ORGANIZATION AND STRUCTURE

Much of the structure of the hose and belting industry is organized around how the product gets to its eventual end user—either in the original equipment (OE) or replacement market. Looking at the automotive market, the OE market is much more straightforward, as most of the products are sold directly to the auto makers.

Sales to the aftermarket, though, are a bit more complicated, going through either a three-step or two-step distribution process. In the three-step process, the manufacturer sells his hose or belting to a wholesale distributor that handles automotive parts lines. The distributor in turn sells the product to what is known as a jobber, an example of which would include the NAPA store chain. The final step is for the jobber to sell the hose and belting to the installer—the repair shop that does work on the automobiles. Some manufacturers have increasingly tried to shorten the process by skipping the initial step and selling right to the jobber.

Historically, this has been the most efficient way to get to market, ensuring that there is plenty of inventory in the aftermarket so that people can get the necessary part for their car at almost any time. Hose and belt manufacturers, however, have had to shift with the times as the places where people get their automobiles serviced have evolved. While the total number of outlets for repair service has remained virtually unchanged, the make-up has changed considerably.

Prior to the growth in popularity of self-serve gasoline stations, about 150,000 gas stations in the United States also offered automotive service, By 1990, however, that number had declined to 100,000. Conversely, the number of repair-only shops had

grown from 110,000 to 140,000. Moreover, import car owners used to be much more likely to get their automobiles fixed at the dealer, but that has changed as repair shops have become more attuned to repairing imports. The number of retail auto stores also increased, from about 27,000 in 1980 to 40,000 a decade later, taking additional volume away from the jobbers.

Through all these changes, the hose and belt makers have had to ensure that their distribution system is getting the parts to the proper outlet in a timely fashion. Distribution also plays an important role in the industrial hose and belt markets. Many of these distributors also serve as fabricators, placing needed attachments and accessories onto the basic hose and belts for their final usage. The distributors in this sector also are more likely to play a role in OE accounts, especially for an account that needs to have local inventory. As for the aftermarket, a major portion of the business is sold through distribution sectors, although some hose and belt makers do sell some product directly to the end user.

Distributors also play a major role in times of overcapacity. While only four to five firms make broad lines across many industries, there are enough niche manufacturers to ensure stiff competition in all product areas. This situation gives the distributor an advantage in getting a lower price on products.

Types of Products. A hose is a flexible pipe or conduit that is intended to serve as a means to move material from one place to another. The three basic elements of a hose are the tube, carcass, and cover. The tube is the part of the hose that comes in contact with the fluid and therefore must be resistant to the material. The reinforcement gives the hose strength to withstand any forces, external or internal, that might be encountered, while the cover protects the product from environmental forces.

Although hoses can be referred to by their usage—such as gasoline, air or garden hose—manufacturers and users generally classify the products by the method of reinforcement. The common hose types include:

Knitted Hose. A flexible product knitted in an open-loop manner, the garden hose is a typical example of this kind of product. This type generally is subjected only to low pressure.

Braided Hose. One of the more common hose types, it is produced when a single or multiple ends of yarn, cord, or wire are woven over the tube. The size and type of reinforcement material, as well as the angle, help establish the strength of the hose. These hose types find a variety of usage, from air, water, garden, spray or low-pressure liquid transfer, to more demanding applications like hydraulic, steam and high-pressure transfer of liquid and gases.

Wrapped Fabric Hose. This type of hose is reinforced with an impregnated woven fabric that can be applied by hand or machine. This makes for a stiff, bulky hose that is commonly used in suction or vacuum applications.

Wire Spiralled Hose. Used for hose facing high impulse pressures. Wires are put on in opposite directions to counter the twisting effect of applying the spiral wire.

Woven Jacket Hose. Looms are used for circular weaving of jackets for the hose; often used for fire hose. The design allows the hose to lie flat when not conveying water, for more efficient storage.

Hand-Built Hose. Used to make large hose that needs great strength and excellent crush resistance. Uses include rotary drill hose and oil suction and discharge hose.

Belting. Power transmission belts are more commonly known as V-belts. Given their name because they transmit power and motion between V-shaped sheaves, the belts are made in numerous sizes and lengths. V-belts are preferred where there is limited space. Major applications are in automotive, industrial, agriculture, fractional horsepower, and recreational uses. In automotive use, though, a poly-V, or serpentine belt, has become much more popular in newer car models.

Flat belting also is used in some limited power transmission applications, but the overwhelming use for these products is in conveying uses. Basic components of conveyor belts include the carcass, which bears the load and is usually made of several plies of rubber-coated textile fabric or a single layer of steel cable; the rubber cover, which must resist wear, cracking, and element pressures; the breaker, which improves adhesion between the carcass and cover; and the skim coating, used to hold the load-bearing plies together.

Conveyer belts are used for a variety of purposes, from the grocery market check-out stand, to coal mines where coal is conveyed from deep within the mine, to growing applications in recycling and waste management programs.

BACKGROUND AND DEVELOPMENT

This industry has undergone significant change over the past several decades. In automotive—the top market for hose and transmission belting—a catalog of about 50 V-belts and 100 hoses covered most of the cars on the road shortly after World War II. Cars became more complicated, however, and smaller cars (requiring smaller engine compartments) assumed increased market share over the 1970s and 1980s. Hose and belt manufacturers responded with products that conformed to the new size and weight demands of the automotive market.

The serpentine belt also made great inroads over the years. While designs at one time had several V-belts in the engine compartment, producers discovered that one serpentine belt could drive a number of operations simultaneously, resulting in savings in weight and space. In 1982 there were approximately 50 sizes of serpentine belts; a decade later that number had increased to between 200 and 250.

Belts and hose also last much longer in the modern era of manufacturing. Such products used to last 10,000 miles. In the modern era, however, hoses and belts commonly last for 40,000 miles or more of use.

CURRENT CONDITIONS

Rubber hose shipments were expected to increase 3.5 percent a year from 1991 to 1996, rising to $1.54 billion a year because of an increase in motor vehicle production and growth in other industrial and construction products. While showing steady growth, a lack of new applications and penetration by alternate materials were expected to keep the growth of rubber hose below the increases made by general industry. Imports, which have been felt in other rubber product markets, could limit growth in this industry sector as well. Commodity hose lines are the most likely to be affected by imports from Southeast Asia. Conversely, domestic hose makers are projected to raise their export sales.

Hydraulic hose shipments were projected to spur much of the industry's growth. In 1991 hydraulic hose accounted for 44 percent of the industrial hose market. But because of the specialty uses of the sector, it is less susceptible to imports and allows for better margins on the pricing side.

The rubber belt market was expected to reach $1.1 billion by 1996. Factors inducing growth were projected to include automobile sales and a growth in the sales of industrial equipment, two major belting markets. Both flat belting and V-belts were projected to enjoy robust growth in the mid-1990s. The latter category makes up nearly two-thirds of belt sales and was expected to grow 4.5 percent a year to $735 million annually. Automobiles will continue to be the largest market, but because rising sales of serpentine belts will hold down growth in this sector, some observers expect the percentage growth in industrial applications to nearly double that of the motor vehicle segment.

Flat belt growth was forecast to be 5.1 percent annually for the five-year period ending in 1996, which would bring the market to $433 million a year. The sector was projected for more growth because of expected new uses in waste recovery and handling systems and food handling equipment, where there is a movement toward increased automation.

INDUSTRY LEADERS

Gates Rubber Co., Dayco Products Inc., and Goodyear Tire & Rubber Co. generally are considered the top three hose and belt manufacturers in the United States.

Founded in 1911, Denver-based Gates has 10 hose and belt plants in the United States, two in Canada, and three in Mexico, as well as another 15 facilities around the world. The firm has a major presence in automotive, industrial and hydraulic markets, and posted worldwide 1993 rubber product sales—mainly from belts and hoses—of $1.12 billion.

Dayco, headquartered near Dayton, Ohio, is the largest operating unit of publicly held Mark IV Industries Inc. Dayco has 27 production facilities worldwide, including 14 in the United States, and has annual sales of about $900 million, a tremendous increase over its sales of $320 million in 1986. This surge has been accomplished through both internal growth and two major acquisitions—hose maker Anchor Swan in 1990 and the power transmission belting business of Italy's Pirelli S.p.A. in 1993.

Goodyear, the leading U.S. tire maker, also operates ten North American hose and belt plants. Although it does not release its hose and belt sales figures, the Akron, Ohio-based firm has major market shares in automotive hose and belts, industrial hose and belts, and heavy duty conveyor belting.

WORK FORCE

Total employment in the industry was estimated at 23,200 in 1992. Of these, about 17,200 were production workers earning about $11.35 an hour, according to government figures. Other occupations include chemists, product designers, engineers, and sales people.

The average number of workers per factory has decreased over the years because of increased productivity traceable to improved processes and automation. In 1972 19 hose and belt plants in the U.S.—about 21 percent of facilities—accounted for 76 percent of em-

ployment and 75 percent of shipments. A decade later, just nine plants employed 500 or more, accounting for 44 percent of employment and 39 percent of shipments. The average number of workers per plant dropped from 354 in 1972 to 187 in 1982 to just 124 in 1987.

AMERICA AND THE WORLD

Importers generally compete more easily in commodity lines than specialty ones, putting pricing pressure on U.S. firms. One trend that increased competition in this industry in the United States was the emergence of transplant auto makers, especially from Japan, in America. As these Japanese firms began production in the United States, it was not uncommon for their traditional domestic suppliers to follow them to America. Examples include power transmission belters MBL (USA) Inc., which located in Illinois, and Bando Manufacturing of America, which built its plant in Kentucky. There also was an increase in the number of joint ventures between Japanese and U.S. firms to supply the transplant car firms.

Some U.S. firms also have done quite well in Europe. One 1994 study showed Gates as the top automotive power transmission and timing belt maker in Europe, with 40 percent of the market, followed by Dayco with 15 percent and Goodyear, which doesn't manufacture the lines in Europe, at 10 percent.

RESEARCH AND TECHNOLOGY

Rubber hose, while still used in the overwhelming majority of industrial hose products, will face increased competition from other materials. Driving the need for new materials are a number of factors, such as the evolution of some of the traditional applications of the product. For example, alternate fuels and higher operating temperatures bring different requirements for hose products. When states begin to require higher alcohol content in fuel in order to reduce emissions, the hose materials must change as well. Specialty rubbers, plastic, Teflon and nylon are among materials expected to challenge commodity rubber.

Like hose, belts will be impacted by the shrinking of auto engine compartments. Because of hotter temperatures, belt makers will be forced to turn to new materials that will withstand the environment in which it is used. Some of the commodity types of rubber also will face competition from specialty rubbers and plastics.

INDUSTRY INFORMATION SOURCES
Babington, Mary, *Freedonia Study #416, Industrial Rubber Products,* Cleveland: Freedonia Group Inc., 1992.

"Belt Makers, Distributors Better Partners," *Rubber & Plastics News,* June 22, 1992.

"Dayco Chief Touts Teamwork," *Rubber & Plastics News,* June 7, 1993.

"Gates' Sales Increase 2.2%," *Rubber & Plastics News,* Feb. 21, 1994.

"Hose, Belts to Expand 2-3%," *Rubber & Plastics News,* January 20, 1992.

Long, Harry, ed., *Basic Compounding and Processing of Rubber,* Akron, OH: American Chemical Society Inc., 1985.

"Plant Sites for U.S.-based Hose, Belt Makers," *Rubber & Plastics News,* June 7, 1993.

Plehwe, Dieter, *Change and Concentration in the World Rubber Industry,* Brussels, Belgium: International Federation of Chemical, Energy and General Workers' Unions.

1987 Census of Manufacturers, Washington, DC: U.S. Department of Commerce, 1987.

"U.S. Dominates Auto Belt Market," *European Rubber Journal,* January 1994.

The Vanderbilt Rubber Handbook, Norwalk, CT: R.T. Vanderbilt Co. Inc., 1990.

—Bruce Meyer

SIC 3053

GASKETS, PACKING AND SEALING DEVICES

This category covers establishments primarily engaged in manufacturing gaskets, gasketing materials, compression packings, mold packings, oil seals, and mechanical seals. It includes gaskets, packing, and sealing devices made of rubber, leather, metal, asbestos, and plastics.

INDUSTRY SNAPSHOT

By definition, a seal is a "device for eliminating or controlling the leakage of liquids and/or gases while preventing the entrance of external contaminants such as dust and dirt," according to John J. Carr in the *Vanderbilt Rubber Handbook.*

Seals are divided into two classifications: static or dynamic. Static seals seal surfaces where there is no relative motion between the surfaces. An example of a static seal would be an engine cylinder-head gasket. Dynamic seals are used wherever relative motion exists between two surfaces, either intermittently or continuously. Examples are engine crank-shaft seals and hydraulic cylinder-rod seals.

There are several basic types of seals. Cup-packings are mainly used as piston-head seals. Previously made from leather, elastomers are now used for low-pressure, smaller-sized cups, while an elastomer/fabric blend is used for high-pressure applications. Cup-packings are particularly effective where clearance between surfaces to be sealed is excessive—for example, when sealing rough metal surfaces.

Gaskets typify the compression-sealing method. They are made from a wide variety of materials, often times used in combination with one another. For example, cork and elastomers are a popular combination in automotive usage because cork's compressibility and rubber's resiliency combine to give excellent results in such uses as engine gaskets. Gaskets can be molded or cut from a sheet. They are installed between two surfaces and pressure from bolting or clamping provides the sealing force.

Elastomeric gaskets are the most common type of non-metallic gasket. They can be made of synthetic rubber or thermoplastic elastomers (TPEs)—materials that have properties similar to rubber but are processed like plastics. Elastomeric gaskets are produced in a variety of sizes, colors, and finishes. They also can be produced to be specially resistant to such things as temperature, oil, chemicals, weathering, aging, and abrasion. With all these variations, as well as the variety of elastomers available, the applications vary tremendously. Simple applications would include such things as plumbing gaskets, while other, more sophisticated gaskets find advanced applications in aerospace products.

The simplest and most common sealing device, O-rings are used in numerous systems. They can be used in static and dynamic applications, depending on the proper design. Among their primary uses are as components in automotive steering and brake systems, off-the-road heavy equipment, aircraft, and other industrial and household items.

Mechanical face ceals are a multi-component sealing device used to create a leakage-free seal between a rotating shaft and a member through which the shaft passes. They are used in automotive water pumps and in the chemical process industries.

Molded packings and seals are mainly used in such things as fluid handling pumps, valves, cylinders, piston-type accumulators, and other equipment. They can be used as seals on the rod, ram, piston, plunger stem, or spool to develop and maintain hydraulic working power. They find their main applications in static sealing uses. Molded seals include squeeze-type ring seals and lip types. Squeeze seals are used in low-pressure applications, with lip seals finding more usage in high-pressure needs.

Radial lip seals are used in dynamic, low-pressure applications. Many are available in standard sizes but the trend is to customized production.

U-packings are pressure-activated sealing devices commonly used in low to moderate dynamic sealing applications. They can be found in such things as pneumatically or hydraulically activated door openers.

Three or more seals are often used together in the low-speed, high-pressure dynamic applications common to V-packings. In one of this type of seal's many end-product uses, V-packings are found in heavy-duty hydraulic cylinders of off-the-road earth-moving equipment.

Gaskets and seals are vital to the operation of many types of equipment. Three markets—transportation equipment, industrial equipment and machinery, and electrical equipment—account for more than 90 percent of total demand. Of this, sales to original equipment manufacturers (OEMs) account for about 40 percent of revenue, and aftermarket sales an additional 60 percent.

Transportation equipment, including automobiles, is the largest OEM customer, accounting for 40 percent of total sales. The cyclical nature of the market resulting from such dependency on automobile sales has been offset by the relative stability of aftermarket demand for industry products.

By 1992, U.S. shipments in the seals and gasket industry were estimated at $2.87 billion, about 72 percent higher than a decade earlier. Gaskets held the greatest share, at $1.38 billion, followed by molded seals, $801 million; shaft seals, $568 million; and compression packings, $116 million.

ORGANIZATION AND STRUCTURE

This industry supports varied manufacturing and other industries, gaining its existence from the end use of its products rather than from the products themselves. Because of the industry's dependency on the health of the economy in general, the demand for gaskets, seals, and packings mirrors the cycles experienced by the makers of the durable goods that utilize such supplies.

Makers of gaskets and seals are also influenced by their customers in areas such as product development, production processes, marketing, and pricing. With the large number of suppliers available, end users can bargain not only for better pricing, but for better service as well.

Other variables outside the control of U.S. gasket and seal manufacturers combine to affect the market.

For example, since the early 1980s, the industry saw a rise not only in the amount of gaskets and seals imported into the U.S., but also in the variety of types of machinery in which such products were used. Varying levels of industrial production have also impacted the market.

Among the three major markets, transportation equipment uses accounted for 46 percent of gasket and seal demand in 1992. The transportation sector used more than $1.38 billion worth of product, nearly double the amount used a decade before. Industrial equipment and machinery accounted for 27 percent of applications, totaling $820 million in 1992. The final major end use, electrical and electronic equipment, took up $577 million, or 19 percent of gasket and seal sales in 1992. A fourth market, instruments, accounted for the remaining 8 percent, posting $91 million in sales in 1992.

Although sales to OEMs were predicted to grow at a faster pace than aftermarket sales, from 1987 to 1992 the aftermarket gained on OEMs as durable goods production was depressed by an economic slump. Traditionally, when economic times are tough, the replacement market generally shows greater increases because companies delay purchases of new equipment and spend money instead on maintenance of existing machinery. But when the economy goes up, this is reversed and OEM sales rise quicker as more new equipment is purchased.

BACKGROUND AND DEVELOPMENT

Historically, a number of different types of seals have been used in general applications. They are: gaskets, U-packings, V-packings, cup packings and O-rings. In time, the uses for seals have multiplied and improvements in materials and technology have allowed seal manufacturers to offer a product with extended life and better performance.

The sealing industry encountered many challenges during the 1980s and '90s as applications for sealing products became more complex. Aeronautical and oil-field consumers were among the first to push for more demanding requirements. Elastomeric seal chemists and engineers were forced to advance technology from a "so-called art," to an "engineering science," according to Kerry C. Smith in *Rubber & Plastics News*.

Traditional materials such as cork, rubber, paper, and felt soon began to give way to specialty materials. For example, rubber gaskets used to be found in low-pressure and temperature uses. However, rubber is not always the material of choice for gaskets, because contact with oil and grease negatively impact its performance in such uses as the automobile aftermarket. The success of rubber in such usage is dependent on proper installation. Higher engine temperatures also negatively impact the selection of rubber for automobile gaskets. Specialty rubbers and TPEs more easily met the newer, more demanding standards and allowed the number of possible gasket applications to grow.

The synthetic rubber category can be broken into three sub-categories: commodity rubbers, medium performance rubbers, and specialty rubbers. The commodity types generally cost the least, but offer less in the area of performance. In the past, these types generally took the largest percentage of elastomeric gasket usage. More recently the trend has been toward the medium-performance and advanced rubbers. Among medium performance types, ethylene-propylene rubber, commonly known as EPDM, has found greater acceptance because it offers better weatherability and abrasion resistance.

Specialty rubbers are usually available in low volume and give the best performance, but at a markedly higher cost. These advanced materials have seen wider applications in head gaskets, manifold gaskets, and oven-door and other appliance gaskets. A number of these elastomers offer higher heat resistance, along with high fuel and oil resistance. Silicone rubber, especially, is being used more and more in aerospace applications.

Various TPEs find gasketing applications because they are resistant to oil and other engine fluids, are light-weight, and offer superior durability. But TPEs haven't achieved greater market share because their heat resistance has not been comparable to some of the specialty rubbers. TPEs are expected to continue to gain in non-critical uses and will grow into more critical areas after their heat resistance is improved.

About 80 percent of the elastomeric gaskets manufactured have been made of various synthetic rubbers, with TPEs accounting for the remainder. Since the early 1980s, however, TPEs have increased their share. By the end of the 1990s, specialty synthetic rubbers are projected to once again show the highest percentage growth.

Examples of increasingly demanding design- and life-requirements in automotive applications have included the ability to seal the non-chlorinated refrigerants that began replacing the chlorofluorinated refrigerants (CFCs) that were historically used. Auto makers looked for near-zero permeation, but also expected seals to last up to 150,000 miles in engines operating at increasingly higher temperatures.

Current Conditions

The transportation equipment sector projected an annual growth rate of 6.6 percent through the end of the 1990s. Industrial equipment and related machinery was expected to have the highest growth, 7.2 percent, with sales forecast to hit $1.6 billion by 1997. The third major market sector, electrical and electronic equipment, expected to attain annual growth of 6.5 percent over the same period.

Such increases were expected to be fueled by better sales of cars and industrial equipment. The shift to more specialty materials—such as carbon and aramid fibers, fluoroplastics, and expanded graphite— were predicted to increase the value of shipments relative to actual unit demand. Advances in auto engineering that resulted in greater engine temperatures also helped such specialty materials gain favor.

Manufacturers of molded seals, gaskets, and packings forecast the fastest growth—shipments totaled $801 million in 1992—because of the service the products provide in both static and dynamic sealing applications. Growth projections for molded seals alone called for annual increases of 7.1 percent, which would make it a $1.1 billion market by 1997. The advantages molded seals have over other seal types and an increase in durable goods production were seen as factors in growth potential. Also contributing to the growth was an effort underway to enact stricter fluid controls in the chemicals and petroleum industries.

An expected recovery by the automobile market and other durable goods makers would allow the growth of nonmetallic gaskets to outpace other industries. Recovering demand in the industrial equipment and machinery market was also expected to help.

O-rings and other ring seals continued to be the most commonly used products in this segment. O-rings and other ring seals accounted for $374 million of the $801 million in molded seals usage in 1992.

OEM sales were projected to increase 7.3 percent a year through 1997, bringing this segment to $1.8 billion in sales. Replacement sales were expected to climb to $2.5 billion in 1997, which would be a 6.4-percent increase annually. Areas expected to receive growth were transportation equipment servicing, manufacturing markets, and the utilities market. Though OEM sales were projected to grow at a more rapid pace, the aftermarket would still provide the majority of sales because of the broad base of existing machinery and equipment that would be serviced.

Specialty materials were expected to see higher growth than traditional commodity materials such as cork and rubber. Because of new applications, studies projected elastomeric gasket usage to rise 7.7 percent a year to $511 million by 1997. Much of the increased usage was expected to involve these higher performing elastomers. By contrast, overall gasket usage was expected to climb just 6.9 percent a year.

INDUSTRY LEADERS

Freudenberg-NOK of Plymouth, Michigan, Detroit-based Federal-Mogul Corp., and CR Industries Inc. in Elgin, Illinois, are among the U.S.-based leaders in this industry. As these firms also derive revenue from other sources, it is difficult to pinpoint their exact sales in this category.

Other firms with a significant presence in the industry include Cleveland-based Parker Hannifin Corp.; Wynn's Precision Inc. of Lebanon, Tennessee; John Crane Inc. in Vandelia, Illinois; and Coltec Industries' Garlock Mechanical Packing Division in Palmyra, New York.

WORK FORCE

Total employment in the industry was about 28,400 according to the latest figures available from the U.S. government. The leading states in terms of employment were California, Illinois, Ohio, and Texas. The range of employment varies extensively, from factory workers producing the products, to chemists and engineer who develop the compounds and design, to the sales force that deals with OEM and aftermarket accounts.

RESEARCH AND TECHNOLOGY

In response to increasing imports, many makers of gaskets and seals took a proactive stance, cutting manufacturing costs, going to advanced production concepts such as computer-aided design, and after-uses that had the opportunity to provide greater than average growth. Examples of such applications are non-asbestos gasketing or seals designed to reduce emissions in process industries. Industry participants also spent to improve product design. These actions helped the industry maintain steady growth since the early 1980s.

Despite their uses in highly complex applications, gasket and seal technology itself is more defined. Developments have come in the form of the new materials being used and demands from customers. Capital costs aren't immense, but investment has been needed to keep up with these continuing shifts.

Firms in the gasket and seal industry that looked ahead at long-term industry prospects needed to be focused toward customer demands and ready to invest in new technology and product development.

INDUSTRY INFORMATION SOURCES

Ita, Paul. *Freedonia Study #516: Gaskets & Seals,* Cleveland: Freedonia Group Inc., 1993.

Carr, John J., contributor. *The Vanderbilt Rubber Handbook,* Norwalk, CT: R. T. Vanderbilt Co. Inc., 1990.

Smith, Kerry C. "Seal Industry Rediscovers Stress Relaxation," *Rubber & Plastics News,* Jan. 31, 1994.

1987 Census of Manufacturers, Washington, DC: U.S. Department of Commerce.

—Bruce Meyer

SIC 3061

MOLDED, EXTRUDED AND LATHE-CUT MECHANICAL RUBBER GOODS

This category covers establishments primarily engaged in manufacturing molded, extruded, and lathe-cut mechanical rubber goods. The products are generally parts for machinery and equipment. Establishments primarily engaged in manufacturing other industrial rubber goods, rubberized fabric and miscellaneous rubber specialties and sundries are classified in **SIC 3069: Fabricated Rubber Products, Not Elsewhere Classified.**

INDUSTRY SNAPSHOT

Molded, extruded, and lathe-cut goods are used in various machinery and equipment. End uses for these products exist in automobiles, oil and gas equipment, appliances, farm equipment, and construction machinery. About 600 firms in the U.S. make molded, extruded, and lathe-cut goods. The market is fragmented due to the diversity of the end uses; no single company has dominated the industry. The sector also faces strong foreign competition. The U.S. and Canadian market alone was estimated at $5.1 billion in 1993, with sales of about $5.8 billion by 1997. Total U.S. employment industry-wide is in the area of 50,000 people.

Much of the products in this segment have been custom-made to various end-user specifications. As such, manufacturers often sell them with a higher profit margin. Such customer orders have helped this sector show a higher rate of growth in shipment value than other industries.

Entering the mid-1990s, the recovery of the U.S. automobile industry was projected to fuel growth in industrial rubber products, which find more than half their end uses in cars. Other areas of growth were expected to be manufacturing, mining, construction, oil and natural gas, appliances and agriculture.

Competition from imports and other materials such as plastics, which cut processing time by eliminating the curing step necessary to rubber production, were expected to hold back overall growth. As auto makers continue to ask for just-in-time delivery to decrease inventories, the advantage of plastics could provide a competitive edge in some uses.

Background and Development

The term ''molded goods'' encompasses a wide-ranging group of products whose shape is determined by the mold in which they are produced. Markets using molded goods include automotive and other types of transportation, appliances, oil and gas fields, off-high-way machinery, and equipment used in such industries as construction, farm, lawn and garden, and mining. Benefits of molded goods include resiliency, insulation, cushioning, flexibility, and vibration- or noise-dampening.

Among the myriad of products produced in this segment of the industry are automotive and off-high-way air springs; chassis bumpers; engine and truck mounts; automotive vibration dampeners; weatherstripping; wiper blades; pedals and pedal pads; rubber marine bearings; bellows, grommets and mounts used in appliances; drill pipe protectors; shock absorber mounts; conveyor wheels; pool table bumpers; and railroad-crossing pads.

The rubber mold, normally made from steel, is the most important component in the molding process; it gives the part its geometry and ensures that it has the proper dimensions, look, and functions. The choice of molding process—compression, transfer, or injection—takes into account many variables because none of the three main methods can handle all applications. Some hybrid processes, combining two of the three molding techniques, have become popular in some uses.

Compression molding is the most widely-used technique due to its relative simplicity. The material is placed in the mold and compressed using hydraulic clamp pressure. When the cycle is completed, the clamp is released and the product removed from the mold. The mold can be virtually any size as long as sufficient clamping pressure exists.

This molding process generally has the least-expensive mold and yields minimal amounts of waste rubber. Drawbacks include having the longest cure time (the cycle it takes for the product to be formed); the number of finishing operations necessary to render the product usable; and the lack of control over meeting exact customer specifications.

Transfer molding is a more precise process. The material is transferred from a pot—normally located above the mold cavities—down to the mold at the desired time. The technique gives better tolerance control; it ensures that the mold is closed before rubber is introduced to eliminate exposure to the environment; it can be used when other items are to be inserted into the rubber product; and it offers a sometimes substantially shorter curing time. Transfer molding, however, leaves more waste, requires moderate secondary operations, and requires a more expensive mold.

Injection molding requires the most expensive press and molds, but often yields the lowest overall cost to produce the part as it gives more options for automation. Material is injected into a closed mold from an injection barrel. One injection system can be used to feed material into several molds, either by having the injector automatically moved to different molds, or by having several molds rotate to a fixed injection unit. The part removal operation also is a good candidate for automation. Other benefits include high-precision parts; lowest rubber-prepping cost; shortest cycle times; and minimal exposure to the environment during the molding process. Drawbacks to injection molding include expensive tooling and the potential for large amounts of waste if proper precautions aren't taken.

An extruder is a power-driven screw enclosed in a cylinder. In the extruded molding process, material goes in one end and is sent through the cylinder by a rotating screw. At the other end, the material is fed through a die, a steel mold designed to produce the desired shape of the product being made. Among the products made using extrusion are cables; wire insulation; door and deck automotive lid seals; window and glass channels in cars; wiper blades; and rubber tubing used in medical, automotive, and appliance applications.

Extruded goods are flexible and good for sealing. They offer the advantage of low-cost permanent tooling and high production rates. Extrusion dies to make prototypes can be produced swiftly and for little cost.

Extruders have been in use for more than 150 years in industry. Originally, the rubber going into the extruder had to be pre-warmed so it could be conveyed through the extruder. This hot-feed extrusion method was time-consuming and required great amounts of labor to complete the warming process.

Earlier this century, however, cold-feed extruders were developed. These machines accept material at room temperature and include components designed to warm and soften the material for final forming. These machines are sometimes three times longer than hot-feed extruders, but they result in faster cycles, lower labor costs, and more uniform products. Recent studies have emphasized new designs for more effective self-feeding of the material and higher output rates.

Lathe-cut goods are by far the smallest segment of the category, accounting for just more than $50 million in business in the U.S. in 1991. Automotive is by far the largest category, accounting for about 80 percent of usage.

Lathe-cut products in automotive include oil filter washers; fuel system components; disc brake washers; and electric and electronic parts. Other areas using these goods are agriculture, communications, filtration, material handling, printing, and pumps and valves used in water systems.

CURRENT CONDITIONS

As auto makers remain the single largest customer of molded, extruded, and lathe-cut products, their demands have a large impact on the industry. During the 1990s, for example, it was common in the automotive industry for manufacturers to reduce their supplier base. While in the past an auto maker may have a bought a single part from many firms, he now became more selective in vendor selection and began buying that part from fewer and fewer vendors. Auto companies became more stringent in their requests for high

quality, on-time delivery, quick response to requests and, as always, competitive pricing.

Auto makers also began to ask suppliers of these products to supply the technical capability to develop a component from conception to finished product. This enabled vehicle manufacturers to cut their own development overhead and leave certain design work to companies with expertise in that particular discipline. Full-service molders and extruders, therefore, were expected to make the most gains.

While there have been an increasing number of companies in this industry gaining size, industry executives agree that there will always be a place for the so-called ''job shops'' which do custom work on products that often are short-run. These firms offer quick turn-around on prototypes and fill niche markets that larger molders can't service cost-effectively. Job shops are often run by entrepreneurial types, carry lower overheads, and are highly flexible. One government study found that single-establishment companies with up to 20 employees accounted for seven percent of the total value of shipments in this category.

Growth prospects for U.S. consumption of molded goods was projected in one study at 7.1 percent a year for the five years leading up to 1996. That would bring the U.S.-only market to $3.8 billion, more than $1.1 billion higher than 1991.

Prices were expected to increase more than commodity items, again due to many of the parts being custom-made. Major end-use markets, including automotive, were expected to be strong. Transportation usage was estimated at $1.5 billion in 1991 ($1.3 billion of that was automotive) and that segment was forecast to grow to $2.06 billion.

Other areas of strong growth were expected to be transportation, off-highway machinery, appliances,

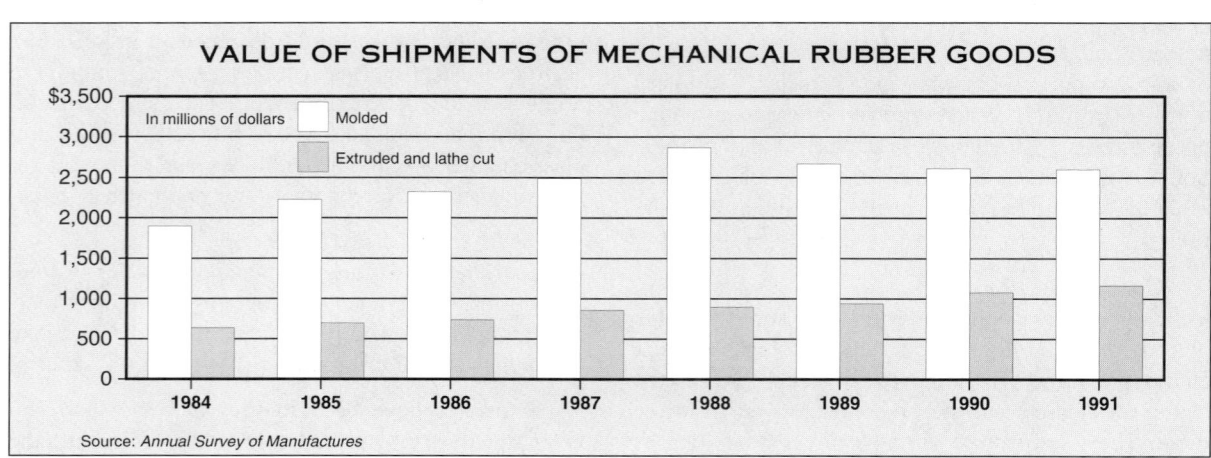

VALUE OF SHIPMENTS OF MECHANICAL RUBBER GOODS

In millions of dollars — Molded; Extruded and lathe cut

Source: *Annual Survey of Manufactures*

and other miscellaneous applications, all above six percent a year. Off-highway machinery parts accounted for $202 million in shipments in 1991 and was projected to reach $290 million in 1996; appliance applications were forecast to rise from $130 million to $190 million in the same time period; and other applications were slated to rise from $775 million to $1.17 billion. Such gains were forecast based on the assumption that capital spending in these areas would grow following the recession of the early 1990s.

Growth in molded products for oil and gas machinery was expected to lag behind, at just 2.1 percent a year. The sector was projected to climb from $83 million to $92 million between 1991 and 1996. The slow growth was expected because U.S. oil production was dropping and natural gas production was expected to go up only slightly.

Strong growth in certain niche markets, including wiper blades and vibration control products, was expected. Use of molded products in the latter area mirrored auto maker's efforts to try to provide smoother-riding vehicles.

Extruded rubber products shipments in the United States were forecast to grow 10.7 percent, jumping to $1.38 billion by 1996. Strong growth of end-use markets was expected to bring extruded product growth of above ten percent on all market. These products were also likely to benefit from solid niche markets and good performance and processing characteristics.

Automotive extrusions, not including tubing, were projected to grow from $425 million to $700 million between 1991 and 1996. Tubing was forecast to rise from $170 million to $285 million. Extrusions for appliances were expected to nearly double, from $88 million to $150 million in 1996. Miscellaneous markets were expected to account for $245 million in business by 1996, compared with just $147 million in 1991.

One niche market expected to rise quickly was weatherstripping, both that used in automobiles and in other markets. The product found favor with consumers and manufacturers alike because of its ability to reduce noise and keep out the elements. Another growing specialty niche was foam rubber for automobile cushioning, which was predicted to rise because of the ever-growing concentration on safety and comfort.

Shipments of lathe-cut goods were forecast to increase 5.7 percent a year, reaching $120 million in 1996. The segment also was expected to benefit from a stronger automotive market and rising spending on industrial equipment. Growth was, however, predicted to be confined by competition from other materials and imports.

INDUSTRY LEADERS

Because of the fragmented nature of the industry, no one firm or small group of firms dominate. Several companies do, however, have a substantial presence.

Akron, Ohio-based GenCorp Inc. had nearly $700 million in rubber product sales in 1992, many of these involving molded and extruded goods for the automotive market. Cleveland-based Standard Products Inc. reported more than $400 million in rubber product sales that year, a good portion coming from automotive sealing and other molded and extruded goods. In addition, Cooper Tire & Rubber Co. in Findlay, Ohio, continued to be a major presence in molded goods for automotive vibration controls.

Michigan-based Freudenberg-NOK General Partnership—a joint venture between a Japanese and a German firm—had $300 million in rubber product sales with production of molded goods at about ten factories in North America. Lord Corp. of Erie, Pennsylvania, posted $140 million in rubber product sales, with most of that in molded mounts and other goods. Clevite Elastomers of Milan, Ohio, and Goshen Rubber Co. Inc. in Goshen, Indiana, also posted annual sales in these areas of about $100 million.

AMERICA AND THE WORLD

Imports from Europe and the Far East have played a significant role in the market. Some U.S. firms, in turn, explored service niche or specialty markets that have traditionally been harder for imports to penetrate than markets for commodity products.

Joint ventures, especially with Japanese-owned companies, also became prevalent. These helped U.S. firms gain business with both foreign auto makers as well as transplant companies that make cars and other products in America.

RESEARCH AND TECHNOLOGY

Plastic products are expected to continue to challenge rubber for end-product applications that require more stringent characteristics. As auto makers design smaller engine compartments in an effort to improve fuel efficiency and work in conjunction with front-wheel drive systems, they will demand better-performing products. As smaller compartments lead to hotter engine temperatures, automotive components will need to be made of materials with higher heat tolerances.

While traditional rubbers have continued to be used, other materials have been tested. Specialty elastomers, a synthetic rubber made for such specific uses, and thermoplastic elastomers, a material that is processed like a plastic but has the properties of rubber, are among the materials vying for increased usage. New fuels, mandated to reduce harmful emissions into the air, will also factor into material selections in the future.

New techniques will continue to evolve. One such predicted growth area is liquid injection molding (LIM) using silicone rubber. This process was unveiled in the late 1970s amid much hype as to how it would simplify life for molders. According to early literature, the liquid material went directly into the machine and the finished product came out—supposedly eliminating the need for several secondary operations necessary with traditional rubber molding.

While the reality of LIM didn't quite meet its promise when it was first introduced, improvements it its technology in the early 1990s increased its popularity. Molders of components for medical devices, especially, adopted the process, with many adding or expanding LIM capability. The draw for medical molders has been the ability to make a clean product—the finished component emerges virtually untouched—that meets tight tolerances.

Cellular manufacturing has also gained in prominence. In this process, molding and secondary finishing operations all take place in one "cell," eliminating the necessity for the product to be moved to different areas of the plant. This improves quality, product flow, and efficiency, and helps reduce staffing requirements as well.

Industry products themselves are expected to continue to evolve. One such area is in the field of vibration control products for automobiles, which have traditionally been passive systems. With use of a rubber mount, engineers can control a single frequency that causes noise or motion of the vehicle. More advanced mounts have been designed to control two frequency-related problems.

Technology is evolving, though, to a future where cars will have adaptive or active vibration control systems. Computer-controlled actuators and sensors will be used in conjunction with the rubber mounts, allowing the product to adapt to numerous frequencies.

INDUSTRY INFORMATION SOURCES

Babington, Mary. *Freedonia Study #416, Industrial Rubber Products,* Cleveland: Freedonia Group Inc., 1992.

"Hot Ticket: Molders Scramble to Expand LIM Capacity," *Rubber & Plastics News,* Feb. 15, 1993.

"Job Shops: Is Bigger Better?" *Rubber & Plastics News,* Nov. 23, 1992.

Long, Harry, ed. *Basic Compounding and Processing of Rubber,* Akron, OH: American Chemical Society Inc. Rubber Division, 1985.

"RMA Projects Slow Growth through 1987," *Rubber & Plastics News,* Nov. 23, 1992.

Smith, Maurice, and James F. Walder, contributors. *The Vanderbilt Rubber Handbook,* Norwalk, CT: R. T. Vanderbilt Co. Inc., 1990.

"U.S. Rubber Industry's Top 50," *Rubber & Plastics News,* July 5, 1993.

1987 Census of Manufacturers, Washington, DC: U.S. Department of Commerce, 1987.

—Bruce Meyer

SIC 3069

FABRICATED RUBBER PRODUCTS, NOT ELSEWHERE CLASSIFIED

This category covers establishments primarily engaged in manufacturing industrial rubber goods, rubberized fabrics and vulcanized rubber clothing, and miscellaneous rubber specialties and sundries, not elsewhere classified. Included in this industry are establishments primarily engaged in reclaiming rubber and rubber articles. Establishments primarily engaged in the wholesale distribution of scrap rubber are classified in **SIC 5093: Scrap and Waste Materials.** Establishments primarily engaged in rebuilding and retreading tires are classified in **SIC 7534: Tire Retreading and Repair Shops;** those manufacturing rubberized clothing from purchased materials are classified in **SIC 2385: Waterproof Outerwear;** and those manufacturing gaskets and packing are classified in **SIC 3053: Gaskets, Packing, and Sealing Devices.**

INDUSTRY SNAPSHOT

This industry includes more than 100 rubber products not classified in other rubber products industries. The total value of U.S. shipments for these products was estimated at $6.7 billion in 1993 and was expected to continue to realize growth of about three percent per year. Since 1987, the value of shipments gradually rose from $5.4 billion to the 1993 level. Only in 1992 did business drop at all, falling two percent.

The main reason for the projected rise was expected growing demand by manufacturers for rubber products, although higher consumer spending also was expected to help. Items used in automobiles and those related to health protection were forecast to show larger percentage increases than the average. With a large number of players in these market segments, firms must continue to focus on improved customer service, product design, and delivery. U.S. firms export a good deal of products to industrialized countries, but also import a considerable amount of low-cost products from developing nations. Manufacturers are expected to continue focusing on flexible, customer-oriented production. Developments of new materials also are forecast to help improve product quality and durability.

About 55,800 people were employed by U.S. companies in this industry in 1993. Of those, production workers accounted for 42,600 jobs, which paid an average of just under $10 an hour. Employment totals remained fairly stable from 1987 to 1993.

CURRENT CONDITIONS

Because this classification includes such wide ranging products as toy balloons, rubber brake linings, rubber rafts and pontoons, and many others, it is not possible to make broad generalizations covering the entire category. What follows is an explanation of some of the products, along with an exploration of some segments that were showing the most activity going into the mid-1990s.

Gloves and condoms. With the AIDS crisis escalating throughout the 1980s and continuing into the 1990s, more attention has been focused on latex gloves and condoms than on any other fabricated rubber product. Both products are made using a dipping process, where a form in the shape of the product desired (such as a hand) is dipped into latex.

Latex condoms have been identified as the best way to prevent the passing of the AIDS virus from one person to another during sexual intercourse. The campaign to increase condom usage has included a plea from a former U.S. surgeon general, along with public service announcements on television featuring sports and entertainment personalities. One study indicated that, because of the sex education campaign, women are buying a larger share of condoms—as many as 20 percent of condoms in 1993.

But while condoms may have received the bulk of the public attention, the role of latex gloves has been perhaps equally as important in the fight against AIDS. The gloves are used in examinations and surgery, and

now are used by virtually all health-care personnel when performing a task that requires contact with a patient. Besides physician's exams, the gloves also are widely used in dental procedures. Despite high expectations, however, neither the glove or condom markets reached the enormous proportions by the mid-1990s that were projected in the 1980s. Exam gloves, for example, were hit by a case of reality not meeting expectations. When demand began to grow to help protect workers from exposure to AIDS, many more plants went into operation than could be supported by the growing use. One official at a glove firm said that from 1986 to 1990 the demand for latex examination gloves may have doubled, but the capacity quadrupled. The situation was not helped by medical institutions that, trying to ensure delivery, placed duplicate orders with multiple distributors, helping to unrealistically raise apparent demand. This situation led to a consolidation in the glove industry, with many start-up firms going out of business and larger, multi-national firms scaling back production.

The U.S. condom market did experience moderate, though not spectacular, growth from 1989 to 1993; sales rose from 398 million to 437 million units. That trend is expected to continue, with sales forecast to hit 490 million by 1999. In dollar terms, the market has performed a bit better; condom sales were valued at $115 million in 1989 and climbed to $147 million in 1993. Compounded growth of 5.6 percent a year was expected to bring the market to $204 million in 1999. The top U.S. condom firms are Carter-Wallace Inc.; Schmid Laboratories Inc., which is owned by London International Group; Ansell Inc.; and Aladan Inc.

Ansell International, the world's largest exam glove firm, closed a plant in Arizona and shifted much of its production to its Asian facilities. Ansell still maintained two U.S. medical glove facilities, and had two such factories in Malaysia, and one in Thailand. Another multi-national, Smith & Nephew Ltd., closed an exam glove plant in Ohio, and decided to concentrate on the more regulated surgical glove market.

U.S. glove firms also face stiff competition in exam gloves from overseas firms, much of it economically driven. Many firms locate plants in Malaysia because the latex is available in that country. Also, the Malaysian government puts duties of five to ten percent on exported liquid latex, but none on exported finished gloves. Malaysia also offers economic incentives and cheaper labor. But even glove firms in Malaysia were hurt by demand not meeting expectations. From 1987 to 1990 the government issued 300 permits for glove factories. By late 1988 only 90 had begun operating and by the end of 1990 only 30 plants remained.

Entering the mid-1990s, glove and condom makers began studying a new problem; the use of alternate materials for people allergic to latex. Reactions to latex range from relatively minor problems, such as localized contact dermatitis, to much more severe difficulties like systemic dermatitis and anaphylactic shock, which can be life-threatening. From October 1988 to April 1992, there were 1,036 severe reactions and 15 deaths related to latex allergies and reported to the U.S. Food and Drug Administration. Populations most exposed to latex, such as operating room nurses, were shown by studies to be more susceptible to latex allergies.

To counter these problems, glove and condom makers were producing more hypoallergenic latex products in 1992, and also trying new materials. A few companies in North America by 1994 were making gloves of thermoplastic elastomers—a material with the characteristics of rubber but processed like a plastic. Also, the FDA in 1993 approved a condom made of polyurethane by London International. A smaller company, Wisconsin Pharmacal, had a polyurethane condom for women approved by the FDA in 1993. None of the non-latex products, though, had made a major impact on the glove and condom market by 1994.

Single-ply rubber roofing. This is another market expected to show tremendous growth that never quite reached the high plateau reserved for it. Rubber roofing finds use in commercial building. The membrane most commonly used was developed in 1963 by Du Pont. Rubber roofing evolved because the roofing materials in use had a higher incidence of early failure, and the energy crisis caused higher material costs for asphalt-based roofs. Roofers were looking for a membrane that would be flexible and have superior weather and water resistance over a longer period of time. Rubber roofing gained favor because it could accommodate movement, was functional at high and low temperatures, resisted environmental elements, and was not subject to the effects of ponded water.

From a small 1980 base of $70 million, rubber roofing demand in the United States quadrupled by 1985 to $287 million, and then doubled by 1991 to an estimated $608 million. Annual growth of 11.1 percent from 1991 to 1996 was expected, which will allow rubber roofing to exceed $1 billion. But growth of rubber roofing staggered early in the 1990s, according to the Rubber Manufacturers Association (RMA), which represents rubber product firms. Single-ply

roofing hit a peak in 1990 and stagnated for the next several years.

The RMA pegged 1990 usage at one billion square feet—the membrane is made in sheet form—but said the market fell to 850 million square feet in 1991 because of a drop in the U.S. economy. Shipments recovered to 910 million square feet in 1992 and 968 million square feet in 1993. The RMA forecast the market in 1994 to total about one billion square feet, still short of 1990 demand.

The rubber roofing market also has seen much consolidation, with many firms entering the fray but later dropping out—especially after a 1983 price war virtually wiped out profits for many of the firms. The two leading firms in the United States are Carlisle SynTec Systems, which pioneered the product's usage, and Firestone Building Products Co., owned by tire maker Bridgestone/Firestone Inc.

Both of the leaders made major acquisitions in 1993. Carlisle bought the roofing business of Goodyear Tire & Rubber Co. after making the product for Goodyear for two years under a private-label arrangement. Firestone then purchased the roofing operations of Colonial Rubber Works Inc.

Rubber-covered rollers. The largest market for these products is for printing rollers used in the graphic arts industry. Other applications are in paper making, plastic film production, printing, steel fabricating, textile manufacturing, metal coating and leather processing. Rubber covered rolls consist of three parts: a metal core; a rubber bonding adhesive applied to the core; and a rubber cover. The graphic arts industry uses rolls in printing presses to convey the ink onto the printing plate. In the paper industry, the rolls are used to squeeze water out of newly formed paper web, so it compresses to the correct thickness. Steel mills use rolls in many strip processing lines because the rubber coverings reduce noise, provide traction, give a wringing action between processes, and protect the metal from corrosion.

Growth of rubber covered rolls has been gradual since 1980. U.S. usage was pegged at $189 million in 1980, growing to $232 million in 1985. Growth slowed a bit as the market was estimated at $244 million in 1991. But shipments were expected to begin climbing faster, as the forecast for 1996 was for $318 million in sales.

Sheet rubber. This rubber product is made using a machine called a calender. A strip of material fed into one side of the machine is flattened and emerges as a rubber sheet, which is used in various industrial applications like packing and lining. The process makes sheet goods in various widths and thicknesses. U.S. consumption of sheet rubber goods has varied since 1980. At that time, shipments were valued at $119 million, a figure that rose to $153 million in 1985. By 1991, though, demand had dropped to $142 million. Usage, however, was projected to pick up by 1996, with a market forecast of $162 million.

Sponge rubber products. Sponge rubber goods can be classified as either open- or closed-cell. Open-cell sponge rubber takes its name from natural occurring sponge. It is, by definition, "an elastic mass made porous by interconnecting cells," G.R. Sprague of Colonial Rubber Works wrote in the *Vanderbilt Rubber Handbook.* Typical open-cell products include carpet underlay, mattress filling and upholstery filling. Closed-cell sponge is different because the cells do not connect. Applications include insulation, automotive weatherstripping, architectural gaskets, swimsuit material, and pipe insulation. It, too, can be used in mattress and upholstery filling.

Hard rubber products. These goods are actually a contradiction to the normal definition of rubber. By definition, rubber products normally are expected to stretch to at least twice their normal dimensions when stress is applied, and then returned to their original form once the stress is removed. Hard rubber products are made so as to not follow this guideline, although the goods do retain many of the qualities of rubber. Typical hard rubber products include steering wheels, caster wheels, electrical insulation, battery boxes and bowling balls.

Rubberized fabrics. The making of rubberized fabric is one of the oldest forms of rubber manufacturing. When latex was discovered, it was spread on a fabric and placed in the sun. When the water evaporated, the resulting product was a type of coated fabric. Historically, makers of rubberized fabrics considered their processes an art and kept their secrets hidden. This meant that only a few manufacturers could make products, and what they produced was highly specialized. More recently, the technology for making coated fabrics has evolved from being an art into a science, and the information has been spread through the industry so that the number of applications has grown tremendously.

Included in the products offered are inflatable safety equipment, such as life vests, life boats, and escape slides carried on aircraft. The process also is common in using polyurethane coatings to simulate leather coatings, especially in the apparel, shoe, and upholstery industries.

INDUSTRY INFORMATION SOURCES

"After the Gold Rush," *Rubber & Plastics News,* August 19, 1991.

"Ansell to Close Arizona Medical Glove Plant," *Rubber & Plastics News,* September 17, 1990.

"Assorted Lines to Post Gains," *Rubber & Plastics News,* January 22, 1990.

Babington, Mary, *Freedonia Study #416, Industrial Rubber Products,* Cleveland: Freedonia Group Inc., 1992.

"Experts Seek Solution to Rising Latex Allergies," *Rubber & Plastics News,* November 23, 1992.

"Fabricated Goods to Rise 3%," *Rubber & Plastics News,* January 17, 1994.

"Fabricated Goods to Rise 3%," *Rubber & Plastics News,* January 18, 1993.

"Firestone to Buy Colonial Roofing Unit," *Rubber & Plastics News,* November 22, 1993.

"Goodyear to Cut 1,000 Worldwide in '92," *Rubber & Plastics News,* February 1, 1993.

"Latex Allergies Spawn Glove, Condom Maker," *Rubber & Plastics News,* February 14, 1994.

Long, Harry, ed., *Basic Compounding and Processing of Rubber,* Akron, Ohio: American Chemical Society Inc., 1985.

Plehwe, Dieter, *Change and Concentration in the World Rubber Industry,* Brussels, Belgium: International Federation of Chemical, Energy and General Workers' Unions, 1991.

"RMA Sees 6.5% Rise in Roofing," *Rubber & Plastics News,* August 23, 1993.

"Smith & Nephew Axing Glove Line, Closing Plant," *Rubber & Plastics News,* September 3, 1990.

"Tactyl Adding Output for Latex-free Gloves," *Rubber & Plastics News,* July 6, 1992.

"Today's Roofing Market Flat As a Board," *Rubber & Plastics News,* April 29, 1991.

The Vanderbilt Rubber Handbook, Norwalk, CT: R.T. Vanderbilt Co. Inc., 1990.

"Single-ply Rubber Roofing," *Rubber & Plastics News,* August 7, 1989.

"U.S. Latex Glove Makers Struggle to Keep Up," *Rubber & Plastics News,* October 1, 1990.

"Unexplored Niche for Condoms," *Rubber & Plastics News,* February 14, 1994.

"View from Above," *Rubber & Plastics News,* August 19, 1991.

—Bruce Meyer

SIC 3081

UNSUPPORTED PLASTICS FILM AND SHEET

Establishments primarily engaged in manufacturing unsupported plastics film and sheet, from purchased resins or from resins produced in the same plant are classified in this industry. Establishments primarily engaged in manufacturing plastics film and sheet for blister and bubble formed packaging are classified in **SIC 3089: Plastics Products, Not Elswhere Classified.**

INDUSTRY SNAPSHOT

The value of shipments in the plastics film and sheet industry in 1991 was $9.17 billion, up from $8.14 billion in 1987 (in current dollars). About 600 establishments operated in the industry, and two-thirds of these establishments had 20 or more employees. The average firm size as measured by the number of production workers per establishment was 73 percent larger than that for the manufacturing sector as a whole.

The plastics film and sheet industry employed 36,000 production workers in 1991, and this number had been fairly constant since 1987. The industry was highly capital-intensive, having over two-and-one-half times as much investment per production worker as that for the manufacturing sector as a whole. The industry's annual hours and hourly wages for production workers came in slightly higher than those in the manufacturing sector at large.

ORGANIZATION AND STRUCTURE

Of the top 15 firms by sales in the plastics film and sheet industry, two were private independents, three public independents, and the remaining ten were subsidiaries and divisions of larger firms. All of these 15 firms had greater than $100 million in sales. Of the remaining 60 firms ranking among the top 75 by sales, 50 percent were private independents.

The states ranking in the top ten by value of shipments were, in order of descending value: Massachusetts, Ohio, South Carolina, New Jersey, California, Illinois, Texas, Pennsylvania, Virginia, and New York. Together these ten states accounted for 60 percent of total shipments and 61 percent of total employment for the industry. The average number of employees per establishment varied widely across these states. South Carolina and Virginia, the states with the highest number of employees per plant, had between five and

ten times as many employees per plant on average, as did New York and California.

The industry was served by the Chemical Fabrics and Film Association, headquartered in Cleveland, Ohio. The association, formerly known as the Plastic Coatings and Film Association, was founded in 1927 and had 23 members. The association published industry standards and an annual directory, and also organized an annual convention. The most important industry periodical was the *Journal of Plastic Film and Sheeting.*

BACKGROUND AND DEVELOPMENT

Though the terms are sometimes used interchangeably, plastics films are generally defined as being less than 0.010 inches in thickness, whereas plastics sheet is thicker. The plastics film and sheet industry had its origins in the rapid growth of the organic chemical industry in the late-nineteenth century. The first commercially successful plastics film was cellulose nitrate. Though this film had many desirable properties, its flammability limited the scope of its use. In his book *Plastic Films*, John Briston called regenerated cellulose, or cellophane, "the most important development in films. . . ." The commercialization of this film followed the development of continuous-process film production machinery for which the Swiss chemist J.E. Brandenburger received his first patents in 1911. Cellophane was initially used for the packaging of luxury and semi-luxury goods, but its use expanded rapidly thereafter.

In the 1992 volume of *Plastic Films: Technology and Packaging Applications*, Osborn and Jenkins summarized the growth of the industry as follows: "The commercialization of cellophane in the 1920s revolutionized the flexible packaging of consumer goods. For the first time, the buyer could see the contents of the package through a film that protected the packaged items from dirt, moisture, and atmospheric gases. Countless items previously packaged in heavy metal or fragile glass containers began to appear in this safe, convenient, light weight film. As a result, the flexible packaging industry grew from a small, paper-based operation into the . . . giant it is today."

Cellophane remained the dominant film in the industry until the commercialization of polyethylene film in the 1950s. One of the key advantages of polyethylene film was its lower cost, which made it possible to use for large tonnage packaging applications. As of 1987, cellulose films made up only seven percent of the industry's product share, compared to 29 percent for polyethylene films. The rapid growth of the prepackaged food industry in the post-World War II period provided an ever-growing demand for polyethylene films. The use of polyethylene films expanded to the packaging of textiles and toys, as well as heavy sacks for industrial and agricultural uses.

The industry introduced polypropylene films in 1959. This film was stiffer than polyethylene film, and thus, readily lent itself to packaging with high-speed machinery. Polypropylene film made up seven percent of the industry's product share in 1987, and was expected to grow more rapidly in use than polyethylene films.

As of 1989, 28 percent of polyethylene and polypropylene film was used for merchandise bags, 25 percent for non-food packaging and trash and can liners, 24 percent for food packaging, seven percent for shrink and stretch wrap, and the remainder for other non-packaging purposes.

The rapid market growth of plastics films was enabled in part by ever-lowering costs. This changed to some extent after the Oil Crisis of 1972, which slowed the growth of the industry. Nonetheless, plastics film continued to grow at the expense of cellophane and other traditional, flexible packaging materials. In their 1992 book *Plastic Films: Technology and Packaging Applications*, Osborn and Jenkins considered the effects of rising energy costs on the plastics film industry. Noting that the production of aluminum foil was up to four times as energy intensive as the production of plastics film, the authors wrote, "Rising energy costs will continue to favor flexible over rigid packaging, plastics films and paper over foil, and may cause a minor shift in the paper/plastics balance in the favor of paper. The latter effect can not be large, since paper has only a few of the many packaging-friendly attributes of plastics." The authors conclude that the diminishing supply of oil and gas will not significantly effect the production of plastics films for two reasons. First, of products produced with oil and gas, plastics have the highest valued-added in the production process. Second, plastics packaging used only one-half percent of all oil and gas consumed in the United States.

One of the relatively new important markets for plastics films was agricultural production. The agricultural industry used plastics films for greenhouses, row covers, irrigation channels, and mulches. Plastics mulches reduced weeds, fungi, and insects, and held in ground moisture. The use of plastics mulches resulted in yield increases of up to 250 percent in certain field tests.

CURRENT CONDITIONS

The value of shipments in the plastics film and sheet industry increased by 13 percent from 1987 to 1991, with 1990 a peak year (in current dollars). Capital investments increased by 24 percent over this same period, with 1991 a peak year, when $520 million in new capital investments were made. The *U.S. Industrial Outlook* for 1994 reported that, "shipments of miscellaneous plastics products . . . are expected to grow by five percent in 1994," and included extruded plastics such as plastic film and sheet among the products with highest expected growth. A 1992 report by the Freedonia Group predicted that the use of all plastics films would grow at an annual rate of 3.4 percent to 1996, with growth strongest for polyethylene and polypropylene films in secondary-packaging and primary-food packaging applications.

In 1993, the TPC Business Research group published a report on thermoformed plastics films, entitled "High-Performance Films in the United States." The report projected an annual average growth rate of 3.8 percent for these films through 1997, implying $2.6 billion in sales by that year. While polyester made up 75 percent of such films in 1993, films made from polycarbonate, nylon, and polyolefin-based resins were expected to grow more rapidly. The use of stretch film was expected to continue growing at double-digit rates.

Employment of production workers was stable from 1987 to 1991. The Bureau of Labor Statistics made employment forecasts at the **SIC 308** level for 30 occupational categories. Based on projected changes from 1990 to 2005, employment was expected to increase in all 30 occupations, with double-digit increases projected for 26 occupations. Projections made for the plastics film and sheet industry alone would have varied from these figures. Yet aside from **SIC 3089: Plastics Products Not Elsewhere Classified**, the plastics film and sheet industry was largest of the industries making up **SIC 308**, comprising 13 percent of total shipments at the **SIC 308** level.

One of the important challenges facing the plastics film and sheet industry was the development and use of more environmentally friendly products and processes. The October 1993 issue of the *Journal of Plastic Film and Sheeting* summarized these factors as follows: "market forces pushing companies to invest in recyclable laminates; present and pending waste disposal regulations; the stress on biodegradability by the end user and its implications for selection of components to be used in a process." Two researchers at Cornell University published a study in 1992 that addressed the issue of the biodegradability of plastics films. The researchers tested 12 films claimed by their manufacturers to be biodegradable and judged that only one of these films, produced by E.I. du Pont de Nemours & Company (DuPont), was truly biodegradable. This film was relatively expensive and may not be economically feasible for such applications as trash bags. Among other films claimed to be biodegradable, the best of them simply broke into small pieces.

Demand for biodegradable and recycled plastics was expected to have a lasting impact on the industry. In a 1992 conference titled ''Greener and Better: Packaging Challenges for the 1990s,'' the subject was addressed by Richard Mayer, CEO of Kraft General Foods Inc.. The January 1993 issue of the *Journal of Plastic Film and Sheeting* summarized his keynote speech as follows: ''Mayer emphasized that unity and partnership are needed by material producers, converters, packagers, wholesalers, and retailers if the industry is to meet the consumer's challenge for better and lighter packages, which use much recycled material. Since consumers are demanding legislative action to obtain source reduction, reuse of packages, and minimum recycling requirements, it is becoming increasingly important that the packaging industry respond with both action and education.''

INDUSTRY LEADERS

The top four firms in the plastics film and sheet industry were: the Packaging and Industrial Products Division of Borden, Inc. in Columbus, Ohio; Envirodyne Industries, Inc. of Oak Brook, Illinois; the ICI Americas, Inc. Films Group of Wilmington, Delaware; and CYRO Industries of Mount Arlington, New Jersey. Together these firms accounted for about 30 percent of total sales for the industry.

Publicly-held Borden, Inc. was founded in 1857. With $1.83 billion in sales in 1992, its Packaging and Industrial Products Division was by far the industry's largest producer. Though highly diversified across industry lines, Borden's two major products were packaged foods and plastics film and other packaging materials. The Packaging and Industrial Products Division made up one-fourth of Borden's total sales. Borden had manufacturing and processing facilities in over 20 countries and in 34 states across the United States.

Envirodyne Industries was founded in 1970, and had $544 million in sales and 4,600 employees in 1992. The firm was a subsidiary of the privately-held Emerald Acquisition, Corp., also of Oak Brook. Envirodyne acquired its plastics production facilities in its 1986 purchases of Union Carbide Corporation's film packaging business and of Filmco International Ltd. The firm produced shrink wrap and plastics film

for food packaging. Though the company's facilities were profitable, it filed Chapter 11 bankruptcy in 1993—the result of debt acquired during a leveraged buyout in 1989.

The ICI Films Group had $300 million in sales and 4,000 employees in 1992. The group was a division of ICI Americas, Inc., a subsidiary of the publicly-held Imperial Chemical Industries PLC, a U.K.-based firm. The firm had long been one of the main technical innovators in the plastics film industry. Among its key developments was low-density polyethylene in 1933. ICI Films started up a new $18 million plant in the U.K. in 1992, and announced in 1993 that it was tripling its capacity for the production of a new polyester film called Kaladex. The demand for Kaladex resulted from the film's great imperviousness to moisture and oxygen.

CYRO Industries had $200 million in sales and 800 employees in 1992. The firm was founded in 1976 as a joint venture with the publicly held American Cyanamid Co. CYRO announced in 1992 that it would expand its capacity of continuously manufactured plastics sheet by 25 percent.

RESEARCH AND TECHNOLOGY

Plastics film and sheet was produced by feeding molten plastics through either a flat or tubular die. After being shaped, the film was cooled or 'quenched,' either by coming into contact with a cooled roller or by being immersed in water. Water quenching more uniformly cools films, and was preferred especially when film clarity was a consideration.

One of the most important outputs of the industry was laminated plastics films. Lamination enabled a film that combined the optimal characteristics of each of the component materials, whether that characteristic be imperviousness, stiffness, clarity, strength, or wrinkle-resistance. Laminates were produced either by adhesive bonding of separately-produced films or by the newer process of coextrusion. In coextrusion, two or more films were simultaneously formed and heat-bonded either by a set of adjacent dies or by a manifold die. By creating laminated plastics films in one continuous process, coextrusion greatly reduced their cost. One of the disadvantages of coextruded films is that it was not possible to print on their protected inside surface, since component layers are formed and bonded almost simultaneously. The quality of print was of great importance for the marketing of packaged food products. New developments in surface printing were underway to address this problem.

The industry developed a number of new products and processes in the 1990s to address the issue of environmental safety. A project undertaken by Dow Plastics and Advanced Environmental Recycling Technologies of Rogers, Arkansas, created a new process to remove dirt and other wastes from recycled polyethylene grocery sacks and stretch film. Grocery and merchandise bags constituted the bulk of recycled plastics film products. DuPont developed a new polyester film, Mylar OL, that enabled dependable seals for packaging with the use of adhesives, making the film more readily recyclable. The Exxon Chemical Co. started up a new film production line in 1993 that was capable of producing seven million pounds of plastics film a year using up to 50 percent post-consumer plastics. Mobil Chemical developed a new low-density polyethylene called 'Super Strength' that enabled films to be produced that were 30 percent thinner, yet just as strong as conventional plastics films. Highly-impervious silica-coated plastics films began to be commercialized in the United States in the 1990s after having been developed in Japan in Europe. Aside from their desirable packaging properties, silica-coated films more readily lent themselves to recycling than laminates containing vinyl-based resins.

Airco Gases of Murray Hill, New Jersey, developed a new cooling technology known as cryogenic bubble cooling. This process eliminated a long-standing bottleneck in the production of plastics films and enabled output increases of up to 60 percent.

INDUSTRY INFORMATION SOURCES

Annual Survey of Manufactures, Washington, D.C.: U.S. Census Bureau, 1991.

Benning, Calvin. *Plastic Films for Packaging,* Lancaster, Pennsylvania: Technomic Publishing Co., 1983.

"Biodegradability of Modified Plastic Films in Controlled Biological Environments," *Environmental Science and Technology,* January 1992.

Briston, John H. *Plastic Films* (2nd ed.), Harlow, England: Longman Scientific and Technical, 1983.

"Critical Issues: Broader Scope for TAPPI," *Journal of Plastic Film and Sheeting,* October 1993.

"Cryogenic Bubble Cooling Could Increase Film Output By Up To 60 Percent," *Modern Plastics,* August 1992.

"CYRO Begins Growth Project," *Glass Magazine,* August 1992.

Daniels, Peggy Kneffel and Carol A. Schwartz, eds. *Encyclopedia of Associations* (28th ed.), Detroit, Michigan: Gale Research Inc., 1994.

Darnay, Arsen J., ed. *Manufacturing USA: Industry Analysis, Statistics, and Leading Companies* (3rd ed.), Detroit, Michigan: Gale Research Inc., 1993.

"Demand for High-Performance Films," *Paper, Film and Foil Converter,* September 1992.

"Donald Kelly Gets Egg On His Face," *Business Week, Industrial Edition,* February 24, 1992.

"Environmental News," *Journal of Plastic Film and Sheeting,* January 1993.

"Exxon Adds Post-Consumer Film Capacity," *Plastic News,* January 11, 1993.

"Marketing Reports," *Journal of Plastic Film and Sheeting,* January 1994.

"Mobil Chemical Makes New Polyethylene Resin," *Journal of Commerce,* April 10, 1992.

Moody's Industrial Manual, New York: Moody's Investors Service Inc., 1993.

"New Films," *Journal of Plastic Film and Sheeting,* January 1993.

Osborn, Kenton and Wilmer Jenkins. *Plastic Films: Technology and Packaging Application,* Lancaster, Pennsylvania: Technomic Publishing Company, Inc., 1992.

"PEN Film Business Emerges As ICI Slates Production," *Chemical Marketing Reporter,* March 16, 1992.

"Plastic Film Demand to Hit 11 Billion Lb by '96," *Packaging U.S.,* August 1992.

"Plastics Units Fuel Envirodyne in Hard Times," *Plastic News,* February 15, 1993.

"Process Efficiencies Bolster Stretch Film," *Modern Plastics,* December 1991.

"Silica-Coated Plastics for Thin Films, Bottles on Edge of U.S. Market," *Paper, Film and Foil Converter,* August 1992.

Sweeting, Orville. *The Science and Technology of Polymer Films,* New York: John Wiley and Sons, Inc., 1968.

"24th National Agricultural Plastics Congress," *Journal of Plastic Film and Sheeting,* January 1994.

U.S. Industrial Outlook, Washington, D.C.: U.S. Department of Commerce, 1994.

Ward's Business Directory of U.S. Private and Public Companies, Detroit, Michigan: Gale Research Inc., 1993.

—David Kucera

SIC 3082

UNSUPPORTED PLASTICS PROFILE SHAPES

This industry covers establishments primarily engaged in manufacturing unsupported plastics profiles, rods, tubes, and other shapes. Establishments primarily engaged in manufacturing plastics hose are classified in **SIC 3052: Rubber and Plastics Hose and Belting.**

The value of shipments in the plastics profile shapes industry in 1991 was $2.80 billion, up from $2.28 billion in 1987. The *U.S. Industrial Outlook* for 1994 projected growth rates of five percent and included molded plastic products such as plastics profile shapes among those products with highest expected growth. There are about 550 establishments in the industry, 56 percent of which had 20 or more employees. Average firm size as measured by the number of production workers per establishment is slightly larger than that for the manufacturing sector as a whole. Annual capital investments ranged from a high of $147 million in 1988 to a low of $121 million in 1991.

The industry employed 20,100 production workers in 1991, up from 19,100 in 1982, but down from a peak of 21,300 in 1989. The industry has 81 percent as much investment per production worker on average as that for the manufacturing sector as a whole. Annual hours worked by production workers in the industry are slightly higher on average than those worked in the manufacturing sector at large, and hourly wages are 20 percent lower. Of the top 12 firms in the industry by sales, 8 are divisions or subsidiaries and 4 are private independents. Of the remaining 13 firms ranking among the top 25, 11 are private independents. The industry had 83 percent as much investment per establishment on average as that for the manufacturing sector as a whole.

The top three firms in the plastics profile shapes industry are Autostyle Inc. of Grand Rapids, Michigan, AutoStyle Plastics Inc., also of Grand Rapids, and Tubed Products Inc. of Easthampton, Massachusetts. Together these firms account for eight percent of total sales for the industry. Autostyle Inc. had $107 million in sales and 1,200 employees in 1992. Founded in 1966, the firm is a private independent. AutoStyle Plastics had $89 million in sales and 950 employees. The firm is a subsidiary of Autostyle Inc. Both firms produce plastic automotive parts. Tubed Products Inc. had $38 million in sales and 825 employees in 1992. Founded in 1947, the firm is a subsidiary of the publicly held McCormick and Co. Inc. of Sparks, Maryland, and manufactures plastic squeeze tubes.

The top products by share in the industry are those made from vinyl (16 percent), polyethylene (16 percent), polypropylene (12 percent), polystyrene (10 percent), nylon (4 percent), acrylates (4 percent), and styrene copolymer (1 percent). The states ranking in the top ten by value of shipments in the industry are, in order of descending value, Ohio, Illinois, Indiana, California, New Jersey, Michigan, Pennsylvania, Texas, Virginia, and New York. Together these ten states accounted for 62 percent of total shipments and 64

percent of total employment for the industry in the United States.

INDUSTRY INFORMATION SOURCES

Annual Survey of Manufactures, Washington, D.C.: U.S. Census Bureau, 1991.

Darnay, Arsen J., editor, *Manufacturing USA: Industry Analysis, Statistics, and Leading Companies* (3rd edition), Detroit, Michigan: Gale Research Inc., 1993.

U.S. Industrial Outlook, Washington, D.C.: U.S. Department of Commerce, 1994.

Ward's Business Directory of U.S. Private and Public Companies, Detroit, Michigan: Gale Research Inc., 1993.

—David Kucera

SIC 3083

LAMINATED PLASTICS PLATE, SHEET, AND PROFILE SHAPES

This category covers establishments primarily engaged in manufacturing laminated plastics plate, sheet, profiles, rods, and tubes. Establishments primarily engaged in manufacturing laminated flexible packaging are classified in paper and paperboard products industries.

INDUSTRY SNAPSHOT

Establishments engaged in the manufacture of plastic plates, sheets, and related products shipped goods valued at $2.3 billion dollars in 1990 (not adjusted for inflation). This figure remained in line with a generally flat trend in the industry in recent years. The total value of shipments increased by seven percent from 1987 to 1990. The industry lagged behind the growth of plastics products in general, which experienced growth in shipments of over 17 percent during the same period.

The relatively flat trend in laminated plastic plate and sheet production has been attributed to several economic forces. Continuing weakness in the manufacturing sector due to the prolonged economic recession undoubtedly contributed to the stagnation in the demand for the industry's products during the late 1980s and early 1990s. On the positive side, however, laminated plastic makers have been able to maintain an advantage over competitors in nonplastic plate and sheet. In addition, research and development has resulted in better products and cheaper methods of production. Continuing advancements in processing technology are opening new markets throughout the world, most notably the recycling market.

ORGANIZATION AND STRUCTURE

In 1989 approximately 224 establishments were engaged in the production of laminated plastic plate and sheet. These establishments employed 83 employees per establishment, 63 of which were production workers. During the same year, the average value added per production worker was $87,858—a figure which compared less than favorably with an overall average of $105,881 for all U.S. manufacturing industries.

In terms of geographic concentration, the largest number of establishments was located in the East North Central region of the United States, followed by the Middle Atlantic region and then the Pacific region (including Alaska and Hawaii). Alternatively, when ranked by the number of establishments per state, California was first with 37, followed by Ohio (21), Illinois (15), New Jersey (14), New York (12), and Pennsylvania (12).

Market concentration was relatively high in the laminated plastics plate and sheet industry. In 1992 it was estimated that the largest eight companies accounted for approximately two-thirds of the industry's $2.8 billion in sales. In descending order of market share, the dominant companies in the laminated plastic plate and sheet industry were: James River Corporation, with a 22 percent market share; Ralph Wilson Plastics Company, (ten percent); Allied-Signal Incorporated (eight percent); Spartech Corporation (6.2 percent); Uniroyal Plastics Acquisition (six percent); Formica Corporation (six percent); Wolverine Technologies, Inc. (4.8 percent); and Nevamar Corporation (four percent). Many of these companies were diversified, so the above figures should be interpreted with caution. While three of the largest companies in the industry, including the James River Corporation, were divisions of larger companies, most of the leading companies were subsidiaries. Only one company in the top ten, Spartech Corporation, was publicly traded. While most of the largest ten competitors were subsidiaries and divisions, of the next 50 corporations, 31 were private companies.

The primary materials consumed by the laminated plastic plate and sheet industry, when ranked by delivered costs (not adjusted for inflation) were: materials, parts, containers and supplies of various kinds, valued at $937 million in 1987; paper and paperboard products, except paperboard boxes, containers, and corrugated paperboard ($235 million); other materials and components, parts, containers and supplies ($179 million); plastic resins consumed in the form of granules, pellets, powders, liquids ($157 million).

The major sources of input for the plastics industry were overwhelmingly from the manufacturing sector, which accounted for nearly 63 percent of sector input. The single major input was plastic materials and resins, which comprised 36.2 percent of inputs. Wholesale trade accounted for 8.5 percent of inputs, while imports (undifferentiated by industry sector) contributed 5.8 percent of sector input.

If disaggregated by total product share, the industry's output was divided among the following product classes: thermosetting products made up approximately 38 percent of the industry's total output in the early 1990s; thermoplastics (29 percent); and other laminates (28 percent). Plastic laminates (excluding flexible packaging), laminated plastics plate, and sheet and profile shapes accounted for the remaining five percent.

The principal sectors responsible for the purchase of miscellaneous plastics products were hospitals, which bought 5.6 percent of sector output, followed by electronic components with 5.2 percent, and personal consumption with 4.3 percent. Exports made up 4.0 percent of total product sales.

BACKGROUND AND DEVELOPMENT

Laminated plastic plate and sheet products are defined, in rather technical terms, as plastic materials consisting of superimposed layers of synthetic resin-impregnated or coated filler which have been bonded together by means of heat and pressure to form a single piece. Plastic sheet is distinguished from plastic film by its thickness; Plastic sheet is defined as a material more than 0.010 of an inch in thickness. Sheet is known for its resistance to corrosion and is used in applications from building construction to production of appliances and other consumer durables. When discrete separate layers of plastics are joined together by an adhesive, heat, or other method, the finished product is called a laminate. The term ''composite'' is used to describe sheets that result when two or more plastics are combined.

Laminates. The history of laminated plastics can perhaps be best understood in the context of the development of the plastics industry in general. Some have referred to the 20th century as the ''plastic century,'' when plastics technology applications were thought, at the time of their inception, to be virtually limitless. In some respects this optimism was justified, as plastic in general began to make vast inroads as a lighter replacement for steel and other natural materials. With the boom in consumer spending following World War II, the idea of what some referred to as a "plastics utopia" was not all that far-fetched. After the mid-1950s, laminated plastic was everywhere, with applications proliferating at an unprecedented rate.

One of the earliest and most famous names in laminated plastics history is Formica, the trade name developed by the Formica Corporation (Formica Laminate) over 80 years ago, spawning a vast array of products. It was during the 1950s that Formica took on its most characteristic use as kitchen counter tops. Formica was sold as a durable nonporous material that required only the wipe of a damp cloth to clean the surface. Eventually, Formica surfaces would be able to imitate any type of surface.

Formica laminate was perfected by two former Westinghouse employees, Daniel J. O'Conor and Herbert A. Faber. They developed a process for making rigid laminated sheets which could be cut into various shapes. The Formica Insulation Company began in Cincinnati in 1913 as a venture of these two enterprising former Westinghouse employees. The new product was called "Formica" to distinguish it from other products such as Westinghouse's "Bakelite-Micarta," which had distinguished itself from the previous "Micarta." While early laminates were dark in color and homogeneous, it wasn't long before Formica's surface could hold any color, pattern, or texture including stone, wood, and textile. Other companies, such as Redmanol Company and Bakelite, founded by plastics pioneer Leo Baekeland, as well as smaller companies such as Continental Fibre and Diamond State Fibre, were all selling virtually the same product in the 1920s and 1930s. Sales of laminates boomed as laminate panels covered interiors of railroad cars, decorative laminates covered lobbies of many buildings, and even the Queen Mary was lined with Formica laminate.

By the 1950s, technological change, lower resin prices, and new thermoplastic materials derived from petroleum led to a massive proliferation of laminates. Technological applications in the consumer appliance industry, including washing machines, vacuum cleaners, and refrigerators all benefitted from Formica parts. It was during this time that Formica took on its most characteristic use as kitchen counter tops. Shortly afterward, the company was making dinette tops and chairs. Industry competition became fierce. By 1950 weekly production of Formica dinette sheets was 55,000 units, compared with just 28,000 units two years earlier.

In the 1950s the plastics industry expanded at an astounding rate—more rapidly than most other American industries. Plastic laminate applications boomed as well, especially in consumer industries. In 1969 Formica ceased production of industrial grade laminate, one of its first applications. And in 1971 they received a patent for the development of a heavy-ink process used as another surface texturing technique. One year later a metallic laminate line was produced. A decade later, in 1982, Formica laminate went three-dimensional by way of ColorCore, a surfacing material that made it possible to achieve volumetric as well as intaglio or cameo effects.

CURRENT CONDITIONS

Since the applications of products in the laminated plastics plate, sheet, and profile shapes industry are widespread, the outlook for the industry depends, for the most part, on the state of the national and global economy. The outlook for the export market for laminated plastics products is relatively optimistic when compared with the rest of the plastics industry. More specifically, while during the 1980s imports of all plastics categories grew six-fold, laminated plastics continued to account for the bulk of industry exports. Most exports go to Canada and Mexico, and are expected to increase with the removal of tariffs and taxes as part of the North American Free Trade Agreement, which went into effect at the beginning of 1994. Meanwhile, the world laminates market in 1990 was increasing at a rate of 20 to 25 percent annually. Predictions for 1995 from some European experts indicate a world market worth of $5 billion.

WORK FORCE

While following a cyclical pattern, total employment in this industry remained relatively flat between 1987 and 1990. Total employment was 17,300 in 1987, rose eight percent to around 18,600 in 1988, then dropped to 17,600 in 1990, for an overall increase of only two percent for the entire period. Production worker employment followed roughly the same trend, rising from 12,900 in 1987 to 14,000 in 1988, and falling to only 13,400 for an overall increase of four percent over the entire period.

Average hourly earnings of production workers in laminated plastics was $9.98 in 1987—which is high relative to other plastics industries. Regional differentials in average wages per hour for production workers ranged from a high of $13.10 in New Jersey to a low of $8.45 in California. New York followed New Jersey at $12.40 per hour, followed by Pennsylvania at $10.40, Ohio at $10.25, Wisconsin at $10.20, and Illinois at $8.60. Between 1987 and 1990, average hourly wages rose ten percent while real wages fell about 4.5 percent over the same period.

RESEARCH AND TECHNOLOGY

U.S. producers were continually developing new products and processes. This effort was reflected during the early and mid-1990s, for the most part, through the computerization of nearly all aspects of the laminated plastics production cycle, including design, manufacture, and distribution. Specifically, this has meant increased applications of computer-aided design and computer aided manufacturing. At the sales level, these innovations include individualized customer design which will lead to shorter delivery times and better quality control. By allowing manufacturers to determine precise product demand, these new methods of production and delivery will allow users of these techniques to achieve quick delivery and short turnover times.

Of course, all of these innovations, while increasing productivity and reducing unit costs, involve major investments in computer automated machinery. As a result, firms have tried to reduce relative labor costs, which remain high relative to other plastics industry groups. With their economies of scale and access to internally generated funds, the larger companies will be better positioned to implement these expensive, large capital commitment operations. This will undoubtedly lead to a pattern of technological change which is anything but uniform across firms in the industry.

Finally, most firms in the industry long ago recognized the trend toward recycling and are devoting considerable research efforts to developing recyclable materials and technologies which hold potentially profitable applications.

INDUSTRY INFORMATION SOURCES

Dubois, Harry, *Plastics History U.S.A.*, Hanover, MA: Halliday Lithographic Company, 1972.

Lewin, Susan Grant, ed., *Formica & Design: From the Counter Top to High Art*, New York: Rizzoli International Publications, 1991.

Manufacturing USA: Industry Analyses, Statistics, and Leading Companies, 3rd Edition, Detroit: Gale Publications.

Pasquale, John A., "Laminating," *Modern Plastics Encyclopedia: Modern Plastics*, October 1991.

Rosato, Dominick V., William K. Fallon, and Donald V. Rosato, *Markets for Plastics*, New York: Van Nostrand, Reinhold Co., 1969.

U.S. Industrial Outlook 1994, Washington, DC: U.S. Department of Commerce, January 1994.

—John A. Sarich

SIC 3084

PLASTICS PIPE

This category covers establishments primarily engaged in manufacturing plastics pipe. Establishments primarily engaged in manufacturing plastics pipe fittings are classified in **SIC 3089: Plastics Products, Not Elsewhere Classified.**

INDUSTRY SNAPSHOT

Establishments manufacturing plastics pipe produced a total of approximately $2.6 billion dollars worth of product in 1990 (in current terms, or not adjusted for inflation). This figure remained in line with a generally flat trend in the industry whose total value of shipments increased by only 6.5 percent from 1987 to 1990. The industry lagged behind the growth of plastics products in general, which experienced growth in shipments of over 17 percent during the same period.

This relatively flat trend in plastics pipe production has been attributed to economic trends. Continuing weakness in the manufacturing sector due to the prolonged economic recession led to stagnation in the demand for the industry's products during this period. On the positive side, however, plastics pipe as a commodity has, in general, been able to maintain a large advantage over competitors in nonplastics piping. Although markets have stagnated since, in the 1980s plastics piping markets grew at a rate four times faster than that of nonplastics markets. In addition, research and development spurred new products and cheaper methods of production. The continuing advancements in processing technology are opening new markets and applications throughout the world.

ORGANIZATION AND STRUCTURE

In 1987, approximately 242 establishments were engaged in the production of plastics pipe. Each establishment employed an average of approximately 54 employees, 41 of which were production workers. For the same year, the average value added per production worker was $61,214. This figure compared less than favorably with an overall average of $105,881 calculated for 459 U.S. manufacturing industries.

In terms of major area of geographic concentration, the largest number of establishments were located in the Pacific region of the United States (including Alaska and Hawaii) followed by the West South Central region. Alternatively, when ranked by the number of establishments per state, California was first with 31; followed by Texas with 27; Ohio with 13; Florida with 12; Alabama and Iowa with 10 each; and Indiana, North Carolina, and Pennsylvania with nine each.

Market concentration was relatively high in the plastics pipe industry. In 1992, it was estimated that the largest 25 companies accounted for approximately $1.3 billion, or over 90 percent of the entire industry's sales. In descending order of market share, the dominant companies in the plastics pipe industry were: Lamson and Sessions Company's Home Products Division, with approximately 18.3 percent of the market; Phillips Driscopipe, Inc., with 9.9 percent; Advanced Drainage Systems, 7.1 percent; Pacific Western Extruded, 6.4 percent; H & W Industries, 5.3 percent; Harsco Corporation's Cantex Division, 4.9 percent; National Pipe Company, 4.2 percent; and Smith Fiberglass Products Inc., Cresline Plastic Pipe Company, Inc., Diamond Plastics Corporation, and Ameron, Inc.'s Fiber Glass Pipe Division, with 3.5 percent each. Many of these companies were diversified companies, so the above figures should be interpreted with caution. While the largest companies in the industry, including Lamson and Sessions Company's Home Products Division were divisions of larger companies, most of the leading companies were private companies. In fact, 26 of the top 48 companies were private companies.

Data available from the input-output tables assembled by the Commerce Department from 1977, 1982, and 1987 indicated that the primary materials consumed by the plastics pipe industry when ranked by delivered costs (again, not adjusted for inflation) were: materials, parts, and containers of various kinds with $1,579.7 million; and plastics resins consumed in the form of granules, pellets, powders, liquids, $940.8 million. The major sources of input supply were overwhelming from the manufacturing sector, which accounted for nearly 63 percent of sector input: the major input was plastics materials and resins which comprised 36.2 percent of inputs. Wholesale trade accounted for 8.5 percent of inputs. Imports accounted for 5.8 percent of sector input.

If desegregated by total product share, the industry's output was divided among the following product classes: water piping made up 32.92 percent of the industry's total output; drain, waste, and vent pipe made up 22.8 percent of output; and sewer pipes had 16.1 percent, while industrial and mining (including chemical processing, food processing), oil and gas piping, and other plastics piping accounted for the remaining 28 or so percent. The principal economic industries responsible for the purchase of plastics pipe were hospitals, which bought 5.6 percent of sector output, electronic components with 5.2 percent, and personal consumption with 4.3 percent. Exports made up 4.0 percent of total product sales.

BACKGROUND AND DEVELOPMENT

Plastics pipe was first manufactured commercially in the United States in 1940, when the Southern California Gas Company used a type of plastics pipe (called butyrate pipe) to distribute natural gas. Prior to that time, polyvinyl chloride pipe had been used in Germany as early as 1930. Then, plastics pipe was being produced as well by several U.S. companies for use in chemical services. Plastics pipe production in the U.S. commenced in 1948 with the development of polyethylene pipe for water services. Initial applications of the new pipe included use on farms for drainage and in the petroleum industry.

Plastics pipe and tubing is the final stage of value added production into consumer or industrial products. In general, plastics manufacturing is as follows: plastics materials (monomers) are chemically altered to produce polymers, which are then mixed with certain materials to impart certain characteristics such as durability, flexibility, and chemical resistance. Then, other manufacturing processes are used to produce final products such as plastics pipe. The production processes specific to plastics pipe manufacturing—processes including a variety of methods such as coating, extrusion, molding, and laminating—allow for continuous production of piping. Plastics pipe have various functions for long and short distance transportation of fluids. Also, plastics pipes have various intermediary purposes for final use in building construction.

The boom in plastics piping in the post-World War II period is intertwined with the boom in plastics manufacturing which has a close relation to the advancement of consumer society in the U.S., most notably the substitution of plastics material for other materials such as copper, aluminum, and steel. This enabled the use of plastics products to seriously challenge metal or alloy applications in such fields as aerospace, transportation, electricity, and engineering industry. In general, the plastics industry is the single, most-important "downstream" industry in the petrochemicals value-added chain. Plastics products are produced by various chemical processes that allow the formation of usable products by heating, milling, or extrusion. Plastics soften but do not melt when heated, thereby allowing them to change shape without losing cohesion. Before the 1930s, industrial products were largely based on coal as the basic chemical feed stock. The surge and rapid expansion of the production and consumption of plastics was directly related to the advent of petroleum as the main chemical feedstock. Thus, the petroleum and plastics industry are intrinsically related and petrochemicals provide the basis for mass production of plastics, and conversely, plastics provided petroleum with their main downstream market.

Retail sales of plastics pipe for various applications were up to $500,000 by 1948 and annual sales volume grew to $10 million by 1952. The new major classes of rigid thermoplastics pipe, namely ABS (acrylonitrile-butadiene-styrene) and PVC (polyvinyl chloride) were introduced in 1949 and 1950, respectively, and became widely used in new markets, competing effectively with other materials such as steel and copper piping. Plastics piping became widely used in drain, waste and vent applications, natural gas distribution, and in chemical industry. By 1956, styrene rubber pipe for sewer and drainage services became common pipe material by around 1956. This was followed by other successful materials thermoplastics piping, acetal, polypropylene, and polyvinyl dichloride. Sales grew to $25 million in 1957, $75 million in 1963, $100 million in 1964, and $120 million in 1965. Thus, from 1948 to 1965 sales of plastics piping grew by nearly two-and-one-half times.

Applications became very wide-spread in construction and building, as piping of all sizes pervaded the economic development of the post World War II period in the U.S. New standards for municipal building codes were being written and new standards were adopted to provide for the now dominant use of plastics pipe. In addition, the competitive effect on other materials products, such as steel and copper pipe producers was such that manufacturers sought to protect their markets by acquiring manufacturers and distributors. This was especially important in oil piping where hundreds of miles of tubular goods are involved.

Plastics pipe's competitive advantage over various metals was the result of many factors, not the least of which was its low cost. In addition, plastics pipe offers other advantages to users in that it is lightweight and resistant to varying environmental conditions, it is relatively easy to install, it minimizes solid deposits, it has low frictional losses, and it has self-insulating characteristics. Its only drawback are its temperature and pressure characteristics where various metal pipes sometimes enjoy an advantage.

Specific among plastics pipe's many applications developed are as follows: water supply and distribution including water utilities, municipal water treatment plants, chemical feed lines, sludge lines, and water distribution; natural gas distribution; drain, waste, and vent services, where plastic is resistant to chemicals; industrial uses especially food and beverage piping, acid and corrosive drain lines, chemical, electric and communication conduits, water and gas service, essentially general drainage; irrigation of farm and ranch systems, including movement of water and gas, fertilizer and insecticide; petroleum, mainly oil field use in salt water disposal systems and crude oil flow lines; public and private utilities, namely water systems, gas transmission, water and gas mains, sewer treatment and disposal and waste transferral.

In any case, the decade of the 1960s and 1970s were boom times for plastics in general and plastics piping in particular. Approximately 55 companies were engaged in the manufacture of plastics pipe by the mid-1970s. From 1964-70 total sales more than doubled from 150.0 million pounds to 345 million pounds. In 1967, sales were 320 million pounds or $240 million dollars. By 1969, of the $5 billion per year total pipe market, plastics pipe accounted for one to two percent and was growing at a rate of about 15 percent per year, about two times as fast as the growth of the chemical industry. The $240 million plastic pipe industry in 1967 topped the half million dollar mark by the mid-1970s. Steel would lose five percent of its market to plastic pipe (over $100 million sales), while copper lost 50 percent and aluminum 20 percent.

CURRENT CONDITIONS

Overall, the plastics products market is expected to grow at a rate of four to five percent per year through the mid-1990s, in real terms, according to U.S. Commerce Department projections. Plastics applications in building and construction (a category which includes not only piping, but also conduits and pipe fittings) comprise the second largest category of consumption, 21.1 percent, behind only packaging, which has 29.6 percent of total plastics markets. The underground piping market is the largest use segment of plastics pipe—water, drain, waste, vent, sewer and drain, gas, irrigation, conduit and pressure—and remains the largest market for plastics piping not only in the U.S. but in the world.

Significant recycling advances have been made in the industry but the portion of total plastics recycled remains low compared with total production or consumption. The industry is responding to public pressure to develop environmentally safer products and to advance recycling into all of its product areas. Efforts are underway between the industry and federal, state, and local governments to evaluate the merits of various policies.

While new technologies will further the trend toward the replacement of non-plastics materials with plastics, there is some concern over the feasibility of plastics recycling which may lead some to shift back to older materials (aluminum, copper, and other metals). From the production side, industry efforts to implement computer-aided design and manufacture (CAD/CAM) is expected to lead to drastic reductions in costs, reductions in turnover time, and decrease some of the environmental concerns by minimizing material waste. These continuing advancements in process technology remain the key factors behind the plastics piping product's success and future growth.

WORK FORCE

Over the period covering 1987-1990, total employment in the plastics pipe industry rose by only 3.2 percent, from 12,500 to 12,900 people. Production worker employment followed roughly the same trend, rising from 9,500 to a peak of 10,000 in 1989 before declining to 9,800 in 1990.

In 1990, the major occupational categories for the plastics products industry (these data relate to the 3-digit SIC industry group for miscellaneous plastics products rather than the specific 4-digit SIC for plastics piping) were: plastics molding machine operators, who made up 17.8 percent of total employment; assemblers and fabricators who made up 8.6 percent, and packers and packagers, which comprised 4.8 percent. Approximately 8.7 percent of occupations were involved in some type of managerial or supervisory function while 6.2 percent were engaged in some type of clerical, transportation, and accounting/financial tasks. The remainder were engaged in some type of production activity.

The Bureau of Labor Statistics has forecasted that all of these occupational categories are expected to grow by the year 2005, reflecting the projected growth in demand for the industry's products. However, the occupation that made up the bulk of the industry's employment in 1987, plastic molding machine operators, is projected to grow 29.5 percent to 2005, trailing 12 other categories in projected job growth. Production workers as a percent of total employment has drifted downward slowly since 1972, to about 78 percent in the late 1980s from 80 percent in 1972.

The job categories with the largest projected growth ranked by projected percentage growth to 2005

were largely nonproduction jobs: sales and related workers were projected to grow by 69 percent by 2005; industrial production managers, with a projected growth of 64.2 percent; industrial machinery mechanics with 50.9 percent; tool & die makers, 44.9 percent. Blue collar worker supervisors; hand packers and packagers; inspectors, testers and graders; freight, stock, and material movers; and extruding and forming machine operators occupations were forecast to grow by 35.8 percent.

On the income distribution side, while average hourly earnings of production workers in plastic pipe production rose from $3.27 in 1972 to $8.43 in 1987, the purchasing power of these money wages actually declined by 10 percent over the same period. General payroll per employee, adjusted for inflation, fell from an average of $18,215 to $17,903 over this same period. From 1987 to 1992, average hourly earnings rose by about 13 percent to $9.63, which, in real terms, translated into a decline of almost 9 percent.

In terms of value added per production worker, money wages per hour rose about two-and-one-half times while the value added per hour by these production workers rose by over three times, indicating a shift in income distribution away from wages and toward profits. Note: When comparing industry figures for plastic piping over time, plastic piping was included as part of **SIC 3079: Miscellaneous Plastics Products** in 1972 and the work force figures were calculated on the 1972 SIC basis.

INDUSTRY INFORMATION SOURCES

Chasis, David A., *Plastic Piping Systems,* Industrial Press, Inc., 1988.

Dubois, Harry, *Plastics History U.S.A.,* Hanover, Massachusetts: Halliday Lithographic Company, 1972.

Manufacturing USA: Industry Analyses, Statistics, and Leading Companies, 3rd Edition, Detroit, Michigan: Gale Publications, 1993.

Penn, W.S., *PVC Technology,* New York: Wiley Interscience, 1972.

Rosato, Dominick V., William K. Fallon, and Donald V. Rosado, *Markets For Plastics,* New York: Van Nostrand, Reinhold Co., 1969.

United Nations Centre on Transnational Corporations, United Nations, *Transnational Corporations in the Plastics Industry,* New York: United Nations, 1990.

U.S. Department of Commerce, International Trade Administration, *U.S. Industrial Outlook 1994,* Washington, D.C.: U.S. Government Printing Office, January, 1994.

Walker, Robert, P.E., ''The Early History of PVC Pipe,'' *Uni-Bell PVC Pipe News,* Summer, 1990.

—John A. Sarich

SIC 3085

PLASTICS BOTTLES

Included in this category are establishments primarily engaged in manufacturing plastics bottles.

INDUSTRY SNAPSHOT

This industry is dependent on nine separate markets, all of which have been showing moderate and steady growth over the last ten years. The use of plastic in bottles has been steadily replacing the use of aluminum and glass because of its convenience and cost effectiveness.

In 1990, plastic bottles comprised 22.7 percent of the container market by material shipments, metal cans 59.1 percent, and glass containers 18.2 percent. A report by the Freedonia Group entitled ''Beverages & Containers: Markets & Materials'' claimed that metal will remain the dominant packaging material for beverages, but plastic will continue to gain market share at the expense of glass throughout the 1990s.

ORGANIZATION AND STRUCTURE

The nine plastic bottle markets in the United States are listed below in descending size order:

Plastic Soft Drink Bottles: In 1992, approximately 7.80 billion units of plastic bottles were sold to the soft drink industry, a 12.0 percent increase over 1991. This segment accounts for approximately 20 percent of all plastic bottles sold in the United States, and is the fastest growing plastic bottle market in the United States. The Beverage Marketing Corporation predicts that demand for polyethylene terephthalate (PET) bottles in the soft drink industry will increase two percent annually over the next five years. After 1997, annual demand is projected to rise again by 2.1 percent.

Plastic Milk Bottles: In 1991, 5.41 billion units of plastic bottles were sold to the milk industry, a 1.1 percent rise from 1989. Plastic milk bottles account for approximately 15.5 percent of all plastic bottles sold in the United States; however, it is the slowest growing market among all nine plastic bottle segments. Plastic accounts for 78 percent of milk packaging according to Market Search Inc. The current recycling rate for HDPE milk jugs is about 14 percent, and analysts believe a rate of 25 percent is achievable by 1995. In 1988, two percent was recycled. The higher recycling rate is due to the rapid growth in curbside programs and neighborhood drop-off centers.

Medicinal Plastic Bottles: In 1991, 4.78 billion units of plastic bottles were sold, accounting for 13.7 percent of all plastic bottles in the United States. It increased 9.2 percent over 1989, making it the third fastest growing market segment.

Plastic Household Chemical Bottles: Approximately 4.61 billion units of plastic bottles were sold in 1991, accounting for 13.2 percent of all plastic bottles in the United States. This segment is the sixth fastest growing market for plastic bottles, rising 6.1 percent from 1989 to 1991.

Plastic Toiletry & Cosmetic Bottles: Approximately 3.71 billion units were sold in 1991, accounting for 10.5 percent of all plastic bottles sold in the United States. This is the second fastest growing market, rising 15.5 percent from 1989 to 1991. Developments in the performance and appearance of plastic containers are slowly eroding the position of glass in the toiletries sector.

Plastic Auto & Marine Bottles: In 1991, 3.22 billion units were sold, accounting for 9.2 percent of all plastic bottles sold in the United States. This is the seventh fastest growing market for plastic bottles, increasing 5.5 percent from 1989 to 1991.

Plastic Juice & Water Bottles: In 1991, 8.9 percent of all plastic bottles sold were to the fruit juice and water market, with 3.13 billion units sold in the United States. This is the fifth fastest growing market, increasing 6.6 percent from 1989 to 1991. Consumer studies showed that there was a desire for clean PET bottles because plastic allows containers in places where bottles are forbidden, like parks, beaches, gyms, and health clubs.

Plastic Food Bottles (excluding milk): In 1991, 2.66 billion units of plastic bottles were sold, representing an increase of 2.9 percent over 1989. This market accounts for 7.6 percent of all plastic bottles sold in the United States.

Industrial Plastic Bottles: In 1991, 521 million units were sold in the U.S, accounting for 1.5 percent of all plastic bottles sold. This is the fourth fastest growth market, rising 9.0 percent from 1989 to 1991.

BACKGROUND AND DEVELOPMENT

The value of plastic bottle shipments by all U.S. producers, as reported from Census and industry data, has gone from $483 million in to nearly $4 billion in

1991. At the heart of this growing industry are the suppliers of plastic resins, which, for the majority of plastic bottles, are one of three types: Polyethylene Terephthalate (PET), High Density Polyethylene (HDPE), and Vinyl.

Bottle demand for PET in the United States was 1.3 billion pounds in 1992, about 70 percent of the total PET market. The largest market for PET is carbonated soft drink containers at 910 million pounds. Single serving carbonated soft drink containers in 12-, 16-, and 20-ounce sizes are now a 225-million-pound market that is growing 25 percent annually.

PET resin producers supply the bulk ingredient to make plastic bottles, and their production in 1991 capacity rose to only 68,000 tons, while demand shot up to 206,000 tons. By 1992 demand had increased to 219,000 tons, while new capacity more than doubled, reaching 140,000 tons. Plants worldwide should be reaching capacities of upwards of 93 percent. Eastman Company plans to expand domestic resin production 300 million pounds in 1993, 300 million in 1994, and 250 million pounds in 1995. In early 1992, PET resin stood at 65-67 cents per pound and fell at the end of 1992 to 62-64 cents per pound. Prices should rise with increased demand for PET resin.

In 1992, PET resin demand from the soft drink industry topped 900 million pounds, and by 1997 it could approach to 1.4 billion pounds. With PET resin bringing higher prices and worldwide demand exceeding supply, lightweighting of plastic bottles is PET manufacturer's highest priority. Environmental and pricing pressures are prompting PET producers to investigate methods for reducing the weight of the two liter bottle below its current weight of 55 grams. A one-gram reduction of PET from the current container would be a 22 million pound savings to the beverage industry and a cost savings of about $15 million per year. One way to achieve this goal is to make all PET bottles with plastic closure finishes instead of aluminum closures. The removal of basecups is also another potential solution. One-piece PET bottles in the United States could fall to 50.5 grams. In Europe, PET producers are marketing a one-way PET bottle that weighs between 48 and 49 grams.

The custom container market is now at 480 million pounds with an annual growth rate of 15 percent. Within this market, sports drink containers took 45 million pounds of PET in 1992 and will grow to 70 million in 1993. Bottled mineral water in 1992 was 28 million pounds and was expected to grow to 35 million pounds in 1993. Technology Forecasts of Westport, Connecticut, projects an eight percent annual growth rate in PET resin use through 1997.

The recycled version of HDPE, the second type of plastic resin, had previously cost more than its virgin plastic, and many packagers have been using recycled HDPE to satisfy environmental concerns. But in 1994, there are indications that the gap between these plastics has significantly narrowed or, in some cases, has disappeared. Important variables between these markets are the availability of high quality, well-sorted HDPE and the degree to which collection is subsidized by municipalities. As state lawmakers and major retailers insist on recycled content packaging, demand will rise for this resin.

Vinyl, the third type of plastic resin, is used mostly for packaging household chemicals, liquid soap, shampoo, edible oils, and bottled water. In Europe, vinyl is the leading packaging material for bottled water, and 36 percent of U.S. and Canadian water bottlers reported that they used one or more sizes. For clean, one-gallon water bottles, vinyl is the leading material. Currently, 200 million pounds of vinyl bottles are produced annually, and that number is expected to grow to 270 million by 1995.

CURRENT CONDITIONS

In 1991, $3.99 billion of plastic bottles were shipped by all U.S. producers, a 2.7 percent increase over the 1990 level of $3.89 billion. 35.01 billion units of plastic bottles were shipped in 1991, a 2.0 percent increase over 1990.

The market research firm SRI International of Menlo Park, California, projects U.S. consumption of recycled PET will increase 12 percent annually through 1996, due mostly to the success of curbside collection efforts. There are now 3,100 community programs in the United States that accept PET in their recycling bins, up from 575 in 1990. Approximately 3.7 billion PET bottles were recycled in 1992. The major soft drink manufacturers now use PET bottles that contain a percentage of recycled resin. Some 19 percent of all plastic bottles were recycled in 1992, led by the 41.5 percent recycling rate of soft drink bottles. In 1991, 14 percent of all plastic bottles were recycled, also led by the 36 percent recycling rate of soft drink bottles.

INDUSTRY LEADERS

For the entire plastic bottle market, Crown, Cork, and Seal of Philadelphia, Pennsylvania, is the industry leader with between 35 and 40 percent market share. Other major players include Eastman Chemical Company, ICI Americas, Hoechst Celanese, and Shell Chemical Company. According to *Investext*, Johnson Controls held a 34 percent market share in the $1.10

billion plastic pop bottle industry in 1991. Constar International held a 32 percent market share, self-manufacturers held 16 percent, U.S. Container seven percent, Silgan six percent, and other independents five percent.

WORK FORCE

In 1991, 28,600 employees worked for an estimated 160 companies in the plastic bottle industry, up 14 percent from 25,100 employees in 1987. Twenty-five thousand of the employees in 1991 were production workers. Average wages in 1991 were $9.72 per hour, up 11.2 percent from the $8.74 per hour wage in 1987. Payroll in 1991 reached $646.7 million, up 29 percent from the level in 1987. In 1991, production hours reached 51.8 million, up 17.7 percent from 44 million hours in 1987.

California is the largest plastic bottle manufacturing state in the United States, with 36 companies shipping more than $340 million worth of bottles. It accounts for 12 percent of industry shipments, and employs approximately 3,000 workers. Other states in the top five are Ohio, with 26 companies shipping $319 million and employing 3,200; New Jersey, with 23 companies shipping $282 million and employing 2,700; Texas, with 22 companies shipping $216 million and employing 1500; and Illinois, with 22 companies shipping $200 million and employing 2,100. The bulk of the nation's plastic bottles come from the Great Lakes region, which represents about 40 percent of total industry shipments.

AMERICA AND THE WORLD

Imports of plastic bottles into the United States reached $52.1 million in 1991, up 4 percent from 1990 and up 8.1 percent from the 1989 level of $48.2 million. Exports of plastic bottles from the United States to the rest of the world reached $131 million in 1991, up 49.7 percent from $87.5 million in 1990, and up 162 percent from the 1989 level of $50 million.

Outside the United States, PET containers are battling glass for market share in the refillable-container soft drink market, especially in Europe where refillable PET is being driven by regulations and in Latin America where it is cost effective to use. Beverage containers account for 80 percent of the PET used in Europe, and just four percent was recycled in 1992. A Pan-European association called Petcore, which was formed by PET resin producers and bottle converters, is aiming to reach a recycling target of at least 15 percent, which would be in line with the European Packaging and Packaging Waste Directives. Petcore will work with public sector groups and industry to increase the recycling of blowmoulded PET containers up to five liters in size. Petcore wants to achieve a recycling target of 30 percent. Petcore's U.S. counterpart, NAPCORE, reached in 1992 a 27 percent recycling level. "Reaching 15 percent in five years will be tough. The problem is not recycling capacity, but getting the PET back from the customer," states Dr. Vince Matthews, coordinator of Petcore.

Since 1991, German law has required manufacturers, distributors and retailers to take back product packaging. Though 64 percent of all plastics must be recycled by 1995, only four percent is recycled now in Germany, but an industry consortium called Duales System Deutschland (DSD) wants to improve that level. All costs of DSD system are internalized and passed along to the consumer, and the estimated yearly per capita cost is $33. By weight, nearly 80 percent of the food and beverage container market in Germany is glass, approximately 18 percent is metal, and 2 percent is plastic. The program cost $6 billion to start and $2.6 billion annually, and has come under criticism from German citizens. A comparable program in the United States could cost $18 billion annually.

RESEARCH AND TECHNOLOGY

Two University of Pittsburgh scientists are designing plastic that can be made without toxic by-products and recycled with help from an enzyme. If the technology can be developed in an economically feasible manner, it could aid in efforts to recycle plastic bottles. Drs. Alan Russell and Eric Beckman are working on developing "bioplastic," which instead of being made with organic solvents is made with carbon dioxide. Carbon dioxide fluid can chemically sort out mixed batches of melted plastic, enabling recyclers to shred plastic and dump the pieces into a high pressure tank of supercritical carbon dioxide. The same type of plastic floats to the top of the tank, usually the lightest. Several companies are considering licensing the technology.

To aid in the recycling of plastic bottles, plastic labels are being widely produced in the same polymer type as the plastic bottle, and closures are also being made increasingly compatible.

The packaging market for stretch blow-molded plastic bottles may also expand. Favorable market potential is attributed to a new thermoplastic polyester resin and a number of new process technologies. The new resin, polyethylene naphthalate, is expected to become available in 1995 in commercial volumes and should develop opportunities for processors looking to replace glass bottles in demanding applications that cannot be accessed by PET.

INDUSTRY INFORMATION SOURCES

Census of Manufacturing Industries, Industry 3085 - Plastics Bottles.

"Crystallized Neck Thread Finish Stymies Heat Distortion: Makes Hot-Filled PET Alluring to More Beverage Processors," *Food Processing,* December 1992.

Humer, Caroline, "Shining Star: Polyethylene Terephthalate Use Increases in Plastic Container Industry," *Chemical Marketing Reporter,* February 15, 1993.

Jabbonsky, Larry, "Some Pretty Diverse Units; Beverage Packaging Industry Statistics," *Beverage World,* June 1993.

Predicasts Basebook, Cleveland, Ohio: Predicasts, SIC 3085.

Prince, Greg, "Recycling from A to Z: An Alphabetic Guide to Recycling Issues," *Beverage World,* June 1993.

Pringle, David, "Petcore to Scan Europe for Waste PET Containers: Pan-European Association Formed by Polyethylene Terephthalate Resin Producers and Bottle Converters," *Packaging Week,* January 6, 1994.

"Recycled/Virgin Cost Gap Shrinks for HDPE Bottles" *Packaging,* January 1994.

Reiter, Jeff, "Recycling Bottleneck: Promoting High Density Polythylene Bottle Recycling," *Dairy Foods Magazine,* July 1992.

Rigdon, Joan, "Technology—In the Lab: Scientists Design Greener Plastic for Recycling by Using Enzymes," *Wall Street Journal,* August 26, 1993.

Sfiligoj, Eric, "Answering the Critics, Recyclable Polyethylene Terephthalate Beverage Containers Are Replacing Glass Bottles," *Beverage World,* June 1992.

Stack, Gifford, "Green Dot Not for U.S.: Germany's Packaging Law Doesn't Make Sense Here," *Beverage Industry,* September 1993.

—William A. Bennett

SIC 3086

PLASTICS FOAM PRODUCTS

This industry covers establishments primarily engaged in manufacturing plastics foam products.

INDUSTRY SNAPSHOT

Approximately 956 establishments were engaged in the manufacture of plastics foam products in 1987. By 1990 the industry produced products estimated at $8,988.2 million. This 1990 figure remained in line with a generally upward production trend in the industry since 1987. Total value of shipments increased by over 30 percent from 1987 to 1990, higher than the increase in plastics products in general, which grew at a 17 percent rate over the same period.

This upward trend in plastics foam products production was due to several economic forces and to new applications for foam products. Consumer spending, especially for durable goods, construction, and health care products, which together make up the bulk of product demand, is expected to grow.

ORGANIZATION AND STRUCTURE

In 1987 approximately 956 establishments were engaged in the production of plastic foam products. These businesses employed approximately 67 employees per establishment, of which 51 were production workers. For the same year, the average value added per production worker was $67,029, a small figure compared to an average of $105,881 calculated for a cross-section of 459 U.S. manufacturing industries.

The largest number of plastic foam products establishments were located in the East North Central region, followed by the Middle Atlantic region and the Pacific region. However, when ranked by the number of establishments per state, California was first with 147, followed by Texas with 55, Pennsylvania with 54, Michigan with 53, Illinois and North Carolina with 51 each, Ohio with 46, and New York with 40. It was estimated that the largest five companies producing plastic foam products accounted for approximately $2.6 billion, or over 59 percent of the entire industry's sales. In descending order of market share, the dominant companies in the plastics foam products industry were: Lamson and Sessions Company's Home Products Division, with approximately 18.3 percent of the market; PMC Inc., with about 22 percent of the market; Dart Container Corporation, with 12.3 percent; E.R. Carpenter Company Inc., with 11.1 percent; Sealed Air Corporation, with 9.2 percent; and Amoco Foam Products Company, with 4.5 percent. Of the top five companies, only Sealed Air Corporation was publicly traded; the vast majority of the top 100 companies were privately held.

The industry's output was divided among various product classes as follows: furniture, and furnishings plastics foam products (including carpet underlay, carpet and rug cushions, and formed and slab stock for pillows, seating, and cushioning), led with 25.25 percent of the industry's total output; consumer and institutional plastics foam products (including cups, plates and bowls, cooler chests, and trays) followed with 18.97 percent; transportation plastics foam products, and packaging plastics foam products, each comprised approximately 15 percent of the output. Building and construction foam products, and other plastics foam products not elsewhere classified, accounted for the remaining 26 or so percent. The principal industries responsible for the purchase of plastics foam products were hospitals, buying 5.6 percent of sector output, electronic components makers, buying 5.2 percent. Personal consumption accounted for 4.3 percent.

BACKGROUND AND DEVELOPMENT

Plastics foams, sometimes called expandable plastics, are versatile materials that were first used in the post-World War II plastics boom. Plastic foam products are used both as original and as replacement materials in industries. Foam products emerge out of a unique chemical process. Foamed plastic is an expanded material with a distinct cellular structure that can be either rigid or flexible. Rigid foam consists of spherical, hollow spheres attached together, while flexible foam has its cells connected, thus giving it a spongy structure. Polystyrene and polyurethanes are used for rigid foams and vinyls, and cellulose acetate. Linear polyurethanes have been traditionally used in flexible foams. By 1969, flexible urethane dominated the market with polystyrene running second, rigid urethane third and polyvinyl chloride fourth.

Following World War II, plastics foam consumption in the United States grew tremendously, increasing more than ten-fold from 1955 to 1970. By 1967, total consumption of plastics foam products rose to 700 million pounds or $60 million. By 1970, output weight was one billion pounds. It took only five years for this figure to double. Over 700 companies in the 1970s were in some way involved in the production of plastics foams, including most major chemical companies, rubber and tire companies, textile mills, and even drug companies.

By the end of the 1960s the threat of oversupply led the industry to step up research and development to improve materials and develop new market outlets, notably tires, sporting goods, advanced military equipment, and highway safety barriers. Rigid urethane and polystyrene were used for industrial purposes such as industrial walls and cold storage insulation. The foams came in many forms—slabs, logs, sheets, rods, tubes, and particles.

In general, plastics are manufactured as follows: plastic materials (monomers) are chemically altered to produce more complex materials called polymers, which are then mixed with certain materials to impart characteristics such as durability, flexibility, and chemical resistance. Subsequent manufacturing processes produce final products such as the rigid and flexible foam used in consumer durable goods, buildings, and refrigerated transport, and so forth. Foam

production processes involve a variety of methods and the output takes the form of slabs, blocks, boards, sheets, molded shapes, and extruded insulation. Foam can also be produced on-site, for building insulation and cushioning applications. Most grades of foam are produced by extrusion and injection molding. Over half of foamed plastic is polyurethane, the rest consisting of expandable polystyrene and vinyl, phenolic, epoxy, urea, and silicone.

The post-World War II boom in plastics foam products is intertwined with the growth in general plastics manufacturing, growth stemming from a burgeoning U.S. consumer base and from the substitution of plastics for materials such as copper, aluminum, and steel. Plastic products seriously challenged metals and alloys in the aerospace, transportation, electricity, and engineering industries. In general, the plastics industry is the single most important "downstream" industry in the petrochemicals value-added chain. Plastics are produced by various chemical processes that allow forming end-products through heating, milling, or extrusion. Plastics soften but do not melt when heated, thereby allowing them to change shape without losing cohesion. Before the 1930s, industrial products were largely based on coal as the basic chemical feed stock. The surge in production and consumption of plastic was directly related to the availability of petroleum—plastic's main chemical feedstock. The petroleum and plastics industry are linked; petrochemicals provide the basis for mass production of plastics and, conversely, plastics provide petroleum with their main downstream market.

Total plastics foam production tripled from 1970 to 1980. Increased production was fueled during this period by skyrocketing demand for consumer goods such as furniture cushioning, mattresses, bedding, and other items that use mostly urethane foams. Rigid foam found growing use in buildings, refrigerated transports, household refrigerators and freezers, dehumidifiers, dishwashers, packaging, and marine salvage.

CURRENT CONDITIONS

The main concern of industry leaders is, of course, market growth and expansion. Of particular interest are consumer durable goods, construction, and health care, which make up a large portion of demand for the industry's products. The early 1990s upturn in consumer spending, especially for durables such as appliances, (which use large quantities of rigid foam and adhesives) buoyed the market for plastic foams; construction, also rigid foam user, underwent similar growth.

The plastics industry faces challenges due to environmental damage caused by its use of certain processes and chemicals. The industry must comply with federal and worldwide environmental rules aimed at banning use of chlorofluorocarbons (CFCs), which are said to deplete the ozone layer. The rules have led to a competitive race to develop replacements for CFCs. In addition, political pressure is forcing companies to develop recycling processes; as of the early 1990s, only a small portion of plastic in general was recyclable.

"We will soon eliminate CFCs from all our products," said Gert Baumann of Miles Inc., and Chairman of the Polyurethane Division of the Society of the Plastics Industry, quoted in *Modern Plastics* in 1992. Industry attention was focussed, for the price of noncompliance was high. Under the Montreal Protocol signed by most industrial countries in 1987, CFCs were to be banned worldwide by the year 2000 and in the United States by 1995. In the United States, tax penalties on CFCs rose from $0.25 per pound at the end of 1992 to $2.65 per pound by 1994.

The industry has devoted significant resources to developing alternatives to CFCs. They have been very successful in the flexible foam sector but less progress has been made by rigid foam makers. For rigid foams, some firms are developing new formulations that use hydrochlorofluorocarbons (HCFCs), which have a lower ozone depletion potential than CFCs, while retaining some of CFCs' desirable properties. Flexible foams are also being reformulated. New machinery has been developed, tailored to the low boiling point agents that are gradually replacing CFCs.

Recycling efforts are also underway. For example, construction board has been made from rigid foam scrap and carpet pad has been produced from auto seating scrap. Though most of the focus in the recycling movement has been on bottles and foamed polystyrene containers, the push is on for polyurethane recycling. The plastics foam products industry and federal, state, and local governments are evaluating the merits of various recycling policies.

Finally, in addition to its recycling efforts, firms in the industry hope to improve the aesthetic of urethane foams, particularly in automobiles. For example, technology is being developed which would reduce foam scorching at high temperatures. And, in another effort, some are attempting to eliminate fogging that occurs on the insides of car windows when sunlight heats up plastics in passenger compartments.

Buoyed by continued growth and innovation, the plastics foam industry seems strong enough to meet the challenge of environmental regulation.

WORK FORCE

Over the period covering 1987-1990, total employment in the plastics products industry overall rose by only 3.2 percent, from 12,500 to 12,900 people. Production worker employment followed roughly the same trend, rising from 9,500 to a peak of 10,000 in 1989 before declining to 9,800 in 1990.

In 1990, the major occupational categories for the plastics products industry total were: plastic molding machine operators, who made up 17.8 percent of total employment; assemblers and fabricators, who made up 8.6 percent, and packers and packagers, who comprised 4.8 percent. Approximately 8.7 percent of industry employees were engaged in some type of managerial or supervisory function, while 6.2 percent were engaged in clerical, transportation, and accounting/financial tasks. The remaining employees were engaged in production activity.

The Bureau of Labor Statistics has forecast that all these occupational categories will grow by the year 2005, reflecting the growth in demand for this industry's products. The occupation making up the bulk of the industry's employment, plastic molding machine operators, should grow 29.5 percent to 2005, trailing 12 other industry categories in projected growth. Production workers as a percentage of total industry employment has drifted downward slowly, falling from 80 percent in 1972 to about 78 percent in the late 1980s.

The industry job categories with the largest projected growth to 2005 were largely non-production jobs: sales and related workers, projected to grow by 69 percent; industrial production managers, 64.2 percent; industrial machinery mechanics, 50.9 percent; and tool & die makers, 44.9 percent. Categories uniformly forecast to grow by 35.8 percent were: blue collar worker supervisors; hand packers and packagers; inspectors, testers and graders; freight, stock, and material movers; and extruding and forming machine operators.

Concerning the industry's income distribution, while average hourly earnings of production workers in plastic products production rose from $3.27 in 1972 to $8.43 in 1987, the purchasing power of these wages actually declined by 10 percent. General payroll per employee, adjusted for inflation, fell from an average of $18,215 to $17,903. From 1987 to 1992, average hourly earnings rose by about 13 percent to $9.63, which, in real terms, translated into a decline of almost nine percent. From 1972 to 1987, in terms of value added per production worker, wages per hour rose about two and one half times, while the value added per hour by these production workers rose by over three times, a shift in income distribution away from wages and toward profits.

INDUSTRY INFORMATION SOURCES

Dubois, Harry, *Plastics History U.S.A.,* Hanover, Massachusetts: Halliday Lithographic Company, 1972.

Graff, Gordon, ''Improving Economics and Replacing CFCs dominate polyurethanes,'' *Modern Plastics,* December, 1992.

Manufacturing USA: Industry Analyses, Statistics, and Leading Companies, 3rd Edition, Michigan: Gale Publications, 1993.

Rosato, Dominick V., William K. Fallon, and Donald V. Rosado. *Markets For Plastics,* New York: Van Nostrand, Reinhold Co., 1969.

United Nations Centre on Transnational Corporations, United Nations. *Transnational Corporations in the Plastics Industry,* New York: United Nations, 1990.

U.S. Department of Commerce, International Trade Administration, *U.S. Industrial Outlook 1994,* Washington, D.C.: U.S. Government Printing Office, January, 1994.

—John A. Sarich

SIC 3087

CUSTOM COMPOUNDING OF PURCHASED PLASTICS RESINS

This category covers establishments primarily engaged in custom compounding of purchased plastics resins. For more information related to this industry, see the **SIC 2821: Plastic Materials, Synthetic Resins, and Nonvulcanizable Elastomers**.

Custom compounding companies purchase plastic resins from plastic manufacturers. They alter and manipulate the resins to form new compounds, which they usually sell to companies that make plastic products. They contribute to the plastic manufacturing process by upgrading the quality and performance of resins, improving the efficiency of the compounding process, and developing entirely new plastic substances. Custom compounding emerged as a separate industry during the 1980s and is credited with increasing the breadth of the U.S. plastics business during that decade. About one-third of all U.S. polymer production undergoes some sort of compounding.

BACKGROUND AND DEVELOPMENT

Plastics are extremely long polymers, or long-chain molecules, which are shaped and molded under heat and pressure to form a resin. Resins typically take the form of pellets, flakes, powder, granules, or liquid. Although many resin manufacturers process their own resins and even make plastic products, they often sell resins to companies that make custom compounds. Custom compounders alter the physical properties of the resins they purchase by: 1) mixing or melt-state blending several resins together; 2) introducing additives, or; 3) adding fillers and reinforcements. An almost infinite number of compounds, each with varying grades and performance characteristics, can be created.

Several categories of additives are used to make compounds. Plasticizers, the most common additives, are chemicals that increase a resin's flexibility. Similarly, impact modifiers increase stress resistance. Plasticizers and impact modifiers are used, for example, to increase the resilience of plastic automobile body panels or to make polyvinyl chloride (PVC) resins used in construction materials. Various stabilizers and antioxidants are used to retard the oxidation and breakdown of resins that results from exposure to heat, light, air, and moisture. Heat stabilizers, for instance, help resins to retain their physical structure during processing. Flame retardants are added to reduce inflammability, and colorants are used to change a resin's hue.

Fillers and reinforcements are used to add texture, strength, and other characteristics to resins without changing their polymer structure. Examples of fillers are cotton and asbestos flocks, glass fibers, chopped monofilaments, carbon fibers, hollow glass spheres, metal powder, and carbon. Glass fiber, which is integrated as whole or chopped mat, and carbon fiber have traditionally accounted for the majority of filler and reinforcement material used in the plastics industry.

Plastic compounding companies work with and create four general grades of resins and compounds. Commodity resins, which receive little attention in this industry, are low-tech plastics made with standardized formulas. Intermediate resins are slightly more advanced. Engineering resins exhibit higher performance characteristics. Advanced resin compounds, the most expensive class, are those most able to withstand exposure to heat, weight, impact, acids, and other forces. They are typically used for applications in aerospace, microelectronics, and other high-tech industries.

The first plastic, a natural material called Keratin, was developed in the early 1700s. Parkesine, the first synthetic plastic, was invented in 1862 by Englishmen

Alexander Parkes; but, it was American John Wyatt who recognized the important plasticizing effect of the Parkesine production process. Wyatt renamed the substance Celluloid in 1870 and is recognized as the founder of modern day plastic making in the United States.

The use of plastics increased rapidly during the early 1900s as new processing techniques, such as molding, evolved. Compounding occurred, but in relatively simple ways. Resins were combined with paints and varnishes, for example, to increase their durability. Not until World War II were more advanced compounding processes used on a broad scale—to make items such as airplane gun turret covers and lightweight field equipment. Huge advances in the chemical additives industry during the 1950s through the 1970s created a strong demand for new compounds with specific characteristics. As compounders learned to make resins more flexible, durable, attractive, and flame retardant, the need for plastics compounds grew. By the early 1980s, the plastics industry was shipping $15 billion worth of resins, about 30 percent of which were compounded by resin manufacturers or plastic goods producers.

During the 1980s, the U.S. plastics industry began to shift its focus from commodity-like resins and compounds to higher grade products that could be used to replace steel, glass, and other natural, more expensive materials. The development of high-tech additives and alloys allowed U.S. producers to retain their global industry lead in spite of fierce foreign competition from low-cost manufacturers. As the need for advanced, efficient compounding processes expanded, custom compounding firms proliferated.

By 1987, custom compounders were processing about 8.5 billion pounds of resins annually and grossing $2.5 billion. And despite a late 1980s recession, production volume jumped to 12.5 billion pounds by 1990 and industry revenues climbed to $3.2 billion, reflecting average annual sales growth of eight percent between 1986 and 1990. As plastics consumers increasingly sought the expertise and efficiency of custom compounding companies, revenues swelled at a rate of approximately seven to ten percent annually during the early 1990s.

CURRENT CONDITIONS

Two dominant trends in the custom compounding industry in the early 1990s included increased competition and a growing demand for specialty and high-tech compounds. For example, fast growing product segments included electrically conductive plastic compounds, specialty color-concentrates, and liquid-crys-

tal polymers. And although most custom compounding companies continued to realize revenue and profit gains in the early 1990s, greater competition was diminishing overall profit growth. Indeed, compounding firms in Taiwan, Singapore, Indonesia, and other low-cost manufacturing countries were vying for U.S. export market share.

Besides greater foreign competition, several major U.S. resin suppliers were entering the custom compounding arena by providing small orders of highly tailored materials. To combat new competition and to reduce costs associated with research, development, and environmental regulations, many custom compounders were acquiring or merging with their competitors. In addition, some commodity resin producers were acquiring custom compounding firms as a means of diversifying their operations.

Despite new competition, compounding revenues were forecast to grow at an annual rate of about nine percent through at least 1994, and some niche market segments were expected to expand 20 percent or more annually. The total volume of resins processed by custom compounders was estimated at about 20 million pounds in 1994. Continued growth in this market is expected to be driven by an ongoing trend toward highly differentiated resins and new plastic goods manufacturing methods. Importantly, new plastic assembly and molding techniques will continue to generate a market for compatible compounds. Likewise, a growing need for environmentally friendly production processes and biodegradable compounds will boost industry activity.

INDUSTRY LEADERS

About 380 companies participated in the custom compounding industry in the early 1990s. Only the top ten achieved sales of more than $5 million in 1991, and all had 150 or fewer employees. The largest custom compounder was Fibre Glass-Evercoat Co. Inc., of Ohio, which had 1991 sales of $40 million and about 100 employees. Insta-Foam Products Inc., of Illinois, was the second largest producer with revenues of $25 million. Other major players included Dennis Chemical Co., of Missouri, and Dexter Corp., of New Jersey.

WORK FORCE

The industry employed about 18,000 workers going into the 1990s. Long-term employment prospects for this and related plastics industries is generally positive, though workers are paid less, on average, than other U.S. manufacturing employees. For more information about jobs and salaries see **SIC 2821:**

Plastic Materials, Synthetic Resins, and Nonvulcanizable Elastomers.

RESEARCH AND TECHNOLOGY

A technological focal point in the mid-1990s was the development of techniques that allowed resin processors to create compounds and alloys while extruding plastic into molds. By melting and mixing compounds during the molding process, processors were able to eliminate problems caused by heating resins twice. Such compound/molding techniques were already resulting in higher performance and less expensive plastic products by the early 1990s. Specifically, new grades of materials created using these new compounding techniques were capable of making products with thinner walls, greater product uniformity, and more even molecular distribution—improvements that allowed for increased use of plastics in automobiles and packaging industries, for example.

Significant expenditures were also being directed toward the development of new-environmentally safe compounds. Companies were striving to meet new chlorofluorocarbon (CFC) emission regulations by developing compounds that would not require hazardous manufacturing processes. Similarly, new additives and compounds were under development in the mid-1990s that would accelerate the natural breakdown of plastics products and reduce landfill waste. Although technologies like weak-link and bacterial polymers showed promise, extremely high production costs made them commercially impractical for most purposes in 1994.

INDUSTRY INFORMATION SOURCES

Ainsworth, Susan J., ''Plastics Additives,'' *Chemical & Engineering News*, August 31, 1992.

Byrne, Harlan S., ''Spartech Corp.,'' *Barron's*, February 1, 1993.

Coombes, Peter, ''Compounders Change Shape,'' *Chemical Week*, April 4, 1990.

Darnay, Arsen J., ed., *Manufacturing USA; Industry Analyses, Statistics, and Leading Companies*, Detroit: Gale Research Inc., 1993.

Kreisher, Keith, ''Compounding's Growth Fosters New Machines, Process Technology,'' *Modern Plastics*, July 1991.

Kreisher, Keith, ''Compounding Goes On-Line with Big Payoff to Users,'' *Modern Plastics*, July 1990.

McCoy, Michael, ''Compounds Credited for Plastics Growth,'' *Chemical Marketing Reporter*, May 18, 1992.

Miller, Bernie, ''Molder-Friendly Resins Keep the Dream Alive,'' *Plastics World*, September 1993.

Modern Plastics Encyclopedia, New York: McGraw-Hill Inc., October 1987.

Smock, Doug, ''Health Concerns Spur New Biocide Uses,'' *Plastics World*, March 1992.

Swain, Robert, ''Ban on Cadmium: Is it Logical?'' *Plastics World*, November 1993.

U.S. Industrial Outlook 1993, Washington, D.C.: U.S. Department of Commerce, January 1993.

Wood, Andrew, ''Plastics Compounding: Restructuring Brings a Different Lineup,'' *Chemical Week*, May 12, 1993.

—Dave Mote

SIC 3088

PLASTICS PLUMBING FIXTURES

This category includes establishments primarily engaged in manufacturing plastics plumbing fixtures. Establishments primarily engaged in assembling plastics plumbing fixture fittings are classified in **SIC 3432: Plumbing Fixture Fittings and Trim.** Establishments primarily engaged in manufacturing plastics plumbing fixture components are classified in **SIC 3089: Plastics Products, Not Elsewhere Classified.** As a result of the 1987 SIC industry reclassification, information is unavailable for the industry prior to 1987 at this level of aggregation.

INDUSTRY SNAPSHOT

In the 1990s, plastics plumbing products included among other items bathtubs, sinks, and lavatories. The value of industry shipments increased from $709 million in 1987 to an estimated $1.12 billion in 1993, in 1987 dollars. The value of shipments in current dollars was an estimated $972 million in 1993, revealing substantial price deflation for the industry's outputs. There were about 170 establishments in the industry. Half of these establishments had 20 or more employees. Average firm size as measured by the number of production workers per establishment was 12 percent larger than that for the manufacturing sector as a whole.

The industry employed an estimated 6,000 production workers in 1993, down from a peak of 7,100 in 1988. The industry was relatively capital-intensive, on average 23 percent higher than the manufacturing sector as a whole, by investment per production worker. Annual hours worked by production workers in the industry were slightly less than those worked in the manufacturing sector at large, and hourly wages were 22 percent lower.

ORGANIZATION AND STRUCTURE

Of the top 30 firms by sales in the plastics plumbing fixtures industry, two-thirds were private independents, the others being exclusively subsidiaries and divisions of larger firms. Only one of the top five firms was a private independent. The top 15 firms had greater than $10 million in sales.

Production was concentrated in the relatively recently industrialized states of the South and Southwest. The states ranking in the top nine by number of establishments were, highest to lowest, California (with 34), Texas (with 18), Florida (with 13), Georgia and Michigan (with 10 each), Illinois (with 8), Ohio (with 7), and Washington and Indiana (with 6 each). Together these nine states accounted for 55 percent of all establishments and 65 percent of total employment for the industry, with California alone accounting for 23 percent of total employment. The average number of employees per establishment varied widely by state. Colorado, with the highest number of employees per plant, averaged nearly six times as many employees per plant as Florida and Ohio.

The industry is served by the Plumbing Manufacturers Institute, headquartered in Glen Ellyn, Illinois. The Institute was founded in 1956 and had 50 members. The Institute, which organizes semiannual conventions, has committees on Codes, Government Affairs, Standards, Intra-Industry, and Statistics.

BACKGROUND AND DEVELOPMENT

The development and use of plumbing fixtures increased rapidly after the introduction of pressurized water supply and sanitary drainage systems in the 1840s. Kitchen sinks and toilets were the first fixtures installed, followed by washtubs and bathtubs. The earliest sinks and tubs were made of wood lined with sheets of metal. Thereafter, cast iron and glazed pottery sinks came into broad use. One significant early improvement in sinks was the built-in overflow.

The 1870s saw the increased popularity of bathing and new techniques of bathtub production. These new tubs were made of enameled cast iron and were mass produced by a New York manufacturer.

The first modern toilet was designed by the Englishman Joseph Bramah in about 1790. Known as a valve closet, this design saw long use in the toilet compartment of railroad cars. The valve closet was followed by the less expensive pan closet, which was in common use from the 1830s to the 1870s. Also developed in England, the pan closet had a lead bowl with a hole in the bottom sealed by a hinged copper pan. In the 1850s, glazed pottery toilets came into use, and in the 1880s the first all earthenware toilets were developed in England.

The early plumbing fixtures were primarily of English design. This changed after the 1880s, when the United States became a center of fixture design. Louis Nielsen describes this change and possible causes for it in his book *Standard Plumbing Engineering Design*. After the 1880s, he writes, ''developments in plumbing fixture design proceeded independently and at an accelerated pace in the United States. Much of this may be attributed to . . . [U.S. industrial expansion and] the continuous increase in population due to waves of immigration, and the tremendous demand for new homes and buildings to house the swelling numbers in industrial centers all over the country.''

Many of the designs and materials developed in the United States around the turn of the century dominated the industry until very recently. Key among these was the development of the washdown toilet, similar in principle to today's toilet. One of the key advantages of this toilet was that it remained sanitary after extended use, thereby rendering earlier toilet designs obsolete. A number of improvements were made to this basic design in the twentieth century. These involved combining the components of the washdown toilet into a single integrated unit, using siphon jets to strengthen the flush, and reducing noise of operation.

As regards materials, one of the key developments around the turn of the century was glazed vitreous chinaware. With its smooth impervious surface, vitreous chinaware was the dominant material for many plumbing fixtures, until the rapid growth in the use of plastic fixtures in recent years. Introduced by plumbing fixture manufacturers in 1952, plastics came to be widely used for toilets, bathtubs, whirlpool baths, shower stalls, utility and laundry sinks, and sink-washtray combinations in bathrooms.

The creation of industry-wide standards was important to the development of the industry. Nationwide standards first appeared just after World War I. Contemporary standards were established by the American National Standards Institute's Committee A112. These standards address both design and materials suitability. Regarding the general quality of fixtures, standards require that fixtures ''shall have smooth impervious surfaces, shall be durable for the uses intended, and shall be free from defects and concealed fouling surfaces.'' The regulations also detailed standard dimensions and other specifications for fixtures.

CURRENT CONDITIONS

Industry conditions suggest future growth. The overall trend in shipments was strongly upward from 1987 to 1993, increasing by 57 percent in real terms over the period, with 1993 a peak year. Capital investments increased even more rapidly, with $15 million invested in 1987, $19 million in 1988, $69 million in 1989, $110 million in 1990, and $91 million in 1991. The value of imports of plastics plumbing fixtures increased from $24 million in 1989 to an estimated $49 million in 1993, while the value of exports increased from $19 million to $48 million for these same years.

Employment of production workers declined overall from 1988 to 1993. The Bureau of Labor Statistics made employment forecasts at the general industry level for 30 occupational categories. For the period from 1990 to 2005, employment was projected to increase in all 30 occupations, with double-digit increases in 26 occupations. These projections were at odds with early 1990s employment patterns in the plastics plumbing fixtures industry, which industry, however, made up only one percent of total employment at this general industry level in 1991.

Plumbing fixtures are primarily made of three materials and are classified into three different industries accordingly. Aside from the plastics plumbing fixtures industry, are **SIC 3261: Vitreous Plumbing Fixtures** and **SIC 3431: Metal Plumbing Fixtures**. The primary demand for plumbing fixtures results from new construction. New construction slumped after the late 1980s and picked up again after 1992, and the fortunes of the plumbing fixtures industries followed accordingly. Recent increases in the number of bathrooms in new housing benefited the industry. From the early 1980s to the early 1990s, the number of newly-built single occupancy homes with two-and-one-half or more baths doubled to 44 percent.

The use of plastic plumbing fixtures grew at the expense of the vitreous and metal plumbing fixtures industries. The *U.S. Industrial Outlook* for 1994 described this development as follows: ''In recent years changing consumer tastes have displaced other materials with plastics for bathtubs, whirlpool baths, and lavatory sinks. Although plastics' share has slipped slightly during the recent contraction of building activity, they still account for 62 percent of bathtubs, 92 percent of whirlpool baths, and 28 percent of lavatories produced. Vitreous materials were used principally for bathroom fixtures - toilet bowls, flush tanks, and lavatories. Metal fixtures (enameled or stainless steel) dominate in the kitchen, and retain a significant portion of the lavatory and bathtub markets.'' While from 1987 to 1993 the real value of shipments suffered overall declines of eight percent for the metal plumbing fixtures industry, and 15 percent for the vitreous plumbing fixtures industry, the real value of shipments of plastic plumbing fixtures increased by 57 percent over these same years.

INDUSTRY LEADERS

The top five firms in the industry in 1992 were Tomkins Industries Inc.-Lasco Products Group of Anaheim, California; Bristol Corp. of Bristol, Indiana; Aqua Glass Corp. of Adamsville, Tennessee; Hancor Co. of Findlay, Ohio; and the Universal-Rundle Corp. Fiberglass Division of New Castle, Pennsylvania. Together these firms accounted for about 50 percent of total sales and over 70 percent of total employment for the industry.

Tomkins Industries Inc.-Lasco Products Group was founded in 1947 and had $160 million in sales and 1,360 employees in 1992. The thirteenth largest producer in the industry, Lasco Bath Fixtures of Cordele, Georgia, was a division of the Lasco Products Group.

The firm's immediate parent was Tomkins Industries Inc. of Dayton, Ohio, a diversified company with sixteen manufacturing operations. Ultimate ownership of the firm was held by Tomkins PLC of the United Kingdom.

The Bristol Corp. was founded in 1947 and had $110 million in sales and 1,300 employees in 1992. The firm was a subsidiary of the privately held Bristol Holding Corp., also of Bristol, Indiana.

The Aqua Glass Corp. was founded in 1969 and had $90 million in sales and 1,000 employees in 1992. The firm became a wholly-owned subsidiary of the publicly held Masco Corp. in 1984. Aqua Glass manufactured acrylic bathtubs, showers, and whirlpools. The firm began marketing its products on the West Coast in the early 1990s and in 1993 announced the opening of its first West Coast office in Klamath Falls, Oregon. The expanded facilities were to include manufacturing and warehousing operations and were expected to employ 300 persons by 1996.

The Hancor Co. was a private independent firm founded in 1902 with $54 million in sales and 600 employees in 1992. Hancor was originally a producer of clay drainage tiles. The firm had fourteen plants in 1992 and announced plans in 1993 to substantially expand its manufacturing facilities.

The Fiberglass Division of the Universal-Rundle Corp. had $41 million in sales and 700 employees in 1992. Universal-Rundle became a wholly-owned subsidiary of the publicly held Nortek Inc. in 1986.

RESEARCH AND TECHNOLOGY

The key areas of industry development concerned water conservation and accommodation of the disabled and elderly. Conventional fixtures were wasteful of water, with waste rates of 70 percent for conventional toilets and 50 percent for conventional showers. The *U.S Industrial Outlook* for 1994 described the development of water-conserving fixtures as follows: "An emerging trend in the market for fixtures and fittings is the increasing popularity of products that use substantially less water. These models, such as water closet bowls that use 1.6 gallons of water or less per flush (about half the amount of typical older models), have been encouraged by water and energy conservation regulations. Industry standards mandating their use in new installations were scheduled for the near future." Among these regulations were the National Plumbing Products Efficiency Act of 1991.

Though water conservation fixtures typically cost up to 30 to 50 percent more than conventional fixtures, they sold well nationwide, but particularly in drought-afflicted California. In 1992 Toto Niki USA introduced a tankless computerized toilet that not only conserved water but flushed quietly. The industry standard for faucets was for flows of 2.5 to 2.7 gallons per minute in 1992. New York State had the nation's strictest regulations regarding faucet flow in 1992, and 90 percent of bath faucets produced met these standards. Yet manufacturers expected to see new regulations that would lower this standard to as low as 2 gallons per minute.

Industry manufacturers, prompted by the Americans with Disabilities Act of 1990, accelerated design and production of fixtures to accommodate the disabled. The Act defines disability broadly, such that some 43 million Americans fall within the definition, and the Act requires owners and tenants of buildings defined as 'public accommodations' to provide sinks, toilets, and drinking fountains that were accessible to those with disabilities. An article in the August 10, 1992 issue of *National Home Center News* reported on the rapid sales growth of plumbing fixtures designed to accommodate the elderly and disabled: "Spurred by demand from an aging population that's growing and a greater focus on the needs of the handicapped, category sales have been growing in the double digits and even faster for many home centers and hardware stores around the country." These fixtures include high-seat toilets, half-pedestal sinks, shower stalls with molded-in seats, and bathtubs with integrated seats that can be automatically raised and lowered.

INDUSTRY INFORMATION SOURCES

"Accessibility Poses New Challenges to Plumbing Design," *Consulting Specifying Engineer,* February, 1993.

Annual Survey of Manufactures, Washington, D.C.: U.S. Census Bureau, 1991.

Breger, Bill, "Pipe Maker Hancor a Long Way from its Clay Foundation," *Plastics News,* March 2, 1992.

Breger, Bill, "Hancor Inc. Building 15th HDPE Pipe Plant," *Plastic News,* September 6, 1993.

"Computerized Toilet is Silent, Tankless," *Design News,* December 21, 1992.

Daniels, Peggy Kneffel and Carol A. Schwartz, eds., *Encyclopedia of Associations* (28th ed.). Detroit, Michigan: Gale Research Inc., 1994.

Darnay, Arsen J., ed., *Manufacturing USA: Industry Analysis, Statistics, and Leading Companies* (3rd ed.), Detroit, Michigan: Gale Research Inc., 1993.

"Elderly a Growing Category for Dealers," *National Home Center News,* August 10, 1992.

"Engineers at the Bar," *Consulting Specifying Engineer,* August 1992.

"Hancor Adds Lines at Four Facilities," *Plastic News,* June 28, 1993.

"Klamath Falls Attracts Aqua Glass Corporation," *Plants, Sites and Parks,* January 1993.

"Make Room for Water-Savers," *Hardware Age,* April 1992.

"Making it Easier to Soak the Elderly," *Wall Street Journal,* January 17, 1992.

Moody's Industrial Manual, New York: Moody's Investors Service Inc., 1993.

Moody's International Manual, New York: Moody's Investors Service Inc., 1993.

Nielsen, Louis S., *Standard Plumbing Engineering Design,* Second Edition, New York: McGraw-Hill Book Co., 1982.

Ruderman, Gary S., "Consumer Backlash to Flood Mandate for Low-Flow Faucets," *National Home Center News,* October 12, 1992.

Standard and Poor's Register of Corporations, Directors and Executives, Vol. I, New York: Standard and Poor's, 1994.

U.S. Industrial Outlook, Washington, D.C.: U.S. Department of Commerce, 1994.

Ward's Business Directory of U.S. Private and Public Companies, Detroit, Michigan: Gale Research Inc., 1993.

—David Kucera

SIC 3089

PLASTICS PRODUCTS, NOT ELSEWHERE CLASSIFIED

This category covers establishments primarily engaged in manufacturing plastics products not classified elsewhere. Establishments primarily engaged in manufacturing artificial leather are classified in **SIC 2295: Coated Fabrics, Not Rubberized.**

Companies in the not elsewhere classified plastics products industry manufacture a multitude of items, ranging from clothespins and air mattresses to shoe soles and septic tanks. This industry accounted for approximately 60 percent of all plastics products sales in the early 1990s. For more information about manufacturing processes and the history of plastics products, see other entries in industry group 308. For information regarding resin manufacturing, see **SIC 2821: Plastics Materials, Synthetic Resins, and Nonvulcanizable Elastomers.**

There are at least 12 major processing techniques used to form plastics goods. A traditional and popular technique is extrusion, which entails melting and compressing plastic granules in a tube. A screw conveyor inside the tube forces the plastic through a nozzle at the end of the tube. The physical characteristics of the plastic can be altered by applying heat or cold to the barrel, adjusting the screw pressure, or by using different types and sizes of screws. Extrusion processes are used to make pipe, sheeting, films, and various forms.

Another popular processing technique is blow-molding, whereby extruded plastic is forced into a bottle-shaped mold. Compressed air inflates the hot plastic and pushes it against the cold sides of the mold, resulting in thin-walled plastic containers. Injection molding, one of the most popular processing operations, entails extruding plastic directly into a mold, where it hardens into a solid form. Sheets of plastic are created through calendaring or film and sheet extrusion. Foam is made in a process called foaming. Other popular plastic processing techniques include film casting, rotational molding, laminating, and casting.

The two main classes of plastics are thermosets and thermoplastics. Thermosets, which account for only ten percent of the material used in this industry, harden by chemical reaction and cannot be melted and reshaped once they are created. Primary products created with thermoset plastics are epoxies and phenol formaldehyde (Bakelite). Epoxies are used to manufacture flooring, protective coatings, adhesives and cements, electrical hardware, and particle board. Bake-

lite is formed into electrical parts, pot handles, and various knobs.

Thermoplastics include acrylics, cellulose proportionate (Forticel), ABS (acrylonitrile-butadiene-styrene), polyphenylene oxide (Noryl), and polysulfone. Acrylics are utilized in the production of windows, signs, vehicle light covers, and textiles. Forticel is applied in the manufacture of items such as pens, typewriter keys, telephone housing, and other applications that require impact strength. ABS, which has very high impact resistance, is used to make drain pipes, automobile parts, and small appliances and tools. Noryl, which combines high impact strength with temperature stability, is used for products like machine parts and equipment housing. Lastly, polysulfone, which is heat resistant, is used in battery casings, smoke alarms, electronic connectors, and shower heads.

Although miscellaneous plastics products markets are extremely fragmented, a few major categories stand out. For instance, miscellaneous plastic packaging, such as caps, food trays, and bubble wrap, constituted a leading 12 percent of shipments in the early 1990s. Fabricated plastics used for vehicles, such as turn indicator housings, also made up 12 percent of the market. Plastics used to make electrical devices accounted for about eight percent of industry sales, and plastic siding contributed two percent of revenues. Other major product groups included doors and window frames, dinnerware and kitchenware, and plastic furniture parts.

BACKGROUND AND DEVELOPMENT

Keratin, a natural plastic, was used in the United States to make lantern windows and other simple items as early as 1740. Gutta Percha, or gum elastic, was first used during the middle 1850s to make billiard balls and ocean cable insulation, Manufacturers borrowed forming and processing techniques from Malayan natives. Shellac plastics, developed by Samuel Speck, also emerged during the middle 1800s, and were used to create goods such as checkers, buttons, and insulators.

Following the invention of the first synthetic plastics in the late 1870s (see **SIC 2821: Plastics Materials, Synthetic Resins, and Nonvulcanizable Elastomers**), plastics products sales began to accelerate. American Dr. Baekland introduced the first moldable plastic, Bakelite, in 1909. Bakelite prompted a flurry of new molding techniques and resins during the early 1900s. Advances during World War II also bolstered the industry. The rampant proliferation of new synthetic chemicals and production processes during the 1950s, 1960s, and 1970s resulted in massive industry expansion. By the late 1970s, plastics products had become a staple of American life and were rapidly displacing conventional materials in a range of applications.

U.S. sales of miscellaneous plastics products expanded rapidly during the 1980s, but increased competition, both at home and abroad, contributed to lagging price growth. Total U.S. plastics products shipments, excluding bottles and plumbing equipment, rose to $58 billion by 1987. About 60 percent—or $33.8 billion—of that total was comprised of miscellaneous goods from this industry. Despite a late 1980s and early 1990s U.S. recession, shipment growth persisted as new additives and processing techniques were introduced. As the industry entered the 1990s, it was grossing $39 billion annually and employing a work force of more than 400,000.

CURRENT CONDITIONS

Stiff competition and weak prices continued to plague manufacturers in the early 1990s, but increased sales of plastic goods for automobiles, packaged goods, and construction materials in 1992 and 1993 boosted margins for many competitors. Output of all plastics products grew 5.7 percent in 1992 and 5.4 percent in 1993, and prices in some important market segments rose an estimated three percent to five percent per year. Sales in some depressed sectors, such as high-tech engineering plastics, were rebounding. Industry receipts were expected to climb at a rate of three percent to six percent annually through the mid-1990s.

In the long term, the use of plastics products will proliferate. But successful manufacturers will be forced to develop and implement improved processing techniques that reduce costs and improve quality. As foreign competition mounts—particularly for commodity-like products—U.S. technological superiority in plastics will become paramount.

As in the early 1990s, many companies will respond to increased competition by acquiring or merging with competitors to reduce research and development costs, establish a global presence, and pool capital investment dollars for expensive new equipment. Some smaller firms with niche expertise will also find growth.

INDUSTRY LEADERS

Despite industry consolidation during the late 1980s and early 1990s, the miscellaneous plastics products industry remained relatively fragmented. About 8,000 companies competed going into the 1990s, down from almost 8,600 in 1987. The average industry participant shipped about $4.7 million worth of goods, or less than 60 percent as much as the average U.S. manufacturer. The majority of producers are small and specialized.

The largest competitor in the early 1990s was Premark International Inc., of Illinois. Premark, a diversified plastics manufacturer, had 1991 sales of $2.7 billion and employed 25,400 workers. The second biggest player was USG Corp., also of Illinois, which had $1.9 billion in 1991 revenues and employed about 12,000 workers. Other industry leaders included: Aeroquip Corp. ($1.4 billion in 1991 sales), of Ohio; Premark International Inc. ($960 million); the Florida-based division of Premark; and Owens-Illinois Closure Inc. ($580 million), of Ohio.

WORK FORCE

The industry's 400,000 member work force will benefit in the future from strong growth in demand for plastics products. However, productivity gains achieved through automation and the integration of more efficient processing techniques will contribute to a lag between shipment growth and new jobs. Opportunities for laborers will likely expand 30 percent to 40 percent between 1990 and 2005, according to the Bureau of Labor Statistics. For example, jobs for molding machine operators—which account for about 17 percent of the work force—will likely grow by 30 percent, as will positions for managers and executives. Better yet, jobs for sales professionals, industrial machine operators, and machinery mechanics will spiral 50 percent to 70 percent by 2005. Unfortunately, workers in this industry receive, on average, only 75 percent of the wages paid in other U.S. manufacturing industries.

AMERICA AND THE WORLD

Although exports and imports have traditionally played a minor role in the plastics products industry, imports (excluding bottles and plumbing) into the United States swelled six-fold during the 1980s to about $3.8 billion by 1991. By the early 1990s, the U.S. plastics products industry trade surplus had been whittled to only $200 million. While a weak dollar and increased industry productivity helped to buoy the trade surplus in 1992 and 1993, foreign competition was expected to increase in the long term.

One of the regions of greatest growth was China. Its plastics products shipments soared more than 200 percent during the 1980s, reaching approximately 4.1 billion tons by 1992 and reflecting average annual growth of about 12.5 percent. Chinese manufacturers suffered, however, from a lack of production equipment and access to processed raw materials. As capacity accelerates to meet demand during the 1990s, China will likely become a formidable competitor in export markets, particularly in fast growing East Asian countries.

Imports may also rise in the wake of the North American Free Trade Agreement, as U.S. manufacturers move production facilities south of the border to take advantage of inexpensive labor and reduced environmental restrictions. After Canada, Mexico was the second biggest importer of plastics goods into the United States during 1993.

RESEARCH AND TECHNOLOGY

Going into the 1990s, major technological trends in the plastics products industry included recyclability and faster concept-to-production cycles. Indeed, many companies were ardently seeking flexible processing, extrusion, and molding techniques that would allow them to design and quickly manufacture new products. One of the most important recycling tactics was "design-for-recycling," whereby plastics products and devices are created in such a way that they can be efficiently ground, melted, and reused. For example, glue and adhesives that can contaminate reground materials were being eliminated from manufactured plastic goods.

The grand prize winner of *Modern Plastics* magazine's design awards in 1993 was the Polaroid Microcan, a microscope-mounted camera for lab use that quickly develops polaroid pictures. The plastic camera was manufactured using design-for-recycling and fast concept-to-production technology. Other contest winners included a new injection-molded lawnmower hood and a high-tech portable computer casing.

INDUSTRY INFORMATION SOURCES

Barlow, Rick Data, "Plastics Prices Up 1%," *Hospitals Materials Management*, November 1992.

Darnay, Arsen J., ed., *Manufacturing USA: Industry Analyses, Statistics, and Leading Companies,* Detroit: Gale Research Inc., 1993.

Dvorak, Paul, "Putting the Brakes on Throwaway Designs," *Machine Design*, February 12, 1993.

Farris, Susan E., "What's Ahead for Plastics?," *Plastics World*, January 1993.

"First Annual Design Awards," *Modern Plastics*, June 1993.

Smock, Doug, "Precise Plastics Targets Special Niches for Growth," December 1992.

U.S. Industrial Outlook 1993, Washington, D.C.: U.S. Department of Commerce, January 1993.

Wood, Andrew, "Plastics '92—Engineered Plastics: Pinning Hopes on Renewed Growth," *Chemical Week*, October 28, 1992.

Zhengxing, Lu, "Look at China's Plastics Market," *Plastics World*, November 1992.

—Dave Mote

LEATHER & LEATHER PRODUCTS

SIC 3111

LEATHER TANNING AND FINISHING

This category includes establishments primarily engaged in tanning, currying, and finishing raw or cured hides and skins into leather. Converters and dealers who buy hides, skins, or leather for processing under contracts with tanners and/or finishers are also included in this category.

INDUSTRY SNAPSHOT

The dollar value of leather tanning and finishing industry shipments increased about one percent in 1992 over 1991, to $2.29 billion from $2.27 billion, according to the 1993 *U.S. Industrial Outlook*. Increased export demand for U.S. leather was the primary reason for the increase. In the United States, shoe and upholstery leather, especially for cars, made up most of the leather market. The number of companies engaged in leather tanning and finishing declined in the 1980s as larger firms acquired smaller ones. The number of establishments in the tanning industry shrank by almost two-thirds in the ten year period from 1982 to 1992, from 342 to 110.

Through the 1990s, leather tanning in the United States was primarily the work of privately-held companies. Eighty-eight percent of the leather processed in the United States is cattlehide, while specialty leathers, including deer, calf, goat, lamb, and other animals and reptiles, makes up the other 12 percent. The largest establishments were in New York, Massachusetts, California, Wisconsin, Pennsylvania, New Jersey, and Texas. Although the number of establishments engaged in tanning leather has contracted, production

expanded by 6 percent in 1992 over 1991 and production employment increased by the same amount. Research support continued to make the industry more cost-effective, and helped it deal with demands made by environmental protection laws passed in the 1980s. In addition to research by individual firms, the industry has maintained a research facility in Ohio.

ORGANIZATION AND STRUCTURE

Leather tanning is a process in which chemical agents and extracts are applied to various kinds of hides and skins. Skins and hides removed at the packing house are salted or soaked in brine to preserve them until they reach the tannery. The first step followed at the tannery is to soak the hides to remove the salt. The primary two methods used to then convert the raw material into leather are chrome tanning and vegetable tanning.

There are four stages hides progress through during the tanning process: Lime Split, Wet-Blue, Crust, and Conditioning and Finishing. At the Eagle Ottawa Leather Company in Wisconsin the stages are performed thusly: After soaking, the hides are split. Then in the Wet-Blue stage the hides are tumbled in large teak wood drums to preserve the hide and add strength and durability. The leather is then "dewatered" and shaved to a uniform thickness. In the Crust stage, the hides are tumbled again in smaller drums where dyes and oils are added to provide the necessary color as well as the softness and durability required of fine leather. Hides are clipped to individual framers and dried to an exact, uniform moisture content. The Conditioning and Finishing stage softens and texturizes the leather. The hides are softened mechanically, final colors are sprayed onto the leather to meet customer requirements, and embossing provides the required texture. The leather is softened again and at a final quality control point the leather is subjected to a variety of tests to ensure that it will meet customer specifications.

BACKGROUND AND DEVELOPMENT

Tanning, the process that turns raw animal hides into the soft, pliable, and enduring material called leather, is one of humankind's oldest industries. Recovered specimens of leather tents and shoes date as far back as 6,000 B.C., and ancient Egyptian carvings show tanners at work. Early Romans used leather not only for shoes, but also for money. From the middle ages through the seventeenth century, the most common additive used in the soaking process to cure or tan the leather were gall nuts, insect eggs laid on parts of the oak tree. Advances in the chemical and mechanical processes of tanning opened up the industry worldwide and helped the growth of the American tanning industry.

The Leather Industry in America. The first English leather worker to come to the New World was a shoemaker named Experience Miller. Miller arrived in Plymouth Colony in 1624, and soon found that the native Americans used bark tanning to preserve cattle and other hides. The abundance of deer hides and water resources in the colonies lead to the development of a flourishing tanning industry in the colonies. By 1650, there were over 50 tanneries in Massachusetts alone. Early colonial tanneries were small and often moved when the vegetable tanning materials or the source of hides in one area were exhausted. The first tanning machine used in the United States was a stone mill used to grind tree bark. It was invented by Peter Minuit, Governor of New Amsterdam. By 1800, there were 2,000 tanneries in the United States.

Technological innovations in the nineteenth century increased production. In 1805, Englishman Sir Humphry Davey discovered that many trees besides oak could be used in the tanning process. The trees he named were the hemlock, mimosa, chestnut and ash—all trees that were in abundance in the United States. An American, Samuel Parker, further advanced the tanning industry in 1809 by inventing a machine to split hides. Before his invention it took one man a whole day to split four hides. With Parker's invention one man could split 100 hides in one day. These developments made leather cheaper and opened the market for leather to all classes. In 1884, August Schultz discovered that chromium salts could be used in the tanning process instead of vegetable material. This method, perfected ten years later by Martin Dennis,

allowed more attractive and flexible leathers to be produced at a faster rate.

Other procedural changes and inventions, including a machine to remove hair and flesh from the skins, gave the U.S. industry a further boost by increasing the supply of leather in the market. By the end of the nineteenth century, tanneries had begun to consolidate. The larger tanneries produced more goods than had the many smaller operations because they could maintain heavy, expensive machinery and a large work force. In 1899, 1,306 tanneries produced leather valued at $204 million versus 6,664 tanneries producing only $40 million worth of leather in 1850. Integration and growth continued into the twentieth century. In 1919, 680 tanneries produced $900 million worth of leather. The number of tanneries continued to shrink with the slowdown of the depression and competition from synthetics after World War II. In the 1970s, the decline in meat eating decreased the available hides for tanning and began the increase in the cost of leather worldwide.

The leather tanning industry began another series of technological innovations in the late 1970s and 1980s in response to the need to assess the effect of tanning chemicals used on the environment. The Leather Industries of America Research Laboratory, based in Cincinnati, Ohio, worked on changes relating to the chemical aspects of hide processing.

CURRENT CONDITIONS

Charles Myers, President of the Leather Industries of America, Inc., an association of leather tanners and related industries noted in 1994 that the tanning industry, which once produced primarily for U.S. markets, had now become an aggressive exporter. He said, "We now export more raw material than finished product to countries that can finish more cheaply than we [can], and we have virtually no domestic customer base. The glovemakers [and] shoemakers that were our customers are now producing abroad."

In 1985, the Environmental Protection Agency (EPA) established new standards to control pre-treatment of the liquid wastes that tanners discharge indirectly to publicly-owned waste treatment facilities. These standards applied to wastes containing sulfides and chromium and to the acidity of the waste. All tanners discharging directly into waterways were required to operate with the EPA-approved National Discharge Elimination System (NDES) permits. The EPA standards for this group required control of conventional pollutants such as solids and biological oxygen as well as sulfides, chromium, and acidity.

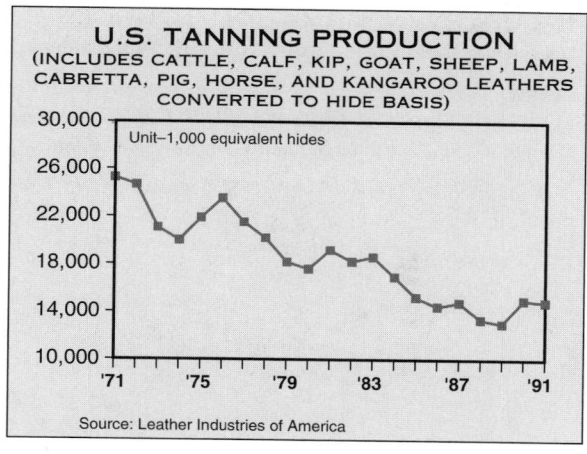

U.S. TANNING PRODUCTION
(INCLUDES CATTLE, CALF, KIP, GOAT, SHEEP, LAMB, CABRETTA, PIG, HORSE, AND KANGAROO LEATHERS CONVERTED TO HIDE BASIS)

Unit—1,000 equivalent hides

Source: Leather Industries of America

In 1992, the waste scrap leather, wet-blue trimmings and shavings, and tannery sludge that contained chromium was exempt from hazardous waste regulation. Tanning systems that recycled chromium had been developed and were widely used throughout the industry to reduce the amount of chromium that appeared in the final effluent. There had been talk of removing the exemption on waste from leather products, which would force the leather industry to come up with new techniques for the disposal of those products. When considering future changes to the process to meet environmental controls, the U.S. Department of Commerce predicted that new waste treatment technology at wet-blue plants would help the tanners to meet the new requirements.

Strict Federal standards curbing the emission of volatile organic compounds into the air have encouraged the industry to develop low-solvent or solvent-free finishing (coating) technologies for the leather. The 1990 Clean Air Act requires a 90 percent reduction by 1994 from the 1987 baseline. In 1992, the EPA planned to initiate a study of tanning in 1994 to determine the need, if any, to further revise guidelines.

As an example of the high priority the industry assigns to environmental standards, the Eagle Ottawa Leather Company published a three-page summary of its environmental achievements in 1992. The company noted its successful reduction of toxic air emissions by 98 percent, minimized use of landfills by recycling waste, minimized chemical use, decreased loadings to waste water treatment plants, and a plan to reduce its use of water overall.

The future of the tanning industry was in contention in the 1990s. "If you remove inflation, the industry has been at a standstill over the last few years," said tanner's association president Myers, "and we will continue to be flat or decline unless something

changes." Myers predicted further consolidation of the industry to fewer players who will concentrate on the upper end leathers, selling those to domestic firms and exporting much of the rest. *U.S. Industrial Outlook,* however, predicted a brighter future, expecting leather shipments to increase in 1993 by about five percent to 16.7 million cattlehide units with a proportionate increase in dollars. The Department of Commerce rated that the long-term outlook for the industry as "good". Continued increases in the hide supply would mean lower prices and would encourage tanners to increase working capital and reduce debt. In addition, *U.S. Industrial Outlook* maintained that U.S. trade negotiations could give the tanning industry greater access to world markets by reducing barriers to U.S. exports.

INDUSTRY LEADERS

The three industry leaders are privately held companies. They are: Albert Trostel and Sons Co. of Milwaukee, Wisconsin; Seton Co. of Norristown, New Jersey; and Feuer Leather Corp. of Hawthorne, New York. Many other firms engaged in leather tanning and finishing were related either corporately or by family ties to these firms.

WORK FORCE

The industry is unionized, but also highly mechanized. The 1987 Census of Manufactures reports employment of 14,600 in the industry, about twenty-five percent below the 19,500 employees reported in 1982. The 1993 *U.S. Industrial Outlook* estimates that there were 10,800 people employed in the industry in 1992, but predicted an increase of 3.1 percent in 1993. The leading states for employment in 1987 were New York, Wisconsin, and Pennsylvania, accounting for thirty-five percent of the industry's employment.

Associated work for the tanning industry lay in the fields of chemistry and environmental management. The outlook for leather workers depends upon the continued demand for the leather product and the availability of hides.

AMERICA AND THE WORLD

According to the 1993 *U.S. Industrial Outlook,* the role of the United States in the export of leather should grow in the 1990s. Import and export in the leather tanning and finishing industry primarily involved the import and export of the raw and wet-blue hides and finished leather. Unlike many countries with abundant hide supplies, the United States did not restrict exports. Restriction of exports lowers the price of hides, making it cheaper to tan and produce leather products with one's own hides. Argentina, Brazil, and India restricted exports to support their tanning industries.

Combined exports of raw and wet-blue cattlehides totaled 22.2 million hides in 1992, according to the U.S. Department of Commerce. The number was down about 7.5 percent from 1991. During the first half of 1992, four countries imported 92 percent of U.S. total exports. These were Korea (46 percent), Japan (21 percent), Mexico (14 percent), and Taiwan (11 percent). Most of those hides sent were from cattle. The United States produced very small quantities of calfskin, but exported virtually all of it. Some domestic sheepskin was exported and some used in the domestic apparel industry.

Leather exports increased in 1992 by about seven percent to $725 million. The weaker U.S. dollar stimulated export demand despite weak economies around the world. Japan was the largest importer of U.S. leather, taking 30 percent of the exports in the first half of 1992. About eighty-five percent of that was automobile leather, which is exempt from the tariff-rate quotas that Japan imposes on other leather goods. Leather imports were also up. Imports increased by about nine percent in 1992 to $624 million, over the $571 million of 1991. About 74 percent of the 1992 imports were cattlehide leather. Argentina was the largest supplier to the United States. From January through March in 1992, 49 percent of the leather imports came from beneficiary developing countries—those that receive tariff concessions from the United States under the Generalized System of Preferences (GSP) section of the Trade Act of 1974.

Both the United States and the European Community continued to address the issue of Japan's tariff-rate quota on leather and leather footwear. In U.S.-Mexico negotiations on a North American Free Trade Agreement (NAFTA), Mexico refused to meet a U.S. request for immediate reciprocal reductions to zero for both U.S. and Mexican tariffs on leather. A compromise led to an agreement to reduce duties over a ten-year period.

In September 1990, the U.S. Department of Commerce determined that Argentine cowhides were selling in Argentina at an artificially low price due to that country's export embargo and proposed a countervailing duty on Argentina's leather. In May 1992, the Government of Argentina responded by revoking its export embargo and replacing that with an export tax which was expected to have the same effect on the export of raw or cured hides as did the embargo.

INDUSTRY INFORMATION SOURCES

Interview with President Charles Myers of Leather Industries of America, Inc.

The Story of American Leather and U.S. Leather Industries Statistics, 1992. Leather Industries of America, 1992.

U.S. Industrial Outlook 1992. U.S. Department of Commerce, 1993.

U.S. Occupational Outlook Handbook. U.S. Department of Labor, 1992.

—Joan Leotta

SIC 3131

BOOT AND SHOE CUT STOCK AND FINDINGS

Establishments that fall under this category are primarily engaged in manufacturing leather soles, inner soles, and other boot and shoe cut stock and findings. The industry also includes finished wood heels. Establishments primarily engaged in manufacturing heels, soiling strips, and soles made of rubber, composition, plastics, and fiber are classified in the major group for for rubber and miscellaneous plastics products.

In 1993, the boot and shoe cut stock findings segment continued to suffer from the growing penetration of relatively low-cost imported footwear into the United States. According to footwear industry statistics, in 1983 the U.S. market for nonrubber footwear totaled 921 million pairs, of which 340 million, or 37 percent, were made in America. By 1992, the market had grown to 1,139 million pairs, but only 165 million, or 14 percent, were of domestic manufacture. The import/export imbalance was even more telling: 974 million pairs were imported, while only 21 million were exported.

In this environment, many footwear plants have been forced to close. Between 1982 and 1992, there was a net loss of 366 nonrubber footwear plants in the United States, and plant openings had slowed to a trickle. Pricing was also under intense pressure: the average factory price for nonrubber footwear increased about 2% to an estimated $21.16 a pair in 1993, the smallest advance in three years, because of competition from imported shoes. In the labor-intensive footwear industry, U.S. makers simply could not compete with manufacturers overseas whose wage rates were far below U.S. levels.

The drop in domestically produced footwear, of course, depressed the business of companies that supply shoe manufacturers. According to government statistics, shipments for the segment in 1991 totaled $379 million, down from $425 million in 1981. Moreover, the number of workers in the segment fell from 7,000 to 5,000 over the same time period. Besides the dramatic increase in shoe imports, leather sole makers also had to contend with a shift by consumers to more casual footwear and the rising cost of leather. While there remained a market for the fine leather shoe, many Americans were no longer dressing up for work and did not require several pairs of dress shoes. Some industry executives worried that the move to casual footwear would become more pronounced in the future.

During the recession of the early 1990s, the repair trade picked up somewhat, as consumers have traditionally mended old shoes when they did not have the money to buy new ones. Some manufacturers thought sales were less robust than in previous recessions, however, because so many white-collar workers were out of work and wearing dress shoes less often. There was also concern about longer-term trends in the repair market. One estimate showed that only eight to 10 percent of consumers made use of shoe repair shops, and the average customer was a relatively advanced 45 years old. The availability of inexpensive imported footwear may also encourage people to simply buy new shoes rather than repair old ones.

INDUSTRY INFORMATION SOURCES

"A Recovery Is No Shoe-In," *Wall Street Journal*, May 28, 1992.

McNally, Pamela, "Vendors Taking Advantage of Manmades' Price and Texture," *Footwear News*, January 25, 1993.

Rieger, Nancy, "North American Exposure: Borders, Barriers and Free Trade," *Footwear News*, October 11, 1993.

Stebbins, John, et al, *Footwear Manual*, Washington: Footwear Industries of America, 1993.

U.S. Industrial Outlook, U.S. Department of Commerce, 1994.

—Bob Schneider

SIC 3142

HOUSE SLIPPERS

This classification includes establishments primarily engaged in manufacturing house slippers of leather or other materials.

The house slippers industry falls under the auspices of the nonrubber footwear industry, which produces all types of footwear except rubber protective and rubber-soled "sneakers." House slippers may be constructed with leather, vinyl, plastic, cloth, or textile uppers or combinations of these materials for both genders and all ages.

The modern structure of the house slippers industry is characterized by several major brand names with primary distribution through department store venues. The leading brand names differentiate themselves by comfort and fashion levels. In 1993 the leading brand names included Dearfoams, by R.G. Barry Corporation, and Isotoners, by Aris. An article in the July, 1993, edition of *Footwear News* indicated, however, that consumers' footwear buying habits had shifted to form, function, and comfort and away from brands. Many consumers were seeking lower-priced house slippers in strip shopping centers and outlet stores instead of in traditional higher-end shopping mall department stores.

A major portion of the house slipper consumer market is represented by house-bound invalids and hospitalized patients. This sector of the market seeks products that are light-weight, comfortable, easy to put on and take off, and unlikely to fall off the feet. *American Salesman* magazine also listed house slippers among the items one should never fail to pack when traveling. Sales people and other frequent travelers opt for house slippers that are fashionable, light-weight, and easy to pack.

In 1993 shipments of house slippers declined about five percent to more than 45 million pairs. Their product value dropped to an estimated $268 million. House slippers accounted for 26 percent of the quantity but only 7.5 percent of the value of nonrubber footwear product shipments, primarily because most slippers are produced from lower-cost vinyls and other textiles. The ratio of imports to apparent consumption for house slippers was approximately 28 percent by quantity. This was the lowest ratio of all areas of the nonrubber footwear industry. Industry experts expect shipments of house slippers to continue to decline moderately throughout the end of the 20th century.

In order to maintain profitability in the face of declining demand, the house slipper industry considers new technology essential to increase productivity and lower costs of manufacturing. Increased use of computers has already integrated design, management, manufacturing, and marketing functions. Overall, the industry emphasizes such non-price factors as quality and quick delivery in competition with imports. The industry has turned to computer-aided design (CAD) and computer-aided manufacturing (CAM). Through these methods, companies can link computer system data to auto-stitchers, milling, and turning machines. The industry has also increased its use of three-dimensional CAD, which produces more accurate slipper patterns and reduces the number of prototypes needed.

INDUSTRY INFORMATION SOURCES

"Industry Responds to Cost-conscious Consumers," *Standard & Poor's Industry Surveys,* New York, NY, 1994.

"Shoe Manufacturing," *Moody's Industry Review,* volume 13, March 11, 1994.

"SIC 314, Leather and Leather Products," *Dunn's Business Rankings,* New York, NY, 1993.

U.S. Industrial Outlook—Other Consumer Non-Durables, 35th edition, Washington, D.C.: U.S. Department of Commerce's International Trade Administration, 1994.

—Wendy Johnson Bilas

SIC 3143

MEN'S FOOTWEAR, EXCEPT ATHLETIC

This category includes establishments primarily engaged in the production of men's footwear designed for dress, street, and work. Establishments primarily engaged in the production of such protective footwear as rubbers, rubber boots, storm shoes, galoshes, and other footwear with rubber soles vulcanized to the uppers are classified in **SIC 3021: Rubber and Plastics Footwear.** Establishments primarily engaged in the production of athletic shoes and youths' and boys' shoes are classified in **SIC 3149: Footwear Except Rubber, Not Elsewhere Classified,** and those manufacturing orthopedic extension shoes are classified in **SIC 3842: Orthopedic, Prosthetic, and Surgical Applliances and Supplies.**

INDUSTRY SNAPSHOT

According to Footwear Industries of America, approximately 200 companies in the United States were involved in the manufacture of nonrubber footwear in 1992. However, that year the American industry controlled less than 14 percent of the domestic market, due to overwhelming competition from imports, which began in the 1960s.

BACKGROUND AND DEVELOPMENT

New England had become the center of a thriving footwear industry as early as 1800, and by 1850, the United States was exporting large quantities of high quality, inexpensive shoes to England and other European countries. Micajah Pratt, who began making and selling shoes in Lynn, Massachusetts, in 1812, was considered an innovator in the industry. He was among the first to use standard patterns and sole cutting machines. Pratt eventually employed about 500 workers—many of whom lived in other towns and worked at home—and produced almost 250,000 pairs of shoes annually.

Shoemaking became industrialized in the early 1860s, prompted by the development of machinery for attaching the leather part of a shoe, known as the upper, to the sole. In 1858, Lyman R. Blake of Abington, Massachusetts, invented a machine that attached the leather uppers with nails and wooden pegs. Soon thereafter, Gordon McKay, also of Abington, improved on Blake's invention by substituting thread for the cumbersome nails and pegs. Recognizing the threat that McKay's sewing machine posed to their livelihood, shoemakers staged the first general strike in the footwear industry in 1859. Nevertheless, by 1864, the Blake sewer was used by most U.S. shoemakers.

The most important technological advance, however, was probably the shoe-lasting machine, invented in 1882 by Jan Ernst Matzeliger, who also worked in a Lynn shoe factory. "Lasting" was the process of shaping the leather upper over a wooden form before attaching it to the sole. Matzeliger's shoe-lasting machine, patented in 1883, allowed shoes to be mass produced for the first time.

CURRENT CONDITIONS

In 1992, U.S. companies produced 168 million pairs of nonrubber footwear, 41 million pairs of which were men's shoes, down from the 642 million pairs of shoes manufactured in 1968, which then accounted for more than 78 percent of the market. Imports rose during the same period by more than 550 percent, from 175 million in 1968 to almost 975 million in 1992. More than half the imports in 1992 came from China, followed by Brazil (11 percent), Indonesia (eight percent), Taiwan (eight percent), and Korea (seven percent). The United States exported about 21 million pairs of nonrubber footwear in 1992, including 5.6

million pairs of men's shoes. The largest importer of U.S. shoes was Mexico, with 13.6 percent of the export market.

The nonrubber footwear industry in general was expected to continue shrinking, especially as more companies began shifting all or part of their manufacturing operations overseas to take advantage of lower labor costs. The exceptions in the men's footwear industry consisted of a few firms that produced top-quality leather dress shoes, or that filled a unique export market, such as bootmaker Tony Lama, Inc. in El Paso, Texas. In 1989, Tony Lama, Jr., then the company's chairperson, told *Nation's Business,* "They don't make original cowboy boots everywhere in the world. [Foreign customers] don't mind spending money on a fine pair of cowboy boots, but its important that they be made in America."

INDUSTRY LEADERS

Florsheim Shoe Co. Chicago-based Florsheim, a subsidiary of Interco, Inc., was perhaps the best-known maker of men's dress shoes in the United States in the early 1990s, accounting for about 20 percent of the market.

Florsheim was founded in 1892 by Milton S. Florsheim, whose father, Sigmund, had operated a shoe store in Chicago since 1856. Milton Florsheim began branding the company name on the sole of every shoe it produced, creating one of the earliest brand names in the shoe industry. In the early 1900s, Florsheim began advertising nationally in magazines such as *The Saturday Evening Post.* Florsheim was one of the first manufacturers to open its own retail stores and was credited with introducing low-cut dress shoes for men.

In the early 1990s, a survey showed consumers associated the Florsheim brand name with high prices. The company responded by reducing prices on four of its most popular styles of men's dress shoes. Florsheim also introduced several new styles that targeted the market for men's casual footwear. Florsheim's Outdoorsman line of hiking and hunting boots was introduced in 1989.

Interco Inc. Florsheim's parent company, Interco, was at one time the largest shoe manufacturer in the United States. Originally known as the International Shoe Company, Interco was created in 1911 by a merger of two St. Louis companies—Roberts, Johnson & Rand Shoe Co. and the Peters Shoe Co.—then two of the oldest and best known names in the industry. International Shoe acquired several other footwear makers in the 1920s, including the McElwain Co. of

Boston, an acquisition that the Federal Trade Commission attempted to block as a violation of the Clayton Antitrust Act. However, the Supreme Court reversed the commission's order in 1930.

In the 1950s, International Shoe was producing more than 55 million pairs of shoes annually. The company, which changed its name to Interco in 1966, also diversified into clothing and furniture. However, the company was among the hardest hit by foreign competition in the 1970s and was forced to sell or close many of its shoe factories. A failed takeover in the late 1980s left the company in financial trouble and resulted in Interco declaring bankruptcy in 1991. Interco was reorganized in 1992.

Timberland Co. The Timberland Co. of Hampton, New Hampshire, maker of rugged, upscale hiking boots and walking shoes, was founded by Russian immigrant Nathan Swartz. Swartz had spent 33 years in the footwear industry when he purchased half interest in the Abington Shoe Co. in 1951. When his partner died four years later, Swartz purchased the rest of the company, and his sons, Herman and Sidney, joined him in the business. For the next 15 years, Abington operated out of a converted warehouse in Boston, producing inexpensive, private-label men's shoes and work boots. The dress shoes were most often sold through discount stores, while the work boots were a staple in Army/Navy surplus stores.

Around 1970, sales of Abington's leather work boots began to increase unexpectedly. Herman Swartz later told *INC.* magazine: "When we visited the stores, we saw that a lot of young people, college students, were buying them. You don't have to be a genius to know that something's going on." Abington had stumbled onto a new fashion trend that incorporated gear generally favored by enthusiasts of the outdoors.

In 1973, Abington, which had relocated to Newmarket, New Hampshire, selected "Timberland" from a list of names suggested by an advertising agency and set up a subsidiary to manufacture a new line of leather boots, insulated and waterproof, with a thick rubber sole. The company turned out just 2,500 pairs of Timberland boots the first year, compared to 490,000 shoes and boots from the Abington line.

At first, Abington marketed Timberland boots the same as it had its Abington line—primarily to hunters and fishermen who shopped the Army/Navy surplus stores—and sales were unimpressive. In 1975, however, a marketing consultant suggested the company position Timberland as a fashion item, selling the boots through upscale department stores and retail outlets; a hefty price increase would pay for an advertising campaign. The first ads for Timberland carried the tagline, "A whole line of fine leather boots that cost plenty, and should" would create the demand. In 1979, Abington officially changed its name to the Timberland Co. That year, the company sold 500,000 pairs of Timberland boots as revenues topped $16 million. Revenues topped $100 million for the first time in 1987.

WORK FORCE

The U.S. nonrubber footwear industry employed 66,200 workers in 1992, a 72 percent decrease since 1968 when employment was 233,400. While workers in the U.S. nonrubber footwear industry earned an average of $9.08 per hour in 1991, those in Indonesia earned the equivalent of 30 cents per hour, and in China the average wage was estimated at the equivalent of 50 cents per hour. Of the major foreign competitors, Taiwan paid the highest average wages, $3.71, which was still less than 41 percent of the U.S. average.

AMERICA AND THE WORLD

The United States was one of the few industrialized nations that did not protect its footwear industry with high import tariffs. The industry therefore faced stiff competition from imports while in effect being locked out of many foreign markets. As a result, imports increased by 556 percent between 1968, when President Lyndon Johnson cut tariff's in half, and 1992, when imports accounted for 87 percent of the U.S. market for nonrubber footwear. According to Footwear Industries of America, more than 2,000 footwear factories were operating in the United States at the start of 1968, and only 376 by the end of 1992, an average of more than 30 plant closings every year.

There were several efforts after 1968 to impose higher import tariffs, most notably the Textile, Apparel and Footwear Act of 1990, which was vetoed by President George Bush. Congress also ultimately rejected similar bills in 1985 and 1988. Also the during this time, the industry filed complaints about unfair trade practices with the International Trade Commission, but in 1984 the ITC ruled that the U.S. footwear industry was not being harmed by imports. The Senate Finance Committee initiated a case with the ITC the following year, which resulted in a recommendation for five years of global quotas, but the plan was tabled in the early 1990s.

After the Textile, Apparel and Footwear Act was vetoed in 1990, the Footwear Industries of America, the trade association that had lobbied for import protection, in effect gave up the fight. Fawn Evenson, then

executive director of the FIA, told *The Journal of Commerce and Commercial* in 1992, "We literally spent millions of dollars on trade cases. We almost went broke trying to protect jobs."

In 1990, the FIA voted to expand its membership to include importers and tacitly supported the North American Free Trade Agreement by focusing its efforts on ensuring that Mexico would not become a trans-ship point for duty free shoes from other countries, most of which imposed tariffs of 25 percent or more on U.S. exports or locked out U.S. companies entirely. Evenson explained, "We are importers. We've stopped quota battles. We're going to spend a lot more time on market access and on exports. We're now going to devote our efforts to companies that are surviving."

INDUSTRY INFORMATION SOURCES

"Background on the Florsheim Shoe Company," Chicago: The Florsheim Company, December 10, 1992.

Bahls, Jane Easter, "U.S. Shoe Firms Thrive in High-Quality Market," *Nation's Business,* February 1989, p. 38.

"Current Highlights of the Nonrubber Footwear Industry," Washington D.C.: Footwear Industries of America, March 15, 1993.

Flax, Steven, "Boot Camp," *INC.,* September 1987, p. 99.

"Florsheim . . . A Century of Quality and Fashion," Chicago: The Florsheim Company, January 7, 1993.

Marriott, Michel, "Out of the Woods," *New York Times,* November 7, 1993, p. V1.

McDowell, Colin, *Shoes: Fashion and Fantasy,* New York: Rizzoli International Publications, Inc., 1989.

Melamed, Dennis, "The Party's Over for US Manufacturers," *Journal of Commerce and Commercial,* May 4, 1992, p. 9A.

Pereira, Joseph, "Sneaker Makers, Hearing Clomp-Clomp of Competition, Launch 'Rugged' Lines," *Wall Street Journal,* September 14, 1993, p. B1.

Rhodes, Lucien, "Sole Success," *INC.,* February 1982, p. 44.

—Dean Boyer

SIC 3144

WOMEN'S FOOTWEAR, EXCEPT ATHLETIC

This category covers establishments engaged in the production of women's footwear designed primarily for dress, street, and work. Establishments engaged in the production of athletic shoes and misses', children's, infants', and babies' footwear are classified in

SIC 3149: Footwear, Except Rubber, Not Else-where Classified. Establishments primarily engaged in the production of rubber or plastic footwear are classified in **SIC 3021: Rubber and Plastics Foot-wear,** and those manufacturing orthopedic extension shoes are classified in **SIC 3842: Orthopedic, Pros-thetic, and Surgical Appliances and Supplies.**

INDUSTRY SNAPSHOT

The women's footwear industry in the United States is dominated by large companies that manufacture and produce a wide variety of shoes each year. Although this category does not include shoe manufacturers whose primary product is rubber protective and rubber-soled (athletic) shoes, it has been influenced greatly by the popularity of the latter. The women's footwear industry is blessed with a steady market of consumers eager for new styles, and that factor combined with the short life span of a pair of shoes can spell lucrative profits for a well-established shoe manufacturer. In 1993 American manufacturers produced and shipped 58 million pairs of women's shoes. The value of these shipments was an estimated $1.3 billion. In relation to the overall shoe industry, women's footwear accounted for 34 percent of all shoes produced by American manufacturers and 35 percent of the value of those shoes. However, the most pressing problem for domestic shoe manufacturers is the foreign-made shoe. Comparably stylish and more affordable imported shoes dominate the shoe market. It was estimated that almost 90 percent of women's shoes sold in the United States in 1993 were imported from major producers such as Mexico, Brazil, and Taiwan. These imports are priced lower than similar American-made styles due to the low labor and production costs in these countries.

ORGANIZATION AND STRUCTURE

The large corporate entities that are predominant in the American shoe industry are constantly engaged in upgrading their product and improving their market share. Part of this is accomplished by offering a vast array of shoes for each season. An important department within a shoe manufacturing company is the design staff, who watch European and American fashion trends and attempt to devise new twists on the basic product. A common way to reduce cost for such companies is to send out much of their manufacturing jobs to foreign factories. There, labor costs are cheaper, and the shoes return to the United States for the final phases of production. The shoes are then sent out to stores nationwide through a comprehensive distribution network. Marketing teams within shoe companies negotiate with retail outlets and department stores to place as much of their company's products on display shelves as possible. Competition is fierce and dramatic shifts within the industry based on the smallest stylistic or structural innovations are commonplace. Much of the industry's design, marketing, and management sectors meet annually at a number of trade shows. The most established fair is the Fashion Footwear Association of New York show, held in New York City in early February. Two other important trade fairs are the National Shoe Fair and Shoes in New York.

CURRENT CONDITIONS

Despite some setbacks, the women's footwear industry continues to show a relatively steady growth pattern. The value of shipments for American shoe manufacturers reached a peak of $1.4 billion in 1988, but began posting major drops from 2 to 9 percent in subsequent years. However, by 1993 the industry seemed to have regained some momentum and showed slight increases in the value of shipments. In 1993 the estimated figure for this category was $1.2 billion, with a 6 percent increase forecasted for the following year. Industry analysts predict a decline in coming years in overall per-capita shoe consumption due to shifting demographic patterns. A forecasted drop in the popularity of athletic shoes may in future years portend an increased demand for the casual shoes whose stylistic and structural components are rooted in the athletic shoe industry. Imports are expected to dominate the women's shoe market into the 21st century, but forecasters predict that U.S. exports will increase slightly in coming years.

INDUSTRY LEADERS

One of the largest American manufacturers of women's footwear is the United States Shoe Corp., based in Cincinnati, Ohio. The publicly held company was founded in 1931 and employs 41,000 people. It is a large diversified manufacturing company that is also a franchiser of retail shoe, apparel, and eyeglass stores. Annual sales for this company totaled $2.65 billion in 1993. Its shoe manufacturing divisions operate under the corporate names Bandolino, Selby, Easy Spirit, Vittorio Ricci, Capezio, Amalfi, Evan Picone, Pappagallo, Texas Boot, and Wrangler Boot. It also operates nationwide retail apparel outlets including August Max Woman, Caren Charles, Pappagallo, and Casual Corner, as well as the optical-goods outlets LensCrafters.

In the early 1990s U.S. Shoe suffered losses to its major competitor Nine West, particularly in the well-established Bandolino division. Bandolino dress and career shoes were targeted at fashion-conscious work-ing women with prices ranging from $55 to $70. For many years this brand occupied a solid niche in the dress and career shoe market, flanked on each side by U.S. Shoe's more moderately-priced Vittorio Ricci line and the upscale Evan Picone segment. Its price points increased in recent years, however, due to U.S. Shoe's reliance on keeping Bandolino manufactured in Italy. An unfavorable exchange rate on the lire drove up prices on Bandolino shoes, while its main competi-tor, Nine West, was providing fresher styles in the same price range. Retailers began discounting Bandolino and the brand suffered from a cheapened product image in the eyes of consumers. Department stores ceded more shelf space to Nine West and U.S. Shoe and Bandolino lost even more ground in the market.

However, the company restructured its operations in 1993, particularly in the Bandolino division, in a strategy to win back market share from Nine West. The most important factor in U.S. Shoe's revitalization program was revising its traditional strategy of manu-facturing all Bandolino products in Spanish and Italian factories; its competitors had long been sourcing out their shoe manufacturing to Brazil and Far East coun-tries, where labor costs are cheaper. To combat this, U.S. Shoe kept its higher-end Bandolino dress shoes made in European factories, but began using Brazilian and Far Eastern production facilities to manufacture the line's more casual shoes.

U.S. Shoe gained sales in the late 1980s and early 1990s with the introduction of its Easy Spirit line of dress shoes. This label attempted to create comfortable women's dress or career pumps. This trend grew out of the practice of legions of working women, who in the 1980s began pairing business attire with sneakers or running shoes for street travel, carrying their pumps in a bag and changing shoes when inside the workplace. Pump sales peaked in the mid-1980s, but after that point began to drop off; they had become less of a fashion staple and more of a basic wardrobe necessity. Additionally, women began diversifying their working wardrobes and incorporating more low-heeled and flat shoes. In the last years of the decade, dress pump sales remained steady around $3.7 billion, while sales of low-heeled and flat shoes jumped as much as 10 per-cent from year to year.

Shoe manufacturers such as U.S. Shoe strove to capitalize on women's unwillingness to torture their feet in high heels for the entire day. The Easy Spirit label, launched in 1988, was typical of this new cate-gory of footwear, featuring low- to medium-heeled pumps with flexible soles and padded linings. The

shoes are made at a company plant in Kentucky. Ad-vertising campaigns depicted women playing basket-ball in the shoes and trumpeted the slogan, ''Looks like a pump, feels like a sneaker.'' The shoes, priced at around $100 a pair, cost more than average pumps but have proven popular with working women.

Nine West, another key player in the women's footwear industry, is a relative newcomer to the field. The publicly held company was founded in 1977 and reported 1992 sales of $461.6 million. Based in Con-necticut, Nine West sources out its shoe manufacturing to factories in Brazil. Its shoes have a high brand recognition and can be found both in department stores and the company's own retail outlets. This strategy has proved successful, and by the early 1990s Nine West stores, which account for 30 percent of company sales, enjoyed one of the highest sales-per-square-foot ratio in the industry. The company's product lines include the Nine West, Calico, and Enzo Angiolini brands, and in pricing its product between $20 and $55 Nine West has appealed to younger working women. The Enzo Angiolini division made strides in the early 1990s against its major competitors in moderately-priced, European-styled dress and career shoes like U.S. Shoe's Bandolino line. Nine West's success in captur-ing a large segment of the women's shoe market was reflected in its announcement of expansion plans in 1993. A key component of this strategy is to gain more market share by launching separate retail outlets for its Enzo Angiolini line.

Another large producer of women's footwear is the Maine-based Dexter Shoe Co. Founded in 1957, it manufacturers both men's and women's shoes and employs 2,000 people. In 1993 Dexter reported annual sales of $140 million. Another relative newcomer to the industry is Kenneth Cole Productions, Inc. The New York City-based company is known for irreverent advertising campaigns showcasing quirky, cutting-edge footwear for both men and women. A private company employing 200, Kenneth Cole's 1990 revenues were reported at $14 million. Part of the company was sold off to a group of investors in 1987 and this sale generated the formation of the What's What shoe company. This separate firm is best known as the producer of the Aerosole, a lightweight casual shoe with a leather upper and a patented flexible sole.

Another upstart company in the women's foot-wear industry is Sam & Libby, Inc. Founded in 1987 by Sam and Libby Edelman, a husband-and-wife team involved in the successful Esprit clothing company in the 1980s, the company is also known for its attention-getting advertising campaigns. The photogenic couple are the main focus of the ads, which are geared toward a young, hip, but price-conscious consumer. The San Carlos, California-based company employs 150 and reported sales of $75 million for 1992, but that figure also encompasses Sam & Libby shoes classified in **SIC 3021: Rubber and Plastics Footwear.** The company was launched to great fanfare around a product line that was a remake of the ballet slipper. The Edelmans had noticed many European women wearing the dance shoe as a casual slip-on, and thought the idea would also appeal to younger American women. Industry experts were skeptical, but the ballet slipper line was launched in 1987 to great success. The all-leather shoe with a large bow was produced in a variety of colors and sold in department stores for around $20. Four years after its introduction the ballet slipper was still accounting for 20 to 25 percent of company sales. Yet Sam & Libby experienced a shaky first few years—sales in the early years were followed by a successful public offering of the company's stock in an expansion move, but steady losses damaged its fiscal reputation by the early 1990s. During this period the company also introduced a line of women's apparel, and in 1992 began a more upscale footwear division under the label Just Libby.

The Stride Rite Corp. is another key player in the women's footwear industry, although its women's division is only one segment of its footwear operations. The Cambridge, Massachusetts, company profited in the 1980s by the re-marketing of its lightweight canvas Keds sneaker, a standard product which had been made by the company for over seventy years. The success of this casual shoe led to the reemergence of a similar product line, the Grasshoppers label, aimed at older women. Footwear in this line included Keds-style canvas casuals, leather casuals, espadrilles, and leather sandals.

The popularity of such casual shoes based on athletic-shoe styling and comfort has led to a burgeoning new segment of the women's footwear category. Shoe manufacturers, including the athletic shoe companies themselves, jumped into this niche in the early 1990s and all began offering quasi-athletic shoes made with leather uppers and an emphasis on unique styling. This trend coincided with a general relaxation of office dress codes and created a new half-casual, half-workplace type of shoe.

One of the first companies to go after this segment was the Oregon-based athletic shoe manufacturer Nike. Its "i.e. by Nike" line was introduced in 1988 to much success and spawned a rash of imitators, such as the Boks line made by Reebok. Nike's label, which changed its name to just "i.e." and then to "i.e. with Nike Air," utilizes athletic-shoe technology in com-

pressed-air pockets placed in the heel and front of the sole, but is designed in a variety of colors and styles to complement casual apparel. The Brazilian-made shoes are priced between $60-$70 and sell in the women's shoe sections of upscale department stores. New Balance has also entered this market with its American Classics Collection, which debuted in 1993. The shoes fall under three separate categories—dress, casual, and outdoor—and are manufactured at New Balance facilities in the United States.

The dramatic changes that have affected the American shoe manufacturers have also left some behind. The recession of the late 1980s and early 1990s particularly ravaged the retail sector of the economy, and mergers, acquisitions, and bankruptcies became common in the industry. Intershoe, Inc., makers of the Nickels line of shoes, filed for bankruptcy in 1992 but was bought by an Italian group.

WORK FORCE

As mentioned previously, U.S. shoe manufacturers have looked overseas to increase their profits, but not by selling their wares in foreign consumer markets. Instead, companies such as Nine West have found a pool of cheap labor in the Third World and source out manufacturing operations to factories there. These countries, such as the Dominican Republic, Mexico, Thailand, India, and China, have relatively few governmental regulatory measures regarding working conditions, health and safety codes, and the right to unionize. This drain has resulted in a steady loss of American jobs since the 1980s, a problem compounded by the increased automation of U.S.-based manufacturing operations.

AMERICA AND THE WORLD

Manufacturers of women's footwear in the United States face strong competition from cheaper imports. The amount of imported shoes on the American market has increased greatly in recent years, from 175 million pairs in 1968 to 941 million in 1986 and an estimated 1 billion in 1993. The majority of these shoes come from the Far East and South America, with China, Brazil, and Italy exporting the largest amount of women's shoes into the United States. To combat this, U.S. manufacturers ship cut footwear patterns to their plants in Third World countries to be either partially or completely assembled. It is cheaper for the footwear to be only partially assembled abroad, since American companies then pay a lower duty (typically 5 percent) on unfinished goods being re-exported to the United States. The final, less labor-intensive manufacturing details are then completed at home, such as bottoming, finishing, and packing. For the first six months of 1993, more than 13 million pairs of partially-completed shoes entered the United States, an increase of around 12 percent from the same period of the previous year.

On the other side of the international trade in women's footwear, American manufacturers shipped over 20 million pairs for sale abroad in 1993. The value of these shipments was $337 million, and the average unit price was around $16.44. Mexico received about 16 percent of this total, followed by Canada at 8 percent. Newly opened markets in the former Eastern Bloc accounted for the rest of the shipments, with Russia and Poland receiving 8 percent each of the 20 million pairs in 1993. Japan, France, and the United Kingdom accounted for the rest of the total.

The North American Free Trade Agreement (NAFTA), ratified in 1993 by the United States, Canada, and Mexico, creates several ramifications for the women's footwear industry in the United States. Under the agreement's guidelines, duties on shoes produced in Mexico would be reduced over a ten-year period, which may result in an increase in imports. However, NAFTA's rules also addressed the origin of shoes produced in Mexico, setting limits on the amount of materials that could be produced in countries in Central and South America with burgeoning shoe industries. These content regulations will help insure that third-country manufacturers will not nominally assemble shoes in Mexico, then ship them to the United States and benefit from the reduced tariffs. Yet these South and Central American countries are also involved in negotiating similar trade agreements with the United States, which could result in lowered or nonexistent tariffs on women's shoes imported into the U.S. in the late 1990s.

RESEARCH AND TECHNOLOGY

Computer technology has played a vital role in the women's footwear industry in the United States. Companies have invested large sums of money to integrate the latest computer technology into all facets of their operations. In the research and development segment, the use of computer-aided design (CAD) is now commonplace, and many companies have managed to integrate CAD with computer-aided manufacturing (CAM) processes. The result means that shoes can be produced quicker and more accurately in America by high-tech machinery, effectively lowering production costs and eliminating jobs. The women's footwear industry has also utilized robotics technology in manufacturing. Robots handle shoes during the production process, facilitating the steps involved in moving the

shoe from one production module to the next. European shoe manufacturers are responsible for many of the advances in this area. Computers are also used extensively in the management section of the women's footwear industry in tracking production figures and coordinating them with distribution and sales.

INDUSTRY INFORMATION SOURCES

Agins, Teri, "Shoemakers Introduce Walking Pumps with Sneaker Comfort, High-Heel Style," *Wall Street Journal,* March 27, 1989.

"Boks by Reebok Get Independent Division Status," *Footwear News,* December 9, 1991.

Byrne, Harlan S., "United States Shoe," *Barron's,* February 17, 1992.

Current Industrial Reports: Footwear, Fourth Quarter 1992, Washington, DC: U.S. Department of Commerce, March, 1993.

Footwear News, January 4, 1993.

Foster, Caryl, and Rich Wilner, "Casuals Widen Athletics' Horizons," *Footwear News,* November 16, 1992.

Foster, Caryl, "Sam & Libby," *Footwear News,* October 7, 1991.

"High Heeled Sneakers," *Time,* May 14, 1990.

Infantino, Vivian, "Fashion Viewpoints," *Footwear News,* December 14, 1992.

Marcial, Gene G., "U.S. Shoe May Be Hot to Trot," *Business Week,* January 21, 1991.

McAllister, Bob. "i.e.: In Other Words . . . Fashionable Technology," *Footwear News,* August 5, 1991.

McNally, Pamela, and Isabelle Sender, "Retail: Nine West Still Dynamic," *Footwear News,* May 24, 1993.

"Nine West Group," *Fortune,* May 3, 1993.

"Nine West to Open 146 Stores," *Footwear News,* July 12, 1993.

Rooney, Ellen, "Marx & Newman Shuffles Management; Retailers Blame Styling, Prices," *Footwear News,* March 15, 1993.

Rooney, "Bandolino Will Pick up Enzo Angiolini Gauntlet," *Footwear News,* December 6, 1993.

"Sam and Libby Try Again," *Forbes,* March 15, 1993.

Sohng, Laurie, "In Praise of Pumps: An Ode to Immortality," *Footwear News,* November 22, 1993.

Tedeschi, Mark, "Keds Wants Grasshoppers to Entice Women over 35," *Footwear News,* July 22, 1991.

U.S. Industrial Outlook 1994, Washington, DC: U.S. Department of Commerce, January 1994.

—Carol Brennan

SIC 3149

FOOTWEAR, EXCEPT RUBBER, NOT ELSEWHERE CLASSIFIED

This classification includes establishments primarily engaged in the production of shoes, not elsewhere classified, such as misses', youths', boys', children's, and infants' footwear and athletic footwear. Establishments primarily engaged in the manufacture of rubber or plastics footwear are classified in **SIC 3021: Rubber and Plastics Footwear,** and those manufacturing orthopedic extension shoes are classified in **SIC 3842: Orthopedic, Prosthetic, and Surgical Appliances and Supplies.**

INDUSTRY SNAPSHOT

The nonrubber footwear industry manufacturedall types of footwear except rubber protective and rubber-soled fabric-upper (the traditional ''sneaker''). Nonrubber footwear may be constructed with leather, vinyl, plastic, or textile uppers or combinations of these materials for all ages and both genders. Men's footwear producers, classified in **SIC 3143: Men's Footwear, Except Athletic**, and women's footwear producers, classified in **SIC 3144: Women's Footwear, Except Athletic**, composed their own independent industries.

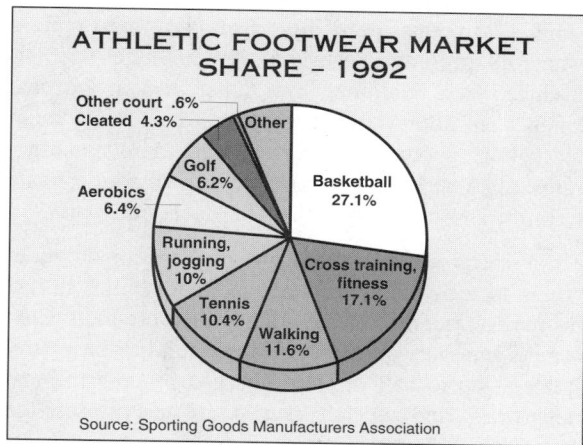

ATHLETIC FOOTWEAR MARKET SHARE – 1992

Other court .6%
Cleated 4.3%
Other
Golf 6.2%
Aerobics 6.4%
Basketball 27.1%
Running, jogging 10%
Cross training, fitness 17.1%
Tennis 10.4%
Walking 11.6%

Source: Sporting Goods Manufacturers Association

As a group, 18 publicly-held U.S. footwear resource companies (companies that either produced footwear domestically or sourced production abroad) reported a 4.8 percent increase in sales in 1992 from 1991 sales, but recorded a 19.5 percent decline in profits. However, 94 percent of the group's total profits came from the two largest athletic footwear producers.

Four companies, including the third largest athletic footwear producer, recorded losses in 1992.

In 1993, shipments of footwear for youths and boys, misses, children, infants and babies, and athletic and other miscellaneous types of footwear, increased approximately three percent to an estimated 25 million pairs. The value of these shipments increased about four percent to $250 million. Shipments of footwear in this group accounted for 15 percent by quantity and seven percent by value of all categories of footwear sold. Production of misses' and athletic footwear increased in 1993, but children's and babies' footwear sales declined.

ORGANIZATION AND STRUCTURE

The 1987 *Census of Manufactures* listed 379 companies operating in 471 establishments in the nonrubber footwear industry. In 1986, approximately 990 factories were in operation. Based on published reports of plants closings, these declines continued from 1987 to the early 1990s. Ten closings were reported in 1992. Many of the plants closed in the early 1990s were owned by the largest manufacturing and retailing companies, which opted to source more footwear from lower-cost producers overseas. In 1993, total employment declined about four percent to an estimated 48,200. Production employment also declined by about five percent.

Nearly half (48 percent) of the nonrubber footwear produced in the United States had leather uppers in 1992. This was down from 51 percent in 1991. Only 31 percent of juvenile types of shoes had leather uppers, while 75 percent of athletic footwear had leather uppers.

Historically, consumers primarily have purchased their footwear at footwear specialty stores and department stores. In the past, customers were strongly brand-loyal and most often selected footwear purchases on the basis of brand recognition and style. During the 1980s, consumers took great interest in their appearance and became slightly extravagant at the sales counter. Personal consumption of footwear and other apparel nearly doubled in the 1980s, with an average annual growth rate of 7.3 percent. Hurt by a recession, weak growth in disposable income, and high unemployment, consumers in the early 1990s became much more frugal.

Along with these economic changes came changes in consumer psychology. Designer names, high-priced shoes and apparel, and frequent shopping sprees became things of the past. Consumers became more value conscious and began purchasing less expensive products at lower-end retail establishments, such as mass merchandisers. *Footwear News* indicated that consumers' footwear buying habits began to shift away from designer brands in 1993. The magazine also reported that many shoe buyers were seeking lower-priced goods in strip shopping centers and outlet stores instead of the higher-end shopping malls. According to *Women's Wear Daily*, department stores' share of all apparel expenditures fell to 24.3 percent in 1993, down from 33.6 percent in 1985. A survey by the *Wall Street Journal* confirmed that women were buying more of their families' shoes and other apparel at mass merchandisers, such as K-Mart and Wal-Mart, and shopping less frequently at department and specialty stores.

In addition to opting for different types of retail establishments, shoppers also selected different types of merchandise by the early 1990s. Basic footwear and moderately priced brand name shoes were often the best selling items. This pattern reflected a more value-oriented consumer, as well as an aging population seeking comfort and less formality in footwear. In the late 1980s and early 1990s, many mass merchandisers added more recognizable national brand names to their in-store inventory. In the past, most brand names were distributed only through department stores.

By the 1990s, formal attire was less popular than it was in the 1980s, and footwear sales reflected this trend. A decrease in the size of the white collar work force and a trend toward more relaxed office attire contributed to a slide in the sale of formal footwear.

Throughout the late 1980s, the ten largest publicly traded apparel companies saw their market share increase by nearly five percent. Part of this growth was attributed to increased demand for these companies' products, but a series of acquisitions and consolidations also was beneficial. This consolidation of the footwear manufacturing industry paralleled developments in the retail industry as a whole. As large department store retailers merged in the late 1980s, they consolidated their buying functions. Larger apparel and footwear manufacturers benefited from this because it became more efficient for the fewer number of buyers to use one vendor rather than several. In response, growth-oriented apparel and footwear manufacturers increased their acquisition activity in search of new brands and broader product offerings.

In addition, the enormous growth of large mass merchandisers drove the industry to consolidate. From 1981 through 1991, Sears, the nation's largest retailer, saw its sales increase rapidly, as did Wal-Mart and K-mart. Savvy footwear manufacturers understood they could increase their sales and market share by offering these retail giants a broad array of brand-name mer-

chandise. Historically, many brand-name manufacturers sold their goods only to department stores, but later sold nearly identical merchandise to mass merchandisers in order to participate in the mass merchandisers' phenomenal growth. Not surprisingly, this affected manufacturers' relationships with department stores, which sought exclusivity in their products. To remedy the situation, many manufacturers began to produce several different categories of brand names, each of which was distributed through a different type of retailer.

Throughout history, retailers and footwear manufacturers have had an adversarial relationship because of issues centered around pricing. By the mid-1990s, pricing was still an important factor, but retailers still wanted more. Storage of inventory was one of the highest expenses a retailer faced. To reduce this expense, retailers increasingly were demanding that manufacturers carry the inventory instead, and make deliveries when the retailers' stock was low. In order for this type of relationship to work, especially when dealing with large quantities of merchandise required by stores such as Wal-Mart or K-mart, retailers and vendors found it necessary to form partnerships. Quick response is the most important aspect of this relationship. Orders must be replenished automatically via computer links called electronic data interchange (EDI).

Retailers also demanded a continual flow of new merchandise. Some footwear manufacturers responded to this need by creating "flow replenishment" programs, in which new products were introduced in a continual flow rather than in seasonal batches. In addition, retailers were demanding more marketing support and other services. Many manufactures, as a result, were creating their own point-of-sale fixtures, and advertising their products nationally.

Experts attributed the growing appeal of outlet stores to the value-conscious shopper. Outlet stores' primary attraction was the price of their products. Customers generally purchased footwear and other apparel items at up to half the cost charged by conventional department and specialty stores. In many cases, the merchandise offered was no longer irregulars, overruns, or odd lots. Often, the merchandise was first-quality, coming from current inventory, although many footwear manufacturers used their own outlet stores to dispense extra or second-quality merchandise. Manufacturers preferred this form of distribution to off-price retailers because they avoided tarnishing their brand names. This risk often occurred when too much merchandise was sold through discounters. In addition, outlet stores also tended to be located far from the selling areas of conventional department and specialty stores. This decreased the chance that the manufacturer's regular retail store lost sales to the outlet store.

CURRENT CONDITIONS

Athletic Footwear. Athletic footwear was the largest-selling category in the footwear industry. Consumption of athletic footwear, including imports and domestic production of rubber-soled "sneakers," reached a peak of about 565 million pairs in 1992, but declined approximately one percent in 1993. Athletic footwear represented about 38 percent of combined nonrubber and rubber-fabric footwear consumption of approximately 1.5 billion pairs in 1993. Imports of juvenile footwear were up about seven percent in the first half of 1993 from the same period in 1992, but imports of athletic nonrubber footwear declined.

The largest selling brand of athletic footwear was Nike with a 26 percent share of the athletic footwear market. Nike was followed by Reebok with 23 percent, L.A. Gear with 13 percent, Converse with five percent, and Avia with four percent.

In 1989, the top three athletic footwear brands paid for 87 percent of the top five's $93.7 million total advertising expenditures. The general target audience was 18- to 34-year olds, and marketers reached them with a mix of sports, lifestyle television programming, and magazine titles. While Nike, Converse, and Avia built strong followings in the performance shoe business, Reebok and L.A. Gear had more of a fashion than a performance-based image. Nike was the top advertising spender in 1989 with $33.3 million. L.A. Gear spent $21.5 million on athletic shoe advertising. Most athletic shoe companies relied on high-priced, prime time television advertisements and major sporting

event television advertisements for most of their media advertisements.

The nation's largest selling footwear company, Kinney Shoe Corporation, launched its own private label of athletic footwear in August 1993 through its Foot Locker sneaker and sports apparel retail chain. The new shoe brand, In the Zone or ITZ, had its own independent marketing budget and was set to compete with the volatile second tier of athletic shoe brands, such as L.A. Gear, Adidas, Converse, and Asics.

Outdoor Footwear. One of the fastest-growing categories in the footwear industry was outdoor footwear. Outdoor footwear included rugged hiking boots and casual outdoor sandals. According to *Sporting Goods Business*, footwear suppliers forecasted that the rugged/casual footwear market would see substantial growth at least to 1995 before levelling off at a ten to 20 percent increase for several years afterward.

Many traditional athletic footwear companies recognized the potential profit in this category and were scrambling to participate. Nike's outdoor division, for example, grew from $60 million for fiscal 1992 to an estimated $130 million for fiscal 1993. Many other traditional athletic brands were trying to find a place in the outdoor market niche, while still maintaining their high-performance athletic images.

In the athletic outdoor shoe category, Teva sandals were one of the most popular styles of footwear in the early 1990s. Deckers was one of the leading manufacturers in this category. In 1994, net income for Deckers was expected to rise 80 percent to $10.6 million, with 90 percent of this increase attributable to Teva sandals.

One of the fastest-growing companies in the outwear shoe category was Timberland Company. Analysts estimated that its 41 percent increase in sales in

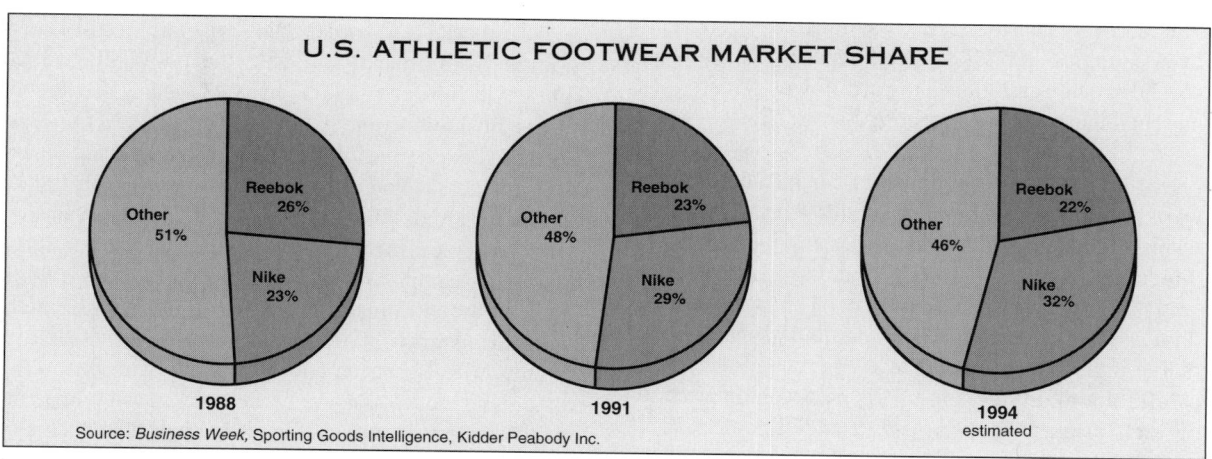

U.S. ATHLETIC FOOTWEAR MARKET SHARE

1988

Other 51%
Reebok 26%
Nike 23%

1991

Other 48%
Reebok 23%
Nike 29%

1994 estimated

Other 46%
Reebok 22%
Nike 32%

Source: *Business Week*, Sporting Goods Intelligence, Kidder Peabody Inc.

1993 was engendered by the shift in Americans' fashion tastes. In addition to streamlining its operations, Timberland cultivated the casual, outdoor fashion that began to increase in popularity in the early 1990s. Many companies were attempting to imitate Timberland's style, but consumers still considered Timberland to be the "original." In *Adweek*, Don Maurer of Mullen Advertising stated that Timberland could become the next Nike.

Safety footwear constituted yet another segment of the footwear industry. This type of footwear was worn mainly by workers with hazardous, physically demanding jobs. This segment included heavy leather work boots with steel toes for extra protection. According to *Occupational Hazards*, safety footwear was beginning to look much more like mainstream retail footwear in the mid-1990s. The article stated that workers cared as much about style and comfort as they did about protection, and that they were more inclined to wear shoes that are aesthetically pleasing. The most successful safety footwear manufacturers were designing shoes that provided a safe environment for the foot with an overall stylish appeal.

Juvenile Footwear. After many years of rapid growth due to the heavy sales demands of the post-war baby boom era, juvenile footwear sales slowed in the early 1990s. Despite reaching the peak of the baby boom, however, competition among this category's competitors was still tight. The undisputed leader in juvenile footwear was Stride Rite. In 1992, the company announced 27 consecutive quarters of increased earnings.

Stride Rite's primary competition in the juvenile footwear industry included Keds (a brand also owned by Stride Rite), Weebok (owned by Reebok), Sebago, Sam & Libby, and Toddler University. As in the case of adult footwear, the industry witnessed a trend away from shopping at higher-priced department stores and specialty shop retailers, toward lower-priced mass merchandisers and outlet stores.

With more and more two-career families, parents were finding less time to take children shopping. As a result, the industry also was witnessing a trend toward direct mail purchasing through catalogs. In 1991, *Catalog Age* reported the founding of many new children's apparel catalogs with particularly aggressive marketing approaches. These merchandisers were careful not to dilute their efforts by focusing attention on their primary footwear merchandise.

AMERICA AND THE WORLD

With limited prospects for domestic growth, many footwear companies in the early 1990s were looking for growth opportunities abroad. For footwear merchandise, market penetration was limited since tastes in fashion apparel differ from one country to the next. Liz Claiborne's efforts to penetrate the United Kingdom and Canadian markets were initially successful, but experts questioned whether this success would carry to the French or German markets, where tastes in fashion differed dramatically from U.S. tastes.

Many manufacturers believed that basic footwear, such as tennis shoes and children's shoes, had the potential for a large international market. Many brand-name products, such as Nike, were being built into major international franchises in the early 1990s. In 1993, Asia contributed about $500 million of Nike's total revenues of $4 billion, which represented a 66 percent jump from the previous year. Such rapidly rising Asian sales were especially important to Nike as it struggled to overcome slow growth in the United States. In China, Nike found that its challenge was to get its shoes into stores and ensure that those stores knew how to display products that were extremely expensive by Chinese standards. In the Philippines, 20 percent of Nike's shoe sales were made by door-to-door salesmen who sold the shoes on credit. Keeping control of its distribution operation and remaining flexible in the face of cultural differences were keys to boosting Nike's sales in the region. According to the *Far Eastern Economic Review*, Nike gained control of its distribution in Taiwan, Hong Kong, Malaysia, China, Singapore, Australia, and New Zealand within a three year period. Nike executives spoke of creating an emotional tie with the consumer in these countries, and as a result, Nike was one of the world's most recognized brand images in the early 1990s.

Timberland Company also was successful in exporting its footwear. In 1983, the company had no interest in foreign markets; in 1993, nearly 40 percent of its business came from overseas markets. Timberland's executives developed an interest in the export business when they joined forces with an Italian consumer goods distributor to establish European operations. Once there, they learned that international marketing campaigns needed to be country-specific to succeed. According to the company's director of international business, Timberland became very sensitive to cultural differences and won many European customers by developing new flexible marketing techniques, which included "concept shops," "specialty shops," and filling retailers orders quickly.

RESEARCH AND TECHNOLOGY

Like most industries, manufacturers in the nonrubber footwear industry were under extreme pressure to limit the size of their work force, while boosting productivity and efficiency at the same time. For that reason, the industry considered new technology essential to increase growth and profitability. In the 1970s and 1980s, the use of computers integrated design, manufacturing, management, and marketing tasks. Computerized production allowed manufacturers to emphasize non-price factors such as quality and quick delivery to compete with imports.

Many footwear producers turned to computer-aided design (CAD) and computer-aided manufacturing (CAM) systems and software. As a result, these manufacturers produced tooling from CAD-generated data and linked it to auto-stitchers, milling, and turning machines. In the early 1990s, the industry witnessed a resurgence of interest in three-dimensional CAD, which produced more accurate shoe patterns and reduced the number of prototypes required to take a new shoe design to the retail level.

In the footwear industry, computers also enabled manufacturers to combine several operations or machines under fewer operators, thereby reducing handling time and the number of employees, while improving quality. The industry also developed computerized robots to handle and transfer operations within and between production modules.

In order to meet the demands of retailers' quick response requirements, more and more manufacturers were utilizing electronic data interchange (EDI). The goal of quick response was to maintain lean inventories and avoid overstocking, while insuring that retailers had the merchandise customers wanted to buy. EDI allowed retailers and manufacturers to link themselves together.

In the EDI system, inter-linked computer systems were placed at every point of the manufacturing and sales process. Through use of an electronic scanner and bar code tagged to the merchandise, retailers recorded which type of footwear was sold at the point of sale. All sales data on the individual products, including details of color and size, were transmitted immediately to the manufacturer. Through this method, the manufacturer kept track of every store's retail sales trends. This first-hand view of consumer purchasing trends allowed manufacturers to produce apparel based directly on customer demand. The information contained in the bar code set automatic re-ordering into motion. The industry also referred to this type of inventory replenishment as ''flow'' or ''just in time.''

In addition to allowing automatic replenishment, EDI also ameliorated distribution and shipping processes. For example, once a shipment was ready to go, the manufacturer created a labelling document, and EDI sent an invoice automatically.

A great deal of this new technology was developed and used in Europe before coming to the United States. Most of it was easily transferred to Far Eastern footwear producers, depending on the availability of capital. For these Far Eastern manufacturers, however, the labor-saving benefits of this new technology were not as great as for producers with higher production costs. Industry experts predicted that the net effect of such technology would reduce the costs of U.S. production relative to Far Eastern production, although the latter would continue to maintain a competitive advantage for most categories of footwear.

INDUSTRY INFORMATION SOURCES

Bednarski, Kate, ''Convincing Male Managers to Target Women customers,'' *Working Woman,* June 993, p. 23.

Gaffney, Andrew, ''Footwear's Future,'' *Sporting Goods Business,* January 1994, p. 44.

Jensen, Jeff, ''Sneaker Ads on the Wrong Track,'' *Advertising Age,* November 29, 1993, p. 3.

Jensen, Jeff, ''Sneaker Giants Are Heeding the Call of the Great Outdoors,'' *Advertising Age,* January 31, 1994, p. 4.

Laabs, Jennifer, ''Family Issues Are a Priority at Stride Rite,'' *Personnel Journal,* July 1993, p. 48.

Maremont, Mark, ''Timberland Comes Out of the Woods,'' *Business Week,* September 13, 1993, p. 78.

Miller, Cyndee, ''Pitch for Sneakers Is Also Campaign to End Violence,'' *Marketing News,* December 6, 1993, p. 13.

Sharkey, Betsy, ''If the Shoe Fits,'' *Adweek,* February 14, 1994, p. 23.

Sloan, Pat, ''Reebok, Nike Look Beyond Sneakers,'' *Advertising Age,* June 28, 1993, p. 8.

—Wendy Johnson Bilas

SIC 3151

LEATHER GLOVES AND MITTENS

This category includes establishments primarily engaged in the manufacture of dress, semi-dress, and work gloves, which are made exclusively of leather or leather with lining of other materials. Excluded are establishments primarily engaged in the manufacture of athletic gloves (**SIC 3949: Sporting and Athletic Goods, Not Elsewhere Classified**), semi-dress and work gloves made primarily of cloth (**SIC 2381: Dress and Work Gloves, Except Knit and All-Leather**), and safety gloves (**SIC 3842: Orthopedic, Prosthetic, and Surgical Appliances and Supplies**).

In 1992, the value of the products shipped declined about five percent from 1991 to $103 million, following a pattern of steady decline since 1988. *Industrial Outlook* attributed the decline in the late 1980s and early 1990s to the recession, which caused a decreased demand for work gloves in manufacturing and construction. But historical data shows that the industry has been shrinking in both output and the number of manufacturers over the last twenty years due to competition from lower-priced imports. *Industrial Outlook* predicted a further decline of 3.5 percent in 1993 for the industry overall, partly due to increased competition from imports.

The U.S. glove industry began about 1760 when Sir William Johnson, founder of Johnstown and Gloversville, New York, brought in a group of glove makers from Perthsire, England to make deerskin mittens and heavy gloves for nearby farmers. Native Americans had shown Johnson how to use the local barks for dying and tanning. The abundant supply of deer hides and the availability of streams and lakes for tanning the hides and transporting the finished gloves to nearby farm communities helped the industry flourish.

Nineteenth-century inventions that mechanized glove cutting and sewing increased productivity in the industry, but the industry still needed skilled workers. In the 1890s, many glove workers came from Italy. Fulton County, where Johnstown and Gloversville are located, remained the U.S. glove-making center, and was home to the now-defunct industry association and union headquarters. Through the 1930s, the U.S. + Department of Labor noted that while men cut most of the materials for gloves in the area's many small factories, most of the sewing was performed by women. Sewing of the heavier work gloves was done in the factories on heavy duty machines, while work on the dress and semi-dress gloves was often done on a piece-work basis in homes.

After World War II, competition from cheaper labor abroad began to cut into the American market. By the early 1990s, most U.S. manufacturers sent some or all of their work off-shore for assembly to provide a lower-priced product, some to contract firms and some to factories owned by the U.S. manufacturer. Fewer than one-third of the gloves under U.S. labels are wholly manufactured in the United States. The 1987 *Census of Manufactures* showed employment in the industry at 3100, twenty-one percent lower than the figure for 1982. New York, Wisconsin, and Illinois

employed the largest number of glove workers. The largest single segment of the U.S. glovemaking industry remained in the Johnstown-Gloversville area of upper New York State.

Work produced in the United States is considered high quality and is often marketed to specialty firms or sold under arrangement to catalog firms such as L.L. Bean. While some U.S.-made gloves are exported as finished products, the majority of exports (70 percent in 1992) consist of cut glove pieces that will be returned to the United States as finished gloves. The United States Department of Commerce divided domestic glove production into two product segments: work gloves, which comprised 85 percent of glove production, and dress and semi-dress gloves, which comprised the remaining 15 percent.

INDUSTRY INFORMATION SOURCES

U.S. Department of Commerce. *U.S. Industrial Outlook 1992*. Washington, DC: Department of Commerce, 1992.

U.S. Department of Labor. *U.S. Occupational Outlook Handbook*, May 1992.

Wards Business Directory of U.S. Private and Public Companies. Detroit, MI: Gale Research, 1993.

World Book Encyclopedia. Chicago: World Book, Inc., 1986.

—Joan Leotta

SIC 3161

LUGGAGE

This category covers establishments primarily engaged in manufacturing luggage of leather or other materials. The luggage industry produces a wide variety of products, including suitcases, briefcases, attache cases, hand luggage, tote bags, trunks, and occupational cases. Materials used in addition to leather include plastics, nylon, cotton, linen, and metals. Many products use a combination of these materials. Construction methods include sewing, molding, and laminating. About 25 percent of U.S.-made luggage products are made of leather, with leather use most common in attache cases and briefcases.

INDUSTRY SNAPSHOT

Luggage shipments increased about 67 percent in 1992, to almost $1.1 billion. Total industry employment declined 3.7 percent, to 13,000 employees, but employment in the area of production increased about 4 percent, to 10,200. This indicated that the industry was lowering overhead labor, while increasing production. There are more than two dozen different types of occupations in the luggage/leather products industry, including sewing machine operators, plastic molding machine operators, leather workers, assemblers, inspectors, and packagers.

In 1992, a moderate economic recovery resulted in slightly more travel and, hence, more demand for luggage. Luggage purchases amounted to $2.2 billion in 1992, up about 12 percent from the previous year. Imports increased about 20 percent, to about $1.3 billion, representing about 59 percent of purchases.

BACKGROUND AND DEVELOPMENT

Luggage—defined as a product designed to carry items by hand from place to place—has been around in some form or another since the beginning of time. Cave men and women likely carried sticks, stones, bones, and furs in small leather sacks or large skins as they moved from cave to cave. Egyptians packed precious objects into casket-shaped trunks and buried them in tombs with their kings and queens. In those early days, separate trunks or chests were used to transport different types of items; there were, for example, jewelry, linen, and wardrobe cases. This practice endured for centuries and is still popular with those who have no need to travel lightly.

From the earliest time, however, how one traveled dictated what type of ''luggage'' one used. When traveling by foot, for example, a simple sack was often sufficient. If beasts of burden were available, items were boxed or bagged and secured atop the animal. Travel by ship or barge made it possible to use large trunks and chests. Of course, the more money one had, the grander the style of travel and the type of luggage. ''Heaven only knows how many people it took to get Cleopatra's barge up the Nile, Marco Polo to China, or Mrs. Vanderbilt across the Atlantic,'' wrote Diane Sustendal in *Showcase*. ''It's only in recent years that hopping the Concorde with a single bag has become a status way to travel. Prior to that, three or more matched pieces of luggage lined up at a dock, train station, or airport said something about the status of the traveler.''

Whole groups of people, she noted, have been identified by the types of luggage they carried. The ''Casket Girls of Louisiana,'' young women sent from France to the colony to marry, carried their belongings in caskets. Carpetbaggers got their name from the bags in which they carried cash and clothing to the South following the Civil War. ''Old Saddlebags'' referred to the early Pony Express riders who carried mail in such pouches on the back of horses. Some types of

luggage have gotten their names from modes of transportation: the coach bag, train case, flight kit, pullman case, and steamer trunk are all examples. The luggage lexicon has also been impacted by war. British soldiers during World War I had their ''kit bag.'' American G.I.s packed their belongings in a ''duffle bag'' or ''furlough bag.''

The luggage industry bubbled with new ideas after World War II. Many materials developed for the wartime effort were put to use in the industry: rip-stop nylon, fiberglass, plastics, simulated fabric, leather, and aluminum. Manufacturers learned to design products that were durable, yet light enough to meet plane travel requirements. Luggage became available in three categories: constructed, or molded luggage; semi-constructed, with such features as side zipper entry and compartments for easy packing; and soft luggage, which is lightweight and collapsible.

Color added a fashion statement previously missing from luggage. Fashionable women travelers could choose from such colors as bright red, pale blue, pink, and cream; men had gray, navy, forest green, and burgundy as alternatives to the more conservative black or brown. In the late 1960s, the colors of luggage mimicked the colors of fashion—hot pink, neon yellow and orange, and bright blue.

By the 1970s, with the idea of space travel no longer a distant reality, luggage resembling space suit fabrics first appeared. During that same time period, ''designer luggage'' became the vogue, and luggage sported designer logos. As plane travel became faster and more efficient, travelers began placing a higher priority on speed. Manufacturers recognized this and devoted more of their attention on carry-on luggage, which permitted passengers to save time by avoiding check-in lines and baggage claim areas. The Mac Pac by Casecraft Inc. illustrated this trend. This European-styled set consisted of a three-suit garment bag, four-zipper expandable boarding case, and 10-inch grooming kit. ''We are targeting those people who want three pieces in one package,'' reported Larry Wiviott, director of sales and marketing for Casecraft, in *Upscale Discounting*.

In the 1980s, an era known for conspicuous consumption, customers demanded that their luggage demonstrate their wealth, status, and personal taste. They looked for classic styling, quality, and high-fashion touches. Leather, tweeds, and stripes were big sellers. ''I think what you'll see is an upscaling of the traditional, meaning a richer, classical look,'' predicted Cathy Lynch, director of marketing at Samsonite, in *Upscale Discounting*. For example, Henry Rosenfeld Travelware introduced several new tweeds and leather designs in 1988. One line of luggage featured interchangeable sets. "One may be a tweed, and one may be a solid, and one may be a tapestry, but they all work together," Barbara Cooke, assistant sales manager for Rosenfeld, noted in *Upscale Discounting.* "You don't have to go with the traditional five-piece set anymore. It all coordinates and works well together." Popular colors included earth tones, blue-black, burgundy, melon, pumpkin, olive green, and deep gold.

Responding to the consumers' increasing interest in quality, name brand luggage, vendors introduced luggage with better fabrics and more features, such as zippers, pockets, and compartments to hold such items as shirts, hair dryers, running shoes, and tennis racquets. "The additional pocket and strap and the feeling of security it gives the consumer are the important element of luggage today," according to Joel Dupre, Action Bags executive, as quoted in *Upscale Discounting.* Peters Bag Corp. introduced a Sasson Executive Style luggage set in 1989, which included a garment bag with full front zippered pocket, adjustable shoulder strap, boarding bag with dual zipper opening, front and side zipper pockets, and a utility kit with a fully-lined interior and two-way zipper.

Many manufacturers used gussets to allow bags to expand to larger proportions. "One of the buzzwords of the '80s has become expandables," noted Sustendal. Even Bob Plath, a Northwest Airlines 747 captain, got into the act. He designed and successfully marketed his own expandable carry-on luggage after years of struggling with bulky carry-ons. The Travelpro Rollaboard, a soft-sided suitcase on wheels, was expandable up to a 120-pound capacity, yet meets size requirements to fit under most airline seats and in overhead bins.

Business Cases. Attache cases or briefcases have been around as long as people have had to call on clients. Scribes and physicians may have been the first to use some form of business case. Blacksmiths, cobblers, carpenters, seamstresses, musicians, and artists used bags, boxes, and small cases to transport the tools of their trade. "In fact, the shape of the bag used by cobblers and blacksmiths is reminiscent of today's medical bag," wrote Sustendal. "The attache, with its hard sides and box-like construction, is a direct descendant of an artist's paint box and the scribe's writing box." Early coverings designed to protect books, letters, sketches, and legal briefs were forerunners of today's portfolios or briefcases.

Throughout the twentieth century, the functions and appearance of the business case have changed frequently and sometimes dramatically. While leather business cases are still popular, there are now more choices than ever before—molded cases of plastic or metal, fashion cases, canvas cases, and cases made of exotic skins, including snake, eel, and crocodile. In the late 1980s, R. F. Kilpatric and Associates even introduced a wooden briefcase from Sweden, available in natural wood and a mahogany color. Briefcases that doubled as luggage also made their appearance. "There's now a new type of briefcase on the market, which is more expansive," John Brandley, marketing research manager for Amity Leather Products, told *Upscale Discounting.* "It can carry more than a regular briefcase because there's room for toiletries and overnight clothing and it's now regulation size."

Like luggage, business cases eventually became available in a variety of colors. Gray, burgundy, tan, forest green, even red, white, and blue became acceptable options for business executives. Such features as contrasting trim, gleaming or burnished hardware, detachable shoulder straps, and retractable handles also became available. Compartments for holding pens, business cards, calculators, checkbooks, cellular phones, computers, and mini-televisions were added to many of the new designs, as were sleeves to accommodate portfolios, notepaper, computer readouts, legal pads, agendas, and reports.

Regardless of what new trends emerge in the 1990s, business cases are expected to retain their traditional flavor. "There will always be something traditional about the business case, for it is not an item of folly," wrote Sustendal. "It connotes seriousness of purpose and gives the carrier a solid, substantial air."

INDUSTRY LEADERS

Samsonite, headquartered in Denver, Colorado, is the world's leading manufacturer of luggage. In 1991, the company had an estimated $300 million in sales. Samsonite was founded in 1910 as the Shwayder Trunk Manufacturing Company. From a one-room business near downtown Denver with 10 employees, Samsonite has grown into a network of 30 manufacturing and distribution centers employing 6,500 individuals throughout the world.

Samsonite established its reputation by producing a product that was extremely durable. The company's original slogan—"Strong enough to stand on"—was first illustrated by a picture of founder Jess Shwayder, his father, and three of his brothers standing on a plank that rested on a Shwayder hardcase. Today Samsonite makes both hardside and softside luggage. Hardside luggage is made by the molding and assembly of plastic components, utilizing either vacuum forming or injection molding techniques. Samsonite's softside luggage involves the manufacturing of hand-assembled luggage made of synthetic fiber materials and steel or plastic frames. The company's hardside luggage sales continued to grow dramatically in the early 1990s, particularly in the European market. Samsonite is the leading manufacturer of hardside luggage in the world.

The second largest U.S. luggage manufacturer is Zero Corporation of Los Angeles, California, which had sales of $170 million in 1991, followed by American Trading & Production, American Tourister Inc., and Hartmann Luggage Co. Major foreign players in the luggage industry include Louis Vuitton, a manufacturer of high quality luggage based in Paris, France, and Delsey Luggage Inc., also based in Paris. Delsey entered the upscale U.S. market in 1985 after establishing itself as the leading manufacturer of hard-side luggage in Europe. "Delsey is considered to be France's largest luggage manufacturer and among the top three worldwide, although well behind industry leader Samsonite," wrote Kurt Kleiner in the *Baltimore Business Journal.* Delsey's worldwide luggage sales were about $100 million a year in 1988, and were growing at about 20 percent a year.

AMERICA AND THE WORLD

The resurgence of pride in America and American-made products in the 1980s prompted many luggage manufacturers to focus on American-made goods and push the "Made in the U.S.A." logo. "We're promoting it on all merchandise that applies," John Gallup, a luggage buyer for K-Mart Corp., told *Upscale Discounting.* "We are putting it into our advertising." Promoting U.S.-made luggage was often challenging, however, since few luggage products are actually made in the United States. "Almost all nylon goods, whether it's Samsonite, American Tourister, Verdi, it's all imported," said Gallup. "It has the good old American name but basically it's an import." According to American Tourister manager Karl Czerny, however, approximately 25 percent of their merchandise is made in the United States. That percentage is made up primarily of their hardside luggage, which is bulky and expensive to import.

Luggage imports rose about 20 percent in 1992, to an estimated $1.3 billion, and represented 59 percent of domestic consumption. Although almost 31 percent of all attache cases and briefcases are made of leather, only about 2 percent of all luggage imports are leather. Prime sources of luggage imports were China, with 59 percent of the total, followed by Taiwan (19 percent), and South Korea (7 percent). In 1992, U.S. luggage exports rose about 44 percent over 1991 to an esti-

mated $157 million. Canada, Japan, and Mexico were the largest export markets.

INDUSTRY INFORMATION SOURCES

Berman, Phyllis, "Is Traveling Well the Best Revenge?," *Forbes,* August 8, 1988.

Dickey, Christopher, "The New King of Luxury," *Newsweek,* August 7, 1989.

Gandee, Charles, "Gandee at Large," *HG,* February 1990.

Goodman, Wendy, "Living with Style," *HG,* March 1992.

Kleiner, Kurt, "Delsey Luggage Enjoys the Sweet Smell of Its Expansion," *Baltimore Business Journal,* June 13, 1988.

LeTellier, George, "Higher Fashion Key in Luggage," *Upscale Discounting,* March 1987.

Richards, Nora, "Putting a Tag on 'U.S. Made,'" *Upscale Discounting,* April 1988.

————, "Quality, Advertising Are Keys to Sales," *Upscale Discounting,* February 1988.

————, "Venders Aim for Creativity in Merchandising," *Upscale Discounting,* March 1988.

————, "Venders Quickly Fill Consumer Needs in Fashion, Function," *Upscale Discounting,* May 1988.

————, "Venders Rely on Exotics & Basics," *Upscale Discounting,* January 1988.

Samsonite Corporation, *Samsonite Annual Report,* Denver, CO: Samsonite Corporation, 1992.

"Smart Sailing," *Forbes,* December 1, 1986.

Statistical Abstract of the United States, Washington, DC: U.S. Bureau of the Census.

Sustendal, Diane, "Where We've Been: A History of Luggage, Business Cases, Personal Leather Goods and Components," *Showcase,* November-December 1988.

U.S. Department of Commerce, *U.S. Industrial Outlook 1993,* Washington, DC: U.S. Department of Commerce, January 1993.

Walsh, John, "Vendors Introducing Better Fabrics and Features in Luggage," *Upscale Discounting,* January 1989.

Zisser, Melinda, "The Flyboy's Bag," *Florida Business Journal,* September 24, 1990.

—Pamela Berry

SIC 3171

WOMEN'S HANDBAGS AND PURSES

This classification includes establishments primarily engaged in manufacturing women's handbags and purses of leather or other materials, except precious metals. Establishments primarily engaged in manufacturing precious metal handbags and purses are classified in **SIC 3911: Jewelry, Precious Metal.**

INDUSTRY SNAPSHOT

The women's handbag and purse industry produces all women's handbags and purses of leather and other materials, except precious metals. Approximately 62 percent of the domestic handbags shipped in the United States in 1993 were made of leather. Handbag production shipments declined about ten percent in 1993 to an estimated $336 million. Total industry employment also dropped approximately five percent to 5,200. Production employment declined ten percent to 3,500. Apparent consumption of handbags and purses in 1993 declined about two percent from 1992 to an estimated $1.2 billion.

BACKGROUND AND DEVELOPMENT

Historically, women have made most of their handbag purchases at boutique specialty stores and department stores. Consumers in the purse and handbag industry most often selected handbag purchases on the basis of designer recognition and style. During the 1980s, consumers took great interest in their appearance and became slightly extravagant at the sales counter. The sales of high-priced and mid-range brands, such as Coach and Dooney and Bourke, proliferated. Personal consumption of handbags and other apparel accessories nearly doubled in the 1980s with an average annual growth rate of 7.3 percent. Then, hurt by the recession, weak growth in disposable income, and high unemployment, consumers became much more cost-conscious.

Along with these economic changes came changes in consumer psychology. Designer names, high-priced accessories, and frequent shopping sprees became much less frequent. Consumers became more value conscious and began purchasing less expensive products at lower-end retail establishments and mass merchandisers. An writer for *Footwear News* indicated that leather buying habits had begun to shift to form, function, and comfort, and away from designer names.

Despite the recessionary economy, however, Coach and Dooney & Bourke lines, which ranged from just below $100 to more than $300 in 1993, remained consistently strong performers. But other high-priced segments of the handbag business have not fared as well. High-priced lines like Liz Claiborne stumbled badly at the retail counters. Many experts attribute the success of Coach and Dooney & Bourke to the lines' classic/casual stylings versus Liz Claiborne's dressier appearance.

Shoppers changed their handbag-buying habits throughout the early 1990s. Consumer purchasing shifted toward the most basic, functional accessories. Rather than purchasing a handbag to match each outfit—the pattern during the first three-quarters of the 20th century—shoppers began purchasing a single handbag versatile enough to match many outfits. This pattern reflects a more value-oriented consumer, as well as an aging population seeking comfort and casualness. In the past several years, many mass merchandisers have added more recognizable national brand names to their in-store inventory. In the past, most brand names were distributed only through department stores.

CURRENT CONDITIONS

In 1992 specialty and department store retailers were optimistic about the growth of the handbag category, according to *Stores Magazine.* At the time, retailers were predicting sales increases on handbags ranging from a low of eight percent a high of 20 percent. The key for sales success was to have the right assortment of handbags, from the moderate-priced to the higher-priced brands, such as Coach and Dooney & Bourke. By 1992, the moderate-priced handbag business had doubled its 1990 sales level. Brand names such as Perry Ellis America, Capezio, and Esprit led the pack in producing fashionable handbags at moderate prices and giving retailers new inventory options.

Besides seeking more basic handbags, many shoppers were seeking lower-priced goods in strip shopping centers and outlet stores instead of the higher-end shopping malls. According to *Women's Wear Daily,* department store share of all apparel expenditures fell to 24.3 percent in 1993, down from 33.6 percent in 1985. A survey by the *Wall Street Journal* confirmed that women were buying more of their handbags and other apparel at mass merchandisers, such as Kmart and Wal-Mart, and shopping less frequently at department and specialty stores. For K-mart and Wal-mart, brand name recognition is still important, and such brands as Chic and Gitano have been particularly successful. Abe Chehebar, president of Gitano handbags, told *Discount Merchandiser* that functional, organizer-style bags have been solid performers for his company. He considers these bags to be "life-style oriented." As a result, shoulder bags and totes continue to be strong performers. Chehebar also considers designer signatures on handbags to be important features because they elevate the accessories as status items.

Storage of inventory is one of the highest expenses a retailer faces. To reduce this expense, retailers are increasingly demanding that a manufacturer carry the inventory instead and make deliveries when the retailers' stock is low. In order for this type of relationship to work, especially when dealing with large quantities of merchandise required by stores such as Wal-Mart or K-mart, retailers and vendors find it necessary to form partnerships. Quick response is the most important aspect of this relationship. Orders must be replenished automatically via computer links called electronic data interchange (EDI).

Experts attribute the growing appeal of outlet stores to the value-conscious shopper. Outlet stores' primary draw is price. Customers can generally purchase footwear and other apparel items at up to half the cost charged by conventional department and specialty stores. In many cases, the merchandise offered is no longer irregulars, overruns, or odd lots. The merchandise is often top quality and comes from current inventory, although many footwear manufacturers use their own outlet stores to move surplus and low-quality merchandise. Manufacturers prefer this form of distribution to off-price retailers because they avoid tarnishing their brand names, which can occur when too much merchandise is sold through discounters. In addition, outlet stores tend to be located too far from the selling areas of conventional department and specialty stores. This decreases the chance that the manufacturer's regular retail customers will lose sales to the outlet stores.

INDUSTRY LEADERS

Throughout the late 1980s, the ten largest publicly traded apparel and accessory companies saw their market share increase by nearly five percent. Part of this growth can be attributed to increased demand for these companies' products. But the remaining growth was a result of acquisitions and consolidations. This consolidation within the footwear manufacturing industry parallels that of the retail industry. As large department store retailers merged in the late 1980s, they consolidated their buying functions. Larger manufacturers benefitted from this because it became more efficient for a fewer number of buyers to use one vendor rather than several. In response, growth-oriented handbag and purse manufacturers increased their acquisition activity in search of new brands and broader product offerings.

In addition, the enormous growth of large mass merchandisers was driving the industry to consolidate going into the mid-1990s. From 1981 through 1991, Sears—the nation's largest retailer—saw its sales increase rapidly, as did Wal-Mart and Kmart. Savvy footwear manufacturers understand that they can increase their sales and market penetration by offering

these retail giants a broad array of brand-name merchandise. Historically, many brand-name manufacturers sold their goods only to department stores, but they soon began selling nearly identical merchandise to mass merchandisers in order to participate in the mass merchandisers' phenomenal growth. Not surprisingly, this affected the manufacturers' relationships with the department stores, who seek exclusivity in their products. To remedy the situation, many manufacturers began to produce several different categories of brand names, each of which is distributed through a different type of retailer. Each retailer has brand exclusivity within its own category.

AMERICA AND THE WORLD

Because labor costs represent such a high proportion of total production costs, handbags and other personal leather goods industries encountered significant import competition in the 1980s and early 1990s. This competition came primarily from developing nations where wage rates are far below those in the United States. China, for example, has rapidly become the dominant supplier to the United States of all these products. Some of the world's leading brands of these goods are now produced in developing countries, a trend that is expected to continue because of the drastic differences in labor costs. Furthermore, because international demand for handbags and other leather goods was rising in the early 1990s, many more developing countries with appropriate supplies of leather and suitable production skills could possibly enter the trade. Most of these developing nations enter by producing travel goods or small leather articles, which tend to stay in fashion longer than women's handbags. This way, the producers have opportunities to establish steady export businesses before turning to the production of the seasonal women's handbags.

U.S. exports of handbags increased about 18 percent to an estimated $41 million in 1993. Mexico was the largest market by quantity, accounting for 51 percent of all U.S. exports. However, most of these exports were cut parts for handbags that were assembled in Mexico and re-exported to the United States as finished goods. Japan was the leading market for finished U.S. handbags with an estimated 38 percent, or nearly $14 million, of purchases in 1993.

The total value of U.S. imports of handbags, luggage, and personal leather goods declined about two percent in 1993. The value of U.S. exports in this industry increased about four percent to $288 million. Handbag imports totaled $906 million, accounting for 76 percent of consumption in 1993. Foreign suppliers with the largest share, by quantity, were China (80 percent), Korea (six percent), and India (four percent).

RESEARCH AND TECHNOLOGY

More than many other industries, production of handbags and purses is heavily labor intensive. Therefore, like most companies, large producers of women's handbags are under extreme pressure to limit their number of employees by boosting productivity and efficiency. The industry considers new technology to be the key to increasing growth and profitability and keeping more production jobs in the United States. In recent decades, increased use of computers has integrated design, manufacturing, management, and marketing functions. Computerized production allows manufacturers to emphasize such non-price factors as quality and quick delivery to compete with imports.

Many handbag producers have turned to computer-aided design (CAD) and computer-aided manufacturing (CAM) systems and software. As a result, these manufacturers can produce tooling from CAD data and link it to auto-stitchers, milling, and turning machines. Computers also enable manufacturers to combine several operations or machines under fewer operators, thereby reducing handling time and number of employees, and improving quality. The industry has also developed computerized robots to handle and transfer operations within and between production modules.

In order to meet the demands of retailers' quick response requirements, more manufacturers are utilizing electronic data interchange (EDI), which allows retailers and manufacturers to communicate data. The goal of quick response is to maintain lean inventories and avoid overstocking, while ensuring that retailers have on hand the merchandise customers want to buy. In the EDI system, interlinked computer systems are placed at every point of the manufacturing and sales process. Through use of an electronic scanner and bar code that has been tagged to the merchandise, retailers record at the point of sale which merchandise has been sold. All sales data on the individual products, including details of color and size, are transmitted immediately to the manufacturer. Through this method, the manufacturer keeps track of every store's retail sales trends. This first-hand view of consumer purchasing trends allows manufacturers to produce handbags based directly on customer demand. The information contained in the bar code sets automatic reordering into motion. The industry also refers to this type of inventory replenishment as "flow" or "just in time." The manufacturer can quickly restock a retailer's shelves, using no more than a computer for communi-

cation. In addition to allowing automatic replenishment, EDI also enhances distribution and shipping. For example, once a shipment is ready to go, the manufacturer creates a labelling document and EDI sends an invoice automatically. In the future, EDI is likely to include electronic funds transfer as well.

A great deal of this new technology was developed and used in Europe before coming to the United States. Most of it can be readily transferred to Far Eastern producers, depending on the availability of capital. For these manufacturers, however, the labor-saving benefits of this new technology will not be as great as for producers with higher costs of production. Industry experts predict that the net effect of such technology will be to reduce the costs of U.S. production relative to Far Eastern production, although the latter will continue to maintain a competitive advantage for most categories of handbags.

Handbag producers are also making breakthroughs environmentally. In late 1993, a company by the name of Holiday Fair began producing handbags made of EEKO, a mainly water-based combination of natural and synthetic rubbers that has the look, feel, and colorability of leather. Holiday Fair's management team hopes this new material will eventually replace leather and leather substitutes. To promote its product, the company is placing heavy emphasis on retail and consumer educational programs that include detailed point-of-purchase literature and a store video. The company also intends to assume responsibility for the safe disposal, recycling, and reuse of all its products by using tags that offer consumers a value coupon toward their next Holiday Fair purchase if they return used handbags to the company. In January 1994 Holiday Fair also began shipping a new line of handbags made of polypropylene EEKO2, a material that emulates cotton for products ranging from tote bags to belts.

INDUSTRY INFORMATION SOURCES

Abend, Jules, "Environmentalism Is in the Bag," *Bobbin,* December 1993, 46.

Corwin, Pat, "Branded Handbags Trending Well," *Discount Merchandiser,* July 1991, 28-30.

Dunn's Business Rankings, New York: Dunn & Bradstreet, 1993.

Reda, Susan, "Handbag Forecast," *Stores,* May 1992, 86-88.

Sauer, Ron, "Leather Goods: Attractive Exports for Developing Countries," *International Trade Forum,* 1993, 22-25.

Standard & Poor's Industry Surveys, New York: Standard & Poor's Corporation, 1994.

U.S. Industrial Outlook 1993, Washington, DC: U.S. Department of Commerce, 1994.

— Wendy Johnson Bilas

SIC 3172

PERSONAL LEATHER GOODS, EXCEPT WOMEN'S HANDBAGS AND PURSES

This category covers establishments primarily engaged in manufacturing small articles normally carried on the person or in a handbag, such as billfolds, key cases, and coin purses of leather or other materials, except precious metal. Establishments primarily engaged in manufacturing similar personal goods or precious metals are classified in **SIC 3911: Jewelry, Precious Metal.**

The overall economic health of the personal leather goods industry is yoked to the status of the domestic leather production industry as a whole. Both this small segment and its parent category are affected by many of the same problems in manufacturing, labor costs, and competition with foreign-made products. The products manufactured by this industry are sometimes referred to as flatgoods due to their small dimensions; they are generally designed to fit into pockets or handbags. Such items include wallets and billfolds, coin purses, and key and cigarette cases; these goods may be manufactured wholly or partially of leather, plastic, or fabric, or from a combination of these materials.

Wallets and billfolds have historically represented the largest production segment of this industry, accounting for almost a third of all goods produced in 1989 and over 75 percent of the total monetary value of shipments. Travel kits are the next largest portion of the flatgoods market, followed by jewelry boxes and small items such as key and eyeglass cases. Typically manufacturers offer several product lines each season in a variety of colors and prices. Many of the products are interrelated—consumers of both sexes can purchase a wallet and accompanying accouterments in a single style at the department store counter, traditionally the largest retailer of such products. This industry category also includes such items as watchbands, compacts, and business cards cases if made from leather.

According to U.S. Department of Commerce estimates, the value of shipments for this segment of the leather manufacturing industry totaled $321 million in 1993. This figure represented a nearly six percent decline from the previous year. Employment figures also dropped six percent from 1992 to a 1993 figure of 5,300. Production workers, which have generally accounted for nearly 80 percent of all workers engaged in the industry, saw a slightly higher decline in employment statistics. The number of firms engaged in the production of flatgoods has been in decline since the early 1970s. Approximately 244 firms were classified as manufacturers in this industry in 1972, but by 1987 that number had declined 15 percent to 208. The majority of firms engaged have been smaller enterprises with less than 20 employees. Only 60 of the 208 firms operating in 1987 reported employing more than 20 workers in total.

Since the early 1970s, the personal leather goods industry in the United States has been dramatically affected by foreign-made products. Due to the skilled nature of the work, labor costs for domestic manufacturers are relatively high—the estimated average hourly wage in the industry was $7.75 for a production worker in 1993. Foreign manufacturers, most notably in China, Korea, India, and Italy, can produce flatgoods at a much reduced cost due to significantly lower wages in these countries. Because of this, the American consumer market for these products has become saturated with imported wallets, key cases, and eyeglass cases that have lower retail prices than their domestically produced counterparts.

In 1993 approximately 49 percent of the $589 million worth of flatgoods purchased by U.S. consumers were imports. The market share held by imports in this industry has continued to rise in the early 1990s, portending a forecast of economic difficulty for American manufacturers engaged in this industry. However, while imports continue to increase, so do exports of domestically produced flatgoods. A strong dollar and increased trade with Japan and Canada have helped to double the amount of exports since 1989. Estimated 1994 figures forecast an increase in exports of over 12 percent from the previous year's totals to $23.1 million.

INDUSTRY INFORMATION SOURCES

1987 Census of Manufactures, Washington, DC: U.S. Department of Commerce, 1987.

Current Industrial Reports: Luggage and Personal Leather Goods 1989, Washington, DC: U.S. Department of Commerce, September 1990.

United States Industrial Outlook 1994, Washington, DC: U.S. Department of Commerce, January 1994.

—Carol Brennan

LEATHER GOODS, NOT ELSEWHERE CLASSIFIED

This category covers establishments primarily engaged in manufacturing leather goods, not elsewhere classified, such as saddlery, harnesses, whips, embossed leather goods, leather desk sets, razor strops, and leather belting. Establishments primarily engaged in manufacturing gaskets and packing are classified in **SIC 3053: Gaskets, Packing, and Sealing Devices.** Establishments primarily engaged in manufacturing leather and sheep-lined clothing are classified in **SIC 2386: Leather and Sheep-Lined Clothing.**

The industry category of manufacturers of miscellaneous leather goods encompasses a broad array of unusual products with somewhat archaic uses. For example, a significant number of items classified relate to the antiquated pursuit of equestrianship and to the former reliance on the horse as a primary form of transportation during the 18th and 19th centuries in the United States. For this reason, the miscellaneous leather goods industry can trace its roots back to the first skilled leather craftspeople who arrived on the North American continent with early European settlers, and before that back to near prehistoric times when militia units roamed much of Eurasia on horseback. The demand for such items as saddles, feed bags, halters and harnesses, riding crops, helmets, and stirrups made from leather later declined with the advent of the industrial era.

The miscellaneous leather goods industry then shifted to manufacturing products for use in factories and other mechanical establishments. Such items made by the industry include textile machinery aprons, machinery belting, and sleeves and leggings for welders. Declines in the manufacturing segment of the economy led to another shift toward consumer products. This area, which dominated the industry in the 1990s, is involved in manufacturing small leather novelty items and includes such goods as leather collars and harnesses for household dogs and cats. A large portion of the industry's overall earnings in contemporary times is derived from the manufacture and sale of leather desk accessories.

According to 1987 U.S. Department of Commerce statistics, this category was comprised of 384 companies engaged in manufacturing miscellaneous leather goods. Most of these establishments were occupied exclusively in producing goods classified under this industry category. Almost three-quarters of those firms were small establishments with less than 20 employees on the payroll. The number of workers in the industry was 6,700 for the same year, with a relatively high percentage of that number, 5,500 jobholders, involved in production work. Payroll costs amounted to $89.7 million, with production workers earning $59.8 million of that figure. The value of shipments for the industry in 1987 totaled $390.6 million, a significant increase from the previous year's figure of $305.2 million.

Yet the industry has been in an overall decline since the mid-1970s, when 532 firms employed 8,600 workers in the industry to produce shipments totaling $284.2 million in 1977. By 1982 7,000 workers at 415 establishments produced goods totaling $327.4 million. The cost of materials used by the industry in manufacturing has remained relatively stable throughout the same period. In 1977 this amount was $154 million, and five years later had risen to just $165.3 million; in 1987 the cost of materials totaled $181.4 million, a somewhat dramatic jump from the previous year's figure of $134.5 million. While finished leather accounts for the majority of material utilized by the miscellaneous leather goods industry, broadwoven fabrics, coated plastics and fabrics, and other forms of plastics are also used in industry production.

INDUSTRY INFORMATION SOURCES
1987 Census of Manufactures, Washington, DC: U.S. Department of Commerce, 1987.

—Carol Brennan

STONE, CLAY, GLASS, & CONCRETE PRODUCTS

FLAT GLASS

This category covers establishments primarily engaged in manufacturing flat glass. This industry also produces laminated glass, but establishments primarily engaged in manufacturing laminated glass from purchased flat glass are classified in **SIC 3231: Glass Products, Made of Purchased Glass**. Manufactured flat glass covered under this industry includes such types as building glass, cathedral glass, insulating glass, optical glass, picture glass, sheet glass, structural glass, and window glass.

INDUSTRY SNAPSHOT

The flat glass manufacturing industry, like many others, is predicated on the general economic well-being of the nation. Inextricably linked with the construction and housing industries, the flat glass industry has been hurt by the general recessionary atmosphere of the late 1980s and early 1990s.

The flat glass manufacturing market is dominated by products intended for use by the office and housing construction industry. The construction market accounts for roughly 54 percent of flat glass industry sales. Approximately 25 percent goes to windshields for the automobile market, and the remainder of industry sales is in the area of specialty products such as mirrors, solar panels, and signs.

Formerly a fairly labor-intensive industry, *Glass Magazine* noted in 1992 that "over the past two decades, the flat glass industry has introduced many automated manufacturing procedures, partly to reduce payroll costs. Reflecting this increased automation in production, the cost of payroll as a percentage of the value of industry shipments has been declining . . . [I]n 1970, the percentage was 29.7; by 1989 . . . the percentage had declined to only 21.6."

The industry, however, has been forced to deal with higher costs in the area of raw materials. The same industry overview in *Glass Magazine* noted that "the cost of materials as a percentage of the value of industry shipments rose from 31.8 percent in 1970 to 38.9 percent in 1989."

Industry observers and players hope that more fortuitous general economic conditions in the 1990s in the realm of housing starts and construction will carry flat glass manufacturing companies to greater financial success.

ORGANIZATION AND STRUCTURE

Flat glass producers fall into two major classes: Makers of raw float glass and secondly, fabricators or companies that treat raw glass with special coatings for finished products. Two popularly used types of treated glasses are tempered and laminated flat glass. Tempered glass is a special form of ordinary glass, heat treated to add strength and resistance to thermal stress. Because broken tempered glass shatters into cube-shaped particles minus the jagged edges, it features a high safety value. This unique safety characteristic makes tempered glass ideal for shower enclosures, storefront doors, fireplace screens, and other heavy contact areas. Because tempered glass cannot be cut, drilled, or edged, it is favored as a security glass in the building construction and motor vehicle industries. Use of tempered glass is limited where building codes require fire resistant glazing. In 1992 the flat glass industry produced 406 million square feet of tempered

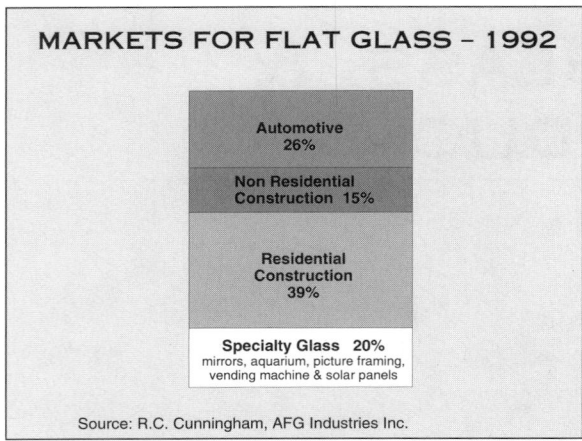

MARKETS FOR FLAT GLASS – 1992

Automotive 26%

Non Residential Construction 15%

Residential Construction 39%

Specialty Glass 20%
mirrors, aquarium, picture framing, vending machine & solar panels

Source: R.C. Cunningham, AFG Industries Inc.

glass, a significant increase over its production of 333 million square feet in the previous year.

Tempered, clear, or tinted glass may be finished via lamination, a process that bonds layers of glass with interlayers of plasticized polyvinyl butyral (PVB). Laminated glass improves sound control, security, solar energy control, glare reduction, and resistance to windblown debris. When the glass is broken, the laminated glass particles stick to the PVB instead of shattering.

Low-emissivity or "low-e" glass is cited as the most energy efficient advance developed over the past two decades. Similar in some of its attributes to aluminum foil, the invisible, colorless, thin metallic coating of low-e glass reflects radiant heat and maintains cool temperatures.

Emissivity is a measurement of the energy-controlling ability of window glass to minimize heat loss during winter conditions. The lower the emissivity, the more energy efficient the product. One study found that use of low-e glass in commercial buildings decreased heating, cooling, and lighting needs by as much as 40 percent. While low emissivity glass transmits most daylight, it also reduces the amount of ultraviolet light that contributes to furniture fading.

After flat glass is manufactured and processed with special coatings, distribution branches to a multi-leveled chain, with sales occurring at all levels. According to *Glass Magazine*, the normal distribution routes for domestic and imported flat glass are (1) directly from domestic or foreign producers to manufacturers, fabricators, and glazing contractors or (2) through independent glass distributors who, in turn, serve manufacturers, fabricators, glazing contractors, and retailers. More glass companies find cost savings by integrating distribution and retailing components as

part of their manufacturing operations. This strategy opens more channels for direct sales to mirror manufacturers or independent glass distributors. One manufacturer sells its products directly to recognized factory buyers in addition to funneling sales through its own distribution centers and service branches.

Product line also determines the distribution route. Distribution of window glass, for example, may extend from producer to door manufacturer or by way of the glass distributor to jobber to retailer. Flat glass for residential windows is shipped directly from glass manufacturers or fabricators, with 10-20 percent purchased by flat glass distributors for sale to low-volume window manufacturers. With these nuances of distribution, smaller retailers and glazing firms sometimes face the higher end of the distributor's price. Searches for the cost-effective products, particularly for non-factory tempered glass buyers, often lead purchasers to imported glass.

Glass wall construction comprises more than 52 percent of contemporary offices and bank buildings. Aesthetic appeal has popularized building facade designs that combine glass with granite or other exterior building materials. According to *Buildings*, the prevalence of glass building exteriors in the southern United States supports solar efficiency of glass. Moreover, the cost of a square foot of glass is less than that of the same size portion of most other building materials. Glass manufacturers hope that these factors will further invigorate the preference for glass building exteriors.

What consumers prefer largely determines what the flat glass industry manufactures. Glass windows are, of course, an integral element of the average architectural structure. Survey polls indicate most consumers select windows on the basis of energy cost savings. Additionally, consumers favor windows that feature reduced condensation, balanced solar protection, ultraviolet radiation (UV), and noise blocking. According to government estimates, window glass accounts for an annual energy loss equivalent to 1.7 billion barrels of oil.

Tinted windows impose special problems for commercial and residential clients. In the South, where glass exteriors are more prevalent, designers control excessive window heat by using tinted reflective glass. Unfortunately, tinting reduces natural light and increases reliance on artificial light, which further adds to utility bills. Tinted solar protection windows have their drawbacks as well, particularly in high rise residential buildings. Unless draperies remain closed, constant exposure to natural solar conditions can harm furnishings and paint. Trials with windowless facilities offer less desirable results. Studies of windowless schools show reduced student productivity and a negative impact on attrition rates. The industry has responded to these issues by embarking on a search for the perfect window, an appealing window capable of balancing solar gain and loss for both heating and cooling purposes.

In the opinion of industry leaders, improved low-e glass may be the ultimate solution. An advanced research and manufacturing program sponsored by Libbey-Owens-Ford Company has produced a hard-coat, low-e glass with performance ratings nearly twice that of existing medium performance pyrolytic technology, according to company officials. Test results indicate the glass reduces emissivity ratings to a new range of 0.15-0.19 as opposed to other low-e ratings from 0.30 to 0.40.

Fire safety glass draws a lot of attention from consumers and commercial clients. Wire glass remains the most popular choice for fire-rated glazing because of its low cost, about $2.50 per square foot at factory cost. As a product used for 60 years, glaziers feel comfortable with the efficacy of wired glass. Most wired glass features a 45-minute fire rating. When broken, the wire holds glass shards in place. Although wire glass is less appealing in appearance than other fire glass, it is fairly effective in preventing fires from spreading and complements visibility as well. Wire glass extends fire security, not security resistance. Consumer Product Safety Commission regulations require that wire glass be installed only in fire-rated doors.

Several new types of fire glass have recently appeared on the market. FireLite, a new glazing option for fire-rated doors, looks, feels, and cuts like glass but is technically not a glass. It is a clear ceramic, similar to the wood stove window. When exposed to heat, FireLite does not expand or break as glass. The material also resists the effects of cold. Underwriters Laboratories, Inc.'s (UL) three-hour rating for a 100-square-inch FireLite glass proves that it outperforms most glasses. The main advantage of FireLite is that it is thin enough to fit into standard fire-rated doors.

BACKGROUND AND DEVELOPMENT

Used as an ancient building material, glass today contains a semblance of the original basic raw materials: Silica sand, soda ash, dolomite, limestone, salt cake, and other materials. Archeological records indicate the beginning of flat glass manufacturing, possibly by the Syrians, around the year 3000 BC. Early glass served aesthetic functions, but limited transpar-

ency, tedious production, and fragility precluded other uses.

Several centuries later, the industrial revolution changed the functional qualities of flat glass. Following the introduction of electric and steam power, mechanization of plate glass production decreased production costs. Flat glass became more functional and by 1925, 42 plants in the United States produced 600 million square feet of sheet glass.

In 1959 the Pilkington Brothers PLC, an England-based firm, perfected the revolutionary float glass manufacturing process that yields a flawless clear or tinted glass, without requiring the cumbersome grind and polish steps previously utilized. Float glass transparency allowed about 75-92 percent transmittance of visible light. Aside from its superior functional qualities, the float glass process offered tremendous manufacturing savings: capital investment costs decreased by 25-50 percent per ton of glass and manufacturing outlays decreased by 15-30 percent. Despite a mid-1970s industry recession that forced numerous closings of sheet glass plants, float glass production increased during this period. In fact, float glass completely dominates the market today for flat glass in thicknesses up to 25 mm.

CURRENT CONDITIONS

According to the U.S. Department of Commerce, flat glass production for 1992 was 4.7 billion square feet, an 8.8 percent increase from the 1991 total of 4.3 billion square feet. Peaks and valleys are common to the industry, dependent as it is on the well-being of other industries. After a steady rise began in 1983, the flat glass industry peaked in 1987 with a $3.5 billion value of product shipments, the highest in 15 years. The shipment value of flat glass products each subsequent year diminished, however, with $2.6 billion recorded in 1992. Although prices remained constant between 1990-91, purchases of flat glass products showed a decline over the last several years. The industry opted for price reductions as a means for stabilizing prices. Such approaches may persist as manufacturers compete to increase gross sales and retain a market share.

Similar to many other industries, the flat glass manufacturing establishment suffered from the late 1980s-early 1990s recessionary conditions, which lowered the level of housing construction, reduced automobile sales, and depressed other markets. Reversal of these industries signals an upturn trend for the flat glass industry. Led by single family housing and public works projects, some analysts predict that total contracting for new construction may grow by as much as eight percent in the latter part of the 1990s. For the glass industry, this increase could translate into as much as a two percent rise in the production and shipment of flat glass. Even with these boosts, however, some observers feel that flat glass output will not match the high levels of the 1986-1987 period.

The industry also faces possible damage from the proposed ASHRAE 90.2 regulation, a standard that would limit fenestration (the arrangement and design of windows and doors in a building) in the design of energy efficient low-rise residential buildings. The American Society of Heating, Refrigeration, and Air Conditioning Engineers proposed the standard. Fenestration area is normally 20 percent of conditioned floor area in a newly constructed single family detached home. The new 15 percent fenestration limitation imposed by the standard ASHRAE 90.2 leads to a projected 2.75 million fewer windows sold for single-family detached homes and 750,000 fewer patio doors. Compliance with the standard thus spells a potential $2.4 billion loss for the glass industry. Several flat glass industry groups have challenged the standard and criticized the lack of flat glass industry input in the development of the standard.

In recent years, the flat glass industry's pricing methods have come under some scrutiny. Glass manufacturers, distributors, and fabricators have traditionally calculated the price of total square footage by rounding up fractional amounts. Apparently tradition permitted continuation of this eighteenth century practice. However, after a California glass retailer complained of unfair pricing due to this method, officials were forced to reexamine the flat glass industry's overall pricing methodology. Proposed alternatives include the adoption of either a unit price method or a fractional-inch computational method. Either method requires manufacturers, wholesalers, and the entire distribution chain to reprogram or recalculate glass costs to the actual fractional-inch square footage.

Members of the flat glass manufacturing industry also face challenges in the 1990s on environmental, energy, and safety fronts. To date the industry has concentrated on compliance with the requirements of several landmark legislative actions handed down by the Environmental Protection Agency (EPA), the Department of Energy, and various local regulatory agencies. The Clean Air Act amendments, promulgated by EPA, specifically address the hazardous rate of air pollutants emitted by specific facilities and processes. The legislation also lists hazardous air pollutants, many of which are substances generic to flat glass production. Flat glass industrial facilities are thus impacted by the Clean Air regulation requirements.

Cost factors connected to the new law, claim industry representatives, may further deflate industry progress. The latest amendments drop consideration of a manufacturer's "economic feasibility" as a determinant for defining the best available control technology. State and regional regulatory agencies still retain some authority in making this decision, but under the new law, the EPA makes the basic decision regarding the best control technology. The industry charges that the acquisition of an EPA permit specifying the manufacturer's operational requirements is too costly, complex, and time-consuming. The new Clean Air regulations also impose penalties for violations. Prison sentences and fines of up to $1 million may be used to penalize actions of negligent release of hazardous air pollutants that place another person in imminent danger. Sums up to $25,000 per day can be levied as administrative penalties.

As a result of a recent consent decree between the United States and Corning, Inc. and partners, Corning is being forced to pay fines totaling $1.825 million for violation of arsenic emission regulations at its glass manufacturing plants. The agreement also requires the companies involved to install automatic and computerized equipment to better control and monitor arsenic emissions. PPG Industries, Inc., a leading flat glass manufacturer, recently received a $31.5 million clean-up bill from New Jersey for chromium contamination at one of its manufacturing locations. Reduction of atmospheric emissions has thus assumed greater importance to the flat glass industry in recent years. The solution, according to industry observers, must find ways to reduce emissions without adversely affecting the chemical composition of flat glass production.

Water pollution and waste recycling pinpoint additional environmental concerns of the flat glass industry. Practically all glass manufacturing uses large amounts of water for cooling, product rinsing, and other processes, although less water is used by newer plants and those utilizing municipal water systems. Waste water from plants without surface discharge systems flows into a sewer system. Waste water pollution originates from manufacturing processes that use fluoride rinses, oil drains from the glass forming machine area, ammonia used for glass frosting, and many other chemicals. In terms of recycling, some glass products are 100-percent recyclable, but mirrors and windows are nonrecyclable.

Public pressure to initiate efforts to stop the greenhouse effect has also placed glass and other building products under scrutiny. Recently Congress reviewed a bill calling for labeling of energy-efficiency windows. Environmental and research groups supported the bill because labeling could facilitate consumer identification of a window brand's energy conservation features. Window trade associations, however, questioned the need for another labeling program when 75 percent of window manufacturers already participate in a voluntary certification program maintained by the American Architectural Manufacturers Association (AAMA). The biggest boost to the labeling initiative came from recent Canadian legislation that instituted specifications regarding product labeling. Because the free trade agreement between the United States and Canada extends to products sold to Canada, U.S. manufacturers might find it wise to initiate glass labeling that meets the legal requirements of both nations.

INDUSTRY LEADERS

Leading North American flat glass manufacturers include the Libbey-Owens-Ford Company, headquartered in Toledo, Ohio; Guardian Industries Corporation of Northville, Michigan; Ford Glass Division of Ford Motor Co., located in Detroit, Michigan; PPG Industries, Inc., of Pittsburgh, Pennsylvania; and AFG Industries, headquartered in Fort Worth, Texas.

Based on operation capacity, PPG ranks first in North America. For 1992 PPG reported a net income of $319.4 million on sales of $5.8 billion. Net income for 1991 was $276.2 million on sales of $5.7 billion. Comparative reports of 1993 and 1992 first quarters show a 40 percent improvement, excluding a one-time net charge for mandated accounting changes.

WORK FORCE

In 1979 the flat glass industry employed about 19,500 workers; by 1991, according to *Glass Magazine*'s 1992 industry overview, the number of total workers had declined to 16,700. The number of production workers experienced a parallel decline, from 15,200 in 1979 to a little more than 13,000 in 1991. Analysts attribute the reduction to manufacturing automation and production trimming. Average hourly earnings for flat glass production workers slightly increased, from $15.90 in 1987 to $16.85 in 1992. Average overtime declined from 7.7 weekly hours in 1988 to 5.9 weekly hours in 1992.

Despite the decline in total employment in the industry in recent years, however, the number of operational flat glass plants in the United States has actually increased, at least in part because of increased automation in the industry. Of the 124 manufacturing facilities operational in 1990, 53 employed more than 20 workers.

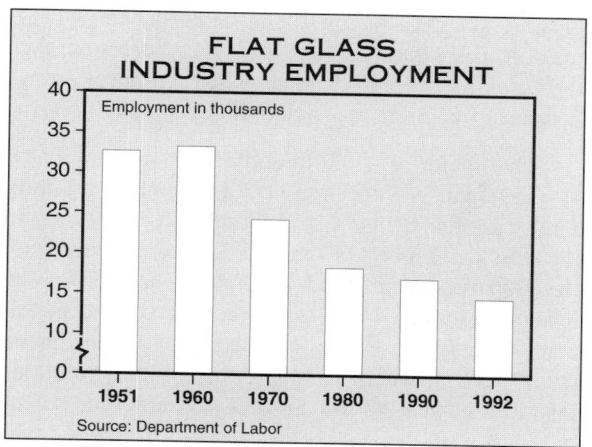

FLAT GLASS INDUSTRY EMPLOYMENT

Employment in thousands

Source: Department of Labor

In 1990 the Bureau of Labor Statistics rated flat glass manufacturing as the nation's 19th most hazardous industry in 1988. *Glass Magazine* noted that the findings, based on state worker compensation data, found that "as in previous years of the survey, injury rates varied widely by company size. Rates for companies with fewer than 50 employees or with more than 1000 employees were lower than the rates for the midsize establishments."

AMERICA AND THE WORLD

Of the top 10 glass export and import markets, Canada consistently remains first in both categories, followed by Mexico and Japan. Between 1989-1991, exports to Canada totaled more than $900 million and imports from that country totaled nearly $430 million. In 1991 Canada accounted for 35 percent of the American international market, followed by Mexico (22 percent), which has dramatically increased the amount of flat glass it purchases from the United States in recent years. The trade in flat glass, however, has also increased from Mexico to the United States. *Glass Magazine*'s 1992 Industry Survey states that "the country which increased its export volume to the United States the most over the past few years is Mexico—from $5.3 million in 1981 to $74.2 million in 1991."

Most U.S. flat glass manufacturers are engaged in some type of international commercial activity, either through joint ventures with foreign firms, licensing of technology to foreign producers, or acquisition of all or part of foreign flat glass manufacturers.

RESEARCH AND TECHNOLOGY

By the year 2000, the demand for flat glass, according to some projections, will result in shipments totaling 6 billion square feet. Tempered glass shipments will continue to outrank shipments of laminated glass. The appeal of low-e glass, introduced in 1982, make it likely that it will be able to capture more than the current 20-percent market share it currently enjoys because of ongoing research and development efforts.

One major research initiative with an anticipated 10-year span is Fenestration 2000, a project jointly funded by the British firm Pilkington Glass Ltd. and the U.S. firm Libbey-Owens-Ford, in conjunction with the Departments of Energy of both countries. The recently completed Phase One consisted of a market context study documenting expectations of designers, developers, and occupants regarding futuristic building fabrics and windows. Phase Two studies the potential energy efficiency benefits versus the cost effectiveness of these concepts. To date, feedback from ongoing project studies at the Lawrence Berkeley Laboratories reveals several exciting new applications. One potentially attractive product is an electrochromic glass capable of changing heat and light transmission via electrical signal. Products under consideration also include windows with passive panels, incorporating color patterns or holographic images. These large-area panels could also house a flat panel television or computer screen.

Companies appear to push their high-tech coatings and glazings more than commodities. Pilkington, the float glass originator, developed another potentially big winner, K glass, a pyrolytically-coated, low-emissivity product offering performance close to that of sputter-coated glasses. In addition to its window treatment use, the glass is also being tested for use on refrigerator and oven doors, where heat reflection can be advantageous.

Utilization of gas filling as a replacement for dry air atmosphere in insulating glass improves both thermal and sound values. Gas filling has been used in Europe for the last 20 years, but only recently has its use been validated in the United States. Heat loss by conduction occurs because of the tendency of heat to flow toward cooler temperatures. Argon gas filling in insulating glass slows the flow of building heat to the outside in winter and reduces the amount of outdoor heat entering the building. U.S. manufacturers continue to study the effectiveness of glass filling, particularly with uncoated glass units.

Another promising product under consideration is switchable glass, a liquid crystal glass that can be wired to any structure's electrical system and operated by flipping a switch. Liquid crystals make the glass cloudy but permit sufficient light without obstructing visibility. The electrical current changes the glass from opaque to clear. Its current use is in interior applications such as partitions and conference rooms, where privacy and optional visibility are desirable.

Melanin, a pigment found in hair, skin, and eyes, can be synthetically produced and is now being tested for use in manufacturing window glass. Melanin gives window glass a yellowish to amberish tint and heightens visibility because the pigment blocks glare-producing blue wavelengths. Because of its high absorption capacity, only a small amount of melanin is needed, thereby reducing the cost.

INDUSTRY INFORMATION SOURCES

Button, David A. "Glass for the Year 2000." *Glass Digest,* January 15, 1990.

"California questions glass measurement practices." *Glass Magazine,* April 1990.

Destefano, James T. "How the Clean Air Act Impacts Glass Producers," *Glass Industry,* May 1992.

Current Industrial Reports: Flat Glass, Summary for 1992. Washington, DC: U.S. Department of Commerce, Bureau of Census, 1991.

"Flat Glass Manufacturing Makes Hazardous Industry List." *Glass Magazine,* November 1990.

"A glass primer," *Glass Magazine,* April 1990.

Miller, John. "Focus on windows." *Buildings,* July 1987.

"National Legislation may Mandate Window Labels." *Glass Magazine,* November 1989.

"Pilkington research forges ahead." *Glass Digest,* February 15, 1990.

"PPG reports on first quarter." *Glass Reflections,* June 1993.

"A Preview of Fenestration in the Year 2000," *Fenestration,* New York: Ashlee Publishing Company, 1989.

"Proposed Residential Design Standard Could Hurt Fenestration Industry." *Fenestration,* New York: Ashlee Publishing Company, 1989.

"Quarterly report on flat glass MQ32A, first quarter 1993." *Current Industrial Reports.* Washington, DC: U.S. Department of Commerce, 1993.

"A Repeat Performance of 1991 is Predicted," *Glass Industry,* January 1992.

Sraeel, Holly. "Glass Building Facades: What's Hot, What's Not," *Buildings,* April 1989.

Sitrin, Todd W. "Glass on the Homefront." *Glass Magazine,* December 1989.

Tooley, Fay V., ed. *The Handbook of Glass Manufacture.* 3rd ed. New York: Ashlee Publishing Company.

"U.S. Flat Glass Outlook: A Repeat Performance of 1991 is Predicted." *Glass Industry,* January 1992.

Williams, Franklin E. "Flat Glass Industry Overview." *Glass Magazine,* September 1992.

————. "Flat Glass Technology." *Construction Review*, March/April 1990.

————. "Flat Glass Trends and Forecasts." *Glass Magazine*, January 1993.

—Attrices Dean Griffin

SIC 3221

GLASS CONTAINERS

This category includes establishments primarily engaged in manufacturing glass containers for commercial packing and bottling, and for home canning. Products include: ampoules; bottles, containers, jars, and jugs for packing, bottling, and canning; carboys; cosmetic jars; fruit jars; medicine bottles; packers' ware; vials; and water bottles.

INDUSTRY SNAPSHOT

When *Packaging* magazine sponsored a survey in 1986 of 2,000 consumers to determine which mode of packaging best preserved the flavor of juice, 36.9 percent of the respondents expressing a preference replied that glass containers were best, 5.3 percent preferred cardboard boxes, while only 2.3 percent stated cans kept the best taste. The survey revealed that consumers preferred glass containers for a range of products including beer, wine, and preserved fruits, cooked pasta, tomato sauce, and beer stew. Though widespread consumer endorsement of glass packaging would seem to please manufacturers of glass containers, the editor of *Packaging* warned that what consumers say and what they buy are two different things.

The *Packaging* survey proves that promotion of glass containers has been successful. For several years, the advertising thrust of glass manufacturers has focused on the positive aspects of glass use. At one point, glass container manufacturers sponsored advertisement campaigns touting their product as a naturally pure, recyclable taste protector. Particularly innovative was the industry's Nickel Solution Trust, formed in 1983 by coalition of labor organizations and glass container manufacturers. Employees of glass container companies pledged a nickel of each hourly pay and the employers contributed matching funds to pay for glass promotions. Since its inception, the trust has expended more than $21 million for recycling program development and management. Despite aggressive promotions such as these, the glass container market remained sluggish. Consequently, the glass container industry has become smaller but also much smarter. Promotion,

however, continues to target those areas where glass retains a winning edge as a premium product.

In the early 1990s, 99 plants manufactured glass containers, six less than in 1987. Of these, 88 have more than 20 employees. Most of the plants are located close to the eastern United States. Manufacturers maintain anywhere from one to thirteen plants. The industry is composed of primary producers who make glass containers originating from the melting process and those who fabricate and supply containers to wholesalers and retailers.

BACKGROUND AND DEVELOPMENT

For centuries, glass objects were made by artisans using hand blowing methods. Many products created by these highly trained craftsmen now adorn art museum collections. Mechanization came to the glass-making industry with the industrial revolution, and the introduction of the pressing machine and other refinements promoted a range of new designs and uses of glass containers. Wide mouth Mason jars became popular in the United States in the early 1900s, while the popularity of narrow neck jars developed more slowly.

M. J. Owens and E. D. Libbey initiated a new process of bottle making by filling and dipping the first or blank mold into hot glass and evacuating the air from the mold. Several years of experimentation finally led to development of an automated bottle machine. By 1920, 200 of these automatic machines accounted for approximately 45 percent of the total U.S. bottle production.

Today, the glass container industry manufactures two basic types of containers: narrow neck and wide mouth containers. The industry further classifies containers by their end use, creating categories of glass designated for food, beverages, beer, liquor, wine; chemical, household, and industrial uses; toiletries and cosmetics; and other uses including medicinal and health supplies. Wide mouth and narrow neck bottles are used interchangeably, depending on the product, but tradition or utility occasionally dictates specific bottle types. For example, milk is normally packaged in wide mouth containers, both wide mouth and narrow neck bottles are used for cosmetics, while narrow neck bottles are more practical for perfumes.

Consumer preferences and marketing strategy often combine to determine whether a product is packaged in a wide mouth or narrow neck container. One company used feedback from consumer focus groups to determine the best container for mustard. Participants expressed preference for a wide-mouth jar that would allow the use of a large serving spoon or spatula. The company's selection of a wide mouth container originated from an entirely different perspective. A smaller jar, in the company's estimation, connoted saving the product for special occasions rather than using it as a special item for everyday meals. Thus the selection of wide-mouth jar satisfied consumer preferences and complemented the company's marketing strategy.

Shape is the most important feature of a bottle. To be practical, a bottle must be able to stand up, have a filling mouth, and withstand a variety of mechanical handling devices such as washing machines, filling tubes, labelers, and conveyors. According to experts, spherical-shaped containers present the most efficient use of glass container weight. Next to the sphere, the most efficient use of glass is a cylinder with similar dimensions of diameter and height. The container industry generally favors glass containers characterized by broad, rounded shoulders, edges, and corners. To ensure maximum strength, the industry avoids the use of square or rectangular shapes, flats or panels, or offsets. Glass containers are also designed to convey a brand image. Clear beveled-edge bottles offer high profile products an advantageous shelf presence and easy handling benefits for consumers.

Even more marketable are glass containers combining eye-catching designs with a functional after-life as decanters or collector items. A few decades ago, small, odd-sized and -shaped bottles were replaced by standardized bottles, in part because manufacturers discovered that standardized bottles could be produced faster using the old machinery. While most odd-shaped bottles have disappeared, they are now prized and traded as antique collectibles. In the 1990s, Dr. Pepper issued a commemorative bottle saluting the involvement of U.S. troops in Operation Desert Storm. In contrast, plastic or aluminum containers rarely offer any collectible value. For the industry, bottle collecting could increase industry share of the beverage market by three percent and rise to account for 25 percent of all glass beverage bottles.

Manufacturers capitalize on designer appeal of glass containers by constantly adding innovative designs. Each year, the Glass Packaging Institute recognizes creative glass containers by making awards in several categories, including food, beverage, package design, label, environmental awareness, and mature product repositioning. In 1989, Fireworks Popcorn captured first place as winner in the overall food category. The award winning package highlighted the product's vivid popcorn colors by using a clear, reusable 15-ounce jar shaped like a home canning jar. In the beverage category, first place honor went to Ocean

Spray's choice of a large, collector-type glass carafe packaging its premium fruit juice.

Changing the design of a glass container entails more than adding a new face. Most design changes create a ripple effect on the overall product manufacturing process, affecting cost and product positioning. Even the slightest modifications—such as ovaling a round food jar or adding a modest blown-in decorative effect—can increase the container's weight by 20 percent. Maintaining lighter weight without reducing container strength highlights one persistent industry concern. One solution to the weight problems appears to be the use of the narrow neck press and blow technology capable of manufacturing more efficient containers at 15-20 percent lighter weights. Another possible solution to weight reduction of glass containers might emerge from development of a process which uniformly maintains glass wall thickness and enhances the container strength through some type of coating. The results would be a 12-ounce capacity container made in the 3-4 ounce weight range. According to an industry spokesperson, once manufacturers improve control over the container production process, weight problems will be alleviated.

Many gloriously designed containers generate both consumer delights and production havoc. For example, Welch's redesign of a popular jelly jar featuring a new ''tear-drop'' shaped container proved popular with consumers but caused countless cost and handling problems. Because the tapered glass jar was smallest at the bottom, with jar-to-jar contact only at the shoulder, containers frequently toppled over on the conveyors. Case packing of the tear-drop jars necessitated manual rather than the usual mechanical handling, thereby adding three packers per shift. Because of the additional costs accompanying the new design, the company redesigned the container by making the container base the same diameter as the shoulders. The slightly heavier jar caused a modest increase in freight costs, but by eliminating the jar's tip-over tendency, case packing increased by 2,000 per shift, thereby eliminating the need for additional production shifts.

For many other products, the image qualities of glass containers combine with other features to convey a unique premium appeal. Glass packaged wine coolers, for example, were tremendously popular in the mid 1980s, with sales as high as three million bottles daily. Analysts attributed the boom in part to the popularity of the single-serving bottle, a concept that was virtually unknown a few years earlier. Successful demonstration of the concept with wine coolers led to single-serve juice beverages and later bottled water. Gatorade, for one, reported a 30 percent sales increase in one year following introduction of a 16-ounce single-serve, wide mouth bottle, conveniently suitable for carrying "at the point of sweat." More than 100 companies later joined the promotion of the single-serve bottles' health advantages. The single-serve concept also motivated distilled spirits producers to carve their niche by introducing spirit coolers in single-serve glass bottles.

CURRENT CONDITIONS

In 1992, production of glass containers amounted to 286.0 million gross and shipments amounted to 282.7 million gross. In 1992, shipments of narrow neck containers amounted to 210.4 million gross and shipments of wide mouth containers were 72.2 million gross. Production and shipment of narrow neck containers consistently outrank those of wide mouth containers by 34 percent. Wide-mouth containers are most popular for food, including dairy products, and have held steady sales and production over the last few years at about 72 million. The lowest shipment and production levels are for narrow neck and wide mouth chemical, household and industrial containers. At best the glass container industry can be described as flat. Bottle shipments, according to analysts, will likely remain flat. Continued overcapacity and the threat of conversion to alternative packaging stands to keep price increases in the 3.0 to 3.5 percent range.

Several factors contribute to the flat conditions of the glass container industry. Since the 1980s, the glass container market has suffered a steady loss of market share to alternate plastic and can packaging. Analysts finger the beer industry as a major factor causing the decline of the glass container industry. More than 85 percent of the decline was due to brewers switching to aluminum cans and the lingering residual of this change still poses an imminently significant threat, in the industry's opinion. Statistics may well support this threat. Although shipment and production of beer bottles remain high, at about 88 million, analysts feared a decline as higher price tags forced consumers to switch to lower-price canned beer.

The glass container industry prioritizes creative glass container promotions. In what was known as the Nickel Project, special groups of glass workers known as Glass Awareness Committees teamed up with distributors and retailers to promote consumer purchases of soft drinks in nonrefillable glass bottles. The chosen promotion sites were all located in glass plant towns and plans were coordinated with local organizations. The summer phase initiative boosted sales by an estimated 111 percent over previous year's totals. The industry planned to continue the program with more emphasis on recyclability as well as the resealable and taste features of glass packaging.

Flexibility may determine the glass container's response to its environmental challenges. Glass is 100 percent recyclable. A used glass container can be melted and repeatedly made in a new glass container. Glass recycling creates no additional waste or by-products. Yet glass recycling ranks lower than that of plastic. The Glass Packaging Institute (GPI), the glass container industry's trade group, questions the Environmental Protection Agency's (EPA) statistics quoting the recycling rate for glass at 10-12 percent, plastic at 20 percent, and aluminum cans at 55 percent. Still, glass retains a positive recyclability perception. In contrast, recyclability of plastic beverage containers is accepted by only 20.7 percent of consumers.

Recent testimony before a Congressional subcommittee by the Glass Packaging Institute cited three major problems for the glass industry's recycling program: (1) because plants are located primarily on the East and West coasts and the Southeast, transporting recycled glass from community collection facilities to these plants proves expensive; (2) recycling of increasing amounts of imported green containers exceeds the domestic demand for these containers; and (3) because of loose quality control at local collection sites, mixing recyclable and nonrecyclable glass damages the manufacturing process. The most viable recycling solution, according to some experts, comes from less packaging. In the last ten years, 16-ounce glass bottles have been reduced by 30 percent, thus lowering the amounts of materials and waste.

One drawback to recycling cited by the Glass Packaging Institute relates to forced deposit laws requiring a consumer to pay a deposit and then return the containers to the store for a refund. The industry perceives such legislation as devastating to the market share of environmentally friendly glass containers and argues that it sways consumers to use plastic. GPI believes the most effective way to reduce solid waste is not forced deposit laws, but comprehensive curbside recycling. The practice of bottle refilling as an alternative to recycling may experience a comeback. A team of several breweries refilled 48 million beer bottles between 1990-91. They reported that bottle refilling saved landfill space equal to a football field 24 feet deep.

The Glass Packaging Institute noted the 1990s began with five major bottling companies switching from plastic to glass containers, citing as reasons consumer preference, environmental climate, and packaging costs. According to investment analysts, however, falling resin prices could be an omen signaling a return to plastic. In 1989, a price differential of 20 percent between plastic and glass caused plastic to lose its market share to glass, primarily in the area of 16-ounce containers. When the differential was closer to five percent or less, plastic regained some of its share. Until the glass container industry develops a more cost-competitive, lighter weight, or break resistant package, analysts foresee fewer gains derived from the anticipated growth of the soft drink market.

Another area in need of attention from the glass container industry involves raw materials leftover from the manufacturing process. According to an industry spokesperson, only 85-90 percent of the melted raw materials are converted to a marketable product. The remaining 10-15 percent of raw material becomes cullet or discarded waste, mostly broken glass. Industry leaders are attempting to devise satisfactory uses for this cullet.

INDUSTRY LEADERS

Among the leading U.S. glass container manufacturers for the 1990s are Owens-Illinois, Anchor Hocking, and Ball-Incon Glass Packaging. Net sales for Owens-Illinois in the early 1990s totaled $2.8 billion, operating income, $393 million, and capital expenditures, $156.8 million. Owens-Illinois began the decade with a $115.7 million decrease in net sales for the glass container segment, though that segment still reported an increase in operating profit. In the specialized glass segment, the $440.5 million net sales remained consistent with the prior year. Higher unit sales volume attributed to a slight increase in net sales of the pharmaceutical packaging and laboratory ware businesses. The increase however was offset by a slight decrease in net sales of the tableware glass business. A 3.7 percent decrease in the combined U.S. dollar sales of Owens-Illinois consolidated foreign affiliates also attributed to a decrease of overall company sales.

Anchor Hocking Glass, manufacturer of tabletop, ovenware, household, and food service glassware, benefitted from a seven percent growth of revenue by expanding product listings with retailers and adding new products. Among the new consumer and food service products, Anchor introduced a line of machine-made lead crystal.

Record net sales for Ball-Incon Glass Packaging, a wholly owned division of Ball Corporation, totaled $583.2 million, an increase of $17 million over the previous year. The rise was attributed to a price increase and an increase in shipments that offset a decrease in total industry shipments. Operating earnings for 1991 increased 8.4 percent and benefitted, according to *Glass Magazine,* from a favorable product mix, stable overhead, and high plant utilization rates. Fruit and juice market segments represented 68 percent of the division's net sales.

Ball-Incon has undergone several management changes after emerging from the 1987 merger between Ball Corporation and InCon Packaging. The new corporation later acquired the glass container businesses and assets of both companies to become a glass container giant. Recognized as a producer of glass containers for the food industry, Ball-Incon employs 5,500 and expects annual sales of more than $550 million. Ball-Incon recently acquired Kerr's four glass container manufacturing plants.

WORK FORCE

The total work force of the glass container industry decreased eight percent between 1988 and 1992. The majority of employees are male, employed in the production category. An average work week is 43.1 hours with overtime consisting of an estimated 5.8 hours weekly. Since 1988, hourly earnings have increased by an average of $1.59 bringing the average weekly earnings to $590.47.

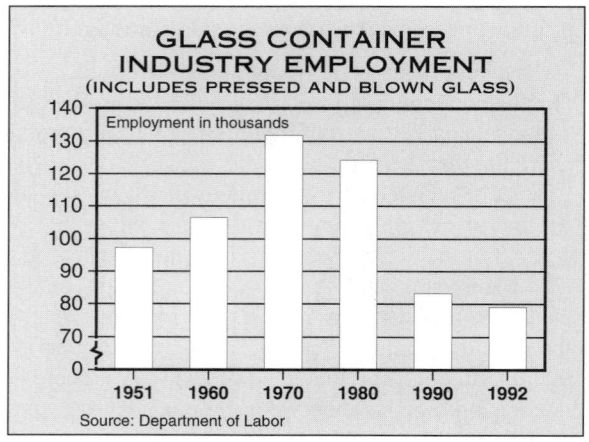

Noting significant improvements in labor productivity per unit, an Owens-Illinois spokesperson added that producing a quality product still requires an excessive amount of labor. Labor constitutes 35 percent of the cost of glass, but only 9 percent and 13 percent for cans and plastic, respectively. Although use of sophisticated control systems in the future will require more operator interpretation rather than intervention, production workers must be better trained and more knowledgeable than most manufacturing employees.

AMERICA AND THE WORLD

In 1992, total exports of glass containers represented 3.3 percent of manufacturers' shipments, while imports represented 4.8 percent of total consumption. Exports during 1991 were less than one percent lower than 1992, but imports remained about the same. At one point, imported beer, regarded for its prestige, image, and flavor, accounted for imports of roughly 1.5 billion bottles per year. The weak dollar may curb beer imports because analysts believe consumers are approaching the price limitations they are willing to pay for imported beer.

RESEARCH AND TECHNOLOGY

In 1975, the EPA promulgated effluent standards and guidelines covering wastewater discharges from glass container manufacturing plants. The regulations targeted oil and grease pollution which originates from soluble oils used in glass shearing, machine lubrication, and condensate from compressed air systems. The problem of oil and grease pollution relates to the biodegradable nature of emulsified oil which subjects cullet quench systems to severe biological growth problems. According to *Glass Magazine,* biological growth within cullet quench systems degrades oil and grease removal efficiency, often resulting in effluent values exceeding regulatory standards. Additionally, the biologically fouled cullet quench system precipitates a potential health hazard from Legionnaire's Disease as well as contributes to unpleasant working conditions.

To date, a few technologies have demonstrated capacity for breaking up oil and grease found in glass container plant wastewater. One technology consists of carbon absorption, a process where wastewater passes through a bed of activated carbon which absorbs the oil and grease. This process is more applicable to small flows with relatively low oil and grease loadings. The process of chemical coagulation followed by dissolved air flotation (DAF) is another process where chemical emulsion breakers and other processes are added to wastewater to break emulsion. DAF has been successfully used and research studies continue to study various emulsion breaking chemistries.

Since 1975, compliance with national standards has enabled glass container manufacturers to make significant improvements in control of oil and grease in wastewater. In the 1990s, research and development emphasis was on technology to upgrade wastewater treatment technology to comply with stringent state and local effluent standards.

In the future, the recyclable features of glass products could play a major role in safe disposal of hazardous waste, according to the editor of *Glass Industry.* The Department of Energy opened a new $1.3-billion Defense Waste Processing Facility in South Carolina designed to test the feasibility of encasing radioactive materials in glass. This process, known as vitrification, entails encasing hazardous waste in "logs" of strong glass, wrapped in steel. Steel cylinders measuring 10-feet high and two feet around each hold 165 gallons of waste.

Parallelling this project is an experiment in process during the 1990s at the California-based Lawrence Livermore National Laboratory on radioactivity release from glass. A computer model was being designed to predict the release of radioactivity, if any, from a nuclear waste repository incorporating glass. To ensure adequate leakage prevention of harmful radioactive material from glass, scientists were performing a variety of laboratory experiments and computer simulations of potential environmental scenarios that might be affected by radioactive leaks. In terms of EPA's hazardous waste management program, vitrification reflects an urgency because, to date, it demonstrates the best available technology for various waste streams.

Large and small glass container manufacturers have spent millions for high tech equipment and computerized operations. Part of the $40 million Anchor Glass expended in the 1990s was for installation of sophisticated quality control equipment on all the company's production lines. Wheaton Glass completed a $10-million investment in manufacturing operations of containers for the parenteral drug and the cosmetics industries. Over a period of three years, Kerr invested in excess of $22 million for improvements such as computerized furnace control systems, high-productivity forming machines, and quality control equipment. The $40 million expended by Liberty Glass gave its one plant the distinction as "the most modern and best-equipped single-service beverage glass production plant in the world," according to the company.

Considerable industry attention now focuses on eliminating weak spots of containers by uniform redistribution of glass. The benefits would be strong, light-weight containers containing less glass produced faster and less expensively. Several companies have achieved outstanding results by improving traditional machinery such as the latest press-and-blow molding. Owens-Illinois's "ten-quad machine" claims to be the fastest forming machine in the United States for glass containers. It operates at speeds well over 450 containers per minute.

Glass coatings remain a significant aspect of research and development. Through a program identified as the Advanced Glass Treatment Systems, various coatings for strength enhancement of glass containers are being studied. Manufacturers are also experimenting with sophisticated hot- and cold-end coatings to reduce breakage and scuffing. These coatings also increase container filling speeds. A New York based company developed a coating procedure identified as the Brandt Color Coat process. The water-based acrylic coating expands colors and textures of glass beverage bottles. Glass can be tinted in a range of desired colors combined with transparent opaque, matte, or frost finishes. The process offers more cost-effectiveness and more scratch-resistance than conventional bottle-tinting methods, plus a resistance to ultraviolet light, normally harmful to beverages such as beer. It also allows bottle labels to be printed with UV-cured inks without fear of harm to the contents. Anchor Glass Container is the only U.S. manufacturer to offer this new product.

INDUSTRY INFORMATION SOURCES

Ashton, Robin, ''Awards Highlight Glass Innovations,'' *Packaging,* April 1989.

''Ball Corporation to Close Santa Ana Factory,'' *Los Angeles Times,* June 25, 1992, D2.

Copperthite, Kimberly G., ''Shipments to Rise Slightly in 1991,'' *Glass Industry,* January 1991.

''Glass Container Promotion Boosts Soft Drink Sales,'' *Glass Industry,* January 1992.

''Glass Containers: Summary for 1992,'' *Current Industrial Reports,* Washington, DC: U.S. Department of Commerce, May 1993.

''Glass Provides a Class Image,'' *Packaging,* July 1987.

Glass Recycling: Why? How?, Washington, DC: Glass Packaging Institute.

Heuer, Ross, ''New Jar Is Key to Packaging Line Upgrading,'' *Packaging,* February 1987.

''How the Industry Fared in 1991,'' *Glass Industry,* June 1992.

Keister, Timothy, ''How to Control Oil and Grease in the Effluent from Glass Container Plants,'' *Glass Industry,* May 1993.

Lang, Nancy A., ''A Touch of Glass,'' *Beverage World,* June 1990.

———, ''Hoisting the Glass,'' *Beverage World,* June 1989.

Larson, Melissa, ''Glass Offers a Clear Alternative,'' *Packaging,* June 1992.

''Market Breakout of the U.S. Glass Manufacturing Industry: 1990 vs. 1987,'' *Glass Industry Fact Sheet,* June 1993.

''Monthly Report on Glass Containers: April 1993,'' *Current Industrial Reports,* Washington, DC: U.S. Department of Commerce, May 1993.

Penberthy, Larry, ''Why Glass Is a Good Host for Hazardous Waste,'' *Glass Industry,* May 1992.

Perrine, Lowell E., ''Glass Could Play Major Role in the Safe Disposal of Hazardous Waste,'' *Glass Industry,* January 1991.

———, ''Glass Problems Conference Features an Industry Status Report,'' *Glass Industry,* January 1991.

''Plants Modernize, Quality Improves,'' *Packaging,* July 1987.

Prince, Greg, ''One for the Ages,'' *Beverage Worldline,* June 1991.

Russo, James R., ''Hidden Strength for Glass Packages,'' *Packages,* August 1986.

Testin, Robert F., and Peter J. Vergano, ''Less Packaging and More Recycling Reduces Waste,'' *Food Review.*

Tooley, Fay V., ed., *The Handbook of Glass Manufacture,* Vol. 2., Ashlee Publishing Co., 1985.

Varshneya, A. K., and K. Frederes, ''How Much Lead Leaches from Crystal Glassware?,'' *Glass Industry,* April 1993.

''Wide-mouth Glass Jar for R. T. French's Dip 'N Spread,'' *Packaging,* October 1987.

—Attrices Dean Griffin

SIC 3229

PRESSED AND BLOWN GLASS AND GLASSWARE, NOT ELSEWHERE CLASSIFIED

This category includes establishments primarily engaged in manufacturing glass and glassware, not elsewhere classified, pressed, blown, or shaped from glass produced in the same establishment. Establishments primarily engaged in manufacturing textile glass fibers are also included in this industry, but establishments primarily engaged in manufacturing glass wool insulation products are classified in **SIC 3296: Mineral Wool.** Establishments primarily engaged in manufacturing fiber optic cables are classified in **SIC 3357: Drawing and Insulating of Nonferrous Wire,** and those manufacturing fiber optic medical devices are classified in the Surgical, Medical, And Dental Instruments and Supplies industries. Establishments primarily engaged in the production of pressed lenses for vehicular lighting, beacons, and lanterns are also included in this industry, but establishments primarily engaged in the production of optical lenses are classified in **SIC 3827: Optical Instruments and**

Lenses. Establishments primarily engaged in manufacturing glass containers are classified in **SIC 3221: Glass Containers,** and those manufacturing complete electric light bulbs are classified in **SIC 3641: Electric Lamp Bulbs and Tubes.**

INDUSTRY SNAPSHOT

The pressed and blown glassware industry manufactured products ranging from television tubes, ashtrays, candlesticks, stemware, tobacco jars, and optical lenses to Christmas tree ornaments. Throughout the 1980s, the industry maintained a steady level of employment at about 37,000 workers, while the value of shipments rose consistently to reach $3.86 billion by 1988. The total number of establishments engaged in the industry also grew during the 1980s, from 331 in 1982 to 403 in 1988. The average establishment employed about twice as many production workers and invested nearly 2.5 times more capital than the national average for manufacturing firms.

ORGANIZATION AND STRUCTURE

The companies involved in the pressed and blown glass industry displayed much diversity in earnings and employment levels. Of the 403 total industry establishments in 1988, 67 percent employed 20 or fewer people. However, the industry was dominated by large companies related in some way to Corning Incorporated: Owens-Corning, Owens-Illinois, and Owens/Corning Fiberglas, for example. Anchor Hocking was another giant in the industry, although dwarfed by the Corning units. Steuben Glass, a Corning company, and Lenox Crystal were among those companies making hand-made stemware, both of which shared the international market with Waterford crystal of Ireland.

Due to the resurgence of interest in glass blowing in America, small craft shops could be found across the country where artisans sold their wares, displayed their techniques, and often taught classes. However, these shops were generally neither involved nor interested in producing the mass quantities of machine-made glassware supplied by the Corning conglomerate.

The product share within the industry was split between six types of goods. Textile glass fiber accounted for 33.7 percent of the overall market; machine-made table, kitchen, art, and novelty glassware claimed 16.8 percent; machine-made lighting and electronic glassware took another 17.2 percent; all other machine-made glassware accounted for 14.2 percent; hand-made pressed and blown glassware claimed 3.5 percent; and pressed and blown glass not specified by kind comprised the remaining 14.6 percent. The materials consumed in the greatest amounts by the industry included plastic film and sheets, unsupported glass, all types of glass sand, and paperboard boxes.

BACKGROUND AND DEVELOPMENT

The Mesopotamians were credited by archaeologists with making the world's first glass, circa 2500 B.C. However, it was not until the Roman Empire that glass making evolved as a standard craft, much like baking and jewelry making. Venice eventually became known as the glass making capital of the world, and remained so through the 1600s. Glass making in America was very much a crude art form until the eighteenth century, and nearly died out several times. Glass items of any quality, such windows or glassware, had to be purchased from England. However, several small shops where glass was blown provided wares for limited customer bases, and eventually larger manufacturers, such as Bakewell and Company of Pittsburgh, entered the marketplace. For the cosmetic enhancement of glass, etching was practiced during the seventeenth and eighteenth centuries. However, the ability to press glass in very large quantities did not develop until the nineteenth century.

The glass industry in America started to boom after the War of 1812. Between 1800 and 1825, America experienced strong demographic, economic, and political growth. Luxury items were in ever-increasing demand, creating a need for machine-made glass products. Glass pressing was already common in Europe by the late 1700s, although the pieces were small and made with waffle-iron-type presses. American inventors developed the first large, hand-operated pressing machine, although the exact date and maker of the machine was not known.

The introduction of glass pressing created a new challenge for glass makers. Only specific glass mixtures were adequate for pressing, which required experimentation. Also, experience was required to know how much molten glass could be placed in a press without scrapping the piece, and how much time was required to produce the glass before it started to cool and crack. By the time these processes were perfected, glass makers started producing molds exhibiting ornate designs, referred to as "lacy glass." Glass pressing continued to evolve during the colonial era, expanding to candlesticks and lamps. The Victorian era heavily influenced glass making, and by the 1880s colored glass was the order of the day. Glass collecting became a pastime for many and an obsession for some, evidenced by collectors willing to pay heavily for early American, lacy, carnival, and depression glassware.

CURRENT CONDITIONS

The pressed and blown glass industry in the mid-1990s experienced low margins, high competition, and high technology. While glass tableware and cooking dishes did not share the high-tech image of fiber optic cables and devices, research and development of better materials for these purposes continued. Likewise, new marketing approaches, such as creative packaging and merchandizing, were constantly investigated.

INDUSTRY LEADERS

Four of the five top-ranking companies in the glass industry, based on 1991 sales, were related to Corning Incorporated of Corning, New York. The parent company had estimated gross sales of $2.09 billion and employed 26,000 people. Anchor-Hocking Corporation of Lancaster, Ohio—which was not affiliated with Corning—grossed $433 million with 6,000 employees.

Corning Incorporated changed its name in 1989 from Corning Glass Works to better recognize its commitment to a number of diverse industries. The founder, Amory Houghton, moved his glass operation from Brooklyn to Corning, New York, in 1868. By 1875, Corning Glass Works was incorporated and Houghton became president of the company, a position he retained until 1911.

The technical expertise of the company was recognized early, as Thomas Edison asked for its help in making electric light bulbs in 1880. In 1912 Corning invented borosilicate, which was used to produce Pyrex in 1915. Pyrex immediately became standard in the scientific community for laboratory equipment, although the consumer markets were not tapped until years later. Another significant milestone for Corning was the 1934 manufacture of a 200-inch diameter mirror for the Mount Palomar telescope. The company surpassed this accomplishment by creating the world's largest single-piece telescope mirror for the Japanese government in 1992. In the 1960s, Corning created the ceramic heat-resisting reentry shields and glass windshields for the Apollo moon program. The most significant research for Corning in past years was in the development of fiber optics. Corning realized the potential of the material in the 1960s and continued research and development although market demand was low, and by 1984 invested $87 million in new fiber optic plant facilities.

Owens-Illinois controlled nearly 33 percent of the domestic and foreign bottle markets in 1988. It was the largest manufacturer of glass bottles in the world and produced other products such as television picture tubes, tableware, and telescope lenses. The company originated through a 1907 merger of Owens Bottle Company and Illinois Glass Company. In 1935 Libbey Glass Company was purchased, adding tableware to the Owens-Illinois product line. In 1956 Owens-Illinois purchased National Container Corporation, which diversified the company into forest products. Also during the 1950s, the company entered the plastics market, creating squeezable bottles for prepared sauces and semi-rigid containers for bleach and laundry detergent. However, glass manufacturing remained the main focus of Owens-Illinois. Owens changed the way beverages were packaged and sold when it created the one-way glass bottle, a thinner version of the deposit bottle.

In the 1970s, Owens-Illinois experienced a downturn due to two factors: beverage manufacturers started making their own bottles, and a world-wide recession curtailed consumer spending. The company increased productivity during this period through extensive modernization, but also closed 48 plants and laid off 17,000 workers. The company was taken over by Kohlberg, Kravis, Roberts and Company in February 1987.

Owens/Corning Fiberglas Corporation (OCF) started when Owens-Illinois converted an idle glass factory into a research and development center to investigate the uses of fiberglass. While the center initially worked on glass fiber replacements for expensive steel wool dust filters for home furnaces, it stumbled onto the discovery of fine glass fibers as a result of a failed attempt to find a new way to melt glass rods. This discovery produced a joint venture with Corning Glass Works in 1935, which became so successful that in 1949 the courts forced the two companies to license patents to competitors and give up control of the operation because they illegally monopolized the fiberglass industry. Building insulation, fiberglass pipes, and automobile body panels were among the first products produced by the venture.

In 1952, OCF went public as a separate entity and over the years aggressively pursued further research and development and acquisitions of high technology companies. However, in 1986 OCF found itself in a difficult position after taking out huge loans to stave off a takeover bid by Wickes Companies. By 1990, however, the company brought the debt down to $1.5 billion and reestablished itself as the world leader in fiberglass products.

Although Corning performed well during the recession of the early 1990s due to its overseas joint ventures, the company's long-standing joint venture with Dow caused its stock price to tumble. Dow Corning was the maker of silicon breast implants, which were banned by the Food and Drug Administration. Each news report covering a new lawsuit against Dow Corning resulted in lower stock prices. The FDA's final decision on the safety of silicon implants could seriously affect all of Corning, because that venture alone was as large as all its other ventures combined.

WORK FORCE

In 1982, 37,600 people were employed in the pressed and blown glass industry, over 78 percent of whom were production workers. Employment levels held steady through 1988, when the industry employed 36,600 people, 83 percent of whom were production workers. Average hourly wages increased by 23 percent over the same period, from $9.41 in 1982 to $12.23 in 1988. The 1988 hourly wage was $1.57 higher than the average for all manufacturing industries.

Projections for the work force in the glass industry were not bright going into the twenty-first century. Every major occupation employed by this industry was expected to decrease in numbers. Those expected to face reductions greater than 30 percent included inspectors, hand packers, furnace operators, assemblers, machine feeders, packaging machine operators, forming machine operators, and secretaries. Those faced with reductions between 20 percent and 30 percent included general laborers, blue-collar worker supervisors, truck and tractor operators, material movers, and precision workers.

INDUSTRY INFORMATION SOURCES

Considine, Douglas M., editor, *Van Nostrand's Scientific Encyclopedia*, New York: Van Nostrand Reinhold, 1976.

Darnay, Arsen J., editor, *Manufacturing USA: Industry Analyses, Statistics, and Leading Companies*, Detroit: Gale Research, 1992.

Ellis, William S., "Glass: Capturing the Dance of Light," *National Geographic*, December 1993.

"Fiberglass Parts Made Faster than a Speeding Bullet," *Ward's Auto World*, February 1993.

Fink, Ronald, "Corning: Bad Breaks," *Financial World*, July 6, 1993.

Hammonds, Keith, "Corning's Class Act: How Jamie Houghton Reinvented the Company," *Business Week*, May 13, 1991.

Hast, Adele, editor, *International Directory of Company Histories*, Chicago: St. James, 1988.

Holusha, John, "A Huge Looking Glass for Japan," *New York Times*, November 25, 1992.

Lang, Sarah, "Corning's Blueprint for Training in the '90s," *Training*, July 1991.

Paul, Cynthia, "Corning Sets Complementary 'Lifestyle' for Mass," *HFD—The Weekly Home Furnishings Newspaper*, May 17, 1993.

Polak, Ada, *Glass: Its Tradition and Its Makers*, New York: Putnam's Sons, 1975.

"Process Produces Practically Perfect Preforms," *Machine Design*, March 26, 1993.

Rogers, Frances, *5000 Years of Glass*, Philadelphia: Lippincott, 1948.

Roush, Gary B., "A Program for Sharing Corporate Intelligence," *Journal of Business Strategy*, January-February 1991.

—Valerie E. Wilson

SIC 3231

GLASS PRODUCTS, MADE OF PURCHASED GLASS

This category covers establishments primarily engaged in manufacturing glass products from purchased glass. Establishments primarily engaged in manufacturing optical lenses, except ophthalmic, are classified in **SIC 3827: Optical Instruments and Lenses,** and those manufacturing ophthalmic lenses are classified in **SIC 3851: Opthalmic Goods.**

ORGANIZATION AND STRUCTURE

Firms in the purchased glass products industry are distinguished from other glass manufacturing firms—known as "primary" glass manufacturers—in that their products are not made directly from raw glass materials but from "secondary" glass purchased from other companies.

The seven principal markets for the glass products industry as a whole in 1991 were flat glass (30 percent), containers (18 percent), lighting (18 percent), fiber glass (11 percent), television and cathode ray tubes (10 percent), miscellaneous products (7 percent), and consumerware (6 percent). Only a few of these markets, however, were served by purchased glass manufacturing firms. The uses for the glass products manufactured by industry firms are diverse—ranging from automotive, pharmaceutical, and scientific/technical applications to household, beverage industry, and other manufacturing uses.

Industry firms manufacture everyday home glass products, such as mirrors, shower doors, bathtub enclosures, picture glass, ash trays, lighting fixture glass, glass top tables, display shelving, window glass, automobile glass, clock glass, patio doors, oven door panels, novelty and souvenir glass items, appliance glass, and cosmetic, drug, and perfume containers. Industry products are also used in an extensive number of industrial, technical, and other non-household applications such as safety and bullet-proof glass, instrument dials, precision glass tubing, stained glass, industrial safety glasses and welding lenses, greenhouse glass, chemical glassware, instrument panels, cathode ray tube screens, and high-tolerance specialty glass products such as elapsed-time indicators and gravity-sensing electrolytic transducers.

Important subgroups of industry products include beverage glasses such as tumblers and stemware, beer glasses, crystal glassware, and casual glassware, and glass fiber used in optical components and for data and non-data transmission (including faceplates, sensors, and glass-based optical coatings).

Product Manufacture. Because industry firms do not manufacture glass from raw materials as primary glass manufacturers do, the methods for manufacturing glass products from purchased glass vary with the specific product. Firms within the industry purchase glass in the following forms: float glass (a type of flat glass manufactured by floating the glass in a bath of molten tin),sheet glass, and plate glass; glass sand; as "cullet" or glass scrap; and in other forms, including manufactured glass tumblers, stemware, and tableware.

Other materials and supplies used in the manufacture of purchased glass products in 1987 included industrial inorganic chemicals, plastic film and sheets, ground or otherwise treated nonmetallic minerals, and sodium carbonate (soda ash) as well as paperboard containers, wood boxes and pallets, and lumber.

Some of the more common glass products, which illustrate different glass manufacturing methods, include laboratory glass, laminated glass, mirror glass, ornamental glass, safety glass, and stained glass.

Laboratory Glassware. Laboratory glass products such as test tubes, beakers, vials, and glass for distilling liquids are often made of borosilicate glass (a combination of boric oxide, silica sand, and other chemicals) because it has a high natural resistance to temperature change and corrosion, making it ideal for scientific, pharmaceutical, and some household uses. A common manufacturing method for laboratory glassware is machine blowing, in which molten glass is fed into a blowing element where jets of air are blown into the liquefied glass, causing it, with the aid of molds, to expand and conform to predetermined dimensions. Another common glass making method is

machine pressing, where molten glass, cut at regular intervals into individual "gobs," is dropped into molds where it is then shifted beneath a plunging or pressing element that gives the glass, when cooled, its final shape.

Laminated Glass. Laminated or compound glass is comprised of two or more sheets of glass and a layer of plastic fused together by heating in a pressurized tank or "autoclave." When laminated glass products such as automobile windshields are broken, they crack rather than shatter because the fragments adhere to the plastic layer, maintaining the glass's transparency and preventing the scattering of shards.

Mirror Glass. Mirrors are made by treating washed float glass with a tin-based solution, then spraying the surface with a "silvering" solution made of silver nitrate and water followed by a "reducing" agent. The combination of the tin solution and the reducing agent creates a reflective silver film on the glass surface, which is then treated with a layer of copper and a protective lacquer and allowed to dry.

Ornamental Glass. Ornamental glass products are manufactured by running sheets of glass through rollers that shape or emboss the glass surface according to the specific (and often trademarked) design of the individual firm. Some types of ornamental glass, each made using different techniques, include light scattering glass, "wave" glass, lined glass, curved or semicircular "roundel" glass, and glass with flower or other decorative impressions.

Safety Glass. Safety or tempered glass is designed to break into small, rounded pieces of a predetermined size when shattered, thus reducing the creation of dangerous sharp fragments. Such glass is manufactured by heating sheets of flat glass, then subjecting them to bursts of cold air, which causes the interior of the glass to cool more slowly than the surface. The physical bond between the interior and external glass layers is such that when the pane is broken, the fragments are small, uniformly sized, and non-injurious.

Stained Glass. Stained glass consists of segments of individually colored panes joined together to create an image or pattern. The three methods for staining glass are painting, fusion with metallic oxides, and enameling. Glass painting involves applying pigments to hardened glass, then permanently burning or baking the pigment on to the surface of the glass in an oven. Alternatively, metallic oxides of varying colors can be added to glass while it is still molten, changing the tint of the glass itself when it cools. Metallic oxides are also used in enameling methods but are applied to hardened rather than molten glass. The enamel coating is then bonded with the glass by firing or baking.

Industry Specialization. Many industry firms manufacture more than one type of glass product. For example, Apogee Enterprises Inc. of Minnesota produces insulating, heat-tempered, laminated, non-glare, picture, automotive, and bullet-resistant glass. A few firms, however, such as American Mirror Company, Inc. (Virginia), Fisher Skylights, Inc. (New York), and Riordan Stained Glass Studio (Illinois), specialize in a single line of glass products. In 1987, 66 industry firms specialized in manufacturing mirrors, 61 specialized in laminated glass manufacture, another 61 made machine pressed and blown glassware, and 14 made hand pressed and blown glassware. Industry specialization in glass product manufacturing is also reflected in the names of some industry firms, such as Artistic Shower Door & Mirror Company Inc., Pilkington Aerospace Inc., National Bullet Proof Inc., and Christmas by Krebs Inc., among others.

End-users. The major users of glass products in the early 1980s (including some non-industry products but excluding containers such as bottles and jars) were: individual consumers of personal goods (15.2 percent of industry output); manufacturers purchasing non-container glass and glass products (9.7 percent); exports to foreign markets (7.8 percent); motor vehicle and car body manufacturers (5.6 percent); restaurants, bars, and other eating and drinking establishments (4.5 percent); automotive repair shops and service businesses (4.4 percent); lighting fixture and equipment manufacturers (3.3 percent); miscellaneous plastics products manufacturers (3.3 percent); hotels and other hospitality businesses (2.8 percent), and electric lamp manufacturers. The remaining 40 percent of glass product purchases was divided among more than 70 business sectors.

CURRENT CONDITIONS

This industry, comprised of 1,325 companies operating 1,429 business establishments, employed 51,100 workers in 1987 and generated $5.4 billion in shipments. The states with the largest number of firms were California (224), New York (113), New Jersey (91), and Texas (82). Industry establishments in Pennsylvania, Ohio, Michigan, California, and North Carolina accounted for almost half the value of U.S. purchased glass product shipments in the late 1980s.

Between 1972 and 1987, the purchased glass products industry experienced continuous solid growth, with the only declines in the value of shipments occurring in the mid-1970s. In that 16-year period, the value of industry shipments more than quadrupled from $1.3 billion to $5.4 billion, the number of industry firms increased 38 percent from 817 to 1,325, and employment grew 52 percent from 33,700 to 51,100. At the same time, the cost of materials and payroll as a percentage of total shipment value declined from 73 to 67 percent industry wide.

Faced with decreased demand for glass products, industry firms entered into joint ventures, introduced new products, and improved facilities in the early 1990s to stimulate sales. Between 1992 and 1994, glass container shipments averaged about 70,000 per quarter, with seasonal fluctuations. Demand for glass fiber products used in automotive and other transportation equipment was expected to increase about three percent per year in the early to mid-1990s to 5.3 billion pounds (with a value of $4.1 billion) by 1995.

INDUSTRY LEADERS

The leading industry firms in 1993 included BP Chemicals Inc. (Ohio), with $1.7 billion in sales and 4,800 employees, Guardian Industries Corp. (Michigan), with $1 billion in sales and 8,000 employees, Harvard Industries Inc. (New Jersey), with $730 million in sales and 8,200 workers, and Ford Motor Company Glass Division (Michigan), with $375 million in sales and 3,500 workers. Other industry leaders include Schott Corp., Pilkington Holdings Inc., FEL Corp., Safelite Glass Corp., and Excel Industries Inc.

Several industry firms, including Dillmeier Industries Inc. (Arkansas), RRR Glassworks Inc. (California), and Glass Products Inc. (Pennsylvania), were exclusively engaged in the manufacture of purchased glass products in the early 1990s. Other firms primarily engaged in purchased glass product manufacture were also active in such industries as local trucking, curtain and drapery manufacture, testing services laboratories, and wood household furniture manufacturing, among others.

WORK FORCE

The glass making occupations with the greatest number of workers in 1990 included glass product assemblers and fabricators (12 percent of glass industry employment); general helpers, laborers, and material movers (eight percent); hand packers and packagers of manufactured products (six percent); glass manufacturing machine feeders and offbearers (workers who deliver raw materials and carry them away from glass manufacturing machines; five percent); and blue collar worker supervisors (five percent). The remaining two-thirds of industry employees consisted of other production workers—such as glass product cutting and slicing machine setters, operators, and tenders; precision glass product inspectors, testers, and graders; glass hand cutters and trimmers; glass furnace, kiln, or kettle operators and tenders; and glass product coating, painting, and spraying machine operators—and non-production administrative positions such as sales staff, general managers and executives, support and clerical staff, and industrial production managers.

Production workers accounted for 77 percent of industry employees in 1987, and the average annual salary for all industry employees was $20,739. The average industry firm in 1989 had 38 employees (30 of whom were production workers), an average payroll per employee of $22,640, and an average annual shipment value of $4.2 million.

AMERICA AND THE WORLD

Over 90 companies in at least 29 countries produced purchased glass products in 1993. Among the world's largest purchased glass manufacturing firms were Schott Glaswerke (Germany), with $3 billion in sales and 31,500 employees, Nippon Sheet Glass Company Ltd. (Japan), with $2.3 billion in sales and 3,860 workers, Hoya Corporation, with $1 billion in sales and 4,350 employees, and Pilkington Glass Ltd., with 569 million in sales and 4,690 workers.

INDUSTRY INFORMATION SOURCES

Berlye, Milton K., *Encyclopedia of Working with Glass,* Dobbs Ferry, NY: Oceana Publications, 1968.

Census of Manufactures, 1987, Washington, DC: U.S. Department of Commerce, 1990.

Ceramic Industry, August, 1992; June, 1993.

Glass Industry, September 1992.

Pfaender, Heinz G., *Schott Guide to Glass,* New York: Van Nostrand & Reinhold, 1983.

—Paul Bodine

SIC 3241

CEMENT, HYDRAULIC

Establishments primarily engaged in manufacturing hydraulic cement, including portland, natural, masonry, and pozzolana cements.

The employment level in the hydraulic cement industry steadily declined throughout the 1980s; in 1982 24,600 people were employed, and by 1990 there were just over 18,000. The value of shipments, on the other hand, increased between 1982 and 1990 by $7 million. In 1982 237 establishments across the nation

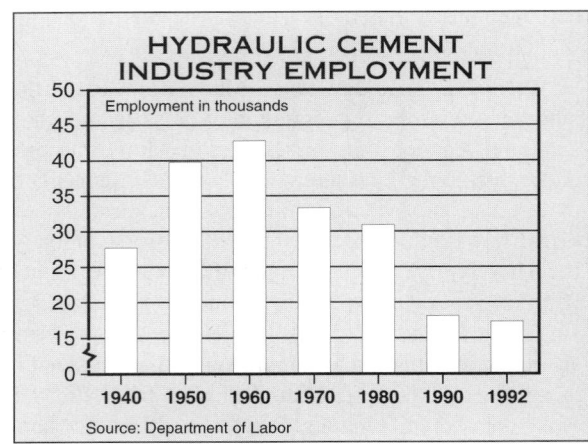

HYDRAULIC CEMENT INDUSTRY EMPLOYMENT

Employment in thousands

Source: Department of Labor

were engaged in this industry, while by 1987, 55 establishments had dropped out, leaving only 182 in business.

In selected ratios, the hydraulic cement industry outperforms the average manufacturing industry by more than three times in areas of wages per establishment, value added per establishment, shipments per establishment, and investment per establishment. While this industry enjoys significantly higher rates of investment, shipments, and value-added processes, it also incurs higher costs, employment levels, and wage rates than most other manufacturing industries.

The total product share is split into nine categories, with portland cements claiming nearly 88 percent of the total market and five market segments in 1987. Normal portland cement ASTM (American Society for Testing and Materials) type I controlled 58.3 percent of industry production. Moderate heat of hydration portland cement ASTM type II controlled 20.9 percent of the market. High early strength ASTM type III portland cement controlled 4.7 percent of the market. Other portland cements, including oil well and waterproof, but excluding white portland and portland slag, controlled 2.4 percent. Masonry cement claimed 7.1 percent; prepared hydraulic, natural, and hydraulic lime cements, 1.4 percent; cement clinker, 0.7 percent; and hydraulic cement, not specified by kind, 2.9 percent of the market.

LaFarge Corporation, based in Reston, Virginia, reported 1991 sales of $1.497 billion and employed 8,200 people, while that same year, Holnam Incorporated of Dundee, Michigan, had revenues of $1 billion and employed 6,000 people in 1991. Also in 1991, Blue Circle Incorporated of Marietta, Georgia, had estimated sales of $740 million and a work force of 1,000 people; Southdown Incorporated of Houston, Texas, reported revenues of $592 million and had 3,300 workers; and Lone Star Industries, based in Stamford, Connecticut, reported sales of $338 million and 5,000 employees.

Approaching the twenty-first century, the hydraulic cement industry was expected to increase employment levels by more than ten percent in three occupations: industrial machinery mechanics, sales workers, and industrial production managers. Most other occupations were expected to face reductions; those most significantly affected were hand packers, furnace operators, secretaries, and crushing and mixing machine operators. Positions for general managers and top executives would possibly decline by more than five percent as the hydraulic cement industry approached the year 2000.

Hourly wages were significantly higher in 1987, when the average wage was $14.08 compared to $10.36, the average wage for all of manufacturing. By 1990 the average hourly wage had risen to $14.22. At an average of $17.60 per hour, the state of Virginia's 400 workers in the hydraulic cement industry enjoyed the highest hourly wage in 1987. Kansas's 700 workers were the closest to Virginia with the average hourly wage being $15.70. Both states contained five hydraulic cement establishments each.

INDUSTRY INFORMATION SOURCES

Darnay, Arsen J., ed. *Manufacturing USA: Industry Analyses, Statistics, and Leading Companies*. Detroit: Gale Research, Inc., 1992.

—Valerie E. Wilson

SIC 3251

BRICK AND STRUCTURAL CLAY TILE

This category covers establishments primarily engaged in manufacturing brick and structural clay tile. Establishments primarily engaged in manufacturing clay firebrick fall under **SIC 3255: Clay Refractories**; those manufacturing nonclay firebrick are grouped under **SIC 3297: Nonclay Refractories**; those manufacturing sand lime brick are classified in **SIC 3299: Nonmetallic Mineral Products, Not Elsewhere Classified**; those manufacturing architectural terra cotta and other miscellaneous structural clay products are classified in **SIC 3259: Structural Clay Products, Not Elsewhere Classified**; and those manufacturing glass brick are classified fall under **SIC 3229: Pressed and Blown Glass and Glassware, Not Elsewhere Classified**.

Products manufactured in this industry are used primarily for their structural properties rather than for decorative or aesthetic qualities; they may generally be divided into solid masonry products, such as most bricks, and hollow masonry products, such as structural tile. Industry products have traditionally been divided into the following groups: building—or common—brick and structural clay tile, and face brick and structural clay tile, with average dimensions of 2 1/4″ × 3 5/8″ × 7 5/8″ (90 percent of value of 1987 shipments); miscellaneous brick and structural clay tile (6.2 percent of value of 1987 shipments); glazed brick and structural hollow tile (2.1 percent); and other brick products—including paving, floor, and sewer brick (1.8 percent).

The characteristics of brick (52 percent of 1991 structural clay industry revenues) and structural clay tile products (less than 48 percent of structural clay industry revenues) vary depending on the type of clay or raw mineral material used, the manner in which they are manufactured, the temperature at which they are burned or baked, their relative absorptive and strength qualities, and the severity of the climates they will be used in. Typical uses for industry products in the early 1980s were the construction and alteration of office buildings, residential one-unit structures, industrial and educational buildings, and several other building construction and maintenance uses.

In its most common form, brick is made from clay that has been mixed with water, formed or ''tempered'' into a rectangular block, dried, and burned in a kiln. Common brick refers to brick in its undifferentiated state as it comes from the kiln and is used as ''backup'' masonry for wall thickness and structural support behind face brick. Face brick is chosen based on its uniformity of appearance for use in the exterior or visible portions of walls and is divided into various grades of color, texture, and perfection. Glazed brick is brick that has been treated with a coating of melted ground glass to repel moisture, engender easy cleaning, and/or create a desired appearance. The standard dimensions of U.S. bricks range between 4″ and 6″ thick, 2 3/4″ and 4″ high, and 8″ and 12″ wide (including surrounding mortar). Other forms of brick manufactured by industry firms include vitrified brick (heat fused into glass or a glassy material), hollow brick, flooring brick, paving brick, and slumped brick (with an expanded base due to settling during curing).

Unlike common ceramic home floor tile which is typically thin and flat, structural tile more resembles concrete construction blocks in that it is hollow or cored and is primarily used for structural support rather than for aesthetic, decorative purposes. Structural clay tile is derived from clay, ceramic, and refractory minerals including kaolin and ball clay, mixed with industrial chemicals, molded into specific dimensions by forcing the raw material through dies, and burned or baked in kilns or ovens.

There are four basic types of structural clay tile. Structural clay load-bearing wall tile is used in the construction of exposed walls or load-bearing walls to bear the weight of floors, roofs, and such facings as stucco or plaster. Structural clay nonload-bearing tile consists of partition tile for use in the construction of partitions in the interior of buildings and for backing up walls made of composites of two or more materials, such as fiberglass and reinforced plastic; furring tile, which is used to line the inside of walls for plaster bases and to provide an "air space" between the plaster and the wall; and fireproofing tile, which is used to protect steel girders, beams, columns, and other structural elements from fire. The third type of structural clay tile is flooring tile used in floor and roof construction (but distinguished from common flat decorative floor tile), and the fourth—structural clay facing tile—is used in exposed or visible interior and exterior walls and partitions. Other specific types of tile manufactured by industry firms include clay book tile, clay radial chimney blocks, corncob tile, clay floor arch tile, and silo tile. Like brick, structural clay tile may be glazed or unglazed depending on its use.

The different types of structural clay tile can be graded in terms of their suitability for climates of varying severity, ease of cleaning, absorptive properties, stain resistance qualities, range of colors, degree of perfection of surface finish, and resistance to chemicals.

The use of uniform or modular standards for brick and structural clay tile by the construction industry and the brick and structural clay tile manufacturing industry has a long history, and industry products are governed by precise specifications with respect to tile length, width, and thickness as well as strength, endurance, and appearance. For example, in the early 1960s there were twelve distinct different modular sizes or specifications for structural load-bearing wall tile. Sizes that become unpopular may be dropped, however, and new ones added as construction industry demand dictates. Traditionally, few manufacturers have produced all the tile sizes accepted as standard by the industry.

Like most other industries, this one is constantly evolving. The manufacture of brick and structural clay tile by industry firms has benefitted from better kiln designs, improved knowledge of brick and tile raw materials and their characteristics, greater use of modern manufacturing technology, and better control over the firing or baking process.

In 1987, 167 companies operating 266 business establishments employed 16,600 workers (81 percent of whom were production workers) and generated $1.25 billion in shipments of brick and structural clay tile products. The average industry establishment in 1989 had 60 employees (49 production workers), an average per employee payroll of $20,820, and shipments with a value of $4,462,921.

The leading brick and structural clay tile industry firms in 1993 were Justin Industries Inc. of Texas ($453 million in sales, 5,102 employees), Boral Bricks Inc. of Georgia ($130 million, 1,900 employees), and Acme Brick Company/Justin Industries of Texas ($100 million, 1,800 employees). The states with the most firms—as well as the most workers—were North Carolina (21 establishments), Texas (29), Ohio (25), and Pennsylvania (15), which together accounted for 39 percent of industry employment.

The brick and structural clay tile industry is significantly effected by fluctuations in the homebuilding and construction industries; in 1991 U.S. demand for common and face brick dropped 21 percent from the 5.4 billion bricks produced in 1990 due to depressed commercial, industrial, and housing construction. Shipments of clay floor and wall tile rose to more than 120 million square feet in the third quarter of 1992, however, and were expected to reach peaks of close to 135 million square feet in mid-1994. The leading issues confronting brick and structural clay tile manufacturers in the early 1990s were conforming to environmental legislation requirements, managing labor costs, coping with fluctuating markets, financing new facilities, and competing with imported products.

INDUSTRY INFORMATION SOURCES

Brick Institute of America, 11490 Commerce Park, Reston, Virginia, 22091.

"Cement and Structural Clay Products," *1987 Census of Manufactures: Industry Series*, Washington, D.C.: U.S. Department of Commerce.

Ceramic Industry, Troy, Michigan: Business News Publishing Co. [monthly].

Masonry, Oak Brook, Illinois: Mason Contractors Association of America [bimonthly].

Technical Notes on Brick Construction, Reston, VA: Brick Institute of America [monthly].

—Paul Bodine

CERAMIC WALL AND FLOOR TILE

This industry covers establishments primarily engaged in manufacturing ceramic wall and floor tile. Establishments primarily engaged in manufacturing structural clay tile are classifed in **SIC 3251: Brick and Structural Clay Tile,** and those manufacturing drain tile are classified in **SIC 3259: Structural Clay Products, Not Elsewhere Classified.**

INDUSTRY SNAPSHOT

Nearly 99 percent of this industry's product share is composed of glazed and unglazed floor tile and wall tile, including quarry tile and ceramic mosaic tile. Because this industry is so focused on decorative tiles, it is completely dependent on the economic health of the construction and remodeling industries.

Clay, ceramic, and refractory materials such as kaolin and ball clay are the raw materials consumed in the manufacture of ceramic tiles. Other industrial chemicals, some lead-based, are also used to produce ceramic tiles. Because of the industry's use and disposal of these lead-based chemicals, ceramic manufacturers are forced to comply with a wide array of Environmental Protection Agency regulations.

This industry experienced growth through the 1980s in terms of establishments, shipments, and employment levels. In 1982 97 establishments were engaged in this industry, 52 of which employed 20 or more employees. By 1988 112 establishments were present, 53 employing 20 or more people. Leading states involved in ceramic wall and floor tile manufacturing included California, Texas, and Ohio. The total work force in 1982 was approximately 7,500, 81 percent of which were production workers. By the end of 1990 the total work force had grown to 10,000, with 83 percent of the employees working in a production capacity. Average wages increased, to $10.05 per hour in 1990, but still fell short of the national average for all manufacturing.

BACKGROUND AND DEVELOPMENT

The evolution of clay tiles stems began with the introduction of roofing tiles, followed by flooring tiles and wall tiles. The Roman historian Pliny wrote that tiles were invented in Greece on the isle of Cyprus by Cinyra, son of Agrippa. However, no dates were assigned to Cinyra's invention. The earliest baked clay roof tiles were excavated near Argos, Greece, which date circa 1800 B.C. The technique for production of this architectural media moved to Southern Italy and Sicily and slowly spread throughout the rest of continental Europe. Until the industrial revolution, when tile making was mechanized somewhat, only the very rich could afford tiled roofs and floors. This is evident in the 89 B.C. Charter of Tarentum, which stated that Senate membership and voting privileges were restricted to those men who owned housing, within Tarentum, roofed with at least 1500 tiles.

As with all industries, the Industrial Revolution forever changed the manufacture of clay tiles. By the 1850s the British led the industry in machinery innovation and heavily influenced production methods in Germany, France, Belgium, Holland, Spain, and Portugal. The introduction of machines to aid in the manufacturing process resulted in dramatically higher production levels and far greater availability of tiles.

The ceramic tile industry in the United States entered its own period of enlightenment in the 1870s. While glazed tiles were produced in the United States approximately 30 years previously, it was not until the Philadelphia International Centennial Exhibition of 1876 that the art form in ceramic tiles developed its own uniquely American twist. This progress is documented by Charles Thomas Davis, writer of *Manufacture of Bricks, Tiles and Terra-Cotta,* published in 1884. He wrote, "Nothing in the history of pottery is so remarkable as the progress which has been made in the manufacture of encaustic and decorative tiles, but especially in the latter, in this country since the Centennial Exposition of 1876. . . . [it] injected into us as a nation new conceptions of the ideal, the natural, and the beautiful in art." However, during 1870 and 1900 many American tiles produced imitated the lifestyle in Victorian Britain, mainly because many of the artisans were trained either in Britain or directly by the British.

A new, distinctly different generation began to infuse the American ceramic tile industry in the early 1900s. These artisans were trained in American potteries and art schools and prided themselves on original, hand-made tiles. The leaders in innovation were the small companies that created a broad diversity in style and technique. This period was struck a deadly blow by the Great Depression of 1929, when the construction industry shuddered to a halt and many small tile firms were forced to close their doors.

The United States then entered World War II and the Art Deco movement again changed the design of ceramic tiles. Screen printing became an important method of coloring tiles and production methods were improved to lend great consistency to final tile products. The tile industry in the United States today is dominated by international conglomerates like Armstrong World Industries, which owns American Olean Tile. However, as in the early 1900s, much of the artistry in the industry is spurred by smaller tile companies.

CURRENT CONDITIONS

The ceramic tile industry is closely tied to the construction industry, both residential and nonresidential. In the first quarter of 1993, residential construction spending was flat and nonresidential started to decline. Due to depressed sales, inventory accumulation caused production of various ceramic products to stall. Likewise, poor weather conditions throughout the United States slowed construction, directly affecting the sales and shipments of ceramic products. During the remainder of 1993, however, clay floor and wall tiles experienced strong growth in shipments because of economic recovery in other industries. Because of lower interest rates and general economic improvement, housing starts are projected to grow at least through the mid-1990s and residential remodeling is also forecast to grow. This growth will serve as a tremendous boon to establishments involved in ceramic wall and floor tile manufacturing.

INDUSTRY LEADERS

American Olean Tile Company of Lansdale, Pennsylvania, is owned by Armstrong World Industries. This acquisition was completed in 1988 in an effort to boost profitability, the first of several restructuring moves for Armstrong, the largest outfit in this industry in terms of sales. Armstrong, a public company that in the early 1990s employed nearly 23,000 workers, posted annual sales of $2.55 billion in the early 1990s.

Dal-Tile Corporation of Dallas, Texas, was acquired in 1990 by AEA Investors for $650 million, making the acquisition the largest ever for AEA. Unfortunately for AEA, a New York-based consortium of former chief executives of America's largest firms, four lawsuits have been filed against either the company or its previous owners for illegal dumping practices. Many of the charges, however, concerned activities undertaken under the company's former ownership (resulting in multi-million dollar fines and other sentences). Dal-Tile Group posted annual sales of more than $500 million in the early 1990s.

Other key companies in this industry include American Biltrite Inc., United States Ceramic Tile Co., and Monarch Industries Inc.

WORK FORCE

Today, the work force engaged in tile manufacture works in a highly mechanized, if not totally automated, setting or works in a small specialty studio setting, creating highly artistic and functional tiles.

The industries producing stone, clay, and mineral products are expected to engage in downsizing efforts across a variety of occupations by the year 2000. The number of hand packers and packagers is expected by some industry observers to be reduced by nearly 25 percent, largely as a result of increasing automation. Other occupations expected to experience work force reductions of between 15 and 20 percent include assemblers and fabricators; furnace, kiln, oven, and kettle operators; crushing and mixing machine operators; precision inspectors, graders, and testers; packaging and filling machine operators; machine feeders and offbearers; hand freight, stock, material movers; secretaries; cutting and slicing machine operators; grinders and polishers; and metal and plastic machine forming operators. Occupations expected to enjoy growth in the industry include sales workers, industrial ma-

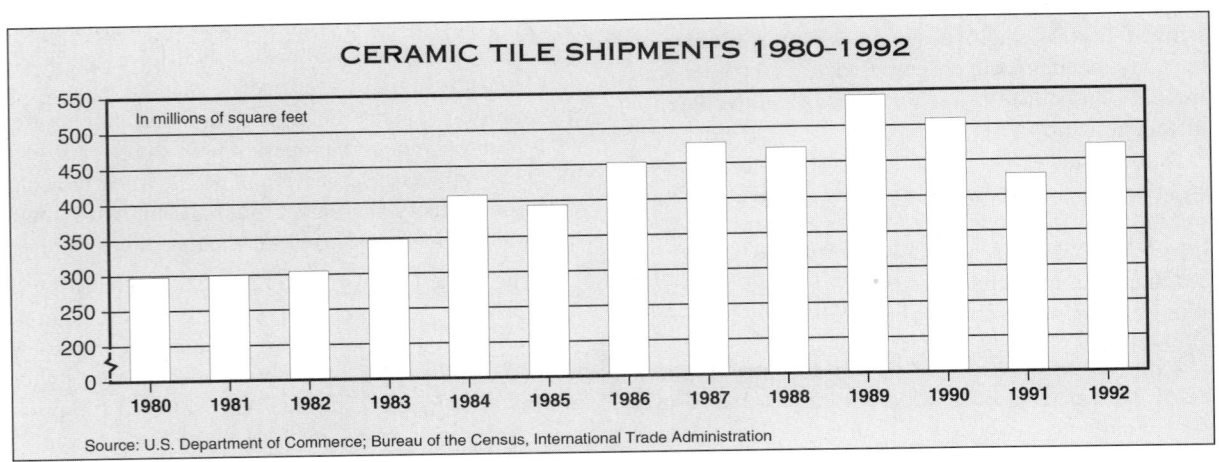

CERAMIC TILE SHIPMENTS 1980–1992

In millions of square feet

Source: U.S. Department of Commerce; Bureau of the Census, International Trade Administration

chinery mechanics, and industrial production managers.

RESEARCH AND TECHNOLOGY

The production methods employed to manufacture ceramic tiles have greatly improved since the end of World War II. Increasing customer demand for greater variety in styles and uses of tiles have broadened the base of techniques used to produce final artistic effects. While clay tile making continues to resemble many of the practices used 1000 years ago, better production methods and materials lend high quality and consistency to the final product. Much of the research today is centered around the historical aspects of clay tile, mainly seen in restoration, conservation, and collection efforts and archaeological pursuits.

INDUSTRY INFORMATION SOURCES

"Florida Tile." *Custom Builder*, November-December 1992.

Belli, Anne. "42 Residents sue tile firm over waste." *Dallas Morning News*, July 10, 1992.

Berss, Marcia. "Slippery Tile." *Forbes*, December 6, 1993.

Brodribb, Gerald. *Roman Brick and Tile*, Wolfeboro, NH: Alan Sutton Publishing Inc., 1989.

Lemmen, Hans van. *Tiles: 1,000 Years of Architectural Decoration*, New York: Harry N. Abrams, Inc., 1993.

Steele, Andrew. "Inventory Glut Haunts Production Levels," *Ceramic Industry*, June, 1993.

———, "Economic Forecast 1993-94," *Ceramic Industry*, July 1993.

———, "Stock market's fast track slows on Main Street," *Ceramic Industry*, October 1993.

—Valerie E. Wilson

SIC 3255

CLAY REFRACTORIES

This category covers establishments primarily engaged in manufacturing clay firebrick and other heat resisting clay products. Establishments primarily engaged in manufacturing nonclay refractories and all graphite refractories, whether of carbon bond or ceramic bond, are classified under **SIC 3297: Nonclay Refractories**.

The refractory industry as a whole was comprised of the following major market divisions in 1991: brick and refractory shapes (56 percent of refractory sales),

ground or bulk and lump refractories (19 percent), insulating ceramic fiber (12 percent, see **SIC 3299: Nonmetallic Products, Not Elsewhere Classified**), and other refractory products (13 percent).

Refractories are mineral- and chemical-based materials with very high heat-resisting properties, which make them ideal for structural uses in the construction of walls, ceilings, and associated elements of iron and steel industry blast furnaces, glass manufacturing tanks, cement kilns, hot stoves, ceramic kilns, open hearth furnaces, nonferrous metallurgical furnaces, ceramic kilns, and steam boilers. Most clay refractory products are manufactured in the form of bricks, but refractory clay may also be formed into special shapes such as the T-sections of refractory pipes or the small stands that support ceramic products during firing in a kiln.

Because of its low cost in comparison to other refractories, fireclay—a mixture of kaolinite clay and silica sand—is the preferred material for clay refractory brick, which is classified as "low," "intermediate," "high," and "superduty" according to the temperature at which it softens when fired or baked. Typical specific uses of fire clay refractory bricks are boiler furnace linings, blast furnace linings, molten iron casting pit refractories, and other applications that do not entail extremely high temperatures.

Plastic fireclays are refractories that are moldable when mixed with water and are often used for furnace linings or as a binding agent in fireclay brick manufacture. Fireclay may be combined with other raw materials to increase its refractoriness and to reduce its shrinkage during firing. Because of improvements in the combustion properties of fuels used in industrial furnaces, performance requirements for refractory materials have continued to be upgraded to extend their operational life and conform to harsher furnace environments. This has led to the development of "superrefractories" which consist of 50 to 80 percent alumina, a form of aluminum oxide found in minerals such as corundum and bauxite and also used in the manufacture of aluminum.

In 1991, over one quarter of the value of industry product shipments consisted of high-alumina (50 percent alumina content or higher) glass-house pots or crucibles for melting and refining glass, tank blocks (blocks of refractory clay used in the lower portions of glass-tank furnaces), feeder parts (for devices that supply the raw refractory material to a preparation machine prior to firing), and other high alumina pouring or casting pit refractories for the casting of molten steel, such as "nozzles" (used in ladles for extracting molten steel), "runners" (refractory-lined channels in which molten iron flows from a blast furnace when tapped), and ladle "gate" parts (such as refractory-lined ladles or pouring spouts for holding molten iron or steel). Nearly one fifth of the value of industry shipments consisted of "castable" (i.e., made from a mixture of refractory clay and cement) high and low alumina (50 percent alumina content or higher) refractories, and insulating castable refractories.

Almost 15 percent of the value of industry shipments consisted of fireclay with some silica sand content, superduty and "bloating" (i.e., expanding when fired) fireclay bricks, fireclay and high alumina pouring or casting pit refractories, clay kiln "furniture" (small heat-resistant supports for bracing pottery-ware during firing in kilns), and other clay refractory shapes. More than 12 percent of industry shipment value consisted of plastic low-alumina clay refractories and "ramming" mixes (for making refractory shapes or for lining furnace walls with pneumatic tools), high alumina plastic clay refractories and ramming mixes, and bonded high-alumina content plastic clay refractories and ramming mixes.

The remaining 25 percent of industry shipment value was divided among high-alumina clay refractory materials sold in lump or ground form either for indirect use by customers inside and outside the refractory industry as a finished product or as an export; insulating clay refractory bricks and shapes with high and low temperature limits; fireclay "gunning" mixes (a refractory powder for repairing furnace linings), including high- and low-alumina insulating and non-insulating gunning mixes; and wet and dry clay and high-alumina content refractory bonding mortars for strengthening refractory brick walls.

Other products manufactured by industry firms include clay refractory cement, refractory tile made out of fire clay, and various refractory elements used in glass manufacturing, such as glasshouse floaters, melting pots, rings, saggers, and stoppers.

Manufacture. In 1987, nearly 60 percent of materials consumed by industry firms in the manufacture of clay refractories consisted of clay, ceramic, and refractory minerals extracted and processed by mining firms (see **Industry Group 145**); more than 17 percent consisted of reprocessed clay and nonclay refractories purchased from other industry firms; 5 percent consisted of industrial chemicals, and the remainder consisted of miscellaneous materials, parts, containers, and supplies. Fuel and labor costs and kiln maintenance account for a large percentage of the cost of refractory manufacture.

One of the most common methods for manufacturing clay refractories is extrusion, in which moist refractory clay is forced by pressure through a die of specific dimensions, creating a rectangular shaft of clay which can then be cut at regular intervals to form bricks. The extruded bricks may then be sent through tunnel driers or dried on hot floors. Another common manufacturing process for noncomplex refractory shapes is power pressing, in which brick presses weighing as much 3,600 tons produce bricks of up to 28 inches in length. Unlike brick extruding machines, brick presses do not require large amounts of water and thus simplify the drying and handling of the bricks. Other methods of refractory manufacture include slip casting, hydrostatic pressing, fusion casting, and hand molding.

After initial forming, clay refractory bricks and shapes are often fired in tunnel-shaped kilns to strengthen the brick or shape and stabilize it at a temperature equal to or higher than it will experience in actual use (often 1800 degrees Fahrenheit or more).

In 1987, 111 companies employing 6,400 employees (4,700 of whom were production workers) generated more than $788 million in shipments. The average payroll per industry employee was $23,469, and the average hourly wage for production workers was $10.69. The average industry firm in 1989 had 47 employees (36 production workers) and $6.2 million worth of shipments. The leading industry firms in 1993 were North American Refractories of Ohio ($290 million in sales, 2,000 employees), Adience Inc. of Pennsylvania ($270 million, 1,500 employees), Dresser Industries Inc./Harbison-Walker Refractories Division of Pennsylvania ($225 million, 1,800 employees), and A. P. Green Industries of Missouri ($168 million, 1,500 employees). The states with the largest number of industry establishments in 1987 were Pennsylvania (30), Ohio (27), California (10), and Alabama (8); these states accounted for 44 percent of all industry shipments and 44 percent of all employment.

Between 1972 and 1987, the clay refractories industry grew from 86 to 111 firms while industry employment fell from 11,200 to 6,400 workers (production and nonproduction). In the same period, the value of industry shipments more than doubled from $336 million to more than $788 million. In the early 1990s, the clay refractories industry experienced steady declines in shipment value, down to $771 million in 1990 and $755 million in 1991 as demand for refractory products decreased.

Trends in the clay refractory industry in the early 1990s included the opening of new plants and facilities, mergers and acquisitions, new seamless refractory furnace linings that reduced air leakage into and out of industrial furnaces, improvements in furnace operation and refractory materials resulting in increases in the number of tons of steel (up to 1 million) that could be produced before refractory linings needed replacing, partnerships between refractory suppliers and steelmakers to develop new refractory materials and techniques, and continuing industry efforts to find purer grades of refractory minerals that will increase the temperature resisting limits of refractory products.

The long-term trend toward increased automation of refractory manufacturing processes (such as automatic brick batching) also continued with the development of robotic and remote control gunning machines for relining furnaces and applying refractory coatings without furnace downtime. The major issues facing refractories producers in the early 1990s were environmental anti-pollution standards, increases in materials costs, and changing markets.

INDUSTRY INFORMATION SOURCES

ProQuest/ABI Inform [business periodical database], Ann Arbor, MI: Bell & Howell Information Company, 1994 [updated periodically].

Ceramic Industry, Troy Michigan: Business News Publishing Co. [monthly].

Dodd, A. E., *Dictionary of Ceramics*, London: George Newnes Limited, 1967.

Norton, F. H., *Refractories*, New York, NY: McGraw-Hill Book Company, 1968.

Refractory News, Pittsburgh, PA: Refractories Institute [monthly].

—Paul Bodine

SIC 3259

STRUCTURAL CLAY PRODUCTS, NOT ELSEWHERE CLASSIFIED

This industry classification includes establishments engaged in the manufacture of clay sewer pipe and structural clay products, not elsewhere classified.

Between 1982 and 1988, this industry realized steady growth in shipment values, except for slight downturns in 1985 and 1987. The industry's 78 establishments shipped $133.6 million in clay products in 1982. By 1988 the value of shipments increased to $175.4 million while the total number of establishments had decreased to less than 70. Employment levels remained relatively flat over the 1980s, with a peak

employment level of 2,700 in 1984, 2,200 of whom were production workers. By 1988 this level was reduced to 2,200, 1,700 of whom were production workers. The wage structure in this industry is lower than the average in other manufacturing industries.

In selected ratios, this industry has posted consistently lower numbers than the national average in payroll, wages, value added, cost, shipments, and investments per employee and establishment in recent years. Performance is less than half the national average in investment and cost per establishment, employee, and production worker. The only ratio where this industry performed higher than the average of all manufacturing was hours per production worker.

The product share of the industry is split into three classifications. Vitrified clay sewer pipes and fittings claimed approximately 50 percent of the total product share in the late 1980s. Other structural clay products, not elsewhere classified, claimed about 35 percent and structural clay products, not specified by kind, claimed around 15 percent of the product share. Other products manufactured by this industry include liner brick for sewers, roofing tile, stove and flue lining, adobe brick, architectural terra cotta, and chimney thimbles.

Pullman Power Products Corporation of Pittsburgh, Pennsylvania, posted sales of $175 million in 1991 while employing 1,000 people. Mission Clay Products Corporation of Whittier, California, tallied an estimated $25 million while employing 300 people in 1991. Other industry leaders included Clay City Pipe Company, Boral Industries Inc. U.S. Tile Co., Superior Clay Corporation, Logan Clay Products Co., and Pacific Clay Products, Inc.

Some industry observers expect significant downsizing in this industry during the next decade. The only occupations expected to increase employment levels include extruding and forming machine operators, industrial machinery mechanics, sales workers, maintenance repairers, truck drivers, industrial production managers, and coating machine operators. Those occupations expected to face reductions are primarily in the realm of assembly/production and include assemblers, furnace operators, crushing and mixing machine operators, inspectors, hand packers, packaging machine operators, machine feeders, material movers, secretaries, cutting machine operators, general machine operators, grinders, and machine forming and machine tool cutting operators.

INDUSTRY INFORMATION SOURCES

Statistics for Industry Groups and Industries, 1991, Washington, DC: U.S. Department of Commerce, 1991.

U.S. Industrial Outlook, 1994, Washington, DC: U.S. Department of Commerce, 1994.

Ward's Business Directory of U.S. Private and Public Companies, 1994, Detroit: Gale, 1994.

—Valerie E. Wilson

SIC 3261

VITREOUS CHINA PLUMBING FIXTURES AND CHINA AND EARTHENWARE FITTINGS AND BATHROOM ACCESSORIES

This industry consists of establishments primarily engaged in manufacturing vitreous china plumbing fixtures and china and earthenware fittings and bathroom accessories. Items manufactured in this industry include flush tanks, lavatories, bidets, urinals, toilet fixtures, closet bowls, drinking fountains, and sinks. Other items include vitreous china and earthenware bolt caps, bathroom accessories, faucet handles, soap dishes, and towel bar holders.

INDUSTRY SNAPSHOT

Manufacturers of vitreous china plumbing products function in the larger plumbing industry. The industry imposes strict standards that regulate everything from the width of pipe holes to the number of gallons used in each toilet flush. The manufacture of U.S. plumbing products suffered during the recession of the late 1980s. Of 156 manufacturing industries rated by the U.S. Department of Commerce, International Trade Administration, this industry was ranked 142 in its compound annual growth rate of -3.9 percent from 1988 to 1993.

Vitreous china is a ceramic product made primarily with specially treated clays and other chemicals including feldspar and silica, then glazed and fired at high temperatures in a kiln. The vitreous product lasts forever, and does not absorb water or other materials. It is a product that changed plumbing throughout the world.

ORGANIZATION AND STRUCTURE

The vitreous china plumbing industry is driven by construction spending. Therefore, when the housing starts and remodeling trends plummeted in the 1980s, the industry suffered tremendously. Since vitreous china plumbing products are needed in both residential and commercial settings, both of those construction industries affect the industry. Foreign-trade conditions also affect the manufacturers, since imports still provide much of the plumbing ware in the United States.

Many manufacturers sell their wares only to distributors, who in turn sell the products to contractors and plumbers. Home centers, which have begun to change the way many Americans furnish or remodel their homes and businesses, have had an effect on the vitreous plumbing industry as well. For example, one large manufacturer, American Standard, sells to independent wholesalers who sell to the trade. They allow their wholesalers to sell American Standard products to home centers and other retailers. Their new line is actually being manufactured in Thailand to be sold in the United States.

Conversely, another major U.S. manufacturer, Kohler Company, still insists on selling its products only through distributors. Even Kohler employees, who receive products at a discount, must go through the middleman. Many manufacturers have begun to sell their wares directly to the home centers in order to prevent competitors from gaining too much market share.

BACKGROUND AND DEVELOPMENT

From the time civilization reached a point at which populations were centralized, plumbing has been an important concern. Typhoid fever and dysentery spread during the Industrial Revolution when sewage systems were still combined with systems for drinking water. Once separate systems were designed, different plumbing fixtures were also used to deliver drinking water and to remove waste materials from buildings.

Thomas Crapper invented the flush toilet, or water closet as it was known in England, in 1884. The mechanism he designed, with its float, valves, and arms that regulate the water in the flush tank, has remained virtually unchanged to the present. The early toilets as well as the earliest bathtubs, washbasins, and drinking fountains, were made from enameled cast iron. Vitreous china plumbing products were not introduced for several more decades.

By 1927 Walter Kohler was making vitreous china lavatories and toilets in his Wisconsin pottery operation, which emerged at that time as the third largest plumbing products company in the United States. As consumers began to customize their bathrooms, Kohler created vitreous china plumbing products in colors that matched the enameled cast iron bathtubs and accessories. In 1964 Kohler began manufacturing a self-rimming lavatory that eliminated the need for a metal frame or rim on the counter.

In the second half of the twentieth century, the American attitude toward the bathroom changed. People were spending more time there, and were using the bathroom not just for hygiene purposes, but also as a bastion of relaxation. Manufacturers also thrived as a result of the increasing numbers of bathrooms being placed in each residential setting.

CURRENT CONDITIONS

Coming out of the slump. Due to the drawn-out slump in housing starts and other new construction in the 1980s, the manufacturers of vitreous plumbing products suffered. The value of shipments of vitreous china plumbing fixtures was almost $790 million in 1992, up slightly from $786 million in 1991, but down from a high of $941 million in shipments in 1988.

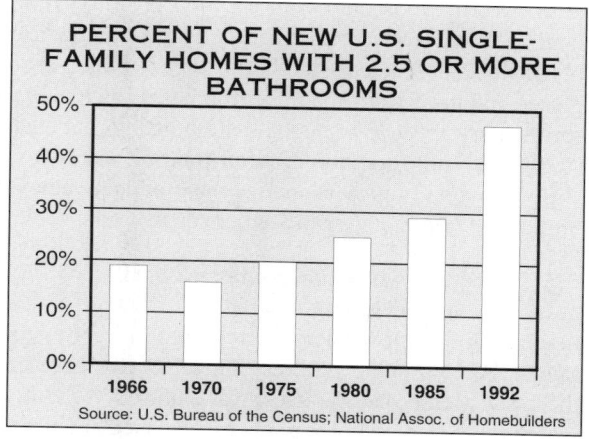

PERCENT OF NEW U.S. SINGLE-FAMILY HOMES WITH 2.5 OR MORE BATHROOMS

Source: U.S. Bureau of the Census; National Assoc. of Homebuilders

As housing starts picked up after the recession, plumbing experts believe their industry is heading toward a substantial recovery. Remodelers and do-it-yourself rehabbers contributed to their optimism. Many manufacturers began to offer their goods for sale through home centers, and some consumers saw this as an opportunity to save money in their remodeling work. There has also been a trend away from intricate luxury items and flashy colors in favor of a back-to-basics look and an emphasis on quality and value. White plumbing fixtures are offered in great number and great variety, with white shades ranging from blue-white to dark beige.

Competition from abroad and from other materials. Imports of foreign vitreous plumbing fixtures have had a harmful impact on U.S.-made products. The U.S. Bureau of the Census measured the apparent consumption of vitreous plumbing fixtures by subtracting exports from the total of imports plus manufacturers'

shipments. This apparent consumption dropped from $880,064,000 to $762,786,000 from 1990 to 1991. The percentage of imports to apparent consumption dropped from 9.1 percent to 8.8 percent. The weaker dollar made imports more difficult in the late 1980s, and made exports more affordable for foreign buyers.

In the early 1990s, the vitreous china plumbing fixtures industry had more competition than ever before from plastics. The value of shipments of plastics plumbing fixtures in 1991 was $888.4 million, while the value of shipments of vitreous plumbing fixtures in 1991 was only $675.1 million. While the compound annual growth of vitreous plumbing fixtures was -0.9 percent from 1990 to 1993, the compound annual growth of plastic plumbing fixtures rose 3.3 percent. This trend was expected to stabilize as materials technology continued to improve the flexibility of style and design in ceramics.

Environmental consciousness. Water conservation became an important issue to the industry beginning in the 1970s. Most water closets used an average of 3.5 gallons per flush (gpf). A federal bill known as the National Plumbing Products Efficiency Act (NPPEA) was signed into law at the end of 1992 as part of the Comprehensive National Energy Policy Act. The bill regulated the amount of water required per flush of a toilet or urinal. It also regulated the flow rate of showerheads and faucets. The American Society of Plumbing Engineers Research Foundation conducted field studies in the early 1990s to explore the possibility of replacing 3.5 gpf toilets with 1.6 gpf fixtures. Despite the fact that they found more clogging in the low-flow fixtures, environmental concerns overrode their criticisms, and the new U.S. code was enacted.

Manufacturers of vitreous plumbing fixtures worked with other plumbing industry advisors to coordinate low-flow products, as well as other new products that were developed in response to consumer concerns. One group of these products featured so-called universal design. These plumbing fixtures were equally accessible by wheelchair-bound and elderly consumers. Another recent trend is toward lead-free plumbing. New requirements for plumbing systems came as a response to several lawsuits involving faucets. California's 1986 law, known as Proposition 65, specified toxic substances that were prohibited from being discharged into drinking water. These changes, which required implementation of lead-free plumbing, meant that entire plumbing systems had to be reworked.

INDUSTRY LEADERS

Most major industry players derive all or most of their sales from plumbing-related products. The most recognized names in the industry in the United States are Kohler Company, which is headquartered in Wisconsin, and American Standard in New York.

Kohler employs more than 14,000 people. It's vitreous china products are manufactured in Kohler, Wisconsin; Spartanburg, South Carolina; and Brownwood, Texas. Kohler purchased Jacob Delafon, a Paris-based manufacturer in 1986, with manufacturing facilities in France, Spain, Morocco, and Egypt. Kohler also opened a vitreous china pottery facility near Monterrey, Mexico, to produce a line of mid-priced plumbing products.

American Standard and its U.S. Plumbing Co. division lead the industry. American Standard also has cultivated an overseas presence, with a holding company known as American Standard Sanitaryware in Thailand, which manufactures much of the vitreous china sold under the American Standard brand name. The company has an estimated market share of 35 to 40 percent in Thailand.

Other key manufacturers of vitreous china plumbing products in the U.S. include Gerber Plumbing Fixtures Corp. in Illinois; Masco Corp. in Indiana; Eljer Industries in Dallas, Texas; Universal-Rundle Corp. of Pennsylvania; and Briggs Industries, Inc. of Tampa, Florida. During the economic downturn of the 1980s, several manufacturers in the industry were forced out. The industry saw many mergers and acquisitions until only the leanest and most successful companies remained.

Because of intense competition, both from here and abroad, manufacturers have had to expand their product lines, innovate with new technology, cut production costs, and improve their relationships with their distributors. Advertising costs have risen as well as consumers exhibited a greater interest in the plumbing fixtures they pay for and use.

WORK FORCE

Average hourly earnings for workers in the vitreous plumbing fixtures industry, most of whom are involved in actual production, rose from $10.26 in 1987 to $12.10 in 1989, but fell to $11.96 in 1990. Wages were expected to recover slightly in the early 1990s. Many of the plants where vitreous china plumbing products are manufactured are unionized. Some belong to the Glass Molders, Pottery, Plastics and Allied Workers International Union (GPPAW), while some factories are part of the local United Auto Workers (UAW). The GPPAW publishes a health and safety manual that identifies potential workplace hazards for manufacturers of vitreous china products. Unions also negotiate wages, certain workplace standards, vacation time, and other benefits for their members.

Many workers in this industry spend their entire careers perfecting one job. Each job in production is unique, from the creation of the special clay mixture, called slip, to the packaging of the final products.

Some plants have a sliphouse, where there are machine operators, mixers, and others who must bring the raw materials to exactly the right consistency before it can be cast. Casters pour the slip into plaster of Paris molds, where it dries for a specified length of time. The porous molds draw moisture out of the slip until a shell forms the outlines of the lavatory, flush tank, or other product. If it sits too long, when the rest of the slip is poured out, the shell will be too thick to be glazed and fired. Each manufacturer has its own recipe for the slip and its own methods for casting, but each step is carefully monitored. After pouring out excess slip, casters and finishers sponge the products, removing coarse edges and seams left over from the mold.

The pottery where the fixtures are cast can be very dusty during the drying operations. During certain hours each day all workers are required to wear respirators. The plumbing fixtures, known at this point in the production process as greenware, must dry, usually overnight, before they are ready to be glazed and fired. Some glazing is still done manually by a glazer, who usually wears a protective mask. Other glazes are applied by glazing machines. In most factories, loaders place greenware onto tiered carts that can be moved from the casting room through the glazing department and directly through the kilns. Kiln operators and loaders become accustomed to the intense heat needed to vitrify the greenware. Glazes and ceramics become melded together, forming the impermeable vitreous china that is necessary for these plumbing fixtures. Kilns reach temperatures of up to 2,300 degrees Fahrenheit; the kilns are almost never shut down, as it would take close to two weeks to get them back up to firing temperature.

Once they emerge from the kiln, the fixtures are checked by inspectors and chosen by selectors. Pieces that are slightly defective are sent back for regrinding, reglazing, and refiring. Some vitreous china fixtures are then specially adorned by decorators. These must also be seen by inspectors before being sent to the packing department.

AMERICA AND THE WORLD

The manufacture of vitreous plumbing fixtures is a labor-intensive business. Costs for U.S. manufacturers have risen dramatically over the last decades, and foreign competition has increased, in part because of the low labor costs that foreign companies incur.

However, statistics charting the industry in the early 1990s show that the weaker dollar may have helped U.S. manufacturers in terms of international trade. The value of imports of vitreous plumbing fixtures in 1989 was $72.6 million. In 1990 it was $71.9 million, and in 1991 it was $64.4 million. The value of exports in 1989 was $41.1 million, rising to $54.1 million in 1990, and falling back to $46.1 million in 1991.

U.S. manufacturers have a number of other concerns as well. Certain products are used much more extensively in other countries than in the United States. Bidets, for example, which are extremely popular in Europe, are used on a limited basis in the United States.

RESEARCH AND TECHNOLOGY

Vitreous china materials and basic toilet designs have not changed significantly in the past half century. Much of the industry's research efforts have concentrated on perfecting current manufacturing methodologies. Quick-dry glazes, for instance, enable manufacturers to upgrade their rate of production. Many experiments in plumbing fixtures have gone by the wayside, while others are constantly being introduced. For example, Kohler recently introduced the Rosario Lite toilet, which flushes automatically when the user closes the lid.

Several foreign companies have proven adept in their aggressive efforts to improve their product line. Toto, one of Japan's largest plumbing products manufacturers, has introduced several new features, not yet available in the United States, for plumbing fixtures. The company's Washlet toilet features hot-water cleaning and hot-air drying. Toto's Sound Princess, developed in response to the practice of many Japanese women of flushing repeatedly during one sitting, plays a recording of flushing water so that the user does not feel compelled to flush in order to mask obtrusive noises. Japanese manufacturers also have produced toilets that send urine for medical tests. Another new product features an armrest that can simultaneously measure one's blood pressure, temperature, and pulse. As the population ages in the U.S. these features might be requested more often, and local manufacturers may begin producing them.

INDUSTRY INFORMATION SOURCES

"Bathroom Products Keep Pace With Consumer Trends," *Professional Builder & Remodeler*, March 1992: 61.

"Bold Craftsmen," Kohler, WI: Kohler Company, 1973.

Ecenbarger, William. "Flushed with success," *Chicago Tribune Magazine,* April 4, 1993: 22-29.

Hardy, Quentin. "We Can Laugh, but Once Again Japan has Forged Ahead of Us," *Wall Street Journal*, November 10, 1992: B1.

Hooper, Larry R. "Clogs cloud use of commercial '1.6' closets," *Contractor,* June 1992: 1.

"Innovative plbg., 'back to white'," *Contractor*, November 1990: 3.

Mahnke, Susan. "Kohler of Kohler of Kohler," *Wisconsin Trails,* Spring 1979.

Sefrin, Eliot. "Plumbing Suppliers Predict 'Comeback' in 1993," *Kitchen & Bath Design News*, February 1993: 20-22.

—Fran Shonfeld Sherman

SIC 3262

VITREOUS CHINA TABLE AND KITCHEN ARTICLES

This industry consists of companies that manufacture vitreous china table and kitchen articles, such as bone china, vitreous china tableware, vitreous china dishes, and china cooking ware. Manufacturers of fine earthenware table and kitchen articles are in **SIC 3263: Fine Earthenware (Whiteware) Table and Kitchen Articles.**

Manufacture of vitreous china table and kitchen articles is an anomaly in 20th-century America. It is a very labor-intensive industry, with skilled craftsmen perfecting work that has extremely high standards of quality. Modern technology has entered the industry, but in many ways, fine china and porcelain are made just as they were centuries ago.

Vitreous china is made of clays that are glazed and fired at extremely high temperatures. The temperatures cause the glaze to fuse with the clay and become nonporous. This china is both delicate and extremely durable. For this reason, it is used in hotels and restaurants more often than the semi-vitreous earthenware manufactured in **SIC 3263.**

The industry is closely tied to economic conditions because many people consider china to be a luxury. Also, since the manufacturers sell to the hotel and restaurant trade, they suffer when there is a slump in new hotel and restaurant openings. The bridal market accounts for a large percentage of sales of bone china and other vitreous china table articles, and when the bridal market suffers, so does the industry. Competition from abroad is intense. Imports account for about half of U.S. market of home ware, kitchenware, and tableware. Some U.S. manufacturers have part of the work done overseas and finish their pieces in this country.

According to the 1991 *Annual Survey of Manufacturers,* 6,000 people were employed in this industry. Of these, 4,800 worked in production. The cost of materials used by the industry was $69.9 million dollars in 1991, a decline from 1990, but the value of industry shipments rose almost $10 million to $355.6 million.

Porcelain was being made in China as early as the 9th century. Many centuries later, the Ohio River valley became the first china manufacturing center in the United States. Here manufacturers had easy access to kaolin, the soft, white clay that is essential to the manufacture of china and porcelain. This was one of the earliest industries in the country.

As consumer confidence recovered following the economic downturn in the 1980s, the industry improved. Manufacturers began to respond to consumer concerns about lead content in chinaware. California's Proposition 65 required labeling on chinaware warning consumers if a product exposed them to more than 0.5 micrograms of lead per day.

Most industry leaders have been in the business for many years. Pfaltzgraff, founded in 1811 and headquartered in York, Pennsylvannia, is said to be the oldest continuously operating pottery in the country. It is owned by a privately held company called Susquehanna Broadcasting. Pfaltzgraff purchased another well-known chinaware manufacturer, Syracuse, in 1983. Lenox China, founded in 1889 in Trenton, New Jersey, was bought by Brown-Forman in 1983. Oneida, which bought Buffalo China in 1983, was originally known for its quality flatware. Homer Laughlin was founded in 1871 in West Virginia.

Industry jobs include machine operators in the sliphouse; mold runners, casters, and jiggermen who shape and form the clay; cutters and finishers who dry and secondary shape; glaze grinders and decorators; kiln firemen and loaders; inspectors, selectors, and stampers, and packers. Average hourly wages for production workers in this industry were $11.27 in 1990. Kiln operators earned hourly wages of $6.06 to $9.26, while molders and casters earned $4.61 to $9.86 per hour.

The U.S. industry endures heavy worldwide competition, especially with Japan, Taiwan, China, and England. However, a weaker dollar has meant that exports from the United States have increased, especially to Taiwan, Canada, and Mexico, while foreign products have become more expensive, making domestic products more attractive at home.

In this industry, much of the technology is the same as it was ages ago. Many glaze recipes, clays, molds, casting, and firing processes have remained unchanged, but potters' wheels are electric and jiggerblades quickly shape the pieces. Some manufacturers were looking in new technological directions to beat foreign competitors.

Pfaltzgraff was the first in the industry to have a Dry Press system, which formed, finished, decorated, glazed, and fired china in one continuous process. It vastly increased productivity. The company also invested in a CAD/CAM system that provided 3-D images of finished china products.

INDUSTRY INFORMATION SOURCES

Altman, Seymour, and Violet Altman, *The Book of Buffalo Pottery,* Atglen, PA: Schiffer, 1987, 19-20.

Belasco, Lisa, ''How Safe are Your Dishes, Glasses, Pots & Pans?'' *Good Housekeeping,* June 1991, 199.

Bill, Andrew, ''Dining with the Masters,'' *Town & Country,* April 1991, 169-71.

''Chinamakers Pressed to Label Wares,'' *Restaurant/Hotel Design International,* January 1992, 13.

Cotter, Wes, ''Local China Factory May Get Second Life,'' *Pittsburgh Business Times,* February 17, 1992, 1.

''CRA Warns about Lead in Service Wares,'' *Nation's Restaurant News,* August 31, 1992, 21.

Durocher, Joseph, ''Fashion Plate,'' *Restaurant Business Manager,* June 10, 1992, 188-90.

''The Fine China and Crystal Story,'' Lawrenceville, NJ: Lenox China, September 1990.

Foley, Denise, ''Case of the 'Anemic' Diagnosis,'' *Prevention Magazine,* September 1991, 106-113.

''Glossary of Fine China and Crystal Terms,'' Lawrenceville, NJ: Lenox China, July 1991.

Hube, Karen, ''Makers Try to Get the Lead Out,'' *HFD, The Weekly Home Furnishings Newspaper,* February 1993, 54.

Lewis, Herschell, and Margo Lewis, *Everybody's Guide to Plate Collecting,* Chicago: Bonus Books, 1988.

Manroe, Candace Ord, ''Earth, Fire, Winds of Time,'' *Country Home,* June 1992, 44-46.

McCoy, Charles, ''California Suits Say Faucet Makers Break Toxics Law,'' *Wall Street Journal,* December 16, 1992, B8.

Nellett, Michelle, "Meet the Generations: Pfaltzgraff," *Gifts & Decorative Accessories,* April 1992, 68.

Oliver, Brian, "The China Syndrome," *Marketing,* July 11, 1991, 26-27.

Pfaltzgraff: America's Potter, York, PA: Historical Society of York County, 1989.

"Tabletop Report 1991," *HFD, The Weekly Home Furnishings Newspaper,* September 23, 1991.

—Fran Shonfeld Sherman

SIC 3263

FINE EARTHENWARE (WHITEWARE) TABLE AND KITCHEN ARTICLES

This industry consists of companies that manufacture semivitreous earthenware table and kitchen articles. These include fine semivitreous whiteware, semivitreous earthenware used for cooking and serving food, and both commercial and household earthenware. Manufacturers of vitreous china table and kitchen articles are included in **SIC 3262: Vitreous China Table and Kitchen Articles.**

Fine earthenware table and kitchen articles have been made for centuries. Earthenware is porous, coarse, and opaque, unlike vitrified porcelain and bone china, which are non-porous and translucent. All are considered to be pottery and begin with clay and other raw materials, but earthenware is fired at lower temperatures and is more breakable.

Although most of the same companies that manufacture earthenware also manufacture vitreous china, far fewer people work directly on these products. According to the 1991 *Annual Survey of Manufacturers,* 1,100 people were employed in this industry, compared with 6,000 in **SIC 3262.** Of the 1,100 workers, 900 worked in production. The value of industry shipments in 1991 was $42 million, whereas shipments of vitreous china table and kitchen articles were valued at $355.6 million.

Many styles and types of earthenware have become very popular as everyday dinnerware. Since earthenware is less expensive than bone china or other vitreous tableware, sales of it were less effected by the economic downturn of the 1980s. China and porcelain products have begun to draw more consumers, however, especially in high-income households headed by 45- to 54-year-olds. The bridal market accounts for a large percentage of retail sales of semivitreous earthenware.

In the early 1990s, manufacturers were also beginning to respond to consumer concerns about lead content in chinaware. Some manufacturers changed the recipes of their glazes to reduce the lead content. Ceramicware imported from other countries was more often to blame, since many countries did not have strict lead-content rules. California's Proposition 65 required labeling on chinaware warning consumers if a product exposes them to more than 0.5 micrograms of lead per day.

Most of the leaders in this industry are well-recognized names. Pfaltzgraff, founded in 1811 and headquartered in York, Pennsylvania, is said to be the oldest continuously operating pottery in the country. It is owned by a privately held company called Susquehanna Broadcasting. Pfaltzgraff purchased another well-known chinaware manufacturer, Syracuse, in 1983. Oneida, which bought Buffalo China in 1983, was originally known for its quality flatware. And Homer Laughlin, founded in 1871 in West Virginia, is another major private company in the industry.

Industry jobs include machine operators in the sliphouse; mold runners, casters, and jiggermen who work to shape and form the clay; cutters and finishers who dry and secondary shape the product; glaze grinders and decorators; kiln firemen and loaders; inspectors, selectors, and stampers, and packers. Average hourly wages for production workers in this industry were $11.27 in 1990. Kiln operators earned hourly wages of $6.06 to $9.26, while molders and casters earned hourly wages of $4.61 to $9.86.

Imports account for about half of the sales in earthenware and kitchenware. Foreign competition comes especially from Japan, Taiwan, China, and England. However, exports to Taiwan, Canada, and Mexico have increased in the last few years as the dollar has weakened.

The oldest form of pottery, earthenware was made in China as early as 9th century, where it was dried in the sun. Kilns have become the source of heat to fire pottery that becomes modern dinnerware, but in the industry as a whole, much of the technology is the same as it was centuries ago. Much has not changed, including the labor-intensive nature of the work, but pottery wheels are electric, and a jiggerblade can speedily shape a plate. Skilled craftsmen are still employed to manufacture products whose standards of quality are very high.

INDUSTRY INFORMATION SOURCES

Altman, Seymour, and Violet Altman, *The Book of Buffalo Pottery,* Atglen, PA: Schiffer, 1987, 19-20.

Belasco, Lisa, "How Safe are Your Dishes, Glasses, Pots & Pans?" *Good Housekeeping,* June 1991, 199.

"Chinamakers Pressed to Label Wares," *Restaurant/Hotel Design International,* January 1992, 13.

Foley, Denise, "Case of the 'Anemic' Diagnosis," *Prevention Magazine,* September 1991, 106-113.

Hube, Karen, "Makers Try to Get the Lead Out," *HFD, The Weekly Home Furnishings Newspaper,* February 1993, 54.

Lewis, Herschell, and Margo Lewis, *Everybody's Guide to Plate Collecting,* Chicago: Bonus Books, 1988.

Manroe, Candace Ord, "Earth, Fire, Winds of Time," *Country Home,* June 1992, 44-46.

McCoy, Charles, "California Suits Say Faucet Makers Break Toxics Law," *Wall Street Journal,* December 16, 1992, B8.

Nellett, Michelle, "Meet the Generations: Pfaltzgraff," *Gifts & Decorative Accessories,* April 1992, 68.

Pfaltzgraff: America's Potter, York, PA: Historical Society of York County, 1989.

Sullivan, Terry, "Plates for Guys," *Gentleman's Quarterly,* September 1992, 106.

"Tabletop Report 1991," *HFD, The Weekly Home Furnishings Newspaper,* September 23, 1991.

—Fran Shonfeld Sherman

SIC 3264

PORCELAIN ELECTRICAL SUPPLIES

This category consists of manufacturers of porcelain electronic insulators, molded porcelain parts for electrical devices, other electrical insulators, ceramic electronic and electrical supplies, and spark plug and steatitic porcelain.

Unlike other pottery-products industries, the porcelain electrical supplies industry is a high-technology industry. Only the base material, the clay, makes it similar to other pottery products. The products manufactured in this industry are ideal insulators for electrical currents because of the way they dissipate heat. The United States has the technological edge in most electronic ceramic components used in the high-performance markets.

According to the *Annual Survey of Manufacturers,* the value of product shipments in this industry rose steadily from $759.1 million in 1987, to a high of $936.5 million in 1990. Due in part to the decrease in U.S. military spending, the value of product shipments dropped to $927.4 million in 1991. Capital expenditures in this industry were quite high. New capital expenditures in 1991 were $57.1 million dollars. Of these, $50.2 million were for machinery and equipment, and only $6.9 million were spent on buildings and other structures. Despite the fact that there were fewer employees in 1991 than in 1990, new capital expenditures rose almost seven million dollars from $50.9 million.

There were 8,700 people working in the porcelain electrical supplies industry in 1991, of whom 6,700 worked in production. In 1990, there were 8,900 workers, of whom 6,900 worked in production. The small reduction in employment was attributed to the U.S. economic downturn as well as to competition from abroad. The payroll for the industry was $238.2 million in 1991, down from $241.8 million in 1990. Professional staff in the industry include inspectors, metrology and process workers, and application engineers.

Many of the companies working in this industry also make engineering supplies that are not porcelain-based. Some of the companies are small job shops making small quantities of a specific product and others are large international corporations. Brush Wellman Inc., for example, makes beryllia ceramics and beryllium alloys used as insulators for microelectronics. These products represent only about ten percent of their business.

The Adolph Coors Company, whose primary business is malt beverages, was also making technical ceramics at a separate facility until late 1992, when the brewery became a separate company. Coors Ceramics Company became a part of the holding company called ACX Technologies. SPS Technologies Inc. has a subsidiary, Arnold Engineering, which makes ferrite magnets used in DC motors in the automotive industry. Ceramics represent only about ten percent of Arnold Engineering's business. A group of advanced ceramics manufacturers and purchasers formed the United States Advanced Ceramics Association in 1985 to promote the industry.

Some of the latest technology employed by manufacturers in this industry includes dry press production equipment, automation such as computerized tool control systems and computer aided design, high volume tunnel kilns, and statistical process control that is integrated on a network. Precision operations include grinding, lapping, and polishing.

INDUSTRY INFORMATION SOURCES

Abraham, Thomas, "U.S. Advanced Ceramic Market Surges Ahead," *Ceramic Industry,* December 1990, pp. 32-35.

"Pottery Deficit Revealed," *Washington Post,* April 20, 1991, p. B1.

Robertson, Jack, ''Broken Ceramics,'' *Electronic News,* January 11, 1993, p. 8.

Stevens, Tim, ''Structures Get Smart,'' *Materials Engineering,* October 1991, pp. 18-20.

—Fran Shonfeld Sherman

SIC 3269

POTTERY PRODUCTS, NOT ELSEWHERE CLASSIFIED

This industry consists of manufacturers of art and ornamental pottery, industrial and laboratory pottery, unglazed earthenware florists' articles, earthenware table and kitchen articles, as well as those establishments primarily engaged in firing and decorating white china and earthenware for the trade.

INDUSTRY SNAPSHOT

The manufacture of pottery products, like the manufacture of vitreous china table and kitchen articles discussed in the article **SIC 3262: Vitreous China Table and Kitchen Articles,** is an anomaly in twentieth-century American industry. It is labor-intensive, and to a large extent involves machinery that has not changed much in the last half-century.

Pottery is made of clays that are mixed with other chemicals. Some pottery products are made on modern versions of potter's wheels, and some are glazed and fired at extremely high temperatures to become vitreous china. Pottery that is glazed and fired in a kiln becomes vitrified, or non-porous and glass-like, when the high temperatures cause the glaze to fuse with the clay. This china is both delicate and extremely durable. For this reason, it is used for fine giftware such as bone china figurines and lamp bases.

Some terms used in this industry can be confusing at first. Earthenware is thick, opaque, porous, and is not vitrified. China and porcelain are translucent and vitrified. Ceramics are clay products that have been molded and fired. Biscuit or bisque is the name given to ware after its first firing but before glaze has been applied.

Competition from abroad is intense in this industry. Pottery products are sold in the United States from Japanese, English, Chinese, and Spanish manufacturers, among others. Imports account for almost three quarters of the U.S. gift market. The weakened dollar has evened the tables somewhat in the last few years, enabling U.S. manufacturers to sell more of their wares in Canada, Taiwan, and Mexico.

The industry is closely tied to economic conditions, as many consumers consider art and ornamental pottery to be a luxury. Although the U.S. economy was recovering in the early 1990s, the upturn in the giftware market was slower than in other industries.

ORGANIZATION AND STRUCTURE

The manufacture of pottery products is led by several manufacturers who also create tableware and kitchenware made of vitreous china and semivitreous earthenware. Much of the equipment used by these manufacturers is the same for all of these products. Glazes and kiln temperatures vary widely, however, and the manufacturers often keep their different lines separate. Some manufacturers, for example, create their unglazed red earthenware lines in a separate plant from their semivitreous tableware lines.

The market for giftware in the form of promotional or commemorative pottery items is central for the manufacturers classified in this classification. Some of these items slid through the recession without suffering, as corporate buyers continued to purchase promotional ceramics at much the same rate.

BACKGROUND AND DEVELOPMENT

Porcelain was being made in China as early as the ninth century. By the seventeenth and eighteenth centuries fine porcelain art objects were being created in Europe as well. These objects reflected the styles of the times, and can be still seen in museums representing styles as diverse as Baroque and Rococo. When waves of immigrants traveled to the United States, they brought their crafting techniques with them. They maintained connections with their old countries through the crafts they had seen and created before leaving. In the United States in the nineteenth century, the Ohio River Valley became the first pottery manufacturing center. Here manufacturers had easy access to kaolin, the soft, white clay that is essential to the manufacture of china and porcelain. This was one of the earliest industries in the country.

The Industrial Revolution changed the manufacture of porcelain products just as it had changed other industries. Around the world, potters who had created hand-thrown ware and then painstakingly decorated their work one piece at a time, began to change the procedures they used. Mass copies of pottery objects became available at lower prices as the processes were speeded up. Some manufacturers objected to the new ways, however, and insisted on maintaining individuality and high quality in their wares.

Some of the early pottery used as homeware included salt-glazed items. Their old-fashioned, unfinished look came from the rock salt that was shoveled into the kiln while the oven was at a very high temperature. The glaze formed by the vaporized salt mixing with the clay was granular in texture and appearance.

Potters in the United States had to adapt to the changing tastes and needs of their communities late in the nineteenth century. They had to compete with increasingly available glass and tin containers, and many of them expanded their product lines to include red earthenware florists' articles and ornamental art pottery. Their flexibility was shown in the increased demand for crocks during the Prohibition era, and the emphasis on the basic flowerpots, which became the only luxury many consumers allowed themselves through World War I and the Depression. For many U.S. potteries, red clay flowerpots were the company staple for decades.

Most craftsmen at the turn of the century worked at other jobs and did their potting either as a hobby or to earn extra money. Since kilns were very expensive, and large potteries were few and far between, some kilns were purchased by entire communities. When a community had a kiln, many local craftsmen would use it by mutual arrangement with the owner.

CURRENT CONDITIONS

According to the *1991 Annual Survey of Manufacturers,* the value of shipments in the industry was $626.3 million, up from $591.7 million in 1990, $519.7 million in 1987, and only $146.9 million in 1972. These figures included the shipments of products that were primary to the industry as well as those that were secondary to the industry. Most of the value of product shipments for this industry came from art and decorative ware made either of china and porcelain, or of earthenware and stoneware.

Giftware in the 1990s was increasingly diverse. New designs of ceramic and pottery items reflected interest in the environment and in multicultural themes. Both wholesalers and retailers displayed collections of pottery and stoneware that were reminiscent of specific cultures, or that were politically correct, environmentally friendly, or both. One popular cookie jar was designed to resemble the earth, complete with raised continents. Certain traditional items, such as elegant china and earthenware figures still sold well.

During the recession of the late 1980s the giftware market suffered. Even affluent consumers who purchased art ware and other stoneware and earthenware items were becoming more price conscious. Manufacturers had to lower prices or develop newer lines to compensate for losses. However, while the retail market was sluggish, many manufacturers covered their losses by responding to increased demand for promotional giftware and tableware. In the dinnerware market (which is also covered in **SIC 3262: Vitreous China Table and Kitchen Articles,** and **SIC 3263: Fine Earthenware (Whiteware) Table and Kitchen Articles**), more than half of sales were through mass merchants and department stores.

As consumer confidence recovered following the downturn in the 1980s, the industry gained ground. Manufacturers were also beginning to respond to consumer concerns about lead content in ceramics. California's Proposition 65 required labeling on chinaware warning consumers if a product exposed them to more than 0.5 micrograms of lead per day. The increasing concern about lead content in earthenware, pottery, and other ceramics led to the establishment of the Coalition of Safe Ceramicware (CSC). In early 1992 the CSC pledged that its members complied with all of the FDA standards regarding safe levels of lead, with Proposition 65, and with the California Tableware Safety Program.

INDUSTRY LEADERS

In 1993, most of the recognized leaders in the manufacture of pottery products also manufactured fine earthenware and/or vitreous china table and kitchen products. Most industry leaders had been in the business for many years. Pfaltzgraff, founded in 1811 and headquartered in York, Pennsylvania, was recognized as the oldest continuously operating pottery in the country. It was owned by a privately held company called Susquehanna Broadcasting and operated by the fifth generation of the Pfaltzgraff family. Pfaltzgraff purchased another well-known manufacturer of pottery products, Syracuse, in 1983. In 1988, Pfaltzgraff bought Treasure Craft, a California company that was known for its giftware and household ceramic products.

Lenox China, founded in 1889 in Trenton, New Jersey, was bought by Brown-Forman in 1983. Its founder, Walter Scott Lenox, formed the Ceramic Art Company, which made table items as well as gift and art pieces including parasol handles, vases, inkstands, and thimbles. Lenox opened a new facility in 1985 in Oxford, North Carolina, expressly for the manufacture of Lenox China giftware. Other Lenox China plants were in Pomona, New Jersey, and Kinston, North Carolina.

A newer manufacturer was Beaver Falls China Company, which was formed when former employees of Mayer China Company reopened a local plant that had put about 100 skilled potters out of work when it closed in 1989. Besides making fine china for the hotel and restaurant industry (**SIC 3262: Vitreous China Table and Kitchen Articles**), the company planned to make pottery ashtrays, salt and pepper shakers, and other earthenware kitchen articles and accessories.

WORK FORCE

Many workers in this industry spend their entire careers perfecting one job. Each job in production is unique, from the creation of the special clay mixture, called slip, to the packaging of the final products. Training a potter takes many years, and most manufacturers in this industry hire production workers with the intention of investing the time required so that the workers learn the craft from top to bottom.

Some plants have a sliphouse, where there are machine operators, mixers, and others who must bring the raw materials to exactly the right consistency before it can be cast. Casters pour the slip into plaster-of-Paris molds where it dries for a specified length of time. The porous molds draw moisture out of the slip until enough of a shell forms the outlines of the product. If it sits too long, when the rest of the slip is poured out, the shell will be too thick to be glazed and fired. Each manufacturer has its own recipe for the slip and its own methods for casting, but each step is carefully monitored.

After pouring out excess slip, casters and finishers sponge the products, removing coarse edges and seams left over from the mold. In some plants, jiggermen work in shaping and forming the clay, and cutters and finishers in drying and secondary shaping. The pottery where the products are cast can be very dusty during the drying operations. During certain hours each day all workers are required to wear respirators. The pottery, then known as greenware, must dry, usually overnight, before it is ready to be glazed and fired.

Most glazing is done by a glazer, who usually wears a protective mask. Glazes are sprayed onto once piece at a time. The industry is still quite labor-intensive. Some glazes are applied by glazing machines. In most factories, loaders place greenware onto tiered carts that can be moved from the casting room through the glazing department and directly through the kilns. Kiln operators and loaders get used to the intense heat needed to vitrify the greenware. Glazes and ceramics become melded together, forming the impermeable vitreous china that is necessary for these plumbing fixtures. Kilns reach temperatures of up to 2,300 degrees Fahrenheit, and therefore are almost never shut down, since it would take close to two weeks to get them back up to firing temperature.

Once they emerge from the kiln, the products are checked by inspectors and chosen by selectors. Pieces that are slightly defective are sent back for regrinding, reglazing, and refiring. Many items, especially in giftware, are then specially adorned by decorators. These must also be seen by inspectors before being sent to the packing department.

The manufacturers also have support departments, including machine shops where machinery can be repaired or cleaned, mold departments, where plaster molds are made and repaired, and warehouses that handle shipping and receiving. They also have administrative departments covering human resources, public relations, corporate development, and other general business needs.

In the early 1990s, many of the plants where pottery products were manufactured were unionized. Some of the organized workers belonged to the Glass Molders, Pottery, Plastics and Allied Workers International Union (GPPAW). At this time, the GPPAW published a health and safety manual that identified potential workplace hazards for manufacturers of dinnerware, chinaware, and other pottery products. This and other unions were also active in negotiating wages, certain workplace standards, vacation time, and other benefits for their members.

According to the *1991 Annual Survey of Manufactures* published by the U.S. Bureau of the Census, 12,500 people worked in the pottery products industry represented by the SIC code 3269. Of these, 9,900 worked in production. According to the *1987 Census of Manufacturers,* there were only 10,500 people working in the industry. The average hourly wage for production workers in 1990 was $11.27. The wages rose from $7.06 in 1987, $5.96 in 1982, and $3.87 in 1977. In the early 1990s kiln operators earned hourly wages of $6.06 to $9.26, while molders and casters earned $4.61 to $9.86 per hour.

AMERICA AND THE WORLD

As it entered the 1990s, the United States was in heavy world competition in this industry, especially with Japan, Taiwan, China, and England. However, the weaker dollar at this time meant that exports from the United States increased, especially to Taiwan, Canada, and Mexico, while foreign products have become more expensive, and made domestic products more attractive at home.

U.S. potteries tried to capitalize on the desire of local consumers to buy products made in their country. They tried to keep close tabs on marketplace trends and to respond with items the American consumers would want. The new Beaver Falls China Company planned to stamp all of their wares "Made in Pennsylvania USA."

RESEARCH AND TECHNOLOGY

In this industry, much of the technology employed in 1993 was the same as it was ages ago. The factories in the early twentieth century used more machinery to produce more pottery, but the essentials remained. For example, hand-throwing techniques were supplemented with hand-jigger machines. Today's potter's wheel is electric, and a jiggerblade is usually used to speedily shape a plate. Salt glazing was gradually replaced by dip-glazing, in which the ware was dipped before firing. In some plants, pottery is currently glazed automatically, while in others, glazers spray glaze onto only one item at a time. Only slight changes have been made in the recipes for clays, the shape and type of molds, casting methods, and firing techniques.

Some manufacturers were looking in new technological directions to keep foreign competitors at bay. Pfaltzgraff was the first in the industry to have a dry press system, which formed, finished, decorated, glazed, and fired pottery products in one continuous process. It vastly increased productivity, especially for plates and small bowls. The company also invested in a CAD/CAM system that provided 3-D images of finished products so that problems could be anticipated and corrected before production began.

The larger changes for the pottery products industry were in the general way business was conducted. In order to survive, these small, family-owned potteries had to become businesses that competed not only in the national but also the international market. It was no longer enough to make a quality product. Manufacturers also had to market and sell their wares, create new innovations, and pass on to a new generation of potters the desire to keep this age-old craft thriving.

INDUSTRY INFORMATION SOURCES

Bill, Andrew. "Dining with the Masters. " *Town and Country,* April 1991, pp. 169-71.

"Ceramicware Group: Makers Meet Lead Norms." *HFD: The Weekly Home Furnishings Newspaper,* March 16, 1992, p. 97.

Cotter, Wes. "Local China Factory May Get Second Life." *Pittsburgh Business Times,* February 17, 1992, p. 1.

The Fine China and Crystal Story. Lawrenceville, NJ: Lenox China, September 1990.

"Gifts, Tableware, Novelties." *Hardware Age,* December 1992, p. 53.

Glossary of Fine China and Crystal Terms. Lawrenceville, NJ: Lenox China, July 1991.

Manroe, Candace Ord. "Earth, Fire, Winds of Time." *Country Home,* June 1992, pp. 44-46.

Nellett, Michelle. "Meet the Generations: Pfaltzgraff." *Gifts and Decorative Accessories,* April 1992, p. 68.

Oliver, Brian. "The China Syndrome." *Marketing,* July 11, 1991, pp. 26-27.

Pfaltzgraff: America's Potter. York, PA: Historical Society of York County, 1989.

"Tabletop Report 1991." *HFD: The Weekly Home Furnishings Newspaper,* September 23, 1991.

—Fran Shonfeld Sherman

SIC 3271

CONCRETE BLOCK AND BRICK

This category covers establishments engaged in manufacturing concrete building block and brick from a combination of cement and aggregate. Contractors engaged in concrete construction work are classified in the construction segments of major groups for building construction—general contractors and operative builders, for heavy construction other than building construction—contractors, and for construction—special trade contractors, while establishments primarily engaged in mixing and delivering ready-mixed concrete are classified in **SIC 3273: Ready-Mixed Concrete.**

In 1992 the concrete block and brick industry had approximately 17,000 employees and the establishments in the industry shipped products with a total value of $2.1 billion. The 17,800 employees in the industry in 1991 earned a total of $461.8 million, for an average of $25,944 per year per employee. The 9,900 production workers earned an average of $10.07 per hour that year. Although the industry has had slow and fluctuating growth in the 1980s and early 1990s, the part of the market which is expected to be strong in the latter 1990s is the public works segment which should be helpful to the concrete block and brick industry.

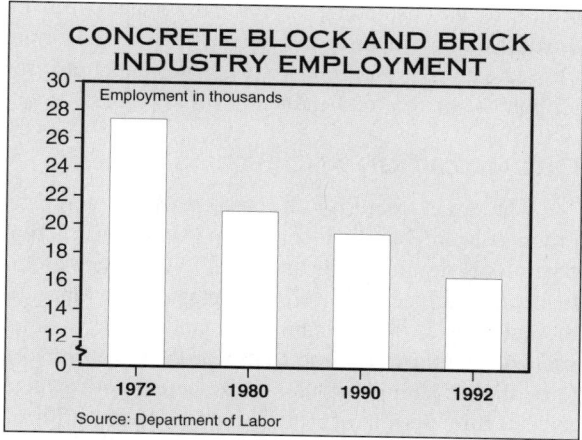

CONCRETE BLOCK AND BRICK INDUSTRY EMPLOYMENT

Employment in thousands

1972 1980 1990 1992

Source: Department of Labor

The first solid concrete block patent was granted in 1832 and the first hollow concrete building block patent was in 1850, both in England. Harmon S. Palmer patented a concrete block machine in 1900 in the United States. Since then, the concrete block has continued to increase in popularity because of the product's durability and economy. The industry has also advanced in terms of product quality, production and distribution methods, and installation procedures. Concrete's fire safety compared to that of wood has been a major factor in its appeal. In the early days, small concrete manufacturing facilities sprouted up rapidly in most urban areas in the United States because they needed to be located near their users' destinations. A block machine could be bought for $100 in 1906, and the business opportunities appealed to entrepreneurial instincts.

The National Concrete Masonry Association (NCMA) was an affiliate of the Portland Cement Association in the 1930s. The NCMA became independent in 1942 and has since supported concrete block producers, machinery manufacturers, and related interests. Since its founding, the NCMA has conducted research and testing on concrete block products and structures.

Establishments in this industry tend to be relatively small, local operations, since it is generally not economical to ship concrete block and brick more than 50 miles because of its weight. For this reason, companies in the industry have grown by organizing or purchasing added concrete block and brick production operations in new areas.

Another factor in the structure of the industry is that most of the companies which produce concrete block and brick also produce other concrete related products, including ready-mixed concrete, concrete pipe, or various precast or prestressed products, such as building structural parts, which can be fabricated

centrally and shipped the locations where they will be installed.

Most concrete block and brick establishments have one or more competitors in their areas, and they compete on matters such as price, location, service, quality, and reliability. They also compete with other building products such as lumber, clay brick, and steel.

The concrete block and brick industry's major expenditures in 1991 were employee compensation $547.3 million; materials 1,072.6 million; fuel 42.9 million; and capital expenditures 48.8 million. While the industry's employment increased 20 percent (15,500 to 118,600) between 1982 and 1987, the number of companies dropped six percent (1,039 to 976), indicating the trend toward mergers and larger, though fewer, companies. In 1987 the annual sales average for the companies in the industry was $2.3 million, and these companies on the average had 19 employees.

None of the larger companies in the concrete industries has concrete block and brick as the primary product line. These larger companies produce concrete block as one part of a group of products in the concrete and other construction related fields. Two of the leading concrete block and brick producers have been Zurn Constructors, Inc. and Concrete Pipe & Products Co., Inc.

Zurn Constructors, Inc. had 500 employees and annual sales at the rate of $160 million in 1992. Its primary field was heavy construction, and concrete block and brick were its secondary product line with plastics pipe as its third area of business. It has been a subsidiary of Zurn Industries Inc., also headquartered in Erie, Pennsylvania, which has been involved in power plant construction, steam generators, and water and air purification systems.

Concrete Pipe & Products Co., Inc.'s sales in 1992 were at the annual rate of $90 million and its employees numbered 850. The company's primary product line is concrete products, except block and brick, and its secondary line is concrete block and brick. It also conducts a wholesale business in construction materials. Concrete Pipe was founded in 1925 and is based in Richmond, Virginia. The company has expanded by many acquisitions since its founding, and has acquired product and process patents which helped further its growth.

Research has continued in the 1990s to improve the characteristics of concrete block as well as to make possible different features to fit varying users' needs and desires. New exterior appearance attributes have been developed such as ribbed, fluted, and split-faced surfaces which have met the needs of innovative architects for the walls of buildings. Blocks of lighter weight have been created by mixing different raw material aggregates with the cement and water. And new uses have been found for concrete blocks, such as in a drainage system. Research has also been conducted in ways in which concrete block might be constructed automatically into building walls.

INDUSTRY INFORMATION SOURCES

Annual Survey of Manufactures Statistics for Industry Groups and Industries, Washington, DC: U.S. Department of Commerce, 1991.

Census of Manufactures Concrete, Plaster, and Cut Stone Products, Washington, DC: U.S. Department of Commerce, 1987.

Nilson, Arthur H., and George Winter, *Design of Concrete Structures,* New York: McGraw-Hill, 1986.

—Douglas B. Hoyt

SIC 3272

CONCRETE PRODUCTS, EXCEPT BLOCK AND BRICK

This category covers establishments primarily engaged in manufacturing concrete products, except block and brick, from a combination of cement and aggregate. Contractors engaged in concrete construction work are classified in the Construction industries, and establishments primarily engaged in mixing and delivering ready-mixed concrete are classified in **SIC 3273: Ready-Mixed Concrete.**

INDUSTRY SNAPSHOT

The products included in this industry were made of concrete, formed and hardened at the cement facility, and shipped in finished form to customers or users. Many of the items were prefabricated parts to be assembled into buildings, bridges, or parking structures. Pipe was another major segment of the industry. Other products included a variety of utilitarian and decorative items, such as burial vaults, septic tanks, monuments, and bird baths.

In contrast to products that were poured on-site, the products of this industry were made in a controlled environment, away from a construction job site. Such controlled production conditions enabled concrete products to be made more structurally sound and in accordance with construction specifications.

In 1991 the concrete products industry employed 61,000 people and shipped products valued at $5.5 billion to its customers. In 1987 the states with the greatest employment in the industry were California, Florida, Pennsylvania, and Texas, which accounted for 35 percent of the total industry employment.

ORGANIZATION AND STRUCTURE

The great majority of customers for concrete products were building contractors and construction firms. This required industry firms to deal with architects and engineers as well as management. Many of the industry's sales comprised standard or off-the-shelf items that were produced, warehoused, and sold to multiple customers. Other items were tailor-made to the specific design of particular buildings, bridges, parking structures, or other facilities. Where products made of plastic or lumber were possible alternatives, precast concrete products were sometimes preferred and selected for environmental reasons.

Companies in the industry tended to grow by acquisitions and mergers. The greater size enabled the companies to spread their marketing, research, and engineering costs over a larger number of activities. Industry firms also joined to form several trade groups, which generally conducted research into materials and methods to improve the products, performed promotion of the product specialty, and represented the industry in governmental matters. These associations included the American Concrete Institute, the American Concrete Pressure Pipe Association, the Concrete Reinforcing Steel Institute, the Post-Tensioning Institute, the Portland Cement Association, the American Segmental Bridge Institute, and the Precast/Prestressed Concrete Institute.

Industry firms continually conducted research to improve the qualities of concrete products. Areas of focus included workability, strength, durability, weight, and insulating ability. Minimum quality standards were established by the American Society for Testing and Materials (ASTM), and were continuously modified as technology developed and changed.

BACKGROUND AND DEVELOPMENT

Concrete was made by mixing together cement, sand, gravel, possibly other aggregates, and water. The concrete then was molded and might be reinforced in a variety of ways to meet its different purposes. Molds were made of wood, fiberglass, concrete, or other materials. Precast concrete was poured into molds of the desired product shapes, in which it was hardened and cured. Reinforced concrete was strengthened by inserting steel rods or mixing in fibers. Prestressed concrete had steel wires or rods inserted and stretched so as to compress the concrete and make it resist tensile stresses. Other qualities of concrete were modified by use of different types of sand, gravel, crushed stone, and cement in differing proportions. All of these factors affected the properties relating to its strength, durability, workability, curing time, resistance to temperature and humidity changes, and appearance.

CURRENT CONDITIONS

In 1967 there were 2,687 companies in the concrete products industry, employing 70,000 workers and shipping products valued at $5.8 billion. By 1982 there were 2,749 companies, employing 20 percent fewer employees and shipping 39 percent less product value. In 1991 the industry purchased $2.7 billion worth of materials and made new capital expenditures amounting to $153 million.

The concrete products industry often experienced cyclical changes along with the construction industries on which it largely depended. The industry's business fluctuations were most apparent in the total number of employees. For example, the industry stood at 58,000 workers in 1975; 66,000 in 1979; 54,200 in 1983; 70,000 in 1987; and 61,000 in 1991.

In the 1990s, analysts predicted that U.S. infrastructure needs would foster a substantial demand for specialized concrete products. For example, a 1992 review judged many of the 600,000 bridges in the Federal Highway Administration's jurisdiction as requiring either replacement or significant repairs. The water distribution system in New York City also broke and caused frequent flood conditions in the 1980s and early 1990s. In response to increased demand, the concrete products industry was expected to continue to enhance concrete's qualities and usefulness through engineering improvements.

INDUSTRY LEADERS

Ameron Inc.'s principal product lines were readymixed concrete, concrete products except block and brick, and concrete block and brick. Started in 1907, the company posted 1992 sales of $465 million with 3,000 workers. Ameron considered itself a leader in pipe technology and was a major pipe supplier in the western United States, with plants in California, Arizona, and Oregon. It also managed pipe manufacturing operations in Colombia and Saudi Arabia.

Based in Atlanta, Georgia, CSR Construction Materials USA Inc. had 2,000 employees and $202 million in sales in 1992, entirely from specialty concrete products. It was a subsidiary of CSR America Inc., also based in Atlanta, which in turn was owned by CSR Limited of Australia, which made and sold building materials and other products throughout Asia, the United Kingdom, Australia, and the United States.

Boral Concrete Products Inc., headquartered in San Bernadino, California, was a subsidiary of Boral Industries Inc. of Ontario. Boral Concrete had sales of $100 million and 500 employees in 1992. Its primary product category was concrete roofing tiles and slabs. Boral Limited was a global concern doing business in 23 countries, mostly in building materials and energy, with 1993 sales exceeding $4 billion.

North Star Concrete Inc., a subsidiary of Condux Corp., was headquartered in St. Paul, Minnesota. The company's 1992 sales were $70 million, and it had 500 employees. Founded in 1988, the company's facilities and marketing area were located in the midwest and eastern parts of the United States.

Spancrete Industries Inc. specialized in a precast, prestressed, hollow core plank or slab that was widely used for floors, roofs, and walls. These planks were made in a variety of shapes and sizes to fit the individual users' needs. The Spancrete process was based on a machine bought in Germany in 1953 by the company's founder. Subsequently, the machines were made and sold by a subsidiary of Spancrete Industries, and their use was supported by an association of companies that purchased the machines under a licensing agreement. Spancrete Industries was based in Milwaukee, Wisconsin, and had 1992 sales of $53 million with 420 employees.

WORK FORCE

The concrete products industry employed 61,000 people in 1991 and earned a total of $1.4 billion, for an average of $23,062 per employee. Almost 74 percent of the industry employees were hourly workers, who earned an average of $9.56 per hour. The industry's white collar jobs encompassed accounting, engineering, estimating, marketing, and management.

RESEARCH AND TECHNOLOGY

Industry firms conducted continuous research throughout the twentieth century to enhance the qualities of concrete products and construction operations and to improve the methods for producing and delivering concrete. Some of the advancements were made by businessmen and managers, as with the adaptation of trucks for deliveries and mixing in the early part of the century.

More and more, dramatic improvements in the strength and other qualities of concrete were made by scientific, engineering, and chemical research and analyses. Technicians in these specialties combined steel with concrete to enable its use in large bridge and skyscraper structural elements, as well as applied computers and automation to control and mix raw material ingredients accurately. Many studies and tests were conducted to determine the effects of different material ingredients, and varying proportions of those ingredients, in producing desired new concrete qualities. These scientific activities were performed by both individual companies—each hoping to improve its own competitive position—and industry supported trade associations and institutes.

The industry's engineers had to make significant efforts to comply with increasingly strict governmental regulations on pollution and other environmental matters. Some of the environmental controls led to changes with other benefits—for example, utilizing used tires as fuel proved cheaper and produced less pollution than other fuels, in addition to reducing unsightly dumps and land fills.

INDUSTRY INFORMATION SOURCES

Annual Survey of Manufactures Statistics for Industry Groups and Industries, Washington, DC: U.S. Department of Commerce, 1991.

Census of Manufactures: Concrete, Plaster, and Cut Stone Products, Washington, DC: U.S. Department of Commerce, 1987.

''Concrete Today—An ENR Special Advertising Section,'' *Engineering News-Record,* May 3, 1993.

The ENR Directory of Construction Information Services, New York: McGraw-Hill, 1993.

Nilson, Arthur H., and George Winter, *Design of Concrete Structures,* New York: McGraw-Hill, 1986.

Waddell, J. J., *Concrete Construction Handbook,* New York: McGraw-Hill, 1968.

—Douglas B. Hoyt

SIC 3273

READY-MIXED CONCRETE

This category covers establishments primarily engaged in manufacturing portland cement concrete manufactured and delivered to a purchaser in a plastic and unhardened state. This industry includes production and sale of central-mixed concrete, shrink-mixed concrete, and truck-mixed concrete.

INDUSTRY SNAPSHOT

A material similar to stone, concrete is made by mixing selected proportions and qualities of cement, sand, gravel, and sometimes other aggregates. Water is added and the soft mixture is formed into shapes of the products desired. Water and cement interact chemically to form a solid mass, binding the ingredient particles together, but the mixture remains soft so that it can be shaped before the cement hardens.

Concrete was a leading material resource for building construction and for various products because of its strength, ability to be molded into any shape, resistance to fire and weather, and because of the availability of materials from which it is made. Concrete's limited strength under tensile stress was substantially overcome by reinforcement with steel and other materials in various ways.

Concrete businesses in the early 1990s furnished much of the basic resources for the construction industries, as well as for road pavements and utilitarian and artistic products like railroad ties and birdbaths. A few of the larger construction contractors manufactured their own concrete materials and products, while others relied on concrete producers to provide the concrete and concrete products they needed.

The ready-mixed concrete industry included businesses that made concrete and delivered it to contractors or other customers for constructing buildings, bridges, roads, sidewalks, or other facilities. The concrete production process involved the use of large scale equipment and machinery located reasonably near to where the concrete was to be used, so that the concrete could be delivered while it was still soft enough to be shaped.

The concrete ready-mixed industry was heavily dependent on its primary customers, which were constructors of homes, industrial and office buildings, highways, and bridges. Consequently, the industry's market generally shadows the cyclical markets served by construction industries. For example, in the early 1990s the market for public works construction was strong while the other building markets were weak. Concrete industries were developing new technologies in the 1980s and 1990s to make concrete building parts stronger and more attractive, which helped the industry to reinforce its market in the construction industries.

In 1991 the ready-mixed concrete industry employed 86,100 people, and shipped products valued at $11.68 billion. The principal states in the industry in 1987 were California, Texas, Florida, and Arizona, which accounted for 31 percent of the industry's employment.

ORGANIZATION AND STRUCTURE

Many ready-mixed concrete companies were relatively small, having customers in one community or a limited region, primarily because soft concrete cannot be delivered beyond about 20 miles from where it is made. Yet to produce the concrete economically requires considerable expenditures for plant and trucking facilities. Most concrete plants were fixed, but some were portable and could be moved close to sites where major construction was to be done. Many of the larger companies have grown by expanding to larger territories as well as by buying smaller local firms. In 1987 there were 3,749 companies in the industry. Each employed an average of 25.8 workers and recorded $3.5 million in sales.

Most of the ready-mixed concrete producers also were involved in related concrete businesses, such as the mining of sand and gravel, the production of crushed stone, cement manufacture, or the manufacture of concrete blocks, pipe, building structural elements, and other concrete products.

Most industry establishments competed against several concrete businesses in a small market area. In addition, several non-concrete products substituted for concrete provided another arena of competition. These alternative resources included lumber, asphalt, brick, and steel.

The National Ready-Mixed Concrete Association (NRMCA) was the primary trade group supporting the industry. Headquartered near Washington, DC, the NRMCA helped its more than 1,000 members by fostering research, training, and product promotion programs, and by representing the industry before federal and professional groups. The NRMCA worked with many other trade associations in the ready-mixed concrete industry including the Portland Cement Association (PCA), the American Concrete Pavement Association (ACPA), the Concrete Reinforcing Steel Institute (CRSI), the Post-Tensioning Institute (PTI), and the American Concrete Institute (ACI).

The American Society for Testing and Materials began providing guidelines for the manufacture and testing of concrete products in 1933. Throughout its existence, the organization continued to revise its specifications as the ready-mixed concrete industry, and the technology it utilized, evolved. These specifications reflected the responsibilities of the various agents concerned, such as concrete manufacturers, contractors, engineers, and owners. Additional organizations, including the American Concrete Institute (ACI) and the National Ready Mixed Concrete Association (NRMCA), published other specifications.

BACKGROUND AND DEVELOPMENT

Though the first use of concrete dates back many centuries, widespread usage did not occur until the 19th century, when improvements in the materials combined to form the cement ingredient were made. In the 20th century, reinforcement techniques were developed that made cement structural components for skyscrapers and large bridges over highways and rivers practical. The development of trucks equipped to mix concrete in transit in the 1920s made it possible for the ready-mixed approach to become the dominant process for concrete usage by the 1990s.

Portland cement was invented in 1824 by Joseph Aspdin, a British engineer, and had strength and water resistance qualities superior to those of previous cements. Limestone and clay were portland cement's principal ingredients. These raw materials were ground finely, combined, and heated in a kiln to form clinkers, which are then pulverized. The name portland came from the Isle of Portland, where limestone was quarried. Portland cement was the primary type of cement used from its origination.

In 1909 concrete was first mixed in transit in a horse drawn wagon with gears from the wheels activating paddles in the mixing process. In 1913 concrete was taken to the work site in a dump truck. The first company to market a revolving horizontal drum mixer was the Paris Mixer Company in 1926. Between 1925 and 1930, the number of ready-mixed concrete plants in the United States increased from 25 to 100. The National Ready Mixed Concrete Association was formed in 1930 and helped to foster the rapid growth of the industry.

Concrete, like stone, has very good compressive strength; it withstands considerable pressure from above without crumbling. However, concrete does not have great tensile strength. A concrete beam between two posts will crack if too much pressure is placed in the middle of the beam. To overcome the tensile limitation, steel rods were placed in the concrete before it hardened, reinforcing its tensile strength. Reinforcing concrete techniques were begun in the first decade of the 20th century. Pre-stressed concrete can withstand even greater tensile stresses by stretching rods or wires before the concrete hardens around them. The released wires or rods then compress the concrete itself, providing additional tensile strength. Pre-stressed technology enabled cement to be used in much greater spans, covering distances required in the construction of larger scale buildings and bridges.

Between 1977 and 1987, the number of employees in the industry increased from 87,900 to 96,900, while the number of companies decreased from 4,317 to 3,749, reflecting a number of acquisitions and mergers.

CURRENT CONDITIONS

Many of the larger ready-mixed concrete companies benefitted from centralized purchasing, marketing, and engineering operations. Many were involved in manufacturing fields related to concrete production, such as making concrete pipe, railroad ties, and construction structural elements. Because of the benefits of size, it was expected that the trend toward larger companies in the industry would continue.

There was steady improvement in the durability, appearance, and other qualities of ready-mixed concrete. Lower production costs and greater quality control also were achieved. These advancements were spurred by competitive forces and aided by the many trade groups conducting research and providing training.

INDUSTRY LEADERS

Lafarge Corp. recorded $1.5 billion in sales in 1992. Headquartered in Reston, Virginia, the company had 7,600 employees in 1992. In 1993 the company operated 15 cement plants, 90 distribution terminals, and 450 construction materials facilities. It was one of the biggest producers of ready-mixed concrete and aggregates in the United States. A 1993 restructuring program consolidated 11 regional units down to six. In 1994 Lafarge was organized into separate geographic divisions. The western and eastern regions were headquartered in Canada. Lafarge's principal stockholder was Lafarge Coppée in Paris, France. The company pioneered innovative cost reduction techniques, using scrap tires for fuel and industrial by-products, such as ash, foundry sands, and paper sludge, for alternative raw materials.

Founded in 1909 and headquartered in Birmingham, Alabama, Vulcan Materials Company had 6,400 employees and annual sales of $1.1 billion in 1992. It was engaged in the mining of construction sand and gravel, the production of crushed limestone, and in the manufacture of ready-mixed concrete, concrete pipe, and several chemical materials. Sixty-four percent of the company's sales was generated by the production of construction materials. The company focused its marketing efforts in the southeastern United States. Its facilities included 129 stone quarries, 13 sand and gravel pits, three slag plants, seven ready-mixed concrete plants, and 19 asphalt plants. The company increased its size through a variety of small acquisitions and a few larger mergers. It also became the country's

largest producer of crushed stone. Ready-mixed concrete sales in 1992 were $12.4 million.

Texas Industries Inc. posted $614 million in sales in 1993 exclusively through the production of steel, cement, and concrete materials and products. Although about two-thirds of these sales were generated by steel products, the balance embraced the full range of concrete products, including sand and gravel, portland cement, ready-mixed concrete, concrete block and brick, pipe, pre-stressed concrete products, and architectural pre-cast concrete panels. Headquartered in Dallas, the company employed 2,700 workers in 1993. It operated one steel mill, 29 ready-mixed concrete plants, and two cement plants in Texas, as well as 13 sand and gravel mine operations, most of which were located in Texas.

Ameron Inc., founded in 1906, was based in Monterey Park, California. The company employed 3,000 workers and reported $465 million in sales in 1992. Ameron's leading product was ready-mixed concrete, followed by other concrete products and concrete blocks. The company also manufactured paints and varnishes, non-cement pipe products, and mined sand.

Florida Rock Industries Inc.'s largest business segment was ready-mixed concrete, but its other primary businesses included a wide range of mining, quarrying, and processing of raw materials for concrete, as well as the sale of various types of sand and stone for use in concrete manufacture. The company also produced concrete block, pre-stressed concrete, and other construction materials. Founded in 1931 and headquartered in Jacksonville, Florida, the company recorded $294 million in sales and employed 2,385 people. In 1993 the company operated 82 ready-mix concrete facilities, 12 concrete block plants, and owned 838 ready-mix and block delivery trucks. Most of its operations and customers were in the southeastern United States, especially Florida, Georgia, Virginia, Maryland, North Carolina, and Washington, D.C.

Lone Star Industries Inc. was formed in 1919. Its 1993 sales of $240 million was almost entirely produced through the sale of concrete-related products. Portland cement was its primary product, followed by ready-mixed concrete, then concrete blocks and other products such as pipe and pre-stressed concrete products. The company also mined for sand and gravel. Based in Stamford, Connecticut, the company employed about 1,600 people in 1993, of which some 1,000 were union members. The company operated facilities throughout the United States and in Canada and Brazil. With 15 cement plants, 17 aggregate plants and quarries, 36 ready-mixed and other concrete products plants, Lone Star generated $30.8 million in ready-mixed concrete sales in 1992. A leading producer of cement in the United States, the company had difficulties resulting from depressed prices for cement in the 1980s. In 1990, the company filed for protection from its creditors under Chapter 11 of the Federal Bankruptcy Code and in 1994 recovered from the bankruptcy process.

WORK FORCE

Most of the employees in the ready-mixed concrete industry were production workers. Larger companies and many smaller companies used computers not only for accounting but for controlling the processes of concrete mixing and other production operations. The larger companies in particular employed skilled engineers to help refine mixing and production processes.

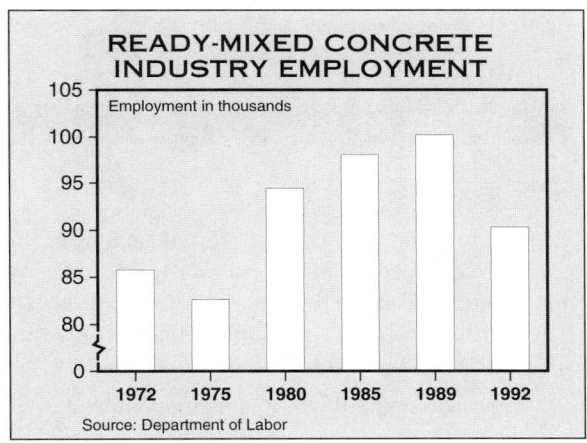

READY-MIXED CONCRETE INDUSTRY EMPLOYMENT

Employment in thousands

Source: Department of Labor

The 86,100 employees in the industry in 1991 earned a total of $2.24 billion in wages, for an average of $26,052 per year per employee. The 62,800 production workers earned an average of $11.19 per hour that year.

AMERICA AND THE WORLD

The principal international relationships of the ready-mixed concrete industry have been that some of the raw materials have been received from overseas, some operations in the United States have been foreign owned, and some American companies have had facilities that produce concrete in other countries.

Concrete transactions between countries were somewhat limited by the fact that ready-mixed concrete production and sales were local operations. Also, hardened concrete products, like pipe and concrete block, were prohibitively expensive to ship overseas because of their weight. However, there have been significant cases of international ownership of ready-mixed and other concrete operations.

In the 1980s, cement from foreign sources filled over 15 percent of U.S. needs. The chairman of Lone Star Industries, Inc. made an effort to achieve restraints against the increasing presence of imported cement. Failing in his bid to reduce import levels, Lone Star then became the largest importer of cement. By 1992, imported cement had dropped to eight percent of consumption in the United States.

Many U.S. cement companies were acquired by foreign interests because reduced profits had made them vulnerable to takeovers. More than 65 percent of U.S. cement production facilities were acquired by foreign interests. The two largest cement producing companies in the United States were foreign owned.

Lafarge Corporation, the largest cement producer in North America and a major manufacturer of ready-mixed concrete, was a subsidiary of a French construction company, Lafarge Coppée. Lafarge Coppée was a major building materials company operating in 35 countries and with sales of $5.8 billion in 1992. Lafarge Corporation reorganized its structure in 1993 into six regional territories. Four of these six regions were headquartered in Canada.

RESEARCH AND TECHNOLOGY

With keen competition forcing ready-mixed concrete companies to improve service and cut costs, many of the larger companies looked toward research and technology to improve the quality of concrete products and reduce their production costs. Lafarge Corporation, for example, used scrap tires as a fuel, which removed the tires from unsightly dumps and reduced detrimental air emissions since tires burn more efficiently than most coals. Lafarge also used industrial by-products such as used refractory bricks and iron mill scale as low cost raw materials for concrete.

For years concrete producers and industry groups endeavored to improve concrete's strength, durability, uniformity, appearance, drying time, and weight. By the early 1990s, concrete's compression strength had been increased to withstand 20,000 pounds per square inch (psi), while laboratory experiments reached the strength of 100,000 psi. In the 1960s, 5,800 psi was considered to be high-strength concrete.

The American Society of Civil Engineers established the Civil Engineering Research Council (CERC) to spearhead a program of construction product improvements the society considers to be essential to meet infrastructure needs for the 21st century. The CERC developed plans to work with government, industry, and trade groups in designing and perfecting higher strength concrete.

Other research was conducted to create new types of concrete that would enable their use in products previously made from ceramics, plastic, or aluminum. Lone Star developed a new product named Pyrament that dried quickly enough to allow traffic on a road four hours after the concrete was laid. Greater strength to weight ratios and improved ability to absorb energy were achieved by incorporating reinforcing materials such as wood, glass, carbon, or steel into concrete.

Computer hardware and software were used by ready-mixed concrete manufacturers in a variety of ways, and also to prepare job estimates, control production processes, and schedule deliveries. In the late 1980s, the major ready-mixed concrete producer located in Seattle, Washington, Lakeside Sand and Gravel, instituted an efficiency and productivity improvement program that included many computer applications, such as computerized vehicle maintenance, dispatching, and an aggregate handling process.

In the late 1980s, Raia Industries Inc., based in Hackensack, New Jersey, applied Command Data software to help control the manufacturing and delivery of concrete. A 200 to 300 percent increase in productivity was reported from the computer system which delivered ingredients, monitored processing operations and moisture content, and also helped to load the trucks.

A faculty member of the Southern Illinois University designed an easy computer program for small concrete contractors to use in preparing estimates. With this program, the contractor entered the quantities of materials needed for a job, then the program applied the unit prices and produced a complete concrete estimate for the customer with all the costs and specifications clearly itemized.

Ready-mixed concrete companies as well as trade groups were continuously seeking more efficient manufacturing and processing approaches. Examples included enabling longer delivery span, reducing truck and equipment maintenance costs, facilitating filling of bags, and automated setting of concrete curbs.

In the late 1980s, Master Builders Inc. developed a technology that slowed the hardening process in the formation of concrete, thus enabling it to be transported over longer periods of time and distances. This technique was called the DELVO system, and was said

not to be detrimental to the strength or other concrete characteristics.

INDUSTRY INFORMATION SOURCES

Annual Survey of Manufactures Statistics for Industry Groups and Industries, Washington: U.S. Department of Commerce, 1991.

Census of Manufactures Concrete, Plaster, and Cut Stone Products, Washington: U.S. Department of Commerce, 1987.

''Concrete Today—an ENR Special Advertising Section,'' *Engineering News-Record,* May 3, 1993.

Nilson, Arthur H., and George Winter, *Design of Concrete Structures,* New York: McGraw-Hill, 1986.

Standard & Poor's Industry Surveys, New York: Standard & Poor's Corporation, 1993.

Waddell, J. J., *Concrete Construction Handbook,* New York: McGraw-Hill, 1968.

—Douglas B. Hoyt

SIC 3274

LIME

The lime industry is comprised of establishments primarily engaged in manufacturing quick-lime, hydrated lime, and miscellaneous lime-related products. It is considered part of the larger concrete, gypsum, and plaster products industry.

Lime, or quick-lime, is calcium oxide derived from naturally occurring calcium carbonate. Lime, one of the oldest products of chemical reaction known to man, is a white or grayish-white solid that is used for numerous applications. Solid lime, for example, is used extensively as a fertilizer and building material. It is also commonly utilized as a chemical neutralizer to treat solid and gaseous wastes. Quick-lime accounted for approximately 72 percent of industry revenues in the early 1990s.

When mixed with water, lime turns into calcium hydroxide, or slaked lime, which is used to make mortars, plasters, and cement. Slacked lime represented about 19 percent of industry output in 1991. Lime is also used to make calcium carbide, which decomposes in water to form the flammable acetylene gas used in welding torches.

Blast furnace operators and steel manufacturers consume the largest amounts lime products to melt and process steel. This important segment consumed about 30 percent of industry output in the early 1990s.

Chemical and industrial applications represented 15 percent of the lime market. Chemical firms, for example, use lime-related products in the production plastic resins. Gas desulfurization uses accounted for 10 percent of sales, and construction industries consumed about eight percent of output, by value.

Lime is considered a commodity, and industry profit margins are typically low. However, new applications for lime allowed the industry to realize steady demand growth throughout the mid-1900s and even through the 1980s. Between 1982 and 1988, for instance, sales of lime expanded 35 percent, from $543 million to about $830 million. Growth faltered in the late 1980s and early 1990s, and lime production dipped to about 17.5 million tons and $720 million in 1991. Markets began recovering in 1993 and 1994, though, and the long-term outlook was favorable.

While some core lime markets remained stagnant going into the mid-1990s, other segments were expected to buoy production volume and industry earnings throughout the 1990s and early 2000s. Plus, as environmental restrictions increase, lime uses related to treating gaseous emissions, solid wastes, and liquid sludge will grow, and other markets will expand as well. In 1992, for example, Chemstar Lime Co. patented a lime-based product that increases the amount of gold that can be extracted from mines. It received a second patent for a lime-based, dust control agent.

A recovering economy and new lime applications will help boost industry employment between 1990 and 2005, according to the Bureau of Labor statistics. Lime manufacturers employed about 4,500 workers in the early 1990s, down from more than 5,500 in the early 1980s. Despite continued productivity gains, however, jobs in most occupations should rise by five to 20 percent by 2005. Truck drivers, which make up about 30 percent of the entire work force, will see their opportunities jump by 13 percent. Industrial production management jobs will grow approximately 23 percent. Sales and marketing positions will likely increase 27 percent.

Only 70 U.S. companies participated in the lime industry in 1990. The largest U.S. lime producer was Edward C. Levy Co. of Michigan. Levy had 1991 sales of $140 million and employed 1,400 workers. Dravo Lime Co., the second biggest competitor, had $120 million in revenues and 700 employees. Other industry leaders included Chemical Lime, Inc. of Texas and Chemstar Lime Co. of Arizona.

INDUSTRY INFORMATION SOURCES

Darnay, Arsen J., ed., *Manufacturing USA; Industry Analyses, Statistics, and Leading Companies*, Detroit: Gale Research Inc., 1993.

Darnay, Arsen J., and Marlita A. Reddy, eds., *Market Share Reporter: An Annual Compilation of Reported Market Share Data on Companies, Products, and Services, 1993*, Detroit: Gale Research Inc., 1993.

Encyclopedia Britannica, Chicago: Encyclopedia Britannica, Inc., 1993.

"Lime is Special," *Chemical Marketing Reporter*, August 31, 1992.

Santos, William, "Lime Demand Strengthens With Squeeze on Waste," *Chemical Marketing Reporter*, May 3, 1993.

Standard & Poor's Industry Surveys, New York: Standard & Poor's Corporation, August 5, 1993.

U.S. Industrial Outlook 1993, Washington, D.C.: U.S. Department of Commerce, January 1993.

—Dave Mote

SIC 3275

GYPSUM PRODUCTS

Companies predominately employed in manufacturing plaster, plasterboard, and other gypsum products constitute the Gypsum Products Industry. Popular industry offerings include acoustical plaster, wallboard, cement, insulating plaster, orthopedic plaster (for casts), plaster of paris, and gypsum rock, lath, and tile.

Gypsum, or hydrated calcium sulfate, has been an important construction material for centuries. It is mined from hardened ocean and saline-lake brine deposits. Natural supplies of the material are abundant, particularly in the United States, Canada, France, Italy, and Britain. The largest U.S. gypsum sources are in New York, Michigan, Texas, and a few other states.

Gypsum is used as a fertilizer, a filler in paper and textiles, and a retarding agent in cement. About 80 percent of total gypsum output, however, is used to make plaster that is formed into building products. When combined with water and additives, plaster becomes a white cementing material that sets and hardens by chemical reaction. It is an excellent construction material for interior walls because it is inexpensive, easy to install, fire retardant, and acts as a noise insulator.

About 40 percent of wallboard products are used in new residential construction. Another 35 percent of industry output is used for remodeling and repair, and 10 percent goes into new commercial construction. The remaining 15 percent of the market consists of numerous miscellaneous applications, such as mobile home walls.

Because the industry is dependent on new residential construction, sales are closely linked to U.S. housing starts. Strong housing markets during the post-World War II U.S. economic expansion pushed industry sales close to $2 billion in the late 1970s. But a housing slump in the early 1980s kept revenues to $2.3 billion in 1982.

A recovery in housing starts boosted gypsum industry sales to a peak of nearly $2.7 billion in 1987. A U.S. economic recession and depressed housing markets in the late 1980s and early 1990s, however, pummeled industry participants. Receipts plunged below $2 billion annually in the early 1990s, and wallboard prices crashed from $127 per thousand square feet in 1985 to $67 in 1992.

After being hammered by brutal markets, gypsum producers experienced a slight reprieve in 1993 as industry revenues rose a tepid 4 percent. Gypsum demand was forecast to rise about 3 percent per year through the mid-1990s. Prices were also expected to recover, albeit very slowly. New manufacturing technologies, mostly aimed at reducing energy consumption, were expected to raise productivity and boost profit margins.

About 90 U.S. firms produced gypsum in the early 1990s. United States Gypsum Co. (USG), of Illinois, was the largest, with over 30 percent of the U.S. wallboard market. The company had $1.5 billion in 1991 sales and about 10,000 employees in its diversified operations. USG was emerging from chapter 11 bankruptcy in 1993. National Gypsum, the second largest producer, was also emerging from bankruptcy in 1993. It had 1991 sales of $1.5 billion and about 6,500 workers. Other major gypsum producers in the early 1990s included Redco II, of California, and Republic Gypsum and Aancor Holdings Inc., both of which are based in Texas.

About 10,500 workers served the industry in the early 1990s. Most employees are blue-collar laborers. The average hourly wage for production workers was $12 in 1989, compared to $10.49 for the average U.S. manufacturing industry laborer. The average number of hours each laborer worked in 1989, however, was significantly higher than in other manufacturing sectors. Employment growth in the long-term will depend on housing starts. Because most mills are al-ready highly automated, future productivity gains will result in negligible workforce reductions.

INDUSTRY INFORMATION SOURCES

Darnay, Arsen J., ed., *Manufacturing USA; Industry Analyses, Statistics, and Leading Companies,* Detroit: Gale Research Inc., 1993.

Barron, Tom, ''Recyclers Find New Uses for Newsprint,'' *Environment Today,* October 1992.

Darnay, Arsen J., and Marlita A. Reddy, eds., *Market Share Reporter: An Annual Compilation of Reported Market Share Data on Companies, Products, and Services, 1993,* Detroit: Gale Research Inc., 1993.

Encyclopaedia Britannica, Chicago: Encyclopedia Britannica, Inc., 1993.

Santos, William, ''Lime Demand Strengthens With Squeeze on Waste,'' *Chemical Marketing Reporter,* May 3, 1993.

Standard & Poor's Industry Surveys, New York: Standard & Poor's Corporation, August 5, 1993.

U.S. Industrial Outlook 1993, Washington, D.C.: U.S. Department of Commerce, January 1993.

—Dave Mote

SIC 3281

CUT STONE AND STONE PRODUCTS

This category covers establishments primarily engaged in cutting, shaping, and finishing granite, marble, limestone, slate, and other stone for building and miscellaneous uses. Establishments primarily engaged in buying or selling partly finished monuments and tombstones, but performing no work on the stones other than lettering, finishing, or shaping to custom order, are classified in either the wholesale or retail trade divisions. The cutting of grindstones, pulpstones, and whetstones at the quarry is classified in the mining division.

INDUSTRY SNAPSHOT

Dimension stone sales expanded steadily during the 1980s as construction markets grew. Sales jumped from $555 million in 1982 to almost $1 billion by 1990. Despite a severe construction industry recession which began in the late 1980s, a trend toward the use of stone in new buildings buoyed industry earnings, as did new technology that delivered productivity gains.

ORGANIZATION AND STRUCTURE

The three main materials utilized in this industry are granite, marble, and limestone. Granite products accounted for more than 50 percent of industry output in the early 1990s. Granite is a light-colored rock—usually found in mountainous regions—that is comprised primarily of varying amounts of quartz and feldspar. About half of all cut granite is used in buildings, the remainder being consumed to create monuments and miscellaneous products. Marble, which represented approximately 19 percent of production during the early 1990s, is also used mostly in buildings. It is metamorphosized limestone, and is usually quarried from the core of young mountains in the Rockies or from the exposed roots of ancient mountains in the Appalachians. The presence of impurities and other minerals during metamorphosis is responsible for the many colors and streaks found in different types of marble. Its strength and appearance make it a popular stone for statuary and decorative applications.

Limestone, a sedimentary rock, is comprised primarily of calcite that resulted from the sedimentation of coral and dead organisms. Limestone varies greatly in texture and color. Although most limestone is crushed for use as agricultural lime or cement, cut limestone is often used as building stone. Limestone products, almost all of which is building stone, accounted for about 9 percent of industry shipments during the early 1990s. Aside from the three major stone products groups, miscellaneous cut stone comprised the remaining 20 percent of sales. Slate, for example, is commonly used in construction and to make items such as billiard tables and chalkboards.

Dimension stone is usually removed from open pits in rectangular blocks, although some rock is mined from tunnel-type quarries. A channeling machine is used to cut softer rocks, such as limestone, marble, and sandstone, into blocks that are removed by cranes and hauled away. The rock may also be cut by wire sawing, which involves pulling a wire surrounded by an abrasive slurry back-and-forth along the stone.

From the quarry, the stone is hauled to a processing plant where it is cut, shaped, polished, and/or coated. Most dimension stone is finished into masonry veneer for use as fascia on buildings. The stone veneer is anchored to a structural frame or backing, often giving the impression that the structure is built with stone blocks. A significant portion of cut stone is shaped and finished into surfaces for floors, walls, tables, and counters.

BACKGROUND AND DEVELOPMENT

Dimension stone was quarried at least as early as Egyptian times. The Egyptian pyramids were built from quarried stone in about 2,800 B.C.; the largest pyramid contains 2.3 million blocks with an average weight of 2.5 tons. The Babylonians used cut stone in 600 B.C. to build the renowned Hanging Gardens. The Greeks and the Romans also used cut and finished stone as construction, decorative, and statuary material. In fact, the Greeks quarried marble as early as 447 B.C.

Stone was quarried in America as a building and paving material before the Revolutionary War. But the U.S. cut stone industry lagged behind European production until the development of a railway system during the mid-1800s. Mechanized cutting and finishing tools and methods during the late 1800s and early 1900s significantly boosted industry activity, as did the building boom of the 1920s. Early U.S. stone structures of import include St. Patrick's Cathedral (1879) and The Cathedral of St. John the Divine (begun in 1892).

Although stone remains an important building material, new construction materials and methods developed during the 20th century have limited its use almost entirely to a finishing element of mostly decorative value. Steel frames and concrete have particularly infringed on conventional uses of stone. Furthermore, new synthetic materials have replaced stone in many decorative and functional applications, such as counter tops, wall coverings, and architectural ornamentation. Many synthetic substitutes with the look and feel of marble or granite are less expensive, more durable, and easier to manufacture, ship, and install than real stone. Nevertheless, stone is still a popular and cost-effective building material for many indoor and outdoor construction projects and consumer products.

Although synthetics and glass became popular building materials during the 1980s, an escalation in commercial construction spurred cut stone industry expansion. Sales climbed from about $555 million in the early 1980s to nearly $900 million by 1988, reflecting average annual growth of more than eight percent. And despite a recession in building activity during the late 1980s, revenues continued to ascend to nearly $1 billion by 1990. Furthermore, increased interest in stone building materials, as opposed to concrete and glass, continued to buoy sales into the early 1990s.

CURRENT CONDITIONS

Many cut stone and stone product companies were crunched by the construction slowdown, which lingered into the early 1990s. As demand slowed, prices dropped and profit margins slipped as a result of overcapacity and increased competition. Most industry segments were stable, however. Granite producers, for example, were achieving greater demand at the expense of marble. Marble had been losing market share since the 1980s when it was determined that most varieties are affected by acid rain. Although granite producers were fighting stiff foreign competition, the use of granite for headstones and monuments remained strong and a construction industry uptick in 1993 and 1994 bolstered the bottom line for many competitors.

Some companies were also benefitting from productivity gains implemented during the 1980s and early 1990s. The industry had succeeded at increasing its work force only 25 percent during the 1980s as its shipment value surged almost 80 percent. New automated cutting and finishing equipment, as well as advanced transportation and information systems, were credited with increasing efficiency. But while some producers had been able to boost profitability through automation, stone cutting remained a labor intensive industry susceptible to imports from low-cost emerging nations. India, for example, made steady inroads into the U.S. granite industry in the early 1990s.

The long term industry outlook was generally lackluster going into 1994. Limited opportunities for further productivity gains coupled with greater foreign competition will hurt many industry sectors. And most traditional domestic markets, such as construction, will realize tepid growth at best. In addition, superior synthetic substitutes will continue to make gains. Because of stone's weight-to-value ratio, moreover, opportunities for U.S. export growth are slim with the exception of niche specialty stones. U.S. producers exported slightly more than one percent of production in 1993.

INDUSTRY LEADERS

Because of its logistical characteristics (i.e. transportation costs), the cut stone industry is highly fragmented into relatively small, local manufacturers. The average cut stone producer generated $1.27 million in revenues in 1989, compared to about $8.43 million for the average U.S. manufacturer. In the early 1990s, 740 companies competed, and only the top 25 had sales of more than $10 million per year. The largest producer was General Crushed Stone Co., of Pennsylvania, which had 1991 sales of $162 million with a work force of 1,500. Davidson Mineral Properties, of Georgia, had 1991 revenues of $110 million and about 900 employees. Other industry leaders included Pluess-Staufer Industries Inc., of Vermont, and Texas Granite Corp.

WORK FORCE

The employment outlook for the cut stone and stone products industry is dismal. In fact, most labor positions are expected to decline in number by about 15 percent to 30 percent between 1990 and 2005, according to the Bureau of Labor Statistics. Jobs for helpers and material handlers, which account for a leading seven percent of the work force, will likely diminish 20 percent by 2005. And work for cutting machine operators, truck drivers, and finishers will fall ten to 20 percent. Even management positions will decline 14 percent or more. Only opportunities for production managers are forecast to increase, though only slightly. The average cut stone industry laborer earned $9.31 in 1989, about $.70 less than the U.S. manufacturing average.

RESEARCH AND TECHNOLOGY

New cutting, finishing, and construction technologies in the mid-1990s were helping the cut stone and stone products industry remain competitive against new synthetics and low-cost imports. For example, advanced construction techniques were used in Washington D.C. in 1992 to create and erect massive 50-foot tall limestone columns for the Market Square Arena. 800,000 cubic feet of limestone was quarried to produce the 80,000 cubic feet of material actually contained in the columns. An advanced horizontal lathe rounded and fluted the huge structures, which were put into place as the concrete frame of the building was poured. The project was indicative of a trend toward greater use of natural stone in restorative building projects.

Cut stone producers were also benefitting from improved quarrying techniques, such as laser rockface profiling and robotic drilling and cutting machines. While much of this technology was being developed for extraction of crushed stone and other minerals, cut stone producers were finding applications for these and related innovations.

INDUSTRY INFORMATION SOURCES

Barna, Ed, "Vermont Mining Companies Stay Grounded," *Vermont Business Magazine,* January 1994.

Bordenaro, Michael, "Weighing Options for Stone Cladding Systems: Careful Assessment of Trusses, Precast Panels, Stick Systems and Other Thin-stone Cladding Methods Can Result in Cost and Structural Benefits," *Building Design and Construction,* July 1992.

Bordenaro, Michael, "New Technology for Traditional Stone," *Building Design and Construction,* May 1992.

Garrett, Rodney, "Technology Addresses Problems and Profits," *Pit and Quarry,* January 1994.

Tuunanen, Ari, "Automation of Hard Rock Drilling Machines," *Pit and Quarry,* January 1994.

—Dave Mote

SIC 3291

ABRASIVE PRODUCTS

This category covers establishments primarily engaged in manufacturing abrasive grinding wheels of natural or synthetic materials, abrasive-coated products, and other abrasive products. The cutting of grindstones, pulpstones, and whetstones at the quarry is classified in the mining industries.

INDUSTRY SNAPSHOT

The value of shipments in 1991 was $3.76 billion, up from $2.75 billion in 1982. In the early 1990s there were approximately 400 establishments in the industry, the same number of establishments in existence during the early 1980s. Half of these 400 establishments had 20 or more employees. Average firm size as measured by the number of production workers per establishment was 14 percent larger than that for the manufacturing sector as a whole.

The industry employed 16,300 production workers in 1991, down from a peak of 17,500 in 1984. The industry had about the same investment per production worker as that for the manufacturing sector as a whole. Annual hours worked by production workers in the industry were about the same as those worked in the manufacturing sector at large, and hourly wages were 12 percent higher.

ORGANIZATION AND STRUCTURE

Ranked by sales, two-thirds of the top 30 firms in the industry were subsidiaries and divisions of larger firms, while the others were private companies. Of the industry's 75 leading companies, 84 percent were private corporations. Each of the industry's leading 30 companies generated more than $10 million and employed 100 or more workers.

The states ranking in the top ten by number of establishments were: Michigan, with 46; New York and California, with 40 each; Ohio, with 38; Illinois, with 36; Massachusetts, with 31; Pennsylvania, with 29; New Jersey, with 22; Texas, with 19; and North Carolina, with 15. Together these ten states accounted for 80 percent of all establishments and over 60 percent of the industry's total employment. The average number of employees per establishment varied widely by state. Missouri and Wisconsin, the states with the highest number of employees per plant, had an average of about ten times as many employees per plant as did Pennsylvania, New Jersey, Michigan and California.

The top four types of abrasive products by product share were nonmetallic coated abrasive products and buffing and polishing wheels (45 percent), nonmetallic sized abrasives (27 percent), other nonmetallic abrasives (23 percent), and metal abrasives (seven percent).

The largest organization serving the industry was the Abrasive Engineering Society, headquartered in Butler, Pennsylvania. The Society was founded in 1957 and had 400 members (its name changed from the American Society for Abrasive Methods in 1975). In addition to an annual technical conference and semiannual educational seminars, the Society published the quarterly *AES Magazine*, circulation 3,000. The industry was also served by smaller organizations, among them the Abrasive Grain Association of Cleveland, the Coated Abrasives Manufacturers Institute of Cleveland, and the Industrial Diamond Manufacturers Association of New York City.

BACKGROUND AND DEVELOPMENT

Abrasives have been vital to the production of metal products since the earliest days of metallurgy in ancient times, but the modern abrasive products industry was largely the result of technical developments achieved during the late 19th century. These developments involved not only the abrasives themselves, but also the binders used to create bonded abrasive products.

A key development for the industry was synthetic abrasives. In 1901, Dr. Acheson synthesized silicon carbide, the first of the synthetic abrasive grains to attain broad, commercial success. The use of fused aluminum oxide abrasives was pioneered by C.B. Jacobs in the 1890s and became a commercially viable product by 1904. Along with the naturally-occurring corundum, garnet and diamond, silicon carbide and fused aluminum oxide dominated the abrasive products market into the 1930s. In 1938, a new technique for producing aluminum oxide was developed, resulting in the most successful abrasive grain for precision grinding that had existed up to that time. In the 1950s, aluminum oxides were produced by non-fusion methods. Fused mixtures of aluminum and zirconium oxides also became commercially viable.

Diamonds gained widespread commercial use as abrasives in the 1930s. This resulted from the creation of the first bonded wheels, which used industrial diamonds, and was accelerated by the need for an extremely hard abrasive to grind tungsten carbide, the use of which became important in the 1930s. Synthetic diamonds were produced in 1960 by General Electric.

Along with cubic boron nitride, diamonds made up the hardest class of abrasives known as "superabrasives."

In 1987, aluminum oxide and silicon carbide, the oldest synthetic abrasives, continued to dominate the industry's output, with $104 million and $51 million in value consumed, respectively. Ranking next in order of value of materials consumed were natural abrasive materials ($30 million), diamond ($27 million), aluminum-zirconium oxide ($23 million) and cubic boron nitride ($7 million).

The development of binders for bonded abrasive products, including grinding and buffing wheels and flexible abrasives such as sandpaper, were as important as the development of synthetic fibers. Rubber was used to bond abrasives for grinding wheels in the 1850s. Sand, corundum and diamond bonded by shellac were used to make grinding wheels in India in the early 19th century. The shellac process was utilized by the Waltham Emery Wheel Company. Rubber and shellac remained the only organic binders until the development of synthetic resins in the 1920s.

Inorganic binders were developed in the late-19th century in an effort to simulate the properties of sandstone. Key among these were the vitrified products commercialized by the Norton Co. of Massachusetts in the late-19th century. In addition to these binders, so-called "active" fillers were used in the construction of grinding wheels. Active fillers enabled cooler grinding, increased wheel porosity, and increased the applications for grinding wheels.

CURRENT CONDITIONS

Overall, the industry's value of shipments increased from 1982 to 1991, peaking in 1988. The value of shipments stagnated after 1988, declining by nearly $300 million in three years. Capital investments remained fairly strong however, totaling slightly less in 1990 than the peak years in 1984 and 1985.

Employment of production workers declined from 1982 to 1991, and was lower in 1991 than in every year in that decade except for 1987. Employment prospects for the industry appeared bleak. The Bureau of Labor Statistics made employment forecasts for 30 occupational categories included within the abrasive products industry. Based on projected changes from 1990 to 2005, employment was expected to decline by double-digit figures in 16 occupations and single-digit figures in 11 other occupations.

A 1990 study of the industry by the Business Communications Co. Inc. projected an annual growth rate of four percent through 1995. Among those materials expected to show declining sales were fused

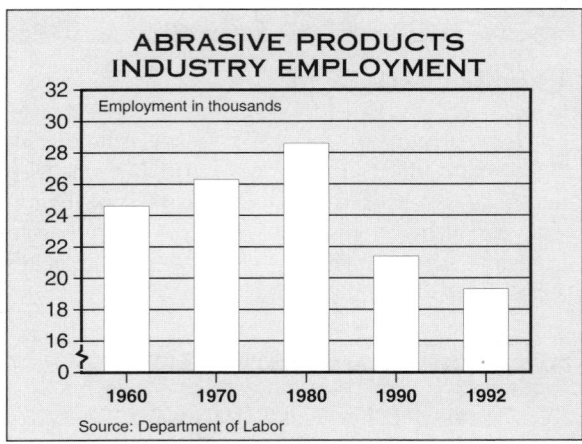

aluminum oxides and metallic abrasives. The use of silicon carbides, aluminum-zirconium oxides and superabrasives was expected to grow, with the most dramatic growth projected for superabrasives. The market share of superabrasives was projected to increase from 31 percent in 1990 to 36.5 percent in 1995. U.S. firms lagged behind their competitors in Europe and the Far East in the use of more high-technology superabrasives.

Theodore L. Giese, business manager of the Abrasive Engineering Society, argued in *AES Magazine* that the future success of the industry was dependent on the development of formal education in abrasives technologies. Noting that only two universities in the United States had recognized programs in these technologies, the University of Connecticut and the University of Massachusetts, Giese wrote: "We have learned that trial-and-error methods for solving problems are inefficient tools for product development and troubleshooting grinding operations. Measurement-oriented strategies such as SPC [statistical process control] are necessary. Control of a grinding operation now requires an understanding of the grinding system and the concepts behind the grinding process. That means . . . a better comprehension of ideas behind the technology we use. All this translates into the need for more education."

In the early 1990s, a cooperative venture between Japanese and American engineers was established in an effort to develop improved methods of production for the industry in both countries. This involved Japanese engineers using the facilities of the University of Connecticut's Center for Grinding Research and Development and sharing their knowledge with the university's staff and students.

INDUSTRY LEADERS

The top four firms in the industry in 1992 were the Norton Co. of Worcester, Massachusetts, Metallurg Inc. of New York City, Armco Worldwide Grinding Systems Inc. of Kansas City, Missouri, and General Electric Superabrasives of Worthington, Ohio. Together these firms accounted for about 70 percent of total sales for the industry.

The Norton Company was founded in 1885 and had $1.4 billion in sales in 1992, making it the largest producer of abrasive products in the world. The firm experienced substantial sales growth and greater profits in the late 1980s. From one quarter in 1987 to the corresponding quarter in 1988, for example, income from operations increased 91 percent and operating profits increased 77 percent. The firm operated a number of divisions within the industry. Among these were Norton Co. Coated Abrasives of Troy, New York, founded in 1928, with $200 million in sales and 1,200 employees, Norton Co. Advanced Ceramics of Worcester, Massachusetts, with roughly $190 million in sales and 2,100 employees, and Norton Co.'s Amplex Corp. of Bloomfield, Connecticut, founded in 1956, with $5.4 million in sales and 100 employees. In July of 1990, the Compagnie de Saint-Gobain of France acquired the majority of the Norton Co.'s common shares. The French firm also owned Norton-affiliated producers of abrasives and ceramics in: Australia, Bermuda, Japan, Germany, Belgium, Luxembourg, the Netherlands, Italy, Spain, Norway, the United Kingdom, Canada and Brazil. Norton Co. underwent substantial restructuring after its acquisition by the Compagnie de Saint-Gobain, including $50 million in modernization investments over three years.

Metallurg Inc., a private corporation founded in 1914, generated $600 million in sales in 1992, and employed 4,600 workers. The firm filed for Chapter 11 bankruptcy in the fall of 1993. As reported in American Metal Market, firm vice-president Michael Banks stated, "We have been operating in a terribly difficult business environment and a deteriorating business situation. . . . Banks blamed plummeting prices during the past two to three years for the weak business environment, and the influx of Russian material and compliance with evermore environmental regulations added to the company's difficult situation."

Armco Worldwide Grinding Systems Inc. was a segment of publicly-held Armco Inc. The firm had $425 million in sales in 1992 and 1,000 employees. In 1991, the firm entered into joint ventures with Donhad Forgings Pty. Ltd. of Australia and Cia Sideruriga de Guadalajata of Mexico. Mineral Reagents International of Midland, Michigan was created as a wholly-owned subsidiary of Worldwide Grinding Systems in 1992.

GE Superabrasives was a division of the publicly-held General Electric Co. Founded in 1957, the firm had $300 million in sales and 1,000 employees in 1992. The firm pioneered the development of synthetic diamonds, one of the key developments in the industry's history. GE Superabrasives offered an interactive software program in 1992 that provided instruction in machining with superabrasives. Together with De Beers Consolidated Mines, GE Superabrasives accounted for 90 percent of the world's industrial diamond market. A suit alleging price fixing was brought against GE Superabrasives and De Beers in 1992.

RESEARCH AND TECHNOLOGY

Much of the research and many of the new technical developments in the industry were related to the increased importance of superabrasives. In Superabrasive Grinding, J.L. Metzger summarized future areas of superabrasives development, "Our experience indicates that major developments are likely to continue - possibly even to accelerate - in the following areas: (1) New, custom-designed, 'hard-to-grind' materials for an ever widening spectrum of industrial applications; (2) Creep feed grinding, also known as plunge or deep feed grinding; (3) High performance, high-speed grinding of hardened steels with CBN-wheels [cubic boron nitride]; (4) Form or profile grinding, in part with electroplated, in part with crushable wheels, in high removal, high precision, high surface quality applications; (5) CNC-control [computer numerically controlled] of production grinding machines, with, possibly, partial adaptive control optimization." Other developments regarding superabrasives included the use of chemical vapor deposition for optimal bonding of diamond coatings. Flexible belt superabrasive products were advocated over bonded wheel superabrasives for the grinding of ceramics on the grounds that flexible products were less inclined to chip and crack ceramics.

Additional areas of technical development for the industry included improvements in coated (sandpaper-like) abrasives, such as new backings, adhesives, grains and joint designs (for belt abrasives) and the use of cushioned belts. These improvements made coated abrasives faster and more economical than traditional grinding and cutting techniques for many applications. Substantial research was also undertaken in an effort to improve the liquid coolants and lubricants that were used in many grinding operations.

INDUSTRY INFORMATION SOURCES

Annual Survey of Manufactures, Washington, D.C.: U.S. Census Bureau, 1991.

Anselment, George, "Guest Editorial," *AES Magazine,* Spring 1991, p. 30.

Coes, L. Jr., *Abrasives,* New York: Springer-Verlag, 1971.

Cohn, Lynne, "Metallurg, Citing Tough Times, Files for Chapter 11 Protection," *American Metal Market,* September 6, 1993.

"Cushioned Abrasives for Off-Hand Finishing," *Metal Finishing,* July 1993.

Daniels, Peggy Kneffel and Carol A. Schwartz, eds. *Encyclopedia of Associations* (28th ed.), Detroit: Gale Research Inc., 1994.

Darnay, Arsen J., ed. *Manufacturing USA: Industry Analysis, Statistics, and Leading Companies* (3rd ed.), Detroit: Gale Research Inc., 1993.

"De Beers and GE are Sued," *New York Times,* May 5, 1992.

"Diamond/CBN Industry Shows Change, Growth," *Ceramics Industry,* January 1992.

"Diamonds and Dirt," *Business Week,* August 10, 1992.

Giese, Theodore L. "Editorial," *AES Magazine,* Summer 1992, p. 31.

"Japanese Scientists Help American Industry," *AES Magazine,* Winter 1991, p. 30.

Metzger, J.L., *Superabrasive Grinding,* London: Butterworth & Co., 1986.

"Mineral Reagents International, Inc.," *Mining Journal,* July 3, 1992.

Moody's Industrial Manual, New York: Moody's Investors Service Inc., 1993.

Moody's International Manual, New York: Moody's Investors Service Inc., 1993.

"Norton Reports Higher Sales and Income," *AES Magazine,* June-July 1988, p. 27.

"Saint-Gobain Bouscule Norton," *Usine Nouvelle,* July 16, 1992.

Standard and Poor's Register of Corporations, Directors and Executives, vol. 1, New York: Standard and Poor's, 1994.

Subramanian, K., "A Bright Future for Superabrasives," *AES Magazine,* Summer 1991, p. 30.

"Superabrasive Use to Increase," *AES Magazine,* Spring 1991, p. 30.

"Superabrasive for Ceramic Grinding, Finishing," *Ceramic Industry,* April 1992.

"Thin-Film Diamond at the Cutting Edge," *Tooling and Production,* July 1993.

"Tooling Guide," *Precision Toolmaker,* February 1992.

Visser, R.G., "Grinding with Flexible Superabrasive Products," *AES Magazine,* Summer 1992, p. 31.

Ward's Business Directory of U.S. Private and Public Companies, Detroit: Gale Research Inc., 1993.

Wellborn, William, "Synthetic Mineral - The Foundation Stone of Modern Abrasive Tools," *AES Magazine,* Spring 1992, p. 31.

—David Kucera

SIC 3292

ASBESTOS PRODUCTS

This category includes establishments primarily engaged in manufacturing asbestos textiles, asbestos building materials, except asbestos paper, insulating materials for covering boilers and pipes, and other products composed wholly or chiefly of asbestos. Establishments primarily engaged in manufacturing asbestos paper are classified in **SIC 2621: Paper Mills,** or those manufacturing gaskets and packing materials, which are classified in **SIC 3053: Gaskets, Packing, and Sealing Devices.**

INDUSTRY SNAPSHOT

The use of asbestos in manufactured products in the United States fell dramatically after studies in the early 1970s linked airborne asbestos fibers to asbestosis, a scarring of the lungs that makes breathing difficult, and mesothelioma, a rare and deadly form of cancer. The Environmental Protection Agency (EPA) banned the use of spray-on asbestos insulation in 1973, and the U.S. tile and floor-covering industry, once a major consumer, voluntarily eliminated use of asbestos by 1986. According to the Census Bureau, the value of asbestos products produced in the United States in 1990 was about $352 million.

In 1989 the EPA issued a ruling that would have eliminated all use of asbestos in the United States by 1996. However, the ban was declared unreasonable by the federal courts, which permitted continued use of asbestos in products that were either being imported or manufactured in the United States as of July, 1989. The courts let stand an EPA ban on any new products containing asbestos.

By 1994 there were fewer than 50 companies in the United States still involved in manufacturing products containing asbestos. The majority made friction products for automobile brakes. The rest were involved in making roofing materials, heat-resistant gaskets, and safety clothing. Most of the asbestos used by

U.S. manufacturers was chrysotile asbestos imported from Canada.

BACKGROUND AND DEVELOPMENT

Asbestos is a group of soft minerals composed of tiny fibers that is nearly impervious to acid, fire, and biological decay, and is a poor conductor of heat and electricity. It was not until the late 1800s, when asbestos was first widely used to insulate boilers, steam pipes, and other high-temperature industrial equipment, that it became known as "white gold," especially in Canada, which was the world's leading supplier.

Since 1900, asbestos has found its way into more than 3,000 different products manufactured in the United States, from safety clothing and automobile brake linings to textured paints and electrical insulation. The most extensive use of asbestos, however, was as insulation in construction. The United States used thousands of tons of asbestos insulation in shipbuilding during World War II. There was another surge in the use of asbestos insulation in the 1960s when it was routinely sprayed on structural beams and roof decks. In the mid-1970s, the United States was using an estimated 700,000 tons of asbestos per year, most of it in insulation products.

Health concerns. The connection between asbestos and respiratory illness was noted by the ancient Greeks, but the first medical studies were not done until the early 1900s when the use of asbestos became widespread. When asbestos fibers are inhaled, they cling to the insides of the lungs. The body reacts by covering the fibers with proteins. As this scar tissues increases, the lungs become clogged and lose their elasticity. The scarring and resulting respiratory complications are called asbestosis. There also was evidence that prolonged exposure to asbestos increased the incidence of cancer, including mesothelioma, which affected the visceral membranes. Exposure to asbestos also greatly increased the risk of lung cancer for cigarettes smokers.

In 1931 Great Britain became the first country to pass laws regulating the exposure to asbestos. (The United States did not pass similar laws until the early 1970s.) In the 1960s Dr. Irving Selikoff, an epidemiologist at Mount Sinai Hospital in New York, studied the incidence of respiratory diseases in men who had worked in the asbestos industry or in the shipyards during World War II. Selikoff also noted an increase of respiratory problems in wives who shook asbestos dust out of their husbands' work clothes. Selikoff's controversial conclusion was that no level of exposure to asbestos could be considered safe. However,

Selikoff's conclusion was disputed by later studies. In the late 1980s, the United Kingdom Health and Safety Commission concluded that the long-term risk to workers in an office building with asbestos insulation was so low that it was comparable to inhaling one puff of cigarette smoke every day for a lifetime.

Federal regulation. The United States began regulating industrial exposure to asbestos dust in the early 1970s. In 1986 the EPA declared that "no level of exposure to asbestos is without risk," and attempted to ban the use of asbestos in consumer products. The EPA order would have phased out almost all use of asbestos by 1996. However, The Asbestos Institute, supported by the Canadian asbestos-mining industry, filed a petition for review of the ban with the U.S. Court of Appeals. In 1991 the court ruled that the ban was unreasonable.

In its ruling, the court said that the EPA had overstepped its authority by attempting to ban all use of asbestos and had failed to consider both the financial costs and the health risks posed by asbestos substitutes. The court said many of the proposed substitutes "actually may increase the risk of injury Americans face." For example, the court said there was "credible evidence that non-asbestos brakes could increase significantly the number of highway fatalities." The court found, based on the EPA's own studies, that "a complete ban would save less than one statistical life [over] 13 years."

Under the court ruling, which was affirmed in 1993, U.S. companies were allowed to continue manufacturing asbestos products that were either being imported or manufactured in the United States at the time the EPA announced the ban in 1989. The court let stand an EPA ban on new uses of asbestos or asbestos products.

Johns-Manville Corporation. The Johns-Manville Corporation was created in 1901 from the merger of two asbestos products companies. In 1969 Clarence Borel, a laborer who had spent more than 30 years installing asbestos insulation, brought suit against Johns-Manville and other asbestos products companies alleging that they had knowingly manufactured a hazardous product (*Borel v. Fibreboard Paper Products Company, et al*). Borel, who was suffering from asbestosis, testified that in all his years as an installer, no one had ever told him that asbestos could make him ill.

In addition to Johns-Manville, the suit named the Pittsburgh Corning Corporation, Owens-Corning Fiberglass Corporation, Union Asbestos & Rubber Company, Combustion Engineering Inc., Eagle-Picher In-

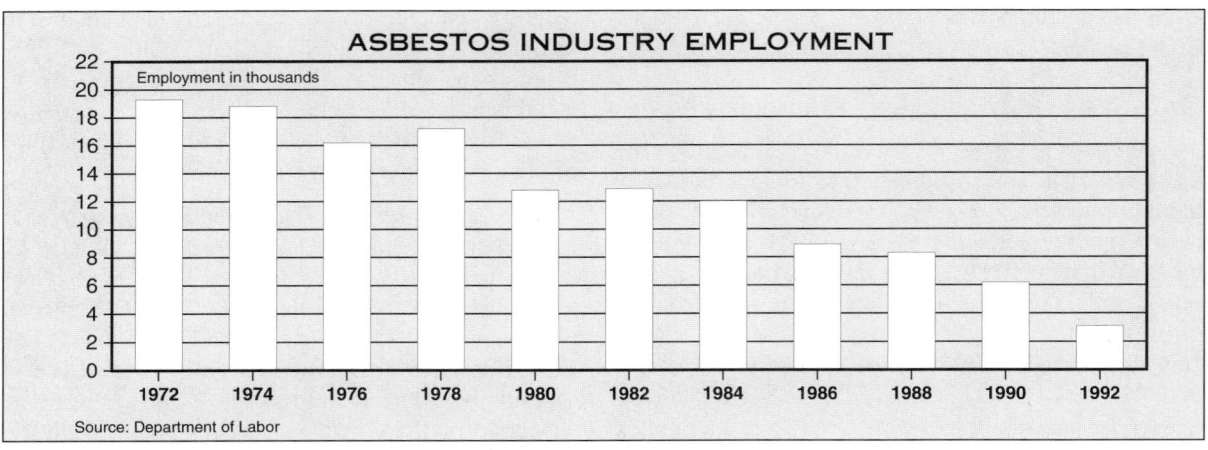

ASBESTOS INDUSTRY EMPLOYMENT

Employment in thousands

Source: Department of Labor

dustries Inc., the Philip Carey Corporation, Armstrong Contracting & Supply Corporation, Rubberoid Company, and the Standard Asbestos Manufacturing & Insulation Company. Those companies produced testimony that most laborers were aware of the dangers but refused to wear the breathing masks provided by insulation contractors. As the industry leader, Johns-Manville argued that it also began putting warning labels on its products in 1964—as soon as it had sufficient evidence that installation workers were at risk.

In the end, the jury found both Borel and the asbestos-products companies guilty of negligence. Borel died in 1970 before the verdict was rendered, and the jury said the asbestos-products companies were liable for his death. The jury awarded Borel's widow nearly $80,000. The decision was upheld in 1973 by the U.S. Court of Appeals, which found that Johns-Manville and the other defendants could have foreseen the dangers to Borel "at the time the products causing Borel's injuries were sold." That ruling opened the floodgates to litigation. By the end of 1981, more than 16,000 lawsuits had been filed against Johns-Manville. Most of the suits were filed by insulation workers and people who had worked in the shipyards during World War II. Johns-Manville put the projected costs of the lawsuits at $2 billion—twice the company's assets at the time—and in 1982, the company filed for protection under Chapter 11 of the U.S. Bankruptcy Code. It was the largest U.S. corporation to ever file for bankruptcy.

Johns-Manville filed a plan for reorganization in 1983. As part of the plan, the company, which changed its name to the Manville Corporation, established a trust fund to pay for asbestos-related claims. The Manville Personal Injury Settlement Fund owned 80 percent of the reorganized company, which also ended

all involvement with asbestos. Initially, the trust was funded at $1 billion. However, as the number of claims increased—to more than 200,000 by 1993—the fund was increased to almost $3 billion. Because asbestosis and other asbestos-related diseases develop over time, the Rand Corporation estimated that claims against the Manville trust and other asbestos-products companies eventually could reach more than $50 billion.

After a decade of court battles, in 1993, two insurance companies, the Chubb Corporation and CNA Financial Corporation, agreed to pay up to $3 billion for asbestos-related claims against the Fibreboard Corporation, which was spun off from Louisiana Pacific in 1988. More than 145,000 people claimed to have been harmed by Fibreboard products. The decision was expected to keep Fibreboard from declaring bankruptcy. However, at least a dozen other asbestos-products companies were forced into bankruptcy by asbestos litigation along with Johns-Manville, including the National Gypsum Company, Celotex Corporation, and Eagle-Picher.

CURRENT CONDITIONS

In 1993 the EPA issued a report on what products were permitted under the court ruling. These included asbestos clothing, roofing materials, gaskets, and friction products for automotive use including brakes, brake linings and clutch facings. Friction products accounted for about 70 percent of the asbestos used by U.S. manufacturers and were of particular concern to the appeals court because several automobile makers testified that non-asbestos brakes were less reliable than brakes with asbestos, especially for trucks and heavier cars. The appeals court found that there was "credible evidence that non-asbestos brakes could increase significantly the number of highway fatalities." After the court ruling, the EPA asked car makers to switch to non-asbestos brakes voluntarily by 1994, but no major manufacturers had agreed to do so in 1993.

The asbestos in those products allowed by the court order was considered ''locked-in'' or ''encapsulated,'' and was not considered a health risk. The asbestos fibers in friction products were mixed with various binders and only a minuscule percentage were released into the air during normal use. Automotive repair shops used special equipment to sweep asbestos fibers from the air. The asbestos fibers in roofing materials and gaskets were surrounded by asphalt, latex, rubber or other resilient material.

INDUSTRY INFORMATION SOURCES

Anderson, Walter D., ''Comments of the Resilient Floor Covering Institute,'' Washington, D.C.: Occupational Safety and Health Administration, December 3, 1990.

Asbestos, Ottawa, Ontario, Canada: Energy, Mines and Resources Canada, 1986.

''Asbestos: Manufacture, Importation, Processing, and Distribution in Commerce Prohibitions; Final Rule,'' Federal Register, July 12, 1989.

''Asbestos Production: The Chrysotile Crisis?'' Industrial Materials, May 1992, 41.

Brodeur, Paul, Outrageous Misconduct: The Asbestos Industry on Trial, New York: Pantheon Books, 1985.

Chrysotile Asbestos: A Material for Today and Tomorrow, Ministry of Energy and Resources, Government of Quebec, 1986.

''Erecting a Firewall Against Asbestos,'' U.S. News & World Report, July 17, 1989, 10.

Galen, Michele, ''The Man Who's Cutting Through the Asbestos Mess,'' Business Week, January 28, 1991, 71.

Guidry, Lori L., ''Asbestos: Tarnished 'White Gold,''' Current Health, February 1988, 28.

''Manville Corporation,'' International Directory of Company Histories, Vol. 7, Detroit: St. James Press, 1993, 291.

Mannin, Margaret, ''The Asbestos Dilemma,'' U.S. News & World Report, January 11, 1991, 57.

Pigg, B. J., ''The Uses of Chrysotile,'' Asbestos Information Association, November 1993.

Powell, Bill, ''The Case for Asbestos,'' Newsweek, September 29, 1986, 40.

Richmond, Louis S., ''Why Throw Money at Asbestos,'' Fortune, June 6, 1988, 57.

Sentes, Ray, ''Poisonous Pits,'' Canadian Dimension, April/May 1990, 43.

Solomon, Stephen, ''The Asbestos Fallout at Johns-Manville,'' Fortune, May 7, 1979, 196.

—Dean Boyer

MINERALS AND EARTHS, GROUND OR OTHERWISE TREATED

This category includes establishments operating without a mine or quarry and primarily engaged in crushing, grinding, pulverizing, or otherwise preparing clay, ceramic, and refractory minerals; barite; and miscellaneous nonmetallic minerals, excluding fuels. Also included in this category are establishments primarily crushing slag and preparing roofing granules. The improvement or preparation of the minerals and metallic ores and the cleaning and grading of coal are classified in Division B, Mining, whether or not the operation is associated with a mine.

Products in this classification include barium, blast furnace slag, clay for petroleum refining, ground clay, activated clay desiccants, diatomaceous earth, filtering clays, Fuller's earth, kaolin, black lead, mica, pulverized earth, pumice roofing granules, talc, and vermiculite. The value of shipments in this industry tended to spike up and down throughout the 1980s, dropping as low as $1.17 billion in 1985 and rising as high as $1.52 billion in 1988. In 1990 the value of shipments was $1.5 billion. No single product dominates this industry. In 1987 activated clays held the largest share of the market, at 11.6 percent, followed closely by lightweight aggregate at 8.9 percent, crushed slag at 8.8 percent, and refractory magnesia at 8.2 percent. A wide range of other materials and earths hold the remaining 62.5 percent of the market.

The products produced by this industry tend to have a relatively low value compared to their weight. As a result, truck transportation and warehousing accounted for 20.6 percent of the inputs used by the minerals and earths industry in 1982—an unusually high percentage compared with other industries. Rail transportation accounted for another 6.5 percent of the inputs used by this industry. Ground or treated minerals accounted for 15.4 percent of all inputs. The power required to process ground mineral and earth products are also important inputs, with gas utilities accounting for 6.7 percent of all inputs and electric utilities accounting for 5.1 percent in 1982.

The petroleum and natural gas well drilling industry is, by far, the largest purchaser of this industry's products, consuming 28.1 percent of all outputs in 1982. Other significant customers include manufacturers of asphalt felts and coatings (9.7 percent), gypsum products manufacturers (8.8 percent), and ready-mixed concrete producers (5.6 percent). Over 30 other industries purchased the remaining 47.8 percent of this industry's products.

The production of ground minerals and earths is concentrated in seven states, with Georgia, Michigan, Pennsylvania, Ohio, Illinois, Louisiana, and New Jersey accounting for 43.5 percent of all product shipments in 1987. Georgia was the largest single producing state, with 10.3 percent of the total. The leading companies in the ground minerals and earths industry include Eagle-Picher Industries; Minerals Technologies Inc. in New York (formerly a unit of Pfizer Inc.); Owl Companies; Engelhard Corp.; English China Clays Inc.; Dry Branch Kaolin; and J. M. Huber Inc. Many of these companies operate out of the southeastern United States, where abundant supplies of clay (kaolin) are located. This industry employed 9,000 people in 1990, ten percent less than it did in 1982. The total industry payroll in 1990 was $241.6 million, with an average hourly wage of $11.49.

INDUSTRY INFORMATION SOURCES

Darnay, Arsen J., editor, *Manufacturing USA: Third Edition,* Detroit, MI: Gale Research Inc., 1993.

Darnay, Arsen J., editor, *Market Share Reporter 1992,* Detroit, MI: Gale Research Inc., 1992.

U.S. Industrial Outlook 1993, Washington, DC: U.S. Department of Commerce, 1993.

—Alan Rooks

SIC 3296

MINERAL WOOL

This category includes establishments primarily engaged in manufacturing mineral wool and mineral wool insulation products made of such siliceous materials as rock, slag, glass, or combinations thereof. Establishments primarily engaged in manufacturing asbestos insulation products are classified in **SIC 3292: Asbestos Products,** and those manufacturing textile glass fibers are classified in **SIC 3229: Pressed and Blown Glass and Glassware, Not Elsewhere Classified.**

Products produced by this industry include mineral wool acoustical board and tile; fiberglass insulation; glass wool; mineral wool roofing mats; and insulation made from rock wool, slag, and silica minerals. The value of shipments in the mineral wool industry grew relatively steadily throughout the 1980s, from $2.3 billion in 1982 to a peak of $3.4 billion in 1988. However, the mineral wool industry—like others in

the U.S.—was hit hard by a major recession in 1989, and by 1991, the industry's value of shipments had fallen back to $3.1 billion.

This industry produced two major product categories: mineral wool for thermal and acoustical envelope insulation, which accounted for 69.3 percent of the market in 1987; and mineral wool for industrial, equipment, and appliance insulation, which accounted for 25 percent.

Within the first category, batt, blanket, and roll insulation products have the largest market share by far, accounting for 35 percent of industry output in 1987. This area includes the familiar fiberglass insulation found in the attics of most homes. The use of fiberglass insulation in the upper stories and ceilings of homes varies by type. In 1991, batts accounted for 44 percent of all installations, while blown fiberglass was a close second at 43 percent. Other forms accounted for the remaining 13 percent. Acoustical mineral wool holds the next highest market share in the mineral wool industry, at 19.1 percent.

Within the second major category—industrial, equipment, and appliance insulation—most of the market is fairly evenly spread among four different categories: special purpose insulation pieces, with nine percent of the total market; an all other category (4.9 percent); flexible blankets (4.5 percent); and pipe insulation (3.73 percent).

The power required to process mineral wools is the single biggest raw material purchased by this industry. In 1982, gas utilities accounted for 11.5 percent of all inputs, while electric utilities accounted for another 9.7 percent. Other major inputs included: wholesale trade (7.7 percent); cyclic crudes and organics (6.5 percent); miscellaneous inorganic chemicals (5.2 percent); paper products, including kraft paper used as backing for fiberglass batts (four percent); plastics (3.8 percent); and mineral wool (3.5 percent).

Because insulation for homes is a consumer product, advertising—such as the "Pink Panther" television spots for Owens-Corning Fiberglas Corporation products—accounted for 2.2 percent of inputs. Adding new insulation to existing buildings was the largest use of mineral wool in 1982, accounting for 16.1 percent of production. Construction of residential homes was the second largest user, consuming 11.5 percent, followed by adding insulation to residential homes (7.7 percent). Other major sectors of the U.S. economy purchasing mineral wool products included office buildings (7.6 percent of production), exports (5.8 percent), new additions to homes (5.1 percent), and machinery, not elsewhere classified (4.1 percent). Over

30 other sectors of the U.S. economy—mostly in manufacturing and construction—are significant users of mineral wool.

The production of mineral wool is concentrated in six states, with Georgia, California, Pennsylvania, Indiana, Texas, and New Jersey accounting for the majority of U.S. production, 51.3 percent. Owens-Corning Fiberglas, Toledo, Ohio, is the leading manufacturer of mineral wool. Other significant players include: Manville Corp., PPG Industries Inc., Glass Group, USG Corp., CertainTeed Corp., Schuller International, and Industrial Acoustics Co.

Employment in the mineral wool industry remained fairly stable throughout the 1980s, dropping slightly from 19,700 in 1982 to 19,000 in 1990. In 1990, the mineral wool industry had a payroll of $582.5 million and an average hourly wage of $14.21.

INDUSTRY INFORMATION SOURCES

Darnay, Arsen J. *Manufacturing USA: Third Edition*, Detroit, Gale Research Inc., 1993.

Darnay, Arsen J. and Marlita A. *Market Share Reporter 1994*, Detroit, Gale Research Inc., 1994.

U.S. Industrial Outlook 1993, Washington, DC: U.S. Department of Commerce, 1993.

Standard Industrial Classification Manual 1987, Washington, DC: Executive Office of the President, Office of Management and Budget, 1987.

—Alan Rooks

SIC 3297

NONCLAY REFRACTORIES

This category includes establishments primarily engaged in manufacturing refractories and crucibles made of materials other than clay. This industry includes establishments primarily engaged in manufacturing all graphite refractories, whether of carbon bond or ceramic bond. Establishments primarily engaged in manufacturing clay refractories are classified in **SIC 3255: Clay Refractories.** As defined in this industry, a refractory is a product such as brick that is resistant to intense heat. The main use of refractories is to create fire-resistant construction materials for industrial buildings. Another use of refractories is to create furnaces and other devices. Crucibles are vessels—made of a substance that will withstand extreme heat—used for melting metals or minerals.

This industry includes establishments primarily engaged in manufacturing all graphite refractories,

whether of carbon bond or ceramic bond. Products produced by the nonclay refractories industry include: alumina-fused refractories; bauxite brick; carbon brick; refractory brick; nonclay castable refractories; high temperature cement; magnesia cement; crucibles made of graphite, chrome, silica, or other nonclay materials; dolomite brick; nonclay gunning mixes; nonclay plastics refractories; nonclay refractory cement; and pyrolytic graphite.

The value of shipments in this industry grew dramatically through most of the 1980s, from $691 million in 1982 to $954.5 million in 1987 and $1.11 billion 1989. In 1990, the industry's value of shipments fell slightly to $1.07 billion as a recession in the United States hurt overall sales.

Materials, parts, containers, and supplies were by far the largest category of materials consumed by the nonclay refractories industry in 1987, with a delivered cost of $367 million. The next highest category—clay, ceramic, and refractory minerals—cost the industry $105.8 million, while dead-burned magnesia or magnesite had a delivered cost of $38.4 million. Clay or nonclay refractories accounted for another $41.4 million worth of materials.

The category called ''all other materials and components, parts containers, and supplies'' cost the industry $117.5 million in 1987, while a separate category called ''materials, parts, containers, and supplies not specified by kind'' accounted for another $53.7 million.

The majority of nonclay refractory products—50.3 percent—were used to construct industrial buildings in 1982. Maintenance of existing buildings accounted for the second highest use of nonclay refractories, at 18 percent of all outputs. Exports were strong, accounting for 12 percent of all outputs in 1982. The manufacturing of iron and steel foundries, together with blast furnaces and steel mills, accounted for just under one percent of this industry's output.

The nonclay refractories industry is concentrated in two states—Ohio and Pennsylvania—which accounted for 44.3 percent of all U.S. production in 1987. The leading companies in this industry are relatively small niche manufacturers. In 1992, none had sales over $170 million, and all but three had sales under $50 million. Leading companies include: Quigley Company, Inc., New York, New York; J.E. Baker Co., York, Pennsylvania; Ferro Corp., Cleveland, Ohio; Resco Products, Inc., Norristown, Pennsylvania; and Carborundum Co., Falconer, New York.

Other leading firms include C-E Minerals, Inc., King of Prussia, Pennsylvania; Corhart Refractories

Corp., Louisville, Kentucky; and Allied Mineral Products Co., Columbus, Ohio.

Unlike many other American industries, the nonclay refractories industry increased employment during the 1980s, moving from 6,800 people in 1982 to 8,500 in 1989. The total industry payroll in 1990 was $240 million, with workers earning an average hourly wage of $12.72.

INDUSTRY INFORMATION SOURCES

Darnay, Arsen J. *Manufacturing USA: Third Edition,* Detroit, Gale Research Inc., 1993.

Darnay, Arsen J. *Market Share Reporter 1992,* Detroit, Gale Research Inc., 1992.

U.S. Industrial Outlook 1993, Washington, DC: U.S. Department of Commerce, 1993.

—Alan Rooks

SIC 3299

NONMETALLIC MINERAL PRODUCTS, NOT ELSEWHERE CLASSIFIED

The Nonmetallic Mineral Products, Not Elsewhere Classified, Industry is comprised of firms that manufacture goods made from plaster of paris, papiermache, sand lime, and other miscellaneous nonmetallic mineral products. Examples of industry output include synthetic stones, clay and plaster plaques, architectural plaster work, plaster of paris sculptures, miniature gypsum images, plaster of paris flower boxes, and gypsum urns. For more information about the background and structure of nonmetallic mineral industries, see related entries in Industry Group 329 (abrasive, asbestos, and miscellaneous nonmetallic mineral products).

Markets for miscellaneous nonmetallic mineral products are extremely fragmented. The largest single industry product category is statuary and art goods, which accounted for about 13 percent of industry output during the early 1990s. The largest consumer of this industry's offerings is the nonferrous wire-drawing industry, which uses tubing made from quartz to produce electrical wire. Other major consumers include: motor and generator makers, which also use quartz tubing; jewelry manufacturers; trophy and plaque producers; and makers of art supplies. About 9 percent of production is exported.

The industry is relatively low-tech and manufactures many commodity-like products. The average amount of value contributed per production worker, for example, was about 65 percent lower than the U.S. manufacturing average in the early 1990s. Likewise, capital investment per employee was a meager 34 percent of the national manufacturing average. As a result, many producers of nonmetallic mineral products are highly susceptible to competition from low-cost foreign producers.

U.S. sales of miscellaneous nonmetallic mineral products topped $400 million in the early 1980s. During the mid-1980s, however, shipment growth slowed compared to the 1960s and 1970s. Although domestic demand for products such as electrical wiring and art supplies increased, foreign competition reduced profit opportunities in many sectors. Revenues increased at a tepid 5 percent annually between 1982 and 1990, slightly lagging inflation. Furthermore, a U.S. recession in the late 1980s and early 1990s stalled expansion—annual sales hovered around $650 million to $700 million.

About 500 companies competed in the industry in the early 1990s. The majority of even the top 25 firms generated revenues of less than $25 million per year. The largest industry participant was Hoechst CeramTec North, of Massachusetts, which had 1991 sales of $110 million. The second largest competitor was Howmet Corp., of Tennessee, with $75 million in revenues. Other industry leaders included Channel Technologies Inc., of California, and Tam Ceramics Inc., of New York.

Miscellaneous nonmetallic mineral product manufacturers employed a work force of about 7,000 in the early 1990s. The average hourly wage for production workers was about $8, or 76 percent of the national manufacturing average. Similarly, the average annual payroll per employee was $19,000, or less than three-quarters of the national average. Future prospects for employment in this industry are generally dismal. Positions for most laborers will likely decline by 20 to 30 percent between 1990 and 2005, according to the Bureau of Labor Statistics. Even jobs for general managers and top executives will plummet by around 15 percent.

INDUSTRY INFORMATION SOURCES

Darnay, Arsen J., ed., *Manufacturing USA; Industry Analyses, Statistics, and Leading Companies*, Detroit: Gale Research Inc., 1993.

U.S. Industrial Outlook 1994, Washington, D.C.: U.S. Department of Commerce, January 1994.

—Dave Mote

PRIMARY METAL INDUSTRIES

STEEL WORKS, BLAST FURNACES (INCLUDING COKE OVENS), AND ROLLING MILLS

This classification includes establishments primarily engaged in manufacturing hot metal, pig iron, and silvery pig iron from iron ore and iron and steel scrap; converting pig iron, scrap iron, and scrap steel into steel; and in hot-rolling iron and steel into basic shapes, such as plates, sheets, strips, rods, bars, and tubing. Merchant blast furnaces and byproduct or beehive coke ovens are also included in this industry. Establishments primarily engaged in manufacturing ferro and nonferrous additive alloys by electrometallurgical processes are classified in **SIC 3313: Electrometallurgical Products, Except Steel.**

INDUSTRY SNAPSHOT

The first steel mill in North America was built in the 1600s, making the industry one of the oldest in the country. By 1992, U.S. steel companies employed about 180,000 people, shipped about $60 billion worth of products, and produced over 90 million tons of steel. The automotive industry alone consumed in excess of 10,000 tons of steel in 1991, and U.S. companies exported 6.3 million tons of steel.

Despite its impressive size, the steel industry began declining in the mid-1970s and suffered a devastating depression between 1982 and 1986. After peaking in 1978 at over 137 million tons, U.S. steel production slipped to less than 90 million tons in 1991. Anemic market growth, expensive labor, increased production costs, and stagnant prices pummeled many manufac-

turers in the industry. In addition, the proliferation of foreign competition and the popularity of substitute materials, such as plastics and aluminum, gouged industry profits.

In response to a more competitive environment, the U.S. steel industry continued to restructure itself in the early 1990s. By 1993, new production techniques and facilities, as well as increased automation, had made U.S. steelmakers among the most productive in the world. Nevertheless, the economic slowdown in the late 1980s and early 1990s, coupled with the problems mentioned above, cast doubt on the future of most steelmakers.

ORGANIZATION AND STRUCTURE

Steel companies are involved in the manufacture of the following products: hot metal, pig iron, and silvery pig iron from iron ore, iron and steel scrap. They are also involved in converting pig iron, scrap iron, and scrap steel into steel as well as hot-rolling iron and steel into plates, sheets, strips, and bars. These end products are purchased by companies in other industries, which usually shape and manipulate the steel to create finished products.

Products offered by steelmakers are classified, according to the manner in which they were processed and their chemical compositions, into five categories. Carbon steels are used mostly for flat rolled products because of their high malleability. Machines, auto bodies, ships, and building structures are made with this type of steel. In fact, carbon steels account for about 88 percent of all U.S. steel production. Alloy steels, which make up about 10 percent of the market, integrate elements into steel to enhance its physical properties. Corrosion resistance, greater strength, and in-

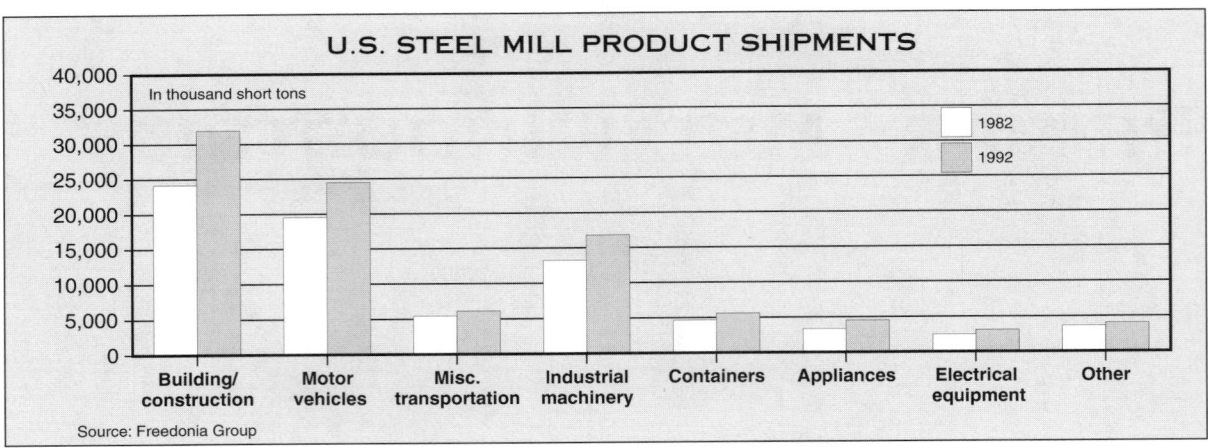

U.S. STEEL MILL PRODUCT SHIPMENTS

In thousand short tons

☐ 1982
▨ 1992

Building/construction · Motor vehicles · Misc. transportation · Industrial machinery · Containers · Appliances · Electrical equipment · Other

Source: Freedonia Group

creased conductivity are a few of the advantages offered by some alloys.

In comparison to carbon and alloy steels, stainless steels are highly resistant to rust and may be stronger or offer resistance to temperature changes. Accounting for 2 percent of the steel market volume, stainless steel is often used in pipes, tanks, and in the medical field. Tool steels and high-strength low alloy (HSLA) steels account for less than 1 percent of industry production, combined. They are used in applications in which strength and weight are critical.

Integrated Manufacturers Versus Minimills. Steel manufacturers can be divided into two camps—traditional integrated mills and non-integrated "mini-mills." Integrated steel mills undertake every step of the steel making process. These facilities typically begin by converting mixtures of iron ore, limestone, and coke (made from coal) into molten iron using a blast furnace. Basic oxygen furnaces (BOFs) are next used to convert the molten iron into steel, which is then cast into ingots. Ingots are then shaped into slabs, billets, or blooms of steel.

Increasing numbers of integrated mills in the early 1990s were using a process called continuous casting to bypass the production of ingots and cast billets, slabs, and blooms directly from molten iron. Steelmakers next convert the finished, or semi-finished, steel into rolls, plates, bars, tubes, rails, or other more marketable products. This final procedure is accomplished at a rolling mill.

In the early 1990s, minimills, or non-integrated facilities, were using the same process as integrated mills with a few exceptions. Rather than process base materials, minimills typically start with scrap iron or steel. The scrap is melted in an electric arc furnace (EAF), rather than a blast or basic oxygen furnace, and

continuously cast into blooms and billets. Minimills typically produced fewer finished products than integrated mills. Although many manufacturers were broadening their offerings to include steel pipes, plates, and sheets, most minimills emphasized rods and bars used in light construction.

Minimills are capable of producing from 100,000 to 500,000 tons of steel per year. In contrast, most integrated mills can generate several million tons of product annually. Minimills are also typically able to produce steel at a much lower cost than their larger cousins. Because minimills do not have to be located near supplies of raw ingredients, for instance, they are able to operate closer to their customers, thus reducing product transport costs. In addition, more minimills are located in the southern United States and benefit from less expensive, non-union labor. Furthermore, mini-mills are more likely to employ more advanced technology, such as continuous casting and EAFs, that reduce production costs and improve quality.

Competitive Structure. In 1992, integrated steelmakers accounted for approximately 75 percent of U.S. steel industry production. At that time, the industry was relatively concentrated and imposed formidable entry barriers, such as high start-up costs and intense competition. The top 75 competitors in the industry, for instance, dominated over 90 percent of the market in 1991, with about $55 billion in shipments. Furthermore, the top 6 firms in the industry accounted for about 40 percent of shipments, or $25 billion worth of product.

On average, minimills realized about $500 in capital costs per ton of steel produced, while integrated mills incurred about $2,000 per ton. Likewise, during the mid-1980s and early 1990s, minimills generated about $32 in operating profit per ton of steel, compared to just $3 per ton for integrated mills. Minimills also shipped an average of 752 tons per employee during that period, compared with 381 tons per worker for integrated producers.

Service and distribution centers consumed approximately 25 percent of U.S. steel production in 1991. The largest steel customer that built consumer products was the automobile industry, which used 10 million tons in 1991, or about 13 percent of total steel production. The construction industry purchased about 11.5 million tons of steel in 1991, and machinery manufacturers used about 2 million tons. Other large steel consumers included oil and gas companies (1.4 million tons in 1991), container manufacturers (4.3 million tons), and various commercial equipment producers (.8 million tons).

BACKGROUND AND DEVELOPMENT

The U.S. steel industry originated in 1645 in Massachusetts, when Saugus ironworks was established. By the beginning of the eighteenth century iron making was underway in almost every other colony. Despite English parliamentary acts that tried to restrict the burgeoning industry, manufacturers in North America continued to build new iron mills, and eventually finished steel mills, throughout the 1700s. Iron production in this early period entailed the use of charcoal fuel or water power, along with a small labor force, to melt iron ore in a blast furnace. Entrepreneurs could start a mill with several hundred dollars. By 1800, approximately 84,000 tons of iron were being produced in North America.

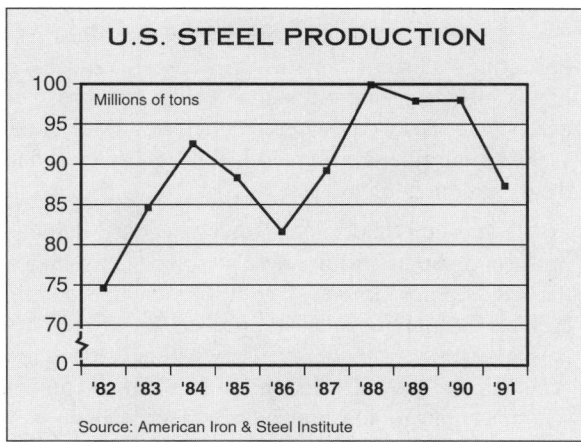

U.S. STEEL PRODUCTION

Millions of tons

Source: American Iron & Steel Institute

The production process changed very little throughout the 1800s, although advances in transportation freed the industry from many geographical constraints. Toward the end of the 1800s, however, the structure of the industry changed as it became more

concentrated and the number of firms dwindled. It was during this era that many of the great steel magnates and companies were born, such as Andrew Carnegie, Henry Clay Frick, Bethlehem Steel, and Illinois Steel Company. It was also during this time that the first steel import tariffs and trade associations were instigated. Many bitter and deadly labor disputes rocked the industry during the late 1800s and early 1900s.

In the early 1900s, the development of the open hearth furnace (OHF) made it possible for companies to produce higher quality steel and to use scrap metal in the production process. Improved steel quality was an important advantage for firms that were striving to serve the needs of the new automobile industry. Indeed, the massive growth in demand for new steel during the early 1900s, particularly in the 1920s, was a boon to the industry. After suffering setbacks during the Great Depression, when over 50 percent of U.S. steel production capacity stood idle, steel markets expanded significantly throughout World War II.

In the 30 years following the World War II, U.S. steelmakers dominated the global steel industry. In addition to the fact that many European and Japanese producers had been stifled by damage during the war, U.S. plants were technologically superior. Additionally, U.S. facilities were also an average of more than three times larger than those in other industrialized nations. In 1950 over 45 percent of the world's raw steel was produced in the United States. American firms produced about 90 million tons of steel, compared to about 30 million tons and less than 5 million tons produced by Europe and Japan, respectively.

Because U.S. firms enjoyed great economies of scale and technological supremacy, their steelworkers were by far the highest paid in the world. U.S. manufacturers enjoyed immediate access to the fastest growing economy in the industrialized world. These and other factors helped to push U.S. steel production from around 90 million tons in 1950 to nearly 140 million tons by the 1970s. Although the U.S. steel industry maintained a significant lead over the European Community (EC) and Japan from the 1950s through the 1970s, companies in those two regions gained quickly on their U.S. counterparts. By 1970, the EC and Japan were producing about 120 million and 90 million tons of steel per year, respectively.

Despite its size and its rapid growth, the U.S. steel industry began experiencing problems in the 1960s and 1970s. In addition to high labor costs, slowing growth in domestic markets, and a declining world market share, the industry was also beginning to pay the price for failing to invest the resources necessary to maintain its technological lead. Most companies, for example, had been slow to convert their operations to more productive basic oxygen furnaces (BOFs), which were replacing the old OHFs. Indeed, by the mid-1970s it was clear that U.S. companies had lost their leadership role in world steel markets—despite a flurry of capital investment by steelmakers in the late 1960s.

Since the Mid-1970s. The U.S. steel industry experienced its first significant reversal in the mid-1970s. A rise in energy prices was one of most significant factors that contributed to the industry's decline. In 1975, after oil prices had jumped from $3 to $12 per barrel in less than two years, U.S. steel production dropped by 20 percent. To make matters worse, U.S. companies had substantially increased their production capacity in the early 1970s in anticipation of strong market growth—a dreadful miscalculation. High labor costs continued to plague U.S. competitors as well, adding to their comparative inefficiency in the global market.

Other miscellaneous factors battered down industry profits. Environmental regulations, for example, forced the industry to spend a peak of nearly $400 million in 1981 to reduce pollutants. Also, government subsidized imported steel was cutting into domestic market revenues. The dumping problem became so bad that the U.S. government enacted Voluntary Restraint Agreements (VRAs) in the early 1980s—which essentially amounted to anti-dumping legislation for 29 importing countries. Finally, steel substitutes were further reducing steel's market share. For instance, the average amount of steel and iron contained in an automobile fell from 2,535 pounds in 1977 to 1,757 pounds in 1992, but the average amount of plastic in an automobile rose from about 180 pounds to 245 pounds.

The proliferation of minimills also added to the woes of large steel producers. Although minimills had originated in the 1960s, by the late 1970s these facilities were beginning to compete directly with large producers in specific market niches. The more efficient and technologically superior minimills particularly benefitted from EAFs, which proved much more productive than even the BOFs in which large manufacturers continued to invest. As a result, the market share of the top 6 producers declined from 64 percent in 1980 to about 50 percent by 1990.

The end result of the problems affecting the industry was decreased production and profits beginning in the late 1970s and continuing throughout most of the 1980s. Total U.S. steel production declined from a peak of 136 million tons in 1979 to a low of about 81.5 million tons in 1986. U.S. manufacturers' share of

world steel production also plummeted from over 17 percent in 1976 to about 11 percent in 1990. Furthermore, industry employment plummeted from about 300,000 in 1982 to less than 190,000 by 1990. Industry profits fell through the floor, declining to a loss of over $1.8 billion in 1985, and a staggering loss of nearly $4.2 billion in 1986. Although industry net income jumped to over $1 billion in 1987, profits remained relatively stagnant throughout the decade.

Industry Restructuring. In response to the metamorphosis of steel markets, U.S. producers launched a major industry restructuring in the 1980s. Companies greatly increased investments in new production technologies. Integrated mills alone invested $23 billion in the 1980s to modernize their plants. The percentage of steel produced in older OHFs, for instance, fell from nearly 20 percent in 1977 to less than 5 percent by 1990. During the same period, steel produced using efficient EAFs increased from just over 20 percent to nearly 40 percent. Most importantly, manufacturers increased the amount of steel that was produced using continuous casting from just 15 percent in 1980 to over 75 percent by 1991—nearing the levels found in the EC and Japanese industries.

U.S. steelmakers made important gains in other areas, too. Investment in pollution controls declined to just over $100 million in 1990, although those costs were beginning to rise again in the early 1990s. Manufacturers also succeeded in stabilizing their labor costs, although it was estimated that labor still represented about 30 percent of the cost of production in the early 1990s and was expected to increase. Large investments in automation, however, had helped to bring labor expenses in line with overseas competitors. Also bolstering industry competitiveness was the success of highly efficient minimills that could produce steel nearly twice as fast as integrated facilities. By the early 1990s, minimills represented a full 25 percent of industry production.

Domestic producers had also succeeded in reducing steel dumping by importers with such legislation as the VRAs. Furthermore, American companies had increased the quality of their products by investing in new production technology. They had developed new products, for instance, that allowed them to compete with many plastic substitutes. New steel products were being offered that had the corrosion resistance and weight advantages of many plastics, yet cost less to create.

CURRENT CONDITIONS

As a result of restructuring during the 1980s, U.S. steel companies in 1992 were among the most productive in the world. Manufacturers had dramatically reduced the average amount of labor required to produce one ton of steel from 11 manhours in 1982 to 3.5 manhours in 1992—less than both Japanese and European producers. At least one study estimated that pretax production costs in the United States were lower than costs in any other major steel producing nation, except Britain. Furthermore, exports had grown to a peak of 8 percent of production by 1992, despite a more than 5 percent decline in foreign demand since the late 1980s. At the same time, a slight upturn in the U.S. economy in 1992 and early 1993 was buoying domestic demand.

Another factor aiding the industry was the success of domestic steelmakers against foreign dumping in the U.S. market. There were 84 anti-dumping suits filed with the Department of Commerce and the International Trade Commission by 12 U.S. companies in 1992. In 1993 the Commerce Department agreed with the charges and imposed severe duties on those importing countries identified in the suits. This development was expected to help increase domestic sales and prices in through the 1990s.

Despite successful restructuring and positive legislation, industry problems persisted in 1993. U.S. companies still faced massive capital investments in the 1990s which were necessary to upgrade outdated operations. For instance, about 40 percent of the industry's coke ovens will need to be replaced at a cost of around $250 million each before the year 2000. In addition to capital requirements, substitute materials, such as glass, ceramics, aluminum, and plastics, continued to threaten steelmakers. The share of the beverage can market held by the steel industry, for example, fell from 100 percent in 1960 to less than 4 percent by 1992. Furthermore, the aluminum content of automobiles was expected to increase dramatically in the 1990s.

Environmental expenditures were also expected to increase through the 1990s. Stringent new amendments to the Clean Air Act were passed in 1990 and were expected to raise production costs. Some industry participants predicted dire consequences for the industry as a result of the new standards. Already, environmental expenditures had grown from 5 percent of industry capital outlays in 1987 to 15 percent in 1991. In addition, a new requirement for toxic coke oven emissions threatened to add $17, or 3 percent of total costs, to each ton of steel produced for integrated companies. Minimills were expected to suffer from provisions affecting electric power plants. Steelmakers hoped to offset some of these increases by boosting the use of recycled steel, which in 1993 was used to produce about 30 percent of industry output.

The new environmental regulations also made it easier to punish business executives for failing to have their companies comply with standards. For example, the maximum fine of $25,000 per day and one year in prison was increased to $250,000 per day for individuals, $500,000 per day for companies, and up to five years in prison for executives. The new amendments also allowed prosecutors to use circumstantial evidence, and increased the number of areas in which individuals could be held liable from four to 15.

Although U.S. steelmakers had made great strides in relation to their foreign counterparts, they continued to struggle toward profitability in the early 1990s. Global steel markets were shrinking and an intensely competitive environment was keeping manufacturers from raising their prices at rates greater than inflation. The top six U.S. producers, for instance, lost $1.5 billion in 1991 and $1 billion in 1992. These companies were expected to post combined profits of $500 million in 1993, however. Industry losses totaled over $2 billion in 1992, though many analysts predicted positive income for 1993. Meanwhile, total global demand for steel actually fell from a peak of 786 million metric tons in 1989 to 714 million in 1992.

The Future of Steel. Steel shipments were expected to rise about 1.5 percent in 1993, to about 84 million tons. Growth was expected to remain sluggish and increase to 87 million tons in 1996. The industry anticipated increased consumption by service centers, automobile manufacturers, and construction firms, at least in the short term, but was not expecting any demand increases from oil and gas producers. Demand from capital goods markets was also expected to increase slightly through 1994, and higher earnings for steelmakers were expected to result from long-awaited price increases, made possible by a recovering economy and anti-dumping legislation.

Integrated steelmakers, which were under severe profit pressure during the 1980s, were expected to reap the most benefits from increased prices. Nevertheless, analysts expected that minimills would continue to gain market share and to significantly outperform integrated facilities throughout the 1990s. Minimills promised to pose a growing threat as they expanded their offerings to include flat-rolled sheet steel and large structural products—currently the domain of integrated producers. Furthermore, rapid advancements in minimill production technology were allowing this sector to compete with integrated manufacturers in a growing number of markets.

Case Study in Quality. In May of 1993, Honda of American Manufacturing granted its American sheet steel supplier, LTV, the first production support quality award ever given to an American steel company. In 1992, LTV made 100 percent of its deliveries on time to Honda, and also met a defect level of .0012 percent. In fact, LTV was replacing Nippon Steel as Honda's supplier of vehicle hood skins because it offered the highest quality. In 1993, Honda of America was likely to become the only auto manufacturer in the U.S. that uses 100 percent U.S. steel—even the Big Three U.S. automakers received some steel from Japan.

Indeed, one of the most visible examples of enhanced U.S. steel quality since the early 1980s has occurred in the auto market. Ford Motor Company, for instance, realized a drop in its rejection rate of steel from 8.8 percent in 1982 to less than 1 percent in 1991. More significantly, steelmakers were increasingly gaining access to Japanese auto manufacturing plants in the U.S. that have traditionally maintained the highest quality standards. Nissan in Tennessee, Honda in Ohio, and AutoAlliance in Michigan (a Mazda/Ford venture) were all receiving nearly 100 percent of their steel from U.S. producers in 1993.

INDUSTRY LEADERS

United States Steel, of Pittsburgh, a subsidiary of USX Corp., is the largest domestic steelmaker. USX's U.S. Steel Group had sales of nearly $5.5 billion and employed 21,500 workers in 1991. The USX corporation suffered losses of $578 million from $17.1 billion in sales in that year. In 1973, this company produced a record 35 million net tons of raw steel. By 1990, however, its total steelmaking capacity had shrunk from 37 million to 19 million tons. The capacity reduction was the result of a restructuring effort in the 1980s that eliminated or modernized its facilities. In 1990, U.S. Steel operated six plants.

The second largest company producing steel, by revenues, in the early 1990s was LTV Corporation, of Dallas. In 1991, this industry giant had sales of $6.1 billion and employed 35,300 people. LTV Steel, LTV Corporation's steelmaking subsidiary, was formed as a result of the merger of Jones & Laughlin and Republic Steel in 1984. Shortly thereafter, following a price collapse in 1985, LTV Steel filed for bankruptcy. Massive capital investments, joint ventures, and automation efforts helped revive the company in the late 1980s, however. From a loss of over $3 billion in 1986, LTV rebounded to a net income of $74 million in 1991. Other large integrated steel producers include ARMCO, Bethlehem Steel Corp., Inland Steel, and National Steel Corp.

Nucor Corp. One of the most progressive and successful steel producers in the early 1990s was Nucor Corporation, of North Carolina. In contrast to the larger producers already mentioned, Nucor produced steel in minimills. With a net income of $64.7 million from operating revenues of $1.5 billion in 1991, this company was the most profitable of the large producers. Established in 1967 with a single mill in South Carolina, Nucor had added 5 plants by 1991 with a production capacity of about 4 million tons per year. Using state-of-the-art technology, such as EAFs and continuous casting, Nucor was able to produce steel from scrap at a fraction of the cost incurred by its larger competitors.

Nucor has also been a leader in expanding the markets served by the minimill sector. In the early 1990s the company was breaking into the flat-rolled steel market, which previously was controlled entirely by integrated producers and accounted for about 45 percent of their production. To produce this sheet steel, Nucor was utilizing a new technique called thin-slab casting. This method was proving much less costly than conventional casting methods. Nucor's thin-slab casting operation became profitable in June 1990, only ten months after it started production, and was operating at its maximum capacity of 800,000 tons-per-year by 1992.

In July of 1992, Nucor opened a new $330-million, one-million-ton-per-year, thin-slab casting sheet plant in Arkansas. The company also announced plans to control 20 percent of the sheet steel market in 2000 by progressing to 8 million tons of capacity. In addition to its attack on the sheet steel market, Nucor also constructed a mill in partnership with Yamato of Japan to roll wide-flange beams—a product produced primarily by integrated mills in the early 1990s.

WORK FORCE

U.S. steel productivity nearly doubled between 1980 and 1993. During the same period, the number of manhours required to produce a unit of steel plummeted more than threefold. These factors, combined with a reduction in demand since the late 1980s, dealt a lethal blow to many jobs in the industry. The trend toward automation was expected to maintain a trend toward fewer workers. Furthermore, workers worried that passage of the North American Free Trade Agreement (NAFTA) would have potentially devastating effects on laborers. Workers in the industry were concerned that producers would be drawn to the low-cost labor and reduced environmental liability offered in Mexico and consequently close numerous U.S. plants.

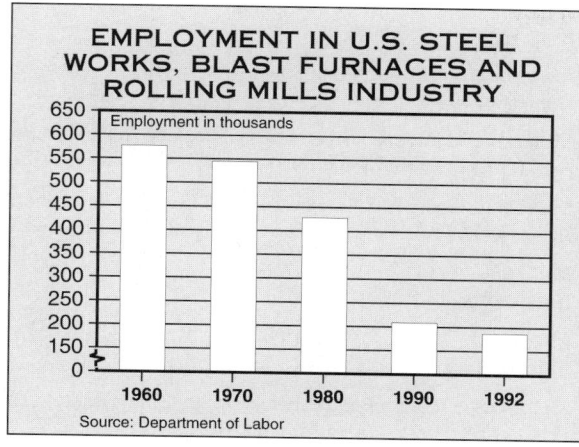

EMPLOYMENT IN U.S. STEEL WORKS, BLAST FURNACES AND ROLLING MILLS INDUSTRY

Employment in thousands

650, 600, 550, 500, 450, 400, 350, 300, 250, 200, 150, 0

1960 1970 1980 1990 1992

Source: Department of Labor

While overall steel employment was likely to decline through the 1990s, new positions were expected in the emerging minimill sector. In fact, employment growth at minimills rose by an average of 19 percent between 1986 and 1991, while employment at integrated companies fell by 30 percent.

Current Contracts. In 1993, *Monthly Labor Review* noted, "the United Steelworkers indicated that it wanted to move away from an adversarial approach to bargaining and would seek innovative agreements with longer durations, less restrictive work rules, and ways to reduce the work force in return for more job security and a greater voice in how the steel companies are run. In reaching agreements with four of the major domestic steelmakers during 1993, the union succeeded in reshaping collective bargaining in the industry." The first settlement was reached with Inland Steel Industries; it gave the union greater job security and decision making input, while management enjoyed a longer term contract with fewer work rules and a reduction in the work force. The union then reached agreement with Bethlehem Steel Corp. and National Steel Corp., and, after protracted discussions, was able to reach agreement with U.S. Steel.

AMERICA AND THE WORLD

U.S. exports of steel reached 6.3 million tons in 1992, representing a record 8 percent of total shipments. Despite moderate export growth and the comparative productivity of U.S. steelmakers, however, the U.S. steel industry still faced huge trade deficits in the early 1990s. Imports in 1992, for instance, exceeded $8.3 billion, versus just $3.8 billion in exports. The only region in which the United States held a surplus was North America, where Canada and Mexico purchased over $2 billion of U.S. steel, versus about $1.8 billion which the U.S. bought from those

two countries. The EC, on the other hand, sold $2.4 billion worth of steel to the United States and purchased only $309 million from domestic steelmakers. Significant deficits also existed with Japan, Asia, and South America. Domestic producers hoped that new anti-dumping legislation would reduce the imbalance.

Total global steel production dropped to 714 million metric tons in 1992, about 3 percent below the 1991 level, and the total value of the world industry hovered around $300 billion. The Commonwealth of Independent States (formerly the U.S.S.R) produced the largest portion of global output, at 111 million metric tons. That region's production had been falling steadily since 1988, however, and had dropped 16 percent in 1991 alone. Japan, the second largest producer, generated 98 million tons of steel in 1992.

The United States ranked third in the world order, with about 83 million metric tons of production. Interestingly, the United States was one of only two large steel producers that increased its total production over 1991 levels. China, which also increased its 1991 production levels by a solid 13 percent, produced 80 million metric tons of steel in 1992. This country threatened to quickly overcome the U.S. steel industry in size. Germany produced about 40 million metric tons of steel in 1992, Korea generated about 30 million tons, Italy pumped out 25 million tons, and Brazil produced 24 million tons of steel.

The International Iron and Steel Institute (ISI) estimates that world production will grow by about 32 million tons by the turn of the century. Most growth was expected to occur in developing nations, where the average growth rate approached 25 percent between 1987 and 1991. Asia, at least in the short term, offered the greatest likelihood of increased consumption.

RESEARCH AND TECHNOLOGY

Rather than expanding production capacity, producers in the late 1980s and 1990s were relying on new technology to help achieve greater efficiency and quality. Because the overall global steel market has matured, companies in the early 1990s could grow only by increasing market share, raising profit margins, or by developing new steel products.

In addition to continuous casting, thin-slab casting, and EAFs, companies were experimenting with a variety of new production techniques. For example, an array of devices were being employed in the early 1990s to help companies spot, map, describe, and classify defects in sheet steel that were as small as .02 inches in diameter. Strobe lights, laser beams, and artificial intelligence systems were all at work insuring higher quality output. Furthermore, continuing advancements in alloys and steel coatings were allowing manufacturers to create new steel products that could compete with advanced plastics and ceramics.

An important development for integrated steel mills in the early 1990s was "direct" steelmaking. Using the direct process, companies were able to combine coke ovens, blast furnaces, and BOFs into one process. Besides lowering production costs by about 10 percent, direct steelmaking also eliminated many harmful emissions. Consequently, this alternative was seen as a way to substantially reduce the amount of capital that companies would have to spend to replace obsolete ovens and furnaces. An experimental facility, built by a government/industry cooperative in 1990, was already operating in Pittsburgh. A second, larger experimental facility was scheduled for completion by 1995, and several foreign competitors were building similar plants.

Besides new production techniques, U.S. steelmakers were also realizing productivity gains in the early 1990s through information technology. Bethlehem Steel, for instance, entered a 10-year contract with Electronic Data Systems, Inc. to coordinate its operations. EDS will eventually provide Bethlehem with all necessary resources for data center management, applications development support, and process control activities. The goal of the effort was to fully integrate all aspects of Bethlehem's operations and to allow the company to concentrate on steelmaking, rather than information management.

INDUSTRY INFORMATION SOURCES

Baker, Stephen. "1993 Industry Outlook: Steel - Striking While the Iron is Hot." *Business Week* (January 11, 1993).

Barnett, Donald F., and Louis Schorsch. *Steel: Upheaval in a Basic Industry.* Cambridge: Ballinger Publishing Company, 1983.

Berry, Bryan. "Japanese Autos: Bodies in Red, White and Blue." *Iron Age* (July 1993).

Darnay, Arsen J., ed. *Manufacturing USA; Industry Analyses, Statistics, and Leading Companies.* Detroit: Gale Research Inc., 1993.

"Green Wave Won't Capsize Steel." *Iron Age* (March 1993).

Hess, George W. "Providing Information Services for Big Steel." *Iron Age* (April 1993).

Hess, George W. "The Eyes Have It." *Iron Age* (July 1993).

Hogan, William Thomas. *Global Steel in the 1990s.* Lexington, Mass.: Lexington Books, 1991.

"Iron Age's Guide to Steel Prices, Production Levels." *Iron Age* (March 1993).

Jacobson, John E. "Minimill Mentality is Key to Survival." *Iron Age* (March 1993).

Jacobson, John E. "Finding Success in the 1990s." *Iron Age* (January 1993).

McKenna, Maureen. "Steelmakers Focus on Survival Strategies." *Iron Age* (August 1993).

McManus, George J. "Integrateds Still Looking for Profits." *Iron Age* (March 1993).

McManus, George J. "The Direct Approach to Making Iron." *Iron Age* (July 1993).

McManus, George J. "Steel Outlook: Bottom's Up." *Iron Age* (January 1993).

McManus, George J. "Demand Up In First Quarter, But Profits Still Down." *Iron Age* (June 1993).

Paskoff, Paul F. *Iron and Steel in the Nineteenth Century.* New York: Bruccoli Clark Layman, Inc., 1989.

Standard & Poor's Industry Surveys. New York: Standard & Poor's Corporation, November 12, 1992.

U.S. Industrial Outlook 1993. Washington, D.C.: U.S. Department of Commerce, January 1993.

—Dave Mote

SIC 3313

ELECTROMETALLURGICAL PRODUCTS, EXCEPT STEEL

The electrometallurgical products industry comprises companies that manufacture metal additive alloys for both ferrous and nonferrous metals using electrometallurgical or metallothermic processes. Establishments primarily engaged in manufacturing electrometallurgical steel are classified in **SIC 3312: Steel Works, Blast Furnaces (Including Coke Ovens), and Rolling Mills.**

The following alloying metals are used most commonly to enhance iron and steel: nickel, molybdenum, manganese, silocon, aluminum, phosphorus, calcium, sulfur, lead, and selenium. Tungsten carbide powder and spiegeleisen are also produced in this industry. Alloys have three main purposes: to eliminate undesired elements in a base metal; to add special characteristics, such as strength, heat resistance, and corrosion resistance; and to neutralize unwanted properties of a metal.

Electrometallurgical companies were shipping about $1.1 billion worth of products per year in the early 1990s. Nickel and molybdenum, the most common alloys produced in the industry, accounted for over $700 million and $175 million of total shipments, respectively. Nickel is used primarily to create stainless steel, while molybdenum is used to strengthen steel for aerospace and other specialty steel applications.

North American metals producers have been strengthening and enhancing iron and steel with alloys since the 1600s. Only since World War II, however, has the mining and production of the alloying metals emerged as a significant industry. Since that time, the federal government has promoted the extraction and processing of various ferrous and nonferrous alloys as a means of insuring reserves for national defense and security.

Demand for alloy metals surged from the 1950s through the 1970s, as the U.S. economy expanded and new alloying technologies broadened the industry's market. The auto and capital equipment industries, particularly, became major consumers of ferroalloys during that period. By the end of the 1970s, the electrometallurgical industry employed about 6,000 workers and was shipping about $700 million worth of products each year.

As maturing markets, high production costs, and metal substitutes reduced U.S. steel production in the 1980s, growth of alloy demand slowed—despite the fact that the percentage of metals that used alloys continued to rise. The value of shipments dropped from $707 million in 1982 to a low of $667 million in 1986, and employment plummeted to 3,600.

As steel and other metal orders rose in the late 1980s the alloy market rebounded, sending the value of shipments past $1.2 billion by 1990. Despite a huge increase in production tonnage, industry profitability sagged as the competitive and glutted market steadily eroded prices. The price of nickel, for instance, fell from $6.49 per pound in 1988 to about $3.00 by 1993. Similarly, molybdenum prices dropped to under $3.00 from $3.50 in 1988. Going into the 1990s, producers of ferrous and nonferrous alloys expected a mild reprieve from glutted markets and faltering prices. Nickel prices were expected to continue falling, though demand was expected to increase slightly.

Producers expected minuscule revenue growth in the mid-1990s as world steel production remained stagnant. Furthermore, western nickel producers carried 68,000 metric tons of inventory in 1993 that would likely reduce any positive effects of new uses for alloys. Exports were also forecast to languish in the 1990s, despite the relatively high productivity of American companies.

Because income growth in the industry comes largely from increased productivity, employment is

expected to decrease. The number of workers employed in most sectors of the industry will likely decline by 10 percent to 30 percent by 2005. Virtually every occupation in the alloy industry was forecast by the Bureau of Labor Statistics to decline between 1990 and 2005. New manufacturing and information technologies that increase automation will yield most of the productivity gains.

The largest producer in the industry in the early 1990s was Shieldalloy Metallurgical Corp. of New Jersey. The company realized an estimated $220 million in sales during 1991, with only 400 employees. Elkem Metals Co. of Pittsburgh, Pennsylvania was the second largest leader in the business, with sales of $190 million and 2,300 employees. Other large electrometallurgical corporations in the early 1990s included: SKW Alloys, Inc. of New York; Climax Performance Materials of Connecticut; and Globe Metallurgical Inc. of Illinois.

INDUSTRY INFORMATION SOURCES

Darnay, Arsen J., ed. *Manufacturing USA; Industry Analyses, Statistics, and Leading Companies*. Detroit: Gale Research Inc., 1993.

Standard & Poor's Industry Surveys. New York: Standard & Poor's Corporation, (November 12, 1992)

Stundza, Tom. ''Slow-Growth Climate Supplants No-Growth.'' *Purchasing* (April 1, 1993).

Stundza, Tom. ''Nonferrous 1992: Recovery, Yes; Bull Markets, No!'' *Purchasing* (March 5, 1993).

Stundza, Tom. ''Glut Smothers Pricing; Hikes Will Be Sluggish.'' *Purchasing* (August 19, 1993).

Stundza, Tom. ''High-Strength Alloys Pursue New Markets.'' *Purchasing* (September 10, 1992).

U.S. Department of Commerce. *U.S. Industrial Outlook 1993*. Washington, D.C.: U.S. Department of Commerce, (January, 1993).

—Dave Mote

SIC 3315

STEEL WIREDRAWING AND STEEL NAILS AND SPIKES

This category covers establishments primarily engaged in drawing wire from purchased iron or steel rods, bars, or wire, as well as those which may be engaged in the further manufacture of products made from wire. Establishments primarily engaged in manufacturing steel nails and spikes from purchased materials are also included in this industry. Rolling mills engaged in the production of ferrous wire from wire rods or hot-rolled bars produced in the same establishment are classified under **SIC 3312: Blast Furnaces and Steel Mills.** Establishments primarily engaged in drawing nonferrous wire are classified in other industry categories.

INDUSTRY SNAPSHOT

The steel wire and related products industry shipped 631,000 tons of product during the first nine months of 1993, a figure down approximately one percent from the first nine months of 1992. After disappointing sales during most of the 1980s, the industry looked forward to improved economic conditions as well as a general strengthening of the automobile, housing, and construction industries, businesses on which steel wire makers relied for sales.

Steel wiredrawing represented approximately one percent of all American steel industry shipments in 1993. Wiredrawing plants manufactured a wide variety of products including barbed and twisted wire, steel baskets, brads, cable, chain link fencing, fence gates, posts and fittings, form ties, horseshoe nails, steel nails, paper clips, spikes, staples, wire cages, tacks, tie wires, wire fabric, wire carts, wire cloth, and wire garment hangers.

As the global economy improved in the mid-1990s, important financial ratios for the industry were also expected to improve. Gross profit margins for 1992 averaged 25.2 percent of sales, down from 26.3 percent in 1991. Net profit margins after tax in 1992 averaged 3.5 percent, up from 2.5 percent in 1991. Return on assets averaged 4.7 percent in 1992, up from 2.9 percent in 1991.

ORGANIZATION AND STRUCTURE

In 1991, industry shipments totaled $3.9 billion, and 865,000 tons of steel wire and related products were shipped. From 1990 to 1991, the dollar value of shipments dropped 5.6 percent, while tonnage shipped dropped 5.8 percent. Due to increased foreign competition and the substitution of other materials for steel, production levels were not expected to return to industry peaks reached during the mid-1960s, when yearly production levels of 3.5 million tons of steel wire and related products were common.

In 1993, approximately 350 companies produced steel wire and related products, and over 200 of these firms retained more than 20 employees. The largest concentration of firms by shipment value were in the Great Lakes region of the United States, with the Southeast and New England regions ranking second

and third, respectively. The largest producing states in descending order of shipments were Illinois, California, Massachusetts, Texas, Pennsylvania, Ohio, and New Jersey.

Seven major classes of steel wire and related products comprised the industry category. Noninsulated ferrous wire rope, cable, and strand manufactured in wiredrawing plants represented approximately 20.2 percent of the dollar value of the steel wire and related products industry shipments in 1990. Steel nails, staples, tacks, spikes, and brads made up approximately 13 percent of this industry's total product shipments. Steel wire not produced in steel mills represented approximately 35.5 percent of total product shipments, while fencing and fence gates made in wiredrawing plants accounted for approximately 6.3 percent. Ferrous wire cloth and other ferrous woven wire products made in wiredrawing plants comprised 2.3 percent of industry shipments. Other fabricated ferrous wire products, except springs, represented 16.5 percent of steel wire product shipments. Steel wire and related products not elsewhere classified made up approximately 6.2 percent of total industry shipments.

BACKGROUND AND DEVELOPMENT

The demand for steel wire evolved from the housing, construction, and automotive industries. To service these markets, steel wire makers bought steel rod from both domestic and foreign mills and drew it into wire and other related products. While steel wiredrawing companies shopped globally for the least expensive sources of steel bar, their ability to buy from foreign sources depended on the trade climate between the United States and its competitors. Protectionist legislation imposed by the U.S. Congress often involved quotas or costly duties on the price of steel bar and wire, increasing expense to manufacturers that may be passed to their customers.

During the 1980s, increases in imports during the recession coupled with high dollar valuations led many domestic steel wire producers to call for extended voluntary restraint arrangements and duties on imported steel wire and products. The high inflation rates, interest rates, and value of the dollar made offshore sources of steel wire attractive and affordable for domestic users. Industry shipments dropped 21.4 percent between 1981 to 1982.

From the mid-1980s to the early 1990s, American steel wire producers charged many countries with unfair trading practices, most notably with dumping product at prices less than the cost to make them. In February 1989, 30 Japanese producers were subject to duties as high as 29.8 percent. The Specialty Steel

Industry of the United States, which represented virtually all U.S. producers of stainless and alloy tool steels and other high technology metals, found that import penetration grew to 20.2 percent of the U.S. market, up from 18.6 percent in 1990. In 1991, Mexico and South Korea accounted for over 75 percent, or 54,599 tons, of steel wire rope imports. In March 1993, the International Trade Commission determined that both countries were guilty of dumping wire rope. Mexico was assessed anti-dumping margins of 111.68 percent, while South Korea was assessed between 0.1 and 1.51 percent. Steel wire rope imports from South Korea totaled $64.1 million in 1991. Antidumping duties of 24.39 percent on stainless wire rod imports from two French producers, and duties placed on three Brazilian producers between 24.63 and 26.50 percent, were also assessed by the International Trade Commission.

CURRENT CONDITIONS

The upturn in the U.S. economy during the last half of 1993 was expected to help domestic wire makers, as demand among automakers, appliance manufacturers, and construction firms increased. At the end of 1993, steel wire makers asked for three percent price increases for finished products, which in most cases were granted. Bookings remained strong through the first quarter of 1994, and further price increases of two to three percent were expected by mid-1994. Due to increased demand, delivery times for steel shipping were extended. As the world economies, particularly in Europe and Japan, slowly improved, some industry analysts predicted shortages of steel wire. Others speculated that higher domestic steel prices could lead to increased use of cheaper, offshore sources of steel.

The optimism among most steel wire makers in the United States was not shared among those on the West Coast, where the extremely soft housing market and the decline in building and construction activity in Southern California prolonged the industry slump. Furthermore, price hikes in the cost of steel rod by domestic suppliers east of the Rockies made it difficult for West Coast steel wire manufacturers to pass along additional raw material costs to customers.

INDUSTRY LEADERS

While the majority of steel wire producers were privately held firms, a relatively large number were subsidiaries or divisions of larger companies. Some of the largest producers by sales and number of employees in 1993 included Cablec Corp. ($370 million in sales and 2,500 employees); National-Standard ($303 million in sales and 2,500 employees); Stanley-Bost ($290 million in sales and 3,400 employees); Duo-Fast ($210 million in sales and 1,200 employees); Bekaert Corp. ($190 million in sales and 1,300 employees); and Davis Walker ($150 million in sales and 800 employees).

Growth in the industry was reflected by Goodyear Tire and Rubber, which planned to spend $4.6 million to expand its steel tire cord plant in Asheboro, North Carolina, where wire for earthmover and truck tires was manufactured. Furthermore, in January 1992, Nucor Corp. made entered the steel wire industry, signing a licensing agreement with Gradic Wire AB, a Swedish firm, for direct wire casting technology. The mini-mill bought exclusive North American rights to G-castings, a patented direct coast wire technique that assured high productivity, low investment cost, high yields, and lower product costs.

WORK FORCE

Employment in the industry peaked in 1979 at 33,800 and then reached an industry low in 1985, with a work force of 20,900. While sharp increases in hiring led to employment figures of 27,000 in 1988, employment has generally fallen steadily since that time. In 1991, the industry's work force totaled 25,200, down 5.6 percent from 1990. Most workers were represented by the United Steel Workers of America.

Total compensation, which included payroll, social security and other legally required payments, and other employer payments and programs, was $846,000 in 1991. During the 1980s, salaries generally declined, while social security and other legally required payments as a percent of total compensation increased. Hours worked fell 8.3 percent to 40.8 million hours between 1990 and 1991. Wages in the U.S. steel wiredrawing and steel nails industry averaged $11.52 in 1991.

Steel wire makers faced several employment issues in the 1990s, including spiraling healthcare costs and the need for fully funded company pension plans. During this time, many smaller companies had health care costs that exceeded earnings.

AMERICA AND THE WORLD

The North American Free Trade Agreement (NAFTA), ratified in the fall of 1993 by President Clinton, was expected to reduce the level of steel wire duties among the United States, Mexico, and Canada. In the early 1990s, steel wire tariffs averaged between ten and 15 percent in Mexico, 1.5 and 5.6 percent in the United States, and 5.7 and 6.8 percent in Canada. For stainless steel wire, tariffs averaged ten percent in Mexico, between 3.3 and 10.6 percent in the United

States, and zero to 12.5 percent in Canada. Under NAFTA, all tariffs on steel wire products shipped within North America would fall to zero in the year 2004, while Mexican tariffs would slowly fall over a ten-year period. Many members of the American Wire Producers Association raised concerns over this discrepancy in phaseout periods.

From 1982 to 1987, imports of steel wire shot up 40 percent from 625,000 tons to 1.04 million tons, reaching a high of 1.18 million tons in 1984. During this period, the relative strength of the dollar held exports to a seven percent increase, or 35,730 tons. However, as the dollar fell in value between 1987 and 1991, exports rose 150 percent. Imports of steel wire and nails in 1991 were 392,000 tons, down 9.3 percent from 1990.

RESEARCH AND TECHNOLOGY

Competition from companies offering specialty metals and new processes posed a continual challenge to the industry, as their traditional markets, such as the automotive and construction industries, looked to use lighter, stronger, and cheaper materials. Seeking to expand its market as well as its sources for raw materials, the industry regarded recycling as a potential important area. Tamco, a rebar manufacturing company in California, tested the recycling of steel wire from discarded steel-belted tires to produce new steel. In addition, 3M introduced a "Never Rust" Wool Soap Pad made from recycled beverage containers.

INDUSTRY INFORMATION SOURCES

Justin, Martin, "Big Steel Loses," *Fortune,* August 23, 1993.

"Schedule of Proposed Tariff Eliminations in the North American Free Trade Agreement," *American-Metal-Market,* September 17, 1992.

Shapiro, Eben, "Minnesota Mining's Wool Pads Grab Sizable Chunk of Business," *Wall Street Journal,* January 13, 1994.

—William A. Bennett

SIC 3316

COLD FINISHING OF STEEL SHAPES

This industry covers establishments primarily engaged in cold-rolling steel sheets and strip from purchased hot-rolled sheets; cold-drawing steel bars and steel shapes from purchased hot-rolled steel bars; and producing other cold finished steel. Establishments primarily engaged in the production of steel, including hot-rolled steel sheets that are then cold-rolled are classified in **SIC 3312: Blast Furnaces and Steel Mills.**

INDUSTRY SNAPSHOT

The demand for cold finished steel comes primarily from the automotive, aerospace, construction, housing, and home appliance industries. In 1993, the U.S. cold finishing steel industry shipped 15.02 million tons of steel, up 2.8 percent from the 14.61 million tons shipped in 1992. Throughout 1993, the industry experienced increased orders, largely due to the recovering domestic economy and a reduction in imported steel. That year, the automobile, appliance, and housing markets strengthened, and steel prices rose for the first time in four years. However, despite the increased demand for cold finished steel, excess capacity for the entire industry remained at 50 percent.

As the industry entered the mid-1990s, it's success hinged on its ability to meet the needs of domestic durable goods customers in a climate of rising competition, business costs, and alternative uses of new metals and plastics. The industry was therefore called upon to improve quality, technology, and productivity while working in partnership with their customers to enhance their prospects for long-term survival.

ORGANIZATION AND STRUCTURE

There were approximately 150 companies producing cold finished steel shapes in 1993. Over 100 of these firms employed more than 20 employees. The largest concentration of firms by shipment value could be found in the Great Lakes region of the United States. The Northeast and West Coast were second and third, respectively. The largest producing states in descending order of shipments were Ohio, Michigan, Connecticut, Illinois, California, Pennsylvania, Indiana, and New York.

Cold-rolling is the process of rolling steel without first reheating it. This method produces a smooth steel surface that reduces thickness and enhances machinability. Cold-rolling gives steel the ability to be stretched and shaped without cracking and provides it with a bright finish. The three main product classes within the industry are steel sheet, steel strip, and steel bars.

Steel sheet and strip are both flat products that are generally less than 1/4-inch thick. Sheet is the wider of the two by 12 inches or more and is produced to less exact thicknesses than strip. In 1992, cold-rolled steel sheet represented approximately 84 percent of this industry group's total shipments in tons and 15.4 percent of all steel shipments made in the United States. Cold-rolled steel strip represented approximately six percent of this group's total shipments in tons and .8 percent of total U.S. steel shipments in 1992. Steelmakers produce most sheet and strip in the form of large coils that the user can cut into pieces of any desired length. Much of the sheet and strip manufactured is used in automobile bodies, but thousands of other products also contain these forms of steel.

Cold finished steel bars represented approximately ten percent of this group's total shipments in tons and 1.4 percent of total U.S. steel shipments in 1992. Steel companies make bars in many sizes and various shapes, including squares, circles, ovals, hexagons, and rectangles. Products made from steel bars include many precision-engineered components that power automobiles, trucks, tractors, hand tools, washing machines, and lawn mowers.

BACKGROUND AND DEVELOPMENT

The production of cold finished steel became industrialized early in the twentieth century, prompted by the mass marketing of automobiles, household appliances, and industrial machinery, all of which required cold finished steel parts. New and more efficient steel production methods ensued at a rapid pace.

During World War II, the American steel industry boomed, while in other countries steel manufacturing facilities sustained considerable damage. Global steel markets were dominated by American firms during the postwar years, and by 1960, American shipments of cold finished steel shapes totaled 17 million tons, rising to 20 million tons by the middle of the decade. During this time, however, Japan and several European countries focused on rebuilding their steel industries, using the most modern facilities and equipment available, while American steelmakers continued to use older, less efficient equipment. Consequently, American shipments fell below 17 million tons in 1970.

Worldwide inflation and high interest rates in the early 1970s curtailed foreign steel production, particularly in developing nations, allowing U.S. shipments to realize significant gains. In 1973, U.S. shipments stood at 24.09 million tons, the highest level experienced by the industry in over two decades. However, economic recession in the United States eventually pushed shipments back down to 20.76 million tons in 1979.

The cold finished steel industry faced intense foreign competition during the 1980s. Due to the high value of the dollar, foreign steel became significantly less expensive than American steel. Furthermore, having rebuilt and improved their facilities, foreign producers were marketing a superior product, and this quality gap widened significantly during the decade. Consequently, American companies operating with outdated equipment and production methods were often priced out of the market. From 1979 to 1980, U.S. shipments of cold finished steel dropped 24 percent. The industry recovered slightly in 1981 with shipments rising eight percent. However, the following year, shipments fell 25 percent to a 30-year low.

Hoping to become more competitive by realizing productivity gains, some American companies began installing completely automated, high-speed production equipment with computer controlled systems. In 1988, industry shipments stood at 16.3 million tons, representing a small increase over previous years. However, the Gulf War and early 1990s economic recession depressed shipments 16 percent in 1991 to 13.63 million tons. 1992 and 1993 offered slight improvements, with shipments rising to 14.61 and 15.02 million tons, respectively.

CURRENT CONDITIONS

Many analysts doubted that cold finished steel makers would again reach the shipment levels enjoyed during the 1960s and 1970s. Steel sheet and bar shipments had apparently peaked in 1973 at 20.38 and 2.25 million tons each, while steel strip shipments peaked earlier, at 1.58 million tons in 1966.

Nevertheless, the industry regarded the 1990s with optimism. As the industry gradually shed its excess capacity, its ability to raise prices in the face of increasing demand was expected to help buoy profits. Steelmakers also relied on investments in new technologies and commitments to reducing costs to increase their chances for survival and long-term profitability.

Cold-rolled steel sheet shipments during the first nine months of 1993 were 9.588 million tons, down .82 percent from the same nine month period in 1992. Steel strip fell 7.5 percent in 1991 to 755,000 tons, down from 816,000 tons in 1990. Prices for steel strip and sheet, which remained 50 percent lower on average than their last peak in 1988-89, were expected to rise by the mid-1990s. In May 1993, cold rolled steel strip and sheet was priced at $440 per ton, a figure that was predicted to rise to at least $460 per ton by the year's end.

Cold-finished steel bar shipments during the first nine months of 1993 rose sharply to 1.152 million tons, up 43.5 percent from the same nine month period in 1992. As the leading auto manufacturers pushed for cost reductions from all parts suppliers, however, some steel bar manufacturers were expected to have difficulty passing along their rising costs. Moreover, bar suppliers still operated at only 60 percent capacity. Nevertheless, Bernard Lashinsky, former economist for Inland Steel Industries Inc. and director of steel consulting for AUS Consultants, projected cold-finished bar shipments reaching 1.7 million tons in 1995. Furthermore, prices were expected to increase from the extremely depressed levels that existed in the 1980s.

INDUSTRY LEADERS

LTV Steel Company of Cleveland, Ohio, was the country's largest cold-finisher of steel shapes, with 16,400 employees in 1993. The company emerged from protection under Chapter 11 of the Federal Bankruptcy Code in June 1993, and its projected sales for 1994 were $4.5 billion. After substantial reorganization, the company's orders stabilized and shipments increased. LTV Steel planned to increase prices on cold-rolled sheet and strip three percent in January 1994.

Worthington Industries of Columbus, Ohio, was a diversified steel company employing 6,500 workers, with cold finishing operations serving the housing, auto, communications, and leisure industries. Sales for 1994 were expected to reach $1.2 billion with profits of $75 million. Another large firm, Steel Technologies of Louisville, Kentucky, expected its sales to reach $235 million in 1994, with net income of $13 million. While the company marketed to appliance manufacturers, and the electrical and communications industries, more than 75 percent of the its sales went to auto makers. Other industry leaders in the early 1990s included J & L Specialty Products of Pittsburgh; Hitachi Metals of Purchase, New York; and Cyclops Industries of Coshocton, Ohio.

WORK FORCE

Approximately 15,800 employees served the industry in 1991. This reflected a three percent drop in employment from 1990 and a 23 percent drop from the industry high in 1978. Production workers numbered 11,000 in 1991, a 3.5 percent decrease from 1990 and a 36 percent drop from the industry high in 1974. In the early 1990s, attrition and early retirement incentives were used more often than layoffs to cut back on labor costs. Flexible assignment of employees helped reduce the number of classes of skilled steel trades.

Average production wages per hour reached $15.91 in 1991. Total compensation reached $713.7 million that year, of which $538.7 million went for payroll, $67.9 for social security and other legally required payments, and $107.1 million for employer payments and other programs. Nearly all nonmanagement employees belong to the United Steelworkers of America (USWA), one of the largest labor unions in the United States.

AMERICA AND THE WORLD

In the early 1990s, the U.S. steel industry filed charges of unfair competition against several foreign firms. Upon review, the U.S. International Trade Commission (ITC) found that 25 of the claims were justified and assessed duties accordingly. Due to the increased potential for duties imposed by the ITC on their steel, many foreign steelmakers reduced their exports to the United States in 1993.

The 1993 passage of the North American Free Trade Agreement (NAFTA) was expected to help eliminate tariffs placed on foreign steel entering America. Mexico, Canada, and the United States were scheduled to drop all tariffs on cold finished steel traded among the three countries before the year 2004. As of 1993, the tariff on steel sheet, strip, and bar exported by Mexico was ten percent. Canada's tariffs on sheet and strip were between 6.8 and 10.2 percent, and on bar between zero and 12.5 percent. The United States tariffs on sheet and strip were between 2.4 and six percent, and on bar between 3.3 and 10.6 percent.

RESEARCH AND TECHNOLOGY

In the early 1990s, the industry was concerned with improving the quality and reputation of steel in the face of aggressive marketing techniques by makers of alternative metals. Manufacturers that purchased steel bar typically looked to obtain straight components, tight tolerances, fast machining rates, and quality surfaces—characteristics that could be furnished by alternative materials such as plastics, aluminum, and brass. The low density of aluminum, for example, was found to lengthen tool life and productivity in machining operations as well as to produce a lighter weight, and thereby more fuel efficient, automobile. Moreover, steep declines in brass and aluminum prices made those materials more attractive to manufacturers. Analysts estimated that by 1995, aluminum and plastic would displace more than 200,000 tons of steel in automotive panels alone.

In order to compete for market share, the steel industry sought a better understanding of the product's end use and to communicate to customers the advantages of steel. By becoming a part of their customers' product problem-solving and supplier development teams, steel firms hoped to win back lost markets and combat the substitution of alternative metals for their cold-finished steel.

INDUSTRY INFORMATION SOURCES

Class, James M., "Metals: Steelmakers are Starting to Shine Again, But Not So Producers of Aluminum, Copper and Nickel," *Forbes,* January 3, 1994.

Justin, Martin, "Big Steel Loses," *Fortune,* August 23, 1993.

Norton, Erle, "Top Steelmakers Welcome 1994 With 3% Price Increase," *The Wall Street Journal,* January 6, 1994.

"Schedule of Proposed Tariff Eliminations in the North American Free Trade Agreement," *American-Metal-Market,* September 17, 1992.

—William A. Bennett

SIC 3317

STEEL PIPE AND TUBES

Included in this category are establishments primarily engaged in the production of welded or seamless steel pipe and tubes and heavy riveted steel pipe from purchased materials. Establishments primarily engaged in the production of steel, including steel skelp or steel blanks, tube rounds, or pierced billets, are classified under **SIC 3312: Blast Furnaces & Steel Mills.**

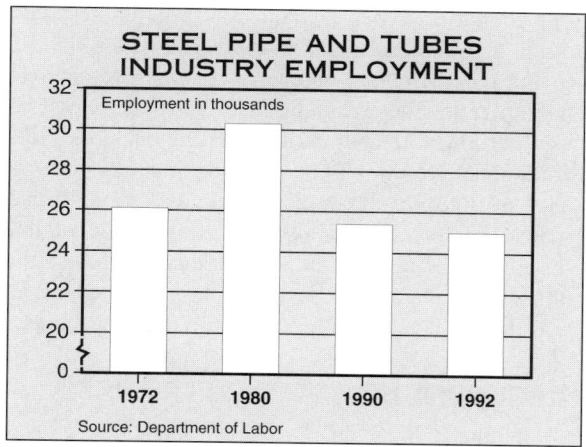

STEEL PIPE AND TUBES INDUSTRY EMPLOYMENT

Employment in thousands

Source: Department of Labor

After some years of declining sales, the American steel pipe and tubes industry appeared to be entering a period of stronger economic growth in the mid-1990s. During the first seven months of 1993, shipments were running 22.1 percent ahead of 1992's first seven months. Total shipments were 3.645 million tons in 1992, down 18.8 percent from the 1991 level of 4,488 million tons. Rising demand and increases in raw material and energy costs drove the prices of seamless carbon tubing up to $973 per ton, welded tubing up to $739 per ton, seamless carbon casing up to $701 per ton, and welded casing up to $560 per ton.

In the United States, the automotive, display fixture, juvenile furniture, and exercise and recreation equipment industries showed healthy increases in demand for steel pipes and tubes. Regionally, the Midwest, mountain, and southern states exhibited high demand, while sales in the northeast and on the West Coast remained stagnant. The U.S. market was expected to reach its peak in 1994-95, while strong global demand was expected as well.

In the steel pipe and tube industry, approximately 221 companies employed 22,700 workers, of which 17,300 were in production, in 1991. That year total compensation reached $677.8 million. The largest producing states in descending order were Ohio, Pennsylvania, Michigan, Illinois, New Jersey, and Arkansas. New capital expenditures on plant and equipment totaled $144.8 million, an increase of over 45 percent from 1990 levels.

The American steel pipe and tube industry exported 753,117 net tons in 1991, a 60 percent increase over the 1990 level of 470,783 tons. Imports of foreign steel pipe and tubes totaled 2.7 million tons, an increase of over 5.6 percent from 1990.

In 1992, the U.S. International Trade Commission and U.S. Commerce Department ruled in favor of many American pipe and tube manufacturers, concluding that foreign countries were dumping their shipments into the U.S. market at less than the cost of production or values sold at home. The countries found guilty of dumping in 1992 (with corresponding duties assessed) were: Brazil (103.38 percent); South Korea (4.9-11.6 percent); Mexico (32.6 percent); Taiwan (19.5-27.7 percent); and Venezuela (52.5 percent).

Also during this time, the Committee on Pipe and Tube Imports was one of the few steel trade associations that supported the North American Free Trade Agreement (NAFTA). The industry believed NAFTA would increase demand for steel pipe and tubes among the United States, Canada, and Mexico. Phaseout of the two percent U.S. tariffs and ten to 15 percent Mexican tariffs would occur under the pact.

The TI Vari-Form operations of Bundy International Corp. of Warren, Michigan, designed a tubular steel closure assembly for the Dodge Ram pickup trucks for the fall of 1993. A new tubing subframe that cradled the car's engine while supporting the front suspension was also slated for Ford's 1995 Topaz and Tempo models. Both developments could increase Bundy's tubular shipments by 12,000 additional tons per year, while also leading to other uses for steel tubing in cars in the future.

INDUSTRY INFORMATION SOURCES

Beirne, Mike, "North Star Increases Tube Price $15 Per Ton," *American-Metal-Market,* September 22, 1993.

Giobbe, Dorothy, "Pipe and Tubing Survey: Cautious Hope Again—On a Stronger Base," *Metal-Center-News,* February 1993.

"Tubular Steel Gets Chrysler Nod: It's for Radiator Part in Ram Pickup Truck," *American-Metal-Market,* August 3, 1993.

Vivani, Laura, "Pipemakers Allege Circumvention," *American-Metal-Market,* April 26, 1993.

Wrigley, Al, "Ford Nod To New Subframe Spurs Use Of Steel Tubing," *American-Metal-Market,* April 2, 1993.

—William A. Bennett

SIC 3321

GRAY AND DUCTILE IRON FOUNDRIES

This classification covers establishments primarily engaged in manufacturing gray and ductile iron castings, including cast iron pressure and soil pipes and fittings.

INDUSTRY SNAPSHOT

The foundry industry as a whole has been cut in half since 1955 when the number of establishments involved in ferrous and non-ferrous casting across the country was 6,000. Only 3,100 establishments remained in 1990, with approximately 700 engaged in casting gray and ductile iron. However, due to technological advancements and capacity gains through consolidations, output per remaining producer rose.

In 1990, total industry shipments were at only 40 percent of the tonnage shipped in 1978. Gray iron suffered a huge decline between 1978 and 1982, from approximately 18.5 million tons to 9.5 million tons. Since 1982, gray iron shipments have continued to decrease. Ductile iron, however, has shown slight growth in shipments since 1982, continuing a trend started in 1966. The growth of ductile iron was largely due to its increasing recognition as more economical and structurally sound than gray and malleable irons.

The metal casting industry was wounded severely in the 1980s. During the 1970s, the industry was filled with back orders that exceeded annual capacity, providing a seller's market. The pricing strategies reflected this, as did profit margins. However, shipment volume was the key issue during the 1970s, not quality, and certainly not price. During the 1980s, foreign competitors emerged who offered timely delivery of better quality castings at lower prices. During the recession of the late 1980s and early 1990s, consumers turned to overseas suppliers, leaving the domestic producers behind. Consequently, U.S. foundries were operating at no more than 50 percent capacity by the mid-1980s.

ORGANIZATION AND STRUCTURE

This industry is heavily engaged in manufacturing pipes and pipe fittings. However, other segments of the industry are growing in response to changing market demands. For example, the automotive industry has switched most engine components to aluminum in response to consumer demands for lighter, more fuel efficient cars. While this move has hurt some gray and ductile iron foundries, it has forced them to find alternative markets. This is apparent in that 52.6 percent of the product share is claimed by other gray iron castings, and 19.9 percent is claimed by other ductile iron castings. Only 3.9 percent of the product share is taken by cast iron pressure and soil pipe and fittings, and 14 percent is taken by ductile iron pressure pipe and fittings.

Historically, the automotive and aerospace industries were the largest customers of gray and ductile iron foundries. When demand was at its highest, each of the Big Three automakers owned several foundries. In the early 1990s, however, consumer demand for lighter, more fuel efficient cars vastly decreased the iron portion of the automotive casting business. Likewise, since the mid-1980s the poor financial performance of both the domestic automotive and aerospace industries forced closings of many self-contained foundries. Companies in these industries found that outsourcing the casting business was a cheaper alternative than under-utilizing plant and labor capacities.

BACKGROUND AND DEVELOPMENT

Humans have been casting metals for at least 5,000 years. This is evidenced by early societies' progression from the Stone Age to the Bronze Age, when people started extracting ores and shaping them by melting or hammering methods. The Iron Age began in Europe circa 1100 B.C. Cast iron came into commercial use in the early 1700s, when a mechanic named Abraham Darby, and some Dutch workmen established a brass foundry in Bristol, England. It was there that Darby and his men started experimenting with iron as a replacement for brass. Because brass and iron are completely different pouring mediums in terms of their reaction with sand and solidification patterns, Darby faced many technical difficulties in his early experiments. With the help of John Thomas, a boy working in his shop, Darby succeeded in casting a complete iron pot. For proprietary reasons, Darby and Thomas entered into an agreement in which the boy was to remain his servant to keep the secret.

Ductile iron was not discovered until after World War II. Laboratory metallurgists at International Nickel Company noticed that the addition of a higher content of magnesium than is normally required for gray iron produced a structurally different material. When observing the material at a microscopic level, researchers noticed that the graphite particles had taken on a spheroidal shape, thus coining the name "nodular iron" in the United States, and "spheroidal graphite cast iron" in Great Britain. The recognition of nodular iron's mechanical strength, and its ability to provide more ductile than other metals in its class, provided it with its more commonly accepted name, ductile iron. Since its release to the marketplace in 1949, ductile iron has gained acceptance as an important engineering material, and replaced many of the previous applications formerly reserved for steels and other irons. The discovery of ductile iron was one of the greatest achievements in the engineering materials community in the twentieth century.

CURRENT CONDITIONS

Companies in the manufacturing industries have traditionally stepped up sales efforts or cut the price of their products in order to catch and keep customers. However, foundries in the early 1990s faced unprecedented competition, shrinking demand, foreign sourcing, and buyer ignorance and indifference. Consequently, the concept of target marketing was becoming a hot topic during this period as more foundries improved their marketing techniques to broaden their customer base.

Another tool used increasingly by the foundry industry was certification through the International Organization for Standardization. This series of certifications, referred to as ISO 9000, offered distinct competitive advantage for those who qualified and passed the certification audit. Although the audit was intensive, the result was the receipt of an internationally recognized benchmark standard, which signified the recipient was paying attention to details and distinguishing itself as a manufacturer of quality castings, engineered with integrity.

INDUSTRY LEADERS

The following companies were the top five gray and ductile foundries in 1991: Amsted Industries, Inc. with sales of $890 million; Ford Motor Company Casting Division with sales of $550 million; Intermet Corporation of Atlanta with sales of $397 million; U.S. Pipe and Foundry Company with estimated sales of $340 million; and Intermet Corporation of Lynchburg with sales of $300 million. The 75 top-selling companies in 1991 reported combined sales of $6.825 billion and employed 63,500 people.

Ford Motor Company's Casting Division fell victim to the recession in the late 1980s. Having reduced its labor force due to huge reported profit losses, the division followed the automaker's trend and began outsourcing much of its casting needs. Likewise, the push toward aluminum auto components implied that significant re-tooling of existing foundries would be necessary. However, Ford's Casting Division remained an industry pioneer in terms of technological advancement. The Casting Division reported great success with its casting simulation systems, which saved the company both time and money.

Intermet Corporation recently launched a joint venture with Comalco Limited of Australia to extend its iron making expertise to aluminum. Intermet built a pilot plant in Lewisport, Kentucky banking on two prevalent trends in the automotive industry: outsourcing and aluminum auto components. The replacement of iron engine blocks with aluminum was expected to greatly exceed the nation's aluminum casting capacity by the year 2000. Without preparation to switch ductile and gray iron operations to incorporate aluminum into the product line, Intermet, along with all other limited foundries, stood to lose market share.

Waupaca Foundry Incorporated, located in Waupaca, Wisconsin, improved its efficiency and quality levels in its cleaning operations through the use of video camera data. The workers who ground excess iron from the castings were empowered with the responsibility to inspect the casting, once cleaned, against a process control sheet which contained a video image of the part and annotations. This innovative method of process control ensured that the grinder/inspector always used the most current work instructions. Waupaca Foundry reported sales of $144 million in 1991.

WORK FORCE

In general, most labor-intensive occupations in the gray and ductile iron foundries expected continued work force reductions through the 1990s. The occupa-

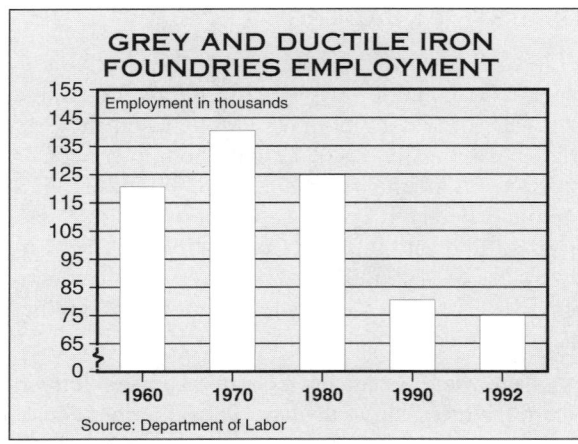

GREY AND DUCTILE IRON FOUNDRIES EMPLOYMENT

Employment in thousands

Source: Department of Labor

tions that faced the most substantial reductions, 20 percent and more, included grinders and polishers, mold assembly and shakeout workers, precision inspectors, metal pourers, assemblers, and hand workers. Other occupations that were facing reductions from 10 percent to 20 percent included general laborers, precision workers, molding machine operators, truck and tractor operators, furnace operators, welders, electricians, material movers, and custodians. The only occupations expecting to gain employment levels were industrial machinery mechanics, sales workers, millwrights, and industrial production managers.

Hourly compensation in this industry was, on average, substantially higher in comparison to other forms of manufacturing. In 1988, the average hourly wage was $13.08 in the gray and ductile iron foundry industry. The average hourly wage of all manufacturing concerns was $10.66. In 1987 Ohio and Michigan, which offered the highest hourly compensation in the industry, were paying hourly wages of $16.67 and $16.21 respectively. These states claimed the highest concentrations of gray and ductile iron foundries, and the highest value of shipments, which represented nearly 30 percent of the entire shipment activity in the United States.

The labor dilemma in the foundry industry did not begin in the late 1980s. In August, 1895, *The Foundry*, a monthly journal, lamented the industry's lack of appeal to young talent. ''American foundries as a rule are not making any longer the high-grade mechanic needed to turn out the best work . . . The smart, intelligent American boy can find more profitable, congenial employment than working in an iron foundry, where he will receive $2.50 a day, more or less — generally less — after he has served a several-year apprenticeship.''

Women started making an impact on the work force at the turn of the twentieth century. According to the March 1899 edition of *The Foundry*, ''the introduction of women into the core room marks an interesting epoch in iron founding. Women are especially adept in the making of small cores, and to this branch of the industry they are always confined. After a six months apprenticeship the girls are able to earn from $7 to $9 per week.'' The effects of World War II dramatically changed the work place as women began fill the roles of men engaged in the War. According to the March 1943 edition of *The Foundry*, ''because the present critical manpower situation seriously threatens production of war goods, the war problems committee of the Wisconsin Chapter of the American Foundryman Association studied the possibility of women replacing men in making castings for ordnance, tanks, armament, navy parts, and other vital war materials. . . . The committee urged the same pay for women for equal jobs, which it felt would inspire better workmanship. . . . It was recommended that women be used as widely as possible.''

AMERICA AND THE WORLD

The foundry industry faced tremendous challenges in the global marketplace in the early 1990s. According to Dr. Gerhard Engels, Chairman of the Association of German Foundry Specialists, West German foundry production increased to 4.3 million tons in 1990, ranking it as the fifth largest foundry producer in the world, behind the Soviet Union, the United States, China, and Japan. It ranked first in the world in terms of production per capita, but this figure began a steady decline in 1990 due to the dramatic political changes that followed the fall of the Berlin Wall. Engels anticipated that only 40 percent of the East German foundries would survive the reunification of East and West Germany.

While the United States was not faced with the accelerated social, political, and industrial changes present in Germany in the early 1990s, it was touched by the same marketplace. The North American Free Trade Agreement (NAFTA) was expected to affect U.S. industries as the EC and Berlin Wall affected West Germany. Also, the financial impact of environmental and safety regulations continued to beleaguer foundries in 1993. For example, Mexico was being pressured by the United States to install air pollution control devices in the early 1990s. However, Mexican laws included a loophole which did not require the devices to operate. In Korea, foundry workers were not provided with safety equipment such as eye protection, hard hats, respiratory devices, or ear plugs. Additionally, workman's compensation and minimum wage were much higher in the United States. The benefits that American workers enjoyed, and often took for granted, added significantly to the costs of U.S. companies. In financial terms, foreign competitors legally had an edge toward profit during the early 1990s.

RESEARCH AND TECHNOLOGY

Conditions in the iron foundry industry, especially ductile iron, were beginning to improve in 1993. The U.S. Government was interested in replacing many forged steel components with cast ductile iron. Particularly, the U.S. Navy was researching the increased lethality of ductile iron projectiles over those made from steel. Other contractors were looking for less expensive alternatives to forged steel components in lower stress applications, where the mechanical properties of ductile iron would suffice. However, more research and development was needed for this material, because other lighter weight materials were replacing ductile iron in lower stress applications. Ductile iron's low production price tag was enticing to both manufacturers and consumers and served as one of the primary incentives for its use.

Cast thermal analysis, also called numerical modeling/simulation, was used to improve quality and productivity in the foundry through pattern design optimization. The benefits of using numerical modeling were substantial, especially in relation to cost savings associated with time and material waste. Computer technology displaced the standard "pour and pray" method of metalcasting, and helped engineers optimize casting designs.

For the foundry industry as a whole, the advent of rapid prototyping technology was perhaps one of the most exciting advancements of the 1990s. Rapid prototyping is a computer integrated method of accelerating the step between design and manufacture of the part. Under normal circumstances, a foundry would take weeks to construct a pattern, and core boxes if necessary, from an original design. With rapid prototyping, this process took only days, in some cases only hours, to create a limited production pattern. The competitive edge this technology offered was substantial, especially considering the accuracy it was expected to lend to the price-quoting process.

INDUSTRY INFORMATION SOURCES

"The Foundry: Reminiscences from Foundry Management & Technology's Pages Past." *Foundry Management & Technology* (March, 1993).

"Foundry Industry History: The Gay Nineties (Part 1 of 12)." *Foundry Management & Technology* (September, 1991).

"Foundry Industry History: World War II (Part 6 of 12)." *Foundry Management & Technology* (February, 1992).

Considine, Douglas M., ed. *Van Nostrand's Scientific Encyclopedia.* New York: Van Nostrand Reinhold Company, 1976.

Darnay, Arsen J., ed. *Manufacturing USA: Industry Analyses, Statistics, and Leading Companies.* Detroit: Gale Research, Inc., 1992.

Dudley, Jeffery A., et al. "Numerical Modeling of Castings in the Production Process." *Modern Casting* (December, 1992).

Engels, Gerhard. "Foundries Challenges are Global in Scope." *Foundry Management & Technology* (June, 1993).

Gordon, Shelley. "ISO 9001 Certification: Was It Worth It?" *Modern Casting* (July, 1993).

Krueger, L.S., "Castings: Commodity or Components?" *Modern Casting* (July, 1993).

Moore, Alan. "Is the Future of Ductile Iron Precarious?" *Foundry Management & Technology* (June, 1992).

Peters, Dean M., ed. "Intermet's Big Push into Aluminum." *Foundry Management & Technology* (June, 1993).

Rauch, A.H., ed. *Source Book on Ductile Iron.* Metals Park, Oh.: American Society for Metals, 1977.

Rodgers, Robert C., ed. "Videos of Castings Simplify Cleaning Operations." *Foundry Management & Technology* (August, 1991).

Uziel, Yehoram. "Functional Prototyping - Has the Future Arrived?" *Foundry Management & Technology* (March, 1993).

Warden, T. Jerry. "Acquiring a Marketing Focus." *Modern Casting* (July, 1993).

—Valerie E. Wilson

SIC 3322

MALLEABLE IRON FOUNDRIES

This industry is made up of establishments primarily engaged in the manufacturing of malleable iron castings.

INDUSTRY SNAPSHOT

The value of 1992 shipments and other receipts of the malleable iron foundry industry totaled $258 million, down 6.7 percent from the production shipment level of $276.5 million in 1991. Twenty-eight companies employed over 4,600 people in the industry, of which 3,300 people worked in production. Together, these companies generated over $1.6 billion in sales.

The industry is in severe decline, and is not expected to return to its glory days of the 1960s. Over a third of the malleable foundries in the United States have been closed since the early 1980s, with further consolidation likely to continue. The factors which have led to this decline are strong foreign competition, the substitution of other metals and materials for malleable iron, rapid changes in technology, and unfavorable domestic economic conditions.

The 1992 production for the malleable foundry industry was 234,900 metric tons (mt). Industry analysts expect these numbers to continue to go down as well, with some analysts expressing the belief that declining industry health could result in production falling to levels as low as 100,000 mt by the year 1997.

ORGANIZATION AND STRUCTURE

Castings are used in 90 percent of all durable goods. In 1992, over 3,200 United States metal foundries made over 100,000 distinct products, posting sales of over $25 billion and producing more than 8.8 billion metric tons of product. Malleable iron casting production represented approximately 2.6 percent of the total United States casting output. Capacity utilization in 1990 for malleable iron foundries was 78 percent, just slightly better than the 75 percent average for the entire foundry industry. This reflected the high rate of disinvestment in plants and equipment that occurred during the 1980s, however, rather good economic health.

As an indication of the decline of this industry, government statisticians now classify malleable iron foundries as job shops. These foundries generally operate on a job or order basis, manufacturing castings for sale to others or for interplant transfer. In the 1970s, half of all malleable iron foundry castings came from in-house or captive plants. But in the 1980s, a major shift occurred when large independent manufacturers of railroad cars, oil-drilling equipment, heavy machinery, automobile, trucks, and major appliances sold off, shut down, or consolidated their captive operations. Today, upwards of 75 percent of all malleable iron castings come from independent or custom casters.

Two types of malleable iron are produced by these foundries: standard malleable iron and pearlitic malleable iron. In 1992 the value of shipments for each of these two product classes of malleable iron castings were 145,800 mt for standard malleable iron (62.1 percent of total) and 89,100 mt for pearlitic malleable

iron (37.9 percent of total). In 1991 the value added of manufacturing for malleable iron foundries—a good measure of net production value—declined 20.8 percent from 1990 levels to $156 million.

Most of the malleable iron foundries are found in the nation's Midwestern and Northeastern states. The largest malleable iron producing states, in descending order of shipments, are Wisconsin, Pennsylvania, Michigan, Connecticut, New York, Ohio, and Illinois.

BACKGROUND AND DEVELOPMENT

Malleable iron foundries are large plants where workers make metal products called castings by pouring molten metal into molds that are left to harden. Malleable iron is made from white cast iron by annealing it at temperatures from 1500 to 1850 degrees Fahrenheit over several days. When annealed, the iron carbide breaks up, producing rosettes of graphite. The iron is known for its shock resistance, strength, machinability, and ductility. Products such as engine blocks, iron ornaments, and valves can be made from malleable iron castings. The automotive, railroad, construction, agricultural implement, and hardware industries have wide uses for malleable iron castings.

Casting molten metal is believed to be one of the most efficient and economical ways of shaping metal products. Even as we approach the mid-1990s, it remains the most widely used metal forming process. Cast iron was first made by the Chinese around the eighth century B.C. However, it wasn't until the invention of the blast furnace by the Europeans in the fourteenth century that large quantities of cast iron were produced. North America's first operational foundry was built in 1642 along the Saugus River, close to Boston. About eight tons per week of grey iron castings were produced at the site.

Malleable iron, which was also called American blackheart iron, replaced grey-iron as the standard cast-metal around 1820, when the commercialization of secondary heat treating of the metal was first used. In 1966 malleable iron castings production in the United States accounted for 50 percent of the total malleable iron cast in the world. However, the year 1967 saw ductile iron castings production surpass malleable iron castings production in the United States. The United States in 1991 accounted for roughly 18 percent of the world's malleable iron castings production.

During the 1960s, average yearly production of malleable iron castings reached its peak at around 983,300 metric tons. Production during the decade of the 1970s remained at respectable average yearly production levels of 854,900 metric tons. However, the 1980s reflected the difficult economic times for the industry, with average yearly production levels shrinking to 346,100 metric tons.

The foundry industry still ranks within the top ten manufacturing segments in the United States. However, it has been battered by technological and competitive forces throughout the last two decades. The high inflation rates, high interest rates, high value of the dollar, and deep recession during the early 1980s hurt this industry tremendously. The largest customers of malleable iron castings, the domestic heavy equipment manufacturers, realized that these economic conditions favored offshore sources of malleable iron castings. Foreign competitors not only had lower prices when compared to American malleable iron sources, but they also had high quality manufacturing capabilities. Consequently, the value of castings shipments in the United States dropped 55 percent from 1977's level of $721.9 million to $323.2 million in 1982.

The high interest rates also raised the industry's cost of capital, which is the price to finance and replace existing operations. This practically shut off any new capital expenditures on plant and equipment in the United States. Capital reinvestment dropped 85 percent between the years 1978 and 1983. The high dollar, high interest rates, and high cost of capital made it very expensive to reinvest in the business of producing malleable iron castings. The lower rates of reinvestment by American malleable iron casters at a time when foreign competitors were raising their levels of casting quality put U.S. foundries at a technological disadvantage. In 1986 the Reagan Administration's decision to not sanction import restrictions further hurt the industry.

Even with the weakened dollar and improved quality of American malleable iron castings in the early 1990s, imports are likely to remain high. The offshore competitors who gained strong inroads to the American market are not likely to give up market share easily. To illustrate the damaging effects of adverse economic conditions and increased foreign competition, total shipments of 1.172 million mt of malleable iron castings in 1969 fell to production levels of 284,000 mt in 1982. A small recovery in the industry occurred in 1984 when production increased to 380,000 mt. However, production soon slid back to 299,000 mt in 1989. The number of establishments producing malleable iron castings decreased from 73 in 1972 to 28 in the mid-1990s. Some observers expect further declines in the number of operators in the industry throughout the 1990s.

CURRENT CONDITIONS

Based on the economic recoveries of the United States, European Community, and Japan, peak shipments for all metalcasting production should be reached in 1994 and 1995. However, in the long-run, changes in technology and global and environmental conditions are expected to hurt U.S. malleable iron foundries. While total growth of metalcasting shipments into the next century are forecast, malleable iron casting production is expected to continue to decline. In 1993, for instance, despite improved domestic demand and dollar valuations favoring domestic exports rather than foreign imports, malleable iron casting production is expected to fall to 226,000 mt, down more than 12 percent from 258,000 mt in 1992. Current challenges facing the malleable iron foundry industry include:

Demand for Cheaper, Lighter, and Stronger Components. Many U.S. end use manufacturers are substituting plastics, ceramics, composites, lighter alloys, and nonferrous castings for malleable iron in appliances, aerospace equipment, builder's hardware, and automotive components to help them compete in a global economy and to meet government regulations. Total iron usage per passenger car and light truck was approximately 600 lbs. in 1978. Industry analysts, however, estimate that usage could drop to 200 pounds before the year 2002. Similarly, it is estimated that 30 percent of passenger car and light truck engine blocks will be made out of aluminum by 1998, a figure that could well rise to more than 50 percent by early in the next decade. Many components that were once castings may now be weldments, forgings, or mechanical assemblies.

Changing Markets. Weakened demand for American made cars, trucks, farm equipment, machine tools, freight cars, and oil field machinery have also hurt the demand for malleable iron castings. While a number of the above industries were enjoying financial upturns entering the mid-1990s, their mixed fortunes of the last number of years impacted significantly on malleable iron foundries, and these outfits have been slow to recover.

Replacement By Ductile Iron Castings. Related to the need for lightweight and high-strength components and parts is the growth in the replacement rate of ductile iron castings for malleable iron castings. Malleable iron competes with ductile and grey iron in the traditional light and heavy industrial manufacturing markets, but ductile iron is lighter than malleable iron. Ductile iron actually doubled its share of the market in the last decade because of its unique compatibility with new casting techniques called ''near-net-shapes.'' This new method of casting allows for thinner-walled castings with intricate and complex shapes and sizes. Secondary finishing like blasting and sanding are virtually eliminated under use of this process. In the automotive industry, ductile iron engine blocks are increasingly replacing malleable iron engine blocks. In the housing industry, ductile iron valve castings are expected to continue to replace malleable iron valves castings because of its superior resistance to shock and impact. Ductile castings are also replacing malleable castings in the farm equipment, electrical fittings, and plumbing fittings markets.

Foreign Competition. In the 1980s overseas competitors adapted more quickly to changes in the industry than did domestic producers. They also used the strong dollar of the early 1980s to gain a foothold in the U.S. market that they have yet to relinquish. Approximately 20 percent of all malleable iron castings used in the United States in 1992 were imported. Thailand has been particularly responsible for the decline in American foundry's market shares in plumbing and electrical fitting castings.

Increasing Customer Demands. Many malleable iron castings customers have shifted from placing large batch type orders of castings to lower castings order levels. Just-in-time delivered high quality parts and the increased technological support that must accompany such inventory practices put pressure on many small domestic malleable iron foundries to meet these changes in the marketplace. Those foundries that cannot make these transitions will not survive.

INDUSTRY LEADERS

The General Motors Corporation Central Foundry Division in Saginaw, Michigan, is the largest facility producing malleable iron castings. Products are mainly produced for their auto and truck markets. Annual sales reached $1.4 billion in the early 1990s, a period when the division employed 11,000 workers. Other leading companies include National Castings of Lisle, Illinois, with $89 million in sales and 900 employees; Wagner Castings of Decatur, Illinois ($85 million, 1,000 employees); Harvard Industries, headquartered in Albion, Michigan ($80 million, 700 employees); Duriron Foundry of Dayton, Ohio ($100 million, 1,000 employees); and Citation Carolina, based in Lufkin, Texas ($50 million, 700 employees).

WORK FORCE

The heavily unionized American foundry industry employed approximately 230,000 people in 1991. Total employment in malleable iron foundries in 1991 was 4,600, representing two percent of total foundry

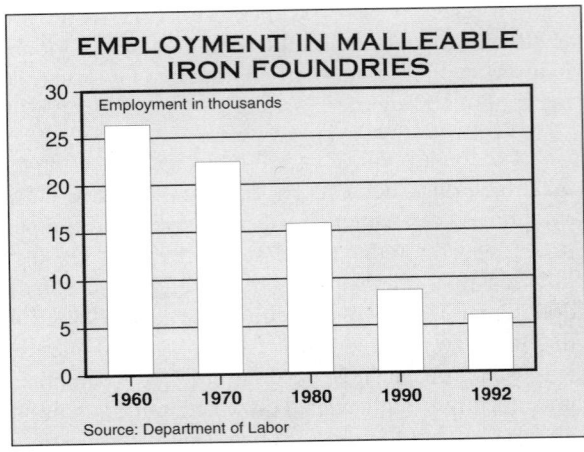

EMPLOYMENT IN MALLEABLE IRON FOUNDRIES

Employment in thousands

Source: Department of Labor

employment. Production workers numbered 3,300, accumulating 6.2 million production hours. Total employment in 1992 rose mildly from the 1991 employment level, to just over 5,000 workers. Employment in the malleable foundry industry reached its peak in 1951 at 32,289, of which 28,388 workers were in production.

Total compensation in 1991 was $191.2 million. Payroll, social security and legally required payments, and employer payments and other programs were $144.0 million, $17.6 million, and $29.6 million, respectively.

AMERICA AND THE WORLD

According to *Modern Castings*' ''Census of World Casting Production,'' the world's production of malleable iron castings was approximately 1.3 million metric tons in 1991. This is roughly a drop of 62 percent from the record production levels of 3.4 million mt reached in 1973.

In 1991 the United States' share of total world production was roughly 18 percent (down from 50 percent in 1966). The largest producer of malleable iron castings was The People's Republic of China, with 32 percent of total world production. Japan's share of world production totaled 17 percent, while Germany tallied 8.7 percent of global production (data for what was formerly the Soviet Union was not available for casting production estimates).

RESEARCH AND TECHNOLOGY

Exotic materials and thin-walled castings are regarded by many industry observers as the wave of the future. Some of the rapid technological changes occurring around malleable iron casters are new mold designs; new metal casting techniques; new computerized casting, finishing and monitoring; and new purchasing procedures by domestic consumer and industrial product manufacturers. The industry is under attack by new-technology parts-making processes, and it has been slow to change to compete with these more efficient casting processes.

For future survival, American malleable iron foundries must keep up with the technological changes in the industry. New investments in operations to improve melting, alloying, metal flow, die and mold filling temperature control, and lubrication will all help in this regard. Today's global marketplace also demands stronger quality control, price restrictions, and tighter specifications. Casting has moved from an art to a science. The days of testing sand moisture by hand are over, for computer controls are what drive the most exacting tolerances today. Partnership arrangements between foundries and their customers and suppliers will help to promote future growth. Pricing, quality assurance, service, and the consolidation of suppliers using just-in-time production practices to keep costs low and response time to customers high will help protect domestic malleable iron casting operations from further market declines.

INDUSTRY INFORMATION SOURCES

Annual Survey of Manufacturers, Washington, DC: Bureau of The Census.

"Cautious Optimism Prevails Among U.S. Metalcasters," Penton Publishing, Cleveland, OH.

Malleable Iron Castings, Malleable Founders Society, The Ann Arbor Press, Inc., 1960.

"Modern Casting Census of World Casting Production," *Modern Casting,* December 1992.

1987 Census of Manufacturers, Washington, DC: Bureau of the Census.

Sanders, Clyde A., *History Cast in Metal,* Cast Metals Institute, American Foundrymen's Society.

Stundza, Tom. "Why Foundries Are Stalled In Neutral," *Purchasing,* October 1989

—William A. Bennett

SIC 3324

STEEL INVESTMENT FOUNDRIES

This classification covers establishments primarily engaged in manufacturing steel investment foundries.

INDUSTRY SNAPSHOT

The steel investment casting business was growing in the early 1990s. The industry was one of the few in which the growth of shipments matched growth in employment. After suffering a fairly small decline in business during 1982, the industry began a steady growth trend. In 1983, shipments were valued at $939.6 million and the size of the total work force was 15,200. By 1988, shipments had grown to $1.47 billion, total employment was at 20,800, and the average hourly wage in the industry was $10.09. The number of establishments dedicated to this type of steel casting grew slowly during the 1980s. In 1982, 132 establishments existed and remained through 1985. In 1986 only 131 establishments were dedicated to this industry, followed by a sharp decrease in 1987 to 112. By 1988, that number jumped to 137, and 99 of all industry firms employed more than 20 people.

In 1987 the product share was split between the following four product classes: high temperature metal castings, which claimed 67.8 percent of the market; stainless steel, which claimed 12.9 percent; carbon steel, which included low carbon alloy steel, claimed 5.5 percent; and alloy steel, including some stainless steel, claimed 4.3 percent. Non-specific steel investment foundries were contained in the remaining 9.4 percent of the industry.

Materials consumed were primarily those used to make steel. The delivered cost of pig iron was withheld from the 1987 Census of Manufacturers for competitive reasons. However, the delivered cost of iron and purchased steel scrap accounted for a collective delivered cost of $10.9 million. Aluminum, copper, magnesium, nickel-based alloys, cobalt-based alloys, ferrochromium, ferrosilicon, and ferromanganese are other primarily consumed alloys which totaled a delivered cost of at least $142.1 million. Delivered costs of ferromanganese, magnesium, and unalloyed aluminum were also withheld for competitive reasons. Of those alloys disclosed, nickel-based alloys accounted for $98.7 million. Sand had a delivered cost of $10.6 million and clay and nonclay refractories had delivered costs of $3.7 million and $4.3 million, respectively. Industrial dies, molds, jigs, and fixtures that were used to produce the wax patterns reported delivered costs of $9.4 million. Grinding wheels and other abrasives had delivered costs of $16.2 million. Electrodes for industrial patterns carried a cost of $1.2 million. Pattern wax had a cost of $7.4 million.

ORGANIZATION AND STRUCTURE

Steel investment foundries are not necessarily in a class of their own. Many foundries practice investment casting regardless of the metal type, and many steel foundries may practice several casting processes beside investment. For example, the art industry used investment casting to create bronze sculptures, and the jewelry industry used investment casting to produce intricate designs. Relatively few steel foundries, with respect to the entire steel foundry industry, exclusively used the investment casting process.

This industry is at the mercy of the entire steel industry. The Environmental Protection Agency and the Occupational Safety and Health Administration also keep watchful eyes on the industry and continually impose regulations. One particular advantage of the investment casting process is that, compared to other casting processes, it is not harmful to the environment. The sand used can be recycled more; and because the process involves no chemical binders, there is no danger of producing hazardous fumes. With less waste and fewer pollutants produced, this process was not severely affected by increasing environmental legislation.

BACKGROUND AND DEVELOPMENT

According to Paul DeGarmo in his work *Materials and Processes in Manufacturing*, "investment casting actually is a very old process. It existed in China for centuries, and Cellini employed a form of it in Italy in the sixteenth century. Dentists have utilized the process since 1897, but it was not until World War II that it attained industrial importance for making jet turbine blades from metals that were not readily machinable. Currently millions of castings are produced by the process each year, its unique characteristics permitting the designer almost unlimited freedom in the complexity and close tolerances he can utilize."

Investment casting is also known as precision casting or the lost wax process. A pattern of wax or other expendable material is created and is attached, sometimes in clusters, to expendable down sprues. This conglomeration is then invested, or surrounded, by a refractory slurry which then dries and hardens at room temperature. The mold is then heated to melt or burn out the wax or other expendable material. In the hollow cavity, molten metal is cast. This casting process is particularly adapted to the production of small, intricate parts using metals of higher melting points than are feasible for use in die casting. Steel is one of the primary metals used in the industry.

Investment casting is a high precision process, and is therefore expensive. The process allows highly complex shapes to be produced, while maintaining good dimensional accuracy and surface finishes. The ability to produce thin wall sections are another advantage to

using the investment casting process. Sections as thin as 0.015 inches, for example, have been cast.

The Investment Casting Institute (ICI) was founded in 1950 and it held its first meeting in 1953. At that time, the organization had 13 member companies. In the early 1990s, 250 companies were affiliated with the organization. The ICI holds semi-annual meetings, a technical meeting in the fall, and a members-only meeting in the spring to discuss management issues. The ICI also provides training in several aspects of the industry.

CURRENT CONDITIONS

The United States had 300 operating steel foundries at the end of 1991. These foundries produced 900,900 metric tons of castings, 31,800 metric tons of which were steel investment castings. There were 358 foundries participating in investment molding, independent of type of metal poured, which accounted for 7 percent of the total castings produced. According to Dean Peters in the September 1992 issue of *Foundry Management & Technology*, "in 1991, the average price of investment castings was eight times higher than prices of all other castings on a weight basis." The process was not fully mechanized and was consequently time-consuming, labor intensive, and costly. Despite their high prices, investment castings continued to have a loyal niche market.

In a survey conducted by *Foundry Management & Technology* magazine, published in 1992, steel producers were optimistic about future business levels. While only 60 steel foundries responded to the survey, casting shipments were up by 3 percent from 1991 and gains of 7.3 percent in 1993 and 12.2 percent in 1994 were anticipated. Capital spending was planned to increase by nearly 30 percent in 1993, with 57 percent of the expenditures to be placed with new equipment and 25.9 percent to be invested in new plants. However, the growth rate of the steel industry was expected to experience slow growth.

Steel investment castings require high quality steel, due to the intricate nature of parts cast using this process. Because extreme precision is required in producing these castings, any inclusions in the metal will ruin a part. The primary quality issue facing the steel industry in the early 1990s was the cleanliness of steel. Clean steel is important to the industry because steel that is free of tramp elements, slag, and dross creates better quality parts. According to John Svoboda, "In the early 1980s a high level management task force representing the steel industry identified oxide macroinclusions as the major factor responsible for the lack of acceptance of steel castings by the design engineering community. This study augmented the already well-known requirements for cast steel to be free from tramp elements, gases, and microinclusions. In short, the mandate for 'clean steel' has been issued.'' By the early 1990s, significant progress had been made in clean steel production. However, future studies were expected to establish a method of quantifying the cleanliness of steel and find the relationship between cleanliness, mechanical properties, and design performance.

INDUSTRY LEADERS

According to the 1991 edition of *Ward's Business Directory of U.S. Private and Public Companies*, the 30 leading companies in this industry grossed total sales of $1.943 billion and employed 24,500 people. The Howmet Corporation of Greenwich, Connecticut reported sales of $900 million and employed 11,000 people. Precision Castparts Corporation of Portland, Oregon reported sales of $457 million and employed 6,700 people. Howmet Corporation of Whitehall, Michigan ranked third with sales of $160 million and total employment of 1,600 people. Arwood Corporation of Rockleigh, New Jersey reported sales of $90 million and employed 1,400 people. Dolphin Incorporated of Phoenix, Arizona reported sales of $39 million and employed 500 people.

The greatest concentration of steel investment foundries were located in the Great Lakes Region in the early 1990s. Wisconsin was the only state to disclose shipment figures. All other states withheld such financial data due to competitive reasons. Wisconsin's ten establishments engaged in this industry employed 1,100 people at an average hourly wage of $9.78, and had shipments of $74 million. This figure represented 5.1 percent of the industry's total shipments. California, with 19 establishments, contained the highest number of facilities dedicated to this industry. Michigan, Ohio, and Texas respectively had 13, 12, and 11 establishments in the industry.

WORK FORCE

The iron and steel foundry industry was facing major reductions in employment approaching the year 2000. The only industry occupations expected to increase employment levels were industrial machinery mechanics, sales workers, millwrights, and industrial production managers. Occupations that were expecting work force reductions of more than 19 percent included grinders and polishers, mold assembly and shakeout operators, inspectors, metal pourers, welders, assemblers, handworkers, and material handlers. The following occupations were expecting reductions between 10 percent and 19 percent: general laborers, precision workers, blue collar worker supervisors, molding machine operators, truck and tractor operators, grinders, furnace operators, electricians, and janitors.

AMERICA AND THE WORLD

Although the market for steel castings made from this process was small, steel investment foundries were operating all over the world in the early 1990s. The national economy, however, has had a much greater impact on the U.S. industry than global competition. The North American Free Trade Agreement (NAFTA), ratified in 1993, was of great concern to the foundry industry. The most vocalized concern from Canada and the United States was fear of job losses. Workers were concerned that U.S. and Canadian businesses would rush to Mexico to take advantage of that country's lower labor costs. In 1993, the average hourly wage for U.S. a manufacturing job, including benefits, was $14.50, while Mexico's average wage was only $2.50 per hour. Canadians were also concerned about loss of market share, because the Canadian economy relied heavily on exports. The agreement was also expected to force Mexico to address its lax environmental regulations. As of 1993, Mexico's steel foundries were controlling only prime, not secondary, emissions.

RESEARCH AND TECHNOLOGY

A major technological advancement in the foundry industry came on the market in the early 1990s. This advancement was known as either Rapid Prototyping or Functional Prototyping. Rapid prototyping is a computerized system that uses stereolithography and selective laser sintering to create a three-dimensional shape that has been drawn on a computer aided drafting station. A computer takes the three dimensional model and mathematically slices it into layers of specific thickness. Each layer is transmitted digitally from the design unit to the production unit where the material of choice is used to build the shape layer by layer. There were several types of these prototyping systems used by the industry in the early 1990s. Using this new technology, a designer could take a customer's idea, design it, and, in several hours or days, depending on the size of the part, have a prototype available for the customer to evaluate. The new technology dramatically reduced both the time and expense of producing intricate designs.

One specific prototyping process was especially suited to the investment casting industry. Soligen Incorporated created direct shell production casting

(DSPC), which created a ceramic shell into which metal could be poured directly. As reported in *Foundry Management & Technology*, this is essentially the final product of the investment casting process, in which a wax part is dipped in a ceramic slurry and is afterwards expended. The DSPC machine was expected to have a retail price of $300,000 in the United States. The layers produced in the production unit will be 0.002 inch thick, with a projected build rate of 350 cubic inches per hour. It was estimated that the total build time would be between 9 and 20 hours and the cost of the final shell would be between $250 and $2,500.

New technologies presented at the 1992 Investment Casting Institute Conference included a dual-track induction melting furnace, an automated cluster assembly machine, the newest PC-based robot, and an automatic wax injection machine. Research papers presented were primarily concerned with the availability of three-dimensional fluid flow and solidification computer models. Other issues of heat transfer behaviors, porosity formation, and gating design parameters were also presented as research papers. The rapid prototyping equipment described in the previous paragraphs was on display at the conference and Sandia National Laboratories, the developer of the machine, gave a presentation on its experiences with rapid prototyping.

INDUSTRY INFORMATION SOURCES

"26th Census of World Casting Production - 1991." *Modern Casting* (December, 1992).

Darnay, Arsen J., ed. *Manufacturing USA: Industry Analyses, Statistics, and Leading Companies.* Detroit: Gale Research, Inc., 1991.

DeGarmo, E. Paul. *Materials and Processes in Manufacturing.* New York: Macmillan Publishing Company, 1979.

Farias, Roberto. "North American Free Trade Agreement: A Perspective from Mexico." *Modern Casting* (December, 1992).

Kanicki, David P., ed. "Fact and Fears About NAFTA." *Modern Casting* (October, 1992).

Kennedy, Donald P. "North American Free Trade Agreement: A Perspective from Canada." *Modern Casting* (October, 1992).

Peters, Dean M., ed. "The Automation of Molding, Moldmaking, and Coremaking." *Foundry Management & Technology* (September, 1992).

Peters, Dean M., ed. "Metalcasters Cautiously Optimistic on Next Year's Growth." *Foundry Management & Technology* (December, 1992).

Rodgers, Robert C., ed. "Foundry Industry Organizations." *Foundry Management & Technology* (September, 1992).

Svoboda, John M. "Clean Steel Technology." *Modern Casting* (October, 1991).

Twarog, Daniel L. "Gains Mark 1992 ICI Gathering." *Modern Casting* (January, 1993).

Uziel, Yehoram. "Functional Prototyping — Has the Future Arrived?" *Foundry Management & Technology* (March, 1993).

—Valerie E. Wilson

SIC 3325

STEEL FOUNDRIES, NOT ELSEWHERE CLASSIFIED

This classification provides coverage of establishments primarily engaged in manufacturing steel castings, not elsewhere classified.

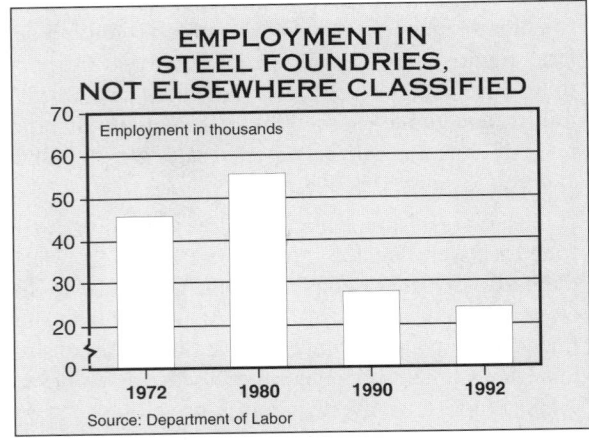

EMPLOYMENT IN STEEL FOUNDRIES, NOT ELSEWHERE CLASSIFIED

Employment in thousands

Source: Department of Labor

Carbon steel castings held 44 percent of the market share in 1987, while high alloy and other alloy steel castings each held just over 22 percent of the market. Approximately 11 percent of the market was non-specific in 1987. On the whole, this industry steadily downsized employment levels between 1982 and 1986, with the highest level being 36,900 and the lowest level being 19,700. Between 1986 and 1988 employment levels grew to 24,800, nearly 81 percent of whom were production workers. In 1991, the top 75 companies grossed annual sales of $2.52 billion and employed 28,800 people. Compared to all other manufacturing industries, this industry maintains lower than average costs, possibly due to very low investment ratios. Production workers comprise the largest percentage of this industry's total work force. Industry shipments fell from $2 billion in 1982 to $1.4 billion in

1986. Between 1986 and 1988 a significant rebound occurred, bringing shipments to over $2 billion for the first time since 1982.

Esco Corporation of Portland, Oregon was the industry leader in 1991 with an estimated $290 million in sales and 3,000 employees. American Steel Foundries of Chicago was ranked second, with an estimated $150 million in sales and 1,800 employees. ABC Rail Company of Chicago was ranked third, with an estimated $140 million in sales and 1,400 employees. Latrobe Steel Company of Latrobe, Pennsylvania was ranked fourth, with $130 million in sales and 1,000 employees. Haynes International of Kokomo, Indiana was ranked fifth, with an estimated $110 million in sales and 1,200 employees.

The Bureau of Labor Statistics has projected a bleak future for this industry's occupations. Except for industrial machinery mechanics, sales workers, millwrights, and industrial production managers, all other occupations are expected to face reductions in employment levels. The many steel foundry occupations expected to face over a 10 percent reduction going into the year 2000 include: general laborers, grinders, precision workers, blue collar worker supervisors, mold assembly and shakeout operators, inspectors, metal pourers, truck operators, grinding machine operators, furnace machine operators, welders, assemblers, hand workers, electricians, material handlers, and janitors.

The Great Lakes area has the heaviest concentration of steel foundries, and Ohio's 28 establishments ranked first in terms of shipments, which amounted to $294 million in 1987. In 1987, Pennsylvania had more foundries than any other state. Its 39 establishments were ranked second, with shipments of $204 million in 1987. Wisconsin was ranked third with $184 million worth of shipments generated by 16 establishments in that same year. Hourly wages between these three states did not vary significantly during this period. Workers in Ohio were paid the highest hourly wage, compared to Pennsylvania and Wisconsin, at $11.23. On the average, Pennsylvania and Wisconsin paid workers $10.35 and $10.25 per hour, respectively. The average compensation throughout the industry in 1987 was $10.63.

INDUSTRY INFORMATION SOURCES

Darnay, Arsen J., ed. *Manufacturing USA: Industry Analyses, Statistics, and Leading Companies.* Detroit: Gale Research, Inc., 1991.

—Valerie E. Wilson

SIC 3331

PRIMARY SMELTING AND REFINING OF COPPER

This industry consists of companies that smelt copper from ore and refine copper by electrolytic or other processes. Those establishments engaged in rolling, drawing, or extruding copper are classified in **SIC 3351: Rolling, Drawing, and Extruding of Copper.**

INDUSTRY SNAPSHOT

Copper has excellent properties that made it useful to many industries. As a base metal, copper is used both alone and in alloyed combinations with other metals. The electrical, communications, and construction industries use copper in many of their products.

The United States is a major producer as well as a major consumer of copper, and U.S. copper smelters thrive on the electrical conductivity and corrosion resistance of copper. In the early 1990s, the average single family home contained about 422 pounds of copper. Most of this was in plumbing tube and building wire. This figure was up from a household average of 230 pounds in 1980. Copper industries have benefitted from increased usage of the metal in other areas as well. In 1981 the average car contained 30 pounds of copper; ten years later each car contained about 50 pounds of copper.

The copper industry in the United States has roots dating back to the earliest days of colonial America. The industry grew and prospered along with the American industrial boom, and came to participate in a worldwide market of miners, producers, smelters, manufacturers, foundries, and consumers.

The value of copper, a mined natural resource, has fluctuated. Copper demand has historically been cyclical, and often rose in the spring when building construction increased. Demand likewise fell when its end-use markets suffered. Tom Stundza, the Markets and Metals Editor for the trade magazine *Purchasing,* noted that, ''a market truism is that nonferrous metals prices overreact to reduced demand from industrial sectors.'' At the same time, occasional spurts of demand surprised the industry. For example, stronger auto sales, while unexpected in the early 1990s, helped copper industries.

Nearing the end of the twentieth century, all of the players in the copper industry were involved in the recyclability of copper. Recycled copper is highly valued—high-grade scrap often has more than 90 percent of the value of newly-mined copper. Both copper production and copper consumption were rising in the early 1990s after suffering in the late 1980s.

ORGANIZATION AND STRUCTURE

Companies engaged in smelting and refining copper create products for a variety of national and international industries. End-use markets for copper and copper alloy were dominated by building construction and electrical and electronic products. These two general industries accounted for more than 65 percent of all copper shipments in 1991. Most of the copper went into building construction, while 24 percent went into electrical and electronic products in 1991. Other end-use markets for copper were industrial machinery and equipment, transportation equipment, and consumer products.

Copper in the United States went from the mines to the smelters. In some cases these were owned by the same company, and in some cases the mining and smelting were performed at nearby facilities. The mining and smelting companies are the producers of copper materials, while the wire rod mills and brass mills and foundries that work copper prepare the metal for delivery to manufacturers in various industries.

Mining companies process copper ores, most of which are retrieved from open-pit mines. These ores are refined and sometimes alloyed with other elements, such as zinc or beryllium. A primary smelting reactor such as a reverberatory furnace produces copper sulfide from concentrated ore. Some reverberatory furnaces were replaced by oxygen/flash smelting, which created less air pollution. The final step in smelting and refining works involves an electrolytic or other refining process. The resulting copper is often close to 100 percent pure.

BACKGROUND AND DEVELOPMENT

Copper mining had origins in the Middle East, but reached its zenith in America. In the mid-eighteenth century miners in the colonies discovered copper ores in what is now the northeastern United States. They mined these ores, but English law prohibited the establishment of smelting works in the colonies, so the ore was sent straight to England for smelting and refining.

After the American Revolution miners and smelters moved to the newly-created United States and began working in American mines and refineries. Copper sheathing began to be used on wooden ships as early as the 1790s. The copper protected the ships from the pressure and corrosive effects of the ocean. Great demand from the shipping industry helped the budding copper industry, but the United States still depended on copper imports from England and South America. In 1806 U.S. importers of copper asked the Congress to exempt copper from customs duty. The protests lodged by copper industry pioneers succeeded in lowering tariffs applied to copper imports.

In the early 1800s U.S. companies began to use blast furnaces for smelting and refining copper. Later, with the rise of American industry, growing copper works created stripping, boiler plates, rivets and other copper-based items that were used in an increasingly diverse number of industries and products. Copper nails replaced cast iron nails in building and the boom in putting up towns and cities across the new nation resulted in a windfall for the copper industry.

The reserves of copper in the United States have not suffered appreciably during the twentieth century. Although copper has been in use for more than 10,000 years, about three-quarters of all copper consumed has been produced since World War II. New deposits have been found and better mining and extracting methods developed by copper companies.

In the 1970s the trend in the copper smelting industry was toward the purchase of smelters, refining companies, and mines by oil companies. In the following decade, almost all of these oil companies sold off their copper companies, leaving them independent again, but this time with a renewed sense of the marketplace. Workers in some of these companies learned new technologies that would enable them to compete in the international copper arena. Instead of the pyrometallurgy of the reverberatory furnaces, many smelters introduced hydrometallurgical processing that produced copper whose purity and quality matched that of the electrolytically refined copper.

The 1980s were not boom years for many players in the various copper-related industries. The three largest U.S. producers of copper—Asarco, Phelps Dodge Corporation, and AMAX, Inc.—lost almost $2.5 billion from 1982 through 1985. These companies, however, remained leaders in the field despite their difficulties. Many other companies in the copper industry went out of business, though. Those that remained made drastic changes to cut operating costs and improve efficiency. These cost-cutting measures at times exacerbated difficulties with labor.

CURRENT CONDITIONS

Copper consumption fell during the late 1980s and early 1990s. The compound growth rate for copper consumption from 1989 through 1993 was -1.3 percent. Copper production dipped too, but by 1992 it was showing strong growth and recorded a compound growth rate of two percent for 1989 through 1993.

U.S. productivity improved and copper consumption was expected to increase towards the year 2000. In 1992 copper consumption increased by more than three percent over the previous year to almost three million metric tons.

The United States maintained its world leadership in copper production in the early 1990s. U.S. companies produced more than 1.7 million metric tons of copper ores and 2.1 million tons of refined copper products in 1992. Consumption of copper throughout the world was expected to increase toward the next century, and some analysts were concerned about supply levels, as mines in Peru, Zaire, and Yugoslavia were expected to face production problems in the late 1990s. Industry executives watched political climates in such countries as Zambia for potential effects on the worldwide copper industry.

Many other metal industries suffered from the worldwide recession of the late-1980s and early 1990s before any of the copper-related industries felt the effects. Entering the mid-1990s, the demand for copper was higher than the supply, which suffered from production problems as well as recessionary woes. In these years, manufacturers have received many of their shipments from existing copper inventories. While copper production was down in Chile, which had been supplying much of the world's copper, U.S. demand was high, creating inventory shortfalls. At the same time, a new consumer, China, responded to the needs of its growing economy by purchasing copper in greater quantities.

The world smelter production of copper was 10,616,200 short tons in 1992, down from a high of 10,806,400 in 1989 according to the American Bureau of Metal Statistics and the U.S. Bureau of Mines. International competition was a factor in the 1990s, as was an increased environmental consciousness in the United States. One copper company declined to build a new smelting facility in Texas after environmental groups protested.

Copper industry executives approached the turn of the century with guarded optimism. They saw successful applications of copper in many existing industries, and were working to expand the use of copper in other industries. One of the key roles of the Copper Development Association (CDA), a leading representative body for the industry, is to work with manufacturers to develop new uses for copper. CDA created programs aimed at increasing the usage of copper in specific industries. CDA executives knew that in Europe, for instance, copper was used four times more than in the U.S. for architectural applications. Copper's efficient conductivity made it useful for fire sprinkler systems and for electrical wiring.

Copper mining and smelting in the United States is also subject to weather-related difficulties. Much of the U.S. copper output is from mines in Arizona (in 1991 Arizona accounted for 63 percent of the aggregate U.S. copper output) and other Western regions. Therefore, when weather in that region is rainier than usual, production is hampered. Heavy rains in the early 1990s added harmful clay to solutions used to separate copper from ores, and also made ores stick to conveyors and trucks.

INDUSTRY LEADERS

In the early 1990s, the primary smelters and refiners of copper that had survived the economic turmoil of the 1980s were expanding. Phelps Dodge Corporation, based in Phoenix, was the largest U.S. copper company. The company suffered from depleted sulfide ore at its Arizona mine, but it was still twice the size of Asarco Inc. Other leaders include Kennecott Corporation and Colonial Metals Co.

Kennecott Corporation invested in a state-of-the-art copper smelter, expanded its copper refinery, and opened a precious-metals plant in Utah. Asarco and Cyprus Minerals also expanded or moved facilities. Asarco had bought the Ray Mine in Hayden, Arizona, from rival Kennecott in 1986 for $72 million. By 1991 it had earned its purchase price more than five times over. Asarco improved its profit margins by adding copper mining to its smelting operations.

Among U.S. copper smelters, production was measured in short tons. Magma Copper Company Smelting and Refining Division, in San Manuel, Arizona, for example, had an annual capacity of 1,050,000 short tons. The Phelps Dodge Corporation's Tyrone Branch facility in Playas, New Mexico, could smelt 750,000 short tons.

Other large smelters in the early 1990s, listed with their owners, their locations, and their annual capacities, included Chino Mines (Phelps Dodge Corporation) in Hurley, New Mexico, 550,000 short tons; Hayden Smelter (Asarco Incorporated) in Hayden, Arizona, 720,000 short tons; El Paso Smelter (Asarco) in El Paso, Texas, 450,000 short tons; Hayden-Ray Smelter (Asarco) in Hayden, Arizona, 360,000 short tons; and Kennecott Utah Copper (Kennecott Corporation) in Garfield, Utah, 643,000 short tons. At the end of 1992, the total annual capacity of U.S. smelters reached more than five million short tons.

AMERICA AND THE WORLD

According to the American Bureau of Metal statistics and the U.S. Bureau of Mines, the United States was still the world leader in smelter production of copper entering the mid-1990s. In 1992, 1,742,000 short tons of copper were smelted in the U.S. In comparison, 1,520,400 short tons were smelted in Chile, the second-ranked country in copper smelter production. During that same year, a little over one million short tons were smelted in the former Soviet Union, 1.3 million short tons were smelted in Japan, and 940 thousand short tons were smelted in all of Africa.

However, according to *Standard and Poor's Industry Surveys* in 1993, U.S. mine production of copper for 1991 was 1,634,000 metric tons, while Chile mined 1,814,000 metric tons. Chile was considered the world's leading copper-producing nation by virtue of the fact that its mines produced more copper than those in the United States. This contrasted with the balance in the mid-1960s, when U.S. companies controlled about 45 percent of copper production in the free world. At that time, U.S. companies owned many of the mines in South America, especially in Chile and Peru. As nationalism took hold in South America many of these mines came under local control, and the balance shifted away from the U.S. companies.

The United States remained the leader in world consumption of refined copper in the early 1990s. In 1991 manufacturers in the United States consumed more than two million metric tons of copper, while Japan consumed 1.6 million metric tons.

The copper industry was becoming increasingly global in its outlook in the 1990s. Smelters and refiners of copper were looking toward developing countries as markets for copper-based products. Those countries that were improving their infrastructures with telecommunications cables, power cables, and other basic building tools needed more copper. The Asian markets of China, Taiwan, and South Korea were hoped to provide large new markets.

In 1993 a politically charged topic in the industry was the General Agreement on Tariffs and Trade (GATT). Copper industry leaders met with U.S. trade officials to request a reduction of Japanese and European tariffs under GATT. Their aim was to eliminate global tariffs on copper to gain better access to foreign markets and argued that the Japanese market was too heavily protected. The U.S. International Trade Commission (ITC) rejected high tariffs on imported metals.

The U.S. formed an International Copper Study Group in the early 1990s in conjunction with 17 other countries involved in the copper industry. Their aim was to allow informational exchanges between producing and consuming countries as well as to increase copper production and consumption. Members included Germany, China, Chile, Peru, and France.

RESEARCH AND TECHNOLOGY

A low-cost method of production being used in the early 1990s in U.S. copper companies was known as SX-EW, or solvent extractionelectrowinning. Solutions of sulfuric acid were applied to dumps of copper-bearing ores, then the dissolved copper was recovered by depositing copper onto electrically-charged cathodes. This was known as electrowinning. SX-EW had fewer steps, and caused less pollution, at a lower cost than early production methods. But only some of the world's ore was able to be processed by this method. Primary sulfide ore, located deeper in mines and combined with other elements, was not eligible for SX-EW. SX-EW was effective for oxide ore and secondary sulfide ore, which were found closer to the mine's surface, where the ore had been oxidized. Unfortunately, the contents of U.S. mines often principally contained primary sulfide ores rather than oxide ores and secondary sulfide ores.

The technical research and market development arm of the copper industry has promoted new technologies that use copper materials in a wide array of applications. Such new applications include the use of copper radiators for the automobile industry. The copper industry emphasizes copper's corrosion resistance and strength, and notes that the new radiators are also lighter and more durable than current copper radiators.

Copper radiators comprised only about 30 percent of the automobile radiator market in the early 1990s. American auto manufacturers were replacing copper radiators with aluminum radiators. However, the Plymouth Neon, created for fuel efficiency, featured copper radiators. There was also an increase in other copper elements used in automobiles, especially due to the expanded use of wiring and electronics in each car.

Other proposed uses of copper included solar energy, nuclear waste disposal canisters, and superconductivity applications. Industrial applications, such as valves, fittings, and power utilities remained steady users of copper. Until 1982 another copper user was the U.S. mint, which coined pennies using a copper alloy. In 1982 the copper alloy used in the production of U.S. pennies was replaced by zinc. Another loss to the industry was the increasing use of fiber optics products, which began to replace some of the copper telecommunications equipment.

Recyclability became increasingly important as copper companies faced the next century. Because copper was more easily recycled than many other metals, more copper was recovered from recycled material than was obtained from newly mined ores. The combination of recycled copper materials and healthy U.S. deposits of copper made the country highly self-sufficient in copper. Aluminum, which competed with copper in many areas, was a more difficult metal for the United States to obtain.

INDUSTRY INFORMATION SOURCES

"Annual Data: 1993: Copper Supply and Consumption, 1972-1992," New York: Copper Development Association Inc., 1993.

"A.T.&T. in Copper Cable Venture in Venezuela," *New York Times,* February 10, 1994, C3.

Charlier, Marj, "Gold Companies Likely to Post Uneven Results; Copper Outlook is Grim," *Wall Street Journal,* October 8, 1993.

"Copper in the USA: Bright Future—Colorful Past," New York: Copper Development Association Inc., 1990.

Getler, Warren, "Copper Futures Rise, but Traders Warn Rally is Likely to be Short-Lived Amid Oversupply, *Wall Street Journal,* October 12, 1993, C18.

Gross, John E., "Copper Market Letter," *Copper Talk.* May 1993, 7.

Jolly, Janice L.W., "Copper Demand Could Exceed Supply in the Next Eight Years," *American Metal Market,* February 17, 1993, 6A.

Payne, Robert M., "Electrical Uses are Big Growth Area for Copper," *American Metal Market,* November 23, 1992, 10A.

Simon, Howard, "Traders hope copper prices will blossom in the spring," *Journal of Commerce and Commercial,* February 16, 1993, 8A.

Stewart, Alan, "CAP-italize on Copper," *Telephone Engineer & Management,* October 1, 1992, 53.

Stundza, Tom, "Cheap Metal, and Plenty of It," *Purchasing,* March 7, 1991, 50.

Taylor, Jeffrey, "U.S. Copper Futures Fall as Available Stocks of the Metal Reach a 15-Year High in London," *Wall Street Journal,* October 27, 1993, C18.

Temes, Judy, "Polish and Tarnish," *Crain's New York Business,* November 12, 1990, 3.

Whiteman, Maxwell, *Copper for America,* New Brunswick: Rutgers University Press, 1971.

Wrigley, Al, "Copper-Brass Comeback," *American Metal Market,* September 20, 1993, 4.

—Fran Shonfeld Sherman

PRIMARY PRODUCTION OF ALUMINUM

This classification includes establishments primarily engaged in producing aluminum from alumina and in refining aluminum by any process. Excluded from this classification are establishments primarily engaged in rolling, drawing, or extruding aluminum, which are classified in the following product groups: **SIC 3353: Aluminum Sheet, Plate and Foil; SIC 3354: Aluminum Extruded Products; SIC 3355: Aluminum Rolling and Drawing Not Elsewhere Classified; SIC 3356: Rolling, Drawing, and Extruding of Nonferrous Metals, Except Copper and Aluminum; and SIC 3357: Drawing and Insulating of Nonferrous Wire.**

INDUSTRY SNAPSHOT

Divided into product groups, the aluminum industry comprises three distinct segments: primary aluminum manufacturers, semi-fabricated aluminum manufacturers, and secondary, or scrap aluminum manufacturers. Of these three segments, the primary aluminum industry is the smallest in terms of number of manufacturers and generates revenues roughly equivalent to the sales recorded by secondary smelting manufacturers. The semi-fabricated aluminum industry, by far, accounts for the greatest amount of revenue within the broader, loosely structured aluminum industry.

To produce aluminum, primary aluminum manufacturers first process bauxite, an ore that is the basic raw material of aluminum, to create alumina. A powerful electric current is then passed through a solution containing alumina to produce aluminum in its most primary form. Aluminum in this form, either as a mass of metal in bar or block shape (referred to as ingot), or as a smaller rectangular bar (referred to as billet), serves as the raw material for manufacturers engaged in producing aluminum products. Primary aluminum manufacturers supply aluminum to semi-fabricated aluminum manufacturers and to a diverse array of manufacturers outside the aluminum industry who utilize aluminum to manufacture their products.

Throughout much of its existence, the primary aluminum industry comprised fewer than ten manufacturers, but as it entered the 1990s approximately 30 manufacturers were involved in producing primary aluminum. Much of the proliferation of manufacturers occurred during the 1980s—especially between 1982 and 1987—a period during which the number of manufacturers climbed from 15 to 34. In 1990, these manufacturers generated $7.03 billion in sales, an aggregate value of shipments primarily derived from the production of aluminum ingot, which accounted for over 75 percent of the industry's total shipments. Billet primary aluminum, the only other type of aluminum produced by the industry that accounted for any appreciable revenue, represented 22.8 percent of the industry's shipments.

These shipments were purchased by the industry's six primary markets: building and construction, containers and packaging, transportation, electrical, consumer durables, and machinery and equipment. In 1992, the bulk of the industry's aluminum was utilized by manufacturers involved in building and construction, container and packaging, and transportation industries, which, together, purchased approximately 60 percent of the industry's total shipments. In ranking order behind the industry's three major markets were electrical manufacturers, consumer durable manufacturers, and machinery and equipment manufacturers. The early 1990s have proven difficult in some respects for members of the aluminum industry, despite dramatic increases in sales to major markets such as automotive. A huge influx of aluminum from Russia, with a dearth of domestic industries to sell to, has dramatically impacted on the profit margins of U.S. aluminum companies. The price of aluminum in 1993 fell to 49 cents a pound, an all-time low when inflation is factored in. In an effort to blunt the impact of the Russian aluminum shipments, *Business Week* notes, "aluminum companies are offering technical and environmental assistance to the Russians, and even an aluminum-foil joint venture in Siberia. North American producers are clearly eager for relief."

ORGANIZATION AND STRUCTURE

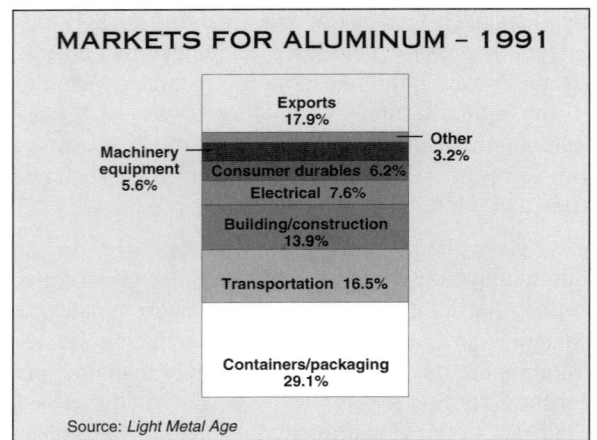

MARKETS FOR ALUMINUM – 1991

Exports 17.9%
Other 3.2%
Machinery equipment 5.6%
Consumer durables 6.2%
Electrical 7.6%
Building/construction 13.9%
Transportation 16.5%
Containers/packaging 29.1%

Source: *Light Metal Age*

Although the industry consists of relatively few manufacturers, the size of a primary aluminum manufacturing facilities, in terms of the number of people employed per establishment, were comparatively large when measured against other manufacturing industries. Of the 52 establishments involved in producing primary aluminum in 1989, which includes all of the manufacturing facilities operated by the approximately 30 companies engaged in the industry during that year, only 13 employed less than 20 people. The average number of employees per facility, however, was more than six times greater than the average of all other manufacturing industries in the United States. In 1989, the typical primary aluminum manufacturing establishment employed 363 people, while the average manufacturing facility in the United States employed 54 people.

Geographically, a majority of the establishments involved in the primary aluminum industry were located in the Pacific Northwest, particularly in the state of Washington, which contained seven facilities that manufactured 25 percent of the industry's total shipments. Ohio, with four facilities, ranked as the second largest concentrated area of primary aluminum manufacturing facilities, followed by three states, Kentucky, New York, and North Carolina, with three facilities each.

The amount of money required to purchase the raw materials for primary aluminum production was considerably higher than the expenditures incurred by the typical facility in all other manufacturing industries. This disparity was primarily due to the tremendous amount of electrical energy required to produce aluminum and because nearly all of the bauxite needed to produce alumina must be imported. Consequently, operating a primary aluminum manufacturing facility is very expensive, frequently 20 times more expensive then operating an average manufacturing establishment. According to 1989 figures, the average cost per establishment in the primary aluminum industry, that is, the average amount of money paid for raw manufacturing materials, was $91 million, significantly more than the $4.5 million averaged by all other manufacturing establishments. The average investment per establishment, or the average expense earmarked for purchasing manufacturing machinery and paying for production retooling, was also significantly higher in the primary aluminum industry. In 1989, primary aluminum manufacturers paid an average of $3.5 million for such expenditures, compared to the $296,864 averaged by all other manufacturing industries in the United States.

BACKGROUND AND DEVELOPMENT

In 1886, the concurrent development in the United States and France of an economical electrolytic process for refining aluminum immediately spawned widespread optimism. Many manufacturers regarded the discovery as the new metal of the future. Aluminum would continue to be regarded as the metal of the future throughout its first century of existence, indeed well past the point its future should have arrived, leading aluminum manufacturers and government officials to overestimate demand for the metal on occasion. But the creation of a process to economically produce aluminum did, in fact, warrant its fair share of hyperbole, even if the expectations associated with its production sometimes ran too high. The metal possessed desirable conductive and thermal properties, was lightweight, and could be used to form many hard, light, corrosion-resistant alloys. As American manufacturing industries slowly effected a move toward creating products that were lighter in weight, aluminum would prove to be an integral component in a wealth of manufacturing processes, eventually establishing a pervasive, global presence that would validate the hopeful projections held by aluminum's early proponents.

But in 1886, there was only the metal and no clear idea of how aluminum could become, in practical terms, the metal of the future. Discovery of the myriad applications for the new wonder metal fell entirely to the only aluminum manufacturing company of any consequence at the time, the Pittsburgh Reduction Company, later renamed the Aluminum Company of America, and more commonly known as Alcoa. Indeed, Alcoa would remain the only manufacturer of any consequence for the aluminum industry's first 60 years, establishing a monopoly over the U.S. aluminum market during the interim and, consequently, solely guiding the industry's direction for the first half of the 20th century.

Under the partial stewardship of Charles Martin Hall, a young chemist who had discovered the more economically feasible process of aluminum production while working in his woodshed, Alcoa faced, during its early years of operation, the daunting chore of creating first a need, then a demand for aluminum. Initially, the company utilized aluminum to manufacture a line of cooking utensils, which later, in 1901, were successful enough to merit the organization of a cookware subsidiary named American Cooking Utensil. The biggest market for aluminum, however, proved to be the automobile industry, a market that would fuel the industry's growth for its first five dec-

ades of operation. By 1915, 65 percent of all new, or primary aluminum was utilized in automotive parts.

At this time, Alcoa still stood alone in the U.S. aluminum market, with the only competition coming from foreign manufacturers, whose penetration of the U.S. market was limited by high tariffs and comparatively higher energy costs. America's entrance into World War I quelled the negligible affect foreign manufacturers had on Alcoa and provided the opportunity for America's uncontested primary aluminum giant to begin exporting aluminum to Great Britain, France, and Italy. On the home front, Alcoa enjoyed commensurate success, supplying the federal government with aluminum for military applications.

By the conclusion of the war in 1918, Alcoa was producing 152 million pounds of aluminum annually and stood poised to further develop export markets it had first penetrated during the war. The manufacturing of aluminum had become a lucrative business, thanks largely to escalating demand during the war and to the fervor with which the automobile industry embraced the still new metal. Alcoa, almost entirely responsible for creating this burgeoning demand, sought to capitalize on the boom wherever it could, spending the 1920s acquiring factories, bauxite mines, and power-generating facilities in Scandinavia, Western Europe, and Canada. Toward the end of the decade, however, Alcoa's ubiquitous presence overseas made efficient management and production too difficult. In 1928, the company divested all of its foreign operations, excluding bauxite mines it owned in Dutch Guiana, which were spun off as Aluminum Limited and later renamed Alcan Aluminum Limited.

Reorganized and focused on domestic production, Alcoa struggled through the Great Depression, during which the company's sales plummeted from $34.4 million to $11.1 million and half of its work force was laid off. Once demand for aluminum returned in 1936, Alcoa quickly recovered from the earlier losses, still maintaining an omnipotent grip on the U.S. aluminum market. This enviable position, however, would not be enjoyed by the company for long, as the end of the 1930s signaled the end of Alcoa's overwhelming command over the production of U.S. aluminum and marked the beginning of a new era of competition in the U.S. primary aluminum industry, although it would be over a decade before competition in the industry would begin in earnest.

Anti-trust suits had been filed against Alcoa by the U.S. Justice Department dating back to 1911 without much success, but in 1937 a suit filed by U.S. Attorney General Homer Cummings, charging Alcoa with monopolization and restraint of trade, initiated proceedings that finally wrested control of the U.S. aluminum market away from Alcoa. The trial lasted from 1938 to 1940 and several appeals were made. Although a district court ruled in Alcoa's favor in 1942, the final decision, in 1945, sustained the government's appeal.

While lawyers for both parties scuttled among various courts, making a series of appeals that made the Alcoa anti-trust suit the largest proceeding in the history of U.S. law at that time, America had entered another war, spurring demand for aluminum. The military applications for aluminum had significantly increased during the 23-year span between World War I and World War II, creating a military appetite for aluminum that Alcoa, still the lone manufacturer in the United States of any consequence, found unable to satiate. Frustrated by Alcoa's inability to supply all the aluminum that was needed, the war department stepped in and financed new plants to provide additional production capacity.

These plants, built and operated by Alcoa, swelled the nation's output of aluminum and enabled the heightened demand to be met. As the war drew to a close and victory appeared assured, government officials were left with the responsibility of what to do with the additional capacity created during the war, which would be superfluous during peacetime. The answer to the problem was the solution of another exigency: How to effectuate an equitable conclusion to the anti-trust suit levied against Alcoa? The decision was made to offer the government-financed aluminum production plants at reduced prices to two fledgling aluminum manufacturers, Reynolds Metals Company and Permanente Metals Corporation, both of which were owned by industrialist Henry Kaiser. In 1950, a district court decree parceled out the U.S. aluminum market among the three manufacturers, giving Alcoa 50.9 percent of the nation's production capacity, Reynolds Metals 30.9 percent, and Permanente Metals, by this time renamed Kaiser Aluminum & Chemical Corporation, 18.2 percent of production capacity.

Although the seven-year debate concerning the redistribution of the U.S. aluminum market did not necessarily spawn an industry comprised of numerous participants, but, instead, left control of the market to a tightly knit cadre of manufacturers, competition was, nevertheless, quick in coming, particularly from Reynolds Metals. The company's aluminum production capacity doubled as a result of acquiring six of the government financed plants, which enhanced its ability to capitalize further on the introduction of its aluminum foil products several years earlier in 1947. Although much smaller in terms of sales volume and production capacity than Alcoa, Reynolds Metals es-

tablished itself as the more aggressive marketer, expanding overseas at a rapid rate, while focusing on developing innovative applications for aluminum that would later help elevate the company's magnitude in relation to Alcoa's.

A postwar housing boom infused the industry with an increased demand for aluminum, but the problem of smelting over-capacity, unresolved by the government's actions following the war, remained as a potential impediment to the industry's continued success. Although the hazards posed by excess supply did not threaten primary aluminum manufacturers to any great extent during the 1950s, the danger still remained. To exacerbate matters, production capacity tripled during the decade, partly due to justifiable increases engendered by the rising demand for aluminum from the housing and construction and transportation industries, but also because of federal orders to augment aluminum production to meet the demand created by the nation's involvement in the Korean War. The industry was insulated from the negative affects of oversupply during the early 1950s thanks to an agreement with the federal authorities that guaranteed the purchase of excess aluminum at market prices by the government, referred to as a ''put.'' But federal intervention merely masked the problem of over capacity, a problem that would plague manufacturers in the years to follow.

Despite their inherently precarious position, primary aluminum manufacturers entered the 1960s rightfully optimistic. The decade would bring with it the development of several new applications for aluminum that would enrich the industry considerably and fuel its growth for the next several decades. The utilization of aluminum to manufacture automobile engines, used in only one model in 1960, became more widespread during the early 1960s, as 1961 commenced with eight automobile models boasting aluminum engines. Further, aluminum bumpers and other new applications for automobiles were being developed, contributing to a rise in the amount of aluminum utilized per automobile to 62.1 pounds by 1961. A year earlier, Reynolds Metals introduced the first aluminum drill pipe, which was met with encouraging enthusiasm by other manufacturing industries, but Reynolds Metals' greatest gift to the future success of the primary aluminum industry came in 1963, with its fabrication of an aluminum beverage can. The utilization of aluminum in beverage cans would increase dramatically for the next 30 years, supporting the industry's growth throughout the 1960s and 1970s, and become a linchpin to primary aluminum manufacturers' survival in the 1990s.

These developments, combined with a housing construction boom and the growing popularity of mobile homes, which contained a large amount of aluminum, drove demand from domestic customers upward, while the industry's export activity accelerated at a rapid rate. Foreign demand for U.S. aluminium tripled between 1959 and 1960, totaling over 500 million pounds in the first year of the decade, and enabling U.S. manufacturers to sidestep the pernicious affects of oversupply.

To foster the further development of overseas markets, U.S. manufacturers of primary aluminum also began striking affiliation agreements with foreign aluminum producers in the early 1960s. In addition to joint ventures already existing at that time in Guinea and elsewhere, primary production facilities were opened in Greece and Australia in 1960, concurrent with the development of a hydroelectric and aluminum project in Ghana.

By aggressively developing new markets for their product, instead of patiently waiting for demand to catch up to supply, which was the general practice in former years, primary aluminum manufacturers had ameliorated their position in the aluminum marketplace. However, as sales climbed for each manufacturer and production increased, industry participants found they were actually recording smaller profits, inducing one manufacturer to describe the industry's performance as characterized by "profitless prosperity." Indeed, profitless prosperity was an apt description, and one that would be equally applicable in the ensuing years. The price of aluminum had deteriorated, shrinking profit margins, and an excessive amount of unused production capacity saddled manufacturers with a growing percentage of operating costs that did not generate revenue. To exacerbate matters, the importation of primary aluminum into the U.S. market saturated a market already sufficiently supplied with aluminum. Consequently, U.S. producers of aluminum were shipping more aluminum, but were reaping reduced earnings. The three largest manufacturers watched with dismay as their combined net profit margins slipped from 10.7 percent in 1956, to 5.2 percent by 1960. Alcoa, for example, which produced 36 percent of all the aluminum manufactured in the United States at this time, posted a sales total within one percent of its record high in 1960, yet lost $40 million, the company's worst profit performance in a decade. Thus, the paradoxical nature of the primary aluminum industry became readily apparent in the early 1960s—innovative applications for primary aluminum promised increased demand and production levels grew, but

manufacturers garnered comparatively prosaic earnings.

By the mid-1960s, the primary aluminum industry was comprised of seven companies operating 23 separate plants. Conditions had improved considerably in the five years since earnings slipped from more lucrative levels, as the industry recorded its fourth consecutive, record year in shipments in 1965. Significant gains were realized in several markets that relied on primary aluminum for manufacturing purposes, most notably the burgeoning demand for aluminum to fabricate trucktrailers, mobile homes, and related equipment. Aluminum usage in this segment of the transportation market soared 32 percent in 1964, complementing an increase in the usage of aluminum per automobile to nearly 70 pounds. The electrical market also provided additional business for aluminum manufacturers, as aluminum usage for underground residential distribution cable, building wire for industrial, commercial, and residential uses, and extra high voltage transmission lines increased 19 percent.

These surges in demand experienced by the primary aluminium industry's key end-use markets were imputable to the concerted search by aluminum manufacturers for new ways in which aluminum could be used. This, however, was nothing new; manufacturers had been exploring aluminum's potential applications for years, beginning with Alcoa's initial research and development efforts back in the 1890s. What was new, and what sparked a resurgence in optimism regarding the primary aluminum industry's future by manufacturers and industry observers alike, was a stabilization of aluminum prices, which previously had fluctuated wildly, glutting production capacity and squeezing profit margins. Also, the affiliations with foreign aluminum manufacturers that were initiated earlier in the decade began to buoy the industry's performance, as manufacturers benefitted from high-volume, global operations. Providing further impetus to the industry's growth was a trend toward incorporating aluminum into many new large-scale construction projects during the mid-1960s, such as in skyscrapers and large ships. These emboldening developments led industry observers to note that, perhaps, the primary aluminum industry was emerging from its protracted adolescence, and had, indeed, become the metal of the future after nearly 80 years of commercial availability.

By the end of the decade, nine manufacturers representing 13 companies were involved in producing primary aluminum. The building and construction market continued to be the largest consuming segment of primary aluminum, accounting for 23 percent of the industry's shipments. The transportation industry ranked second, purchasing 20 percent, followed by the electrical market, which accounted for 13 percent, and the rapidly growing packaging and containing market, enlarged by the increasing popularity of aluminum beverage cans, accounted for ten percent. During the 1960s, aluminum shipments increased by an annual average rate of roughly nine percent and the price of aluminum continued to remain stable. The estimated average price index for primary aluminum in 1969 reflected only a four percent increase from the 1960 level.

In the early and mid-1970s, an energy crises touched off recessive economic conditions that sent many manufacturing industries' earnings spiraling downward. For primary aluminum manufacturers, the deleterious affects of the energy crises were particularly harsh, since their production facilities were the most energy-intensive of all manufacturing activities. Aluminum manufacturers consumed four percent of all the electric power generated in the United States, the purchase of which represented greater than a third of the total manufacturing cost of aluminum. Consequently, when the price of electricity soared, primary aluminum manufacturers suffered the brunt of the damage engendered by escalating energy costs. In 1975, the nadir of the recession, primary aluminum operating capacity dropped to 75 percent and the industry's total shipments plummeted 28 percent from the previous year's total.

Despite the decline in shipments, primary aluminum inventories swelled during the recession. It took two years to work off the aluminum ferreted away during the general economic decline once the economic scene improved, prolonging the industry's recovery. Not surprisingly, primary aluminum manufacturers intensified their efforts toward developing primary aluminum processes that reduced their dependence on electricity. Laudable achievements already had been achieved toward this objective; the energy consumption required to produce aluminum had dropped from 12 kilowatt hours per pound of aluminum following World War II, to roughly eight kilowatt hours by this time. But after the recessive mid-1970s, manufacturers invested more time and money into developing alternative methods to produce aluminum. Additionally, a majority of primary aluminum manufacturers began concentrating more on the secondary smelting of aluminum, which required far less electric power.

Once the industry recovered from the negative affects of the energy crises in the late 1970s, manufacturers were unable to meet the rising demand for aluminum, as conditions within the industry quickly reversed. The transformation was only temporary, however, for demand just as quickly disappeared in the early 1980s, due, in part, to a significant decline in housing and construction activity. Compounding the situation, aluminum prices plummeted, causing the closure of a substantial percentage of production capacity. Despite the diminished production capacity, total operating smelter capacity in the United States fell to 72 percent, three percentage points below the low recorded in 1975. By the mid-1980s, key aluminum markets had become saturated, with foreign aluminum manufacturers carving a 21 percent share of the U.S. primary and fabricated aluminum market, up from the nine percent market share they secured in 1980.

Sales in the U.S. aluminum market grew at twice the rate of the gross national product during the 1960s and 1970s, but in the 1980s the expansion into new, untapped markets was no longer possible. Buffeted by a rapidly growing scrap aluminum industry that benefitted from the trend toward recycling and an increasing use of plastic instead of aluminum for beverage containers, primary aluminum manufacturers faced unfavorable prospects as the industry faltered in its tenth decade of existence. The fabrication end of the aluminum industry, which generated 80 percent of the overall aluminum industry's revenues by the mid-1980s, began to attract more primary aluminum manufacturers as the decade drew to a close, while primary production facilities sprouted up overseas, signaling, for some, the beginning of a new era in U.S. aluminum production.

CURRENT CONDITIONS

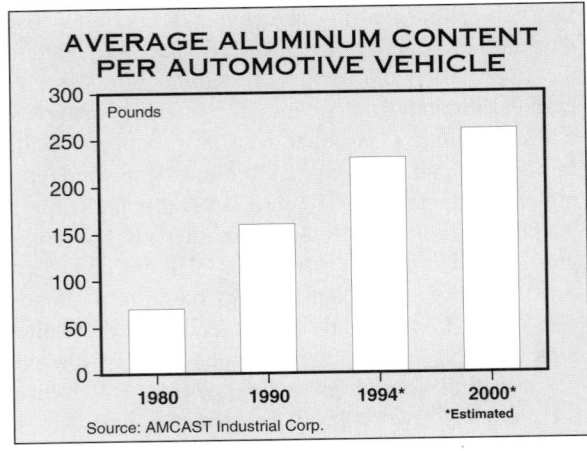

AVERAGE ALUMINUM CONTENT PER AUTOMOTIVE VEHICLE

Source: AMCAST Industrial Corp.

Faced with the relatively high cost of electricity in the United States, manufacturers of primary aluminum were forced, in the late 1980s and early 1990s, to halt further domestic construction of new smelting capacity and, instead, channeled additional smelting capacity construction to other countries where energy costs were lower. Entering the early 1990s, manufacturers attempted to take advantage of the comparatively inexpensive reserves of natural gas in the Middle East and hydroelectric power in other countries. The domestic construction of new smelting capacity was also limited by the amended Clean Air Act of 1990, which, in part, required electric utilities to reduce sulfur dioxide emissions. The costs incurred by electric utilities in making these emission reductions were, in turn, passed to primary aluminum manufacturers, which widened the gulf between foreign and domestic energy costs further. Additionally, future attempts to bridle potential climate changes engendered by the production of greenhouse gases could adversely affect the primary aluminum industry's main source of energy. Roughly 50 percent of the U.S. smelters in operation in 1993 were supplied electricity from coal burning power plants, a principal source of greenhouse gas emissions.

To maintain demand for primary aluminum production, manufacturers continued their long tradition of searching for innovative uses of aluminum and augmenting the proportional use of aluminum for existing applications. For decades, manufacturers of primary aluminum have looked toward the automobile industry to boost the demand for aluminum, knowing that each incremental increase in the amount of aluminum utilized per automobile signaled an appreciable rise in aluminum demand. Looking forward from 1993, primary aluminum manufacturers were encouraged by the automobile industry's projections that the utilization of aluminum in automobiles was expected to increase by 30 percent during the next decade to 210 pounds of aluminum per automobile. Aside from the conventional applications for aluminum in automobiles, such as in automobile frames, structural members, and body frames, automobile manufacturers were also utilizing precision aluminum parts produced by the powder metallurgy (P/M) process to an increasing extent. Requiring less machining and less handling, P/M parts were, in 1993, considered by automobile manufacturers to be part of the solution toward improving quality, reducing vehicle weight, and lowering manufacturing costs. Accordingly, the utilization of P/M parts, which totaled 25 pounds per automobile in 1993, was expected to increase in the coming years and help bolster aluminum demand in the United States.

Supported by the beverage can market, the largest end use of aluminum in the United States, the primary aluminum industry was expected to increase its shipments at a compound annual rate of just under three percent from 1993 to 1997. With consumption of beer in the United States slowing, and large plastic bottles emerging as an increasingly popular receptacle for pop producers, growth in this area is expected to remain modest. Moreover, as *Business Week* noted in 1993, "canmakers are working with ever-thinner grades of aluminum, which means slimmer shipments . . . In an attempt to secure its market for can-sheet, Reynolds has announced plans to buy Miller Brewing Co.'s can plants."

INDUSTRY LEADERS

In terms of sales volume, the two largest competitors in the primary aluminum industry in 1992 were Alcoa and Reynolds Metals, each a major contributor to the advancement of the industry. Indeed, for the first 60 years of the industry, primary aluminum production meant Alcoa. Starting with a jump start on its competitors, Alcoa owned the patent for the electrolytic process that first made the production of aluminum commercially feasible. Reynolds Metals, joining the fray during World War, established itself as a leading primary aluminum manufacturer from the outset, aggressively pursuing the development of innovative applications for aluminum and expanding into foreign markets.

Negatively affected by overall slide of the primary aluminum industry during the 1980s, Alcoa and Reynolds Metals diversified their operations to mitigate their losses from the decline and placed a lesser emphasis on the production of primary aluminum. Instead, both companies concentrated more on the fabrication end of the aluminum industry and smelting secondary aluminum harvested from recycled aluminum. In 1992, Alcoa recorded a loss of $1.14 billion on revenue of $9.49 billion. Reynolds Metals, for the same year, lost $748.8 million on revenue of $5.66 billion.

WORK FORCE

Total employment in the primary aluminum industry declined throughout much of the 1980s, then stabilized toward the latter end of the decade. The most precipitous decline occurred between 1984 and 1986, when total employment fell from 22,500 to 16,900. By 1988, the industry's employment base had rebounded to nearly 19,000, and approached 20,000 by the beginning of the 1990s. Clearly, further reductions in the industry's production capacity will have a commensurate effect on the industry's employment level. The trend toward relocating smelting facilities abroad to realize lower energy costs that began during the 1980s

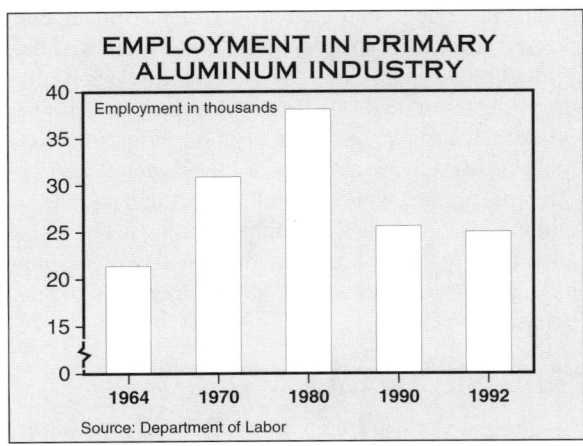

EMPLOYMENT IN PRIMARY ALUMINUM INDUSTRY

Employment in thousands

Source: Department of Labor

will likely erode into the industry's total employment level if this burgeoning movement to foreign soil continues throughout the 1990s.

Of the 25,000 people employed in the primary aluminum industry in 1990, an overwhelming majority were employed as production workers. Salaried employees, or those performing managerial, administrative, or technical duties, composed the balance of the industry's work force. The typical primary aluminum manufacturing facility employed 287 production workers and 76 salaried employees.

Generally, production workers were employed by the industry on a full-time basis, averaging two percent more hours per year than the typical production worker employed by all other manufacturing industries. Average hourly wages in the primary aluminum industry were considerably higher than the average amount earned by production workers employed by all other manufacturing industries. In 1989, production workers in the industry were paid $17.69 per hour, 69 percent more than the $10.49 per hour paid to all other production workers. In 1990, primary aluminum production workers' hourly wage slipped to $17.50, while salaried employees were paid an average of $45,939 a year.

As a consequence of the comparatively high hourly wage paid to production workers in the industry, the personnel costs per manufacturing facility, including both production workers' wages and salaries paid to managerial, administrative, and technical staff, were nearly 900 percent higher the personnel costs incurred by the average of all other manufacturing industries. In 1989, the average payroll per establishment in the primary aluminum industry was $13,788,462, compared to $1,398,674 recorded by the average manufacturing facility.

Prognostications for the industry's work force in the year 2005 suggested a general decline for nearly every occupation employed by the primary metals industry, of which the primary aluminum industry is a subdivision. According to U.S. Bureau of Labor estimates, only primary metal salespeople and industrial production managers were expected to proportionately increase their representation in the industry between 1990 and 2005. Occupations expected to be affected most severely were machine tool cutting and forming workers, metal molding machine operators, machine workers, and hand workers, each of which were expected to decline by 27 to 33 percent by 2005.

AMERICA AND THE WORLD

In 1993, aluminum prices plunged to their lowest real level in history, as cheaper, foreign produced metal flooded the U.S. market and led to the accusation by domestic manufacturers that foreign competitors were "dumping" aluminum, or selling their products at artificially low prices in the United States to increase their market share. By the beginning of 1994, domestic producers were considering filing "anti-dumping" charges with the U.S. government to stem the flow of imports entering their markets.

These imports originated from several fronts, most notably from Japan and Taiwan, but the situation was exacerbated for U.S. manufacturers by the collapse of the Soviet Union in the early 1990s. Before the collapse, Soviet aluminum was almost entirely channeled to the Soviet defense industry, but when the country's military needs faded, its aluminum entered the U.S. market, saturating a market already filled with a surfeit of aluminum. From 1989 to 1993, the amount of aluminum originating from the former Soviet Union and entering the United States ballooned from 250,000 metric tons to 1.6 million metric tons. *Business Week* commented in 1993 that, "since the Russian avalanche began in late 1990, U.S. aluminum makers have cut production by 796,000 metric tons, or 20% of capacity, and laid off 1,300 employees. But prices continue to fall. Meanwhile, the European Community, after cutting production by 320,000 metric tons, is trying to limit shipments from Russia to Europe—detouring more of the metal to North America."

Consequently, America's position as the world leader in primary aluminum production appeared threatened in the early 1990s, with the prospects for the industry's future resting on either lowering the manufacturing costs of aluminum or quelling the formidable wave of foreign-produced aluminum from entering the U.S. market.

INDUSTRY INFORMATION SOURCES

"Aluminum Fights Off a Double Whammy," *Business Week,* January 25, 1982, 28.

"The Aluminum Glut: It Points Up the Pitfalls of Government Planning," *Barron's,* October 16, 1961, 1.

"Aluminum in the Seventies," *Wall Street Transcript,* July 27, 1970, 21, 291.

"Aluminum Industry Gears for Growth," *Steel,* July 26, 1965, 94-99.

"Autopsy," *Forbes,* April 1, 1961, 15.

Baker, Stephen, "Suddenly, There's Aluminum Everywhere," *Business Week,* October 25, 1993, 46.

Boericke, William F., "Important Non-Ferrous Metals Picture for 1961," *The Magazine of Wall Street,* January 28, 1961, 506-526.

"Metal of the Future Is Getting There," *Business Week,* June 24, 1967, 116-123.

"Metals," *Forbes,* January 1, 1962, 37.

Milbank, Dana, "Alcoa Posts Loss of $80 million for 4th Quarter," *Wall Street Journal,* January 13, 1993, A6.

Miles, Gregory L., "That Crunching You Hear Is the U.S. Aluminum Industry," *Business Week,* July 8, 1985, 52A.

Miller, Gay Sands, "U.S. Aluminum Makers Say More Imports Will Be Needed to Avoid Future Shortages," *Wall Street Journal,* February 21, 1978, 48.

Nag, Amal, "Aluminum Makers Push Search for Ways to Slash Energy Use," *Wall Street Journal,* December 26, 1980, 9.

Regan, Bob, "Aluminum Smelters Make 72,938 Tons of Extra Metal in '91," *American Metal Market,* January 14, 1992.

"Reynolds Metals Posts Loss of $152.1 Million," *Wall Street Journal,* January 19, 1993, C21.

"Sales Boom Spurs New Wave of Aluminum Plant Projects," *Chemical Week,* July 20, 1963, 26-29.

U.S. Industrial Outlook, Washington, D.C.: U.S. Department of Commerce, 1960-1993.

—Jeffrey L. Covell

SIC 3339

PRIMARY SMELTING AND REFINING OF NONFERROUS METALS, EXCEPT COPPER AND ALUMINUM

This classification covers establishments primarily engaged in smelting and refining nonferrous metals, except copper and aluminum. Establishments primarily engaged in rolling, drawing, and extruding these nonferrous primary metals are classified in **SIC 3356: Rolling, Drawing, and Extruding of Nonferrous Metals, Except Copper and Aluminum,** and the production of bullion at the site of the mine is classified in various mining classifications.

This industry supplies nonferrous metals for further consumption to secondary smelting and refining establishments. The metals refined include antimony, babbitt, beryllium, bismuth, cadmium, chromium, cobalt, columbium, germanium, gold, iridium, lead, magnesium, nickel, platinum, rhenium, selenium, silicon, silver, tantalum, tellurium, tin, titanium, zinc, and zirconium. These metals are extracted from their ores and poured into basic shapes, such as slabs, pig molds, or ingots.

After experiencing a steady drop in shipments between 1983 and 1986 from $3.465 billion to $2.569 billion, the industry rebounded to $4.286 billion in shipments by 1988. Employment levels, however, do not mirror shipment levels. In 1982 13,400 total employees worked in this industry, 9,200 of whom were production workers. By 1988 10,100 employees remained, 7,500 of whom were production workers. In general, when compared to the average of all other manufacturing, workers in this industry are well paid.

Magnesium Refining. Due to the lower weight and comparable strength of magnesium components when compared to aluminum, magnesium is increasingly utilized as a manufacturing material. Because of this popularity, magnesium die casting has grown an average of 18 percent per year between 1983 and 1993. However, the worldwide demand for magnesium has only grown at two percent per year. Moreover, domestic magnesium manufacturers have been hurt by increased imports, especially those from the Commonwealth of Independent States (CIS). The former Soviet Union was restricted from entering the free world magnesium markets due to trade barriers imposed, but by the second half of 1992 these barriers were lifted and the CIS was allowed to participate. The Commerce Department estimated that American imports of magnesium from the CIS would more than quadruple in 1993 compared to 1992.

Precious Metals Refining. The short-term outlook for precious metal smelting and refining is somewhat mixed. A recent *Barron's* feature discussed the prospects of these metals. According to Jeff Christian of CPM Group, gold prices are expected to increase, and the strengthening U.S. economy can support these prices. George Milling-Stanley of Lehman Brothers suggested the outlook for silver is not as strong, because a glut of silver is available on the market due to depressed demand. Also, silver is used primarily in industrial applications, and is dependent on growth rates in industrialized countries, and while the United States' economic picture appears solid entering the mid-1990s, other industrialized nations continue to struggle to extricate themselves from recessionary conditions.

Leading Companies. Significant companies in this industry in the early 1990s included Handy and Harman Co. and Horsehead Industries Inc., both in New York City; Johnson Matthey Inc., based in Wayne, Pennsylvania; Cookson America Inc. of Providence, Rhode Island; and Brush Wellman Inc., headquartered in Cleveland, Ohio.

Technological Advances. Late in October 1993 researchers at the National Institute of Standards and Technology in Boulder, Colorado, announced they had developed a new alloy. The alloy is a combination of nickel, chromium, manganese, molybdenum, copper, nitrogen, and iron. It can withstand temperatures below -269 degrees celsius (-516 degrees fahrenheit), and is expected to find use in fusion energy studies, superconducting magnets, and physics experiments funded by the U.S. government. The importance of the alloy will lie in welding seams in superconducting magnets, which must resist fracture in such low temperatures.

INDUSTRY INFORMATION SOURCES

Barron's, November 15, 1993, 10-11.

Cohn, Lynne M., *American Metal Market*, October 13, 1993, 1.

Haflich, Frank. *American Metal Market*, November 23, 1993, 2.

U.S. Industrial Outlook 1994, Washington, DC: U.S. Department of Commerce, 1994.

—Valerie E. Wilson

SIC 3341

SECONDARY SMELTING AND REFINING OF NONFERROUS METALS

This classification comprises establishments primarily engaged in recovering nonferrous metals and alloys from new and used scrap and dross, or in producing alloys from purchased refined metals. This industry includes establishments engaged in both the recovery and alloying of precious metals. Also included in this industry are plants involved in the recovery of tin through secondary smelting and refining, as well as by chemical processes. Excluded from the classification of this industry are establishments primarily engaged in assembling, sorting, and breaking up scrap metal without smelting and refining the metal. These establishments are classified in **SIC 5093: Scrap and Waste Materials.**

INDUSTRY SNAPSHOT

Metal, utilized by nearly every manufacturing industry in the United States and abroad, is produced through two basic production methods: primary and secondary. Primary manufacturers produce metal by subjecting particular extracted ores to various metallurgical processes, creating metal in large block or bar form, while secondary manufacturers smelt, refine, and sometimes blend metal recovered from either the shaping and trimming of primary metal during production and fabrication, or from recycled metal. The secondary smelting and refining of nonferrous metals, as defined by **SIC 3341**, comprises the secondary production of metals that do not contain iron, such as aluminum, copper, gold, lead, nickel, silver, tin, and zinc. These metals are used in a wide variety of manufactured products, including ammunition, beverage cans, coins, automobiles, household appliances and a wealth of other products that nearly encompass the breadth of U.S. manufacturing activity.

Copper, possessing superior electrical conductivity, is a strong, durable metal used in a variety of structural applications and for power, lighting, and communications transmissions. Domestically, the major markets for copper are construction, electrical and electronics, and industrial machinery and equipment.

Aluminum, the most widely used nonferrous metal, possesses several attributes, such as light weight, corrosion resistance, and high electrical and thermal conductivity that makes the metal suitable for a variety of applications. Container and packaging manufacturers purchase a majority of the domestically produced aluminum, while other major end-use markets include the transportation sector, the buildings and construction sector, and the electrical sector.

Lead is primarily used in the manufacturing of storage batteries, which in turn are incorporated into automobile ignition starters, uninterruptible power supplies for computer systems, and standby power supplies for emergency lighting systems and telephones. Other marker sectors that purchase lead include paint and glass manufacturers and building products manufacturers.

Zinc is primarily used to galvanize products found in the automobile, steel, and construction industries, but a greater percentage of secondary zinc is used to produce brass and bronze, as well as assorted chemicals and dusts. Additional applications include the blending of zinc-based, die-cast alloys and brass alloys.

Approximately 350 companies in the United States were involved in the secondary smelting and refining industry in 1990. These manufacturers recorded $6.13 billion in sales for products included in the **SIC 3341** classification, an aggregate value of shipments primarily derived from the production of the industry's five key products: secondary aluminum, secondary precious metals (gold, silver, platinum), secondary copper, secondary lead, and secondary zinc. Although the secondary smelting and refining industry produces other metals, such as nickel and tin, these five metals accounted for the bulk of the industry's total shipments. Of all the metals produced by the industry, secondary aluminum represented the largest product category, accounting for 38.5 percent of the industry's aggregate shipments. Precious metals were the industry's second largest product category, representing 17.6 percent of total shipments, followed by secondary copper, which accounted for 12.8 percent. Percentage share for the production of secondary lead and zinc is impossible to gauge because pertinent data was withheld by the respective manufacturers to prevent disclosure of competitive information.

ORGANIZATION AND STRUCTURE

In terms of the number of people employed per establishment, the secondary smelting and refining industry has been, historically, predominately populated by relatively small manufacturing facilities. Of the 383 secondary smelting and refining establishments in operation in 1989, 207 employed less than 20 people, while the remaining 176 employed 20 people or more. These 383 establishments represented all of the individual production facilities operated by the approximately 350 companies engaged in smelting and refining secondary aluminum in 1989. When the secondary smelting and refining industry is compared against all other manufacturing industries in the United States, a clearer picture of the industry's size is provided. In 1989, the average number of employees per establishment for all U.S. manufacturing industries was 54, or 29 percent more than the average number of employees per establishment in the secondary smelting and refining industry.

Geographically, a majority of the secondary smelting and refining production facilities in the late

1980s was located in the four state area comprising Michigan, Illinois, Indiana, and Ohio. Together, these states contained 110 production facilities. The Middle Atlantic states of Pennsylvania, New York, and New Jersey formed the second largest regional concentration of facilities, with 74 establishments, followed by the Pacific region, which ranked as the third largest area of production solely by virtue of the 43 establishments located in California, the greatest number located in any one state and the only state within the region that contained any secondary smelting and refining facilities. Ranked according to the number of establishments per state, California was followed by Ohio, with 36 production facilities, and Pennsylvania, which contained 32 establishments. The 11 manufacturing facilities in Alabama exceeded the production output of all other states, despite being dwarfed by the 43 facilities in California. The facilities in Alabama eclipsed the shipment volume of California by a tenth of a percentage point, accounting for 12.3 percent of the industry's total shipments and recording $543.6 million in sales, five million more than California's revenue total.

The expenses incurred from operating a secondary smelting and refining facility were substantially higher than the amount of money required to operate the average manufacturing facility in the United States. This disparity was most evident in the average cost per establishment, that is, the average amount of money paid for raw manufacturing materials. According to 1989 figures, the average cost per establishment in the secondary smelting and refining industry was $13.9 million, more than three times greater than the $4.5 million averaged by all other manufacturing industries. The average investment per establishment in the secondary smelting and refining industry for production machinery and other equipment necessary in the recovery of primary metal, however, was five percent lower than the average investment per establishment in all other manufacturing industries. The average investment per establishment in the secondary smelting and refining industry was $282,768, while the typical manufacturing establishment required an investment of $296,864.

BACKGROUND AND DEVELOPMENT

In the historiography of secondary smelting and refining, one chronicler traces the origins of recovering scrap metal to the seventh descendent of Adam, back to the founder of the iron and steel industry, and by implication, the founder of the scrap metal industry—Tubal-Cain. The writer then proceeds to chart the utilization of scrap metal throughout the span of civilization, making references along the way to documented accounts of scrap metal usage by such notable personages as Moses, Chaucer, Shakespeare, Paul Revere, Captain Kidd, and Thoreau. While this exploration into the depths of scrap metal's history may strike some as overindulgent, it does indicate the pervasiveness and integrality of secondary metal in the history of human existence. It also suggests that scrap metal has been used as long as metal has been used by mankind.

But, obviously, the processing of scrap in the days of Tubal-Cain bore no resemblance to the modern secondary metal industry. The smelting and refining of scrap metal as an organized and structured industry, the type of industry that operated in the 1990s, was a modern creation in the United States. It formed in the early 1900s, as secondary smelting and refining manufacturers began to shed their image as junk peddlers, and gradually became regarded as legitimate operators of an enterprise essential to the existence of modern manufacturing industries. This transition was hastened by the formation of the National Association of Waste Material Dealers, in 1913, which gave manufacturers, for the first time, formalized rules of operation, a code of ethics, and uniform specifications for scrap metal production. The creation of this governing body, renamed the National Association of Secondary Material Industries (NASMI) in 1960, lent cohesion to a loosely structured group of manufacturers struggling to attain order in a rapidly changing manufacturing environment.

Although the advent of NASMI helped define and shape the industry, the smelting and refining of secondary nonferrous metals had been occurring in an industrial setting for quite some time before NASMI came into existence. No statistical record of scrap consumption in the United States exists prior to 1900, but in 1900, the first year figures were recorded, U.S. manufacturers consumed 5.1 million gross tons of ferrous and nonferrous secondary metal. Indeed, the first American scrap metal company, Cline & Bernheim, based in Nashville, Tennessee, had begun operating nearly 40 years before industry-wide consumption figures were recorded in 1862. Following the records, the first market coverage of the scrap industry was published in 1865, when the *Commercial Bulletin of Boston* began providing scrap metal prices. And even further back in time, the first commercial use of scrap metal in the United States occurred at an iron works in Lynn, Massachusetts in 1642.

Although some of these early uses of scrap metal were of the ferrous variety, the tradition of scrap metal usage had its roots stretching back to the founding of

the United States. Accordingly, the scrap metal industry had gathered more than a modicum of momentum by the time NASMI emerged. Once it did emerge, though, the modern version of the secondary nonferrous metal industry began and the recovery, smelting, and refining of such metals became distinguished from the production of primary metals, rather than lumped together under the more general and generic metal industry umbrella.

Following the founding of NASMI, secondary non-ferrous production occurred at a predictable, steady rate, devoid of any significant impulse from external market forces that, otherwise, would have proportionately boosted the industry's production volume. Military build-up during World War I, which had a positive affect on many manufacturing industries, provided less than its expected impact on secondary metal producers, largely due to the conspicuous absence of wartime scrap metal drives. A tremendous increase in secondary nonferrous metal production did occur, however, as a result of America's entrance into World War II. By early summer in 1942, the first summer after the Japanese bombed Pearl Harbor, the nation embarked on a virtually uninterrupted campaign to recover scrap metal, elevating the importance of secondary producers in the metal manufacturing industry.

During the immediate post-war years, a majority of American manufacturing industries flourished, and the secondary nonferrous metal industry, as a supplier of the raw material for much of the accelerated production, shared in the explosive growth of the American economy. By 1950, primary manufacturers of nonferrous metals held a commanding lead in the global market, producing nearly half of the world's supply of refined copper, aluminum, and zinc, and more than 25 percent of the world's supply of lead. Secondary producers of these metals, who literally benefitted from the crumbs of the prodigious production volume, were well positioned to profit from the increased demand for nonferrous metals, converting "old" scrap, or metal recovered from recycled products, and converting "new" scrap gleaned from the trimming and shaping of primary nonferrous ingot (referred to as "home" scrap).

This closely knit, interdependent relationship secondary producers maintained within the nonferrous metal industry, which had matured and strengthened in the roughly four decades since the establishment of NASMI, invigorated production during robust economic conditions, but also made industry participants vulnerable to the vagaries of the overall metal industry. Although conditions were favorable in the 1950s, several portentous developments arose during this time that augured a somewhat bleaker future for all manufacturers of nonferrous metal.

The consumption of nonferrous metals had increased exponentially since the turn of the century, fueled by a rapidly growing population and its needs for products manufactured with nonferrous metals. By the time the United States entered World War II, this increased demand had depleted the country's metal ore reserves to the extent that the self-sufficient production of several key nonferrous metals, such as zinc and lead, was no longer possible, while the manufacturing of another key nonferrous metal, aluminum, required an ore more commonly found in countries other than the United States. During the 1950s, this development had persuaded many primary manufacturers of nonferrous metals to affiliate with foreign metal manufacturers to meet existing U.S. demand, or to establish wholly owned operations overseas, where ore deposits were plentiful. While this expansion into foreign metal markets narrowed the gap between supply and demand and sparked the overall metal industry's growth, it also fostered the growth of the global nonferrous metal market, establishing, for the first time, manufacturing facilities in less-developed countries and encouraging output in more sophisticated, foreign markets. Repercussions from this shift overseas were not immediate, but in the years ahead, the evolution of a genuine global metal industry would engender a sharply contested nonferrous metal market.

Although the scarcity of particular ore deposits in the United States would affect primary manufacturers of nonferrous metals more severely than secondary producers, the fortunes of both sectors of the nonferrous metal industry were intertwined to the extent that neither entirely escaped the troubles of the other. But a technological innovation developed by primary manufacturers in the 1950s promised to impinge directly on the demand for secondary nonferrous metal, while reducing the manufacturing costs incurred by primary producers, which pitted these two, often complementary, industry segments against each other. The basic principle behind this innovation was relatively simple: introduce oxygen into the furnaces in which pig iron is converted to steel. The addition of oxygen quickened the conversion process, reducing the energy requirements of metal production, and most harmful to secondary producers, the new process needed far less scrap metal with which to manufacture ingot. Without oxygen, primary manufacturers needed a high percentage of scrap metal to efficiently produce metal, but with oxygen the proportion of scrap metal dropped to as low as 40 percent. Initially, steel manufacturers

employed this new process, but by the mid and late 1960s, the utilization of oxygen in the production of nonferrous metals had begun, as aluminum manufacturers adopted the process. Of course, the use of oxygen also reduced the conversion time in the production of secondary metals, but the losses suffered as a result of the diminished role scrap metal played in the manufacturing of primary metal were significant.

Fortunately for secondary metal producers, the popularity of this new production method was roughly concurrent with the birth of widespread recycling efforts, which bolstered the industry's production output and marked the beginning of a movement that would serve as a linchpin to the industry's existence and success into the 1990s. To varying degrees, the recycling of used products and materials had been occurring for many decades prior to the late 1960s and early 1970s—the existence of the secondary metal industry itself, comprised of former junk peddlers, was testament to the long tradition of recycling—but these efforts were intensified due to the growing outcry against pollution and waste, as landfills dotting the nation's landscape brimmed with refuse. Also, recycling had been generally limited to the recovery of industrial, or commercial by-products, not the recycling of consumer products, such as storage batteries and aluminum and tin cans.

Once recycling began in earnest, secondary producers of nonferrous metals began to play a more dominant role in the overall nonferrous metals industry, outpacing primary manufacturers in terms of production volume and capitalizing on governmental efforts aimed at reducing the amount of national waste. Federally led and financed attempts to reduce waste received an initial push from the creation of the Office of Solid Waste Management in 1965, which was strengthened in 1970 by the promulgation of the Resource Recovery Act. The Resource Recovery Act authorized a three-year budget of $461 million, but, most important to secondary nonferrous metal producers, the Act changed the Office of Solid Waste Management's primary objective from the sanitary dumping of solid wastes to recycling those wastes. In a short time, the effect of this concerted push toward recovering solid wastes ameliorated the secondary nonferrous industry's position, driving scrap manufacturer's production output upwards. By 1971, the secondary production of lead accounted for roughly 50 percent of the total lead consumption in the United States and the proportional representation of other secondary nonferrous metals were no less impressive: secondary copper accounted for approximately 45 percent; secondary aluminum, 35 percent; secondary zinc, 23 percent.

By the mid-1970s, however, a recession and a worldwide energy crisis nearly crippled all sectors of the ferrous and nonferrous metal industry, as successive oil shocks quaked the foundations of an industry that relied on relatively large amounts of energy to exist. Indeed, the deleterious affects of the energy crises plagued metal manufacturers for the rest of the decade and stood as a turning point for the health of metal manufacturers worldwide. The annual growth rates in the consumption of nonferrous metals from 1979 to 1988 stood well below the pace recorded from 1950 to 1974: the annual consumption rate of aluminum, worldwide, from 1950 to 1974 was nine percent, while from 1979 to 1988 the rate dropped to 2.3 percent; copper fell from 3.9 percent to 1.1 percent; lead from 2.7 percent to 0.5 percent; and zinc from 3.9 percent to 1.2 percent.

As the secondary smelting and refining industry entered the 1980s, a period of corporate restructuring began, as companies purchased, sold, and merged operations to enhance their competitiveness, while the key metals within the industry were each affected, either negatively or positively, by conditions peculiar to their markets. The production of secondary copper suffered a decline in total shipments in the early 1980s after effecting a rebound from the pernicious 1970s. By 1989, however, shipments eclipsed the one year surge experienced at the start of the decade, as manufacturers combated difficulties associated with aging production facilities and environmental regulations. Over the entire decade, secondary production accounted for 26 percent of the total U.S. copper production, a more encouraging representation than the 20 percent recorded from 1975 to 1979.

Secondary aluminum production fared comparatively better during the 1980s, increasing 40 percent over the decade. Hampered by decreasing primary production of aluminum in the United States and a nearly glutted beverage can market, secondary aluminum manufacturers also experienced capricious fluctuations in demand during much of the decade. Nevertheless, secondary aluminum producers concluded the 1980s with three solid years of production output, during which they recorded much of the production growth of the decade.

Primary lead manufacturers, struggling with the sharply decreased demand for tetraethyl lead (TEL), which is used to produce leaded gasoline, witnessed secondary manufacturers of lead increase their representation of total lead consumption during the 1980s. The reclamation of lead acid storage batteries, the

largest market for lead and typically recyclable, elevated the importance of the secondary lead industry. In 1980, primary and secondary lead production was roughly equally split, with secondary producers supplying half of nation's total lead. By the end of the decade, secondary lead manufacturers supplied approximately 65 percent of the total lead consumed in the United States.

Secondary zinc manufacturers also figured more prominently within their nonferrous metal niche during the 1980s. The demand for zinc, both from primary and secondary suppliers, increased throughout much of the decade, excluding a temporary decline in 1982. Overall consumption rose 21 percent over the course of the decade, while secondary zinc producers increased their share of the total zinc production to 23 percent.

CURRENT CONDITIONS

As the secondary smelting and refining industry entered the mid-1990s, intensified recycling by both the consumer and industrial sectors buoyed the production output of industry participants despite recessive economic conditions during the early 1990s and the losses suffered by primary producers. Each of the metals within the industry were expected to demonstrate positive growth into the late 1990s, a forecast largely predicated on the expected increase in the reclamation of industrial and consumer solid waste. Additional success in this direction will continue to elevate the industry's importance within the overall nonferrous metal industry and fuel its future growth.

From 1993 to 1997, the consumption rate of aluminum, zinc, and copper was expected to increase two percent annually for each metal. Lead consumption was expected to experience slower growth during this period, increasing one percent annually, but secondary producers were expected to increase their share of total lead production. By the end of the four year period, the secondary production of lead was expected to account for 74 percent of the total lead production in the United States.

INDUSTRY LEADERS

Ranked according to sales volume, the two largest manufacturers in the secondary smelting and refining industry in the early 1990s were Connell Limited Partnership, located in Boston, Massachusetts, and U.S. Reduction Company, located in Munster, Indiana, both of which were privately-owned.

Connell, a holding company with operations involved in fabricating special dies, plate work, and metal forming machine tools, as well as sheet metal production, is engaged in the secondary smelting and refining industry through its Wabash Alloys division, the leading producer of aluminum casting alloys in the United States. Deriving a majority of its business from the automobile industry, Wabash converts aluminum scrap into aluminum casting alloys, which are then sold to major automobile manufacturers or to die-casting companies that cater to the automobile industry. Approximately 70 percent of the scrap processed by the company is related to the automobile industry.

With 750 employees and six manufacturing plants in North America, Wabash generated an estimated $300 million in 1992, while Connell recorded roughly $1.2 billion in sales.

U.S. Reduction Company, a more diversified producer of secondary nonferrous metals than Wabash, garnered approximately $310 million in sales in 1992 and employed 400 people.

WORK FORCE

Total employment in the secondary smelting and refining industry dropped throughout much of the 1980s, effecting a slight rise in the late 1980s and into the early 1990s. In 1982, the industry's total employment stood at 19,200, then slipped to 12,500 by 1987, experiencing the most precipitous drops from 1982 to 1983 and from 1986 to 1987. After 1987, the nadir of the industry's employment decline, total employment increased by an average of 800 per year, climbing to 14,600 by the end of the decade. In 1990, the industry's employment base continued to rise, although at a less robust pace than during the late 1980s, reaching 14,700 by the end of the year.

Of the 14,700 people employed in the secondary smelting and refining industry in 1990, 3,900 were salaried employees, or those performing managerial, administrative, or technical duties, while the balance of the industry's work force comprised 10,800 production workers. A typical secondary smelting and refining facility in 1989 employed 27 production workers and 11 salaried employees.

Generally, production workers are employed on a full-time basis, averaging 12 percent more hours per year than the average number of hours worked by production workers in all other manufacturing industries. On average, production workers employed by the secondary smelting and refining industry earn slightly more than the typical production worker. In 1989, a typical production worker employed by a manufacturing industry earned $10.49 per hour, while production workers involved in the secondary smelting and re-fining industry earned $10.63. In 1990, salaried employees earned an average of $43,951 per year.

Prognostications for the industry's work force in the year 2005 suggested a general decline for nearly every occupation employed by the primary metals industry, of which the secondary smelting and refining industry is a subdivision. According to U.S. Bureau of Labor estimates, only primary metal salespeople and industrial production managers were expected to proportionately increase their representation in the industry between 1990 and 2005. Occupations expected to be affected most severely were machine tool cutting and forming workers, metal molding machine operators, machine workers, and hand workers, each of which were expected to decline by 27 to 33 percent by 2005.

AMERICA AND THE WORLD

The U.S. nonferrous metal industry, once the preeminent, global leader in production volume, entered the 1990s harried by a combination of domestic exigencies, such as escalating production costs and mounting foreign competition. Consequently, foreign manufacturers of nonferrous metals, some of whom were located in less developed countries rich in metal ore deposits, were able to gain ground on domestic manufacturers during the 1980s, and with certain metals, supplant the U.S. as the leading metal manufacturer. This situation was further exacerbated for U.S. manufacturers because some of the foreign manufacturing companies, particularly in the less developed countries, were state-owned operations, financed and directed by local government, which muddled the global, nonferrous metal picture because these companies frequently pursued political goals, rather than economic objectives. These developments affected domestic manufacturers of primary nonferrous metals more severely than secondary producers, although any significant cutbacks in primary production eventually and inevitably affect secondary producers.

Despite the increasing competition and the flight of primary manufacturing facilities, secondary producers in the United States maintained a leading position in the international, nonferrous market as they entered the 1990s. With five secondary smelters, two electrolytic refineries and six fire refineries operating in 1990, the U.S. secondary copper industry ranked as the largest producer in the world, accounting for 31 percent of the 1.5 million metric tonnes of secondary copper produced by all countries with market economies, that is, all non-socialist world (NSW) countries. West Germany ranked as the second largest producer, supplying 16 percent of the NSW's copper, followed by Japan, which accounted for ten percent. Other prominent secondary copper-producing nations and their market share percentages were: Belgium (six percent), Italy (five percent), United Kingdom (five percent), Brazil (three percent), South Korea (three percent), Yugoslavia (three percent), and Canada (three percent).

U.S. secondary aluminum producers held a larger lead in the NSW secondary aluminum market than their copper counterparts, manufacturing 41 percent of the 5.4 million metric tonnes produced in 1988. America's closest rival, Japan, produced 20 percent of the total, 10 percent more than the NSW's third largest producer, West Germany. In descending order after West Germany were: Italy (seven percent), France (four percent), United Kingdom (two percent), Netherlands (two percent), Australia (two percent), Canada (two percent), and Spain (two percent).

U.S. secondary lead producers enjoyed an equally sizeable advantage in the NSW secondary lead market, producing 33 percent of the 2.1 million metric tonnes produced by NSW countries in 1988. Trailing the U.S. by a considerable margin were the United Kingdom, West Germany, and Japan, which produced 10 percent, eight percent, and six percent of the NSW supply, respectively. These manufacturing countries were closely followed by France and Italy, which each produced five percent of the total production. Other lead producing countries and their market share percentages were: Canada (four percent), Brazil (three percent), Spain (three percent), and South Korea (two percent).

The international secondary zinc market was sharply contested in the late 1980s, as the United States maintained a precarious lead over its two strongest competitors, Australia and Japan. Of the 400,000 metric tonnes of zinc produced in the NSW in 1988, the United States controlled 20 percent of the market, followed by Australia and Japan, which each accounted for 18 percent of total production. West Germany, the only other major producer of secondary zinc in the NSW, supplied nine percent of the international market.

INDUSTRY INFORMATION SOURCES

"Aluminum Gets Hot with Oxygen," *Business Week*, August 10, 1968, pp. 80-81.

"Aluminum Plants Set Record," *American Metal Market*, March 22, 1991, p. 7.

Barringer, Edwin C., *The Story of Scrap*, Washington, DC: Institute of Scrap Iron & Steel Inc., 1954.

Cardwell, Nancy, "Copper Processors Curtailing Operations, Doubtful Phase 4 Will Make Scrap Available," *The Wall Street Journal*, July 23, 1973, p. 4.

Codero, Harry G. and Tarring, Leslie H., *Babylon to Birmingham*, London: Quin Press Ltd., 1961.

"Copper-base Scrap Use in '87 at 1,576,620 Tons," *American Metal Market*, March 17, 1988, p. 9.

"Industry Looks Up to Copper Mine in the Sky," *Business Week*, September 16, 1967, pp. 177-182.

Klein, Frederick C., "Russia Exports Scrap Aluminum to the U.S., Rousing Concern Here," *The Wall Street Journal*, January 25, 1966, p. 15.

"Metals Outlook," *Material Engineering*, January 1970, p. 29.

Miller, Herbert John, *Non-ferrous Metals Industry*, New York: United Nations, no. 1, 1969.

Newman, Barry, "Recycling Backlash," *The Wall Street Journal*, May 9, 1973, p. 1.

"New Drive to Get Rid of Trash," *U.S. News & World Report*, June 7, 1971, pp. 65-68.

O'Sullivan, Orla, "Zinc Recovery to Rise as '80s Autos Recycle," *American Metal Market*, February 24, 1993, p. 1.

"Process to Convert Scrap without Melting Disclosed," *The Wall Street Journal*, June 26, 1970, p. 18.

Rosenberg, Joseph, "Off the Scrap Heap," *Barron's*, April 17, 1972, p. 11.

Schroeder, Norman, "Small Secondary Lead Smelters Seen Cutting Environment Safeguard Cost," *American Metal Market*, November 15, 1988, p. 1.

Suisman, Michael and Rasher, Howard WM., eds., *Non-ferrous Scrap Metal Guidebook*, New York: National Association of Secondary Material Industries, 1960.

Tsukasa, Furukawa and Gloria LaRue, "Foreign Nickel Buyers Shielded," *American Metal Market*, March 17, 1988, p. 1.

"Turning Junk and Trash into a Resource," *Business Week*, October 10, 1970, pp. 66-75.

U.S. Congress, Office of Technology Assessment, *Non-ferrous Metals: Industry Structure—Background Paper*, Washington, DC: U.S. Government Printing Office, 1990.

U.S. Industrial Outlook, Washington, DC: U.S. Department of Commerce, 1960-1993.

Warden, Ed, "ARA: Specification Ingot Shipments Up," *American Metal Market*, March 6, 1989, p. 2.

—Jeffrey L. Covell

SIC 3351

ROLLING, DRAWING, AND EXTRUDING OF COPPER

This industry consists of establishments that roll, draw, or extrude copper, brass, bronze, and other copper-based alloys. These establishments create basic shapes such as plate, sheet, strip, bar, and tubing.

INDUSTRY SNAPSHOT

The companies of this industry are known as copper fabricators, whose role in the larger copper industry is to create the strip, sheet, plate, rod, bar and other copper products used in a myriad of products and industries. These companies receive smelted and refined copper from newly mined copper ore and copper scrap and turn them into products used in industries in the realm of building construction and electrical and electronic product manufacturing. Wire rod mills and brass mills comprised more than 85 percent of the fabricators in the United States. Copper foundries are discussed in **SIC 3366: Copper Foundries.**

During the economic downturn of the 1980s, there was a high degree of consolidation in the industry. Buyouts and mergers led to a leaner field of companies. Large, multi-product wire and cable mills used to be tied to mining companies. Many of these mining companies spun off their fabricators in order to be more efficient. Some refining companies, however, added continuous cast wire rod mills to the end of their production process, thereby effectively opening their own millworks.

Most brass mills in the United States had three areas of production. One division produced rod, bar, and shapes; another division produced strip, sheet, and plate; and the third division produced commercial and plumbing tube. Brass rod and brass strip, two of the most popular copper alloys produced in the industry, had the kind of corrosion resistance, machinability, and electrical properties that enabled them to be used under adverse climatic conditions. Air-conditioning tube and plumbing tube were two examples of the unalloyed copper and high-copper alloys that comprised another major segment of the mill's output.

ORGANIZATION AND STRUCTURE

Copper that is rolled, drawn, and extruded is utilized by many different industries. End-use markets for copper and copper alloy were dominated by building construction and electrical and electronic products manufacturing. These two general industries accounted for more than 65 percent of all copper shipments in 1991. Other end-use markets for copper were industrial machinery and equipment, transportation equipment, and consumer products.

Copper in the United States passes from the mines to the smelters. In some cases these facilities were owned by the same company, and in some cases the mining and smelting were performed at nearby locations. The mining and smelting companies were the producers of copper, and the wire rod mills, brass mills, and foundries were the consumers of copper who prepared the metal for delivery to manufacturers in various industries.

Mining companies processed copper ores, most of which were retrieved from open-pit mines. These ores were refined and sometimes alloyed with other elements, such as zinc or beryllium. The percentage of copper and copper alloys that went to wire rod mills was 49 percent, while 40 percent went to brass mills and seven percent went to foundries. All of these fabricators created copper-based products used throughout U.S. industry.

Several associations concerned with various facets of copper production have emerged over the years. One of the mainstays of the U.S. copper industry was the Copper and Brass Development Association (CDA). CDA tracked market statistics and published handbooks, reports, and bulletins. It also sought to broaden copper markets in this country and abroad. The Copper and Brass Servicenter Association served as a sales arm for brass mills and as a warehouse for manufacturers' inventory. The American Copper Council was another trade organization central to the copper industry.

BACKGROUND AND DEVELOPMENT

Copper mining had origins in the Middle East, but reached its zenith in the American West. Small mining operations allowed prosperous towns to grow up in Michigan and Arizona. In the mid-eighteenth century miners in the colonies discovered copper ores in what is now the northeastern United States. They mined these ores, but English law prohibited the establishment of smelting works in the colonies, so the ore was sent straight to England for smelting and refining.

After the American Revolution many copper workers moved to the newly-created United States. Copper sheathing began to be used on wooden ships as early as the 1790s. The copper protected the ships from the pressure and corrosive effects of the ocean. Great demand from the shipping industry helped the budding copper industry, but the U.S. still depended on copper imports from England and South America. In 1806 U.S. importers of copper asked Congress to exempt copper from customs duty. The protests lodged by copper industry pioneers succeeded in lowering tariffs applied to copper imports.

Fulton's steamships had copper parts by this time, as copper was better than pinewood boilers at containing steam. Later, with the rise of American industry, growing copper fabricators created stripping, boiler plates, rivets and other copper-based items that were used in an increasingly diverse number of industries and products. Copper nails replaced cast iron nails in building and the boom in putting up towns and cities across the new nation resulted in a windfall for the copper industry.

By the beginning of the twentieth century, due to "the development of efficient flotation processes around the turn of the century," according to the Copper Development Association, "open-pit mining techniques were developed . . . and the United States quickly became the world's largest producer of copper."

The brass mill industry began in the early days of colonial America in Connecticut. Copper mills could be found from Waterbury south to Ansonia. Melting and rolling techniques were tested and developed here. While little of this industry remains in Connecticut, it remains centered in the eastern United States.

CURRENT CONDITIONS

The economic upheavals in the U.S. in the 1980s affected the copper industry only belatedly. Copper prices fell as a result of overstocks, and companies were forced to confront inventory problems. According to the American Bureau of Metal Statistics, copper shipments rose 7.6 percent in the summer of 1993 over the summer of 1992. In fact cathode and bar suppliers were selling out and trying to keep up with demand for their products. But brass mill executives were concerned that the downward trend in copper prices did not bode well for copper in the future. Competing materials, such as plastics, also caused industry leaders to focus on quality and cost effectiveness.

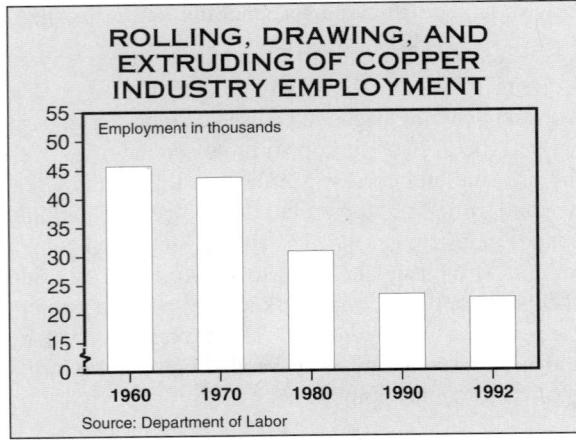

ROLLING, DRAWING, AND EXTRUDING OF COPPER INDUSTRY EMPLOYMENT

Source: Department of Labor

According to an article in the trade magazine *Copper Talk,* in the summer of 1993, overall shipments of strip, sheet, and plate declined in the 1980s, but demand for copper products increased slightly. Shipments to the electrical and electronic products markets grew to represent 36 percent of shipments. This was an increase of 12 percentage points from just two years earlier, according to Copper Development Association statistics. The percentage of copper mill products that were consumed by the building construction industry was more than 40 percent in 1991. Electrical and electronic products industries received 24 percent, and the industrial machinery industry accounted for 13 percent.

INDUSTRY LEADERS

Major companies engaged in copper rolling, drawing, and extrusion processes include Mueller Industries Inc., a public company based in Wichita, Kansas; Marmon Group Inc., a privately-owned firm headquartered in Chicago, Illinois; Outokumu Copper Inc. of Stamford, Connecticut; and Gaston Copper Recycling, based in Gaston, South Carolina.

WORK FORCE

In 1990 there were 93,754 extruding and forming machine operators. They worked in many different industries, including the copper industries. While jobs in this industry fluctuated with the health of the economy and the strength of the particular metal industry, many manufacturers were adapting their equipment and their business to enable them to continue to employ workers. From 1990 through the year 2005, the expected percent change in the number of extruding and forming machine operators was only down 1.1 percent. While there were better areas of the manufacturing sector in growth potential, this outlook was not nearly as bleak as that in other copper-related industries. The number of mining, quarrying, and tunneling occupations, for instance, was expected by some observers to fall by almost 20 percent, while the number of foundry mold assembly and shakeout workers was expected to fall by more than 20 percent.

AMERICA AND THE WORLD

Exports from the brass mill industry were increasing through the 1990s while imports were decreasing. The chief markets for the export of these goods were Mexico, Canada, and Japan. Many copper industry executives were expecting more Mexican consumption of brass mill items such as commercial and plumbing tube, strip, sheet, and plate, and rod, and bars after the passage of the North American Free Trade

Agreement (NAFTA). Industry players hope rising Mexican incomes spur increased demand for copper supplies.

The copper industry was becoming increasingly global in its outlook in the 1990s. Those countries that were improving their infrastructures with telecommunications cables, power cables, and other basic building tools needed more copper. The Asian markets of China, Taiwan, and South Korea were hoped to provide large new markets. Copper tends to be sensitive to supply constraints, however, and political and financial troubles in copper-producing nations can wreak havoc with the usually-stable balance of supply and demand.

In the early 1990s there were still legislative paths for concerned copper industry executives to take when faced with international competition that was viewed as unfair. Foreign manufacturers of brass sheet and strip, for instance, were watched carefully for charges of dumping products below market costs.

The U.S. formed an International Copper Study Group in the early 1990s in conjunction with 17 other countries involved in the copper industry. Their aim was to allow informational exchanges between producing and consuming countries as well as to increase copper production and consumption. Members included Germany, China, Chile, Peru, and France.

RESEARCH AND TECHNOLOGY

Patricia Foley, a copper executive writing in the trade magazine *Copper Talk,* said, ''In the late 1980s, most strip and sheet producers invested to serve the growing electronic markets. They installed automatic gauge control and statistical process control capabilities to enable them to produce strip with consistent and close tolerances.'' The emphasis on these new precise technologies was apparent in most of the companies involved in the rolling, drawing, and extruding of copper. In order for them to remain competitive in the market, their products needed to meet a higher standard of excellence and precision.

INDUSTRY INFORMATION SOURCES

''Annual Data: 1993: Copper Supply and Consumption, 1972-1992,'' New York: Copper Development Association Inc., 1993.

''A.T.&T. in Copper Cable Venture in Venezuela,'' *New York Times,* February 10, 1994, C3.

Caney, Derek J. ''Servicecenters Ship Less Copper,'' *American Metal Market,* September 2, 1993, 3.

———, ''Copper Rod Demand Strengthens,'' *American Metal Market,* October 21, 1993, 1.

''Copper in the USA: Bright Future—Colorful Past,'' New York: Copper Development Association Inc., 1990.

Gross, John E. ''Copper Market Letter,'' *Copper Talk,* May 1993, 7.

Stundza, Tom. ''Purchasing deluge will ebb slightly in '93,'' *Purchasing,* March 4, 1993, 34.

Taylor, Jeffrey. ''U.S. Copper Futures Fall as Available Stocks of the Metal Reach a 15-Year High in London,'' *Wall Street Journal,* October 27, 1993, C18.

Temes, Judy. ''Polish and tarnish,'' *Crain's New York Business,* November 12, 1990, 3.

Whiteman, Maxwell. *Copper for America,* New Brunswick: Rutgers University Press, 1971.

—Fran Shonfeld Sherman

SIC 3353

ALUMINUM SHEET, PLATE, AND FOIL

This classification covers establishments primarily engaged in flat rolling aluminum and aluminum-alloy basic shapes, such as sheet, plate, and foil, including establishments producing welded tube. Also included are establishments primarily producing similar products by continuous casting.

INDUSTRY SNAPSHOT

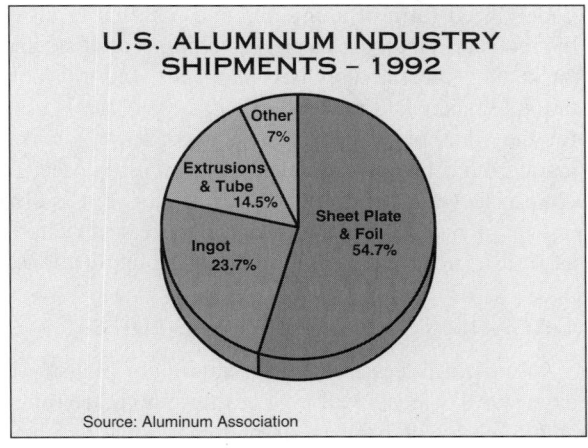

U.S. ALUMINUM INDUSTRY SHIPMENTS – 1992

Other 7%
Extrusions & Tube 14.5%
Sheet Plate & Foil 54.7%
Ingot 23.7%

Source: Aluminum Association

The condition of the major aluminum producers in 1993 was unhappily ironic. Despite business moves generally regarded as sound, many producers continued to lose money. Over the past several decades, aluminum makers had been successful in developing new products and taking market share from competitors like steel. Much of the industry's gains could be traced to the intrinsic qualities of the metal—aluminum is strong, lightweight, and eminently recyclable, all qualities that remain highly prized in the 1990s. Skilled management and smart marketing, however, had also been significant factors in the industry's advance. Thus it had come to dominate the beverage can market and had established an increasing presence in automobile manufacturing.

While the industry had done an excellent job in spurring demand, it was under severe pressure owing to extremely high aluminum exports from Russia. Given the worldwide recession that continued to hang over many Western economies through 1993, the growth in supply weakened prices and eroded margins. Therefore, despite the industry's successes in many markets, it was forced to close plants and lay off workers to stem operating losses. Longer term, however, producers remained optimistic that aluminum's traits give it a bright future as the metal of choice in a growing variety of applications.

Aluminum sheet, plate, and foil represent the industry's major product group and account for the majority of shipments from aluminum producers. To make them, aluminum is first produced in the form of sheet ingot. These ingots, which may weigh as much as 20 tons, are flat rolled and re-rolled until the desired thickness, or gauge, is achieved. The gauge determines what product has been produced: plate is a quarter-inch thick or more; sheet is .006 inch to .249 inch; and foil is less than .006 inch. Sheet is by far the most widely used form of aluminum and is found in all of the industry's major markets, including containers and packaging (most notably beverage cans) and transportation (eg, panels for automobile bodies). Plate is used for the skins of jetliners and to make storage tanks, among other heavy-duty applications. Foil is used, of course, to wrap the Thanksgiving turkey, but is also utilized in building insulation and electrical capacitors, as well as a wide variety of packaging applications.

ORGANIZATION AND STRUCTURE

Vertical integration in the aluminum industry is extensive—it goes well beyond the mining, refining, and smelting of primary aluminum (including sheet ingot, casting ingot, and extrusion billet) to the production of semifabricated and fabricated products downstream, including sheet, plate, and foil offerings. Four major producers—Alcoa, Alcan of Canada (which was part of Alcoa earlier in the century), Reynolds Metals, and Alumax (which was spun off from AMAX in 1993)—dominate the North American aluminum industry and thus dominate the market for sheet, plate, and foil. Alcoa, Alcan, and Reynolds combined have a

78 percent share of the key can sheet market that accounts for about half of all sheet, plate, and foil shipments.

BACKGROUND AND DEVELOPMENT

The aluminum industry is relatively young. The first major application, cast cooking utensils, did not appear until the 1890s. Following the turn of the century, however, prices fell, production rose, and applications grew. World War I greatly expanded use of the metal, as armies searched for lightweight, durable materials for military equipment. In the 1920s high-strength alloys were developed that were used in the development of the commercial airline industry in the 1930s. In World War II, aluminum output grew spectacularly, primarily to build warplanes, but also to package soldiers' rations. While consumption dropped briefly right after the war, consumer demand soon picked up the slack. The Korean War in the early 1950s produced another surge in aluminum shipments. As consumer demand grew in the postwar prosperity, the range of applications increased accordingly. Use of aluminum building products in commercial and residential construction expanded, and aluminum foil became a staple of the American kitchen.

The advent of a strong environmental movement gave new prominence to the industry, since aluminum was particularly suited to recycling. To produce aluminum from recycled scrap requires only five percent of the huge amount of energy that it takes to make it from scratch. Since the economics of recycling make so much sense, industry participants have supported the efforts of environmentalists in this area. Moreover, as governments pressure automakers to increase gas mileage of their vehicles and thus save energy, lightweight aluminum is gaining favor among manufacturers in a variety of applications.

CURRENT CONDITIONS

Aluminum is a notoriously cyclical business, and after a very strong performance at the end of the 1980s a few lean years might have been expected. The extent of the downturn, however, has been an alarming one for industry participants and well beyond expectations. In the early 1990s the aluminum industry became one of the unintended victims of the Cold War's aftermath. Russia no longer needed much aluminum for its defense sector, but it did hunger for export earnings. Before the fall of the Berlin Wall in 1989, Russia sent about 250,000 metric tons of aluminum overseas each year; by 1993, they were shipping aluminum at an annual rate of 1.2 million metric tons. As Clifford Gaddy, a Brookings Institution economist, told the

Wall Street Journal, "We were used to a world in which one of the biggest commodity producers was the most stable and predictable—everything was planned five years ahead with the absolute minimum of surprise. Now it's switched to the exact opposite, where even their own government doesn't know what's happening."

While the immediate casualty of unchecked exports was ingot quotes (almost all of Russia's shipments are in ingot form), after a short time lag the overflow depressed prices of semifabricated products like sheet, plate, and foil. By the third quarter of 1993, U.S. producers had idled about 800,000 metric tons of industry capacity to cope with the worldwide glut, but prices were still depressed near year-end. Besides slashing output and laying off production workers, major companies like Alcoa were also cutting research and development budgets, or, as with Reynolds, selling off nonstrategic businesses. The industry did welcome Congress's decision to eliminate President Clinton's proposed energy tax in 1993, since energy accounts for 30 percent of the average producer's costs. Nevertheless, the industry will still have to contend with the requirements of the 1990 Clean Air Act, which may add as much as five percent to the cost of coal-fired electricity by the year 2000.

As for demand, the industry's efforts to develop new products and expand its share of existing markets continued to pay off. According to statistics of the Aluminum Association, sheet, plate, and foil volume rose five percent in 1992 to 9.7 billion pounds. At that level, the three products accounted for 55 percent of the industry's total shipments. Demand for sheet rose six percent to 8.4 billion pounds; plate was down two percent to 0.3 billion pounds; and foil production rose five percent to 0.9 billion pounds. Demand for aluminum products remained steady through much of 1993, rising slightly above 1992 levels, although orders for can sheet were lackluster.

Aggregate shipments of sheet products in 1992 were higher in each of the industry's major markets: containers and packaging (52 percent of total sheet shipments); building and construction (14 percent); exports (13 percent); transportation (eight percent); consumer durables (five percent); machinery and equipment (four percent); and electrical (three percent). The transportation segment recorded the largest gain, with sheet shipments up 16 percent; some observers believe that this sector holds the greatest promise for the industry. Nearly all plate shipments go to the transportation sector, where demand was about equal to that in 1991. More than 60 percent of all foil shipments go to container and packaging markets; de-

mand from the transportation and consumer durable sectors is also significant. Better results in all three sectors contributed to the gain in foil shipments during 1992.

Can Sheet Production. In 1963 almost no beverage cans were made from aluminum; 30 years later, 97 percent were constructed from the metal. Can sheet has thus become the industry's most important market, dominated by a few large producers: Alcoa and Alcan together have a 62 percent share, while Reynolds has about 16 percent. Shipments of can sheet rose steadily throughout the 1980s and early 1990s, increasing from 2.9 billion bounds in 1982 to 4.3 billion pounds in 1992—24 percent of the aluminum industry's total shipments. In both 1992 and 1993, however, growth in beverage can demand slowed. Moreover, substantial overcapacity has hurt profit margins, and with another eight percent rise in capacity forecast for 1994, the market may become even more competitive. With aluminum already so dominant in the market, the small gains in market share stemming from softer aluminum quotes have been small compensation for lower prices.

Aluminum makers have taken all of the beer can materials business from its steel rivals and have lost few sales to bottle makers. Nevertheless, total beer can shipments are declining, as the number of 18- to 34-year-olds in America falls. Through the first nine months of 1993, demand was down by 2.6 percent, following declines of 1.6 percent in 1992 and 0.8 percent in 1991. In a move designed to lock in markets for its can sheet, Reynolds purchased Miller Brewing's string of five can and can-end plants; formerly, Kaiser Aluminum was the top supplier of can sheet for the plants.

Demand for soft-drink cans remained strong, rising about five percent through most of 1993. Can makers, however, have adopted smaller lid designs and are using thinner aluminum. As a consequence, manufacturing of each can requires smaller amounts of aluminum than in past years. Thus, greater unit demand for cans does not necessarily translate into an equal rise in aluminum requirements. Additionally, there appears to be a trend toward the more economical large, plastic bottle, as well as the so-called New Age drinks that tend to be packaged in glass. Producers are hopeful that overseas beverage can markets, where aluminum's penetration has on average been much lower than in the United States, will pick up the slack.

Automotive. The aluminum industry has invested substantial resources in both research and development and marketing to displace steel as the metal of choice in automobiles, and over the past several years it has made significant progress toward that goal. According to industry estimates, in 1991 the average Ford contained 219 pounds of aluminum; for GM, the figure was 197 pounds; and for Chrysler it was 156 pounds (an average car weighs perhaps 3,000 pounds). All told, the aluminum content of domestic cars was up 40-50 percent in a decade, and perhaps 135 percent in two decades. Estimates of the proportion of aluminum usage in cars by the year 2000 vary widely, but some observers put the figure at 350 to 400 pounds. General Motors's Aurora cars, expected to be introduced during 1994, are expected to contain more than 300 pounds of aluminum apiece. The large producers are optimistic that aluminum usage in cars will increase steadily. For example, in 1992 Reynolds had 28 auto-related plants, representing a $500-million business; it forecast that automotive sales would generate $2.5 billion in revenue by 1997, about the size of its key packaging division.

In the automotive market, as in others, aluminum's advantages are its recyclability (at a time when governments and environmentalists are aiming for a totally recyclable car) and its light weight (which improves fuel economy). The development of higher strength alloys has also increased aluminum's attractiveness in recent years. Some observers believe that the Japanese auto industry has a particular interest in incorporating aluminum into vehicles because of the high price of gasoline in Japan and the high proportion of imported raw materials. One drawback of aluminum is the relatively high cost, which has led some observers to believe that luxury models will use a relatively high ratio of the metal. Others believe that the electric car is the most promising market for aluminum because such automobiles must be light to compensate for the presence of heavy batteries. Shorter term, however, the metal may make more extensive inroads in all auto market segments because of the sharp drop in aluminum prices (although volatility in aluminum quotes is a negative for the automakers, which seek materials with stable costs).

While the majority of the aluminum used in cars is in the form of castings, sheet volume is expected to increase at a faster rate. The amount of aluminum sheet used in U.S. auto applications in 1993 totaled about 295 million pounds, up 15 percent from the prior-year level. The sheet is used for the body, hoods, deck lids, and doors; heat exchangers and bumper reinforcements are among the fastest-growing applications. One estimate puts the total amount of sheet volume for automotive applications in the year 2000 at 650 million pounds, more than double levels posted in 1993.

Aerospace. The aluminum industry has aggressively penetrated the aerospace market; nearly all defense planes have an aluminum content of 70 to 90 percent. Demand for aluminum from the aerospace segment was strong during the 1980s, as both defense spending and commercial aircraft orders were buoyant. By the early 1990s, however, the aerospace segment was in decline. The airlines cancelled or delayed orders as their profits disappeared, and with the Cold War over the government cut outlays for the military. According to Aluminum Association statistics, annual shipments of both heat-treatable sheet and heat-treatable plate, which are primarily used in defense and aerospace applications, fell 23 percent and 19 percent, respectively, between 1989 and 1992. By the second half of 1993, lead times at mills were as short as eight weeks, versus a more normal 10 to 12 weeks. In early 1994 some industry participants thought a bottoming out had been reached and that this industry niche would recover a bit.

Although the fortunes of aluminum producers in aerospace fell significantly, they continued to maintain a dominant role in the aircraft market. In the 1980s proponents of nonmetallic advanced composites claimed that by the second half of the 1990s they would account for up to 80 percent of commercial airframe weight. In 1994 those predictions appeared overblown. Aluminum in the newest commercial transport, the Boeing 777, accounted for about 65 percent of total weight, down from previous generations of airliners but nowhere near the 20-25 percent level that some pessimistic observers had forecast. The composites have made the most headway in the plane's tail, which in the 777 represents a loss of about 25,000 pounds of aluminum products.

Meanwhile, the industry continues to work on new alloys and new processes. Despite cutbacks in its budget, the Pentagon remains committed to maintaining its technological edge, which encourages aluminum companies to make new investments in research and development to service the military's needs. Aluminum producers are also reallocating resources to service the existing market. For example, in 1993 Alcoa expanded its aircraft sheet facility in Irvine, California, to meet the growing demand for just-in-time delivery to commercial transport builders, which helps them keep delivery to a bare minimum. On the other hand, it reduced manpower at its main facility in Riverside, Iowa, by about ten percent.

Marine. Another market where aluminum has strong potential is in specialized marine crafts. Textron Marine Systems recently won a contract to build the first-ever all-aluminum high-speed rescue boats to be used by the U.S. Coast Guard. Each boat uses about seven tons of aluminum. Because of aluminum's lightweight characteristics, the new boats will be twice as fast as those they will replace, which have steel hulls. The crafts are also designed to survive 360-degree side rollovers and end-over flips and to handle hurricane-force winds. A further marine application for aluminum is high-speed catamaran vessels, where the light weight of aluminum is again a key factor.

Bridges. According to the Federal Highway Administration, some 100,000 of the nation's 500,000 to 600,000 bridges are in need of repair, and about 5,000 to 7,000 bridge decks need to be replaced quickly. While aluminum will probably not be chosen for most of these decks, even a relatively small share of the market would bring producers significant sales, since each bridge deck replacement that does utilize aluminum may require as much as 50,000 pounds of the metal. Although aluminum is relatively costly compared with other suitable materials, its advocates believe that the initial high investment is offset by lower costs in the fabrication, maintenance, and erection of the bridge. They also say that using prefabricated aluminum bridge deck material could cut the time a bridge is closed for reconstruction to two to four weeks from the three to four months generally required for concrete and carbon steel bridge building.

The first use of aluminum in bridge decking was at Pittsburgh's Smithfield Bridge in 1930. That deck was replaced by another that combined aluminum plate with extrusions and was still in use in the early 1990s. An aluminum plate girder railroad bridge with a 100-foot-long span was built in Massena, New York, in 1946, and between 1958 and 1963 a half-dozen other aluminum bridges were built in the United States and Canada. The Aluminum Association industry trade group hopes to reignite interest in aluminum bridge construction through sponsorship of a project to replace a concrete bridge deck in Tazewell County, Virginia, with an aluminum one. The Association will document the full cost of building the bridge and carefully monitor the bridge's performance to acquire the detailed data necessary for promoting aluminum use in this market.

INDUSTRY LEADERS

The largest aluminum producer in the world is Alcoa (Aluminum Co. of America). Indeed, in the early part of the century it was the only aluminum producer of consequence in North America. In 1928 it spun off its foreign operations into Alcan, the large Canadian producer, as it continued to dominate the U.S. market. In 1950, Alcoa's domestic monopoly—which had already been somewhat diluted by the federal government's efforts to create competitors during

and following World War II—came to an end as the courts dismantled the company.

In the early 1960s the reconfigured company began to produce more semifabricated and fabricated products as it expanded output of can stock and products for the aerospace industry. In the late 1980s, after a quick nod to diversification earlier in the decade, the company refocused on its aluminum business. Alcoa stresses the importance of safety in its operations, and in the early 1990s had the best safety record of the major producers. The company also made strides in its labor relations, introducing a new profit-sharing plant. Nevertheless, the unprecedented size of Russia's exports have taken their toll on the company. In June 1993 the company cut a quarter of its capacity and laid off 750 workers, two percent of its domestic work force. Third-quarter earnings were down 36 percent to $28 million, and those profits came from nonaluminum business. Alcoa remains a powerful contender in most aluminum markets, however; notably, it supplies some 90 percent of Boeing's aluminum needs.

Reynolds Metal Co. has been a leader in developing new aluminum products, from baseball bats to grain bins. It introduced the aluminum beverage can in 1963, when steelmakers had a lock on that market. Reynolds' two-piece can took about one-fifth the time to make and used 40 percent less metal than the three-piece can of its steel rivals, which it quickly displaced. In 1968 the company pioneered the huge can recycling program that gave makers a cheap source of aluminum and cheered environmentalists.

Reynolds had the wisdom to stick with its famous aluminum foil when it was a money-loser. It has built on the popularity of its foil by expanding into plastic and paper household packaging products. Non-aluminum business accounts for 15-20 percent of sales, and about 25 percent of sales are in overseas markets. Despite the company's strengths, it has not been able to escape the broader problems of the aluminum manufacturing industry, posting losses in 1993.

Alcan was formed in 1928 when Alcoa spun off its foreign operations to form the Canadian company. For more than 20 years thereafter, however, the same individuals controlled both firms. In 1950 the courts ordered investors to sell their shares of one company or the other, and the ownership ties between the two firms were severed. At that time Alcan's focus was on the primary aluminum market, but in the late 1950s it decided to expand significantly its fabricating operations. Alcan established semifabricating plants of its own in the United States that afforded stable outlets for its ingot. In 1971, for the first time, Alcan shipped more semifabricated and fabricated tonnage than ingot, and these products now account for about two-thirds of sales. Alcan posted losses through much of 1993 as well.

AMAX was a mining, metal, and energy company whose origins date from the late nineteenth century. The company began aluminum operations in 1962 when it purchased two Midwestern aluminum companies. At one point the company sold half its aluminum business to Mitsui & Co., but in the late 1980s rebought it. In 1993 AMAX merged with Cypress Metals while spinning off all of its aluminum operations to create Alumax, which is now the third-largest aluminum company in America. Alumax produces a wide range of sheet, plate, and foil products, a significant portion of which are marketed through distributors. About 40 percent of its total sales are to the building and construction markets.

WORK FORCE

The manufacturing work force of the major aluminum companies is heavily unionized. The industry's two major unions are the United Steelworkers and the Aluminum, Brick, and Glass Workers. In June 1993 new three-year aluminum pacts were reached covering 27 aluminum plants of Alcoa and Reynolds with an aggregate payroll of 17,000 workers. Some provisions of the new contract included a new managed health care program, a $0.25 increase in base hourly wage rates in the first year, and improved benefits. The agreements at Alcoa and Reynolds are noteworthy because they set the pattern for thousands of other workers at smaller aluminum companies throughout the industry (according to Aluminum Association statistics, the aluminum industry as a whole has about 130,000 workers). The major producers pay, on average, about 10 to 20 percent more than smaller companies. [American and the World]

The U.S. aluminum industry has historically been adept at expanding overseas and capitalizing on its foreign assets. Indeed, the aluminum industry has a greater presence abroad than many other U.S. industries. In 1992 some 40 percent of Alcoa's sales and 43 percent of its identifiable assets were located overseas; the comparable figures for Reynolds Metals were 25 percent and 36 percent.

In the early 1990s, however, international developments were the source of the industry's major problems. While shipments in the U.S. in 1992 were healthy as the economy pulled out of recession, conditions in Europe and Japan remained depressed; meanwhile, Russia was rapidly increasing its aluminum exports. Since 1978, the price of aluminum ingot

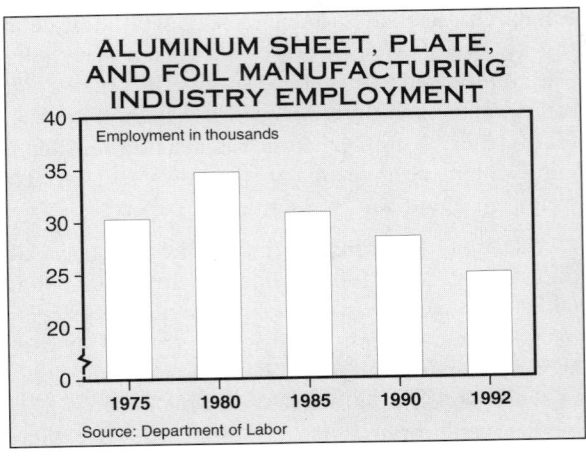

ALUMINUM SHEET, PLATE, AND FOIL MANUFACTURING INDUSTRY EMPLOYMENT

Employment in thousands

Source: Department of Labor

(which is eventually reflected in sheet, plate, and foil quotes) has been set on the London Metal Exchange (LME): it fell from above a peak of $1.65 in 1988 to $.50 in late 1993. With the international supply/demand equation unbalanced, producers worldwide were suffering. As Lloyd T. O'Connell, Reynolds Metals's chief economist, told the *Wall Street Journal:* "If the demand is weak abroad, it's almost as bad as if demand is weak domestically. The LME doesn't care where the metal is."

According to statistics of the Aluminum Association, exports of sheet and plate rose about 12 percent in 1992 to 1.094 billion pounds; foil shipments increased 11 percent to 68 million pounds. The strong advance in sheet and plate shipments reflects increased demand for can stock, especially from Japan. Sheet and plate imports to the United States in 1992, meanwhile, rose 10 percent to 749 million pounds, while foil imports declined eight percent to 49 million pounds. Canada accounts for over 60 percent of sheet and plate exports to the United States, while Japan, the next largest exporter, accounts for about six percent.

In recent years, U.S. producers have strengthened ties with Japanese aluminum and steel companies. In September 1990, Alcoa and Kobe Steel announced a strategic alliance to exploit worldwide opportunities in aluminum that has resulted in four joint ventures in the United States and Japan. The agreement was particularly noteworthy because the steelmaker has strong relationships with the automobile industry. One venture, however, is directed toward the beverage can market in Japan, where aluminum has a far smaller usage rate than in the United States.

While the Alcoa-Kobe alliance is by far the most notable of the U.S.-Japan collaborations, there have been others. Reynolds has joined with Sumitomo Metals for technical collaboration on rolled products for the auto industry. While demand for automotive aluminum in Japan leveled off in 1992 since the economy remained depressed, aluminum producers have strong hopes for the future. Since gasoline costs are high in Japan (perhaps three times U.S. levels) and the country has few natural resources, easily recyclable, lightweight aluminum would appear to be an excellent material for this market.

RESEARCH AND TECHNOLOGY

The enormous strides that aluminum has made in displacing steel and other materials in the container/packaging, automotive, aerospace, and construction markets demonstrates the substantial investment it has made in research and development. This effort has been instrumental in developing a wide range of new aluminum products including beverage cans, baseball bats, grain bins, roofing, windows, appliance parts, and semitrailers; it has also yielded stronger, lighter, cheaper alloys and improved production processes. A comment of David Moison, a consultant at Resource Strategies, to the *Wall Street Journal* is telling: "People in aluminum don't have the belief somebody's going to use it just because they make it. They've had to fight like hell to convert people to aluminum."

Producers have also made remarkable strides in improving productivity, which has advanced from 15 man-hours per ton in the 1960s to six man-hours per ton in the early 1990s. Since aluminum by weight costs six times as much as steel and is so energy-intensive, the industry has had to strive constantly to reduce its costs to remain competitive. The effort to increase productivity takes many forms. Kaiser Aluminum spent $250-million to modernize its Trentwood Works in Spokane, Washington; the improvements are credited with helping Kaiser post strong profits in 1992. Reynolds worked with Westinghouse Commercial Systems to develop a computerized tracking system that cut its cost of transportation as a percentage of sales from 8.1 percent in 1984 to 6.1 percent in 1991. Alcoa employed computer simulation to make improvements to its aluminum coil handling and storage costs, saving it $12 million a year. And Alcan and other aluminum sheet producers are using automatic surface inspection that can capture, interpret, and report detailed surface defect information while the sheet moves at high speeds on the line.

INDUSTRY INFORMATION SOURCES

Alcoa Update, no. 1, Pittsburgh: Alcoa, 1993.

Alumax 1992 Annual Report, Atlanta: Alumax, 1993.

"Aluminum Distribution Is Growing," *Purchasing*, October 7, 1993.

"Nothing Common about this Market," *Purchasing*, November 5, 1992.

Aluminum Statistical Review for 1992, Washington, DC: The Aluminum Association, 1993.

Ambrosia, John, "Aluminum Tries to Recycle its Past Success," *Iron Age*, June 1992.

———, "Defense Cuts Won't Ground Lightweight Metals," *Iron Age*, April 1993.

———, "Trentwood: A Study in Modern Maturity," *Iron Age*, February 1993.

Metal Statistics 1993, New York: Chilton Publications, 1993.

Auguston, Karen A., "How Simulation Helped Alcoa Save $12 Million a Year," *Modern Materials Handling*, March 1993.

Baade, Jeffrey, "Metals & Mining (Diversified) Industry," *Value Line Investment Survey*, November 5, 1993.

Baker, Steve, "Suddenly, There's Aluminum Everywhere," *Business Week*, October 25, 1993.

Bellini, E. Vincent, et al. "Plant Automation Improves Product Quality and Efficiency," *Industrial Engineering*, June 1992.

Blesada, Alexandra, and McGough, Robert, "A Game of Chicken," *Financial World*, February 18, 1992.

Bonney, Joseph, "Shipper-Controlled Cargo Tracking," *American Shipper*, February 1992.

Bourke, William O. "Aluminum: Pleased with the '80s, Looking Forward to the '90s," *Engineering & Mining Journal*, February 1990.

Burgert, Philip, "Producers Try to Bridge the Infrastructure Gap," *American Metal Market*, November 11, 1993.

Canby, Thomas, "Aluminum, The Magic Metal," *National Geographic*, August 1978.

Choe, Boum-Jong, "After the Metals Market Boom," *Finance & Development*, June 1990.

Fuqua, Don, "Aerospace Industry Hits Turbulence," *American Metal Market*, April 7, 1993.

Hoover's Handbook of American Business 1993, Austin, TX: Reference Press, 1993.

Hoover's Handbook of World Business 1993, Austin, TX: Reference Press, 1993.

Klebnikobv, Paul, "Absolutely Trashed," *Forbes*, April 12, 1993.

McManus, George, "Another Set of Eyes for Quality," *Iron Age*, May 1992.

Mallory, Maria, and Michael Schroeder, "How the USW hit Mark Rich Where It Hurts," *Business Week*, May 11, 1992.

Milbank, Dana, "Labor Jitters Unsettle Market for Aluminum," *Wall Street Journal*, April 2, 1992.

———, "Aluminum Firms' Glut Problems Mount," *Wall Street Journal*, January 21, 1992.

———, "U.S. Aluminum Makers Hit Downside of Going Global," *Wall Street Journal,* March 22, 1993.

———, "Aluminum Producers, Agile and Aggressive, Outfight Steelmakers," *Wall Street Journal,* July 1, 1992.

Moberly, John, "Aluminum: More of the Same," *Engineering and Mining Journal,* March 1993.

Norton, Erle, "Alcoa Will Cut Output by 25%, Trim U.S. Force," *Wall Street Journal,* June 29, 1993.

Plunkert, Patricia, and Errol Sehnke, "Aluminum, Bauxite, & Alumina," *Minerals Yearbook,* vol. 1, Washington: U.S. Department of the Interior, 1992.

Regan, Bob, "Aircraft Aluminum Goes into Tailspin," *American Metal Market,* April 7, 1993.

———, "Aluminum Volume Gains Come with Little Reward," *American Metal Market,* September 6, 1993.

———, "The Beverage Can Stock Market Goes Flat," *American Metal Market,* November 11, 1993.

Rescigno, Richard, "Silver Lining to Aluminum," *Barron's,* October 5, 1992.

Reynolds Metals 1992 Annual Report, Richmond, VA: Reynolds, 1993.

Sorrentino, Anthony, "Aluminum: Oversupply to Keep Prices Under Pressure," *Standard & Poor's Industry Surveys,* October 29, 1992.

Stewart, Thomas A., "A New Way to Wake Up a Giant," *Fortune,* October 22, 1990.

The Story and Uses of Aluminum, Washington, DC: Aluminum Association, 1984.

Stuckey, John A., *Vertical Integration and Joint Ventures in the Aluminum Industry,* Cambridge, MA: Harvard University Press, 1983.

Stundza, Tom, "Global Factors Keep Supply Up, Prices Down," *Purchasing,* November 7, 1991.

U.S. Industrial Outlook, 1993, Washington, DC: U.S. Department of Commerce, 1993.

Winter, Drew, "It's Standing Room Only at Aluminum Seminar," *Ward's Auto World,* December 1991.

—Bob Schneider

SIC 3354

ALUMINUM EXTRUDED PRODUCTS

This classification covers establishments primarily engaged in extruding aluminum and aluminum-base alloy basic shapes, such as rod and bar, pipe and tube, and tube blooms, including establishments producing tube by drawing.

INDUSTRY SNAPSHOT

The process of extruding aluminum has been compared to squeezing toothpaste from a tube, with the metal (initially in the form of extrusion billet) taking the shape of the die through which it has been pressed. While commercially pure aluminum is used in some extrusion applications, more often the aluminum is mixed with other metals—particularly magnesium and silicon—to form alloys. Aluminum extrusions are used to make windows, doors, and gates; as components in cars, trucks, and jet aircraft; in the manufacture of major appliances, furniture, and electrical equipment; and in a host of other applications, ranging from cranes to athletic goods.

As in other segments of the aluminum industry, in the early 1990s the steep increase in Russia's aluminum exports had a substantial impact on the extruding operations of the major integrated producers. Extruders also had to contend with substantial competition in many of their major markets from competing materials, like vinyl, wood, roll-formed steel, and aluminum and manganese die castings. But after several years of declining demand, sales began to rebound in 1992, and the industry consolidated those gains in 1993. Longer term, producers looked to a stronger economy, a better housing market, and increased use of extrusions in automotive applications to sustain demand.

ORGANIZATION AND STRUCTURE

According to a report by Hydro Aluminum of Norway released in 1992, there were approximately 1,000 extruding firms worldwide, operating some 3,500 presses with annual capacity of 6.5 million metric tons. The world's leading producer was the Ministry of Aviation of Russia, with 400,000 metric tons of capacity; the top-ten list also included three Japanese firms. The 10 extruders control about one-third of total worldwide capacity. In 1991 they extruded 1.9 million tons of shapes, tubes, and bar products, more than 35 percent of estimated worldwide output of 5.2 million tons.

All four of the major integrated North American producers—Alcan of Canada, Alcoa, Reynolds, and Alumax—were among the top ten extruders. Nevertheless, there is significantly less concentration in the U.S. extrusion market compared with other important industry segments. For example, while five or six producers account for nearly all sales of can sheet, the aluminum industry's most important product, about a dozen integrated mills and independent producers control perhaps two-thirds of the extrusion market.

To some extent, the extrusion segment may be divided between the commodity-like output of large producers, which may be said to be sold by the pound, and specialty production of smaller makers, sold by the part. As in other industries, extruders have their areas of specialization. Some work primarily in certain alloy series, while others specialize in close tolerances, miniature shapes, or extremely large shapes.

BACKGROUND AND DEVELOPMENT

The first aluminum extrusion press in North America was opened by Alcoa in New Kensington, Pennsylvania, in 1904. During the 1930s large strides were made in the extrusion process, permitting the formation of virtually any type of aluminum cross section for a wide variety of applications. During World War II the use of aluminum in aerospace applications grew rapidly, as the strength of Allied air forces was key to the war effort. In the postwar period, extruders continued to expand, benefitting from the growth in the residential housing sector. Demand for the industry's products peaked in 1987, with shipments that year totaling some 2.5 billion pounds, according to Aluminum Association statistics.

CURRENT CONDITIONS

Following the dissolution of the Soviet Union and the end of the Cold War, the aluminum industry in Russia suffered a major contraction in its major markets, as both defense orders and consumer demand fell sharply. Desperately in need of export earnings, Russian producers began to ship huge quantities of ingot to the West. The subsequent overhang in worldwide supply was soon reflected in lower ingot quotes, and the glut produced price cuts that eventually spread throughout the industry's major markets, including extrusions. The decline in extrusion prices generally had a greater impact on the large integrated firms, with their huge investments in primary production facilities, than on extruders who buy their billet from primary producers. While in some respects the price cuts represented an opportunity for extruders to pick up market share against manufacturers of competing materials, they also served as an unpleasant reminder of the volatility and unpredictability of aluminum prices.

Since 1987, the extruders had been faced with declining demand for its products in the key building and construction market, reflecting substitution of competing materials and, in the early 1990s, a weak housing market. Since over half of all extruded aluminum shapes are shipped (either directly or through distributors) to the building products market, the loss of share in major products like windows and doors has hurt. During this period there was a significant shakeout in the industry, with the number of extruders falling 20 to 30 percent. Small- and medium-sized firms that were thinly capitalized were the most vulnerable.

Industry statistics for 1992 and 1993, however, showed some improvement in the level of demand. According to statistics based on end use compiled by the Aluminum Extruders Council, total shipments in 1992 were up 10.7 percent over 1991 levels. Shipment increases were posted in a number of market areas, including building and construction (three percent); transportation (17 percent); consumer durables (ten percent); and machinery and equipment (38 percent). Only shipments in the electric sector were down, falling by three percent. According to Aluminum Association statistics, during the first ten months of 1993 sales continued to improve, rising ten percent from year-earlier levels to 2.3 billion pounds. As 1994 began, healthy improvements in the U.S. economy and the domestic housing market were hopeful signs that industry conditions would continue to improve.

Some extruders are providing customers with an increasing number of value-added services downstream. By offering a variety of machines for extra processing, extruders can help their customers get new products to market more quickly and save them the costs of investing in the equipment themselves. It also reduces questions of accountability for poor quality, since the customer doesn't have to send the parts on to a fabricator or finisher before using them. While some observers note that providing additional services hasn't always resulted in increased profitability, they add that it has helped in developing customer loyalty.

Window and Door. Shipments of extrusions for window and door applications were only 555 million pounds in 1991, compared with 680 million pounds in 1990 and 902 million pounds in the peak year of 1986. While industry participants hope that the dramatic increase in housing starts entering the mid-1950s will translate into increased sales for aluminum extruded products producers, it should be noted that sales of frames made from vinyl plastics rose from 5.1 million units in 1986 to 8.6 million in 1990 while operating under the same economic conditions. In 1992 aluminum extrusions held a 28 percent share of the window and door market, versus a 58 percent portion a decade earlier. According to one industry participant, extrusions have been losing share because of (1) volatility in aluminum pricing (aluminum prices rose when vinyl was beginning to gain market share in the mid-1980s); and (2) vinyl and wood are perceived to be much more energy efficient. While some in the industry were hopeful of a turnaround, others suspect that vinyl and other products will continue to take share from aluminum in this market.

Automotive. Extruders were much more optimistic about the outlook for aluminum usage in automobiles. While applications for use of extrusions in family vehicles produced in North America increased only slightly during the early 1990s, many industry observers thought that aluminum extrusions would record solid gains in the decade ahead. Since aluminum is lighter than steel, iron, and copper and easily recyclable, the metal fits well with a strategy of reducing energy consumption. Thus the prospects for extrusion applications—bumper beams, radiator tubing, evaporators, air-conditioning, compressor parts, among others—have steadily improved. Aluminum extrusions accounted for about 14 to 16 pounds of the typical 1993 model, up from about six to nine pounds a decade earlier. Total aluminum content in American cars is thought to be about 190 pounds, but that could rise to 350 or 400 pounds by the year 2000. In Japan, where the use of aluminum in cars is particularly attractive because of the lack of raw materials and high gas prices, automotive extrusion demand had grown from 26,600 metric tons in 1982 to 92,700 one decade later.

One application that particularly excites producers is the spaceframe, where aluminum extrusions are used to make the skeletal system of the car's structure. A single spaceframe might eventually include 100 to 200 pounds or more of extruded parts. In 1993 Alcoa was building a $70-million plant in Soest, Germany, for producing structural space frames in quantity; its first customer will be Volkswagen's Audi. Rather than spot welding as many 300 stamped steel components, less than 100 aluminum extrusions and interconnecting die-cast nodes are robotically welded to form the spaceframe. The spaceframe offers a weight saving of about 35 percent over steel bodies. Alcoa envisions that output at this plant, which may eventually produce enough material for 100,000 cars a year, will be the forerunner of several facilities overseas and in the United States to produce spaceframe components.

Chevrolet has already produced the world's first aluminum extrusion-based subframe in a production car. The substitution of an aluminum stamping design for the rear subframe of its 1993 Corvette reduced tooling expenses and overall costs, and shaved four pounds from the vehicle. Reynolds Metals is also working on a prototype for a spaceframe with Ford Motor.

Aircraft. The market for aircraft aluminum extrusions was depressed during the early 1990s because of the decline in U.S. military spending and a drop in orders for commercial airplanes. The segment underwent a shakeup in 1992 as one of the largest makers of small press aerospace alloy shapes, International Light Metals, went out of business; the company had at one time accounted for as much as 35 percent of aircraft extrusions less than 5-inch circle size. The two major surviving producers were Alcoa, by far the largest maker, and Universal Alloy. In a bid to find a niche between industry giant Alcoa and the distributors (who have traditionally accounted for most shipments to end users), Universal Alloy decided to sell the bulk of its shapes directly to end-users or their contractors.

Bridges. Extruders have been eyeing the infrastructure market for new demand, including the tens of thousands of bridges that need to be refurbished. While most of the work will probably go to producers of other materials, with each repair requiring perhaps 50,000 pounds of aluminum, even a small share of the market would generate significant sales. One factor weighing in favor of aluminum extrusions is that processes are now available to tailor parts to individual bridge design; they can then be quickly assembled and virtually snapped together, significantly reducing the time the bridge has to be closed for reconstruction.

INDUSTRY LEADERS

According to Hydro Aluminum's survey, the largest producer of extrusions in America was Alcoa, with 200,000 tons of capacity. At that level, it was the fifth largest producer in the world. Reynolds Metals had about the same amount of capacity, while Alumax had 150,000 tons. Alcan of Canada was the largest North American producer, with 250,000 tons of capacity. The four companies represent the major integrated producers that dominate the North American aluminum industry. While extrusion operations are important to all four companies, they are a relatively small portion of the firms' operations, somewhat overshadowed by the primary production of ingot and semifabricated products like aluminum sheet. According to Aluminum Association statistics, extrusions and tube represented 14.5 percent of industry shipments in 1992 compared with 13.4 percent in 1991.

WORK FORCE

The manufacturing facilities of the major producers are heavily unionized; the two major unions are the Aluminum, Brick, and Glass Workers and the United Steelworkers. Contract talks between these unions and Alcoa and Reynolds, which in 1993 were concluded without a strike, have a significant influence on pay rates throughout the industry. In general, wages at the major firms are about 10 to 20 percent above pay rates at smaller companies.

AMERICA AND THE WORLD

According to statistics compiled by the Aluminum Association, total imports of angles and shapes (ie, extruded products) was 10.8 million pounds in 1992, with about two-thirds of the total coming from Canada. In the five-year, 1988-1992 period, imports have fluctuated widely, ranging from 20.1 million pounds in 1988 to 4.8 million in 1991.

Exports of U.S.-produced aluminum extruded products totaled 67.1 million pounds in 1992, with Canada taking in 19 percent of that total, Korea receiving 16 percent, and Mexico importing 13 percent. In recent years U.S. exports have been on an upward curve, rising from 25.8 million pounds in 1988 to 71.6 million in 1991, before dropping slightly in 1992.

RESEARCH AND TECHNOLOGY

During 1993, a major research and development initiative was begun at the New York State Center for Advanced Technology in Automation & Robotics at Rensselaer Polytechnic Institute. The program grew out of a joint task force that included representatives of the university, the Aluminum Association, and the Aluminum Extruders Council. The research agenda includes basic metallurgical studies; die surface enhancement through plasma spraying and other processes; projections of metal flow and extrudability; and sensor utilization for inspection and process control. A long-term research goal of the program is to develop intelligent process-control techniques by combining process physics with artificial intelligence to improve process yield and quality. The emphasis will be on research that can assist companies in succeeding in the global economy. The program is funded by the New York State Science and Technology Foundation, federal agencies, and corporate donors.

INDUSTRY INFORMATION SOURCES

"Aircraft Aluminum Exclusions in a Market Remake," *American Metal Market,* June 25, 1993.

"Alcoa to Build Spaceframe Plant in Germany," *Purchasing,* January 16, 1992.

Aluminum Statistical Review for 1992, Washington, DC: Aluminum Association, 1993.

Courter, Eileen, "Extrusions Tackle the Technical Hurdles," *American Metal Market,* September 9, 1993.

Demmier, Al, "Aluminum Spaceframes," *Automotive Engineering,* January 1992.

DiGuiseppe, T.J., "Hydro Outfits Corvettes with Extruded Subframe," *American Metal Market,* September 9, 1993.

Extrusion Spotlight: Competitive Materials, Wauconda, IL: Aluminum Extruders Council, 1989.

Furukawa, Tsukasa, "Recession Chills Ardor for Aluminum in Japan but Direction Is Still Up," *American Metal Market,* September 9, 1993.

Grzelka, Constance, "Window Market Closing for Extruders," *American Metal Market,* March 19, 1993.

Puffer, Raymond, "Aluminum Extrusion R&D Is Under Way," *American Metal Market,* March 19, 1993.

Sterner, Bob, "Extruders Plunge into Downstream Processing." *American Metal Market,* March 19, 1993.

The Story and Use of Aluminum, Washington, DC: Aluminum Association, 1984.

Stundza, Tom, "Buyers Keep Switching to Alternate Materials," *American Metal Market,* August 13, 1992.

Wrigley, Al, "Detroit Weighs New Uses for Extrusions," *American Metal Market,* March 19, 1993.

—Bob Schneider

SIC 3355

ALUMINUM ROLLING AND DRAWING, NOT ELSEWHERE CLASSIFIED

This classification refers to establishments primarily engaged in rolling, drawing, and other operations resulting in the production of aluminum ingot, including extrusion ingot, and aluminum and aluminum-base alloy basic shapes, not elsewhere classified, such as rolled and continuous cast rod and bar. Establishments primarily engaged in producing aluminum powder, flake, and paste are classified in **SIC 3399: Primary Metal Products, Not Elsewhere Classified,** and those producing aluminum wire and cable from purchased wire bars, rods, or wire are classified in **SIC 3357: Drawing and Insulating of Nonferrous Wire.**

Rod, bar, and wire products are often grouped together in a single product category. Wire is made from rod or bar, and by definition is less than three-eighths inches in diameter, while rod and bar are larger. Electrical transmission lines represent by far the major end-use of rod/bar/wire products. Rod and bar are also used to make rivets, nails, screws, and bolts, and parts of machinery and equipment. According to the Aluminum Association, rod, bar, and wire shipments rose 1.5 percent during the first ten months of 1993 to 259 million pounds, representing 1.9 percent of total aluminum industry shipments.

Rod, bar, and wire production slumped during the late 1980s and early 1990s. Demand for electrical transmission lines fell, as new construction was lackluster and electricity usage remained flat. Several of the major aluminum companies thus elected to retreat from the electrical conductor market. After 40 years in the business, Reynolds sold the bulk of its operations to BICC in 1992. Alcoa gradually withdrew from the market over a period of six years, finally competing its exit in 1993.

As in other sectors of the aluminum business, prices for rod, bar, and wire have deteriorated owing to the enormous increases in Russian exports, which have depressed quotes throughout the industry. One bright spot, however, at least on the demand side of the equation, has been the automotive sector. The passenger car market for aluminum rod and bar products grew to 29 million pounds in 1992 from just 9 million pounds in 1982. Aluminum's light weight and recyclability are making it an attractive material for automakers; applications like automotive electrical harnesses are therefore creating increased demand for rod and bar. Rod and bar makers are continuing to pursue research and development (R&D) efforts designed to give them a greater presence in the automotive market.

Leading companies in this manufacturing sector in the early 1990s included Intalco Aluminum Corporation, a Ferndale, Washington-based company that posted sales of more than $200 million in 1992; Precision Interconnect Corp., headquartered in Portland, Oregon; Rea Wire Industries Inc., a private firm based in Fort Wayne, Indiana; and Spectrulite Consortium Inc., a privately-owned company in Madison, Illinois.

INDUSTRY INFORMATION SOURCES

Aluminum Situation, Washington, DC: Aluminum Association, December 1993.

Aluminum Statistical Review for 1992, Washington, DC: Aluminum Association, 1993.

Demmier, Al, ''Tech Briefs—Wear-Resistant Aluminum,'' *Automotive Engineering,* January 1992.

Regan, Bob, ''Alcoa Completes End of Electrical Rods,'' *American Metal Market,* November 22, 1993.

———, ''BICC To Pay $100M for Reynolds Cable,'' *American Metal Market,* June 18, 1992.

The Story and Uses of Aluminum, Washington, DC: Aluminum Association, 1993.

—Bob Schneider

SIC 3356

ROLLING, DRAWING, AND EXTRUDING OF NONFERROUS METALS, EXCEPT COPPER AND ALUMINUM

This classification covers establishments primarily engaged in rolling, drawing, and extruding nonferrous metals other than copper and aluminum. The products of this industry are in the form of basic shapes, such as plate, sheet, strip, bar, and tubing. Excluded from this classification are establishments primarily engaged in recovering nonferrous metals and alloys from scrap or dross. Such establishments are classified in **SIC 3341: Secondary Smelting and Refining of Nonferrous Metals.** Those establishments primarily engaged in manufacturing gold, silver, tin, and other foils, except aluminum, are classified in **SIC 3497: Metal Foil and Leaf;** those establishments manufacturing aluminum foil are classified in **SIC 3353: Aluminum Sheet, Plate, and Foil.**

INDUSTRY SNAPSHOT

Nonferrous metals are utilized by nearly every manufacturing industry in the United States and abroad, their existence critical to the production of a broad spectrum of products, from tin cans to semiconductors. The metals used by manufacturers to produce their products are purchased from three types of metal manufacturers, the three primary segments of the metal industry. Depending on the particular needs of the buyer, metal can be obtained from primary metal manufacturers, secondary metal manufacturers, and semi-fabricated metal manufacturers, each of which share an interdependent relationship with the other. Primary manufacturers produce metal by subjecting particular extracted ores to various metallurgical processes, thereby creating metal in its most basic form. Secondary manufacturers smelt, refine, and sometimes blend metal recovered from the shaping and trimming of primary metal during production and fabrication, or from recycled metal. The metal produced by these two types of manufacturers leaves the production site in either large bar or block form, a form known as ingot. As ingot, the metal exists in a convenient and efficient state for storage or shipping, ready for delivery to manufacturers requiring metal cast in this form, or ready to be shipped to a facility equipped to further shape or extrude the metal.

These latter facilities, the manufacturing establishments classified in this industry, take metal in its basic form, then roll, draw, or extrude the massive bar or block ingot into various shapes to make the metal suitable for a wide variety of applications. As semi-finished products, the metal is formed into plate, sheet, strip, bar, or tubing, then delivered to manufacturers involved in a multitude of industries.

The membership of this industry are involved in shaping and forming precious metals, nickel, titanium, magnesium, lead, zinc, and other nonferrous metals. Copper and aluminum are not included. Of all the metal products manufactured by semi-fabricators in the United States, precious metal mill shapes constitute the greatest percentage of the industry's shipments, representing 28 percent. Magnesium, lead, and zinc mill shapes compose the industry's second largest product category, accounting for 24 percent of the industry's shipments, while nickel and titanium mill shapes represent the industry's third and fourth largest product category, accounting for 22 percent and 18 percent, respectively.

By manufacturing these and other products of lesser importance, the industry generated $3.48 billion in sales in 1990, following a decade of rather unimpressive performance. In fact, the industry's revenue total in 1990 barely surpassed the sum recorded eight years earlier in 1982, when it posted $3.41 billion in revenue. Through the first half of the decade, aggregate sales declined, reaching a nadir of $3 billion in 1986, then slowly effecting a recovery during the late 1980s to reach $3.63 billion in 1989.

ORGANIZATION AND STRUCTURE

In 1990 approximately 140 companies derived the bulk of their revenue from the rolling, drawing, or extrusion of nonferrous metals other than aluminum and copper. These companies, some of which owned several manufacturing facilities, operated roughly 160 separate establishments.

In terms of the number of people employed per establishment, the semi-fabricated metal industry was characterized during the early 1990s by relatively large manufacturing establishments, particularly when compared to the average size of all other manufacturing establishments in the United States and to other branches of the metal industry. More than half of the manufacturing establishments in operation in 1990 in this industrial sector employed 20 people or more, while the typical establishment employed 118 workers, more than twice the size of the average manufacturing establishment involved in all other manufacturing industries.

Geographically, semi-fabricated metal manufacturing establishments were concentrated primarily in the three-state region of New York, New Jersey, and Pennsylvania during the early 1990s; more than 50 establishments involved in rolling, drawing, and extruding of nonferrous metals (except copper and aluminum) made their home in this region. The second most densely populated region comprised the five-state region of Wisconsin, Michigan, Illinois, Indiana, and Ohio, with 39 establishments. Although the Midwest and Northeast were home to the bulk of the industry's manufacturing establishments, the Western United States also contained a significant number of manufacturing facilities.

As with the other branches of the metal industry, the operating costs in the semi-fabricated metal industry are significantly higher than the costs incurred by the average manufacturing establishment. In 1989 the average cost per establishment in the semi-fabricated metal industry, that is, the average amount earmarked for raw materials, was $13.6 million, three times greater than the average expense incurred by other manufacturing industries.

BACKGROUND AND DEVELOPMENT

Historically, growth in the semi-fabricated metal industry has been contingent on the vagaries of the metal market as a whole; if demand for particular metals experience an increase, then semi-fabricators generally enjoy a commensurate upswing in business. Since the market for both ferrous and nonferrous metals is cyclical in nature, frequently falling and rising by appreciable measures within the same year, the semi-fabricated metal industry's existence also has been characterized by bursts of growth and periodic declines. Essentially then, the industry's history has mirrored the growth and decline of primary and secondary nonferrous metal producers, functioning as a dependent arm of the metal manufacturing industry and realizing earnings from the sundry markets that spur activity in the primary and secondary metal manufacturing industries.

Following World War II, however, a number of technological developments directly benefitted semi-fabricated, nonferrous metal manufacturers working with metals other than aluminum and copper took place. These stand as noteworthy achievements peculiar to the industry, developments that enabled manufacturers to play a more prominent role in the metal industry.

One of these technological advances made two of the less widely used metals more popular in the semi-fabricated metal industry. In 1964, after the conclusion of a seven-year research and development program financed by the U.S. Air Force and conducted by Republic Aviation Corp., a method was found by which titanium could be extruded more thinly than previously had been possible and at significantly lower costs, a capability that greatly enhanced titanium's applicability to the then burgeoning jet airplane and aerospace industries. In 1963, one year before the extrusion process was fully developed, 5,000 tons of titanium were consumed in the United States. Five years later, U.S. consumption had climbed to 25,000 tons and showed no signs of slowing down. During this five year period enormous technological strides were achieved in the production of titanium under the aegis of Reactive Metals Inc. and Titanium Metals Corporation of America in a joint venture to resolve the major problems associated with extracting the metal from its ores.

As the production of a supersonic transport aircraft neared completion in the late 1960s, domestic titanium consumption approached 80,000 tons annually, largely because supersonic transports and other high-speed aircraft required an appreciably greater percentage of titanium than slower aircraft because of temperature resistance qualities. Consequently, supersonic transports were 80 percent titanium, while slower aircraft such as Boeing Company's 727, were manufactured with less than two percent titanium. As the nation's space program intensified, the applications for titanium broadened, leading to widespread use of titanium in the aviation and aerospace industries in the early 1990s.

Shortly after the titanium extrusion process was developed, another nonferrous metal began a similar rise in popularity, once again as result of an extensive research and development program. This time, however, the work was conducted outside U.S. borders by Canada's Cominco, Ltd., the world's largest producer of refined lead and zinc during the late 1960s. In 1964, concurrent with the conclusion of the U.S. Air Force's titanium research program, Cominco began exploring possible methods to improve the extrusion technology of zinc. Five years later, a suitable method was discovered that enabled zinc to be extruded without tearing, cracking, or sticking to the dies, problems that had restricted the use of zinc by the semi-fabricated metal industry. Prior to Cominco's discovery, zinc occasionally had been rolled or drawn, but it was more commonly known in the metal industry for its galvanizing and die casting properties. The capability to extrude the metal, however, greatly improved the metal's suitability for a host of component parts used in the production of automobiles and appliances. By using zinc, manufacturers could match colors more accurately, giving zinc an aesthetic advantage over aluminum and other metals. Consequently, the use of zinc by semi-

fabricated metal manufacturers began in earnest during the 1970s, eventually becoming one of the key metals utilized by the industry in the early 1990s.

CURRENT CONDITIONS

Essentially affected by the same market factors that dictate the economic health of primary and secondary metal manufacturers, semi-fabricated metal manufacturers entered the mid-1990s bolstered by the strong performance of some metals and negatively affected by the static performance of others. Rarely is the industry's future easy to ascertain since its overall performance is dependent on the separate markets for individual metals, which frequently experience divergent bouts of growth and decline.

Emerging from the recessive early 1990s, however, the semi-fabricated metal industry's future was shaped by the encouraging strength of the lead market and a weakening titanium market. Reduced military spending and a flagging commercial aviation market sent the demand for semi-fabricated titanium mill products spiraling downward. These two market segments together accounted for 75 percent of the semi-fabricated titanium market, a market that dictates to a large extent the health of the overall industry. Prognostications for the recovery of these two markets were not encouraging, particularly the military aerospace market, as defense spending cuts during the early and mid-1990s portended a leaner military budget for the near future.

The lead market, on the other hand, demonstrated encouraging vitality during this period. Following three years of successive declines in consumption, the lead market experienced a resurgence in 1993 when consumption increased 4.7 percent. This increase was largely attributable to an increase in storage battery production, the primary end-use of lead and a component of the semi-fabricated metal industry. Storage batteries accounted for 81.1 percent of the total domestic lead demand in 1993, significantly more than 12 years earlier, when storage batteries represented 60 percent of the domestic demand. Providing a boon to semi-fabricated metal manufacturers, the increase in storage battery production reflected a commensurate increase in the production of battery metal, one of the multitude of products manufactured by the semi-fabricated metal industry. Some industry analysts in 1993 projected a 1.4 percent annual increase in lead consumption to 1998, which should benefit semi-fabricated metal manufacturers, but any optimism must be tempered by taking into account the possibility of future governmental efforts to curb lead usage. The Lead Reduction Act of 1993, for instance, was a legislative action—unpopular in the industry—that sought to address health concerns linked to lead exposure.

INDUSTRY LEADERS

Ranked according to sales volume, the three largest semi-fabricated metal manufacturers in 1993 were Inco Alloys International Inc., Titanium Metals Corp., and RMI Titanium Co., which generated more than $600 million in combined revenue. The balance of the industry's manufacturers each recorded less than $100 million in revenue, with the majority of the companies posting less than $5 million in annual revenue.

The industry's largest manufacturer, Inco Alloys, focused primarily on the production of nickel products to generate $342.8 million in sales in 1993. Employing 1,740 workers, Inco Alloys operated as a subsidiary of Inco United States Inc., a holding company that posted $885 million in revenue in 1993.

Titanium Metals Corp., the industry's second largest manufacturer, recorded $140 million in sales in 1993 primarily through the production of titanium tubing. A subsidiary of Tremont Corp., Titanium Metals also produced titanium sponge, an intermediate product from which titanium metal is derived, making the company one of the leading integrated titanium producers in the United States

RMI Titanium Co. became the largest nonintegrated producer of titanium mill products in the United States in 1993 when its 10,000 tons-per-year titanium sponge plant in Ashtabula, Ohio, was permanently closed in February of that year. Through the production of titanium metal products and titanium powder, a product classified in **SIC 3499: Fabricated Metal Products, Not Elsewhere Classified,** RMI generated $135.6 million in 1993.

WORK FORCE

Total employment in the semi-fabricated metal industry fluctuated throughout the 1980s, effecting slight, sporadic gains, then suffering proportionate declines. In 1982 the industry employed 20,000 and by the beginning of the 1990s the total had fallen to 18,600, largely due to the attrition of 1,200 salaried positions in the industry. Despite this modest decline in the number of the industry's production workers, employees recorded more hours in 1990 than in 1982.

Production workers are generally employed on a full-time basis and earn more per hour than their counterparts in other manufacturing industries, averaging, in 1989, $13.73 per hour compared to the manufacturing standard that year of $10.49. By 1990, the average hourly wage had risen to $14.57, while salaried employees (those performing administrative, technical, or managerial duties) earned $38,565 per year.

INDUSTRY INFORMATION SOURCES

Annual Survey of Manufactures, Washington, DC: U.S. Department of Commerce.

"An Overlooked Metal Broadens its Appeal," *Business Week,* May 17, 1969, 124.

Statistical Abstract of the United States: 1993, 113th ed., Washington, DC: U.S. Bureau of the Census, 1993.

"Titanium Extrusion Knowhow Gets Big Boost," *Steel,* December 21, 1964.

Walker, Robert, "Titanium Sales Poised for a Take-Off," *New York Times,* January 14, 1968, F1.

U.S. Industrial Outlook, Washington, DC: U.S. Department of Commerce, 1964-1994.

—Jeffrey L. Covell

SIC 3357

DRAWING AND INSULATING OF NONFERROUS WIRE

This classification covers establishments primarily engaged in drawing, drawing and insulating, and insulating wire and cable of nonferrous metals from purchased wire bars, rods, or wire. Also included are establishments primarily engaged in manufacturing insulated fiber optic cable. Establishments primarily engaged in manufacturing glass fiber optic materials are included in **SIC 3229: Pressed and Blown Glass and Glassware, Not Elsewhere Classified,** while those manufacturing fabricated wire products from purchased wire are classified in **SIC 3496: Miscellaneous Fabricated Wire Products.**

INDUSTRY SNAPSHOT

Manufacturers involved in drawing and extruding nonferrous wire and cable supply five primary markets with various types of products manufactured from aluminum and copper, the two most widely utilized nonferrous metals, and other nonferrous metals. These products, ranging from fiber optic cable to insect wire screening, are drawn or extruded from wire bars or rods, a process that essentially winnows the larger bar and rod shapes into wire or cable. The wire and cable is then insulated with assorted materials such as paper or rubber or other materials, including polyethylene and polyvinyl chloride, for use in an assortment of applications, including wiring for residential and commercial buildings, communication networks, power distribution, automobiles, and appliances.

Historically, the five primary markets for the industry's products have been communication industries; electric utilities; automobile, truck, and boat manufacturers; the construction industry; and manufacturers of home appliances and industrial machinery. Since the conclusion of World War II, the composition of the industry's primary markets has remained unchanged, although the order of importance of each market to the industry has changed somewhat, according to market forces that have elevated certain markets, while depressing others. In the early 1990s, the construction industry stood as the industry's largest market, accounting for 18 percent of its total shipments, while telephone and telegraph wire and cable and electronic wire and cable each represented 14 percent of the industry's shipments. The fourth largest market, power wire and cable for the distribution of electricity, accounted for 11 percent of the industry's shipments, and wire and cords for appliances and machinery, the industry's fifth largest market, accounted for nearly eight percent.

By producing products for these and other markets, manufacturers generated $11.68 billion in revenue in 1991, marking the second consecutive year that the industry's sales volume had declined. During the 1980s, the industry's revenue total climbed steadily, from $8.22 billion in 1982 to $9.05 billion in 1986, peaking at $13.45 billion in 1989. For the next two years, as a global recession neared, revenue fell, dropping to $12.48 billion in 1990, then slipping again to the 1991 total.

ORGANIZATION AND STRUCTURE

As the nonferrous wire drawing and insulating industry entered the 1990s, approximately 340 companies in the United States were deriving the bulk of their revenue from the fabrication and insulation of wire and cable. These companies, many of which owned more than one manufacturing establishment, operated roughly 470 separate manufacturing facilities, 30 more than were in existence a decade earlier. Of these 470 establishments, 348, or nearly 75 percent, employed 20 or more workers, while the average size of a wire drawing and insulating establishment, in terms of the number of employees per establishment, was more than twice the size of the average manufacturing establishment.

Geographically, a majority of the industry's manufacturing establishments were located in the northeastern United States, particularly in Massachusetts, Rhode Island, Connecticut, Vermont, and New Hamp-

shire. In terms of the greatest number of establishments located in one state, California led all other states with 53 manufacturing establishments, although the 10 establishments in Georgia employed more workers than those in California and generated more than twice as much revenue.

Manufacturing establishments in this industry have historically been relatively costly to operate, by far exceeding the national average. This has been primarily attributable to the high price of raw materials needed to operate a wire drawing and insulation manufacturing establishment. The production machinery required to operate a wire drawing and insulation manufacturing establishment also was appreciably more expensive than the national standard posted by other manufacturing establishments.

BACKGROUND AND DEVELOPMENT

The wire and cable manufacturing industry has changed enormously over the years because of technological progress both in its own operations and in the systems and needs of its customers. The modern wire and cable manufacturing industry emerged in the late nineteenth century and the early twentieth century, a time during which the industrialization of the United States created a need for wire and cable products and provided a means for their production.

Once America became an industrialized nation, wire became a fundamental product underpinning the nation's growth, both industrially and commercially. For years, copper had been the preferred metal for a majority of the wire and cable manufacturing industry's products, its high conductivity elevating the metal above all others. Aluminum, which would eventually gain widespread acceptance in the industry, was first introduced as a cable conductor during the 1930s, but did not represent an appreciable portion of the market until the 1950s, when a tightened supply of copper, combined with the rising cost of that metal, forced manufacturers to search for an alternative.

Manufacturers' selection of aluminum to augment their copper supply came at an opportune time in the country's development: the population was rapidly expanding, creating a housing boom; televisions and radios were being manufactured at unprecedented levels; a community antennae television (CATV) market was burgeoning; more and more automobiles were being manufactured; and electric power generation in the country was about to begin two decades of exponential growth. Wire and cable manufacturers served each of these markets, experiencing enviable growth as the nation enjoyed an age of prosperity. By the beginning of the 1970s, the industry had evolved into a

$3 billion entity, primarily due to the growth of the national economy over the previous two decades.

The use of aluminum by the industry's products, however, particularly in the wiring of residential homes, caused considerable anxiety for some manufacturers when the U.S. Consumer Product Safety Commission (CPSC) filed a lawsuit against 26 manufacturers in 1977. Charging that 1.5 million homes wired with aluminum between 1965 and 1973 were in danger of catching fire, the CPSC sought to force those manufacturers responsible for producing the wire to pay for the rewiring of each home, at an estimated cost of $300 per home.

The potential for fire stemmed from the poorer conductivity of aluminum when compared to copper. Since aluminum was less conductive than copper, more aluminum was required to form a wire, which created a thicker stock that wire installers were unable to fit tightly into wall outlets. This led to loose connections that, in turn, caused the wiring to overheat. The problem was corrected for all homes wired after 1973, but the scare sent aluminum's share of the wiring market cascading downward from 17 percent to 1.4 percent during the 1970s.

CPSC's revelation, however, did not dissuade manufacturers from eschewing aluminum as a key raw material in the production of wire and cable. By the late 1980s, manufacturers purchased more primary aluminum than any other nonferrous metal to produce wire and cable products.

CURRENT CONDITIONS

As the wire drawing and insulating industry entered the mid-1990s, manufacturing activity resumed its pre-recession levels, thanks largely to the recovery of the construction industry. Increases in private residential housing starts augured well for manufacturers involved in producing building wire. Other wire and cable markets effected recoveries as well, enabling the industry to stanch its shrinking revenue volume. While the general upswing in the national economy was encouraging to manufacturers, perhaps the brightest prospect for the industry's future lay in the growth of the fiber optics industry, for which the wire drawing and insulating industry supplies fiber optic cable.

From 1989 to 1993 U.S. shipments of fiber optic equipment, which includes optical fiber and cable as well as other products excluded from the wire drawing and insulating manufacturing industry, increased 13 percent annually, with prognostications calling for still greater growth later in the decade. In 1993 the world market for fiber optic equipment was estimated to be

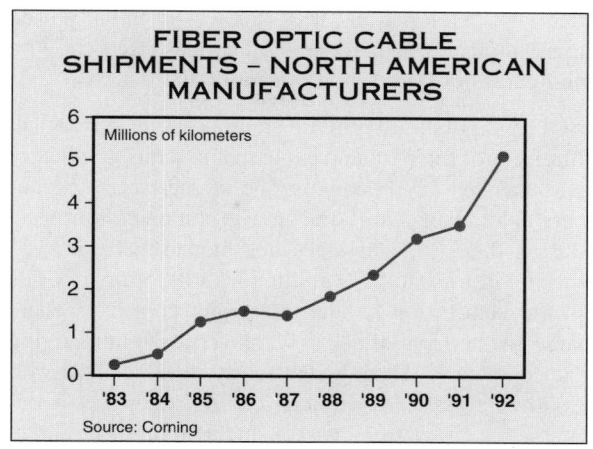

FIBER OPTIC CABLE SHIPMENTS – NORTH AMERICAN MANUFACTURERS

Source: Corning

$5 billion, a market in which U.S. manufacturers maintained a lead over European and Japanese producers, although the gap separating the United States from other manufacturers was closing in early 1994. Some observers expect this market to double in value by the end of the decade, promising lucrative profit potential for manufacturers of fiber optic cable. As the conventional markets supporting cable and wire manufacturers' core business once again fueled the industry's growth, those manufacturers able to afford the costly nature of exploring "next-generation" technology began turning to the production of fiber optic cable in increasing numbers.

INDUSTRY LEADERS

Ranked according to sales volume, the two largest wire and cable manufacturers during the early 1990s were Southwire Company Inc., based in Carrollton, Georgia, and Raychem Corp., based in Menlo Park, California. Southwire and Raychem became leaders in the industry despite the better-financed and more entrenched presence of giants in the metal industry such as Anaconda, Kaiser, and Reynolds Metals.

A long-time presence in the industry, Southwire was initially founded by Roy Richards to manufacture wire for his primary business pursuit at the time, Roy Richards Construction Company. His wire business quickly dwarfed his construction interests, however, and Richards further buttressed his wire manufacturing business with several innovations, including one in which a machine was developed that could continuously cast aluminum rod. Southwire than sought to deliver a similar process for copper rod, a more difficult task given copper's troublesome metallurgical properties. After five years of research under a joint agreement with Western Electric Co., however, a process called the Southwire Continuous Rod (SCR) system was developed in 1963; this was eventually used to manufacture 90 percent of all copper electrical wire and cable produced in major industrial nations.

By this time Southwire stood at the technological forefront of the wire and cable manufacturing industry and was steadily becoming one of the largest producers in terms of sales volume. The company flourished during the 1970s; annual sales increased from $123 million in 1970 to $723 million by 1980 primarily due to the acquisition of aluminum and copper smelters and other efforts aimed toward vertically integrating the company. During the early 1980s, however, Southwire's success shuddered to a stop, as a depressed construction market and automobile market combined with an imprudent capital expansion program, saddled the company with excessive debt and led to successive annual net losses in 1981, 1982, and 1983. By 1984, the elimination of inefficient and unprofitable operations improved the profitability of the company, while a recovery of the construction market and automobile market buoyed sales. Two years later a diversification program was initiated, leading to the acquisition of a building wire and cable plant in Utah and the purchase three years later, in 1989, of Hi-Tech Cable Corporation, one of the largest copper wire and cable production facilities in the United States. In 1991 the company purchased the assets of AT&T Nassau Metals Corporation, from which Gaston Copper Recycling Corporation was formed, making Southwire the largest recycler of copper in the United States. The following year, Integral Corporation, a manufacturer of cable-in-conduit, was purchased, enabling Southwire to post $1.30 billion in revenue for the year. In 1993, sales climbed slightly to $1.33 billion.

Raychem Corp., founded in 1957, manufactured, during the early 1990s, electronic heat tracing systems and telephone cable splice closures in addition to its core manufacturing business—the production of wire and cable. With its Sigaform Division, which manufactured plastic tubing and injected molded parts, Raychem generated $1.29 billion in revenue in 1993, lagging only slightly behind Southwire.

Other leading companies involved in the drawing and insulating of nonferrous wire include Essex Group Inc., Carol Cable Company Inc., Siecor Corp., Cooper, and Penn Central Corp.

WORK FORCE

Total employment in the wire drawing and insulation industry declined throughout the 1980s. A large percentage of this decline was attributable to diminishing number of production jobs; in 1982 there were 50,000 production workers employed by the industry, but by 1990 their numbers had fallen to 44,600.

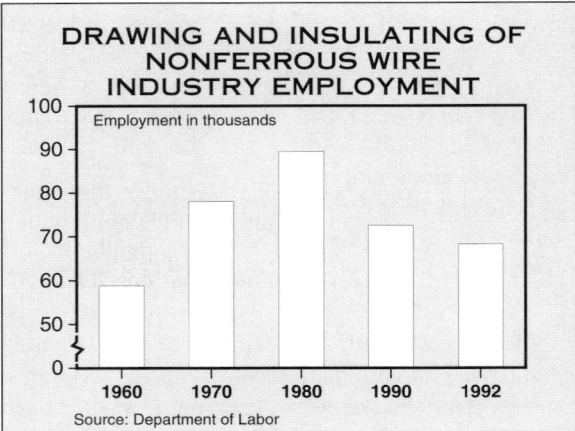

DRAWING AND INSULATING OF NONFERROUS WIRE INDUSTRY EMPLOYMENT

Employment in thousands

Source: Department of Labor

INDUSTRY INFORMATION SOURCES

"Aluminum Gaining on Copper in Electric Transformer Race," *Industry Week,* March 2, 1970, 18.

Annual Survey of Manufactures, Washington, DC: U.S. Department of Commerce.

Corwin, Phillip, "All Along the Line," *Barron's,* April 4, 1966, 11.

Donnelly, Richard A., "Hotter Lines," *Barron's,* May 1, 1972, 11.

"Electrical Cable Using Sodium as Conductor Appears to Pass Tests," *Wall Street Journal,* February 2, 1966, 4.

"Electrical Equipment Is Prime for Growth," *Industry Week,* November 30, 1970, 68.

Miller, Gay Sands, "Electric Debate," *Wall Street Journal,* January 11, 1978, 1.

"Most Defendants Plead No Contest in Wiring Case," *Wall Street Journal,* December 8, 1977, 16.

"Nonferrous Metals: Try Living without Them," *Nation's Business,* August 1979, 65.

Statistical Abstract of the United States: 1993, 113th ed., Washington, DC: U.S. Bureau of the Census, 1993.

U.S. Industrial Outlook, Washington, DC: U.S. Department of Commerce, 1964-1994.

"Wire and Cable Business Up Despite Cutback in Home Building," *Electrical World,* April 17, 1967, 119.

—Jeffrey L. Covell

SIC 3363

ALUMINUM DIE-CASTINGS

This classification is comprised of establishments primarily engaged in manufacturing die-castings of aluminum (including alloys).

Aluminum die-castings differ from other types of aluminum castings based on the type of mold used and the process by which the molten metal is delivered to the die. Whereas casting molds may be made of many different materials including sand, plaster, iron, steel, and polystyrene, dies are made only of metal, most frequently steel. In die-casting, the die is typically filled with molten metal forced into it under pressure, unlike other casting processes where liquid metal is generally poured by gravity. Die-casting techniques are typically used to produce greater volumes of cast products than other types of casting.

In 1990, U.S. shipments of aluminum die-castings totaled 1,368.3 million pounds. Die-castings accounted for 64.1 percent of all aluminum castings, which totaled 2,134 million pounds. Of the aluminum die-castings produced, 848.5 million pounds were manufactured for sale and 519.8 million pounds represented die-castings made for use by their manufacturer. Nearly half the die-castings sold in the U.S. were sold to the automotive industry.

The first commercially produced aluminum die-castings in the United States were manufactured in 1915. In 1946, the U.S. Department of Commerce reported that aluminum die-casting production totaled 73 million pounds, representing about 16 percent of the total die-casting production for all metals that year. Prior to the late 1960s, zinc was used in a majority of die-cast products, but in 1967, aluminum production surpassed that of zinc. Throughout the 1970s aluminum production continued to expand dramatically, and by 1988, aluminum die-casting production reached the 1.5 billion pound mark.

As the die-casting industry entered the 1990s, aluminum remained in the top position. Its chemical and physical properties offered many advantages to industrial users. For example, aluminum die-castings weighed about 60 percent less than identical iron products, they resisted corrosion, and they were stronger than permanent mold or sand castings. Automated production methods produced high quantities at low, per-unit costs. Industry analysts expected shipments to reach 1.7 billion pounds by 1994.

One of the largest aluminum die-casters in the United States was Doehler-Jarvis. Doehler-Jarvis was founded by Herman Doehler, who developed the first die-casting machine around the turn of the century. During its long history, the company boasted many ''firsts'' in die-casting technology including the first transmission case casing, the first die-cast oil pan, and the first automotive cylinder block. Doehler-Jarvis also was a pioneer in computer assisted design (CAD). In 1979, the company introduced CAD, a technology which permitted dies to be made with electronic information and eliminate the need to make blueprints.

In 1980, Doehler-Jarvis introduced the ''doehlercore system,'' a patented and proprietary process using expendable cores in high pressure castings. This process enabled the company to cast parts with complex internal shapes.

By the early 1990s, Doehler-Jarvis operated three casting centers with combined manufacturing space totaling two million square feet. The company reported annual shipments of 75,000 tons valued at $300 million. In 1992, Doehler-Jarvis employed 2,500 workers.

INDUSTRY INFORMATION SOURCES

The Aluminum Association, *Aluminum Statistical Review for 1991*, Washington, DC: Aluminum Association, 1992.

''Aluminum Castings Shipments to Reach $6.5 Billion by 1994,'' *Foundry Management & Technology*, March 1991.

''Die Casting Demand Seen Rising,'' *American Metal Market*, May 18, 1992.

Doehler-Jarvis, *Aluminum Casting Alloys Fact Book*, Toledo, OH: Doehler, 1991.

Doehler-Jarvis, *Diecaster to the World*, Toledo, OH: Doehler, 1992.

Miske, Jack C., ''A Progress Report on Diecasting,'' *Foundry Management & Technology*, August 1990.

—Karen Bellenir

SIC 3364

NONFERROUS DIE-CASTINGS EXCEPT ALUMINUM

This classification is comprised of establishments primarily involved in manufacturing die-castings from nonferrous metals and alloys other than aluminum. Establishments primarily engaged in manufacturing die-castings from aluminum and aluminum alloys are classified in **SIC 3363: Aluminum Die-Castings**.

According to figures released by the U.S. Bureau of the Census, zinc die-castings represented the largest category of die-castings other than aluminum. In 1988, domestic production totaled 482 million pounds. Magnesium, another important non-aluminum die-casting metal, represented almost 30 million pounds.

Die-casting techniques, which relied on injecting molten metal into steel molds under pressure, were developed around the turn of the twentieth century. Industrial development and needs spawned by both World Wars brought increased use of die-castings.

In 1946, shipments of die-castings approximated 460 million pounds. Of this total, 376 million pounds represented die-castings fabricated with zinc. Zinc remained the top metal for die-casters until it was surpassed by aluminum in 1967. The 1970s and 1980s brought additional challenges to zinc die-casters when auto makers began replacing zinc components with plastic products, and domestic manufacturers faced increased challenges from imported products. Improvements in the ability to cast zinc parts using thin-wall technology were expected to help zinc recapture some of its lost market share.

As the die-casting industry prepared for the 1990s, the North American Die Casting Association (NADCA) predicted that technological improvements would increase demand for die-cast products. In addition to refinements in zinc production, the ability to work with magnesium held promise.

Innovations permitted fabricators to purify magnesium of contaminants associated with poor corrosion resistance. Refined magnesium possessed qualities making it competitive with aluminum, steel, plastics, and other traditional materials. These improvements resulted in dramatic increases in magnesium die-casting shipments. For example, in 1983, magnesium shipments totaled 4,800 metric tons. By 1990, the figure had increased to 15,800 metric tons. Although magnesium shipments dropped slightly in 1991 to 15,200 metric tons, industry analysts expected sales to rebound. Some extended estimates predicted a doubling or tripling by 1996 or 1997.

The largest user of magnesium die-castings was the automotive industry. According to a 1992 estimate, 75 to 80 percent of the nation's magnesium die-castings were produced for vehicle use. Magnesium parts for cars included various housings, brackets, and steering column components. Other users of magnesium castings included manufacturers of appliances, power tools, computer equipment, and consumer goods.

Another metal receiving increased interest during the early 1990s was titanium. Titanium possessed low weight, high strength, and good corrosion resistance. Although it had been used since the early 1950s in

aerospace applications, widespread acceptance failed to develop because of the high costs associated with titanium production. Innovations developed during the 1980s, however, opened the door to expanded use. In 1991, producers shipped approximately two million pounds of titanium castings.

INDUSTRY INFORMATION SOURCES

Ambrosia, John, "Magnesium Packs Heavy Punch in Auto Market," *Iron Age*, August 1992.

"Diecastings Second Largest Consumer of Magnesium," *Foundry Management & Technology*, May 1991.

Heine, Hans J., "Casting Development Technology Opens Doors to New Titanium Applications," *Foundry Management & Technology*, March 1991.

Hilsdorf, Robert, "Technology Helps Zinc Regain Uses," *American Metal Market*, October 19, 1987.

"Magnesium Die Castings for Appliance Parts," *Appliance Manufacturer*, April 1991.

Miske, Jack C., "A Progress Report on Diecasting," *Foundry Management & Technology*, August 1990.

"U.S. Zinc Diecasting Industry Hit by Indirect Imports," *Foundry Management & Technology*, January 1991.

—Karen Bellenir

SIC 3365

ALUMINUM FOUNDRIES

This category includes establishments primarily engaged in manufacturing aluminum (including alloys) castings, except die-castings, which are classified in **SIC 3363: Aluminum Die-Castings.**

INDUSTRY SNAPSHOT

Aluminum foundries create castings by pouring heated, liquified metal into hollowed out molds. As the molten metal within a mold cools, it hardens and assumes the shape created by the mold's cavity. Aluminum foundries typically work with metal purchased in the form of ingots from primary producers or from secondary aluminum recyclers. Some foundries located in close proximity to primary smelters obtain aluminum in molten form.

According to figures published by the Aluminum Association, 2.1 billion pounds of aluminum castings were shipped during 1991. The total represented a 0.9 percent drop from levels attained in 1990 and a decrease of 8.7 percent from the 2.3 billion pounds recorded in 1988, the industry's peak year.

The largest user of aluminum castings was the automotive industry. Some analysts expected to see demand from the automotive sector expand as car designers turned increasingly to aluminum products to help reduce vehicle weight and meet federally mandated fuel efficiency standards. Demand in another historically significant cast aluminum market, however, was declining. Shipments for cast aluminum cookware, which had totaled 206 million pounds in 1983, fell to 120 million pounds in 1990 and dropped even further to 117 million pounds in 1991.

Overall, industry analysts predicted that shipments of aluminum castings would increase by 2.8 percent per year and reach 2.5 billion pounds by 1994. The two technologies expected to yield the highest production increases were investment casting and expendable pattern casting.

BACKGROUND AND DEVELOPMENT

Aluminum is the most abundant metal in the earth's crust, but it never occurs naturally in isolation. It is a component of many gem stones such as rubies, turquoise, and jade, and it exists in the mineral bauxite. Clays with high aluminum content were used to make pottery in prehistoric times, and aluminum compounds were used by several ancient civilizations. The ability to break the chemical bonds between aluminum and other elements to produce the isolated metal was first achieved during the 1800s.

Bauxite, the source for virtually all modern aluminum, was first discovered in Lex Baux, France in 1821. Advances made during the nineteenth century in chemistry and electrolysis made the commercial production of aluminum metal from bauxite practical. In 1855, aluminum cost $115 per pound, but improvements in chemical production led to price reductions. By 1859, the price had dropped to $17 per pound.

Although falling prices permitted the introduction of some aluminum products, such as surgical instruments and novelty items, they were still too high to permit widespread industrial use of aluminum. The most important breakthrough came later in the century when Charles Martin Hall in the United States and Paul L. T. Héroult in France independently developed commercial aluminum production methods based on electrolysis. As a result, by the turn of the twentieth century, aluminum prices had dropped to $0.33 per pound.

One of the most famous aluminum castings in the United States was placed on the tip of the Washington Monument in 1884. The first aluminum household utensils were created during the 1890s and gained popularity during the early 1900s. By the mid 1960s, over half of the cookware on the U.S. market was aluminum. In 1903, aluminum reached new heights when the Wilbur and Orville Wright launched their Kitty Hawk Flyer. Its converted engine contained 30 pounds of aluminum parts.

During World War I, items such as canteens, mess kits, ammunition cases, and tent pins were made from cast aluminum. The emerging automotive industry required engines, manifolds, crankcases, oil pans, and valve covers. World War II increased aluminum casting demands by the military, and brought growing needs within the aeronautic industry.

Modern casting techniques. During the second half of the twentieth century, aluminum foundries relied on several different casting technologies to meet the diverse demands of their customers. The casting techniques are differentiated by the type of mold used and the process by which the molds are filled. One of the most common types of casting is called ''sand casting.'' Sand castings are created using molds formed from a precise blends of sands, clays, and moisture. After a mold is formed, molten aluminum is poured into it. When the aluminum hardens, the sand is removed. The advantages of sand casting are its versatility and low cost for producing small quantities. Its principle disadvantage is its slowness compared to other casting methods.

Shell mold casting is a type of sand casting that relies on a thin mold made of preformed, baked sand. Plaster mold casting is similar to sand casting but molds are fabricated from plaster instead of sand. Plaster mold casting produces products with an improved surface finish.

Permanent mold castings employ molds made of iron or steel into which aluminum is poured. Although aluminum die-casting also uses permanent steel molds, it differs from permanent mold casting because, instead of relying on gravity, pressure is used to force the molten aluminum into the dies. Permanent mold casting technology produces the strongest castings.

Investment casting is a complex type of casting in which two or more permanent molds are assembled with an intervening wax lining or in which a wax shape is formed and dipped into a special liquid ceramic. When dried, the ceramic creates a shell around the shape. In both cases, the wax is heated and drained to create a hollow for the liquid aluminum. Because the melted wax is drained out of the mold, investment casting is sometimes referred to as the ''lost wax'' method. After cooling, the mold is broken and an exact aluminum replica of the former wax image remains.

One advantage of investment casting is its ability to duplicate intricate patterns.

One of the most recently developed casting processes is called expendable pattern casting, sometimes referred to as "lost foam casting" or "evaporative foam pattern casting." Expendable pattern casting employs a polystyrene pattern made from fused polystyrene beads surrounded by a special sand pack. When liquid aluminum is poured into the mold the polystyrene vaporizes. The procedure yields a casting of the same dimensions as the pattern. The process holds many advantages such as a reduction in finishing costs and an improved ability to make more complicated designs. According to one estimate, production cost savings associated with expendable pattern casting are as much as 50 percent over traditional casting techniques.

Why aluminum? Many industrial users favor aluminum because of its physical and chemical properties. Aluminum reflects light, conducts heat and electricity, is non-magnetic, non-toxic, and naturally resistant to corrosion, and weighs only one third as much as an equal volume of steel. Cast aluminum products are made of pure aluminum or aluminum alloys. Pure industrial aluminum is defined as aluminum containing less than one percent impurities. Many of the alloying elements often incorporated into aluminum are added to improve the mixture's hardness, tensile strength, or corrosion resistance. Binary aluminum alloys are made of aluminum plus one other element, while complex alloys contain two or more other elements. The most frequently used metals in aluminum alloys include copper, magnesium, manganese, and zinc. Another element frequently alloyed with aluminum is silicon. Alloys of aluminum with silicon have a lower melting point which results in improved castability.

CURRENT CONDITIONS

One of the most rapidly growing areas of aluminum castings use during the early 1990s was within the automotive industry. According to a study commissioned by the Aluminum Association, the average 1991 North American car contained 191 pounds of aluminum parts. Castings represented 66 percent of the total aluminum. Excluding wheels, an estimated 90 percent of the automotive aluminum castings were made with recycled aluminum.

The increased use of aluminum in automobiles is the result of an increased emphasis on making cars lighter to achieve improved fuel efficiency. In 1992, the Aluminum Association stated, "If all cars in the U.S. fleet of about 150 million applied the use of aluminum components available today, annual gasoline savings would be about 275 million barrels—roughly 13 percent of annual U.S. gasoline consumption." In addition to fuel savings, the Association cited other benefits of increasing reliance on aluminum, including better acceleration, improved stopping, enhanced handling, and less vibration.

Some critics claimed that the cast aluminum industry was too dependent on the automotive industry. Because of slack auto sales during the late 1980s and early 1990s, casting production capacity exceeded product demand. Although optimistic reports suggested a rebound during the early 1990s as car sales improved, less optimistic projections predicted that the automotive industry would not increase its aluminum use. Because of continuing pressure to produce cars with better fuel efficiency, some industry watchers predicted that the automotive industry would instead turn to components made with even lighter weight materials.

Another concern facing the aluminum casting industry was the problem of waste disposal. In 1991, *Foundry Management & Technology* reported that foundry solid wastes totaled more than 9 million tons per year. Of this total, 7.2 million tons were sand. Annual disposal costs were estimated at $451 million annually. The problem was expected to escalate as per-ton disposal costs increased. Forecasters predicted a possible doubling of dumping charges by 2001.

In response, the casting industry began investigating ways of reducing the amount of waste generated through programs such as sand reclamation and reuse. Some governmental jurisdictions instituted studies to evaluate potential applications for foundry waste. Proposed uses included fill for highway embankments, sub-base materials for concrete slabs, and raw material for making construction products such as bricks.

INDUSTRY LEADERS

One of the largest aluminum foundries in the United States was Amcast Industrial Corporation. Amcast began its corporate life during the 1860s as Dayton Malleable Iron Company, a manufacturer of cast iron products. In 1983, the company reorganized, changed its name to Amcast, and centered its focus on producing aluminum components. In 1992, the company reported that 96 percent of its revenues were derived from products it had acquired or developed within the previous decade. Amcast's largest customer group was comprised of automobile makers. The company provided products such as wheels, anti-lock brake system parts, and suspension system components to General Motors, Ford, Chrysler, BMW, and

Toyota. Amcast also supplied castings to both commercial and military aircraft manufacturers.

Another major aluminum foundry in the United States was Fort Wayne Foundry Corporation. Fort Wayne operated two foundries in Indiana. The original plant, located in Ft. Wayne, consisted of a 50,000 square foot foundry. Its more modern facility, a $10 million plant occupying a 13-acre site, opened in 1985 in Columbia City. The Columbia City plant pioneered the use of a vacuum molding system capable of producing castings of higher quality with closer tolerances than traditional casting methods.

Fort Wayne's principle customer was General Motors. The company provided aluminum covers and engine parts for GM's Chevrolet-Pontiac-Canada division and cam components for Buick-Oldsmobile-Cadillac engines. In 1987, combined shipments from both Fort Wayne production plants were estimated at 40 million pounds.

WORK FORCE

Aluminum foundries employed a wide variety of skilled and unskilled workers. Typical employees with specialized skills included technicians, engineers, and chemists. Other specialists included patternmakers (who produce the patterns necessary to create castings), molders (who make the sand molds), and coremakers (who make sand cores). Aluminum foundries also employed many workers with skills not specific to metalcasting. These included industrial hygienists, electricians, and millwrights.

According to the American Foundrymen's Society (AFS), 28 universities in the United States offered Cast Metals Studies programs. In addition, the Cast Metals Institute, established by the AFS in 1957, provided ongoing training to individuals within the industry.

Among employees in aluminum foundries, burns were one of the leading causes of work-related injuries. To help protect workers from the inherent dangers involved in handling hot, liquid metal, the Aluminum Association published *Guidelines for Handling Molten Aluminum*. Recommended safety precautions included the use of shields and the establishment of areas in which personnel must wear protective equipment. Special protective clothing for workers directly exposed to molten aluminum was deemed essential because some types of fabrics were subject to igniting or melting upon contact with the liquid metal. As a result, industry standards required wrist to ankle coverage and mandated the use of special footwear, gloves, headgear, and safety glasses.

RESEARCH AND TECHNOLOGY

Ongoing research efforts within the cast aluminum industry were aimed at alleviating specific casting problems and producing castings of a better quality. Because aluminum shrinks as it cools, casting were sometimes prone to "hot tears," a type of fracture caused by the stresses created during solidification. Breaks in the finished product caused by insufficient metal flow during the casting process led to another problem. These types of deficiencies were termed "shrinkage cracks."

One of the biggest challenges, however, was the elimination of hydrogen-induced porosity in cast products. Under certain conditions, hydrogen, which was soluble in aluminum, could cause tiny pores within a casting's metal structure. According to Hans J. Heine, International Editor of *Foundry Management & Technology*, these tiny holes represented "a primary cause for rejection of an aluminum casting."

To help reduce hydrogen-induced porosity, a method was developed to pass nitrogen gas through the molten aluminum solution. The nitrogen was not soluble in aluminum and the action of its presence helped the mixture release trapped hydrogen prior to casting. Some researchers experimented with refinements using argon, freon, and chlorine. Although these methods were deemed effective, industry analysts judged them to be too expensive. Another promising method of reducing hydrogen induced-porosity involved degassing the molten aluminum under a partial vacuum. Pressurized conditions caused the gas to float to the surface of the molten mixture.

To produce castings with specific qualities, sometimes heat treatments were used. When a cast product was heated and cooled under precise conditions, it developed a uniform internal structure, removed stresses, and improved its strength, stability, and hardness. One type of heat treatment, called annealing, involved heating a casting to a temperature above the point where its metal crystals would melt and then cooling it to recrystallize the metal.

INDUSTRY INFORMATION SOURCES

Aluminum Association, "Aluminum: Know the Facts," Washington, DC: Aluminum Association, October 1992.

————, *Aluminum Statistical Review for 1991,* Washington, DC: Aluminum Association, 1992.

————, *Aluminum: How It's Made and Where It's Used,* New York: Aluminum Association, 1968.

————, *The Story and Uses of Aluminum,* Washington DC: Aluminum Association.

————, "Study to Determine the Net Weight of Aluminum in North American Car Production," Washington, DC: Aluminum Association.

"Aluminum Castings Shipments to Reach $6.5 billion by 1994," *Foundry Management & Technology,* March 1991.

AMCAST Industrial Corporation, *Annual Report,* Dayton, OH: Amcast, 1992.

American Foundrymen's Society, *Metalcasting: An Art . . . Science . . . Career!,* Des Plaines, IL: American Foundrymen's Society.

Ammen, C. W., *Casting Aluminum,* Blue Ridge Summit, PA: Tab Books, 1985.

East, William R., "Solid Waste—No Place to Go," *Foundry Management & Technology,* May 1991.

Heine, Hans J., "Reducing Porosity," *Foundry Management & Technology,* February 1992.

Leitch, Robert R., "Making Aluminum Alloy Wheels in Permanent Molds," *Foundry Management & Technology,* February 1989.

Monks, Howard, "Ancient Casting Process Waxing in Modern Times," *American Metal Market,* October 19, 1987.

Rodgers, Robert C., "Fort Wayne Foundry Corp. Triples Size to Match Sales," *Foundry Management & Technology,* August 1987.

————, "Quality Aluminum Casting Expands Its Capabilities," *Foundry Management & Technology,* September 1990.

Sasser, B. J., "Guidelines for Personal Protection with Molten Aluminum," *Foundry Management & Technology,* October 1990.

Stundaz, Tom, "Too Much Reliance on Automotive," *Purchasing,* July 18, 1991.

Tenaglia, Richard D., "Evaporative Casting Study Yields Solid Improvements," *American Metal Market,* October 19, 1987.

—Karen Bellenir

SIC 3366

COPPER FOUNDRIES

This industry consists of companies primarily engaged in manufacturing copper and copper-alloy castings, except die-castings. Establishments that produce copper castings and also are engaged in fabricating operations for a specific product are classified in the industry of the specific product. Therefore, some of the companies considered to be a part of the copper foundry industry are not included in this classification, although some of the statistics covering the copper foundry industry do include these "captive" foundry departments of manufacturers.

According to the "1992 Census of World Casting Production" compiled by the trade magazine *Modern Casting,* there were approximately 2,100 foundries of nonferrous metal in the United States operating in 1992. These foundries produced 261,000 metric tons of copper and copper-alloys. Foundries in the United States produced more copper-based castings than foundries anywhere else in the world.

Approximately 25 to 30 percent of the castings output in the U.S. came from the captive foundry producers in the early 1990s. Some of these made copper castings, but the statistical data covering their output was scattered in coverage of other industries such as motor vehicles (**SIC 3711: Motor Vehicles and Passenger Car Bodies**), plumbing fixtures (**SIC 3432: Plumbing Fixture Fittings and Trim**), agricultural equipment (**SIC 3523: Farm Machinery and Equipment**), and machine tools (**SIC 3541: Machine Tools, Metal Cutting Types**).

The copper industry is made up of producers such as mining, smelting, and refining companies, and fabricators such as foundries and brass and wire rod mills. Copper is mined and refined before alloys are added to it. Copper and copper alloys are sold to fabricators who create such products as forgings, rods, bars, and tubes that are used in the construction industry, telecommunications industry, and in various manufacturing industries.

Copper is renowned for its corrosion resistance, electrical and thermal conductivity, machinability, color, and ease of finishing. Foundries combined copper with several other elements to create alloys with a wide range of qualities. Copper-based castings are strong and corrosion-resistant, making them essential as a basic tool in the building, plumbing, and automobile industries.

Foundries cast copper in many different ways. The most common of these are sand casting, centrifugal casting, continuous casting, investment casting, permanent mold casting, and shell mold casting. Sand casting, in which molten metal is poured into a sand mold, is the most widely used method of producing large quantities of copper and copper alloy castings. One of its primary assets is that the cost of the mold patterns is usually reasonably low.

Centrifugal casting consists of pouring molten metal into a revolving or rotating mold. The molten metal is poured into a spinning mold cavity and the metal is held against the wall by centrifugal force. This method is often utilized for casting bearings, gears, or machinery pieces. In continuous casting molten copper alloy is fed through an open-ended mold to yield bar, tube, or other shape cables.

Investment casting, also called precision casting, was still used in the late twentieth century for decorative copper applications. The method was also used to make aircraft parts. Investment casting, also known as precision casting, has a long history that predates the Egyptian pyramids.

One of the mainstays of the U.S. copper industry is the Copper and Brass Development Association (CDA). Its members include the primary copper producers, miners and smelters, described in **SIC 3331: Primary Smelting and Refining of Copper;** manufacturers of mill products such as sheet, strip, rod, bar, tube, and pipe described in **SIC 3351: Rolling, Drawing, and Extruding of Copper;** as well as the copper foundries of this industry. CDA tracks market statistics and published handbooks, reports, and bulletins as part of its efforts to broaden copper markets in this country and abroad.

The American Foundrymen's Society (AFS) comprises the foundries of the United States, Canada, and Mexico. It is a professional, technical, and management association that works with government leadership to influence Congress on legislative issues, prepare educational programs, and perform research for its members and interested laypeople. With almost 14,000 members in more than 47 countries, it is the leading metalcasting association in North America.

Historical Use. Copper-based castings have a long history. Copper artifacts have been dated back to 8700 BC, and smelting was performed by 5000 BC. Casting, especially sand casting, is one of the oldest known methods of producing metal components. As agricultural equipment, shipping equipment, and plumbing developed, so did the need for advanced castings. Nonferrous castings, including copper-based castings, also became essential to the modern world with the proliferation of automobiles, televisions, airplanes, and telecommunications equipment.

In the 1950s and 1960s induction furnaces were used in most foundries to melt brass and other copper alloys. Core or channel furnaces and coreless or crucible furnaces were both induction furnaces in which current was induced into the metal before it was melted. The temperature of the metal to be poured was carefully measured. Pyrometers, which measured the metal temperature, became increasingly accurate and easier to read as the technology improved.

There were tremendous advances in technology and environmental science from the 1960s through the 1980s. As foundry practices began to adapt to these advances, the improvements saved money, increased efficiency, and assisted U.S. foundries in maintaining world leadership in the field, an increasingly difficult task with the emergence of casting producers in foreign countries. Many of these outfits boasted state-of-the-art facilities, low labor costs, and subsidized work, and many U.S. foundries accused their foreign counterparts of dumping products below costs.

The metalcasting industry is a basic component of all industrial societies, but the economic upheavals in the 1970s and 1980s brought tremendous change to the industry. Many foundries had to close their doors, and many more merged into larger companies.

Copper foundries relied on the health of the U.S. economy and the success of their customers in the manufacturing industries in order to prosper. As the business environment improved in the early 1990s the copper-related industries also improved. Some foundries that survived the changes decided to invest in new plants and equipment to accommodate the new technology. Many cut their labor forces, aiming for cost effectiveness. Surviving foundries increasingly worked with users of their end products to customize castings.

Some of the leading copper foundries in the United States include Babcock Thorn Ltd., Carbone of America, Outokumpu, and Olin Corporation. Foundries that are divisions or subsidiaries of larger corporations include Brass Group and AJ Oster Company Inc. Some of the country's leading privately held foundries were SW Centrifugal Inc., Ampco Metal Inc., and R. Lavin and Sons Inc.

Most U.S. foundries are small by the relative standards of U.S. industry. Eighty percent of American foundries employed fewer than 100 people. In 1991 there were more than 1,000 foundries of nonferrous metals employing fewer than 20 people, while another 800 nonferrous metals foundries employed 25 to 100 people. The number of workers in the nonferrous foundry industries (including copper foundries) fell from 89,300 in 1984 to 78,000 in 1992. The number of hours worked in these foundries each week fell from 42 in 1984 to 41.1 in 1992. Hourly pay, according to the Bureau of Labor Statistics, rose from $9.04 in 1984 to $10.86 in 1992.

INDUSTRY INFORMATION SOURCES

"Annual Data: 1993: Copper Supply and Consumption, 1972-1992," New York: Copper Development Association Inc., 1993.

Copper-Base Alloys Foundry Practice, Des Plaines, IL: American Foundrymen's Society, 1965.

"Copper in the USA: Bright Future—Colorful Past," New York: Copper Development Association Inc., 1990.

Getler, Warren. "Copper Futures Rise, but Traders Warn Rally is Likely to be Short-Lived Amid Oversupply, *Wall Street Journal,* October 12, 1993, C18.

Kanicki, David P. "World Foundry Congress Highlights Computer Applications," *Modern Casting,* December 1993, 26.

Orogo, Constantine D., et al. "A Vision of Computer-Aided Casting in the Year 2000," *Modern Casting,* October 1993, 20.

Stundza, Tom. "Purchasing deluge will ebb slightly in '93," *Purchasing,* March 4, 1993, 34.

Taylor, Jeffrey. "U.S. Copper Futures Fall as Available Stocks of the Metal Reach a 15-Year High in London," *Wall Street Journal,* October 27, 1993, C18.

Temes, Judy. "Polish and Tarnish," *Crain's New York Business,* November 12, 1990, p. 3.

Whiteman, Maxwell. *Copper for America,* New Brunswick: Rutgers University Press, 1971.

—Fran Shonfeld Sherman

SIC 3369

NONFERROUS FOUNDRIES, EXCEPT ALUMINUM AND COPPER

The available statistics on this industry are relatively new, as a reclassification took place in 1987. The product share in 1987 was distributed between zinc castings with 3.8% of the total share; magnesium and magnesium-base alloy cast in sand mold claimed 16.9%; magnesium and magnesium-base alloys cast in permanent and semi-permanent molds claimed 4.8%; titanium and other nonferrous castings covered 66.6%, while the other 7.9% of the market share was held by non-specific nonferrous foundries.

Between 1982 and 1986, the value of shipments increased slightly from $916 million to $1.23 billion. Once the industry was reclassified in 1987, the value of shipments was adjusted to $339.9 million and rose to $366.8 million in 1988. Likewise, employment data was adjusted due to the reclassification. Employment grew from 14,900 in 1982 to 15,500 in 1986. In 1987, this level was adjusted to 4,000 and grew to 4,400 by the end of 1988. In 1982 358 establishments were engaged in this industry. By 1986, this figure dropped to 318. In 1987, the number of establishments was adjusted to 24, which increased to 56 by 1988. Nearly 50 percent of all establishments in this industry employ less than 20 people, however the average employ-

ment level per establishment is 79 employees. Wages per hour increased between 1982 and 1986 from $8.11 to $9.71. In 1987 wages per hour were $11.36, but fell to $10.88 by the end of 1988.

Comparatively, employees in this industry are paid just above the national average for all manufacturing, which was $10.66 per hour in 1988. Nonferrous foundries also ranked higher than the manufacturing average in ratios of employees per establishment, payroll, production workers, wages, and value added per establishment. Other ratios indicate this industry has a lower cost structure than other types of manufacturing. However, ratios of shipments per establishment, as well as employee and production worker ratios, are significantly lower than the manufacturing average.

The top 69 companies engaged in this industry grossed sales of $903.7 million in 1991 and employed 9,600 people. Prime Alloy Castings Inc. of Port Hueneme, California is a private company which grossed an estimated $57 million in sales while employing 400 in 1991. NGK Materials Corporation of Reading, Pennsylvania grossed sales of $55 million and employed 500 in 1991. SMP Incorporated of Wickliffe, Ohio grossed sales of $50 million and employed 500 in 1991. Nuclear Metals Incorporated of Concord, Massachusetts grossed sales of $50 million and employed 600 people in 1991. MacDonald's Industrial of Grand Rapids, Michigan grossed sales of $41 million and employed 400 in 1991.

Going into the next century, the occupational outlook for this industry is bright compared to other manufacturing industries. Employment levels are expected to drop by less than 2% for grinders and polishers, inspectors, mold assembly and shakeout workers, metal pourers, assemblers, metal machine operators, machine forming operators, and secretaries. Those occupations expected to grow more than 20% include machinists, combination machine tool operators, tool and die makers, industrial machinery mechanics, maintenance repairers, sales workers, and industrial production managers.

INDUSTRY INFORMATION SOURCES

Darnay, Arsen J., ed. *Manufacturing USA: Industry Analyses, Statistics, and Leading Companies*, Detroit: Gale Research, Inc., 1992.

—Valerie E. Wilson

SIC 3398

METAL HEAT TREATING

This category covers establishments primarily engaged in heat treating of metal for the trade.

The metal heat treating industry provides a service to the trades requiring annealed, brazed, burned, hardened, tempered, and shot-peened metals. By nature of this, it is classified as a primary metal product industry. The metal heat treating industry experienced significant growth in shipments during the 1980s. In 1982 shipments were valued at $1.13 billion. By 1988, shipments had grown to $1.76 billion. During this time the number of establishments decreased from 758 to 703, yet the number of establishments employing more than 20 increased 9 percent from 289 in 1982 to 316 in 1988. Total employment increased from 17,700 in 1982 to 19,300 in 1988. Wages increased nearly 15 percent during the 1980s, from $8.05 in 1982 to $9.52 in 1988. However, $9.52 per hour is low compared to all manufacturing industries, which averaged $10.66 in 1988. Fairly large outlays in capital investment were made between 1984 and 1987, averaging $79.35 million per year. Comparatively, capital investment in 1983 was $26.8 million and $49.8 million in 1988.

The leading 75 companies engaged in this industry grossed sales of $727.2 million in 1991 and employed 7,700. Metal Improvement Company of Paramus, New Jersey, had estimated sales of $96 million in 1991 while employing 900 people. Lindberg Corporation of Chicago, Illinois, reported sales of $79 million and employed 1,000 people in 1991. Paulo Products Company of St. Louis, Missouri, reported sales of $50 million and employed 300 people. Cooperheat Incorporated of Somerset, New Jersey, was estimated to have grossed $43 million in sales while employing 400 people. Hinderliter Heat Treating Incorporated of Dallas, Texas, reported sales of $25 million and employed 400 people.

As the 21st century approaches, the employment levels of many occupations in the primary metal products industry, which includes heat treatment facilities, are expected to decrease. Those occupations expected to face reductions of more than 25 percent include miscellaneous hand workers, electricians, metal pourers, metal/plastic machine workers, furnace operators, and welders. Those occupations expected to face reductions between 10 and 25 percent include blue collar worker supervisors, general laborers, heat treating machine operators, furnace operators, truck and tractor operators, crushing and mixing machine operators, inspectors, crane operators, material movers, machine tool workers, secretaries, machine feeders, science and mathematics technicians, material moving equipment operators, and metal molding machine operators. Sales workers will be in demand, as the employment level in this occupation is expected to increase by 12.5 percent by the year 2000.

Michigan claims the highest number of establishments engaged in this industry, and the most value in shipments. Michigan's 119 establishments shipped $272.7 million in heat treated products, which was 19.5 percent of the total in the United States. Of the total U.S. work force engaged in this industry, 18.3 percent were employed in Michigan, which accounts for 3,300 employees who averaged $10.08 per hour in 1987. New York's heat treatment facilities reported total shipments of $155 million in 1987 while employing 1,400 people who averaged $11.74 per hour. Ohio's 85 establishments engaged in this industry reported shipments of $149.6 million and employed 2,100 who averaged hourly earnings of $8.94. Tennessee's employees averaged the lowest hourly wage at $8.

INDUSTRY INFORMATION SOURCES

Darnay, Arsen J., editor, *Manufacturing USA: Industry Analyses, Statistics, and Leading Companies,* Detroit: Gale Research, Inc., 1992.

—Valerie E. Wilson

SIC 3399

PRIMARY METAL PRODUCTS, NOT ELSEWHERE CLASSIFIED

This category covers establishments primarily engaged in manufacturing primary metal products, not elsewhere classified, such as nonferrous nails, brads, and spikes, and metal powder, flakes, and paste.

Total product share of the primary metal products industry is split into three major groups: metal powders, paste, and flakes claim 68.8 percent of the industry; other primary metal products, not elsewhere classified, claim 20.6 percent of the industry; and primary metal products, not specified by kind, claim 10.6 percent of the industry. The value of shipments grew from $938 million in 1982 to $1.76 billion in 1988. Capital investment averaged $47.5 million between 1982 and 1987, but jumped to $101.8 million in 1988.

Average hourly wages did not continually climb during the 1980s. In 1982 the average hourly wage was $9.57, which increased to $10.91 by 1985. In 1986 this wage fell to $10.48, climbing to $10.77 by the end of 1987. However, the average hourly wage reported in 1988 fell to $10.22, its lowest since 1983. The total number of establishments in 1982 was 249, 80 of which employed 20 or more employees. The total number of establishments fell to 187 in 1986, but the number of establishments employing more that 20 grew to 93. By 1988, the number of establishments rebounded to 258, 112 of which employed more than 20.

Seventy-four of the leading companies engaged in this industry in 1991 realized total sales of $1.51 billion and employed 12,900 people. The Hoeganaes Corporation of Riverton, New Jersey, had an estimated sales volume of $130 million in 1991 while employing 500 people. Keystone Carbon Company of St. Marys, Pennsylvania, reported sales of $100 million and employment of 1,300 people. SSI Technologies Incorporated of Janesville, Wisconsin, reported sales of $70 million and employed 600 people. Eutectic Corporation of Flushing, New York, reported sales of $65 million and employed 500 in 1991. Federal-Mogul Corporation of Romulus, Michigan, reported sales of $60 million and employed 600 people.

As the 21st century approached, the employment levels of many occupations in the primary metal products industry, which includes nonferrous foundries and heat treatment facilities, are expected to decrease. Those occupations expected to face reductions of more than 25 percent include miscellaneous hand workers, electricians, metal pourers, metal/plastic machine workers, furnace operators, and welders. Those occupations expected to face reductions between 10 percent and 25 percent include blue collar worker supervisors, general laborers, heat treating machine operators, furnace operators, truck and tractor operators, crushing and mixing machine operators, inspectors, crane operators, material movers, machine tool workers, secretaries, machine feeders, science and mathematics technicians, material moving equipment operators, and metal molding machine operators. Sales workers will be in demand, as the employment level in this occupation is expected to increase by 12.5 percent by the year 2000.

Pennsylvania's 23 establishments shipped $197.8 million in primary metal products during 1987 and employed 2,100 people, earning an average of $12.00 per hour. Michigan's 15 establishments shipped $48.8 million and employed 400 people, averaging $10.40 per hour. Tennessee's 6 establishments shipped $45.8 million and employed 500 people, earning $6.86 per hour.

INDUSTRY INFORMATION SOURCES

Darnay, Arsen J., editor, *Manufacturing USA: Industry Analyses, Statistics, and Leading Companies,* Detroit: Gale Research, Inc., 1992.

—Valerie E. Wilson

Fabricated Metal Products, Except Machinery/Transportation Equipment

METAL CANS AND SHIPPING CONTAINERS

The metal can and shipping container industry includes companies engaged in the manufacture of metal cans from purchased materials, primarily steel and aluminum. The majority of the cans and containers produced in this industry are used to package various foods and beverages. Foil containers are excluded from this classification.

INDUSTRY SNAPSHOT

In 1992 U.S. metal can manufacturers produced over 125 billion cans, worth approximately $13 billion, and paid about $1.3 billion in salaries to over 35,000 U.S. workers. In the early 1990s, can manufacturers experienced slow overall growth in a weak domestic economy, and while aluminum can shipments rose steadily, steel can production stagnated. The long term outlook for the maturing metal can industry was generally optimistic in the mid-1990s. In an effort to boost profits, competitors were striving to exploit burgeoning foreign markets, new production technologies, and recycling opportunities. Employment in the industry, however, was expected to decline as producers automated production and moved facilities to foreign countries in which labor was less expensive.

ORGANIZATION AND STRUCTURE

The metal can industry was divided along the lines of the raw material used in manufacturing: steel and aluminum. Of the two types of cans, steel proved less expensive to produce, easier to heat, and stronger, while aluminum offered a greater strength-to-weight ratio, making it less expensive to transport. Moreover, consumers generally preferred aluminum cans over steel for some products, particularly beverages. Technological advances in the recycling industry generally applied to aluminum rather than steel cans.

The manufacture of steel cans typically involved three pieces—a top, bottom, and body. The body of the can was rolled and then soldered, welded, or cemented at the seam, and the can's top and bottom were later mounted to the ends of the body. Tin-plated steel cans, on the other hand, were generally constructed from two pieces, including a body and bottom, which were stamped and drawn from one piece of metal, and a top that was later attached. Aluminum cans were also produced from two pieces of metal, but usually featured a slight ''neck'' at the top of the body, which reduced the amount of material needed.

Because of its packaging properties, steel was used to produce about 95 percent of all food cans and containers made from metal in the early 1990s. steel also comprised about 50 percent of all non-food metal containers and about four percent of beverage cans. During this time, steel can manufacturers created about 30 to 35 billion cans from four million tons of steel per year. Eight billion vegetable cans, which accounted for 25 percent of the entire steel can market, were the largest single segment. The second largest market for steel cans was pet food, which required about 3.8 billion steel cans per year. Other significant market segments included: soft drinks (nine percent of steel can demand); aerosol cans (eight percent); fruit and fruit juices (eight percent); seafoods (five percent); and baby food (3.1 percent).

Aluminum cans were used primarily as beverage containers, largely because they were recyclable and held a greater appeal for consumers. In the early 1990s, aluminum can manufacturers annually produced about 95 billion containers weighing over 1.5 million tons. Aluminum can manufacturers used more aluminum than any other U.S. industry, providing 97 percent of all metal cans used in the beverage industry. Of containers used by soft drink manufacturers, 50 percent were made of aluminum, while about 45 percent of the beer industry's containers were aluminum. Less than three percent of the aluminum cans manufactured were used to contain food items, such as fruit juices, pet foods, and meat products.

Recycled cans provided an important source of production material for manufacturers. In 1992, the equivalent of 68 percent of all aluminum cans and 50 percent of steel cans produced in the U.S. were recycled. While both steel and aluminum cans were nearly 100 percent recyclable, aluminum can manufacturers favored the process due to the high price of new aluminum, which was nearly double that of steel. For example, the production of one pound of aluminum typically required an energy intensive process and four to five pounds of bauxite. Recycling, on the other hand, saved 95 percent of the energy necessary to produce finished aluminum, and eliminated altogether the mining, shipping, refining, and reduction processes. While new steel production was a less expensive process, many steel can producers were also using recycled materials, given its cost-effectiveness and the country's increasing concern for environmental conservation.

BACKGROUND AND DEVELOPMENT

The canning industry traces its origins to 1809, when French confectioner Nicolas Appert developed a method for preserving food, using glass jars that had been boiled in water. The ability to keep raw food from spoiling over long periods of time proved an important discovery, of particular benefit to French troops at war during this time. The basic canning principles developed by Appert closely resembled canning processes still used in many applications in the 1990s; carefully prepared raw food was sealed in a container, heated to a predetermined temperature to destroy spoilage organisms, and then cooled.

The glass bottle was eventually replaced by the tin can in a procedure patented in England by Peter Durand. While canning technology reached the United States in 1820, the tin-coated steel container did not gain widespread use in America until 1939. In 1861, Isaac Solomon discovered that adding sodium chloride to the preserving and canning process allowed for a longer shelf life. Subsequent advancements in canning during the Civil War hastened industry growth.

The canning industry experienced rapid proliferation beginning in the early 1900s, when advancements in can and glass jar technology lowered costs and improved canning reliability. For instance, soldered seams, which sometimes contaminated the food, were replaced by more reliable welding techniques during this time. Furthermore, the development of new machinery allowed producers to manufacture and fill mass quantities of cans.

Progress in can coatings and preservatives during the 1950s, among other technological breakthroughs, helped establish the United States as a world leader in the canning industry. By 1965, in fact, the United States was producing about 1.7 billion cans per year. The canning industry continued to enjoy high growth rates over the next two decades, as potential uses for the traditional steel can increased dramatically, most notably perhaps as A container for carbonated bever-

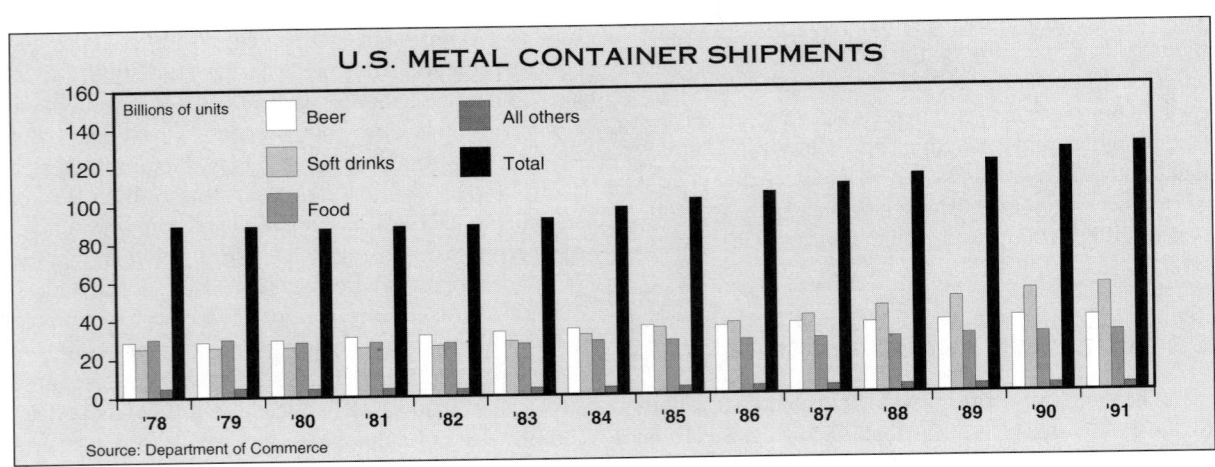

U.S. METAL CONTAINER SHIPMENTS

Billions of units

Beer   All others   Soft drinks   Total   Food

Source: Department of Commerce

ages. Although carbonated beverages constituted a negligible market for cans in the 1960s, by 1975 manufacturers were producing over 26 billion beverage cans per year, eclipsing the use of cans for food.

However, while the market for cans expanded, alternative packaging methods began offering stiff competition. Plastic and aluminum containers, which were developed into viable canning techniques during the early 1960s, began to enjoy widespread use in the 1970s. Because they offered price, weight, and convenience advantages important to beverage producers, aluminum cans quickly began to overtake that market segment. Furthermore, in 1974, Reynold's Metals Co. developed a pull tab for the aluminum can that remained attached to the can after opening. This innovation proved safer than the traditional steel pull-tab and also produced less litter, making the aluminum can especially attractive to the beverage market.

The market for metal beverage cans continued to escalate in the 1980s—from about 50 billion cans produced in 1980 to nearly 95 billion by 1990—and aluminum cans captured an increasing share of the market. Having entered the industry in 1961, aluminum's market share reached 79 percent by 1975, 82 percent by 1980, and over 95 percent by 1990. Furthermore, the beverage can market had grown to dominate the entire can industry. By the early 1990s, nearly three times more aluminum cans than steel cans were being produced. Plastic containers, which accounted for more than 25 percent of all food container production, were also competing for can consumers.

During this time, the introduction of the aluminum can recycling industry augmented the popularity of the aluminum can. The amount of aluminum cans recycled annually leapt from about 300 million pounds in 1979 to over one billion in 1981 and to nearly two billion by 1991.

Although they had effectively been nudged out of the beverage can industry, steel can manufacturers continued to control the food and consumer products can market. Throughout the 1980s and early 1990s, steel cans represented approximately 95 percent of that market. By the mid-1990s, however, steel container revenues were in decline, due largely to increased competition from microwave and frozen food products that utilized plastic packaging. During this time, shipments of steel cans and containers stagnated between 4.1 and 4.5 billion tons.

CURRENT CONDITIONS

U.S. aluminum can manufacturers faced a slow economy and a mature domestic market in the mid-1990s. Growth in this segment of the industry slowed to 3.9 percent in 1990, 2.5 percent in 1991, and just over three percent in 1992. Furthermore, beer sales, which accounted for about 50 percent of aluminum can demand in 1993, were expected to drop throughout the decade, and the use of new plastic 12- and 16-ounce containers threatened to replace the aluminum can in other markets. Nevertheless, aluminum can makers were encouraged by low aluminum prices that prevailed in the early 1990s—the result of an influx of cheap foreign ingot and sheet aluminum.

In addition to the industry-wide maturation of markets, steel can manufacturers in particular were challenged by slight gains experienced by producers of aluminum and plastic containers. Shipments of steel containers posted disappointing declines of 4.4 percent in 1991 and 5.7 percent in 1992, following nearly a decade of stagnation. The most notable blow to the industry was delivered in 1993, when Bev-Pak Inc., one of the nation's largest remaining producers of steel beverage cans, announced plans to switch to aluminum cans. Weirton Steel Corp. also announced its decision to end marketing efforts of steel cans.

In addressing the effects of a mature domestic market for metal cans, manufacturers tried several tactics, including: increasing productivity through new automation processes and information systems; exploiting international markets; diversifying existing product lines to appeal to niche market groups; and developing new product technologies that would broaden metal can markets. Diversification of existing product lines proliferated in the early 1990s, as companies began offering new container designs—such as cans with fluted sides or smaller tops—that helped differentiate products on the market.

INDUSTRY LEADERS

The largest U.S. manufacturer of metal cans in the early 1990s was the American National Can Co., based in Chicago. With 20,000 employees and sales of $4.5 billion in 1991, American National was the industry's undisputed leader. Crown Cork and Seal Co., Inc., of Philadelphia, was the second largest firm, with annual sales in excess of $3 billion and over 17,000 workers. Reynold's Metals Co., of Richmond, Virginia, which had sales of $1.9 billion in 1991, edged out the fourth place competitor, Ball Corp., of Muncie, Indiana. Ball garnered $1.4 billion in 1991 sales and employed 12,500 workers in its diversified operations.

Although these four companies were much larger than any of their competitors, their revenues represented a wide variety of operations outside of metal can manufacturing. The metal can industry as a whole remained relatively diversified, supporting several firms that generated revenues of less than $50 million and employed fewer than 500 employees. Like other maturing business sectors, however, the industry was becoming more consolidated in the early 1990s. Between 1982 and 1991 the number of metal can manufacturing companies declined from 397 to 345.

WORK FORCE

Increased productivity in the industry prompted a reduced work force, and between 1982 and 1990, industry employment declined from about 50,000 to around 35,000. This trend was expected to continue through the 1990s, fueled by increased automation and the movement of production facilities to loosely regulated, low-wage paying countries, such as Mexico. Jobs for machinery mechanics, which accounted for ten percent of the work force in 1993, were expected to decline by about 20 percent between 1990 and 2005. Positions for machine forming operators and tenders (7.4 percent of the work force) were expected to see declines in work force of over 45 percent during the same period. In fact, every occupation in the industry would likely plunge by ten to 50 percent, with most job opportunities—including those for top executives and managers—decreasing by at least 30 percent.

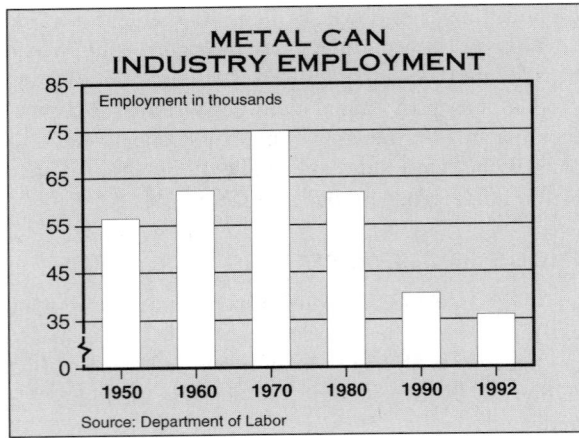

METAL CAN INDUSTRY EMPLOYMENT

Employment in thousands

Source: Department of Labor

Nevertheless, in the early 1990s, the metal can industry was more productive, paid higher wages, and invested more money in new products and facilities than most other U.S. manufacturing industries. Wages per hour, for instance, averaged over $15 in the late 1980s, compared to an average of just over $10 per hour offered by many manufacturing industries. Moreover, investment per worker neared $10,000, while all manufacturing industries averaged just $5,500.

AMERICA AND THE WORLD

Foreign food and beverage markets offered huge growth potential for U.S. canners, particularly aluminum can producers, who stood to benefit from the global shift away from steel cans. While 50 percent of all beverage cans produced outside the U.S. were steel in 1992, U.S. aluminum canners, operating the most technologically advanced and productive plants in the world, were poised to gain market share as other countries sought the environmental benefits associated with aluminum.

Foreign markets provided excellent opportunities for savvy U.S. exporters. Total U.S. food and beverage exports grew 23 percent between 1990 and 1992. Exports of some commonly canned items, including condensed milk, tripled. During this time, soft drink and carbonated water exports shot up over 63 percent, overall beverage exports represented growth of 48 percent, and preserved fruit and vegetable exports increased by about 32 percent.

RESEARCH AND TECHNOLOGY

One of the most notable advances among metal can manufacturers in the early 1990s was the development of thinner aluminum. By adjusting can shapes and production methods, manufacturers were successfully "lightweighting" and "downgauging" cans that were cheaper to produce and transport. The fluted can body was one example of an innovation in this area, as was the "202" beverage can, which sported a top that was one quarter of an inch smaller than most beverage cans used in 1993. Furthermore, Ball Corp. developed a spin-flow necking process that slimmed down both ends of its aluminum cans and thereby reduced the amount of aluminum required for manufacture as well as the amount of energy required in the production process.

Several steel beverage can developments also occurred in the early 1990s, as some producers tried to revive that market. The Japanese introduced a coffee can with a transparent window and steel cans with built-in self-heating mechanisms. In 1992, one Japanese firm introduced the "Toyo Ultimate Can," a two-piece steel can that was lighter than conventional steel cans and had a polyester rust-free coating. Despite this and other advances in steel can technology, however, most countries, including Japan, were switching to aluminum in the mid-1990s.

INDUSTRY INFORMATION SOURCES

"821 Billion Cans Can't Be Wrong," *Beverage World,* October 1993.

Boustead, I., and G. F. Hancock, *Energy and Packaging.* New York: John Wiley & Sons, 1981.

"Canmaking: Ball Puts a New Spin on Lightweighting Cans," *Packaging Digest,* September 1993.

Can Shipment Report 1988. Washington, D.C.: Can Manufacturers Institute, 1988.

"Japan Brews Up New Packages," *Prepared Foods,* May 1993.

Larson, Melissa, "New Marketing Ideas Come in Cans," *Packaging,* April 1993.

Levandoski, Robert C., "Here Comes the Light-Weight 202 Narrow-Neck Soft Drink Can," *Beverage Industry,* April 1993.

Levandoski, Robert C., "It's a Packaging War," *Beverage Industry,* July 1993.

Oman, Bruce, "Who Didn't Know That," *Beverage World,* May 1993.

"Packaging Outlook," *Purchasing World,* April 1990.

Sfiligoj, Eric, "Metal Cans: Supply-Side Economics," *Beverage World,* June 1992.

"Steel and Aluminum Cans," *Packaging,* July 1990.

Stundza, Tom, "Metal Cans: Lusting for Market Share," *Purchasing,* February 22, 1990.

Suda, Rieko, "Japan Beverage Firms Tilt to Aluminum," *Journal of Commerce and Commercial,* December 7, 1992.

"Time to Sing the Requiem of the Can of Steel?" *Beverage World's Periscope,* June 30, 1993.

Walker, Tracey L., "Japanese Unveil 'Ultimate' Beverage Can at Bev-Pak," *Beverage Industry,* June 1992.

—Dave Mote

SIC 3412

METAL SHIPPING BARRELS, DRUMS, KEGS, AND PAILS

This category includes establishments primarily engaged in manufacturing metal shipping barrels, drums, kegs, and pails.

This metal shipping barrels, drums, kegs, and pails industry has changed little since 1982. The value of shipments has remained fairly flat, while employment levels have dropped slightly. There were 161 establishments in the industry in 1988, employing 8,200 people, of which 77 percent were production workers. When compared to other forms of manufacturing, this industry paid lower-than-average hourly wages of $9.74 in 1988 (the average was $10.66). Carbon and alloy steels are the most heavily consumed

materials, while aluminum claims a small portion of the market. Steel shipping barrels and drums account for nearly 65 percent of the industry's market share, with steel pails claiming 18.5 percent of the market. The remainder of the market is split between non-specific barrels, drums, and pails.

The top 59 companies in this industry employed 7,100 people and had a combined total sales of $962.5 million in 1991. The top five industry leaders are spread throughout the United States. Container Products Incorporated of Southfield, Michigan reported sales of $85 million and employed 500 people. Imacc Corporation of Oakland, California employed 600 people and reported sales of $70 million. Evans Industry Incorporated of Harvey, Louisiana reported $63 million in sales and employed 300 people. Nesco Steel Barrel Company of Granite City, Illinois reported sales of $49 million and employed less than 100 people. Myers Container Corporation of Oakland, California reported sales of $45 million and employed 300 people.

Five states hold the majority of the industry's establishments and sales. Ohio's 21 establishments shipped $150.4 million worth barrels, drums, and pails in 1987, while employing 1,300 people. Employing 1,000 people, New Jersey's nine establishments shipped $115.5 million. California's 15 establishments shipped $106.1 million and employed 800 people. Texas's 13 establishments shipped $104.7 million and employed 700 people. Pennsylvania's 11 establishments shipped $66.2 million and employed 400 people. California workers averaged the highest wages in 1987, at $11.64 per hour. Texas hourly workers were paid the lowest, at $7.62 per hour.

Employment levels of most occupations in this industry are expected to decline approaching the year 2000. Those facing reductions of over 17 percent are machine forming operators, general laborers, machine feeders, blue collar worker supervisors, inspectors, truck operators, metal/plastic workers, machine tool workers, assemblers, hand packers, packaging machine operators, punching machine operators, material handlers, secretaries, miscellaneous machine operators, welding machine setters, and sheet metal workers.

With increased global competition, cost cutting and customer service have become industry-wide priorities. As a response to these new priorities, Kraft General Food's Atlantic Gelatin Division recently implemented a new shipping drum design, engineered by the Greif Brothers Corporation. The design departs from the traditional cylindrical style with a cube-shaped drum. The new drums have convex sides with rounded corners. Kraft's division has reported savings of hundreds of thousands of dollars in shipping costs, because truck trailers can hold 640 cubic drums, opposed to 500 cylindrical drums. Storage is another area where cubic drums find financial advantage.

INDUSTRY INFORMATION SOURCES

Darnay, Arsen J., ed., *Manufacturing USA: Industry Analyses, Statistics, and Leading Companies,* Detroit: Gale Research, Inc., 1991.

Eckhouse, Kimberly, "Shaped-up Shippers More Space and Cost Efficient," *Food Processing,* May 1993.

—Valerie E. Wilson

SIC 3421

CUTLERY

This category includes establishments primarily engaged in the manufacture of items such as pocket knives, safety razors, razor blades, straight razors, table cutlery, scissors, shears, manicure tools, kitchen and butcher knives, and artisans' knives. Establishments primarily engaged in manufacturing precious metal cutlery and table cutlery with handles of metal are classified **SIC 3914: Sliverware, Plated Ware, and Stainless Steel Ware;** those manufacturing electric razors, knives, or scissors are classified in **SIC 3634: Electric Housewares and Fans;** those manufacturing hair clippers for human use are classified in **SIC 3999: Manufacturing Industries, Not Elsewhere Classified** and for animal use in **SIC 3523: Farm Machinery and Equipment;** and those manufacturing power hedge shears and trimmers are classified in **SIC 3524: Lawn and Garden Tractors and Home Lawn and Garden Equipment.**

INDUSTRY SNAPSHOT

Rated in 1872 by J.B. Hyde as one of America's "great industries," cutlery manufacturing has witnessed significant change during the 20th century. Instead of small craft shops producing innovative but simple utensils, modern cutlery firms are more likely to be mass producers of one or two extremely simple products which can be sold anywhere in the world. However, sales of the various cutlery products showed steady growth throughout the century, increasing form $37,002 in 1921 to $1.1 billion in 1987.

ORGANIZATION AND STRUCTURE

The industry can be divided into two main components: kitchen and table cutlery, and non-electric razors and razor blades. Shears and scissors comprise a third, but proportionately tiny segment of the industry.

Traditionally, the industry was centered in the New England area. In 1860 Massachusetts and Connecticut produced 81 percent of all cutlery manufactured in the United States. While still major players in the industry as late as 1987, these states dropped in rank behind Pennsylvania, New Jersey, New York, California, and Ohio according to the 1987 *Census of Manufactures,* published by the U.S. Department of Commerce.

The 1987 census forecasted 123 active companies with 126 establishments for 1988, but the industry underwent a major reorganization during the early 1990s, with many companies either merging with competitors or leaving the market. The census forecast called for shipments of $1.1 billion in 1988.

Most cutlery products are sold by retail chain stores, warehouse clubs, specialty stores or catalogue operations. Manufacturers supported retail sales with national advertising campaigns, promotional offers, and sales training programs.

Mass merchandisers like Wal-Mart, K-mart, Target and Bradlees accounted for 49 percent of all kitchen and table cutlery sales according to a 1993 *Weekly Home Furnishings Newspaper* article. Sales for that year were estimated at $350 million.

In 1993, disposable razors held 60 percent of the razor market, which hovered around $800 million. Scissors and shears manufacturing declined during the early 1990s. Half of the 12 companies operating in 1987 ceased operations by 1993. Their shipments totaled $51.8 million in 1987, but by 1993 two out of every three pairs of scissors or shears sold in the United States were imported.

BACKGROUND AND DEVELOPMENT

The production of quality cutting tools required skilled artisans, most of whom worked in the communities of Sheffield, England and Solingen, Germany. Because the cost to transport the finished product was small, early American efforts could not compete with the quality or price of imported products. The American industry was helped by a 20 percent ad valorem tax imposed in 1792 and an innovative machine-forged knife introduced in 1844. The U.S. industry continued to push for even higher tariffs in the 1890s with some success, but its greatest victory came during World War I. Between 1914 and 1919, all German products disappeared from the Americas along with most British manufactures. Tariff increases in 1922 solidified the industry gain, ensuring prosperity for the industry and high consumer prices, although the 1930s saw a shift in demand to lower-priced products.

One of the biggest problems for the industry was the quality of steel available. Sheffield set the standard with its invention of crucible steel in 1740. That process took imported Swedish ''blister'' steel, known for its consistent quality, and melted it in clay crucibles along with precise amounts of manganese, carbon, and other materials. The result was a steel well suited for knives and other blades. American firms imported this steel, thereby increasing their production costs, until late in the 19th century. At the time, American crucible steel proved unreliable and experiments with cold and hot rolled carbon steel produced an inferior product. In 1910 stainless steel in the form of an alloy of cobalt, chromium, and steel made its debut as the ''rustless steel,'' but the lack of accurate measuring instruments, like pyrometers and thermometers, along with the scarcity of skilled annealers to judge the preparation of the metal, often resulted in brittle knives or soft edges. However, technology and demand continued to evolve, and by 1930 a consistent material became available and competition prompted its almost universal use in many product lines. Half of all cutlery produced during the early 1930s used the new stainless steel mixtures of steel, chromium, and cobalt, molybdenum, silicon, vanadium or magnesium. Electric smelting furnaces provided the control necessary to produce high-quality steel consistently.

Meanwhile, the American mass production system made inroads into the cutlery plant, displacing expensive, hard-to-find craftsmen like grinders with automated machinery that required no special skills to operate. Generally firms specialized in a narrow range of products like butchers' knives or ax heads, but with excess manufacturing capacity available, especially just after World War I, many new firms entered the industry and produced cheaper knock-offs of the original products. The competition forced the established firms to expand their product lines and reduce inventory stock. At the same time, new product designs came and went as technology helped the product evolve.

The industry fought the competition and falling prices with manufacturers' associations like the American Cutlers Association, which was founded in 1870 in Greenfield, Connecticut. It established uniform pricing, discount rates, and a method of absorbing freight costs into the price structure. The result was the continued dominance of East Coast firms as the market expanded westward. After fading for a few years, the association reappeared during World War II as a government lobbying group.

The post-war period saw an influx of inexpensive Japanese and Chinese cutlery, along with a gradual reduction of import tariffs in the 1950s. The traditional centers of skilled trade for the industry gradually eroded as mass production techniques flooded the world markets. In the United States before tariff reductions, fifty domestic manufacturers supplied almost the entire country's demand for shears and scissors. By 1993, only six firms operated in the United States. Traditionally, cutlery manufacturers operated small plants in established rural communities, drawing on a base of family artisans. In 1933, more than half of all cutlery produced in the United States came from cities of less than 500,000 people; most of those communities had fewer than 2,500 people. However, new industrial strategies gave the advantage to large cities with sizable pools of unskilled labor. Even so, some older firms like those in the Connecticut Valley retained a large portion of the market for certain specialty knives and other quality cutlery.

CURRENT CONDITIONS

During the latter part of the 20th century, small firms continued to join or be absorbed by large, diversified corporations. By 1987, only 61 establishments in the cutlery industry listed any form of cutlery as their primary product, according to the *Census of Manufactures*. The other 80 produced cutlery as a secondary or even tertiary product line.

The industry saw signs of an upturn during the 1980s, however, as a newly favored domestic lifestyle promised increased demand for products like cutlery, particularly high-tech innovative products that emphasized increased convenience. ''Never-sharpen'' knife sets with a $50 to $100 price range set the pace, but consumers quickly showed a predilection for mid-range products. For instance, good-quality stainless steel flatware became the preferred alternative to silverware. At the same time, consumers insisted on brand-name products, but refused to pay high-end prices.

Industry reacted by consolidating production with universal products and reducing product lines to specialty, high-value, high-tech merchandise. In 1994, Gillette Company, the largest American razor manufacturer, announced it would reorganize its production arrangements by laying off 2,000 workers, or 6 percent of its work force, while hiring an equivalent number to increase production at other plants around the world. This strategy eliminated multi-product facilities, dedicating each plant to a specific product. Gillette's chairman and chief executive, Alfred Zeien, claimed the move was a continuation of his efforts to position the company as a global enterprise by producing universally accepted products which could be produced in large numbers and sold worldwide.

Other American cutlery firms became aware of the need to consider their global position with the introduction of ISO 9000 standards. Developed by the International Organization for Standardization, which was formed in Switzerland in 1946, the guidelines sought to reach across political boundaries and homogenize such industrial procedures as design, manufacturing, inspection, packaging, marketing, quality control, and measurement. European industry quickly moved to adopt ISO 9000 as the new international standard, but acceptance was slower in the United States.

INDUSTRY LEADERS

Most companies in this category were relatively small operations, with larger firms usually producing items in addition to cutlery. Some of the larger firms in the industry group include Gillette Company and American Safety Razor for the razor segment, Fiskars' Gerber Legendary Blades and Buck Knives for knife manufacturing, and Fiskars Inc. for scissors.

Gillette Company, the largest in the category, commanded a 65 percent share of the razor market as of 1991. Based in Boston, the firm began operations in 1901. Gillette employed 31,200 workers for total sales of $3.8 billion in 1991, with its shaver division bringing in sales of $290 million.

American Safety Razor of Verona, Virginia, was founded in 1989. It employed 900 people to produce sales of $142 million in 1991. Fiskars Inc. of Wassau, Wisconsin was founded in 1978 and employed 1,000 for scissors sales of $140 million in 1991. Its subsidiary, Fiskars Inc. Gerber Division produced $35 million worth of knives in 1991 under the name Gerber Legendary Blades. It was established in Portland, Oregon, in 1939.

WORK FORCE

Employment in the cutlery industry declined from 13,400 in 1972 to 10,500 in 1987. Meanwhile production increased from $428 million in 1972 to $1.1 billion in 1987. In its infancy, the cutlery industry had great difficulty in finding sufficient skilled artisans in the Americas. Instead it turned to Europe, particularly the cities of Sheffield and Solingen, to encourage the immigration of craftspersons. After 1900, the flow

dried up because wages had equalized between Europe and the United States and because such technical innovations as the grinding machine made the need for skilled workers less pressing. Because the trade required years of apprenticeship and intensive training, companies often contracted with experienced workers rather than train their own. In that system, a skilled artisan contracted with a cutlery manufacturer to produce an agreed upon quantity of product for a specified price. He then hired his own workers and purchased his own materials. That allowed many contracting artisans to apprentice their own children in the trade. The system later fell into disrepute and was criticized as a method of reducing costs to the company while forcing the worker into sweatshop-like conditions. Trade unions vehemently opposed the system.

Trade unionism began to flourish in the early 1880s as a depression in the industry prompted manufacturers to attempt to reduce wages. In 1884, workers began to strike, although no official union backed the labor action at that time. Unofficially, the Knights of Labor Assembly was commonly accused of inflaming the workers. Despite intense labor organization and decades of strikes, the cutlery manufacturers associations managed to resist unionization and its demands by standardizing wage and hiring policies throughout the industry. The final blow to skilled labor came with the industry-wide use of the grinding machine, which made the specialized artisans' skills obsolete.

AMERICA AND THE WORLD

The nature of the typical cutlery firm had changed dramatically by the 1990s. The small shop still existed, but was rare. Despite complaints of unfair competition and ''dumping'' from the traditional centers of the industry, accompanied by demands for ever-higher tariff protection, mass marketing firms in countries like China, Japan, Brazil, and Korea made steady inroads and forced the old firms to reassess their operations. Many failed, but some, like Westall Richardson of Britain, succeeded. Westall Richardson became Europe's largest producer of kitchen knives by 1987 and captured 33 percent of the British market. Most of its 400 employees were unskilled laborers; the company concentrated its expertise in engineering and marketing.

By the late 1980s the mecca of the industry, Sheffield, could only support a small number of specialized firms as well as an equally small collection of master cutlers, known as ''little Mesters.'' In the late 1980s, one of the few remaining cutlery factories in Sheffield, the Globe Works, received a £1.5 million historic restoration grant. Because the center was built as an integrated factory in 1825, it included facilities for every part of the cutlery manufacturing process, from charcoal-burning furnaces to grinding and finishing workshops. The grant was used to restore the workshops and manager's residence destroyed in a fire in 1970. Completion of the project was scheduled for spring of 1989. The restored works provided a site where the vanishing skills of the little Mesters could be passed on to later generations of crafters. Plans call for the complex to become a showplace for the industry and a training facility for the British Cutlery and Silverware Association.

Certainly the concept of specialization worked for the Swiss firm, Victorinox. The makers of the internationally renowned Swiss Army knife produced at least 4 million of their distinctive pocket knives annually as of 1984. Actual sales figures are a closely guarded secret. In addition to pocket knives, Victorinox makes kitchen and butcher's knives. Even Victorinox, however, felt threatened by foreign competition from mass-production factories. Cheap knock-offs of the original Swiss pocket knife appeared routinely in Taiwan and Japan, and the Far East, West Germany, Austria, and the United States were just as likely to have firms copying and marketing look-alike products. Even the Swiss Helvetia Cross appeared on the copies. Such copyright infringement invariably brought diplomatic protests, but the company found its only effective protection was to clearly brand "Victorinox, Switzerland, Stainless, and Rostfrie" on every knife it made.

Such careful branding, which also included date and place of manufacture, helped create the hobby of pocket knife collecting, which became one of the hottest new crazes in American antique collecting in the 1990s. With each knife clearly identified, value and collectibility could be determined and agreed upon easily.

RESEARCH AND TECHNOLOGY

The 20th century began with the introduction of stainless steel as the preferred metal in cutlery manufacturing. That led to mass production machinery and plant specialization as the old skills of the trade, geared to old metals, became increasingly obsolete. By the end of the century, stainless steel also faced the possibility of obsolescence as the industry sought high-tech replacement materials for increasingly rare and expensive natural resources like iron and aluminum. The new, computer-designed substances offered the advantages of being stronger, lighter, more durable, and easier to work with, which reduced the skill-level needed to form the finished product. As Robert

Newnham, professor of solid-state science at Pennsylvania State University, told *Time* magazine, "At one time, we had to settle for whatever Mother Nature gave us. Now if we're not satisfied we can go out and create our own materials." The materials were beginning to appear in 1990 in such products as ceramic scissors which never rusted and never got dull. The United States led the world in materials research for much of the century but by the last decade the Japanese were forging ahead. The American preoccupation with military and aerospace applications restricted research for industrial and consumer applications, but the Japanese targeted those areas specifically.

INDUSTRY INFORMATION SOURCES

"A New Edge for Cutlery," *Economist,* April 4, 1987, 48.

Census of Manufactures, 1987, Washington, DC: U.S. Department of Commerce, 1990.

"Cutlery: Slicing It Up," *Weekly Home Furnishing Newspaper,* April 19, 1993, C1.

Darnay, Arsen J., ed., *Manufacturing USA,* 2nd edition, Detroit: Gale Research, 1989.

"Disposable Razors Retain Their Broad Appeal," *Chain Drug Review,* November 22, 1993, 8.

"Gillette's Sensor Gets $175 Million Worldwide Launch," *Cosmetics International,* November 10, 1989.

Jacobson, Philip, "A Cutthroat Business," *Connoisseur,* December, 1984, 56.

McCarrol, Thomas, "Solid as Steel, Light as a Cushion," *Time,* November 26, 1990, 94-95.

Pereira, Joseph, "Gillette to Realign Global Facilities; Change Is Slated," *Wall Street Journal,* January 14, 1994, C17.

Rifkin, Glen, "Gillette Will Cut 2,000 Jobs during Next 2 Years," *New York Times,* January 11, 1994, D4.

Taber, Martha Van Hoesen, *A History of the Cutlery Industry in the Connecticut Valley,* Northhampton, MA: Smith College Dept. of History, 1955.

Uchitelle, Louis, "Gillette's World New: One Blade Fits All," *New York Times,* January 3, 1994, C3.

"U.S. Lags on Rigorous New Quality Standards," *American Cutlery Manufacturers Association Newsletter,* winter/spring, 1993.

Weisselberg, Tim, "'Little Mesters' Re-forged," *History Today,* December, 1988, 3-4.

White, Richard, "Pocketknives: The Newest Collecting Craze," *Antiques & Collecting Hobbies,* October 1990.

—Al Cook

SIC 3423

HAND AND EDGE TOOLS

Firms in this industry manufacture simple, edged hand-tools like files, axes, chisels, prying bars, rulers, soldering irons, tongs, rakes, and cutters for metal-working and woodworking. Saws and saw blades are manufactured in **SIC 3425: Saw Blades and Handsaws**, while metal cutting dies and power driven hand tools, attachments, and accessories appear under the major group for industrial and commercial machinery and computer equipment.

The industry provides basic hand tools for domestic use and for professional mechanics. In 1987, industry shipments reached $1.4 billion, according to the 1987 *Census of Manufactures*. The *Census* also lists 703 companies operating 773 establishments—186 of them with more than 50 employees. Only one firm had more than 1,000 employees.

Traditionally, production in this industry was centered in the New England area, paralleling the development of the cutlery industry, SIC 3421. In the early 1900s, Massachusetts and Connecticut commanded 47 percent of the hand and edge tool and cutlery industries. However, the shift toward mass-production techniques and away from a reliance on skilled craftsmen resulted in the establishment of the hand and edge tool industry in heartland states. The industry tended to follow the source of cheap materials and markets, differentiating it from cutlery by its marked westward migration. In 1987, the four main states producing hand and edge tools were Ohio, Minnesota, Connecticut, and South Carolina.

INDUSTRY LEADERS

Three of the largest companies by sales volume in the Hand and Edge Tool industry in 1993 were Stanley Works of New Britain, Connecticut, Snap-on Tools Corp. of Kenosha, Wisconsin, and Danahar Corp. of Washington D.C. In 1993 Stanley Works, founded in 1843, manufactured a variety of hardware and electrical products in several industries. Stanley employed 17,420 workers for total sales of $1.9 billion. Hand and edge tools were produced by its Stanley Air Tools Division.

Snap-on Tools, established in 1920, also produced a variety of tools and furniture. Snap-on Tools employed 7,200 workers in 1993 and grossed $881 million. And Danahar Corporation, founded in 1978, was manufacturing a variety of automotive and air conditioning parts and tools, testing equipment and indus-

trial measuring systems, and voting machines in 1993. Danaher employed 7,500 people and made total sales of $837 million.

Employment in the industry peaked in 1979 at 51,100, then dropped to 40,00 in 1983 before recovering to 42,000 by 1988. According to *Manufacturing USA*, the industry employed an average of 54 workers per establishment in 1988. That drop from a 1923 average of 79 employees per establishment indicated the growth of automation in the industry, as well as more efficient production techniques.

INDUSTRY INFORMATION SOURCES

Darnay, Arsen J., ed., *Manufacturing USA: Industry Analyses, Statistics, and Leading Companies*, Detroit: Gale Research Inc., 1989.

Taber, Martha Van Hoesen, *A History of the Cutler Industry in the Connecticut Valley*, Northhampton, MA: Smith College, 1955.

1987 Census of Manufactures: Industry Series, Washington: U.S. Department of Commerce, 1987.

— Al Cook

SIC 3425

SAW BLADES AND HANDSAWS

This category covers establishments primarily engaged in manufacturing handsaws and saw blades for hand and power driven saws. Establishments primarily engaged in manufacturing power driven sawing machines are classified in the major group for industrial and commercial machinery and computer equipment.

Shipments for the saw blades and handsaws industry in 1987 reached $682.5 million, according to the 1987 *Census of Manufacturers*. The 1987 Census lists 128 companies operating 139 establishments in this industry, 61 with more than 20 employees. Only two had more than 500 employees. Firms in this industry averaged 58 employees per establishment, according to *Manufacturing USA*.

Traditionally, production in the saw blades and handsaws industry was centered in the New England area of the United States, paralleling the development of **SIC 3421: Cutlery.** The shift towards mass-production techniques and away from a reliance on skilled craftsman resulted in the establishment of the industry in heartland states. The industry tended to follow the source of cheap materials and markets, differentiating it from cutlery by its marked westward migration. In 1987 the four main states producing saws and saw blades were Massachusetts, Oregon, Kentucky, and Virginia. They accounted for 45 percent of the employment in the industry.

Three of the largest companies by sales volume in the saw blades and handsaws industry in 1993 were Blount Inc. Oregon Cutting Systems of Portland, Oregon; Kasco Corp. of St. Louis, Missouri; and Rule Industries of Burlington, Massachusetts. Their listings in *Dunn & Bradstreet* indicate that Blount Inc. Oregon Cutting Systems, founded in 1947 as a subsidiary of Blount Inc. of Montgomery, Alabama, manufactured chain saws and accessories. It employed 1,000 workers for total sales of $180 million. Kasco Corp., founded in 1901 as a subsidiary of Bairnco Corp., manufactured $58.9 million worth of band saw blades for cutting meat and fish. It employed 486 workers. Rule Industries, founded in 1963, made a variety of saw blades, fasteners, hardware, electrical switches, and pump and pumping equipment. It employed 493 workers for total sales of $52 million.

Employment in the industry peaked in 1981 at 9,400 and again in 1986 at 9,300, but generally averaged about 8,000. According to *Manufacturing USA,* the industry employed an average of 58 workers per establishment in 1988. The challenge to the industry towards the end of the 20th century was to maintain a high level of precision for the cutting edges and to produce new metals and composites to cut the increasingly diverse range of hard-to-cut man-made materials. Modern blades must be able to last long periods of time, operating in unmanned, automatic feed industrial applications.

Sales in the saw industry were tied closely to the health of such industries as steel, housing, and lumbering, which used large quantities of saw blades and handsaws. Generally, in both America and Japan, the production of saws and blades increased steadily after World War II. Japanese exports went mainly to Asia, but North America took 27 percent of its production in 1990.

INDUSTRY INFORMATION SOURCES

Darnay, Arsen J., editor, *Manufacturing USA: Industry Analyses, Statistics, and Leading Companies,* Detroit: Gale Research Inc., 1989.

Morikawa, Naohide, *Business Japan,* "Continued Steady Growth for Saw/Knife Industry," January 1991, 52-53; "Industrial Saw and Knife Industry Regains Smooth Growth Pattern," January 1990, 100.

1987 Census of Manufactures—Industry Series, Washington, DC: U.S. Department of Commerce, 1987.

Taber, Martha Van Hoesen, *A History of the Cutlery Industry in the Connecticut Valley,* Northhampton, MA: Smith College, Department of History, 1955.

—Al Cook

SIC 3429

HARDWARE, NOT ELSEWHERE CLASSIFIED

This category covers establishments primarily engaged in manufacturing miscellaneous metal products usually termed hardware, not elsewhere classified. Establishments primarily engaged in manufacturing nuts and bolts are classifed in **SIC 3452: Bolts, Nuts, Screws, Rivets, and Washers;** those manufacturing nails and spikes are classified in the major group for primary metal industries; those manufacturing cutlery are classified in **SIC 3421: Cutlery;** those manufacturing hand tools are classified in **SIC 3423: Hand and Edge Tools, Except Machine Tools and Handsaws;** and those manufacturing pole line and transmission hardware are classified in industry group 364 (electric lighting and wiring equipment).

This industry manufactures a diverse range of products, including brackets, clamps, couplings, door locks, fireplace equipment, handcuffs, nut crackers, and piano hardware. In 1988 industry shipments reached $8.4 billion, according to *Manufacturing USA.* The 1987 *Census of Manufactures* lists 1,128 companies operating 1,240 establishments; 180 had more than 100 employees, and one had more than 1,000 employees. Firms in this industry averaged 70 employees per establishment, which is several more than the industrial average of 58.

Traditionally, production in this industry was centered in the New England area. Many small blacksmith shops produced simple but useful household items, known as "Yankee notions," of low grade iron and steel. The availability of rail and ship transport allowed for rapid distribution along the Eastern seaboard and the central United States. However, the shift toward mass production techniques and away from a reliance on skilled craftsman resulted in the migration of the industry to the Midwest. The industry tended to follow the source of cheap materials and markets, differentiating it from cutlery by its marked westward migration. The industry has adapted its production methods to the use of numerical control production (NC) with great success in both productivity and precision. In 1987, the four main states producing hardware in this industry were California, Michigan, Ohio and Illinois.

Three of the largest companies by sales volume in this industry in 1993 were Schlage Lock Company of San Francisco, California, Yale Security of Inc. of Charlotte, North Carolina, and Master Lock Co. of Milwaukee, Wisconsin. Schlage Lock Company, founded in 1974, manufactured $300 million worth of locks and lock sets in 1993 and employed 3,000 workers. Master Lock Co., a subsidiary of Masterbrand Industries, was founded in 1976. It manufactured $150.9 million worth of padlocks, locks, lock-sets, door locks, bolts, and checks in 1993 and employed 1,860 workers. Yale Security Inc. is a subsidiary of Yale & Valor Limited. Founded in 1987, it had sales of $189 million and employed 2,300 workers in 1993. It manufactured locks and lock sets as well as non-electric door opening and closing devices.

Both employment and sales in the industry increased steadily throughout the 1980s, but declined substantially with the general economic downturn near the end of the decade. The industry was particularly hurt by the soft housing market, since businesses in that sector use a substantial amount of hardware. By 1992, the hardware industry showed signs of recovery with an 11.7 percent increase in September sales over September 1991 and a 6.6 percent increase for the first nine months of 1992. Unemployment figures also showed signs of improvement.

INDUSTRY INFORMATION SOURCES

Census of Manufactures, 1987, Washington, DC: U.S. Department of Commerce, 1990.

Darnay, Arsen J., *Manufacturing USA,* 2nd edition, Detroit: Gale Research, Inc., 1989.

Gallagher, Terrence V., "Have We Turned the Corner?" *Hardware Age,* January, 1993, 11.

Taber, Martha Van Hoesen, *A History of the Cutlery Industry in the Connecticut Valley,* Northhampton, MA: Smith College Department of History, 1955.

—Al Cook

SIC 3431

ENAMELED IRON AND METAL SANITARY WARE

This category includes establishments primarily engaged in manufacturing enameled iron, cast iron, or pressed metal sanitary wares, such as bathtubs, sinks, toilets, and other bathroom and household plumbing fixtures. Non-metallic plumbing products are listed in **SIC 3088: Plastic Plumbing Fixtures, SIC 3261:** **Vitreous Sanitary Ware,** and **SIC 3469: Porcelain Enameled Kitchen, Household, and Hospital Ware.**

INDUSTRY SNAPSHOT

Metal sanitary ware manufacturers compete in the household, commercial, and industrial plumbing product markets, producing products made of cast iron, enameled iron and steel, and stainless steel. Traditionally, these markets have been directly influenced by the nation's construction markets and, therefore, are extremely cyclical. U.S. manufacturers' sales of plumbing fixtures totaled approximately $2.5 billion in the early 1990s. Iron and steel plumbing products accounted for 36 percent of the total market, with sales of approximately $900 million in 1987.

In recent years, the increased usage of plastic and fiberglass plumbing products has reduced the demand for iron and steel plumbing products. In response to this change, manufacturers have developed composite materials that combine the strength and durability of metal with the light weight and rust-proof features of plastic and fiberglass products. A steady demand for stainless steel products, especially kitchen sinks, has kept approximately 100 manufacturers in business since the 1980s, despite two severe slumps in the U.S. construction market.

ORGANIZATION AND STRUCTURE

Nearly a quarter of the 100 metal sanitary ware manufacturing establishments in the early 1990s were located in California. Other leading states included Ohio, Florida, Indiana, Illinois, and Texas. The industry employed approximately 7,300 people, producing an annual payroll of more than $200 million.

Traditional wholesale distribution of plumbing products to building contractors is supplemented by retail distribution of plumbing products to the do-it-yourself market. Traditionally, metal sanitary ware manufacturers distributed their products through independent wholesale distributors of building products. Any advertising was of a technical nature and was aimed at the knowledgeable plumbing professional. Recently, the growth of replacement/remodeling markets for building products has increased profitability of plumbing products marketed directly to the consumer. In response, manufacturers have expanded their marketing efforts, focussing on a consumer more concerned with function and style than with the technical specifications of the product.

BACKGROUND AND DEVELOPMENT

The fate of the plumbing producer is most directly tied to the health of the nation's new construction markets. The demand for new construction is labeled a leading indicator by economists because it provides insight into the future conditions of the overall economy. Hence, a decline in the demand for new construction usually precedes a slowdown in the nation's gross national product (GNP) growth. This held true in the recessions of 1982 and 1991, as construction activity began to decline a year before the rest of the economy slid into recession. Metal sanitary ware manufacturers felt the recessions early as well, as demand for metal sanitary wares fell with slowed construction activity.

During the 1980s, several trends in the construction industry impacted metal sanitary ware producers. Severe declines in construction activity in 1980 and 1982 caused many manufacturers to shut down. The number of metal sanitary ware manufacturing establishments dropped to 77 in 1982. However, after a severe decline, construction demand boomed in 1983 and 1984, as consumer optimism fueled demand for new houses. In addition, an unprecedented cut in the tax on capital gains implemented by President Ronald Reagan's administration suddenly made business investment in commercial offices, stores, residential condominiums, and apartments extremely attractive. As a result, demand for both residential and commercial plumbing products boomed in the mid-1980s. By 1987, 107 metal sanitary ware manufacturing establishments were in operation.

By the end of 1990, however, the construction industry suffered a serious decline, as housing starts fell to near record lows. The cause of the decline was primarily attributed to an oversupply of commercial office space and residential housing caused by the building spree of the middle of the decade. Analysts suggested that this glut in the supply of newly constructed properties would take many years to clear, holding down construction growth into the mid-1990s.

While metal sanitary ware manufacturers suffered through the latest downturn in construction, their decline was not as deep as was expected. This was attributed to plumbing ware manufacturers' success in the less cyclical home remodeling market. Expenditures for residential improvement, maintenance, and repairs grew rapidly during the second half of the 1980s, nearly doubling in only five years. The category continued to grow in 1991, despite an overall recession.

CURRENT CONDITIONS

Entering the 1990s, metal sanitary ware manufacturers faced a construction market in which slow growth was predicted for several years. This forced the industry to seek growth through other markets—mainly, the replacement and remodeling plumbing fixtures market. In addition, plumbing manufacturers faced a more environmentally-concerned consumer who demanded efficient, water conserving plumbing products.

An influence on the growth in remodeling and replacement markets for plumbing products was attributed to the increasing desire for homeowners to entertain within the home. This phenomenon, called "cocooning," was expected to affect plumbing ware manufacturers for many years to come. Especially fruitful for metal sanitary ware manufacturers was the increased emphasis on the kitchen and the basement in the scheme of the house. Stainless steel was the most popular material for kitchen and bar sinks primarily because of low-price and ease of installation for the do-it-yourself homeowner.

In the late 1980s, remodeling projects and do-it-yourself repairs became popular hobbies for many homeowners. Disgust over the high cost of plumbing repairs and the urge to modernize their bathrooms and kitchens led many people to undertake plumbing projects they would have avoided only a few years earlier. As a result, manufacturers often market installation guides to consumers in the form of books or videos.

On the other hand, the move toward larger bathrooms with jacuzzis and whirlpools threatened metal sanitary ware manufacturers' bathtub market. Shower stall and wall-surround bathtubs with whirlpool technology are not feasibly made using cast iron and enameled steel. In response, several metal sanitary ware manufacturers developed composite materials that combine the features of steel and cast iron with the light weight and ease of transportation and installation of plastics and fiberglass products. Acceptance of these composite materials should allow metal sanitary ware manufacturers to take advantage of demand for more luxurious bathtub products. The industry was successful in shifting its focus from bathtubs to the kitchen and sink markets. In fact, sales for the industry doubled in the 1980s, despite a fall in bathtub market share from 62 percent to 38 percent during the decade.

Stainless steel kitchen sink demand offset the decline in cast iron and enameled steel bathtub demand. While sales nearly doubled during 1980s, profit margins for the industry declined steadily. As a percentage of total costs, material costs grew from 42 percent to 52 percent during the decade. The decline in profit margins was the direct result of a skyrocketing increase in the cost of materials for stainless steel production.

Concern for the environment challenged metal sanitary ware manufacturers to use recycled metals and to provide more efficient products. Many states, for example, passed legislation requiring that all new toilets use only 1.6 gallons of water per flush as opposed to the traditional 3.5 gallons per flush.

INDUSTRY LEADERS

The two largest plumbing ware manufacturers, Kohler Company and American Standard, are private. Kohler has been private since its founding in 1873, while investors led a leveraged employee buy-out to privatize American Standard in 1988. Both companies produce a full line of plumbing products in all types of materials. Kohler Company produces the majority of its metal sanitary ware products at its corporate headquarters in Wisconsin. American Standard has subsidized it cast iron and enameled steel products with a composite material called "Americast."

The two companies have pushed the demand for luxurious bathroom items into increasingly expensive products. Each company offers computerized whirlpool systems that cost more than $30,000. In addition, these companies have extensive distribution systems to market their products throughout the world. These products are either exported from U.S. factories or produced in company-owned factories in other countries.

Other plumbing ware manufacturers include American Brands, Inc., Black & Decker Corporation, Eljer Industries, Inc., Elkay Manufacturing Co., Masco Corporation, Nortex, Inc., and UNR Industries. Elkay Manufacturing and UNR Industries compete almost solely in the stainless steel sink markets, while the others offer several lines of plumbing products.

WORK FORCE

The industry employed approximately 7,300 workers into the 1990s, 5,700 of whom were involved in production. The decrease in profit margins has caused production workers' wages to remain stagnant. Despite yearly productivity gains, workers' wages have barely kept up with inflation. Payroll costs as a percentage of total costs declined during the 1980s from 24 percent to 21 percent. Production workers' hourly wages have hovered around $11.00 since 1985.

AMERICA AND THE WORLD

The U.S. market for plumbing ware fixtures does not include a large percentage of imported products. The added cost of shipping large cast iron and enameled steel products overseas usually makes imports too expensive for the U.S. market. This lack of import competition has given U.S. producers of plumbing ware products a luxury that many other industries do not enjoy. On the other hand, metal sanitary ware manufacturers are limited in their exports for the same reasons. This makes U.S. producers highly vulnerable to the fluctuations of the domestic market for plumbing products.

The majority of U.S. trade in metal sanitary ware products occurs with Canada and Mexico. Transportation costs to these markets are minimal. Companies in the United States also compete in many overseas markets through foreign production in proximity to the particular market. Either through direct ownership of a plant on foreign soil, or through licensing agreements with foreign manufacturers, U.S. companies participate in foreign markets while eliminating expensive shipping costs.

The protection of U.S. metal sanitary ware producers has saved many domestic manufacturing jobs. Primarily, production job declines have been caused by productivity improvements. However, two significant occurrences threaten to change this in the 1990s. First, the stainless steel sink market is more open to foreign competition because these products are lightweight and, therefore, do not incur the high shipping costs of cast iron and enameled steel products. Secondly, the North American Free Trade Agreement (NAFTA) would give metal sanitary ware manufacturers access to low wage production workers without the large addition in shipping costs usually associated with foreign production.

INDUSTRY INFORMATION SOURCES

Krause, Clifford, "Conference Committee Approves an Energy Bill," *New York Times,* October 1, 1992.

Lehman, H. Jane, "Proposals Seek to Set Plumbing Product Standards," *Washington Post,* August 8, 1992.

"A New Use for Old Toilets," *New York Times,* April 7, 1991.

Stipp, David, "Cheap Retrofit Kits Save Toilet Water," *Wall Street Journal,* February 21, 1991.

U.S. Department of Commerce, *U.S. Industrial Outlook 1992,* Washington, DC: U.S. Department of Commerce, January 1992.

—Philip Jones

SIC 3432

PLUMBING FIXTURES AND FITTINGS

Companies that produce metal plumbing fixtures and parts make up the plumbing fixture and fittings industry. This classification also encompasses establishments engaged in the assembly of plastic components into fixtures and fittings. Companies that manufacture plastic, ceramic, earthenware, and other types of plumbing fixtures are classified in separate industries, as are firms that make steam or water line valves.

INDUSTRY SNAPSHOT

Although advanced plumbing systems have existed since 2000 B.C., metal pipes and fittings were not commonplace in the United States until the early 1900s, when they began playing an important role in the development of industrialized society. By 1993, sales of metal plumbing fittings approached $3 billion, representing industry employment of about 15,500.

As fixture manufacturers approached the close of the twentieth century, they looked forward to sustained market growth and increased profits. The industry had enjoyed steady expansion since the 1970s, despite economic recessions. To maintain profitability in 1993, competitors were introducing new products, increasing productivity, and taking advantage of propitious demographic trends.

ORGANIZATION AND STRUCTURE

Plumbing refers to the system of pipes, fixtures, and other apparatus in a structure that supplies water and removes liquid and waterborne wastes. The foremost role of an integrated plumbing system is to safely deliver and remove water, and fixtures and fittings must therefore conform to strict codes, regulations, and trade standards. Manufacturers of fixtures are also concerned with producing styles that appeal to consumers by reflecting current trends in home decoration.

Most plumbing fixtures and fittings are built for residential use. Primary residential applications include kitchens, bathrooms, gardens, and utility rooms. Fixtures also complement various commercial, industrial, and institutional plumbing systems. Manufacturing metals used by the industry include copper, brass, bronze, and iron. Most fixtures and fittings may be divided into one of four groups: traps, tubes, and drains; pipe fittings; faucets and toilets; and shower fixtures.

Basin drains usually incorporate traps or tubes. Traps are essentially drainage pipes with a bend, or trap, beneath the drain for holding water and preventing odors and gases from backing up out of the drain. P, J, and S shaped traps are commonly used for sinks, while drum and bottle-type traps, which are typically used for bathtub and kitchen drains, consist of a cylindrical metal box or settling basin attached to the waste pipe. Other types of traps include grease, laundry tray, and slop sink. Most traps incorporate a clean-out plug or screw to remove debris that is caught in the trap. Tubes are used to connect traps, garbage disposals, dishwasher drains, and other drains and devices. They come in a variety of shapes and materials to suit all applications and configurations.

Pipe fittings are used to connect pipes and tubes, and come in a multitude of shapes and sizes. Several categories of fittings exist. Nipples are used to extend a pipe and to provide proper threading for connection to other pipes. Couplings are used to join standard sizes of pipe. Similarly, floor flanges connect pipes to a wall, floor, or other flat surface. Elbow fittings make it possible to change the direction of a straight pipe. Reducers, when incorporated with couplings, provide a means of connecting different sized pipes. Three- and four-way tees allow a pipe to branch out into two or three other pipes, often of smaller size. Other common fitting types include return bends, flair and compression fittings, wye (Y) bends, slip joints, and ground joint unions.

Toilet fixtures and fittings include levers and other parts that control the flush and water inlet valves. The ballcock assembly is the primary mechanism that controls water supply in the tank and toilet. Faucets are available in several different forms. Compression faucets, common in residential plumbing, use a washer to control water flow and are operated by turning a lever, moving a ball, or shifting a handle. Fuller ball faucets work similarly, but use a ball stopper instead of a washer mechanism. Ground-key faucets use a copper plunger to regulate water flow. Sill cocks, which are designed to resist freezing, are heavy duty exterior faucets.

Standard shower heads are typically made of chrome-plated brass or plastic, and offer adjustable spray, swivel-ball joints, and self-cleaning rims. Massaging showerheads incorporate a diverting valve that allows for a pulsating action. Continental showers allow the shower head to be removed and used as a hand shower. Popular shower head enhancements include water-saving flow control mechanisms and anti-scald valves. Some regional building codes mandate inclusion of anti-scald valves in public facilities, as well as for showers in multi-family structures.

Sundry devices include water fountain heads, lawn hose nozzles and sprinklers, shower rods, various plumber's tools and supplies, water-saving devices, and anti-scald bath and shower valves. Special equipment of more durable material and incorporating a higher degree of technology is produced for hospitals, industrial plants, laboratories, and other niche markets.

Residential markets accounted for over 60 percent of the metal plumbing fixtures and fittings market in the 1980s. About 40 percent of that amount was attributable to maintenance, repair, additions, and alterations of single-family dwellings. Maintenance and repair of buildings represented about 12 percent of the market, while the remaining 27 percent of sales were divided amongst multiple commercial, industrial, and institutional sectors. Exports commanded around four percent of the market in the early 1990s.

Single lever sink and bathtub/shower controls represented 22 percent of industry production in the late 1980s. Two and three handle bath and shower fittings accounted for an additional nine percent of output. Miscellaneous lavatory fittings made up over 12 percent of the market, and sink faucets accounted for about ten percent. Drains and overflow devices made up only one percent of sales. Miscellaneous fittings, trim, and fixtures accounted for about 45 percent of industry shipments.

BACKGROUND AND DEVELOPMENT

Latrine-like receptacles with crude drains are known to have existed as long ago as 8,000 B.C. Advanced plumbing systems built of terra cotta and burned brick were used as early as 2,500 B.C. The first latrine with a water flushing reservoir dates back to 2,000 B.C. in the royal palace of the Minoans. Clay plumbing pipes were introduced by the Greeks in about 200 B.C., and, later, the Romans began developing complex plumbing infrastructure that incorporated the use of lead pipes. By 300 A.D., the Roman system was carrying over 50 million gallons of water per day to residents.

Advancements in plumbing technology languished after the fall of the Roman Empire until the seventeenth and eighteenth centuries. While cast iron pipes were introduced into plumbing in London in 1619, metal plumbing systems were not used on a significant scale in the United States until the nineteenth century. Between 1850 and 1900, the industry expanded rapidly, and by 1900, almost all U.S. towns with more than 2,000 residents had relatively advanced plumbing systems.

During the economic expansion that occurred in the United States after World War II, demand for metal fixtures and fittings escalated. Over the next three decades, massive increases in new single family homes, as well as growth in commercial and institutional structures, prompted a huge demand for all types of faucets, drains, fittings, and other fixtures. As the U.S. population skyrocketed, the percentage of families owning their own home also increased from about 45 percent in 1940 to nearly 65 percent by the late 1970s. By 1980, metal pluming fixture manufacturers were shipping about $1 billion worth of products each year.

Growth in the industry slowed in the late 1970s and 1980s, due to higher interest rates, demographic shifts, and other economic factors. Nevertheless, plumbing fitting and fixture manufacturers continued to report gains during the 1980s. Furthermore, the amount of plumbing fixtures used to build the average house during this time rose steadily. While most homes built prior to 1960 had only one bathroom, for instance, most homes built in the 1980s featured at least two baths. Moreover, kitchens became larger and utilized more elaborate fixtures than earlier homes, and new amenities, such as hot tubs and dual sink decks also helped the industry to sustain growth during this time. Importantly, the replacement market for existing home fixtures and fittings augmented the new home market.

From $1.3 billion in shipments in 1982, industry sales steadily rose to about $3 billion by 1991, representing an average annual growth rate of more than seven percent. At the same time, productivity in the industry increased. While industry employment remained stable at about 15,000, dollar shipments per worker jumped over 230 percent. Many producers were able to supplement sales of traditional metal fittings and fixtures with new synthetic fixtures, including plastics, which are classified in other standard industry categories.

CURRENT CONDITIONS

Faced with economic recession in 1989 and 1990, metal plumbing fixture and fitting manufacturers suffered temporary setbacks, and sales in 1990 grew only one percent over 1989 levels. Nevertheless, over the next two years, growth resumed a healthy eight percent per year. In the mid-1990s, manufacturers looked forward to several industry developments that promised to boost their earnings.

Renewed growth in housing starts was particularly encouraging for producers, as 1992 showed a 20 percent rise in new home construction—the first increase in five years. Furthermore, the trend toward larger and more luxurious bath and kitchen amenities appeared to be proliferating. The average new home in the early 1990s included 2.5 baths, while the master bath was generally 30 percent larger than those of 25 years ago. Moreover, a 1993 *Builder* magazine survey of new home buyers indicated that consumers were seeking more distinctive bath and kitchen fixtures.

Renewed growth in maintenance, alteration, and additions markets also contributed to growth in the industry. General home improvement expenditures by consumers rose 5.4 percent in 1992, and were expected to rise an average of 6.5 percent through 1997. Home remodeling expenditures were expected to grow by about five percent in 1993.

Manufacturers hoped that 1992 legislation would boost replacement market sales, as well as sales of new water-flow devices. The National Energy Policy Act, passed by Congress in 1992, set maximum water-flow rates allowed for residential and commercial fixtures. Residential regulations, which were scheduled to take effect in 1993, allowed only 1.6 gallons-per-flush (gpf) for water closets, 1 gpf for urinals, and 2.5 gallons per minute for faucets and showerheads. Similar commercial regulations would take effect in 1996.

Fixture and fitting producers were also benefitting in the mid-1990s from new distribution channels. Discount hardware and home center warehouse stores were quickly becoming a primary outlet for consumer sales, as increasing numbers of consumers sought to install and repair plumbing themselves in order to avoid large mark-ups charged by plumbers and traditional hardware stores. HQ, Home Depot, Menards, and Builder's Square were a few of the massive warehouse chains that were bringing new buyers into the market.

Despite general optimism in the industry in the 1990s, some manufacturers faced potentially harmful publicity. Lawsuits filed in 1992 against 16 faucet manufacturers were brought to court the following year. Two environmental groups and the California attorney's office sued American Standard, B&K Industries, U.S. Brass, Kohler, and several other large fixture and fitting companies, charging that 19 brands of faucets leached lead into drinking water, violating California's drinking water laws.

Metal plumbing fitting and fixture manufacturers were expected to sustain the moderate growth they achieved throughout the 1980s. Industry analysts suggested that continued low interest rates, combined with a mild economic recovery, would boost home construction and renovation activity, resulting in stronger sales. Nevertheless, the growing popularity of plastic fixtures demanded that metal fixture manufacturers diversify their product lines or risk losing valuable market share.

Foreign trade was also expected to play a slightly greater role in the industry. By 1992, exports had grown to represent approximately four percent of American sales, a trend that manufacturers hoped would continue throughout the decade. At the same time, manufacturers faced the possibility of increased competition from imported fixtures and fittings, particularly from Canada, Mexico, and the Pacific Rim.

INDUSTRY LEADERS

Masco Corp. and its Delta Faucet division, the largest company participating in the industry, generated over $3.5 billion in 1991 sales from its diversified operations. The Michigan-based company employed over 42,000 workers. Kohler, of Wisconsin, was the second largest producer in the industry with $1.24 billion in sales and about 14,000 employees. Nibco Inc., of Indiana, placed third with revenues of $240 million and 2,700 workers. Other leading competitors included Moen Inc., of Ohio, Black and Decker Corp., of California, and Sterling Plumbing Group Inc., of Illinois.

WORK FORCE

In the early 1990s, about 170 companies employed approximately 16,000 workers in the metal plumbing fixture and fitting industry. Several of the larger companies in the industry, however, were highly diversified and manufactured products in several industry classifications. In comparison to many other manufacturing sectors, the plumbing fixture and fitting industry was specialized and protected from new entrants by high start-up costs and established brand names.

Although total employment decreased between one and five percent per year between 1987 and 1991, the work force grew by nearly eight percent in 1992. Similar job growth was predicted for 1993. Despite these increases, however, the average wage climbed only .5 and one percent in 1991 and 1992, respectively. Furthermore, The Bureau of Labor Statistics estimated that most manufacturing jobs in the industry would decline by ten to 25 percent between 1990 and 2005, due to increased automation and the movement of some manufacturing operations to foreign countries. Jobs for assemblers and most machine operators were expected to realize the greatest decreases. However, the number of available positions for some machinists sales staff were expected to rise.

RESEARCH AND TECHNOLOGY

Fitting and fixture manufacturers introduced new products and designs to keep up with changing consumer tastes and to conform with new regulations and standards. In the mid-1990s, some of the most important developments included water-saving devices, such as aerators and restrictors. One product, called ''Flush Wise,'' allowed a toilet to flush using only a preset fraction of the water actually held in the toilet tank. The easily installed device operated without reducing the pressure or scouring action of the water, according to the manufacturer.

New fixture packaging designs were also helping sales in 1993. Price Pfister Inc. was able to drastically reduce a 30 percent rejection rate for its packaged parts, caused by pieces that were scratched during shipping. The new boxes reduced damage and allowed consumers to fully view the parts before purchasing them. Moen, Inc. also developed a new packaging system.

Other products introduced in 1993 included faucets with built-in soap dispensers, urinals with integrated electronic flushing devices, faucet systems with infrared sensors for water control, digital temperature readout showers, and new ''push-on'' fixtures.

INDUSTRY INFORMATION SOURCES

Arnold, Don, ''Record Crowds See Latest HVAC/Plbg Electronics,'' *Contractor*, June 1993.

''Buying Imports vs. Waving Old Glory'' *Contractor*, May 1992.

Cory, Jim, ''Big Chains Move into Small Markets,'' *Hardware Age*, July 1993.

Fletcher, June, ''Kitchens & Master Suites,'' *Builder*, November 1993.

Halverston, Richard, ''Water-Saving Devices Offer Growth Potential,'' *Discount Store News*, August 17, 1993.

''Home Centers: Source or Scourge,'' *Contractor*, June 1993.

''Home Improvement Market Growth Projected at 6.5% Annually,'' *Contractor*, August 1993.

Hooper, Larry R., ''Energy Bill Would Conserve Water, Even Cold Water,'' *Contractor*, July 1992.

Hoover, Jon, ''Building Sales with the Basics,'' *Hardware Age*, April 1993.

Inlow, Alan R., ''Plumbing Steps that Save Water,'' *Journal of Property Management*, September/October 1992.

''New Box, Cushioning Helps Faucets Arrive Safely,'' *Packaging*, October 1993.

''Plumbing Supplies,'' *Do-It-Yourself Retailing*, May 1992.

Smith, Roy, ''Electronics Take Over Plumbing at ISH,'' *Contractor*, June 1993.

U.S. Industrial Outlook 1993, Washington, D.C.: U.S. Department of Commerce, January 1993.

—Dave Mote

SIC 3433

HEATING EQUIPMENT, EXCEPT ELECTRIC AND WARM AIR FURNACES

This category covers establishments primarily engaged in manufacturing heating equipment, except electric and warm air furnaces, including gas, oil, and stoker coal fired equipment for the automatic utilization of gaseous, liquid, and solid fuels. Establishments primarily engaged in manufacturing warm air furnaces are classified in **SIC 3585: Air-Conditioning and Warm Air Heating Equipments and Commercial and Industrial Refrigeration Equipment;** cooking stoves and ranges are classified in **SIC 3631: Household Cooking Equipment;** boiler shops primarily engaged in the production of industrial, power, and marine boilers are classified in **SIC 3443: Fabricated Plate Work (Boiler Shops);** and those manufacturing industrial process furnaces and ovens are classified in **SIC 3567: Industrial Process Furnaces and Ovens.**

INDUSTRY SNAPSHOT

The heating equipment industry is comprised of firms primarily engaged in manufacturing heating devices other than electric equipment and warm air furnaces. Residential and low-pressure boilers are included in this classification, as are steam and hot water furnaces, fireplaces, room heaters, heating stoves, and other mechanisms. Making fire and building devices to utilize the resultant heat were among man's earliest and most noteworthy achievements. Indeed, stove, furnace, and other equipment designs implemented as early as 600 B.C. were still in use throughout the world in the twentieth century.

By the early 1990s, the U.S. heating equipment industry was shipping about $2 billion worth of products each year—a figure which had changed little in over a decade. The industry was characterized by maturity, consolidation, and increasing foreign competition. To remain competitive, industry participants in the 1980s and early 1990s were reducing employment, increasing productivity, and moving manufacturing facilities abroad.

ORGANIZATION AND STRUCTURE

The heating equipment industry generally encompasses all non-electric devices used to heat spaces in homes, buildings, and industrial structures. Such heaters are powered by coal, oil, gas, wood, or solar power. In addition to their different energy sources, industry offerings can be categorized as fireplaces and wood burning stoves; supplemental heaters; or low-pressure steam and hot water boilers and furnaces. Warm-air furnaces and high-pressure steam and hot water systems, which are often used as central heating systems for larger structures, are included in **SIC 3585: Air-Conditioning and Warm Air Heating Equipments and Commercial and Industrial Refrigeration Equipment** and **SIC 3443: Fabricated Plate Work (Boiler Shops),** respectively.

Low-Pressure Boilers. Low-pressure steam and hot-water boilers differ from other industry offerings in that they are often used as central heating devices to warm several spaces within a structure. A hot-water system usually consists of a centrally located cast-iron boiler and a network of steel or copper pipes that are connected to satellite radiators. Water is heated in the boiler and transferred up through the pipes to the radiators. As the water travels through the metal radiator, it releases heat, becomes more dense, and falls back down to the boiler where it is reheated. Motor driven pumps are used to increase pressure and to allow rooms below the boiler to receive heat.

Steam heating systems work similarly to hot water systems. Because steam is a gas, however, it cannot hold heat as well as water and it is more susceptible to sharp temperature fluctuations. As a result, steam systems generally require more apparatus and are less efficient for many residential, as well as some commercial, applications.

Supplemental Heaters. Non-electric supplemental heaters are used to heat spaces that are not connected to centralized heating systems, such as garages and warehouses. In addition, they are often used for ''zone'' heating, a complement to a central heating system that can reduce overall energy costs. Space heaters typically run on natural gas and oil.

Kerosene space heaters have traditionally been a popular residential device. Although they are cost-efficient and relatively easy to operate, safety concerns have reduced the desirability of these heaters in relation to competing products. Open flame kerosene heaters deplete oxygen and emit carbon monoxide. In addition, they can become a fire hazard if misused. As a result, some local ordinances have banned kerosene heaters.

Gas and liquid propane (LP) supplemental heaters are of three types: infrared-radiant, which transfer most of their heat through direct infrared radiation from the heater to the objects in a room; convection, which heat and recirculate air, and; catalytic, which produce heat when gas is distributed and ignited over a platinum-plated grid. Gas and LP heaters are comparatively clean-burning and inexpensive to operate. They also require little or no ventilation.

Portable forced-air heaters are commonly used to heat work areas, such as outdoor construction sites. Although they are fueled by oil, kerosene, or gas, they may also use electric fans to disperse the heat. Industrial forced-air systems can supply as much as 600,000 British thermal units (BTUs) of heat. Other supplemental heating devices include baseboard units, duct fans, solar heaters, and various oil-filled heaters—many of which incorporate electrical devices.

Fireplaces and Woodburning Stoves. Because they use a relatively inexpensive and renewable energy source, fireplaces and woodburning stoves are a popular alternative to boiler and supplemental heating systems. Wood-fueled heat, however, is relatively inefficient and emits more pollution than oil, gas, or LP. A standard fireplace, for instance, is only 5 percent to 15 percent energy efficient when a fire is burning, and -5 percent to -10 percent inefficient when the fire is dying. Although many woodburning stoves are 40 percent to 65 percent energy efficient, most other heaters are much more efficient and pollution-free. Many furnaces, for example, offer greater than 70 percent efficiency.

The three principal types of woodburning stoves are; traditional box (radiant), airtight (circulating), and pellet-fed. Airtight stoves have a sealed firebox, a tight-fitting door, and a manually or thermostatically controlled air intake damper that controls burning. Pellet-fed stoves burn processed wood pellets that are fed into the stove's combustion chamber electronically, allowing greater heat control and efficiency.

Fireplace heating products offered by manufacturers in the industry include artificial gas fireplaces and various heat-saving accessories. Heat recovery systems, for instance, generate heat through convection and radiation using energy from an open fire. Tube grates pull cool air out of the room and blow hot air back out. Similarly, heat extractors, which are often installed in a chimney, heat and circulate air in a room using energy from the fireplace.

Market Structure. In the early 1990s, cast-iron boilers, radiators, and convectors used in steam and hot water systems accounted for about 25 percent of industry sales—this represented the largest single industry segment. Floor and wall systems, unit heaters, infrared heaters, and stokers accounted for about 16 percent of production. Of that 16 percent, supplemental unit heaters made up about half. Domestic heating stoves of all fuel types represented about 13 percent of industry output. Various miscellaneous heating equipment accounted for about 45 percent of production. Such devices included fireplace accessories, parts and attachments for boiler systems, and domestic stoves, forced-air devices, and specialty oil-burning heaters.

Residential and personal uses accounted for about 32 percent of heating equipment expenditures in the early 1990s. Office buildings consumed about ten percent of production, and miscellaneous farm, industrial, and commercial uses accounted for about 51 percent of the market. Exports consumed the remaining seven percent of production.

BACKGROUND AND DEVELOPMENT

Woodburning stoves, believed to be the first heating devices, were first used by the Chinese in 600 B.C. Central heat was first used in 350 B.C., when the Greeks began building flues beneath building floors to heat rooms. The Romans developed more complex central heating systems called hypocausts in the early Christian era. These systems transferred heat from a furnace using conduction, convection, and radiation. Although the chimney was not developed until the 14th century, heating systems designed for European castles in the 11th and 12th centuries were important precursors to the flue and other space heating contraptions.

Woodburning and coalburning stove technology continued to advance before and during the middle ages. In fact, stoves similar in design to the earliest Chinese units were still in use throughout Russia and parts of Europe in the 1990s. The first manufactured cast-iron stove, which was essentially an iron box, was produced in Lynn, Massachusetts, in 1642. Benjamin Franklin improved this design in 1744 by joining the stove to a fireplace. The first round cast-iron stoves, which became popular in the 19th century, were built in Pennsylvania in 1800 by Isaac Orr.

Central heating system technology, in contrast to advances in stove systems, languished after the fall of the Roman Empire. The first central hot-water system that used pipes to heat a building, for instance, was created in 1792 to heat the Bank of England. Not until 1840, moreover, did similar technology reach the

United States. Central steam heaters were also developed in the late 1700s and were implemented in the United States in the late 1800s. John H. Mills made important contributions to the advancement of steam heat in the United States. Not until the early 20th century were hot air systems, similar to those used in the Roman hypocausts, revived for practical use.

In addition to new heat delivery methods, such as steam and hot water, central furnaces, and iron stoves, the burgeoning U.S. heating equipment industry also benefitted from the commercial application of new fuels in the 19th and 20th centuries. In the early 1900s, particularly in the 1920s, heating devices which could efficiently utilize gas and oil increased the scope of the market served by traditional woodburning and coalburning device manufacturers. Likewise, the availability of liquified propane in the 1940s significantly boosted demand for gas-powered heaters.

Gas- and oil-powered heating equipment, as well as electrical equipment classified in other industries, proliferated during the 1940s through the 1970s. As a result, the share of the heating equipment market represented by coalburning and woodburning devices declined. Nevertheless, shipments of nearly all types of heating equipment ballooned in the postwar economic boom. As housing starts swelled in the 1950, 1960s, and 1970s, the demand for space heaters, stoves, and fireplace accessories blossomed. Booming commercial, industrial, and institutional markets hiked the production of boiler and radiator systems. The even faster proliferation of warm-air furnaces and electric heating equipment, however, cannibalized growth in some industry segments.

Despite solid market growth throughout much of the 1970s, manufacturers realized by the end of that decade that the heating equipment industry had entered maturity. Although fluctuations in energy prices caused temporary spurts in demand in various industry segments, the overall demand for heating equipment had stabilized. Throughout the 1980s the value of industry shipments stagnated at about $2.1 billion in shipments. Although energy shortages in the late 1970s and early 1980s aroused interest in some alternative heating equipment, such as solar-powered systems, sales from these segments collapsed in the mid-1980s as energy costs stabilized and alternative-energy tax incentives faded.

Although some manufacturers were able to take advantage of budding foreign markets during the 1980s, domestic producers generally found themselves under increasing pressure from foreign rivals in their core U.S. market. Stagnant revenue growth and declining profit margins plagued many producers throughout the decade.

CURRENT CONDITIONS

In response to idle markets and downward pressure on margins, heating equipment manufacturers in the early 1990s were continuing two trends which they started in the early 1980s—consolidation and increased productivity. Like companies in other mature businesses, heating equipment producers were consolidating the industry through merger and acquisition, or by exiting the market and abandoning market share. The primary benefits for competitors of mergers and acquisitions were related to multiple economies of scale and increased financial strength.

Increasing productivity, the second trend, was being achieved primarily through automation and work force reduction. Between 1980 and 1990, the total number of workers employed in the industry had declined nearly 30 percent, from over 26,000 to about 18,500. Some producers had also realized gains by exporting some production activities and by increasing their use of foreign parts. By 1991, for instance, imported parts accounted for a full 35 percent of materials used by heating equipment producers.

Going into the mid-1990s, manufacturers were facing a slight reprieve from the tepid growth that had plagued them for more than a decade. This growth represented marked improvements over sales in the early 1990s. For instance, total unit sales of all types of heating equipment fell from 2.35 million in 1989 to only 2.15 in 1990. In 1992, conversely, sales of residential boilers jumped 8.7 percent to 321,942 units; this jump followed five successive years of decline. Furthermore, boiler sales growth of five percent or more was expected for 1993.

Sales of residential baseboard and covector devices jumped too in 1993, by an estimated 13.7 percent. Miscellaneous room heater sales were expected to rise by a less dramatic nine percent in 1993. Increases in residential markets, caused by a surge in homebuilding activity, were partially offset by commercial and industrial sectors. Demand for nonresidential boilers, for instance, was projected to continue its steady two percent per year decline in 1993.

Demand for heating equipment will likely remain relatively stagnant in the near future, though growth will be markedly improved over recessed 1990 and 1991 levels. The replacement market for boilers, which grew from a 69 percent share of the overall boiler market in 1987 to a whopping 80 percent by 1991, will recede in relation to the demand for new

installations. This trend was already underway in 1992 and 1993.

Sales of gas-powered equipment will likely increase, as natural gas prices remain low and the threat of increases in fuel-oil prices looms. Space heating consumption of gas, which already represented the largest single market for natural gas, was expected to increase slightly. Because 88 percent of all gas customers already use gas for space heating, however, growth potential in this market is limited. Instead, producers will be forced look for growth overseas.

Productivity gains achieved in the 1980s will not be sustainable in the 1990s. Producers may be able to increase margins by moving production to other countries, such as Mexico. Passage of the North American Free Trade Agreement in 1993 elevated the likelihood of this occurrence.

Low energy prices will dilute opportunities for sales growth of high-tech, energy efficient products. Indeed, the energy intensive, comparatively low-tech nature of heating equipment minimized opportunities for technological breakthroughs that might otherwise spur large numbers of replacement sales. However, producers in 1993 continued to make technological strides in several areas. The "zero-clearance" fireplace, which inserts into a traditional fireplace, promised up to 90 percent efficiency and reduced emissions of pollutants. Similarly, developers of "thermoformers," which use catalytic gas-fired infrared heaters, claimed their innovation could save up to 80 percent on electrical costs.

INDUSTRY LEADERS

Despite intensive consolidation efforts during the 1980s, the heating equipment industry remained highly fragmented going into the mid-1990s. The industry was comprised of a multitude of small companies, most of which produced a narrow line of products. Only the top five competitors generated more than $75 million in sales in 1991. The majority of the 50 largest firms employed fewer than 300 workers. In the early 1990s, fewer than 450 companies were competing in the industry—down from over 900 as recently as 1980.

The largest U.S. manufacturer of heating equipment in 1991 was Amtrol Inc. of Rhode Island. With fewer than 1,000 workers, Amtrol boasted estimated sales of $150 million. Tampella Power Corp. of Pennsylvania, followed closely with $125 million in sales and about 300 employees. Mestek Inc. of Massachusetts, generated about $110 million in sales with 1,400 workers. Other large firms included Riley Consolidated Inc. of Massachusetts, Martin Industries Inc. of Alabama, and Eclipse Inc. of Illinois.

Sellers Engineering Company of Danville, Kentucky, is representative of many firms in the industry. Founded in the mid-1930s, the boiler making company increased its sales to $5 million annually by 1993. It marketed it products to contractors through a network of sales representatives at 77 locations. The company was forced to change its products in the 1970s to include oil-fired equipment, as the demand for gas-fired boilers waned in the wake of the energy crises. "Competition can be stiff in the commercial and industrial boiler and water heater market," noted President Tom Sellers in the March 1993 issue of *Lane Report.*

WORK FORCE

Employment prospects in the heating equipment industry were bleak going into the mid-1990s. The Bureau of Labor Statistics estimates that employment in most heating equipment manufacturing positions will decline by 15 percent to 25 percent between 1990 and 2005. Positions for assemblers and fabricators, which account for a leading 15 percent of total jobs in the industry, were expected to decline by 23 percent. Jobs for grinders and polishers, machine tool workers, and lathe operators will also decline by over 20 percent. Manufacturing opportunities will arise, however, for some machinists, sheet metal workers, and tool and die makers. Furthermore, sales positions are expected to increase by over 22 percent.

Workers in the industry are paid less than the average for all U.S. manufacturing industries. In 1991 the average hourly production wage was $9.50—about $1 less than the national average. Furthermore, the average wage increased only about 25 percent between 1980 and 1990. In the future, increased automation and movement of some production activities overseas will likely exert downward pressure on wage growth for traditional heating equipment manufacturing jobs.

INDUSTRY INFORMATION SOURCES

Browne, Dan, *Alternative Home Heating,* New York: Holt, Rinehart and Winston, 1980.

"Comfort and Construction," *Air Conditioning, Heating & Refrigeration News,* March 30, 1992.

"Heating and Cooling," *Do-It-Yourself Retailing,* May 1992.

Lindsay, Karen F., "Heaters Said to Cut Thermoforming Energy Costs By As Much as 80%," *Modern Plastics,* May 1993.

"Replacement Market," *Air Conditioning, Heating & Refrigeration News,* March 29, 1993.

Reynolds, Sharon M., "Business is Heating up for Sellers," *Lane Report,* March 1993.

Russ, Lynch, "Solar Company Sees Brighter Future," *Honolulu Star-Bulletin,* December 3, 1992.

Standard & Poor's Industry Surveys, New York: Standard & Poor's Corporation, December 31, 1993.

"Statistical Panorama," *Air Conditioning, Heating & Refrigeration News,* March 29, 1993.

"Heating," *Air Conditioning, Heating & Refrigeration News,* March 29, 1993.

U.S. Industrial Outlook 1993, Washington, D.C.: U.S. Department of Commerce, January 1993.

Wasik, John F., "Fireplaces: Burning Better," *Popular Science,* February 1993.

—Dave Mote

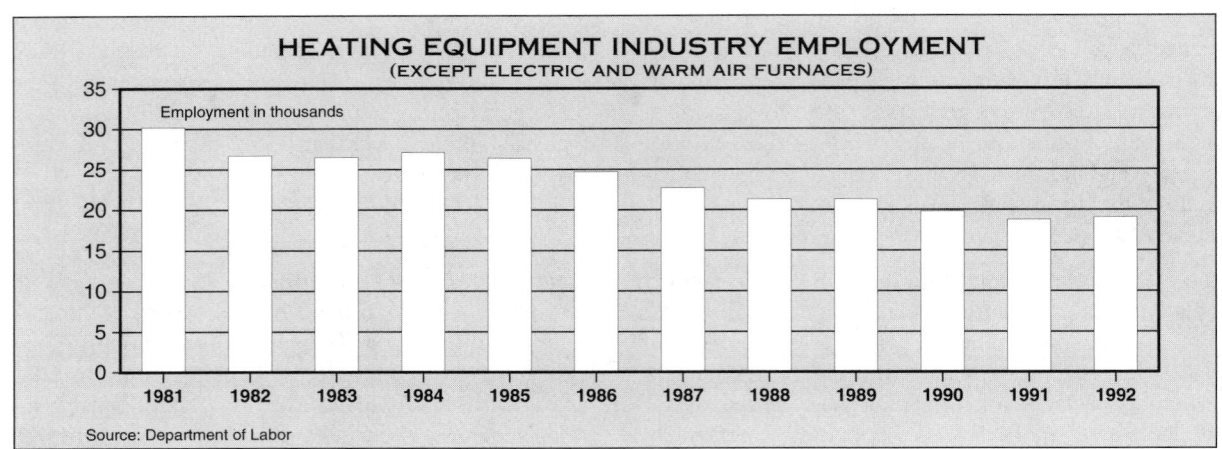

HEATING EQUIPMENT INDUSTRY EMPLOYMENT
(EXCEPT ELECTRIC AND WARM AIR FURNACES)

Employment in thousands

Source: Department of Labor

SIC 3441

FABRICATED STRUCTURAL METAL

This classification includes establishments primarily engaged in fabricating iron and steel or other metal for structural purposes, such as bridges, buildings, and sections for ships, boats, and barges. Establishments primarily engaged in manufacturing metal doors, sash, frames, molding, and trim are classified in **SIC 3442: Metal Doors, Sash, Frames, Molding, and Trim;** and establishments doing fabrication work at the site of construction are classified in the Construction industries.

INDUSTRY SNAPSHOT

Industry shipment and employment levels remained fairly constant between 1982 and 1990. In 1982 the value of shipments was $8.84 billion. By 1990 this value had dropped to $8.63 billion. The lowest point was reached in 1983, when the value of shipments was $7.95 billion. The highest point was reached in 1988, when shipments were valued at $9.02 billion. In 1982 103,500 people were employed by this industry, 75,400 of whom were employed as production workers. The total employment level dropped to a low of 80,300 in 1987, then rebounded to 83,000 in 1989, only to drop again in 1990 to 82,000. Production worker employment levels were at their lowest level of 57,800 in 1986. This level increased in 1989 to 60,000, and remained at that level through 1990.

The fabricated structural metal industry's products were divided into four categories. Fabricated structural metal for buildings accounted for 55.1 percent of the industry's shipments, structural metal for bridges accounted for 7.1 percent, other fabricated structural metal accounted for 22 percent, and fabricated structural metal, not specified by kind accounted for 15.8 percent.

Average hourly wages in this industry were slightly lower than the average recorded by all manufacturing industries. In 1982, average pay was $8.56 per hour. This steadily increased to $10.80 per hour by 1990. In 1988, the average for this industry was $10.20 per hour, which was slightly lower than the national standard of $10.66 per hour.

ORGANIZATION AND STRUCTURE

Only Wyoming, Alaska, and Hawaii did not contain any fabricated structural metal manufacturing establishments. California's 251 establishments led the nation in value of shipments in 1987, reaching $809.5 million. This accounted for 9.3 percent of total U.S. shipments that year. California's 7,100 employees earned an average of $13.03 per hour, ranking second in pay to Connecticut's $14.50 per hour average.

BACKGROUND AND DEVELOPMENT

At first, metals were hammered into shape, then when fire was found to alter the structure of the ores, furnaces were built and metals were cast into useful shapes. The use of ferrous metals, however, did not emerge until 7000 years after copper and bronze were first smelted. Once technology advanced and iron smelting began, iron rapidly replaced copper for tools and weapons. By 100 B.C. the use of iron as a semi-structural material was recognized.

By the 1990s the kiln, hammer, and anvil had been replaced with blast furnaces and multi-ton presses. Structural shapes were continuously cast and forged, later to be cut to standard lengths. Although greater understanding of the metallurgical properties of metals occurred over the course of the industry's development, and manufacturing processes evolved, lending uniformity and structural integrity to the final product, working conditions in the industry changed little. Although steel and iron mills were much safer places to work in the early 1990s, thanks largely to the Occupational Safety and Health Act and the Environmental Protection Agency, the hazards remained, making mill work a fairly dangerous occupation in comparison to other manufacturing occupations.

CURRENT CONDITIONS

Foreign competition forced the fabricated structural metal industry to focus on quality and reducing costs. During the 1980s, fabricated iron and steel products became so expensive because of labor and other overhead costs, that many purchasers started buying products from foreign manufacturers. Increasing government regulations concerning environmental and safety issues also helped to increase production costs in the United States. Without similar government restrictions and regulations, developing countries stood as serious, competitive threats to U.S. manufacturers.

Although foreign competition adversely affected businesses in the 1980s, and a recession toward the end of the decade hindered capital investment, several signs indicated the United States was effecting a turnaround. The productivity of American workers was increasing, and corporate reorganization of most companies helped to reduce costs. Capital investments in new equipment and advancing technology bolstered quality levels, while keeping costs in check. Leading companies, like Nucor Corporation, served as examples of the profitability possible in what were thought to be mature industries. Diversification was another strategy being employed by major structural metal producers, like Bethlehem Steel, which looked for new opportunities in related markets.

INDUSTRY LEADERS

In 1991, the leading 75 companies in this industry recorded $6.39 billion in sales and employed 47,400 people. The leader in terms of sales, Babcock Industries, Incorporated, based in Fairfield, Connecticut, recorded $800 million in sales and employed 8,000 workers. Second to Babcock was Valmont Industries, Incorporated, based in Valley, Nevada. Valmont generated $790 million in sales and employed 4,400 workers. Ranking third was Stewart & Stevenson Services of Houston, Texas, which reported $605 million in sales and employed 2,600 people. Everett Smith Investment Company, based in Milwaukee, Wisconsin ranked fourth, with $225 million in sales. Carolina Steel Corporation, based in Greensboro, North Carolina, ranked fifth, with $190 million in sales.

Nucor Corporation of Charlotte, North Carolina made considerable capital investments in late 1993. Its Jewett, Texas mill received a continuous caster, online in June 1994. The company's Hickman, Arkansas hot-rolled sheet mill received a $35 million thin-slab caster, expected to be operational soon after July 1994. This caster was expected to increase productivity from 1.2 million tons to two million tons per year, and increase the work force by up to 50 people. These investments toward expansion helped Nucor record a 59 percent rise in profits in 1993. But even with profits soaring, in August 1993 Standard & Poor's Corporation's CreditWatch listed Nucor as a company to watch because its debt had "negative implications."

WORK FORCE

Several occupations were expected to increase their representation in the industry by the end of the 1990s. The number of combination machine tool operators was expected to grow by just over eight percent. Cost estimators were expected to increase 12.6 percent. Industrial production managers were expected to increase 15.5 percent. Machinists were expected to increase 6.6 percent. Light and heavy truck drivers were expected to increase 7.3 percent. Sales workers were expected to experience the highest hiring gain in the industry, increasing their numbers 18 percent.

AMERICA AND THE WORLD

In July 1993 Nucor Corporation engaged in a study with Nippon Steel Corporation and the Industrial

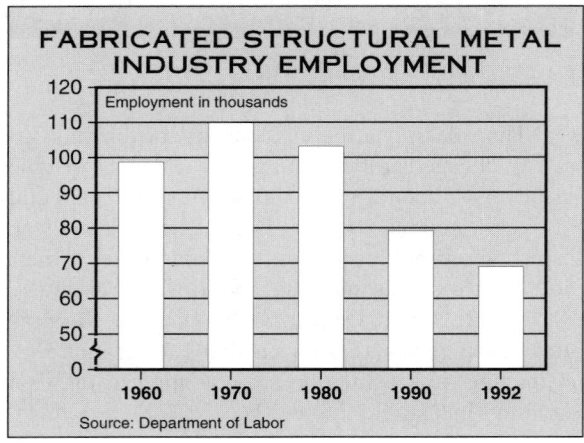

FABRICATED STRUCTURAL METAL INDUSTRY EMPLOYMENT

Employment in thousands

Source: Department of Labor

Bank of Japan, planning to build a thin slab casting mill in Malaysia. The $400 million coil mill, if found to be feasible, would produce one million tons of hot-rolled steel per year. All the production would be consumed within Malaysia, and none would require exportation. This move followed Nucor's January 1993 announcement to build its first facility on foreign ground. The $60 million facility will be located in the Republic of Trinidad and will be built with the aim of reducing dependence on steel scrap. Nucor will employ 50 workers to pioneer a new manufacturing process that converts iron ore to iron carbide with natural gas, producing quality steel with less scrap and pollutants

Closely following Nucor's success was Inland Steel Company. Inland used various cost-cutting measures, such as work force reduction and equipment upgrades, to reduce production costs with the goal of meeting Nucor's costs per ton. Inland also was engaged in a joint venture with Nippon Steel in New Carlisle, Indiana. These developments were expected to boost steel production from 4.5 million tons to six million tons per year.

RESEARCH AND TECHNOLOGY

Innovations in casting technology boosted the productivity of structural metal manufacturers. One manufacturer of casting equipment and systems, Rokop Corporation, was experiencing growth as a result of two companies' capital investments. Nucor Corporation requested another continuous caster, making it the fourth piece of such equipment installed in its facilities. Rokop planned to complete the equipment installation in June 1994.

The other company making a capital investment with Rokop was Tennessee Valley Steel Corporation. This project added a dual-stream ladle sequencing system, the fourth ladle system project for Rokop, two of which were sold to casters in China and Hungary. A fifth system similar to this was sold to Keystone Steel & Wire Company.

Rokop Corporation's projects were indicative of a trend in the structural metal industry to modernize facilities. Steel mills and iron casters have been around for centuries, while the principal technology has changed little. However, controlling processes to improve quality and reduce costs enabled great technological innovations. Bethlehem Steel was participating in this strategy by investing $100 million in modernization of its new subsidiary, Bethlehem Structural Products, which was a leading supplier of structural steel and sheet-piling to the construction industry. The aim of this three-year project was to increase productivity, cut costs, and improve quality.

INDUSTRY INFORMATION SOURCES

Aeppel, Timothy, ''Armco Inc. Posts Loss on a Charge; Nucor Net up 59%,'' *Wall Street Journal,* October 22, 1993.

Bierne, Mike, ''Carolina Plan to Avail Bondholders,'' *American Metal Market,* September 1, 1993.

''Carolina Gains Financing,'' *American Metal Market,* September 2, 1993.

''Debt of Nucor, USX Placed Under Review by Rating Agencies,'' *Wall Street Journal,* August 12, 1993.

Fitch, John A., *The Steel Workers: From Conspiracy to Collective Bargaining,* New York: Arno & The New York Times, 1969.

Knauth, Percy, *The Metalsmiths,* New York: Time-Life Books, 1974.

—Valerie A. Wilson

SIC 3442

METAL DOORS, SASH, FRAMES, MOLDING, AND TRIM

Companies in this industry are engaged primarily in manufacturing ferrous and nonferrous metal doors, sash, window and door frames and screens, molding, and trim. Establishments primarily engaged in manufacuturing metal covered wood doors, windows, sash, door frames, molding, and trim are classified in **SIC 2431: Millwork**.

INDUSTRY SNAPSHOT

The metal doors, sash, frames, molding, and trim industry has experienced moderate but steady growth in shipments since 1982. Shipments were valued at $4.685 billion that year. By 1988, shipments had grown to $6.952 billion. Employment levels grew slightly in the early 1980s, but flattened between 1986 and 1988. In 1982 approximately 66,300 people were employed by this industry, 47,600 of those being production workers. These figures grew to 74,000 total employees and 54,300 production workers by 1988.

Workers are paid poorly in this industry compared to average pay in all manufacturing industries combined. In 1982, the average hourly wage was $6.61; the figure had grown to $7.92 by the end of 1988. That same year the average hourly wage for all manufacturing workers was $10.66. Other comparative ratios indicate this industry rates below the manufacturing average in terms of value added, cost, shipments, investment per establishment, employee, and production worker. In fact, in terms of investment this industry ranks nearly two-thirds below the average manufacturing industry.

ORGANIZATION AND STRUCTURE

This industry is dominated by small businesses with fewer than 20 employees. In 1982, of the 1,738 establishments engaged in this industry, only 673 employed more than 20 people. By 1988 the total number of establishments fell to 1,531, while those employing more than 20 people grew slightly to 680.

The product share is divided into six areas. Metal doors and frames, except storm doors, held 40.1 percent of the total market share in 1987. Metal window sash and frames, except storm sash, held 25.1 percent; metal molding and trim and store fronts held 5.7 percent; metal combination screen, storm sash, and storm doors held 6.9 percent; metal window and door screens and metal weather strip held 3.8 percent; and metal doors, sash, and trim, not specified by kind, held 18.3 percent of the market share in 1987.

In 1987 California contained 208 establishments engaged in the manufacture of metal doors, sash, frames, molding, and trim. These establishments shipped 11.2 percent of the U.S. total in this industry, amounting to $738.9 million for that year. The total number employed in California was 8,800, averaging 42 people per establishment. These workers earned an average of $7.97 per hour. Ohio's 73 establishments shipped $604.9 million worth of product and employed 4,400. These employees earned an average $8.52 per hour. Pennsylvania's 78 establishments had gross revenues of $445.7 million and employed 5,700 who earned an average $8.35 per hour. Texas's 124 firms engaged in this industry shipped $436.2 million worth of product and employed 5,200 workers who earned an average $6.99 per hour. Florida's 111 companies had sales of $335.8 million and employed 4,700 who earned an average $6.40 per hour. Maryland's 700 employees earned the highest average wage of any state's workers engaged in this industry—$9.10 per hour—during 1987. By contrast, metal door, etc. workers in South Carolina earned an average $6.17 per hour, the lowest average hourly wage for any state in the United States.

CURRENT CONDITIONS

This industry is a natural fit for glass, aluminum, or building materials manufacturers wishing to diversify their operations. During 1993 the furnishings supplier LaSalle was acquired by the British building materials group Heywood Williams. The LaSalle purchase was considered a lucrative gain because operating profits for the company nearly doubled between 1991 and 1992, rising from $3.3 million to $6.4 million. Furnishings for manufactured houses was LaSalle's specialty.

Entrepreneurs seeking to get involved in this industry, analysts warn, should realize that it is an extremely competitive, low profit margin industry. Firms that succeed will have a clear idea of their market and use innovative marketing strategies to win and keep customers.

INDUSTRY LEADERS

The top 75 companies engaged in this industry grossed total sales of $6.066 billion and employed 66,300 people in 1991. The leading company was Phillips Industries Inc. of Dayton, Ohio, which had sales of $927 million and employed 9,700 that year. Following Phillips was Dallas Corporation of Dallas, Texas. Dallas grossed $323 million and employed 3,100 people in 1991. Ranking third was Keller Industries Inc. of Miami, Florida, which grossed $240 million in sales and employed 3,500 people. International Aluminum Company of Monterey Park, California grossed $220 million and employed 2,000 people in 1991. Elixir Industries of Gardena, California grossed an estimated $210 million and employed 1,400 people.

WORK FORCE

Approaching the year 2000, several skilled trade positions employed by this industry can look forward to increased demand. The number of combination machine tool operators is expected to grow by just over eight percent. Cost estimators should add 12.6 percent to present levels, and industrial production managers can expect to add 15.5 percent to current employment levels. Machinists should expand the employment

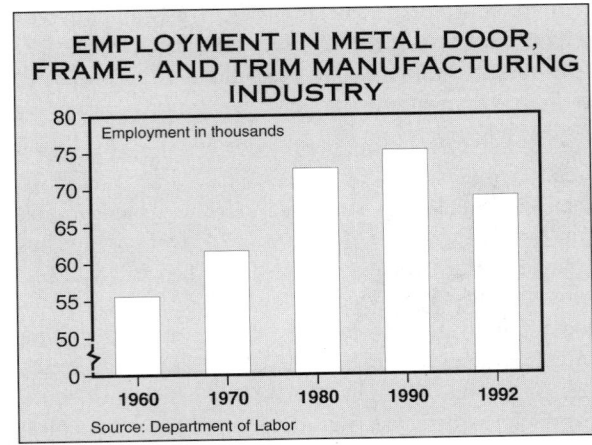

EMPLOYMENT IN METAL DOOR, FRAME, AND TRIM MANUFACTURING INDUSTRY

Employment in thousands

Source: Department of Labor

level by 6.6 percent. Light and heavy truck drivers should experience increased demand of 7.3 percent. Sales workers are expected to see the highest hiring gain in this industry, at 18 percent.

Other positions should experience reductions in workforce. Coating, painting, and spraying machine operators are expected to be reduced by more than 23 percent, which is the sharpest decline estimated for this industry. Other occupations expected to be reduced between 10 and 20 percent include the following: assemblers and fabricators; welders and cutters; metal fabricators; welding machine setters; metal and plastic machine forming operators; structural metal precision fitters; secretaries; freight, stock and material movers; and precision inspectors.

RESEARCH AND TECHNOLOGY

A process has recently been developed that fuses glass and metal. The result of this innovation is called UNI-SAN 6500, available in viewing windows from Jacoby-Tarbox. The process is reported to eliminate common causes of window breakage through its improved strength. Increased safety and durability are key to these single-unit windows.

INDUSTRY INFORMATION SOURCES

Darnay, Arsen J., ed. *Manufacturing USA: Industry Analyses, Statistics, and Leading Companies*, Detroit: Gale Research, Inc., 1992.

—Valerie E. Wilson

SIC 3443

FABRICATED PLATE WORK—BOILER SHOPS

This classification includes establishments primarily engaged in manufacturing power and marine boilers, pressure and nonpressure tanks, processing and storage vessels, heat exchangers, and weldments and similar products; these are made by cutting, forming, and joining metal plates, shapes, bars, sheet, pipe mill products, and tubing to custom or standard design for factory or field assembly. Excluded from this category are establishments primarily involved in manufacturing warm air heating furnaces, which are classified in **SIC 3585: Refrigeration and Heating Equipment.** Those establishments primarily engaged in manufacturing nonelectric heating apparatus other than power boilers are classified in **SIC 3433: Heating Equipments, Except Electric.** Also excluded from the fabricated plate work classification are manufacturers of household cooking apparatus and those manufacturing industrial process furnaces and ovens. The former are covered in **SIC 3631: Household Cooking Equipment,** and the latter are listed under **SIC 3567: Industrial Furnaces and Ovens.**

INDUSTRY SNAPSHOT

Plating—the application of a thin metal layer on a surface to enhance wearing quality, to prevent leakage, and to protect against corrosion—is used in the fabrication of many products. The manufacturing process is generally consigned to manufacturers involved in the fabricated plate work industry. Although the bulk of the industry's shipments comprise a multitude of products manufactured through plating processes, the core of the fabricated plate work industry essentially includes the manufacturing of power and marine boilers and various types of plate tanks and storage vessels.

Power boilers, as classified by the American Society of Mechanical Engineers, operate at greater than 15-psig steam pressure and are intended for stationary service, which excludes locomotive boilers from the scope of the fabricated plate work industry. Boilers operating at 15-psig steam pressure or lower, known as low-pressure heating boilers, are classified in **SIC 3433: Heating Equipment, Except Electric.** Power boilers, designed to operate at high pressures and temperatures, generate steam to provide power for utility companies and for various industrial processes. The boiler itself consists of two principal parts: the furnace, which provides heat, usually by burning fuel, and the boiler proper, in which water is converted to steam by the heat piped in from the furnace. A steam engine derives its power from steam generated under pressure in a boiler. Marine boilers are designed and fabricated for use aboard a wide range of vessels, including tugboats, ocean liners, oil drilling barges, freighters, and aircraft carriers.

ORGANIZATION AND STRUCTURE

The fabricated plate work industry is comprised of large and small manufacturing facilities. Of the 1,561 fabricated plate work establishments in existence in 1989, nearly half employed fewer than 20 people, while the industry average was 47 employees.

Geographically, fabricated plate work manufacturing occurs throughout much of the United States, with 38 states containing five or more manufacturing facilities. The bulk of manufacturing activity in the early 1990s took place in the five-state region comprising Michigan, Wisconsin, Illinois, Indiana, and Ohio. Together, these states contained 361 manufacturing establishments, which generated $1.47 billion in sales and accounted for 16.9 percent of the total domestic shipments delivered by the industry. The 290 establishments in New York, Pennsylvania, and New Jersey ranked as the second greatest regional concentration of manufacturing facilities, posting $1.30 billion in revenue and accounting for 19.2 percent of the nation's aggregate shipments. Texas, Oklahoma, Arkansas, and Louisiana represented the United States' third greatest regional concentration of fabricated plate work establishments, largely due to the prodigious production output registered by the 168 establishments located in Texas. Together, these four states contained 289 manufacturing establishments, recorded $1.02 billion in revenue, and accounted for 15.4 percent of domestic shipments.

California, with 174 establishments, contained the greatest number of fabricated plate work manufacturing facilities in any one state, followed by the 168 in Texas and the 130 establishments located in Pennsylvania. Pennsylvania, however, surpassed Texas and California in terms of total revenue collected and in shipment volume, posting $748.5 million in sales and accounting for 11 percent of the industry's total shipments.

Operating a manufacturing establishment in the fabricated plate work industry is generally a less expensive venture than operating other typical manufacturing establishments, particularly in the area of average costs incurred. In 1989, the average cost incurred from purchasing the necessary raw materials for manufacturing fabricated plate work per establishment was $2.65 million, 41 percent lower than the average recorded by all other manufacturing industries. A greater difference is found in the area of average investment per establishment. In 1989, the average expenditure for manufacturing machinery and retooling in the fabricated plate work industry was $93,466, or nearly 70 percent below the $296,864 incurred by a typical manufacturing facility.

BACKGROUND AND DEVELOPMENT

The origins of the fabricated plate work industry may be traced to the early development of boilers, which began in the Middle Ages, when scientists, engineers, and inventors experimented with the idea of harnessing the power of steam. For centuries, improvements were made in both the theory of deriving power from steam and in steam generators themselves. Seventeenth-century inventor Giovanni Battista della Porta was the first to discover that when steam condensed in a closed vessel it created a vacuum that could draw up water. Thomas Savery, an English engineer working in the late seventeenth century, created the first machine to provide mechanical power by utilizing steam. By 1800, vast improvements had been made in designing steam engines and boilers, but the expense involved in developing prototypes was prohibitive.

In 1800, a landmark development in the history of boiler development occurred when Richard Trevithick put together a steam engine and boiler, which, eventually, through the addition of tubes carrying gases from a fire, increased the heating surface and efficiency of the boiler. Several decades after Trevithick's achievements, John Stevens, an American engineer, developed one of the first boilers in which tubes carried water to be converted to steam, instead of gases from a fire. This "water-tube" boiler represented the culmination of roughly 50 years of work by Stevens in his efforts toward constructing an efficient steam system to power ships along the Hudson River. By the mid-nineteenth century, further improvements had been made in the water-tube design, which allowed the water to circulate more easily, provided more heating surface, and lowered the risk of boiler explosions.

During this time, boiler design was fostered by the industrialization of Great Britain. The shift from an agrarian and commercial society to an industrial society was prompting a similar transition in the United States, shaping that country into a modern manufacturing nation. Steam powered both of these industrialization movements; the power it provided proved intrinsic to the movement toward large and distinct manufacturing industries. In the United States, residences and local industries were the primary users of these steam generators until the latter half of the century, when the applications for steam power broadened and spurred the emergence of a market segment for the fabricated plate work industry that would fuel its growth throughout the twentieth century.

The unveiling of this new use for steam took place at the 1876 U.S. Centennial Exhibition in Philadelphia, during which the practicality of generating electricity by steam power was demonstrated to the attending public. Five years later, four boilers were powering the Brush Electric Light and Power Co. in Philadelphia, the nation's first commercial electric generating station, marking the beginning of a new era for both the United States in general and boiler manufacturers in particular. From this time forward, power boilers in mills and factories appeared with increasing frequency, particularly in sugar refining companies, as the industrialization of the United States neared its greatest intensity.

Similar advances had been made with marine boilers, another integral product that bolstered the U.S. fabricated plate work manufacturers, helping them to form a genuine, organized industry after the turn of the century. Beginning with the *Great Britain* in the early nineteenth century, marine engineers began exploring the possibilities of providing power to becalmed ships through steam. Eventually sails and masts were discarded and boilers became the sole source of power for ships of all classes and sizes, from the 1,154-ton *Britannica*, which "sailed" from Liverpool to Boston in 1840, to the *Monitor* and the *Virginia*, two iron-hulled steamboats pitted against each other during the American Civil War.

By the time that boilers had become common in American industry, marine boilers were also fueling a majority of the U.S. vessels on water. Accordingly, by the end of the nineteenth century, fabricated plate work manufacturing, essentially comprising the fabrication of power and marine boilers, was being conducted in earnest. In 1889, the American Boiler Manufacturers' Association (ABMA) was chartered with the stated purpose of elevating the standards of boiler design and manufacture and preventing the production and sale of boilers deemed unfit for safe operation. Moreover, the establishment of a national association for boiler manufacturers cohered a loosely organized group of manufacturers into a more structured body, marking the formal beginnings of the boiler shop, or fabricated plate work, industry in the United States.

Before the fledgling industry could emerge as an integrated and uniform group of manufacturers, nationwide boiler manufacturing standards needed to be created and the alarming frequency of boiler explosions needed to be quelled, something the formation of the ABMA had failed to do. Another association with a vested interest in the production of boilers, the American Society of Mechanical Engineers (ASME), had also failed to curb the number of accidents related to boiler explosions, despite formulating a code entitled "Standard Method for Steam Boiler Trials" in 1884. In 1914, a committee under the purview of ASME published the "Boiler and Pressure Vessel Code," which provided manufacturers with standard specifications for the design, fabrication, installation, and inspection of boilers and pressure vessels. The adoption of nationwide standards helped curtail the number of boiler explosions, while providing manufacturers with a universal manufacturing language to communicate with and enabling them to produce higher-quality boilers that conformed to the diverse needs their customers.

Once ASME's Boiler Code gained widespread acceptance, many of the fabricated plate work industry's internal, organizational problems were resolved, or at least made more manageable, facilitating, and in some cases invigorating, the industry's growth. Technological improvements in the design of boilers followed at a rapid pace, as the onus of spearheading future design and production innovations fell to the companies involved in the industry, rather than to the independent engineers.

Several historic achievements followed the publication of the Boiler Code, the first of which involved the opening of the Edgar Steam Electric Station in Weymouth, Massachusetts. The electric station, operated under the aegis of the Boston Edison Company, opened in 1925 with a high-efficiency turbine and boiler system able to produce electricity at the rate of one kilowatt hour per one pound of coal. For its time, this ratio represented a considerable leap in efficiency—conventional power plants competing on the vanguard of technology were consuming five to ten pounds per kilowatt hour—and the station remained a model of efficiency until it was dismantled and sold to a South American power company in the 1970s.

Thirty-three years after the Edgar Electric Steam Station demonstrated to the world the efficiency of steam generated electrical stations, President Dwight D. Eisenhower tripped a switch that activated the first North American commercial central electric-generating station to utilize nuclear energy. Located in Shippingport, a town northwest of Pittsburgh, the Shippingport Atomic Power Station was designed by the Westinghouse Electric Corporation and the Division of Naval Reactors of the Atomic Energy Commission for the Department of Energy and the Duquesne Light Company. Generating 60,000 kilowatts of electricity,

the Shippingport Station was small compared to the generating capacity of similar electric stations to follow, but it heralded the advent of a new method for generating electricity, a process that incorporated the use of boilers.

In 1960, the first commercial geothermal electric-generating station in North America began operating in Sonoma County, California, north of San Francisco. This geothermal field, from which generators received naturally produced steam, was first discovered in 1847 and then tapped in the early 1920s, but the steam and hot water billowing from the earth proved too corrosive for pipes and other equipment of the 1920s. By the late 1950s, however, significant advances in anti-corrosion technology had enabled the Pacific Gas and Electric Company to successfully generate steam from the Sonoma field, which further broadened the applications for boilers in the production of energy.

These benchmark events in the development of additional uses for boilers, coupled with the increasing utilization of boilers by the industrial sector, accelerated the growth of the fabricated plate work industry. By the early 1960s, boiler shop manufacturers—producing power and marine boilers, pressure and non-pressure tanks, processing and storage vessels, heat exchangers, weldments, and sundry other plate products—represented a $1.5 billion a year industry. Consistent improvements in design and the increased requirements of U.S. industry led to the fabrication of massive boilers, some of which were able to generate 6.5 million pounds of steam per hour, heated by furnaces approximating the size of 40 medium-sized houses. In the electrical power field, the use of boilers in thermal power plants, which accounted for roughly 80 percent of all electrical power generated in the nation, was pervasive, as boiler manufacturers benefitted from their position as suppliers of equipment essential to a diverse customer base.

As the industry entered the 1970s, the demand for power boilers remained strong, stronger than manufacturers were able to satisfy. However, growing concern for the potentially harmful effects of additional electrical generating facilities on the environment began to make the selection of future power plant sites difficult. Consequently, an electrical production deficit existed during the late 1960s, which sparked a wave of concern by utility operators regarding the availability of the equipment necessary to construct additional facilities, as demand outpaced supply. During the 1960s, this gap between production and consumption created a commensurate gap between new orders for power boilers and the production of power boilers. This gap narrowed by the beginning of the 1970s, when electric utility operators began ordering steam generating equipment in advance as a hedge against an anticipated shortage of power boilers. For manufacturers in the fabricated plate work industry, particularly those focusing on the fabrication of power boilers, this panic boosted sales volume. The value of power boiler shipments increased 18 percent from 1969 to 1970, the culmination of a decade that saw industry-wide power boiler revenue climb from $341 million in 1963 to $631 million in 1970.

The 1970s, however, marked a turning point for the fabricated plate work industry. During the mid-1970s, utility companies became increasingly concerned about the availability of fuel, environmental exigencies, and future demand for energy, resulting in an energy crisis. Energy conservation efforts and soaring energy costs sharply reduced new orders for utility boilers. The fabricated plate industry also experienced slackened reflecting the losses incurred by nearly every manufacturing industry in the United States during the energy crunch.

Revenue garnered from the production of power boilers fell from over $1 billion in 1974 to $860 million by 1978, while total boiler production fell from 90 million pounds of capacity to 36.5 million pounds, prompting manufacturers to plead for federal intervention. In response, the National Energy Act and the Industrial Fuel Use Act were passed in 1978. While the government hoped such measures would reduce the number of industrial boilers dependent on gas and oil for fuel, the fabricated plate work industry hoped they would invigorate the stagnant boiler market. Neither occurred, as both manufacturers and their customers became confused about which fuel was to be used, an understandable predicament considering the government's vacillating position on the issue.

As a result of the somewhat bleak prospects facing manufacturers in the industry, expected profit margins were reduced in the early 1980s, and competition intensified for the dwindling number of new orders. To mitigate their losses, some manufacturers exited the business entirely, while others began concentrating more on retrofitting and converting existing boilers. Although these latter manufacturers were able to stave off the negative affects of the six-year downturn, their strategy did not preclude serious losses. Nationwide energy conservation by both of the industry's primary markets—industrial and utility—imposed, in effect, a limit on the extent to which boiler manufacturers could recover. In 1980, the Department of Energy estimated that the concerted movement toward conservation had reduced the growth in energy demand to half the growth rate of the Gross National Product, an

unsettling discovery considering that the two growth rates, historically, had been roughly equal.

Consequently, manufacturers entered the mid-1980s struggling to maintain their precarious presence in the boiler and fabricated plate work market. Electric utilities at this time were operating old electric generating equipment approaching the end of its economic life, but boiler manufacturers did not expect to realize any significant wave of new orders until the early 1990s, as electric utility operators forestalled the purchase of new equipment as long as possible. An increasing percentage of the industry's work continued to be the rebuilding and refurbishing of older units, but for a considerable number of manufacturers this type of work did not generate enough money to sustain operations, and the roster of fabricated plate work manufacturers shrank.

By the late 1980s, conditions had not improved greatly. Manufacturing operations were consolidated and some facilities were shut down due to decreased demand. As manufacturers looked toward the future, a reversal of the depressed state of the industry was largely predicated on the equipment purchasing decisions by electric utility companies and a return to more aggressive capital expansion programs by the industrial sector, both of which were stunted by the recessive economic conditions of the early 1990s.

CURRENT CONDITIONS

Approximately 1,500 companies in the United States were involved in producing fabricated plate work in 1990. This figure reflected the latest of a decade-long decline in the number of manufacturers engaged in the industry. The sharpest decline occurred from 1982 to 1987, when the number of participants dropped from 1,743 to 1,584. Total revenue garnered by the industry during the 1980s declined as well, dropping from $8.23 billion in 1982 to as low as $6.15 billion in 1986. In the late 1980s, however, the industry's performance improved, as revenue increased for three consecutive years to concluded what otherwise had been a decade of consistent decline. In 1987, the industry's revenue total increased to $6.79 billion, then leapt to $7.81 billion the following year.

As the industry entered the 1990s, its sales volume eclipsed the total recorded in 1982, climbing to $8.65 billion in 1990, an aggregate value of shipments predominately derived from the industry's five primary product groups: heat exchangers and steam condensers; fabricated steel plate; steel power boilers, parts, and attachments; metal tanks and vessels (custom fabricated at the factory); and fabricated plate work not conforming to the parameters of standard fabricated plate work. This last product category, attesting to the wide range of products manufactured by the industry, was the most abundantly produced product by fabricated plate work manufacturers, accounting for 20.1 percent of the industry's total shipments. Standard fabricated plate work represented the industry's second largest product category, accounting for 16.7 percent of total shipments, followed by heat exchangers and steam condensers, which accounted for 14.4 percent. Steel power boilers and their parts and attachments represented 10.3 percent of the industry's shipments, and were closely trailed by metal tanks and vessels manufactured in a factory setting and according to customer specifications, which represented 10.2 percent. The remainder of the industry's products comprised storage tanks (5.3 percent), nuclear reactor stream supply systems (5.5 percent), and gas cylinders (3.7 percent).

INDUSTRY LEADERS

Ranked according to sales volume, the two largest companies involved in the fabricated plate work industry in the early 1990s were McDermott Inc., based in New Orleans, Louisiana, and CBI Industries Inc., based in Oak Brook, Illinois.

McDermott Inc., controlled by McDermott International Inc., earned its position largely through a merger in 1978 with The Babcock & Wilcox Company, arguably the progenitor of all boiler manufacturing and fabricated plate work companies in the United States. Formed in 1867 as Babcock, Wilcox and Co., the company's roots actually stretched back to 1856, when a 26 year-old engineer from Rhode Island, Stephen Wilcox, applied his knowledge of water circulation theory to perfect a new boiler concept utilizing inclined water tubes. Later referred to by Thomas Edison as "the best boiler God has permitted man yet to make," the success of Wilcox's system persuaded him and his friend George Herman Babcock to form Babcock, Wilcox and Co.

Initially, the two partners sold a majority of their boilers to sugar refineries. Then, in 1881, the company began supplying the boilers for the country's first central electric power station at the Brush Electric Light and Power Co. in Philadelphia. In the following years, Babcock & Wilcox boilers would continue to represent the vanguard of power generation technology, pioneering significant advances in utility steam generation design and marine boiler development. Moreover, the company helped to shape the industry by playing an instrumental role in the development of the American Society of Mechanical Engineers' Boiler and Pressure Vessel Code in 1914.

In the early 1990s, Babcock & Wilcox, as a leading subsidiary within McDermott's power generation systems and equipment division, continued to set the pace for other companies involved in the industry, thriving as a major supplier of nuclear steam generating equipment, critical heat exchanges, and replacement recirculating steam generators. Employing approximately 16,500 workers, McDermott Inc. garnered $1.52 billion in 1993 through the sale of power generation equipment, representing 77 percent of the company's $1.96 billion total revenue.

CBI Industries, Inc. was formed in 1979 to become the holding company of Chicago Bridge & Iron Co. and other subsidiaries. Divided into three primary business segments, including contracting services, industrial gases, and investments, CBI was by the early 1990s involved in oil and refined product storage, and oil and gas production, as well as in providing engineering, design, and fabrication services. Chicago Bridge & Iron, the parent company of the contracting services segment, owned ten principal production plants in the United States, Canada, and Australia. The contracting services segment, the largest business segment within CBI in terms of total sales collected, posted $793 million in revenue in 1992, nearly half of the $1.67 billion recorded by all the subsidiaries owned by the company.

WORK FORCE

Total employment in the fabricated plate work industry declined sharply during the 1980s, falling most precipitously, from 103,200 to 71,200, between 1982 and 1986, a period during which the industry's aggregate revenue total experienced a commensurate decline. Toward the latter half of the decade, as sales recovered slightly, the industry's employment base grew. As the industry entered the 1990s, employment

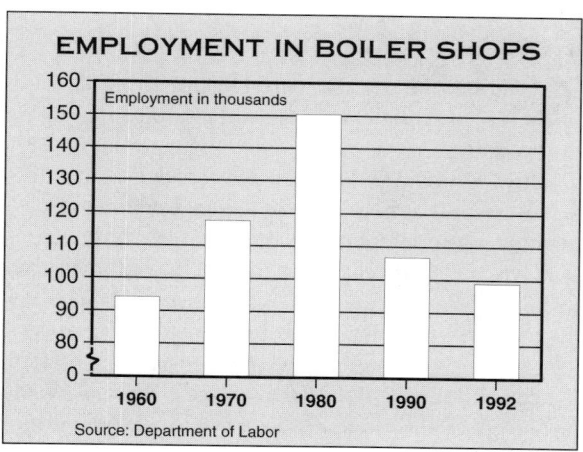

EMPLOYMENT IN BOILER SHOPS

Employment in thousands

Source: Department of Labor

was buoyed but was still far below the employment total of the early 1980s.

Of the people employed in the industry in 1990, an overwhelming majority were employed as production workers, while salaried employees—those performing managerial, administrative, or technical duties—composed the balance of the industry's work force. In 1989, the typical fabricated plate work manufacturing establishment employed 33 production workers and 14 salaried employees.

In general, production workers in the fabricated plate work industry are employed on a full-time basis, averaging, in 1989, two percent more hours per year than a production worker employed by a typical manufacturing industry. These workers also earned more per hour than their counterparts in the manufacturing field, averaging $11.57 per hour in 1989, while production workers in all other manufacturing industries averaged $10.49 per hour. In 1990, productions workers' hourly wage increased to $11.93, at which time salaried employees earned an average of $36,274 per year.

In terms of the total payroll per establishment, the fabricated plate work industry's work force expenditures were roughly equal to the average payroll expenditures for all other manufacturing industries, largely because the fabricated plate work industry employed fewer workers per establishment than the average of all other manufacturing industries. In 1989, the average payroll per establishment in the industry was $1,261,819, ten percent below the payroll costs incurred by a other types of manufacturing establishments. The typical fabricated plate work manufacturing establishment did, however, employ 13 percent fewer workers than the average manufacturing establishment, which accounted for, in part, the relatively lower payroll expenditures in the fabricated plate work industry.

RESEARCH AND TECHNOLOGY

During the 1980s, two technological developments in particular enabled manufacturers in the industry to increase production efficiency and improve the quality of their products. One of these advances, acoustic emissions technology, had been available to manufacturers of metal related products for centuries, but was not utilized in the production of fabricated plate work in a widespread fashion until much later. The other, computer-aided design, or CAD, technology, was developed in the 1980s, as an inevitable extension of the rapid technological advancements achieved by the computer industry as a whole during the decade. The use of acoustic emission technology

and computers promised to figure prominently in the development of more reliable and more efficient products.

The use of acoustic emissions technology emerged during the 1980s as a viable and effective means to gauge the quality of plate work, and its adoption by manufacturers quickly spread. Acoustic emission, the sound produced by various types of materials during production processes, was first used commercially by those involved in the production of pottery. Potters relied on the audible cracking sounds clay pots produced while cooling in a kiln. These sounds enabled the practiced listener to determine which pots would eventually crack. An application more closely related to the type employed by fabricated plate work manufacturers, however, was used by tin manufacturers, who listened to the sounds of smelted tin, known as "tin cry," to detect structural flaws in the manufactured metal. For manufacturers involved in the fabricated plate work industry, acoustic emissions provided similar information in identifying the inherent structural weaknesses of their products.

Perhaps the most valuable contribution that monitoring acoustic emissions provided was the ability of manufacturers to determine the rate of deterioration of their products, rather than merely the condition of the metal at the time of inspection. Moreover, the structural integrity of metal could be determined without cutting into it, which conventional methods required. By the late 1980s, acoustic emission technology was embraced by manufacturers throughout the United States and regarded in the industry as the most reliable method of monitoring the structural defects of fabricated plate work during production.

Complementing the emergence of acoustic emission technology, the fabricated plate work industry also benefitted from the increasing advancements in computer design and software applications during the 1980s, helping manufacturers to reduce the operating and production costs of their products and to improve their designs. The advent of Computer Aided Design (CAD), in particular, provided manufacturers with an invaluable tool to determine the most economical and efficient design of power boilers and other products manufactured by the industry. Additional software applications—designed for use in industrial settings and able to perform tasks that previously had consumed a considerable portion of research and development expenditures—reinforced the industry's dependence on computers to effectively compete in a market that demanded the most sophisticated resources available.

INDUSTRY INFORMATION SOURCES

Bennett, K. W., "Tank Industry: Lonely Bull Kicks Its Heels Up-High," *Iron Age,* June 11, 1970, 83.

"A Bureaucrat in Your Tank," *The Economist,* March 23, 1985, 31.

"Consent Decree to Tell Trade Groups to Certify Foreign-Made Boilers," *Wall Street Journal,* June 14, 1972, 38.

"Court Releases Pressure on Imported Equipment," *Chemical Week,* September 27, 1972, 28.

Cross, Wilbur, *The Code: An Authorized History of the ASME Boiler and Pressure Vessel Code,* New York: American Society of Mechanical Engineers, 1990.

"EPA Proposes New Standards for Hazardous-Waste Storage Tanks," *Chemical Engineering,* July 8, 1985, 20.

Irving, R. R., "Wanted: Rupture-Proof Tanks," *Iron Age,* September 24, 1970, 73-75.

Kleinhans, Frank B., *Boiler Construction,* New York: The Locomotive Publishing Co., 1904.

"One Hundred Pounds of Plastic in Every 1990 Car?" *Iron Age,* November 6, 1978, 88.

"Optimized Pre-Fab Panels Cut Boiler Erection Time, Labor Requirements," *Electrical World,* November 17, 1969, 40.

"Regulatory Confusion Stymies Boiler Sales," *Industry Week,* February 19, 1979, 92.

Sheilds, Carl D., *Boilers: Types, Characteristics, and Functions,* New York: F.W. Dodge Corporation, 1961.

"Two Engineers' Groups Face Antitrust Charges," *Wall Street Journal,* July 23, 1970, 3.

—Jeffrey L. Covell

SIC 3444

SHEET METAL WORK

This classification covers establishments primarily engaged in manufacturing sheet metal work for buildings (not including fabrication work done by construction contractors at the place of construction), and manufacturing stovepipes, light tanks, and other products of sheet metal.

INDUSTRY SNAPSHOT

In 1987, 4,073 companies involved in the sheet metal work industry employed 100,300 workers, 75 percent of whom were production workers, and generated $9.7 billion in revenue. More than a third of all employees in the industry worked in California, Texas, Ohio, and New York. The states with the largest number of industry establishments in 1987 were California, with 669, Texas, with 308, New York, with 273, and

Florida, with 233. In 1989, the average industry establishment employed 25 workers, had an average annual payroll of $23,925, and recorded $2.56 million in annual sales.

ORGANIZATION AND STRUCTURE

Sheet metal forming was one of the most basic and pervasive manufacturing processes in U.S. industry. In general, sheet metal products manufactured by industry firms had thin walls, both simple and complex designs, greater surface area in relation to their thickness, and were generally lighter in weight and possessed greater versatility compared to metal products formed and shaped through casting and forging manufacturing processes. The manufacture of sheet metal products was generally characterized by low to moderate labor, equipment, and die costs.

Industry sheet metal products were manufactured with a wide range of metal forming machine tools, utilizing several different methods. Several different techniques were used to produce the same sheet metal part. The factors determining that method was used included the cost of the die, the amount of labor available, the number of sheet metal parts to be made, and the speed of production, among other factors. Deep drawing methods, for example, involved more complicated machinery and cost more than other methods, but they were also faster and were more cost-effective for jobs involving the manufacture of many parts.

The sheet metal industry required billions of dollars worth of materials and supplies annually in order to operate. In 1987, for example, industry expenditures for materials and supplies amounted to more than half the value of the industry's shipments. The principal sources for the materials and supplies used by industry firms were blast furnaces and steel mills, and aluminum rolling and drawing companies. Other secondary sources for raw material included fabricated structural metal companies, metal coating and allied services companies, and over 50 other business sectors. Low-carbon steel was the most widely used metal for sheet metal processes because of its low cost and high strength and formability properties.

More than 50 percent of the value of all sheet metal industry products used or purchased in the early 1980s was for additions and alterations to residential structures, structural maintenance in residential structures, and for the construction of highways, streets, one-unit residential structures, office buildings, electric utility facilities, and industrial buildings. Industry products also were used in the manufacture of general structural metal products, electronic computing equipment, and outdoor signs. The remaining products, composing approximately 48 percent of the value of industry shipments, were purchased by customers in more than 50 other construction and manufacturing sectors.

CURRENT CONDITIONS

From 1972 to 1987, the sheet metal work industry experienced steady, uninterrupted growth. The number of firms grew from 2,960 to 4,073, and the value of shipments nearly quadrupled from $2.68 billion to $9.7 billion. In the same period, employment grew from 74,000 to 100,000.

California, Texas, New York, Florida, and Pennsylvania, the states in which the most industry firms were located, accounted for one third of the dollar value of industry shipments in 1987. Other leading states in shipment value were Ohio, which produced $1.14 billion worth of shipments, Illinois, which produced $554 million worth, and New Jersey, which produced $541 million worth.

In 1993, the sheet steel industry segment was characterized by expectations of stronger sales, price increases, as well as uncertainty on the part of some sheet steel product buyers concerning the availability of an adequate supply of sheet steel products. The consumption of sheet steel was expected to decline to 49.4 million tons in 1993 because of inventory surpluses from 1992, and then rise to 49.9 million tons in 1994. Between 1993 and 1994 industry firms were expected to raise wholesale prices for sheet metal work products.

INDUSTRY LEADERS

The leading sheet metal work firms in the early 1990s included Robertson-Ceco Corporation, with $651 million in 1993 sales and 4,288 employees, Lane Enterprises Inc., with $500 million in sales and 250 employees, and Stolle Corporation, with $480 million in sales and 4,600 employees. Several industry firms, such as ESI Metals Corporation, Stelmatic Industries Inc., and Panagraphics Inc., were exclusively engaged in the manufacture of sheet metal work in the early 1990s. Firms such as Lomanco Inc., United States Aluminum & Steel Highway Products Corporation, and Associated Materials Inc. were primarily engaged in sheet metal product manufacturing, but also were engaged in industries such as roofing, siding and insulation material distribution, plastics pipe manufacturing, and electric houseware and household fan manufacturing. A significant number of firms derived their principal business revenues from non-industry activi-

ties and performed sheet metal work as a secondary business.

WORK FORCE

There were approximately 92,000 sheet metal workers in the United States in 1992, although the vast majority worked for non-industry firms such as plumbing, heating and air conditioning contractors, and on-site construction contractors. Sheet metal workers often learned their trade through apprenticeships involving four to five years of combined classroom and on-the-job training, and many became members of the Sheet Metal Workers' International Association union. Because sheet metal products were used primarily in building construction and maintenance, opportunities for growth in sheet metal work was dependent on the economic vitality of the residential, commercial, and industrial building and construction industries.

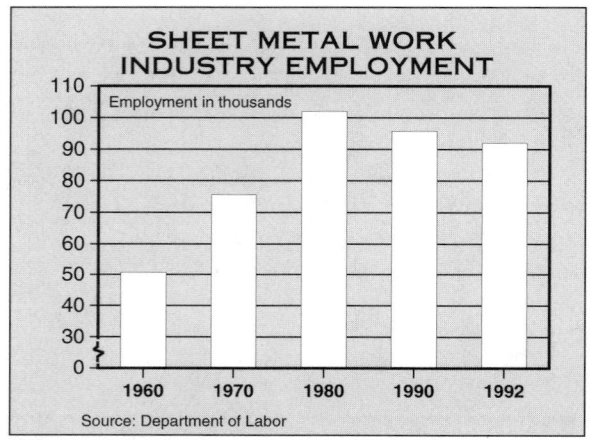

AMERICA AND THE WORLD

At least 87 companies in 25 countries (excluding the United States) manufactured sheet metal products in the early 1990s. The nations containing the greatest number of industry firms were the United Kingdom, Canada, Germany, and Denmark. Some the largest international sheet metal producers in 1993 were GKN Plc, based in the United Kingdom, with $3.56 billion in annual sales, The Rugby Group Plc, also based in the United Kingdom, with $1.02 billion in annual sales, and Zeuna-Staerker Gmbh & Company KG, based in Germany, with $222 million in annual sales.

RESEARCH AND TECHNOLOGY

Technological advances in the sheet metal work industry centered on improving tools, dies, and other equipment, employing greater use of automated machinery, and increasing the use of computer and software. Electromechanically-operated industrial robots were operated continuously, repeating precise machining motions with greater accuracy than manual methods allowed. Although in the early 1990s Japanese and European firms led U.S. manufacturers in the use of laser-cutting technology for cutting sheet metal to product specifications, as the decade progressed, the United States was gaining ground on its foreign competitors. Generally speaking, automation of sheet metal manufacturing processes required resilient equipment and quick programming, startup, and retooling times to take advantage of the efficiencies that automation offered. In response to the need to cut costs and increase equipment durability, some industry firms in the early 1990s turned to plastics, epoxy, and polyurethane to replace traditionally metallic tools and dies.

Finite element analysis (FEA) software programs enabled product designers to predict the effectiveness of sheet metal stamping dies for the manufacture of products with intricate surfaces and identified potential strains and stresses in the sheet metal. FEA also enabled manufacturers to accurately predict potential problems in sheet metal bending operations before any metal was actually machined. Software packages such as ''PE/Sheet Advisor'' used a combination of ''expert system'' logic and three-dimensional modeling to enable sheet metal product manufacturers to incorporate data gathered from manufacturing operations into the design of new products. A FEA program called ''SHEETS'' was designed to reduce the amount of time designers spent analyzing the formability of sheet metal before manufacturing a sheet metal product.

Large sheet metal operations employed central computers to direct all sheet metal forming operations. This ''systems approach'' managed entire sheet metal processes using vast ''unified'' databases containing information on materials, tool and die parameters, and mechanical properties of the variables of the sheet metal manufacturing process. In some systems, a ''master production compiler'' assembled the data for all sheet metal parts on the production timetable, arranged it according to material specifications, then established the optimal layout for the various sheet metal sizes, and generated the appropriate machine language code. In the early 1990s, it was estimated the efficiency of such computer-aided-manufacturing (CAM) and computer-aided-design (CAD) systems was four to five times greater than traditional methods. Small- to medium-sized firms that could not afford the costs of a truly integrated and centralized sheet metal CAM sys-

tem purchased simulation or modeling CAD software to eliminate the costly trial-and-error methods for developing and manufacturing new sheet metal products.

INDUSTRY INFORMATION SOURCES

Census of Manufactures: Fabricated Structural Metal Products, Washington: Bureau of the Census, 1987.

Kalpakjian, Serope, *Manufacturing Engineering and Technology,*

Reading: Addison-Wesley Publishing Company, 1989.

Sheet Metal Work, Omaha: American Business Directories, Inc., 1993.

—Paul Bodine

SIC 3446

ARCHITECTURAL AND ORNAMENTAL METAL WORK

This category includes establishments primarily engaged in manufacturing architectural and ornamental metal work, such as stairs and staircases, open steel flooring (grating), fire escapes, grilles, railings, and fences and gates, except those made from wire.

Manufacturers in the architectural and ornamental metal work industry provide construction contractors with building and finishing materials for all divisions of the development market. Product offerings include bank fixtures, guide rails for stairways and ramps, permanent ladders and stairways, lamp posts, flag poles, metal grates, fire escapes, decorative fences and posts, brass fixtures, and various metal adornments. Classified in other industries are firms that specialize in producing wire fences, prefabricated metal buildings and parts, and miscellaneous metal work.

Metal working is one of the world's oldest trades. It originated in about 2500 B.C. when bronze was discovered, although smiths prior to that time had produced architectural ornaments using gold. Not until the discovery of iron in 1200 B.C., however, did the craft of structural metal work develop. The industry in the United States flourished when architectural styles progressed from the applied ornament period in the 19th century to the organic, or functional, ornament period in the 1900s. U.S. economic boom periods in the 1920s, 1950s, and 1960s all served to increase the size and scope of the industry.

Architectural and ornamental metal work firms realized steady market growth during most of the 1980s as a result of an active construction market.

Shipments climbed from less than $1.5 billion in 1982 to $2.5 billion by 1990. During the same period, industry employment rose from about 23,000 to 30,000. The total number of companies serving the market declined during the 1980s, reflecting a trend toward consolidation. This tendency was evidenced by a 30 percent increase in companies employing more than 20 employees.

Despite a construction lull in the late 1980s that stymied growth in the industry until 1990, shipments were again increasing and employers were adding to their payrolls by 1991. While building markets still sagged in 1993, architecture and ornamental metal work firms were benefitting from a combination of increased public construction spending, renovation work mandated by the Americans with Disabilities Act, and an increase in the popularity of metal ornament in some building sectors. Products most in demand in 1990 were stairways, fences, railings, and gates, which accounted for a combined total of more than 17 percent of the market. Open flooring, grating, and studs made up about 13 percent of the market, and grilles, registers, and air diffusers represented another 12.5 percent of demand.

The industry is dominated by small private firms. In fact, in 1991 most of the top 75 firms employed 100 or fewer people. Furthermore, over two-thirds of those companies generated revenues of less than $10 million. The largest producer in the industry in 1991 was Harsco Corp. of Camp Hill, Pennsylvania. Twenty-eight percent of its $1.8 billion in sales in 1991 were attributable to ornamental metal work. The next largest player was Kawneer Company, Inc. of Norcross, Georgia, with sales of $250 million.

Growth in architectural metal work will likely remain average or below average compared to other U.S. industries throughout the 1990s and early 2000s. Jobs in metal work are projected to decline, however, as new manufacturing technology allows employers to automate many labor positions. Furthermore, new, less expensive synthetic materials will garner increasing shares of the ornamental metal market. While sales jobs, for instance, are expected to increase 7.6 percent between 1991 and 2005, positions for assemblers and fabricators will likely decline by more than 32 percent.

INDUSTRY INFORMATION SOURCES

Braun-Feldweg. *Metal Design and Technique*. London: B. T. Batsford Ltd., 1975.

Darnay, Arsen J., ed. *Manufacturing USA; Industry Analyses, Statistics, and Leading Companies*. Detroit: Gale Research, Inc., 1993.

Darnay, Arsen J., and Marlita A. Reddy, eds. *Market Share Reporter: An Annual Compilation of Reported Market Share Data on Companies, Products, and Services, 1993*. Detroit: Gale Research, Inc., 1993.

Encyclopaedia Britannica. Chicago, IL: Encyclopedia Britannica, Inc., 1968.

Geerlings, Gerald K. *Metal Crafts In Architecture*. New York: Charles Scribner's Sons, 1929.

"Metals Products," *Architectural Record*, December 1992.

"On Their Metal," *Building*, 17 July 1992.

Standard & Poor's Industry Corporate Descriptions. New York: Standard & Poor's Corporation, 14 February 1993.

—Dave Mote

SIC 3448

PREFABRICATED METAL BUILDINGS AND COMPONENTS

This category covers establishments primarily engaged in manufacturing portable and other prefabricated metal buildings and parts and prefabricated exterior metal panels.

The prefabricated metal buildings industry manufactures such products as portable buildings and houses, silos, greenhouses, carports and garages, and other prefabricated metal buildings. Total product share is split between nine products. Prefabricated metal building systems, excluding farm service buildings, residential buildings, and parts, claimed 57.5 percent of the product share. Other prefabricated and portable metal buildings and parts claimed 21.5 percent. Grain storage buildings, including farm and commercial types fabricated of steel and aluminum, claimed 2.3 percent. Other farm service buildings claimed 1.5 percent. Steel and aluminum greenhouses claimed 2.4 percent. Dwellings, including vacation homes and camps, claimed 0.9 percent. Small utility buildings, including tool sheds, cabanas, and storage houses, claimed 3.7 percent. Other prefabricated metal buildings, including garages, claimed 3.9 percent. And metal buildings, not specified by kind, accounted for 21.0 percent of the product share.

The value of shipments in this industry was $2.32 billion in 1982 and peaked at $3.47 billion in 1989. This figure slipped to $3.42 billion in 1990. Employment levels steadily climbed over the 1980s, growing from 23,500 in 1982 to 30,000 in 1990. The total number of establishments declined from 569 in 1982 to 493 in 1986. By 1988 the total increased to 545, 250 of which employed more than 20. Wages per hour steadily increased between 1982 and 1990, beginning at $8.13 and ending at $9.50. Compared to the average of all manufacturing, this industry pays less, adds less value to the raw materials, ships less, invests less, and enjoys a lower cost structure.

Total sales of $4.45 billion and total employment of 35,700 were reported by the leading 75 companies in this industry in 1991. United Dominion Industries of Charlotte, North Carolina, employed 10,000 and grossed sales of $1.40 billion in 1991. Butler Manufacturing Company of Kansas City, Missouri, grossed sales of $580 million and employed 3,600. Champion Home Builders of Dryden, Michigan, grossed sales of $250 million and employed 2,500. AMCA International Corporation of Memphis, Tennessee, grossed sales of $200 million and employed 1,800, and American Buildings Company of Eufaula, Alabama, grossed sales of $180 million and employed 1,300.

Most occupations in this industry will face reductions as the 21st century nears. Coating and painting machine operators should expect the sharpest reduction, nearly 24 percent. Other occupations facing work force reductions include assemblers, sheet metal workers, welders, metal fabricators, welding machine setters, machine forming operators, structural metal fitters, secretaries, material movers, and inspectors. Those occupations expected to see increases in work force levels include sales workers, truck drivers, machinists, industrial production managers, cost estimators, and combination machine tool operators.

The highest concentration of prefabricated metal buildings manufacturers was found in southeastern coastal states. However, Texas's 64 establishments shipped $316.5 million in 1991, which was 10 percent of the total shipments in the United States. These establishments employed 3,100, averaging 48 employees per establishment earning an average $8.81 per hour. Illinois's 20 establishments shipped $243.4 million in 1991 and employed 1,500 people whose average hourly wage was $10.67. California's 61 establishments shipped $242.6 million and employed 2,200 people, earning $8.97 on average. And North Carolina's 19 establishments shipped $198 million and employed 1,500 people, earning $9.52 on average.

INDUSTRY INFORMATION SOURCES

Darnay, Arsen J., editor, *Manufacturing USA: Industry Analyses, Statistics, and Leading Companies,* Detroit: Gale Research Inc., 1992.

—Valerie E. Wilson

MISCELLANEOUS STRUCTURAL METAL WORK

The category includes establishments primarily engaged in manufacturing miscellaneous structural metal work, such as metal plaster bases, fabricated bar joists, and concrete reinforcing bars. Also included in this industry are establishments primarily engaged in custom roll forming of metal.

According to the 1987 *Census of Manufacturers,* nearly 40 percent of the United States structural metal work industry was engaged in manufacturing custom roll-formed metals. Another 35 percent of the industry manufactured fabricated bar joists and concrete reinforcing bars. The other 25 percent was split between manufacturing metal plaster bases, curtain walls, and other miscellaneous metal work. Closely related to the construction and automobile industries, structural metal work manufacturers were heavily affected by the recession of the late 1980s and early 1990s, after seeing a $1 billion boom in shipments between 1986 and 1988.

One reason for this decline was the industry trade deficit between the United States and its foreign competitors. During a speech in 1993, the Atlantic Chapter President of the American Institute for International Steel stated that the customers of the steel producing firms were adversely affected by the amount of complaints filed by U.S. firms against foreign steel manufacturers concerning this trade deficit. The deficit situation, combined with U.S. steel producers' protests, caused diminished business at U.S. ports, higher prices for steel products, and the shortage of specialty plate and sheet products previously supplied by foreign suppliers. The danger in this situation was some U.S. steel-using firms were contemplating relocation to Canada, Mexico, and other Pacific Rim countries.

Concentrated in the eastern regions of the continental United States, this industry segment grew to employ over 25,000 people by 1988, paying average earnings of over $10 per hour. Selected ratios reveal that this industry typically employs fewer people per establishment and pays average wages when compared to all other forms of manufacturing. According to *Ward's Business Directory of U.S. Private and Public Companies,* the industry leader in 1991 in terms of gross sales was Superior Metal Products, Inc. based in Lima, Ohio with $58 million in sales.

With increased automation, the face of the industry is expected to change into the year 2000. Heavy reductions in employment of assemblers, fabricators, welders, welding machine setters, machine forming operators, secretaries, material handlers, and painting/ spraying machine operators are expected. However, job prospects for sales personnel, industrial production managers, and cost estimators are expected to increase.

The research and development segment of the industry has been active, aiming primarily at cost reduction through process improvement and materials research. In 1993, CF&I Corporation invented a new process which can produce rails continuously for 1/4 mile, reducing the need for welding and reducing construction costs. Ford Motor Company, in partnership with Alcan Rolled Products Company, is experimenting with the effects of hybrid aluminum-steel sheet metal on an automobile's fuel economy, durability, service, and performance. However, other segments of the aluminum, steel, and copper industries are mired in uncertainty over the economy. The economic factor known as consumer confidence greatly affects these related industries, due to their reliance on construction and automobile industries.

INDUSTRY INFORMATION SOURCES

Buelte, Horst, ''Trade Law Must Reflect Current Reality,'' *American Metal Market,* May 7, 1993.

Darnay, Arsen J., ed., *Manufacturing USA: Industry Analyses, Statistics, and Leading Companies,* Detroit: Gale Research, Inc., 1989.

Rizzuto, A. B., et al., ''Metals & Mining Industry—Industry Report,'' *Bear, Stearns, & Co. Inc.,* March 17, 1993.

Scolieri, Peter, ''Continuous Rails Patented,'' *American Metal Market,* April 16, 1993.

Wrigley, Al, ''Ford Tests Aluminum Friendly,'' *American Metal Market,* February 15, 1993.

—Valerie E. Wilson

SIC 3451

SCREW MACHINE PRODUCTS

This category includes establishments primarily engaged in manufacturing automatic or hand screw machine products from rod, bar, or tube stock of metal, fiber, plastics, or other material. The products of this industry consist of a wide variety of unassembled parts and are usually manufactured on a job or order basis. Establishments included in this industry may perform assembly of some parts manufactured in the same establishment, but establishments primarily engaged in producing assembled components are classified ac-

cording to the nature of the components. Establishments primarily engaged in manufacturing standard bolts, nuts, rivets, screws, and other industrial fasteners on headers, threaders, and nut forming machines are classified in **SIC 3452: Bolts, Nuts, Screws, Rivets, and Washers.**

INDUSTRY SNAPSHOT

The screw machine products industry is defined more by the process of manufacture than by any specific product. Although screw machine products manufacturers produce a wide variety of products for many types of industries—ranging from ball holders for ball-point pens to precise components for medical equipment to gears and other parts for the automotive industry—they all use a variation on the screw machine, a large, usually cam-driven piece of machinery that allows roughly cylindrical material to be subjected to a variety of tooling and machining operations as the material is turned about its axis. Screw machines may have as many as eight spindles that act upon the part being machined, and are able to produce highly precise parts quickly The screw machine, by insuring the interchangeability of manufactured parts, was a major contributor to the development of modern manufacturing and assembly processes.

Screw machine products manufacturers are located primarily in the industrialized sectors of the Northeast and Midwest and near aerospace manufacturers in the West. According to *U.S. Industrial Outlook 1993,* fewer than 2,000 manufacturers produced an estimated $3.16 billion dollars worth of goods in 1992. The industry is dominated by smaller companies employing less than 50 workers, most of whom are highly-skilled machinists. Many of the shops are privately-owned, and most are located close to the industries to which they supply parts. In addition, many larger companies that use screw machine products manufacture those products in-house. The major purchaser of screw machine products is the automotive industry, but, as screw machine products form an integral part of all manufactured items, they are used by hundreds of other industries.

ORGANIZATION AND STRUCTURE

The vast majority of screw machine products are manufactured on a job or order basis. The purchaser of a product provides the manufacturer with a precise description of the part desired, and the manufacturer then sets up its machines to produce that part. Part runs may call for the manufacture of as few as a hundred or as many as a million parts, requiring a single screw machine or a shop full of machines to produce the part on time. Because of the nature of their business, screw machine products manufacturers rely on the flexibility of their equipment and their employees to accommodate the different needs of the various screw machine products purchasers.

Three types of screw machines are used by manufacturers: Swiss, single-spindle, and multiple-spindle machines. Using these machines, a machinist may perform up to 32 different types of cutting and forming operations. Fred W. Lewis, discussing the screw machine products industry in the *Handbook of Product Design for Manufacturing,* stated, "The amount of work done is limited only by the number of tool positions available and the tool layout engineer's ingenuity." The tool layout engineer designs the cams that control the various machining operations and sets up the machine, which is then capable of producing millions of identical pieces. Many manufacturers are turning to computer-controlled rather than cam-controlled operations, because of the longer set-up time required for cam-driven machines and the level of expertise required to operate them. Computer-controlled screw machines, however, are not necessarily more productive than cam-driven machines.

The flexibility inherent in both machine and machinist allows screw machine products manufacturers to produce parts for many types of industries. While larger manufacturers have diversified their production, smaller companies have tended toward specialization, and may produce as much as 80 percent of their total output for one company. This degree of commitment means small manufacturers experience whatever economic downturns or upturns the industry they are captive to experiences. The actual screw machines account for the major capital expenditures of manufacturers in this industry. The screw machine is a remarkably durable piece of machinery, however; it can be rebuilt and overhauled, and computer controls can be added to enhance the machine's flexibility, thus spreading capital outlay out over a long period of time.

BACKGROUND AND DEVELOPMENT

Although the first machine-cut screws were produced in 1800, at the dawn of the first industrial age, the concept of a screw dates back as far the third century B.C., when the Greek mathematician Archimedes designed a water-powered, screw-driven system to lift water. Much later, in the middle 1400s, Leonardo da Vinci drew plans for a screw-cutting lathe. But it was Henry Maudslay, an English mechanic, who in 1800 first cut a piece of lead on a lathe into the helical pattern we know as a screw. Early screw manufacturers were hampered by the lack of any stan-

dards for measuring their products or insuring their uniformity. Thus each producer made a different size and pitch of screw, making it very difficult to replace parts when needed.

The early manufacture of machined metal parts in the United States occurred primarily in the increasingly industrialized Northeast states, where small shops produced parts for the machines that would drive American economic growth. Such shops used belt-driven lathes that were powered by water or, occasionally, an ox tied to a treadmill outside the factory. It was not until the middle of the nineteenth century, however, that a small group of machinists centered around Windsor, Vermont created the machine tools that preceded today's screw machines. Out of this innovative environment of skilled inventors and machinists, which included Francis A. Pratt, Richard Lawrence, and James Hartness, all pioneers in machine tool development, came Christopher Spencer, who in 1873 created the Hartford Automatic Screw Machine.

According to Donald E. Wood, editor of *Automatic Machining* and author of *From Archimedes to Automation: The History of the Screw Machine,* Spencer's automatic screw machine was "the prototype for all single-spindle machines in use today." This machine was manufactured by the Hartford Machine Screw Co., which is the oldest continuing screw product manufacturer in the country. Soon Pratt & Whitney Co. of Hartford, Connecticut and Brown & Sharpe Manufacturing Co. of Providence, Rhode Island began manufacturing screw machines that were famed for their precision and accuracy. The creation of precision screw machines contributed greatly to the development of modern manufacturing, as screw machines made products for the growing automotive industry and other developing industries. According to Wood, "the mass production of consumer goods, and its parallel problem, precise interchangeability of goods components, came only after machine tools had been devised which could make products alike in a rapid manner, and standardization of measurement had been established."

Although the screw machine was initially designed to produce threaded fasteners, users of the machine soon recognized that it was capable of producing a vast number of products. In fact, standardized screw thread manufacturers soon turned to a different process, called cold-heading, and this industry is now classified as **SIC 3452: Bolts, Nuts, Screws, Rivets, and Washers.** Because the screw machine could machine any roughly cylindrical, symmetrical piece of stock, it soon was used to manufacture gears, pulleys, push rods, rollers, and other products. By 1960, over 1500 screw machine product manufacturers employed over 30,000 workers and operated over 40,000 screw machines to produce nearly one billion dollars in annual sales of special component parts.

CURRENT CONDITIONS

Though the screw machine product industry generally feels the effects of national economic downturns, it nevertheless fared relatively well in the overall economic downturn of the early 1990s. While the value of shipments for the industry was relatively stagnant between 1988 and 1991, shipments increased eight percent in 1992 to $3.156 billion dollars. *U.S. Industrial Outlook 1993* predicted that shipments would increase another four percent from 1992 to 1993. These increases were tied to the strong recovery of the domestic automobile industry, which sought to cut costs even if this meant purchasing screw machine products from independent manufacturers rather than captive screw machine departments. Despite increased shipments, total employment declined into the early 1990s. From a high of 44,800 total employees in 1989, the industry employed 40,100 people in 1992.

As American manufacturing concentrated in the midwestern states of Michigan, Illinois, and Ohio, so did the screw machine products industry. The largest number of screw machine products manufacturers gathered around automotive production facilities in Michigan, which according to the 1982 Census of Manufactures was home to 262 industry establishments employing 6,000 workers, or 14.4 percent of the U.S. work force. Michigan manufacturers generated $430 million in shipments in 1982, 19.8 percent of the U.S. total. Illinois followed closely behind with 247 establishments, 6,000 employees, and $317 million in shipments; Ohio had 175 establishments, 4,500 employees, and $239 million in shipments. New York, California, and Connecticut were also major centers for the screw machine products industry; each of these states shipped more than $130 million in goods in 1982.

The screw machine products industry is characterized by a high degree of structural stability: the machinery it uses, the processes involved in manufacture, and the kinds of products it produces have remained essentially the same for nearly one hundred years. Many manufacturers use screw machines that are decades old. Most employees learn their trade through hands-on training or a form of apprenticeship, though workers are increasingly receiving training in vocational education programs. Thus, the screw machine operator of two generations ago would recognize many

of the operations being conducted in today's shop, though the old timer might be surprised to see young operators, who had not gone through an apprenticeship, programming computer-controlled screw machines to work on plastics and fibers as well as metals.

INDUSTRY LEADERS

There are few giants in the screw machine products industry; most manufacturers employ fewer than 50 workers and operate less than a dozen screw machines. A few large, diversified companies do play major roles within the industry, however. According to *Ward's Business Directory of U.S. Private and Public Companies 1993,* the largest employer and sales leader is the Hi-Shear Corporation of Torrance, California, which employed 800 workers and produced $75 million in goods in 1993. ITW Ramset/Red Head, a division of the highly-diversified Illinois Tool Works, employs 200 people in its Wood Dale, Illinois plant, and shipped $50 million in goods. Other manufacturers with more than $30 million in sales in 1993 are Kelco Industries of Woodstock, Illinois; Huron Inc., of Lexington, Michigan; B. and G. Manufacturing Co. of Hatfield, Pennsylvania; IW Industries Inc. of Melville, New York; and Atlas Bolt and Screw Co. of Ashland, Ohio.

WORK FORCE

Manufacturers of screw machine products have traditionally employed a highly-skilled workforce, though the aging of highly-trained employees and the availability of more accessible computer-controlled machines suggests that the work force of the future will be somewhat less skilled and younger. Because learning to set up a cam-controlled screw machine takes years of training, finding qualified employees has been one of the industry's biggest problems. Operators

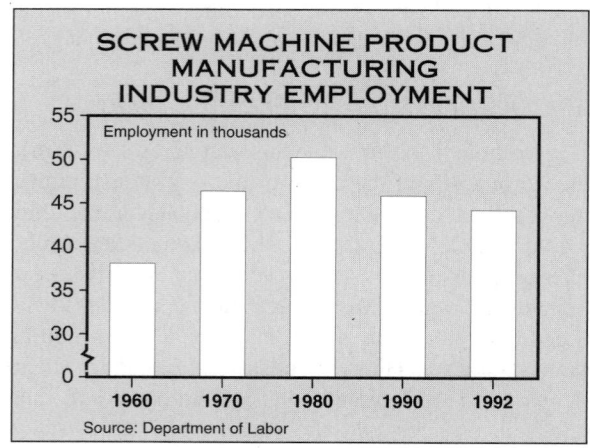

SCREW MACHINE PRODUCT MANUFACTURING INDUSTRY EMPLOYMENT

traditionally learned the intricacies of setting up a machine through an apprenticeship, but vocational training programs and on-the-job training have now supplanted formal apprenticeships. In addition, the National Screw Machine Products Association, located near Cleveland, Ohio, provides training manuals, videos, and seminars for its members. The industry's move to greater computerization is driven less by the inherent machining benefits of computer control than by the greater ease of training that computers allow.

Most employees in the screw machine products industry are machinists of some sort. Because manufacturers are provided with design specifications for their products, they employ no designers. Manufacturing engineers specify the machining operations and cams required to produce the job based on the design they are given and machinists set up the machines and supervise their operation. In many smaller firms the principal owner is also the head engineer. The Bureau of Labor Statistics predicted that the industry would experience a 12.8 percent decline in employment opportunities for machinists of all sorts between the years 1986 and 2000. *U.S. Industrial Outlook 1993* listed the average wage within the screw machine products industry as $10.13 an hour in 1990, noting steady increases of close to 3.5 percent for the preceding three years.

INDUSTRY INFORMATION SOURCES

Darnay, Arsen J., ed., *Manufacturing USA,* Detroit: Gale Research Inc., 1989.

Lewis, Fred W., "Screw Machine Products." In *Handbook of Product Design for Manufacturing: A Practical Guide to Low-Cost Production,* ed. James G. Bralla, 4.21-4.31, New York: McGraw-Hill, 1986.

U.S. Department of Commerce, *1987 Census of Manufactures,* Washington, DC: U.S. Department of Commerce, 1987.

U.S. Department of Commerce, *U.S. Industrial Outlook 1993,* Washington, DC: U.S. Department of Commerce, January 1993.

Ward's Business Directory of U.S. Private and Public Companies, Detroit: Gale Research Inc., 1993.

Wood, Donald E., *From Archimedes to Automation: The History of the Screw Machine,* Brecksville, OH: National Screw Machine Products Association.

—Tom Pendergast

SIC 3452

BOLTS, NUTS, SCREWS, RIVETS, AND WASHERS

This category includes establishments primarily engaged in manufacturing metal bolts, nuts, screws, rivets, washers, formed and threaded wire goods, and special industrial fasteners. Rolling mills engaged in manufacturing similar products are classified in the major group for primary metal industries; establishments primarily engaged in manufacturing screw machine products are classified in **SIC 3451: Screw Machine Products;** and those manufacturing plastics fasteners are classified in **SIC 3089: Plastics Products, Not Elsewhere Classified.**

INDUSTRY SNAPSHOT

Manufacturers in **SIC 3452** produce the materials that hold American industry together: bolts, nuts, screws, rivets, and washers. Producing these items in lots as small as 1,000 and as large as 20 million, manufacturers make both custom-ordered and standard fasteners using processes quite different from that of the screw machine product industry, **SIC 3451,** with which it otherwise shares many similarities. While screw machine product manufacturers produce their goods using some form of screw machine that cuts into a metal product to produce the needed tooling, fastener manufacturers use a variety of cold-forming and rolling processes to produce simpler parts with greater strength. Both industries trace their beginnings to the early stages of industrialization, which was made possible by innovations in the field of fastener engineering.

The fastener industry is remarkably decentralized, with hundreds of small shops producing the majority of fasteners. Manufacturers in the fastener industry have tended to cluster around the industries which purchase its products, traditionally the automotive, defense, and aerospace industries. The industry is therefore concentrated in the auto-producing states of the upper Midwest and the defense and aerospace-oriented regions of California. But such dependence has had its costs. Slumps in the auto industry in the 1980s posed severe challenges to fastener manufacturers, and defense downsizing in the 1990s posed an equally significant threat. Domestic fastener manufacturers were also seriously threatened by an influx of cheap, foreign-made fasteners in the 1970s and 1980s. The Fastener Quality Act of 1990, passed in response to complaints about poor quality and fraud on the part of foreign fastener manufacturers, promised some protection for the domestic industry.

ORGANIZATION AND STRUCTURE

Manufacturers within **SIC 3452** produce a wide and ever-changing variety of products that fall under the general name "industrial fasteners." According to the Industrial Fastener Institute, the trade association for the industry, a fastener is "a mechanical device for holding two or more bodies in definite position with respect to each other. A high percentage of fasteners have threads as part of their design, but unthreaded items such as rivets, clevis pins, machine pins, etc., are considered fasteners as well." The industry produces fasteners using the primary manufacturing operations of heading, upsetting, forming, forging and extruding. Fasteners use primarily ferrous metals for their products, usually carbon and alloy steels. Most fasteners begin as wire, rod, or bar, which is cut to length, headed, and then threaded.

A typical hex-head bolt begins as a shaft of metal whose length is a number of times larger than its diameter. This shaft is placed in a die, a metal holder that maintains the shafts position when it is struck by a punch, which is designed to impart the hexagonal shape of a bolt head to the shaft. Multiple punches are sometimes used to impart more intricate head shapes or to form harder metals. The headed shaft is then given an external thread in another cold-forming process called thread-rolling. In thread-rolling, the headed shaft is pressed between stationary and moving hardened-steel dies, which squeeze the material into the desired thread form. The nut that accompanies this bolt may also be cold-formed using a thread-forming tap that displaces rather than removes metal to form the interior thread. These and other processes like them constitute the major means by which industrial manufacturers produce their goods.

According to the *Manufacturers' Capability Guide,* published by the Industrial Fastener Institute, "Cold forming is a high-speed, high-volume production process, with economical production rates determined by part size, design complexity, and degree of forming required—all factors that determine the number of blows required to form the part and thus the complexity of the tooling and equipment required." Cold-forming has the advantage of allowing the manufacturer to produce many thousands of products an hour; according to John E. Neely and Richard R. Kibbe, authors of *Modern Materials and Manufacturing Processes,* "Production rates on upsetting machines can be as high as 36,000/hr for small unpierced rivets, and No. 8 size screw blanks can be made at

27,000/hr." Such economies of scale allow manufacturers to offset the very high costs of cold-forming equipment. Cold-forming also has the advantage of wasting no material, since the metal is pressed into shape rather than trimmed away by machining, and of allowing the metal grain to form in continuous unbroken lines, improving tensile and shear strengths and resistance to fatigue.

BACKGROUND AND DEVELOPMENT

According to *The Heritage of Mechanical Fasteners,* a publication produced by the Industrial Fastener Institute, "Man's conquest of nature has depended upon his ability to fasten useful things together." Ever since they bound an axle to a wheel to provide the means of moving a cart, humans have been using fasteners to make their lives easier. People were fashioning nails as early as 2800 B.C., and the first screw appeared around 250 B.C., but it was not until the fifteenth century that what we now know as threaded fasteners began to appear in common usage. In this century, the first printing press was held together and run by a screw, tiny screws held Swiss-made watches together, and French mathematician Jacques Besson designed the first practical machine for cutting screws.

The Industrial Revolution, which swept the Western world after the middle of the eighteenth century, brought about many of the technological innovations that gave birth to the modern fastener industry. In 1760, Job and William Wyatt became the first known manufacturers of threaded fasteners. The English brothers employed 59 people in their water-powered factory, producing 1,200 gross of wood-screws a week. Screw makers started up throughout England and America, but purchasers of their products were faced with a serious problem. Because fastener makers shared no common rules for size and thread pitch, a nut from one shop had little chance of fitting a bolt from another. Nuts and bolts had to be carefully paired, for once separated they were practically useless.

"The one man most responsible for starting threaded fasteners on their way to becoming the high-precision, freely interchangeable, taken-for-granted components we know today was the English inventor Henry Maudslay," according to *The Heritage of Mechanical Fasteners.* Maudslay invented a bar lathe capable of making highly accurate and duplicatable threads, and his ideas led others, including American inventor David Wilkinson, to design machines that would form the basis for the new machine tool industry. Most early threads were cut on a screw machine, but in 1836 William Keane of New York invented a process known as thread-rolling that formed threads without cutting away material. That process, which later became prevalent, differentiates the fastener industry (**SIC 3452**) from the screw machine product industry (**SIC 3451**).

In 1834, the C. Read & Co. of Providence, Rhode Island became the first significant manufacturer of screws in the United States. Within 10 years, the small firm had a number of competitors, including the A. P. Plant Co. of Plantsville, Connecticut, which in 1842 became the first company to issue a price list and discount large orders. The 1840s saw an explosion of advances in the industry: in 1844, Julius B. Savage introduced machine-made nuts; and in 1847, William E. Ward patented the first automatic cold-heading machine.

Fastener manufacturers benefitted from the Civil War, when all of American industry was mobilized in the production of firearms, machinery, and railroad equipment to feed a war that devoured machinery as fast as it did men. Shortly after the war, the center of the American fastener industry shifted from the Northeast to the Midwest (then referred to as the West) in order to stay close to the expanding railroads and growing iron and steel production facilities. By the end of the nineteenth century, Cleveland, Ohio was the capital of the American fastener industry, and most of the processes for creating its products had been created.

Fastener manufacturers benefitted greatly from the screw-thread standardization that began in 1864, when the United States adopted the Sellers thread system over the Whitworth screw-thread used by the British. Having different thread systems posed no problem for the two countries, until it came time for them to cooperate during World War I. American manufacturers were not equipped to manufacture the British threads, and field repairs of machinery were disastrous. The fiasco was nearly repeated in World War II, but temporary adjustments helped avert disaster. In 1964, the International Organization for Standardization (ISO) announced two universal thread systems: ISO Inch and ISO Metric. Despite occasional efforts to convert manufacturers to the metric system, the United States remains the only country in the world still tied to the inch system. This practice leads to dual manufacturing facilities and inventories, but American manufacturers and the American public have resisted conversion to the metric system.

By 1969, the U.S. fastener industry had reached its peak of production. In that year, 450 companies operating 600 plants and employing over 50,000 employees manufactured over two billion fasteners a year. By 1984, however, the industry had decreased in size—to 250 manufacturers operating 350 plants and employing 35,000 people—because of severe challenges from foreign competition and dramatic changes in the requirements of original equipment manufacturers (OEMs). The biggest challenge came from foreign fastener producers, who took advantage of inexpensive third-world labor and material costs to produce cheap ''standards,'' or fasteners that met nationally recognized product standards. The Industrial Fastener Institute reported that domestic manufacturers went from supplying 80 percent of American bolts, nuts, and large screws in 1969 to just 44 percent in 1984. During the same period, OEMs, especially automobile manufacturers, were pressing fastener manufacturers to develop specialized products at lower costs. The production of these items sustained many companies, but it drove the smaller, less technologically developed companies out of the industry.

Beginning in the mid-1980s, the American fastener industry began to rebound. Many manufacturers had allied themselves with companies in need of technically sophisticated products rather than simple standardized commodities, and the falling value of the U.S. dollar drove the prices of foreign products up. Then, in 1985, reports began surfacing in newspapers across the country of ''bogus bolts,'' bolts that were graded to withstand high loads but were failing in service, leading to the destruction of property and, in one case, the loss of life. The Industrial Fastener Institute began an investigation, and in 1986, urged an investigation by the U.S. Customs Service.

In 1988, after an 18-month investigation, a U.S. House subcommittee published a report entitled *The Threat from Substandard Fasteners: Is America Losing Its Grip?* The report stated that ''the failure of substandard and often counterfeit fasteners has killed people, reduced our defense readiness, and cost both the American taxpayer and the American industry untold millions in breakdowns, downtime, reconstruction, and other unnecessary inefficiencies.'' The subcommittee concluded that the substandard and counterfeit fasteners at fault were largely foreign made. The ''bogus bolts'' controversy ended in the passage of Public Law 101-592, the Fastener Quality Act, in 1990. This act provided for the ''testing, certification, and distribution of certain fasteners used in commerce within the United States.'' Perhaps more important than the law, the investigation challenged the quality of the fasteners imported from abroad while affirming the quality of fasteners made in the United States.

CURRENT CONDITIONS

The industrial fastener industry experienced little or no growth through the late 1980s and into the early 1990s. Value of shipments, expressed in 1987 dollars, rose just slightly from $5,084 million in 1987 to a forecast $5,127 million in 1993. From 1987 to 1992, employment within the industry dropped from 38,700 to 34,600 production workers, according to *U.S. Industrial Outlook 1993*. According to analyst Richard Reise, "Industrial fastener companies are feeling the effects of efforts by major equipment and machinery manufacturers, particularly the U.S. automobile manufacturers, to cut costs of components and supplies. This means lower prices and tighter profit margins for fastener suppliers." Such pressures may continue to drive small- and medium-sized fastener companies from the industry, since they have little choice but to comply with the requests of purchasers who may buy the vast majority of their products. Other challenges to the fastener industry in the 1990s came from decreases in defense spending and soft demand from domestic aircraft manufacturers.

Though domestic consumption of fasteners is expected to grow at an average annual rate of two to three percent through 1997, the fastener industry is expected to benefit from increased export opportunities, especially in South America and Western Europe. According to Reise, "U.S. fastener companies are becoming more aggressive in searching out export markets, rather than just responding to unsolicited export orders. U.S.-made fasteners that offer the best prospects for export are high-quality, high-price, low-weight products." The top five export destinations for U.S. companies in 1991 were Canada (53 percent), Mexico (13.6 percent), the United Kingdom (6.8 percent), France (3.1 percent), and Japan (3.0 percent). Passage of the North American Free Trade Agreement (NAFTA) promised further growth in exports.

The United States has been a major consumer of foreign made fasteners for decades, especially of the cheaply made "standards" used in many areas of the automotive and residential construction industries. Taiwan was the major importer of fasteners for the first half of 1993, shipping 381 million pounds of fasteners worth over $245 million or 45.7 percent of total imports. Japan was the second largest importer (19.9 percent), followed by Canada (16.7 percent), China (4.3 percent), and numerous other importers. The adoption of regulations stemming from the Fastener Quality Act is expected to change the import market as manufacturers of low-quality products are forced to comply with more stringent fastener specifications and

as U.S. Customs officials crack-down on price-fixing and product-dumping.

INDUSTRY LEADERS

Fastener manufacturers have long congregated near the industries that buy their products, and according to Industrial Fastener Institute sources, the major purchasers are automobile manufacturers, the federal government, electronics, machinery, aerospace, and appliance manufacturers. For this reason, Illinois, Ohio, Michigan, and Pennsylvania lead all states in fastener production. California, home to major players in the defense and aerospace industries, is also a major producer of fasteners. Illinois Tool Works, with headquarters in Glenview, Illinois, is by far the largest producer of industrial fasteners in the United States, with $2.64 billion in 1991 sales and nearly 20,000 employees. Other major manufacturers are Microdot, Inc. of Fullerton, California, and Black & Decker Corp. Fastening Systems Group of Towson, Maryland. The majority of manufacturers listed in *Ward's Business Directory of U.S. Private and Public Companies 1993* employ just a few hundred workers and bring in less than $50 million in annual income.

INDUSTRY INFORMATION SOURCES

"Cold Formed Parts Yield Impressive Benefits," *Manufacturing Engineering*, November 1984.

Darnay, Arsen J., ed., *Manufacturing USA*, Detroit: Gale Research Inc., 1989.

Engineering Staff, Teledyne Landis Machine, James G. Bralla, ed., "Screw Threads," *Handbook of Product Design for Manufacturing: A Practical Guide to Low-Cost Production*, New York: McGraw-Hill, 1986.

The Heritage of Mechanical Fasteners, Cleveland, OH: Industrial Fastener Institute, 1991.

Industrial Fastener Institute, "Fastener Application Advisory," Cleveland, OH: Industrial Fastener Institute, May 1993.

Industrial Fastener Institute, "Fastener Application Advisory: The Fastener Quality Act, Public Law 101-592," Cleveland, OH: Industrial Fastener Institute, May 1993.

"Industrial Fastener Shipments to Grow 6% Per Year as Markets Recover," *Fastener Industry News*, April 22, 1993.

"Manufacturers' Capability Guide. Division 2, Small Products: Fasteners & Accessories," Cleveland, OH: Industrial Fastener Institute, 1987.

Neely, John E., and Richard R. Kibbe, *Modern Materials and Manufacturing Processes*, New York: John Wiley & Sons, 1987.

U.S. Congress House Committee on Energy and Commerce, Subcommittee on Oversight and Investigations, *The Threat from Substandard Fasteners: Is America Losing Its Grip?* 100th Cong., 2d sess., 1988, Committee Print 100-Y.

U.S. Department of Commerce, *1987 Census of Manufactures*, Washington, DC: U.S. Department of Commerce, 1987.

U.S. Department of Commerce, *U.S. Industrial Outlook 1993*, Washington, DC: U.S. Department of Commerce, January 1993.

Ward's Business Directory of U.S. Private and Public Companies, Detroit: Gale Research Inc., 1993.

Wick, Charles, James G. Bralla, ed., ''Cold-Headed Parts,'' *Handbook of Product Design for Manufacturing: A Practical Guide to Low-Cost Production*, New York: McGraw-Hill, 1986.

Wood, Donald E., *From Archimedes to Automation: The History of the Screw Machine*, Brecksville, OH: National Screw Machine Products Association.

—Tom Pendergast

SIC 3462

IRON AND STEEL FORGINGS

This industry includes establishments primarily engaged in manufacturing iron and steel forgings, with or without the use of dies. These establishments generally operate on a job or order basis, manufacturing forgings for sale to others or for interplant transfer. Establishments that produce metal forgings for incorporation in end products produced in the same establishment are classified on the basis of the end product. Establishments further processing forgings are classified according to the particular product or process.

INDUSTRY SNAPSHOT

The forging processes of the iron and steel forging industry characterize the industry rather than the industry's end products. Forging reconfigures a substance by pressing, hammering, or constricting it with a great deal of pressure. Most substances are forged after they have been heated, but not melted. Liquefying metals to make parts is called casting.

There are three main processes for forging metal: closed die or impression die forging, which compresses a metal between two dies that contain an impression of the end product; open die forging, which hammers metal between two flat dies but moves the piece between blows to shape the end product; and seamless rolled ring forging, which punches a hole in the work piece and then rolls and squeezes it into a thin, seamless ring.

All forging processes make very strong parts known as forgings. Forgings are strong because forging processes create a grain flow in the parts of the finished product that require maximum strength. Forging processes also impart beneficial metallurgical properties, such as ductility, resistance properties, dimensional stability, and absence of porosity. Although companies may forge many types of metal, in 1993 the most common forged metal was carbon steel; the second most common was alloy steel.

Establishments in the iron and steel forging industry are concentrated in the Midwest and Northeast, with the highest number of establishments in Ohio, Illinois, Michigan, and Pennsylvania. Of the entire forging industry, Ohio, Pennsylvania, and Illinois hold over 40 percent of U.S. forging plants. In 1992 there were 13 states which did not have any forging establishments. Those states were Alaska, Delaware, Florida, Hawaii, Idaho, Maine, Montana, New Hampshire, New Mexico, North and South Dakota, Utah, and Wyoming.

In addition to the establishments that concentrate their efforts on forging iron and steel in the United States, many companies produce their own forgings for manufacture of their primary products. Shipments were valued at $3 billion for companies in this industry in 1987. But when other SIC groups were taken into account, the Department of Commerce's *Census of Manufactures* found that other companies shipped $0.2 billion worth of products considered primary to this industry classification.

Purchases of forgings came from industries concentrated in the same general regions as the forging companies, even though forging companies market their products nationally and internationally. The largest purchasers of forged products are the aerospace, national defense, and automotive industries, as well as agricultural, construction, mining, material handling, and general industrial equipment manufacturers.

In 1992 the Clinton Administration ordered substantial support for industry growth through research and technology with a mandate to the Department of Commerce's National Institute of Standards and Technology (NIST). The mandate required NIST to be more vigorous in its efforts to solve commercial sector problems. The government involvement in research and technology will allow small, regional companies to access more sources of information to increase their competitive abilities and help larger companies defray the cost of high-risk, long-term research on new technologies.

BACKGROUND AND DEVELOPMENT

Humans first forged metals by hand-hammering them. The steam hammer automated the forging industry in 1843; the steam raised the hammer, but the weight of the hammer was the only pressure used to shape the metal. By 1888, a double-acting hammer used steam to supplement the pressure exerted by the falling hammer. Technology continued to advance the industry.

A census taken by *Forging* reported that two forging methods dominated the industry in 1992: closed die and open die methods. The closed die method was used by 248 companies, while the open die method was used by 109 companies, a margin of more than two-to-one. The ring rolling method was used as a primary method by 16 plants; 13 plants in the census cited other unnamed primary methods of forging. (The *Forging* census included 32 Canadian companies and companies classified in **SIC 3463: Nonferrous Forgings.**)

Forging developed as more of an art than a science, and even in the 1990s, when most forging was almost completely mechanized, forging processes could not be completely predicted with scientific methods. The unique problems posed by forging are the result of the many factors manufacturers must take into account. The most common factors to consider are the properties of the metal to be transformed, the strain or amount of pressure required to shape the metal, the rate at which the pressure can be applied to the metal for deformation, and the appropriate temperature for the deformation to occur without scaling or breaking the material. All the factors must be balanced to achieve consistently desired results from any of the forging processes.

Even with advances in technology, the complexity of some forging problems have not been solved. Determining the kind of die lubricant to use for forging operations is an example. Before the industrial revolution, animal oils, coal, soapstone, and crude oils were used because the products were "simple" and the processes requiring lubricants were "minimal," according to *Forging*. The advent of the steam-hammer demanded new lubricants, which were developed by the end of the nineteenth century. The new lubricants were steam-refined mineral oils, sawdust, salt water, fatty soap solutions, and oil and graphite flake combinations.

The oil and graphite mixtures proved to be effective as forging speeds increased with automation, but because those mixtures were explosive, other lubricants needed to be developed. Mixtures of water and

graphite replaced the oil-based mixtures by 1970. In response to health related problems caused by graphite lubricants, research on synthetic lubricants began in the 1970s. In 1993 *Forging* reported that "water-based graphites make up about 60 percent of the forging industry sales, synthetics 15 percent, and oil-based graphites 15 percent."

The success of the forging process relies on the effectiveness of the lubricant, but no simple method for selecting a lubricant exists. Each lubricant has advantages as well as disadvantages. Oil and graphite applies easily and works well at many temperatures, but is explosive and expensive. Water and graphite costs less and helps cool dies, but requires careful application to work; in addition, graphite dust can collect in the work area and cause problems for workers. Synthetic lubricants are cost effective and less hazardous but must be applied through spraying, may impede metal flow, and are ineffective to use for forging complex shapes.

From 1982 to 1986 the iron and steel forging industry's costs as well as profits declined slightly. The cost of materials lowered to 90 percent ($1.4 billion) of 1982 costs ($1.5 billion), but the value of shipments also dipped to 88 percent ($2.6 billion) of 1982 values ($2.9 billion). In addition, the value added by manufacture dropped by eight percent to $1.2 billion. Interestingly, the industry's capital investment amounted to only 47 percent ($74.4 million) of that which was invested in 1982 ($158.4 million). The total number of establishments, workers, and production hours also declined by 1986.

CURRENT CONDITIONS

There are three types of forging orders: custom forgings, which are made at the request of a customer; captive forgings, which are made for the company's own internal use; and catalog forgings, which are standard parts that are resold through various sources. Forged products range from precision aircraft parts to everyday hammer heads and wrenches. The forging industry's sales mostly come from custom forgings. In the entire forging industry, which includes **SIC 3463: Nonferrous Forgings,** 1992 sales of custom forgings were more than $4 billion, according to the Forging Industry Association (figures include 250 companies in the United States and Canada).

In a separate study of sales, the FIA gathered annual sales of custom forgings in 1992. The study included 130 North American companies and all types of metals. Sales figures were reported according to the type of forging process. Closed die forgings amounted to $2.8 billion in sales, a 0.5 percent increase over sales in 1991. Open die forging sales dropped 11 percent from 1991 figures to $658 million.

FIA's census, as reported in *Forging*, showed slight gains in production in the early 1990s. Orders for both impression die forging and open die forgings rose from 1991 to 1992, by one percent and nine percent, respectively.

INDUSTRY LEADERS

The majority of the most successful forging companies are privately held. The top ten iron and steel forgings companies in 1993 were Brenlin Group of Akron, Ohio, with $496 million in sales and 3,400 employees; Lancer Industries Inc. of New York, New York, with $315 million in sales and 2,000 employees; Ladish Company Inc. of Cudahy, Wisconsin, with an estimated $230 million in sales and 2,200 employees; Masco Corp. Forming Technology Division of Royal Oak, Michigan, with $105 million in sales and 300 employees; Janberg Industries Inc. of Chicago, Illinois, with $92 million in sales and 600 employees; Can-Am Industries Inc., part of Titan Wheel International Inc., of Quincy, Illinois, with an estimated $80 million in sales and 400 employees; and Keller Group Inc. of Northfield, Illinois, with $80 million in sales and 400 employees.

WORK FORCE

Forging requires large amounts of capital investments to maintain the expensive equipment, but the industry sustains companies in a wide variety of sizes. Typical companies have an employee range of 50 to 250 employees, but can have as few as 10 employees or as many as 1000 employees. Machine forming operators make up the largest part of the work force in the industry. Employment in the industry was reported by the U.S. Department of Labor to be around 30,000 in 1992.

RESEARCH AND TECHNOLOGY

New funding for research and technology will spur growth in the forging industry for 30 years past 1993. $80 billion worth of federal funding was made available to American manufacturers by a mandate from the Clinton Administration. NIST expected a 1994 budget of $47.2 million, an increase of $6.6 million, to help it increase American industry competitiveness through development of new technologies, according to *Forging*. Roger W. Werne, the associate director for engineering and technology transfer for Lawrence Livermore National Laboratory, noted in *Forging* that under the Clinton Administration's increased funding for national laboratories, the labs can act as an "'insurance policy' that can enhance the probability of success of a U.S. company or consortium of companies that decides to push the limit of their technology beyond existing boundaries." About the development of new technologies, the executive editor of *Forging*, John R. Wright, stated that "America is on the verge of wholesale new areas of technology development. We are close to breakthroughs—a technology blast that will carry this country for the next 30 years."

INDUSTRY INFORMATION SOURCES

"Federal Spending to Highlight Research." *Forging*, Spring 1993: 8.

"Forging Industry Fact Sheet." Cleveland, OH: Forging Industry Association, August 1992.

"1992 Sales Shown in FIA Survey." *Forging*, Summer 1993: 8.

"Sowing the Seeds of Tomorrow's Technology." *Forging*, Spring 1993: 20-21.

"Taking a Tally of the U.S. Forging Industry." *Forging*, Summer 1993: 23-25.

1987 Census of Manufactures. Washington, DC: U.S. Department of Commerce, 1987.

Werne, Roger W. "Grand Challenges for Industrial Competitiveness." *Forging*, Summer 1993: 34-36.

Wright, John R. "Tapping into Technology." *Forging*, Summer 1993: 5.

—Sara Pendergast

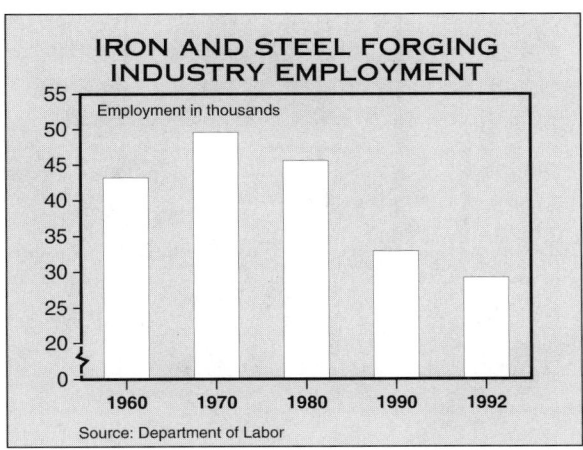

IRON AND STEEL FORGING INDUSTRY EMPLOYMENT

Employment in thousands

Source: Department of Labor

SIC 3463

NONFERROUS FORGINGS

This category includes establishments primarily engaged in manufacturing nonferrous forgings, with or without the use of dies. These establishments generally operate on a job or order basis, manufacturing forgings for sale to others or for interplant transfer. Establishments that produce metal forgings for incorporation in end products produced in the same establishment are classified on the basis of the end product. Establishments further processing forgings are classified according to the particular product or process.

The forging industry as a whole, which includes **SIC 3462: Iron and Steel Forgings,** is characterized by its forging processes rather than its end products. Because many companies forge many types of metals, including both ferrous and nonferrous, industry information for this industry classification and **SIC 3462: Iron and Steel Forgings** are often reported together. The Forging Industry Association, for example, does not distinguish between the two SICs, presenting information on sales for the entire industry. Therefore, this entry will focus on the unique characteristics of the nonferrous forgings industry, and general information on forging can be found in the essay on **SIC 3462: Iron and Steel Forgings.**

The number of companies engaged in primarily manufacturing nonferrous forgings is only one-fifth the number of companies engaged in forging iron and steel. In 1986 60 companies primarily used nonferrous metals to manufacture their forgings, a decrease of four companies since 1982. Capital investment within the industry slid in 1986 to 44 percent ($43.8 million) of that which was invested in 1982. Production in value of shipments also declined during that period by one percent, to $1,086.1 million. As the value of shipments fell, however, the cost of materials and the value added by manufacture increased, by three and eight percent to $586.1 million and $497.8 million, respectively.

In the 1990s, the nonferrous forging industry continued to be a small part of the total forging industry. In a 1993 census taken by *Forging,* 40 of 386 plants across the United States and Canada concentrated their efforts on forging aluminum, while 13 facilities concentrated on titanium and 12 on copper base alloys. The forging of nonferrous metals is not limited to only these companies, however. The total number of plants that engage in nonferrous metal forging to some degree is significantly higher. When asked all the types of metals a company forged, the number of plants that indicated that they engaged in at least a modicum of aluminum forging rose to 89, while those engaged in titanium forging reached 55, and those forging copper base alloys increased to 51.

Compared with other manufacturing establishments, the nonferrous forging industry is labor-intensive. The industry employs more than twice as many employees per company than other manufacturers, with 132 workers per establishment on average as opposed to 61. The 1987 *Census of Manufactures* reported that the nonferrous forgings industry employed 7,300 employees, a drop of eight percent since 1982.

Aluminum is the metal most often forged in this industry classification. It is ''the most forgeable of all metals,'' according to *Forging.* Aluminum and its alloys can be forged into many different shapes and sizes. The metal is unique because it can be heated to the same temperature as the dies that will form it. The hardness of the dies is also lower than dies used for forging steel. The most common lubricant for forging aluminum is a graphite-water solution with some soap to help the flow of the metal. Aluminum can also be forged into precision parts that need no further machining for use. Gravity or drop hammers are used for open die forgings, mechanical presses for closed die forgings, and hydraulic presses for complex pieces.

Other nonferrous forgings are made from magnesium and its alloys, whose coarse grains require that the metal be forged slowly in hydraulic presses; copper and its alloys, including brass and bronze; and titanium and its alloys, which are very sensitive to temperature changes but are extremely strong and resistant to corrosion.

INDUSTRY INFORMATION SOURCES

''Boeing Chooses Ti for 777 Designs.'' *Forging,* Summer 1993: 8-9.

''Metals and Alloys.'' *Forging,* Spring 1993: 25-34.

1987 Census of Manufactures. Washington, DC: U.S. Department of Commerce, 1987.

''Taking a Tally of the U.S. Forging Industry.'' *Forging,* Summer 1993: 23-25.

—Sara Pendergast

AUTOMOTIVE STAMPINGS

This category includes establishments that primarily manufacture metal auto parts, such as body panels, hubs and trim pieces, usually for sale to other manufacturers or for use in assembly facilities located off-site. Those firms which utilize the stamped products in the manufacture of end products in the same establishment are categorized by that end-product.

INDUSTRY SNAPSHOT

The automotive stamping industry remains closely dependant on the health of the domestic U.S. automobile market. With the decline of domestic car and truck production after 1988, the demand for stampings also decreased. According to *U.S. Industrial Outlook- 1991*, the value of shipments for the industry showed no change between 1987 and 1991 when expressed in 1987 dollars; the industry stagnated at approximately $16 billion. The industry employed 117,100 in 1988. The technical expertise of industry production workers is increasing rapidly as the industry adapts to new production techniques and strategies, the challenges of new metal alloys, and the competition of plastic alternatives.

ORGANIZATION AND STRUCTURE

As with all manufacturers of automotive parts, stamping firms produce for two major market components: the original equipment manufacturer (OEM) and the after-market or replacement parts sector. Typical components include fenders, roofs, floor pans, exhaust systems, brake shoes and trim pieces. Such large pieces require a considerable investment in tooling and scale of operation. Consequently, businesses engaged in their manufacture are usually operated by the major automotive manufacturers or contracted by them. Small components, such as brackets, valves and hangers, do not require the same level of sophisticated engineering investment, which allows small, independent firms to specialize in such items. As a rule of thumb, automotive manufacturers contract out any stamped part needed in volumes below 200,000 pieces annually.

Stamping plants tend to be large operations employing many production workers. In 1982, 82 percent of all such establishments employed more than 100 workers. However, between 1972 and 1987 the number of production workers employed dropped three percent from 103,000 to 99,900, after dipping to 74,500 in 1982. At the same time the number of

establishments rose by 57 percent, from 453 to 713. The average firm employed 135 workers in 1982, compared with 166 in 1988. Because the automotive stamping industry is a major supplier to automotive manufacturers, firms in SIC 3465 are concentrated in Michigan, Ohio, and Indiana, near the major U.S. automakers.

BACKGROUND AND DEVELOPMENT

The process or art of stamping metal to form hundreds or even thousands of identical parts evolved with the automotive industry. In 1912, Philadelphian Edward Budd convinced the Hupp Motor Co., the Oakland Motor Co., and Garford Motors to begin incorporating metal into the design of their car bodies instead of the traditional wood. For the next few years, cars were made using a combination of both materials. In 1914, however, the Dodge brothers moved the automotive and the stamping industries into the modern era of industrial manufacturing with an order for 5,000 all-steel touring sedan bodies.

Stamping, or cold-forming, involves the use of power-operated clamping devices. A moving die, or forming-tool, presses into a sheet of metal and against a fixed die. The metal undergoes what is known as plastic deformation to take on the desired shape and thickness. Until the 1930s, the method was more art than science. Skilled artisans would produce relatively simple dies and use their collective experience to effectively produce parts mainly by trial and error. They often used an array of special tools and rituals to trick the sheet metal into shape.

As the industry needed to produce more sophisticated components, the unitized body which eventually replaced the frame entirely on domestic automobiles was developed. With the unitized body, once the die design, the metal material, and the blank sheet dimensions were chosen and found to be correct, the tool-system could create thousands of duplications under the supervision of relatively unskilled labor. That cost-saving attribute appealed to the needs of mass production manufacturers and overcame the disadvantage of the time-consuming process of die development. The new stamping process would require each individual component of the process to have a unique set of custom-designed dies.

A major advancement in press design came in the 1950s with the use of numerical controls. They made the new presses more accurate, faster, and easier to set up, allowing the industry to begin manufacturing a new range of products including mufflers, oil filler caps, some gears, engine mounts and brackets. By the 1970s, this technology gave way to computer numerical controls. The computer allowed the presses to run faster and operate more precisely, creating a need for automatic systems and robot loaders and unloaders.

The growing popularity of fuel-efficient Japanese-built cars challenged the mass-production philosophy of the American automotive manufacturers, particularly in the 1980s. The stamping industry felt the pressure directly. Its manufacturing philosophy prescribed large, regional facilities supplying several assembly plants in various geographic locations. However, the number of car models being produced, including foreign models, was steadily climbing. In 1986, there were 51 models sold in the United States; by 1990 there were 90. The capacity of press lines in operation had increased as older lines were replaced with more modern, efficient systems, which meant competition increased along with the number of required die changes.

Increased foreign competition also meant the domestic manufacturers had to improve the quality of their product. They needed new metals with better corrosion resistance. Instead of the standard 0.040-inch-thick carbon steel the industry had been using, manufacturers began specifying Zincrometal, one-sided and two-sided galvanized and coated alloy-steels. In addition, customers became far less tolerant of part variations which showed up as poor fit and finish. In 1981, many firms introduced Statistical Process Control and begin to implement Just-In-Time manufacturing systems in order to tighten the production belt. The resulting retrenching turned into downsizing and a massive reduction in production employment. Between 1972 and 1982, the number of production workers in the industry dropped from 103,000 to 74,500.

A major impediment to improved efficiencies in American stamping plants was the age of the equipment inventory. According to the 13th *American Machinist* inventory of metalworking machinery, almost one-half of all American metalforming equipment was at least 20 years old in 1983. Much of this equipment was cumbersome, designed for long production runs with long periods of shut down for maintenance and die replacement. During the 1980s, rebuilt and upgraded parts for these presses rose to 29 percent of all machine tool manufacturer's shipments. Even with the efforts to modernize, however, some machines could not be made competitive with the newer, more flexible Japanese technologies.

CURRENT CONDITIONS

One of the most important battles for the American industry to win was the challenge of the rapid die change. Traditionally, American stampers took hours and sometimes days to change the dies in their machines. With the lines shut down for maintenance, one shift out of three working, and a warehouse full of finished product inventory in case of an unexpected breakdown, such long change-out times had not been a problem. However, with Just-In-Time production methods, inventories shrank to only hours of reserve parts and the number of die-changes increased to several per day. In contrast, in Japan during the early 1980s, die-changes took ten minutes, using small armies of workers. By 1991, Hirotec Corp of Hiroshima could consistently change a die set in 80-to-90 seconds using just three men.

The difference between the United States and Japanese stamping processes was equipment design and planning. Older American machines required the complete removal of the old die before a new one could be installed. To do that, workers had to unfasten bolts and brackets. Having placed the new die, they would then set the piston stroke height and adjust the die position. Japanese presses use hydraulic clamps to hold standardized dies, and have openings on either side to allow the new die to be inserted as the old is withdrawn.

To remain competitive, in the early 1990s the Big Three U.S. automakers (Ford Motor Company, General Motors Corporation, and Chrysler Corporation) spent billions for new presses and new stamping plants tied to particular assembly facilities. The on-site stamping plant produces all the major parts required for the assembly of a specific car, cutting down on transportation costs and increasing the efficiency of shorter production runs. However, in 1991 the Big Three still had 22 major regional facilities which would be expensive to abandon and replace.

To increase the efficiency of those older plants, the industry began to standardize the die heights and improve the die designs and body panel designs so as to reduce the number of strokes needed to complete the forming process and reduce the amount of scrap steel produced. Formed parts almost always require multiple hits by the die or a series of dies to take the desired finished shape. Reducing the number of strokes required increases the rate of production and the life of the die. American molds typically average five and one-half hits per panel compared to less than three and one-half for Japanese systems.

During the early 1990s, the competitive need for higher efficiency through better quality control and increased flexibility drove the auto-makers to rethink their stamping arrangements and manufacturing philosophies. The traditional method of sourcing parts from several suppliers working from a manufacturer-supplied design gave way to a more cooperative and interactive approach. Copying the Japanese method, the manufacturers began to involve specific suppliers early on in the design stage and to require them to provide much of the engineering expertise, which reduced costs to the manufacturer and allowed the supplier to maintain an economy of scale in its actual production. It also meant fewer but larger suppliers. At the same time, manufacturers moved to on-site stamping plants equipped with sophisticated technology which effectively automated the process from start to finish. The increased efficiencies allowed the industry to compete effectively with foreign firms and to resist pressure from other materials like aluminum and plastics.

INDUSTRY LEADERS

The largest stamping firms in the OEM portion of the industry remain the automotive manufacturers themselves, but those firms farm-out about 25 percent of their new-car stamping requirements to independent firms. The largest of the independent stamping firms is The Budd Company of Troy Michigan, employing 9,000 workers in 36 facilities to produce $1.4 billion in sales in 1991. Founded in 1912, the company pioneered the development of metal stampings throughout the early part of the century, racking up such firsts as the first four-door, all steel sedan body (Dodge), the first all-steel unitized body (Nash), stainless steel ''streamliner'' trains of the 1930s, the Navy's Conestoga RB-1 stainless steel cargo plane built during World War II, the prototype for the French Citroen, and the all-plastic-bodied 1954 Studebaker Coupe.

Metal stampings make up more than 50 percent of the company's sales, but it also manufactures fiberglass and plastic composite body panels, truck brake and wheel components, iron castings, and cold weather products like engine block heaters and interior car warmers. The German steel manufacturer and stamping firm, Thyssen AG, bought Budd Co. in 1978. The American firm had extended itself into many non-automotive areas like aerospace and nuclear energy, reaching an employment high of 21,500, but it was loosing money. Thyssen propped up the company with influxes of capital, trimmed company operations, and limited operations to the automotive business to help it through the recession of the 1980s.

The second largest independent metal stamper, Douglas & Lomason Co., headquartered in Farmington Hills, Michigan, began operations in 1902 as a carriage rail maker. It produces seat systems and trim components for the Big Three and the Japanese

transplants at 21 facilities using 5,300 employees. Most of its business comes from domestic car manufacturers. In 1992, Chrysler accounted for 43 percent of Douglas & Lomason's automotive sales. Ford made up 28 percent and General Motors, 20 percent. Its 1991 total sales volume exceeded $425 million.

The Active Tool and Manufacturing Company of Roseville, Michigan is the third largest stamping firm. It supplies both the OEM and the after-market sectors of the stamping industry. Founded in 1929, it employs 1,500 at three manufacturing sites, a research facility and its Tooling Center. Sales for 1992 exceeded $110 million.

WORK FORCE

Traditionally, the large stamping plants, using large quantities of relatively unskilled workers, have operated with union labor. The main unions are the United Auto Workers (UAW) in the United States and the Canadian Automobile Aerospace and Agricultural Implement Workers (CAW) in Canada. However, many transplant operations have tried to use non-union labor throughout their operations including the on-site stamping plants.

With the shift to advanced automation at the newer plants, the traditional union stance of clearly defined job descriptions and classifications is giving way to more flexible arrangements like Ford's Modern Operating Agreement at its Wayne, Michigan on-site stamping facility. Under that agreement, only one category of production worker exists. Each worker receives training on the entire manufacturing process to produce a teamwork approach. Displaced by sophisticated automation, the number of unskilled operators continues to decline. In their place, skilled tradesmen and craft-workers design and maintain the complicated production machinery and its robot servers.

Manufacturers and a growing number of labor leaders see automation as the key to preventing manufacturing facilities from relocating in Mexico with the advent of the North American Free Trade Agreement (NAFTA). Without the competitive edge of tireless automation, the lower wages accepted by Mexican workers would force manufacturers to relocate to stay competitive.

AMERICA AND THE WORLD

The American stamping industry in the 1990s has been playing catch-up with their European and Japanese counterparts. American plants typically wasted twice as much material, used more press operations, and ran presses at half the speed of foreign plants with production runs five times as long. Body panel sets costing $300 in a Japanese plant could cost $700 in its American counterpart. By building newer, more flexible plants and up-grading old presses where possible, American manufacturers are slowly overcoming their impediments.

RESEARCH AND TECHNOLOGY

Modern stamping plants are using advanced technology to redefine themselves. Once the labor-intensive blacksmith shop of the auto industry, stamping now taps the skills and ingenuity of its workers to produce machines and computer monitoring systems to do repetitive work. At a fully automated plant like Ford's $600-million Wayne, Michigan stamping plant, for example, human operators are used only to load raw steel into the plant and to remove the finished product at the end of the production line. Automatic guided vehicles follow roadways of wires embedded in the factory floor carrying bar-coded metal to the correct storage area or the next press that needs that particular type of material. Transfer presses pass the metal down lines of six or eight similar machines to form complicated components. The completed parts exit the production area, and enter the transfer area where operators manually check them and rack them on a conveyor. Their next stop is the assembly facility.

Transfer presses need less production floor room, but often achieve only 25-30 percent operating efficiency because of their complexity. Simpler, easier to repair robot systems may become the technology of choice where the need for flexibility dominates. Robot systems appeal to small-batch producers like Budd Company. A ''hard-tooled'' automation system like a transfer press line may need expensive retooling every few years, but a ''soft-tooled'' robotic system can be upgraded by reprogramming and minor physical relocations.

The computer has also improved new die design and raw material usage, reducing both the production costs due to wastage and the design time needed for the evolution of a new car. Such programs can reduce the skilled man-hours needed for die face design by 50 percent, die face manufacture by 30 percent, and die tryout and corrective modification by 30 percent. Such improvements went a long way in reducing the traditional domestic car manufacturers' five-year new car design period, putting it in line with Japanese design periods of two or three years.

INDUSTRY INFORMATION SOURCES

''Active Tool and Manufacturing Co.'' *Chilton's Automotive Industries*, June 1993.

Advances and Trends in Automotive Sheet Steel Stamping. Detroit, MI: SAE International Congress & Exposition, 1988.

''Automakers Cut Steel Costs by Improving Stamping Operations.'' *Iron Age*, May 1988.

Belli, Colleen. ''Celebrating 60 years on the East Side.'' *Automotive News*, 7 October 1985.

Berry, Bryan. ''Chrysler Drawn to Galvannealed.'' *Iron Age*, April 1990.

———. ''For Steelmakers, Quality Is Job Won.'' *Iron Age*, July 1992.

———. ''U.S. Automakers Overhaul Stamping.'' *Iron Age*, April 1987.

Brooke, Lindsay. ''At Arm's Length.'' *Chilton's Automotive Industries*, June 1993.

———. ''Japan's Stamping Master.'' *Chilton's Automotive Industries*, November 1991.

''The Budd Company.'' *Chilton's Automotive Industries*, June 1993.

Byrne, Harlan S. ''Douglas & Lomason.'' *Barron's*, 30 November 1992.

Callahan, Joseph. ''Defying the Doomsayers.'' *Automotive Industries*, November 1989.

Coffman, Cathy. ''Zeroing in on Automotive.'' *Automotive Industries*, July 1989.

Davie, Michael. ''Stelco Quality 'Leadership' Gets Nod from Chrysler.'' *Hamilton Spectator*, 22 June 1993.

''Douglas & Lomason Co.'' *Chilton's Automotive Industries*, June 1993.

Fleming, Al. ''Budd Looks to Future after Weathering Bad Times.'' *Automotive News*, 2 February 1987.

———. ''Team Player.'' *Automotive News*, 9 July 1990.

Gould, Les and Karen Auguston. ''GM's Oshawa Stamping Plant: Integrated Automation at Its Best.'' *Modern Materials Handling*, November 1989.

Harbour, Jim. ''How to Cut Stamping Costs.'' *Automotive Industries*, May 1989.

———. ''On-Site Stamping.'' *Automotive Industries*, September 1991.

Huber, Robert R. ''Technology Keeps Forming Competitive.'' *Production*, August 1990.

Iliescu, Constantin, ed. *Cold-Pressing Technology.* New York: Elsevier Science Publishing Company Inc., 1990.

Manjii, James F. ''GM Oshawa Meets Foreign Competition with Systems Integration.'' *Automation*, October 1991.

McElroy, John. ''Toyota's Stamping Break-Through.'' *Chilton's Automotive Industries*, May 1990.

Noaker, Paula M. ''Revamp Your Stamping Strategy—Not Just the Line.'' *Manufacturing Technologies*, March 1989.

''Taking the Plunge.'' *Ward's Auto World*, July 1986.

"Trends of Labor Productivity in Metal Stamping Industries." *Monthly Labor Review*, May 1986.

Vasilash, Gary S. "Competing." *Production*, December 1992.

————. "Who Says Only the Young Are Innovatively Aggressive?" *Production*, February 1989.

Witt, Clyde E. "First for Ford." *Material Handling Engineering*, December 1989.

—Al Cook

SIC 3466

CROWNS AND CLOSURES

This category covers establishments primarily engaged in manufacturing metal crowns and closures, including bottle caps and jar crowns and tops.

INDUSTRY SNAPSHOT

The crowns and closures industrial classification is a small portion of the stamped metals industry that is fading into a highly segmented industry. As bottlers shift from glass to plastic containers, plastic closures are becoming preferred over metal. Shipments in this industry slipped between 1986 and 1988 from $914.5 million to $700.8 million. Shipments rose in 1989 to $702.4 million, and again in 1990 to $720.2 million. Employment, however, has fallen since 1983, with the sharpest decline between 1987 and 1988. In 1983, this industry employed 7,100 people, 5,700 of whom were production workers. By 1990, this total was 4,400, with 3,500 production workers.

In comparison to other manufacturing industries, the companies engaged in the crowns and closures industry boast higher investment, shipments, and greater value added per establishment. More employees and higher payrolls per establishment were reported in 1989, with 34 of the 53 establishments employing more than 20 people.

Indiana's six companies claimed the highest shipments of any other state. These shipments, valued at $160 million, represented 19.5 percent of the total in the United States. Approximately 1,200 people were employed by Indiana's crown and closure manufacturers, which represents 19.7 percent of all American workers employed by this industry. Approximately 200 employees per establishment were reported, earning an average hourly wage of $10.05. California's seven firms reported shipments valued at $66 million, representing 8.1 percent of the U.S. total. Connecticut's six establishments tied this percentage.

Approximately 500 people were employed by California's establishments, each averaging 71 people paid an average of $11.25 per hour. Connecticut's companies employed 900, with each firm averaging 150 people paid an average of $9.57 per hour. Other states with crown and closures firms include: Illinois with six, Pennsylvania with six, New York with four, New Jersey with three, Oklahoma with three, and Texas with one.

ORGANIZATION AND STRUCTURE

The product share of this industry is split into three sections. Metal commercial closures and metal home canning closures comprise 84.39 percent of the total market, and metal crowns for glass and metal containers represent 14.08 percent. The remaining 1.53 percent is represented by non specific crowns and closures. Aluminum, in the form of sheet, plate, and foil, is proportionately the industry's largest input. Tin plate, tin free steel, terneplate, and blackplate represent the second most highly consumed materials. Carbon steel sheet and strips are also used.

Bottled and canned soft drink manufacturers use up 22.3 percent of the industry's outputs. Malt beverage makers use 10.6 percent, pickles, sauces, and salad dressings consume 10.5 percent, and canned fruits and vegetables take 7.7 percent of the industry's outputs. The industry's products are also used in the packaging of roasted coffee, wines, brandy, brandy spirits, toilet preparations, and confectionery products.

INDUSTRY LEADERS

The Anchor Hocking Packaging Company was ranked as the industry leader in sales in 1992. Of the twelve companies reporting over $1 million in sales, Anchor Hocking of Lancaster, Ohio reported $130 million. Continental Can Company of Downers Grove, Illinois, was ranked second with estimated sales of $120 million. Specialty Packaging Products of Richmond, Virginia, was ranked third with sales of $66 million. Other industry leaders include Aluminum Company of America (ALCOA) and Phoenix Closures Inc. For the top twelve companies engaged in this industry, total sales were $474 million in 1992 and 5,000 people were employed.

Shortly after the turn of the century, a new business named Continental Can Company (CCC) was started in Syracuse, New York. This company survived the Great Depression, two world wars, and other economic booms and busts, emerging as an entity boasting $5 billion in sales by 1982. In 1984, CCC was sold and broken into separate businesses. Meanwhile, in 1983, CCC's president, Donald Bainton, retired and joined Viatech, Inc. as chairman. Viatech then acquired several overseas packaging companies, and by 1991 it purchased Continental Plastic Containers, Inc., the last remaining division of the original CCC. By 1992, Viatech acquired the right to use the Continental Can Company name and triple-C logo.

Viatech then formally changed its name to Continental Can Company, and it was first listed on the New York Stock Exchange in 1992. That same year, the company diversified through the purchase of Merrywood Inc.'s 50 percent interest in Plastic Containers, Inc. Plastic Containers Inc. is the holding company for Continental Plastic Containers, Inc. The primary focus of the company is long term growth and profitability in domestic and international operations.

CCC's sales improved by 65 percent in 1992 to $511 million from $310 million in 1991. However, third quarter results in 1993 showed a drop of income by 45 percent. Foreign currency translations and the weak European economy were blamed for the results, primarily attributable to the company's operations in Germany, France, and Spain.

ALCOA's 1992 annual report defines its corporate mission as "creating value for customers, employees and shareholders through innovation, technology and operational expertise. ALCOA will be the best aluminum company in the world, and a leader in other businesses in which we choose to compete." The cover of the annual report shows numerous bottle caps sporting the logos of 7UP, Vess, Michelob, All Sport, Coca-Cola, and Clearly Canadian, among others. The report states, "Over 20 billion ALCOA closures—produced in 14 plants on four continents—capped beverages and other consumer products in more than 50 countries during 1992." Packaging accounted for 30 percent of ALCOA's total 1992 revenues. However, ALCOA's sales have dropped significantly since 1989, when $10.91 billion was reported. By 1992, this figure dropped to $9.49 billion. A net loss of $1.14 billion was reported that same year. Mandatory changes in accounting for employee and retiree health benefits were cited as the cause for this substantial loss. In addition, the reduced cost of aluminum caused sales and operating revenues to be lower than 1991 levels by $400 million.

WORK FORCE

Dramatic decreases in employment levels in the metal forging and stamping industries are predicted to take place as the year 2005 approaches. Metal and plastic machine forming operators and tenders are expected to face a nearly 40 percent reduction. Metal and plastic machine tool cutting operators are also expected to lose nearly 40 percent of current staffing. Other occupations expected to lose between 30 and 40 percent of current levels include: machine tool cutting and forming operators; assemblers and fabricators; and punch press operators. Those occupations expected to downsize 20 to 30 percent include: material handlers; general managers and top executives; machine feeders and offbearers; metal and plastic machine setters; janitors and housekeepers; general utility maintenance repairers; and secretaries. Occupations being reduced less than 20 percent include: blue collar worker supervisors; precision inspectors, testers, and graders; welding machine setters; industrial machinery mechanics; industrial truck and tractor operators; machinists; welders and cutters; sheet metal workers; traffic, shipping, and receiving clerks; freight, stock, and material movers; and precision metal workers.

Industry workers are paid better than the average production worker employed in other manufacturing industries. The average wage for all manufacturing in 1989 was $10.49 per hour, whereas hourly workers employed by this industry averaged $11.92 per hour. The average hourly wage increased to $12.27 in 1990.

AMERICA AND THE WORLD

According to ALCOA's *1992 Annual Report,* the entrance of Central European and former Soviet companies into the world market has served to create an oversupply of aluminum products. This glut in the market has driven prices down. In addition, the presence of more competitors in a sluggish world economy has forced existing manufacturers to emphasize quality and cut costs as much as possible.

INDUSTRY INFORMATION SOURCES

Aluminum Company of America (ALCOA), *1992 Annual Report,* 1993.

"Business Briefs: Continental Can Co.," *Wall Street Journal,* October 4, 1993.

Continental Can Company, Inc. (CCC), *1992 Annual Report,* 1993.

Darnay, Arsen J., ed., *Manufacturing USA,* 3rd edition, Detroit: Gale, 1993.

—Valerie E. Wilson

METAL STAMPINGS, NOT ELSEWHERE CLASSIFIED

This category includes establishments primarily engaged in manufacturing metal stampings and spun products, not elsewhere classified, including porcelain enameled products. Products of this industry include household appliance housings and parts, cooking and kitchen utensils, and other nonautomotive job stampings.

Over 2,700 companies were engaged in the metal stamping industry in 1988. That year, the industry employed 97,000 people at an average hourly wage of $9.65. The value of shipments increased $2 billion between 1982 and 1988, while employment levels remained stable. A large reason for the increase in shipment values was the rising cost of materials.

The largest portion of the industry stamps metal for motor homes, aviation, agricultural equipment, computers, electrical appliances, radios, televisions, kitchen appliances, and laundry equipment. Cooking and kitchen utensils, such as tea kettles, metal spoons, baking pans, and stainless steel mixing bowls, claim a distinct majority of the industry's product base.

Significant reductions in the labor pool are expected in several production line occupations by the year 2000. The largest segment of employment in the industry is occupied by metal and plastic forming machine operators. However, this segment is expected to be one of the hardest hit, with over 19 percent of the positions being eliminated. Other occupations facing similar reductions include assemblers and fabricators, precision inspectors, welding machine setters, truck and tractor operators, cutting tool operators, machine feeders, material movers, welders and cutters, and sheet metal workers. The only occupations expected to grow more than ten percent include sales workers and industrial machinery mechanics.

The top 75 companies booked sales of $4.13 billion in 1991 while employing 37,700 people. The top five industry leaders are Hexcel Corporation, Tempel Steel Company, JSJ Corporation, Desco Corporation, and Ekco Group Incorporated. Hexcel, located in Dublin, California, booked sales in 1991 of $411 million while employing 3,500 people. Tempel, located in Niles, Illinois, booked sales of $210 million while employing 1,200 people. JSJ, located in Grand Haven, Michigan, booked sales of $175 million while employing 2,000 people. Desco, located in Colliers, West Virginia, had estimated sales of $170 million while employing 200 people. Ekco, located in Nashua, New Hampshire, booked sales of $167 million while employing 1,700 people.

The stamping industry is currently entering into a new age of technology. Although computer aided drafting and manufacturing tools have been used to great advantage in the metal cutting industry, the related metal forming industries have not used available software tools. Specialized software is being developed to add precision to the processes. Not only does the software design better stamping dies, but it can be interfaced with the machinery to tell the operator when the die is beginning to dull, or when the machine itself is beginning to malfunction.

The implementation of computer technology helps manufacturers to reduce costs throughout machining operations. For larger production lines, the area of specialty tooling is gaining importance as more companies cut costs and competition grows. With specialty tooling, several operations can be combined by using unique punch dies. Louver, countersink, embossing, lettering, and lance-and-form tools are gaining popularity as more industry leaders seek to improve product quality and cost through process redesign.

INDUSTRY INFORMATION SOURCES

Gettelman, Ken. "Pressworking Joins the Computer Revolution." *Modern Machine Shop*, March 1992.

Sheridan, Gary. "Creative Tooling for Punch Presses." *Modern Machine Shop*, March 1992.

U.S. Industrial Outlook 1993. Washington, DC: U.S. Department of Commerce, 1993.

—Valerie E. Wilson

ELECTROPLATING, PLATING, POLISHING, ANODIZING AND COLORING

Establishments primarily engaged in all types of electroplating, plating, anodizing, coloring, and finishing of metals and formed products for the trade. Also included in this industry were establishments that perform these types of activities on their own account, on purchased metals or formed products. Establishments that both manufacture and finish products were classified according to the products.

INDUSTRY SNAPSHOT

The value of the industry's shipments in 1990 were just over $4.5 billion, up from $2.7 billion in 1982. There were roughly 3,200 firms in the industry in 1989, 34 percent of which had 20 or more employees, up from 26 percent in 1982. Average firm size in the industry as measured by production workers per establishment was 51 percent lower than the typical manufacturing industry.

The industry employed 73,000 workers in 1990, up from 62,000 in 1982. The industry was relatively labor-intensive, having an average of only 36 percent of the investment per production worker as that for the manufacturing sector as a whole. Annual hours worked by production workers in the industry were about the same as those averaged by production workers in a typical manufacturing industry, while hourly wages were 20 percent lower.

ORGANIZATION AND STRUCTURE

Essentially there were two types of firms in the industry, small, private corporations and large, publicly-held companies that were either subsidiaries or divisions of larger parent corporations. Of the top four firms in the industry in 1992, two were subsidiaries and two were divisions, while 79 percent of the leading 75 firms were private corporations.

While larger firms often were more diversified in the number of electroplating and finishing processes they utilized, smaller firms tended to specialize in one or two types of finishing processes. During the 1950s and 1960s, many companies established their own finishing operations, but with the increased environmental regulation of the industry beginning in the 1970s, many manufacturing firms opted to subcontract for finishing services, thus avoiding the added costs of waste treatment. Entering the 1990s, the trend once again was for manufacturing firms to own and operate their own finishing operations, often integrating production and finishing processes.

Capital investment in the industry was very low compared to the average capital expenditure in all other manufacturing industries. In 1989, the average investment per establishment in the metal finishing industry was 82 percent below the national standard for manufacturing industries. This enabled relatively easy entry into the industry and accounted for the large number of small, often family-owned, private firms.

In the mid-1970s, about three-fourths of a finishing firm's business came from within a 50- to 75-mile radius of the firm. Since finishers needed to be near their customers, their operations were located in the same areas as producers of durable goods.

The states ranking in the top ten by value of shipments in the late 1980s were, in ranking order: California, Michigan, Ohio, Illinois, New York, Connecticut, Massachusetts, Pennsylvania, Indiana, and Missouri. Together these states accounted for 70 percent of the industry's total shipments and 68 percent of its total employment.

BACKGROUND AND DEVELOPMENT

Historically, the most important activity in this industry was electroplating. Electroplating entailed adhering a thin metal coating on an object by immersing it into an electrically-charged solvent containing the dissolved plating metal. Metals commonly used in plating included copper, nickel, chromium, zinc, lead, cadmium, tin, brass, and bronze, as well as precious metals such as gold, silver, and platinum. Electroplating served a number of functions, such as protecting from corrosion and wear, as decoration, and as electrical shielding.

Alessandro Volta's creation of the battery in 1800 made electroplating possible for the first time. Commercial electroplating began around 1840. Before the development of commercial nickel plating in the 1910s, the metals most commonly used for plating were silver, gold, and brass. Nickel plating tarnished and developed green corrosion, but this problem was eradicated in the late 1920s with the development of commercially-practical chromium plating. This was one of the key developments in the history of the industry, especially in regard to plating applications for the automobile and appliance industries. Though nonmetallic materials had been electroplated since the mid-19th century, they became increasingly important for the industry after the development in 1963 of ABS plastic, which lent itself to electroplating.

Of increasing importance for the industry in the 1980s and early 1990s was plating utilized as electrical shielding, particularly for the plastic housings of computers. The Crown City Plating Co., based in El Monte, California developed the electroless process used for such shielding around 1970. Robert Coombes, the company's president and CEO, attributed the increased sales of the firm to computer manufacturers' shift from metal housings to cheaper plastic housings, which required a metal coating to provide adequate shielding.

The solvents used to dissolve plating metals often were highly toxic. Cyanide, for example, was a commonly used solvent. In addition to being one of the most toxic of commonly found pollutants, its toxicity was heightened when mixed with certain plating metals. Cyanide also interfered with water treatment processes and formed a toxic gas when converted to an acid. Of the plating metals, cadmium, chromium and lead were the most problematic. The increasing regulation of the use of such toxins was of central importance to the industry's development.

Key pieces of legislation affecting the industry included the Federal Water Pollution Control Act Amendments of 1972, the Resource Conservation and Recovery Act of 1976, the Clean Water Act of 1977, and the Comprehensive Environmental Response, Compensation and Liability Act of 1980, better known as Superfund. The number of enforcement actions by the Environmental Protection Agency (EPA) increased steadily from the late 1980s into the 1990s. Total fines imposed by the EPA and Justice Department for violation of the Resource Conservation and Recovery Act in the first half of 1993 exceeded the total for 1992, suggesting that pollution abatement would continue to be a key issue for the industry.

The industry's trade organization was the National Association of Metal Finishers, located in Chicago. Founded in 1955, the association had 940 members in the early 1990s who were managing executives of firms in the industry. The significant effect of environmental and safety regulations on the industry was suggested by the composition of the association's committees. Of ten committees, eight were devoted to issues of regulation.

Firms in the metal finishing industry were studied in the mid-1970s to determine the key problems facing both individual firms and the industry as a whole. For both categories, respondents put the same three problems at the top of list: increasing production costs, excessive competition, and a shortage of experienced employees. Excessive competition was also listed as a severe problem in a 1967 survey. Such competition had a number of important implications, one of which was the relatively slow rate of productivity growth in the industry. From 1958 to 1974, the value added per production worker hour more than quadrupled for computers and related machines and doubled for motor vehicles and parts and household laundry equipment. During this same period, the metal finishing industry experienced only a 17 percent increase. As of 1989, the valued added per production worker in the plating industry was less than half as much for the manufacturing sector as a whole.

CURRENT CONDITIONS

A 1992 study of the industry's future concluded that the significant developments for the industry lay in environmental regulations as well as future demand for more sophisticated finishes. As parts to be finished became larger and more complex, finishing processes also became more complex.

Demand for the industry's products was dependent on the demand for durable goods, the manufacture of which nearly encompassed American industry. Accordingly growth in the metal finishing industry was dependent on growth in the manufacturing sector at large. Growth and profitability were also dependent on the development of environmentally safe manufacturing techniques. The pace of technical change was brisk entering the 1990s, which suggested that the industry could meet environmental and safety regulations in a cost-effective manner. Some of the most promising technologies, such as the dry application of metal powders, were classified in **SIC 3479: Metal Coating & Allied Services.** The success of such techniques was expected to lead to a shift in production away from the plating industry.

The relative ease of entry into the industry made for highly competitive conditions in which small, independent companies were positioned between large suppliers of finishing machinery and materials and large corporations for which they provided services. This meant relatively low profits for small manufacturers.

Entering the 1990s, theoretical, rather than empirical, knowledge became increasingly important. Many new techniques in the industry were developed by suppliers of equipment and materials for the industry. Thus, smaller firms were able to employ some of the same innovations as the larger firms. Given the greater purchasing power enjoyed by large manufacturers, however, suppliers allocated a disproportionate amount of their research and technical support to such firms.

The problem smaller firms have of keeping up with innovative techniques was exacerbated by their need to accommodate a host environmental regulations. The problem was not limited to financial constraints alone, but was intensified by the less sophisticated control procedures many smaller companies were able to utilize. One example of this was in the use of low-cyanide zinc electroplating solutions, or in solutions using no cyanide. Unlike processes using high-cyanide solutions, quality finishes could only be obtained through a highly sophisticated process.

INDUSTRY LEADERS

Entering the 1990s, the three largest firms in the industry entering the 1990s were USS-Posco Industries, based in Pittsburg, California, the Metallurgical Materials Division of Texas Instruments Inc., based in Attleboro, Massachusetts, and Dyna-Craft Inc., based in Santa Clara, California. Together these three firms accounted for 16 percent of total sales for the industry.

USS-Posco, a subsidiary of the USX Corp., was created from a 1986 joint venture with the Korean Pohang Iron and Steel Corp. With roughly $480 million in annual sales and 1,200 employees, it was by far the largest firm in the industry. After paying for a $450 million modernization in 1989, the firm had yet to record a profit by 1992, but hoped to be operating at near full capacity by 1993. The success of its operations was dependent, however, on the outcome of a dispute with other U.S. steel producers over the firm's use of Korean steel from Pohang in its operations.

The Metallurgical Materials Division of Texas Instruments Inc., with 2,200 employees, generated approximately $150-million in annual sales in the early 1990s. Dyna-Craft Inc. was the third largest producer in the industry, with about $100 million in annual sales and 1,500 employees. The firm was a subsidiary of the National Semi-Conductor Corp.

RESEARCH AND TECHNOLOGY

As it entered the 1990s, many of the most significant technical developments in the industry were in response to environmental regulation. Sandia National Laboratories in Albuquerque developed methods for gold-plating onto microelectronic devices that did not use cyanide. Metal-ceramic coatings were substituted for cadmium coatings for certain high-price parts. Handy and Harman, the ninth largest firm in the industry, developed a formable silver-tin oxide as a replacement for silver-cadmium oxide for coating electrical contacts. Previously used silver-tin oxides were not formable, so the process of applying them was more labor-intensive and costly. In addition to their reduced environmental hazard, silver-tin oxides were also more highly conductive.

GE Research and Development devised a new method for nickel-plating plastics to shield computer housings. This process did not use chromium (unlike Crown City Plating Co.'s process) and was applied with a water-based solution.

INDUSTRY INFORMATION SOURCES

Abrahamson, Peggy, "EPA Sets Record for Case Actions," *American-Metal-Market,* December 13, 1991.

"Anodizing Protects Aircraft," *Defense-News,* November 29, 1992.

Arnett, Harold E. and Donald N. Smith, *The Metal Finishing Industry: A Framework for Success,* Ann Arbor: University of Michigan, 1977.

Brenner, Abner, *Electrodeposition of Alloys: Principles and Practice,* New York: Academic Press, 1963.

Cherry, Kenneth F, *Plating Waste Treatment,* Ann Arbor, Michigan: Ann Arbor Science Publishers, Inc., 1982.

Daniels, Peggy Kneffel and Carol A. Schwartz, eds. *Encyclopedia of Associations* (28th ed.), Detroit: Gale Research Inc., 1994.

Darnay, Arsen J., ed. *Manufacturing USA: Industry Analyses, Statistics, and Leading Companies* (3rd ed.). Detroit, Michigan: Gale Research Inc., 1993.

Dubpernell, George, *Electrodeposition of Chromium from Chromic Acid Solutions,* New York: Pergamon Press Inc., 1977.

Haflich, Frank, "USS-Posco Eyes Full Capacity Output, Profits," *American Metal Market,* December 16, 1991.

"Impingement: The Key to Effective Aqueous Cleaning," *Metal-Finishing,* August, 1992.

"Industry Activities: An Advanced Vapor Degreasing Technology," *Metal-Finishing,* July 1993.

Industry Norms and Key Business Ratios, New York: Dun and Bradstreet Information Services, 1982/83-1992/93.

Institute of Metal Finishing, *Nickel-Chromium Plating,* Teddington: Robert Draper Ltd., 1961.

"Mass Finishing in the '90s," *Metal-Finishing,* March 1992.

"Metal Finishing Not Bright," *Chemical Week,* April 14, 1993.

"Metallic-Ceramic Coating Replacing Plating with Cadmium for Expensive Parts," *Machine Design,* July 23, 1993.

Moody's Industrial Manual, New York: Moody's Investors Service, Inc., 1988, 1990, 1992.

O'Sullivan, Orla, "New H&H Alloy Makes Gains," *American Metal Market,* January 20, 1993.

"Plating Polycarbonate," *Appliance Manufacturer,* August 1992.

Raub, E. and K. Muller, *Fundamentals of Metal Deposition,* Amsterdam: Elsevier Publishing Company, 1967.

"RCRA Settlements Garner $6 Million More," *Chemical and Engineering News,* May 24, 1993.

Ross, Robert B, *Handbook of Metal Treatments and Testing,* London: E. & F. N. Spon Ltd., 1977.

"Sandia Develops Safer Microelectronic Plating Process," *Mechanical-Engineering,* December 1991.

Sterner, Bob. "Electronic Shielding Process Uses Chromium," *American Metal Market,* August 6, 1992.

"US Steelmakers' Complaint Imperils Korean Venture," *Journal of Commerce,* July 8, 1992.

Viani, Laura, "Parties Squabble Over Posco Policy," *American Metal Market,* July 2, 1993.

—David Kucera

SIC 3479

COATING, ENGRAVING, AND ALLIED SERVICES, NOT ELSEWHERE CLASSIFIED

This industry includes establishments primarily engaged in performing the following types of services on metals, for the trade: (1) enameling, lacquering, and varnishing metal products; (2) hot dip galvanizing of mill sheets, plates and bars, castings, and formed products fabricated of iron and steel; hot dip coating such items with aluminum, lead, or zinc; retinning cans and utensils; (3) engraving, chasing, and etching jewelry, silverware, notarial, and other seals, and other metal products for purposes other than printing; and (4) other metal services not elsewhere classified. Also included in this industry were establishments which perform these types of activities on their own account on purchased metals or formed products. Establishments that both manufacture and finish products were classified according to the products.

INDUSTRY SNAPSHOT

The value of shipments in 1990 was just over $4.9 billion, up from $2.4 billion in 1982. The industry consisted of about 1,700 firms in 1989, 38 percent of these having 20 or more employees, up from 31 percent in 1982. Yet, average firm size as measured by production workers per establishment remained relatively small, 56 percent of that for manufacturing as a whole.

The industry employed 44,000 workers in 1990, up from 35,000 in 1982. The industry was relatively labor-intensive, having an average of only 47 percent of the investment per production worker as that for the manufacturing sector as a whole. Annual hours worked by production workers in the industry were somewhat higher than those worked in manufacturing at large, and hourly wages were 12 percent lower.

Growth of output and employment stagnated entering the 1990s, but profit rates remained close to the average for the period 1982 to 1992. The industry stood to benefit from projected growth in the use of galvanized steel and in the use of alternatives to electroplating that it offered.

ORGANIZATION AND STRUCTURE

There were, by and large, two types of firms in the industry—the small independents and the large captive firms that were either subsidiaries or divisions of yet larger parent firms. Of the top four firms in the industry, three were subsidiaries and one a public independent. Of the top 75 firms in the industry, 49 percent were private independents in the early-1990s.

Whereas larger firms were often more diversified in their finishing activities, independents tended to specialize in one or two types of finishing. There was a tendency for manufacturing firms to set up their own finishing operations during the 1950s and 1960s. With the increased environmental regulation of the industry beginning in the 1970s, many manufacturing firms opted to subcontract for finishing services, thus getting around the added costs of waste treatment. Entering the 1990s, the tendency was once again for manufacturing firms to undertake finishing operations, often integrating production and finishing processes.

The capital requirements of the industry were low compared to the average for manufacturing. Average investment per establishment was only 27 percent that for the manufacturing sector as a whole in 1989. This enabled relatively easy entry into the industry, and accounted for the large number of small private firms, often family proprietorships.

Parts to be finished were typically shipped to finishing firms by their customers, after which they were shipped back. As of the mid-1970s, about three-fourths of a finishing firm's business came from within a 50-to-75-mile radius of the firm. Since finishers needed to be near their customers, their operations were located in the same areas as producers of durable goods.

The states ranking in the top ten by value of shipments in the late-1980s were, in order of descending value: Ohio, California, Illinois, Pennsylvania, Texas, Indiana, New York, New Jersey, Massachusetts, and Connecticut. Together these states accounted for 74 percent of total shipments and 65 percent of total employment.

The outputs of the metal-coating industry were dispersed somewhat more widely across industry lines than the outputs of the metal-plating industry. The top ten industries buying the outputs of the metal-coating industry in 1982 made up 50 percent of the total output sold. Those industries were: prefabricated metal buildings (ten percent), sheet metal work (6.2 percent), crowns and closures (5.4 percent), electronic components not elsewhere classified (5.1 percent), fabricated structural metal (4.9 percent), blast furnaces and steel mills (4.5 percent), metal cans (3.8 percent), x-ray apparatus and tubes (3.7 percent), motor vehicles and car bodies (3.3 percent), and metal coating and allied services (3.1 percent).

BACKGROUND AND DEVELOPMENT

Just over one-half the output of this industry consisted of the application of organic coatings such as paints, varnishes, and lacquers. Though metals had been coated by like means since ancient times, their modern application was dependent on the development of phosphating as a surface preparation. Phosphating involved treating a metal, usually steel, with phosphoric acid. This greatly improved the adhesion and durability of coatings. Phosphating alone was also used as an anti-corrosive coating on steel in conditions where the potential for corrosion was not high. Though phosphating was developed in the 1860s, treatment times were exceedingly long until iron filings were added to the phosphoric acid bath after 1906 (following Thomas Watts Coslett's patent), shortening treatment time to about two-and-one-half hours. The treatment time was shortened to ten minutes by the addition of copper salts in 1929, after which the process became generally used as a surface preparation for organic coatings. More recent developments lowered treatment times to five seconds.

Next to the application of organic coatings, galvanizing was the largest activity in the industry, and made up 22 percent of output. Metal coating and allied services not specified by kind made up 21 percent of output, and the remaining six percent consisted of engraved and etched products.

Galvanizing is the process of dipping steel or iron into a bath of molten zinc. The zinc coating served as a corrosion prohibitor, and was applied to structural parts, sheeting, pipe, various containers, and hardware. During this process, the metal to be coated was immersed until it reached the same temperature as the bath (typically 1,562 degrees fahrenheit). Thus, the process could not be used on springs or other objects in which desirable properties would be lost by such exposure to heat. Since uniformity of thickness was not readily controllable in hot dip processes, galvanizing was limited to applications in which such uniformity was not required. Electroplating with zinc was sometimes also referred to as galvanizing or electrogalvanizing. This process was done cold, and could assure high uniformity of thickness, getting around the above-mentioned problems. (This process was not included in the metal-coating industry, but rather in the metal-plating industry.)

As with all metal-coating processes, it was vital that parts were thoroughly cleaned before being galvanized. This typically involved treating the parts to be galvanized in an acid bath, after which they were fluxed, a process that generally used hydrochloric acid. The wastes produced by such pre-treatment were toxic, as were the solvents used in the organic coatings processes. The minimization of such wastes continued to be central issues for the industry, as did the development of alternative solvents.

The industry was served by the National Association of Metal Finishers, located in Chicago, Illinois. Founded in 1955, the Association had 940 members in the early 1990s, who were managing executives of firms in the industry.

Firms in the metal-finishing industries were surveyed in the mid-1970s to determine the key problems facing both individual firms and the industries at large. For both categories, respondents put the same three problems at the top of list: increasing production costs, excessive competition, and a shortage of experienced employees. Excessive competition was also listed as a severe problem in a 1967 survey. Such competition had a number of important implications. Key among these was the relatively slow productivity growth of the industry, both in relation to the industries it served and to the manufacturing sector as a whole. From 1958 to 1974, value-added per production worker hour increased by over fourfold for computers and related machines, and by twofold for motor vehicles and parts and household laundry equipment. During the same span of years, this measure of productivity growth increased by only 17 percent for the metal-finishing industries. As of 1989, value added per production worker in the coating industry was only 62 percent of that added for the manufacturing sector as a whole.

CURRENT CONDITIONS

Growth prospects for firms involved in galvanizing appeared promising entering the mid-1990s. By 1995 or 1996, the vast majority of automobiles with steel bodies were expected to feature two-sided galvanized steel. The Intermodal Surface Transportation Efficiency Act of 1991 required that all highways, bridges, and tunnels built with federal funds take into account the costs of materials over their life-cycles. This strongly favored the use of galvanized metals. The American Galvanizers Association estimated in 1992 that use of galvanized steel would double through the 1990s, largely as a result of increased use for highways, bridges, and wastewater treatment systems.

A number of large firms responded to these growth prospects by expanding capacity. The Precoat Metals division of the Sequa Corp. (the number eight producer in the industry) announced in 1993 that it would have a new plant operating in Jackson, Mississippi, in 1994 with 120,000-ton-per-year capacity. The plant resulted from a partnership with the nearby Double G Coating, Inc., a joint-venture galvanizing line of the Bethlehem Steel Corp. and the National Steel Corp. Precoat Metals also planned to serve other steel producers. Consolidated Systems, a South Carolina-based firm, announced in 1993 that it would have new a galvanizing line operational in 1994 with 160,000-ton-per-year capacity.

Consolidated Systems' new line was planned to serve the construction industry. The Kinark Corp. of Tulsa, Oklahoma, the nation's largest, hot-dip galvanizing company, was also expanding its capacity as it entered the 1990s.

The most promising of the environmentally friendlier alternatives to electroplating were the application of metal powders and vacuum deposition, processes that were projected to become increasingly important. Thus, the effects of environmental regulation provided substantial benefits to the industry, and growth prospects appeared promising. From the perspective of the firms, the question remained whether plating or coating firms could more readily diversify into these technologies.

A 1992 study of the industry's future concluded that the significant developments in the industry would result from environmental regulations, demand for more sophisticated finishes, and from the integration of finishing into production processes. As parts to be finished became larger and more complex, the study noted that finishing processes would also become more complex.

The relative ease of entry into the industry made for highly competitive conditions in which small independents were sandwiched between the large suppliers of finishing machinery and materials and the large firms for which they provided services. This meant relatively low profits for independents. Profit rates varied greatly among firms in the industry. Taking rates of return on equity, a firm ranking at the median had less than half the profitability of a firm ranking at the upper quartile (the rate from 1982 to 1992 averaged about 37 percent for the upper quartile firm and 17 percent for the median firm).

Entering the 1990s, theoretical knowledge, as opposed to knowledge that could be readily gained empirically, rapidly increased in importance. Equipment and material suppliers developed many new techniques in the industry. Thus, smaller firms were able to obtain some of the same innovations as larger firms. Nonetheless, given the greater purchasing power of the captive and large independent firms, suppliers allocated a disproportionate amount of their research and technical support to such firms.

Another issue inhibiting investment by smaller firms in more capital-intensive techniques was that, unlike large captive firms, they were less able to absorb the losses resulting from excess capacity in the face of an economic downturn. Because the greater profitability of the more successful firms could be used to finance techniques that were more productive and sophisticated, the gap between large captive firms and smaller independents was likely to remain, if not widen.

Industry Leaders

As of the early-1990s, the three largest firms in the industry were: the Ransburg Corp. of Indianapolis, Indiana, Praxair Surface Technologies of Indianapolis, and the Material Sciences Corp. of Elk Grove Village, Illinois. Together these three firms accounted for 13 percent of total sales for the industry.

The Ransburg Corp. became a wholly-owned subsidiary of Illinois Tool Works, Inc. in 1989. The firm had annual sales of about $320 million in the early-1990s, and had 2,500 employees.

Praxair Surface Technologies was known as Union Carbide Coatings Service until 1992. It was a subsidiary of Praxair, Inc., whose primary activity was the production of industrial gases. The firm had annual sales of about $200 million in the early-1990s and had 2,000 employees.

The Material Sciences Corp. was incorporated in 1983, and was a public independent. It owned Pre Finish Metals, Inc., another large producer in the industry, and had 700 employees. Material Sciences lost $30 million in fiscal year 1990, a result of unprofitable acquisitions and heavy debt burden. The firm also had to contend with environmental sanctions at two Superfund sites. After trying and failing to sell itself, the firm's fortunes turned around in the early-1990s. Its earnings rose fourfold in the quarter ending May 31, 1992, and sales were $156 million in the year prior to March 1993, up from $143 the year before. The firm was involved not only in coating, but also in electroplating operations. (In 1984, the firm entered into a joint venture with Bethlehem Steel Corp. and the Inland Steel Co. to pursue electroplating production.)

Aside from its two Illinois plants, the firm had four other plants in California, Ohio, and Pennsylvania.

RESEARCH AND TECHNOLOGY

As with the metal-plating industry, a number of innovations in the metal-coating industry were motivated by increasingly pressing environmental regulations. For the process of stripping coatings from rejected parts, blasting with plastic particles was seen as a viable alternative to the more toxic methods of chemical stripping and incineration. This method of stripping was advocated in the trade journal *Metal-Finishing* on the basis of its greater environmental friendliness. In the early-1990s, Whirlpool Corp. installed a pre-treating line in its Evanston, Illinois, plant that made use of a safer alternative to traditional phosphating. The line used a chrome-free rinse and cleaners that lessened the production of heavy metal wastes. The new line also improved the quality of coatings and consumed less energy.

New developments in the deposition of metal coatings were expected to possibly cause a shift away from electroplating to alternative methods, such as new forms of vacuum deposition. This process involved reducing pressure in a closed container to produce a vacuum in which pure metals could be vaporized at low temperatures and then allowed to condense on a surface. Laboratory tests of new vacuum methods produced high-quality coatings with fast coating times. Vacuum coating also had the significant advantage that it did not generate the toxic sludges of electroplating processes. Another technology of increasing importance was the application of metal powders by spraying or through the use of centrifugal force. A 1993 study projected that the use of powder coatings for metal finishing would grow at the high annual rate of 12 percent. As with vacuum deposition, such applications of metal powders had the significant advantage that they did not produce toxic sludges.

While the initial costs of pollution abatement technologies may have been prohibitive to some firms, a number of these technologies could lower production costs. The BASF Corp. reported that pollution abatement measures at two of its coating plants saved it $1.3 million in 1991, and that the payback period after initial investments ranged from 15 to 20 months. New technologies in the application of powder coatings made them not only an environmentally friendlier, but also a cost-effective alternative to electroplating.

INDUSTRY INFORMATION SOURCES

"A Safe and Cost-Efficient Method of Stripping Rejected Parts," *Metal-Finishing*, April 1992.

Arnett, Harold E. and Donald N. Smith. *The Metal Finishing Industry: A Framework for Success,* Ann Arbor, Michigan: University of Michigan, 1977.

Cage, W.E. Jr. "Specialty Chemical Conference - Industry Report," *Wheat First Butcher & Singer, Inc.,* March 24, 1992.

Daniels, Peggy Kneffel and Carol A. Schwartz, eds. *Encyclopedia of Associations* (28th ed.), Detroit, Michigan: Gale Research Inc., 1994.

Darnay, Arsen J., ed. *Manufacturing USA: Industry Analyses, Statistics, and Leading Companies* (3rd ed.), Detroit, Michigan: Gale Research Inc., 1993.

Freeman, D.B. *Phosphating and Metal Pre-Treatment: A Guide to Modern Processes and Practice,* New York: Industrial Press Inc., 1986.

Gannon, Virginia. "Highway Bill's Life-Cycle Clause May Boost Galvanizing," *American-Metal-Market,* July 14, 1992.

"Green Powder Coatings Come to the Forefront," *Performance Chemicals,* March 1992.

Industry Norms and Key Business Ratios, New York: Dun and Bradstreet Information Services, 1982/83-1992/93.

"Mass Finishing in the '90s," *Metal-Finishing,* March 1992.

Moody's Industrial Manual, New York: Moody's Investors Service, Inc., 1993.

Murphy, H. Lee. "Material Eyes Stock Deal," *Crain's Chicago Business,* July 12, 1992.

"New Arc Method Could Spark Shift to Vacuum Coatings," *Research-and-Development,* June 1992.

Prentice-Hall Editorial Staff. *Encyclopedic Dictionary of Production and Production Control,* Engelwood Cliffs, New Jersey: Prentice-Hall, Inc., 1964.

"The Road to Faultless Finishing," *Appliance-Manufacturer,* April 1993.

Ross, Robert B. *Handbook of Metal Treatments and Testing,* London: E. & F. N. Spon Ltd., 1977.

Scolieri, Peter. "Two Coating Lines Planned: 1994 Start-Up Set by Precoat Metals, Consolidated Systems," *American-Metal-Market,* October 5, 1992.

U.S. Industrial Outlook 1993, Washington, D.C.: U.S. Department of Commerce, 1993.

"U.S. Powder Coatings Industry Growing Strong," *Paint-and-Coatings Industry,* June 1993.

"Waste Minimization Pays Off at BASF Coatings Facilities," *Modern-Paint-and-Coatings,* July 1992.

—David Kucera

SMALL ARMS AMMUNITION

Establishments primarily engaged in manufacturing ammunition for small arms having a bore of 30 mm (or 1.18 inch) or less. Establishments primarily engaged in manufacturing ammunition, except for small arms, are classified in **SIC 3483: Ammunition, Except for Small Arms;** those manufacturing blasting and detonating caps and safety fuses are classified in **SIC 2892: Explosives;** and those manufacturing fireworks are classified in **SIC 2899: Chemicals and Chemical Preparations, Not Elsewhere Classified.**

INDUSTRY SNAPSHOT

The use of projectiles propelled by gunpowder, which began in the early 1300s, played an important role in the settling, and subsequent defense, of the United States since the first Europeans landed on American soil. By the 1990s, spurred by sport, defense, and construction markets, the U.S. small arms ammunition industry had grown into a $900 million business, employing about 8,500 workers. Although the ammunition industry approximated the size of the firearms industry, ammunition producers operated in relative obscurity.

Heading into the mid-1990s, ammo makers were engaged in fierce competition to maintain their share of a mature industry characterized by homogenous products. To boost sales and differentiate their products, manufacturers were offering specialized merchandise that appealed to niche market segments. They were also striving to increase productivity through automation.

ORGANIZATION AND STRUCTURE

Ammunition producers manufacture both cartridges and shells. The two types of cartridges, used in rifles and pistols, are rimfire and centerfire. Rimfire cartridges are comprised of a bullet usually made of lead, a bullet casing that is most often made of brass, and gunpowder. The bullet is discharged by striking the rim of the cartridge.

Centerfire cartridges are similar to rimfires, but they have a primer mounted in the center of the end of the cartridge. A firing pin strikes the primer, which ignites the gunpowder and discharges the bullet. Shotgun shells also use primers, but are filled with steel or lead buckshot and are usually packed in a plastic and brass shell. In addition to cartridges and shells, the small arms ammunition industry also includes the

manufacture of BBs and pellets, which are most commonly fired from spring- or pneumatic- powered pistols and rifles.

Rimfire cartridges are typically used for smaller bore pistols and rifles, and account for about eight percent of industry sales. Centerfire pistol cartridges, including ammo that can be interchanged between pistols and rifles, represent about 14 percent of revenues. Centerfire rifle ammunition makes up an additional 12 percent of sales, while shotgun shells account for about 22 percent of industry shipments. Primers and other ammunition components sold separately garner about a 13 percent share of the market. Miscellaneous ammo products account for the remaining 30 percent of industry revenues. A significant portion of miscellaneous ammo is ramset shells, used in the construction industry to drive nails into concrete.

The average cartridge was sold for about 15 cents in 1992, though prices vary widely by size and type. Specialty ammunition used to hunt large game can cost as much as five dollars per round. Other specialty ammunition, designed to explode on impact or penetrate protective gear, commonly runs as high as 50 cents or one dollar per round. BBs and pellets, in contrast, cost a fraction of a cent per piece.

Small arms ammunition is produced primarily for three types of firearms: handguns, including both semi-automatics and revolvers; shotguns; and rifles. In addition to these categories, smaller markets exist for fully-automatic rifles and handguns, as well as for BB and pellet guns. When using a revolver, encased bullets, or cartridges or rounds of ammunition, are loaded into a carousel. As the trigger is pulled the carousel rotates, exposing a new bullet which the hammer strikes. To fire again, the shooter must release and then pull the trigger through a full motion, which exposes a new bullet and cocks and releases the hammer.

Most semi-automatic guns hold rounds of ammunition in a spring-loaded clip. When the trigger is pulled and a round is fired, residual pressure created by the explosion quickly expels the empty bullet casing, places a new round in the chamber, and cocks the hammer. The shooter can fire again by disengaging the trigger and then pulling it through a half motion that releases the hammer. Fully-automatic weapons, or machine guns, fire ammunition similarly to semi-automatics, except that they continue to fire and reload rounds as long as the shooter does not release the trigger.

Ammo Consumers and Trade Representatives. Ammunition sold to the general public represented about 40 percent of industry sales in the 1980s. Sales to the federal government for military and other uses accounted for about 20 percent of sales, a figure that fell to about 15 percent in the early 1990s. Exports, the third largest category, consumed approximately 10 percent of production. Cement and hydraulic industries made up about 6 percent of market share, while state and local governments and police accounted for about 5 percent. Various industrial and construction industries accounted for the remaining 20 percent of sales.

Hunters purchase 80 percent of the ammunition sold to the general public, or about 30 percent of total industry output. In addition to the use of rifles and shotguns for sport purposes, about 60 percent of hunters also own handguns, making people in that group significant consumers of pistol ammunition.

There are three industry and consumer groups that represent ammunition interests in the United States. Most ammunition industry executives are affiliated with the National Shooting Sports Federation (NSSF), which promotes hunting and target shooting. The NSSF's sister organization, the Sporting Arms and Ammunition Manufacturers Institute (SAAMI), sets voluntary national standards for ammunition and firearm design. These groups rarely participate in political lobbying efforts, although ammo producers have traditionally donated money to support game populations and preserve hunting areas. The third and best-known organization, the National Rifle Association (NRA), is heavily involved in lobbying efforts, most of which are of interest to ammo manufacturers and users. Only 12 percent of all hunters, however, belong to this organization.

An Obscure Industry. The ammunition industry is about 70 percent as large as the entire firearms industry that it complements. The comparably high-profile firearm industry receives large amounts of press and is often the target of state and federal regulatory initiatives. Ammunition makers, however, operate in relative obscurity, with little publicity, regulation, or outside analysis of their industry.

One reason that the industry has such a low profile is that most of its products are very homogenous, resulting in an undynamic commodity-like business environment. In addition, the largest producers in the industry are owned by massive conglomerates that view their ammo operations as relatively small sideline businesses.

BACKGROUND AND DEVELOPMENT

The use of gunpowder to propel projectiles dates back to fourteenth century Europe. Iron darts with brass fittings were mounted on shafts, much like

crossbow arrows of the time. The shaft held the gunpowder and was wrapped with leather to keep gases from the burning powder from leaking out of the sides of the shaft.

During the fourteenth, fifteenth, and sixteenth centuries, armies experimented with a variety of projectiles. Gunpowder was used to fire rocks in the 1300s, though metal balls became the ammunition of choice by the 1400s. Hot shot, or heated metal balls, added a deadly twist to this technique.

The invention of rifled guns created a demand for new types of ammunition. Although round metal balls were first used in the rifled barrels, the spinning effect caused by the rifled barrel had a negligible effect on the ball. Because elongated projectiles benefitted most from the rifling technique, this type of ammunition grew in popularity throughout the 19th and 20th centuries.

Muskets, which fire rounded lead balls and similar projectiles, dominated the North American landscape throughout most of the 19th century. Following the U.S. Civil War, though, several developments changed ammunition. The mass production of rifles and pistols in the late 1800s and early 1900s made elongated bullets the dominant form of ammunition in the United States.

Winchester rifles, Colt revolvers, and other famous weaponry created markets for a variety of new ammunition during the westward U.S. expansion. Widespread use of smokeless gunpowder, which was perfected in the late 1880s, hastened ammunition industry growth. Most importantly, advances in ammunition and firearms during both world wars broadened the scope of the industry to include specialized ammunition for automatic weapons and other new firearms.

In addition to a huge demand for ammunition by the military, ammunition producers in the United States enjoyed a large market for hunting products throughout the 20th century. Except during times of war, in fact, hunters remained the largest consumers of all types of small arms ammunition throughout the 19th and 20th centuries.

The 1970s and 1980s. Following steady growth in commercial sales during the first half of the twentieth century and throughout the 1960s, the general public's demand for ammo began to slip in the 1970s. Although military consumption provided sporadic boosts in sales, the industry's core market, hunters, stagnated.

Stalled growth in hunting impeded the expansion of profits for some manufacturers throughout the 1970s and early 1980s. After Ronald Reagan was elected to office in 1980, however, an increase in ammo sales to the military boosted revenues. Profits were further buoyed by an increase in target shooting. By the mid-1980s the military was consuming nearly 30 percent of industry production, and handgun and target shooters had become the primary growth market for manufacturers.

The value of ammo sales gradually edged upward from about $800 million in 1982 to approximately $920 million in 1985 and 1986. An increase in the cost of lead that caused inflated ammo prices was partially responsible for this rise, however. A decline in military consumption in the late 1980s reduced shipments to about $840 million by 1990, despite another jump in the cost of lead in 1989 and 1990. Depressed construction markets also quelled revenue growth, as the demand for ramset shells and other industrial products decreased.

The small arms ammunition business represented a mature industry throughout the 1980s and early 1990s. It was characterized by stagnant growth, homogenous products, and low profit margins. As they entered the 1990s, producers sought means of increasing profits and maintaining market share.

CURRENT CONDITIONS

To boost profits in the 1990s, small ammo producers were slowly raising productivity, selling through new marketing channels, and offering new niche products. Manufacturers plowed an average of $25 million per year into production facilities in the 1980s, a very low investment compared to most other industries. Despite that low figure, industry employment fell from about 7.4 million to 6.3 million workers during the decade, at the same time that overall production increased.

Winchester, for instance, installed computer-controlled cartridge loading machines that allowed the company to produce 9-millimeter cartridges and other popular ammo at a rate of up to 450 units per minute. Despite industry efforts at low-cost, high volume production in some areas, most manufacturers still used some very old production techniques. Even at Winchester many low-volume products in 1993 were still loaded at rates of 40 to 60 per minute using machines the company acquired in 1931. Lead shot, moreover, was produced using a two-century old process.

Besides moderate productivity gains, producers were benefitting in the early 1990s from new marketing channels. Sporting goods stores and gun shops continued to account for a declining share of total ammo sales, as they had since the 1980s. Instead, such discount stores as Wal-Mart and Kmart, accounted for

30 percent to 50 percent of commercial sales by 1992. In addition, mail order catalog sales were becoming an increasingly important channel of distribution. One of the largest ammunition catalogers, AcuSport Corp., of Ohio, increased mail order sales from $30 million in 1988 to over $75 million by 1992.

Many producers were also developing new bullet types to appeal to niche market segments. These unique items offered higher profit margins than popular commodity ammo. Police and handgun owners, for instance, had proved a viable market for sales of specialty bullets. The Black Talon, for example, was a bullet designed to enter a person's body, spread out, and extend tiny razors that stopped the bullet inside the body. Other ammo was designed to explode on impact and release tiny pellets into its target, or pierce metal plate or protective gear.

As the mid-1990s approached, an area of potential growth for industry competitors was the export market. Productivity gains realized in the 1980s allowed U.S. producers to stem an influx of cheap import ammunition from Brazil and the Far East during that decade. As their production costs became more globally competitive, some manufacturers began eyeing burgeoning foreign ammo markets. Exports already accounted for more than 10 percent of total U.S. production in the early 1990s. Foreign producers had captured less than 20 percent of the U.S. ammo market by 1992, and import growth seemed to have stabilized.

Regulatory Efforts. Although the ammo industry in 1993 remained loosely regulated in comparison to other weapons-related industries, federal and state initiatives sought to tether the industry in the early 1990s. New York City already required people purchasing ammo to display to the seller a legal permit to use the gun that would fire the ammunition. That law was loosely enforced, and critics on both sides of the gun-control issue agreed that the information required by the law was of little help in criminal investigations. A similar federal proposal was defeated by Congress in 1986.

Congress, with the support of the NRA, had succeeded in banning certain types of ''cop-killer'' bullets, designed to penetrate bullet-proof vests. That ban represented the only piece of legislation ever passed to directly limit the sale of small arms ammunition.

Senator Patrick Moynihan (New York) had unsuccessfully tried to pass legislation in the early 1990s banning the sale of 9 millimeter, .25 caliber, and .32 caliber ammunition, which together accounted for 50 percent of the bullets fired at police officers. Critics argued that the law could not be enforced and would have a negligible effect on crime. Nevertheless, the Clinton administration had indicated support for similar types of legislation.

INDUSTRY LEADERS

The largest producer of small arms ammunition in the United States in 1992 was Winchester, of Illinois. The company manufactured about 350 different cartridges, totaling well over one billion rounds per year. Winchester's main rival in the early 1990s was Remington Arms Company Inc., a subsidiary of E.I. du Pont de Nemours & Company. Remington was producing about 1.5 billion rounds per year while also producing traditional firearms.

The third major U.S. producer was Federal Cartridge Co., of Minnesota. Federal is a subsidiary of Pentair Corp., and is engaged primarily in small arms ammo production. In 1992, Federal generated $46 million in revenues with 900 employees. Winchester, Remington, Federal, and CCI, which specializes in .22 caliber ammunition, accounted for the majority of industry sales.

The other approximately 80 companies that make up the industry are comparatively small. Most of them employ fewer than 100 workers and have sales of less than $1 million per year. Several companies specialize in producing specialty cartridges, construction industry products, and reused rounds.

WORK FORCE

Employment in the small arms ammunition industry is expected to plummet between 1990 and 2005, according to the Bureau of Labor Statistics. Productivity gains, movement of production facilities to low-cost countries, and stagnant domestic market growth will contribute to this trend. Jobs for assemblers and fabricators, which represent a leading 14 percent of industry positions, had been forecasted to fall by more than 50 percent. Other manufacturing positions, which account for the bulk of industry employment, are expected to decline by 25 percent to 50 percent. Even general management and executive positions should drop by more than 40 percent. Workers already employed in the industry, however, continued to enjoy higher wages than workers in most other U.S. manufacturing industries in 1992.

INDUSTRY INFORMATION SOURCES

Darnay, Arsen J., and Marlita A. Reddy, eds., *Market Share Reporter: An Annual Compilation of Reported Market Share Data on Companies, Products, and Services,* Detroit: Gale Research Inc., 1993.

Darnay, Arsen J., ed., *Manufacturing USA: Industry Analyses, Statistics, and Leading Companies,* Detroit: Gale Research Inc., 1993.

Encyclopaedia Britannica, Chicago: Encyclopedia Britannica, Inc., 1968.

Farnham, Alan, "A Bang That's Worth Ten Billion Bucks," *Fortune,* March 19, 1992.

Jones, Maggie, "Gunmakers target women," *Working Woman,* July 1993.

Feder, Barnaby J., "Moynihan Wages Battle on 2d Front of Gun War," *New York Times,* March 20, 1992.

———, "As Gun Debate Rages, Ammunition Makers Are Quietly, and Busily, At Work," *New York Times,* March 20, 1992.

Gilbert, Nathaniel, "Careful Planning Keeps Olin Lucky," *Financier,* August 1991.

Lubove, Seth, "No More Adventures," *Forbes,* December 7, 1992.

Miller, Paul, "AcuSport Corp," *Catalog Age,* November 1992.

Standard & Poor's Industry Surveys, New York: Standard & Poor's Corporation, December 31, 1993.

U.S. Industrial Outlook 1993, Washington, DC: U.S. Department of Commerce, January 1993.

—Dave Mote

SIC 3483

AMMUNITION, EXCEPT FOR SMALL ARMS

This category covers establishments primarily engaged in manufacturing ammunition, not elsewhere classified, or in loading and assembling ammunition more than 30 mm. (or more than 1.18 inch), including component parts. This industry also includes establishments primarily engaged in manufacturing bombs, mines, torpedoes, grenades, depth charges, chemical warfare projectiles, and their component parts. Establishments primarily engaged in manufacturing small arms are classified in **SIC 3482: Small Arms Ammunition;** those manufacturing explosives are classified in **SIC 2892: Explosives;** and those manufacturing military pyrotechnics are classified in **SIC 2899: Chemicals and Chemical Preparations, Not Elsewhere Classified.**

About 45 percent of U.S. large ammunition industry output in the early 1990s was bombs. An additional 40 percent of production included miscellaneous bullets and other projectiles, casings, and components. Rockets made up the remaining 30 percent of shipments. Nearly 80 percent of all sales in 1991 were sold under U.S. government contract, mostly to the armed services. Another 15 percent of industry output was exported, and about five percent was consumed by various manufacturing sectors. Examples of manufacturing uses include demolition and mining.

Gunpowder was first employed to project missiles early in the 14th century, when large dart-like objects were propelled through the air during medieval battles. Darts were soon replaced by more reliable rounded projectiles that were fired from canon-type devices. Napoleon III released one of the first written works about artillery that included large ammunition in 1338, entitled *Etudes Sur . . . l'artillerie.* Stone shot was replaced by iron shot in the mid-1300s, as iron allowed greater penetration of stone walls. Soon thereafter, shells were invented that could be filled with gunpowder, fired from canons, and made to explode. Rounded metal balls and shells remained the principal types of large ammunition from the 15th through the 19th century.

The large ammunition industry in the United States arose as a result of both internal and external military conflicts, particularly the Civil War and both world wars. Development of the rifled artillery barrel and smokeless gunpowder in the 19th century lead to the proliferation of elongated bullets and shells. This ammunition type dominated production throughout most of the 20th century.

Although production of some large ammunition types peaked during World War II, the manufacture of other types of projectiles and explosives proliferated between 1950 and the late 1980s. Nuclear bombs and guided missiles, particularly, contributed to industry growth throughout the Cold War. By 1988, the industry employed 26,000 workers and was producing a record $4.3 billion in shipments per year. During the Reagan presidency alone, the ammunition industry had grown from just $1.8 billion in shipments and 16,000 workers.

The end of the Cold War in the late 1980s, punctuated by the demise of the Soviet Union, pummeled the large ammunition industry. As defense purchases plunged, sales dropped to $3.1 billion in 1990, and continued to plummet in 1991 and 1992. Likewise, industry employment crashed to about 14,500. Adding to employee woes were moderate increases in manufacturing productivity—the result of over $600 million in capital investments by producers in the early and mid-1980s.

Going into the mid-1990s, large ammunition manufacturers were expecting continued cuts in U.S. defense expenditures by the Clinton administration. Em-

ployment in every position in the industry was forecast to fall by 25 percent to 50 percent. For example, jobs for assemblers and fabricators, which accounted for a leading 14 percent of all workers, were expected to fall 51 percent between 1990 and 2005. Even white collar jobs were forecast to decline by over 40 percent during that period. Companies were counting on export growth to partially offset domestic declines.

The industry is highly concentrated and encompassed fewer than 70 firms in the early 1990s. Honeywell Inc. of Minnesota, the largest producer, earned over $1.5 billion in 1991 and employed more than 11,000 workers. The next largest competitor in 1991 was EG and G Rocky Flats Inc. of Golden Colorado. That enterprise generated $375 million in revenues and employed about 1,300. Other industry leaders in the early 1990s included Olin Corporation of Florida, Mason Company Inc., of Kentucky, and Grumman Corp. of New York.

INDUSTRY INFORMATION SOURCES

Ambrosia, John, ''Defense Cuts Won't Ground Lightweight Metals,'' *Iron Age,* April 1993.

Chakravarty, Subrata N., ''Sink or Swim,'' *Forbes,* October 14, 1991.

Farnham, Alan, ''A Bang That's Worth Ten Billion Bucks,'' *Fortune,* March 19, 1992.

Gilbert, Nathaniel, ''Careful Planning Keeps Olin Lucky,'' *Financier,* August 1991.

Inglesby, Tom, and Elaine West, ''Boom! On Time, All the Time,'' *Manufacturing Systems,* February 12, 1992.

Rapoport, Carla, ''Japan's Rising Defense Industry,'' *Fortune,* April 24, 1989.

Standard & Poor's Industry Surveys, New York: Standard & Poor's Corporation, December 31, 1993.

—Dave Mote

SIC 3484

SMALL ARMS

This category includes establishments primarily engaged in manufacturing small firearms or parts for small firearms. Small firearms, defined as having a bore of 30 mm or less, include pistols, revolvers, rifles, shotguns, and submachine guns. This category also includes establishments that manufacturer weapons with bores greater than 30 mm but which nevertheless are carried and employed by individuals, including grenade launchers and heavy field machine guns. Establishments primarily engaged in manufacturing artillery and mortars having bores greater than 30 mm are classified in **SIC 3489: Ordnance and Accessories, Not Elsewhere Classified.**

INDUSTRY SNAPSHOT

In 1987, there were 144 companies engaged in manufacturing small arms in the United States. This number was about the same as 1982, despite a 30 percent decrease in gun sales and rising anti-gun sentiment in the early 1980s. The 1987 number represented an increase of nearly 100 percent over the 1972 number, however. These manufacturers shipped $1.1 billion worth of small arms in 1987, having regained about ten percent of the sales lost in the early 1980s. Most major manufacturers indicated steady growth and a strengthening market from 1987 into 1993. Historically, the small arms industry has been extremely cyclical and subject to many external pressures, including the general state of the economy, worldwide military conflicts, and public opinion about private ownership of guns. Entering the mid-1990s, public debate about private ownership of firearms reached new heights. Gun control proponents pointed to the appalling level of firearm violence committed annually in the United States, while the National Rifle Association (NRA) and others argued that such gun-control efforts were misguided and flew in the face of rights guaranteed in the Constitution (though some legal scholars hold that the oft-quoted Second Amendment provides no such guarantee).

More than 13,000 people were employed by the small arms industry in 1987, nearly three quarters of whom were involved in production. This was a 35 percent decline since employment peaked at a little more than 20,000 in 1980. The decline in employment was due in part to lost sales in the early 1980s, corporate reorganization, and extensive modernization and improvement in productivity by major manufacturers. Employment statistics for the entire gun manufacturing industry, including ammunition manufacturers, indicate that the work force remained in 1992 at about the same level as 1982—about 65,000 employees.

ORGANIZATION AND STRUCTURE

Many small-arms companies trace their beginnings to the late nineteenth century and the Connecticut River Valley between Hartford and Springfield, Massachusetts, known as Gun Valley because of the concentration of armories. Because of this long tradition, several small arms companies that no longer have manufacturing facilities in Gun Valley still maintain headquarters there in the late twentieth century.

Following the Great Depression of the 1930s, many surviving small arms companies diversified or were purchased by large corporations. The trend towards amalgamation reversed itself in the 1980s when two of the largest corporations in the industry, Colt Industries and the Olin Corporation, divested themselves of poorly performing firearms divisions to form stand-alone companies. One of those new companies, the U.S. Repeating Arms Co., maker of Winchester rifles, was then sold to Belgian firearms conglomerate Fabrique Nationale Herstal, and then acquired by the French government-owned GIAT Industries. Fabrique Nationale and Italian firearms maker Pietro Beretta Fabbrica Amri also had large manufacturing facilities in the United States.

BACKGROUND AND DEVELOPMENT

The small arms industry has played an important part in the historical development of the United States, and in the myths and ideals that accompanied that development. Historians of the Industrial Revolution acknowledge the important role that the small arms industry played in teaching American manufacturers about the virtues of interchangeable standardized parts. Moreover, guns bearing the names Remington, Winchester, and Colt are associated with the settlement of the Old West, Manifest Destiny, and the development of the United States into a world power.

Although many prominent craftsmen produced firearms in colonial America, gunmaking as an industry really began in 1775 when the Continental Congress established the Committee of Safety, whose responsibilities included ensuring that the Continental Army had sufficient firearms. The Committee of Safety established specifications for manufacturing flintlock muskets and awarded contracts to various American gunmakers. In 1794, Congress established a national armory at Springfield, Massachusetts which not only stored but manufactured muskets for military use. A second armory was established at Harper's Ferry, Virginia in 1796. The armory at Harper's Ferry would eventually be burned deliberately in 1861 to keep it out of the hands of Confederate forces. The Springfield armory was in operation until 1975.

In 1808, as tensions mounted between the United States and England which would eventually erupt into the War of 1812, the federal armories tooled up to manufacture 40,000 muskets a year. Private gunmakers were also awarded contracts to manufacture between 2,500 and 10,000 muskets each, with the goal of supplying nearly 100,000 militiamen. The federal armories provided "pattern" muskets for the private manufacturers to copy.

Early innovators. One of the early gunmakers to receive a government contract was Eli Whitney, best known as the inventor of the cotton gin, who had established an armory in New Haven, Connecticut in 1798. Whitney was a Yale-educated engineer who realized that the most efficient and cost-effective way to make guns was to manufacture interchangeable parts that could then be assembled by unskilled workers. Although Whitney was far from being the most successful gunmaker of the day, he amazed government officials inspecting his plant by assembling muskets from parts chosen at random. Whitney was the first U.S. industrialist to manufacture interchangeable parts and was considered the father of mass production long before Henry Ford began building cars. By the 1850s, his "American System" of manufacturing was known throughout Europe. The Whitney Armory continued to manufacture guns until 1888.

Although rifles were invented in the early 1500s, and the famous Pennsylvania-made Kentucky rifles were used by some militiamen during the American Revolution, smooth-bore muskets remained the most common firearm well into the nineteenth century. Despite their inaccuracy, they were easier to load and fire than the rifle. Then in 1810, an American gunsmith, John H. Hall, invented a breech-loading flintlock rifle that could be loaded quickly using a paper cartridge containing ball and powder. The U.S. Army ordered 200 rifles in 1818 for experimentation, and Hall supervised their construction at the federal armory at Harpers Ferry. The rifles performed well, but the military continued to rely on muskets up until the Civil War. The Springfield Armory did not begin manufacturing rifles until 1858, but had produced more than 840,000 by the end of 1865. On the other hand, hunters and frontiersmen who favored accuracy switched to breech-loading rifles much sooner. The 200 Hall rifles built in 1818 were also the first firearms manufactured in a government armory using interchangeable parts.

Samuel Colt. Samuel Colt was the first great American gunmaker. He was born in Hartford, Connecticut in 1814, and left school at the age of ten to work in his father's silk mill in Ware, Massachusetts. At the age of 16, he joined the crew of a ship bound for London and Calcutta. In London, Colt apparently saw a display of early attempts at designing repeating firearms. During the voyage home, and possibly inspired by the ship's clutch-controlled rotating capstan, he whittled a crude wooden model of a pistol with a revolving cylinder.

Between 1832 and 1835, Colt financed development of his revolving pistol as a lecturer and "practical chemist," billing himself as "the celebrated Dr. S.

Coult of London and Calcutta" and giving demonstrations of laughing gas in the United States and Canada. He sent money and ideas for improvements in his design to John Pearson, a Baltimore gunsmith, who created a working model. Colt received patents on his design from England and France in 1835, and from the United States in 1836. The most radical feature of Colt's design was a ratchet that rotated and locked the cylinder in place when the gun was cocked.

Colt established the Patent Arms Manufacturing Company in Paterson, New Jersey in 1836 to produce revolving pistols and rifles. However, the head of U.S. Army Ordnance was not impressed with a demonstration and the company failed to receive a military contract. Although the Army eventually did order about 100 rifles and a few five-shot revolvers for fighting the Seminole Indians in Florida, Colt was forced to close down his company in 1842.

At the start of the Mexican War in 1846, General Zachary Taylor, who had used an early Paterson-model Colt revolver, asked Colt for 1,000 revolvers to be delivered within three months. Captain Samuel Walker of the Texas Rangers, which had used Colt revolvers to fight the Comanches, also asked for guns, only Walker wanted a larger caliber revolver that would fire six shots. Colt designed a gun to Walker's specifications, but without a factory of his own he subcontracted the manufacturing to Eli Whitney Jr., who was then running the armory his father had founded and was the Army's primary contractor for muskets. Colt personally supervised the manufacturing. The .44 caliber six-shooter became known as the Walker gun. Tragically, Walker was killed in action four days after he received a set of Walker-model revolvers from Colt.

In 1847, the Army ordered another 1,000 revolvers and Colt set up the renamed Colt's Patent Arms Manufacturing Co. in leased space in his hometown of Hartford. He also hired a talented machinist, Elisha K. Root, to manage the operation. Root, who received twice his former salary at a farm-implements company, was given a free hand in setting up the factory. He designed belt-driven machinery for turning gun stocks, boring rifling barrels, and making cartridges. Under Root's direction the Colt armory became a showplace for Eli Whitney's "American System."

In 1853, Colt became the first American manufacturer to establish a foreign branch when he opened a factory on the Thames River in London to supply guns to the British government. Colt became known as gunmaker to the world and successfully defended his patents against infringement until they expired in 1856. When he died six years later, a new factory he had built in Hartford in 1855 was the largest private armory in the world and Colt was one of the wealthiest men in America with an estate valued at $15 million.

Gatling, Maxim, and Browning. The Civil War was the proving ground for many advances in firearms and ordnance, including the famous Sharpes carbine, more than 80,000 of which were produced for the Northern troops by the Sharpes Rifle Manufacturing Co. But no development was more dramatic than the introduction of the first practical machine gun, patented in 1862 by Richard J. Gatling.

Gatling was the son of a North Carolina planter who spent most of his career improving agricultural methods and inventing farm machinery. His hand-cranked machine gun actually performed erratically during the Civil War, but with some mechanical improvements the design was officially adopted by the U.S. Army in 1866. Gatling later sold his patent to the Colt's Patent Arms Manufacturing Co.

In 1884, another American inventor, Sir Hiram Stevens Maxim, developed the first semi-automatic rifle when he modified a Winchester rifle so the power of the recoil would eject the spent cartridge and load the next round. In 1889, Maxim also developed the first fully automatic machine gun. Maxim's designs were adopted by every major power in the world between 1900 and the World War I. English models of the Maxim machine gun, known as the Vickers, were used by both sides in World War II, and the North Koreans employed outdated Maxim machine guns in the Korean War.

Maxim also experimented with internal combustion engines, steam-powered flight, and electric lights, losing a critical patent lawsuit to Thomas Edison. A native of Maine, Maxim moved to England and became a British citizen in 1900. He was knighted in 1901. His son, Hiram Percy Maxim, invented the silencer, which mutes the report of a gunshot.

Jonathon M. Browning, the son of a Utah gunsmith, was the most prolific and successful American gun designer in history. He developed one of the earliest semi-automatic pistols and the first gas-operated machine gun. Browning sold or licensed most of his designs to the Colt Patent Arms Manufacturing Co., including several machine gun designs. He also licensed designs to the Winchester Repeating Arms Company, including the first lever-action rifle strong enough to use the high-power cartridges of the day. This rifle, named Model 1886, made Winchester the best-known name among American rifle makers.

In 1888, when no American companies expressed interest in his semi-automatic pistol, Browning licensed the design to the Belgian gunmaking firm of Fabrique Nationale Herstal. He also licensed the Browning name for use outside of North America. Browning and Nationale Fabrique later collaborated on some of the most famous firearms in history, including the Browning Automatic Rifle, or BAR, used during World War I and World War II. Fabrique Nationale purchased controlling interest in Browning Arms in 1977.

Browning also designed the first successful gas-operated machine gun. In 1890, he sold the design Colt, which produced the Colt Machine Gun Model 1895, the first fully automatic machine gun used by U.S. military forces. In 1990, Colt also became the first U.S. company to produce an automatic pistol, also based on a Browning design.

CURRENT CONDITIONS

Sales of small arms in the United States rose sharply in the early 1990s, in part because of gun control legislation passed in 1994. The Brady Bill, which calls for a five-day waiting period (and background check) before a customer can purchase a handgun, was passed in 1994 after bitter debate. A ban on 19 types of assault weapons was passed shortly thereafter in a dramatic 216-214 vote in the House of Representatives (the measure passed the Senate by a comfortable margin). In analyzing the vote, *Time* noted that "the gun lobby has recently collided with . . . an increased fear of violent crime. Twenty-two cities had a record number of homicides last year. That has left many citizens feeling vulnerable and increasingly unsympathetic to those who interpret the Second Amendment as protecting the rights of Americans to own guns . . . Polls showed that people supported the [assault weapon] ban by ratios as lopsided as 4 to 1; a much quoted statistic by proponents of the measure held that though assault weapons may constitute only one percent of the firearms in the U.S., they are responsible for eight percent of the killings." Ironically, however, the measures actually spurred gun sales across the country as buyers sought to make their purchases before the new laws took affect. Anti-gun sentiment also caused several retail outlets to stop selling guns and convinced some large corporations to improve their public image by divesting gun-manufacturing divisions.

Less costly foreign imports also affected U.S. manufacturing, reducing the profit margin on the sale of guns. Foreign imports were less costly because of higher U.S. wages and the fact that many gun factories were among the oldest industrial facilities in the United States. Also to blame was the high cost of product liability insurance in the United States, which some manufacturers considered a greater long-term threat to the industry than efforts to ban or restrict firearms. Nearly all major gun manufacturers were hit with multi-million dollar lawsuits in the 1980s.

Foreign gunmakers also established manufacturing facilities in the United States in the 1980s to avoid restrictions on imports, including Italy's Pietro Beretta Fabbrica Amri and Belgium's Fabrique Nationale. In 1985, Beretta USA signed a contract to provide 9mm handguns to the U.S. Army, ending Colt's 100-year dominance of military sidearms. Three years later, Fabrique Nationale wrested the Army contract for the M-16 automatic rifle away from Colt. The losses were a major reason that Colt Industries eventually sold its firearms division to a group of private investors. Two other famous names in American gunmaking, Winchester and Smith & Wesson, was also sold in the 1980s to avoid bankruptcy.

INDUSTRY LEADERS

Remington Arms Company, Inc. In 1993, Remington was a subsidiary of E.I. du Pont de Nemours and Company. Based in Wilmington, Delaware, Remington was the leading manufacturer of shotguns, producing more than 262,000 in 1991, or about one-third of all shotguns made in the United States. Remington, with revenues of $250 million, was also a leading manufacturer of rifles and ammunition and marketed a line of hunting apparel.

Remington traces its heritage to Eliphalet Remington, an early American gunsmith who produced his first flintlock rifle in 1816. Raised in Central New York, Remington purchased land along the Erie Canal in 1828 and established an armory. The town that developed around the armory became known as Remington's Corners until Eliphalet Remington insisted the town change the name to Ilion. Remington's manufacturing facilities were still in Ilion in 1993. The company was known as E. Remington & Sons during the Civil War. The Depression of 1884 forced the company into bankruptcy, and it was reorganized in 1888 as the Remington Arms Co. Du Pont purchased Remington in 1933 during the Great Depression.

Remington is considered a leader in introducing new technology and production techniques. After World War II, Remington began manufacturing parts that were interchangeable between models. The company also simplified the shape and design of many gun parts, which initially caused gun enthusiasts who were used to the elaborate showpieces of the past to treat newer Remington models with scorn. Some parts designed in the early 1950s were still being used on models introduced in the 1980s.

In the late 1980s, Remington became one of the first gunmakers to install computer-aided design/computer-aided manufacturing equipment (CAD/CAM) to reduce costs and increase its ability to respond to consumer trends. Paradoxically, the new manufacturing process produced parts by traditional machine tooling rather than stamping or casting, which most companies had turned to in the middle of the twentieth century to save money. The Remington plant in Ilion was considered one of the most advanced metal-work facilities in the United States.

O.F. Mossberg & Sons, Inc. O.F. Mossberg is the second leading maker of shotguns in the United States, manufacturing more than 209,000 in 1991. The New Haven, Conn.-based company had revenues of $20 million. Oliver F. Mossberg was a Swedish immigrant who worked for several U.S. gunmakers before he began making .22 caliber "novelty guns" in his spare time to put his sons, Iver and Harold, through college. In 1919, the Mossbergs formed O.F. Mossberg & Sons. Between 1919 and 1932, they produced about 37,000 .22 caliber "Brownie" pistols. They began manufacturing .22 caliber rifles in 1922. Oliver Mossberg died in 1937.

The company continued to produce .22 caliber pistols and rifles after World War II, but also expanded into bolt-action shotguns. The first pump-action Mossberg shotguns were introduced in 1957. In 1986, Mossberg ended production of all rifles and pistols to concentrate solely on shotguns. Mossberg shotguns are widely used in law enforcement and the military. Mossberg claims to be the oldest family-owned and operated firearms manufacturer in the United States. In 1993, Alan I. Mossberg, grandson of the founder, was president and CEO.

U.S. Repeating Arms Co., Inc. The U.S. Repeating Arms Co. (USRAC) is a major manufacturer of shotguns and rifles under the legendary Winchester brand name. In 1991, USRAC produced more than 126,000 shotguns and 113,000 rifles, generating revenues of $74 million. The company was owned by GIAT Industries, a private company wholly owned by the French government.

The Winchester Repeating Arms Company was founded by Oliver F. Winchester in New Haven, Connecticut, in 1866. Winchester was a shirtmaker by trade, but became involved in gunmaking when he purchased the assets of the defunct Volcanic Repeating Arms Co. Volcanic had been founded in 1855 by

Horace Smith and Daniel B. Wesson, later of Smith & Wesson fame. Winchester was an early investor in the company, which went bankrupt in 1857. The Winchester Model 1866 was the first successful lever-action repeating rifle. Later models made the Winchester name synonymous with American-made rifles.

When the market for guns collapsed during the Depression, Winchester was purchased by the Olin Corporation. In 1981, a group of Olin employees purchased the Winchester gun division in a leveraged buyout, calling the new company the U.S. Repeating Arms Co., and licensing the Winchester name from Olin. Unfortunately, gun sales in the United States plummeted in the early 1980s, and USRAC filed for bankruptcy. USRAC was then purchased in 1987 by a group of investors led by Fabrique Nationale, a Belgium gunmaker and at one time the largest private arms company in the world. Fabrique Nationale became the sole owner in 1990, and was purchased by GIAT Industries in 1992.

Sturm, Ruger & Company, Inc. Sturm, Ruger & Co. is the largest maker of small arms in the United States, accounting for nearly 15 percent of the industry. It was the only U.S. gunmaker active in all four small arms categories of rifles, shotguns, revolvers and pistols. In 1991, Sturm, Ruger produced more than 240,000 rifles, more than any other U.S. gunmaker. The company also manufactured 170,000 pistols, 85,000 revolvers, and 8,000 shotguns. Based in Southport, Connecticut, Sturm, Ruger had sales of $156 million in 1992.

Sturm, Ruger was founded in 1948 by William Batterman Ruger with a $50,000 stake from Alexander Sturm, a family friend and gun collector. Ruger had been a firearms designer for the U.S. government's Springfield Armory and the Auto Ordnance Corporation. Sturm, Ruger started by manufacturing a .22 caliber target pistol designed by Ruger, but gained special favor with gun enthusiasts in the early 1950s when it began producing Old West-style six-shooters that capitalized on the popularity of adult TV Westerns. Sturm, Ruger also utilized a manufacturing process known as investment casting. Rather than machine-tooling parts for its guns, Sturm, Ruger cast parts from molten steel. The parts were not only cheaper to produce, they were stronger.

Between 1982 and 1992, when sales of small arms in the United States fell by almost 50 percent, Sturm, Ruger increased sales by nearly 75 percent. In 1986, Sturm, Ruger forced its distributors to choose between its guns and those made by Smith & Wesson. About half chose to stay with Sturm, Ruger.

In 1992, *Forbes* called Sturm, Ruger one of the 200 Best Small Companies in the United States. However, a discordant note was sounded by the *Wall Street Journal* in 1993 when the newspaper reported that more than 600 people had been injured and 40 killed in accidental shootings involving Sturm, Ruger's Old West-style revolvers. Between 1953 and 1972, Sturm, Ruger produced more than 1.5 million of the single-action revolvers patterned after the legendary 1873 Colt Peacemaker. Like the original Peacemaker, however, Sturm, Ruger six-shooters often discharged accidentally if the gun was dropped or the hammer struck. Although Sturm, Ruger refused to release exact numbers, the *Wall Street Journal* reported that the company lost at least 20 lawsuits and settled hundreds more that never went to trial.

Sturm, Ruger redesigned its Old West revolvers in 1972 to make them safer. In 1982, Sturm, Ruger offered to retrofit older models with a safety device at no cost to their owners. However, fewer than ten percent of the 1.2 million Old Model revolvers were modified. The company also ran a series of ads from 1981 to 1983 urging gun owners to load revolvers with only five bullets and leave the hammer resting on an empty chamber.

The Marlin Firearms Co. Marlin Firearms was the second leading manufacturer of rifles in the United States, and the largest maker of .22 caliber rifles. The privately-owned Marlin Firearms had revenues of $50 million in 1991. Marlin was founded in New Haven, Connecticut in 1870 by John Mahlon Marlin, who had worked for the Colt Patent Firearms Co. during the Civil War. Trick shooter Annie Oakley used a specially-made Marlin Model 1889 in Buffalo Bill Cody's Wild West show in the 1890s. Marlin was also known for its Colt-Browning machine guns and military rifles made during World War I, when it was known as the Marlin Rockwell Corporation. After the war, Rockwell had no interest in sporting guns and auctioned off the firearms division. Frank Kenna, whose family owned and operated Marlin Firearms into the 1990s, purchased the business for $100. In addition to firearms, Marlin produced razor blades from 1936 until the 1960s.

Smith & Wesson Corporation. Smith & Wesson is the leading manufacturer of revolvers in the United States, producing more than 256,000 in 1991. The company also manufactured more than 168,000 pistols, making it the second largest small arms company in the United States.

Smith & Wesson's most popular revolver is the .38 Special, widely used by police officers. The company also manufactures the .44 Magnum revolver used by Clint Eastwood in the ''Dirty Harry'' movies. In the late 1980s, Smith & Wesson became a leader in the emerging market for hand guns designed especially for women with the Lady Smith. The Lady Smith was a .357 Magnum with a grip and trigger mechanism designed for smaller hands. Many women's magazines refused to run ads for Lady Smith when it was introduced in 1988.

Horace Smith and Daniel B. Wesson formed their first partnership in 1851, creating the Volcanic Repeating Arms Co., which they later sold to Oliver F. Winchester. In 1856, when the Colt patents expired, Wesson developed a revolver that used a metallic rim-fire cartridge. He and Smith then formed Smith & Wesson in Springfield, Massachusetts in 1856. Smith retired from the business in 1873, but Wesson and his descendants continued to run the company until 1967, when it was purchased by the Bangor Punta Corporation. In 1984, the company became part of the Lear Siegler Holdings Corporation. Lear Siegler sold the company to F.H. Tompkins PLC, a British manufacturer of plumbing supplies and lawn mowers, in 1987. In 1992, the company had revenues of $140 million.

Colt Manufacturing Company. At one time the largest and most important gunmaker in the United States, the Colt Manufacturing Co. was a relatively small maker of rifles and pistols in the early 1990s, producing 70,000 pistols and 38,000 rifles in 1991. Colt was owned by an investment group that included the United Auto Workers Union and the State of Connecticut. It had revenues of about $100 million.

Colt's Patent Arms Manufacturing Company, founded by inventor Samuel Colt in 1847, provided the Union Army with more than 107,000 revolvers during the Civil War. The famed Peacemaker, a six-shooter used in the Old West, was introduced in 1873 and manufactured continuously until 1941, and Colt produced commemorative Peacemakers after World War II.

The Colt family owned the company until 1901, when it was sold to a group of investors. The company suffered several setbacks in the 1920s and 1930s, beginning with its decision to stop manufacturing the Thompson submachine gun because it had become popular with gangsters. Nearly two million of the popular Tommy guns, as they were called, were produced during World War II by another contractor. Ironically, 60 years later Colt ended production of the AR-15, a popular semi-automatic civilian model of the military's M-16, in part because it was being used by drug dealers.

Like most other small arms manufacturers, Colt was hard hit by the Great Depression. Its difficulties were compounded by a violent strike in 1935, during which the home of its then-president Sam Stone was firebombed, and a hurricane in 1936, which destroyed most of what was left of the Colt Manufacturing Co. The company seemingly rebounded during World War II, but mismanagement later led to a financial crisis and manufacturing stopped altogether between 1945 and 1947.

In 1955, Colt was purchased by the Penn-Texas Corporation, a corporate raider who was expected to dismantle the company. In 1962, a stockholder's revolt forced out Penn-Texas and the company was reorganized as Colt Industries. In 1963, Colt became the sole contractor for the Army's new M-16 automatic assault rifle.

After nearly two decades of growth, during which Colt Industries became a diversified billion-dollar corporation, the Firearms Division suffered another series of market defeats in the 1980s. In 1985, the U.S. government dropped the Colt .45, standard military issue since 1911, and adopted a 9mm semi-automatic pistol in its place. Colt lost the contract to the Beretta USA Corporation. Then in 1986, the United Auto Workers struck the Colt plant in Hartford. Replacement workers were hired, but the lingering strike and concerns about quality may have caused Colt to lose the M-16 contract in 1988, when an order for 500,000 rifles went to FN Manufacturing, the American manufacturing subsidiary of Fabrique Nationale. Several unionized police departments also refused to buy from Colt during the strike.

In 1990, a group of investors that included the State of Connecticut purchased the Firearms Division from Colt Industries. The UAW agreed to end the strike in exchange for rehiring striking workers and an 11 percent share of the company. The division was renamed the Colt Manufacturing Co. The new owners almost immediately found themselves embroiled in an old controversy when Colt announced plans in 1991 to a market a rifle similar to the discontinued AR-15. At the time, Connecticut, with a 47 percent stake in the company and $25 million of its employee pension funds at risk, was considering a ban on all assault-style rifles.

INDUSTRY INFORMATION SOURCES

''A Belgium Arms Maker Bids for Browning,'' *Business Week*, August 22, 1977, 27.

Carey, A. Merwyn, *American Firearms Makers,* New York: Thomas Y. Crowell Co., 1953.

Carmichel, Jim, "New Guns the Way They Used to Be," *Outdoor Life,* May 1988, 68.

Chant, Christopher, *New Encyclopedia of Handguns,* New York: Gallery Books, 1986.

Clede, Bill, "U.S. Repeating Arms Co.," *Shooting Industry,* n.d., 104.

Grant, Ellsworth S., "Gunmaker to the World," *American Heritage,* June 1968.

Greene, Richard, "Under the Gun," *Forbes,* March 2, 1981, 98.

Gresham, Grits, "Winchester Rides Again," *Sports Afield,* November 1992.

"The History of Marlin Firearms," North Haven, CT: Marlin Firearms Company.

Holusha, John, "Colt to Sell Unit that Won the West," *New York Times,* April 29, 1989, 33.

Isikoff, Michael, "New Colt Assault Rifle Revives Debate," *Washington Post,* April 19, 1990, A3.

Johnson, Kirk, "Gun Valley Tries to Adapt to the Winds of Change," *New York Times,* March 21, 1989, B1.

———, "Gun Import Ban Enriches Small U.S. Arms Makers," *New York Times,* July 14, 1989, A1.

———, "Emotions and History Tied to Colt Abandonment of Semiautomatics," *New York Times,* March 17, 1989, A18.

———, "Connecticut Debates Stake in Gun Maker It Saved," *New York Times,* April 26, 1990, A1.

King, Resa W., "United States Gunmakers: The Casualties Pile Up," *Business Week,* May 19, 1986, 77.

Larson, Erik, "Wild West Legacy: Ruger Gun Often Fires if Dropped, but Firm Sees No Need for Recall," *Wall Street Journal,* June 24, 1993, 1.

"Lethal Weapon 2," *Time,* May 16, 1994, 40-43.

Lockett, Bob, "Colt: What Went Wrong in Hartford?" *Shooting Industry,* July 1992, 34.

Maines, John, "Can Females Be Friends with Firearms?," *American Demographics,* June 1992, 22.

Matunas, Edward A., "U.S. Repeating Arms Company: On the Road to Glory," *Shooting Industry,* July 1988, 46.

Millman, Joel, "Steady Finger on the Trigger," *Forbes,* November 9, 1992, 188.

Moreton, Dave, "60 Years of History and Big Plans for the Future," *American Firearms Industry,* August 1979.

"Mossberg's Unchanging Target: Development and Growth," *Connecticut Industry,* October 1967, 6.

Peterson, Harold, *Encyclopedia of Firearms,* New York: E.P. Dutton, 1964.

Sobel, Robert, and David B. Sicilia, *The Entrepreneurs: An American Adventure,* Boston: Houghton Mifflin, 1986.

Stevenson, Richard W., "Smith & Wesson Is Sold to Britons," *New York Times,* May 23, 1987, 33.

Sturm, Ruger and Company, Inc., *1992 Annual Report,* Southport, CT: Sturm, Ruger and Company, Inc., 1993.

Walter, John, *The Rifle Book,* London: Arms & Armour Press, 1990.

"Why the Firearms Business Has Tired Blood," *Business Week,* November 27, 1978, 107.

Wilson, R. L., *The Colt Heritage,* New York: Simon and Schuster, 1979.

"Winchester Purchaser Sees Huge Potential," *New York Times,* December 31, 1987, D2.

Wyman, Stephen H., "Colt Loses Firepower in Weapons Industry," *Washington Post,* March 17, 1989, B12.

—Dean Boyer

SIC 3489

ORDNANCE AND ACCESSORIES, NOT ELSEWHERE CLASSIFIED

This category covers establishments primarily engaged in manufacturing ordnance and accessories, not elsewhere classified, such as naval, aircraft, antiaircraft, tank, coast, and field artillery having a bore more than 30 mm. (or more than 1.18 inch), and components. Establishments primarily engaged in manufacturing small arms and parts 30 mm. or less are classified in **SIC 3484: Small Arms;** those manufacturing tanks are classified in **SIC 3795: Tanks and Tank Components;** and those manufacturing guided missiles are classified in Industry Group 376 (Guided Missiles and Space Vehicles and Parts).

The value of shipments in the ordnance and accessories industry was $1.48 billion in 1991. Shipments declined every year from 1988 to 1991, and were lower in 1991 than in all years back to 1983. 1984 was a peak year with $1.93 billion in shipments. Annual capital investments were $13 million in 1991, lower than all years in the prior decade. 1987 was a peak year, with $50 million invested.

The industry employed 9,300 production workers in 1991, fewer than all years back to 1982. As with the value of shipments, 1984 was a peak year, with 14,700 production workers employed. The Bureau of Labor Statistics made employment forecasts at the SIC 348 (Ordnance and Accessories, Except Vehicles and Guided Missiles) level for 27 occupational categories. Based on projected changes from 1990 to 2005, employment was expected to decline by double-digit figures in all 27 occupations and by over 30 percent in 21 of these occupations.

The industry is highly labor intensive, having only 22 percent as much investment per production worker as that for the manufacturing sector as a whole. Annual hours worked by production workers in the industry are slightly lower on average than those worked in the manufacturing sector at large, and hourly wages are 50 percent higher. There are about 60 establishments in the ordnance industry, just over half of which had 20 or more employees. Average firm size as measured by the number of production workers per establishment is over five times as large as for the manufacturing sector as a whole.

Of the top 12 firms by sales in the industry in 1992, the largest, Alliant TechSystems Inc., is publicly held, while the remainder are either subsidiaries or divisions. All of the top 12 firms have $25 million or more in sales and 200 or more employees. Of the remaining 13 firms ranking among the top 25 by sales in 1992, just over half were private independents. Average investment per establishment is 11 percent higher than for the manufacturing sector as a whole. The top three firms in the ordnance and accessories industry are Alliant TechSystems Inc. of Edina, Minnesota, SCI Technology of Huntsville, Alabama, and the FMC Corp. Naval Systems Division of Minneapolis, Minnesota.

Alliant Techsystems was founded in 1990 upon its acquisition of the Defense and Marine Systems Business of Honeywell Inc. The publicly held firm had $1.19 billion in sales and 6,700 employees in 1992. SCI Technology was founded in 1961 and had $660 million in sales and 7,000 employees in 1992. The firm is a subsidiary of the publicly held SCI Systems Inc., also of Huntsville. The Naval Systems Division of the publicly held FMC Corp. was founded in 1964 and had $270 million in sales and 2,500 employees in 1992.

The states ranking in the top four by number of establishments in the industry are California (with 8), Ohio (with 4), and Minnesota and Texas (with 3 each). Together these four states account for about one-third of all industry establishments in the United States. The top five industries and sectors buying the outputs of the ordnance and accessories industry are listed as follows: federal government purchase, national defense, with a 72.0 percent share; exports, with a 24.4 percent share; ordnance and accessories, not elsewhere classified, with a 2.4 percent share; change in business inventories, with a 1.0 percent share; and small arms ammunition, with a 0.2 percent share.

INDUSTRY INFORMATION SOURCES

"Alliant Announces Layoffs in Spring," *Defense News,* March 2, 1992.

"Alliant Techsystems Lowers Profit Forecast," *Interavia Air Letter,* November 23, 1992.

Annual Survey of Manufactures, Washington, D.C.: U.S. Census Bureau, 1991.

Darnay, Arsen J., editor, *Manufacturing USA: Industry Analysis, Statistics, and Leading Companies* (3rd edition), Detroit, Michigan: Gale Research Inc., 1993.

Lashinsky, Adam, "FMC Girds for Waning of Defense Business," *Crain's Chicago Business,* May 10, 1992.

Moody's Industrial Manual, New York: Moody's Investors Service Inc., 1993.

Ward's Business Directory of U.S. Private and Public Companies, Detroit, Michigan: Gale Research Inc., 1993.

—David Kucera

SIC 3491

INDUSTRIAL VALVES

This category covers establishments primarily engaged in manufacturing industrial valves. Establishments primarily engaged in manufacturing fluid power valves are classified in **SIC 3492: Fluid Power Valves and Hose Fittings;** those manufacturing plumbing fixture fittings and trim are classified in **SIC 3432: Plumbing Fixture Fittings and Trim;** and those manufacturing plumbing and heating valves are classified in **SIC 3494: Valves and Pipe Fittings, Not Elsewhere Classified.**

INDUSTRY SNAPSHOT

Segments of the valve industry were reclassified in 1987, and therefore data prior to 1987 is unavailable. However, between 1987 and 1990 the industry's level of shipments increased from nearly $4.60 billion to $5.75 billion, while the level of employment remained relatively flat. In 1990, 30,300 of the total 46,400 people employed by this industry were production workers. Average wages across the industry were higher than the average for all U.S. manufacturers in 1989 at $11.45 per hour, compared to $10.49 for all manufacturing. By 1990, the average hourly wage for employees in this industry was $12.15.

Compared to other manufacturing industries, the industrial valves segment is labor intensive. Comparative ratios of employees, production workers, wages, and hours worked per establishment are much higher than in other manufacturing industries. Value added, cost, shipments, and investment per establishment are also higher than the manufacturing average. In 1989,

279 of the 380 total establishments in this classification employed more than 20 people.

The industry consumed $1.62 billion in materials, parts, containers, and miscellaneous supplies in 1987. Gray and malleable iron castings accounted for most consumption at $142.6 million. Steel casting consumption ran second to iron, costing $127.7 million. Copper and copper-based alloy castings cost $50.1 million, while aluminum and aluminum-based alloy castings cost $37.8 million. Other materials consumed include mill shapes such as sheet, plate, and bars of carbon and stainless steel, copper, and aluminum. Fabricated rubber, plastics, and wire products, ball and roller bearings, screw machine products, including bolts, nuts, screws, and rivets, and electric motors also contributed greatly to the list of products consumed.

ORGANIZATION AND STRUCTURE

Industry market share is spread amongst ten product groups: The largest share, 27.26 percent, is automatic valves (regulating and control type) and parts; gates, globes, and check valves represent 16.12 percent; industrial valves, not elsewhere classified, (15.22); ball valves (12.20); valves for water works (9.43); solenoid valves (7.03); plug valves (5.00); butterfly valves (4.59); nuclear valves (2.03); and industrial valves, unspecified, (1.13).

Valve producers rely heavily on a number of economic sectors and industries for manufacturing input. The highest percentage of input is provided by blast furnaces and steel mills (19.6 percent). Other inputs include imported materials (13.8 percent); wholesale trade (8.1); iron and steel foundries (7.5); and pipe, valves, and pipe fittings (3.2). The remaining 50 percent includes services such as advertising, banking, transportation, communication, and legal.

Benefactors of the industrial valves industry are numerous. Industrial buildings demand the greatest amount of output from this industry at 12.2 percent. Gross private fixed investment consumes 11.7 percent of production. Approximately 7.8 percent of production is exported. Maintenance of nonfarm buildings consumes 5.5 percent, while crude petroleum and natural gas require four percent. Other consuming sectors of industrial valves include sewer system construction, household laundry equipment, paper mills, and oil field machinery.

CURRENT CONDITIONS

The metal fabricating industry faced sluggish growth going into the mid-1990s. This is a result of heavy reliance on the industrial sector of the economy, which was recovering from a recession. Increased activity in automotive, oil exploration, and farming were expected to boost industry sales through 1997. And long range prospects for industrial valves are promising, as plant and equipment spending for the petroleum industry will likely increase. Also, plant and equipment expenditures by electric utilities and pulp and paper companies are projected to rebound.

Eventually, the power industry is expected to renovate existing plants. International sales continue to be key to survival. Also, an increased focus on research and development is likely. According to *U.S. Industrial Outlook,* "Product shipments of valves and pipe fittings could grow at an average annual rate of between two and three percent through 1996. Exports in particular should register large increases during this period. To comply with Clean Air Act, many U.S. manufacturers and power producers will need to apply advanced valve technology, which will lead to expanded orders."

INDUSTRY LEADERS

The top 75 competitors all grossed over $5 million and had total sales of $2.57 billion in 1992. Total employment by these 75 companies was 25,100. The top ten companies include Mueller Company, Fisher Controls International, Stockham Valves and Fittings, Vesuvius U.S.A., Vesuvius U.S.A. Flo-Con, Cooper Industries, DeZurik Incorporated, Mark Controls Corporation, Crosby Valve and Gage Company, and Dresser Industries.

Mueller Company had estimated sales of $21 million. Monsanto sold Fisher Controls International in 1992 to Emerson Electric Company for $1.28 billion. Monsanto claimed it wanted to focus on its primary operations, which include pharmaceutical, agricultural products, chemicals and food ingredients. Fisher's earnings contributions were low, causing analysts to view it as Monsanto's weak link. Likewise, analysts never believed Fisher was a good fit for Monsanto.

In 1975 Tyco Laboratories purchased Grinell Corporation from International Telephone and Telegraph (ITT) with $14 million and the promise to pay 40 percent of Grinell's net earnings for the next ten years. This purchase, forced by federal courts on anti-trust grounds, was a boost for Tyco. In 1975 Tyco's sales were $58 million, compared to Grinell's $1.07 million. Grinell was incorporated in 1892 as the General Fire Extinguisher Company. The company dominated the fire protection equipment industry to the point of becoming a monopoly, bringing a 1961 antitrust suit against itself and three subsidiaries. Eventually Grinell divested itself of the three subsidiaries and merged with ITT in 1969. According to its 1993 annual report, "Tyco Laboratories, Inc. is a global manufacturer and distributor of industrial products with leadership positions in each of its four core businesses: fire protection, flow control, electrical and electronic components, and packaging materials." With its fiscal year ending June 30,1993, sales were $3.11 billion compared to $3.06 billion in 1992. Tyco's major flow control products include a "wide range of valves and fittings, pipe and tubing. Pipe hangers and castings. Butterfly valves and ball valves, sampling devices, and other products for industrial/process control." The major markets served included, "construction, utilities, water and gas distribution companies, food, beverage, chemical, automotive and other industrial markets."

Like other successful competitors, Stockham Valves and Fittings of Birmingham, Alabama continued to expand operations. In 1991, it established cast products and flow control divisions. Later, in 1993, a joint venture was announced between Stockham and FICOTECH, a manufacturer of fire safety equipment. The two will sell fire safety actuators which are designed to mount on Stockham valves, serving industries where fire or explosions are legitimate hazards. To expand overseas operations, Stockham acquired the Triangle Valve Company of England.

WORK FORCE

While this industry faces significant downsizing in some occupations, other occupations are expected to grow by the year 2005. Combination machine tool operators are expected to add nearly 23 percent to the current work force between 1990 and 2005, for example. Jobs for sales workers will also increase, by nearly 20 percent. Demand for industrial production managers should also increase, by 15 percent. Jobs for mechanical engineers will jump 12 percent. Other occupations expected to grow include machinists, welding machine setters, industrial machinery mechanics, tool and die makers, sheet metal workers, and precision metal workers.

Occupations expected to face major reductions (over 25 percent) include: assemblers and fabricators, machine forming operators, machine tool cutting operators, and bookkeepers. Reductions between ten and 25 percent include: machine tool cutting and forming workers; metal and plastic machine setters; helpers, laborers, and material movers; lathe and turning machine operators; and secretaries. Other occupations expected to face reductions include: blue collar worker supervisors; inspectors, testers, and graders; general managers and top executives; welders and cutters; traffic, shipping and receiving clerks; hand packers; general office clerks; freight, stock, and material movers; industrial truck and tractor operators; production, planning, and expediting clerks; and general utility maintenance repairers.

AMERICA AND THE WORLD

International shipments in 1992 fell to 14 percent of total sales. Political instability in Venezuela and a weak European economy were cited as primary reasons for reduced shipment levels. Sales volumes did increase in some Middle Eastern countries. Furthermore, opportunities for valve manufacturers in overseas markets should increase as a result of increased concern over air and water quality, and Eastern Europe's antiquated technologies in production and distribution, particularly in the oil industry. These factors, combined with worldwide reductions in trade barriers, should provide an important avenue for growth.

RESEARCH AND TECHNOLOGY

Equipment leaks have become the focus of the U.S. Environmental Protection Agency (EPA), particularly in the area of air purification. With the implementation of the Clean Air Act Amendment of 1990, the National Emission Standard for Equipment Leaks became regulation. Emission concentration levels below 500 parts per million are now practical due to Fisher Controls' Enviro-Seal packing system for control valves. Similarly, Mark Controls patented a valve packing design that helps customers comply with the Clean Air Act. Work was in progress in 1992 to improve high pressure valve applications.

INDUSTRY INFORMATION SOURCES

Darnay, Arsen J., ed., *Manufacturing USA: Industry Analyses, Statistics, and Leading Companies,* Detroit: Gale Research, Inc., 1993.

"Casting a Vote for Amcast," *Forbes,* August 17, 1992.

"Fisher Controls Ushers in Enviro-Seal Packing and Enviro-Service Maintenance to Meet Tough New Environmental Regulations," *Plant Engineering,* November 19, 1992.

International Directory of Company Histories, Chicago: St. James Press, 1991.

Leach, Mark, "Higher Profit Is Seen by Amcast Industrial for Its Fiscal Year," *Wall Street Journal,* July 23, 1993.

"Monsanto to Sell Fisher Controls Subsidiary," *Chemical and Engineering News,* August 10, 1992.

"Monsanto Surprises with Fisher Sell-Off," *European Chemical News,* August 10, 1992.

"Service/Suppliers: Stockham Valves & Fittings," *Oil & Gas Journal,* August 9, 1993.

"Service/Suppliers: Stockham Valves & Fittings," *Oil & Gas Journal,* January 11, 1993.

"Service/Suppliers: Stockham Valves & Fittings," *Oil & Gas Journal,* September 9, 1991.

Soloman, Caleb, "Forecast Spurs Dive in Cooper Industries Stock," *Wall Street Journal,* January 26, 1994.

Tyco Laboratories, Inc. 1993 Annual Report, Exeter, NH: Tyco Laboratories, 1994.

U.S. Industrial Outlook 1992, Washington, DC: U.S. Department of Commerce, January 1992.

"Wyman-Gordon Co.: Pact Is Reached to Acquire Cooper Industries Division," *Wall Street Journal,* January 18, 1994.

—Valerie E. Wilson

SIC 3492

FLUID POWER VALVES AND HOSE FITTINGS

This classification covers establishments primarily engaged in manufacturing hydraulic and pneumatic valves, hose and tube fittings, and hose assemblies for fluid power systems. Establishments primarily engaged in manufacturing fluid power cylinders are classified in **SIC 3593: Fluid Power Cylinders and Actuators;** those manufacturing fluid power pumps are classified in **SIC 3594: Fluid Power Pumps and Motors;** and those manufacturing hydraulic intake and exhaust motor vehicle valves are classified in **SIC 3592: Carburetors, Pistons, Piston Rings, and Valves.**

INDUSTRY SNAPSHOT

Industry data before 1987 is not available for this classification because it was not established as a separate category until that year. Between 1987 and 1990 the value of fluid power valves and hose fittings shipped by U.S. producers increased from $2.5 billion to $3.3 billion. Employment remained relatively flat, growing from 27,900 in 1987 to 30,900 in 1990. Nearly 66 percent of the work force was comprised of production workers in 1987. This percentage grew only one point by 1990. The wages of these workers were higher than the average of all manufacturing; in 1989 the average hourly wage for all manufacturing workers was $10.49 per hour, while this industry managed to pay an average of $11.62. This rate increased to an average of $12.46 per hour in 1990.

ORGANIZATION AND STRUCTURE

Most of the establishments engaged in this industry employ more than 20 people. Therefore, this industry is characterized by larger businesses and labor intensive processes. The amount of employees per establishment was higher than the average of all manufacturing. Payroll, hours worked, and wage statistics were also higher than the average manufacturing firm. However, in terms of value added, shipments, and investment per establishment, this industry ranked lower than average.

Product share is split between eight manufactured items. The largest segment (19 percent in 1992) was hydraulic and pneumatic hose or tube end fittings and assemblies. Hydraulic valves represented nine percent of the total market. Fittings for metal and plastics tubing used in fluid power transfer systems claimed 16 percent of the total market. Aerospace type hydraulic and pneumatic valves represented 14 percent of sales, and pneumatic valves claimed 14 percent of the total. Aerospace type hydraulic and pneumatic hose or tube end fittings and assemblies represented 11 percent of sales. Six percent was claimed by parts for fluid power valves.

Fluid power valves rely heavily on a number of economic sectors and industries for the inputs to business. The highest percentage of input is provided by blast furnaces and steel mills, at 20 percent in 1992. Imported materials claimed 14 percent of inputs, while wholesale trade claimed eight percent. Iron and steel foundries contributed eight percent, and pipe, valves, and pipe fittings made up three percent of the inputs required for manufacture. The remaining 50 percent included contributors such as advertising and banking, transportation services, communication and legal services, and other heavy industrial suppliers.

The benefactors of the fluid power valves and hose fittings segment are varied. Industrial buildings demanded the greatest amount of outputs from this industry in the early 1990s, at 12 percent—slightly more than Gross private fixed investment. Approximately eight percent of production was exported. Maintenance of nonfarm buildings consumed six percent of the output, while crude petroleum and natural gas required four percent. Other consumers of fluid power valves and pipe fittings include sewer system construction, household laundry equipment, paper mills, and oil field machinery.

CURRENT CONDITIONS

Industries supporting the machinery industries should expect renewed growth due to the turnaround in the U.S. economy which began in 1993. An economic stimulus package in Japan, if approved by voters, could particularly benefit some major U.S. producers. In fact, long term forecasts looking past 1996 and 1998 are favorable for the industry. Although consumer confidence in the economy and earning potential was pessimistic going into the mid-1990s, lower financing terms made automobiles and housing more affordable and attractive which is good for the support industries like fluid power valves. Overseas, the outlook was much more grim. Europe's recession and turbulence over economic unification, added to Japan's slowed economy, caused forecasters to be cautious.

INDUSTRY LEADERS

The top 75 companies engaged in this industry grossed over $5 Billion in 1992 and employed 50,600 people. Each of the companies reported sales over $4 million in revenues. The top five competitors included: Fisher Controls of St. Louis, Missouri; Vickers of Troy, Michigan; Keystone International of Houston, Texas; Applied Power of Milwaukee, Wisconsin; and Duriron Company of Dayton, Ohio. Finishing out the list of the top ten were Watts Regulator Company, Watts Industries, Dover Diversified, Emerson Electric, and Xomox Corporation.

ITT Fluid Technology Corporation was ranked as the industry leader with sales of $1.1 billion and 8000 employees in 1991. Fisher Controls International Inc. was ranked second with sales of $928 million and 9600 employees. Vickers was ranked third with sales of $820 million and 7500 employees. SPX Corporation was ranked fourth with sales of $801 million and 5200 employees. Keystone International Inc. was ranked fifth with sales of $528.4 million and 4100 employees.

Vickers was founded in 1921 by Harry Vickers of Los Angeles. Due to its relationship with the auto industry, Vickers moved to Detroit in 1929. By 1937 Vickers was sold to Sperry, and continued its diversified operations by producing hydraulic pumps, transmissions, valves, and controls. Harry Vickers remained with Sperry, eventually becoming president in 1954. In 1955, Sperry merged with Remington Rand and created Sperry Rand of which Harry Vickers was CEO, and later Chairman until 1967. The company shortened its name in 1979 to Sperry Corporation. The recession in the early 1980s forced Sperry to place Vickers on the block. Libbey Owens Ford purchased Vickers in 1984, adding another non-glass manufacturer to its list of subsidiaries. In 1986 Libbey Owens Ford completed the sale of its glass facilities and adopted the name Trinova to represent Aeroquip Corporation, Vickers, and Sterling Engineered Products. Sterling was later spun-off as its own division, leaving Aeroquip and Vickers to create the variety of power and motion control components for military, aerospace, and general industrial uses. As of 1991, 80 percent of Trinova's sales were generated by power and motion control systems.

Duriron reported net sales of $300 million in 1992, up from $296 million in 1991. According to its 1992 *Annual Report,* "Duriron's 1992 operating performance fell short of expectations as the Company earned $1.42 per share with record sales of $300 million." The president and CEO, John S. Haddick retired and was replaced by William Jordon in February of 1992. Haddick said of the transition, "We set some tough goals during my eight years as CEO and achieved many of them. I'm proud of the team that made it happen. Yet, these accomplishments will certainly pale compared with the opportunities that lie ahead. We've got the leadership in place to get the job done." Duriron's product lines include: centrifugal process and chemical injection metering pumps, automatic control valves, rotary valves and associated automation equipment, filtration equipment and complete waste water systems; laboratory drainage pipe and fittings, and high alloy castings.

Applied Power Inc. showed a slight improvement in net sales for 1993 over years past. In 1993, net sales were $361 million compared to $357 million in 1992 and $359 million in 1991. The world economy, particularly in Europe and Japan, was cited as a significant influence in net results. Applied Power defines itself as "a holding company managing a balanced portfolio of autonomous operating businesses primarily serving industrial markets. We seek to own and develop businesses with intrinsic competitive advantages that serve a variety of end-user markets in different geographic regions, with an emphasis on investment." The companies held are divided into two groups, the first being the Distributed Products Group which contains Enerpac and GB Electrical, and the second being the Engineered Solutions Group which contains Barry Controls and Power-Packer/APITECH.

Keystone International's sales increased from $521 million in 1991 to $528 million in 1992. Keystone is genuinely an international company, with 57 percent of 1992 sales coming from overseas. The United States represented 42 percent of 1992 sales, while Europe, the Middle East, and Africa represented 33 percent. Asia-Pacific made up about 18 percent, and North and South America outside the United States represented 6.4 percent. According to the 1992 *Annual Report,* "Keystone International, Inc. is a leader in the manufacturing and marketing of flow control equipment in virtually every industrial and geographical market worldwide. With 30 manufacturing plants located in 16 countries and 4100 employees around the world, Keystone's presence in global markets is unmatched by any other company in our industry.'' Keystone attributes part of its success to the long-range restructuring plan of dividing operations into strategic business units. The objectives of this strategy are to reduce costs and consolidate six of the companies, representing 11 distinct product lines, which were acquired over six years. As in the case of Keystone Controls, good customer relations are built through selling to the end user, rather than valve manufacturer. This guarantees the control will fit the valve equipment, no matter who manufactured the equipment.

WORK FORCE

While this industry faces significant downsizing in some occupations, other occupations are expected to grow by the year 2005. Machine tool operators, for example, are expected to boost their work force by 23 percent between 1990 and 2005. Sales workers will also increase current employment levels, by nearly 20 percent. Jobs for industrial production managers should also increase, by 15 percent. Jobs for mechanical engineers will likely rise 12 percent. Other occupations expected to grow include machinists, welding machine setters, industrial machinery mechanics, tool and die makers, sheet metal workers, and precision metal workers.

Occupational groups expected to face the most major reductions (over 25 percent) include: assemblers and fabricators, machine forming operators, machine tool cutting operators, and bookkeepers. Reductions between ten and 25 percent include: machine tool cutting and forming workers, metal and plastic machine setters; helpers, laborers, and material movers; lathe and turning machine operators; and secretaries. Other occupations expected to face reductions include: blue collar work supervisors; inspectors, testers, and graders; general managers and top executives; welders and cutters; traffic, shipping and receiving clerks; hand packers; general office clerks; freight, stock, and material movers; industrial truck and tractor operators; production, planning, and expediting clerks; and general utility maintenance repairers.

AMERICA AND THE WORLD

According to Duriron's 1992 *Annual Report,* acquisitions are part of the strategy of overcoming weak world-wide economic conditions. ''Despite the concerns of a slumping world economy, we moved aggressively ahead this past year, acquiring Kammer, a European-based, growth-oriented, automated valve company, significantly expanding our manufacturing, sales and service capabilities in Europe, Australia, and the Asia-Pacific, introducing new products to help cus-

tomers meet changing process and environmental needs, and continuing to implement our world class manufacturing program throughout the organization.'' Another goal set by the company was to grow international business until it represents half the total sales volume. This is to be accomplished by 2000 by expanding existing overseas capacities, acquiring new operations around the world, and developing customer partnerships. It is part of the strategy that affected net earnings in 1992, but the effect is viewed as a positive move for the future. According to the annual report, ''Implementation of the European free trade agreement, the potential impact of the North American free trade pact, and the anticipated establishment of trading blocs in the Asia-Pacific attest to the dramatic changes taking place in our markets. Coupled with accelerated overseas growth in the process industries, these changes, without question, demonstrate that the international marketplace offers Duriron an excellent opportunity for dynamic and sustained growth. Through the diligent use of the tools at our disposal, including total quality assurance, improved productivity and consistent customer satisfaction, we will be successful.''

RESEARCH AND TECHNOLOGY

The biggest changes in valve technology are in the micromachines markets. The Pentagon's Defense Advanced Research Projects Agency (DARPA), is currently working on the fabrication of a ''tiny valve on a silicon chip that can replace bigger, costlier metal valves. One possible use: controlling the flow of samples into a small gas chromatograph that detects poisons in the environment.''

INDUSTRY INFORMATION SOURCES

Applied Power, Inc. 1993 Annual Report, Milwaukee, WI: Applied Power Inc., 1994.

Autry, Ret, ''Companies to Watch: Keystone International,'' *Fortune,* May 6, 1991.

Carey, John, ''Meet the Champion of the Micro Age,'' *Business Week,* April 26, 1993.

Darnay, Arsen J., ed, *Manufacturing USA: Industry Analyses, Statistics, and Leading Companies,* Detroit: Gale Research, Inc., 1993.

Duriron Company 1992 Annual Report, Dayton, OH: Duriron, 1993.

International Directory of Company Histories, Detroit: St. James Press, 1991.

Keystone International, Inc. 1992 Annual Report, Houston, TX: Keystone International Inc., 1993.

''Keystone on Its Keister,'' *Forbes,* August 30, 1993.

Reimer, David M., ''Machinery Industry,'' *The Value Line Investment Survey,* February 11, 1994.

''Services/Suppliers: Keystone International,'' *Oil & Gas Journal,* May 18, 1992.

—Valerie E. Wilson

SIC 3493

STEEL SPRINGS, EXCEPT WIRE

This category includes establishments primarily engaged in manufacturing leaf springs, hot wound springs, and coiled flat springs. Establishments primarily engaged in manufacturing wire springs are classified in **SIC 3495: Wire Springs.**

The spring manufacturing industry does not differentiate between the standard industrial codes of steel springs, except wire and wire springs. Instead, the Spring Manufacturers Institute, Inc. (SMI) analyses the industry as one unit. In 1992, SMI reported that the industry generated almost $1.9 billion in sales and employed 20,735 people. Separate figures for SIC 3493 from the previous year revealed that the steel springs, except wire group makes up a small portion of the entire spring industry; it had industry shipments valued at $523.4 million and employed 5,600 people, according to the *1991 Annual Survey of Manufactures.* For more information on the spring manufacturing industry as a whole, consult the essay on **SIC 3495: Wire Springs.**

The automotive industry is the largest customer for steel springs. SMI reported that sales to automotive customers accounted for the largest portion, 41.3 percent, of industry sales in 1992, followed by industrial equipment customers, which accounted for 8.8 percent of sales. Alloy, carbon, and stainless steels were the most commonly used spring materials because of their strength. Titanium was gaining popularity in the early 1990s because of its superior strength, light weight, and resistance to corrosion. Titanium's high cost had been prohibitive but new titanium alloys expanded its use.

Advances in technology have boosted the production capabilities of some spring manufacturers, but are not a requirement for survival in the industry. Tecknow Education Services Inc. president George Keremedjiev noted in *Springs* that spring manufacturing companies were using anything from ''state-of-the-art electronics in tooling to machinery and tooling that seemingly is frozen in time back in the 1950s.'' The technology employed can run the gamut from old machines fitted with electronic sensors that check spring positioning to the Spring Manufacturers Institute, Inc.'s (SMI) Spring Design software program, which enables the most novice engineer to successfully design springs. Hindering greater implementation of technology has been the lack of nationalized standards for spring making.

Because the capital investments required for advances in technology are high, companies must consider the competitive advantages of modernization. If a company is able to maintain or increase sales volume with old assets, it may not be beneficial to modernize its machinery because of the cost involved. SMI's *1992 Annual Market Summary* noted that modernization would be an inefficient use of assets unless it helped ''to produce a higher profit percentage on net sales.'' Nevertheless, Keremedjiev predicted in *Springs* that modern methods of production are needed for a spring manufacturer ''to achieve world class quality in the production process.'' And, according to Scott Rankin of Vulcan Spring in *Springs,* there is ''universal recognition'' that technology will change the industry. Springmaking, once known as the ''Black Art'' because of its difficulty, can now be mastered by a ''springmaker with a month's knowledge and the ability to type numbers on a keyboard,'' noted Rankin.

As trade barriers are removed throughout the world, the American spring industry has had to compete for foreign manufacturing customers. Supplying American springs to foreign customers will keep the industry competitive because, according to SMI president Pete Peterson in *Springs,* ''We don't worry too much about Japanese springs landing in America. But we must worry about the finished products coming here.'' To compete globally, Bud Peterson noted in *Springs* that some American springmakers counteract manufacturers' preferences for national suppliers by forming joint ventures with prominent foreign springmakers. One such joint venture allowed America's largest springmaker, Associated Spring of Bristol, Connecticut, to establish relationships with Japanese automakers through its association with NHK Spring Co., Ltd. of Japan, Japan's largest springmaker.

INDUSTRY INFORMATION SOURCES

Keremedjiev, George, ''Sensors and Electronics in Spring Manufacture . . . the Key to Savings and Quality,'' *Springs,* May 1993, 27-28.

''Looking Ahead—Not Back—as SMI Celebrates its 60th Anniversary,'' *Springs,* October 1993, 54.

Peterson, Bud, ''The Family Tree of Springmakers Withstands the Winds of Change,'' *Springs,* May 1993, 77-85.

"Petersons Stamp Success on Spring Industry," *Springs,* October 1993.

"Removing the Veil of the "Black Art," Newcomers Share Their Enthusiasm for the Springs Industry," *Springs,* October 1992.

"Spring Design Enters New Era," *Springs,* October 1992, 11-12.

U.S. Census Bureau, *Annual Survey of Manufactures,* Washington, DC: U.S. Census Bureau, 1991.

Additional information provided by the Spring Manufacturers Institute, Inc.

—Sara Pendergast

SIC 3494

VALVES AND PIPE FITTINGS, NOT ELSEWHERE CLASSIFIED

This category includes establishments primarily engaged in manufacturing metal valves and pipe fittings, not elsewhere classified, such as plumbing and heating valves, and pipe fittings, flanges, and unions, except from purchased pipes. Establishments primarily engaged in manufacturing plastics pipe fittings are classified in **SIC 3089: Plastics Products, Not Elsewhere Classified;** those manufacturing plumbing fixture fittings and trim are classified in **SIC 3432: Plumbing Fixture Fittings and Trim;** and those manufacturing fittings and couplings for garden hose are classified in **SIC 3429: Hardware, Not Elsewhere Classified.**

Approximately 59 percent of the metal valve and pipe fitting industry was engaged in producing metal fittings, flanges, and unions for piping systems, according to the 1987 Census of Manufacturing. Nearly another 20 percent of the industry was engaged in producing plumbing and heating valves. The industry is heavily reliant on both the oil and construction industries. While the domestic oil industry has been depressed since the mid-1980s, however, the retrofitting of pipes in housing has served to maintain a level of stability in this industry.

Growth in the industry was assured because of changes in fire sprinkler laws. A fire in a Puerto Rico hotel in the early 1990s caused the federal government to review and change laws regarding automatic fire sprinkler systems in buildings exceeding six stories. Additionally, a low-rise hotel fire in Chicago, which killed 15 people in 1993, caused the federal automatic fire sprinkler laws to change regarding buildings lower than seven stories. As a result, many buildings will start retrofitting to comply with new safety regulations. In 1993, Merrill Lynch expected the retrofit market to top $10 billion.

As of 1988, the industry employed nearly 27,000 people in the United States, whose earnings averaged $10.31 per hour. The primary occupation of the industry was assemblers and fabricators. However, the total number of people employed in this field is expected to decrease by over 12 percent going into the year 2000. Other occupations expected to be reduced include machine forming operators, precision inspectors, welding machine setters, metal/plastic machine workers, welders and cutters, secretaries, and packagers. Sales workers and industrial machinery mechanics are expected to increase employment levels by over 20 percent, and industrial production managers are expected to increase by over 17.6 percent going into the next century.

Due to a reclassification of the industrial code, the data available for the industry since 1987 is remarkably different from that of the previous decade. However, preliminary data for the late 1980s suggests that the industry was experiencing moderate business growth. Selected ratios for the industry suggest it is a labor intensive, high paying, low cost, low investment business segment when compared to other manufacturing industries.

Two of the industry leaders are Crane Company and Cameron Iron Works, a division of Cooper Industries. According to Crane's 1991 annual report, it booked $1.3 billion in sales that year with over 9000 employees. Cameron Iron Works recorded $850 million in sales in 1991, with 5900 employees. At the end of 1992, Crane's business strategy was to maintain a balanced business mix and avoid capital intensive, cyclical businesses. During a speech in 1992 at Lehman Brothers' Tenth Annual Diversified Companies Seminar, Crane's chairman and chief executive officer, R. S. Evans, planned to focus the company on niche businesses with high market shares. This strategy would include its valve and pipe fitting interests.

INDUSTRY INFORMATION SOURCES

Darnay, Arsen J., ed., *Manufacturing USA: Industry Analyses, Statistics, and Leading Companies,* Detroit: Gale Research, 1989.

Crane Company, *Annual Report,* Stamford, CT: Crane Company, 1991.

Heller, S. J., "Crane Company—Company Report," Sherson Lehman Brothers, Inc., December 17, 1992.

Neves, C. P., "Tyco Laboratories—Company Report," Merrill Lynch Capital Markets, March 18, 1993.

—Valerie E. Wilson

SIC 3495

WIRE SPRINGS

This industry consists of establishments primarily engaged in manufacturing wire springs from purchased wire. Establishments primarily engaged in assembling wire bedsprings or seats are classified in the Furniture and Fixtures industries.

INDUSTRY SNAPSHOT

The 1991 value of shipments in the wire springs industry—which includes the production of furniture, mechanical, clock, gun, instrument, sash balance, and hair springs—was $1.83 billion, up from $1.10 billion in 1982 (in current dollars). There were about 400 establishments in the industry, 55 percent of these having 20 or more employees. Average firm size as measured by the number of production workers per establishment was 13 percent larger than that for the manufacturing sector as a whole.

The industry employed 16,300 production workers in 1991, about the same number it employed in 1983, but down from a peak of 18,500 production workers in 1985. The industry was relatively labor-intensive, having an average of only 37 percent of the investment per production worker as that for the manufacturing sector as a whole. Annual hours worked by production workers in the industry were about the same as those worked in manufacturing at large, and hourly wages were 11 percent lower.

ORGANIZATION AND STRUCTURE

A full 80 percent of the top 75 firms in the industry were private independents. The capital requirements for the industry were relatively low, with the average investment per establishment 41 percent of that for the manufacturing sector as a whole. Prior to the 1980s, it was rare for firms to cooperate in the production of springs, but this changed in more recent years. Firms learned to cooperate on a number of bases. For example, some firms developed expertise in grinding springs at high tolerances, while others developed high levels of efficiency in looping the wire on the ends of springs. Other spring-producing firms found it advantageous to hire these firms for such operations.

The smallest firms had fewer than 25 employees, and generally did not design the springs they produced, relying instead on specifications provided by their customers. They typically produced small batches of springs made from larger wires (up to about 3/8 inches in diameter), as well as batches both large and small from smaller diameter wires (up to about 0.08 inches in diameter). These versatile firms typically had one or two hand-operated spring coilers and several automatic spring coilers, in addition to a lathe or two for coiling heavier wires. Also, these small firms typically had a number of machines devoted to the other processes necessary for spring production, including grinders, spring testers, baking ovens, and various machine tools.

Medium-size plants had 25 to 100 employees, and these made up the largest share of firms in the industry. Three-fourths of the top 75 firms in the industry had 100 or fewer employees. These firms typically employed engineers to design and test springs. Medium-size firms either specialized in producing coil springs in large batches or were diversified in the production of a large number of spring types. These firms employed similar processes as smaller firms, and the main distinctions regarding capital goods were the number and size of machines. These firms also typically had a greater variety of machines to supplement core production processes, such as electroplating equipment. The increased use of computers in the design and production of springs after the 1980s lead to greater qualitative distinctions in the production processes of smaller and larger firms.

Large firms had more than 100 employees. There were about 15 such firms in the United States in the early-1990s. These firms typically had a greater number of technical and scientific staff. In addition to engineers, such firms employed metallurgists and highly-trained inspectors. These firms also devoted substantial resources to specialized research equipment, such as fatigue testers and wire twisting machines. These large establishments were typically diversified in the production of all major spring types and were often diversified across industry lines.

In the years just after World War II, production of springs was tightly concentrated in the northeast states of Connecticut, New York, Pennsylvania, Illinois, and Ohio. The states ranking in the top ten by value of shipments in the late-1980s were, in order of descending value: Illinois, Michigan, Indiana, California, Ohio, Pennsylvania, Kentucky, North Carolina, Tennessee, and Connecticut, indicating a proportional shift in regional production. Together these ten states accounted for 64 percent of total shipments and 65 percent of total employment. Some plants in the midwest produced principally for the automobile industry, while some in California and Pennsylvania produced principally for the aircraft and railroad industries, respectively.

The outputs of the wire springs industry were widely dispersed across industry and sector lines, reflecting the great extent to which the industry was dependent not only on the production of manufactures, but on the production of the economy at large. The top ten industries and sectors buying the outputs of the industry were: mattresses and bedsprings (5.8 percent); logging camps and logging contractors (5.1 percent); concrete products, not elsewhere classified (four percent); tires and inner tubes (3.2 percent); construction machinery and equipment (three percent); personal consumption expenditures (2.9 percent); exports (2.9 percent); office buildings (2.7 percent); retail trade, except eating and drinking (2.5 percent); and highway and street construction (2.4 percent). The top five types of springs by product share were: unassembled upholstery and furniture springs (43 percent), and precision mechanical springs of the compression (19 percent), extension (ten percent), and torsion (six percent) types.

BACKGROUND AND DEVELOPMENT

The wire spring manufacturing industry grew rapidly in the post-World War II period. The number of plants producing precision springs increased by about six-fold from 1940 to 1980. Membership in the Spring Manufacturers Institute increased from 40 in 1940 to 350 in the 1990s.

The Spring Manufacturers Institute was founded in 1933 (its name changed from the Spring Manufactures Association in 1961). It had a staff of four in the mid-1990s, and was headquartered in Rolling Meadows, Illinois. The institute published two periodicals, the quarterly *Coiler's Gazette* (circulation 750) and the semi-annual *Springs: The Magazine of Spring Technology* (circulation 7,000), as well as the books, *Handbook of Spring Design, Spring Materials, Specification Cross Reference,* and *Mechanical Springs.* In addition, the institute produced the software program "Spring Design." The industry was also served by the American Society of Mechanical Engineers in New York, New York, the American Society for Testing and Material in Philadelphia, Pennsylvania, and the American Society for Metals in Metals Park, Ohio.

Their are three primary types of wire springs: compression springs absorb energy as they are compressed, extension springs as they are extended, and torsion springs as they are twisted. The design and production of wire springs has been referred to as a "Black Art" because of the complexity of interactive variables that must be taken into account. The industry used about 100 types of metals in the production of springs. The choice of the optimal metal depends on such conditions as the potential for corrosion, conductivity, the loads to be borne by the spring, the temperature ranges to which the spring will be exposed, the desired working-life of the spring, and by size constraints. The basic types of metals included high-carbon steels, steel alloys, stainless steels, and copper and nickel-based alloys. Since the cost of range of materials can very from one to hundreds of dollars per pound, and since safety was often a factor (in production of vehicles, for instance), the optimal choice of materials was vital.

The production process begins with the operation of coiling metal wire. For smaller batches (several hundred or less), the manufacturer used a hand-operated coiler or a lathe. Larger batches used automatic coilers. Whereas in the mid-1970s, many coilers produced at the rate of 3,000 to 5,000 springs per hour, by the 1980s, machines were sold that coiled up to 18,000 springs per hour. After being coiled, springs were baked to stabilize their shape. Thereafter, they were compressed to remove any set that would accumulate during usage. Lastly, the ends of the springs were shaped (in the case of extension and torsion springs) and ground. Precision grinding was among the most time-consuming and expensive operations in the production of springs. After they were thus formed, springs were typically finished by either oiling, painting, electroplating, or oxidizing.

In addition to the more common wire spring types are hairsprings. These are spiral springs made from very fine flattened wire (as thin as 0.0002 inches). These springs were used in clocks and watches, as well as specialized precision instruments. Hairsprings were produced by only a few firms.

CURRENT CONDITIONS

The value of shipments continued to increase after 1985, though at a slower pace than in the early-1980s. There were $54 million in capital investments made in 1991, down from a peak of $71 million in 1984. Employment of production workers peaked in 1985 and declined thereafter. The Bureau of Labor Statistics made employment forecasts for 30 occupational categories in the miscellaneous fabricated metal products industries. Based on projected changes from years 1990 to 2005, employment was expected to decline by double-digit figures in nine occupations (occupations accounting for 30 percent total employment in 1990) and single-digit figures in ten other occupations. Only three occupations were projected to show double digit increases to 2005 (occupations accounting for only six percent of total employment in 1990). Thus, overall employment prospects for the industry did not appear promising. Projections made for the wire spring industry alone would have varied from these figures, but the trend toward automation of spring production suggested consistency with projections made at the larger industry level.

Four top executives in the industry were interviewed in the October 1992 issue of *Springs: The Magazine of Spring Technology* regarding the current state and future of the industry. They regarded the industry as highly fragmented, with an excessive number of small firms. One executive stated, "Most companies are under five million dollars and a handful show ten million dollars in sales. It's ironic because I believe the critical size, at least five million dollars, is necessary to survive in the coming years." In the same light, another executive stated, "We'll need to investigate strategic alliances, the shrinking number of companies serving our industry plus more joint ventures." Executives described the industry as being excessively price competitive. Two of them noted that firms' marketing and price strategies should emphasize the degree of engineering and the tight tolerances required for the production of springs. The impact of technological change and diffusion was expected to be of ever-increasing importance in coming years, and the possibility of the increased viability of plastic springs in the future was noted.

INDUSTRY LEADERS

The three largest firms in the industry in 1992 were Associated Spring of Bristol, Connecticut; American Spring Wire Corp. of Bedford Heights, Ohio; and Peterson Spring of Southfield, Michigan. Together these firms accounted for about 20 percent of total sales for the industry.

Associated Spring was a division of the Barnes Group, Inc. With about $185 million in sales and 2,000 employees in 1992, the firm was by far the largest in the industry. Associated Spring, incorporated in 1925, extended its operations widely across the United States and the world, with facilities in ten states as well as in Mexico, the United Kingdom, Singapore, Canada, Brazil, and France.

The firm suffered declining sales and net losses entering the 1990s, and it announced in 1992 that it would close two of its plants as part of a broader consolidation strategy. William R. Fenoglio, president and CEO of the Barnes Group, stated that the concen-

tration of manufacturing facilities in fewer locations would enable the firm to lower costs. In 1993, Associated Spring invested in new technologies using computer-aided design. An article in the July 23, 1993 issue of *Machine-Design* reported, "Associated Spring plans on taking an industry that has traditionally been low technology and bringing it into the twenty-first century, according to Andre Papillon, senior product design engineer for Associated Spring."

American Spring Wire, founded in 1968, was a private corporation, and had about $80 million in sales and 300 employees in 1992. The firm purchased the equipment and inventory of J and S Metals, Inc. in 1991, thus expanding its operations by backwards integration.

Peterson Spring was a division of Peterson American, a private corporation. Peterson Spring generated about $75 million in sales and had 600 employees in 1992. The firm was founded in 1929, and had 20 manufacturing plants, 14 U.S. offices and seven foreign offices. A large portion of the firm's production was purchased by the automobile industry. The firm's plants were given several awards for quality production by its customers in the 1990s. Peterson Spring's Ontario plant received the Chrysler Quality Excellence Award in 1992, and its Windsor plant was awarded the GM Mark of Excellence Award in 1993.

RESEARCH AND TECHNOLOGY

The two key areas of development in the industry were the use of computers and electronics in the production and design of springs and the development of new materials. The Spring Manufacturers Institute developed a software program for the design of compression, extension, and torsion springs. The program was based on parameters drawn from the *SMI Handbook of Spring Design*, and enabled those with little experience to design springs that were optimal under various sets of constraints. The program was expected to be useful not only to spring manufacturers, but also to spring buyers. These buyers could better design their products with prior knowledge of the spring configurations their products would require.

The production process was substantially altered in recent years with the increased viability of Computer Numerically Controlled (CNC) spring-making equipment. The implementation of these technologies in spring-making lagged behind the machine tool industry both because of the relatively small size of the wire spring industry and because of the complex set of operations required for the production of springs. The newest CNC technologies made possible the increased speed of production, lesser setup and training times, greater precision, and lower costs. The increased use of electronic sensors was also advocated as a means of modernizing production.

Springs made from titanium alloys weighed half those made from steel and were also highly resistant to corrosion. The cost of titanium alloys had been prohibitive for many applications, but new and less costly titanium alloys enabled their rapidly expanded use.

INDUSTRY INFORMATION SOURCES

Annual Survey of Manufactures, Washington, D.C.: U.S. Census Bureau, 1991.

''Barnes Group: Will Close Two Spring Production Plants and a Distribution Facility,'' *The Wall Street Journal,* December 2, 1992.

Carlson, Harold. *Spring Manufacturing Handbook,* New York, New York: Marcel Dekker, Inc., 1982.

Daniels, Peggy Kneffel and Carol A. Schwartz, eds. *Encyclopedia of Associations* (28th ed.), Detroit, Michigan: Gale Research Inc., 1994.

Darnay, Arsen J., ed. *Manufacturing USA: Industry Analysis, Statistics, and Leading Companies* (3rd ed.), Detroit, Michigan: Gale Research Inc., 1993.

Directory of Leading Private Companies (7th ed.), Wilmette, Illinois: National Register Reference Publishing, 1992.

''Firm Will Post Loss for Year After Charge of $40.7 Million,'' *The Wall Street Journal,* January 27, 1993.

Godfrey, Loren. ''Justifying New Technologies; As CNC Machines Come of Age,'' *Springs: The Magazine of Spring Technology,* May 1993.

''Investing in the Future with Analysis,'' *Machine-Design,* July 23, 1993.

Keremedjiev, George. ''Sensors and Electronics in Spring Manufacture . . . The Key to Savings and Quality,'' *Springs: The Magazine of Spring Technology,* May 1993.

Lanke, Ed. ''Spring Design Enters New Era,'' *Springs: The Magazine of Spring Technology,* October 1992.

Moody's Industrial Manual, New York: Moody's Investors Service Inc., 1993.

''Plant News,'' *Springs: The Magazine of Spring Technology,* October 1992.

''Plant News,'' *Springs: The Magazine of Spring Technology,* May 1993.

''Removing the Veil of the 'Black Art,' Newcomers Share Their Enthusiasm for Springs Industry,'' *Springs: The Magazine of Spring Technology,* October 1992.

Sommer, Chris. ''Titanium Offers Heavy-Weight Potential for Spring Makers,'' *Springs: The Magazine of Spring Technology,* October 1993.

Viani, Laura. ''American Spring Wire Buys J&S Equipment, Inventory,'' *American Metal Market,* June 5, 1991.

Ward's Business Directory of U.S. Private and Public Companies, Detroit, Michigan: Gale Research Inc., 1993.

—David Kucera

SIC 3496

MISCELLANEOUS FABRICATED WIRE PRODUCTS

This category includes establishments primarily engaged in manufacturing miscellaneous fabricated wire products from purchased wire, such as noninsulated wire rope and cable; fencing; screening, netting, paper machine wire cloth; hangers, paper clips, kitchenware, and wire carts. Rolling mills engaged in manufacturing wire products are classified in the Primary Metal Industries. Establishments primarily engaged in manufacturing steel nails and spikes from purchased wire or rod are classified in **SIC 3315: Steel Wiredrawing and Steel Nails and Spikes;** those manufacturing nonferrous wire nails and spikes from purchased wire or rod are classified in **SIC 3399: Primary Metal Products, Not Elsewhere Classified**; those drawing and insulating nonferrous wire are classified in **SIC 3357: Drawing and Insulating of Nonferrous Wire;** and those manufacturing wire springs are classified in **SIC 3495: Wire Springs.**

The miscellaneous fabricated wire products industry produces a wide variety of wire-based goods, from barbed wire to bird cages to conveyor belts to hog rings to paper clips. The largest single product produced by the industry is noninsulated ferrous wire rope and cable, representing 13.2 percent of the product share in 1987, according to *Manufacturing U.S.A.* While ferrous and nonferrous wire cloth, ferrous woven wire products, fencing, and fence gates all claim significant shares of the market, the production of the majority of products produced by this industry is too limited to be represented statistically. The materials consumed by the industry include wire, steel castings, plastics, and bolts. Steel wire is the most heavily consumed category of wire, with a delivered cost to the industry of $284.5 million in 1987. Stainless steel, copper, and aluminum wires are also consumed.

The decade of the 1980s saw the number of establishments involved in this industry drop while the value of shipments and the number of employees remained steady or rose slightly. Shipments rose appreciably between 1982 and 1988, from $2.357 billion to $2.963 billion. The industry work force remained stable, rising slightly from 36,800 employees in 1982 to 37,000 by 1988. In 1988, the 28,000 production workers in this industry averaged $8.14 per hour.

Barbed wire, the most famous of miscellaneous fabricated wire products, changed the course of American history. According to Henry D. and Frances T. McCallum, authors of *The Wire that Fenced the West,* "The introduction of barbed wire in the 1870s had remarkable social and economic consequences. Before the wire's invention, fences were intended to keep animals and trespassers out. Because barbed wire effectively kept animals in, the landholding concepts of cattlemen and small settlers changed radically with the new power that barbed wire gave them.''

Before the invention of barbed wire, ranchers used plain wire, wooden fences, and natural hedges to mark their territory. However, these boundaries were generally impractical, labor intensive, and highly penetrable. When a rancher had only his family to tend the animals, maintaining a fence around the perimeter of hundreds or thousands of acres was out of the question. Having such a problem to deal with, the rancher kept his stock to a low, manageable number. Getting rich in the West off of cattle and horses required an investment in cow hands and a steady cash flow to keep them. The invention of barbed wire paved the way for large herds of cattle that needed little supervision. Credit for the invention is generally given to Isaac Ellwood and Joseph Glidden, who saw a sample of a wooden fence with sharp wire projections on display at the 1873 DeKalb (Illinois) County Fair, and quickly set about patenting and manufacturing barbed wire.

Barbed wire also changed the way war was fought. Barbed wire was first used as a war defense system during the Russo-Japanese War of 1904-1905. In 1914, the American Steel & Wire Division of United States Steel Corporation and many other U.S. manufacturers sent mile after mile of barbed wire to Europe, where it was tangled into barriers that were impenetrable by ground forces. In World War II, a new military occupation was invented as a result of barbed wire's use. "Frogmen" were trained to cut clearings for submarines and ship propellers through the carloads of barbed wire dumped by the Japanese into the sea.

The top 75 manufacturers in the United States sold $2.8 billion in miscellaneous wire products in 1991 and employed 29,500 people. Ranking first in sales was AXIA Incorporated of Oak Brook, Illinois. AXIA sold an estimated $180 million worth of wire products and employed 1,200 people. MMI Products, Incorporated of Houston, Texas reported sales of $125 million and employed 1,000 people. Acco International of Wheeling, Illinois had estimated sales of $95 million

and employed 1,100 people. Master Halco Incorporated of La Habra, California ranked fourth with sales of $81 million and employed 900 people. American Spring Wire Corporation of Bedford, Ohio sold $75 million and employed 300 people.

The Great Lakes region traditionally led the nation in shipments of miscellaneous fabricated wire products, thanks to its access to raw materials. Pennsylvania's 77 establishments ranked first in shipments for an individual state, however. Pennsylvania's shipments of $241 million worth of goods represented nine percent of the value of all wire products in the United States. The states 2,800 workers averaged $9.13 per hour. California's 140 establishments shipped $232.8 million and employed 2,900 people at an average hourly wage of $7.70. Illinois ranked third in shipments, shipping $205.2 million. Illinois' 98 establishments employed 2,700 people at an average wage of $8.02 per hour. Ohio's 62 establishments shipped $142.4 million in goods. The 2,100 wire workers in Ohio averaged $8.53 per hour. New Jersey's 61 establishments shipped $130.4 million and employed a total 1,700 people at an average hourly wage of $8.12 per hour.

INDUSTRY INFORMATION SOURCES

Darnay, Arsen J., ed., *Manufacturing U.S.A.: Industry Analyses, Statistics, and Leading Companies,* Detroit: Gale Research, Inc., 1991.

McCallum, Henry D., and Frances T. McCallum, *The Wire that Fenced the West,* Norman: University of Oklahoma Press, 1985.

—Valerie E. Wilson

SIC 3497

METAL FOIL AND LEAF

This category covers establishments primarily engaged in manufacturing gold, silver, tin, and other metal foil (including converted metal foil) and leaf. Also included are establishments primarily engaged in converting metal foil (including aluminum) into wrappers, cookware, dinnerware, and containers, except bags and liners. Establishments primarily engaged in manufacturing plain aluminum foil are classified in **SIC 3353: Aluminum Sheet, Plate, and Foil.**

INDUSTRY SNAPSHOT

The value of shipments in 1991 was $2.74 billion in the metal foil and leaf industry, up from $1.83

billion in 1982 (in current dollars). About 120 establishments operated in the industry, up from about 100 in 1982. Of these 120 establishments, 57 percent had more than 20 employees. The number of establishments with more than 20 employees remained about the same over this same time period, implying that the new firms in the industry were quite small. Nonetheless, average firm size remained large. As measured by the number of production workers per establishment, average firm size was 83 percent larger than that for the manufacturing sector as a whole.

The industry employed 7,700 production workers in 1991, about the same number it employed in 1983, but down from a peak of 8,500 production workers in 1984. The industry was relatively capital-intensive, on average 29 percent higher than the manufacturing sector as a whole by investment per production worker. Annual hours worked by production workers in the industry were 12 percent higher than those worked in manufacturing at large, and wages were 24 percent higher.

ORGANIZATION AND STRUCTURE

The states ranking in the top ten by number of establishments in the late-1980s were, in order of descending value: California and New Jersey (with 19 each), Ohio and Kentucky (with ten each), Illinois (with nine), New York and North Carolina (with six each), Missouri and Pennsylvania (with four each) and Virginia (with three). Together these ten states accounted for 76 percent of all establishments and 90 percent of total employment for the industry. The average number of employees per plant varied widely by state. Virginia, the state with the highest number of employees per plant, had 16 times as many employees per plant as California and New York, and eight times as many as Kentucky and New Jersey.

The top ten industries and sectors buying the outputs of the metal foil and leaf industry were: personal consumption expenditures (23.4 percent); frozen fruits, fruit juices and vegetables (13.2 percent); commercial printing (5.2 percent); cigarettes (4.8 percent); food preparations, not elsewhere classified (4.4 percent); frozen specialties (4.2 percent); metal foil and leaf (3.3 percent); paperboard containers and boxes (3.1 percent); exports (2.9 percent); and cheese, natural and processed (2.8 percent).

A very large proportion of the industry's output was used for packaging and preparing foods. This was manifested not only by the above list, but by a consideration of the remaining 34 industries and sectors buying a 0.1 percent or greater share of the metal foil

industry's output, 53 percent of which were directly food-related.

The top three industries providing inputs into the metal foil and leaf industry were: first, aluminum rolling and drawing, with a 36.5 percent share; second, paperboard containers and boxes, with a 10.3 percent share; and third, fabricated metal products not elsewhere classified, with a 10.2 percent share.

Aluminum foil, the bulk of which was converted into food containers and packaging for food and other products, is a major component for this industry, and purchases of inputs reflect this. A full 43 percent of the industry's output consisted of laminated aluminum foil rolls and sheets for flexible packaging uses (with the bulk of this being foil-paper laminate). Another 34 percent of the industry's output consisted of converted, unmounted aluminum foil packaging products (not laminated to other materials). As a consequence, the fortunes of the industry were closely tied to the prosperity of the food packaging industry. The remaining 23 percent of the industry's output consisted of unconverted metal foil and leaf and converted foil for non-packaging applications.

Firms involved in the production of metal foil and leaf were not generally involved in the production of metals. As Hamilton Bowman wrote in his *Handbook of Precision Sheet, Strip and Foil,* a foil producer's ''operations are generally confined to the cold rolling, heat treating, flattening, slitting, and edge conditioning of coils of flat-rolled metal produced for him by a basic mill.'' The scope of operations in the industry have widened considerably in recent years as the use of foil for containers, packaging, electronics, and holograms became increasingly important.

The industry was served by the Aluminum Foil Container Manufacturers Association, headquartered in Savannah, Georgia. The association was founded in 1955, and had a staff of two and a membership of 12. Their journal, *Paper, Film and Foil Converter,* provided information to producers in the industry.

BACKGROUND AND DEVELOPMENT

Metalsmiths have produced flat metal sheets for many centuries. In its earliest forms, metal foil was produced by hammering malleable metals against a flat surface. As early as the seventeenth century, metal foils were produced by hand-operated rolling mills. These early mills made use of two parallel iron cylinders through which metals were passed in a number of successive stages, depending on the thickness of foil desired. Though hammering techniques are still used in the production of gold leaf and foil, the use of parallel cylinders remains the dominant method of foil production. By the mid-nineteenth century, a great many powered rolling mills were in use in Europe and the United States. At that time, thinner products were referred to as sheet and thicker products as plate.

By the end of the nineteenth century, continuous-process roller mills came into use. These mills differed substantially from their predecessors. Instead of reducing the metal to desired thicknesses by making a series of passes, continuous-process mills operated on a longer piece of metal that was flattened to desired thickness by being passed once through a series of roller pairs set at ever-closer distances to each other. These mills substantially reduced the costs of production by optimizing the flow of materials and reducing set-up times.

Until the mid-1920s, continuous-process mills (also referred to as tandem or strip mills) were not able to produce widths of greater than 24 inches. More powerful mills were developed at that time that could accommodate greater widths, and subsequently, narrower widths were produced by slitting broader widths of material.

A wide variety of metal was converted to foils, among them copper, gold, lead, magnesium, nickel, platinum, silver, tin, and zinc. Foil is generally defined as being 0.005 inches or less in thickness. Foil producers also often produced precision sheet and strip, materials between 0.015 and 0.005 inches in thickness. Thicker products were generally produced at basic mills.

The cold rolling of foil and precision sheet and strip required much greater precision than the cold rolling of thicker sheets. Variations in thickness, temper, and finish needed to be much more controlled. Consequently, foil was produced at much slower speeds than thicker sheets, and complex systems were required to monitor variation. Key developments in the post-World War II period included the use of smaller diameter rollers, the more rigid mounting of rollers and more sophisticated drive mechanisms and systems of control.

Larger diameter rollers had the disadvantage that they make greater surface contact with the rolled metal. Consequently, greater force was required to overcome the greater frictional resistance of large rollers. Thus, for any given amount of energy used, large rollers could reduce sheet thicknesses by lesser amounts than smaller rollers. The greater flexibility of smaller rollers required that they be backed up by large adjacent rollers, called backup or support rolls. In four-high mills, each contact roller was backed up by a

single support roll. In cluster mills, each contact roller was typically backed by nine support rolls. Steckel mills are four-high mills in which the rolls are not driven. Metal sheet was instead pulled through the rolls, permitting a great deal of thickness control, though somewhat less reduction per pass than a standard four-high mill. Large-diameter, two-high mills permitted reductions of only ten percent per pass, whereas four-high mills permitted reductions of 50 to 60 percent, and cluster mills reductions of 75 percent per pass. Smaller contact rollers enabled not only greater reductions, but also lesser variations in foil thickness.

Cold rolling makes metal harder and more brittle. Depending on the thickness of foil desired, cold rolled metals needed to be heat treated, or annealed, in order to soften them for further reduction. Reductions obtained through cycles of annealing and cold rolling are constrained only by the mechanical limitations of the rolling machinery and by handling considerations.

The development of the industry was based on these basic technologies. In his book *Handbook of Precision Sheet, Strip, and Foil*, Hamilton Bowman wrote that the growth of the industry since the 1960s resulted "as designers have come to appreciate the unique advantages of economy, weight saving, and dimensional precision inherent in these metals."

CURRENT CONDITIONS

The overall trend value of shipments from 1982 to 1991 was upward, with sales being particularly strong in 1987 and 1988. The value of shipments stagnated after 1989, however, and declined by just over $100 million from 1990 to 1991. Capital investment remained strong, nonetheless, and 1991 was a peak year with $100 million invested. Capital investments rose strongly and steadily from 1982, in which $40 million were invested. Indeed, capital investment rose 148 percent from 1982 to 1991, compared to overall growth of 50 percent for the value of shipments in these same years. This suggested that capitalists had a substantial amount of confidence in the prospects of some if not all of the industry's outputs.

Employment growth was stagnant from 1982 to 1991 and declined every year from 1988 to 1991. The patterns in employment, value of shipments, and investment indicated a substantial amount of capital intensification in the industry. Based on projected changes from years 1990 to 2005, employment was expected to decline by double-digit figures in nine occupations (occupations accounting for 30 percent of total employment in 1990) and single-digit figures in ten other occupations. Only three occupations were projected to show double-digit increases to 2005 (occupations accounting for only six percent of total employment in 1990). Thus, overall employment prospects for the industry did not appear promising.

The future of the industry was dependent in large part on technical developments within and without the industry. A number of materials were developed in the 1990s that were viable substitutes to metal foil laminates, the most important product of the industry. Among these materials were metallized polypropylene, metallized paper, polyethyene, and ethylene vinyl alcohol. On the other hand, new products such as extremely thin steel foils and improved foil baking products suggested the possibility of continued growth for the core products of the industry.

INDUSTRY LEADERS

The top four firms in the industry in 1992 were: Gould, Inc. and its Foil Division of Eastlake, Ohio; Circuit Foil USA, Inc. of Bordentown, New Jersey; Transfer Print Foils, Inc. of East Brunswick, New Jersey; and Alumax Foils, Inc. of St. Louis, Missouri. Together these firms accounted for about 21 percent of total sales for the industry and about 60 percent of total employment.

Gould, Inc. was incorporated in 1928 as the National Battery Co. and acquired its present name in 1969. The company entered into a joint venture in 1981 with Nippon Mining Ltd. (Nikko). This undertaking resulted in the opening of a plant in Japan for the production of copper foil using Gould's thin foil technology (producing foils of 0.0007 inches and less in thickness). These foils were used in the production of circuit boards for computers and telecommunications devices. In the late 1980s, the firm had 53 plants in 15 states across the United States and 14 plants in 11 foreign countries. Gould's fortunes took a turn for the worse after the mid-1980s, with the firm suffering net losses in 1985 through 1987. These losses resulted in part from a $13.4 million dollar settlement the company paid out in 1986 for a worker injury case, involving a lead smelter the firm operated in the 1970s. The firm was bought out in 1988 by Nippon Mining for a sum of $1.1 billion. In that year Gould held a 33 percent share of the world's market for copper foil. The firm had sales of $407 million and 4,600 employees in 1992, down from sales of $450 million and 5,000 employees in 1991. Nippon Mining announced in the fall of 1993 that it would write off $860 million in an effort to liquidate Gould, Inc. Nippon Mining planned to sell Gould's assets to two new companies, Gould Electronics, Inc. and Gould Instrument Systems, Inc.

Circuit Foil USA, Inc. generated $40 million in sales and had 300 employees in 1992. Transfer Print Foils, Inc. was a privately-owned independent. The firm produced holographic products and generated $30 million in sales with 100 employees in 1992. Its scope of operations were highly vertically integrated, enabling great efficiency in product development and production, as well as lowering costs by eliminating middlemen. The use of holograms increased rapidly after the 1980s, the result of increased demand for security purposes and of applications for consumer-oriented goods. The quality and price of holograms also improved as a result of computerized design, new materials, and lower-cost production processes. Transfer Print Foils announced in 1993 that it would move to a larger plant to expand its operations.

Alumax Foils, Inc. generated $26 million in sales and had 300 employees in 1992. The firm was a division of the aluminum producer Alumax, Inc. Alumax, Inc. was a wholly owned subsidiary of metal and energy producer AMAX, Inc. from 1986 to 1993. Though Alumax, Inc.'s shipments increased by 23 percent in 1992, the firm suffered record losses, in large part because of depressed aluminum prices. These low prices resulted from large exports of aluminum from Russian smelters. After the 1993 merger of Cyprus Mineral Co. and AMAX, Inc., Alumax Inc. became a publicly-held independent. Alumax retained $1.2 billion of debt resulting primarily from production of a smelter in Quebec, Canada in 1992.

INDUSTRY INFORMATION SOURCES

"Aluminum: Banner Output, Record Losses," *Chemical Engineering,* April 1993.

Annual Survey of Manufactures. Washington, D.C.: U.S. Census Bureau, 1991.

Bowman, Hamilton B. *Handbook of Precision Sheet, Strip and Foil,* Metals Park, Ohio: American Society for Metals, 1980.

Daniels, Peggy Kneffel and Carol A. Schwartz, eds. *Encyclopedia of Associations* (28th ed.), Detroit, Michigan: Gale research Inc., 1994.

Darnay, Arsen J., ed. *Manufacturing USA: Industry Analyses, Statistics, and Leading Companies* (3rd ed.), Detroit, Michigan: Gale Research Inc., 1993.

"Handi-Foil Baking Lines Set," *HFD,* December 16, 1991.

"Holograms Making Inroads Into Converted Products," *Paper, Film and Foil Converter,* March 1993.

"Innovative Containers Give Foodservice a Boost," *Packaging US,* March 1993.

"Lead Astray," *Beverage World,* November 1991.

"Merger Will Create a Mining Giant," *The New York Times,* May 26, 1993.

Moody's Industrial Manual. New York: Moody's Investors Service Inc., 1988, 1933.

"New On the Menu," *Packaging US,* March 1993.

"Nikko Kyodo Draws Flak for Decision to Dissolve Gould," *Nikkei Weekly,* September 13, 1993.

"Packaging - Industry Report," *The First Boston Corporation,* June 7, 1993.

Pollack, Andrew. "$865 Million Write-Off Over Gould," *The New York Times,* September 8, 1993.

Regan, Bob. "Amax '90s Strategy: Navigating the Rocks," *American Metal Market,* November 23, 1992.

Thurston, Scott. "Norcross Aluminum Products Maker to be Spun Off After Parent's Merger," *Atlanta Constitution,* May 28, 1993.

Ward's Business Directory of U.S. Private and Public Companies. Detroit, Michigan: Gale Research Inc., 1993.

"Will Profit Squeeze Offset Growth for Metallizers?" *Paper, Film and Foil Converter,* March 1993.

Worden, Andrew. "Insurance to Pay for Lead Injuries," *American Metal Market,* October 12, 1992.

— David Kucera

SIC 3498

FABRICATED PIPE AND PIPE FITTINGS

This industry covers establishments primarily engaged in fabricating pipe and pipe fittings from purchased metal pipe, by processes such as cutting, threading, and bending. Establishments primarily engaged in manufacturing cast iron pipe and fittings, including cast and forged pipe fittings that have been machined and threaded, are classified in **SIC 3321: Gray and Ductile Iron Foundries;** those manufacturing welded and heavy riveted pipe and seamless steel pipe are classified in **SIC 3317: Steel Pipe and Tubes;** and those manufacturing products such as banisters, railings, and guards from pipe are classified in **SIC 3446: Architecture and Ornamental Metal Work.**

Industry shipments in 1991 for the approximately 600 companies involved in this area of manufacturing fell to $2.27 billion, a 2.6 percent drop from the $2.33 billion level reached in 1990. The U.S. fabricated pipe and pipe fitting industry is strongly dependent on the health of the domestic construction industry, which, after enduring rough economic conditions in the early 1990s, showed signs of rebounding entering the mid-1990s; players in the fabricated pipe industry hope to ride the coattails of that larger industry to increased prosperity throughout the remainder of the 1990s.

Industry shipments reached a high of $3.035 billion in 1982. However, the early 1980s recession, the strong American dollar, and increased foreign competition hurt the industry badly. Shipments declined five years in a row to a low of $1.75 billion.

Improvements in the domestic as well as international economic climate, along with the replacement of old manufacturing processes, helped the industry rebound during the latter part of the 1980s and weather the downturn of the early 1990s. For pipe, valve, and fitting manufacturers, the last two years have seen marked gains in the industry's ability to meet the steady demand for fire protection flow control products. The industry's recent positive fortunes have also been due in part to increased global competitiveness. Overseas producers have been chased away from the U.S. market by increased domestic quality, lower dollar valuations, and some strong anti-dumping legislation. Industry leaders include Davis Water Co. of Georgia, Tyler Pipe Industries of Texas, Berg Steel Pipe Co. of Florida, Victaulic Co. of Pennsylvania, and Parker Hannifin, located in Ohio.

The fabricated pipe and fittings industry employed 20,500 in 1991, 15,000 of whom were production workers. This was a decrease of roughly 6.4 percent from the employment level of 1990. Employment highs in the industry were recorded in 1979, when 32,900 employees worked in fabricated pipe manufacturing facilities. Average annual wages per employee were $25,405, with average weekly wages of $489, in 1991.

INDUSTRY INFORMATION SOURCES

"UA professor's research helps Birmingham company," *Modern Casting,* June 1992.

U.S. Census of Manufactures, 1987, Washington, DC: U.S. Department of Commerce, 1987.

—William A. Bennett

SIC 3499

FABRICATED METAL PRODUCTS, NOT ELSEWHERE CLASSIFIED

The Fabricated Metal Products, Not Elsewhere Classified (NEC), Industry encompasses establishments that manufacture a plethora of miscellaneous metal goods for both commercial and residential applications. Examples of industry output include metal ladders, ironing boards, steel safes, toilet fixtures, trophies, lawnmower wheels, chairs, barricades, ammunition boxes, and automobile seat frames. For more information about miscellaneous fabricated metal products, see other entries in this industry group.

Although the industry is extremely fragmented, a few product segments stand out. Flat metal straps used for shipping and anchoring, for example, accounted for a leading 7 percent of industry revenues in the early 1990s. Steel safes and vaults made up 6 percent of the market. Metal ladders represented about 4% of shipments. Other major product groups in this industry included magnets (3 percent of sales), steel boxes (2 percent), railroad switches and crossings (1.4 percent), and stamped metal wheels (1 percent). About 10 percent of production was exported in the early '90s.

The background and development of the miscellaneous fabricated metal products NEC industry varies by product category. However, a general surge in demand characterized the overall industry during the post-World War II U.S. economic expansion. Going into the 1980s, industry participants were churning out about $4.4 billion worth of goods per year and employing a work force of 65,000 people. Healthy economic growth during most of the 1980s, moreover, boosted sales and profits. A surge in housing starts, for example, boosted shipments of metal furniture parts and ladders. Likewise, bank and vault manufacturers benefitted from growth in the savings and loan industry.

By 1989, miscellaneous metal products NEC sales had reached $6.95 billion, representing average annual revenue growth of 7 percent per year since 1983. Contrary to many other manufacturing sectors, both the number of employees and companies in the industry grew during the decade, to 80,000 and 900, respectively. Unfortunately, however, economic recess in the early 1990s stalled expansion. Revenues actually declined about 1 percent in 1990 and remained flat throughout 1991 and 1992. Shipments of metal containers, for example, dropped about 6 percent in 1992, and purchases by the ailing savings and loan industry remained depressed. An uptick in housing and auto-

mobile markets going into the mid-1990s, though, renewed optimism in some segments.

Because of its specialized nature, the miscellaneous metal products NEC industry is highly fragmented. The average industry participant grossed 27 percent as much as the average U.S. manufacturer in the early 1990s, and employed about half as many workers. Even the majority of the top 50 companies had sales of less than $50 million in 1991 and employed fewer than 500 workers. The largest competitor was Steel Technologies, of Kentucky, which had 1991 sales of $141 million and 400 workers. Abex Corp., of Virginia, was the second biggest player with $140 million in revenues and 1,600 employees. Other industry leaders included R.D. Werner Company Inc., of Pennsylvania, and Inter Innovation Lefebure Inc., of Iowa.

Despite steady sales and employment growth throughout the 1980s, job prospects for the overall miscellaneous fabricated metal products industry are dim. Automation and the movement of manufacturing facilities outside the United States will curtail job growth. Openings for most positions will decline by 10 percent to 30 percent between 1990 and 2005, according to the Bureau of Labor Statistics. Jobs for assemblers and fabricators, which make up a leading 10 percent of the work force, will decline by about 25 percent, as will positions for machine operators. Even jobs for top executives should fall by about 8 percent. In contrast, positions for sales professionals and mechanical engineers should rise by 19 percent and 12 percent, respectively.

INDUSTRY INFORMATION SOURCES

Darnay, Arsen J., ed., *Manufacturing USA; Industry Analyses, Statistics, and Leading Companies*, Detroit: Gale Research Inc., 1993.

Standard & Poor's Industry Surveys, New York: Standard & Poor's Corporation, December 24, 1992.

U.S. Industrial Outlook 1993, Washington, D.C.: U.S. Department of Commerce, January 1993.

—Dave Mote

INDUSTRIAL & COMMERCIAL MACHINERY & COMPUTER EQUIPMENT

SIC 3511

STEAM, GAS, AND HYDRAULIC TURBINES, AND TURBINE GENERATOR SET UNITS

This industry covers establishments primarily engaged in manufacturing steam turbines; hydraulic turbines; gas turbines, except aircraft; and complete steam, gas, and hydraulic turbine generator set units. Also included in this industry are the manufacture of wind and solar powered turbine generators and windmills for generating electric power. Establishments engaged in manufacturing nonautomotive type generators are classified in **SIC 3621: Motors and Generators;** those manufacturing aircraft turbines are classified in **SIC 3724: Aircraft Engines and Engine Parts;** and those manufacturing windmill heads and towers for pumping water for agricultural use are classified in **SIC 3523: Farm Machinery and Equipment.**

INDUSTRY SNAPSHOT

The turbine sector has made a strong comeback since its slump in the 1980s. Throughout most of the decade, demand for power by electrical utilities had remained at low levels, and sales of traditional steam-powered turbines had stalled. The development of gas turbines that are relatively inexpensive and are adaptable to the power industry's fluctuating needs was a boon for turbine makers in the early 1990s. The sector also benefited from the growth in overseas markets, particularly in Asia, where demand for additional capacity has outpaced that of the United States market.

Some observers also forecast a turnaround for the wind-power industry. After much enthusiasm for wind as an alternative energy source was voiced in the 1970s, the industry collapsed in the late 1980s as oil prices dropped and tax credits expired. But improved wind technologies, greater environmental awareness, and continuing uncertainty about the cost and availability of fossil fuels gave hope to the industry's supporters.

BACKGROUND AND DEVELOPMENT

The modern steam turbine was developed in the late nineteenth century. By 1910 the largest steam turbine-generator unit could produce 30,000 kilowatts, compared with just 1,200 kilowatts ten years earlier. Steam turbines thus became the prime movers in power plants early in the twentieth century. By 1940 single turbine units with a capacity of 100,000 kilowatts were in general use. During the 1950s and 1960s, steam turbines continued to dominate an expanding power-generation market, as fossil fuel prices remained low and ever-larger steam turbines were brought on line. In the 1980s, however, additions to the power capacity of utilities slowed because of erratic growth in consumption and the difficult political climate for utilities in many states.

Wind Power. Small wind turbines were set up in rural areas of the Midwest during the early twentieth century, but power from utilities largely displaced them during the 1930s. As oil prices surged in the 1970s, however, renewable energy resources came in vogue, and the wind industry was resuscitated. Tax relief was offered for wind farms, and research was greatly expanded. About 14,000 wind turbines were installed between 1980 and 1985, the vast majority of them in California. When oil prices dropped below $20 a barrel and tax incentives were eliminated, however, much of the domestic wind industry collapsed.

CURRENT CONDITIONS

The manufacture of steam and gas turbines is concentrated among a few electrical giants. In the United States, the two historical competitors have been General Electric and Westinghouse. Other large international rivals include Siemens AG of Germany and Asea Brown Boveri of Switzerland. In 1990 the major producers of gas turbines for utilities were General Electric, Asea Brown Boveri, and Kraftwerk. According to government estimates for 1991, the turbine industry as a whole employed 22,000 workers, including 13,000 production workers.

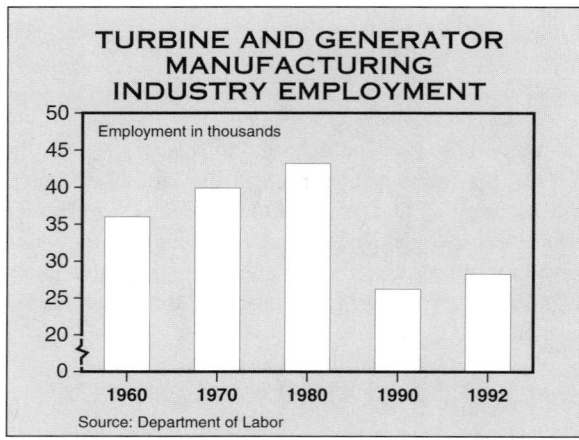

TURBINE AND GENERATOR
MANUFACTURING
INDUSTRY EMPLOYMENT

Employment in thousands

Source: Department of Labor

Most of the companies that entered the wind turbine business in the early 1980s, when the industry was in its heyday, many of them undercapitalized and heavily in debt, have simply disappeared. By 1987, only three manufacturers of the larger-scale turbines used by utilities were still in business, and only one was producing turbines in significant numbers. The number of companies making small wind turbines for stand-alone power has also contracted substantially, although the remaining firms have done relatively well by expanding exports.

Since growth in electricity consumption was expected to remain depressed in the 1990s, many utilities were not eager to make large-scale additions to their generating capacity, especially in light of the tough regulatory climate. Nevertheless, since their facilities had expanded little in the second half of the 1980s and there was some erratic growth in demand, the power companies needed a flexible and economical way to generate more electricity. The gas turbine proved to be the answer for many utilities. The upgraded models introduced in the late 1980s were much smaller than steam turbines; they were easy to switch on and off and could be installed in a modular fashion. They also ran

at high temperatures, allowing them to function more efficiently. The new gas turbine models were ideal for utilities seeking to fine tune their generating capacity to meet varying power needs.

Domestic markets for wind turbines, however, remained weak in the early 1990s, in part because of the fatigue life of a turbine's major components—five years—and their costly replacement costs. Even though demand for new wind turbines remained soft, however, wind power still produced one percent of California's electricity, enough to meet the needs of a city the size of San Francisco. And while there has been relatively little activity in the contiguous United States, overseas markets have become stronger. Small wind turbine makers have managed to increase exports significantly to expanding European markets, thereby compensating for the downturn at home. Supporters contend that important advances in wind-powered turbine design and maintenance techniques are making wind a more attractive energy alternative as well. In 1992 the cost of generating electricity from existing turbines had fallen to seven cents per kilowatt hour; for new equipment, the cost fell to only five to six cents. Moreover, the industry appears to be making some headway in combatting a reputation for technical problems and unreliable equipment. In the early 1990s, the 16,500 wind-powered turbines in the United states reached a level wherein they produced power 90 percent of the time, compared with only 50 percent several years earlier.

INDUSTRY LEADERS

General Electric, the market leader, has staged a remarkable recovery since the mid-1980s. At that point, consumption of electricity was growing only slowly and turbines were thus wearing out less quickly. The fall in the oil price had also hurt GE's markets in the Middle East. The company found itself losing money in what had been its most profitable business. In 1986, however, the company introduced a new series of advanced gas-fired turbines that turned around its power systems segment. GE's relatively small and inexpensive gas turbines were ideal for utilities seeking to adjust to fluctuating demand by adding capacity selectively. Increased penetration of overseas markets was also key to the turnaround. Since U.S. demand was weak, the company sought and found new customers abroad, including a major sale of 14 gas turbines for Tokyo Electric Power's Futtsu power plant for $750 million. It also concluded agreements with Korea Electric Power and Taiwan Electric Power. GE continues to emphasize overseas markets, which are projected to grow faster than domestic demand. It is licensing its gas-turbine technology to companies like Sumitomo Corporation of Japan, which in turn is exporting GE-type turbines to Indonesia. The company has also improved its manufacturing and warehousing techniques. By 1993, the power systems segment was turning over its $1.2-billion inventory five times annually, twice the 1991 level. Between 1989 and 1993 the company also spent $1 billion to upgrade its turbine plant at Greenville, South Carolina. The surge in turbine sales and manufacturing improvements has had a big impact on GE's profitability: operating profit from the company's power systems segment more than doubled between 1988 and 1992, growing from $471 million to more than $1.037 billion on over $6 billion in sales.

Other leading manufacturers include Babcock and Wilcox Co., Sequa Corporation, Howmet Corp., Solar Turbines Inc., Stewart and Stevenson Services, Inc., and New Elliott Corporation.

AMERICA AND THE WORLD

During the early 1990s, the turbine market increasingly became international in scope. Major American and European manufacturers strengthened their presence in each other's backyard. In 1991 GE and its European partners won 56 percent of gas turbine orders in Europe. Building on that strength, in 1992 General Electric formed a new European subsidiary for sales and service of its turbines. Meanwhile, the German industrial conglomerate Siemens AG took over a spin-off of Allis-Chalmers Co., known as A-C Equipment of Wisconsin, and invested $30 million in its Milwaukee plant. In 1992 it shipped its first U.S.-manufactured gas turbine to Taiwan. Both U.S. and European makers recognized, however, that growth would be strongest in non-Western nations. In 1992 GE estimated that the Asia-Pacific market had represented about 30 percent of all recent additions to world generating capacity, with the United States and Europe accounting for 20 percent each. Longer-term growth was expected to remain strongest outside the traditional Western markets.

In overseas markets, Denmark, Germany. and Britain have been in the forefront of developing wind energy. In 1992 wind energy accounted for less than 0.1 percent of Europe's total power generation. Nevertheless, the wind industry in Europe enjoys government subsidies and is growing quickly; it has also been a pioneer in developing wind farms offshore. Some observers believe that small wind turbines may prove an excellent source of electricity in areas of developing countries where there are no existing power grids. In 1992 the World Bank sponsored projects in Mexico, India, and Indonesia that would utilize wind turbines in providing power to local villages.

RESEARCH AND TECHNOLOGY

Many of the advances in gas turbines over the past decade have their roots in jet engine technology, as manufacturers have adopted techniques perfected for the airlines and the Pentagon to power generation. Older gas turbines have a thermal efficiency of 25 percent—they capture and convert to electricity about one-quarter of the energy value of their fuel—versus a 33 percent thermal efficiency posted by steam turbines. Using the technologies developed for aircraft, however, some newer gas turbines have reached thermal efficiencies of 40 percent. Other recently developed gas turbines have achieved even higher efficiency levels through combined cycle generation, in which the turbines use the exhaust gases from the turbine to boil water into steam, which is then used in a steam turbine to generate additional electricity. A variation of this method is to boil water with the exhaust gases and inject some of the steam back into the gas turbine, so it is running on a combination of gases and steam. Some industry participants believe that gas-fired and combined-cycle power systems will be the leading technologies of the 1990s, representing about half of all new capacity additions worldwide. Fossil-fueled steam turbines, hydroelectric power, and nuclear plants will account for the balance.

The wind industry has made progress on several fronts that have historically hampered its growth. One major problem for the industry has been the variability and intermittent nature of wind. Traditional, fixed-speed wind turbines have had a relatively low capacity factor compared with other energy sources because they have not been able to take advantage of the full range of wind velocities. Improvements in wind turbine design and technologies, however, have allowed finer control of power output at both low and high wind speeds. Other advances, including more accurate weather forecasting, improved methods of picking the best sites for wind farms, and blades that can better cope with the destructive effects of dead insects, have contributed to more efficient wind energy production.

INDUSTRY INFORMATION SOURCES

Brennan, Robert J., "GE Forms Unit in Europe to Serve Turbine Market," *Wall Street Journal,* October 13, 1992.

Collins, Steven, "Small Gas Turbines Post Gain in Performance," *Power,* October 1992.

Frank, Deborah, "Blowing in the Wind," *Popular Mechanics,* August 1991.

General Electric Annual Report, 1992, Fairfield, CT: General Electric, 1993.

Kirchen, Rick, ''Siemens Transforms Former A-C Unit into a Powerhouse,'' *Business Journal-Milwaukee,* October 3, 1992.

Quickel, Stephen, ''Bootstrap,'' *Financial World,* June 12, 1990.

''The Quixotic Technology: Is Wind Energy an Impossible Dream?'' *The Economist,* November 14, 1992.

Rickert, Lu, ''Combined Cycle Power Plants,'' *Global Gas Turbine News,* May 1993.

''Siemens Exports First U.S.-Manufactured Gas Turbine to Taiwan,'' *Electrical World,* June 1992.

Smart, Tim, et al. ''A Big Offshore Surge for GE's Juice Factory.'' *Business Week,* June 21, 1993.

''Turbines in a Spin,'' *The Economist,* July 19, 1986.

U.S. Industrial Outlook 1993, Washington DC: U.S. Department of Commerce, 1993.

Vogel, Shawna, ''Wind Power,'' *Discover,* May 1989.

Wald, Matthew L., ''Better Ways to Make Electricity,'' *New York Times,* April 11, 1990.

—Bob Schneider

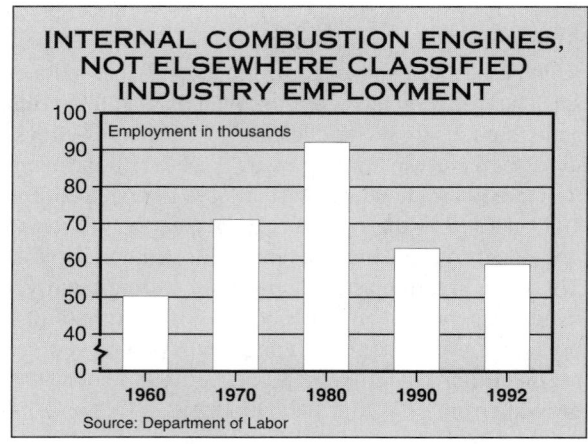

operators and truck makers, which may decide to make an engine standard on a specific line.

SIC 3519

INTERNAL COMBUSTION ENGINES, NOT ELSEWHERE CLASSIFIED

This industry includes establishments primarily engaged in manufacturing diesel, semidiesel, or other internal combustion engines, not elsewhere classified, for stationary, marine, traction, and other uses. Establishments primarily engaged in manufacturing aircraft engines are classified in **SIC 3724: Aircraft Engines and Engine Parts,** and those manufacturing automotive engines, except diesel, are classified in **SIC 3714: Motor Vehicle Parts and Accessories.**

Diesel engines are used primarily in large trucks and buses, high-powered farm tractors, and in heavy construction machinery. In Europe there are significant numbers of diesel autos, which get better mileage than gasoline-powered cars. In the United States, however, diesel cars have had limited appeal because they produce high levels of soot and nitric oxides and have thus run afoul of anti-pollution laws.

The fortunes of U.S. diesel engine makers depend heavily on the highly cyclical market for heavy-duty trucks. The end-user has the option of choosing his own engine, so companies must impress both truck

The leading diesel engine makers are Cummins Engine Corporation, Caterpillar Inc., and Detroit Diesel. Detroit Diesel is a relative newcomer to the spotlight in the industry. In 1988 former auto racer Roger Penske bought control of the company from General Motors and proceeded to raise its share of the $3 billion market for U.S. diesel truck engines from three percent in 1987 to over 25 percent in 1992. Much of Detroit Diesel's turnaround is ascribed to its Series 60 engine, which provided far better fuel efficiency than previous models, as well as computerized features that could diagnose mechanical problems and monitor driver productivity. As Detroit Diesel advanced, Cummins receded: it lost ten points of market share in two years and posted substantial losses in 1990 and 1991. The company had already suffered through tough times in the mid-1980s, when the firm cut both its prices and profitability to defend its markets against Japanese manufacturers. By the first quarter of 1992, however, Cummins had made a strong recovery. It took about 40 percent of the diesel truck engine market, up five points from the year-earlier level, and recorded its first quarterly profit since 1989. The return to profitability reflected a strong upturn in demand for heavy-duty trucks, a more competitive product line, corporate downsizing, and an increased emphasis on establishing a presence in other diesel engine markets, including that for recreational vehicles.

All of the Big Three, as the leading diesel-engine makers are known, are pursuing alliances with foreign manufacturers to enter Japanese and European markets—which, at $6 billion, are double the size of the domestic market. Many of these foreign manufacturers are located in countries that have only recently toughened their pollution standards, and many of these manufacturers still use older emission control technologies. U.S. makers have already coped with tough emission control laws at home, and they use this experience as a bargaining chip in gaining access to new markets.

INDUSTRY INFORMATION SOURCES

"Cummins Wins 90% of Growing Class A Diesel Market." *RV Business*, July 22, 1991.

Feder, Barnaby. "A Diesel Maker's Comeback Route." *New York Times*, June 11, 1992.

———. "Cummins Engine Is Tuned Up for the Boom in the Truck Market." *New York Times*, February 18, 1993.

Kelly, Kevin. "Does Cummins Have the Oomph to Climb This Hill?" *Business Week*, November 4, 1991.

———. "The Rising Rumble of American Diesels." *Business Week*, September 6, 1993.

Stipp, David. "Diesel Designers Try to Lighten Dark Clouds." *Wall Street Journal*, July 23, 1991.

White, Joseph. "Revved Up: How Detroit Diesel, Out from Under GM, Turned Around Fast." *Wall Street Journal*, August 16, 1991.

—Bob Schneider

SIC 3523

FARM MACHINERY AND EQUIPMENT

This category covers establishments primarily manufacturing farm machinery and equipment, including wheel tractors, for use in the preparation and maintenance of the soil; planting and harvesting of the crop; preparing crops for market on the farm; or for use in performing other farm operations and processes. Included in this industry are establishments primarily engaged in manufacturing commercial mowing and other turf and grounds care equipment. Establishments primarily engaged in manufacturing farm handtools are classified as the Cutlery, Handtools, and General Hardware industries, and those manufacturing garden tractors, lawnmowers, and other lawn and garden equipment are classified in **SIC 3524: Lawn and Garden Tractors and Home Lawn and Garden Equipment.**

INDUSTRY SNAPSHOT

Beginning in the mid-19th century, major advances in agricultural equipment technology allowed vast expanses of often intractable American land to be farmed. In the process, and as agricultural equipment grew in variety, complexity, and size, farming itself was transformed, until most of it was conducted on a vast scale with highly specialized machinery.

In *Farm Chemicals* Dale L. Little noted that although "much of the scientific knowledge needed for high-yield agriculture was available in the 1930s, the economic malaise of the Great Depression delayed its implementation." Thereafter, productivity rose enormously. In 1940, according to Little, "U.S. farmers produced 56 million tons of corn on about 76.5 million acres, with an average yield of only 26 bushels per acre," as compared to 1992, when "about 230 million tons of corn were produced on just 69 million acres, with an average yield of nearly 119 bushels per acre."

Such a level of efficiency created chronic excess supply; the extent and fertility of the land available, in combination with sophisticated planting and cultivation techniques, caused American farmers to produce on a scale typically exceeding market demand. With any surplus driving prices down, farmers could not make sufficient money to maintain or upgrade their equipment, which meant that the agricultural implement manufacturers were victims of their customers' efficiency.

The financial success of such manufacturers was also tied to farming profits in other ways. Unusually bad weather diminished farmers' yields, and unusually good weather merely underscored the tendency toward chronic excess supply. Equally unpredictable, political crises in various parts of the world often had an effect on market demand. All of these hazards affected the manufacturers of agricultural equipment by putting the livelihood of many American farmers at risk at the same time.

ORGANIZATION AND STRUCTURE

Among other financial difficulties affecting many American farmers throughout the 1980s, was the major problem of surplus inventories created by unexpected reductions in demand. Carol Ann Gregg in *Implement & Tractor* noted, "Farmers look at machinery costs in terms of bushels of corn, pounds of milk or bushels of wheat. They just can't buy a tractor for the same number of bushels today as they did ten years ago." But equipment still had to be maintained and replaced somehow, "Farmers used to figure on purchasing a new tractor every three to five years. Now it's more like every ten years. When new equipment doesn't move, the supply of quality used equipment shrinks."

Just as farmers struggled to locate secondhand machinery, so did manufacturers struggle with valuable inventories of new equipment sitting idle for long periods. Summarizing the financial troubles that plagued one particular company, J.I. Case, when it badly misjudged the difference between booked sales and actual dealership sales, *Business Week* noted, "like other farm-equipment manufacturers, [Case] books the sale when it ships a piece of equipment to a dealer, even though it doesn't get paid until the dealer sells the goods, often at a discount. Some Case rivals, such as Deere & Co., immediately adjust sales figures downward by as much as 20 percent off their list prices. By comparison, Case often adjusted downward by a much smaller percentage." As a result, the effect of unusually slow-moving inventory was disguised and the dimensions of the problem did not become apparent as early as they might have.

Tom Pharr, president of Powell Manufacturing Company, the largest manufacturer of tobacco mechanization equipment in the world, stressed his own business' determination to avoid any such inventory-related problems, "We don't really want our dealers to keep an extensive inventory. . . . Manufacturers and dealers got into trouble in the '80s because of large inventories. Inventory will run you bankrupt if you don't keep it under control." Pharr explained how traffic from manufacturers to dealers, then to customers, could be structured in a less risky way, "By building customer loyalty, Powell dealers can encourage customers to order equipment that is not kept in inventory. They like to do demonstrations on farms and then take orders, rather than keeping enough equipment in inventory to satisfy immediate customer demand. We encourage our customers to shop early and place an order. They know if they put their money with us they can depend on getting the machine when they need it along with after-sales parts and service."

Not all concerns about structure and organization in the American farm-equipment industry focused on inventory-related problems. Mike Brezonick in *Diesel Progress Engines & Drives*, explained how John Deere had sought innovative ways to improve and speed up product development for its sophisticated 7000 series tractors. The lynchpin of the new approach was a determination to include as many interested parties as possible at the earliest stages, "While the team approach is nothing new, the make-up of the teams was a little different. . . . Purchasing analysts, buyers, materials personnel and in some cases, key suppliers, were in on initial design discussions."

In addition to avoiding the pitfalls of clogged inventories and in seeking better overall communication among interested parties, the American farm equipment manufacturing industry faced structural change in responding to heightened ecological aware-ness and Environmental Protection Agency (EPA) rulings. Hembree Brandon in *Implement & Tractor* noted new EPA standards concerning exhaust emissions were designed to take effect for engines of over 750 horsepower in the year 2000, for those of 50 to 100 horsepower in 1998, for those of 100 to 175 horsepower in 1997, and for those of 175 to 750 horsepower in 1996. According to *Implement & Tractor*, clean air legislation creating new diesel fuel standards was seen as making viable an otherwise too expensive diesel blend containing soy oil, and leading to a decline in carbon monoxide and hydrocarbon emissions. From the point of view of farmers, this cleaner fuel was seen as having no consequences for torque output, even if it did lead to small reductions in horsepower.

BACKGROUND AND DEVELOPMENT

The major expansion period for U.S. agriculture came during the late 19th century. A total of 408 million acres had been farmed prior to 1870, and in the next 30 years an additional 431 million acres were newly cultivated. As the scale of U.S. agriculture dramatically increased, so did its complexity, with locally-oriented farmers later engaged in an international system of storing, shipping, and selling engendered by increased mechanization, cash crops, and stock trading in commodities.

In the emergence of these developments, the most significant role was played by the largest farming enterprises. Heralding increased mechanization, greater crop specialization, and a trend towards farming on a large scale, the 40,000-acre or more farms were run with the same kind of military efficiency that characterized the lumber industry.

The pace of mechanization was so rapid and extended into so many areas of farming technology that, in 1860 alone, the U.S. Patent Office issued new patents for corn shellers, corn huskers, corn cultivators, corn-shock binders, cornstalk shocking machines, cornstalk cutters, corn cleaners, corn and cob crushers, seed drills, corn harvesters, rotary harrows, corn and cob mills, smut machines and hundreds of corn planters.

The types of plows used since the earliest development of agriculture proved to be unsuitable in dense, heavy prairie, so new designs were essential. A first step came in the form of an adaptation of Jethro Wood's 1814 iron plow, a "prairie breaker" that was very heavy, clogged easily, and moved slowly, even when pulled by a team of oxen. In 1837, a blacksmith in Grand Detour, Illinois developed the first "singing plow" by combining a wrought iron moldboard with a steel share scavenged from a broken band saw, enabling a far more thorough and clog-free scouring of the prairie. By the 1850s, this blacksmith was manufacturing approximately ten thousand examples of his invention annually at his mass-production plant in Moline, Illinois.

But better and better plows alone were not sufficient for all the needs of American farmers during the rapid escalation of agriculture in the late 19th century. Other key developments included design improvements for tractors, harrows, corn planters, and combine harvesters.

Though Hart and Parr Charles were responsible for pioneering the gasoline tractor in 1901, most American farmers were unable to afford the new machine until the advent of Henry Ford's Fordson tractor in 1917, priced at $397. A critical new development came seven years later with International Harvester's Farmall tractor, its innovative addition of removable attachments making the machine highly versatile.

During the nineteenth century, harrows rapidly became stronger and more complex. Before the introduction of the tractor, these had to be dragged by animals. The first designs, hoes and brush harrows, were outmoded in the 1840s by the Geddes, a hinged triangular construction of wood with teeth made of iron, which, in turn, was outmoded several decades later by an all iron and steel model. This design also was outmoded by a harrow called the Nishwitz rotary disk harrow, which through rollers or clod-crushers, sifted and tamped down the soil.

The planting of corn was both time consuming and inaccurate until technological advances permitted the mechanization of the planting and the measuring involved as well. In Galsburg, Illinois in the 1850s, George W. Brown pioneered a semi-mechanized method of corn planting with a horse-drawn vehicle that dropped seed by hand. Next, shoes or "furrow openers" were added to the front of the vehicle for better preparation of the soil, and the seed-dropping mechanism was refined, permitting vehicle operators to divide the tasks of driving and navigating. The latter improvement enabled operators to pay closer attention to where the corn was being dropped.

Developments in combine harvesting technology took a slower and more interrupted course than did those of the other forms of farming equipment. The steam-driven reaping and threshing machines introduced in the 1880s were replaced by the versatility of the Farmall tractor. The Second World War delayed the full implementation of the technological advances marked by Allis Chalmers' All-Crop Harvester of 1936, a gleaner equipped with a special corn-head attachment. With the resumption of peace, the versatile and efficient but expensive combines initially took a back seat to the much cheaper picker-sheller machinery. Only with the proliferation of silos and their efficient storage of vast quantities did the diesel-driven combines' capacity for mass-harvesting give them an unbeatable advantage.

CURRENT CONDITIONS

Summarizing the hard times suffered by many American farmers during the 1980s, *The Economist* observed that "the biggest losers, apart from the grain farmers themselves, are makers of farm machinery. They have gone through a prolonged lean patch. Their American customers have in recent years bought only about 20,000 big tractors a year, compared with the 50,000 or so they used to buy a decade ago. Combine harvesters have fared no better. Only 130,000 were sold in the 1980s versus 300,000 in the 1970s." But as the same magazine noted, an overall improvement in the fortunes of U.S. agriculture by the beginning of the 1990s was not sufficient in itself to reverse this trend, because farmers remained hostage to a variety of short-term hazards, including excess supply, aided by exceptionally good weather, and leading to reductions in price, "John Deere, J.I. Case and other leading producers of farm machinery had hoped the recent decline in the burden of farmers' debts (to about 15 percent of farm assets) would revive demand for their products. Their hopes are being dashed by the prospect of lower incomes for . . . farmers."

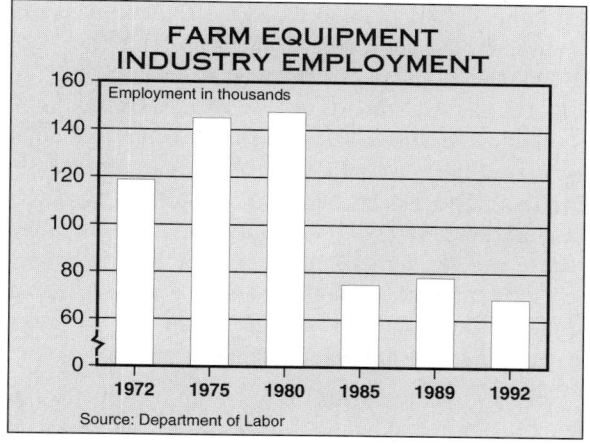

Among the short-term hazards affecting farmers and manufacturers of agricultural equipment were unsettling political events, such as Iraq's invasion of Kuwait in August 1990. The immediate effect of the Persian Gulf War was that showroom traffic disappeared and the swift rebound anticipated by J. I. Case did not occur, which meant the company faced a swollen inventory in early 1991.

Thus, the industry's emergence from grave doldrums in the 1980s was not accompanied by any immediate or secure upswing in profitability. According to *Implement & Tractor* retail sales for two-wheel and four-wheel tractors dropped between 1987 and 1989 from 108,184 to 106,570, then increased to 108,350 in 1990, only to drop once more to 93,974 in 1991.

Forecasting to 2005, the U.S. Department of Labor saw signs of health for the agricultural equipment industry, noting that farmers had generally recovered from the losses and excessive debts incurred during the 1980s. Farmers were expected to replace machinery that they had been unable to replace when times were hardest, and to invest in new machinery, taking advantage of improvements brought about by advanced technology.

INDUSTRY LEADERS

In 1993, John Deere of Moline, Illinois, had sales of $7 billion and 36,500 employees. J. I. Case, of Racine, Wisconsin, had sales of $3.7 billion, with 7,000 employees. Ford New Holland Americas, of New Holland, Pennsylvania, had sales of $2.8 billion, and Allied Products, based in Chicago, had sales of $324 million and 3,200 employees.

AMERICA AND THE WORLD

According to *Implement & Tractor*, the total value of farm equipment imported to the United States rose between 1986 and 1990, from $1.63 billion to $2.50 billion, but dropped in 1991 to $1.88 billion. The chief sources of these imports in 1991 were Germany ($437 million), Canada ($340 million), the United Kingdom ($301 million), Italy ($145 million), and France ($99 million). The highest value imports in 1991 were agricultural tractors ($971 million), parts for agricultural tractors ($200 million), mowers other than lawn mowers ($59 million), certain types of harvesting machines ($55 million), and parts of harrows, cultivators, weeders, and similar equipment ($55 million).

The total value of U.S. farm (and industrial) equipment exports followed the same pattern as imports, rising between 1987 and 1990, from $1.57 billion to $2.50 billion, but dropping in 1991 to $2.23 billion. The chief destinations for these exports in 1991 were Canada ($670 million), Mexico ($189 million), Germany ($151 million), Saudi Arabia ($123 million), and France ($122 million). The highest value exports in 1991 were various farm tractors ($434 million),

agricultural sprayers, including parts ($432 million), parts for farm tractors ($424 million), self-propelled combines ($163 million), and hay balers ($58 million).

INDUSTRY INFORMATION SOURCES

Brandon, Hembree, "Machinery Sales Pace Quickens," *Implement & Tractor,* November/December 1993, p. 3.

Brezonick, Mike, "How Deere Designed Its New Ag Tractors," *Diesel Progress Engines & Drives,* April 1993, p. 12.

Fussell, Betty, *The Story of Corn,* New York: Knopf, 1992.

Gregg, Carol Ann, "Dealer Adjust to Farm Changes," *Implement & Tractor,* November/December 1993, p. 13.

Hudson, Jim, "Builders Listening to Buyers," *Implement & Tractor,* November/December 1993, p. 1.

Hudson, Jim, "Export Sales Likely Success Key," *Implement & Tractor,* January/February 1993, pp. 1-3.

Hudson, Jim, "Manufacturer Sees '94 as 'Real Comeback Year,'" *Implement & Tractor,* November/December 1993, p. 1.

"I&T 55th Annual Market Statistics," *Implement & Tractor,* January/February 1993, pp. 18-21.

Ivey, Mark and Kelly, Kevin, "As J.I. Case Sowed, So Shall It Reap," *Business Week,* 22 July 1991, p. 27.

Little, Dale L. "Legacy of Science," *Farm Chemicals,* July 1993, p. 8.

"Mexico Wide Open to Traders," *Implement & Tractor,* January/February, 1993, p. 22.

Schlereth, Thomas J., *Victorian America,* New York: HarperCollins, 1991.

"Soyoil in Diesel Helps Cut Pollution," *Implement & Tractor,* August/September 1993, p. 6.

"U.S. Farm Wheel Tractor Retail Sales, 1987-1991," *Implement & Tractor,* January/February 1993, p. 22.

"The Weather's Too Damn Nice," *The Economist,* 13 July 1991, p. 29.

Yengst, Charles R., "Trendlines," *Diesel Progress Engines & Drives,* December 1993, p. 4.

—Richard Hillyer

SIC 3524

LAWN AND GARDEN TRACTORS AND HOME LAWN AND GARDEN EQUIPMENT

This entry discusses establishments primarily engaged in manufacturing lawn mowers, lawn and garden tractors, and other lawn and garden equipment used for home lawn and garden care. It also includes establishments primarily engaged in manufacturing snowblowers and throwers for residential use. Other equipment classified here includes: wagons and carts for lawn and garden use, lawn mower grass catchers, power hedge trimmers, power lawn edgers, loaders for garden tractors, mulchers, plow attachments for garden tractors, rototillers, seeders, and residential lawn vacuums.

Establishments primarily engaged in manufacturing farm equipment and machinery are classified in **SIC 3523: Farm Machinery and Equipment**. Those manufacturing hand lawn and garden shears and pruners are classified in **SIC 3421: Cutlery** and those manufacturing other garden handtools are classified in **SIC 3423: Hand and Edge Tools, Except Machine Tools and Handsaws**.

INDUSTRY SNAPSHOT

In 1992, the lawn and garden equipment industry generated approximately $4.25 billion in revenues. Americans spent nearly $3.7 billion on products for their 25 to 30 million acres of lawns in 1992, and U.S. exports of lawn and garden equipment exceeded $592 million.

The industry both benefitted and was hurt by the economic recession of the first part of the 1990s. More people were taking care of their own lawns rather than hiring professional landscaping companies, and that meant homeowners were buying equipment. But with consumer confidence down, homeowners were restrained in their purchases. A drop in housing starts also negatively affected purchases of outdoor power equipment for lawns.

In the early 1990s the industry was forced to reduce pollution caused by its gas-powered machinery. California began the nationwide trend of introducing strict guidelines, calling for limits on air and noise pollution. This was followed by a 1994 announcement by the Environmental Protection Agency that is was introducing the first national emission standards for lawn mowers and other gas-powered gardening equipment.

Concern for the environment also powered the latest trend in lawn mowers—mulching. Many states banned lawn and garden cuttings from landfills, and in response, consumers snapped up mulching mowers and attachments. Mulching cuts each blade of grass many times and forces the particles back into the soil to nourish it.

Manufacturers expected that the North American Free Trade Agreement with Canada and Mexico would boost export sales and that the European market would open up as well with the relaxation of trade barriers.

ORGANIZATION AND STRUCTURE

*Distribution.*Many of the manufacturers in this industry relied on a two-step distribution system involving licensed dealers to market their equipment. However, many were turning directly to the mass merchandisers such as Builders Square, Wal-Mart, Home Depot, and others to sell lawn and garden equipment.

In order to maintain good relations with their traditional distributors and dealers, some manufacturers sold several lines of merchandise under different brand names. While the less expensive lines could be found in home centers and discount stores, the higher-priced models had to be purchased at dealerships. Homelite segmented its market into mass market, dealers, and professional landscapers.

The major manufacturers and their dealers were facing heavy competition from the companies that produced inexpensive power mowers for $39 to $159, especially during the recession in the early 1990s.

Dealers for some companies, such as Ariens, were functioning more as manufacturers' representatives than as independent dealers or wholesale distributors. Rather than stocking large inventories they were being paid commissions for direct-shipped orders.

White Outdoor Products Co., a division of MTD, absorbed another MTD division, Yard-Man Co., and the Yard-Man brand was due to be dropped. This consolidation brought about a change in distribution too. While retailers ordered Yard-Man products from a distributor, White products were ordered directly from the company. The company was expected to continue direct-order distribution to retailers, except in the South and on the coasts where a distributor network would be established.

Outdoor Power Equipment Institute. The Lawn Mower Institute was formed in the early 1950s as an association of lawn mower companies. Its purpose at the time was to develop a voice for the industry, especially in dealings with the government. By 1960, recognizing that the industry was diversifying into a broad array of power equipment, the association became the Outdoor Power Equipment Institute (OPEI). Its member companies were producing riding lawn mowers, tillers, garden tractors and trimmers.

In the early 1970s, the industry feared that the newly-formed Consumer Product Safety Commission (CPSC) would write safety standards that the manufacturers would not be able to meet. OPEI, acting as a voice for the industry, opened up communication with the CPSC and adopted voluntary safety standards before the CPSC issued its mandatory standards, which were less stringent than the industry had feared. OPEI continued to function as a spokesgroup for the entire outdoor power equipment industry.

BACKGROUND AND DEVELOPMENT

Lawn mower development. The nation's zest for lawn maintenance is relatively new, although the lawn mower, developed in England, has been in existence since the 1830s. According to some accounts, the push mower was considered an excellent exercise machine. Lawn mowers were familiar to American children since before the Civil War.

In the 1930s, lawn mower sales in the United States amounted to about 50,000 units a year. After World War II, however, Americans migrated to the suburbs and began to take pride in tending their new lawns, hedges, and gardens. New types of grass were developed to produce plush lawns, and with this passion for the perfect lawn came a burst in sales of new lawn mowers.

The reel mowers were the standard cutting tool until the 1950s, when the gas-powered rotary mower finally became more than a rough cutting tool. By the end of the decade, power mowers outsold reel mowers by a nine to one margin. Unfortunately, the rise in popularity of the power mower was accompanied by a surge in lawn mowing accidents—especially toe and finger amputations and wounds from flying debris.

In 1954, the Outdoor Power Equipment Institute began working with the American National Standards Institute (formerly the American Standards Association) to formulate safety standards for power mowers. Since its beginnings OPEI's member companies have worked to improve mower safety while preventing prices from skyrocketing due to expensive safety features.

Some of the first safety measures included attaching decks to handles with bolt-on brackets instead of cotter pins and positioning the starter cord away from the discharge chute. The OPEI also launched public relations campaigns concerning mower safety.

A new era of consumer activism began in 1969 with Ralph Nader's book *Unsafe at Any Speed,* which was concerned with auto industry negligence pertaining to safety issues. In 1972, the federal Consumer Product Safety Act created a Consumer Products Safety Commission (CPSC). The power lawn mower industry was one of that agency's first concerns because of a report that 77,000 people a year were injured by the whirling blades. It took ten years of data-gathering and testimony from experts and consumers before the CPSC issued its first safety requirements: the dead-man control and blade housing and shield designs that prevented foot injury.

The deadman control prevents hand injuries that occurred when operators attempted to clear the chute of wet grass without shutting down the machine. With a deadman control, the lawn mower blade stops turning within three seconds of the operator's release of the spring-loaded control on the handle. The operator cannot get around to the chute before the blade stops turning, eliminating the risk of losing a finger if he or she attempts to clear a clogged chute. Less expensive mowers feature a simple control that shuts down the entire engine when an operator releases the handle. More expensive models stop the blade but allow the engine to keep running.

The second regulation was designed to prevent foot injuries that often occurred when power mowers were operated. The regulation called for blade housings and shields to prevent the operator's foot from fitting under the deck and slipping into the blade. Mower manufacturers must perform a standard "foot-probe test" to ensure that their mower designs meet the requirement.

The industry itself devised the safety standard that requires debris to be deflected onto the ground rather than flying out of the chute and potentially hitting bystanders. The manufacturers perform structural-integrity and thrown-objects tests to be sure the mower design meets the established safety standards. For both tests, steel balls and common nails are fed into the mower housing with its blades turning. To pass the structural-integrity test, the mower housing and the grass catcher must be able to prevent the ejection of hard objects the mower picks up. If a steel ball bends any part of the housing or breaks halfway through any surface, or if a ball or nail that the mower picks up hits a bystander target or operator target, the mower fails the test. The thrown-objects test for mowers without grass catchers requires the mower to pass over 200 nails and stipulates that only a small percentage of ejected nails may strike above a designated height on a bystander target.

These safety features added more than $25 to the cost of each mower. In addition, liability insurance for power mower manufacturers pushed prices even higher. The price of a power mower nearly doubled between 1980 and 1990.

By 1990, 6.7 million power mowers a year were being sold, including 1.1 million riding mowers. Front engine riding mowers have been showing the most growth in sales in recent years. Only about 100,000 reel mowers are sold annually.

Environmental requirements. For decades, people bagged their grass clippings and put them out on the curb to be taken to the landfill as garbage. As landfill space became scarce and expensive in the 1970s and 1980s, yard and garden waste became a major concern of environmentalists and industry analysts. By 1990, yard waste was responsible for about 18 percent of garbage by weight, and when compressed it accounted for 10 percent by volume. Most of the yard waste was grass clippings.

States and municipalities across the country banned organic waste such as grass and leaves from landfills. This ban led to increased sales of mulching mowers or mulcher attachments, as well as blower vacuums and hand-held shredders that grind leaves and small twigs. Mulching mowers became the best-selling mowers during the early 1990s, as they enabled people to turn grass clippings and other organic materials into mulch for gardens and under trees and bushes.

In the early 1990s, manufacturers offered models that mulched only, as well as kits that could convert side-discharge or rear-bagging mowers into mulchers. Mulching kits added $15 to $40 to mower prices. Some companies were offering mulching blades that they claimed could be substituted on mowers with no modifications to the mower deck.

Because mulching mowers are not effective if the grass is too high, a convertible mower that could mulch or mow offered consumers some flexibility depending upon the conditions. Conversions between bagging and mulching operations have become easier on many new-model walk-behinds.

CURRENT CONDITIONS

Though mulchers were selling better than any other mowers in 1992, sales of lawn and garden equipment were still slow.

The industry expected sales to pick up when housing starts increased in 1992. Manufacturers also predicted that sales would rise as baby boomers hit middle age and were at the peak of their earning power. They expected that the baby boomers would either move to bigger homes with bigger lawns, or undertake lawn improvement projects at their existing homes.

Weather. This industry is greatly influenced by the weather. Wet weather generally increases sales of lawn mowers and other lawn equipment. The cold summer of 1992 slowed grass growth and consequently lawn mower sales. Recent winters with heavy snowfall, however, gave snowblower sales a boost.

Environment. Environmental concerns were also expected to perk up sales during the second half of the 1990s. New products that met California's stringent noise and air pollution laws were predicted to sell well in other parts of the country even before the EPA's announcement of new emission-reducing regulations. In 1992 the Environmental Protection Agency (EPA) and the National Consortium for Emissions Reductions in Lawn Care, comprised mainly of electric company representatives, traded 1,000 cordless electric lawn mowers (valued at $400 each) for consumers' old gasoline-powered machines. The EPA collected the gas mowers to test their emissions and to help the agency determine how to reduce pollution. After its studies, the EPA estimated that about ten percent of the nation's air pollution comes from the country's lawn mowers, garden tractors, chain saws, and other gas-powered garden equipment.

The 1990 Clear Air Act called for national emission standards for non-road engines, which included two- and four-stroke outdoor equipment. That legislation, coupled with the EPA's proposals, may be easier for manufacturers to deal with as they would enable companies to design mowers that would meet any state's environmental regulations.

Manufacturers were uncertain about the technology that new environment-friendly mowers and other machinery might use. While willing to consider alternatives, such as propane or even solar-powered engines, manufacturers were concerned that consumers would not accept the price increases associated with cost of the new technological enhancements.

INDUSTRY LEADERS

The big names in lawn mowers and other outdoor power equipment included Fuqua Industries Inc. of Georgia, Murray Ohio Manufacturing Co., based in Tennessee, Toro Company of Minnesota, Deere Inc., and Black and Decker Corp., based in Maryland. Honda riding mowers have also become a popular choice in the United States.

Toro Company. Toro Company, founded in 1914, had sales of $635 million in 1992, including sales of irrigation equipment. Its lawn mowers and snow removal equipment were considered high quality products. In 1989, Toro introduced a "highly maneuverable rider" series with front wheels that turned 80 degrees in either direction, providing a four-inch turning radius. This was one of the first of a new generation of riding mowers that could make tight turns and was easy to drive.

Toro was disappointed in its entry into the mass merchandising world of Sears Roebuck & Co. and Montgomery Ward & Co. In 1991, the company anticipated sales of $25 to $30 million from those two chains for Lawn Boy mowers, but actual sales reached about $17 million.

Like other manufacturers in the industry, Toro was looking for ways to cut costs and streamline operations, especially with the economy in a slowdown. In 1992, it announced it was closing its riding-products plant in South Bend, Indiana, and moving the operations to its plants in Windom, Minnesota, and Tomah, Wisconsin. It also shut down a distribution center in Mountain Top, Pennsylvania, eliminating 270 jobs there.

Fuqua's Snapper mowers. Fuqua produced Snapper mowers, both riding and walk-behinds, which were usually number two in sales just behind Toro mowers. The Snapper mowers, however, sold for between $189 and $6,000. Even its low-end mowers were at a disadvantage because many of its rivals sold mowers for as low as $89 in discount outlets.

Fuqua was struggling in 1989 and 1990 and took serious measures, cutting its corporate staff from 41 to 18 people and consolidating three plants into one. Dry weather and a recession that hit the home building industry hard also hurt Fuqua and its lawn equipment competitors. Fuqua had sales of almost $925 million in 1991; however, that figure included revenue from its other businesses as well, including sporting equipment, clothing and accessories and photofinishing. Its Snapper unit had an operating loss of $51 million that year.

In 1991, Fuqua president Charles Scott said the company needed to develop other distribution channels besides the lawn and garden dealer. The company also needed another product line besides Snapper, he told *Financial World.* The Snapper division made a profit in 1992, but news articles indicated that Fuqua would consider selling the division if the price was right.

Murray Ohio Manufacturing Co. Murray Ohio Manufacturing Co., a bicycle manufacturer that has been in existence since 1919, has also been producing lawn mowers since 1968. The company sold $300 million worth of lawn and garden equipment in 1991, which represented nearly half of its total revenues for the year.

Deere & Company. Deere & Company, the country's leading manufacturer of farm equipment, was also a leader in sales of lawn and garden equipment, selling riding mowers, small tractors, and walk-behind mowers. Its lawn and grounds equipment, including golf course equipment, accounted for about $780 million of its $6.9 billion in sales in 1991.

Black and Decker Corp. Black and Decker, the leading manufacturer of power tools, also produced outdoor power equipment such as lawn trimmers and blowers and marketed them under the brand names: Lawn Genie, Lawn Raker, Groom N'Edge, Vac'N'Mulch and YardCleaner. Outdoor products usually account for about 10 percent of the company's total revenues which were nearly $4.8 billion in 1992.

Ariens Co. The Ariens Co. of Wisconsin, a small but well-known manufacturer of garden tractors, tillers and power mowers had sales of $75 million in its 1991 fiscal year. The family-run company followed an aggressive acquisition strategy in the 1980s. In 1982, it purchased Gravely International, a heavy-duty equipment manufacturer. Three years later, Ariens acquired Promark, which produced large commercial shredders and other equipment for the tree industry. Its 1989 maneuverings brought Ariens a chance to broaden its home-use market. To do so, Ariens acquired the North American rights to manufacture and distribute handheld, two-stroke machinery for a Japanese company, Tanaka Kogyo. That same year, Ariens purchased TurfVac and began marketing its leaf removal equipment through the Promark division.

Great States Corp. and American Lawn Mower Co. Most of the reel mowers marketed in recent years were made by Great States Corp. and American Lawn Mower Co. of Indiana. Establishments which market reel mowers under their own names simply put their own label on Great States and American Mower products.

AMERICA AND THE WORLD

In 1992, exports increased by $53 million to $592 million. Imports were valued at $76 million, a $2-million increase from the previous year. The largest export market was Canada which received approximately 27 percent of the U.S. export market. About 15 percent of exports were shipped to France and 8 percent to Germany.

Imports had declined for four years until 1992 when they started to rise again. The decline, however, had been largely attributable to an increase in production at foreign-owned facilities located in the United States. Equipment from Japan and Canada led the import market. Imports from Japan rose by 19 percent between 1991 and 1992 and accounted for 46 percent of all U.S. lawn and garden equipment imports. Imports from Canada fell by about 17 percent in 1992, but still accounted for about 25 percent of total industry imports. Japanese and Swedish companies were building lawn and garden equipment with engines made by the U.S. firm Briggs and Stratton, a leading small engine manufacturer.

The elimination of tariffs under the North American Free Trade Agreement was expected to boost exports, as would the unified European Community standards which became effective in 1993.

RESEARCH AND TECHNOLOGY

Until recently, consumers had two choices in outdoor power equipment. They could buy gas-powered machinery that was loud and generated such pollutants as hydrocarbons and carbon monoxide. Or they could buy the less powerful electric models with their long, unwieldy power cords.

The worst culprits in terms of pollution have been the hand-held equipment with two-stroke engines. These engines generate a relatively high amount of pollution because every downward stroke of the piston generates power. The piston compresses air and fuel in the cylinder and raw fuel sometimes leaks out the exhaust with the used air. The engine also requires a very rich fuel and oil mixture which may not burn completely.

According to the California Air Resources Board (CARB), the 4.6 million small utility engines in the state, which included 2.1 million lawn mowers and almost one million trimmers, were responsible for five percent of the hydrocarbons and four percent of the carbon monoxide released into the air annually. CARB also said a dirty lawn mower operated for half an hour emitted as many ozone-destructive pollutants as a car driven 172 miles.

CARB issued strict regulations to go into effect in two stages, the first in 1994 and the second in 1999. By 1994, the emissions had to be cut by 46 percent and by 1999, another 55 percent. The 1994 regulations differentiated between two-stroke and four-stroke engines, calling for different restrictions on emissions. The 1999 regulations, however, require two-stroke engines that are not hand-held to meet the four-stroke emissions standards.

The national Clean Air Act amendment of 1990 also called for investigation of the emissions of non-road equipment, including not only power equipment but boat motors and agricultural and construction machinery. The EPA issued new regulations for diesel-fueled machinery operating at 50 horsepower or above (which included tractors, forklifts, and earth-moving equipment) in 1993 and announced emission limits for

chain saw and lawn and garden equipment manufacturers in mid-1994. The two-step phase-in of these new regulations begins to go into effect August 1, 1996.

The pressure to eliminate the polluting gas-powered hand-held equipment ignited a small revolution in design of lawn and garden power tools. Manufacturers began testing gas-powered equipment that burned more cleanly, equipment powered by built-in batteries, and even sun-, propane-, or methanol-powered machinery.

INDUSTRY INFORMATION SOURCES

Baldo, Anthony, ''Red Alert Time,'' *Financial World,* September 3, 1991, 24-6.

Kimber, Robert, ''Pushing Toward Safety,'' *Horticulture,* May 1990, 70-73.

Konrad, Walecia, ''Fuqua Runs into a Patch of Tall Weeds,'' *Business Week*, August 5, 1991, 52.

Markovich, Bob, ''Chipping Away,'' *Home Mechanix,* October 1990, 74-80.

Patton, Phil, ''The Only Way to Mow,'' *Esquire,* July 1990, 32.

Samuelson, Robert, ''The Joys of Mowing,'' *Newsweek,* April 29, 1991, 49.

Yeaple, Judith Anne, ''Greener Pastures,'' *Popular Science,* July 1992, 85-92.

SIC 3531

CONSTRUCTION MACHINERY AND EQUIPMENT

This industry includes establishments primarily engaged in manufacturing heavy machinery and equipment used primarily by the construction industries, such as bulldozers; cranes, except industrial plant overhead and truck-type cranes; dredging machinery; pavers; self-propelled backfillers; backhoes; aggregate spreaders; construction plows; and power shovels. This industry also includes establishments primarily engaged in manufacturing forestry equipment and certain specialized equipment, not elsewhere classified, similar to that used by the construction industries, such as elevating platforms, ship cranes and capstans, aerial work platforms, and automobile wrecker hoists. Establishments primarily engaged in manufacturing mining equipment are included in **SIC 3532: Mining Machinery and Equipment, Except Oil and Gas Field Machinery and Equipment**; those manufacturing industrial plant overhead traveling cranes are classified under **SIC 3536: Overhead Traveling Cranes,**

Hoists, and Monorail Systems; and those establishments manufacturing industrial truck-type cranes are classified under **SIC 3537: Industrial Trucks, Tractors, Trailers, and Stackers**.

INDUSTRY SNAPSHOT

The U.S. construction equipment industry consists of about 700 manufacturers; however, in 1992 only six companies controlled 70 percent of worldwide sales. Leading companies include Caterpillar Inc., J.I. Case Co., Komatsu-Dresser Co., Clark Equipment Co., Deere & Co., Terex Corp., and the Ingersoll-Rand Co.

Weak American and overseas economies have hurt the construction equipment industry in recent years, as sales of equipment are directly related to the health of the construction industry. Many analysts feel, however, that at least a modest turnaround in the industry's fortunes is imminent. As *Standard & Poors Industry Surveys* indicated, "in all likelihood, 1991 probably represented a trough; total construction spending peaked in 1986 at $421.4 billion and declined without interruption through 1991." *Industry Surveys* noted in 1992 that, thus far, "the recovery in construction spending . . . has been confined to private spending for residential buildings and government spending for public construction. Expenditures for nonresidential buildings have continued to decline. Categories such as industrial, office, hotel, and motel reported double-digit declines through August." *U.S. Industrial Outlook 1993* stated, however, that "assuming the economic recovery gains strength both in the United States and abroad, the construction machinery industry is expected to grow in constant dollars by about 3 percent. This also assumes that highway and bridge reconstruction and repair will continue at a strong pace, along with home building. Higher levels of metal and coal strip mining also will ensure a stronger demand for construction machinery. The improved sales by dealers during 1992 will stimulate shipments by factories in 1993."

ORGANIZATION AND STRUCTURE

This industry provides several major categories of equipment for use by the larger construction industry.

Earthmoving machinery is utilized by companies involved in residential and commercial construction, as well as those involved in highway construction and dambuilding, As *U.S. Industrial Outlook 1993* notes, "Passage of the Intermodal Surface Transportation efficiency Act in late 1991 provided state governments with over $16 billion in Federal funds for highway projects during 1992. This funding along with state expenditures for roads improved demand for highway construction equipment in many regions of the United States." Caterpillar Inc. is the industry leader in the production of earthmoving machinery, historically the cornerstone of its product line.

Excavators and cranes are utilized in a variety of construction areas. Excavators are used in most construction jobs and come in a wide variety of sizes and configurations, from small tractor-mounted backhoes to large power shovels. Cranes are used for bridge, highway, and large commercial or industrial construction jobs. They are also used in offshore oil drilling.

Other construction equipment includes underground mining machinery, asphalt and concrete pavers, air compressors and tools, pumps, hoists, and rock-crushing and screening equipment. Figgie International is a leading producer of concrete mixing trucks, while Ingersoll-Rand is a leader in the production of compactors and compressors.

CURRENT CONDITIONS

Sales of new equipment were down during the early 1990s, but sales of repair and replacement parts improved. Construction machinery manufacturing companies remain hopeful that mounting concern about the state of the nation's infrastructure will translate into increased sales over the course of the 1990s. Serious efforts to repair and resurface the nation's highways and bridges would stimulate sales. The U.S. Department of Commerce has estimated that more than half the country's major highways and one-third of its bridges are in need of some repair, and notes that such work will require highly automated bituminous and concrete paving equipment, milling machinery, and high-powered pavement breakers. Manufacturers also anticipate opportunity for growth through new construction projects as more communities build pollution control facilities, such as solid waste disposal and wastewater treatment facilities. In addition, the major earthquake that devastated vast portions of the Los Angeles transportation system will undoubtedly require major reconstruction efforts.

Recessions abroad also hurt the U.S. construction machinery industry well into the 1990s, as many construction projects and mining expansions were postponed until economies improved. In 1992, for instance, U.S. exports in the area of construction machinery declined by approximately 14 percent. This situation did nothing to improve the fortunes of domestic producers, since about one-fourth of sales of U.S. construction equipment companies were generated by exports. Many U.S. manufacturers participated in joint ventures or sales agreements with foreign companies, especially companies in Europe and Japan.

These partnerships allowed U.S. companies to shift production when costs of labor, raw materials, and currency values changed.

INDUSTRY LEADERS

The world's leading manufacturer of construction equipment is Caterpillar Inc., with total revenues in 1992 of more than $22 billion. Originally incorporated in 1925 as the Caterpillar Tractor Company, the company boasts more than two dozen major production facilities worldwide. After suffering significant losses during the 1980s, the company embarked on a series of changes to regain their previous form. As *Everybody's Business: A Field Guide to the 400 Leading Companies in America* notes, Caterpillar "closed 9 plants, completely overhauled the remaining 30, cut their work force from 90,000 to 60,000, introduced new machinery and moved aggressively into foreign markets." The transformation was at times a painful one, particularly in the area of labor (a sector that continues to trouble the company), but analysis by industry observers such as *Standard & Poors Industry Surveys* feel that Caterpillar has regained its footing, citing "higher volume and firmer prices stemming from better end markets in the U.S., the absence of restructuring charges, and favorable adjustments to inventory. The company also reported that its operations had reached the point where the benefits of its factory modernization program exceeded its costs."

Deere & Co., a familiar name in farm machinery and lawn and garden equipment, was also a leading manufacturer of construction equipment such as backhoe loaders, crawler dozers, excavators, and log skidders. Other industry leaders include J.I. Case, a subsidiary of Tenneco Inc., Clark Equipment, Ingersoll-Rand, and Dresser Industries.

WORK FORCE

For domestic construction equipment manufacturers, labor is a huge part of operating expenses for leading manufacturers such as Deere & Co. and Caterpillar. Labor at both companies is represented by the United Auto Workers, and both companies have had their share of labor disputes in recent years. The most recent battle of consequence, between the UAW and Caterpillar, has been a particularly bitter one. Intermittent strikes and lock-outs have marked the strike, which began in early 1992. The acrimonious dispute was still going strong in mid-1994.

RESEARCH AND TECHNOLOGY

Caterpillar and other construction equipment companies have spent billions of dollars in recent

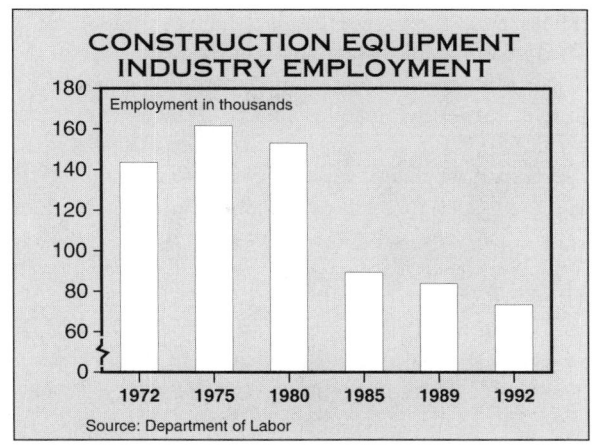

CONSTRUCTION EQUIPMENT INDUSTRY EMPLOYMENT

Employment in thousands

Source: Department of Labor

years to upgrade factories and dealer networks. Caterpillar's seven-year, $2-billion plan introduced in the 1980s was intended to link the company's plants, its suppliers, and dealers. Its new streamlined production featured computers that could adjust machine tools in seconds, a process that ordinarily would have taken a day. With plants reconfigured into "cells," workers could handle several manufacturing processes at one time. A Caterpillar plant in France began to use an "intelligent" crane that did not require a human operator to transport large steel slabs to a special area to be drilled by a computerized flame cutter. With the new system in place, the time it took to fill an order for a replacement part was cut from 20 days to 8 days.

Construction equipment itself has often been considered relatively "low-tech," but "intelligent" machinery is increasingly being developed for field work. Kraft TeleRobotics of Kansas, for instance is testing Haz-Trak, an excavator and materials handler that can be operated by remote control hundreds of yards away, allowing operators to handle dangerous materials such as radioactive waste from a safe distance. The excavator, it is hoped, can eventually be operated from even greater distances.

AMERICA AND THE WORLD

The construction machinery industry is truly a global one, with U.S. manufacturers marketing their equipment all over the world to industrialized and developing countries. Competition is international, with Komatsu Ltd. of Japan Caterpillar's major competitor.

Komatsu has invested in both European and U.S. companies to improve its market presence worldwide. Komatsu invested heavily in Dresser Industries, based in Dallas, Texas, in 1988. Komatsu was to run manufacturing and develop product technology, while

Dresser would provide the plants and the marketing, as the two companies sought to challenge industry leader Caterpillar, Inc. The new joint company made a full line of earthmoving equipment with prices that ranged from $50,000 to $1.5 million. Komatsu Dresser spent $200 million to convert some Dresser plants in the United States to Japanese manufacturing techniques. The joint venture was not very profitable, however, with Komatsu Dresser Co.'s market share slipping from just over 20 percent in 1988 to 18 percent in 1991 and Caterpillar picking up market share. Dresser announced it would sell off its share in the venture to shareholders and concentrate on oil and gas services.

In 1993 Komatsu announced that it would also enter into a joint venture with Cummins Engine Co., the nation's largest manufacturer of diesel engines. Cummins was expected to provide Komatsu with diesel engines for its off-highway machinery and save Komatsu the huge expense of developing its own diesel-emission control equipment to meet pollution requirements in California and probably Europe within a few years.

INDUSTRY INFORMATION SOURCES

Bremner, Brian. "Can Caterpillar Inch Its Way Back to Heftier Profits?" *Business Week*. September 25, 1989: 75.

"End Markets Begin to Recover in 1992." *Standard and Poor's Industry Surveys*. December 24, 1992: S36-8.

Flint, Jerry. "The Enemy of My Enemy." *Forbes*. November 14, 1988.

Kelly, Kevin. "Labor's Metamorphosis: The High Stakes at Caterpillar." *Commonweal*. January 15, 1993.

Langreth, Robert. "Smart Shovel." *Popular Science*. June 1992: 82-4, 108-109.

Moskowitz, Milton, Robert Levering and Michael Katz. *Everybody's Business, A Field Guide to the 400 Leading Companies in America*. New York: Doubleday, 1990.

Slutsker, Gary. "What's Good for Caterpillar. . . ." *Forbes*. December 7, 1992: 108-10.

SIC 3532

MINING MACHINERY

This category includes establishments primarily engaged in manufacturing heavy machinery and equipment used by the mining industries, such as coal breakers, mine cars, mineral cleaning machinery, concentration machinery, core drills, coal cutters, portable rock drills, and rock crushing machinery. Establishments primarily engaged in manufacturing construc-

tion machinery are classified in **SIC 3531: Construction Machinery and Equipment;** those manufacturing welldrilling machinery are classified in **SIC 3533: Oil and Gas Field Machinery and Equipment;** and those manufacturing coal and ore conveyors are classified in **SIC 3535: Conveyors and Conveying Equipment.**

INDUSTRY SNAPSHOT

The mining equipment industry suffered a substantial drop in shipments during 1982 and has been recovering ever since. At the beginning of 1982, shipments were valued at $2.11 billion. By 1983 they had dropped to $1.51 billion and had only recovered to $1.95 billion by 1991. The employment level in this industry dropped sharply during 1982 and again between 1984 and 1987. Since 1987, the employment level has remained virtually flat. Diminishing demand for domestically produced minerals fueled the decline, decreasing mining activity substantially. To combat weakened demand, mining equipment companies have relied on the export market for business opportunities, but this market has been far from stable. Foreign manufacturers gained ground against U.S. manufacturers in the 1980s, thanks to improved quality and lower prices. All of these factors have pushed U.S. mining equipment companies to step up cost cutting measures and look to innovation as the key to success.

ORGANIZATION AND STRUCTURE

The mining equipment industry is highly dependent on mining activity in the United States and the world. When demand for mined materials is high, mine operators order new machinery; when demand is low, orders fall off. Mining machinery manufacturers are cushioned somewhat from demand cycles because different kinds of mines use similar machinery. Thus a decline in coal mining, for example, may be offset by a boom in salt mining, as both mining industries use the same machinery.

The market share of this industry is split between six categories. Underground mining machinery claims 15.4 percent of the industry. Crushing, pulverizing, and screening machinery claim 11.0 percent. Drills and other mining machinery, not elsewhere classified, claim 9.4 percent. Mineral processing machinery claims 4.9 percent. Parts and attachments for mining machinery and equipment claim 50.1 percent of the industry. Mining machinery, not specified by kind, claims the remaining 9.2 percent of the industry market.

The mining machinery industry draws its supplies from a variety of sources. Mill shapes and forms made from carbon, alloy, and stainless steels, copper, and aluminum are the most highly consumed materials. Castings from gray and malleable iron, steel, aluminum, and copper, and forgings from iron and steel are also heavily consumed. Fabricated structural metal products, speed changers, gears, industrial high-speed drives, and roller bearings constitute other significant materials consumed by the industry.

BACKGROUND AND DEVELOPMENT

Mining came late to the United States, for early surveyors assumed that there were no significant mineral resources to be found in the country. Politicians and statesmen arguing over currency shortly after the Revolutionary War ruled out gold and silver because the United States supposedly did not have the resources to produce this type of exchange. Benjamin Franklin said, "Gold and silver are not the produce of North America, which has no mines." Another eighteenth-century observer, Cornelius de Pauw of the Netherlands, remarked that "in all the extent of America there are found but few mines of iron, and these so inferior in quality to those of the old continent that it cannot even be used for nails." As history has shown, these remarks proved wildly presumptuous. Explorers moving westward across the country in the nineteenth century discovered rich reserves of gold, silver, lead, copper, iron, nickel, coal, and many other ores and minerals. The country proved far richer than any of the original settlers had imagined.

The first mechanisms to dig and extract mineral resources from the earth were hammers, chisels, shovels, and buckets. More advanced operations used single cars on rail ways to convey materials to the surface of underground mines. The hammer and chisel were the first instruments to be replaced by pneumatically-powered cutting devices. British inventors were nearly one decade ahead of the Americans in the development of mechanical power to cut into the ground. In 1850, a Glasgow mine owner proved compressed air could be used to power underground machinery. By 1853, a cutting chain machine was developed which matured into a machine called the Gartsherrie, patented in 1864. The Gartsherrie is considered the precursor of modern coal cutters.

A rock drill was invented and patented by Simon Ingersoll in 1870. After Ingersoll's patent changed hands several times and improvements to his invention had been made, Addison Rand was able to persuade mining companies to use his new technology instead of hammers and chisels. The two inventors came together in 1905 and advertised themselves as "the largest builder of air power machinery in the world."

Ingersoll's side of the operation specialized in construction work, while Rand's specialized in underground mining. Today, Ingersoll-Rand is a highly diversified company with many interests, most of which are related to its origins in mining.

Though the industrial revolution was dependent on abundant supplies of coal to generate power, the coal mining industry lagged far behind others in using machinery to ease the work of men. Men manually shovelled coal into coal cars well into the twentieth century. Keith Dix, author of *What's a Coal Miner to Do?*, wrote: "It is ironic that the advance in technology and management, which gave modern industry its momentum, bypassed the one industry on which most others depended." By 1948, roughly 33 percent of the country's underground coal continued to be loaded by hand.

Joseph Joy, who was responsible for the mechanization of coal loading, is considered the single most significant inventor in this industry; he was awarded 106 patents between 1904 and 1944. Joy developed the Joy Loader in response to two insistent demands: American industry's demand for an increasing supply of coal and newly-organized mineworkers' demand for improvements in working conditions that were frequently subhuman. Following the development of the Joy Loader, men would no longer need to shovel coal by hand, though many would lose their jobs as a result. The Joy Manufacturing Company, known today as Joy Technologies Incorporated, claimed that Joy Loaders accounted for 72 percent of all coal loaded mechanically by 1954.

During the 1970s, the U.S. Government pushed the development of new mining technologies through legislation on health and safety, air and water pollution, and environmental protection of the land mined. Such efforts changed the face of the mining industry, requiring skilled staff to operate and maintain mechanized production. Productivity in underground coal mines was hampered due to additional resources required to prevent accidents, black lung disease, and acid-runoff. In surface mining, additional resources were necessary to meet land restoration standards and to negotiate with those who claimed the land for agricultural purposes. Mining machinery manufacturers sought to capitalize on the changing industry by providing machines to do the required jobs.

CURRENT CONDITIONS

By the 1980s, U.S. Government interest in mining was concerned with addressing import-export imbalances. A 1986 report suggested that foreign penetration of the U.S. machinery market was primarily due to the strength of the dollar, high domestic material and capital costs, and generous financing and credit terms offered by some foreign governments to support export sales. The report projected that U.S. mining equipment manufacturers would face a steadily growing export market, shifting to Latin America, Asia, and Africa. Current world events, such as the North American Free Trade Agreement, the emergence of Korean and Taiwanese manufacturers, and the plea from South Africa, a major mining country, to lift trade sanctions, underscore the significance of these projections and the importance for U.S. manufacturers of developing the export market.

Due to the high price of mining machinery, the used-machinery market is very healthy, especially outside the United States. This demand creates an incentive for thieves to steal equipment, which is a relatively easy task. Machinery is usually left in unsecured areas, and is easy to start, difficult to trace, and easy to sell. The increase in equipment thefts in the early 1980s spurred Deere & Company to issue a Manufacturer's Certificate of Origin (MCO), which was adopted by the Construction Industry Manufacturers Association in 1983. Since then more than 20 manufacturers have used the MCO, which has reduced the thefts of certain machinery. As used-equipment buyers become more aware of the frequency of machinery theft, more MCOs have been requested upon the purchase of used-equipment.

U.S. manufacturers maintained a significant, though not a leading, share of the world mining machinery industry in the early 1990s. The strongest competitors in the world market were Japan, Germany, France, Canada, South Korea, Taiwan, and South Africa. While mining in the United States had dropped sharply due to a worldwide surplus of metal and mineral supplies, mining abroad has expanded quickly, opening new markets for U.S. manufacturers. The largest potential market was the former Soviet Union, which had vast amounts of natural resources. Although much of this marketplace was speculative in the early 1990s, analysts suggested that the way to jump-start the economy of Russia and the other nations was to enter the world marketplace through the sale of these resources. Many of the former Soviet Union's mines were in dire need of modernization and capital investment, providing a ready market for U.S. mining machinery equipment.

INDUSTRY LEADERS

According to the 1994 *Ward's Business Directory of U.S. Private and Public Companies,* the 88 companies listed for the industry had combined sales of $4.22

billion with a total employment figure of 31,300. Joy Technologies of Pittsburgh, Pennsylvania, the industry leader, had sales of $581 million and employed 3,900 people. INDRESCO Inc., located in Dallas, Texas, ranked second with sales of $559 million, while retaining 2,800 employees. The Chicago, Illinois company Jupiter Industries Inc. held third place with $500 million in sales, followed by Harnischfeger Corporation of Milwaukee, Wisconsin, with a sales figure of $442 million. Longyear Company of Salt Lake City, Utah, rounded out the top five with sales of $275 million.

WORK FORCE

U.S. Department of Labor projections for the year 2005 indicate that the workforce of the mining machinery industry will change significantly. Welders and cutters, who account for the largest segment in this industry, are expected to reduce their numbers by 11.1 percent. Others facing reductions of ten percent or more include assemblers, welding machine setters, machine builders, secretaries, inspectors, truck and tractor operators, and material handlers. Machinists are expected to increase employment levels by 6.8 percent, sales workers by 18.2 percent, mechanical engineers by 9.5 percent, numerically controlled machine tool operators by 9.5 percent, industrial machinery mechanics by 18.3 percent, industrial production managers by 15.7 percent, engineering technicians by 6.0 percent, combination machine tool operators by 8.3 percent, and coating/painting/spraying machine operators by 7.5 percent.

Pennsylvania's 40 establishments and Virginia's 32 establishments employed and shipped significantly more than any other states in 1987. Pennsylvania's mining machinery establishments employed 2,400 people and paid them an average of $12.21 per hour.

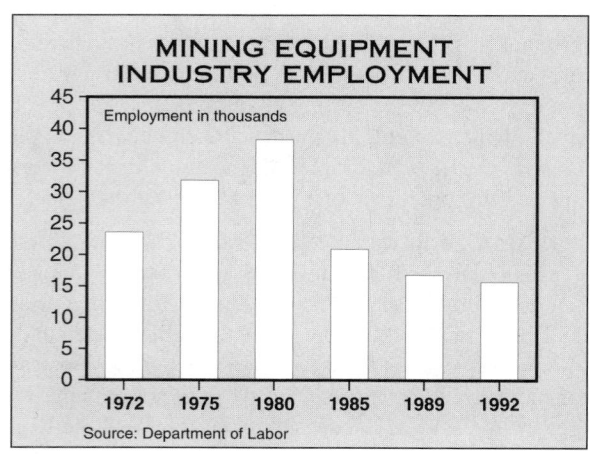

MINING EQUIPMENT INDUSTRY EMPLOYMENT

Employment in thousands

Source: Department of Labor

Shipments from that state exceeded $287 million in 1987. Virginia's establishments employed 2,200 and paid an average of $10.23 per hour. Total shipments from that state topped $260 million in 1987. West Virginia and Ohio also contributed significantly to the industry.

RESEARCH AND TECHNOLOGY

Mining equipment is considered mature in terms of design and innovation. Therefore, any improvements rely on research and development of new materials and advanced sensing, control, and computer techniques. Innovations in technology have typically sought to achieve gains in productivity or worker safety. The dangers of underground mining have prompted underground machinery designers to develop remote controlled and automated mining systems. These systems reduce production costs, increase productivity, and increase worker safety. The United Kingdom and Germany have made improvements in remote control and automated systems. But because such systems are expensive and the market has been volatile since the 1980s, the development of such systems has proceeded slowly.

Surface mining is much safer and more productive because larger machinery can be used. Sensing and control systems are frequently installed in surface equipment. Blast hole drills employ automated systems that regulate the speed and feet rate of the drill bit. Mining shovels have on-board microprocessors which relay information and record data. Because they can be added to existing equipment, these technologies have been developed by many manufacturers.

INDUSTRY INFORMATION SOURCES

Darnay, Arsen J., ed., *Manufacturing U.S.A.: Industry Analyses, Statistics, and Leading Companies,* Detroit: Gale Research, 1991.

Brady, T. M., and T. W. Martin, ''Metal Mining Equipment,'' *Mining Engineering,* May 1989.

———, ''Metal Mining Equipment,'' *Mining Engineering,* May 1990.

———, ''Metal Mining Equipment,'' *Mining Engineering,* May 1991.

''Caterpillar Opens New Conference and Training Facility in Arizona,'' *Mining Engineering,* August 1991.

Dagdelen, K., ''Open Pit Mining,'' *Mining Engineering,* May 1991.

''Developments to Watch,'' *Coal Age,* April 1987.

Dix, Keith, *What's a Coal Miner to Do?,* Pittsburgh: University of Pittsburgh Press, 1988.

''Exports Forecasted to Dominate Mining Equipment Market,'' *Mining Engineering,* October 1985.

Hast, Adele, ed., *International Directory of Company Histories,* Vol. 3, Chicago: St. James Press, 1988.

Huhta, Richard S., ''Highlights of Hillhead,'' *Rock Products,* September 1987.

———, ''Highlights of Hillhead '91,'' *Rock Products,* September 1991.

Kapp, William K., ''Opportunities Improving for Machinery Exports,'' *American Mining Congress Journal,* March 27, 1985.

O'Neil, Tim, ''Finnish Mining and Technology,'' *Mining Engineering,* October 1988.

Peterson, Carl R., ''Innovation in Mining Technology,'' *Mechanical Engineering,* August 1986.

''Protecting Equipment from Thieves,'' *Coal Age,* April 1987.

Rickard, Thomas A., *A History of American Mining,* New York: McGraw-Hill, 1932.

Tough, J. Brian, and Carl L. Livesay, ''Innovation Key to Competitiveness in Equipment Market,'' *American Mining Congress Journal,* March 27, 1985.

U.S. Department of Commerce, International Trade Administration, *A Competitive Assessment of the U.S. Mining Machinery Industry,* Washington, DC: GPO, October 1986.

U.S. Department of Labor, Bureau of Labor Statistics, *Technological Change and its Labor Impact in Five Energy Industries,* Washington, DC: GPO, April 1979.

von Lobenstein, J. G., Eduardo Julia, and Richard G. Hite, ''Expanding and Mechanizing El Soldado,'' *Energy & Mining Journal,* March 1988.

—Valerie E. Wilson

SIC 3533

OIL FIELD MACHINERY

This category covers establishments primarily engaged in manufacturing machinery and equipment for use in oil and gas fields or for drilling water wells, including portable drilling rigs. Establishments primarily engaged in manufacturing offshore oil and gas well drilling and production platforms are classified in **SIC 3731: Ship Building and Repairing.**

INDUSTRY SNAPSHOT

In the early 1990s the condition of the the oil and gas field machinery industry was dismal. As oil prices continued to remain depressed, the costs of drilling for oil did not prove profitable. Therefore, with little drilling activity, there was little need to produce the support machinery. Industry investment reports published by Merrill Lynch and Standard and Poor's shared the same opinion: oil and gas prices would remain relatively flat—compared to the early 1980s—throughout the remainder of the twentieth century. As a result, the activity in other support industries would stagnate and possibly whither away, unless viable diversification strategies could be successfully implemented.

In 1991, the top 75 companies claimed total sales of $12.1 billion, employing 103,500 people. The business establishments were located primarily in the southern United States, with Texas being the industry hub. As well as manufacturing oil and gas field machinery, the businesses involved in the industry were segmented as to the type machinery produced. Manufacturers of production machinery and equipment controlled 38.8 percent of the market share, while manufacturers of rotary oil and gas field drilling machinery and equipment controlled a 29.6 percent market share. Portable drilling rigs and parts claimed a ten-percent share, while oil and gas field derricks and well surveying machinery claimed 4.3 percent. Approximately another 17 percent of the market was classified as nonspecific oil support machinery and equipment.

ORGANIZATION AND STRUCTURE

The oil and gas field machinery industry includes field tools, oil derricks, drilling rigs and tools, well logging and surveying equipment, and general gas well and oil field machinery and equipment. Many companies exist in the United States that make specialty drilling equipment and other related machinery. Other companies, such as machine tool makers, produce smaller parts either for assembly at the more specialized companies or replacement needs while the rig is in service. The companies producing drilling rigs usually maintain a field service department, however private consultant-type firms also specialize in field repair of all oil field related equipment.

By 1993 the entire oil industry was controlled, regulated, and lobbied for or against, to a certain degree, by organizations like the Organization of Petroleum Exporting Countries (OPEC) and the American Petroleum Institute. Yet, domestically, the industry was ultimately controlled through regulations imposed by the U.S. government and the governments of international competitors. The Environmental Protection Agency had begun to place stringent restrictions on companies selling crude oil, which ultimately affected the cost of producing oil. This drove down profits making oil drilling a losing proposition with low selling costs being the standard. Given these conditions, oil drilling was performed mostly by major oil-

selling companies, like Exxon, Texaco, and Citgo. This was in sharp contrast to the early 1980s, when drilling rigs had been common sights in the front yards of southern and midwestern private homes.

The decrease in drilling activity world-wide adversely affected the oil and gas field machinery industry. Smaller support machinery businesses that thrived in the early 1980s either went out of business or were bought out and became a division of a parent company. By the 1990s, the organization and structure of this industry primarily consisted of very large, well-diversified companies. For example, the only remaining wholly owned domestic manufacturer of oil field pumping units was Lufkin Industries, which was ranked twelfth in the industry (by dollar sales) by Ward's Business Directory of U.S. Private and Public Companies. Lufkin accomplished this through purchasing the inventory of its only domestic competitor, American Industries, when American closed its doors in the summer of 1992. Having cornered this market, Lufkin continued to realize low sales volumes and reduced capacity in this segment of its business.

BACKGROUND AND DEVELOPMENT

In the United States, oil drilling evolved as a result of seeking salt brine. Without refrigeration, one of the few means of preserving meat was through packing it with salt. Therefore, salt brine was a heavily demanded commodity. In 1806 two brothers, David and Joseph Ruffner, established a business supplying settlers near Charleston, West Virginia, with salt brine. Quickly, the demand for the salt became so great that the brothers devised a way to drill a hole to intercept the flow of the brine seepage. This well, responsible for developing the spring pole and drilling line, was the first well drilled in America with tools. From this point, other types of wells were drilled in the Ruffner fashion. In 1814 near Burkesville, Kentucky, was drilled the "American Well," which was 475 feet deep and supposedly produced 1,000 barrels of oil per day.

The invention of the steam engine in tandem with cable tools changed the nature of oil and gas drilling from 1860 to 1930. During this time, crude oil was gaining favor as an illuminant, replacing whale oil used for lamps. Also, the use of machinery to aid man's endeavors was more widely spread, and crude oil was known to be an excellent lubricant. Its use as a fuel was gaining popularity too. These three developments created a demand for oil drilling; thus the industry gained momentum. The first well drilled in America strictly for oil production to supply the machinery industry was the Drake well. Following the Drake well, patent applications were filed in abundance for a wide assortment of tools, rigs, and machines to support oil drilling activities. Among these patents were predecessors to common modern oil industry machinery, including rolling cutter rock bits, an offshore drilling rig, and rotary and percussion motion devices.

From this point, the oil boom was upon the world. An oil field in Corsicana, Texas, was the first well to catapult the blooming industry into the powerful economic prominence it holds today. In this oil field, the Lucas Spindletop well "blew" January 10, 1901. Once it was contained, it produced approximately 75,000 to 80,000 barrels per day. Exploratory drilling in the Gulf Coastal Plain areas of Texas and Louisiana became commonplace and produced abundant supplies of oil. Likewise, oil fields in California and the midwestern plain states were cropping up.

It was not until the 1930s that the oil drilling really became a science. Although the American Petroleum Institute organized its first equipment standardization committee in 1925, the industry did not really become specialized for another five to ten years. Before the 1930s, the parts of an oil drilling rig were made for other machines. While these makeshift rigs were practical and effective enough to achieve the purpose intended, vast improvements were necessary to efficiently produce oil with less waste. Mechanical engineers and petroleum engineers started designing oil field machinery and tools. From these efforts the following were created: better tooth and ball bearing designs of rock bits, roller bearing enclosed engines, automatic controls for steam generating plants, and gas engine electric generator sets with motors. Also, drilling rig personnel were becoming more educated about their profession and safety practices.

Basically, the same principles are employed today as in the past. Aside from the demise of oil derricks which have given way to pumping units, and the offshore drilling methods used along the coast lines, the industry has not radically changed since its inception. The oil drilling industry can be summarized as an evolution of improved techniques, which will continue as long as oil lies beneath the earth's surface.

CURRENT CONDITIONS

Standard & Poor's March 1993 *Industry Survey* reported that crude oil prices were expected to maintain the downward trend throughout the rest of the 1990s at a rate of two percent to four percent. This was due to current production levels being higher than worldwide demand levels. Historical data showed U.S. light sweet crude oil prices fluctuated between $25 and $30 per barrel during 1983 and 1985. Suddenly, prices plummeted to record low levels in 1986, with a barrel

of oil commanding between six and ten dollars. Prices crept back up, only to fall again in 1988. Once the Persian Gulf War started, U.S. light sweet crude prices jumped from about $13 per barrel to over $35 at the end of 1990, only to plummet again to the pre-war price range by the end of first quarter 1991. The first quarter of 1993 did not lend any comfort to oil investors, as oil prices continued the downward trend started in the second half of 1992.

As a result of the oil prices, the oil drilling industry was expected to continue its downward trend as long as oil prices remained lower than the cost of drilling. With no chance of profits on the horizon, the entire oil field machinery industry was depressed. This phenomenon might have been difficult for the average consumer to understand, as gasoline prices had not reflected sharp decreases in the price for a barrel of oil. The "pass the buck" policy was imposed at the gasoline pump, for any motorist who filled his or her tank was helping oil refineries pay for the costs of being a good environmentally-minded neighbor. Environmental regulations would continue to grow stiffer, as the Clinton Administration embraced environmental policies. This added cost of doing business threatened many oil producers and transporters while barrel prices remained low. The profit margins would continue to diminish as long as added Environmental Protection Agency regulations were imposed. According to Standard & Poor's, "Oil companies are finding it cheaper to import refined products than to manufacture those same products in the United States. The major oil refiners, for example, are adding to their refining capacity in the Pacific Rim, where environmental regulations are more hospitable."

Baker Hughes, an oil field machinery manufacturer, reported the domestic rig count at the end of 1992 was 935 working units. This is a 15 percent increase from the year before. Standard & Poor's attributes this to the warmer winter, but colder-than-normal spring temperatures compounded with the offshore drilling devastation caused by Hurricane Andrew created an extremely volatile oil price base. The second reason was that Congress passed laws ending special tax credits for those drilling in what are considered unconventional natural gas fields. These credits were created to encourage drilling through subsidizing the activity. Before the laws went into effect, the drillers stepped up production to take every last possible drop before taxes were imposed. This added to the volatility of oil prices in 1992.

Cleaner burning gasolines and policies such as the BTU (British thermal unit) tax were gaining support in the early 1990s in efforts to simultaneously purify the environment and eradicate the national debt. Gasoline producers were facing a reformulation of their product that included higher amounts of oxygenates in response to the Clean Air Act Amendments. This would help reduce smog, while increasing the efficiency of automobile engines. The effects of this reformulation would be seen by the consumer at the gasoline pump. The Btu tax, or some similar energy tax which would tax consumers' usage of oil, oil products, natural gas, and coal, was expected to be passed by Congress in 1993. An increase in utility bills could encourage consumers to practice conservation, decreasing the demand for those mentioned taxable products.

INDUSTRY LEADERS

In 1991 the top five companies in terms of sales were Dresser Industries, Baker Hughes, Cameron Iron Works, Otis Engineering, and Vetco Gray. Of the 75 leading companies listed in this directory, nearly 63 percent of the top manufacturers of oil field machinery resided in Texas. Only Dresser Industries and Baker Hughes reported sales in the billions, $3.9 billion and $2.3 billion respectively, while the others reported sales in the millions.

The parent company of Cameron Iron Works was Cooper Industries, based in Houston, Texas. Cooper, owning over 60 companies and product lines including Champion Spark Plug and McGraw-Edison, reported revenues of $6.2 billion. Thirty-three percent of Cooper Industry's 1991 operating revenues came from petroleum and industrial equipment.

Lufkin Industries opened its doors in December 1902 as Lufkin Foundry and Machine Company (LFMC) to meet the need for boiler and sawmill repair in east Texas. Within a few years, the company branched into the design, manufacture, and repair of sawmill equipment. By 1920, oil was a major industry in Texas and LFMC headed in a new direction. The original design of the standard oil rig lent itself to frequent breakdowns and was very undependable. This presented an opportunity for LFMC to redesign the rig and corner the pumping unit market. Meeting this challenge, LFMC radically altered the shape and function of the standard oil rig by designing the first enclosed gear, crank-balanced oil well pumping unit. This first unit was put into service during the winter of 1923 on a Humble Oil Company well at Goose Creek, Texas. In just a short time the company was acknowledged as a world leader in the production of oil field pumping units.

In 1991 Lufkin's total company sales climbed to $193 million. Perhaps the most noticeable achievement of the year was the expansion of Lufkin's inter-

national market, primarily in Russia, for oil field pumping units. Soon, over 66 percent of the company's pumping unit shipments were sent to locations outside the United States. In 1993, although U.S. drilling activity was at an all-time low, the opportunity for growth in the international arena remained strong. The company became the dominant domestic manufacturer of oil field pumping units when it purchased its only remaining direct competitors: GEO Churchill in 1991 and American Industries in 1992. However, in May 1993, the closing of GEO Churchill was announced due to low business levels and under-utilized capacity at the Texas facilities. During the same week, another local Lufkin facility's closing was announced, with the intent to consolidate the two fabrication facilities into one also due to low business levels.

WORK FORCE

Between 1982 and 1987, nearly half of the establishments in this industry either went out of business or were consumed by larger companies. In 1982 industry shipments were in excess of nine billion dollars, dropping to a decade low below three billion dollars in 1987. This figure steadily improved to four billion dollars by the end of 1991. The employment statistics showed similar movement compared to the shipments. In 1982, the industry employed over 90,000 people. By 1987 this figure had fallen to under 25,000 employees. Between 1987 and 1991, the employment level improved slightly, although the trend remained fairly flat. Wages increased steadily from 1987 to 1991, with the industry average pay being $13.12 per hour. This industry paid approximately 27 percent higher wages than the average for all other manufacturing, which paid approximately $10.66 per hour.

The industry was primarily composed of blue collar workers, namely welders, assemblers, machin-

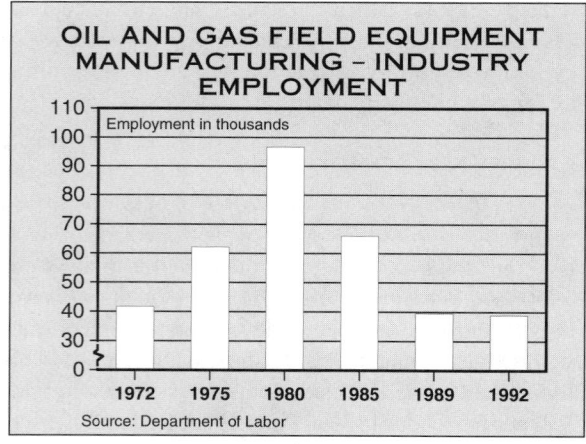

OIL AND GAS FIELD EQUIPMENT MANUFACTURING – INDUSTRY EMPLOYMENT

Employment in thousands

Source: Department of Labor

ists, and machine builders. Mechanical engineers held a prominent position in the industry, and accounted for 2.4 percent of the total work force. This figure was expected to grow by 9.5 percent by 2000. The hottest occupations in the industry were sales, industrial production managers, and industrial machinery mechanics each expected to grow by over 15 percent by 2000. The occupations expected to decrease more than ten percent from present levels were welders/cutters, assemblers, welding machine setters, machine builders, secretaries, inspectors, and material handlers.

As of 1987, 65.7 percent of the industry's employees were based in Texas, averaging $13.47 per hour. In Oklahoma, 13.3 percent of the industry's employees reside, with average earnings of $12.57. New Mexico, with 0.8 percent of the industry work force, offered an average of $15.00 per hour, the highest reported in the industry.

AMERICA AND THE WORLD

The influence of the OPEC nations cannot be ignored, because the cartel plays a huge role in the world economy. At no time was this more evident than during the Persian Gulf War of 1990-1991, when the absence of Iraqi and Kuwati oil sent the world economy reeling. These two countries accounted for 6.5 percent of the world supply of oil. The countries involved in OPEC are Saudi Arabia, Iran, Kuwait, Iraq, and Venezuela.

Another world region in limbo was the former Soviet Union, the world's largest oil producer. It has been asserted that this area sits upon a large lake of oil, compared to the small pond beneath the Middle East. Chevron signed a deal to develop the Tenghiz field near the Caspian Sea in Kazakhstan. The field was first measured with inaccurate Soviet tools, which showed the field to contain 4.5 billion barrels of oil. Chevron intended to remeasure the field, and anticipated a value of possibly ten times the original estimate. Additionally, several tracts in the former Soviet Union had not been explored. The economic turmoil in this fragmenting giant was vitally linked to the production of oil; the doom of one would surely result in the doom of the other. In Russia, oil was the only commercial product. Russia's economic survival was dependent on its oil production, and a total collapse would be felt all over the world. Yet, the former Soviets realized the health of their economy was totally dependent on the export of oil for foreign currency. In 1993, the total oil production was expected to fall to eight million barrels per day, in contrast to 10.5 million and nine million barrels per day in 1991 and 1992, respectively.

The European Community (EC) was another area of concern, mainly because the monetary system was not standardized, with no definite time-frame for standardization established. Europe both produced and consumed much of the world's oil, thereby making it of concern world-wide. While the EC was stable politically, compared with the Middle East and Russia, the monetary/commercial situation was not. As of January 1, 1993, commerce was united with regulations imposed on banking, airline, transportation, food, taxes, and certain utility industries. According to Standard & Poor's, ''The problem with the EC commercial union and its dealings with oil is that oil is bought in dollars and refined products are sold in each country's local currency. Thus, currency volatility exacerbates the erratic nature of crude oil prices.'' It was believed that once European currencies were unified, the oil industry and its price structure would stabilize. This, in turn, would increase capital investment.

The Pacific Rim was an economically expanding area, due to the growth of manufacturing related industry. Heavy manufacturing required oil-related products to run the machines used in the business, increasing the demand for oil. It was expected that Singapore's and Japan's refining and distribution centers would expand, as industrialization efforts continued.

RESEARCH AND TECHNOLOGY

With limited resources for capital investment, research and development in oil related industries was limited. However, as competition increases the need to cut unnecessary costs and produce oil more efficiently would continue to be the top priority. Therefore, the major oil companies who produced the product would apply pressure to the machinery and equipment manufacturers to produce more efficiently operating products. Although the method of drawing oil from the ground had not changed significantly in theory or principle over time, the design of higher performance drilling rigs had. For example, Lufkin Industries bought a patent allowing them to produce a windmill pumping unit. The unit operated on the same principle as an ordinary windmill used to pump water from the ground. The advantage of this unit is that across the plains of Texas, Oklahoma, and Kansas, where the wind never seems to stop blowing, a constant source of power is available free of charge. By reducing the production costs, this type of innovation could encourage domestic drilling activity. Meanwhile, the search continued for alternative fuel sources. If significant breakthroughs were found, and allowed to be marketed by the oil industry lobbyists, the demand for oil and its related products would continue to decrease. However, if the amount of oil in the former Soviet Union is as large as anticipated, the push for alternative fuels may subside until the resources have been completely exhausted.

INDUSTRY INFORMATION SOURCES

Brantly, J.E. *History of Oil Well Drilling.* Houston: Gulf Publishing Company, 1971.

Darnay, Arsen J., ed. *Manufacturing USA: Industry Analyses, Statistics, and Leading Companies.* Detroit: Gale Research, 1989.

Graves, Edward. "Oil: Changes and Challenges for Clinton." *Standard & Poor's Industry Surveys,* March 4, 1993.

Hayes, Thomas C. "Cooper Industries is Looking for a New Conquest." *New York Times,* June 9, 1992.

McCann, J. "Global Capital Goods Group—Industry Report." *Merrill Lynch Capital Markets,* March 4, 1993.

McGinty, J. E. "Cooper Industries Inc. Company Report," *The First Boston Corporation,* February 5, 1993.

—Valerie E. Wilson

SIC 3534

ELEVATORS AND MOVING STAIRWAYS

This classification comprises establishments primarily engaged in manufacturing passenger or freight elevators, automobile lifts, dumbwaiters, and moving stairways. Establishments primarily involved in manufacturing commercial conveyor systems and equipment are classified in **SIC 3535: Conveyors and Conveying Equipment,** and those manufacturing farm elevators are classified in **SIC 3523: Farm Machinery and Equipment.**

INDUSTRY SNAPSHOT

The elevator and moving stairway industry manufactured a series of products designed for the vertical transportation of both materials and passengers. The various types of machinery manufactured for the exclusive purpose of moving materials, such as freight elevators and automobile lifts, comprised a small niche of the wide-ranging materials handling market. While the industry produced a variety of products that served this capacity, it generated the majority of its revenues from manufacturing passenger elevators and escalators, as well as from producing parts required for elevator renovation and modernization.

In 1991, 175 establishments were engaged in manufacturing elevators and moving stairways, gener-

ating over $1.8 billion in shipments. Elevators and moving stairways accounted for roughly 75 percent of total shipments, while parts and attachments produced for separate sale comprised 18 percent of this figure. Electric and hydraulic passenger elevators, which combined for roughly 45 percent of the industry's total shipments, were the largest product groups within the industry. Automobile lifts, which comprised 10 percent of the total figure, were the next largest group, followed by freight elevators, other types of non-farm elevators, and moving stairways and escalators, which each accounted for less than 6 percent of total shipments.

ORGANIZATION AND STRUCTURE

Establishments in the elevator and moving stairway industry employed an average of 57 people, approximately 3 less than the average for all establishments producing construction and related machinery. Of the 175 establishments operating in 1991, 55 percent employed less than 20 workers. However, 69 percent of all employees in the industry were concentrated in establishments employing more than 100 people. While several of the industry's leading companies were subsidiaries of public companies, 31 of the 49 companies generating the highest revenues in the 1990s were privately owned.

Establishments engaged in the production of elevators and moving stairways could be found throughout the United States, with the greatest concentration of employees being located in the East. New York posted the greatest concentration of any state with 20 locations and 765 total employees, and the three-state region that also included Pennsylvania and New Jersey operated 24 percent of all establishments and employed 18 percent of the industry's total work force. Other strong contingencies of elevator and escalator producers could be found in Ohio, Illinois, Michigan, and California.

In 1991, this industry as a whole spent over $712 million on raw materials, which translated to about $4 million per establishment, roughly 12 percent below the average for all construction and related machinery establishments. New capital expenditures, at $28.5 million for the industry as a whole, or roughly $163,000 per establishment, also fell well below the larger industry group average of $230,000 per establishment.

BACKGROUND AND DEVELOPMENT

The genesis and evolution of the elevator industry closely paralleled the historical development of the Otis Elevator Company. The company was founded by

Elisha Otis, the inventor of the first "safe" hoist, a technological development that generated public confidence in the elevator for the first time and laid the foundation for the elaborate vertical transportation systems of the twentieth century. An innovative advertiser as well as a skillful engineer, Otis brought his new invention to the Crystal Palace Exposition in New York City in 1854. During the middle of his demonstration, Otis stunned the crowd by cutting the rope that held up the hoist platform on which he stood, only to be kept securely in place by the release of the wagon spring safety mechanism he had invented. While Otis himself died before he was able to realize the financial rewards of his inventions, the company he founded reached the $1 million mark in sales in 1870 through the leadership of his sons, Charles and Norton.

As technology made the construction of taller buildings possible, the Otis-dominated elevator industry kept pace with developments of its own, introducing the hydraulic elevator in 1878, the electric elevator in 1889, and the gearless traction electric elevator in 1903. These innovations would later become the backbone of the industry, enabling passengers to be transported safely at greater speeds and to greater heights in buildings such as the 102-floor Empire State Building and the 110-floor World Trade Center.

As the volume of passengers and the number of taller buildings increased, the need arose for federal safety codes regulating the industry. In 1922, the American standard safety requirements for elevators were established, codifying the informal laws that had previously governed the industry. By keeping such concerns at the forefront, the industry was able to maintain an excellent record of safety, strengthening consumer confidence and paving the way for the public acceptance of new technologies in future years.

As elevator speeds reached 700 feet per minute, the need for an automated control system became more evident. Consequently, in 1924 Otis developed the Signal Control System, which took the guesswork away from the operator by automatically slowing down the elevator as passengers on various floors pushed call buttons. The system was further refined with the invention of Peak Period Control, a control device which automated the job of the elevator starter, further increasing efficiency.

The widespread use of electronics in World War II ushered in a new era of technological advance in the elevator industry. In addition to providing improvements in safety devices, such as the development of a sensor that automatically returned the elevator doors to the open position when a person occupied the doorway, electronics technology finally eliminated the need for elevator operators and starters. With Otis's development and refinement of Autotronics, a system that electronically controlled when elevator doors should be opened and closed, most commercial elevators were fully automated by the mid-1950s.

The next two decades were marked by continued refinement of the automatic control systems developed in the 1950s. By 1970, for instance, solid state circuitry, which contained hundreds of printed circuit boards per system, was applied to the elevator industry. This innovation significantly reduced the size and weight of the control system, while improving its reliability and ease of maintenance in comparison to earlier models. New methods of production were introduced as well, such as the concept of the pre-engineered elevator, which brought forth the mass production of uniformly designed elevators. This manufacturing philosophy not only lowered production costs, but, by providing the architect with the exact hoistway dimensions and other elevator specifications, eliminated much of the arduous work required in designing elevators to fit individual construction projects. Such innovations enabled the industry to surpass the $1 billion mark in shipments by 1982, more than twice the total of a decade earlier.

As the 1980s progressed, however, the pattern of growth characteristic of earlier years was not sustained. An increased demand for escalators in shopping malls and other public building throughout the country was not enough to overcome the slowdown in the elevator market, a direct result of the severe decline in multi-story building. At the close of 1991, total shipments of $1.18 billion were recorded, reflecting only a 5 percent increase over the previous 10 years. In a similar fashion, new capital expenditures fell from $31.2 million to $16.3 million, nearly a 48 percent decline.

CURRENT CONDITIONS

In an attempt to combat the recessive economic conditions of the early 1990s, the elevator industry attempted to fill the void in large new elevator contracts by shifting its attention to the renovation and modernization of models installed 20 or more years ago. By replacing older modelled control panels with solid state machinery and computer technology, the elevator industry hoped to survive the effects of the glutted real estate market. Elevator manufacturers also looked to take advantage of the new opportunities for renovation made available by legislation passed during the early 1990s requiring that elevators be updated to provide greater handicapped accessibility in public and private buildings.

The entrance of modern technology into the elevator industry also fostered greater competition between major contractors who were also engaged in manufacturing new elevators, and smaller independent firms who derived their business exclusively from the service market. In an effort to guarantee future service and renovation contracts on the elevators they manufactured, many of the larger companies in the industry attempted to guard the technical data governing their elevators so that outside contractors lacking proper access codes would be unable to service their product. Although this form of proprietization was frowned upon by governing organizations such as the National Association of Elevator Contractors (NAEC), the small profit margin on new elevators—roughly 5 percent according to industry leaders—encouraged companies to protect their large capital investments in this manner.

While the future of the industry largely depended on the condition of the real estate and construction markets, it would also be influenced by firms' ability to sell clients on new technological developments, particularly those implementing the use of computerized control systems, which promised to revolutionize the industry in the 1990s. With the advent of various types of new computer technology, the future of the industry would largely be determined by the ability of elevator manufacturers to convince consumers that extensive modernization projects were indeed necessary. Without the support of a strong U.S. economy in the future, it appeared doubtful that such expenses would be justified by companies attempting to cut costs wherever they could.

INDUSTRY LEADERS

As was the case from the inception of the vertical transportation industry, Otis Elevator Company was the world's leader in manufacturing and servicing elevators and escalators. A wholly owned subsidiary of United Technologies Corporation since 1976, Otis employed 47,500 people while generating annual sales of $5.3 billion in the early 1990s, over twice that of its nearest competitor, Dover Corporation. While the domestic market for new elevators faltered, Otis extended its long-held interest in foreign markets, investing in new partnerships with companies in China, Vietnam, Poland, Czechoslovakia, and Russia in the early 1990s. The largest of its international operations were found in its Paris division, which was responsible for 53 percent of Otis's total sales in 1991.

Otis's continued success in the market could also be attributed to its ongoing commitment to research and development. Investing more than $1 billion in a system-level redesign of its products, the company replaced its electromechanical systems with third-generation solid-state controls. Otis renovated and modernized products made by other companies as well as its own, servicing over 730,000 elevators worldwide, an increase of over 250,000 in the last decade. With promising new developments in the mid-1990s, such as its "fuzzy" logic computer control system, which promised to improve the efficiency of elevators throughout the world, Otis was expected to maintain its position at the top of the industry.

Otis's major domestic competitor was New York based Dover, which generated annual sales of over $2.2 billion in the early 1990s while employing 18,800 people. It was the largest producer of new elevators in the United States, the second-largest in Canada, and the third-largest in the United Kingdom. Other leading companies included Schindler Elevator Corporation, located in Morristown, New Jersey, which achieved annual sales of $910 million with 8,500 employees; and Montgomery Elevator Company, based in Moline, Illinois, which posted sales of $710 million with 6,300 employees.

WORK FORCE

Total employment in the elevator and escalator industry encountered a period of gradual decline in the early and mid-1980s. After reaching a decade high of 13,000 total employees in 1982, employment figures declined to 10,200 in 1987. This pattern of slow decrease continued into the early 1990s, culminating in the 1991 figure of 8,900, a 31.5 percent decline from 1982.

Of the 8,900 employed by the industry in 1991, 5,800 were production workers, while the remaining 3,100 held technical, managerial, or administrative positions. Both white- and blue-collar workers suffered from the general decline of the industry during the mid and late-1980s. White-collar workers faced a greater rate of attrition, losing 41.5 percent of its work force between 1982 and 1991, while blue-collar positions were reduced by only 25 percent during the same period.

Most likely to be employed on a full-time basis, the average production employee in the elevator and moving stairway industry worked roughly 41 hours a week—about 5 percent more than the average for all production workers employed in the larger industrial machinery and equipment manufacturing industry. Production workers in the elevator and moving stairway industry received roughly the same wages as those employed in the larger industry group, averaging $12.74 an hour. White-collar workers, however, employed at an average annual salary of $36,968, acquired wages roughly 6 percent below the average for related industrial machinery fields.

As elevator and moving stairway establishments continued to downsize their work forces to accommodate the shift towards modernization and renovation and away from the manufacturing of new units, the education requirements for working in the industry promised to change as well. As evidenced by the NAEC's early campaign to improve the training of field personnel and recruit more people with computer experience, the introduction of more sophisticated computerized technology into the industry demanded a larger percentage of workers with a strong college or trade school background in computers.

RESEARCH AND TECHNOLOGY

While the Japanese centered their efforts on the production of faster elevators during the 1990s, U.S. companies focused on making them run ''smarter,'' or more efficiently, in relation to the needs of their patrons. One of the most promising developments in domestic elevator technology came in Otis's introduction of a new type of computer software that used what was known as ''fuzzy logic'' to decide upon the best way to accommodate the various traffic needs of a modern office building. This type of artificial intelligence software distinguished itself from the standard computer logic governing conventional modern elevators by its ability to process uncertainties of information more efficiently. Rather than simply sending the closest elevator when a patron signalled, fuzzy logic took into account the number of people waiting for elevators throughout the building, hoping to avoid the common problem of sending an elevator to service one individual at the expense of several left waiting somewhere else. While Otis's innovative system, first installed in Japan in 1993, encountered some problems, it held great potential for the future of the industry. Otis hoped to improve its product with the addition of neural network technology, a computer system that could be taught to learn from its mistakes, and usher the elevator industry into a new technological era by the end of the century.

INDUSTRY INFORMATION SOURCES

Alborghetti, Marci, ''UTC Divisions Rise to Occasion,'' *Connecticut Post,* December 10, 1993.

Anderson, Paul, editor, *Tell Me About Elevators,* Farmington, Connecticut: Otis Elevator Company, 1978.

Annual Survey of Manufactures, Washington, D.C.: U.S. Department of Commerce, 1991.

Census of Manufactures, Washington, D.C.: U.S. Department of Commerce, 1987.

Chartrand, Sabra, ''Computer Software from Otis Uses Fuzzy Logic to Make Elevators Smarter and More Efficient,'' *New York Times,* September 13, 1993.

County Business Patterns, Washington, D.C.: U.S. Department of Commerce, 1991.

Darnay, Arsen J., editor, *Manufacturing USA,* Detroit: Gale Research, 1992.

Edgar, Susan E., editor, *Ward's Business Directory of U.S. Private and Public Companies,* Detroit: Gale Research, 1994.

Hast, Adele, editor, *International Directory of Company Histories,* Chicago: St. James Press, 1994.

McManamy, Rob, ''Contractors Rise on Modernizations,'' *Engineering News Record,* July 26, 1990.

''Otis Seizes the High Ground,'' *International Management,* November 1992.

Patton, Robert, ''Mag Lift: Japan's Engineers Push the Envelope for Elevators,'' *Scientific American,* October 1993.

Philpot, Jerry, ''Escalators into the Deep,'' *Mass Transit,* April 1992.

Pinder, Jeanne B., ''Fuzzy Thinking Has Merits When It Comes to Elevators,'' *New York Times,* September 22, 1993.

Pollack, Andrew, ''Fastest, Maybe Smoothest, Trip Up,'' *New York Times,* September 22, 1993.

Umlauf, Elyse, ''Control Logic Makes Elevators 'Smarter,''' *Building Design and Construction,* May 1992.

—Jason Gallman

SIC 3535

CONVEYORS AND CONVEYING EQUIPMENT

This category covers establishments primarily engaged in manufacturing conveyors and conveying equipment for installation in factories, warehouses, mines, and other industrial and commercial establishments. Establishments primarily engaged in manufacturing farm elevators and conveyors are classified in **SIC 3523: Farm Machinery and Equipment;** those manufacturing passenger or freight elevators, dumbwaiters, and moving stairways are classified in **SIC 3534: Elevators and Moving Stairways;** and those manufacturing overhead traveling cranes and monorail systems are classified in **SIC 3536: Overhead Traveling Cranes, Hoists, and Monorail Systems.**

INDUSTRY SNAPSHOT

Conveying systems have been an integral part of mining operations for nearly a century, but manufacturing industries have also become dependent on them. Regulations mandated by the Occupational Safety and Hazard Administration have limited human exposure to certain harmful materials, requiring more extensive machine automation. With increased automation, conveying systems become an absolutely necessary part of operating a manufacturing plant.

Global competition has forced business owners to look for ways to cut costs and improve productivity. In industrial firms, one way to reach this goal is to automate some processes in the production activities. While this varies for the type of business and to what degree the production processes are repeatable, most manufacturing firms have looked at material handling systems as a possible answer. It is for these reasons material handling systems manufacturers have experienced considerable growth during the profit-driven 1980s, and the cost-cutting 1990s.

However, as with most mining and manufacturing support industries, builders of conveyors and conveying equipment are limited to industry-related economic cycles. The installation of non-value added equipment is heavily scrutinized by senior management officials, who are directly accountable to stockholders. Such investment is often viewed as an unnecessary expense, especially when the company's financial health is in question. Therefore, the conveying system industry is reliant on a company's willingness to invest in itself.

ORGANIZATION AND STRUCTURE

The conveying system industry is highly specialized, and therefore almost totally self-contained. While the industry relies heavily on suppliers for many of the materials consumed, the design of the systems and their assembly is usually performed at one facility. Armed with design engineers and production facilities, the industry is capable of meeting individual material movement challenges in industries ranging from mining, to heavy manufacturing, to the airline industry. Standard equipment is produced in the pre-engineered sector of the industry.

Over 50 percent of the manufactured products in this industry are dedicated to unit handling conveyors and conveying systems, with nearly four percent dedicated to these systems' parts, attachments, and accessories. Another 25 percent of the product share is dedicated to bulk material handling conveyors and conveying systems, with nearly another ten percent dedicated to these systems' parts, attachments, and accessories. The remainder of the industry is non-specific to any particular type of conveying system.

BACKGROUND AND DEVELOPMENT

The first conveying systems were developed to draw water from wells in the ground. This method was used in various applications over the centuries, but conveying systems really gained importance through the mining industry. In the beginning of the mining industry, mine cars were used as buckets to haul coal or other ores to the earth's surface. Mine cars have been replaced with continuous conveying systems such as belt conveyors, steel-apron conveyors, and chain-conveyors, which are used to haul as much as 5,000 tons per hour on lower grade slopes, and 1,300 tons per hour in high angle conditions. Since wages account for most of the production costs in the mining industry, mechanization was necessary. Likewise, as the government began to regulate worker safety and workman's compensation claims, the initial expense of installing a mechanized system seemed like a good investment because the systems could minimize workers' contact with hazardous materials and reduce workers' physical strain.

Although mining has long been the greatest force in the conveying system industry, the growing presence of production lines since Henry Ford's development of the assembly line has expanded the industry. The industry expansion brought new challenges. As machines were created to perform at higher capacities, the conveying systems delivering the materials to the machines have had to meet these capacities. For example, in some beverage industries today, conveying systems are required to maintain a flow of up to 1600 units per minute.

CURRENT CONDITIONS

The world recession of the late 1980s and early 1990s affected the mining industry significantly. In countries where commodities prices have fallen, some mining operations ceased due to production costs exceeding the market value of the extracted raw materials. Naturally, capital expenditures in this area have fallen, with investment in conveying systems being an unjustifiable expenditure.

As one component of the greater material handling industry, conveyers found new importance in the Flexible Manufacturing Systems (FMS) methodology during the 1980s. However, as this theoretical approach was moving in one direction, manufacturers were concentrating more on productivity in terms of cost reduction. The installation of FMS was often cost prohibitive and limiting to companies reliant on reacting quickly to changing market needs. Yet in terms of lowering costs through increased quality and efficiency to increase profitability, the material handling improvements through FMS were justifiable costs. Companies with existing conveying systems that wished to increase productivity through improved material handling techniques provided a market for the retrofitting segment. Manufacturing industries, particularly where machining is a large portion of value-added production, employ palletization work-holding principles in everyday operations. These principles transfer materials from one machining center to another on the same work-holding device, eliminating setup time.

INDUSTRY LEADERS

The top five companies, in terms of 1991 sales, were Interlake Corporation, with $913 million in sales and 7,100 employees, Litton Industrial Automation, with sales of $730 million and 3,500 employees, Jervis B. Webb Company Incorporated, with sales of $350 million 2,500 employees, Smith International Incorporated, with $312 million in sales and 2,900 employees, and Fuller Company, with $164 million in sales and 1,000 employees. The top 75 companies had combined total sales of $4.792 billion, and employed 35,700 people.

The Litton Conveyor Systems Operations plant is the primary engineering and manufacturing facility for Litton Pre-Engineered Products. The products produced at this facility range from single conveyor units to complex multi-million dollar unit handling systems. With Service Centers located in Los Angeles, Dallas, and Atlanta, Litton boasts that over 80 percent of the U.S. market is within an overnight shipment from one of its service centers. Litton's distribution system for pre-engineered products is extensive, with 80 authorized distributors throughout the United States.

Midwest Conveyor Company Incorporated ranked eighth in the industry in 1991 in sales, with $80 million and 400 employees. In March 1993, Midwest announced it had developed a high capacity conveyor system, capable of transporting up to 5000 tons of product per hour. The Matchappel Quick-set Folding Conveyor System is reportedly easy to install and extend, using belts ranging from 1050 to 1600 millimeters wide. It is used in many coal mining and quarrying operations in Australia, including Wambo Mining Corporation Proprietary Limited. Hoping to extend its international markets, Midwest Conveyor is attempting to acquire licensing agreements in Europe and Canada.

Continental Conveyor and Equipment Company ranked ninth in the industry in 1991 in sales, with $70 million and 500 employees. In October 1992, Continental announced it received two significant orders for its High Angle Conveyors (HAC). The first order originated from an underground coal mine in Illinois, with a vertical lift of 104 meters, planning to replace a 590 ton per hour Flexowall system with a 1360 ton per hour HAC. The second order was from a coal company in South Africa with a vertical lift requirement of 13.3 meters; this company requested three 400 ton-per-hour and two 600 ton-per-hour HACs.

WORK FORCE

According to the *Annual Survey of Manufacturers,* employment levels in this industry are dropping as automation increases. In 1982, employment was around 36,000 nationwide. By 1988, this fell to just under 32,000. However, Department of Labor figures indicate that this level of employment has remained steady in recent years.

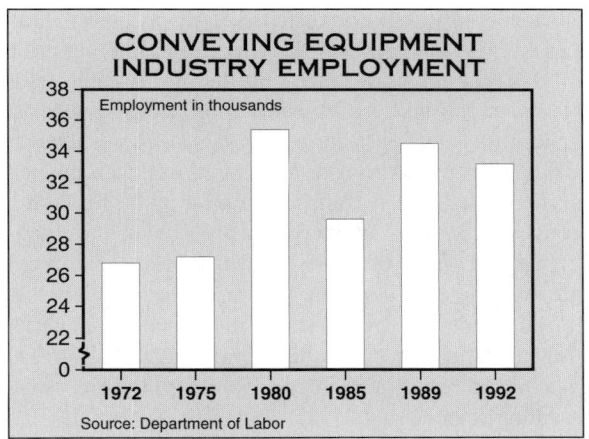

With average earnings of $10.28 per hour in 1988, employees were paid four percent under the average reported by all other forms of manufacturing in the nation. However, workers were spending four percent more time on the job than most other manufacturing workers, which implies overtime compensation was granted.

In terms of employment, the face of the industry is expected to change significantly in some occupations by the year 2000. Those fields expected to encounter employment reductions of ten percent or more include, welders and cutters, assemblers, welding machine setters, machine builders, secretaries, precision inspectors, and material handlers. Other occupations expected to grow at a healthy rate include machinists, sales workers, mechanical engineers, numerically controlled machine tool operators, machinery mechanics, production managers, engineering technicians, combination machine tool operators, and coating/painting machine operators.

AMERICA AND THE WORLD

In mining, the former Soviet Union had not implemented conveying systems until the early 1990s. Rather, inefficient trucks remained the material handling equipment of choice at mining pits and quarries. Demand for conveying technology has increased in response to increased demand for fuel efficiency. Various combinations of dead-end and lateral-field conveyors are being used for maximum fuel efficiency. The ex-Soviets also enjoyed productivity increases of between 11 and 25 percent which were accomplished by implementing a material storage location mid-way through the conveying system. Other benefits enjoyed are increased worker safety by the automated equipment and decreased labor costs.

Conveying systems are used extensively by the Japanese, who have invested heavily in automation. Japan's use of high-tech systems caught the attention of U.S. manufacturers, who by the mid-to-late 1980s started experimenting with new approaches to material handling. One application that has become a buzzword in manufacturing is palletization. In automated systems, material is transported on a pallet through a conveying system. When pallets are designed as workholding devices, personnel and machining resources are maximized and productivity increases. Leaving the machine operator free to set up machines, the material flow is refined because both horizontal and vertical machining centers can interface with palletized workholding devices.

While the economy provides one set of influences on making business decisions, the U.S. government provides another. The Occupational Safety and Health Administration continues to impose regulations concerning worker safety, which often leave automation as the only choice for some production processes. In applications where hazardous waste or dangerous fumes are employed, robotics and automated machining centers are the only solution for meeting government regulations. According to the Robotic Industries Association, 831 new installations of robots for assembly were reported in the United States in 1989, up from 701 in 1988. This figure represents approximately 21 percent of total robot installations.

While the Europeans and Asians do not regulate worker safety to the same degree the United States does, they do investigate ways to increase quality and productivity at minimal costs. The Japanese government provides programs for funding robot application development, education, tax credits, and loans to purchase the equipment.

RESEARCH AND TECHNOLOGY

The food and beverage industries employ conveying systems primarily as a function of labor savings. Speed, reliability, and performance are emphasized as being top priorities of beverage production lines. Production machines are continually being improved to perform at faster rates. However, the production rate of a machine is moot unless the conveyor system can deliver the containers on time. Because bottling companies are demanding higher production rates from their machines, in some cases as much as 1,600 units per minute or more, material handling equipment manufacturers have had to redesign their products to meet the higher speeds. Computerized process flows have made the industry more sophisticated, allowing for variable speed control through ''intelligent'' software that accepts feedback from key points in the system.

Although conveyor manufacturers often specialize in designing and installing specialized conveying systems, some companies choose to build the system with their internal engineering staff, using pre-engineered components. One such company is Richards-Wilcox Manufacturing Company, a builder of file and shelving products. In March 1993, Richards-Wilcox announced that it built a monorail conveyor system, which was proving to be cost effective. The system, called the ZIG-ZAG, is used specifically for heavy components, sometimes weighing as much as a human is allowed to lift by law. The ZIG-ZAG is a continuous loop system that automatically loads and transports the file and shelving components through a final coating process at a rate of 22 feet per minute. At the end of the cycle, the system unloads the components. The system features an overhead transport and assembly system, which saves shop floor space.

Despite the tight world economy, some mining companies have chosen to invest in better conveying systems in light of the potential operational cost-savings. Due to many problems in the early 1970s, Neyveli Lignite Corporation, in India, tried this approach in 1974. As a result Neyveli was very successful through the 1980s. Again faced with problems common to the lignite mining industry, Neyveli announced in 1993 that it had installed a sophisticated system of belt conveyors which operate 24 hours a day. Through this system, Neyveli reported increased production capability, which improved its financial outlook.

Another mining advancement in recent years is Butterley Engineering's Moving Car Bunker system. The system keeps coal mine conveyor belts running at a constant rate through surge control technology. The surge control system is activated when the trunk belt becomes overloaded and coal starts to build up. This is an alternative to conventional design, which build trunk belts to respond to peak tonnage. The bunker is designed with open-bottom storage units, coupled together. These units are capable of hauling as much as 3,000 tons of coal.

INDUSTRY INFORMATION SOURCES

"Bottling for Dollars," *Dairy Foods,* October 1992.

Butkevich, G. R., "Conveyor Transport: A Viewpoint from Russia," *Pit & Quarry,* November 1992.

"Components Conveyed to Smooth Finish with Richards-Wilcox," *Industrial Engineering,* March 1993.

Darnay, Arsen J., ed., *Manufacturing USA: Industry Analyses, Statistics, and Leading Companies,* Detroit: Gale Research, Inc., 1992.

Geppert, Hans, "Palletization: The Best Lesson from the FMS Experiment," *Modern Machine Shop,* May 1992.

"Game, Set, and Matchappel," *World Mining Equipment,* March 1993.

"High Angle News from Continental," *World Mining Equipment,* October 1992.

Horton, Nick, "Conveyor Systems and Their Maintenance," *World Mining Equipment,* October 1992.

Kasturi, T. S., "Progress through Perseverance: The Story of Neyveli Lignite's Conveyor System," *World Mining Equipment,* March 1993.

Leone, Paul, "Merrily They Roll Along," *Beverage World,* December 1992.

Schreiber, Rita R., "Assembly Robots Build Quality," *Manufacturing Engineering,* June 1991.

Swenson, Peter W., "Automated Machining," *Manufacturing Engineering,* December 1990.

—Valerie E. Wilson

SIC 3536

OVERHEAD TRAVELING CRANES, HOISTS, AND MONORAIL SYSTEMS

This classification comprises establishments primarily engaged in manufacturing overhead traveling cranes, hoists, and monorail systems for installation in factories, warehouses, marinas, and other industrial and commercial establishments. Excluded from this classification are establishments primarily engaged in manufacturing cranes except industrial types, automobile wrecker hoists, and aerial work platforms, which are classified in **SIC 3531: Construction Machinery**. Also excluded from this industry are those manufacturing aircraft loading hoists, which are classified in **SIC 3537: Industrial Trucks, Tractors, Trailers, and Stackers**.

INDUSTRY SNAPSHOT

The overhead traveling crane, hoist, and monorail system industry includes a diverse assortment of products that fit within a narrowly defined segment of the materials handling equipment industry. Not to be confused with various types of mobile cranes used in construction projects, overhead cranes are variously structured machines that "travel" along a runway structure or pair of tracks located above the work floor of a plant or factory. They are further characterized by the presence of a fixed or trolley-mounted hoisting system that is connected to the tracks by a bridge structure, which consists of either a single or double girder.

The industry manufactures three basic kinds of overhead traveling cranes that accommodate the vast majority of materials handling needs. The first type is the overhead bridge crane, which is fixed to an overhead beam running the length of the building. Generally regarded as the most rugged of all overhead traveling cranes, this class of crane is noted for its ability to cover the entire width and length of a plant. The jib crane is the second variety of crane produced by the industry. It is usually mounted to a wall or pillar and is used to service a smaller area of a plant, usually the area of a single workstation. Gantry cranes, which are mounted overhead and are able to service a particular bay or workstation, comprise the third category.

While overhead travelling cranes are sometimes operated manually, they are usually powered by electricity and can be interfaced with automatic guided vehicles, stacker cranes, and monorails for increased efficiency. Accordingly, hoists and monorails, the other major segments of this industrial classification, are often manufactured for use in conjunction with overhead traveling cranes. Employed mainly in an industrial capacity, products in this industry are also employed in stone and concrete pre-casting yards, steel fabricating shops, and storage facilities.

According to *County Business Patterns,* 160 establishments, employing over 7,300 people, engaged in the manufacturing of hoists, overhead cranes, and monorail systems in 1991. These companies combined for more than $1.2 billion in industry shipments, according to the *Annual Survey of Manufactures* for the same year, a 20 percent increase from 1990. The manufacturing of overhead traveling cranes and monorail systems accounted for 57 percent of total shipments, while the production of various types of hoists comprised 34 percent. These figures are representative of the industry's growing emphasis on traveling cranes and monorails, which were responsible for only 40 percent of total revenues in 1987.

ORGANIZATION AND STRUCTURE

The average number of employees per establishment in the hoist, crane, and monorail industry is 31 percent higher than the average for all establishments engaged in the manufacturing of industrial machinery and equipment, according to 1991 *County Business Patterns* statistics. While the average establishment employs 46 people, more than half of all employees in the industry work for facilities that are comprised of 100 to 500 people.

Geographically, the greatest concentration of hoist, crane, and monorail manufacturing takes place in the five-state region of Ohio, Michigan, Pennsylvania, Illinois, and Wisconsin, where more than a third of all the industry's establishments are located and 45 percent of its employees work. The 18 establishments in Texas, however, account for the greatest number of establishments located in one state. Ohio, the state employing the most people in the industry, and California each have 17 locations.

As a whole, the industry spent $519 million on raw materials in 1991, which translates to about $3.24 million per establishment, roughly 28 percent below the average for all construction and related machinery manufacturing establishments, according to the *Annual Survey of Manufactures*. New capital expenditures, just over $178,000 per establishment, also fell well below the larger industry group average of $230,000.

BACKGROUND AND DEVELOPMENT

While various types of jib cranes and other lifting devices were installed in foundries during the late 18th century, and the overhead traveling bridge crane existed as early as 1860, materials handling systems were not widely used in the United States until its entrance into World War II in 1941. During the 1940s, however, firms that had previously been hesitant to make the large capital investment necessary for implementing an extensive materials handling system were forced to do so in order to meet the production demands of their war materials contracts. The fact that the implementation of materials handling systems actually lowered production costs in many cases was only a by-product of the more pressing concern of supplying the military with the necessary weaponry and machinery for winning the war.

The new levels of production volume and efficiency demonstrated during the war through the use of materials handling systems led to a phenomenal increase in the use of various types of overhead traveling cranes, hoists, and monorails in the years immediately following the war. Having demonstrated its potential for lowering production costs during the war, materials handling emerged as the most effective tool for offsetting the rising costs of labor and materials. During this period, materials handling research and development efforts evolved into an integral segment of industrial management and engineering education programs as well, legitimizing the discipline of materials handling within both academic and industrial settings.

As technology—especially in the field of electronics—progressed during the 1950s and 1960s, gradual improvements were made in overhead traveling cranes, hoists, and monorail systems, enabling the industry to carve a profitable niche in the larger spectrum of materials handling equipment. As industries were being pressured to increase production while employing the same amount of floor space, equipment that could move materials overhead offered several advantages over its competitors in the broadly defined materials handling industry. While most types of conveyor systems, for instance, occupied a considerable amount of floor space, overhead cranes kept this space free for other production activities. Offering this ergonomic advantage, the hoist, crane, and monorail industry grew into a $500 million a year business by the early 1970s, employing over 16,000 people, according to *Census of Manufactures* statistics.

As the 1970s progressed, the introduction of computer technology revolutionized the field. While the development of solid-state logic had signalled the end of many of the bulky relay-type controls of earlier years in storage-retrieval systems, the same technology could not be applied to complex one-of-a-kind systems without a relatively high capital investment. The widespread availability of microcomputers, however, solved this problem, enabling cranes to be regulated by programmable controllers. Rather than investing tremendous amounts of capital to perform specialized tasks requiring automation, companies were often able to use their existing hardware for a variety of tasks, changing only the computer software to accommodate the desired new function. Largely through the improvements in efficiency engendered by these technological advances, the overhead traveling crane, hoist, and monorail industry more than doubled the value of its annual shipments by the end of the decade, while increasing its production work force by only seven percent.

Although the 1981 passage of the Economic Recovery Tax—which offered incentives to companies that invested in the modernization and expansion of their production facilities—held promise for a strong decade for the materials handling business as a whole, such expectations did not hold true for most segments of the broad industry group. While the conveyor and conveying equipment industry enjoyed steady increases in revenues during the early and mid-1980s, the hoist, crane, and monorail industry lagged behind, suffering nearly a 50 percent decrease in revenue between 1981—the industry's best year of production with over $1.4 billion in shipping—and 1987, according to Census of Manufactures information. The increased use of robotics, the fastest growing segment of the materials handling industry in the 1980s, was partially responsible for this decline. Revenues for the hoist, crane, and monorail industry steadily improved during the late 1980s, however, as the nation's economy grew, enabling businesses to purchase materials handling equipment they had put off buying earlier in the decade.

CURRENT CONDITIONS

The volume of materials handling equipment is generally thought to be closely correlated to the conditions of the U.S. economy as a whole. Accordingly, the recessive conditions of the early 1990s resulted in sluggish patterns of growth for all segments of the materials handling market during this period. Lacking the cash flow to justify new purchases of equipment, most companies relied on their existing machinery to handle their materials handling needs. The hoist, crane, and monorail industry, however, went against this general trend. While shipments for the industry's counterparts in the conveyor and conveying equipment and industrial truck and tractors industries fell five percent and nearly 12 percent, respectively, manufacturers of hoists, cranes, and monorails enjoyed a 20 percent increase in shipments between 1990 and 1991, according to the Annual Survey of Manufactures.

Analysts have exhibited a guarded optimism for the future of both the hoist, crane, and monorail market and the larger materials handling industry. As segments of the U.S. economy crucial to the materials handling market, such as the construction industry, are expected to recover, sales of new equipment are expected to increase. This expected pattern of growth will also be dependent on a continued reduction in the foreign trade deficit for materials handling equipment, which should benefit from the opening up of markets in Eastern Europe for retooling and rebuilding factories. The growth expected from these factors during the mid-1990s, however, may be offset by the fact that many companies made heavy purchases of materials handling equipment in the late 1980s and may not need new equipment until the end of the century. Taking into account these various considerations, an analyst for Manufacturing Automation predicts that the materials handling industry as a whole will boost sales 40 percent by the year 2000. Growth in the hoist, crane, and monorail segment is expected to lag behind the rest of the industry and should reach only 20 percent.

INDUSTRY LEADERS

Various companies have led the hoist, crane, and monorail industry in recent years, demonstrating the parity of this segment of the materials handling industry. Amdura Corporation—formerly known as American Hoist and Derrick—was easily the industry leader in late 1980s, averaging $625 million in sales, according to Ward's Business Directory of U.S. Private and Public Companies 1991. However, faced with severe cash flow problems in the early 1990s, the company disappeared from the list of industry leaders, opening up its market share to a host of both new and experienced competitors.

While long-time producers of materials handling equipment Columbus McKinnon Corporation and JLG Industries Incorporated all raised their sales figures in Amdura's absence, Chatwins Group Incorporated, a privately owned company founded in 1988, took the lead in the early 1990s. Generating an average of $130 million in annual sales between 1990 and 1993, Chatwins edged out Columbus McKinnon and JLG Industries, which registered sales figures of $120 million and $111 million, respectively, according to the 1994 Ward's Business Directory of U.S. Private and Public Companies.

WORK FORCE

Total employment in the hoist, crane, and monorail industry declined sharply in the early and mid-1980s, according to labor statistics compiled in the 1987 Census of Manufactures. After reaching a high of 18,700 in 1981, employment figures steadily declined to 7,900 in 1987. After reporting a slight increase in the last years of the decade, the Annual Survey of Manufactures showed that, by 1991, total employment in the industry had climbed to 8,400. This trend, however, was not sustained, as demonstrated by the

Department of Labor's report for the third quarter of 1993, which showed employment at only 7,400.

Of the total number of people employed by hoist, crane, and monorail establishments in 1991, 5,000 were classified as production workers, while the remaining 3,400 were engaged in technical, managerial, or administrative duties. The pattern of decline in the 1980s proved to be more damaging to the blue-collar work force, which suffered a 62 percent decrease between 1981 and 1987, compared to white-collar positions which were reduced by 48 percent.

For the most part, production workers were employed on a full-time basis in 1991, according to the *Annual Survey of Manufactures*, averaging 39.6 hours a week, just above the 39.1 average for all production workers in the industrial machinery and equipment industry. Averaging $13.45 per hour, production workers in the hoist, crane, and monorail industry earned wages 6 percent higher than their counterparts in the larger industry classification. White-collar workers in the hoist, crane, and monorail industry, however, typically earned 7.6 percent less than others in related industrial machinery fields, averaging an annual salary of $36,559 in 1991.

While the expected recovery of the U.S. economy may signal better times for the materials handling work force as a whole in the later 1990s, blue-collar employment prospects in the hoist, crane, and monorail industry may suffer from the very durability of the products they manufacture. With a life-span of 30 years or more, cranes installed in the 1980s may not need to be replaced until well into the twenty-first century. As they face the need for new materials handling functions, companies in the future are expected to "retrofit," or modernize, their older model equipment to cut costs. Consequently, the strongest employment opportunities in the industry in future years will be found, most likely, in the fields of service and technical support rather than in the production of new units.

RESEARCH AND TECHNOLOGY

For an industry whose fundamental hardware components originated more than a century ago, new developments in product technology have, for the most part, occurred gradually over a number of years as the country's material handling needs have changed. According to Clyde E. Witt, senior editor for *Material Handling Engineering*, "Crane technology has been stimulated through innovative thinking and creative efforts of manufacturers as well as users. Mechanical and technological advances have been a process of evolution, not revolution or major breakthroughs."

This is not to say, however, that significant technological innovations have not been made in this segment of the materials handling industry.

The most significant of these changes in recent years, has occurred, similar to other manufacturing industries, as a result of the development and advancement of solid state logic and computer technology. Whereas overhead traveling cranes of the past were controlled by bulky relay-type systems, models developed since the 1970s are regulated by highly developed solid-state logic and computer regulated control systems. Although older control systems were sufficient for simple storage and retrieval tasks, they were less successful when applied to production functions, which often required the crane to perform a variety of precise movements by several different components. The development of these new forms of technology enabled overhead cranes to perform these complex production tasks more efficiently by reducing the size of control system hardware and improving its flexibility and durability.

In the 1980s and early 1990s, control mechanisms for overhead traveling cranes and other types of equipment within this industrial classification were further refined and modernized to accommodate the changing needs of their users. The major developments in this period have involved the increased efficiency and wider range of applications for automated cranes regulated by programmable controllers or other computers. Such improvements have brought forth the introduction of automated cranes to a wide range of manufacturing environments, servicing locations as varied as an aerospace plant and a textile factory. The widespread acceptance of automated control systems has also facilitated a variety of interfacing applications, linking overhead cranes with other types of materials handling equipment, such as monorails, robots, and automated guided vehicles.

INDUSTRY INFORMATION SOURCES

Annual Survey of Manufactures, Washington, D.C: U.S. Department of Commerce, 1991.

Census of Manufactures, Washington, D.C: U.S. Department of Commerce, 1987.

County Business Patterns, Washington, D.C.: U.S. Department of Commerce, 1991.

"Cranes, Hoists, Winches and Productivity," *Marine Log*, October 1993.

Darnay, Arsen J., ed., *Manufacturing USA*, Detroit: Gale Research Inc., 1993.

Edgar, Susan E., *Ward's Business Directory of U.S. Private and Public Companies 1994*, Detroit: Gale, 1994.

Holzhauer, Ron, "Bridge and Gantry Cranes: Masters of Overhead Handling," *Plant Engineering*, April 13, 1989, 82-89.

"Matching Cranes to Your Handling Needs," *Modern Materials Handling*, July 1987, 76-79.

"New Reports Cite MH Market Trends," *Material Handling Engineering*, September 1983, 13.

Semling, Harold V., "Commerce Predicts Good MH Sales Year," *Material Handling Engineering*, March 1982, 45-46.

Shapiro, Howard I., Jay P. Shapiro, and Lawrence K. Shapiro, *Cranes and Derricks*, New York: McGraw-Hill, 1991.

Totu, A.R., "Guidelines for Overhead Crane Safety," *Plant Engineering*, April 4, 1991, 45-48.

Trade and Employment, Washington, D.C: U.S. Department of Commerce, 1993.

"U.S. Manufactures' Sales of Material Handling Equipment to Top $12 Billion By Year 2000," *Manufacturing Automation*, June 1992.

"What Computers Can Do For Overhead Cranes," *Modern Materials Handling*, May 1977, 60-61.

Witt, Clyde E., "Partnering Gets Lift from Crane Manufacturers," *Material Handling Engineering*, January 1992, 65-67.

—Jason Gallman

SIC 3537

INDUSTRIAL TRUCKS, TRACTORS, TRAILERS, AND STACKERS

This classification comprises establishments primarily engaged in manufacturing industrial trucks, tractors, trailers, stackers (truck type), and related equipment used for handling materials on floors and paved surfaces in and around industrial and commercial plants, depots, docks, airports, and terminals. Excluded from this classification are establishments primarily involved in manufacturing motor vehicles and motor vehicle type trailers, which are classified in **Industry Group 371: Transportation Equipment**, and those manufacturing farm type wheel tractors, which are classified in **SIC 3523: Farm Machinery & Equipment**. Also excluded from this industry are establishments primarily engaged in manufacturing tractor shovel loaders and tracklaying tractors, which are classified in **SIC 3531: Construction Machinery**, and those manufacturing wood pallets and skids, which are classified in **SIC 2448: Wood Pallets & Skids**.

INDUSTRY SNAPSHOT

The industrial truck and tractor industry includes a narrowly defined yet diverse assortment of products that are part of a larger industrial classification commonly known as the material handling equipment industry. Equipment within the smaller industrial truck and tractor category is utilized to move, package, and store both finished products and the raw materials used to manufacture finished products. Accordingly, industrial truck and tractor products are used in nearly every industrial setting, from supermarkets to missile manufacturing installations.

More than 400 companies in the United States were involved in manufacturing industrial trucks and tractors in 1990. These companies generated $2.72 billion in revenues for products included in this classification. This figure represents an aggregate value of shipments largely derived from the production of forklift trucks and other work trucks fitted with lifting or handling equipment machines—the largest product group within the industry. Self-propelled models of these types of machines accounted for 43.8 percent of the industry's total shipments. The other primary product group was comprised of parts and attachments for industrial trucks and tractors, which composed 19 percent of the industry's total shipments. The balance of the industry's shipments consisted of various material handling machinery, such as work trucks and tractors not fitted with lifting or handling equipment, mobile straddle carriers and cranes, and portable elevators and stackers.

ORGANIZATION AND STRUCTURE

The average staff size of establishments in the truck and tractor industry is 15 percent lower than that of all other manufacturing industries. The industry is predominately comprised of establishments employing less than 20 people. Of the 451 establishments in operation in 1989, 193 employed 20 or more workers.

Geographically, the greatest concentration of industrial truck and tractor manufacturing establishments is in the five-state region of Michigan, Wisconsin, Indiana, Ohio, and Illinois, which together operated 139 manufacturing establishments in the early 1990s. Washington, Oregon, and Alaska composed the nation's second most populated industrial truck and tractor industry region, with 74 manufacturing establishments. The 53 establishments in California represented the greatest number of industry businesses located in one state, followed by 44 in Ohio, and 39 in Michigan.

In 1989, the average cost per establishment, that is, the average amount paid for raw manufacturing materials, was 20 percent lower than the average recorded by all other manufacturing industries. A typical firm in the truck and tractor industry spent $3,649,446 on these materials, while firms in all other manufacturing industries spent an average of $4,542,893. Likewise, the average amount spent on manufacturing machinery and production retooling for an industrial truck and tractor establishment was considerably lower than the average recorded by all other manufacturing industries. In 1989, the average investment per establishment in the industrial truck and tractor industry was $117,517, or 40 percent lower than the average of $296,864 spent by firms in all other manufacturing industries.

BACKGROUND AND DEVELOPMENT

America's entrance into World War II in 1941 signaled the beginning of a four-year surge in business activity that defined the future of many U.S. industries. The frenetic pace of production required to support the country's war efforts rejuvenated some industries that had been wallowing in inertia, engendered the genesis of others, and launched many more toward exponentially higher production and sales volumes. For the industrial truck and tractor industry, the dramatically increased demand for manufactured goods created a commensurately heightened demand for material handling equipment; as the country manufactured more products, there was a growing need to move, stack, and store them quickly and efficiently. Consequently, the industrial truck and tractor industry was swept up into the expansion of U.S. industry as a whole, benefiting from the increased business activity enjoyed by the individual companies which it served.

Augmenting this demand from the industry's traditional, industrial customers was a vast government market that opened up during the war, as industrial truck and tractor manufacturers answered the sundry material handling needs of the military itself. The combination of these two factors fostered a rapid growth rate for the industry, amplifying the importance of industrial truck and tractor products in the successful operation of any manufacturing plant or military installation. During this period truck and tractor products enabled manufacturers to approach production and sales volumes proportionate to levels recorded 50 years later, in the 1990s. Though its foundation was established before the war, the industry's modern structure was not fully defined until the 1950s and 1960s, when industrial establishments nationwide were transformed by the trend toward automation.

To be sure, the onset of World War II did not mark the formal beginning of the industrial truck and tractor industry, but the robust growth experienced as a result of the war and the increased applications for the industry's products prompted by the automation of U.S. industry following the war, created an industrial community much more dependent upon the industrial truck and tractor industry for effective operation. These were formative years for the industry, a period during which industrial truck and tractor manufacturing companies began to resemble their descendants much more than their predecessors and began to record production and sales levels that distinguished the industry from other segments within the material handling equipment industry.

During the 1950s and 1960s, when the industrial truck and tractor industry became a measurably distinct segment of the broader, loosely structured material handling equipment industry, accurate measurements of the industry's magnitude could be taken. In the early the 1960s, the sale of industrial trucks and tractors and related products accounted for approximately $389 million of the nearly $1 billion generated by the material handling equipment industry.

The leading manufacturers involved in the industry at this time were primarily publicly-held companies engaged in the manufacture of other products included in the material handling industry, such as conveyor and monorail systems, but derived the majority of their revenue from the sale of industrial truck and tractor equipment, particularly from the sale of forklifts. The largest of these manufacturers, Clark Equipment Co. of Battle Creek, Michigan, posted annual sales of approximately $200 million in the late 1950s and early 1960s, far exceeding the sales volumes of its nearest competitors. These competitors, however, compensated for their more diminutive size by developing industrial truck and tractor equipment for more diverse applications, focusing on manufacturing equipment that increased efficiency in the industrial workplace.

Initially, the pace of the industry's growth was largely determined by the amount other businesses were spending on capital expansion, but by the early 1960s U.S. industry as a whole began to focus on increasing the efficiency of manufacturing facilities. Manufacturers realized that industrial truck and tractor equipment could help them make great strides toward this goal. Decreasing the turning radius of a forklift, for example, allowed a manufacturer to reduce the distance between storage aisles and therefore increase inventory space without realizing any increase in land costs. Accordingly, many manufacturers, both large and small, were developing industrial truck and tractor products during the early 1960s that would eventually become integral components of modern manufacturing establishments.

Despite its relatively unimpressive revenue total of $49 million in 1960, Hyster Co. of Portland, Oregon, was, nevertheless, contributing to the industry's technological advancement by designing prototypes of forklifts that automatically weighed loads to be lifted and adjusted their operating speed accordingly. If a load was light, this sensing system enabled the forklift to operate at a higher speed than was normally achieved by earlier forklifts that operated at set speeds, regardless of load weight. Similar advancements were being made by other manufacturers. For instance, Barrett-Cravens Co.'s "Guide-o-matic" system controlled industrial tractors by a buried wire, enabling them to function without an operator.

The popularity of innovative products such as these fueled the industry's growth during the 1960s, as manufacturers increasingly began to look toward the industrial truck and tractor industry for solutions to problems associated with moving, stacking, and storing their manufactured products, and to aid in their transformation toward automated operation. This represented a significant shift in the nature of the needs that this industry's products filled. Instead of supplying equipment solely to manufacturers expanding the size of their plants, industrial truck and tractor manufacturing companies now could rely on business from companies that were streamlining their operations or automating their production processes.

Along with its move toward manufacturing more sophisticated products and designing complete material handling systems, the industry was enjoying increased demand for its newly developed large steel and aluminum containers. "Containerization," or the utilization of trailer-sized steel and aluminum containers for shipping purposes, was, in the early 1960s, one of the relatively recent innovations developed by the industry to help its customers cut costs. These containers, sometimes referred to as "ambulatory vaults," had been used by an increasing number of manufacturers in the 1950s because they reduced handling costs and allowed for quicker delivery.

Two developments in the early 1960s organized the manufacturing end of container production and ensured that manufacturers could continue to rely on large containers to generate additional business. In early 1961 industry-wide standards were established for the production of containers, specifying that all containers in the future must be 8 feet in width and

height and either 10, 20, or 40 feet in length. Following the establishment of these specifications, the Federal Maritime Board ordered that only ships built to accommodate these new, standardized containers would be eligible for government subsidies or government-insured mortgages.

By the mid-1960s the industry's annual value of shipments had eclipsed $500 million, making it the largest segment within the overall material handling industry. Growth continued to be spurred by the industry's development of innovative products, which persuaded some of its customers to apportion a larger percentage of their capital investment budget toward material handling needs, and others to scrap their existing machinery and invest in more sophisticated equipment. A considerable amount of the industry's growth, however, came through capital expansion programs initiated by its customers. While this presented no problem to industrial truck and tractor manufacturers when economic conditions were particularly favorable, this dependency on the health of the U.S. economy in general made the industry vulnerable to general economic downturns. Despite the industry's efforts aimed at decreasing its reliance on the vagaries of widespread capital expansion, industrial truck and tractor manufacturers still found themselves monitoring the growth of other industries with a wary eye.

By the close of the decade, however, the overall U.S. economy had proven strong enough to support the continued growth of the industrial truck and tractor industry. Revenues for the industry exceeded $1 billion by 1970, representing an average annual growth rate of greater than 11 percent during the previous decade. While no single dramatic technological advancement launched the industry toward higher revenues, each year customer demands were stimulated by new products that incorporated innovative designs and functions.

Over the course of the next several years, as the nation's economy spiraled downward in reaction to a shortage of oil and petroleum products, the industrial truck and tractor industry's performance began to flag. The industrial sector of the U.S. economy operated below capacity throughout the recession, causing the cancellation or postponement of many manufacturers' expansion plans. Because these investments represented a major source of industrial truck and tractor manufacturers' revenues, business faltered, demonstrating the volatility of the industry's market. With the industrial sector of the nation's economy operating at 70 percent of its capacity, the industrial truck and tractor industry's revenues dropped from $1.53 billion in 1974 to $1.30 billion in 1975.

The industry slowly recovered from the losses of the early and mid-1970s, generating revenues of $1.91 billion in 1977. By the end of the decade, however, industry revenues skyrocketed to nearly $3 billion, but this growth masked the emergence of a pernicious force that threatened to derail the industry's leading companies from their meteoric recovery.

For years, industrial truck and tractor manufacturers' command of the U.S. market was virtually unassailable; foreign manufacturers had relegated themselves to producing inexpensive equipment and left the manufacturing of higher-priced, more sophisticated equipment, which was by far the more lucrative segment of the global industrial truck and tractor market, to American companies. But by the late 1970s, domestic manufactures had become lulled into complacency by decades of dominance, and foreign manufacturers, particularly the Japanese, began to woo customers away from U.S. manufacturers. Ironically, the reason for this rise in demand for Japanese products was attributable largely to the success domestic manufacturers had enjoyed for the past several decades. Each year new designs and features were incorporated into U.S.-produced equipment, creating, by the late 1970s, an assortment of highly-sophisticated equipment. The incremental advances in technology had, by this time, spawned equipment too advanced and too costly for the basic material handling needs of U.S. industries. Concurrently, an increasing number of industrial truck and tractor customers found the cheaper Japanese equipment suitable for their basic material handling tasks, a revelation that led to reduced operating costs for customers and to an erosion of U.S. industrial truck and tractor manufacturers' market share. American truck and trucking equipment had simply become too sophisticated for the needs of its average customers.

By the early 1980s, the price advantage afforded to purchasers of Japanese industrial truck and tractor equipment had widened to as much as 30 percent. Still, in the face of this burgeoning trend toward more inexpensive, less sophisticated equipment, U.S. manufacturers were slow to respond. As conditions worsened, domestic manufacturers attempted to stave off mounting foreign competition by designing even more sophisticated products, which further aggravated their losses. Clark Equipment, for example, spent $25 million on the design of a high-technology lift truck equipped with oil-cooled brakes that failed miserably when it was introduced in 1982.

When the U.S. forklift market plummeted in 1982 and 1983, many domestic manufacturers were poorly positioned to sustain further losses. Caterpillar, bereft of its once commanding lead over the industry, sought cheaper manufacturing sites for its production of industrial trucks and tractors, and, in 1983, the company moved the majority of its lift truck production to Korea under the aegis of a South Korean company, Daewoo Heavy Industries Ltd. Similarly, Clark Equipment relocated from Michigan to more inexpensive Kentucky, and, in 1986, Clark eventually followed Caterpillar's lead by signing a ten-year production accord with Samsung Group in Korea.

Among the industry's leaders, Hyster Co. was the one notable exception to domestic manufacturers' disregard toward the shifting market demands. Introducing an inexpensive "XL" line of forklifts in 1981, that matched the Japanese in terms of price and accounted for $44 million in sales in 18 months, Hyster avoided the debilitating losses suffered by its largest competitors. Moreover, Hyster revamped its design, engineering, and manufacturing methods to assimilate the cross-functional and more efficient style of Japanese production, enabling the company to manufacture as many industrial truck and tractor products by the end of the 1980s as it had ten years earlier, with half as many employees. Consequently, Hyster was the only U.S. industrial truck and tractor manufacture among the industry's three largest producers to remain profitable during the 1980s, further underscoring the imprudence of Clark Equipment's and Caterpillar's continued focus on producing technologically advanced equipment in the early 1980s.

The relocation of key manufacturing responsibilities to Korea by Clark Equipment and Caterpillar failed to arrest the precipitous plunge of their integral fork lift operations. Korean wages tripled during the 1980s, erasing any benefits that would have been otherwise realized by relocating, and the dollar declined 24 percent against the Korean won between 1986 and 1989, further increasing the severity of their losses. By the early 1990s, the cumulative effect of the previous decade's failures forced Clark Equipment and Caterpillar to divest their core industrial truck and tractor businesses. In 1992, Clark Equipment sold its forklift operations to Terex Corp. for $95 million. Later that year, Caterpillar signed a joint venture agreement with Mitsubishi Heavy Industries Ltd. that ceded 80 percent of its fork lift business to the Japanese company.

CURRENT CONDITIONS

The industrial truck and tractor industry was slowly adjusting to the changing needs of its customers as it entered the mid-1990s. Sparked by the recessive economic conditions of the early 1990s, U.S. industry as a whole was experiencing changes and many businesses reduced their work force and streamlined their operations. This trend is expected to continue as manufacturers try to meet changing market demands. Industry analysts expect that material handling equipment will likely garner the bulk of the industry's sales in the mid-1990s.

The concerted movement toward manufacturing a proportionately higher number of electric lift trucks initiated by the Japanese in 1992, prompted a parallel response by U.S. manufacturers. These electrically powered lift trucks were more profitable for industrial truck and tractor manufacturers than gas-powered lift trucks and they showed signs of becoming the industry's most popular product in the mid-1990s. Whether the mistakes of the early 1980s will be repeated in the mid-1990s will depend largely on the ability of U.S. industrial truck and tractor manufacturers to produce simplified products that can effectively compete with imposing foreign competition.

INDUSTRY LEADERS

Shaken by the volatile economic conditions of the 1980s, the industrial truck and tractor industry's leading companies entered the 1990s searching for a way to return to their former preeminent positions within the industry. Both Caterpillar, with $10.19 billion in revenues in 1992, and Clark Equipment, with $802 million in revenues in 1992, suffered disastrous losses during the 1980s, which left their presence in the industrial truck and tractor market considerably diminished. Hyster Co., which had been the industry's third largest company, demonstrated comparatively robust performance during the 1980s, which elevated the Portland, Oregon-based manufacturer to the fore of the industrial truck and tractor industry. Indeed, Hyster became the model of a successful industrial truck and tractor manufacturer for other companies in the industry to emulate, as it streamlined its operations and focused on producing low-cost, reliable equipment. Still, other manufacturers continued to concentrate on the high-end market and to operate with a surfeit of employees.

In the early 1990s, Clark Equipment and Caterpillar turned their attention toward designing and manufacturing industrial truck and tractor products that could effectively compete with Japanese equipment. With the economic might of Caterpillar and Clark Equipment's long tradition of introducing innovative products, the two former powerhouses of the industrial truck and tractor industry possess the necessary tools to strengthen their position within the industry, but their recovery depends upon whether they can become

more responsive to their customers' needs in the mid-1990s.

WORK FORCE

Total employment in the industrial trucks and tractors industry declined during the 1980s, slipping to a low of 19,900 in 1986. Following a slight rebound in 1987, the industry's employment total remained below 25,000 in the early 1990s.

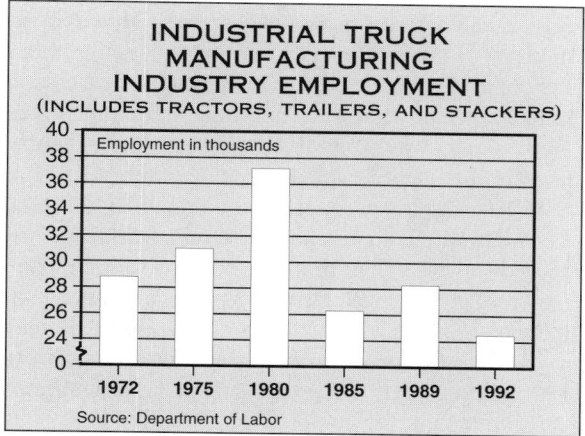

INDUSTRIAL TRUCK MANUFACTURING INDUSTRY EMPLOYMENT (INCLUDES TRACTORS, TRAILERS, AND STACKERS)
Employment in thousands
Source: Department of Labor

Of the approximately 25,000 people employed by the industry, about 13,000 are production workers, while the remaining employees perform technical, managerial, or administrative duties. Although the number of production workers declined during the 1980s, falling from 14,300 in 1982 to 13,200 in 1990, white-collar positions suffered a greater rate of attrition, dropping from 9,700 in 1982 to 6,900 in 1990.

Typically, production workers are employed on a full-time basis, averaging 1,993 hours annually, only slightly below the 1,996 hours averaged by production workers employed in all other manufacturing industries. Average hourly wages of workers in the industrial truck and tractor industry were slightly higher than those of workers in all other manufacturing industries. In 1990, production workers in the industrial truck and tractor industry earned an average hourly wage of $11.00, while white-collar employees earned an average annual salary of $33,478.

Prospects in the industry's work force remained bleak in 1990, according to U.S. Bureau of Labor projections. Between 1990 and 2005, positions for general manufacturing assemblers and fabricators employed by the construction and related machinery industry, of which the industrial truck and tractor industry is a subdivision, were expected to decline 28.1

percent. Predicted to be equally hard hit were positions for machine tool cutting operators, which were expected to drop 28 percent. Other job categories projected to decline by more than 20 percent were lathe and turning machine tool operators and drilling and boring machine operators.

AMERICA AND THE WORLD

As U.S. manufacturers of industrial trucks and tractors entered the mid-1990s, competition from foreign manufacturers posed the greatest threat to the industry's future. For years, U.S. manufacturers held the domestic market largely to themselves; businesses in need of industrial truck and tractor equipment generally shied away from purchasing products manufactured abroad, fearing a lack of spare parts and service. By 1970, imports accounted for a mere $13 million of $1 billion U.S. industrial truck and tractor market. Moreover, the $13 million recorded by foreign manufacturers in 1970 reflected a 72 percent increase from the total posted two years earlier. Likewise, U.S. manufacturers explored profit potentials overseas. By 1970, the value of U.S. exports neared $100 million a year, with parts and complete trucks and tractors being shipped to Europe, South America, and Asia.

By the end of the 1970s, however, the commanding position that U.S. manufacturers held over foreign manufacturers was quickly reversed, largely due to the gains achieved by Japanese manufacturers. By concentrating on supplying inexpensive, yet sturdy industrial truck and tractor products, the Japanese were able to secure a formidable presence in the U.S. market. Competition became fierce, leading one of the few large U.S. manufacturers of industrial truck and tractor products that fared well during the 1980s, Hyster Co., to petition the International Trade Commission in 1986, charging that Japan was selling equipment in the U.S. at prices below the cost of production in the U.S. Two years later, the International Trade Commission ruled in Hyster's favor and applied import duties of up to 51.3 percent to Japanese products entering the U.S. market. Although these import duties provided a much needed respite from increasing Japanese competition, Japanese manufacturers began establishing assembly plants in the U.S. soon after the ruling to circumvent the tariff payments. Entering the 1990s, the Japanese continued to maintain a roughly 50 percent share of the U.S. market.

INDUSTRY INFORMATION SOURCES

Darnay, Arsen J., ed., *Manufacturing USA*, Detroit: Gale Research Inc., 1993.

Drugan, Cheryl G., "Repairing," *Handling & Shipping Management*, March 1982, 36-40.

Guiles, Roger A., "Industry's Trucks: Will Next Stop Be Last Stop?" *Iron Age*, February 1, 1973, 40-41.

"Harnessing Air to Do Warehousing Chores," *Business Week*, June 18, 1966, 172.

Kelly, Kevin, "How U.S. Forklift Makers Dropped the Goods," *Business Week*, June 15, 1992.

Loehwing, David A., "Forklift Pick-Up," *Barron's*, June 5, 1961, 3, 15-17.

"Materials Handling Enjoying a Big Lift," *Business Week*, May 29, 1965, 60.

"Materials Handling Industry," *The Wall Street Transcript*, March 19, 1973, 32,260.

Rohan, Thomas M., "Making 'Em Overseas," *Industry Week*, December 12, 1983, 28.

Rutter, Richard, "Automation Helps Material Handling," *The New York Times*, May 3, 1964, F1.

Schwind, Gene, "Clark Brings a Clear Sheet Approval to Narrow Aisles," *Material Handling Engineering*, April 1993, 20.

Thomas, Dana L., "Good for the Long Haul," *Barron's*, September 9, 1963, 3-12.

U.S. Industrial Outlook, Washington, D.C.: U.S. Department of Commerce, 1960-1980.

"Wall Street Roundup," *The Wall Street Transcript*, October 4, 1976, 44, 857.

—Jeffrey L. Covell

SIC 3541

MACHINE TOOLS, METAL CUTTING TYPES

This industry details establishments primarily engaged in manufacturing metal cutting type machine tools, not supported in the hands of an operator when in use, that shape metal by cutting or use of electrical techniques; the rebuilding of such machine tools; and the manufacture of replacement parts for them. Also included in this industry are metalworking machine tools designed primarily for home workshops. Establishments primarily engaged in the manufacture of electrical and gas welding and soldering equipment are classified in **SIC 3548: Electric and Gas Welding and Soldering Equipment**; those establishments manufacturing portable power-driven handtools are classified in **SIC 3546: Power-Driven Handtools**.

INDUSTRY SNAPSHOT

The metal cutting industry is concerned with the removal of metal from a larger piece of metal to create a desired shape. Metal cutting, also referred to as machining, is performed on most manufactured items. The uses range from low-precision machining, such as grinding undesired protrusions from a rough casting, to high-precision machining, which involves working tolerances of less than half the thickness of a human hair (0.0001 inch). Classic metal cutting produces scrap pieces, called chips, which are relatively useless and generally cannot be reused through remelting or pressing. Both the environmental and economic consequences of such waste has created new processes referred to as chipless machining. General machining processes include turning, shaping, milling, drilling, sawing, abrasive machining, and broaching.

The machine tool industry as a whole is closely tied to national and world economic conditions. The total shipments of metal cutting machine tools dropped sharply between 1982 to 1983 from $5 billion to below $3 billion. From that point, shipments remained steady between $3 and $4 billion. The world-wide recession of the late 1980s and early 1990s created a trough in machine tool-related sales. The machine tool industry is hopeful, however, that anticipated economic upswings in the mid-1990s will carry their industry along as well. Sales finally started to climb toward the end of 1992, with profitability lagging behind. Pricing strategies were renewed, generating more attractive profits for the industry.

The prices for metal cutting machine tools range from under $100,000 to several million dollars, depending on the sophistication and purpose of the tool. Multiple machining centers, capable of performing several metal cutting processes, are becoming more popular with larger companies interested in decreasing the amount of time handling materials between machining stations.

As worldwide competition increases in areas of quality and precision, U.S. machine shops will be forced to update or totally replace machine tools with those that possess higher levels of technical innovation. However, a downward trend in employment levels was forming in the early 1990s as machine tool manufacturers cut direct labor costs. This trend, a disheartening one for those seeking employment in this industry, infers higher levels of automation throughout all related industries and will require the manufacture of more automated machine tools.

ORGANIZATION AND STRUCTURE

Four major categories are represented in this industry: 1) classic machine tools; 2) automated machine tools; 3) expendable tools; and 4) machine tool repair. Classic metal cutting machine tools are characterized by manually operated, power driven (usually electric) stationary machines. These machines are operated by skilled machinists with relatively good trigonometry skills. The demand for these machines has dropped, giving way to the use of automated machine tools.

Automated machine tools are more commonly known as numerically controlled (NC) machine tools. NC machines use a generated program of coordinate values (numerics) to machine parts quickly, with consistency and precision. Downtime between tool changes is minimized, compared to classic machining methods. The information is loaded into the machine by punched tape, punched cards, or magnetic tape that has been generated by a computer program written by an NC programmer. The NC machines have given way to Computer Numerically Controlled (CNC) machines due to the affordability of microcomputers. The next wave of NC machines is expected to include Downloadable Numerically Controlled (DNC) machines, which are network-based CNC machines. This technology reduces the steps between design engineering and manufacturing. All NC machines have created a large market for manufacturers of machine controls, and have increased microcomputer markets. Chipless machining processes implement some form of NC capabilities to their various machine configurations.

Expendable tools are the actual cutting pieces that wear as a result of use. Therefore, this segment of the industry is closely tied to client industry levels of activity. Although many of these tools can be re-sharpened and re-used, many machine shops find it more economical to replace the tool once it is worn. When industry success is high, this segment of the industry experiences increased sales.

Machine tool repair has become a more specialized segment due to the increased popularity of NC machines. The nature of this business category requires that repair technicians have adequate computer hardware/software trouble-shooting skills. Machine tool repair in the modern manufacturing era is thus closely related to computer electronics as well as mechanics.

BACKGROUND AND DEVELOPMENT

Various machine tools have been crafted through the centuries to address man's specific needs, but it was the invention of the clock in 1364 that created a need for higher precision machining methods. Clocks require accurately turned arbors, machine-cut gears, and screw threads. The concepts of precision and consistency in product quality thus pushed machine tool technology to the point that, by the seventeenth century, clock making was regarded as a particularly painstaking craft.

During the second half of the eighteenth century, the barriers between pure science and workshop technology were breaking down. Scientists began interacting more closely with mechanical engineers, spawning new ideas for improved machining techniques. The steam engine was born from this interaction, an invention that drastically increased the potential of the machine tool in the minds of the industrial leaders of the day. The industrial age was afoot. This period was greatly influenced by Henry Maudslay, who is known as the man responsible for the introduction of many of the early engineering machine tools.

Maudslay introduced the concept of precision to heavy machinery, which before that time had been only the concern of watch and scientific instrument makers. In the early 1800s he made the first screw-cutting lathe, a device that has remained the standard even today. His second great contribution was in the creation of a method of finishing a plane surface with a surface plate, marking compound, and hand scraper. Maudslay also constructed a micrometer in 1805 that enabled machinists to measure their work to one ten-thousandths of an inch. Maudslay's successors furthered his craft and assisted in the evolution of machine tools, thus encouraging the industrial revolution.

Today, metal cutting tools remain very similar to those used in the nineteenth century. The implementation of computers has increased the precision and time efficiency of the metal cutting tools, but the basic processes have not changed significantly. However, new metal cutting advances are gaining acceptance and applicability in industry, whereby metal is eroded by chemical discharges, electric discharges, water jets, and laser beams. These advances could again bring significant changes to the methods employed to cut metal to achieve a desired shape.

CURRENT CONDITIONS

Soft pricing policies have depressed the profitability of the metal cutting machine tool industry. As pricing is dependent on volume of sales, it is expected the industry should return to profitability by the mid-1990s. According to Standard & Poor's *Industry Surveys*, "Extensive industry restructuring has lowered break-even points, thereby making it possible for com-

panies to achieve higher earnings on lower volumes and prices than in past cyclical recoveries."

The industries placing the most orders with metal cutting machine tool manufacturers have limited orders due to large financial losses. The auto industry accounts for approximately one-third of the metal cutting tool industry. Increased orders from any of the Big Three automakers are predicated on their performance. While recent signals for that industry are promising, the past two decades have not been banner ones for the domestic auto manufacturers. Decreases in spending by farming and construction industries in the late 1980s and early 1990s were offset by the aerospace industry. However, this industry too has suffered due to the financial instability of various airline companies, as well as military spending cutbacks. Military orders account for approximately five percent of the metal cutting tool industry's business.

The metal cutting tool industry is also hoping that proposed increases in U.S. infrastructure spending, increased spending on the part of former Soviet-bloc countries, and reinvestment in machinery by U.S. companies will help to offset the uncertain status of those industries that have traditionally placed the bulk of orders with metal cutting tool manufacturers.

INDUSTRY LEADERS

According to *Dun's Business Rankings*, the top three domestic manufacturers of metal cutting machine tools are Cincinnati Milacron, Ingersoll International Inc., and Giddings & Lewis. Cincinnati Milacron and Ingersoll International are heavily diversified in other industries and each report annual sales in excess of $500 million. Cincinnati Milacron held a rare position in the early 1990s by reporting profits at a time when other metal cutting machine tool manufacturers were suffering losses. This is largely due to Milacron's diversified interests outside the machine tool industry. Plastics machinery accounts for 35 percent of Milacron's sales, while computer controls, measurement and inspection equipment, and grinding wheels account for the rest. Cincinnati Milacron employs 7,300 people worldwide; Ingersoll employs 4,800 worldwide. Giddings & Lewis reports annual sales of $243 million and employs 5,400 people worldwide.

The industry leaders in NC machine tools are General Electric and Allen-Bradley, both of which primarily manufacture control systems. Expendable tools, such as drills, taps, chucks, and reamers are produced by TRW Geometric Tools, Acme-Cleveland, and National Twist Drill, among others.

WORK FORCE

Roughly one-quarter of the entire metal cutting industry employs machinists and tooling and die makers. The rest of the industry is split between other jobs, such as managers and supervisors, machine tool operators, assemblers, drafters, accountants, and traffic clerks. Employment of machine tool cutting operators, assemblers, machine builders, inspectors, and secretarial personnel is expected to decline beyond the year 2000.

Most people employed by this industry reside in the Great Lakes region and the Northeastern United States. More than 100 metal cutting related establishments call Michigan home, with 21 percent of all American machine tool shipments originating in that state. The establishments in states with the highest concentration of employees were paying more than $13 per hour, on the average, at the end of the 1980s.

AMERICA AND THE WORLD

Throughout the 1980s, the Japanese provided stiff competition for American manufacturers of metal cutting tools. Back in 1974, The U.S. enjoyed a machine tool trade surplus relative to the Japanese. In 1991 that surplus had been transformed into a $1 billion trade deficit. As a result, seven of the world's largest machine tool companies were based in Japan in the early 1990s. An increasing German presence also threatens the U.S. metal cutting industry, as German companies produce some of the leading specialty CNC machines.

In a survey conducted by *Ward's Auto World* in 1992, 52 percent of the responding automobile manufacturing executives stated that U.S. machine tools are the world's best. U.S. tools won accolades for their durability, flexibility, ease of repair, and leading-edge technology. Twenty-five percent of the respondents preferred Japanese machine tools, regarded as the best products for stamping and welding. Twenty percent preferred European machine tools, stating they were the best tools for painting and precision machining.

RESEARCH AND TECHNOLOGY

Due to the limitations and adverse side-effects of traditional machining, chipless machining processes have been developed. These processes are primarily concerned with chemical, electrochemical, electrodischarge, water jet, and laser machining techniques. Intricate parts require non-traditional machining methods, and the advent of the computer age has hastened the research and development of chipless machining processes. As NC controls become more sophisticated, environmental laws grow more stringent, and technology advances, the need for chipless machining processes is expected to increase.

INDUSTRY INFORMATION SOURCES

Brophy, Theresa. "Machine Tool Industry," *The Value Line Investment Survey,* February 12, 1993.

DeGarmo, E. Paul. *Materials and Processes in Manufacturing.* New York: Macmillan, 1979.

Dun's Business Rankings. Parsippany, NJ: Dun & Bradstreet Corporation, 1992.

Murray, Charles. "Automation Comes to Airframes." *Design News,* September 21, 1992.

Nugent, Thomas M., ed. "Steel and Heavy Machinery: Basic Analysis," *Standard & Poor's Industry Surveys,* December 24, 1992.

O'Boyle, Thomas F. "Alleged Links of Kennametal to Iraq Studied," *Wall Street Journal,* April 24, 1992.

Plumb, Stephen E. "Machine Tool Trade Deficit Overlooked in US/Japan Dialogue," *Ward's Auto World,* May 1992.

Rolt, L.T.C. *A Short History of Machine Tools.* Cambridge, MA: M.I.T. Press, 1967.

Schiller, Zachary. "One Takes the High-end Road, the Other Takes the Low: Giddings: Bring on the Bells and Whistles." *Business Week,* May 18, 1992.

Winter, Drew. "'US Machine Tools Are Still the Best," *Ward's Auto World,* July 1992.

—Valerie E. Wilson

SIC 3542

MACHINE TOOLS, METAL FORMING TYPES

This industry covers establishments primarily engaged in manufacturing metal forming machine tools, not supported in the hands of an operator while in use, for pressing, hammering, extruding, shearing, die-casting, or otherwise forming metal into shape. This industry also includes the rebuilding of such machine tools and the manufacture of repair parts for them. Establishments primarily engaged in the manufacture of electric and gas welding equipment and soldering equipment are classified in **SIC 3548: Electric and Gas Welding and Soldering Equipment**; those manufacturing portable power-driven handtools are classified in **SIC 3546: Power-Driven Handtools**; those manufacturing rolling mill machinery and equipment are detailed in **SIC 3547: Rolling Mill Machinery and Equipment**.

The metal forming machine tool industry is very closely related to the metal cutting industry. Many machine shops employ both types of machine tools.

The primary difference between metal cutting and metal forming concerns the removal of metal. Metal forming is a process by which a piece of metal, generally flat sheet stock or a rod, is forced into another shape by means of pressing the material beyond its present yield strength condition. Because most metals can be formed in this way, the metal forming industry is significant to major industries thoughout the United States. According to Standard & Poor's *Industry Surveys*, "The automotive industry is the largest single market for metal-forming machinery."

Most manufacturers of metal cutting tools also produce metal forming tools. Among the most notable are: Ingersoll International Inc., Wean Incorporated, and National Machinery. The domestic number of shipments far outweighed the foreign number of shipments of complete metal forming tools in the 1980s. This trend is static, as foreign competitors have rallied for a share of the metal cutting tool market rather than the metal forming machine tool market. In the U.S. market, punching, shearing, and bending machines hold 24 percent of the total metal forming tool industry; presses hold 20 percent, metal forming machine tools hold 22 percent, and parts for metal forming machine tools hold 28 percent.

At the conclusion of the 1980s, the average worker in the metal forming tool industry was earning more than $13 per hour. At that point in time, approximately 14,600 people were employed in this industry. Machinists and tool and die makers account for 25 percent of the entire labor force. The industry is projected to encounter a negative personnel growth rate into 2000, as restructuring, cost-cutting measures, and automation reduce the work force. The occupations in the industry likely to be hardest hit are precision metal workers, secretaries, metal cutting machine tool operators, machine builders, inspectors, and forming machine operators.

The primary concentration of metal forming companies is around the Great Lakes region and some northeastern states. Another smaller concentration of metal forming interests lies along the West Coast and Alaska. Thirty-seven establishments are located in Michigan that ship a total $190.8 million worth of metal forming equipment. Illinois is home to 27 such establishments, which ship $322.5 million domestically and internationally. Ohio also claims 27 establishments, shipping $303.3 million.

Since the metal forming industry is linked so closely to the automotive industry, growth in the industry is closely linked to the health of domestic car manufacturers. It follows, then, that the metal forming machine tool industry did not enjoy extraordinary suc-cess in the 1970s and 1980s. However, public demand for American-made products has encouraged automakers, even those held by Japanese firms operating in the United States, to purchase American-made tooling whenever possible. Those metal forming equipment manufacturers in the United States hope to benefit from this movement.

INDUSTRY INFORMATION SOURCES

DeGarmo, E. Paul. *Materials and Processes in Manufacturing*. New York: Macmillan, 1979.

Nugent, Thomas M., ed. "Steel and Heavy Machinery: Basic Analysis," *Standard & Poor's Industry Surveys*, December 24, 1992.

—Valerie E. Wilson

SIC 3543

INDUSTRIAL PATTERNS

This category covers establishments primarily engaged in manufacturing industrial patterns.

Industrial patternmaking companies make patterns for forming and molding metal. These patterns are used by other companies to produce metal ornaments, tools, automobile parts, cutlery, and other goods. The largest consumer of industrial patterns is the architectural metalworking industry, which consumed more than 20 percent of industry output in the early 1990s. Producers of pipes, valves, and fittings represented roughly 12 percent of the market. Miscellaneous repair shops purchased 27 percent of output. Other specialized industries purchased patterns to make engineering and scientific apparatus, prefabricated structural metal, car parts, railroad equipment, and other metal products.

Industrial patterns are often used in foundries to create molds and dies for iron, steel, and other metal. Foundries typically melt scrap in an electric furnace. The liquid is poured into a mold which is usually formed from sand, metal, or ceramic. The metal cools and solidifies into any number of complicated shapes, such as an engine block, a turbine blade, or surgical instrument.

Copper was the first material that metallurgists learned to melt and form. By 4000 B.C. smiths had developed sophisticated smelting (melting and molding) techniques. Iron ore was first smelted in 1500 B.C. to make utensils and weapons. The advancement of the blast furnace, which was invented in 1323, was hastened by the industrial revolution in 18th century England. Advanced metallurgical and patternmaking techniques evolved during the 1800s and particularly during the 1900s, in the wake of both world wars.

U.S. industrial patternmaking emerged as a separate industry during the 1950s, 1960s, and 1970s. Patternmakers continued to enjoy relatively healthy growth during most of the 1980s as the demand for metal products, such as architectural metalwork and automotive parts, swelled. By 1988, the industry was generating revenues of about $719 million per year and employing a work force of 10,500. A real estate depression in the late 1980s that reduced demand for architectural metals, coupled with a general U.S. recession, hurt competitors in the late 1980s and early 1990s. Sales slipped to about $530 million in 1990 and employment plunged to 8,100. A slight recovery was restoring margins for some competitors going into the mid-1990s.

The industry is comprised of approximately 700 companies, most of which are privately owned and located in the Midwest. The average patternmaker employed 12 workers in the late 1980s and garnered revenues of about $750,000. The largest competitor in the early 1990s was Cole Pattern and Engineering, of Indiana, which had 1991 sales of $98 million and employed a work force of 700. D And F Corp., the second largest player, had revenues of $16 million and 100 employees. Other industry leaders included Progress Pattern Corp., of Michigan, and FAI Inc., of Wisconsin.

Despite an economic boost going into the mid-1990s, the long term employment outlook for the overall metalworking industry is dismal. Jobs for most laborers are expected to decline 20 to 30 percent between 1990 and 2005, according to the Bureau of Labor Statistics. The demand for machine tool cutting operators, for example, will plummet about 27 percent by 2005. Jobs for machine tool cutting and forming workers will fall by about 19 percent. Positions for engineers and sales professionals, in contrast, should rise ten to 20 percent. The average patternmaking industry employee earned about 14 percent more than the average U.S. manufacturing worker in the early 1990s.

INDUSTRY INFORMATION SOURCES

Darnay, Arsen J., ed., *Manufacturing USA; Industry Analyses, Statistics, and Leading Companies*, Detroit: Gale Research Inc., 1993.

Grolier's Encyclopedia, Danbury, CT: Grolier's Inc., 1993.

Occupational Outlook Handbook, 1992-1993 Edition, Washington, D.C.: U.S. Department of Labor, 1992.

U.S. Industrial Outlook 1993, Washington, D.C.: U.S. Department of Commerce, January 1993.

—Dave Mote

SIC 3544

SPECIAL DIES AND TOOLS, DIE SETS, JIGS AND FIXTURES, AND INDUSTRIAL MOLDS

This classification includes establishments commonly known as contract tool and die shops primarily engaged in manufacturing, on a job or order basis, special tools and fixtures for use with machine tools, hammers, die-casting machines, and presses. The products of establishments classified in this industry include a wide variety of special tooling, such as dies; punches; diesets and components, and sub-presses; jigs and fixtures; and special checking devices. Establishments primarily engaged in manufacturing molds for die-casting and foundry casting; metal molds for plaster working, rubber working, plastics working, glass working and similar machinery are also included. Establishments primarily engaged in manufacturing molds for heavy steel ingots are classified in **SIC 3321: Gray and Ductile Iron Foundries,** and those manufacturing cutting dies, except metal cutting, are classified in **SIC 3423: Hand and Edge Tools, Except Machine Tools and Handsaws.**

INDUSTRY SNAPSHOT

The value of shipments in the tool and die industry in 1993 was an estimated $9.99 billion, up from $5.37 billion in 1982. The value of shipments increased by 32 percent from 1987 to 1993 in current dollars but by only 14 percent in real terms, implying substantial price inflation for the industry's products. In the early 1990s, there were a very large number of establishments in the industry, about 7000. Only 24 percent of these establishments had 20 or more employees. Average firm size as measured by the number of production workers per establishment was 64 percent smaller than that for the manufacturing sector as a whole.

The tool and die industry employed an estimated 88,800 production workers in 1993, down from a peak of 94,700 in 1989. The industry was relatively labor-intensive, with only half as much investment per production worker as that for the manufacturing sector as a whole. Annual hours worked by production workers in the industry were seven percent higher on average than those worked in the manufacturing sector at large, and hourly wages for production workers were 26 percent higher.

ORGANIZATION AND STRUCTURE

There were, by and large, two types of firms in the tool and die industry: the small independents and the large firms that were either subsidiaries or divisions of yet larger parent firms. Of the top ten firms in the industry, eight were either subsidiaries or divisions. Of the remaining 65 firms ranking among the top 75 by sales, 74 percent were private independents. The capital requirements for the industry were very low, with average investment per establishment only 19 percent of that for the manufacturing sector as a whole.

The states ranking in the industry top ten by value of shipments were, in order of descending value, Michigan, Ohio, Illinois, Pennsylvania, California, Indiana, Wisconsin, New York, New Jersey, and Connecticut. Together these ten states accounted for 83 percent of total shipments and 81 percent of total employment for the industry. Michigan was the most important state for tool and die production, accounting for 29 percent of total shipments and 24 percent of total employment for the industry. Of the top five firms in the industry, three were located in Michigan. This reflected firms' proximity to centers of automotive design and production. The automobile industry has long provided tool and die producers with one of their most important markets. Annual expenditures on tools and dies by General Motors, Ford Motor Co., Chrysler, and American Motors increased from $800 million in 1962 to nearly $2 billion in 1974.

A very large share of the tool and die industry's output was purchased for gross private fixed investment and by the metal working industries. The top five industries and sectors buying the outputs of the industry were: gross private fixed investment (43 percent), motor vehicles and car bodies (4.6), export (4.4), aircraft (4.3), and special dies and tools and machine tool accessories (3.6).

The top three types of product by share were dies, tools, and die sets (61 percent), industrial molds and mold boxes (30 percent), and jigs and fixtures (nine percent). Most firms in the industry were highly specialized in their production. This specialization extended beyond the three product types noted above and included the size of dies or molds produced by a tool and die shop.

The industry was served by the National Tooling and Machining Association of Fort Washington, Maryland, known as the National Tool and Die Manufacturers Association until 1960 and the National Tool,

Die and Precision Machining Association until 1980. The Association was founded in 1943 and had 3,100 members and a staff of 40, making it among the largest trade associations in the United States. Among the Association's publications were the annual *Buyers Guide of Special Tooling and Precision Machining Services, Basic Diemaking,* and *Advanced Diemaking.* The Association organized an annual convention and semi-annual conferences. The industry was also served by the Tooling and Manufacturing Association of Chicago and the Michigan Tooling Association of Dearborn. The latter Association of 600 members was founded in 1933 and published the periodical *Tool Talk.* Other industry journals included *Tooling and Production, Modern Machine Shop, Precision Toolmaker,* and *American Machinist.*

The International Union of Tool, Die and Mold Makers, based in Rahway, New Jersey, was founded in 1972 and had 275 members and a staff of two. The Union absorbed the Tool, Die and Mold Makers Guild in 1975.

BACKGROUND AND DEVELOPMENT

There are essentially two types of dies, pressworking dies and molding dies. Pressworking dies (also called stamping dies) are used to cut and shape sheet metals with electrical or hydraulic presses ranging in size from bench presses to the three-story high giants used to stamp automotive body parts. A pressworking die set consists of two components, the upper part attached to the press ram, called a punch, and the lower part attached to the press bed, called a die (though die sets were often simply referred to as dies). Molding dies are used to form both metals and plastics. The most common type consists of two units that when closed form a cavity into which molten material is poured.

The development of the tool and die industry was central to the development of interchangeable parts and mass production technologies in manufacturing. As the *U.S. Industrial Outlook* for 1994 reported, "Nearly every manufacturer that mass produces a product relies to some degree on contract manufacturing support provided by the small business companies that make up the special tooling and machining industry in the United States." A key historical figure in the industry was Eli Whitney, who used jigs and fixtures to assure the uniformity and thus interchangeability of component parts of firearms used during the War of 1812.

The rapid growth of mass production technologies after the late-19th century led to the development of a great number of tool and die shops, most of them small independent contractors. The number of tool and die producing establishments increased from 5,209 in 1954 to 6,616 in 1972 and 6,983 in 1989. Of the total number of establishments in 1989, 1,665 had 20 or more employees.

In their 1975 book *The Tool and Die Industry,* Harold E. Arnett and Donald N. Smith described the special characteristics of the tool and die industry. They wrote: "While mass production is made possible by tooling, the principal tools themselves cannot be mass produced. Tool making, and especially mold and diemaking, is one of the few activities connected with modern large-scale industry in which there has not been a general substitution of machinery for basic skills. These tools are custom-made, one-at-a-time by skilled artisans who patiently and precisely machine, finish, and construct the complicated devices. Only one die, or set of dies, is needed for the manufacture of many thousands, and sometimes millions, of automobile fenders or hoods of a given design."

There was substantial evidence that the characteristics of tool and die production as described by Arnett and Smith were undergoing significant change in the 1980s and 1990s. While the output of the industry increased by 14 percent in real terms from 1987 to 1993, the employment of production workers increased by only 1.25 percent. Such labor displacement was partially the result of computerized production technologies. The flexibility of these technologies also enabled tool and die producers to undertake a broader range of operations. A number of industry observers predicted the consolidation of tool and die firms, resulting in fewer and larger firms.

CURRENT CONDITIONS

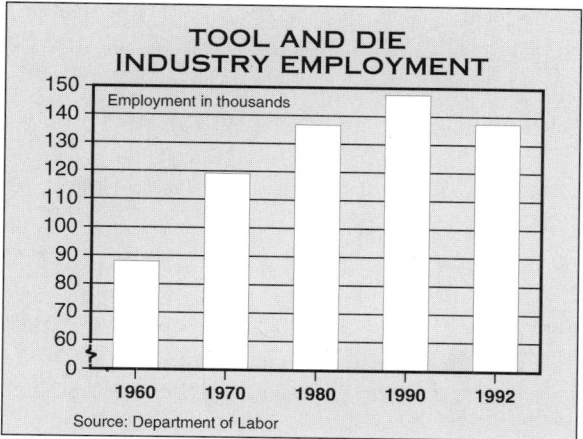

TOOL AND DIE INDUSTRY EMPLOYMENT

Employment in thousands

Source: Department of Labor

The value of shipments in the tool and die industry increased by an estimated 14 percent in real terms from 1987 to 1993, with 1989 being a peak year. Capital investments grew from $233 million in 1982 to $413 million in 1991.

A report in *U.S. Industrial Outlook* for 1994 summarized conditions in the industry as follows: "Orders expanded modestly in 1993, by about 7 percent, although companies serving the defense and aerospace industries saw sales decline by 5 percent due to defense industry cutbacks and softness in the commercial aerospace market. In particular, small contract manufacturers along the Atlantic and Pacific coasts were hit hard by the weak markets and cutbacks in defense spending. . . . The industry is expected to continue to enjoy modest growth in the 3-5 percent range in 1994." The report noted that following the passage of the North American Free Trade Agreement (NAFTA), a number of U.S. tool and die producers were looking to export markets for growth. These producers hoped to serve both Mexican and Canadian manufacturers and also to benefit from the expanded export sales of U.S. manufacturers. The report also noted the rapidly expanding use of computer-numerically-controlled (CNC) machine tools and computer-aided-design (CAD) in the industry, emphasizing the increasingly important role of education for both workers and managers. Most of the education for the industry was provided privately by the Tooling and Manufacturing Association and by local chapters of the National Tooling and Machining Association.

A number of large manufacturing firms were reducing or eliminating their in-house tool and die operations during the 1990s, creating new possibilities for independent producers. Among these was General Motors, which announced in 1993 that it expected to eliminate four of its 11 tool and die shops.

Though the number of production workers employed increased overall from 1982 to 1993, it declined by about 6,000 from peak year 1989 to 1993. The trend toward the automation of production in the industry suggested that employment may decline further.

INDUSTRY LEADERS

The top five firms in the tool and die industry were Connell LP Danly Die Set of Chicago, the Fairchild Corp. D-M-E Co. of Madison Heights, Michigan, the Johnson Controls Inc. Plastic Machinery Division of Manchester, Michigan, Plastic Engineered Components Inc. of New Berlin, Wisconsin, and the Autodie Corp. of Grand Rapids, Michigan. Together these firms accounted for about 6 percent of total sales for the industry.

Danly Die Set was founded in 1922 and had $170 million in sales and 700 employees in 1992. The firm was a division of privately-held Connell Limited Partnership of Boston. Related divisions of Connell L.P. were Danly Punchrite of Cleveland, also a producer of die sets, with $13 million in sales and 60 employees in 1992, and Danly Machine of Chicago, a producer of metal-forming machine tools (see **SIC 3542: Machine Tools, Metal Forming Types**).

The Fairchild Corp. D-M-E Co. was founded in 1943 and had $130 million in sales and 750 employees in 1992. The firm was a division of the publicly held Fairchild Corp. of Chantilly, Virginia. The Fairchild Corp. was also involved in the aerospace and communications industries and had facilities in 15 countries and throughout the United States.

The Plastic Machinery Division of the publicly held Johnson Controls Inc. had $83 million in sales and 400 employees in 1992. Created in 1985, the Division specialized in the production of dies for the molding of plastics. Johnson Controls Inc. (Johnson Service Co. until 1974) was established in 1885. The firm diversified into the production of plastic products in the late-1970s and had plastics-related facilities in Italy, Belgium and the United Kingdom as well as in 23 states across America. Among its plastic products were beverage bottles, car seats, and automotive battery casings. In the four quarters leading up to March 1993, sales for Johnson Controls increased by 18 percent and net profit increased by 31 percent. The firm bought out the Plastics U.S.A. Corp. in 1992.

Plastic Engineered Components Inc. was a private independent founded in 1911. The firm had $80 million in sales and 850 employees in 1992. As with Johnson Controls, Plastic Engineered Components was not only a producer of dies for the production of plastic products, but also a producer of plastic goods themselves, with three divisions producing various plastic products.

The Autodie Corp. was a privately-held firm with $76 million in sales and 375 employees in 1992. Autodie lost $63 million in fiscal year 1991. The firm filed Chapter 11 bankruptcy in August of 1992 and was bought by AD Acquisition, a unit of Progressive Tool & Industries, in November of 1992 for $33.8 million. Autobond was a subsidiary of Autodie that was also purchased by AD Acquisition. Autodie primarily produced large-scale dies and molds for the auto industry whereas Progressive Tool produced tooling for both the auto and aerospace industries.

RESEARCH AND TECHNOLOGY

The key area of research and technical change in the tool and die industry in the 1990s involved CAD/CAM technologies. The journal *Plastics Technology* surveyed 700 producers of industrial molds regarding their use of CAD. These producers used CAD for 10 percent of their tooling in 1992 and aimed to increase this to 40 to 50 percent in the future. In 1993, Solingen Inc. of Northridge, California introduced a manufacturing process called direct shell production casting, which enabled the casting of metal parts directly from a three-dimensional image on a computer screen. Among the leading producers of software for the industry were the Roland Digital Group and Delcam International PLC.

INDUSTRY INFORMATION SOURCES

Annual Survey of Manufactures, Washington, DC: U.S. Census Bureau, 1991.

Arnett, Harold, and Donald Smith, *The Tool and Die Industry: Problems and Prospects,* Ann Arbor, MI: University of Michigan School of Business Administration, 1975.

Chase, Herbert, *Die Castings: Their Design, Composition, Application Specification, Testing and Finishing,* New York: John Wiley & Sons, 1934.

"Closing of Autodie Felt Throughout Local Economy," *Grand Rapids Press,* August 9, 1992.

"Commitment to Design Technology Market," *Precision Toolmaker,* January/February, 1994.

Darnay, Arsen J., ed., *Manufacturing USA: Industry Analysis, Statistics, and Leading Companies,* 3rd edition, Detroit: Gale Research, Inc., 1993.

Dickin, Peter, "Jack of All Trades or Master of None?" *Precision Toolmaker,* April/May, 1993.

Frame, Phil, "GM Expected to Shut 4 Tool and Die Shops," *Automotive News,* March 1, 1993.

Goldsberry, Clare, "New Metal Casting Process May Mean Faster Mold Making," *Plastic News,* January 4, 1993.

"JCI Buys Blow Molding Machinery Firm," *Plastic News,* July 13, 1992.

King, Angela, "New Offer for Autodie," *Crain's Detroit Business,* December 6, 1992.

"Mining Money in Mature Markets," *Fortune,* March 22, 1993.

Moody's Industrial Manual, New York: Moody's Investors Service, 1993.

Ostergaard, D. Eugene, *Basic Diemaking,* New York: McGraw-Hill, 1963.

Ostergaard, *Advanced Diemaking,* New York: McGraw-Hill, 1967.

"Patience Pays," *Forbes,* August 17, 1992.

"700 Readers Say: Mold Analysis Makes the Grade," *Plastics Technology,* April, 1992.

U.S. Industrial Outlook 1994, Washington, DC: U.S. Department of Commerce, January 1994.

Ward's Business Directory of U.S. Private and Public Companies, Detroit: Gale Research, Inc., 1993.

—David Kucera

SIC 3545

CUTTING TOOLS, MACHINE TOOL ACCESSORIES, AND MACHINIST'S PRECISION MEASURING DEVICES

This category covers establishments primarily engaged in manufacturing cutting tools, machinists' precision measuring tools, and attachments and accessories for machine tools and for other metalworking machinery, not elsewhere classified. Establishments primarily engaged in manufacturing handtools, except power-driven types, are classified in the Cutlery, Handtools, and General Hardware industries.

INDUSTRY SNAPSHOT

The cutting tools, machine tool accessories, and precision measuring devices industry is facing transition. Increased global competition in all aspects of manufacturing have created demand for better, longer-lasting tools and accessories. Extensive development of tougher cutting tool materials and coatings has been the driving force of change in this industry, along with improved cutting tool design that lends extended performance. The quality control movement is affecting the measuring device segment through demand for electronic gauges that link to statistical process control software packages. Modular tooling designs have affected the accessories segment.

Ironically, while this industry has paced itself to match industry demand for productivity improvements, it also has met with its own problems. The influx of foreign competitors to this market has been staggering, forcing cutting tool and measuring device manufacturers to look introspectively at their own operations. Process improvements and increased development became commonplace practices to remain profitable.

ORGANIZATION AND STRUCTURE

The organization of this industry is changing as more companies are merging or being acquired. While the close relation between machine tools and cutting tools is apparent, the industries were mostly kept separate, primarily because the production philosophies were different. Machine tools, especially today's computer numerically controlled machining centers, are not generally mass-production items. However, cutting tools are produced in large quantities, because they are disposable items. Yet, the attraction of gaining diversification through complementary product lines has prompted larger companies to seek others that offer stability in the economy's cyclical path. The recession hurt the machine tool industry greatly, as many companies either postponed purchases of new equipment, or invested in used equipment. Since profits became losses for most machine tool manufacturers, the attraction to the cutting tool industry was enhanced. This was evidenced in early 1993, when Cincinnati Milacron Inc. acquired Valenite Inc..

The precision measuring device segment remains substantially self-contained. The industry leader domestically is L. S. Starett Co., a foremost producer of micrometers and other manual measuring devices. Brand recognition is Starett's greatest asset, however, strong competition from foreign suppliers, like Mitutoyo, remains a threat to continued financial strength.

BACKGROUND AND DEVELOPMENT

The background and development of cutting tools, accessories, and measuring devices is closely tied to the history of machine tool development. The first gear-cutting mechanism was designed by Leonardo da Vinci, however, no evidence indicates it was ever built. Through the clock making industry, the demand for precision gears and precision measuring devices grew. As time-keeping devices became more popular, production techniques were developed to meet the increasing demand. Metal removing devices were available with very small teeth, which served more as rotary files than chip-forming, cutting tools. Yet, it was not until the mid-1800s that the first cutting tool was developed.

The Phoenix Iron Works of Hartford, Connecticut, created the first tool to really form a metal chip, thereby cutting the metal. The tool had 56 teeth placed around its nearly three-inch diameter. The teeth were chipped by a hammer and chisel. While effective, the tool required too much labor when it needed sharpening. In 1864, the Brown & Sharpe Company, later the Brown & Sharpe Manufacturing Company, developed the first cutter that could be sharpened by grinding the face, without altering its shape. To date, the elements of this design are still in use.

CURRENT CONDITIONS

The current downturn in the machine tool industry does not necessarily correlate to the health of the cutting tool industry. Generally, cutting tool sales are viewed as an economic indicator of the nation's manufacturing productivity level. The difference is primarily a capital expense. A corporation may decide to purchase a used machine tool over a new one in recessionary times. However, if a company is cutting metal, the cutting tools wear or break, and must be sharpened or replaced with new cutting tools. Therefore, the productivity of a metal cutting company is generally directly related to the purchasing levels of machine tools. However, longer lasting cutting tools are being manufactured with specialized coatings which extend the wear life of the tool—sometimes as much as four times the normal wear. With improved cutting tool materials and geometry, the volume of machine tool sales will inevitably drop, because the tools are designed to reduce the frequency of replacement. Likewise, improved engineering design of metal castings intentionally reduce the amount of removable machine stock, requiring less cutting tool activity.

Improved tool coatings are also driving end mill innovation. Cubic boron nitride (CBN) coated tooling inserts are gaining ground on carbide and ceramic inserts in areas like high production milling of cast iron. Polycrystalline diamond (PCD) coated inserts are also expected to gain acceptance, largely due to research and development efforts in PCD film technology. PCD is especially suited for ultrahard cutting applications. Titanium Nitride (TiN) coatings can also provide significant benefits, including lower machining cost per part, longer tool life, higher feeds and speeds, improved finished part quality, and reduced tool deflection.

Another example of improved tool wear through coating is polycrystalline cubic boron nitride (PCBN). This innovation, when applied to turning inserts, threatens to replace many grinding operations. Used to machine hardened-steel, PCBN turning inserts have no equal. Referred to as hard turning, the insert comes within or surpasses the accuracy and surface finish once reserved for grinding operations. The surface is improved because hard turning burnishes the surface, ending in a cleaner, rust- and crack-inhibitive surface. It has been estimated that a $150 million international market exists for hardened-steel machining. Approximately 50 percent of Sumitomo Electric Industries' PCBN use was reserved for turning hardened-steel automotive and machine parts. This use was growing at a rate of 25 percent annually. While Sumitomo observes PCBN probably will never fully replace grinding, in applications where repeatable perpendicularity are required, grinding cannot compete.

End mill design is evolving into more specialized geometries for certain material applications. For example, when milling aluminum, a standard, two-flute, high-speed, steel end mill was used. However, studies show that using a three-flute end mill on aluminum grants ample space for chip formation, while allowing a feed rate increase of up to 50 percent. The tool design change increases productivity by allowing aluminum to be machined faster, without increased tool breakage.

Quick change and modular tools are making inroads. Flexibility and adaptability have been emphasized by customers over the years, which these tooling configurations offer. Rapid precise tool changes save downtime and enable tailoring production schedules, thus using personnel and machine tools more efficiently. Modular tooling systems standardize spindle-to-tool interface connections, offering reduced hardware inventories. According to Charles R. Brown, Kennametal Incorporated's application engineering systems manager, "These systems move a process that for centuries has been manual into the age of automation. It's a quantum leap."

Statistical process control (SPC) is taking a new turn through increased use of electronic gauges on the shop floor. Wired to a computer, the gauges show digital readout of the measurement. This reading is input to the SPC software, which creates process control charts. The operator/inspector no longer shuffles through paperwork and calculations, and the readings are much more accurate. Such "real-time" information is beneficial in seeing trends, such as tool wear, before any parts are scrapped. The major trend in SPC today is moving measuring devices from the quality assurance department to the shop floor. Coordinate measuring machines and computer-linked electronic gauges are two examples of measurement equipment moving to the source to gain better control through improving response time, when a problem arises on the SPC charts. The biggest drawback to implementing use of electronic gauges is the initial cost involved. Purchasing the computer equipment, special gauges, training employees in the use of the software and hardware, and specialized calibration require such an outlay of money that many machine shops are intimidated, while remaining skeptical of any additional cost savings. Mitutoyo/MTI Corporation studied the level of electronic gauge use in industry in 1989. They found 61 percent of the surveyed machine shops used both dial and electronic gauges, while 31 percent did not use electronic gauges at all. Only 1.5 percent of the machine shops surveyed were totally committed to electronic gauge use.

INDUSTRY LEADERS

In 1991, the top five companies, in terms of sales, were: Blount Incorporated with $684 million, Valenite Inc. with an estimated $340 million, Black & Decker Corporation with an estimated $190 million, Brown & Sharpe Manufacturing Company with $188 million, and L. S. Starrett Co. with $184 million. Pooled together, the top 75 companies engaged in this industry grossed sales of $3.708 billion in 1991, while employing 37,400 people.

Black & Decker was incorporated in 1910 with an investment of $1,800. Originally a machine shop manufacturing other companies products, Black & Decker expanded into the electric-powered tool market in 1916. The success of the company was based on its innovative universal motor design and trigger switch. When these two innovations were teamed with a pistol grip, the company introduced a one-half-inch portable drill for the low price of $230. The design of the drill became a standard for all other portable drills. Since that time, Black & Decker became an international force in do-it-yourself tools and accessories. Although Black & Decker's business has not always been in a state of constant growth, the company is dominant in this industry, as well as in the small hardware appliances industry. Black & Decker has sought to avoid cyclical economic trends through diversifying its product line with complimentary product groups. Therefore, while the cutting tools and machine tool accessory markets are fairly volatile, Black & Decker's success is not determined by sales in this category.

Valenite Inc. was acquired in February 1993 by Cincinnati Milacron Inc. for $80 million, plus Valenite's debts. This acquisition should help Milacron's financial position, in light of the downturn in machine tool sales. According to *Standard & Poor's Industry Surveys*, machine tools should account for approximately 33 percent of Milacron's sales in 1993, as opposed to 48 percent in 1992 and 51 percent in 1991.

WORK FORCE

In 1988, employees working in this industry earned an average of $10.72 per hour compared to the $10.66 average of all other manufacturing-based industries. In 1987, employees in Michigan averaged $12, where the greatest concentration of cutting tool manufacturers can be found. Employees in Missouri were paid the highest average hourly wage in 1987, at $13.40. The state offering the lowest compensation in the United States for this industry was South Carolina.

Many occupations in this industry will be reduced as the country moves toward the next century. Those facing the most significant reductions, over ten percent, include tool cutting operators, assemblers and fabricators, secretaries, machine builders, precision inspectors, and metal forming operators. Small increases in a few occupations are expected. These include industrial production managers, mechanical engineers, combination machine tool operators, numerically controlled machine operators, and machinists.

According to the American Society for Training and Development, U.S. companies spend approximately $210 billion annually on training—$30 billion on formal programs and $180 billion on informal. A 1989 study of Fortune 500 companies found that 70 percent planned to increase their expenditures for training that year. While $210 billion seems like a very large amount of money to spend on training, U.S. companies spend ten percent of the initial cost of equipment on machine maintenance, but spend less than two percent on maintaining the skills of its work force.

AMERICA AND THE WORLD

Competition and cost are the battle cries of the 1990s. Global competition is fierce, and only those who master cost savings measures will beat the competitors. Nowhere is this more evident than in the auto industry. Although the Americans have experienced difficulty in the marketplace where Japanese cars reign supreme, the Europeans face greater challenges. Nissan's plant in Sunderland, England lags one hour behind normal production time in Nissan's Japanese plants—18 man-hours vs. 17 man-hours per car. However, European plants, on the average, produce a car in 30 to 35 man-hours. German automakers generally require 40 man-hours per car. In terms of cost cutting, it has been estimated that 150,000 jobs too many exist as a result of this inefficiency. Although work ethics differ between the cultures, so does the level of sophisticated machine tools and cutting tools. In order to bridge this gap, European manufacturers may order higher standard machine tools, cutting tools, and accessories, increasing the order quantities.

The latest wave in quality improvement is a series of certifications known as ISO 9000. ISO stands for the International Organization for Standardization, which over 100 European countries have adopted as official. When business is viewed in a global perspective, the ISO certifications are becoming increasingly necessary to obtain. In the United States, many of the larger companies/organizations—such as Caterpillar, York International, and American Petroleum Institute—

have developed their own quality standards. Once a company becomes a potential supplier for the larger company, a quality audit is performed at the potential supplier's facility. Depending on the customer-supplier base, it would be possible for a company to hold several quality certifications, each with their own unique requirements. The benefit to obtaining ISO certification is to achieve a quality level that is understood throughout the world. The ISO certification is reviewed and reaudited every six months. While this is relatively new and fairly controversial in the United States, over 15,000 certifications are held in Britain alone. The cost of compliance is one of the major obstacles to applying for certification—$15,000 to $20,000 for average-sized companies. However, the cost of non-compliance in the future could mean fewer business opportunities, as ISO could become a general requirement for contract awards both domestically and internationally.

RESEARCH AND TECHNOLOGY

Cryogenic treatment, or deep freezing, of cutting tools is currently a relatively unexplored process. It has little technical data available to support the successes in increased tool life as a result of the process. For years, one small tooling and die company in Arcadia, Ohio, experimented with dropping several materials, like metals and nylon, to 320 degrees below zero Fahrenheit, or 77 degrees Kelvin. The results have been outstanding. Carbide inserts seem to last two- to eight-times longer than untreated inserts. Blades for cutting abrasive rubber are lasting up to 37 times longer. Carbide dies stay in service for months, rather than weeks, before needing sharpened. Even nylon stockings seem better able to resist runners. The National Science Foundation has approved a research grant for the company to investigate the effect of cryogenic treatment on the wear life and microstructure of steel. If the research leads to significant findings, deep freezing may become another significant option for improvement of tool life.

INDUSTRY INFORMATION SOURCES

Albert, Mark. "Cutting Tools in the Deep Freeze," *Modern Machine Shop,* January 1992.

Beard, Tom, ed. "Fast and Good," *Modern Machine Shop,* June 1993.

Darnay, Arsen J., ed. *Manufacturing USA: Industry Analyses, Statistics, and Leading Companies,* Detroit: Gale Research, Inc., 1992.

Fruit, Robert. "Move SPC to the Shop Floor," *Modern Machine Shop,* April 1993.

Hast, Adele, ed. "Black & Decker Corporation," *International Directory of Company Histories,* Chicago: St. James Press, 1988.

Koepfer, Chris. "Getting Ready for ISO 9000," *Modern Machine Shop,* April 1993.

Miska, Kurt H. "Tools, Workholding & Machine Accessories," *Manufacturing Engineering,* August 1990.

Noaker, Paula M. "Hard Facts on Hard Turning," *Manufacturing Engineering,* February 1992.

Owen, Jean. "Gaging Quality," *Manufacturing Engineering,* April 1990.

Owen, Jean. "Inspection/Quality Assurance," *Manufacturing Engineering,* August 1990.

Owen, Jean. "Moving to Modular," *Manufacturing Engineering,* February 1992.

Peterson, Gary J. "Survival Training for the '90s," *Manufacturing Engineering,* August 1990.

"Steel & Heavy Machinery," *Standard & Poor's Industry Surveys,* April 8, 1993.

Woodbury, Robert S. *Studies in the History of Machine Tools,* Cambridge, Massachusetts: The MIT Press, 1972.

—Valerie E. Wilson

SIC 3546

HANDTOOLS

This industry includes establishments primarily engaged in manufacturing power-driven hand-tools, such as drills and drilling tools, pneumatic and snagging grinders, and electric hammers. Establishments primarily engaged in manufacturing metal cutting type and metal forming type machines (including home workshop tools) which are not supported in the hands of an operator are classified in **SIC 3541: Machine Tools, Metal Cutting Types** and **SIC 3542: Machine Tools, Metal Forming Types;** and those primarily manufacturing power-driven heavy construction or mining hand-tools are classified in a range of construction machinery and equipment industries.

INDUSTRY SNAPSHOT

The U.S. power-driven handtool industry includes professional and non-professional tools like electric drills, portable chain saws, portable electric sanders, and pneumatic hammers. The industry's value of shipments was approximately $2.354 billion in 1992. The recession seriously hurt the handtool industry and future growth depends upon upturns in the construction of residential dwellings, commercial buildings, and home repair and improvements. The United States is a net importer of power-driven handtools. In 1992 exports totaled $618 million while imports totaled $811 million. However, this imbalance was closing in the early 1990s.

Pneumatic hand tools, driven by compressed air, are produced for industrial and professional customers. The non-professional consumer handtool market, however, has become a significant sector in the industry's sales. Non-professional home improvement sales represented half of the electric handtool market in the early 1990s. The portable chain saw market, however, has experienced flat sales for over a decade due to declining timber harvests. Cordless tools were an expanding area for power-driven handtool manufacturers. In 1992 they accounted for nearly 30 percent of the industry's sales.

ORGANIZATION AND STRUCTURE

Success for the power-driven handtool industry depends upon a variety of economic factors that influence industrial and consumer spending. Capital spending by business and industry directly affects power-driven handtool manufacturers, particularly in their manufacture of pneumatic power tools. Pneumatic handtools operate by forcing compressed air through rotor blades. They are lightweight, durable, high performance tools that are used in demanding industrial situations. Pneumatic handtools comprised 24 percent of the industry's total shipments in the early 1990s. Examples of pneumatic products include: drills, grinders (metalworking machinery), pneumatic chip removal guns, hammers, ratchet wrenches, and sanders.

Retail sales to the do-it-yourself consumer sector, which accounted for nearly 50 percent of the industry's total shipments in 1993, have become a major influence upon the success of the industry. Black & Decker, for example, receives between 25 percent and 35 percent of its revenues from the do-it-yourself market. According to *U.S. Industrial Outlook*, the industry is also highly sensitive to sales of new and existing residential units and spending trends for home improvement, maintenance, and repair. Electric power handtools dominated these sectors because they were generally less expensive than pneumatic tools. The cordless battery powered handtool market also gave a boost to the industry in the early 1990s. In 1992, cordless tools (of all classes) represented 30 percent of the industry's total value of shipments. The cordless tool sector was expected to grab a larger percentage of the industry's sales as technology improves battery power and charge duration. Examples of electric power handtools include: buffing machines, chipping

hammers, drills, grinders, hammers, sanders, saws, and screwdrivers.

The power-driven handtool industry also includes gasoline powered chain saws. This product class is directly tied to the success of the timber industry. Lower timber harvests, due in part to environmental concerns, have become a serious problem for chain saw manufacturers. Moreover, lower consumer purchases due to a declining use of firewood for home heating contributed to a decade of flat sales. Gasoline powered chain saws comprised an estimated 13.3 percent of the industry's total shipments in 1992.

BACKGROUND AND DEVELOPMENT

The power-driven handtool industry developed in conjunction with the rest of the United States' industrial growth. U.S. manufacturers often started as small operations producing specific power tools for local markets. As the United States grew into a world economic leader, the power-driven handtool industry likewise expanded internationally.

The Black & Decker Corporation, for example, was founded in 1910 by S. Duncan Black and Alonzo G. Decker in Baltimore. The company first began manufacturing milk-bottle-cap machines and candy dippers. By 1917 Black & Decker patented the first pistol grip, trigger switch electric drill. The company's success enabled it to begin international operations by 1918. According to *Hoover's Handbook of American Business*, Black & Decker developed products that defined the power tool industry. For example, Black & Decker introduced the first portable screwdriver in 1923, the first electric hammer in 1936, and the first portable electric drill for the consumer in 1946. In 1993 Black & Decker was the world's leading power-driven handtool manufacturer.

The Ingersoll-Rand Company, founded in 1905 in New York, sold pneumatic handtools to the mining industry. Another contemporary industry leader, The Stanley Works, founded in 1852 in New Britain, Connecticut, had international operations before it began manufacturing electric tools in 1929.

CURRENT CONDITIONS

According to *U.S. Industrial Outlook*, the recession seriously hurt the handtool industry in 1990 and 1991. The value of shipments dropped by $163 million (6.9 percent) in 1991. Overall employment dropped by 900 employees (4.9 percent) in 1991 to a total of 17,400. Bankruptcies of retail establishments resulted in a fall in retail sales. The chain saw segment experienced a decade of flat sales due to lower timber harvests and reduced home fire wood consumption. However, exports increased steadily during the 1980s, while imports declined during the same period.

The industry recovered during 1992 due to a 10 percent increase in residential home-improvement purchases. The industry's value of shipments jumped 6.9 percent from $2.202 billion in 1991 to $2.354 billion in 1992. Employment levels declined at a slower rate in 1992, by 300 employees or 2 percent. In addition, the proliferation of large home centers gave manufactures additional markets to sell their products. Moreover, technology gave a boost to the power-driven handtool industry by opening new markets for cordless tools. Cordless tools accounted for 30 percent of the industry in 1992. The destruction caused by Hurricane Andrew spurred demand for chain saws in 1992. This sector increased by 5 percent, to 1.42 million units in 1992 from 1.35 million units in 1991. During 1992, however, the import-export deficit was $193 million; although U.S. exports increased by 5.6 percent to $618 million, imports rose by 11.6 percent to $811 million. Additional export increases depend upon a world economic recovery, and expanding sales to new markets in Eastern Europe, the former Soviet Union, and the developing world.

Near-term Conditions. In 1993 the home improvement sector was expected to rise by 5 percent, while sales in the home repair and maintenance sector were expected to rise by 4 percent. These sectors helped increase the industry's value of shipments by 5.3 percent to $2.478 billion. The destruction of residential and commercial buildings in the Midwest during the Mississippi flooding was also likely bolster the industry in the short-term. The import-export deficit was projected to decline to $129 million in 1993. Exports were expected to rise by 6.5 percent to $658 million, while imports should decline by 3 percent to $787 million.

Long-term Conditions. The U.S. power-driven handtool industry was expected to experience annual growth of 1.5 percent from 1993 to 1998. Industry growth depends upon increased expenditures in the home improvement, home repair and maintenance, and residential and commercial construction sectors. In addition, new battery technology was expected to help the industry to expand the market for advanced cordless tools.

INDUSTRY LEADERS

Black & Decker Corporation dominated the U.S. power-driven handtool industry. Other U.S. industry leaders in 1993 included: the Ingersoll-Rand Co., The Stanley Works, and the Chicago Pneumatic Tool Co.

In 1993, Black & Decker was the largest power-driven handtool manufacturer in the world. The Towson, Maryland-based company employed 38,600 people in 1991 and had $4.637 billion in sales. Its power tool division had sales of $1.095 billion, accounting for 24 percent of the company's total sales. According to *Hoover's Handbook of American Business*, Black & Decker eventually set the pace for the industry by introducing innovative power-tools like the first portable screwdriver in 1922 and portable electric drills in 1946. In the early 1990s Black & Decker was an international company that carried the seventh most recognized brand name in the United States. Its brand recognition was also among the top twenty in Europe.

The second largest U.S. power-driven handtool manufacturer in 1993 was the Ingersoll-Rand Co. The Woodcliff Lake, New Jersey-based company was founded in 1905 when the Ingersoll Rock Drill Co. and the Rand Drill Co. merged to form Ingersoll-Rand. The company had sales of $3.586 billion and employed 31,117 people in 1991. Its bearings, locks, and tools division had total sales of $1.647 billion, accounting for 46 percent of the company's total sales. Foreign sales comprised 40 percent of Ingersoll-Rand's total sales.

The Stanley Works was the third largest manufacturer of power-driven handtools in the United States. Based in New Britain, Connecticut, the company was founded in 1843 by Frederick T. Stanley as a bolt manufacturer. In 1991, The Stanley Works had total sales of $1.962 billion and had 17,420 employees. According to *Hoover's Handbook of American Business*, the company's home improvement and consumer products division (hand tools, hardware, and residential door systems) comprised 52 percent of the company's sales. The company's industrial and professional products division also manufactured electric and hydraulic tools for industry.

The Chicago Pneumatic Tool Co., based in New York, was a leading U.S. manufacturer of pneumatic handtools for industrial purposes in the 1980s. In 1985 tools and equipment represented 20 percent of the company's sales. The company had $400.2 million in sales and employed 4,001 people. The Danaher Corp. bought the Chicago Pneumatic Tool Company in December, 1986.

Other major U.S. power-driven handtool leaders included: the Thiokol Corp. ($1.3 billion in sales), U.S. Power Tools Inc. ($1.07 billion in sales), the Danaher Corp. ($948.9 million in sales), and the Snap-on Tools Corp. ($881.0 million in sales).

WORK FORCE

According to the Bureau of Labor Statistics, the U.S. power-driven handtool industry employed 17,100 people. In 1989, production workers represented 11,700 of the 17,100 employees and earned an average weekly salary of $401.97. Occupations in the power-driven handtool industry included: tool and die makers, machinists, mechanical engineers, drafters, blue collar worker supervisors, and stock clerks.

AMERICA AND THE WORLD

The United States is a world leader in the manufacture of power-driven handtools, and most U.S. manufacturers were significant exporters in the early 1990s. Black & Decker, for example, had total export sales (for all products) of $2.038 billion in 1991. Although the United States still had an import-export deficit in the early 1990s, U.S. exports increased steadily during the 1980's, while imports declined during the same period. During 1992 exports increased by 5.6 percent to $618 million, while imports rose by 11.6 percent to $811 million, resulting in a net deficit of $193 million. In 1992, the Black & Decker Corporation filed a complaint with the Department of Commerce, alleging that its Japanese competitors were illegally dumping power tools in the United States.

Major U.S. competitors included Germany, Japan, and Great Britain. The Robert Bosch Company, with its headquarters in Stuttgart, Germany, sold $3.308 million (from all divisions) in the United States. The company had total sales of $33.6 billion in 1991 and employed 181,498 people. Another large German power tool manufacturer is the Stihl Andreas Co. It manufactures chain saws, hand saws, and replacement parts. The company had total sales of $1.15 billion in 1991 and had 5,666 employees.

Sumitomo Electric Industries LTD of Osaka, Japan exported $126.113 million in 1992. The company had total sales of $1.157 billion in 1992 and had 14,833 employees. Another large U.S. competitor in Japan is Ryobi Limited, which exported $66,054,000 worth of products in 1992. Power tools and other hardware products accounted for 41 percent of Ryobi's 1992 revenues. The company had total sales of $212.8 billion and 2,390 employees in 1992.

In Great Britain, Dobson Park Industries exported $73,600 to the United States in 1992. Its power tool sales were $19,849 in 1992, totaling 9 percent of the company's 1992 revenues.

Other large power-driven handtool manufacturers include: the Hitachi Koki Co. (Japan), the Makita Corp. (Japan), the Shibaura Engineering Works Co. (Japan), the Hilti Ag Co. (Switzerland), Johnson Electric Holdings Ltd. (Hong Kong), and the Kanematsu-Nnk Corp. (Japan).

RESEARCH AND TECHNOLOGY

Most research in the power-driven handtool industry in the early 1990s was directed toward ergonomics and portability. Ergonomic designs involve creating tools that are more comfortable and efficient for the user. Long term use of poorly designed power-driven handtools can have serious consequences to workers' health and safety. According to John Bonnanzio in *Industrial Distribution*, injuries caused by constant exposure to noise and vibrations can cause such injuries as hearing loss, carpal tunnel syndrome, and hand-arm vibration syndrome (HAVS). Injuries of this type cost companies an estimated $100 billion annually. Improved ergonomic designs can significantly reduce injuries caused by long term use of power-driven hand tools.

The power-driven handtool industry was changing due to the development of cordless battery operated tools. According to *Business Week*, the key advantages of cordless tools are indoor safety and outdoor convenience. Cordless tools were an expanding area for power-driven handtool manufacturers in the early 1990s. In 1992 they accounted for nearly 30 percent of the industry.

INDUSTRY INFORMATION SOURCES

Avery, Susan. "Power Tools Take a Pounding." *Purchasing* Vol. 113 (October 22, 1992): 57-58.

Bonnanzio, John. "Designs That Sell." *Industrial Distribution* Vol. 79 (June 1990): 27-28.

"Distribution of Sales by Class of Customer." *1987 Census of Manufactures. Subject Series. Vol. S-4*. Washington, D.C.: U.S. Department of Commerce, 1987.

Eastman, Martin. "Vibration Shakes Workers: Nerves and Blood Vessels Can Suffer Irreversible Damage from Prolonged or Repeated Motion." *Safety & Health* Vol. 143 (May 1991): 32-35.

Employment, Hours, and Earnings, United States, 1909-90, Vol. 1. Washington, D.C.: U.S. Department of Labor , 1991.

"Gerneral Summary." *1987 Census of Manufactures. Subject Series. Vol. S-1*. Washington, D.C.: U.S. Department of Commerce, 1987.

Hoover, Gary, Alta Campbell, and Patrick J. Spain, eds. *Hoover's Handbook of American Business 1992*. Emeryville, Cal.: Publishers Group West, 1992.

Industry Surveys. Vol. 2 M-Z. Standard & Poor's Corporation, 1993.

"Metalworking Machinery and Equipment." *1987 Census of Manufactures. Industry Series. Vol. 35-C.* Washington, D.C.: U.S. Department of Commerce, 1987.

"The 'Do It Yourself' Stocks." *Financial World.* Vol. 144 (July 23, 1975): 15.

Towell, Julie E., senior ed., *Ward's Business Directory.* Vols. 1, 2, 3. Detroit: Gale Research Inc., 1992.

U.S. Industrial Outlook 1993. Washington, D.C.: U.S. Department of Commerce, 1993.

Warner, Joan. "Charged-up Cordless Tools." *Business Week* (March 29, 1993): 100.

—Scott Plamondon

SIC 3547

ROLLING MILL MACHINERY

This category covers establishments primarily engaged in manufacturing rolling mill machinery and processing equipment for metal production, such as cold forming mills, structural mills, and finishing equipment.

The value of shipments in the rolling mill machinery industry in 1991 was $487 million, down from $503 million in 1982. 1989 was a peak year with $605 million in shipments. There are about 80 establishments in the industry. Forty percent of these establishments have 20 or more employees. Average firm size as measured by the number of production workers per establishment is 19 percent smaller than that for the manufacturing sector as a whole. Annual capital investments were $12 million in 1991, second only to the $15 million invested in peak year 1982.

The rolling mill machinery industry employed 2,300 production workers in 1991, down from a peak of 5,100 in 1982. The industry is relatively labor-intensive, having 30 percent as much investment per production worker as that for the manufacturing sector as a whole. Annual hours worked by production workers in the industry are 9 percent higher on average than those worked in the manufacturing sector at large, and hourly wages are 18 percent higher. Of the top 22 firms by sales in the industry, 68 percent are private independents. The capital requirements for the industry are relatively low, with average investment per establishment 25 percent of that for the manufacturing sector as a whole.

The top three firms in the rolling mill machinery industry are RB and W Corp. of Mentor, Ohio; Wean Inc. of Pittsburgh, Pennsylvania; and Morgan Construction Co. of Worcester, Massachusetts. Together these firms account for nearly two-thirds of total sales for the industry. RB and W had $164 million in sales and 1,100 employees in 1992. The publicly held firm was founded in 1929. In addition to producing rolling mill machinery, RB and W produces cold formed metal products, including automotive parts. Publicly held Wean Inc. had $76 million in sales and 456 employees in 1992. The firm produces hot dip galvanizing lines. Wean's Industries Division of Youngstown, Ohio, is the industry's fourth-largest producer, with $65 million in sales and 345 employees in 1992. Wean suffered net losses of $23 million in 1992. Morgan Construction had $70 million in sales and 510 employees in 1992. The privately held firm was founded in 1888 and produces steel rolling and drawing machinery.

The top rolling mill machinery products by share are hot rolling mill machinery (43 percent), rolling mill machinery, not elsewhere classified, including tube mill machinery, processing lines, and machined rolls for rolling mills (34 percent), and cold rolling mill machinery (17 percent). The states ranking in the top five by number of establishments in the industry are Ohio (with 15), Pennsylvania (with 8), Illinois (with 7), Massachusetts (with 5), and Indiana (with 3). Together these five states account for 79 percent of total employment for the industry in the United States. Ohio by itself accounts for 31 percent of total employment in the industry.

The top five industries and sectors buying the outputs of the industry are: gross fixed private investment, with a 75.4 percent share; exports, with a 17.8 percent share; change in business inventories, with a 3.7 percent share; rolling mill machinery, with a 2.6 percent share; and federal government purchases, for national defense, with a 0.1 percent share.

INDUSTRY INFORMATION SOURCES

Annual Survey of Manufactures, Washington, D.C.: U.S. Census Bureau, 1991.

Darnay, Arsen J., editor, *Manufacturing USA: Industry Analysis, Statistics, and Leading Companies* (3rd edition), Detroit, MI: Gale Research Inc., 1993.

U.S. Industrial Outlook, Washington, D.C.: U.S. Department of Commerce, 1994.

Ward's Business Directory of U.S. Private and Public Companies, Detroit, MI: Gale Research Inc., 1993.

"Wean Doesn't Expect to Make Debt Payout," *American Metal Market,* March 2, 1993.

—David Kucera

SIC 3548

ELECTRIC AND GAS WELDING AND SOLDERING EQUIPMENT

This industry includes establishments primarily engaged in manufacturing electric and gas welding and soldering equipment and accessories. Also included are establishments primarily engaged in coating welding wire from purchased wire or from wire drawn in the same establishment. Establishments primarily engaged in manufacturing handheld soldering irons are classified in **SIC 3423: Hand and Edge Tools, Except Machine Tools and Handsaws,** and those manufacturing electron beam, ultrasonic, and laser welding equipment are classified in **SIC 3699: Electrical Machinery, Equipment, and Supplies, Not Elsewhere Classified.**

Welding and soldering equipment manufacturers, as a whole, experienced an increase of more than a $1 billion increase in shipments between 1987 and 1991. In 1988, the industry employed over 12,000 people, and paid significantly higher wages than other forms of manufacturing. The average compensation for an hourly worker was $12.58, compared to a total manufacturing average of $10.66 per hour.

Although industry employment levels were relatively stable toward the end of the 1980s, certain occupations were expected to face reductions going into the year 2000. These included secretaries, metal and plastic machine forming operators, precision inspectors, machine builders, assemblers and fabricators, and metal and plastic machine tool cutting operators. The only occupations expected to increase by over nine percent into the year 2000 are sales workers and industrial production managers.

Approximately 31 percent of the industry's manufacturers produce arc welding machines and their components and accessories, while another 27 percent make arc welding electrodes. The rest of the industry is split between manufacturing resistance welders, gas welding and cutting equipment, welding apparatus, and miscellaneous welding equipment.

Of the 219 companies engaged in this business, most are concentrated in the Great Lakes region, supporting the automotive industry. Michigan claims 48 manufacturers and 16.4 percent of the industry shipment volume, by dollar amount. However, Ohio, with its 21 welding equipment manufacturers, claims 28.2 percent of the industry shipment volume. Additionally, workers in Ohio averaged $14.71 per hour in 1987, while workers in Michigan averaged $12.78 per hour.

Lincoln Electric Company, the industry leader in terms of sales volume, is located in Cleveland, Ohio. Employing approximately 2,600 people in 1991, the company sold an estimated $620 million worth of welding equipment. Lincoln's pay structure and bonus-incentive plans have created a source of study for management researchers and motivational theorists. At Lincoln, an open-door policy exists that encourages communication between various employee levels. Rather than resorting to layoffs as the only course of down-sizing, Lincoln practices hiring freezes and voluntary layoffs. Lincoln credits its outstanding production volumes to this type of management-worker relationship.

Big Three Industries, located in Houston, Texas, employed 2,000 people in 1991, and recorded sales of $534 million. The company has gained some of its financial strength through the installation of a satellite network system that manages its databases. Big Three was formerly spending over $286,000 annually on telecommunications expenses between business locations; the investment in the satellite network has saved the company $23,000 per month since its installation in 1990.

Miller Electric Manufacturing Company, located in Appleton, Wisconsin, generated sales of an estimated $170 million in 1991. The company was able to increase product quality and worker productivity through the installation of a thermal storage air conditioning system. The thermal storage system has also reduced the company's electricity bills, because the system produces ice at night when utility rates are low.

INDUSTRY INFORMATION SOURCES

"Big Three Saves $23,000 a Month." *Communication News* (September, 1990).

Castronovo-Fusco, Mary Ann. "Dealing with Recession: Twenty-five Ways HR Executives are Leading Their Companies." *Employment Relations Today* (Spring, 1991).

Darnay, Arsen J., ed. *Manufacturing USA: Industry Analyses, Statistics, and Leading Companies.* Detroit: Gale Research, Inc., 1989.

Porteus, Evan L., et al. "On Manufacturing / Marketing Incentives." *Management Science* (September, 1991).

Schwed, Robert L. "Plant Cooling Increases Quality, Productivity." *Air Conditioning, Heating & Refrigeration News* (October 12, 1992).

— Valerie E. Wilson

SIC 3549

METALWORKING MACHINERY, NOT ELSEWHERE CLASSIFIED

This classification covers establishments primarily engaged in manufacturing metalworking machinery, not elsewhere classified. Establishments primarily engaged in manufacturing automotive maintenance equipment are classified in **SIC 3559: Special Industry Machinery, Not Elsewhere Classified.**

This industry includes special purpose machinery such as robotics machinery, which alone encompasses a growing trend in manufacturing. As industry continues to automate repetitive and often dangerous tasks, the use of assembly machines is expected to increase. The growth in this industrial classification during the early-to-mid 1980s has been a testament to this trend. The employment and shipment statistical data for this code is somewhat limited, due to reclassification of the content in 1987. However, an upward trend is apparent both before and after 1987, although the level of employment and shipments dropped significantly when the reclassification took place.

The product share of this classification is split between assembly machinery with 51 percent, coiling, cut-to-length, and slitting line metalworking machinery with 33 percent, and miscellaneous metalworking machinery with 16 percent. In 1991, total sales in this industry were $872.2 million. The Universal Instruments Corporation of Binghamton, New York was the largest business in the industry; the company sold an estimated $140 million worth of machinery and employed 1,500 people in 1991. The closest competitor, Detroit Tool & Engineering of Lebanon, Missouri, had $68 million in sales and employed 600 people. The third highest selling machinery company in 1991 was Allen Group Incorporated of Westland, Michigan. Allen sold $60 million in machinery and employed 500 people. Weldun International Incorporated of Bridgman, Michigan reported $60 million in sales and employed 400 people. The fifth highest selling company in 1991 was the Olofsson Corporation of Lansing, Michigan. Olofsson reported $40 million in sales and employed 300 people.

Although this industry is showing growth in sales, certain employment levels are expected to decline by the year 2000. Those occupations expected to be downsized by 18 percent to 19 percent include assemblers, secretaries, machine builders, inspectors, and machine forming operators. Machine tool cutting operators are expected to be reduced by 14 percent. Staffing in the following occupations is expected to be reduced by less than 10 percent: tool and die makers, general managers and top executives, blue collar worker supervisors, machine tool workers, precision metal workers, grinding machine workers, turning machine operators, general office clerks, bookkeepers, drafters, drilling machine tool workers, janitors, traffic clerks, and financial managers. Increases in employment levels are expected in only six occupations in the industry. Machinists are expected to increase in employment levels by 1.3 percent, sales workers by 12 percent, numerically controlled machine operators by nearly 4 percent, industrial production managers by nearly 10 percent, combination machine tool operators by almost 3 percent, and mechanical engineers by 5.5 percent.

In the early 1990s, Michigan had the highest number of establishments involved in this industry. In 1987, Michigan's 50 establishments sold $244 million worth of machinery, which accounted for 23.6 percent of the industry's total shipments. Approximately 2,200 people in Michigan were employed in this industry, receiving average hourly wages of $12.68. Illinois was ranked second in terms of shipments, reporting over $136 million in 1987. Approximately 1,600 Illinois residents were employed by this industry at an average wage of $11.84 per hour. Wisconsin was the highest paying state in this industry in 1987. Reporting $99.6 million in sales and employing 1,200 people, Wisconsin's establishments paid workers an average hourly wage of $14.86.

INDUSTRY INFORMATION SOURCES

Darnay, Arsen J., ed. *Manufacturing USA: Industry Analyses, Statistics, and Leading Companies*. Detroit: Gale Research, Inc., 1991.

—Valerie E. Wilson

SIC 3552

TEXTILE MACHINERY

This industry deals with establishments primarily engaged in manufacturing machinery for the textile industries, including parts, attachments, and accessories. Establishments primarily engaged in manufacturing industrial sewing machines are classified in **SIC 3559: Special Industry Machinery, Not Elsewhere Classified,** and those manufacturing household sewing machines are classified in **SIC 3639: Household Appliances, Not Elsewhere Classified.**

INDUSTRY SNAPSHOT

Between 1985 and 1991, the textile machinery industry doubled its shipment values from $1 billion to $2 billion. However, the number of employees and establishments engaged in the industry dropped slightly during that period. Between 1987 and 1990, textile manufacturers' capacity utilization dropped sharply from approximately 92 percent to below 82 percent, directly depressing the machinery industry. However, a strong resurgence was seen between 1990 and 1992, as capacity utilization increased from below 82 percent to nearly 90 percent. Inventories also grew significantly between 1985 and 1993, rising from a value of nearly $4.5 billion to $6 billion.

These figures indicate that textile manufacturers of the early 1990s were secure in a potentially growing market. The development of machinery to support this industry mirrors the outlook of the entire retail industry. Likewise, technological developments in machinery that offer textile manufacturers a competitive edge in terms of cost savings, increased productivity, and better quality, also serve to stimulate the machinery side of the textile industry.

ORGANIZATION AND STRUCTURE

The textile machinery industry encompasses all machinery used from the start of the yarn-making process through weaving the cloth and eventually final treatments and dyeing. Most fabrics produced by weaving or knitting must undergo a number of further processing treatments before they are ready for sale. In the finishing operations, the fabric is subjected to mechanical and chemical treatment whereby its appearance and quality are improved and its commercial value is enhanced. Each of these processes requires different machinery, thus the scope of textile machinery is very broad.

The industry is comprised of every machine needed in all stages of the development of textiles, from yarn spinning to final dressing. The term "finishing" or "dressing" is collectively applied to the various finishing treatments required for each type of fabric. For example, textiles produced from vegetable fibers require different treatment—raising, singeing, dyeing, printing—than those produced from animal or synthetic fibers. These procedures require mechanical treatment and processing by chemicals to improve the glaze, shape-retaining properties, crease resistance, smoothness, and drape of the material. Additionally, depending on the kind of material and the purpose for which it is to be used, a textile can be made shrinkproof, water-repellent, supple, soft, or heavy. Mechanical finishing treatments may consist of mangling, pressing, rolling, milling, shearing, calendering, raising, and singeing. Before undergoing these treatments, the material is passed through liquid baths or steam baths in which various substances, such as starch, vegetable gums, glues, gelatins, and mucilages are added to the fabric. Each type of machinery, as well as parts, attachments, and accessories, are included in this industrial classification.

In terms of product share, parts and attachments for principle machines represent 39.5 percent of the machinery produced. Fiber-to-fabric textile machinery holds a 15.7 percent product share. Fabric machinery for weaving, knitting, embroidering, braiding, tufting, and lace making comprises 8.1 percent of the industry. Finishing machinery claims a 5.3 percent product share. Machines used for bleaching, mercerizing, and dyeing claim 4.5 percent of the product share. Machinery for drying stocks, yarns, cloth, carpet, and other non-woven materials represents 3.1 percent of the product share. Non-specific machinery represents the remaining 19.5 percent of the products manufactured by the industry.

BACKGROUND AND DEVELOPMENT

The first hand weaving looms are thought to date back to 4000 B.C. Although the East is credited with the first horizontally arranged weaving plane, its date of origin is unknown. A shedding mechanism, which originated in China, was not introduced in Europe until the third or fourth century A.D. Only minor advances were made with the hand loom over the next millennium. The first major development occurred in 1733, when the flying shuttle was introduced. Designed by an Englishman, the shuttle came equipped with wheels, which reduced resistance as the shuttle passed through the fibers. This considerably decreased the time constraints of producing woven fabrics and expanded the capabilities of the hand loom.

Several blueprints for power looms were submitted during the sixteenth, seventeenth, and eighteenth centuries. Circa 1500, Leonardo da Vinci sketched a hydraulic-driven power loom. This idea was repeated in 1678, and later in 1745; however, none of these were built. It was not until 1784 that an English parson designed the first manufacturable and functional power loom. A short while after the parson's machine went into limited production of fabrics, another stride was made for this machinery industry. In 1796 an automatic loom stopping system, called the "shuttle stop motion," was developed. The theory behind this system is still in use today. In 1822, an English engineer made further improvements to the power loom, which prompted the manufacture of the first large series of power looms.

The oldest known patterning device is drawn in a Chinese book, which dates back to the twelfth century A.D. Much later, in 1725, a punched cardboard card served as the first dobby, a device used for creating unusual weaves. The first patterning machine was created by J. M. Jacquard in 1805, variations of this machine still bear his name. Another significant advance occurred in 1835, when a shuttle was developed that enabled different thread colors to be inserted into the fabric weave.

CURRENT CONDITIONS

According to *Standard & Poor's Industrial Surveys*, the Department of Commerce reported that the value of domestic textile manufacturers' shipments hit a record high in 1992 for the second consecutive year. Shipments rose 7.1 percent to $72.5 billion, up from $67.7 billion in 1991. Due to higher sales volumes and increased efficiencies from capital investment in machinery, profits in the textiles industry have exploded. Record profits of $ 1.9 billion were reported in 1992, rising from $882 million in 1991, and $433 million in 1990. Additionally, inventory values were $500 million higher than they were in 1991. While the explosive growth in profits is not expected to continue, sales are expected to increase in anticipation of higher consumer confidence levels.

Continued investment in textile machinery has reflected textile manufacturers' optimism toward the industry's future. Between 1991 and 1992 manufacturers increased their capital expenditures by 7 percent, raising their investments to $2.08 billion. Buyer demands for higher quality apparel and home furnishings at lower prices have encouraged this capital investment trend. Manufacturers have also been shifting to automated processes in lieu of labor intensive operations that drive costs.

INDUSTRY LEADERS

The following five companies led the industry in sales in 1991: John Brown Incorporated, with $210 million; John D. Hollingsworth, with $79 million; Platt-Saco-Lowell Corporation, with $78 million; Steel Heddle Manufacturing Company, with $70 million; and A. B. Carter Incorporated, with $65 million. Combined, the 75 top-selling companies employed 15,400 people and had sales of $1.41 3 billion in 1991.

The United Kingdom Division of Platt-Saco-Lowell, which is a subsidiary of John D. Hollingsworth on Wheels, suffered severe financial

losses during the global economic recession of the early 1990s. Having entered into Chapter 11 proceedings, the company was ordered by its creditors to find a buyer no later than May 1,1993. Reporting unadjusted losses in 1992 of 1.28 million pounds sterling on 10.16 million pounds of sales and unsecured debts of 3.47 million pounds, Platt continued its four-year-long downward profit spiral. The most serious blow issued to Platt was the removal of Hollingsworth's orders for Platt's Model 2000 card; approximately 71 percent of Platt's sales depended on Hollingsworth's business.

Other textile machinery manufacturers fared better than Platt during the early 1990s. Industry leader Steel Heddle, for example, has been praised for its strength in quality control, which it obtains through high-speed motion analysis technology. Combining this technology with other quality control and testing techniques, Steel Heddle has been able to improve the quality of its loom accessory products. Heddle uses Eastman Kodak Company's EktaPro motion analyzer to perform motion analysis which locates and diagnoses stresses in Heddle's own stainless steel wire that it uses to make its heddle products. The motion analyzer has saved the company money, increased customer satisfaction, improved product designs, and is also configured for a variety of other applications, including research and development. Such diagnostic tools have also been useful in finding the location of technical problems that previously could only have been deduced from trial and error testing and engineering calculations.

Heddle also improved its product line by using plastic instead of aluminum in its harness frames. Modern high-speed weaving machines often put too much stress on aluminum harness frames. The new plastic frames weigh less than the aluminum ones, but are still able to provide greater stiffness and structural stability. Steel Heddle's other advancements in material conversions include riderless and rider-design carbon-fiber harness frames made for water and air jet weaving machines. With these lightweight frames, Heddle has reduced machine wear and achieved significant energy savings.

WORK FORCE

The employment level in the textile machinery industry has declined since 1982. By 1991, 17,200 people were employed in the industry, down from 19,400 in 1981. In 1988, the average hourly wage of industry employees was $9.86, which was slightly below the average wage of $10.66 earned by employees of all other manufacturing industries. Workers in New York received the highest wage in the industry, earning $11.50 an hour. South Carolina workers earned the lowest wage in the industry in 1987, receiving $8.93 an hour. All textile companies are located east of the Mississippi River, and most are based in the Carolinas.

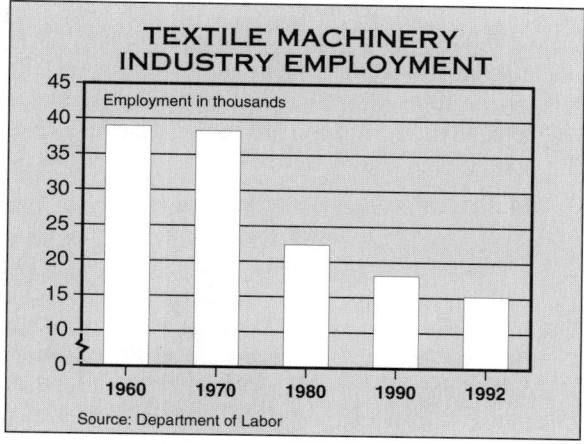

TEXTILE MACHINERY INDUSTRY EMPLOYMENT

Employment in thousands

Source: Department of Labor

The industry is expected to make significant reductions in several occupations in the late 1990s. Those occupations anticipating cuts in excess of 10 percent include machine builders, assemblers, secretaries, welders, sheet metal workers, precision inspectors, welding machine setters, and machine tool cutting operators. However, job opportunities in many occupations are expected to grow by over 10 percent. These positions include sales workers, production managers, machinery mechanics, engineering and science managers, and electrical and electronics engineers.

AMERICA AND THE WORLD

The textile machinery industry is ultimately driven by the retail buying habits of American shoppers. Through the 1980s and early 1990s, retail sales, as a percentage of disposable income, declined from 50 percent in 1980 to approximately 44 percent in 1992. Lagging consumer confidence has been cited as the main reason for this trend. However, such factors as decreasing leisure time and increased bargain shopping have also contributed to the decline in retail sales. Consequently, the industry suffered from decreasing domestic demand in the early 1990s.

According to *Standard & Poor's Industry Surveys*, the ratification of the North American Free Trade Agreement (NAFTA) is expected to create a huge new market for the textile industry. Subsequently, this extended market could offset some of the ongoing sales volume losses caused by cheaper imports. Additionally, NAFTA proposes a "rule of origin" clause that

could serve to benefit the textile industry. The rule of origin makes allowances for Canada, Mexico, and the United States to waive duties and quotas on products made from raw materials that were produced in one of the three nations. This would give U.S., Mexican, and Canadian manufacturers a competitive advantage over Taiwanese and Korean textile producers. Some analysts believe that U.S. apparel makers will try to reap additional benefits by moving their facilities to Mexico, where labor costs are low. In turn, if additional plants are built in Mexico or Canada, the textile machinery industry would benefit.

The dramatic political and economic changes in Europe and the former Soviet Union could also create new markets for textile machinery. While many machinery suppliers exist within Europe, their technology is inferior to that of the West and Japan. Consequently, textile producers in these European countries may look to U.S. manufacturers for assistance in modernizing their facilities.

RESEARCH AND TECHNOLOGY

While Steel Heddle has reported advances in quality control techniques and material use, three other companies are leading the industry in technical innovation. The John D. Hollingsworth Company, for example, has developed an automatic bale opening system, and Marshall & Williams has developed an improved pen tinter and incineration system. Hollingsworth's new Rotomix is a state-of-the-art automatic bale opening system. It employs counter-rotating heads that blend the top, middle, and bottom of the bales to achieve a superior blend over other bale mixing equipment. The Rotomix can open three different bale sizes and boasts a maximum production speed of 1,500 kilograms per hour. However, operation at this speed does not maximize efficiency; a production speed of 1,200 kilograms per hour is recommended for peak efficiency.

Another innovative company is Marshall & Williams (M&W), which reported sales of $20 million in 1991. M&W has developed a better dye pen that operates in a vertical orientation. The pen offers the control and accuracy normally reserved for horizontally orientated pens, while achieving efficiency characteristic of vertically oriented pens. Heat-treated, powdered steel alloy components give the pen equipment durability and stability and enable it to achieve a superior pen line. Additionally, the pen's close-return design features an offset for the return track and reduces nozzle-to-cloth distance. Another innovation developed by M&W is an internal incineration system. The system consists of small incinerators which are placed in several oven zones. Oven exhaust air is drawn into the incinerators, where it is heated to between 1,000 and 1,500 degrees Fahrenheit. That temperature is maintained until all volatile organic compounds in the exhaust have been destroyed; and finally, clean exhaust is passed through a heat exchanger before it is released from the oven. Demand for this system is expected to grow dramatically as manufacturers strive to meet increasingly strict regulations imposed by the Environmental Protection Agency.

INDUSTRY INFORMATION SOURCES

Darnay, Arsen J., ed., *Manufacturing USA: Industry Analyses Statistics and Leading Companies*, Detroit: Gale Research, Inc., 1992.

Fallon, James, "Creditors Give Platt-Saco-Lowell Until May to Find a Buyer," *Daily News Record*, April 22, 1993.

"Marshall & Williams: Vertical Tinter System," *Textile World*, April 1993.

McAllister, Isaacs, III, "Combing Resurgence Rides New Technology Fast Track," *Textile World*, February 1992.

Pinto, Akiva, "Hollingsworth: Rotomix Automated Bale Opening System," *Textile World*, April 1993.

"Steel Heddle: Carbon Fiber Harness Frames," *Textile World*, April 1992.

"Steel Heddle Uses High-Tech Motion Analysis," *Industrial Engineering*, June 1992.

Talavá ek, Oldřich, and Vladimír Svatý, *Shuttleless Weaving Machines*, Amsterdam: Elsevier Scientific Publishing Company, 1981.

Vandeventer, Elizabeth, "Textiles, Apparel & Home Furnishings: Current Analysis," *Standard & Poor's Industry Surveys*, March 18, 1993.

Witkin, Philip M., "Marshall & Williams: Internal Incineration for Finishing Ovens," *Textile World*, April 1992.

—Valerie E. Wilson

SIC 3553

WOODWORKING MACHINERY

This category includes establishments primarily engaged in manufacturing machinery for sawmills, for making particleboard and similar products, and for otherwise working or producing wood products. Establishments primarily engaged in manufacturing hand tools are classified in cutlery, handtools, and general hardware manufacturing industries, while those engaged in manufacturing portable power-driven hand tools are classified in **SIC 3546: Power-Driven Handtools.**

In 1990, there were approximately 280 companies primarily engaged in manufacturing woodworking machinery used by the forest products industry. Less than 100 of those companies employed more than 20 people, but they accounted for nearly 85 percent of the industry's output. In 1987, the industry shipped $885 million worth of machinery and employed approximately 9,000 people. Most woodworking machinery manufacturers were located in North Carolina, Ohio, Oregon, or Tennessee. Equipment made by the industry included machinery used in cutting, shaping, sanding, gluing, laminating and finishing wood products.

In the 1980s, the woodworking machinery industry was affected by a slowdown in the housing industry and a general recession in the U.S. economy. In the early 1990s, the industry was further affected by cutting limits imposed on the logging industry in the Pacific Northwest. However, in 1992, George Delaney, then president of the Wood Machinery Manufacturers of America (WMMA), which represented more than 100 companies in the industry, said the number one issue facing the organization's membership was product-liability reform legislation. Woodworking machinery manufacturers often paid as much as 10 percent of their annual sales for liability insurance, a cost that foreign competitors did not face.

In the early 1990s, the woodworking machinery industry benefited from legislation that required woodworking companies to reduce the amount of dust in the air of their factories. Several companies in the industry increased their revenues by manufacturing dust-reduction equipment. Environmental concerns over logging also prompted production of new machinery. With stricter limits on logging, the forest products industry was buying updated equipment that reduced the amount of waste in manufacturing wood products.

The Coe Manufacturing Co., founded in 1852, was one of the first companies to manufacture computerized woodworking machinery, introducing a computer-controlled veneer lathe in 1977. The company operates manufacturing facilities in Tigard, Oregon and Painesville, Ohio, where its headquarters are located. In 1992, Coe, a privately held company, employed approximately 760 workers and had revenues of $80 million. Most of Coe's woodworking machinery is sold to plywood manufacturers.

Founded in 1919, Delta International Machinery Corp. was the largest manufacturer of general purpose woodworking machinery and accessories in the United States. The company operates manufacturing facilities in Tupelo, Mississippi and Limeira, Brazil and has headquarters in Pittsburgh, Pennsylvania. In 1992, the company, a subsidiary of Pentair, Inc., employed approximately 1,000 workers and had revenues of $100 million.

U.S. Natural Resources, Inc., formed in 1928, has expanded its business by acquiring woodworking machinery manufacturers. By 1993 several companies had come under the company's aegis. The oldest company was Irvington Forest Industries, a saw manufacturer founded in 1907 and acquired by U.S. Natural Resources in 1969. Other companies included the Moore Dry Kiln Co., founded in 1910 and acquired in 1968; Schurman Machine Works, founded in 1934 and acquired in 1975; and Applied Theory Associates, a consulting firm founded in 1969 and acquired in 1982. Based in Vancouver, Washington, U.S. Natural Resources employed approximately 800 workers and had sales of $84 million in 1992.

INDUSTRY INFORMATION SOURCES

"American Technology in Action," *Furniture Design & Manufacturing*, June 1992.

Anderson, Michael A., "Coe Helping the Wood Industry to Computerize," *Portland Business Journal*, March 24, 1986, 23.

"IWF '90 Packs 'em in: 32,000 People, 903 Exhibits," *Forest Industries*, October 1990, 7.

1993 Buyer's Guide and Directory, Philadelphia: Wood Machinery Manufacturers of America, 1993.

—Dean Boyer

SIC 3554

PAPER INDUSTRIES MACHINERY

This category covers establishments primarily engaged in manufacturing machinery used in the pulp, paper, and paper products industries. Establishments primarily engaged in manufacturing printing trades machinery are classified in **SIC 3555: Printing Trades Machinery and Equipment.**

The United States is the world's leading producer of paper-making machinery. In 1992, approximately 230 U.S. companies were involved in manufacturing machinery used in the pulp, paper, and paper products industries. These companies shipped nearly $2.4 billion worth of equipment in 1992. The Department of Commerce estimated that shipments peaked at $2.8 billion in 1990, after five years of steady growth. Shipments subsequently declined by 7 percent, however, during the global recession of the early 1990s.

This growth during the 1980s was the result of several factors, including a demand for de-inking sys-

tems and other equipment used in recycling newspapers, magazines and corrugated containers. Despite lower shipments in 1992, strong demand for machinery capable of meeting environmental standards was expected to continue. In addition, economic reform and the spread of democracy in Eastern Europe and the former Soviet Union were expected to create an expanded overseas market for U.S. manufacturers of paper industries machinery. In fact, exports accounted for about 45 percent of all shipments of paper industries machinery in 1992.

The growing free market in Eastern Europe also resulted in a 25 percent increase in the export of U.S. paper products in 1991, further increasing demand for new or rebuilt paper industries machinery at home. According to industry figures, parts for rebuilt machines accounted for as much as 70 percent of the paper-making machinery market. There also was a growing market for used machinery, particularly in the specialties paper industry.

Historical Development. The first machines used for making paper were invented in France in the late eighteenth century. In 1799, Frenchman Nicholas Louis Robert received a patent on a machine that could produce a continuous roll of paper. Several years later, London stationers Henry and Sealy Fourdrinier financed improvements in Robert's paper-making machine, which eventually came to bear their name. Manufacturers began using the Fourdrinier machine for the commercial production of paper in England in 1812. Eventually, the Fourdrinier machine became the foundation of the paper-making industry.

The first Fourdrinier machine used in the U.S. was imported from England in 1827 and put into operation at a paper mill in Saugerties, New York. However, by 1829, an American company, Phelps & Spafford, began manufacturing Fourdrinier machines, the first of which was installed at Norwich, Connecticut. Phelps & Spafford reorganized after the recession of 1837 as Smith and Winchester, and continued to operate into the twentieth century. Several other U.S. manufacturers of paper machinery were also founded prior to the Civil War, including the Merrill Machine Company and the Bakers Falls Iron Machine Works, both of which were still leading companies in 1993, although under different names.

Pulping. Until the mid-1800s, paper was made principally from rags rather than wood. Then, between 1840 and 1860, several mechanical processes were developed that produced wood pulp suitable for making rough-grained paper. One of these pulp grinders was known as the Jordan refiner. Invented in 1858 by two Americans, Joseph Jordan and Thomas Eustace, the Jordan refiner was the principal pulping machine until it was replaced in the early twentieth century by disk refiners. In 1867, American chemist Benjamin Tilghman found that pulp could also be produced by dissolving wood in a solution of sulfuric acid. A German chemist, Carl Dahl, perfected chemical pulping in the late 1880s. Mechanical pulping was extremely efficient, converting as much as 90 percent of the basic raw material into usable pulp. Although chemical pulping was considerably less efficient, the pulp generated by this process could be used to produce a higher grade of paper. Newsprint was generally a blend of about 25 percent mechanical pulp and 75 percent chemical pulp. Top quality stationery was still made from rag pulp. Many of the machines manufactured by the paper machinery industry during this period, such as barkers, chippers, and refiners, were used for the pulping processes.

Exports. Historically, the United States has been a net exporter of paper industries machinery, with Canada, the United Kingdom, Mexico and Australia being its most important foreign markets. However, imports began growing in relation to exports during the 1970s, and in 1979 the balance tipped in favor of imports. Before the rise of imports, nearly 90 percent of all new paper-making machines installed in the United States came from U.S.-based manufacturers. By the early 1980s, however, 50 percent of the new machines came from foreign manufacturers.

Much of the imported machinery came from Germany, the leading exporter of paper industries machinery in the world. Finland, Sweden, Switzerland, and Japan have also sold significant amounts of paper-making machinery in the U.S. market. There was a brief recovery in 1982, when exports exceeded imports by about $110 million. However, the downward trend returned in 1983, and by 1987 the industry's trade deficit had grown to almost $300 million. Exports began to improve in the late 1980s and early 1990s, and the Department of Commerce estimated that the U.S. industry would again be a net exporter in 1993.

The Wisconsin-based Beloit Corporation was the largest U.S. producer of machinery for the paper industry with sales of $483 million in 1985. Founded in 1858 as the Merrill Machine Company, the company's name was changed in 1885 to the Beloit Iron Works. The company achieved some fame in 1893 when it built a paper-making machine that was displayed at the Chicago World's Fair. The name Beloit Corp. was adopted in 1961. In 1986, the company was acquired by the Milwaukee-based Harnischfeger Corporation. In addition to its U.S. facilities, the company has

manufacturing operations in the United Kingdom, Canada, Italy, and Brazil.

Another industry leader, the Black Clawson Company, was founded in 1893 and is best known as a producer of systems for bleaching or whitening wood pulp. In 1987, the New York-based company had sales of about $170 million, and operated plants in New York and Ohio.

The Sandy Hill Corporation was founded in upstate New York in 1858 as the Bakers Falls Iron Machine Works. The name was changed almost immediately to the Sandy Hill Iron & Brass Works, reflecting the original name of the community where it was located. Sandy Hill Corp. is primarily involved in producing parts for rebuilding machinery. In addition to its New York plant, the company also has facilities in Canada. In 1987, the company had sales of approximately $35 million.

INDUSTRY INFORMATION SOURCES

Abrahams, Edward D., *A Competitive Assessment of the U.S. Paper Machinery Industry*, Washington, D.C.: U.S. Department of Commerce, 1989.

Press, Falls Church, V.A.: American Paper Machinery Association, May 1993.

Special Industry Machinery, 1987 Census of Manufacturers, Washington, D.C.: U.S. Department of Commerce, 1990.

U.S. Industrial Outlook 1993, Washington, D.C.: U.S. Department of Commerce, 1993.

—Dean Boyer

SIC 3555

PRINTING TRADES MACHINERY AND EQUIPMENT

This category covers establishments primarily engaged in manufacturing machinery and equipment used by the printing and bookbinding trades, including printing presses, bookbinding machines, typesetting and photoengraving equipment, and a variety of specialized tools for the printing trades.

INDUSTRY SNAPSHOT

There were approximately 400 companies involved in making machinery for the printing trades industry in the early 1990s. In 1987, these manufacturers shipped slightly more than $3 billion worth of equipment. In 1992, shipments had declined to $2.7 billion, which reflected generally slow growth in the printing trades industry. However, orders for new equipment typically were placed six months in advance, and industry analysts expected shipments to increase as much as 18 percent in 1993. About 40 percent of the industry's output in 1992, or $1.1 billion, was exported to foreign countries, which was about equal to the value of U.S. imports of printing trades machinery. Major foreign purchasers of U.S. machinery were Canada, Mexico, the United Kingdom, Germany, and Japan. Most imports came from Germany and Japan.

The printing machinery industry began undergoing tremendous change in the 1970s as computer technology replaced or significantly changed the type of machinery used by the printing trades. This included developments in phototypesetting and photocomposition, and greater automation of traditional printing press operations. Employment in the printing machinery industry declined from about 27,000 in 1987 to 21,000 in 1992.

ORGANIZATION AND STRUCTURE

In 1993, the printing machinery industry included many companies that had been founded nearly a century before, such as Linotype-Hell Company, Heidelberg Harris, Inc., and Monotype, Inc. It also included dozens of newer companies that were founded since the late 1960s, accompanying the rapid growth of phototypesetting, photocomposition, and computer-controlled presses.

The largest printing machinery industry association was NPES The Association for Suppliers of Printing and Publishing Technologies. In 1993, NPES had more than 300 members, which included computer manufacturers and software companies, as well as traditional printing machinery manufacturers. NPES conducted market research and promoted international trade on behalf of its members. NPES was founded in 1933 as the National Printing Equipment Association. The name was changed to the National Printing Equipment and Supply Association in 1978, and changed again in 1991 to NPES. James C. Gould, then chairman of NPES, said the name acknowledged the "continuing change and new directions in our industry."

BACKGROUND AND DEVELOPMENT

Letterpress printing, using raised images to print on paper, was an ancient art developed by the Babylonians as early as 2000 B.C. for producing playing cards. However, the first printing presses were derived from machines used to press grapes and cheese and were not invented until the early fifteenth century, more than 3,000 years later. The modern printing in-

dustry was generally considered to date from the mid fifteenth century with the invention of moveable type by a German printer, Johannes Gutenberg. The Gutenberg press used a flat wooden plate, or platen, to press a single sheet of soft paper against a form containing letters cast in metal from clay molds.

The printing press changed very little over the next 400 years. When Stephen Daye established the first publishing house in the American Colonies in 1639, his English-made press was not significantly different from Gutenberg's. Christopher Sauer, Jr. of Cambridge, Massachusetts also followed the Gutenberg model when he manufactured the first press built in the American Colonies in 1750. However, printing machinery technology began to change radically in the early 1800s, with many of the advancements developed by American manufacturers. Among the most important U.S. contributions to printing machinery were the development of the Columbian press, the rotary press, the Linotype machine, and the offset press. The United States was the leading manufacturer of printing presses from about the time of the Civil War until after World War II, when Germany began to challenge the U.S. dominance.

Columbian Press. In 1813, George Clymer, a printer in Philadelphia, replaced the cumbersome screw mechanism of the Gutenberg press with a much faster system of levers that allowed press operators to achieve sufficient pressure for printing. The elaborate system had a long handle known in the printing trades as "the devil's tail." Clymer's Columbian Press was cast from iron and was noted for its intricate metal work that included dolphins, flowers, and an intimidating American eagle perched on top. Unfortunately for Clymer, with Western expansion of the United States, many American printers preferred wooden presses that were lighter and could be transported more easily. Clymer moved to England in 1817 where Clymer & Company manufactured presses until 1851.

Rotary press. The rotary press was an American adaptation of the cylinder press. Friedrich Koenig, a German clockmaker who had emigrated to England, developed the first practical cylinder press about 1811. Koenig replaced the flat platen with a cylinder that allowed press operators to maintain a uniform pressure as the type bed was moved horizontally. The first Koenig press, which could print about 1,100 sheets per hour, was installed at *The Times of London* in 1816. Koenig later returned to Germany where he established the first printing press factory. The Koenig press, however, cost about 10 times as much as other presses and never became popular.

Richard March Hoe, a New York City manufacturer, built the first cylinder press in the United States in 1830. Hoe also realized that the greatest limitation to Koenig's press was the time it took to move the massive type bed back and forth. In 1846, R. Hoe & Company developed the first rotary press. Instead of using a flat type bed, Hoe mounted type around the outside of a huge cylinder. This cylinder was surrounded by four smaller platen cylinders. Instead of the back and forth motion of the Koenig press, the Hoe type cylinder revolved in a continuous motion. Each of the four hand-fed platen cylinders could print about 2,000 sheets per hour. This gave the Hoe rotary press a capacity of 8,000 copies per hour. The speed was later increased to 20,000 sheets. The first Hoe rotary press was installed at *The Philadelphia Public Ledger*. Hoe & Co. continued to manufacture presses and other printing machinery until 1968, when it declared bankruptcy.

William Bullock, a Philadelphia printer, perfected the first rotary press able to print on both sides of the paper. In 1880, he also developed the first high-speed press to print from a continuous roll of paper. The Goss Printing Company, founded in Chicago in 1885, was the first company to combine multiple high-speed rotary presses into a single machine that could print entire newspapers in one press run. In 1889, Goss installed a set of six presses for *The New York Herald* that could print 72,000 newspapers per hour. Hoe also developed a machine for cutting and folding newspapers that were printed on continuous-roll web presses.

Typesetting. For 400 years after Gutenberg invented moveable type, printers composed lines of type by hand, one letter at a time. When the printing was completed, the letters were returned to a type case. It was a tedious process, and one that resisted all attempts at mechanization. *American History Illustrated* once called it "the century's most perplexing invention problem." By one account, more than 200 inventors attempted to solve the enormous engineering problem posed by typesetting. Most ended up frustrated, and many ended up broke. Mark Twain lost most of his fortune backing the Paige Compositor, which turned out to be an impractical failure. An examiner in the U.S. Patent Office reportedly went insane trying to cope with the technical complexity of the many patents filed on mechanical typesetters in the late 1880s.

In 1884, Ottmar Mergenthaler, an immigrant German clockmaker working for a scientific instruments company in Baltimore, invented a machine he named the Linotype. The Linotype allowed an operator sitting at a keyboard to compose lines of type from brass molds, or matrices. Separate lines of type were then cast in metal and slid into galleys for printing. The brass matrices returned to their original position until they were needed again. After printing, the type was melted down and the metal could be reused.

The Linotype, which Thomas Edison called "the eighth wonder of the world," solved several critical problems. First, because the brass matrices were immediately reusable, there was no need for a large precast supply of type. Since every line of type was newly cast from an alloy of lead, tin and antimony, printers always received a quality impression. The Linotype also justified each line of type automatically by sliding wedge-shaped pieces of metal between each word. The first 12 Linotypes were installed at *The New York Tribune* in 1886. Within ten years, there were Linotypes in use throughout Europe and as far west as Hawaii.

The Monotype, a machine similar to the Linotype, was invented in 1887 by an American, Tolbert Lanston. The Monotype cast individual letters from brass matrices and was especially popular with book publishers because it could cast special symbols or non-Latin alphabets. Additionally, corrections could be made by changing a single letter rather than an entire line of type.

The first phototypesetting machines were patented about 1880, but did not become practical until after World War II when the graphic arts industry began to grow. Linotype and Monotype typesetters were used almost universally by commercial printers until phototypesetting machines began to replace them in the 1970s. By the mid 1980s, most major and newspapers had switched from "hot lead" to "cold type."

In 1992, *The New York Times* printed a story about "The Last Yiddish Linotype in America." Linotype machine No. 23,211 was one of nine made for the *Jewish Daily Forward* in New York in 1918. Outfitted with Hebrew letters and converted to compose type right to left, Linotype No. 23,211 was in operation until 1991, when the 3,000 pound machine and a host of other equipment were replaced by a single desktop computer. In 1993, the NPES forecast that nearly all published materials would originate on computer-based systems by the end of the century.

Other American developments in printing machinery included the halftone screen. Used to create an engraving for printing pictures, the halftone screen was perfected in the 1880s by Max and Louis Levy. Offset printing on paper is often attributed to an American printer named Ira Rubel. Offset lithography had been used since the 1880s to print labels directly on tin containers. In 1905, Rubel was operating a rotary press when he unintentionally transferred an image onto the rubber impression cylinders. When he then fed paper through the press he noticed that the images left by the rubber cylinders were much sharper than the direct image left by the raised type. For many years, offset printing was used for high-quality work. In the 1970s, offset presses also began to replace letter presses for high-speed printing such as newspapers.

National Associations. Leading members of the printing equipment industry banded together in 1910 to form the Printing Press Manufacturers Association (PPMA), whose stated purpose was to convince Congress to pass laws protecting the industry from foreign imports. However, the PPMA disbanded in 1922, after the death of two leading members and in the wake of an investigation by the newly formed Federal Trade Commission, which found that many such industry organizations were illegally exchanging price information.

In 1933, 26 manufacturers of printing presses, bindery equipment, typesetting machinery, and specialty printing equipment formed the National Printing Equipment Association (NPEA) to work with President Franklin Roosevelt's National Recovery Administration (NRA). The NRA was created by the National Industrial Recovery Act of 1933 to help pull the country out of the Great Depression by enforcing codes of fair competition for business and industry, including minimum wages and standard work weeks. The printing equipment industry estimated that manufacturers sold more than $100 million worth of printing equipment in 1928, a year before the stock market crash that plunged the economy into depression. By 1933, sales had dropped to about $18 million and employment had been cut in half, from 18,000 to 9,000. In addition to establishing a code of fair competition for the industry, the manufacturers also hoped to control the market for used equipment. More than 100 commercial printing plants failed between 1929 and 1933, flooding the market with used equipment.

The industry code proposed by the NPEA was accepted by the National Recovery Administration in 1934, but in 1935, a unanimous U.S. Supreme Court ruled that the National Industrial Recovery Act was unconstitutional. Although the NPEA code of fair competition was invalidated, the organization voted to continue as a source of information and education for the printing equipment industry.

New York World Fair. In 1939, more than 100,000 people visited a display of printing machinery technology at the New York World Fair, including the original Stephen Daye Press, then owned by the Vermont His-

torical Society. More than 200 companies participated in the exhibition, which covered 50,000 square feet in the Grand Central Palace. Mayor Fiorello LaGuardia declared the last week in September to be ''Printing Industry Week,'' and the U.S. Post Office issued a 3-cent stamp commemorating the 300th anniversary of printing in the United States.

World War II. Rationing of critical supplies such as steel and rubber practically shut down the printing machinery industry during World War II. However, many manufacturers compensated by accepting government contracts to build weapons. As early as 1939, even before the U.S. entered the war, the Goss Printing Company turned down a major contract with the *St. Louis Post Dispatch* because the newspaper was unwilling to accept a clause that would excuse Goss if the war prevented it from fulfilling the contract. However, Goss did negotiate a contract with the U.S. Navy to build gun mounts, sighting mechanisms and other weapons machinery.

After the U.S. entered the war, the War Production Board (WPB) halted the manufacture of all printing equipment for civilian use. By July 1942, nearly the entire industry had been converted to the production of war material. Other industry leaders, in addition to Goss, R. Hoe & Company and the ATF-Webendorfer Company, were building recoil mechanisms for anti-aircraft guns. Mergenthaler Linotype Company was making fire-control instruments, F.P. Rosback Company was also making parts for anti-aircraft guns and wing tips for P-38 airplanes, and the Miehle Printing Press & Manufacturing Company was making shell casing and naval ordnance.

Eventually, the WPB allocated some material for manufacturing spare parts for printing equipment, but between 1943 and 1945 the printing machinery industry nearly quadrupled its pre-war output—and more than 80 percent was for the war effort. The WPB later reported, ''no other segment of the metal-working industry showed a higher degree of conversion to war work.'' According to the WPB, 22 printing machinery manufacturers were awarded the Army-Navy ''E'' for production excellence, including every manufacturer of printing presses.

Xerography. After World War II, the printing machinery industry began to face increased competition from foreign manufacturers, especially German companies who received favorable trade agreements as part of the European rebuilding. The industry also began to change with the rapid development of phototypesetting and photocomposition. However, a process of transferring images invented in the 1938 by Chester F. Carlson may ultimately prove to have an even greater impact on the printing machinery industry. Carlson, a patent attorney in New York with a degree in physics, called his process "electrophotography." The Battelle Memorial Institute, a non-profit research organization, and the Haloid Co., a producer of photo supplies founded in 1906, later renamed the process "xerography." In 1961, Haloid became the Xerox Corporation. Xerography began replacing job presses for many printing functions in the 1970s.

CURRENT CONDITIONS

With the development of phototypesetting, photo-composition, and non-impact printing, the printing trades were evolving from a craft to a high-technology industry. Consequently, the printing machinery industry evolved as well. In the early 1990s, there was still a need for the massive presses that dominated the industry and the equipment necessary to run them. However, just as Linotypes gave way to computer typesetters, industry leaders were predicting that non-impact printing would someday replace the huge presses. In 1992, AM International Inc., a Chicago-based manufacturer of printing machinery, unveiled the Electrobook Press, a non-impact press based on electrostatic imaging. The Electrobook Press was developed jointly by AM International, publisher McGraw-Hill Inc., and commercial printer R.R. Donnelly & Sons. McGraw-Hill expected to use the new press to publish customized textbooks for university professors. The press was too slow in 1993, however, to be used by newspapers.

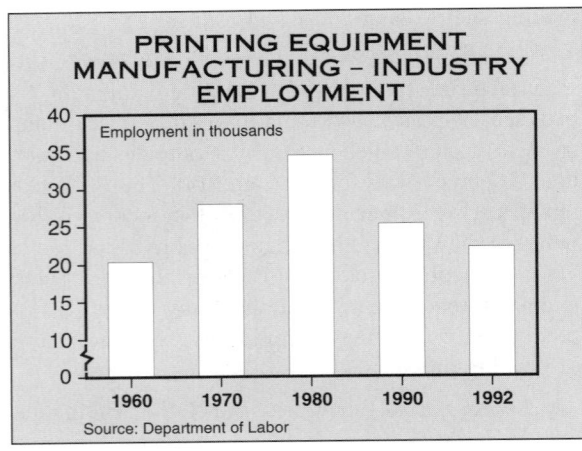

PRINTING EQUIPMENT MANUFACTURING – INDUSTRY EMPLOYMENT

Employment in thousands

Source: Department of Labor

INDUSTRY LEADERS

Leading companies in the printing trades machinery industry include Rockwell Graphic Systems in Westmont, Illinois; AM International Inc. in Dayton, Ohio; AB Dick Co. of Niles, Illinois; Baldwin Technology Company Inc. of Rowayton, Connecticut; and Markem Corp. in Keene, New Hampshire.

INDUSTRY INFORMATION SOURCES

"An Idea Looking for a Company." *Appliance Manufacturer* (November 1988): 33.

Angrist, Stanley W. "The Last Yiddish Linotype." *The Wall Street Journal* (March 5, 1992): A12.

Arnold, Edmund. *Ink on Paper.* New York: Harper & Row, 1963.

Gustaitis, Joseph. "Ottmar Mergenthaler's Wonderful Machine." *American History Illustrated* (June 1986): 28.

Marketing Handbook For Printing & Publishing Technologies. Reston, Va.: NPES The Association for Suppliers of Printing and Publishing Technologies, 1993.

McKeon, John J. *Challenge, Change and Opportunity: A History of NPES.* Reston, Va.: NPES The Association for Suppliers of Printing and Publishing Technologies, 1993 (unpublished manuscript).

Moran, James. *Printing Presses: History and Development from the Fifteenth Century to Modern Times.* Berkeley: University of California Press, 1973.

Oswald, John Clyde. *Printing in the Americas.* Port Washington, N.Y.: Kennikat Press, Inc., 1937.

Reilly, Patrick M. "Digital Press Is Introduced By Three Firms," *The Wall Street Journal* (April 14, 1992): B6.

—Dean Boyer

SIC 3556

FOOD PRODUCTS MACHINERY

This industry covers establishments primarily engaged in manufacturing machinery for use by the food products and beverage manufacturing industries and similar machinery for use in manufacturing animal foods. Establishments primarily engaged in manufacturing food packaging machinery are classified in **SIC 3565: Packaging Machinery;** those manufacturing industrial refrigeration machinery are classified in **SIC 3585: Air-Conditioning and Warm Air Heating Equipment and Commercial and Industrial Refrigeration Equipment.**

INDUSTRY SNAPSHOT

In 1988, over 500 establishments engaged in the U.S. food processing machinery industry, employing nearly 13,000 people and shipping nearly $3 billion of equipment that year. According to a United Nations report, approximately $904 million of manufactured machinery was exported to over 120 overseas markets in 1988. Domestically, nearly 20,000 food processing plants exist, which shipped $321 billion of processed food in 1988 and $345 billion in 1989. According to *Standard & Poor's Industry Survey*, U.S. citizens spent 11.5 percent of their disposable personal income on food in 1991, totalling $485.8 billion. The machinery industry as a whole is stable, and growing in certain segments. The presence of foreign-made machinery, however, was increasing in the early 1990s.

The food products machinery industry and the processed food industry enjoy a very strong relationship. This is illustrated by the presence of engineering departments within large food processing corporations. For their own specialized applications, many of which may be considered proprietary, patents may be obtained. Often, the level of this cooperation depends on the sophistication of the processing operations and the equipment required to carry out those steps.

ORGANIZATION AND STRUCTURE

Food products machinery and packaging equipment were included in the same industrial code until 1987, and much of the literature and data from the 1970s and 1980s combines the two industries into one category. The 1987 classification split the two types of businesses into separate categories, recognizing that the industries were serving divergent business niches.

In terms of product share, in 1991, 34 percent of the machinery industry made commercial food products machinery, excluding packaging machinery and food cooking and warming equipment. Another 31 percent of the industry manufactured industrial machinery and equipment for manufacturing or processing foods, beverages, and animal or fowl feed. Nearly 15 percent of the industry manufactured dairy and milk products plant machinery and equipment. The remaining 20 percent manufactured non-specific food products machinery.

According to a 1991 United Nations report, the industrial production of food processing machinery in North America was characterized by the following features: (1) A still large but declining part of manufacturing takes place in small and medium sized independent firms; (2) Production is usually based on orders received; (3) The markets for many types of machines are restricted; (4) Equipment production is heterogeneous; (5) Production series are relatively small; (6) Concentration similar to that in food industries is taking place; and (7) Internationalization is accelerating. In the United States, over 500 establishments shipped processing equipment, which had an estimated total value of $3 billion in 1991. The smaller, specialized equipment manufacturers produced nearly 80 percent of all food processing equipment in the United States, while the 12 largest companies in the industry supplied the remaining 20 percent.

CURRENT CONDITIONS

The trend for Americans to eat healthier has had a direct impact on this industry. For example, demand for lower fat meats such as poultry and seafood has increased, while annual per capita beef consumption has dropped significantly. Likewise, changing demographics have radically changed the entire food industry. The most significant demographic change affecting the food industry has been the increasing number of women in the work force. Double income families have driven consumer demand for foods that can be prepared quickly and easily.

Indications of an improving economy in the 1990s provided optimistic news for the food and beverage industry in general. Yet, even in during the recession of the late 1980s and early 1990s, the food industries did not suffer heavy losses. Price stability, a direct impact of the recession on the cost side of the industry, provided stable prices for consumers and steady wages for employees. The wage increases across the food industry were comparable to inflation, at about 3 percent. As long as food stocks such as agricultural commodities and meat production remain strong, the entire food industry is expected to remain healthy.

In developed countries, demographic trends determine the focus of the food industry. According to a UN report, "longer lives, earlier marriages, more divorces, and fewer children are giving rise to new population patterns, where more one- and two-person households are establishing new consumer patterns, for example eating out more often and buying convenience foods. A new structure in age distribution—more people in the over 60 group—leads to new demand patterns, as the requirements from aged people differ from those of the younger. For example old people eat smaller portions but need a higher concentration of essential proteins, vitamins, etc. in those portions."

The increasing number of women in the work force is perhaps the most important of the demographic trends affecting the industry, as women have been the traditional food preparers in the family unit. Working women have less time to fix meals for their families and consequently purchase food that requires little preparation. The effects of this trend can be seen especially in meat processing, where secondary operations are employed in response to consumer eating habits. Both the processing and packaging industries have been influenced by the trend, because meats in the fresh chilled form, already marinated, skinned, and sectioned, are growing in availability. There is also an increasing variety of frozen foods available.

New technological innovations in the house, such as microwave ovens, have also led to new consumption patterns. These differences are directly influencing the development and design of food processing equipment, especially where secondary operations may be employed. The complexity of more highly developed food systems may be illustrated by the number of new food products introduced in the U.S. food system between 1983 and 1988.

INDUSTRY LEADERS

The top 75 companies in the industry reported combined sales of $5.395 billion and employed 53,900 people. In 1987, the highest concentration of shipments were originated from Ohio's 36 food processing machinery establishments. Ohio shipments, valued at $324.2 million, represented 16.4 percent of the nation's total shipments. Illinois's 53 establishments shipped $259.1 million worth of equipment, claiming 13.1 percent of the nation's total shipments. California, which has 82 establishments engaged in this industry, claimed an 8.9 percent share of the market with $175.9 million in shipments.

In 1991, Premark International Incorporated, located in Deerfield, Illinois, was the industry leader with estimated sales of $1.06 billion and a work force of 10,000. PMI Food Equipment Group, located in Troy, Ohio, ranked second with estimated sales of $800 million and a work force of 10,600. Premark International Incorporated's division located in Troy, Ohio again makes a showing with a third-place ranking. The Troy division grossed an estimated $740 million in sales with a work force of 7,000. Ranking fourth in the nation was APV Consolidated Incorporated, located in Chicago, Illinois, with estimated sales of $360 million in food products machinery and a work force of 3,000. The fifth-ranked company in terms of sales was FMC Corporation, located in Chicago. FMC was estimated to have sold equipment valued at $310 million with a work force of 3,000.

Premark International is a new company; it was created in 1986 after the failed Dart & Kraft merger. Kraft, feeling its earnings were stifled by the Dart interests, returned alone to its primary concern, food products. The Dart companies formed Premark, which consisted of Tupperware products, Ralph Wilson Plastics, and West Bend. Premark also obtained Hobart, which was acquired by the Dart & Kraft group. The Tupperware operations lost $57.9 million for Premark in its first year, and continued to lose money. In 1992,

Premark announced it would close the Tennessee factory that makes Tupperware products.

The Hobart line is the core of Premark's food equipment group. Hobart was acquired by Dart & Kraft in 1981 after a hostile takeover attempt by Canadian Pacific Enterprises failed. Canadian Pacific offered a reported $300 million for Hobart's operations, but Hobart, preferring independence, declined. Congressmen supported Hobart and appealed to Treasury Secretary Donald Regan to prohibit the takeover on grounds of breaching national security. Hobart finally sold out to Dart & Kraft for $460 million, having realized it probably did not have the strength to battle future takeover attempts alone.

American's changing lifestyles and eating habits boosted Premark's food equipment sales. Fast food menus began changing in the mid-1980s and required new equipment, such as catalytic chicken fryers and grooved griddles for fajitas. Take home foods, such as bakery products from grocery stores, were more readily available for consumers as 2,500 in-store bakeries were built in 1987. These bakeries generally cost $130,000 to equip with the necessary machinery, although some cost as much as $300,000. International lifestyles and eating habits were changing too, as the English started eating more pizza and the Japanese started eating more hamburgers. Improved sales of these foods helped the food equipment group to contribute $57.8 million to Premark's profits in 1988.

Since 1985, the United Kingdom branches of APV have been involved in joint venture agreements with the former Soviet Union countries Bulgaria and Hungary. In Bulgaria, efforts include engineering and consulting in biotechnology, refrigeration, air-conditioning, and food processing. In Hungary, the manufacture of food processing machinery and equipment is of primary concern to the venture. Food production is a primary concern in the former U.S.S.R., as much of the present equipment is old and in need of replacement. Equipment where sanitation is critical, such as dairy and meat processing machinery, are receiving the greatest emphasis.

WORK FORCE

Productivity in the food products machinery industry, as measured by output per production worker man-hour, increased somewhat between 1972 and 1986. The average value of shipments per production worker man-hour rose from $51.0 in 1972 to $61.4 in 1986. After industry shipment peaked in 1978, productivity declined. Productivity has grown annually since 1981, largely owing to the increased automation of plants and equipment. The industry has been quick to adopt new technology, especially computer technology, to improve efficiency and create new product lines, and the capital to labor ratio has risen significantly since 1972.

While the industry's stock of machinery and equipment has grown in the late 1980s and early 1990s, the number of production worker man-hours has decreased steadily. Increased competition from imports has been a motivating force, as has consumer demand for a broader range of food products. Industry shipments decreased by about 5 percent, from $2.09 billion in 1985 to $1.985 in 1986. Estimated industry shipments for 1987 showed a modest increase to $2.06 billion, followed by a projected increase to $2.17 billion in 1988.

While the average hourly wage for an employee in this industry was $11.27 in 1987, those employed in Illinois enjoyed substantially higher wages of $14.71. Those employed in Connecticut received an average of $14.67 per hour; in Washington, $14.33; in Indiana, $14.13. Those states that offered average hourly wages between $11 and $14 were Ohio, Michigan, New York, Virginia, Missouri, and New Jersey.

As previously mentioned, the employment outlook for the industry is expected to change going into the twenty-first century. Significant staff reductions of greater than 17 percent are expected in occupations such as machine builders, assemblers, secretaries, precision inspectors, welding machine setters, and machine assemblers. The employment outlook for other industry occupations looks much brighter, as increases of greater than 10 percent are expected for sales workers, production managers, machinery mechanics, engineering and science managers, and electrical and electronics engineers.

AMERICA AND THE WORLD

According to a UN report, the low relative U.S. dollar value spurred competitiveness in this industry during the 1980s and helped many U.S. manufacturers increase market share. Throughout the world, the U.S. share of food-product machinery peaked in 1981 and 1982 at about 19.7 percent, declining steadily through 1986. The Federal Republic of Germany has lost market share since 1978, when it claimed the largest share of the world market at 28.9 percent. Many food-product machinery companies have begun to focus on international markets, and some have established production facilities abroad. While Austria, Italy, Japan, and the Netherlands have reported great increases in their market shares, they now face increasing competition from some of the newly industrialized countries, notably Mexico, Brazil, and Taiwan. The North American Free Trade Agreement is expected to have a significant impact on the industry.

The United States's greatest export customers for food processing machinery in 1988 were Canada, with a 15.1 percent share, and the United Kingdom, with a 9.2 percent share. However, Mexico followed closely behind Canada with an 8 percent share. Other major export markets were western Europe, Australia, Japan, China, and Venezuela. China was the only nation that the United States increased exports to between 1980 and 1986. In contrast, U.S. importing activity has grown steadily between 1980 and 1988. The Germans and Italians have been dominant suppliers throughout the 1980s, while Japan and the United Kingdom were the third and fourth leading suppliers by 1988. According to a UN report, "Food-product and packaging machinery imported from the Federal Republic of Germany in 1988 amounted to $284 million, a 190 percent increase over the 1980 figure. United States imports from Italy amounted to $216 million in 1988, over 300 percent higher than the 1980 value."

The UN report also states, "The largest food-processing machinery import categories in value terms for 1988 were: wrapping and packaging machinery ($213M), bakery machinery ($56M), chocolate and confectionery machinery ($41M), and meat processing equipment ($28M). All these import categories registered strong growth between 1980 and 1986."

RESEARCH AND TECHNOLOGY

The development of new food-processing and packaging technologies is based on external factors such as economic and political swings and internal factors such as eating trends and technological breakthroughs. In the early 1990s, the industry expected a continuing proliferation of new products in the marketplace. As consumer eating habits change, technology will undoubtedly change to satisfy these trends. Most forecasts have shown that the popularity of convenience foods in the United States will continue to grow.

As many more countries have begun establishing industrialized economies, the subsequent standard of living advancements are expected to create a demand for more nutritional, sterile, and convenient foods. The United Nations' Economic Commission for Europe reports that "the world's most populous countries, China, the Soviet Union, and India, are starting to improve their processing, preserving, and distribution systems to produce better quality foods. The recent reforms in the USSR will dramatically increase the level of funding for new food-processing technology and equipment. Current plans call for expenditures of up to $63 billion through 1995. The USSR's Government and food industry will look increasingly to the West for much needed new technology.'' In the early 1990s, the United States was in an excellent position to exert its influence in this industry, as the standards placed on domestically produced machinery were attractive to foreign purchasers.

INDUSTRY INFORMATION SOURCES

Darnay, Arsen J., ed. *Manufacturing USA: Industry Analyses, Statistics, and Leading Companies.* Detroit: Gale Research, Inc., 1992.

Hast, Adele, ed. *International Directory of Company Histories.* Volume III. Chicago: St. James Press, 1988.

''Premark Will Take Charge to Shut Plant for Tupperware Line.'' *Wall Street Journal* (October 12, 1992).

Shea, Kenneth. *Industry Surveys.* Standard & Poor's Corporation, (August 6, 1992).

United Nations. Economic Commission for Europe. *Food-Processing Machinery.* New York: United Nations, 1991.

— Valerie E. Wilson

SIC 3559

SPECIAL INDUSTRY MACHINERY, NOT ELSEWHERE CLASSIFIED

This classification covers establishments primarily engaged in manufacturing special industry machinery, not elsewhere classified, such as smelting and refining equipment, cement making, clay working, cotton ginning, glass making, hat making, incandescent lamp making, leather working, paint making, rubber working, cigar and cigarette making, tobacco working, shoe making, and stone working machinery, industrial sewing machines, and automotive maintenance machinery and equipment.

INDUSTRY SNAPSHOT

The special industry machinery industry was comprised of companies that manufactured a variety of miscellaneous machines used to produce goods in other industries. Numerous product offerings ranged from broom making contraptions to zipper makers, although semiconductor manufacturing equipment accounted for the majority of the classification's output.

The number and production volume of machines classified in this industry increased substantially during the industrial revolution, and particularly after World War II. By the early 1980s, about $5 billion in annual U.S. machinery sales were attributed to miscellaneous equipment in this sector. Although overall U.S. industrial machinery sales growth slowed during the 1980s, a surging demand for high-tech semiconductor manufacturing equipment more than doubled industry revenues to more than $10 billion by 1989.

While a U.S. recession in the late 1980s and early 1990s depressed many industrial machinery segments, semiconductor machine sales continued to balloon—to about $6 billion by 1993. Renewed U.S. competitiveness in high-tech equipment manufacturing allowed domestic competitors to thwart their Japanese contenders. In addition, increased semiconductor demand from industries such as telecommunications augmented growth. Output was expected to expand throughout the mid-1990s.

ORGANIZATION AND STRUCTURE

The miscellaneous special machinery industry encompassed a plethora of devices, including: tire retreading machinery, stone tumblers, tile making equipment, automotive frame straighteners, lumber drying kilns, cork cutters, brick makers, shoe repair equipment, leather-working devices, and plastic molding machines.

Despite growth in some segments, such as pharmaceutical machinery, semiconductor equipment represented the largest and fastest growing sector of the industry throughout most of the 1980s and early 1990s. In 1993, semiconductor machines accounted for about 50 percent of production. The next largest segment of this diversified industry was chemical making equipment, which accounted for about 5 percent of shipments.

Semiconductor Manufacturing Process. Semiconductor production involved a sequence of more than 200 steps using numerous machines. Although the manufacturing process varied depending on the type of chip produced, four basic functions were typically performed to complete a semiconductor wafer, or circuit: 1) deposition of thin film on the (usually silicon) wafer; 2) impurity doping, when selected impurities were introduced that controlled conductivity; 3) lithographic patterning, which determined the geometric features and layout of the circuit; and 4) etching, which removed coating material to reveal the structure patterned in the lithographic process. These steps were repeated sequentially until the semiconductor wafer was complete. After the semiconductor was created using ''front-end'' fabrication equipment, ''back-end'' machines were used to test and assemble the chips. Back-end devices included three categories of machines: material handling, process diagnostics and testing, and assembly.

Semiconductor Equipment Markets. Global semiconductor machinery sales totaled approximately $12 billion in 1993. U.S. producers captured about 51 percent of that market. Front-end fabricating machinery made up approximately 46 percent, or $5.5 billion, of global semiconductor shipments in 1993. Deposition equipment represented 34 percent, or $1.9 billion, and lithographic machinery accounted for 28 percent. Etching and doping devices represented 18 percent and 10 percent, respectively, of front-end equipment sales. Miscellaneous devices accounted for the remainder of front-end shipments.

Back-end fabricating machinery made up about 34 percent, or $4 billion, of semiconductor equipment revenues in 1993. Automatic test equipment constituted 36 percent, or $1.45 billion, and assembly machines accounted for 31 percent. Diagnostic and material handling devices represented 20 percent and 15 percent, respectively, of back-end machine sales. In addition to front-end and back-end equipment, spare parts comprised about $2.4 billion, or 20 percent, of global semiconductor machinery shipments.

BACKGROUND AND DEVELOPMENT

The history of miscellaneous special industry machinery varied by product group. One of the earliest and most renowned machines in this industry was the cotton gin, which Eli Whitney invented in 1793. The gin removed seed from cotton by pulling the fiber through a set of wire teeth mounted on a revolving cylinder. Because the device could be powered by man, animal, or water, it received immediate and widespread acceptance and made cotton a staple of nineteenth century southern life.

The development and widespread dissemination of electric power during the late nineteenth and early twentieth centuries resulted in the introduction of a multitude of machinery for miscellaneous industries. Likewise, post-war U.S. economic expansion propelled product introductions and sales throughout the mid-1900s. A pivotal breakthrough was Bell Laboratory's introduction in 1947 of the solid-state transistor, which utilized semiconductors. By the 1960s a market for semiconductor manufacturing equipment began to emerge.

Spurred by important chip advances like Intel Corporation's 1971 introduction of the memory integrated circuit, U.S. producers took the early lead in producing semiconductor manufacturing equipment. The mass production of chips allowed by these high-

tech machines resulted in dramatic semiconductor price reductions. As a result, the demand for chips surged as semiconductors were integrated into all types of electronic consumer and business devices. Importantly, the use of semiconductors in personal computers caused chip manufacturing equipment sales to balloon during much of the 1980s.

The 1980s. Although domestic manufacturers took the early lead, Japanese semiconductor machinery makers successfully captured much of the global market during the 1980s. The Japanese particularly excelled at delivering equipment for high-volume commodity chips. To combat Japanese strengths, U.S. semiconductor producers restructured, increased their manufacturing efficiency, and concentrated on developing new technologies during the mid-1980s. As the U.S. chip industry made a transition from commodity to proprietary chip production, it ceded a 45 percent share of the global semiconductor equipment market to its arch-rival.

Despite a loss of market share, chip machinery makers increased sales substantially during the 1980s. However, most other miscellaneous special industry machinery producers suffered. Capital spending on new equipment by other industries declined or grew at a slow pace in comparison to pre-1980 expenditures. Spending on new equipment by the transportation industry stagnated, for example, as did equipment purchases by the important petroleum and coal sector. Nevertheless, growth of semiconductor equipment demand helped double industry revenues to more than $10 billion by 1990.

CURRENT CONDITIONS

Strategies adopted by U.S. semiconductor manufacturers in the 1980s began to pay off in the early 1990s. Aided by a weak dollar and a recession in Japan, domestic producers boosted revenues to $5.8 billion in 1991. Although sales dropped 3 percent in 1992, shipments climbed an impressive 18 percent in 1993 to about $6 billion. Assisted by a technological lead in growing product segments and newfound productivity, U.S. manufacturers were able to recover a 4 percent share of the global market from Japan. In 1993 they held 51 percent, compared to 41 percent controlled by Japan.

Also boosting U.S. semiconductor equipment competitiveness was fallout from SEMATECH, a joint private sector-government funded research and development consortium. SEMATECH was formed in 1987 to combat increasingly competitive Japanese semiconductor producers. In addition, industry participants on both sides of the Pacific benefitted from technology exchanges and partnerships with foreign and domestic competitors. Indeed, U.S. firms learned from the Japanese that traditional methods of developing and producing manufacturing technology in isolation from competitors were no longer feasible.

Front-end equipment sales led industry growth going into the mid-1990s. Most importantly, shipments of deposition equipment rose 17 percent in 1993. U.S. producers held the lead in deposition technology, and benefitted from a proliferating trend toward smaller, more integrated chips that required more complex deposition. A shift toward the production of high-profit, application-specific, integrated circuits (ASIC) also boosted sales of U.S. front-end manufacturing devices. In contrast, sales of lithographic machinery, of which the U.S. supplied only a 16 percent global share in 1993, plummeted in the early 1990s.

Back-end equipment sales also rose at a steady clip. Global shipments of test equipment gained 14 percent in 1993, and sales of material handling and diagnostic machines increased about 13 percent. Production of assembly devices, of which the U.S. made 30 percent globally, jumped 15 percent.

Long-term prospects. Growth in the special industry machinery business should continue to be dominated by semiconductor manufacturing equipment. Although some other industry segments gained slightly in 1992 and 1993 as a result of industry restructuring and a weak U.S. dollar, most sectors remained stagnant or depressed. Excluding semiconductor equipment, increased industry efficiency and demand would likely be partially offset by low-cost foreign producers and the movement of production facilities outside U.S. borders.

In contrast, demand for U.S.-built semiconductor machinery should continue to expand throughout the 1990s at a rate of about 13 percent annually. Market expansion was expected to be propelled by the need for cutting-edge equipment that could manufacture constantly improving chips. In addition, increased demand for semiconductors from communications and computer industries should boost chip production volume. Partnering was expected to become an important industry dynamic as firms strove to reduce development costs.

INDUSTRY LEADERS

Over 2000 companies participated in the miscellaneous special industry machinery business in the early 1990s. Semiconductor equipment manufacturers dominated the top spots. Applied Materials Inc. of Califor-

nia was the largest producer, with 1992 net income of $37 million from $794 million in sales. This company was also the largest semiconductor machine maker in the world going into the mid-1990s.

Under the direction of CEO James C. Morgan, Applied Materials realized average revenue growth of 20 percent per year between 1988 and 1992 and maintained profitability throughout the recession. High quality and continuous improvement were company mainstays. Morgan emphasized a broad product line, the capability to enter new markets quickly, and the expertise to rapidly take new technologies to the global marketplace. Over 55 percent of Applied Materials' revenues in 1992 were garnered from exports. The company strove to become the first $1 billion semiconductor equipment company in the world.

Other U.S. industry leaders included Teradyne, with 1992 sales of $278 million; Varian, with $263 million; and General Signal, with $214 million. Of the top 10 global leaders, however, six were Japanese. Tokyo Electron was the second largest world competitor with 1992 sales of $677 million. Nikon, Canon, and Advantest took the succeeding slots.

WORK FORCE

Despite expectations of healthy growth, employment in the special industry machinery business appeared likely to decline significantly between 1990 and 2005, according to the Bureau of Labor Statistics. Even during the 1980s, when production more than doubled, the work force grew by only about 10 percent. Continued restructuring and the movement of some manufacturing activities to low-cost countries should accelerate this trend.

Although semiconductor machinery employment appeared likely to stabilize, overall special industry machinery employment was expected to decline by 15 to 30 percent for most labor occupations. However, jobs for trained machinists and machine tool operators should rise, as should opportunities for production managers and electrical engineers. Industry wages were about 20 percent above the U.S. manufacturing industry average.

AMERICA AND THE WORLD

U.S. semiconductor machinery producers increased their share of the global market from 35 percent in 1991 to 42 percent in 1992 and 51 percent in 1993. Japan supplied 41 percent of worldwide equipment demand in 1993, while Europe controlled about 8 percent of the market. The United States, which purchased 37 percent of global production in 1993, was also the biggest consumer of chip making machinery. Japan consumed 33 percent of worldwide output, down from 43 percent in 1990. European and Southeast Asian countries comprised most of the remainder of the market.

U.S. producers exported 40 percent of their chip machinery in 1993. They shipped $756 million, or about 33 percent, of their exports to Japan, a 15 percent increase over 1992. South Korea and Taiwan, the second- and third-largest importers of U.S. chip machinery, bought about $295 million worth of goods. Total exports to Asia (excluding Japan) climbed 13 percent in 1993, and exports to Europe swelled in response to decreasingly competitive producers on that continent. The U.S. imported only 20 percent of its semiconductor equipment, most of which came from Japan.

With the exception of lithography equipment, U.S. producers held a technological and market lead in front-end machinery. They also led in the production of testing equipment, though Japan was stronger in assembly and material handling markets. Going into the mid-1990s, the United States was positioned to take advantage of the fastest growing and most technologically advanced equipment segments. However, Japan was expected to again emerge as the world's largest semiconductor equipment consumer following its recession.

In the long run, partnerships between Japanese and U.S. equipment firms were expected to blur national distinctions. Demand for semiconductor manufacturing equipment in emerging markets should provide strong growth for producers in both countries. Purchases of equipment in China, for example, swelled 140 percent 1993. U.S. overseas sales appeared likely to grow faster between 1994 and 1998 than in the previous five years.

RESEARCH AND TECHNOLOGY

Semiconductor equipment manufacturers were heavily dependent upon research and technology to sustain competitiveness. Applied Materials, for example, injected about 10 percent of its total revenues into capital investments in the early 1990s. For comparison, the average capital investment for all U.S. manufacturers was closer to 4 percent of gross sales. In contrast, capital spending by other firms in the special industry machinery business were much lower than even the national average.

U.S. semiconductor machinery makers invested heavily in productivity, quality, customer service programs, and new plants and equipment during the 1980s and early 1990s. Most importantly, though, research and development outlays allowed them to sharpen their competitive edge in the development of high-tech, value-added machinery. They especially advanced in the fast-growing market for chemical and physical vapor deposition equipment, which was expected to lead industry growth throughout the mid-1990s. They also stretched their lead in automatic test equipment technology.

In the latter half of the 1990s, development efforts were expected to emphasize, among other technologies, machinery for advanced multichip modules, which mounted multiple integrated circuits on one unit. The Advanced Research Projects Agency (ARPA), a high-tech consortium, already provided funding for this research in the early 1990s. Equipment for manufacturing liquid crystal displays (LCDs) should also be a priority. LCDs were used for flat-panel displays on portable computers, and were manufactured using a process similar to that utilized to make chips. The U.S. Display Consortium, which included ARPA and several equipment and display providers, was formed in 1993 to further LCD manufacturing technology.

GaAs. Another technology advancing in the mid-1990s that offered significant potential for equipment producers was gallium arsenide (GaAs), which was developed as a synthetic alternative to silicon. GaAs was first touted as a breakthrough replacement for silicon in the early 1980s. GaAs proponents cited its advantages of high speed, superior temperature tolerance, and low power requirements, among others. In addition, GaAs could emit light, making it useful in fiber optical communications systems.

Unfortunately, GaAs was slow to emerge as a viable technology and commanded a meager share of semiconductor equipment shipments. It was very brittle and difficult to handle. Only 50 percent of the chips produced per batch were usable, compared to 70 percent or more for most silicon chips. As a result, GaAs chips typically cost five times more to produce than similar silicon circuits. Although some analysts predicted GaAs sales to surpass $5 billion, by 1990 actual shipments were less than $300 million and were forecast to reach only about $600 million by 1994.

Despite the problems, intense military and aerospace applications for GaAs chips kept the technology afloat in the mid-1990s. In addition, some producers achieved increased batch yields by using manufacturing equipment built for silicon chips. They also improved the compatibility of silicon and GaAs chips. A strong potential still existed for GaAs semiconductors, which operated at least twice as fast as silicon chips.

INDUSTRY INFORMATION SOURCES

Darnay, Arsen J., editor, *Manufacturing USA: Industry Analyses, Statistics, and Leading Companies,* Detroit: Gale Research, 1993.

Dorsch, Jeff, "Fab Gear to Grow Modestly in '92 to $10.4 Billion," *Electronic News,* January 6, 1992.

Robertson, Jack, "Japan Surpasses Foreign Semicon 20 Percent Share Target," *Electronic News,* March 22, 1993.

Standard & Poor's Industry Surveys, New York: Standard & Poor's, June 10, 1993.

Thompson, Terrence, "The Americans Are Back in the Semi Equipment Business," *Electronic Business,* July 1993.

Ristelhueber, Robert, "IC Makers Brace for a Slowdown," *Electronic Business Buyer,* January 1994.

U.S. Industrial Outlook 1994, Washington, D.C.: U.S. Department of Commerce, January 1994.

Willet, Hugh G., "Chips: National Semiconductor; View from the Top," *Electronic Business,* January 13, 1992.

—Dave Mote

SIC 3561

PUMPS AND PUMPING EQUIPMENT

This category covers firms primarily engaged in manufacturing pumps and related equipment for general industrial, commercial or household use. It does not cover manufacturers of fluid power pumps or motors (**SIC 3594**), manufacturers of measuring and dispensing pumps for gasoline service stations (**SIC 3586**), non-laboratory-use vacuum pumps (**SIC 3563**), laboratory vacuum pumps (**SIC 3821**), or motor vehicle pumps (**SIC 3714**). The category does include domestic water and sump pump manufacturers.

INDUSTRY SNAPSHOT

Pumps are one of the most common machines used by industry today, second only to electric motors. As such the health of the pump manufacturing industry depends to a great extent on the general health of industrial America. Particularly important are the petrochemical and the pulp and paper industries, but steel making, electric power generation, oil and gas wells, fields and pipelines, sewage system construction, and general housing and commercial construction also depend on a variety of special purpose pumps.

Such pumps, which can be abrasive by nature themselves, often wear quickly because they frequently move materials contaminated with abrasives in challenging climatic and environmental conditions.

This requires frequent replacement or repair, making the replacement parts segment of the industry particularly important.

ORGANIZATION AND STRUCTURE

Some 613 establishments manufactured pumps and pump equipment in 1977, an increase of ten percent over the 1972 census figures. However, this number dropped to 528 by 1987 and an administrative redistribution of SIC codes left the industry with only 405 establishments at the end of 1987. The other 123 establishments were reclassified into **SIC 3594: Fluid Power Pumps and Motors.**

Historically, manufacturing in this industry has been heavily concentrated; in 1977 more than half the industry's employees worked in the four largest facilities, and 79 percent of all facilities employed fewer than 100 workers. By 1987 this had changed slightly with 75 percent of all facilities employing fewer than 100, but diffusion was more evident in the larger firms. The 1987 Census showed the largest 41 firms employing 52.6 percent of all workers.

BACKGROUND AND DEVELOPMENT

The world's first pump was probably the force or air pump built by Ktesibios of Alexandria about 270 B.C. He used a cylinder and plunger arrangement to pump air through pipes of various lengths, creating the first water organ. The water was used to maintain a steady air pressure in the system. Simple pumps became common fairly quickly for domestic use and as fire extinguishers. Roman ruins yield examples of pumps used for fire control and for lifting water in wells. The famed Roman aqueducts were probably not fed with pumps, but rather used water wheels to lift water from reservoirs directly to the piping system.

A major advancement in pumping technology came in 1698 with the issuing of a British patent to Thomas Savery for a steam powered pump for use in coal mines. The device was later adapted to provide water to some country houses. This pump was effectively replaced by the Newcomen engine, patented in 1712, which placed the steam boilers and piston assembly at the top of the mine shaft instead of at the bottom. The concept introduced the now familiar working or balance beam to transfer power to the pump mechanism in the mine.

The industrial revolution found many uses for the now-powered pump, including industrial processing and domestic distribution of water. However, the 20th century introduced a new refinement, electrification. The first American factory to replace its central steam plant and its maze-like system of pulleys and belts with electric motors was a cotton mill in 1894. All new factories used the new technology.

Economic and technological expansion in the 1960s stimulated pump production and encouraged the adoption of new manufacturing techniques. The industry adopted specially designed milling machines and combination machines that could perform milling, radial drilling and facing (smoothing) in one operation. Automatic tool changing devices operated by numerical control tape programs increased production efficiency.

In general the pump industry manufactures large specialty items to meet a client's specific needs. To accommodate such a need for flexibility, the industry quickly adopted numerically controlled machine tools and computer numerical controls. This shifted the center of production control to the firm's engineering department and away from the craftsmen on the shop floor. Computer assisted drafting and modelling programs have further increased design efficiency.

CURRENT CONDITIONS

The general industrial slowdown of the 1980s hit the pump industry hard. Major clients like the nuclear power industry, the oil well and pipeline industry, and the construction industry cut back on orders for new equipment and idled existing components. A strong U.S. dollar made American products uncompetitive in foreign markets.

By 1988, this began to change. A weakening dollar increased exports and a general pickup in the manufacturing climate sparked new domestic orders in almost all sectors. The industry continued to modernize production by consolidating facilities and adopting sophisticated CAD/CAM systems and metalworking and casting technologies. New materials and designs were explored to extend the life of components in corrosive environments and to increase reliability. *U.S. Industrial Outlook—1990* predicted a 2.6 percent growth in the industry until 1994, assuming it could continue to compete with increasingly innovative foreign manufacturers.

The *Monthly Labor Review,* 1982, noted that one of the largest users of pumps was the chemical industry, taking about 10 percent of the pump industry's output. Pumps for this market used special materials like fiberglass, plastics and stainless steel to accommodate salt solutions, acids and chlorine.

Steel mills and blast furnaces took about seven percent of output to move liquid fuels and water for coolant. The move in the steel industry away from open-hearth furnaces to oxygen and electric furnaces and to continuous casting instead of slabbing mills necessitated larger, more powerful pumps to provide higher volumes of coolant water. This meant the development of higher-output centrifugal pumps.

The oil-well and pipeline industries took 18 percent of output. Demand in this sector dropped off dramatically in the 1960s but recovered after that. This industry bought reciprocal pumps for mud circulation, submersible centrifugal units for lifting crude oil and standard centrifugal pumps to maintain pressure with water-flooding. Pipelines require high-horsepower centrifugal pumps. In the 1960s the average pipeline diameter was enlarged by 33 percent, requiring much larger pumps to move the higher volumes of petroleum products.

Between 1969 and 1979, the proportion of electric generating facilities producing more than 500,000 kilowatts increased from three percent to 12 percent. The larger generating facilities, nuclear and gas-turbine, required proportionately larger pumps.

Construction took 18 percent of output including centrifugal pumps and trash pumps which can accommodate up to 25 percent small solids in the pumped liquid. New sewage plant construction to accommodate increasingly stringent environmental regulations was expected to increase the demand for pumps. In the 1990s, infrastructure replacement and up-grading was expected to do the same.

INDUSTRY LEADERS

The three top firms by sales in the pumps and pumping equipment industry in 1993 were Goulds Pumps Inc. of Seneca Falls, New York; Commercial Intertech Corp. of Youngstown, Ohio; and BWIP International Inc. of Long Beach, California. Their listings in Dunn and Bradstreet show that: Goulds was established in 1844 and employs 4,300 workers to produce $566 million in annual sales. Its subsidiaries include G&H Castings Division, Municipal Business Unit Division, Texas Division, and Vertical Pump Division. Commercial Intertech Corp. was established in 1920 and employs 4,000 workers to produce $436 million in annual sales. It has one subsidiary, Oildyne Division. BWIP International was a subsidiary of BWIP Holdings Inc. It was established in 1987 and employs 3,000 workers to produce $378 million in annual sales. Its subsidiaries include Borg-Warner Industrial Products Division, and Centrifugal Pumps Division.

WORK FORCE

The *Monthly Labor Review,* 1982, noted that the general industrial machinery group generally used a high proportion of skilled trades, about 30 percent of all production workers compared to the 26 percent proportion in all manufacturing. Pump production made up about 29 percent of all labor in the industrial machinery group. Metal working craftsmen and machinists were three times more common in this industry than in manufacturing as a whole while laborers were half as common. Average wages were ten percent higher in this industry, indicating a higher degree of necessary skill. This disparity continued as late as 1988 when the pump industry paid an average hourly wage of $12.35 compared to the manufacturing average of $10.66. The industry also employed a high proportion of non-production workers, indicating a reliance on mechanical engineers. This employment group was three times more common in the pump industry than in general manufacturing.

Industry-Occupation Matrix, Bureau of Labor Statistics, projected a continuation of this trend with its estimate of employment changes until the year 2000. It expected double digit increases for industrial machinery mechanics, sales workers, engineering and science managers, industrial production managers, NC tool operators for both plastics and metals, mechanical engineers, combination machine tool operators, machinists, and engineering technicians. Total employment in the industry sat at 55,100 in 1988, a 57 percent increase from the 35,200 employed in 1987 when the industry was redefined.

AMERICA AND THE WORLD

Pumps and pumping equipment were manufactured to international standards allowing American manufacturers to compete effectively in the international market. These same standards, however, also made the United States vulnerable to foreign competition, particularly on price and quality. During the early half of the 1980s, the strong American dollar made such competition particularly difficult, undermining an already weak industrial climate in American manufacturing. As a result, the U.S. merchandise trade deficit quadrupled between 1982 and 1984, reaching $145 billion. This effect showed up in the pump manufacturing industry, but was delayed. In 1985 the industry showed a trade surplus, but by 1987 it had become a $1.9 billion deficit. The drop of the value of the U.S. dollar which began in March of 1985 provided new impetus for the pump industry. By 1987, the average export price expressed in foreign currency of pumps and other machinery had fallen 23.1 percent. By 1990,

even though domestic prices increased an average of five percent each year, the foreign currency price of pumps and components had dropped more than 11 percent. This made American operations more profitable, increased export volumes and discouraged imports. It also encouraged foreign firms to establish manufacturing and assembly facilities in the United States.

In 1990, exports approached $1.1 billion while imports exceeded $.7 billion. Major markets for American products included Canada, Mexico, the United Kingdom, Saudi Arabia, West Germany, Venezuela, and Japan. The top importers included Japan, West Germany, Canada, and the United Kingdom. China appeared poised to become a major market in the late 1980s with a push for industrial modernization, but a lack of foreign currency dampened demand. Firms like Bingham-Willamette Co. of Portland and Goulds Pumps of Seneca Falls, New York, hoped to sell large quantities of sophisticated pumping equipment to China. In 1985, Bingham-Willamette sold six pumps valued at $600,000 and expected to up that to 200 pumps per year, but the business dwindled within two years. Goulds, in 1988, signed a joint-venture agreement with Nanjing Deep Well Company to produce 600 pump units for four petrochemical plants, a deal worth several millions at each plant.

RESEARCH AND TECHNOLOGY

The majority of pumps manufactured are custom made to a client's specific requirements for use in complex applications where the failure of the pump could be disastrous. Consequently, manufacturing innovation has stressed flexibility and reliability. Major innovations included the adoption of numerical and computer control manufacturing systems and the reliance on engineering expertise assisted by computer modelling software to custom design components for short run production. New corrosion resistant materials have been developed and refinements to old processes adopted. Specially designed metal-forming machines were created for the industry, including combination milling, radial drilling and facing machines, variable setting grinders which automatically form tapered shafts, and automatic tool changing devices controlled by NC tapes or computer software. Foundry operations for production of pump casings and core-making have advanced with rapid-cycle machinery, synchronous fabricating machinery and a no-bake molding process using a resin binder and catalyst. Closer tolerances were achieved in components by replacing wooden molds and cores with ceramic.

Demands for higher efficiency pumps meant an industry shift from fixed displacement pumps to variable displacement because they do not waste energy by venting excess pumped material through a relief valve. A variable displacement pump adjusts its own flow rate to match demand.

INDUSTRY INFORMATION SOURCES

"Dollar's Fall Boosts U.S. Machinery Exports, 1985-90," *Monthly Labor Review,* July 1991.

"Expert System Lets Users Configure Pumps on a PC," *Machine Design,* October 12, 1989.

Kranzberg, Melvin, and Carroll W. Pursel, Jr., eds., *Technology in Western Civilization,* Volume 1, New York: Oxford University Press, 1967.

Margus, Edward, "Nonmetallic Pumps for Corrosive/Erosive Services," *Plant Engineering,* October 22, 1992.

1982 Census of Manufacturers, Washington, D.C.: Department of Commerce, 1987.

"Productivity in the Pump and Compressor Industry," *Monthly Labor Review,* December, 1982.

Renner, Kevin, "Bingham Shifts Tactics; Will Close Plant," *Business Journal,* March 24, 1986.

Segelken, Jane Baker, "Seeing Red Puts This Company in the Black," *Central New York Business Journal,* February, 1988.

U.S. Industrial Outlook 1980, Washington: U.S. Department of Commerce, 1989.

U.S. Industrial Outlook 1990, Washington: U.S. Department of Commerce, 1990.

Usher, Abbot Payson, *A History of Mechanical Inventions,* Boston: Beacon Press, 1929.

Villaume, John M., "Sale of Six Pumps to China Buoys Bingham-Willamette," *Business Journal,* June 24, 1988.

—Al Cook

SIC 3562

BALL AND ROLLER BEARINGS

This industry covers establishments primarily engaged in manufacturing ball and roller bearings (including ball or roller bearing pillow block, flange, takeup cartridge and hangar units) and parts. Establishments primarily engaged in manufacturing plain bearings are classified in **SIC 3568: Mechanical Power Transmission Equipment, Not Elsewhere Classified.**

INDUSTRY SNAPSHOT

The ball and roller bearing industry is very large, but mature. It touches everything from the space shuttle, to household appliances, automobiles, dentist drills, roller skates, and computer disk drives. Ball and roller bearings are used in anything that slides, glides, or rolls and in some cases are as large as 15 meters in diameter. Two general classes of bearings exist: commodity and precision. Commodity bearings are used in rotating elements that have relatively low revolutions per minute and do not face extreme stresses. Precision bearings, on the other hand, are highly accurate in terms of material quality, consistency of finish and diameter, and repeatability of tolerance levels. These bearings go through rigorous tests that check their internal structure for failure tendencies and measure their diameters to within one-millionth of an inch. Because the bearing industry has achieved such high product standards, it is widely respected for its ability to ensure an extraordinarily high level of quality control.

Product share within the industry is split into six categories. In 1987, unmounted ball bearings accounted for 37 percent of the product share, while unmounted tapered roller bearings accounted for 21 percent. Roller bearings that were neither mounted nor tapered accounted for 20.3 percent of the product share. Mounted bearings held 8.4 percent and parts for ball and roller bearings held 11.8 percent of the product share. Non-specific ball and roller bearings accounted for the remaining 1.5 percent. In terms of delivered cost, balls, rollers, cages, collars, races, and other antifriction bearing components and parts represented $350.1 million to the industry in 1987.

The materials consumed by the industry primarily include alloy steel mill shapes. However, cold steel and iron forgings are also widely used in the bearing industry. Other materials and devices used by the industry include raw and composite ceramics, electric motors, machine cutting tools, grinding wheels, powdered metals, copper wire, stainless steel sheets, carbon steel bars, and iron, steel, and copper scrap.

Approximately 31 percent of the roller bearings and 38 percent of the ball bearings produced by the industry are consumed by manufacturers of motor vehicles and related parts. General industry and machinery consume nearly 10 percent of the industry's roller bearings and just over 9 percent of its ball bearings. Construction and farm machinery together consume 17.2 percent of the industry's roller bearings and 16.1 percent of its ball bearings. The mining, oil drilling, and metalworking industries are also heavy consumers of antifriction bearings. Additionally, bearings of various types and sizes are widely used in refrigeration and heating equipment, motors and generators, aircraft and related parts, and railroad equipment.

Issues facing the bearings industry are complex. As a secondary steel product manufacturing industry, it is in the middle of the production chain. However, policies favoring the steel industry may not be in the best interest of the bearings industry, and vice versa. Because bearings are essential components of military and civilian machinery and equipment, the federal government has historically been a major customer of the industry. However, high labor and production costs have caused the bearings industry to lose business to foreign competitors who have been able to sell bearings of equal quality at lower prices.

ORGANIZATION AND STRUCTURE

The ball and roller bearing business is unusual because it is strictly a component manufacturing industry. The industry accommodates its markets by selling loose or packaged bearings; packaged bearings are installed in races that allow manufacturers to interchange complete bearing components. The industry has continued to evolve by developing new materials and lubricants and researching alternative uses for bearings. Bearings have been found to have almost limitless applications and are expected to be in demand as long as machines are manufactured.

Ball bearings are spherical in shape, while roller bearings are cylindrical and may be tapered on one end or flattened to resemble needles. Generally, a ball bearing is used when speed is important; a roller bearing is used more often when load is most important. The manufacture of antifriction bearings starts from rod or wire. In a typical production process, pieces of wire are cut off in a press, placed between dies, and pressed into the shape of a ball or roller. Large rollers are produced by machining turning processes. The fin of surplus material that forms in the pressing process is removed between rotating file discs, and the diameter of the bearings is reduced through grinding and tumbling processes. Roundness specifications and surface finish improvements are also attained during grinding and tumbling. The bearings are then hardened, tempered, and given a high polish by further tumbling with a polishing agent. Finally, the elements are graded according to diameter.

Antifriction bearings offer several advantages to machine designers. The friction placed on the bearings due to loads exerted is much lower than for other types of bearings. It is the lack of bearing friction that prevents excessive wear and abrasions on machines that start and stop while loads are applied. Automobile parts are examples of elements that benefit from less friction and wear. Roller bearings, in particular, are easily lubricated, can carry heavy loads relative to their size, and remain accurately aligned over extended periods of use. For these reasons, the huge market for antifriction bearings is stable and nearly recession proof.

BACKGROUND AND DEVELOPMENT

Since the invention of the wheel, the theory of bearing movement has been understood as a powerful phenomenon. The transfer of power to a rolling element has allowed societies to develop increasingly sophisticated structures and innovative machinery. As engines became more advanced and technology and production techniques improved, bearing manufacturing itself became a high-precision trade. Because virtually anything that rolls or spins uses bearings, the performance of the moving part is directly related to the bearing component. As such sophisticated machinery as military and commercial aircraft and nuclear-powered submarines have demanded increasingly high levels of precision and performance, bearing technology has evolved as a science and industry of its own.

In the mid-1980s, bearing manufacturers were subjected to a marketing tactic known as dumping. Dumping is a strategy, most commonly associated with the Japanese, which involves selling products in foreign countries at prices lower than the cost of manufacture in the parent country. The strategy is designed to allow a manufacturer to gain market share in a foreign country by providing a product at a price that is too low for competitors to match. Eventually competitors will be forced out of business, and the foreign competitor can command much higher prices because the competition has died.

Between 1968 and 1986 market share of imported bearings in the United States rose from 30 percent to 64 percent. After experiencing significant market share losses, Timken Company and the Anti-Friction Bearing Manufacturers Association (AFBMA) petitioned the Department of Commerce to conduct an investigation of import practices in 1987. The Trade Expansion Act of 1962 makes provisions for such investigations if the industry has been eroded to the point that it cannot compete internationally and if the nation's security is at risk. Until this appeal in 1987, only two other appeals had met with any success. The first case was related to the oil industry during the Kennedy administration and the second involved negotiating voluntary restraint concessions for the U.S. machine tools industry in 1986.

Because bearings are used in missile guidance systems, aircraft engines, tanks, and machine guns, dependence on foreign suppliers could leave this military equipment vulnerable to sabotage. Moreover, because U.S. equipment manufacturers do not have control over foreign companies' schedules they could be limited in their response to a surge in production and mobilization demands during wartime.

While many accused the bearing industry of being bad sports, the Department of Commerce was motivated to listen to Timken and the AFBMA when additional evidence of dumping was presented. Although the yen had gained value against the dollar, Japanese companies were unwilling to raise prices to compensate for this rise. The Japanese preferred to sell their bearings at a loss by absorbing costs, rather than losing market share. Timken and the AFBMA won the petition and the Department of Commerce instructed U.S. Customs to collect duties on shipments from Great Britain, Sweden, Italy, France, West Germany, Japan, Romania, Singapore, and Thailand. However, because SKF of Sweden, FAG of Germany, Koyo Seiko and Nippon Seiko of Japan already owned plants in the United States at the time of this decision, they were free from import duties. The Defense Department, however, supported domestic manufacturers by issuing a buy-American policy for antifriction bearing purchases.

The purchasers' side of the issue is quite different from that of the manufacturers. As prices began to climb, purchasers were incensed. Although the decision to impose duties only affected imported antifriction bearings, distributors took this as an opportunity to implement across-the-board increases. By 1989, a coalition of original equipment manufacturers called the American Manufacturers for Trade in Bearings (AMTB) took a stand against the duties levied. The AMTB, which included Black & Decker, 3M, AT&T, IBM, Briggs & Stratton, Emerson Electric, GE, Hewlett-Packard, Westinghouse, and Xerox, represented manufacturers that collectively purchased over 200 million ball bearings annually. This amounted to two-thirds the consumption of commodity ball bearings and double the amount produced by U.S. bearing manufacturers. The AMTB claimed that domestic bearing manufacturers were unable to meet U.S. demand for commodity ball bearings since the early 1980s and argued that the imports made-up for this shortfall.

The specific bearings the AMTB was fighting for were commodity ball bearings, which have specific applications. Five models are the most popular in this line, which collectively account for over 50 percent of the commodity bearings sold in the United States. Their primary applications are in power tools, appliances, automobiles, office equipment, and computer components. According to the director of commodities purchasing at Black & Decker, only three companies in the United States were capable of producing commodity ball bearings at the time of this decision.

CURRENT CONDITIONS

In the early 1990s, domestic bearing manufacturers were devising creative cost-cutting strategies to beat the competition. The director of purchasing and logistics at the Timken Company, for example, has placed emphasis on a coordinated sourcing strategy that would help the company compete globally. In this strategy, the purchasing function is more integrated with the rest of the company. This allows the purchasers to make buying decisions based on quality of materials, rather than price alone. Since Timken uses a fairly broad range of bearings and bearing components, company purchasers are divided into teams that correspond to their individual level of expertise. Additionally, Timken purchasers do not wait for suppliers to visit them; instead, they go to visit the suppliers. Moreover, Timken looks for value-added materials, which will facilitate other operations rather than produce more work.

Because bearings are vital components of machinery, the market shows no signs of vanishing. While employment levels may drop as a reaction to increased automation of manufacturing processes, the shipment levels are not expected to drop. However, domestic manufacturers in the early 1990s were not investing the capital necessary to keep up with technical advances. New non-destructive quality control methods, such as using eddy currents to measure surface variance, monitoring interior surface integrity with x-rays, and verifying chemical composition through gas, are innovations that have improved the quality of bearings. As production and testing techniques improve, domestic manufacturers will be expected to implement this technology in order to compete. However, the buy-American push implemented by the Defense Department and other manufacturers should allow bearing manufacturers to enjoy stability, and even expansion, through the year 2000.

Counterfeit bearings have posed another threat to the bearing industry. In February 1988, certain sellers were found guilty of deceiving buyers with counterfeit maximum capacity bearings. Although the bearings arrived in the same packaging as the authentic bearings and had the correct marking on the outer ring, purchasers noticed that the inner ring was marked by a different manufacturer. The main victims to fall prey to this scheme were those who did not purchase the bearings from authorized distributors.

INDUSTRY LEADERS

The highest regional concentration of bearings manufacturers was in the Great Lakes area. In terms of shipments, however, South Carolina ranked first. Its 10 bearing establishments shipped $482.8 million worth of bearings in 1987, which accounted for 13 percent of the total bearings shipments in the United States. In 1987, South Carolina employed 4,900 in this industry, who received an average hourly wage of $9.12 per hour. Connecticut ranked second in terms of shipments. Its 21 establishments shipped $406.8 million worth of bearings, which accounted for 10.9 percent of the nation's total bearing shipments. Approximately 5,100 people were employed by the bearing industry in Connecticut during 1987 and had average wages of $12.61 per hour. Seventeen establishments were located in New York, which collectively shipped $227.4 million in bearings in 1987. The 2,400 people employed by these manufacturers received an average hourly wage of $12.49, which was the highest average hourly wage in the industry. Indiana's 10 establishments shipped $194 million; Illinois's 12 establishments shipped $132.3 million; New Jersey's 8 establishments shipped $75.9 million; and, California's 13 establishments shipped $64.0 million.

In 1991, Ingersoll-Rand led the industry in sales. Based in Woodcliff Lake, New Jersey, Ingersoll boasted sales of $3.45 billion and employed 31,600 people. The Timken Company of Canton Ohio was ranked second, with 17,200 employees and sales of $1.53 billion in 1991. The Torrington Company of Torrington, Connecticut was ranked third with estimated sales of $850 million and a work force of 12,000. SKF U.S.A Incorporated, located in King of Prussia, Pennsylvania, was ranked fourth with estimated sales of $430 million and 4,500 employees. Ranked fifth was the Hoover Group Incorporated of Alpharetta, Georgia, which had sales of $220 million and a staff of 2,000. In 1991, the top 75 bearing manufacturers had combined sales of $9.258 billion and employed 95,500 people.

Since its beginning in 1905, Ingersoll-Rand was primarily an engineering products firm that specialized in coal mining equipment and air compressors. However, by the 1960s, the company was searching for diversified product lines that would complement existing products. In 1968 Ingersoll-Rand entered the bear-

ings industry through the acquisition of the Torrington Company. This placed Ingersoll-Rand in the business of making needle and roller bearings as well as knitting needles, metal-forming machines, universal joints, and roller clutches. This investment turned out to be extremely beneficial to Ingersoll-Rand, as it protected the company from the cyclical downturns of the mining equipment market.

Timken has been perfecting its tapered roller bearings since 1898, and by the early 1990s the company offered 26,000 different bearing combinations. Boasting that it is the world's largest tapered roller bearing producer, Timken attributes part of this success to international trade. After establishing a sales office in Japan in 1974, in an effort to serve Asian distributors, Timken finally made inroads with Japanese automobile manufacturers in 1987. The currency exchange rate and political climates contributed to the company's success in 1987, but the company received an important image boost primarily by maintaining a good reputation for quality when other U.S. goods were perceived as being inferior to Japanese products. While price competitiveness was not possible, technical expertise from Timken's side won praise from Japanese design engineers who started specifying tapered roller bearings for their products. With patience and expertise, Timken started supplying Nissan Motor Company and Mazda Motor Corporation with wheel bearings.

Due to the recession, however, Timken was forced to temporarily cut salaries and reduce work weeks for production workers in many plants in August 1991. The company's financial status worsened, and by December Timken was forced to lay-off approximately 300 workers at six plants in Canton, Ohio. During these difficult times, Timken was able to arrange temporary price cuts from vendors. Reportedly, over 95 percent of the company's suppliers agreed to negotiate temporary price cuts to allow Timken to remain strong through the recession.

Sweden-based SKF, which was incorporated in 1907, is the acknowledged leader of the world's roller bearing industry. In 1988, SKF controlled 20 percent of the world market in bearings, which was more than twice the market share held by its closest competitors. The company's entrance into the bearings market was motivated by its frustration with the poor quality and high cost of other bearings. The parent company, Gamlestadens Fabriker, a textile manufacturer, granted funds for research into producing bearings. Subsequently, the founder of SKF, Sven Wingquist, went on to develop the double row, self-aligning ball bearing which introduced SKF as a leader and innovator in the industry. From the onset, SKF aligned itself with the automotive industry and pushed its operations into France and the United Kingdom in order to compete directly with German manufacturers. In 1916 SKF expanded by acquiring another Swedish ball bearing producer as well as a steel works company to increase its steel supply for its bearings. During the 1920s, SKF furthered its reputation for innovation when it introduced spherical and taper roller bearings.

By the 1970s SKF faced serious competitive threats in its European market due to the influx of Japanese bearing makers like NTN, NSK, and Koyo Seiko. In response, SKF began to place more emphasis on bearing quality in an effort to retain customer loyalty. The company introduced a global forecasting and supply system, which allowed all of its European plants to be aware of demand. Additionally, the company was able to expand product lines by increasing its funding of product research and development. In 1986 SKF formed a 50-50 joint venture with Koyo Seiko, making it the first foreign bearings manufacturer to participate in the Japanese market. While Koyo Seiko was interested in SKF's technology, SKF was interested in the Japanese company's 20-percent stake in Toyota and the booming market in Southeast Asia.

WORK FORCE

Although shipments have climbed steadily since 1983, employment levels have been declining since 1984. The total employment level in the industry dropped 15.5 percent between 1982 and 1987, from 43,700 to 36,900. That level rose 4.9 percent in 1988 to 38,800. Production workers, who have traditionally made up between two-thirds and three-quarters of the industry's entire work force, suffered fewer layoffs than other industry workers in the 1980s and made larger gains when manufacturers began rehiring in the early 1990s. The number of production workers fell 12.8 percent between 1982 and 1987, from 33,500 to 29,200. However, in 1988 the production work force enjoyed a 7 percent gain, reaching an employment level of 31,400. In 1991 the top 75 bearing manufacturers employed a work force of nearly 95,500 people. Just over 60,000 of these employees worked at the top three manufacturers, Ingersoll-Rand, Timken, and Torrington. In 1988, the average hourly wage in the industry was reported to be $12.18, which was higher than the $10.88 hourly rate reported as the average wage for all manufacturing positions.

As a reflection of global competition, the work force is expected to change significantly in the late 1990s. While certain occupations are expected to decline in numbers, others are expected to grow. Those facing reductions include assemblers, inspectors, secretaries, machine tool cutting operators, machine builders, welders, sheet metal workers, machine assemblers, machine forming operators, and welding machine setters. Those occupations expected to increase by 20 percent or more include sales workers, industrial machinery mechanics, industrial production managers, and engineering and science managers. Those occupations expected to increase by 12 percent to 15 percent include machinists, mechanical engineers, numerically controlled machine tool operators, and combination machine tool operators. Occupations expected to increase at levels between 5 percent and 11 percent include precision woodworkers, production and inventory control clerks, traffic clerks, general office clerks, and engineering technicians.

One company that is highly respected in the industry is Industrial Tectonics. At Industrial Tectonics employees are empowered to be responsible for bearing quality by three basic ethics. The first ethic is that the employees must be able to measure everything produced. The second ethic is an assurance that verifiable quality control systems are in place. The third is related to employees improving themselves and participating in these quality control efforts. Industrial Tectonics confers responsibility and accountability to all employees, forcing them to understand quality-related issues. Machinists gage the parts they produce and correct problems when statistical control trends show correction is necessary. Employees are expected to engage in practical and theoretical applications classes both on company time and on their own time. The company takes comprehensive skills inventories to decide what types of job-related training would benefit employees. For this type of involvement, Industrial Tectonics rewards employees with promotions and other incentive programs. Due to such an emphasis on quality and investment in human resources, Industrial Tectonics is the only bearing manufacturer to supply master balls to the National Bureau of Standards. Additionally, the U.S. Navy has selected Industrial Tectonics as a supplier of precision ball bearings for nuclear use. The company has also shipped millions of flow control parts to General Motors for over two years without one reject.

AMERICA AND THE WORLD

In 1987, the U.S. Air Force and Army launched the Engine Bearing Technology Modernization Program in an effort to support U.S. bearing manufacturers. This program came as a response to the U.S. Department of Commerce's findings that foreign manufacturers were dumping their bearings in the U.S.

market and potentially jeopardizing national security. In a December 1987 *Mechanical Engineering* article James Dill wrote, "Competition in the international bearing industry is fierce and profit margins are small. Because U.S. plants tend to be older and economic conditions have been unfavorable for reinvestment, overseas suppliers have captured much of the higher-profit, lower-performance bearing business. U.S. suppliers have been left with the specialized, high-precision portion of the bearing market. With their production base reduced, U.S. suppliers have found it increasingly difficult to invest in modernizing their precision bearing plants, and there is a growing concern that this sector of the business may also be lost to overseas suppliers."

While the Japanese may appear to pose the most significant threat to U.S. bearing manufacturers, Singapore and Korea are mounting strong competitive campaigns against the Japanese. Also contending for world market share are the Europeans and some countries from the former Soviet Union. The impact of the North American Free Trade Agreement will certainly affect the bearing industry, as new plants are built in Mexico and lower manufacturing costs are realized.

According to a 1985 Department of Commerce report, the following free world countries were supplying bearings: West Germany, with 24 percent of the total market; Japan, with 18 percent; the United States, with 12 percent; France, with 10 percent; United Kingdom, with 10 percent; Italy and Sweden, with 6 percent each; and, Austria and Switzerland, with 3 percent each. As for U.S. imports, Japan held 43 percent of the import market, West Germany 17 percent, Canada 13 percent, and Singapore 6 percent. Romania entered the U.S. import market in the early 1980s, and by 1983 held 4 percent of the market, primarily supplying tapered roller bearings. Hungary held 2 percent of the market when it began importing tapered roller bearings to the United States in 1983. Hungary bearings were used predominately for truck and trailers and were priced between 22 percent and 29 percent lower than comparable U.S. products.

RESEARCH AND TECHNOLOGY

The production of precision bearings is changing quickly, as technology allows greater and more accurate measurements to be taken. In 1989 it was announced that the Timken Company developed production equipment, gages, and methods of manufacture to produce bearings called Precision Plus. The Precision Plus bearings boast a radial run-out of less than 40 millionths of an inch. Radial run-out is a measure of how closely the bearings will run in a perfect circle in a

given bearing-ring path. Timken was able to create this new class of bearings through assessing grinding wheel variables such as type, speed of the wheel, feed rate into the wheel, coolant type, coolant temperature, and wheel dressing techniques. When bearings are produced to precision units of a millionth of an inch, shelf-life becomes a factor. If bearings sit on a shelf for less than six months, the diameter can change several millionths of an inch. In high precision applications, this is unsatisfactory. Therefore, Timken developed a proprietary heat treatment process which prevents dimensional changes from occurring over time. The Precision Plus bearings are available in standard sizes ranging from 3/8 inch to 12 inches in diameter.

Silicon Nitride that has been through a process called Hot Isostatic Pressing (HIPing) is one of the best-suited materials for producing high-quality bearings. Standard bearings are typically made of steel, and are consequently subject to wear. In the early 1990s, however, researchers were experimenting with hybrid steel/ceramic bearings and all-ceramic bearings. The Japanese were leading the way in this investigation, having found methods for producing ceramic components with consistency and accuracy. Ceramic bearings are attractive to manufacturers for several reasons: they exert less centrifugal force on the outer race; they can operate at higher temperatures and speeds; and, they provide better control and more accuracy in given applications. Japanese manufacturers have tested ceramic bearings in aircraft engines with no appreciable wear observed.

The Japanese are also aggressively researching alternative processing techniques and methods for improving corrosion resistance in aircraft quality bearings. New forms of failure analysis are also lending insights to the behavior of bearings under specific conditions. In both the United States and Japan, x-ray and gas chromatography are becoming more common non-destructive testing methods. High temperature applications are also under aggressive study abroad at Japanese Universities and bearing manufacturers. Solid lubrication is an area where the United States leads the way in research, and the Japanese have shown keen interest in the findings.

Although the bearing industry generally implements very precise test sequences, some purchasers of bearings are finding that acceptance testing is necessary before shipping a product that uses ball or roller bearings. The reason for this is that each bearing is individually produced, and therefore unique. The U.S. Army, for example, had an embarrassing and expensive mishap with a tank's firing mechanism due to problems with its bearing components. Therefore, acceptance testing by original equipment manufacturers is a growing trend in manufacturing.

One of the most innovative applications for bearings is in anti-lock braking (ABS) and traction control systems. ABS operates through electronically controlled bearings, which act as sensors. The sensors are able to relay information about wheel speeds to the car control system. In a January 9, 1992 *Machine Design* article Michael Courtright commented, "Wheel-bearing hubs are an optimum location for monitoring wheel speed for two reasons: bearings and hubs are mechanically precise and close to the wheel." The ABS computer receives information about the wheel speeds and decides if the regulation of brake fluid to one wheel will be necessary to prevent lock-up. General Motors' Delco Chassis Division innovated this approach, and currently Timken and SKF Bearings supply instrumented bearing packages to automakers. However, the product is not standardized across the auto industry and presently lacks support of some executives who feel the life of the sensors is much more volatile than the life of the hub. Consequently, when a sensor fails the entire hub must be replaced, making the system potentially expensive in maintenance terms. More standardization is needed to ensure ABS is successful. However, government regulations could force the issue of instrumented bearings and ABS in all cars.

INDUSTRY INFORMATION SOURCES

Avery, Susan, "Bearing Makers: First the Good News," *Purchasing,* February 11, 1988.

A Competitive Assessment of the U.S. Ball and Roller Bearings Industry, U. S. Department of Commerce, International Trade Administration, Washington, D.C.: GPO, February 1988.

Courtright, Michael L., "Instrumented Bearings Get Rolling with ABS," *Machine Design,* January 9, 1992.

Darnay, Arsen J., ed., *Manufacturing U.S.A: Industry Analyses, Statistics, and Leading Companies,* Detroit: Gale Research, Inc., 1991.

Dill, James F., "Sizing Up the Japanese," *Mechanical Engineering,* December 1987.

"Dumping Case Trips Bearing Price Hikes," *Purchasing,* December 15, 1988.

Hast, Adele, ed., *International Directory of Company Histories, Vol. III.* Chicago: St. James Press, 1988.

Hosang, G.W., "Experimental and Computed Performance Characteristics of High-Speed Silicon Nitride Hybrid Ball Bearings," *Journal of Engineering for Gas Turbines and Power,* October 1991.

Imberman, Woodruff, "Improve: Upgrade: Innovate," *Modern Machine Shop,* February 1988.

"Industry Group Seeks Quotas on Bearing Imports," *Industrial Distribution,* September 1987.

Mason, Fred, "6-Spindle Automatics Get CNC," *American Machinist & Automated Manufacturing,* March 1987.

Platt, Stephen E., "Timken is No Stranger to the Japanese," *Ward's Auto World,* September 1988.

Purchase, Michael, "Acceptance Testing for Bearings," *Machine Design,* March 23, 1989.

Raia, Ernie, "Buyers Fight Ball Bearings Dumping Claim," *Purchasing*, May 4, 1989.

"Tapered Roller Bearings Made to Highest Precision Ever," *Machine Design,* March 23, 1989.

West, Bartlett, "Three Quality Ethics Spell Success," *Modern Machine Shop,* May 1988.

Zimmerman, Susan, "Competition Changes the Buying Landscape," *Purchasing,* February 6, 1992.

—Valerie E. Wilson

SIC 3563

AIR AND GAS COMPRESSORS

This category covers firms primarily engaged in manufacturing air and gas compressors for general industrial use, and non-agricultural spraying and dusting equipment. It does not include manufacturers of refrigeration and air-conditioning compressors (**SIC 3585: Air-Conditioning and Warm Air Heating Equipment and Commercial and Industrial Refrigeration Equipment**), pneumatic pumps and motors for fluid power transmission (**SIC 3594: Fluid Power Pumps and Motors**), agricultural spraying and dusting equipment (**SIC 3523: Farm Machinery and Equipment**), or laboratory vacuum pumps (**SIC 3821: Laboratory Apparatus and Furniture**).

INDUSTRY SNAPSHOT

Compressors provide one of the most versatile forms of energy used by industry today. Compressed air as a power source ranks as most commonly used behind only electricity, gas and water. In addition, compressors provide the motive force needed to economically transport gas and other materials in pipelines. Since compressors are required to operate in difficult environments and conditions, they wear quickly. As a result, the replacement parts portion of the industry composed a significant portion of shipments, 20 percent in 1977 according to the census. Other major markets included the chemical industry, steel mills and blast furnaces, energy-related extraction industries, pipelines and well-drilling, and general construction.

ORGANIZATION AND STRUCTURE

Some 175 establishments manufactured air and gas compressors in 1977, an increase of more than 100 percent over the 1972 census figure. This number reached 259 by 1987. Historically, manufacturing in this industry has been heavily concentrated; in 1977 more than half the industry's employees worked in the four largest facilities, and 79 percent of all facilities employed fewer than 100 workers. By 1987 this had changed slightly. While 75 percent of all facilities still employed fewer than 100, diffusion was more evident in the larger firms. The 1987 Census showed the largest 136 firms employing 52.5 percent of all workers.

The use of compressed air and gas can be divided into three major categories, according to the *Compressed Air and Gas Handbook:* compressed air and gas for process services, compressed air for power, and compressed air for general industrial applications.

Process services include chemical alterations like combustion, nitrogen fixation, polymerization, hydrogenation and alkylation; and change of state operations like quenching, drying, and atomization. Products that result from these types of procedures include liquid fuels, plastics, synthetic rubber, ammonia and fertilizers.

Power uses utilize the potential energy of stored compressed air to directly perform work. The tools and devices powered by compressed air are termed pneumatic. They generally perform more slowly than electric tools but faster than hydraulic and provide smooth power application. The energy potential can be translated into rotation and torque with the use of rotary air motors, vanes or air turbines. Reciprocating motion and direct force provide easily controllable presses, clamps and feeding devices. Air pressure can be used to accelerate a mass such as a pile driver or pavement breaker. Blow guns use the air pressure stream directly to move materials such as chips, debris and paint. Air can displace fluids, semi-fluids and solids to drive materials through pipelines. When air and liquid are mixed, the resulting bubbling action provides agitation, mixing and aeration.

Industry uses of compressed air include plant maintenance and the powering of pneumatic tools for production line work. This has been especially important for automation of thread-tightening, pressing, hammering, feeding, positioning and safety-control sensors.

BACKGROUND AND DEVELOPMENT

The world's first pump was probably the force or air pump built by Ktesibios of Alexandria about 270 B.C. He used a cylinder and plunger arrangement to pump air through pipes of various lengths, creating the first water organ. The water was used to maintain a steady air pressure in the system. Simple air pumps and bellows provided low-pressure compressed air for such devices as organs and black-smith furnaces, but major advancements in compressor technology had to wait until the arrival of the Industrial Revolution.

Generally the term compressor was applied to any blower which produced compressed air in excess of 40 psi. Below that pressure, the device is simply called a blower or industrial fan. With new industrial processes came new demands for flexibility of power sources. Coupling the air pump to a steam engine showed the potential of air power. By 1900, the stationary air compressor was a common tool for industry, albeit a massive one requiring bulky, space-consuming foundations. In 1900, the portable compressor made its debut by the simple expedient of placing wheels under some of the smaller stationary engines. Until 1910, the most common power for such compressors was the steam engine or an oil engine. The main application for the devices was for rock-drilling. The invention of a light-weight air drill spurred development of the portable compressor.

Major advances came in the 1930s, when the two-stage, air-cooled compressor appeared, followed by multi-speed regulation by the end of the decade. The 1950s saw the introduction of the rotary-screw compressor in the United States which allowed for considerably higher operating speeds in smaller, lighter units. Continued improvements made possible the now-common truck-mounted diesel-powered units used by utilities and construction companies everywhere as a completely portable and flexible power source.

One industry to especially benefit from the new technology was oil exploration and drilling. In 1938 some oil companies began experimenting with air-powered drills. The technique used a rotating bit and pumped either mud or air through holes in the bit to clear the cutting face. New booster compressors producing 1500 psi were developed specifically for the industry. By the end of World War II, portable drilling rigs were quickly and efficiently boring shallow wells.

The construction industry borrowed the technology for its blast-hole drillers in 1946. In 1954 it developed its own bottom-hole tool which used 100 psi compressed air to rotate a carbide-tipped tool. Water-well-drills used 250 psi air to clear water from the hole while drilling.

The two most common types of compressors are the positive-displacement and the velocity or dynamic. Positive-displacement machines trap air in a confined space and then reduce the volume of that space to increase the pressure. The bicycle pump is a familiar example of this type of compressor. It need not use a piston assembly, a rotating gear, or a screw mechanism. Such compressors can be powered by electric motors, oil or gas engines, or steam engines or turbines. The most common applications for these compressors are off-shore oil drilling, construction applications, locomotives, ships, mining, and smaller units in machine shops, bakeries, dry cleaning plants, food processing plants, furniture factories, printing plants, textile mills, automotive service shops, and other industrial and commercial applications using compressed air.

The dynamic system uses a fan or turbine mechanism to force the air or gas against the casing by centrifugal force. Such systems often use several stages or series of compression to achieve high pressures. The systems can be either axial, expelling gas along the line of its impeller axis, or radial, expelling gas against the casing by centrifugal force. The most common applications for these devices are in refineries, petrochemical plants, steel mills, ammonia plants, sewage aeration, pipeline boosters, wind tunnels and supercharging diesel engines.

CURRENT CONDITIONS

The general industrial slowdown of the 1980s hit the compressor industry hard. Major clients like the nuclear power industry, oil well and pipeline industry, and the construction industry cut back on orders for new equipment and idled existing components. A strong U.S. dollar made American products uncompetitive in foreign markets.

By 1988, this started to change. A weakening dollar spurred exports and a general pickup in the manufacturing climate sparked new domestic orders in almost all sectors. The industry continued to modernize production by consolidating facilities and adopting sophisticated CAD/CAM systems and metalworking and casting technologies. New materials and designs were explored to extend the life of components in corrosive environments and to increase reliability. *U.S. Industrial Outlook—1990* predicted a 2.6 percent growth in the industry until 1994, assuming it could continue to compete with increasingly innovative foreign manufacturers.

The *Monthly Labor Review* noted in 1982 that one of the largest users of compressors was the chemical industry, taking about ten percent of the compressor industry's output. Steel mills and blast furnaces took about seven percent of output. The oil-well and pipeline industries took 18 percent of output. Demand in this sector dropped off dramatically in the 1960s but steadily recovered. Compressors are used in both oil drilling and oil field maintenance operations, particularly for secondary recovery efforts. Construction took 18 percent of output. Particularly important in this market category were the sales of portable compressors used to drive pneumatic tools on the construction site where other sources of energy might be restricted.

INDUSTRY LEADERS

Three of the top firms by sales in the air and gas compressor industry in 1993 were Thomas Industries of Louisville, Kentucky; Cooper Industries Inc. Energy Services Group of Mt. Vernon, Ohio; and Calmar Spraying Systems Inc. of City of Industry, California. Thomas Industries was established in 1928 and employs 3,530 workers to produce $408 million in annual sales. It has one subsidiary, Power Air Division. Cooper Industries Energy Services Group is one of several divisions of Cooper Industries producing pumps and compressors for various applications. It was established in 1833 and 3,300 workers produce $330 million in annual sales. Calmar Spraying Systems Inc. was a subsidiary of CSS Holding Inc. It was established in 1983 and employs 3,020 workers to produce annual sales of $290 million. It has one subsidiary, Calmar Inc.

WORK FORCE

The *Monthly Labor Review,* 1982, noted that the general industrial machinery group generally used a high proportion of skilled trades, about 30 percent of all production workers compared to the 26 percent proportion in all manufacturing. Compressor and pump production made up about 29 percent of all labor in the industrial machinery group. Metal working craftsmen and machinists were three times more common in this industry than in manufacturing as a whole while laborers were half as common. Average wages were ten percent higher in this industry indicating a higher degree of necessary skill. This disparity continued as late as 1988 when the compressor industry paid an average hourly wage of $12.68 compared to the manufacturing average of $10.66. The industry also employed a high proportion of non-production workers, indicating a reliance on mechanical engineers. This employment group was three times more common in the compressor industry than in general manufacturing.

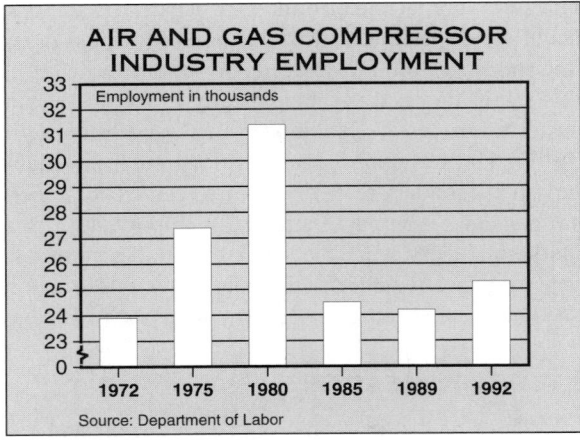

AIR AND GAS COMPRESSOR INDUSTRY EMPLOYMENT

Employment in thousands

Source: Department of Labor

The Bureau of Labor Statistics projected a continuation of this trend with its estimate of employment changes until the year 2000. It expected double digit increases for industrial machinery mechanics, sales workers, engineering and science managers, industrial production managers, NC tool operators for both plastics and metals, mechanical engineers, combination machine tool operators, machinists, and engineering technicians. Total employment sat at 24,400 in 1989, a 32 percent drop from the 32,100 employed in 1982. In the same time period, the value of shipments increased from $3.3 billion to $3.5 billion as estimated by *U.S. Industrial Outlook—1990.*

AMERICA AND THE WORLD

Air and gas compressors were manufactured to international standards allowing American manufacturers to compete effectively in the international market. These same standards also made the United States vulnerable to foreign competition, particularly on price and quality. During the early half of the 1980s, the strong American dollar made such competition particularly difficult, undermining an already weak industrial climate in American manufacturing. As a result, the U.S. merchandise trade deficit quadrupled between 1982 and 1984, reaching $145 billion. This effect showed up in the compressor manufacturing industry, but was delayed. In 1985 this industry showed a trade surplus, but by 1987 it had become a $1.9 billion deficit. The drop of the value of the U.S. dollar which began in March of 1985 provided new impetus for the compressor industry. By 1987, the average export price expressed in foreign currency of compressors and other machinery had fallen 23.1 percent. By 1990,

even though domestic prices increased an average of five percent each year, the foreign currency price of compressors and replacement parts had dropped more than 11 percent. That made American operations more profitable, increased export volumes, and discouraged imports. It also encouraged foreign firms to establish manufacturing and assembly facilities in the United States.

In 1990, exports approached $770 million while imports exceeded $520 million. Major markets for American products included Canada, Mexico, the United Kingdom, Saudi Arabia, West Germany, Venezuela, and Japan. The top importers included Japan, West Germany, Canada, and the United Kingdom.

RESEARCH AND TECHNOLOGY

The majority of compressors manufactured are custom made to a client's specific requirements for use in complex applications where the failure of the compressor could be disastrous. Consequently, manufacturing innovation has stressed flexibility and reliability. Major innovations included the adoption of numerical and computer control manufacturing systems and the reliance on engineering expertise assisted by computer modelling software to custom design components for short run production. New corrosion resistant materials were developed and refinements to old processes adopted. Specially designed metal-forming machines were created for the industry, including combination milling, radial drilling and facing machines, variable setting grinders which automatically form tapered shafts, and automatic tool changing devices controlled by NC tapes or computer software. Foundry operations for production of compressor casings and core-making advanced with rapid-cycle machinery, synchronous fabricating machinery and a no-bake molding process using a resin binder and catalyst. Closer tolerances were achieved in components by replacing wooden molds and cores with ceramic. Increasing concern over energy efficiency dictated more advanced compressor designs with larger displacements.

INDUSTRY INFORMATION SOURCES

"Build Your Working Knowledge of Process Compressors," *Chemical Engineering Progress,* February, 1993.

Compressed Air and Gas Handbook, New York: Compressed Air and Gas Institute, 1973.

"Compressor Diagnostics Software Being Developed," *Oil & Gas Journal,* September 28, 1992.

"Dollar's Fall Boosts U.S. Machinery Exports, 1985-90," *Monthly Labor Review,* July 1991.

Hanlon, Paul, "Plastics Fight Friction in Reciprocating Compressors," *Machine Design,* April 9, 1992.

Kirsch, F. William, *Waste Minimization Assessment for a Manufacturer of Compressed Air Equipment Components,* Cincinnati, Ohio: U.S. Environmental Protection Agency, 1991.

Kranzberg, Melvin, and Carroll W. Pursel, Jr., eds., *Technology in Western Civilization,* Volume 1, New York: Oxford University Press, 1967.

1982 Census of Manufacturers, Washington, D.C.: Department of Commerce, 1987.

"Productivity in the Pump and Compressor Industry," *Monthly Labor Review,* December 1982.

Scheel, Lyman F., *Gas and Air Compression Machinery,* New York: McGraw-Hill, 1961.

U.S. Industrial Outlook 1980, Washington, D.C.: U.S. Department of Commerce, 1989.

U.S. Industrial Outlook 1990, Washington, D.C.: U.S. Department of Commerce, 1990.

Usher, Abbot Payson, *A History of Mechanical Inventions,* Boston: Beacon Press, 1929.

—Al Cook

SIC 3564

INDUSTRIAL AND COMMERCIAL FANS AND BLOWERS AND AIR PURIFICATION EQUIPMENT

This category covers firms primarily engaged in manufacturing blowers for general industrial and commercial use, and commercial exhaust fans, ventilating fans and attic fans. Also included are manufacturers of duct collection equipment and other air purification equipment for heating and air conditioning systems and equipment for industrial gas cleaning systems. It does not include manufacturers of refrigeration and air-conditioning components (**SIC 3585**), or small household fans, kitchen and bath ventilation fans, or other domestic fan components (**SIC 3634**).

INDUSTRY SNAPSHOT

American industry depends on the low-pressure, high-volume movement of air. Without it, much industrial and commercial activity would quickly suffocate. Consequently, the fan can be found in applications as diverse as huge blowers used to bubble air through sewage water and industrial waste, to street cleaners and industrial leaf blowers. In modern shopping centers and commercial/industrial strip malls, unnoticed roof ventilators silently exchange contaminated air for fresh; the attic fan performs the same function for residential buildings. Heating and air conditioning systems depend on fans to move heat away from coils and heat exchangers and into the structure, and to feed the fossil fuel combustion processes with large quantities of oxygen-bearing air. Exhaust systems push the products of this combustion outside the structure or extract grease and heat from commercial cooking appliances and industrial ovens.

The fan's ability to move large quantities of air makes it the base component of the rapidly expanding air pollution control industry. Starting with the plant, the device has been harnessed to help trap and remove pollutants like dust and metal particles, carbon monoxide, nitrous oxides, sulphur dioxide, sulfuric acid and hydrocarbon solvents in a variety of filters and traps. In 1990 *Current Reports* estimated shipments of such pollution abatement equipment reached $899 million.

ORGANIZATION AND STRUCTURE

Some 445 establishments manufactured fans and blowers at 502 locations, according to the 1987 Census. This showed a marked increase in the number of firms from 360 in 1972, but the total employment in the industry remained somewhat constant at 23,500 in 1977 and 24,800 in 1987. Historically, manufacturing in this industry has been heavily concentrated; in 1987 more than three-quarters of the industry's employees worked in the largest 25 percent of facilities, and more than 75 percent of all facilities employed fewer than 50 workers. Ohio, New York, California, and North Carolina led the industry in employment, capturing 37 percent between them in 1987.

Fans and blowers belong to the same family of devices as compressors and pumps. A pump moves liquids, while the others move gases. A compressor will provide a means of increasing the pressure of the gas to more than 40 psi. That gas can then either be delivered directly to the application or stored for metered use. A blower can also increase the pressure of the gas to as much as 40 psi, but delivers it directly to the application through an area of high resistance like a pipeline. Fans provide large volumes of uncompressed gas and operate in low-resistance environments which could also include ducting systems. Technically, an increase in gas density of less than seven percent between inlet and outlet defines the gas as uncompressed.

The main uses of fans and blowers, according to the *Compressed Air and Gas Handbook,* are for process services (including chemical alterations like combustion, nitrogen fixation, polymerization, hydrogenation and alkylation), and for change of state operations (including quenching, drying, and atomization). Products that result from these types of procedures include liquid fuels, plastics, synthetic rubber, ammonia and fertilizers.

BACKGROUND AND DEVELOPMENT

The world's first pump was probably the force or air pump built by Ktesibios of Alexandria about 270 B.C. He used a cylinder and plunger arrangement to pump air through pipes of various lengths, creating the first water organ. The water was used to maintain a steady air pressure in the system. Simple air pumps and bellows provided low-pressure ''compressed'' air for such devices as organs and black-smith furnaces, but major advancements in fan technology had to wait until the arrival of the Industrial Revolution.

The two most common types of fans and blowers are the axial and the centrifugal. Axial fans are used in applications that produce low resistance to air flow. The gas is moved in the same direction as the fans axis of rotation, much as a water wheel on a classic mill or paddle steamer. In the centrifugal fan, the gas moves perpendicular to the fans axis of rotation. Most domestic fans use angled and curved blades to produce the centrifugal effect at low pressure. Centrifugal blowers and fans are used in relatively high resistance application and usually provide quieter operation than axial units. All fans and blowers fall into the general compressor classification of dynamic.

CURRENT CONDITIONS

The general industrial slowdown of the 1980s hit the fan and blower industry hard. Major clients like the petrochemical industry; heating, ventilation and air conditioning industry; and the construction industry cut back on orders for new equipment and idled existing components. A strong U.S. dollar made American products uncompetitive in foreign markets.

By 1988, this started to change. A weakening dollar stimulated exports and a general pickup in the manufacturing climate sparked new domestic orders in almost all sectors. The industry continued to modernize production by consolidating facilities and adopting sophisticated CAD/CAM systems and metalworking and casting technologies. New materials and designs were explored to extend the life of components in corrosive environments and to increase reliability.

New environmental regulations like the Clean Air Act domestically and its counterparts in other countries spurred the development and sale of air pollution abatement equipment. Two major products in this category were particle emission collectors with shipments of $513 million in 1990 and gaseous emission control units with sales of $220 million that year, according to *U.S. Industrial Outlook—1993.* In 1990, the major clients for such products were steam electric power generators, $90 million; industrial steam plants, $72 million; pulp and paper mills, $65 million; chemical and fertilizer producers, $44 million; and petroleum refiners, $23 million. Demand for such products continued to accelerate towards a total expected yearly sales level of $8.7 billion in the year 2000. Steel mills increased purchases to $62.82 million in 1991. By 1992, the pulp and paper industry accounted for 9.9 percent of all sales of air pollution control equipment and U.S. utilities projected a five year sales spree of six billion dollars worth of flue gas desulfurization equipment.

INDUSTRY LEADERS

Three of the top firms by sales in the blower and fan industry in 1993 were Snyder-General Corp. of Dallas, Texas; Air & Water Technologies Corp. of Somerville, New Jersey; and Ampco-Pittsburgh Corp. of Pittsburgh, Pennsylvania. Snyder-General was founded in 1982 and employs 7,000 workers to produce $750 million in sales. Its subsidiaries include American Air Filter Division, which ranks as third largest in this category on its own; Comfortmaker Division; and Filtration Products Division. Air & Water Technologies was established in 1987 and employees 3,430 workers to produce $657 million in sales. It has one subsidiary, Air Base Construction Equipment. Ampco-Pittsburgh was established in 1929 and employs 2,100 to produce $221 million in annual sales.

WORK FORCE

The *Monthly Labor Review,* 1982, noted that compressor and pump production made up about 29 percent of all labor in the industrial machinery group. Metal working craftsmen and machinists were three times more common in this industry than in manufacturing as a whole, while laborers were half as common. Average wages were ten percent higher in this industry indicating a higher degree of necessary skill. This disparity continued as late as 1988 when the compressor industry paid an average hourly wage of $12.68 compared to the manufacturing average of $10.66. The fan and blower section of the industrial machine category showed a lower hourly wage, $9.60 in 1988, indicating that this sector used a higher percentage of traditional unskilled labor.

Total employment in the industry sat at 24,200 in 1988, a 19 percent drop from the 29,800 employed in 1982. In the same time period, the value of shipments increased from $2.2 billion to $2.4 billion as estimated by *U.S. Industrial Outlook—1990.*

AMERICA AND THE WORLD

Blowers and fans and the increasingly important air pollution abatement equipment were manufactured to international standards allowing American manufacturers to compete effectively on the international market. These same standards, however, also made the United States vulnerable to foreign competition, particularly on price and quality. During the early half of the 1980s, the strong American dollar made such competition particularly difficult, undermining an already weak industrial climate in American manufacturing. As a result, the U.S. merchandise trade deficit quadrupled between 1982 and 1984, reaching $145 billion. This effect showed up in the blower manufacturing industry, but was delayed. In 1985 this industry showed a trade surplus, but by 1987 it had become a $1.9 billion deficit. The drop of the value of the U.S. dollar, which began in March of 1985, provided new impetus for the blower industry. By 1987, the average export price expressed in foreign currency of blowers and other machinery had fallen 23.1 percent. By 1990, even though domestic prices increased an average of five percent each year, the foreign currency price of blowers had dropped more than 11 percent. This made American operations more profitable, increased export volumes, and discouraged imports. It also encouraged foreign firms to establish manufacturing and assembly facilities in the United States.

Such globalization trends were particularly important in the air pollution abatement equipment (APC) sector. U.S. and European multinationals used direct investment, cross-border mergers, acquisitions, joint ventures and foreign collaboration to gain entry to each other's markets and to other markets around the world. The main target markets for such equipment in the early 1990s were Asia, Eastern Europe, the former Soviet Union, and Latin America. Many firms prefer to license foreign manufacturers instead of competing directly, creating a brisk trade in environmental technology.

The United States exported 16 percent of its production of APC equipment in 1992. This market had grown rapidly in the 1980s, reaching $100 million by 1989, but dropped off after that because of a slowdown of the world economy and a temporary saturation of the market. The main markets were the Pacific Basin, Canada, Mexico and Europe. American industry imported about 26 percent of its APC needs in 1992, mainly from Europe and Japan.

RESEARCH AND TECHNOLOGY

New and more stringent environmental regulations in the United States and around the world encouraged research into new air pollution abatement technology. With a projected annual growth of three to four percent between 1993 and 1997, resulting in a total market of more than $250 billion, the industry looked forward to a period of innovative research. This was especially true since some regulations called for pollution limitations in excess of what was technically possible at the time.

However, the industry also found ways of applying the old technologies in new ways. Some major areas of research included electrostatic precipitators with the addition of high-voltage direct-current pulses to capture fly-ash, filter bags treated with microporous films or membranes to keep dust cake out of the filter material, conditioning flue gas streams with sulfur trioxide or ammonia before filtering to improve the life of the filter, the development of sulfur trioxide generators to convert flue gases without the need of adding the chemical, new plastic materials to extend the concept of flue gas cooling with water beyond the wood products industry, and sorbent injection of such materials as carbon, char, and sodium sulfide to capture heavy metals like mercury.

INDUSTRY INFORMATION SOURCES

Bouley, Jeffrey, ''Fans & Blowers,'' *Pollution Engineering,* April 15, 1993.

Compressed Air and Gas Handbook, New York: Compressed Air and Gas Institute, 1973.

''Dollar's Fall Boosts U.S. Machinery Exports, 1985-90,'' *Monthly Labor Review,* July 1991.

Kirsch, F. William, *Waste Minimization Assessment for a Manufacturer of Compressed Air Equipment Components,* Cincinnati, Ohio: U.S. Environmental Protection Agency, 1991.

Kranzberg, Melvin, and Carroll W. Pursel, Jr., eds., *Technology in Western Civilization,* Volume 1, New York: Oxford University Press, 1967.

1982 Census of Manufacturers. Washington, D.C.: Department of Commerce, 1987.

Nudo, Lori, ''Capturing Heavy Metals,'' *Pollution Engineering,* September 1993.

''Productivity in the Pump and Compressor Industry,'' *Monthly Labor Review,* December 1982.

Scheel, Lyman F., *Gas and Air Compression Machinery,* New York: McGraw-Hill, 1961.

U.S. Industrial Outlook 1993, Washington, D.C.: U.S. Department of Commerce, 1989.

"U.S. Utilities Will Commit $6 Billion More for Flue Gas Desulfurization (FGD) Systems," *Environmental Science Technology,* January 1992.

Usher, Abbot Payson, *A History of Mechanical Inventions,* Boston: Beacon Press, 1929.

—Al Cook

SIC 3565

PACKAGING MACHINERY

Firms in this industry manufacture machinery used in packaging, wrapping and bottling.

Since the statistical reorganization of the industry in 1987, packaging equipment showed a steady increase in production along with a slight decline in employment as manufacturing automation increased. Shipments rose from $2.2 billion in 1987 to $2.65 billion in 1991. Employment in the same period dropped from 22,600 to 22,000.

The industry found itself challenged to change and innovate in the late 1980s and early 1990s as industry shifted to leaner production methods requiring just-in-time (JIT) inventory management and consumers rebelled against excessive and expensive product packaging. This meant new technology to manufacture smaller, more flexible machinery and more packaging options for manufacturers.

To meet the demand, the industry introduced programmable logic controllers, robotics, self-diagnostic systems, microprocessor controls, automated testing, vision inspection systems, and built-in fault correction devices. Hydraulic and pneumatic actuators reduced clamping time and sped line changeover rates. Modern lines could shift from producing one part to an entirely different component in minutes instead of the previously common hours.

Illinois, Ohio, California, and New Jersey led the country in production of packaging equipment in 1987, according to the *1987 Census of Manufactures.* These states accounted for 43 percent of the nation's total employment in the industry. The average firm employed 49 workers in 1988, according to *Manufacturing USA,* but nearly half of the total 431 establishments had fewer than 20 employees.

Three of the largest firms by sales in the Packaging Machinery industry in 1993 were Signode Corp. of Glenview, Illinois; Figgie International Inc., Meyer World Packaging Manufacturing Co. of Charleston, South Carolina; and Videojet Systems International Inc. of Wood Dale, Illinois. Their listings in Dunn and Bradstreet indicate that: Signode was established in 1989 and employed 1,500 workers to produce $400 million in annual sales. Meyer World Packaging was a subsidiary of Figgie International Inc. It was established in 1904 and employed 110 workers to produce $150 million in annual sales. Videojet was a subsidiary of Dick A B Co. Inc. It was established in 1980 and employed 1,100 workers to produce $165 million in sales.

Exports formed an important part of the industry's market with 24 percent of its 1992 production shipped to about 140 foreign countries. This represented $647 million in sales, a six percent increase over 1991 figures, and the seventh consecutive yearly rise in exports. The largest purchaser of American equipment was Canada followed by Europe, the Asia-Pacific region, and Central and South America. *U.S. Industrial Outlook 1993* identified five exceptional growth markets: Japan, South Korea, Taiwan, Germany, and France.

Imports out-paced exports in 1989, but with only two percent increases averaging only 1.9 percent, *U.S. Industrial Outlook* expected exports and imports to even out by 1992. The largest importers were Germany and Italy, accounting for 50 percent of all sales by foreign companies, followed by Japan, Canada, Sweden, Switzerland, and the United Kingdom. The major products included wrapping machines for candy and tobacco.

The industry faced major challenges by environmental and energy concerns both in the United States and in foreign countries, especially Europe. The demands for recyclable and reusable materials and containers prompted more than 500 legislative proposals in fifty states to control solid waste. Other countries instituted their own measures. Concerns over conflicting regulations prompted interest in such measures as the ISO 9000 international machinery standard which would define the rules of manufacture and prevent such national or state standards from becoming non-tariff barriers to trade.

At the same time, industry was demanding lighter materials both in the actual packaging and the machinery, to reduce energy costs in transportation. Responding to JIT philosophies, packaging equipment companies were beginning to use air freight to speed delivery time.

INDUSTRY INFORMATION SOURCES

"Exporting Pays Off," *Business America,* October 7, 1991.

"Fluid Power in Action: Packaging Equipment," *Hydraulics & Pneumatics,* September 1991.

1987 Census of Manufactures—Industry Series, Washington, D.C.: U.S. Department of Commerce, 1988.

"Simple Is Better for Packaging Machine Manufacturer," *Modern Machine Shop,* May 1992.

U.S. Industrial Outlook 1993, Washington, D.C.: U.S. Department of Commerce, 1993.

—Al Cook

SIC 3566

SPEED CHANGERS, INDUSTRIAL HIGH-SPEED DRIVES, AND GEARS

Firms in this industry manufacture speed changers, industrial high-speed drives and gears. Products not covered by this classification include hydrostatic drives (**SIC 3594**), automatic transmissions (**SIC 3714**), and aircraft power-transmission devices (**SIC 3728**).

The industry provides basic mechanical power transmission components used in most industrial machinery. In 1987, industry shipments reached $1.5 billion, according to the *1987 Census of Manufactures.* The 1987 Census lists 250 companies operating 276 establishments, most with less than 50 employees. Only one had more than 1,000 employees. Firms in this industry averaged 73 employees per establishment according to *Manufacturing USA.* Most production centered in the industrial heartland with Wisconsin, Illinois, Indiana, and Pennsylvania leading in total employment.

Typical manufacturing includes metal grinding, cutting, degreasing, and surface finishing (including hardening). Such material working includes basic metal shaping, heat treatment, and metallurgic modifications using chemicals during processing.

In America, the technology and the expertise of local artisans to produce quality gears lagged behind Europe until near the end of the nineteenth century. According to Robert S. Woodbury, this changed when G.B. Grant developed the first successful machine to cut teeth in a rotating gear blank with a rotating hob. In 1896, F.W. Fellows patented a gear-shaping machine that could turn out a wide variety of gears quickly and cheaply. The rise of the "American System" of mass manufacturing on an assembly line made such tools quickly popular, displacing the traditional hand chiselled and filed gears of Europe. These two machine concepts became the dominant technology used in the manufacture of almost all gears in the United States and elsewhere.

By the 1990s, however, the advantages of mass production faded in the face of demands for more flexibility in the design and delivery of individual part orders. Gear manufacturers shifted to heavily automated production systems using Statistical Process Control (SPC), Computerized Numerical Control (CNC) and Just-In-Time (JIT) philosophies. These systems allowed greater precision and faster production shifts. Three-dimensional computer digitized master components maintain closer tolerances than can be achieved even with a skilled craftsman and allow the same master to be used as a benchmark at production facilities around the globe.

Three of the largest companies by sales volume in the speed changers, industrial high-speed drives, and gears industry in 1993 were Ross Hill Controls Corp. of Houston, Texas; Baldor Electric Co. of Fort Smith, Arkansas; and Allen Bradley Company Inc. Motion Control Division of Brown Deer, Wisconsin. Ross Hill was established in 1971 and employed 350 workers to produce $320 million in annual sales. Baldor Electric was established in 1920 and employed 2,975 to produce sales of $286 million. Motion Control was a subsidiary of Allen Bradley Company, itself a Rockwell-International company. It was established in 1972 and employed 800 to produce sales of $190 million.

Employment in the industry peaked in 1974 at 27,000, then dropped to 17,400 in 1986 before recovering to 19,300 by 1988. The 1988 hourly wage rate of $12.30 made this industry one of the higher paid, according to *Manufacturing USA.*

Since the industrial process of making large quantities of gears produces large amounts of waste by-products, the Environmental Protection Agency targeted the industry as a waste minimization opportunity in 1992. In particular, it noted that the use of trichloroethane as a degreasing agent might need to be replaced with more advanced technology like ultrasonics. The chemical is one of 17 listed by the EPA as an industrial toxic. International agencies have identified trichloroethane as an ozone depleting substance contributing to global warming.

Exports became an increasingly important market for the industry and for industrial machines in general as the 1980s progressed. Most of the market success of the industry came as a result of the weakening of the U.S. dollar relative to foreign currencies. Even though industry costs pushed domestic prices up, the declining value of the dollar between 1985 and 1987 reduced those prices in terms of foreign currency by 23.1 percent according to *Monthly Labor Review.* At the same time, the effective price of foreign products sold in the United States increased by 47.9 percent despite price cutting by manufacturers. As a result, America's $1.9 billion trade deficit of 1985 became a surplus in both 1989 and 1990.

INDUSTRY INFORMATION SOURCES

Craven, Jill, and Allan Gouchenour, "Dollar's Fall Boosts U.S. Machinery Exports, 1985-90," *Monthly Labor Review,* July 1991.

Kranzber, Melvin, and Carroll W. Pursell, Jr. *Technology in Western Civilization,* New York: Oxford University Press, 1967.

Manufacturing USA, Detroit: Gale Research, 1989.

1987 Census of Manufactures, Washington, D.C.: U.S. Department of Commerce, 1988.

Owen, Jean, "Gearing Up," *Manufacturing Engineering,* September 1993.

Ulbrecht, Alan, *Waste Reduction Activities and Options for a Manufacturer of Hardened Steel Gears,* Cincinnati: U.S. Environmental Protection Agency, Risk Reduction Engineering Laboratory, 1992.

Usher, Abbott Payson, *A History of Mechanical Inventions,* Boston: Beacon Press, 1959.

—Al Cook

SIC 3567

INDUSTRIAL PROCESS FURNACES AND OVENS

Firms in this industry are primarily engaged in manufacturing industrial process furnaces, ovens, induction and dielectric heating equipment and related devices. Products not included in the classification include bakery ovens (**SIC 3556**), cement, wood and chemical kilns (**SIC 3559**), cremating ovens (**SIC 3569**), and laboratory furnaces and ovens (**SIC 3821**).

Between 1983 and 1988, the industry showed steady growth in both production and employment with shipments rising from $54.2 million to $1,697.6 million and employment jumping from 16,100 to 18,200. The average wage, however, did not follow the same trend. Production worker hourly compensation peaked in 1987 at $10.25 then fell to $9.81 in 1988.

The concept of using heat to modify a material in some desirable manner originated very early in human history. Its application gave us names for eras like the

Bronze Age and the Iron Age, as scientific advancement combined furnace design and fuels to achieve higher and more controllable temperatures and chemical reactions within the combustion or heating chambers. The Industrial Revolution brought the biggest advancements and launched the Steel Age as industry abandoned charcoal as the most common fuel and adopted coal and coke. By the end of the 20th century natural gas and electricity were displacing much solid fuel use.

Near the end of the century, though, many of the industry's prime customers did not utilize the new technologies. For instance, the steel industry used the Bessemer process which involved blowing large volumes of heated air through molten iron in a furnace. The American steel industry began using the process in the 1860s. The open hearth method, developed in the same decade, produced larger volumes of steel over longer periods of time, allowing for better quality control. By 1907, the open hearth method was more popular than the Bessemer. In the 1950s, however, furnace designers found they could improve the performance of the Bessemer furnace by using oxygen instead of air and the Bessemer furnace once again took the lead. By 1990, U.S. steel producers were using the Bessemer oxygen furnace for 59.7 percent of production, the open hearth method for 3.5 percent and electric furnaces had grabbed 36.8 percent of the market, according to *Market Share Reporter.*

This was only after more efficient foreign competition forced U.S. steel manufacturers to close outdated smelters and blast furnaces across the country. The area around Pittsburgh once supported 80,000 steel manufacturing jobs, but by 1990 fewer than 4,000 remained as the industry shut down and shifted production to newer mini-mill facilities.

Robert J. Pasquarelli, president of New Jersey Steel Corp., summarized the trend in *Iron Age:* "I think what's going on in the flat-rolled [steel] business is tantamount to what happened with Bessemer in the last century. I think the whole industry's going to be reconfigured in the next ten years." In the 1990s, concern over air quality prompted passage of the Clean Air Act which mandated reductions of nitrous oxide emissions from such facilities as smelters and blast furnaces and designated such facilities as prime areas of concern. The legislation required special operating permits and monitoring provisions.

Three of the largest firms by sales volume in the Industrial Furnaces and Ovens industry in 1993 were Ogden Projects Inc. of Fairfield, New Jersey; Inductotherm Industries Inc. of Rancocas, New Jersey; and Emerson Electric Co., E.L. Wiegand Division of

Pittsburgh, Pennsylvania. According to Dun and Bradstreet, Ogden Projects was established in 1984 and employs 403 workers to produce $364 million in annual sales. It was a subsidiary of Ogden Corp. Inductotherm was established in 1953 and employs 4,200 to produce sales of $431 million. Its subsidiaries include Inductoheat, Inductotherm Corp. and Induction Process Equipment Corp. E.L. Wiegland was a subsidiary of Emerson Electric Co. It was established in 1917 and employed 2,100 workers to produce $200 million in annual sales.

INDUSTRY INFORMATION SOURCES

"Industrial Archeology: Monument to a Blast-Furnace," *Economist,* February 3, 1990.

Kranzberg, Melvin, and Carroll W. Pursel, Jr., eds., *Technology in Western Civilization,* Volume 1, New York: Oxford University Press, 1967.

Manufacturing USA, 2nd Edition, Detroit: Gale Research, 1989.

McManus, George, "High-Voltage Spending by the Electric Steelmakers," *Iron Age,* September 1993.

"Modelling and Optimization of the NO Formation in an Industrial Glass Furnace," *Journal of Engineering for Industry,* November 1992.

1987 Census of Manufactures—Industry Series, Washington, D.C.: U.S. Department of Commerce, 1988.

—Al Cook

SIC 3568

MECHANICAL POWER TRANSMISSION EQUIPMENT, NOT ELSEWHERE CLASSIFIED

This industry is comprised of companies that manufacture mechanical power transmission equipment and parts for industrial machinery. Products include ball joints, pulleys, bearings, drive chains, sprockets, shafts, couplings, and other parts. Companies that make transmission devices for vehicles and aircraft are classified in **SIC 3714: Motor Vehicle Parts and Accessories** and **SIC 3728: Aircraft Parts and Auxiliary Equipment, Not Elsewhere Classified,** respectively.

Bearings and bushings accounted for 18 percent of industry sales in the early 1990s. Clutches and brakes made up 15 percent of revenues, and chains for sprocket drives represented about ten percent of the transmission equipment market. Pulleys, sprockets, and chains accounted for ten percent of sales, and couplings and joints each made up seven percent.

Equipment for outboard and inboard marine engines delivered five percent of industry revenues.

The market for miscellaneous transmission equipment is fragmented. Motor vehicle manufacturers were the largest buying sector, accounting for ten percent of industry revenues in the early 1990s. The construction and farm machinery industries consumed six percent and four percent, respectively, of output. Motorcycle and bicycle makers purchased about four percent of production. Other significant markets for transmission equipment included shipbuilders, steelmakers, the missile industry, and logging companies. About eight percent of production is exported.

Power transmission refers to the transfer of power through mechanical devices. The invention of the steam engine by James Watt in 1765 and the development of the internal combustion engine during the mid-1800s greatly expanded applications for power transmission equipment and played an important role in the industrial revolution. The industry realized greatest growth during the U.S. economic expansion of the post-World War II era. Indeed by the early 1980s, makers of miscellaneous transmission equipment were shipping about $2 billion worth of goods annually.

Industry sales and profit growth slowed during the 1980s as capital spending by U.S. manufacturing sectors stagnated. Revenues climbed an average of about six percent annually during the decade, barely keeping pace with inflation. Only increased capital investments by nondurable goods producers and nonmanufacturing industries were able to buoy earnings. By 1990, annual sales of miscellaneous transmission equipment had climbed to about $2.6 billion.

In an effort to sustain profitability, miscellaneous transmission manufacturers increased productivity during the 1980s through automation and restructuring. As real output rose, the industry work force shrank more than 13 percent during the decade, from over 27,000 to about 24,000. Despite efficiency gains, a recession in the late 1980s and early 1990s reduced profits for many competitors. Sales dropped about 2.5 percent in 1992. Nevertheless, reviving markets offered hope going into the mid-1990s.

The largest competitor in the early 1990s by far was Ifint USA, of New York, which had 1991 sales of $915 million. U.S. Tsubaki Inc., of Illinois, placed second with about $100 million in sales. Third-place Funk Manufacturing Co., of Kansas, boasted revenues of $70 million. About 300 companies competed in the industry in the early 1990s, but only the top ten reached sales of over $30 million.

Future employment prospects are dim. Productivity gains and the movement of some production facilities across U.S. borders has resulted in continued work force reductions. Most labor opportunities have declined and will continue declining by about 20 percent to 30 percent by the year 2005, according to the Bureau of Labor Statistics. Even jobs for managers will decline significantly. Sales and marketing positions, however, will likely increase slightly.

INDUSTRY INFORMATION SOURCES

Avery, Susan, ''Power Transmission Recovers; Manufacturers Hike Prices,'' *Purchasing*, June 17, 1993.

Darnay, Arsen J., ed., *Manufacturing USA; Industry Analyses, Statistics, and Leading Companies*, Detroit: Gale Research Inc., 1993.

U.S. Industrial Outlook 1994, Washington, D.C.: U.S. Department of Commerce, January 1994.

—Dave Mote

SIC 3569

GENERAL INDUSTRIAL MACHINERY AND EQUIPMENT, NOT ELSEWHERE CLASSIFIED

This category covers establishments primarily engaged in manufacturing machinery, equipment, and components for general industrial use, and for which no special classification is provided. Machine shops primarily engaged in producing machine and equipment parts, usually on a job or order basis, are classified in **SIC 3599: Industrial and Commercial Machinery and Equipment, Not Elsewhere Classified.**

Companies in the not elsewhere classified general industrial machinery and equipment industry produce miscellaneous manufacturing equipment. The plethora of industry offerings includes items such as altitude testing chambers, hydraulic bridge machinery, industrial centrifuges, cremating ovens, industrial fluid filters, swimming pool heaters, fire hoses, hydraulic jacks, and fire sprinkler systems.

The industry is heavily dependent upon sales to other manufacturing businesses and to construction industries. In addition, about 30 percent of revenues are derived from exports. Intense capital investments during the U.S. industrial boom of the mid-1900s resulted in steady demand growth for all types of industrial machinery. By the early 1980s, in fact, domestic producers of miscellaneous industrial machines were shipping about $4.5 billion worth of products each year and employing a work force of 65,000.

Rampant growth in U.S. capital spending slowed in the 1980s, as foreign-manufactured goods reduced U.S. producers' share of capital goods markets. Machinery purchases by transportation industries were particularly slow. As a result, sales of miscellaneous machinery stagnated. Industry revenues lagged as a result of inflation and climbed at an average rate of about two percent per year during the 1980s to about $5.36 billion. Recessed commercial and residential construction markets added to industry woes in the late 1980s and early 1990s. Ailing manufacturers scrambled to sustain profitability by raising productivity, cutting their work force, and merging with or acquiring competitors.

Going into the mid-1990s, producers of miscellaneous machinery hoped to benefit from increased capital spending by the Clinton administration, an uptick in capital equipment replacements, and a devalued dollar which was boosting exports. In addition, sales of machinery to some sectors showed signs of increasing. Construction equipment sales, for example, rose about

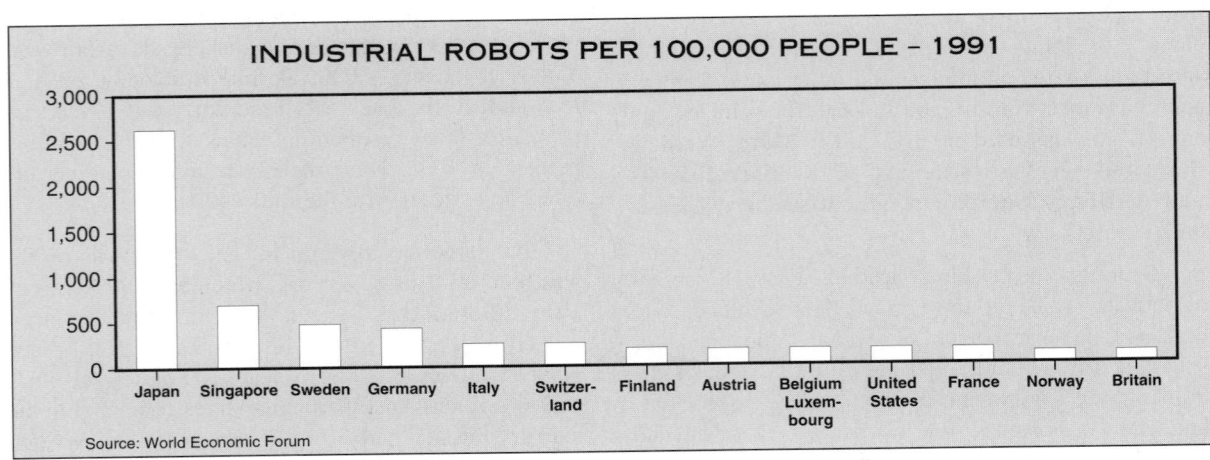

INDUSTRIAL ROBOTS PER 100,000 PEOPLE – 1991

Source: World Economic Forum

three percent. However, spending on new manufacturing facilities and infrastructure was expected to remain flat at least through the mid-1990s.

The industry is dominated by numerous specialty manufacturers. Despite industry consolidation, over 1,000 companies competed going into the 1990s. Of the top 75 competitors, over half had sales of less than $40 million and employed fewer than 300 workers. The top producer was Tyco Laboratories of New Hampshire, which had 1991 sales of $2.1 billion from its diversified operations. Grinnell Corp., which is also based in New Hampshire, had revenues of $1.6 billion. Other major manufacturers of miscellaneous industrial machinery included Figgie International, Inc., of Ohio, and Pall Corp., of New York.

As companies continue to automate production facilities and move manufacturing operations across U.S. borders, general industrial machinery industry employment will continue to plummet. The miscellaneous equipment work force had already plunged to about 47,000 by 1990, despite an increase in production. Likewise, employment for most occupations will drop by ten to 30 percent between 1990 and 2005, according to the Bureau of Labor Statistics. Jobs for assemblers and fabricators, which make up over ten percent of the work force, will likely decline 32 percent by 2005, as will positions for machinists. Management opportunities will also deteriorate significantly. Sales and marketing positions, on the other hand, will increase slightly.

INDUSTRY INFORMATION SOURCES

Darnay, Arsen J., ed., *Manufacturing USA; Industry Analyses, Statistics, and Leading Companies*, Detroit: Gale Research Inc., 1993.

Standard & Poor's Industry Surveys, New York: Standard & Poor's Corporation, December 24, 1992.

U.S. Industrial Outlook 1993, Washington, D.C.: U.S. Department of Commerce, January 1993.

—Dave Mote

SIC 3571

ELECTRONIC COMPUTERS

The electronic computer industry encompasses companies primarily engaged in manufacturing supercomputers, mainframes, workstations, mid-range systems, and various personal computers. Electronic computers are machines which: 1) store the processing program or programs and the data immediately neces-

sary for execution of the program; 2) can be freely programmed in accordance with the requirements of the user; 3) perform arithmetical computations specified by the user; and 4) execute, without human intervention, a processing program which requires them to modify their execution by logical decision during the processing run. Included in this industry are digital computers, analog computers, and hybrid digital/analog computers. Establishments primarily engaged in manufacturing machinery or equipment which incorporate computers or a central processing unit for the purpose of performing functions such as measuring, displaying, or controlling process variables are classified based on the manufactured end product.

INDUSTRY SNAPSHOT

In 1992, the total worldwide value of U.S. manufacturers' equipment and service sales for all computer-related industries, much of which was part of the electronic computer industry, amounted to over $175 billion. Sales of personal computers alone topped $33 billion in 1992. For comparison, the U.S. motor vehicle and parts industries combined represented sales of about $200 billion in 1992.

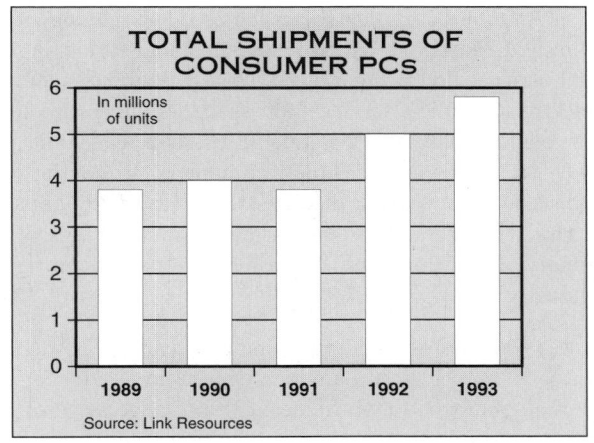

TOTAL SHIPMENTS OF CONSUMER PCs

In millions of units

Source: Link Resources

Industry statistics in the early 1990s represented the culmination of rampant growth in the use of computers which occurred during the 1970s and 1980s. In the early 1990s, however, the overall industry was battered by a downturn in sales and a shift in the general dynamics of computer and information technology markets. Indeed, the total dollar value of shipments actually decreased between 1989 and 1990, and industry employment continued to fall steadily as it had since 1988. The general outlook for most segments of the industry, however, was positive going into the mid-1990s, in part because of anticipated benefits stemming from passage of the North American Free Trade Agreement (NAFTA). In the first quarter of 1994, Compaq Computer Corp. took the lead in world market share for personal computer shipments, surpassing traditional leaders International Business Machines Corp. (IBM) and Apple Computer Inc. for the first time. "The share numbers lend credence to Compaq's own assertions that it will dethrone IBM and Apple in full-year sales. Compaq had said that would happen by 1996. However, analysts said both IBM and Apple should come on stronger later in the year after a typically slow start," observed the *Wall Street Journal.*

ORGANIZATION AND STRUCTURE

Electronic computers are defined as machines which: (1) store the processing program or programs and the data immediately necessary for execution of the program; (2) can be freely programmed in accordance with the requirements of the user; (3) perform arithmetical computations specified by the user; and (4) execute, without human intervention, a processing program which requires them to modify their execution by logical decision during the processing run.

All computers can be categorized as analog or digital. In addition, "hybrid" computers combine digital and analog technology. Analog computers are electromechanical devices whose operation is based on continuously variable quantities such as lengths, weights, or voltages. Digital computers, in contrast, operate by processing discrete quantities of digits or characters. Digital computers that process strings of binary digits dominate the computer manufacturing industry.

Products. The computer industry can be divided into five types of devices, including: (1) supercomputers; (2) mainframes; (3) midrange systems; (4) workstations; and (5) personal computers, which include laptops, notebooks, and hand-held devices.

Supercomputers are high-speed number crunchers that allow scientists, engineers, and businesses to process and manipulate massive amounts of data very quickly. Their performance is typically measured in terms of billions of floating point operations per second, or gigaflops (GFLOPS), as opposed to millions of instructions per second (MIPS) assigned to most other types of computers. These technological taskmasters are used to complete complex feats, such as forecasting weather, designing ships and automobiles, conducting nuclear research, and carrying out advanced simulations.

An important distinction exists between traditional high-powered "vector," and low-powered "parallel" supercomputers. The newer parallel devices join as many as tens of thousands of cheap microprocessors to accomplish what vector systems achieve with a handful of more expensive processors. Though usually less expensive, systems that use Massively Parallel Processing (MPP) technology can perform many tasks faster than traditional vector systems.

Mainframe computers generally offer less raw computational power than supercomputers, and are most often used to handle large volumes of general purpose business or institutional applications. Users access the mainframe through satellite terminals that are connected to the system. Some mainframes also offer add-on features that make them competitive with low-end supercomputers. Systems typically cost more than $1 million, and may cost as much as $30 million. In 1992, mainframe processing speeds ranged from approximately 50 MIPS to over 350 MIPS.

Midrange computers serve anywhere from a few to several hundred users, either locally or at remote locations. Small to medium-sized businesses, company departments, and manufacturing facilities commonly use midrange systems for communications processing, automation, reporting, and networking. Midrange systems often employ vendor-developed proprietary applications which are tailored to the organization's needs. Newer "open" systems, though, allow the use of standardized operating systems and applications. Midrange computers can range in price from $10,000 to about $1 million.

Workstations are high-powered single-user computer systems. Unlike the systems mentioned above that serve users at satellite terminals, workstations are self-contained units. Because of technological advances in the 1980s, many workstations are capable of performing intensive research, engineering, and graphics tasks that allow them to compete with low-end supercomputers and mainframes. High-performance microprocessors allow many workstations to employ high-resolution or 3-D graphic interfaces, sophisticated multi-task software, and advanced communication capabilities. Workstation prices can range from $3,000 to over $100,000.

Personal computers (PCs), like workstations, are predominantly single-user, self-contained units. They offer the least raw computing power of any segment of the industry, but provide the greatest amount of flexibility, diversity, and portability. Although PCs are well-suited for home and personal use, about two-thirds of all units sold in the early 1990s were used for business and professional purposes. Prices ranged from $250 for low-powered clones to more than $25,000 for fully configured systems with advanced graphic and communications capabilities. This segment includes laptop and notebook computers, the latter of which were effectively replacing the slightly larger laptop designs in 1993.

Market Structure. In 1992, 13.9 million PCs were sold for $33 billion by U.S. manufacturers. Of this amount, $24 billion was garnered from desktop units, $6 billion from laptop sales, $3 billion from notebook computers, and about $300 million was made from hand-held devices. Although PC sales were greater than sales in any other industry segment, low producer concentration and a commodity-like environment in 1993 resulted in the lowest profit margins in the computer industry. For instance, while margins on PCs were typically between 5 percent and 30 percent, mainframe producers often earned a mark-up of 50 percent to 70 percent.

Leading edge companies that delivered the latest technology to the market supplied most of the expensive high-end PC products. Less-expensive, though high-quality, PCs were supplied by manufacturers that lagged behind the technological wave and stressed value. Approximately 50 percent of all units were sold through dealers, 18 percent were distributed through resellers, 16 percent were sold by direct sales or mail order, and the remaining 16 percent of sales were made by volume merchants. The top five companies, all of which were American, served about 45 percent of the U.S. PC market.

U.S. electronic computer manufacturers shipped approximately 700,000 workstations in 1992, which had a combined worth of $11 billion. The top five manufacturers in the world, all of which were American, garnered over 80 percent of the global market and about 90 percent of the domestic market. Sun Microsystems, the largest workstation producer, served 40 percent of the world market alone in 1991. Shipping $26 billion worth of midrange systems in 1992, U.S. firms also controlled about 60 percent of the global market. About 25 percent of all midrange computers sold in 1992 were open systems.

U.S. mainframe manufacturers generated about $12.5 billion in U.S. sales in 1992, and garnered about 65 percent of the $27 billion world market. U.S. supercomputer manufacturers cornered about 90 percent of the $1.8 billion world market in 1992. MPP systems accounted for approximately $300 million of supercomputer sales. Revenues for each industry segment include subordinate sales of peripherals and services that are not necessarily included in this industry classification.

BACKGROUND AND DEVELOPMENT

The abacus, the first significant computational tool in history, was likely invented in the Middle East. Thousands of years later, in seventeenth-century Europe, the first mechanical calculating devices were built. The English mathematician Charles Babbage carried that concept a step further in the nineteenth century with the design of the Analytical Engine, the first digital computer. The Engine design showed how programs could be stored on punched cards similar to those used by French looms. Although the Analytical Engine was never built, it influenced the first digital mechanical computers and helped pave the way of the computer revolution that changed the world.

The few computers in existence in the 1940s were primarily used to grind out tables of complex mathematical functions. Researchers that understood the potential of more advanced devices, however, were successful in securing sizable U.S. government and military grants to fund further development. The first general-purpose electronic computer, ENIAC, was completed in 1946. ENIAC, which stands for electronic numerical integrator and calculator, required partial rewiring in order to program it for different tasks. The first operational stored-program electronic digital computer, similar in function to computers of today, was completed in 1949 at the University of Cambridge. Although various analog devices were also developed and tested in the 1930s and 1940s, analog computers played a relatively minor role in the development of the industry.

The electromechanical computers of the mid-1940s had already been replaced by the early 1950s with more powerful and flexible electronic versions. The UNIVAC system, developed for the U.S. Bureau of the Census, and a similar system used by the General Electric Company were two of the first commercially viable electronic computers put into use. By the end of the 1950s, business, government, and scientific communities began to view the computer as a dependable and potentially effective tool for an enormous variety of tasks.

Timesharing systems, pioneered at the Massachusetts Institute of Technology, allowed public and private entities to gain extensive access to large, expensive mainframe computer systems in the 1960s. Timesharing allowed several users at remote locations to simultaneously use a single machine. Users were charged for the amount of time that they were actually connected to the computer by cables or telephone lines. Although timeshare technology was first used primarily for scientific and technical endeavors, business and industry participants soon learned that they, too, could benefit from access to centralized processors.

By the end of the 1960s the computer industry was poised for rapid growth. Computers in the 1960s were already up to 100 times faster than their counterparts of the 1950s—and computer memory and speed continued to rise at an increasing rate. Furthermore, the first minicomputer was installed in 1965, breaking ground for an entirely new segment of the industry. The number of digital computers had increased from less than 15 in 1950 to over 40,000 by the late 1960s. Going into the 1970s, though, all sectors of society were beginning to seek the computational power offered by supercomputers and mainframes to handle labor-intensive tasks. In addition, industry leaders were continually striving to expand their market by increasing computer access to end-users, rather than only trained computer professionals.

Development of the microprocessor in 1971 allowed the entire central processor of a computer to be placed on a single silicone chip. It was this development that led to subsequent rapid expansion and transformation of the industry. In addition to the proliferation of supercomputers, mainframes, and midrange systems that took advantage of new chip technology, workstations and personal computer devices began to emerge. By the early 1980s, over 500,000 general-purpose computers had been installed in North America. Furthermore, the market was growing at an annual rate of about 20 percent.

The 1980s. In the early 1980s, the computer industry consisted of several niches, each dominated by one or two manufacturers that had been the first to successfully exploit an opening in the market. International Business Machines (IBM), Sperry, Wang, Unisys, and Digital Equipment Corporation (DEC) were among the many companies that generated immense revenues during the decade. For the most part, these companies succeeded by developing proprietary hardware and operating systems that effectively prohibited customers from switching to a competitor's product.

Manufacturers often enjoyed profit margins of 70 percent to 90 percent on sales of various mainframe and minicomputer installations. Demand ballooned throughout the decade as business, industry, and the public sector invested billions of dollars to computerize and automate information management, manufacturing, computationally-intensive research, and other activities. As many mainframe companies settled into their respective niches, however, the rapid advancement of microprocessor technology caused a market shift that took many industry leaders by surprise.

While the pattern of events is easy to recognize in hindsight, many industry participants failed to foresee the dominance of personal computers, workstations, and some midrange systems. Within a period of a few years, in fact, technological innovations turned the slow and limited microcomputer of the early 1980s into a relatively low-cost, powerful, and speedy contender. Furthermore, by networking these smaller devices, users were able to develop cost-effective systems that could handle tasks that were previously performed only by mainframes and powerful minicomputers.

Many mainframe and minicomputer manufacturers initially avoided the personal computer market for a number of reasons. Besides being viewed as technologically inferior, personal computers offered lower profit margins than larger systems. For this reason, the new segment required the use of sales and distribution channels unfamiliar to many manufacturers. Furthermore, most personal computers were open-based systems, rather than proprietary. Because open-based systems allow users to employ commercially available software and standard operating systems, opportunities for follow-up sales and service profits were comparatively limited.

Although the demand for mainframe and supercomputer sales advanced throughout most of the decade, manufacturers that focused solely on those products and failed to respond to the inevitable dominance of workstations and PCs found themselves in serious financial trouble in the mid-1980s. The number of PCs purchased by Americans rose from fewer than 500,000 PCs in 1980 to approximately 7 million in 1984. By 1989, annual PC sales approached 10 million. Sales of workstations, which were not introduced to the market until 1983, were also growing at a phenomenal rate (over 110 percent annually between 1986 and 1988).

Large-scale systems held 12.6 percent of all computer-related industry revenues in 1987. By 1991, however, this share had fallen to just 9.5 percent. During the same period, PCs increased their share of the entire computer-related market from 10.6 percent to 15.2 percent. Moreover, workstation manufacturers' market share, which was nonexistent in 1983, leapt to 4.7 percent in 1991. Going into the early 1990s, PCs and workstation companies seemed prepared to continue their advancement, while many large-scale manufacturers retrenched, or shifted their focus.

CURRENT CONDITIONS

Strong growth and solid profits enjoyed by most electronic computer manufacturers during the 1980s faded in the early 1990s, as the industry realized a serious reduction in the overall growth of domestic demand. Several factors contributed to the downturn. In addition to the global recession of the late 1980s and early 1990s, manufacturers were beginning to confront the fact that the U.S. computer market was becoming saturated. In addition, the shift from high-profit, large-scale proprietary systems to low-margin, open architecture, desktop computers was reducing profit opportunities.

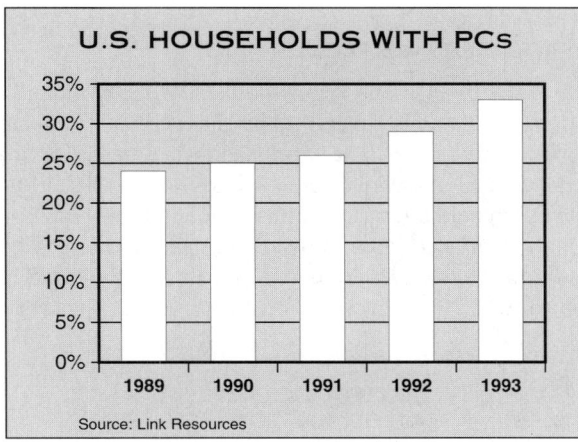

U.S. HOUSEHOLDS WITH PCs

Source: Link Resources

Indeed, cheap personal systems that offered computing power similar to that offered by the mainframes of the early 1980s were now viewed as a commodity by many consumers. Rather than purchasing a personal computer system from a retail outlet at a price of $4,000 or $5,000, many customers in the early 1990s began purchasing more advanced systems through the mail or at discount warehouses for approximately $1,000 to $2,000. Furthermore, many newer systems came preloaded with software that would have cost thousands of dollars only a few years earlier.

Competition intensified as continual technological breakthroughs allowed the industry to produce cheaper and smaller devices. In addition, improvements in networking technology were allowing large customers to build powerful and flexible systems at historically low costs. The value of all computer and peripheral devices shipped by domestic manufacturers in the United States fell from a peak of $54.9 billion in 1989 to about $51.6 billion in 1991. Likewise, employment by those companies dropped from 290,000 in 1988 to an estimated 224,000 by 1992. Importantly, however, the annual volume of units sold by the industry continued to climb throughout the early 1990s.

In response to the new environment of the 1990s almost all companies, and especially older competi-

tors, were slashing prices in an effort to boost sales volume; emphasizing smaller, cheaper systems; increasing sales of services and software; forming alliances; and downsizing their work force. Companies were forming alliances to achieve increased economies of scale and broaden distribution channels. Some of the larger alliances in the early 1990s included Toshiba and IBM, Apple and Toshiba, and DEC and Olivetti. Mergers and acquisitions were expected to multiply as companies battled growing product development expenses in the face of suppressed profit margins.

Employee reduction was being accomplished primarily through industry automation. Computer firms laid off a total of 191,729 workers worldwide between 1988 and 1992. The number of U.S. production workers, alone, declined 4.7 percent in 1992, to 84,000. Although cutbacks were the combined result of plant closings, automation, and the contracting out of some manufacturing operations to foreign producers, they reflected a greater investment in automation per worker than any other U.S. industry. In 1989, for instance, computer and office equipment industries invested a combined total of $1.7 billion in automation, or 5.3 percent of the entire U.S. total.

Industry Segment Status. Supercomputer company sales effectively stagnated in 1989, resulting in the departure of a number of manufacturers from the industry. Although domestic sales revenue increased 5 percent in 1992, to $1.8 billion, the segment lost market share, and profits were hampered by increased volume at reduced prices. On the bright side, sales of less expensive parallel systems rose 34 percent to about $300 million in 1992. This trend was expected to continue in 1993, though total industry sales were projected to increase by about 8 percent. A decline in domestic defense research computer spending should keep annual revenue growth at approximately 12 percent in the mid-1990s, despite a strong rise in demand in the civilian sector. Future growth is dependent on an increase in the availability of standardized software packages for MPP systems.

Mainframe computers in use around the world actually declined from about 26,588 in 1990 to 25,923 in 1992, resulting in the deterioration of several industry leaders. Consolidation of corporate mainframe sites contributed to the decrease in demand. Although the value of U.S. shipments surged 2 percent in 1992 to $12.6 billion, heavy discounting curbed profits for many competitors. Furthermore, increased competition from Japanese companies reduced the U.S. industry's share of the world market to 65 percent in 1992. Although midrange systems and workstations are expected to continue to devour mainframe sales in the mid-1990s, more powerful mainframe products will likely help this segment sustain moderate growth. Systems with as much as 40 percent greater performance, combined with open architecture that allows users to access standardized operating systems, should tentatively keep the mainframe market alive. Integration of parallel processing technology into mainframe products may also boost revenues in this segment.

Midrange computer manufacturers maintained annual revenues of approximately $26 billion in the early 1990s. Unlike supercomputers and mainframes, however, unit sales also remained relatively stable. Although workstations and PC networks will increasingly compete for midrange customers, market share stolen from the mainframe industry should keep revenues steady. Midrange manufacturers will continue to supplement equipment sales by increasing software and service offerings. The trend toward open-systems, which should command 30 percent of the midrange market by 1996, will persist as well.

Workstation manufacturer sales jumped 25 percent in 1992 to $11 billion. This segment, which shipped 700,000 units in 1992, was the fastest growing sector of the entire electronic computing industry. U.S. suppliers also dominated 88 percent of the foreign market, which grew three-fold between 1987 and 1991 to $8.7 billion. Strong demand from governments, scientists, engineers, and businesses was expected to increase as users continue to shift from mainframes and midrange systems to high-performance workstations. Revenues in the industry were expected to rise nearly 30 percent in 1993, to $14 billion, and were projected to exceed $35 billion before 2000. Commercial and educational demand will eventually exceed the science and engineering market. Lower priced workstations will also begin to compete with top-of-the-line PC products in the 1990s.

Desktop PC revenues rose 9 percent in 1992, to $24 billion from 11.1 million units shipped. These figures, though, reflected a maturing and saturated market. Most desktop manufacturers were ailing from severe price erosion caused by drastic discounting in the commodity-like environment. Profits were battered by intense price wars that began in 1991, and these declines were exacerbated by the growing popularity of notebook computers. Despite technological advances in performance, buyers were taking a wait-and-see attitude about replacing their old systems with newer technology. Even the laptop market increased only 1 percent in 1992, to about $6 billion.

Smaller notebook computers, whose market grew 55 percent in 1992 to $3 billion, were destroying the sales of their larger cousins, but were also keeping the PC industry afloat. Notebook sales were expected to continue booming in 1993 as smaller, denser, and more efficient units made them even more attractive. "Subnotebooks" were also appearing on the market in greater quantities in 1993, and the total notebook unit volume was expected be nearly double that of 1992. As in other segments of the electronic computer industry, however, price erosion is expected to keep profit gains below market growth in the mid-1990s. Moreover, portable computers are projected to represent over 50 percent of the PCs on the market by 1997.

INDUSTRY LEADERS

The diverse and segmented electronic computing industry contains several major players that dominate particular niches. The workstation segment, for instance, is dominated by Sun Microsystems of California. Sun held over 40 percent of the world workstation market in 1991 and enjoyed sales in excess of $2.5 billion. Hewlett-Packard of California followed Sun with a 17.2 percent share of the workstation market.

GLOBAL COMPUTER HARDWARE REVENUES

Source: McKinsey & Co.

The midrange segment was dominated by IBM, of New York, and DEC, of Vermont, which held 18 percent and 11 percent of the world market in 1991, respectively. IBM was also the largest mainframe producer, with 47 percent of the world market share in 1991. This figure was down from 52 percent in 1990, however. Cray Research, of Minnesota, owned over 90 percent of the supercomputer market in 1991. Cray benefitted from the exit of Control Data Corp. from that industry in 1989. Control Data held about 25 percent of the market, but was unwilling to continue its massive research and development expenditures.

Although IBM held the largest share of the PC market in 1991, its market share in that fiercely competitive environment is not what it once was. From 27 percent in 1985, IBM's share of that market plummeted to less than 14 percent by 1992. Apple Computer, of California, also held about 14 percent of the PC market in 1992. Up-and-coming competitors in the PC market in the early 1990s included Packard Bell, Gateway 2000, AST, and Everex.

Perhaps the greatest threat to IBM and Apple in the PC arena, however, is Compaq Computer Corp. Compaq, according to industry analyst Dataquest Inc., shipped about 980,000 PCs worldwide in the first quarter of 1994. IBM, meanwhile, shipped 955,000 and Apple sent out 865,000. These figures mark the first time that a company other than IBM and Apple has reached such a position in the PC market. The company also took the lead in the first quarter of 1994 in U.S. sales, garnering 12.4 percent of the market (Apple secured 10.4 percent, IBM, 10.1 percent). ''Compaq's surge over IBM and Apple is all the more dramatic,'' noted the *Wall Street Journal,* ''given the fact that it has built a business around making IBM-compatible PCs and following the technical advances of those rivals.'' Compaq's ability to hold on to the number one spot for any significant length of time, however, will surely be tested by IBM, Apple, and other rivals.

Many companies which led the computer industry in the 1980s suffered massive financial losses in the early 1990s. Wang Laboratories, for instance, declared bankruptcy after posting an $11 million loss on $1.2 billion in sales. IBM, which suffered the most severe losses, managed to accrue more losses in 1992 than most industry leaders generated in sales revenue.

Big Blue. IBM, or Big Blue as it is often called, remains the unmitigated mammoth of the global electronic computing industry. Its revenues were more than ten times greater than any other participant in the industry in 1992. The company was founded in 1910 by Charles Ranlett Flint under the company name of Calculating-Tabulating-Recording (CTR), and got its start by utilizing punch-card technology invented by Herman Hollerith to develop tabulating machines.

IBM grew quickly by stressing large-scale, custom-built systems, and by leasing, rather than selling, its products to most of its customers. From sales of $4.2 million in 1910, IBM's annual revenues grew to $141.7 million by the mid-1940s. Government orders during World War II were largely responsible for the company's rapid growth during the 1940s. It was during this period, in fact, that IBM developed the Mark I—the first computer capable of retaining a set of rules that could be applied to information that was input at a later time.

IBM's dominance of the computer market persisted throughout the post-war years. Although other competitors innovated new technologies and were able to capture market niches, IBM successfully countered their advances with its own products. By the mid-1960s, IBM owned 65 percent of the U.S. computer market. IBM's mainframe models 360 and 370 generated massive profits for the company during the 1970s. As sales climbed, profits roared to $3 billion by 1980. Although IBM continued to grow through the mid-1980s, the company began to lose focus. Its hesitation to take the PC market seriously in the late 1970s and early 1980s was recognized as a major miscalculation by the mid-1980s. Earnings faltered in the late 1980s and IBM scrambled to revive its unwieldy and massive enterprise. Between 1985 and 1992, IBM dismissed 100,000 employees and restructured its operations several times.

Although IBM's 370 still held 70 percent of the U.S. mainframe market in the early 1990s, the shrinking significance of mainframe systems was leaving the company vulnerable to viciously competitive small systems producers. IBM had sales of about $70 billion in 1992, approximately 60 percent of which was from exports. Losses in that year, however, grew to $4.75 billion. For comparison, Apple Computers, one of IBM's closest competitors, had revenues of about $5.5 billion in 1991.

WORK FORCE

The electronic computer industry employs large numbers of electrical engineers, programmers, assemblers, and technicians. In fact, these occupations represent about 30 percent of the industry total. Companies also hire large numbers of people for miscellaneous management, sales, and clerical positions. In 1993, total employment in the entire computer industry, of which electronic computer manufacturers represented about 50 percent, totaled about 220,000. Employment was significantly down from the industry peak in the mid-1980s, when electronic computer manufacturers employed over 150,000 workers.

Despite an expected increase in the total number of units shipped and a general rise in the value of U.S. and global computer markets, the job outlook for the industry is poor. Companies are expected to continue to introduce labor-saving automation and to outsource manufacturing activities to low-cost foreign producers. Furthermore, corporate alliances should moderate the demand for research and development professionals.

While the demand for programmers in the industry is expected to rise slightly—about 8 percent between 1992 and 2005—the demand for other occupations will likely fall, according to the Bureau of Labor Statistics. The demand for engineers, for instance, will slip about 3.5 percent by 2005. Likewise, technician and engineering management jobs will fall by 2 percent to 5 percent. Manufacturing jobs, especially, will disappear. The demand for electrical and electronic assemblers, for example, will likely plummet 55 percent by 2005. Analysts project that assemblers and fabricator positions will decline by about 37 percent, while the demand for production planning professionals will fall over 20 percent.

Management executive positions are expected to decrease as well—by an estimated 22 percent. Even the number of lower level management jobs is expected to fall by about 20 percent by 2005. The one bright spot in the job picture is an expected 47 percent increase in the demand for systems analysts and computer scientists. This group currently accounts for only about 2.4 percent of employment in the computer and office equipment industries.

AMERICA AND THE WORLD

U.S. electronic computer companies continued to dominate the world equipment industry in the early 1990s, though they had been gradually losing market share since the mid-1980s. In 1991, for instance, U.S. firms captured about 60 percent of the entire $290 billion world computer equipment and services market—down from about 75 percent in 1984. Despite loss of market share, revenue from exports continued to grow steadily as the world market ballooned from just $132 billion in 1984. Imports were becoming an important source of profit for some companies as growth in the U.S. market, which accounted for 35 percent of global demand, slowed. Passage of the North American Free Trade Agreement, which took effect January 1, 1994, was expected to open a lucrative market in Mexico for American-made computers and software. NAFTA eliminates 70 percent of Mexican tariffs on U.S. computer equipment and a ten percent tariff on U.S. software.

Despite export growth in some industry segments, the U.S. industry posted a $5 billion trade deficit in 1992—its second deficit in history. While exports increased 2 percent in 1992, imports jumped 15 percent. Imports accounted for approximately 50 percent of all U.S. computer sales in 1992 as computer and peripheral imports jumped 18 percent over 1991 levels. U.S. firms maintained decisive leadership in midrange, PC, and workstation equipment markets. For instance, the United States served 88 percent of the global workstation market in 1992. Small scale systems were expec-

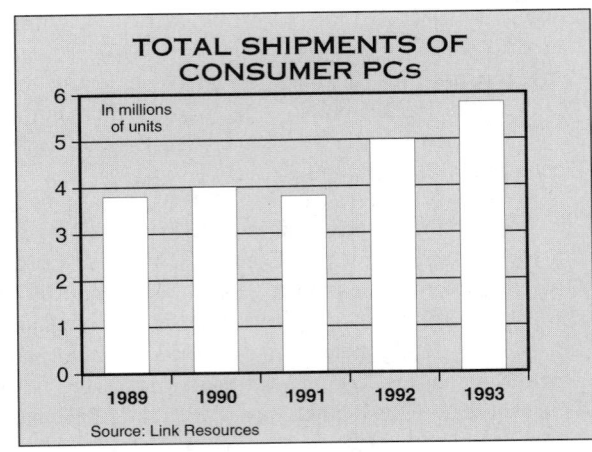

ted to provide the greatest overseas growth opportunities for U.S. manufacturers.

Although the United States still maintained a technological advantage in large-scale systems and workstations, some Japanese competitors had made significant strides in those segments. Japanese firms owned 25 percent of the mainframe market in 1992, for instance, though much of that share was attributable to sales in domestic, protected markets. Although Japanese companies were trying to infiltrate the supercomputer market, over 90 percent of which was controlled by U.S. companies, their systems offered limited performance and lagged in MPP technology. Acquisition of U.S. and European firms, in addition to their own research and development, will likely make Japanese manufacturers contenders for supercomputer market share in the future.

Indeed, the greatest source of competition in all computer segments for U.S. firms came from Japan. Firms in that country enjoyed access to domestic markets (over 20 percent of the world market) that were significantly protected from U.S. competition. In other words, U.S. manufacturers were not allowed to compete effectively in some sectors of the fastest growing and second largest equipment market in the world. In contrast, Japanese companies were able to increase their share of the comparatively open world market to about 20 percent by 1991. U.S. and Japanese representatives did sign a trade agreement in 1992, however, which became fully effective in April of 1993. The intent of the pact was to help open the Japanese public sector to foreign computer suppliers. U.S. companies did supply over 60 percent of the Japanese workstation market in 1992, and held significant market share in some other niches.

RESEARCH AND TECHNOLOGY

The U.S. computer industry spent more money on research and development in the early 1990s than any other major industrial sector. The growth in annual research spending in the industry began to slow in the 1990s, however, as industry profitability declined. In addition, many companies were reducing their overall product development expenditures through alliances with their competitors and with companies in other industries. For instance, Honeywell, AT&T, IBM, and General Electric teamed up in 1992 to form the Optoelectronic Technology Consortium. The U.S. government provided funding for the consortium as well.

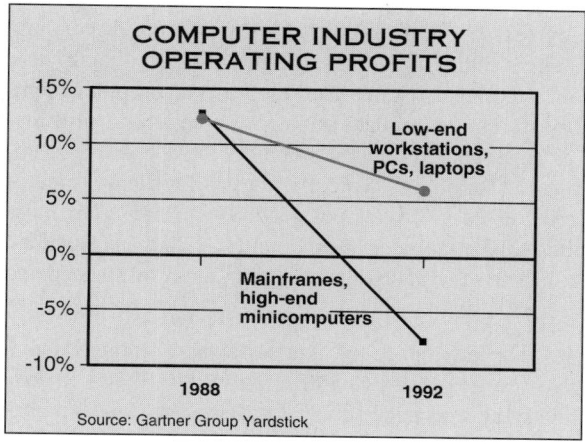

COMPUTER INDUSTRY OPERATING PROFITS

Low-end workstations, PCs, laptops

Mainframes, high-end minicomputers

Source: Gartner Group Yardstick

Government dollars were funding industry research and development for a multitude of activities that were directly tied to the electronic computing industry. The federal government's High Performance Computing and Communications Initiative (HPCCI), for instance, received $657 million in government funds in 1992 alone. Part of that money will be used to develop a parallel computer system that will operate at one trillion floating point operations per second (teraflops). Going into the mid-1990s, several industry and government leaders were seeking research and development tax credits for computer firms, and were trying to establish greater cooperation between public and private sectors.

In its quest to assume a leadership role in the global computing industry, Japan, too, was investing heavily in research in the early 1990s. As it ended its 11-year, $415-million Fifth Generation Computer Project in 1992, the Japanese government began the 10-year, $450-million Real World Computing Project. This project will assemble a group of both domestic and foreign manufacturers to research MPP systems,

voice recognition, and "fuzzy" logic. Fuzzy logic, an industry catch-phrase in the 1990s, referred to the ability of computers to learn from mistakes and to mimic the human thought process. Japan already held the lead in semiconductors, digital imaging, data storage, and optoelectronics.

Technological innovations before the year 2000 that may impact the industry include the possible development of a fiber optic communications superhighway, 3-D holographic devices, and advance MPP systems. A trend toward smaller, faster, cheaper machines with greater memory will continue. This long-time dominant trend will be overshadowed, however, with an increased emphasis on initiatives such as fuzzy logic and virtual reality—technology which will expand the role of the industry in all segments of modern society.

An example of such new devices is the Scanning Probe Microscope (SPM), which effectively combines a computer with an advanced microscope, that allows scientists to create 3-D images of a compound's atomic structure. Several U.S. manufacturers were developing and selling SPMs in 1993, and the Japanese government was funding a $250 million Atom Manipulation project to advance the technology. New miniature hand-held computing and communication devices are also expected to extend the scope of the industry.

INDUSTRY INFORMATION SOURCES

Carlton, Jim, "Compaq PCs Outsold IBM and Apple World-Wide During the First Quarter," *Wall Street Journal,* May 25, 1994.

Darnay, Arsen J., ed., *Manufacturing USA; Industry Analyses, Statistics, and Leading Companies,* Detroit: Gale Research Inc., 1993.

Gross, Neil, Emily Smith, and John Carey, "Windows on the World of Atoms," *Business Week,* August 30, 1993.

Guterl, Fred, "The Sleeper of Supercomputers," *Business Week,* August 9, 1993.

Hast, Adele, ed., *International Directory of Company Histories, Volume III,* Chicago: St. James Press, 1991.

Occupational Outlook Handbook, 1992-93 Edition, Washington, D.C.: U.S. Department of Labor, 1992.

Rebello, Cathy, and Peter Burrows, "Apple's Uncertain Harvest," *Business Week,* August 9, 1993.

Standard & Poor's Industry Surveys, New York: Standard & Poor's Corporation, December 31, 1993.

U.S. Industrial Outlook 1993, Washington, D.C.: U.S. Department of Commerce, January 1993.

"U.S. Workstations Are Really Working in Japan," *Business Week,* August 9, 1993.

Verity, John, "The Parallel Universe Grows," *Business Week*, August 16, 1993.

—Dave Mote

SIC 3572

COMPUTER STORAGE DEVICES

This classification covers establishments primarily engaged in manufacturing computer storage devices.

INDUSTRY SNAPSHOT

The computer memory storage device industry is comprised of firms that manufacture tape, magnetic, and optical memory components that are used with computers. CD-ROM diskette drives, floppy disk drives, and hard disk drives are a few of the products represented by industry participants.

Memory storage devices played a critical role in the development of the computer industry during the twentieth century. By the early 1990s, memory storage manufacturers represented 15 percent of the entire U.S. computer products and services industry, with over $9 billion in domestic shipments. Furthermore, in 1992 U.S. firms generated over $18 billion in worldwide hard disk drive sales, alone, which accounted for over 75 percent of global demand in that sector. The top 75 companies in the industry employed over 125,000 workers.

Going into the mid-1990s, memory storage companies were focusing on new product development in a dynamic industry characterized by short product life cycles and intense price competition. Most makers of magnetic disk drives, for instance, were struggling to overcome the effects of severe price reductions in a commodity-like environment that had developed in the early 1990s. The most profitable companies were those that were successfully developing and delivering cutting edge technologies, such as CD-ROM, RAID, and flash cards.

ORGANIZATION AND STRUCTURE

Most computer memory storage devices can be classified as either optical or magnetic. In 1992, about 70 million magnetic devices were being shipped annually by U.S. manufacturers. Newer optical components, in contrast, were being shipped at a rate of about 3.5 million units per year. In addition to optical and magnetic storage, semiconductor memory chips that store data and programs in the form of digital impulses were gaining recognition as a viable new technology in the early 1990s.

Magnetic Storage. Magnetic devices record information in the form of magnetized spots that represent a binary code (a series of digits represented by either 1 or 0). A magnetized head suspended slightly above the surface of a medium reads and writes information on the disk. To record information, electrical charges are delivered through the head that register a pattern on the surface of the magnetically sensitive medium. To read data, the same head detects and converts spots into electrical impulses. The data can be retained indefinitely, or erased and replaced with new magnetic spots.

The three primary classes of magnetic storage devices are hard disk drives, floppy disk drives, and magnetic tape machines. Magnetic tapes, which were once the most widely used method of computer memory storage, store data on 1/2-inch-wide or 8 millimeter tape coated with a magnetically sensitive compound. Tape units typically read and write at a rate of 183 to 722 kilobytes per second, and can store more than 270 gigabytes. Some units, called autoloaders, combine several tape cartridges to maximize speed and capacity.

The advantage of magnetic tape storage is that massive quantities of information can be stored in a relatively compact space. Furthermore, tape devices have historically been the fastest method of reading and writing large amounts of data. The drawback of tape systems, however, is that the tape must be read from one end to the other in order to retrieve and store information. For this reason, magnetic tape is most often used to copy, or backup, large amounts of data stored on a network or mainframe system (or for other purposes in which stored data can be sequentially accessed). In 1992, about 2 million magnetic tape storage components were sold by U.S. manufacturers.

A hard disk magnetic storage device resembles a stack of small metal plates that rotate at a constant speed. Between each plate, a magnetic head is positioned on an arm that sweeps across the disk's surface. Each plate is coated on both sides with a magnetically sensitive compound on which a head can read or write information. Every bit of information stored on the disks is accessible by the heads each time the stack rotates.

The advantage of hard drives is that they can quickly retrieve information nonsequentially. Furthermore, because they are compact they make excellent storage devices for micro computers. Most of the 37 million hard drives sold in 1992 held 200 megabytes or less of information. Disk drives with greater capacities are commonly used in workstations, minicomputers, local area networks (LANs), and mainframes.

Hard drives used for larger computer systems are generally 14-inch, 10-inch, or 8-inch drives. Microcomputers typically have 5.25-inch, 3.5-inch, 2.5-inch, or 1.8-inch drives. Smaller disks usually hold one to two megabytes of information. In 1992, 26.5 million 3.5-inch drives were sold by U.S. firms. Sales of older 5.25-inch drives lagged at about 6.4 million units, while sales of newer 2.5-inch drives increased to sales of about 5.7 million. Approximately 300,000 cutting edge 1.8-inch were sold in 1992.

Computers communicate, or interface, with disk drives through a controller. Most drives comply with high-performance interface standards such as the Enhanced Small Drive Interface (ESDI) or the Small Computer Systems Interface (SCSI). SCSI drives are more easily integrated into other manufacturers' products; consequently, they are the most common type of drive.

Floppy diskette drives read and write information to a single rotating disk that can be removed from the drive. They are used to transfer and temporarily store information on 3.5-inch or 5.25-inch diskettes. Floppy drive technology is essentially the same as that used in hard disk drives, but floppy disks are made of coated synthetic material rather than metal. Although some U.S. manufacturers produce floppy drives, the domestic magnetic drive industry emphasizes hard drive production.

Optical Storage. Compact Disk - Read Only Memory (CD-ROM) drives use laser beams to read information on a rotating synthetic disk. Most consumer disks are composed of three layers: an overcoat that protects the information on the disk; the dye layer, where the information is recorded as digital bits of information; and a mirrored base that reflects the laser back to its source. CD-Write Once Read Many (CD-WORM) drives and disks also allow users to store their own information on a diskette, though that data cannot be erased and replaced with new information.

The advantage of optical storage is that comparatively massive amounts of information can be inexpensively stored on a small, portable medium. Because a single CD can store up to 300,000 pages of information, CD-ROM is often used for storing such memory intensive applications as information databases or programs with elaborate graphics. The name and phone number of every household in the United States, for instance, was available on three CDs in 1992 for less than $200.

The disadvantage of CD-ROM is that information retrieval is significantly slower than that of magnetic devices. Also, optical storage is relatively inflexible because it does not allow users to easily write and erase information. In 1992 U.S. firms sold 2.3 million CD-ROM drives, and about 250,000 CD-WORM drives.

Semiconductor Memory. Manufacturers in the early 1990s were also delivering computer storage on innovative new semiconductor memory chips called flash cards. Flash memory stores programs and data in the form of digital impulses. Data can be easily read, written, and erased on cards that hold two to four megabytes of data. The cards can be inserted and removed from a flash card slot just like a floppy diskette. Flash cards perform much faster than magnetic devices, however, and require much less power to operate.

Because flash memory is nonvolatile and requires no moving parts, a user can turn off his computer, turn it back on later, and find himself at the same place he was when he powered down. Because of its advantages, flash memory technology is popular with manufacturers of notebook, pen-based, and hand-held computers. The Personal Computer Memory Card International Association (PCMCIA) represents the interests of this industry segment and strives to maintain manufacturing standards.

Competitive Structure. A multitude of different organizational structures are represented in the computer memory storage industry. The industry is highly fragmented and is characterized by technological volatility. Firms that do not develop and produce breakthrough products are often forced to compete in a high-volume, low-margin, commodity-like market environment. Cutting-edge firms, in contrast, can reap huge short-term profits as a result of innovation. These firms, though, must often risk large research and development expenditures to generate new technology for rapidly shifting, unpredictable markets.

Original equipment manufacturers, such as IBM, Digital, and Hewlett-Packard, produce or purchase devices that are integrated into their own computers. Other large vendors, such as Seagate Technologies and Conner Peripherals, produce devices that are installed in, or used with, other computer manufacturers' products. These companies tend to purchase few of their components from other companies. In contrast to the more vertically integrated companies just described, several companies utilize foreign manufacturers to produce their drives or to manufacture many of the components that go into their storage devices.

BACKGROUND AND DEVELOPMENT

The punch card, the first storage mechanism used with a mechanical computer, was introduced by Herman Hollerith in 1886 to help the U.S. Bureau of the Census calculate demographic data. The punch card concept was actually developed by Charles Babbage and was demonstrated in his 1833 design of the Analytical Engine. Although Babbage's engine was never built, it provided a model for Hollerith and others. Punch cards allowed computer operators to automatically repeat arithmetic operations on numbers that were represented by holes punched into successive cards.

In 1944, International Business Machines (IBM) developed the first large-scale automatic digital computer, which was conceived by Howard H. Aiken of Harvard University. The Automatic Sequence Controlled Calculator (nicknamed the Mark I) utilized over 750,000 parts and relied on punched cards and punched tape to store data. The contraption was used to compute ballistic data for defense purposes, and could calculate three additions per second. In 1946, Bell Telephone Laboratories developed a similar computer that stored and read sequences of instructions on loops of paper tape.

The Electronic Numerical Integrator and Calculator (ENIAC), which was completed in 1945, stored numbers and computing instructions entirely by electronic circuits containing over 18,000 vacuum tubes. Although ENIAC still used punched cards for input and output data, the computer could electronically store 20 numbers. The computer had to be programmed by tedious rewiring in order to accomplish different tasks. Despite its limitations, the computer was used until 1956.

During the mid-1940s researchers realized that a major hurdle in the advancement of computer technology was a lack of adequate resident memory storage capacity. During the 1940s and 1950s, four storage techniques were developed: acoustic delay lines; magnetic drums; electrostatic devices; and magnetic cores. Mathematician John von Neumann was one of the most influential developers of storage technology during this era.

The first magnetic core computer, the Whirlwind, was developed at the Massachusetts Institute of Technology in 1953. By the mid-1950s magnetic core memory had become the principal storage system. At this point, many companies realized that computer production and design had the potential to be a viable industry. IBM, Sperry, Rand, Burroughs, RCA, General Electric, and other companies quickly began introducing computers for a variety of commercial and institutional applications. By 1960, in fact, approximately 5,000 stored-program computers were operating in the United States. Throughout the 1960s this number doubled every two to three years.

As the computer industry expanded during 1960s and 1970s, the need for mass memory storage devices that could hold programs and backup data drove the development of a variety of mechanisms. Some of the most successful storage devices used magnetic "Winchester" technology. These devices, which were developed by IBM in 1956, evolved into what is now the magnetic hard disk drive.

The 1980s. During the 1980s the use of Winchester drives began dominate the memory storage industry. Prior to disk storage, magnetic tape was the industry's primary information storage medium. Advancements in disk technology, though, quickly outpaced the speed and efficiency of tape systems—resulting in the obsolescence of tape for most applications.

Augmenting growth of both hard disk and floppy disk drives in the 1980s was the proliferation of the microcomputer. Throughout the 1980s these personal computers (PCs) relied solely on magnetic disk technology for memory storage. As sales of PCs skyrocketed from less than 500,000 per year in 1980 to 10 million in 1990, the demand for disk storage devices soared. Growth in workstations, microcomputers, and mainframes also spurred demand. By 1990 manufacturers were shipping over 26 million Winchester hard drives and about 40 million floppy drives per year.

Despite the decline of market share attributable to magnetic tape drives, this segment experienced steady growth during the 1980s and early 1990s. By 1989, manufacturers were shipping about 1.6 million tape drives per year, most of which were being used to backup hard disks and network systems. Furthermore, tape drive sales were expected to grow at an annual rate of approximately 8 percent in the early 1990s.

As computer memory storage device manufacturers entered the 1990s, new storage technology was beginning to widespread attention by the industry and consumers. Optical memory, which had been viewed essentially as an experimental or specialty technology during the late 1980s, was beginning to establish itself in mainstream business and consumer markets. There was also an increasing interest in semiconductor memory.

The Early 1990s. Magnetic disk drives continued to dominate industry offerings in the early 1990s. The number of hard drives sold, for instance, climbed steadily to 31 million in 1991 and to 37 million by 1992. Floppy drive sales volume also climbed, much as it had during the 1980s, to about 45 million per year by 1993. Despite a massive shakeout in the PC market, which was placing severe downward price pressure on PC manufacturers, many storage device producers enjoyed solid profit growth in 1991 and 1992. This was partly a result of PC industry price wars that were boosting PC unit shipments.

As is often the case with high-tech products, the price of most individual drives continued to decline in the early 1990s. In fact, the price of the average magnetic disk drive typically falls 3 percent to 5 percent every three months. This phenomenon occurs as a specific drive technology becomes obsolete when a new product is introduced.

Only in unique instances will producers realize gains rather than losses in profit margins on individual components. This situation occurred in the PC hard drive market during 1992 for several reasons. Most importantly, a jump in the use of new memory-consuming PC operating systems caused a surge in demand for larger PC hard drives. As a result, producers were able to realize significant price gains after several years of deteriorating margins. The average price of 3.5-inch 40 megabyte drives, for instance, vaulted to $165—18 percent higher than the average 1991 price.

CURRENT CONDITIONS

The size of the magnetic disk drive industry continued to grow in 1993. The market for hard drives, for instance, grew from $24.2 billion 1991 to $26.2 billion in 1992, and to approximately $27 billion in 1993. Nevertheless, increasing competition was depressing profits in the magnetic drive segment of the storage industry. Though PC price wars buoyed drive manufacturers' earnings in 1992, plummeting prices decreased profits in 1993. Between February and June of 1993, for example, disk drive prices dropped 25 percent.

Following impressive gains in 1992, the stock price of larger producers tumbled in 1993 and forecasted earnings also fell. Conner Peripherals' stock, for instance, fell 52 percent in price, and Wall Street analysts projected a 22 percent decline in 1993 earnings. The price of Western Digital's stock plunged 49 percent, and the company's expected earnings were 26 percent below those of 1992. Even Seagate Technology, which some analysts believed was best prepared to compete in the mid-1990s environment, expected its earnings to fall by 14 percent. Most memory storage device manufacturers were accustomed to volatile

markets, however, and were only mildly phased by the temporary setbacks.

To counter the commodity-like environment that characterized most segments of the magnetic storage industry in the mid-1990s, many companies were trying to expand their development and production of technologically superior products that offered higher profit margins. Some firms were banking on 2.5-inch and 1.8-inch hard disk drives that could be used in notebook computers to stimulate sales. Although the market for 2.5-inch drives leapt from about 2 million in 1991 to 3 million in 1992, demand for that sector was not growing at the rate that many manufacturers had expected. The number of shipments of newer 1.8-inch drives rose from about 300,000 in 1992 to an estimated 850,000 in 1993, and was expected to reach 9 million by 1995.

Casting doubt on analysts' predictions for 1.8-inch and 2.5-inch hard drive shipments was the unveiling of an even smaller drive in 1992. Hewlett-Packard disclosed its 1.3-inch, 20 megabyte, matchbox-sized hard disk drive. The company expects to direct the product toward the burgeoning hand-held and sub-notebook computer market. Similarly, Areal Technology Inc. announced its development of a 2.5-inch drive platter that could store 91.5 megabytes—more than any other drive plate on the market. Another breakthrough included a 3.5-inch hard drive with a memory capacity of 1.47 gigabytes, which was developed by Conner Peripherals. Seagate, IBM, and DEC, among others, were striving to develop competing 3.5-inch drives with capacities of 1.6 to 2 gigabytes.

Another new technology affecting magnetic drive makers was data compression software that could effectively double the storage capacity of a computer's hard disk. For many users, this development meant that they could postpone the purchase of a larger hard drive (or a new computer) and still take advantage of new operating systems and applications that required extensive memory capabilities.

RAID Delivers. A major new technology boosting magnetic memory device manufacturers in the mid-1990s involved Redundant Arrays of Inexpensive Disks (RAIDs), which were first introduced in 1987. RAIDs allow several hard drives to work in concert as a single, high-capacity, relatively inexpensive, and dependable memory backup device. Applications include backup storage for mainframes, networks, and other high-end systems. 1993 RAID systems offered storage capacity of as much as 183 gigabytes.

Worldwide shipments of RAIDs grew from 16,000 units in 1991 to 30,000 in 1992, worth an estimated $1.2 billion. Moreover, the market for RAIDs was expected to boom to $2.4 billion in 1993, $4.1 billion in 1994, and to more than $5 billion by 1995. RAIDs will likely dominate the high-end storage device market by the late 1990s. Although IBM held the largest share of the RAID market in 1993, at 17.4 percent, a vast number of companies were racing to capture market share in the mid-1990s—reflecting the viability of this highly profitable and competitive segment.

CDs Proliferate. As the demand for magnetic drives grew in the early and mid-1990s, CD-ROM and CD-WORM optical devices were expanding the scope of the memory storage industry and augmenting producer revenues. During the late 1980s and early 1990s, manufacturers worked to establish the new technology in commercial markets. Primary users included libraries, law and accounting firms, and other entities that could afford the relatively expensive technology. By 1993, though, CD-ROM was also making its way into the mass consumer market.

Small businesses, game players, and home computer users were embracing CD-ROM, and a plethora of new disk titles were prompting consumers to buy the devices. Many computer manufacturers were beginning to build CD drives into their PCs; furthermore, optical drive prices were falling. In 1992, for instance, peripheral CD-ROM drives typically sold for $300. By 1993, though, the price had fallen to between $200 and $300, while the cost of an internal CD-ROM drive was as low as $100. As CD-ROM technology gained acceptance, sales soared. Worldwide shipments of CD-ROM drives rose to about 1.4 million in 1991, according to Disk Trend, Inc. Shipments jumped to about 2.3 million in 1992, and they reached an estimated 4.8 million in 1993. Analysts predicted annual shipments to approach 6.5 million in 1994, over 8 million in 1995, and over 13 million by 1997.

Optical memory products posed little immediate threat to magnetic device manufacturers in 1993. Optical products were still relatively slow and were best suited for memory intensive applications that magnetic devices couldn't handle. Developers were improving optical technology, however, and were racing to create fast CD drives that could read, write, and erase information with the same speed and ease of magnetic drives—a goal that, if reached, could quash magnetic technology. Some companies were already offering ''double-speed'' CD-ROM drives in 1993 at an average price of $700 per unit, and much faster drives were under development.

Disk Trend estimates that 34 percent of CD-ROM drives will be used for games in 1994, while educa-

tional and entertainment uses will represent about 30 percent of demand. Although CD-ROM use by commercial and institutional sectors will continue to balloon, the 36 percent share of the market that they represent will likely decrease in the late 1990s as drive prices fall.

Some analysts were reluctant to project the long-term popularity of CD memory technology—likening it to beta technology that floundered in the 1980s. Nevertheless, developers had poured over $3 billion into research and development of the technology by 1992. Although total revenues from this segment were still lower than the $3 billion investment, IBM, Apple Computers, Sony, and other large producers were working to promote optical memory devices. IBM, for instance, was busy developing a magneto-optical rewriting technology that would allow drives to erase and store information. Likewise, Apple was preparing to promote a line of computers that provided CD-ROM drives as a standard feature.

Flashcards. Technologically superior semiconductor flash memory technology, which was still in its commercial infancy, offered one of the greatest opportunities for growth in the computer memory storage industry. The compact, energy efficient, high-capacity devices proved to be weighty contenders in the bid to serve the rapidly expanding notebook and pen-based computer markets. Several major semiconductor and disk producers were investing large sums in the development of the new technology.

Intel, which served 85 percent of the world market for flash memory cards in 1993, had been marketing the technology since 1990. Intel teamed up with disk giant Conner Peripherals in 1992 to advance flash card technology, and unveiled a line of 20 cards. Analysts expected flash memory to become a dominant force in computer and telecommunications memory storage in the future. Falling prices, enforcement of PCMCIA standards, even faster chips, and increased card capacity are expected to propel market growth in the late 1990s.

INDUSTRY LEADERS

The largest company engaged primarily in the manufacture of computer storage devices in 1993 was Seagate Technologies Inc., of Scotts Valley, California. The company earned revenues of $2.3 billion in 1991 and $3 billion in 1992, and employed approximately 40,000 workers. Projected sales for 1993 were estimated at $2.6 billion. Despite a temporary setback in earnings, Seagate was relatively well positioned to increase its market share in the future. The company is recognized as one of the most vertically integrated firms in the industry. In fact, Seagate manufactures most of the parts that go into its drives.

Conner Peripherals, the second largest competitor, earned about $1.6 billion in 1991, approximately $2 billion in 1992 and had nearly 9,500 employees. Earnings for 1993, however, were forecast to drop back to about $1.6 billion. In 1992 the California-based company, which specializes in hard drive production, announced plans to expand into the entire storage market. Accordingly, it purchased the largest producer of magnetic tape backup systems in the United States. Conner led the industry in important 3.5-inch hard drive capacity technology.

Other industry leaders in the early 1990s included: Imprimis Technology Inc. of Minnesota, which had $1.2 billion in revenue in 1991; Storage Technology of Colorado, with 1991 sales of $1.1 billion; Quantum Corp. of California ($878 million); Maxtor Corp. of California ($500 million); and TBG. Inc. of New York ($400 million). In addition to storage industry participants, computer vendors like IBM, Compaq, and DEC were major suppliers of storage devices. In the RAID drive market, for instance, IBM, DEC, Compaq, and Hewlett-Packard owned over 50 percent of the market.

WORK FORCE

The computer storage industry work force includes a higher proportion of electrical and electronics engineers than most other U.S. industries. The industry also hires large numbers of trained precision assemblers, as well as a significant number of parts assemblers and fabricators.

As with most segments of the computer and computer services industry, analysts expect little or no employment growth with storage device manufacturers throughout the end of the 1990s and during the early 2000s. In fact, demand for almost every occupation in the industry will decline significantly. Between 1990 and 1993, alone, total computer industry employment plummeted 50,000 to about 214,500. Massive productivity gains were largely to blame.

The number of both precision and parts assemblers employed by manufacturers, for instance, is expected to decline between 40 percent and 55 percent from 1990 to 2005. Automation, as well as outsourcing of labor tasks to foreign countries, will account for much of this loss. Clerical positions will also decline drastically, by about 30 percent. Even the demand for engineers will fall by 1 percent or 2 percent by 2005, as companies form corporate alliances that allow them to reduce overlapping research and development expenditures.

On the bright side, the demand for systems analysts and computer scientists is expected to increase by about 40 percent between 1990 and 2005. Furthermore, opportunities will become available to professionals who can help develop cutting edge technologies, particularly for optical and semiconductor products.

AMERICA AND THE WORLD

U.S. computer storage device firms held the definitive lead in the world market in the mid-1990s, and still maintained a solid lead over their arch rival, Japan. U.S. firms served 75 percent of the $24-billion global hard drive market in 1993, for instance, while Japan only held about 15 percent. Japanese firms, though, play an important role in the hard drive sector by supplying most of the spindle motors, bearings, and other parts that U.S. firms incorporate into the drives that they build.

Although Japanese firms dominate the world floppy drive market, U.S. companies manufacture about 44 percent of the floppy diskettes used worldwide. Japanese firms have invested heavily in American companies that produce drives and diskettes, however. Japan also maintains a technological lead in the burgeoning CD-ROM market, with Sony, Hitachi, and Toshiba leading industry advancements. Philips NV, a Netherlands competitor, was also a major force in this segment. Intel, however, garnered the dominant share of the semiconductor market for America in the mid-1990s.

One factor thwarting global progress for American exporters was the inaccessibility of one of the largest computer storage device markets in the world—Japan. Despite relatively open U.S. markets, shrewd Japanese trading tactics were succeeding in leaving U.S. producers out of many segments of that market. Japan accounted for about 20 percent of the global demand for all computer equipment and services in 1993.

RESEARCH AND TECHNOLOGY

Industry research and development will increasingly result both from strategic alliances and from government initiatives. For example, General Electric, AT&T, Honeywell, and IBM established the Optoelectronic Technology Consortium (OTC) in July 1992 to advance domestic optical technology. Consortium members will share research already completed on their own, and will release their combined findings to other U.S. computer and semiconductor firms. The OTC was scheduled to continue for 30 months, and was backed by $8 million in initial funding. Half of the funding for the OTC was supplied by the Federal Defense Advanced Research Projects Agency (DARPA).

In addition to the OTC, the Microelectronics and Computer Technology Corp. (MCC), also an industry consortium, began a five-year research project on holographic mass-storage subsystems. This effort was backed by $10.3 million in federal grants and $12.7 million from consortium members. A similar government/private enterprise effort was underway in California that involved the National Institute of Standards and Technology and several universities. Its purpose was to integrate optical technology into a prototype computer that might eventually lead to a desktop supercomputer.

Finally, the High Performance Computing and Communications Initiative (HPCCI), which was the major federal computing research project underway in the early 1990s, was expected to result in residual advancements in storage technology. The HPCCI received $657 million in federal funds in 1992.

The Future. Memory storage devices will continue to play a leading role in the advancement of computer technology, as they have since the birth of the computer industry. The role of the memory storage device industry will become increasingly blurred, however, as the computer, telecommunications, consumer electronics, information, and entertainment industries converge into a massive multimedia industry that interconnects various technologies and services. Multimedia, by its most basic definition, will combine data, audio, and video signals into one digital stream.

The dominant technologies that will drive this metamorphosis are data processing, storage, interface, fiber optics, wireless, compression, and digital broadband switching. As a result, companies from many industries will find themselves competing and cooperating with firms in completely separate industries. Firms that once delivered memory storage solely for the computer industry will be selling their technology to a wide range of markets. The advancement of flash memory technology provides evidence of this trend. In 1993, semiconductor and disk storage companies were already cooperating to develop flash memory storage products not only for computers, but also for telephones, automobiles, and other industries.

Optical memory will likely play an integral role in the future of multimedia because of its capacity to store text, images, animation, and video. Virtual reality products represent another area in which optical technology can be applied. CD drives were already in production in 1993 that could read and write to laser discs that held twice as much memory as disks sold in 1992. These disks also delivered information at twice the speed of the earlier disks. As it did with flash cards, the implementation of industry standards will likely propel this technology to center stage.

INDUSTRY INFORMATION SOURCES

Booker, Ellis, ''When Storage Is State of the Art,'' *Computerworld*, May 17, 1993.

Darnay, Arsen J., ed., *Manufacturing USA; Industry Analyses, Statistics, and Leading Companies*, Detroit: Gale Research Inc., 1993.

Darnay, Arsen J., and Marlita A. Reddy, eds., *Market Share Reporter: An Annual Compilation of Reported Market Share Data on Companies, Products, and Services, 1993*, Detroit: Gale Research Inc., 1993.

''Eking Out More Space for Data on PC Disks,'' *Electronic Business*, May 1993.

Encyclopaedia Britannica, Chicago: Encyclopaedia Britannica, Inc., 1989.

Ferelli, Mark, ''Do-It-Yourself CD-R Impacts Bottom Line,'' *Computer Technology Review*, August 1993.

———, ''Don't Wait For A Disaster Before Autoloading Backup,'' *Computer Technology Review*, August 1993.

———, ''CD-ROMs Board and Storm The LAN,'' *Computer Technology Review*, August 1993.

Jorgensen, Barbara, ''CD-ROM Leaps into the Consumer Market,'' *Electronic Business*, July 1993.

Lee, Yvonne, ''PCMCIA Spec Debated,'' *InfoWorld*, May 31, 1993.

Quickel, Stephen W., ''The Worst is Yet to Come,'' *Electronic Business*, June 1993.

Rose, John, ''New Competitors Will Scramble the Opportunities,'' *Electronic Business*, July 1993.

''Socket and Card Services,'' *Machine Design*, June 11, 1993.

Standard & Poor's Industry Surveys, New York: Standard & Poor's Corporation, December 31, 1992.

U.S. Industrial Outlook 1993, Washington, D.C.: U.S. Department of Commerce, January 1993.

''Where Have All the High-Tech Jobs Gone?'' *Electronic Business*, August 1993.

—Dave Mote

SIC 3575

COMPUTER TERMINALS

Companies primarily engaged in manufacturing computer terminals, teleprinters, and multistation

CRTs (cathode ray tube) make up the computer terminal industry. Personal computers, workstations, minicomputers, and other systems that contain central processing units (CPUs) are classified in the electronic computer industry. Establishments primarily engaged in manufacturing point-of-sale, funds transfer, and automatic teller machines are classified in **SIC 3578: Calculating and Accounting Machines, Except Electronic Computers.**

A computer terminal acts as an interface between a user and a system server that has a CPU and storage capacity. Typically, a network of terminals are attached to the server. While some network systems allow terminals to have unimpeded access to the server, most systems require users to share the processor. As a result, such ''timeshare'' servers operate more slowly as more users access the processor.

Terminals were first used to access large mainframe systems that became popular in the 1970s. As the speed and memory capacity of computers increased and prices of desktop computers fell during the 1980s, the popularity of systems that used terminals declined in relation to computers.

Despite some limitations, systems that use network terminals offer several advantages over computers. For instance, microcomputers and workstations run applications locally, and therefore require more memory and an operating system. Many terminals, on the other hand, run only the display part of a computer application locally, and rely on the server to handle data processing and storage. As a result, terminals offer advantages in costs, centralized control, and security.

Although sales of network servers and systems remained strong in the late 1980s and early 1990s, terminal sales lagged. Unlike other sectors of the computer hardware industry, terminal manufacturers' shipments fell from $2.3 billion in 1988 to about $1.9 billion in the early 1990s. Furthermore, industry employment had fallen from about 18,000 in 1988 to 12,000 by 1990.

Much of the industry's decline was a result of increased competition from personal computers (PCs). As PC prices plummeted, consumers increasingly networked low-cost PCs with servers to achieve the advantages of both desktop and terminal systems. In contrast to the declining sales of terminals, sales of PCs approached $30 billion in 1992.

Going into the mid-1990s, terminal manufacturers were hoping to stabilize revenues with new products, such as X-terminals. X-terminals contain internal software, and therefore allow the interaction of concurrent

applications running in the popular ''WINDOWS'' environment. X-terminals cost several thousand dollars less than workstations, and slightly less than many microcomputers in the early 1990s. X-terminals also offered higher resolution, larger screens, and greater networking capabilities than many desktop and workstation computers. X-terminal manufacturers had sales of $300 million in 1991, and sales were expected to double every year until 1995.

Anacomp Inc., of Indiana, was the largest manufacturer of computer terminals in 1992, with sales of $652 million and about 5,000 employees. Wyse Technology, of California, a major producer of X-terminals, was the second largest competitor, with $300 million in sales and 2,000 workers. Other industry leaders in the early 1990s included Radius Inc., of California ($110 million in sales), Ampex Corp., of California ($100 million), and Emerson Computer Corp., of New Jersey ($75 million).

The majority of the top 50 companies in the industry employed fewer than 100 workers and generated less than $20 million in annual revenues in the early 1990s. Employment prospects in the computer terminal manufacturing industry are bleak, according to the Bureau of Labor Statistics. Employment for most occupations in the industry is expected to fall by 10 percent to 40 percent between 1993 and 2005.

INDUSTRY INFORMATION SOURCES

Francis, Bob, ''A Smart Look for Dumb Terminals,'' *Datamation*, September 1, 1992.

Kinnucan, Paul, ''Jury Still Out on X-Terminals,'' *Systems Integration*, October 1990.

Pinella, Paul, ''WYSE Technology,'' *Datamation*, June 15, 1992.

Shaffer, Richard A., ''The Story of X,'' *Forbes*, August 3, 1992.

Yager, Tom, ''X Terminals for Workstation Power at PC Prices,'' *Byte*, May 1991.

—Dave Mote

SIC 3577

COMPUTER PERIPHERAL EQUIPMENT, NOT ELSEWHERE CLASSIFIED

Computer peripheral equipment not elsewhere classified includes miscellaneous computer accessories that support the activities of a computer's central processing unit (CPU). Companies in this industry manufacture a variety of products, including printers, plotters, graphic displays, optical scanners, and more. Not included in this industry segment are computer terminals, storage devices, modems and other communications devices, or computer-driven office machines. For information on computer peripheral equipment classified elsewhere, see **SIC 3571: Electronic Computers, 3572: Computer Storage Devices, 3575: Computer Terminals,** and **3579: Office Machines, Not Elsewhere Classified.**

INDUSTRY SNAPSHOT

Peripheral equipment accounted for a major share of U.S. computer industry revenues. In 1992, for instance, computer peripherals from all industries represented about $65 billion, or 20 percent, of the global computer equipment and services market. U.S. sales of printers alone exceeded $11 billion that year. The peripherals industry was expected to grow faster than most other industries throughout the 1990s.

Peripheral manufacturers benefitted from new markets created by technological advancements in the computer industry. Faster, less expensive personal computers with greater memory capacity boosted peripheral sales, as did the increasing interest in multimedia equipment, which incorporated the capabilities of computers, telephones, video display terminals, and fax machines. In the early 1990s, industry competitors hastened to bring out new technology that could take advantage of computer advancements and could broaden the scope of the peripheral market.

ORGANIZATION AND STRUCTURE

Facilitating communication with the CPU, peripheral equipment was used with supercomputers, mainframes, minicomputers, workstations, and personal computers. The three largest categories of peripherals were graphic displays, printers, and scanners. In addition to the major peripheral categories, numerous miscellaneous products included: computer sound systems, magnetic ink recognition devices, graphic and technical plotters, graphics production equipment, and various multimedia devices.

Graphic Displays. The most popular types of graphic displays were traditional cathode ray tube (CRT) monitors and flat panel Liquid Crystal Displays (LCDs). Although some CRTs were built into computers or terminals, most were offered as peripheral devices that may be added to a personal computer or network terminal. A video card was used as an interface between the CRT and the CPU, allowing compatibility for specific monitors and computer systems.

CRTs provided either monochrome (black-and-white) or color graphics. CRT displays were also offered with a variety of graphics capabilities that allowed monitors to deliver varying degrees of flexibility, performance, resolution quality, and size. Low resolution monitors, for instance, contained 640 x 480 pixels per inch, while higher resolution CRTs could deliver 1,280 x 1,024, 1,600 x 1,200, or more pixels per inch. Most CRTs measured between ten and 17 inches diagonally. In 1992, over 11 million CRTs were sold for use with new personal desktop computers, a figure that did not include sales of monitors used with larger computers or networks. CRT prices ranged from $50 for monochrome displays to several thousand dollars for large, high-definition color monitors.

Among the fastest growing and most dynamic segments of the graphic display market was the LCD. Because LCDs were flat, they were the display of choice for the rapidly growing notebook computer industry. Although far fewer LCDs than CRTs were purchased in the early 1990s, LCDs provided manufacturers with much larger profit margins than older, commodity-like CRTs. Global LCD sales grew to over $3.1 billion in 1992.

Monochrome displays accounted for over 70 percent of LCD revenues in 1992. The remaining 30 percent of sales represented a variety of color LCDs. About 75 percent of all color LCDs sold were passive-matrix displays, also called super-twisted nematic (STN). Active-matrix displays, also called thin-film transistors (TFTs), made up the remaining 25 percent of color LCDs. TFTs provided the highest graphic quality in this segment, and mimicked large semiconductors in which many transistors functioned as a cohesive unit. High-tech TFTs sold for an average price of $1,200 in 1992—about twice as much as passive-matrix LCDs. Most LCD screen sizes ranged from 8.5 to 10.4 inches.

Printers. The three principal printer types were dot-matrix, ink-jet, and laser. Dot matrix printers were one of the first responses to demands by computer users for an output device that offered more flexibility than impact character printers. Dot-matrix devices dominated the printer market and continued to account for over 50 percent of unit sales in the early 1990s. However, by the 1990s the dot-matrix printer was largely being replaced since it offered smaller profit margins in relation to newer technology. Dot-matrix prices typically ranged from $75 to $200.

Ink-jet printers, which averaged about $400 in price, featured much higher resolution and flexibility than dot-matrix technology. Ink-jets commonly offered resolution of 300 to 600 dots per inch (DPI) in

1993 and provided several fonts and graphic capabilities. Ink-jets captured 18 percent of total U.S. printer revenues in 1992, and those featuring color graphics accounted for about 22 percent of all ink-jets shipped.

Laser printers ranged in price from about $700 for low-end personal devices to between $1,500 and $3,000 for heavy-duty business printers in 1993. Like the ink-jet printer, laser printers typically offered 300 to 600 DPI resolution. However, laser printers were typically faster and more flexible that ink-jets and usually had a greater paper handling capacity. In 1992, laser printers accounted for about 28 percent of all printer shipments.

Scanners. Peripheral scanners were used to translate optical images to electronic signals. Able to recognize characters, line art, and gray-scale images, scanners used photosensitive arrays that reflected light in order to digitize printed information. The three types of scanners common in the early 1990s were handheld, desktop, and drum. Drum scanners were not considered peripheral equipment, however, because they were a high-end tool used primarily in the printing industry.

Desktop, or flatbed, scanners were the most common device. Using optical character recognition (OCR) technology, these scanners were most often used to quickly translate stacks of printed pages into a word processing document that could be viewed, searched, and manipulated using a word processor. Typical flatbed scanners had a resolution of 300 to 600 dots per inch (DPI). Handheld scanners were priced much lower than flatbeds and were regarded as more useful for scanning small graphics. They also delivered lower resolution and limited OCR compatibility. In 1992, approximately $1 billion worth of scanners were sold worldwide.

BACKGROUND AND DEVELOPMENT

The miscellaneous peripherals industry emerged from the commercial computer industry in the 1970s. Not until the creation and subsequent widespread acceptance of desktop and personal computers (PCs) in the 1980s, however, did the industry capture a significant share of all computer-related expenditures. PCs extended the market for peripherals to the mass consumer market and generated a demand for numerous computer add-on products.

Some of the early peripherals included card punching and sorting machines, microfilm output units, plotter controls, tabulators, tape cleaners, and tape print units. During the 1980s, however, scanners, printers, and displays that complemented PCs, work-

stations, and network systems grew to dominate the market. As the speed and memory storage capacity of desktop computers increased, so did the capabilities of peripherals. By the mid-1980s, peripherals accounted for 20 percent of all computer industry revenues.

Global computer equipment and services sales escalated from $243 billion in 1988 to about $280 billion in 1990. Despite an overall slowdown in computer industry growth in the early 1990s, revenues from peripherals continued their spiral to $290 billion in 1991, reaching nearly $320 billion in 1992. Throughout this period the market for peripherals, including storage devices as well as some other peripherals classified in other industries, maintained about a 20 percent share of the total market—peaking at about $65 billion by 1992. Peripherals not elsewhere classified captured an estimated $18 billion of that amount.

CURRENT CONDITIONS

In the early 1990s, the peripherals industry exceeded growth in other computer equipment industry segments, largely due to the severe price slashing by PC vendors effected during this time. As PC manufacturers' revenues fell in the early 1990s, the number of units shipped increased substantially, prompting a greater demand for all types of add-on peripherals.

Annual sales of scanners and other electronic imaging peripherals grew at a rate of nearly 20 percent in 1992 to about $2 billion. Furthermore, this segment of the peripherals industry enjoyed relatively high profit margins, and analysts predicted that annual scanner sales would increase 100 percent by 1997. Falling prices, more powerful and simple imaging software and technology, the proliferation of color scanners, and advances in computer memory storage techniques were expected to be the dominant factors driving market growth in this segment, while flatbed scanners would continue to account for the majority of product sales.

Printer sales jumped 10.7 percent in 1992 to about $11.2 billion, representing about 11 million units. This growth rate was expected to hold during 1993, boosting revenues past $12.4 billion from 12.9 million units. Although unit shipments of printers rose in the early 1990s, low-end printers of all types, particularly the dot matrix printer, had become low-profit commodity items by 1993. In the early 1990s, ink-jet printers and low-end laser printers followed a course similar to that of dot matrix devices—as prices and profit margins declined. Laser printers remained profitable, however, as did both low and high-end color printers. Printer shipments were expected to jump to about 24 million by 1998 worth nearly $19 billion, representing an estimated annual growth rate of about 7.5 percent. By 1998, laser printers would likely hold a 50 percent share of the printer market, while ink-jets would represent over 30 percent.

CRT displays utilized technology that had been changed only slightly during the past decade—resulting in a price-intensive commodity environment for CRT vendors. LCDs, in contrast, still offered solid growth and profit opportunities. Sales and prices of color LCDs were particularly competitive. From $917 million in 1992, color LCD sales were expected to reach over $2.7 billion by 1996. Advances in LCD technology were expected to keep profit margins relatively high through the mid-1990s, though technology available in 1993 was expected to quickly be outdated. TFT displays that cost $1,150 in 1993, for example, were expected to drop in price to about $700 by 1995.

Sales of multimedia peripherals, such as computer sound-systems, were expected to post strong gains throughout the 1990s. Creative Technology Ltd., which led the industry in 1993 sales of add-on sound boards that could digitally recreate human speech, offered evidence of this sector's viability. The company's earnings jumped 327 percent in 1992 to $22.3 million on revenues of $85.6 million. It was also quick to develop computer add-ons called circuit cards that could give PCs the ability to show full-motion video.

INDUSTRY LEADERS

The largest producer of peripheral computer equipment in the world in the early 1990s was International Business Machines (IBM), of New York. IBM held a 12.6 percent share of the global peripheral market in 1992. Although the company generated $64.5 billion in revenues in 1992, it lost $6.87 billion. Peripheral equipment accounted for about 12.5 percent, or $8 billion, of the company's sales. IBM's share of the world peripheral market declined in 1992, as revenues from that division fell nearly 23 percent.

The second largest supplier of peripherals in 1992 was Hewlett-Packard Co., of California, which accounted for 7.3 percent of global peripheral revenues. About 36 percent of the company's $12.7 billion in revenues was derived from peripheral sales. Hewlett-Packard was the largest U.S. supplier of printers and was an important market innovator in the early 1990s. The introduction of new ink-jet and laser technology during this time helped the company reap huge profits from printer sales, and thrust the company to a 40 to 50 percent share of the entire printer market. However, the corporation's profits declined by 27 percent to $549 million in 1992.

The next three largest peripheral suppliers in the world were Canon, Hitachi, and Fujitsu—all Japanese firms. These three competitors accounted for a combined total of 16.5 percent of the peripherals market in 1992 and had increased their revenues from that segment of their business an average of 12.6 percent. Other large American peripheral manufacturers included Digital Equipment Corporation, Xerox, AT&T, Quantum, and Apple.

WORK FORCE

Like most other computer-related segments, the peripheral industry was expected to realize a significant reduction in its work force during the 1990s. This downsizing was expected to occur even among the industry's more successful companies, due to increased productivity gains and mergers effected to benefit from economies of scale. For more information about jobs and opportunities in the computer hardware industry, see **SIC 3571: Electronic Computers.**

AMERICA AND THE WORLD

Although U.S. companies lead the world in most segments of the peripherals industry, foreign competitors were rapidly gaining in the early 1990s. Japanese firms, in particular, were increasing market share and vying for industry dominance.

Between 1984 and 1991, Japanese companies increased their share of all computer-related revenues from nine to 27 percent, while the U.S. market share declined from 79 to 62 percent. Moreover, in 1992, five of the top 15 firms in the peripherals industry were Japanese-owned and operated. These five firms increased their share to 23.1 percent of the global market in 1992. While U.S. firms lead in sales of printers and scanners in the early 1990s, Japanese-based Panasonic and Canon held significant shares of the printer industry, and Japan also lead the industry in LCD screen production. Furthermore, many U.S. producers purchased many of their parts from Japanese manufacturers.

RESEARCH AND TECHNOLOGY

U.S. firms were on the leading edge of almost every peripheral technology in the industry in the mid-1990s. At least two efforts were underway during this time to advance the role of U.S. firms in the production of the rapidly growing color LCD market. One was a joint venture between Motorola Inc. and In Focus Systems, called Motif. Motif sought to develop high-quality LCDs that could be manufactured inexpensively. The other effort was initiated by the Defense Advanced Research Projects Agency (DARPA).

DARPA planned to provide $15 million in seed money for a consortium of large and small companies that would assemble the framework necessary to effectively compete in the color LCD market.

Scanner and printer manufacturers were striving toward similar technological and productivity goals. The demand for higher resolution, faster input and output, lower production costs, and greater flexibility were driving investment and development in both printer categories. In 1993, manufacturers were already delivering low-end laser printers capable of printing 600 DPI or greater.

In the future, the computer peripheral industry expected to become increasingly integrated into complementary industries, as data processing, interface, storage, fiber optics, wireless, and digital broadband switching technologies converged into a massive multimedia industry. Scanners, printers, and displays would also likely be used in conjunction with other communications and information equipment.

INDUSTRY INFORMATION SOURCES

Arnold, Bill, ''Color LCDs: From Famine to Feast,'' *Electronic Business,* April 1993.

Brandt, Richard, ''Sound Blaster Hears the Blare of Competition,'' *Business Week,* April 12, 1992.

Braun, Ellen, ''Computer Printers: More Power, Less Cost,'' *Office Systems,* March 1992.

Braun, Ellen, ''Scanners Give PCs New Eyes,'' *Office Systems,* August 1993.

''Electronic Imaging Collides with Health Care Cost Control,'' *Electronic Business,* July 1993.

McCracken, Ted, ''Video Amplifier Keying Performance,'' *Computer Technology Review,* August 1993.

McNamara, George, ''Will Scanners Ride Image Management's Breaking Wave?'' *Computer Technology Review,* August 1993.

Rose, John, ''New Competitors Will Scramble the Opportunities,'' *Electronic Business,* July 1993.

Ryan, Kimberly, ''Peripherals: Powerful, Plentiful and Colorful,'' *Datamation,* January 15, 1993.

Schlak, Mark, ''The New IT Industry Takes Shape,'' *Datamation,* June 15, 1993.

Siatt, Wayne, ''Lasers, Ink-Jets Pack Practical Printing Power,'' *Office Products Development,* July 1993.

Thomas, Mike, ''Electronic Imaging Posts Impressive Gains,'' *The Office,* January 1993.

Trowbridge, Dave, ''Multifunctional Peripherals Will Overcome,'' *Computer Technology Review,* December 1990.

Trowbridge, Dave, ''OmniScan Aims to Reverse Slump in Fortunes of Handheld Scanners,'' *Computer Technology Review,* August 1993.

''Where Have All the High-Tech Jobs Gone?'' *Electronic Business,* August 1993.

—Dave Mote

SIC 3578

CALCULATING AND ACCOUNTING MACHINES, EXCEPT ELECTRONIC COMPUTERS

This industry covers establishments primarily engaged in manufacturing point-of-sale devices, fund transfer devices, and other calculating and accounting machines, except electronic computers. Included are electronic calculating and accounting machines which must be paced by operator intervention, even when augmented by attachments. These machines may include program control or have input/output capabilities.

Charles Xavier Thomas, of France, is credited with starting the industry when he introduced the arithmometer in the 1870s. Frank Baldwin and William S. Burroughs were also major innovators in early calculating machine technology. During the industrial revolution and until the mid-1900s, mechanical and electrical adding machines dominated industry offerings. The invention of the hand-held calculator in 1948 and the integrated circuit in the late 1960s, however, initiated the demise of traditional adding machines.

Although 3.5 million desk-top and hand-held calculators were sold in 1990 for a total of about $700 million, both products had essentially become commodity items by the 1980s. Electronic cash registers, an offshoot of calculating machines, offered higher profit margins for manufacturers. Scanning technology and the demand for related inventory tracking systems in the 1980s and early 1990s spurred the development of new ''high-tech'' cash registers that buoyed profits for some prior producers of traditional calculating machines. Other competitors exited the market or shifted to production of other equipment.

ATMs and POSs, which were added to industry offerings in the 1980s, quickly eclipsed sales of cash registers and adding machines. Sales of ATMs, which store cash and are used primarily by bank customers to conduct account transactions, skyrocketed past a total of 90,000 units by 1993. Less expensive POS devices, which allow consumers to conduct electronic account transactions from a purchase point such as a gas station or supermarket, numbered about 300,000 in 1993.

By the early 1990s, the market for ATMs was becoming saturated in comparison to the 1980s. Manufacturers' earnings, however, were expected to rise as industry analysts projected a growing demand for replacement machines and a 20 percent rise in the number of ATM installations between 1993 and 1997. The number of POS devices sold, on the other hand, is expected to balloon to over 1.1 million by 1997 as an increasing number of retailers adopt this method of accepting payment.

In 1992, the top 25 companies in the industry generated about $1.6 billion in sales from all adding and calculating machines. Diebold Inc., which produced over half of all ATMs sold in 1992, was the largest producer—with $476 million in sales and 3,800 employees. The Minnesota-based National Computer Systems was the second largest company in the industry with $300 million in sales and 3,000 employees. Most companies in the industry, however, are small. Only the top ten competitors, for example, employed more than 100 people or generated over $15 million in revenues.

Manufacturers hoped to increase ATM sales in the mid-1990s by integrating video-conferencing and imaging capabilities into their products. Some banks were also experimenting with selling mutual fund shares through ATMs. Cash register manufacturers were striving to jump-start lagging sales by integrating advanced inventory tracking and information systems technology into new product offerings.

Despite the popularity of ATMs and POS devices in the United States, the technology has been slow to catch on overseas. Only about 40,000 ATMs, for example, have been installed outside the United States. Combined, Spain and the United Kingdom have approximately 10,000 ATMs, while Austria, Denmark, Germany, Ireland, Norway, and Sweden have none. ATMs in Japan are available for use only in the daytime.

INDUSTRY INFORMATION SOURCES

Angel, Abcede, "Marketers Total ECR Costs, Benefits," *National Petroleum News*, March 1993.

Barthel, Matt, "Point of Sale Devices Seen Outpacing ATMs," *American Banker*, July 19, 1993.

Cody, Angela, "Calculators + PCs = Performance," *Today's Office*, August 1990.

Cope, Debra, "Equity Funds by ATM Seen as Wave of Future," *American Banker*, August 17, 1993.

Darnay, Arsen J., ed., *Manufacturing USA; Industry Analyses, Statistics, and Leading Companies*, Detroit: Gale Research Inc., 1993.

Darnay, Arsen J., and Marlita A. Reddy, eds., *Market Share Reporter: An Annual Compilation of Reported Market Share Data on Companies, Products, and Services, 1993*, Detroit: Gale Research Inc., 1993.

"Don't Bank on ATMs Abroad," *Money*, April 1993.

Encyclopaedia Britannica, Chicago: Encyclopaedia Britannica, Inc., 1989.

Mitchell, Richard, "ATM Sales Rise with Bank Profits," *Bank Management*, May 1993.

Rehr, Darryl C., "Calculators: You Can Count on Them," *Office*, July 1991.

—Dave Mote

SIC 3579

OFFICE MACHINES, NOT ELSEWHERE CLASSIFIED

Companies principally engaged in manufacturing miscellaneous office machines and devices comprise the office machines, not elsewhere classified, industry. Such devices include typewriting, mail room, dictation, and facsimile machines. In addition, a multitude of companies in the industry produce specialty products, such as paper shredders, envelope stuffing machines, ticket counters, and coin wrapping machines. Establishments primarily engaged in manufacturing modems and other communications interface equipment are classified in **SIC 3661: Telephone and Telegraph Apparatus.**

INDUSTRY SNAPSHOT

In the early 1990s, sales of miscellaneous office machines were estimated at $3.5 to $4 billion per year. This figure was down from a peak of over $5 billion in 1985 and about $4.3 billion in 1989. Furthermore, industry employment plummeted from nearly 50,000 in the early 1980s to about 30,000 by the early 1990s. Contributing to the decline of industry sales and employment were several factors, including: increased use of computers, foreign competition, lackluster economic growth, increased productivity, reduced corporate spending, and U.S. demographic changes.

Manufacturers were responding to the more competitive environment of the 1990s by integrating the latest technology into new product offerings, infiltrating new channels of distribution and targeting home offices. Although industry employment was expected to plummet during the 1990s and profits remained stagnant for many companies in the mid-1990s, some opportunities, such as the North American Free Trade Agreement (NAFTA), offered hope for manufacturers.

ORGANIZATION AND STRUCTURE

Typewriters. Typewriters and word processing machines accounted for the largest segment of the miscellaneous business machines industry in 1992, representing over 40 percent of total shipments. While most of the units sold were electronic typewriters, some companies were still marketing electromechanical typewriters, which resembled traditional manual typewriters, but used electricity to reduce the effort required by the typist and to increase the quality of type.

Electronic typewriters took the electromechanical concept a step further by reducing the number of moving parts and featuring advanced capabilities. For instance, many electronic typewriters could recall a series of pressed keys and then delete those characters from a sheet of paper on command. Some units also allowed the typist to store a word or phrase in the machine's memory, which would automatically recall and print on command.

A third model of typewriter was the personal word processor (PWP). PWPs allowed the typist to view text on a screen before it was actually transferred to paper, much like a personal computer (PC). Most PWPs were simply an electronic typewriter with a liquid crystal display, or CRT, and a central processing unit attached. Unlike PCs, PWPs usually offered access only to internally stored proprietary software programs. Many PWPs were also equipped with spreadsheet software, and some advanced units offered disk drives, DOS compatibility, and hand-held scanners.

Typewriters and PWPs were less expensive and regarded as easier to use than most PCs. Compact electronic typewriters typically sold for $250 to $700 in 1993, while the most advanced PWP models sold for $2,000 to $6,000.

Other Products. Making up the remaining 50 to 60 percent of the miscellaneous office machines industry were a variety of specialty devices. Dictation machines, for instance, were used by professionals and executives, for whom certain jobs required the recording of their voices for later transcription. Depending on the features offered, dictaphones ranged in price from $150 to $2,500 in 1993.

Shredders, used to destroy internal printed documents, also accounted for a slim segment of the market. In the mid-1990s, personal shredders used by small companies and professional practices ranged widely in options and prices. Inexpensive shredders could be purchased for as little as $500, while larger shredders usually started at about $5,000 and industrial, full-featured shredders were available for as much as $100,000. The more expensive models featured conveyer belts and were capable of shredding boxes, metal binders, and entire wastebaskets.

The facsimile machine, or fax, was also an important and popular product in the industry. The fax scanned a document and produced electrical signals that were sent to another fax machine, which converted the signals into a copy of the original document. In the mid-1990s, the average large company sent 260 faxes per day, while mid-sized firms sent about 40 faxes per day.

A fifth major segment of the industry consisted of mailroom equipment. In fact, various mail machines accounted for about 25 percent of industry sales in 1992. Designed to meter, sort, and track mail, such machines were used by the postal service, as well as private organizations. While sorting machines could mean an initial cost of anywhere from $5,000 to $500,000, they greatly reduced the cost of sorting mail manually from $35 per thousand to less than $3 per thousand. The most advanced sorters utilized optical character recognition (OCR) to read addresses and USPS bar codes.

BACKGROUND AND DEVELOPMENT

The business machine industry emerged from the industrial revolution in the latter part of the nineteenth century. As the need to record and manage business information grew, several products, including the typewriter, were developed to meet demands. Although the typewriter was invented in 1714 by Henry Mill, a London engineer, the most famous devices were developed in the late 1800s. The Remington typewriter, first offered to the public in 1874, was one of the more popular early machines.

The first electromechanical typewriter was invented by Thomas Edison in 1872, though practical application of this device did not occur until the twentieth century. One of the first electric models, the Electromatic, was purchased by International Business Machines in 1933; after World War II, several other companies introduced electric typewriters. During the post-war era, the business machine industry flourished. A booming economy and new technology soon prompted the development of a plethora of labor-saving devices.

Although an early version of the facsimile machine was introduced in 1843 by Scottish inventor Alexander Bain, this device did not have any practical application in the United States until 1925. That year, the American Telephone & Telegraph Company introduced a wirephoto service. The following year, RCA opened the first transatlantic radiophoto circuit for commercial use, which used fax technology. Advances in production technology, which drastically reduced the price of fax machines, made the fax machine available to the general public during the late 1970s and 1980s.

While dictation machines also gained widespread public acceptance during the mid-1900s, the invention of the integrated circuit in the 1960s brought hand-held recording devices into the professional mainstream. Dictaphones remained the primary means of recording information for doctors, lawyers, and business executives throughout the 1970s and much of the 1980s. The advent of personal computers, notebook computers, and cellular telephone technology adversely affected sales of dictation equipment in the 1980s, and by the early 1990s, dictation machines were largely being replaced with machines featuring alternative technologies.

As increasingly inexpensive computer and cellular technology was rendering dictaphones and typewriters obsolete, many business machine companies struggled to adapt to evolving market demands.

Nevertheless, technological advances were opening new markets for other miscellaneous business machines, particularly postal equipment, in demand due to increased postal volume and new postal requirements for addresses.

CURRENT CONDITIONS

Shipments of miscellaneous business machines peaked in 1985 at over $5 billion. After that time, however, several factors combined to deflate revenues and profit margins for manufacturers. Most importantly, the popularity of superior computer technology was affecting revenues from industry staples such as typewriters and dictation equipment. Although business machine manufacturers countered with PWPs and other low-cost, higher technology products, computers threatened to eventually deplete the market for even those items.

At the same time that computers and cellular phones were making industry waves, the U.S. business machine market experienced an economic recession in the late 1980s. Revenues from miscellaneous business machines fell to about $3.2 billion in 1987. Although

sales picked up in 1988 and 1989, shipments only reached $3.5 to $4 billion per year before slumping again in the early 1990s. Reduced expenditures by large businesses were a primary cause for the decrease.

In addition to alternative technologies and the recession, manufacturers were also facing a more competitive market in the 1980s and early 1990s. Many products, such as typewriters and facsimile machines, had become low-cost commodity items that offered slim profit margins. In response to price competition from both domestic and foreign manufacturers, U.S. companies moved their production operations overseas or increased automation in domestic facilities. As a result, industry employment in the United States plummeted from about 45,000 in 1982 to about 30,000 in the early 1990s.

Industry Response. In response to inclement market conditions, manufacturers scrambled to buoy profits and remain competitive. Besides diverting investments into competing industries, such as computer-related office products, producers tailored product offerings to appeal to the growth market of the 1990s—small business.

In 1989, industry analysts predicted that 25 million home offices would exist by 1993. Instead, about 40 million home offices emerged, representing an increase in 1992 of 2.2 million. Furthermore, analysts anticipated that by 1995 some 42.5 million home offices would be in operation. Because the average home office spent $40 to $50 per week on business supplies, manufacturers were increasingly catering to this segment.

In an effort to reach small businesses and home office buyers, manufacturers were also adjusting their marketing and distribution strategies in the mid-1990s. While producers once sold products primarily through dedicated office device resellers, many companies were using 50 or more different types of retailers to move their equipment in the 1990s.

One of the fastest growing distribution channels during this time was the discount superstore and business center, such as Wal-Mart, Office Depot, and K-Mart. In 1993, manufacturers distributed an estimated seven to ten percent of their shipments through these retail chains, and some industry participants suggested that this figure would eventually exceed 20 or 30 percent. The number of U.S. office products superstores increased from 19 in 1988 to over 800 by 1993. Furthermore, sales of business equipment and supplies at these outlets grew from $230 million to about $3 billion by 1992, providing a viable channel for many manufacturers.

Manufacturers were also boosting sales by emphasizing distribution through equipment leasing companies. Many businesses favored the lease agreement in order to take advantage of changing technology and certain tax benefits. In addition, leasing allowed companies to reduce their capital equipment investment—an important point in the capital-starved environment of the 1990s.

Some manufacturers looked forward to increased sales in Mexico as a result of NAFTA, which was expected to increase capital spending in that nation. Furthermore, some competitors hoped to shore up their bottom line by moving manufacturing facilities south, where they could take advantage of inexpensive labor and a loosely regulated manufacturing environment.

INDUSTRY LEADERS

The largest supplier of miscellaneous business machines in the United States in 1992 was the Xerox Corp. of Connecticut. The company had sales of about $18 billion, most of which derived from business equipment classified in other industries, such as photocopiers. Pitney Bowes, also of Connecticut, placed second with sales of $3.2 billion in 1992, much of which was garnered from products outside the industry. Other large competitors included Toshiba America Information of California (with $900 million in sales and 1,800 employees), Simplex Time Recorder Co. of Massachusetts ($510 million), and Smith Corona Corp. of Connecticut ($493 million).

Employment by miscellaneous business equipment manufacturers, like employment in most other business equipment and computer-related industries, was expected to decline during the 1990s and into the next century. Advances in productivity and automation, outsourcing of manufacturing activities to foreign firms, and stagnation in demand for traditional equipment such as typewriters were likely to contribute to the decline.

Analysts predicted an employment decline of 20 to 50 percent among most manufacturers between 1993 and 2005. Electric and electronic assemblage positions, which accounted for ten percent of industry jobs in 1992, were expected to fall by about 55 percent. Similarly, positions for general assemblers and fabricators were projected to decline by nearly 40 percent.

Moreover, positions on the higher end of the pay scale, including those of engineer, technician, and management support, were expected to fall by four to 15 percent by 2005, and executive and managerial positions would likely decline by about 20 percent. On the other hand, experts speculated that sales jobs and computer programming positions would increase by about one percent, and information systems jobs, which accounted for 2.5 percent of total industry employment in 1993, would experience growth of about 44 percent by 2005.

RESEARCH AND TECHNOLOGY

Manufacturers sought to retain market share and revenues by delivering new products and technology in the early 1990s. PWPs represented efforts by typewriter companies to combat the dominance of PCs. New typewriters by Lexmark International Inc., a division of IBM, sought to combine the best features of typewriters and computers. Eight models introduced in late 1993 offered advanced text editing, long-term storage, and word processing features—functions which helped make typewriters the tool of choice for some activities like individual envelope typing, invoicing, and labeling.

Competitors were also improving fax machines, often combining the functions of copiers, electronic mail, scanners, and computers into a single unit. In 1993, Sharp Electronics introduced the first two-sided, or duplex, fax machine, which could scan, collate, and fax a set of two-sided documents. Major advances were also occurring in the large postal machine market. Datatech, for instance, offered a new machine in 1993 designed to address business envelopes with Delivery Point Barcodes—a feature that helped reduce postal rates.

INDUSTRY INFORMATION SOURCES

"Buyers Find Savings by Leasing Equipment," *Purchasing,* August 19, 1993.

Carbonara, Joseph, "Home Office Market: Has it Delivered?," *Office Products Distribution,* May 1993.

Cosgrove, Nancy Dunn, "The Paperless Office: Still a Myth in the Nineties," *The Office,* April 1993.

Cosgrove, Nancy, "Typewriters Adapt: They're Here to Stay," *The Office,* January 1993.

Gragg, Ellen, "Shredders Give Protection from Espionage and Gossip," *Office Systems,* July 1993.

Johnson, Leone, "Dictation Machines Seek to Specialize," *The Office,* January 1993.

LeGallee, Julie, "Typewriters: Are Computers Driving Them to Pasture," *The Office,* August 1993.

"Low Cost Printer Does #10 Envelopes," *Purchasing,* July 15, 1993.

"New Typewriter Complements PC Office Environment," *Purchasing,* September 23, 1993.

"Range of Equipment to Meet USPS Rules," *Purchasing,* September 23, 1993.

Sopko, Sandra, "The Well-Connected, Efficient & High-Tech," *The Office,* September 1993.

Thomas, Howard, and David Stockwell, "Office Products Marketing: The Next Generation," *Office Products Distribution,* May 1993.

"Use of Plain Paper Faxes Rise," *Purchasing,* July 15, 1993.

—Dave Mote

SIC 3581

AUTOMATIC VENDING MACHINES

This industry consists of establishments primarily engaged in manufacturing automatic vending machines and coin-operated mechanisms for such machines.

INDUSTRY SNAPSHOT

Over $26 billion worth of merchandise was purchased from automatic vending machines in the United States in 1992. That figure does not include revenue from non-merchandise vending machines, such as games or laundry equipment. That year, about 4.5 million vending machines were in operation across the United States. In 1990, manufacturers' shipments of automatic vending machines had a total value of $741.7 million. About 72 percent of that total, or $524.6 million, came from coin-operated machines. The remainder of products shipped were primarily coin-operated mechanisms and parts for vending machines. In 1992, 704,394 coin-operated vending machines were built. Beverage machines and snack machines were the most common, making up about equal shares of the total manufactured, with snack machines leading slightly in quantity, and the more expensive beverage machines leading in shipment value.

ORGANIZATION AND STRUCTURE

Vending was essentially a three step process involving three separate industries: manufacturing companies, distributors, and vending machine operators. SIC 3581 covers only the manufacturing step in this multi-stage industrial sequence.

About 90 U.S. companies produced automatic vending machines or parts for them in 1993. Although a vast majority of vending machines were manufactured by large companies, the industry did sustain quite a few smaller firms. In 1990, 24 companies with fewer than five employees were in operation. Another 33 companies had between five and 19 employees, while 22 companies employed anywhere from 20 to 250 workers. Geographically, California and Illinois had the highest concentrations in the industry, with 17 and 14 establishments respectively.

The U.S. Department of Commerce counted 47 companies engaged in manufacturing coin-operated vending machines in 1992. Of these, 14 produced beverage machines, 18 made machines that sold food and confections, and 32 manufactured other types of vending machines, including those selling cigarettes, water, and postage stamps. Canned and bottled soft drink machines made up by far the largest share of beverage machines manufactured, totaling 221,804 units in 1992. Among confection and food vending machines, those that sold bulk confections and charms predominated, totaling 151,870 shipped in 1992. Bagged snacks and confections made up another significant share at 86,539.

The National Automatic Merchandising Association (NAMA) was the most important trade organization in the vending industry in the 1990s. The NAMA represented companies involved in every facet of vending, from machine manufacturers to suppliers of vended products. Founded in 1936, the NAMA compiled a broad range of statistics and produced several periodic publications, including a regular industry newsletter, a review of pertinent state legislation, and a labor issues bulletin. Headquartered in Chicago, the organization had 2,400 members, 32 state groups, and an annual budget of about $2.5 million in 1993.

The National Bulk Vendors Association (NBVA) concentratrd specifically on the manufacture and operation of bulk vending equipment, such as machines that distribute a handful of peanuts. The NBVA was founded in 1949 and was also based in Chicago.

BACKGROUND AND DEVELOPMENT

The idea of the vending machine has existed since at least 215 B.C., when the mathematician Hero described and illustrated a number of inventions conceived by himself and his teacher, Tesibius, in a book called *Pneumatika*. Included in the book was the plan for a completely automatic coin-operated machine that dispensed a small amount of sacrificial water when a five-drachma coin was deposited. It is unlikely that the machine was used on a large scale, and there is no evidence to suggest that anything was sold automatically again for centuries.

Coin-operated machines that sold snuff and tobacco began to appear in English taverns around 1615. These machines were actually cruder than Hero's device and required the proprietor to shut the lid after each use. Usually made of brass, the machines were portable and were carried from customer to customer.

In the nineteenth century, vending machines began to appear in much greater variety and quantity. An early incarnation of the newspaper machine appeared in England in 1822. The device was the brainchild of Richard Carlile, a bookseller trying to avoid arrest for peddling copies of banned works such as Thomas Paine's *The Age of Reason.* While his machine worked, he didn't escape arrest.

The first known patent for a vending machine was issued in 1857 to Simeon Denham for a penny postage stamp device. Over the next couple of decades, inventors began showing up at patent offices all over the world with coin-operated machines that sold candy, cigarettes, handkerchiefs, and other small items. In 1884, the first U.S. vending machine patent was issued to W. H. Fruen for a contraption remarkably similar to Hero's holy water machine.

The American vending machine industry was truly born in 1888, when Thomas Adams of the Adams Gum Company began selling his Tutti-Frutti gum out of machines on the platforms of New York's elevated rail system. These machines were an immediate success, and towards the end of the century, postage stamp machines also became more common. The Automatic Machine Company of Buffalo, New York, was the first company to sell stamps automatically on a large scale, beginning in 1891. Bulk vending machines began to appear around the turn of the century. The Mills Novelty Company introduced the first of these, which sold a pre-set amount of peanuts for a penny, at the Pan American Exposition in 1901. The following year, the Horn & Hardart Baking Company revolutionized vending in the United States by opening its first Automat restaurant in Philadelphia.

Prior to 1908, beverage vending machines dispensed only the beverages themselves, which the customer then drank out of a common cup. That year, with public awareness of sanitation growing, the Public Cup Vendor Company of New York (later to become the Dixie Cup Company) unveiled a machine that dispensed water in individual paper cups.

By the 1920s, the vending industry had been divided into manufacturers and operators. The Doehler Die Casting company, for example, developed machines for vending a diverse range of products that included Life Savers, lighter fluid, and sanitary napkins. Another industry revolution took place in 1925, when three new machines were developed, all of which sold cigarettes. Candy machines that offered customers a choice of products began to spread in the

1930s. Nathaniel Leverone, the founder of the Canteen Company, was a pioneer in the development of this type of machine.

The manufacture of vending machines was suspended during World War II, but at the war's conclusion the industry regained its momentum. Among the machines that appeared during this time were the first hot coffee venders and a hot dog machine. In the first decade after World War II, hundreds of small manufacturing companies entered the vending machine arena, and vast improvements were made in design, especially in the area of coin mechanisms. In 1960, paper money changers came into widespread use. When machines for vending canned soft drinks were introduced in 1961, vending sales soared.

Since 1960, the vending machine industry has been consolidating to a great degree. Manufacturing has become increasingly dominated by large companies. At the same time, advances in electronic components, which first appeared in vending machines in 1980, have made machines "smarter," enabling them to keep records and diagnose glitches. The variety of products vended automatically has continued to grow explosively, as items specifically created for machine vending, such as microwave popcorn, have made their appearances.

CURRENT CONDITIONS

In the early 1990s, vending machine manufacturing appeared to be entering a new era. The emergence of "smart" machines was certain to affect every part of the industry. The availability of full-service machines that could handle a variety of products and perform their own record keeping was enabling bottling companies to take over many of the chores that were previously handed over to third party operators. This represented the reversal of a trend that began in the 1950s, when bottlers began to remove themselves from the day-to-day servicing of machines. In addition, the replacement of moving parts by electronic components was expected to contribute to a further concentration of manufacturing companies, since the demand for spare parts was sure to decline sharply.

The new generation of smart vending machines was also expected to give manufacturers a healthy boost. Since the beginning of the 1990s, the slumping U.S. economy had led operators to seek ways to hold their costs in check. Frequently, this meant refurbishing old machines rather than purchasing new ones. Dixie-Narco Inc., for example, saw its sales drop by about 18 percent in 1990, while its parts business was actually more active than usual. The improved security and record keeping capabilities offered by newer machines, and their potential to save operators money in the long-run, might provide operators an incentive to invest in the latest equipment.

Several other profound changes were taking place in the vending industry in the 1990s. Some resulted from new technology, while others stemmed more directly from changes taking place in American society in general. New machines developed during this time were capable of vending food of much higher quality than was previously possible. This ability was having a particularly noticeable effect in the workplace, as corporate downsizing necessitated the replacement of many company cafeterias by vending areas. With a new emphasis on hot, nutritious foods, the major manufacturers began producing machines to sell such items as French fries, fresh pizza slices, and a much broader line of microwaveable frozen foods.

The sharp decline in cigarette smoking in the United States in the early 1990s also had a dramatic impact on the vending industry. Once a huge seller as one of the four C's of vending (cold drinks, candy, confections, and cigarettes), cigarettes generated only 5.7 percent of vending operators' revenue in 1993, compared with 45.5 percent in 1960.

Inflation in the 1990s affected the vending industry adversely as well. The convenience of dropping coins into a machine in exchange for merchandise disappeared when the price of an item exceeded the amount of change reasonably accommodated in a pocket. Manufacturers reacted to this problem in two ways. One involved the introduction of debit cards, which first appeared in 1985. Debit cards eliminated the need to carry change, enabling regular users of a vending area to pre-pay for several dollars worth of merchandise at a time. Mechanized dollar bill acceptors, notoriously fussy and uncooperative, had also improved somewhat by the mid-1990s. The other angle from which the industry attacked the inflation problem was by lobbying for the reintroduction of a dollar coin. The issue of such a coin would probably benefit the vending industry immensely, especially given the growing presence of upscale items like cappuccino in vending machines.

INDUSTRY LEADERS

Dixie-Narco Inc., a division of Maytag Corporation, was the nation's leading manufacturer of automatic vending machines in 1993. Founded in 1957 and headquartered in Williston, South Carolina, Dixie-Narco employed 1,230 workers, and reported annual sales of about $150 million in 1993. Rowe International Inc. of Whippany, New Jersey, was a privately-held company with annual sales of $99 million and about 1,200 employees, and IMI Cornelius Inc.—a subsidiary of IMI PLC—had annual sales of $89 million and employed 725. Other large vending machine manufacturers included Mars Inc. Electronics International ($67 million), the machine manufacturing arm of candy giant Mars Inc.; and Crane Co. National Vendors of Bridgeton, Missouri ($65 million).

WORK FORCE

Employment in the vending machine manufacturing industry declined from 1984-94. In 1990, about 7,500 workers were employed in the industry. The total payroll for its work force that year was about $181 million. At its peak in 1984, 8,300 people worked in the industry, earning a total payroll of $157 million. In 1990, the industry had 5,200 production workers, whose average hourly wage was $9.62. Among the occupations most frequently employed by the vending industry were machine assemblers, sheet metal workers, machine tool cutting and forming workers, and welders.

AMERICA AND THE WORLD

The United States was not alone in its obsession with the convenience offered by vending machines. Industry leader Dixie-Narco, for example, was selling a complete line of models in over 30 countries by 1990. The company began to emphasize exports even more around that time, tailoring machines for the specific needs of its foreign markets rather than merely making small adjustments in its existing models.

The popularity of the vending machine proved even stronger in Japan. Half of Japan's $24 billion in retail soft drink sales in 1990 came through vending machines, and this market share was expected to increase. In Japan, the machines lined the sidewalks, playing music and offering a wide variety of merchandise, including beer, sushi, and panty hose. One advantage that vending operators in Japan had over their American counterparts was that vandalism was almost unheard of in that country in the 1990s.

The enthusiasm for vended goods was not global, however. Although American manufacturers sold machines successfully in Europe for years, the machines were not always welcome. Café proprietors in Bordeaux, France, for example, refused to serve Coca Cola for a period in 1990 in protest of the placement of 60 Coke machines on public sidewalks in their city— an offense to both their sense of good taste and fair competition.

RESEARCH AND TECHNOLOGY

Flexibility and security are two areas in which engineers in the vending industry were making great strides. The Merlin 2000 series developed by a company called InterBev in 1989 provided a good example of the flexibility built into the new generation of vending machines. The Merlin 2000 machines could sell both soda and juice from one machine, with an improved mechanism for adjusting prices from one selection to the next.

Furthermore, electronic bill and coin changing mechanisms made fraud much more difficult, since they were harder to fool than the old systems. One common form of vandalism—the injection of salt water into coin mechanisms, which put some machines into a ''jackpot'' mode by shorting out electronic parts—was circumvented by an improved shielding of components. Programmable security code devices were also being installed on many new machines to prevent unauthorized individuals from tampering with pricing and from removing money or merchandise. Other new security measures included locking money bags and heavier doors that were more resistant to vandalism.

Since the reliability of equipment often determines an operator's profitability, manufacturers continued to look for ways to reduce the need for service on their machines. Vendo Co., for example, unveiled a machine called UniVendor in 1990. With half as many moving parts as other models, Vendo's UniVendor was able to simplify maintenance by reducing the margin for error.

State-of-the-art technology led to the appearance of a huge range of specialized vending machines at trade shows in the 1990s. Many of these machines sold food that was cooked right in the machine. French fry machines, for example, used a special hot-air cooking process, and pizza machines not only cooked the pizza fresh using infrared heat, but also automatically called the manufacturer when a malfunction occurred. Other innovations included a machine that printed business cards automatically and one that vended pre-peeled oranges.

INDUSTRY INFORMATION SOURCES

Batdorf, Tracey L., ''Vending: Money Making Machines Keep Improving,'' *Beverage Industry,* May 1990.

Brotman, Barbara, ''Demand for Quality Exacts Change from Vending Industry,'' *Chicago Tribune,* October 8, 1993.

Colmer, Michael, *The Great Vending Machine Book,* Chicago: Contemporary Books, 1977.

Current Industrial Reports: Vending Machines (Coin-Operated), Washington, D.C.: U.S. Department of Commerce, 1993.

Fitzell, Phil, ''Opening the Floodgates,'' *Beverage World,* January 1990.

Fitzell, Phil, ''Whistlin' Dixie,'' *Beverage World,* October 1991.

Hall, Trish, ''Vending Machines: The Next Generation in Dining,'' *New York Times,* September 9, 1992.

Henry, Anne, ''High-Tech Vending,'' *Appliance,* December 1991.

Remich, Norman C., Jr., ''Coin to Replace $1 Bill?'' *Appliance Manufacturer,* July 1992.

Schreiber, G. R., *Automatic Selling,* New York: John Wiley & Sons, 1954.

Schreiber, G. R., *A Concise History of Vending in the U.S.A.,* Chicago: National Automatic Merchandising Association, 1990.

Sfiligoj, Eric, and Laurie MacDonald, ''Splendor in the Vendor,'' *Beverage World,* February 1992.

Tanzer, Andrew, ''War of the Sales Robots,'' *Forbes,* January 7, 1991.

Walker, Tracey L., ''Defending Your Vendors,'' *Beverage Industry,* January 1991.

Woutat, Donald, ''Sizzlers in the Vending Machine,'' *Los Angeles Times,* November 22, 1990.

—Robert R. Jacobson

SIC 3582

COMMERCIAL LAUNDRY EQUIPMENT

The Commercial Laundry, Dry Cleaning, and Pressing Machine Industry encompasses companies primarily engaged in manufacturing nonresidential laundry equipment. Coin-operated machines are classified in **SIC 3633: Household Laundry Equipment Industry.**

The largest product group in this industry is washers and extractors, which account for almost 40 percent of sales. Commercial dryers and presses make up about 16 percent and 11 percent, respectively, of output. Dry cleaning equipment accounts for an additional 11 percent of production, while parts, attachments, and miscellaneous equipment represent the remainder of sales.

Hotels, hospitals, and contract laundry services that serve commercial and institutional customers were the biggest consumers of commercial laundry equipment in the early 1990s. Dry cleaners represented about 17 percent of the market. Government institutions, including the armed services, prisons, schools, and hospitals, bought about 11 percent of industry output, and 12 percent of production was exported.

Maytag Corp. introduced the first electric washing machine in 1907. Not until the 1950s, however, did commercial laundry equipment producers achieve widespread market penetration. The proliferation of hotels, hospitals, and government institutions during the post-World War II U.S. economic boom pushed industry revenues to almost $300 million per year by the end of the 1970s. Continued growth in demand during the 1980s, particularly in hotel and hospital markets, increased sales to $587 million by 1988.

The commercial laundry industry faltered in the late 1980s and early 1990s as recession gripped the U.S. economy. Sales plummeted to $480 million during 1989 and bobbed up to only $526 million in 1990. Although commercial construction markets remained sluggish in the early and mid-1990s, increased sales to institutional consumers helped some manufacturers stabilize their earnings. An increase in new construction in 1993 and 1994, moreover, partially renewed industry optimism.

Manufacturers in the mid-1990s were striving to boost profits by building machines that were more energy efficient, conserved water, and offered more features. Pellerin Milnor Corp., for example, introduced a valve that allowed commercial washing machines to reuse water. Speed Queen designed a line of commercial laundry machines that took more time, effort, and noise to steal. The machines also increased dryer airflow and allowed easier loading and servicing.

The largest U.S. company primarily engaged in the production of commercial laundry equipment in the early 1990s was Pellerin Milnor Corp., of Louisiana. Pellerin had sales of $100 million in 1991 and employed about 800 workers. Cissell Manufacturing Co., of Kentucky, was the second largest competitor. It boasted revenues of $40 million and had about 400 employees. Other major players included Unimac Company Inc., of Florida, and American Dryer Corp., of Massachusetts. Approximately 70 companies were included in the industry in the early 1990s.

Although sales and unit shipments grew by more than 50 percent during the 1980s, industry employment rose less than 10 percent, to about 5,200. Industry consolidation, company restructuring, manufacturing productivity gains, and the movement of production facilities to Mexico all contributed to stagnant job growth. Employment in this industry should decline considerably during the 1990s, as more manufacturers

move south of the border and productivity rises. Most positions, in fact, should decline by 15 percent to 40 percent between 1990 and 2005, according to the Bureau of Labor Statistics.

INDUSTRY INFORMATION SOURCES

Colliers Encyclopedia, New York: P.F. Collier, Inc., 1988.

Darnay, Arsen J., ed., *Manufacturing USA; Industry Analyses, Statistics, and Leading Companies,* Detroit: Gale Research Inc., 1993.

"Laundry Suppliers Move to Improve Savings, Efficiency," *Hotel & Motel Management,* November 22, 1993.

Remich, Norman C. Jr., "Maytag at 100," *Appliance Manufacturer,* November 1993.

Remich, Norman C., Jr., "Security One Key to Commercial Line," *Appliance Manufacturer,* May 1993.

Remich, Norman C. Jr., "Shipments Show Strength," *Appliance Manufacturer,* November 1993.

—Dave Mote

SIC 3585

REFRIGERATION AND HEATING EQUIPMENT

This category includes establishments primarily engaged in the manufacture of commercial or industrial refrigeration equipment or domestic, commercial, or industrial air conditioning units. Other equipment manufactured under this classification includes warm air furnaces, humidifiers and dehumidifiers, soda fountains, and beer dispensing machines. Some equipment not covered by this category household refrigerators and freezers, and electric space heaters and portable humidifiers and dehumidifiers.

INDUSTRY SNAPSHOT

A trip to the local supermarket provides graphic evidence of the importance of the heating, refrigeration and air conditioning industry (HVAC) on modern American society. Many of the products found in the air-conditioned aisles, like fresh fruits or live fish, could never have been transported without cooling technology. The Air Conditioning and Refrigeration Institute (ARI) estimates that more than three-fourths of all foods consumed by Americans have been produced, packaged, shipped, stored, or preserved by refrigeration. Temperature control systems have also become common in shopping malls, commercial office buildings, and hospitals. In 1992, 77 percent of all new houses in the United States were built with central air conditioning.

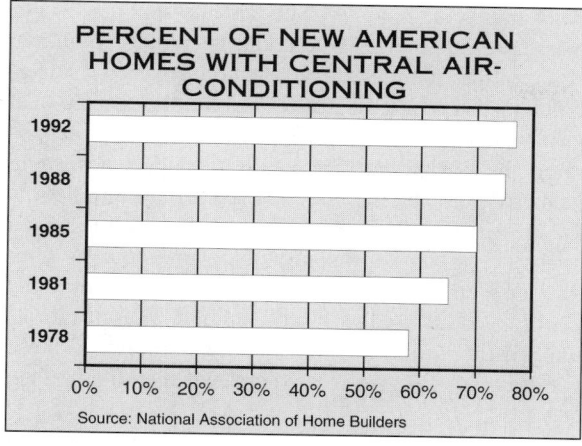

PERCENT OF NEW AMERICAN HOMES WITH CENTRAL AIR-CONDITIONING

Source: National Association of Home Builders

BACKGROUND AND DEVELOPMENT

Until the industrial revolution, refrigeration depended on the natural mediums of ice, snow, and water. The early Chinese harvested winter ice and packed it in dried straw for use in the summer. The Egyptians used porous earthenware jugs placed on their rooftops at night to cool their liquid contents by the natural process of evaporation. Since changing a liquid to a gas requires a considerable amount of heat energy, the liquid remaining in the containers became much cooler by morning. During colonial times, the ice hut was a familiar part of the landscape. It used the Chinese concept of harvesting ice to preserve food during the summer. Well into the 1800s, Americans sold ice to foreign countries as a natural refrigerant. The periodic home deliveries of ice were a commonplace experience for most Americans during the early part of the twentieth century.

The first attempts to find an industrial method to duplicate and improve on nature came in 1748 from Dr. William Cullen of Scotland. However, Dr. John Gorrie, director of the U.S. Marine Hospital at Apalachicola, Florida built the first commercial machine, receiving U.S. Patent 8080 for it in 1851. By 1880, the fledgling industry had developed reciprocating compressors which made possible such things as commercial ice making, brewing, meat packing and fish processing. In 1904, 70 of the pioneers formed the American Society of Refrigeration Engineers, officially creating a new profession.

In 1911, Willis H. Carrier presented the mathematical bases for the now-standard psychometric charts, which define the theoretical properties of heat transfer through air. This advancement and his later work earned Carrier the title of "the father of air-conditioning." In 1922, he invented the centrifugal refrigeration compressor. During World War II, he contributed to the building of a 10,000,000 cubic foot wind tunnel which could be cooled to -67 degrees Fahrenheit. The most notable use of the new air-conditioning technology was in the motion picture theaters of the 1920s. New York City theaters, including the Rivoli, Paramount, Roxy, and Lowe's in Times Square, lead the innovation. By the end of the decade hundreds of theaters across the country offered a controlled climate along with their feature film.

The heating industry refined the early concept of the open fire by enclosing the fire with brick or stone structures equipped with chimneys. These dirty and inefficient first efforts generally heated only the room they occupied but could also be used for cooking and provided a central focus to the household. Throughout the nineteenth century, developments in metallurgy

However, high interest rates and a sluggish economy slowed new construction in the late 1980s and early 1990s. The slowdown in construction softened the demand for new heating, refrigeration, and air conditioning equipment, but spurred the repair and upgrade replacement segment of the industry. Much of the housing built in the 1950s, 1960s, and 1970s needed replacement equipment since the average domestic furnace or air conditioner had a useful life of twenty years. Many American power utilities promoted energy conservation and higher efficiency upgrades. These activities held industry shipments in 1991 to about $18 billion (expressed in 1987 dollars).

The Clean Air Act of 1990, which introduced extensive air-quality standards and the incremental reduction and eventual banning of chlorofluorocarbons (CFCs) by the year 2000, challenged the industry to improve its technology. The challenge caused uncertainty in the industry as new systems were developed, using chemicals which were not compatible with the old refrigerants. In the early 1990s, the fear of products becoming obsolete caused the industry to stagnate, while alternative refrigerants were researched.

The number of firms in the industry rose slowly in the 1980s from 730 companies operating 865 establishments in 1982 to 736 operating 865 in 1987. Of those companies, the largest seven accounted for 72 percent of the U.S. market, according to *Market Share Reporter*. Worldwide, the largest twelve international manufacturers split 66 percent of the market in 1990, continuing a trend noted by the *Monthly Labor Review*, which observed an intensification of market share concentration between 1963 and 1977. In 1977, the eight largest companies shared 51 percent of the industry's total shipments.

and forging promoted the use of remote water boilers attached to radiators by metal piping. These sturdy contrivances often used layers of asbestos to retain the heat in the water.

The warm-air furnace reduced the cost of heating, making the concept of central heating more available. Early systems were usually coal-fired, cast-iron machines that filled whole basements. They distributed the heat by means of "gravity" through large metal ducts attached to ornate grills in floors and walls. Like any other material when heated, air becomes lighter and tends to be pushed upwards by the cooler air surrounding it. The gravity is actually "working" on the cooler air, pushing it down to displace the lighter warm air. Later, electric fans attached to the heaters created the first forced-air systems. Cast-iron heaters have been replaced by compact sheet-metal cabinets, which contain burner, blower, and filter.

Burning Alternatives. A more integral change occurred in the fuel being burned. The early machines used coal or even wood or charcoal. Such material required large storage areas and considerable labor in feeding the furnace and cleaning out the burnt residue of cinders and ash. The fire produced great amounts of air pollution in the form of sooty smoke and smog. London's famous pea-soup fogs of Victorian days disappeared when the British parliament banned the burning of coal within the city limits.

The first technological revolution in modern heating fuel technology came with the use of fuel oil as a replacement for coal. The Gilbert and Barker company claim to have produced the first industrial oil burner in North America in 1889, but patents for several burners were not issued until 1892. These early machines were often called range burners because they were primarily used for the kitchen stove. New heat resistant metals made the use of fuel oil as a furnace fuel both practical and desirable by the late 1920s. That began a shift in consumer fuel preference which virtually eliminated coal as a domestic fuel by the late 1950s. A second fuel revolution came with the OPEC oil embargoes of the 1970s. Once cheap and plentiful, fuel oil quickly rose in price and scientists began predicting a world-wide oil shortage and depletion of reserves by the year 2000. To compensate, the industry shifted to domestically-available natural gas and, to some extent, electricity. By 1992, with the cost of generating electricity escalating, natural gas became the clear preference of most American consumers, reaching a market penetration of 65 percent, according to the *Detroit Free Press.*

Modern refrigeration and air conditioning work on essentially the same principle. Both collect heat from one area and transfer it to another where it dissi-

pates into some medium. The basic system consists of a compressor driven by an electric motor and two coils. In the first coil, called the condenser, the refrigerant gas is compressed into a liquid, discharging heat as it changes state. In the second coil, called the evaporator, the refrigerant becomes a gas again, absorbing heat from outside the coil. The essential ingredient is the refrigerant gas. Early refrigerant materials included air, water, butane, propane, ether, ammonia, sulphur dioxide and methyl chloride. Some, like ammonia, continue to be used in large commercial applications like skating rinks and ice factories. Many of these materials were highly toxic, corrosive, and flammable.

In 1930, Thomas Midgely of the DuPont Company developed the first fluorocarbon refrigerant and demonstrated his faith in its safety at a company press conference by inhaling a stream of the gas and blowing out a candle with it. In 1956, the industry adopted DuPont's numbering system for all fluorocarbon refrigerants. The most common used in the 1990s were the chlorofluorocarbons R-12 for automotive and appliance applications and R-502 for commercial and industrial applications. A second generation of refrigerant compound displaced CFCs in many applications. The hydrochlorofluorocarbon (HCFC) R-22 dominated the domestic central air conditioning market and was gaining popularity for some commercial applications.

Until 1953, water remained the most common cooling medium for air conditioning and refrigeration. Systems of that day used municipal water supplies or cooling towers, making the technology difficult for most domestic applications. The introduction of air-cooled systems in 1953, followed by the now-familiar split-system, launched the concept of controlled cooling into national acceptance. By 1973, 75 percent of industry sales were residential units. The development of electrically activated refrigerant reversing valves allowed cooling systems to be used for heating as well. The heat pump concept pioneered in the 1960s exchanged the functions of the two coils, as the evaporator became the condenser and the condenser acted as an evaporator. The systems scavenged usable heat out of the fall and winter air and pumped it into the building. Early models operated inefficiently in unsuitable climates, earning the technology a bad reputation with consumers. In 1960, only 28 percent of new homes were installed with central air conditioning, but by 1992, the technology was included in 77 percent of new homes.

The technology sparked development of the commercial rooftop combination heating and cooling unit. Placing the heating and cooling equipment in a single box on the roof freed up valuable commercial space and simplified servicing and installation. In addition, improvements in compressor design, particularly the hermetic or sealed compressor, allowed the size and capacity of industrial refrigeration machines to increase and spurred the advancement of the chiller systems that dominated the large building and industrial markets.

CURRENT CONDITIONS

The 1990s marked a decade of revolutionary change for the HVAC industry. By 1990, the American economy was experiencing a severe recession with only dim prospects for recovery over the following five years. New housing construction dropped to an eight-year low and dragged furnace and air conditioner sales with them. Foreign manufacturers, especially the Japanese, were commandeering increasing market share worldwide with innovative products that threatened to displace American designs. Office building operators across the country were reporting cases of "sick-building syndrome," in which workers developed debilitating symptoms from a build-up of pollution levels in sealed, air conditioned buildings. In 1993, Congress passed a new energy bill which mandated higher efficiency standards for heating and air conditioning appliances and promised to make the requirements stricter in 1998. But the event most devastating to the HVAC industry was the discovery of a seven-million-square-kilometer hole in the ozone layer above the south pole, and the scientific evidence which linked that phenomenon to the release of chlorofluorocarbons (CFCs) into the atmosphere. That revelation threatened the basic component of the HVAC industry. Midgley's supposedly safe refrigerant, around which the industry was designed, had become an unacceptable pollutant.

Global Warming and Ozone Depletion. The first rumblings of environmental damage started with the British scientist, James Lovelock. In 1973, Lovelock wrote that carbon dioxide and CFCs in the atmosphere created a "greenhouse" effect by trapping heat in the lower atmosphere. Although few scientists argued the physics, the expected warming did not materialize as predicted. Other factors intervened, making it clear that the atmosphere and its energy transmission characteristics were too complicated to be fully understood as of yet. In 1991, the National Oceanic & Atmospheric Administration noted that historic temperature readings indicated a consistent rise in night time minimum temperatures. University of Virginia climatologist Patrick J. Michaels saw that as a positive trend. "If the nights warm up," he said in *Science &*

Technology, "the growing season will be longer. Instead of apocalypse, we may end up with a more beneficial climate." By 1992, the *ASHRAE Journal* discounted CFC's direct role in global warming, but it cautioned that refrigerant systems in general contribute indirectly through the energy they consume. Vicki Norberg-Bohm noted in *Environment* that energy consumption in domestic and commercial buildings accounts for 34 percent of American carbon dioxide emissions.

The depletion of the ozone layer presented a more immediately serious problem. First noted in 1973 by British scientist Sherry Rowland, the phenomenon threatened to undermine the food chain by killing off basic marine creatures with overdoses of ultraviolet radiation normally intercepted by ozone in the atmosphere. The rising radiation could also cause an epidemic of skin cancer. The essential problem is the chlorine component of the CFC. Chlorine atoms destroy ozone molecules in the high atmosphere through a complicated series of chemical reactions. Each chlorine atom destroys one ozone molecule every minute for about one year.

In 1973, the industrial world was dumping almost one megaton of CFCs into the atmosphere every year. CFC production was a $2-billion-a-year business. Its leaders resisted the scientific theories, calling for extensive studies and time to develop replacement materials. Eventually Sweden, Norway, and Canada banned CFCs used in aerosol cans, but nothing further happened until the British Antarctic Survey discovered a hole in the ozone layer half the size of Antarctica. In 1987, 24 industrialized countries signed the Montreal Protocol, calling for a 50-percent reduction in CFC production by the year 2000.

In June 1990, the protocol timetable was amended. CFC production in developed nations was banned by the year 2000 but developing nations could continue to produce them until 2010. As a temporary replacement refrigerant, hydrochlorofluorocarbons (HCFC) were scheduled for phase-out in 2030. This answered a concern by developing nations that the ban would work to the advantage of European and American firms who had the money to invest in alternative refrigerant technology. Manufacturers in those two regions produced two-thirds of the world's CFCs at that time.

Also in 1990, the refrigeration industry petitioned the Environmental Protection Agency to develop and issue uniform national recycling standards and requirements in anticipation of the large quantities of old refrigerant which would need to be removed from refurbished machinery. In 1992, ARI estimated the existing stock of refrigeration and air conditioning equipment in the United States exceeded $135 billion. In February, 1992, President George Bush reset the Montreal Protocol timetable, moving its requirements ahead by four years and calling for other nations to follow suit.

The problem for the industry revolved around finding a suitable replacement refrigerant which could be produced quickly enough to meet the phase-out schedule. To make the ban effective, that technology would have to be shared with developing nations in order to persuade them not to continue building their own CFC industry. Refrigerant engineers looked for chemical combinations which were not flammable, corrosive, or toxic and which would operate reasonably well in existing equipment. The lubricants in the old systems had to be compatible with the new gases and in some cases new lubricants had to be found. In addition, the new designs had to meet the higher energy efficiency standards of 1993. Most of the new chemicals worked reasonably well but not as efficiently as CFCs. That meant other equipment redesigns were needed to meet the necessary efficiency ratings. The research and new technology added to the cost of the machinery at a time when sales of refrigeration equipment were at best stagnant. Moreover, another round of higher energy requirements were slated to go into effect in 1998, but the industry could not build towards that higher target because the standard was still being developed in 1993.

The process of replacing CFCs required a shift to HCFC-22, which was the only proven substitute for CFC refrigerants in 1993. Other HCFCs were being developed for release later in the decade. At the same time, chlorine free alternatives were coming off the drawing board, notably DuPont's "Suva" HP62 (HFC) which, in 1993, appeared to be an excellent, zero-ozone-depleting alternative to R-502, the most common industrial refrigerant. Equipment manufacturers were redesigning compressors to match the characteristics of the new gases. However, HCFC was a stop-gap, an attempt to abandon CFCs as quickly as possible while developing the third generation refrigerant to answer all the environmental and technical challenges.

A hasty decision on an appropriate alternative could be expensive and prove a risk to consumers. One chemical under consideration for use in home refrigerators and window air conditioners in 1992 was R-152A (difluoroethane). The EPA was considering mandating its use in place of R-12 because its alternative, R-134A, was itself a mild greenhouse gas. DuPont, which had invested heavily in a R-134A pro-

duction facility, opposed the use of R-152A because that gas was extremely flammable. Its tests showed a leak from the soft copper or plastic refrigerant tubing could turn the appliance into an incendiary bomb under certain circumstances. In the 1990s, modern HVAC systems were designed to isolate the indoor environment from an increasingly polluted urban world. With the rising cost of energy after the OPEC oil shocks, consumers sought to minimize consumption through energy conservation. The first and most obvious method was to tighten homes and buildings to prevent heat loss through the use of insulation and thermal window glass. In some cases, overzealous efforts had deadly consequences when the structures became too tight and the heating equipment burned up all the available oxygen. Instead of air, the occupants found they were breathing high concentrations of carbon dioxide or, even more deadly, carbon monoxide. In 1986, the Consumer Products Safety Commission reported that more than 200 Americans died each year from carbon monoxide poisoning in their homes. To combat the problem the industry promoted sealed combustion appliances, high-efficiency, chimney-less furnaces and outside-air-intake devices called make-up-air units.

In large buildings the problem surfaced as the "sick-building syndrome," first noted in the 1970s. Workers complained of tiredness, headaches, eye and respiratory-tract irritations, excessive colds, and dry, itchy skin. Investigators discovered air-borne asbestos particles, bacteria, chemicals, carcinogenic tobacco residues and fungus in the forced air systems. The EPA reported the presence of asbestos in 733,000 public and commercial buildings in 1988. Legionnaires disease developed from bacteria carried by aerosols in ventilation systems. As with the atmospheric environment, the building micro-environment was a complicated system requiring careful scientific evaluation and monitoring to keep it safe for human occupation.

The American HVAC market of the 1990s was saturated. New construction had slowed, and older housing, commercial, and industrial buildings were already retrofitted with HVAC systems. Much of this equipment was aging and needed replacing by the mid-1990s. In the housing sector, replacement work reached 60 percent of the domestic market in 1991. For the commercial segment, that share was over 45 percent. The effect on the industry was a shift away from dependance on the cyclical construction industry to a more stable and long-cycled replacement industry.

INDUSTRY LEADERS

At the close of World War II, America's clear leader in the HVAC industry was Carrier Corp., which held 90 percent of the market. By the 1990s, Carrier Corp., by then a subsidiary of United Technologies Corp., no longer held a stable lead in the industry. Decades of under-investment in research and development, poor quality control, and inconsistent dealer relations coupled with a decision to terminate its marketing agreement with the department store giant, Sears Roebuck and Co., cut Carrier's market share to 37 percent in 1991. The company began to fight back by selling off unrelated business ventures, trimming white collar workers and concentrating on new product development. It targeted 75 percent of its product line for replacement with high-tech innovations. Carrier spent $90 million on research and development in 1990, but other major firms like Lennox and York were beating Carrier to the marketplace, forcing it to play catch-up. Cutting energy costs, noise levels, and developing CFC-free equipment in automated factories became the market strategy of the 1990s.

Carrier held an 11 percent worldwide market-share, with its primary success in Europe. It was the only U.S. firm to break into Japan, where it had a one-percent foothold. To expand its sales in Japan and to protect its 17-percent share of the Asian market, Carrier invested $30 million into specialized research and development in Japan and doubled its research staff there to 40 in 1989. Headquartered in Farmington, Connecticut, the company employs 28,000 to produce sales of $3.8 billion.

ASI Holding Corp. was the second largest firm in SIC 3585 in 1992. It controlled American Standard Inc., which in turn operated Trane Commercial Systems Group. American Standard, the leading U.S. bathroom fixture firm, and Trane, the largest U.S. producer of air conditioners, joined forces in 1983. The companies then restructured in 1988 to form ASI Holding Corp. Trane specialized in custom-built heavy refrigeration and cooling equipment for large buildings, but expanded into the domestic air conditioning market with the purchase of General Electric's air conditioning division. The move was intended to stave off an unfriendly take-over bid by IC Industries, but it also made Trane attractive to American Standard. Standard had tried to enter the air conditioning business in the 1960s but found the competition too stiff. Trane employed 13,000 workers to produce 1991 sales of $1.42 billion.

Another major competitor in the industry in 1992 was York International Corp., formed in 1986 when its parent company, Borg-Warner, tired of three years of constant losses. In 1988, an investor group took over the new company in a leveraged buy-out. York started its air-conditioning business in 1981 when it purchased Westinghouse Electric's air conditioning division. It developed a distinctive, technically sophisticated product and sold it through exclusive dealerships. By 1992, the company was doing well even with the slump in new housing starts and the declining economy. Much of its success came from its export business, which made up 40 percent of total sales, and its concentration on commercial refrigeration, which accounted for 70 percent of sales. Future marketing strategies targeted Pacific Rim and Latin American countries as prime growth areas. In 1992, it operated its head office at York, Pennsylvania, employing 11,500 to produce total sales of $1.6 billion.

WORK FORCE

Traditionally, the heating, refrigeration and air-conditioning manufacturing industry has been highly labor intensive. In 1988, the average number of production workers at an establishment in the industry was 111, compared to the average of 37 workers in all manufacturing. Much of the assembly work was done by hand fitting many small parts and cutting metal shapes with the use of templates. By the mid-1980s, the industry was shifting towards more automated production with the use of numerical control machining tools and welding robots. Eventually computerized control led to fully automated plants such as Rheem's Texarcana air conditioning facility. Consequently, even though shipments increased between 1982 and 1990 from $12.39 billion to $21.939 billion, production worker employment stayed relatively stable, remaining around 120,000 from 1980 to 1992.

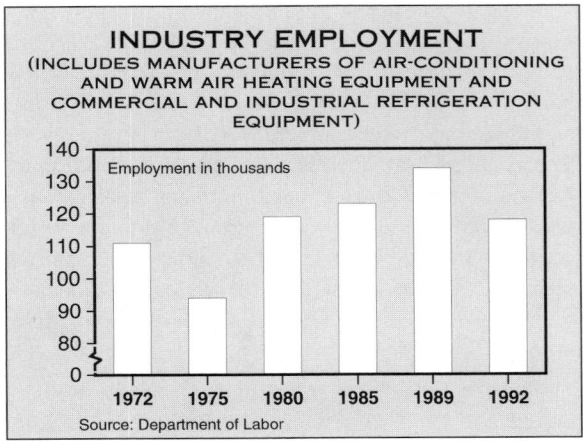

INDUSTRY EMPLOYMENT
(INCLUDES MANUFACTURERS OF AIR-CONDITIONING AND WARM AIR HEATING EQUIPMENT AND COMMERCIAL AND INDUSTRIAL REFRIGERATION EQUIPMENT)

Employment in thousands

Source: Department of Labor

The Bureau of Labor Statistics predicted that employment in occupations like assemblers, fabricators, solderers, and brazers would decline by about 6.5 percent by the year 2000. Electrical and electronic assemblers faced a 41.6 percent drop because of the increasing use of solid state circuit board systems. On the other hand, general labor categories and support staffs showed moderate gains. Mechanical engineers were the group that was expected to be in the highest demand in the industry.

AMERICA AND THE WORLD

The domestic American market represented 45 percent of the world's air conditioning and refrigeration demand in 1991, but the industry was clearly global. American firms, applying flexible manufacturing philosophies and taking advantage of foreign currency exchange fluctuations, built manufacturing facilities in Asia, Europe, Latin America, and the Middle East, moving much of their production capacity offshore. Japanese manufacturers, America's primary foreign competition, built two compressor plants in the United States in 1990 for many of the same reasons. Generally, the industry had a positive balance of trade which increased in 1991 when imports declined ten percent. The industry exported $3.274 billion in 1991 compared to imports of $1.78 billion. The top export markets were Canada (26 percent), Mexico (13 percent) and Saudi Arabia (6 percent), according to U.S. Industrial Outlook.

The market competition was much tighter on a global scale. In 1990, American manufacturers held 37 percent of world market-share compared with 38 percent held by Japanese manufacturers. Inside Japan itself, Carrier Corp. was the only American producer to make any inroads, where it held a one percent market share.

The Japanese market demanded a different technology than that common in the United States. Ironically, Japanese firms produced primarily what is known as a ductless-split, which was first developed and abandoned in the United States during the 1960s. The system looks much like a window air conditioner, but the compressor is housed in a separate condenser box placed outside the structure. Refrigerant tubing connects the two coils and their independent fan assemblies. The Japanese saw the concept as ideal for their relatively compact homes and perfected the technology.

In the 1990s, Japanese manufacturers used the system to earn a 55 percent market-share in Asia, the world's fastest growing market, compared to the American 22-percent share. They also began an assault on the European and American markets. In Europe, the Japanese models made air conditioning available to many older buildings equipped with boiler heating systems where installing a duct system would be impractical. The Japanese models also worked well in small computer-room applications. American manufacturers responded to the threat of foreign competition and a softening domestic market with massive influxes of capital into their own research and development and co-operative ventures with Japanese and other foreign competitors to take advantage of specialized expertise.

The 1991 worldwide HVAC industry enjoyed a $60-billion market which was growing at a rate of about 1-to-2 percent per year. The American portion of that market was about $22 billion. Writing for the ASHRAE Journal, Richard Biederman and Jaroslav Wurm predicted that the world market would continue to grow to about eight times that size before it reached saturation. The challenges of the early 1990s caused the industry to begin considering alternative technologies. Concerns over indoor air quality made it clear that heating, ventilation, humidification, and air cleaning could not be considered as separate fields of endeavor, but instead all must be integrated into the design of new buildings to become part of the essential operational architecture of an organic system. The Munich (Germany) Airport Center provided an excellent example of the incorporation of all these systems. The structure was designed with its energy and ventilation needs in mind as part of the original concept. Using glass and fabric panels in the roof structure, the architects avoided the need for heating or air conditioning equipment and reduced the amount of artificial lighting required. Design of the building relied heavily on computer modelling to predict how the system would work under extreme conditions.

The efficiency of the Munich Airport Center illustrates how the use of microelectronics for computer modelling and for control systems revolutionized the HVAC industry and promoted the system concept. They allowed more sophisticated designs and more accurate control to deliver energy savings and increased health and comfort levels. In 1993, 20,000 French families lived in fully automated houses, a concept catching on in America. The system controls lighting, heating, security and entertainment devices. New HVAC systems were making the home more independent and self-sufficient. The new technology called cogeneration devices used basic refrigeration technology to cool or heat the structure, produce hot water, and generate enough electricity to run the house. Simpler systems sacrificed the cooling function by eliminating the refrigerant circuit. In both cases, a natural gas engine drives the generator to produce the electricity. The heat from the exhaust gas is reclaimed by water in the system's heating circuit. The full heat-pump system, which also gathers heat from outside the house, uses only one-half the gas needed by a conventional furnace or two-thirds used in a high-efficiency condensing furnace.

Space has always been a problem in the commercial world, and finding room and the right location for a noisy air conditioning system was often difficult for mall builders and for architects designing space-saving housing developments. One answer promoted in the 1990s was computer generated "antinoise." By analyzing and matching the sound waves created by the HVAC equipment, the computer could order up an exact counter-wave. The result was actual silence, not just a deadening of noise behind bulky sound barriers.

In addition to antinoise, the industry also considered some older technologies abandoned in earlier, more wasteful days. Solar heating, particularly for domestic hot water, made a comeback in the 1990s after losing favor in the 1970s. About 1.5 million homes in America used solar-powered hot water heaters to displace up to one-quarter of their domestic energy needs. Solar pool heaters also gained popularity. Another surprising but effective old technology involved using heat from burning natural gas to cool a structure. The concept uses an absorbent, usually lithium bromide, and water to produce the refrigeration effect. Early models were bulky and not easily understood, but advancements in Japan made this environmentally friendly system a prime alternative to traditional CFC systems.

Another modern reworking of an old concept which gained popularity in the 1990s was thermal storage. The effectiveness of this strategy relied on the use of off-peak electricity rates or alternative, cheaper fuel sources to power industrial air-conditioning chillers or ice-making machines during evening or weekend hours. Instead of using the machines to directly cool the structure, the designers channelled the refrigerant output to large tanks of water to make ice. During normal operating hours, the ice absorbed heat from the building, providing effective cooling. This allowed the designers to select smaller equipment than would be needed to cool the structure on demand. They could also use naturally-occurring ammonia as a refrigerant rather than CFC. Ammonia lost favor with the introduction of CFC because of its toxicity and flammability. The HVAC industry continued to improve technology to reduce environmental degradation and energy loss into the 1990s.

Industry Information Sources

Alper, Joe. "Antinoise Creates the Sounds of Silence." *Science* 252 (2 April 1991).

Barlas, Stephen. "Congress/Bush Approve Energy Bill." *Appliance*, November 1992.

Beddows, Norman A. "Concerns About Indoor Air Quality Warrant Review of HVAC Systems." *Occupational Health & Safety* 59 (May 1990).

Brand, Horst, and Clyde Huffstutler. "Productivity in Making Air Conditioners, Refrigeration Equipment, and Furnaces." *Monthly Labor Review* 107 (December 1984).

Carey, John. "Is the World Heating Up? Well, Just Listen." *Business Week*, 4 February 1991.

Chege, James M., ed. *Refrigeration and Air-Conditioning.* Englewood Cliffs, NJ: Prentice-Hall Inc., 1979.

Clifford, Mark. "Back to Basics." *Forbes*, 30 June 1986.

Cox, J.E., and Charles R. Miro. "Worsening Ozone Layer Outlook Points to Quicker CFC Ban." *ASHRAE Journal* 34 (February 1992).

Dickson, David, and Eliot Marshall. "Europe Recognizes the Ozone Threat." *Science* 243 (10 March 1989).

Edelson, Edward. "The Man Who Knew Too Much." *Popular Science* 234 (January 1989).

Eklund, Christopher S. "Stan Hiller Is Old-Fashioned: He Fixes Broken Companies." *Business Week*, 31 March 1986.

Geake, Elisabeth. "Dial C for Central Heating, D for Dishwasher . . ." *New Scientist* 132 (14 December 1991).

James, C. S. *Information Bulletin TC72-24: Fuel Oils and Burning Equipment.* Toronto, Ontario: Imperial Oil Limited, 1973.

Konrad, Wally. "Solar Energy's New Place in the Sun." *Business Week*, 7 October 1991.

Lemonick, Michael D. "Deadly Danger in a Spray Can." *Time*, 2 January 1989.

Lueders, David. "Cooling a Modern Plant for a Week at a Time with Ice." *Control Engineering* 39 (Mid-March 1992).

Marcial, Gene G. "A Cooling Play That's Heating Up." *Business Week*, 2 March 1992.

"1993 HVAC&R Technology Review." *ASHRAE Journal* 35 (January 1993).

Norberg-Bohm, Vicki. "From the Inside Out: Reducing CO2 Emissions in the Buildings Sector." *Environment* 33 (April 1991).

Perry, Chris, and Todd Vogel. "How Japan is Beating the Others Cold." *Business Week*, 3 September 1990.

Remich, Norman C. et al. "Industry Backs Bush on CFC-ban Speedup." *Appliance Manufacturer*, April 1992.

Russell, James S. "A Model of Efficiency." *Architectural Record* 180 (April 1992).

Samuel, Peter. "Will Your Next Refrigerator Explode?" *Consumers' Research* 75 (July 1992).

Stepanek, Steven. "Air Apparents: Emerging HVAC Technologies May Rule Replacement Decisions." *Buildings* 85 (November 1991).

Szerlag, Hanz. "By the Numbers: Houses Get Cooler." *Detroit Free Press*, 27 June 1993.

———. "By the Numbers: Gassing Up." *Detroit Free Press*, 4 July 1993.

"Total CFC Ban Needed to Halt Global Warming." *New Scientist* 127 (8 September 1990).

"Trane Has Finally Found a Refuge." *Business Week*, 19 December 1983.

U.S. Department of Commerce. *U.S. Industrial Outlook.* Washington, DC: U.S. Department of Commerce, 1991, 1992.

Vogel, Todd. "Can Carrier Corp. Turn up the Juice?" *Business Week*, 3 September 1990.

"What's Next in Home Energy." *Popular Science* 237 (November 1990).

Wison, Alex. "Combustion Gases, an Indoor Threat." *Home Mechanix*, October 1991.

Wurm, Jaroslav, and Richard Biederman. "Status of the HVAC Industry." *ASHRAE Journal* 34 (January 1992).

— Al Cook

SIC 3586

MEASURING AND DISPENSING PUMPS

The Measuring and Dispensing Pumps Industry is comprised of establishments primarily engaged in manufacturing pumps used in service stations for dispensing gas, oil, and grease. This category also includes grease guns. Industrial pumps are classified in **SIC 3561: Pumps and Pumping Equipment**.

In the early 1990s, multi-pump units, which offer several grades of gasoline from the same pump, accounted for about 22 percent of industry sales. More traditional single-pump units still held a 19 percent share of the market. Lubricating oil pumps represented about 4 percent of output, and grease guns made up 3 percent of sales. Approximately 30 percent of industry revenues were made from the sale of parts and attachments, such as vapor recovery systems and replacement hoses.

Non-industrial gas, oil, and grease pumps are a corollary of the proliferation of cars and trucks during the early and mid-1900s. As American society became increasingly mobile, markets for service station pumps expanded rapidly. Indeed, by the late 1970s the service station pump industry was shipping more than $600 million worth of products per year and employing about 8,000 workers.

Despite an oil shortage in the United States in the late 1970s and a recession in the early 1980s, industry revenues climbed sporadically to $1.14 billion by 1988. Although growth of demand for new gas, oil, and grease pumps waned in comparison to growth in previous decades, other product segments prospered. Importantly, environmental regulations forced service stations in many states to equip their pumps with costly new vapor recovery systems and safety devices.

A U.S. economic recession in the late 1980s and early 1990s suppressed pump sales to about $1.03 billion per year in the early 1990s. As sales faltered, industry employment plummeted from a high of 9,400 in 1987 to about 8,000 by 1990. An upturn in the U.S. economy in 1993 offered a slight reprieve for many ailing manufacturers, though long term growth prospects remained questionable in light of saturated markets.

Going into the mid-1990s, pump manufacturers scrambled to revive profits by introducing new gas pump systems, focusing on the multi-pump market, and incorporating computer technology into their machines. New pumps with point-of-sale credit card devices, for example, allowed customers to fill a vehicle with gas and pay without leaving their car, thus reducing labor costs. Likewise, to help service stations comply with Federal "Stage II" vapor recovery guidelines, producers of vapor recovery pumps and attachments were introducing a variety of new systems and designs.

The largest U.S. company primarily engaged in the production of service station pumps and equipment in the early 1990s was Graco Inc., of Minneapolis, Minnesota. Graco boasted 1991 sales of $321 million with 2,400 employees. Tokheim Corp., of Indiana, placed second with $217 million in sales. Other major players included Gilbarco Inc., of North Carolina, and Dresser Industries Wayne Division, of Maryland. In all, about 80 companies were classified in the industry in the early 1990s.

Industry participants were able to increase production yet keep a lid on employment growth during the 1980s primarily through productivity gains. The movement of some manufacturing activities overseas also reduced work force gains. The future of employment in this industry was uncertain going into the mid-1990s. However, the outlook for job growth in the overall service machinery sector was generally positive through 2005, according to the Bureau of Labor Statistics.

INDUSTRY INFORMATION SOURCES

Darnay, Arsen J., ed., *Manufacturing USA; Industry Analyses, Statistics, and Leading Companies*, Detroit: Gale Research Inc., 1993.

Shook, Phil, "Stage II Equipment: Meeting the Challenge," *National Petroleum News*, July 1993.

U.S. Industrial Outlook 1993, Washington, D.C.: U.S. Department of Commerce, January 1994.

Upton, Howard, "When the Feds Controlled Pump Prices," *National Petroleum News*, July 1993.

—Dave Mote

SIC 3589

SERVICE INDUSTRY MACHINERY, NOT ELSEWHERE CLASSIFIED

Companies in this classification are principally engaged in manufacturing miscellaneous equipment for use in service businesses. Examples of industry products are floor sanding machines, cafeteria food warmers, commercial fryers, sludge processors, sewage treatment equipment, mop wringers, and commercial corn poppers. Household appliances and machinery are classified elsewhere. For more information on the history and structure of U.S. machinery industries, see **SIC 3552: Textile Machinery** through **SIC 3559: Special Industry Machinery, Not Elsewhere Classified**.

The largest segment of the miscellaneous service machine industry is food service equipment, which accounted for about 28 percent of industry revenues in the early 1990s. Commercial ranges, stoves, and broilers made up the bulk of that group. Industrial floor and carpet cleaning equipment represented ten percent of the market, as did miscellaneous sewage treatment products. Parts for water heaters and softeners accounted for eight percent of sales. Other major categories included commercial car and bus washing equipment, commercial dishwashers, sand blasting machines, and industrial vacuum systems. Only two percent of output was exported in 1992.

General industry expansion between 1950 and 1980 resulted in aggregate shipments of more than $2.5 billion by the early 1980s. Steady growth of service industries during the 1980s, particularly food services, resulted in rapid growth. Sales went from about $2.6 billion in 1983 to $3.4 billion by 1986, and to $4.9 billion by 1990. As revenues grew at an average annual pace of almost nine percent per year, industry employment jumped from 31,000 in the early 1980s to about 39,000 by the early 1990s.

Despite U.S. economic malaise in the early 1990s, most service machinery manufacturers sustained moderate growth. Sales of food service products, for example, grew at a rate of five to six percent per year in 1992 and 1993, and overall U.S. production machinery shipments increased four to six percent per year between 1991 and 1993. In addition, manufacturing productivity gains and industry consolidation boosted profit margins for many competitors.

The miscellaneous service machinery industry is extremely fragmented and is dominated by relatively small, specialty manufacturers. The average industry participant employed only 25 workers in 1992, compared to an average of 37 for all other U.S. manufacturers. Furthermore, of the approximately 900 competitors in 1992, only five had more than $100 million in sales. Most of the top 100 companies had less than $30 million in revenues and fewer than 200 workers. The largest company in the industry was Alco Food Systems Inc., of Pennsylvania. Alco had 1991 sales of $300 million and employed about 1,100 workers. Culligan International Co., of Illinois, employed 2,200 workers and generated 1991 sales of $290 million. Other leaders included Bissell Inc., of Michigan, and Tennant Co., of Minnesota.

Despite continued productivity increases and the movement of some manufacturing facilities to foreign countries, employment prospects for the overall service machinery industry were positive. Opportunities for most occupations were expected to swell by 10 to 20 percent between 1990 and 2005, according to the Bureau of Labor Statistics. Jobs for assembler and fabricators, which account for about 25 percent of the work force, will likely decline slightly. However, the number of labor positions should grow. Openings for some workers, such as sales and marketing professionals, will likely increase by as much as 50 percent.

INDUSTRY INFORMATION SOURCES

Darnay, Arsen J., ed., *Manufacturing USA; Industry Analyses, Statistics, and Leading Companies*, Detroit: Gale Research Inc., 1993.

Standard & Poor's Industry Surveys, New York: Standard & Poor's Corporation, December 24, 1992.

U.S. Industrial Outlook 1993, Washington, D.C.: U.S. Department of Commerce, January 1993.

—Dave Mote

SIC 3592

CARBURETORS, PISTONS, RINGS, AND VALVES

This category includes establishments primarily engaged in manufacturing carburetors, pistons, piston rings, and engine intake and exhaust valves. Establishments primarily engaged in manufacturing metallic packing are classified in **SIC 3053: Gaskets, Packing, and Sealing Devices,** and those primarily engaged in manufacturing machine repair and equipment parts (except electric), on a job or order basis for others, are classified in **SIC 3599: Industrial and Commercial Machinery and Equipment, Not Elsewhere Classified.**

INDUSTRY SNAPSHOT

The late 1980s were difficult times for the carburetors, pistons, rings, and valves industry, as shipments declined from a high of $3.096 billion in 1984 to just $2.042 billion in 1990. Changes in employment levels were equally dismal, peaking in 1984 at 33,400 only to fall to 20,600 by the end of 1990. Of these 20,600 employees, 16,500 were production workers. The greatest factors contributing to this long decline were the growth of overseas parts manufacturing capabilities and the rise of the Japanese automakers, who have captured a larger percentage of the U.S. automotive market. Despite this decline, workers in this industry averaged $13.83 per hour in 1989, well above the average of $10.49 recorded by all manufacturing industries.

The industry tends to be dominated by larger companies, employing an average of 148 workers in 1989. The materials consumed by the industry cover most of the materials used in manufacturing: ferrous and non-ferrous stock, ceramics, rubber, and plastic. The industry supplies carburetors, pistons, rings, and valves either as original equipment for manufacturers of new products or as replacement parts for older products. The industry's product share is broken into three major categories, each with several subcategories. New and rebuilt carburetors claimed 45.48 percent of the total industry production in 1987, with new carburetors alone accounting for 31.19 percent. Pistons, piston rings, and piston pins claimed 31.94 percent of the total share. Engine intake and exhaust valves claimed 19.78 percent. In each segment, the majority of parts were manufactured for use in motor vehicle engines.

The leading purchasers of carburetors, pistons, rings, and valves are the motor vehicle parts and accessories industry, the motor vehicles and car bodies industry, and the internal combustion engines, not elsewhere classified, industry, with 34.3, 16.9, and 14.3 percent shares respectively. Other major purchasers include the farm machinery and equipment industry, the automotive repair shops and services industry, and a variety of other consumers of automotive parts.

CURRENT CONDITIONS

Having rebounded slightly from one of the worst recessions in the auto industry, a sluggish economy, and the ever-present Japanese threat, the U.S. auto industry continues to play a game of catchup in the early 1990s. Long-term growth in the general auto industry is not expected to be greater than four percent per year and negative growth is expected through 1996 for SIC 3592 and other auto parts industries. Maintenance repairs should stimulate after-market growth.

According to the *U.S. Industrial Outlook 1992,* "The aftermarket also stands to benefit from the 20 percent increase in vehicle financing periods that occurred during the 1980s. This factor will have significant beneficial consequences for aftermarket sales during 1992-1996. The extension of the financing—and thus the ownership—period of both new and used vehicles has tended to keep vehicles in operation longer, increase the average age of vehicles, and cause older age categories to account for a growing percent of total vehicles in operation."

While the aftermarket looks good for the automotive parts industry, original equipment suppliers will continue to fight for survival. One tried and true strategy is to become heavily involved in the early design of automobiles, forming alliances with auto manufacturers. The Japanese in particular support this trend and have chosen specific suppliers that are involved in the initial design to exclusively supply parts.

INDUSTRY LEADERS

The top 36 companies in SIC 3592 recorded total sales of $1.54 billion and employed 15,700 people in 1991, according to *Ward's Business Directory of U.S. Private and Public Companies.* Sealed Power Technologies of Muskegon, Michigan, the industry leader, had sales of $325 million in 1991 and employed 3,100 people. Dana Corporation of Greensville, South Carolina, grossed $200 million in sales and employed 1,400 people. Walbro Corporation of Cass City, Michigan, grossed $167 million and employed 1,700 people. Goetze Corporation of Muskegon, Michigan, had sales of $100 million and employed 1,100 people. Zollner Corporation of Fort Wayne, Indiana, grossed $95 million and employed 1,000 people.

Sealed Power Corporation was incorporated in 1912 as the Piston Ring Company by two men who combined their life savings, $3000 total, and borrowed more. The first order was placed by Continental Motors Corporation, and the Piston Ring Company's business boomed. In its first year the company produced 348,000 rings. A foundry was added the next year, and by 1921 the company expanded into the auto replacement market. International sales were started in 1925, and within a year 38 countries were importing the company's wares. By 1932, the company formally changed its name to Sealed Power and launched both advertising and acquisition campaigns.

World War II was good for Sealed Power because expansion was necessary to meet military demand. Likewise, recessions did not hurt the company due to consumer tendencies to repair cars, rather than replace them. Sealed Power divides its operations into four segments: replacement parts, powered products, service products, and industrial supplies. In 1993, Federal-Mogul Corporation acquired the replacement division from parent company SPX for $150 million. A trademark agreement was also signed giving exclusive rights to Federal-Mogul for the distribution of Sealed Power and Speed-Pro brand engine and chassis parts. However, in 1994 SPX Corporation agreed to acquire 49 percent interest in Sealed Power Technologies Limited Partnership from Riken Corporation of Tokyo. Valued at $239 million, this deal would give SPX a 98 percent holding of Sealed Power Technologies Partnership.

Dana Corporation defines itself as "a global leader in the manufacturing and marketing of vehicular and industrial components." At the end of 1992 Dana reported sales of $4.87 billion, an increase from $4.40 billion the year before. Employing more than 35,000 people worldwide, Dana had $2.9 billion in original equipment sales and $1.9 billion in distribution of automotive and truck parts. Dana chairman Southwood J. Morcott said, "Much of Dana's improvement in 1992 stemmed from a solid rebound in our markets, particularly the light truck segment which constitutes more than one-fourth of our business." With joint ventures and subsidiaries in the United States, France, Japan, Korea, Mexico, Brazil, and Singapore, Walbro increased net sales from $200 million in 1991 to $241 million in 1992.

AMERICA AND THE WORLD

U.S. auto parts companies continue to pursue overseas markets largely through overseas expansions of existing operations. According to an industry survey in 1991, major auto parts firms attribute their survival to overseas markets. Supplier families have been formed, which are joint operations between parts manufacturers. Although parts exports represent a growing share of industry shipments, the overall trade performance since the late 1970s has diminished greatly. While Canada, Europe, and Mexico contain subsidiaries of many U.S. auto parts firms, U.S. firms have not been able to penetrate Japan's domestic parts market. According to *U.S. Industrial Outlook 1992,* "As recently as 1982, U.S. auto parts suppliers generated a $1.5 billion surplus in parts trade with the rest of the world, despite a parts trade deficit of $1.7 billion with Japan. But by 1990, the industry's trade performance had undergone a complete turnaround, recording a deficit that reflected a large trade imbalance with Japan while U.S. trade with the rest of the world showed a surplus."

The globalization of the industry is predicted to continue, especially as the Japanese continue to engage in joint ventures with U.S. firms. Japanese manufacturers are becoming more willing to share the risk of business, as many have encountered losses or have not become profitable in a timely manner. Therefore, foreign mergers and acquisitions will continue in an attempt to distribute more thinly the costs of product research and development. The trade imbalance may be counteracted by growing exports to Canada, Europe, and Mexico. Trade with Mexico is expected to grow substantially, as the vehicular market in that country is projected to increase significantly. However, the situation with Japan is expected to deteriorate unless the labor shortages and high land costs in Japan continue to cramp their domestic industries.

RESEARCH AND TECHNOLOGY

While many of the advancements in this industry are driven by the automotive industry, concern for public safety and the liabilities involved also pushes contributions to research and technology. One example of this is the field testing conducted in Iowa which helped analyze the failure of piston skirts in diesel engines that drive emergency generators for nuclear power plants. Two similar failures occurred within one month at a Pennsylvania plant run by the municipal electric utility company. The failure was analyzed using state-of-the-art computer modeling systems, which were then supported by field tests with a similar diesel generator in Iowa. The detrimental design feature of the piston skirt was changed and new data from the field tests was input to the databases accessed by the computer modeling systems.

Current developments in the automotive industry concerning valves and pistons are aimed at pollution control, reliability, performance, and fuel efficiency. The 1993 "Excellence in Design" award, granted by *Design News* magazine, went to an engineer who developed an exhaust-gas recirculation and idle-air control valve which simplifies the implementation of smog-control equipment. Due to the development of airflow analysis, the combustion rate for different engines with different cylinder heads can be analyzed, thereby helping engineers to improve engine performance.

The challenge in the automotive parts industries is to deliver performance and fuel economy to the consumer, while protecting the environment. With increasing government regulations such as the Clean Air Act and fuel efficiency standards, automotive engineers are kept busy in laboratories and racing pits. Additionally, the media is skeptical of automobile makers since fuel efficiency claims were inflated in the early 1980s. "And as a result, the press and the public remain convinced that the 100-mpg carburetor and the low-cost catalytic converter are sitting in a locked vault in Highland Park, Dearborn, or Warren." said Jack Keebler, engineering editor of *Automotive News*. With current technologies, fuel efficiency becomes a trade-off against low cost, good driveability, low noise, low emissions, and 100,000-mile durability. More research into these factors is being performed by teams all over the world.

INDUSTRY INFORMATION SOURCES

"Business Briefs: Federal-Mogul Corp.," *Wall Street Journal*, September 17, 1993.

"Business Briefs: SPX Corp.," *Wall Street Journal*, January 17, 1994.

"Combustion Effects of Asymmetric Valve Strategies," *Automotive Engineering*, December 1993.

Dana Corporation, *1992 Annual Report*, Greenville, SC: Dana Corp., 1993.

Darnay, Arsen J., ed., *Manufacturing U.S.A.: Industry Analyses, Statistics, and Leading Companies*, Detroit: Gale Research, Inc., 1993.

"1st National of Chicago in Deal to Fund SPX," *American Banker*, February 18, 1994.

Graddage, M.J., "Field Testing to Validate Models Used in Explaining a Piston Problem in a Large Diesel Engine," *Journal of Engineering for Gas Turbines and Power*, October 1993.

Hast, Adele, ed., *International Directory of Company Histories*, Chicago: St. James Press, 1991.

Keebler, Jack, "Those New 'Miracle' Engines Must Pass Five Stiff Tests," *Automotive News*, August 26, 1991.

Lynch, Terrence, "Integrated Valve Meters EGR and Idle Air," *Design News*, February 22, 1993.

O'Conner, Leo, "A New Turn for Rotary-valve Engines," *Mechanical Engineering*, January 1993.

U.S. Department of Commerce, *U.S. Industrial Outlook 1992: Business Forecasts for 350 Industries*, Washington, DC: U.S. Department of Commerce, 1992.

Walbro Corporation, *1992 Annual Report*, Cass City, MI: Walbro Corp., 1993.

—Valerie E. Wilson

SIC 3593

FLUID POWER CYLINDERS AND ACTUATORS

This classification covers establishments primarily engaged in manufacturing hydraulic and pneumatic cylinders and actuators for use in fluid power systems.

Companies in the fluid power cylinders and actuators industry manufacture fluid (and pneumatic) cylinders used in various hydraulic and pneumatic devices, such as jacks, lifters, and machine tools. These devices are used to exert massive amounts of force in a controlled manner. They exploit Pascal's law, which states that pressure exerted upon a liquid is evenly transmitted in all directions. One of the simplest machines that uses a fluid power cylinder is the hydraulic press, which is used, for example, to press plastics into forms.

The three primary types of hydraulic cylinders are single-acting, double-acting, and differential. Single-acting devices consist of a large plunger, or piston, into which oil (air in a pneumatic cylinder) is pumped. A valve keeps the oil from backing up into the pump and allows a controlled release of the pressure. Double-acting cylinders work similarly, but oil is pushed against one side of the cylinder, thus allowing a push or pull motion; these cylinders are used for hoisting equipment (such as cranes) and earth-moving machines. A differential cylinder has a large piston that requires a greater amount of oil to displace the cylinder, thus allowing greater uniformity of force than a typical single-acting cylinder.

Although hydraulic pumps for powering hydraulic cylinders were developed in the nineteenth century, it was not until the twentieth century that fluid power devices became a widespread means of energy transmission. By 1987, the first year in which this industry was classified separately by the federal government, fluid power cylinder manufacturers were generating sales of about $1.9 billion. Although receipts rose to more than $2.2 billion by 1989, a recession in the late 1980s and early 1990s reduced demand from industrial sectors such that sales slipped below $2 billion annually during the early 1990s.

Industry participants in the mid-1990s have benefitted from a gradual U.S. economic recovery. However, continued slack demand from the important aerospace and defense industries boded poorly for future earnings growth in the industry. As domestic market growth waned, manufacturers were looking to exports and advanced technology to boost sales. New pumps in 1994 were smaller, faster, more efficient, and lighter than their predecessors. Furthermore, manufacturing processes were increasingly being automated, resulting in greater productivity and U.S. competitiveness.

About 360 companies competed in this industry going into the early 1990s. The largest, by far, was Parker Hannifin Corp., of Ohio. This diversified giant had 1991 sales of $2.5 billion and a work force of over 30,000. Other industry leaders in 1991 revenues included Allied-Signal Aerospace Co. ($500 million), Rexroth Corp. ($80 million), and Duff-Norton Co. ($50 million, estimated).

Although industry sales were expected to remain stable or increase slightly throughout the 1990s, manufacturing productivity gains and the movement of some production activities overseas will significantly reduce employment opportunities, according to the Department of Labor Statistics. Labor positions in miscellaneous industrial machinery industries, in general, will fall by 15 percent to 30 percent for most occupations between 1990 and 2005. Even the demand for engineers and managers will likely decline or increase only marginally.

INDUSTRY INFORMATION SOURCES

Banks, Howard, Jason Zweig, Alyssa A. Lappen, Philip Glouchevitch, and Julie Pitta, "Annual Report on American Industry," *Forbes,* January 8, 1990.

Darnay, Arsen J., ed., *Manufacturing USA: Industry Analyses, Statistics, and Leading Companies,* 3rd edition, Detroit: Gale Research Inc., 1993.

Green, Larry, "Hydrostatics: Back to Basics," *Equipment Management,* May 1990.

"Power Input and Storage," *Machine Design,* June 1990.

Smith, A. C., "Control System Basics," *Equipment Management,* October 1990.

—Dave Mote

SIC 3594

FLUID POWER PUMPS & MOTORS

This classification covers establishments primarily engaged in manufacturing hydraulic and pneumatic fluid power pumps and motors, including hydrostatic transmissions. Establishments primarily engaged in manufacturing pumps for motor vehicles are classified in **SIC 3714: Motor Vehicle Parts and Accessories**.

Manufacturers in this industry produce pumps and drives for fluid (hydraulic), and some pneumatic (air), power mechanisms, primarily for use in industrial and aerospace applications. Because fluid power devices exert (sometimes massive mounts of) controlled pressure, they are commonly utilized to power aircraft landing gear, industrial presses and lifts, heavy earth-moving equipment, and other heavy-duty equipment. They are also often integrated into smaller machines that require precise power transfer.

Fluid power systems combine cylinders, couplings, valves, and pumps and motors. A positive displacement hydraulic pump, such as a piston pump, is the part of the system that delivers the oil required to drive or control hydraulic machinery. It creates pressure in a series of short bursts. In contrast, impulse pumps, such as the centrifugal pump, deliver steady, continuous oil pressure with less vibration. Hydraulic motors typically operate in conjunction with pumps and are often used to precisely vary the rotational speed of various machines.

Pascal's law, which states that pressure exerted upon a liquid is evenly transmitted in all directions, was posited in the mid-1600s. However, pumps that could efficiently deliver high and controlled pressure were not introduced until the 1800s. Not until the mid-1900s, in fact, did hydraulic pumps and motors become a common means of power transfer. By 1987, the first year in which this industry was separately classified by the Federal Government, sales of fluid power pumps and motors approached $1.5 billion. Although industry revenues increased to nearly $1.8 billion by 1990, a U.S. recession quashed sales and earnings growth for most competitors throughout the early 1990s.

Industry participants in the mid-1990s have benefitting from a moderate upturn in the U.S. and global economy that was boosting pump and motor demand in the industrial sector. Unfortunately, vital aerospace and defense markets remained depressed and proffered little hope for gains in the near future. The most successful competitors countered market malaise with productivity gains and the introduction of cutting edge, high-performance equipment. Many also looked to increased demand in overseas markets for high-tech U.S. pumps and motors. Demand was expected to grow about six percent in 1994 and 1995.

About 150 companies served this industry going into the 1990s, the largest of which was Trinova Corp., of Ohio. This diversified producer garnered 1991 sales of nearly $2 billion and employed a work force of more than 19,000. Mannesmann Capital Corp., of New York, was the second largest competitor with 1991 revenues of $1.7 billion. The majority of the top 50 companies, however, generated 1991 sales of less than $15 million and employed fewer than 50 workers.

Although in the early 1990s the industry employed about 15,000 Americans—in relatively high-wage positions compared to other U.S. manufacturing industries—long-term-employment prospects are bleak, according to the Bureau of Labor Statistics. Increased foreign competition and continued productivity gains, through automation and restructuring, will curtail opportunities for labor and white-collar workers alike.

INDUSTRY INFORMATION SOURCES

American Academic Encyclopedia, Danbury, CT: Groliers Inc., 1994.

Avery, Susan, "Fluid Power Takes Off," *Purchasing,* June 17, 1993.

Darnay, Arsen J., ed., *Manufacturing USA: Industry Analyses, Statistics, and Leading Companies,* 3rd edition, Detroit: Gale Research Inc., 1993.

Nuck, Frank, and John Plout, "Composite Cylinder Tubes Cut Weight, Costs," *Machine Design,* November 12, 1993.

Smith, A. C., "Control System Basics," *Equipment Management,* October 1990.

—Dave Mote

SIC 3596

SCALES AND BALANCES, EXCEPT LABORATORY

The Scales and Balances, Except Laboratory, Industry is comprised of companies that manufacture household and industrial weighing scales. Industry offerings include baby and bathroom scales, truck and railroad scales, and various commercial measuring devices. Scientific scales are included in **SIC 3821: Laboratory Apparatus and Furniture**.

About one-third of this industry's revenues in the early 1990s were earned from sales of industrial scales. These devices are used in applications such as weighing food before it is packaged, or weighing loads or bags of grain. Truck scales, variously used to weigh items such as cement trucks or freight haulers, accounted for roughly six percent of industry output, and railroad car scales represented less than one percent of production value. Household scales made up 14 percent of this industry's market in the early 1990s. Retail and commercial equipment, such as grocery store produce balances, as well as postal scales, accounted for about ten percent of production. Miscellaneous scales and attachments comprised the remainder of the market.

Growth in the Scales and Balances Industry in the United States occurred mostly during the 20th century. The demand for manufacturing and packaging scales in the wake of the industrial revolution, the emergence of a market for vehicle and railroad scales, and the introduction of the household bathroom scale in the mid-1900s were major catalysts for industry expansion. By the 1980s, U.S. manufacturers were shipping over $600 million worth of products and employing more than 6,000 workers.

Industry revenues topped $725 million in 1988. Economic recess in the late 1980s, however, pushed sales as low as $650 million. Revenues climbed back up to about $680 million in the early 1990s, and producers were benefitting from a moderate economic recovery going into the mid-1990s. Saturated markets and expectations of torpid economic growth, however, cast doubt on the future expansion of the scale industry.

The largest U.S. company primarily engaged in the production of scales in the early 1990s was Mettler Instrument Inc., of New Jersey. Mettler had $150 million in revenues and employed about 300 workers in 1991. Chronos Richardson Inc., also of New Jersey, had 1991 sales of $86 million and about 100 employees. Other leaders included Fairbanks Inc., of Missouri, and Weight-Tronix Inc., of Minnesota.

The more than 100 firms that competed in this industry in the early 1990s employed about 6,300 workers. Employment was forecast to fall significantly, however. Productivity gains and the movement of production facilities across U.S. borders were estimated to contribute to a contraction in most scale manufacturing occupations of 5 to 30 percent between 1990 and 2005, according to the Bureau of Labor Statistics.

To boost sales and profits, scale producers going into the mid-1990s were striving to develop new and better machines. The newest industrial packaging scales in 1993, for example, could make up to 1,200 weighs-per-minute and were accurate to within one gram. Likewise, new electronic on-board loader scales were boosting the safety, ease-of-use, and accuracy of traditional truck scales. Mettler was selling high-tech, computerized grain weighers in 1993 that weighed grain bags as they moved along a conveyor belt. New self-service scales that were being marketed to grocery stores allowed consumers to weigh and label their own produce. A new pocket-sized postal scale was introduced in 1992 that could weigh letters up to four ounces.

INDUSTRY INFORMATION SOURCES

"A Pocket-Sized Postal Scale," *Consumer Reports*, October 1992.

"Bathroom Scales," *Consumer Reports*, January 1993.

Darnay, Arsen J., ed., *Manufacturing USA; Industry Analyses, Statistics, and Leading Companies*, Detroit: Gale Research Inc., 1993.

Drake, Bob, "Controlling Truck Loads One Bucket at a Time," *Pit & Quarry*, September 1992.

"In-Motion Checkweigher Pays for Itself in 1 Month," *Modern Materials Handling*, September 1993.

Spaulding, Mark, "New Weigh Systems Raise Overall Productivity: Latest Units Offer Higher Accuracy, Faster Speeds and Less Giveaway for a Better Bottom Line," *Packaging*, June 1993.

Weston, Cael, "New Self-Service Scales Weighing In," *Supermarket News*, January 25, 1993.

—Dave Mote

SIC 3599

INDUSTRIAL AND COMMERCIAL MACHINERY AND EQUIPMENT, NOT ELSEWHERE CLASSIFIED

This industry is made up of firms that manufacture miscellaneous machinery and equipment not elsewhere classified. It also encompasses establishments primarily engaged in producing or repairing machinery and equipment on a job or order basis for other companies. Examples of industry output include carnival amusement rides, catapults, sludge tables, flexible tubes and hoses, weather vanes, and non-vehicle engine filters. Motor vehicle engine filter manufacturers are classified separately in **SIC 3714: Motor Vehicle Parts and Accessories** and those manufacturing coin-operated amusement machines are classified in **SIC 3999: Manufacturing Industries, Not Elsewhere Classified**.

Machine shop service receipts account for a significant portion of industry revenues, although reliable statistics for that segment were unavailable in the early 1990s. The largest product group in this fragmented industry is flexible metal hosing and tubing, which accounted for 2.2 percent of sales in the late 1980s. Metal bellows represented less than one percent of the market for miscellaneous industrial machinery, and carnival equipment made up about 0.2 percent of sales.

The industry exported a significant portion of its output—about 30 percent in the early 1990s. Approximately 55 percent of sales were the result of capital spending by domestic manufacturers. The remaining 15 percent of production was consumed by numerous market niches. The armed forces, for example, purchased about 2.5 percent of output in the late 1980s, and communication service industries made up slightly less than one percent of the market.

The history of this industry varies by product segment. An overall expansion of the industrial sector during the post-World War II U.S. economic boom, pushed sales of miscellaneous machinery to the $12 billion mark by 1980. A slowdown in capital spending by durable goods manufacturers during the 1980s dampened sales and profit growth in comparison to the 1960s and 1970s. Revenue growth averaged only four percent annually between 1982 and 1990, mirroring capital spending increases. By 1990, miscellaneous industrial machinery producers were delivering about $17 billion worth of goods and machine shop services annually.

In an effort to combat foreign competition, sluggish markets, and thinning profit margins, many producers implemented work force reductions and restructured their management systems. Some producers also moved production activities to low-cost countries in Southeast Asia and South America. Despite resulting productivity gains, a global recession in the late 1980s and early 1990s suppressed profits for most industrial machine manufacturers. However, recovering domestic markets and improved global competitiveness was encouraging many producers in the mid-1990s.

The industry is extremely fragmented. Average shipments per company are less than one-tenth the U.S. manufacturing average. And, of the approximately 20,000 firms participating in this industry, none had revenues of more than $100 million. In fact the largest producer, Anamet Inc., of Connecticut, had 1991 sales of only $65 million. Springfield Remanufacturing, of Missouri, and Remmele Engineering Inc., of Minnesota, were the next largest industry participants with 1991 sales of $60 million each.

Although U.S. shipment volume of industrial machinery was expected to stabilize or increase through 2000, productivity gains continued to contribute to work force reductions. During the 1980s, industry employment remained steady at 250,000 despite an increase in output. Opportunities for most workers were expected to decline significantly between 1990 and 2005, according to the Bureau of Labor Statistics. Jobs for machine tool operators, for example, were expected to diminish by 20 to 30 percent by 2005. Only positions for skilled machinists, sales and marketing professionals, production managers, and mechanical engineers were expected to increase, but only slightly.

INDUSTRY INFORMATION SOURCES

Darnay, Arsen J., ed., *Manufacturing USA; Industry Analyses, Statistics, and Leading Companies*, Detroit: Gale Research Inc., 1993.

Standard & Poor's Industry Surveys, New York: Standard & Poor's Corporation, December 31, 1993.

U.S. Industrial Outlook 1994, Washington, D.C.: U.S. Department of Commerce, January 1994.

—Dave Mote

ELECTRONIC & OTHER ELECTRICAL EQUIPMENT & COMPONENTS, EXCEPT COMPUTERS

POWER, DISTRIBUTION, AND SPECIALTY TRANSFORMERS

This category covers establishments primarily engaged in manufacturing power, distribution, instrument, and specialty transformers. Radio frequency or voice frequency electronic transformers, coils, and chokes are classified in **SIC 3677: Electronic Coils, Transformers, and Other Inductors**, and resistance welder transformers are part of **SIC 3548: Electric and Gas Welding and Soldering Equipment**.

A transformer is used to reduce or increase the voltage, or electromotive force, of electricity traveling through a wire. It accomplishes this by transferring electric energy from one coil or winding to another coil through electromagnetic induction. As an illustration, electricity-generating plants use generator transformers to "step-up," or increase, voltage that is transferred through power lines. When the high voltage electricity reaches a community, a step-down transformer reduces its power. A distribution transformer makes a final step-down in voltage by diminishing the force of the electricity to a level usable in homes and businesses. Some electrical devices, such as doorbells and small appliances, use additional step-down transformers to decrease voltage.

A typical transformer has two windings, or coils of wire, that are insulated from each other. The two coils are wound on a common magnetic circuit of laminated sheet metal, called the core. Each end of the primary coil is connected to the incoming alternating current (AC) power source. Each end of the secondary coil, which receives the energy, is connected to the outgoing power line. The ratio between the number of windings in each coil determines whether the voltage will be boosted or diminished.

Two types of transformers are core- and shell-type. In core-type equipment the windings surround the laminated metal core. In shell-type transformers the metal core surrounds the windings. Distribution transformers are usually core-type, while more advanced high-voltage devices are often shell-type. Transformers can also be classified according to the type of cooling system they use; smaller transformers are usually cooled by air and larger equipment is oil-cooled. Finally, transformers are either single-phase or polyphase. Polyphase devices typically have a three-legged core that can produce at least three different voltages.

The majority of apparatus manufactured in this industry are power and distribution transformers purchased by electric utilities. These devices accounted for about 55 percent of industry sales in the early 1990s. Because most transformers are simple and rugged, they often last as long as 40 years. Therefore, producers are largely dependent on purchases by utilities that are expanding service. Shipments of distribution transformers, for instance, are closely linked to new housing starts. But demand is also influenced by conversion to more efficient or aesthetically pleasing transformers.

The other 45 percent of the transformer market is primarily comprised of step-down equipment integrated into individual electrical devices. Fluorescent lamp ballasts, for instance, represented approximately 17 percent of production in the early 1990s. Various specialty transformers, such as machine tool and high-intensity light transformers, accounted for nine percent of sales. Other popular industry offerings include transformers for electric furnaces, rectifiers, ignition systems, consumer electronics, and toys.

BACKGROUND AND DEVELOPMENT

Transformer operation is based on a principle posited in 1830 by Joseph Henry which stated that electrical energy can be moved efficiently from one coil to another through electromagnetic induction. Michael Faraday and Henry independently observed in 1831 that a magnet moved through a closed coil of wire induces a current. When Faraday replaced the magnet with a charged electromagnet, he had built the first transformer. The value of the transformer was not fully understood until later in the 19th century, when devices that used alternating current became popular.

As the demand for electricity swelled during the late 1800s and early 20th century, the need for electrical transforming devices emerged. As the United States built its massive electrical distribution infrastructure during the early part of the century, transformer sales ballooned. During the post-World War II economic expansion, moreover, the industry benefitted from aggressive government attempts to bring electricity to every American home. The Rural Electrification Administration was established in 1935, for example, and was charged with distributing power to even the most remote regions and communities of the nation. In addition, electricity demand swelled during the mid-1900s as new applications for electricity, such as air-conditioning, became popular.

By the early 1980s, the transformer industry was shipping about $3 billion worth of equipment annually and employing a work force of 40,000. Growth slowed throughout the 1980s as the demand for new infrastructure equipment leveled. Total U.S. electric utility capacity rose roughly 20 percent between 1978 and 1991—tepid growth in comparison to the increases of the 1950s and 1960s. However, manufacturers were aided by healthy housing starts during the mid-1980s and the development of more efficient transformers that boosted replacement demand. Industry revenues climbed at an average annual rate of six percent between 1983 and 1990, to about $4.2 billion.

CURRENT CONDITIONS

Low housing starts and a general U.S. recession stalled transformer demand in the early 1990s, as sales slipped to about $4.1 billion in 1991. While demand for the very largest transformers increased, shipments of most industry offerings declined. Utility construction activity declined, and the number of new genera-

tion and transmission projects built by utilities was expected to recede during the late 1990s.

Despite the lack of new utility projects, manufacturers hoped to benefit from other industry trends. Of the high-voltage and distribution transformers already in service, many were scheduled for replacement during the 1990s and early 2000s. In addition, many utilities were replacing good units with newer, more efficient designs. Newer transformers integrated advanced silicon low-loss steel or amorphous metal cores, for instance, and offered greater serviceability. Likewise, the market for overhead transformers, typically mounted on unsightly poles, was being displaced by newer ground units.

While replacements were expected to ease slack sales, transformer industry revenues were expected to grow at a lackluster one to two percent through the year 2000. The North American Electric Reliability Council estimated that existing transmission systems will be generally adequate to meet demand throughout the 1990s. The need for smaller units from the private sector was expected to grow slowly. The consequence to manufacturers of controversial electric and magnetic fields (EMFs) was still undetermined. (EMFs are created by transmission lines and equipment and are said to create health hazards such as cancer.)

U.S. producers were also expecting to suffer from an influx of transformer imports from Mexico. International competition traditionally had made a minimal impact on this industry because of the high weight-to-value ratio of larger transformers and the propensity of some utilities to purchase American products. But the North American Free Trade Agreement (NAFTA) was anticipated to boost exports from nearby Mexico, which was already the largest industry importer, having delivered 40 percent, or $235 million, of all foreign transformers into the United States during 1991. Domestic producers exported $380 million worth of transformers in 1992, mostly to Mexico and Canada.

INDUSTRY LEADERS

Only 270 companies participated in this consolidated industry going into the 1990s, and only a few dominated. Westinghouse Electric Corp., of Pennsylvania, for example, had 1991 sales of nearly $13 billion and employed a work force of 116,000. Cooper Industries, of Texas, was the second largest manufacturer with revenues of $6.2 billion in 1991 and about 58,000 workers. Siemens Energy, the third largest player, shipped $1 billion worth of goods and employed 7,000. Other industry leaders included ABB Power T and D Co. Inc., of Pennsylvania, and Valmont Industries Inc., of Nebraska.

The long term employment outlook for manufacturers of transformers and related equipment is pitiful. The work force had already shriveled 25 percent during the 1980s, to about 30,000 by 1992, and cutbacks were expected to continue. Increased automation and management restructuring was expected to further downsizing. The Bureau of Labor Statistics estimated that jobs in this sector for assemblers and fabricators, which accounted for roughly 20 percent of the electric distribution equipment work force, would plummet by nearly 50 percent between 1990 and 2005. Other labor positions were expected to decline similarly. However, opportunities for sales professionals, engineers, and industrial production managers were anticipated to expand about 15 percent by the year 2005.

RESEARCH AND TECHNOLOGY

Transformer manufacturers invested relatively little in development of new products and plants. The industry expended just $2,238 per employee on capital investments annually in the late 1980s, compared to $5,524 spent by the average U.S. manufacturer. Industry-related technical innovations in the early 1990s included new transformer test equipment that allows operators to select and apply test voltage to any leg of a transformer winding, thereby eliminating the need to disconnect the leads. Also, new insulating materials were allowing companies to refurbish old transformers and boost their efficiency, a development that was anticipated to reduce demand for new, more efficient replacement units.

INDUSTRY INFORMATION SOURCES

Darnay, Arsen J., ed., *Manufacturing USA; Industry Analyses, Statistics, and Leading Companies*, Detroit: Gale Research Inc., 1993.

Reason, John, "How Electric Utilities Buy Quality When They Buy Transformers," *Electric World*, May 1992.

Reason, John, "Transformer Rebuild Increases Load Capacity," *Electrical World*, February 1994.

Standard & Poor's Industry Surveys, New York: Standard & Poor's Corporation, December 31, 1993.

U.S. Industrial Outlook 1993, Washington, D.C.: U.S. Department of Commerce, June 10, 1993.

Whitlow, Alan W., "Portable Test Box Saves Time on Transformer Checks," *Transmission & Distribution*, January 1993.

—Dave Mote

SWITCHGEAR AND SWITCHBOARD APPARATUS

This category covers establishments primarily engaged in manufacturing switchgear and switchboard apparatus. Important products of this industry include power switches, circuit breakers, power switching equipment, and similar switchgear for general industrial application; also, switchboards and cubicles, control and metering panels, fuses and fuse mountings, and similar switchboard apparatus and supplies. Relays and switches in electronic devices and industrial controls are classified elsewhere.

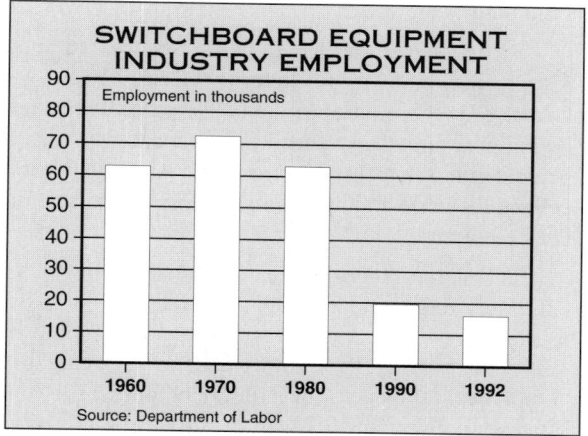

SWITCHBOARD EQUIPMENT INDUSTRY EMPLOYMENT

Employment in thousands

Source: Department of Labor

A switchgear is used to interrupt or reestablish the flow of electricity in a circuit. It is generally used in combination with metering, protective, and regulating equipment to protect and control motors, generators, transformers, and transmission and distribution lines. A switchboard is comprised of one or more panels with various switches and indicators that are used to route electricity and operate circuits.

Switchgears are typically concentrated at points where electrical systems make significant changes in power, current, or routing, such as electrical supply substations and control centers. Switchgear assemblies range in size from smaller, ground-mounted units to large walk-in installations and can be classified as outdoor or indoor units. Commercial and industrial assemblies are usually indoors, while utilities and co-generation facilities are more likely to have outdoor gear. Manufactured for a variety of functions and power levels, all switchgear conforms to standards set by the Institute of Electrical and Electronic Engineers (IEEE), the American National Standards Institute

(ANSI), or the National Electrical Manufacturers Association (NEMA).

Metal-clad switchgear assemblies are the most common devices used in electricity distribution. They usually contain: circuit breakers, which can be deactivated; primary circuits, such as transformers; insulating materials; interlocks, which ensure that circuit breakers can be safely inserted into and removed from the assembly; and, instrument panels that control the assembly. Metal-clad power center switchgear is used to regulate and route power in high-voltage applications. Similarly, medium-voltage vac-clad switchgear is used in circuits involving transmission and distribution lines and motors. Other common types of assemblies used in electrical distribution include metal-clad interrupter, low voltage, and station-type cubicle switching gear.

Switchboards and panelboards represented about 33 percent of industry revenues in the early 1990s, and circuit breakers made up about 30 percent of sales. Switchgear units and fuses accounted for about 28 percent and 7 percent of shipments, respectively. Miscellaneous parts and apparatus comprised the remainder of output.

The market for switchgear and related apparatus is extremely fragmented. About 20 percent of purchases in the early 1990s were classified as fixed capital investments, mostly by utilities and power generation companies. Six percent of industry output was used in office buildings, and industrial building applications consumed approximately five percent of production. Other significant market segments included refrigeration and heating equipment manufacturers, residential home builders, and communications industries. About 30 percent of production was exported.

BACKGROUND AND DEVELOPMENT

Power transformation technology was conceived as early as 1830 by Michael Faraday and Joseph Henry, who discovered the theory of electromagnetic induction. But the first commercially practical manual switching systems emerged during the late 1800s to service the flourishing telephone industry. By the late 1880s, shortly after Alexander Graham Bell's invention of the telephone in 1876, the telephone switchboard had evolved to a state where thousands of calls could be switched and connected at the same time. The first automatic switching system was introduced at the 1881 Paris Electrical Exposition, and a workable system had been patented by 1889. A similar device was installed in New Jersey in 1914. Using electrical impulses, it raised and rotated a shaft in a series of movements to make a contact.

The need for gear that would protect and control high-power electric circuits, which constitutes most of the equipment in this industry, resulted from advances in electricity during the early 1900s. Lee De Forest's 1906 invention of the electron tube and a plethora of subsequent breakthroughs spawned a huge demand for electricity in the United States. As the country built its massive electrical power infrastructure, sales of fuses, control panels, and all types of switchgear soared. Notably, the Rural Electrification Administration, which was established in 1935, and other government initiatives expended massive funds to try to bring electricity into every American home.

Electricity demand swelled during the mid-1900s as new applications for electric power, such as air-conditioning and television, became popular. In addition, post-World War II U.S. economic growth resulted in a great demand from industry for circuit control and protection apparatus. Equipment also improved as manufacturers developed means of reducing arcing (damaging sparks that occur when switches are activated), and integrated circuits were applied to switchboards and control devices. By the late 1970s, manufacturers of switchgear and switchboard equipment were shipping about $5 billion worth of goods annually and employing a work force of more than 66,000.

CURRENT CONDITIONS

Industry sales effectively stagnated during the 1980s, continuing a trend started in the 1970s. Indeed, the rampant expansion of the U.S. electric power infrastructure had subsided. Total U.S. electric utility capacity increased a modest 20 percent between 1978 and 1990—pitiful in comparison to growth during the 1950s and 1960s. Industry revenue growth was well below inflation rates during the early 1980s, rising to only $5.5 billion by 1986. Official industry content was changed in 1987, reducing sales volume to about $4.9 billion. Sales continued to slightly increase at an annual rate of less than 2 percent during the late 1980s, to about $5.5 billion by 1990.

Slack demand for new electric power infrastructure, recessed construction sectors, weak industrial demand, and a generally despondent U.S. economy hindered many industry participants in the early 1990s. Sales slipped in 1991 and fell again in 1992—by one percent in inflation-adjusted terms. Likewise, shipments were expected to rise only two percent in 1993, despite an overall U.S. economic recovery and a surge in new construction. Furthermore, the long term industry outlook was lamentable going into the mid-1990s. Domestic demand for new switchgear was expected to likely decline further, or stagnate, and because most switchgear was rugged and durable, replacement activity offered limited profit opportunities. Overall, the industry was expected to grow at a rate of only one to two percent annually between 1993 and 1997.

Despite lackluster performance overall, opportunities for savvy U.S. exporters remained strong in the early and mid-1990s, particularly in Mexico and East Asia. Export activity was 18 percent in early 1992, bolstered by a weak dollar and a growing demand for reputable U.S. equipment by developing countries. Sales were especially swift to Mexico, which accounted for approximately 30 percent, or $454 million, of all cross-border sales in 1991. Also, exports to Mexico were expected to jump in the wake the North American Free Trade Agreement (NAFTA). Other major importers of U.S. switchgear were Canada ($224 million), the United Kingdom ($95 million), and Japan ($81 million). The United States imported about $1.7 billion worth of switchgear in the early 1990s, most of which came from Mexico, Japan, and Canada.

INDUSTRY LEADERS

There were only about 450 industry participants in the early 1990s, reflecting consolidation efforts characteristic of many slow-growth industries. As competition increased during the 1980s, consolidation proliferated as companies merged with and acquired rivals in an effort to boost capital and take advantage of other economies of scale. About 650 companies were engaged in this industry in the early 1980s, but about 100 of those were reclassified in other sectors in 1987.

The biggest manufacturers of switchgear and switchboard equipment were large, diversified communications and power equipment conglomerates, such as General Electric and Honeywell. One of the largest companies primarily engaged in this industry in the early 1990s was Square D Co., of Illinois. This company, which is a major supplier of load-interrupting and metal-clad switchgear, had 1991 sales of $1.6 billion and employed 17,500 workers. Challenger Electric, another industry leader, had 1991 revenues of $200 million and employed 2,200 people. Other major manufacturers included Schlumberger Industries Inc., of Georgia, Liebert Corp., of Ohio, and C and K Components Inc., of Massachusetts.

WORK FORCE

Approximately 42,000 workers served this industry going into the 1990s. In addition to slack demand, productivity gains contributed to work force reductions during the 1980s and early 1990s. Specifically, factory automation and advanced information systems allowed many manufacturers to boost international competitiveness and retain profits in spite of stagnant markets. Likewise, the long term employment outlook for makers of switchgear was generally poor. The number of jobs for assemblers and fabricators, which make up almost 30 percent of the work force, was expected to decline by more than 40 percent between 1990 and 2005, according to the Bureau of Labor Statistics. Most labor positions were expected to fall 10 to 30 percent. Opportunities for engineers and sales professionals, on the other hand, were expanding and an increase by approximately 15 percent by the year 2005 was expected.

RESEARCH AND TECHNOLOGY

The switchgear and switchboard industry invests relatively little in research and development. In the early 1990s, for example, companies invested an average of $2,720 per employee back into their business, compared to about $5,520 spent by the average U.S. manufacturer. One of the most important areas of technological advancement in the early 1990s was switchgear that integrated sulfur hexafloride gas (SF6). SF6 has insulation and arc-quenching properties that could be used to reduce damage caused by arcing. The newer switches are safer, more reliable and require less maintenance than conventional switchgear.

INDUSTRY INFORMATION SOURCES

Darnay, Arsen J., ed., *Manufacturing USA; Industry Analyses, Statistics, and Leading Companies*, Detroit: Gale Research Inc., 1993.

Lazar, Irwin, ''Understanding Switchgear and Its Specifications,'' *Consulting-Specifying Engineer*, February 1992.

Lazar, Irwin, ''Specifying Switchgear for Maximum Reliability,'' *Consulting-Specifying Engineer*, August 1989.

Palko, Ed, ''Taking Advantage of Fused Interrupter Switchgear,'' *Plant Engineering*, May 2, 1991.

Reason, John, ''SF6: Revolution in Switchgear,'' *Electrical World*, December 1989.

U.S. Industrial Outlook 1993, Washington, D.C.: U.S. Department of Commerce, June 10, 1993.

—Dave Mote

SIC 3621

MOTORS AND GENERATORS

This classification comprises establishments primarily engaged in manufacturing power generators, motor generator sets, and electric motors, excluding engine-starting motors. Also covered in this classification are establishments primarily involved in manufacturing railway motors and control equipment, as well as motors, generators, and control equipment for gasoline, electric, and oil-electric buses and trucks.

Establishments primarily engaged in manufacturing turbogenerators are classified in **SIC 3511: Steam, Gas, and Hydraulic Turbines, and Turbine Generator Set Units**, and those manufacturing starting motors and battery-charging generators for internal combustion engines are grouped in **SIC 3694: Electric Equipment for Internal Combustion Engines.** Establishments primarily engaged in manufacturing generators for welding equipment are classified in **SIC 3548: Electric and Gas Welding and Soldering Equipment.**

INDUSTRY SNAPSHOT

Approximately 350 companies in the United States were involved in manufacturing motors and generators in 1992. These companies recorded more than $7.5 billion in sales for products included in the SIC 3621 classification, which consisted of four primary product groups: fractional horsepower motors, integral horsepower motors and generators, prime mover generator sets, and parts and supplies for motors and generators. Other products manufactured by the industry included land transportation motors and fractional and integral motor generator sets. Of these products, fractional horsepower motors represented nearly 50 percent of the industry's shipments, followed by integral horsepower motors and generators, which accounted for 18.5 percent. Prime mover generator sets accounted for another 11.2 percent of the industry's shipments, while parts and supplies for motors and generators represented nearly 8 percent.

Motor and generator manufacturers were heavily dependent on the health of several industrial markets to sustain their growth. Fractional horsepower motors were used in various household appliances—including refrigerators, freezers, air conditioners, automatic dishwashers, and microwave ovens—as well as other products that required a small horsepower motor, such as computer disk drives. Consequently, fluctuations in the residential construction market and changes in consumer spending were shadowed by the fractional motor market.

Integral horsepower motors were best suited for industrial uses, where greater horsepower was required. Integral motors powered vehicles used in large construction projects and provided the necessary power for many different types of manufacturing facilities. Any significant changes in nonresidential construction activity or capital expenditures in the industrial sector generally had parallel affects on integral motor production.

In addition to these market dependencies, motor and generator sales were affected by the vacillating costs of raw materials. Steel, an essential element in the production of motors, generators, and their related parts and supplies, was subject to pernicious price swings that could impinge on the industry's profit margin. Other materials, such as wire and brushes used in the manufacturing of motors and generators, also demonstrated a propensity for erratic jumps in price and had an appreciable affect on the motor and generator industry.

ORGANIZATION AND STRUCTURE

The motor and generator industry was predominantly populated by medium- and large-sized companies, or those employing more than 20 people. Of the 467 manufacturing facilities operated by the approximately 350 companies involved in the industry in 1989, only 160 employed less than 20 people. In fact, the 75 largest establishments employed an average of 6,742 people. While this figure included employees engaged in manufacturing or managing the production of some other types of goods, it is indicative of the relatively large size of facilities involved in the industry. On average, a motor and generator establishment employed 163 people, or more than three times the number of people employed in a typical manufacturing facility for all other U.S. industries.

Geographically, motor and generator production occurred throughout much of the nation, according to 1987 *Census of Manufacturers* studies, but was particularly concentrated in the eastern half of the United States. Industry production took place in 30 states, with the majority of the manufacturing establishments located in Michigan, Wisconsin, Illinois, Indiana, and Ohio. Together, these five states contained 149 of the 462 establishments that existed in 1987. The second-largest area of regional concentration was the Middle Atlantic states—New York, New Jersey, and Pennsylvania—which accounted for 73 establishments. The Pacific region stood as the nation's third-largest region of motor and generator production solely by virtue of the 46 establishments located in California, the only state within the Pacific region to contain any facilities. Ranked according to the number of facilities per individual state, California ranked first and was closely followed by Illinois with 40 and Ohio with 36.

The costs involved in establishing and operating a motor and generator manufacturing facility were substantially higher than the average manufacturing facility. In 1989, the average cost per establishment for raw manufacturing materials was $8.14 million in the motor and generator industry, compared to $4.54 million for the average of all manufacturing industries. The average investment for purchasing manufacturing machinery and paying for production retooling was $461,456 in the motor and generator industry, 55 percent higher than the average for other industries.

The relatively expensive nature of conducting business in the motor and generator industry tended to discourage the entry of small manufacturing companies. Since manufacturers frequently encountered expensive retooling costs—when a particular product became obsolete and was replaced by a new product, for example, or when a significant technological advancement dictated the implementation of a new production process—many companies manufactured a diverse line of products, some of which were excluded from the boundaries of the SIC 3621 classification. This diversity helped to insulate companies from potentially deleterious financial conditions affecting the motor and generator industry.

BACKGROUND AND DEVELOPMENT

The principle of the electric motor was first developed by Michael Faraday in 1821, but a diverse group of scientists and lay innovators quickly followed Faraday's lead and began experimenting with amended designs. Improvements on Faraday's design followed in quick succession, as inventors of the nineteenth century were swept up by the inspiring and momentous technological advancements that characterized the era. This work helped pave the way toward developing the type of electric motor that became an integral component in twentieth-century factories, stores, and homes.

Sixteen years after Faraday first announced his discovery, Thomas Davenport, a blacksmith from Vermont, developed a motor that successfully powered a printing press. This invention marked one of the earliest uses of the electric motor for commercial purposes, and Davenport was granted Patent No. 132 for it. Not to be outdone, Moses Farmer, another Yankee pioneer in the development of the electric motor, created a miniature electric railway as an exhibit for country fairs. Charles G. Page used this application of the electric motor on a larger scale in 1857, when he made an experimental run with a full-sized locomotive from Washington to Baltimore.

While these developments were encouraging and marked significant technological advancements, the design of these early motors limited the ways in which they could be used. Since they derived energy from

large, expensive batteries, these early versions were essentially suitable only for demonstration purposes; to utilize them in a commercial or industrial setting on a daily basis was still impractical. But this shortcoming disappeared with the advent of practical dynamos, or direct-current generators. No longer fettered by cumbersome batteries, early models of these smaller, cheaper-to-operate motors appeared at the Electrical Exhibition and National Conference of Electricians in Philadelphia in 1884. These were electrically driven rather than battery-powered motors, and their development greatly increased the potential applications for the electric motor. By 1887, there were already 15 well-known manufacturers of small electric motors in the United States, and more than 10,000 electric motors of 15 horsepower or less had been produced.

The development of direct-current generators greatly enhanced the economic feasibility of electric motors in the workplace and the home. However, even though the technology was in place, the fledgling industry's growth suffered from the shortsightedness of some business leaders. The individuals spearheading the movement towards electrification focused their efforts on employing electricity to generate light rather than on the vast industrial and commercial applications for the electric motor. In fact, the majority of early electric utilities were established as lighting businesses. As a result, other uses for electric motors were lost in the rush. But the incorporation of the first practical dynamo into the operation of the electric motor slowly drew the attention of more than a few enterprising individuals, and the industry formally began to experience a substantial demand for its products.

As the nation entered a new century, two companies became established as pioneers in the industrial and commercial development of electric motors. General Electric Company (GE), created to market and manufacture the innovations developed by Thomas Edison, entered into the electric motor field through mergers and acquisitions. Emerson Electric Manufacturing Company, formed to explore applications for the newly developed alternating current electric motor, entered the market with manufacturing processes it had developed specifically to use electrically driven motors. Both of these companies figured prominently throughout the course of the industry's history and helped catapult the use of electric motors and generators toward the pervasive levels of the 1990s.

The nation slowly became electrified during the first half of the twentieth century. It took until the 1950s for certain segments of the country to have the necessary electrical wire strung to enable the transmission of electricity. GE manufactured a broad assortment of electric motors and generators to run cement, paper, and steel manufacturing facilities, and also spent considerable effort on developing electric-powered locomotive engines. Emerson, meanwhile, concentrated on producing electric motors for use in home appliances such as sewing machines, water pumps, and fans, and also carved a niche in the growing market for electric motors within products intended for business offices.

Emerson and GE were joined by many other manufacturers of motors and generators during these pre-World War II decades, as the relatively new technology beckoned entrepreneurs into the market and expanded the size of the industry. Rural Electrification Administration crews were constantly stringing transmission wire, convincing observers that electrification of the entire nation was inevitable. For those contemplating a foray into the electric motor and generator industry, this development translated into encouraging prospects for the future. Manufacturing facilities mechanized their processes to be powered by electricity, if they had not already done so, and appliances used in the home increasingly depended on electricity for power.

When the postwar economic boom of the 1950s exponentially increased consumer spending and invigorated both residential and nonresidential construction, the motor and generator industry gained a solid foundation. Every American home aspired to own at least two modern appliances, which marked the dawn of a new era and infused motor and generator manufacturers with increased business. Manufacturing activity in general increased as well, with electrically driven production lines becoming the norm.

The lucrative conditions characterizing the market attracted more and more manufacturers, and by the end of the decade competition became intense within the industry. In addition, the nature of the competition changed gradually during this period. The smattering of smaller companies that had proliferated before World War II began consolidating into large conglomerates.

In the 1960s, Emerson and GE competed for market share against such manufacturers as Reliance Electric & Engineering Co., Wagner Electric Co., and Westinghouse Electric Corp. This competition resulted in a significant decline in the price of fractional horsepower motors, the primary product within the motor and generator industry. Exacerbating the effect of the shrinking profit margins was the increasing cost of raw materials used in the production of fractional motors, particularly of magnetic wire. By the middle of the

decade, a majority of the leading companies raised their prices for fractional motors in an attempt to stave off the debilitating effects of rising raw material expenditures.

At this time, there were approximately 325 companies competing in the industry, operating more than 400 establishments and employing slightly more than 100,000 workers. Despite the shrinking profit margins and other problems associated with the rapid pace at which the industry was maturing, the demand for electric motors continued to increase, attracting more and more competitors. Growth of the industry primarily stemmed from demand for fractional motors, which far outpaced other motor and generator products in terms of proportional representation of industry shipments. Fractional motors accounted for over 36 percent of total industry shipments by the mid-1960s, up from less than 30 percent in the 1950s, and this percentage would increase in the coming years. The reasons for this growth were as numerous as the different types of household items and appliances that were sold to consumers each year. Fractional motors were used in such diverse items as electric lawn mowers and hedge trimmers, electric toothbrushes, refrigerators, and washing machines.

Other products classified in the motor and generator industry recorded respectable sales figures, but their growth was less dramatic than the increasing demand for fractional motors. Products such as small generating sets powered by diesel and other internal-combustion engines benefitted from stable demand from the farming and transportation industries, while shipments of integral horsepower motors spiraled downward during the late 1950s and early 1960s. Integral motors could be reconditioned, whereas fractional motors were rarely rebuilt. This, in part, accounted for an increasing disparity between fractional and integral motor shipments. In 1958, the value of shipments for fractional and integral motors was approximately even, at $430 million. Six years later, the value of shipments of fractional motors had soared to nearly $600 million, while integral motor shipments had fallen to roughly $375 million.

This period in the history of the motor and generator industry also witnessed the increasing encroachment of foreign manufacturers into the U.S. market. In 1963, five million units of motor and generator products were imported into the U.S., but this figure nearly quintupled four years later when more than 23 million imported units were sold. This growth in total imports was occasioned by significant increases in the value of shipments recorded by two countries—the United Kingdom and Japan. The United Kingdom increased motor and generator product shipments to the United States from $1.5 million in 1963 to $18.4 million by 1967. But this was a one-time surge for U.K. producers: five years later shipments dropped to $12.6 million, and by the end of the 1970s U.K. imports slipped below $10 million. Japan, on the other hand, went from negligible shipments in 1963 to over $15 million worth four years later, and this continued to increase to $27.8 million by 1972 and $67 million by the end of the decade.

High inflation in the early 1970s negatively affected manufacturers of motors and generators, as residential and nonresidential construction declined and many consumers delayed purchasing appliances. The total value of industry shipments declined by five percent between 1974 and 1975 to $3.12 billion, while production worker employment within the industry decreased from 77,700 to 60,600. Hoping to escape the rising costs of materials and supplies occurring at this time, many manufacturers overstocked their inventories. This led to a later downward adjustment in production, further eroding the industry's profit margins. Once consumer appliance purchases returned to normal levels and construction picked up in the late 1970s, however, the industry exhibited robust growth again. Shipment values increased by 12 percent between 1977 and 1978 to $5 billion, and approached $6 billion by the beginning of the 1980s.

Entering the 1980s, however, high inflation continued to inflict damage on the motor and generator industry, particularly due to reduced capital expenditure programs initiated by other industries. In the absence of vigorous, nationwide plant expansion and the consequent orders for motors and generators, the industry was forced to look elsewhere for money. Since major retooling of production machinery was prohibitively expensive, many manufacturers streamlined their operations, relying on more efficient production procedures to help them withstand the decline in business. Part of this effort to economize resulted in a reduction of the industry's labor force. From 1981 to 1982, employment of production workers dropped from 93,400 to 84,100, the latest of a series of significant declines from the 107,000 high recorded in 1979.

In the meantime, the value of import shipments entering the United States continued to increase dramatically during the 1970s, and by the early 1980s foreign competition stood as a formidable force. The value of all import shipments classified in the motor and generator industry in 1972 was $181 million, but this figure ballooned to $801 million ten years later. U.S. manufacturers, however, had simultaneously intensified their efforts to increase exports in order to combat escalating material costs and declining business. Consequently, domestic exports, a majority of which were shipped to Canada and Mexico, also grew substantially. Between 1979 and 1981, the value of export shipments increased from $887 million to nearly $1.4 billion, maintaining a favorable trade balance for U.S. manufacturers.

CURRENT CONDITIONS

The motor and generator industry was expected to expand at a compound annual rate of two percent from 1993 to 1997, suggesting the beginning of a recovery from the pernicious effects of a recession in the early 1990s. During the recession, flagging consumer spending and a decline in housing and industrial construction compounded the existing difficulties associated with foreign competition, excess industry capacity, and cascading prices. The restoration of these integral markets was anticipated to improve the industry's condition as it moved into the twenty-first century, but additional challenges loomed on the horizon.

Escalating energy costs, coupled with federal regulations requiring new energy efficiency standards, made the development of new technology and manufacturing processes intrinsic to any manufacturer's future profitability. The motor and generator industry made progress in this direction during the 1980s, including the development of a highly efficient fractional motor in 1985 that enabled appliances to operate more quietly and at lower cost. However, the industry needed further advances in the 1990s to ensure its viability. In 1992, GE unveiled a variable-speed motor for air conditioning and heating equipment that operated 20 percent more efficiently than other motors used at the time. Manufacturers able to produce equally innovative and energy efficient products would most likely figure prominently in the industry's future.

INDUSTRY LEADERS

Ranked according to sales volume, the two largest companies engaged in the motor and generator industry in 1992 were General Electric Company and Emerson Electric Company. These companies began competing for market share before the turn of the century and have managed to lead the motor and generator industry through much of its history.

Emerson Electric, with about 70,000 employees, recorded roughly $8 billion in revenues in 1992—a considerable gain in magnitude from its origin as small, regional manufacturer of fans and electric motors. Founded in 1890 in St. Louis, Missouri, by judge John Wesley Emerson, Emerson Electric at first engaged in the production of alternating current electric motors. The company enjoyed considerable success well into the twentieth century incorporating electric motors into sundry household appliances. By the 1920s, electric fans became the company's primary product, accounting for 40 percent of total sales.

Following the Great Depression in the 1930s—when sales plummeted, stock dividend payments were halted, and hotly contested labor disputes threatened to bankrupt the company—Emerson Electric's financial condition was buoyed by military contracts obtained during World War II. The company manufactured a variety of war-related products, including gun turrets installed in Air Force bombers such as the B-17, B-25, and B-26. Combined with its other contributions toward the war effort, these products infused the company with $100 million annually.

Defense-related work continued to support Emerson Electric following the war, although during the immediate postwar years military contracts dropped to as low as $1.5 million. But defense-related work picked up again in the 1950s, when the Air Force modernized its bomber fleet, elevating sales from military contracts to 30 percent of the company's total. To supplement its armament production, company management also decided to branch out into the engineering and development of electronics and avionics.

By the end of the 1950s, however, Emerson Electric's management grew fearful of the company's dependence on the military for such a considerable portion of its revenues. To address this, they began an aggressive acquisition program in the 1960s, averaging one acquisition per year throughout the decade. These additional companies enabled Emerson Electric to increase its presence in consumer markets, diversifying the company's product mix to include such items as lighting fixtures, door chimes, and intercom units, and providing for a more stable future. Acquisitions and diversification continued into the 1970s and 1980s, as Emerson Electric became a leader in both consumer and industrial markets. By the 1990s, Emerson Electric's products were sold to commercial and industrial businesses involved in a wide assortment of factory automation and process control enterprises.

General Electric posted $62.2 billion in revenues in 1992, with enough employees to populate many cities in the nation (284,000). Growing from a storied past, it became one of the handful of behemoth corporations that dictated the health of the national economy. In fact, GE's history charted some of the most significant technological discoveries and advancements of the twentieth century. From Thomas Edison's development of the light bulb, to advances in turbine engines, to the refinement of nuclear power production processes, GE has stood as a pioneer in the engineering and manufacturing world for over 100 years.

While this impressive past elevated the company into the upper echelon of international businesses, GE's more recent achievements, especially in the motor and generator industry, have been comparatively dismal. During the 1970s and 1980s, the company suffered increasing losses from foreign competition, labor disputes, and "indirect imports" (finished products that were assembled with electric motors already included). These mounting difficulties forced GE to close several motor and generator manufacturing plants in the late 1980s and to lay off a considerable percentage of its work force. In 1987, for example, GE discontinued production of large-horsepower integral motors, ranging in size from 800 to 8,000 horsepower, which left 825 workers without employment. GE judged the heavy-duty industrial market for these motors to be oversaturated, unattractive due to low prices, and unlikely to recover in the foreseeable future. Harder hit by these market-wide developments than rival Emerson Electric, GE began to slip from its almost unassailable position atop the motor and generator industry in the late 1980s and early 1990s.

WORK FORCE

Total employment in the motor and generator industry decreased through much of the 1980s. This trend continued into the 1990s, as a nationwide recession weakened the motor and generator market. Beyond the negative effects of market fluctuations, manufacturing industries as a whole continued to streamline their operations by eliminating layers of managerial staff and altering production processes to reduce the number of workers required to perform certain tasks. This general movement toward fewer employees per manufacturing facility made future reductions of the motor and generator industry employment base likely.

Of the 72,600 total people employed in the motor and generator industry, 55,100 were production workers. Managerial, administrative, and technical employees composed the remainder of the industry's work force. Generally, production workers were employed on a full-time basis and worked the same average number of hours per year as workers in other manufacturing industries. At $10.35 per hour, compensation for production workers in the motor and generator industry was slightly below the average of $10.49 for other manufacturing industries. In terms of total payroll per manufacturing facility, however, which encompassed both production workers and salaried

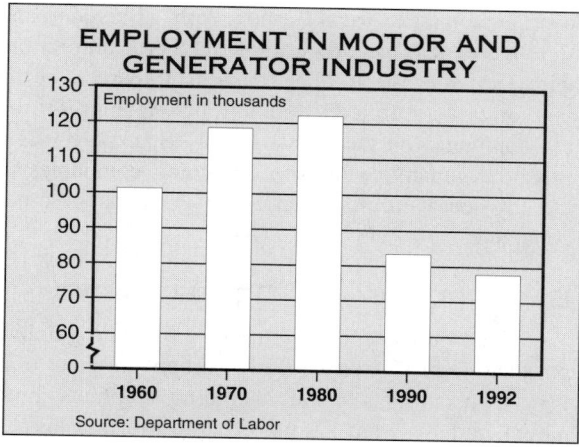

EMPLOYMENT IN MOTOR AND GENERATOR INDUSTRY

Employment in thousands

Source: Department of Labor

employees, 1989 labor costs in the motor and generator industry were considerably higher at $3,887,152 than the average of $1,398,674. This disparity was due, in part, to the greater number of employees per establishment in the motor and generator industry, but also reflected the high salaries paid to managerial, administrative, and technical personnel. In 1990, salaried employees earned an average of $93,476 per year in the industry.

AMERICA AND THE WORLD

The international market for motors and generators was intensely competitive, with Japan, Mexico, Canada, Germany, and the United Kingdom shipping just over $2 billion worth of products to the United States in 1991. Canada and Mexico combined for a 30.1 percent share of the U.S. import market, followed by the European Community with a 24 percent share, and Japan with a 22.4 percent share.

Exports from the United States totalled $2.016 billion in 1991, $15 million greater than the import total. The primary markets for motors and generators manufactured in the United States were Canada, Mexico, Nigeria, South Korea, and the Netherlands. Canada and Mexico accounted for the greatest share of U.S. exports at 31.4 percent, followed by East Asia at 19.9 percent, the European Community at 15.4 percent, and South America at 5.8 percent. The largest disparity between U.S. import and export totals in 1991 existed with Japan. For the year, Japan shipped $449 million worth of motor and generator products to the United States, compared to the $48 million worth of products the United States shipped to Japan.

INDUSTRY INFORMATION SOURCES

Darnay, Arsen J., editor, *Manufacturing USA,* Detroit: Gale Research Inc., 1993.

"Electric Motor Price Rises Set by Some Makers," *Wall Street Journal,* January 20, 1966, p.4.

"Engineering the Electric Century: Motor Development Creates New Loads for Utilities, Changes Industrial Practice," *Electrical World,* August 15, 1973, pp. 38-40.

Gates, Ward, "Electronics Industry Finally Entering Growth Stage," *Magazine of Wall Street,* March 23, 1963, pp. 26-29, 51-53.

"GE Electric Motors Will Feature the Use of Superconductors," *Wall Street Journal,* July 9, 1976, p.3.

"GE Introduces a Motor that Is More Efficient," *Wall Street Journal,* July 1, 1992, p. B6.

Glaberson, William, "An Uneasy Alliance in Smokestack U.S.A.," *New York Times,* March 13, 1988, pp. F1, F11.

"Going on the Straight and Narrow," *Business Week,* January 20, 1968, pp. 134-138.

"Putting Customer Demands First," *Business Week,* November 28, 1970, pp. 62-63.

Rifkin, Glenn, "Using Spin to Power Electric Cars," *New York Times,* November 11, 1992, p. D5.

Stipp, David, "Big Advance in Power Making Works Wonderfully in Theory," *Wall Street Journal,* January 17, 1986, p. 21.

U.S. Industrial Outlook, Washington, DC: U.S. Department of Commerce, 1960-1993.

Weimer, George A., "Power Transmission: A Drive for Efficiency," *Iron Age,* May 26, 1980, pp. 32-37.

—Jeffrey L. Covell

SIC 3624

CARBON AND GRAPHITE PRODUCTS

This category covers establishments primarily engaged in manufacturing carbon, graphite, and metal-graphite brushes and brush stock; carbon or graphite electrodes for thermal and electrolytic uses; carbon and graphite fibers; and other carbon, graphite, and metal-graphite products.

INDUSTRY SNAPSHOT

Carbon and graphite products manufacturing establishments were responsible for shipments worth an estimated $1.16 billion in 1990. Total value of shipments during the 1980s reached a peak of $1.30 billion in 1988 before declining by 11 percent to $1.16 billion in 1990.

Although the industry demonstrated signs of renewed life in the early 1990s, carbon and graphite products output slowly declined in the early 1980s.

The lackluster performance of the industry was attributed to the effect of several economic forces that created product oversupply and excess capacity in the industry. One of the main causes cited for the decade-long stagnation of the industry was the decline of the steel industry, a prime market for the industry's products. In addition, world demand for carbon and graphite electrodes plummeted, also a result of more efficient electrode performance in steel production. The decline in demand for carbon and graphite electrodes for use in steel production, coupled with the strength of the dollar in the mid-1980s, which helped rival foreign producers to increase their presence in the U.S. market, adversely affected the industry's output and profitability.

On the positive side, structural changes in the industry led to a rebound in the 1990s, including slight growth in some export markets. Although the industry was a perennial net importer of carbon and graphite products, the volume of carbon and graphite exports increased 27 percent from 1990 to 1991.

ORGANIZATION AND STRUCTURE

In 1989 approximately 93 establishments were engaged in the production of carbon and graphite products. These establishments employed approximately 108 workers each, 76 of which were employed as production workers. For the same year, the average value added per production worker was $81,620. This figure was small compared to the national standard of $105,881.

Geographically, the greatest number of establishments producing carbon and graphite products in 1987 were located in a region comprising Michigan, Ohio, Indiana, Illinois, and Wisconsin. Ranked by the number of establishments per state, Pennsylvania and Ohio ranked first with 12 each, followed by California with nine, New York with seven, Michigan with six, and North Carolina and South Carolina with four each.

The bulk of the industry's revenue was garnered by a limited number of manufacturers. It was estimated that Stackpole Corporation's various operations, with sales of $420 million, accounted for nearly 40 percent of industry sales in 1992. Moreover, the leading 15 companies accounted for well over 90 percent of the industry's output in 1992. Ranked according to market share, the dominant companies in the carbon and graphite products industry were: Great Lakes Carbon Corporation of Briarcliff Manor, New York with a 12 percent share; Union Carbide Corporation, with 7.7 percent; Stackpole Corporation's Kane, Pennsylvania operation, with 5.1 percent; Stackpole Corporation's Coudersport, Pennsylvania operation, with 4.3 per-

cent; National Electrical Carbon, with 4.1 percent; and Pure Industries, Inc. and Carbone U.S.A. Corporation, with 3.7 percent each. The remaining 19 percent of the market was controlled by about 20 companies. Of the top companies in the industry, only Stackpole was a private company, while the remaining companies in the top ten were subsidiaries or divisions of other companies.

BACKGROUND AND DEVELOPMENT

The products composing the carbon and graphite products industry were mostly carbon products of a very high carbon content, including graphites, both natural and synthetic. Carbon's hardest form is known as diamond; graphite is its softest form. Graphite appears naturally in three forms: amorphous, which is the last stage of the coalification process, crystalline flake, which is used in brake linings and pencils, and lump, used mostly in batteries and found primarily in Sri Lanka.

Synthetic carbon and graphite comes in three basic product categories. Electrodes composed the industry's largest product category. Making up over half of the industry's products, electrodes were used in all types of electric furnaces. Graphite fibers were the second largest category of graphite products. Synthetic powder, made from scraps that are pulverized into a powder, make up the bulk of the remainder of synthetic products.

Industrial uses of graphite and carbon began in the early 1800s. In 1800, Sir Humphrey utilized carbon in the electric arc, which used an electrode made out of charcoal. By 1857, after seven years of experiments with new electrodes yielding a purer carbon, De Grasses B. Fowler patented the process of making carbon plates by mixing ground coke with tar and shaping the mixture under pressure in molds. Soon after, in 1877, Charles F. Brush and Washington H. Laurence of Cleveland began to experiment with carbon electrodes, and, by 1878, Brush was manufacturing electrodes.

By 1896 E.G. Atcheson patented a process which transformed amorphous carbon to synthetic graphite by heat treatment, which laid the foundation for the modern graphite industry. A succession of inventions followed in the electrothermal field, all of which required electrodes of carbon or graphite for their applications. For example, in 1896, H.Y. Castner patented a process that involved the heating of carbon electrodes by means of electricity so that a graphite-like form of carbon was produced. By 1899, the Atcheson Graphite Company was formed in Niagara Falls, New York, producing electrodes for Castner's electrochemical processes, with much of the output going to Europe, the center of the industry at the time.

In 1906, the first steel made with electric power was manufactured in the United States by the Holcomb Steel Company in Syracuse, New York using German electrodes. As the industry progressed, larger and larger electrodes were needed. By 1914 there was a vast expansion in electric furnace capacity and in the electrochemical industry, leading to a rise in the demand for electrodes of all varieties. The 30-inch carbon electrode came in 1927 and the 40-inch carbon electrode followed a year later. Graphite electrodes progressed similarly, but at a slightly slower pace, with the 14-inch electrode introduced between 1914 and 1918. By 1937, the size of graphite electrodes reached 20 inches. At that time, Germany, England, France, Italy and Sweden made graphite and amorphous electrodes. Carbon products were made in most countries in Europe and Japan.

By 1959 many new products followed. Filamentary carbon was made into graphite cloth and eventually carbon and graphite cloth, felt, yarn, tape and fibers were to follow. These products had the desirable properties of not melting at high temperatures and under high pressures. Such applications for carbon and graphite increased exponentially, with many new firms capitalizing on the thermal stability, electrical conductivity, thermal conductivity, and corrosion resistance of carbon and graphite fibers.

By the early 1980s, however, world demand began to collapse because of the decline in consumption of graphite electrodes, particularly by the steel industry. This decline was attributed to improved electrode performance as well as lower priced electrode imports. By 1985, leading producer Union Carbide suspended production at its Clarksville, Tennessee plant when market conditions favored meeting demand for electrodes from a combination of its facilities in Yabucoa, Puerto Rico and Columbia Tennessee. They reopened the Clarksville facility in 1987.

At that time costs were rising, and carbon products firms were experiencing poor profitability. Union Carbide was not the only firm experiencing poor profitability and excess capacity. Fierce domestic and foreign competition was making it hard to meet costs in new carbon electrode plants. Declining demand led to over-capacity in electrodes due mostly to low operating rates in steel mills. Coupled with this was the decline in the U.S. steel industry caused by heightened competition from foreign producers. Another key factor was the increased costs of fuels, such as natural gas used to carbonize coal to make carbon and graphite. Foreign competition was strengthened further by the strength of the dollar at the time, which raised prices of U.S. goods in relation to foreign goods, and enabled consumers to purchase lower priced products from rival producers, especially Italian and Japanese companies. Lastly, alternative products (titanium diboride electrodes were substituted for carbon or graphite) provided 25 percent savings on electrical energy, a major expense in aluminum smelting. Accordingly, key aluminum producers, such as Kaiser Aluminum, Alcoa, and Alcan began using titanium diboride instead of carbon or graphite.

CURRENT CONDITIONS

According to the Bureau of Mines, production of manufactured graphite and graphite fibers decreased ten percent and 14 percent, respectively. In the late 1980s and early 1990s, mergers and acquisitions consolidated the industry, which shed some of its excess capacity. One of the largest mergers in the early 1990s was the joint formation of Horsehead Industries and Hoechst AG of Germany in 1992. This merger combined Horsehead Industries carbon and graphite operations in its graphite products division. SGL Carbon operated plants in Europe and throughout North America. Sales of the newly formed graphite products company were expected to total $750 million per year.

WORK FORCE

From 1987 to 1990, total employment in carbon and graphite production fell from 9,800 to 8,600 people. Production worker employment fell from 8,500 in 1982, to 7,300 in 1985, before rising to 7,400 in 1988 and declining to 6,300 in 1990. Overall, the 1980s witnessed a 7.1 percent decline in industry and a 7.4 percent drop in production employment.

Average hourly earnings of production workers in carbon and graphite production rose steadily from $4.25 in 1972 to $11.21 in 1987. However, the purchasing power of production workers declined by about three percent over the same period.

INDUSTRY INFORMATION SOURCES

''Carbide Plans Major Expansion Program,'' *The Journal of Commerce,* March 15, 1977.

Duffy, Hazel, ''BOC Subsidiary Expands U.S. Graphite Production,'' *Financial Times,* September 15, 1979.

Glynn, Don, and Jones, Susan R., ''At the Brink in Niagara Falls,'' *Chemical Week,* June 5, 1985.

''Great Lakes Carton, Sigri Merge Operations,'' *Ceramic Industry,* March 1992.

Henry, David K., and Richard Oliver, ''The Defense Buildup, 1977-85: Effects on Production and Employment,'' *Monthly Labor Review,* August 1987.

"Horsehead and Hoechst Merge Two Subsidiaries," *Modern Casting,* April 1992.

"Horsehead and Hoechst To Form Joint Company," *Modern Casting,* November 1991.

Mantell, Charles L., *Carbon and Graphite Handbook,* Huntington, New York: Robert E. Krieger Publishing Company, 1979.

Manufacturing USA: Industry Analyses, Statistics, and Leading Companies, 3rd Edition, Detroit: Gale Research Inc., 1993.

"Sigri Great Lakes Carbon to be Formed via Merger of Great Lakes Carbon Division and Sigri," *Light Metal Age,* February 1992.

Taylor, Harold A. Jr., "Graphite," *Mineral Facts and Problems 1985 Edition,* Washington: U.S. Government Printing Office, 1985.

Taylor, Harold, A. Jr., "Graphite," *Minerals Yearbook,* Washington: U.S. Government Printing Office, 1991.

U.S. Department of Commerce, Bureau of the Census, *Census of Manufactures: Electrical Transmission and Distribution Equipment and Electrical Industrial Apparatus,* Washington: U.S. Government Printing Office, May 1990.

U.S. Department of Commerce, International Trade Administration, *U.S. Industrial Outlook 1994,* Washington: U.S. Government Printing Office, January 1994.

—John A. Sarich

SIC 3625

RELAYS AND INDUSTRIAL CONTROLS

This category covers establishments primarily engaged in manufacturing electronic relays and industrial controls used for starting, regulating, stopping, and protecting circuits and electric motors. Mechanical switches and relays are classified elsewhere.

This industry encompasses two major categories: electronic relays and industrial controls. Electronic relays are used in circuitry for computers, communications equipment, and a multitude of other electronic devices. A relay is basically a switch that is used to open or close a circuit. It controls the flow of electricity to create a desired result. Most industrial controls are essentially switches, as well, but of a more complex nature. They are usually associated with the control of electric motors and systems. Industrial controls include contraptions such as motor starters, contractors, control centers, and programmable logic controllers.

A conventional electronic relay contains a solenoid, which is a coil of wire with an enclosed, fixed iron core. When electricity passes through the wire a magnetic field is created that energizes the core. An armature connected to the core allows it to move and activate, or trip, the relay. Smaller relays used in transistorized equipment work similarly, but are much smaller and require a fraction of the power consumed by electromechanical relays. The tiny reed relay, for example, is made with two flat magnetic strips. The separated strips are sealed in a capsule filled with an inert gas (to prevent corrosion), which sits inside a coil. When electricity is applied to the coil the two magnetic strips are drawn to each other, thus completing a circuit. Finally, miniaturized solid-state relays are not magnetically activated, but are instead triggered by electrical pulses.

Relays made up only about 15 percent of industry shipments in the early 1990s. A wide range of industrial controls, many of which incorporate electromechanical and solid-state relays, constituted the remainder of shipments. Two standards for industrial controls are administered by the International Electrotechnical Commission (IEC) and the National Electrical Manufacturers Association (NEMA). IEC-approved controls conform to standards which have brought them a reputation for compactness and affordability. Controls rated by NEMA, while considered less streamlined, are generally perceived by users to be more reliable and serviceable for heavy industrial uses.

The largest consumer of relays and industrial controls in the early 1990s was the computer equipment industry, which purchased 14 percent of production. Most of the remaining output was consumed by various manufacturing industries. Machine tool producers, for example, made up about three percent of the market, and manufacturers of heating and air-conditioning equipment represented two percent of industry revenues. Other consumers of industrial controls included producers of mining machinery, automobiles, railroad equipment, aircraft, and construction equipment.

BACKGROUND AND DEVELOPMENT

One of the first practical applications of electrical relay technology was the telegraph, which was patented by Samuel F.B. Morse in 1844. Relays that were used to operate electronic devices were not developed on a significant scale until late in the 19th century, following Thomas Edison's work with the electronic vacuum tube. As the demand for lighting, phonograph, and other electrical devices flourished during the early 1900s, the need for relays surged. Importantly, U.S. investments in electronics research during World War II spawned significant advancements in all types of electronic components.

When integrated circuits were introduced in 1958, many manufacturers of relays and other electromechanical devices feared that the new solid-state components would make some conventional products obsolete. But the development of miniaturized relays served to expand the breadth of the industry and culminated in demand growth for both traditional and new devices during the 1960s and 1970s. Demand for relays boomed as a result of expanding consumer electronics, business machine, computer, and communications markets. Likewise, industrial controls evolved from relatively simple relay and switch devices used to start and control motors into complex, high-tech mechanisms used to regulate speed, pressure, timing, and other mechanical characteristics.

Overall demand for electronic components grew during the 1980s, bolstered by the proliferation of personal computers and peripherals, telecommunications equipment, and the integration of electronics into industrial and consumer products. Worldwide sales of integrated circuits, for example, jumped 464 percent during the decade. Shipments of many conventional relay products stagnated or declined, largely as a result of foreign competition. But the demand for new high-tech industrial controls, as well as some types of relays, thrived. By 1987, the peak of the 1980s economic expansion, industry sales reached $6.1 billion and employment topped 66,000.

CURRENT CONDITIONS

While the United States slumped into a recession during the late 1980s and early 1990s, sales of relays and industrial controls continued to climb at a healthy pace of nine percent annually through 1991—the industry generated revenues of more than $8 billion that year. In addition to strong demand, manufacturers benefitted from industry consolidation and increased efficiency which had characterized electrical component manufacturers during the 1980s. Indeed, as shipments grew during late 1980s producers continued to reduce employment through automation and restructuring.

The relays and industrial controls industry began to feel the pinch of recession in the early 1990s. Conventional relay shipments, which had already dropped 2.7 percent in 1991, were hit hardest. Nevertheless, overall sales climbed about three percent in both 1992 and 1993, and growth in some segments remained strong. Three primary factors were contributing to the success of relay and industrial control makers going into the mid-1990s: 1) the recovery of industries that purchased their products, 2) increased global competitiveness, which was the result of productivity gains

and a devalued U.S. dollar, and 3) technological advances that were broadening the market for industrial controls.

Long term industry gains will partially depend on U.S. export growth. While exports accounted for only about six percent of sales in 1992, they made up the fastest growing market segment and offered lucrative long term potential for sales of high-tech industrial controls. Canada and Mexico were the largest foreign consumers of U.S. exports and represented about 30 percent of cross-border revenues. European nations also consumed 30 percent of U.S. exports. But the regions of fastest growth were the East Asian countries, which purchased only 14 percent of exports in the early 1990s. The United States imported a total of $650 billion worth of relays and controls annually in the early 1990s, more than 40 percent of which came from Japan.

INDUSTRY LEADERS

Despite steady consolidation in electronics components industries during the 1980s and early 1990s, the relay and industrial controls industry remained relatively fragmented in the early 1990s with about 1,000 competitors. Most companies built industrial controls and specialized in a specific industry niche. The largest competitor in the early 1990s was Allen-Bradley Company Inc., of Wisconsin, a producer of diverse electromechanical goods. The company generated sales of $1.4 billion during 1991 and employed 13,000 workers. During the early 1990s, Allen-Bradley implemented a major restructuring effort based on its benchmarking, or comparison, of other companies. It built a 27,000-square-foot, high-tech production facility that emphasized efficiency and the ability to quickly bring new products to market. The effort had successfully lowered development and manufacturing costs by 1993.

The second largest competitor was Teleflex Inc., of Pennsylvania, which had $444 million in 1991 revenues and employed a work force of 5,800. Other major players included: Woodward Governor Co. ($340 million in 1991 revenues), of Illinois; Potter and Brumfield ($310 million), of Indiana, and; Square D Co. ($279 million), of North Carolina. In 1991 Square D Co. was purchased by French-based control manufacturer Schneider S.A., reflecting an ongoing interest by foreign companies in purchasing U.S. controls technology.

WORK FORCE

Despite a generally positive outlook for most companies in this industry, long term job prospects are less pleasant. Productivity gains and imports of some commodity-like relays and controls will continue to diminish opportunities, particularly for laborers. Jobs for assemblers and fabricators, which account for about 25 percent of the U.S. electrical apparatus work force, was predicted to decline by 30 to 50 percent between 1990 and 2005, according to the Bureau of Labor Statistics. Even positions for white collar managers and top executives expected to see cuts by about ten percent. Only jobs for sales professionals and engineers will increase, though slightly.

RESEARCH AND TECHNOLOGY

Advanced industrial controls represented roughly 20 percent of industry shipments going into the mid-1990s and is expected to continue to provide the greatest profit opportunities for U.S. firms throughout the decade. Electronic and computer-based controls were seen as eventually displacing conventional equipment, and devices based on the IEC standard were expected to replace NEMA-rated products in an increasing number of applications. Regardless of high-tech trends, U.S. producers in this industry lagged behind most other industrial sectors in capital investments, research, and development expenditures during the late 1980s and early 1990s.

One of the most prolific industry trends in the mid-1990s was the integration of fuzzy-logic into control systems. Fuzzy-logic employs the chaos theory, which holds that there are identifiable tendencies of movement amid apparently random patterns. Fuzzy-logic industrial controls are particularly well-suited for complex systems that are heavily dependent on human supervision. In addition to U.S. initiatives, Siemens Corp., of Germany, and several Japanese firms were investing heavily in this new technology.

INDUSTRY INFORMATION SOURCES

Avery, Susan, "What Buyers Need to Know About Industrial Controls," *Purchasing*, June 20, 1991.

Bergstrom, Robin P., "Where Fuzzy Thinking Isn't Wrongheaded," *Production*, August 1991.

Burrows, Peter, "Back to Basics Strategy Revives Control Maker Oak Industries," *Electronic Business*, March 1993.

Darnay, Arsen J., ed., *Manufacturing USA; Industry Analyses, Statistics, and Leading Companies*, Detroit: Gale Research Inc., 1993.

"Fuzzy Coprocessor Sharpens Industrial Controls," *Machine Design*, July 23, 1993.

U.S. Industrial Outlook 1993, Washington, D.C.: U.S. Department of Commerce, June 10, 1993.

Vasilash, Gary S., "A Singular Device," *Production*, June 1993.

Wexler, Joanie, "Users Grapple With New Option for Switched Data," *Network World*, February 14, 1994.

Yost, Larry, "The Allen-Bradley Story," *Journal of Business Strategy*, May/June 1993.

—Dave Mote

SIC 3629

ELECTRICAL INDUSTRIAL APPARATUS, NOT ELSEWHERE CLASSIFIED

This category covers establishments primarily engaged in manufacturing industrial and commercial electric apparatus, such as fixed and variable capacitors and rectifiers for industrial applications.

Examples of products manufactured in the miscellaneous electrical industrial apparatus industry include battery chargers, nonelectronic condensers, nonelectric rectifiers, surge suppressors, and thermoelectric generators. Companies that produce capacitors and rectifiers are classified elsewhere.

Nonelectric rectifying apparatus that is used to convert alternating current to direct current accounted for about 50 percent of industry output in the early 1990s. Nonelectric capacitor equipment made up about 12 percent of revenues. Other major product groups included coil windings (3.65 percent of sales), solenoids (2.53 percent), and cathodic protection equipment (1.7 percent). About 50 percent of output was sold to other manufacturing industries, and 30 percent was produced for the U.S. armed forces. Federal nondefense purchases contributed ten percent of revenues. The remainder of output was shipped to several other sectors, such as automotive repair services and communications industries.

History. American Lee DeForest's patent in 1906 of an electrical vacuum tube, which was based on a design by Thomas Edison, marked the beginning of practical electronics applications. Inventions during both world wars delivered pivotal technological breakthroughs that vastly broadened the scope of the electronics industry. As electrical apparatus sales surged during the post-World War II U.S. economic expansion, miscellaneous electrical industrial apparatus shipments swelled. By the beginning of the 1980s, the industry was generating revenues of about $1.1 billion per year and employing a work force of more than 16,000.

Industry Outlook. Industry growth lagged during the 1980s, partly as a result of an influx of foreign goods into the United States that integrated apparatus manufactured overseas. In addition, increasingly popular solid state components reduced the demand for some types of traditional electromechanical equipment produced in this industry. Even a major jump in U.S. defense spending was insufficient to impel growth. Sales increased to just $1.5 billion by the end of the decade, reflecting a decline in inflation-adjusted revenues since 1980. Although competitors were beginning to emerge from a U.S. recession in the mid-1990s, the long term outlook remained generally poor.

Top Players. There were more than 450 companies competing in the miscellaneous electrical industrial apparatus industry in the late 1980s. The largest player was Exide Electronics Group Inc., of North Carolina, which had 1991 sales of $139 million and about 1,300 workers. Acme Electric Corp., of New York, shipped $91 million worth of goods in 1991 and employed 1,000. Other industry leaders included Maxwell Laboratories Inc., of California, and Camco Products and Service, of Oklahoma. Most competitors were small, specialized manufacturers. Even most of the top 50 companies employed fewer than 100 workers.

Future employment prospects for this industry were predicted to be dismal. Total employment plummeted 11 percent between 1982 and 1990 to 14,600. Continued productivity gains, achieved through automation and restructuring, were expected to continue to whittle the work force through the 1990s. Positions for electrical assemblers, which accounted for about 20 percent of electrical apparatus industry employment, were predicted to plunge by about 48 percent between 1990 and 2005, according to the Bureau of Labor Statistics. Likewise, jobs for machine operators, coil winders, and most other labor workers will also drop significantly. Only positions for engineers and sales professionals were expected to increase, but only slightly.

INDUSTRY INFORMATION SOURCES

Darnay, Arsen J., ed., *Manufacturing USA; Industry Analyses, Statistics, and Leading Companies*, Detroit: Gale Research Inc., 1993.

U.S. Industrial Outlook 1993, Washington, D.C.: U.S. Department of Commerce, January 1993.

—Dave Mote

SIC 3631

HOUSEHOLD COOKING EQUIPMENT

This category covers establishments primarily engaged in manufacturing household electric and non-electric cooking equipment, such as stoves, ranges, and ovens, except portable electric appliances. This industry includes establishments primarily engaged in manufacturing microwave and convection ovens, including portable. Establishments primarily engaged in manufacturing other electric household cooking appliances, such as portable ovens, hot plates, grills, percolators, and toasters, are classified in **SIC 3634: Electric Housewares and Fans.** Establishments primarily engaged in manufacturing commercial cooking equipment are classified in **SIC 3589: Service Industry Machinery, Not Elsewhere Classified.**

INDUSTRY SNAPSHOT

Household cooking equipment is part of the estimated $17 billion appliance market that includes white goods—washing machines, refrigerators, and other long-term appliances—in the United States. Like white goods, household cooking equipment is dependent on the housing economy and previous housing slumps have impacted the industry rather severely. This category also is described as a "mature" industry, with much consolidation occurring among the major appliance manufacturers. Demand for replacements of old and worn-out appliances drives the market, since most major appliances last ten to 15 years.

White goods sales peaked in 1987 with 38 million units sold, but the industry endured a slowdown during the early 1990s. Overall product shipments of appliances grew three percent in 1993 to $17.7 billion, while housing starts only increased about four percent during the same period of time, according to the *1994 U.S. Industrial Outlook*. Household cooking equipment represented an estimated $3.3 million worth of shipments or about 20 million units in 1993.

Five major corporations dominate the household appliance industry and imports make up more than 50 percent of the domestic market in many categories of small appliances like coffeemakers. An objective of many of the main appliance manufacturers is to expand their markets globally. Many firms accomplished this by opening factories in Europe and Asia.

Appliance shipments were expected to increase four percent in 1994, reported the *U.S. Industrial Outlook*. The North American Free Trade Agreement may also help expand U.S. exports of home appliances to Mexico. In terms of five-year growth, shipments were projected to increase about two percent every year due in part to the fact that appliances are a mature industry. Most appliances are purchased for new housing, replacement, or remodeling. Consequently, private housing starts were predicted to increase four percent in 1994, as well, and the number of occupied housing units was expected to grow about one percent annually.

ORGANIZATION AND STRUCTURE

The top industry leaders of household cooking equipment were: Whirlpool Corp., General Electric Company (GE), White Consolidated Industries Inc., Sony Electronics, Inc., Maytag Corp., Sharp Electronics Corp., Washington Energy Co., and Sunbeam-Oster Company, Inc. Whirlpool is the largest major appliance manufacturer in the world, and dominates the industry. For example, Whirlpool has been the major supplier of Sears, Roebuck & Co.'s Kenmore household cooking range line.

These main manufacturers produce the following brand name household cooking appliances: Whirlpool Corp. produces Kenmore, KitchenAid, and Whirlpool ranges; Maytag Corp. produces Magic Chef, Maytag, Admiral, Hardwick, and Jenn-Air ranges; General Electric produces GE, Hotpoint, and RCA electric ranges; White Consolidated Industries produces Frigidaire, Tappan, White-Westinghouse, and Gibson ranges.

BACKGROUND AND DEVELOPMENT

A roaring fire in the chimney or pot bellied stove had been the only way to cook food until Benjamin Franklin tried to tame the unpredictability of the flame with the Franklin stove. But his stove was only an iron box with flues and not a "range" as we know it—his invention only slightly improved open hearth cooking.

The development of cast iron ranges that burned coal or wood led the next improvement during the 19th century, but the heat source was also unpredictable and food had to be monitored constantly to prevent cooking disasters. While this type of device enabled a variety of foods to be cooked at once, these stoves were still dirty and often a fire hazard.

To the rescue were the gas burning stoves, developed in the mid-nineteenth century. The first use of gas to cook food in the home was demonstrated by James Sharp in Northhampton, England, between 1830 and 1832, states Lawrence Wright in his book *Home Fires Burning, the History of Domestic Heating and Cooking*. Gas burners concentrated heat at the cooking source and ensured that food was cooked more evenly and all the way through. The transition to gas cooking, however, required a major plumbing overhaul as pipes had to be hooked up to a stove. Middle class and wealthy housewives initially used the first gas stoves. Thermostatically controlled gas ovens began appearing in 1915, and essentially, freed cooks from the kitchen. Cooks could finally leave food unattended for brief periods of time without major incident.

Eventually, tabletops, cabinets, and drawers were added to gas burning stoves, which transformed the devices into "kitchen furniture." Because of the gas stove, cooking utensils evolved from wood to heavy cast iron and tin to lightweight aluminum, tempered glass and ceramic. Shirley Abbott and Bonnie Slotnick in *American Heritage Magazine* wrote that by the 1920s, gas ranges were made of white porcelain enamel, and within a decade, were produced in decorative colors to match other kitchen appliances and cabinetry. "The look of the American kitchen was thus set for the rest of the century," they wrote, ". . . light, spotless, efficient." Gas ranges revolutionized cooking, making it more sanitary and time saving, even despite the advances made in electric ranges. Gas ranges were still a preferred method of cooking in the latter twentieth century.

Attempts to use electricity in home cooking occurred as early as the late nineteenth century. The 1893 Columbian Exhibition at Chicago featured a "Model Electric Kitchen." In 1905, the "General Electric Range," equipped with its own switchboard, sat on metal legs with the oven well above the cooking surface. But until 1912, most electric ranges were converted gas cookers made of cast-iron and some insulation. In this type of range, all the heating elements were sealed in airtight containers to keep from burning out. Electric cookers relied on the "Bastian heater," or a wire spiral contained inside a quartz tube. Other improvements on this theme consisted of the Dowsing Electric Fire (with sausage lamps), resistance wires of nickel and chromium that heated without oxidization. But early electric cooking overloaded circuits, and was not made efficient until power companies were able to supply more electricity to homes.

Electric ranges did not compete with gas or solid fuel ranges until the 1930s. Consumers favor gas ranges over electric ovens because food can be cooked faster on a gas range, and gas ovens do not interfere with other electrical appliances. A gas range also does not leave residual heat. On the other hand, an electric range does not need to be lit. According to Wright, ". . . most have more useful cooking space in their ovens; some will simmer when the lid of the pan is on;

all have or can have, automatic oven timers and more have spits. . . . So if you are particularly keen on instant control of the heat, you will choose gas, if on cleanliness, and a wide choice of extras, electricity.'' However, improvements made on both types of ranges make them competitive in the market place.

In 1945, Percy L. Spencer, a researcher at Raytheon Co., invented the microwave oven. Spencer looked for a way to cook by radio waves. But it wasn't until he was working around a magnetron that he discovered that a candy bar melted in his pocket even though he had not felt any heat. He placed Indian corn in front of the magnetron and witnessed kernels popping.

Spencer later added a cabinet with trays to the machine and created the first ''radar range.'' Microwave ovens were first used commercially before entering the home cooking market. Raytheon and Litton Industries Inc., both defense contractors, tried to sell microwave ovens in the United States, but did not meet with much success. Most consumers thought it was unnecessary to use a microwave in addition to a gas or electric range.

The Japanese entered the market, and became one of the first big manufacturers of microwave ovens, in part because the appliances fit the Japanese lifestyle perfectly. Japanese cooking requires reheating. And with Japanese houses and kitchens being smaller, microwave ovens were the perfect space savers. Japan exported microwaves to the United States in the 1970s, and five years later, the market had swelled to 2.2 million microwaves. American appliance manufacturers didn't try to reenter the market until the late 1970s. However, by this time, the Japanese had already controlled 25 percent of the market.

Korean manufacturers like Samsung began entering the American market in the early 1980s, by supplying merchandisers like J.C. Penney Company, Inc. with inexpensive microwave ovens. Eventually U.S. manufacturers began producing microwave ovens that would compete directly with other imported models. Americans soon began to perceive microwave ovens as an adjunct to the kitchen. Microwave ovens can reheat leftover food and frozen items quickly, cleanly, and conveniently making meal preparation less of an ordeal. The development of such models like General Electric's Spacesaver oven have made microwave ovens a valuable asset to the kitchen. However, conventional convection ovens (gas or electric) have not been completely replaced. Studies conducted in the late 1980s show that convection ovens are used to prepare the main meal or to cook meals from scratch.

CURRENT CONDITIONS

Industry reports projected 14.3 million units of household cooking equipment were expected to be shipped in the first quarter of 1994. And according to *Appliance Magazine*, ''. . . cooking appliance trends continue to emphasize cleanability, convenience, and sophisticated design, with a growing concern for energy efficiency.'' Major manufacturers focused on improving the overall product with new engineering. Consumers, the magazine stated, are becoming more interested in convection cooking appliances like wall ovens. And gas ranges may be gaining in more popularity as improvements in technology catch up with electric range and microwave ovens. Also, the glass ''cook tops'' that cover burners and electric coil eyelets became more popular, as well as combined microwave/oven arrangements that save space and are more energy efficient.

INDUSTRY LEADERS

The top ten leading manufacturers of household cooking equipment are in order of ranking: Whirlpool Corp., $7,097 million; Sony Electronics, Inc., $5,500 million; General Electric Company (GE Appliances), $5,451 million; White Consolidated Industries, Inc., $4,820 million; Maytag Corp., $3,041.2 million; Sharp Electronics Corp., $2,200 million; Washington Energy Co., $967.2 million; Sunbeam-Oster Company, Inc., $590 million; and Whirlpool Corp. Findlay Division, $400 million.

Market share differs among the industry leaders depending on the household equipment category, although Whirlpool has been cited as the world leader in overall market share in core appliances including gas and electric ranges. Whirlpool's marketing strategy has been to produce specific appliances to serve a widening global consumer base. For example, it sells a 42-inch oven to African markets large enough to cook a whole sheep or goat.

General Electric, in second place in 1992, lost market share due to losses in electric and gas ranges. Maytag improved its share in electric ranges and dishwashers.

In terms of gas ranges, Maytag had held the most market share of this category with about 25 percent, followed by General Electric, and White Consolidated Industries with 24 percent each. But Maytag's share has been slipping according to a Lehman Brother's 1993 industry report. It stated the company endured problems with a gas valve problem in its Magic Chef ranges in 1992. GE increased in market share from 17 percent in 1990 to 24 percent in 1991, after the acquisition of Roper's manufacturing facilities. GE also made gas ranges in Mexico, and had the capacity to produce more than its one million unit per year rate. Raytheon's Amana brand lost two percentage points from 21 percent in 1992.

Market share in electric ranges experienced more shifts in share. GE leads here, but lost four percentage points to 39 percent in 1992—the first time in ten years the company has fallen below 40 percent market share, according to a 1993 Lehman Brothers industry report. Whirlpool moved up one point to 19 percent of the electric range market, followed by White Consolidated Industries with 18 percent, while Maytag had 14 percent and Raytheon had five percent in 1992.

WORK FORCE

Total employment for the household appliance industry was 106,000 in 1993, down from 117,000 in 1987. Production workers, however, numbered about 85,700 compared to 92,500 in 1987. Government sources also projected that workers in this industry would earn hourly wages averaging $11.29 in 1993, compared with $10.75 an hour in 1987. Employees in this category represented a total payroll of about $442.2 million in 1989.

AMERICA AND THE WORLD

Many appliances are American-made, however, other countries like Japan and South Korea became leading suppliers of white goods to the United States. The supplying other countries are Mexico, China, and Taiwan.

Imports and exports of appliances increased at nearly the same rate, according to the *1994 U.S. Industrial Outlook*—about seven percent to $4.1 billion for imports and six percent to $2.5 billion for exports. American appliance manufacturers like General Electric formed joint partnerships with foreign companies to make stoves and microwave ovens overseas for the American market. Many of these foreign-made appliances then come under an American label. The *U.S. Industrial Outlook* stated that "Mexico is expected to increase its lead regardless of the fate of the North American Free Trade Agreement, because of the growing integration of its appliance industry with that of the United States." Countries with traditionally lower wages, like South Korea and China, will continue to be major suppliers of small appliances. Microwave ovens still represent the majority of imported appliances, but in recent years, demand for microwaves has tapered off.

American manufacturers expanded their markets to be global leaders in the industry. Whirlpool led the way by owing a 70 percent stake in Inglis of Canada and in an Italian company. Whirlpool also has developed joint ventures with Indian and Mexican companies. In 1988, the company formed a joint venture with N.V. Philips of the Netherlands to make appliance for international markets. The leading markets for American appliances are Canada, Mexico, Japan, Germany, and Saudi Arabia, respectively. The lowering of tariffs between countries, for example, resulted in the doubling of exports to Canada since 1990. American exports to Mexico also doubled in the early-1990s because of such tariff reductions.

RESEARCH AND TECHNOLOGY

As mentioned earlier, household cooking equipment has undergone a gradual evolution since man discovered fire. But what is startling is that recent leaps and bounds in technology occurred within the last decade. Gas ranges used a basic grate and burner as the basic heating element needed to cook food. And although the microwave oven had been invented in the mid-1940s, it did not become widely used until the mid-1980s. Consumers only used gas or electric ranges (electric heating coils and or disks) for cooking.

In 1987, the National Appliance Energy Conversation Act established national efficiency standards for major household appliances including kitchen ranges and ovens. The law authorized the U.S. Department of Energy to propose standards in 1994. After a comment period, final standards were expected to be published in late 1994, and become effective by 1997.

This national mandate comes in the wake of such improvements in technology that offer new options such as convection, induction, halogen, sealed burners, solid black glass and ceramic cooktops, and downdraft and radiant heating techniques—an array of options never available before. The new technologies have made ovens "self-cleaning," more fuel and energy efficient, safer, and even streamlined for decorative purposes. A consumer can reheat, thaw, barbecue, broil, grill, griddle, bake, boil, and poach food at the same time, on the same appliance, and in less time.

INDUSTRY INFORMATION SOURCES
Abbott, Shirley, and Slotnick, Bonnie. "The Gas Range," *American Heritage,* May/June 1991, p. 30.

"As the Temperature Cools Down, Cooking Products Begin to Heat Up," *HFD-Weekly Home Furnishings,* Nov. 4, 1991, p. 122.

Beaulieu, Brian. "Appliance Turnaround by Fourth Quarter," *Appliance Manufacturer,* April 1991, p. 18.

Betty, Gerry. "Cooking Products Outlook: Technology Gains Acceptance," *HFD-Weekly Home Furnishings,* June 4, 1990, p. 195.

Cayer, Shirley. "White Goods Wars Continued," *Purchasing,* May 7, 1992, p. 69.

"Cookware Heats Up With Induction," *Chain Store Age,* February 1987, p. 83.

Cornell, R.T. et al. "Monthly Appliance Shipment Forecast-Industry Report," *Lehman Brothers, Inc.,* Oct. 29, 1993.

Darnay, Arsen, ed. *Gale's Service Industries USA,* Detroit: Gale Research, 1992.

Flint, Jerry. "Consumer Durables," *Forbes,* Jan. 8, 1994, p. 142.

"Global Growth Strategies," *Appliance Manufacturer,* January 1992, p. 13.

"Gas Ranges Cooking; Hot in Sept., 9 Months," *HFD-Weekly Home Furnishings,* Nov. 5, 1990, p. 144.

Hardman, Adrienne. "Whirlpool: Set to Cycle," *Financial World,* Oct. 13, 1992, p. 18.

Harris, John M. "Household Appliances," *U.S. Industrial Outlook, 1994,* p. 36-11.

"In Praise of Mighty Microwave Oven, FF Leaders Call for Standardization," *Quick Frozen Foods International,* January 1988, p. 108.

Magaziner, Ira C., and Patinkin, Mark. "Fast Heat: How Korea Won the Microwave War," *Harvard Business Review,* January-February 1989, p. 83.

"Microwave Ovens Are Making Macro Advances," *Nation's Restaurant Business News,* Oct. 18, 1993, p. 58.

"Microwaves, Bakeware Plateau," *Chain Store Age,* General Merchandise Trends, August 1987, p. 30.

Predicasts Forecasts, 1993, Foster City, CA: Information Access Co., Annual Issue No. 32, 4th Quarter.

Predicasts Forecasts, 1994, Foster City, CA: Information Access Co., Annual Issue No. 134, Jan. 18, 1994, 2nd Quarter.

Queisser, Wolfgang K.H. "From Components to a Cooking System," *Appliance Manufacturer,* May 1988, p. 76.

Remich, Norman C. Jr. "Good News for Majors," *Appliance Manufacturer,* July 1991, p. 7.

Remich, Norman C. Jr. "What's Hot in Majors," *Appliance Manufacturer,* April 1987, p. 44.

"Three New England Inventions that Changed Parties Everywhere," *Yankee,* January 1993, p. 30.

Underwood, Elaine. "Manufacturers Look for New Frontiers," *AdWeek's Marketing Week, Superbrands* 1990 supplement, September 1990.

Wright, Lawrence. *Home Fires Burning, the History of Domestic Heating and Cooking,* London: Routledge & Kegan Paul, 1964.

—Evelyn S. Dorman

SIC 3632

HOUSEHOLD REFRIGERATORS AND HOME AND FARM FREEZERS

This entry discusses establishments primarily engaged in manufacturing household refrigerators and home and farm freezers. Establishments primarily engaged in manufacturing commercial and industrial refrigeration equipment are categorized in **SIC 3585: Air-Conditioning and Warm Air Heating Equipment and Commercial and Industrial Refrigeration Equipment.**

INDUSTRY SNAPSHOT

As the household refrigerator and freezer industry (and the appliance industry in general) entered the 1990s, it was dominated in the United States by five companies—Whirlpool, General Electric, Maytag, Electrolux (Frigidaire), and Raytheon (Amana). Most of these companies, however, sold appliances under many other brand names, many of which had been around since home refrigeration finally became feasible in the late 1920s.

By the beginning of the 1990s, several decades of consolidation had left an industry with little room for growth domestically. There were no smaller companies left for the large corporations to buy, and it was a mature industry with 99.9 percent of American households possessing refrigerators, according to *Appliance* magazine. About 33 percent of homes contained a freezer. The refrigerator industry, however, had a steady market for replacements and units for new homes. The manufacturers' best opportunities for growth in a low-growth industry were to expand their profit margin, either by raising prices or cutting production costs and operating expenses, and to increase sales abroad.

Each company sold appliances at three different price ranges, with low-end products the least profitable and high-end products offering the best profit margin. With the shaky economy in the early 1990s, sales of low-end refrigerators performed more strongly than top-of-the line models.

The big five of this industry had all instituted programs to improve productivity, and the industry was considered one of the most efficient in the country, leaving little room for foreign products to take any significant market share as they had in the car and electronics industries. In addition, prices of American refrigerators and freezers had remained reasonable. Several stylish European appliances found a small market in the United States but they were unlikely to take any significant market share because of their expense.

U.S. manufacturers shipped more than 7.2 million refrigerators, with a value of almost four billion dollars, and more than 1.4 million freezers in 1991. (Both figures include exports.) The U.S. Department of Commerce predicted that shipments of household appliances would increase by about 2.5 percent a year through 1996.

Whirlpool and General Electric each produced 30 to 35 percent of all appliances shipped, followed by Frigidaire, Maytag, and Amana. These five companies produced more than 95 percent of all appliances made in the United States. Shipment of refrigerators represents the largest share of the appliance industry and General Electric was the leader in that category, followed by Whirlpool. According to Standard and Poor's industry survey, brand loyalty was strong in the replacement appliance market, and although percentages shifted from year to year, it was unlikely that any manufacturer would take a serious bite out of another manufacturers' market shares.

U.S. manufacturers were under serious environmental pressure in the 1990s to increase recyclability of refrigerators, reduce energy consumption and eliminate chlorofluorocarbons as the refrigerant in refrigerators and freezers.

ORGANIZATION AND STRUCTURE

Both the manufacturers and appliance distributors were busy consolidating in the 1970s and 1980s. As the distributors became larger, they wanted more pricing and service concessions. This put pressure on manufacturers as they had to keep taking tighter and tighter profit margins. The manufacturers were better able to provide concessions through their own consolidation which streamlined operations. This consolidation enabled them to produce more efficiently and maintain tight profit margins despite large volume discounts to giant distributors and mega-retailers

Home Furnishings Daily wrote that ten retailers handled more than 44 percent of the appliance market in 1992. The largest was Sears with a 29 percent share of the market. The large retailers deal directly with the manufacturers rather than with a middleperson, the distributor. In a slow economy, manufacturers try to streamline marketing and distribution and one way to do this is to cut out the distributor.

This trend towards selling directly to mass merchandisers hurt many distributors who had exclusive contracts with particular manufacturers. Many smaller

distributors were driven out of business because they heavily depended upon a particular manufacturer for most of their inventory or they depended upon a few large retailers, who suddenly decided to deal directly with the manufacturer, for most of their sales. Meanwhile, small retailers were concerned that they were too small to have much clout dealing directly with the manufacturer and needed distributors to represent them.

But some manufacturers were also becoming disenchanted with their direct marketing to large retailers, finding that brand loyalty and profits were declining, and loyal distributors and dealers were going out of business. GE network of small dealers was down from 50 percent of sales in 1981 to only 35 percent ten years later. In response, GE let its dealers electronically tap into the company's production schedules and place direct orders with a guarantee of two-day delivery.

Traditionally, dealers maintained large inventories of products; however, this trend was changing, and there was some speculation that retailer outlets would become showrooms, and products would be shipped directly from the manufacturer to the customer. In response, manufacturers would have to be able to guarantee delivery of appliances within a two- or three-day period. Appliance companies were also restructuring their sales departments to offer greater exposure of their entire product lines to more distributors or retailers.

The big appliance companies sold refrigerators and freezers in a broad array of brands, a reminder of the consolidation that has occurred. Whirlpool manufactured Estate, KitchenAid, Roper, and Whirlpool products in the United States. General Electric sold appliances under its own name, as well as the RCA and Hotpoint brands. At the beginning of the 1980s, Maytag did not even make refrigerators. But by the close of the decade, the company was making Admiral, Jen-Air, Magic Chef, Norge, and Maytag refrigerators.

Some of the most familiar names in refrigerators and freezers were actually owned by Electrolux of Sweden: Frigidaire, Kelvinator, White-Westinghouse, Gibson, and Tappan. Raytheon, primarily a defense contractor, acquired Amana in 1965 and produced refrigerators and other appliances under that very established brand name.

BACKGROUND AND DEVELOPMENT

The history of electric refrigerators is relatively short. It was not until the 1930s that refrigeration became a large industry. In the 1920s, few American households had refrigerators. Ice and ice boxes were the norm for keeping items cold. The ice box was an insulated box or cabinet in which a block of ice was set to keep items cool inside. The ice could keep for several days if the box was well insulated and well sealed. Every few days, the ice had to be replaced.

During the mid-nineteenth century, many inventors patented their own versions of mechanical refrigerating machines that could make ice and others that could keep things cool in a large compartment. In the northeast, natural ice was available during the winter months; however, selling manufactured ice became a big business in the southeastern United States by the 1890s and a few years later in the north as well. Breweries all over the country had adopted refrigeration. Cold storage buildings became common in the cities, meat packers were using refrigeration units, and even railroad cars and ships provided refrigerated transportation. But home refrigeration would wait several decades; the refrigeration required a bulky cooling system that was not practical for home use.

The quest for an effective mechanical refrigeration system for the home was widespread. Large companies as well as individual inventors could see how popular home refrigerators would be. People working to develop a refrigerator were often backed by large manufacturers who could see that if their inventors were successful, the invention would be worth millions since the market was so vast. Cities in the United States and abroad were expanding and people lived farther and farther from the places where food was produced. They needed to keep more supplies on hand, but they needed a place to preserve them. Use of ice boxes was widespread, but a refrigerator would be more convenient.

Building and marketing a home refrigerator had many restrictions that the commercial units did not. The home unit had to be small enough to fit easily into the house; it had to be automatic and not require an operator as the commercial units did. It also had to use safer chemicals than the highly toxic or flammable ones used in commercial units. And even if those requirements were met, the unit had to be affordable, which meant mass production had to be possible.

During the beginning of the twentieth century, two avenues of development were being pursued— compression technology and absorption technology. Compression required electricity to power a pump called a compressor. Absorption required gas power and did not even need a motor. The first functional household refrigerator was produced in Chicago in 1912; it was called the Domelre. Six years later, Amer-

ican Nathaniel Wales designed a unit called the Kelvinator, which employed compression technology. The Kelvinator became the first mass-produced home refrigerator. In 1919, General Motors bought a small refrigerator company called Frigidaire, which also made compression refrigerators. By 1920, about 75,000 homes had refrigerators.

Since gas was the most widely used energy source, the absorption refrigerator would have seemed a better choice than compression. Yet, dozens of companies were involved in refrigerators development, the few that had substantial corporate backing were working on compression machines.

General Electric had been working on commercial and household refrigerator development for many years, but it wasn't until 1923 that it put substantial resources into development of the home version. Officials at the company realized that refrigerators already on the market had certainly not been perfected and that whoever solved some of the early problems could dominate the market. Refrigerators were expensive. They had dropped in price but still cost $450 for the most inexpensive model, a lot of money in a time when most people had annual incomes of less than $2,000. These early compression models used as refrigerants ammonia, sulphur dioxide, or methyl chloride which carried danger of explosion or poisonous leaks. The refrigerators also had a short life since these refrigerants were corrosive.

The first home refrigerators were also noisy and needed servicing every few months. Fortunately, the noisy motor was separate from the cooling box. The motor could be put in the basement or elsewhere. But the separation of the two parts also forced the compressor to work harder to pump the refrigerant to the cooling box in the kitchen.

Considering the government requirements in the 1990s calling for refrigerators that run on less electricity, it is ironic that in the 1920s, a compelling reason to pursue compression technology was that it required electricity 24 hours a day and therefore, would use a lot of power. It was clear that most homes would soon have either gas or electric power. Electricity was in its infancy, but GE was betting that electricity would win out over gas. General Electric was also watching out for the interests of the electric utility companies, their main customers.

In 1927, General Electric began marketing the first refrigerator with a hermetically-sealed motor and an attached cooling box. It was called the "Monitor Top," because the motor was in a circular box on top of the cooling compartment. By 1929 the company had sold an astonishing 50,000 Monitor Tops. That same year, GE replaced the wood cabinet with steel and brought out its first all-steel refrigerators. In 1931, GE produced its one millionth Monitor Top refrigerator.

In the 1930s, General Motors' Frigidaire company developed the first use of chlorofluorocarbons as a refrigerant, technology which became the standard for decades and which essentially eliminated the danger of fire and poisoning. In 1939, GE produced the first refrigerator that had a freezer compartment as well as a cooling compartment.

The absorption unit was not completely out of the picture. Inventors were still working on improved versions, and once perfected they would have offered many advantages over the compression machines: they were not as noisy, they had few movable parts, and in many places gas was cheaper than electricity. But slowly, the companies developing these machines went out of business; they had received very little development or promotional capital from the gas companies or other corporations. Between 1926 and 1957, only one large company, Servel, manufactured and marketed absorption refrigerators. By 1940, there were four major manufacturers of compression refrigerators, and each was associated with a large corporation: General Electric, Westinghouse, American Motors' Kelvinator, and General Motors' Frigidaire.

Ice boxes remained common well into the 1930s and even into the 1940s, but refrigerators were becoming a large industry by the 1930s, despite the Depression. Prices had come down with improved mass production, and consumers were also offered the opportunity to buy the appliance on an installment plan. The industry grew large as refrigerator motors and refrigerant systems were made smaller and safer for home use. The refrigerator was constantly being improved, with features such as automatic defrost, ice makers, and redesigned interior shelving.

The freezer has not been nearly as successful as the refrigerator. The process for quick-freezing food started to take off in 1925, and families bought frozen food to keep in their new freezers. In the 1940s and 1950s, freezers and the convenience of frozen food were in their heyday; families could save money by purchasing meat, frozen vegetables, and other items in large quantities. However, the freezer never quite caught on. They were expensive to run, which offset any savings from bulk purchases of food.

Until the early 1980s, there were 15 to 30 domestic appliance manufacturers. Consolidation whittled them down to the five major companies.

CURRENT CONDITIONS

Market factors. Sales of refrigerators and freezers depend upon many factors. About 75 percent of appliance sales were for replacements due to serious repairs, redecorating, or moving. Compression refrigerators built in the previous few decades had an average life span of about 16 years. Because 99.9 percent of American homes had refrigerators in the 1990s, there was a steady market for replacement units. Only about a third of American homes contained freezers, however, so although the replacement market was smaller, there was also room for expansion.

Refrigerator sales were also dependent upon housing starts. About 25 percent of appliance sales were linked to new construction of houses and apartment buildings. However, because of its steady replacement market, refrigerators were less dependent than other appliances upon housing starts.

The state of the economy also had a direct effect on refrigerator-freezer sales. Consumers were less likely to make purchases of replacement appliances, unless absolutely necessary, during difficult economic periods.

Manufacturers had not made any significant price increases and the average prices remained constant for the seven years between 1985 and 1992. Although Whirlpool tried to raise prices in 1992, none of the other manufacturers followed suit, forcing Whirlpool to lower prices again.

Environmental impact. Refrigerator and freezer makers faced strict new guidelines from the Department of Energy for 1993. The guidelines required higher efficiency standards, and manufacturers were making small changes to meet the energy-use goals, such as improving insulation, compressors, motors, and door gaskets. Interior dimensions on some machines were to be smaller to allow for thicker walls and doors. Another set of guidelines calling for even stricter energy efficiency was likely with a possible target date of 1998 for full implementation. Manufacturers were concerned that they would not be able to meet those requirements.

For the typical home of the early 1990s, a frost-free refrigerator or freezer was the second most expensive home appliance to operate besides the water heater. Appliance makers were required to include labels listing an estimate of the cost per year of running each appliance so that consumers could compare costs and energy usage.

The refrigerator and freezer industry was also under pressure to find an alternative coolant to chlorofluorocarbons (CFCs) which were believed to cause depletion of the ozone layer that protects the planet from dangerous cancer-causing ultraviolet rays. An agreement called the Montreal Protocol called for complete elimination of the use of CFCs by the year 2000; however, officials and environmentalists from many countries were pushing for elimination of CFCs by 1996 because of evidence that the level of CFCs in the stratosphere over North America was even worse than had originally been reported. (See the **Research and Technology** section for more on the redesign of refrigerators and freezers.)

Congressional bills called for manufacturers to recycle both packaging and the products themselves. The bills stipulated that new products had to be easier to disassemble for recycling and that some packaging had to be reusable.

INDUSTRY LEADERS

General Electric was the number one refrigerator maker in 1992, with Whirlpool a distant second. Between the two of them, however, they controlled 61 percent of the domestic market for all appliances.

Whirlpool, which started out making washing machines only, became a full-line appliance manufacturer in the 1950s and 1960s. At that time, it also became the principal supplier of the Sears Kenmore brand and still was in 1993. Sears accounted for about 19 percent of Whirlpool's revenues in 1991. Between 1981 and 1991, Whirlpool's revenues shot up from $2.4 billion to $6.8 billion. Refrigeration equipment accounted for $2.3 billion in 1991.

In 1986, Whirlpool acquired KitchenAid, a high-end producer of appliances, including refrigerators. In 1991, Whirlpool completed its acquisition of Philips, the second largest appliance company in Europe. It also had partners in Eastern Europe, Brazil, Argentina, Mexico, Italy, and India. The Philips acquisition boosted Whirlpool's global presence and made Whirlpool one of the top two appliance makers in the world, along with Electrolux.

General Electric was a huge American conglomerate with revenues of more than $59 billion in 1992. Sales of major appliances accounted for about $5.5 billion. GE spent $120 million to build a new automated plant in Columbia, Tennessee, to make rotary compressors for refrigerators and establish a center at which employees would learn the skills to operate the high tech plant. GE bought a 50 percent share in a British appliance company in order to increase its European presence.

At the beginning of the 1980s, Maytag was a small company making top-of-the-line washers and dryers in Newton, Iowa. But with the decade of consolidation beginning, Maytag saw that it either had to expand its product line or risk being taken over. When the decade ended, Maytag was making refrigerators, freezers, stoves, washers, driers, microwaves, and even soft-drink vending machines and dollar-bill changers. It had plants in eight states and eight foreign countries. Sales of major appliances accounted for $2.8 billion in 1991.

Maytag's acquisition of Hoover gave the company an instant presence overseas. In the United States, Hoover was known as a vacuum cleaner company, but overseas it also made refrigerators, as well as washers, driers, and dishwashers. Of Hoover's sales of $1.4 billion, 60 percent was generated abroad.

Between 1970 and 1985, Electrolux, a Swedish company, bought more than 300 companies in 40 countries. Through its 1987 acquisition of White Consolidated Industries in the United States it acquired rights to sell refrigerators and other appliances under the familiar American brand names.

Raytheon, an aerospace company, joined the appliance business through its acquisition of Amana in 1965. Amana was a cooperatively-owned company run by the Amana Society, a German religious sect that had emigrated to Iowa. The society began making refrigerators in 1934. Raytheon also acquired two other appliance makers, Caloric and Speed Queen. In the early 1990s, there was speculation about the fates of Raytheon's Amana division and General Electric's appliance divisions. Because appliances made up a very small share of either company's business, industry observers wondered if the appliance divisions of these two corporate giants would be sold to foreign companies.

WORK FORCE

General Electric employed about 30,000 people at 12 domestic appliance plants in the early 1990s. The company was at the forefront of innovative workplace programs. With its "Work-Out" program, teams of 50 to 60 people, including suppliers, customers, production workers, engineers, marketing and sales people, met to brainstorm and come up with recommendations to the business staff.

Whirlpool was involving workers in a different way. It was trying a special incentive program at one of its appliance plants in order to improve production. Improved productivity translated into an extra $2,700 in annual pay to raise average annual wages for production workers to $26,400 in 1991. The more productive the plant, the larger the pool of money for the workers to share. The improvements in productivity reduced costs for the company and boosted profits; quality also improved at the plant, with fewer mistakes or bad parts. The plant also opened a new training center. As part of its program to involve production workers more in the total process, the company offered workers the opportunity to see how the components they made were used in the finished appliance. Other Whirlpool plants were also achieving higher productivity and lower costs.

Maytag established "focus groups" to improve its manufacturing productivity. All products in a category were to be produced at one plant; therefore, all refrigerators in all price ranges would be developed in one plant to improve design and efficiency.

AMERICA AND THE WORLD

Domestic appliance makers became more active in the European market as another avenue for growth. In 1991, Europe accounted for about a third of Whirlpool's sales and 15 percent of Maytag's sales. Whirlpool also acquired partners in eastern Europe and South America to continue to stretch its market.

In the early 1990s, the European market was still fragmented among many small manufacturers, much like the U.S. industry before consolidation. Many of the smaller companies made only one kind of appliance, such as refrigerators, or marketed their products in one country only. U.S. manufacturers saw great opportunity in Europe, especially in eastern Europe. However, consolidation was also beginning to happen in western Europe, and it was likely that these consolidated companies would begin to market the same refrigerators across the continent, rather than making country-specific brands, each with its own advertising and marketing campaigns. An additional consideration for U.S. marketers was that European demands differed from American demands in appliances; European appliances tended to be smaller and more stylish.

Southeast Asia was a tough market which U.S. makers for the most part had left alone since it was dominated by three Japanese businesses: Matsushita, Hitachi, and Toshiba. However, American companies were beginning to show more interest in this market. American manufacturers also looked to Latin America as a growing market.

There was little concern that foreign manufacturers would gain any significant hold on the U.S. refrigerator-freezer market because the U.S. industry offered good value, service, and durability. Electrolux, the parent company to Frigidaire and other brands, was a Swedish company but it was the only foreign presence in the American market and it was selling American-made brands. Any increase of imports of refrigerators and other appliances was largely attributable to the ownership interests of U.S. companies in foreign concerns. The industry expected that implementation of the North American Free Trade Agreement would result in more imports of American-brand products from Mexico since labor and transportation costs would be lower.

The leading export markets for U.S. appliances were Canada, Mexico, Taiwan, Germany and Saudi Arabia. The complete lifting of any tariff on appliances between the U.S. and Canada was scheduled for 1998, and the gradual reduction in tariffs in the meantime, brought increased sales there.

RESEARCH AND TECHNOLOGY

The refrigerator and freezer industry was scrambling in order to come up with a new technology to replace CFCs by 1996. In fact, a national consortium of electric utilities and the Natural Resources Defense Council established the Super Efficient Refrigerator Program to offer a $30-million prize to the U.S. company that produced the most environmentally-clean and cost-efficient refrigerator. The winning model had to be 25 to 50 percent more efficient than 1993 models, as well as be free of chlorofluorocarbon refrigerant.

A typical 15-year old refrigerator consumed about 1,700 kilowatts of electricity, for an average cost of $136 based on a cost of eight cents a kilowatt-hour. That meant a consumer would pay five or six times the price of the refrigerator in energy costs over the refrigerator's lifetime.

More recent models consumed less than half that many kilowatts, generally about 700 kilowatts annually. The winning refrigerator would consume between 350 and 525 kilowatts a year. According to the Environmental Protection Agency, that represented an annual savings for American consumers of half a billion dollars or more in electrical bills. This reduction in energy costs would translate into a reduction in use of the fuels that generate electricity—coal, oil, and nuclear materials. The EPA estimated that widespread adoption of the new refrigerators would save the country three billion to six billion kilowatt-hours a year, which would require from five to ten million barrels of oil to generate. According to utility companies, refrigerators and freezers consume 20 percent of the electricity used in a home. Development of more efficient refrigerators would reduce demand for electricity and even curtail the need for new power plants.

The model that won the contest also had to remove CFCs completely from the coolant system of the refrigerator. The entrants in this contest as well as scientists around the world were exploring alternate refrigeration technologies. Some scientists were experimenting with the use of other chemical substances to replace the commonly used Freon, the CFC that circulates in refrigerators, freezers, and air conditioners.

Here's how a compression refrigerator works. The refrigerant, a liquid chemical, is pumped through the tubes in the cooling cabinet. It evaporates there and pulls heat from the air. The gas is pumped out of the cabinet and into the compressor and condenser where the heat is expelled into the room. The evaporator chemical becomes liquid again and is pumped back into the food area.

Chemical companies, such as DuPont, as well as refrigerator makers and environmentalists were involved in the development of alternative refrigerants. One of the alternative refrigerants being suggested was a hydrofluorocarbon (HFC). Use of an alternate substance such as this would allow refrigerator makers to retain the current technology of the vapor-compressor refrigerator. One of the other proposed refrigerants was said to be dangerous because it posed a risk of fire or toxic fumes, while environmentalists claimed that another posed an environmental threat because, although it was not harmful to the ozone, it might contribute to the greenhouse effect. Furthermore, because CFCs were also used in refrigerator insulation, several possible replacements would require new liner materials.

Another approach was represented by the work of U.S. physicist Steven L. Garrett who was developing a thermo-acoustic refrigerator that used sound instead of CFCs to transfer heat. This technology, which was first designed for military satellites, would be less harmful to the environment than any substance in a vapor-compressor refrigerator. Even so, thermo-acoustics would require big changes by manufacturers to retool their facilities or send their production workers back to school to learn a new technology. Alternative refrigerants would not require these changes.

Researchers financed in part by the Environmental Protection Agency built demonstration CFC-free refrigerators that were eight percent to sixteen percent more energy-efficient than existing refrigerators cooled by CFC. These test refrigerators also cooled freezer and refrigerator sections separately instead of using the same air to cool both sections, as traditional models did.

German scientists were working on a refrigerator that used a mixture of propane and butane in place of CFCs. The unit they were working on, however, had no freezer compartment and used more electricity than that used by a typical refrigerator cooled by CFC vapor compression. Italian scientists used the same vapor-compression technology that is found in CFC-refrigerators, but they substituted a hydrofluorocarbon—HFC-134a. The refrigerator had two modules for refrigeration and one for freezing; the modules were made from polystyrene and made recycling and manufacture easier. The power pack was easily removable for recycling or repairs.

INDUSTRY INFORMATION SOURCES

Bergstrom, Robin. "It's Not by Magic." *Production*, February 1991, p. 36-9.

Cohen, Daniel. *The Last Hundred Years: Household Technology*. New York: M. Evans, 1982.

Cowan, Ruth Schwartz. *More Work for Mother*. New York: Basic Books, 1983.

Enders, John. "The Race for a Safer Fridge Heats Up." *Syracuse Herald-American,* June 13, 1993.

McCoy, Charles. "Two Big Firms to Vie to Build a Better Fridge." *Wall Street Journal*, December 8, 1992, p. B1.

Moskowitz, Milton, Robert Levering, and Michael Katz. *Everybody's Business: A Field Guide to the 400 Leading Companies in America*. New York: Doubleday, 1990.

Samuel, Peter. "Will Your Next Refrigerator Explode?" *Consumers' Research*, July 1992, p.16.

Tannenbaum, Jeffrey A. "Enterprise: Amana Refrigeration Fights Tiny Distributor." *Wall Street Journal*, February 26, 1992, p. B2.

Tannenbaum, Jeffrey A. "Enterprise: Distributors' Links to Producers Grow More Fragile." *Wall Street Journal*, October 28, 1992, p.B2.

Wartzman, Rick. "Sharing Gains: A Whirlpool Factory Raises Productivity." *Wall Street Journal*, May 4, 1992, p. A1.

—Wendy J. Stein

SIC 3633

HOUSEHOLD LAUNDRY EQUIPMENT

This classification covers establishments primarily engaged in manufacturing laundry equipment, such as washing machines, dryers, and ironers, for household use, including coin-operated equipment. Establishments primarily engaged in manufacturing commercial laundry equipment are classified in **SIC 3582:**

Commercial Laundry, Drycleaning, and Pressing Machines, while those manufacturing portable electric irons are classified in **SIC 3634: Electric Housewares and Fans.**

INDUSTRY SNAPSHOT

Although mechanical washing contraptions existed before the start of the twentieth century, only since the 1950s have gas and electric-powered laundry equipment achieved widespread use. By the early 1990s, over 70 percent of all U.S. homes had both a washer and a dryer. Furthermore, producers were shipping about 12 million new units each year with a market value of approximately $3 billion. Over 16,000 Americans were employed in the industry in 1993.

Positive demographic trends and healthy housing starts helped boost household laundry equipment sales by more than 50 percent between 1980 and 1990. Although industry participants suffered the effects of recessed construction markets and economic malaise in the early 1990s, sales were rebounding going into the mid-1990s and analysts predicted that shipments would continue to grow at a rate of one percent to three percent through the end of the decade.

To boost sales and profits, washer and dryer manufacturers in 1994 were striving to develop new and better appliances which would spur replacement sales, while also scrambling to comply with new federal environmental regulations. In addition, most were seeking growth overseas, in regions such as Asia and Mexico.

ORGANIZATION AND STRUCTURE

Household laundry equipment represented about 17 percent of the overall U.S. household appliance industry in the early 1990s. It is America's second largest appliance segment, by revenues, following refrigerators. Although ironers and mangles, or pressing machines, account for a small portion of industry sales, washers and dryers make up the lion's share of production.

Nearly 80 percent of all household laundry equipment is purchased by individuals for home use. An additional six percent of industry output is consumed by laundromats, dry cleaners, and other services that use domestic laundry equipment. The remainder of the U.S. market is comprised of state, local, and federal government institutions, such as the armed forces and prisons. Over seven percent of U.S. production in the early 1990s was exported.

The market for first-time purchasers of washers and dryers is relatively saturated, with the exception of first-time home buyers. As a result, the industry is highly dependent upon sales of replacement appliances. Most laundry equipment has a life span of 10 to 16 years. However, several factors may influence the replacement rate of washers and dryers. An increase in sales of existing homes, for example, boosts replacements because new occupants are more likely to buy new appliances. Likewise, heightened remodeling activity also spurs replacements.

Changes in home trends may also spawn premature replacements. As laundry equipment was increasingly moved out of basements and closer to living areas in the 1980s, for instance, the need for quieter and more attractive washers and dryers caused an influx of consumers to upgrade. Increases in repair costs in relation to price of new units can also shorten replacement cycles. Finally, because appliances are discretionary purchases that can be postponed, industry revenues are closely tied to the health of the overall economy.

Types of Products. The three major household laundry product categories are electric washing machines, electric dryers, and gas dryers. Washers are of two types; top-load and front-load. Top-load washers have an agitator in the center of the wash tub that thrashes the water and the fabric. Front-load, or tumble-type, washers lift and drop the laundry into the wash water as the tub spins. Both washer types wring out excess water by spinning.

Although many top-loading machines are easier to access, tumble-type washers require less water and detergent to clean a load of laundry. Both types of washers are differentiated primarily by their features, which include washing actions, capacity, water temperature combinations, water levels, and noise levels. Most top-load washers range in price from $400 to $550, while front-load machines usually cost an additional $100. In 1992 U.S. producers sold 6.5 million washers, most of which were top-load.

Dryers are basically revolving drums which tumble clothes through heated air. Different features and product quality result in a price range of $400 to $800. More expensive dryers offer as many as three different heating cycles, extended tumble cycles, wrinkle-remove features, and sturdier construction, such as porcelain coated drums and tops. Although gas dryers are typically more expensive to purchase initially, they are often significantly cheaper to operate. In 1992 U.S. manufacturers shipped about 1.2 million gas and 3.5 million electric dryers.

BACKGROUND AND DEVELOPMENT

Numerous washer and dryer devices, ranging from washboards to hand-cranked wringers, were used to clean laundry prior to the twentieth century. The first electric washing machine was introduced in 1907 by the Maytag Company. But not until after World War II, during the post-war U.S. economic expansion, did electric washing machines, and later dryers, realize mainstream acceptance. As the demand for all types of appliances proliferated during the 1950s, 1960s, and 1970s, the laundry equipment industry grew rapidly. The introduction of fully automatic washers and dryers in the mid-1960s rocketed the industry to prominence during the following decade, as washers and dryers became standard household amenities.

By the early 1980s, the laundry equipment industry was shipping over $2 billion worth of goods annually and employing over 16,000 workers. Well over 50 percent of U.S. households had both a washer and a dryer. Strong home construction and appliance replacement markets, moreover, allowed producers to enjoy solid gains throughout the 1980s. Indeed, industry revenues grew at an average annual rate of over five percent between 1982 and 1990, despite an economic slowdown in the late 1980s. Sales surged past $3.2 billion in 1990, stagnated in 1991, and grew about three percent in 1992.

An important dynamic which characterized the laundry equipment industry during the 1980s was consolidation. As the vigorous growth of the late 1960s, 1970s, and early 1980s waned, producers tried to achieve economies of scale though merger and acquisition. By the end of the 1980s only 16 competitors remained, compared to over 25 at the start of the decade. In fact, the top two companies controlled nearly 70 percent of the market, and the top four manufacturers accounted for about 80 percent of sales. Antitrust laws enacted during the 1980s succeeded in slowing the rate of consolidation by the early 1990s.

CURRENT CONDITIONS

Laundry industry sales grew about three percent in 1993. Unit volume, moreover, leapt by nearly six percent. Although unit sales of washing machines rose only 4.2 percent in 1993, to about 6.23 million, gas dryer shipments grew a healthy 6.5 percent, to 1.04 million, and electric dryer deliveries bounded 8.2 percent to approximately 3.25 million. Increased sales were largely the result of an uptick in housing starts and escalating consumer expenditures following the recession.

Manufacturers were able to boost unit shipments faster than revenues and retain profit growth through productivity gains. Indeed, hefty capital investments in automation and information systems during the 1980s helped the appliance industry become one of the most efficient businesses in the United States. As the value of washer and dryer shipments grew 50 percent during the 1980s, unit prices remained stable in real dollars and unit volume soared. Despite a huge surge in real output, industry employment actually declined slightly during the decade. Efficiency gains contributed to the industry's dominance of the domestic market, of which it controlled a whopping 85 percent.

In addition to short term economic factors and production efficiencies, laundry equipment manufacturers in the mid-1990s also benefitted from long-term demographic factors and buying patterns. Importantly, the baby boom generation, aged 35 to 54 years, was becoming wealthier and was investing a greater share of its income in home-related goods. Because this important market segment was also spending an increasing amount of time working and having children, analysts expected boomers to begin spending a greater proportion of their income on conveniences, such as washers and dryers.

Augmenting renewed sales were new distribution and customer service programs which manufacturers were initiating. Many producers, for example, were strengthening their support for retailers with training and service programs. Likewise, customer relationship initiatives were helping manufacturers cultivate consumer loyalty. Whirlpool, for example, announced early in 1994 that it was going to replace its system of independent distributors with factory-direct distribution.

Federal Regulation. As manufacturers fought to overcome price pressures and economic malaise in the mid-1990s, they waged battle on a second front—Increasing federal regulations were forcing washer and dryer producers to comply with costly new standards aimed at reducing environmental damage. New Department of Energy Standards (DOE) initiatives, which took affect in May of 1994, required machine makers to lower rinse-water temperatures, reduce water consumption, and install energy-efficient motors and insulation. More standards were scheduled to go into effect in 1997.

Manufacturers were also under pressure to increase the recyclability of their machines. Two Congressional bills that failed to pass in 1992 would have mandated product material content, recycling rates, and packaging. In anticipation of new laws, some producers were striving to improve the recyclability of their machines by making components that can be recovered, restored, and reused.

Future Growth. Besides baby-boom patterns, overall U.S. household formations are expected to rise during the 1990s, from 93.1 million in 1990 to 106 million in 2000. This should result in steady growth of first-time appliance buyers. Furthermore, because a large percentage of existing washers and dryers were purchased in the early 1980s, some observers expect replacement sales to increase in the latter part of the 1990s as old machines wear. The industry is also expected to benefit from low interest rates, a reduction in inventories in 1994, more strategic inventory management in the future, and export growth. Greater demand for compact washers and dryers that suit smaller living spaces will offer a high-growth, yet small, niche.

INDUSTRY LEADERS

The laundry equipment industry is highly consolidated. The top four companies account for about 80 percent of all shipments. Whirlpool, the industry behemoth, captured over 50 percent of the U.S. washer and dryer market in 1993. General Electric Corp. and Maytag Corp. each garnered about 17 percent of overall sales. Electrolux, of Sweden, met approximately 13 percent of U.S. demand.

Maytag is credited with giving birth to the industry, and has a proven reputation for supplying high quality washers and dryers. Maytag began by selling farm equipment, but invented electric laundry machines in the early 1900s. In 1966 Maytag introduced full automatic washers, and in 1976 it brought out a complimentary line of dryers. It maintained a focused product line until the 1980s, when it acquired Hardwick Stove in 1981, Jenn-Air in 1982, and Magic Chef in 1986. In an effort to expand its overseas operations, Maytag formed a strategic alliance with Germany's Bosch-Siemens in 1993. Maytag and Siemens will share design and process technologies.

Whirlpool overtook General Electric in 1993 to become the world's largest appliance manufacturer. Leading edge production techniques and improved product quality helped Whirlpool achieve a record $205 million profit in 1992 from $6.3 billion in sales. After realizing growth of 14 percent annually during the 1980s, Whirlpool was concentrating on global expansion in the 1990s, and was investing heavily in Asian and European markets.

WORK FORCE

Although the top four laundry equipment producers expected to increase production throughout the 1990s, many analysts expect industry employment in the United States to decline. Heightened campaigns for greater productivity, the likely movement of some manufacturing activities to Mexico, and continued management restructuring may diminish opportunities for workers in the industry.

Assemblers and fabricator positions, which account for about 40 percent of the entire workforce, will plummet by as much as 37 percent between 1990 and 2005, according to the Bureau of Labor Statistics. Other blue-collar jobs in this manufacturing sector will drop by 15 percent to 50 percent. Management and support opportunities are expected to decline as well. In fact, only jobs for sales and marketing workers were expected to increase. Despite workforce reductions, in the early 1990s laborers in this industry earned wages approximately 25 percent greater than the average of all other U.S. manufacturing industries.

AMERICA AND THE WORLD

U.S. washer and dryer makers supplied about 30 percent of global demand going into the mid-1990s. Although they exported less than ten percent of total production, domestic producers were avidly seeking to capture a grater share of the world export market. Overall appliance exports grew 16 percent in 1992, continuing a trend started in the 1980s. The leading foreign markets were Canada, Mexico, Taiwan, Germany, and Saudi Arabia.

In the early 1990s a weak U.S. dollar boosted exports, particularly to Europe and Japan. In addition, exports to Mexico grew a healthy 18 percent, though imports from that country soared an estimated 40 percent as U.S.-Mexican joint ventures proliferated. While U.S. producers were benefitting from cheap Mexican labor, low-cost appliance manufacturers in other emerging regions, especially in Asia, posed a threat to future U.S. export growth.

Whirlpool, which derived about one-third of its revenues from overseas sales, had been the most successful U.S. exporter. It was thriving in Europe and maintained substantial interests in South American countries, such as Brazil and Argentina. Maytag was also advancing in Europe in the 1990s, and was garnering about 15 percent of its revenues from foreign operations. U.S. manufacturers have enjoyed less success in the Asian arena, which was dominated by three major Japanese appliance conglomerates.

Although U.S. washer and dryer makers held a stranglehold on domestic markets, their dominance was expected to wane in the wake of increased imports from Mexico. Passage of the North American Free Trade Agreement (NAFTA) in 1994 was expected to accelerate the movement of production facilities across U.S. borders—a trend which should increase corporate earnings and reduce domestic employment and payrolls.

RESEARCH AND TECHNOLOGY

Capital investments during the mid-1990s were being used to develop more efficient production and distribution methods and to achieve compliance with environmental regulations and pressures. They were also being used to create better and less-expensive products. For example, control software that was being incorporated in machines optimized wash and dry cycles for different types of laundry, adjusted temperature and water levels during a cycle, and allowed machines to talk to users. These microprocessors were also making possible many advanced features, such as self-diagnostic systems, delayed-start timers, and touch controls with cycle programming. New features were also being designed to maximize energy efficiency—an improvement which could expedite replacement sales.

One of the most advanced innovations under development in the mid-1990s involves the study of washing machines that can use "fuzzy-logic." In 1993 South Korea's Goldstar Co. claimed to have invented the first consumer product that exploited the chaos theory, which holds that there are identifiable tendencies of movement amid the apparent randomness of patterns. Goldstar analyzed the movements of water in a standard washing machine, identified those that produced cleaner and less-tangled clothes, and then designed a washing machine that mimicked the movements. Whirlpool was integrating similar technology into some of its models.

INDUSTRY INFORMATION SOURCES

Babyak, Richard, "Team Effort," *Appliance Manufacturer*, April 1993.

Berardinis, Lawrence A., "It Washes! It Rinses! It Talks!" *Machine Design*, September 12, 1991.

"Clothes Dryers," *Consumer Reports*, July 1993.

Crystal, Charlotte, "How Not to Move to Mexico," *International Business*, September 1993.

Koselka, Rita, "Red Faces in Michigan," *Forbes*, August 2, 1993.

Darnay, Arsen J., ed. *Manufacturing USA; Industry Analyses, Statistics, and Leading Companies*. Detroit: Gale, 1993.

"Factory Unit Shipments," *Appliance*, February 1994.

Holding, Robert L., "Anticipating 1994 for Home Appliances," *Appliances*, January 1994.

Kindel, Stephen, "World Washer: Why Whirlpool Leads in Appliances, Not Some Japanese Outfit," *Financial World*, March 20, 1990.

Nevin, Frederick, "Demand Building for Feature-Laden Laundry Appliances," *HFD-The Weekly Home Furnishings Newspaper*, March 16, 1992.

Remich, Norman C., Jr., "Maytag at 100," *Appliance Manufacturer*, November 1993.

———, "Shipments Show Strength," *Appliance Manufacturer*, November 1993.

Somheil, Timothy, "1994: The Key Word is Improvement," *Appliance*, January 1994.

Stewart, Thomas A., "A Heartland Industry Takes On the World," *Fortune*, March 12, 1990.

U.S. Industrial Outlook 1993, Washington, DC: U.S. Department of Commerce, 1994.

"Washing Machines: Front-loader or top-loader," *Consumer Reports*, November 1993.

—Dave Mote

SIC 3634

ELECTRIC HOUSEWARES AND FANS

This category includes establishments primarily engaged in manufacturing electric housewares for heating, cooking, and other purposes; and electric household fans, except attic fans. Important products of this industry include household-type ventilation and exhaust fans; portable household cooking appliances, except convection and microwave ovens; electric space heaters; electrically heated bedcoverings, electric scissors; and portable humidifiers and dehumidifiers. Establishments primarily engaged in manufacturing attic fans and industrial and commercial exhaust and ventilation fans are classified in **SIC 3564: Industrial and Commercial Fans and Blowers and Air Purification Equipment;** and those manufacturing room air-conditioners and humidifying and dehumidifying equipment, except portable, are classified in **SIC 3585: Air-Conditioning and Warm Air Heating Equipment and Commercial and Industrial Refrigeration Equipment.**

INDUSTRY SNAPSHOT

Electric housewares and fans comprise a major portion of the widely diverse products of the general housewares category, ranking second in shipments only to household laundry equipment in 1987. In that year, the industry shipped $2.8 billion worth of product and employed 25.2 thousand workers, a 35 percent decrease from 1982. Like the other sectors of the housewares industry, the economic success of this industry is tied to the health of the housing industry and to general consumer confidence levels.

ORGANIZATION AND STRUCTURE

The 1987 *Census of Manufactures* reported a total of 201 firms operating 230 establishments for this industry. Geographically, employment was highest in North Carolina, Tennessee, Wisconsin, and Missouri. Over half of the establishments (130) had less than 20 employees, while only 59 had more than 100 employees. The largest 36 firms produced 77 percent of the industry's output and employed 74 percent of the workers.

By the 1990s, little product was sold directly to the consumer. Instead, manufacturers sold to major mass distribution networks wholesale, using account representatives who not only knew their company's product line but also the best way to market and promote sales. These account representatives replaced the earlier door-to-door salesman of the industry's infancy. At first, sales representatives were company employees working directly for the manufacturing firm, but in the early 1990s some firms started to contract out the sales representative function to independent marketing firms who could specialize in product promotion.

To support new marketing activities, manufacturers engaged in national advertising and promotion campaigns, headlining the product and directing customers to major retail chains. One very successful medium for the industry was the infomercial. Manufacturers discovered that by packaging their advertising material as a television talk show and featuring celebrity guest appearances, they could capture consumer attention and raise awareness of their new products dramatically. Consumers seemed to like the option of gaining detailed information on a product without the pressure of dealing directly with a salesperson. Infomercials were used to target specific television audiences as a direct sales pitch or to supplement national advertising campaigns. They also appeared in the stores themselves as part of point-of-purchase displays.

BACKGROUND AND DEVELOPMENT

Housewares in general evolved with the changing needs of the modernizing kitchen and the growing demand for more efficient, less labor-intensive work spaces and appliances. In *The Housewares Story,* Earl Lifshey describes the transition from wasteful disorder to luxurious convenience. An important part of the progress was the advent of the first electric houseware, the electric iron. The first iron patent was issued on June 6, 1882, but the power to run it was not available until 1890. Generating companies had to first be convinced to keep their generators on during the day. A more successful iron followed in 1905 when Earl Richardson, an electric company plant supervisor and meter reader, developed the first iron with the heating elements concentrated at the point. He marketed the new concept, developed with input from homemakers, under the trademark ''Hotpoint,'' according to Lifshey.

Many of the early housewares designs met with manufacturer resistance. The inventors needed a marketing network, and the most logical one was the power generating and distributing companies themselves. Often, to gain a foothold, the inventors would offer free samples to homeowners and then take these field test results to the utilities as proof of the existence of a market as much as the quality of the product itself. Eventually, utilities realized the market potential of electric housewares and bought into the concept of load building as a way to increase profitability. They began offering appliances directly to homeowners, allowing them to finance their purchases through their utility billings.

Some major electric appliance contributions were Landers, Frary & Clark's 1908 introduction of the ''universal'' coffee percolator, General Electric and Westinghouse's 1909 marketing of the first electric toaster, Westinghouse's first electric frying pan introduction in 1911, Landers, Frary & Clark's 1918 introduction of an electric waffle iron which plugged into a light socket, and A. F. Dormeyer's 1927 introduction of an electric household beater which featured a detachable motor for cleaning.

The proliferation of products in the industry prompted retailers to consider the future of electric appliances. The first to adopt a marketing strategy to promote them was Wanamaker's in New York. In October 1906, it opened its ''Electro-Domestic Science'' exposition. Continuing a decades-long tradition, the department store placed the display in its basement, the poorly-lit, badly-ventilated, unevenly-heated space which had become associated with housewares. However, it was not long before the department found itself displaced upwards by the Bargain Basement concept and into the mainstream of department store marketing. Other marketers, like hardware and drug stores and discount and wholesale outlets, quickly entered the arena, but with the poor transportation facilities of the day, they provided essentially local and somewhat isolated markets. To grow into a mass-production industry, electric housewares needed a mass-distribution system. The "drummer" or travelling salesman, so named because of the huge drums of product he carried around, could only begin to tap the potential of the market.

The mail order catalogue was already a success by the turn of the century. Mail order companies provided an excellent alternative to travelling salesmen because they bought large volumes of goods cheaply and distributed them by means of the mail system. By 1972, mail order comprised $261 million worth of retail sales in general housewares.

CURRENT CONDITIONS

The recession years of the 1980s and early 1990s hit the electric housewares industry hard. Production peaked in 1984 at $3.2 billion according to *Manufacturing USA*. By 1987, it had dropped to $2.8 billion. The Freedonia Group projected sales of electric housewares to grow 4.6 percent annually from 1990 to 1995, however, reaching an eventual high of $6.4 billion.

During the mid-to-late 1980s, many of the long-time industry giants were beginning to falter or fail. In 1985, the biggest name in the industry, General Electric, sold its housewares division to Black and Decker Corporation, but that was only one of many deals which rearranged the list of major players in the industry throughout the 1980s. Much of the activity was driven by a shift from traditional mass-production and inventory systems to more time-sensitive "just-in-time" production. Some poorly capitalized corporations could not handle the erratic production schedules of the latter method and provide reliable product delivery. The result was a concentration of production in fewer larger companies using modern production techniques. Between 1972 and 1987, the number of establishments dropped from 299 to 230. At the same time, automation and more efficient production techniques reduced the number of production workers from 41,000 to 19,300.

In 1988, the leading firm in the electric housewares industry, Allegheny International (AI), filed for Chapter 11 bankruptcy and began a long series of maneuvers to recapitalize. At one point, AI accepted an offer from Black and Decker which would have given that company 63 percent of the iron market, 59 percent of hand-held mixers, and almost 40 percent of food processors. That seemed to be too much concentration for the industry and a campaign of determined opposition scuttled the deal. AI eventually emerged

from Chapter 11 as Sunbeam-Oster Corp. in 1990.

As the economy began to pick up in the early 1990s, consumer confidence buoyed industry production, but the consolidation trend continued. By 1992, three of the largest firms, the revitalized Sunbeam-Oster Inc., Rival Co., and Toastmaster Inc., had each successfully floated large initial public offerings and intended to spend at least some of that capital on corporate acquisitions. They targeted firms with less than $10 million in sales since those companies would be having difficulty meeting the increasingly demanding shipment requirements of the major retailing chains. Some of the $299 million raised was to be used to retire debt incurred during the 1980s and some was earmarked for new product development.

New product may have been the real driving force of the early 1990s for the electric housewares industry as baby-boomers began to cocoon, retreating into their homes and looking for ways to optimize comfort and style. Sunbeam estimated that 24 percent of its 1992 sales came from products introduced for the first time within the preceding four years.

The old "new and improved" tag took on the added qualifiers of "healthy" and "energy efficient" and "environmentally friendly." Color and shape became important criteria as consumers demanded innovation in form as well as function. Products included the "Robochef," which used microprocessor technology to computerize food preparation from raw ingredients to finished meal, West Bend's "Chip Factory," which automatically prepared and dispensed customized potato chips for the home consumer, and completely automatic bread makers which also prepared dough for cookies, pies, and pasta. One area which came of age in the 1990s was the fan portion of the electric housewares industry. The Vornado fan, with its modernistic styling and quiet but high-volume air moving capabilities, revitalized the domestic circulation fan business for many retailers. At the same time, the ceiling fan, most popular in the southern United States, changed from the functional, low-priced favorite of the mass-merchandiser to an up-scale designer product. Style and color as well as quiet, efficient and variable operation became important selling features.

The Freedonia Group estimated sales of fans would increase an average of 2.2 percent per year from 1980 to 1995, boosting production from $741 million to $1.2 billion. Sixty percent of the 16 million fans sold in 1992 included some type of light fixture, and many of those were of the chandelier style, incorporating French glass, lead cut crystal, and solid Italian brass.

INDUSTRY LEADERS

The 1992 *Ward's Business Directory of U.S. Private and Public Companies,* listed Allegheny International Inc. as the largest firm in the electric housewares industry. However, that firm has since passed through a difficult two-year bankruptcy struggle to re-emerge as Sunbeam-Oster Company, Inc. The new firm is headquartered in Providence, Rhode Island. In 1991, it reported $886 million in sales and employed 10,000 people.

By 1993, Black & Decker U.S. Inc. of Baltimore, Maryland, was no longer the largest electric housewares manufacturer, relinquishing its title to Sunbeam-Oster. Even so, in the 1993 Dun's *Million Dollar Directory,* it reported annual sales of $718 million and a work force of 8,500. In the 1992 *Business Rankings Annual,* Black & Decker is ranked as the largest producer of electric irons and portable electric mixers, holding 48 percent and 36 percent market shares, respectively. The firm was created in 1978 as a subsidiary of the parent company, Black & Decker Corp., which was founded in 1910.

The 1990 merger of Hamilton Beach and Proctor-Silex moved those companies into position as the third largest electric housewares manufacturer. Headquartered in Glen Allen, Virginia, the company reported sales of $350 million and employment of 2,800 in the 1993 Dun's *Million Dollar Directory.* The company is a subsidiary of HB-PS Holding Co., Inc. According to the 1992 *Business Rankings Annual,* it led the industry in sales of electric toasters, commanding a 30 percent market share.

WORK FORCE

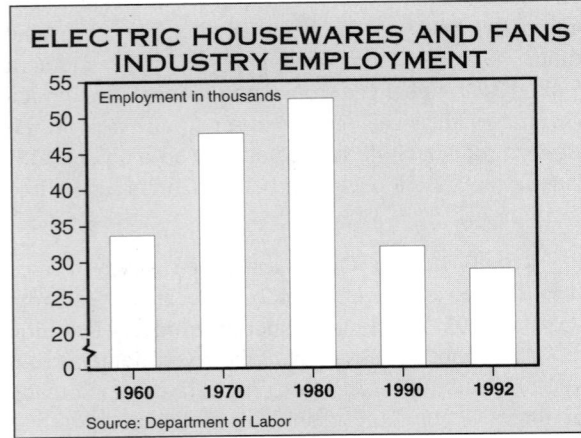

ELECTRIC HOUSEWARES AND FANS INDUSTRY EMPLOYMENT

Employment in thousands

Source: Department of Labor

In 1972, the average production worker in the electric housewares industry earned $3.03 per hour and added $11.58 worth of value to the product for each production hour. By 1987, that wage had jumped to $7.58 per hour and the workers were adding $37.25 value per hour. According to the 1987 *Census of Manufactures,* workers in this industry earned 71 percent of the average industrial hourly wage. In 1992 there were 28,700 people employed in this industry, earning an average hourly salary of $7.96.

AMERICA AND THE WORLD

The industry slowdown of the 1980s prompted some firms to look beyond the United States for future markets. As the U.S. dollar weakened compared to European and Japanese currencies, American exports cut into the market share of European products by pushing their relative costs up by as much as 25 percent. Much product already flowed freely into Canada by the early 1990s because of the Canada-U.S. Free Trade Agreement and the similar cultural and living standards found in each country.

Sunbeam-Oster already operated and marketed its products in more than 60 countries by 1992. In Latin America, the Oster brand often claims more than 75 percent market share. Sunbeam operates offices and some manufacturing facilities in Peru, Venezuela, and Mexico.

It named Europe as the prime target for expansion throughout the remaining part of the decade. To help in broaden its markets, it opened marketing offices in Germany, France, and the United Kingdom. Generally, American products have more features than the equivalent European design although the Europeans traditionally excel on styling.

RESEARCH AND TECHNOLOGY

The kitchen of tomorrow will be smarter looking, with stylish innovative shapes that belie the function, and smarter working, drawing on microprocessor technology to automate food preparation. Those machines will even be able to learn. Once shown a task, or recipe, they will memorize it and be ready to perform it flawlessly whenever needed. They will be easier on the environment, using less electricity than earlier models and featuring replaceable components made of recyclable materials.

One dilemma for the industry remains the effect of electromagnetic fields from power lines and electric appliances. Suggested links between those fields and cancer prompted some manufacturers to abandon the electric blanket market in 1988. However, Sunbeam opted instead to reduce the devices electromagnetic field by 97 percent and rename the product "automatic warming blankets." A 1993 study monitoring the effects of power lines on 36,000 electric utility workers in Southern California showed no evidence of any danger, thus making this less of a concern.

INDUSTRY INFORMATION SOURCES

Adler, Sam, "Warming Up to Other Lines," *HFD: The Weekly Home Furnishings Newspaper,* July 27, 1992.

"B&D to Buy Unit from AI, Draws Fire: Rivals, Creditors Hit Oster-Sunbeam Sale," *HFD: The Weekly Home Furnishings Newspaper,* January 23, 1989.

"Effecting Efficiency: Hamilton Beach/Proctor-Silex Stages a Turnaround with Cost Controls and Price Positioning," *HFD: The Weekly Home Furnishings Newspaper,* February 1, 1993.

"Emerson's AirDesign Division Fans Upward," *HFD: The Weekly Home Furnishings Newspaper,* September 30, 1991.

Employment, Hours, and Earnings—United States, 1981-93, Washington, DC: U.S. Department of Labor, Bureau of Labor Statistics, 1993.

Farnsworth, Steve, "Sunbeam-Oster Sets Expansion; Company Plots Strategy to Bolster Sales in International Markets," *HFD: The Weekly Home Furnishings Newspaper,* July 6, 1992.

"Healthy-cooking Trend, Print, TV Ads Head Up Food Steamer Category," *HFD: The Weekly Home Furnishings Newspaper,* April 12, 1993.

"Inside-out Motor Design," *Appliance,* December 1992.

"Life after Chapter 11 for Six Big Survivors," *Fortune,* February 11, 1991.

Lifshey, Earl, *The Housewares Story: A History of the American Housewares Industry,* Chicago: National Housewares Manufacturers Association, 1973.

Maio, Patrick, "Falling Dollar Boosts State's Exporters," *Baltimore Business Journal,* September 11, 1992.

Maras, Eliot, "Changes Needed to Build Electrics Trade," *Housewares,* November 21, 1990.

Murphy, H. Lee, "Fan Makers See Strong '92 Sales; Extreme Heat, Drought Lead to Depletion of Retail Stocks; New Products Abound," *HFD: The Weekly Home Furnishings Newspaper,* August 26, 1991.

Ostroff, Jim, "U.S. Places Duties on Imports from Several Chinese Fan Makers," *HFD: The Weekly Home Furnishings Newspaper,* November 11, 1991.

Patton, Phil, "Way Cool Breeze," *Esquire,* July 1991.

"Power Lines Revisited," *Time,* March 29, 1993.

Purpura, Linda, "The Future Is Now as Food Cookers Go High Tech," *HFD: The Weekly Home Furnishings Newspaper,* January 27, 1992.

Ratliff, Duke, "Electrics Vendors See Infomercials Continuing to Drive the Category," *HFD: The Weekly Home Furnishings Newspaper,* May 17, 1993.

Santorelli, Dina, "Fan-tastic: Ceiling Fans Come of Age through Style and Innovation," *HFD: The Weekly Home Furnishings Newspaper,* March 22, 1993.

Schifrin, Matthew, "Hidden Value," *Forbes,* May 11, 1992.

Schroeder, Michael, "Allegheny's Battle to Come Back from the Abyss," *Business Week,* June 26, 1989.

"Small-appliance Makers Hot," *HFD: The Weekly Home Furnishings Newspaper,* September 14, 1992.

"U.S. Small Appliance Sales to Increase 2.8 Percent Annually through 1995," *Appliance,* September 1991.

Weber, Joseph, "The Screws Are Tightening at Black & Decker," *Business Week,* September 23, 1991.

—Al Cook

SIC 3635

HOUSEHOLD VACUUM CLEANERS

This classification covers establishments primarily engaged in manufacturing vacuum cleaners for household use. Establishments primarily engaged in manufacturing vacuum cleaners for industrial use are classified in **SIC 3589: Service Industry Machinery, Not Elsewhere Classified.** Establishments primarily engaged in installation of central vacuum cleaner systems are classified in **SIC 1796: Installation or Erection of Building Equipment, Not Elsewhere Classified.**

The four primary categories of household vacuums are upright, canister, stick, and handheld models. The upright vacuum cleaner, which was the first vacuum to gain widespread acceptance in the United States, descended from the manual carpet sweeper. Uprights come in two styles, those with a vertically-mounted soft collector bag and those with an exterior plastic shell that contains the bag. Because they have a rotating brush, uprights are usually better at cleaning carpets. Their limited suction makes them less efficient at cleaning upholstery and bare surfaces, however. U.S. manufacturers sold nearly nine million upright cleaners in 1993, according to *Appliance* magazine in 1994, up from about 7.8 million in 1992.

Canister vacuums have more suction and are easier to use on stairs. But they are generally difficult to store, have a small collector bag, and require the user to pull the canister along the floor behind the nozzle. About 1.8 million canister vacuums were shipped in 1993, down from more than two million in 1992.

Appliance predicts this downward trend will continue in 1994. Stick vacuums are similar to upright cleaners, but they usually lack a rotating brush and are less adept at cleaning than either canister or uprights. Stick vacuums, though, are usually light-weight, easy to store, and inexpensive. About 1.6 million stick vacuums were sold by U.S. producers in 1993, up from 1.5 million in 1992.

The two types of handheld vacuums are electric and rechargeable. About 3.3 million and 2.2 million electric and rechargeable units, respectively, were shipped in 1993 according to *Appliance*. These figures mark a slippage in shipments from 1992, when 3.6 million electric and 2.7 million rechargeable units were sold.

Following solid industry growth during the 1960s and 1970s, the household vacuum cleaner industry realized steady expansion during the 1980s. Prodded by new product introductions and positive demographic trends, vacuum cleaner sales rocketed from $775 million in 1982 to $1.87 billion in 1990, reflecting an average annual growth rate of more than ten percent. Stick and handheld vacuums were the fastest growing product segments during this period.

Economic recess sent industry revenues tumbling below $1.7 billion in the early 1990s. A recovery entering the mid-1990s, however, buoyed earnings and promised to revive struggling manufacturers. Overall unit shipments were forecast by some observers to rise as much as four percent in 1994, with stick and upright vacuums leading industry growth.

About 25 U.S. companies manufactured vacuums in the early 1990s. The largest manufacturer was the American division of Electrolux Corp. This Georgia-based competitor generated 1991 sales of almost $2 billion from its diversified operations, and employed 18,000 workers. Hoover Co., of Ohio, was the second largest producer. It had sales of $1.6 billion from all of its divisions and about 14,000 workers. Other industry leaders included Scott Fetzer Co., of Ohio, and Eureka Co., of Illinois.

In the mid-1990s, vacuum makers were trying to boost sales with new high-tech products. Eureka, for example, introduced a line of environmentally-friendly vacuums that were designed to filter out 99 percent of the dust and dirt that enters the vacuum. Philips Home Products Corp. brought out Blue Magic, a high-tech vacuum with a turbo-compressor that operates by fuzzy logic. Blue Magic also has a silencing mechanism and can be operated with a remote control. Another technological highlight included new polymers,

which were allowing vacuum manufacturers to reduce unit costs and weight and improve quality.

INDUSTRY INFORMATION SOURCES

Holding, Robert L., "Anticipating 1994 for Home Appliances," *Appliance*, January 1994.

Leaversuch, Robert D., "Vacuum-Cleaner Upgrades: A Fertile Polymer Market," *Modern Plastics*, May 1993.

Remich, Norman C., Jr., "Clean Comfort," *Appliance Manufacturer*, June 1993.

———, "Industry Outlook," *Appliance Manufacturer*, January 1994.

———, "World Vac More Than Floor Care," *Appliance Manufacture*, June 1993.

Somheil, Timothy, "1994: The Key Word is Improvement," *Appliance*, January 1994.

U.S. Industrial Outlook 1993. Washington, D.C.: U.S. Department of Commerce, January 1994.

"Vacuum Cleaners," *Consumer Reports*, February 1993.

—Dave Mote

SIC 3639

HOUSEHOLD APPLIANCES, NOT ELSEWHERE CLASSIFIED

This industry includes establishments primarily engaged in manufacturing household appliances, not elsewhere classified, such as water heaters, dishwashers, food waste disposal units, and household sewing machines. Major product groups include water heaters, dishwashers, food disposers, trash compactors, floor waxers, and sewing machines. Laundry equipment, refrigerators, and other major household goods are classified separately, as are commercial appliances.

INDUSTRY SNAPSHOT

A uniquely American innovation, electric and gas household appliances became commonplace in U.S. homes during the post-war economic expansion of the 1950s, 1960s, and 1970s. By the early 1980s, miscellaneous appliance makers in the United States were shipping about $1.5 billion worth of goods each year and employing a work force of more than 14,000. Continued rapid growth in the 1980s, moreover, pushed industry sales past $3.2 billion by the early 1990s.

Although manufacturers suffered during an economic recession in the early 1990s, sales began to pick up entering the mid-1990s. Export growth was augmenting the domestic recovery and promised to provide an avenue for long-term expansion. Furthermore, positive demographic trends and U.S. replacement markets were expected to buoy domestic revenues throughout the decade. Challenges faced by competitors in the early 1990s included federal regulations designed to address environmental concerns and a lack of major new product lines.

ORGANIZATION AND STRUCTURE

Miscellaneous appliances represent about eight percent of the overall U.S. appliance manufacturing industry, which generated 1991 revenues of about $18.5 billion. The largest segment of this business category is water heater manufacturing, which accounts for roughly 40 percent of industry sales. Dishwashers, the second largest product category, are trailed by sewing machines, trash compactors, disposers, floor waxers, and related supplies and attachments.

About 26 percent of industry revenues in the early 1990s was garnered from individual consumer purchases. Residential builders consumed about 20 percent of aggregate output, while commercial and institutional developers made up approximately 24 percent of the market. Roughly five percent of production was exported. The remaining 25 percent of sales were made to the armed forces, state and local governments, mobile home builders, and other sectors.

Appliance sales are driven primarily by three factors: replacement sales; product market penetration, particularly in the case of completely new appliances; and new construction, which generates demand by builders that perform first-time installations. Because most product categories have achieved almost full market penetration, miscellaneous appliance sales are highly dependent upon replacement sales and new construction, and are closely linked to housing starts and economic growth.

The appliance industry can be differentiated from other manufacturing sectors by its production characteristics. Appliance manufacturing is essentially an assembly-line process whereby ready-made components are assembled. Because it has low fixed-costs and is labor-intensive, appliance production offers abundant opportunities for manufacturing efficiency gains. This characteristic contributes to a high weight-to-value ratio that limits overseas appliance imports into the United States, and has caused prices to remain effectively fixed during the 1980s and early 1990s.

Products. The two main types of water heaters are electric- and gas-powered. Gas heaters made up nearly 60 percent of all water heater sales in the early 1990s. Although electric heaters are often priced lower, gas heaters usually operate less expensively. Most water heaters consist of a tank that is made of galvanized iron or aluminum alloys and holds between 20 and 140 gallons. A glass or plastic liner is used to reduce corrosion inside the tank. Water temperature can be adjusted between 100 and 200 degrees Fahrenheit. In 1993 U.S. producers sold about 7.3 million water heaters.

The two main categories of household dishwashers are portable and built-in. Of 3.5 million dishwashers shipped in 1993, only 180,500 were portable units. Most dishwashers use pumps and impellers to throw the same water against dishes over and over to clean them. Fresh rinse water is then used. The cycle is typically completed by heat-drying the dishes. About 50 percent of all U.S. homes had a dishwasher in the early 1990s, up from 45 percent in 1980.

Garbage disposal units are motor-operated grinders that are installed in kitchen sinks. These devices allow food to be washed down the drain. Approximately 50 percent of all U.S. homes were equipped with a disposal unit in the early 1990s, and nearly four million units were sold in 1993. Only 114,000 trash compactors were shipped in 1993, representing a negligible share of the appliance market. Sewing machines also accounted for a meager share of U.S. miscellaneous appliance output (70 percent of these machines are manufactured in Japan).

BACKGROUND AND DEVELOPMENT

Many of the appliances classified in this industry have existed for centuries. Not until the twentieth century, however, did self-contained electric- and gas-powered household appliances appear. A primary impetus for the development of such tools was the almost total disappearance of full-time domestic servants.

Appliances available in the early 1900s included electric clothes washers, water heaters, refrigerators, and sewing machines. In the second half of the century, during rapid post-war U.S. economic growth, a demand emerged for dishwashers, clothes dryers, food disposers, floor polishers, and similar devices of convenience. A rise in discretionary income, growth in the number of U.S. households, and a desire for more recreational time were major factors contributing to the rise of the miscellaneous appliance industry from the 1950s to the 1970s.

By the early 1980s, miscellaneous appliance manufacturers were shipping about $1.5 billion worth of goods each year, and employing over 14,000 workers. Strong industry growth continued during the 1980s as housing starts surged and growing home renovation markets spurred replacement sales. In addition, an increase in the number of working women boosted market penetration by some products.

Although industry revenues shot up over 100 percent between 1982 and 1990, to about $3.3 billion, unit shipments grew at an even faster rate and industry profits climbed. Manufacturers were able to achieve such growth through economies-of-scale and productivity gains. Indeed, as revenues and shipments more than doubled during the 1980s, industry employment remained steady. Hefty investments in automation and information systems permitted these efficiency gains.

Economies of scale were attained primarily through mergers and acquisitions, which characterized almost all appliance sectors throughout the 1980s and early 1990s. As manufacturers joined forces to increase investment capital and reduce research and production expenditures, the number of competitors in the miscellaneous appliances industry lessened. Anti-trust legislation enacted during the 1980s slowed the rate of consolidation by the early 1990s.

CURRENT CONDITIONS

Sluggish economic conditions, which suppressed housing starts and replacement sales, battered manufacturers of miscellaneous appliances in 1990. Home building and consumer expenditures picked up in 1992, though, prodded by low interest rates and pent-up demand. After plunging to $3.1 billion in 1990, industry revenues climbed to $3.3 billion in 1991 and grew about four percent annually during 1992 and 1993. Unit sales volume climbed even faster. Dishwasher shipments, for example, jumped almost eight percent in 1993, and water heater orders increased by about six percent.

Although appliance makers lacked major new product offerings that could broaden their industry, they were having some success enticing new buyers to the market by adding new features to established products. Manufacturers were also benefitting from generally positive demographic trends. For instance, aging baby-boomers were investing an increasing proportion of their income into their homes. In addition, large numbers of appliances sold in the early 1980s were rapidly approaching replacement age.

Although the strong growth that miscellaneous appliance makers enjoyed during the 1980s was un-

likely to occur in the 1990s, observers expect steady modest growth for the next several years. In addition, some industry niches, such as portable dishwashers, may realize periods of faster growth. Furthermore, continued gains in manufacturing productivity should boost bottom-line profits throughout the decade.

In an effort to exceed forecasts, producers in the mid-1990s were striving to accelerate replacement sales by developing more energy-efficient, convenient, and versatile machines. They were also hoping to expand export sales. Encouraging industry participants were the likelihood of continued low interest rates, diminishing inventories, steady annual growth in consumer spending, and the potential of completely new product introductions.

New government environmental regulations were one of the greatest hurdles facing appliance makers in the mid-1990s. The Department of Energy's (DOE's) National Appliance Energy Conservation Act of 1987, for example, set new standards that limit energy consumption by new appliances. The act requires manufacturers to cut energy consumption by their products by 25 percent every five years. DOE mandates that became effective in May 1994 also required dishwasher manufacturers to build machines that use less water and make more efficient use of electric energy. Likewise, new regulations that may be implemented by the DOE in 1997 encompass water heaters. Other regulatory initiatives were aimed at making appliances more recyclable.

Most industry participants expected to achieve compliance with all regulations on schedule, and some manufacturers even hoped to boost sales with environmentally-friendly products. Nevertheless, some appliance makers resented the new regulations, citing the capital investments required to meet the stipulations of such legislation.

INDUSTRY LEADERS

The appliance industry is highly consolidated; five major firms supply over 90 percent of all U.S. appliances. The biggest players in the miscellaneous appliance market are General Electric (GE) and Whirlpool. GE produced over 40 percent of all dishwashers sold in America in 1993, for example, while Whirlpool products accounted for another 30 percent of that total. Some smaller product segments, however, are dominated by niche firms. In-Sink-Erator, for example, controlled 60 percent of the U.S. disposal market in 1993.

The largest company primarily engaged in the production of miscellaneous appliances in the early 1990s was Nortek Inc., of Rhode Island. Nortek gener-

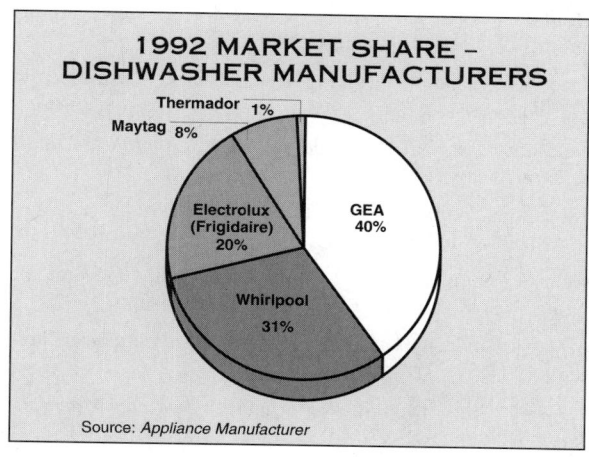

1992 MARKET SHARE – DISHWASHER MANUFACTURERS

Thermador 1%
Maytag 8%
Electrolux (Frigidaire) 20%
GEA 40%
Whirlpool 31%

Source: *Appliance Manufacturer*

ated sales of $1.04 billion in 1991 and employed over 8,500 workers. SSMC Inc., of New Jersey, another major company that primarily produced appliances in this industry, had 1991 sales of $992 million. State Industries Inc., of Tennessee, garnered $280 million in sales during 1991 and employed 2,600 workers. Other major miscellaneous appliance producers included Mor-Flo Industries, Inc. ($213 million in 1991 sales), Emerson Electric Co. ($190 million), and A.O. Smith Corp. ($165 million).

WORK FORCE

Although productivity gains allowed manufacturers to boost shipments, revenues, and earnings during the 1980s, the workforce suffered cutbacks as a result of those gains. Continued advances in efficiency combined with the movement of manufacturing facilities overseas during the 1990s could significantly curtail industry job prospects in the future. In fact, most blue-collar workers will realize cutbacks of 20 to 40 percent between 1990 and 2005, according to the Bureau of Labor Statistics.

AMERICA AND THE WORLD

The United States is the largest consumer and producer of appliances in the world. It produces and consumes more than 30 percent of global output of most product segments and maintains the highest level of market saturation in virtually every major line of appliances. While 50 percent of U.S. households had a dishwasher in 1993, for example, only 35 percent of French homes were so equipped, and just 15 percent of households in the United Kingdom had dishwashers. Generally low penetration of major appliances in comparison to the United States reflects higher energy costs, less space, and lower living standards characteristic of other countries.

Exports. Because manufacturers have achieved close to maximum market penetration with most miscellaneous appliances in the United States, they have increasingly focused their expansion efforts in the 1990s on foreign markets that offered a greater potential for growth. Europe proffered the greatest prospects for profits. Appliance industries on that continent were still fragmented, leaving the market open for massive U.S. conglomerates. Sweden's Electrolux, the largest European competitor, controlled only 20 percent of the market in 1993, and Germany's Bosch-Siemens held just 12 percent. Whirlpool had already captured more than ten percent of the European market by 1994 and was rapidly expanding its presence. Like Whirlpool, GE was advancing in Europe and was positioning itself to take advantage of burgeoning Eastern European economies.

While opportunities prevailed in rapidly unfurling Asian markets, U.S. producers were largely avoiding that region. Three successful Japanese conglomerates—Hitachi, Toshiba, and Matsushita—had established a strong grip on much of the Asian market and posed formidable entry barriers to even the most savvy American competitors. Likewise, Japanese producers were avoiding North American markets for fear of their U.S. counterparts, which maintained a lead in production efficiency, distribution, and marketing know-how—U.S. producers supplied over 75 percent of domestic demand for all types of appliances in 1993. Japanese companies had succeeded in penetrating the sewing machine market, though, and were supplying over 70 percent of global demand for that appliance going into 1994.

U.S. appliance exports jumped 16 percent in 1992. Canada and Mexico consumed about 46 percent of those shipments, while the European Community purchased about 15 percent. East Asian and South American consumers accounted for 12 percent and six percent of U.S. exports, respectively. In the short term, Canada and Mexico will continue to offer strong growth opportunities, particularly in the wake of the North American Free Trade Agreement (NAFTA) that Congress passed in 1994. Exports to Mexico leapt 18 percent in 1993, while shipments to Canada ballooned 20 percent following a 1992 reduction in tariffs.

Imports. As domestic appliance makers continued to boost exports, imports into the United States surged. Imports increased by an uncharacteristically high 28 percent in 1992, despite a weak U.S. dollar, and imports were forecast to rise steadily during the 1990s and early 2000s. The main reason for import growth was the proliferation of U.S.-owned manufacturing plants in foreign countries. U.S. producers were shifting production to low-cost countries, such as Mexico and China, that offered cheap labor and materials. Imports from Mexico, for example, grew by 40 percent in 1993 and were expected to expand further with the passage of NAFTA.

RESEARCH AND TECHNOLOGY

Technological advancements in the mid-1990s centered around compliance with environmental regulations and the development of more efficient appliances. Producers were striving to retain the cleansing power of dishwashers, for example, while reducing water usage. Meanwhile, water heater manufacturers continued to search for more efficient heating, insulation, and distribution technology.

European manufacturers were involved in production of a noise-free dishwasher in the early 1990s. Although the cleansing power of such machines was not yet acceptable to U.S. consumers, manufacturers from all continents were trying to develop a soundless machine. Frigidaire, for example, was offering three sound-blanketing packages with its dishwashers which incorporated vinyl-backed fiberglass, quilted foil-backed fiberglass, and asphaltic sound-damping materials. Manufacturers were also experimenting with quieter motors and noise-cancellation frequency generators.

Advancements related to all types of appliances were being achieved through the increased use of plastics. New thermoplastics, for example, were being used to reduce heat loss that occurs in appliances encased in metal. Other plastics were helping manufacturers reduce shipping weight and increase the strength and durability of their products. Waste King Inc., for instance, switched from a stainless steel housing on a garbage disposal to one made of an engineered polymer compound. It reduced the unit's weight by five ounces, made it smaller, and decreased its noise level by five decibels.

INDUSTRY INFORMATION SOURCES

Bendall, Daniel, "Waste Handling," *Restaurant Hospitality*, March 1990.

Darnay, Arsen J., ed. *Manufacturing USA; Industry Analyses, Statistics, and Leading Companies*. Detroit: Gale, 1993.

Dzierwa, Richard, "The Energy & Intensity," *Appliance*, February 1994.

"Factory Unit Shipments," *Appliance*, February 1994.

Heil, Timothy W., "A Variety of Design Factors Govern Water Heater Choices," *Consulting-Specifying Engineer*, January 1991.

Holding, Robert L., "Anticipating 1994 for Home Appliances," *Appliances*, January 1994.

Jaccoma, Richard, "Talking Dishwashers," *Dealerscope Merchandising*, August 1992.

Jancsurak, Joe, "Plastics Take the Heat," *Appliance Manufacturer*, May 1991.

Nagahama, Yuji, "Trends of the Domestic & Industrial Sewing Machine Industry," *Japan 21st*, December 1992.

Remich, Norman C., Jr., "Next Dishwasher Generation: Noise-Free?" *Appliance Manufacturer*, February 1992.

———, "Industry Outlook," *Appliance Manufacturer*, January 1994.

———, "Shipments Show Strength," *Appliance Manufacturer*, November 1993.

Somheil, Timothy, "1994: The Key Word is Improvement," *Appliance*, January 1994.

Stewart, Thomas A., "A Heartland Industry Takes On the World," *Fortune*, March 12, 1990.

U.S. Industrial Outlook 1993. Washington, D.C.: U.S. Department of Commerce.

Yasui, Nobuyuki, and Motoi Sekiguchi. "Sewing Machine Industry to Form New Organization; Japan's Industrial Sewing Machine Industry Dominates World Market," *Business Japan*, December 1991.

—Dave Mote

SIC 3641

ELECTRIC LAMP BULBS AND TUBES

This industry classification covers establishments primarily engaged in manufacturing electric bulbs, tubes, and related light sources. Important products of this industry include incandescent filament lamps, vapor and fluorescent lamps, photoflash and photoflood lamps, and electrotherapeutic lamp units for ultraviolet and infrared radiation. Establishments primarily engaged in manufacturing glass blanks for bulbs are classified in **SIC 3229: Pressed and Blown Glass and Glassware, Not Elsewhere Classified.**

INDUSTRY SNAPSHOT

The first practical light bulbs were invented in 1878. A bulb industry emerged early in the twentieth century as an infrastructure capable of carrying electricity to the general population evolved. By the early 1980s, about 70 U.S. firms were selling over $2 billion worth of bulbs and tubes each year. Erratic market growth during the 1980s pushed industry sales to approximately $3 billion per year by the early 1990s. American electric lamp manufacturers employed nearly 20,000 workers and were shipping about $180 million worth of exports annually in the early 1990s.

Going into the mid-1990s, U.S. bulb producers were battling a sluggish domestic economy. Sales were down and many market segments had matured. Some manufacturers, however, were boosting profits with high-tech lamps and bulbs that could burn longer, brighter, and more efficiently. Other producers were striving to capture a greater share of the global bulb market—worldwide bulb demand topped $9 billion in 1990 and was growing at a rate of three to four percent annually going into the mid-1990s.

ORGANIZATION AND STRUCTURE

The light bulb and electric lamp industry provides a practical means of converting electric energy into usable light. In the early 1990s about 25 percent of all the electricity sold in the U.S. was used for lighting. Besides illuminating businesses, schools, and homes, light bulbs are used in a plethora of applications and products, including automobiles, flashlights, sports fields, medical equipment, airport runways, and emergency exit signs.

The industry produces thousands of different bulbs, tubes, strobes, and flashes. But the three primary products sold by U.S. electric lamp manufacturers are incandescent, fluorescent, and electric-discharge lights and bulbs.

Incandescent bulbs produce light by heating a filament to a high temperature. The filament, which is usually composed of tungsten, emits a yellowish glow as electricity flows through it. The bulb is filled with an inert gas, such as argon, to keep the filament from melting and evaporating. Most incandescent bulbs are designed to operate at between 30 and 150 watts of power and at 120 volts of electricity. They typically produce between 750 and 2,500 lumens of light (a lumen is the amount of light that falls on each square foot of a 1-foot radius sphere when a candle is placed at the center).

One reason that incandescent bulbs are popular is because they are inexpensive to purchase. A standard bulb usually costs less than $1 and provides about 750 hours of light. Incandescent bulbs are also relatively compact, operate well at low temperatures, and offer a high degree of optical control. The primary disadvantage of this type of lamp, however, is low efficiency. A typical 100-watt bulb, for example, dissipates about 95 percent of its electric current as heat. Less than five percent is actually converted to light, resulting in high-operating temperatures and superfluous energy consumption.

A second type of incandescent bulb is the halogen lamp, which became popular during the 1980s. Halogen bulbs are filled with iodine or bromine gas, which prolongs the filament's life by reducing tungsten evaporation. A standard halogen bulb lasts about 3,000 hours. Some halogen lamps also consume less energy. Because these bulbs emit ultraviolet radiation and can get extremely hot, however, they are often encased in a heat resistant material, like quartz, within the outer bulb. For this and other reasons, halogen lamps cost as much as five or even ten times more than traditional tungsten bulbs.

The second major category of electric bulbs is the fluorescent bulb and tube sector, which serves as the primary electric light source in the United States. Most fluorescent lamps are tube shaped, have a tungsten filament or tungsten coils, and are filled with mercury vapor and argon gas. When electricity is applied to the lamp, an electrode at one end emits electrons that travel through the bulb, react with the mercury, and emit ultraviolet radiation. The radiation reacts with a phosphor coating on the inside of the bulb to produce visible light. Fluorescent lamps are usually tubular, but also come in compact rod, ring, and globe shapes.

Although they are larger than incandescent bulbs and cost more to produce, fluorescent lamps are more energy efficient and have a longer life. Compact florescent lamps that can be substituted for standard incandescent bulbs, for example, produce between 35 and 70 lumens-per-watt. Incandescent bulbs, in contrast, deliver only 14 to 18 lumens-per-watt. While compact fluorescent bulbs typically cost between $15 and $30 each, their overall cost is lower. In 1992 it cost an average of approximately $33 to buy and burn a compact fluorescent bulb for 10,000 hours; by contrast, operation of ten 60-watt incandescent bulbs for the same amount of time cost $58.

Electric-discharge lamps, the third major industry category, produce light through a gas or a metallic vapor. The color and intensity of the light can be altered by using different types of gas and varying the pressure in the bulb. Gases such as neon, argon, krypton, mercury, and xenon allow electric-discharge lamps to be used in a variety of applications. Mercury lamps, which deliver an efficient 65 lumens-per-watt, are widely used to light industrial spaces and roadways. Although electric-discharge lamps are expensive, slow-starting, and usually produce an unappealing bluish-greenish glow, they are long-lasting, energy efficient, and compact.

Markets. About 40 percent of light bulb industry revenues in the early 1990s were derived from sales to individual consumers. State and local governments, including schools, purchased about six percent of industry output. Hotels and hospitals each accounted for roughly 3.5 percent of lamp sales. The remainder of the market was highly fragmented. Motor vehicle manufacturers, for example, consumed about 2.3 percent of production, as did electric utilities.

BACKGROUND AND DEVELOPMENT

Oil lamps were used for illumination in the earliest known civilizations, and were a common artificial light source for over 6000 years. Gas lamps became popular early in the nineteenth century, particularly in Europe. Neither gas nor oil lamps, however, were sufficient to light entire rooms or mimic daylight.

The first incandescent electric lamp was produced in 1802 by Humphrey Davy, an English chemist. Davy heated strips of platinum in the open air using an electric current. The strips soon burned up, and the lack of a satisfactory source of electric power made the concept impracticable. Similar efforts during the succeeding 70 years caused some scientists to declare the development of a long-burning electric lamp impossible.

Good vacuum pumps that removed air from glass bulbs made possible the creation of the first commercially viable incandescent lamps. Joseph Wilson Swan, of England, and Thomas Edison, of the United States, separately invented the first successful light bulbs in 1878. Both lamps used carbon filaments in evacuated glass bulbs. Edison received most of the credit for the invention, however, because he subsequently invented much of the equipment needed to implement his lamp in a practical lighting system.

Edison's first lamp provided the same amount of light as 16 candles, and produced about 1.4 lumens-per-watt. But technological advancements soon improved Edison's original bulb. Notably, in 1911 tungsten was introduced as a filament. In 1913 filaments were coiled for the first time and bulbs were filled with inert gas. Beginning in 1925, bulbs were frosted on the inside to emit a diffused glow instead of a glaring brightness. Improvements in energy flow and bulb pressure helped boost standard 40-watt bulbs to 1,000 hours of life and 14 lumens-per-watt by the early 1960s. Incandescent lamps with more power had developed by the 1960s as well.

The first electric arc lamp was patented in 1845 by Thomas Wright. Wright's carbon-arc lamp led to the development in the late 1800s of electric-discharge bulbs that could produce ten times the light emitted by carbon-filament incandescent lamps. These early bulbs were largely limited to use as heavy-duty street lights,

however, because they had to be continuously fed with carbon rods. The mercury-arc lamp, developed in 1901, eliminated many drawbacks of early electric-discharge bulbs. Likewise, the introduction of neon tubes in 1920 led to the popularization of electric-discharge lamps for advertising signs. Sodium lamps that were developed during the 1930s became popular for various outdoor and industrial applications.

The fluorescent lamp was invented by Frenchman Alexandre Edmond Becquerel in 1859, but was not introduced commercially in the United States until 1938. By the early 1950s, though, fluorescent lamps had overtaken incandescent bulbs as the primary source of artificial light in the United States. Superior efficiency, long life, and greater light output drove the growth of this important industry segment. By the 1960s, in fact, manufacturers were offering more than 50 shapes and sizes of fluorescent lamps ranging from four to 240 watts in power.

Booms in residential, commercial, and institutional construction from the 1950s to the 1970s vastly expanded U.S. light bulb markets. By the early 1980s, in fact, about 60 U.S. producers were shipping $2 billion worth of various electric lamps, and were employing more than 22,000 workers. Following a development lull in the late 1970s and early 1980s, renewed demand pressed industry sales past an impressive $2.8 billion per year by 1986. This figure reflected average annual growth of nearly ten percent between 1982 and 1986. Although sales increased at a more tepid pace through 1988, to about $3.2 billion, a U.S. recession in the late 1980s and early 1990s depressed industry revenues back below $3 billion.

CURRENT CONDITIONS

Going into the mid-1990s, U.S. electric lamp manufacturers were hoping to benefit from slowly strengthening commercial and residential construction industries. Nevertheless, demand from builders was expected to remain suppressed indefinitely. Instead, bulb makers were focusing on increasing profits through sales of advanced lamps that could reduce energy consumption, improve lighting, boost longevity, and minimize adverse environmental impacts. Compact fluorescent and halogen bulbs, particularly, offered solid growth potential.

The National Energy Security Act of 1992 effectively mandated the use of such advanced bulbs. That act sought to prevent the sale of inefficient fluorescent light bulbs beginning in 1994, and other energy-inefficient bulbs by 1995. It banned most standard four- and eight-foot fluorescent light tubes, some incandescent reflector lamps, and many types of flood lamps. Likewise, the Environmental Protection Agency's (EPA's) "Green Lights" voluntary conservation program was designed to encourage corporations to install new lighting. Full national participation, according to the EPA, could reduce total U.S. electric consumption by ten percent and slash lighting electricity requirements by 50 percent, resulting in an annual $18.6 billion savings.

Sales of advanced high-profit-margin lamps were already ballooning in the early 1990s. Consumers were increasingly switching to long-lasting halogen bulbs that cost as much as $20. In addition, energy-efficient compact fluorescent bulbs that could be screwed into standard bulb sockets were realizing widespread appeal. In fact, many utility companies were spurring demand for the new bulbs by purchasing and reselling them to consumers at reduced prices. Several major utilities were also offering valuable rebates and incentives to large electricity consumers that installed more efficient lighting systems. Utility managers reasoned that such efforts would reduce energy waste.

INDUSTRY LEADERS

About 70 companies participated in the U.S. electric lamp manufacturing industry in the early 1990s. The majority of companies had less than $1 million in sales and fewer than 100 employees. Even most of the top 25 companies garnered less than $20 million in sales and employed fewer than 300 workers.

The two largest industry participants are GTE Products Corporation and General Electric Co. GTE enjoyed 1991 sales of over $2 billion and employed 26,000 workers in its diversified operations. General Electric, the recognized light bulb industry leader, had 1991 sales of about $1.2 billion and over 12,000 employees. North American Philips Corp., of New Jersey, was the third largest company in the business, with $620 million in revenues and 7,500 U.S. workers. Other major competitors included Duro-Test Corp. ($92 million in 1991 sales), Alsy Manufacturing Inc. ($68 million), Venture Lighting ($43 million), and Voltarc Lighting ($29 million).

WORK FORCE

Although sales and production volume increased for most industry participants during the 1980s, aggregate employment actually dropped about 12 percent, to less than 20,000, in the early 1990s. Manufacturing productivity gains and management restructuring were the primary culprits of recessed employment figures. Industry observers cite further productivity jumps, combined with the transfer of some manufacturing activities overseas, as reason to believe that employ-

ment in the industry may fall further in the next several years.

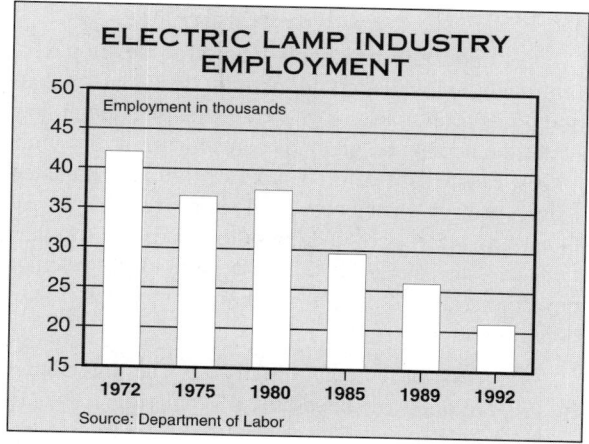

ELECTRIC LAMP INDUSTRY EMPLOYMENT

Employment in thousands

Source: Department of Labor

Jobs for assemblers and fabricators, which accounted for a leading 24 percent of this industry's work force in the early 1990s, will likely decline by about 25 percent between 1990 and 2005, according to the Bureau of Labor Statistics. Jobs for machine operators of all types should fall similarly. Even secretarial and clerical positions are expected to decline, by 15 to 20 percent. On the bright side, the Bureau of Labor Statistics expects employment of sales and marketing professionals to rise by nearly 40 percent, while jobs for material handlers and packers will likely expand 10 to 15 percent by 2005. The average payroll per worker in the industry is roughly equivalent to the mean for all U.S. manufacturing sectors.

AMERICA AND THE WORLD

Besides domestic sales, many manufacturers were also striving to take advantage of growth opportunities overseas. Global electric lamp sales were estimated at about $9 billion in 1993 and were expected to increase to about $11.5 billion by the turn of the century. U.S. producers met nearly 30 percent of worldwide demand in the early 1990s and hoped to further boost their global market share. Although low-cost foreign manufacturers posed significant obstacles to exporters of traditional, commodity-like incandescent bulbs, U.S. manufacturers maintained a decided advantage in markets for high-tech lamps.

General Electric Co. took the lead in foreign expansion in 1990 when it purchased Hungarian light bulb maker Tungsram Co. Tungsram lost money in the early 1990s, but GE invested $90 million in the operation between 1990 and 1993 to increase productivity and cut costs. GE planned to build Tungsram into the cornerstone of its European lighting business.

RESEARCH AND TECHNOLOGY

As light bulb producers labored to develop new, high-tech lamps that could increase their market share and boost profit margins, a steady stream of technological advancements greeted consumers in the mid-1990s. Most bulbs offered superior lighting characteristics, greater efficiency, and improved longevity. Other advances were making bulbs more environmentally safe for disposal; this is a particularly relevant development in the case of fluorescent bulbs, which contain mercury.

One notable breakthrough was the Intersource bulb, developed by Intersource Technologies Inc. in 1993 and scheduled for sale in 1994. The Intersource light bulb, or E-lamp, uses radio-wave technology to produce light, and does not use a tungsten filament. It emits much less heat and consumes up to 75 percent less energy than conventional incandescent bulbs. The 20,000-hour E-lamp was priced at $15 to $20, fits normal bulb sockets, and is designed to provide 20 years of normal service.

INDUSTRY INFORMATION SOURCES

Annual Survey of Manufactures, Washington, DC: U.S. Department of Commerce.

"Bright Ideas in Light Bulbs," *Consumer Reports*, October 1992.

Burgert, Philip, "This Bright Idea May Dim Lighting Filament Market," *American Metal Market*, August 31, 1993.

Cross, Michael, "Eternal Life for Light Bulbs," *New Scientist*, February 20, 1993.

Dinley, Brigg, "The What, Where and Why of Bulbs," *HFD-The Weekly Home Furnishings Newspaper*, August 17, 1992.

Elson, Joel, "Halogens in the Spotlight," *Supermarket News*, May 17, 1993.

———, "Bulbs in Bulk," *Supermarket News*, July 19, 1993.

"Energy Act Sets New Light Bulb Standards," *Hardware Age*, December 1992.

Frickel, Fred, "Energy and Cost Savings with Compact Fluorescent," *Journal of Property Management*, January/February 1992.

"How the New Energy Law Affects the Lighting Buy," *Purchasing*, April 1, 1993.

Miller, William H., "The 20-Year Light Bulb Clicks On," *Industry Week*, November 16, 1993.

Schares, Gail E., "GE Gropes For the On-Switch in Hungary," *Business Week*, April 26, 1993.

Snyder, Glenn, "Shedding Light on Bulb Sales," *Progressive Grocer*, June 1993.

Sun, Marjorie, "Bright Sparks with Bulbs," *Far Eastern Economic Review*, January 24, 1991.

U.S. Industrial Outlook 1994, Washington, DC: U.S. Department of Commerce, January 1994.

Verespej, Michael A., "The $20 Light Bulb: A Start-up Challenges GE with Technology GE Rejected," *Industry Week*, February 15, 1993.

—Dave Mote

SIC 3643

CURRENT-CARRYING WIRING DEVICES

The Current-Carrying Wiring Devices Industry is comprised of establishments principally engaged in manufacturing interior electrical components used to connect equipment to a power source. Popular industry offerings are lampholders, power outlets, connector bodies, switches, dimmers, fluorescent starters, and wire connectors. Numerous miscellaneous products encompass trolley line materials and lightning protectors.

In 1729 Stephen Gray, an English Physicist, was one of the first to discover that some substances could carry electricity from one location to another. These substances were called conductors. In 1820, Danish physicist Hans Christian Oersted found that a wire carrying a current of electricity would cause a compass needle to change direction. Georg Simon Ohm was credited with developing the theory of electric circuits in 1825. Subsequent advances gave birth to manufactured current-carrying wiring devices.

Rapid development of residential, commercial, and institutional structures in the United States between 1945 and 1980 propelled industry revenues past $2.5 billion per year. Strong development markets during most of the 1980s, moreover, resulted in average annual growth of about 8 percent. By 1989, sales of current-carrying devices had surged to about $4.4 billion. Economic recess in 1990 stalled industry growth, as sales dropped nearly 2 percent. Stagnant construction markets repressed growth throughout the early 1990s, though an uptick in housing starts in 1993 boosted shipments 2 percent, to about $4.5 billion.

Going into the middle-1990s, wiring device manufacturers were benefitting from steady residential construction markets. Besides new home building, an upsurge in renovations buoyed device sales. In addition, new government building regulations mandated the use of some wiring products. The National Electrical Code (NEC) that was implemented in the early '90s, for example, required the installation of special ground-fault circuit interrupters (GFCIs) that detect ground faults and shut off power to protected circuits. Industry shipments were expected to grow at a rate of about 2 percent throughout the decade.

To compensate for slow domestic sales, some industry participants were capitalizing on expanding export demand, which was rising as a result of a weak U.S. dollar. Exports gained 14 percent in 1991, reaching a record $1.4 billion, or nearly 30 percent of total shipments. However, imports of current-carrying devices ballooned a threatening 21 percent early in 1992, cutting into manufacturer's domestic market share. Major importers into the United States were Japan, Mexico, Taiwan, and Germany. Imports from Mexico were expected to continue swelling in the mid-1990s, particularly in light of the North American Free Trade Agreement (NAFTA).

The industry is extremely fragmented, with over 420 companies vying for market share in the early 1990s. The largest competitor was Leviton Manufacturing Co. Inc., of New York, which boasted 1991 revenues of $800 million and about 5,000 employees. Hubbell Inc., of Connecticut, was the second largest producer with $719 million in 1991 sales and about 5,500 workers. Other industry leaders included Thomas and Betts Corp., of New Jersey, Group Dekko International Inc., of Indiana, and Cherry Corp., of Illinois. The majority of the top 100 companies in the industry have sales of less than $40 million and fewer than 300 employees.

Prospects for most occupations in this industry are weak throughout 2005, according the Bureau of Labor Statistics. Aggregate industry employment fell slightly during the 1980s, despite output growth. Continued productivity gains will contribute to a declines of 15 percent to 40 percent for many labor positions between 1990 and 2005. But some positions, such as those for sales and marketing professionals, are forecast to grow as much as 38 percent.

INDUSTRY INFORMATION SOURCES

Darnay, Arsen J., ed., *Manufacturing USA; Industry Analyses, Statistics, and Leading Companies.* Detroit: Gale Research Inc., 1993.

U.S. Industrial Outlook 1993. Washington, D.C.: U.S. Department of Commerce, January 1993.

—Dave Mote

SIC 3644

NONCURRENT-CARRYING WIRING DEVICES

The Noncurrent-Carrying Wiring Devices industry is made up of companies that primarily manufacture hardware used to support electrical systems. Popular products include electrical conduits and fittings, boxes for outlets, switches, fuses, and pole and transmission line devices. Insulators are also included in this industry, with the exception of those made from glass or ceramics. For information about the history of electrical systems, **see SICs 3641: Electric Lamp Bulbs and Tubes and 3643: Current-Carrying Wiring Devices**.

Most noncurrent-carrying wiring products are consumed by the nonresidential construction sector. A leading 14 percent of industry output in the early 1990s was pole and transmission line hardware, which was purchased by cable television and utility companies. The remainder of the market is highly fragmented. Store and restaurant construction, for example, accounted for just more than one percent of sales, as did construction related to mobile homes. About .8 percent of shipments was integrated into warehouses, and another .8 percent was used to manufacture cooking equipment. Other industry offerings were used for highway and street construction, sewer system development, industrial controls, and lawn and garden equipment.

Rampant infrastructure growth and commercial development during the post-World War II U.S. economic boom resulted in noncurrent-carrying wiring device sales of more than $2 billion by the late 1970s. Steady market growth during the 1980s, moreover, generated average annual revenue growth of about 4.5 percent. By 1989, industry participants were shipping about $3.4 billion worth of goods per year.

A severe depression in commercial development and stagnant institutional construction markets contributed to industry decline in the early 1990s. Sales slipped about 2.5 percent in 1990 and continued to fade about 1.5 percent per year through 1993. Weak residential and utility markets added to manufacturers' woes. Going into the middle part of the decade, analysts expected only a slight reprieve from lackluster markets. Sales were forecast to grow at a measly 1.5 percent per year between 1993 and 1997, lagging inflation.

About 200 companies competed in the noncurrent-carrying wiring device industry in the early '90s. The majority of the top 50 producers had sales of less than $20 million and employed fewer than 200 workers. The average company had 113 employees in 1989, 78 of which were production workers. Wages are high in comparison to other U.S. manufacturing sectors. The average payroll per employee, for example, was $26,554 in 1989, compared to an average of $26,000 for all other U.S. manufacturers.

The largest competitor was FL Industries, which is comprised of two separate companies in New Jersey and Tennessee. The companies had combined revenues of $1.02 billion in 1991, and employed 9,000 workers. Lamson and Sessions Co., of Ohio, was the second largest competitor, with sales of $318 million and about 1,800 workers. Grinnell Corp., also of Ohio, had 1991 revenues of $270 million and 900 employees. Other leaders included Hoffman Engineering Co., of Illinois, and Appleton Electric Co., of Minnesota.

Prospects for employment in this industry are relatively poor. Although output increased during the 1980s, employment declined from about 26,000 in the early 1980s to around 22,000 a decade later. Productivity gains, management restructuring, and the movement of some manufacturing activities to foreign countries were primary reasons for work force reductions. Although many labor positions will be eliminated between 1990 and 2005, according to the Bureau of Labor Statistics, some jobs, such as those for sales and marketing professionals, will likely increase.

INDUSTRY INFORMATION SOURCES

Darnay, Arsen J., ed., *Manufacturing USA; Industry Analyses, Statistics, and Leading Companies*, Detroit: Gale Research Inc., 1993.

U.S. Industrial Outlook 1993, Washington, D.C.: U.S. Department of Commerce, January 1993.

—Dave Mote

SIC 3645

RESIDENTIAL ELECTRIC LIGHTING FIGURES

The Residential Electric Lighting Fixtures Industry encompasses manufacturers that produce a variety of equipment and components for home use. Popular offerings include chandeliers, desk and floor lamps, glass and metal lamp shades, yard lights, and wall-mounted lighting fixtures. Light bulbs, cloth and plastic lamp shades, flashlights, and lanterns are classified in other industries.

About 50 percent of industry revenues in the early 1990s were derived from stationary, or mounted, fix-

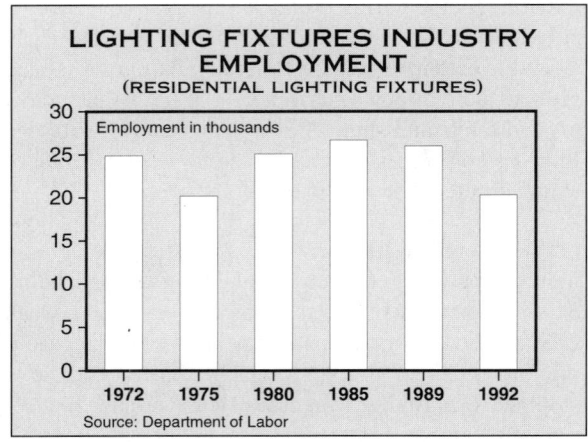

LIGHTING FIXTURES INDUSTRY EMPLOYMENT
(RESIDENTIAL LIGHTING FIXTURES)

Source: Department of Labor

tures, such as ceiling and wall lamps. Portable lamps, like movable desk and floor lamps, accounted for about 35 percent of shipments. The remainder of revenues were garnered from the sale of lamp shades and related parts and accessories. A significant portion of industry output was used in industrial and office buildings, hospitals, restaurants, and other commercial and institutional structures. Five percent of production was exported.

Oil lamps were used in Mesopotamia prior to 2,500 B.C. The first electric lamp pre-dates the light bulb—In 1650 German Otto von Guericke produced a luminous glow from a spinning globe of sulfur. The evolution of modern day lamps and fixtures parallels the popularization of the electric light bulb, which Thomas Edison invented in 1879. Rapid demand growth for all types of lighting devices helped the residential lighting fixture industry grow to a $1.4 billion business by the early 1980s.

Industry revenues grew sluggishly during the 1980s, despite healthy residential and construction markets. Stiff foreign competition was a primary reason for stagnant sales. Although revenues sputtered up to about $1.8 billion by 1988, a severe commercial development depression and stalled housing starts hammered the industry in the late 1980s. Sales plummeted about 16 percent between 1988 and 1990, to $1.56 billion.

New home construction buoyed sales to about $1.64 billion in 1992 and to an estimated $1.7 billion by 1993. Nevertheless, lackluster expansion of about 1.5 percent per year was expected to plague manufacturers throughout the decade. The savviest competitors were hoping to rejuvenate lagging margins with sales of fixtures for energy-saving lighting equipment. Others were seeking profit growth through merger and acquisitions. Indeed, the number of industry participants had dwindled from about 650 in the early 1980s to about 500 by the early 1990s, as companies combined forces to survive withering demand.

Despite consolidation, the residential lighting fixture industry remained fragmented in the early 1990s. The majority of the top 50 competitors had sales of less than $25 million in 1991, and employed fewer than 400 workers. The largest producer was GTE Products Corp., of Massachusetts, which had sales of $1.56 billion from its diversified operations and employed about 16,000 workers. Genlyte Group, Inc., of New Jersey, was the second largest competitor with $492 million in sales and 3,900 workers. Other industry leaders included Lightoloier Inc., of New Jersey, and Metalux Lighting Co., of Georgia.

Job growth for most occupations in this industry will remain stagnant through the early 2000s. Aggregate employment had already plummeted from about 22,000 in the early 1880s to less than 18,000 in the early 1990s—the result of work force reductions and manufacturing productivity gains. Jobs for assemblers and fasteners, which account for more than 30 percent of the work force, will decline by 15 percent to 40 percent between 1990 and 2005, according to the Bureau of Labor Statistics. Only selected positions, such as those for sales professionals and machinists, were expected to increase in number.

INDUSTRY INFORMATION SOURCES

Darnay, Arsen J., ed., *Manufacturing USA; Industry Analyses, Statistics, and Leading Companies*, Detroit: Gale Research Inc., 1993.

U.S. Industrial Outlook 1993, Washington, D.C.: U.S. Department of Commerce, January 1993.

—Dave Mote

SIC 3646

COMMERCIAL, INDUSTRIAL, AND INSTITUTIONAL ELECTRIC LIGHTING FIXTURES

The Commercial Lighting Fixture Industry is comprised of establishments primarily engaged in manufacturing electric lighting fixtures for commercial, industrial, and institutional customers. Popular industry offerings include hotel and restaurant chandeliers, desk and floor lamps for offices, luminous ceiling panels, and industrial fluorescent lighting fixtures.

About 80 percent of industry output in the early 1990s was used for commercial and institutional purposes, and 15 percent was utilized in industrial applications. Approximately five percent of production was exported. The largest single market for commercial lighting devices was office buildings, which purchased about ten percent of all fixtures produced by both residential and commercial fixture manufacturers. The remainder of the market was highly fragmented. Hospitals, for example, received about 3.1 percent of shipments and parking garages consumed one percent of production.

The use of lighting fixtures in commercial applications followed Thomas Edison's invention of the light bulb in 1879. During the industrial revolution in the late 1880s and early 1900s, electric light fixtures became common in factories, hospitals, hotels, and other commercial structures. Fixtures for fluorescent bulbs, which were introduced in 1938 and were more energy-efficient than previous bulbs, became the industry emphasis by the 1950s. Steady market growth during the post-World War II U.S. economic expansion pushed sales of commercial fixtures past $1.5 billion by the early 1980s.

Healthy commercial development throughout most of the 1980s resulted in average annual revenue growth of nearly eight percent for the commercial fixture industry. By 1990, sales topped $3.2 billion per year. Despite a severe downturn in commercial development in 1989 and the early 1990s, sales dipped only one percent in 1991 before increasing an encouraging four percent in 1992. Healthy institutional demand and sales of fixtures for new energy-saving bulbs continued to buoy earnings in 1993, as industry revenues climbed an estimated 3.5 percent to around $3.4 billion. For comparison, total U.S. light bulb sales were about $3 billion in 1993.

Going into the middle 1990s, U.S. commercial lighting fixture producers expected to benefit from government initiatives that were encouraging businesses to replace existing lights and fixtures with new energy-saving devices. They were also boosting profits through cost-cutting programs and productivity gains. In light of increasing foreign competition, many manufacturers were forming joint ventures with overseas producers and moving production facilities outside the United States. Valmont Electric, for example, moved 25 percent of its manufacturing operations to Mexico in 1992. Shipments by both residential and commercial fixture producers were expected to grow at a rate of between two and three percent through mid-decade.

About 250 U.S. companies competed in the commercial lighting fixture industry in the early 1990s.

The majority of the top 50 producers had less than $50 million in sales and fewer than 200 employees. The largest industry participant was National Service Industries Inc., of Georgia, which had sales of about $2.2 billion from its diversified operations. Rank America, Inc., also in Georgia, had sales of $500 million and employed 300 workers. Other industry leaders included USI Lighting Inc. and Lights of America Inc., both of which are based in California.

Although industry employment rose from 19,000 in the early 1980s to 23,000 by the early 1990s, future employment prospects in this industry are not encouraging. Many manufacturing positions should decline significantly between 1990 and 2005, according to the Bureau of Labor Statistics, in the wake of productivity gains and the movement of production facilities overseas. However, sales positions and some specialized machinist occupations, which account for a relatively small share of this industry's work force, will probably increase.

INDUSTRY INFORMATION SOURCES

Darnay, Arsen J., ed., *Manufacturing USA; Industry Analyses, Statistics, and Leading Companies*, Detroit: Gale Research Inc., 1993.

U.S. Industrial Outlook 1993, Washington, D.C.: U.S. Department of Commerce, January 1993.

—Dave Mote

SIC 3647

VEHICULAR LIGHTING EQUIPMENT

This category includes establishments primarily engaged in manufacturing vehicular lighting equipment. Establishments primarily engaged in manufacturing sealed-beam lamps are classified in **SIC 3641: Electric Light Bulbs and Tubes.**

The world has come a long way since the first driver of a horseless carriage attached two kerosene lamps to his vehicle to light his way at night. Aftermarket electric lighting systems were available for vehicles as early as the turn of the century, and acetylene headlamps started appearing on cars around 1905, but it was not until 1912 that Cadillac featured electric lights as standard equipment on its cars. Lights for airplanes were also an afterthought, first appearing some years after the Wright Brothers flew their aircraft at Kitty Hawk. Vehicular lighting is now standard equipment on aircraft, automobiles, boats, bikes, motorcycles, and locomotives, and is even used on roller skates and baby buggies. Vehicular lights flash, flicker, and give signals; their messages have become an integral part of our daily lives.

Companies that manufacture vehicular lighting equipment generally do so for a wide range of vehicles, including automobiles, airplanes, trains, boats, bicycles, motorcycles, and amusement rides. Also, companies frequently work together on the same lighting project, often on a contractor-subcontractor basis. According to *Manufacturing U.S.A.*, the value of the vehicular lighting equipment industry is approximately $3 billion and employs approximately 18,000 people. The vehicular lighting equipment industry is just a small part of the large automotive parts and accessories industry, whose shipment reached $90.8 billion in 1993, according to *U.S. Industrial Outlook*.

From the simple use of lights to show the way, the vehicle lighting industry has developed increasingly sophisticated lighting for myriad purposes. *Motor Trend* reported a new type of brake-light system being developed by David L. Camperon, a researcher at Embry Riddle Aeronautical University in Daytona Beach, Florida, that would improve driver response time at night. According to *Popular Science*, Ultralux in Sweden has developed ultraviolet headlights that do not blind oncoming drivers and can penetrate fog. *Bicycling* magazine reported the development of Scandinavian Trading Tess lights that increase vision and visibility while riding. And according to *Aviation Week and Space Technology*, manufacturers are working on the development of "smart skin" systems that feature electronics built into the fuselages and wing surfaces of aircraft.

Among the leading companies in the vehicular lighting equipment industry are GTE Products Corp., Peterson Manufacturing Company, Truck-Lite Co., Inc., and North American Lighting. GTE is involved with Sylvania automation and miniature lighting and has estimated sales of $130 million and employs 1,600 people. Peterson, a leading manufacturer of vehicle lights, reflectors, and mirrors for the automotive and trucking industry, has sales of $100 million and employs 1,200 people. Truck-Lite's sales are $66 million, and the company employs 502 people, while North American Lighting's sales are estimated at $63 million, with 700 employees.

The United States was expected to import more automotive parts and accessories, including vehicular lighting equipment, than it exports through the middle of the 1990s. This trade imbalance is due chiefly to increased shipments from Japan. Overall, however, *U.S. Industrial Outlook* projects that U.S. parts exports should increase slowly. Other opportunities exist for

U.S. manufacturers, however. Some U.S. companies are looking to Mexico for increased export business, mainly because of the North American Free Trade Agreement. Others, including Allied-Signal and Federal-Mogul Corp., are exploring joint ventures with foreign manufacturers and acquiring overseas manufacturing facilities. Foreign investment in the U.S. parts industry is also expected to grow slowly.

INDUSTRY INFORMATION SOURCES

''Allied-Signal, Chrysler Contract,'' *Wall Street Journal,* February 2, 1993.

''Buck Rogers Lights: Tess,'' *Bicycling,* November 1992, 31.

Darnay, Arsen J., ed., *Manufacturing USA,* 2d ed., Detroit: Gale Research Inc., 1989.

Henderson, Breck W., ''FAA: Aircraft Strobe Lights May Fall Short of Standard,'' *Aviation Week and Space Technology,* September 14, 1992, 42.

Lynch, Terrence P., ''Aircraft Beacon Design Eliminates Fresnel Lens,'' *Design News,* November 18, 1991, 99-100.

''Portable Lights,'' *Bicycling,* January 1992, 26-28.

Scott, David, ''Safety Headlights,'' *Popular Science,* March 1993, 49.

Scott, William B., ''Companies Pursue Conformal Electronics for Civil and Military Applications,'' *Aviation Week and Space Technology,* January 29, 1990, 56-58.

Siuru, Bill, ''Lighting Up the Road of Tomorrow,'' *Mechanical Engineering,* August 1991, 64-67.

''Taillight Change?'' *Motor Trend,* January 1993, 32.

U.S. Department of Commerce, *U.S. Industrial Outlook 1993,* Washington, DC: U.S. Department of Commerce, January 1993.

—Ron Schultz

SIC 3648

LIGHTING EQUIPMENT, NOT ELSEWHERE CLASSIFIED

This classification covers establishments primarily engaged in manufacturing miscellaneous lighting fixtures and equipment, electric and nonelectric, not elsewhere classified. Examples of such products include flashlights and similar portable lamps, searchlights, ultraviolet lamp fixtures, and infrared lamp fixtures. Establishments primarily engaged in manufacturing electric light bulbs, tubes, and related light sources are classified in **SIC 3641: Electric Lamp Bulbs and Tubes.** Those establishments pro-

ducing glassware for lighting fixtures are classified in various glass manufacturing industries. Those establishments manufacturing traffic signals are classified in SIC 3669: Communications Equipment, Not Elsewhere Classified.

Outdoor lighting equipment constituted 55 percent of industry output in the early 1990s, while flashlight manufacturing comprised an additional 15 percent of industry production. The remainder of the market was highly fragmented amongst various electric and nonelectric devices. Personal consumption expenditures represented about 16 percent of consumption, and four percent of the industry's output was exported. Numerous institutional and commercial sectors accounted for the majority of sales.

Late 1980s revenues of over $1.8 billion per year for the miscellaneous lighting equipment industry (approximately 20 to 25 percent of total lighting equipment industry total) represented an average annual growth rate of more than eight percent between 1988 and 1982, when sales were about $1 billion. Strong commercial and residential construction markets boosted shipments during the decade, as did general economic expansion. Growth faltered in the early 1990s, however, as the effects of economic malaise and depressed construction sectors pinched profits. Recovering residential building and remodeling markets boosted demand in 1992 and 1993, however, a condition that industry players hope to see continue through the mid-1990s.

Miscellaneous lighting equipment manufacturers were hoping to overcome analysts' predictions of slow 1990s growth by introducing new and better fixtures. Much of the emphasis was on devices that could reduce energy consumption and accommodate new high-tech bulbs. The National Energy Security Act of 1992 even mandated the use of more efficient bulbs and equipment. In addition, the Environmental Protection Agency's voluntary ''Green Light'' conservation program was encouraging corporations to install new energy-efficient equipment and fixtures.

The largest company participating in this industry in the early 1990s was Coleman Outdoor Products. This Kansas-based outfit generated 1991 sales of $180 million from its operations, and had about 1,900 employees. Stabler Company Inc., headquartered in Pennsylvania, had sales of $100 million and about 1,500 workers. Juno-Lighting, based in Illinois, the third biggest competitor, had sales of $86 million with 600 employees. Other leaders included Dual-Lite Inc. of Connecticut, Osram Corp. of New York, Trans-Industries Inc. in Michigan, and LightAlarms' Electronics Corp., based in New York.

Although industry employment grew from about 8,500 to more than 9,500 during the 1980s, the outlook for employment growth was poor through the early 2000s. Productivity gains and the transfer of some manufacturing activities to low-cost producers in other countries are expected to contribute to job losses for several occupations. Positions for assemblers and fabricators, which account for over 25 percent of the work force, will likely decline by 15 to 30 percent between 1990 and 2005, according to the Bureau of Labor Statistics. While most blue-collar opportunities will wane, jobs for selected groups such as sales and marketing professionals could rise significantly.

INDUSTRY INFORMATION SOURCES

Darnay, Arsen J., ed. *Manufacturing USA,* Detroit: Gale, 1993.

"Energy Act Sets New Lightbulb Standards," *Hardware Age*, December 1992.

"How the New Energy Law Affects the Lighting Buy," *Purchasing*, April 1, 1993.

U.S. Industrial Outlook 1994, Washington, DC: U.S. Department of Commerce, 1994.

—Dave Mote

SIC 3651

HOUSEHOLD AUDIO AND VIDEO EQUIPMENT

This category includes establishments primarily engaged in manufacturing electronic audio and video equipment for use at home or in automobiles, such as televisions, video recorders and players, radio receivers and amplifiers, phonographs, cassette tape players, and compact disc (CD) players. This industry also includes companies that manufacture microphones, speakers, and public address systems.

INDUSTRY SNAPSHOT

In 1991, U.S. manufacturers produced an estimated $7.7 billion worth of household audio and video equipment. The industry employed more than 21,000 workers in manufacturing jobs and another 8,000 people in marketing, distribution, and support positions. U.S. manufacturers concentrated almost solely on high-end televisions and speakers. Nearly all other consumer electronics products sold in the United States, including videocassette recorders (VCRs), radios, tape players, camcorders, and CD players, were manufactured abroad. In 1991, the United States imported more than $13 billion worth of household audio

and video equipment while exporting less than $2.3 billion.

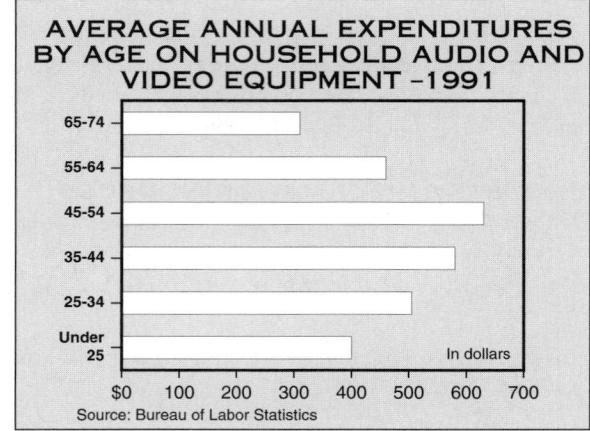

AVERAGE ANNUAL EXPENDITURES BY AGE ON HOUSEHOLD AUDIO AND VIDEO EQUIPMENT –1991

Source: Bureau of Labor Statistics

Approximately 350 companies manufactured household audio and video equipment in the United States in the early 1990s, down from a peak of more than 550 companies in the late 1970s. The decline was due in large part to intense foreign competition, primarily from Japan and South Korea, which forced many U.S. manufacturers to abandon consumer electronics altogether.

ORGANIZATION AND STRUCTURE

The household audio and video manufacturing industry in the United States was dominated in the early 1990s by American subsidiaries of Japanese companies, who used technologies developed by American companies. These subsidiaries assembled color televisions and high-fidelity audio equipment from components imported from Japan or from Japanese-owned manufacturing facilities in other countries. The exception was speaker systems, where U.S.-owned companies were recognized as market leaders worldwide. The Zenith Electronics Corporation in Glenview, Illinois was the only major U.S.-owned company still manufacturing color televisions in 1993. Zenith controlled about ten percent of the U.S. market.

BACKGROUND AND DEVELOPMENT

American manufacturers dominated the household audio and video industry from the first experimental radio and television broadcasts until the 1980s, when many U.S.-owned companies were forced out of manufacturing by foreign competition. The first radios to be mass-manufactured were developed by RCA in the 1920s, which also pioneered television manufacturing in the 1930s. For years, American manufacturers like RCA, Westinghouse, General Electric, Motorola, Philco, and Zenith dominated the industry.

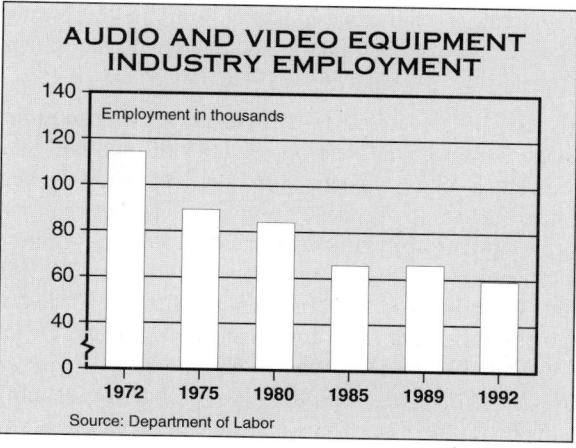

AUDIO AND VIDEO EQUIPMENT INDUSTRY EMPLOYMENT

Employment in thousands

1972 1975 1980 1985 1989 1992

Source: Department of Labor

Television manufacturing. Although the nature of television manufacturing in the United States began to change in the late 1960s, the stage was set more than a decade earlier when several major Japanese manufacturers formed the Home Electronic Appliance Market Stabilization Council. Despite opposition from the Japanese Fair Trade Commission, this cartel successfully lobbied the Japanese government to establish tariffs and other trade barriers that protected the manufacturers from foreign competition. This allowed the cartel to establish minimum prices and control their domestic market. In addition, U.S. companies locked out of the Japanese market began to license advanced technology to the Japanese. In 1962, RCA Corporation became the first company to license color technology to the Japanese manufacturers.

In 1963, the Japanese manufacturers began to export televisions to the United States, using the profits from their protected domestic market to subsidized below-cost sales in the United States, in violation of U.S. trade laws. In addition, a Department of Justice investigation later revealed that the Japanese gave American importers, including Sears, Roebuck & Co., illegal rebates on every Japanese television they sold in the United States. Sales of Japanese-made televisions soared while U.S. companies suffered.

The United States Electronic Industry Association filed a complaint about the illegal "dumping" in 1968. However, Japanese manufacturers stonewalled the investigation for more than three years. In addition, the U.S. government was not eager to upset trade negotiations with Japan and proceeded with the investigation reluctantly. In 1971, the Treasury Department ruled that the Japanese companies had violated U.S.

law and owed millions of dollars in anti-dumping levies. Nine years passed before a settlement was reached, however, and the Japanese paid about one-tenth of what they owed. The damage to U.S. television manufacturers was irreversible.

In 1968, there were 28 U.S.-owned companies manufacturing televisions in this country. By 1976, there were only six. More than 20,000 jobs were eliminated. Several financially strapped U.S. companies were purchased by Japanese or European competitors, while others simply went out of business. Matsushita Electric Industrial Company, the largest consumer electronics company in the world, purchased Motorola's Consumer Products Division. Magnavox was purchased by N.V. Philips, S.A., a Dutch manufacturer. Among the brand names to disappear were Admiral and Dumont. In addition, dozens of smaller manufacturers making parts for U.S.-made televisions also failed.

In 1977, the Japanese manufacturers signed an Orderly Marketing Agreement limiting exports to the United States to 1.5 million sets annually. However, the agreement allowed the Japanese to manufacture televisions in the United States in excess of the quotas. Three of the five largest Japanese companies, Matsushita, the Sony Corporation, and Sanyo Electric Company, had already established manufacturing facilities in the United States, and Hitachi and Tokyo Shibaura Electric soon followed suit. The Japanese also established manufacturing facilities in other countries with abundant, low-cost labor such as Mexico and Argentina to circumvent the limits on imports from Japan. In addition, Taiwan and South Korea began exporting televisions to the United States. Taiwanese imports more than doubled in 1977, increasing that country's share of the U.S. market from 7 to 14 percent. Some Taiwanese imports were apparently Japanese televisions illegally transshipped from Taiwan.

An investigation later revealed that Robert Strauss, the former Democratic Party chairman who had been appointed by President Carter as special trade representative to Japan, also signed a secret agreement in which he promised that the United States would settle financial claims against the Japanese manufacturers "expeditiously," and would limit an International Trade Commission investigation into further allegations of illegal dumping. Strauss also promised that the Carter Administration would appeal a ruling court decision in favor of Zenith, which had won a $400 million predatory pricing suit against Matsushita. The award would have been trebled under U.S. antitrust law to $1.2 billion. Finally, Strauss agreed to ignore official Japanese government policies that prevented U.S. companies from competing in the protected Japanese home electronics market.

Congress did not learn of the secret agreement until 1979, but nevertheless agreed to honor the commitment. Under the Strauss agreement, the Japanese eventually paid about $66 million of the $500 million the Treasury Department said they owed for illegal dumping; the anti-trust suit filed by Zenith was eventually dismissed by the Supreme Court. Meanwhile, the Japanese solidified their hold on the U.S. television market.

At least one U.S. company, however, blamed irrational cost-cutting by U.S. market leaders as much as the Japanese for the decline of U.S. manufacturing. Robert J. O'Neil, then president of GTE Consumer Electronics Co., told *Business Week* in 1978 that "RCA and Zenith are the biggest problem in the industry." RCA and Zenith were then battling each other for the number one position in sales of color TVs in the United States. According to O'Neil, cost cutting by RCA and Zenith forced other U.S. companies to lower their prices to unprofitable levels. In dismissing the antitrust suit against Matsushita, the Supreme Court noted that Zenith and RCA were still the leading TV makers in the United States, with more than 40 percent of the market between them, despite 20 years of Japanese competition. GTE eventually sold its consumer electronics company, including the Sylvania and Philco brand names, to the Dutch company that purchased Magnavox, N.V. Philips.

Among the last major U.S.-owned companies to manufacture televisions were the General Electric Corporation and the RCA Corporation, which together accounted for about 45 percent of all color television sets sold in the United States in 1980. General Electric quit manufacturing televisions in 1984, and began importing sets made by Matsushita with the GE brand name. In 1985, General Electric temporarily re-entered the market when it purchased RCA. However, despite a 23 percent share of the market for color TVs in the United States, and 17 percent of the market for VCRs, the RCA consumer electronics division was losing money. In 1986, General Electric sold the RCA consumer products division to Thomson, S.A., a French electronics corporation second only to Matsushita in size. The sale left the United States without a single American-owned firm manufacturing VCRs.

Audio equipment. The experience of the audio equipment manufacturing industry in the United States was similar to that of television manufacturers. Until the mid-1960s, most of the leading manufacturers in the world were U.S.-owned companies with such well known brand names as Fisher, Bose, Sherwood, and Marantz. The first Japanese brand to appear in the annual *Stereo/Hi-Fi Directory and Buyers Guide* was Kenwood, in 1965. However, over the next five years, the number of Japanese brands sold in the United States increased dramatically. Sony, Pioneer, and Sansui were introduced in 1968, JVC in 1970.

By 1980, most U.S.-owned companies had either moved their manufacturing facilities off-shore to take advantage of cheap labor, or they had licensed their brand names to Japanese companies and become distributors for foreign manufacturers. Many Japanese companies eventually built manufacturing facilities in the United States. It soon became difficult to distinguish U.S.-made from foreign-made products. Or, as William Livingstone, then editor-in-chief of *Stereo Review Magazine,* wrote in 1986, "Do you give more support to the labor force and overall economy of the United States by buying a component manufactured in Hong Kong for an American company or by buying one made by American hands in a Japanese-owned factory in California or Tennessee?"

VCRs, camcorders, CD players. With the exception of RCA, major American manufacturers disdained entering the market for VCRs, camcorders, and CD players as those technologies were developed in the 1980s. In many cases, U.S. companies apparently underestimated the tremendous markets that developed. But economist Pat Choate, writing in the *Washington Post,* pointed out that the loss of U.S. television manufacturing also hamstrung U.S. manufacturers ability to enter these new fields by undermining the companies that produced high-technology components. U.S. companies were relegated to a marketing role, rather than manufacturing, which helped create a huge trade deficit in consumer electronics in the 1980s.

CURRENT CONDITIONS

In 1989, the New York attorney general charged Matsushita, whose products sold in the United States under the Panasonic and Technics brand names, with price-fixing. Although the company denied any wrongdoing, it agreed to pay an $18 million fine. This indicated to some industry analysts that Japanese manufacturers, having virtually eliminated American competition through predatory pricing policies, now intended to squeeze larger profit margins from the U.S. market.

However, a lingering recession was also affecting the industry. Ironically, many of the same Japanese companies that established U.S. manufacturing facilities in the 1970s to avoid restrictions on imports were beginning to move their operations to Mexico, where labor costs were considerably lower. Televisions made

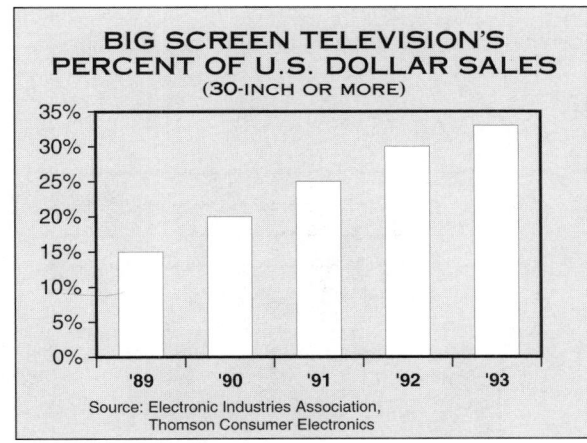

BIG SCREEN TELEVISION'S PERCENT OF U.S. DOLLAR SALES
(30-INCH OR MORE)

Source: Electronic Industries Association, Thomson Consumer Electronics

in Mexico by foreign companies went almost exclusively into the U.S. market. The North American Free Trade Agreement (NAFTA) endorsed by President Clinton in 1993 was expected to hasten this movement to Mexico.

Increased competition from Korean and Taiwanese manufacturers also continued to affect the U.S. consumer electronics manufacturing in the mid-1980s. Reminiscent of Japan's entry into the U.S. market, Goldstar Electronics, a leading Korean television manufacturer, was found guilty in 1984 of selling its TVs in the United States for 20 percent less than those same sets sold for in Korea. To avoid paying a 20-percent anti-dumping tariff, Goldstar began beefing up production at a plant it opened in Alabama in 1981.

In 1993, several major corporations, including Zenith and General Instruments, were waiting for the Federal Communications Commission to set technological protocols for High Definition Television (HDTV) in the United States. These companies, and a third partnership led by Thomson, Philips, and NBC, were hopeful that HDTV would help revitalize the U.S. electronics manufacturing industry. However, after considerable activity in the late 1980s, interest in HDTV appeared to be waning. Meanwhile, to maximize profits, U.S.-based manufacturers were beginning to concentrate on large-screen TVs and home-theater units, leaving low-margin color TV to be manufactured elsewhere. There also were persistent rumors in the early 1990s that Zenith was looking to sell its television division.

INDUSTRY LEADERS

The leading makers of household audio and video equipment in the United States were subsidiaries of foreign-owned companies, including the Japanese-owned Sony Corporation of America, with 1992 sales

of $5.5 billion, and Matsushita Electric Corporation of America, with sales of $2.5 billion. Thomson Consumer Electronics, the U.S. subsidiary of French-owned Thomson, S.A., had sales of $6 billion. Sales figures for each of these companies included consumer electronics products not included in this industry classification.

RESEARCH AND TECHNOLOGY

In early 1994 the HG Digital Conference, a committee representing 50 electronics companies in Europe, Asia, and the United States, agreed on a proposed standard for VCRs that will use digital technology. The agreement was reached in part to avoid future format battles such as the one that took place in the 1980s between Beta and VHS systems. This new technology, which is expected to provide manufacturers with the ability to increase image quality, involves storing tape images in the ones and zeroes of computer code rather than the current wave-like form. These new VCRs are expected to use video tapes that are one-quarter inch wide, half the width of existing VHS tapes. As noted in the *New York Times,* "some industry experts think it will take a few years for costs to come down enough for such machines to become popular. Initial estimates range up to $3,000, which is up to 10 times the cost of some current VCR models."

INDUSTRY INFORMATION SOURCES

Blair, Roger D., et. al, "An Economic Analysis of Matsushita," *Antitrust Bulletin,* Summer 1991, 355.

Choate, Pat, "Japan and the Big Squeeze," *Washington Post,* September 30, 1990, D1.

Dreyfack, Kenneth, "Japan Can't Make a Quick Yen in the U.S. Anymore," *Business Week,* February 23, 1987, 120.

Dumaine, Brian, "Goldstar's U.S. Debut," *Fortune,* October 15, 1984, 141.

Fantel, Hans, "American Speakers—Loud and Clear," *New York Times,* June 2, 1991, H36.

Gall, Norman, "Close the Door, They Come in the Window," *Forbes,* February 15, 1982, 80.

Greene, Richard, "One to Watch," *Forbes,* February 13, 1984, 114.

Hirsch, Julian, "Is American Audio Technology Dead?," *Stereo Review,* June 1987, 24.

"Hot Duel over Dumping," *Time,* March 26, 1979, 64.

"Imports Fuzz the Future of Color TV Makers," *Business Week,* May 26, 1980, 51.

Kallen, Barbara, "Down the Tube?," *Forbes,* June 3, 1985, 186.

"Kickbacks in Living Color," *Time,* June 13, 1977, 63.

Livingstone, William, "Audio in America," *Stereo Review,* June 1986, 8.

"No Happy Ending," *Forbes,* December 11, 1978, 35.

Pearlman, Jerry K., "Save the Lectures, Give Us Some Help," *New York Times,* December 14, 1986.

Petre, Peter, "GE's Gamble on American-Made TVs," *Fortune,* July 6, 1987, 50.

Pollack, Andrew, "Technology Pact Prepares for Digital VCR Production," *Detroit Free Press,* April 16, 1994 (from the *New York Times*).

"Tactics to Outwit U.S. Protectionists," *Business Week,* March 28, 1977, 36.

Therrien, Lois, "Zenith Is Sticking Its Neck Out in a Cutthroat Market," *Business Week,* August 17, 1987.

"The TV-set Competition That Won't Go Away," *Business Week,* May 8, 1978, 86.

Verespej, Michael A., "Un-American Activities," *Industry Week,* September 7, 1987, 32.

—Dean Boyer

SIC 3652

PHONOGRAPH RECORDS AND PRERECORDED AUDIO TAPES AND DISKS

This category includes establishments primarily engaged in manufacturing phonograph records and prerecorded audio tapes and disks. Establishments primarily engaged in the design, development, and production of prepackaged computer software are classified in Computer Programming, Data Processing, and Other Computer Related Services; and those reproducing prerecorded video tape cassettes and disks are classified in the Motion Picture industries.

INDUSTRY SNAPSHOT

"When Thomas Edison invented practical phonograph recording in 1877 he could hardly have anticipated the powerful mass entertainment medium it would become," wrote Michael Fink in his *Inside the Music Business.* After a rocky start in the first decades of the twentieth century, the business of recording and selling music has grown into an international industry worth many billions of dollars. Analysts from the International Federation of the Phonographic Industry (IFPF) estimated that in 1990 international record sales, a category that includes audiotapes and disks, grossed $24.1 billion. Though five major companies dominate the industry, the nature of the music business

has always guaranteed a place for the small record company attuned to new forms of popular music.

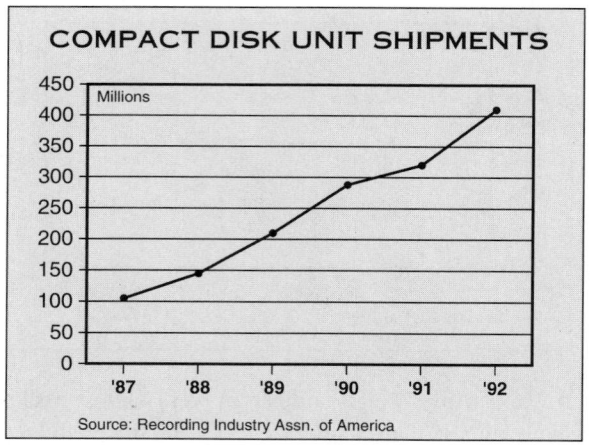

COMPACT DISK UNIT SHIPMENTS

Source: Recording Industry Assn. of America

ORGANIZATION AND STRUCTURE

The business of producing recorded music is like digging for gold—a record company has to pan many streams before it hits the jackpot. The principle work of each recording company consists of locating promising musical acts, producing them in the most commercial way, promoting them to fit into a rapidly changing market, and providing efficient distribution. Record companies lose money on albums that do not sell as well as anticipated, but those that become "hits" provide such immense profits that they make up for the failures.

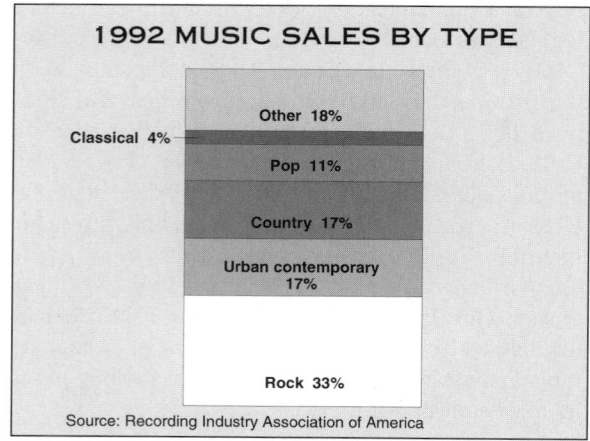

1992 MUSIC SALES BY TYPE

Source: Recording Industry Association of America

Industry organization. Although the Recording Industry Association of America (RIAA) claims 220 members, five of those corporations account for over 90 percent of the market. In November of 1992, *Music and Media* reported that PolyGram held 27 percent of the market, Sony Music Entertainment Inc. held 17.8 percent, Time Warner and Thorn/EMI both held 16.7 percent, and the Bertelsmann Music Group held 15.3 percent. The smaller companies, called independent labels, together accounted for only 6.5 percent of the market.

Recording companies are often referred to as ''labels,'' though that terms became less accurate when large companies began marketing music under several different ''labels,'' or brands. Originally, the ''label'' was synonymous with the company, for each recording company had one label that identified its records. During the years, however, big companies have bought little companies, and single firms have come to own several smaller companies and their labels. When CBS bought the American Record Corporation in 1938, for example, they acquired both the Brunswick and Vocalion labels. After the very large corporate mergers and buyouts of the late 1980s and early 1990s, each one of the five companies that dominated the market owned many labels: PolyGram had twenty seven and Sony had twenty five. These companies are known as the major labels, or simply ''the majors.'' Many of the individual labels owned by a large corporation retain their own staff, which enables the large companies to maintain better and more personal relations with the artists, who record on only one label. Independent record companies are usually still identified with a single label and are referred to as ''the independents'' or ''the indies.''

Single labels often produce only one kind of music. For example, Deutche Grammophone is a classical music label, Mercury carries country-western music, and Motown is a rhythm and blues (R&B) label; all are owned by PolyGram. Occasionally, a major label will create, rather than buy, a new label to produce one specific genre, as when Warner launched Warner Western in 1992 to record western (i.e. cowboy) music. On the other hand, not all labels are thus limited. Koch International, an independent label, produces classical, country, pop, and jazz.

Company Organization. The first job of any recording company is to sign up musicians. This job is handled by the A&R (Artists and Repertoire) department, which scouts for and signs contracts with new talent, finds them songs if they do not write their own, and finds the right producer to oversee their records. In the first few decades of the industry, the A&R department hired a singer, found new songs for this singer to perform, and produced the record. These functions made the A&R department one of the largest and most powerful in any recording company.

Rock and Roll music changed much of the music industry and affected A&R departments more than any. Rock musicians often wrote their own songs and found their own producers. As Steve Chapple and Reebee Garofalo explain in *Rock 'n' Roll Is Here to Pay: The History and Politics of the Music Industry,* ''In the fifties the bulk of music was produced with staff producers who were assigned by the all-powerful A&R heads to record several of a company's acts. But these men often did not understand the new music. What's more, since many new groups wrote their own material, an A&R person was not needed to bring publisher and performer together. As conflicts between staff producers and groups increased, and as company A&R men proved for the most part unable to recognize underground talent, record companies turned to independent producers.'' Today the role of the A&R department is much more limited than what it was, and relies heavily on the independent producer for the sound of the final product.

The producer of a record, as the name implies, oversees the production of the master recording. The producer serves as the artistic director and the business manager for the recording. The record company, through the A&R department, contracts with the artist and producer and provides the advance money for both. The producer then handles the main business aspects of getting the album recorded. This includes budgeting for the project, arranging the copyright licenses when necessary, booking the recording studio, and hiring any extra musicians and equipment as needed. While recording companies frequently own studios, independent studios are also used for a variety of reasons, including the local musical styles of an area. Most records are still made in one of the three major musical cities, Los Angeles, New York, and Nashville, but the studios of smaller cities with unique musical roots are often hired for their unique sounds.

The producer also oversees the rehearsing, recording, and mixing of the musical tracks. Depending on the musicians involved, the producer sometimes has an enormous artistic role in the recording. The producer may hire out or write an arrangement, choosing how the accompaniment will sound. Working with the musicians in rehearsal, the producer frequently contributes to the musical interpretation. ''My job is to help writers,'' Chris Thomas, rock star Elton John's producer, told *Billboard* in 1993. ''That's the reason you're there: to help them get their song realized in recorded form.'' Thomas defines producing as ''filling in the colors of a picture.'' No matter the size of the group, each instrument and voice is recorded separately on its own track. The producer oversees the mixdown of the tracks, combining the individual instruments into the final ensemble sound. "Recording basic tracks is a game. It's fun. It's easy," said Thomas. "Mixing is much harder because you can't always fix it tomorrow. . . . You've got to balance it very carefully." The final balance of instruments and voices, as well as the use of different electronic effects such as tone-quality filters, reverberation, delay, and echo, are determined by the producer. Musicians today who want complete control over their own artistic productions will sometimes produce their own work, but many recordings are still governed by producers who are trained in sound engineering.

After the master recording is made and delivered to the record company, the production and promotion departments take over. The production department will make the physical items that the consumers will buy, both the recording and, just as importantly, the packaging. Both the producer and the promotion department may have roles in the artwork for the packaging. Music videos, a major form of promotion on MTV and other music television networks, may have the same producer as the album, or a different one.

Since the ultimate goal of record companies is to sell a record, the marketing department is frequently the largest and most important. In this intensely competitive industry, promotion and marketing play a large part in the final success of any recording. Marketing departments use two primary avenues of publicity: radio promotion and media advertising.

Airplay is the most effective form of promotion for any popular recording, whether it be on radio or television, and having a new record programmed onto the playlist is the goal of all promoters. While there are several thousand music-format radio stations across the United States, only several hundred are important. Record promoters may send promotional copies to all stations, but they concentrate their personal efforts on the important few. These are the stations that determine the poll lists in the trade publications, such as Billboard's Top Ten. Most radio stations, however, usually play less than 40 songs in rotation in a week. Since the recording industry produces several hundred new albums each week, the competition for these spots is fierce. Since the early 1960s, "payola," or money paid to radio stations to play music, has been outlawed, but legal giveaways to radio station program directors and other personnel include albums, T-shirts, tickets to concerts, and invitations to press parties. Music television works much the same way. To become a hit, a song now must not only be played on the radio, but also be shown in video format on television.

Since 1957, when Dick Clark introduced hit after hit on his dance show, American Bandstand, television has been an effective promotional tool to supplement radio. In 1981, Warner Amex Cable Communications, which has since become Time Warner, introduced rock music programming to cable television in the form of MTV, and music videos revolutionized the industry. During the first few years, when not every pop musician made videos, MTV provided an avenue for new artists to reach audiences. By the middle of the 1980s, however, MTV became as play-list oriented as radio, and competition to have a video shown became as fierce as on any top-40 radio station. Other channels have also shown music videos, including VH-1, the adult-oriented MTV spin-off, Video Music Channel, Country Music TV, the Nashville Network, and NBC's Friday Night Videos. Videos have become essential to music promotion, and, as Michael Fink wrote in his 1989 book on the music industry, "[any] new record/tape release with aspirations to be a hit must have a music video clip to accompany it."

Publicity and advertising departments also cultivate the popular music press when releasing albums. Press kits for new artists include carefully prepared biographies presenting the most profitable image for the artist. Old and new artists alike go on publicity tours, although the rising costs of concert tours have kept record companies from providing full financial support for this element of publicity. In the late 1980s, retail outlets began to sponsor in-house concerts of relatively unknown artists as part of the promotional package. Radio and television interviews, both national and local, help to publicize new releases; music critics receive advance copies of the new albums with the hopes that favorable reviews will sell disks. Music trade publications carry much advertising for artists and their recent releases.

Large companies distribute their records through branch distributors, independent distributors, and mail-order record clubs. In the big cities, branch offices of the recording company distribute their recordings locally in conjunction with local promoters and advertising specialists. In smaller areas not covered by branch offices, record companies use the services of independent distributors, one-stops, and rack jobbers, who deal with many different record companies and distribute to record stores, department stores, and other record outlets (see **SIC 5735: Record and Prerecorded Tape Stores**). While retailing is considered a different industry altogether, some of the major labels own retail outlets; they do not limit their distribution to these stores, of course.

The first company foray into record-company-owned retail was the formation of record clubs, pioneered by Columbia Records when they formed Columbia House in the mid 1950s. RCA soon followed, and both have remained the biggest sponsors of direct-mail distribution. Since direct mail avoids middle-man costs, the companies can make more profit while still giving consumers a discounted price. From their inception, record clubs have proved profitable for the majors. Shortly after Sony bought CBS records in the late 1980s, they entered into an agreement with Time Warner, owners of Warner Records, to jointly operate Columbia House Records. In 1993, the two conglomerates announced a new joint ownership and operation of two other direct-mail operations, Warner's Music Sound Exchange for the U.S. market, and Sony's Music $ More in Germany.

Corporate Structure of Independents. Independent labels, while varying greatly in size and complexity, generally have few of the administrative capabilities of the major labels. Their forté is signing and producing new music, and they often contract out other elements of their business. The small companies, like the rap-music label Flavor Unit Records, which released its first recording in December of 1992, have a skeletal administrative and production staffs. Major label Epic Records agreed to promote and distribute Flavor Units' records. The benefit to the small company of such an arrangement is the access to the publicity power of a major label; the larger company reaps the benefits of an expanding market without much company investment. "Epic hasn't ventured that deep into rap," Epic executive vice-president Richard Griffith told *Billboard*. "We've been looking for people to be our partners as experts." Small labels that do not connect with major labels often hire out for such services, contracting with independent public relations firms, distributors, studios, and disk factories.

BACKGROUND AND DEVELOPMENT

A few years after Thomas Edison invented phonograph recording using wax cylinders in 1877, Emile Berliner developed the disk format of recording. These two formats competed in popularity for a few years, but by the beginning of the twentieth century, the disk format had won. The earliest music recorded was classical opera and popular tin-pan alley and Broadway songs. In 1917, the first jazz recordings were made, and in 1920, the first blues were recorded. These recordings signalled the industry's discovery of the "race" market, a term used to describe music performed by and for African-Americans. "Race" records were to influence the industry and American

popular music greatly throughout the century. In the 1940s, the term was replaced by the "rhythm and blues" category.

From the outset, the industry has been dominated by a few large companies. The two earliest recording companies have remained among the majors throughout the century. The Victor Talking Machine Company formed as an offshoot of the English Gramophone and Typewriter Company in 1901, and eventually became RCA records; the Columbia Gramophone Company became Columbia Records in the late 1930s. Together, RCA and Columbia have shared the majority of the market for decades and, although by the early 1990s they were owned by different corporations, they still belong to the majors. The industry grew rapidly after 1900, peaking in 1921 with sales of $106 million.

By 1922, however, radio had destroyed the market with the free music it offered over the airwaves. Sales fell throughout the entire decade, and when the stock market crashed in 1929, most of the smaller companies either went out of business or were bought by the two larger companies.

Just as radio almost destroyed the industry in the 1920s, radio saved it in the 1930s. The two rival radio networks, Radio Corporation of America and Columbia Broadcasting System, bought the rival record firms, Victor and Columbia Gramophone, respectively. The large profits from the radio industry financed recorded music. New technologies developed for radio, such as the electronic microphone, enhanced music recording as well. Record stars became radio stars and radio became the main promotional tool for selling records. In the mid-1930s, when Jack Kapp of the newly-formed independent label Decca reduced the price of records from 75 cents to 35 cents and people could afford to buy them again, the demand for recordings began to pick up. Music popular in the late thirties and early forties included big-band jazz and popular Broadway and movie songs, and in limited but growing regional markets, hillbilly music (now known as country music), and rhythm and blues (formerly "race" records). The record format during these early years was shellac disks playing at 78 rotations per minute (rpm) with only one song on each side (singles).

The social and economic changes accompanying World War II created changes in the music world that would impact the industry forever. Because of the war-induced shortages of shellac, RCA and CBS limited their record production to mainstream popular music for white audiences, leaving a hole in the R&B and country market. Small independent labels grew to fill the gap left by the majors.

At the same time, new industrial labor opportunities opened up to Blacks, causing a migration of Black families from southern rural areas to northern cities. Poor white families from the South, the region that loved hillbilly music, moved north as well. As their financial prospects brightened, the demand for their music on record grew. Radio stepped in to fill the gap between supply and demand: some stations began programming rhythm and blues (R&B) between the white-oriented pop music programs, some began to program country music, and new stations formed to play only R&B or country. While both country and R&B records had previously sold only in small and isolated areas of the country, both could now be heard everywhere on radio by anyone, white or black. A few companies, like Capitol Records, continued to produce both country and R&B, and succeeded in spreading this music into the pop market. Young people, mostly teenagers, began buying all three R&B, country, and pop. The market was diversifying. Record formats changed from the 78 rpm single to the 45 rpm single with better sound, and the 33 1/3 rpm Long Playing album started gaining popularity as well, especially for classical music.

The kids who listened to a variety of popular music in the 1940s became the musicians of the 1950s who played a new kind of music that synthesized all three: rock and roll. Elvis Presley's "Heart Break Hotel," an early rock and roll hit, topped all three charts, pop, R&B, and country. This new music drew even bigger teenage audiences, who were, in the affluence of the 1950s, able to spend more on luxuries like records than their predecessors. Sales soared. The new music, with its stronger rhythms and stronger lyrics than Broadway pop tunes, scandalized white conservative critics and frightened the major labels. Independent labels cashed in on the new music, growing more numerous and larger than ever before, while the majors tried to control the market by making records of their contracted popular crooners singing the new hits. By the end of the decade the frenzy for the new music had subsided, and the majors were moving back onto the charts with their watered-down versions of the rock songs, thanks in part to Dick Clark and his dance show, American Bandstand, which captivated thousands of white teenagers by bringing the recording stars into their homes through the medium of television.

The arrival of The Beatles in the early 1960s injected a new fever of activity into the industry, benefiting the independents and majors alike. Independent

producers, who seemed to understand the new music better than the staff producers of the major companies, became the "wizards" of the industry, discovering and recording the new talents that fed the business. Sales patterns began to change as well. Albums began to replace singles as the dominant format. A wide spectrum of popular musical styles flourished, and FM radio grew in popularity as it played and promoted the different types of rock and pop.

Even with the economic recession of the 1970s, which slowed record sales down and bankrupted many of the smallest independents, the market has continued to grow since the advent of rock and roll. In an effort to produce something for everyone at great profits, record companies have expanded the types of popular music available. As Michael Fink wrote in *Inside the Music Business,* "American taste and the U.S. market for records and tapes has splintered and broadened to an extreme degree in the 1980s. A 1984 report issued by the Recording Industry Association of America (RIAA), covering the years 1979-1983, identified no fewer than ten distinct 'music types': rock, country, pop/easy listening, black/dance, gospel, classical, show/soundtracks, jazz, children's, and other (ethnic, nostalgia, folk, Latin, and so forth)." As the decade progressed, some of these categories splintered further; black/dance includes rap and hiphop, while rock includes acid, punk, techno, and fusion, just to name a few.

The introduction of the compact disc (CD), with its greater durability and much higher fidelity, brought new profits to the industries. Sales jumped as consumers began to replace their vinyl collections with the better sounding product, and new markets for older records opened up as companies began reissuing older albums in the new format. By the end of the 1980s, sales of vinyl records had almost completely died out, and most companies stopped producing the older format completely in the early 1990s.

The late 1980s and early 1990s saw the absorption of the biggest independent companies into huge conglomerates, as large electronics firms bought up record labels. Sony Corporation started the trend in 1987 when it bought CBS records for $2 billion, an unheard of figure. Two years later, EMI, Philips, and Bertelsmann Music Group led bidding wars for the largest independent labels like A&M and Motown, which eventually went to Philips' PolyGram division.

AMERICA AND THE WORLD

While American music enjoys wide-spread popularity even in non-English speaking countries, after the large electronic conglomerates bought out the major and independent labels, America no longer dominated the industry. While most of the labels were still American, the biggest of the majors—were European and Japanese. Sony, the firm that bought CBS records and owns over 20 labels, is a Japanese electronics conglomerate. Philips N.V., a Dutch electronics firm, owns 80 percent of PolyGram, which carries the American labels Motown and A&M, and also owns European labels like Deutche Grammophone. Thorn/EMI of England owns Capitol, an American label. The German Bertelsmann Music Group bought RCA and Arista in 1986, and the Japanese company Matsushita, bought MCA in 1991. All companies, of course, have international distribution. Time Warner, the only American company among the majors, continues to increase international distribution to remain competitive. In 1992, they signed a deal with Starstream Communications Group Inc. to begin distributing their records in Eastern Europe.

CURRENT CONDITIONS

After several years of sluggish sales due to economic recession, 1992 record industry sales figures began to recover. While unit sales were down 7.5 percent in 1991, they bounced back up 6.7 percent in 1992, with total gross income up 11 percent, the strongest gain since 1987. In 1992, Sony recorded $3.5 billion in sales, PolyGram had $3.3 billion, and Warner $3.2 billion.

Despite such healthy sales figures, the industry began to fear and fight a new retail trend: the used CD market. Because of the CD's durability and high price tag in relation to previous vinyl and contemporary cassette prices, several of the largest music retail chains in the United States began selling used CDs. Previously, only small locally-owned stores sold used products. Rather than lowering the prices on CDs, which retailers had been requesting for years, the industry leaders fought back by withholding cooperative advertising dollars (distributors and retailers share some publicity costs at the local level). Artists began to get involved in the fray when country music superstar Garth Brooks declared that he would refuse to distribute his albums, the best-selling country albums at the time, to any store selling used CDs. Such tactics had little effect. One store in Oregon even held a ''Garth Brooks Barbecue,'' burning his records in protest. As Russ Solomon, the owner of the large chain Tower Records, told *Newsweek*, ''This is crazy. Who the hell knows where this will end? or whether music fans will be forgotten in the heat of the argument.'' Independent record retailers responded by filing lawsuits against the four major distributors that instituted the punitive poli-

cies at roughly the same time that the Federal Trade Commission announced that it was launching an investigation into the policies. The distributors quickly retreated from their hard line stance, putting an end to the confrontation.

INDUSTRY LEADERS

Today the industry is dominated by five huge conglomerates, called the majors. Each owns many different record labels, and each produce hundreds of new potential ''hit'' records each month.

The Japanese electronics firm Sony established the largest record producer when it formed its subsidiary, Sony Music Entertainment International, and bought CBS records in 1987. The Columbia Broadcasting System, which had been formed in the late 1920s as a separate entity from Columbia Phonograph, entered the record business in 1938 when it purchased the American Record Corporation; their new record division then became Columbia Recording Corporation, or Columbia Records. The record group remained a profitable arm of CBS, and a major presence in the industry for decades. It grew from just several labels in the early 1940s to acquire many more through the years. In the 1980s, when CBS began faltering in the television ratings and losing revenues, CBS sacrificed their record group. Despite the fact that CBS Records was the best selling record company in the America, they sold it to Sony Corporation in 1987.

Sony Corporation, one of the best known names in consumer electronics, was established shortly after World War II. Their early products, tape recorders and transistor radios, sold well. In the 1960s they led the international electronics industry with their miniaturized products based on the transistor. The company grew, creating subsidiaries to reduce the companies dependence on outside suppliers. After faltering sales growth in the mid 1970s due to increasing competition, in 1978 Sony once again came to dominate the market with their introduction of the portable stereo system, the Walkman. Within another three years, they broke new sound ground again when they developed and introduced the Compact Disc (CD) in conjunction with the Dutch electronics firm, Philips.

In 1987, Sony bought CBS records, the largest producer of records and tapes, and entered the majors. Sony wanted to gain better control over the sales of new formats by producing both the hardware (equipment) and the software (recordings). As the *International Directory of Company Histories* suggests, ''The acquisition marked less of a diversification for Sony than an evolution towards dominance in a specific market.'' In 1992, Sony Music Entertainment International led the majors by grossing $3.5 billion in sales of over 25 record labels.

Warner Communications Inc. is the only American-owned conglomerate in the majors. The Warner brothers, Jack, Albert, Harry, and Sam, established a successful film production and distribution company in the 1910s. The company made movie history with their film *The Jazz Singer* (1927), which was the first talky to gain nation-wide distribution. The company remained strong well into the 1950s, when television began to change consumer entertainment patterns and cut into the film market. In 1966, the last Warner brother sold the company to Seven Arts Productions, which was more interested in selling television rights to old movies than making new movies, and the company continued to decline.

Warner Brothers-Seven Arts first got into the record business in 1969, when they bought the large independent Atlantic Records. In 1971, after being purchased by Stephen Ross, the company was renamed Warner Communications. Under the new director, the company once again flourished, and began buying up smaller record labels and launching new ones. They acquired contracts for many of the hottest musical acts in the business and became a prominent force in the industry.

In 1989, Warner was purchased by Time Inc., and became Time Warner, a colossal media conglomerate. By 1992, when record sales for Time Warner reached the $3 billion mark, the company owned some of the most profitable labels, including Atlantic, Elektra, Warner Bros., and Giant/Reprise. The company has continued to grow by creating new labels for new markets, such as Warner Western, which was launched in 1992 to produce cowboy music.

RESEARCH AND TECHNOLOGY

Because the industry is highly reliant on electronics technology, research and technological development in the electronics industry always has a great impact on the recording industry. Radio, the first major advance after the invention of recording, nearly killed the industry and then later saved it. The developments with the greatest impact have been newer electronic formats with greater sound fidelity.

In the 1940s, a better sound resulted from the development of the Long Play records (LPs); as sound quality improved, customers seemed willing to spend more on the product. In the 1960s, Philips introduced the cassette format, which was more durable and portable than the LP; when Sony introduced the Walkman personal stereo in the 1980s, which used cassettes and

allowed consumers to carry music everywhere, the cassette market really took off. In the 1980s, the new format of the CD again presented a quantum leap in sound quality, so much so that many audiophiles replaced their entire collection of vinyl recordings with the new format. As record companies issued older recordings in the new format, previously out-of-print recordings, especially old jazz favorites, became available to new generations of listeners, and the market expanded again.

In the early 1990s, two new formats were introduced, the mini disc and the digital audio tape. Both of these formats brought CD quality fidelity to home recording. Industry analysts in 1992 claimed the new formats would benefit long term growth prospects, encouraging customers once again to replace their older recordings in the new format. The new formats worried many in the industry, however, and artists and companies alike feared the loss of copyright revenues from home recordings; piracy has always been the major form of income loss. In 1992, however, the consumer electronics industry worked out compromise legislation with congress and industry leaders which provides compensation for prospective copies done on the digital machines by imposing royalty fees on the equipment sales. By early 1993, both formats had been released. Due to high initial equipment costs, sales started slow, but analysts agreed that once prices come down, both formats would do well. While all agreed that one or the other of the formats would eventually predominate over the other, none could predict which format would win.

INDUSTRY INFORMATION SOURCES

Bakker, Machgiel, ''PolyGram Continues EHR Top 40 Reign,'' *Music and Media,* November 7, 1992.

Chapple, Steve, and Reebee Garofalo, *Rock 'n' Roll Is Here to Pay: The History and Politics of the Music Industry,* Chicago: Nelson-Hall, 1977.

Christman, Ed, ''Majors Lash Out at Used-CD Biz,'' *Billboard,* March 20, 1993, 1.

———, and Catherine Applefeld, ''Courting the Classical Consumer,'' *Billboard,* October 31, 1992, 75.

Cromer, Ben, ''Chris Thomas: The One Helping Guide Elton's Sound,'' *Billboard,* January 9, 1993, 50.

Denisoff, R. Serge, *Tarnished Gold: The Record Industry Revisited,* New Brunswick, NJ: Transaction Books, 1986.

Fink, Michael, *Inside the Music Business: Music in Contemporary Life,* New York: Schirmer Books, 1989.

Gubernick, Lisa, and Kate Bohnen, ''Garth's Barbecue,'' *Forbes,* August 2, 1993, 120.

International Directory of Company Histories, Chicago: St. James Press, 1988-1991.

Knoedelseder, William K., Jr., ''Back in the Groove,'' *Los Angeles Times,* April 17, 1989.

McGuire, Stryker, ''Why Garth Brooks Feels Used,'' *Newsweek,* July 26, 1993, 41.

Nelson, Havelock, ''Latifa Label Brings Rap Flavor to Epic,'' *Billboard,* December 19, 1992, 12.

Newcomb, Peter, ''I Heard It at the Record Store,'' *Forbes,* July 8, 1991, 88.

Standard & Poors Industry Surveys, New York: Standard & Poors Corporation, 1993.

U.S. Department of Commerce, *U.S. Industrial Outlook 1993,* Washington, DC: U.S. Department of Commerce, 1993.

''With FTC Inquiry Under Way, Suits Mount in Used-CD Fray,'' *Billboard,* August 14, 1993.

—Robin Armstrong

SIC 3661

TELEPHONE AND TELEGRAPH APPARATUS

This industry covers establishments primarily engaged in manufacturing wire telephone and telegraph equipment are included in this industry. Included are establishments manufacturing modems and other telephone and telegraph interface equipment. Establishments primarily engaged in manufacturing cellular radio telephones are classified in **SIC 3663: Radio and Television Broadcasting and Communications Equipment.**

INDUSTRY SNAPSHOT

The North American Telecommunications Association (NATA) forecasted that the total annual market for telecommunications equipment would grow from $39 billion in 1991 to $58.2 billion in 1996 for an overall estimated growth rate of 49.2 percent. This growth rate follows a 6.8 percent compound annual growth rate between 1985 and 1991.

Network equipment grew from $7.2 billion in 1985 to $10.2 billion in 1991, while customer premise equipment reached the $11.1 billion mark in 1991. The data communications market grew from $2.9 billion in 1985 to $7.2 billion in 1991, and was expected to approach $9.6 billion in 1996. Voice processing systems were expected to lead all categories in growth with a 154 percent growth rate forecast between 1991 and 1996. Equipment manufacturers sold nearly $1.3 billion in voice processing software and hardware in 1991.

More than a thousand companies provide network and customer premise to the public switched network and to private users across the nation. The two largest U.S. equipment manufacturers are the American Telephone and Telegraph Company (AT&T of New York and the Motorola Corporation of Illinois. These two companies ranked second and seventh, respectively, in 1991 worldwide equipment sales revenue. Alcatel Corporation of France was the largest worldwide equipment seller capturing 10.3 percent of the 1991 market.

The U.S. Bureau of Labor anticipated an overall decline in employment in this sector with the category of electric and electronic assemblers forecast to fall by 51 percent between 1990 and 2005. Due to a substantial reengineering of the workflow in this industry, many traditional jobs were predicted to become automated and downsizing would occur across the various employment classifications. Positions unaffected by this downsizing were computer programmers and sales/marketing personnel. This group was expected to grow by 17 percent during this timeframe.

ORGANIZATION AND STRUCTURE

The organization and structure of the telephone and telegraph equipment market is broken down into two broad categories: network equipment manufacturers, who sell telephone switching and switchboard equipment primarily to local and long distance phone companies; and end-user or terminal equipment manufacturers, who sell data and voice communications equipment, facsimile equipment, call/voice processing equipment, consumer communications electronics, private branch exchanges (PBX), and videoconferencing equipment to both large and small businesses and residential users. The breakdown of equipment sales in these market segments for 1993 and their respective market shares based on 1993 sales were: network equipment, with $12.6 billion and 39.3 percent; datacom equipment, with $8.2 billion and 25.6 percent; facsimile equipment, with $3.3 billion and 10.4 percent; call/voice processing, with $3.2 billion and 10.1 percent; consumer electronics, with $2.3 billion and 7.3 percent; private branch exchanges, with $2.1 billion and 6.7 percent; and videoconferencing, with $223 million and 0.7 percent.

BACKGROUND AND DEVELOPMENT

In the wake of the deregulation of telecommunications in the United States and worldwide, the business user faced a bewildering choice of services and equipment. The growing importance of voice, data, and text communication links for the conduct of everyday business demanded that information about telecommunications networks and equipment and the costs involved find its way out of the specialist departments and into the hands of business managers and residential users. Access to information and reliable communication links are vital.

In the past, business telecommunications were more or less a straightforward matter. Services were provided by AT&T with its undisputed monopoly as carrier of voice, data, and text communications. Large business users had private branch exchanges, or PBXs, for internal and external voice traffic, telex machines for instantaneous transmission of text, and dedicated data lines for communications with their mainframe computers. Small businesses used key telephone systems and facsimile machines.

Progress in microelectronics and the deregulation of the telecommunications structure in the United States have changed all that. The boundaries between computing and telecommunications have become blurred. With the advent of the Integrated Service Digital Network, or ISDN, the telecommunications network would no longer distinguish between voice, text, data, and image traffic. Everything went over the wire or the fiber optic cable in bits. There would be a uniform ISDN plug for telephones, computers, and fax machines. Personal computers not only become immensely powerful, they also double as telex and data communications terminals, as fax machines, as telephones and telephone answering machines. Electronic data interchange would eventually do away with forms completed in duplicate and triplicates. Videophones would bring the person at the other end of the line right into the office. In short, the management of the flow of, and access to, communication takes an ever more important place in the organization and the running of a modern business, independent of its size.

Telecommunications equipment and services swamped the market, which became ever more complicated for the ordinary business person. Manufacturers announced new products and services almost daily. The talk moved towards digital networks and equipment linked by fiber optic; ISDN and electronic mail, fax, videotext, and mobile communications; and networking, voice data integration, and compatibility.

Knowing what these terms mean, how they relate to the plethora of products available on the market and how to use them for business, will become as indispensable to the manager of a small business as familiarity with the personal computer. Because it is not the telecommunications equipment itself, but its judicious use which will be instrumental in a company's success.

Changes in telecommunications regulations since the early 1980s transformed the way telecommunications can be used. Competition in network provision has improved the quality of traditional services. Waiting lists for business and residential voice and data lines has fallen dramatically. Telecommunication and equipment prices have also declined. New telecommunication based services have sprung up, bringing revenue not only to telecommunication operators and the information providers, but also generally enhancing the value of business operations. Even domestic users with touch tone telephones are beginning to avail themselves of network-based facilities which ten years ago only users with sophisticated communications equipment could afford.

The proliferation of the equipment market not only means greater choice at lower prices for the user, it also opens up more possibilities of creative use of telecommunications in the way business is conducted. A PBX offering direct dial-in could route facsimile as well as telephone traffic. Therefore, businesses would find it unnecessary to install a separate fax line. The availability of electronic mail services opened up the world of telex and text-based fax to the users of personal computers without the need for expensive terminal equipment.

CURRENT CONDITIONS

Central Office Switching Systems. The real value of the United States' telecommunications system lies in its ability to access a wide range of users wherever they our located (Universal Service). This is the role of telephone switching systems.

When large scale integrated circuits were perfected in the 1970s, it became technically feasible to develop a digital-switching network to replace the electronic network in central offices. The current state-of-the-art of central office technology has a digital switching network controlled by a programmable central processor. Most modern switching equipment, ranging from small PBXs to large toll tandem switches that can handle thousands of trunks, used this technology. Further research was underway to develop even less costly switching systems capable of switching light streams rather than electrical pulses.

Switching systems route calls between themselves and selected terminating stations by addressing. Station addresses in the United States consist of a three digit area code and a seven digit telephone number. From overseas locations, a country code is added.

Centrex. Before the arrival of micro-electronics and stored program control private branch exchanges, large companies were reluctant to place switching systems on their premises to provide private branch exchange service. Centrex is a PBX-like service furnished by the local telephone company through equipment located in the central office. Centrex features allow direct inward dialing (DID) to a telephone number and direct outward dialing (DOD) from a number without operator intervention. For calls into the Centrex, the service is equivalent to individual line service. Outgoing calls differ from individual line service only in the requirement that the caller dials an individual access code (usually 9). Calls between stations in the Centrex group require four or five digits instead of the seven digits required for ordinary calls. An attendant position located on the customer's premises is linked to the central office over a separate circuit. Centrex service provides PBX features without locating a switching system on the user's premises.

The demand for Centrex service provided by the Regional Bell Operating Companies was expected to grow by four to five percent annually. Small business Centrex service (less than 100 lines) experienced five to ten percent growth rates, while the intermediate to large line size segments experienced flat or negative growth rates. The distribution of the current eight-million-line Centrex installed base is as follows: less than 100 company lines, 1.4 million total lines; 100 to 399 company lines, one million total lines; 400 to 1,000 company lines, 1.55 million total lines; 1,000 or more company lines, 4.05 million total lines.

Customer Premise Equipment. It was forecasted that sales of telephone products would grow by 7.3 percent annually from $3.1 billion in 1992 to almost $4.1 billion in 1996. This category includes telephone sets, cordless telephones, and answering machines. The projected increase in this group was due primarily to a jump in marketshare for cordless phones from 41.9 percent in 1992 to 49.4 percent in 1996, and an expected growth in telephone answering systems from 31.9 percent in 1992 to 36.7 percent in 1996. The market share for one and two-line phones was forecasted to decline from 21 percent to 10.9 percent for single line units and 4.4 percent to three percent for two-line phones between 1992 and 1996.

In recent years, cordless telephones have gained wide consumer acceptance with an estimated 40 percent household penetration in the United States. Cordless phones were projected to account for 17 percent of the wireless communications equipment market by 1997. These instruments use a low-powered radio link between a base unit and the portable telephone. In 1992, sales of cordless phones reached $1.34 billion, a 6.6 percent growth rate from 1991 levels. Manufac-

turer sales approached the 20 million unit level in 1992 with the average unit price dropping from $85 to $76 dollars during this timeframe. Leading manufacturers AT&T, General Electric Company, and Sony Corporation expected continued price declines in this category.

The latest generation of cordless telephones were multibutton units which could be assigned to outside lines, intercom paths, or system features such as speed dial. The handset and base could talk on any of the channels, and the user could accept the channel with the best reception. Standard key features such as transfer and hold were activated from the cordless unit.

The sale of telephone answering equipment experienced significant growth in 1992, reaching the $1 billion dollar sales level on an eight percent growth rate. Answering apparatus once provided exclusively by the local exchange companies, or LECs, were widely available from leading suppliers AT&T, Panasonic Co., and Sharp Corporation. Unit sales for this product reached the $14.5 million mark with manufacturers distributing their stock primarily through mass merchants and electronic and appliance stores.

The telephone answering machine market will continue to grow, but technological innovation will replace the traditional stand-alone telephone answering machine connected to a telephone with integrated telephone answering devices. These units will include telephone answering devices incorporated into every piece of communications equipment from basic telephones to cordless integrated answering telephone devices to personal computer systems.

The market offers two categories of telephone sets: general purpose sets or corded phones and special purpose telephones, such as coin operated telephones. The sale of corded phones grew 9.2 percent in 1992 to achieve $654 million in dollar sales. Unit sales were up five million to reach 26.1 million units in 1992. Leading suppliers AT&T, General Electric, and Conair Corp. distributed their products primarily through electronics/appliance stores and mass merchant outlets.

The price of general purpose sets is often a clue to their quality. Many inexpensive instruments provide poor transmission quality and fail when dropped. At the high end of the scale, price usually is a function of features or looks. Two-line phone sets were expected to show only modest unit growth (3.9 percent) through the mid-1990s with an overall decline in total dollar sales due to average price declines in manufacturer prices. Single-line phone sets will be replaced by feature phones with many more characteristics and capabilities than existing models.

Coin Telephones. The advent of the customer-owned coin operated telephone (COCOT) is another byproduct of divestiture that is confusing to many users. In the first few years following the dissolution of the Bell System, many private companies saw COCOTs as a potentially lucrative business. The companies that ventured into this market with less than adequate equipment, however, quickly discovered what the local exchange companies, or LECs, have long understood: the risks and administrative costs of coin telephones are high, and the companies that enter this market without understanding the hazards can lose large amounts. The two major risks are fraud and vandalism. These can be combatted with durable instruments and by building defenses into the telephone.

The North American Telecommunication Association estimated that there were 265,000 COCOTs in service competing against 1.88 million telephone company-owned pay phones. This number was expected to reach 340,000 by 1996. The average gross revenue per unit is forecast at $1,004 annually. Equipment manufacturers for this category sell close to $210 million a year in pay phone instruments to telephone and COCOT companies, and increased growth was forecasted due to an expanding market.

Key Telephone Systems. Key Telephone Systems (KTS) are not high-technology products compared to radio, satellite, and fiber optics, and they don't have the technical appeal of a PBX, but they are the workhorses of American business. Like other customer premise products, KTSs have evolved from wired logic and electromechanical operation to stored program or firmware control. In the process, they adopted many features that were once the exclusive province of PBX. The difference between the PBX and the key system was indistinct enough that the industry used the term, ''hybrid,'' to describe one class of system that has elements of both.

The demand for key telephone systems is substantial as small businesses and even some residences wanting several in-house lines purchase these products. Key telephone set manufacturers had 1991 revenues of $1.3 billion. AT&T accounted for 40 percent of this market with Tie/Communications, Inc. and Executone Information Systems accounting for 15 percent and 12 percent respectively. The top sales in this category by company market share in 1991: AT&T had 40 percent, Tie/Communications, Inc. had 15 percent, Executone Information Systems had 12 percent, Cortelco PBX Systems Corp. had eight percent and Toshiba America, Inc. had seven percent.

The Electronic Key Telephone System offers most of the features of a PBX, especially the hybrid version, which is a cross between a PBX and a Key System. The distinction between the KTSs and PBXs is becoming more blurred as technology brings more intelligence to the KTS. Further blurring the trend between Key Systems and PBXs is the propensity of some manufacturers to make their Key Telephone instrument lines compatible with their PBX lines, allowing a company to grow out of its KTS and into a larger, more sophisticated PBX.

Private Branch Exchanges. Many organizations operate private telecommunications systems. These systems range in size from the Federal Telephone System, which is larger than the telecommunications systems in many countries, to small Private Branch Exchanges (PBXs). As of December 1992, an installed base of 28.5 million PBX stations were in operation with AT&T responsible for 30 percent of this market, Northern Telecom, 20 percent, and Siemens/Rolm, 18 percent.

Although AT&T is the leading equipment manufacturer in this category, it has lost marketshare to foreign competitors, particularly Northern Telecom of Canada, over the last several years. In 1992, 4.4 million PBX stations were shipped worldwide, with AT&T controlling 26 percent marketshare, down from 28 percent in 1991. Northern Telecom was responsible for 25 percent of these shipments, up three percent from 1991 for an increase of 132,000 stations shipped.

The market for low-end PBXs (systems with less than 100 lines) generated $2.6 billion in revenue in 1991. Mitel Corporation controlled 24 percent of this market, or $624 million, with AT&T and Northern Telecom responsible for 20 percent and ten percent of marketshare, respectively.

Nearly every business with more than 30 to 100 stations is in the market for a PBX, or its central office counterpart, Centrex (a service by the local phone companies through which the guts of the system are located on the local phone company premise). PBXs are economical for some very small businesses that need features that most key systems do not provide such as restriction and least cost routing. They are also economical for very large businesses that have PBXs using central office switching systems of a size that rivals many metropolitan public networks. Most PBXs can be mounted in a cabinet on the business user's premises and can operate without air conditioning in an ordinary office environment.

The office PBX increasingly controls private voice networks. As the network evolves into all-digital, so does the PBX in all but the low end systems of 100 stations or fewer, which remain analog. The advent of the T-1 carrier as the preferred transmission medium is the principle force driving the evolution of the PBX. The long distance carriers make it increasingly attractive for business users to bypass the local central office with T-1 trunks directly to the long distance carrier's central office. The cost of T-1 service for PBX lines is particularly advantageous when data transmission facilities parallel the route of voice. The integration of voice and data reduces the cost of access lines to the outside world.

Call/Voice Processing Equipment. Several converging forces have increased the importance of incoming call management systems. First, there is the increasing use of telemarketing. A telemarketing center typically has banks of 800-numbers with different numbers associated with different product lines or promotions, and different agents with access to various databases to handle callers' questions. A caller distribution system is needed in this case to direct incoming calls to the appropriate agent. Secondly, most incoming 800-calls are delivered via T-1 technology. With this technology, calls need to be routed to the appropriate party when they reach the customer premise. Finally, call distribution technology has advanced to the point where it is basically a merger of telephone and computer operations. Any organization with more than a few answering positions finds that the cost of some machine-controlled call distribution pays for itself quickly.

Call/voice processing systems accounted for 10.1 percent or $3.2 billion of all telecommunication and data equipment sales for 1993. This figure was up $329 million or 11.33 percent from 1992. Sales of U.S. call processing equipment were forecasted to grow at an annual compound rate of 21 percent between 1992 and 1998 to $8.2 billion. This category consists of uniform call distribution systems, call sequencers, automatic call distributors, and voice processing systems.

A uniform call distribution system (UCD), a standard feature of many PBXs, often significantly improves call handling. The stand-alone counterpart of a UCD is the call sequencer. This device may work with a PBX or key telephone system, or it may be connected directly to incoming lines. Unlike the UCD, a call sequencer does not direct calls, but alerts agents to the presence of incoming calls. The most sophisticated device is an automatic call distributor (ACD), which can either stand alone or integrate with a PBX. An ACD routes calls to the least busy agent to equalize the work load. The ACD administrator typically has a video display terminal that presents call statistics in real time, and has many management tools that monitor and improve service and measure the agent's effec-

tiveness. Any organization that has a large number of incoming calls targeted for service positions is a potential ACD user. This includes departments that handle mail orders, literary delivery, inquiries, field service, credit, and collections.

The marriage of computer and telecommunications technologies brought a family of equipment collectively known as voice processing systems to the market. Three classes of equipment comprise voice processing: voice mail, automated attendant, and voice response or audiotex equipment. Octel Communications controls 17 percent of the voice messaging market with Northern Telecom registering 14 percent and AT&T with 13 percent of overall market sales. Five other companies—VMX, Rolm, Centigram, Active Voice, and Boston Technology—make up the remainder with less than ten percent of the market each.

Facsimile Equipment. Since the early 1980s facsimile equipment (FAX) has become an indispensable business machine essential to the every day transactions of most businesses. The FAX machine works by scanning the printed page, encoding it, and transmitting a facsimile of the images in shades of black and white without identifying individual characters. Facsimile can convey both text and graphic information, source documents can be retransmitted without rekeying, and facsimile transmission is affected less by transmission errors than other types of data communication. Facsimile is also fast. Some facsimile machines also double as printers and copiers.

The sale of home facsimile equipment grew 12.3 percent to $247 million in 1992. Although unit sales grew an estimated 30 percent from 1991 levels, overall dollar sales volume declined due to a drop in the average unit sales price from $550 in 1991 to $475 in 1992. Leading suppliers Canon USA, Muratec, and Sharp accounted for 89 percent of 1992 sales volume in this category.

Data Communications Equipment. Like other types of telecommunications equipment, modems have become faster, cheaper, and smarter. The ready availability of inexpensive personal computers has expanded the demand for modems, and basically two types of modems exist in the market: dial-up modems and private line modems. Dial-up modems either plug into a personal computer slot, or are self contained devices that plug into the computer's serial port. Many of the modem's features are designed to emulate a telephone. These features include: dial tone recognition, automatic tone and dial pulse dialing, monitoring call progress tones such as busy and reorder, automatic answer, and call termination. These items are priced on a commodity type basis and use the public network for the transmission of information. Private line modems work exclusively with voice and data private lines, and although it has the same functions as a dial-up modem, it is not as popular as the dial-up modem.

Many data applications, by their nature, are incapable of fully using a data circuit. Rather than flowing in a steady stream, data usually flows in steady, short bursts with long, idle periods intervening. To make use of this idle capacity, data multiplexers are employed to collect data from multiple stations and combine it into a single, high-speed bit stream.

Data multiplexers come in two types: time division multiplexers (TDM) and statistical multiplexers (statmux). In a TDM, each station is assigned a time slot, and the multiplexer collects data from each station in turn. If a station has no data to send, its time slot goes unused. A statmux makes use of the idle time periods in a data circuit by assigning time slots to pairs of stations according to the amount of traffic they have to send. The multiplexer collects data from the terminal and sends it to the distant end, with the address of the receiving terminal minimizing idle times between transactions.

Analog or frequency division multiplexers are also available to divide a voice channel into multiple segments for data transmission. Their primary use is to connect multiple, slow-speed data terminals over voice channels. A concentrator is similar to a multiplexer except that it is usually a single-ended device which connects directly to a host computer. The primary application for multiplexers is in data networks that use asynchronous terminals. Since many of these items cannot be addressed and have no error correction capability, they are of limited use by themselves in remote locations. The multiplexer provides end-to-end error checking and correction and circuit sharing to support multiple terminals.

INDUSTRY LEADERS

More than a thousand companies provide network and terminal equipment to the public switched network and to private users across the nation. American Telephone and Telegraph Company of New York is the largest of these manufacturers with $64 billion in sales and net income of $3.8 billion. AT&T sells switching and transmission systems through its AT&T Taiwan Telecommunications affiliate, switching systems through its Network Systems Group, and equipment through its Communication Products Group. AT&T ranked second in the world behind Alcatel Corporation of France with 10.3 percent of 1991 worldwide equipment sales revenues.

Motorola Corporation was the second largest U.S. producer of telecommunications equipment worldwide, accounting for 6.6 percent of 1991 worldwide revenues, which placed it seventh on the list of telecommunications equipment producers worldwide. The company was the leading maker of data communications equipment such as modems and multiplexers through its Codex and Universal Systems operations. Motorola had over $13.3 billion in sales in 1992.

Rockwell International of Seal Beach, California, had 1992 sales of $10.9 billion. Rockwell's telecommunications business is the world's largest manufacturer of modems for fax machines and computers.

A number of other multinational conglomerates also provide communication equipment used in the telephone network such as: International Business Machines Corporation, or IBM, provider of data storage, communication devices, and network systems; Digital Equipment Corporation, maker of network and communication products; GTE Corporation, a PBX manufacturer; and Hewlett-Packard Company, manufacturer of optelectronic devices and analytical instruments.

Harris Corporation of Florida sold $496 million in communications products in 1992, primarily digital telephone switches. Reliance Electric Company of Ohio is a leading provider of equipment and services to the central office switched network with over $402 million in sales in 1992. These companies constitute only a small percentage of all the manufacturers in this industry, but account for a large proportion of overall equipment sales.

WORK FORCE

The increase in technology was forecast to eradicate many of the traditional positions associated with the manufacture of telephone equipment and apparatus. A study by the U.S. Bureau of Labor anticipated a 51 percent decline in electrical and electronic assemblers between the years 1990 and 2005. This group accounted for 16.5 percent of the employees of manufacturers of telephone equipment and apparatus. A related group of electrical and electronic engineers, who accounted for 8.2 percent of the work force, was expected to grow by 5.7 percent over this timeframe.

On the whole, there will be a substantial reengineering of the workflow in this industry, with many traditional jobs becoming automated and a downsizing in administrative and support staff. An increase of 17 percent was expected for computer programmers, and sales/marketing personnel would be needed to sell the products in a market driven by price/features.

AMERICA AND THE WORLD

Historically, the United States has been the leader in telecommunications equipment technology and innovation. This was due primarily to the monopoly that AT&T (the Bell System) had on the nation's telephone system for the first 100 years of its existence. The breakup of the Bell System in 1984 created a new playing field for telecommunication equipment manufacturers worldwide. Since telephone technology is not drastically different from computer technology, and in fact, many of the same components and techniques are used in both, the race to compete in this market became a global endeavor. This factor coupled with the regulatory barriers harnessing the former Bell Operating Companies resulted in the United States losing this 100 year advantage almost overnight.

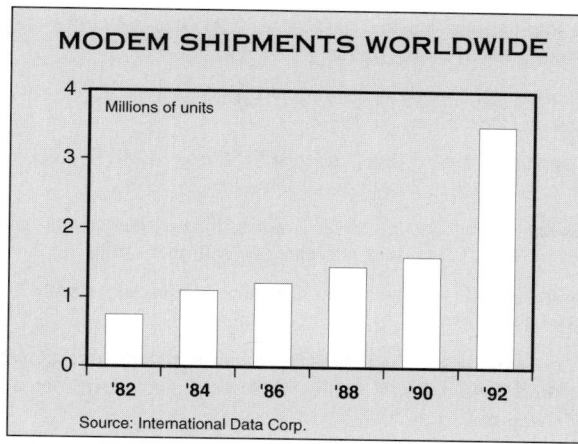

MODEM SHIPMENTS WORLDWIDE

Millions of units

Source: International Data Corp.

Between the years 1983 to 1989, the United States' export of telecommunication equipment increased at a compound annual rate of 15 percent. During this same timeframe, imports of telecommunication equipment grew by 30 percent. In 1989, the U.S. telecommunication equipment industry had a trade deficit of $2.7 billion, which improved 15 percent in 1990 to $2.4 billion. Low technology terminal equipment (i.e. telephones) accounted for the largest component of foreign imports. Foreign producers in the Far East were able to capture this market through lower manufacturing costs. China, Malaysia, and Thailand contributed the most to this market. Japan accounted for almost 34 percent of the U.S. imports of telecom equipment in 1992, down from 47 percent in 1982. This trend was due primarily to the United States' shift to Canada and Western Europe for high technology

switching equipment. The U.S. Senate, in response to these developments, passed the Telecommunications Equipment Research and Manufacturing Act of 1991 in an attempt to make the market more competitive.

Although the United States is no longer the dominant manufacturer in the telecommunications equipment market, it is currently reestablishing itself as an international force. Despite an enormous trade deficit with Japan and other Far Eastern suppliers, the United States is the largest manufacturer of foreign-produced equipment in Japan. From 1987 to 1990, the United States had a trade surplus with Europe exceeding $700 million.

Only two out of the top 15 telecommunications equipment manufacturers worldwide in 1991 were U.S. companies. Alcatel Corporation of France led this list with 15.5 percent of the market, followed by AT&T (United States) with 10.3 percent, Siemens (Germany) with 9.9 percent, Northern Telecom (Canada) with 8.2 percent, NEC Corporation (Japan) and L.M. Ericsson (Sweden) with 6.7 percent each, and Motorola, Inc. (United States) with 6.6 percent.

RESEARCH AND TECHNOLOGY

All of the trends involving computers and communications ultimately converge at the desktop. Higher-speed processors, more powerful and higher capacity networks, and more flexible software and management systems are redefining the way we utilize communication products at our work space. While voice, video, and data communications have each evolved independently, they were starting to come together into a ''multimedia'' environment to make future communications more efficient, effective, and user-friendly.

While the personal computer revolution has been thoroughly documented over the past decade, the familiar telephone instrument found virtually everywhere has undergone a transformation of its own. This piece of communications equipment has been dramatically rethought, redesigned, and reequipped to accomplish a new role in the communications revolution. The standard telephone is becoming a voice terminal in a market where voice, video, and data applications are being formed into integrated communication systems.

The 1990s saw the emergence of Integrated Service Digital Network, or ISDN, as mode of interfacing in this new communications environment. This interface is an important step toward achieving universal compatibility among different manufacturers.

In addition to the deployment of ISDN technology, an entirely new level of integration between telephones and computing is being developed on hardware and software systems called application programming interfaces, or APIs. APIs will enable the user to integrate his personal computer and voice terminal into one instrument. The personal computer's processing and memory-storage capabilities offer the potential for a new dimension of multimedia communications capabilities at the desktop. As this technology evolves, the basic telephone will be transformed from a stand-alone voice terminal to a device that integrates voice, data, text, fax, and video services. Eventually, push-button dial pads and handsets will be replaced by voice-activated terminals with integrated speaker and microphone capabilities.

The revolution in communications technology occurring at the desktop has also been taking place in the switched networks. Electromechanical switching will all but disappear by the year 2000. Around the mid-1990s, the country reached the crossover point between analog and digital switching with more than half the lines in the United States being served by digital central offices. The local exchange companies or LECs are basing their networks on ISDN technology, which uses circuit switched technology, and it was estimated that most PBX manufacturers will retain circuit switching as well. The technology with the most intriguing future is photonic switching, estimated to be 1,000 times faster than present switching products. As fiber-optic cable extends to the desktops with a photonic switch in the network, users can link high-bandwidth facilities around the world presenting businesses with a myriad of communication opportunities for the future.

INDUSTRY INFORMATION SOURCES

"American Telephone and Telegraph Corporation," *Hoover's Handbook of American Business,* January 1, 1994.

Bellamy, John C. *Digital Telephony,* New York: John Wiley & Sons, 1982.

Beyda, William J. *Basic Data Communications-A Comprehensive Overview,* Englewood Cliffs, NJ: Prentice-Hall, 1989.

Brewster, R.L. *Communication Systems and Computer Networks,* New York: John Wiley & Sons, 1989.

Connelly, Joanne. "U.S. Computer Hardware up Four Percent '92 Forecast," *Electronic News,* January 6, 1992.

"Consumer Electronics Sales for '92 up 7.9 Percent; Electronics '92 Statistical Report," *HFD - The Weekly Home Furnishings Newspaper,* March 15, 1993.

"Cordless, TADS top $4 Billion Phone Market; Cordless Telephones; Telephone Answering Devices; Computers, Business Systems & Office Products," *Purchasing,* December 16, 1993.

Darnay, Arsen J. and Redding, Marlita A. *Market Share Reporter: An Annual Compilation of Reported Market Share Data on Companies, Products, and Services 1994,* Detroit, MI: Gale Research, Inc., 1994.

Darney, Arsen J. *Manufacturing USA. Industry Analysis, Statistics and Leading Companies 3rd Edition Volume II,* Detroit, MI: Gale Research, Inc., 1994.

"Digital Equipment Corporation," *Hoover's Handbook of American Business,* January 1, 1994.

Dordick, H.S. *Understanding Modern Telecommunications,* New York: McGraw-Hill, 1986.

Elbert, Bruce R. *Private Telecommunications Networks,* Norwood, MA: Artech House, 1987.

Frenzel, Louise, Jr. *Communication Electronics,* New York: McGraw-Hill, 1989.

Gasman, Lawrence, D. *Manager's Guide to the New Telecommunications Network,* Norwood, MA: Artech House, 1988.

"GTE Corporation," *Hoover's Handbook of American Business,* January 1, 1994.

"International Business Machines," *Hoover's Handbook of American Business,* January 1, 1994.

Kace, Ong. "The Big Business in Small Offices," *The Strait Times,* December 28, 1993.

Kendall, Peter. "Independents Nibble on Bell Pay-Phone Pie," *The Chicago Tribune,* February 21, 1993.

Keen, Peter G. *Competing in Time: Using Telecommunications For Competitive Advantage,* Ballinger, 1988.

Labate, John. "Companies to Watch," *Fortune,* March 21, 1994.

Leibowitz, Ed. "The Great Dumb Switch Debate-Part One: Dumb Switches and Intelligent Switches; An OAI Focus," *Teleconnect,* July 1992.

McKay, Deborah. "Technology Explosion Brings Flood of New Equipment," *The Financial Post,* November 13, 1993.

"Motorola, Inc.," *Hoover's Handbook of American Business,* January 1, 1994.

Noll, A. Michael. *Introduction to Telephones and Telephone Systems,* Norwood, MA: Artech House, 1988.

"Reliance Electric Company," *Hoover's Handbook of American Business,* January 1, 1994.

Robinson, Brian. "Telephone Services Make Their Way Into LAN," *Network World,* October 4, 1993.

"Rockwell International Corporation," *Hoover's Handbook of American Business,* January 1, 1994.

"States Vary Widely in Regulation of Pay Phone Marketplace," *State Telephone Regulation Report,* November 3, 1993.

Sulkin, Allan. "Centrex Providers Discover that Small Can Be Beautiful," *Business Communications Review,* April 1992.

"TADS, Cordless to Drive Phones; Cordless Telephones and Telephone Answering Devices to be Major Factors in Consumer Telephone Market; BIS Strategic Decisions Report," *HFD - The Weekly Home Furnishings Newspaper,* November 29, 1993.

Tissot, Anthony F. "The Changing Role of The PBX in Today's Office Environment," *Telecommunications,* November 1993.

"Toshiba Launches Small Digital Key Telephone System," *RBOC Update,* April 1993.

"U.S. Call Processing Markets to Triple and Top $8 Billion," *Telephone IP News,* March 1994.

"U.S. Telecommunications Equipment Market To Reach $58.2 billion by 1996," *RBOC Update,* July 1992.

"Vanguard's Voice Processing Industry Temperature Check," *Voice Technology News,* April 6, 1993.

Waite, Andrew, J. *The Inbound Telephone Call Center,* New York: Telecom Library, 1989.

—Andrew Burke

SIC 3663

RADIO AND TELEVISION BROADCASTING AND COMMUNICATIONS EQUIPMENT

This industry manufactures radio and television broadcasting and communications equipment. Important products of this industry are closed-circuit and cable television equipment; studio audio and video equipment; light communications equipment; transmitters, transceivers, and receivers (except household and automotive); cellular radio telephones; fiber optics equipment; communication antennas; RF power amplifiers; satellite communications systems (space and ground segments); and fixed and mobile radio systems. Establishments primarily engaged in manufacturing household audio and communications equipment are classified in **SIC 3651: Household Audio and Video Equipment;** those manufacturing intercommunications equipment are classified in **SIC 3669: Communications Equipment, Not Elsewhere Classified;** and those manufacturing consumer radio and television receiving antennas are classified in **SIC 3679: Electronic Components, Not Elsewhere Classified.**

INDUSTRY SNAPSHOT

This industry covers a range of interrelated and sometimes competing communications systems. The industry continues to reinvent itself as individual segments grow. The emerging structure is being shaped by consumer trends, regulations, technological advances, and corporate decisions. The electromagnetic spectrum, through which the wireless communications companies of this industry transmit signals, is controlled by the Federal Government, which has exerted profound influence over this industry in recent years with new regulations and legislation.

Because communications systems are rapidly being transformed by the demand for customized, interconnected, and wireless services, products leading growth in this industry include wireless communication systems (pagers, cellular phones, personal communications systems), mobile communications equipment, and satellite communications devices.

ORGANIZATION AND STRUCTURE

This category contains several different types of communications technologies. Connectivity between these technologies is increasing, resulting in hybridized products and systems. This is reflected in the fact that the players in this industry include cable television, cellular, electronics, telephone, computer, and satellite communications companies. Wireless communications services include cellular, paging, and specialized mobile radio. Cellular and paging, the largest segments of this market, generated more than $10 billion in industry sales in 1992.

Historically, high-technology consumer electronics equipment becomes less expensive in the years after introduction. This has been true in the case of many products offered by this industry, and it has helped drive growth by attracting new consumer markets. The average wholesale price of cellular phones, for example, decreased to about $280 in 1993, when about five million cellular telephones were sold in the United States, up 13 percent over 1992.

Pagers. Significant growth in the paging industry has been attributed to increasingly sophisticated and lower-priced products and services. The number of paging subscribers in the United States reached approximately 17 million at the beginning of 1994, up from 14 million at the beginning of 1993. In 1992 revenues were $2.3 billion. Some of this growth can be attributed to a trend toward non-business use. Whereas a decade ago pagers were most commonly found on doctors and other busy professionals "on call," they are now likely to be found on parents trying to contact their children, or waiters who need to know when their orders are ready.

Consumers have taken to pagers because a new generation of models offers new services, such as phone numbers, text messages, customized stock prices, news flashes, and sports scores. There is also a developing consumer trend toward integrating and customizing communications services that contributes to growth and reduces competition among different communication services. For example, about 20 percent of cellular subscribers use paging in conjunction with their cellular service to mediate costs because being paged is less expensive than receiving an incoming call on a cellular phone.

Cellular telephones. Cellular telephones get their name from the small regions (cells) into which service areas are divided. Each cell contains a base station with a low-power transmitter/receiver. Base stations are connected to mobile telephone switching offices (MTSOs) either by telephone wire or microwave transmission. A computer at the switching office coordinates calls for the service area, and monitors a call's signal strength. When the signal loses strength because the caller is exiting the cell, the MTSO switches the call to the next cell. Cells sometimes overlap one another or have gaps between them because of topographical obstructions.

Cellular subscribers are expected to number about 20 million in 1994, drawn by enhancements such as improved capacity, seamless networking, and personal 800 service. Cumulative capital investment and revenues from cellular services are both expected to continue increasing through the 1990s. Equipment sales should continue to rise, to the benefit of companies in this category, as operators add to their analog capacity and some begin the transition to digital technology. This transition is critical to the cellular industry's competitiveness. A digital cellular system transmits a caller's voice by converting the sound waves into a numerical code, rather than a wave pattern, as in analog systems. Calling capacity is expected to increase by a factor of three or more with digital cell sites. In addition to increased capacity, the conversion to digital offers other advantages: lower unit costs; better quality and increased privacy; and the promise of advanced services and data transmission. Several domestic suppliers, including Ericsson, Hughes, and Motorola, offer dual-mode digital/analog cellular telephones.

Business users still account for the majority of cellular users, but much of the growth in cellular, as with paging, has come from the consumer market since the equipment has become more affordable. A decrease in prices may drive down average revenues per consumer but should not hamper overall growth, because of increased volume and product innovations. Technological innovations in electronic circuitry and in the intelligence built into the cellular network have resulted in new features which make cellular more attractive. Short messaging can be displayed on an alphanumeric display, for example. Some companies have introduced cellular phones which can also handle regular wired calls, faxes, or modems.

Another development affecting the structure of the cellular industry is the creation, by Independent Telecommunications Network, Inc. (ITN), of a nationwide Signaling System 7 backbone network to transport cellular calls between cell sites. A Signaling System 7 is an advanced network protocol which manages traffic flow through a telephone network. This is significant because it will eliminate charges related to "roaming" agreements between operators and special access codes that now complicate the use of a cellular phones outside of home service regions. Cellular carriers are trying to capitalize on the increasing mobility of business people by moving into data transmission. In 1992, nine major cellular carriers teamed up with IBM to provide a data network called CelluPlan II over existing analog cellular networks. Their competition comes primarily from two major providers of mobile data services: Ardis, a joint venture between IBM and Motorola, and RAM Mobile Data, a creation of BellSouth and RAM Broadcasting. These networks are independent of the cellular network and serve businesses only via radio waves.

The involvement of BellSouth, a long-distance wireline telephone company, in a cellular venture is not unusual. Several major long-distance wireline telephone companies have staked a claim in the cellular market by buying cellular companies—Sprint acquired Centel Corporation in 1993, and AT&T acquired McCaw Cellular. In addition to giving the wireline companies the chance to join rather than compete with wireless services, this gives the cellular companies access to the huge marketing resources of their parent companies.

Personal Communications Services. Personal communications networks, or services, (PCS) describes low-powered microcellular technology that operates in the 900 MHz band. Although available to consumers in Europe and tested in the United States, PCS systems are not widely available in the United States. PCS are expected to make a person carrying a pocket-sized phone available at the same number no matter where the person goes. They transmit calls via radio waves to base stations clustered in many service areas. The system is digital and is expected to be cheaper than existing cellular once it's widely available to consumers. Some analysts believe that it would be ideally suited for telecommuters because digital technology allows PCS to provide data and video services as well as voice, and will give employees the ability to hook up to office computers or fax machines while travelling.

On September 23, 1993 the Federal Communications Commission (FCC) authorized 160 MHz of spectrum for PCS. Starting in 1994, the FCC will begin auctioning PCS licenses, which could generate $10.2 billion for the Federal Government and stimulate the creation of a new generation of wireless services and products. More than one hundred companies have applied to the FCC to operate PCS systems. Carriers are expected to invest in new transceivers, and consumers will purchase feature-rich new phones and wireless portable devices such as personal digital assistants. At the time of its decision, the FCC did not approve a national PCS license. However, once licenses are auctioned a nationwide roaming consortium will likely be formed by groups of licensees that will allow seamless service nationwide. As with existing cellular, there is no consensus on PCS standards. The Telecommunications Industry Association is attempting to develop them, which may enable the fledgling industry to avoid the confusion of multiple standards with which the cellular industry currently contends.

Microwave and Satellite Systems. This is a more mature technology than others in this category. Microwave transmission can be achieved via terrestrial or satellite systems. Terrestrial, or ground systems, work by sending very high frequency signals from transmitters to repeater stations and back to receivers. For these systems to work, there must be no obstructions, such as mountains, between stations. Satellite transmission works similarly but the repeater station is placed in orbit, usually with the region it serves. Because satellites don't have the geographic constraints of terrestrial systems, they are better suited for long-distance, point-to-multipoint transmissions such as television broadcasts. Microwave and satellite systems can also be used to transmit audio, video, and data.

Microwave systems can be categorized as long-haul (transmission distances greater than five miles) or short-haul applications. Long haul microwave equipment is used by common carriers, oil companies, electric utilities, broadcast and cable television operators, pipeline industries, and government agencies. Almost 90 percent of public and private television stations transmit signals via satellite. Short haul customers include universities, institutions, corporations, hotel chains, hospitals, local area networks, cellular phone networks, and local governments. According to the FCC, the majority of users of the 36,538 existing private microwave networks are industrial. Public services hold about 22 percent of private microwave network licenses.

Shipments of land-based microwave systems increased to about $1 billion in 1993, while component sales increased moderately to almost $1.3 billion. The growth is mostly in short-haul applications, such as computer LANs (local-area networks) and video conferencing.

BACKGROUND AND DEVELOPMENT

This industry has developed by continually shedding its old identity as new technologies come along. For example, Motorola, one of the giants in the industry, began in the car radio business. The company sold Handie-Talkies to the Army in World War II and later installed radios in police cars. Many of the companies in this category have been defense contractors.

In the early 1980s, when cellular phones were introduced, AT&T predicted that by the year 2000 about 900,000 mobile phones would be in use in the United States. By 1993, that prediction had already been exceeded a dozen times. In the early 1990s cordless phones began to outsell corded phones. Much of this activity would have been inconceivable before the Justice Department filed suit against AT&T and the Bell monopoly was broken up in the early 1980s. Until 1957, when the courts ruled that telephone customers had the right to use non-AT&T telephone equipment as long as it didn't interfere with the public network, everyone used AT&T equipment and service. AT&T's dominant position as the primary U.S. carrier was finally challenged in 1969 by a company using newly developed microwave technology. That company would become MCI Communications Corporation. The industry did not undergo complete restructuring, however, until the Justice Department officially broke the monopoly in 1984, making way for new communications technologies, equipment, and services.

Some industry observers believe the shift from wireline to wireless communications could be as profound as the shift from gaslight to electric light bulbs. After first underestimating the market for wireless communications, major communications, computers, electronics, and data companies have begun investing heavily in it. AT&T's deal to pay $12.6 billion for McCaw Cellular is one of many examples. A highly publicized health scare in 1993, in which a Florida widower claimed that cellular phone use caused his wife's brain cancer, has spurred research into a possible cellular/cancer link. Long-term impact on the growth of the market will be negligible unless a link is found. The FCC decision to reallocate 200 MHz of spectrum to make way for emerging PCS technologies is vital to the development of the industry and will likely be considered a landmark decision in the future.

CURRENT CONDITIONS

The current status of this industry is healthy and dynamic. Because of excitement surrounding the idea of a national "information superhighway" and growth in new communications technologies, companies in this industry are keenly watched by Wall Street. The Clinton Administration's technologically-friendly position should foster industry growth. Clinton has proposed a broad 10-year plan to force the Pentagon and other federal agencies to cede control of a big block of the nation's airwaves and make them available for new commercial technologies. This comes in addition to the FCC's 1993 decision to reallocate the public airwaves. Even the older, less cutting-edge areas of this industry are profitable. Domestic output of television sets and picture tubes, for example, has increased due to demand from Mexico, Canada, Europe, Asia, and Central and South America. While the biggest revenues are anticipated in wireless communications services, rather than in equipment, some analysts predict a $1.6 billion hardware market by 2000.

The value of shipments of radio and television broadcasting and communications equipment increased to $18 billion in 1993, from $17.8 billion in 1992. Shipment value was forecast to increase to $18.4 billion in 1994. The accelerating development of wireless personal communications services will continue to fuel the demand for radio base station equipment, antennas, low earth orbit satellite systems, and wireless equipment. An important development in the cellular segment is the gradual replacement of analog cellular technology with digital cellular technology. Because there hasn't yet been a decision on which of two rival digital standards—time division multiple access (TDMA) and code division multiple access (CDMA) will be the industry standard—there is currently a market for products which support multiple interfaces. Generic base station transceivers which handle calls using all modulation standards, including U.S. and foreign, analog and digital, voice and data, may also be available for use with a variety of wireless networks, including paging and PCS.

Technological advances like Cellular Digital Packet Data (CPCD) for cellular service were introduced to help analog cellular systems compete with new digital systems. CPCD has been adopted by companies with analog systems to make them more competitive with digital systems. The FCC decision regarding the reallocation of spectrum is a powerful one for this industry because it means companies have a chance at gaining more transmission access. Ultimately, it will translate into money. As a result of the FCC decision green-lighting PCS, the formulation of strategic alliances, the valuation of desired PCN territories, and the sale and purchase of cellular holdings will occur furiously as companies try to maneuver into the emerging PCS market.

A National PCS Consortium was formed in 1993 by 16 companies. Their diversity indicates the broad range of interest in PCS. They include cellular, cable television, specialized mobile radio, and alternative access providers. This group will be the first to conduct national PCS trials. MCI has also formed a consortium, comprising more than 150 cable television, cellular, and publishing companies, seeking a stake in the future of PCS.

The FCC decision to reallocate 220 MHz of spectrum previously occupied by fixed microwave users will boost microwave equipment sales by allowing fixed microwave users to relocate to higher frequencies, and by freeing 200 MHz of formerly government-occupied spectrum for private sector use. Rather than take business from the existing cellular market, some analysts believe PCS may enhance it. Innovations in digital and microcellular technologies, as well as market stimulation from PCS, are likely to push new equipment purchases by cellular carriers and customers until the end of the decade. Other industry observers predict that PCS will threaten to supercede both cellular and wired service.

In order to compete with the emerging PCS market, cellular carriers are developing new systems. Southwestern Bell Mobile Systems' FreedomLink Personal Communications System is a new wireless business phone service based on cellular technology. AccessLine Technologies is marketing a form of personal communications using existing technologies and spectrum through programmable networking and call processing. It's able to replace landline, cellular, fax, pager, and voice mail numbers with a single "smart" telephone number. As cellular systems have expanded, they have fueled the growth of microwave systems for backup or for remote-access areas. Microwave communications technology has been increasingly incorporated into cellular networks in the United States and overseas.

New business applications for wireless data technologies are currently being explored in many areas. Executives were the first to adopt cellular phones, but repair and service people have also found that they can increase productivity with wireless devices. Copier-repair technicians from Pitney-Bowes now carry $2,500 wireless data terminals connected to the wireless Ardis network, a creation of Motorola and IBM, which tells them everything they need to know about their assignments and even allows them to order parts. Motorola predicts that by 2000 the market for such two-way wireless systems could reach $5 billion.

INDUSTRY LEADERS

The massive capital requirements of building unique telecommunications systems guarantees that the companies involved will be large and powerful ones. The biggest players in the computer, communications, and information industries are all maneuvering for the anticipated wireless revolution. Motorola is the leader in this industry, with $13 billion in sales and more than 100,000 employees. Motorola has a broad product line compatible with most standards and long-standing experience in radio electronics. It is the world's leading supplier of pagers, two-way radios, and dispatch systems for commercial fleets. Motorola has the largest segment of the global cellular telephone market, according to U.S. International Trade Commission (ITC) reports. In addition to its strong position on the equipment side, it is buying radio frequencies around the world. Motorola is also developing the Iridium project, a proposed $3.8 billion system which will use 77 small satellites in low earth orbit to connect calls around the world.

One of Motorola's biggest competitors is AT&T, the long-distance giant which invested heavily in the cellular business through its purchase of McCaw Cellular Communications, the nation's largest cellular telephone carrier. AT&T also plans to be heavily involved with PCS. Other major companies in this industry include General Electric Co., General Signal Corporation, GTE Government Systems Corporation, Scientific-Atlanta Inc., McDonnell Douglas Corporation, General Instrument Corporation, Harris Corporation, and Ericsson. None of the top ten companies in this category have sales of less than $380 million or fewer than 3,600 employees.

WORK FORCE

Employment in this industry remained steady in the early 1990s at approximately 123,000. Mergers and consolidations among manufacturers, as well as improved productivity and technology, may mean employment declines in the future. However, this effect may be countered by the growing demand in certain segments of the industry.

Average hourly earnings are estimated at $12.75. Electrical and electronic assemblers, engineers, and technicians accounted for 30 percent of the employment in this industry as of 1990. By 2005, it is esti-

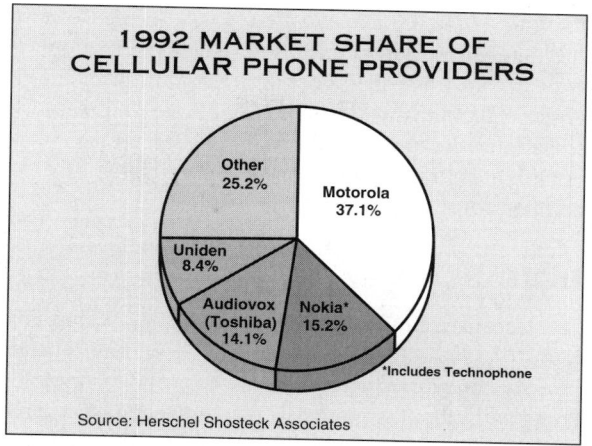

1992 MARKET SHARE OF CELLULAR PHONE PROVIDERS

Other 25.2%
Motorola 37.1%
Uniden 8.4%
Audiovox (Toshiba) 14.1%
Nokia* 15.2%
*Includes Technophone

Source: Herschel Shosteck Associates

mated that the need for electrical and electronic assemblers will decrease by about half.

AMERICA AND THE WORLD

This industry is positioned to take advantage of demand from developing markets abroad, such as Eastern Europe, Central and South America, and China. American companies are increasingly linking up with overseas competitors to create global partnerships. For example, in the personal communicator market (which includes wireless communication devices such as Apple Computer's Newton and Motorola's digital personal communicator), AT&T has joined Matsushita and Olivetti. Intel has joined Ericsson, the Swedish phone-equipment maker, in a similar venture.

At mid-1993, the number of cellular subscribers worldwide reached 27 million, with the United States accounting for about half of them. An estimated 40 percent of cellular phones purchased in the United States are imported. In 1993, imports were valued at more than $400 million for two million units. While this is more units than in 1992, the average price per imported phone decreased.

In 1993, the largest export markets for U.S. telecommunications products were Canada and Mexico. East Asia is the source of about 65 percent of total imports to the United States. Parts exports of $1.6 billion represented more than a third of exports for the first half of 1993, whereas parts imports accounted for only about a quarter of total imports for this period. Radio transceivers are the leading export category, followed by parts for radio equipment.

The U.S. cellular industry is highly competitive in cellular licenses awarded to foreign operators. About 70 percent of the total licenses to operate cellular systems abroad have been awarded to U.S. firms. Because the number of European cellular subscribers alone is expected to more than double to 13 million by 1996, American companies should continue to dominate international cellular operations. However, the lack of a common digital standard has hindered sales of U.S. cellular network equipment abroad.

RESEARCH AND TECHNOLOGY

Because of the high-technology orientation of this industry, research and technology are a continual, high priority concern. Much of the research and technology being carried out is intended to achieve one of several goals: to maximize an existing technology, such as CDPD; to combine existing technologies for enhanced competitiveness across technologies, such as PCN; and to improve technology in existing products to attract consumers with next-generation models, like a new generation of pagers.

INDUSTRY INFORMATION SOURCES

Andrews, Edmund L., ''U.S. Seeks Airwaves of Military,'' *New York Times,* February 10, 1994.

Burrows, Peter, ''The 1993 Up & Comers,'' *Electronic Business,* March 1993.

Cray, Dan, ''Hughes Readies Handsets,'' *Electronic News,* May 4, 1992.

Cringely, Robert X., ''Who, What, and Wireless,'' *Forbes ASAP,* 1993.

''Dimensions of U.S.-based TV Industry,'' *Television Digest,* August 16, 1993.

Gilder, George, ''George Gilder's Telecosm,'' *Forbes ASAP,* March 29, 1993.

Moody's Industrial Manual, New York: Moody's Investors Service, 1993.

Slutsker, Gary, ''The Company That Likes to Obsolete Itself,'' *Forbes,* September 13, 1993.

Slutsker, Gary, ''The Taxicab as Phone Company,'' *Forbes,* January 6, 1992.

Slutsker, Gary, ''The Tortoise and the Hare,'' *Forbes,* February 1, 1993.

Standard & Poor's Industry Surveys, New York: Standard & Poor's Corporation, 1993.

Therrien, Lois, ''Pagers Start to Deliver More Than Phone Numbers,'' *Business Week,* November 15, 1993.

U.S. Industrial Outlook 1994, Washington, DC: U.S. Department of Commerce, January 1994.

Ziegler, Bart, et al., ''Building a Wireless Future,'' *Business Week,* April 5, 1993.

—Leslee York

COMMUNICATION EQUIPMENT NOT ELSEWHERE CLASSIFIED

This classification covers companies primarily engaged in manufacturing communications and related equipment, not elsewhere classified. Important products of this industry include intercommunication equipment, traffic signaling equipment, and fire and burglar alarm apparatus. Establishments that provide security systems monitoring and maintenance are discussed in **SIC 7382: Security Systems Services.**

While this miscellaneous communications equipment industry includes a number of visible and important products, such as railroad signaling devices and various traffic control equipment, the revenue accrued in this industry is traceable largely to security and smoke/fire alarm systems.

Alarm Systems. The United States has long dominated the alarm manufacturing and alarm monitoring industries worldwide. Myriad alarm manufacturers have been able to establish themselves over the years; in the early 1990s the National Burglar and Fire Alarm Association estimated that more than 13,000 local installation companies were operating in America. The popularity of the product has enabled both manufacturers and monitoring services to thrive. STAT Resources Inc. estimated in 1992 that one in 11 households in the country is equipped with a monitoring system, while other statistics indicate that more than 18.5 million burglar alarm systems are in use in the United States. Expensive alarm systems are especially popular, a result, most observers say, of increased public concern about safety. *Security Distributing & Marketing* reported that sales of residential security systems grew at a rate of 37 percent in 1993.

Manufacturers of alarm systems typically produce two kinds of component systems—perimeter and interior alarms. Perimeter systems may include contacts that detect the opening of doors and windows, detectors that pick up cutting and breaking of glass, and alarm screens that allow windows to be opened for fresh air, but activate an alarm if the screen is tampered with. Interior systems usually include infra-red motion detectors located in strategic areas, fire alarms, panic buttons that can be operated manually to alert the monitoring station, and a key pad to operate the system. In recent years manufacturers have created new alarm systems capable of operating in concert with other home automation features so that homeowners can manipulate their surveillance system as well as their entertainment systems and heating and cooling systems. The factors that determine price are the size of the area being defended, the number of apertures that need to be protected, and the quantity and nature of the devices installed. The average family home can be protected for between $800 and $1500. Over the last several years prices for such goods have fallen significantly and basic systems could be purchased in the early 1990s for as little as $200.

Fire Systems. There are two smoke-sensing technologies commonly used in residential smoke detectors—photoelectric and ionization. Both are available in 9-volt battery and 110-volt house current models. Photoelectric detectors are more sensitive and provide a quicker alarm to slow smoldering fires. Ionization debtors respond to fast burning fires such as stove grease or burning newspapers.

Pittway Corporation of Chicago, Illinois has long reigned as a leader in the smoke alarm manufacturing arena via its Ademco Security Group. Swayed by the high-growth security alarm sector, however, Pittway has increasingly concentrated on security system manufacturing opportunities, though Pittway's System Technology Group is the leading manufacturer of automatic fire alarm control systems. Pittway had 1993 sales of $650 million and a work force of 4,800 employees.

ADT Ltd. of Boca Raton, Florida, is the nation's second largest provider of electronic security alarm systems, with net income of $85.6 million on $1.3 billion in sales in 1992. ADT's services include the sale, installation, monitoring and service of fire detection systems.

INDUSTRY INFORMATION SOURCES

Nix, Shann, "Homeowners Focus on Security Systems," *Orlando Sentinel,* June 5, 1993.

Rossi, Douglas, "A Bell Goes Off, and a Business Blooms," *Newsday,* February 28, 1994.

Schulman, Robert, "All About Home Alarm Systems: Burglar, Fire, Flood—Name It, You Can Guard Against It," *New York Times,* January 10, 1993.

Shiver, Jube, Jr., "Alarmed Industry Reacts to a Threat," *Los Angeles Times,* May 6, 1994.

U.S. Industrial Outlook 1994, Washington, DC: U.S. Department of Commerce, 1994.

—Andrew Burke

SIC 3671

ELECTRON TUBES

This category covers establishments primarily engaged in manufacturing electron tubes and tube parts. Establishments primarily engaged in manufacturing X-ray tubes and parts are classified in **SIC 3844: X-Ray Apparatus and Tubes and Related Irradiation Apparatus.**

INDUSTRY SNAPSHOT

In 1987, 102 companies operated 121 business establishments in the electron tube industry and generated $2.74 billion in shipments. The industry employed 28,400 workers, 72 percent of whom were involved in production activities. After sales declines in the early 1990s, exacerbated by reduced purchases of electron tubes by the Defense Department, the value of industry shipments was expected to rise seven percent to $3.1 billion in 1994. Long-term prospects for cathode ray tubes in multimedia entertainment systems and high-definition televisions offered new growth markets for industry firms.

ORGANIZATION AND STRUCTURE

The two most recognizable types of electron tubes were the ordinary television and computer tube and the once-common vacuum tube used in radios and other electronic equipment. Generally speaking, electron tubes were sealed glass, enamel, or metallic tubes of varying sizes into which electrons were fired for the purpose of displaying images or conducting, transmitting, or multiplying light for nondisplay purposes. Examples of electron tubes included microwave tubes, television sets, computer displays, camera tubes, Geiger counters, radar screens, and vacuum tubes, in addition to a variety of industrial, military, and specialized electron tubes.

Electron tubes varied according to the extent to which they were evacuated or emptied of gases and vapors, the capability and type of the electron source, and the number and configuration of electrodes they contained. The amount of power used in electron tubes ranged from milliwatts to hundreds of megawatts, and the frequency of operation ranged between zero and ten to the eleventh power Hertz depending on the type of tube.

Traditionally, industry products were divided into three broad groups: transmittal, industrial, and special-purpose electron tubes, which accounted for 41.6 percent of the total value of industry shipments in 1987;

receiving-type electron tubes, including new and rebuilt cathode ray tubes, which totalled 36.7 percent of shipments; and electron tube parts, which claimed 6.2 percent of shipments. The major transmittal, industrial, and special-purpose electron tube product types included high vacuum tubes, gas and vapor tubes, microwave tubes, electrooptical tubes, and miscellaneous special-purpose tubes. The principal receiving-type electron tubes included cathode ray picture tubes for television and other uses. Electron tube parts included products such as cathodes, "headers," "bases," electron guns, and "getters" (for removing residual gas molecules from electron tubes).

Cathode ray tubes (CRT) were used in video displays, televisions, computer and multimedia monitors, oscilloscope displays, and other measuring and testing equipment, and were the most widely used electron tube product in the United States. CRTs with high-resolution displays were commonly used in graphics and publishing applications, but since the mid-1980s the production of computer-based CRTs of ever-increasing color capability and image quality for residential as well as industrial and office applications grew exponentially.

In general, CRTs operated by focusing a beam of electrons of varying intensities on a display surface such as a phosphor screen, which formed patterns of light that took the form of characters or images. The three basic components of a CRT were the "envelope," the electron gun, and the phosphor screen. The envelope, which was usually made of glass, was a funnel-shaped element through which the electrons were fired toward the faceplate on the broad end of the envelope. The electron gun was the source of the electrons, which, when heated and formed into a beam, were directed at an element behind the phosphor screen where they were deflected in changing patterns to controlled locations on the screen. The phosphor screen itself consisted of a layer of luminescent material that coated the inner surface of the CRT's glass faceplate. Color CRTs used a screen made up of luminous materials that emitted red, green, and blue colors, varying according to how often and how intensely they were struck by the electron beam. While monochrome CRT screens employed one electron gun, color screens typically employed three.

Electrooptical tubes included camera tubes, photo cells and other photo-conductive and photo-emissive tubes, and—for their major end-use—airport bomb detector picture tubes. Other product types included image intensifiers, converters, and photo-multipliers. Demand for these electron tubes was largely dependent on the upgrade, replacement, and expansion of airport security equipment.

Gas tubes—a category of transmittal, industrial, and special-purpose electron tubes—were used primarily in industrial applications because of their efficiency and ability to handle high levels of power or current at generally low frequency levels. Product types included diodes, rectifiers, control-type industrial triodes, hydrogen and nonhydrogen thyratons, and other gas and vapor tubes. High-power tubes were also used in broadcasting transmitters. Vacuum tubes, once the primary element in electrical circuits, were primarily used in applications where low noise and high frequency were involved. Since the late 1940s, they were mostly replaced by semiconductor circuits.

Microwave tubes, unlike low-frequency power electron tubes, were primarily used in high and ultrahigh frequency applications such as radars, telecommunications equipment, military communication and control systems, high-frequency microwave ovens, scientific research equipment, FM radio transmitters, and industrial heating equipment. Traveling wave tubes, which were divided into forward and backward wave electron tubes with power output ranges from less than 10 watts up to 1 kilowatt or more, accounted for about two-thirds of the microwave electron tubes produced in 1992. Microwave tubes as a whole comprised roughly 40 percent of the power and special-purpose tube market.

BACKGROUND AND DEVELOPMENT

Electron tubes were the principal components of almost all electronic circuits and equipment until semiconductors were developed and began to replace them in the late 1940s and 1950s. The first application of cathode ray tube technology was for an oscilloscope in 1897, and the first television using a cathode ray tube was developed in the late 1920s. Commercial production of monochrome television picture tubes began in the late 1940s. After World War II, U.S. electron tube manufacturers found a diverse and lucrative market in defense applications—ranging from radar to communication and control equipment—which in the early 1990s began to be supplanted by multiplying commercial uses such as computer screen tubes and television picture tubes.

CURRENT CONDITIONS

After 3.3 percent growth in the value of industry product shipments from 1988 to 1989, the electron tube manufacturing industry experienced a 15.4 percent decrease in 1990, followed by another drop of 0.1 percent in 1991. However, shipment value was expected to grow between 6 and 7 percent annually through 1994, fueled primarily by commercial demand for CRTs for television tubes, computers, and other video displays. Moreover, growing markets for high-definition televisions and multimedia computer tubes were expected to offer expanded nonmilitary markets for CRTs. Due to sharp cuts in military spending and the substitution of power semiconductors for power electron tubes, the market for power and special-purpose electron tubes in the mid-1990s was expected to be dependent on demand for spares and replacement parts rather than new equipment purchases.

The average industry firm in 1987 generated $17.6 million in shipments and employed 161 workers, with an average payroll per employee of $29,248. The states of California, Pennsylvania, and New Jersey combined accounted for $1.42 billion, or 52 percent, of industry shipments.

INDUSTRY LEADERS

The leaders in the electron tube industry in the early 1990s included Varian Associates Inc. of California, which posted 1992 sales of $1.27 billion and had 10,200 employees; Zenith Electronics Corporation—Rauland Division of Illinois, with $269 million and 2,400 employees; and Philips Display Components Company of Michigan, with $180 million and 2,200 employees. Other prominent industry firms included Litton Systems Inc.—Electron Devices Division, Toshiba Display Devices Inc., Hughes Aircraft Company—Electron Dynamics Division, and Richardson Electronics Ltd.

Varian Associates Inc. was the preponderant sales leader in the electron tube manufacturing industry in the early 1990s, with end-users in the communications, radar, electronic warfare countermeasures, scientific, medical, and industrial sectors. In 1993, its Electron Devices segment generated $278 million in sales, or 21 percent of the company's total, and was comprised of eight facilities in California, Arizona, Massachusetts, and Ontario, Canada. These facilities manufactured products across the spectrum of industry technology, including power-grid tube products, crossed-field and receiver protector products, microwave products, traveling wave tube products, coupled cavity tube products, and printed circuit board assembly. Research and development expenditures represented between 2.8 and 4.5 percent of Varian's electron tube sales between 1991 and 1993, and the company was involved in research and development efforts with the Lawrence Livermore National Laboratory to design high-power, high-frequency microwave tubes for use in fusion energy applications.

AMERICA AND THE WORLD

Exports of electron tube products—valued at $771 million—accounted for nearly 12 percent of the end-use of industry products in the early 1980s. Over half of U.S. electron tube exports in 1992 went to Mexico and Canada, which purchased 39.9 percent and 10.6 percent respectively, with Japan, South Korea, and the United Kingdom representing the next three largest markets.

The United States imported $928 million of electron tubes in 1992, a 14 percent increase over 1991, with Japan accounting for 63.7 percent of that amount. The other nations producing electron tubes for import to the United States included Mexico, Taiwan, France, and Germany.

RESEARCH AND TECHNOLOGY

The growing demand for computer monitors for use in homes and offices starting in the 1980s forced industry firms to develop more user-friendly monitor designs, such as the "flat square CRT," in which the curvature of the CRT's screen was greatly reduced. CRT display technology also continued to evolve in the areas of unit price and color display capabilities. For example, in the early 1990s, software programs began to be marketed that enabled users of CRT displays to create nuances of color and shade that accurately matched standardized printer's color swatches. And in 1992, Zenith began producing higher-resolution, larger-screen, "flat tension mask" color computer monitors, which it also expected to use in its television models. Although high-definition television was not expected to become a reality until the year 2000, trends in standard television tubes in the early 1990s were toward increasingly larger sizes. In 1992, for example, Zenith introduced 13 new giant-screen, "home theater" color TV models, which ranged in size from 32- and 35-inch "direct view" models and 46- to 52-inch rear-projection models to 10-foot diagonal front-projection systems with expanded dark shades for greater picture depth and richer color.

The application of multifunctional CRT displays in the instrument panels of military and—to a lesser degree—commercial aircraft also continued in the early 1990s. However, the inherent disadvantages of CRTs—limited screen size, unwieldy shape, high power requirements, and fragility—led manufacturers to investigate alternatives to CRT technology, such as light-emitting diodes and flat panel/liquid crystal displays (LCD). Improvements in LCDs, which were thinner and lighter than CRTs, enabled them to compete in price with CRT-based, large-screen, video-data projectors while offering roughly two to four times their brightness. In aircraft cockpit applications in particular—where limited space and high levels of glare diminished the usefulness of CRTs—flat panel displays increasingly emerged as the favored display technology. Another emergent technology— structurally less complex than LCDs and even thinner in size—that threatened to displace the CRT electron tube was the field emission display, which was based on vacuum microelectronics and combined the advantages of the old vacuum tube technology with the benefits of computer chips.

In the early 1990s, advances in research and technology also continued in non-CRT product categories. So-called direct broadcast satellites for noncable, high-definition television transmissions (among other uses) were developed that used electron tubes, such as traveling wave tubes, for satellite tubes and uplink stations and achieved tube lifetimes of 15 years.

INDUSTRY INFORMATION SOURCES

Census of Manufactures: Electronic Components, Washington, D.C.: U.S. Department of Commerce, 1990.

Darnay, Arsen J., editor, *Manufacturing U.S.A.: Industry Analyses, Statistics, and Leading Companies,* Detroit: Gale Research, 1992.

DuFlon, Ray, "Color Display Systems Achieve Color Consistency," *Computer Technology Review,* July 1990.

House, William R., "Electron Tubes in Ku-Band DBS," *Satellite Communications,* February 1991.

"INFOCOMM Showcases Latest AV Goodies," *Training,* April 1992.

Johnstone, Bob, "Flat Out for Profits," *Far Eastern Economic Review,* April 19, 1990.

U.S. Industrial Outlook 1994, Washington, D.C.: U.S. Department of Commerce, 1994.

Varian Associates, Inc., Annual Report, Palo Alto, California: Varian Associates, 1993.

Ward's Business Directory of U.S. Private and Public Companies, Detroit: Gale Research, 1992.

Zenith Electronics Corporation, Annual Report, Melrose Park, Illinois: Zenith Electronics, 1993.

—Paul Bodine

SIC 3672

PRINTED CIRCUIT BOARDS

This category includes establishments primarily engaged in the manufacture of printed circuit boards, sometimes referred to as printed wiring boards.

A printed circuit board (PCB) is a thin piece of insulating material onto which tiny electrical wiring pathways or "traces" have been printed, usually by a photoengraving process. PCBs provide the physical structure for mounting electronic components, such as semiconductors; the printed traces then serve to interconnect the components, forming an electronic system. PCBs are used in a wide range of electronic products, including computers, telecommunications equipment, electronic instruments, and automobiles.

According to the Institute of Interconnecting and Packaging Electronic Circuits (IPC), approximately 750 to 800 independent companies produced PCBs in the United States in 1992. Yet independent manufacturers accounted for only 66 percent of the entire market. So-called "captive" PCB-makers, primarily large original equipment manufacturers (OEMs) who make their own boards, comprised the remaining 34 percent. Though the largest market for OEM boards was in computer applications, captive board makers also served a large number of communications and government/military users as well.

U.S. PCB production reached $5.3 billion in 1991, according to IPC, while worldwide sales of PCBs reached $20.2 billion in 1992, according to the Electronic Outlook Corp. Total value of the industry, including bare boards, components, and various activities involved in the assembly of boards, was estimated at $60 billion.

Computer makers were the major consumers of independently produced PCBs in 1991, when over 43 percent of overall independent board production went to computer companies. Communications constituted the second major market for independently produced PCBs with more than 17 percent. The role of independent PCB manufacturers has increased steadily over the years. Though more than 90 percent of independent PCB-makers reported annual sales of less than $10 million in 1991, OEMs were increasingly relying on them to supply boards for their products, and industry observers expected this trend to continue.

Printed circuit board assembly companies (PCBAs) comprise a growing, specialized segment of the PCB industry. More than just contract assemblers, PCBAs provide design services, global procurement, cost reduction services, and access to advanced technology. The early 1990s saw a dramatic growth in the use of PCBAs, and industry observers expected that trend to continue because of the cost savings these companies provided. There were nearly 800 PCBAs in operation in the United States in 1992 with an estimated total value of $5.9 billion. PCBAs employed approximately 80,000 workers in 1991, while independent board makers employed about 70,000.

At the start of the 1990s, PCB makers were adapting to two important industry trends: increasing use of smaller circuitry products and greater demand for surface mount technology. The seemingly inexorable drive among electronics firms toward smaller components has been cited as part of the cause of a decline in PCB usage from 1988 to 1991. Smaller components required less space on the PCB and smaller or fewer boards.

Spurred by the demand for smaller, higher-performance PCBs, the industry moved quickly toward surface mount technology. Surface mounting involves the soldering of components directly onto the surface of a board. The process allows components to be mounted closer together and even on both sides of a board. In 1989, less than 12 percent of boards included surface mounted components; by 1992 more than half of all PCBs were assembled with one or more surface-mounted components.

Though the domestic PCB industry continued to remain globally competitive in utilizing advanced manufacturing technologies, increasing overseas production resulted in a significant decrease in the U.S. share of the world PCB market from 40 percent in 1980 to 29 percent in 1990. In 1991, Japan ranked first in worldwide production of rigid PCBs with 33.8 percent of the market; the U.S. ranked second with 26.9 percent. Germany, Taiwan, the United Kingdom, and Hong Kong ranked third through sixth, respectively.

The U.S. printed circuit board industry was expected to grow about seven percent in 1993, and was considered by observers to be on a solid upswing. Long-term prospects for the industry hinged on its ability to cut costs and improve competitiveness with Asian board producers. Also, observers predicted the industry would continue to experience significant consolidation.

INDUSTRY INFORMATION SOURCES

Bylinsky, Gene, *High Tech: Window to the Future,* Hong Kong: Intercontinental Publishing Corporation Ltd., 1985.

Standard & Poor's Industry Surveys, New York: Standard & Poor's Corporation, 1993.

U.S. Industrial Outlook 1993, Washington, DC: U.S. Department of Commerce, 1993.

—John K. Waters

SIC 3674

SEMICONDUCTORS AND RELATED DEVICES

This category covers establishments primarily engaged in manufacturing semiconductors and related solid-state devices. Important products of this industry are semiconductor diodes and stacks, including rectifiers, integrated microcircuits (semiconductor networks), transistors, solar cells, and light sensing and emitting semiconductor (solid-state) devices.

INDUSTRY SNAPSHOT

The U.S. semiconductor industry experienced generally sluggish conditions during the mid-1980s, but seemed to be entering a period of renewed growth in the early 1990s. Worldwide sales of semiconductors and semiconductor products exceeded $21 billion in 1991; by 1992, the U.S. Department of Commerce was predicting a strong recovery for the industry, with the overall value of shipments reaching nearly $30 billion.

According to the Semiconductor Industry Association, semiconductor companies employed more than 200,000 Americans in 1991. That figure is expected to fluctuate over the next several years. The health of the semiconductor industry remains closely tied to three other economically sensitive and cyclical industries: computers, automobiles, and consumer electronics. Consequently, the industry has a history of erratic earnings.

Industry observers predicted an especially profitable rebound for semiconductors in the mid-1990s due to several factors. Inventories were at historically low levels in 1992, while the U.S. economy surged upward in 1993, signaling improved financial outlooks for key industry customers such as the automotive manufacturers. New generations of semiconductors were proving popular as well, selling at higher average prices and wider margins. Finally, sales of electronic equipment in general were accelerating worldwide, with the semiconductor content of that equipment increasing.

The early 1990s also saw the continuation of the trend toward strategic alliances and corporate partnering among semiconductor companies. This trend was fast becoming an important competitive tool, allowing individual firms to share the ever-increasing costs of production. Entering the mid-1990s, U.S. semiconductor manufacturers were shifting their attention from commodity products to the development of innovative proprietary products, which they have begun vigorously protecting with the help of new patent legislation.

ORGANIZATION AND STRUCTURE

Sometimes referred to as "the crude oil of the information age," semiconductors are a pervasive but generally unseen aspect of everyday life. The tiny electronic circuits etched on chips of silicon are critical to the operation of virtually all electronics, from automatic coffee makers and anti-lock braking systems to cellular phones and supercomputers.

The computer industry is by far the largest market for semiconductors. In 1991 sales to computer manufacturers and related enterprises accounted for 41 percent of overall sales of semiconductors in this country. Consumer electronics and the automotive industry are also important users of semiconductors and related products. Sales to these two industries combined accounted for 25 percent of total sales in that same year.

Semiconductor chips are manufactured in "fabs," which is short for fabrication facilities, in "clean rooms" utterly free of contaminating dust. In those facilities, thin, round silicon wafers are processed in batches. Chipmakers buy polished blank wafers from companies that specialize in growing silicon crystals, from which the wafers are cut. Each wafer is about half a millimeter thick. Microelectronics circuits are built up on the wafer layer by layer.

Circuit patterns—the collection of transistors, capacitors, and associated components and their interconnections—are inscribed on large glass plates called photomasks. The photomasks are later reduced and photolithographically projected onto the silicon wafers. Each mask comprises a total integrated circuit design.

As *Industry Surveys* notes, semiconductor companies design and manufacture primarily two types of products: integrated circuits (ICs) and discrete devices. A discrete semiconductor is an individual circuit that performs a single function affecting the flow of electrical current. For example, a transistor, one of the most common types of discrete devices, amplifies electrical signals; rectifiers and diodes generally convert alternating current into direct current; capacitors block the flow of alternating current at controlled levels; and resistors limit current flow and divide or drop current.

Integrated Circuits. Also called "chips," integrated circuits are a collection of microminiaturized electronic components, such as transistors and capacitors, placed on a tiny rectangle of silicon. A single integrated circuit can perform the functions of thousands of discrete transistors, diodes, capacitors, and resistors. There are three basic types of integrated circuits currently produced by American semiconductor manufacturers: memory components, which are used to store data or computer programs; logic devices, which perform such operations as mathematical calculations; and components which combine the two. This latter category of integrated circuit is the most sophisticated and includes microprocessors, the computer "brain" which manipulates a wide range of data, and microcontrollers, which perform repetitive tasks.

The two largest selling types of memory integrated circuits, notes *Industry Surveys,* are DRAMs and SRAMs. A DRAM (dynamic random access memories; pronounced DEE-ram), stores digital information and provides high-speed storage and retrieval of data. It is called a "dynamic" circuit because the data is stored in a temporary medium that allows it to fade, and so must be constantly refreshed electronically.

SRAMs (static random access memories; pronounced ESS-rams) perform many of the same functions as DRAMs, but at higher speeds. Unlike DRAMs, they do not require constant electronic refreshing, hence the term "static." They also contain more electronic circuitry and are more expensive to produce than DRAMs.

Both of these integrated circuit products are manufactured in large quantities, and so are considered to be "process drivers." That is, the manufacturing processes used to produce them are constantly being refined, and those refinements often affect manufacturing processes of other products.

Two other important semiconductor memory products are EPROMs (erasable programmable read-only memories) and EEPROMs (electrically erasable read-only memories). EPROMs are used to store computer programs. Unlike older read-only memories (ROMs), which carried fixed programs, commented *Industry Surveys,* EPROMs are programmed by the customer. EEPROMs are easier and faster to update than EPROMs because they are programmed using electricity. While EPROMs are usually programmed only once, EEPROMs can be reprogrammed without removing them from their applications, so they can be updated virtually anytime.

ASICS. Most logic semiconductors are now customized products tailored to the specific needs of each customer. In fact, ASICS (application-specific integrated circuits) have become the most commonly manufactured non-microcomponent logic semiconductors.

There are four basic classes of ASICs; each class has a different degree of customization of the chip. Full-custom ASICs are designed from scratch; standard cells are designed by combining modular cells from a cell library; semi-custom chips are customized in only one or two areas; and programmable logic devices are programmed by blowing fuses in a device to alter the logic function. Because of high design costs and the often limited quantities produced, ASICs tend to be more expensive than integrated circuits built from off-the-shelf components. But because they combine several specialized functions on a single chip, they offer some important advantages: they're smaller, simpler, and fewer of them are needed; they allow for a greater degree of integration, which leads to more efficient use of circuitry; and, since they contain less circuitry, fewer interconnections are needed and overall performance is enhanced.

Microprocessors and Controllers. Microprocessors (MPUs) are the central processing units in all microcomputer-based systems. These products perform a variety of tasks by manipulating data within a system and controlling input, output, peripherals, and memory devices.

The two major types of MPUs are CISCs (complex instruction set computing) and RISCs (reduced instruction set computing). Though CISCs used to be the basis for all MPU operations, RISCs have became increasingly popular in recent years because of their faster operating speeds, their ability to run more sophisticated software, and their ability to deliver better graphics. MPUs are used in local area networks (linked personal computers and workstations; called LANs) and satellites. The latest generation of these circuits operate at speeds of from 40 to 50 million cycles per second.

Microcontrollers (MCUs), which combine a microprocessor, memory circuits, and input/output circuitry, are used as embedded controllers in virtually every electronic product. They perform such repetitive tasks as controlling the antilock brake systems in automobiles.

BACKGROUND AND DEVELOPMENT

Semiconductors were invented in the United States in the late 1950s, but the invention that truly began the electronics revolution appeared nearly 50 years earlier. The three-element vacuum tube was invented by Lee de Forest in Palo Alto, California, in 1906. Called the audion, the tube was used as a sound amplifier and generator of electromagnetic waves; its invention laid the foundation for the development of radio, television, radar, computers and many other ground-breaking electronic devices. These early tubes, however, were bulky and fragile. For example, ENIAC (Electronic Numerical Integrator and Computer), the world's first large electronic computer, ran on 18,000 vacuum tubes and was the size of a house.

The tubes also played a vital role in the development of early telephone communications networks. But as those networks expanded across the United States, the unreliability of the tubes became intolerable. Consequently, the main push for a replacement for the vacuum tube came from researchers at AT&T Bell Laboratories in New Jersey.

For a number of years, the company had been studying potential uses of solid materials that were poor conductors of electricity, primarily silicon and germanium. Silicon, one of the world's most plentiful elements, is found in the earth's crust as silica and silicate and is the principal component of sand, quartz, and glass. In its pure form, silicon is a very poor conductor, but Bell Lab researchers found that it could be treated, or "doped," with other materials to act as a conductor under some conditions and an insulator under others.

These new "semiconductors" allowed for the development in 1947 of the transistor, which marked the beginning of the age of solid-state electronics. In 1956 William Shockley, John Bardeen, and Walter H. Brattain, the Bell Labs research team responsible for the development and refinement of the transistor, received the Nobel Prize for their invention. The same year he was awarded the Nobel Prize, Shockley returned to his boyhood home of Palo Alto, California, and established his own semiconductor manufacturing operation. To staff his new company, Shockley recruited many of the country's brightest young scientists and engineers.

Disagreements eventually led seven of Shockley's recruits to set out on their own. The company they founded, Fairchild Semiconductor, would become "the mother of semiconductor companies." According to the Semiconductor Industry Association, more than 23 semiconductor and related enterprises can trace their origins back to Fairchild. Among them were such important and well-known companies as Intel, Advanced Micro Devices, and National Semiconductor.

Probably the most important technological development to come out of Fairchild was the integrated circuit or "chip." Both the head of Fairchild, MIT graduate Robert N. Noyce, and Texas Instruments researcher Jack Kilby are credited with inventing the integrated circuit almost simultaneously in 1958. The original Texas Instruments version of the chip required the soldering of tiny gold wires on the outside to connect the components. The Fairchild version, on the other hand, relied on a thin layer of metal conducting film, which was sprayed onto the chip like paint. Roadways were then cut by lithography into this metallic layer to create the desired pattern of connections between elements of the circuit. This version of the chip was more readily manufacturable, and Fairchild soon emerged as the early leader of the semiconductor industry.

Noyce left Fairchild in 1968, along with Gordon E. Moore, a respected physical chemist. Together, they formed Intel Corporation and set out to manufacture a computer memory chip. Intel eventually came to dominate the industry as the undisputed leader in semiconductor technology. In addition to the first memory chips, Intel was responsible for pioneering the development of the microprocessor, the so-called "computer-on-a-chip."

U.S. manufacturers continued to dominate the semiconductor industry until the 1980s, when foreign industrial targeting and illegal dumping practices combined to erode U.S. worldwide market share. This "blood bath," as it was referred to in industry publications at the time, drove Intel, Motorola, National Semiconductor, Advanced Micro Devices, and Mostek out of the dynamic random access memory (DRAM) market altogether. Japanese manufacturers, however, who utilized investment cost advantages to conquer the DRAM market, saw that market plunge at the onset of the 1990s. As *Forbes* noted in 1991, DRAM sales in 1990 "contracted instead of growing, plunging 24%— or roughly $2 billion in annual revenues."

Consequently, U.S. semiconductor manufacturers began to refocus their efforts on proprietary products during the early 1990s, capitalizing on their well-known strengths in design and innovation, and moving away from commodity products. According to industry observers, two Congressional actions were instrumental in paving the way for this development.

The first was the establishment in 1982 of the U.S. Court of Appeals for Federal Circuit in Washington, D.C., a court specifically formed to hear patent cases. Previously, patent cases had been tried in federal district courts, where an estimated 70 percent of patents were successfully challenged. With the new court, however, that statistic was reversed, with about two-thirds of patents upheld.

The second was the Semiconductor Chip Protection Act, passed by Congress in 1984. The new law specifically protected semiconductor design, or "mask work," for up to 10 years. As electronics firms began to exercise their rights, the courts continued to provide stronger legal protection for proprietary chip designs. In 1991 Congress extended the Act until 1995.

CURRENT CONDITIONS

In late 1992, industry observers began to note signs of an economic rebound for U.S. semiconductor manufacturers. In June of that year, a price war in the personal computer market gave the industry a much-needed boost. By November, orders were outpacing shipments and the industry was clearly expanding.

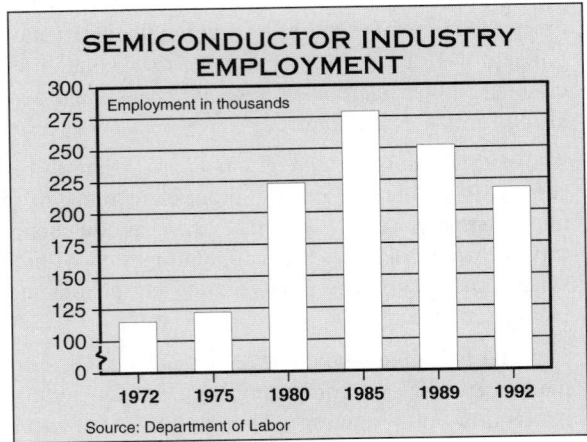

SEMICONDUCTOR INDUSTRY EMPLOYMENT

Source: Department of Labor

As 1993 drew to a close, the U.S. semiconductor industry was experiencing a strong upturn. Worldwide semiconductor sales had increased nine percent in 1992. According to *Standard & Poor's 1993 Industry Surveys,* growth of worldwide semiconductor sales was expected to accelerate between 18 and 20 percent in 1993, an increase of eight percent from the previous year.

The strategic shift among U.S. chipmakers away from commodity products in favor of the higher priced proprietary products was expected to yield increased profits and fuel a continuation of the 1992 rebound, although a temporary reduction in revenues was expected as older facilities and products were phased out. In fact, the industry saw itself on the path of solid growth through 1997. The increasingly robust recovery of the U.S. economy, as well as improvements in Japanese consumer electronics markets, were also expected to positively influence the industry's growth.

Two additional factors were expected to contribute to the continued growth of the semiconductor industry: overall increases in worldwide sales of electronic equipment, and the increasing semiconductor content of electronic products. Integrated Circuit Engineering Corp. (ICE), a market research firm based in Scottsdale, Arizona, forecast an increase in worldwide electronics sales from $595 billion in 1992 to $900 billion by 1997. ICE also projected an increase in the semiconductor content of electronic equipment—from 12.5 percent in 1992 to 15.3 percent in 1997. This growth is driven by the increasingly sophisticated nature of consumer electronics. Manufacturers of fax machines, notebook computers, and camcorders, for example, used semiconductors in these products to perform increasingly complex operations.

Despite the industry's anticipated overall rebound, evidence suggested that growth would vary considerably among market segments. For example, while sales of memory products experienced a deep recession, microprocessors grew rapidly; while some companies reported serious losses, others reported record earnings.

Military demand for semiconductors was weak in 1992 because of cutbacks in U.S. defense spending. Semiconductor sales to the military, which accounted for five percent of sales in 1988, accounted for only three percent of sales in 1992. Also, sales of consumer electronics worldwide grew only five percent in 1992. One reason was probably the severe recession in the Japanese consumer electronics industry.

In 1992 product distributors benefited from the stronger industry conditions, posting sales of $10.2 billion in 1992, up 12.4 percent from the previous year. However, the capital equipment segment of the industry had a weak year. According to *Standard & Poor's 1993 Industry Surveys,* worldwide semiconductor capital spending declined 6.3 percent in 1992, a fall traceable to a steep 33 percent decrease in spending by Japanese manufacturers.

The continuing development of the Integrated Services Digital Network (ISDN) is expected to provide an important new market for chipmakers in the future. The ISDN is a fully digital communications network capable of carrying voice, data, and video signals simultaneously over existing telephone lines. The network, which was being installed in certain markets in 1993, requires large numbers of semiconductors.

Another factor in the industry is the shrinking number of production options available to players in the field. Many companies that have emerged in recent years in this realm have farmed out production to other facilities with spare capacity in their wafer-fabrication plants. As *Business Week* noted, by using these facilities, "U.S. entrepreneurs avoided the main hurdle for a chip startup: the tens or hundreds of millions in wafer-fabrication costs. A new venture could thus devote its resouces to innovative designs . . . By pioneering these cutting-edge products, fabless companies grew faster and earned higher returns than established chipmak-

ers—giving them clout way beyond their 5% share of the $77 billion world chip market.'' In the mid-1990s, however, that capacity glut has disappeared and companies without their own production facilities are feeling increasingly cramped and may be forced to invest to secure guaranteed access to production facilities.

INDUSTRY LEADERS

With worldwide sales reaching well over $5 billion in 1992, Intel Corporation was the largest manufacturer of semiconductors in the United States. Intel was founded in what would become California's Silicon Valley in 1968 by industry pioneers Robert N. Noyce, Gordon E. Moore, and Andrew S. Grove. Starting with 12 employees, Intel pursued research that led to the development of the first computer chip. The company also played an instrumental role in the development of metal oxide semiconductor (MOS) technology.

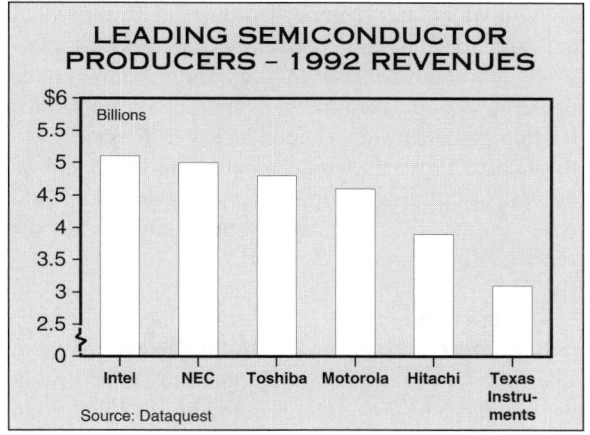

LEADING SEMICONDUCTOR PRODUCERS – 1992 REVENUES
Source: Dataquest

Originally a supplier of semiconductor memory for mainframe computers and mini-computers, Intel eventually became a leading suppler of microcomputers. The company sells its microcomputer components, modules, and systems directly to companies that incorporate them into their products. These are primarily computer systems manufacturers, but also include makers of automobiles and a wide range of industrial and telecommunications equipment. The company also sells personal computer enhancements and networking products through distributors, resellers, and retail stores worldwide. The company sells supercomputers directly to end users. Intel has design, development, production, and administration facilities throughout the Western United States, Europe, and Asia. In 1992, the company employed some 24,000 people around the world.

The Semiconductor Products Sector of Motorola posted sales of $4.47 billion in 1992, making that company the second largest American chipmaker. Motorola employs approximately 107,000 people worldwide and is among the 40 largest industrial companies in the United States ranked by total sales.

Motorola was founded in 1928 in Chicago, Illinois, by Paul V. Galvin. As the Galvin Manufacturing Corp., the company's first product was a "battery eliminator" that allowed consumers to operate radios directly from household current instead of the batteries supplied with early models. In the 1930s the company successfully commercialized car radios under the brand name "Motorola." The company's name was changed to Motorola, Inc., in 1947, the same year it began research into solid-state electronics.

The company's semiconductor division designs and produces a broad line of discrete semiconductors and integrated circuits, including microprocessors, microcomputers, and memory products. These products are sold to computer, consumer, automotive, industrial, federal government/military and telecommunications markets. In addition to being one of the world's leading providers of semiconductor technology, Motorola also provides wireless communication and advanced electronics equipment and services to worldwide markets. The company maintains sales and service offices around the world.

Texas Instruments, Incorporated, is the country's third largest chipmaker, with 1992 semiconductor sales of $3.14 billion. Headquartered in Dallas, Texas, the company has manufacturing facilities in 18 countries and marketing or engineering services in more than 30 countries.

The company was founded in 1930 as the "Geophysical Service" by J. Clarence "Doc" Karcher and Eugene McDermott. It was the first independent contractor to specialize in reflection seismograph methods of exploration. The firm's name was changed to Texas Instruments, better known as TI, in 1951. The company entered the semiconductor business in 1952 with the purchase of a license from Western Electric Company to manufacture transistors.

In addition to semiconductors, TI products and services include defense electronics systems, software productivity tools, computer and peripheral products, custom engineering and manufacturing services, electrical controls, metallurgical materials, and consumer electronics products.

AMERICA AND THE WORLD

According to *U.S. Industrial Outlook 1993,* the recovering U.S. market was becoming a magnet for imports of semiconductors. The country's semiconductor trade deficit in 1991 was $2.1 billion. Sales of semiconductors in the United States, Canada, and Mexico were much stronger than other regional markets.

The Japanese electronics industry was the world's largest producer of memory chips and the U.S.'s greatest competitor in semiconductor sales. But in the early 1990s the Japanese consumer electronics industry was in a severe slump and the country's overall economy was growing at only 1.5 percent. Consequently, there was a 6.3 percent drop in Japanese semiconductor sales.

In 1992 the market for North American chipmakers' products outgrew Japan's for the first time since 1985. The European market also grew, boosted by the weaker dollar. In fact, these factors led to an overall shift in worldwide market share for the semiconductor industry. North American companies' share increased to 30 percent in 1992, up from 28 percent the previous year. European firms held on to a steady 19 percent market share. Meanwhile, Japanese market share fell from 38 percent in 1991 to 33 percent in 1992. Many observers expect this trend to continue in the mid-1990s, as companies in the United States and smaller countries grow rapidly and Japan struggles to regain its momentum.

The 1992 domestic industry rebound resulted in increased capital spending on the part of U.S. semiconductor manufacturers. By contrast, capital spending among Japanese companies dropped from the previous year's levels, due to the difficult economic condition and overcapacity for DRAMs, a product niche the Japanese largely control.

In an effort to reduce costs and lower financial risks, Japanese chipmakers entered into alliances with foreign companies. Since 1989 Japan has entered into about 88 such alliances, ranging from manufacturing joint ventures to joint product development agreements. These alliances have focused primarily on high definition television (HDTV) chip development, microprocessor development, ASIC development, and computer-aided design projects.

In 1986 the United States and Japan entered into an agreement—called the U.S.-Japan Semiconductor Arrangement—designed to eliminate dumping of Japanese products in world markets and to increase market access for foreign semiconductor manufacturers in the Japanese market. In 1991 the follow-on agreement to the 1986 agreement went into effect. According to *U.S. Industrial Outlook 1993,* the new agreement reflects the U.S. expectations that more than 20 percent share of the Japanese market can be captured by foreign suppliers by the end of 1992 through the efforts of government and industry.

While U.S. semiconductor companies were consolidating in the early 1990s, companies in the so-called dynamic Asian economies (DAEs) were expanding. DAE countries include South Korea, Taiwan, Hong Kong, China, Singapore, and Malaysia. DAE countries dominated U.S. semiconductor imports in 1992. Southeastern Asian markets present extensive opportunities for U.S. chip exporters as well, since most of the world's major electronics companies have established operations there, and more electronic products means more need for semiconductors. The re-establishment of trade relations with Vietnam in 1994 also presents U.S. companies with still another market to explore.

According to data compiled by the World Semiconductor Statistics organization, the European market for semiconductors was expected to grow by 7.7 percent in 1992, making Europe approximately 19 percent of the world market. The European market was considered a battleground for competition among the global electronics giants. Both South Korean and Japanese semiconductor companies increased their presence in Europe, but American companies still held 44 percent of market share in 1991.

RESEARCH AND TECHNOLOGY

According to Dataquest, a market research company based in San Jose, California, about one-third of U.S. semiconductor industry revenues is spent on technology development and capital; 14 percent of revenues is spent on research and development (R&D) alone. Costs for new semiconductor fabrication facilities (fabs), a major capital consideration for many companies, range from $600 million to $900 million.

A number of products and technology developments on the horizon in 1994 were likely to contribute to the growth of the semiconductor industry.

High Definition Television. One of the most talked-about of these developments was high definition television (HDTV). HDTV produces pictures that are four to five times clearer than the standard television picture, approximating the clarity of a 35mm slide. In addition to commercial broadcast television, the first of which were expected by the mid-1990s, HDTV technology could also find applications in areas such as medical imaging and computer graphics. Since

the sets require a huge number of semiconductors, they are expected to be a major new market for chipmakers.

Fuzzy Logic. Another emerging semiconductor technology expected to create important future markets is called "fuzzy logic." As *Standard & Poor's Industry Surveys* notes, "currently led by Japanese manufacturers, fuzzy logic allows microcontrollers to create gray areas between the yes/no, on/off choices of the binary world. The result is that engineers can design microprocessors that allow machinery to operate with gradual refinements."

INDUSTRY INFORMATION SOURCES

Alster, Norm. "Drowning in DRAMs," *Forbes,* November 11, 1991.

Braun, Ernest, and Stuart MacDonald, *Revolution in Miniature; The History and Impact of Semiconductor Electronics,* New York: The Press Syndicate of the University of Cambridge, 1978.

Bylinsky, Gene, *High Tech: Window to the Future,* Hong Kong: Intercontinental Publishing Corporation Ltd., 1985.

Fletcher, Peter, and Andrew Rosenbaum. "Europe's in the Chips," *Electronics,* August 1990.

Hof, Robert D., "'Real Men Have Fabs,'" *Business Week,* April 11, 1994.

Pitta, Julie, "Score one for vertical integration," *Forbes,* January 18, 1993.

Queisser, Hans, *The Conquest of the Microchip,* London, England: Harvard University Press, 1988.

Reid, T.R., *The Chip; How Two Americans Invented the Microchip & Launched a Revolution,* New York: Simon and Schuster, 1984.

Renmore, C.D., *Silicon Chips and You,* New York: Beaufort Books, 1980.

Rosch, Winn L., "The Evolution of the PC Microprocessor," *PC Magazine,* January 31, 1989.

Sexton, Jean Deitz, *Silicon Valley: Inventing the Future,* Chatsworth, CA: Windsor Publications, Inc., 1992.

Standard & Poor's Industry Surveys, New York: Standard & Poor's Corporation, 1993.

U.S. Industrial Outlook 1993, Washington, DC: U.S. Department of Commerce, 1993.

U.S. Industrial Outlook 1994, Washington, DC: U.S. Department of Commerce, 1993.

Weber, Samuel. "For chip maker, 'another year of blah growth,'" *Electronics,* January 1992.

—John K. Waters

SIC 3675

ELECTRONIC CAPACITORS

This category covers establishments primarily engaged in manufacturing electronic capacitors. Establishments primarily engaged in manufacturing electrical capacitors are classified in **SIC 3629: Electrical Industrial Apparatus, Not Elsewhere Classified.**

INDUSTRY SNAPSHOT

The value of shipments in the electronic capacitors industry in 1993 was an estimated $1.7 billion, up from $1.2 billion in 1982. There were about 135 establishments in the industry, three-fourths of which had 20 or more employees. Average firm size as measured by the number of production workers per establishment was over three times as large as that for the manufacturing sector as a whole.

Employment of production workers in the industry declined from 21,600 in 1982 to 13,500 in 1991. The industry was relatively labor intensive, having 44 percent as much investment per production worker as that for the manufacturing sector as a whole. Annual hours worked by production workers in the industry were slightly lower on average than those worked in the manufacturing sector at large, and hourly wages were 23 percent lower.

ORGANIZATION AND STRUCTURE

Of the top ten firms by sales in the electronic capacitor industry in 1992, two were private independents, two were publicly held, and the remainder were either subsidiaries or divisions of larger firms. Of the remaining 40 firms ranking among the top 50 by sales in the industry, 21 were private independents. Though average investment per production worker was relatively low for the industry, capital requirements were relatively high, with average investment per establishment 39 percent greater than that for the manufacturing sector as a whole. The *U.S. Industrial Outlook* for 1994 described organizational changes in the industry: "The U.S. capacitor market is dominated by foreign-owned subsidiaries, reflecting major consolidation and numerous buyouts over the past 5 years. There are fewer, but bigger, companies." Of the top five firms in the industry, two of them, the AVX Corp. and the Murata Erie North America Inc. State College Division, were owned by Japanese firms.

The states ranking in the top nine by employment in the electronic capacitor industry were, in order of descent, South Carolina, California, New York,

Maine, Massachusetts, North Carolina, Connecticut, Florida, and Pennsylvania. Together these nine states accounted for 79 percent of total employment, over 75 percent of total shipments, and about 73 percent of all establishments for the industry in the United States. The top two firms by sales in the industry, the AVX Corp. and the Kemet Electronics Corp., were both based in South Carolina. The average number of employees per establishment varied widely across these states. Maine, with the highest number of employees per establishment, had an average of nearly ten times as many employees per establishment as did California and Pennsylvania.

The top four types of capacitors by product share in 1992 were those made from ceramic, at 48 percent, tantalum, at 26 percent, paper and film, at 16 percent, and aluminum, at 9 percent. The share of ceramic capacitors increased from 39 percent in 1983 whereas the share of paper and film and aluminum capacitors declined from 19 and 13 percent respectively. The share of tantalum capacitors held steadily during the 1990s.

Among the largest of the several trade organizations serving the industry are the Electronic Industries Association of Washington, D.C., and the American Electronics Association of Santa Clara, California. The Electronic Industries Association was founded in 1924 and has 1,200 members, a staff of 150, and an annual budget of $26 million. The association produces a number of publications, catalogued in its semiannual *EAI Publications Index.* The American Electronics Association was founded in 1943 and has 3,500 members and a staff of 140. In addition to organizing an annual convention, the Association publishes the monthly *American Electronics Association-Update*, with a circulation of 35,000, as well as a number of handbooks, among them *Government Affairs Bulletin, Benchmark Wage and Salary Survey,* and *Operating Ratios Survey.*

BACKGROUND AND DEVELOPMENT

In his *Basic Electricity and Electronics,* Delton T. Horn defined capacitors and capacitance: "A capacitor is a device capable of storing charge in a circuit, and typically consists of two metal plates separated by an insulator, called a *dielectric.* Capacitance is directly proportional to the area of the plates and the dielectric constant of the insulator and is inversely proportional to the distance between the plates." Capacitors can store charges from voltage sources for a wide range of time, to be released as needed. The classification of capacitor types by material such as paper, ceramic, or tantalum refer to the insulating dielectric. Electronic capacitors are part of a class of electronic components called passive components. They differ from active components, such as vacuum tubes and transistors, in that they can neither distinguish voltage polarity nor amplify a signal.

The first capacitor was the Leyden Jar, invented independently in the mid-1740s by Germans Dean von Kleist and Peter von Muschenbrock. A glass jar acted as the insulating material. The mica capacitor was developed in Germany in 1874 by M. Bauer. Mica had advantages over glass in that it better withstood shocks and that the same capacitance could be produced with a smaller capacitor. The paper capacitor was patented by D. G. Fitzgerald in the United Kingdom in 1876. Ceramic capacitors were first produced in 1900 by L. Lombardi in Italy. Ceramic capacitors have the advantage that they can withstand extreme temperatures and are highly stable. The tubular glass capacitor was produced in 1904 by I. Moscicki in the United Kingdom. It was this capacitor that Marconi used in his early experiments with radio communication.

World War I provided an important catalyst for technical change in electronic communications, during which new radio tubes and circuits were developed. The interwar years saw the rapid growth of radio, and millions of radios were in use worldwide on the eve of World War II. Paper dielectric capacitors enclosed in cardboard tubes and bakelite-enclosed stacked mica capacitors were the types in most common use in the interwar period.

During the World War II years, substantial developments were made in communications electronics, radio astronomy, xerography, and radar and computer technology as well as in miniaturization and improving the energy efficiency of components. The harsh conditions and importance of reliability imposed by the war led to the development of metal-cased and metalized paper dielectric capacitors as well improvements in ceramic capacitors. The tantalum capacitor was produced in 1956 by D. McLean and F. Power of the United States, after which it became among the most widely used capacitor types.

Among the most significant developments in electronic components in the postwar period were the transistor and integrated circuit. Transistors are based on solid-state technology, serving as substitutes for the older triode vacuum tube active components, developed by de Forest in 1906. The transistor (whose name derives from *trans*ferred res*istor*) was developed by the Bell Laboratories in 1948 and enabled electronic equipment to be produced in increasingly smaller sizes. The first integrated circuit was produced by Texas Instruments in 1959. This device made use of

transistors and other components mounted on a semiconductor chip to form an entire electronic circuit. Prior to the development of integrated circuits, electronic circuits were made exclusively of discreet and separable components—combinations of vacuum tubes or transistors and passive components. Since capacitors with high capacitance values were relatively large, they were generally not produced within an integrated circuit but rather added externally.

Chip capacitors are surface-mounted to circuit boards, in contrast to traditional capacitors with wire leads. Though chip capacitors are generally higher-priced than those with leads, the price gap decreased in recent years. Chip capacitors came into increasing use during the 1990s, especially in equipment such as portable phones, video cameras, and electronic notebooks, items for which space constraints were a prime consideration. The *U.S. Industrial Outlook* for 1994 described these developments: "Trends in the capacitor industry are toward surface mounting and the miniaturization of multilayer capacitor chips. Capacitors were one of the first components to become available as surface-mount or chip components and have led the miniaturization drive in passive components. . . . Ceramic and tantalum chip capacitors are two of the largest passive component products in the North American market. . . . More than 80 percent of tantalum electrolytic capacitors produced are surface-mount devices, which is above average for the capacitor industry." The sales of multilayer ceramic chip capacitors increased by 20 percent in real terms in 1991.

CURRENT CONDITIONS

The value of shipments in the electronic capacitor industry declined from $1.7 billion in 1988 to $1.5 billion in 1990. This pattern reversed itself in the 1990s, with $1.6 billion in shipments in 1992, an estimated $1.7 billion in 1993, and a projected $1.8 billion in 1994. Annual capital investments were $95 million in 1988, $52 million in 1990, and $57 million in 1991.

The *U.S. Industrial Outlook* for 1994 summarized recent developments in the electronic capacitor industry: "Due to the prospect of continuing moderate sales, defense-spending cutbacks, economic slowdown in several key markets, and vendor reduction, capacitor makers are striving to differentiate themselves within a small but highly competitive group of manufacturers. This requires increased service and a continual search for the right product mix. Vendors report growing demand from telecommunications and surface-mount product lines. The successful companies in 1993 have reduced cycle times, and have employed just-in-time (JIT), dock-to-stock delivery, with supplier-managed inventories.''

INDUSTRY LEADERS

The top five firms in the electronic capacitor industry in 1992 were the AVX Corp. of Myrtle Beach, South Carolina, the Kemet Electronics Corp. of Greenville, South Carolina, the Sprague Electric Co. of Stamford, Connecticut, the General Electric Co. Capacitor and Power Protection Operation of Fort Edward, New York, and the Murata Erie North America Inc. State College Division of State College, Pennsylvania.

AVX Corp. was founded in 1972 and had $568 million in sales and 8,174 employees in 1992. The firm produces ceramic and tantalum capacitors. The firm became a subsidiary of Kyocera America Inc. of San Diego as a result of a 1990 merger, with ultimate ownership held by the Kyocera Corp. of Japan (previously the Kyoto Ceramic Co.). AVX announced in 1993 that it was building a new R&D facility in Myrtle Beach.

The Kemet Electronics Corp., a privately held firm, was founded in 1954 and had $530 million in sales and 6,500 employees in 1992. Kemet was a key supplier to the Zeus/Semicap Division formed by Zeus Components Inc. in 1992, thus enabling Zeus Components to provide its original equipment manufacturers (OEMs) with a full line of Kemet's tantalum and ceramic capacitors.

The Sprague Electric Co. had $294 million in sales and 935 employees in 1992. The firm produced electronic resistors (classified in **SIC 3676: Electronic Resistors**) as well as electronic capacitors. Sprague is a subsidiary of the publicly held STI Group Inc. of Stamford, Connecticut. Sprague's tantalum capacitor division was bought out by publicly held Vishay Intertechnology Inc. of Malvern, Pennsylvania, in 1992. Sprague represented part of Vishay's strategy of acquiring electronic components producers around the world and selling components under their original brand names.

The General Electric Co. Capacitor and Power Protection Operation was founded in 1903 and had $200 million in sales and 2,000 employees in 1992. The firm is a division of the publicly held General Electric Co. of Fairfield, Connecticut. The Murata Erie North America Inc. State College Division was founded in 1981 and had $87 million in sales and 1,000 employees in 1992. In addition to producing capacitors, the firm also produces televisions and radios. The firm is a division of Murata Erie North America Inc., of Smyrna, Georgia, whose primary activity was the production of electronic resistors. Murata Erie North America Inc. is a subsidiary of the Murata Manufacturing Co., Ltd. of Japan. Murata Erie North America entered into a distribution agreement with TTI Inc. in 1992 in which TTI would provide Murata's capacitors to OEMs on a nationwide basis.

AMERICA AND THE WORLD

The United States had a trade surplus in electronic capacitors of $47 million in 1991, declining to $36 million in 1992. The five largest export markets for U.S. capacitors are, in order of descent, Mexico, Singapore, Hong Kong, Germany, and the United Kingdom. Mexico, which has a $40 million trade deficit in capacitors with the United States, by itself accounts for the total U.S. trade surplus and for one-third of total U.S. capacitor exports in 1992. Capacitor sales to Mexico increased by 21 percent from the first half of 1992 to the first half of 1993. Singapore was the most dynamic of the United States's major capacitor markets, with sales increasing 66 percent from the first half of 1992 to the first half of 1993. Sales to Hong Kong and Germany declined over these same periods while sales to the United Kingdom increased moderately.

The five largest importers of electronic capacitors into the United States are, in order of descent, Japan, Mexico, Taiwan, Germany, and the United Kingdom. Japanese-produced capacitors accounted for 41 percent of all capacitor imports in 1992, with a 10 percent increase from the first half of 1992 to the first half of 1993. Japan remained the dominant producer of chip capacitors for the world market, and affected the U.S. capacitor market not only through import sales but through its ownership of top U.S.-based producers. Most Mexican-produced capacitor imports into the United States came from plants run by East-Asian firms in export-processing zones. These capacitors accounted for 29 percent of all capacitor imports into the United States in 1992, with a six percent decline from the first half of 1992 to the first half of 1993. Though capacitor imports from Taiwan, Germany, and the United Kingdom made up small shares of total capacitor imports into the United States, these imports grew rapidly from the first half of 1992 to the first half of 1993, by rates of 64, 31, and 29 percent respectively.

RESEARCH AND TECHNOLOGY

Among the key technical developments in the electronic capacitor industry in the 1990s was the use of new insulating, or dielectric, materials. Voltronic received a patent in 1993 for a capacitor with a Teflon dielectric. This device achieved capacitance to size ratios four to ten times greater than previously existing capacitors. Electrocube announced in 1993 the development of a capacitor with a polyester and metal-foil dielectric that was available in smaller sizes than other capacitor types. Both Voltronic's and Electrocube's capacitors are representative of the strong trend toward miniaturization of electronic components. The Toshiba Marcon Electronics America Corp. developed a capacitor with an organic dielectric that it hoped would be a viable alternative to tantalum capacitors.

INDUSTRY INFORMATION SOURCES

Annual Survey of Manufactures, Washington, D.C.: U.S. Census Bureau, 1991.

Burrill, G. Steven and Stephen E. Almassy, *Electronics 90: The New Competitive Priorities,* San Francisco, California: Ernst & Young, 1990.

Daniels, Peggy Kneffel and Carol A. Schwartz, editors, *Encyclopedia of Associations* (28th edition), Detroit, Michigan: Gale Research Inc., 1994.

Darnay, Arsen J., editor, *Manufacturing USA: Industry Analysis, Statistics, and Leading Companies* (3rd edition), Detroit, Michigan: Gale Research Inc., 1993.

Dummer, G. W. A., *Electronic Inventions and Discoveries: Electronics from its Earliest Beginnings to the Present Day* (3rd edition), Headington Hill Hall, England: Pergamon Press Ltd., 1983.

Dunn, Darrell, "Murata Erie Adds Another National to Its Roster," *Electronic Buyers' News,* March 9, 1992.

EIA Marketing Services Department, *1993 Edition Electronic Market Data Book,* Washington, D.C.: Electronic Industries Association, 1993.

Horn, Delton T., *Basic Electricity and Electronics,* Westerville, Ohio: Glencoe Division, 1993.

Jorgensen, Barbara, "Vishnay Opens Direct Sales Office," *Electronic Buyers' News,* October 18, 1993.

Kozicki, Michael N., *Modern Electronics Guidebook: An Overview,* New York, New York: Van Nostrand Reinhold, 1991.

Levine, Sy, *Basic Concepts and Passive Components,* Plainview, New York: Electro-Horizons Publications, 1986.

McKeefry, Hailey, "Toshiba Gives Traditional Capacitor Technology an Organic Twist," *Electronic Buyers' News,* September 27, 1993.

Moody's Industrial Manual, New York: Moody's Investors Service Inc., 1993.

Moody's International Manual, New York: Moody's Investors Service Inc., 1992.

"Polyester Capacitors Conserve Real Estate," *Electronic Engineering Times,* July 5, 1993.

"Progress Continues in Capacitor Technology," *American Ceramic Society Bulletin,* March 1993.

U.S. Industrial Outlook, Washington, D.C.: U.S. Department of Commerce, 1994.

"Vishnay Gets Bigger, Concentrates on Big Customers," *Electronic Business Buyer,* September 1993.

"Voltronics Wins Trimmer Patent," *Microwave and RF,* November 1993.

Votapka, Timothy, *Electronic Buyers' News,* "Zeus Eyes More Passives," April 6, 1992; "AVX to Build R&D Center," April 12, 1993.

Ward's Business Directory of U.S. Private and Public Companies, Detroit, Michigan: Gale Research Inc., 1993.

—David Kucera

SIC 3676

ELECTRONIC RESISTORS

This category covers establishments primarily engaged in manufacturing electronic resistors. Establishments primarily engaged in manufacturing resistors for telephone and telegraph apparatus are classified in **SIC 3661: Telephone and Telegraph Apparatus.**

INDUSTRY SNAPSHOT

The value of shipments in the electronic resistors industry in 1992 was an estimated $797 million, up only slightly from $766 million in 1982. 1984 was a peak year, with $983 million in shipments. There are just over 100 establishments in the industry, 85 percent of which have 20 or more employees. The number of establishments and the percentage of these with more than 20 employees was stable throughout the 1980s. Average firm size as measured by the number of production workers per establishment is over three times as large as for the manufacturing sector as a whole.

Employment of production workers in the industry declined from 12,400 in 1982 to 8,600 in 1991. The industry is relatively labor intensive, having 60 percent as much investment per production worker as that for the manufacturing sector as a whole. Annual hours worked by production workers in the industry are 10 percent lower on average than those worked in the manufacturing sector at large, and hourly wages are 31 percent lower.

ORGANIZATION AND STRUCTURE

Of the top ten firms by sales in the electronic resistors industry in 1992, three were private independents and the remaining seven were either subsidiaries or divisions of larger firms. Of the remaining 25 firms ranking among the top 35 by sales in the industry, 17 (or 68 percent) were private independents. Though average investment per production worker is relatively low for the industry, capital requirements are relatively high, with average investment per establishment 88 percent greater than that for the manufacturing sector as a whole.

The states ranking in the top ten by employment in the electronic resistors industry are California (with 2,500 employees), Indiana (with 1,900), Texas, North Carolina, and Nebraska (with 1,700 employees each), New Hampshire (with 1,000), Illinois, Massachusetts, and New York (with 700 employees each), and Florida (with 600). Together these ten states account for 84 percent of total employment and about 73 percent of all establishments for the industry in the United States. The average number of employees per establishment varies widely across these states. The average establishment in Nebraska and North Carolina, with the highest number of employees per establishment, has between 6 and 14 times as many employees per establishment as does the average establishment in New Jersey and Connecticut.

The top ten industries and sectors buying the outputs of the electronic components and accessories industries are: radio and TV communication equipment, which purchases a 13.5 percent share of the industry; exports, with a 9.8 percent share; telephone and telegraph apparatus, with a 9.6 percent share; electronic computing equipment, with a 9.4 percent share; electronic components, not elsewhere classified, with a 9.1 percent share; radio and TV receiving sets, with a 5.8 percent share; guided missiles and space vehicles, with a 3.2 percent share; personal consumption expenditures, with a 2.9 percent share; X-ray apparatus and tubes, with a 2.6 percent share; and aircraft, with a 2.2 percent share.

There are three basic classes of resistors: fixed resistors, variable resistors, and resistor networks. The most important of these classes by product share in 1991 were fixed resistors, with a 34 percent share, followed by variable resistors, with a 27 percent share, and resistor networks, with a 21 percent share. Fixed resistors grew by product share from 1990 to 1991 at the expense of variable resistors, while the share of resistor networks remained stable.

Within the class of fixed resistors, the four types by product share in 1991 were metal and other film, at 39 percent, wirewound, at 33 percent, chip, at 16 percent, and carbon composition and carbon film, at 12 percent. Metal and other film and chip fixed resistors grew by product share from 1990 to 1991 at the expense of wirewound and carbon composition and carbon film fixed resistors. Within the class of variable resistors, the share of non-wirewound and wirewound devices remained stable from 1990 to 1991 at 71 and 29 percent respectively. Within the class of resistor networks, the top three types by product share in 1991 were SIP (single in-line package), at 41 percent, surface mount, at 29 percent, and DIP (dual in-line package), at 16 percent. The product share of surface mount resistor networks grew by fully 38 percent from 1990 to 1991, a dramatic increase in product share at the expense of other resistor network types. The product share of surface mount resistor networks in relation to all electronic resistors increased by 33 percent from 1990 to 1991.

Among the largest of the several trade organizations serving the industry is the Electronic Industries Association of Washington, D.C., founded in 1924; it has 1,200 members, a staff of 150, and an annual budget of $26 million. Another large trade organization serving the industry is the American Electronics Association of Santa Clara, California, founded in 1943; it has 3,500 members and a staff of 140.

BACKGROUND AND DEVELOPMENT

In his *Basic Electricity and Electronics,* Delton T. Horn defined resistors and resistance: ''A resistor is a device which opposes current in a dc [direct current] circuit; a measure of this opposition is called *resistance,* measured in ohms. . . . Ohms's Law, the relationship between voltage, current, and resistance, states that current is directly proportional to voltage and inversely proportional to resistance in a circuit.'' Resistance is one of the three variables of Ohm's Law, and is thus a necessary pre-condition for any functioning circuit. Resistors are either fixed, with a designated ohm value, or variable, with a designated range of ohm values. Variable resistors are either potentiometers, which control voltage, or rheostats, which directly control resistance. Electronic transistors are part of a class of electronic components called passive components. They differ from active components, such as vacuum tubes and transistors, in that they can neither distinguish voltage polarity nor amplify a signal.

The first electronic resistor was patented in the United Kingdom by C. S. Bradley in 1885. This was a molded carbon composition resistor made of a carbon-rubber mixture. The earliest carbon film resistor was produced in the United Kingdom by T. E. Gambrell and A. F. Harris in 1897. As with the carbon composition resistor, this device preceded the development of broadcasting by a number of years. The first thin metal film resistor was developed in the United Kingdom by W. F. Swann in 1913. The first high-resistance metal film resistor was produced in Germany by F. Kruger in 1919.

The first cracked carbon resistor was produced by Germans Siemens and Halske in 1925. Siemens produced so many of these resistors that they became commonly referred to as "Siemens resistors." The first sprayed metal film resistor was developed in Germany by S. Loewe in 1926. This was produced by spraying an atomized solution of platinum impregnated with resin, after which the sprayed form was heated. In his *Electronic Inventions and Discoveries,* G. W. A. Dummer described developments in the industry around this time: "It might be considered that this period (the early 1920s) saw the birth of the components industry. Resistors were produced in large quantities and used as grid leaks, anode loads, etc., and consisted of carbon compositions of many kinds compressed into tubular containers and fitted with end caps. . . . Cracked-carbon film-type resistors were introduced from Germany . . . and by 1934 were being manufactured in quantity in the United Kingdom." An ever-growing market for resistors and other electronic components in the period between the World Wars was provided by the rapidly expanding use of radio and other forms of electronic communication.

During the early 1950s electronic engineers realized that the working portion of a resistor was only a small fraction of the total volume. For plastic-molded carbon film resistors, for example, only 3.6 percent of the total volume was actually used. This realization led to the development of early thick film and thin film circuits. One of the most important of these was the nickel-chromium (or nichrome) thin film resistor, produced in the United Kingdom by R. H. Alderton and F. Ashworth in 1957. This became the most widely used type of thin film resistor in recent years. It was also in the 1950s that automation techniques were developed for attaching traditional electronic components with wire leads to circuit boards. These processes could produce up to 10,000 finished circuit boards per day. A key development in the production of thick film resistors was the use of lasers for trimming in the late 1960s.

The first integrated circuit was produced by Texas Instruments in 1959. This device made use of components mounted on a semiconductor chip to form an entire electronic circuit. Prior to the development of integrated circuits, electronic circuits were made exclusively of discreet and separable components—combinations of vacuum or transistors and passive components. In *Electronic Inventions and Discoveries,* Dummer wrote, "The present explosion of integrated circuits in the form of VLSI [very large-scale integra-

tion] and VHSIC [very high-speed integrated circuit] has been the most important development in the history of electronics."

The mass production and widespread commercial viability of integrated circuits was made possible by the planar process of production, developed in the United States in 1959 by Jean Hoerni, a Swiss physicist, and Robert Noyce, an American physicist. Chip resistors are surface-mounted to circuit boards, in contrast to traditional resistors with wire leads running through circuit boards. Surface mount resistor types became of ever-increasing importance in the 1990s.

Current Conditions

Though technical change remained dynamic in the electronic resistors industry, growth prospects do not appear promising. The value of shipments in the electronic capacitor industry declined from $890 million in 1989 to an estimated $797 million in 1992. Capital investments declined from $56 million in 1989 to $34 million 1991. Employment of production workers declined from 11,700 in 1989 to 8,600 in 1991. The peak year for employment of production workers was 1984, with 13,000 employed.

The *U.S. Industrial Outlook* for 1994 noted, "Overall, the U.S. resistor industry is mature, and profit margins are slim." The 1990s saw substantial consolidation of electronic components distributors (**SIC 5065: Electronic Parts and Equipment, Not Elsewhere Classified**). The December 12, 1991, issue of *Electronic News* noted the possible effects of this consolidation on suppliers of electronic components: "So much consolidation could expectedly be accompanied by a feverish degree of franchise shuffling as suppliers attempted to shore up their distributor networks against a persistent recessionary climate."

Industry Leaders

The top five firms by sales in the electronic resistors industry in 1992 were Bourns Inc. of Riverside, California, Dale Electronic Inc. of Columbus, Nebraska, Murata Erie North America Inc. of Smyrna, Georgia, Beckman Industrial Corp. of Fullerton, California, and IRC Inc. of Boone, North Carolina. Bourns Inc. is a privately held firm founded in 1946 with $360 million in sales and 4,500 employees in 1992. The firm's products are distributed across North America and in 12 European countries by the ITT Corporation's Electronic Components Distribution unit. Bourns underwent a streamlining operation in 1991, which resulted in the elimination of a number of managerial positions. The firm entered into a cooperative agreement with number five producer IRC Inc. in early

1992. By mid-1992, between 50 and 100 thousand thin-film precision resistor networks were being produced each month under the agreement. Bourns announced in 1992 that it was diversifying into the production of miniature electronic switches (**SIC 3679: Electronic Components, Not Elsewhere Classified**).

Dale Electronics Inc. was founded in 1951 and had $180 million in sales and 4,500 employees in 1992. In addition to electronic resistors, the firm also produces electronic capacitors (**SIC 3675: Electronic Capacitors**) and non-electronic power transformers (**SIC 3612: Power, Distribution, and Specialty Transformers**). Dale Electronics is a subsidiary of Dale Holdings Inc., itself a subsidiary of Vishay Intertechnology Inc. of Malvern, Pennsylvania. Vishay Intertechnology is a manufacturer of resistor-based stress measurement sensors (**SIC 3829: Measuring and Controlling Devices, Not Elsewhere Classified**), inductors (**SIC 3677: Electronic Coils, Transformers, and Other Inductors**), and specialized connectors (**SIC 3678: Electronic Connectors**). Dale Electronics represented part of Vishnay's strategy of acquiring electronic components producers around the world and selling components under their original brand names.

Murata Erie North America Inc. was founded in 1981 and had $130 million in sales and 1,704 employees in 1992. The firm is a subsidiary of the Murata Manufacturing Co. Ltd. of Japan and in addition to producing electronic resistors produces electronic capacitors. Beckman Industrial Corp. was founded in 1952 and had $100 million in sales and 350 employees in 1992. Beckman manufactures electronic resistors for industrial and military networks as well as electronic test and measuring equipment (**SIC 3825: Instruments for Measuring and Testing of Electricity and Electrical Signals**). The firm is a subsidiary of the publicly held Emerson Electric Co. of St. Louis, which produces electric motors (**SIC 3621: Motors and Generators**) and electric relays (**SIC 3625: Relays and Industrial Controls**). Beckman sold its $30 million per year Instrumentation Products Division to Wavetek in 1992. IRC Inc. (also International Resistive Co. Inc.) was founded in 1973 and had $50 million in sales and 1,000 employees in 1992. In 1990 the firm became a subsidiary of Crystalate Electronics Inc., a subsidiary of the TT Group PLC.

AMERICA AND THE WORLD

The United States had a trade deficit in electronic resistors of $170 million in 1992. Exports of electronic resistors produced in the United States increased by an estimated five percent in 1993, to $254 million. Chip resistors were expected to experience the most rapid export growth in coming years. The three largest export markets for resistors produced in the United States are, in order of descent, Mexico, Canada, and Japan. Mexico and Canada by themselves account for 34 percent of all U.S. resistor exports in 1992. Among the most rapidly growing export markets for U.S. resistors are Malaysia, Singapore, and Mexico, with growth rates in the first half of 1993 at 65, 57, and 24 percent respectively.

Imports of electronic resistors into the United States increased by 15 percent in 1992, to $411 million. Imports from Japan accounted for 37 percent of this total. In the first half of 1993, imports of electronic resistors into the United States increased by 40 percent for Japan and 19 percent for Mexico.

RESEARCH AND TECHNOLOGY

The Electronic Industries Association's *1993 Edition Electronic Market Data Book* described recent technical developments in the electronic resistors industry: ''The move to surface mount resistor chips is the dominant technology trend in the resistor industry. A strong link is developing between the expansion of the automotive industry's use of printed circuit boards (PCBs) and the increased use of surface mounted resistor chips. Product developments trends in resistors are primarily toward thin- and thick-film resistor networks.'' Resistor networks combine a set of electronic components, such as integrated circuits and resistors, to carry out coordinated functions. These networks have come to replace individual resistors, a trend that was expected to continue.

As of 1992, approximately ten percent of trimming potentiometers, variable resistors used in high-volume PCB applications, were surface mounted types. A marketing manager at Bourns Inc., the industry's largest producer, expected this share to reach 25 to 30 percent by the late 1990s. Trimming potentiometers were the most important class of potentiometers. In 1992, Ohmtek Inc., a division of Vishay Intertechnology Inc., announced the development of its Quick-Net program, which reduced lead times for the production and delivery of resistor network prototypes to two weeks. Previously, it typically took 10 to 12 weeks for a firm to complete this process.

INDUSTRY INFORMATION SOURCES

Annual Survey of Manufactures, Washington, D.C.: U.S. Census Bureau, 1991.

Burrill, G. Steven and Stephen E. Almassy, *Electronics 90: The New Competitive Priorities,* San Francisco, California: Ernst & Young, 1990.

"Coming: Speed, 'Catchy Name,'" *Electronic Buyers' News,* July 20, 1992.

"Consolidation Breeding Competition," *Electronic Buyers' News,* October 25, 1993.

Daniels, Peggy Kneffel and Carol A. Schwartz, editors, *Encyclopedia of Associations* (28th edition), Detroit, Michigan: Gale Research Inc., 1994.

Darnay, Arsen J., editor, *Manufacturing USA: Industry Analysis, Statistics, and Leading Companies* (3rd edition), Detroit, Michigan: Gale Research Inc., 1993.

"Distribution Trends 1992: The Year in Review," *Electronic News,* December 12, 1991.

Dummer, G. W. A., *Electronic Inventions and Discoveries: Electronics from Its Earliest Beginnings to the Present Day* (3rd edition), Headington Hill Hall, England: Pergamon Press Ltd., 1983.

Dunn, Darrell, "Pact Payoff Expected," *Electronic Buyers' News,* June 1, 1992.

EIA Marketing Services Department, *1993 Edition Electronic Market Data Book,* Washington, D.C.: Electronic Industries Association, 1993.

Horn, Delton T., *Basic Electricity and Electronics,* Westerville, Ohio: Glencoe Division, 1993.

Kozicki, Michael N., *Modern Electronics Guidebook: An Overview,* New York, New York: Van Nostrand Reinhold, 1991.

Levine, Sy, *Basic Concepts and Passive Components,* Plainview, New York: Electro-Horizons Publications, 1986.

McKeefry, Haily, "Pots Are Surfacing Everywhere," *Electronic Buyers' News,* June 15, 1992.

Million Dollar Directory, Parsippany, New Jersey: Dun & Bradstreet, Inc., 1993.

Moody's Industrial Manual, New York: Moody's Investors Service Inc., 1993.

Norman, Diane, "Bourns in Strategy Switch," *Electronic Buyers' News,* November 23, 1992.

Thryft, Ann, "More Changes at Bourns: Streamlining Continues, New Markets Are Tried," *Electronic Buyers' News,* April 27, 1992.

U.S. Industrial Outlook, Washington, D.C.: U.S. Department of Commerce, 1994.

"Vishnay Gets Bigger, Concentrates on Big Customers," *Electronic Business Buyer,* September 1993.

Ward's Business Directory of U.S. Private and Public Companies, Detroit, Michigan: Gale Research Inc., 1993.

"Wavetek Acquires Division," *Microwaves and RF,* November 1992.

—David Kucera

SIC 3677

ELECTRONIC COILS, TRANSFORMERS, AND OTHER INDUCTORS

Establishments primarily engaged in manufacturing electronic coils, transformers, and inductors. Establishments primarily engaged in manufacturing electrical transformers are classified in Industry **3612: Power, Distribution, and Specialty Transformers;** those manufacturing transformers and inductors for telephone and telegraph apparatus are classified in Industry **3661: Telephone and Telegraph Apparatus;** and those manufacturing semiconductors and related devices are classified in Industry **3674: Semiconductors and Related Devices.**

INDUSTRY SNAPSHOT

The value of shipments in the electronic coils and transformers industry was an estimated $1.1 billion in 1993, up only slightly from $1.0 billion in 1983. The peak year was 1988, with $1.3 billion in shipments (in current dollars). There were just under 400 establishments in the industry, 61 percent of which had 20 or more employees. Average firm size as measured by the number of production workers per establishment was 27 larger than for the manufacturing sector as a whole.

Employment of production workers in the industry declined from a peak of 21,200 in 1983 to 16,600 in 1991. Employment of production workers was lower in 1991 than in all years in the prior decade. The industry was highly labor-intensive, having only 19 percent as much investment per production worker as that for the manufacturing sector as a whole. Annual hours worked by production workers in the industry were 10 percent lower on average than those worked in the manufacturing sector at large, and hourly wages were 34 percent lower.

ORGANIZATION AND STRUCTURE

Of the top ten firms by sales in the electronic coils and transformers industry in 1992, five were private independents, four were subsidiaries, and one was publicly-held. Of the remaining 90 firms ranking among the top 100 by sales in the industry, 77 percent were private independents. Capital requirements were relatively low for the industry, with average investment per establishment 25 percent that for the manufacturing sector as a whole.

The states ranking in the top ten by employment in the industry were Illinois (with 3,200 employees), New York (with more than 2,500) California (with

2,500), Indiana (with 2,300), Massachusetts and Virginia (with 1,700 employees each), New Jersey (with 1,300), Minnesota (with 900), and Florida and Connecticut (with 800 employees each). Together these ten states accounted for more than 75 percent of total employment and more than 69 percent of all establishments for the industry in the United States. The average number of employees per establishment varied widely across these states. Virginia, with the highest number of employees per establishment, had an average of 9 times as many employees per establishment as Florida and 13 times as many as California. Of the top six firms by sales in the industry in 1992, five were from either Illinois or New York.

The top nine types of coils and transformers by product share in 1991 were, in order of descent, pulse transformers, computer and other (at 15.5 percent), plate and filament transformers (at 13.5 percent), toroidal windings (at 10.7 percent), audio transformers (at 9.2 percent), radio frequency coils (at 4.8 percent), radio frequency chokes (at 4.7 percent), low frequency chokes (at 3.9 percent), IF transformers (at 2.2 percent), and TV transformers and reactors (at 2.2 percent). The coil and transformer types that experienced growing product shares from 1982 to 1991 are shown in bold letters. (The ''other'' category accounted for 33.2 percent of product share in 1991, up from 22.9 percent in 1982.)

Among the largest of the several trade organizations serving the industry were the Electronic Industries Association of Washington, D.C. and the American Electronics Association of Santa Clara, California. The Electronic Industries Association was founded in 1924 and had 1,200 members, a staff of 150, and an annual budget of $26 million. The Association produced a number of publications, catalogued in its semiannual *EAI Publications Index*. The American Electronics Association was founded in 1943 and had 3,500 members and a staff of 140. In addition to organizing an annual convention, the Association published the monthly *American Electronics Association-Update*, with a circulation of 35,000, as well as a number of handbooks, among them *Government Affairs Bulletin*, *Benchmark Wage and Salary Survey*, and *Operating Ratios Survey*.

BACKGROUND AND DEVELOPMENT

''Inductor'' is a generic term for an electronic coil, sometimes also referred to as an electronic choke. Inductors function to either filter or select certain frequencies within AC or pulsating DC circuits. In his *Basic Electricity and Electronics*, Delton Horn defines inductors and inductance as follows: ''An inductor is a device capable of storing magnetic energy in a circuit. Typically it consists of a coil of wire around some type of core, which may be magnetic or nonmagnetic. Inductance is directly proportional to the square of the number of turns [of wire]. An inductor opposes changes in current. It also opposes current, and this opposition increases as the frequency of the signal increases.'' Coil wire must be coated with an insulating material, usually varnish, lacquer or enamel, to prevent turns of wire from coming into electrical contact. The greater the ferrous content of the core, the greater the coil's inductance. Coils with non-ferrous cores are referred to as ''air core'' inductors.

In his *Basic Concepts and Passive Components*, Levine defines transformers as follows: ''A *transformer* is a component consisting of a group of separate and unconnected lengths of wire wound around a common core. Its purpose is to provide an efficient transfer of electrical power between circuits connected to its various sections while maintaining electrical isolation between them. This transfer of power is accomplished magnetically.'' Transformers serve a number of functions, and transformer types are defined by function. Among the most important of these types are power transformers, output transformers, radio frequency (RF) transformers, and pulse transformers. Power transformers function to transfer power from an AC power source to a rectifier section, which changes AC to pulsating DC, isolating and changing the level of that power as needed. Output transformers function to transfer signals from an audio amplifier to a loudspeaker. RF transformers function to transfer signals between stages of radio frequency amplification circuits. Pulse transformers functions to transfer signals between stages of digital electronic systems.

Electronic coils and transformers are part of a class of electronic components called passive components (SICs 3675-3679). They differ from active components, such as vacuum tubes and transistors, in that they can neither distinguish voltage polarity nor amplify a signal.

The pioneering figure in the industry was Michael Faraday, the English chemist and physicist (1791-1867). Faraday is credited with discovering the phenomenon of electromagnetic induction in 1831 and was the first to use a magnetic circuit to connect two electric circuits. In his experiments with induction, Faraday developed an early version of the transformer. The earliest patent for a power transformer was granted to C. Zipernowski, O. Blathy and M. Deri of Budapest in 1885. Deri was also granted the first patent for a distribution transformer in 1885.

The *U.S. Industrial Outlook* for 1994 reports, "The chief end uses of coils and transformers are in stereos and other home entertainment equipment, computers, telecommunications equipment, and industrial and control instruments." As with other electronic components, the growth of the coil and transformer industry was tied up with the growth of radio broadcasting after World War I. Stringent demands were made on all electronic components during World War II. This led to a large number of technological improvements, among them standardization, energy efficiency, miniaturization, ease of maintenance, and reliability, especially in the face of mechanical shocks, vibration, temperature extremes, humidity, and high altitude. During these years, resin-encased transformers were developed, as were oil-filled transformers sealed in metal housings.

The most important recent trends in coil and transformer production were continued miniaturization and weight reduction as well as surface mounting. Surface mounted components (or SMD for surface mounted device) offered a number of advantages over traditional components with wire leads mounted through circuit boards. Since SMDs could be placed on both sides of a circuit board, they optimized space. SMDs were lighter than components with wire leads and enabled faster assembly techniques and less expensive manufacture of circuit boards, which, with SMDs, did not require hole drilling. SMDs made possible shorter distances between components, which reduced circuit capacitance and resistance and minimized interference.

As a result of size constraints, coils with high levels of inductance were very difficult to produce in integrated circuits. Nonetheless, the pace of technical change in the industry was brisk, suggesting that such integration problems might be overcome. Integrated coils were generally produced by forming flat spirals of metal on the face of a circuit.

CURRENT CONDITIONS

The value of shipments in the electronic coils and transformers industry declined every year from 1988 to 1991. This pattern appears to have been broken in more recent years, however, with the estimated value of shipments growing by three percent in 1993. The *U.S. Industrial Outlook* for 1994 noted that export growth may play an important role for the industry. It reported as follows: "Since the primary end market for coils and transformers are consumer electronic products, such as television sets, U.S. exports will grow in conjunction with increased production in the major consumer electronics [industries] in Mexico, Japan,

Singapore, Hong Kong, and Taiwan. China is expected to be a strong long-term growth market for U.S. exports." Annual capital investments showed consecutive declines from 1989 to 1991. Annual capital investments exceeded $30 million in 1982 and 1983 but in no year thereafter up to 1991 (all values in current dollars).

Employment of production workers declined from 19,100 in 1988 to 16,600 in 1991, with consecutive declines through these years. The Bureau of Labor Statistics made employment forecasts at the SIC 367 level for 20 occupational categories. Based on projected changes from 1990 to 2005, employment was expected to decline by double-digit figures in five occupations, which accounted for 27 percent of total employment in 1990. Nine occupations were projected to show double-digit increases to 2005—occupations accounting for 23 percent of total employment in 1990. The occupations with projected declines were those directly associated with production processes, while those with projected increases included managerial, technical, and sales personnel. Projections made for the electronic capacitors industry alone would have varied from these figures, but past employment trends in the industry suggested consistency with projections made at the SIC 367 level.

In their *1993 Edition Electronic Market Data Book*, the Electronic Industries Association published their forecast for sales of defense-related electronics for years 1993 to 2002. The Association summarized their forecast as follows: "Despite the forecast of a flat budget for defense procurement, there will be increasing purchases of electronic equipment, with contractors the winners. Production will be limited to the most advanced weapon systems and high technology will be inserted into existing equipment through modifications and upgrades. In addition, a majority of the research and development investment will be in electronics. Suppliers of state-of-the-art electronic systems can therefore expect modest growth in their defense market."

INDUSTRY LEADERS

The top five firms by sales in the electronic coils and transformers industry in 1992 were, in order of descent, Kearney-National Inc. of White Plains, New York; the Basler Electric Co. of Highland, Illinois; the Electro-Mechanical Corp. of Bristol, Virginia; the Products Unlimited Corp. of Sterling, Illinois; and American Precision Industries Inc. of Buffalo, New York.

Kearney-National was founded in 1843 and had $180 million in sales and 2,300 employees in 1992. In addition to producing electronic transformers, the firm produced electrical systems for automobiles. Kearney-National was a subsidiary of the privately-held Dyson-Kissner-Moran Corp., a holding company based in New York City.

Basler Electric was a privately-held firm founded in 1947, with $76 million in sales and 1,300 employees in 1992. In addition to producing electronic inductors and power transformers, the firm produced electrical relays and industrial controls.

The privately-held Electro-Mechanical Corp. was founded in 1958 and had $61 million in sales and 750 employees in 1992. In addition to producing electronic transformers, the firm manufactured and repaired electrical transformers, switchgear, and other control systems.

The Products Unlimited Corp. was a privately-held firm founded in 1978, with $57 million in sales and 700 employees in 1992. The firm purchased a line of electrical contactors (SIC 3622) from Cooper Industries in 1992.

American Precision Industries Inc. was founded in 1946 and had $52 million in sales and 640 employees in 1992. The publicly-held firm's secondary activities included the manufacture of heat transfer products, electromagnetic clutches and brakes used in rotary control applications.

AMERICA AND THE WORLD

The United States had a trade surplus in electronic coils and transformers of $101 million in 1992, compared to a deficit of $3.11 billion for all passive components (SICs 3675-3679) for that year. Exports of electronic resistors produced in the United States increased by eight percent in 1992, to $501 million. Mexico was by far the largest export market for electronic coils and transformers produced in the United States, accounting for 67 percent of U.S. exports in 1992. The United States ran a $140 million surplus with Mexico in electronic coils and transformers in that year. Other important export markets included Canada, Singapore, Taiwan, Hong Kong, and Japan.

Imports of electronic coils and transformers into the United States increased by 23 percent in the first half of 1993. The three largest importers of electronic coils and transformers into the United States were, in order of descent, Mexico, Japan, and Taiwan. In the first half of 1993, imports from Japan increased by 39 percent whereas imports from Taiwan decreased by 18 percent.

RESEARCH AND TECHNOLOGY

There was a considerable amount of new product development in the electronic coil and transformer industry in the 1990s. Beta Transformer Technology introduced a series of surface-mount transformers that were only 0.13 inch thick. The J.R. Miller Division of Bell Industries began the production of four new series of surface-mount inductors. Schaffer EMC announced the development of a new series of toroidal inductors. Ohmite Manufacturing, primarily a producer of electronic resistors, began production of miniature high-current radio-frequency inductors. The Signal Transformer Co. announced its development of a high-power transformer that was the first in its class to meet international certification standards.

Significant developments were made in the production of thermoplastic encapsulated coils, which the May 1993 issue of *Appliance* describes as follows: "Recent developments include the first successful encapsulation of integrated circuit chips in an electrical device; further increases in the production of thermoplastic-encapsulated solenoids, sensors, transformers, motor components and other coil devices; new wire-friendly nylon resins that minimize magnet wire corrosion; and direct encapsulation of components with crimped connections as a low-cost alternative to the potting of complex circuits." Thermoplastic encapsulated coils were one of the more promising products the industry had to offer, and demand for these devices was rising.

The U.S. Department of Energy's Argonne National Laboratory and the Intermagnetics General Corp. announced the development in 1993 of a superconducting coil with a magnetic field 50 thousand times as strong as that produced by the Earth. The American Superconductor Co. received a $1.9 million, three-year contract from the Department of Commerce in 1992 to manufacture superconducting magnetic coils.

INDUSTRY INFORMATION SOURCES

"AC Power Line EMI Suppression Chokes," *Electronic Buyers' News*, March 29, 1993.

"Appliance Coil Winding: Advances in Thermoplastic Encapsulation of Transformers and Small Wound Coils," *Appliance*, May 1993.

Annual Survey of Manufactures, Washington, D.C.: U.S. Census Bureau, 1991.

Burrill, G. Steven and Stephen E. Almassy, *Electronics 90: The New Competitive Priorities*, San Francisco: Ernst & Young, 1990.

Daniels, Peggy Kneffel and Carol A. Schwartz, eds. *Encyclopedia of Associations*, 28th ed., Detroit: Gale Research Inc., 1994.

Darnay, Arsen J., ed. *Manufacturing USA: Industry Analysis, Statistics, and Leading Companies*, 3rd ed., Detroit: Gale Research Inc., 1993.

"Dry Transformers Aren't All Wet," *PIMA*, August 1992.

Dummer, G.W.A. *Electronic Inventions and Discoveries: Electronics from its Earliest Beginnings to the Present Day*, 3rd ed., Headington Hill Hall, England: Pergamon Press Ltd., 1983.

1993 Edition Electronic Market Data Book, Washington, DC: Electronic Industries Association, 1993.

Horn, Delton T., *Basic Electricity and Electronics*, Westerville, Ohio: Glencoe Division, 1993.

Kozicki, Michael N., *Modern Electronics Guidebook: An Overview*. New York: Van Nostrand Reinhold, 1991.

Levine, Sy, *Basic Concepts and Passive Components*, Plainview, New York: Electro-Horizons Publications, 1986.

Moody's Industrial Manual, New York: Moody's Investors Service Inc., 1993.

Norman, Diane, "Ohmite Adds Components," *Electronic Buyers' News*, January 13, 1992.

"Products Unlimited Buys Arrow Line," *Appliance Manufacturer*, March 1992.

"Public-Private Collaboration Produces Strongest Field by High-Tc Coil," *JOM*, October, 1993.

"Superconducting Coils to be Developed for Electric Motor," *Power Engineering*, July 1992.

"Surface-Mount Inductors Have Ratings to 2.6 A," *Electronic Buyers' News*, September 27, 1993.

U.S. Industrial Outlook, Washington, D.C.: U.S. Department of Commerce, 1994.

Votapka, Timothy, "Low-Profile Transformer," *Electronic Buyers' News*, April 11, 1993; "Approval Pending: Signal's Transformers Await International OK," *Electronic Buyers' News*, June 21, 1993.

Ward's Business Directory of U.S. Private and Public Companies, Detroit: Gale Research Inc., 1993.

— David Kucera

SIC 3678

ELECTRONIC CONNECTORS

This industry is comprised of manufacturers of electronic connectors, e.g. coaxial, cylindrical, rack and panel, and printed circuit connectors. Establishments primarily engaged in manufacturing electrical connectors are classified in **SIC 3643: Current-Carrying Wiring Devices;** those manufacturing electronic capacitors are classified in **SIC 3675: Electronic Capacitors;** and those manufacturing electronic coils, transformers, and other inductors are classified in **SIC 3677: Electronic Coils, Transformers, and Other Inductors.**

INDUSTRY SNAPSHOT

The health of the electronic connectors industry is tied to that of electronic equipment and other finished-product (e.g. automobile) manufacturers. A cutback in military spending and a depression in the prices of personal computers (PCs) has reduced the number of connector manufacturers through closures and mergers. The most successful companies, such as AMP Inc. and Molex, have traditionally invested heavily in research and development, effectively differentiating their products in a competitive environment.

ORGANIZATION AND STRUCTURE

Makers of electronic connectors and other passive electronic components must rely on manufacturers of finished products to maintain favorable prices and provide a market for their goods. As is the case in most components industries, military markets generally require the most advanced products, which are usually the most expensive. When an industry such as the PC industry slows or is forced to reduce its prices, as was the case worldwide in the late 1980s and early 1990s, connector manufacturers have difficulty maintaining profits.

Throughout the 1980s and 1990s, the connector industry was overcrowded, with approximately 800 manufacturers worldwide. Consolidations and mergers reduced the number of players in the United States considerably by the mid-1990s. A notable departure was that of Du Pont, which sold its connector business for approximately $400 million in 1993.

BACKGROUND AND DEVELOPMENT

The beginnings of the electronic connectors industry can be traced to products such as the solderless electrical connectors AMP Inc. manufactured for use in aircraft and boats in the 1940s, and the introduction of the printed wiring board in 1936 by Dr. Paul Eisner. The increased use of electronic components, particularly in military applications, in the 1980s was ironically foreshadowed by growth in demand for electrical components in military ships and aircraft during World War II. At the end of the War, contract terminations eliminated many shops. However, the postwar explosion of the semiconductor-related industries eventually made the connectors field more attractive, so that by the 1990s the number of connector manufacturers had risen to approximately 800.

CURRENT CONDITIONS

Electronic connectors accounted for approximately $18 billion in worldwide sales in 1992, essentially the same as 1991. In fact, they had not risen since 1987. The United States produced an estimated $3.7 billion worth of connectors in 1992. Due to the lingering slow market, vendors became more responsive, improving service—AMP Inc. increased on-time deliveries from 65 percent in 1986 to 93 percent in 1992—and typically investing heavily in research and development.

Several factors were expected to spur growth in the connector market six percent to nine percent per year in the mid-1990s. One was the worldwide recovery of electronics industries. Japanese producers, in particular, continued to improve from their decline of 1992. However, European electronics industries were expected to remain weak. The United States had shown signs of recovery, although military orders continued to drop sharply. Personal computer prices were expected to climb again by 1995, thereby improving market conditions for the connectors.

A promising long-term trend was the proliferation of electronics in such varied industries as automobiles and telecommunications. Automotive electronics, desktop units, network, and miscellaneous wiring were expected to spur demand for newer connector technologies. Surface-mount connectors were expected to show the strongest growth as the new technology gained acceptance.

INDUSTRY LEADERS

The worldwide connector industry has been dominated by AMP Inc. of Harrisburg, Pa., with Molex a distant second. Notable competitors include Thomas and Betts, Augat, and Samtec. In 1993, AMP had sales of $873 million, up 3.4 percent from the previous year, and a market share of about 18 percent. Growth in U.S. and Asian markets, with the exception of Japan, boosted AMP's expansion. The company had $3.3 billion in sales in 1992 and employed 26,000 workers in 35 countries.

AMP, originally known as Aircraft Marine Products, was founded by Uncas A. Whitaker in 1941. Whitaker, trained as a mechanical and electrical engineer, started the company after working for Westinghouse Electric, the Hoover Company, and American Machine & Foundry (now known as AMF Inc.). The company's chief products were solderless electrical connectors used in aircraft and boat production. These allowed electrical connections to be made quickly with only a crimping tool, rather than a soldering iron. The company thrived on war production orders as electrical components became increasingly important in aircraft and boat design.

The roots of AMP's international success can be traced to 1957, when it began operations with Japanese companies. It obtained a monopoly in the Japanese automotive market for electrical connectors that has kept it the largest passive components manufacturer in Japan into the 1990s. 30 foreign subsidiaries, most with engineering and production capability, helped AMP remain responsive to the needs of overseas clients. In 1990, the company achieved 54 percent of sales and 59 percent of pre-tax income outside of North America.

AMP experienced its greatest growth, about 15 percent per year, between going public in 1956 and a slowdown in the electronics industry in 1989. After this slowdown, the number of AMP Inc. manufacturing facilities fell from about 140 in the mid-1980s to approximately 100 in 1990. During the same period, the company cut back its work force by 4,000. An emphasis on developing new products has helped AMP maintain its position as the top-ranked connector manufacturer. The company won 277 patents in 1992, spending nine percent of sales in research and development. AMP has moved its strategies from marketing connectors to marketing complete harnesses, sensing customers' desires to do as little assembly as possible, and reducing labor costs. It has also provided software for customers to see how AMP products fit with their own via CAD programs.

Another industry leader with strong international connections is Molex Inc. of Lisle, Ill. Over 70 percent of this company's sales and profits in 1993 were garnered outside the United States. The fact that the company has factories in 19 countries was cited as a factor in its continued overall success in the early 1990s. The company's annual revenues were approximately $900 million in 1991, with about five percent to six percent of the world market—second only to AMP Inc. This was a great increase from a decade earlier, when Molex ranked tenth in terms of world market share. Like AMP, Molex has invested heavily in research and development. It invested $110 million in 1993.

Augat followed a similar strategy as that of AMP in its move to become more of a full-service supplier with the acquisition of National Industries in 1991. After the acquisition of National, a well-established maker of wire harnesses for the automotive industry,

40 percent of Augat's sales were to car makers, compared with 30 percent before the acquisition. Augat's sales topped $282 million in 1991, with profits of $22.1 million.

Another U.S. company that has had success abroad is Samtec Inc. of New Albany, Ind., which was established in 1976. In 1984, it initiated marketing channels in Europe which led to the establishment of a manufacturing facility in Cumbernauld, Scotland. In 1992, sales increased 75 percent in Europe. Executives at Samtec credited the company's European success with an emphasis on fast service facilitated by the plant in Scotland. Samtec also opened a facility in Singapore in 1991.

AMERICA AND THE WORLD

The U.S. trade deficit in electronic connectors continued to grow in 1992. Imports were valued at $533 million, more than ever before; exports were valued at $129 million. Canada, Japan, Singapore, Mexico, and Germany were the top markets for the U.S. connectors. Mexico, Germany, and Singapore showed promise to grow as export markets in the future; exports to Mexico more than tripled in the first half of 1993. Mexico, Taiwan, and Japan led in exporting connectors to the United States; Mexico exported $129 million to the United States in 1992. Canada and Germany were also considerable suppliers for the U.S. market.

RESEARCH AND TECHNOLOGY

About one-third of electronic connectors sold in the United States are printed circuit boards. Printed circuit boards experienced growth of approximately 2.5 percent worldwide, with sales reaching $20.2 billion in 1991. Cylindrical, rack and panel, planar hermetic sealed, and fiber optic connectors divide the rest of the electronic connector market, with fiber optic connectors showing a strong potential for growth. The demand for increasing miniaturization will drive technological advances in the future. Specialized military and commercial applications will also fuel research.

Surface mounting, a technology originally developed for the camcorder industry, had gained acceptance by the 1990s, becoming utilized in approximately 24 percent of all integrated circuits (ICs) in 1990 and 43 percent of all ICs in 1992. In printed circuit boards, components are traditionally soldered to the board by means of small connecting leads that are inserted into holes in the board before being soldered. However, surface mounting is a process whereby the components are soldered directly onto the board. This results in a great deal of space savings—

up to 40 percent when only one side of the board is used. In addition, with surface mounting components can be mounted on both sides of the board, allowing for a total space savings of up to 60 percent and a weight savings of up to 90 percent over conventionally-mounted circuit boards. The process also lends itself to cost-reducing automation. Reliability is improved, as well.

It has been estimated that by 1997, 76 percent of all ICs will feature surface mounting. The automotive industry has become the main user of surface mounting, along with other markets where miniaturization is important, such as consumer electronic, avionics, and space applications.

Westinghouse and Lockheed Sanders, suppliers of military aircraft (the AH-64 helicopter and F-22 fighter, respectively) went one step further than circuit mounting to improve reliability. Citing the failure of solder joints under fatigue as a causative factor in avionics failures, Westinghouse introduced Solder Free Interconnects (secured by cantilever spring clips) and Lockheed Sanders introduced folding printed circuit boards with flexible printed wiring. Although some aspects of the emerging technology made manufacturing less labor-intensive, others, particularly the small size of the components, required heavy investments in specialized machines able to handle the process.

The drive for miniaturization was also fueled by the laptop computer industry, which required in 1994 high density interconnections for such next-generation components as miniaturized memory cards and 1.8-inch disk drives, and connectors for linking the laptops with networks and desk-based PCs. Specialty Electronics marketed two-millimeter and one-millimeter connectors for use in the smallest of computers and electronic devices, such as pagers.

Connectors designed to operate in high-current applications were offered by Panduit Electronics Group of Tinely Park, Il., for use in computers, appliances, and other heavy-duty applications. Panduit utilized "hertz stress" theory to determine the optimum arrangement of dimples used to make the contact in the connector.

Apple planned to introduce a new high-speed serial standard called "Firewire" in 1995 to replace the existing connectors on Macintosh computers. The new system was planned to faster transmission of data. The technology featured other advances, too, such as greatly simplified use and an improved capacity for handling real-time video. IBM and other computer manufacturers had endorsed the standard as of 1994, helping to insure its success.

Challenging operational environments of industry and the military continued to provide a demand for specialized connectors. In 1991, Ocean Design Inc. introduced an oil-filled, pressurized connector for military and petroleum industry use underseas and in damp conditions. This connector could be mated underwater without shutting off power. The design relied on a thin layer of a specially engineered thermoplastic to strengthen its protective epoxy layer. Another specialized connector with military applications was the BetaFlex circuit board connector. This connector was developed to meet a need for very fast data transmission in the high vibration environment of avionics. At the core of this design was a nickel-titanium memory alloy. Pave Technology Co. introduced a radiation-resistant "push-through" connector, allowing workers to replace its connection without entering a sealed chamber.

Not content with the connector's status as the weak link in the signal chain, W.L. Gore & Associates of Newark, De. introduced a coaxial connector-and-cable assembly in which the connectors as well as the cable were shielded, preventing signal loss of as much as 30 percent. In addition, the connector assembly featured a four-beam contact, providing more surface area than the standard two-beam contact. In 1992 AMP Inc. introduced a hybrid called the Active Eurocard Connector. This high speed connector featured a small printed circuit board on which microchips could be placed, freeing motherboard space. The design was said to allow space to be utilized more efficiently and to dramatically increase bus speed. Highly controlled impedance was a feature of all these high-density connectors.

Providing standards for the vast number of new technologies remained a problem going into the mid-1990s, although some manufacturers preferred proprietary standards, forcing customers to purchase many different components from one source. A trend of working closely with suppliers to develop customized connectors developed in the 1990s, which was expected to provide somewhat higher profit margins.

INDUSTRY INFORMATION SOURCES

"AMP," *Machine Design,* November 26, 1993.

"AMP Inc.: Fourth-Quarter Net Rose Despite International Woes," *Wall Street Journal,* January 27, 1994.

Avery, Susan, "Interconnects May Get Rise Out of Buyers," *Purchasing,* April 2, 1992.

Barrett, Amy, "Intimations of Mortality," *FW,* September 18, 1990.

Brothers, J.T., "Historical Development of Component Parts Field," *Proceedings of the I.R.E.,* May 1968.

Byrne, Harlan S., "Molex: Global Connection Protects Its Business," *Barron's,* October 25, 1993.

Byrne, Harlan S., "Augat Inc.: A Confident Bet on Autos," *Barron's,* May 25, 1992.

Coombs, Clyde F., ed., *Printed Circuits Handbook,* New York: McGraw Hill, 1988.

Electronic Components: Gaps in Technology, Paris: Organisation for Economic Cooperation and Development, 1968.

Erdman, Andrew, "Staying Ahead of 800 Competitors," *Fortune,* June 1, 1992.

"Hicks Muse to Acquire Unit of Du Pont for $400 Million Cash, Preferred Stock," *Wall Street Journal,* November 10, 1992.

"Interconnections," *Machine Design,* June 1993.

International Directory of Company Histories, volume 2, Chicago: St. James Press, 1990.

Leventon, William, "Connectors Close the Reliability Gap," *Design News,* December 21, 1992.

Levine, Bernard, "Passive Components Outlook: U.S. on Course; Offshore Adrift," *Electronic News,* January 4, 1993.

Lineback, J. Robert, "Connector Makers Fight a Price Plunge," *Electronic Business Buyer,* January 1994.

McClenahen, John S., "Samtec's European Connection," *Industry Week,* October 4, 1993.

Murray, Charles J., "Hermetic Connector Improves Glovebox Safety," *Design News,* December 16, 1991.

Nordwall, Bruce D., "Companies Reduce Solder to Increase Reliability," *Aviation Week & Space Technology,* December 6, 1993.

Norr, Henry, "SCSI Gets Burned: Apple's New Firewire Technology Promises Faster Connections," *MacUser,* March 1994.

Peppler, Michael, "When 'Less' is More: Epoxyless Fiber-Optic Connectors Can Reduce Premises Cabling Costs Significantly," *Telephone Engineer & Management,* February 1, 1994.

"Shape-Memory Alloys Aid Mil-Spec Connector," *Design News,* January 21, 1991.

"Thermosets Strengthen Undersea Connectors," *Design News,* January 21, 1991.

"Vendors Find Size Challenge in Notebook CPUs," *Electronic News,* October 7, 1991.

—Frederick C. Ingram

SIC 3679

ELECTRONICS COMPONENTS NOT ELSEWHERE CLASSIFIED

The Electronic Components Not Elsewhere Classified Industry is comprised of firms primarily engaged in manufacturing a multitude of miscellaneous electronic devices. Examples of more popular industry offerings include automobile antennas, oscillators, mechanical rectifiers, solenoids, quartz crystals, and electronic switches. For information on semiconductors, resistors, capacitors, connectors, and coils, see related electronic component industries.

INDUSTRY SNAPSHOT

Since its inception in 1883, the electronics industry has emerged as one of the most encompassing and significant industries of the modern era—worldwide equipment sales approached a staggering $600 billion in the early 1990s. Although U.S. electronic component shipments rose rapidly during the 1980s and early 1990s, miscellaneous equipment classified in this industry, which includes many low-tech commodity devices, experienced tepid growth. Industry revenues climbed at a meager pace of less than two percent per year during the 1980s to about $17 billion, not even keeping up with inflation.

Going into the mid-1990s, U.S. miscellaneous electronic component manufacturers were struggling to overcome intense competition from low-cost foreign producers. Makers of many traditional products were also striving to retain market share in the face of increasingly popular solid state components. Nevertheless, rising exports and gains in selected product lines were predicted to allow participants in this industry to maintain growth of two percent per year throughout the decade.

ORGANIZATION AND STRUCTURE

Miscellaneous electronic component manufacturers supply products for five broad areas: communications, such as radios, televisions, and satellite systems; computers and calculators; scientific instruments; military applications, particularly missile and radar systems; and power control and manufacturing equipment, such as machine controllers and industrial robots.

The single largest market for electronic components, not elsewhere classified, in the early 1990s was radio and television transmission equipment producers, which consumed about 14 percent of industry

output. Telephone and telegraph communications equipment makers purchased about 10 percent of shipments, and computer manufacturers represented nine percent of the market.

Other major market segments included: radio and TV receiving equipment (which made up six percent of sales); guided missiles, space, and aircraft components (seven percent); X-ray apparatus (three percent); and individual consumers (five percent). Ten percent of production was exported, and the remainder of output was used in numerous niche markets, such as musical instruments, surgical equipment, children's toys, and surveillance devices.

Products. Most miscellaneous electronic components are used to accomplish or support the primary electronic functions of rectification, amplification, oscillation, and switching and timing. In addition, this industry encompasses several peripheral products, such as headphones and phonograph needles. Finally, some unrelated odds and ends are lumped into this industry, such as hermetic seals for equipment, record cutting styli, and video triggers (except those on remote control devices).

In comparison to the leading edge semiconductors and circuits manufactured in other electronic sectors, the majority of components classified in this industry are low-tech, commodity-like products. The major product groups listed below, for example, were developed during the birth of the electronics industry and remain similar in function to their earliest predecessors. For example rectifiers, which are used to convert alternating current (AC) to direct current (DC), were one of the first electronic components developed.

Piezoelectric devices, like oscillators, are used in clocks, pressure gauges, communications equipment, and other contraptions. They utilize materials, such as slivers of quartz, that can convert high-frequency AC into ultrasonic waves of the same frequency. They can also change a mechanical vibration into an electrical signal. Properly cut quartz crystals, for instance, are used as frequency controls in radios and televisions.

Switches and relays are devices that open and close electronic and electrical circuits. Common switches, which are manually operated, include pushbutton, rotary, slide, and toggle mechanisms. Types of relays, which are triggered electronically, are timing, electromechanical, and reed. Solid state relays are excluded from this industry. Relays are often activated by a solenoid, which is a uniformly wound coil of wire in the form of a cylinder. Passage of DC through the wire creates a magnetic field that moves a metal (usually iron) core that actuates the relay.

Liquid crystal displays (LCDs) represent one of the few high-growth segments of this industry. LCDs combine fluidity characteristic of light oils with the orientation properties of crystals to modify ambient light. LCDs are used in calculators and watches, but are primarily utilized in the production of flat-panel displays for lap-top computers.

BACKGROUND AND DEVELOPMENT

Thomas Edison gave birth to the electronics industry in 1883, 10 years after he invented the light bulb, when he induced electrons to jump from a carbon filament to a metal plate inside a vacuum tube. Edison's discovery was not put into use at the time. Lee De Forest, another American, patented a tube based on Edison's concept in 1906. De Forest's discovery marked the beginning of practical applications in electronics.

Many of the products in the miscellaneous components industry, such as piezoelectric devices, relays, and rectifiers, were developed during the initial stages of the electronics revolution. Wireless communication systems, for example, were pioneered by the British Marconi Company. The National Electric Signaling Company of the U.S. General Electric Company, which was formed by Edison interests, led the development of lighting, phonograph, and other electrical equipment. Later, Westinghouse and the Radio Corporation of America made significant contributions to component advancements.

Intense development efforts during World War I spurred electronic component improvements. Piezoelectricity, for example, had been discovered in 1880. Not until World War I, however, was it applied—piezoelectric devices were used to produce underwater acoustic waves in an early form of submarine-detecting sonar, and later as control devices in radios.

The popularization of the radio after World War I, combined with the proliferation of commercial broadcasting, generated a huge demand by the general public for radio components during the 1920s and 1930s. Although television was invented during the late 1920s and 1930s, World War II delayed the introduction of television broadcasting to the general public. But World War II did spawn huge advancements in new electronic components, such as radar, as electronic research expenditures reached $1.5 billion per year.

Integrated circuits that were introduced in 1958, as well as other advanced semiconductors that were popularized during the 1960s and 1970s, threatened to displace some components that were electromechanical or moved electrons by heat. Instead, these devices served to expand the breadth of the electronics industry, resulting in demand growth for most traditional electronic components.

The proliferation of military electronics, particularly during the Korean War, and of consumer electronics during the 1950s resulted in massive industry expansion. Likewise, the introduction of microwave communications, computers, electronic scientific apparatus, and aerospace equipment during the 1960s and 1970s resulted in huge new markets for all types of switches, rectifiers, piezoelectric devices, and other miscellaneous components. Indeed, as new applications for electronic components mushroomed, industry revenues surged to about $13 billion by the late 1970s.

The 1980s. Demand for all electronic components mushroomed during the 1980s, ramrodded by the global explosion of personal computers and peripherals, telecommunications equipment, and the integration of electronics into a plethora of industrial and consumer products. Worldwide sales of integrated circuits, for example, swelled 464 percent during the decade. U.S. shipment growth of the miscellaneous electronic components in this classification, however, stagnated.

As high-tech semiconductors encroached upon their market share, manufacturers of miscellaneous components realized aggregate expansion of only two percent per year throughout the 1980s, not even keeping up with inflation or increases in materials costs. The industry fared better than many analysts had predicted it would, though, in the face of falling prices and fierce foreign competition from low-cost producers. Industry revenues surged as high as $19 billion in 1984, but then waffled between $15 and $17 billion throughout the remainder of the decade and into the early 1990s.

Realizing that profit opportunities from traditional miscellaneous components were dwindling, many U.S. manufacturers simply abandoned the industry or switched their emphasis to related growing segments of the electronics industry. Other producers maintained profitability through vast manufacturing productivity gains. Importantly, many makers of traditional components maintained a resilient market presence by developing and introducing miniaturized products with greater reliability.

The dominant feature of this industry during the 1980s, which reflected the three trends above, was consolidation. In an effort to maximize efficiency, take advantage of new manufacturing processes, and increase capital, companies rapidly merged with or acquired their competitors. In fact, the number of industry participants plummeted from over 3,700 in the early 1980s to less than 2,500 by the late 1980s.

CURRENT CONDITIONS

Miscellaneous electronic component producers enjoyed encouraging revenue gains of between three and five percent per year between 1988 and 1990. Economic recess caught up with the industry in 1991, however, when sales rose a tepid 2.2 percent. Shipments of filter devices, for example, increased 2.2 percent, as did piezoelectric components. Sales of piezoelectric mechanisms, though, had fallen dramatically from a peak of $295 million in 1987 to about $238 million in 1991. Bucking analysts predictions, relay sales declined only 2.7 percent in 1991, to $495 million, as solid state devices encroached on their market dominance.

As domestic sales of miscellaneous devices continued to sputter in the early 1990s, manufacturers were increasingly looking to exports to buoy thinning profit margins. Export growth had been consistently strong since 1989, and cross-border sales had grown to more than $2 billion by the early 1990s. The strongest export markets were Canada, Mexico, Japan, and the U.K. The largest importers to the U.S., which were increasingly grasping domestic market share, were Japan, Taiwan, Singapore, Mexico, and Canada. Japan dominated U.S. miscellaneous component imports with a staggering 53 percent share.

Going into the mid-1990s, economic recovery in the U.S. and abroad was expected to boost worldwide demand for passive components, which also includes some items outside of this industry. Sales were forecast to surge 10 percent in 1993, though U.S. shipment growth was projected at a modest four percent. Although integrated circuits and other advanced devices will continue to cannibalize miscellaneous component market share, slow expansion through the mid-1990s will be fueled by strengthening computer, telecommunications, and automotive industries.

Exports will offer growth opportunities, as well, boosted by the weak dollar and the passage of the North American Free Trade Agreement (NAFTA) in 1994. Imports, though, may rise significantly as U.S. manufacturers move production to low-cost production regions, particularly Mexico and the Pacific Rim.

One Company's Response. In 1989, Oak Industries, Inc. of Massachusetts, implemented a major restructuring in an effort to shore up shrinking profits and growth. Oak divested its cable box business, dumped entertainment investments, and focused its resources on its core businesses of controls, solenoids,

and switches. It slashed its work force by 25 percent (to 1,500) and cut its corporate staff to 22 from 47. Oak also acquired components-maker Gilbert Engineering Co. to help it attain an advantage over smaller industrial controls producers. In 1991, Oak Industries was ranked twenty-fourth by revenues. By 1993, the company had more than doubled its sales per employee and had boosted annual revenues to over $200 million.

INDUSTRY LEADERS

Because of the breadth and diversity of its offerings, the miscellaneous electronic component industry is still fragmented, despite consolidation. Over 2,000 firms participated going into the mid-1990s. Even most of the top 75 firms in the industry had less than $100 million in sales in the early 1990s, and fewer than 1,000 workers. Some companies, such as FEI Microwave, Inc. and Electro-Scan, Inc., specialize in producing a few niche proprietary products. Companies like Texas Instruments and Motorola, which are primarily engaged in producing products in other electronics segments, manufacture miscellaneous components to support other product lines. Other companies produce high-volume commodity components for sale to other manufacturers, like auto makers and appliance manufacturers.

The largest U.S. manufacturer of electronic components, not elsewhere classified, in the early 1990s was the Harris Corporation of Florida. Harris generated 1991 revenues of more than $3 billion from its diversified operations, and employed 33,400 workers. Ford Motor Company was the second largest component manufacturer in the early 1990s. It produced huge quantities of antennas, radio components, and devices which utilized miscellaneous electronic components. Other major manufacturers included General Instrument Corp. of Alabama (with 1991 sales of $1.4 billion from all operations), SCI Systems of New York ($1.2 billion), and Magnavox Government of Indiana ($620 million).

WORK FORCE

Industry employment peaked in 1984 at 243,000. Productivity gains, company consolidation, and the movement of some manufacturing activities outside the U.S. contributed to significant work force reductions after that year, though. Employment plummeted to about 160,000 by the late 1980s, a decline of about 35 percent, and was stable going into the early 1990s.

Despite shipment growth, production jobs in the overall electronic components industry was forecast to fall considerably between 1990 and 2005, according to the Bureau of Labor Statistics. Past trends indicated that sales of miscellaneous components would decline at a much faster rate, however. Jobs for electrical assemblers, which comprise a leading 20 percent of the overall electronic component work force, will likely decline by about 40 percent by 2005. However, employment prospects for management and sales professionals and engineers were less discouraging.

RESEARCH AND TECHNOLOGY

The most rapid technological advancements in the electronic components industry were occurring in integrated circuit and advanced semiconductor sectors. However, some producers of traditional miscellaneous components were striving to combat high-tech components with improved devices of their own. Smaller and more dependable relays, for example, had allowed electromechanical relay manufacturers to maintain a 96 percent share of that market, despite jumps in solid state relay sales in the early 1990s.

Some segments of the miscellaneous component industry were experiencing pivotal breakthroughs. For example, U.S. manufacturers were racing to establish a presence in the swelling global LCD industry, of which Japan controlled an impressive 95 percent. In 1994, new U.S., European, and Israeli joint ventures planned to begin shipping LCDs that could compete with advanced Japanese flat-panel products. Despite their domination of LCD markets, however, Japanese LCD manufacturers continued to improve their products and cut production costs, and planned to introduce several lines of improved LCDs in 1994. In contrast to most other miscellaneous electronic components, worldwide LCD sales were forecast to jump 25 percent in both 1994 and 1995, from $4.3 billion in 1993.

INDUSTRY INFORMATION SOURCES

1993 Britannica Book of the Year, Chicago: Encyclopedia Britannica, Inc., 1993.

Burrows, Peter, ''Back to Basics Strategy Revives Control Maker Oak Industries,'' *Electronic Business*, March 1993.

Darnay, Arsen J., and Marlita A. Reddy, eds., *Market Share Reporter: An Annual Compilation of Reported Market Share Data on Companies, Products, and Services, 1993*, Detroit: Gale Research Inc., 1993.

Darnay, Arsen J., ed., *Manufacturing USA; Industry Analyses, Statistics, and Leading Companies*, Detroit: Gale Research Inc., 1993.

Gross, Neil, ''Japan's Liquid-Crystal Gold Rush,'' *Business Week*, January 17, 1994.

Lineback, J. Robert, ''LCD Glut Doesn't Scare New Players,'' *Electronic Business Buyer*, December 1993.

Standard & Poor's Industry Surveys, New York: Standard & Poor's Corporation, December 31, 1993.

Tessler, Franklin N., ''Input Alternatives,'' *Macworld*, June 1992.

U.S. Industrial Outlook 1993, Washington, D.C.: U.S. Department of Commerce, June 10, 1993.

—Dave Mote

SIC 3691

STORAGE BATTERIES

This category is comprised of establishments primarily engaged in manufacturing storage batteries, including alkaline cell storage batteries, rechargeable batteries, lead acid storage batteries, nickel cadmium storage batteries, and other types of storage batteries.

INDUSTRY SNAPSHOT

The storage battery industry is driven by industry needs for small, long-lasting, cost-effective storage, or rechargeable, batteries. Batteries have been named as the limiting factor in the design of products ranging from laptop computers to electric automobiles. They are important in supplying starting and lighting power for conventionally-fueled vehicles, supplying emergency power for various applications, for load-leveling or supplying additional power during peak demand as part of electrical utility systems, and as a supplement to solar, wave, or wind power. Uninterruptable power supply systems, usually designed to combat drops in power for personal computers (PCs), have created a new market for storage batteries. In all of these applications, the main feature of the storage battery is that it can retain energy supplied from an external electrical charge, whereas the electrochemical reaction within primary batteries cannot be reversed.

ORGANIZATION AND STRUCTURE

Approximately 50 major U.S. establishments competed in the storage battery industry in 1990. Smaller shops abounded—5,000 by one estimate. Regional producers accounted for about 13 percent of sales of automotive and specialized storage batteries. The overall market was dominated by very large primary battery manufacturers such as Duracell International, Eveready Battery Co., and Rayovac Corp., and by companies specializing in SLI (starting, lighting, and ignition) and industrial storage batteries, such as Exide Corp. and Gates Energy Products. These latter companies have gained market share through acquisitions of related manufacturers since the earliest days of the industry.

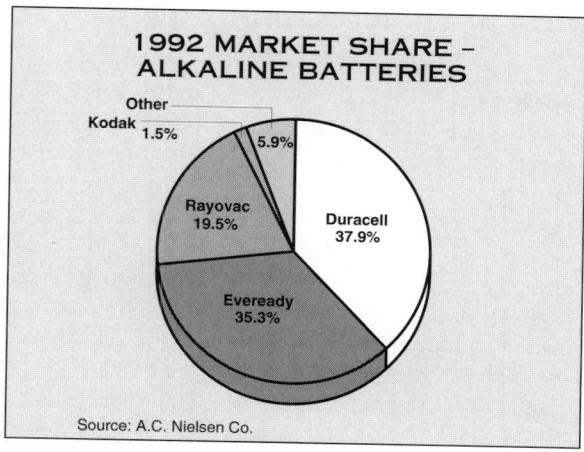

1992 MARKET SHARE –
ALKALINE BATTERIES

Other
Kodak 1.5%   5.9%
Rayovac 19.5%
Duracell 37.9%
Eveready 35.3%

Source: A.C. Nielsen Co.

BACKGROUND AND DEVELOPMENT

Credit for the invention of the first true storage battery has been given to Gaston Planté for a lead-acid battery he developed in 1859. It was made of two coiled lead strips separated by a cloth. However, his storage battery required charging by primary cells, a process taking months to years. The introduction of the French ''Faure Electric Accumulator'' two decades later generated excitement in continental Europe, Great Britain, and the United States. It was conceived that the devices would be delivered to homes and businesses daily, like milk deliveries. Demand for electric, rather than gas, streetlights was strong from the beginning, and electrical lighting in the home gradually became a status symbol. However, similar designs of batteries patented by Faure, a Frenchman, and Charles Brush, an American, resulted in patent litigation which paralyzed American storage battery manufacturers for four years.

Electricity was not readily available on a large scale until the 1880s. This gave impetus to the development of storage batteries, used for over thirty-five years while alternating current systems were being developed and perfected. The batteries used were large enough to power over two million homes for an hour. Although AC power began to carry more of the load, storage batteries continued to be used in the operation of electrical switches in the power networks. The appearance of ''horseless carriages'' in the 1890s also fueled demand for storage batteries.

In the early days of the automobile, storage batteries were seriously considered as an alternative to horses and internal combustion engines. Storage batteries had powered racing horseless carriages and electric cabs. However, the batteries could not compete in long distance travel and their use declined with an increase in better roads. However, they continued to be well-suited for town travel; gasoline vehicles of the day had to be hand-cranked, a risky prospect. Storage batteries helped provide a solution for this difficulty, thereby relegating the electric passenger car to obsolescence. The first automobile to use an electric starter as standard equipment was the 1912 Cadillac.

The use of electric street trucks continued into the 1930s. By this time, storage batteries had powered household appliances, boats, and the first submarines. In World War II they also powered torpedoes, aircraft radios, and commercial broadcast stations. They were also used to power local telephone exchanges and intercontinental repeater stations. Storage batteries excelled in other industrial uses, such as powering electric shuttles in mines and battery-powered trains, which became quite popular in Germany. Golf carts provided an important market for the batteries as well.

CURRENT CONDITIONS

The market for automotive, commercial, and industrial storage batteries had long been considered mature and highly competitive by the 1990s. This competition drove many smaller manufacturers out of business as prices fell because of excess capacity. Successful producers of these types of batteries sought to maximize economies of scale. Replacement batteries made up over 80 percent of the automotive battery market. An emphasis on technological improvement was most evident with suppliers for military and space programs, electric vehicles, laptop computers and cellular phones, and power management accessories.

Environmental legislation has forced carmakers to develop electric vehicles. Laws were introduced in California for carmakers selling over 30,000 units annually that would require that at least two percent of sales to consist of totally emissionless vehicles. The limiting factor in efforts to create such vehicles was the creation of storage batteries that were light and powerful, yet cost effective. Recycling efforts were another important theme in the storage battery industry, as many metals (e.g. cadmium) used posed health and environmental risks. The recycled metals also form an important part of commodity supplies, particularly recovered lead.

INDUSTRY LEADERS

Notable storage battery companies include Duracell International Inc., the largest U.S. storage battery company, with $1.6 billion in sales and 8,000 employees. Eveready Battery Co. (owned by Ralston-Purina) was second with sales of $1.5 billion, and Rayovac Corp., with sales of $520 million, was the third largest manufacturer in America.

WORK FORCE

The top 500 industry competitors employed about 60,000 workers in the early 1990s. In 1994 Exide employed 1,501 salaried employees and 3,791 hourly employees. It reported that 40 percent of its salaried employees were engaged in sales, service, and marketing, and 30 percent were engaged in engineering and manufacturing. Of its hourly employees, 32 percent were represented by unions, with whom the company claimed good relations.

AMERICA AND THE WORLD

Japan has been slow to embrace the electric car, perhaps because its environmental lobbies have lacked the clout of those in the United States and Europe. Great Britain and Germany have generally embraced battery-powered vehicles. However, in 1991 three production models and twelve prototype designs were displayed by Japanese manufacturers at the Tokyo Motor Show, though the number of these vehicles on the road remained negligible. In the same year, Japan's Ministry of International Trade & Industry called for 200,000 electric cars to be on the roads of Japan by the end of the century, promoting its vision with low-interest loans and tax discounts for buyers of the vehicles.

Japan Storage Battery, Tokyo Electric Power (Tepco), and Nissan formed a coalition in the early 1990s to produce a workable electric car system. Japan Storage Battery and Nissan worked together to research an electrical equivalent of the "fuel pump," a high-current device for partially recharging batteries in a few minutes. Most electric car batteries must be charged overnight. Tepco planned to install 12 of these rapid chargers in Tokyo to service its fleet of 45 service vehicles. Kansai Electric Power of Osaka had also been in partnership with Japan Storage Battery. Japan Storage Battery has also sponsored recycling collection efforts for nicad batteries.

In 1992, total production of storage batteries in Japan was valued at Y357.2 million. Lead storage batteries (manufactured by Yuasa, Japan Storage Battery Co., Matsushita Storage Battery, and others) accounted for Y207.4 million; alkaline types, Y149.7 million (Sanyo Battery Co. and Matsushita control over 90 percent of Japan's nicad market). Industrial sales were down 5.7 percent from 1991 to Y44.5 million; automotive batteries were down 8.0 percent to 13.0 million pieces; 11.4 million replacement batteries were sold (down 2.1 percent), and 2.0 million were exported. Storage batteries for consumer electronics fell 6.3 percent to Y168.3 million.

RESEARCH AND TECHNOLOGY

Most SLI batteries have been of the lead-acid variety developed in the late 19th century. They are an excellent potential power supply for other applications because of their low cost and availability. They are also easy to recycle. Specialized military and aviation-related applications have called for nickel-cadmium cells, which were popularized through portable radios and other consumer devices. Their cost remained prohibitive for automotive use, however, due to the high cost of cadmium compared to lead—a nicad cell for a car cost $11,400 in 1991. Nickel-cadmium cells accounted for seven percent of total battery sales in the West in the 1980s and 82 percent of alkaline secondary battery sales. As used in vehicles, they offer somewhat higher performance than lead-acid batteries but are equally as heavy and much more difficult to recycle.

A similar type of battery to the nickel-cadmium, the iron-nickel oxide alkaline battery, was invented by Thomas Edison and patented in the United States in 1901—the same year as Jungner's nickel-cadmium battery. Due to poor performance, the iron-nickel oxide batteries did not meet with the same success of the Nicads.

Nickel hydrogen batteries have been introduced as an alternative to nicads. They possess a greater capacity and boast environmental benefits since they do not contain cadmium. Sanyo Electric has been the leader in developing and producing these cells, used in portable telephones, laptop computers, and camcorders, in the early 1990s. Other types of secondary cells invented at the end of the 19th century included those utilizing zinc as an electrode. These have been used in satellites, military aircraft, submarines, and assorted military equipment. On satellites, they have generally been used in conjunction with solar power.

Nickel-metal-hydrides (NiMH) batteries showed great promise in the 1990s for applications involving laptop computers. But nickel-cadmium and nickel-metal-hydride (NiMH) batteries deteriorate if they are overcharged. A strategy to combat this has been to install integrated circuits capable of monitoring battery voltage, charge/discharge current, and cell case temperature. The goal in the mid-1990s was to recharge a typical laptop battery in 15 minutes. Toshiba Battery Co. planned to market nickel-hydrogen storage batteries in cooperation with Duracell Inc. and Valta Battery A.G., a German company.

Sony introduced a lithium ion secondary storage battery for use in portable telephones and camcorders. It featured twice the capacity of a hydrogen storage cell and one-third the weight. An innovation among consumer battery manufacturers was announced by Rayovac in 1993: reusable alkaline batteries, a concept traditionally thought unworkable. The company claimed its batteries could hold a charge for up to five years, compared to three months for nicads. In 1993, toy manufacturer SLM International introduced a controversial recharger for ordinary alkaline batteries. In 1994, Duracell Inc. announced its Advanced Battery-Pack Interconnect for nickel-metal-hydride connections, which featured an automatic battery contact cleaner and other refinements.

Consumer demand, environmental legislation, and other factors made electric car research a high priority in the last quarter of the 20th century. Electric utility companies supported research in electric cars, partially to encourage the more consistent electricity use that would occur from the vehicles being charged at night, during off-peak hours. Vehicle traction batteries, the kind used to drive vehicles, have been produced in various configurations. Lead-acid batteries were found not to be powerful enough or light enough for the task. However, due to their low cost, availability, and ease of recycling, General Motors chose them for their "Impact" all-electric sports car under development in the 1990s, which, it was claimed, could accelerate from 0 to 100 kph in eight seconds. Zinc-nickel oxide, zinc-chlorine oxide, sodium-sulphur, and lithium-iron sulfide batteries also seemed likely candidates for electric vehicles in the 1990s. The latter two are high-temperature cells requiring pre-heating, and seem best suited for railway or load leveling applications.

Other more complex electric vehicle options included hybrid systems involving a battery in addition to an internal combustion engine. It was hoped that a practical vehicle of this type, not immediately foreseeable by the mid-1990s, would also allow increased efficiency by means such as regenerative braking. Hybrid battery types were also considered, such as a lead-acid battery for acceleration and a zinc-oxide one for cruising.

INDUSTRY INFORMATION SOURCES

Brothers, J.T., "Historical Development of Component Parts Field," *Proceedings of the I.R.E.*, May 1968.

Ferelli, Mark, "Power Protection Plays Its UPS Card," *Computer Technology Review*, June 1992.

Frankel, Doris, "Lead-Acid Batteries Seen as Wave of the Future in Electric Vehicles," *Journal of Commerce and Commercial*, December 13, 1993.

Hooper, Laurence, "A Movable Feast: Power to the People," *Wall Street Journal*, November 16, 1992.

Horwitt, Elisabeth, "Software Checks UPS Pulse," *Computerworld*, June 14, 1993.

Jacobs, Karen J., "Rayovac Corp. Unveils Reusable Alkaline Batteries," *Wall Street Journal*, June 16, 1993.

Johnstone, Bob, "More Power to Electric Cars," *Far Eastern Economic Review*, November 7, 1991.

Kerridge, Brian, "Battery-Management ICs," *EDN*, May 13, 1993.

Levingston, Stephen E., "SLM Seeks Added Spark with Recharger," *Wall Street Journal*, February 8, 1993.

Malinak, David, "NiMH Battery-Pack Interconnect Advances Standardization," *Electronic Design*, December 2, 1993.

Negishi, Shigeru, "Production Figures for the Storage Battery Industry," *Japan 21st*, October 1993.

"New Type of Secondary Storage Battery Draws Attention—a Key Device Following Semiconductors and Panel Displays," *Japan 21st*, October 1993.

Rolph, S. Wyman, *Exide: The Development of an Engineering Idea*, New York: The Newcomen Society in North America, 1951.

Schimpf, Mark, "Portable Power for the 1990s," *Telephony*, August 30, 1993.

Shipman, Alan, "Power Struggle," *International Management*, April 1993.

Sullivan, Kristina B., "Environmental Concerns Linger for Battery Safety," *PC Week*, June 28, 1993.

Vincent, Colin A., Bruno Scrosati, Mario Lazzari, and Franco Bonino, *Modern Batteries: An Introduction to Electrochemical Power Sources*, London: Edward Arnold, 1984.

Wrigley, Al, "Nickel Batteries Seen for Electric Cars, Vans," *American Metal Market*, December 16, 1991.

—Frederick C. Ingram

SIC 3692

PRIMARY BATTERIES, DRY AND WET

This industry covers establishments primarily engaged in manufacturing primary batteries, dry or wet.

INDUSTRY SNAPSHOT

In the early 1990s, demand for primary (i.e., disposable, nonrechargeable) batteries remained healthy owing to the expanding use of portable electronic products. Longer-lasting alkaline batteries, introduced in the 1980s, continued to take the major share of the U.S. retail (household) market, which was growing at a rate of five to eight percent per year. The industry had also met the challenge of producing a mercury-free battery that satisfied environmental concerns. The two major primary battery manufacturers, Duracell and Eveready, were faced with some competition from the rechargeable sector, where significant strides in R&D have been made. Given their relative convenience and low initial cost, however, disposable batteries were expected to remain dominant in the household sector to the year 2000.

ORGANIZATION AND STRUCTURE

Duracell International, Eveready Battery (a division of Ralston-Purina), and Rayovac are considered the "Big Three" of disposable batteries, representing 90 percent or more of U.S. sales. One estimate of market share for 1993 showed Duracell with 43 percent; Eveready, 35 percent; and Rayovac, 13 percent. Other significant participants included Kodak and Panasonic, made by Matsushita of Japan. Both Duracell and Eveready are powerful players in the European and other international markets.

BACKGROUND AND DEVELOPMENT

The first battery was constructed by Alessandro Volta in about 1800. The Leclanché cell, developed by the French engineer Georges Leclanché in 1866, immediately became a commercial success in large sizes because its component materials were easily available. Until fairly recently, however, the major use for primary batteries in the home was in flashlights. The strong growth in primary battery sales began to accelerate in the 1950s, with expanding demand for transistor radios. The continuing introduction of new electronic products (including boom boxes, toys, and cameras) and the increasing desire for portability has fueled the growth in sales for primary batteries. Zinc chloride batteries, which are similar to Leclanché cells, but produce more energy, were dominant in the U.S. market in the 1970s and the early 1980s, when longer-lasting alkalines began to overtake them. According to one estimate, alkaline batteries accounted for 82 percent of the U.S. consumer battery market in 1993.

Other important primary batteries include silver oxide-zinc cells, which are used in watches, hearing aids, and cameras. Lithium cells have attracted the most research in recent years; they are particularly suited for such applications as personal paging systems, heart pacers, and automated cameras.

CURRENT CONDITIONS

In the early 1990s, annual household battery sales in the United States totaled approximately 2.7 billion units, representing a $3 billion plus market. The great majority of these sales—some 90 to 94 percent—were primary batteries (also known as single-use batteries, disposables, or throwaways). According to one estimate, portable/audio applications accounted for 40 percent of all purchases; toys/games, 21 percent; flashlights, 17 percent; photo, 12 percent; and miscellaneous, 10 percent.

While disposables remained dominant, however, sales of rechargeables were expanding at a faster pace—perhaps twice as fast. The increasing popularity of the rechargeables stems from several developments. First, compared with the first rechargeables introduced in the 1960s, the new offerings were less expensive and could hold their charge for a much longer time. Proponents of rechargeables also emphasized the environmental benefits of a cell that could be used over and over and contained no mercury.

A variety of new technologies benefitted the rechargeable makers, as well. Notably, in 1993, Rayovac introduced a rechargeable alkaline battery, named Renewal, in the standard AAA, AA, C, and D sizes, putting it in direct competition with disposable alkaline products. The company said that its Renewal batteries would last up to three times longer than fully charged nickel cadmium batteries and could be reused at least 25 times. In the same year, SLM International, a maker of toys and sporting goods, announced that it would market the first recharger that would be safe for both alkaline and rechargeable nickel cadmium batteries. The company said its Buddy L. Charger could simultaneously recharge up to four alkaline or nickel cadmium batteries from any manufacturer.

Nevertheless, most observers did not believe that throwaways would soon be obsolete, or even lose their dominant position in the market. The initial investment in rechargeables was still considerable: for example, the Renewal brand initially sold for $5 to $6 per pack, plus $15 to $30 for the power station to recharge them. Many consumers will still prefer the convenience of throwaways, even if they could ultimately save a few dollars by consistently using rechargeables. Some of the supposed environmental benefits of rechargeables were also open to question, since primary batteries, while numerous, represented less than one percent of all municipal solid waste. Battery makers are making additional efforts to cut their waste products: Panasonic, for example, designed new packaging for its batteries that was made of high-density polyethylene and was therefore recyclable through 6,000 service centers nationwide.

Another argument for rechargeables had been that the throwaways contained relatively high levels of mercury, which is said to damage the nervous system and increase the risk of cancer when ingested in even small quantities. As of 1992, six states had passed laws requiring that all batteries be "mercury-free" by 1996; at least 20 others had similar legislation pending. Such laws soon became moot, however. The major producers had been working on eliminating mercury from their offerings for some time, and nearly all the major brands quickly fell within the allowed limits. While some producers remained skeptical that so-called green marketing would actually help sales, the industry recognized that a mercury-free product was necessary to compete at all.

The Big Three battle fiercely for the consumer's dollar, especially at Christmas time, when batteries are needed for toys, games, and other electronic gifts. Indeed, some 35 to 40 percent of all household battery sales are made in the final quarter of the year. To distinguish their brands and maintain or expand share, the major firms spend huge sums on advertising: in 1993, outlays for their fall campaigns were estimated at over $90 million. Commercials like those featuring Eveready's Energizer Bunny have thus become familiar to millions of Americans.

Besides struggling to gain the consumer's attention, the companies also jockey for shelf space in consumer outlets (particularly near the checkout counter, where last-minute purchases are made). Indeed, Duracell has attributed much of its growth to increased distribution at mass merchandisers and warehouse clubs. The manufacturers walk a fine line as they try to woo new distributors without offending old ones. Safeway, the large supermarket chain, stopped carrying Eveready batteries in 1992, explaining that the battery maker was giving special price breaks to the warehouse clubs.

INDUSTRY LEADERS

According to some estimates, Duracell is the world's leading producer of alkaline batteries, which represented 82 percent of its fiscal 1993 (ended June 30) sales. All of its batteries are marketed under the Duracell trademark. Duracell's packaging is distinguished by the Copper Top tester, introduced in 1991, which allows consumers to test the strength of their batteries. Duracell is also a leading producer of lithium batteries for consumer applications and zinc air batteries, most of which are so-called button cells, which are used in hearing aids and medical equipment.

In 1988, a leveraged buyout (LBO) led by Kohlberg Kravis Roberts (KKR) took Duracell private. While leveraged buyouts have come under attack for weakening strong companies by saddling them with debt, Duracell's LBO has been generally judged a success. The company completed an initial public

offering in 1991 that reduced its $1.6 billion of debt by one-third, and it once again became profitable in fiscal 1992. While some sales growth continued to come from the U.S. market, the company was looking to develop overseas markets for additional revenue increases. Sales of its Other International Markets segment, which includes operations in Latin America, the Pacific Rim, the Middle East, and Africa, rose at more than twice the rate of its traditional U.S. and European markets. About 40 percent of the company's earnings came from outside the United States.

Eveready is one of the oldest battery companies, with origins in the nineteenth century. Eveready was sold by Union Carbide in 1986 to Ralston-Purina, which also markets pet foods (e.g., Purina Cat Chow), bakery goods (e.g., Hostess Twinkies), and other consumer and agricultural products. Eveready manufactures a full-line of battery products in five categories: alkaline, carbon zinc, miniature, and rechargeable batteries, and certain lighting devices. It operates 46 plants and markets its products in over 160 countries. Eveready has significantly enhanced its European operations by buying Paris-based Mazda-Wonder in 1989; Madrid-based Tudor in 1992; and, also in 1992, Ever Ready of the United Kingdom (from which it had been separated decades earlier). The company markets its products principally under the trademarks Eveready and Energizer.

In fiscal 1993 ended September 30, Ralston's battery sales totaled about $2 billion, or about 25 percent of total revenue. Worldwide battery revenue was up 10 percent, while alkaline sales rose 14 percent. During the year the company also completed implementation of its zero-mercury alkaline program and introduced an AA lithium battery.

AMERICA AND THE WORLD

The widespread diffusion of portable electronic products in Europe has, as in the U.S., been accompanied by strong sales of batteries to operate them. Demand for the smaller AAA and AA batteries has outstripped that for C and D cells, and now accounts for two-thirds of sales. There has been a similar move toward more-powerful alkaline batteries from zinc-chloride cells, partly due to the marketing efforts of Duracell. According to one estimate, by 1992 alkalines had captured 58 percent of the consumer market in France; 54 percent in Italy; 53 percent in the U.K.; 46 percent in Germany; and 25 percent in the rest of Europe. Duracell controls about half of the European alkaline market, but Eveready provided substantial competition after purchasing several European makers. Varta of Germany is the only European brand that has managed to maintain its lead in its home market. Panasonic and Rayovac, though small players, have nonetheless managed to record steady sales increases in this market, as well.

Rechargeables have been gaining some ground in Europe, but in 1993 they still only accounted for about two percent of consumer sales; one forecast showed their share rising to about five percent by the end of the century. Lithium cells are also appearing in the primary market. Eveready markets its AA product and Panasonic and Kodak offer three and nine-volt lithium cells for cameras. Like America, the EC has enacted environmental legislation that has had the effect of nearly eliminating sales of mercury batteries.

In 1993, annual consumer battery sales in the United Kingdom were running at a $500 million plus level. In the 1970s, Ever Ready owned most of the market, but Duracell became the leader in the 1980s as its alkaline brands recorded growth rates of more than 20 percent per year. Ever Ready had been acquired by the conglomerate Hanson in 1982, which soon sold off the company's operations on the continent to Duracell. In 1992, Hanson sold the rest of Ever Ready to Ralston-Purina, owner of Eveready, and thus the company that had been split years before was, in some sense, reunited. Ralston quickly replaced the lagging Gold Seal alkaline brand with its own Energizer, and began promoting the brand strongly in the hope of becoming a meaningful competitor to well-established Duracell. In August 1993, the British company Kleeneze Group introduced a battery recharger that allowed users to recharge conventional disposables up to 20 times.

Sales of alkaline batteries have risen sharply in Japan, from 276 million units in 1987 to 424 million units in 1991, and were continuing to grow at a rate of about 10 percent per year. Unlike the U.S. and Europe, however, zinc carbon and zinc chloride batteries still account for more than half of the household battery market. Japan also produces large quantities of silver oxide batteries for watches, air button cells for hearing aids and pagers, and lithium batteries for cameras. According to government statistics, Japan produced 4.3 billion primary batteries in 1991, up four percent from the prior year. The growth rate was slightly below the five percent recorded in each of the prior three years, which may have reflected the onset of recession in Japan.

About a third of the batteries produced were exported. Some 37 percent of overseas shipments went to other countries in Asia; Europe and North America each received about 25 percent. As in the U.S. and Europe, Japanese battery makers have successfully completed the transition to no-mercury cells and are in compliance with government regulations.

RESEARCH AND TECHNOLOGY

One major focus of R&D in the early 1990s was the effort to produce mercury-free alkaline batteries. By 1994, researchers had been able to reduce mercury levels that had one time been as high as six to eight percent to merely trace elements. With the goal of mercury-free batteries largely accomplished, manufacturers have been able to concentrate on producing lighter, more powerful and longer-lasting batteries. As electronics makers produced ever-smaller and smarter products, traditional batteries account for an increasing proportion of total weight. Thus, the development of lithium batteries has been emphasized, since these cells have the advantages of extremely high-energy density and long shelf life.

INDUSTRY INFORMATION SOURCES

Duracell Annual Report and 10-K, 1993, Bethel, CT: Duracell, 1993.

Elliott, Stuart, ''The Big Three in Batteries Start Up New Campaigns,'' *The New York Times*, September 29, 1993.

Encyclopedia Britannica, Macropedia 18:393-400, Chicago: Encyclopedia Britannica, 1993.

''Eveready and Konami Join Forces for Promotion,'' *Playthings*, July 1991.

Farnham, Alan, ''What's Sparking Duracell,'' *Fortune*, July 16, 1990.

Ikegami, Akira, ''Primary Batteries Meet Changing Demand of Technology,'' *Business Japan*, January 1991.

Jacobs, Karen, ''Rayovac Corp. Unveils Reusable Alkaline Batteries,'' *Wall Street Journal*, June 16, 1993.

Kavanagh, Michael, ''Duracell Jumps onto Rechargeable Wagon,'' *Marketing*, October 14, 1993.

Lefton, Terry, ''Beating the Green Rap,'' *Adweek's Marketing Week*, January 27, 1992.

Liesse, Julie, ''Batteries Getting Greener,'' *Advertising Age*, February 17, 1992.

Nayyar, Seema, ''Ralston Unit Alienates Retailers,'' *Brandweek*, August 10, 1992.

Oliver, Joyce, ''Duracell CEO Charged Up About His Company,'' *Marketing News*, November 11, 1991.

''Portable Electronics Buoy Market,'' *Supermarket News*, November 8, 1993.

''Recharged,'' *The Economist*, May 2, 1991.

Sasakura, Jun, ''Current Conditions and the Future of Japan's Primary Battery Industry,'' *Japan 21st Century*, January 1993.

Ralston-Purina Annual Report and 10-K, 1993, St. Louis: Ralston-Purina, 1993.

"Rechargeables Take on Primary Battery Market," *HFD*, January 6, 1992.

Shipman, Alan, "Power Struggle," *International Management*, April 1993.

Simmons, Jacqueline, "Rayovac Ads Power Rechargeable Battery," *Wall Street Journal*, December 23, 1993.

Tilsner, Julie, "Duracell Looks Abroad for More Juice," *Business Week*, December 21, 1992.

Toor, Mat, "Energizer: The Birth of a Brand," *Marketing* (U.K.), March 4, 1993.

—Bob Schneider

SIC 3694

ELECTRICAL EQUIPMENT FOR INTERNAL COMBUSTION ENGINES

Establishments primarily engaged in manufacturing electrical equipment for internal combustion engines. Important products of this industry include armatures, starting motors, alternators, and generators for automobiles and aircraft; and ignition apparatus for internal combustion engines, including spark plugs, magnetos, coils, and distributors.

INDUSTRY SNAPSHOT

The automobile electrical-parts sector made a comeback in 1993 as sales of new vehicles approached almost $14 billion. Both the automakers and their industry suppliers got high grades for improvements in quality by consumers who began purchasing an increasing number of American cars.

The movement back to the Big Three—General Motors, Ford, and Chrysler—was key for U.S. electrical equipment producers due to the automakers' reliance upon either their own components divisions or domestic parts-makers to supply the U.S. market. While the Japanese greatly increased procurement from U.S. suppliers during the same period, the cars they marketed in the United States were still less likely to have U.S.-made parts. The trade imbalance in auto parts and the willingness of Japanese automakers to use U.S. suppliers, both in Japan and the United States, became the subjects of heated controversy between the two nations.

Electrical-equipment makers were also trying to adapt to the restructuring of the auto industry. The Big Three were cutting the number of suppliers they dealt with and concentrating their business on a select group of component manufacturers. The automakers were giving these suppliers more responsibility for design and engineering; in turn, suppliers were granted longer contracts, often for the entire life of the model rather than for one or two years. In addition, the Big Three were shedding their non-core parts operations in favor of buying more parts from outside vendors, thereby avoiding the overhead costs for plant and material necessary for in-house manufacture. There was also a movement toward standardization of parts across model lines.

The aftermarket segment of the electrical auto-parts business devoted to repair and maintenance of existing automobiles presented a mixed picture. The tendency of car owners to keep their vehicles longer and the increasing push for tougher auto-emission standards augured well for the future. But longer-lasting and better-made parts also decreased the need for replacements. The long-term trend toward imported vehicles also hurt U.S. suppliers in the aftermarket, since their share of the business for these cars was relatively small. The do-it-yourself (DIY) segment was also hurt by the consumer's wariness of doing any work on the increasingly sophisticated electrical systems in new vehicles.

ORGANIZATION AND STRUCTURE

According to government statistics, sales of electrical equipment for internal combustion engines accounted for about 9 percent of the $100 billion U.S. parts industry in the early 1990s. The industry can essentially be divided into two parts: original equipment manufacturing (OEM) and the automotive aftermarket. OEM manufacturing is for new autos; the aftermarket is for used ones. In both segments, the manufacturers comprise (1) the components groups or affiliates of the large automakers, and (2) independent parts makers, which themselves may be divisions of much larger industrial entities. As Japanese companies took an increasing share of the U.S. market, Japanese-affiliated suppliers began to open local branches; by 1993, almost 300 such companies were located in the United States.

BACKGROUND AND DEVELOPMENT

The application of electronics in automobiles has become increasingly sophisticated since commercial production of the automobile began in the early twentieth century. The first electric starter appeared on a 1912 model and, by the 1930s, six-volt electrical systems were standard. Electrical requirements grew as engines became larger and additional features—for example, radios and multispeed windshield wipers—were added; by the late 1950s, 12-volt systems had replaced six-volt systems as a requirement. In the 1970s, electrical, or transistorized, ignition systems, that required less maintenance and were more reliable than mechanical breaker-point systems, were introduced. In the 1990s, distributorless ignition systems (DIS) were gaining popularity: rather than distributors, they use a small ignition coil for each spark plug. The ignition computer triggers the coils individually, using engine sensors to time the pulses correctly.

CURRENT CONDITIONS

The OEM parts industry, which had been depressed since 1989, began to pick up in 1992 and improved steadily through 1993. New-car and light truck sales were buoyant, rising eight percent to an estimated 13.9 million units, following a 4.5 percent gain in 1992. Moreover, a greater portion of the new vehicles were American, rather than Japanese and German. The Japanese share of the U.S. market fell for the second straight year to 23.1 percent; moreover, the Japanese were far behind in the light trucks category, where sales were expanding rapidly. More American-made cars meant greater demand for American-made starters, alternators, spark plugs, and other electrical equipment in new vehicles.

The improvement in sales of American-made autos reflected both a recovering economy and a perception that the Big Three were producing better quality cars. According to J. D. Power & Associates, in 1987, new owners of American cars reported 50 percent more defects than those who had bought Japanese automobiles; five years later, in 1992, the spread was down to ten percent, and was even less for some models. The strengthening of the Japanese yen gave the Big Three a huge advantage in pricing—as much as $2,500 per vehicle, according to one estimate. The strong yen also gave a boost to domestic auto suppliers, since Japanese makers were eager to avoid high-cost production in their own country. Nevertheless, many American parts-makers were concerned that the transplants were avoiding their commitment to source most of their parts in the United States. They claimed that Japanese automakers overstated the local content in their products, and that the close relationship between Japanese automakers and Japanese suppliers extended across the Pacific, preventing American companies from gaining much-needed business.

The U.S. affiliates of Japanese suppliers were not thriving, however. Indeed, in 1993 there were reports that many of them were in fact losing money because their plants were operating below capacity. Most of these affiliates were still importing some components from Japan, and at a yen/dollar rate of 110:1 that was often not a profitable activity. Moreover, these companies had sometimes set up shop in America under financial plans that called for gaining significant business from the Big Three. While they had some moderate success in wresting business from American companies, gaining greater share would prove difficult, since U.S. suppliers had already bridged the quality gap that had caused the big automakers to look for alternatives. Nevertheless, it was feared that the additional capacity that the Japanese created could act as a drag on profitability for all makers if sales of new vehicles did not remain healthy.

The tremendous financial pressure that the Big Three came under during the early 1990s made them rethink the way they were doing business. They gave their top suppliers greater responsibility for design and engineering. In return for taking on these greater burdens, the supplier received a longer contract—often for the life of the model, rather than one to three years. The automakers, wishing to reduce the number of suppliers they dealt with, began awarding contracts for entire components or subassemblies to so-called Tier 1 suppliers. For example, in its North American operations, Ford reduced the number of suppliers it dealt with from 2,400 in 1980 to 1,400 in 1993, and planned to deal with only 1,000 suppliers by the year 2000 or earlier. The Tier 1 companies gainer the added responsibility of dealing with smaller sub-contractors that had previously provided goods and services directly with the automakers themselves.

Automakers also moved towards the standardization of more parts and components across model lines. Rather than customizing each component for a specific car or truck, the manufacturers planned to use common designs for a variety of models. Electrical components, as examples of parts that consumer don't perceive as distinguishing one model from another, are especially likely candidates for standardization. Suppliers would be able to amortize research and development costs and expenses connected to tooling over larger volumes; they would also be able to reduce the wide variety of low-volume parts in held inventory to satisfy infrequent orders.

For smaller suppliers, however, these trends were more portents of the increasing consolidation in the industry. According to one estimate, the number of auto parts makers in the United States fell from 3,000 to 2,000 during the years 1983 to 1992.

The Big Three also sought to reduce the proportion of auto parts that they manufactured themselves. In the early 1990s, General Motors made about 70 percent of its components; Ford, 45 percent,; and Chrysler, 30 percent. In the effort to increase outsourcing, the Big Three were selling off sections of their parts-making operations. In early 1994, for example, Chrysler sold a large portion of its Acustar parts-making subsidiary to Yamazaki of Japan, including eight plants in Mexico that made electrical wiring systems for cars and trucks. It was the third piece of Acustar that Chrysler had sold in two years; in 1988, it had wanted to sell the entire subsidiary, but reconsidered after the United Auto Workers Union (UAW) protested the proposed sale. Chrysler planned to continue receiving wiring systems from the old plants, however, under a long-term agreement it signed with Yamazaki.

In the aftermarket segment of the industry, business trends were mixed. Consumers continued to hold on to their cars longer; in fact, there was some evidence that the recovery in auto sales in 1992-93 partly stemmed from consumers finally being forced to replace old cars that could no longer be repaired. Registration data for 1992 indicated that the average age of the U.S. automobile had reached the highest level in years. Automobiles in the seven- to eleven-year category represented 28.6 percent of all cars on the road that year, compared with 27.7 percent in 1991 and 26.3 percent in 1990. According to some observers, automobile price increases had far surpassed the rise in consumer incomes, contributing to the trend of keeping the family car longer. The average age of an auto rose from 6.8 years in the mid-'80s to nearly eight years in 1993. If, as was predicted, consumers continued to hold on to their cars longer, overall automobile maintenance and repair expenditures were expected to increase.

The legislative environment has also favored replacement part companies, since tougher emission standards related to the Clean Air Act of 1990 and other environmental legislation acted together to add to consumer demand. California emission standards, considered to be the most stringent in the nation, were adapted in various forms in up to a dozen other states; in all, from one-third to one-half of all registrations in 1992 were covered by tougher environmental standards. Efforts by several states to enhance their emission inspection programs were expected to contribute to improved vehicle-maintenance practices. The Environmental Protection Agency estimates that the 20 percent of all vehicles that fail emission tests are responsible for some 60 percent of all toxic emissions. The cost of bringing them up to required standards was estimated to run into billions of dollars, much of which would flow to parts companies.

It should be emphasized, however, that growth in unit sales in the aftermarket segment continued to be slow throughout the 1980s and into the 1990s. According to one estimate, sales of spark plugs and ignition parts rose only 0.7 percent in 1992. Manufacturers utilized technological advances that allowed them to build parts and components with extended life-expectancies—most electronically driven systems proved to be very reliable and consequently needed less maintenance. Moreover, parts were made of better, longer-lasting materials, a fact which also lengthened the time periods necessary between maintenance or replacement. For some engine parts, quality had so improved that, barring an automobile accident, they would never be replaced during the auto's lifetime. New technologies had superannuated much traditional auto maintenance: few cars needed such items as breaker points, and the annual tune-up had become a relic of the past. On the other hand, as environmental regulations become tougher, older cars might in fact require more tune-ups. While bigger vehicles were beginning to stage a comeback in the 1990s, the movement during the 1970s and early 1980s toward cars with fewer cylinders had significantly reduced spark-plug demand in the industry's aftermarket.

Moreover, the nature of the aftermarket business was changing: the increasing sophistication of the engine's electrical system had made many consumers skeptical of doing work themselves rather than taking their car to a trained mechanic. As systems became more complex, strong technical training became an important factor for professionals and DIYers alike. Some observers also commented that, as in other consumer products, brand loyalty was declining among many auto owners who were more concerned with buying quality parts at a competitive price.

Parts counterfeiting was another challenge for the aftermarket industry. In 1993, the Federal Trade Commission estimated that auto-parts counterfeiting was a $3 billion-a-year business in the United States. General Motors contended that it and it suppliers were losing $1.2 billion annually to counterfeits; among the parts most copied were electronic ignition modules. Although Congress attempted to deal with the problem in 1984 by passing the Trademark Counterfeiting Act, the counterfeiting business continued to thrive.

The incursion of foreign cars into the U.S. auto market also had a negative impact on U.S. parts makers in the aftermarket. According to one 1990 estimate, the average domestic parts manufacturer obtained only ten percent of its sales from parts for imports, even though they accounted for 25 percent or more of vehicles in use. Some professional installers and do-it-yourselfers working on import vehicles continued to feel that, at least in certain applications, it was better to use original-equipment-version (OEV) products than the aftermarket offerings of U.S. parts manufacturers. In addition, some potential DIYers were reluctant to work on their imported vehicles, and thus were more likely to bring their cars to dealer service departments that used OEV parts. Despite this hesitancy, however, since the early 1980s—when sales for imported vehicles accounted for only one percent of revenue— domestic parts-makers have made important strides in supplying the import aftermarket.

Just as the introduction of electronic ignition systems erased demand for points and condensers, the advent of the distributorless ignition system (DIS) has resulted in a shrinking market for distributor caps and rotors. On the other hand, some spark-plug makers predicted that DIS systems would result in more plug sales because their higher voltage requirements would shorten the plug's life. Actually, since the 1970s, sales of spark plugs have stabilized. The introduction of the emission-reducing catalytic converter tended to prolong the life of spark plugs because of its requirement of unleaded fuel. In addition, smaller, four-cylinder engines, which require fewer plugs than their six- and eight-cylinder counterparts, became more prevalent. The spark-plug sector of the industry therefore welcomed the higher sales levels of larger vehicles during the early 1990s, as gas became cheap and plentiful. On the downside, however, the compact engine departments of many recent larger vehicles tend to discourage plug-changing, which some contend now require the abilities of a contortionist.

INDUSTRY LEADERS

General Motors's Automotive Components Group is the top OEM manufacturer in the United States; in 1992, it employed about 180,000 people and had $24 billion in worldwide revenue. The group sold off many of its loss-making units, like most of its Delco Chassis division, and emphasized businesses where it believed it could be globally competitive: ignition and control systems, starting motors, and generators. Many of these products are made by the Delco-Remy division, which pioneered the self-starter, battery ignition, and alternators with internal regulators.

Like General Motors, Ford's components group also took steps to reduce its non-core operations. An important manufacturer of electrical systems, Ford reported worldwide sales of $9 billion in 1992. Nippondenso America, a components company making electrical systems for Toyota and other automakers, was the fifth-largest OEM automotive supplier in 1992.

Many large conglomerates have significant automotive electrical equipment operations; these companies include United Technologies, ITT, Allied-Signal, Rockwell, and Siemens. In 1993, Cooper Industries consolidated its automotive operations in a new company called Cooper Automotive. The company includes both Belden Automotive Wire & Cable and Champion Spark Plug, two leading names in the industry.

One of the largest electrical components companies in the world was founded in 1886 by Robert Bosch, a German engineer. In 1992, the eponymous company had over $12 billion in OEM automotive sales, a little over ten percent of which were in the United States. Bosch has been credited with developing the first electronic fuel-injection system, used on the 1967 Volkswagen. The company as a whole has over 13,000 people working on Research & Development. It is the thirteenth-largest company in Germany and supplies most of the top European makers.

Perhaps the largest company making products almost exclusively for the automotive aftermarket is Echlin. A little less than a third of its $1.8 billion sales in fiscal 1992 came from engine-system parts, distributor coils, ignition coils, electronic voltage regulators, electronic fuel-injection systems, and other such offerings. The company's products are primarily sold as replacement products for use by professional mechanics; OEM sales have amounted to only five percent of total revenue. Echlin performed very well in the early 1990s, doubling its earnings between 1991 and 1993. International sales represent about 32 percent of total revenue.

WORK FORCE

Pay levels in auto-parts manufacturing can vary widely for basically the same type of work. According to one estimate, hourly employees at General Motors cost the company about $42 an hour in 1993, more than double the wage rate for the typical U.S. component manufacturer. The UAW expressed repeated concern over the Big Three's outsourcing plans and has made them a major issue in contract negotiations. Ford threatened to close an in-house fuel injector plant that employed 2,000 workers, but eventually agreed to keep the plant open for the life of the contract. General Motors's outsourcing plans also came under fire, especially in light of the company's moves to sell off entire divisions.

AMERICA AND THE WORLD

While America's trade imbalance with Japan in auto parts made headlines in 1993, it is important to

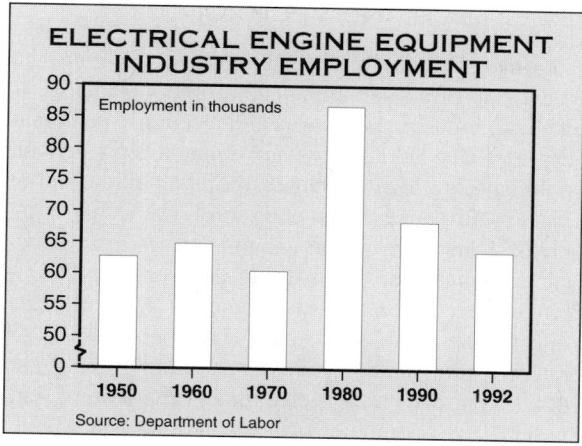

ELECTRICAL ENGINE EQUIPMENT INDUSTRY EMPLOYMENT

Employment in thousands

Source: Department of Labor

recognize that the total deficit in auto parts actually shrunk to $3.7 billion, far below the $14.6 billion recorded in 1989 and the lowest level since 1985. From 1985 to 1993, U.S. exports of automotive parts more than doubled to an estimated $34.4 billion. The surplus in parts trade with Canada was some $8.8 billion, and the trade equation with Mexico was also positive. The North American Free Trade Agreement (NAFTA) passed by Congress in 1993 after much debate was welcomed by both OEM manufacturers and aftermarket suppliers who saw that it would expand their trade opportunities in North America. The passage of the General Agreement on Tariffs and Trade (GATT) was expected to eventually enhance their access to Asian markets now dominated by the Japanese.

In 1994, the long-simmering dispute between the United States and Japan on their trade imbalance became significantly more confrontational. U.S. and Japanese negotiators were unable to conclude a new trade agreement, and soon thereafter President Clinton reinstated Section 301 legislation, which called for a series of steps that would eventually result in much higher tariffs on imported Japanese auto parts. At the heart of the trade dispute was the gross imbalance in auto trade between the two nations. Of the $48 billion trade deficit between the two countries, the auto industry as a whole represented some 60 percent, and a third of that figure, or 20 percent, stemmed from the imbalance in auto parts. The deficit was especially significant in automotive electrical parts, with U.S. imports of spark plugs, ignition coils, starters, and other parts often many times as large as corresponding exports.

By some accounts, however, Japanese auto companies were making significant progress in procuring more parts from American makers. Purchases by Japanese makers from U.S. suppliers for production both in

Japan and in the United States totaled $13 billion in 1992, a 44-percent increase in two years. Toyota purchased about $4.0 billion from U.S. suppliers for its domestic and U.S. factories in the fiscal year ending March 1993, compared with just a little over $1 billion in fiscal 1988. In 1993, General Motors increased its total sales to the Japanese to $600 million, versus $400 million the year before and almost nil in 1986. The Japanese companies were also opening up U.S. technical centers to test U.S.-made parts. In 1990, a U.S.-made part submitted to Toyota went to Japan for testing, a process that could take six months. In 1993, it went to Ann Arbor, Michigan, and the supplier would have the evaluation in less than a week.

While the Japanese were increasing their purchases of American-made auto parts, however, the overall trade deficit in automobiles and parts nonetheless remained huge. Somewhat ironically, the decline in the Japanese share of the U.S. auto market had made matters worse, since much of the anticipated increase in procurement from American suppliers depended on buoyant demand for Japanese autos made in the United States. The strength of the yen does increase the incentive for plants in Japan to buy parts made in America. Critics of Japanese trade practices noted, however, the continuing difficulties that American firms were having in selling parts to these plants: according to one estimate, exports of U.S. parts represented only about one percent of the $100 billion Japanese parts market. They also pointed out that the American-made parts used in factories in Japan tended to be items like carpets, rather than technologically sophisticated parts like electronic controls that represent much of the value of the car.

U.S. parts companies have also argued that much of the "American" parts purchased by Japanese firms for U.S. production were from Japanese-owned suppliers who set up shop in the United States. Indeed, what constituted an American car, or indeed an American company, was a continuing source of controversy with no easy answers. Toyota contended that the Camrys built in the United States are 75-percent domestic content, but Ford believed they were only 50 percent. Of 63 parts-suppliers for the Camry, 32 were U.S.-owned, 14 were U.S.-Japan joint ventures, nine were owned whole or in part by Toyota, five are U.S. operations of a non-Toyota Japanese parent, and three were Canadian- or European-owned.

U.S. parts makers took steps to increase sales to plants in Japan. Ford Motor opened a $16 million electronics research center in Hiroshima that would be staffed by 40 technicians. Hiroshima is the home of Mazda Motors, 25 percent owned by Ford and its major components customer in Japan. The new center was expected to develop and produce engine control units and electronic components. Ford also planned to spend $50 million to build a technical center in Yokohama, near Tokyo, that was scheduled to open in mid-1995. General Motors opened a similar facility in 1991 that increased its component sales 50 percent since start-up. General Motors had the advantage of being on the cutting edge of emissions-control technology, which continued to be much demand as emission standards toughened.

Japanese automakers generally produced only 20 percent to 30 percent of their own parts. There are about 500 principal parts makers, but there are a very large number of secondary and tertiary makers that sell to the principal makers. According to the Japan Auto Parts Industry Association, production of electric parts for engines rose to $9 billion in fiscal 1991 ending March 1992, up 17.5 percent from the prior year. According to Japanese government statistics, total exports of electric parts for internal combustion engines in calendar 1992 amounted to $1.3 billion, up about six percent from the previous year. Like their American counterparts, the Japanese automakers, which were notorious for having numerous varieties of parts in a single model, tried to standardize their parts requirements across model lines and aimed to reduce the total number of part types they used by 20 percent to 45 percent.

Germany has some 3,000 parts makers employing 750,000 people with annual sales of $80 billion. The top 100 account for about four-fifths of all sales. German automakers have lowered the proportion of the car they produce themselves from 40 percent to 35 percent since 1981, but several other European makers make less than 30 percent. Germany's high wage scales and manufacturing costs forced much of its car industry to look at cheaper production facilities overseas. Both BMW and Mercedes-Benz planned to open up plants in the United States during the 1990s, offering greater opportunities to local suppliers. BMW spokesmen said that the vehicles it intended to build at its South Carolina plant would be 80-percent domestic content. While much of the engine may still be made in Germany, ITT won a contract to make copper-intensive ignition switches, multi-function electrical switches, and wiper systems for the plant. Some companies have also moved their production facilities within Europe: Robert Bosch, for example, began producing alternators in Wales and Spain that used to be made in Germany.

RESEARCH AND TECHNOLOGY

The drive to control automotive emissions and reduce air pollution remained a primary challenge for the auto industry as a whole and electronic parts makers in particular. The three government-regulated auto pollutants are hydrocarbon, carbon monoxide, and oxides of nitrogen exhaust emissions. The catalysts that break them down in the exhaust stream must have a carefully balanced chemistry to work properly. Essential to this process is electronically controlled fuel injection and ignition systems with feedback from various sensors. Some makers have tried to provide additional controls through electronic valve-timing, individual cylinder control, and combustion-quality sensors.

Other factors being equal, older cars—especially those with more than 100,000 miles—pollute more than new vehicles because exhaust gases become dirtier as spark timing and other factors begin to vary. The environmental regulations that require ignition designers to build more efficient combustion systems have led them to scrap the traditional rotor-based distributor and use a distributorless, all-electronic ignition system (DIS). General Motors introduced the first DIS in 1984.

DIS systems do away with the small variations in spark timing that develop as the mechanical distributors wear. Misfirings are sensed by the DIS, which compensates by signaling corrections in the fuel/air mixture and in timing, which is controlled by a microprocessor. While DIS eliminates the distributor, it does add one coil for each pair of cylinders. But in cost/benefit terms, improvements in gas mileage and reduced emissions offset the expense of additional coils and semiconductors. In 1992, about 25 percent of the ignition systems in new cars operated without distributors. Many industry observers expected that number to rise to 100 percent within a few years.

INDUSTRY INFORMATION SOURCES

"Aftermarket Megatrends," *Motor Age,* August 1991.

"Along the Pipeline: Cooper Industries," *Ward's Auto World,* August 1992.

"Auto Parts (Replacement) Industry," *Value Line, Ratings & Report,* December 17, 1993.

Aylward, Larry. "Category Still Has Spark," *Aftermarket Business,* June 1, 1993.

Aylward, Larry. "Import Parts Not So Foreign," *Aftermarket Business,* April 1993.

Chappell, Lindsay. "Parts Deficit with Japan Won't Rise or Fall, Study Predicts," *Automotive News,* August 23, 1993.

Chappell, Lindsay. "Transplant Supplier Wave Now Down to a Trickle," *Automotive News,* October 25, 1993.

"Components: Robert Bosch," *Financial World,* April 14, 1992.

"Corporate Profiles: AC-Delco," *Automotive Marketing,* December 1992.

Diem, William R. "New Kids in Town," *Automotive News Insight,* November 23, 1992.

Echlin Inc. Annual Report, Branford, CT: Echlin, 1993.

"Fall & Winter Selling Guide," *Automotive Marketing,* September 1993.

"Ford Seeks Big Share of Japan Parts," *Automotive News,* November 8, 1993.

Frame, Phil. "All the World's a Market for GM Cars," *Automobile News,* July 26, 1993.

Frame, Phil. "GM Units Break with Tradition for Push on Aftermarket Parts," *Automobile News,* October 18, 1993.

Franzreb, John J. "Auto Parts (Replacement) Industry," *Value Line, Reports & Ratings,* December 17, 1993.

Gross, Neil. "How Many Parts Makers Can Stomach the Lopez Diet?" *Business Week,* June 28, 1993.

Gyorki, John. "More Cars Go Distributorless," *Machine Design,* September 12, 1991.

Harmon, Amy. "Auto Supply Companies Face a Rough Road," *Los Angeles Times* August 30, 1992.

Henry, Jim. "'93 Sales Top 13.9 Million, Best since '89," *Automotive News,* January 10, 1994.

"Japan Discovers Openness." *Economist,* October 16, 1993.

"Japanese Parts Purchases Increase," *Automotive Aftermarket,* March 1993.

Johnson, Richard. "Ford Seeks Big Share of Japanese Parts," *Automotive News,* November 8, 1993.

Johnson, Richard. "GM Parts Win an Edge in Japan," *Automotive News,* February 17, 1992.

Katcher, Philip. "Parts Counterfeiting: The Problem that Won't Go Away," *Automotive Marketing,* November 1993.

Kaufman, Edward. "Some Changes in the Import Parts Market," *Automotive Marketing,* August 1991.

Keebler, Jack. "Emissions Balancing Act Gets Electronic Boost," *Automotive News Insight,* November 23, 1992.

Levin, Doron. "Slimming Further, GM Is Selling Delco Units," *New York Times,* September 29, 1993.

"Lots of Mileage Left: Sizing up the Prospects of the Makers of Auto Parts." *Barron's,* May 17, 1993.

"Meeting the Automotive Environmental Challenge," *Business Week,* November 1. 1993.

Montgomery, Leland. "Moment of Truth," *Financial World,* July 21, 1992.

Nauss, Donald. "Japan Shaving the Trade Gap in U.S. Parts," *Los Angeles Times,* May 10, 1993.

"Parts Unit Sale Is Set By Chrysler." *New York Times,* February 24, 1994.

Plumb, Stephen. "Components Shakeout Will Have Big Impact on Suppliers, OEMs," *Ward's Auto World,* July 1993.

Pollack, Andrew. "Ford Chief Says Japanese Still Lag on Parts Purchases," *New York Times,* December 5, 1992.

Pollack, Andrew. "Trade in Auto Parts Favors Japan Despite Gains by the U.S." *New York Times,* July 1, 1993.

Prendgast, Matt. "Troubleshooting & Adjusting DIS Using Standard Tools," *Motor Age,* September 1991.

Robinson, Gail. "Integrated Ignition IGBT Takes Up Less Space," *Design News,* October 4, 1993.

"Sales Benefit from Transition," *Aftermarket Business,* April 1, 1991.

Salomon, R. S. "Profits in Parts," *Forbes,* April 26, 1993.

"Sparking Sales Through Ignition Parts," *Aftermarket Business,* February 1, 1991.

Standard & Poor's Industry Surveys, New York: Standard & Poor's Corporation, 1993.

Suris, Oscar. "BMW Expects U.S.-Made Cars to Have 80% Level of North American Content," *Wall Street Journal,* August 5, 1993.

Suris, Oscar. "GM's Suppliers' Hopes for Better Times Rests on Speech by Lopez's Successor," *Wall Street Journal,* August 6, 1993.

Tanaka, Masato. "Conditions for the Auto Parts Industry in Japan," *Japan 21st Century,* October 1993.

Templeman, John. "How Many Parts Suppliers Can Stomach the Lopez Diet?" *Business Week,* June 28, 1993.

Templin, Neal. "Japan Auto Makers Buy More U.S. Parts," *Wall Street Journal,* August 24, 1993.

"Top 50 Automotive Suppliers to North America," *Automotive News,* April 26, 1993.

Treece, James. "Toyota's Camry: Made in the U.S.—Sort Of," *Business Week,* November 22, 1993.

U.S. Industrial Outlook 1993, Washington DC: U.S. Department of Commerce, 1993.

—Bob Schneider

SIC 3695

MAGNETIC AND OPTICAL RECORDING MEDIA

This classification comprises establishments primarily engaged in manufacturing blank tape, disk, or cassette magnetic or optical recording media for use in recording audio, video, or other signals. Excluded from this classification are establishments primarily engaged in manufacturing blank or recorded records and prerecorded audio tapes, which are included within the scope of **SIC 3652: Prerecorded Records & Tapes.** Also excluded are establishments primarily engaged in manufacturing prepackaged computer software and those establishments manufacturing prerecorded video tape cassettes and disks. The former are classified in **SIC 7372: Prepackaged Software** and the latter are classified in **Industry Group 78: Motion Pictures.**

INDUSTRY SNAPSHOT

The magnetic and optical recording media industry manufactures blank audio and video recording tape, computer tape, and both rigid and floppy computer disks, utilizing either magnetic or optical recording technology. To an extent, the magnetic and optical methods of recording data, images, and sound are competing technologies: the magnetic method offers the user quick retrieval of recorded material, while the optical method benefits those with large storage requirements. Consumers and businesses must chose between the two according to their needs.

Before 1987, the U.S. Census Bureau did not recognize manufacturers of blank audio and video tapes, and floppy and rigid computer disk manufacturers, as composing a distinct industry; instead, these manufacturers were grouped together with manufacturers of such products as phonograph needles, radio headphones, and microwave components. In 1987 the U.S. Census Bureau began separately tracking the recording the industry, which had emerged as a significant force, generating $3.50 billion in revenue and comprising 181 manufacturing companies scattered throughout the United States.

The industry's growth from 1987 to the mid-1990s was remarkable, not in terms of its sales volume—only modest gains were recorded from 1987 to the mid-1990s—but rather, remarkable growth in the form of technological progress. With announcements of improvements in both the production of data storage products and the production of audio and video tape occurring almost monthly during the late 1980s and early 1990s, the industry underwent repeated periods of flux. Predictions for the industry called either for its collapse due to the discovery of a competing technology that would render magnetic and optical recording technology obsolete, or industry forecasts promised a meteoric rise in sales. Rarely did industry observers or participants predict modest gains in revenue or a continuation of the status quo. But in fact, despite the leaps

manufacturers achieved in the technological sophistication of their products, industry-wide sales figures did not enjoy a proportionate increase. To be sure, the bulk of the industry's products experienced between 11 and 13 percent annual growth rates during the early 1990s—an enviable rate of growth for any industry—but when the industry's actual revenue growth was measured against its predicted growth, reality fell short of expectations.

Nevertheless, manufacturers of magnetic and optical recording media were involved in a robust industry in the mid-1990s, poised to garner an appreciable share of the revenue realized from the enormous popularity of home audio and video entertainment and the increasing necessity of computers for both professional and personal needs. Financial success in the industry is predicated on the manufacturer remaining at the forefront of technology, consistently developing new products to stimulate public interest and to meet the increasingly sophisticated demands of audio, video, and computer equipment. It is an industry characterized by frenetically evolving technologies that, some have argued, are still in their nascence. Thus, manufacturers in the industry during the early 1990s were challenged by not only an undetermined future, but often by an undecided present as well.

ORGANIZATION AND STRUCTURE

Approximately 180 companies in the United States were involved in manufacturing magnetic and optical recording media in the early 1990s. In 1990, these companies, many of which owned more than one plant, operated approximately 215 manufacturing establishments in the United States and recorded $4.03 billion in revenue. This sales volume represented an increase of $528 million from the total generated in 1987, the bulk of which was realized in 1990, when aggregate sales increased by nearly $388 million.

The top seven companies, ranked according to sales volume, earned $100 million or more each in annual revenue, while the majority of the industry's manufacturers, approximately 170 of the 180 total companies, garnered under $50 million each in annual sales. The industry leader, BASF Corp., by far outranked its nearest competitor in sales volume, recording $5.4 billion in sales in 1993, compared to the $327 million posted by Komag Inc., the industry's second largest manufacturer.

Of the approximately 215 manufacturing establishments in operation during the early 1990s, less than half employed 20 or more workers. Although this suggests an industry populated by relatively small manufacturing establishments, a truer picture emerges when the average size of all magnetic and optical recording media manufacturing establishments is considered against the average size of manufacturing establishments in all other industries. In the early 1990s, the average manufacturing establishment in the United States employed 54 workers, less than the half the total averaged by the magnetic and optical recording media industry, which employed an average of 118 workers.

In the early 1990s, the greatest geographic concentration of magnetic and optical recording media manufacturing establishments was in California. California, with 76 manufacturing establishments, produced 35 percent of the industry's total shipments, employed 38 percent of the industry's total work force, and generated $1.22 billion in revenue. The second greatest concentration of manufacturing establishments was found in Massachusetts, Maine, and New Hampshire. Together, these states contained 17 manufacturing establishments. Despite the predominance of manufacturing establishments in the Western and Northeastern United States, industry activity was fairly widespread throughout the country, with manufacturing establishments located in 21 states.

BACKGROUND AND DEVELOPMENT

The magnetic and optical recording media industry is a modern phenomenon, its emergence stemming from technological advancements that began following World War II. First came dictating and audio recording machines, which required blank audio tapes. Next, computers and video tape recorders created a need for tape for recording information. As equipment relying on magnetic media became more advanced, magnetic media evolved as well, with improvements in both sound, image, and data recording capabilities occurring alongside advances in the way the tape itself was housed: first on reels, then inside cassettes and cartridges. Eventually, during the 1970s, magnetic recording technology advanced to disks, a response to the advent of personal computers.

Just as the pursuit of better ways to manufacture magnetic media created entirely new forms of magnetic media, the push for progress also led to the discovery of an entirely new method of recording and storing data, images, and sounds: optical recording. Emerging during the 1970s, but experiencing its most appreciable growth during the 1980s, optical recording technology promised to greatly increase recording and storage possibilities for the industry and enrich manufacturers along the way.

The origin of magnetic recording technology dates back more than fifty years before magnetic media became a commercially viable product in the

1950s. The principle of magnetic recording was first developed in 1893 by a Danish inventor named Valdemar Poulsen. Poulsen's encouraging discovery led to the formation of a U.S. company twelve years later called the American Telegraphon Co., organized expressly to manufacture Poulsen's recording machines. This initial attempt to employ magnetic recording technology failed, however, largely because the wire Poulsen's design used tended to become twisted, which produced unsatisfactory and irregular results.

For the next half century, magnetic recording development stood at a relative standstill, at least in the United States. In Germany, however, experiments continued, particularly during the two decades bridging World War I and World War II, when Karl Bauer and A. Nasavischwily designed a machine called the "Magnetophone," a recording machine that used magnetized plastic tape.

Toward the end of World War II, U.S. soldiers discovered the German Magnetophones and brought them back to the United States, recognizing that the German recording machines were capable of much higher fidelity than the wire recorders used in the United States. Once the German tape recorders became the property of the U.S. Government, they were given to the Brush Development Co. to begin production of the far superior tape recorders. Brush Development began marketing tape recorders in 1946, which, obviously, created a need for magnetic tape, a need first filled by Minnesota Mining & Manufacturing (3M) one year later, when the company introduced its Scotch brand magnetic recording tape.

Once 3M began producing magnetic recording tape, formally launching the magnetic media industry in the United States, other manufacturers soon joined the fray. By the end of the decade, three years after 3M began manufacturing magnetic tape, the industry's ranks included four manufacturers, four companies which would lead the industry for roughly the next decade and produce virtually all magnetic tape sold in the United States. These four manufacturers were Reeves Soundcraft Corp., which started producing magnetic tape in 1950, Audio Devices, Inc., Reeves Soundcraft, of Orradio Industries, whose president, Herbert Orr, was one of the military officers who discovered the Magnetophones in Germany, and, finally, the industry's pioneer, 3M.

As these manufacturers entered the 1950s, a decade of exponential growth, the magnetic tape market represented a $500,000 a year business. Although a recent innovation, magnetic tape already had many applications. Initially, its use as instrumentation tape outstripped its sound recording applications, as manufacturers of enormous room-size computers, missiles, satellites, and aircraft purchased magnetic tape to monitor production and performance of their products. The petroleum industry used magnetic tape in geophysical exploration equipment, telephone companies used tape to record toll calls, and a host of diverse industries used magnetic tape in automation equipment. In addition to these instrumentation uses, magnetic tape was also used to record radio programs and was purchased by consumers to use with their audio equipment.

By the mid-1950s, the magnetic tape industry had grown considerably, not in terms of the number of manufacturers producing magnetic tape, for 3M, Audio Devices, Reeves Soundcraft, and Orradio Industries still produced nearly all the tape in the country, but in terms of its sales volume, which had increased nearly 30 fold. From $500,000 in 1950, the industry's annual revenue soared to nearly $15 million by the middle of the decade, largely due to the increasing number of applications for magnetic tape in industrial settings, and also to the growing popularity of home stereo systems and recorders. More than three million home audio units existed at this time and unit sales were increasing by more than 500,000 annually, providing blank audio tape manufacturers with a burgeoning customer base. Music connoisseurs had discovered that magnetic tape offered better sound quality than phonograph records. But perhaps the most significant development during the 1950s occurred in 1957, when Ampex Corporation, a manufacturer of recorders and instrumentation machines and 25 percent owner of Orradio Industries, developed the first practical video tape recorder.

Ampex' discovery would soon ignite demand for blank video tape, an entirely new market for tape manufacturers. While television producers explored the possibilities of taping television programs, the industry demonstrated a robust vitality throughout the late 1950s and early 1960s, growing 35 percent to 40 percent annually in revenue volume. By the mid-1960s, the magnetic tape industry represented a $100 million business, which now included blank video tape as one of its primary products, in addition to audio and instrumentation tape. Television had switched from live to taped broadcasts, creating a nearly insatiable demand for blank video tape, while automobiles outfitted with cassette decks spurred the sales of blank audio tapes. Competition for this lucrative market had intensified since the 1950s: approximately 30 manufacturers now vied for market share, a competition in which 3M still held a commanding lead. Controlling roughly 50 percent of the market during the 1950s, 3M contin-

ued to account for half of the industry's sales during the 1960s, thanks in part to its early lead in both the blank video and audio tape production markets.

Despite the greater number of manufacturers in the industry, its leading companies, with a few exceptions, were the same companies that led the industry in the early 1950s. Reeves Soundcraft still ranked among the industry's top five manufacturers, as did Audio Devices, and, of course, 3M. Ampex Corp., by virtue of its partial ownership of Orradio Industries, and its development of the video recorder, now ranked as the second largest manufacturer, while a relatively new player, Memorex Corporation, had quickly ascended to the industry's upper echelon. Founded in 1961, Memorex was formed by a group of former 3M and Ampex employees, and owed its rise to concentrating on computer tape production, which by now accounted for the largest segment of the magnetic tape market. The lucrative magnetic tape market also attracted much larger manufacturers, such as Radio Corporation of America, and Eastman Kodak, but these companies did not derive enough revenue directly from the manufacture of magnetic tape to rank as industry leaders.

As these manufacturers entered the 1970s, they kept pace with the growing sophistication of audio and video equipment by producing higher quality tape and offering consumers various types of blank tape. In addition to choices in tape length, consumers could now opt for low noise or high noise tape, high energy or low energy tape, or ferri-chrome tape—a selection process many found confusing. This problem would continue to plague manufacturers into the 1990s, but the industry's sales volume swelled nevertheless, climbing to approximately $350 million by the early 1970s.

In 1975, North American Philips Corp., through its subsidiary Magnavox Co., unveiled, in a joint venture with MCA and its subsidiary MCA Disco-Vision Inc., an optical video-disk system for the home. This system employed a light beam rather than a needle or stylus to transmit images and sound from a disk to a television screen. Although it would be several years before optical disk production represented an appreciable portion of industry shipments, the advent of optical media broadened the industry's scope and provided a new breed of competition.

As the industry entered the 1980s, the prospects for further growth were encouraging. Personal desktop computers began to emerge as a popular product, creating a need for magnetic media disks, and the blank video tape market exploded. Blank audio tape, now almost entirely sold in cassette form, also realized exponential growth fueled primarily by the popularity of automobile stereo systems. Consumers continued to be confused by the array of audio tapes from which to choose, a problem now shared by blank video tape manufacturers, who produced tapes for either Beta or VHS video equipment in addition to low-bias and high-bias tape. To combat the confusion, manufacturers began color-coding their products, but assisting consumers in their selection was not of paramount importance during the early 1980s, particularly for blank video tape manufacturers, as the most pressing problem facing consumers was simply locating tape. Blank video tape sales to duplicators, who then sold cassettes of prerecorded programs, were growing as fast as sales to consumers during the early 1980s, creating a shortage of blank tape at the retail level. Capital expansion programs initiated by several large manufacturers aggravated the problem. As manufacturers added production capacity, some facilities had to reduce their output due to the construction, leaving few blank tapes for neighborhood stores. This problem, however, was only temporary and underscored the vitality of the video market. The market continued to expand at an accelerated rate throughout the decade as the sales of video cassette recorders ballooned.

The strong steady growth of the blank audio and video tape markets, however, did not overshadow equally encouraging developments in another segment of the magnetic and optical recording media industry, a segment that promised to greatly increase financial rewards. Several years earlier, in 1973, IBM developed the Winchester computer drive, a magnetic disk housed in an air-tight container. Earlier computer drives were housed in containers that could open and shut to allow the removal of a disk, but the Winchester was permanently sealed in its container, free from dust particles. The air pressure inside the container kept the lightweight recording and writing head a fraction of a millimeter above the spinning disk, enabling the drive that held the head in place to manipulate the magnetic field on the disk's surface with unprecedented precision. The development of the Winchester was a historic event, allowing computer users to store far more data than had been possible with data tape; manufacturers now stood to benefit enormously from the fledgling personal computer market.

As recording media manufacturers charted their course through the remainder of the 1980s, the computer market came to the fore, making the production of computer disks a fiercely contested and lucrative segment of the industry. The increasing number of personal computers spurred the sale of 5.25-inch floppy disks, at first one-sided, then double-sided and high density, and had a matching effect on the sale of

3.5-inch rigid disks, developed after the introduction of 5.25-inch disks. Improvements in optical disk storage by the middle of the decade gave optical systems a decided advantage over magnetic systems for particular tasks, such as searching databases of fingerprints to solve criminal cases, but optical disk storage was unsuitable for many other chores and needed further refinement before gaining widespread usage. In the latter part of the decade, 3.5-inch disks eclipsed 5.25-inch disks as the industry's biggest seller, while the price of personal computers continued a decade-long price decline, causing more and more consumers to become disk consumers.

CURRENT CONDITIONS

The late 1980s and early 1990s witnessed the emergence of several new forms of magnetic and optical recording media. Manufacturers, put in the position of predicting which products would fuel the industry's growth five or ten years into the future, gambled to a certain extent on the development of particular technologies and products, hoping to gain an early lead. Each year new products utilizing innovative technology led some observers to state that advances in optical recording technology would make magnetic media obsolete, while others announced that optical recording technology would never match magnetic media's importance in the industry. Finally, others foresaw a confluence of the two technologies into hybrid products utilizing both magnetic and optical recording technologies.

Against this backdrop, the industry demonstrated vitality, recording enviable growth in the early 1990s despite recessive economic conditions. The high-grade video tape market, which represented 30 percent of the blank video tape market in 1993, grew 12 to 13 percent annually during the early 1990s, while regular grade tape sales demonstrated more robust growth, increasing 20 percent in 1992 despite only a five percent increase in video hardware sales. The trend in video tape production during the early 1990s aped the audio tape trend during the 1980s, as manufacturers sought to increase their market share by producing tapes of greater length. BASF, the industry's leading company in the early 1990s, marketed the first nine-hour video cassette in 1991, then introduced a 10-hour cassette the following year, paving the way for other manufacturers to follow. Although long-length tapes represented a relatively small portion of the video tape market, sales grew steadily in 1993 and early 1994, these tapes increasing their proportional representation in the video tape market.

Although blank video tape sales rose in the early 1990s, this growth did not necessarily translate into increased profits. The retail price of video cassettes plunged during the 1980s, dropping from nearly $25 per cassette in the late 1970s, to below two dollars per cassette by the beginning of the 1990s. Larger manufacturers with financial interests in businesses unrelated to blank video tape production could offset this decline in profit margin with their larger cash reserves and thus gain market share from smaller manufacturers wholly dependent on blank video tape production for revenue. Yet as these larger manufacturers entered the mid-1990s, the decline of video tape prices at the retail level formed a formidable obstacle to future profit growth in the video tape market.

Three new audio recording formats developed in the late 1980s and early 1990s provided a glimpse of the market's future, as the drive for higher quality recording technology spawned Digital Audio Tape (DAT), Digital Compact Cassette (DCC), and Mini-Disc (MD). Each of these products were still in their infancy during the early 1990s, both in terms of consumer product awareness and the manufacturers' marketing efforts, and, consequently, represented only a small part of the blank audio tape market. However, each was predicted to play a more significant role as the decade progressed. DAT was developed to provide sound quality equal to the high quality of compact disks, but on a medium that could record as well as play back. DAT was also adapted for use with computers, proving to be an ideal medium to back up large capacity hard disk drives.

By 1993, nearly every manufacturer participating in the blank audio tape market had plans to market DCC or MD products, roughly a year and a half after BASF became the first independent blank media company to engage in large-scale DCC tape production. MD products entered the market in early 1993 through Sony 's Recording Media division, which, later in the year, adapted the 2.5-inch audio disk for use as computer data storage, much like the adaptation of DAT technology. As the industry entered the mid-1990s, Sony, with its audio MD, and Philips, with its DCC, were pitted against each other in a battle that could likely determine the future success of each product, according to the International Association of Magnetic and Optical Media Manufacturers and Related Industries, the industry's trade organization.

Sales of floppy disks reached a record high in 1992, with more than 1.6 billion units sold. Continuing the trend established during the late 1980s, sales of 5.25-inch disks declined, while sales of 3.5-inch disks increased, accounting for over 64 percent of units sold.

DATs, initially developed for audio play back and recording, emerged as the fastest growing data recording product in the magnetic media market segment, sales projected to quadruple by 1996 from the five million units sold in 1992. The advent of CD-ROM technology created additional optimism for manufacturers in the industry, intensifying the debate between proponents of magnetic media and those predicting the future domination of optical media.

Mounting foreign competition in the global computer disk market, particularly from China, dampened what otherwise were encouraging developments in the early 1990s. With more than 60 factories manufacturing computer disks, China's growing prominence threatened to wrest market share from U.S. manufacturers in an industry already dominated by foreign manufacturers. Although disks made in China were inferior those made in the United States during the mid-1990s, their effect on domestic disk prices was an unpleasant development for U.S. manufacturers.

INDUSTRY LEADERS

Ranked according to sales volume, the three largest manufacturers of magnetic and optical recording media in the early 1990s were BASF Corporation, and Sony Recording Media of America. Together, these companies generated more than six billion dollars in revenue, led by the $5.4 billion recorded by BASF Corporation.

Formed as a U.S. subsidiary of BASF Group, an enormous German conglomerate based in Ludwigshaafen with interests in pharmaceuticals, chemicals, cosmetics, and electronics, BASF Corporation gained prominence in the magnetic and optical recording media industry by pioneering long-length audio and video tapes. Backed by the massive financial resources of its parent corporation, which posted nearly $32 billion dollars in sales in 1993, BASF Corporation was able to withstand the dramatic decline in retail prices of blank video tapes during the 1980s, while smaller manufacturers ceded market share. Another U.S. subsidiary of BASF Group, BASF Information Systems, which operated as a subsidiary of BASF Corporation, ranked as the industry's fourth largest manufacturer, recording $300 million in sales in 1993.

Positioned in between these two subsidiary companies of BASF Group were Komag Inc. and Sony Recording Media of America. Komag, the lone U.S. representative in the industry's top four, posted $327 million in 1993 primarily through the production of thin magnetic films for disk drives. Based in Milpitas, California, Komag unseated Sony Recording Media of America, as the industry's second largest manufacturer in 1993. Sony Recording Media of America, the U.S. subsidiary of Tokyo-based Sony Corporation, generated $300 million in revenue in 1993.

WORK FORCE

In 1990, 24,000 people were employed by the magnetic and optical recording media industry in the United States, representing a decline of 1,300 from the previous year's total and a drop of 1,600 from the total recorded in 1987. Of the 24,000 people employed in 1990, a majority were employed as production workers, a segment of the work force that increased its proportional representation in the industry during the decline in total employment. In 1990, there were 16,100 production workers employed by the industry, while the balance of the industry's work force was composed of 7,900 salaried employees, or those performing managerial, technical, or administrative duties.

Typically, production workers are employed on a full-time basis, but average three percent fewer hours per year than production workers employed by other manufacturing industries. Production workers in the magnetic and optical recording media industry earn more per hour than their counterparts in other manufacturing industries, averaging $10.78 per hour in 1989 compared to the national average of $10.49 per hour. In 1990, the hourly wage for production workers employed by the magnetic and optical recording media industry increased to $11.29, at which time salaried employees averaged $37,644 per year.

Predictions in the early 1990s by the U.S. Bureau of Labor for the future of the industry's work force were generally optimistic, although several occupations were expected to suffer severe declines in their proportional representation. From 1990 to 2005, the number of electronic assemblers and precision electronic equipment assemblers were expected to decline by 40 percent and 41 percent, respectively. Those occupations projected to experience the greatest proportional growth were electronic engineers, salespeople, and electronic technicians, each of which were expected to increase in number by more than 29 percent.

INDUSTRY INFORMATION SOURCES

"BASF Video Promotions Lead the Industry," *Dealerscope Merchandising,* February 1990, p. 48.

"Better-Than-Expected Sales Raise Threat of Blank Videotape Shortages," *Merchandising,* July 1980, p. 87.

"Blank Audio, Videotape Suppliers Set Promos, Debut New Packaging," *Merchandising,* March 1981, p. 52.

Cornell, Christopher, "Kicking Off the New Season," *Dealerscope Merchandising,* January 1993, p. 142.

————, "A Tough Room," *Dealerscope Merchandising,* May 1992, p. 22.

————, "Turn, Turn, Turn," *Dealerscope Merchandising,* November 1992, p. 28.

————, "Twelve DCC Issues Raised at ITA," *Dealerscope Merchandising,* May 1991, p. 32.

————, "A Wake-Up Call," *Dealerscope Merchandising,* April 1993, p. 16.

————, "The Way They See It," *Dealerscope Merchandising,* April 1993, p. 32.

Darney, Arsen J., editor, *Manufacturing USA,* Detroit: Gale Research Inc., 1993.

Endrijonas, Janet, "Magnetic Media Changed Our World in 11 Years," *The Office,* February 1992, p. 20.

Finaly, Douglas, "Optical Disk: Good but Not Dominating," *The Office,* October 1992, p. 18.

Gelfand, Michael, "Blank Tapes: Untangling the Market," *Dealerscope Merchandising,* April 1992, p. 66.

————, "Blank Videotape Update," *Dealerscope Merchandising,* March 1993, p. 70.

Goldston, Terry, "Nowhere to Go but Up," *Dealerscope Merchandising,* November 1990, p. 34.

————, "Unraveling Magnetic Media," *Dealerscope Merchandising,* March 1991, p. 50.

"A Groovy Way of Stretching Computer Memories," *The Economist,* April 25, 1981, p. 99.

Hammer, Richard G., "Magnetic Tape," *Barron's,* July 21, 1958, p. 5.

Harvey, David A., "State of the Media," *Byte,* November 1990, p. 275.

"Heading for $100-Million Year," *Business Week,* February 14, 1959, p. 103.

Kalow, Samuel Jay, "Magnetic Media Still Continues to Innovate," *The Office,* April 1990, p. 79.

Lion, Karina, "DAT's a Solution," *Byte,* November 1990, p. 323.

"The Little Floppies That Could," *Dealerscope Merchandising,* March 1991, p. 44.

"Magnetic Tape - Growth Industry," *Financial World,* March 30, 1966, p. 10.

"A Maturing Market Takes Hold," *Dealerscope Merchandising,* April 1990, p. 39.

Roth, Cliff, "A Day for Crystal Gazing," *Dealerscope Merchandising,* January 1993, p. 118.

Ryan, Bob, "Entering a New Phase," *Byte,* November 1990, p. 289.

————, "The Once and Future King," *Byte,* November 1990, p. 301.

Shidaker, Geoff, "Demise of Low-End Cassette Boosts Premium Tape Sales," *Merchandising Week,* August 19, 1974, p. 3.

"Tape Winds Up for Bigger Role," *Business Week,* July 19, 1958, p. 106.

Tazelbar, Jane Morill, "Magnetic vs. Optical," *Byte,* November 1990, p. 272.

U.S. Bureau of the Census, *Statistical Abstract of the United States: 1993* (113th edition), Washington, DC, 1993.

U.S. Industrial Outlook, Washington, DC: U.S. Department of Commerce, 1994.

—Jeffrey L. Covell

SIC 3699

ELECTRICAL MACHINERY, EQUIPMENT, AND SUPPLIES, NOT ELSEWHERE CLASSIFIED

This classification comprises establishments primarily engaged in manufacturing electrical machinery, equipment, and supplies, not elsewhere classified, including high energy particle acceleration systems and equipment, electronic simulators, appliance and extension cords, bells and chimes, and insect traps.

INDUSTRY SNAPSHOT

Industries classified in the *Standard Industrial Classification Manual* as including products "not elsewhere classified" essentially are comprised of a collection of miscellaneous products that share a broadly defined similarity, but rarely are produced by the same type of manufacturers. These "not elsewhere classified" industries (usually abbreviated as NEC) are created as such to retain the integrity or homogeneity of other industries, which otherwise would become muddled by the inclusion of products that are instead consigned to NEC industries. Consequently, NEC industries frequently include distinctly separate types of manufacturers, competing in entirely different markets, and manufacturing a diverse assortment of products.

SIC 3699: Electrical Machinery, Equipment, and Supplies, Not Elsewhere Classified includes various types of amplifiers, such as magnetic and pulse amplifiers, maser amplifiers, DC amplifiers, and differential and facsimile amplifiers, but excludes audio or video amplifiers. This category also includes various types of particle accelerators (also known as atom smashers), scientific electronic equipment, electronic kits to be assembled by purchaser, and consumer electronic equipment. As the industry entered the 1990s, this segment accounted for roughly 30 percent of the industry's shipments.

The products within the electronic teaching machines, teaching aids, trainers, and simulators category represented approximately 21 percent of the industry's shipments, primarily through the manufacture of electronic trainers and simulators. According to 1987 U.S. census figures, electronic trainers and simulators accounted for $1.11 billion of the $1.16 billion generated by the entire product category, a total largely derived from the manufacture of flight simulators.

The laser systems and equipment, except communication, product category includes laser designator/ranging equipment, laser instrumentation equipment such as laboratory alignment devices and surveying equipment, industrial laser equipment, and medical laser equipment. In the early 1990s, this category accounted for roughly 15 percent of the industry's shipments.

The electrical products, NEC category includes a host of diverse products such as electric gongs, bells, and chimes, electric Christmas tree lighting sets, electric insect killers, automatic garage door openers, electric fence chargers, and electric outboard motors for boats. Automatic garage door openers accounted for the bulk of the industry's shipments within this product category, which represented approximately 13 percent of the industry's shipments.

The apparatus wire and cordage product category includes appliance cords manufactured primarily from purchased insulated wire for various household appliances, including electric irons, grills, and waffle irons. This category accounted for approximately four percent of the industry's shipments.

The smallest product category within the industry, ultrasonic equipment, except for medical and dental use, includes ultrasonic equipment manufactured for industrial applications, such as ultrasonic cleaners, drills, welders, and solderers. This category accounted for roughly one percent of the industry's shipments in the early 1990s.

Although this classification includes a multitude of diverse products the majority of the products that constitute the industry's core businesses were added to its classification in 1987, when **SIC 3699: Electrical Machinery, Equipment, and Supplies, Not Elsewhere Classified** was reclassified. Added to the industry's classification were particle accelerators, flight simulators, laser equipment, and ultrasonic equipment, as well as other, less significant, products. The effect of this reclassification on the industry's revenue total was enormous; in 1986, the miscellaneous electrical equipment and supplies industry represented a $1.76

billion business and the following year, after it was reclassified, it represented a $5.05 billion business.

ORGANIZATION AND STRUCTURE

The miscellaneous electrical equipment and supplies industry became a much more densely populated industry following its reclassification in 1987. Prior to that year, approximately 700 companies in the United States were involved in manufacturing products ascribed to the industry. Once reclassified, the industry's roster nearly doubled to include 1,324 manufacturers and 1,379 individual manufacturing establishments, more than twice as many individual, separate manufacturing establishments in operation the previous year. From 1987 to the beginning of the 1990s, the number of manufacturers in the industry declined, falling to approximately 1,200. The number of individual manufacturing establishments dropped as well, totaling 1,249 in 1990.

During the 1980s, the industry's sales volume rose steadily before and after the reclassification, but realized a greater rate of growth before being reclassified. From 1982 to 1986, aggregate revenue increased nearly 30 percent, more than twice as much as the percentage increase from 1987 to 1990. In 1990, the industry's sales volume reached $5.84 billion, an increase of $792 million from the total recorded in 1987. Individual manufacturing establishments averaged, at the beginning of the 1990s, $4.5 million in annual revenue, slightly more than half of the sales volume generated by the typical manufacturing establishment.

Of the approximately 1,200 manufacturing establishments operating in the industry during the early 1990s, nearly 700 employed less than 20 workers. The typical manufacturing establishment employed 47 workers, half of whom performed managerial, technical, or administrative duties, while the balance of the average establishment's work force consisted of production workers. Compared to the typical manufacturing establishment in the United States, this industry's manufacturing establishments were 12 percent smaller in terms of the number of employees per establishment than the national standard, and employed a greater proportion of salaried employees. In 1989, the typical manufacturing establishment in the United States employed 69 percent of its work force as production workers, while in this industry the typical establishment's work force was virtually evenly divided between production workers and salaried employees.

Geographically, the bulk of the industry's manufacturing activity took place in California, which employed 20 percent of the industry's work force and accounted for 20 percent of the industry's sales volume. With 291 manufacturing establishments, California contained the most manufacturing establishments of any one state, distantly followed by New York, which contained 94 facilities. The third greatest concentration of manufacturing establishments in the early 1990s was found in Texas, although the 84 facilities in Texas accounted for a smaller percentage of the industry's shipments than the 74 located in Florida, which together generated $528 million in sales, or 10 percent of the industry's shipments. Aside from these four states, where the greatest amount of manufacturing activity occurred, production facilities were located throughout the United States by the 1990s, with 29 states containing manufacturing establishments.

BACKGROUND AND DEVELOPMENT

Each product segment composing the miscellaneous electrical machinery and equipment industry possesses a history distinct from the other products grouped into this classification. For the most part, the manufacturers of these disparate product categories have little in common with each other and rarely compete in the same market. Manufacturers of flight simulators, for example, have little in common with manufacturers of automatic garage door openers and compete for market share in entirely different markets. Essentially then, the miscellaneous electrical machinery and equipment industry includes six smaller, subsidiary industries—three of lesser importance and three of greater importance—each of which has experienced different paths of development.

These subsidiary industries do share, however, one common thread; their products depend on electricity and a branch of science and engineering closely related to the science of electronics. Some of the products within the industry rely solely on electricity to operate, but generally these products are of lesser importance to the growth of the industry as a whole. Rather, many of the more important products that contribute significantly to the industry's growth rely on electronic technology, particularly those products added to the industry after the 1987 reclassification. Accordingly, without electrical power and, perhaps more important, without the emergence of electronics, the miscellaneous electrical equipment and supplies industry would not exist.

Before the electrical machinery industry could emerge as representing an appreciable portion of all manufacturing activity in the United States, sufficient electrical power had to be developed. By the beginning of the 20th century enough electrical power was being generated in the United States—2.2 billion kilowatt hours in 1902—to engender the electrical machinery industry as a viable sector of U.S. manufacturing. At this time, the electrical machinery industry accounted for roughly one percent of the total manufacturing activity in the country, a proportion that would increase to 4.5 percent by 1929 and reach 6.6 percent by the beginning of the 1960s. During these six decades of growth, the electrical machinery industry expanded more than six times as rapidly as American industry as a whole, and the level of technological sophistication in the country had increased sufficiently to encourage the production of electronic products in earnest.

In 1907, American inventor Lee DeForest ushered in the electronic age with his development of a three-electrode vacuum tube, which he called an audion, making it possible to amplify weak radio signals and transmit them over long distances, a capability earlier vacuum tubes failed to provide. From this discovery, the world was introduced to the radio, creating a small but lucrative market for a new breed of manufacturer—radio makers. The number of radio manufacturers flourished during the 1920s and 1930s, but their numbers began to dwindle as the United States neared involvement in World War II. Infused with orders from the U.S. government for electronic equipment to aid in the war effort, the electronic industry was buoyed for several years during the war, but at its conclusion the small group of electronics manufacturers still represented only slightly more than a fledgling industry, employing relatively few people, contributing a comparatively small amount to the national economy, and amounting to little more than $500 million at the factory level.

The industry's growth during its first 40 years of existence only appeared lackluster in retrospect, however, for in the ten years following the war the industry expanded at a tremendous pace, becoming the fifth largest industrial segment of the national economy by the late 1950s, employing more than one million people, and comprising more than 2,500 large and small manufacturers. By 1957, the industry's annual sales volume at the manufacturers' level had increased 14 times in the previous ten years, reaching $7 billion, considered at the time to be the most prolific growth rate in the shortest time span of any industry in U.S. history. This prodigious growth witnessed the development of many innovative electronic applications, which inspired a host of sophisticated products for commercial, industrial, and consumer use, including the primary products in the miscellaneous electrical machinery and equipment industry. During this decade, flight simulators, an assortment of consumer elec-

tronic products, particle accelerators, and lasers each emerged as substantial, revenue-generating products.

Two U.S. physicists, Arthur L. Schawlow and Charles H. Townes, first propounded the theory of the laser (an acronym for light amplification by stimulated emission of radiation) in 1958, which was based on Townes' development of the maser (microwave amplification by stimulated emission of radiation) roughly eight years earlier, when the electronics industry was beginning to exponentially expand. Two years after the idea was born, the first laser, a ruby laser, was constructed by Theodore H. Maiman in 1960. Particle accelerators, first developed by John D. Cockcroft and Ernest T.S. Walton in 1932, did not become commercially viable products until the 1950s, their evolution as such largely attributable to the work of Robert J. Van de Graaff and the company he helped found in 1946, High Voltage Engineering Corporation. During the 1950s, a decade of enormous growth in the electronics industry, flight simulators also appeared as a commercially viable product although they had been in existence for a number of years. Receiving a significant boost from their military applications during World War II, flight simulators gained the attention of the burgeoning commercial airline industry, creating an incentive for electronics manufacturers to convert their facilities to the production of simulators.

From the 1950s forward, then, the major product categories of the miscellaneous electrical machinery industry were generating appreciable amounts of revenue, albeit from different markets, signaling the genesis of the industry itself.

By the late 1950s, there were eight manufacturers in the world producing particle accelerators. The largest of these, Van de Graaff's High Voltage Engineering Corporation, controlled 40 percent of the $20 million global market. Although still a comparatively small market, industry pundits foresaw the market for particle accelerators increasing to nearly $80 million dollars by the mid-1960s. This optimism stemmed from the various and remarkable industrial applications for particle accelerators, which were then beginning to overshadow their scientific contributions, or at least command more of the limelight.

Functioning as a machine that synthetically produced radiation energy, particle accelerators were used in various production processes, from sterilizing surgical sutures after they had been packaged, to irradiating wire and cable insulation used in missiles and jet aircraft as well as other electronic gear exposed to high temperatures. Particle accelerators could also perform other feats, such as converting sawdust into digestible feed for livestock, transforming sugar into acid, and waterproofing shoe leather.

The main obstacle facing particle accelerator manufacturers as they entered the 1960s was the expensive nature of their business and the high price of their products. Some units sold for up to $150 million each, limiting the manufacturers' clientele to only those businesses for which the high price tag and operating costs of particle accelerators were offset by their ability to perform a task that otherwise could not be completed. Consequently, there were only 250 particle accelerators in existence in the world by the beginning of the 1960s, but prices were coming down rapidly as manufacturers augmented the world supply by producing 40 to 45 units per year.

As the push toward reducing the manufacturing cost and operating cost of particle accelerators progressed—the cost per kilowatt hour, for example, was cut in third in just two years—scientists also sought to construct bigger and bigger units. The bigger the accelerator, the greater the speed at which particles could be slammed against each other, providing scientists with more information about the basic laws of matter with each incremental increase in size and power. Particle accelerator power, measured by the number of electron volts produced by the accelerated particles, increased throughout the 1960s and 1970s, standing at 30 billion electron volts at the beginning of the 1960s, then increasing to 500 billion electron volts by the beginning of the 1970s. These and further advances in power and research broadened the particle accelerator's applicability for industrial and medical use, particularly in the form of powerful x-ray machines used to detect hidden flaws in metal castings and in the production of semiconductors as well as to diagnose and treat cancer.

From the first primitive trainers manufactured in the 1940s by Singer-Link to the early 1990s, the market for flight simulators, marine simulators, and other electronic training devices managed to remain a vital component of the miscellaneous electrical machinery and equipment industry, despite being heavily dependent on military spending, which has fluctuated dramatically since their emergence. Military sales, both to the U.S. government and to other countries, essentially created the industry during World War II and fueled its growth into the 1950s. The growth of the civilian aircraft industry and the airline industry during the 1950s added to this existing business. Yet another market segment for flight simulator manufacturers emerged during the decade, when the Soviet Union launched the world's first space satellite in 1957 and formally christened the Space Age. Thus, in quick succession three primary markets for the flight simulator industry were created, inducing a growing number of simulator manufacturers to replicate as best they could the rapid technological advancements taking place in the burgeoning aerospace industry.

The bulk of flight simulator manufacturers' space simulation business came soon after the Soviets launched their satellite, when the frenetic race to put man on the moon began. In the early 1960s, the U.S. government earmarked $65 billion to be spent over a seven-year period to win such a race, $300 million of which simulator manufacturers could expect to garner. Initially, more 200 space simulators were ordered, as NASA sought to simulate each stage of a moon voyage.

While space simulators were intended to provide training for hypothetical equipment traveling in a hypothetical environment, flight simulators for military and civilian aircraft replicated actual, existing aircraft and would prove to be the linchpin of simulator manufacturers' financial stability in the years to come. As the costs of operating aircraft increased dramatically, spurred by the rapidly advancing technology they utilized, simulating the flight without having to pay for fuel and ground support—or the possibility that the plane could be destroyed—became a desirable alternative. Consequently, any significant decline in military spending usually had an insignificant effect on simulator manufacturers, since their products could be construed as cost-saving purchases. For the industry's commercial clientele, the same rationale held true, particularly during the energy crises in the early and mid-1970s. With the rising cost of fuel, many airlines opted for simulators to augment their traditional pilot and crew training. To be sure, simulator manufacturers were negatively affected by the usual economic exigencies, and their market was comparatively small, but their business was not affected as severely when economic conditions soured as other manufacturers dependent on the aerospace industry.

Simulator manufacturers' role in the civilian aircraft industry received a tremendous boost in 1981, when the Federal Aviation Administration authorized the training of pilots by Braniff Airlines without the pilots recording any actual flight time. Instead, pilots trained in a Rediffusion 747 simulator manufactured by U.K.-based Rediffusion. With this edict, the simulator industry reached "total realism," spurring the industry's growth for the decade.

CURRENT CONDITIONS

Entering the mid-1990s, two product categories within this industry were facing defining moments in the history of their development. Perhaps the most disheartening news for industry participants was the announcement in October 1993 that the 54-mile-long particle accelerator known as the Superconducting Super Collider would not be completed. First proposed as a $4.4 billion project in 1983, construction costs escalated over the years, climbing to $5.6 billion, then $8.2 billion, and finally to roughly $11 billion by 1993, a price that the U.S. House of Representatives deemed too steep. In a 282 to 143 vote the House canceled the project—after more than two billion dollars had been spent to finish roughly 20 percent of the accelerator—and allotted $615 million to formally terminate construction.

Prognostications for flight simulator manufacturers were more encouraging, however, as the industry emerged from the economically recessive early 1990s virtually unscathed. Increases in the size of the world's aircraft transport fleet through the year 2005 were predicted, which led industry observers to project a nearly 150 percent increase in the demand for full-flight simulators. In Asia and the Pacific region, aircraft operators during this period were expected to require 200 percent more simulators than they possessed in 1992, while Western European aircraft operators were predicted to require 155 percent more simulators, along with just slightly smaller percentage increases by North American and Latin American operators. Driving this increased demand, which promised to greatly expand the size of the simulator industry, was a projected growth in demand for very-long-range aircraft, or those aircraft designed to fly distances greater than 5,500 nautical miles.

INDUSTRY LEADERS

In the early 1990s, six companies in the industry recorded more than $100 million in annual sales. These manufacturers composed the industry's leadership entering the mid-1990s and were reflective of the eclectic nature of this industry. Two of the leading five companies were involved in manufacturing flight simulators, one company produced lasers, another manufactured extension cords and appliance cords for household electrical equipment, and of the remaining two, one manufactured electrical equipment, while the other manufactured electronic products. Together, these six companies generated $1.35 billion in revenue in 1993. In ranking order these manufacturers were CAE-Link Corp., Coherent, Inc., Thomson Corporation of America, Edwards Company Inc., Core Industries Inc., and Woods Wire Products Inc.

Founded in 1947 as CAE Electronics Ltd., a Montreal-based electronics firm, CAE-Link became one of

the first all-Canadian electronic companies to be established. Initially, the company specialized in repairing and overhauling electronic and electro-mechanical equipment and devices, but shortly after its inception, during the early 1950s, the company began to design and manufacture flight, radar, and weapons simulators for Canadian military training. A decade later, this diversification into simulated training aids developed into the company's primary business, with military orders for simulators coming not only from Canada, but also from North Atlantic Treaty Organization (NATO) countries.

Although CAE flourished during the late 1950s and early 1960s, its dependence on military orders, frequently a capricious market segment, worried the company's management. Defense-oriented business accounted for 99 percent of sales in 1962. In that year, CAE's management decided it was time to wean the company from dependence on the military market, and so it began a diversification and acquisition program. The following year, CAE Industries Ltd. was established as a parent company to project the company's intent on expanding into other fields.

Roughly 15 years after the diversification effort was initiated, CAE achieved considerable success. Military orders now accounted for 20 percent of the company's total sales, and the CAE organization had grown enormously, expanding to 16 divisions involved in a number of activities, including the manufacture of high-technology electronic, aerospace, and metal products for the world market; the distribution of machine tools, industrial, forestry, and construction equipment; and the design and manufacture of flight and marine simulators. CAE Electronics still represented CAE Industries' largest subsidiary and primary business activity, fueling, in the mid-1970s, the company's most prodigious growth, as the number of employees increased from 500 to 1,400 during a four-year period and sales increased from $15 million to $50 million.

Over the course of the 1980s, CAE Industries once again became dependent on military sales, primarily through its U.S. subsidiary CAE-Link Corp., which acquired the Singer Company's Link Flight Simulation Division in 1988. Through its U.S. subsidiary, CAE Industries manufactured military flight and mission simulators for the U.S. Air Force F-117A stealth fighter, the B-2, and various U.S. Army helicopter models. Also, the U.S. subsidiary manufactured simulators for the F-16, antisubmarine warfare simulators for the U.S. Navy P-2 and S-3 aircraft, simulation trainers for Navy surface and undersea vessels, and several U.S. Army command and control systems.

By the end of the decade, CAE Industries' annual sales had eclipsed one billion dollars, with military products accounting for 92 percent of total sales and 79 percent of operating income. In 1992, CAE-Link Corp., the company's U.S. subsidiary, and Bicoastal Corp., the successor to the Singer Co. and the second largest manufacturer in the industry, agreed to pay the U.S. government $55 million in a civil settlement relating to charges that the two manufacturers had overcharged the Pentagon for flight simulators. At that time Bicoastal was in Chapter 11 bankruptcy, its collapse imminent. Other manufacturers in the industry were able to fill the void created by Bicoastal's financial difficulties and, as the industry entered 1993, the composition of the industry's leading six positions was established for the mid-1990s.

Despite its problems with the U.S. government, CAE-Link remained the industry's largest manufacturer in the early-1990s, posting $415 million in sales in 1993. As a result of Bicoastal's collapse, Coherent, Inc., a designer and manufacturer of scientific, medical, and industrial lasers based in Santa Clara, California, became the industry's second largest manufacturer, with $215 million in sales in 1993.

The industry's third position was occupied by Thomson Corporation of America, the U.S. subsidiary of the fourth largest consumer electronics company in the world, the French government-owned Thomson SA. In addition to manufacturing electronic tubes and circuits, Thomson Corporation of America also manufactured flight simulators, which helped the company to post $200 million in sales in 1993.

The industry's fourth largest manufacturer, Edwards Company Inc., manufactured electrical equipment and alarm systems. A division of General Signal Corp., Edwards Co. was based in Farmington, Connecticut and recorded $190 million in sales in 1993.

The fifth and sixth largest manufacturers were Core Industries Inc. and Woods Wire Products Inc., respectively. Core Industries, based in Bloomfield Hills, Michigan, manufactured electrical products, farm equipment, and fluid controls equipment, generating $184 million in sales in 1993. Woods Wire Products, a subsidiary of Pentland USA Inc. based in Carmel, Indiana, manufactured extension cords and appliance cords for household electrical equipment. In 1993, Woods Wire Products recorded $110 million in sales.

WORK FORCE

In 1986, 24,700 people were employed by the industry, the majority of whom were employed as pro-

duction workers. One year later, after the reclassification, the industry's payroll swelled to include 60,300 employees and comprised nearly as many salaried employees as production workers. Before the reclassification, approximately 75 percent of the industry's work force were employed as production workers, while the remaining 25 percent were employed as salaried workers performing administrative, technical, or managerial duties. After the inclusion of manufacturers involved in producing sophisticated, high-technology products the following year, the composition of the industry's work force was nearly evenly divided between the two types of employees, with 47 percent working as salaried employees and 53 percent employed in production.

Following the reclassification, which more than doubled the size of the industry's work force, total employment declined, dropping below 60,000 by the end of the 1980s. Production workers bore the brunt of this decline, as 3,800 lost their jobs. By 1990, when total employment amounted to 58,400, these hourly wage employees no longer composed a majority of the industry's work force.

Generally, production workers are employed on a full-time basis, working, in the late 1980s, three percent fewer hours per year than the typical production worker, while earning slightly more per hour than the typical production worker. In 1989, production workers employed by all other manufacturing industries averaged $10.49 per hour, compared to the $10.50 per hour averaged by production workers employed by the miscellaneous electrical equipment and supplies industry. This hourly wage fell to $10.11 in 1990, when salaried employees earned an average of $37,864 per year.

INDUSTRY INFORMATION SOURCES

"Biggest Atom Smasher Rises on Illinois Prairie," *Engineering News-Record,* August 6, 1970, 60.

"CAE-Link, Bicoastal to Pay $55.5 Million in Fraud Settlement," *Aviation Week & Space Technology,* July 20, 1992, 26.

Crawford, Wilby, "New Technology Keeps Costs Down," *Interavia Aerospace Review,* August 1991, 15.

Dornheim, Michael A., "Low-Cost Simulation Likely to Reshape Market," *Aviation Week & Space Technology,* September 2, 1991, 38.

"Extra Zip for Atom Smashers," *Business Week,* March 27, 1981, 78.

"First Industrial Laser Retired to Smithsonian," *Iron Age,* September 24, 1979, 9.

Gutman, Walter K., "Atomic Alchemy," *Barron's,* October 19, 1959, 5.

"House Backs Funding of 'Big Science' Projects," *Chemical & Engineering News,* June 17, 1991, 6.

"Hurrah for Second Thoughts," *The Economist,* June 27, 1970, 73.

Kolcum, Edward H., "Gulf War Training Deficiencies to Dictate Future of Simulation," *Aviation Week & Space Technology,* December 16-23, 1991, 51.

Kolcum, "Simulator Market to Stay Strong Despite Budget Cuts," *Aviation Week & Space Technology,* November 12, 1990, 24.

"Link Flight Simulation Consolidating Military Programs to Cut Costs," *Aviation Week & Space Technology,* November 12, 1990, 71.

McKenna, James T., "Very-Long-Range Aircraft Seen Driving 150% Rise in Simulator Demand," *Aviation Week & Space Technology,* July 20, 1992, 36.

Moorman, Robert W., "From the Beginning," *Air Transport World,* August, 1992, 62.

Nelms, Douglas W., "Changing Times," *Air Transport World,* April 1991, 92.

"The New Business of Space Simulation," *Steel,* July 9, 1962, 59.

Nordwall, Bruce D., "Airline Demand for Flight Simulators to Outstrip Growth in Transport Fleets," *Aviation Week & Space Technology,* August 3, 1992, 55.

"Push for Biggest Atom Smasher," *Business Week,* April 8, 1961, 29.

"Radiation for Industry," *Chemical Week,* May 5, 1962, 51.

Stein, Kenneth J., "New Technology Spurs Simulator Gains," *Aviation Week & Space Technology,* November 30, 1981, 129.

"Wanted: Bigger Atom Smashers," *Business Week,* September 10, 1960, 75.

Whitehead, Ross, "Rapid Growth Ahead for Industrial Lasers," *Industry Week,* April 28, 1980, 95.

Willmot, May, "CAE Moves up in Simulators," *Interavia,* April, 1979, 319.

—Jeffrey L. Covell

TRANSPORTATION EQUIPMENT

MOTOR VEHICLES AND PASSENGER CAR BODIES

This industry classification is comprised of establishments primarily engaged in manufacturing or assembling complete automobiles, trucks, commercial vehicles, and buses as well as specialty motor vehicles intended for highway use such as ambulances, armored cars, hearses, fire department vehicles, snow plows, and tow trucks. This classification also includes establishments involved in manufacturing passenger car bodies and all types of vehicle chassis. Although some establishments within the industry also manufacture motor vehicle parts, establishments primarily involved in manufacturing motor vehicle parts (other than chassis and passenger car bodies) are classified in **SIC 3714: Motor Vehicle Parts and Accessories.**

Establishments primarily engaged in the manufacture of truck and bus bodies, or in the assembly of completed trucks and buses on purchased chassis, are classified in **SIC 3713: Truck and Bus Bodies.** Establishments primarily engaged in the manufacture of truck trailers are classified in **SIC 3715: Truck Trailers.** Other motor vehicle classifications include motor homes assembled on purchased chassis (**SIC 3716: Motor Homes**), motorcycles (**SIC 3751: Motorcycles, Bicycles, and Parts**), off-highway tractors (**SIC 3523: Farm Machinery and Equipment**), industrial tractors (**SIC 3537: Industrial Trucks, Tractors, Trailers, and Stackers**), combat tanks (**SIC 3795: Tanks and Tank Components**) and stamped passenger car body parts (**SIC 3465: Automotive Stampings**).

INDUSTRY SNAPSHOT

The motor vehicle industry represents one of the largest segments within the U.S. economy. In 1991, for instance, sales of cars and trucks totaled $189 billion, representing 3.3 percent of the nation's Gross Domestic Product. In 1993 the "Big Three" auto companies (General Motors, Ford, and Chrysler) produced 14.2 million cars and trucks, the most since 1989 and a figure indicative of the turnaround the three Detroit-based automakers have enjoyed in the early 1990s. By the first quarter of 1994, Chrysler was posting a profit-per-vehicle-sold in North America of $1,203, while Ford tallied $656 of profit for every vehicle sold and General Motors posted $355 of profit for every car sold.

Forecasters predicted increasing strength within the auto industry during its rebound. Many observers expect sales of more than 15 million cars and trucks in 1994, as government analysts have predicted an 8.5 percent increase in passenger car sales and a 5.7 percent increase in light truck sales. Some industry watchers expect annual vehicle sales to reach a high of 17 million units by 1996, breaking a record set ten years earlier. The average age of cars and the availability of money were cited as two reasons for such optimism. During the late 1980s and early 1990s many consumers postponed auto purchases. As a result, the average age of passenger cars on U.S. roads increased to 7.9 years, and an estimated 35 percent of the nation's passenger car fleet was nine or more years old. Declining interest rates and debt restructuring made more money available for vehicle purchases.

Minivan sales represented one of the fastest growing market segments in the United States and Europe. *Business Week* estimated U.S. minivan sales at 1.1

million units in 1993 and forecasted annual sales of 1.3 million by 1995. According to one report, European minivan sales held the potential to grow by as much as 230 percent by 1996. Manufacturers favored minivans because their price range of $14,000 to $28,000 brought profits of about $4,000 per vehicle.

Although analysts forecasted short-term growth within the automotive industry, long-term projections offered less promise. The U.S. Department of Commerce concluded that the domestic market and other major markets around the world were saturated, holding little prospect for long-term annual growth rates of more than one or two percent. In addition, analysts noted growing price resistance among consumers. As new vehicles became more reliable and more expensive, replacement cycles lengthened. Purchases were viewed as discretionary rather than necessary. Increasingly, the automakers have countered such market realities through restrained pricing strategies and other steps. Coupled with an economic outlook in 1994 wherein interest rates were low, players in the industry hope the strides made in recent years can be sustained.

ORGANIZATION AND STRUCTURE

In the United States, auto production is dominated by three manufacturers, General Motors, Ford, and Chrysler. Together, these establishments are referred to as the ''Big Three.'' In 1993, they were the only three remaining members of the American Automobile Manufacturers Association (AAMA). The AAMA, formerly the Motor Vehicle Manufacturers Association (MVMA), was originally founded as the National Automobile Chamber of Commerce in 1915. Its purpose was to administer the cross licensing of patents, and during the 1930s the organization established a code of fair competition.

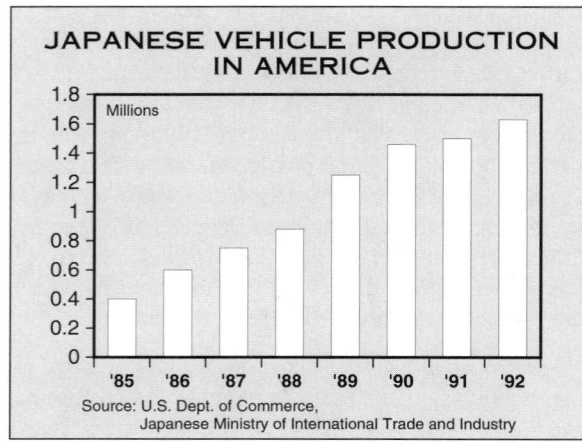

JAPANESE VEHICLE PRODUCTION IN AMERICA

Source: U.S. Dept. of Commerce, Japanese Ministry of International Trade and Industry

The MVMA changed its name to the AAMA and moved its offices from Detroit to Washington following the ouster of its foreign members (Honda of America Manufacturing, Inc. and Volvo Cars of North America) in 1992. The restructured AAMA promised to better serve the common interests of domestic car makers, to serve as a lobbying agent, and to oversee cooperative research ventures undertaken by domestic auto makers.

BACKGROUND AND DEVELOPMENT

The modern automobile was not invented by any single person. Many people in many nations contributed the ideas, inventions, and innovations required to assemble useful motor vehicles. Roger Bacon, the thirteenth-century English philosopher and scientist, prophesied its development. Leonardo da Vinci envisioned plans for its construction. A Frenchman, Nicholas Joseph Cugnot, constructed the first functioning self-propelled unit. Cugnot's vehicle, built in 1769, had three wheels and was powered with a steam engine. In the United States the first patent for a self-propelled vehicle was awarded to Oliver Evans by the state of Maryland in 1787. The newly organized Federal Patent Office awarded its first patent for a self-propelled landcarriage to Nathan Read in 1791. By 1891 the country had seen more than 100 renderings of motorized vehicles.

The first internal combustion engine was developed by the Belgian inventor, Etienne Lenoir. He used it to power a car during a demonstration in Paris in 1862. A German, Nicholas Otto, developed a quieter four-stroke coal-gas engine in 1878. The first gasoline vehicles were developed in 1885 by two Germans working independently, Karl Benz and Gottlieb Daimler. The world's first motor vehicles built for commercial sale were offered in France by Armand Peugeot in 1889, and Panhard and Levassor in 1890. The French are also credited with coining the term ''automobile,'' formed from two Latin words meaning self-moving.

During the early 1890s many people in the United States were working separately on producing better ''horseless carriages.'' According to some accounts two brothers, Charles and Frank Duryea of Springfield, Massachusetts, developed the first successful American gasoline automobile. The Duryea model was based on Benz's work as reported in *Scientific American.* Other contenders for the honor of producing the first American motor-car included Gottfried Schloemer of Milwaukee, Wisconsin, Henry Nadig of Allentown, Pennsylvania, Charles H. Black of Indianapolis, Indiana, and John W. Lambert of Ohio City, Ohio.

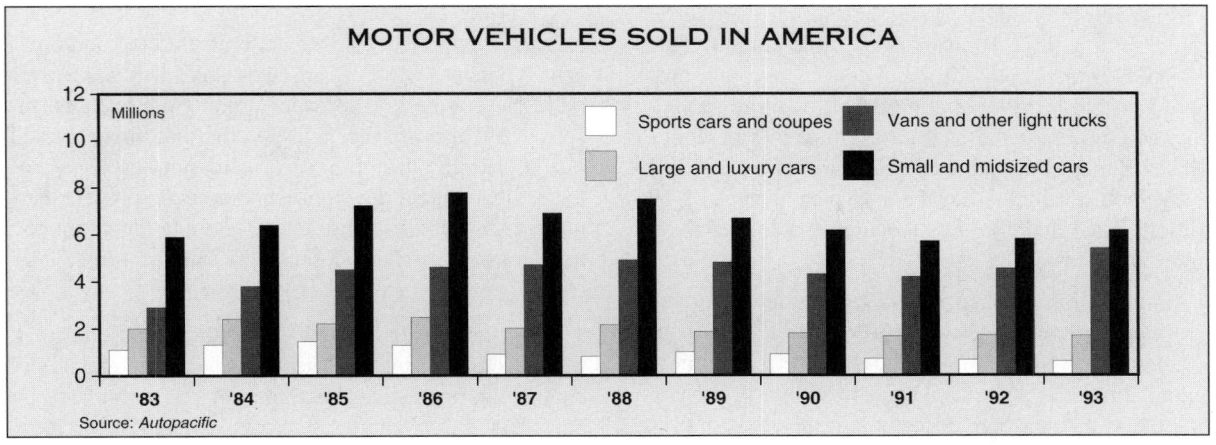

MOTOR VEHICLES SOLD IN AMERICA

Sports cars and coupes · Vans and other light trucks · Large and luxury cars · Small and midsized cars

Source: *Autopacific*

The 1890s brought commercial automobile production to the United States. Elwood Haynes and Edgar and Elmer Apperson were among the first entrepreneurs of the new technology. They built Haynes-Apperson vehicles in a machine shop located in Kokomo, Indiana. By 1899, 30 motor vehicle producers were offering electric, steam, and gasoline powered vehicles. The 1900 U.S. Census listed motor vehicle manufacturers under "Miscellaneous Manufactures."

Among the long list of early automotive pioneers, the best remembered is undoubtedly Henry Ford. Henry Ford built his first car, called a "quadricycle," in 1896. He established the Detroit Automobile Company in 1899—the venture failed. Ford's second company, the Henry Ford Company, founded in 1901, also failed. He finally achieved success with his third organization, the Ford Motor Company, officially founded on June 10, 1903.

Many other popularly known names in automotive history entered the industry during the last decade of the nineteenth century and the first decades of the twentieth century. Studebaker, originally a manufacturer of wagons, carriages, and horse-drawn vehicles, entered the automotive industry in 1897. Packard Motor Company was founded in 1899 and produced its first car in 1900. Ransom Eli Olds established the Olds Motor Vehicle Company in 1897. The company was later reorganized to form the Olds Motor Works, and by 1904 Olds was producing 5,000 "Olds-mobiles" annually. Cadillac Motor Car was established in 1902 with the help of financial backers who abandoned Henry Ford's earlier efforts. Buick Motor Car Company was founded by David D. Buick in 1903 and later sold to William Durant, the founder of General Motors. Louis Chevrolet, born in Switzerland, came to the United States in 1905 and began his automotive career as a race car driver for Buick. Walter P. Chrysler

purchased his first car in 1908. Following a career at Buick Motor Car Company he assumed the presidency of the Chrysler Corporation, formed from the remnants of the Maxwell Motor Car Company on June 6, 1925.

Throughout the early decades of the 20th century, Ford dominated the industry. He achieved nearly legendary status by introducing the automotive industry to the benefits of automated production and by providing an automobile at a price that most people could afford. In 1908, Ford decided to focus his company's efforts on the construction of only one model—the Model T. To help lower costs and speed production, he began moving toward assembly line production.

In 1913 a moving belt was installed in Ford's magneto department. (A magneto was a part that provided the electric current required for ignition.) After its installation, the moving belt enabled each worker to perform a single task rather than assemble a completed magneto. Production experienced a four-fold increase and Ford transferred moving assembly lines to other parts of the plant. In its first complete year of assembly line production, the company built 248,000 cars (compared with 78,000 the previous year). In 1915, Ford's annual production reached 500,000 and prices fell. The 1912 Model T sold for $600, the 1914 cost $490, a 1915 touring car cost $440, and the price of the 1925 model dropped to $290. By 1920, an estimated three-fifths of U.S. cars and 50 percent of all the cars in the world were Model Ts. Although its sales diminished as consumers turned to more modern offerings, the Model T earned its place in history. When Model T production was halted in 1927 an estimated 11 of every 20 cars on American roads were Model Ts. Fifteen million units had been sold. No other single model surpassed Model T sales until the 1960s, when the record fell to the Volkswagen Beetle.

During the mid-1920s the automobile market became saturated. To bolster sales, auto manufactures aimed their marketing efforts at creating two-car families. To help families make purchases more quickly, they offered financing, and an estimated 75 percent of all new cars were purchased on installment in 1925. By 1929 motor vehicles had been driven a total of 198 billion miles and the average motorist logged 7,500 miles per year.

Auto sales dropped in 1929, an indication of the coming depression. As the 1930s opened, auto output was down 37 percent. Production in 1931 tumbled again, down 30 percent. The auto industry fell from first place, as measured according to the value of products sold, to fourth in the national economy, and its decline created a ripple effect through the nation's entire economic infrastructure. Automakers, however, were among the first to emerge from the depression years. By 1936, for example, General Motors was close to its pre-Depression profits.

The late 1930s brought technical innovations to the automotive industry. Automatic transmissions became common, increased precision enabled manufacturers to produce better cars, and attention to styling and aerodynamics improved stability and fuel efficiency. Post-depression era work projects also improved the nation's highway system and the mileage of paved roads more than doubled between 1933 and 1941. The Pennsylvania Turnpike opened in 1940, and although initial estimates projected the toll road would carry 715 vehicles per day, within two weeks 26,000 vehicles per day were using the new roadway.

When World War II arrived, the nation refocused its attention on producing items for the war effort; civilian car production stopped in 1942. One of the most popular cars developed for military use was the "Jeep." Although not all historians agree, some contend that the name "Jeep" was coined from the initials GP, taken from the military lexicon where the "General Purpose Vehicle" had become a "GP." After the war's end, the Jeep was redesigned for civilian use and designated a "Civilian Jeep" or "CJ" model.

American automakers found an eager market in the post-war years. Half of the nation's 25.8 million registered cars were ten or more years old, and people were ready to purchase new cars. Between 1946 and 1950 21.4 million new cars were sold. Production in 1949 topped the five million mark for the first time since the pre-Depression era. The dominance of car and truck transportation was further assured in 1958, when the National Highway Act was passed. This legislation provided funds for significant construction to improve the nation's highway system.

During the 1950s the look of a car assumed greater importance. Car buyers preferred big and powerful vehicles, which resulted in advertising that emphasized engine horsepower. Ornamental tail fins, inspired by aircraft fuselages, were first incorporated into a Cadillac design and came to symbolize cars of the era. Technical developments included power steering, power brakes, and improvements in automatic transmissions—all necessary to help control large cars.

By the 1960s the new car market was saturated. Manufacturers relied on promotions and annual model changes to boost sales. The market was dominated by the "Big Three" and American Motors Corporation, which had been formed following the merger of two independent producers (Hudson and Nash) in the post-war years. Imported cars, led by the Volkswagen Beetle, began to make an impact on the American market during this period. In 1968 ten percent of all auto sales were captured by foreign manufacturers. The two largest Japanese manufacturers, Toyota and Nissan (Datsun), had entered the U.S. market during the late 1950s and saw rapid growth during the 1960s. By 1970 Toyota was the nation's number two import; Datsun was number three. That year imports accounted for 15 percent of the U.S. passenger car market.

In addition to increased competition, the 1960s brought the auto industry rising criticism. Ralph Nadar's *Unsafe at Any Speed: The Designed-in Dangers of the American Automobile* was published in 1965 and inaugurated a crusade for safer cars. In 1966 Congress passed the National Traffic and Motor Vehicle Safety Act which mandated improvements in passenger safety, driver visibility, and braking. The Act also required public announcement of recalls to correct safety defects. During the first ten years of regulation, 52 million cars and trucks were recalled. Safety was not the only arena for critics; cars were also identified as a source of air pollution. In 1965 Congress passed the Vehicle Air Pollution and Control Act setting mandatory pollution standards. And the 1970s opened with another anti-pollution effort—Congress passed the Clean Air Act which mandated a 90 percent reduction in auto emissions within six years.

Concerns about fuel efficiency dominated the 1970s. In 1973, General Motor's cars averaged less than 12 miles per gallon and other domestic car makers offerings were only slightly better. Two oil crises during the decade brought the nation increased gas prices, local shortages, a 55 miles-per-hour speed limit, and federally mandated fuel efficiency. The Energy Policy and Conservation Act, passed in 1975, specified that car manufacturers must meet a sales-weighted "Corporate Average Fuel Economy'' (CAFE) standard of 20 miles per gallon by the 1980 model year and 27.5 miles per gallon by the 1985 model year.

During the early 1980s domestic auto makers found themselves unprepared for the sudden surge in the small car market, and as a result they lost substantial ground to imports. A growing sense that the products coming out of Detroit were inferior to those of imports further exacerbated the slide of the domestic automotive manufacturers. Chrysler Corporation wavered on the brink of bankruptcy and secured a federal loan guarantee of $1.5 billion to survive. A resurgence during the middle of the decade failed to provide long-term stability. The auto industry achieved record sales of 16.3 million units in 1986, but new light vehicle sales fell in four out of the five years between 1986 and 1991. In 1990 the ''Big Three'' suffered considerable losses, and General Motors was in particularly bad shape. During 1991 U.S. production facilities operated at only 60 to 65 percent of their capacity.

CURRENT CONDITIONS

U.S. auto makers' profitability suffered during the economic slowdown of the late 1980s and early 1990s, but vehicle sales during 1992 and 1993 indicated that the industry was rebounding. In the fall of 1993, *Fortune* reported that domestic production was up six percent. Lower costs and improved productivity helped bolster the industry's profit picture. Cars were manufactured more efficiently and manufacturing processes had less environmental impact.

Environmental concerns, however, continued to influence the industry. California introduced stringent clean air standards in 1990. The legislation required auto makers to begin offering Zero Emission Vehicles (ZEV) in 1998. The regulations also called for incremental increases in the percentage of ZEV cars sold,

beginning with two percent in 1998, moving to five percent in 2001, and expanding to ten percent in 2003. Other states were considering adopting California-style legislation. Moreover, the federal government continued to insist on compliance with the CAFE standards previously established by the Energy Policy and Conservation Act. New passenger cars were required to average 27.5 miles per gallon and light trucks to average 20.2 miles per gallon. Non-compliance by a manufacturer brought penalties of as much as $7,700 per vehicle. According to EPA statistics, the U.S. passenger car fleet averaged 26.9 miles per gallon in 1992; U.S. light trucks averaged 20.4 miles per gallon. Imported passenger cars averaged 29 miles per gallon and imported light trucks averaged 22.4 miles per gallon.

Some critics in the industry charged that fuel efficiency standards were contradictory to safety requirements. The Coalition for Vehicle Choice (CVC) was formed to counter legislative attempts to increase CAFE requirements to 40 miles per gallon. The CVC argued that high CAFE standards reduced the availability of family-sized vehicles and impeded efforts aimed at enhancing auto safety. To speed efforts at increasing vehicle safety, Congress passed the Intermodal Surface Transportation Efficiency Act in 1992. Its requirements included the installation of driver and front seat air bags in passenger cars by 1998 and in trucks, minivans, and sport/utility vehicles by 1999. The legislation also established rules concerning rollovers, brakes, child booster seats, head-injury protection, and side impact protection.

Another issue facing domestic auto makers during the early 1990s was the continued impact of foreign competition. Entering the mid-1990s, however, it is the Japanese manufacturers on the defensive. ''Why are the Big Three suddenly so hot?,'' asked *Business*

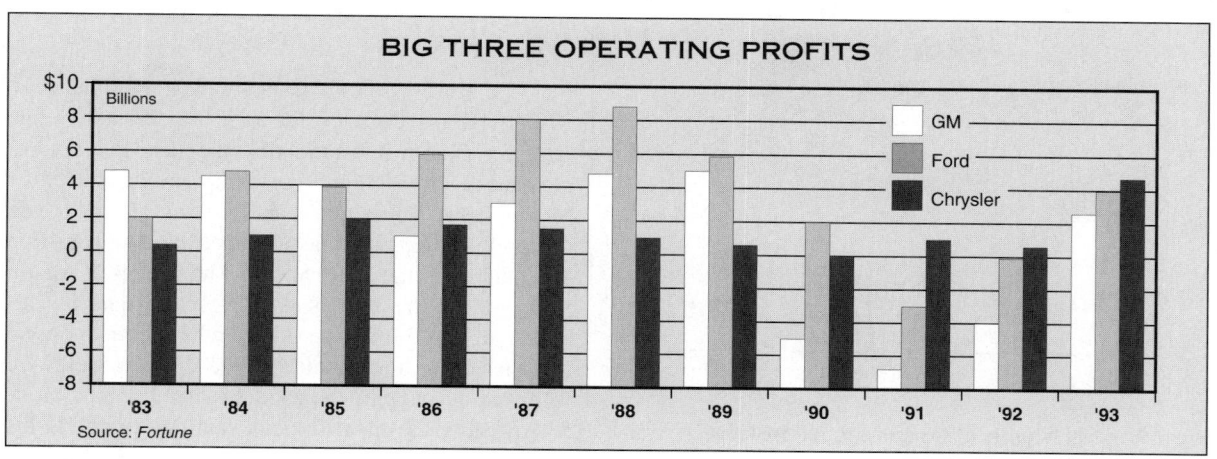

Source: *Fortune*

Week in 1993. "One reason is that the yen has risen sky-high, notes Chrysler Corp. President Robert A. Lutz and 'exchange rates are really working against [Japanese companies] big time.' Quality [of the domestic fleet] is also way up, Buy American sentiment is strong, and slumping profits are forcing the Japanese to raise prices to boost margins." The magazine also noted that, contrary to past recoveries, the Big Three are showing restraint in their pricing strategies. Another factor is that "major new product launches should keep customer interest high. GM, Ford, and Chrysler are all introducing new small and intermediate-size cars, noted *Fortune* in 1994.

Still another reason for the success enjoyed by Ford, GM, and Chrysler was in the realm of truck sales. As *Automotive Industries* observed in May 1994, "trucks are the single biggest reason the Big Three are re-capturing market share. The numbers tell the story. While car sales increased 312,000 units in 1993, truck sales shot up by 725,000 units—more than twice as much. And the Japanese automakers collectively sell less than 10 percent of the trucks sold in America." While the quality of the American products is one reason for their success, America's 25 percent tariff on imported trucks is another important factor.

INDUSTRY LEADERS

General Motors. In 1993 the world's largest full-line vehicle manufacturer was General Motors Corporation. General Motors (GM) offered domestic automobiles under the nameplates Chevrolet, Pontiac, Oldsmobile, Buick, Cadillac, GMC Truck, and Saturn. International products included Opel, Vauxhall, Saab, Lotus, and Isuzu.

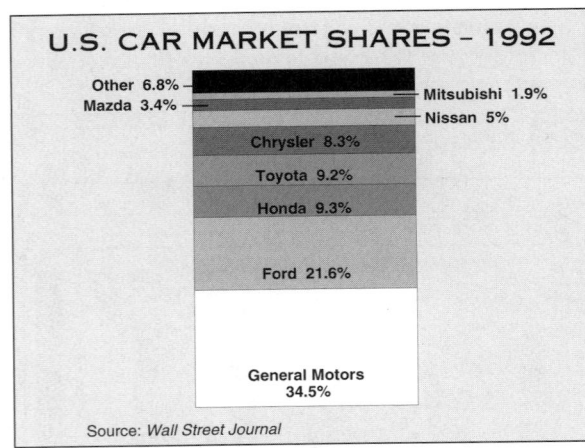

U.S. CAR MARKET SHARES – 1992

Other 6.8%
Mazda 3.4%
Mitsubishi 1.9%
Nissan 5%
Chrysler 8.3%
Toyota 9.2%
Honda 9.3%
Ford 21.6%
General Motors 34.5%

Source: *Wall Street Journal*

General Motors was incorporated in 1908 by William C. Durant. Its first components were Oldsmobile

and Buick. The company acquired two more manufacturers in 1909, Oakland and Cadillac, and between 1910 and 1920 Durant obtained more than thirty companies. The unit that would go on to become GM's largest division, Chevrolet, was acquired in 1918 and accounted for 49 percent of GM's sales in 1992. Although it remained the largest auto manufacturer, GM saw its market share drop during the 1980s and early 1990s.

In 1992 GM reported sales of 7,146,000 units valued in excess of $118.5 billion. Worldwide GM employment stood at 571,000. When workers at the company's subsidiaries were included, the company's employment totaled 750,000 (a figure that has steadily dropped in the last couple of years as GM fights to control production costs). In 1993 General Motors posted higher sales than any company in America—$138 billion. The company parlayed that into $1.176 billion in earnings. While still struggling in some areas, GM enters the mid-1990s in better financial condition than it has seen in several years.

Ford. The second largest auto manufacturer in the United States and in the world in the mid-1990s is the Ford Motor Company. In 1992 Ford sold 3.17 million units under its domestic nameplates Ford, Lincoln, and Mercury, and the company's Taurus was the best-selling car in the United States. Ford represented the corporation's largest division, accounting for 81.8 percent of sales. In addition to its own units, the company owned 25 percent of Mazda (Japan), 10 percent of Kai Motors (South Korea), 100 percent of Jaguar (United Kingdom), and 75 percent of Aston Martin (United Kingdom). In 1992 Ford's worldwide factory sales totaled 5.76 million units. In 1993 the company reported earnings of $2.5 billion (on $108.5 billion in total sales), a $3 billion turnaround from the year before, and attributed the good numbers to dramatically improved car and truck sales in the United States, worldwide cost-cutting, and the performance of its financial subsidiaries.

The Ford Motor Company was established in 1903 by Henry Ford, whose early models bore alphabetic designations. His first offering, the Model A, was introduced in 1903, and the company introduced the Model C the following year. Looking for a car with mass appeal that could be produced at a low cost, Ford continued making innovations. The Model N was introduced for the 1906 and 1907 season and boasted speeds up to 45 miles per hour and a fuel economy of 20 miles per gallon. It sold for $600. The Model N was followed by an upgraded Model R and a refined Model S. Arguably the most famous car in automotive history, Ford's Model T was introduced for the 1908 and

1909 season. Ford's ninth model in six years, the Model T achieved nearly legendary status and dominated the industry for 18 years.

Chrysler. The third company of the U.S. "Big Three" is the Chrysler Corporation. Chrysler was formed out of remnants of the Maxwell Motor Car Co. in 1925 by Walter P. Chrysler. It's first line of cars, the "Chrysler Six," were aimed at the medium priced market. A year later Chrysler rose from 57th in industry sales to fifth and expanded its operations into Canada. By 1929, the company was counted as one of the "Big Three."

Chrysler experienced high sales during the early 1970s, but events later in the decade pushed the company to the brink of bankruptcy. The challenge of rebuilding the company was taken on by Lee A. Iacocca, who became Chrysler's President in 1978 and Chairman in 1979. To help ensure Chrysler's survival, Congress passed the Chrysler Corporation Loan Guarantee Act, which provided the company with $1.5 billion in federal loan guarantees. Chrysler's new line of K-cars helped create the momentum necessary for a return to profitability, enabling the company to pay off its federal loan guarantees seven years early.

Chrysler's pioneering efforts in the minivan market also helped the company achieve success. The Dodge Caravan and the Plymouth Voyager, both introduced in 1983, gave Chrysler leadership within the new market. Chrysler remained the nation's minivan market leader throughout the remainder of the decade and into the 1990s.

By 1991 Chrysler's worldwide employment was 123,000. The company's products were sold in 80 countries through a network of 8,000 dealers and sales of 2,175,447 cars and trucks in 1992 totaled $36.9 billion. The Dodge nameplate accounted for almost half the company's sales and other nameplates included Chrysler, Plymouth, Jeep and Eagle. In addition, Chrysler owned a 15.6 percent interest in Maserati. In 1993 Chrysler continued its sharp recent performance, pulling in $3.8 billion in pretax operating profits—more than four more times more than in 1992—and $2.41 billion in after-tax profits. Chrysler's total sales for 1993 reached $43.6 billion.

WORK FORCE

During the early 1990s approximately one of every seven jobs in the U.S. domestic economy related to the production, sale, operation, or maintenance of motor vehicles. As the *Detroit Free Press* noted in 1993, "the U.S. auto industry was a major force in the creation of new jobs for many years, with employment

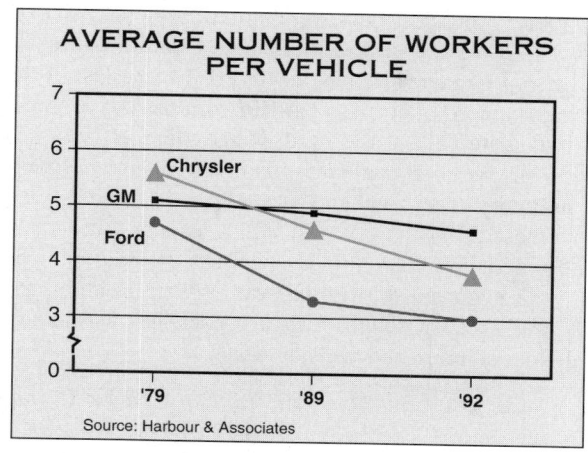

AVERAGE NUMBER OF WORKERS PER VEHICLE

Source: Harbour & Associates

peaking in 1978 at more than one million workers. But since then employment has slid and the industry is no longer a source of new jobs." The *Free Press* went on to point out that auto industry employment in 1992 was 812,200 jobs, of which a little over 413,000 were hourly positions. This is in part a result of increasing productivity per worker at the "Big Three" manufacturing plants—one of the primary reasons for the dramatic upswing in fortunes for Ford, GM, and Chrysler in the early 1990s. According to the U.S. Department of Commerce and the Federal Reserve Bank of Chicago, GM, Ford and Chrysler have all, from 1980 to 1991, cut by at least one-third the number of worker-hours required to assemble a vehicle.

Unions in the Automotive Industry. The United Auto Workers (UAW) union represents many employees within the automotive industry. UAW membership peaked in 1979 with 1.5 million members and fell to 900,000 members in 1993. The largest employer of UAW members was General Motors. Organization of auto workers began in the post-Depression era. During the Depression, growing labor unrest resulted as companies cut workers' pay, shortened work weeks, fired people irrespective of their seniority, and rehired only younger workers. Workers also expressed job dissatisfaction as companies increased the pressure to speed productivity. In 1933 Congress passed the National Industrial Recovery Act, which gave labor the right to organize and bargain collectively. Although the act was declared unconstitutional in 1935, the rights to bargain collectively and insure union elections were again secured when Congress passed the Wagner-Connery Act (Wagner Act), establishing the National Labor Relations Board.

In 1936, the American Federation of Labor (AFL) granted the United Automobile Workers of America its charter. The union later became the United Automobile, Aerospace and Agricultural Implement Workers (UAW) and affiliated with the Committee for Industrial Organizations (CIO). Ford was the last of the major auto producers to bargain with the UAW. Elections were held at the Ford Rouge plant in 1941 following years of conflict, sometimes violent, between union organizers and anti-union forces. Union activity increased following World War II as auto production resumed. Workers joined together to maintain pay levels achieved during the war. Walter Reuther, the UAW's leader, fought for wage packages with a cost of living index and pension plans.

Current Contracts. The *Monthly Labor Review* observed in 1994 that "after picking Ford Motor Co. as its settlement target for the 1993 round of auto negotiations, the United Automobile Workers appeared about to sign a 6-year contract with the automaker that would guarantee fully paid health care coverage and job and income security to current employees in return for more flexible work rules and a lower starting rate for new hires. . . . but the agreement unraveled, apparently because the union believed that it would be too costly in terms of plant closings and consolidations. The ensuing settlement broke little new ground, basically preserving existing contract terms. In the eyes of some observers, the parties lost an opportunity to restructure labor costs in the industry and become more competitive with Japanese automakers and their American transplants." Instead, Ford and the UAW reached agreement on a three-year deal that "preserved employees' health care coverage and job and income security arrangements, improved employees' pension benefits, strengthened the union's position on subcontracting work, and gave the company more advantageous provisions regarding new hires." Subsequent settlements with Chrysler and General Motors followed the same basic pattern as the one consummated with Ford.

AMERICA AND THE WORLD

In 1991 the U.S. Department of Commerce estimated that 48.5 million motor vehicles were produced worldwide, an indication of its long-time presence in all corners of the world. Indeed, the automobile industry, almost from its inception, has been international in scope. Ford began assembly in Britain in 1911 and by 1914 was the largest British producer. General Motors established an export company in 1911 to sell the company's products overseas. Following World War I, Ford built assembly plants in Denmark, France, Germany, Italy, Spain and Sweden. General Motors purchased existing corporations such as Vauxhall in Britain and Opel in Germany. Ford and General Motors

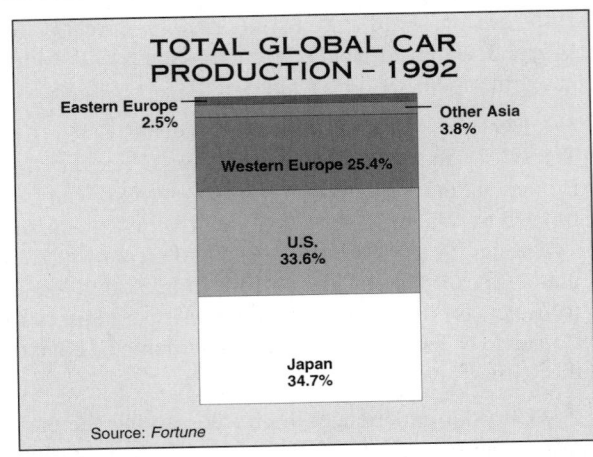

TOTAL GLOBAL CAR PRODUCTION - 1992

Eastern Europe 2.5%

Other Asia 3.8%

Western Europe 25.4%

U.S. 33.6%

Japan 34.7%

Source: *Fortune*

entered the Japanese market in 1925 and 1927 respectively. And Chrysler established Chrysler de Mexico in 1938 to import and distribute Chrysler products south of the border.

The first foreign companies to sell products in the United States offered luxury and sport models such as Rolls-Royce, Mercedes, Jaguar and Porsche. In 1950, imports sales totaled less than half percent of total car sales. The first foreign car to penetrate the mainstream market with a small family car was the Volkswagen Beetle. By 1968, Volkswagen accounted for 62 percent of all imports, but the German manufacturer began losing ground to Japanese producers.

In early 1993 Japan was the world's top producer of automobiles, accounting for 34.7 percent of the units sold worldwide. The United States was second with 33.6 percent, followed by Western Europe with 25.4 percent. Within the U.S. market, analysts expected increased exports for the revitalized domestic producers, in part because of the passage of the North American Free Trade Agreement (NAFTA), which in its first few months has already pushed a dramatic surge in U.S. car sales to Mexico. At the same time, Japanese manufacturers are battling difficult exchange rates in their efforts to sell cars and trucks in America. The result has been a decreased U.S. market share for Japanese companies in the early 1990s. "In 1993, for the second straight year, their share of the U.S. market for cars and light trucks fell—this time to 23.2 percent, off 2.6 points since 1991." noted *Business Week*. "Beleaguered by the strong yen and deep slumps in the Japanese and European auto markets, Japan's car companies are sounding ever more content to back off the market-share race." Japanese manufacturers have nonetheless attempted to address the mid-1990s environment, cutting into overhead costs, introducing new models in areas of traditional weakness (such as minivans), and shifting production increasingly to facilities in America, where production costs are lower.

Many Japanese firms have established production facilities in the United States. Honda, Toyota, Nissan, Mazda, Mitsubishi, and Subaru-Isuzu all built plants in the United States during the 1980s. By 1992, these "transplant" facilities were producing 1.6 million units annually, about 17 percent of the total light vehicle output. Approximately 200,000 units were produced under contract for the "Big Three" manufacturers. According to one estimate, by 1993 half of the sales of Japanese vehicles in the United States may be units assembled in the United States. Forecasters predicted that foreign capacity on U.S. soil would increase to 2.4 million cars and light trucks before the decade's end. Additional investments were expected to be made by Honda, Nissan, Toyota, Suzuki, and the South Korean manufacturer, Hyundai. In addition, BMW announced its intention to establish a plant in South Carolina with the ability to produce 75,000 units per year beginning in 1995. Other companies expected to add production in either the United States or Mexico were Volkswagen and Mercedes-Benz.

The proliferation of foreign car manufacturing on U.S. soil led to increased concern regarding distinctions between domestic and foreign built automobiles. In response, the U.S. Congress passed the American Automobile Labeling Law. The legislation, scheduled to go into effect on October 1, 1994, required new vehicle stickers to contain information relating to the automobile's domestic content.

RESEARCH AND TECHNOLOGY

In the fierce competitive environment of the international automotive industry, any edge in design, engineering, or technology assumes tremendous importance and can result in shifts of market share worth millions of dollars. Timely research and swift technological adaptation are vital in a wide array of automotive niche markets. A typical example of this dynamic can be seen through an examination of the diesel pickup truck market. Until recently Ford enjoyed a huge edge in market share in diesel pickups, approximately 12 percent of the total sales of pickups in the United States. Ford's position, however, has fallen from a commanding 75 percent stake to around 40 percent by the beginning of 1994. As the *Detroit Free Press* noted, "Ford owned the market for most of the '80s. General Motors had developed a lousy reputation for diesel engines when it tried to convert gasoline engines into diesels for passenger cars during the late '70s. And Chrysler only became a player in the diesel market in 1987 when it began buying diesel engines

from Cummins. With the much-revered Cummins engine under the hood, Dodge quickly began taking diesel market share from Ford. Its penetration peaked at 36 percent in 1991, just as GM came back with a new turbocharged 6.5-liter engine for its diesel trucks. . . . Now Ford, having stood by while its lead all but evaporated, is out with the latest advancement, a massive 7.3-liter turbocharged, direct-injection diesel from Navistar that gives it a competitive edge in horsepower, hauling and fuel economy." Thus the search for the competitive advantage in technology and design remains a central bulwark of the industry mentality.

As the automotive industry entered the 1990s private industrial research and government funded research focused on improving fuel efficiency, developing alternative fuels, reducing vehicle emissions, developing environmentally friendly manufacturing processes, and recycling junked vehicles. Alternative fuels, such as ethanol and methanol mixtures, liquid natural gas (LNG) and liquid petroleum gas (LPG) were under investigation as clean-burning energy sources. Researchers were also working on developing a viable electric car.

The U.S. Advanced Battery Consortium (USABC) was developed by the "Big Three" and the U.S. Department of Energy to work on new battery technology. Battery types other than conventional lead-acid batteries included nickel-cadmium, sodium-sulfur, zinc-air, nickel-hydride, lithium polymer, and hydrogen fuel cells. Nickel-cadmium batteries were preferred by Japanese manufacturers, although some critics claimed they were unsuited for mass production because cadmium was a scarce mineral and highly toxic.

Solar Car Corporation in Melbourne, Florida, was one of the country's pioneering organizations in the construction of hybrid solar/electric vehicles. Hybrid vehicles contained a small auxiliary engine powered by gasoline or other alternative fuel to assist in recharging batteries or extending a vehicle's range. Solar panels helped supplement the battery and extend its life from two to three years to five to six years. According to company statements, its electric vehicles were capable of attaining top speeds of 75 miles per hour and able to travel 50 to 80 miles before recharging.

Another type of alternate vehicle under development by the automotive industry was fueled by natural gas. According to the American Gas Association, an estimated 30,000 natural-gas vehicles (NGVs) were operating in the United States in 1993. Some projections anticipated as many as 500,000 NGVs in the United States by the year 2000. Already in 1993, an estimated 700,000 were in use worldwide. Natural gas proponents cite several advantages the fuel holds over conventional gasoline: It costs 25 to 30 percent less than gasoline, produces 90 percent less carbon monoxide and 50 percent less hydrocarbons, and spurs increased engine efficiency. In addition, because of deep domestic reserves, natural gas holds the potential to help the United States reduce its dependance on imported oil.

Researchers within the automotive industry were also working on creating safer ways to manage traffic. To help further the advancement of traffic management, reduce traffic congestion, and lessen the number of accidents in congested urban regions, Congress appropriated $660 million to be spent during fiscal years 1992 through 1997 on a study of "Intelligent Vehicle Highway Systems" (IVHS). Potential IVHS technologies included radar, microwave, ultrasonics, and video. Its aim was to assist with driver tasks such as visibility and navigational assistance. Necessary ingredients included anti-lock brakes, better traction control, improved steering responses, refined suspension systems, and the ability to monitor tire pressure.

INDUSTRY INFORMATION SOURCES

Adler, Alan L., "Competitive Torque," *Detroit Free Press*, April 4, 1994.

Armstrong, Larry, Kathleen Kerwin, and Bill Spindle, "Trying to Rev Up," *Business Week*, January 24, 1994.

"The Big Three Are Learning to Hold a Lead," *Business Week*, April 26, 1993.

Bolan, Nelson, *How Detroit Changed History*, Lawrenceville, VA: Brunswick, 1987.

Brady, Howard, "Company Profile: Solar Car Corporation," *Brevard Technical Journal*, March 1993.

1992 Chrysler Corporation Report to Shareholders, Highland Park, MI: Chrysler Corporation, 1993.

"Chrysler Corporation Fact Sheet," Highland Park: Chrysler Corporation, February 9, 1993.

"Chrysler Sees Record U.S. Auto Sales by 1996," *New York Times*, July 16, 1993.

Cimini, Michael H., Susan L. Behrmann, and Eric M. Johnson, "Labor-management Bargaining in 1993," *Monthly Labor Review*, January 1994.

Dammann, George H., *Seventy Years of Chrysler*, Sarasota, FL: Crestline Publishing, 1974.

Gates, Max, "Labeling Law Comes at a Cost," *Automotive News*, December 21, 1992.

Gates, Max, and Lindsay Chappell, "MVMA Kicks Out Honda's U.S. Arm," *Automotive News*, November 30, 1992.

General Motors Annual Report 1992 Detroit: General Motors Corporation, 1993.

General Motors Annual Report Form 10K for Year Ended December 31, 1992, Detroit: General Motors, 1993.

General Motors: The First 75 Years of Transportation Products, Princeton, NJ and Detroit: *Automobile Quarterly* and General Motors Corporation, 1983.

"How Federal Officials Ignored Auto Safety," *Consumer's Research*, April 1992.

Langworth, Richard M., *The Complete History of Ford Motor Company*, New York: Beekman House, 1987.

Ludel, Moses, "The Jeep Legend Lives!," *Off-Road*, August 1992.

Matthews, Harry W., Jr., "100 Year Dash," *Automotive News*, May 3, 1992.

McCann, Hugh, and David C. Smith, "NGV's: Natural Gas Nears Lead in Alternate Fuel Race," *WARD's Auto World*, June 1993.

McElroy, John, "The Lesson of '78," *Automotive Industries*, May 1994.

Muller, Joann, "Ford Makes $3-Billion Turnaround," *Detroit Free Press*, February 10, 1994.

1987 Census of Manufactures, Washington, D.C.: Bureau of the Census, 1990.

Rae, John B., *The American Automobile Industry*, Boston: Twayne Publishers, 1984.

Sears, Stephen W., *The Automobile in America*, New York: American Heritage Publishing, 1977.

Sherman, Don, "Blink of an Eye," *Motor Trend*, May 1993.

Simanaitis, Dennis, "Electric Vehicles," *Road & Track*, May 1992.

Sorge, Marjorie, "UAW Walks a Tightrope between Old and New Jobs," *WARD's Auto World*, June 1993.

Swan, Tony, "Jeep Thrills," *Popular Mechanics*, January 1991.

Taylor, Alex, "Why Electric Cars Make No Sense," *Fortune*, July 26, 1993.

————, "U.S. Automakers Go Flat Out," *Fortune*, February 21, 1994.

U.S. Industrial Outlook 1993. Washington, D.C.: U.S. Department of Commerce, 1993.

Ward's Automotive Yearbook. Detroit: Ward's Communications, 1993.

Woodruff, David, "The Minivan Free-For-All," *Business Week*, July 26, 1993.

Woods, Wilton, "The World's Top Automakers Change Lanes," *Fortune*, October 4, 1993.

Wysner, John, *Rays of Hope . . . A Critical (and Hopeful) Cultural History of the American Automotive Business*, Los Angeles: Authors Unlimited, 1991.

—Karen Bellenir

TRUCK AND BUS BODIES

This industry is comprised of establishments primarily involved in the manufacture of truck and bus bodies. Some establishments also provide complete vehicles by assembling the bodies they make onto purchased chassis. Establishments engaged in the manufacture of vehicle chassis are classified in **SIC 3711: Motor Behicles and Passenger Car Bodies.** Establishments primarily engaged in the manufacture of truck trailers and demountable cargo containers are classified in **SIC 3715: Truck Trailers.**

Other related motor vehicle classifications include establishments primarily engaged in the assembly of motor homes on purchased chassis (**SIC 3716: Motor Homes**), stamped body parts for trucks and buses (**SIC 3465: Automotive Stampings**), cabs for agricultural tractors (**SIC 3523: Farm Machinery and Equipment**), cabs for industrial tractors (**SIC 3537: Industrial Trucks, Tractors, Trailers, and Stackers**), and cabs for off-highway construction tractors (**SIC 3531: Construction Machinery and Equipment**).

INDUSTRY SNAPSHOT

According to figures reported by the U.S. Department of Commerce, **SIC 3713: Truck and Bus Bodies** shipped products valued at $4.6 billion in 1987. Of this total, $4.2 billion represented products considered primary to the industry. Secondary products were valued at $184.7 million, and $222.9 million represented miscellaneous transactions. These figures yielded a specialization ratio of 96 percent, an increase from the 93 percent reported in 1982.

Truck sales tended to be volatile because they were subject to cyclical changes in the overall economy. The nation's industrial sector created the largest portion of freight tonnage, and changes in the volume of industrial freight shipments led to parallel shifts in total truck sales. Interest rates and fuel costs also impacted the industry.

Medium- and heavy-duty truck makers marked their most productive year in 1988 when the industry sold 334,000 units. Sales tumbled in subsequent years, however; and in 1991, heavy-duty truck makers recorded their worst year since 1983. An improving national economy helped sales begin to rebound in 1992. During that year, combined heavy-duty and medium-duty truck sales rose 11 percent over 1991, reaching 246,000 units.

Government forecasters and industry watchers predicted continued expansion during the middle years of the 1990s. Although initial orders showed faster growth within the heavy-duty truck segment, some analysts expected long-term demand for medium-duty trucks to outpace the heavier vehicles. Reasons cited included "just-in-time" inventory practices and a growing number of service industries. Service industries typically required smaller vehicles than manufacturing industries, and "just-in-time" inventory practices required smaller, more frequent deliveries, making the lighter trucks more economical.

BACKGROUND AND DEVELOPMENT

Established guidelines in the United States categorized on-road trucks and buses into one of eight classes according to their gross vehicle weight. As a group, Classes 1 through 3 were referred to as light-duty trucks; Classes 4 through 7 were referred to as medium-duty trucks; and Class 8 vehicles were referred to as heavy-duty trucks. Most buses fell into the medium-duty classification. Light-duty trucks included personal pickups, minivans, and sport/utility vehicles. Class 1 vehicles were those weighing up to 6,000 pounds; Class 2 vehicles weighed between 6,001 and 10,000 pounds; and Class 3 vehicles weighed between 10,001 and 14,000 pounds. Medium-duty trucks included service or local delivery vehicles, some types of construction vehicles, school buses, and refuse collection vehicles. Class 4 vehicles weighed between 14,001 and 16,000 pounds; Class 5 vehicles weighed between 16,001 and 19,500 pounds; Class 6 vehicles weighed between 19,501 and 26,000 pounds; and Class 7 vehicles weighed between 26,001 and 33,000. Purchasers of medium-duty trucks tended to be small to medium-sized businesses. Heavy-duty trucks, listed as Class 8, were the largest type of on-road vehicle sold in the United States. Class 8 vehicles weighed more than 33,000 pounds and were primarily purchased by large industrial manufacturers and interstate fleet operators.

Trucks and buses were made up of three primary parts: the chassis, the body, and the engine. The chassis contained the wheels, axles, and fuel tank as well as all the structural elements necessary to provide support to the body and engine. Manufacturers often used one single chassis style with many different body types.

Truck and bus body makers provided a variety of body styles to meet different hauling requirements. Van bodies were used to transport enclosed cargo and types of vans varied. For example, refrigerated vans were air tight while livestock vans featured vents to allow for air flow. Tank bodies were used to transport liquids. Hoppers were a special type of tank used to carry chemicals, salt, wheat and cement. Flat bed truck bodies were designed to carry large, heavy loads such as machinery, steel beams, and telephone poles.

Other factors also distinguished different types of trucks. "Straight" or "rigid" trucks were mounted on a single chassis, with their cab and load areas forming one unit. "Semi" or "tractor trailer" trucks were mounted on two chassis, with their cab and load areas forming two separate units. The units were attached with a device located behind the cab on the tractor called a "fifth wheel."

Straight trucks, semi-trucks, and buses were available in two basic configurations termed "conventional" and "cab-over." In conventional designs, the vehicle's engine was located under a traditional hood in front of the driver cab. In cab-over designs, the driver cab was mounted directly over the engine. The cab-over design permitted manufacturers to make shorter cabs. In areas where total vehicle length was limited by law, cab-over tractors permitted drivers to pull longer cargo trailers.

Another type of truck designation, based on numerical references, was used to describe how many wheels a vehicle possessed and how many of its wheels were powered by the engine. For example, a 4x2 truck was one with four wheels, two of which were drive wheels. A 4x4 vehicle had four wheels and all four were drive wheels. A 6x4 truck had a total of six wheels and four of them were drive wheels.

In the United States, many truck engines differed from automobile engines because they ran on diesel fuel rather than gasoline. Diesel engines, invented by Rudolf Diesel in 1897, were a type of internal combustion engine powered by the controlled explosion of fuel sprayed into a cylinder under pressure. Diesel engine design was simpler than gasoline engine design and required no spark plug. Diesel fuel also cost less than gasoline and did not burn as readily if spilled. Diesel engines, however, were more expensive to construct because they required heavier gears to accommodate a more powerful stroke. Because diesel engines were especially suited for heavy-duty hauling and long-distance running they gained popularity in cartage vehicles in the United States.

Trucks developed in response to the need to transport goods. John B. Rae, automotive historian and author of *The American Automobile Industry,* wrote, "At the beginning of the nineteenth century the cost of moving goods thirty miles inland by road in the United States was as great as the cost of carrying the same goods across the Atlantic." Although steam locomotives helped provide alternatives to animal power during the middle and late 1800s, railroads could not offer "door-to-door" service.

As the emerging automotive industry began to supply people with self-propelled vehicles for personal transportation, enterprising innovators began to apply the technology toward the development of commercial vehicles. The popular Model T chassis, introduced in 1908, found itself used in a variety of applications. Ford Motor Company offered it as an Ice Cream truck, as an urban delivery truck, and as a farm vehicle.

One of the first types of specialty trucks was the twin boom wrecker, designed by Ernest Holmes in 1914. The truck's twin booms featured cables powered by the vehicle's engine. One cable could be deployed to rescue or lift a disabled vehicle; the other cable could be hooked to a tree to provide additional support. Other truck innovations made during the early decades of the 20th century included four-wheel drive, four-wheel steering, and an improved clutch system.

With the coming of World War I, unfavorable front-line driving conditions compelled truck designers to make other improvements and refinements. One popular truck developed during the war era was the Mack AC. The Mack AC earned itself the nickname "Bulldog" because of its blunt-nose and reputation for toughness. To help it perform in mud, the Bulldog's engine was connected to the vehicle's rear wheels with a drive train and the truck's solid rubber tires were puncture-proof. The Mack Truck Company honored the Bulldog by incorporating the image of a bulldog in the organization's official logo.

During the period between World War I and World War II, truck makers turned increasingly to pneumatic tires. Pneumatic tires were filled with air and provided a smoother ride. Truck designers made larger vehicles capable of carrying heavier loads, making additional wheels necessary to distribute their weight more evenly and avoid damaging tires and road surfaces.

During the 1920s "semi-truck" designs were introduced. Semi-trucks featured a tractor front end which was used to pull a trailer section behind. Semi-trucks were better able to turn tight corners, and they replaced large, rigid, single-section trucks. In addition to the improved maneuverability, semi construction provided for more efficient tractor use. Because the trailer could be detached for cargo loading and unloading, the tractor was freed for other tasks. The 1920s also saw the introduction of modern motor buses. In 1923, two brothers, Frank P. and William B. Fageol, organized the Twin Coach Company. Twin Motor Coach buses were the first to offer underneath engines.

By 1930, the number of trucks on American roads had grown to 3.6 million, up from 1.1 million in 1920. An estimated one in four were farm owned and the era saw vast improvements in farm-to-market roadways. Although many pioneering truck manufacturers were also involved in making automobiles, the different economies of scale involved in producing the two types of vehicles resulted in a different mix of major manufacturers. Passenger car makers relied on capital-intensive mass production technology. This led to industry consolidation and the emergence of the "Big Three" companies (Ford, Chrysler, and General Motors). Truck makers, however, built a variety of vehicles, each type customized to perform a special task. As a result, a greater number of smaller companies were able to compete. During the 1930s the nation's principle truck manufacturers were the White Motor Company, Mack International, Autocar Company, and International Harvester.

During World War II, auto makers and truck makers focused their energies on providing military vehicles. Special-task trucks, missile carriers, troop transports, and cargo haulers were all necessary to the war effort. Manufacturers, working under government contract, intensified research and development projects aimed at building better, more reliable trucks. Following the war, the knowledge gained was transferred to civilian undertakings and the 1950s saw tremendous expansion in the trucking industry.

Improvements in the nation's highway system also played a role. In 1956, Congress passed the Interstate Highway Act, which authorized the construction of 41,000 miles of interstate highways and offered to fund 90 percent of the project with money from the Highway Trust Fund. As the nation's infrastructure improved, long-distance trucking became more feasible. Prior to the 1950s most of the nation's long distance freight shipments were made by rail and trucks were used primarily to provide local delivery to and from rail stations. Unloading and re-loading cargo for rail-to-truck transfers increased the cost of moving goods and provided an economic incentive for shippers to switch to long-distance over-the-road transport. The percentage of freight deliveries made by truck increased from about 17 percent of all deliveries in 1950 to almost 25 percent by the end of the decade.

Another national phenomenon, suburban growth, increased the importance of trucks to American life. Decentralized, suburban lifestyles required the kind of flexible freight transport trucks provided. Trucks made suburban development possible, and suburban devel-

opment increased the demand for trucks. Trucks served the construction industry as it built suburbs; trucks carried household possessions as families moved into the suburbs; and trucks served the businesses that moved from the central city to outlying areas.

During the 1960s and 1970s the increased presence of large trucks on American roads led to increased concern about their safety. Semi-trucks were notorious for their tendency to jackknife under adverse braking conditions. When the trailer's wheels locked during breaking, it pushed the trailer forward causing the vehicle's two parts to bend into a jackknife position and skid. To help prevent jackknifing, anti-lock brake systems were investigated. The Federal Motor Vehicle Safety Standard 121, enacted in 1975, set performance standards for vehicles with air brakes and mandated the use of anti-lock braking systems through its stipulation of minimum stopping distances. Unfortunately, available technology was not able to meet the standard.

Anti-lock brakes worked by modulating the amount of air applied to the brakes. When a sensor indicated that a wheel was in danger of locking, it applied air pressure in a pulsing manner. The pulsing pressure enabled the wheel to keep rolling and prevented it from skidding. During the 1970s, however, available computer technology was too slow to immediately interpret sensor input. The resulting time lag caused brake failure. In April of 1978, the Ninth U.S. Circuit Court of Appeals struck down the "no-lock" and minimum stopping distance requirements.

The 1980s brought renewed efforts at making trucks safer. A study done by AAA of Michigan found that in car-truck accidents motorists sustained a higher percentage of fatalities because trucks were becoming longer, wider, and heavier, while cars were getting smaller and lighter. Researchers investigated ways of preventing small vehicles from underriding trucks during crashes. Congress mandated a study of truck brake systems and legislators enacted regulations establishing national standards for licensing truck drivers and sharing driver information among the fifty states.

CURRENT CONDITIONS

During the late 1980s and early 1990s, truck manufacturers suffered the effects of a nationwide economic slow down. In 1992, however, sales and orders began to show improvement. According to the *1993 Ward's Automotive Yearbook,* overall truck sales in 1992 were 12.8 percent higher than those for 1991. Medium-duty trucks in Classes 4 through 7 posted a 6.5 percent gain, and heavy-duty Class 8 truck sales increased 20.6 percent.

The recovery extended into 1993. In January of 1993, Class 8 sales were 44.7 percent higher than those for January of 1992. Production continued to be high during the early months of the year and industry watchers estimated that Class 8 factory sales would hit 160,000 by the year's end. Although increases in medium-duty truck sales lagged behind heavy-duty sales in the early months of 1993, the medium-duty segment began to catch up during the middle of the year.

According to a report in *Automotive News,* the truck market was expected to continue improving through 1994. The rebound was attributed to a better economic climate and the effect of an aging national truck fleet. Another factor bolstering expectations among truck makers was a government announcement of plans to spend $15 billion to upgrade the nation's infrastructure. Planners predicted an increased demand for vehicles such as dumpers, haulers, and mixers needed to construct and repair road surfaces.

Within the motor coach segment of the industry, manufacturers placed an ever-increasing emphasis on luxury. Motor coaches offered amenities such as VCR systems, kitchens, and larger bathroom facilities. Buses were also available in a wide variety of vehicle sizes, ranging from small 20 seat mini-buses to large vehicles capable of seating 76 passengers.

One segment of the industry unique to Canada and the United States was the manufacture of school buses for student transport. School bus models, however, because they were simpler and less expensive than other types of buses, were a common export item. In developing countries such as Costa Rica, Nicaragua, Columbia, Venezuela, and Bolivia they were used to provide community transportation.

Safety issues continued to be a primary concern within the industry. The 1990s brought a newly designed anti-lock braking system based on digital computer technology. Advanced computer capabilities helped anti-lock brakes overcome some of the problems associated with earlier systems. The National Highway Traffic Safety Administration (NHTSA) began studying the new anti-lock brake systems and was expected to complete its tests by June of 1994. New regulations were expected to go into effect during 1996.

Underride regulations were also forthcoming. In an effort to reduce traffic fatalities resulting from cars striking the rear-ends of trucks and truck trailers, NHTSA was considering mandating design modifications. One possible future alteration was a change in bumper heights. Some researchers argued that if collisions occurred at the car's frame elevation, occupants would be better protected by the controlled-crush design features of the automobile.

In environmental matters, truck makers were preparing to meet newer, more stringent emission standards. Many medium- and heavy-duty trucks burned diesel fuel. Diesel exhaust contained pollutants such as nitrogen oxides, hydrocarbons, carbon monoxide, and particulate matter visible as black smoke. Between 1988 and 1991, emissions of nitrogen oxides had been cut by more than half. New emission standards were scheduled to begin in 1994 and 1998. The 1994 standards required that levels of particulates be cut by more than fifty percent; the 1998 standards required a further 25 percent cut in emissions of nitrogen oxide.

INDUSTRY LEADERS

One of the largest truck makers was Ford Truck Operations, a division of Ford Motor Company. Ford Truck, with headquarters in Dearborn, Michigan, was the number one producer of medium-duty trucks and the number two producer in combined medium-duty and heavy-duty units. In 1992, Ford reported sales of 44,996 units in Classes 4 through 7 and sales of 13,798 units in Class 8 vehicles.

Another truck maker affiliated with one of the "Big Three" auto makers was GM Truck and Bus, a division of General Motors. GM participated in only the medium-duty truck market, primarily within Classes 6 and 7. The company offered vehicles under the GMC and Chevrolet nameplates. GM's market share fell from 25 percent in 1990 to 23.5 percent in 1991. In 1992, GMC held 15.6 percent of the medium-duty market and Chevrolet held 8.5 percent, giving GM a combined market share of 24 percent.

GM's involvement in Class 8 trucks changed in 1988 with the establishment of Volvo GM Heavy Truck Corporation. Volvo GM was formed as a joint venture between GM and the heavy truck divisions of the Swedish firm Volvo—White Motor Trucks and Autocar. Although GM initially retained a 27 percent interest in Volvo GM, it later sold some of its interest to Volvo, giving Volvo a total of 83 percent of the venture.

In 1992, Volvo GM held 6.2 percent of the total medium- and heavy-duty truck market. Within the medium-duty segment, however, the company participated only in Class 7 vehicles. Its primary focus was in the Class 8 market where it sold 14,641 units. Volvo GM sales within the United States accounted for approximately 33 percent of Volvo's medium- and heavy-duty truck deliveries worldwide.

The number one market-share holder for total truck sales within the combined medium-duty and heavy-duty classifications was Navistar International Transportation Corporation, a wholly owned subsidiary of Navistar International Corporation. Navistar's products encompassed many types of trucks in Classes 5 through 8. The company's diesel-powered products were marketed under the ''International'' brand.

Navistar was also the nation's leading supplier of school bus chassis, a position it had held for more than two decades. Navistar sold bus chassis to body manufacturers who completed the buses and delivered them to end consumers. In addition, the company manufactured chassis for small capacity buses such as those operated to provide service to disabled students. American Transportation Corporation, maker of Ward brand school bus bodies, was partly owned by Navistar.

Navistar's roots can be traced back to the first decade of the 20th century. The company, headquartered in Chicago, Illinois, was built on a foundation laid by International Harvester. International Harvester was founded in 1907 and played a leading role in the development of the industry through the early decades of the 1900s.

In the early 1990s, Navistar operated seven manufacturing and assembly plants in the United States and one in Canada. The eight plants provided the company with eight million square feet of assembly floor space. Navistar products were sold through 949 dealer and distribution outlets, and the company's customers included common carriers, private carriers, government and service organizations, the construction industry, the energy and petroleum industries, and student transportation services.

In 1992, according to figures published by *Ward's Automotive Yearbook,* Navistar produced 38,559 medium-duty and 25,283 heavy-duty trucks. Although its combined sales of medium-duty and heavy-duty trucks gave the company a total market share of 25.6 percent, the highest in the industry, Navistar held neither individual number one position. In the medium-duty segment it placed second behind Ford Motor Company. In the heavy-duty segment Navistar occupied the number one position for 28 years, but in 1992 the company dropped to the number two position and Freightliner climbed to number one.

Navistar faced serious financial difficulties during 1992. The company posted its third consecutive year of losses and found itself entangled in a legal challenge by the UAW over retiree health-care costs. The company claimed that without an agreement to restructure

the costs it would have to file for bankruptcy. In order to provide the cash necessary to fund post-retirement health care benefits and to provide money for working capital, Navistar filed a registration statement with the Securities and Exchange Commission on September 20, 1993, to offer 22 million shares of common stock. Through the stock offering the company planned to raise $500 million.

Freightliner, the company that unseated Navistar from its previously held position as the number one heavy-duty truck manufacturer, was a subsidiary of Dailmer-Benz AG with U.S. offices in Portland, Oregon. Freightliner's 1992 sales of 27,491 heavy-duty trucks earned it a 23.1 percent share of the Class 8 market. The company's sales within the medium-duty market, however, were much less with 1992 marking Freightliner's initial offering of vehicles within the medium-duty market. Although the company posted sales of 1,912 units within Classes 6 and 7, it captured only 1.5 percent of the medium-duty market.

Some industry analysts doubted whether Freightliner would be able to substantially increase its participation in the medium-duty truck market during 1994 because of construction capacity limitations. Freightliner built both medium-duty and heavy-duty trucks at the same plants and demand for its Class 8 vehicles constrained the company's ability to produce additional medium-duty trucks. To help increase production, Freightliner announced plans to build additional plant capacity for Class 6 and 7 trucks. Freightliner also owned an 80 percent interest in a Mexican joint venture to assemble its products.

Another major participant in the truck manufacturing industry was PACCAR, Inc. PACCAR, a domestic corporation with headquarters in Bellevue, Washington, offered two truck nameplates, Kenworth and Peterbilt. Combined, Kenworth and Peterbilt captured 20.6 percent of the Class 8 market in 1992. Their market share, however, represented a decrease from 21.4 percent in 1991 and 22 percent in 1990.

Perhaps one of the best known names within the truck-making industry was Mack Trucks, Inc. Mack achieved popularity during World War I when its ''Bulldog'' truck was acclaimed for toughness and the phrase ''built like a Mack Truck'' entered the American lexicon. Mack built trucks in Classes 6, 7, and 8, but most of the company's total 1992 production of 13,375 units fell into the heavy duty segment where Mack held 10.1 percent of the market. In the worldwide market, Mack's heavy-duty and medium-duty diesel products were sold in more than 65 countries. Although Mack Trucks had a long history of truck making in the United States, the company was not U.S.

owned. In 1979 the French Renault Vehicles Industriels SA began purchasing an interest in Mack. Renault's ownership totaled 46 percent in 1985, and in 1990 the French firm purchased the remainder, acquiring complete ownership.

Mack encountered serious financial difficulties during the late 1980s and early 1990s. In 1992, Mack posted its fourth consecutive year of losses. Cost cutting measures, employee reductions, and an emphasis on improved productivity were aimed at helping the company return to profitability. Between 1990 and 1993, the company reduced its work force by more than 25 percent, down to 4,800 employees. In May of 1993, Mack announced plans to permanently close its assembly plant in Oakville, Ontario, idling an additional 250 workers. The Oakville plant made Mack's RD model which was used for construction, ready-mix, logging and refuse applications. Mack planned to transfer its Oakville assembly to the company's plant in Macungie, Pennsylvania.

Another company with a long history in the American truck-making industry was Oshkosh Truck Corporation. Oshkosh Truck focused on providing specialized trucks and transport equipment for specific market niches. The company's product line included heavy-duty commercial trucks, military vehicles, buses, and walk-in delivery vans as well as equipment for heavy snow removal and specialized refuse pickup.

Oshkosh Truck traced its beginnings back to two inventors, William R. Besserdich and Bernhard A. Mosling. Besserdich and Mosling held patents for innovations necessary to produce four-wheel drive vehicles. One patent was for a method of transferring the engine's power to all four vehicle wheels using an automatic locking differential. A differential enabled the wheels on the axle to go around corners at different speeds. The other patent improved the front axle's steering and drive abilities. In 1915 Besserdich and Mosling approached several major car manufacturers but were turned away. They incorporated their own company, Wisconsin Duplex Auto Company, in 1917. Wisconsin Duplex later moved to Oshkosh and became Oshkosh Truck. The company's first vehicle, nicknamed ''Old Betsy,'' had a three-speed transmission, one-ton hauling capacity, and weighed 3,280 pounds.

WORK FORCE

According to government statistics, the truck and bus body industry employed 37,800 workers in 1987. This total represented a 35 percent increase over the employment of 28,100 reported in 1982 and an increase of 14 percent over 1986. Top states in employment were Pennsylvania, Indiana, Ohio, and California. Single-establishment companies with 20 or fewer employees accounted for 14 percent of shipments as measured by value.

AMERICA AND THE WORLD

During the early 1990s, North America was the world's largest combined medium- and heavy-duty truck market. As a result, the region attracted interest from overseas establishments and the U.S. market experienced an increasing presence of foreign-owned participants. Three large foreign-owned companies with domestic manufacturing facilities (Freightliner, Volvo GM, and Mack Trucks) increased their combined market share from about 20 percent in 1990 to about 22 percent in 1991. Japanese manufacturers (Isuzu Truck of America, Hino Diesel Trucks USA, Nissan Truck of America, and Mitsubishi Fuso Truck of America) boosted their U.S. sales by 31 percent between 1991 and 1992.

Imported vehicles represented 11 percent of vehicles sold in the medium-duty classes during 1991, up from 3.1 percent in 1986. Within the Class 8 segment, however, imports captured less than one percent of 1991's total sales. According to a Hino representative, differences between the heavy-duty truck markets in the United States and Japan made the shipment of Class 8 trucks from Japanese manufacturers into the United States impractical. The U.S. market was unique because trucks were custom manufactured using a combination of in-house and outsourced components in accordance with a particular customer's specifications.

American exports of medium- and heavy-duty trucks totaled $1.1 billion in 1991, an increase over the $951 million recorded in 1990. The ability of U.S. companies to compete overseas was bolstered by a drop in the value of the dollar in relationship to the yen and European currencies. U.S. opportunities in the European Community, however, were limited by import duties ranging from 17 to 22 percent of the vehicles' landed value. Talks were underway to negotiate a more favorable tariff situation.

The biggest U.S. trading partner in heavy and medium-duty trucks was Canada. Canada received 43 percent of U.S. exports and supplied 73 percent of U.S. imports. Some analysts expected Mexico to be the fastest growing market for U.S. medium- and heavy-duty trucks. Other growing overseas markets included South and Central America, Eastern Europe and nations formed following the break-up of the former Soviet Union.

RESEARCH AND TECHNOLOGY

During the early 1990s, truck and bus makers were facing many challenges to improve their environmental and safety records. Research toward improving the industry's environmental impact focused on reducing vehicle emissions, improving fuel economy, and developing alternative fuels.

The Clean Air Act Amendments of 1990 imposed increasing reductions in vehicle emissions creating a need for expanded research in clean-burning diesel technology. Efforts were also underway to make vehicles with increased fuel economy. Designers worked toward making lighter trucks with smaller dimensions, better aerodynamic styling, and improved engine performance. In a similar vein, some groups were advocating the development of alternate fuels. One of the most promising alternate fuels was natural gas. Many environmental groups favored natural gas over gasoline and diesel fuels because it emitted 90 percent less carbon monoxide and 50 percent less hydrocarbons.

Safety issues under investigation included searches for innovative designs offering improved driver visibility, better braking systems, and the development of collision avoidance technologies. Greyhound Lines, Inc. planned to provide radar collision-avoidance on buses by the middle of the 1990s. The system under development used a light and buzzer to alert drivers when other vehicles got too close.

Other changes were also being studied. Manufacturers investigated possible alterations to improve driving and sleeping accommodations for truck operators. They were also developing advanced drive-trains to permit the construction of trailers capable of carrying more cargo.

INDUSTRY INFORMATION SOURCES

Berg, Tom, "What's This? Fleets Now Asking for ABS?," *Modern Tire Dealer,* June 1993.

Bohn, Joseph, "Alarm Sounded on Truck Fatalities: New Laws on Books; More Analysis of Problems Proposed," *Automotive News,* December 29, 1986.

Bohn, Joseph, "Big Trucks Make Strong Start in '93," *Automotive News,* February 22, 1993.

Bohn, Joseph, "Class 8 Sales Fire Spreads to Medium-Duties," *Automotive News,* April 26, 1993.

Bolan, Nelson, *How Detroit Changed History,* Lawrenceville, VA: Brunswick, 1987.

Bradley, Peter, "Medium Trucks: Safe, Lean, Clean Machines," *Purchasing,* February 18, 1993.

"DRI Predicts 6% Drop in West Europe Sales," *WARD's Auto World,* July 1992.

Field, Mike, "Building a Better Bus; Inspired by European Designs, the Industry Is Upgrading Its Vehicles and Its Image," *Travel Weekly,* March 29, 1990.

"From Four-Wheel Drive to Ten-Wheel Drive," *Communication,* December 1992.

Jefferis, David, *Giants of the Road: The History of Land Transportation,* New York: Franklin Watts, 1991.

Kahn, Helen, "Dual Trucker Licenses Banned," *Automotive News,* June 8, 1987.

Kahn, Helen, "NHTSA Urges Better Brakes to Cut Heavy-Truck Accidents," *Automotive News,* June 8, 1987.

Keaton, Joanne, "Back to School," *Indiana Business Magazine,* September 1992.

Langworth, Richard M., *The Complete History of Ford Motor Company,* New York: Beekman House, 1987.

"Mack Closing Ontario Plant," *Automotive News,* May 17, 1993.

"Mack Ready for Rebound in Heavy-Duty Truck Market," Allentown, PA: Mack Trucks Inc., January 1993.

McCann, Hugh, and David C. Smith, "NGV's: Natural Gas Nears Lead in Alternate Fuel Race," *WARD's Auto World,* June 1993.

Moore, Walt, "A Second Chance for Anti-Lock Brakes," *Construction Equipment,* October 1990.

"Navistar Files Registration with SEC, Offering 22 Million Shares of Common Stock," News Release, September 20, 1993.

"Navistar International Corporation" *Prospectus,* Chicago: Navistar, 1993.

1987 Census of Manufactures, Washington, D.C.: Bureau of the Census, 1990.

"Oshkosh Truck Corporation," *Annual Report for the Year Ended September 30, 1992.* Oshkosh, WI: Oshkosh Truck, 1992.

Paccar Annual Report 1992, Bellevue, WA: Paccar Inc., 1993.

"Paccar Reports Earnings," *Automotive News,* February 1, 1993.

Plumb, Stephen E., "EC '92 Creates Opportunity and Consolidation," *WARD's Auto World,* July 1992.

Rae, John B., *The American Automobile Industry,* Boston: Twayne Publishers, 1984.

Schine, Eric, Mark Maremont, and Christina Del Valle, "Here Comes the Thinking Car," *Business Week,* May 25, 1992.

Sears, Stephen W., *History of the Automobile in America,* New York: American Heritage Publishing, 1977.

Ward's Automotive Yearbook, Detroit: Ward's Communications, 1993.

U.S. Industrial Outlook 1993. Washington, D.C.: U.S. Department of Commerce, 1993.

Zim, Herbert S., and James R. Skelly, *Trucks,* New York: Morrow, 1970.

—Karen Bellenir

SIC 3714

MOTOR VEHICLE PARTS AND ACCESSORIES

This industry includes establishments primarily engaged in manufacturing motor vehicle parts and accessories, but not engaged in manufacturing complete motor vehicles or passenger car bodies. Establishments primarily engaged in manufacturing or assembling complete automobiles and trucks are classified in **SIC 3711: Motor Vehicles and Passenger Car Bodies**; those manufacturing tires and inner tubes are classified in **SIC 3011: Tires and Inner Tubes**; those manufacturing automobile stampings are classified in **SIC 3465: Automotive Stampings**; those manufacturing vehicular lighting equipment are classified in **SIC 3647: Vehicular Lighting Equipment**; those manufacturing ignition systems are classified in **SIC 3694**; those manufacturing storage batteries are classified in **SIC 3691**; and those manufacturing carburetors, pistons, piston rings, and engine intake and exhaust valves are classified in **SIC 2592: Carburetors, Pistons, Piston Rings, and Valves**.

INDUSTRY SNAPSHOT

An estimated 15,000 parts and accessories are used in the production of motor vehicles. These parts represent the principle products of about 2,500 companies and a portion of the output of thousands of others. The annual production of motor vehicle parts and accessories within the United States is valued at over $90 billion. The Motor Equipment Manufacturers Association (MEMA) is the leading industry trade organization and compiles industry statistics.

ORGANIZATION AND STRUCTURE

The auto parts industry is divided into two principle segments: original equipment (OE) suppliers and aftermarket suppliers.

Original Equipment Suppliers. Original equipment suppliers sell parts and components directly to automobile manufacturers to be used in the production of new vehicles. Consequently, sales in the OE market depend on the number, size, and complexity of new vehicles produced. Primary products include wheels, frames, axles, transmissions, transaxles, bearings, springs, bumpers, brake systems, fuel injectors, seats, seat belts, airbags, cushioning, and safety padding materials. For many large suppliers, OE parts provide the majority of sales, although most suppliers also produce parts for aftermarket sales. Companies that supply both OE and aftermarket parts can generally cover development and tooling costs on the OE sales volume and supply the aftermarket at higher volumes than pure aftermarket suppliers. Furthermore, spreading research, development, and tool and die outlays over several contracts with different manufacturers provides OE suppliers a cost advantage over the in-house parts divisions of vehicle manufacturers. OE suppliers typically concentrate on a few components and systems requiring a high degree of technological skill and manufacturing efficiency. By supplying parts for new vehicles, OE manufacturers are generally on the leading edge of technology, and vehicle manufactures have begun to turn to suppliers for increased engineering and development responsibilities. Auto makers also look to leading suppliers for financing and services related to inventory management, logistics, and tooling.

Aftermarket Suppliers. Aftermarket parts suppliers manufacture and sell replacement products for used vehicles. Primary products include spark plugs, shock absorbers, struts, springs, brakes pads, rotors, filters, wiper blades, and exhaust systems. Aftermarket parts are distributed through a few major parts distributors and thousands of small jobbers and local firms for sale by auto dealers, service stations, repair shops, auto parts stores, tire stores, department stores, discount stores, and home and do-it-yourself stores. Aftermaket sales tend to be more stable than OE sales, particularly during recessionary times. As owners put off the purchase of new autos, they tend to extend the life of their current vehicles through increased maintenance and parts replacement.

BACKGROUND AND DEVELOPMENT

The automotive parts industry began with the development of the automobile at the turn of the century, and the growth in the parts industry followed that of the automotive industry. By 1970, automobiles were manufactured in long production runs of few vehicle models. The vehicle population consisted of a fairly homogenous group of cars that were not known to be particularly well made. Automobiles of the era were easy to repair, and, with nearly all of the 225,000 service stations in operation providing repair services, mechanics were abundant. Parts suppliers found it easy to predict the demand for a relatively narrow range of parts and profited from their manufacture.

Beginning in the 1970s, several trends in the U.S. automobile industry started to affect domestic parts producers. The number of vehicle models produced began to expand, buoyed mostly by the increased sales of Japanese automobiles in the U.S. market. The continued proliferation of models and the shortening of model lives increased the number of parts required for vehicle manufacture and repair while lowering the volume of individual part production. Lowered economies of scale began to dampen the profits of parts suppliers, while growing product lines increased the number of niche suppliers.

During the 1980s, small trucks began to sell more rapidly than passenger cars, requiring an increased production of parts for the truck population. During this time, the increasing market share gained by foreign vehicle manufacturers—whose OE and replacement parts were principally supplied by foreign parts producers—resulted in a decrease in the overall market for domestic parts.

Responding to this global competition, U.S. vehicle manufacturers placed a stronger emphasis on quality and reliability. However, more reliable new cars led to fewer repairs, slowing growth in aftermarket parts sales. In addition, the increased technical complexity of newer vehicles made performing repairs more difficult. Of the roughly 130,000 service stations in existence in 1990, only about 50 percent still performed repair services, with dealers and independent service facilities gaining a share of repair services. The increased cost of repairing more complex systems, the inability of do-it-yourselfers to perform their own repairs, and the decreased number of service stations performing routine checks led to an underperformance of maintenance and repair. These effects were counteracted to a limited extent by the aging automobile population. While the number of cars under three years old remained relatively constant between 1970 and 1991, the number of cars greater than three years old increased significantly, and the aging vehicle population provided a growing market for vehicle repair and parts replacement.

CURRENT CONDITIONS

In the late 1980s and early 1990s, parts manufacturers were forced to respond to major changes in technological advances, relationships with vehicle manufacturers, and the impact of Japanese auto makers.

Technology. Parts makers have worked to meet the increased technological sophistication of new automobiles. Protective airbags were installed in 51 percent of 1992 model year cars, compared to almost none

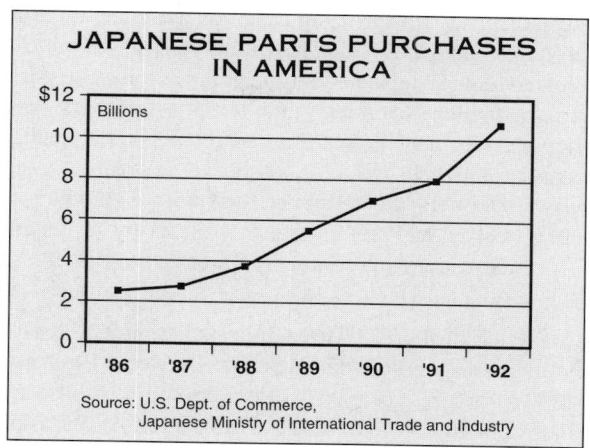

JAPANESE PARTS PURCHASES IN AMERICA

Source: U.S. Dept. of Commerce, Japanese Ministry of International Trade and Industry

in 1989. With regulations requiring the use of passive restraints, airbags are expected to be standard equipment on almost all cars and light trucks by 1998. Antilock braking systems were installed on 32 percent of new automobiles in the 1992 model year, and traction control systems and innovative suspensions are gaining in popularity. By the year 2000, the use of electronic components, currently employed in engine management, climate control, braking, convenience, and other vehicle systems, is expected to grow by 200 percent compared to 1987 levels. Additional developments are underway to increase the use of lighter weight materials throughout new vehicles. While increasing research and development costs, the use of complex and expensive components and systems has improved opportunities for revenue and profit increases for parts suppliers. Further opportunities are provided by new clean air regulations. More stringent regulations will increase the complexity of engine control and emissions systems, and a required increase in inspection programs may lead to more repair and parts replacement opportunities for aftermarket suppliers.

Relationship with the Auto Makers. With an influx of auto makers, the United States has become the most competitive automotive market in the world. To meet the demands of increased competition, the "Big Three" U.S. auto makers (General Motors, Ford, and Chrysler) have focused efforts on quality improvement, cost reduction, and strategic sourcing—reducing the number of primary suppliers while increasing their responsibilities. These efforts have had tremendous impact on parts manufacturers. In the past, OE parts were sold largely on annual contracts covering the model year. In a move to improve supplier relationships, vehicle manufacturer began to award contracts for the life of a vehicle model. In addition, auto makers are reducing the number of suppliers they deal with directly, awarding primary suppliers more responsibility for the design and development of entire systems and subassemblies. Primary suppliers are expected to integrate and coordinate the purchase of parts from smaller secondary and tertiary suppliers, and suppliers of all levels are urged to raise their quality standards while reducing costs. In response, many parts suppliers are reducing the number of vendors they deal with. Parts suppliers most likely to benefit from these trends are large suppliers able to increase the services they offer to vehicle manufacturers.

Each of the Big Three auto makers initiated programs for supplier management. Between 1980 and 1991, Ford reduced its worldwide supplier base by half, and in 1991, it began a restructuring plan that included increased supplier reductions. The company also asked suppliers to cut costs by one percent annually until 1997 and opened up its bidding system so that outside suppliers competed evenly against Ford Automotive Components Group, which supplied about 50 percent of the companies parts in the early 1990s.

Chrysler implemented its SCORE (supplier cost-reduction effort) program, urging suppliers to come up with ideas for improvements and cost savings in manufacturing, scheduling, inventory, and shipping. Chrysler has attempted to establish longer term relationships with suppliers by naming suppliers for specific commodities. The company had fewer than 2,500 suppliers in 1992, down from more than 3,000 in the late 1980s, and it has a goal of eventually reducing the number of suppliers it deals with to 750. The company's 1993 LH model uses 170 suppliers, compared to 600 to 800 suppliers for cars of earlier model years.

General Motors initiated the industry's most controversial supplier management plan with its PICOS (purchased input concept optimization with suppliers) program, which demanded significant price reductions from suppliers given long term contracts. Under the program, GM sent teams of engineers, designers, and purchasing cost accountants to meet with parts suppliers at their plants to investigate production inefficiencies and propose solutions leading to cost reductions. The program also allowed GM to accept unsolicited bids from worldwide suppliers for contracts it had already negotiated for future models, and it stripped away advantages to GM's Automotive Components Group. In addition, the company offered suppliers the opportunity to lease factory space in GM plants and a supply of labor from idled workers.

In 1992, the Big Three announced a plan to develop a standardized quality assessment program for suppliers. Such a move, which would reduce the time and paperwork required in undergoing several quality audits by different auto makers, is expected to eventually save suppliers $160 million annually. A first step toward a common standard was taken by eliminating a major source of redundancy in quality auditing. Previously, first tier suppliers were required to audit second and third tier suppliers from whom they purchased parts. However, because many companies acting as second and third tier suppliers also sell parts directly to one of the Big Three, they were already required to be audited under either the Ford Q101, Chrysler Supplier Quality Assessment, or GM Target for Excellence quality program. With the new arrangement, suppliers that have already been qualified through one of the Big Three are no longer required to be audited by a primary supplier. The agreement is expected to save the supplier industry $500,000 a year.

The Impact of Japanese Auto Makers. Increased sales of Japanese automobiles has affected the operations of both OE and aftermarket parts manufacturers. Because most Japanese aftermarket parts are furnished by Japanese OE suppliers, the volumes of replacement parts for domestic parts suppliers has dropped as Japanese vehicles increased their market share in the United States. Domestic parts suppliers have begun to increase their offerings of replacements parts for Japanese vehicles, but at the same time, Japanese suppliers are starting to seek the higher profit margins through the supply of aftermarket parts for U.S. vehicles.

While Japanese manufacturers have increased their production of cars within the United States, the move has not significantly improved the opportunities for domestic parts manufacturers. Foreign vehicles manufactured in the United States have significantly fewer domestic suppliers than Big Three cars. Domestic OE suppliers have argued that the Japanese plants in the United States continue to purchase parts from suppliers based in Japan and the growing number of Japanese suppliers operating in the United States. Furthermore, with the increased capacity of many American factories manufacturing Japanese cars, Japanese suppliers have begun to compete for OE contracts with the Big Three. Some suppliers believe that their industry could be permanently suppressed by these developments.

Some domestic parts suppliers have claimed that they have been hampered by the Japanese keiretsu system, the close relationship between auto makers and their suppliers, arguing that the system impinges on their ability to supply parts to Japanese vehicle manufacturers in North America and Japan. At the request of U.S. suppliers, the Federal Trade Commission (FTC) began an investigation of alleged antitrust violations by Japanese auto producers in the United States. Japanese producers have argued that they purchase from suppliers that meet their needs, and so far the FTC has concluded that there is no clear evidence of collusion among Japanese companies. During President Bush's 1992 trade mission to Japan, Japanese auto makers pledged to purchase $19 billion worth of U.S. auto parts annually by 1995. During 1992 and 1993, Japanese purchases of U.S. auto parts began to increase. The rising value of the Yen relative to the dollar has made shipments of parts from Japan more expensive, encouraging Japanese transplant manufacturers to purchase more U.S. parts.

INDUSTRY LEADERS

For many leading automotive parts suppliers, including Allied-Signal, Eaton, ITT, Rockwell, and TRW, motor vehicle supply provides only a portion of the sales of a much larger organization. These diverse manufacturers often supply components and systems to other transportation industries such as aerospace and defense. For other large suppliers, including Dana and Federal-Mogul, automotive supply is the primary business.

WORK FORCE

Vehicle manufacturers generally have higher labor costs than parts suppliers, who are able to employ more non-union workers. The percentage of workers at aftermarket supply businesses represented by the United Auto Workers (UAW) declined from 50 percent in 1978 to 25 percent in 1990. In 1992, total employment in the U.S. parts industry, including domestic and foreign-owned suppliers, was an estimated 624,000, an increase of seven percent over 1991. Of those employees, 507,000 were production workers, representing an increase of almost ten percent over 1991. The increase in employment in 1992 followed a three-year decline resulting from supplier consolidations.

AMERICA AND THE WORLD

U.S. parts manufacturers have been forced to match the growth in global operations of domestic auto makers to maintain their primary supply relationships. Additionally, international growth has been spurred by the desire to gain supply contracts with overseas vehicle manufacturers. Most leading domestic producers have established manufacturing facilities in the principle auto producing regions of the world, including Canada, Europe, and Mexico. In Europe alone, seven leading U.S. parts manufacturers have combined annual sales exceeding $1 billion. The global integration of the auto industry has led many suppliers to develop joint ventures with foreign parts producers. As the industry continues to globalize, increased U.S. supplier investments are expected in Mexico, Asia, and Europe.

The United States has posted a trade deficit in automotive parts since 1983, primarily due to a large deficit with Japan. Between 1989 and 1992, the parts trade deficit with Japan remained between $9 billion and $10 billion, accounting for one fifth of the overall trade deficit with Japan. Canada is the only major nation with which the United States has maintained a trade surplus, and Canada remains the leading trading partner of U.S. firms. Between 1985 and 1991, Canada received over 60 percent of total U.S. parts exports and supplied one third of total imports.

The number of foreign firms producing parts in the United States increased dramatically throughout the 1980s and early 1990s. In 1992, approximately 350 wholly owned foreign part plants, and over 120 joint ventures, operated in the United States. Japanese suppliers owned 167 U.S. parts plants and were part of 123 joint ventures. European firms, led by German manufacturers, owned 168 plants in the United States, and Canadian firms owned 17, with one joint venture. While fairly well established in Europe and Canada, U.S. penetration of the Japanese domestic market remained weak. In 1992 one wholly owned U.S. parts plant, and a few joint ventures, were operating in Japan.

Continued consolidation and increasing global competition are forecast for the automotive parts industry. The future prospects for large domestic producers are likely to depend on their ability to obtain contracts with Japanese transplant manufacturers as well as to retain contracts with the Big Three against competition from Japanese suppliers. For smaller second and third tier suppliers, the key is likely to be establishing strong relationships with primary suppliers.

INDUSTRY INFORMATION SOURCES

Standard and Poor's Industry Surveys. New York: Standard & Poor's, 1993.

U.S. Industrial Outlook 1993. Washington, DC: U.S. Department of Commerce, 1993.

Templin, Neal. "Japan Auto Makers Buy More U.S. Parts," *The Wall Street Journal,* August 24, 1993.

Ward's Automotive Yearbook, 1993.

—Paolo Motta

TRUCK TRAILERS

This industry covers establishments primarily engaged in manufacturing truck trailers, truck trailer chassis for sale separately, detachable trailer bodies (cargo containers) for sale separately, and detachable trailer (cargo container) chassis for sale separately.

Like heavy trucks, truck trailers are purchased for specific applications and are therefore manufactured in a variety of styles and types. Van, container chassis, and flatbed trailers comprise the majority of trailer shipments, while the remainder consists of a small number of more specialized trailer types. Both the number of axles and length of trailers vary, with the most popular trailers having two axles, followed by single axle designs and trailers with three or more axles. Popular trailer lengths are 48 feet and 28 feet.

In the early 1980s, in response to an increase in intermodal shipments of goods—a system using two or more methods of transport, including trucks, trains, and ships—container chassis trailer shipments increased. The demand for a variety of trailer types, including custom designs, prompted the establishment of several original equipment manufacturers (OEMs) in the trailer industry. Furthermore, increased competition arose from deregulation of the industry in 1980, making manufacturers leaner and more efficient. Many trailer manufacturers are small businesses serving local areas, often employing 50 or fewer workers. In 1984 approximately 400 truck trailer manufacturers were operating in the United States, employing almost 28,000 workers. Approximately 214,000 trailers were shipped that year for total sales of $3.31 billion. In 1992, consolidation and a decline in shipments reduced the industry workforce to an estimated 24,300 workers, of which 19,000 were production workers. Trailer shipments totaled 187,000 units in 1992, and total industry sales were estimated at $3.47 billion. The industry was operating below capacity during the early 1990s.

The market for exporting truck trailers was expected to expand throughout the 1990s. The United States maintains a trade surplus in truck trailers, and in 1991 the value of exports for the truck trailer industry was $175 million, while the value of imports was only $23.9 million. These figures were expected to reach $250 million and $45 million, respectively, by the mid-1990s.

Truck trailers are manufactured in most of the 50 states. Texas, California, and Pennsylvania lead the nation in the number of manufacturing establishments per state. In 1992 Great Dane Trailers, Wabash National, and Fruehauf Trailer were the leading manufacturers of truck trailers of truck trailers.

INDUSTRY INFORMATION SOURCES

U.S. Industrial Outlook 1993, Washington, DC: U.S. Department of Commerce, 1993.

—Paolo Motta

MOTOR HOMES

This category covers establishments primarily engaged in manufacturing self-contained motor homes on purchased chassis. Establishments engaged in manufacturing self-contained motor homes on chassis manufactured in the same establishment are classified in **Industry 3711: Motor Vehicles and Passenger Car Bodies.** Establishments primarily engaged in manufacturing mobile homes are classified in **Industry 2451: Mobile Homes;** and those manufacturing travel trailers and pickup campers are classified in **Industry 3792: Travel Trailers and Campers**. Establishments primarily engaged in van conversion on a custom basis are classified in Services, **Industry 7532: Top, Body, and Upholstery Repair Shops and Paint Shops.**

INDUSTRY SNAPSHOT

After facing contracting markets in the recession of the early 1990s, the motor home industry staged a solid recovery in 1993. Prospects for continued strong sales were excellent, as demographic, economic, and cultural factors were weighted heavily in the industry's favor. The U.S. population is aging, and it is older, more affluent Americans who are the industry's best customers. Many urbanites of all ages seem eager to spend their free time out in the country, and they are showing a strong preference for vehicles that also provided lodging. Interest rates, though starting to rise in early 1994, were at low levels, making financing of new motor homes relatively easy; at the same time, the tax code offered substantial benefits to many owners. Gasoline shortages, which had hurt the business badly in the late 1970s, were nowhere in sight, and fuel prices remained low. Even prospects for the small export market were improving, given a weaker dollar and the popularity in Europe of U.S.-made motor homes loaded with creature comforts.

ORGANIZATION AND STRUCTURE

The recreational vehicle (RV) industry can be divided into two groups—towables, which include conventional and fifth-wheel travel trailers, folding camping trailers, and truck campers; and motorized vehicles, which include motor homes and van conversions. The overwhelming majority of motor homes sold in the United States are built on chassis that have been purchased from an outside manufacturer. The two key manufacturers of gasoline-powered chassis for motor homes are General Motors's Chevrolet division and Ford Motor Co., while Spartan and Oshkosh Truck Corporation are two important names in the smaller diesel segment.

Motor homes are classified as either Class A, B, or C models. A Class A vehicle is probably what most people think of when they hear the term "motor home": it is a living unit entirely constructed on a bare, specially designed motor vehicle chassis, and the driver sits within the vehicle itself. Class A models have been the most popular: in 1993 they represented about 60 percent of all motor homes shipped (and more in terms of dollar value). Class C models are smaller vehicles wherein the driver usually sits inside a separate cab; they accounted for about 34 percent of unit shipments. A Class B motor home, also called a van camper, is defined by the Recreational Vehicle Industry Association (RVIA) as "a panel-type truck to which the RV manufacturer adds any two of the following conveniences: sleeping, kitchen, and toilet facilities." Class B vehicles represented about 6 percent of 1993 shipments.

The two largest manufacturers in the industry, Fleetwood and Winnebago Industries Inc., held about half of the motor home market in 1992. Together, the ten largest makers accounted for over 80 percent of all sales. In aggregate, there were about 20 to 30 manufacturers of each class of motor home. Total retail sales of all motor homes in 1993 were about $2.7 billion.

The RVIA defines a van conversion as "a completed or incomplete automotive van chassis modified decoratively or aesthetically in appearance by the RV manufacturer for transportation and recreational purposes. These changes may include windows, paneling, seats, sofas, and accessories." The top van converter is the privately owned Mark III, which converted more than 54,000 units in 1993; other top companies include Glaval and Tiara. The industry includes dozens of small converters who convert 300 or fewer vehicles a year. Chevrolet, Ford, Dodge, and GMC Truck all supply van chassis to the converters. Both Chevrolet and Ford have made efforts to reduce the number of converters they supply, and it is likely that there will be continued consolidation in the industry.

BACKGROUND AND DEVELOPMENT

According to one source, the first motor home in the United States was built to take tourists out West for the San Francisco Exposition of 1915. Although its promoters claimed that it had all the advantages of an ocean cruiser—with hot running water and electric lights—testimony confirming the comfort of the journey does not appear in any historical record. Wealthy industrialists, notably Henry Ford and Thomas Edison, were among the pioneers of the motor home industry; they built relatively luxurious caravans with amenities like leather swivel chairs and refrigerators. The well-to-do were imitated by the middle class, who bolted boxes to the backs of Model Ts and fastened a bed and dresser inside to create what was then called a "house car." American individualism soon made itself felt, and by the late 1920s house cars that looked like log cabins, miniature mansions, and even airplanes could be seen on the highways.

The early motor home riders stayed overnight at farms and ranches, but eventually large campgrounds were built that could hold over 1,000 vehicles. The sites were often overcrowded and unsanitary, and a far cry from the outdoor life these early RV users sought. Driving the first professionally built motor homes was not much fun either. They were made with heavy materials that overtaxed the chassis and gave poor weight distribution; insulation was poor, and the vehicles were not suited to the existing roads. Thus, until the 1960s the towable trailer was the more popular form of RV.

In the mid-1950s some small companies began to build what might be called motorized trailers. While they represented a significant improvement, they were still overweight and underpowered. A few years later, however, Winnebago began to introduce its innovative products, which became very popular in the late 1960s and early 1970s. The company developed a special wall construction called Thermo-Panel that had the required structural strength and offered good insulation; at the same time, it was light enough to raise gas mileage and engine performance. Moreover, once Winnebago introduced assembly line production, it was able to make its motor homes a lot cheaper than the competition could.

CURRENT CONDITIONS

According to a survey performed by the RVIA in 1993, about 69 percent of motor home purchasers have a gross income of between $50,000 and $100,000 a year, while 59 percent have been in the same job or the same industry for ten years or more. Nevertheless, because buying a motor home represented a major commitment—in 1994 the average price of a Class A motor home was more than $62,000—customers must feel financially secure before they will purchase. In late 1992, as GNP began to expand more sharply and consumer confidence rose, the motor home buyer once again returned to the market.

The industry was thus able to post impressive results in 1993. According to *RV Business,* unit shipments of all motor homes were up 13 percent from 1992 levels to about 53,140 units. Notably, shipments in the important Class A category were up a solid 17 percent to about 32,130 units; Class C vehicles registered a 7 percent gain to 17,940, while Class B models rose 5 percent to 3,070. The strong performance of motorized vehicles followed through to the first two months of 1994, when motor home shipments rose 8 percent overall, including a 16 percent jump in Class A vehicles. Although shipments in 1993 continued to be below peak 1988 levels, the motor home industry had undoubtedly recovered from the slowdown in the early 1990s. Business in the van conversion segment was also better; sales had begun to pick up in 1992 and continued to improve in 1993, when shipments rose 7.1 percent to 193,960 units.

While sales in most of the country had revived by 1993, conditions in the important California market remained lackluster. The recession badly hurt the state's RV industry, which lost 155 dealerships between 1990 and 1992, or nearly one-third of the entire dealer body. Los Angeles and Orange counties were particularly hard-hit: during the downturn the number of dealerships fell by half, from 50 to 25. Though in early 1994 there were signs that California's economy was improving, its motor home market remained among the weakest in the country.

Overall, however, industry participants in 1994 were cheerful about prospects for the both the short and long term. The essential economic ingredients appeared to be in place—expanding economy, low interest rates, and falling unemployment—while demographic trends were on the industry's side. The prime buyers of motor homes were people 50 years of age or older, a cohort that was expanding with the aging of the U.S. population. At the same time, those between the age of 30 and 49 were entering the RV market in large numbers. While they tended to buy inexpensive towables—shipments of folding camping trailers were up 36 percent in 1993—their purchases signaled that they liked the RV lifestyle and would be ready to trade up to a motor home when they had more

leisure time and more money. Some also believed that the growing preference of consumers for "car substitutes" like light trucks would make the prospect of tooling around in a 40-foot Class A motor home less formidable.

INDUSTRY LEADERS

Fleetwood Enterprises is the largest motor home manufacturer with about 35 percent of the market. Total revenues in fiscal 1993 were $1.9 billion, about 32 percent of which came from motor homes; the company also has a large manufactured-housing operation, which accounted for about 40 percent of its sales. Most of the remaining revenue was derived from sales of other RVs. Earnings peaked in fiscal 1989 at $70-million and then turned downward; by 1993, however, they had returned to the $57 million level, up 43 percent from the year before.

Fleetwood has a reputation for innovation that is embodied in its Bounder model, the company's best-selling motor home. Introduced in the late 1980s, the Bounder offered a basement-like storage compartment that gave owners a place for storing items like golf bags and suitcases, while raising the level of the living quarters to that of the driver. The company has also built customer loyalty from its excellent aftersales support: every buyer of a Fleetwood product is called to get feedback and suggestions for improvement.

Winnebago, the industry's second-largest company, is almost a generic term for motor home. Some 85 percent of its fiscal 1993 revenues of $327 million came from sales of motor homes; Class A models accounted for 75 percent of the approximately 8,000 units sold. Founded in 1958, the firm posted increasingly strong sales and profits in the late 1960s and early 1970s. Afterward, however, recessions, gas shortages, and, some say, poor management cost the company market share and hurt profitability. Between 1989 to 1992 the company lost money each year. In fiscal 1993, however, Winnebago benefitted from a new line of motor homes that was well received, as well as reduced costs and greater automation of production. These factors, coupled with the improving economy and low interest rates, pushed the company into the black for the year. Winnebago had also begun to recover some market share in the important Class A segment: after falling to a low of 13 percent in fiscal 1990, it had risen to over 17 percent in early 1994.

AMERICA AND THE WORLD

While U.S. exports of motor homes remained scant during the early 1990s, some observers thought that overseas sales would become more important to the industry. European markets, where "caravanning" (as it is known) is a popular pastime, seemed to offer the most promise: workers are relatively affluent; they typically get four to six weeks of vacation per year; and the fall of communism in Eastern Europe makes travel easier and more appealing. Much of the interest focused on Germany, Europe's leading motor home market, with total unit sales of approximately 18,000 in 1990. Several factors favored American makers in the European market: the weakness of the dollar, which makes American-made goods cheaper abroad; the relatively powerful engines and automatic transmissions that American products feature; and the added luxuries, such as air conditioning and microwave ovens, that U.S.-built motor homes offer. In 1992 industry leader Fleetwood Enterprises showed its commitment to Europe by buying most of Niesmann & Bischoff GmbH, a relatively small but well respected German firm.

U.S. makers also have made some inroads into the Japanese market. While American manufacturers do not appear to have encountered unreasonable trade barriers in Japan, they still have had to modify their product to comply with automotive specifications and plumbing and electrical standards. Despite some small successes, many in the industry thought that Japan would remain a relatively small market for U.S. motor home makers, amounting to perhaps 1,000 or so units per year.

INDUSTRY INFORMATION SOURCES

Bergsman, Steve, "RV Firms Rally, But Stock Analysts Stay Cautious," *RV Business,* July 1993.

Braun, Bob, "A Few Key Converters Dominate Market," *RV Business,* October 21, 1991.

Byrne, Harlan, "Winnebago Industries," *Barron's,* January 17, 1994.

Cummings, Tim, "History also Rides an RV in Excursion through Time," *Sheridan Press,* August 30, 1989.

Dysart, Joe, "Rental Dealers See Rousing 1993," *RV Business,* April 1993.

"European Writer Seeks Information on U.S. RV Manufacturing," *RV Business,* July 1993.

Fleetwood Enterprises, 10-K, Riverside, CA: Fleetwood Enterprises, 1993.

Flint, Jerry, "John Crean's Recipe for Success," *Forbes,* October 25, 1993.

Goldenberg, Sherman, "Downsized Coach Niche Continues to Shrink," *RV Business,* July 1992.

Keech, Mike, "Dealer Numbers Drop by Over 20% Since '90," *RV Business,* March 1993.

Kovell, Hank, "Seeing America by RV," *Los Angeles Times,* February 13, 1994.

Kurowski, Jeff, *RV Business,* "Exporters Eye Europe," August 5, 1991; "RV Prices Shock Potential Buyers, Harris Survey Says," January 1994; "U.S. RV Manufacturers Build Sales in Japanese Market," April 1992.

"Let the Good Times Roll," *RV Business,* December 1992.

Longsdorf, Robert, Jr., *RV Business,* "A Giant Shakes the Aftermarket," December 1993; "Al Yoder: Straight Talk on Tangled Issues," August 1993.

"Motorhome Strength Persists in November," *RV Business,* February 1994.

"Motorhomes Offer Independence on the Open Road," *Columbia Record,* February 2, 1988.

Norland, Jim, "RV Body-Building," *RV Business,* June 1992.

Petruno, Tom, "Fleetwood Insider Is Buying Despite RV Sales Worries," *Los Angeles Times,* June 28, 1993.

Reingold, Jennifer, "Fleetwood Enterprises: Movin' On Up," *Financial World,* October 26, 1993.

Rescigno, Richard, "Revved Up for Recovery," *Barron's,* June 27, 1991.

"RV Types & Terms," Reston, VA: Recreation Vehicle Industry Association.

"RVIA's Annual Survey Profiles RV Buyers," *RV Business,* September 1993.

Sharma, Katherine, "1992 Sees Growth of Supplier Interest in European Market," *RV Business,* April 1992.

"Shipment Trends," *RV Business,* March 1994.

Strohbücker, Franz-Peter, "Fleetwood German Partner Ranks High in Europe," *RV Business,* October 1992.

Taylor, Alex, III, "Days of Happy Trailers," *Fortune,* September 6, 1993.

"Uneven '92 Sales Fail to Unseat Market Leaders," *RV Business,* April 1993.

Williams, Rolla, "Going Camping on Wheels," *San Diego Union,* July 2, 1988.

Winnebago Annual Report, 1994, Forest City, IA: Winnebago, 1993.

—Bob Schneider

SIC 3721

AIRCRAFT

This category includes establishments primarily engaged in manufacturing or assembling complete aircraft. This industry also includes estabishments owned by aircraft manufacturers and primarily engaged in research and development on aircraft, whether from enterprise funds or on a contract or fee basis. Also included are establishments engaged in repairing and rebuilding aircraft on a factory basis. Establishments primarily engaged in manufacturing engines and other aircraft parts and auxiliary equipment are classified in **SIC 3724: Aircraft Engines and Engine Parts** and **SIC 3728: Aircraft Parts and Auxiliary Equipment, Not Elsewhere Classified**. Establishments primarily engaged in the repair of aircraft, except on a factory basis, are classified in **SIC 4581: Airports, Flying Fields, and Airport Terminal Services;** and research and development on aircraft by establishments not owned by aircraft manufacturers are classified in **SIC 8731: Commercial Physical and Biological Research.**

INDUSTRY SNAPSHOT

Aircraft manufacturing has been one of the most consistently profitable and successful of American industries. Led by companies such as Boeing, McDonnell Douglas, and Lockheed, the $100-billion aircraft industry collects a higher amount of export earnings than any other American industry. Until recently, no foreign manufacturer has been able to keep up with the pace of technological achievement or brute output achieved by American firms. Airbus Industries, an European consortium, moved into competition with the American giants in the 1980s, however, and growing companies in the Far East, especially Japan, threaten to encroach further on the once distinctly American industry. Industry analysts suggest that future growth in the aircraft manufacturing industry will pay no heed to national borders as more and more companies engage in joint ventures with competitors from around the world, taking advantage of the strengths of the individual companies to provide the most competitive product available.

ORGANIZATION AND STRUCTURE

American aircraft companies have provided airplanes for three distinct markets, the military, commercial aviation, and general aviation. From the end of World War II until the collapse of the Soviet threat in 1989, the American military services had a voracious appetite for sophisticated aircraft which American aircraft and aerospace firms sought to satisfy. This 45-year boom in military spending not only guaranteed the health of many manufacturers, but it also allowed those manufacturers to devote resources to research and development, ensuring that American aircraft would be the most technologically advanced in the world. The end of the Cold War, which has reduced military spending in the United States and around the world, has provided the greatest challenge for American aircraft manufacturers, who had grown accustomed to lucrative Department of Defense contracts. The military aircraft industry seems destined to shrink through the 1990s, though the United States government has sought to guarantee U.S. technological dominance through continued funding of research and development.

The development of commercial aircraft poses far greater risks than that of military aircraft. The development process for a passenger airliner capable of carrying several hundred people is both lengthy and costly, requiring manufacturers to anticipate the needs of airlines far in advance and to gamble vast amounts of money on the product's success. Manufacturers typically have designed new or modified aircraft in response to the demands of carriers, who have typically asked for more fuel efficiency and more seating rather than major redesigns. The *Economist* estimated that a new medium-sized airliner costs over $2 billion to develop, with engines costing another $1.5 billion, and noted that "aerospace companies bet their futures on each product."

As a result of the risks involved, commercial aircraft manufacturers have been rather conservative, pursuing modifications on existing airframes rather than reinventing complete aircraft and most existing commercial airliners have changed little since the 1960s. Given the tremendous financial risks associated with developing new aircraft, many manufacturers today work cooperatively, jointly developing a design and dividing work among partners if the design is successful. The development of a new aircraft might involve many dozens of companies, each contributing some portion of a plane that they have perfected. The two dominant manufacturers of large commercial aircraft are the Boeing Company of Seattle, Washington, and the McDonnell Douglas Company of St. Louis, Missouri.

Though military and commercial aircraft manufacturers dominate the industry, American companies also produce a number of aircraft for the general aviation and helicopter market segments, which includes fixed wing aircraft and rotorcraft for business transportation, regional airline service, recreation, specialized uses such as ambulance service and agricultural spraying, and training. According to *U.S. Industrial Outlook 1993,* American manufacturers have produced about 60 percent of the world's general aviation aircraft and 30 percent of the helicopters. Major U.S. manufacturers of general aviation aircraft include the Beech Aircraft Corp., the Fairchild Aircraft Corp., the Cessna Aircraft Co., Gulfstream Aerospace, and the Learjet

Corp.

Most aircraft manufacturers derive a significant proportion of their profits from the production of replacement and upgrade parts for their airplanes. Since large commercial jets represent such a large investment—a new twin-engine passenger jet may cost several hundred million dollars—airline companies try to keep them in the air for many years. Moreover, the Federal Aviation Administration (FAA) sets stringent guidelines on repair and replacement procedures for passenger aircraft. Manufacturers provide parts through a network of suppliers and subcontractors, which comprise **SIC 3728: Aircraft Parts, Not Elsewhere Classified.**

BACKGROUND AND DEVELOPMENT

The American aircraft manufacturing industry dates its origin to one of the seminal events of the twentieth century: the Wright Brothers' first powered flight in 1903. While many others had flown with gliders, balloons and dirigibles, Wilbur and Orville Wright marked a tremendous breakthrough with powered flight, because they proved the dynamics of flying a wing. In cross section, a wing is flat on the bottom but curved on top. As a wing moves through the air, air passing over the wing is forced to travel a greater distance than air passing under the wing. This causes a pocket of low pressure that literally sucks the wing up into the air. In order to work, the wing must be driven forward, or powered. These principles were described years before the Wrights' flight by Samuel P. Langley, a luckless professor whose aviation experiments were either ignored or witnessed in failure.

The Wrights originally hoped to sell airplanes to the United States Army as battlefield reconnaissance devices. The idea of employing aircraft to attack or drop bombs had not yet occurred to anyone. One of those on hand to witness the Wright Brothers' first demonstration for the Army was a young conscript named Donald Douglas. Despite several impressive flights, Army officials were unmoved. The Wrights took their show to Europe, where they flew for the German, French and British armies. In the process, they prompted interest with such European aviation pioneers as Louis Blériot, Willy Messerschmidt, Anthony Fokker and Marcel Dassault.

Aviation was immediately embraced in Europe as a powerful new force in warfare, but it also made for good entertainment. Blériot and others such as Louis Paulhan built their own airplanes and began touring flying circuses. During 1910 and 1911, these European aviators toured the United States, flying before garage tinkerers like Glenn Martin, Clyde Cessna, Glenn

Curtiss and Bill Boeing. Curtiss, a motorcycle repairman, was immediately drawn to flight, and he had access to the lightweight engines needed to power aircraft. Curtiss was one of the first to mount a propeller on the front of the aircraft in a ''tractor'' design. Until that time, propellers had been rear-mounted ''pusher'' models.

After several of the Army's Wright planes crashed, killing the pilots, the Army found a new supplier in Curtiss, who escaped the enforcement of the Wrights' patents by incorporating the first ailerons. Curtiss thus emerged as the nation's leading aircraft manufacturer and the new supplier of choice to the Army.

Wilbur Wright died in 1912, leaving his brother in charge of their company. A poor manager, Orville Wright naively sold the company and its patents to a group of financiers led by William Boyce Thompson.

With the outbreak of war in Europe in 1914, Germany and France were quick to apply aviation to the battlefield, producing the world's first aces, Roland Garros and Manfred von Richtofen. The United States Army embraced air power in 1914 by creating an aviation group within the Signal Corps. One of its first members was Donald Douglas. Douglas, an engineering graduate of the Massachusetts Institute of Technology, was briefly employed by Glenn Martin, who had experimented with gliders since 1905. He built his first powered aircraft near Los Angeles about 1909, having been bankrolled by another aviation enthusiast, inventor Alexander Graham Bell. Douglas helped Martin develop his first production aircraft, the TT trainer, before he was dispatched to Washington to oversee the government's aviation program. Thompson's group later purchased Martin's company to form an aircraft combine called the Wright-Martin Company.

By 1918, the government had shown its interest in aviation through expansion of an air squadron and active intervention in the industry. Having seen the effect of air power in Europe during World War I, it was determined not to see American air power stunted by legal wrangling or patent hoarders. What emerged was a loosely policed competition for government contracts, primarily military and later air mail business. Hundreds of airplane builders emerged from garages and warehouses.

Automobile executives were chosen to head the government's ambitious 22,000-plane military aeronautics program. Favored for their companies' ability to turn out huge quantities of a standardized product, these executives openly conspired to keep aircraft builders out of the industry. But Douglas, a member of the government board, fed information on the aeronautics program to other aircraft designers. Finally, upset with the performance of the Army's air squadron, and disgusted with government bureaucracy, Douglas resigned in 1919 and moved to Los Angeles to start his own company.

In 1919, automotive interests led by Delco persuaded Orville Wright to lend his name to another venture called Dayton-Wright. Wright was retained only for his venerable name and its ability to draw investment dollars. As an automotive venture, Dayton-Wright built only aircraft engines, and later fell under the control of General Motors. At the close of World War I, the government canceled 90 percent of the aircraft it had ordered, forcing many airplane builders to close. An investigation later revealed criminal collusion and widespread scandal among those who were empowered to grant contracts. However, virtually all involved escaped without prosecution.

Having briefly regained the services of Donald Douglas, Glenn Martin abandoned Thompson's company and struck up an important relationship with General Billy Mitchell, the Army's most powerful advocate of air power. With Mitchell's backing, Martin won a contract to build 20 MB-2 bombers, which Mitchell subsequently used in a spectacular demonstration off the Virginia Capes, sinking the supposedly unsinkable captured German battleship *Ostfriesland.*

A separate aircraft concern was established in 1914 by Allan and Malcolm Loughead. The brothers built their first aircraft in a small garage in San Francisco with financial backing from Max Mamlock and his Alco Cab company. After crashing it, and scaring away Mamlock and his money, the brothers began flying exhibitions and sold Curtiss airplanes to raise money. The Lougheads, intent on military applications for aircraft, embarked on the construction of a large bomber at a site near Santa Barbara. There they met a young builder with an understanding of mathematics named Jack Northrop, whom they asked to join the company as chief engineer.

President Coolidge appointed Dwight Morrow to devise a government program for measured development of the industry in 1925. The resulting Air Commerce Act of 1926 set annual procurement levels for 2,600 military aircraft. Loughead and Northrop, who had drifted for six years, suddenly regained their market and managed to secure financial backing from a Los Angeles venture capitalist named Fred Keeler. As a condition, however, Keeler demanded that Loughead change the spelling of his Scotch-Irish name to accurately match its proper pronunciation. Apparently tired of being addressed as ''Mr. Lug Head,'' Allan

relented, and the new company was called Lockheed. The company later completed an all-metal, single-skin model called the Vega. This model, based on a design by Holland's Anthony Fokker, was developed by Northrop, who then left the company to work for Donald Douglas.

Douglas, whose business was growing on the strength of government sales, had been approached by David R. Davis, who offered to invest $40,000 for a transcontinental airliner. With Northrop's help, Douglas produced the Cloudster, of which the government ordered several hundred for military use. Davis, fearing the risk, bailed out immediately. The Cloudster, however, led Douglas to a series of successful designs, including the DT series torpedo planes and Douglas World Cruiser. Between 1921 and 1928, Douglas' annual production grew from six aircraft to more than 300.

The growing aircraft industry received a tremendous boost in 1927 when Charles Lindbergh completed the first successful cross-Atlantic flight using a modified Ryan Aeronautical tri-motor. Lindbergh's daring and nearly suicidal stunt revived interest in aviation so strongly that investors began pumping millions of dollars into aircraft companies. The following year, Martin relocated to Baltimore to be closer to his customers in Washington. Building bombers, he purchased the engine business of Louis Chevrolet, whose automobile business had been acquired by General Motors.

United Aircraft was the creation of Bill Boeing, a rich Seattle forester who purchased his first plane in 1910 from Glenn Martin and took flying lessons from the builder himself. Boeing and his partner Conrad Westerveldt built a number of early floatplane models for maritime postal delivery. After producing aircraft for the military during World War I, Boeing was persuaded by a customer named Ed Hubbard to form an airline service. In 1920, Boeing won a contract to haul mail between Chicago and Seattle. For the job, he developed a new design, the Model 40, fitted with a Pratt & Whitney engine. Boeing's association with Pratt & Whitney brought him the acquaintance of that company's president, Frederick Rentschler.

The Kelly Airmail Act of 1925 returned airmail service to private bidders after a series of bloody crashes by the government's own air service. Postmaster William Folger Brown actively encouraged the formation of large airline companies by carefully awarding profitable air mail contracts. Boeing acquired numerous private airmail companies and their lucrative contract rights, and in 1928 banded them together to form the National Air Transport

Company. The following year, Boeing and Rentschler merged their airframe and engine businesses to form the United Aircraft & Transportation Company. By the end of 1929 the company had taken over two propeller makers as well as Northrop's Avion company, and laid out an air transportation network that later became United Air Lines.

In August of 1929, Allan Loughead (who retained his own name) and Fred Keeler sold the Lockheed company to a group of automotive investors organized as the Detroit Aircraft company. The company drew tremendous investor interest after aviatrix Amelia Earhart crossed the Atlantic with one of the company's Vegas planes. Only one month later, world financial markets were buffeted by a stock market crash that plunged the nation into the Great Depression. Aviation company stocks, valued at more than $1 billion on total earnings of more than $9 billion, were decimated.

Detroit Aircraft, whose share price had tumbled from $15 to 12.5 cents, failed in 1932. The Lockheed operation was purchased out of receivership for $40,000 by Robert and Courtlandt Gross. The acquisition included an important new design, the Orion. Meanwhile, Allan Loughead had returned to his original real estate business. Jack Northrop, however, returned to Douglas, where he established yet another company as a subsidiary of the Douglas enterprise.

Douglas was associated with an aviation combine similar to Boeing's, called North American Aviation. This company controlled Eastern Airlines and TWA. As a result of this relationship, Douglas, who had grown rich on military contracts, was now called upon to develop commercial airliners for his parent company. The first of these, the Douglas Commercial One or DC-1, emerged during the worst years of the Depression. In February of 1934, the government reduced its subsidy to airmail carriers, creating a sudden demand for faster, more efficient aircraft. Douglas refined his DC design to meet this demand, and in 1935 produced the DC-3, an extremely versatile craft that nearly rendered competitors such as the Boeing's 247 obsolete. The Gross Brothers and their Lockheed company likewise improved upon earlier designs and emerged with the Electra.

Even Glenn Martin, spurned by the War Department, was brought into the commercial market. The devout Republican was forced to mortgage his plant under a Democratic New Deal program. Desperate for business, Martin built a luxurious flying boat, called the China Clipper, for Pan American's trans-Pacific routes. But when Martin only managed to sell three Clippers, the government was forced to support his

business by purchasing the company's newly developed B-10 bomber.

The Depression would have destroyed the aircraft industry were it not for government support. It became official policy to award contracts to an increasingly privileged club of manufacturers, so that their expertise may be preserved and developed for military purposes. This policy hardened the cycle of concentration promoted by Brown. American aviation was controlled by three huge vertical monopolies, each maintaining huge airframe and engine manufacturing facilities and airline services.

In 1934, Senator Hugo Black completed an investigation of improprieties in these aviation investment trusts, which included United Aircraft, North American Aviation, and a third group called the Aviation Corporation of the Americas, or Avco. Several magnates were called to testify at hearings, including Bill Boeing, Donald Douglas and Glenn Martin. All admitted huge profiteering from aviation activities but, in view of the absence of laws against these practices, no prosecution could result. Boeing, however, was so incensed by the nature of the investigation that he sold all his aviation interests and retired.

The combines were eventually dealt a more serious blow. They were dissolved on antitrust grounds, creating an enduring line of business restriction in American aviation. Airframe, engine and airline companies could not now be associated in any way. Boeing's conglomerate was divided into the Boeing Company in Seattle, United Aircraft in Connecticut, and United Air Lines, headquartered in Chicago. Likewise, North American Aviation lost its association with TWA and Eastern Airlines, and Avco lost American Airlines and Pan Am. Martin and Lockheed remained intact, as did Consolidated Aircraft, a company whose growth sprung from its acquisition of the defunct Dayton-Wright's designs.

By 1937, the emergence of the DC-3 and Electra enabled airlines to make money from passenger services alone, ending the reliance on airmail. The efficiency of these aircraft was recognized by belligerents in the small wars being fought in Europe and Asia. Unbeknownst to them, Lockheed, Douglas and Martin frequently sold aircraft to fictional airline companies and other front organizations for the Japanese and German armed forces. The discovery of this trade led to neutrality laws which prescribed an aircraft embargo to any belligerent. But the demand for aircraft, particularly from Britain and France, was so great that the Roosevelt Administration created loopholes designed to allow the export of aircraft to American allies. This enabled the industry to fund development of new designs from large, lucrative export orders.

Much of this development was highly experimental. Northrop, whose subsidiary had been consolidated by Douglas in 1937, formed another company in 1939 with backing from LaMotte Cohu. After raiding Douglas of dozens of engineers, he resumed work on his radical flying wing project. Lockheed produced an equally strange design, a triple-hull fighter called the P-38 Lightning, while Boeing began work on its large B-17 bomber.

Several other smaller manufacturers gained admission to the defense industry club during this time. Grumman, a company established in 1929 to build naval aircraft, grew quickly after winning a contract to supply folding-wing F4F Wildcats to the Navy. By 1941 the company, established by Leroy Grumman and Leon Swirbul, had become the primary supplier to the Navy, overtaking even Martin. McDonnell Aircraft began building aircraft on a large scale in 1939, producing fighters for the Army Air Force. Meanwhile, Consolidated merged with the Vultee Company, forming a huge manufacturing operation in Texas called Convair.

While military preparations were stepped up in 1940 and 1941, the event that sparked tremendous growth in the aircraft industry was the Japanese attack on Pearl Harbor. Huge amounts of government money were poured into engineering and production facilities. President Roosevelt ordered 60,000 aircraft in 1942, and 125,000 the year after. Douglas converted its DC-3 into military cargo planes and bombers, more than 10,000 of which were built. Other manufacturers were suddenly able to complete new designs. Convair produced the B-24 Liberator, and Martin the B-26 and A-30 Baltimore bombers and 70-ton Mars freighter. North American turned out the B-25 Mitchell bomber and the P-51 Mustang, while Douglas added the A-20 Havoc and SBD Dauntless dive bomber. The newly reconstituted Curtiss company returned with its C-46 cargo craft. Grumman provided the Navy with its Widgeon, TBF Avenger and F6F Hellcat.

Boeing, which at one point turned out 16 bombers every day, went into production on its B-29 Super Fortress. Even Ford, which exited the aircraft business during the Depression, was pressed into service, building B-24s. Northrop got his flying wing, the B-49, to fly. With every surface of the craft devoted to creating lift, it was capable of tremendous payloads. The Army, however, refused to develop the boomerang-shaped bomber, fearing possible instability in flight and the use of electronic, rather than cable, controls.

Small airplane builders, such as Beech Aircraft, Cessna and Piper, also participated in the war effort. But due to their limited manufacturing facilities and lack of advanced engineering talent, they were relegated to building support aircraft and parts for other manufacturers. Employment in the industry peaked at 1.3 million people in 1943, as every manufacturer participated in some way in the war effort.

The war completely changed the aircraft industry. In addition to demonstrating the power and strategic importance of aerial combat, it established the parallel relationship between investment and technological development. The war allowed the perfection of strategic bombing tactics, carpet bombing, dogfighting, naval attack bombing and, in the last days of the war, atomic bombing. Wars that were previously fought with tanks and battleships now were waged from above. By the end of the war, work had begun on a new generation of aircraft: jets. Larry Bell's Bell Aircraft Company, Lockheed and McDonnell were the first to experiment with jet power, having gained volumes of captured German jet airframe research.

While the military threat from Germany and Japan had been vanquished, a new adversary emerged in the Soviet Union and became the focus of continued government investment in aviation. The development that occurred during World War II was scaled down, but concentrated in promising new technologies. Development centered on long-range strategic bombers for delivering nuclear bombs to targets in the Soviet Union and speedy fighters to intercept a similar threat from Soviet bombers.

Transition to a peacetime economy was considerably better managed than after World War I, due to the Contract Settlement Act of 1944. Still, the entire industry was forced to choose between commercial and military manufacturing. North American, Grumman, McDonnell, Northrop and Vought chose to develop only military craft, while Douglas pursued commercial designs. Boeing, Martin, Lockheed and Convair elected to develop commercial as well as military designs.

The most important postwar commercial entries were the four-engine Douglas DC-4, the Boeing 377 Stratocruiser and the triple-finned Lockheed Constellation, designed by Howard Hughes for TWA. Having emerged from the war with tremendous manufacturing capacity and engineering talent, these three companies dominated the commercial aircraft industry. Competitors, including Curtiss, Martin and Convair, were forced to exit the market in rapid succession, taking refuge in the more secure military businesses. Hughes Aircraft, famed for its massive Spruce Goose amphibian freighter, failed to break into the production market. After building a few experimental designs, it became the plaything of its owner, millionaire Howard Hughes. Hughes Aircraft later retreated into the missile and aviation controls business.

Boeing and Lockheed also became leading defense suppliers after the war. Lockheed extended its lead in jet fighter designs during the Korean War with its F-94 interceptor and, later, F-104 Starfighter. Boeing developed a family of huge intercontinental bombers, including the B-57, B-50 and B-52. Meanwhile, Convair introduced its B-36, with six pusher propellers, and supersonic B-58 Hustler.

On the recommendations of the Finletter Air Policy Commission, the government made air power the crux of its military establishment. While tremendous competition existed for seemingly open-ended military contracts, manufacturers found new ways to commercialize military designs. Boeing was the first to develop an entirely new passenger aircraft with technologies gained from a jet bomber. Boeing requested permission to use government-funded technologies from its successful eight-engine B-52 to develop a new four-engine jetliner called the 707. Eager to prevent a European monopoly in passenger jets—DeHavilland had just introduced its sleek Comet—the government agreed.

Soon after the 707 flew in 1954, American Airlines, a good Douglas customer, announced plans to buy 30 of Boeing's new jets. Douglas, which had put off introduction of a jet in favor of its DC-6s and DC-7s, was forced to rush a similar design into production or risk following Curtiss and Martin into oblivion. Douglas emerged the following year with highly similar jet design called the DC-8. Ironically, United Air Lines, historically associated with Boeing, placed the first order for the DC-8. Boeing, however, had eclipsed Douglas as the premier American aircraft builder.

Two new jet designs emerged from Europe during the early 1960s, the Sud Aviation Caravelle and Hawker Siddeley Trident. These jetliners featured engines tucked onto the rear of the fuselage, rather than under the wings. At the request of Eastern Airlines, Boeing pursued a three-engine 727, delivered in 1964, while Douglas built a more economical two-engine DC-9, delivered in 1965. Boeing introduced a smaller twin-engine jetliner, the 737, in 1967.

Tremendous consolidation occurred in the aircraft industry during this period. Convair was acquired by General Dynamics in 1952. Martin, which had abandoned aircraft production during the 1950s to concentrate on missiles and aircraft parts, was acquired by the

American Marietta Corporation in 1961. North American, a builder of Air Force fighters, was thrown into deep disarray in 1967 after a fire destroyed one of its Apollo space capsules, killing three astronauts. The company was taken over that year by the machinery manufacturer Rockwell Standard. Also that year, financial difficulties resulting from the DC-8 and DC-9 finally caught up with Douglas. Unable to keep up with the demand for its aircraft, Douglas neared bankruptcy. Eventually, McDonnell Aircraft, a manufacturer of fighter jets and space capsules, prevailed in its bid to acquire Douglas.

The 1960s were a period of feverish development in military aviation, due to continued investments by the Defense Department in new technologies and academic programs, and the creation of the National Aeronautics and Space Administration (NASA). Some of the major accomplishments of this period were in the development of supersonic and rocket-powered aircraft. North American built a six-engine, triple sonic delta wing bomber called the B-70. Obsolete before its first flight, this aircraft evolved into the B-1 Bomber a dozen years later. Lockheed marked two great achievements, with its ultra high-altitude U-2 and triplesonic SR-71 spy planes. Developed in 1964 at Lockheed's super-secret "skunk works," this aircraft remains the fastest jet ever to fly in the American arsenal.

After abandoning research on a revolutionary nuclear-powered bomber, General Dynamics' Convair group became involved in the development of a multi-use fighter/bomber called the F-111 and the F-16 fighter. During the 1960s, McDonnell, Douglas, Martin, Boeing, Grumman and Convair became major participants in the space program. Other manufacturers were reduced to production of single-mission aircraft, such as Vought, with its A-7 Corsair, and Fairchild, with its A-10 Warthog. Northrop began work mainly as a subcontractor to McDonnell Douglas, building the F-18.

A postwar boom in private aviation greatly expanded the fortunes of small aircraft manufacturers such as Cessna, Beech and Piper. After this trend peaked during the 1950s, many turned to production of aircraft for business executives. In 1969 aviation engineer Bill Lear introduced the first private jet, which Cessna and Beech later imitated. A wave of personal injury lawsuits later restricted the growth of these manufacturers, who remain on the fringes of the industry. Fairchild and Beech Aircraft became active in the small airliner market, defined as 19 seats or less. Fairchild, which built the Fokker 27 under contract, developed the Metro airliner. Beech introduced its

King Air, followed some years later by its Model 1900. These craft were operated on small airline "feeder" routes.

In commercial circles, a new market was emerging for larger 300- to 400-passenger jumbo jets. Boeing and McDonnell Douglas, eager to maintain their passenger jet franchises, began the extremely costly development of their 747 and DC-10, respectively. Surprisingly, Lockheed re-entered the market after 20 years, building a three-engine jumbo called the L-1011 Tristar. Boeing was nearly ruined by its four-engine behemoth, and at one point was forced to lay off two-thirds of its work force. McDonnell Douglas fared little better, and Lockheed, mired in huge cost overruns from its massive C-5 Galaxy military cargo plane, required a federal loan guarantee to remain solvent.

The 747 and Tristar hit the market in 1970, and the DC-10 followed in 1971. These aircraft revolutionized air travel by offering airlines the capability to move as many as 400 passengers over distances of up to 5,000 miles. While sales of the DC-10 gained slowly, the 747 soon dominated the skies.

The Airline Deregulation Act, meanwhile, was signed in 1978. This legislation had a tremendous impact on airlines across the country, and plane manufacturers soon felt its repercussions as well. Major national carriers were unprepared for the newly competitive environment created by the Act and found themselves with fleets of Boeing 707s and McDonnell Douglas DC-8s that, because of fuel costs, became prohibitively expensive. In the meantime, new regional carriers utilized fuel-efficient aircraft that fit their needs. The national trunks were forced to examine their fleet configurations and make significant new purchases. Even then, however, analysts charge that the carriers were sluggish in responding. In many cases orders for new aircraft were not made to Boeing or McDonnell Douglas or any other manufacturers until well into the 1980s. The backlog of orders subsequently reached all-time levels, with waiting periods for delivery of new aircraft ranging as long as seven years by 1986.

Similar efforts to build a supersonic transport, or SST, were abandoned by Lockheed and Boeing in 1970 after the market evaporated and the government refused to cover skyrocketing development costs. A European consortium succeeded in building a jet capable of breaking the speed of sound, but the plane proved so costly to build and operate, and its sonic boom so disruptive, that flights were severely curtailed and the planes operated at a loss.

On the success of its F-4 Phantom in Vietnam, McDonnell Douglas developed a family of new military aircraft during the 1970s, including the F-15 Eagle and A-4 Skyhawk. Boeing developed its venerable 707 into tankers and powerful AWACs airborne radar platforms, while Lockheed built large new military cargo craft, such as the C-130 and the Galaxy. Northrop remained a strong player in the military market with aging entries such as its F-5, and failed designs such as the export-intended F-20 Tigershark. Grumman did extremely well in the 1970s with its F-14 Tomcat and a smaller version of the AWACs, the E-2C Hawkeye.

The American military aircraft arsenal gained a huge boost in 1980. The industry, starved for investment since Vietnam, was the primary beneficiary of a massive armament program started by President Carter and trebled by President Reagan. Reagan resurrected Rockwell's $200 million-dollar B-1 bomber, canceled by Carter in 1977, and ordered development of a range of new radar-evading aircraft. Pentagon funding poured into these super secret "black projects." One of the beneficiaries was Lockheed, whose success with the SR-71 won it the right to develop the tiny diamond-shaped F-117 Stealth Fighter. Another was not revealed until 1988, when Northrop unveiled its sinister-looking B-2 Stealth Bomber. A flying wing, the B-2 represented the culmination of the late Jack Northrop's life-long dream. It also emerged, along with the B-1, as the replacement for the elderly but still devastating B-52 and the versatile F-111.

The flood of investment into military aircraft resulted in a series of scandals unrivaled since World War I. Several companies were investigated for vastly overcharging the Pentagon and misappropriating funds. In response, the government began shifting contracts away from offenders and forcing them to compete for business they had earlier taken for granted. In one of the few signs of growth, a consortium of Lockheed, Boeing and General Dynamics was chosen to develop the Advanced Tactical Fighter. In a period of decline for the defense industry, the ATF is one of the few large military projects remaining.

Significant activity also occurred in the commercial airliner market during the 1980s. Boeing introduced several upgraded versions of its hugely profitable 747, and a new series of economical, large twin-engine aircraft, the 757 and widebody 767. These aircraft finished off Lockheed's otherwise excellent L-1011 which, with three engines and a larger crew, was discontinued in 1981. Unable to design entirely new aircraft, McDonnell Douglas upgraded its DC-9 into the MD-80 series, and offered a similarly improved DC-10, called the MD-11.

The late 1980s and early 1990s saw manufacturers seeking partnerships to develop commercial aircraft. McDonnell Douglas failed to establish a limited merger with Taiwan Aerospace in 1990, and was seeking a partner to share development costs of a new four-engine MD-12 jetliner. Boeing, meanwhile, investigated a partnership with Deutsche Airbus, the disaffected German member of Boeing's arch rival, Airbus. Similarly, Boeing is seeking a partner for a planned 1000-passenger super jumbo craft. Given the billions of dollars necessary to develop a new jet, it remains questionable which of these projects will ever make it into the air.

CURRENT CONDITIONS

Aircraft industry analysts expect that the 1990s will see a period of great change in aircraft manufacturing. For years the industry had been propelled by ever-increasing military budgets and ever-increasing numbers of commercial airline passengers, but both of those stimuli changed in the 1990s. U.S. government military expenditures peaked in 1987, when aircraft manufacturers supplied over 1200 planes. By 1994, according to *U.S. Industrial Outlook 1994*, "U.S. manufacturers expect to ship only 540 [military] aircraft or $7.9 billion in sales in 1994, less than half the number shipped in 1987." According to the *U.S. Industrial Outlook 1993*, "the latest DOD [Department of Defense] budget request indicated a cumulative real decline in DOD budget authority of 37 percent since 1985." These budget cuts have prompted corresponding reductions in employment by military aircraft manufacturers. During 1992, McDonnell Douglas, General Dynamics, Northrop, Lockheed, Rockwell, and Grumman cut over 29,000 jobs and were expected to cut another 20,000 jobs during the following two years. The increased competition for scarce military dollars is expected to reduce the number of military aircraft providers or possibly force industry consolidation. Deputy Defense Secretary William Perry told *Interavia* that the "DOD budget will not come back. . . . The companies that succeed are those that will plan accordingly in accepting the new reality despite the hardships it will cost to down-size."

"While procurement of aircraft has declined significantly," noted *U.S. Industrial Outlook 1993*, "research, development, testing, and evaluation funding has remained somewhat stable, providing some haven for U.S. providers of advanced military aircraft technologies." In 1993, the Clinton administration took steps to protect the U.S. aerospace industry's long-held technological superiority, increasing NASA's research and development budget, maintaining the DOD's re-search and development budget, and creating the National Commission to Ensure a Strong, Competitive Airline Industry, which has attempted to challenge the subsidies provided by European Community countries to their aircraft manufacturers. Such efforts are expected to maintain the technological superiority of the American aircraft manufacturing base even while the number of manufacturers shrinks.

While military aircraft manufacturers struggle to adjust to changing military budgets, commercial aircraft manufacturers must adjust to declining demand for aircraft by major carriers, production overcapacity, and government-supported foreign competition. These challenges were made all the more pressing in 1991, when for the first time in history the number of passengers riding on commercial airlines declined. This drop in air travel prompted many airlines to cancel or postpone orders for aircraft, leaving manufacturers with an excess of inventory. According to *U.S. Industrial Outlook 1993*, "U.S. manufacturers are forecast to ship 480 large transport aircraft valued at $26 billion in 1993, down from their peak of 567 aircraft valued at $27 billion in 1987." Both Boeing and McDonnell Douglas have reduced production and laid off nearly 10,000 employees each.

According to *Interavia* contributor John Crampton, "Aerospace manufacturers are learning to live with a whole new set of rules brought about by the industry-wide recession and the peace dividend." Manufacturers are adjusting to this changed marketplace in a number of ways. Most notable has been a trend toward industry consolidation and cooperation. Many of the smaller manufacturers in the industry have been eliminated by the recession, and those that have survived have increasingly banded together to share the risk of developing new products. For both Boeing and McDonnell Douglas, this has meant teaming with Asian manufacturers in order to better penetrate the rapidly expanding Asian market. Industry analysts believe that those manufacturers best able to form working partnerships will be the ones to succeed in the 1990s. In order to remain competitive, aircraft manufacturers must also reduce costs by as much as 30 percent, concluded Crampton. Technological advances will pave the way for some cost reduction, as manufacturers increasingly turn to computer-assisted design mock-ups and paperless workplaces as ways of reducing costly experimentation and excess paperwork.

Analysts predict that the aircraft industry will continue to struggle through the mid-1990s. Anthony L. Velocci, Jr., writing in *Aviation Week & Space Technology*, predicted a 15-percent decline in real-dollar sales for the global aerospace industry, from $157 billion in 1991 to $135 billion in 1996. The industry is expected to rebound by the end of the 1990s, however, with industry sales returning to 1991 levels by the year 2000. Forces expected to affect the industry turnaround include anticipated increases in air travel, especially in underdeveloped markets, and the retirement of aging aircraft, prompting an increase in orders.

The aerospace industry as a whole ranked sixth in value of shipments and fourteenth in employment among all U.S. industries in 1991, and was the nation's leading exporter of manufactured goods, sending abroad products worth $43 billion in 1991 to 135 countries, according to *U.S. Industrial Outlook 1993*. The industry also led the nation in research and development expenditures. Of this total, SIC 3721 accounted for $55,120 million dollars in shipments in 1991, the last year for which complete data is available. In that year, the industry had total employment of 264,000 workers, 126,000 of whom were involved in production, and a trade surplus of over $20 million, leading American industry.

INDUSTRY LEADERS

U.S. manufacturers Boeing and McDonnell Douglas are two of the top three aircraft manufacturing companies in the world, joined with the European Communities Airbus Industries. Since Boeing was founded in 1916 it has sold over 6,500 jet airliners, more than all other manufacturers in the western world combined, according to the *Economist*. Employing nearly 150,000 people around the world, Boeing controls approximately 50 percent of world airline sales. Airbus Industries, founded in 1971 as an experiment in European collaboration, accounts for 30 percent of world airline sales with its range of Airbus planes. Airbus's American competitors complain that the consortium survives only because of hefty subsidies paid by European governments, but efforts at ending those subsidies in the mid-1990s should prove whether Airbus is capable of surviving on its profits. McDonnell Douglas accounts for 17 percent of world airline sales and employs close to 100,000 workers. Though the company has had to be satisfied with a declining share of the market, potential cooperation with Airbus on the construction of a jumbo jet might allow the venerable firm to recapture some of Boeing's market share.

The U.S. general aviation market has seen years of decline, as shipments of its aircraft have fallen from 17,817 in 1978 to just 780 in 1992. The decline has been blamed primarily on tough American product-liability laws, which have required manufacturers to purchase costly insurance in case their products are

implicated in accidents. Rising fuel costs and the decreasing cost of flying on commercial airlines also contributed to the decline of this segment of the industry. This market segment decline drove Piper, one of the largest manufacturers of light aircraft, from the industry in 1991, and forced Cessna, long the industry leader, to reduce the size of its workforce from 16,000 employees in 1979 to just 3,600 in 1988. Cessna has built nearly half of the aircraft flying in the free world, according to the *Economist*. Other manufacturers of general aviation aircraft include Beechcraft, Fairchild, Gulfstream, and Learjet. The military market is dominated by Lockheed, General Dynamics, Northrop, Rockwell, and Grumman, as well as Boeing and McDonnell Douglas.

The leading moneymakers in this industry are in the military and commercial sectors. Boeing posted sales in 1993 of more than $25 billion on the strength of commercial sales and contracts for the F-22 fighter plane and the RAH-66 Commanche helicopter. United Technologies posted total sales of $20 billion in 1993, partly on the strength of helicopter and aircraft sales. But according to *Fortune* in 1993, the "severely depressed airline market will force [United Technologies'] Pratt & Whitney division to cut 11,000 jobs by end of '94."

Another leading company is McDonnell Douglas. A top military supplier, the company posted sales of $14.5 billion in 1993. Lockheed garnered sales of $13 billion that same year, in part because of its F-22 and F-16 military aircraft. Martin Marietta posted 1993 sales of $9.4 billion, but lost out on its bid to merge with Grumman Corp. in 1994 because of Northrop Corp.'s late bid. Northrop, which had sales of more than $5 billion in 1993, topped Marietta's bid for Grumman with its own $2.11 billion offer. Northrop's $62-per-share bid overmatched Marietta's bid of $55-per-share. The combined company, with total annual revenues of more than $13 billion, is to be called Northrop Grumman Corp. The battle for control of Grumman reflected the merger/acquisition trend prevalent in the industry in response to the shrinking military market.

Other aerospace leaders include Allied Signal ($11.8 billion in 1993 sales), Textron ($8.7 billion), and General Dynamics ($4.6 billion).

WORK FORCE

As the *Monthly Labor Review* observed in 1994, "in 1993, negotiators in the aerospace industry faced a tough bargaining environment brought about by reductions in defense spending, cuts in aircraft purchases by troubled commercial airline carriers, and the elimination of thousands of jobs in the industry. As a result, most of the settlements [in union negotiations] featured lump-sum bonuses in lieu of general wage increases, health care cost containment arrangements, enhanced job security provisions, and more attractive retirement programs.''

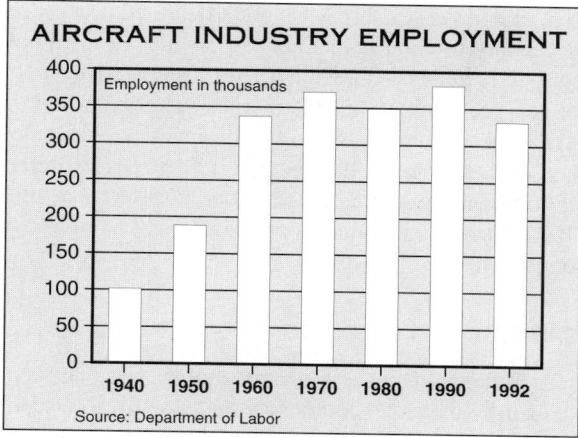

AIRCRAFT INDUSTRY EMPLOYMENT

Employment in thousands

Source: Department of Labor

The shaky financial situation of many of the country's leading carriers, industry analysts note, has cast a shadow over the industry's current work force, for labor costs are regarded as a significant drag on the airlines' ability to reverse their economic fortunes. Even airlines such as Trans World Airlines, whose work force owns 45% of the company's stock, are pondering layoffs. As *Business Week* notes, "TWA's woes have broad implications for the airline industry, which looks increasingly to employee ownership as a way of reducing costs. UAL Corp., parent of United Airlines Inc., has agreed with its unions to exchange 55% of the company's shares for wage and benefit concessions. And most analysts believe Delta Air Lines Inc. and USAir Inc. will make similar deals.''

AMERICA AND THE WORLD

While the worldwide market for military aircraft continues to be a tepid one in the early 1990s because of overcapacity and diminished demand, the market for commercial aircraft is expected to rebound somewhat in the coming years. As *U.S. Industrial Outlook 1994* notes, "demand in world commercial markets, particularly the expanding economies of Asia and the Pacific Rim, is expected to show increases over the next 10 to 15 years. In fact, the larger share of the commercial transport market is now overseas. The U.S. share, as a percentage of the world market, will shrink. Airline traffic, especially international traffic, is expected to show strong growth throughout the rest

of the decade and the industry expects to deliver more than 14,000 aircraft over the next 20 years.''

INDUSTRY INFORMATION SOURCES

Biddle, Wayne. *Barons of the Sky.* New York: Simon & Schuster, 1991.

Bilstein, Roger E. *Flight in America 1900-1983: From the Wrights to the Astronauts.* Baltimore, MD: Johns Hopkins University Press, 1984.

Blay, Roy, ed. *Lockheed Horizons.* Burbank, CA: Lockheed Corporation, 1983.

"Civil Aerospace." *Economist*, 3 September 1988, S1-S28.

Crampton, John. "Going Back to Basics." *Interavia*, November 1993, 18-20.

Donohue, Nancy, and Pankaj Ghemawat, "The U.S. Airline Industry, 1987-1988," Boston, MA: Harvard Business School, 1989.

Franklin, Roger. *The Defender: The Story of General Dynamics.* New York: Harper, 1986.

"How the Top Defense Contractors Stack Up," *Fortune.* February 22, 1993.

Industry & Trade Summary: Aircraft, Spacecraft, and Related Equipment. Washington, DC: Office of Industries, November 1991.

Kaplan, Ellen, ed. *In the Company of Eagles.* Stamford, CT: Pratt & Whitney, 1990.

Mattera, Philip. *Inside U.S. Business: A Concise Encyclopedia of Leading Industries.* Homewood, IL: Dow Jones-Irwin, 1987.

O'Lone, Richard G. "U.S. Airframe Outlook Bright Despite Gloomy 1991 Results." *Aviation Week & Space Technology*, 16 March 1992, 53-55.

Ropelewski, Robert, and Bill Sweetman. "US Government, Industry Seek Competitive Solutions." *Interavia*, August 1993, 23-27.

Solberg, Carl. *Conquest of the Skies.* Boston: Little, Brown, 1979.

Thruelsen, Richard. *The Grumman Story.* New York: Praeger, 1976.

U.S. Industrial Outlook 1993. Washington, DC: U.S. Department of Commerce, 1993.

U.S. Industrial Outlook 1994, Washington, DC: U.S. Department of Commerce, 1994.

Velocci, Jr., Anthony L. "Fewer Players to See Late-Decade Upturn." *Aviation Week & Space Technology*, 15 March 1993, 38-39.

Ward's Business Directory of U.S. Private and Public Companies. Detroit: Gale Research Inc., 1993.

Whitehouse, Arthur. *The Sky's the Limit.* London: Macmillan, 1979.

—John Simley

SIC 3724

AIRCRAFT ENGINES AND ENGINE PARTS

This industry includes establishments primarily engaged in manufacturing aircraft engines and engine parts. This industry also includes establishments owned by aircraft engine manufacturers and primarily engaged in research and development on aircraft engines and engine parts, whether from enterprise funds or on a contract or fee basis. Also included are establishments engaged in repairing and rebuilding aircraft engines on a factory basis. Establishments primarily engaged in manufacturing guided missile and space vehicle propulsion units and parts are classified in **SIC 3764: Guided Missile and Space Vehicle Propulsion Units and Propulsion Unit Parts;** those manufacturing aircraft intake and exhaust valves and pistons are classified in **SIC 3592: Carburetors, Pistons, Piston Rings, and Valves;** and those manufacturing aircraft internal combustion engine filters are classified in **SIC 3714: Motor Vehicle Parts and Accessories.** Establishments primarily engaged in the repair of aircraft engines, except on a factory basis, are classified in **SIC 4581: Airports, Flying Fields, and Airport Terminal Services;** and research and development on aircraft engines on a contract or fee basis by establishments not owned by aircraft engine manufacturers are classified in **SIC 8731: Commercial Physical and Biological Research.**

INDUSTRY SNAPSHOT

The world aircraft engine industry is dominated by three companies: General Electric (GE), Pratt & Whitney, which is a division of United Technologies, and Rolls-Royce. Each of these companies achieved their leading role through the successful development of jet engine models for commercial aircraft, though GE and Pratt & Whitney maintain significant interest in the development of engines for military aircraft. The big three offer jet engines in nearly every thrust range and compete with each other for use on commercial aircraft produced by Boeing, McDonnell Douglas, and Airbus Industries. Several other engine manufacturers, including Allison, Garrett and Lycoming, are involved primarily with small jet turbines and piston engines, which power propeller-driven aircraft. The U.S. aircraft engine industry had 1993 shipments valued at $22,312 million.

Aircraft engine manufacturers had enjoyed a long period of industry growth from the end of World War II until the first years of the 1990s, when changes in military spending and changing commercial air travel patterns caused dramatic shifts in industry planning and expectations. Industry analysts predict that engine manufacturers will struggle to adjust to an industry-wide recession through the mid-1990s, when a revitalized commercial air travel market will increase orders for aircraft engines. The future of the aircraft engine market seems likely to depend on the development of big engines with thrust of 60,000 pounds or more, according to *Interavia.* Each of the big three engine manufacturers is expected to take steps to develop engines to compete in this market category, which is expected to generate $210 billion in sales of engines and parts between 1992 and 2012. Total engine delivery rates are expected to be about 1,700 a year after 1995, turning short-range pessimism into long-range optimism.

ORGANIZATION AND STRUCTURE

The manufacture of aircraft engines was once controlled by the same companies that assembled aircraft and operated airlines, but industry regulation initiated in 1934 forced aircraft engine manufacturers to work independently of aircraft manufacturers. This antitrust legislation is partly responsible for the intense competition that characterizes the aircraft engine industry, in which each of the big three engine makers seeks to provide engines to fit the requirements of a wide range of aircraft. Engine companies are typically chosen to design an engine at the concept stage of a new aircraft. Once the engine is developed, the engine builder may try to adapt the design for other aircraft. In fact, it is common to find the same engine on a variety of competing aircraft. Rarely do engine manufacturers develop an engine that is not capable of multiple applications.

For decades following the end of World War II, military funding supplied much of the research and development money that allowed U.S. manufacturers to continually upgrade their engines. Technical breakthroughs achieved on military projects found their way into commercial engine applications, thus allowing engine manufacturers to achieve substantial profits from commercial engine sales. This arrangement has changed significantly since the end of the Cold War, when the U.S. military budget decreased dramatically. Though the Clinton administration has promised to continue providing research and development funding to the aerospace industry, engine manufacturers are increasingly faced with incorporating the cost of research and development spending into the price of their engines. Bob Leduc, director of strategic planning at Pratt & Whitney, told *Interavia* that his company will need to spend close to $6 billion in development spending to compete for the large engine market, costs that will require the manufacturer to recover $1.3 million per engine just to cover engineering and development costs. Such prohibitive costs may force manufacturers to remove themselves from competition in some market segments.

All of the American aircraft engine manufacturers are divisions of larger corporations. Pratt & Whitney is a division of United Technologies, GE Aircraft Engines is a unit of General Electric, Allison is owned by General Motors, Garrett is a part of Allied Signal, and Lycoming is part of Textron. Pratt & Whitney and GE are thought to possess an advantage over their British competitor, Rolls-Royce, because of their corporate support, which allows them to better weather industry cycles. While the Pratt & Whitney Power Group contributes approximately 32 percent of United Technologies revenue, and GE Aircraft Engines supplies 12 percent of GE's revenue, the aircraft engine portion of Rolls-Royce totals 60 percent of that company's turnover.

BACKGROUND AND DEVELOPMENT

The development of powered aviation, which began with the Wright Brothers in 1903, fell mainly to those who understood engines, rather than those who understood flight. In fact, aeronautical scientists—such as Samuel P. Langley, who was perhaps the first to describe the dynamics of lift over a wing—had very little to do with powered aircraft. Instead, a pair of bicycle mechanics, Wilbur and Orville Wright, and a motorcycle mechanic named Glenn Curtiss were the first to demonstrate propeller-driven aircraft. In fact, Curtiss gained an early lead over the Wrights and a third aviator, Glenn Martin, precisely because he knew how to build lighter, more powerful motors. The first ten years of motorized flight was pioneered by eccentric inventors working out of their garages by night and flying in air shows by day. These barnstormers relied on show earnings to fund their building efforts, and many died in the process.

Industrial support for aviation did not materialize until European aviators demonstrated the strategic use of aircraft in World War I. Major industrial involvement in the United States occurred only after the U.S. Army requested funding for aviation projects. Financiers and industrial magnates were drawn to the industry not by their love of aviation, but by the opportunity to enrich themselves with government contracts. Some of the earliest investors in aircraft ventures were automobile manufacturers and automobile fleet owners. They sponsored specific aircraft builders and later

pulled dishonest financial stunts to take control of aircraft builders' fledgling companies.

Edward Deeds, founder of Delco and the first to commercialize an electric starter, formed a one-sided partnership with the well-known Orville Wright called the Dayton-Wright Company. The company built engines, but no aircraft. The company was later acquired by William Boyce Thompson, who established the first American aircraft combine. Thompson acquired the patents owned by Wright and later Martin; he purchased the rights to a light, European-designed engine called the Hispano-Suiza; and he acquired the facilities of the Simplex Automobile Company to build his engines. Shut out from the management of the company by Thompson and unhappy at only building engines, Wright retired and Martin simply started another company.

Unwilling to allow any single group of financiers to corner the aviation industry, U.S. government officials created the Aircraft Production Board to oversee the development of the American aviation industry. This Board was soon dominated by the automobile industry, which assembled an industrial federation called the Manufacturers Aircraft Association. Auto manufacturers, led by the Packard and Hall-Scott Motor Car companies, convinced the Aircraft Production Board to support the mass production of a single type of aircraft motor, a 400-horsepower, 8-cylinder model called the ''Liberty.'' As evidence of the industry's widespread complicity, this huge water-cooled engine featured an unnecessary electronic ignition system supplied by Delco. Completely inappropriate for use on existing aircraft designs, the monstrosity was better suited for a truck or a boat than an aircraft.

Under pressure from auto manufacturers, the government ordered the production of 11,000 Libertys. This so infuriated Donald Douglas, the leading aircraft designer on the board, that he resigned his position and went back to making airplanes for Glenn Martin. Confident of the program's failure, he, like many other aircraft manufacturers, simply ignored the Liberty. Despite problems with Delco's starter, and with the reconfiguration of the Liberty into an even larger 12-cylinder engine, the government remained perfectly comfortable entrusting the future of aviation to such experienced transportation pioneers as Packard, Hudson, Nash, and Ford.

An Indianapolis, Indiana engine builder named Jim Allison recognized the futility of placing the huge Liberty motor in the light aircraft of the day, and decided to build a light engine of his own. As he pursued the development of lighter engines, he stumbled across a variety of high-quality manufacturing techniques. Engines, he discovered, ran most efficiently at about 30,000 rotations per minute, while propellers generated the greatest amount of thrust at about 2,000 rotations. What was required was a precisely-machined reduction gear. Allison was the first major manufacturer to perfect an engine and clutch mechanism with acceptable tolerances. His lead in this area greatly advanced the Allison reputation and provided the company with hundreds of profitable orders.

Another engine builder of the day was Frederick Rentschler, one of the original founders of Wright Aeronautical. Rentschler grew increasingly weary of managerial interference from automobile magnates, whom he thought were interested only in short-term profit. The development of engines required years of expensive and often fruitless experimentation. Rentschler resigned from Wright in 1924 and began searching for a factory and financial backing to develop better engines. Like Douglas and Allison, Rentschler knew the Liberty design was a failure. He learned from a naval officer that the service would soon announce a competition for a powerful, lightweight air-cooled design.

In 1925, Rentschler acquired the Pratt & Whitney company, a small machine tool manufacturer located in Hartford, Connecticut. Rentschler raided the Wright company of its best engineering talent and enlisted the help of Chance Vought, an aircraft builder. By Christmas of that year, Pratt & Whitney completed its first air-cooled radial engine, the 425-horsepower Wasp. The radial design meant that the cylinders were arranged in a circular fashion around the prop shaft, rather than being lined up along the shaft as in an automobile. This allowed the cylinders to be directly exposed to the thrust of air generated by the propeller. As a result, there was no need for a bulky radiator or heavy liquid coolant, as in the Liberty. Barely a year old, the new Pratt & Whitney company secured an order from the Navy for 200 Wasps. This provided the capital needed to develop an even larger, 525-horsepower engine, the Hornet.

In 1929, automotive interests organized yet another company, Curtiss-Wright, bearing the name of aviation's first pioneers. While neither Glenn Curtiss nor Orville Wright were active in the company, it did manage to turn out a successful product, the Cyclone radial engine. General Motors made the switch to air-cooled engines when its Dutch designer, Anthony Fokker, chose Pratt & Whitney's Wasp engine for his aircraft. Ford, meanwhile, dropped out of the aircraft business to concentrate on automobiles. The Lycoming Foundry and Machine Shop, established in Williamsport, Pennsylvania in 1908, began building

aircraft engines during the late 1920s. Its position in the industry was secured by the success of its nine-cylinder R-680 radial engine, which was standard on many aircraft.

Pratt & Whitney gained dominance in the industry when it gained the attention of Bill Boeing, an aircraft builder based in Seattle, Washington. Boeing, too, was looking for a replacement for the Liberty and considered the Wasp to be the perfect engine for his fighters and mailplanes. When Boeing married the Wasp to his Model 40 mailplane, he discovered the craft could carry an additional 500 pounds of mail, or even passengers, making it extremely profitable. Boeing, Rentschler and Vought later merged their companies into what became America's most powerful aeronautical combine. The new company, called United Aircraft & Transportation, acquired the amphibious airplane builder Sikorsky, the light aircraft manufacturer Stearman, Jack Northrop's Avion experimental aircraft company, propeller makers Hamilton and Standard Steel, and a combination of small airline companies.

United Aircraft grew at an extremely fast pace. While the Great Depression virtually destroyed the industry, United Aircraft continued to expand, taking over the routes of defunct airline companies and providing a stream of exclusive Pratt & Whitney-driven aircraft for the military. In 1934, Senator Hugo Black led an investigation of the industry that resulted in legislation that broke up the aircraft combines. The Boeing Company was separated from United Aircraft, as were the airline services, which were reincorporated as United Airlines in Chicago. Pratt & Whitney, however, remained a division of United Aircraft.

The importance of efficient, powerful engines was well understood by manufacturers in Germany and Japan, who embraced aviation as an instrument of warfare during the mid-1930s. Companies such as Daimler-Benz and Mitsubishi closely studied the advancements in American engine designs and were heavily sponsored by their governments. As a result, during the years leading up to World War II, Japanese and German aircraft advanced beyond the capabilities of American designs. By 1940, however, with the war raging in Europe, the United States government began a massive mobilization of its war industries.

Pratt & Whitney, which had developed a new 2,000-horsepower Double Wasp engine, was required to vastly expand its production capacity. Still unable to meet the demand for nearly 8,000 of these engines, Pratt & Whitney licensed production of its designs to Ford, Buick, Chevrolet, and Nash-Kelvinator. By the end of the war, Pratt & Whitney and its licensees produced a staggering 363,619 aircraft engines, representing half of all the horsepower used by the United States military during the war.

Meanwhile, Curtiss-Wright's R1820 Cyclone was used to power the Boeing B-17 bomber, the Douglas Dauntless dive bomber, and a number of DC-3s. A second design, the R3350, powered Boeing's B-29 bomber and, later, Lockheed's Constellation airliner. Curtiss-Wright provided 35 percent of American wartime horsepower. Allison occupied a special position during the war, producing 70,000 of its V1710 engines for aircraft such as the Lockheed P-38 and Curtiss P-40 Tomahawk. Lycoming, now a division of Avco, built only smaller engines, one of which powered Sikorsky's first helicopter in 1939.

Another manufacturer, the Garrett Corporation, was drawn into engine manufacture during the war. Garrett entered the market first by building intercoolers and turbochargers, devices that heated and concentrated the mix of oxygen and fuel in the combustion chamber for higher engine performance. Garrett turbochargers were fitted to existing engines on American aircraft, vastly improving their performance. Garrett also was active in the production of air conditioning systems and flight controls. Established in 1935 by Cliff Garrett, the company emerged from the war with an excellent reputation among airframe builders and later launched an aggressive diversification that included the development of engines. Garrett's first engine design was the 575-horsepower Model 331 gas turbine, intended for use on helicopters and light aircraft. This engine was later used to power the Beechcraft 18, Aero Commander and Mitsubishi models.

Curtiss-Wright emerged from the war as the number two engine builder in the industry, a position it did not hold for long. Rather than plow its substantial earnings back into product development, Curtiss-Wright chose to invest its profits in other businesses, thus ceding its position to more enlightened competitors such as Pratt & Whitney and General Electric.

During the war, government war procurement officials had designated Pratt & Whitney, Curtiss-Wright and Allison to produce only piston-driven engines. Meanwhile, the development of jet engines was given to Allis Chalmers, General Electric and Westinghouse, which were experienced with steam turbines. The introduction of the jet engine was the most significant development in aviation since the Wright Brothers' first flight. Existing engines used fuel to drive pistons down, turning a shaft while driving other pistons up for another firing. Jet engines used an entirely different principle: air was scooped into a chamber and compressed by a series of turbine blades. Behind these blades, a highly refined fuel was sprayed into the compressed air and ignited. The resulting blast was channeled out the rear of the engine, where it drove a second turbine that powered the intake compressors. With their enormous thrust, jet engines could propel an aircraft at much greater speeds than conventional propellers.

The first jet engines were successfully built in Germany and England. Britain's Rolls-Royce held a strong lead in jet engine technology, due to the work of the inventor Frank Whittle. It was several years before American companies assumed leadership in jet technology, using Whittle's designs. General Electric, whose experience in turbine technology originated with steam-driven electrical generators, was given a government contract to develop Whittle's engine for a new jet, the Bell Aircraft XP-59A, which first flew in 1942. A practical jet engine emerged only after the war, however, with the J33 and J35, which were used to power the Boeing B-47 and Northrop B-49 flying wing. GE turned over its licenses for these designs to Allison in 1946.

Westinghouse scored an early coup in jet technology by building the first axial flow engine; earlier models used less efficient centrifugal compression. But Westinghouse lost its early lead in jet technology when the Navy changed its weight specifications for the engines and canceled millions of dollars worth of orders for Westinghouse engines. Unable to adapt quickly, Westinghouse simply abandoned the jet engine market.

Pratt & Whitney was first introduced to jet engines as a subcontractor to Westinghouse. Later, because American law required that foreign designs for military craft be manufactured domestically, Pratt & Whitney built versions of Rolls-Royce's Nene and Tay jet engines, which saw action during the Korean War. Pratt & Whitney's future was secured when it achieved a major engineering breakthrough. General Electric had been planning engines with up to 7,000 pounds of thrust, but Pratt & Whitney decided to leapfrog other competitors by building an engine that would produce 10,000 pounds of thrust. The result, the J57/JT3, was used to power the F-100, F-101 and F-102 fighters while eight of the engines were used on Boeing's massive new B-52 bomber. Thus the continuing battle for ever increasing amounts of jet thrust was born.

General Motors' Allison division, initially paralyzed by postwar labor action, pursued jet engine development with GE's J33 design. Allison manufactured 15,525 of these engines for a variety of fighter aircraft, and secured its position in the postwar engine market. Lycoming capitalized on its involvement with helicopters after the war. Under the direction of Dr. Anselm Franz, the company built the T53, the first jet engine designed specifically for helicopters. Nearly 20,000 were produced.

Following World War II, government-led industry coordination ended and free market competition, fueled by Cold War military budgets, began. As a result GE terminated its technological partnership with Allison and began work on the J47, which drove the North American F-86 in combat over Korea. A later model, the high-performance J79, powered Convair's B-58, the Lockheed F-104 and McDonnell F-4 Phantom. As in the airframe industry, many of the advancements earned from wartime engine development were applied to commercial markets. Thousands of airliners were retrofitted with more efficient turbo-powered engines.

The advent of jet-powered bombers gave aircraft builders the experience necessary to create jet airliners. After Britain's DeHavilland built the first commercial jet, the Comet, Boeing, Douglas and Convair scrambled to develop their own jetliners. When Boeing's 707 was introduced in 1954, it was powered by four Pratt & Whitney JT3s. Douglas' DC-8, which took to the air in 1955, used the same engine. A commercial version of GE's J79 powered Convair's short-lived 880 and 990 jetliners.

While jet engine companies had successfully converted military engines to civilian uses, the Defense Department continued to press for even greater advancements in propulsion technology. The leading manufacturers began testing ramjets, engines that were designed for such high-speed flight that they required no compressor fans. General Electric was given a contract to build a nuclear-powered jet engine, and Pratt & Whitney was asked to develop liquid hydrogen-fueled rocket motors. Allison built a counter-rotating propeller engine for Convair's vertical takeoff and landing "Pogo Stick" airplane. All the projects were successful, though only the rocket technology was developed.

Within the conventional jet engine arena, General Electric built a massive new J93 engine in 1963. This boron-fueled engine, rated at 30,000 pounds thrust, was developed for North American's brilliant but obsolete Mach-3 B-70 bomber. Pratt & Whitney had better luck in triplesonic flight, developing the J58 engine for Lockheed's SR-71. Capable of crossing the United States in only 68 minutes, the SR-71 established numerous performance records. Pratt & Whitney also built the J75 for Lockheed's high altitude U-2 spy plane. The J52, however, was the company's military mainstay. In production for 30 years, the J52 powered a long line of naval aircraft.

Among the smaller manufacturers, Curtiss-Wright's sales were declining rapidly by 1960. In 1963, as part of a scheme to bolster its position in the market and acquire a staff of talented engineers, Curtiss-Wright launched a hostile takeover bid for Garrett. Garrett's management remained deeply suspicious of its suitor, however, and enlisted the support of Signal Oil & Gas, a company with the financial resources to thwart Curtiss-Wright's bid. Signal acquired Garrett in 1964, permitting the company to operate autonomously. Garrett was firmly established as a manufacturer of auxiliary power units, small engines that are used to provide power to start main engines. Garrett built this business into a series of successful small propulsion engines, principally the TFE731, which powered the Learjet 25, Cessna Citation and Hawker Siddeley 125 business jets.

Lycoming regained its position in the fixed wing market in the mid-1960s, after developing its own small turbofan. This design evolved into the ALF502 which, like Garrett's design, was popular with a variety of business jets. The engine was chosen to power the Hawker Siddeley 146, which eventually emerged as the popular British Aerospace BAe 146 commuter jet.

In the airliner market, Allison briefly extended the life of turboprops by developing a T56 powerplant for a family of Convair airliners, the 440, 540, and 580. Meanwhile Boeing was developing a new medium-range trijet called the 727 and asked for an engine similar to Rolls-Royce's Spey. Allison formed a partnership with Rolls-Royce, but lost the 727 business to Pratt & Whitney, whose JT8D became a best-seller in the industry. In addition to the 727, the versatile engine was used on four twinjets: the Boeing 737, Douglas DC-9, Sud Aviation Caravelle and Dassault Mercure.

While Pratt & Whitney and its JT8D dominated the commercial market, General Electric's J79 derivative declined with the increasingly unpopular Convair jetliners. But General Electric expanded its market for jet engines well beyond the aircraft industry. Variations on the company's engines powered missiles, helicopters, hovercraft, speedboats and even electrical power generators. GE's J85 series became a favorite among the growing ranks of private jet manufacturers. The company scored a major coup in 1965 when it was chosen to develop the engines for Lockheed's super transport, the C-5 Galaxy. To lift the massive freighter into the sky, GE had to develop a more efficient high-bypass "turbofan" engine.

With early turbofans, about half the air taken into an engine passed concentrically around its combustion chamber, providing additional thrust and allowing the engine to operate more efficiently. GE's high-bypass design, the TF39, increased the bypass ratio to eight to one. Four of the engines, which generated 41,100 pounds of thrust, would enable the C-5 to carry 132 tons of cargo. Airline companies immediately embraced the quieter, more fuel-efficient turbofan, which was perfectly suited for subsonic passenger aircraft. But because the engines were considerably fatter, it was impossible to retrofit the thousands of existing aircraft that were designed for the long, skinny JT8D turbojet. Instead, turbofans were reserved for the new line of jumbo jets. The TF39 gave GE the lead in engines for large passenger aircraft such as Boeing's 747, McDonnell Douglas' DC-10 and Lockheed's L-1011. A commercial version of the high-bypass turbofan, the CF6, was developed for the DC-10 in 1971 and Airbus' A300 in 1974.

Pratt & Whitney began development of its own high-bypass engine in 1960. The company's TF30 was used aboard General Dynamics' F-111 and Grumman F-14, and led to a civilian version, the JT9D, which could generate more than 43,000 pounds of thrust. The JT9D entered service with the 747 in 1969, and was the only 747 powerplant until 1975, when GE developed a CF6 for the jumbo jet.

Meanwhile, Lockheed's L-1011 Tristar, a competitor to the DC-10 and 747, was powered by RB211 engines from Rolls-Royce. Allison, Rolls-Royce's American partner, wisely elected to steer clear of the RB211, sure that its pricing was flawed. When problems later arose with the engine, Allison avoided the brush with bankruptcy that nearly ruined Rolls-Royce and Lockheed. Allison did, however, convert its production of Rolls-Royce's Spey into its own TF41, which went on to power Vought's A-7 Corsair. In addition, Allison's T56 turboprop was chosen for the Lockheed C-130 transport, Grumman E-2C and Lockheed Orion.

During the late 1960s, GE was asked to apply its experience with the J93 toward the development of an engine for Boeing's supersonic transport. The resulting design, the GE4, generated nearly 70,000 pounds of thrust. Four of these engines would enable the SST to reach 1,800 miles per hour. However, Boeing canceled the program after airlines lost interest in the SST.

General Electric was awarded a contract to develop a new engine for Rockwell's B-1 bomber in 1970. Unlike the B-52, which the bomber would replace, the B-1 was fitted with afterburners. A common feature of fighter jets, the afterburner was a mechanism that detonated a second spray of fuel into an engine's exhaust thrust. The resulting blast could add as much as 50 percent more power to an engine. The B-1, and the F101 engine GE developed for it, were canceled in 1977. But the engine went back into production when the B-1 program was revived in 1981.

Engine manufacturers benefitted greatly from drastically increased defense spending under the Reagan administration. But the heavy investment in defense industries during those years led to several scandal-ridden cases of overcharging and non-performance. While few of these cases involved engine manufacturers, the laws put in place to correct the abuses still applied to them. These laws were meant to extract more economical and responsible development by mandating strict competitions for government business, particularly between General Electric and Pratt & Whitney.

General Electric's F404 engine, developed for McDonnell Douglas' F-18 fighter, was fitted to Grumman's X-29, an experimental high-maneuverability aircraft with forward swept wings. The engine was later used for Lockheed's F-117 Stealth fighter, which flew secretly as early as 1981, and SAAB's Gripen fighter.

Pratt & Whitney developed the F100 in 1970 for McDonnell Douglas' F-15. The engine, which could send an F-15 to 98,000 feet in only three minutes, was later fitted to General Dynamics' F-16. However, turbine wear on the F100 took years to correct, enabling General Electric to step in with an alternative. GE combined the finest elements of the F101 and F404 to produce the versatile F110. This engine powered all of America's leading fighter jets, including the F-15, F-16 and F-14. Eventually, GE's F110 gained 75 percent of the F100's market.

The loss convinced Pratt & Whitney to pay closer attention to the Pentagon's needs. The company developed variants with special new capabilities, and by 1990 had won back a quarter of the government's Fighter Engine Competition business. Meanwhile, Pratt & Whitney developed a second derivative of its F101, the F118, which was chosen to power Northrop's B-2 Stealth bomber.

Strong growth in airline traffic during the 1970s led aircraft manufacturers to create a new family of airliners to replace the aging DC-8, DC-9 and 727. Boeing designed two large twin-jets, the 757 and 767. The European Airbus consortium introduced a new line of A310, A320 and A330 aircraft. McDonnell Douglas, however, elected to update its existing models. The DC-9 became the MD-80, and the DC-10 became the MD-11. Development centered on improved avionics and control functions, but the greatest advancement occurred with engines, which were now quieter and far more fuel efficient.

Pratt & Whitney's position in the commercial markets had begun to wane in the 1980s. The company was reviled for its growing arrogance and lack of customer focus, and had rested too long on the laurels of its successful JT8D. General Electric's deliveries surpassed Pratt & Whitney's in 1986. General Electric captured a large portion of the new market through its CF6 series and a partnership with the French engine manufacturer SNECMA called CFM International. The company's CFM56 was used to re-engine the old fuel-guzzling DC-8 and military versions of the 707, and was the standard engine on Airbus' A320. In 1987, GE formed a second partnership with Garrett called the CFE Company. This company developed the CFE738, a 6,000–pound thrust turbofan for the small jet market, specifically the Dassault Falcon 2000 business jet.

Eager to remain in the game, Pratt & Whitney established its own international partnership with the German Motoren und Turbinen Union and Italy's Fiat Avianzione. The company developed the PW2037 for Boeing's 757, and the PW4000—designed specifically to compete with the CF6—for the 747. The PW2037 caused General Electric to abandon its entry for the 757, but Pratt & Whitney still faced competition from a modified version of Rolls-Royce's RB211. Pratt & Whitney later formed a second consortium, called International Aero Engines, with MTU, Fiat, Rolls-Royce and Japanese Aero Engines. The company's V2500 engine was used to power Airbus' A320. The partnerships helped preserve Pratt & Whitney's position in the industry until it could mend its relations with airline companies and aircraft manufacturers.

While manufacturers were often able to convert military engines into commercial versions, the two markets held fundamentally different requirements. Airline companies wanted highly reliable, fuel-efficient engines that were quiet and did not pollute. The military, on the other hand, wanted powerful lightweight engines that remained cool enough to avoid detection by enemy tracking. During the mid-1980s, demand grew for a new type of commercial engine with little or no use for the military. Conventional high-bypass jet engines burned too much fuel for the increasingly cost-conscious airline industry, which requested development of a new hybrid propjet.

General Electric and Pratt & Whitney immediately began work on elaborate jet engines whose turbines drove two rear-mounted counter-rotating propellers with crescent-shaped blades. This "propfan," while slightly slower than conventional engines, was twice as fuel efficient as turbofans. The propfan was an unducted pusher propeller design, intended for installation on the rear fuselage of aircraft. Accordingly, Boeing and McDonnell Douglas tested propfans on a 727 and MD-80, and began development of two new twin-propfan designs, the 7J7 and MD-91. In England, Rolls-Royce began work on a ducted propfan, with its blades enclosed within a large shell, called the contrafan. Such a propfan would be suitable for the thousands of aircraft whose engines were wing-mounted.

During the late 1980s, a vicious cycle of competition drove airlines into near bankruptcy while fuel prices dropped. Airline companies canceled orders for hundreds of new aircraft, choosing instead to squeeze a few more years of service out of their existing fleets. As a result, airframe and engine manufacturers were forced to shelve the propfan indefinitely. Despite this, Boeing began planning a larger super twinjet, the 777, intended to compete with the MD-11. Pratt & Whitney's PW4000 was chosen as the launch customer for the 777. Meanwhile, McDonnell Douglas has begun planning a four-engine MD-12, intended to compete with the 747, but has yet to name an engine for the design.

CURRENT CONDITIONS

The early 1990s saw one of the biggest shakeups in aerospace industry history, as military budgets shrank and fewer people chose to fly. Commercial airlines canceled or postponed their orders for airplanes, and aircraft manufacturers in turn canceled their orders for aircraft engines. The industry recession proved particularly challenging for the aircraft engine industry, which was in the process of developing a number of engines for the expected orders of large jet-powered aircraft. General Electric, which had been pouring money into the development of its GE90 engine for the Boeing 777 aircraft, was the most severely affected of the big three engine manufacturers, but all three companies faced dismal short-term prospects.

Industry analysts wondered if the intense competition that had characterized the aircraft engine industry through the 1980s could continue through the 1990s. *Air Transport World* contributor J. A. Donoghue noted that "all three major manufacturers say they are committed to a battle across a broad front; the trend is for competitive offerings to increase as the defense market continues its decline. Airlines undoubtedly are the beneficiaries of these aggressive competitive matchups virtually across the board. The key question is whether this level of competitiveness is sustainable." The biggest drain on the competitors is likely to be research and development costs, which following the end of the Cold War are no longer boosted by Department of Defense dollars. Robert Ropelewski, editor-in-chief of *Interavia* magazine, said the engine builders battle "may end with no winners, but only losers in the current marketplace for large commercial turbine engines."

One difficulty, wrote *Interavia* contributor Pierre Condom, is that "engine manufacturers live in a world where the time unit is not the year, but the decade." Condom suggested that dozens of years are needed to develop an engine and expand it across a wide range of aircraft, and dozens more to realize that engine's impact on the market. Luckily, engine manufacturers are rewarded for successful development by a lucrative spare parts and upgrade market. Since aircraft engines represent such a large investment for airlines, those airlines seek to extend engine life up to 25 years through frequent maintenance and upgrading. According to *Interavia*, "Pratt & Whitney derives about 40 percent of its pre-tax earnings from commercial engine spares sales," a figure characteristic of the industry.

Industry forecasts are much more optimistic when they are extended into the twenty-first century. "Forecasters estimate that between 1992 and 2012, about $330 billion in engines and spare parts will be sold to commercial carriers outside of the former Soviet Union, with $200 billion of the quantity directly attributable to engine sales," wrote *Aviation Week & Space Technology*'s Stanley Kandebo. According to estimates, 54 percent of this money will be spent on engines with thrust greater than 45,000 pounds, 32 percent on engines with thrust less than 30,000 pounds, and the remainder on mid-range engines. The anticipated boom in engine sales is expected to begin after 1995 and continue for at least a decade as airlines retire their older aircraft and trade up to larger aircraft capable to carrying over 200 passengers.

Meanwhile, in the military arena, the Pentagon is sponsoring a competition for a new Advanced Tactical Fighter, or ATF, between Northrop and Lockheed. Similarly, General Electric and Pratt & Whitney were asked to compete for the engine to drive the ATF. In this test, Pratt & Whitney's F119 will challenge GE's F120. The successful model could be worth more than a billion dollars to the winner.

INDUSTRY LEADERS

Though there are more than a dozen companies with significant aircraft engine businesses, only General Electric, Pratt & Whitney, and Rolls-Royce have access to the global market. GE leads the big three with 1992 engines and spare parts sales of $7.4 billion,

followed by Pratt & Whitney's sales of $6.9 billion, and Rolls-Royce's sales of $3.8 billion. Though Rolls-Royce's sales were significantly smaller, 1992 orders put the British firm in close competition with the American giants. Garrett, Allison and Lycoming continue to operate on the fringes of the industry, supplying smaller turbine engines and piston-driven engines for commuter and private aircraft.

Each of the big three engines makers responded to the early-1990s recession with significant cuts in employment and reductions in production. GE Aircraft Engines cut employment from 41,000 people in 1987 to just 26,000 in 1993, while substantially shifting its focus from military to commercial applications. GE was expected to produce between 500 and 600 large commercial engines in 1993. Pratt & Whitney's employment dropped from 46,000 in 1990 to 33,000 in 1993, according to *Interavia*, and 1993 production stood at 400 engines. The smallest of the big three, Rolls-Royce, saw the smallest drops in employment, from 29,500 to 24,500 employees expected by 1994. Rolls-Royce produced just 200 large engines in 1993.

INDUSTRY INFORMATION SOURCES

Biddle, Wayne. *Barons of the Sky*. New York: Simon & Schuster, 1991.

"Civil Aerospace." *Economist*, 3 September 1988, S1-S28.

Condom, Pierre. "Engine Manufacturers Slug It Out." *Interavia*, November 1993, 48-50.

Donoghue, J. A. "A Broad Battle on Many Fronts." *Air Transport World*, November 1992, 65-68.

Flint, Perry. "Big Engine, Big Risk. Big Payoff?" *Air Transport World*, August 1993, 38-59.

General Electric. *Propulsion*. Cincinnati, OH: GE Aircraft Engines, 1991.

Green, William. *Modern Commercial Aircraft*. New York: Portland House, 1987.

Kandebo, Stanley W. "Engine Makers Predict Improved Industry Health over Long Term." *Aviation Week & Space Technology*, 16 March 1992, 59-60.

————. "Manufacturers Predict $50-Billion Engine Market During Next Decade." *Aviation Week & Space Technology*, 20 March 1989, 218-220.

————. "Stable Engine Sales Seen in Late 1994." *Aviation Week & Space Technology*, 15 March 1993, 77-78.

Kaplan, Ellen, ed. *In the Company of Eagles*. Stamford, CT: Pratt & Whitney, 1990.

Mattera, Philip. *Inside U.S. Business: A Concise Encyclopedia of Leading Industries*. Homewood, IL: Dow Jones-Irwin, 1987.

Solberg, Carl. *Conquest of the Skies*. Boston: Little, Brown, 1979.

Sonnenberg, Paul. *Allison: Power of Excellence.* Malibu, CA: Coastline Publishers, 1990.

Textron Corporation. *Company Profile.* Stratford, CT: Textron Lycoming, 1993.

U.S. Department of Commerce. *U.S. Industrial Outlook 1993.* Washington, DC: U.S. Department of Commerce, January 1993.

Ward's Business Directory of U.S. Private and Public Companies. Detroit: Gale Research Inc., 1993.

Whitehouse, Arthur. *The Sky's the Limit.* London: Macmillan, 1979.

—John Simley

SIC 3728

AIRCRAFT PARTS AND AUXILIARY EQUIPMENT, NOT ELSEWHERE CLASSIFIED

This category includes establishments primarily engaged in manufacturing aircraft parts and auxiliary equipment, not elsewhere classified. This industry also includes establishments owned by manufacturers of aircraft parts and auxiliary equipment and primarily engaged in research and development on aircraft parts, whether from enterprise funds or on a contract or fee basis. Establishments primarily engaged in manufacturing or assembling complete aircraft are classified in **SIC 3721: Aircraft;** those manufacturing aircraft engines and parts are classified in **SIC 3724: Aircraft Engines and Engine Parts;** those manufacturing aeronautical instruments are classified in **SIC 3812: Search, Detection, Navigation, Guidance, Aeronautical, and Nautical Systems and Instruments;** those manufacturing aircraft engine electrical equipment are classified in **SIC 3694: Electrical Equipment for Internal Combustion Engines;** and those manufacturing guided missile and space vehicle parts and auxiliary equipment are classified in **SIC 3769: Guided Missile and Space Vehicle Parts and Auxiliary Equipment, Not Elsewhere Classified.** Establishments not owned by manufacturers or aircraft parts but primarily engaged in research and development on aircraft parts on a contract or fee basis are classified in **SIC 8731: Commercial and Biological Research.**

INDUSTRY SNAPSHOT

The American aircraft industry may be divided into four segments. In one segment, manufacturers such as Boeing, McDonnell Douglas, and Lockheed build the wings and fuselages that comprise the airframe. Meanwhile, companies such as General Electric and Pratt & Whitney manufacture the engines that propel aircraft. The third segment covers flight instrumentation, an area where the most profound advances in aviation have taken place. But the fourth segment, broadly defined by industrial classification as "aircraft parts not otherwise classified," includes manufacturers of surface control and cabin pressurization systems, landing gear, lighting, galley equipment, and general use products such nuts and bolts. This highly diversified industry generated shipments valued at $20,215 million in 1992 and regularly runs a $6,000 million trade surplus, contributing significantly to the greater aerospace industry, which ranks sixth in the United States in overall value of shipments and first in exports.

ORGANIZATION AND STRUCTURE

Aircraft manufacturers rely on a broad base of suppliers to provide the thousands of subsystems and parts that make up their products. There are more than 4000 suppliers contributing parts to the aerospace industry, including rubber companies, refrigerator makers, appliance manufacturers and general electronics enterprises. This diversity is necessary because in most cases it is simply uneconomical for an aircraft manufacturer to establish, for example, its own landing light operation. The internal demand for such a specialized product is insufficient to justify the creation of an independent manufacturing division.

Aircraft manufacturers have found it cheaper and more efficient to purchase secondary products from other manufacturers, who may sell similar products to other aircraft companies, as well as automotive manufacturers, railroad signal makers, locomotive and ship builders, and a variety of other customers. For example, an airplane builder such as Boeing, Grumman, or Beech is likely to purchase landing lights from a light bulb maker such as General Electric. Such subcontractors supply a surprisingly large portion of the entire aircraft. On the typical commercial aircraft, a lead manufacturer such as McDonnell Douglas may actually manufacture less than half of the aircraft, though it is responsible for the design and assembly of the final product.

When a major manufacturer discontinues an aircraft design, as Lockheed did with its L-1011 Tristar, a ripple effect is caused that affects every manufacturer that supplied parts for that aircraft. Therefore, parts suppliers strive to diversify their customer base to ensure that the decline of one manufacturer will be tempered by continued sales to others. Given the unstable nature of the industry, parts manufacturers also attempt to find customers outside of the aircraft business as well.

BACKGROUND AND DEVELOPMENT

Aircraft parts manufacturing may be said to predate the invention of powered aircraft. The Wright Brothers' first airplane, little more than a propeller-driven kite, was equipped with cables, chains and an engine that were built by others. In the purest sense, Orville and Wilbur Wright merely designed and assembled their aircraft from existing parts. The same was true of innovator Glenn Curtiss, a motorcycle repairman from upstate New York. While Curtiss had access to the lightweight engines required for flight, he began to experiment with flight controls and invented the aileron, a movable surface on the trailing edge of a wing that revolutionized handling characteristics. The Wrights had clearly invented the airplane, but Curtiss had undoubtedly developed a key control mechanism that made flight practical.

American aviation remained the provence of tinkerers from the Wrights' first flight in 1903 until 1916, when European combatants in World War I demonstrated the utility of aircraft as strategic battlefield weapons. The government hastily created an aviation program within the Army Signal Corps and held a competition for the right to supply more than 20,000 aircraft. Hundreds of amateur flyers, including Glenn Martin, Bill Boeing, Donald Douglas, and Allan and Malcolm Loughead, rushed into the business. Limited in their resources and working out of garages, these pioneers were forced to incorporate whatever parts they could find into their aircraft. The designs of these aircraft were simple, often consisting of fabric stretched over a wooden frame and manipulated with cables and hinges. But the most important part of these aircraft was the engine.

At the time, automobile manufacturers held a virtual monopoly on advanced engine designs. They also had the manufacturing capacity to mass produce the thousands of aircraft the government wanted. As a result, automobile executives easily muscled their way into control of the nation's aviation industry. While this arrangement bred only bad designs and corruption, it established an enduring organizational structure in the aviation industry. General Motors, Ford, Nash, and Packard had long subcontracted manufacturing of parts for its automobiles to independent manufacturers. Unwilling to build manufacturing facilities for something as speculative as aircraft, these manufacturers simply turned to the established automotive supply network for items such as glass, wheels, instrumentation, and seats.

As quickly as they had entered, automobile companies abandoned aviation after the government canceled its 20,000-plane order at the end of World War I. Aircraft designers were once again in charge of their destinies as manufacturers. But they continued to be supplied by the very same parts network that served the automobile industry. Aviation enterprises floundered until 1927, when Charles Lindbergh's daring cross-Atlantic flight inspired tremendous investment in the industry. This growth was choked off after 1929, however, as the nation sunk into the depths of the Great Depression. Traumatized by changes in the industry, aviation companies continued to make small advances on the strength of military sales and a growing air mail business. Eventually this led to the formation of three enormous aviation combines, the largest of which, United Aircraft, might one day have rivaled General Motors in size.

United Aircraft consisted of four airframe builders, Boeing, Vought, Northrop, and Stearman, the engine maker Pratt & Whitney, and a series of airline companies that later became United Air Lines. This powerful organization took over two propeller makers and numerous other manufacturers and began manufacturing a greater proportion of its own parts. The other two monopolies, North American Aviation and the Aviation Corporation of the Americas, were in the process of building similar organizations when, in 1934, the government stepped in with antitrust investigation that broke up the combines and decentralized aircraft manufacturing.

This breakup provided new growth opportunities for a wide variety of potential suppliers. Companies that had previously never even considered the aircraft parts business suddenly discovered the viability of extending their product line into aviation. The driving force behind this expansion was technology. Where aviators were once limited to day flight, lighting and instruments enabled them to fly in darkness. Where navigation had once required visual landmarks, such as railroad tracks, now there were radio and gyroscopes. And where flying was once limited to lower elevations, now there were cabin pressurization systems and oxygen supplements.

The greatest advances in aviation took place during World War II, when heavy government investment in the industry enabled new technologies to be developed that enabled aircraft to fly higher, faster and with more agility than ever before. This placed new stresses on conventional parts and encouraged the development of specialized engineering. Jet aircraft, first tested in 1942, provide the best example of this. While airframes had to be fundamentally redesigned to handle the rigors of jet flight, so too did items such as terminal wiring, indicator lamps, pumps and fluid systems. Repeated exposure to vibration and powerful G-forces caused many conventional parts to break apart. As a result, the development of high-performance aircraft was hampered as much by weak light bulb filaments and rivets as by weak airframes.

The specialized engineering required for postwar aviation necessitated tremendous research funding and elevated manufacturing occupations to fine sciences. Companies that were ill-prepared for this new type of work were forced out of the market or into consolidation with other, stronger manufacturers. Aircraft contractors necessarily became fewer, and the prices of their products grew higher.

Generally, navigation and communications systems were handled by companies that specialized in instrumentation, such as Sperry, Lear and Motorola. Meanwhile, with a few notable exceptions, heating, hydraulics and pressurization systems were handled by engine manufacturers such as Pratt & Whitney, Curtiss-Wright, Allison and General Electric. Manufacturers such as Garrett, Teledyne, Litton, and Dowty manufactured adjunct systems that provided compressed air, temperature regulation, cabin pressurization and hydraulic pressure. Other companies historically associated with the automotive industry, such as BF Goodrich, Bendix and Cleveland Pneumatic, provided products such as wheel assemblies, pumps, hoses, gaskets, and even window seals.

A large constituent in the industry consisted of companies that were already associated with aviation, including United Aircraft, Boeing, Lockheed, and Douglas. Other smaller manufacturers, such as Cessna and Beech, also found a place in the market as suppliers of specialized parts. As a result of bad management, Curtiss-Wright was slowly forced out of engine manufacturing during the 1950s. But the company managed to maintain a leading position in the parts industry, particularly with propellers and a series of wing actuator systems.

Heavy government investment in aviation, primarily through military programs and a budding space agency, continued to result in ever more advanced aircraft. North American Aviation's B-70 bomber and Lockheed's SR-71 reconnaissance jet established new triplesonic speed records, while a variety of other craft managed to climb to more than 100,000 feet. Such planes required paint that exhibited special heat deflection properties. Even landing tires required coating with aluminum paints and inflation with lithium. Windshields were required to withstand tremendous impacts, such as collision with a bird at 2,200 miles per hour. In each case, aircraft parts suppliers never led development of new aircraft. Instead, lead manufacturers conceived of new designs and issued required specifications, and parts manufacturers filled their requirements.

While the Cold War confrontation with the Soviet Union provided the justification for new weapons, American involvement in Vietnam often provided the testing ground. New military designs enabled aircraft manufacturers to develop a further variety of new aircraft, including a supersonic passenger transport, jumbo jets and huge freighters. Advances funded by military dollars helped lower the costs of commercial flight and allowed airline companies to offer passengers more sophisticated in-flight services, including radio headphone entertainment and movies. In addition, galley service became more efficient, incorporating microwave as well as convection heat sources and complex food storage conveyors and dumbwaiters. As aircraft became ever more complex, the aircraft parts industry grew proportionally, until it numbered almost 11,000 suppliers.

CURRENT CONDITIONS

The entire aerospace industry had enjoyed nearly fifty years of growth following the end of World War II, but an industry recession beginning in the late 1980s and early 1990s caused major shifts in the industry. Military spending peaked in 1987 and dropped precipitously following the end of Cold War tensions in 1989, forcing many military-oriented parts suppliers to leave the market. According to *U.S. Industrial Outlook 1993,* about 15,000 suppliers left the aerospace defense market between 1982 and 1987, a decrease that continued into the 1990s, though at a slower rate. A similar decrease occurred in the commercial aircraft parts industry, as the supplier base dropped from 11,000 to 4,000, driven by aircraft manufacturer's demands for greater efficiency. ''For parts suppliers, this streamlining has meant that only the most efficient and highest quality manufacturers have been able to stay in this market,'' noted *U.S. Industrial Outlook 1993.*

Exacerbating the effects of industry streamlining has been the increasing competition from foreign parts suppliers. In order to penetrate international markets, U.S. aircraft and aircraft engine makers have entered into international teaming agreements that specify that a certain proportion of parts are purchased from overseas suppliers. Such agreements have helped foster advances in the aerospace industries of many countries, particularly in the Far East, but have contributed to the shrinkage of the U.S. aircraft parts industry.

Employment in SIC 3728 fell 13 percent between 1990 and 1992, and an additional 6 percent decline was expected in 1993. Total employment numbered 166,000 people in 1993. According to *U.S. Industrial Outlook 1993,* "long-term prospects are for continued declines on the military side, and stabilizing employment on the commercial side."

The late 1980s saw a rash of problems associated with the manufacture of faulty and inadequate parts. The Federal Aviation Administration sets guidelines for the quality and precision of airline parts and certifies the acceptability of manufacturers, but prior to the appearance of bogus parts in the late 1980s it had no measures in place to enforce conformity with these standards. When aircraft mechanics discovered that parts of inferior quality had infiltrated the spare parts marketplace, several task forces set about to establish more stringent means of identifying and monitoring parts. Such guidelines are expected to be in place by 1994. According to *Aviation Week & Space Technology,* most of the manufacturers of defective parts are "small companies, in the $3-10 million range. The companies have been immediately suspended from doing business with the government, and could be debarred for three to five years." Thanks to the high standards of aircraft mechanics, none of the bogus parts have been implicated in aircraft accidents.

INDUSTRY LEADERS

The largest supplier of aircraft parts is Sundstrand, a Rockford, Illinois-based defense electronics company that broke into the aviation market during World War II. The company established a leading position in hydraulics and generators that paved the way for its involvement in jet aircraft technologies during the 1960s. Sundstrand's aviation supply operations expanded rapidly after 1967, due to an aggressive acquisition campaign that gave it the ability to manufacture instrumentation, entertainment systems, temperature controls, and gear drives.

The company's earnings from aircraft parts grew rapidly during the 1980s as a result of generous defense budgets. Sundstrand acquired several more aviation supply companies that broadened its position as a military contractor and provided new opportunities in civilian aviation. Accused of fraud in 1988, Sundstrand was fined and temporarily suspended from bidding on government contracts. The company later endured reverses from a rapid decline in defense spending. However, Sundstrand managed to realign its operations toward more stable civilian work, supplying products to Boeing, Airbus, McDonnell Douglas, and other customers. Sundstrand is the largest parts

manufacturer, comprising nine percent of the segment's total sales.

The second largest manufacturer in this category is Coltec Industries, a former coal and coke supplier in Pennsylvania. The company entered the aviation products industry during a diversification campaign in the 1950s, when it purchased a fuel control systems manufacturer and the Colt firearms business. Known as Colt Industries after 1964, the company's rapid rise in the aircraft parts market occurred only after 1977, when it took over a landing gear manufacturer and a flight control systems company. In 1983, well into the defense build-up that so benefitted Sundstrand, Colt branched into fuel nozzles and other jet engine components, and later turbine engine parts and cockpit indicators and sensors. The company divested much of its non-aerospace operations, including Colt firearms, in 1990. It changed its name to Coltec, and presently accounts for about seven percent of sales in the industry.

The steel conglomerate LTV is also a major manufacturer of aircraft parts, accounting for about five percent of the segment's output. This company was founded by Jim Ling, whose circuitry business merged with Temco Electronics in 1960 to form a leading defense company. The following year, the company acquired Chance Vought Aviation from United Aircraft, giving the company the third letter in its name and enabling it to become deeply involved in the development of aircraft electronics and missile systems. LTV invested heavily in declining steel businesses during the 1980s. The company's only bright spot was its aerospace division. Still, LTV was forced into an eight-year bankruptcy that ended only in 1993. During this time the company sold Vought, but retained much of its parts manufacturing operations, which are concentrated in naval aircraft systems.

In fourth place, with virtually the same market share as LTV, is Lucas Aerospace, an American subsidiary of the British company Lucas Industries. This company gained its expertise in aviation products early, adapting its core automotive parts line for British aircraft manufacturers during World War I. Lucas was introduced to American aviation in the 1930s through a partnership with Bendix called Rotax. Rotax was closely involved with jet engine technologies, and manufactured a variety of electronic and fuel control systems in the post-World War II period. Rotax became Lucas Aerospace in 1971, and prospered from its parent company's involvement with British Aerospace and the Airbus consortium. Due to the fact that Lucas is foreign-controlled, its sales are mainly confined to the civilian aircraft market.

BF Goodrich, with four percent of total parts sales, began as a supplier in 1909, providing the wheels for Glenn Curtiss' early designs. The company subsequently branched into de-icing systems, flight suits, self-sealing fuel tanks, and later inflatable aircraft evacuation slides. BF Goodrich sold its tire operations to Michelin in 1986 specifically to concentrate on the aircraft supply market. Through a series of acquisitions, the company expanded into engine and fuel systems, test equipment and flight instruments. In 1993 BF Goodrich took over Cleveland Pneumatic, a supplier of landing gear for the 747, 767, MD-11, and B-2 bomber. Fairchild remains active in the market through its association with the now defunct Republic Aircraft company. Allied-Signal also plays a major role, stemming from its acquisition of Garrett, as does Boeing, by virtue of its leading role in the airframe industry.

INDUSTRY INFORMATION SOURCES

BF Goodrich. *Company Profile*. Akron, OH: BF Goodrich, 1993.

Biddle, Wayne. *Barons of the Sky*. New York: Simon & Schuster, 1991.

Coltec Holdings, Inc. *Annual Report*. New York: Coltec Holdings, Inc., 1993.

Henderson, Breck W. ''Aircraft Parts Firms Facing U.S. Charges.'' *Aviation Week & Space Technology*, 21 September 1992, 31.

LTV Corporation. *Looking Ahead*. Dallas: LTV Corporation, 1980.

Ott, James. ''Crackdown on 'Bogus' Aircraft Parts Irks Maintenance Industry Officials.'' *Aviation Week & Space Technology*, 16-23 December 1991, 36-38.

———. ''Faulty, Bogus Part Evades Safety Net and Sparks Probe.'' *Aviation Week & Space Technology*, 20 January 1992, 32-34.

———. ''Twin Task Forces to Battle Bogus Parts.'' *Aviation Week & Space Technology*, 15 March 1993, 33.

''Shortage of Replacement Parts May Delay Aging Aircraft Repairs.'' *Aviation Week & Space Technology*, 2 July 1990, 68-72.

Solberg, Carl. *Conquest of the Skies*. Boston: Little Brown, 1979.

Sundstrand Corporation. *A History of the Company*. Rockford, IL: Sundstrand Corporation, 1992.

U.S. Department of Commerce. *U.S. Industrial Outlook 1993*. Washington, DC: U.S. Department of Commerce, January 1993.

Whitehouse, Arthur. *The Sky's the Limit*. London: Macmillan, 1979.

—John Simley

SIC 3731

SHIP BUILDING AND REPAIRING

This category covers establishments primarily engaged in building and repairing ships, barges, lighters, whether self-propelled or towed by other craft. This industry also includes the conversion and alteration of ships and the manufacture of off-shore oil and gas well drilling and production platforms (whether or not self-propelled). Establishments primarily engaged in fabricating structural assemblies or components for ships, or subcontractors engaged in ship painting, joinery, carpentry work, and electrical wiring installation, are classified in other industries. Boat building and repairing are excluded as they are in a separate category, **SIC 3732: Boat Building and Repairing.**

INDUSTRY SNAPSHOT

The United States commercial shipbuilding and repair industry, unlike its counterparts in most major shipbuilding nations, is not a major factor in the world market. Virtually all merchant tonnage is built for domestic customers under a subsidy program or under the protection of the Merchant Marine Act of 1920, the Jones Act, which specifies that all intercoastal traffic must move in U.S. built vessels. The navy has been the largest customer of the industry. As a result, American yards have a greater capability to build one-of-a-kind sophisticated ships than to mass produce less complex large merchant vessels. U.S. shipyards build about 1.1 percent of the yearly world commercial deadweight tonnage (dwt-measure of ship carrying capacity), which is well below that produced by Japan, Korea, China and several other countries. An illustration of the decline of the United States in the world shipping market can be measured as a percentage of world vessel tonnage under order.

With the end of the Cold War, the U.S. military industrial base is shrinking dramatically, as is the nation's shipbuilding industry. In January of 1990, an American shipbuilding concern received the first order for a commercial ocean-going vessel since 1984. Shippers, including American companies, have favored foreign shipyards because of cheaper prices and faster order turn around time. Government subsidies in Japan, Korea, and Germany range from 20 to 30 percent of the cost of the ship, enabling these builders to capture almost all of the commercial shipbuilding business.

Unless foreign shipbuilding and repair subsidies are eliminated, U.S. shipbuilders will not participate in the forecasted replacement of the world's aging merchant fleet during the 1990s. With the downsizing of the U.S. Naval fleet and the lockout of U.S. shipbuilders from the commercial market in the face of government-subsidized competition, the future of the U.S. shipbuilding and repair industry looks bleak. The industry is currently facing massive layoffs and yard closures in this uncompetitive market. Current legislation is on the docket which would require new ships built in subsidized foreign yards to pay high duties to enter American ports. The success of the U.S. shipbuilding industry in the commercial arena is dependent upon this type of mandate.

ORGANIZATION AND STRUCTURE

The United States has four shipbuilding regions: the Atlantic Coast, Gulf Coast, Pacific Coast, and Great Lakes. All four have capabilities to construct commercial and military ships. The Great Lakes yards, however, can export only ships that fit within the constraints of the Welland Canal and the St. Lawrence Seaway. For this reason, the Great Lakes shipbuilding employment is only a small percentage of the industry total in the United States. Peterson Builders, Inc. is the last major shipbuilder in the area with less than five percent of the shipbuilding industry's work force. The Atlantic Coast has the largest percent of total employment, followed by the Gulf Coast, with the Pacific Coast third.

In the United States, most major shipbuilding yards are owned by conglomerates or are divisions of large corporations. The Bethlehem Steel Corporation is an example of this type of entity with BethShip as its shipbuilding unit located in Port Author, Texas and Sparrows Point, Maryland. One of the problems with this type of alignment is that the shipbuilding division is in competition with other divisions of the corporation for investment dollars for expansion, modernization, or other purposes. With an average return on equity of six percent in the shipbuilding industry, the divisions have been losing the fight for corporate resources. An argument in behalf of this structure is that the parent corporation may have more success in obtaining favorable financing than a relatively small subdivision would have if it were independent.

The shipbuilding and repair industry is a capital intensive business with an extensive initial capital outlay required to enter the industry and meet subsequent outfitting and technological requirements. These factors provide substantial barriers to entry especially since the industry is not a very profitable one. The protection of the Shipping Act of 1916 is important to the survival of the members of this industry by helping them consistently attract sufficient cargo to cover initial outlays and fixed costs. This was achieved by the creation of the conference system. Through agreements enforced among the member groups, the conference system stabilized freight rates and the production of new commercial vessels. The stability of this system is necessary because of the individual shipbuilder's cost structure and pricing policy.

As compared with the shipbuilding industry overseas, there is relatively little cooperation among the yards in the United States. In Norway and Sweden for example, research is sponsored jointly by the major shipyards. Other shipbuilding and shipping organizations abroad jointly sponsor computer programming and economic studies for the common benefit. The U.S. shipyards are as independent as they are competitive in seeking contracts. Limited though these exchanges may be, they have stimulated programs of research, ship computer programming, and ship construction techniques.

Despite the strong government ties to the industry of the Maritime Administration and the Navy-supported programs, there is little government intervention in industry-wide planning, quotas and other programs. This restraint reflects the policies of anti-trust legislation as well as the traditions of free, competitive enterprise. Unfortunately, U.S. shipyards are denied many benefits they could acquire from cooperation, such as the use of standard parts and components as employed profitably by Japanese shipbuilders. Benefits could also be gained from exchanges of engineering and other technical information. If U.S. yards hope to compete in the world market, a pooling of information and talent would seem to be a prerequisite.

The basic production facilities of the industry are the shipbuilding positions, either shipways or docks, together with work areas, essential supporting shops, and engineering and design capability. Heavy duty equipment is used for bending, rolling, forming, cutting, and welding plates and shapes; for forming pipe and sheet metal; and for performing a wide range of machining operations. In addition, yards require storage facilities—open areas for steel, piping, subassemblies and other items requiring minimal protection, and shelters for machinery, equipment, stores, outfit and other items requiring protection from rain, sun or pilferage. Facilities for the assembly of heavy steel include large cranes and handling and conveying equipment. The shipyard must also have piers where the ships can be outfitted after launching. These piers are equipped completely with service facilities such as fire mains, electrical power supply, compressed air, and fresh water.

Ship Repair. Ship repair is a sustaining element in the maritime industry. It has enabled many shipbuilders to ride the storm in a capital intensive and cyclical industry. Selection of a repair facility depends upon the magnitude and type of work, the preference of the ship or boat owners, and the proximity of the repair facility to the ship or boat. Periodic and emergency maintenance and repair work are essential to keep vessels operable. A report by the Ocean Shipping Consultants, an industry trade group, predicts a positive outlook for the repair industry throughout the 1990s. This trend can be attributed to the aging fleet of operational ships and the decision by shipowners to extend their useful life.

Repair crews are also called into action when it becomes necessary to break out mothballed merchant and naval ships from the reserve fleets located strategically on Atlantic, Gulf, and Pacific Coasts. All vessels must also undergo special surveys every five years in addition to regular repairs to remain seaworthy. The rapid growth in tank deliveries between 1973 and 1975 should result in a 17 percent increase in mandatory repair work in 1994. Economically, many shipowners have found it more profitable to increase the life of their existing fleet due to the high building costs of a new vessel. The results are increased surveys and repair work for the yards. Finally, environmental issues arising as a result of several accidents and oil spills have put pressure on shipowners to improve maintenance standards.

A critical requirement for a successful repair yard is its ability to meet schedules and complete work rapidly and satisfactorily. Many shipbuilding facilities have repair yards capable of dry-docking vessels of 400 feet or more. These firms handle a majority of the repair dollar volume, with the rest going to smaller docks or pier facilities. The balance are shops that do special or limited repairs, transporting labor or material to the work site. Repair firms without dry docking facilities do not work on such underwater parts as the hull and the propeller. An integrated repair yard uses extensive waterfront acreage with facilities capable of dry-docking and berthing large ships. These integrated yards, as well as smaller repair facilities, cluster around active ports.

Repair yards also require a heavy financial investment. Dry docks are expensive and most of the integrated yards have two or more piers, about 1000 feet long and 40 feet wide. These features are in addition to the cranes, electrical, and mechanical facilities. All such yards have warehouses to stock and shops to process raw materials. In addition, each must have a wider variety of tools than shipbuilders require, since each repair job can be unique. Ship repair yards have not invested capital as heavily as shipbuilding yards. Most of the investments are connected directly with the prospect of using these facilities for ship construction. This long-range planning will help the shipbuilder manage the business when shipbuilding demands have abated.

The Shipbuilders Council of America, the one industry body that functions for the private yards as a group, is the basic source of industry planning. This organization's membership covers most but not all of the major shipbuilding and repair yards and major segments of the allied industries that supply materials and equipment. As a trade association, the Council informs and appropriately presents the views of its members concerning pertinent legislative, executive, and judicial government actions and worldwide industrial and economic trends as they affect the maintenance of the private shipbuilding industry in support of the national needs for ships.

BACKGROUND AND DEVELOPMENT

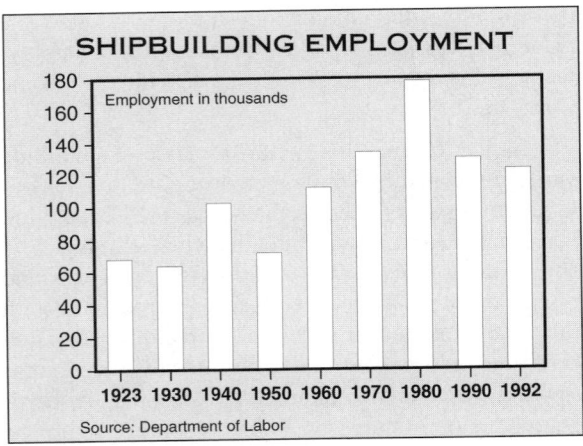

SHIPBUILDING EMPLOYMENT

Employment in thousands

Source: Department of Labor

The colonists came to North America with strong maritime backgrounds, which were reflected by their government. Shipping and shipbuilding, since colonial days, have exerted a powerful influence on the development of the United States. With few exceptions, population clustered at seaports or river ports. The transport of people and commodities until late in the 19th century was accomplished most easily and expeditiously by water. During its early history, moreover, the country imported many of its finished goods and industrial products from Europe and exported raw materials and agricultural products. And the coastal forests provided an apparently inexhaustible supply of inexpensive virgin timber for the construction of the many ships needed.

Legislation by the first Congress of the United States was similar in intent to modern maritime subsidies. The first tariff, enacted in 1789, stipulated a ten percent reduction in custom duties for goods imported in American vessels and a tonnage tax in favor of American shipping. The first literal subsidy by the government was paid in 1845, when Congress authorized the Postmaster General to award mail subsidies, with preference to steamships which could be converted into vessels of war. These subsidies were subsequently discontinued in 1858 as an unnecessary drain on the Treasury.

Infant maritime industries flourished. By 1850, American clipper ships were showing the flag in most ports of the world and were widely considered to be the best sailing vessels in the world at that time. The American merchant marine was second in size only to England's. Although coastwise shipping was protected from foreign flag competition by the Navigation Act of 1817, the American merchant fleet received little else in the way of government assistance before 1845 other than discriminatory duties or taxes and periodic contracts for mail. Essentially throughout this successful era, the maritime industries of the United States were strictly private enterprises.

The Civil War started the decline of the American foreign-trade merchant fleet. As vessels were lost as prizes, American vessels shifted to foreign registry to lessen the risk of capture and to avoid exorbitant insurance rates. Vessels so transferred were not permitted to return to the U.S. registry. Even more far reaching in its effects than the war itself was the development of steel-hull, steam-propelled ships. The advanced technology of England and of other European countries gave foreign builders a considerable advantage in the cost of building iron vessels. Since it was prohibited by law to register foreign-built ships under U.S. documentation, the high cost of domestically-built ships demanded a heavier capital investment for American-flag ships than for ships built abroad. The capital costs reduced potential earnings in foreign trade to a point were investment in American transoceanic shipping was unattractive. Under these conditions, private capital was not attracted to the highly competitive field of shipping. The American merchant marine declined from its once prominent position to a level in 1914 where only nine percent of the value of foreign commerce, imports and exports, was carried in American bottoms.

Awareness of the inadequacy of the U.S. merchant fleet led to attempts to reduce shipbuilding costs

by removing tariffs from imported materials, but these measures were essentially ineffective. Between 1900 and 1914 Congress made several attempts to expand and strengthen the U.S. merchant marine fleet by enacting various subsidy programs and establishing a Merchant Marine Commission in 1904. All of these efforts failed as U.S. merchant tonnage fell to a historical low as a percentage of foreign-flag tonnage.

The outbreak of war in Europe in 1914 finally aroused the country to correct this imbalance in its merchant fleet as American ports were glutted with cargo for export with no way to go. That year emergency legislation permitted foreign-built vessels of any age to be documented by the United States for use in foreign trade. The Shipping Act of 1916 was enacted, which established a Shipping Board of Commissioners to oversee the acquisition of vessels by purchase, to regulate the use of these vessels through liner and conference agreements, and to provide general instructions for the sale or disposal of vessels to U.S. citizens. The Act was modified in 1918 to prohibit the sale or lease of ships, shipyard, or dry dock to a foreigner in time of national emergency. It provided further that no U.S. shipyard could build for a foreign account. This was the first piece of comprehensive maritime legislation of the 20th century and it remains current law in the U.S. shipping industry.

Under the Act, the United States embarked upon its largest shipbuilding program up to that time to yield 2300 vessels. The American merchant fleet grew from 6.8 percent of the world's total in gross tons in 1914 to 22.2 percent in 1920. The Merchant Marine Act of 1920 was established after the Shipping Act to facilitate the disposal of surplus government owned vessels, to settle claims among carriers, to provide assistance to the U.S. merchant marine, and to regulate foreign commerce. The goal of the United States was to establish a merchant marine fleet which could meet all of the country's commerce and military needs. Congress ultimately wanted this fleet to be owned and operated privately by U.S. citizens, and enacted provisions such as tax savings and subsidy assistance to stimulate the transfer of the Government-owned fleet to private firms. Disposal of the ships to private citizens under the Act of 1916 and later under the Act of 1920 progressed slowly and most of the fleet operated under the direction of the Shipping Board.

The disposal of ships to the private sector fluctuated from year to year with most of the surplus ships sold at prices below cost. At the same time, the opening of the Panama Canal expanded the development of intercostal shipping. Availability of ships at low prices, fluctuations in the volume of foreign commerce, and the inability of the U.S. ships built under war-time conditions to compete with swift, modern foreign flag tonnage resulted in a decline in foreign trade for the United States. This backdrop, combined with Congressional dissatisfaction with mail-contract payments to the industry, resulted in the passage of the Merchant Marine Act of 1936. This Act set the congressional foundation on which modern-day maritime policy rests and was the first attempt to set down a comprehensive maritime policy in the post-1916 Act period.

The Merchant Marine Act of 1936 provided subsidies to private U.S. shipowners on essential foreign trade routes. It also provided for the payment of subsidies to cover differentials in construction costs of foreign and domestic builders of vessels ordered for private operators for use on these routes. In addition, the Act authorized the government to build and charter vessels for operation on trade routes when private enterprise was unwilling to fill this role. Other provisions of the Act required subsidized lines to establish special funds to replace older-aged vessels and to provide for loans and mortgage insurance, established citizen requirement for crews, required the establishment of manning scales and conditions for living and working on subsidized vessels, and authorized the establishment of a training program.

Under this Act, a building program of 50 ships a year over a ten year period was planned to rehabilitate the dry-cargo tonnage of the merchant marine. This program turned out to be of inestimable value. At the outbreak of World War II, a substantial number of ships under construction provided an impetus to the required expansion of the shipbuilding industry with high quality ships of proven design and performance for wartime service. The U.S. shipbuilding industry reached a peak of ship production by the end of World War II having built 5,700 vessels during the war. Fifty-seven major private shipyards were in operation—23 on the Atlantic Coast, 22 on the Pacific Coast, and 12 on the Gulf Coast. In addition to achieving high production levels, these yards were innovative and brought new concepts to the industry, including multiple production of standardized designs, a switch from riveted to welded shipbuilding, and techniques for fabricating large subassemblies.

When it became apparent that World War II was drawing to a close in March of 1946, the Ship Sales Act was passed. The objective of the Ship Sales Act was to dispose of surplus tonnage of ocean vessels while promoting the national policy of maintaining a merchant marine owned and operated by private citizens of the United States and to avoid some of the

mistakes of the past. It provided for the sale, over a limited period of time, of war-built vessels to citizens and foreigners alike on a fixed-price basis. Charter of war-built vessels to foreigners was not permitted, but U.S. citizens could charter vessels on a short-term basis.

The postwar period began the decline of the U.S. shipbuilding industry. The downturn was interrupted by four spurts of orders. The first program began in the late 1940s and carried into 1950. It grew primarily out of the need for replacement tonnage which could not be met sufficiently by foreign yards, in part because the German and Japanese yards and component manufacturers could not operate on or near capacity. The second program was sparked by the Korean conflict and continued into 1954. The third program began in 1956 with the Suez crisis and the fourth began in 1961 with the beginning of the deliveries under the Maritime Administration cargo vessel replacement program. The wide fluctuation in demand over the postwar period, coupled with ambitious spending plans by U.S. shipyards to increase automation and an increasingly competitive environment resulted in the decline of the U.S. shipbuilding industry.

In an effort to maintain a certain number of yards operating, the U.S. Government parcelled out its orders among several yards, rather then giving a single yard the run of a specific ship. In effect, this has put shipbuilders in the position of contractors, building small numbers of ships to individual specifications, rather than manufacturers producing large quantities of identical items. The shipbuilders were unable to profit from learning curve benefits which accrue with long runs, and although the government's intentions were good, their actions killed the incentive of shipbuilders to diversify and they lost their competitive edge. The government subsidies which supported the industry and paid for a small number of expensive vessels discouraged capital investment among the shipbuilders and expansion of their yards. The resulting shipyards had a high ratio of labor to capital, making the industry labor-intensive and cost prohibitive. The industry became dependent on government subsidies and Naval construction for its survival.

The industry has been hurt by overcapacity since the 1970s, which was driven by the lack of linkage between supply and demand. Shipping companies, which were not forced to suspend operations, moved to United States trades to attract high-valued cargo. As a result of the influx of carriers the U.S. flag shipping was hit especially hard. A more recent threat posed by open conferences is the entry of state-controlled carriers in world trade. These carriers do not operate in pursuit of profit. Rather, they exist to promote their country's national shipping policies and to earn foreign exchange. The subsidies provided in many of these countries created an artificially high supply of ships which were later sold at low prices. In addition, the rates charged by these carriers were substantially lower than conference rates and resulted in the foreign carriers siphoning off high-rated freight. The U.S. shipbuilding industry had not made the conversion from the military to civilian markets and was effectively shut out of this area because of the foreign subsidies. Even if there was a curb on foreign subsidies, it is still uncertain whether U.S. shipyards could make the transition to the civilian markets. The industry structured the shipyards around the complexity of the navy projects and they were not prepared for the simplicity of design, speed of delivery, and low cost requirements of the commercial sector.

In the early 1980s, the Reagan administration eliminated the direct federal subsidies of about $200 million each year that had made U.S. shipyards competitive with their foreign competitors. Almost all commercial shipbuilding moved overseas. At the same time, however, the President called for a 25 percent expansion in the Navy to increase the fleet to 600 ships. The defense build-up was enough to insulate the shipbuilding industry for the time being, but the industry was working from a much smaller base. In 1979, U.S. shipyards employed 150,000 workers and had 166 ocean-going vessels under construction, 67 of which were commercial ships. In the last ten years, employment has dropped to 72,000 workers and 45 yards have closed, leaving only 17 yards capable of building ocean-going vessels. In 1990, 96 Navy ships and one commercial vessel were under construction at American shipyards. The shipbuilders that have survived relied on the Naval building program which increased its fleet from roughly 450 ships in 1980 to more than 580. In 1990, 95 percent of the business in the shipbuilding industry was Navy construction, overhaul, and repair, with ship repairs accounting for the remaining portion.

With the end of the Cold War, the U.S. military-industrial base is shrinking dramatically, and so is the nation's shipbuilding industry. In January of 1990, an American shipbuilding concern received the first order for a commercial ocean-going vessel since 1984. This despite the fact that cabotage laws remain in effect which require that container ships serving only U.S. ports must be manufactured in a domestic yard. Shippers, including American companies, have favored foreign shipyards because of cheaper prices and faster order turn around time. Government subsidies in Japan, Korea, and Germany range from 20 to 30 percent of the cost of the ship, enabling those builders to capture almost all of the business. In 1989 the Bush Administration failed in a year-long effort to persuade foreigners to end their subsidies. Current legislation is on the docket which would require new ships built in subsidized foreign yards to pay high duties to enter American ports.

CURRENT CONDITIONS

The shipbuilding down cycle of the 1980s was unusually severe because it had been preceded by a period of massive speculative overbuilding. During the early part of that decade, governments of most shipbuilding countries in the world made decisions to pour money into their commercial shipyards. The lone exception was the United States, which terminated its shipbuilding subsidies instead. This decision by the Reagan Administration coupled with the "Section 615" waivers which encouraged American shipbuilders to buy overseas devastated commercial shipbuilding in the United States. These yards then became dependent on the U.S. Government's defense budget for their survival. Because of the cuts in the defense budget and reduced requirements for Navy ships for the remainder of the 1990s, the Shipbuilders Council of America estimates that most of the private shipyards in the U.S. will have to close. The transition to commercial shipbuilding by the shipbuilders cannot be accomplished on the current playing field because of the practice of foreign governments to subsidize their shipbuilding industries and encourage them to dump ships on the world market. The Shipbuilders Council of America estimates that by 1998, 180,000 Americans will lose their jobs in this industry.

Although the world shipbuilding market began to turn around in 1988, foreign yards continued to depend on government support to capture contracts and build ships. They received government payments to modernize their facilities through restructuring and investment aid, indirectly benefited from government-supported ship financing provided to their export and domestic customers from export and home credits, and realized special tax benefits. In addition, many of these foreign yards were awarded government grants to capture shipbuilding and repair contracts, and benefited from government-aided research and development of advanced manufacturing technology. U.S. shipyards have none of these advantages.

Throughout most of the 1980s, the justification for foreign shipbuilding subsidies was low demand. In the 1990s so far, however, the reluctance of many foreign shipbuilders to let go of government subsidies is caused by the desire to capture as many contracts as possible while demand is high, and while denying market access to U.S. shipyards. The U.S. shipyards have been losing the battle to the international commercial shipbuilding market during the last ten years as measured in the number of new merchant vessels under construction or on order at U.S. private shipyards.

INDUSTRY LEADERS

The four leading U.S. shipbuilders as measured by shipyard capabilities and employment level are Newport News Shipbuilding and Drydock located in Virginia, Bath Iron Works in Maine, Avondale in Louisiana, and Tampa Ship in Florida. The remaining nine major shipyards are clustered on the Atlantic, Pacific, and Gulf Coasts. Peterson Builders, Inc. is the last major shipbuilder serving the midwest region.

Newport News Shipbuilding is the largest, most diversified shipyard in the United States. It is strategically located in Newport, Virginia, with deep water access to major shipping lines served by all major airlines and rail transportation. It has the resources to accommodate major overhaul and repair work, new construction, conversion, and routine maintenance work. In addition, it's Sperry Marine subsidiary develops, designs, and markets marine instrumentation and communication systems.

The shipyard of Bath Iron Works, located in Bath, Maine, is on the Kennebec River fifteen miles from the Gulf of Maine and its fabrication facility is located eight miles west in Brunswick. Bath Iron works is renowned for its design and construction of the Arleigh Burke Class guided missile destroyer, but is also capable of building high tech commercial vessels.

Avondale Shipyards, a division of Avondale Industries, Inc., is located on the Gulf Coast in Avondale, Louisiana. The shipyard uses computer aided design and modern series and modular construction methods to build a variety of military and complex commercial vessels.

Tampa Ship, a subsidiary of the American Ship Building Company, is a full service shipyard located in Tampa, Florida. The shipyard has the facilities to construct, convert, and repair a wide range of ships and cargo vessels. It has both inwater and offshore facilities for repair and conversion work and new construction work.

WORK FORCE

The shipbuilding and repair industry employed 118,000 workers in 1989, excluding U.S. Navy yards.

On average, 221 workers were employed in each of the 75 establishment with 163 of these people working in the production end of the business. Average earnings for a production worker were $24,853 per anum with a 2018 hour work year at an hourly wage of $12.31. Many of these workers have special skills such as welding, cutting, assembling and fabricating, blue collar supervising, shipfitting and a host of other important trades necessary for the completion of the shipbuilding task. Most of the 15 major yards are also active in repair and conversion. The balance of the industry is engaged in the construction or repair of small ships, drill rigs, and small specialized commercial craft.

The basic skill requirements for the repair industry are generally higher than those required for shipbuilding. In yards that do both construction and repair, it is common practice to assign the same workers either to building or repair as the workload shifts. These floating assignments help maintain the continuity of employment at a stable level. Other workers may migrate between shipbuilding yards and repair yards. Although supervisory and planning skills for repair and construction differ distinctly, both sets of skills may be learned and used by the same person.

Industry Problems. The first and foremost problem of a shipbuilder is that of utilizing the resources at his command to produce a reasonable return on investment. Within this context, as with any commercial enterprise, the shipbuilder has the problem of maintaining an adequate orderbook, obtaining necessary financing, obtaining and retaining competent personnel, establishing and maintaining suitable facilities, obtaining and utilizing the proper materials, and maintaining an organization which will use these resources properly and efficiently.

One of the most difficult and important problems is the maintenance of a stable orderbook. All of the foregoing considerations, from finance through organization, are strongly supported by stability in the orderbook and suffer severely from instability. The beneficial effects and the efficiency of the enterprise are materially enhanced if the orders are repetitive, to permit series production. The need for an assured market, of course, is implicit throughout all considerations.

In the United States, the problem of obtaining series production is more difficult then in countries where the government, consortia, and individual yards by mutual agreement can allocate particular types of construction to specific yards. Antitrust provisions prevent this type of rationalization in the United States. U.S. yards therefore have to compete with each other for series production and attempt to obtain series production and develop special capabilities for the types of vessels they prefer to build. The industry's reliance on Naval orders has put them at a competitive disadvantage because they are building smaller numbers of ships to individual specifications, rather then producing large quantities of identical items.

Finance for needed expansion has not been difficult to obtain in the past. However, the current massive demands on the capital markets for other needs of the industry may pose future restrictive problems. This factor, coupled with past overbuilding trends in the industry and the current competitive climate facing U.S. shipbuilders, has resulted in a lack of capital available to shipbuilders.

The matter of obtaining and retaining competent personnel has also been a difficult problem for most shipyards. This problem is chiefly due to the cyclic nature of the orderbooks and the work flow. Compounding the problem is the work availability in the construction industry at higher levels of pay. A workload with a reasonable promise of continuing stability is the most significant factor in the attraction and retention of competent personnel.

The establishment and the upgrading of facilities to improve operating efficiency is always under consideration by a shipbuilder. Again, such commitments are only practical with reasonable assurance or high expectation of a market sufficient to produce an adequate return on investment. The cost and availability of material similarly is always important to a shipbuilder since material constitutes about half the cost of the usual commercial vessel. The small demand for material and equipment from the shipbuilding industry leaves the shipbuilder with little bargaining power to improve prices and delivery. The industry's position would be improved by a stability in its purchases by virtue of a stable orderbook and by series production.

AMERICA AND THE WORLD

The building of ocean-going ships is practiced throughout the world. All nations engaged in major shipbuilding participate heavily in world trade. Many build ships as a significant export commodity and their economies are closely tied to the success of this industry. The areas responsible for most of the ship production are grouped broadly into three sectors: the United States, the Far East, and Europe. The European membership is represented by the Association of Western European Shipbuilders and includes Belgium, Denmark, Finland, France, West Germany, Italy, Netherlands, Norway, Spain, Sweden, and the United Kingdom. The industry has been dominated by the Far East

sector with Japan and South Korea controlling over 50 percent of the orders of commercial vessel tonnage. The U.S. yards are not a factor in international competition with only 1.1 percent of the commercial tonnage under construction at U.S. shipyards in 1992. This factor is due primarily to foreign subsidized shipbuilding practices.

RESEARCH AND TECHNOLOGY

The U.S. shipbuilding industry is a leader in the design and development of both complex naval ships and commercial vessel technology. It is responsible for pioneering the technology of nuclear power to submarines and surface ships and in other technical disciplines such as noise attenuation silencing, fully-submerged hydrofoils, streamline submarine hull forms, applying missile system technologies to ships, advanced electronic communications and countermeasures, and logistic support. These advancements are representative of the U.S. shipbuilding industry leadership in high technology design and production. These capabilities are being utilized in the design and manufacture of environmentally-safe commercial vessels.

INDUSTRY INFORMATION SOURCES

All about Shipbuilders Council of America, Fairfax, VA: Shipbuilders Council of America, 1983

"All about Shipbuilding; After a Long Slump, World Shipping Is Embarking on a Modest Recovery," *New York Times,* May 6, 1990.

"All Ashore That's Goin Ashore—The Era of Bargain Prices for Ocean Shipping Services Is Slowly Coming to an End," *Purchasing,* November 9, 1989, 66-69.

"American Ship Can It Survive?," *St. Petersburg Times,* July 12, 1992, Section 1, 1.

Beazer, Cox, and Harvey Watkins, *U.S. Shipbuilding in the 1970's,* Lexington, MA: Lexington Books, D.C. Heath and Company, 1972.

Bringing Back America's Shipyards—A Major Step toward Bringing Back America's Independence. Fairfax: Shipbuilders Council of America, 1988.

"Corporate Profiles '93: NASSCO," *San Diego Daily Transcript,* January 11, 1993.

"Cycle Set to Bottom Out," *Straits Times,* June 20, 1993.

"Department of Transportation: Federal Highway Administration," *Environmental Law Reporter,* 1992.

International Shipbuilding Aid June 1993. Fairfax: Shipbuilders Council of America, June 1993.

"Longer Lives for Aging Cargo Ships," *New York Times,* January 1, 1990, Section 1, 31.

Mack-Forlist, Newman, *The Conversion of Shipbuilding from Military to Civilian Markets,* New York: Praeger Publishers, 1970.

McCoy, Cynthia Y., "The Sinking Ship Industry," *5 Journal of International Law and Business 99,* Evanston, IL: Northwestern School of Law, 1983.

1989-1990 in Review Ship Construction Report, July 1991. Fairfax: Shipbuilders Council of America, 1990.

"Prime Time for Hunters Point Was during World War II, Korea," *San Francisco Chronicle,* April 13, 1991.

Shertz, A., "The Shipping Act of 1984: A Return to Antitrust Immunity," *14 Transportation Law Journal 153,* Denver, CO: University of Denver, 1985.

"Ship Maker Can't Get Under Way," *Houston Chronicle,* July 18, 1993.

Shipbuilders Council of America 1974 Annual Report, Fairfax: Shipbuilders Council of America, 1974.

Shipbuilders Council of America Annual Report 1981, Fairfax: Shipbuilders Council of America, 1982.

"Shipbuilding: Talks on Phasing Out Aids at a Standstill," *European Report,* March 21, 1990.

"Shipping; Pushed in at the Deep End," *Economist,* June 5, 1982, 32.

"The Shipping Revival Has Not Extended to the Shipbuilding Industry," *Lloyds List,* January 31, 1989.

"Shiprepair Sector Ready to Pick Up," *Lloyds List,* October 6, 1992.

"Waiting for Better Times at America's Shipyards," *New York Times,* Section 3, 11.

"World Annual Report on Shipbuilding," *Lloyds List,* March 22, 1989.

—Andrew Burke

SIC 3732

BOAT BUILDING AND REPAIRING

This industry consists of establishments primarily engaged in building and repairing boats. Establishments primarily engaged in operating marinas and which perform incidental boat repair are classified in **SIC 4493: Marinas.** Membership yacht clubs are classified under **SIC 7997: Membership Sports and Recreation Clubs** and outboard motor repair is classified under **SIC 7699: Repair Shops and Related Services, Not Elsewhere Classified.**

INDUSTRY SNAPSHOT

Approximately 17 million pleasure boats were owned by Americans in 1993. Because boats are luxury items, though, the industry that produces them is at the mercy of the economy which generates the disposable income required for their purchase. The boat building industry was in the earliest stages of recovery in the early 1990s from a devastating industry-wide slump that had lasted since about 1989. The value of industry shipments grew to about $4.8 billion in 1992, the first increase since 1988, when shipments peaked at over $5.9 billion. Like many industries that produce durable goods, the boat building industry has experienced a fair amount of downsizing in recent years. The industry employs in the neighborhood of 400,000 workers, nearly a third less than the 1988 peak total.

ORGANIZATION AND STRUCTURE

Repairing accounts for only about a four percent share of the boat building and repairing industry's revenue. In 1987, in the thick of the industry's boom period, 151 of the 2,176 establishments in this classification were engaged primarily in repairing boats. These establishments employed 3,500 workers, and generated $223 million in shipment value. There is some evidence that slow sales of new boats in recent years has provided a bit of a spark to the repair business. Boat yards specializing in refurbishing older boats in the early 1990s charged in the range of $50 to $60 an hour for semi-skilled labor on repairs.

Types of Boats Manufactured. Outboard boats make up the largest category of boats built in the United States. 47.2 percent of all pleasure boats owned are of the outboard variety. In 1992, about 192,000 outboard boats were sold, a slight drop from the previous year and a 40-year low. Aluminum and fiberglass are the most common materials used in the construction of outboard boats. The kinds of boats in this category include runabouts, bass boats, utility boats, offshore fishboats, and pontoons. 148 companies specialized in the manufacture of outboard boats in 1987. The value of outboard boats shipped that year was $1.173 million and about eight million of these boats are currently owned in the United States.

Inboard/outdrive (I/O) boats, also known as sterndrive boats, account for nearly 11 percent of U.S. pleasure boats. 93 companies specialized in I/O boats in 1987. Larger, higher-priced sterndrive boats are among those that have suffered particularly harsh sales declines since the late 1980s. As a result, manufacturers have attempted to attract buyers by lowering prices significantly. This resulted in a 2,000 unit increase in sales of sterndrive boats in 1992.

Inboard boats consist mainly of cabin cruisers and sportboats. The inboard cruiser business has been hit hard by the recession and the ten percent excise tax on

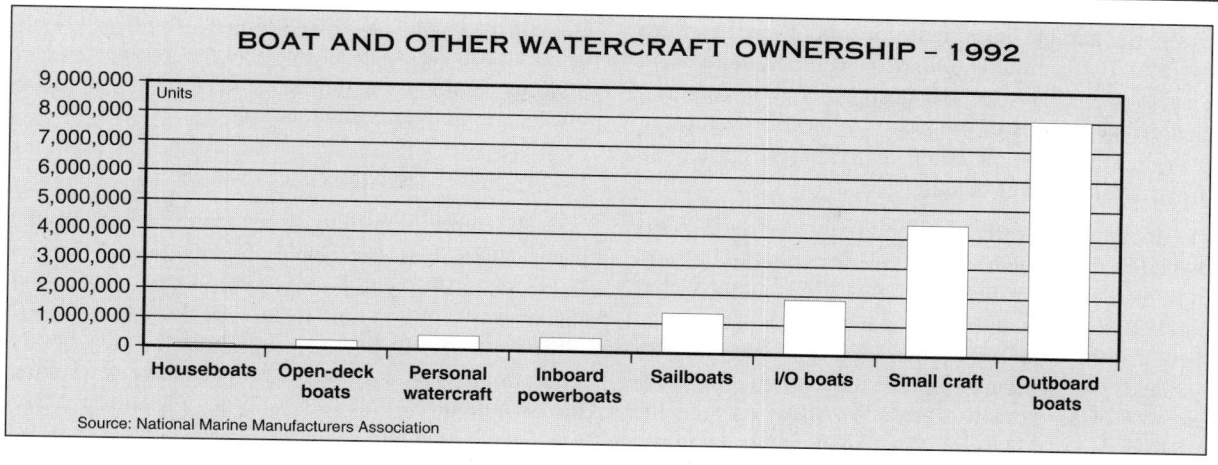

BOAT AND OTHER WATERCRAFT OWNERSHIP – 1992

Source: National Marine Manufacturers Association

luxury boats that took effect in 1991 (but was repealed by the Clinton administration in 1993). Largely due to the tax, inboard cruiser sales were cut in half in 1991, and have yet to recover. Ski boats account for 88 percent of the inboard sportboats manufactured. Other inboard sportboats include runabouts, which represent about nine percent of the market, and inboard fishing boats (under 25 feet).

Eight percent of the boats owned in the United States (about 1.37 million units) are sailboats. This includes both non-powered sailboats (1.3 million) and auxiliary-powered craft (70,000). Altogether, sailboats represent about four percent of the boats being manufactured. The vast majority of sailboats built are in the 12 to 19 foot range. This class accounts for about two-thirds of the sailboats sold. Since 1991 sales of larger sailboats have plummeted, largely attributable to the excise tax on luxury boats. Remaining types of boats include unregistered small craft (canoes, rowboats, dinghies, etc.), personal watercraft, open-deck boats (deck-style monohull runabouts and aluminum pontoons), and houseboats.

Establishment Distribution and Size. Boats are built primarily where there is a lot of water. Geographically, Florida and California dominate the boat building and repairing industry. $1.1 billion in product shipments, about 21 percent of the U.S. total, originate in Florida, where over 400 establishments are located. California is home to about 250 establishments in this industry. Washington and Texas also have over 100 establishments each within their borders.

Boat building and repairing concerns can vary dramatically in size. About half of the over 2,000 establishments in the industry employ only one to four people. The largest share of revenue, however, is generated by more sizeable operations, especially the approximately 100 companies with between 100 and 500

employees. This group accounts for about half of the dollar value of the industry's shipments.

BACKGROUND AND DEVELOPMENT

Prior to the mid-19th century, boats in the United States were built primarily by the people who used them. Most were workboats designed for specific uses. These included whaling boats for the Arctic seas, dories for the Grand Banks, log canoes used by oystermen, and a huge variety of skiffs and other small craft. Eventually the boats became more versatile. The Whitehall was a pulling boat first used in New York harbor as sort of a water taxi. A classic rowing boat, the Whitehall was found to be well-suited as a sailing vessel as well, and it began to appear in other harbors on both coasts, both with and without sails, sometimes used for fishing.

Around 1850, recreational boating began to grow significantly in the United States. Boat builders throughout the Northeast, previously makers of workboats, were now in demand for the production of leisure boats for weekend amateurs. This led to a proliferation of Whitehalls, guide boats, and Saint Lawrence skiffs on lakes from New England to the Midwest. The popularity of rowing boats dropped when the gasoline engine appeared in the United States in 1878. Fishermen, both professional and recreational, began using boats with motors.

Some of the companies that entered the early motorboat industry were automobile manufacturers. One such company was the Lozier Motor Company, which began building boats around the turn of the century. Another important company by the early 1900s was the Electric Boat Company of Bayonne, New Jersey, which manufactured a wide range of boats that included tiny launches and huge luxury cruisers by the time of the company's demise around 1950. Chris-

Craft was another important powerboat manufacturer by 1930. By the middle of the 20th century, there was a renaissance of classic boat designs. New boats modeled on the vessels of the past were constructed using fiberglass and other modern materials. To an extent, this trend has never ceased.

In the 1950s, the number of recreational boats owned in the United States more than doubled, reaching over seven million by 1961. This number has climbed slowly and steadily for the most part since then. In the mid-1980s, the pleasure boat industry boomed, with product shipments growing at an average rate of 13 percent a year. In 1989, however, the economy soured, sending boat manufacturing into a tailspin from which it has yet to emerge. The industry's problems were compounded in 1991 when a ten percent Federal tax on boats retailing for over $100,000 was enacted. Largely as a result of the tax, the share of the pleasure boat market by dollar value accounted for by boats in that high-price bracket slipped from 33 percent to 25 percent in one year.

CURRENT CONDITIONS

Three factors can probably be blamed for the major drop in the demand for boats in the United States between 1989 and 1991. One is the reluctance on the part of consumers to take on additional debt on top of that incurred during the industry's boom years of 1982 through 1988. Another factor has been the decline in the overall economy during this period. As disposable personal income declines, pleasure boats, being large and unnecessary purchases, are among the first items deleted from shopping lists during economic downturns. A third factor has been the ten percent federal luxury tax on pleasure boats with price tags over $100,000. The tax has generally taken the blame for the departure of several luxury boat builders from the market, and the loss of thousands of industry jobs.

Signs of Recovery. The earliest signs of a recovery emerged in 1992. The 1993 repeal of the luxury tax is expected to assist in making the recovery more complete. Part of the increase in orders that took place was to rebuild dealers' inventories, which reached the lowest levels in history by the beginning of 1992. Nevertheless, most manufacturers reported improving conditions, and some began rehiring laid-off workers. Viking Yacht (a maker of high-end vessels), for example, began rehiring after seeing its work force plunge to 65 employees from its 1990 level of 1,500. Industry analysts expect the recovery to continue at the modest pace of 3.5 percent annual real growth through the 1990s. In order to affect the expected recovery, the boating industry must meet the challenge of restoring

consumer demand. Manufacturers are hopeful that the rapidly growing 35 to 54-year-old age group will live up to its demographic billing as big spenders on relaxing leisure activities such as boating.

INDUSTRY LEADERS

The world's leading boat manufacturer in the early 1990s was Brunswick Corporation, based in Lake Forest, Illinois. Brunswick's annual sales were just over two billion dollars, after peaking at over $3.2 billion in 1988 at the end of the boat industry boom. The company had about 17,000 employees. Among the boat brands Brunswick built were Mercury, Mariner, Force, Bayliner, and Ray. Brunswick was founded in 1845, and for much of its history was principally a maker of billiards and bowling equipment. In the early 1960s, the popularity of bowling declined, and the company diversified. By the following decade, Brunswick was building boats on a large scale. In 1986, Brunswick bought two important boat companies, Bayliner and Ray Industries. Between 1982 and 1991, the share of company sales contributed by boating rose from 42 to 66 percent. Since 1989, however, Brunswick has cut 40 percent of its work force and closed 18 of its 49 boat building plants.

Outboard Marine Corporation (OMC), based in Waukegan, Illinois, was another important establishment in the boat building industry. OMC, founded in 1929, had annual sales of just over one billion dollars. This company specialized in low- and medium-priced craft. The well-known Chris-Craft brand is a division of OMC, which employed 8,410 workers overall. Another major boat manufacturer was Genmar Industries Inc., with sales of $230 million. Founded in 1985, Genmar is based in Minneapolis, Minnesota, and employs 2,500.

WORK FORCE

About 43,000 people in the United States were employed in boat building and repairing in the early 1990s, about one-third less than at the 1988 peak. The total payroll for workers in the industry in 1987 was a little over $1 billion. That year, the average payroll per employee was $18,316. Production workers, who made up 82 percent of the total industry employment, earned an average of $8.13 an hour. Welders and cutters made up the largest occupation class, accounting for 7.4 percent of the industry's employment in 1990. Blue collar worker supervisors and shipfitters each accounted for 5.4 percent of the industry's workers. A variety of skilled and semi-skilled occupations each contributed between two and four percent of the work force. Workers in these jobs included carpenters, machinists, electricians, riggers, and sheet metal workers. The rest of the industry's workers were primarily engineers, painters, clerks, managers, mechanics, and helpers.

AMERICA AND THE WORLD

The boat industry in the United States exported $774 million in products in 1991, compared with $207 million in imports. This favorable balance of trade continued in 1992, in spite of a decrease of over $100 million in exports of pleasure boats. Imports of pleasure boats grew by $46 million in 1992, largely due to rebuilding inventories of small and medium size boats on the part of dealers. The decline in exports was traceable to a generally slowed growth rate in most of the major foreign markets for pleasure boats made in the United States.

The largest foreign markets for the U.S. boat industry are Canada and Japan. Exports to Canada were valued at $131 million in 1991, and grew an estimated 22 percent the following year. Two factors contributed to this increase: the U.S.-Canada Free Trade Agreement; and, ironically, the industry-wide recession, which put several Canadian manufacturers out of business and opened the market for U.S. firms.

Exports to Japan have been on the decline, dropping 41 percent to $71 million in 1992, following a period of dramatic growth in that country's pleasure boat market in 1989 and 1990. Other major markets for U.S.-made boats are Germany, Italy, France, and Spain. Spain was the only country other than Canada in the top ten to increase its imports of U.S. boats in 1992.

Canada is also the largest supplier of foreign-made pleasure boats to the United States. In 1992, shipments from Canada totalled about $150 million in value, an 84 percent increase over the previous year. Taiwan and Japan also ship significant numbers of boats to the United States.

Two international developments may help to sustain the growth of U.S. pleasure boat exports in the coming years. First, a united European Community is likely to adopt safety standards that are being adopted in the United States. Second, the approval of the North American Free Trade Agreement (NAFTA) by Congress would cause the disappearance of a 20 percent Mexican tariff on pleasure boats, opening that market for potential exports.

RESEARCH AND TECHNOLOGY

Boat builders look to both the past and the future when it comes to designing their products. Many innovations involve incorporating new materials into classic designs. One example is the use of fiberglass on tin hulls. Since 1990, manufacturers have also sought ways to combine the features of different types of boats into one model. This was illustrated by the 1991 introduction by OMC and other companies of deck-style boats that are roomy like pontoons while performing more like runabouts.

Some of the most impressive innovations in the boat industry in recent years have been in electronics. VHF (very high frequency) radios, among the most common pieces of boating equipment, have evolved from heavy, permanently installed instruments to hand-held, portable devices. Advances have also been made in atmosphere sensor technology, including equipment for detecting carbon monoxide. Another major technological development in boating was the Global Positioning System (GPS), a satellite-based navigational system. GPS was originally developed by the Defense Department for use in deploying weapons. The system, which is available to the public in a semi-crippled form, can be used for navigating on land and in the air as well as at sea.

The boat repair industry has also benefited from technological advances of recent years. Computer-based inventory systems have enabled companies to keep their inventories smaller while at the same time improving the efficiency of parts delivery.

INDUSTRY INFORMATION SOURCES

Banse, Tim, ''The Parts Game: Is There a Computer in Your Future?,'' *Boating Industry,* May 1993.

Boating 1992, Chicago: National Marine Manufacturers Association, 1992.

''The Boating Business,'' *Boating Industry,* January 1993.

Bongiorno, Lori, ''Profits Ahoy!,'' *Business Week,* August 30, 1993.

The Classic Boat, Alexandria, VA: Time-Life Books, 1977.

Harper, Doug, ''Electronic Systems Run Aground,'' *Journal of Commerce,* October 1, 1992.

Henick, Arthur R., ''Tampering with Tradition: Builders Float New Models,'' *Boating Industry,* August 1991.

Lawrence, Richard, ''Politics, Boat Sales Make Strange Bedfellows,'' *Journal of Commerce,* October 1, 1992.

Palmer, Jay, ''Rough Seas,'' *Barron's,* October 14, 1991.

Platt, Gordon, ''Used-Boat Market Riding Tidal Wave,'' *Journal of Commerce,* October 1, 1992.

—Robert R. Jacobson

SIC 3743

RAILROAD EQUIPMENT

This classification covers establishments primarily engaged in building and rebuilding locomotives (including frames and parts not elsewhere classified) of any type or gauge; and railroad, street, and rapid transit cars and car equipment for operations on rails for freight and passenger service. Establishments primarily engaged in manufacturing mining cars are classified in **SIC 3532: Mining Machinery and Equipment, Except Oil and Gas Field Machinery and Equipment.** Repair shops owned and operated by railroads or local transit companies that repair locomotives or cars for their own use are classified in various transportation industries. Establishments primarily engaged in repairing railroad cars on a contract or fee basis are classified in **SIC 4789: Transportation Services, Not Elsewhere Classified;** and those repairing locomotive engines on a contract or fee basis are classified in **SIC 7699: Repair Shops and Related Services, Not Elsewhere Classified.**

INDUSTRY SNAPSHOT

In 1991 the railway supply industry sold over $14 billion in equipment, supplies, and services to the nation's rail systems. The industry employs more than 150,000 persons and includes more than 1,000 companies ranging in size from major conglomerates to small- and medium-size businesses. Railroad equipment manufacturers sell their products not only to the railroads, but also to leasing companies, manufacturing concerns, farmers, and other entities which use the rails for the transportation of their commodities.

The railroad equipment manufacturers that supply the nations' railroads with cars and track are slowly recovering from several decades that have not been kind. Despite new light-rail projects being developed across the nation and an increase in federal money targeted toward mass transit projects, domestic demand has not been regarded as sufficiently strong to attract new American manufacturers to the business until recently. As part of an effort to shore up the industry, the Department of Transportation has promulgated a "Buy America" program which requires rail passenger vehicles purchased with federal funds from foreign companies to have a "domestic content" of 60 percent. Also of great import to the manufacturers of rail equipment is the improved financial performance of several major rail carriers in the early 1990s.

Forbes discussed the "railcar glut that had developed in the late 1970s and early 1980s. In normal years maybe 60,000 railcars were built. But then railcars were marketed as tax shelters; in 1980, 85,000 were built, and industry capacity had exploded to 150,000. . . . When the shelters were curbed in 1981, some 400,000 cars—a six- or seven-year supply— were sitting on sidings unused." By the end of the 1980s, however, as *Forbes* notes, "the number of freight cars in use had declined from 1.8 million to 1.2 million, and industry capacity had dropped to 50,000 cars a year." The stage was set for an upsurge in the industry's fortunes. A major indicator of the railroad equipment industry's health is the number of new freight cars delivered. In 1993 approximately 35,000 railcars were delivered, a significant increase over the 25,000 freight cars delivered in 1992. Moreover, industry observers expect this trend to continue through 1994. This forecast is based primarily on equipment shortages and the age of the current fleet (railways and private owners are currently retiring 60,000 to 80,000 cars a year which have been in service for over twenty years), as well as improved performance by major railroad lines.

The nation's domestic rail passenger car industry, however, has not rebounded in the manner enjoyed by freight car manufacturers. Whereas half a dozen manufacturers were engaged in such production 25 years ago, only one United States-owned manufacturer, Morrison-Knudsen, makes rail passenger cars today.

ORGANIZATION AND STRUCTURE

The nation's freight railroads carry more than one-third of all intercity ton-miles of freight. Their rails are used for all commuter rail traffic and for Amtrak's long-distance passenger traffic, except for the Northeast corridor, which Amtrak owns. The railroads rely upon suppliers to provide equipment, supplies, many services, and the research and development required to help them improve productivity.

Unlike flatcars and boxcars, which are purchased or leased by the railroads, rail tank cars are owned primarily by chemical manufacturers and other manufacturers such as food and fabricated metal products/ machinery companies who use the rails to transport their goods on a regular basis. Recent proposals by the Department of Transportation requiring more expensive, better protected cars for the transportation of hazardous waste has caused concern among the nation's railroad carriers, who worry that forcing the shippers to pay for more expensive, better protected cars will force them to use trucks as their first choice of transport. Rail market share has already suffered attrition at the hands of the trucking industry and other transportation sectors. Since 1945 the railroads' share of the freight business has fallen by almost 50 percent to 37 percent, while the truckers' share has climbed to more than 25 percent from five percent.

The rail industry is the transport method of choice for commodities that are not "time-sensitive" like perishable products and for goods that need to be transported over distances greater than 500 miles. For short-haul food shipments, trucks have captured most of the traffic in the freight market. Recently, there has been an increase in intermodal transportation where manufacturers use the railways to transport their goods for a leg of the journey via trailers and containers and then switch to another form of transport such as trucks or ships. Intermodal loading has almost doubled in capacity since 1980.

Industry Representation. The Railway Progress Institute (RPI), originally founded as the Railway Business Association in 1908, is the international trade association of suppliers to the nation's freight railroads and rail passenger systems. Headquartered in Alexandria, Virginia, it has more than 100 members. The association's objectives are threefold: to support and promote a strong nationwide free enterprise system of railroads for the United States; to support and promote rail rapid transit and light rail systems in major metropolitan areas; and to represent and further RPI members' interests.

In 1992 the Rail Supply and Service Coalition (RSSC) was formed to act as a lobbying group to Washington and state governments. The group consists of the National Railroad Construction and Maintenance Association, the Railway Engineering-Maintenance Suppliers Association, the Railway Supply Association, and Railway Systems Suppliers, Inc. The coalition actively represents the interests of its member groups to further their bargaining position on federal and state issues effecting the industry.

BACKGROUND AND DEVELOPMENT

The railroads were one of the nation's first big businesses. With their intricate network of lines, these companies gave inland points access to navigable waters and joined these waters to the seaboard, linked farms and villages to the rising industrial cities, opened millions of acres of land to cultivation, provided the means to ship raw materials and finished goods quickly and cheaply, and created billions of dollars in capital to be reinvested in the nation's economy.

At the outset of the 1830s the steam locomotive made its arrival. On Christmas Day 1830 the *Best*

Friend of Charleston, the first locomotive built for sale in the United States, made its maiden run. The nation's rail system grew rapidly during the next several decades. The lines largely served cities along the Atlantic coast; New England and the mid-Atlantic states had over 50 percent of the total track mileage in the United States. American railroads, however, did not have a uniform track gauge (distance between the rails). This confusion of gauges necessitated expensive and inefficient trans-shipment of goods where lines of different gauges intersected.

Early Advances. Throughout this time period, the companies constantly improved their tracking and rolling equipment. The first railroads had been built on tracks of iron straps or bars fastened to wooden rails that were attached to blocks of stone embedded in the earth. The iron straps often broke loose under the weight of the passing trains and damaged the bottom of the cars. In response to this, the iron T-rail was developed and wooden ties replaced the stone underneath the rails. A roadbed surface covered with crushed stone or gravel supported the track. Originally most of the engines were imported from England, but Philadelphia jewelry manufacturer Matthias Baldwin entered the business in the 1830s and soon thereafter other locomotive builders emerged in the Northeast. Passenger cars which had been nothing more than stagecoaches with railroad wheels quickly evolved into more spacious, comfortable accommodations. Diminutive four-wheeled freight cars were replaced by longer and heavier eight-wheeled cars with greater carrying capacity. Thus the railways spawned auxiliary enterprises in T-rail manufacturing, locomotive works, and car and wheel shops, and gave impetus to the lumber industry which furnished the wooden ties.

During the 1840s and 1850s there was a proliferation of railroad construction. By 1860 many of the shorter railway lines consolidated through the merger of regional railroad companies. The federal government supported this expansion through land grants and other forms of financial incentives to the railroad companies. Land grants became the major form of financial assistance offered to the railroad companies to encourage the development of railroads to the west in advance of settlement. Revelations of corruption and bribery caused public opinion to demand that such assistance be ended. By the 1870s, most direct federal aid to the railroads had terminated, with most state and local support stopping within the next decade. But government aid, in any case, was relatively small in comparison with investment by private capital in the form of stocks and bonds in rail companies. With the continued growth of the railway industry, companies that provided needed equipment to that industry remained prosperous.

By 1880 the carriers had standardized their gauge to 4 feet 8 1/2 inches as the railroads had established transcontinental operations. To further facilitate the interchange of railroad traffic, the railroad companies required standerized coupling devices, car trucks, bills of lading, and classification of products. Larger locomotives and freight cars with increased carrying capacities required that steel rails be implemented in place of the iron rails. The steel rails provided a smoother, safer, and faster track and lasted much longer than wrought iron, saving the railroads significant maintenance costs. The link-and-pin couplers long-utilized to engage railcars together had over the years cost thousands of men their fingers; these were replaced by effective automatic safety couplers. Similarly, the hand brake system that required men to run along the top of cars to set the devices were replaced by an air brake system mandated by federal law in 1893.

The railroad industry continued as the primary transportation mode throughout the first half of the twentieth century in America. Throughout the 1920s and 1930s, the railroads generally improved and modernized their operations. New steam locomotive designs were introduced by the major builders— Baldwin, Lima, and the American Locomotive Company. These designs increased efficiency, raised average speeds for passenger and freight trains, and reduced the need for double-headed trains and pusher locomotives in mountainous terrain. Capital improvement programs were begun which increased freight car capacities, length of freight trains, and the net tonnage capable of being carried by the average train. Many of the infrastructure systems installed at this time remained for many years as well. The rise of the automobile and air transportation, however, dramatically impacted on the fortunes of rail lines and affiliated industries.

By 1940, the heyday for railroads was over and many of the railroads were in receivership. Industries that had long had the railroad companies as their primary clients suffered accordingly. The Railroad Credit Corporation was created to aid the carriers, but the problems surpassed this emergency type of legislation. The entry of the United States into World War II temporarily alleviated this problem and brought much needed liquidity to the railroads. During this timeframe, the Offices of Defense Transportation coordinated the operations of the railroads. Between 1942-1945, the railroads moved more freight each year than they had since 1918, although they did so with fewer freight and passenger cars, locomotives, and employees. The vast increase in traffic produced record profits for the railroads and allowed them to reduce their debts and establish financial health.

Rise of the Diesel. By 1945 many of the carriers had dieselized their locomotive fleets. The Electro-Motive Division of General Motors developed separate locomotive units for freight service which was adopted by several railroads. Diesel locomotives cost far more than steam power locomotives to acquire, but operational savings came quickly. The diesels did not need the vast amounts of water that steam locomotives required, a significant factor in parts of the West where water was scarce. Diesels also required far less maintenance, had a high level of availability, were fuel efficient, and could operate for many miles without servicing. The diesel also was less harmful to railroad tracks than the steam engine and when placed in reverse could act as a dynamic braking system. This saved the railroad millions of dollars in freight car brake shoes. By 1955 the carriers had spent $3.3 billion for 21,000 diesel locomotives from Electro-Motive, American Locomotive Company, Fairbanks-Morse, and Baldwin Locomotive Works. These manufacturers provided the carriers with a wide range of diesel products to choose from for passenger and freight service.

The revolution in transportation opportunities available to the general public, however, made these railroad advancements seem insignificant. The internal-combustion engine placed the automobile in the hands of virtually every family and as a result, the long-distance passenger train almost died. The diverse railroad-reliant industries suffered as well from the emergence of airlines, which provided speedy service between major cities. Pipelines, barges, trucks, and intercoastal shipping companies carried a larger percentage of commodity products as well.

By the 1960s the rail industry as a whole was in a state of decline. In 1971 Congress created the National Railroad Passenger Corporation, known as Amtrak, to operate virtually all of the nation's remaining rail passenger services. In 1976 the federal government created the Consolidated Rail Corporation (Conrail) to salvage Penn Central and other bankrupt lines in the Northeast. Several carriers prospered by focusing on long-haul freight lines and piggyback trailer traffic.

The railroads survived by scrambling for market share, often establishing services for special product niches. Carriers introduced unit trains dedicated to one cargo—coal, wheat, sulfer, or chemicals that moved in continuous runs from the production site to docks, generators, or factories. The unit trains often utilized specially designed equipment to accommodate the transport of different commodities such as grain or liquid chemicals resulting in reduced freight rates. Railroads also established "run through trains" which stopped for only crew changes and retained the locomotives of the original carriers. To succeed, the carriers acquired pipelines, barge lines, and trucking companies and invested in air freight forwarding to obtain a total intermodal position.

Dieselization, the utilization of new technologies, the introduction of new services, the renewed emphasis on marketing, and the end of money-losing passenger business failed to prevent a massive restructuring of the nation's railroads. The Staggers Act of 1980 provided significant relief for the railroads in rate development as the federal government moved into an era of deregulation. This brought giant mergers, massive line abandonments, and shrinking locomotive and equipment fleets. Railway managers in an era of deregulation continued line rationalization, sought new technologies, and placed a major emphasis on marketing transportation.

CURRENT CONDITIONS

The railroad equipment manufacturers that supply the nations' railroads with cars and track and other equipment are slowly recovering from the lean decade of the 1980s. Capital expenditures by the railroads for equipment contracted from $2.3 billion in 1980 to 995 million in 1990 for a total decline of 58 percent. Moreover, carriers were not purchasing new locomotives; 70 percent of locomotives in operation in 1990 were more than 15 years old, with another 15 percent constructed prior to 1984. The number of freight cars in service dropped as well, falling almost 30 percent between 1980 and 1990, from 1.7 million to 1.2 million.

Over the last five years, the railways steady return to health has helped the equipment manufacturers supporting the industry climb out of a prolonged slump, although it will be difficult for the industry to reach 1980 levels of production, when more than 93,000 railcars were built. Carbuilders' deliveries, considered a benchmark of the industry's health, climbed to 35,00 new freight cars in 1993, up from 25,000 in 1992. Some industry experts predict car orders to increase to 30,000 to 40,000 cars by 1995 due to equipment shortages and the age of the current rail fleet.

The upturn in equipment manufacturing is reflected more in subtle design changes to existing technology and car types that provide the shipper with rapid loading and unloading capabilities, sanitary cleanout, and a large carrying capacity. The three major types of cars currently in demand are covered hopper cars, intermodal cars, and tank cars. Most of the design changes in the last several years have occurred in the tank car manufacturing arena, and were brought about by concerns about environmental safety and product liability. Changes in the tank car design include sloping bottoms, improved heater systems, better gates and hatches, new kinds of insulation, and better interior coating. These changes help to protect the product from contamination while also serving to insulate the tanker from corrusion.

INDUSTRY LEADERS

Only three American companies currently engage in locomotive manufacturing. Morrison-Knudsen Corp., long a major producer of other rail equipment, announced in 1993 that it would produce a prototype engine powered by liquified natural gas. Morrison-Knudsen thus joins General Electric and General Motors, the only other domestic locomotive manufacturers, in the locomotive market.

Leading companies in other areas of railroad equipment manufacturing include ABB Traction, Trinity Industries, and Duchossois Industries Inc. and its Thrall Car Manufacturing Co. subsidiary.

ABB Traction, Inc., an Elmira Heights, New York, privately-held company that manufacturers light rail vehicles, commuter railcars, and high-speed trains. ABB Traction also produces sub-system components including advanced AC propulsion, railcar shells, and trucks.

Thrall Car Manufacturing Company of Chicago Heights, Illinois, is the leading manufacturer of freight cars including intermodal equipment, auto racks, aluminium coal cars, and centerbeam, coiled steel, pressured differential, plastics, and woodchip cars. The Company is privately owned and operates five plants in Illinois and Georgia.

Trinity Industries is a Dallas, Texas-based public corporation with 1992 sales of $1.2 billion. Trinity Industries, the nation's largest car builder, manufacturers, leases, and sells all types of railroad freight and tank cars as well as parts and axles.

AMERICA AND THE WORLD

Overseas, European and Japanese manufacturers have developed extensive rail lines using high-speed rail technology. This thriving domestic market has provided these countries with a industrial base which they have used to expand internationally. This manufacturing base has enabled these countries to capture a large percentage of the U.S. freight and passanger car market. In North America, for instance, the Canadian company Bombardier Corporation has had a virtual monopoly on the U.S. passenger railcar business. Morrison-Knudsen, based in Boise, Idaho, has recently reentered the passenger railcar business, however, and has recently secured several domestic contracts. Included in those was a contract from Amtrak for 50 sleeping cars that was valued at $100 million. As *The Washington Post* noted in December 1992, Morrison-Knudsen's coup was "a blow to Bombardier . . . which has plants in the United States [and] bought the rights to the last U.S. passenger car designs from Pullman Standard Co. and Budd Co. when they went out of business."

The U.S. government, mindful of the systems in place in Europe, is currently exploring high-speed rail iniatives for America's railways. Proposals are aimed at creating an industrial base for high-speed train equipment utilizing traditional railroad equipment suppliers and the defense and aerospace industries.

In regards to international legislation, the railroad industry as a whole supported passage of the North American Free Trade Agreement (NAFTA). The agreement is expected to dramatically increase railroad traffic into Mexico in the coming years, a plus both to carriers and railroad equipment manufacturers.

RESEARCH AND TECHNOLOGY

The United States intermodal rail system is undergoing significant change through the use of information technology. The carriers are going high-tech with innovative electronics equipment and computers designed to improve tracking of shipments and make the railroads increasingly user friendly for commodity transfer. Information technology changes are proposed for nearly every aspect of the railroad industry. Some of these changes include:

Automated Equipment Identification. This program mandates that all railroad equipment be outfitted with electronic identification tags that will allow each freight container to be identified by a trackside laser scanner. This system will track freight container shipments among multiple carriers and eliminate the need for rairoad staff to visually identify containers and manually type in shipment information.

Interline Service Management. The United States rail network is divided into various regional carriers. When a customer books a coast-to-coast shipment he/she must deal with several carriers who will bill that customer separately and track the freight only within their individual rail system. Interline service management is designed to link the communication systems of the different carriers and provide an apparently "seamless" service to the customer.

Computer Systems. Railroads are working together to create a single computer hardware package that will allow customers to communicate with all their carriers. In addition, railroad locomotives are currently being outfitted with computers that communicate via wireless technology with the railroad's mainframe or central computer. It's hoped that data radio technology will improve shipment information and increase operational efficiency and productivity.

On-Board Locomotive Diagnostics. This technology will help to identify potential mechanical/electronic problems and to correct them before the locomotive breaks down. This system will reduce shipment delays and increase reliability.

In addition to innovations in information technology, changes in the industry's traditional hardware such as locomotives, freight cars, air brakes, and couplers has taken place or are currently undergoing redesign. For example, locomotives once powered by diesel fuel are being powered by liquid methane. Natural gas is less expensive, less polluting, and easier on engine parts than is diesel fuel. A new rack-and-loader system is being used to load autos, truck, and ship containers onto intermodal cars for easier transport via flatcars. Modern lightweight aluminium grain and coal hoppers are being employed in freight transport.

Advances in Tank Car Safety. The nation's rail system is currently used to transport a wide range of hazardous materials. The Railway Progress Institute noted that in 1991, "U.S. railroads delivered more than 1.9 million carloads of hazardous materials, an 80 percent increase since 1979." As *Chemical Week* noted as far back as 1978, however, "concern about carrier safety has been mounting in chemical traffic circles for several years. Nearly half of the total 100 billion ton-miles registered annually by chemical movements are carried by rail." Efforts were increased to buttress the safety of rail transport of chemicals. In 1989 *The New York Times* noted that the "Association of American Railroads says that from 1980 to 1987, the number of rail accidents in which there was a release of hazardous materials dropped by 61 percent." The *Times* went on, however, to note that, according to the Illinois Public Action Council, a nonprofit advocacy group, "although the number of railroad accidents involving hazardous materials has been declining, the severity of the accidents has been worsening. In 1987, the number of accidents involving evacuations was twice as high as five years earlier. The number of cars that released hazardous materials increased, as did the percentage of all accidents involving toxic chemicals."

In response to these continuing environmental concerns, many older tank cars have been retrofitted and new ones outfitted with safety devices to prevent accidents in the transportation of these materials. New technology and research into tank car safety has helped to identify safety issues to address in tank car design. Shelf couplers which prevent car couplers from overriding one another and puncturing the ends of tank cars in a derailment or sudden stop are currently in use. Head shields, constructed with 1/2 inch steel, are attached to the ends of tank cars to protect against head punctures. Shields are currently required for cars carrying liquified flammable gases, anhydrous amonia, or ethylene oxide. Tank cars are also being designed with thermal protection to help keep the tank's lading cool enough to avoid or delay explosions in fires. General-service tank cars have added bottom outlet protection devices which protect the outlets from being sheared off during an accident. All these advances have contributed to progress in the industry's safety record. The Railway Progress Institute, an association of industry suppliers, noted that, according to the Federal Railroad Administration, more than 99.99 percent of hazardous material carloads in 1991 reached their destination safely.

INDUSTRY INFORMATION SOURCES

Ainsworth, Don, Asaph Hall, Richard Briggs, et al, *Railroad Research Study Background Papers,* Federal Railroad Administration, U.S. Department of Transportation, 1975.

Allen, Leslie J., "Rail-Supply Industry Gets Back On Track," *St. Louis Post Dispatch,* March 5, 1989.

Boselovic, Len, "Aging Rail Cars Should Help This Company Pick-Up Steam," *Pittsburgh Post-Gazette,* September 19, 1993.

Challenges Accepted-The Story of Railroading, Association of American Railroads, n.d.

Cushman, John Jr., "Chemicals on Rails: A Growing Peril," *The New York Times,* August 2, 1989.

An Integrated Transportation Policy For An Era Of Rising Expectations, Association of American Railroads, 1989.

Flint, Jerry, "A Market Cleared," *Forbes,* June 6, 1994.

"Freight-Car Demand Finally Picks-Up Speed," *Business Week,* May 15, 1978.

Johnson, Gregory, "Five Rail Associations Establish Coalition," *Journal Of Commerce,* May 27, 1992.

Jouzaitis, Carol, "Rail Suppliers Back On Track After Slump," *Chicago Tribune,* September 26, 1988.

Parrish, Michael, "Hazardous Spill Rate Rises For Thin-Skin Tank Cars;Freight: Railroads Say Safety Is Improving But Accidents Have Potential For Large Catastrophe," *Los Angeles Times,* September 22, 1992.

Pena, Federico, "The Ice-Train Cometh; Technology Could Fit Industries Changing From Defense To Civilian Production," *St. Louis Post-Dispatch,* September 21, 1993.

Phillips, Don, "Morrison Knudsen Receives $100 Million Amtrak Order," *The Washington Post,* December 4, 1992.

Phillips, Don, "Getting U.S. Back On Track; Transit Agency Uses Economic Muscle To Revive Pullman Rail Car Legacy," *The Washington Post,* May 24, 1992.

Railroad Facts, Association of American Railroads, September 1991.

Sanchez, Jesus, "Domestic Rail Car Industry Has Virtually Disappeared," *Los Angeles Times,* January 24, 1992.

Suppliers and Railroads-On the Same Track, 1992 Annual Report and Membership Directory, The Railway Progress Institute, 1992.

Wald, Matthew L., "Railroads Are A Growth Industry, For A Change," *New York Times,* June 20, 1993.

Ziemba, Stanley, "Rail-Car Firm Doesn't Trail In Importance," *Chicago Tribune,* March 23, 1992.

————, "Hardware and Software Innovations On Track-Natural Gas Powers Locomotives; Computers Can Follow Every Train," *Chicago Tribune,* November 1, 1992.

—Andrew Burke

SIC 3751

MOTORCYCLES, BICYCLES, AND PARTS

This category includes establishments primarily engaged in manufacturing motorcycles, bicycles, and similar equipment, and parts. Establishments primarily engaged in manufacturing children's vehicles, except bicycles, are classified in **SIC 3944: Games, Toys, and Children's Vehicles, Except Dolls and Bicycles.** Establishments primarily engaged in manufacturing golf carts and other similar personnel carriers are classified in **SIC 3799: Transportation Equipment, Not Elsewhere Classified.**

INDUSTRY SNAPSHOT

In one form or another, the two-wheeled personal vehicle has played an important part in U.S. transportation systems. In 1990, Americans bought more bicycles than cars: 10.8 million compared to 9.3 million. Worldwide, the bicycle outnumbered the automobile two-to-one, although in the United States the car still maintained a numerical lead, 139 million to 103 million. Ninety-three million Americans reported riding a bicycle at least once in 1990, according to the Bicycle Institute of America. More than 28 million rode every week, making cycling America's third most popular sporting activity, according to the National Sporting Goods Association. Bicycling is a sport for all ages; according to the National Sporting Goods Association, ten percent of Americans over age 65 cycle. In 1992, bicycle sales topped $3.2 billion. The exploding mountain bike market accounted for 60 percent of that revenue.

Sales of small commuter motorcycles fell in the late 1980s. Motorcycle registrations dropped from 5.6 million in 1980 to 4.2 million in 1989. Reported commuter-miles ridden plummeted 32 percent during the same period, from a total of 3.1 million to 2.1 million miles. In the early 1990s, the "heavyweight" motorcycle, with engines larger than 700 cubic centimeters (cc) displacement, sparked renewed interest among potential buyers. Harley-Davidson, America's only remaining major motorcycle manufacturer, grabbed a 63.2 percent share of that $600 million market, primarily by catering to nostalgia for the 1950s with safe, reliable replicas of older models. These bikes evoked the image of a "wilder" lifestyle, an image which caught the imagination of middle-aged baby-boomers with disposable incomes. Known in the industry as RUBs (Rich Urban Bikers), they are targeted as the prime consumers of larger motorcycles well into the twenty-first century.

ORGANIZATION AND STRUCTURE

Harley-Davidson Inc. of Milwaukee, Wisconsin knows it is selling more than "bikes." The image of the Harley as America's motorcycle has become integral to its marketing success. Its extensive national dealer network sells motorcycles, parts, and service, but also promotes Harley-Davidson's own line of "Motorclothes" in "designer stores." The company sponsors a motorcycle enthusiast club, the Harley Owners Group (H.O.G.), and organizes rallies and product demonstration outings.

Japanese motorcycle makers Honda and Kawasaki built manufacturing facilities in Ohio and Nebraska, respectively, in the early 1980s. Like other Japanese and European motorcycle manufacturers, they maintain their own dealer networks and generally enjoy a price advantage over comparable Harley models. Even so, the effectiveness of the Harley-Davidson life-style marketing campaign has made the "Hog," as the Harley-Davidson is affectionately known, a desirable status symbol in the biking world.

The bicycle segment of the industry also sells much of its product through specialized dealer networks. These dealer networks generally carry the sophisticated, higher-priced models for the cycling enthusiast. Bikes in this category, like Schwinn's

Paramount line, can sell for more than $5,000. In 1990, 125 brand names produced by relatively small manufacturers battled for market share through the traditional bike-shop medium. However, 70 percent of all bikes sold that year in United States were moved by mass merchandisers like Sears, K-Mart, and Toys 'R' Us, where prices started as low as $100.

Cut-throat competition and rapid innovation in the bicycle segment of the industry has forced many firms out of the market. Chicago, once the world's bike manufacturing capital with more than 90 manufacturers, now has only Schwinn left, and that in name only. Schwinn, established in 1895, sold 25 percent of America's bikes during the 1960s, earning it the reputation as America's bicycle manufacturer even though it was never the largest. A 1981 labor dispute prompted Schwinn to phase out its U.S. manufacturing operations in favor of overseas facilities. That move created a new competitor, Giant Bicycles of Taiwan, which eventually drove Schwinn out of the market after supplying 70 percent of Schwinn's product in 1984. In 1991, Scwhinn filed for bankruptcy. Scott USA of Ketchum, Idaho bought its remaining assets, including the Schwinn trademark, for $41 million in 1993.

BACKGROUND AND DEVELOPMENT

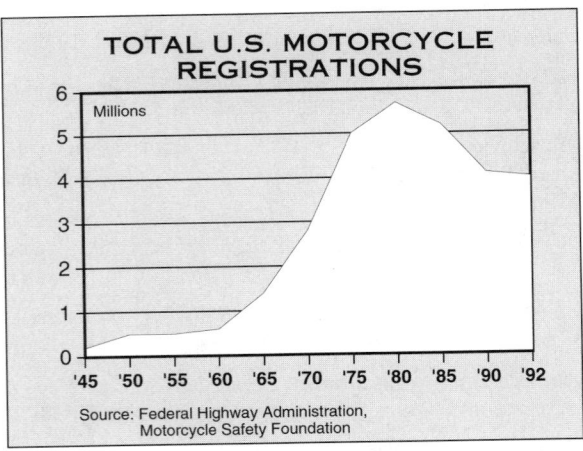

TOTAL U.S. MOTORCYCLE REGISTRATIONS

Source: Federal Highway Administration, Motorcycle Safety Foundation

Bicycles. The bicycle originated in France when Paris carriage maker Pierre Michaux fitted cranks to the front wheel of the German designed draisienne, or hobby horse. By 1867, a bicycle craze was sweeping Europe. According to David A. Hounshell, author of *From the American System to Mass Production: 1800-1932,* the Boston merchant Albert A. Pope deserves credit for introducing the device to America. Pope began importing the British High-Wheel, sometimes known as the ordinary or "Penny-Farthing," in 1876.

By 1878, he was producing his own version at the Weed Sewing Machine plant at Hartford, Connecticut.

The new product tapped a growing demand in America for increased mobility and provided work for the idling American arms industry. Much of the industrial expertise developed for the weapons industry during the Civil War found useful employment in the production of bicycle components. In 1890, 27 bicycle manufacturers produced 40,000 "safety" bicycles, featuring two equal sized wheels.

By 1897, production had increased to 1.2 million annually. Then demand evaporated as the horseless carriage began to make its impact felt. Auto manufacturer Hiram Percy Maxim noted that the bicycle revealed the advantage of quicker personal transportation but failed to answer the challenge. According to Maxim, the bicycle created the demand for the automobile and provided the technology needed to mass produce it.

Bicycles retained a steady but small popularity through the first half of the twentieth century, but it was the baby-boomer generation which fueled the resurgence of the bicycle starting in the 1950s. The single-speed child's bike gave way to multiple speed versions and, eventually, the popular light-weight 10-speed. Throughout the 1970s, the 10-speed dominated the market with a market share hovering around 56 percent. However, an American innovation, the mountain bike, changed all that. Initially designed for climbing the scrubby hills north of San Francisco, mountain bikes and all-terrain-bikes sported fat tires, heavy frames, and multiple gears. By 1991, they had boomed in popularity even in areas miles from any mountain and commandeered a 50-percent market share.

Many traditional firms like Schwinn and Murray failed to react quickly enough to the popularity of the mountain bike, leaving the door open to the small innovators to carve out a niche and for large foreign firms like Taiwan's Giant and China's CBC to gain control of trademarks. The showroom models still sport familiar brand names, but many are foreign-made while others use components no longer made in America. Those firms that did react, like Trek and Cannondale, are enjoying great success in the export market, especially in Europe and Japan.

Motorcycles. The motorcycle represented a first step from the bicycle to the automobile. The simple expedient of attaching a gasoline-powered engine to a bicycle frame produced a device which was at once exotic and affordable. During the first decade of the twentieth century, over 100 companies began manufacturing motorcycles, including Harley-Davidson, In-

dian, Orient, Excelsior, Cyclone, Henderson, and Marsh. By 1915, they produced models which could exceed 100 mph. The 1915 Cyclone, designed specifically for racing, had one speed, which reached speeds of 124 mph, but had no throttle and no brakes. Harley-Davidson began production of its first model, the Silent Grey Fellow, in 1903, the same year Henry Ford unveiled the Model A. When Ford introduced his mass-produced Model T in 1913 and sold it for $500, most motorcycle manufacturers could not compete. After World War I, only Harley-Davidson, Indian, and Excelsior remained. In 1953, only Harley-Davidson was left.

With the OPEC oil-embargo of the early 1970s, motorcycles became popular for commuting—but not the Harley. Consumers wanted cheap, reliable, peppy bikes, and those came from Japan. In 1973, sales of motorcycles reached an all-time peak of 1.5 million. In 1983, Harley-Davidson sought and received tariff protection from the Reagan administration to help it battle Japanese competition. Even with the 45-percent tariff protection, the company was almost bankrupt by 1985 because of poor quality and inefficient production. By applying Japanese management techniques, Harley-Davidson finally reversed its situation and asked for the tariff to be removed one year before it was due to expire. Meanwhile, Honda miscalculated the heavy-weight motorcycle market, concentrating instead on small bikes and high-priced, high-tech super-bikes. Honda's market share dropped from 44 percent in 1985 to 32 percent in 1989.

CURRENT CONDITIONS

According to *American Demographics,* the typical motorcycle rider of the 1990s looks little like the stereotypical biker depicted in popular movies like *Easy Rider.* The 1990s biker will most likely be married, be about 32.5 years old, earn an average income, and could as easily be a white-collar worker as a blue-collar-worker. The West boasts the highest percentage of women riders and the best educated bikers in the country. The Midwest contributes one-third of all riders, but most bikes are sold in the East. The South has the fewest motorcycles.

A continued small growth in shipments of motorcycles and parts will be fueled by continuing strong exports throughout the 1990s. An upswing in domestic consumption should accompany this growth late in the decade if the industry can overcome the public's negative impression of motorcycle safety with current accident statistics. According to the Motorcycle Safety Foundation, rider education programs have helped reduce the accident rate. A 1990 study showed a 22-

percent drop from the 1985 peak of 253 accidents per 10,000 registered motorcycles. The industry intends to target its marketing at the baby-boomer generation as it moves into the 45-to-54-year-old age group during the middle of the 1990s.

The motorcycle sector of the industry will be competing with the bicycle sector as it targets the same audience, playing on that group's high level of activity in physical fitness. Increased pressure to use bicycles for environmentally-friendly commuting in congested cities may also continue to push the domestic market. Strong demand in foreign countries will push exports up, especially if the North American Free Trade Agreement succeeds in reducing tariff barriers to the sizeable Mexican market. At the same time, since bicycle manufacturing is labor intensive, NAFTA would also encourage firms to relocate to Mexico to take advantage of cheap labor.

INDUSTRY LEADERS

Huffy Bicycles, of Celina, Ohio sold more bicycles than any other American manufacturer in 1992, capturing 30 percent of the market. Established in 1928 as part of the Huffman Manufacturing Company, the diversified corporation employs more than 2,200 people in its bicycle division. It is one of the few manufacturers to produce its entire volume domestically. Huffy's sales topped $449 million in 1991.

Second-ranked Murray Ohio Manufacturing of Brentwood, Tennessee commanded 13 percent of bicycle market share in 1991. Murray was particularly affected by pressure from foreign competition in the 1980s, and lost money on every bike it sold in 1987. The company invested $10 million in plant up-grades in 1989 to modernize production methods, which should help it remain competitive. Founded in 1919, it employs 2,800 workers in a variety of manufacturing endeavors.

America's motorcycle giant, Harley-Davidson of Milwaukee, Wisconsin, reported $678.5 million in sales for its motorcycle division in 1991, capturing 63.2 percent share of the domestic heavyweight market, according to the company's 1991 annual report. Harley-Davidson ships motorcycles to 30 foreign countries, earning one-third of its total revenues from exports. Founded in 1903, the company employs 5,300 workers throughout its operations.

AMERICA AND THE WORLD

Compared to the weak growth in domestic consumption, the expansion of exports in both bicycles and motorcycles throughout the late 1980s and early 1990s has been phenomenal. Between 1986 and 1991, motorcycle exports rose 41 percent annually. Bicycle exports increased 87 percent annually between 1987 and 1989, and 134 percent in 1990. Much of the bicycle's success resulted from the introduction of the mountain bike to Europe and other countries. In 1990, American mountain bikes easily accounted for 50 percent of Europe's $5.2 billion bicycle market.

Japan, Canada, and Germany formed the largest markets for U.S. bikes in 1991, but demand was strengthening in Mexico, the Netherlands, and Italy. U.S. manufacturers face continuing pressure from foreign producers, particularly where labor costs are low. Taiwan, Japan, and Mainland China traditionally supply a major part of the U.S. market and are shifting production to higher quality mountain bikes to compete in the mass merchandiser market.

The major importers of American motorcycles are Germany, with $117 million in 1991, and Japan, with $51 million. Canada, the Netherlands, and the United Kingdom also figure prominently in the market. Demand for large motorcycles exceeded supply in the early 1990s, prompting a brisk trade in refurbished Harley-Davidsons and other large bikes for export. The trend has helped reduce the industry trade deficit from $812 million in 1986 to $86 million in 1991. However, Harley-Davidson has barely begun to penetrate the potential market, racking up market share numbers in the low teens in most countries. Domestically, all manufacturers sold a total of 462,000 motorcycles, scooters, and all-terrain vehicles in 1990. In comparison, Japan's motorcycle manufacturers built 5.78 million motorcycles for worldwide sale in 1988, many of them 50-cc scooters.

RESEARCH AND TECHNOLOGY

The manufacturing expertise of Harley-Davidson has come a long way since its first 1903 model, which used a tomato can for a carburetor. Faced with sophisticated competition from Japanese manufactures in the 1980s, the company adopted modern Just-In-Time inventory management and computerized information systems. It retrained its production workers to use statistical monitoring methods, and re-educated managers to work as team leaders instead of bosses. New production line techniques included a state-of-the-art robot assembly system and a $23-million paint center at York, Pennsylvania. The result was the vastly improved quality and productivity needed to overcome Harley-Davidson's reputation as unreliable and expensive.

The mountain bike continued the technological revolution begun with the 10-speed bicycle, reducing cost, and increasing comfort levels. Innovators in bicycle design use new materials and electronic gadgets to bring the century-old "safety" bicycle into the computer age. The molded carbon fiber metals that made stronger lighter frames possible, for example, come from missile technology, while Special Bicycle Components' new three-spoke wheel, which combines carbon fiber, epoxy resin, Kevlar, and aluminum, was designed on the Cray Supercomputer. In addition, hydraulic brakes are replacing the familiar cable systems, and electronic shifters make changing gears a snap. Some manufacturers are investigating a new enclosed automatic transmission system, which could banish "gear-fear" forever. The most visible innovation in bicycling may be a complete new design. The new recumbent bicycle places the rider in a sitting position with the pedals in front, providing a low center of gravity, improving cornering, and pedaling efficiency.

Foreign manufacturers are changing the way they do things too. National Bicycle Industrial Co., a subsidiary of Matsushita, builds its bikes one at a time. Using robots and computer tracking, its 20 employees custom manufacture the product from the individual customer's order. From a base of 18 models of racing, road, and mountain bikes, they can build 11,231,862 variations in 199 color patterns.

INDUSTRY INFORMATION SOURCES

Bahniuk, Douglas E., "Bicycles Become Featherweights," *Machine Design,* November 10, 1988.

Beals, Vaughn L., "Operation Recovery: How Customers Helped Us Turn Around Harley-Davidson," *Success,* January/February 1989.

"Bicycle Transmission Eliminates Shifters, Levers," *Design News,* April 6, 1992.

Brown, Christie, "Then and the Art of Motorcycle Maintenance," *Forbes,* March 4, 1991.

Castro, Janice, "Rock and Roll," *Time,* August 19, 1991.

Clapp, Wallace L., Jr., "Insuring the New Breed of RV," *Rough Notes,* September 1992.

Collingwood, Harris, "For Schwinn, Fewer Bumps Ahead," *Business Week,* February 1, 1993.

Feder, Barnaby, "Schwinn Ready to Sell Most Assets," *New York Times,* January 2, 1993.

Friedman, Dorian, and Sara Collins, "Pedaling for Profits," *U.S. News & World Report,* August 26, 1991.

Hannon, Kerry, "Lots of Eggs, Several Baskets," *Forbes,* April 20, 1987.

Harley-Davidson, Inc., *1991 Annual Report,* Milwaukee, WI: Harley-Davidson, Inc. 1992.

"Harley-Davidson Net Doubled in 4th Period as Sales Climbed 31 Percent," *Wall Street Journal,* February 22, 1993.

"Harley-Davidson: Ready to Ride on Its Own," *Newsweek,* March 30, 1987.

"Harmony in Hog Heaven," *Time,* February 25, 1991.

Hounshell, David A., *From the American System to Mass Production: 1800-1932,* Baltimore: John Hopkins University Press, 1984.

"How Harley Beat Back the Japanese," *Fortune,* September 25, 1989.

Huffy Corporation, *Annual Report,* Dayton, OH: Huffy Corporation, 1991-1992.

"Japanese Motorcycles: Mean Machines?," *Nation's Business,* January 1983.

Kim, Irene, "Racer, Rough Riders, and Recumbents," *Mechanical Engineering,* May 1990.

King, Julia, "Harley-Davidson Revs Up IS Teamwork," *Computerworld,* February 3, 1992.

Lowe, Marcia, "Reinventing the Wheel," *Technology Review,* May/June 1990.

Marvel, Mark, "The Gentrified Hog," *Esquire,* July 1989.

Moffat, Susan, "Japan's New Personalized Production," *Fortune,* October 22, 1990.

"Mounting the Drive for Quality," *Manufacturing Engineering,* January 1992.

Okubo, Toshihiko, "Motorcycle Production Recovers from Slump." *Business Japan,* July 1989.

Phillips, Stephen, "That Vroom You Hear Is Honda Motorcycles," *Business Week,* September 3, 1990.

Pruzzin, Daniel R., "Born to Verruckt," *World Trade,* May 1992.

Shao, Maria, "Mountain Bikes Just Keep on Climbing," *Business Week,* January 7, 1991.

Stern, Richard, L., "The Graying Wild Ones," *Forbes,* January 6, 1992.

Stodghill, Ron, II, "Joe Montgomery's Wild Ride," *Business Week,* April 19, 1993.

Tanzer, Andrew, "Bury Thy Teacher," *Forbes,* December 21, 1992.

Waldrup, Judith, "The Pace Setters," *American Demographics,* May 1991.

Williams, Linda, "Reinventing the Wheel," *Time,* May 7, 1990.

Wilson, David Gordon, "A Short History of Human-Powered Vehicles," *American Scientist,* July/August 1986.

—Al Cook

SIC 3761

MANUFACTURERS OF GUIDED MISSILES AND SPACE VEHICLES

This category covers establishments primarily engaged in manufacturing guided missiles and space vehicles. This industry also includes establishments owned by guided missile and space vehicle manufacturers and primarily engaged in research and development on these products, whether from enterprise funds or on a contract or gee basis. Establishments primarily engaged in manufacturing guided missile and space vehicle propulsion units and propulsion unit parts are classified in **SIC 3764: Guided Missile and Space Vehicle Propulsion Units and Propulsion Unit Parts;** those manufacturing space satellites are classified in **SIC 3669: Communications Equipment, Not Elsewhere Classified;** those manufacturing guided missile and space vehicle airborne and ground guidance, checkout, and launch electronic systems and components are classified in **SIC 3812: Search, Detection, Navigation, Guidance, Aeronautical, and Nautical Systems and Instruments;** and those manufacturing guided missile and space vehicle airframes, nose cones, and space capsules are classified in **SIC 3769: Guided Missile and Space Vehicle Parts and Auxiliary Equipment, Not Elsewhere Classified.** Research and development on guided missiles and space vehicles, on a contract or fee basis, by establishments not owned by guided missile or space vehicle manufacturers are classified in **SIC 8731: Commercial Physical and Biological Research.**

INDUSTRY SNAPSHOT

In 1992, the United States had 110 establishments in this industry, with total gross sales of just over $19 billion. About 20 percent of this industry's production was for complete guided missiles, 32 percent for space vehicles, 20 percent for research and development of guided missiles, six percent for research and development of space vehicles, and most of the remaining production (roughly 20 percent) went toward services on these products.

This industry's history and growth depend on world political affairs, which define America's military needs, and technological developments, which define the country's military and space exploration capabilities and international competitiveness.

This industry's largest customer has long been the United States government. However, the government's market share started to decrease in the late 1980s with the end of the Cold War, reducing defense needs and a rapidly growing commercial market dominated by foreign-owned companies.

ORGANIZATION AND STRUCTURE

This industry is a large part of the aerospace industry, which is made up of roughly 4,000 companies. In 1990, the production of missiles accounted for 20 percent of sales in the aerospace industry, and space vehicles (along with related equipment) accounted for 25 percent of sales.

Of the companies in the aerospace industry, only 60 were primary contractors, mostly in the guided missile and space vehicle sectors. These establishments regularly hired subcontractors in other sectors of the aerospace industry. Due to the size and technical scope of aerospace programs, many primary contractors also were subcontractors in cases where they were not the primary contractor.

This industry is also categorized by the type of manufacturing workload an establishment undertakes. Basically, three types of manufacturing establishments exist in this industry: manufacturers of conventional, battlefield, and short- to medium- range guided missiles; producers of strategic (including ballistic missiles), antiballistic, and long-range missiles; and manufacturers of space vehicles (subdivided into launch vehicles and spacecraft).

Establishments rely on state-of-the-art systems management, in which a subcontractor, often the major computer hardware supplier, supervises hundreds of companies at one time. (The development of systems management in the United States has been credited to this industry.)

BACKGROUND AND DEVELOPMENT

The history of this industry is characterized by the world political climate and technological developments. Wars and American foreign policy directly affected the production of guided missiles, while the space race with the Soviet Union advanced America's production of space vehicles. Technological advances have shaped the growth of this industry with two major advances: the gas turbine engine developed in the late 1940s, for supersonic speed, and the ballistic missile first developed in the late 1950s, for long-range capabilities in war and space exploration.

The aerospace industry emerged from the aftermath of the second World War, which introduced jet rockets and atomic weaponry. These developments added to the already growing aviation industry. Aviation properly started in the late 1920s with the success of Charles Lindburgh's flight across the Atlantic; many companies that entered the aviation business later made the transition into aerospace technology, manufacturing missiles for the U.S. military during the war.

Space vehicles entered this industry later, during the mid- 1950s, with the Cold War placing America into the space race against the Soviet Union. Initially, most manufacturing of space vehicles was for exploration of the earth's upper atmosphere and the moon. Man's first trip to the moon sparked new interest in space technology, which peaked in the late 1960s.

The 1960s also marked tremendous growth in the development of guided missiles. Missiles manufactured in the United States were being sold to the Middle East and other troubled areas of the world at that time.

Both the production of missiles and space vehicles decreased during the mid to late 1970s, because of the end of the Vietnam War and the economic recession. The number of satellites used for military surveillance decreased, and those used for communications increased substantially. However, during this period, major projects involving stealth sea vessels and aircraft were initiated.

During the 1980s, the guided missile portion of this industry hit its all-time peak as a result of renewed defense spending. Under the Reagan administration, fears of an escalating Cold War increased missile sales from just over $10 billion in 1983 to nearly $14 billion in 1988 (according to the Electronic Industries Association). President Reagan proposed the development of antiballistic strategic defenses, commonly known as Star Wars initiatives, to counter possible Soviet attack.

However, by the end of the 1980s, yet another dramatic shift occurred in this industry. With the dissolution of the Soviet Union and the end of the Reagan administration, America's defense spending was greatly reduced. From 1987 to 1992, U.S. Defense Department outlays for aircraft dropped from over $30 billion to just over $23 billion. Similarly, the government budget for research and development in defense and space technology dropped significantly. This was also due to the explosion of the *Challenger* space shuttle, in which seven astronauts perished.

Products. Among the types of guided missiles this industry manufactures are antitank and assault, antiship, air-to-surface, air-to-air and surface-to-air. Antitank and assault missiles were developed in the United States after World War II (though some accounts have Germany developing these missiles near the end of the war). These missiles were first installed on light trucks and helicopters and equipped with warheads to penetrate armor. In early models, tracking was visual, with commands controlled by a hand-operated system transmitted by wire. Later, antitank missiles transmitted commands by radio and laser and infrared homing techniques. By the 1980s, optical fibers became the standard guidance device for these missiles.

Antiship missiles were designed to fight against the heavy armor of warships. These types of guided missiles received little attention by United States manufacturers after World War II, because the Americans and British had used torpedoes, bombs, and unguided rockets to attack naval targets. However, in response to Soviet development of antiship missiles, the United States countered with turbojet-powered missiles, such as the Harpoon, which weighed about 1,200 pounds and carried a warhead weighing 420 pounds. Later, the U.S. Navy Tomahawk introduced a new type of antiship missile, a long-range cruise missile intended for strategic nuclear defense. Its antiship version carried a modified Harpoon guidance system. By the 1980s, antiship missiles were developed for stealth aircraft with visual, infrared, and radar tracking.

Air-to-surface missiles became standard in United States combat by the late 1950s with the AGM-12 Bullpup, a rocket-powered tracking missile with visual tracking and radio transmitted commands. After several variations of the AGM-type missiles were employed during the Vietnam War, the Bullpup was replaced by the AGM-64/65 Maverick group of rocket-powered missiles, which first used television tracking, and later, infrared devices.

Air-to-air missiles were first developed in the United States in the late 1940s with the subsonic Firebird, a radar-guided missile. However, this particular missile become obsolete within a few years, being replaced by supersonic missiles, such as the Falcon, the Sidewinder, and the Sparrow. The Sidewinder became the most used of these missile types; later versions of this missile had highly sensitive emission seekers. Tactical demands saw significant improvements in air-to-air technology, which resulted in long-range air-interception missiles and missiles with higher maneuverability.

Surface-to-air missiles were first introduced by the Germans during World War II, but were not widely used until the 1950s and 1960s. The most important American-produced, surface-to-air missile was the Hawk; this missile was extremely effective in targeting low-flying aircraft. In the mid 1980s, the Hawk was replaced by the Patriot, which gained popularity as a result of the Persian Gulf War.

The missiles described above are also classified as conventional or strategic. Strategic missiles refer to long-range missiles, especially those with nuclear warheads, and include ballistic and cruise missiles. Ballistic missiles are rocket-propelled systems that are launched either from land or sea and move by the launch rocket momentum. Cruise missiles are powered continuously by air-breathing jet engines. These types of missiles are aided by guidance systems and early warning devices on satellites.

Three basic types of space vehicles exist in this industry: space capsules with rocket boosters, reentry vehicles, and satellites. These space vehicles are made of two basic components—the launch vehicle and the spacecraft, also referred to as the payload. The launch vehicle provides the propulsion to send the space craft into space. While the spacecraft itself is basically unpowered, it relies on the initial velocity provided by the launch vehicle, and either enters an orbit around the earth or continues to a further destination.

Space capsules with rocket boosters were first designed and tested in the United States in the mid-1950s with the intent of sending a man into outer space. These capsules are environmentally controlled containers for living organisms. After a few flights in the early 1960s, animals were preferred over humans. The rockets attached to the space capsule are used for launching the space vehicle and later separate from the capsule.

Reentry vehicles, such as space shuttles, were first launched by the United States in 1981. These space vehicles were designed to go into the earth's orbit, drop off a payload, such as a satellite, and return to earth by making a gliding landing. Shuttles are made of three basic components: a winged orbiter that houses crew and cargo, an external tank containing fuel and liquid oxygen, and booster rockets, which separate from the space craft and return to earth. By 1990, the United States had used four shuttles, many on repeated missions, but also with much difficulty. Technical and design problems frequently delayed launches, and the worst of the problems caused the explosion of the *Challenger* space shuttle in 1986.

Satellites are spacecraft that revolve around planets and are used for communications, weather forecasting, scientific research, and military reconnaissance. The first satellite was launched in 1957 by the Soviet Union. By the end of the 1980s, there were hundreds of satellites orbiting the earth and nearby planets. In the early 1990s, an estimated three billion dollars annually went into the manufacturing of communications satellites in America alone.

CURRENT CONDITIONS

By the 1990s, the end of the Cold War initiated cuts in defense spending, drastically affecting the manufacturing of guided missiles and military-employed space vehicles. However, with the view that America needs to retain its technological base in defense, an increase in funding for research and development occurred. This trend was expected to continue with 57 percent of procurement going towards research and development by 1997, compared with 30 percent in 1985. New products have been manufactured only as a limited number of prototypes, which are taken to a full-scale production on the basis of need and available funding.

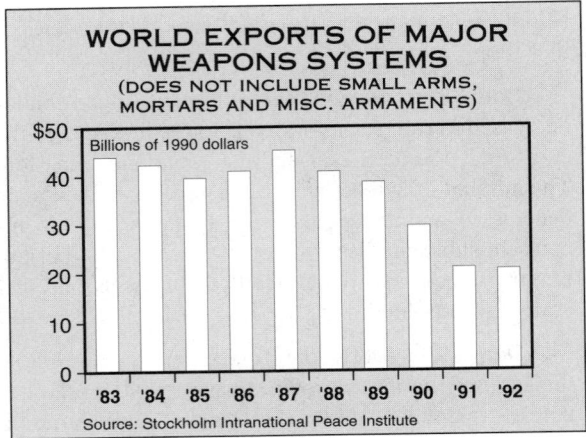

WORLD EXPORTS OF MAJOR WEAPONS SYSTEMS (DOES NOT INCLUDE SMALL ARMS, MORTARS AND MISC. ARMAMENTS)

Billions of 1990 dollars

Source: Stockholm Intranational Peace Institute

This industry was further affected by the signing of the Strategic Arms Reduction Treaty (START) in July 1991. According to the treaty, guided missiles with nuclear warheads would no longer be produced while 30 percent of existing ones would be destroyed.

The end of the twentieth century also started a new phase in the production of space vehicles, whereby space exploration would be trimmed while a new commercial industry would open up. As a result of the *Challenger* disaster and other highly publicized space failures costing millions of dollars, Congress reduced NASA's budget. NASA has flown fewer flights annually, but with larger and more expensive payloads, subsequently producing greater financial risks. For example, in 1993, the loss of the *Mars Observer*, a space vehicle equipped to map the surface of Mars, cost at least $1 billion dollars. Such problems were a factor in space vehicle manufacturers' move away from government projects and into the commercial market. According to Otis Port of *Business Week*, ''Thanks mainly to advances in technology, aerospace companies and some in Washington think they see a chance to make space travel an airline-type business.'' Port added that the goal has become ''to stimulate private enterprise in space.'' The high cost of producing space vehicles since the beginning of the space program was to see a turnaround as commercial business saw a potential market and foreign competition meant NASA no longer monopolized space travel. The trend has now been to fund space projects with greater relevance to living on earth than early space explorations; the orbiting of communication satellites and the construction of the *Freedom* space station are new priorities for the continued presence of America's space program.

Throughout this industry, establishments responded to these developments by diversifying and consolidating. Some companies manufacturing satellites diversified into producing spacecraft electronic components, thereby expanding their roles in the telecommunications industry. Other companies in aerospace developed new areas of scientific and technological research, such as designing medical laboratory equipment usable in specialized environments and software for growing industries in the communications field.

The industry as a whole is expected to undergo restructuring as a result of these changes. According to industry leaders, by the end of the century, the industry will either be small, but with a few strong companies, or would retain its many companies, but on a much smaller production scale. The first type of industry would be better able to invest in research, while the second would be geared more towards low-cost commercial ventures in a highly competitive market.

INDUSTRY LEADERS

In 1992, the three industry leaders in the production of guided missiles and space vehicles were: Rockwell International, with $12.3 billion in gross sales; Lockheed Corp., with $10.2 billion in sales; and Martin Marietta Corp., with $4.7 billion in gross sales. Other key companies in the manufacture of guided missile systems included GM Hughes Electronics Corporation and Raytheon Company.

Rockwell International had its origins in 1919 as Rockwell-Standard, a manufacturer of truck axles. By the late 1960s, the company had evolved into producing industrial machinery and vehicle parts. In 1967, Rockwell merged with North American Aviation, a company that had been in the aviation business since the late 1920s and later played a major role in producing rockets and spacecraft for the United States space program. Prior to its merger with Rockwell, North American Aviation was nearly bankrupt as a result of

an electrical fire in an Apollo space capsule, in which three astronauts were killed. This incident cost North American a large legal settlement and a bruised reputation.

After the merger, the company was called North American Rockwell. With its new name and Rockwell's established history, the company regained its reputation in the aerospace industry. The new company extended beyond government contracts into the private sector, manufacturing a wide range of automotive parts, household appliances, and electric instruments for aviation. In aerospace, the company developed the Saturn V rocket engines used for later Apollo missions. By the early 1970s, the company, now called Rockwell International, was the largest NASA contractor and NASA's primary contractor of space shuttles.

In the late 1970s, Rockwell experienced severe financial setbacks due in part to management problems, but also as a result of the government shifting away from the development of bombers, which Rockwell was in the middle of producing. But the company retained its defense contracts, including the production of the MX ''Peacekeeper'' missiles and five space shuttles.

With a reduction in space shuttle contracts and defense systems in general, Rockwell International entered the 1990s starting commercial ventures with foreign-owned companies. In 1993, the company employed over 105,000 workers and retained its principle subsidiaries in Canada and Great Britain.

Lockheed Corp. began as the Loughead Aircraft Manufacturing Company in 1916 (but the company soon changed its name to Lockheed to reflect the correct pronunciation). This company started with the development of their twin-engine, F-1 flying boats. By 1927, Lockheed became widely known for its planes, including the Lockheed Vega, flown by Amilia Earhart.

Lockheed entered the defense industry in 1938, when commissioned to built reconnaissance bombers for the British. Lockheed went on to produce a wide range of military planes and early cruise missiles during World War II, including the Harpoon. By the end of the war, the company had produced over nine percent of America's military aircraft.

After the war, Lockheed established its missile and space division, starting with submarine launched missiles. During the Cold War, Lockheed developed guided missiles for the Pentagon, including its U-2 spy plane, which had notable success during the Cuban missile crisis in 1962. In addition to military contracts,

Lockheed stayed in the commercial aircraft business, manufacturing jetliners; however, this division nearly placed the company into bankruptcy by the early 1970s. The company finally gained some success in jetliners in the foreign market, but at the expense of being involved in an international scandal. Lockheed was implicated in accepting bribes from several countries, including Iran and Japan.

During the 1980s, Lockheed led the industry in government defense contracts, primarily in building F-19 stealth bombers and the Trident II missiles, and in servicing NASA's space shuttles. During the early 1990s, the company remained successful in defense technology, with its stealth fighters being used in the Persian Gulf War. After an unsuccessful expansion of its commercial divisions, Lockheed reversed course to attempt to become the nation's largest defense contractor. In 1993, the company employed 81,300 workers, and predicted a ten percent increase in its earnings.

Martin Marietta Corp., like other industry leaders, had its origins in airplane production in the early days of aviation. Glenn Martin, the company's founder, ran a small airline business from the early 1900s until World War I, when he began developing bombers for the military. Martin's company grew during World War II with the production of bombers and aircraft, both for the military and the commercial airline industry.

Soon after World War II, the Martin Co. had financial difficulties as a result of incomplete aircraft projects in a competitive airliner market, and the hiring of hundreds of unskilled workers who needed training. But, during the 1950s, the company reestablished itself under new management and by expanding its production into rockets and missiles—one of its early projects in aerospace included the Vanguard missile and the Titan II rocket. After 1960, this company produced only missiles for the government, including the Bullpup and the Pershing. In 1961, the company diversified with the purchase of American-Marietta Corp., primarily a manufacturer of chemical products and construction materials. The company was then renamed Martin Marietta.

Martin Marietta grew in the aerospace industry with the production of the Viking capsules for the 1976 Mars mission, the construction of fuel tanks for several NASA space shuttles, and in the 1980s with the Pershing II and Patriot missiles. However, this company experienced serious losses in its production of space vehicles. The *Challenger* shuttle disaster in 1986, the failures of two earth observation satellites in 1993, and the missing *Mars Observer* in 1993 had damaged Martin Marietta's reputation and ability to stay strong in an uncertain industry.

Martin Marietta entered the 1990s as a major contractor for the American space station and for the Federal Aviation Administration's air traffic management system. In 1993, the company employed 69,000 workers.

WORK FORCE

In 1992 this industry employed more than 100,000 workers. Of these, nearly 53,000 worked in production, with the remaining workers mostly in research and development. For both production and research and development, the main occupations needed for this industry are engineers, scientists, and technicians. Engineers usually specialize as either aeronautical engineers, working with aircraft, or astronautical engineers, working with space vehicles. In 1992, engineers in the aerospace industry started with an average annual salary of $30,000 if they possessed a bachelors degree, $35,000 with a master's, and $47,000 with a Ph.D. Scientists in this industry included astronomers, mathematicians, physicists, metallurgists, and chemists—all of these occupations required Ph.D.s, and offered salaries between $45,000 to $70,000, depending on specialty. Technicians working in this industry include laboratory technicians, electrical technicians, and draftsmen, with an annual starting salary of $50,000. Other occupations required by this industry include technical writers, machinists, assembly workers, system managers, worker supervisors, computer programmers, and various clerical workers.

AMERICA AND THE WORLD

America's production of guided missiles and space vehicles and the political environment after World War II have made America the world's leading exporter of these products. In 1992, U.S. exports of missile systems totaled over $600 million in sales, with air-to-air missiles representing the largest portion of sales. However, this strength in the air-to-air sector of the market has been challenged since 1992, when the European Advanced Short Range Air-to-Air Missile program began.

The countries of the former Soviet Union, which had invested more money and resources in air defense systems than any other nation in the world, have been America's greatest competitor for arms sales to other countries. Upon entering the 1990s, France and Great Britain rapidly became two other leading competitors in the production of missiles.

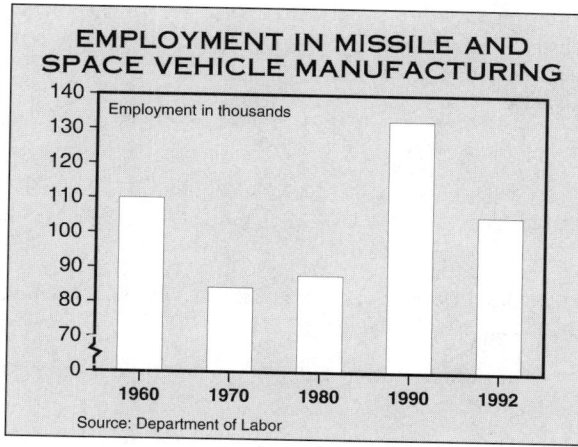

EMPLOYMENT IN MISSILE AND
SPACE VEHICLE MANUFACTURING

Employment in thousands

Source: Department of Labor

The production of strategic missiles, given their nuclear capabilities, were originally restricted to the United States and the Soviet Union. However, since the end of the Cold War, there has been worldwide concern that the superpowers would sell their stockpile of weapons and possibly new weapons to third world countries. Other countries that developed missile technology became somewhat successful in ballistic missiles, but less so with cruise missiles. Ballistic missiles do not require the sophisticated guidance system of cruise missiles and adapt to chemical weaponry more easily.

The end of the Cold War, coupled with worldwide economic recession, gave rise to change in the international market for space programs. An industry first monopolized by America and the former Soviet Union entered into competition with the European Space Agency, the People's Republic of China, and Japan. The new political and economic climate allowed for more cooperative efforts in space. NASA considered Russian contributions to America's *Freedom* space station and other ventures. In the commercial market, plans were made for the International Maritime Satellite Organization, an international consortium, to use a Russian-made rocket to launch its satellites.

Since the late 1980s, foreign competition remained strong for selling space satellites. Arianespace, a European joint venture, dominated the commercial satellite business, and Russia's space agency began shifting its investment to the commercial marketplace. According to the *Wall Street Journal*, in 1993 America built about 75 percent of the world's satellites, but only launched 30 percent, because it had not manufactured the rocket systems to launch the spacecraft.

America also imports guided missiles and space vehicles, but only on a small scale and mostly for research and development. In 1992, United States imports in this industry totaled $2.4 million.

RESEARCH AND TECHNOLOGY

Manufacturers of guided missiles and space vehicles depend on research and development of new technologies, most of which are produced within the industry itself. The three main forces shaping the future of this industry were the development of ballistic missiles, low-cost space vehicles, and the construction and operation of the *Freedom* space station.

Ballistic and anti-ballistic missiles have been continuously developed in order to compete with defense technology of foreign countries. Since the late 1980s, the market for these types of missiles at low prices developed from economic crises in the Soviet Union and other countries, who sold conventional and nuclear weapons to third world countries no longer wanting to rely on superpowers to protect them. This market was met by research and development in low-cost manufacturing of relatively small ballistic and antiballistic missiles, a variety of surface-to-air ballistic missiles, and medium-range ballistic missiles that can be adapted for many uses. Since the Persian Gulf War, researchers of these types of missiles directed their interests toward weapons like those used in the war, but with improved high-precision strike capabilities.

Of low-cost space vehicles, expendable launch vehicles (ELV) were expected to replace the failed space shuttle programs. Research for these vehicles focused on unmanned operations to launch mostly commercial payloads. Given the cost factor, the aim was to launch larger and heavier payloads on each trip. NASA and the U.S. Defense Department are developing an Advanced Launch System to be in operation early in the twentieth century. In the early 1990s, launch capacity exceeded demand, and the industry became concerned that improved technology would increase the life of satellites—both factors would reduce the need for new space vehicle launches.

Another technological development aimed at reducing costs has been work on a reentry vehicle that takes off and lands vertically. In 1993, McDonnell Douglas Corporation began experimental launches of their Delta Clipper, which would, if successful, land vertically. This launch vehicle costs $10 million to build, with an estimated cost of $1,000 per kg to launch into a low earth orbit, compared with NASA's space shuttles, which cost $500 million to produce and $21,000 per kg to launch.

Other innovations in launch vehicles include new airplanes designed to carry spacecraft into orbit. In the

United States, Boeing Defense and Space Group proposed the use of a supersonic carrier the size of a 747 airplane. Similar designs are being developed by the British and Germans. Like other new developments in space technology, these aim to reduce costs. Boeing's proposed system would cost roughly $600 per pound to place a spacecraft into orbit.

To compete with the commercial satellite market, research into a new rocket to carry satellites and other types of spacecraft was proposed in 1993. Five major aerospace companies—Boeing Co., General Dynamics Corp., Lockheed Corp., Martin Marietta Corp., and Rockwell International—sought alliance with NASA to produce a rocket to meet the market needs of commercial launches. With the same goal in mind, alternatives to rockets have been suggested for launching small commercial satellites, such as the use of electromagnetic guns and laser-powered launchers.

The *Freedom* space station, first proposed in 1984, is one of NASA's most important endeavors. Since its origins, the project has been mostly downsized to where it will cost $30 billion. The structure will be 300 feet long with a permanent crew of four astronauts. The first components of the station are due to be launched in early 1996, and a permanent crew will reside in it as early as the year 2000. Many elements under development for the space station include habitation and working modules, free-flying platforms, and highly sophisticated electrical systems.

INDUSTRY INFORMATION SOURCES

Asker, James R. "NASA Struggles With Station Redesign," *Aviation Week and Space Technology,* April 12, 1993.

Banks, Howard. "Preparing for Even More Draconian Cuts in Defense Spending, Suppliers are Cutting Jobs and Costs," *Forbes,* January 6, 1992.

Bright, Charles D. *The Jet Makers: The Aerospace Industry from 1945-1972,* Lawrence, Kansas: Regents Press, 1978.

Corcoran, Elizabeth and Tim Beardsley. "The New Space Race," *Scientific American,* July 1990.

Covault, Craig. "Ambitious Decade Ahead for Europe's Space Effort," *Aviation Week and Space Technology,* March 15, 1993.

Curry, Malcolm R. "Expert Opinion: Peace is Transforming Aerospace and Military Industries," *IEEE Spectrum,* January 1993.

Dornheim, Michael A. "U.S. Navy Unveils Sea Shadow Stealth Vessel," *Aviation Week and Space Technology,* April 26, 1993.

"F-16, EA-6B to Fire Missiles Cued by Intelligence Satellites," *Aviation Week and Space Technology,* April 19, 1993.

Fulghum, David A. "Ballistic Missile Defense Shaping Industry Future," *Aviation Week and Space Technology,* September 7, 1992.

Lavitt, Michael O. "Market Forces," *Aviation Week and Space Technology,* April 5, 1993.

Lenorovitz, Jeffery M. "Steady Growth Seen For Commercial Space," *Aviation Week and Space Technology,* March 15, 1993.

"Lockheed Develops Low-End Launch Vehicle," *Aviation Week and Space Technology,* May 10, 1993.

"Out of a Motherplane's Belly—And Into Orbit," *Business Week,* June 21, 1993.

Payne, Seth. "Can't Afford NASA? Call Rent-A-Rocket," *Business Week,* March 12, 1990.

Port, Otis. "Is Buck Rogers' Ship Coming In?" *Business Week,* June 21, 1993.

Ricks, Thomas E. "Unit of LTV Pleads Guilty in 'Ill Wind' Case," *Wall Street Journal,* May 19, 1993.

Rosewicz, Barbara. "Aerospace Firms Seek Alliance on New Rocket," *Wall Street Journal,* May 6, 1993.

"Russian Proton Booster Offered in Indonesian Launch Competition," *Aviation Week And Space Technology,* April 12, 1993.

"Russian Proton to Launch Inmarsat-3 Satellite in 1995," *Aviation Week and Space Technology,* April 19, 1993.

Rybak, Boris. "Feeble Russian Economy Hinders Space Efforts," *Aviation Week and Space Technology,* March 15, 1993.

Sawyer, Kathy. "Silence at Red Planet Reverberates on Earth," *Washington Post,* November 13, 1993.

Schine, Eric. "Lockheed Sticks to Its Guns," *Business Week,* April 26, 1993.

Scovell, Dawn. "Solid Rockets," *Aerospace America,* December 1992.

Smith, Bruce A. "U.S. Firms Face Long Adjustment," *Aviation Week and Space Technology,* March 15, 1993.

"U.S. Entrepreneurs Seek Russian SLBMs," *Aviation Week and Space Technology,* April 19, 1993.

Velocci, Anthony L. Jr. "Fewer Players to See Late-Decade Upturn," *Aviation Week and Space Technology,* March 15, 1993.

—Paola Trimarco

SIC 3764

GUIDED MISSILE AND SPACE VEHICLE PROPULSION UNITS AND PROPULSION UNIT PARTS

This industry consists of establishments primarily engaged in manufacturing guided missile propulsion units and propulsion unit parts. This industry also includes establishments owned by manufacturers of guided missile and space vehicle propulsion units and parts and primarily engaged in research and development on such products, whether from enterprise funds or on a contract or fee basis. Research and development on guided missile and space propulsion units, on a contract or fee basis by establishments not owned by manufacturers of guided missile and space vehicle propulsion units and parts are classified in **SIC 8731: Commercial Physical and Biological Research.**

INDUSTRY SNAPSHOT

In 1992, American manufacturers of propulsion units, jet engines and propulsion unit parts for guided missiles and space vehicles recorded $6.6 billion in gross sales. In the same year, 53 percent of the industry's shipments consisted of guided missile and space vehicle propulsion units, while 23 percent comprised engine and propulsion unit parts. The remaining 24 percent of the industry's shipments were classified as research and development products.

In the 1990s, there were two basic types of propulsion systems used for guided missiles and space vehicles: solid-fuelled and liquid-fuelled engines. Solid-fuelled engines were the more commonly used of the two because liquid fuels needed to be stored at very low temperatures. Other rockets produced by this industry included hybrid rockets (which use a combination of solid and liquid fuel systems), small propellant rockets for adjusting the altitude of space vehicles, and rockets for track-borne research sheds.

ORGANIZATION AND STRUCTURE

Establishments in this industry were generally subcontractors for producers of complete guided missiles and space vehicles. Primary contractors and subcontractors were hired by a single customer. In 1992, roughly 88 percent of the industry's shipments were manufactured under government contracts, primarily for the U.S. Department of Defense and NASA. The balance of the industry's shipments were manufactured for companies in the private sector, involved

primarily in producing propulsion and engine systems to launch commercial satellites.

BACKGROUND AND DEVELOPMENT

Propulsion units and engines were derived from and often referred to as ''rockets.'' Rockets were believed to have originated in China during the 13th century, soon after the invention of gunpowder. Rockets appeared in Europe in the early 14th century, but did not see regular military use until the War of 1812 and the Napoleonic Wars. Rockets during this period still used some form of gunpowder for propulsion. It was not until the late-19th and early 20th century that modern rocketry, using stored fuels, was first developed.

World War II witnessed the first guided missiles and military aircraft which were powered by propulsion systems. During the war, only the Germans used propulsion guided missiles, though other countries did possess the technological capabilities. It was not until after the war that other countries, including the United States, developed these systems.

The development of the propulsion units used in ballistic missiles led to the development of systems that enabled the launching of the first space vehicles into orbit by the end of the 1950s. Another significant development in propulsion systems came in the 1970s, concurrent with the first designs for space shuttles. These engines were built with propulsion units that jettisoned off the spacecraft, as well as with permanently fixed units that were reusable.

Rockets using nuclear and solar fuel sources also were tested for space missions. Nuclear propulsion was first developed in the 1960s and was considered, twenty years later, for missions to Mars, but concerns about space debris kept this system in the experimental stages. Solar propulsion was investigated for its ability to run an engine at tremendous cost savings.

CURRENT CONDITIONS

Entering the 1990s, the guided missile and space vehicle propulsion industry, like other aerospace industries, was down-sizing its operations, but trying to retain a strong base in research and development. With the end of the Cold War, new propulsion systems for military and space exploration programs were limited to prototypes, which were then taken to full-scale production on the basis of need and available funding.

With federal cut-backs, a number of fixed-price contracts created losses for companies in the late 1980s and early 1990s. In the late 1980s, the Air Force proposed the ''SRMU stabilization program'', a development of the Titan 4 Launcher, but did not fund the implementation of the program. Both the contractor, Martin Marietta Corp., and the subcontractor, Hercules, Inc., invested substantially in the program, and both ended up suing each other over contract terms as a result. In 1993, the U.S. Government agreed to appropriate funds for some of the losses.

The end of the 20th century also began a new phase in the production of space vehicles, as a new commercial industry was emerged. For the guided missile and space vehicle propulsion industry, this meant producing more lower-cost propulsion systems instead of more expensive systems.

Like other industries in aerospace, the guided missile and space vehicle propulsion industry was expected to undergo restructuring as a result of federal defense budget cuts. According to industry leaders, by the end of the century, the industry was expected to be smaller, with many individual companies having a larger market share than they did in the mid-1980s.

INDUSTRY LEADERS

In 1992, the three leaders of the guided missile and space vehicle propulsion industry accounted for nearly 60 percent of all industry sales. GenCorp, Inc. recorded $1.7 billion in sales, Thiokol Corp. had nearly $1.2 billion in sales, and Hercules, Inc. reported $1 billion in sales.

GenCorp, Inc. was established in 1915 as General Rubber Manufacturing Co. By 1992, GenCorp had 11 Aerojet plants in the United States and employed over 13,000 workers. GenCorp's propulsion systems division, Aerojet, accounted for 68 percent of GenCorp's operating profit in 1992. In addition to producing solid and liquid propulsion systems, and their related parts, Aerojet manufactured sensors, warheads and munitions used in the aerospace industry. Aerojet was most widely known for its Titan IV engines and its second stage Delta engines, which allowed spacecraft to maneuver in orbit.

Thiokol Corp. was established in 1969 as Morton-Norwich Products, Inc., and changed its name later that year to Morton Thiokol, Inc. This company was engaged in research and development, and production of solid-fuelled propulsion systems. In 1992, Thiokol was America's largest producer of rocket propulsion systems, with six plants in the United States manufacturing propulsion units. In the same year, 96 percent of this company's sales came from government contracts, including providing propulsion units for NASA's space shuttle programs and the military's Trident and Patriot missiles. In 1992, Thiokol employed over 11,000 workers.

Hercules, Inc. was established in 1915 as Hercules Powder Co.

This company was an international producer of propulsion systems and a wide range of chemicals and materials used in food products. The company's foreign operations accounted for 31 percent of its total sales. In 1992, the aerospace segment of Hercules owned six plants in the United States and operated an additional two plants for the government. In 1992, aerospace products contributed 26 percent of the company's income, which was down five percent from the previous year. However, Hercules' prospects in aerospace were more optimistic, as the company expanded its role in the production of the Trident IV rocket and other U.S. Defense Department programs. In 1992, Hercules employed over 15,400 employees in the United States.

WORK FORCE

In 1992, the guided missile and space vehicle propulsion industry employed roughly 83,000 workers in the United States. Of these, an estimated 25 percent were engineers, mainly aeronautical, astronautical, electronic, and industrial engineers. Other occupations needed in the manufacturing of guided missile and space vehicle propulsion systems included systems analysts, computer scientists, specialized technicians, production managers and machinists.

Overall, employment in this industry was expected to drop considerably by 2005. The largest decline was expected to be in jobs related to the inspection and testing of products. Computer scientists, however, were expected to increase their representation in this industry to facilitate the development of computerized prototypes to replace full-scale testing of new products.

AMERICA AND THE WORLD

Manufacturers of guided missile and space vehicle propulsion and engine systems were affected by developments in foreign countries. In 1992, American companies in this industry exported directly over 15 percent of their products, and through the government, exported indirectly an additional 36 percent.

In the mid-1990s, the superpowers no longer competed solely between themselves for the defense- and space-related business of smaller nations. Other nations, such as France, Great Britain, Australia, Canada, China, Germany, and Japan entered this market. Entering the 1990s, France and Great Britain were leading competitors with America in the production of missiles. The European conglomerate, Arianespace, was the world leader in the production of commercial satellites.

The change in America's relationship with the former Soviet Union also helped to create a highly competitive international market for commercially operated communication satellites and low-budget commercial satellites. Another factor in creating this market was an economic recession in the early 1990s, which forced smaller nations to invest in joint ventures in science and industry.

RESEARCH AND TECHNOLOGY

With a growing interest in the commercial space market, manufacturers of guided missile and space vehicle propulsion systems were focusing on low-cost technology. Engines that could be manufactured for less money and carry heavier payloads for fewer trips were the goals of the industry's research efforts.

In the early 1990s, industry leaders were developing Advanced Launch Systems using cryogenic fuels, as opposed to stored fuels. These systems were also capable of carrying extremely heavy payloads. Another development that met the demand for sending heavy payloads into space was the use of highly successful ballistic missile propulsion units on launch vehicles. In 1993, Lockheed Corp. proposed developing engines for space vehicles similar to its solid-fuelled sea-launched missiles.

From the 1970s to the early 1990s, there was strong interest in electronic propulsion systems, but given the cost of this research and the success of solid-fuel systems, research efforts were limited until the 1990s, when cost-cutting objectives renewed interest in this area. According to *Aviation Week and Space Technology*, "to put payloads into their proper orbits, chemical rockets require more fuel than EP (electronic propulsion) systems to do the same job." These systems required burning fuels, but two to three times less than solid-fuelled propulsion systems.

INDUSTRY INFORMATION SOURCES

Bright, Charles D, *The Jet Makers: The Aerospace Industry 1945-1972,* Lawrence: Regents Press, 1978.

Corcoran, Elizabeth and Tim Beardsley, "The New Space Race," *Scientific American,* July 1990.

Covault, Craig, "Ambitious Decade Ahead for Europe's Space Effort," *Aviation Week and Space Technology,* March 15, 1993.

Dornheim, Michael A., "USAF May Pay Hercules For SRMU Losses," *Aviation Week and Space Technology,* March 1, 1993.

Kandebo, Stanley W., "France Records Advances in Scramjet Program," *Aviation Week and Space Technology,* January 4, 1993.

Lavitt, Michael O., "Market Forces," *Aviation Week and Space Technology,* April 5, 1993.

Lenorovitz, Jeffery M., "Task Force Urges SSME Safety Improvements," *Aviation Week and Space Technology,* March 8, 1993.

"Lockheed Develops Low-End Launch Vehicle," *Aviation Week and Space Technology,* May 10, 1993.

"McDonnell Douglas Posts Record First-Quarter Earnings," *Aviation Week and Space Technology,* April 26, 1993.

Payne, Seth, "Can't Afford NASA? Call Rent-A-Rocket," *Business Week,* March 12, 1990.

"Potential Launch Cost Reduction Spurs Electrical Propulsion Tests," *Aviation Week and Space Technology,* December 14/21, 1992.

"Russian Proton Booster Offered in Indonesian Launch Competition," *Aviation Week And Space Technology,* April 12, 1993.

Schine, Eric, "Lockheed Sticks to Its Guns," *Business Week,* April 26, 1993.

Scovell, Dawn, "Solid Rockets," *Aerospace America,* December 1992.

"Steady Growth Seen For Commercial Space," *Aviation Week and Space Technology,* March 15, 1993.

—Paola Trimarco

SIC 3769

SPACE VEHICLE EQUIPMENT, NOT ELSEWHERE CLASSIFIED

This category covers establishments primarily engaged in manufacturing guided missile and space vehicle parts and auxiliary equipment, not elsewhere classified. This industry also includes establishments owned by manufacturers of guided missile and space vehicle parts and auxiliary equipment, not elsewhere classified, and primarily engaged in research and development on such products, whether from enterprise funds or on a contract or fee basis. Establishments primarily engaged in manufacturing navigational and guidance systems are classified in **SIC 3812: Search, Detection, Navigation, Guidance, Aeronautical, and Nautical Systems and Instruments.** Research and Development on guided missile and space vehicle parts, on a contract or fee basis by establishments not owned by manufacturers of such products, are classified in **SIC 8731: Commercial Physical and Biological Research.**

Products manufactured by this industry are mostly airframe assemblies for guided missiles, castings for missiles and missile components, nose cones for guided missiles, and space capsules for space vehicles. In the early 1990s, roughly 70 percent of this industry's production went towards manufacturing these types of products and the remaining 30 percent went towards research and development.

In 1992, this industry's sales were valued at $1.6 billion, a considerable drop from 1.8 billion in sales in 1988, at the height of the larger aerospace industry's production. The U.S. government is this industry's largest customer, with over 65 percent of the market.

The number of workers in this industry also dropped during this time period from 19,400 in 1988 to 9,800 in 1992. Over half of this industry's work force consisted of production workers. Engineers made up the largest occupation employed by this industry, with roughly equal numbers of aeronautical, electrical, and industrial engineers. Other major occupations found in this industry include aeronautical and electrical technicians and astronomical scientists.

The growth and stability of this industry is dependent on manufacturers of complete guided missiles and space vehicles (**SIC 3761: Manufacturers of Guided Missiles and Space Vehicles**), who act as primary contractors in the manufacturing of these products. Both industries rely largely on the world political situation, which dictated military needs, and since the late 1980s, on the competitiveness of the world market for space exploration and commercial space ventures, mainly in launching communications satellites.

Like other sectors of the aerospace industry, establishments in this industry have been primarily exporters in international trade. In 1992, this industry exported over one billion dollars in equipment to overseas markets. In the same year, this industry only imported $95,000 in products.

In 1992, the industry was lead by Pneumo Abex Corp., with $824 million in gross sales, followed by Martin Marietta Corporation's Manned Space Systems, with $818 million in sales, and Ferranti Defense with $300 million in sales.

Research and development in the production of guided missile and space vehicle equipment and auxiliary parts followed the trend of the aerospace industry as a whole in focusing on reduced-cost reusable products. In the early 1990s, new developments to emerge from this industry included pressurized lockers for space research on space shuttles, external vehicle tanks for manned missions, and equipment for materials processing by commercial industries.

INDUSTRY INFORMATION SOURCES

Asker, James R. "NASA Leases Spacehab for $184 Million for Commercial Experiments on Shuttle," *Aviation Week and Space Technology,* December 10, 1990.

Kolcum, Edward H. "Martin Marietta Poised to Adapt External Tank for NLS Core Vehicles," *Aviation Week and Space Technology,* August 26, 1991.

Lavitt, Michael O. "Market Focus," *Aviation Week and Space Technology,* April 5, 1993.

—Paola Trimarco

SIC 3792

TRAVEL TRAILERS AND CAMPERS

This industry consists of establishments primarily engaged in the manufacture of travel trailers and chassis and campers for attachment to motor vehicles, pickup coaches and caps, covers and canopies for mounting on pick-up trucks, and tent camping trailers. This classification includes travel trailers of up to 35 feet long and 8 feet wide (with storage facilities for waste and water), but excludes mobile home manufacturers. Mobile home manufacturers are classified in **SIC 3716: Motor Homes**.

Upon entering the 1990s this industry's tow-trailer leaders included Fleetwood Enterprises Inc., with approximately 20 percent of the market, followed by a pack of other companies jockeying for position in the five to eight percent market share range. These establishments include Jayco Inc., Skyline Corp., Coachman Industries Inc., Starcraft Corporation, and Mallard Coach Company, Inc.

Fleetwood is also the leader in folding trailer manufacturing, with more than 30 percent of the market and $72 million in sales in 1992; Jayco is a distant second with approximately 17 percent of the market.

In the United States there are approximately 100 establishments in this industry. Most are private subsidiaries of companies that manufacture a range of recreational vehicles. Manufacturers of trailers and campers often assemble chassis made elsewhere on to their products; these chassis are produced by large auto makers such as Ford and General Motors.

Travel trailers and pick-up cabs were introduced in the early 1930s, with camper attachments entering the market in the late 1940s. The emergence of mobile homes, also in the late 1940s, shifted manufacturers' emphasis away from travel trailers and camper attachments. However, while mobile homes dominated the recreational vehicle market in the 1950s and 1960s, the market for travel trailers and camper attachments continued to grow.

The economic recessions of the 1970s and 1980s dramatically reduced sales and manufacturing in this industry. Also, during that time some travel trailer and chassis producers were negatively effected by recalls of their products; over 10,000 units of small mobile homes attached to Toyota pick-up truck chassis were recalled.

The future for the industry is an uncertain one. The recreational vehicle field is an increasingly competitive and crowded one. Some analysts feel that the continued development of other types of recreational vehicles bodes ill for this segment of the transportation manufacturing industry. Richard Rescigno of *Barron's*, however, has predicted that sales of small campers and travel trailers might actually improve in the 1990s since such products are at the inexpensive end of the recreational vehicle market. Rescigno reasons that such products would appeal to the growing number of retirees on limited incomes.

INDUSTRY INFORMATION SOURCES

Callahan, Joseph M. "Winnebago's Hanson: Building Up, Up, Up," *Automotive Industries*, November 1984.

Rescigno, Richard. "Revved Up For Recovery: Recreational-Vehicle Makers Seem Ready To Roll Again," *Barron's*, June 17, 1991.

RV Business, April 5, 1991: 1.

—Paola Trimarco

SIC 3795

TANKS AND TANK COMPONENTS

This category covers establishments primarily engaged in manufacturing complete tanks, specialized components for tanks, and self-propelled weapons. Establishments primarily engaged in manufacturing military vehicles, except tanks and self propelled weapons, are classified in Industry Group 371, and those manufacturing tank engines are classified in Industry Group 351.

INDUSTRY SNAPSHOT

The reduction in the United States military budget has had a severe impact on the defense industry. Goods and services purchased by the U.S. Department of Defense is expected to fall by $28.3 billion to $122.3 billion or 18 percent between the years 1987 and 1997. Lower defense spending has resulted in the consolidation and closure of many defense-related manufacturers and subcontractors with further structural adjustments needed to accommodate the proposed cutbacks. The tank manufacturing and component industry will receive the largest drop in funding as the Pentagon expects spending to drop from $2.5 billion to $491 million over this time period resulting in an 80 percent decline in overall procurement.

The two largest U.S. tank manufacturers, General Dynamics Corporation of Virginia and FMC Corporation of Illinois, have adopted different corporate strategies to survive in this uncertain environment. In two years General Dynamics shed over $3 billion in assets and refocused its businesses into three main areas: nuclear submarine, spacecraft, and armored vehicles. The FMC Corporation, on the other hand, has pursued a diversification strategy into performance chemicals and machine and equipment. FMC's defense systems unit has also placed a greater emphasis on foreign sales to achieve a global base for its products and services.

ORGANIZATION AND STRUCTURE

Despite the decline in defense spending that began in the late 1980s, there remains a market for tanks and tank components in most parts of the world; many countries—including the United States—have considerable amounts of antiquated equipment that will eventually either have to be replaced or modernized. The tank manufacturing and component industry has relied mostly on government procurement trends to fund both the development and production of military armor. With few exceptions, defense manufacturers are privately held. General Dynamics Corporation of Falls Church, Virginia and FMC Corporation of Chicago are the two largest armored tank producers in the United States.

Most of the contracts issued by the U.S. Department of Defense are fixed-price contracts that cover both the research/development and production of armored vehicles. These contracts have been problematic for manufacturers because they require considerable investment during the development stage. Even though many of these contracts are multi-year and provide compensation if cancelled, such payments usually do not cover the price of new machinery and plants. As a result, there has been a consolidation of players in the defense industry with many manufacturers having to shed facilities and workers to remain competitive in an uncertain defense spending environment.

Plants that manufacture tanks and tank components vary between those that are contractor owned and others that are government owned and contractor operated. In the latter case, a plant may close but the facilities remain for possible future mobilization. It is extremely expensive, however, to mothball such facilities and then reopen them.

The tank plants in Detroit, Michigan and Lima, Ohio are government owned and operated by General Dynamics, Land System Division. Both facilities are capable of assembling completed tanks (the Lima plant produces tank components as well). While the Detroit and Lima plants are responsible for the assembly of the M1A1 and M1A2 tanks, they rely on countless subcontractors across the United States to supply them with key components in the tank assembly process. BMY Combat Systems in York, Pennsylvania is the only factory in the United States making self-propelled artillery systems (M109s) and the FMC Corporations, Ground Systems Division at San Jose, California is the only factory making armored personnel carriers (APCs) such as the M2/M3 Bradley and the M113 series.

Concerns exist that the United States is only considering cost-cutting procedures in the early 1990s without taking into account the possibility of future needs in the defense industry.

Some manufacturers of tanks and tank components have invested their own money in private venture developments either for the home market or, more often, for the export market. (For instance, the Royal Thai Army ordered Textrons' Cadillac Gage Stingray, a full tracked armored vehicle.) When a vehicle is built as a private venture, the entire development, test, and production cycles are compressed. While there is an obvious element of risk in this type of program, the user gets his vehicles much sooner and cheaper. In 1992 the United States exported a total of 1,241 tanks: 577 to Turkey, 492 to Greece, 96 to Spain, 75 to Egypt, and one to Singapore.

The reduction in U.S. military spending has hindered the ability of defense manufacturers to negotiate and complete private ventures. Minimal levels of Pentagon procurement of tank and tank components are required for the survival of U.S. tank production facilities until the proposed production of the next-generation Block III tank in 1997. The defense industry requires a sound and profitable production base for future investment and to attract potential foreign orders by maintaining stable cost/pricing levels.

The keys to achieving a stable industrial base are keeping the two major tank facilities in Detroit and Lima up and running—to guarantee a stable production environment which allows for controlled planning and balanced pricing levels—-and investment in research and technology to ensure state- of-the-art equipment.

BACKGROUND AND DEVELOPMENT

The tank, a British invention from World War I, had the mission of advancing on the static German defense lines in northern France. It was developed to flatten thick coils of barbed wire, fend off machine-gun fire, and to rumble over previously inviolable trenches. In short, the tank was to do what great waves of infantry men had failed to do—break the stalemate of trench warfare.

The tank performed as required during World War I but was viewed by most strategists as merely a precursor for infantry attack. That sentiment was ultimately put to rest by the German *blitzkrieg* into Poland in September of 1939, when a Polish brigade of cavalry vainly attacked an onrushing wedge of German tanks.

In June of 1920 the U.S. National Defense Act was passed into law. This act disbanded the army's tank corps, a unit created three years previously, and placed all tanks under the command of the infantry branch. Further, the act stipulated that no new branch of the army, such as a revived tank corps, could be created without congressional approval. This decision was based on the army's conclusion that the tank corps had failed to provide either a doctrine or a justification for itself as an independent arm of the American war effort.

The early perception was that the tank-based armies of the 20th century were slower then the foot soldier's marching rate of a century before. This speculation concerning tank warfare inhibited its role as a support weapon for the infantry for years.

Following World War I, the most plausible threat to United States security was a naval war in the Pacific against Japan. In the following decade, Congress reduced the military budget. Senior officers cut costs by halting production and maintenance of equipment. Inevitably, tanks suffered from this policy, and the U.S. Army had no large tank formations during this interwar period.

The beginning of the mechanization of the U.S. Army began in 1928 after Secretary of War Dwight D.

Davies' observed the British Army's Experimental Mechanical Armed Force. In response, the United States developed the Christie, complete with a modern suspension system and capable of speeds approaching 40 miles per hour. It was during this period that the war department recognized that the development of future armies depended on the proliferation of a mechanized force. The tank was, for the first time, perceived as an offensive power in its own right.

In the spring of 1939, America's main battle tanks were still the M1917 and the Mark VIII of World War I vintage. In the previous several years the army had produced several hundred tanks, the majority of these being experimental models of light tanks armored with only machine guns. Although some effort had been made to keep the United States abreast of mechanized warfare, until the outbreak of World War II the American experience of armor hardly existed.

Following the collapse of France in June of 1940, Congress passed a munitions program to provide material for an army of 1.2 million. Supplemental defense appropriations acts authorized $5 billion for armed forces expenditure. By the end of 1940 the country had produced only 331 tanks. By the end of 1941 it had outproduced Germany with 4,052 tanks, while tank production for the next two years was 24,997 and 29,497 tanks respectively. By the end of the war in Europe, American industry had produced 88,410 tanks, of which 57,027 were medium tanks. More than 8,000 subcontractors working in some 850 different towns and cities throughout the United States had a hand in the production of these tanks.

By 1943, the U.S. Army had created 16 armored divisions and 65 independent tank battalions. Each of these armored divisions consisted of 10,937 men and 2,650 vehicles, of which 248 were tanks. Tanks were used as a highly mobile force for pursuit, exploitation, and disruption of unarmored forces, rather than as an arm of attack against other armored formations. This doctrine had important consequences for American tank design and development. The first of the wartime tanks, the M3 Stuart light tank and M3 Grant/Lee medium tank were developed from pre-war designs. The main American battle tank of the war, the M4 Sherman, was first planned in March of 1941 and produced a year later. Weighing approximately 33 tons and equipped with a 75mm dual-purpose gun, it was highly maneuverable and reliable and boasted a road speed of just under 30 miles per hour (mph).

The U.S. responded to Germans' Panther and Tiger tanks by producing the M26 Pershing. This tank held a 90mm gun, weighed 42.5 tons, and had a top speed of 25 mph. This tank, however, played a rela-

tively small role in the war because it had less speed and maneuverability than the M4 Sherman and because tactical air power was generally used to halt the German armored thrust. By 1947, due to the success of air power and the invention of atomic weapons, the role of the tank had again come into question.

During the Korean War, American tanks proved less than perfect. The M26 Pershing was underpowered for Korea's mountainous terrain, and the army at first was compelled to rely upon its Shermans. The army eventually added the more powerful M46 and M47 Patton tanks to its lineup. Yet, the Korean War confirmed the tank's role as an essential part of the U.S. fighting forces. The heavier armor developed during this conflict changed the tank's principal role to fighting and destroying other tanks.

Throughout the 1950s and early 1960s, the U.S. Army continued to regard its armored forces as central to its fighting doctrine. When U.S. forces were committed to Vietnam in 1965, however, armor had a reduced role. Still, the M48 tanks' firepower and mobility were valuable assets in creating quick reaction teams for preventing infiltration by enemy units. But to work well, the teams had to be part of an all arms-formation; for without helicopters, air and artillery support, and infantry, the armored units could be unwieldy, noisy, and less then effective. Roles such as route security, convoy escort, and border protection were successfully carried out by tank battalions.

The were no major developments in tanks during the 1970s. The anti-war movement of the late 1960s and early 1970s—coupled with the perception that the United States had fought a losing battle—resulted in the redeployment of government resources into domestic endeavors. In 1980, however, President Reagan vowed to rearm America with an unprecedented $1.6 trillion defense spending program over the next six years. The Defense Department's renewed interest in planning and multi-year funding of contracts boosted the sagging defense industry. The tanks and tank component sector of the defense industry was expected to grow by 12.6 percent over this period with nondefense growth hovering at 4.5 percent.

The army's M-1 tank benefited greatly from the increased defense expenditures. A heavy tank with a combat load of 54.5 tons, the M-1 was able to carry a crew of four and had a maximum speed of 45 mph on the road and 30 mph cross country. The tank's road range stood at 275 miles and it main armament was a 105mm gun. The M-1 tank was criticized for transmission malfunctions and the need frequent maintenance of other components during the test process. In addition, the M-1 was found to be incapable of digging itself into a hull-down battle position without the assistance of bulldozers. Nonetheless, the Defense Department budgeted for 7,058 M-1s at a cost of roughly $19 billion.

By 1986, defense budget outlays had grown to $200 million annually. These high levels of defense spending stimulated many U.S. industries. In 1986, 75 sectors of the economy produced at least five percent of their output for defense purposes and 13 sectors produced at least 30 percent of their output for delivery to the U.S. Department of Defense. The passage of the Gramm-Rudman deficit reduction bill as well as reduced government research and development budgets, however, resulted in declines in defense production throughout the remainder of the 1980s.

CURRENT CONDITIONS

The multi-year structure of rearmature programs from the 1980s temporarily insulated the defense industry from budget cuts. In the wake of reduced defense expenditures, many manufacturers began to look to foreign markets to maintain and expand their production base. In 1989 General Dynamics Land System Division was awarded a letter contract for manufacturing technical assistance to support the coproduction of M1A1 tanks in Egypt—a program expected to be worth $1.2 billion to General Dynamics over ten years.

The trend toward private venture projects and cooperative agreements with foreign countries is necessary for the survival of U.S. defense manufacturers. In a 1989 statement, General Dynamics Corporation indicated that even with these agreements the fate of its two tank assembly facilities in Sterling Heights, Michigan and Lima, Ohio was tied to the extension of the M1A1 multi-year contract in 1991. The closure of the Warren, Michigan plant alone would result in the layoff of 1,300 workers.

Significant events in the 1990s that had a major impact on defense forces and their supporting industries include the departure of Soviet forces from Eastern Europe; the dismantling of the Warsaw Pact; the reunification of East and West Germany; the successful eviction of Iraq from Kuwait by the Allied coalition forces; and various United Nations peace-keeping efforts. The very success of Operation Desert Storm prompted questioning in the U.S. legislature about the rationale behind developing new, costly weapons systems. (The ground war lasted just 100 hours with little loss of life or equipment on the Allied Coalition side while Iraqi forces suffered massive losses in both men and equipment.)

In 1990 the army received $14.3 billion to purchase weapon systems; this figure fell to $10.6 billion in 1991 and was expected to fall to $8.7 billion in 1992 and $8.4 billion in 1993. Army officials expected the decline in procurement funding to slip to $6 billion by the mid-1990s. These cuts were expected severely impact the army's armor modernization plans, particularly the development of the Block III battle tank. The fielding of this tank was delayed from 1997 to 2001.

The reduction in the U.S. military budget has also had a direct effected on the ability of defense manufacturers to compete in foreign markets. Foreign sales of tank and tank components are an essential element in the survival of U.S. tank production facilities. The defense industry requires a sound and profitable production base in order to invest in the future and to maintain current cost/pricing levels. The U.S. Army's 1990 proposal to slice its purchase of General Dynamics M1A2 tanks to 62 from the formally planned 3,000 and to terminate the procurement of M1A1 has introduced an element of pricing uncertainty in completed foreign tank sales contracts and has also cast doubt on the U.S. manufacturers' ability to meet future foreign demand. The reduced production capacity of General Dynamics M1A2 tanks is expected to increase costs from about $3 million to $4.5 million per tank, inducing foreign buyers to pursue cheaper markets for these products.

A 1991 Defense Department report projected that its purchases for goods and services would fall by $28.3 billion to $122.3 billion between 1989 and 1997—an overall decline of 18 percent. The tanks and tank component manufacturing industry was expected to experience a drop from $2.5 billion to $491 million over this same period.

In 1992 the Army received appropriations of $225 million for tank upgrades. (Army officials predicted that roughly $250 million annually for the following five to six years was needed to promote a reasonable modernization program.) Congress has increased pressure on Army officials to upgrade the older M1 tanks with new armor, electronics, and more powerful firepower. This upgrade was expected to spread defense spending proportionally among component suppliers.

INDUSTRY LEADERS

General Dynamics Corporation, the Falls Church, Virginia-based company is the nation's fourth largest defense contractor and produces a wide range of major weapons systems for all branches of the armed forces. In 1992 the company had $3.4 billion in military sales. Of this total, 94 percent of military sales was to the U.S. government with the remaining six percent or

$210 million to foreign countries. In the early 1990s the company has sold off $3 billion in assets and refocused its businesses into three main areas: nuclear submarines, spacecraft, and armored vehicles. The armored vehicles division produces the M1 series main battle tank and in 1992 delivered 401 M1 tanks for sales of $1.2 billion, 36 percent of the company's total sales.

Chicago-based FMC Corporation produces the Bradley armored tank. FMC recently merged with Harsco Corporation in a 60-40 venture which combined their defense businesses. The new company's products include armored tanks, artillery systems, and naval guns. In 1992 the company had total sales of $3.9 billion with defense systems accounting for $1.1 billion or 28 percent of total sales. Foreign sales account for 24 percent of FMC's revenues, and the company views foreign expansion as the key to future growth.

Subcontractors make up the remainder of the industry players in the tank and tank components industry. This group includes not only many of the top ten defense manufacturers, but also hundreds of smaller entities which produce more specialized and highly sophisticated subsystem equipment. Companies that fall into this category include Texas Instruments which produces electrical and electronic control devices and electronic control systems; Textron, Inc.'s Cadillac Gage Division which constructs armored vehicles and propulsion systems; Control Data Corporation which assembles flat panel display systems and ground-based fire control systems; Raytheon Company which produces radar and sonar systems; and Martin Marietta Corporation which manufactures advanced computer systems for military applications.

WORK FORCE

Employment in defense-related industries has fallen by 334,000 jobs or 23 percent since the winding down of the procurement policies of the early to mid-1980s. In the tank and tank components industry, approximately 25 percent of the plant labor force is directly engaged in production, while the remaining 75 percent is engaged in management and support functions.

AMERICA AND THE WORLD

The United States' tank and tank components industry is the largest and most technically advanced in the world. The health of the industry is closely tied to its ability to forge international cooperative agreements with the larger arms-producing countries such as Russia, Germany, Britain, France, and China and to

increase foreign military sales of tanks and tank conversion kits. In 1992, the United States exported 1,241 tanks; he success of these programs depends on the ability of the United States to effectively maintain its industrial base. The reduction in the U.S. military budget has had a direct impact on the ability of defense manufacturers to compete in foreign markets. Foreign sales of tank and tank components are an essential element in the survival of U.S. tank production facilities. In order to achieve this goal, the industry requires a sound and profitable production base to invest in the future and to maintain current cost/pricing levels. By protecting the industrial base, the United States will be able to honor pricing levels in completed foreign tank sales contracts and to assure foreigners of the U.S. manufacturers' ability to meet future demand at competitive pricing levels.

RESEARCH AND TECHNOLOGY

Much of the production in the defense industries is inherently inefficient because high volume, mass production techniques are not applicable. Except for the turret and hull components of a tank, most of the production involves small batch processing of relatively complex items with frequent modifications or changes in design. In this type of low volume manufacturing, specialized equipment is under utilized and inventories are relatively high.

Although computer-aided automation has moved slowly into the tank production process, computer-controlled machine tools are standard fixtures in machining operations. Examples of these processes include automated spray systems used for coating metals; automated inspection and optical measuring systems; and computer-aided manufacturing applications used for forging and electron beam welding in tank production. Other areas of the production process which have been computerized consist of process modelling, performance measurement, and on-line production information systems.

Many of the technological changes which have taken place in tank manufacturing involve metalworking. Automated metal cutting systems are in place which use computer-controlled laser machining techniques. Computer-integrated welding systems are in place which make use of sensory process controls. The technology is available to transform the manufacturing system of tank production facilities into a totally computer-integrated process, but the economies of scale associated with expensive outlays in plant and equipment have deterred the manufacturers from pursuing this option.

In the mid-1990s main battle tanks possessed nuclear, biological and chemical (NBC) systems which regulate the environment within the tank in case of this type of warfare. The Department of Defense has made land navigational systems a priority for improvement and installation in all tank subsystems. In the wake of Operation Desert Storm, more emphasis is being placed in the development of friend or foe devices to reduce friendly fire causalities. Such technology will become a part of the tank's vehicle protection system which already includes threat displays, sensors, and decoy launchers.

Other areas of research include ways to construct smaller and lighter main battle tanks, armored turrets to protect the vulnerable top of the tank, development of more powerful cannons, experimentation into a common chassis for futuristic combat vehicles, guns that will utilize electromagnetic and electrothermal cannons. Electromagnetic guns use electric currents as their power source and can power a round farther and faster than a conventional cannon. Electrothermal guns use hot gases and a high energy charge to propel artillery with comparable results.

INDUSTRY INFORMATION SOURCES

Baker, Caleb, "Army Weapon Budget Shortfall Hits Armor Modernization Plan Budget," *Defense News*, 1990.

————, "Revised ASM Plan Emphasizes Support Vehicles Over Tanks," *Defense News*, 1991.

Belloc, Hilaire, *The Elements of the Great War*, Hearts International Library Company, 1970.

Egyptian Defense Minister on Arms Production and Purchases, The British Broadcasting Corporation, 1987.

"Employment, More Than 334,000 Jobs Were Lost In Defense-Related Industries since 1986," *Daily Report For Executives*, 1993.

"General Dynamic Gets First Egyptian M1A1 Coproduction Contract," *Aerospace Daily*, 1989.

Graham, George, and Martin Dickson, "U.S. Rethinks Arms Procurement Philosophy," *Financial Times*, 1992.

Humble, Richard, *Tanks*, Weidenfeld & Nicolson, 1977.

"Industrial Base, Pentagon Report Projects Defense Spending by Industry, State," *Federal Contracts Report*, 1991.

"Is Industry Ready For Defense Buildup?" *Business Week*, 1982.

Jane's Armour and Artillery, London: Janes Info Group, 1987.

Kelly, Orr, *King of the Killing Zone*, New York: W.W. Norton, 1989.

"Levin Says Warren Tank Plant Threatened," United Press International, 1988.

Mackay, Robert, "Saudi Arabia to Buy 315 Next-generation Tanks," United Press International, 1990.

Middleton, Drew, "British Expert Says M-1 Tank May Be Hailed As Innovation," *New York Times*, 1982.

Morrison, David, "Base Concerns-As the Services Scale Back Their Weapon Buys, The Health of the Defense Industrial Base is Bound to Suffer," *Government Executive*, 1992.

Munro, Neil, "U.S. Army Hurries Tank Upgrade Plans," *Defense News*, 1992.

"Pentagon Issues Report Projecting Defense Spending Industry-By-Industry," *Daily Report For Executives*, 1991.

Silverberg, David, "U.S. Army Tank Cuts Put Foreign Sales in Doubt," *Defense News*, 1990.

Simpkin, Richard, *Tank Warfare: An Analysis of Soviet and Nato Tank Philosophy*, New York: Crane Russak, 1979.

"Take Time For Take Research," *Defense News*, 1990.

"Turkey: U.S. Tank," *Defense and Foreign Affairs*, 1986.

"U.N. Lists Big Tank Imports By Greece and Turkey," Reuters, Limited, 1993.

—Andrew Burke

SIC 3799

TRANSPORTATION EQUIPMENT, NOT ELSEWHERE CLASSIFIED

This industry consists of establishments primarily engaged in manufacturing transportation equipment, not elsewhere classified. The transportation equipment classified under this industry includes specialty vehicles and all-terrain vehicles for military, industrial and agricultural purposes; towing bars and systems and trailers for transporting animals; recreational vehicles, such as snowmobiles, water jet-skis, golf carts and recreational all-terrain vehicles; boat trailers; and wheelbarrows. Associated establishments involved in manufacturing industrial vehicles are discussed in **SIC 3537: Industrial Trucks, Tractors, Trailers, and Stackers.**

In 1993 the leading establishments in the most important sections of this industry were Stewart and Stevenson Services, Inc., manufacturers of military transport and aircraft towing equipment; TriMas Corp., manufacturers of industrial trailer system products; and Polaris Industries, L.P., manufacturer of snowmobiles and recreational all-terrain vehicles.

All-terrain vehicles, built with wide tires for driving over difficult terrain and road conditions, are produced primarily for military purposes. For this reason, the prosperity and growth of this segment of the industry is dependent on government defense spending. With the decreases in defense spending for the 1990s, manufacturers of all-terrain vehicles began to diversify; Oshkosh Truck Corp., which in 1991 had sales of over $600 million (due mainly to the Persian Gulf War), responded to a reduction in military orders and defense spending proposals by diversifying into hauling trucks and cement mixers.

All-terrain recreational vehicles carry only a small portion of the recreational vehicle market. Snowmobiles dominate the market. In 1954, Polaris Industries, L.P. became the first American manufacturer to produce snowmobiles. In the United States, snowmobile sales reached their peak in 1971, when over 500,000 were sold. In the late 1970s and early 1980s, snowmobile sales decreased dramatically, the ''victims of higher energy costs, recessions, a few snowless winters, and a serious rash of overbuilding by manufactur-

ers,'' said *Forbes*. By 1983 only 87,000 snowmobiles were sold in the United States. At the beginning of the 1990s, sales figures and profits began to increase again, with Polaris controlling 30 percent of the market, followed closely by Arctco, Inc., manufacturer of the Arctic Cat product line.

INDUSTRY INFORMATION SOURCES

Byrne, Harlan S. ''Oshkosh Truck Corp.: A Bright Outlook Despite Pentagon Cutbacks,'' *Barron's,* January 20, 1992.

Dubashi, Jagannath. ''Designer Trucks,'' *Financial World,* May 18, 1987.

Harris, John. ''Noisemakers,'' *Forbes,* October 29, 1990.

''Kawasaki's Newest Addition is Stubborn as a Mule 4X4,'' *Purchasing,* September 14, 1989.

Winter, Don. ''Air Cushion Vehicle Looks for a Federally Funded Niche,'' *Traffic World,* September 18, 1989.

—Paola Trimarco

MEASURING, ANALYZING & CONTROLLING INSTRUMENTS

SIC 3812

SEARCH, DETECTION, NAVIGATION, GUIDANCE, AERONAUTICAL, AND NAUTICAL SYSTEMS AND INSTRUMENTS

This category includes establishments primarily engaged in manufacturing search, detection, navigation, guidance, aeronautical, and nautical systems and instruments. Important products of this industry are radar systems and equipment; sonar systems and equipment; navigation systems and equipment; countermeasures equipment; aircraft and missile control systems and equipment; flight and navigation sensors, transmitters, and displays; gyroscopes; airframe equipment instruments; and speed, pitch, and roll navigational instruments and systems. Establishments primarily engaged in manufacturing aircraft engine instruments or meteorological systems and equipment, including weather tracking equipment, are classified in **SIC 3829: Measuring and Controlling Devices, Not Elsewhere Classified.**

INDUSTRY SNAPSHOT

More than 200 companies manufactured search and navigation systems and instruments in 1991. Together, these establishments generated over $34.4 billion in shipments. As a result of decreasing defense budgets starting in the mid-1980s, the end of the Cold War, and diminished commercial aircraft industry purchases as a result of the recession of the early 1990s, the search and navigation industry experienced declines in shipments in the early 1990s. Sharp reductions in the military-related expenditures that formed the backbone of industry profits hastened restructuring

and globalization trends already evident in the industry. In order to remain profitable in an economically straitened and increasingly competitive global marketplace, manufacturers in this industry took steps that included: divestiture of low profit divisions; diversification of product lines into nonmilitary markets; workforce cutbacks; new techniques for improving productivity; and increased acquisition, merger, and joint venture activity.

ORGANIZATION AND STRUCTURE

With few exceptions, the principle suppliers of search and navigation equipment are the same contractors who comprise the larger U.S. aerospace industry. The search and navigation equipment industry accounted for about one-quarter of aerospace industry shipments ($129 billion) in 1991, which in turn represented about two-thirds of the worldwide aerospace industry. Many of the largest and most recognizable corporations in the United States—including AT&T, Boeing, Chrysler, General Electric, General Motors, and IBM—manufacture search and navigation industry products for the domestic and international defense and commercial markets.

Along with such aerospace sectors as the business and commercial jet, helicopter, aircraft maintenance, and spare parts industries, the search and navigation industry comprises a so-called ''niche segment'' of the larger aerospace manufacturing group. A substantial majority of the industry's product types fall into the ''avionics''—aviation electronics—product classification, which includes aeronautic radar systems, air traffic control systems, weaponry sighting and fire control systems, and autopilots. Product groups traditionally associated with the avionics industry but excluded from the search and navigation industry include flight trainers and simulators (**SIC 3699: Electrical Machinery, Equipment, and Supplies, Not Elsewhere Classified**) and radio communications equipment and telemetry systems and equipment (**SIC 3663: Radio and Television Broadcasting and Communications Equipment**). Conversely, product groups classified as search and navigation industry products but excluded from the avionics industry's product mix include such nautical instruments as fathometers, hydrophones, sonabuoys, marine sextants, sonar fish finders and other sonar systems, and taffrail logs (i.e., torpedo-shaped instruments dragged behind ships to determine distance traveled or speed).

Historically, the primary customer for industry products has been the U.S. government and in particular the Department of Defense, Federal Aviation Authority, and National Aeronautics and Space Administration. Industry sales to other commercial establishments adhere to the traditional terms and conditions of the business marketplace, and products are evaluated in terms of competitive value for technical superiority, reputation, price, delivery schedule, financing, and reliability. Sales to the federal government, however, tend to follow a highly specialized and structured set of procedures.

Government Procurement. Funds for government search and navigation equipment contracts are authorized by Congress based on budget requests submitted by the executive branch for the end-user agency or department. Congress appropriates specific funding for programs on an annual basis, which often means that programs originally approved for development over several years are subject to adjustments or outright cancellation on a yearly basis. Contractors submit bids to government officials at bidding conferences attended by "prime" contractors—firms or consortia who submit the final integrated system directly to the end-user agency—and subcontractors who attend the conferences to seek out prime contractors with whom to team.

Contracts may be awarded to a single contractor in a "winner-take-all" competition or divided among several contractors or consortia as a percentage of the total awarded contract. Contracts may cover specific phases of the product development process: the concept/design or project definition stage, the prototype or demonstration/validation stage, or the execution or large-scale production stage. Government contracts are also awarded according to the method by which the contractor is paid. In cost reimbursement contracts, the contractor is paid for allowable or "allocable" costs such as engineering and manufacturing expenses, special tooling and test equipment costs,

marketing and administrative expenditures, and the cost of the bid proposal itself. Cost plus fixed fee contracts involve payments to the contractor by the government of a preestablished fee regardless of the firm's actual final costs. Such contracts award contractors who deliver systems below the contracted price and penalize contractors who experience cost overruns. In cost plus incentive fee contracts, the government reimburses the contractor based on the firm's ability to meet certain targets such as cost guidelines, "mission success" parameters, and delivery time constraints.

The average industry "win rate"—the ratio of contracts awarded to total contracts bid on—is about 25 percent in the aerospace and thus the search and navigation industry as a whole. Some firms, however, achieve win rates nearly twice as high.

Contractors are generally paid through periodic "progress payments" for work performed, with a final payment for remaining costs paid upon delivery of the product. Contracts may be extended through "replenishment" and "follow on" orders by the government customer and may be terminated without cause at the sole discretion of the government. Disputes regarding unpaid or overpaid amounts are handled by a Defense Contract Management District Termination Contracting Officer to whom settlement proposals are submitted by the contractor for claimed expenses and "termination costs." The Contracting Officer may award the contractor for work performed prior to the contract's termination or may require that the contractor reimburse funds paid out for canceled work.

The "monopsonic"—or single customer—nature of the government procurement market has led to a unique bifurcation of operations in the search and navigation industry: one set of rules and procedures for commercial clients and a second, completely segregated set of rules and procedures for government contracts. The purpose of the complex government procurement apparatus is to protect the government's interest in fair and reasonable prices, to eliminate contractor fraud, to ensure equal access by all bidders, and to guarantee that the federal funds appropriated for government contracts reflect the economic and social priorities of the government. As a result, the process of bidding on federal contracts entails separate data collection and accounting procedures, conformance to supplier network requirements, adherence to hiring and personnel guidelines, and the disclosure of the contractor's corporate financial information to government auditors. These and other requirements regarding contractor certification and auditing and oversight conformance have resulted in historical labor costs for the industry three times higher for federal contracts (as a percentage of sales) than for equivalent commercial contracts.

Procurement Agencies. Several government agencies perform oversight and other procurement-related functions that directly affect search and navigation industry activities. The Defense Contract Audit Agency oversees expense, scheduling, and product performance reviews of industry contractors and specifies guidelines for planning and implementing federal contracts. The Government Accounting Office (GAO) and Office of Federal Procurement Policy of the Office of Management and Budget perform watchdog reviews of government contracts. "First tier" contractors—firms whose products are delivered directly to a prime contractor—may experience as many as 100 government audits in a single year for pricing, quality, and safety reviews. Similarly, an "operational readiness review" administered by a defense department branch can involve as many as 50 auditors assigned to a single contractor plant at one time.

Contractors may be temporarily suspended or permanently debarred from bidding on government contracts if they are found to be in violation of employment practice laws, standard accounting procedures, or product pricing guidelines. A contractor, for example, who falsely claims that a delivered product has passed more tests than it actually has may be given a "not a responsible contractor" designation and debarred from government bids. In 1989, the GAO guaranteed Litton Industries, a producer of guidance and control systems, a percentage of a production contract for a radar warning receiver when it determined that Loral Corporation had improperly obtained a Litton briefing book outlining Litton's estimated costs. Four years later, the GAO was asked to reconsider a contract awarded to Westinghouse Electric for an anti-submarine warfare sonar system because the contract had been awarded based on a bid that was almost 50 percent lower than the actual cost that the contract's other bidder had incurred for the same work the previous year.

Improper enhancement of a product's capabilities in order to inflate the contractor's bill is termed "goldplating" and represents another significant area of potential abuse which government procurement oversight agencies are charged to monitor.

Other agencies, such as the Navy's Operational Test and Evaluation Force and the Department of Defense's Operational Test and Evaluation Office, perform the tests that gauge the delivered system's adherence to contracted performance specifications. Federal projects like the Army's Contractor Performance Cer-

tification Program recognize contractors who consistently deliver quality products, and the NASA-funded National Technology Transfer Center serves as a medium for sharing federal research project advances with firms in the industry.

Prime Contractors vs. Subcontractors. In 1984, in response to concerns that government contracts were inadequately available to all potential contractors, Congress passed the Competition in Contracting Act, which liberalized the eligibility qualifications of firms submitting bids on federal contracts. Despite such legislation, a senior official of a flight controls subcontractor testified before Congress in 1989 that government procurement policies were freezing subcontractors out of the federal defense market. He cited "decreased progress payment rates, unreasonable profit ceilings, . . . the criminalization of honest mistakes, . . . overzealous audits and increased oversight procedures" as factors preventing subcontractors from competing profitably for government contracts.

Establishments in the search and navigation industry can be classified in terms of their place in the product delivery hierarchy for government procurement contracts. The major prime contractors dominate the industry and are themselves the greatest source of competition for the subcontractors. The influence prime contractors have on subcontractors' profits is reflected in the announcement in the early 1990s by a major prime contractor, Allied Signal, that it planned to reduce its pool of 9,500 suppliers by 79 percent in just two years. Historically, about half of the worth of government contracts to prime contractors is channeled through subcontracts with firms supplying the "primes," and of this amount roughly 50 percent is divided between divisions of other prime contractors and the smaller subcontractors. Government procurement trends fluctuate between an emphasis on "single sourcing"—awarding whole contracts to a major prime contractor—and "multiple sourcing"—distributing procurement funds more evenly through the industry structure.

Business Environment. The unique nature of the government procurement environment entails business trends uncommon in other U.S. industries. Although industry profit rates as a percentage of sales have historically been less than for other industries, profits measured in terms of rate of return on investment are comparable to rates enjoyed by other manufacturing sectors. Search and navigation firms, like other defense sector businesses, may invest in plant and equipment at half the rate of firms in other industries because government contracts often reimburse firms for aging or obsolescent equipment, make available government-owned plants and equipment to the contractor, and offer no guarantee that the plant or equipment utilized for the procured product will ever be contracted for again. Moreover, government progress payments generally cover only "certified costs" and make few allowances for contractor investment in new facilities. Like members of other defense industries, search and navigation contractors require less working capital because they can rely on regular government progress payments instead of depending on unpredictable commercial revenues.

The search and navigation industry is subject to business risks not shared by other American industries. These include unusually high costs for obtaining skilled employees, intense domestic and international competition, continual need to retrain employees and retool facilities, inevitable cost overruns resulting from untried technologies and advanced designs, and instability in the price of raw materials and supplies. Because defense-related products are driven by the requirement of continuing technological improvement and superiority, the rate of obsolescence for industry products is much higher and much more unpredictable than in other American industries.

BACKGROUND AND DEVELOPMENT

Before the invention of the floating gimball gyroscope in the first years of the twentieth century, sea navigators had relied on celestial azimuths, star tables, the sextant, timekeeping instruments, and dead reckoning (a type of inferential estimation) with a magnetic compass.

Rudimentary radio direction-finders consisting of large manually-rotated loop antennas for receiving the homing signals of coastal radio beacons came into wide use in the years before World War I. With the discovery that radio waves striking seagoing vessels produced measurable echoes, radar technology became possible, and by the 1930s, the first on-board VHF radars were installed on ocean liners and naval vessels. By the close of World War II, every capital ship in the U.S. fleet was equipped with a radar unit.

The invention of radar, however, had its greatest impact in air operations and immediately began to play a critical role in the European and Pacific theaters. Prior to its invention, pilots had navigated using magnetic compasses, airspeed instruments, and direction-finding gyros. Radio beacons that enabled pilots to plot their position relative to intercepted radio signals came into use in the late 1920s. These early developments were followed by advances in flight control technology, including General Electric's first flight control

system in 1931 and Honeywell Inc.'s first electric autopilot in 1941.

During World War II, radar proved most effective as a fighter-interceptor tool, a strategic early warning device, an anti-submarine weapon, and as a navigation resource for bombardiers approaching enemy targets. Raytheon Company emerged as the leading producer of radar tubes and systems during the war, and General Electric Company produced more than 50 different types of radar for the U.S. armed services. A precursor of Texas Instruments developed the first anti-submarine detection system in 1941.

Sonar—based on the principal that transmitted sound waves deflecting against underwater objects could be used for detection and identification purposes—had been invented by the U.S. Navy in 1922, and by World War II had become a strategic weapon for airborne, surface ship, and underwater surveillance. Electronic warfare and countermeasures technology grew out of the discovery that radars could be "spoofed" or "jammed" into misinterpreting returning signals. Strips of aluminum foil called "chaff" or "windows" proved to be effective anti-radar measures and led scientists to modify radar technology to overcome such obstacles. Most major radar technology breakthroughs since World War II, such as pulse and phased array, have been attempts to overcome existing or projected jamming or countermeasure technologies.

The development of search and navigation systems in the post-War years was driven by revolutionary advances in jet aircraft, missile technology, satellite systems, digital computers, miniaturization of electronic components, and the specialized needs of the space program. The 1950s witnessed the emergence of the first inertial guidance systems for missiles and submarines. By 1958, the submarine Nautilus was able to successfully navigate underwater to the North Pole using inertial guidance systems modified from Air Force cruise missiles. In 1955, a tactical air navigation system (TACAN) had been introduced, and a year later the first efforts at developing an air collision avoidance system began.

In 1960, Litton Industries introduced an inertial navigation system using a central integrated digital computer for attack aircraft. Four years later, the Navy's Navigational Satellite System became operational with the launching of the Transit satellite. In the 1960s, sonar technology evolved beyond surface ship and submarine applications to networks of fixed sonar systems capable of identifying and tracking vessels from the ocean floor. The decade also saw the emergence of the modern automatic flight control system for aircraft. General Electric's systems for the F-105,

F-111, and F-4 used sensors and computerized components that issued automatic commands to the aircraft's flight control surfaces for stabilization and control. In 1967, the first automatic landing using guidance systems designed for low visibility landing approaches was made at JFK Airport, and Texas Instruments developed the first solid state radar using semiconducting materials and components. Two years later, Texas Instruments delivered its first laser-guided missile systems to the United States Air Force.

During the 1970s, the Global Positioning System satellite network, which is expected eventually to become the dominant source of navigational coordinates, first came under development. Inertial navigators using digital computers also became common on civil and military aircraft. In the early part of the decade, Sundstrand Corporation developed a multimode radar for mapping terrain and seeking airborne targets. The late 1970s and early 1980s saw the emergence of radical new "stealth" or radar-evading "low observable" technologies in the form of the B-1, F-117, and B-2 aircraft. Using radar absorbing materials, innovative airframe shapes, and a variety of other design techniques, the radar "signature" of the B-2 bomber on enemy radar screens was estimated to be the equivalent of a large insect. The emergence of stealth technology—and the likelihood that eventually it would become available to potentially hostile nations—compelled search and navigation manufacturers to investigate alternative technologies to radar detection—such as infrared, ultraviolet, and electro-optical detection—and to search for new, more sensitive radar technologies capable of counteracting stealth "invisibility."

Space programs begun by NASA in the 1960s generated new navigation technologies for satellites, interplanetary probes, lunar landing and "roving" vehicles, and, in the 1980s, the Space Shuttle. In 1985, Texas Instruments developed a new phased array radar technology that offered greater sensitivity and versatility over previous radar systems, and in the latter part of the decade, land navigation systems for automobiles, emergency vehicles, and rental cars began to be developed for complex urban environments. In 1989, the first five Global Positioning System satellites were launched, offering unprecedented accuracies up to a few yards to system users.

The Gulf War between Iraq and a coalition of international forces demonstrated the degree to which search and navigation industry products could influence the outcome of military conflicts. The so-called "Microchip War" was the first conflict fought directly with real-time support from satellite surveillance and communications systems, and Raytheon's Patriot missile—a ground-to-air defensive missile system employing advanced seeking technology—proved itself as a reliable and effective weapon system.

CURRENT CONDITIONS

The search and navigation industry produced more than $34 billion in shipments in 1991 and employed 220,400 workers in early 1993. As a result of the reductions in defense spending of the late 1980s and early 1990s, several establishments in the search and navigation industry committed themselves to reducing the percentage of their contracts dependent on government funds. In 1992, Westinghouse Electric Company's percentage of revenues stemming from government projects was 73 percent, Sundstrand Corporation's was 78 percent, and Martin Marietta's 1989 ratio of government contracts to total contracts was 80 percent. In 1992, Raytheon Company and Westinghouse Electric Company, two of the industry's most prominent manufacturers, announced plans to strive for a 50-50 government/commercial business mix by the mid-1990s.

Product Groups. Search and navigation products can be divided into two broad divisions and several subcategories. Search and detection systems and navigation and guidance systems and equipment ($31.762 billion in 1991 shipments) constitutes about 90 percent of the total search and navigation market and includes the following product groups: light reconnaissance and surveillance systems; identification-friend-or-foe equipment; proximity fuses; radar systems and equipment; sonar search, detection, tracking, and communications equipment; specialized command and control data processing and display equipment; electronic warfare systems and equipment; and navigation systems and equipment, including navigational aids for aircraft, ships, and navigation applications.

The remaining ten percent of the industry's market ($2.656 billion in 1991) consists of aeronautical, nautical, and navigational instruments (excluding aircraft engine instruments) and includes the following product groups: flight and navigation sensors, transmitters, and displays; gyroscopes; airframe equipment instruments; thermocouple and thermocouple lead wire; nautical instruments; other aerospace flight instruments; and parts and components.

Light Reconnaissance and Surveillance Systems. This product group includes infrared, ultraviolet, and visible light reconnaissance systems excluding radar systems such as bomber-defense equipment, weapon fire control equipment, infrared fuses, infrared detection and warning systems, and such night vision equipment as sniperscopes, snooperscopes, and night driving equipment.

Radar Systems and Equipment. This category includes airborne, ship-based, and ground-based radar systems such as early warning radar, air defense and fighter control radar, harbor control radar, meteorological radar, highway speed control radar, bomber navigational radar, space satellite tracking radar, precision approach radar, and other forms of tracking radar technology.

Sonar Systems. This product group consists of airborne-, surface ship-, and submarine-based sonar systems including depth-finding equipment, guidance hydrophones, sonabuoys, sonar fish finders, navigation and mapping sonar, and anti-submarine sonar equipment.

Electronic Warfare Equipment. Electronic warfare systems include such missile-borne and non-missile-borne "countermeasures" equipment as radar jamming devices, underwater countermeasures technology, beam-riders, infrared homing systems, specialized signal processing and intelligence equipment, and other "active" countermeasures equipment (excluding such passive systems as chaff and windows).

Navigation Systems and Equipment. Included in this category are such navigational aids as beacons, transponders, collision warning systems, inertial navigation systems, radio compasses and direction-finders, autopilots, data systems/flight recorders, distance measuring equipment, pilots' "head-up" instrument displays (HUD), aircraft proximity warning systems, flight directors/situation displays, and ship and submarine navigational systems.

Flight and navigation sensors, transmitters, and displays. This product group includes altimeters, compasses, artificial horizon instruments, and airspeed, acceleration, rate-of-climb, angle-of-attack, and bank and turn indicators.

Airframe Equipment Instruments. This category includes position indicators for landing gear and cowl flaps, hydraulic systems for liquid level and temperature indicators, and cabin environmental instruments such as air conditioning, cabin pressure, oxygen, and heating.

INDUSTRY LEADERS

Many of the largest search and navigation industry firms are prominent Fortune 500 multinational corporations whose highly diversified corporate activities cover a wide range of industry groups including heavy construction equipment, engineering services, electronic components, business credit services, office fur-

niture, ship construction, oil and gas services, semiconductors, computers, and radio and television equipment. In 1992, the top ten industry firms accounted for $54 million in sales and employed over 4.5 million workers.

Broad product diversification, aggressive market share protection and expansion strategies, and innovative managerial techniques are among the characteristics of the industry's largest and most dynamic firms. Many of the industry's most recognizable establishments stand at the forefront of American industry's attempts to adopt novel methods for increasing productivity, streamlining corporate decision-making processes, and reshaping rigid organizational structures.

Sundstrand Corporation, a leading producer of commercial and military avionics equipment, adapted to decreased revenues from government military purchases by implementing lower business overhead strategies, cutting back on excess manufacturing capacity, and enhancing employee performance through self-directed work teams and "continuous improvement" programs. Despite the smaller and more competitive market, Sundstrand's 1992 sales were roughly equal to its 1991 levels.

Westinghouse Electronic Systems Group, which manufactures airborne fire control radar, electro-optical and infrared detection systems, anti-submarine combat systems, and command, control, and communications equipment, is the only U.S. company to have implemented "Total Quality Management" techniques in all manufacturing and design phases of product development. Partly as a result of these efforts to make the traditionally separate operations of engineering and manufacturing part of a single unified process, Westinghouse posted total sales and operating revenues of $2.78 billion in 1992.

General Electric Company, a producer of technologies in virtually every product group of the search and navigation industry, implemented a number of strategies in the late 1980s and early 1990s aimed at "empowering" employees and increasing productivity. Three-day employee "Work-Out" seminars and anti-hierarchical programs such as "Boundarylessness" and "co-location," helped GE increase consolidated revenues from 1991 to 1992 by three percent while increasing earnings by seven percent.

Texas Instruments, a leading manufacturer of anti-radar weapons and seekers, electronic warfare systems, and anti-submarine systems, was the first defense contractor to receive the Malcolm Baldridge Quality Award for manufacturing in 1992. Self-directed and cross-functional work teams represent one of Texas Instruments' attempts to implement a "flatter," more quality-driven organizational structure and helped the company achieve 1992 net revenues of $7.44 billion—an increase of over $650 million from 1991.

WORK FORCE

Employment by search and navigation industry firms declined steadily in the late 1980s and early 1990s. From 369,400 employees in 1987, industry employment fell to 314,000 in 1990 and to 220,400 in early 1993. Cutbacks in government defense contracts were the primary reason for these declines although companies with large "backlogs" of awarded but still uncompleted projects continued to hire even despite diminished prospects for new contracts.

In 1993, 32 percent of the industry's employees were classified as production workers. Women comprised 30 percent of the industry workforce in 1990. Establishments in four states—California, New York, Texas, and Florida—employed 53 percent of the industry's workforce in 1987.

Average pay across all occupational categories was $38,491 in early 1993 and average hourly earnings were $15.95. The industry product groups with the highest concentration of employers were missile-borne and space vehicle systems and equipment with 45 establishments, specialized electronic and communication equipment with 44 employers, and light reconnaissance and surveillance systems and equipment with 39 establishments in 1991.

Occupational categories employed in the industry included production workers such as machinists and assemblers, administrative support staff, administrators and executives, and engineers and other technical personnel. The industry employed a wide variety of engineering professionals—from aeronautical, civil, electrical, mechanical, quality assurance, and manufacturing engineers to computer and digital systems, hardware, software, logistical, and algorithm systems engineers. Salaries for degreed engineers ranged between $18,000 and $78,000 per year depending on experience, professional specialization, job responsibilities, and other variables.

The concentration of technical employees in the industry is higher than in many American manufacturing industries. At Westinghouse Electronic Systems Group, for example, almost one-quarter of the firm's 22,000 employees were degreed engineers and scientists in 1992. At E-Systems, Inc., nearly 50 percent of the company's 18,000 employees consisted of engineers, scientists, and other technical professionals. The

company employed 1,500 software engineers alone to design and maintain programming code in 1992.

Because the search and navigation industry historically has been dependent on multi-million dollar, large-scale, limited duration government contracts, fluctuations in employment can be severe. In the early 1990s, for example, Hughes Aircraft Company released 60,000 workers in a single layoff. Layoffs of 8,000 workers or less, however, are more common.

AMERICA AND THE WORLD

The United States continues to lead the world in developing and manufacturing search and navigation instruments and systems. This global dominance is reflected in U.S. export and import superiority relative to other leading nations. In 1992, the search and navigation industry exported about $2.1 billion in shipments. By contrast, Japan, the next leading exporting nation, shipped $301 million in shipments in 1992, followed by Canada ($213 million in shipments), the United Kingdom ($212 million), and France ($168 million). Similarly, while U.S. imports of search and navigation instruments and systems rose to $990 million in 1992, America's closest foreign competitors imported $196 million (Canada), $111 million (the United Kingdom), and $107 million (Japan) in 1992.

Historically, the U.S. search and navigation industry has experienced trade surpluses reflecting its advantage in developing advanced technology. In 1991, however, the U.S. trade surplus in search and navigation equipment declined for the first time—by more than 14 percent over 1990. This unprecedented decline reflected the weakness of the dollar overseas and the increasingly aggressive and competitive global search and navigation market.

Foreign Markets. Prior to an industry-wide slump in the early 1990s, the avionics product groups, which comprise the broad majority of the industry's products, experienced increased demand from democratizing Eastern European nations, growing industrial states in Southeast Asia, and Middle Eastern allies of the United States seeking military avionics upgrades. In the straitened climate of the early 1990s, demand for U.S. search and navigation equipment centered on radar equipment and parts (25 percent of U.S. industry exports in 1992) and avionics equipment for civil aircraft and space navigation applications (20 percent of industry exports in 1992). Potential export markets for U.S. search and navigation instruments include NATO bases in Europe, which were being evaluated for possible conversion into dual-use civil/military facilities, South and Central American nations considering purchases of surveillance equipment for drug interdiction, and Middle Eastern allies reassessing their defense and avionics needs in the post-Gulf War environment.

Air traffic control systems represented the product group with the largest export growth potential for U.S. search and navigation firms. Although the U.S. domestic market was the largest air traffic control market in the world in the early 1990s, contracts for most of its systems and technology upgrades had already been awarded in 1992. U.S. search and navigation firms looked to anticipated upgrades of aging overseas air facilities and new airports planned in such nations as China, Mexico, Iran, Turkey, India, and the former republics of the Soviet Union. Global air traffic control business, which was expected to center on radars, transponders, and integrated control systems, was estimated to total $6.3 billion in 1991 and grow to $14.4 billion by 2002. Air traffic control needs for the former Soviet states was estimated at $12.5 billion alone in 1992.

Joint Ventures. The globalization of the search and navigation market offered the potential for enhanced efficiency, improved market access, and increased worldwide competition. Rationalization, standardization, and interoperability of technology and the growing number of international business arrangements resulted from an increasingly interlinked global marketplace for search and navigation equipment. Joint ventures, in which a technologically superior U.S. manufacturer typically teams up with a less advanced foreign partner firm, are the most common industry business arrangement and often hinge on the U.S. firm's willingness to surrender technology to the foreign producer in exchange for cheaper labor costs, larger markets, or some other "sweetener." In offset agreements, an exporter agrees to obtain domestic markets for the products of the purchaser, and in some cases the exporter is obliged to buy products within the purchasing nation equal to a certain percentage of the contract's value. Offset agreements may also require the production of the product in the purchasing country or some form of co-production under a licensing arrangement. Although some degree of joint venture or co-production between U.S. firms and other nations in the larger defense industry began in the early 1950s, the number, variety, and geographic breadth of such arrangements continues to grow.

Government Intervention. Some domestic aerospace and defense contractors have claimed that the historical unwillingness of the U.S. government to imitate foreign governments by actively intervening to aid exporting companies has weakened U.S. competitiveness. Competitive financing of exports by govern-

ment bodies (such as the United States Export Import Bank), federal funding of "blended" commercial/military foreign sales, or government guarantees of commercial financing for military products are among the remedies advocated by some industry leaders to increase the U.S. position internationally in search and navigation and other defense sectors.

In 1993, the Clinton Administration signed into law a National Cooperative Production Amendments Act that modifies U.S. antitrust law so that penalties imposed on U.S. firms for engaging in joint ventures are reduced. The legislation also includes provisions allowing industry firms to share technology, pool resources, and share the burden of risks associated with equipment and research and development costs. The Act also enables foreign firms to engage in joint ventures with U.S. firms if equal treatment to U.S. firms is extended by their home country.

International Activity. The extent of foreign activity by U.S. search and navigation firms is reflected in the international projects of the Raytheon Company, one of the industry's largest producers. In the early 1990s, Raytheon teamed with Litton Industries to win a radar jamming contract for the government of Greece, entered into a co-production agreement with a Japanese company for development of a version of the Patriot missile, initiated a similar program with Taiwan, gained a contract with the Egyptian navy for minehunting sonar systems, formed a joint venture with Deutsche Aerospace AG to pursue international missile projects, and through its International Air Traffic Control division landed contracts for airports in India, the Netherlands, Germany, and Norway. Raytheon's contract with Saudi Arabia for a Patriot missile defense system in 1992 represented the largest single foreign sale ($327 million) in the company's history.

RESEARCH AND TECHNOLOGY

Research and development (R&D) costs for new technology in the search and navigation industry are assumed by both the federal government and industry contractors. General Electric Company, for example, reported that in 1992 corporate spending on R&D consisted of $1.35 billion of company funds and $543 million in "customer" funds, which largely consisted of federal monies. Texas Instruments invested about $2 billion in R&D between 1987 and 1992, and Raytheon Company invested nearly $290 million in 1992. Of the $162 million Sundstrand Corporation invested in R&D for all its divisions in 1992, about $47 million consisted of funds from customers, especially the U.S. government.

As the amount of R&D subsidized by the U.S. government decreased in the early 1990s, industry firms either began to replace that support with company funds or simply reduced R&D investment. In 1992, for example, General Electric received $127 million less for long-term R&D from the government and other customers but chose to increase its own R&D investment by $157 million. Faced with its own reduction in federal contract funds, however, Sundstrand elected to decrease R&D investment by $17 million from 1991 to 1992. While Raytheon Company's annual investment in R&D continued to grow in the early 1990s, the ratio of its R&D funding to total operating expenses declined from 1983 to 1992.

Long-term R&D contracts made by industry firms with the federal government are often undertaken with no expectation of immediate profit. These so-called "loss contracts" sometimes involve the granting of exclusive data or technical rights to the contractor, which enable the firm to become the sole producer of the technology should it eventually reach a production phase.

The search and navigation industry is one of the most technologically sophisticated sectors of American industry. Major advances in virtually every product group continue to occur at a rapid rate because unlike many other industries, search and navigation and other defense sectors are driven not only by intrinsic market competition but by a government-sponsored national security mandate to produce technologies superior to future projected threats as well as existing ones.

New Technologies. Overall trends in search and navigation systems include increased reliability, "fault-tolerance" (i.e. ability to operate through system failures), and reduced size, cost, weight, and power consumption of system components. Specific innovations now operational or under development in the area of flight control and guidance include night-vision helmets for pilots in which flight instrument data are displayed on a visor; "three-dimensional" synthesized cockpit voices that help pilots visualize threats surrounding the aircraft; aircraft optical sensors that can imitate the processes of the human optic nerve for increased sensitivity and responsiveness to external threats; and windshear warning systems that can give pilots up to 90 seconds advance notice of dangerous conditions. Other advances include moving map displays projected onto the cockpit windscreen for navigation, voice-controlled avionics that respond to pilots' verbal commands, and on-board "Stormscope" systems that can detect lightning threatening commercial aircraft.

Outside the cockpit, search and navigation technologies under development or in operation include small inertial guidance systems built into air-launched weapons, ground-based radar systems that can distinguish between hostile and friendly fire while prioritizing enemy targets, infrared systems that can overcome hidden aircraft exhaust heat by making subtle thermal distinctions between the target and the background sky, airborne laser sensors that can detect illegal drug laboratories by their chemical effluents, and radar that can "see" through foliage and under five to ten meters of soil.

Advances in nautical and marine search and detection technology include new minehunting sonar systems, vessel alert systems for oil tanker navigation in dangerous seas, sonar fish finders that project live-action sonar images onto display screens, and digital sonar systems that can see through large ocean-bottom objects to detect severed cables or an aircraft's submerged "black box."

INDUSTRY INFORMATION SOURCES

Aerospace Industries Association, *AIA Member Company Product Directory, 1993-94,* Washington, DC: AIA, 1993.

Ball, Nicole, and Milton Leitenberg, eds., *The Structure of the Defense Industry,* New York: St. Martin's Press, 1983.

Current Industrial Reports: Selected Instruments and Related Products, Washington, DC: U.S. Department of Commerce, 1992.

"Internationalization of the Aerospace Industry," *Hearing Before the Subcommittee on Economic Stabilization, United States Congress,* Washington, DC: Government Printing Office, 1989.

Kayton, Myron, ed., *Navigation: Land, Sea, Air and Space,* New York: IEEE Press, 1989.

Nordwall, Bruce, "Broadening Base for Avionics," *Aviation Week & Space Technology,* March 15, 1993.

"Swedish-Developed Radar to Penetrate Foliage, Ground," *Aviation Week & Space Technology,* January 18, 1993.

U.S. Industrial Outlook 1993, Washington, DC: U.S. Department of Commerce, 1993.

Velocci, Anthony L., Jr., "Fewer Players to See Late-Decade Upturn," *Aviation Week & Space Technology,* March 15, 1993.

Ward's Business Directory of U.S. Private and Public Companies 1993, Detroit: Gale Research, 1993.

—Paul Bodine

SIC 3821

LABORATORY APPARATUS AND FURNITURE

Establishments in this industry are primarily engaged in manufacturing laboratory apparatus and furniture. The main products of this industry include baths and melting point apparatus, accounting for 36 percent of products manufactured, laboratory furniture such as furnaces and ovens (20 percent), component parts and accessories for instruments (20 percent), and centrifuges (seven percent).

The laboratory apparatus and furniture industry in America is a stable domestic industry, with a small, but growing market for international trade. In 1992 this industry was valued at $2.1 billion, which presented a three percent increase over its value in 1991. This increase has been attributed to growth in exports, which totaled $236 million in sales in 1992, and to an increase in medical and scientific research.

In the United States approximately 60 companies employing roughly 22,500 workers provide laboratory furniture and apparatus manufacturing services. The industry leaders are Henley Group, Inc., which is based in Hampton, New Hampshire; Medline Industries, Inc., of Mundelein, Illinois; and Hamilton Industries, Inc., based in Two Rivers, Wisconsin. Henley Group, Inc. reported over $1.8 billion in sales revenues in 1992, while other industry leaders averaged $200 million.

Some of the smaller companies in this industry, such as Labconco, Inc., with sales of $28 million in 1990, and Parr Instrument Co., with sales of approximately $30 million in 1992, have experienced rapid growth since the mid-1980s by developing their export markets. These companies have found the largest markets for their products in Canada, Germany and Japan. Indeed, exports are widely regarded as a vital element in spurring expected industry growth in the near future. The export market for this industry has not been dominated by any one customer; 50 percent of exports in 1991 went to Japan, Canada, Mexico, Germany, and South Korea. Imports in this industry, meanwhile, were estimated at $134 million in 1992, with Germany, Japan and Switzerland supplying the bulk of these products.

Technological Advances. New apparatus needs and the need to make laboratory costs more efficient have increased several product lines in this industry. Autosamplers, which separate chemicals within a liquid sample, have been in high demand as environmental, pharmaceutical, and biological applications have

increased. According to *Research and Development*, most manufacturers of autosamplers have developed these apparatus for use with their own analytical instruments and are making the apparatus more useable to laboratory personnel without formal training. In 1992 autosamplers were priced at between $8,000 and $15,000, which is moderate for laboratory apparatus and furniture.

Controlling laboratory costs have resulted in numerous product developments, which are also better for the environment. Heto Lab Equipment of Denmark has designed several new lines of equipment for laboratory use, including a vacuum pump that recirculates water, saving up to five tons of water daily.

INDUSTRY INFORMATION SOURCES

"Exporting Pays Off," *Business America*, February 13, 1989.

Hyatt, Joshua, "The G Factor," *Inc.*, January 1992.

Jones, Robert R., "Electrical and Electronic Instrument Markets Strong," *Research and Development*, February 1990.

"Making Your Lab Greener," *Research and Development*, April 1992.

Mosbacher, C. J., "Use of Electrical and Electronic Instruments," *Research and Development*, April 1988.

Studt, Tim. "Autosamplers Do Much More Than Take Samples," *Research and Development*, February 1992.

SIC 3822

AUTOMATIC CONTROLS FOR REGULATING RESIDENTIAL AND COMMERCIAL ENVIRONMENTS AND APPLIANCES

Establishments in this industry are primarily engaged in manufacturing temperature and related controls for heating and air-conditioning installations and refrigeration applications, which are electrically, electronically, or pneumatically actuated, and which measure and control variables such as temperature and humidity; and automatic regulators used as components of household appliances. Automatic controls for regulating residential and commercial environments include HVAC (heating, ventilating, air-conditioning) unit controls and building monitoring controls for temperature and humidity modulation. Automatic controls for appliances include oven temperature controls, dryness controls for clothes dryers, controls for gas burners, and refrigeration thermostats and pressure controls. Establishments primarily engaged in manufacturing industrial process controls are classified in

SIC 3823: Industrial Instruments for Measurement, Display, and Control of Process Variables; and Related Products; those manufacturing motor control switches are classified in **SIC 3625: Relays and Industrial Controls**; those manufacturing switches for household appliances are classified in **SIC 3643: Current-Carrying Wiring Devices**; and those manufacturing appliance timers are classified in **SIC 3873: Watches, Clocks, Clockwork Operated Devices, and Parts**.

INDUSTRY SNAPSHOT

In America there are more than 110 establishments in this industry, which in 1992 totaled $2.4 billion in shipments. The leading establishments include General Electric Co. and its Industrial and Power Systems division, Honeywell, Inc., and Johnson Controls, Inc.

Customers for these products are primarily equipment and appliance manufacturers, electrical contractors, and large industrial users. The market for environmental controls is principally affected by activity in residential and commercial construction. In addition, the market for American manufacturers is greatly affected by foreign competition, which has been rising since the 1980s.

ORGANIZATION AND STRUCTURE

This industry is composed of two groups: manufacturers of automatic controls used in residential and commercial HVAC units and manufacturers of automatic controls used in household appliances and industrial equipment.

Manufacturers of automatic controls for HVAC units distribute their products mainly to suppliers for building construction and contracting firms. For industrial upgrades of HVAC systems, the controls are also sold directly to end users.

Manufacturers of automatic controls for household appliances and industrial equipment are typically subsidiaries or divisions of large establishments, where other subsidiaries or divisions of the same establishment use the controls to assemble appliances and equipment.

BACKGROUND AND DEVELOPMENT

Major Products. Controls for HVAC units are this industry's major product. These controls are produced for residential and commercial buildings and in a variety of styles to meet industrial needs. Factories that use temperature and humidity-sensitive chemicals and materials require highly sophisticated environmental

controlling systems. In the printing industry, computerized HVAC monitoring and controlling have made some printing plants more efficient; these systems provide information for facility operators to electrically monitor HVAC operations from a central location and independently provide cooling and heating of water pumps in ways that save energy.

Another major product line for this industry consists of automatic igniters and thermostats for appliances and equipment. These controls include gas-fired igniters used for water-heaters and gas stoves in the food-service industry; thermostats used in office equipment, such as photocopiers; and custom-designed thermostats for medical equipment, such as blood analyzers and respiratory humidifiers, and kitchen appliances for the home.

As environmental control equipment has grown in size and sophistication, basic designs of automatic controls have undergone considerable changes. Heavy wiring and cables have been replaced by hydraulic systems and low-voltage ignition starters. Electrical controls have also been used increasingly for their high sensitivity and fast response abilities. In laboratories and factories, pneumatic controls used in exhaust and ventilating systems have been replaced by digital controls, which are basically electronic versions of the original pneumatic devices.

Environmental and Energy Concerns. Concerns about the environment, and the resulting legislation, have helped this industry. Environmental issues have created an increased demand for controlling systems that control air quality and conserve energy. In the early 1990s companies in the United States have invested significant capital on devices to lower air, water, and solid waste pollution. Factories from a variety of industries are continuing to monitor and control pollution through the purchase and implementation of highly sensitive control systems.

With conservation of energy, energy management systems (EMS) have also kept this industry active in redesigning and improving their products. Energy management systems are computerized control systems implemented mostly by the utility industry, but also by large manufacturers with their own power stations. Automatic controls have been altered and redesigned for energy efficiency to work within these systems and for the HVAC units in the buildings in which they are stored.

Computerized energy management systems on a smaller scale are also being installed in commercial buildings as a result of the Comprehensive National Energy Policy Act, which was passed in 1993. These systems combine monitoring and controlling of HVAC units with security, lighting, and fire safety systems.

Hotels, department stores, and grocery stores, all large users of energy, began implementing energy management systems in the 1980s. In hotels, automatic controls on heating and air-conditioning units are regulated by sensors in individual rooms that detect whether the rooms are occupied; the controls are also linked up with the hotel's front desk in order to respond to check-ins and check-outs. For hotel owners, these systems cost an average of $120,000 in 1991, but their energy-cost savings were estimated at $30,000 annually. Similarly, energy management systems have saved energy and money for department and grocery stores. In these cases, computerized systems are monitored for a chain of stores by a centralized network. According to Steve Thompson of McRae's department stores, "(the) automated system has not only maintained the chain's standards for temperature and humidity, but has also strengthened them."

CURRENT CONDITIONS

This industry entered the 1990s experiencing small growth following the decline in construction of residential and commercial buildings. This modest growth, along with small sales margins, has limited research and development in new technologies and investment in new facilities.

In addition, as a result of the weak economy, many companies have chosen to upgrade their existing HVAC systems. This has increased commercial repair and maintenance while sales of new HVAC systems dropped by three percent in 1991 and 1992; sales are expected to decline at approximately this rate until late 1993.

INDUSTRY LEADERS

General Electric Industrial Power and Systems is the industry leader with $11.5 billion in sales reported in 1992. The parent company, General Electric Co., is the world's biggest electric conglomerate, and for many years had no real competition. This allowed General Electric to diversify from making household appliances to manufacturing television sets, air-conditioners, and aircraft engines. But in the 1980s competition from Japan and the company's own internal problems with changes in leadership dramatically reduced the company's sales. By 1987 General Electric was increasing productivity by only 1.5 percent annually compared with its Japanese competitors' eight percent average. General Electric responded by moving away from making smaller products like tin-openers to mak-

ing expensive equipment like gas turbines. Its Industry and Power Systems division starting producing fewer automatic controls for their home appliances division; instead, they entered the 1990s expanding their control production operations for large industrial equipment and food-service industry appliances.

Honeywell, Inc., this industry's second largest establishment in terms of sales, reported $6.3 billion in sales in 1992. Honeywell manufacturers products for three segments within this industry: homes and buildings, industry, and space and aviation. For homes and buildings, Honeywell makes thermostats, gas valves, and other residential heating and cooling controls. For industry, the company provides HVAC controls and digital control systems for use with computerized energy management systems. The space and aviation segment, the newest addition to Honeywell's product line, manufactures environmental controls and guidance system controls.

WORK FORCE

In 1992 over 40,000 workers were employed in this industry. Nearly 60 percent of these were production workers, including electricians and assembly line workers; their salaries averaged $440 per week. The remaining 40 percent were employed in administration and management and sales capacities; their salaries varied greatly depending on the size of the company.

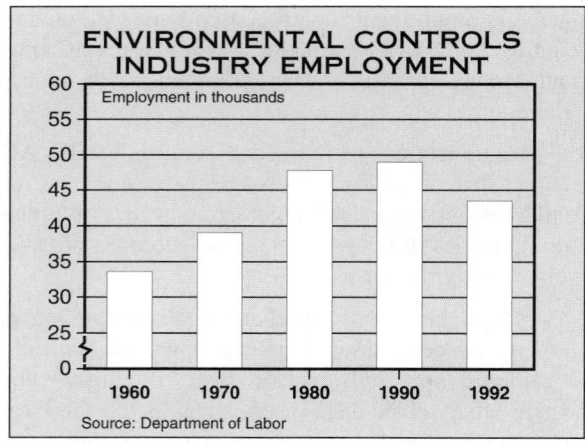

For establishments that sell products directly to end users, additional personnel are sometimes needed in heating and air-conditioning service and maintenance. In 1993 salaries for these service and maintenance technicians averaged between $400 to $600 per week, with their apprentices starting at 50 percent of those salaries. A steady increase in employment is predicted for the rest of the 1990s.

AMERICA AND THE WORLD

This industry is competitive in international trade in both exporting and importing capacities and boasts a trade surplus that has continued to grow into the 1990s. In 1992 exports increased by 8 percent to $4.4 billion and imports increased by 13 percent to $2.4 billion.

Canada is the largest market for exports of automatic controls made in the United States, making up nearly 59 percent of this industry's exports. Exports of these products to Canada increased five times from 1989 to 1993, mostly as a result of the U.S.-Canada Free Trade Agreement, enacted in 1989. This market is expected to continue to grow as Canadian manufacturers address environmental concerns, such as energy savings, through modernized and improved controls.

Mexico is the second largest market for exports in this industry, holding 21 percent of the export market in 1992. Exports to Mexico are expected to increase further when the North American Free Trade Agreement (NAFTA) is fully implemented in the mid-1990s.

East Asian countries make up a substantial portion of this industry's export market. In 1992 Japan accounted for over six percent of the exports of American automatic controls and China, Singapore, and South Korea combined for more than ten percent of the overseas market. Combined, these East Asian countries purchased $65 million in automatic controls made in the United States in 1992.

Mexico is the largest exporter of automatic controls imported to the United States, accounting for nearly 19 percent of all imported automatic controls. Over 20 percent of imports come from European Community members, roughly 16 percent from Japan, and another 16 percent from Canada.

RESEARCH AND TECHNOLOGY

With the downturn in the real estate market in the late 1980s and early 1990s, building owners and developers have become interested in automated building systems as a way of cutting overhead costs and as a marketing device to showcase cost savings and modernization. Upon entering the 1990s, technology in these systems included management-regulated HVAC controls to lower energy costs.

Automated building systems are also being developed for in-home use, combining heating and air-conditioning control with security and fire and smoke detector systems. Honeywell's TotalHome, an automated home control system, uses remote control to program room temperature, appliances, lights and locks. More research is expected in this area as consumer interests in these systems increases.

Continued research is also predicted for automatic controls within energy management systems. Some of these projects involve the use of artificial intelligence and complex information systems.

INDUSTRY INFORMATION SOURCES

Babyak, Richard J. "Multi-Function Ignition Controls," *Appliance Manufacturer* (July 1991).

————."Mini-Igniter Speeds Gas-Fired Hot Water Booster," *Appliance Manufacturer* (July 1991).

"Custom Temperature Sensors Simplify Assembly," *Appliance Manufacturer* (December 1991).

Hauprich, Jerry. "How to Save Energy the Easy Way," *Lodging Hospitality* (February 1992).

Horenovsky, Mirek. "Facility Custom-Designed for Energy Control Center," *Electrical World* (April 1991).

"Hot-Surface Ignition Without Warmup," *Appliance Manufacturer* (May 1991).

Jaben, Jan. "Owners, Tenants More Concerned With Automated Building Systems," *National Real Estate Investor* (June 1991).

Jancsurak, Joe. "Thermostats Rise to Meet Market Demands," *Appliance Manufacturer* (May 1991).

Jesitus, John. "Energy Savings Beckon," *Hotel and Motel Management* (December 16, 1991).

"Learning Curve: The Evolution of System Control," *Electrical World* (September 1990).

Maczka, John R. "EMS Designed for Future Expansion," *Electrical World* (March 1992).

Paoli, A. Delli, Jr., and G. Thomas Saunders, "Design Your Exhaust System to Meet Your Lab's Real Needs," *Research and Development* (August 1987).

Reinbach, Andrew. "The Buzz About Energy Controls," *Buildings* (October 1992).

Selwitz, Robert. "Managing Energy," *Hotel and Motel Management* (December 16, 1991).

"Staying in Control," *American Printer* (June 1992).

"System Exchanges for EMS," *Electrical World* (February 1992).

"System Reduces Energy Costs at McRae's," *Chain Store Age Executive* (January 1992).

Tichy, Noel, and Stratford Sherman. *Control Your Destiny or Someone Else Will*. New York: Doubleday, 1993.

Zelenko, Laura. "Empty Homes Get Cozy by Computer," *American Demographics* (October 1992).

—Paola Trimarco

SIC 3823

INDUSTRIAL INSTRUMENTS FOR MEASUREMENT, DISPLAY, AND CONTROL OF PROCESS VARIABLES, AND RELATED PRODUCTS

This category includes establishments primarily engaged in manufacturing industrial instruments and related products for measuring, displaying (indicating and/or recording), transmitting, and controlling process variables in manufacturing, energy conversion, and public service utilities. These instruments operate mechanically, pneumatically, electronically, or electrically to measure process variables such as temperature, humidity, pressure, vacuum, combustion, flow, level, viscosity, density, acidity, alkalinity, specific gravity, gas and liquid concentration, sequence, time interval, mechanical motion, and rotation. Establishments primarily engaged in manufacturing electrical integrating meters are classified in **SIC 3825: Instruments for Measuring and Testing of Electricity and Electrical Signals;** those manufacturing residential and commercial comfort controls are classified in **SIC 3822: Automatic Controls for Regulating Residential and Commercial Environments and Appliances;** those manufacturing all liquid-in-glass and bimetal thermometers and glass hydrometers are classified in **SIC 3829: Measuring and Controlling Devices, Not Elsewhere Classified;** those manufacturing recorder charts are classified in the Commercial Printing industries; and those manufacturing analytical and optical instruments are classified in **SIC 3826: Laboratory Analytical Instruments** and **SIC 3827: Optical Instruments and Lenses.**

Establishments primarily engaged in manufacturing electrical integrating meters are classified in **SIC 3825: Instruments for Measuring and Testing of Electricity and Electrical Systems;** those manufacturing pressure transducers and all liquid-in-glass and bimetal thermometers and glass hydrometers are classified in **SIC 3829: Measuring and Controlling Devices, Not Elsewhere Classified;** those manufacturing recorder charts are classified in Industry Group 275 (commercial printing); those manufacturing industrial process relays and gauge and programmable controllers are classified in **SIC 3625: Relays and Industrial Controls;** those manufacturing computer software programs for industrial process applications are classified in Industry Group 737 (computer programming, data processing, and other computer-related services); and those manufacturing analytical and optical instru-

ments are classified in **SIC 3826: Laboratory Analytical Instruments.**

INDUSTRY SNAPSHOT

More than 400 companies manufactured process control instruments (PCIs) in 1992, generating $6.2 billion in shipments, or roughly one percent more than in 1991. Diminished investment by end-user industries in new plant and equipment resulted in slim profit margins for industry producers and decreased funding for product research and development. However, because of the industry's technology-intensive product base, wide variety of product types, and the tendency of end-user industries to continue to invest in process improvements even during recessions, PCI manufacturers were expected to weather the economic downturn of the early 1990s and experience solid growth in the latter part of the decade.

Shipments of general industrial process display/control instruments and temperature measuring instruments—the two fastest growing product groups—were expected to grow at an annual rate of 13.6 and 10.8 percent respectively between 1987 and 1995. Formidable competition from foreign PCI manufacturers challenged U.S. producers at home while growing markets in Asia, Eastern Europe, and the former Soviet Union offered U.S. producers opportunities to expand their leading role in the international PCI marketplace.

ORGANIZATION AND STRUCTURE

At the heart of industrial process control is the measurement of the variables, such as temperature and pressure, used in manufacturing processes to transform raw materials into finished products. Measurements made by sensors, meters, or other measuring instruments on the manufacturing process line are sent by a transmitting device to an indicator or recorder for display and/or to a controller where the data is compared to a preestablished set of parameters. The controller calculates the difference between the measured data and the programmed "setpoint" values and, if necessary, adjusts the process variables to conform to the desired parameters. This feedback-and-response cycle is called a loop, and continuous, repeating loops are performed during the industrial process to ensure product quality, efficient use of raw materials, and process safety. Processes typically involving control include reacting, heating and cooling, distilling, petroleum refining, and pulp and paper manufacturing.

PCI end-users. The PCI industry is tightly linked to its end-user industries and to the process or "wet" industries in particular. Capital expenditure by these industries on plant and process improvements has a direct effect on the profits of PCI manufacturers. The process industries use raw materials in fluid or bulk solid form for product manufacture and include the chemical, petroleum, petrochemical, pharmaceutical, pulp and paper, food processing, plastics, and municipal water and waste treatment industries.

Historically, the process industries account for almost two-thirds of all PCI purchases. The chemical industry alone purchases 25 percent of all PCI shipments, followed by the petroleum (19 percent), pulp and paper (10.5 percent), and food processing industries (6.5 percent). Other important purchasers include: non-process or discrete-piece manufacturing industries, which manufacture iron, steel, and non-ferrous metals (such as aluminum and copper), glass and ceramic products, textiles, and machine tools; mining industries; and electric and gas utilities.

Competitive structure. In spite of historically strong growth performance and high technology product groups, the PCI industry has traditionally been undervalued by the financial community, producing low historical stock-price/book-value ratios. This has sometimes prevented PCI companies from attracting the capital necessary to maintain growth and has made firms in the industry ideal targets for acquisition by foreign and domestic companies.

Although changes in the industry's structure are challenging the traditional hold of the largest companies, such major producers as EG&G Inc., Rosemount Inc., ITT Corporation, and Honeywell Inc. dominate the industry and are the preponderant leaders in sales and employment. Due to advances in digital technology, however, PCI system integratibility and product compatibility has increased considerably in recent years. As a result, manufacturers who formerly dominated the industry now face competition from firms whose products can be tied into larger manufacturers' systems, thereby allowing these smaller firms to penetrate closed markets.

An increasing number of end-user manufacturers seek PCI vendors who can provide them with complete integrated systems for their process control applications. Instrument manufacturers who formerly produced only components have thus been forced to broaden their product lines. Despite increasing system compatibility, PCI vendors still compete in the areas of price, quality, added features, delivery, reputation, reliability, and service.

Legislation. Anti-pollution regulations by the Environmental Protection Agency—the largest single regulatory influence on the PCI industry—require manufacturers to purchase instruments to monitor and control their industrial waste levels. Mandated spending to comply with Occupational Safety and Health Administration plant safety regulations is the next largest regulatory action affecting PCI purchases. PCI producers are also affected by Food and Drug Administration policies regulating the manufacture of pharmaceuticals. While government regulation stimulates the sale of anti-pollution-related PCI products, it also reduces capital available for new projects that would increase sales of PCIs.

Product groups. The products of the PCI industry can be divided into several broad groups: general-purpose control system instruments (1991 shipments: $1.5 billion); flow and level instruments ($871.5 million); pressure instruments ($411.3 million); temperature and primary temperature instruments ($547.8 million); gas and liquid analyzers ($362.3 million); humidity instruments ($21.2 million); instruments for process variables such as speed, weight, density, and specific gravity ($105.2 million); and other PCI instruments and spare parts, supplies, accessories, and related products ($950.9 million).

General-purpose control system instruments. The largest-selling type of PCIs, general-purpose control system instruments include multifunction computer control systems as well as general instruments for measuring, displaying, transmitting, and controlling process variables. General-purpose measuring instruments operate electronically or pneumatically to register and quantify process variable conditions in the manufacturing process. The measurement is transformed into a signal that is displayed or sent to the controller for comparison with process variable setpoints. Indicators receive the data gathered by the measuring sensor and present it to the operator in digital or analog form. Analog indicators may represent process variable data through a bar-graph display device, a rotating drum counter, or a scale or dial. Digital indicators represent process variable data in discrete numerical or alphanumerical form on a liquid-crystal or light-emitting diode display or through a cathode ray tube or other display.

Recorders are used for graphing or permanently storing process variable measurements. Early recorders used pen-and-ink mechanisms to mark rolled strips of paper or circular charts. Computer technology has enabled measurements to be recorded digitally in computer memory for later display in printed form or on computer graphics programs.

Controllers receive data signals remotely or directly from measuring or transmitting instruments and send instructions or ''error signals'' to actuating valves or other components on the process line if the signals indicate that the process variables are diverging from desired conditions.

Flow and level instruments. Flowmeters constitute one of the largest sources of industry revenue. Although there are over 100 meter types, the most common are differential-pressure, turbine, mass-flow, variable-area, magnetic, and positive-displacement meters. Flowmeters are used to measure the rates of flow of fluid chemicals, gases, liquids containing particulate matter (slurries), water, sewage, and gas, among other applications. Level instruments can be used to determine the amount of raw materials available for production purposes or the number of items manufactured by the process. Level instruments are typically installed in tanks, bins, hoppers, or other storage devices to monitor levels of materials such as gasoline, milk, solvents, plastic granules, coal, or oil.

Pressure instruments. The vast majority of products manufactured by industry are the result of processes that use pressure to perform work. Punch presses and boilers are typical pressure-based industrial process machines. Pressure measuring instruments such as gauges and pressure transmitters operate hydraulically, pneumatically, or electronically to measure pressure, absolute pressure, vacuum pressure, or draft pressure. The two most common types of pressure gauges are liquid-filled columns or tubes (similar to household barometers) and elastic pressure elements, which operate on spring-action, diaphragm, or bellows principles.

Temperature and primary temperature instruments. More than half of all measured process variables undergo some form of temperature measurement during the manufacturing process. Accurate temperature measurements are important in many industrial processes but are critical in processes like rubber curing, food processing, and medical sterilization, where slight temperature variances can destroy final product quality. The four basic temperature measuring instrument types are thermocouples, resistance thermometers, thermal radiation meters, and non-glass filled systems, such as industrial mercury-filled thermometers. Primary temperature instruments are the sensors that receive and measure the initial temperature data in the process control loop.

Gas and liquid analyzers. Analyzers of gas and liquid in continuous on-stream industrial processes are often classified according to the nature of the interaction between the gas and liquid to be measured and an external source of energy. Analyzers allow molecular-level measurement of process materials without interruption of the process for sample extraction. Analyzers are used to measure industrial effluents and waste products, viscosity of liquids used in mixing processes and food processing, the acidity or alkalinity of process materials, and the octane number in petroleum refining, among other applications. In addition to gas and liquid analyzers, the most common instrument types are oxygen, chromatographic, infrared, and pH analyzers.

Humidity instruments. Instruments such as hygrometers and psychrometers measure the water vapor content of air in such industrial applications as test chambers, pharmaceutical and food packaging, heat treating, and industrial drying. Wet-bulb/dry-bulb humidity, relative humidity, vapor pressure, and dew point are the most common types of measurements performed by industrial humidity instruments.

Other process control instruments. This category includes instruments for measuring such process variables as specific gravity, density, viscosity, weight, or force. Instruments in this category are used in such specialized applications as determining the "freeness" of pulp and paper products, the size of particulate solids in slurries, or the boiling point in petroleum refining. Spare parts, accessories, and PCIs not included in other categories comprised the industry's second largest product group in terms of sales in 1991.

BACKGROUND AND DEVELOPMENT

The modern process controls industry grew out of three historical developments: the emergence of mass production technology, the evolution of instruments for measuring and analyzing process variables, and the development of computer technology in process control applications.

Eli Whitney's invention of the interchangeable part in 1800 represented an important early milestone in the evolution of mass production manufacturing techniques. In the early 1800s, Oliver Evans developed the principle of the automatic manufacturing sequence, which was followed later in the century by advances in machine tooling and the gradual transition from rudimentary assembly-line manufacturing methods to true industrial mechanization.

The nineteenth century also saw fundamental progress in the measurement of properties like temperature, pressure, and fluid flow. In 1822, Thomas J. Seebeck's development of the principle of continuous electrical current flow across metals of differing temperatures laid the foundation for the modern industrial thermocouple. Contemporary thermistor technology grew out of Michael Faraday's discovery of the principles of temperature resistance in the 1830s. E. Bourdon's invention in 1852 of a method for measuring pressure based on the effect of internal pressure variations on the closed end of a curved tube remains a common pressure instrument technology, and the production of the first commercial venturi tube flowmeter in 1887 marked a major advance in fluid meter technology that was still in wide use in the 1990s.

The first commercial industrial controller using newly developed computational procedures, or algorithms, for regulating processes was marketed in 1936. The earliest form of process control was performed solely by the operator who read data from a measuring gauge on the process line, determined whether the measurement varied from some desired setpoint value, and turned a valve if the process variable required adjusting. Later controllers were pneumatically- or electrically-powered devices designed to maintain constant, hard-wired setpoints and sometimes contained both the component for measuring process variables and the component for actuating the regulating valves.

The earliest computer-based control systems appeared in the mid-1950s. Digital computer technology allowed controllers to communicate with other PCIs (such as measuring sensors) as well as a central control room computer. These controllers contained a computer-driven version of a control algorithm for indicating, controlling, and actuating control components. In addition to allowing process set-points to be altered remotely and automatically through a computer terminal, computerized controllers offered lower cost, greater control speed, and increased reliability in comparison to earlier analog systems.

The first automated industrial process plants were constructed in the 1950s, and by 1965 over 1,000 industrial plants worldwide were computer-controlled to some extent. The evolution of computer operation—from vacuum tubes to transistors, then from integrated circuits to microchips—led to the introduction of faster and smaller microprocessing computers in the 1970s. Identical microprocessor-based controllers located at different points on the process line—so-called "distributed" control systems—quickly began to replace centralized control computers. This generation of high-powered, reprogrammable controllers gave operators more control over the process by giving them direct control over more process loops and also enabled them to reconfigure control programs for new processes or applications.

WORK FORCE

The PCI industry employed approximately 60,000 people in 1992. Companies in four states—

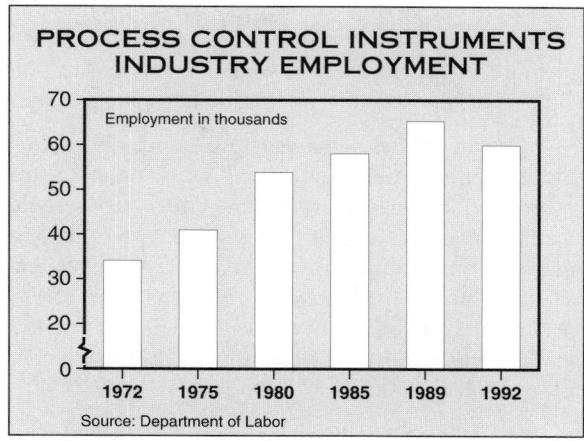

PROCESS CONTROL INSTRUMENTS INDUSTRY EMPLOYMENT

Employment in thousands

Source: Department of Labor

Pennsylvania, California, Massachusetts, and Illinois—accounted for 46 percent of the industry's employment in 1987. Although the number of establishments in the industry has been growing steadily since 1972 (more than 400 companies in 1992 compared to 175 in 1972), the size of the industry's work force has declined since a peak in 1989.

Production positions accounted for more than half of the industry's employment in 1992. The production positions most representative of the industry included machinists, precision electrical and electronic assemblers, and instrument-makers. Workers in these categories build and integrate the components that constitute the industry's product groups and in some applications fabricate instruments requiring accuracies of one ten-millionth of an inch. Instrument-makers earned an average of $24,400 a year in the early 1990s, but the outlook for many PCI production job categories through 2005 was for slower than average growth.

Mechanical and electrical engineers—the industry's most representative non-production positions—design new instruments and systems, formulate product performance requirements, and create maintenance schedules. Some engineers also become involved in production operations, technical sales, and administrative and managerial work. Salaries for engineers range between $31,000 and $93,000 per year depending on specific professional specialization, job responsibilities, experience, industry, and size of plant. Some engineering job classifications were projected to experience 40 to 50 percent total growth between 1991 and 2005.

Several job categories are specific to the instrument manufacturing industries. Instrument engineering technicians and instrument technicians/technologists often assist instrument engineers in formulating the specifications, functional design, and dimensions of process control instrumentation. Their specific functions depend on the unique requirements of the instrument under development as well as the mix of responsibilities of the design team to which they are assigned.

Instrument field engineers are responsible for the installation, start-up, and initial servicing of instruments and systems after they have been delivered to the customer. Instrument field service representatives, maintenance technicians, and service specialists analyze and adjust instrument malfunctions, train service personnel, handle sales of replacement or spare parts to the customer, and ensure the regular operation of the instrument or system.

Independent contractors. Some PCI end-users sign "turnkey" contracts with independent contractors or consultants located in the area in which a new plant is being constructed. These contractors then handle the entire installation and system configuration process at the plant site. Independent contractors often work on a cost-plus-fixed-fee basis and are more commonly used during peak construction periods when many instrumentation projects are active simultaneously.

AMERICA AND THE WORLD

U.S. companies have always played a leading role in the worldwide PCI marketplace. However, foreign PCI industries—led by Germany, Japan, and the United Kingdom—have made significant inroads into the U.S. domestic and overseas markets.

Foreign involvement. Imports of foreign-made PCIs rose to over $1 billion in 1993, representing a 21 percent increase over the previous year. Between 1989 and 1993 alone, imports of PCIs rose 65 percent. Comparatively lower foreign labor costs, subsidy of foreign PCI manufacturers by their governments, and the ability of some foreign manufacturers to bring research breakthroughs to commercial use sooner than U.S. firms all contributed to increased PCI imports. Moreover, some foreign PCI manufacturers have responded to the focus by many U.S. companies on quarter-to-quarter profits by adopting long-term market penetration strategies, which allow them to absorb short-term losses.

Although the United States leads the world in new PCI technology, American engineers have historically tended to focus on revolutionary breakthroughs in technology while foreign research has concentrated on gradual, evolutionary innovation. At the same time, foreign manufacturers' readiness to embrace new technologies has enabled them to market PCI innovations sooner than traditionally more cautious U.S. producers. While U.S. funding of industrial research and development, for example, has favored product development two-to-one over improvements in industrial processes, Japanese funding has been the reverse—thus contributing to Japan's competitiveness in new process control technology.

In 1989, 23 firms from seven countries—led by the United Kingdom and Germany—manufactured PCIs in the United States. Foreign firms looking for acquisition targets have been drawn to PCI industry firms because of the industry's history of continual growth, its high technology base, and its generally undervalued stock-price and book-value.

Exports and free trade. Despite the success of foreign companies in penetrating the U.S. market, the United States has continued to show a trade surplus in PCIs, aided by continuing U.S. advances in new technology and the weakness of the dollar overseas. In 1993, U.S. exports rose to over $2 billion, compared with imports of $1 billion. Historically, one-fifth to one-quarter of PCI shipments have gone to the export market, with the highest concentrations in high technology products like computer controllers and process analyzers.

Efforts to ease international trade barriers and open foreign markets—such as the General Agreement on Tariffs and Trade—offer U.S. PCI producers potential new opportunities overseas. The North American Free Trade Agreement in particular was projected to increase substantially the markets for U.S. PCIs in Mexico and Canada, which ranked first and third, respectively, in imports of U.S. PCIs in 1992. The opening of the Eastern bloc and former Soviet states to increased U.S. trade provided larger potential markets for U.S. instruments. Other leading foreign markets for U.S. PCIs included the European Community, Asia, and South America.

RESEARCH AND TECHNOLOGY

The major developments in PCI technology involve advances in the power and usefulness of the computers used in process control applications, the continued evolution of Artificial Intelligence software applications for process control, and the development of international standards for communicating between components in process control systems.

PCI computer hardware. The PCI industry is the most computer-automated segment of the combined measuring and control industry group. Computers used in industrial process control continue to increase in power, speed, memory, and ease-of-use. Advances in microchip technology have allowed PCI producers to offer a wider range of functions in smaller, lighter, and cheaper instrument packages. Personal computers are increasingly used as process monitors, as workstations for configuring control systems, and as a means for gathering process data and coordinating controllers. Microchip technology has also resulted in microprocessor-based "smart" instruments with self-learning and self-tuning capabilities. The development of parallel processing computing technology and the emergence of cheaper supercomputers offers the opportunity for even faster computation of process control operations.

PCI computer software. Many of the research advances benefitting the PCI industry involve "Artificial Intelligence" software used in experimentation, analysis, design, and prototyping of process control systems. Computer graphics modeling or simulation programs allow designers of process control systems to simulate complex manufacturing processes before they are actually created. Because they can also predict the final properties of raw material mixtures, these systems can also be used in the formulation of new products. Some programs also permit simulated process system models to be tested through on-line interaction with the sensors and actuators that measure and control the variables in the manufacturing process. Self-diagnosing systems are capable of analyzing their own operation, anticipating future conditions, and making changes before problems arise.

Knowledge-based or expert systems use alogical, inductive reasoning and pattern recognition techniques to simulate the imprecise and unpredictable nature of manufacturing processes. These and related "fuzzy logic" programs learn from process events, make qualitative instead of purely logical adjustments to process conditions, and can evaluate and compensate for faults in the process design. In addition to optimizing efficient use of process variables, such software programs allow end-users to more accurately predict the final properties of process mixtures. Because expert systems are programmed to learn and "think" independently, they are able to make instantaneous changes in the quantity and quality of the raw materials introduced into the process without the intervention of human operators.

Communication standards. Fieldbus, an international standard or protocol for linking all data communication between process control components regardless of design or manufacturer, is expected to have a profound effect on the structure of the process controls industry. Fieldbus will allow the immediate conversion of data from traditionally analog-operating process sensors into digital signals, thus greatly expanding the integratibility or interoperability of PCIs. Such open or "transparent" architecture will allow end-users to mix and match system components, resulting in less expensive system expansion, improved performance, and enhanced reliability. Fieldbus was projected to be available by the end of the 1990s.

INDUSTRY INFORMATION SOURCES

Caro, Robert H., "The Fifth Generation Process Control Architecture," *ISA Transactions* 28 (4), 1989, 23-28.

Considine, Douglas, and Glenn D. Considine, eds., *Process Instruments and Controls Handbook,* 3d ed., New York: McGraw-Hill, 1985.

Fardo, Stephen W., and Dale R. Patrick, *Industrial Process Control Systems,* Englewood Cliffs, NJ: Prentice-Hall, 1985.

Frost & Sullivan, *The Process Control Equipment Market (1978-89),* New York: Frost & Sullivan, 1990.

Hopke, William E., ed., *The Encyclopedia of Careers and Vocational Guidance,* Chicago: J. G. Ferguson, 1990.

Maczka, Walter J., ed., "1991 Process Control Industry Outlook," *Intech,* January 1991, 22-28.

Migliorini, Ron, "The Future of Instrumentation," *Process Engineering,* January 1991, 75.

Pinto, Gay, "Prospects Are Promising for Process Controls Market," *I&CS,* January 1987, 28-30.

Stephanopoulos, George, "Process Control with a Computer," *Chemtech,* April 1987, 251-256

U. S. Department of Commerce, *Current Industrial Reports, "Selected Instruments and Related Products," 1991,* Washington, DC: U.S. Government Printing Office, 1992.

————, *U.S. Industrial Outlook 1993,* Washington, DC: U.S. Government Printing Office, 1993.

Ward's Business Directory of U.S. Private and Public Companies 1993, Detroit: Gale Research, 1993.

—Paul Bodine

SIC 3824

TOTALIZING FLUID METERS AND COUNTING DEVICES

This category includes establishments primarily engaged in manufacturing meters for registering or tallying quantities of fluids, motor vehicle measuring instruments, and instruments for counting the frequency of items or events. This category includes establishments that manufacture domestic, commercial, and industrial gas and water meters; meters for measuring speed, distance traveled, and other variables for the motor vehicle industry; and counters and timers for quantifying production rates in industrial processes. Establishments primarily engaged in manufacturing electricity integrating meters and electronic frequency counters are classified in **SIC 3825: Instruments for Measuring and Testing of Electricity and Electrical Signals.** Establishments primarily engaged in manufacturing flowmeters for industrial process control and other industrial process instruments are classified in **SIC 3823: Industrial Instruments for Measurement, Display, and Control of Process Variables; and Related Products.**

More than 150 companies manufactured totalizing fluid meters and counting devices in 1992. These establishments generated over $1.7 billion in sales and employed over 16,000 people. Annual shipments of totalizing fluid meters and counting devices have been decreasing steadily in constant dollar terms since 1988, with a three percent decrease in shipments between 1991 and 1992. This trend reflects general economic stagnation as well as decreased production in the industries that purchase these instruments.

Nearly one-half of the industry's shipments consist of totalizing fluid meters for gas, water, and other liquids, liquid fuel dispensing meters (except service station pumps), and related parts and components. Totalizing fluid meters measure fluids in quantity terms (such as gallons or cubic feet) and indicate total fluid volume rather than the rates of flow indicated by flow meters used in industrial process control. The most common type of totalizing fluid meter is the positive-displacement meter, which takes a variety of forms depending on its design. These meters operate by allowing the fluid to enter a chamber where the force of fluid motion causes a diaphragm, disk, vane, or other element to move or rotate. Each cycle of the rotating or moving element generates a signal that is sent to the registering component of the meter, which tallies or indicates the total fluid quantity.

Small positive-displacement meters used for registering consumption of water in households or businesses claim the largest portion of the industry's market share for meters, followed by meters for registering residential gas consumption. Other significant product groups include registering or totalizing gas meters for commercial or industrial use, impeller meters and consumption registering rotary and turbine gas meters, gauges for computing pressure and temperature corrections in industrial processes, and liquid meters used in industrial bulk plants and pipelines. Totalizing fluid meters have improved rapidly in recent years particularly with respect to reliability, accuracy, and range of measurable flow rates.

About one-quarter of the industry's shipments consist of motor vehicle instruments such as speedometers, tachometers, odometers, fuel level gauges, water temperature gauges, ammeters, oil pressure gauges, and other motor vehicle instruments. One-fifth of the industry's shipments consist of parking meters, taximeters (for determining taxicab fares), and mechanical, electrical, electronic, and electromechanical counting and timing instruments for use in industrial processes. Counters and timers are used in a wide variety of manufacturing applications and typically indicate how many items have been fed into a machine, how fast a machine is operating, how many items have been produced, how long it will take to perform a process, or what time a specific event will occur.

Firms in four states—California, Connecticut, Illinois, and Pennsylvania—accounted for 36 percent of the total number of establishments in the industry in 1987. Two-thirds of the work force consisted of production workers in 1992, and the largest nonproduction employee group in the industry were electrical and electronic engineers. Stewart-Warner Corporation, Daniel Industries Inc., Moorco International Inc., Badger Meter Inc., and American Meter Company were among the industry's leaders in shipments and employment.

INDUSTRY INFORMATION SOURCES

U.S. Department of Commerce, *Census of Manufactures, 1992. Industry Series—Instruments and Related Products,* Washington, DC: U.S. Department of Commerce, 1992.

Considine, Douglas M., ed., *Process Instruments and Controls Handbook,* 2d ed., New York: McGraw-Hill, 1974.

Darnay, Arsen J., ed., *Manufacturing USA,* Detroit, MI: Gale Research, 1989.

Miller, R. W., *Flow Measurement Engineering Handbook,* New York: McGraw-Hill, 1983.

Novellino, John, "Counter-Timers Advance into the Digital Age." *Electronic Design,* September 3, 1992, 81-82.

"Counters and Timers: Keeping Pace in Manufacturing." *Production Engineering,* July 1984, 54-56.

U.S. Department of Commerce, *U. S. Industrial Outlook 1993,* Washington, DC: U.S. Department of Commerce, 1993.

Ward's Business Directory of U. S. Private and Public Companies 1993, Detroit, MI: Gale Research, 1993.

—Paul Bodine

SIC 3825

INSTRUMENTS FOR MEASURING AND TESTING OF ELECTRICITY AND ELECTRICAL SIGNALS

The Instruments for Measuring and Testing of Electricity and Electrical Signals Industry is made up of companies that manufacture a multitude of analytical devices. Examples of industry output include voltmeters, ammeters, wattmeters, watt-hour meters, semiconductor test equipment, and circuit testers. Establishments that produce monitoring and testing equipment for navigational, radar, and sonar systems are described in **SIC 3812: Search, Detection, Navigation, Guidance, Aeronautical, and Nautical Systems and Instruments**.

INDUSTRY SNAPSHOT

Discoveries related to electrical properties gave birth to the electrical testing and measuring (T&M) device industry during the middle 1800s. Technological advancements in the U.S., particularly during both world wars, allowed domestic producers to assume a global leadership position during the middle-1900s. By the 1980s, U.S. companies were shipping over $7 billion worth of goods per year, employing more than 90,000 workers, and exporting equipment valued at about $2 billion annually.

Moderate sales growth which characterized the industry during the 1980s slowed in the early 1990s in the wake of economic recess. But growth resumed in the mid-1990s, bolstered by demand for automatic test equipment (ATE), a devalued U.S. dollar, and shipments of high-tech devices to telecommunications industries. Despite increased foreign competition, the United States widened its $2 billion trade surplus in 1993 and was poised for steady global expansion into the 21st century.

ORGANIZATION AND STRUCTURE

The electrical T&M instruments industry encompasses eight major product groups. ATE, the largest industry segment, represented about 25 percent of sales going into the early 1990s. ATE includes T&M instruments for semiconductors, circuit boards, and computer disk drives. Communications test equipment, the second-ranked product group, constituted approximately seven percent of revenues. This group includes T&M devices for landline, wireless, and fiber-optic communications gear.

Other major industry categories include: signal generators (six percent of sales in the early 1990s), electrical integrating instruments (five percent), multimeters (two percent), oscilloscopes (one percent), and spectrum analyzers (.7 percent). Each of these product groups is comprised of a plethora of different devices. In addition, the remaining 60 percent of industry revenues are garnered from a wide range of miscellaneous T&M instruments, such as: tube testers, impedance measurers, frequency meters, battery testers, stroboscopes, tachometers, oscilloscopes, reflectometers, ammeters, and ohmmeters.

A few of the most common T&M devices warrant description. Ohmmeters, a common and traditional industry offering, are used to measure the amount of electrical resistance in a circuit. Likewise, watt-hour meters are most often used to measure and meter the amount of power that is used by a utility customer—Watt-hour meters are mounted on the exterior of most homes and buildings. Potentiometers are used to precisely measure direct current or voltage. They belong to a broad class of devices called indicating instruments, which includes various voltmeters and ammeters. The galvanometer, another indicating instrument, indicates extremely small currents. Reflectometers measure the amount of light or energy reflected from a surface. An oscilloscope converts electron motion into a visual display on a cathode-ray tube.

More than 50 percent of electrical T&M device industry output in the early 1990s was purchased by private industry for use in manufacturing. The Federal Government consumed about eight percent of production, mostly for defense-related endeavors. Companies within the electrical measuring instrument industry accounted for six percent of sales, and radio and television businesses consumed approximately two percent of production. Miscellaneous markets that each accounted for less than one percent of consumption included utilities, natural gas and petroleum companies, and state and local governments. Exports represented almost 30 percent of sales.

About 850 U.S. companies produced electrical T&M equipment in the early 1990s, up from 750 in the early 1980s. Only the top ten industry participants generated revenues of more than $150 million. The majority of the top 75 firms had sales of less than $50 million and employed fewer than 500 workers. Most companies are niche-oriented and specialize in a single product or category.

T&M manufacturers invest more money in their companies than most other U.S. manufactures. In the early 1990s, the average T&M producer made about $330,000 in capital investments, compared to less than

$290,000 for the average U.S. manufacturer. The industry invests heavily in manufacturing productivity.

Nearly one-third of the companies in the industry, representing almost 25 percent total sales, were located in California in the early 1990s—the result of large defense, semiconductor, and telecommunications industries in that state.

BACKGROUND AND DEVELOPMENT

In 1833, Englishman Carl Friedrich Gauss was the first to show that magnetic quantities could be measured in terms of mechanical units. Wilhelm Weber, also of England, defined a system of electrical units in 1851 which lead to the development of the ohm, a measure of electrical resistance, in 1864. The ampere, a unit used to measure electrical current, soon followed. The United States made the ohm and ampere legal units of electrical measurement in 1894.

Early measuring devices were functional, though generally unreliable for precise readings. The earliest device that would deliver a standard for voltage (electromotive force) for measuring instruments, which was built in 1836, was reproducible only to about one percent accuracy. The Clark Cell of 1872, which was used to establish a standard voltage measurement, also proved unreliable. The Weston Cell, introduced in 1892, became the first device to successfully provide a standard for electrical measuring devices.

Following the development of electrical units and credible standards, numerous electricity measuring devices emerged during the early 1900s. Among the first devices were instruments used to measure electrical resistance, such as ohmmeters. In addition, power meters, or wattmeters, became industry mainstays. One of the largest classes of early devices was indicating instruments, such as voltmeters and ammeters.

Many of the first indicating instruments were iron-vane devices, which utilized a plate of steel, a spring pointer, and a damper to form the vane, or moving elements of the meter. As electricity passed through a magnetic coil, the vane tipped to provide a reading. These rugged instruments remained the primary indicating devices for much of the twentieth century, despite the development of more advanced meters. Electrodynamic instruments, which were much more precise than iron-vane mechanisms, were also developed in the early part of the 20th century. These indicating instruments utilized two sets of coils and became popular for laboratory applications.

The development of the transistor in 1947 by Bell Telephone laboratories lead to a profusion of extremely accurate electrical T&M equipment during the latter half of the century. Tube-type and electromechanical instruments were soon replaced by devices accurate to within one-millionth of a unit. As the number of applications for solid-state electronics ballooned, the demand for various T&M equipment flourished throughout the 1950s, 1960s, and 1970s.

By the end of the 1970s, electrical T&M equipment manufacturers were shipping about $6 billion worth of goods per year. Although industry growth had decelerated during the past decade, shipments continued to increase and U.S. manufacturers maintained a significant technological lead over their global counterparts. In 1982 the industry boasted sales of $6.1 billion and a work force of 90,000 employees.

As the T&M industry recovered from a major recession in the late 1970s and early 1980s, revenues jumped to $6.5 billion in 1983 and to a whopping $7.8 billion in 1984. Increased defense spending, growth in telecommunications, and a general proliferation in computers and other electronic devices also contributed to growth. In the mid-1980s, however, foreign competition cut into industry profits, as the share of electronic devices produced overseas swelled. Indeed, revenues grew to only $7.9 billion per year by the end of the decade.

In an effort to maintain profitability and combat low-cost foreign producers, U.S. T&M instrument companies initiated aggressive productivity programs during the 1980s, and stepped-up research and development efforts in high-tech fields. As a result, industry employment plunged to 82,000 by 1989, and the United States retained its significant technological lead in high-profit T&M devices, such as ATE and telecommunications testing equipment.

CURRENT CONDITIONS

An inexpensive U.S. dollar and a resurgence in domestic semiconductor manufacturing spurred electrical T&M device receipts up six percent in 1990, to $8.4 billion. Although a global recession pushed sales down one percent in 1991, revenues lurched upward six percent in 1992 and four percent in 1993, to $9.2 billion. Analysts expected sales to jump past $9.5 billion in 1994.

In addition to healthy demand, producers were also reaping the benefits of massive productivity gains achieved during the 1980s and early 1990s. Despite shipment growth, industry employment continued to decline between 1990 and 1992, by 12 percent. Improved efficiency was allowing some domestic producers to compete in markets for low-priced, traditional equipment. At the same time, however, many companies were striving to move their low-tech production facilities overseas.

Many analysts were surprised at the impressive performance of industry participants in the early 1990s, particularly in light of drastically reduced spending in the defense sector and overall U.S. economic malaise. But sales of advanced T&M devices were ballooning fast enough to make up for sluggish traditional markets. Shipments of digital oscilloscopes and multimeters that were priced to compete with their analog cousins, for instance, offered significant profit opportunities. Likewise, new products related to wireless communications displayed exemplary growth.

Exports also bolstered profits, as foreign demand for price-competitive, high-tech equipment rose. Overseas shipments vaulted ten percent in 1991, seven percent in 1992, and four percent in 1993. At the same time, import growth stagnated as U.S. firms pelted their competition with efficiency gains and advanced product introductions. U.S. exports were expected to rise four percent in 1993, to $2.8 billion, resulting in a healthy industry trade surplus of more than $2 billion.

The fastest growth sector of the electrical T&M device industry in the early 1990s was ATE. After ceding market share to Japanese semiconductor manufacturers in the previous decade, U.S. chip producers were turning the tables by dominating the market for a new generation of high-speed semiconductors (called application specific integrated circuits). T&M device makers benefitted as U.S. semiconductor shipments rocketed from $14 billion in 1990 to an estimated $28 billion in 1994.

Sales of these high-tech, high-profit ATE instruments had grown at a rate of 11 percent per year between 1987 and 1992, and were forecast to increase at an annual pace of 12 percent to 13 percent between 1992 and 1997. U.S. producers controlled nearly 65 percent of the global ATE market in 1993, compared to 35 percent held by Japan.

INDUSTRY LEADERS

The giant of the electrical T&M industry is Hewlett-Packard Company, of California. It was founded in 1938 by William Hewlett and David Packard, graduates of Stanford University's electrical engineering program. With $538 in start-up funds, the two entrepreneurs developed an audio-testing oscillator. Walt Disney was their first customer.

Hewlett-Packard realized steady growth during World War II and the 1940s by developing and selling various electrical T&M gear. Their first major break-

through was the HP-524A. Introduced in 1951, this device reduced the time required to measure radio frequencies from ten minutes to about two seconds.

Hewlett-Packard went public in 1957, and had 1958 sales of $51 million. It expanded into Japan in 1963, and became heavily involved in computers and calculators during the 1970s and 1980s. The industry behemoth generated 1993 net profits of $840 million from $17 billion in revenues. These figures include sales of goods classified outside of this industry. The company employed about 90,000 workers.

The second largest industry participant in the early 1990s was Tektronix Inc., of Oregon. Tektronix had sales of about $1.4 billion per year and 14,000 workers. Axel Johnson Inc., of New York, was the third largest industry competitor with revenues of around $700 million and 1,600 employees. Other industry leaders included Dynatech Corp. and Teradyne Inc., both of Massachusetts.

Despite analysts' expectation of future growth, employment prospects in the electrical T&M device business were bleak going into the mid-1990s. Continued productivity gains and the movement of manufacturing facilities overseas will result in diminished opportunities for virtually every occupation in the industry. Jobs for most production workers are expected to decline 20 percent to 50 percent between 1990 and 2005, according to the Bureau of Labor Statistics. Jobs for general managers and executives will likely realize a 20 percent reduction. Even positions for research engineers and technicians will decrease by one percent to three percent by 2005.

AMERICA AND THE WORLD

U.S. electrical T&M device manufacturers are the most technologically advanced in the world, as evidenced by their strong trade surplus. Their primary competitive advantage is the ability to develop and manufacture high-tech, high-profit devices, such as ATE and telecommunications instruments. U.S. exports of telecommunications devices, for example, ballooned 21 percent in 1992 and about 13 percent in 1993. In contrast, many firms have licensed their low-end technology to regions such as China and India, where production costs are low.

Japan is by far the leading importer of U.S. T&M instruments, accounting for more than 16 percent, or about $430 million, of U.S. overseas sales in 1993. Canada and the United Kingdom each represented eight percent of the U.S. export market. Germany and Mexico purchased seven percent and 5.5 percent, respectively, of U.S. exports. The European Community commanded 36 percent of overseas shipments, and East Asia (not including China) purchased 22 percent. Japan was also the largest exporter of T&M to the United States, exporting about $175 million worth of equipment to this country in 1993.

Although competition was increasing in the middle 1990s, particularly from Europe and Japan, U.S. manufacturers in this industry should be able to maintain their technological lead into the 21st century. Sales to the viable domestic semiconductor industry will be augmented by strong growth in demand from burgeoning wireless telecommunications industries, in which the United States also maintains a technological edge.

RESEARCH AND TECHNOLOGY

U.S. electrical T&M producers were ardently pursuing technological advances in the mid-1990s that would allow them to sharpen their competitive edge at home and abroad. Several emerging industry segments, such as wireless data communications and digital transmission, offered solid growth opportunities for companies on the cutting edge. One of the fastest growing fields that required new types of T&M instruments was thin film transistor liquid crystal displays (LCDs), which are commonly used on portable computers. Although Japan dominated LCD markets, several U.S. producers were developing T&M devices and were communicating with Japanese LCD manufacturers.

Another emerging industry technology was virtual instruments. These are T&M instruments that combine computer software and instrumentation hardware. The instrument appears on a personal computer screen and provides readings as would a T&M device. In fact, an exact replica of the device is displayed on the computer screen, complete with tuning knobs, meters, and digital readout. Instrumentation hardware is used to take readings that are fed into the computer, analyzed by the software, and displayed on the screen. An important advantage of virtual instruments is that they are easily upgraded with new software, as opposed to T&M devices that become obsolete and must be scrapped.

A multitude of other advances in the mid-1990s included miniature, battery-powered, hand-held oscilloscopes. These devices were being used by automotive technicians, for example, to easily monitor electronic modules in cars and trucks. Similarly, Sentech Systems Inc., of Pennsylvania, introduced a device in 1993 that employs laser-based optics to measure the distortion of a turbine shaft. The technology held promise for like applications in the power generation

industry. Also in 1993, Motorola Inc., of Illinois, introduced a sensor that monitors a vehicle's intake manifold to compute the amount of fuel required for each cylinder.

INDUSTRY INFORMATION SOURCES

Andrews, Walter, "U.S. to Lead ATE's in Boom," *Electronic News*, January 3, 1994.

1993 Britannica Book of the Year, Chicago: Encyclopedia Britannica, Inc., 1994.

Britannica Encyclopaedia, Chicago: Encyclopedia Britannica, Inc., 1968.

Darnay, Arsen J., ed., *Manufacturing USA; Industry Analyses, Statistics, and Leading Companies*, Detroit: Gale Research Inc., 1993.

Dehne, Tim, "Virtual Instruments—What They Are, Where They're At," *Electronic Products*, July 1993.

"Electronic Business 200," *Electronic Business*, July 1993.

Hast, Adele, ed., *International Directory of Company Histories, Volume III*, Chicago: St. James Press, 1991.

Holden, Daniel, "Test Equipment: Back on Track," *Electronic News*, January 4, 1993.

Martin, Thomas W., "SCSI Test Systems Are Changing," *Electronic Products*, July 1993.

Mockry, Scott, "No Code Diagnostics: Using a Handheld Digitizing Oscilloscope for Automotive Diagnostics," *Motor Age*, October 1993.

Schneck, Marcus, "High-Tech Firm Introduces Next Generation of Optical Sensing," *Central Penn Business Journal*, January 13, 1993.

"Sensors and Transducers," *Electronic Products*, June 1993.

Strassberg, Dan, "Analog/Digital Scopes Offer the Best of Two Worlds," *EDN*, March 18, 1993.

U.S. Industrial Outlook 1993, Washington, D.C.: U.S. Department of Commerce, June 10, 1993.

—Dave Mote

SIC 3826

LABORATORY ANALYTICAL INSTRUMENTS

This group covers establishments primarily engaged in manufacturing laboratory instruments and instrumentation systems for chemical or physical analysis of the composition or concentration of samples of solid, fluid, gaseous, or composite material. Establishments primarily engaged in manufacturing instruments for monitoring and analyzing continuous samples from medical patients are classified in **SIC 3845: Elec-**

tromedical and **Electrotherapeutic Apparatus;** and from industrial process streams are classified in **SIC 3823: Industrial Instruments for Measurement, Display, and Control of Process Variables; and Related Products.**

INDUSTRY SNAPSHOT

Laboratory analytical instruments manufactured by this industry were used to conduct physical and chemical analyses. Major product groups included clinical laboratory, chromatographic, and spectrophotometric instruments, and mass spectrometers. Industry shipments were worth nearly $6 billion in 1993, and the industry's work force numbered about 40,000. This high-technology sector exported 30 percent of its output in the early 1990s, resulting in a $1 billion trade surplus.

Devices used to measure the purity of gold date back to the 4th century B.C. The term "analysis," in the chemical sense, was first posited in the 1660s. A series of breakthroughs in chemical measuring methods occurred during the 1800s that preceded the development of more advanced analytic instruments later in the 19th century. But not until the 20th century did the industry begin to resemble its state in the early 1990s.

Laboratory analytical instrument sales swelled to about $3.5 billion in 1987, the first year in which this industry was recognized as a separate business. Entering the mid-1990s, revenues were expected to continue expanding through the end of the decade. U.S. technological superiority and increasing demand for analytical instruments made this an important growth industry.

One of the two largest product segments in this industry was chromatographic equipment used to separate chemical substances to determine their content, or to prepare them for further testing. Chromatography instruments were used in oil refineries and on space vehicles to analyze atmospheres on other planets. Chromatograph equipment accounted for 16 percent of industry sales in 1992.

Spectrophotometric equipment, which also represented 16 percent of the industry's shipments in 1992, was used to view, meter, and record spectrums of light or forms of radiated energy. Spectrochemical analysis usually involved the examination of the emission of radiation by molecules that have been heated or excited by some other form of energy, or the absorption of radiation of particular wavelengths by certain molecules.

Mass spectrometry equipment composed about five percent of industry shipments in the early 1990s.

This type of equipment analyzed chemicals by sorting gaseous ions in electric and magnetic fields. The two major types of mass spectroscopes were spectrographs, which used non-electric means to detect the sorted ions, and spectrometers, which measured ions electrically.

In addition to the three major product segments, 60 percent of industry sales were derived from many other devices. A wide range of instruments made for clinical laboratories, for instance, accounted for about 23 percent of production, while parts and accessories represented 17 percent of output. Specialized instruments represented about 18 percent of the industry's sales. Examples of other specialized devices included: titrimeters, which measured the concentration of a substance in a solution; densitometers, which gauged the optical density of a material; coulometric analyzers, which detected the amount of a substance released during electrolysis; and turbidimeters, which were used to measure the scattering of a light beam through a solution that contains suspended particulate matter.

ORGANIZATION AND STRUCTURE

The laboratory analytical instruments industry was an international business dominated by large, innovative companies. In addition, numerous small firms competed by forming alliances or operating in niche markets. The industry was characterized by high-profits, an emphasis on advanced technology, and sporadic growth. Companies typically sell their products directly to research laboratories in pharmaceutical firms, food companies, hospitals, and other establishments that work with chemicals or analyze substances.

Roughly 40 percent of industry sales in the early 1990s were classified as private sector fixed investments, mostly by laboratories of U.S. companies. About 30 percent of production was exported. The federal government purchased eight percent of output, while engineering and scientific instrument manufacturers consumed five percent of production. Other significant markets were aerospace and communications industries, and state and local governments.

BACKGROUND AND DEVELOPMENT

Rudimentary analytical instruments and measuring devices predate the birth of Christ. Naturalist Robert Boyle of England was credited with introducing the term "analysis," in the chemical sense, in his book *The Sceptical Chymist*, published in 1661. In 1669, Isaac Newton conducted light spectrum experiments that eventually lead to the development of the spectroscope. Also in the 17th century, the first precise gravi-metric analysis equipment (used to measure specific gravity) was believed to have been created by Friedreich Hoffman, a German physician and chemist. Numerous key inventions and discoveries during the 18th century included the flame test for alkali metals, qualitative analysis techniques, and titrimetric analy-sis.

Most instruments and methods before the 18th century yielded qualitative analyses. But in the 19th century, French chemist Antoine-Laurent Lavoisier ushered in quantitative analysis, or the determination of the amounts and proportions of chemicals or ele-ments in a substance or gas. Major breakthroughs in analytical instruments and methods during the 1800s included electrochemical analysis methods and gas analysis. In addition, German chemists Gustav Robert Kirchoff and Robert Bunsen introduced the first practi-cal spectroscope in 1859. This important development lead to the discovery of new elements. Spectrographic equipment improved greatly during the late 1800s and early 1900s with the introduction of mass spectrogra-phy, in 1920, flame photometry, in 1928, and radio-chemical methods developed after World War II.

Perhaps the greatest innovations in the history of this industry related to the development of chromatog-raphy. Although first conceived in 1903, workable chromatography equipment was not built until the early 1940s. Gas chromatography and other advanced techniques that emerged during the 1950s significantly expanded the breadth of the analytical instrument in-dustry. These pivotal innovations, combined with steady market growth during the post-World War II economic expansion, resulted in healthy revenue gains for instrument manufacturers. The U.S. assumed a global technological lead it enjoyed throughout the 1960s and 1970s.

Although shipments of all types of U.S. laboratory equipment surged during the 1980s, not until 1987 did the U.S. government classify analytical instruments as a separate industry. By that time, sales of goods in this sector had grown to about $3.5 billion and were rising rapidly compared to most laboratory equipment indus-tries. Indeed, sales jumped 11.5 percent in both 1988 and 1989, and in 1990, as the U.S. economy slumped into a recession, shipments bulged 14 percent to almost $5 billion. In addition to steady growth in domestic demand, U.S. producers benefitted from a global inter-est in their high-technology products. While imports hovered at about $700 million between 1989 and 1992, U.S. exports ballooned from $1.3 billion to $1.7 bil-lion.

CURRENT CONDITIONS

The laboratory analytical instruments industry continued to benefit during the early 1990s from four key factors: 1) the increased concern over the spread of viruses, such as acquired immune deficiency syndrome (AIDS); 2) an intensified quest for new drugs by phar-maceutical companies; 3) a proliferation of environ-mental concerns and regulations, and; 4) strong de-mand overseas for high-technology, high-profit instruments. As a result, industry shipments rose ap-proximately 20 percent between 1990 and 1993 to almost $6 billion. Furthermore, exports, bolstered by a weak U.S. dollar, bulged about six percent in 1993 to an estimated $1.8 billion.

At the same time that manufacturers in this indus-try were boosting sales and profit margins on high-technology items, many were also increasing their profits through gains in productivity. Increased auto-mation, advanced information systems, and manage-ment restructuring allowed many competitors to cut costs. Thus, as the amount of value added during the manufacturing process increased 30 percent between 1987 and 1990, for the average industry participant, the size of the work force grew less than 20 percent, to approximately 38,000. Gains in productivity were partly offset by higher research and development costs, however.

Entering the mid-1990s, manufacturers focused on product quality and customer service to help them regain the rampant growth they enjoyed during the late 1980s. They also emphasized new product introduc-tions. Environmental and pharmaceutical markets of-fered the strongest growth domestically. But demand from food processing, biotechnology, and chemical industries remained relatively healthy.

In the long term, makers of laboratory analytical instruments were predicted to become increasingly dependent on sales of advanced technology products utilized by highly industrialized nations. Gas chroma-tography and mass spectrometry equipment were an-ticipated to be major growth segments, as were several newer niche product groups, such as capillary electro-phoresis devices. Markets for low-technology products were expected to be controlled by low-cost producers in emerging regions, such as Mexico and East Asia.

INDUSTRY LEADERS

Market share in the laboratory analytical instru-ments industry was concentrated, with a few industry leaders controlling the market. High start-up costs and rigid technological requirements discouraged new en-trants. Perkin-Elmer Corp., the largest manufacturer, generated roughly $840 million in sales in 1991 and employed 6,400 workers. The company reorganized three times between 1988 and 1993, and formed alliances with corporate giants such as Dow Chemical and Hoffmann-La Roche. Despite a drop in earnings in 1993 caused by an accounting change, Perkin-Elmer was positioned for growth during the mid-1990s. In 1993, for example, the company introduced a breakthrough system of medical testing. The testing system integrated an advanced method of replicating DNA, which was more accurate and less expensive than competing systems.

Beckman Instruments Inc., of California, was the second largest company with 1991 sales of $815 million and about 7,100 workers. Beckman developed an instrument in the early 1990s that analyzed extremely small amounts of rare genetic and other biochemical materials. Other industry leaders in the early 1990s included: Fisher Scientific, with $450 million in 1991 sales; Curtin Matheson Scientific Inc., with $350 million in sales; and Millipore Corp., with $300 million in sales. The majority of the leading 75 firms had annual sales of less than $25 million and employed fewer than 100 workers in the early 1990s.

WORK FORCE

Despite expectations for market growth, future employment opportunities in this industry were questionable. The overall outlook for U.S. measuring and controlling device industries was bleak, with most labor positions expected to decline 15 percent to 50 percent between 1990 and 2005, according to the U.S. Bureau of Labor.

Positions for managers, engineers, and sales professionals were forecasted to diminish about ten percent. Although workers in the laboratory analytical instruments business were expected to fare better than their counterparts in related industries, continued productivity gains, consolidation, and the movement of some manufacturing activities overseas would likely thwart long term job growth.

AMERICA AND THE WORLD

The U.S. laboratory analytical industry was the most advanced and productive in the world. As exports surged to roughly $1.8 billion in 1993, its trade surplus grew to a healthy $1 billion. In Japan, U.S. producers achieved an impressive $170 million annual surplus by 1991. Foreign demand for advanced proprietary gear remained strong going into the mid-1990s. Furthermore, the export market for U.S. goods was extremely fragmented, suggesting solid long term growth potential. Product categories realizing the greatest overseas

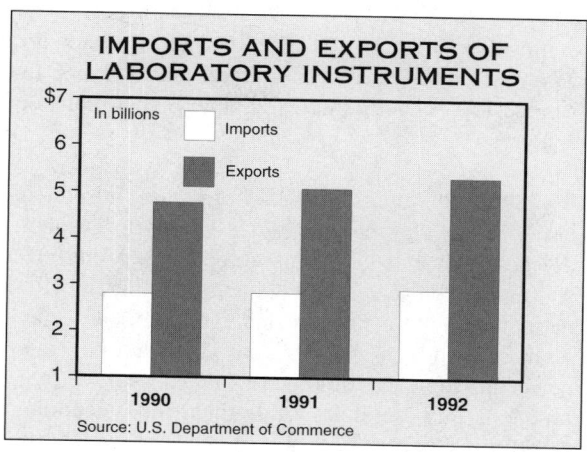

IMPORTS AND EXPORTS OF LABORATORY INSTRUMENTS

Source: U.S. Department of Commerce

demand in the early 1990s included chromatographs and electrophoresis instruments, general chemical instruments, and viscosity measuring devices.

The largest importer of U.S. instruments was Canada, which purchased only 13 percent of all cross-border shipments in 1991. Other major buyers included Japan (12 percent of U.S. exports), Germany (10 percent), the United Kingdom (seven percent), and France (seven percent). Exports to France climbed a whopping 65 percent between 1988 and 1991. Combined sales to Europe totaled $680 million in 1992, representing 40 percent of all exports. Japan was the biggest importer into the United States, supplying $31 million worth of instruments. Japan was followed by Germany, the United Kingdom, and Switzerland.

While global markets were expected to offer opportunities, many competitors in the mid-1990s felt that a global industry presence was a necessity in light of rising development costs and maturing domestic markets.

RESEARCH AND TECHNOLOGY

Major technological trends entering the mid-1990s included the proliferation of combined equipment, such as single units that integrated both chromatograph and spectrometer functions; smaller instruments, particularly portable environmental field equipment, increased quality and precision, and growth in information systems and robotics. The growth in information systems and robotics was evidenced by rising installations of laboratory information management systems (LIMS), as well as a growing demand for automated sample preparation systems for bio-pharmaceutical applications. A new system introduced in 1993, for example, handled multiple sample preparation tasks and was operated by Windows-based personal computer software for easy use. Several other automation and robotics systems, offered by companies such as CRS Plus Inc. and Zymark Inc., were aimed at relatively inexperienced users that wanted to conduct complex sample preparations and analyses.

Similarly, manufacturers were also introducing easier-to-use chromatography and mass spectrometry devices. Advanced systems automatically optimized and tuned themselves during operation, thereby eliminating much of the practice and guess-work associated with conventional instruments. In addition, many newer instruments combined as many as three major functions into one unit. While these high-technology workhorses were regularly priced at more than $200,000, they were typically easier to operate and less expensive than two or more side-by-side units with commensurate capabilities.

INDUSTRY INFORMATION SOURCES

"$3 Billion From Underseas in Decade," *American Metal Market,* January 12, 1994.

Darnay, Arsen J., ed., *Manufacturing USA; Industry Analyses, Statistics, and Leading Companies,* Detroit: Gale Research Inc., 1993.

DeYoung, H. Garrett, "Managing Technology at Warp Speed," *Electronic Business,* January 21, 1991.

"DOC Forecasts Modest Increase in Instruments," *R & D,* February 1992.

"Dow, Perkin-Elmer Sign Process Technology Pact," *Chemical & Engineering News,* May 10, 1993.

Harlans S., Byrne, "Perkin-Elmer: Fine tuning product line leads to improved performance," *Barron's,* June 21, 1993.

"Instrumentation '94," *Chemical & Engineering News,* March 14, 1994.

"P-E Turns $13.8M Profit in Q3," *Electronic News,* May 25, 1992.

Resa, King, "A gene machine starts cloning cash; Roche and Perkin-Elmer are ready to reap big rewards from PCR," *Business Week,* November 22, 1993.

U.S. Industrial Outlook 1993, Washington: U.S. Department of Commerce, June 10, 1993.

Wolf, Kenneth, "France is Major market for American Scientific Gear," *Journal of Commerce and Commercial,* October 15, 1992.

—Dave Mote

OPTICAL INSTRUMENTS AND LENSES

This category covers establishments primarily engaged in manufacturing instruments and apparatus that measure an optical property and optically project, measure, or magnify an image, such as binoculars, microscopes, prisms, and lenses. Included are establishments primarily engaged in manufacturing optical sighting and fire control equipment.

Companies in this industry manufacture a plethora of devices, including: weapon firing control mechanisms, optical laser sighting systems, binoculars, borescopes, cameras lenses, contour projection apparatus, gun sights, opera glasses, interferometers, microscopes, telescopes, periscopes, and spyglasses. Most devices in this industry use lenses. But some products that don't utilize lenses, such as rifle aiming circles and some types of surveying equipment, simply help users to align or measure objects. Electronic optical devices that don't use glass or plastic lenses, like the electron microscope, are classified elsewhere.

The largest segment of this industry is sighting, tracking, and fire control equipment, much of which is used in missile systems, combat aircraft, and other defense applications. These advanced products accounted for about 30 percent of industry revenues in the early 1990s. Optical test and inspection equipment, which made up about seven percent of sales, includes a variety of mechanisms. Much of it is used by other industries, like automobiles and steel, for quality control and other purposes. four percent of industry output was in the form of binoculars and astronomical instruments, and about three percent consisted of microscopes. The remaining 50 percent of sales was garnered from numerous miscellaneous devices.

Most products in the industry use compound lens systems. A series of several convex and/or concave lenses is often used to magnify light reflected from an image. Although a single convex lens will theoretically focus incoming light, such a system typically suffers from defects which cause blurring and distortion. Therefore, many lens systems, such as those in cameras, use eight or more lenses in series or cemented together to reduce aberration, coma (blurring), and distortion.

Lenses are typically manufactured from glass in a process called grinding. First, the glass is cast in blocks, strips, panes, and rods, or may be molded into a rough lens form. Then it is cut and rough-ground using a diamond abrasive on a grinding wheel. Fine grinding is accomplished using a silicon carbide or emery abrasive. For fine optical instruments, final polishing may take several hours using a precise lapping tool. Finally, the edge of the lens is ground so that its axis is precisely centered. Sometimes the lens is coated with a substance that reduces distortion. In addition to glass, transparent plastics are also used for lenses. They are simply molded, rather than ground.

BACKGROUND AND DEVELOPMENT

Modification of simple glass lenses has been practiced since ancient times. But the development of compound lens devices did not occur until 1600. Dutch lensmaker Hans Jannsen and his son, Zacharias, mounted sliding lenses in a tube in 1600 to form the first simple microscope. In 1611, a compound system which used a convex lens in the microscope's eyepiece was built by Johannes Kepler.

Historians often credit Hans Lippershey of Holland with inventing the telescope in 1608. Lippershey accidentally aligned two lenses of opposite curvature and different focal length. The concept may have been understood by Roger Bacon in the 13th century, however. Galileo Galilei developed the first lens, or refracting, astronomical telescope in 1609. Christian Huygens improved his design soon afterward with a telescope that reduced aberration. While these simple devices suffered a variety of defects, they achieved useful results.

During the remainder of the 17th century, compound optical instruments were vastly improved to increase magnifying power and reduce distortion. Important developments included Isaac Newton's design in 1668 of a reflecting telescope that used mirrors to reduce aberration. Innovations during the 18th century largely reduced aberration and distortion in both telescopes and microscopes, resulting in apparatus which closely resemble the instruments commonly used during most of the 20th century.

Early during the 20th century, optical apparatus manufacturers focused on increasing power, or magnification. New lens manufacturing and mounting techniques allowed significant gains. Telescopes, for example, with refracting lenses of 36″ and 40″ and reflectors of 150″ were eventually built in the largest observatories. But conventional glass lens magnifying technology was approaching its limit. Large refracting lenses suffered from distortion caused by sagging under their own weight. After World War II, scientists began searching for optical instruments that used alternatives to glass lenses, such as radio waves and magnetic lenses, to improve microscope and telescope devices.

In addition to the development of optical devices that don't use glass lenses, new types of optical devices emerged during the mid-1900s. Optical apparatus that could be used to control laser beams, for example, became an important industry offering. And the creation of new electro-optical devices opened up entirely new markets in other industries. By the 1980s, electro-optical equipment was being used to analyze and control manufacturing processes, guide missiles, operate audio-visual systems, and to perform many other functions. Optical interferometers, for example, were developed to measure wavelengths, and optical metallographs were created to study the structure of metals and their compounds.

CURRENT CONDITIONS

By the late 1980s, manufacturers of optical instruments and lenses were shipping about $2 billion worth of goods annually. Increased defense spending, an upsurge in exports, and general economic growth significantly bolstered industry revenues during the early- and mid-1980s. Exports had played a particularly important role in earnings growth. Indeed, by the early 1990s exports represented nearly 50 percent of total U.S. optical instrument sales, reflecting an annual increase in overseas demand of nine percent between 1989 and 1992.

Although sales continued to grow at a rate of about four percent annually between 1989 and 1991, shipments slipped about eight percent in 1992 to $2.2 billion and were expected to stagnate or grow slowly in the near future. Decreased U.S. defense expenditures were one reason for the slowdown. Importantly, though, greater competition from low-cost foreign producers was diminishing U.S. sales of binoculars, microscopes, and other conventional devices. In addition, advanced products from manufacturers in Germany and Japan were displacing U.S. exports of some high-tech goods.

Although U.S. export growth had slowed some in the middle 1990s, manufacturers had made sizable gains during the previous decade—U.S. optical industry imports had grown at a rate of about one percent per year during the 1980s, to about $900 million. And U.S. producers were poised for growth in certain technological arenas. Overseas demand was greatest for advanced laser-optics and new liquid crystal devices, which accounted for a combined 35 percent of U.S. exports.

INDUSTRY LEADERS

About 270 companies were classified in the U.S. optical instruments and lenses industry in the early

1990s. Many of these organizations are subsidiaries or divisions of large conglomerates, such as ITT. The largest competitor in the early 1990s was Leica Inc., of Illinois. This diversified optics producer had 1991 sales of about $130 million and employed a work force of 400. Contraves USA Inc., of Pennsylvania, had 1991 revenues of about $100 million. The third largest player was Hughes Danbury Optical, of Connecticut, which also shipped $100 million worth of goods.

Industry participants employed about 22,000 workers in the early 1990s at an average annual payroll of about $30,000, 14 percent higher than the U.S. manufacturing average. Laborers averaged $12.34 per hour going into 1990, compared to the manufacturing hourly average of $10.50. Although the industry pays well, the long term employment outlook for people employed in this and related industries is generally poor. Increased automation combined with the movement of some low-tech manufacturing activities overseas will likely reduce job opportunities. Work for assemblers and fabricators, for example, will decline by 35 percent to 50 percent between 1990 and 2005, according to the Bureau of Labor Statistics. High-tech engineering and research occupations are more apt to provide new opportunities.

RESEARCH AND TECHNOLOGY

Long term growth will depend on the ability of U.S. companies to introduce new, high-profit optical technologies. While the demand for U.S. produced conventional products will stagnate or decline, sales of new manufacturing and laboratory optical equipment should expand at a healthy pace. For example, the Automated Imaging Association estimates that the North American market for new machine visions systems, which includes some products in this industry group, will grow 14 percent per year between 1990 and 1995 to $906 million. Sales of electro-optical systems used in production and quality control were already estimated at about $900 million in 1993.

Japanese competitors lead their U.S. counterparts in some technologies. A breakthrough advance in that country was achieved in 1978 by Hitachi Corporation's Akira Tonomura. Tonomura invented one of the world's most powerful optical devices, the field-emission electron microscope. But U.S. optics manufacturers continued to invest in new products—the average company made capital investments of about $270,000 annually in the early 1990s—and had delivered numerous cutting edge products to market.

Insitec Measurement Systems Inc. introduced a laser-optical instrument that significantly sped up laboratory particle analysis and could be used in difficult environments. Electro-optical instruments were increasingly finding application in industry, as well. Paper manufacturers, for example, were using advanced U.S. optical process control technology in the early 1990s to measure strength, surface, and structural properties of their output. Likewise, high-tech contour projectors and optical comparators were being utilized in businesses, such as tool manufacturing, to inspect and ensure accuracy and quality.

INDUSTRY INFORMATION SOURCES

Bureau, William H., "Properties in Perspective," *Graphic Arts Monthly*, March 1991.

Darnay, Arsen J., ed., *Manufacturing USA; Industry Analyses, Statistics, and Leading Companies*, Detroit: Gale Research Inc., 1993.

Grolier's Encyclopedia. Danbury, CT: Grolier's Inc., 1993.

Holve, Donald J. "Sizing Particles With a Laser," *R&D*, March 1991.

Owen, Jean V., "Seeing the Unseen," *Manufacturing Engineering*, April 1993.

Polidor, Edward T., "Noncontact: Faster Measurement Data," *Quality*, August 1991.

Port, Otis and Neil Gross, "Japan: Scientists," *Business Week*, June 15, 1990.

Stout, Gail, "Machine Visions Systems," *Quality*, January 1993.

U.S. Industrial Outlook 1993, Washington, D.C.: U.S. Department of Commerce, June 10, 1993.

—Dave Mote

SIC 3829

MEASURING AND CONTROLLING DEVICES, NOT ELSEWHERE CLASSIFIED

The Measuring and Controlling Devices, Not Elsewhere Classified industry is comprised of companies primarily engaged in manufacturing a multitude of miscellaneous monitoring instruments. Major industry product segments include aircraft engine instruments (15 percent of industry sales in the early 1990s), nuclear radiation detection devices (18 percent), and geophysical and meteorological equipment (25 percent). This industry also encompasses companies that produce selected surveying and drafting supplies (7 percent), such as transits, slide rules, and T-squares.

Rising demand for measuring and controlling devices by aerospace, nuclear, and petroleum industries after 1950 pushed industry revenues to about $2 billion by the end of the 1970s. Likewise, increased defense spending and general U.S. economic growth, combined with steady export gains, almost doubled revenues during the 1980s. Indeed, as aerospace and nuclear device sales proliferated, overall industry sales grew at an average rate of 7 percent between 1982 and 1990, to more than $4 billion. And exports represented a whopping 40 percent of shipments.

Sharp cutbacks in defense spending and the virtual cessation of new nuclear facility construction in the United States rattled industry participants in the early 1990s. Despite some domestic setbacks, the demand for meteorological measuring devices continued to grow, and exports surged. Sales increased an encouraging 4 percent in 1993 to about $4.6 billion, despite lingering economic malaise. In addition, U.S. producers increased the industry's trade surplus to $1.2 billion. Sales of nuclear detection devices and geophysical instrumentation lead export gains.

In the long term, the miscellaneous measuring and controlling devices industry will likely realize tepid growth. Low interest in domestic nuclear facility development and reduced defense expenditures will severely curtail industry expansion. Japan, South Korea, and Taiwan, which will offer major export markets for radiation testing devices, should partially offset a slowdown in major domestic segments. And demand for geophysical and meteorological devices should remain strong. Two percent growth was forecast for 1994.

The industry is fragmented in comparison to other U.S. manufacturing sectors, with about 850 companies competing in the early 1990s. The average industry participant employed only 24 workers in 1991, compared to 37 for all other U.S. manufacturing firms. Most firms are specialized. Of the top 50 companies, most had revenues of less than $50 million per year in the early 1990s and employed fewer than 400 workers. The largest producer was Imo Industries Inc., of New Jersey, which had 1991 sales of $1 billion from its diversified operations. Ametek Inc., of Pennsylvania, boasted 1991 sales of $661 million, and third-ranked Vishay Intertechnology, also of Pennsylvania, had revenues of $446 million. Other leaders included Sun Electric Corp., of Illinois, and EG and G Energy, of Nevada.

Although industry employment remained steady during the 1980s, at about 37,000 workers, increased automation and the movement of some manufacturing activities overseas will likely result in work force cutbacks during the 1990s. Most labor jobs, such as those for assemblers and material handlers, will decline by 30 percent to 50 percent between 1990 and

2005, according to the Bureau of Labor Statistics. Likewise, executive and managerial support positions will fall 10 percent to 20 percent. Only openings for sales and marketing professionals were forecast to rise—by a slim 2.5 percent by 2005.

INDUSTRY INFORMATION SOURCES

Darnay, Arsen J., ed., *Manufacturing USA; Industry Analyses, Statistics, and Leading Companies*, Detroit: Gale Research Inc., 1993.

Standard & Poor's Industry Surveys, New York: Standard & Poor's Corporation, December 24, 1992.

U.S. Industrial Outlook 1993, Washington, D.C.: U.S. Department of Commerce, January 1993.

—Dave Mote

SIC 3841

SURGICAL AND MEDICAL INSTRUMENTS AND APPARATUS

This category covers establishments primarily engaged in manufacturing medical, surgical, ophthalmic, and veterinary instruments and apparatus. Establishments primarily engaged in manufacturing surgical and orthopedic appliances are classified in **SIC 3842: Orthopedic, Prosthetic, and Surgical Appliances and Supplies;** those manufacturing electrotherapeutic and electromedical apparatus are classified in **SIC 3845: Electromedical and Electrotherapeutic Apparatus;** and those manufacturing X-ray apparatus are classified in **SIC 3844: X-ray Apparatus and Tubes and Related Irradiation Apparatus.**

INDUSTRY SNAPSHOT

The first medical instruments of precision were used in the 17th century. Not until the 18th century was surgery raised to the level of a definite branch of science. Rapid advances which took place in the 20th century resulted in the evolution of a $13 billion U.S. surgical instrument industry by the early 1990s. Indeed, the U.S. maintains the most advanced surgical device industry in the world. Besides serving a critical role in the care of Americans' health, the medical and surgical instrument industry employed 100,000 workers and exported over $2.5 billion worth of products in 1993.

In the early 1990s manufacturers continued to enjoy the fruits of their success. Revenues increased at an average rate of over nine percent in 1990, 1991, and 1992, and were expected to rise similarly in 1993.

Profit growth mimicked this trend. Growth in 1993 exports, moreover, was estimated at ten percent. And, notwithstanding productivity gains, industry employment had grown at approximately five percent per year in the early 1990s.

Despite an overall positive industry environment, medical instrument producers faced several hurdles going into the mid-1990s. Reduced availability of capital for research and development (R&D), a frustrating slowdown in Food and Drug Administration (FDA) new product approvals, and the promise of a nationalized health care system under the Clinton administration were the major issues concerning competitors. Several segments of the industry appeared to be reaching maturity, indicating that overall profit growth might begin slowing in the future.

ORGANIZATION AND STRUCTURE

Total U.S. health care expenditures in 1993 were expected to reach $940 billion, or about 14 percent of U.S. gross domestic product (GDP). Of that amount, the five medical equipment supplies industries represented about 4.3 percent, or $39.5 billion. The surgical, medical, and ophthalmic device industry classified here accounted for 34 percent, or about $13.4 billion, of that amount—this represents just over 1.4 percent of total U.S. health care costs. Complementary segments of the overall medical equipment supplies industry include surgical appliances (35 percent of the market); electromedical equipment (19 percent); X-ray apparatus and tubes (eight percent); and dental equipment (four percent).

Major consumers of industry output in the early 1990s, in order of market size, included foreign consumers, the federal government, medical and health services, doctors and dentists, hospitals, individuals consumers, and drug companies. Sixty-three percent of all industry revenues were classified as gross private fixed investment in 1991.

Over 20,000 medical device manufacturers were registered in the U.S. in 1993. Fewer than 1,500 of these firms, however, were engaged primarily in this industry. The western United States had the highest concentration of competitors, at about 34 percent. In fact, about 20 percent of all firms active in the industry are located in California. Furthermore, California boasted nearly twice as many start-up medical device firms in 1992 as Florida, which had the second greatest number of industry entrants.

The industry is relatively unconcentrated, partly because it is in a stage of growth and has not matured. Barriers to entry are significant, however, unlike many other high-growth businesses. Companies often must incur huge start-up costs to cover research and product development costs. Furthermore, acute technical expertise is typically needed to develop proprietary knowledge necessary to differentiate products from others in the marketplace, and to obtain approvals and patents. Companies that overcome these hurdles, however, often reap large profits if their products succeed.

Products. **SIC 3841: Surgical and Medical Instruments and Apparatus** encompasses a plethora of non-electric diagnostic and therapeutic surgical devices. "Diagnostic" refers to equipment used to identify physical problems based on signs and symptoms. Therapeutic devices are used to actually treat ailments and illnesses. Some of the largest general categories of equipment are hand instruments, monitoring equipment, intravenous apparatus, syringes, and catheters.

Examples of hand instruments include forceps, knives, saws, retractors, clamps, bone drills, and other products. Forceps are used to grasp, pull, and hold objects during delicate operations. Several monitoring devices exist. Gastroscopes, for instance, are used to view the interior of the stomach. Cystoscopes provide a view of the interior of the bladder. Likewise, a laryngoscope is used to study the larynx and vocal cords. Ophthalmoscopes permit inspection of the retina, and stethoscopes are used to listen to internal organs, particularly the heart and lungs. Intravenous equipment basically consists of IV transfusion apparatus, which transfer blood or other fluids into the body.

Catheters, an important industry segment, are tubes that are inserted into various body cavities to drain liquids or remove material. Cardiac catheterization, for instance, involves introducing a small catheter into a vein and then passing it into the heart. This procedure allows doctors to get accurate diagnostic measurements or to clear blocked arteries. A more advanced procedure, called angioplasty, incorporates a tiny balloon into the procedure. As an ultra-thin catheter is slipped into an artery, the balloon is inflated, thereby widening clogged arteries. Catheters are also used to drain urine and other bodily fluids.

Some other miscellaneous devices produced in the industry include tonometers, speculums, skin grafting equipment, sphygmomanometers, silt lamps, hypodermic rifles, surgical probes, operating tables, needle holders, inhalators, and bone plates and screws.

In the late 1980s catheters accounted for the single largest segment of surgical and medical instrument and apparatus shipments. About 14 percent of sales were attributable to this category. Surgical instruments, which represented ten percent of sales, were the second largest segment. Syringes accounted for over eight percent of revenues and diagnostic apparatus held nearly a seven percent share of the market. Blood transfusion devices and anesthesia apparatus represented about six percent and four percent of sales, respectively. Replacement parts accounted for five percent of industry output. Hospital furniture, such as operating room tables, were responsible for over six percent of revenues. Miscellaneous instruments and devices accounted for the remaining 40 percent of shipments.

Federal Regulation. An important dynamic influencing the industry's production and profitability is FDA regulation. The FDA is responsible for insuring that all products sold in the industry comply with federal safety standards. The FDA possesses the authority to recall products, temporarily suspend devices it deems high-risk, and impose monetary penalties for violations.

The 1990 Safe Medical Devices Act (SMDA), which defined procedures for bringing medical products to the market, is one of the most significant pieces of legislation governing producers. Among other stipulations, the SMDA requires certain manufacturers to track patients that should be notified in the case of product failure; submit follow-up reviews for certain implants and devices; and, when applying for pre-market clearance, provide a summary of safety and effectiveness data for each device.

The FDA reviews medical devices under one of two procedures. Firms introducing completely new devices are required to submit a Product Marketing Application (PMA). The PMA must demonstrate the devices' safety, as well as its diagnostic or therapeutic benefit. Detailed documentation of extensive animal and human tests must be provided to the FDA to support manufacturer claims. New devices that resemble products already on the market are reviewed under a less stringent procedure called "501(k) pre-market notification." In 1992 about 2,500 new products were approved under the 501(k) procedure. Conversely, only 12 PMAs were approved in that year.

BACKGROUND AND DEVELOPMENT

In the early 1600s, Sanctorious, an Italian professor, was the first physician to employ diagnostic instruments of precision in the practice of medicine. Using a pendulum made from a cord and a weight, he was able to measure people's pulse rate by adjusting the weight until it swung at an even tempo with the patient's pulse. Sanctorious later implemented a type of thermometer that could measure a patient's weight and temperature. Both inventions were influenced by his friend Galileo.

Although crude forms of surgery had been practiced prior to that time, the 17th and 18th centuries produced several advancements in surgical and anatomical knowledge. Noted physicians, such as Englishmen William Harvey, John Monro, Robert Sibbald, and Archibald Pitcairne, contributed to the science and helped to establish some of the first formal educational institutions for doctors. Microscopes, injection needles, and instruments of dissection were a few of the tools that allowed researchers of that period to gain a comprehensive understanding of the internal human structure, as well as of physiological processes.

An important American contribution to the advancement of surgery was anesthetic devices, which were introduced in the mid-1800s. Crawford Long, Gardner Colton, and Horace Wells shared credit for breakthroughs in ether and nitrous oxide anesthetics. The 19th century also brought important inventions such as the ophthalmoscope, the sphygmomanometer (for measuring blood pressure), and the stethoscope. The first stethoscope, which was invented in 1816, consisted of a perforated wooden cylinder that transmitted sounds from the patient's chest to the doctor's ear. Perhaps more important than new instruments, though, was a gradual understanding of germs during the 1800s. This evolution led to the use of antiseptics, as well as surgical caps, masks, and rubber gloves in the 1890s.

While surgical tools and techniques advanced throughout the 18th and 19th centuries, surgery remained a relatively crude science up until the early 1900s. Even by the turn of the century, surgery more closely resembled a craft than a science. Forceful, hearty surgeons of the time viewed themselves as omniscient pioneers heralding in a new age. Armed with antiseptics, they were prepared to tackle any challenge.

Despite their knowledge of germs, most surgeons before 1910 continued to operate without gloves, masks, or caps. They commonly wore the same smock until it was caked with blood from several surgeries, and would continue using instruments that had been dropped on a bloody floor. Surgery was usually performed in a theater-type setting before an audience as the patient lay on a narrow wooden table. Instruments were usually forged steel, without plating, and had wooden or ivory handles. Because amputation was one of the most common procedures, the saw was a favored tool.

The 20th century, particularly the first 40 years, ushered in an entirely new era of medicine. Better anesthetics, more highly educated and specialized surgeons, and X-ray machines prompted a transition to more scientific surgery and the demand for new types of instruments. New materials, such as stainless steel and plastics, broadened the scope of the device and apparatus industry. Catheters, suction devices, intravenous infusion apparatus, and various mechanical and electrical diagnostic devices were a few of the important inventions that occurred prior to 1930. This new equipment opened up entirely new surgical specialties, such as neurosurgery and cardiac and urinary tract surgery.

Instruments and apparatus introduced in the postwar period were numerous. Inactive metals, such as vitalium and tantalum, were used to create wire and mesh devices that could be left inside the body. Likewise, nylon thread and special plastics, orlon tubing used in place of arteries, plastic sponges that patched heart defects, and other indwelling devices were introduced. In addition, the vast array of diagnostic and therapeutic equipment that comprised industry offerings by the 1980s was gradually developed in the 1950s, 1960s, and 1970s to complement ever-increasing medical knowledge.

By 1980, the medical instrument and apparatus industry was shipping nearly $4 billion worth of products each year. Stellar sales growth since the 1960s was attributable to several factors. Employer-sponsored health care systems developed after World War II offered few incentives for providers to control costs. As a result, expenditures on instruments and apparatus, as well as other health care products and services, ballooned. In fact, throughout the 1970s and 1980s, U.S. health care expenditures rose at a rate of more than ten percent per year.

Other factors that contributed to growth in expenditures—particularly during the 1970s and 1980s—included a burgeoning elderly population and a general increase in demand for health care. General demand growth was largely a result of the development of new, more advanced procedures and equipment designed to deliver more comprehensive and higher quality care. Indeed, between 1965 and 1990, the percentage of the GDP Americans spent on health care jumped from six percent to over 15 percent. Some of the fastest growing segments included instruments for angioplasty, cardiac catheterization, and orthopedic operations.

As expenditures leapt during the 1980s, development and sales of instruments and apparatus blossomed. While manufacturers made massive investments in new product research and development, expenditures on industry products averaged jumps of more than ten percent annually between 1980 and 1990. Furthermore, exports continued to grow as foreign markets looked to the United States as a source of state-of-the-art surgical instruments and apparatus. Throughout the 1980s, in fact, U.S. firms dominated over 50 percent of the world market for surgical supplies.

By 1990, industry participants were generating over $10.2 billion in revenues per year, employing nearly 90,000 workers, and exporting over $1.8 billion in shipments. Besides providing a trade surplus of more than $1 billion annually, the industry was a comparatively non-polluting member of the manufacturing community and was a source of many high-wage jobs.

CURRENT CONDITIONS

Surgical and medical instrument and apparatus manufacturers continued to post solid gains in the early 1990s, in light of a generally sluggish U.S. and global economy. Revenues ascended about ten percent in both 1991 and 1992 and were projected to grow by over eight percent in 1993. Exports, moreover, jumped an average of 14 percent per year between 1989 and 1993.

As the industry's sales volume clambered past an impressive $13 billion, employment surged to over 100,000 in 1993. Success was partially attributable to massive industry investments, which amounted to about 6.5 percent of revenues in the early 1990s. The average investment for other U.S. industries was about 3.6 percent of sales. Medical device firms in the European Community and Japan, moreover, reinvested only five percent and six percent, respectively.

Leading growth in the 1990s was a promising new sphere of "minimally invasive" surgical instruments. These devices allowed surgeons to conduct complex operations without the pain, time, and expense associated with conventional procedures. Laparoscopic and endoscopic devices, for instance, involved the insertion of narrow tubes, called trocars, into a patient's abdomen. A laparoscope inserted into the tube is used to take pictures of the patient's inner organs, and miniature devices sent through the tube are used to perform complex surgical procedures. The market for minimally invasive devices was expected to explode in the 1990s and 2000s.

Another leading growth segment in the early 1990s was angioplasty catheters. In 1992 about 400,000 angioplasty procedures were performed at a cost of $550 million. This compared with 184,000 such operations in 1987 and only 82,000 in 1982. The procedure provided an important alternative to heart by-pass surgery in many cases.

Indeed, because of the changing dynamics of the health care market, cost-containment pressures were driving the growth of new money-saving procedures like angioplasty and laparoscopy. As purchasing decisions in the 1980s and 1990s shifted from physicians to hospitals and managed care facilities, producers were being forced to demonstrate the cost effectiveness of their products. Devices that could reduce hospital stays, increase labor productivity, and facilitate patient care in less expensive settings had become the dominant growth market by 1993.

Industry executives maintained an expectedly rosy outlook going into the mid-1990s, according to a 1993 survey of 242 company presidents and CEOs in *Medical Device & Diagnostic Industry* (*MDDI*). The survey indicated that 80 percent of respondents predicted that their business would improve in 1993, while only two percent expected a decline. Eighty percent of the respondents believed that new product introduction and overall increased unit sales would spur growth, while 21 percent were relying on price growth to boost profits. About 66 percent of the respondents planned to increase research and development expenditures, while less than one percent planned a reduction.

Challenges. Despite strong growth and optimism, competitors were facing significant obstacles to continued profitability as they entered the mid-1990s. Growing regulatory costs and barriers, decreased access to investment capital, and increased competition in the health care industry all posed formidable challenges. Furthermore, some large segments, such as catheters, appeared to be entering a stage of maturity—meaning slower growth and reduced profit margins.

Inadequate funding for growth and research and development was the primary concern of industry executives in 1993, according to the *MDDI* survey. A decline in venture capital, traditionally a significant source of medical device research and development funding, was a major reason for the shortfall. As FDA regulations increased, venture capitalists viewed new projects as riskier. Furthermore, the promise of nationalized health care by the Clinton administration had created a perception of industry instability in the minds of many lenders.

The impact of reduced funding was made most apparent by the reduction in the growth of new start-up companies. After increasing 12 percent in 1991, the number of new start-up firms grew only seven percent in 1992. "Companies looking for venture capital to fund research and development for a breakthrough product that has yet to see its first dollar of sales should look for something else to do," said Brent Rider, a venture capitalist, in *MDDI*.

Besides decreasing research and development capital, President Clinton's national health care proposal in 1993 boded poorly for manufacturers. Clinton backed a system during his campaign which emphasized comprehensive national care—a plan which would add 35 million people to the U.S. medical device market. The proposal that the Clinton administration was preparing to deliver to Congress in 1994, however, incorporated sweeping government controls that implied some negatives for manufacturers. Specifically, the use of high-priced exotic devices would decline, and less-expensive drug therapy would increase in proportion to procedures requiring surgical implements.

Most important, though, analysts feared that the "health care review board" and price controls proposed by the plan would debilitate new product development, crush capital investment in the industry, curb the demand for high-tech products, and reduce foreign demand for advanced U.S. exports. The review board, rather than the market, would be authorized to decide on the cost effectiveness of new technology. It would also determine the eligibility of products for insurance reimbursement. Industry representatives were rigorously opposed to the plan.

FDA Stymies New Products. Besides a capital shortage and the threat of nationalized health care, the most prolific problem facing manufacturers in the early 1990s was a slowdown in FDA product approvals. In 1993 producers were still scrambling to learn how to comply with stringent new product standards imposed by the SMDA of 1990. And, the FDA seemed unable to efficiently process applications for approvals. Device executives labeled this dilemma the number two concern facing the industry in 1993.

After the FDA's initiation of the SMDA, approvals for new products fell dramatically. Although the FDA received 5,000 501(k) applications in 1991 and 1992, the number of approved products slipped from 3,000 in 1991 to just 2,500 in 1992. Furthermore, in mid-1993 the FDA had a backlog of 1,400 applications that had been pending for over three months— the historical norm is closer to 20. PMAs showed even greater declines. Usually submitted at a rate of 60 to 70 per year, PMA approvals fell from 47 in 1990 to 27 in 1991, and to only 12 in 1992. The FDA was also under

Congressional order to review 130 products that went on sale prior to 1976.

In an effort to speed the process, the medical device industry began supporting proposed user fees. Under the proposal, firms would be required to pay a fee for each application processed by the FDA. A similar fee system implemented in 1993 for pharmaceutical firms was costing that industry approximately $36 million per year. However, the FDA had reason for caution. It came under fire in the 1980s and 1990s for approving a heart-valve connected with 300 deaths and for permitting the sale of silicon breast implants.

In response to FDA initiatives, the Medical Device Manufacturers Association (MDMA) was formed in November of 1992. It succeeded the Small Manufacturers Medical Device Association that was established in 1980. The organization's focus was to insure that FDA regulations did not adversely affect the industry, particularly smaller manufacturers.

The Future. Barring adverse federal entanglement, medical and surgical instrument manufacturers should continue to achieve solid growth through the 1990s and beyond. Historically significant industry segments, such as catheters and syringes, will offer less profit potential as markets for those products mature and become more competitive. Market growth for leading-edge minimally invasive surgical tools and devices, however, will supplant profits from declining segments.

Although growth attained in the 1970s and 1980s will likely wane, shipments are expected to grow at a healthy six percent per year (above inflation) through 1997. The market for endoscopic instruments, for example, was expected to grow from $550 million in 1992 to over $3 billion by 1996. Laparoscopic surgery, moreover, will likely account for 80 percent of all abdominal surgery performed by the turn of the century.

An aging population that requires more health care will augment overall growth. In addition, U.S. firms were well positioned to take advantage of emerging foreign markets going into the mid-1990s. Increased efficiency of the new FDA approval process should eventually diminish that industry hurdle, though possibly at a significant cost to competitors.

INDUSTRY LEADERS

The largest manufacturer of surgical and medical instruments and apparatus in the early 1990s was Baxter International Inc. and its subsidiary, Baxter Healthcare Corp. Based in Illinois, this industry giant racked up over $8.1 billion in 1991 revenues and employed over 40,000 workers. For more information

about Baxter, see **SIC 3842: Orthopedic, Prosthetic, and Surgical Appliances and Supplies.**

Siemens Medical Systems, Inc., of New Jersey, was the second largest producer of instruments and apparatus. Siemens, whose parent company is based in Germany, generated $3 billion in 1991 sales from its diversified operations, and employed 7,000 workers. National Medical Care Inc., of Massachusetts, placed third in the industry with sales of more than $1.2 billion in 1991 and over 10,000 employees.

Despite the dominance of a few massive competitors, such as Baxter and Siemens, the industry remained relatively unconcentrated in the mid-1990s. Like most growth industries, revenues are spread among a multitude of niche firms that have developed proprietary products or production techniques, or excel at marketing or distribution. The majority of the top 75 firms competing in the industry in the early 1990s, for instance, each produced revenue of less than $100 million and employed fewer than 1,000 workers.

WORK FORCE

Although a total of more than 21,000 companies were licensed to produce medical devices in 1993, only about 1,200 of those firms were primarily engaged in producing surgical and medical instruments and apparatus. Those firms employed over 100,000 in 1993. An undetermined number of workers were engaged in making products that fit this industry classification but were produced by companies primarily engaged in other industries.

Assemblers and fabricators comprised 14 percent of this industry's work force in the early 1990s. Inspectors, testers, and graders accounted for 3.4 percent of employment, and manufacturing supervisors made up 3.3 percent. Other blue-collar manufacturing posi-

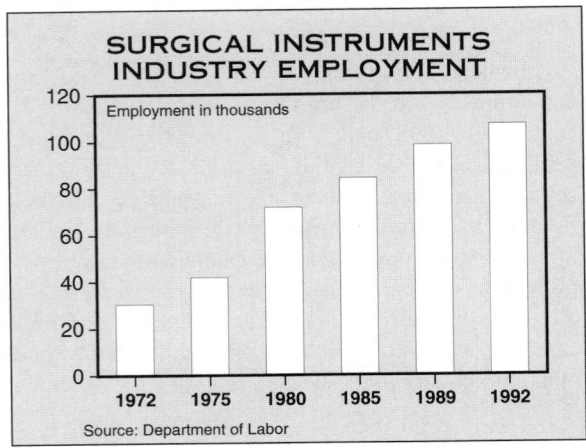

SURGICAL INSTRUMENTS
INDUSTRY EMPLOYMENT

Employment in thousands

Source: Department of Labor

tions represented an additional 60 percent of the work force. Salespersons accounted for six percent of nonlabor workers, while secretaries and clerical staff accounted for about five percent. Relatively high-paying engineering positions accounted for over six percent of the work force, while white collar managers and executives represented about 3.3 percent.

Fifteen percent of industry executives indicated a desire to move manufacturing facilities to foreign countries in 1993, and many competitors were seeking increased productivity through automation. Despite these facts, employment prospects were positive going into the 1990s. The Bureau of Labor Statistics estimated that most occupations in the industry would grow significantly through 2000. Jobs for engineers, for instance, were expected to grow by 60 to 70 percent between 1990 and 2005. Sales and marketing positions, moreover, were forecast to rise by more than 70 percent. Most management jobs will increase by around 40 percent by 2005.

Although blue-collar production jobs will generally rise, the jump will be less substantial. Inspection, supervision, packaging, and shipping positions will rise by 30 to 50 percent by 2005. However, the number of jobs related to parts assembly, which account for about 18 percent the industry's work force, will stagnate or decline.

AMERICA AND THE WORLD

U.S. firms exported an estimated $2.6 billion worth of medical and surgical instruments in 1993, representing ten percent growth since 1992 and commanding a record 19 percent of industry output. Furthermore, the industry's trade surplus rose 5.2 percent to $1.2 billion. Although the U.S. share of the entire global medical device market fell from 60 percent in 1980 to about 50 percent in 1993, rapid expansion of global markets allowed domestic producers to sustain record export growth throughout that period. America's share of the world market was expected to decline to 40 percent by 2000, though export sales volume should rise steadily, even outpacing domestic growth.

The United States remained the world leader in medical device technology and maintained an especially dominant role in medical and dental instruments and supplies. This role was threatened, however, by an increasingly competitive global industry. Japanese and German producers had made significant strides in some market segments, such as high-tech electromedical equipment and some diagnostic machines. Furthermore, Japan planned to double its investment in medical device research and development in 1993 in an effort to catch up with capital expenditures made by their U.S. and German counterparts during the 1980s and early 1990s.

Although Japan maintained the second largest market for medical devices in the world, the United States held a meager 12 percent share of that market in the early 1990s. Japan, in contrast, enjoyed relatively free access to American markets and accounted for over 20 percent of U.S. imports. Surgical and medical instrument imports into the United States in 1993, though, captured less than nine percent of that market. The European Community delivered about 29 percent of U.S. imports in the early 1990s, Mexico and Canada sold 16 percent, and East Asian firms garnered about 14 percent of import revenues. Miscellaneous countries captured the remaining 20 percent. The largest buyer of U.S. goods was Canada, followed closely by Japan, and then Germany. Those three countries, combined with France and Mexico, consumed 50 percent of all industry exports.

Improving U.S. manufacturer prospects in the global instruments and apparatus market were two important international agreements that were hammered out in 1993. In July, seven major industrialized nations agreed to remove all inter-country tariffs on drugs and medical equipment, contingent on passage of the larger General Agreement on Trade and Tariffs (GATT). This development was expected to save U.S. medical industries $400 million per year. If the European Community agreed on a similar proposal, U.S. firms would benefit by only having to file for one permit to sell each product, rather than one for each of the 12 nations.

The second major agreement expected to boost sales was the North American Free Trade Agreement (NAFTA), which Congress passed in November of 1993. NAFTA was expected to save companies in the industry $100 million annually from eliminated tariffs. In addition, investment restrictions on companies seeking to do business in Mexico were eliminated. The agreement also insured that the Mexican government, which made 70 percent of all national health care purchases, would open procurement processes to U.S. bidders.

In the *MDDI* survey, industry executives identified their most promising export growth markets, in order of importance, as Canada, Europe, Japan, the Pacific Rim, Mexico, and Latin American.

RESEARCH AND TECHNOLOGY

The medical and surgical device and apparatus industry is heavily driven by technological advances. In fact, much of the growth in U.S. health care expenditures which occurred during the 1960s, 1970s, and 1980s is attributable to the introduction of costly, high-tech equipment. For manufacturers that have devised new and better devices to help remedy ailments and illnesses, care providers have afforded an enthusiastic market. Life-saving procedures that were unheard of before 1970, such as angioplasty and coronary by-pass, were commonplace in the early 1990s. Industry profits were booming partially as a result of the increased demand for these new procedures.

Although U.S. producers already invested nearly seven percent of their revenues into research and development in the early 1990s, industry executives indicated their intent to boost this figure in the mid-1990s. Furthermore, additional money for research was expected to flow from government sources. The Clinton administration's "Defense Reinvestment and Conversion Initiative," which was developed in 1993, made available half a billion dollars for business partnerships designed to integrate America's high-tech defense industries into the civilian marketplace.

Although some industry analysts believed that medical device companies could be major benefactors of the program, similar efforts in the past had yielded mixed results. Efforts to use NASA technology in the industry, for example, were credited with development of only 100 devices between 1976 and 1990. The Defense Technology Conversion Council (DTCC), a consortium of five federal agencies that was formed in 1993, hoped to improve the transfer of technology to the private sector with its Technology Reinvestment Project. The DTCC selected health care as one of its 11 focus areas. Clinton had proposed a $20 billion DTCC package.

Besides new product development, manufacturers were also concentrating on increased productivity going into the mid-1990s. A number of new flexible computer-integrated manufacturing techniques were being implemented. These techniques promised to synthesize manufacturing operations and promote international production standards. New information software had been developed, for instance, that helped device manufacturers integrate and manage software development, design changes, and testing data. The primary goal of such techniques was to reduce labor costs and increase productivity. Other companies were experimenting with cost-saving approaches like cellular manufacturing. By assigning a cell, or team, of workers responsibility for production of each product, some companies had increased productivity by 25 percent and improved product quality.

New and improved products in the early 1990s were numerous. Shape-memory polymers, for instance, are polyurethane-based polymers that, when exposed to heat, can undergo and retain dramatic changes in hardness, flexibility, elasticity, and vapor permeability. Among other uses, the resins were being used to form catheters that would remain stiff until inserted into the body. Similarly, new plastic springs offered an alternative to metal components in operations requiring resistance to corrosion and static charges.

Silicone balloon cuffs that could be manufactured through extrusion, rather than molding, were offering producers of laparoscopic and other devices the advantage of reduced production costs. Likewise, new injection-molded components were offering more efficient prototyping of new instruments and devices. Other new or improved products included miniature cables, high-tensile wire, heat-shrinking tubing, and a variety of minimally invasive instruments. Major product innovations were also occurring in the area of disposable devices, which were dominating many market segments in 1993 because of their convenience.

INDUSTRY INFORMATION SOURCES

"Beating Swords into Medical Devices," *Medical Device & Diagnostic Industry,* May 1993.

"Capital Slump Hits Device Start-Ups," *Medical Device & Diagnostic Industry,* August 1993.

Darnay, Arsen J., ed., *Manufacturing USA; Industry Analyses, Statistics, and Leading Companies,* Detroit: Gale Research Inc., 1993.

Henke, Cliff, "1993 Business Outlook: Growing at Home and Abroad," *Medical Device & Diagnostic Industry,* March 1993.

"Industrial Outlook Positive Again," *Medical Device & Diagnostic Industry,* February 1993.

"Industry Weighs Long-Term Promise of NAFTA," *Medical Device & Diagnostic Industry,* January 1993.

Jereski, Laura, "Block That Innovation!" *Forbes,* January 18, 1993.

McGlynn, J. Casey, "Preparing for Health Care's New World Order," *Medical Device & Diagnostic Industry,* October 1993.

McVay, Patrick W., and Benjamin L. Hochman, "Federal Consortium Offers New Opportunities for Developing Medical Technologies," *Medical Device & Diagnostic Industry,* June 1993.

Moukheiber, Zina, "Dopey Ducks Revenge," *Forbes,* September 27, 1993.

Perle, Richard, and Martin Cannon, "Turning Swords into Market Shares," *Chief Executive,* May 1993.

"Putting the Lock on Medical Device Costs," *Industrial Engineering,* April 1993.

''Readers' Choice: The Year's Top 20 Products & Services,'' *Medical Device & Diagnostic Industry,* July 1993.

Rogers, Gregg, ''Sites in the Sum: Device Start-Ups Find Warmth in California and Florida,'' *Medical Device & Diagnostic Industry,* May 1993.

Schooleman, Susan, ''Industry Forecast Is That FDA Regulations Will Slow U.S. Market Growth During This Decade,'' *Health Industry Today,* December 1992.

Schooleman, Susan, ''OR Industry Split on Merits of Disposable/Reusable Instruments,'' *Health Industry Today,* May 1993.

Standard & Poor's Industry Surveys, New York: Standard & Poor's Corporation, December 31, 1993.

U.S. Industrial Outlook 1993, Washington, D.C.: U.S. Department of Commerce, January 1993.

U.S. Leader in Key International Standard, New Study Says,'' *Medical Device & Diagnostic Industry,* February 1993.

—Dave Mote

SIC 3842

ORTHOPEDIC, PROSTHETIC, AND SURGICAL APPLIANCES AND SUPPLIES

This classification covers establishments primarily engaged in manufacturing orthopedic, prosthetic, and surgical appliances and supplies, arch supports, and other foot appliances; fracture appliances, elastic hosiery, abdominal supporters, braces, and trusses; bandages; surgical gauze and dressings; sutures; adhesive tapes and medicated plasters; and personal safety appliances and equipment. Establishments primarily engaged in manufacturing surgical and medical instruments are classified in **SIC 3841: Surgical and Medical Instruments and Apparatus.** Establishments primarily engaged in the retail sale of orthopedic or prosthetic appliances and in the personal fitting to the individual prescription by a physician are classified in **SIC 5999: Miscellaneous Retail Stores, Not Elsewhere Classified.**

INDUSTRY SNAPSHOT

The orthopedic, prosthetic, and surgical appliances and supplies industry is comprised of companies predominantly employed in manufacturing items such as artificial limbs and joints, splints, trusses, arch supports, surgical dressings, and related supplies. It also includes some miscellaneous items such as wheelchairs and hearing aids. In addition, personal safety devices, such as snake bite kits, are classified in this industry.

Artificial limbs were used as early as 600 B.C., and orthopedic surgery has existed as a medical specialty since the early 1700s. During the twentieth century, rapid medical advances spawned a huge market for all types of surgical and medical appliances and supplies. By the early 1990s, makers of devices classified in this industry were generating over $13 billion in annual sales and employing over 90,000 workers. Furthermore, they maintained a nearly $1 billion trade surplus.

Going into the mid-1990s, surgical appliance and supplies manufacturers hoped to benefit from solid market growth which had characterized the industry for over two decades. Several issues clouded the industry's future, however. Slow product approvals from the Food and Drug Administration (FDA), the potential overhaul of the nation's health care industry, and reduced availability of outside investment capital were chief concerns for many competitors going into 1994. In addition, several major players in the industry agreed to pay a total of $4.7 billion to as many as two million women who have had breast implants, which have been blamed for a variety of illnesses. Demographic factors and export opportunities, however, are regarded as sources of optimism for the industry.

ORGANIZATION AND STRUCTURE

The entire medical device industry, which is divided into six sub-industries, shipped about $42 billion worth of products in 1993. The surgical appliances industry described in this entry is the largest of those divisions, accounting for about 33 percent, or approximately $14 billion, of total medical product sales. Other segments of the medical supply manufacturing business include surgical and medical instruments (32

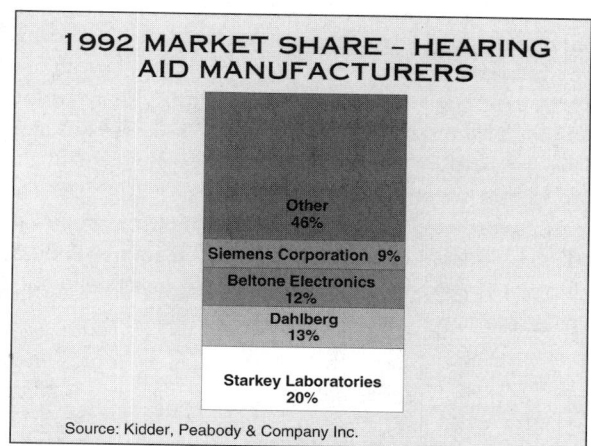

1992 MARKET SHARE – HEARING AID MANUFACTURERS

Other 46%

Siemens Corporation 9%

Beltone Electronics 12%

Dahlberg 13%

Starkey Laboratories 20%

Source: Kidder, Peabody & Company Inc.

percent of sales), electromedical equipment (17 percent), X-ray apparatus and tubes (eight percent), in vitro diagnostic supplies (six percent), and dental equipment (four percent).

The surgical supplies and appliance industry is fragmented, as revenues are distributed among more than 1,400 competitors. The majority of the top 75 firms in the industry, for instance, garnered less than $25 million in revenues in 1991, while only five companies had sales of more than $500 million. These figures, moreover, included some goods produced for other industries.

The industry was still experiencing overall growth, large capital investment, and high profit margins in the early 1990s, indicating that it had not yet reached maturity. While high-tech devices led revenue and profit, though, other segments offered limited opportunities. For example, personal safety equipment and some appliances, such as wheelchairs and crutches, represented sectors of modest growth. Some surgical dressings, like bandages and gauze, were also considered mature products.

Personal consumption expenditures accounted for about 22 percent of industry sales in the 1980s. Government purchases, including purchases through health care facilities and hospitals, consumed about 15 percent of industry output. Hospitals represented an additional 14 percent of the market, and doctors and dentists purchased about four percent of manufacturers goods. Approximately 14 percent of sales were attributable to exports, and 12 percent of industry revenues were classified as gross private fixed investment in the early 1990s. Miscellaneous consumers, which accounted for the remaining 19 percent of sales, included child care services, construction industries, correctional and educational institutions, the Department of Defense, and police departments.

Products. Surgical, orthopedic, and therapeutic appliances and supplies accounted for over 88 percent of industry output in the late 1980s. Orthopedic and prosthetic appliances made up the lion's share of this figure. Orthopedic equipment refers to devices used in the preservation, restoration, and development of the form and function of the extremities and spine. The term prosthetic appliances, in this industry, refers to devices related to artificial limbs and joints. Popular hip and knee replacement devices, for instance, reduce pain and allow patients to regain mobility.

Prosthetic and orthopedic appliances represented approximately 20 percent of industry sales in the late 1980s. Artificial joints, the largest single segment, accounted for about 6.5 percent of total sales, while artificial limbs made up less than .5 percent of shipments. Electronic hearing aids represented over 3 percent of revenues, and elastic braces and supports represented about 1.2 percent of shipments. Additionally, arch supports accounted for 1.5 percent of sales, and replacement and add-on parts for orthopedic and prosthetic devices accounted for 12 percent of industry shipments. This industry segment also includes the following products: bone plates, screws, and nails; mechanical braces; elastic stockings; surgical corsets; splints and trusses, and; intraocular lenses, or lens implants.

Therapeutic appliances and related supplies include a wide array of surgical dressings and devices. Surgical dressings, which include elastic bandages, plaster, gauze, and cotton swabs, represented nearly 13 percent of total industry sales in the late 1980s. Bedpads, adult diapers, and incontinent pads constituted an additional six percent share, and wheelchairs and other patient transport appliances accounted for about 2.5 percent of shipments. Examples of other products in this category are surgical kits, tongue depressors, breathing devices, and therapeutic whirlpool baths.

In addition to the 88 percent of the market represented by the products described above, this industry also encompasses a variety of personal and industrial safety equipment. This type of equipment includes protective clothing, welders hoods, motorcycle and racing helmets, firefighting suits and breathing apparatus, safety gloves, bullet-proof vests, ear and nose plugs, safety goggles, and space suits.

BACKGROUND AND DEVELOPMENT

Prosthetics date as far back as 600 B.C. to the Roman Empire, when artificial legs were used to help amputees regain mobility. It was not until the sixteenth century, through the efforts of French surgeon Ambroise Pare, that prosthetics became a science. His work lead to the development during the sixteenth and seventeenth centuries of replacements for upper extremities. Metal hands, some of which contained moving parts and springs, became popular prosthetics in Europe during the 1600s. They were replaced in the 1700s by two innovations—a single hook, or a leather-covered, nonfunctioning hand attached to the forearm by a leather or wooden shell.

Public acceptance of prostheses, as well as improvements in design, paralleled major wars during the eighteenth, nineteenth, and twentieth centuries. In particular, World War I and World War II boosted the use of prosthetics, which benefited from the integration of new light-weight metals and better mechanical joints.

Advances in materials and mechanical design were rampant during the post-World War II era. Importantly, the development of indwelling materials, such as coated steel, inactive metals, and durable synthetics, gave specialists new ways to replace or mend body joints and parts. New materials and mechanisms also made possible the creation of artificial limbs that more closely mimicked the natural body.

The term orthopedics was given to that specialty in 1741 by Nicholas Andre, a Frenchman. Orthopedic surgery originally applied only to the prevention and care of deformities in children. However, the branch soon grew to encompass treatment of extremities, spine, and associated structures of all humans. The first institute dedicated to the treatment of skeletal deformities was established in Switzerland in the eighteenth century. One of the first notable devices introduced by the industry was the Thomas Splint, which was used for leg fractures. An important U.S. leader in the development of therapeutic orthopedic devices was F. H. Albee (1876-1945), who developed the motor bone saw in 1909.

Rapid advances in medical technology caused a shift in orthopedic treatment during the twentieth century from the use of braces, splints, and other mechanical devices, to surgical procedures. Such procedures incorporated implants and devices which helped surgeons perform advanced operations, like spinal reconstruction, skin grafts, tendon transplants, limb lengthening, restoration of shattered bones and joints, and bone grafts.

Surgical advances in the twentieth century, which paralleled both orthopedic and prosthetic breakthroughs, greatly increased the demand for procedures and treatments that required apparatus developed and manufactured by the surgical appliance industry. In addition, generous employer-sponsored health care plans made large sums of insurance money available for such equipment. Indeed, as a result of overall increased U.S. expenditures on health care during the 1950s, 1960s, and 1970s, sales of orthopedic and prosthetic appliances skyrocketed. Sellers of surgical dressings and other supplies realized similar gains.

The 1980s. By 1980, the surgical appliance and supply business had grown into a $5 billion industry that employed over 40,000 workers. This growth epitomized the immense proliferation of U.S. health care expenditures, which rose at an annual rate of more than 15 percent throughout most of the 1960s and 1970s. By the early 1980s, in fact, American's were spending over ten percent of their gross domestic product on health care. The demand for surgical appliances and supplies continued to balloon throughout the 1980s, as

money spent on health care soared. Between 1982 and 1990, industry revenues grew an average of 8.6 percent annually. Moreover, despite manufacturing productivity gains, industry employment leapt over 25 percent during the same period to exceed 85,000.

Driving revenue and profit growth during the decade was the development of high-tech, high-cost prosthetic and orthopedic devices. Better and stronger artificial joints, limbs, and associated devices allowed specialists to deliver treatments unheard of just a few years earlier. As surgical procedures in general increased, the demand for surgical dressings, drapes, and other supplies grew as well. Exports, too, provided significant profit opportunities.

CURRENT CONDITIONS

Notwithstanding a U.S. economic downturn, surgical appliance and supply manufacturers continued to post solid gains in the early 1990s. Though growth appeared to be slowing in comparison to the 1980s, revenues increased an average of 7.4 percent annually between 1990 and 1992. Furthermore, 1993 growth jumped back up to approximately 8.5 percent, signaling a possible economic rebound. Employment grew by a total of about six percent between 1990 and 1993, to around 92,000.

Despite strong markets, competitors were facing several hurdles to continued success. Concerns about a lack of outside investment capital necessary to fund research and development of new products emerged, as analysts pointed to the uncertainties associated with various health care reform initiatives. Industry participants were also suffering from cost-containment pressures, which particularly affected low-tech items such as surgical dressings, drapes, and sutures. Increasingly cost-conscious hospitals were working to ensure that prices of conventional supplies remained near the overall inflation rate. At the same time, domestic sales of personal and industrial safety equipment were down—a result of recessed construction and manufacturing activity in the early 1990s.

Cost-containment pressures were also hindering makers of orthopedic and prosthetic supplies. The average orthopedic implant, for instance, cost more than $2,400 in 1993. Many manufacturers of such high-tech products, however, were even more concerned with a slowdown in FDA new product approvals. New stringent approval requirements were keeping some new products out of the market and diminishing outside investment in new product development.

The Future. Industry sales will likely rise at an average annual rate of seven percent between 1993 and

1998. A rise in services and procedures provided in outpatient settings will stimulate demand, as will an aging U.S., and world, population. The home health care market, for instance, was expected to grow ten percent in 1993. The need for new specialized surgical appliances that provide end-users with cost savings will offer some of the greatest growth opportunities. Such appliances include kidney dialysis items than can be used in outpatient settings, implantable infusion pumps, and nutritional therapy products. Export growth is also expected to play an important role. Congressional acceptance of the North American Free Trade Agreement in 1993, for instance, was expected to significantly increase profit opportunities in Mexico.

Silicone Implant Settlement. In 1994 eight companies that manufacture silicone breast implants agreed to pay nearly $4.7 billion into a fund for two million women worldwide who have had the implants. The agreement marked the single largest product liability settlement in U.S. history. The fund is expected to cover routine testing, medical care, and surgery (including implant removal), for the next 30 years. As the *Detroit Free Press* noted, ''the settlement attempts to resolve two and a half years of bitter controversy and one of the stormiest chapters in U.S. medical history.'' Companies making the largest contributions to the settlement were Bristol Myers-Squibb Co., Baxter Healthcare Corp., and Dow Corning Corp., once the country's foremost producer of implants.

INDUSTRY LEADERS

The largest company competing in the surgical appliances and supplies industry in the early 1990s was Baxter Healthcare Corp., of California. The company is a division of Illinois-based Baxter International. Baxter was incorporated in 1931 by Ralph Falk and Don Baxter, who began his career selling intravenous solutions in the Midwest. By 1991, the Baxter Healthcare Corp. division was generating annual sales of $1.6 billion and employing over 8,000 workers in its diversified operations. Other leading international companies with divisions in this industry include Dow Corning Corp., Bristol Myers-Squibb Co., and Union Carbide Corp.

Most companies in the industry are small compared to Baxter. Other large industry participants, however, include: Kendall Co., of Massachusetts, which had sales of approximately $900 million in 1991 and 9,000 employees; Zimmer, Inc., of Indiana, which had 4,000 workers and revenues of $700 million in 1991, and; Ethicon, Inc., of New Jersey, with $540 million in sales and 5,000 employees.

WORK FORCE

The 1,400 companies primarily engaged in the industry employed about 91,000 workers in 1992, representing a jump from less than 70,000 in the early 1980s. In addition, several companies classified in other industries employed workers who produced products covered in this industrial classification. Employment rose 2.2 percent in 1992, despite productivity gains which increased average output per worker. About 66 percent of the work force held production jobs in 1992, up 3.8 percent from 1991. Assemblers and fabricators comprised about 15 percent of the work force, for example. Positions in sales and marketing accounted for seven percent of industry employment, and white collar administration jobs accounted for less than three percent.

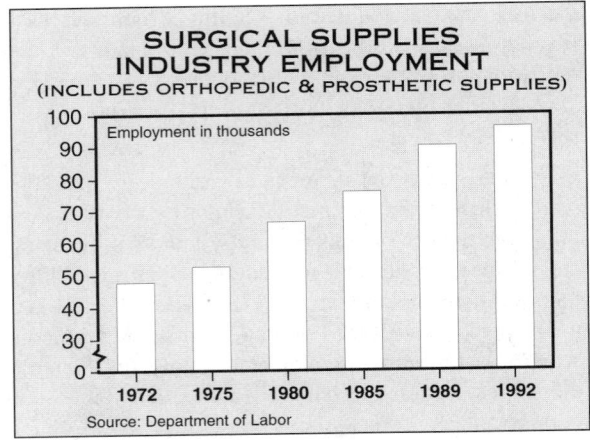

The industry's work force was expected to grow throughout the 1990s. Manufacturing positions, for example, were expected to rise by ten percent to 50 percent between 1990 and 2005, according to the Bureau of Labor Statistics. A few positions, however, such as those for electrical and electronic assemblers, are expected to fall by over 25 percent. Jobs in sales and marketing will likely rise by more than 70 percent, and positions related to engineering, math, and science will leap by 50 percent to 65 percent.

AMERICA AND THE WORLD

As domestic prices and market growth declined in the early 1990s, competitors were increasingly looking overseas to boost profits. Because U.S. medical equipment producers offered the most advanced products in the world, they controlled approximately 50 percent of the world export market in 1990. Although they were losing ground to foreign competitors, particularly the Germans and Japanese, the rapid growth of outside markets was allowing U.S. firms to expand their overseas activities. The demand for high-tech implantable devices led the export surge.

In 1989, surgical appliance and supplies producers exported less than 10 percent of their output. Between 1990 and 1993, though, competitors increased their annual exports by an average of 18.3 percent. By 1993 the industry was shipping nearly 14 percent, or $1.87 billion, of its total production overseas. Canada, Mexico, and Germany purchased about 50 percent of all U.S. exports. In contrast, importers served less that seven percent of the U.S. market in 1993. Of the six medical supply industries, in fact, surgical and appliance manufacturers maintained the greatest trade surplus in the early 1990s. The surplus increased 8.4 percent in 1992, to about $855 million.

Rapid export growth was expected to continue in the 1990s and early 2000s. Standardization of European Community (EC) medical device regulations will cause producers to emphasize sales in that region, which already consumed 36 percent of U.S. exports in 1992. The Far East, Latin America, and Eastern Europe are also expected to provide new opportunities. Popular export items to the EC will continue to include respiratory products, orthopedic equipment and supplies, and artificial joints. Exports of implantable devices to Japan are also anticipated to grow significantly.

RESEARCH AND TECHNOLOGY

Many surgical appliance and supply manufacturers relied heavily on development of new technology to create high-profit products and to increase market share—particularly for orthopedic and prosthetic devices. An example of an innovation in the early 1990s was porous hips and knee replacements that allowed bone to grow directly into the metal implant. Similarly, the Variable Geometry Orthosis, an invention of the early 1990s, was an all-plastic, lightweight orthopedic brace that offered a better fit and greater mobility.

In the late 1990s and 2000s, research will likely emphasize development of better metals and plastics, new non-metallic plastic and ceramic products, and new synthetics that can be used to create implants. Although outside investment capital for new product development waned in the early 1990s, various government partnering programs promised to boost research and development funding. For instance, the Clinton administration backed programs, such as the Defense Technology Conversion Council, that were trying to transfer military and other public technology to the private sector.

INDUSTRY INFORMATION SOURCES

Anstett, Patricia, "3 Breast Implant Firms Settle," *Detroit Free Press,* March 24, 1994.

"Beating Swords into Medical Devices," *Medical Device & Diagnostic Industry*, May 1993.

"Capital Slump Hits Device Start-Ups," *Medical Device & Diagnostic Industry*, August 1993.

"5 More Implant Makers Join Settlement," *Detroit Free Press,* March 25, 1994.

Henke, Cliff, "1993 Business Outlook: Growing at Home and Abroad," *Medical Device & Diagnostic Industry*, March 1993.

"Industrial Outlook Positive Again," *Medical Device & Diagnostic Industry*, February 1993.

"Industry Weighs Long-Term Promise of NAFTA," *Medical Device & Diagnostic Industry*, January 1993.

McVay, Patrick W., and Benjamin L. Hochman, "Federal Consortium Offers New Opportunities for Developing Medical Technologies," *Medical Device & Diagnostic Industry*, June 1993.

Perle, Richard, and Martin Cannon, "Turning Swords into Market Shares," *Chief Executive*, May 1993.

Schooleman, Susan, "Industry Forecast Is That FDA Regulations Will Slow U.S. Market Growth During This Decade," *Health Industry Today*, December 1992.

Standard & Poor's Industry Surveys, New York: Standard & Poor's Corporation, December 31, 1993.

U.S. Industrial Outlook 1993, Washington, D.C.: U.S. Department of Commerce, January 1993.

—Dave Mote

SIC 3843

DENTAL EQUIPMENT AND SUPPLIES

This classification comprises establishments primarily engaged in manufacturing artificial teeth, dental metals, alloys, and amalgams, as well as a wide variety of equipment, instruments, and supplies used by dentists, dental laboratories, and dental colleges. Excluded from this classification are dental laboratories that construct artificial dentures, bridges, inlays, and other dental restorations on specifications from dentists; these are classified in **SIC 8072: Dental Laboratories.**

INDUSTRY SNAPSHOT

As the smallest industry within the medical and dental equipment category, accounting for less than ten percent of the group's total shipments, the dental equipment and supply industry represents a modestly sized market, but it is an industry that is nevertheless essential to the practice of dentistry. The two product segments of the industry, dental equipment and dental supplies, are regarded as separate markets, with some companies manufacturing only supplies, others manufacturing only equipment, and others, generally the larger companies in the industry, manufacturing both equipment and supplies. These products are then sold to dentists, dental laboratories, and dental colleges.

Products manufactured by industry participants include dental chairs, dental hand instruments, and drills, which are considered equipment, and plaster, amalgams (alloyed metals used for filling cavities), and cements, which are considered supplies. Other products, more than 25,000 of them, include abrasive points, wheels, and disks, dental cabinets, denture materials, orthodontic appliances, and artificial teeth not made in dental laboratories.

By manufacturing these and other products, dental equipment and supply manufacturers recorded $1.43 billion in revenue in 1992. The production of equipment and supplies for dentists, particularly dental chairs, instrument delivery systems, dental hand instruments, and dental cements and metals, contributed most heavily to the industry's total revenue, accounting for 51 percent of total shipments. Shipments of dental laboratory equipment and supplies to dental laboratories ranked as the industry's second largest market, accounting for 31 percent of its total shipments.

ORGANIZATION AND STRUCTURE

In the early 1990s, approximately 500 companies in the United States were manufacturing dental equipment and supplies as their primary business. The majority of these manufacturers were small and medium-size companies, with only 25 percent of the total employing 20 or more employees. The typical dental equipment and supply manufacturing establishment was half the size of the typical manufacturing establishment in all other U.S. manufacturing industries, employing 26 people compared to the national standard of 54 employees per establishment.

The bulk of the industry's manufacturing establishments were located in California, which contained 108 facilities in the late 1980s, by far leading all other states in dental equipment and supply production. New York ranked second with 47 manufacturing establishments, followed by Illinois with 37 facilities. Aside from the concentration of facilities on the West Coast, in the Northeast, and in the Great Lakes region, dental equipment and supply production was scattered

throughout the country, with 18 states containing manufacturing establishments.

BACKGROUND AND DEVELOPMENT

Manufacturers of dental equipment and dental supplies first emerged as an appreciable component of American industry in the 1890s, although the first manufacturers of such products undoubtedly originated much earlier, appearing during the genesis of the nation itself, when the practice of dentistry first began in the United States. In fact, the earliest progenitors of the dental equipment and supply industry were the dentists themselves, who made their own equipment in workshops adjoining their public offices. Over the ensuing decades, as the nation's population grew and the magnitude of the country's commerce increased, the production of dental equipment and supplies became distinct from the practice of dentistry, leading to the emergence small, independent dental manufacturing companies by the latter half of the 19th century.

Once the manufacture of dental equipment and supplies became a distinct segment of the dental industry, characterized by small, frequently family-owned businesses, many of which appeared in the decade leading up to the turn of the 20th century, the formal beginning of the dental equipment and supply industry can be said to have begun. But for roughly the next half century, the industry remained small, comprised of companies that, combined, generated a negligible amount of revenue, at least in contrast to the larger manufacturing industries in the country and even when compared to other manufacturers in the broadly defined medical industry. The modern version of the dental equipment and supply industry, which began to assume the characteristics of the industry in existence during the 1990s, would not emerge until after World War II, specifically during the 1960s, when a combination of developments engendered a new breed of dental equipment and supply manufacturer.

During the earliest days of the nation's history, dentists manufactured dental equipment and supplies, then small manufacturing establishments appeared as a natural response to the country's growth, but during both of these phases of the dental industry's development, whether a dentist or a manufacturer was producing the equipment, the list of products manufactured was a short one. This was primarily attributable to the nature of dentistry at the time, a branch of medicine that was essentially consigned to extracting teeth or affixing bridge work. Years before biannual visits to a dentist were recommended, indeed years before dental hygiene was even a common concern, preventive measures to forestall tooth loss or decay were seldom employed, and dentists merely responded to emergency or near emergency situations. Once dentistry became a preventive science following World War II, engendered in large part by the growing affluence of the American populace and the emergence of federally subsidized dental insurance, the nature of dentistry changed dramatically, transforming the dental equipment and supply industry into a much more sophisticated business.

By the 1960s, the scope of the dental equipment and supply industry had widened considerably and its market had matured significantly, drawing the attention of would-be manufacturers and investors. The shift toward preventive dentistry had altered the complexion of the dental equipment and supply industry, but it had not significantly changed the composition of the industry, at least not yet. Still primarily comprised of small, independent manufacturing companies, roughly 500 of them in the early 1960s, the industry continued in many ways to resemble itself 50 years earlier. Its sales volume still represented a modest sum, amounting to roughly $150 million per year as the movement toward preventive dentistry gained momentum, and it had not yet attracted large manufacturing concerns; its largest manufacturer, S. S. White Dental Manufacturing Co., generated $40 million in sales in 1961. The optimism pervading the industry, therefore, was not so much attributable to a dramatic transformation of the industry, but rather stemmed from the expectation of a future transformation.

Essentially, these prognostications called for a dental equipment and supply industry of much larger magnitude, predictions that, when sketched out on paper, appeared highly plausible. During the early 1960s, American families on average were spending twice as much per year on dental care as they had ten years earlier, the natural extension of a society growing increasingly more affluent, while the number of prepaid dental plans had multiplied during the same period, covering approximately 700,000 Americans in 1960. These prepaid plans, coming from either private insurance plans or union-employer agreements, would grow exponentially throughout the decade and into the 1970s, fueling much of the optimism articulated by manufacturers and industry pundits during this twenty year period. Union-sponsored dental care plans proliferated after the landmark agreement reached between the International Longshoremen's & Warehousemen's Union and the Washington State Dental Association in 1954, when the first such program was initiated.

By the mid-1960s, thanks in large part to the growth of union dental care plans, the number of Americans provided with an opportunity for dental care had increased to three million from the 700,000 covered roughly five years earlier. Also, Medicare, a U.S. government health insurance program for those over 65 years of age, and Medicaid, a program that provided medical care to those who could not pay for it, both came into existence in 1965 and promised to extend dental coverage throughout the country in a sweeping fashion. By the end of the decade, the number of Americans covered by dental care plans had doubled again in a five year period and now included more than six million people, the result of a growing awareness of preventive dental care and a surge in the number of dental care coverage plans.

The increase in the number of potential dental care customers that was sparking much of the interest in the dental equipment and supply industry during the 1960s, persuaded larger, conglomerate manufacturing companies with no previous vested interest in the dental field to begin dental equipment production. Many of the smaller, independent manufacturing concerns were absorbed by the incursion of these larger companies, altering the composition of the industry. Meanwhile, those manufacturers already in the industry were diversifying, applying the same technology used in the production of dental equipment to the manufacture of non-dental products. Consequently, as this period of mergers and diversification occurred into the late 1960s, the typical manufacturer in the industry changed from a small, independent company, almost entirely devoted to the production of dental-related products, to a larger, more diversified manufacturer.

This transformation did not, however, have an equally significant effect on the industry's sales volume. From the $150 million generated by U.S. manufacturers at the beginning of the decade, the industry's sales volume had only increased to roughly $280 million by the beginning of the 1970s, a total that seemed to belie the industry's growth in other areas over the course of the decade. Dental equipment manufacturers had supplied two revolutionary pieces of equipment during the dental industry's emergence as a more visible sector of the health care field: the air-driven, high-speed drill and the reclining dentist's chair, both of which proved to be linchpins in the dental industry's climb to the fore, yet revenue totals had not responded in kind.

The reasons for this rather stagnant revenue growth became apparent shortly. By the mid-1970s, approximately 30 million Americans were covered under some sort of dental care plan, reflecting a tremendous increase during the previous 15 years, but when this figure was analyzed to reflect the number of those who actually visited dentists, rather than the number who were provided the opportunity to visit a dentist, the reason for the industry's laggard growth in sales volume became readily apparent. Of all the people receiving dental care in the United States, only 15 percent were covered by dental insurance, compared to more than 90 percent for health care. Since a large proportion of the people covered by dental insurance opted not to receive dental care, the number of people insured in the country, which over the past twenty years had inspired much of the optimism within the dental equipment and supply industry, proved to be a misleading figure, at least to the extent that the more people covered would directly translate into an increase in the industry's sales volume.

Once this misleading measure of the industry's potential growth was removed, a clearer estimation of its true position within the larger health care field showed a relatively small industry—generating roughly $670 million in revenue in 1975—that nevertheless played an essential role in the dental arena. To be sure, the nearly $700 million posted in 1975 by all manufacturers in the United States represented robust growth from a decade earlier, more than trebling in volume during that time, and the percentage of people covered by dental insurance who actually visited dentists would increase as public awareness of dental hygiene grew, but the dental equipment industry had not expanded to the degree that prognosticators had earlier envisaged, and neither did a realistic assessment of its future call for a dramatically different type of industry to emerge. Instead, the dental equipment and supply industry was destined to record more modest growth, from roughly five to ten percent annually in aggregate sales, a rate of growth not prodigious enough to spawn the optimism of the 1960s, but a rate of growth that nonetheless supported the existence of manufacturers into the future.

As the industry progressed past the mid-1970s, when it was mired for several years in a global recession, its growth during the 1980s continued at a moderate rate. By 1982, the industry's sales volume had increased to $1.11 billion, having eclipsed the one billion dollar mark three years earlier. In the face of a sharp decline in the number of labor contract agreements that included dental care coverage, the industry's sales volume increased only marginally by the end of the decade, reaching $1.27 billion.

CURRENT CONDITIONS

Ambiguity about U.S. health care reform and its effect on dentistry coupled with deleterious economic conditions during the early 1990s stunted the dental equipment and supply industry's growth in 1993,

causing the value of its shipments to increase by only two percent to $1.8 billion, compared to the five percent annual growth recorded between 1989 and 1991. Projections for the industry's growth called for a three percent increase in aggregate revenue from 1995 to 1998, fueled in part by the growth of certain fledgling areas of dentistry, such as periodontal surgery, treatment with lasers, and cosmetic dentistry.

INDUSTRY LEADERS

Ranked according to sales volume, the three largest manufacturers of dental equipment and supplies in the United States during the early 1990s were Block Drug Company, Inc., based in Jersey City, New Jersey, Sybron Corporation, based in Milwaukee, Wisconsin, and Dentsply International Inc., based in Rockford, Illinois.

Block Drug, perhaps better known as the marketer of Polident, a widely popular brand name most closely tied to denture care products, recorded $563 million in sales in 1993. Sybron Corp., a perennial industry leader in existence during the emergence of the modern dental equipment and supply industry during the 1960s, generated $383 million in 1993 and, like Block Drug, was a publicly held company. The industry's highest ranking privately owned manufacturer, Dentsply International, the former Dentists' Supply Co. and long-time competitor of Sybron, posted an estimated $260 million in sales in 1993.

WORK FORCE

In 1991 total employment in the dental equipment and supply industry stood at 11,300, marking a decade-long decline in the industry's employment base. This decline, which witnessed the industry's total employment drop from 15,500 to the 1991 level, represented a nearly equal decline in the number of production workers and salaried employees. Of the 11,300 people employed by the industry in 1991, 7,300 were production workers, while the remainder were salaried employees who performed administrative, technical, or managerial duties.

Production workers in the dental equipment and supply industry generally earn slightly less than the national standard for production workers employed by manufacturing industries. In 1989, this difference amounted to 18 cents per hour, with the typical production worker earning $10.49 per hour compared to the $10.31 per hour averaged by production workers in the dental equipment and supply industry. In 1990, the hourly wage for production workers in the dental equipment and supply industry climbed to $11.34, at which time salaried employees in the industry earned an average of $43,441 per year.

AMERICA AND THE WORLD

The international market for dental equipment and supplies in 1993 totaled $5.5 billion, of which U.S. manufacturers enjoyed a commanding share, controlling roughly 50 percent of the market. This lead in the global dental equipment and supply market, largely predicated on the ability of U.S. manufacturers to incorporate high technology into the production of their merchandise, garnered the country a $258 million trade surplus in 1993, with 35 percent of the industry's shipments going overseas. The dental equipment and supply markets in Canada, Germany, Japan, Italy, and France proved to be the strongest export destinations for U.S. manufacturers, while manufacturers in Germany, Japan, Switzerland, Italy, and France posed the greatest threat to the overwhelming lead of U.S. manufacturers in the global market.

INDUSTRY INFORMATION SOURCES

Darnay, Arsen J., ed., *Manufacturing USA,* 3rd edition, Detroit: Gale Research, Inc., 1993.

"Dental Equipment Firms Are Still in Recession," *Industry Week,* September 6, 1976, 92.

"Dental Equipment Picks up Pace," *Business Week,* November 15, 1969, 142.

"Dental Suppliers: Expanded Markets," *Financial World,* June 24, 1970, 40.

Jones, Stacy, "Metal Bonded Directly to Teeth," *New York Times,* October 8, 1966, 37.

Prial, Frank J., "The Denture Venture: Bootleg False Teeth Cutting into Market, *Wall Street Journal,* May 4, 1966, 1.

Rutter, Richard, "Dentists to View Newest Supplies," *New York Times,* December 3, 1961, F1.

"Sullivan Deal," *Barron's,* February 10, 1992, 13.

Sullivan, Michael B., "Painless Extraction," *Barron's,* November 16, 1964, 11.

"Sybron in '82 to Close Ritter Dental Plant; 250 Will Face Layoffs," *Wall Street Journal,* November 5, 1981, 20.

U.S. Industrial Outlook, Washington, DC: U.S. Department of Commerce, 1960-1993.

Wheeler, George, "Nor Poor Mouth," *Barron's,* August 23, 1969, 11.

Willatt, Norris, "That Certain Smile," *Barron's,* March 21, 1966, 11.

—Jeffrey L. Covell

X-RAY APPARATUS AND X-RAY TUBES

Firms in this industry engage primarily in the manufacture of radiographic X-ray, fluoroscopic X-ray, and therapeutic X-ray equipment and tubes for use in medical, industrial and research applications. They also produce irradiation equipment using gamma-ray and beta-ray technology.

INDUSTRY SNAPSHOT

Four consecutive years of double-digit growth made X-Ray Apparatus and Tubes one of America's fastest growing industries in the early 1990s. Its 1992 shipments grew 11.2 percent over the previous year to reach $3.1 billion. Much of its success came from the growing sophistication and portability of its products. The massive machines of hospital X-ray departments still had their place, but now miniaturized versions found every-day use in doctors' and dentists' offices nationwide. In addition, the industry discovered new uses for the non-destructive technology that both increased efficiency and quality of manufacturing processes. With the fall of communism and the relaxation of U.S. technology bans, the industry found vast new and expanding markets in Eastern Europe and other portions of the former Soviet Union.

ORGANIZATION AND STRUCTURE

Approximately one-half of all sales in this industry went to hospital end-users, with the medical profession in general making up the majority of all shipments. Research facilities provided another avenue for sales of major pieces of often experimental equipment. However, the industry was growing increasingly interested in the non-destructive and non-intrusive nature of the imaging technologies.

According to the 1987 Census, 69 firms operating 75 establishments produced $1.5 billion in sales. Sales of primary products, those directly covered by the industry classification, reached $1.3 billion. Secondary products accounted for $74.3 million, and miscellaneous contract work and resales totalled $138.8 million yielding a product specialization ratio for the industry of 95 percent. The coverage ratio, the amount of product sold by those firms classified in the industry, reached only 86 percent.

Geographically, California, with thirteen, hosted the largest number of firms, followed by Illinois with twelve, New York with 7, Wisconsin with 6, and

Massachusetts and Connecticut each hosting five firms.

BACKGROUND AND DEVELOPMENT

The discovery of the X-ray was an accident. In 1895 Wilhelm Conrad Roentgen, experimenting with electrical discharges in an evacuated tube called a Crookes' tube, discovered that the invisible rays given off from his experiment could penetrate a human hand and project a skeletal image onto a florescent screen. Later he substituted photographic film to make a permanent record. Since then, scientists have discovered that X-rays are a type of electromagnetic radiation. An x-ray's wavelength of 0.01 to 300 angstroms is shorter than visible light, lying between and partially over the ultraviolet and gamma-ray segments of the electromagnetic spectrum. They are produced by the collision of high-energy particles with other charged particles.

American scientist, William D. Coolidge, developed the first efficient X-ray tube, called a Coolidge tube, in 1913. Modern tubes fire electrons from a tungsten filament cathode at a target anode, usually made of tungsten, molybdenum or copper and coated with a thin film of gold.

The speed of passage of the x-radiation through a body depends on density. Relatively dense material, like bone, yielded white images, while less-dense material like lungs appeared black. Doctors found the phenomenon invaluable for accurately diagnosing such things as tuberculosis, miners' black lung, and broken bones. However, it only provided a two-dimensional image of the problem area, superimposing layers of body components one on top of another without any indication of depth. One solution to that problem was to use a contrast medium like liquid barium to high-light the esophagus, stomach and intestine. By using a fluoroscope, which produces real-time images on a video screen, the physician tracked the medium through the digestive system, pinpointing any problem areas.

The late-1960s saw a major advancement in the effective use of X-rays for medical diagnosis. By linking the computer to a moving X-ray emitter inside a doughnut-shaped machine, Geoffrey Hounsfield of EMI produced a three-dimensional image of an entire object. Instead of a few X-ray photographs, the computer-aided-tomograph (CAT) took hundreds of thousands of carefully directed, slice-like images which the computer reassembled. Tomograph comes from the Greek word for slice. The results, startlingly clear, could be manipulated to highlight specific areas. CAT scans could locate bleeding inside a brain, find and measure tumors, or help to evaluate injuries anywhere in the body.

Concerns over the amount of radiation a patient would be exposed to and over the cost and sheer physical immensity of the equipment led to the development of ultrasound tomograph which did not use X-rays. By the mid-1980s, the ultrasound systems were beginning to gain popularity. Ultrasound systems are classified under **SIC 3845: Electromedical Apparatus**.

Magnetic Resonance Imaging (MRI) uses a powerful magnet to align the hydrogen atoms in a patient's body. When the magnetic field is released, the atoms return to their original orientation, but different tissues realign at different rates. By using a computer to clock the relative rates of change, physicians can map joints, tumors, post-surgical changes in the chest, abdomen, pelvis, brain and spinal cord.

The safety and effectiveness of all medical devices became the responsibility of the Food and Drug Administration (FDA) in 1938. Radiation emitting devices were specifically targeted in 1968 by the Radiation Control for Health and Safety Act and, in 1976, by the Medical Device Amendments to the Food, Drug and Cosmetic Act.

CURRENT CONDITIONS

Even though other, safer technologies were displacing X-rays by the 1990s in their traditional medical applications, radiation proved useful in unique ways. The fluoroscope could show movement within the body like the operation of the heart and the intestines. It facilitated angioplasty, providing the physician with a real-time way of guiding a balloon-tipped catheter down a blood vessel to the point where the balloon insert could be expanded with the greatest effect. Radiation oncology used X-rays or gamma-rays to attack cancerous tumors without damaging surrounding tissue. With this technique a linear accelerator, betatron or cobalt machine is used to direct a beam of radiation from outside the patient's body at the pinpointed tumor.

Initial investigations of the radiation in the research laboratory led to many useful applications for the non-visible light energy. X-ray crystallography led to X-ray microscopes. Crystal structures direct and control X-rays much as lenses do with normal light energy. Using this principle, researchers were able to delve ever-deeper into the structure of crystals. The fact that X-rays are absorbed by material led to absorption spectroscopy, which studies metals in living systems. The industry began using lithography to produce densely packed computer chips. Holography made it possible to glimpse the world within a living cell.

Scientists also used the radiation to look beyond this world. By launching satellites equipped with X-ray detectors, they were able to observe and theorize about the structure of the universe. The first such satellite, UHURU, was launched from a site near Kenya in 1970 and was followed by an international series of successors. Gamma-ray astronomy extended the reach of X-ray astronomy, making visible the processes of the destruction and creation of chemical elements throughout the universe.

Archeology and paleontology also benefitted from the use of X-ray technology. Previously, the study of such ancient artifacts as mummies and fossilized bones required the systematic destruction or at least the disassembly of the scientific treasures. Using a CAT scan, often tied to a supercomputer, researchers in the late 1980s could get clear three-dimensional images without reducing the artifact to dust. Such scans often revealed surprising facts about the subject giving a glimpse of what life, society, disease, nutrition and intrigue was like in historically distant times.

X-rays also proved invaluable in probing modern-day intrigues. In the 1980s and 1990s, plane hijackings and bombings brought terror to the skies, and advances in weapons technology threatened to make conventional X-ray scanners ineffective in preventing them. Although all metals show up clearly on an X-ray scan, lighter materials like plastics do not. Plastic explosives and the mostly-plastic handgun, the Glock 17, could be smuggled through security inspections undetected. Specially designed innovations like American Science & Engineering Inc.'s Model Z scanner sought ways to tighten security. The Z-scanner concentrates a high intensity beam of X-rays onto the carry-on luggage to compensate for the low absorption rate of softer materials. It then displays both the normal X-ray image which would pick up metals and the Z-image which catches plastics. In 1991, France extended that technology for use in its massive cargo inspection facility at Paris' Charles de Gaulle airport. Their building-size X-ray machine examines entire pallet loads of luggage or entire vehicles at once, producing a sophisticated, easily read image.

By increasing the power and size of the X-ray equipment, industry businesses were able to probe though several feet of metal to map interior details. Defense sub-contractors used CAT scans to inspect MX missiles and Saturn rockets looking for cracks, poor material bonds, migration of fuel or coolants, integrity of castings, and gaps in insulation. In traditional CAT scans, the object to be probed sits within the doughnut shaped emitter ring, but in the late 1980s industry leaders developed a new innovation on the technology, backscatter imaging tomography (BIT). By capturing only the portion of the beams which are reflected back, BIT machinery allowed operators to probe objects even if they could only access one side.

The process provided an efficient method for checking quality of manufactured parts and allowed inspectors to certify and document such critical items as pipe welds in nuclear reactors. X-rays have also been used to examine the nation's highways by detecting early signs of failure and allowing preventative maintenance in place of major periodic rebuilding. They also certified new construction.

Because the industry still sold most of its output in the medical community, changes in Medicare allowances scheduled for 1993 caused some concern. *U.S. Industrial Outlook - 1993* suggested that tightening Medicare reimbursements would tend to limit the expansion of new X-ray technology in larger hospitals.

INDUSTRY LEADERS

Among the industry's top companies are Diasonics Inc., Siemens-Gammasonics Inc, and Gendex Corp.

The largest was the young, aggressive Diasonics. Founded in 1977, it shook up the industry by pioneering and promoting new technologies to improve the versatility and cost-effectiveness of imaging technology. Its digital subtraction angiography, introduced in 1981, enhanced conventional X-ray images and promised to eliminate the need for X-ray film. By 1984, Diasonics decided to abandon the system, taking a huge write-down loss, because of poor product performance. It tried MRI with some success, but sold that product line to Toshiba in 1989 for $204 million. Despite these disappointments, Diasonics posted sales of $286 million in 1992, half of which were made overseas. Headquartered in Milpitas, California, the company had 1,635 employees in 1992.

The German conglomerate Siemens Aktiengesellschaft wanted to buy Diasonics in 1980, but early market conquests by that company put it beyond reach. Diasonics terminated a European marketing arrangement with Siemens in 1982 when it gained a 20-percent share of the American ultrasound market. In 1990, Siemens formed Siemens-Gammasonics as a subsidiary of Siemens Medical Systems Inc. In 1992, the subsidiary had sales of $175 million and employed 900. Siemens-Gammasonics centers its operations in Schaumburg, Illinois.

Founded in 1983, Gendex Corp. of Des Plaines, Illinois employed 600 in 1992 to produce sales of $54.5 million.

WORK FORCE

X-ray equipment manufacturing facilities tend to be large, high-tech facilities. In 1988, the average establishment employed 117 compared to the manufacturing average of 57. Wages accordingly ran about 20 percent higher than average reaching $12.49 per hour in 1988 compared to the average hourly wage in all manufacturing firms of $10.66, according to *Manufacturing USA, 2nd Edition*. Total employment in the industry increased throughout the late 1980s and early 1990s reaching 13,740 in 1992 according to *U.S. Industrial Outlook*. Production workers made up 51.7 percent of the industry's work force. The users of X-ray equipment are radiologists. In the United States, they must take four-to-seven years of specialized training after graduating from medical school.

AMERICA AND THE WORLD

Foreign imports of X-ray equipment accounted for 42 percent of industry sales in 1992 according to *U.S. Industrial Outlook - 1993*, higher than any other segment of the medical industry group. America's largest competitors were Japan and Germany, contributing 60 percent. Overall, the American X-ray industry ran a trade deficit with 1992 imports of $1.1 billion compared to exports of $783 million.

However, imports declined 2.7 percent that year, the first decline in five years. The main export markets for American products were Japan, Germany, and Canada but exports to Eastern Europe tripled their 1991 level reaching $8 million and making that region a prime future growth area.

RESEARCH AND TECHNOLOGY

The uses of X-ray technology and its spin-offs continued to grow in the early 1990s. Medical advancements included such procedures as mammograms which allowed physicians to detect cancerous tumors in women's breasts, before they became apparent by traditional methods. Even so, the technology had its limitations. In 1993, a Canadian study revealed that mammograms were ineffective in predicting breast cancer for women younger than 50. The relatively dense tissue in younger women's breasts hid developing tumors resulting in no difference in diagnosis rates for women who received mammograms and those who did not.

Tomography has also found its way into agriculture to observe harvesting techniques for fruits and vegetables and find out when and why crop damage occurred. The rays showed distribution patterns of pesticides and rates of water absorption by different types of roots and different soil-seed combinations.

Micro-tomography opened the miniature world of ceramics and plastics to the researcher and quality control inspector. By using high-energy sources like synchrotron radiation, industry researchers could analyze the internal structures of rocks and minerals like coal and oil-bearing shales, aiding companies like Exxon in their search for new oil and coal fields. Synchrotron radiation is produced by accelerating particles like electrons to nearly the speed of light within a magnetic field. The result is an intense white light. By channeling that light, researchers can create pencil-thick concentrated beams of x-radiation, ultraviolet, and infrared radiation.

This tunable radiation source could map chemical elements within an object. Exxon has used the technology to map elements within copper, nickel and iron. Biomedical researchers have used the technology to study calcium to gain more knowledge of the makeup of human bones. Intense X-rays could look within the walls of living cells to study their structure and watch the movements of elements like calcium within a body; however, the individual cells targeted by the X-rays would be killed.

A gamma-ray version of the CAT scan—Positron-emission-topography (PET)—measured brain activity. Areas of the brain engaged in thought processes absorbed glucose tagged with positron radiation. Decaying positrons gave off gamma-rays which receptors picked up and translated into a light-and-dark image of the brain. Brains which showed higher IQ levels in standard tests showed less activity than those which scored lower. Researchers theorized that the more intelligent brain was "wired" more efficiently and so used less of its capacity to solve a problem. PET was also used for diagnosing cancer and Alzheimer's disease and in evaluating epileptic patients.

Another recent advance also used gamma-rays. The single photon emission computed tomograph (SPECT) also tracked radioactive isotopes through the body and used a computer to build an image of a metabolic function. It was particularly useful for monitoring heart functions.

Researchers used the technology to examine the internal structure of the earth and to test the "Global Warming" hypothesis. Using seismic waves, rather than X-rays, they mapped the boundary between the earth's core and its mantle. In 1991, researchers began sending a series of sound waves from Heard Island in Antarctica through the naturally stable environment of deep ocean water. Scientists will need to continue this research for several years in order to obtain accurate and meaningful information.

INDUSTRY INFORMATION SOURCES

Begley, Sharon. "How to Tell If You're Smart." *Newsweek* (February 29, 1988): 64.

Carey, John. "Is the World Heating Up? Well, Just Listen." *Business Week* (February 4, 1991): 82.

"CAT Scratches into 3-D." *High Technology Business* (September-October, 1989): 5.

"Core Questions." *Scientific American* 256 (February 1, 1987).

Devaney, Anthony J. "Ultrasound Tomography." *Physics Today* 37 (January 8, 1984): S-37-8.

"Diagnosing Ailing Highways." *USA Today*, Dec. 12, 1989.

Drew, Glen. "Medical devices: A Primer on Medical Device Regulation." *FDA Consumer* (May, 1986): 24-7.

Fox, Jeffrey L. "PET Scan Controversy Aired." *Science* 224 (April 13, 1984): 143-44.

Gregory, William. "Medical X-ray Measuring Device Finds Use in Explosive Detection." *Aviation Week & Space Technology* 124 (April 28, 1986): 31.

Hall, Nina. "X-rays Slice into the Heart of Matter." *New Scientist* 116 (October 15, 1987): 54-6.

Henderson, Breck W. "USAF Seeks Aerospace Applications for Innovative X-ray Tomography." *Aviation Week & Space Technology* 131 (July 31, 1989): 93, 97, 99.

Leitch, Andrew. "Leave Them Bones Alone." *Discover* (March, 1992).

Lenorovitz, Jeffrey M. "France Nears Service Introduction of X-ray-Based Cargo Inspection System." *Aviation Week & Space Technology* 134 (March 25, 1991): 64.

Magnet, Myron. "Diasonics' Winning Ways to Look Inside You." *Fortune* (May 16, 1983): 170-72, 174, 176.

Marcial, Gene G. "Why the Buybacks at Diasonics?" *Business Week* (February 4, 1991): 80.

Merrifield, John T. "USAF Considers Using Computed Tomography Inspection for MX." *Aviation Week & Space Technology* 124 (March 3, 1986): 81, 83.

Monastersky, Richard. "Climate Test: Hum Heard 'round the World." *Science News* 139 (January 26, 1991): 53.

Moss, Carol. "Scanning Ancient Egypt." *Science 85* (January/February, 1985): 82-4.

"New Questions about Mammograms." *Newsweek* (March 8, 1993).

Pomerantz, Martin A. "Gamma-Ray Astronomy." *Grolier's Academic American Encyclopedia*. Compuserve AAE.

Stein, Harry and Keri J. Sperry. "X-rays." *Grolier's Academic American Encyclopedia*. Compuserve AAE.

Stern, Richard L. "Solid as a Rock?" *Forbes* (February 27, 1984): 89-90.

Thomsen, Dietrick E. "A Most Powerful X-ray Machine." *Science News* 132 (October 31, 1987).

Tracy, Eleanor Johnson. "A New X-ray Scanner to Hinder Hijackers." *Fortune* (April 28, 1986): 146.

Weiss, Rick. "You Say Tomato, They Say Tomography." *Science News* 132 (Sept 12, 1987).

—Al Cook

SIC 3845

ELECTROMEDICAL AND ELECTROTHERAPEUTIC APPARATUS

This classification comprises establishments primarily engaged in manufacturing electromedical and electrotherapeutic apparatus. Establishments primarily engaged in manufacturing electrotherapeutic lamp units for ultraviolet and infrared radiation are classified in **SIC 3641: Electric Lamp Bulbs and Tubes.**

INDUSTRY SNAPSHOT

In the half century following World War II, the electromedical industry recorded greater growth than the four other industries composing the medical and dental industrial category, outpacing the revenue growth of the surgical and medical instruments industry, the surgical appliances and supplies industry, the dental equipment and supplies industry, and the x-ray apparatus and tubes industry. The rise of the electromedical industry to a position of prominence within the medical and dental category was attributable primarily to the revolutionary nature of the products manufactured under its purview, a diverse selection of technologically sophisticated medical devices that greatly ameliorated the art of medicine not only in the United States, but throughout the world.

Born from the rapid technological advances that occurred in the electronics field following the war, specifically from the technological achievements that spawned the semiconductor and computer industries, the list of products manufactured by companies within the electromedical industry comprises a host of medical devices regarded in the 1990s as indispensable to the practice of medicine. These products include pacemakers, heart defibrillators, magnetic resonance imaging (MRI) devices, ultrasonic scanning devices, computerized axial tomography (CAT) scanners, and cardiographs, as well as a number of other medical devices equally essential to the diagnosis and treatment of diseases.

Although classified as a distinct industry by the U.S. government's *Standard Industrial Classification Manual* in the 1990s, the electromedical industry was not always regarded as such, functioning for roughly the first 25 years of its existence in an ancillary position to the then-larger x-ray apparatus and tubes industry. From the early 1960s to 1987, electromedical industry statistics were combined with those of the x-ray apparatus and tubes industry. During this time, the electromedical industry evolved from a group of manufacturers representing a modestly sized market into a genuine industry of it own. The classification "X-Ray Apparatus and Tubes; Electromedical and Electrotherapeutic Apparatus," initially was a logical combination of what would later become two separate industries, primarily because the x-ray apparatus segment overshadowed the smaller electromedical segment, generating the bulk of the industry's revenue and representing a more formidable economic force.

In 1987, when many industries were reclassified to more accurately reflect the true nature of American industry, the x-ray apparatus and tubes segment of the classification "X-Ray Apparatus and Tubes; Electromedical and Electrotherapeutic Apparatus," became **SIC 3844: X-ray Apparatus and Tubes and Related Irradiation Apparatus,** while the electromedical segment, by then a larger industry than the x-ray apparatus industry, became **SIC 3845: Electromedical and Electrotherapeutic Apparatus.** This reclassification by the *Standard Industrial Classification Manual,* however, came more than a decade after the electromedical industry had eclipsed the x-ray apparatus industry in magnitude, serving as a somewhat belated recognition of the electromedical industry's force. Consequently, during the electromedical industry's prolific rise to the fore in the 1970s, all of the statistics that tell the story of its growth are somewhat inflated due to the inclusion of the statistical information generated by x-ray apparatus manufacturers.

Growth, which came quickly during the 1970s, slowed during the 1980s. Circumstances within the medical industry, specifically the reduced capital expenditures of more budget-conscious hospitals and the maturation of the electromedical market itself, brought annual revenue growth down to approximately eight percent, half of the annual percentage increase realized during the 1970s. Despite the slower pace, the electromedical industry continued to enjoy enviable revenue growth during the late 1980s and early 1990s,

increasing its value of shipments from $3.57 billion in 1987 to $5.90 billion in 1992 and recording positive growth in each of these years except 1991.

ORGANIZATION AND STRUCTURE

Approximately 200 companies in the United States manufactured electromedical or electrotherapeutic devices as their primary business in the early 1990s. Of the approximately 230 manufacturing establishments operated by the industry's manufacturers, roughly 150 employed 20 or more workers. Compared to the typical size of a manufacturing facility in the United States, the electromedical industry exceeded the national standard by 155 percent, employing 137 workers per establishment compared to the 54 employed on average by all other manufacturing industries.

California led all other states in electromedical device production, manufacturing 24 percent of the industry's total shipments and employing 21 percent of the industry's total work force. With its 39 manufacturing facilities, California contained more than twice as many facilities as the second and third ranking states, Massachusetts and New York, which both contained 15 manufacturing facilities. Other states with a significant number of manufacturing facilities were Texas and Illinois with 13 each, Pennsylvania with 11, and Wisconsin, Florida, and Minnesota with 10 manufacturing establishments each. All totaled, 23 states contained electromedical device manufacturing establishments.

BACKGROUND AND DEVELOPMENT

Truly a product of a technologically modern society, the electromedical industry owes its emergence largely to research and development conducted in the 1950s by scientists and manufacturers in the then-nascent semiconductor and computer industries. From these two technological staging grounds, combined with advancements in the electronic field resulting from the enormous effort put forth by the nation's space program, the process by which electronic technology developed was greatly accelerated. The knowledge gained from these three components of American industry, each heavily dependent on electronic technology, proved to be a boon to other industries as well, strengthening some, while enabling the outright creation of others. Such was the case with the electromedical industry, which emerged during the 1960s.

To be sure, there were precursors to electromedical devices before the 1960s. Electrical pulsing as means to treat a variety of ailments had been employed since before the turn of the 20th century, but these early devices were more curiosities than representative of a genuine industry. Instead, perhaps the first piece of equipment that could justify prognostications for the emergence of a future electromedical industry appeared in the late 1950s, when Earl Bakken, chairman of a bio-medical company named Medtronic, and cardiologists from the University of Minnesota developed one of the first workable cardiac pacemakers.

Nothing more than a automobile battery resting on a dolly and attached to the patient's chest through wire cables, this first pacemaker was rather primitive, but led to further ameliorations and the emergence of much smaller versions that soon were regarded as viable medical devices suitable for implantation. As improvements were made in pacemakers, additional products that would later compose the electromedical industry, such as ultrasonic medical equipment and cardiographs, were developed as well. Their development would take time, but the developmental challenges, though formidable, were not the major obstacles barring the appearance of the electromedical industry. Instead, marketing these new products posed the greatest challenge to the fledgling electromedical manufacturers, as industry participants found it difficult to convince the medical community that electromedical devices provided in many cases a preferable alternative to extant medical equipment. This took time as well, but eventually doctors and hospital administrators embraced the new electronic equipment, and by the end of the 1960s, the industry began to emerge as a recognizable economic force.

For electromedical manufacturers, the rewards were worth the wait. The industry quickly flourished, its growth fueled by the widespread acceptance of all kinds of electromedical equipment throughout U.S. health care institutions. Sales amounted to a modest $233 million in 1967, particularly small considering electromedical manufacturers were responsible for generating only a fraction of the total, overshadowed by their larger cousins, x-ray apparatus manufacturers. But the electromedical industry would not be cast in this supportive role for long, and indeed from this point forward, growth of the electromedical industry would outpace that of the x-ray apparatus industry and thereby fuel the growth of the industry as whole. When, five years later, total sales climbed to $429 million, the leap was even more pronounced for electromedical manufacturers, having started from much below the $233 million figure in 1967, yet accounting for a large part of the nearly $200 million increase.

By 1974, the electromedical industry had closed the gap separating its revenue production with that of the x-ray apparatus industry and drew even, with each segment accounting for half of the $650 million in sales recorded that year. With slightly less than 100 x-ray apparatus and electromedical device manufacturers in the country at that time, the number of manufacturers would swell to nearly 240 in two years, a dramatic increase once again reflective mainly of the electromedical industry's rapid rate of growth. From 1974 to the end of the decade, the electromedical industry's revenue volume skyrocketed at a compound annual rate of 31 percent, an increase that dropped to a less prolific 16.4 percent when adjusted for inflation, yet still represented robust vitality.

Still benefiting from further improvements and from the continued acceptance of their products, which by the mid-1970s had firmly established the electromedical industry as a major player in the broadly defined medical industry, electromedical manufacturers had gained great strides since the first awkward and rudimentary pacemaker appeared in the late 1950s. No longer attached via cable or measuring as large as a hat box, pacemakers were now roughly the size of a fingertip and enjoyed widespread demand. In 1970, 53,000 pacemakers were implanted, and by 1976 the yearly implants had increased to 175,000, representing a quarter of a billion dollars in sales. At this time, the prospects for further sales appeared almost guaranteed, as a development of great significance augured a dramatic increase in the number of pacemakers installed each year. Powered by mercury-zinc batteries, pacemakers typically needed to be replaced at least three times during a patient's life span, but the use of lithium-powered batteries, a development that promised to reshape the market for pacemakers, reduced the average replacement expectation of pacemakers to one per patient. Although the switch to lithium-powered batteries would sharply reduce the industry's replacement sales, the prospect of undergoing fewer surgical procedures induced more patients to opt for pacemaker implants, which drove sales upward.

By 1976, the electromedical and x-ray apparatus industry's aggregate revenue neared the one billion dollar mark, then shot past it the following year, increasing 86 percent to reach $1.88 billion. Underpinned by strong pacemaker sales and even stronger ultrasonic equipment sales, which were increasing 18 percent annually, the electromedical industry approached the end of its decade of prodigious growth nearing $2.5 billion in sales. Success came slower in the early 1980s, but only in contrast to the dramatic growth of the 1970s. Sales eclipsed five billion dollars in 1984, then began to suffer in the ensuing years, falling 2.7 percent in 1985 and increasing only marginally thereafter, as flat demand, a buildup of inventories, and strong competition from imports combined to arrest the industry's expansion.

In 1987, the electromedical industry was separated at last from the x-ray apparatus industry, their respective statistics no longer pooled together. In the last year of their combination, total sales were estimated to be $5 billion; their separation gave, for the first time, a clear indication of their individual magnitude. The electromedical industry emerged as a $3.57 billion industry, employing 29,200 workers, while the x-ray apparatus industry's value of shipments amounted to $1.55 billion and its work force totaled 8,700.

As the electromedical industry entered the late 1980s, manufacturers attempted to effect a recovery from the mid-1980s, a downturn that was exacerbated by the increasingly cost-conscious health care industry. By 1989, price increases at the manufacturer level had averaged only three percent in the previous four years, as increased competition and production overcapacity limited the manufacturers' ability to raise prices. Profits suffered as a result, but revenue continued to grow, sending many manufacturers overseas to forge joint ventures with other companies to lessen the financial constraints of a capital-intensive business.

CURRENT CONDITIONS

After recording double-digit growth between 1987 and 1990, the electromedical industry entered the early 1990s watching its inspiring growth shudder to a stop, particularly in 1993, when sales were flat. In 1994, the industry's revenue total was an estimated $6.23 billion. The industry-wide stagnation of the early 1990s was attributable largely to a sharp decline in MRI shipments, which plummeted nearly 20 percent compared to shipment increases of pacemakers and ultrasonic scanning devices of three percent and five percent, respectively. The decline in MRI shipments, more capital-intensive than pacemakers or ultrasonic scanning devices, was attributed primarily to recessive economic conditions during the early 1990s. As the industry entered the mid-1990s, these uncertainties and their eventual resolution promised to have great import on the future of the industry.

Looking forward from the mid-1990s, prognostications for the electromedical industry were predicated on the further technological development of MRIs, and generally on advancements emanating from the diagnostic side of the electromedical industry. With improved imaging systems, operating at significantly higher speeds, this type of electromedical equipment provided the industry's best answer to the health care industry's need for cost-cutting, more efficient equipment in the 1990s.

INDUSTRY LEADERS

The largest manufacturer in the electromedical industry during the mid-1990s, General Electric's Medical Systems Group based in Milwaukee, Wisconsin, stood as classic example of the electromedical industry's efforts to further penetrate the international electromedical market and reduce the production costs of its products. With joint ventures scattered across Asia, General Electric's Medical Systems Group entered into a joint venture with a personal computer manufacturer, Wipro Ltd., in India in 1990 to produce and sell a wide variety of ultrasound devices. By forging such ties, the Medical Systems Group became one of General Electric's most profitable divisions in the mid-1990s, recording more than $5 billion in sales in 1993.

In ranking order behind General Electric's Medical Systems Group in 1993 were IMCERA Group Inc., based in Northbrook, Illinois, with $1.70 billion in sales, and Picker International Inc., based in Highland Heights, Ohio, with $1.18 billion in sales.

WORK FORCE

Total employment during the electromedical industry's history generally paralleled its pattern of revenue growth, climbing while sales increased and leveling off when revenue growth became less prolific. In 1974, when the industry already was experiencing a phenomenal surge of growth and its total employment included employees involved in the production of x-ray apparatus, there were 13,000 employees composing its work force. Two years later, total employment vaulted to 30,900, largely due to the growth of the electromedical segment of the industry. This figure continued to increase, reaching 41,500 by 1981, then climbing to 48,800 by 1984, at which time total employment in the industry began to record successive annual declines as manufacturers streamlined their operations. By 1988, total employment had fallen to 31,400, then began to increase once again, rising to 34,400 by 1991.

Of the 34,400 people employed by the electromedical industry in 1991, less than half were production workers, an atypical ratio of production workers to salaried employees in American manufacturing industry. The greater proportional representation of salaried employees, those performing managerial, administrative, or technical duties, was primarily due to the technological sophistication of the products manufactured by the industry, which, as the level of sophistication increased over the course of the industry's existence, winnowed the ranks of production workers in the industry.

Generally, production workers were employed on a full-time basis during the early 1990s, averaging four percent more hours per year than the typical production worker employed by other manufacturing industries. Production workers in the electromedical industry generally earned more per hour than their counterparts as well, averaging $10.91 per hour in 1989, compared to the national average of $10.49 per hour. In 1990, this average hourly wage increased to $11.49, at which time salaried employees earned an average of $44,182 per year.

AMERICA AND THE WORLD

Historically, the electromedical industry's international presence has been a major source of its strength, providing manufacturers with ample room to market their highly sophisticated products in markets bereft of similar equipment. In 1993, this presence continued to support the industry at a time when domestic conditions had soured. In that year, U.S. exports of electromedical equipment increased eight percent to $2.4 billion, giving U.S. manufacturers a $1.1 billion trade surplus. Much of this business was attributable to the strong sales performance of electrodiagnostic devices, ultrasonic scanners, and patient monitoring systems. These products were sold chiefly to European Community countries, Japan, and Canada.

INDUSTRY INFORMATION SOURCES

Darnay, Arsen J., editor, *Manufacturing USA,* 3rd edition, Detroit: Gale, 1993.

''Electronic Age of Medicine,'' *Financial World,* September 9, 1964, 10.

Engardio, Pete, ''An Ultrasound Foothold in Asia,'' *Business Week,* November 8, 1993, 68.

Greene, Joan, ''Ya Gotta Have Heart,'' *Barron's,* December 27, 1976, 11.

Loehwing, David A., ''Best of Health: Biomedical Technology—All Systems Are Go,'' *Barron's,* November 5, 1973, 3.

Loehwing, '''Ya Gotta Have Heart': Bio-Medicine Abounds in Risks as Well as Rewards,'' *Barron's,* November 12, 1973, 5.

''Medical Market Turns to Non-Invasive Products,'' *Business Marketing,* October 1983, 18.

U.S. Industrial Outlook, Washington, DC: U.S. Department of Commerce, 1975-1993.

—Jeffrey L. Covell

OPHTHALMIC GOODS

This classification includes establishments primarily engaged in manufacturing ophthalmic frames, lenses, contact lenses, and sunglass lenses. Establishments involved in manufacturing molded glass blanks are included in **SIC 3229: Pressed and Blown Glass and Glassware, Not Elsewhere Classified;** and businesses engaged in grinding lenses and fitting glasses to prescriptions are classified in **SIC 5995: Optical Goods Stores.**

INDUSTRY SNAPSHOT

Approximately 500 companies in the United States were involved in manufacturing ophthalmic goods in 1990. These companies recorded $2.27 billion in sales for products covered in this industry classification. This figure represents an aggregate value of shipments largely derived from the production of the four primary products in the ophthalmic goods industry: ophthalmic lenses and frames, sunglasses, industrial eyewear, and contact lenses. Contact lenses, by far the dominant ophthalmic goods product, accounted for over 31 percent of the total shipments delivered by the industry, with soft contact lenses representing 22 percent of the contact lens product share. Plastic ophthalmic focus lenses accounted for approximately 15 percent of the industry's shipments while ophthalmic frames and industrial eyewear each accounted for 6 percent of the product share. Non-prescription sunglasses represented 4 percent of the total shipments delivered by the industry. Other products within the ophthalmic goods industry include underwater goggles, reading and simple magnifiers, and ophthalmic lens coating.

Except for a temporary downturn in the mid-1980s, the ophthalmic goods industry entered the 1990s after a decade of solid growth. The value of shipments manufactured by the industry rose from $1.28 billion in 1982 to $2.27 billion in 1990, an increase partly attributable to the increasing popularity of sunglasses and to technological innovations in the development of contact lenses.

ORGANIZATION AND STRUCTURE

The ophthalmic goods industry is predominantly populated by relatively small manufacturing operations. Of the 517 establishments involved in producing ophthalmic goods in 1989, nearly 360, or 68 percent of all the facilities engaged in the industry, employed less than 20 people. Together, these 517 establishments represented all of the facilities operating in the industry that were operated by the approximately 500 companies engaged in manufacturing ophthalmic goods. Typically, the larger companies do not solely manufacture ophthalmic goods, but rely on manufacturing a diverse line of products to generate sales. For example, the leading company in the industry, Bausch & Lomb Inc., garnered over 60 percent of its sales in 1991 from health-care products.

A majority of the facilities engaged in manufacturing ophthalmic goods are located in the eastern United States, although California has the greatest number of establishments located in any one state. In terms of regional concentration, New York, New Jersey, and Pennsylvania, contain the most ophthalmic goods facilities, with 103 establishments. The Pacific region, including Alaska and Hawaii, ranks as the second most populated area of ophthalmic goods manufacturing facilities, solely by virtue of the 74 establishments located in California, the only state within the region to contain manufacturing facilities. Michigan, Illinois, and Ohio, home to 64 establishments, represent the nation's third largest regional concentration of ophthalmic facilities.

During the 1980s, the cost of conducting business in the ophthalmic goods industry rose sharply, far outpacing the increase in sales during the decade. In 1982, the industry recorded $1.28 billion in sales and spent $41 million on capital investment. By 1990, sales had climbed to $2.27 billion, but capital investment had more than tripled to $137 million. Despite this exponential increase in capital outlays, the average investment of ophthalmic goods facilities is comparatively less expensive than the average investment of facilities in all other manufacturing industries. The average investment required to operate an ophthalmic facility in 1989 was $282,398, which was five percent below the average investment per establishment of $296,864 for all other manufacturing industries. A more dramatic difference is shown in the cost per establishment. In 1989, $1,284,526 was the average cost for facilities operating in the ophthalmic goods industry, 72 percent below the $4,542,893 averaged by establishments in all other manufacturing industries.

BACKGROUND AND DEVELOPMENT

Until the 1960s, growth in the ophthalmic goods industry had occurred at a steady, predictable rate, largely dictated by the rate of population growth in the United States. During the 1960s, however, an increased demand for ophthalmic products elevated the production and sales levels of manufacturers to an unprecedented height. A combination of several factors prompted this remarkable surge in growth, including a dramatic rise in the nation's population and an increase in the availability of eye examinations. The advent of contact lenses in the 1950s as a genuine alternative to conventional corrective eyewear, however, contributed most significantly to the growth of the ophthalmic goods industry.

Although extraordinary gains were achieved by contact lens manufacturers and retailers during the first years of quantifiable production in the 1950s, certain difficulties associated with the early development of contact lenses slowed the public's acceptance of the new product. On average, a pair of contact lenses sold for $200, an exceedingly high price to pay for many consumers, and the discomfort caused by wearing the hard, hydrophobic lenses, which initially covered most of the exposed eyeball, dissuaded a considerable percentage of consumers from making a long-term conversion to contact lenses. According to industry estimates, roughly half of the people who began fittings for contact lenses reverted back to conventional corrective eyewear, a rate of attrition that would continue to plague contact lens manufacturers into the 1970s.

Despite the high cost of these lenses and the discomfort they often caused, consumers purchased enough contact lenses to push annual sales from $2 million in 1950 to $60 million by 1959. The number of contact lens manufacturers, the majority of which were small, privately-owned companies, also increased at a commensurate rate during the decade, climbing from 20 in 1950 to more than 400 by 1960. This proliferation of contact lens manufacturers led to a rash of deceptive advertising complaints issued by the Federal Trade Commission (FTC) and sparked several fiercely contested patent disputes, as the excitement generated by the creation of a new, potentially lucrative market within the ophthalmic goods industry attracted increased competition. Complaints filed by the FTC, 15 of which were recorded in 1961 compared to only four prior to 1960, patent disputes, along with issues such as whether only ophthalmologists and oculists should be allowed to prescribe and fit contact lenses, caused the sales of contact lenses to stagnate at the close of the decade. But these were problems generally associated with the nascence of the market and, as such, inflicted only a temporary setback on the burgeoning industry.

By the mid-1960s, improvements had been made in contact lenses, although their cost still hovered around $200 a pair. The thickness of the plastic used to manufacture the lenses had been reduced, alleviating some of the irritation experienced when a contact lens wearer's eyelid passed over the lens, and the diameter of the lenses had also been reduced so that they only covered the iris and the pupil, rather than the entire exposed eyeball. Shortly before these improvements were made, however, a discovery of lasting importance for the future of the contact lens market overshadowed the technological strides made by the industry in hard contact lens design—although it would be years before its impact would be felt by manufacturers and retailers. In 1965, two Czechoslovakian scientists, Otto Wichterle and Drahoslav Lim, were awarded a patent for their invention, five years earlier, of a soft plastic suitable for body implants that could also be used to produce contact lenses. Marking the beginning of soft contact lenses, which would eventually account for an overwhelming percentage of contact lens sales, the pliable, hydrophilic material absorbed tears rather than shedding them, as did hard contact lenses, and virtually eliminated any sensation of the eyelid passing over the lens.

Concurrent with the encouraging development of soft contact lenses, the rest of the ophthalmic goods industry was expanding at a robust rate, exceeding the rate of growth in the nation's population. From 1955 to 1965 the population over the age of five increased 18.4 percent, while the number of corrective eyewear users rose by 30 percent. This growth was primarily attributable to a greater portion of the population undergoing complete eye examinations, a trend facilitated by Medicare and Medicaid health programs, increased screening for vision acuity in public school systems, and states requiring mandatory eye examinations for people applying for driving licenses. The increasing number of union optical plans coupled with a greater number of corrective lens wearers purchasing more than one pair of ophthalmic lenses and frames also fueled the expansion of the ophthalmic market in the 1960s.

New product developments in the conventional corrective eyewear field contributed as well to the gains achieved by the ophthalmic industry in the 1960s. One of the four leading publicly-held companies engaged in the ophthalmic goods industry at the time, American Optical Corp., introduced a new single vision lens that provided increased visual sharpness and less distortion from peripheral angles of view. Another leader in the industry, Univis, developed bifocal lenses in 1964 without a visible line separating each half of the lens. Plastic, shatterproof and lightweight lenses, also made their debut in the 1960s. Accounting for only 5 percent of the total corrective lens sales by the mid-1960s, plastic lens sales, nevertheless, had been growing faster than the industry itself during the decade.

Sunglasses also experienced a surge in sales during the 1960s, further accelerating the rapid pace at which the ophthalmic goods industry was expanding. During the 1960s, sunglasses became fashionable accessories worn throughout the year and no longer were considered seasonal products. The product in the ophthalmic goods industry most sensitive to fashion trends, sunglasses quickly became a lucrative product to manufacture and sell, as unit sales rose from 60 million pairs in 1960 to 175 million pairs in 1966. By the end of the decade, the sunglass market had leapt 70 percent from the sales volume recorded in 1965, to approximately $200 million.

Conspicuously absent from the contact lens market during the 1960s were the leading manufacturers in the ophthalmic goods industry. American Optical Company and Bausch & Lomb Inc., which together controlled over 90 percent of the conventional eyeglass market, had eschewed entrance into the contact lens market primarily because the directors of the companies perceived the competition to be too intense. Moreover, neither company felt it had developed a technological innovation in the product encouraging enough to warrant a foray into the market. In 1966, however, Bausch & Lomb acquired the exclusive rights to manufacture and sell the soft, hydrophilic lenses developed by the two Czechoslovakian scientists, and by 1972 had begun distributing soft contact lenses nationwide.

In the 1970s, the ophthalmic goods industry continued to benefit from the population growth, as the prodigious sales increases of the 1960s continued. Wholesale billings for the optical industry as a whole increased from $400 million in 1959 to $900 million by 1969, then doubled to nearly $2 billion by the end of the 1970s. The success of the industry attracted the attention of the FTC once again, in 1974, when it began investigating restraints on price advertising in the optical industry. In the course of its investigation, the FTC found a significant discrepancy in the price of eyewear throughout the nation, with the average price of eyewear running 25 percent higher in states where advertising was illegal and varying by as much as 300 percent within the same state. In 1978, the same year in which eyeglass coverage became mandatory under Medicaid, the FTC lifted the restrictions on advertising with the hope of saving consumers as much as $400 million annually. Consequently, competition within the ophthalmic goods industry intensified as pricing strategies became of paramount importance.

Along with this transformation of the retail side of the optical industry, ophthalmic goods manufacturers continued to experience growth, engendered in part by the expansion of the sunglass market. In the early 1980s, sunglass sales dropped, with unit demand slipping 15 percent in 1981 and 1982, but sales began rising as the decade progressed. Indicative of the product's dependency on fashion trends, the increase in sales was partly attributable to the popularity of several films during the early 1980s that featured well-known actors wearing sunglasses. For example, perhaps the greatest boost from the motion picture industry came when a pair of Bausch & Lomb's Ray-Ban Wayfarer sunglasses were prominently featured in *Risky Business*. In 1981, 18,000 pairs of the Wayfarer sunglasses were sold; however, after the film was released in 1983, unit sales ballooned to 330,000 pairs. Retail sales in the sunglass market rose from $361 million in 1985 to $1.5 billion by the end of the decade, reflecting a 100 percent increase from 1980.

CURRENT CONDITIONS

Although the number of contact lens wearers in the United States tapered off at approximately 24 million in the four or five years prior to 1992, the dynamics within this segment of the ophthalmic goods industry were rapidly changing in the early 1990s. Disposable soft contact lenses, first marketed by Johnson & Johnson in 1988, grabbed the attention of consumers during the product's first years of availability and were expected to woo many contact lens wearers away from conventional contact lenses in the future. Projected to represent half of the contact lens market by 1995, disposable lenses appear to be the product of the future in the ophthalmic goods industry. Consequently, the ability of contact lens manufacturers to respond to this development could determine their success in the future.

Severely affected by the global recession in the early 1990s, the sunglass market plummeted 36 percent from $1.76 billion in sales in 1991 to $961 million in 1992. Especially sensitive to the health of the national economy, the sunglass market also suffered from its robust growth during the 1980s, as the proliferation of sunglass manufacturers exacerbated the effect of the stagnant economy and saturated the market. The surfeit of manufacturers entering the U. S. market from both the domestic and international fronts does not bode well for the immediate future of sunglass sales, but the growing trend of purchasing sunglasses for protection from ultra-violet rays could expand the market somewhat.

Additionally, pending legislation regarding the restructuring of the nation's healthcare system will undoubtedly affect individuals' ophthalmology coverage, and will in turn have a significant impact on ophthalmic goods manufacturers. Doubts concerning what provisions will be included for the optical industry, which ranks below the medical and dental industries in terms of size and strength, characterized the industry's anxiety the last time national health care legislation was seriously considered in the early and mid-1970s. These same concerns were revisited as the industry entered the mid-1990s.

Another factor in the eye-care industry is the emerging struggle featuring optometrists and manufacturers who have joined together against mail-order outlets and, to a lesser degree, other discount outlets, who have sought to gain a share of the market in recent years. Many manufacturers, including the giants of the industry, refuse to sell lenses to mail-order companies or discount outlets that don't have eye-care professionals on-site.

INDUSTRY LEADERS

With over 13,000 employees and manufacturing or marketing operations in 26 countries, Bausch & Lomb is the dominant company operating in the ophthalmic goods industry. A leader in the industry since its inception in 1853, Bausch & Lomb secured a lasting foothold in the optical field by developing the first rubber eyeglass frames, contributing significantly to the advancement of microscope and telescope technology, and through the creation of Aviator-style Ray-Ban sunglasses. The acquisition of the rights to manufacture and sell soft contact lenses in 1966 and the subsequent Federal Drug Administration (FDA) approval to market the lenses in 1971, coupled with the company's diversification in the early 1980s into health care and biomedical business lines, have contributed most appreciably to the company's success in the 1980s and 1990s. With optical products accounting for less than half of the company's sales, Bausch & Lomb posted $1.70 billion in sales in 1992, compared to the $510 million recorded ten years earlier.

The second largest company in the ophthalmic goods industry is Allergan Inc., a manufacturer and marketer of contact lenses and a broad assortment of other ophthalmic products not included in this industry classification. Allergan employed approximately 5,100 people and garnered $897 million in sales in 1992, representing a volume of sales that had more than doubled in the previous six years.

Other leading companies in this industry include CIBA-Vision Optics, a unit of CIBA-Geigy, and Vistakon, a subsidiary of Johnson & Johnson.

WORK FORCE

The ophthalmic goods industry employed 28,000 people in 1990, 19,800 of whom were production workers, with the remaining 8,200 performing administrative, technical, or managerial duties. Employment within the industry shrank during the mid-1980s to a low of 21,700, but rebounded by the end of the decade to surpass levels established during the early 1980s.

Typically, production workers in the ophthalmic goods industry are employed on a full-time basis, averaging 2 percent more hours per year than the average of production workers employed by other U.S. industries. However, they earn on average 20 percent less than other production workers. In 1989, the average hourly wage for production workers in the ophthalmic goods industry was $8.36, while the average wage in all other manufacturing industries was $10.49. The average annual salary of employees holding administrative, technical, or managerial positions in the industry was $31,416 in 1989.

INDUSTRY INFORMATION SOURCES

Collins, Steve, "Optical Firms Look to Rosier Future," *The Commercial and Financial Chronicle*, November 18, 1974.

"Contact-Lens Sellers Just Don't See Eye-To-Eye," *Business Week*, July 12, 1993.

"Curbs on Eyeglass-Price Ads Are Studied by FTC for Possible Antitrust Violations," *The Wall Street Journal*, September 24, 1975.

"Eye, the Jury," *Time*, May 31, 1971.

"The Eyeglass Industry," *The Wall Street Transcript*, May 20, 1968.

"Foresight Saga," *Barron's*, June 8, 1970.

"Future Focus," *The Economist*, July 4, 1987.

Golman, Kevin, "Market for Pricey Sunglasses Heats Up," *The Wall Street Journal*, March 22, 1993.

Grey, David, "Contact Lens Makers Run into Sales Snag; Ads Also Under Fire," *The Wall Street Journal*, February 2, 1961.

"Growth in Optical Field," *Financial World*, August 25, 1965.

Jacob, Rahul, "Trust the Locals Win Worldwide," *Fortune*, May 4, 1992.

Jones, Stacy V., "Lenses Made Pliable by Plastic," *New York Times*, November 27, 1965.

Kuntz, Mary, "Eye Contact," *Forbes*, January 27, 1986.

Lyons, Richard D., "F.T.C. Orders an End to Restraints on Advertising of Eyeglass Prices," *New York Times*, May 25, 1978.

Menzies, Hugh D., "The Hard Fight in Soft Lenses," *Fortune*, July 27, 1981.

"New Under the Sun," *Chemical Week*, June 10, 1967.

"Ophthalmic Companies: Reflections on the Golden Eye," *The Magazine of Wall Street*, March 3, 1972.

Pouschine, Tatiana, "Cruising on Ray-Bans," *Forbes*, August 3, 1992.

Rudolph, Barbara, "Shades of Discontent," *Forbes*, July 18, 1983.

"Shades of the Present," *Investor's Reader*, May 20, 1970.

Walker, Kelly, "Looks That Can Kill," *Forbes*, August 27, 1984.

Wright, Robert A., "Contact Lenses Evoke Wall Street Courtship," *New York Times*, February 26, 1968.

—Jeffrey L. Covell

SIC 3861

PHOTOGRAPHIC EQUIPMENT AND SUPPLIES

This classification includes establishments primarily engaged in manufacturing photographic apparatus, equipment, parts, attachments, and accessories utilized in both still and motion photography. Also covered in this classification are establishments primarily involved in manufacturing photocopy and microfilm equipment, blueprinting and diazotype (white printing) apparatus and equipment, sensitized film, paper, cloth, and plates, and prepared photographic chemicals.

Those establishments involved in manufacturing products that are related to the photographic industry, but are not grouped in the photographic equipment and supplies classification, include manufacturers of unsensitized photographic paper stock, and paper mats, mounts, easels, and folders utilized for photographic purposes. These establishments are classified within the paper and allied products industry. Photographic lens manufacturers are classified in **SIC 3827: Optical Instruments and Lenses** and manufacturers of photographic glass are delineated in the stone, clay, glass, and concrete products industry. Also excluded are manufacturers of chemicals produced for technical purposes that are not specifically prepared and packaged for use in photography, and those manufacturing photographic flash, flood, enlarger, and projection lamp bulbs. The former are classified within chemicals and allied products, and the latter are classified in **SIC 3641: Electric Lamp Bulbs and Tubes.**

INDUSTRY SNAPSHOT

Approximately 700 companies were involved in manufacturing photographic equipment and supplies in the United States in 1992. These companies together recorded $23.5 billion in sales for products included in the classification. The aggregate value of shipments predominantly derived from the industry's six primary product groups: sensitized photographic film, paper, and plates; photocopy equipment; prepared photographic chemicals; still picture equipment; and motion picture equipment. Of the various products, sensitized film, paper, and plates accounted for greater than a third of the industry's shipments, largely due to the commanding lead still picture film enjoyed in the photographic market. Ranked next was photocopying equipment, which represented just under a third of the industry's total shipments, followed by prepared photographic chemicals, still picture equipment, microfilming equipment, and motion picture equipment, each accounting for less than ten percent of the total shipments.

Growth in the photographic equipment and supplies industry was usually fueled by the introduction of new products utilizing innovative technology. Historically, the emergence of a new product into the market invigorated sales, which, in the case of still and motion camera equipment, also increased sales of film and related supplies. Since a majority of the products manufactured in the photographic equipment and supplies industry were considered leisure or non-essential goods, they were particularly sensitive to economic conditions and tended to suffer as a consequence of reduced consumer spending. However, its broad range of products insulated the industry from the effects of vacillating demand to some extent. For example, still picture film and photocopying equipment typically sold consistently despite economic downturns.

ORGANIZATION AND STRUCTURE

The photographic equipment and supplies industry was comprised mostly of small manufacturing operations. Of the 806 facilities operated by the approximately 725 companies involved in the industry in 1989, nearly 500 employed less than 20 people. However, facilities engaged in manufacturing photographic equipment and supplies employed an average of 108 people each—twice the average of 54 people per facility found in all manufacturing industries.

The majority of the industry's manufacturing facilities were located in the Middle Atlantic states of New York, New Jersey, and Pennsylvania. Together, these three states boasted more than 200 establishments, with New York accounting for roughly half that total. The West comprised the nation's second-largest regional concentration, with 147 establishments in California (the greatest number in any one state) and 11 in Oregon. The third-largest concentration was found in the Midwestern states of Michigan, Wisconsin, Illinois, Indiana, and Ohio, with 142 total establishments.

The operating costs associated with a photographic equipment and supplies facility, at $8.6 million, were 89 percent higher than the average manufacturing facility in 1989. The average investment per establishment showed an even greater disparity; photographic equipment and supplies facilities, at an average of $1.25 million, were 320 percent more costly than the $296,864 average per facility for all manufacturing industries. This gulf was likely to widen as electronic imaging products, which required more expensive equipment to manufacture than conventional photographic products, gained in popularity and caused more manufacturers to convert their facilities.

BACKGROUND AND DEVELOPMENT

Although photographic equipment and supplies first became available to consumers in the 1880s, it was not until the 1950s that the industry's sales grew rapidly toward modern proportions. The confluence of several developments occasioned this defining decade for the photographic industry: a significant increase in consumers' disposable income; the emergence of photocopying and microfilming products as lucrative components within the industry; and the development of still cameras that were very easy to operate.

Of course, several remarkable technological achievements that occurred much earlier enabled the industry to experience this formative surge in growth during the 1950s. These innovations took place primarily under the aegis of the industry's leader—the Eastman Kodak Company. Perhaps the most significant contribution to the industry's evolution came from Kodak's founder, George Eastman. In the late 1870s, Eastman adapted a photographic process then being used in Britain that replaced wet-plate developing chemicals and equipment with a dry-plate process. Less cumbersome, cleaner to operate, and generally easier to use than wet-plate cameras, Eastman's dry-plate system represented the industry's first step toward making photographic equipment available to all consumers. In Eastman's words, he intended to make the camera "as convenient as the pencil"—affordable and operable for every stratum of society. Eastman followed this innovation with the introduction of roll-film in the 1890s, a product first developed by film and camera manufacturer Rev. Hannibal Goodwin, but initially marketed by Kodak.

In a bid to capture the nation's interest in photography, manufacturers of this era labored to improve the performance of cameras and the quality of film. A giant leap toward this goal was taken in 1900 when Kodak introduced the first model of its popular, inexpensive, and easy-to-operate Brownie line of cameras. Retailing for one dollar, the first Brownie signaled the beginning of affordable cameras with mass-market appeal. Having achieved its first appreciable market penetration with the Brownie, Kodak later began to develop products aimed at diversifying the applications of photographic equipment. The first 8-millimeter motion picture system designed for the amateur photographer entered the market in 1932, followed by the advent of color film three years later.

Additional products intended to spark interest in amateur photography emerged before the onset of World War II, but in the immediate postwar years a discovery by the founder of Polaroid Corporation, Dr. Edwin H. Land, overshadowed the recent product innovations and forever changed the dynamics of the photographic industry. In 1947, Dr. Land announced the development of a process to instantly develop film, thereby giving birth to the first instant camera and film. When it became available later that year, the product would pique the buying public's interest and catapult Polaroid toward a multi-billion dollar sales volume.

By this time, manufacturers had ameliorated the performance of their products and consumers had grown accustomed to using photographic equipment. As these two market conditions dove-tailed following the war, the economic and population boom of the 1950s ignited photographic sales. According to industry estimates, purchases of photographic products more than doubled during the decade, jumping from under $500 million in 1950 to $1.2 billion by 1960. This prodigious growth of the industry was partly attributable to the robust national economy following the war, which translated into an increase in the amount of disposable income possessed by many of the nation's consumers. The high birth-rate also persuaded a considerable segment of the population to purchase cameras and film in order to photograph newborn babies and young children, the object of approximately 55 percent of the 2.2 billion photographs taken in 1960.

Kodak held a virtual monopoly of the photographic industry from the turn of the century through this period, perennially controlling roughly 90 percent of the film market and an equally overwhelming share of the camera market. By the early 1950s, the federal government began to intervene, filing an antitrust suit against Kodak that eventually resulted in a consent decree in 1954. Part of Kodak's dominance before the consent decree was attributable to a film processing fee that was automatically included with every Kodak film purchase. By including a built-in processing fee, Kodak in effect cornered the processing end of the industry, and consequently discouraged any competition for its film manufacturing business—the dearth of alternative processing facilities inhibited film sales by manufacturers other than Kodak. This practice, however, ended in 1954 when Kodak agreed to sell film without a processing charge and to license other processing companies to develop Kodak film and prints. Although the 1954 consent decree did not appreciably lessen Kodak's grip on the industry, it did enable interested parties to enter a market that previously was essentially closed to outside competition. It also provided those few film manufacturers engaged in the industry before 1954 with a much-needed respite from Kodak's stranglehold.

As competition intensified in the film manufacturing market, competitors scurried to secure a foothold in the fledgling photocopying market, which also promised to be a lucrative enterprise. Although total photocopying sales did not exceed $100 million until 1958, this figure increased rapidly when a product was developed for office use. Photocopiers were primarily targeted toward industrial users during the 1950s, but manufacturers developed new technology to enable the production of smaller machines that would grab the business community's attention. Each of the market leaders manufactured photocopiers that utilized a different photocopying process. Controlling roughly a third of the market, Minnesota Mining and Manufacturing and Kodak used Thermofax and Verifax processes, respectively, while American Photocopy Equipment Company, the third-largest manufacturer, used a diffusion transfer process. In the end, however, these types proved inferior to the process marketed by Xerox Corporation. Xerography featured electrostatic dry copying that replaced the chemicals required by the other photocopying machines with a cleaner process requiring no specially manufactured paper.

Photocopiers utilizing xerography grew from one percent of Xerox's total sales in 1950 to over 60 percent in 1960, infusing not only Xerox but the industry as a whole with exponential growth. Other companies that followed Xerox's lead into electrostatic copying included American Photocopy, Charles Bruning, BBM Photocopy, and Smith-Corona, launching the market toward an eventual multi-billion dollar sales volume. The pace of this growth quickened with the introduction of the Xerox 914 office copier in 1960, which enabled rapid duplication of small quantities of original-source documents for business offices—a task that previously had to be completed manually. Three years after the introduction of the 914, Xerox's sales more than tripled and the industry as a whole soared to $500 million per year. By this time the market was heavily contested among more than 100 competitors, many of whom were still not convinced of xerography's merits and continued to manufacture wet-type machines. But this issue was soon settled by the response of the industry's business customers, and photocopiers rapidly became an indispensable accessory for nearly every office in the United States.

Equally dramatic events took place simultaneously in the photographic market, as the momentum generated in the 1950s carried over into the 1960s. Once again an innovative product emerged to invigorate the market—the Instamatic camera. First marketed by Kodak in 1963, the Instamatic camera and film formed a completely integrated system that afforded several attractive features to make photography simpler for a mass market. The system used a film cartridge that popped into the camera's back, so the task of threading film into the camera was no longer required. The camera was also notable for a rapid-action lever that advanced the film and automatically positioned it for each exposure, eliminating the inaccurate and awkward winding knob found on previous camera models. Some of the key innovations of the camera and film had been developed as far back as the 1940s, but never before had so many convenient features been combined into a single product.

Mysteriously named Project 13, the development of Kodak's Instamatic was shrouded in secrecy, catching all of its competitors by surprise and heightening the camera's popularity. Within the camera's first two years of availability, approximately 7.5 million units were sold, and the effect on Kodak's film sales was similarly positive. According to estimates by Kodak, the average camera owner purchased four rolls of film a year, but with the easy-to-use Instamatic, camera owners increased their purchases to eight rolls a year.

Buoyed by the additional sales generated by Kodak's Instamatic, the photographic industry also experienced a considerable boost from industrial and government purchases. As photographic technology advanced, the useful applications of photographic equipment in factories and for high-technology purposes broadened, making the development of more sophisticated products almost as lucrative as the development of simplistic products. High-speed photographic equipment, taking as many as 5,000 photographs per second, was used to identify product inconsistencies occurring along production lines and to improve the design of industrial products. Cameras were also used inside missiles to photograph foreign countries for military purposes, inside layer cakes to improve leavening agents manufactured by chemical companies, and aboard rockets to record details of the moon's surface. Such diverse applications combined to increase sales to the industrial and government sectors from $360 million in 1959 to $630 million in 1964, which represented nearly half of the $1.4 billion photographic industry for that year.

As the photographic equipment and supplies industry entered the 1970s, each component continued to generate a larger sales volume. The photocopying market had become a $1 billion a year business, with Xerox sitting atop the field ever since its introduction of the 914 photocopier. In 1963 Xerox followed the 914 with a smaller version, the 813, and subsequent models entered the market throughout the rest of the decade. Photocopying technology advanced rapidly during these years—increasing the production output of the machines and reducing their size—which heightened the popularity of photocopiers in business and government offices.

Xerox began marketing the Model 4000 photocopier in May 1970, which turned out to be a timely response to IBM's announcement a month earlier that it intended to enter the photocopying market. The Model 4000 churned out 45 copies a minute, or 2,700 an hour, compared to the approximately 1,000 copies the 914 could produce in a day. It contained two paper trays capable of holding different sizes and types of paper, and was the first photocopier able to automatically copy both sides of a single sheet of paper. Xerox was not the only pioneer in the photocopying equipment market, however, and consumer demand increased as other manufacturers developed attractive features for their machines. This in turn meant both more revenue for industry participants and more competition from companies involved in related businesses. Competition intensified for the remainder of the decade, and Xerox began to cede a large portion of its commanding lead to domestic and foreign competitors.

The microfilm market also expanded during the early 1970s, fueled by the growing utilization of computer systems in the business and government sectors. Computers became capable of storing massive amounts of data: one reel of magnetic computer tape stored enough information to fill 3,500 pages of paper, a task that took impact printers nearly four hours to complete. However, this new technology proved a perfect match for micrographic technology's ability to reduce documents to a fraction of their original size, since the same amount of information could be placed on microfilm in 12 minutes. This process, a fusion of micrographics and computer technology known as computer-output microfilm (COM), promised to provide a considerable boost to the microfilm market. Sales were sluggish until Minnesota Mining and Manufacturing and Kodak, two of the leading companies involved in the microfilm market, opened a network of regional COM centers in 1971 that met with positive response. By the early 1990s, industry estimates indicated that greater than one third of all computer output in the United States was generated on COM.

Micropublishing was another area in which microfilming equipment performed well in the 1970s. Although micropublishing represented only a $50 million a year business in 1970, a myriad of possibilities for micrographics existed in a nation that produced and stored documents at an ever-accelerating rate. Bank checks were microfilmed, newspapers and periodicals were microfilmed for storage in libraries, and many businesses needed to consolidate the plethora of documents they produced each year—all of which combined to invigorate sales of microfilming equipment. In the early 1970s, the microfilm market grew at a rate of 18 percent annually and evolved into a $500 million a year business. This decade established the foundation for future growth, as computer usage became more pervasive and the nation moved into the information age.

Entering the 1980s, manufacturers of conventional film, paper, and cameras began to suffer the effects of a saturated market and foreign competition. Nearly every leading company involved in the industry initiated a major reorganization, as corporate strategies shifted in an attempt to capitalize on the trend toward electronic imaging products. Several early versions of products utilizing the new technology emerged in the mid-1980s—including Sony Corporation's electronic still camera called the Mavica, Canon Incorporated's Xapshot, and Fuji Photo Film Company's Fujix—but sales were disappointing. One product that did sell well, however, was the camcorder, which was introduced in 1983 and quickly offered encouragement to proponents of electronic imaging. In its first two years of availability, 500,000 units were sold, a remarkable success considering each unit sold for an average of $1,000. The popularity of camcorders continued to increase through the end of the decade, laying the foundation for the buying public's acceptance of electronic imaging products. By 1990, unit sales exceeded three million.

CURRENT CONDITIONS

As the photographic equipment and supplies industry moved toward the mid-1990s, it entered a period of technological transformation that was expected to have significant effects in both the manufacturing and retail segments. The advent of electronic imaging—a technology that utilized semiconductor sensors instead of film to record images and then displayed the images on television screens or computer monitors rather than paper—threatened to radically affect the sales of photographic equipment and supplies. Industry observers' and participants' reactions ranged from worry that the new format would entirely supplant conventional photographic equipment and supplies, to less severe predictions that electronic imaging would merely augment the existing market. Initially, much of this debate was academic; electronic imaging products were prohibitively expensive and the quality of images were far inferior to those generated via film. However, as the technology improved and attracted the attention of an increasing number of consumers, concern increased as to which direction the photographic industry would follow. Whatever the outcome of this technologically divisive issue, the $1 billion in sales generated by electronic imaging products in 1990 underscored the need for photographic equipment and supplies manufacturers to adjust to the rapidly changing dynamics of the industry.

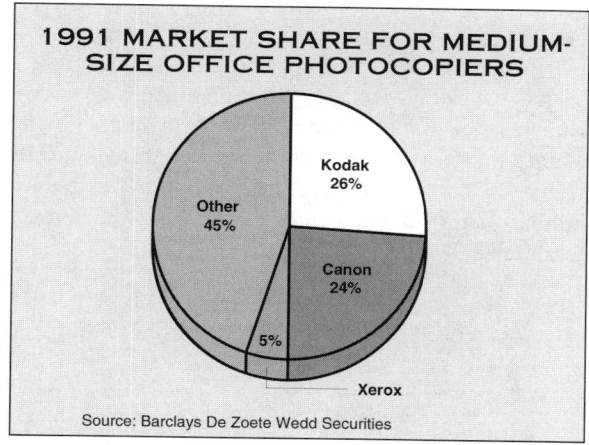

1991 MARKET SHARE FOR MEDIUM-SIZE OFFICE PHOTOCOPIERS

Kodak 26%

Other 45%

Canon 24%

5%

Xerox

Source: Barclays De Zoete Wedd Securities

INDUSTRY LEADERS

Ranked according to sales volume, the two largest companies engaged in the photographic equipment and supplies industry were Eastman Kodak Company and Polaroid Corporation. Kodak, the long-standing leader in the industry, posted a net income of $1.1 billion on $20.2 billion in revenues in 1992, an astronomical increase from the $17 million it earned in

1991. The low profit figure for 1991, however, was primarily the result of an $873 million patent infringement payment to Polaroid.

Incorporated in 1889, Kodak enjoyed enviable success throughout much of the century. However, the industry giant struggled with the growing popularity of electronic imaging, restructuring its organization on four separate occasions in the 1980s and early 1990s. In a bid to enter the race for share in the electronic imaging market, Kodak unveiled its Photo CD system in 1992, which enabled purchasers to transfer images captured on conventional film to a digital disk for display on a television screen or computer. Following the introduction of its Photo CD system, Kodak offered 20 new products in early 1993, the largest number introduced at one time in the company's storied history. The products were designed and marketed primarily for children and elderly people, with the hope of expanding what Kodak perceived as a sated market in the 25- to 40-year-old age group.

Photocopiers were consistent losers for Kodak in the late 1980s and early 1990s, a situation that was exacerbated as the company fell behind its competition technologically. A pressing concern for Kodak was the successful development of a digital color copier that would enable the company to respond to the significant trend in that direction.

Despite these problems and the concerns revolving around the impact of electronic imaging—on which the company had spent over $1 billion in research by 1993—Kodak still maintained a considerable lead over its competitors as it planned for the twenty-first century. The company controlled an estimated 75 percent of the market for film and photographic paper in the United States, and 50 percent worldwide.

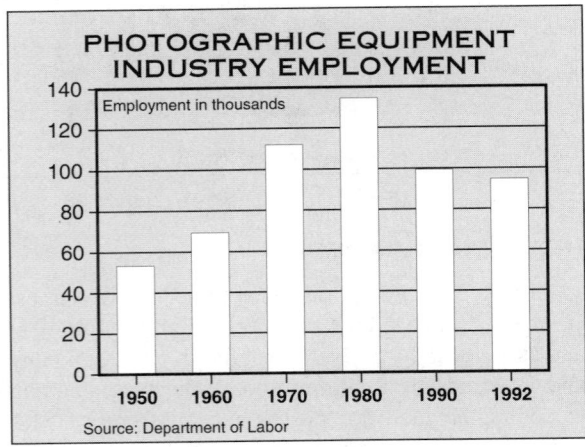

PHOTOGRAPHIC EQUIPMENT INDUSTRY EMPLOYMENT

Employment in thousands

Source: Department of Labor

Polaroid, the world's leading manufacturer of instant cameras and film, recorded $2.15 billion in sales in 1992. The company was established in 1923 by Edwin H. Land, who left college after beginning the research that eventually led to the development of the first synthetic light polarizing material. Polaroid experienced its first considerable growth spurt during World War II, when sales skyrocketed from $1 million in 1941 to $15 million in 1945. Since this exponential leap in sales was primarily attributable to the company's work for the military, which utilized Land's discovery for a variety of purposes, sales returned to their prewar levels afterward, falling to $1.5 million in 1947. In that same year, Land introduced his first instant-picture camera and sales ballooned once again.

After enjoying considerable success with subsequent instant-developing film and camera models, Polaroid's revenues declined in the early 1970s due to unexpectedly low demand for its SX-70 camera. But the company's sales revived in 1975 with the introduction of its inexpensive Pronto camera, six million units of which were sold in the first year. Kodak introduced an array of instant cameras in that same year, touching off a hotly contested and long drawn out patent infringement lawsuit filed by Polaroid.

Polaroid's sales plummeted once again during the 1980s, while the company streamlined its operations to invigorate profits and forestall a hostile takeover attempt by Shamrock Holdings. The company's Spectra camera and film, introduced in 1986, provided a much-needed boost to revenues and brightened what was generally a disappointing decade of performance. The company began manufacturing conventional film for the first time in 1989, and two years later it finally received $873 million from the patent infringement lawsuit it filed against Kodak 16 years earlier.

WORK FORCE

Total employment in the photographic equipment and supplies industry declined during the 1980s, as corporate restructuring, consolidations, and layoffs established a decade-long trend of employment instability. From over 130,000 employees in 1980, employment dropped to 100,00 by 1990. Of the more than 90,000 people employed in the photographic equipment and supplies industry in 1992, there was a fairly even split between production workers and were salaried employees (or those performing managerial, administrative, or technical duties). A proportionately larger number of production jobs were lost during the decade of employment decline, which narrowed the discrepancy between production and salaried positions in the industry to nearly equal representation.

Generally, production workers were employed on a full-time basis, averaging 11 percent more hours per year than the average for production workers in all manufacturing industries. Production workers in the photographic equipment and supplies industry earned $13.41 per hour in 1989, 28 percent more than the average of $10.49 per hour for other industries. This hourly wage increased in 1992 to $14.70, at which time salaried employees earned an average of $44,111 a year.

AMERICA AND THE WORLD

Historically, foreign manufacturers of photographic equipment and supplies have enjoyed considerable success competing in the U.S. market. This tradition continued in the early 1990s, as a global recession exacerbated the competition for flagging consumer spending and retarded the sales of U.S. products overseas. Exports of domestic photographic products were flat in 1992, at an estimated $3.8 billion, after a ten percent increase in 1991. Film, paper, and plates, accounting for 45 percent of all photographic exports, declined two percent in 1992 to $1.7 billion. Motion picture equipment sales incurred the most precipitous decline, slipping 15 percent to $60 million, while photocopying and microfilm equipment sales contributed to the overall stagnation of photographic exports by dipping three percent to approximately $940 million. Counteracting these losses were significant gains from the sale of still picture equipment, which rose 14 percent to $800 million, and from the sale of photographic chemicals, which increased 12 percent to $300 million.

Europe accounted for 45 percent of all domestic photographic sales overseas, the largest export market for U.S. manufacturers. Sales to Eastern Europe declined in 1992 after demonstrating encouraging results the previous year, especially in photocopying equipment sales. Exports to East and West Europe combined fell two percent in 1992, following a six percent increase in 1991. The Asia-Pacific region ranked second behind Europe as an export market for U.S. manufacturers, accounting for 24 percent of international sales, followed by Canada with 16 percent and Latin America with 15 percent.

Imports of photographic equipment and supplies to the United States increased seven percent in 1991 to $5.8 billion, and were expected to rise to $6 billion in 1992. Consumers in the United States purchased fewer foreign-made still picture products, causing import sales to drop to $1.3 billion. Imported motion picture equipment also suffered a decline in demand, though not as severe. Total imports were buoyed by a sharp increase in photocopying and microfilming equipment sales, which jumped 12 percent and represented 44 percent of all imports. Photographic chemicals experienced a more dramatic sales increase, climbing 18 percent, while sensitized film, paper, and plates rose three percent.

The majority of U.S. imports were manufactured in Japan, which continually increased its international presence since supplanting West Germany in 1962 as the world's second-largest exporter. Japanese manufacturers attained their commanding position in the international photographic industry by producing inexpensive, reliable photographic equipment that employed the latest technological advancements. Japan used these two marketing and manufacturing strategies to increase its share of the international photographic market since the early 1960s, and gained a solid position as the United States' major competitor. In 1992, Japan accounted for 64 percent of the import total in the United States. Reunified Germany was no longer a major contender in the U.S. import market, replaced by Canada and the Netherlands, which each supplied five percent of the total.

Although the trade deficit for photographic products increased 14 percent in 1992 to $2.3 billion, prospects for the mid-1990s were encouraging and could narrow the gap or at least prevent further increases between imports and exports in the United States. The expected economic recovery of international markets, particularly in Europe, could ameliorate overseas sales, especially considering the low saturation level of photographic equipment in Eastern Europe and the European Community. Moreover, any reduction of the tariff and trade barriers among European Community countries could have a positive effect on U.S. export performance as well. Within North America, the North American Free Trade Agreement (NAFTA) could ease the traffic of photographic products among Mexico, Canada, and the United States, an arrangement that promised to benefit photographic equipment and supplies manufacturers in the United States. Photographic trade between the United States and Canada was valued at an estimated $900 million in 1992, while two-way trade between Mexico and the United States was an estimated $400 million.

INDUSTRY INFORMATION SOURCES

Bart, Peter, "Spectrum Widens in Film Field," *New York Times,* July 9, 1961.

Bernstein, Peter W., "Polaroid Struggles to Get Back in Focus," *Fortune,* April 7, 1980.

"Cameras Focus on U.S. Buffs," *Business Week,* March 23, 1963.

Chakravarty, Subrata, N., "Xerox—Back on the Road to Success," *Forbes,* July 7, 1980.

Darnay, Arsen J., editor, *Manufacturing USA,* Detroit: Gale Research Inc., 1993.

"Disposable Cameras?," *Forbes,* March 1, 1970.

Driscoll, Lisa, "The New, New Thinking at Xerox," *Business Week,* June 22, 1992.

"Honeywell Discloses Electronic Focus Device," *Wall Street Journal,* September 23, 1975.

"Janofsky, Michael, "Kodak Adds 20 Products in Big Shift," *New York Times,* February 11, 1993.

Maremont, Mark, "Getting the Picture," *Business Week,* February 1, 1993.

"Microfilm Looks for a Booming Market," *Business Week,* May 29, 1971.

"New Life for Photocopiers," *Financial World,* January 29, 1964.

"The New Look of Photography," *Forbes,* July 1, 1991.

"Office Copier Industry Rumbles with Reports That IBM Is Coming," *Wall Street Journal,* April 14, 1970.

Palmer, Jay, "The Picture Brightens: At Eastman Kodak, Things Are Looking Up at All Divisions," *Barron's,* June 25, 1990.

"Photo Industry Changes Its Image," *Discount Store News,* February 3, 1992.

"Polaroid Profit Fell 10 Percent in Third Quarter, But Sales Climbed 4 Percent," *Wall Street Journal,* October 20, 1993.

Sheehan, Robert, "Picture—Sunshine and Shadow," *Fortune,* May 1965.

"Rich Market in Copying," *Moody's Stock Survey,* September 18, 1961.

"Shooting the Works," *Time,* January 17, 1964.

U.S. Industrial Outlook 1993, Washington, DC: U.S. Department of Commerce, 1993.

"Xerox Introduces the Most Advanced Unit Company Has Produced Yet," *Wall Street Journal,* May 20, 1970.

—Jeffrey L. Covell

SIC 3873

WATCHES, CLOCKS, CLOCKWORK OPERATED DEVICES, AND PARTS

This segment covers establishments primarily engaged in manufacturing clocks (including electric) watches, watchcases, mechanisms for clockwork operated devices and clock, and watch parts. This industry includes establishments primarily engaged in assembling clocks and watches from purchased move-

ments and cases. Establishments primarily engaged in manufacturing timeclocks are classified in **SIC 3579: Office Machines, Not Elsewhere Classified;** those manufacturing glass crystals are classified in **SIC 3231: Glass Products, Made of Purchased Glass;** and those manufacturing plastic crystals are classified in **SIC 3089: Plastics Products, Not Elsewhere Classified.**

INDUSTRY SNAPSHOT

The watch and clock industry has always been small compared to other industries, and since the late 1980s and early 1990s, the number of manufacturers has declined. This is due in large part to the movement—begun in the 1970s—of watch parts manufacture from the continental United States to offshore facilities. The popularity of quartz watches, which are produced primarily in Asia, as well as cheaper labor and Japanese competition are some of the factors that prompted the shift to offshore facilities. The largest company in the industry is Timex Enterprises Inc., with estimated 1993 sales of $850 million as compared to SMH (US) Inc., a subsidiary of the Swiss company that makes Swatch watches, following at a distance with $200 million in sales.

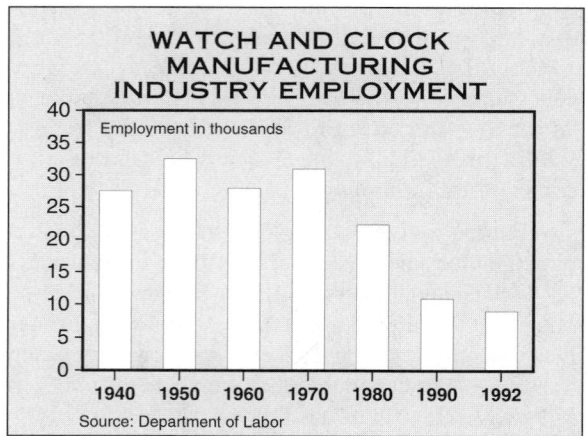

WATCH AND CLOCK MANUFACTURING INDUSTRY EMPLOYMENT

Employment in thousands

Source: Department of Labor

Although the components of the watches are mainly manufactured overseas, assembly takes place in plants in the United States. While the number of people employed in the U.S. watch and clock industry has been steadily declining since 1970, wages have been growing. Production workers were earning $8.69 per hour in 1990, compared to figures from the previous year showing hourly wages at $8.06.

In 1991, according to the U.S. Department of Commerce, watchcases; watch straps; bands and bracelets; and movements were imported from Switzerland, Japan, Hong Kong, Thailand, and several other countries. However, the trend in the industry is toward having both the manufacture of the parts and the assembly of the watches done overseas. Most of the major clock companies still produce their parts domestically.

BACKGROUND AND DEVELOPMENT

The clock industry has existed in the United States since pre-revolutionary days, but the industry did not begin to flourish until the early 1800s when such companies as Ingraham Clock Company and Chelsea Clock Co. were established. The first clocks manufactured for home use were pendulum clocks that, despite their excellent time-keeping, were rather cumbersome. Whether a huge mantle clock or a floor clock, the instrument had to be set perfectly plumb to keep time accurately. Such clocks were hand-made, and the cost was prohibitive. A clock was considered an investment and bought with the understanding that it would be passed from generation to generation. With the advent of the Industrial Revolution new technologies were developed, clocks became less cumbersome and expensive, and watch manufacturing began.

Prior to the 1920s almost all watches were carried in the pocket or purse. Some women's watches were designed as pieces of jewelry in the form of brooches or integrated into necklaces. The first watches were analog—the time was displayed via hands pointing at markers or numerals. In addition, the watches were mechanical, powered by a coiled mainspring that required manual winding.

The industry grew as further technological advances were made. In the 1950s the first battery powered watch was introduced, ushering in the electronic age in personal timekeepers. The spring mechanism was replaced by vibrating quartz crystals that contained a battery powered silicon chip, and the use of integrated circuits led to the development of the digital watch.

The first digital watch, the Pulsar by Hamilton, was launched in the 1970s. Two types of digital watches were introduced—the LCD (Liquid Crystal Display), which required light to read the numerals, and the LED (Light Emitting Diode), which required the wearer to push a button to light it and read the time. Neither gained true acceptance because the LCD was not practical at night, and the LED battery was short lived. The main reason digital watches did not become popular, however, was the reluctance of consumers to accept it. People felt more comfortable with a watch that gave a visual indication of the time remaining until a meeting or appointment.

The digital clock fared much better than the digital watch. The clock companies solved the problems with LCD and LED displays by designing a digital clock run by an electronic chip that called for a light to plug directly into the line cord, stay lit, and give a constant display. The result is that approximately 40 percent of all bedside alarm clocks have digital readouts.

While the digital watch was not a success, the quartz watch was. In the 1980s the production of the mechanical watch fell and watches with quartz chip movements became popular. The vanguard of the industry was the analog quartz watch—more than half are sold in North America, western Europe, and Japan.

AMERICA AND THE WORLD

he 1980s saw a profound change take place in the watch industry. The Swiss industry had hit hard times—production was down and the industry was in trouble. A turnaround occurred in 1983, however, when Nicolas G. Hayek, chairman of SMH Group, introduced the Swatch watch. This inexpensive, trendy watch in a plastic case was a deviation from the traditional high-priced luxury watch usually associated with the Swiss industry. The Swatch was an immediate success and sparked a continuing interest in inexpensive fashion watches. The analog quartz watch, once the industry weakling, had become its mainstay—more than 500 million were produced in 1992. Despite its impact, the Swatch did not re-establish Switzerland as the leading watch producer. For the past decade Japan has led the field in production with Hong Kong second and Switzerland third. Figures from 1992 indicated Japan's production accounted for roughly 44 percent of total global output, Hong Kong was responsible for about 20 percent, and Switzerland contributed approximately 17 percent. U.S. production had little impact on total global figures.

The United States, the biggest single market, has a large trade deficit in watches—1991 exports totaled $73.4 million compared to an import total of $1.84 billion. Japan led in the import of quartz watches, accounting for 32 percent of that category. Switzerland, however, was responsible for by far the largest number of imported of mechanical watches. While production of mechanical timepieces had been steadily declining, small gains were made in the early 1990s in conjunction with rising value that was attributed to increased demand for the high-end models. In the area of watch and clock parts, 1990 statistics showed imports of clock movements valued at $22.1 billion; watch movement imports totaled $13.2 billion; imports of watch straps, bands, and bracelets reached $43.2 billion; and $26.7 billion of watch cases were imported. Overall growth in the watch market has slowed from double-digit to single-digit figures. Nonetheless, production is expected to reach the one billion mark by the end of the 1990s, aided by the entrance of such nations as China, India, and Thailand into the field.

With the advent of the 1990s the global watch industry began to assess its ecological impact, and in 1992 watchmakers pledged to support and aid environmental efforts. Among the steps taken were the development of watch batteries with life spans of ten to 20 years and the use of recycled biodegradable materials for packaging, catalogs, press material and publica-

tions. In light of such advances, the industry's future looks promising.

INDUSTRY INFORMATION SOURCES

Fuhrman, Peter, ''Jewelry for the Wrist,'' *Forbes,* November 23, 1992, 173-78.

Shuster, William George, ''Watches: Global Recession Beaters,'' *Jewelers' Circular-Keystone,* August 1993, 95-99.

Thompson, Joe, ''The Watch World in Figures,'' *Modern Jeweler,* August 1992, 65-67.

''Watches & Clocks,'' *Jewelers' Circular-Keystone,* July 1993, 649-51.

—Annabelle McIlnay

Miscellaneous Manufacturing Industries

JEWELRY, PRECIOUS METAL

This category encompasses those establishments primarily engaged in manufacturing jewelry and other articles worn on or carried about the person, made of precious metals such as platinum, gold, and silver (including base metals clad or rolled with precious metals), with or without stones. In addition to personal jewelry, products of this industry include cigarette cases and lighters, vanity cases and compacts; trimmings for umbrellas and canes; and jewel settings and mountings. Establishments primarily engaged in manufacturing costume jewelry from nonprecious metals and other materials are classified in **SIC 3961: Costume Jewelry and Costume Novelties, Except Precious Metal.**

In 1990 the U.S. Department of Commerce identified 2,147 manufacturers of precious metal in the United States. The industry employed approximately 35,000 people in 1993.

Despite the lingering recessionary conditions of the early 1990s and fierce international competition, the industry managed to grow slightly. The estimated value of precious metal jewelry shipments in 1992 was $3,750 million, an increase of 0.9 percent from the 1991 figures. The 1993 figures were expected to reach $3,900 million. Nonetheless, some retailers experienced sales decreases because of lowered consumer confidence and decreased discretionary income. Expectations of an improved economy, and the hope that customers would begin indulging in long-deferred purchases led to an optimistic view of the industry's future.

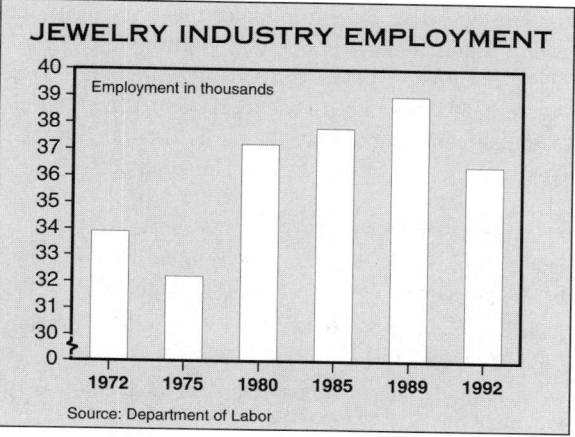

JEWELRY INDUSTRY EMPLOYMENT

Employment in thousands

Source: Department of Labor

The precious metal jewelry industry encompasses retailers, wholesalers, manufacturers, and suppliers, including lapidaries, refiners, stone dealers, findings manufacturers (manufacturers of the small parts used in making jewelry, such as clasps and other items), and subcontractors who provide services such as polishing and electroplating. Manufacturing firms in the precious metal jewelry industry tend to be small establishments and are concentrated in the New York City area. The industry's major expenses are the costs of raw materials and highly-skilled workers.

Two major issues of concern to the precious metal jewelry industry are the ten percent luxury tax imposed on jewelry sales exceeding $10,000 and environmental regulations related to manufacturing processes. Regulations concerning the removal of toxic levels of metals used in electroplating have added financial burdens to many manufacturers and subcontractors. Beginning in May of 1993, products that were made with ozone-depleting chemicals were required to carry identifying labels.

Despite the falling value of the U.S. dollar abroad, the United States maintained an unfavorable trade balance in 1992. Italy, one of the United States' major competitors, supplied 40 percent of all precious metal jewelry imports in 1992. Thailand, Israel, and Hong Kong were also key suppliers. Thailand and Israel both benefitted from the Generalized System of Preferences (GSP), a program that permits developing countries to export some products to the United States duty-free.

The main markets for U.S. exports of precious metal jewelry in 1992 were Switzerland, Japan, and Thailand. Exports to Mexico were expected to increase after ratification of the North American Free Trade Agreement, which enables American goods to enter Mexico duty-free. Most Mexican goods already enter the United States duty-free under the GSP; tariffs between Canada and the United States were already being eliminated under the U.S.-Canada Free Trade Agreement. Some industry experts also hoped that the establishment of product standards for the European Community would benefit the United States.

INDUSTRY INFORMATION SOURCES

Frankovich, George R., *The Jewelry Industry*, Providence, RI: Manufacturing Jewelers and Silversmiths of America.

Jewelers' Circular-Keystone, *1993-94 Jewelers' Almanac*, July, 1993, 602, 605, 613, 646.

Occupational Outlook Handbook, 1992-93 Edition, Washington DC: U.S. Department of Labor, 1992.

U.S. Industrial Outlook 1993, Washington, DC: U.S. Department of Commerce, January 1993.

—Patricia G. Huerster

SIC 3914

SILVERWARE, PLATED WARE, AND STAINLESS STEEL WARE

This category includes businesses whose primary activities consist of manufacturing flatware (including knives, forks, and spoons), hollowware, ecclesiastical ware, trophies, trays, and related products made of sterling silver; metal plated with silver, gold, or other metal; nickel silver; pewter; or stainless steel. The category also includes establishments primarily engaged in manufacturing table flatware with blades and handles of metal. Establishments primarily engaged in manufacturing other metal cutlery are classified in **SIC 3421: Cutlery**, and those manufacturing metal trophies, trays and toilet ware made of metals other than silver, nickel silver, pewter, stainless steel, and plated, are classified in **SIC 3499: Fabricated Metal Products, Not Elsewhere Classified**.

The total value of shipments for the tabletop market in 1992, according to *HFD*, reached $3.544 billion. Of this, dinnerware accounted for $1.491 billion and flatware accounted for $628 million (the remaining total went to crystal and glassware, with $1.425 billion). The 1990 preliminary estimates by the U.S. Department of Commerce indicated that manufacturers of silverware and plated ware employed 7.3 thousand workers.

The early 1990s found the industry still struggling to counter the effects of a lingering recession and changes in consumer preferences, which particularly affected the sterling silver segment of the industry. While manufacturers and retailers hoped to improve sales of sterling silver through aggressive advertising campaigns, many producers of sterling were also introducing new stainless steel lines to augment their business.

In the early 1990s, American manufacturers were producing approximately 20 percent of the world's silverware. Other major producers include Japan, Korea, France, and Italy.

Sterling silver is a term used by the U.S. government to describe a silver alloy consisting of 92.5 percent silver and 7.5 percent of another metal, such as copper. The baser metal is used to add strength to silver, which in its pure state is too soft to be practical. Silverplate, which also includes hollowware or hotelware, describes products made from silver bonded onto a baser metal, such as brass or copper. Silverplating creates a material which is far cheaper to produce than sterling silver and yet gives a similar appearance. It is not, however, as durable as sterling silver, as the plating will eventually wear off. Stainless steel consists of steel alloyed to another metal such as chromium to produce a strong, rust-resistant, and easy-care metal.

The three leading suppliers of flatware in the United States are Gorham, Oneida, and Wallace Silversmiths. Each of these businesses offers flatware patterns in both sterling silver and flatware, although Gorham and Wallace are better known for their sterling and Oneida is best known for its silver plate products and for its stainless steel flatware. Other well-known American manufacturers in the industry include Reed & Barton, Towle, and Dansk. Most U.S. manufacturers are located in the northeast section of the country. Although the principal manufacturers of flatware also produce silver or silver-plated jewelry or decorative products such as bowls, goblets, mugs, etc., flatware is typically the mainstay of the business.

Department stores are the most common point of sales for products in this industry, accounting for 28 percent of flatware sales and 30 percent of dinnerware sales in 1991.

INDUSTRY INFORMATION SOURCES

"Housewares: '92 Statistical Report — Dinnerware." *Home Furnishings Daily* (March 15, 1993): 60.

Hube, Karen. "Steel Cuts into Silver Flatware." *Home Furnishings Daily* (December 21, 1992): 71, 76.

Jewelers' Circular-Keystone. *1993-1994 Jewelers' Almanac* (July, 1993): 646, 652-53.

Neiss, Doug. "Economy's Woes Temper Small Industry Gains." *Home Furnishings Daily* (September 21, 1992): 4-7, 10, 13.

"Spotlighting Silver as a Sterling Investment." *Home Furnishings Daily* (February 15, 1993): 62-3.

—Patricia G. Huerster

SIC 3915

JEWELERS' FINDINGS AND MATERIALS, AND LAPIDARY WORK

This category cover establishments primarily engaged in manufacturing unassembled jewelry parts and stock jewelers' materials such as wire, tubing and sheeting; and establishments of lapidaries primarily engaged in cutting, slabbing, tumbling, carving, engraving, polishing, or faceting stones from natural or manmade precious or semiprecious gem raw materials, either for sale or on a contract basis for the trade; in recutting repolishing, and setting gem stones; or in drilling, cutting, or otherwise preparing jewels for instruments, dies, watches, chronometers, and other industrial uses. This industry includes the drilling, sawing, and peeling of real or cultured pearls. Establishments primarily engaged in manufacturing synthetic stones for gem stones and industrial used are classified **SIC 3299: Nonmetallic Mineral Products, Not Elsewhere Classified,** and those manufacturing artificial pearls are classified in **SIC 3961: Costume Jewelry and Costume Novelties, Except Precious Metal.**

In 1988 industry shipments reached $920.5 million, according to *Manufacturing USA,* down from the 1987 figure of $947.3 million. As of 1987, 437 compa-

nies in this industry operated 442 establishments; 73 had more than 20 employees. Firms in this industry averaged 18 employees per establishment, considerably less than the industrial average of 58.

Production in this industry is centered in the New England area. In 1987 the five main states producing jewelers' findings and lapidary work were New Jersey, Pennsylvania, New York, Rhode Island and Massachusetts. At least 334 of the 442 establishments in the industry operated in those states in 1987.

Three of the largest companies by sales volume in the jewelers' findings and lapidary industry in 1993 were Lazare Kaplan International Inc. of New York, Antwerp Diamond Distributing Inc. of New York, and Vigor Company of Austell, Georgia. Lazare Kaplan, founded in 1984, reported sales of $133 million and employed 197 people in 1993. It specialized in diamond cutting and polishing. A downturn in the diamond market forced the company into Chapter 11 in 1983, but its new owners, Maurice and Leon Tempelsman, spent at least $6 million on advertising and established a unique marketing strategy to lure buyers back. They laser-engraved the Lazare logo and an optional message directly onto the diamond along with a registered identification number. The markings were invisible to the naked eye.

Antwerp Diamond Distributing, founded in 1950, reported sales of $23 million and employed 30 workers in 1993. Vigor Company, founded in 1929, also manufactured chemical products. It reported sales of $20 million in 1993 and employed 70 workers that year.

Diamond cutting takes careful planning and entails a certain amount of risk. Marvin Samuels of Premier Gem Corp. of New York spent four years planning the cutting of what could have been the largest finished diamond in the world. At that time, that title belonged to Cullinan I, one of the British Crown jewels with a weight of 530.2 carats. Shape and surface problems meant choosing between the largest cut diamond with flaws or the second largest but perfectly finished diamond. Samuels chose the latter, finishing the cutting in early 1988 with a stone weighing 407.43 carats.

The jewelry industry in general suffered with the economic downturn of the late 1980s. One-carat diamonds once valued at $60,000 sold for $12,000. Many large chain dealers entered Chapter 11 reorganization and shut down stores across the country. These included Zale Corporation, the country's largest jeweler, and Barry's Jewelers Inc., the third largest. These bankruptcies, closings, and reorganizations sent shock waves through the industry. Many unsecured manufacturers and suppliers in the findings and lapidary segment toppled. That trend was aggravated by a 10-percent luxury tax on jewelry over $10,000, though the tax affected only a small portion of the industry.

The worldwide downturn depressed prices on many gems along with gold and silver, but the DeBeers' Central Selling Organization restricted the supply of diamonds along with sapphires, emeralds, and rubies to keep prices up. By 1986, it was supporting diamond sales in the United States with a $35 million advertising campaign. Even so, the worldwide down-sizing continued. In Antwerp, where diamonds make up six percent of Belgium's imports and exports, the number of diamond workers dropped from more than 19,000 in the 1970s to around 7,500 by 1986. Much of the polishing and grinding business traditionally commanded by that city went to lower-cost shops in Bombay, India.

The U.S. industry exported large amounts of cut, un-set diamonds—$944 million in 1990 according to *Market Share Reporter*. The major markets for U.S. exports were Hong Kong (22.4 percent), Japan (19.9), Israel (18.8), Belgium (18.3), Switzerland (13.2), Britain (4.6), and Canada (2.9).

Another major material used in the lapidary industry was ivory. Worldwide consumption in 1988 reached 453.3 tons. Most of that went to Hong Kong (60.6 percent) and Japan (24.4), but the United States took the bulk of the remaining 15 percent.

INDUSTRY INFORMATION SOURCES

"Belgium Facets," *Economist*, February 1, 1986, 78.

Census of Manufactures, 1987, Washington, DC: U.S. Department of Commerce, 1990.

Kluge, Paul Frederick, "A Diamond as Big as the Ritz—Well, Just about That Big," *Smithsonian*, May, 1988, 72-74.

Koselka, Rita, "Brand Name Diamonds?" *Forbes*, April 28, 1986, 64.

Darnay, Arsen J., ed., *Manufacturing USA*, 2nd edition, Detroit: Gale Research, Inc., 1989.

U.S. Industrial Outlook 1992, Washington, DC: U.S. Department of Commerce, 1992.

U.S. Industrial Outlook 1993, Washington, DC: U.S. Department of Commerce, 1993.

—Al Cook

SIC 3931

MUSICAL INSTRUMENTS

This category covers establishments primarily engaged in manufacturing musical instruments and parts and accessories for musical instruments. The primary products in this category are pianos, with or without player attachments, and organs. This industry also includes all other musical instruments.

INDUSTRY SNAPSHOT

At one time, the ability to play a musical instrument was considered an essential part of a person's basic education. During the later half of the 20th century, however, electronic advances like video games and music-playback machines combined with increasingly hectic lifestyles to make the effort of mastering a musical instrument somewhat less appealing. Nevertheless, in 1987 more than 25 million people in the United States played some sort of keyboard instrument, and sales of all musical instruments, both domestic and imported, reached $1.2 billion.

As part of the personal consumer durables category, musical instrument purchases depend greatly on consumer confidence. Such purchases are made with disposable personal income. In addition, in times of recession discretionary spending for school bands and orchestras, personal music lessons, and high-end instruments become the first casualties of austerity budgets.

ORGANIZATION AND STRUCTURE

Traditionally, the musical instruments industry has been dominated by the production of pianos, player pianos, organs, and parts for those products. According to the 1987 census those instruments accounted for $295.5 million in shipments out of a total of $814.1 million. Seven firms listed pianos as their primary product and shipped $184.9 million worth in 1987. The three product categories made up 37.7 percent of the entire industry.

The cost of building quality pianos soared during the later half of the 20th century, however, and demand stagnated. A good piano uses more than 8,000 moving parts, many of which require rare super-quality materials like ten-grain-per-inch spruce and highest-grade wool. Foreign competitors pushed into the market with innovative man-made materials and mass-production techniques that dramatically lowered the cost and increased the flexibility of the instruments.

Between 1972 and 1987, industry firms increased in number from 310 to 402, but halved their work force. Employment levels fell from 24,500 to 12,200. By 1990, the industry retained only 11,000 workers. In 1987, only 30 firms employed more than 100 workers while 192 had fewer than five. Indiana led the nation in production of musical instruments, contributing 12.8 percent of the total, followed by Pennsylvania (10.3), New York (8.9), Wisconsin (4.1), Illinois (4.0), and Connecticut (1.9).

BACKGROUND AND DEVELOPMENT

The Victorian era (1830-1880) saw the enthroning of music, especially piano music, as an essential stabilizing element of society and particularly the family. In 1881, the *Chambers' Journal* reported: "In every house there is an altar devoted to Saint Cecilia, and all are taught to serve her to the best of their ability. The altar is the pianoforte."

The expected devotees of music were mainly women. In 1922, the Music Teachers National Conference noted that 75 percent of all concert audiences were women and 85 percent of music students were female. In 1978, 57 percent of all music students were female and 79 percent of all piano students were as well. As early as 1840, the American "piano girl" was a recognizable stereotype; at the time, musical ability was thought to enhance a woman's social prestige.

The piano brought families together to play and listen, becoming the centerpiece of the Victorian family and an avidly sought after item in the growing industrialization of hectic post-World War I America. The musical instruments industry sought to capitalize on that interest and place a piano in every parlor in the nation.

Before 1800, all pianos were grand pianos that required a lot of space, but that year saw the development of the John Hawkins's Portable Grand Piano, the precursor of the now-familiar upright piano. That innovation allowed the piano into the parlors of the middle class, a development paralleled by the refinement of the music box, particularly after 1815. This device provided good quality music without the needed effort of the piano or other instrument. These two trends in musical instruments continued throughout the century, with the appeal of passive listening becoming more important in 20th century America. The first electro-mechanical piano, the Telharmonium by Thaddeus Cahill, appeared around 1896.

Playing a piano well required effort and practice. Few could develop the talent to any great degree, a fact that prompted piano manufacturers to look seriously at self-playing pianos. These devices held the promise of combining the social values associated with piano ownership with the pleasures of passive listening. The French led the way in 1863 with a patent on music rolls, but like the German versions they never worked well. The American Angelus player-piano of 1897 achieved the first commercial success, followed by the Pianola in 1898 and the Apollo in 1900. By 1918 it was estimated that more than 800,000 player pianos were in operation in America east of the Mississippi alone and that 75,000 piano rolls were sold every month in Philadelphia. Most played popular ragtime pieces but many delivered concert-quality renditions of classics "recorded" on cylinder by famous concert pianists from America and Europe. More than 100,000 coin-operated electric pianos produced by Wurlitzer and the J.P Seeburg Piano Company were distributed throughout the country and automatic self-playing pianos became common in many movie houses.

Despite manufacturer claims that anyone could play a player-piano, even a child, proper operation required careful and consistent operation of the foot pedals. By 1923, player-piano sales peaked at 56 percent of all pianos sold. The automated devices could not compete with the growing popularity of radios and phonographs, however, which provided simple, reliable listening and took up far less room in the family parlor.

Faced with the evaporation of its market, the industry reversed itself, promoting active piano playing with National Music Week, which encouraged awareness of music in general and music lessons in public schools. In 1928, 358 schools provided piano lessons; that figure jumped to 2,004 by 1930. The National Piano Manufacturers Association, founded in 1901, stressed the joys of active piano playing and encouraged group instruction.

The industry also had to fight an image problem, as mass production techniques led to marketing abuses. The American industrial system of mass production and standardized parts coupled with the expansion of the railroad transportation system near the end of the 19th century sparked a realignment of the traditional piano craft shop. The corporation became the common business structure and manufacturers often bought components to assemble a finished product without the need of a manufacturing facility at all. This was a similar development to what was happening in the automotive industry, with small firms becoming adept at supplying specific component elements to an assembly and marketing firm. The result was, according to Frank L. Wing of Wing & Sons Piano Company, the manufacturing of the world's best pianos as well as the world's worst. Wing & Sons produced three distinct grades of pianos: professional instruments bought by wealthy middle class clients for about $600 in 1916, commercial pianos which provided reasonable sound quality and durability for $400, and the low-grade "assembled" piano which sold for about $200. Many of the last category were "stencil" pianos that did not carry the name of the manufacturer or assembler anywhere on the instrument. Dealers usually stenciled their own names onto the casings after delivery and often used names similar to those found on top quality instruments, such as "Baldin" for "Baldwin."

A major innovation in the production of the American piano was the introduction of the console piano in 1935. This smaller, more streamlined instrument fit better with modern American architecture, blending with the living room decor instead of dominating it. The console piano and the new electronic organ formed a major part of the rising post-war demand of the mid-1940s.

CURRENT CONDITIONS

In 1969 Baldwin Piano executive Morley Thompson predicted piano sales would double by 1980, but instead they dropped by 30 percent. The industry once again faced the problem of lack of interest in pianos in the home and a decline of music instruction in the schools. Other, less expensive instruments, like acoustic guitars and electronic instruments, gobbled up market share while many consumers opted for computer synthesizers or video games.

The baby-boomer generation entered the 35-to-54 age group in the 1990s, bringing with it a pent-up demand from recent recessions and considerable purchasing power. The instruments of choice for this generation were the acoustic guitar and similar instruments. At the same time, austerity budgets at schools trimmed music classes, bands, and orchestras before making any other cuts. Meanwhile, music dealers continued to push instruments with price-cuts and "blowout sales" rather than promote music production with education and innovation.

The industry was expected to pick up slightly during the 1990s, with growth of about two percent annually. That depends on continued increases in consumer confidence, an increased domestic demand spurred by a one percent annual increase in the number of children attending school, reduction of austerity budgets at schools and the accompanying reinstitution of music funding, integration of American, Mexican, and Canadian markets under the North American Free Trade Agreement, and the ability of American industry to fend off foreign competition.

INDUSTRY LEADERS

At the beginning of the 20th century, the American musical instruments industry was dominated by a few big names like Baldwin, Steinway, Aeolian, American, Kimball, Wurlitzer, Steger, and Kohler. By the mid-1990s, after a century of reorganization, merger, takeover, and bankruptcies, many of these once-famous names melded into the two giants that remained at the top of the heap: Baldwin and Steinway.

Baldwin Piano and Organ Co. of Loveland, Ohio, survived dropping sales and rising interest rates by getting into the finance business: it bought and sold loan agreements on its pianos and organs. In 1993, it employed 1,600 workers to produce $110 million in sales. The company was established in 1862 by Dwight Hamilton Baldwin, a retail dealer of pianos and organs in Cincinnati. Its later success resulted from the takeover of many small piano manufacturers and the development of a consignment-based dealership contract arrangement. The system, actually begun by the W. W. Kimball Co. of Chicago, put pianos in showrooms across the country without major investments from the dealer and made pianos available to consumers on monthly payment terms. The dealer paid all local expenses, including freight for the product from the factory, but kept the down-payment and the interest portion of the monthly installment, which the customer paid directly to Baldwin. That interest often amounted to 25 to 30 percent. Baldwin's success prompted a Steinway spokesman to remark in *City of Cincinnati and Its Resources* that "the business of D. H. Baldwin & Co. is the model upon which the entire piano and organ trade of the country should be done."

Steinway has also built a reputation as a maker of quality instruments. Established in 1853 in New York, the firm developed and maintained that image with a refusal to promote its product through sales, with international endorsements by concert pianists, with national concert tours featuring those pianists playing Steinways, and with award-winning national advertising campaigns. In 1983, it became Steinway Musical Properties Inc. and in 1985 it spun off the subsidiary, Steinway Inc. of New York. The company employs 1,000 people to produce sales of $81 million.

A leader in the guitar portion of the industry is Fender Musical Instruments Corp. of Scottsdale, Arizona. Founded in 1985, it employs 700 workers for sales of $100 million.

WORK FORCE

The musical instrument industry has consistently downsized its work force since the 1970s. The industry employed 24,500 in 1972, but only 8,600 in 1991. However, the hourly wage increased from about $3.25 to $9.23 during the same period. Much of the loss of employment resulted from automation and a switch to materials that were easier to work with. This trend was expected to continue at least until 2000, with a projected 49.7 percent loss of electrical and electronic assemblers and double-digit losses in most other production positions. Notable exceptions to the trend include plastic molding machine operators (projected 0.7 percent increase), screen printing machine operators (0.6 percent increase), carpenters (0.7 percent increase) and sales workers (10.7 percent increase).

AMERICA AND THE WORLD

In the early 1990s, exports of American musical instruments were a bright spot for the industry, with six straight years of increased shipments. Sales increased seven percent in 1992 to reach $330 million worth of acoustic guitars, acoustic pianos, brasswinds, and woodwinds, and $360 million in sales were expected for 1993. More than half those exports went to Japan, Germany, United Kingdom, Canada, and Mexico, supported by a favorable currency exchange.

Many of the instruments imported into the United States come from Japan, who supplies 47 percent of the imported electronic instruments, synthesizers, portable keyboards, acoustic guitars and band instruments. Along with Korea and Taiwan, Japan provided 72 percent of the 1991 imports to the United States. Germany contributed 7 percent while imports from Mexico doubled between 1989 and 1992 as American companies established manufacturing facilities in that country to take advantage of lower wages.

RESEARCH AND TECHNOLOGY

The electronic revolution had a great effect on the musical instrument industry. Between 1981 and 1986 the price of an acoustic piano doubled because of increasing labor and material costs, while sales dropped from 282,172 units in 1978 to 166,555 units in 1986. Compare that with a 40 percent increase in the sales of electronic keyboard instruments between 1985 and 1986. In fact, Americans bought twice as many keyboards in 1986 (206 million) than in 1985 and more than four times as many as in 1984. Sales of synthesizers jumped from 220,000 in 1985 to 350,000 in 1986. All that was driven by the increased power and flexibility of computer-assisted music production and a drop in the price of such electronic equipment.

Robert Moog introduced the synthesizer concept in 1964, but his company folded in 1977 and Moog moved to Kurzweil Music Systems Incorporated. The company's Kurzweil 250 used computer memory to reproduce the sounds of any musical instrument. The real breakthrough, however, came in 1983 with the musical instrument digital interface (MIDI), which allowed musicians and composers to connect synthesizers, instruments, and even computers together and have electronic signals successfully pass between them. Computer hardware and accompanying MIDI software sales jumped to $500 million in 1987. The computerized equipment allows composers and musicians to master new instruments quickly and to develop new music faster and more efficiently. They can also incorporate other, non-musical sounds into their compositions and performances. The system breaks down the barriers between composer, performer, music printer, and instrument builder, allowing the musician full control of the creative process.

The technology, however, brings a new set of problems. It allows a musician to ''sample'' sounds from anywhere and anyone and then modify the sound to fit the need. Entire orchestras can be synthesized by one person, and other performers can be used to computer-produce totally new performances. That has led to copyright battles and fears of lack of work for live-performance musicians. In addition, the old fear that plagued the piano industry during the heyday of player-pianos—that the technology will displace the art—has returned.

Another advancement in musical technology is the use of virtual reality. Peter Williams of Virtual S of London experimented with a virtual-reality keyboard in the shape of a checkerboard and bouncing ball. Each square could be a specific instrument or effect controlled by filters and other electronic controllers. The effect is a random music piece accompanied by the visual representation of the bouncing ball on the checkerboard. ''This is one class of music programming that you couldn't do in the real world,'' said Williams in *New Scientist*. ''We're not trying to replace violins and other instruments; this is a different way of doing it.''

Other developments in the industry include a new process for making a plastic clarinet, which was developed by an English clarinetist and teacher along with an industrial designer. By fusing two molded halves instead of injection-molding a single piece, they eliminated the traditional tone problems of earlier plastic clarinets. Traditionally clarinets are made from African hardwoods usually found in endangered rainforests. Consequently the price of such wooden instruments was skyrocketing. The inventors hoped to begin using the same molding technique in the production of saxophones.

INDUSTRY INFORMATION SOURCES

Bloch, Georges, "Will the 'Piano' of the Year 2000 Be Intelligent?," *Impact of Science on Society,* No. 147, 1987, 269-76.

Bode, Harald, "History of Electronic Sound Modification," *Journal of the Audio Engineering Society,* October, 1984, 730-39.

Census of Manufacturers, 1987, Washington, DC: U.S. Department of Commerce, 1990.

Darnay, Arsen J., ed., *Manufacturing USA,* 2nd edition, Detroit: Gale Research, Inc., 1989.

Geake, Elisabeth, "And Hello to Playing Music without Keys," *New Scientist,* August 14, 1993, 17.

Hirokazu, Sayama, "Efforts to Promote Sales Pay off for Musical Instrument Business," *Business Japan,* January, 1984, 95.

Pearsall, Ronald, "Music by Proxy: The Invention and Evolution of Mechanical Music," *Impact of Science on Society,* No. 147, 1987, 261-67.

Roell, Craig H., *The Piano in America, 1890-1940,* Chapel Hill, NC: University of North Carolina Press, 1989.

Saunders, Laura, "Mood Indigo," *Forbes,* August 29, 1983, 50-52.

Sauttaur, Omar, "Plastic Molds the Clarinet to Children's Needs," *New Scientist,* December 28, 1991, 14.

Stern, Richard, and Paul Bornstein, "What Happens When the Music Stops?," *Forbes,* December 20, 1982, 31-33.

Thompson, Terri, "Music Is Alive with the Sound of High Tech," *Business Week,* October 26, 1987, 114-16.

U.S. Industrial Outlook 1992, Washington, DC: U.S. Department of Commerce, 1992.

U.S. Industrial Outlook 1993, Washington, DC: U.S. Department of Commerce, 1993.

—Al Cook

SIC 3942

DOLLS AND STUFFED TOYS

This category covers establishments primarily engaged in manufacturing dolls, doll parts, and doll clothing, except doll wigs. Establishments primarily engaged in manufacturing stuffed toys are also included in this industry. Doll wigs are classified under **SIC 3999: Manufacturing Industries, Not Elsewhere Classified.**

In 1991 industry shipments in the dolls and stuffed toys industry reached an estimated $338 million, according to the *U.S. Industrial Outlook 1992.* That represented a three percent increase over 1990 production and marked returning confidence in the market after slow sales in 1991. Total wholesale sales of dolls approached $1 billion in 1989, according to the New York-based trade group Toy Manufacturers of America. Employment also grew by .6 percent to 34,900 workers, and wages increased slightly to an average of $5.72 per hour.

Most of the American demand for dolls and stuffed animals was supplied by Japan, China, Taiwan, and South Korea; in 1991 $1.9 billion worth were imported. Imports from China alone grew 170 percent between 1987 and 1990 after that country gained "Most Favored Nation" status in 1980. That country supplied 21.8 percent of the world's $21.97 billion toy market in 1989, according to *Market Share Reporter.* The ratio of imported dolls to apparent consumption was 88 percent in 1991 and was expected to grow as the 1990s progressed. The American export market took 24 percent of U.S. production in 1991, but much of that was shipment of partially completed products to Mexico for finishing and eventual re-import into the American market.

One of the biggest names in doll manufacturing is Mattel, Inc., maker of the ever-famous Barbie doll. That one product alone is responsible for almost half of Mattel's 1992 sales of $2.1 billion. In its first year of distribution in 1992, the "Totally Hair" version of Barbie sold more than $100 million. On the average, American girls own eight Barbie dolls, and 95 percent of all American girls have at least one. Mattel hoped to achieve similar market penetration overseas; Mattel chairman John Amerman stated in *Forbes:* "Children's wants and desires, their play patterns, are the same around the world."

In America, however, the traditional caucasian, blonde, fashion-model Barbie attracted some serious competition from a growing collection of ethnic dolls. So Mattel introduced an African-American Barbie in 1980, but only the coloring—not the doll's features—was modified. In 1991 the company introduced a line of dolls designed to "reflect the natural beauty of the African-American woman." The "Shani" line represented a reaction to demographic reality in the United States, where in 1990 15 percent of children under the age of 10 were African-American, 14 percent were Hispanic, and three percent were Asian or Pacific Islander. The ethnic dolls produced by the major toy manufacturers only imitated products already being marketed by minority entrepreneurs.

Mattel, Inc., of El Segundo, California, was founded in 1945 and in 1991 employed 12,500 workers to produce sales of $1.6 billion. Its closest competitor in the doll industry is Hasbro, Inc., of Pawtucket, Rhode Island, with its Playskool Division. That company, founded in 1912, reported total 1991 sales of $2.1 billion for such products as dolls and stuffed toys, games, clothing, baby pacifiers, and rubber and plastic. Tyco Industries Inc. of Mount Laurel, New Jersey, reported sales of $296 million for such products as toy automobiles and trucks, games and toys, and dolls and stuffed animals. It employed 600 workers.

The social effect of dolls cannot be ignored. In 1983 Matthew Mansfield in *Advertising Age* noted that "the first Barbie children are, or are about to be mothers." The plastic figurine has been the role model for a significant portion of a generation currently it its 20s and 30s. That fact concerned researchers at the University of Nevada, Reno. They studied Barbie's form mathematically and discovered that a 5-foot-6-inch woman with Barbie's form would have a waist as little as 17 inches in circumference. Elaine Pedersen and Nancy Markee in *Perceptual and Motor Skills* concluded: "The fashion dolls' proportions, including those of Barbie, did not represent either the Greek ideal or the fashion model's body proportions. They do not represent a healthy individual's body proportions. . . . While Mattel, the makers of Barbie, have said they visualize the doll as being an aspirational role model, the question should be asked—do girls playing with fashion dolls perceive these dolls' bodies as the ideal to be achieved?" Also not comfortable with Barbie's influence on young girls were mathematicians, scientists, and women's groups, who in 1992 protested when Mattel released a talking Barbie who lamented that "Math class is tough."

The doll itself has undergone a transformation as the 20th century proceeded. The "play doll" intended for girls four to ten years old has given way to doll sets. To keep entry-point pricing below $10, manufacturers sell dolls and accessories separately and introduce new-model releases periodically. That led to accessories like specialty clothing and toys based on the doll's created lifestyle. It also encouraged collecting. As prices of antique dolls soared, modern dolls, especially Barbie dolls, became more appealing as "modern collectibles." By 1983, that segment of the market was estimated at $30 million retail. Out of that grew dolls designed specifically for adult collectors with price tags as high as $1,000. The average collector in 1983 owned 200 to 400 dolls and spent $600 annually. In 1991 G.I. Joe's nurse, circa 1950, was trading for $12,000.

INDUSTRY INFORMATION SOURCES

Bryant, June Smith, "More Dolls of Color," *Black Enterprise,* December 1991, 18.

Darnay, Arsen, J., editor, *Manufacturing USA,* Detroit: Gale Research Inc., 1989.

Darnay, Arsen, J., editor, *Market Share Reporter,* Detroit: Gale Research Inc., 1992.

Dunn, Don, "See Those Mouse Ears? They're Worth a Mint," *Business Week,* December 30, 1991, 157.

Dunn, William, "The Move Toward Ethnic Marketing," *Nation's Business,* July 1992, 39-41.

Fitzgerald, Kate, "Barbie Grows Up," *Advertising Age,* June 1, 1992, 30.

Mansfield, Matthew R., "Dolls Aren't Merely Child's Play," *Advertising Age,* June 20, 1983, M4-5.

"Mathematicians Talk Tough to New Barbie," *Science,* October 16, 1992, 396.

Miller, Cyndee, "Toy Companies Release 'Ethnically Correct' Dolls," *Marketing News,* September 30, 1991, 1-2.

Morgenson, Gretchen, "Barbie Does Budapest," *Forbes,* June 7, 1991, 66-69.

1987 Census of Manufactures—Industry Series, Washington, DC: U.S. Department of Commerce.

Pedersen, Elaine L. and Nancy I. Markee, "Fashion Dolls: Representations of Ideals of Beauty," *Perceptual and Motor Skills,* August 1991, 93-94.

Stark, Ellen, "Barbie Looks Like a Million Bucks," *Money,* May 1993, 982.

U.S. Industrial Outlook 1992, Washington, DC: U.S. Department of Commerce, 1992.

—Al Cook

SIC 3944

GAMES, TOYS, AND CHILDREN'S VEHICLES

This entry consists of establishments primarily engaged in manufacturing games and game sets for adults and children, and mechanical and non-mechanical toys. Important industry products include games; toy furniture; doll carriages and carts; construction sets; mechanical trains; toy guns and rifles; baby carriages and strollers; children's tricycles, coaster wagons, play cars, sleds and other children's outdoor wheel goods and vehicles, except bicycles. Also included are establishments primarily engaged in manufacturing electronic board games; electronic toys; and electronic game machines, except coin-operated. Establishments primarily involved in manufacturing dolls and stuffed toys are included in **SIC 3942: Dolls and Stuffed Toys.**

INDUSTRY SNAPSHOT

The U.S. toy industry is a fast-paced industry. Product-driven, it rides the crest of a fad until the next fad happens through a combination of product merit, marketing, and luck. Although the classics, such as Monopoly, Scrabble and Slinky have demonstrated strong, long-term sales performance, few toys or games stay on the shelves for more than a year or two. The early 1990s were healthy years for the toy industry, although the fortunes of various companies have swung wildly. Several factors make the toy industry a risky business, including boom or bust sales patterns, short product life, and only one major selling season, Christmas, which historically has accounted for 50 to 60 percent of annual sales.

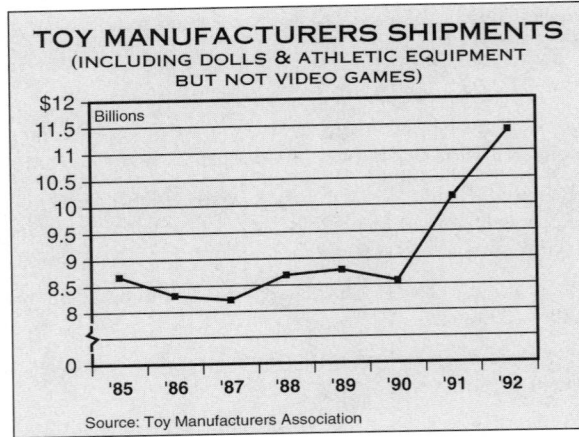

TOY MANUFACTURERS SHIPMENTS
(INCLUDING DOLLS & ATHLETIC EQUIPMENT BUT NOT VIDEO GAMES)

Source: Toy Manufacturers Association

Game makers think of themselves more as publishers than toy makers because many games have a longer sales life than most toys and sell at a fairly predictable level. But game publishers also were subject to the instability of the market, with some games failing and others, such as Trivial Pursuit and Pictionary, experiencing unpredictable success. The game segment used to be a relatively staid component within the toy industry until Trivial Pursuit's sudden success tipped the market upside down and showed that games were not just products for children. Soon, other companies were also looking for the key to success in the adult game market.

ORGANIZATION AND STRUCTURE

Because the industry was heavily dependent on capricious trends, miscalculation or misjudgment at times resulted in enormous losses. The life span of even the most successful toys was often brief, with sales dropping as quickly as they rose. Typically, companies counted themselves among the fortunate if they had one product that sold well for a year. Even if a product remained popular after its debut year, it was likely to be copied, since toy manufacturers often attempted to replicate each other's successful products.

The Toy Manufacturers of America (TMA), the industry's trade organization, was founded shortly after the United States entered World War I, when toy makers faced severe shortages of materials, and Congress was considering an embargo on the buying and selling of Christmas presents to conserve materials needed for the war. TMA formed and successfully lobbied Congress concerning the need to continue to produce toys for America's children despite the war. A few years later, TMA convinced representatives to impose large tariffs on toy imports to protect the American toy industry. TMA continued to lobby and compile information and statistics for the toy industry in the early 1990s.

Ideas for games and toys may originate in-house, but the industry also relied heavily on the ideas of freelance inventors. A company may pour thousands, even hundreds of thousands of dollars into market testing before committing to production. During the course of its development, the concept may change drastically. Most toy manufacturers also subscribed to Toy Retail Sales Tracing Service for quantitative market research revealing trends, product performance, and competition. Qualitative market research involved product testing, usually with small focus groups of children. Toy development was risky and speculative. Until it is officially previewed at the annual American International Toy Fair, a project could be aborted at any stage if it did not meet expectations or if buyers did not express much interest.

Historically, distributors and wholesalers were the toy manufacturers' biggest customers, but in the early 1990s large retail chains ordered directly from the toy makers. Smaller toy stores looked to regional distributors, but for the most part distributors were a dying breed.

According to some industry sources, Toys 'R' Us accounted for as much as 20 percent of the toy market in the United States during the early 1990s. The rest of the toy market comprised national and regional toy store chains, mass merchandisers, wholesalers, catalog showrooms, variety stores, discount stores, department stores, drugstores, local chains, and independent toy stores. There were also "jobbers" who bought closeout merchandise from toy makers to sell to retailers. Mass merchandisers, such as Kmart and Wal-Mart, did not carry as wide a range of merchandise as the large toy stores, but these retailers had tremendous clout with toy makers. The national distribution and volume buying that these stores and others, such as Sears and Service Merchandise, offered, helped them negotiate beneficial deals with toy makers.

Although law prohibits manufacturers from selling merchandise to different customers at different prices, in reality, the larger the customer, the larger the volume discount. The purchasing power of the customer also affected many other negotiable terms, including credit against future sales, and extra merchandise from the manufacturer. These discounts and special terms resulted in widely varying retail prices. Powerful customers also were able to receive markdown money from manufacturers of products that failed so badly retailers were forced to sell them below cost.

BACKGROUND AND DEVELOPMENT

The first American toy manufacturer was established in the 1830s. The company, Tower Toy Company produced doll furniture, toy tools and toy boats. In 1860, Milton Bradley established a publishing and lithography business, but as financial problems plagued the company, Bradley diversified by inventing and publishing The Checkered Game of Life, the precursor of The Game of Life, still popular in the early 1990s. The Civil War slowed the toy industry somewhat, although toy guns were popular, as were Milton Bradley's portable editions of chess, checkers, and dominoes.

In 1883, 16 year-old George S. Parker started his own game company. When his brothers joined him, the company became Parker Brothers. It became the publisher of many games popular in the early 1990s, including the perennial number one selling board game, Monopoly, as well as Sorry!, Risk, and Clue.

Around the turn of the century, the "Golden Age of Toys" brought walking and talking dolls, toy pianos, friction motorized vehicles, steam-powered toys, the Erector Set, the Flexible Flyer sled, Lionel toy trains, and Crayola crayons. In 1906, the Teddy bear craze began with the stuffed animals named for Teddy Roosevelt because he refused to shoot a trapped bear cub during a hunting trip. Between 1900 and 1910, American toy production doubled. During the next decade, it grew 500 percent, largely because World War I had halted the import of European toys. In 1923, Hasbro Inc.. It would become the largest American toy maker, with products such as Mr. Potato Head in the 1950s and Lite Brite and G.I. Joe in the 1960s.

Surprisingly, the Great Depression did not devastate the game and toy industry. Toys and games were inexpensive entertainment to the millions of people out of work. It was during the Great Depression that Parker Brothers brought out its classic real estate game, Monopoly, and Milton Bradley introduced Easy Money, both games that allowed players to imagine being rich by making deals with play dollars. In 1930, Herman G. Fisher and Irving R. Price established the very successful Fisher-Price Toys, which in the early 1990s was the biggest name in infant and preschool toys and merchandise.

World War II slowed the toy industry's growth because of labor and material shortages, but the post-war years brought prosperity to the entire country, and the toy industry reaped the benefits as well. Following World War II, the toy world was revolutionized with the introduction of plastic.

Television Advertising. In 1955, an advertising move by Mattel changed the way toys and games were marketed and also launched the promotional toy business. The nascent American Broadcasting Company (ABC) television network approached Mattel about weekly national advertising on its new show, Walt Disney's "The Mickey Mouse Club" beginning in November, just as the Christmas shopping season opened. To the surprise of many, Mattel took a big financial risk and paid half a million dollars to become a sponsor. Before this bold move, most advertising money was spent on catalogs and trade ads during the Christmas season and an occasional local TV ad to promote the most promising items. With this advertising agreement between Mattel and ABC, Mattel's famous slogan was born—"You can tell it's Mattel, it's swell"—and the power of weekly advertising to kids was launched. The product Mattel had advertised, the Burp Gun, was sold out and the promotional toy business was on its way.

Promotional toys were products advertised on television directly to the consumers—the kids. Television became the number one advertising force in the toy industry. With the line between advertising and entertainment blurred in the late 1980s and early 1990s, entire shows became based on the exploits of a line of characters invented or promoted by a toy company. In 1969, Mattel underwrote a program based on its very successful Hot Wheels line. When a competitor complained, the Federal Communications Commission (FCC) banned it, calling it a "program-length commercial." In 1983 the FCC ruled that the marketplace should determine programming. This change of policy cleared the way for toy-based programming. By the 1986-1987 season, more than 40 toy-based programs were on the air.

According to Sydney Stern and Ted Schoenhaus in *Toyland, The High Stakes Game of the Toy Industry*, television changed the very nature of toys by allowing the toy industry to sell toys that they could never sell before because they could now demonstrate the features of the product. Products that could do something—walk, talk, move, crash—had existed for a long time, but now they began to come to life on television and soon dominated the market. Advertising even began to dictate product development. Products were developed on the basis of how well they would lend themselves to television commercials. Television also allowed the toy makers to create a fantasy around the product, so that children were not only demanding a toy, they were buying into the fantasy which made that particular toy unique. By the 1980s, for some products the commercial was more important than the product itself because it was the commercial that created the concept and the product actually did little on its own. Retailers, trying to anticipate what toys kids would want, paid close attention to the manufacturers' ads and ad budgets in making their purchasing decisions during the early 1990s. At toy fairs for buyers, toy manufacturers previewed the commercials as well as the toys.

A second "revolution" in toy making began with the first video games. In 1972, Nolan Bushnell and a friend invested $250 each to found Atari and produce Pong, a simple video table tennis game. It became a coin-operated hit in bars and arcades, and in 1975 Bushnell began marketing a home version to compete with Odyssey, a video game system being produced by Magnavox. Atari was sold to Warner Communications in 1976. Mattel followed with Intellivision in late 1979 and Coleco brought out ColecoVision in 1983.

The Advent of Video Games. Soon, the industry was licensing the most popular arcade games for home video systems. Video games were bringing in hundreds of millions of dollars. Many new companies formed just to manufacture and sell cartridges for Atari and other game systems, thus taking valuable profits from the systems' developers. Large and small toy companies rushed to produce their own video systems. In a few short years, however, the video game and cartridge fad ran out of steam. Warner lost $539 million on its consumer electronics segment in 1983, and it ended up burying truckloads of game cartridges. Warner, Mattel and Coleco sold their video game businesses during the next two years.

Nintendo, a Japanese electronics company, learned from the mistakes of its predecessors. In the late 1980s, Nintendo was generating sales of more than $1 billion in the United States alone. It was making this money at the expense of other traditional toys and games, taking market share from industry leaders Hasbro and Mattel. Nintendo controlled licensing and sales of all game cartridges so that it would not meet the same fate as Atari.

Sega, another Japanese company, challenged Nintendo in the United States during the early 1990s. In 1991, Sega introduced its Genesis system, and Nintendo responded with Super Nintendo.

CURRENT CONDITIONS

Because toy manufacturers sell to children, their ads were designed to appeal to children, thus generating much controversy about ethics in children's advertising. Children are easily exploited, contended children's advocates; they lack the experience to discern poorly-made products or recognize that a commercial has presented a fantasy world rather than the reality of a particular toy. Action for Children's Television unsuccessfully tried to convince the FCC that toy-based shows were 30-minute commercials and should be purchased as advertising time. Critics of children's television and its ads also continued to protest the promotion of violence through toy-based shows and the weaponry toys advertised, as well as gender stereotyping reflected in many shows and advertised toys.

In the 1980s, television networks ABC, NBC and CBS required that the last five seconds of a toy commercial show the product all alone so that children could see what they are really getting. The networks also limited animation of the ad to one-third of the total time. However, independent stations had no such restrictions, and with the widespread use of cable, the independents were becoming more important advertising channels for toy makers during the early 1990s.

Video games continued to represent a threat to the traditional toy market in the 1990s. Nintendo and Sega were the video leaders, and unlike other toy trends, which soared then saw sales drop dramatically, this generation of electronic games remained popular with sales expected to keep rising. During the early 1990s, traditional toy makers were considering whether to compete for market share with traditional, non-video toys, or enter the video market themselves.

The toy industry turned to more intensive brand management during the early 1990s, focusing on either extending existing lines of products, or spending more money marketing the "classics". For example, Hasbro added new products to the Nerf line of foam sports toys, including Nerf Turbo Football and Nerf

Bow 'n' Arrow. The company augmented its Monopoly line of products with the introduction of Monopoly Junior.

American companies were seeking to expand sales and profits by marketing more aggressively abroad in 1992. Tyco opened four European subsidiaries and Hasbro expanded its operations in a number of Asian countries, including acquiring a small Japanese game and toy company in order to enter the Japanese toy market, which was the second largest in the world behind the United States in the early 1990s. Mattel began selling its merchandise directly rather than dealing with distributors in foreign countries.

Although the industry was dominated by several giants, small companies also had opportunities for success. Some smaller companies acquired rights to products that the big companies had retired, such as Erector Sets and Creepy Crawlers, or launched their own new products. The toy and game industry was attractive to small businesses because start-up costs remained low when manufacturing was subcontracted. Smaller companies could be innovative since they did not have the layers of bureaucracy characteristic of the larger companies, and they did not have to generate as much income. Consolidation also reduced the likelihood that a large company would take a chance on an item able to generate only one or two million dollars. By the early 1990s, large manufacturers needed $10 million products to justify spending their advertising dollars.

INDUSTRY LEADERS

The toy industry underwent extensive consolidation after the video game era began. Some of the most familiar brands lost their independence and became part of large toy corporations such as Hasbro.

Hasbro Inc., a small company in the early 1980s, became the largest U.S. toy manufacturer in 1985, by eschewing the video market and benefitting from widely popular products such as G.I Joe, Transformers, and My Little Pony. In 1984, Hasbro bought the Milton Bradley company, the fourth largest company in the toy industry. With Milton Bradley came the rights to The Game of Life, Twister, and other solid-selling games. By 1988, Milton Bradley accounted for 20 percent of Hasbro's sales. In 1992 Hasbro had sales of more than $2.5 billion. Hasbro also acquired Coleco and then Tonka just as each was headed for bankruptcy. Tonka had owned Kenner and Parker Brothers, so the acquisition of Tonka also brought a second famous game company into the Hasbro empire. Hasbro decided to leave the two separate divisions with their own identities.

The second largest U.S. toy company was Mattel Inc. with 1992 sales of more than $1.8 billion. Mattel built a strong alliance with Walt Disney Co., and Mattel's president called its Disney-related products ''the second cornerstone of our company'' (its primary ''cornerstone'' was Barbie and Barbie-related products). Mattel also made an exclusive licensing agreement to produce toys based on Hanna-Barbera characters, such as Flintstones, Scooby Doo, Jetsons, and Yogi Bear.

Tyco Toys Inc. generated $768 million in sales in 1992, and in 1993, bought Universal Matchbox and ViewMaster-Ideal Group Ltd., further consolidating the industry. Fisher-Price Inc. had sales of $694 million.

INDUSTRY INFORMATION SOURCES

Darrow, Barbara, ''Engineering in Toyland,'' *Design News,* December 12, 1987, p.66.

''Disney, Mattel to Strengthen Ties in Toyland,'' *The Wall Street Journal,* November 12, 1991, p. B1.

''Hot Products Give Toy Industry Strong Year,'' *Standard and Poor's Industry Surveys,* March 11, 1993.

Levy, Richard and Ronald O. Weingartner, *Inside Santa's Workshop,* New York: Henry Holt and Company, 1990.

Rudnitsky, ''Bang, Mom, You're Dead,'' *Forbes,* June 16, 1986,86-7.

Sheff, David, *Game Over: How Nintendo Zapped an American Industry, Captured Your Dollars, and Enslaved Your Children,* New York: Random House, 1993.

Stern, Sydney Ladensohn and Ted Schoenhaus, *Toyland, The High-Stakes Game of the Toy Industry,* Chicago: Contemporary Books, 1990.

''Warfare in Toyland,'' *Maclean's,* December 15, 1986,p. 38.

Yoshihashi, Pauline, ''Hanna-Barbera Reaches Toy Pact with Mattel Inc.,'' *The Wall Street Journal,* November 22, 1991.

—Wendy J. Stein

SIC 3949

SPORTING AND ATHLETIC GOODS, NOT ELSEWHERE CLASSIFIED

This industry covers establishments primarily engaged in manufacturing sporting and athletic goods not elsewhere classified, such as fishing tackle; golf and tennis goods; baseball, football, basketball, and boxing equipment; roller skates and ice skates; gymnasium and playground equipment; billiard and pool tables; and bowling alleys and equipment. Establishments primarily engaged in manufacturing athletic apparel are classified in major group for apparel and other finished products made from fabrics and similar materials; those manufacturing athletic footwear are classified in **SIC 3021: Rubber and Plastics Footwear** and **SIC 3149: Footwear, Except Rubber, Not Elsewhere Classified;** those manufacturing small arms ammunition are classified in **SIC 3482: Small Arms Ammunition;** and those manufacturing small arms are classified in **SIC 3484: Small Arms.**

INDUSTRY SNAPSHOT

After a decade of strong growth, the U.S. sports equipment industry slowed in the early 1990s because of the recession and, for some sports, the wrong weather. Toward the end of 1992, however, as the economy began to pick up, the sector's sales rebounded. The outlook for the industry in the second half of the 1990s remained largely positive, despite concern about product liability exposures and cuts in school sports programs. Some industry observers believed that by the year 2000 Americans would devote 1.3 percent of their disposable income to sports products, up from one percent in 1989. While the American population was aging, much of the postwar baby-boom generation remained committed to staying fit. Growing numbers of women were becoming sports enthusiasts, and manufacturers were designing offerings specifically for their needs (rather than simply painting existing products in pastels). In general, companies were creating new demand by appealing to specific market segments (e.g. basketballs and backboards especially designed for children). And overseas markets were becoming more attractive because of, among other reasons, liberalized trade regulations and a weak U.S. dollar.

Performance among the industry's numerous segments continued to vary significantly in 1993, as a sport's popularity waxed or waned depending on demographics, economics, marketing skill, and fads. In-line skating remained a stand-out performer, although there were signs that its dramatic sales growth was finally slowing. The golf and fitness segments were doing well because of technologically improved products and new adherents among an older population. Recreational fishing, in contrast, was hurt by the lack of new offerings and fewer young anglers. Skiing had recovered modestly with more snowy weather, but the number of skiers was still flat. Sales of team sports equipment, like basketball, baseball, football, and soc-

cer, strengthened as sports stars gave the segment's marketing a boost.

ORGANIZATION AND STRUCTURE

The sporting goods industry encompasses a wide variety of businesses and products, and there are hundreds of participants. Within a specific segment, however, a few large companies may dominate. In tennis rackets, for example, Prince and Wilson had 70 percent of the market in 1993, and the top six companies together had 98 percent. The top firms in the industry as a whole are often parts of conglomerates that engage in a variety of business activities. Wilson Sporting Goods, for example, which offers a broad range of sporting goods equipment, is owned by the Amer Group, a Finnish company that also makes paper envelopes and textbooks, among other products.

The sporting goods sector offers stunning success stories, as a new or substantially improved product, or even an entirely new sport, can capture the public's fancy and produce spectacular returns for the originator. The growth rates of CML Group, the maker of the NordickTrack exercise machine, and Callaway, producer of Big Bertha golf clubs, have been among the fastest growing of all U.S. firms. But for every Rollerblade, a successful company that makes in-line skates, there are dozens of failures. As John Riddle, president of the Sporting Goods Manufacturers Association told *Nation's Business,* "Having a good idea is ten percent of the trick, albeit no easy feat. The other 90 percent is in getting enough capital behind your product and marketing it correctly. A little luck never hurts either.''

BACKGROUND AND DEVELOPMENT

Albert G. Spalding, the man often misidentified as the inventor of baseball, was actually one of the pioneers of the sporting goods industry. After pitching his team, the Boston Red Stockings, to victory in three consecutive National Professional Association pennant races in the early 1870s, Spalding helped found the National League in 1876. In 1878 he opened a sporting goods store with his brother in Chicago. The company expanded from two to 14 stores within two years, and soon afterwards began selling products it manufactured directly to other retail dealers. Spalding is given much of the credit for introducing gloves to baseball; after developing a sore arm from pitching, he switched to first base in 1877 and started wearing highly visible black gloves. (Cynics have suggested, however, that Spalding's interest in wearing gloves was not unrelated to his desire to sell them.)

Spalding also figures prominently in the history of basketball. James Naismith, the inventor of the game, commissioned him to create the world's first basketball in 1892. Spalding Co. balls are still the official ball of the National Basketball Association (NBA).

Another important sporting goods company with a colorful history is Wilson. The firm was originally known as the Ashland Manufacturing Company and was a subsidiary of a meat-packing firm. It sold violin strings, surgical sutures, and strings for tennis products, all by-products of animal gut. In 1914 the company was forced into receivership and taken over by New York bankers. They picked Thomas Wilson to manage the company, partly because of his name— President Woodrow Wilson was then at the height of his popularity, and the owners hoped to capitalize on the association in the consumer's mind. The new firm became Wilson & Company. The firm soon expanded into tennis rackets, hunting and camping equipment, and fishing tackle. It continued to be one of the top manufacturers in the 1990s, with a full line of sports equipment.

A more modern, but already legendary, figure in the history of sports equipment is Scott Olson. Olson was a 19-year-old goaltender with a minor-league hockey team in 1980 when he found a pair of roller skates on which the wheels were arranged in a single row. While the skates felt slow and clumsy, they gave him the sense of skating on ice that traditional roller skates did not. Olson contacted the manufacturer, who had stopped making the line, and bought up the back stock. He put the blades on good skate boots and began selling them out of his house. In 1983 he quit pro hockey, bought up the existing patents, and started the company that would eventually become Rollerblade. While Olson was forced out of the business in 1985, he continued to design and develop new products, including a lightweight golf bag with wheels and a built-in pull handle.

CURRENT CONDITIONS

According to government statistics, shipments of sporting goods in constant dollars grew about four percent in 1993, about the same increase recorded in 1992. Total shipments were $7.3 billion. The outlook for the industry remained strong in 1994. The economy was surging, demographic trends and healthy lifestyles were boosting demand in the over-40 age group, more women were playing sports, and enactment of the North American Free Trade Agreement and other pacts liberalizing trade augured well for overseas business.

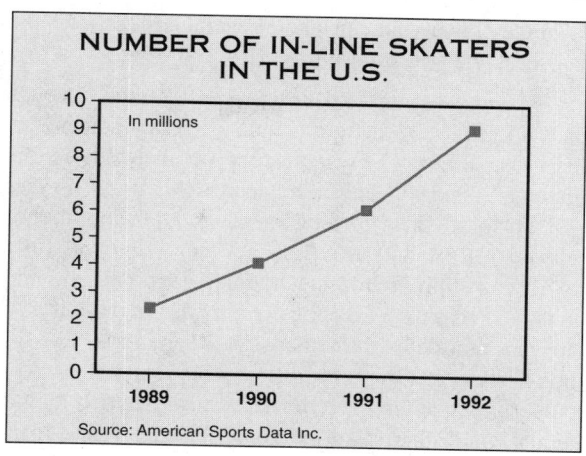

NUMBER OF IN-LINE SKATERS IN THE U.S.

Source: American Sports Data Inc.

While the overall industry was healthy, however, it has faced several problems, most notably product liability costs. These expenses ran so high that manufacturers were discontinuing production of certain products. The number of football helmet manufacturers, for example, fell from 18 in 1970 to two in 1993. While the industry was hopeful that product liability legislation would pass Congress in 1994, it faced vigorous opposition, most notably from the Trial Lawyers Association.

For individual companies, the positives and negatives of the industry as a whole are often overshadowed by the environment in its particular segment. The following paragraphs discuss business conditions in important sports.

Golf. According to the government, in 1993 shipments of golfing equipment in constant dollars were up six percent to $1.7 billion. Golfing continued to attract older, more affluent players. In 1992, in fact, 30 percent of all golfers had incomes of $50,000 to $74,000, the highest proportion for any sport. They had the means to buy the technologically improved products that were introduced in the late 1980s and early 1990s, such as clubs with graphite shafts, oversized heads, and beryllium copper facings. At Callaway, demand for Big Bertha metal oversized woods produced truly astonishing growth, as sales rose from $5 million to $200 million in five years. Whether better clubs have actually helped the golfer's game is questioned by some observers. They note that the average reported handicap remained steady at about 16 from 1980 through 1992. And according to some Professional Golfers Association (PGA) statistics, there was no notable improvement in the scores of professional golfers either. Others argue, though, that the new clubs make disastrous hooks and slices less likely for the average player, and can shave several strokes from the score of the weekend duffer.

Tennis. In notable contrast to golf, tennis has been in a slump. Sales of tennis balls, a good indicator of participation, fell seven percent (annualized) in the first half of 1993 and were also down for full-year 1992. Moreover, according to one study, the number of players fell by half-a-million between 1989 and 1992 to 13.7 million. While the sluggish economy and bad weather were partly responsible for the decline, it also appears that people are choosing other sports, like in-line skating or fitness training, rather than tennis. Apparently, some tennis enthusiasts have decided they'd rather watch than play the game, since revenue from the four tournaments (including the U.S. Open) run by the U.S. Tennis Association were up 16 percent in 1992 from 1991 levels.

In-Line Skating. The growth of in-line skating has been truly astonishing. According to one estimate, in 1992 some 9.4 million people were playing the sport, three times the level in 1989. In less than a decade, sales grew from nearly nothing to $300-million in 1992. Sales have been spurred by the interest in roller hockey, which has become one of the fastest growing sports in the country. Some observers estimate that 15 percent to 20 percent of all in-line sales are now made for roller hockey.

Nevertheless, skate makers did face significant problems. First, the huge popularity of the sport had attracted many new entrants. In the late 1980s, high-priced skates selling for $150 or more and produced primarily by Rollerbade dominated the business. By 1993, however, cheaper skates selling for $75 or so, made by 30 or more manufacturers, had taken more than 40 percent of the market. Even in the high-end of the business Rollerblade faced significant competition from skates produced by two well established ski manufacturers, K2 and Atomic. Moreover, some observers predicted that the number of in-line skaters would rise 16 percent in 1993—still a healthy rate, but nearly half the approximately 30 percent advance recorded in 1992.

Skiing. After five years of decline, sales of skiing equipment and apparel rose 20 percent in 1992. Lots of snowy weather and a healthier economy helped make the 1992-1993 season one of the best in years, with total skier days numbering some 54 million. Nevertheless, the skiing industry still had to contend with the long-term trend of slow expansion. The 54 million figure was up just eight percent from the level recorded 14 years earlier. The decline in cross-country skiing was particularly notable during the dry winters of the late 1980s and early 1990s, since few of these trails

have snow making capabilities. Even with recovery the effects of the downturn linger, since retailers have become much more conservative in ordering inventory.

While U.S. manufacturers had a sizable portion of the market for skis and boots from World War II until the 1970s, in recent years European makers dominated. By 1994, when American skiers went out to buy downhill skis, the odds were three-to-one they would get a European ski. Actually, while the total number of U.S. skiers, estimated at 10 to 12 million, is sizeable, on a per capita basis Americans are much less likely to ski than Europeans (excluding the British) or Japanese. K2 is the largest U.S. producer, with about a 20 percent share of domestic business and ten percent worldwide.

The popularity of snowboarding (akin to skate boarding) has been growing steadily, however, with over 1.5 million enjoying the sport in 1991. Actually, the decline in skiing during the clear-weather years was something of a boon to snowboarders, since desperate ski operators began to open their slopes to them. While many snowboarders do not fit the caricature of a 21-year-old grunge-band enthusiast who skateboards in summer, it is true that they tend to be under 25; most prefer snowboard parks, which have natural and artificial obstacles where they can do the kind of tricks that make parents nervous. Between 260,000 and 300,000 boards were sold during the 1992-93 season, including those of French producer Rossignol and U.S. maker K2.

Fitness Equipment. The desire of an aging American population to keep fit conveniently has supported sales of the fitness equipment segment. According to one estimate, sales of fitness products totaled $2.05 billion in 1992, up 72 percent from 1987 levels but down three percent from the 1991 total. Changing health fashions have boosted the popularity of some products while others have faded. Sales of stair-climbers, used primarily by women wanting to trim their hips, were up 44 percent in 1991. Treadmills, favored by those over 40, recorded a 19 percent gain. Revenue from rowers plunged from $245 million in 1985 to $38 million in 1991, however, apparently because many found them boring and thought they put too much strain on their backs.

One standout performer has been the so-called cross-country skiing machine, sales of which increased 123 percent in 1991. The most successful of these products has been the NordickTrack, made by CML Group, which exercises the entire body rather than just the lower half, the chief shortcoming of treadmills, stationary bikes, and step-exercisers. So-called "infomercials" and television shopping networks have also given a big boost to sales of fitness equipment. In one weekend's worth of such programming, Tony Little, a former Mr. America contender, sold as many 15,000 skiing machines, 10,000 mini-steppers, and 4,000 treadmills.

Team Sports. Despite significant cuts in school athletic budgets for team sports, this category remained relatively healthy owing to the continued popularity of traditional games like football, baseball, and basketball, and a rising interest in sports like soccer and lacrosse. Much of the slack caused by budget cutbacks was picked up by parents, who raise capital for school teams and usually buy their kids equipment at local retailers.

Basketball has benefitted from the successes of the so-called Dream Team, the 1992 Summer Olympics U.S. men's basketball team, as well as the excitement generated by stars like Shaquille O'Neal, who has helped make Spalding's Shaq Attaq basketballs best sellers. Baseball and softball sales have received a boost from the formation of new teams, including women's teams, around the country, as well as from bat and mitt introductions that have improved technologies and materials. Meanwhile, soccer ball makers, who continued to record steady sales increases, hoped that the staging of World Cup 1994 in the United States would bring a new level of interest to the sport.

Fishing. According to government statistics, sales of fishing equipment were $807 million in 1993, barely unchanged from 1992 levels. Although 61 million people spent at least one day fishing in 1992, that was down 11 percent from 1990 levels. And while fishing remained a popular activity of those over 55, one of the fastest growing age groups, it appears that fewer young people are taking up the sport. Industry participants complain that many adults, especially single parents and career couples, just don't have time to take their kids fishing anymore. Some observers blamed the lack of exciting new products (i.e., items that incorporate new technology or are likely to catch the fisherman's fancy). Others believe that sports like golf were taking business from the segment. During 1992 and 1993, sales were also hurt by bad weather conditions for fishing in many parts of the country.

INDUSTRY LEADERS

Brunswick is among the largest sporting goods companies. The company is a leading name in bowling, and the products of its Zebco division are well known to fishermen. The firm also makes billiard tables and golf equipment. In total, the company's so-called recreation segment accounted for about one-third of the firm's sales of $2 billion in 1993. The balance of the company's revenues mostly came from sales of boats and outboard motors. The company's recreation segment performed well in 1993, with sales rising 17 percent and operating earnings up 23 percent. Sales of the Brunswick division (which includes bowling, billiard, and golfing equipment) were strong, partly owing to increased demand for bowling products in overseas markets, particularly Asia.

The sporting goods division of Amer Group of Finland encompasses both Wilson Sporting Goods, a leading producer of golf, racquet, and team sports equipment, and MacGregor Golf, which makes golf equipment and clothing. Total sales of the sporting goods division were about $700 million, about half of the Group's total sales. Sales of the two divisions were up about four percent in dollar terms in 1993, but growth in the (much smaller) MacGregor segment was up 29 percent, owing to successful new products like "Mad Mac" metal woods.

Spalding, one of the most famous names in sporting equipment, makes a complete line of golf and team sports equipment. As a private company it does not offer financial information to the public. But sales of sporting goods, its primary business, have been estimated at several hundred million dollars.

Callaway's Big Bertha line has made it the largest maker of metal golf woods in the world. During the early 1990s the company grew astonishingly fast, with revenues doubling and net income tripling every year. The company went public in March of 1992 at about $15 a share, and by October of 1993 it was selling for $60. While some believe that state-of-the-art stainless steel clubs will ultimately prove to be just one more in a long line of golf fads, others are convinced that worldwide demand will remain strong for the company's clubs.

While by 1994 Rollerblade had lost much market share to cheaper competitors, it still had annual sales of about $130 million, or about half of the total market. The company's owner, Robert O. Naegele, Jr., sold a 50 percent stake in the business to the Benetton family's Nordica S.p.A., a large Italian ski boot supplier. The company was hopeful that products incorporating its Advanced Braking Technology, which is supposed to make braking much easier (especially for beginners), would help shore up sales.

NordicTrack is a division of CML Corporation. Its primary offering continues to be the cross-country ski-exerciser, which has been called the Mercedes of the fitness business. For the fiscal year ended July 1993, the segment's sales rose 42 percent to $378 million (about 60 percent of the corporate total), compared with just $74 million in 1989. NordicTrack markets its fitness equipment through direct response marketing and mail order (69 percent of 1993 sales) and its own proprietary retail stores (31 percent). These marketing methods, coupled with the premium prices that its products can command, have given the segment operating margins that have at times exceeded 30 percent.

Rawlings, a leading maker of baseball gloves, football shoulder pads, and hockey gloves, is a division of the conglomerate Figgie International. In 1993, its sales were about $140 million. According to press reports, in early 1994 Figgie was planning to spin off Rawlings through a public sale of stock.

AMERICA AND THE WORLD

In recent years, U.S. sporting goods companies have done well in overseas markets. According to government estimates, U.S. exports of sporting goods rose 13 percent in 1993 to about $1.5 billion. Between 1987 and 1993, overseas shipments advanced at an annual rate of approximately 15 percent. The broad penetration of U.S. culture overseas has been a boon to the sporting goods industry. Often there is a dynamic interplay between the popularity of the American lifestyle, the star-quality of American athletes, and the marketing savvy of American industry. For example, the growing popularity of basketball among kids in Europe has been linked to the NBA's Shaquille O'Neal, who they know solely through watching Pepsi commercials. U.S. sporting goods products are thus valued in some countries simply because they are made in the United States. Consumers believe they are participating in the American lifestyle by purchasing them.

The perception that U.S. sporting goods are of unusually high quality in certain product categories has also spurred sales. Shipments to Japan, the largest overseas market for U.S. sporting goods, rose 20 percent in 1993. The strong performance in the face of continuing Japanese recession has been linked to the high quality and technological superiority of U.S. golf equipment. The Japanese are avid golfers, and they are often willing to pay extra for the best equipment available. The strength of the Japanese Yen has also helped American manufacturers, since it makes U.S. goods cheaper to buy in Tokyo or Osaka. In general, U.S. sporting goods makers have been aided in recent years by the weakness of the dollar against the major world currencies.

U.S. manufacturers have high hopes for trade within their own hemisphere. Canada is the second most important destination for U.S. sporting goods; its imports from the United States rose five percent in 1993 to $231-million, about half of which was exercise and golf equipment. To the south, exports to Mexico have grown at a compound annual rate of 31 percent since 1987. U.S. shipments to both countries have been supported by reduced tariffs and trade liberalization. The passage of the North American Free Trade Agreement in 1993 should further support shipments to America's neighbors.

U.S. manufacturers were also eyeing South American markets. The restoration of democracy to many Latin American governments had been accompanied by better economic conditions, giving consumers more spending power. Moreover, the trend toward freer trade has been marked, as Argentina and Brazil have sharply reduced trade barriers to overseas goods. While Latin Americans have always been passionate about soccer, they have started to take up typically American sports like basketball and in-line skating, where U.S. companies hold an edge.

Imports of sporting goods to the United States grew five percent in 1993. The manufacture of many sporting goods is labor-intensive, so U.S. companies have shifted much of their production to East Asia, where wage rates are generally lower. Taiwan and South Korea were the prime areas for locating production facilities, and they accounted for 55 percent of U.S. imports in 1989. By 1993, their share had fallen to 34 percent, as China's percentage grew from four percent in 1987 to 18 percent in 1993. Thailand has also become an important exporter, with its share of U.S. imports rising to five percent in 1993 from less than one percent in 1989.

RESEARCH AND TECHNOLOGY

New technology plays a vital role in the sports market. Consumers are often driven to buy new equipment because of the real or perceived advantages of product introductions. On the other hand, tradition also has a hallowed place in sports, and participants have to feel comfortable that their equipment is in the historical spirit of the game. Additionally, innovative manufacturers can create substantially new sports through their products.

In some sports there have been revolutionary changes in equipment over the past 20 or 30 years. The traditional wooden tennis racket had pretty much stayed the same until the 1960s, when manufacturers began to redesign it in an effort to improve performance and ease of play. The introduction of durable metal and fiber-reinforced-composite rackets was followed by oversized and wide body models. More recently, finely balanced rackets that have shock- and vibration-damping handles and new string bed patterns for greater accuracy have been introduced. Compared with the classic wooden model that weighed 14 ounces and had a hitting area of 68 square inches, rackets sold in the early 1990s were 35 percent to 40 percent lighter, with the weight redistributed for better performance, and had a hitting area of 120 square inches.

Intriguingly, engineers have also had stunning successes in overhauling the humble bowling ball. Several new urethane and reactive resin bowling ball shells and complex inner core configurations—designed to vary the ball's rotation as it goes down the lane—have substantially altered the ball's hook as it approaches the pocket. According to some observers, the sharp rise in the number of perfect games—17,654 during the 1992-93 season versus 14,889 during the prior year—is closely related to the improvements in ball designs.

Smart entrepreneurs have also developed innovative products for niche markets. Passengers on cruise ships used to drive thousands of regulation golf balls into the sea. But in 1990 the International Maritime Organization banned the practice as part of its effort to protect sea life. Responding to opportunity, Patrick Kane of Bonita, California, developed a golf ball that flies almost as well as a traditional ball but is made of materials that decompose quickly and can be consumed safely by fish and other marine life. He told the *New York Times* that "It's basically fish food . . . you can market it on the basis of sympathy for the environmentalists."

The sporting goods industry is also working on improving its technology in the more mundane, but nonetheless important, areas of inventory and delivery systems. Better information systems allow manufacturers to keep retailers stocked in goods that are selling well and reduce their own inventories of slow-moving items. Manufacturers can also alert stores to overall sales patterns so that retailers can better react to market trends. Sporting goods companies have also worked to develop packaging that is more environmentally friendly. The packaging for Wilson's 1993 line of footballs, for example, is made from 100 percent recycled paper and uses soy-based inks in printing. It also uses 30% less paper than previous football packaging.

INDUSTRY INFORMATION SOURCES

Ashley, Steven, "High-Tech Rackets Hold Court," *Mechanical Engineering,* August 1993.

Bergstrom, Robin, "All This So You Can Have Fun," *Production,* July 1991.

Booth, Stephen, "Eco Impact: Re-Packaging," *Sporting Goods Business,* August 1993.

Brown, Paul B., "Bats, Balls, & Bucks," *Financial World,* September 15, 1992.

Castle, Ken, "South America: A Slam Dunk for Sports," *Sporting Goods Business,* September 1993.

Charlier, Marj, "Ski Firms, Riding Lift, Predict Big Jump," *Wall Street Journal,* March 25, 1993.

Chernoff, Allan, "Short-Term Profits Rise as Long-Term Interest Declines," *New York Times,* September 12, 1993.

Clay, Bobby, "It *Is* The Shoes," *Black Enterprise,* March 1993.

Corman, Linda, "The Slopes Battle a Bad Economy and the Wrong Weather," *New York Times,* December 6, 1992.

Falcioni, John, "Striking at the Core of Bowling Balls," *Mechanical Engineering,* August 1993.

Ferguson, Tim, "U.S. Ski Makers Lost Their Edge," *Wall Street Journal,* February 15, 1994.

"Fitness Boxing Takes Swing into Retail," *Sporting Goods Business,* October 1993.

"The Fitness Industry: Snow Motion," *The Economist,* March 27, 1993.

"Football Caps Reduce Impact," *Machine Design,* January 8, 1993.

Gerlach, Rex, "AFTMA '92 Preview," *Sporting Goods Business,* July 1992.

Gerlach, Rex, "Stormy Weather," *Sporting Goods Business,* July 1993.

Getler, Warren, "New Golf Shares Flourish Under Callaway's Shadow," *Wall Street Journal,* October 11, 1993.

Halverson, Richard, "Aging Baby Boomers Will Focus on Fitness & Leisure Activities," *Discount Store News,* December 7, 1992.

"Increased Emphasis on Having Fun in Japan Creates More Opportunity for U.S. Vendors," *Sporting Goods Business,* November 1991.

Jensen, Dave, "Often Up in Down Times, Sporting Goods Firms Face Whole New Ballgame," *Milwaukee Business Journal,* March 9, 1992.

Kopp, George, "Trade Winds," *Sporting Goods Business,* September 1993.

Lustigman, Alyssa, "Growing Up," *Sporting Goods Business,* May 1993.

McEvoy, Christopher, "Headway Sizing Up the Helmet Market," *Sporting Goods Business,* July 1993.

McKenna, Joseph, "Jack Curran: Up Against an All-Star Lineup," *Industry Week,* September 6, 1993.

Macnow, Glen, "New Ideas Get a Sporting Chance," *Nation's Business,* December 1992.

"Market Watch: Product Liability Top Issue in SGMA Study," *Sporting Goods Business,* October 1993.

March, Barbara, "Small Fish in the Tackle Business Are Trying New Lures," *Wall Street Journal,* June 23, 1993.

Marks, Peter, "Perfect Pitch: Tony Little's Infomercials Keep the Fitness Gear Moving," *New York Times,* May 9, 1994.

Martin, Justin, "What Fits Better Than a Glove?" *Across the Board,* September 1992.

Moffat, Terrence, "SGB Market Survey: Soccer," *Sporting Goods Business,* April 1993.

Moffat, Terence, "String Fling," *Sporting Goods Business,* February 1993.

Oliver, Peter, "A Prophet Prophecy," *STN,* December 1993.

"Orders Up, But Don't Overlook the Trends," *STN,* November 1993.

Parry, John, "Players' Market," *International Management,* July/August 1991.

Pearlstein, Steven, "It Don't Mean a Thing If You Ain't Got That Swing," *Washington Post,* September 1, 1993.

Pesky, Greg, "Net Gains," *Sporting Goods Business,* September 1993.

Pesky, Greg, "Regaining," *Sporting Goods Business,* October 1992.

Pesky, Greg, "Scoring Points," *Sporting Goods Business,* October 1993.

Pesky, Greg, "Shaq Basketballs Scoring for Spalding," *Sporting Goods Business,* July 1993.

Pesky, Greg, "Teaming Up All Season," *Sporting Goods Business,* February 1993.

Pesky, Greg, "The SGB Interview: Rollerblade—John Hetterick, President & CEO," *Sporting Goods Business,* November 1993.

Pesky, Greg, "Tools of Summer," *Sporting Goods Business,* June 1992.

Reza, H.G, "Lots of Stock—with a Clink," *Los Angeles Times,* December 30, 1993.

Selz, Michael, "Once-Rolling In-Line Skate Makers Skid Amid Rivalry," *Wall Street Journal,* November 30, 1993.

"SIA Stats Support Snowboarding Jump," *Sporting Goods Business,* October, 1993.

"Slower Sales Seen in Next Millenium," *Sporting Goods Business,* March 1992.

Smith, Timothy, "U.S. High-Tech Sports Gap Is All Henry Ford's Fault," *Wall Street Journal,* August 5, 1992.

The Sporting Goods Market in 1993, Mt. Prospect, IL: National Sporting Goods Association, 1993.

Sports Participation in 1992, Mt. Prospect, IL: National Sporting Goods Association, 1993.

Tomkinson, Sharon, "All Things American," *Sporting Goods Business,* September 1993.

Tyler, Gretchen, "Different Strokes for Different Folks," *Indiana Business Magazine,* May 1991.

U.S. Industrial Outlook 1994, Washington, DC: U.S. Commerce Department, January 1994.

—Bob Schneider

SIC 3951

PENS, MECHANICAL PENCILS AND PARTS

This industry contains establishments primarily engaged in manufacturing pens (including ball point pens), refill cartridges, mechanical pencils, fine and broad tipped markers, and parts.

INDUSTRY SNAPSHOT

Sales of all writing instruments hit an all-time high in 1990 at $3.4 billion. This record can be attributed to the increasing diversity of products, the growing popularity of highlighting markers, and the newfound interest in high-end fountain pens.

Nearly 50 companies manufacture writing instruments that are sold in the United States and throughout the world. The ball point pen, introduced to the U.S. market in 1945, continues to dominate writing instrument sales. Newly created roller ball pens and highlighters also have been selling well.

ORGANIZATION AND STRUCTURE

Manufacturers and suppliers of pens and other writing instruments generally have been large public companies, such as BIC Corporation, the largest supplier of ball point pens in the United States. Some are conglomerates like the Gillette Company, which sells writing instruments and other non-writing related products.

Writing instruments are sold to wholesalers and retailers and then are resold to consumers through fine jewelry stores, stationery and office supply stores, department stores, discounters, mass merchandisers, catalogue showrooms, and specialty stores. Pen manufacturers not only produce writing instruments but also are responsible for selling and marketing these products to retailers and consumers.

BACKGROUND AND DEVELOPMENT

The Pen. The earliest writing instruments were developed during the ancient civilizations of China, Greece, Egypt, and Mesopotamia nearly 5,000 years ago. The Egyptians used hollow reeds to apply ink on sheets of papyrus, while the Chinese drew ideograms with brushes made from animal hair.

The Europeans began to use goose quills as ink pens in the sixth century, and this practice grew rapidly during the Middle Ages. Flocks of geese were specifically bred for their feathers as quill production became an important industry throughout Europe. For nearly 1,000 years the quill pen remained the most popular writing instrument.

In the 19th century, however, the steel pen replaced the quill. The steel pen point (or nib) first appeared in England sometime between 1790 and 1803, but this product was not manufactured efficiently or economically until the 1830s. In another 50 years American inventor Lewis Edmon Waterman created the fountain pen with its own self-contained ink supply. Waterman's product ushered in a new generation of writing instruments that dominated the first half of the 20th century. His basic design, which includes a metal nib, a built-in ink supply and an outer shell, are still the main components of fountain pens today.

Ball Point Pens. The ball point pen also dates back to the late 19th century. This type of pen consists of a metal ball housed in a socket that rotates freely. The ball, constantly covered in ink from a reservoir, rolls across a writing surface.

Commercial models of ball point pens appeared in 1895 and the first satisfactory model was patented in Argentina by Hungarian Lazlo Biro. His ball point pen, commonly called the "biro," soon became popular in Great Britain during the late 1930s and 1940s. The ball point pen was introduced to the U.S. market in 1945. American manufacturers quickly adopted the new design and soon dominated production in the ball point industry. Today more than three billion ball point pens are manufactured each year in a variety of styles, point sizes, colors, with prices ranging from no-frills disposables selling for $1.00 a dozen to state-of-the-art, solid gold retractables costing hundreds of dollars.

The Felt-Tip Pen. In 1964 the porous-point or "felt-tip" pen was developed in Japan. Papermate's Flair was among the first felt-tip pens to hit the U.S. market in the 1960s, and it has been the leader ever since. Following their initial success with felt-tips, manufacturers branched out with a variety of fiber-tipped instruments, including newly popular highlighters.

Roller Ball Pens. The most recent large-scale innovation in the writing instrument industry has been the introduction of the roller ball pen in the early 1980s. Unlike the thick ink used in a conventional ball point, roller ball pens employ a mobile ball and liquid ink to produce a smoother line. Technological advances achieved during the late 1980s and early 1990s

have greatly improved the roller ball's overall performance.

CURRENT CONDITIONS

Sales of writing instruments soared to an all-time high of $3.4 billion in 1990, according to statistics available as of July 1993. Product diversification has been one explanation for the rise in sales. Besides the various categories of pens and pencils, the writing instruments market includes highlighters, markers, and any other device used to mark a document. Product mix projected by the Department of Commerce for 1997 is 47.8 percent pens, 28.3 percent pencils, 21.1 percent markers, and 2.7 percent desk sets, according to *The Office.*

The Fountain Pen Market. Although totaling less than five percent of all writing instrument sales, fountain pens have shown a tremendous resurgence in popularity and usage. By 1990 fountain pen sales had reached 25.5 million units, a dramatic rise from the all-time low of 6.4 million units in 1978. By 1991 sales at the wholesale level rose 16 percent to $79 million, nearly double the wholesale figures in 1986.

According to retailers, the most popular fountain pens have been bought by individuals and corporations for use as business gifts and promotional items. Two reasons for the pen's popularity have been its association as a status symbol and its improved technology, especially with the creation of replacement ink cartridges.

"The fountain pen market is hot, and promises to get hotter," reported Joshua Levine in a 1992 issue of *Forbes.* "Like wearing a prestige watch, carrying and publicly wielding a prestige fountain pen has become an 'in' thing," added Levine.

Nearly two dozen firms have attempted to gain a piece of the growing fountain pen market, especially the high-end sector. For example, A. T. Cross, known for its prestigious ball point pens, has been pushing its newly created Townsend line of larger, thicker pens. However, the upper-end fountain pen leader continues to be the German Montblanc, selling half of all pens costing more than $100. Second place Parker Pen has a 25 percent market share.

The Ball Point Market. Despite the recent surge in popularity of the fountain pen, the ball point pen continues to be the leader of the writing instrument market. Known for its low price and reliability, the ball point pen has accounted for nearly one-third of industry sales. Three billion ball point pens are manufactured annually. The BIC Corporation alone has sold more than seven billion pens in the United States since 1983.

The Roller Ball Pen. Roller ball pens brought in sales totaling $201 million in 1989, a 51 percent increase over sales figures just two years earlier. This segment makes up nearly 14 percent of the writing instruments market and has been growing at 10 percent since 1990.

The Highlighter Market. The marker and the highlighter market has been considered a separate entity from the porous-point pen industry and posted sales of $232 million in 1989. Felt-tip highlighters have been one of the fastest growing products in the writing instruments business with sales of 260 million units in 1990, up from 70 million units in 1985.

The Pencil Market. Another 25 percent of overall writing instrument sales has come from the pencil market, both woodcased (represented in **SIC 3952: Lead Pencils, Crayons, and Artists' Materials**) and mechanical (included in this classification). The overall pencil market was a $215.9 million industry in the early 1990s.

INDUSTRY LEADERS

BIC Corporation. The Connecticut-based BIC Corporation has been the largest manufacturer and distributor of ball point pens in North America. BIC pens have made up approximately 40 percent of the office products market in the United States and 60 percent of the over-the-counter market. BIC ball point pens are available in non-retractable, non-refillable models and retractable, refillable models, and in various ink and barrel colors and point sizes. BIC also manufactures highlighting markers and roller pens and distributes mechanical pencils.

In 1992 BIC Corp. posted its highest sales and earnings in company history. Total sales increased to nearly $417.4 million from approximately $369.2 in 1991. Its growth included revenues, profits, and profit margins in all of its core businesses, including the Stationery Products division (formerly known as Writing Instruments).

During 1992 BIC began marketing Soft Feel, a retractable pen with a rubberized barrel. BIC also introduced Body Heat pens, which have heat-sensitive barrels that change colors when held. Body Heat pens are part of BIC Wavelengths, a line of fashionable ball pens and mechanical pencils. The company also has extended its holiday line of Halloween and Christmas pens to include Valentine's Day.

During 1993 the company expanded its production capacity and now operates three facilities in South

Carolina. BIC also moved both its research and development divisions to a suburb of Greenville, South Carolina, its market production to Gaffney, South Carolina, and expanded its Wavelengths production in Spartanburg, South Carolina.

BIC's international operations have consisted of subsidiaries located in Canada, Mexico, Puerto Rico, and Guatemala. Sales by foreign subsidiaries were approximately 16 percent of consolidated net sales in 1992 and 1991, and 15 percent in 1990.

Gillette Company. More commonly associated with men's shaving products, Boston-based Gillette has become a leader in the writing instruments industry. With the low-price Paper Mate, mid-price Parker, and high-end Waterman franchises, Gillette has established a strong position in the industry at all price levels, distribution channels, and geographic areas.

Gillette built its leadership position in the writing instruments market through the acquisition of Waterman in 1987 and Parker Pen Holdings Ltd. in 1993. After its purchase, Gillette soon began to sell Waterman fountain pens at discount outlets in the United States. Francine Gomez, then chief executive of Waterman S.A. and a third-generation family operator, was displeased with this decision. Although sales increased by 40 percent since the Gillette takeover, Gomez argued that the company's marketing strategy in the United States devalued the luxury image of Waterman in France. Gomez resigned from the company in 1988.

Meanwhile, the Parker Pen acquisition should increase Gillette's share of the $5 billion international writing instruments market to approximately 15 percent from eight percent. Gillette may face possible antitrust problems in some European countries since its market share of refillable pens may be as high as 60 percent. Nonetheless, market analysts have applauded the Parker Pen acquisition as a strategically sound move to foster global expansion for the company. Gillette's manufacturing operations for all of its products have been conducted at 62 facilities in 28 countries.

A. T. Cross. Based in Lincoln, Rhode Island, A. T. Cross Company has been a major international manufacturer of fine writing instruments sold to the consumer gift market through stores worldwide, and to the business market via a network of companies specializing in recognition and awards programs. Cross products include ball point pens, mechanical pencils, rolling ball/porous-point pens, and fountain pens.

A. T. Cross has been long known for its slim gold-filled and sterling silver pens and mechanical pencils, which once dominated the high end of the U.S. luxury pen market. Led by these products, the company earned $36 million in 1989.

Consumer tastes changed in late 1980s as increasing numbers of high-end customers starting buying larger pens like Montblanc. A failure to keep up with this trend was reflected in Cross' drop in earnings to $8 million in 1993. Stock prices followed from a high of 41 per share in 1989 to 15.5 in mid-1994.

In 1990 Cross attempted to reenter the high-end market with its pricy Signature line, but the recession of the early 1990s defeated this product. By 1992, under the direction of new company president Russell Boss, the company tried again to regain market share with the introduction of its Townsend line. This product line offers larger, heavier pens, including ball point and fountain models, selling for $50 to $150 each. The line has been selling well and two more pen lines should be introduced by Cross by late 1995.

A. T. Cross manufacturing plants are located in Lincoln, Rhode Island and Ballinasloe, Republic of Ireland. The company's primary foreign markets have been Europe and the Far East, bringing in 34 percent of total sales.

WORK FORCE

According to *Manufacturing USA,* 46 companies produce writing instruments in the United States, employing 19,300 workers. A large percentage of these establishments have been located in California, New Jersey and New York. The largest number of employees at pen manufacturing companies have been assembly workers and fabricators, comprising 15.6 percent of total employment in 1990. Second were sales staff and related workers at 4.3 percent and blue collar worker supervisors at 4.2 percent. The most significant projection for employment in this industry has been the 18.7 percent decline in assembly workers and the 30.1 percent increase in sales personnel by the year 2005.

RESEARCH AND TECHNOLOGY

Research and technology has affected both company operations and product development in the writing instruments industry. Retailers have begun to expect more from pen manufacturers, and companies such as BIC have turned to electronic data exchange (EDI) to keep up with retailers' demands. EDI, which now accounts for 40 percent of BIC's core U.S. business, has allowed company representatives to communicate directly with their customers' computers. BIC also has assisted retailers' with their inventory management, providing a computer-controlled automatic inventory replenishment system.

Technological advances have also affected the design and manufacture of writing instruments. Research at Gillette has produced the Dynagrip refillable ball point pen. The key feature of this pen has been its patented grip, which is formed by molding a soft, flexible material called elastomer. Pockets of air are trapped within the grip, creating tiny air cushions. Manual pressure on the walls surrounding the air pockets causes the wall to change shape, the air pockets to deflate, and the elastomer material to compress. This creates a comfortable writing grip with sufficient resiliency for control. When the grip is released, the elastomer returns to its original shape.

Less high-tech but equally revolutionary has been the creation of environmentally friendly writing instruments. Paris-based Recife has produced a line of pens encased in ebonite, a vulcanized rubber "tapped harmlessly" from trees found in the rain forest. "Unlike plastic pens, whose shells scratch and dull, ebonite pens become more beautiful with age, as their natural sheen richens from contact with skin oils," reported Lesley Alderman in *Money.* These fountain, roller ball, and ball point pens sell for $78 to $200 each, with five percent of Recife's annual sales donated to a rainforest conservation group.

INDUSTRY INFORMATION SOURCES

Alderman, Lesley, "Green Pens," *Money,* May, 1992.

Curry, Gloria M., "Versatile Is the World for Today's Writing Instruments," *The Office,* November 1989.

Darnay, Arsen J., ed., *Manufacturing USA,* 3rd edition, Detroit: Gale Research, Inc., 1993.

Elsberry, Richard B., "Returning to Writing Basics," *Office Systems,* April 1993.

"Gillette Agrees to Buy Parker Pen Holdings for $562.3 Million," *Corporate Growth Report,* September 21, 1992.

Glennon, Anthony J., "A. T. Cross," *Value Line Investment Survey,* February 19, 1993.

LeGallee, Julie, "Writing Instruments Are Key Business Communications Tools," *The Office,* July 1993.

Levine, Joshua, "Pen Wars," *Forbes,* January 6, 1992.

Mancini, Richard, "Writing Instruments: Tried, True and New," *The Office,* August 1991.

Maremont, Mark, and Paula Dwyer, "How Gillette Is Honing Its Edge," *Business Week,* September 28, 1992.

Schuman, Michael, "Thin Is out, Fat Is In," *Forbes,* May 9, 1994.

Wise, Deborah, "Waterman Rift: A Tearful Farewell," *New York Times,* December 16, 1988.

—Catherine A. Quagliana

SIC 3952

LEAD PENCILS, CRAYONS AND ARTISTS' MATERIALS

This category includes establishments primarily engaged in manufacturing lead pencils, pencil leads, and crayons; and materials and equipment for artwork, such as airbrushes, drawing tables and boards, palettes, sketch boxes, pantographs, artists' colors and waxes, pyrography goods, drawing inks, and drafting materials. Establishments primarily engaged in manufacturing mechanical pencils are classified in **SIC 3951: Pens, Mechanical Pencils, and Parts,** and those manufacturing drafting instruments are classified in **SIC 3829: Measuring and Controlling Devices, Not Elsewhere Classified.**

INDUSTRY SNAPSHOT

According to U.S. Commerce Department figures, there were 1,013 establishments under SIC Code 395 in 1987. Under SIC 3952, the Dun & Bradstreet Corp. data base listed 21 major companies. The industry trade association, meanwhile, formerly known as the Pencil Makers Association (PMA), and located in Marlton, New Jersey, lists eight members, including five firms not listed by Dun & Bradstreet. The PMA merged with the Writing Instruments Manufacturers Association (WIMA) in January 1994. WIMA represents both pencil manufacturers and makers of markers, mechanical pencils, and pens.

This industry is best known for the No. 2 pencil. First developed and marketed near the ancient German city of Nuremberg in 1761 by Kasper Faber, the pencil continues to be manufactured in Newark by a company, Faber-Castell Corp., which until recently was controlled by a Faber descendant. Moreover, many pencil companies remain in the hands of the families that started them generations ago.

The Smithsonian Institution has estimated that America's 100 billionth pencil was produced in 1976, and by the early 1990s U.S. companies produced the seven-inch-long, two-for-a-quarter writing utensils at the rate of 2.5 billion per year. Shipments of pencils have steadily increased since records were first compiled in 1950. WIMA reported $148 million in whole-sale pencil shipments in 1992, up from $138 million in 1991, $134 million in 1990, and $124 million in 1989.

Even though shipments have increased, there have been threats to the U.S. manufacturers' hold on the international pencil trade. WIMA claims that low-priced pencils from Thailand and China have made competition impossible for domestic manufacturers, whose WIMA membership figures have declined from ten pencil manufacturers ten years ago to eight in the early 1990s. Domestically, the pencil trade has been threatened by the increased use of computers. The Educational Testing Service, for example, decided to use computers instead of the No. 2 pencil for the Graduate Record Examination by the 1996-97 school year.

ORGANIZATION AND STRUCTURE

The industry association unifies the industry. The Pencil Makers Association, founded in August 1919, and a similar group, the Lead Pencil Manufacturers Association, founded in 1949, merged in November 1970 to promote fair practices in the industry, conduct research, promote wood-cased pencils, and represent the industry before government. The group's first and only international convention was held in San Francisco in 1976, attracting pencil makers from 25 nations.

Among the largest firms in this industry are Binney & Smith, Inc., of Easton, Pennsylvania, makers of the popular Crayola crayons, with $300 million in sales in 1993; Berol Corp., of Brentwood, Tennessee, with $250 million in sales; and Faber-Castell Corp., of Parsippany, New Jersey, which makes a third of the pencils produced in the United States annually, and reported $210 million in 1993 sales.

BACKGROUND AND DEVELOPMENT

Cedar and graphite are the most important materials for making pencils. Cedar accounts for 98 percent of the wood in wood-cased pencils. Wood for the pencil industry came first from the Florida Keys, then Tennessee, and finally California. The wood for pencils was taken from fences, barns, and houses, according to William Ecenberger in an PMA publication. Graphite, meanwhile, has been obtained over the years from mines in a variety of countries, such as England, Sri Lanka, and Mexico.

The image of pencils was tarnished in 1971 when a child who chewed pencils was found to have lead poisoning, and the media blamed the pencil "lead." Even though pencils were made with graphite not lead, the story pushed the industry to start a product certification program open to any pencil manufacturer.

In 1988, Congress passed the Labelling of Hazardous Art Materials Act (Public Law 100-695), with the PMA's full support. The law required that all art materials be reviewed to determine the potential for causing a chronic hazard and that appropriate warning labels be placed on those materials. The artists' materials law was finalized in October 1992 with CPSC's issuance of definitions of chronic toxicity and the codification of ASTM D-4238 as a mandatory regulation.

When the lead in crayons became an issue in the industry in 1994, the problem was easily solved. Hazardous amounts of lead were found in the yellow and orange color crayons imported from China by Concord Enterprises. On March 22, 1994, when the U.S. Consumer Product Safety Commission and Concord Enterprises announced the recall of the crayons because of a lead poisoning hazard, parents were instructed to buy only crayons and children's art materials labelled with ''Conforms to ASTM D-4236,'' indicating that the materials had been approved by a toxicologist and labelled appropriately.

A recall of a different sort occurred in August 1991, when two importers, the Brandy Trading Corp. and Mirage Imports, announced they no longer would sell novelty pencils that resembled hypodermic syringes. The Taiwan-made ''Gold Doctor'' pencils were sending the wrong message to schoolchildren, parents and teachers had complained.

Alternatives to Pencils. The Educational Testing Service took a major step toward eliminating the standardized pencil test with the introduction of a new computerized version of the Graduate Record Exam. Paper and pencil remained an option, but the ETS said that by the 1996-97 school year, all 400,000 students taking the G.R.E. for admission to graduate school would do so on a computer. Instead of sitting in a room with hundreds of other people on one of five annual test dates, they will go to a computer center to take the G.R.E. on any of several days during the week; instead of waiting four to six weeks for test results, they will receive their scores immediately after the exam.

AMERICA AND THE WORLD

In November 1993, the Pencil Makers Association, which represents eight manufacturers, complained that low-priced pencils from Thailand and the People's Republic of China were being sold at less than fair value prices. Imports of pencils from these two nations had risen to 3.5 million gross in 1992 from

53,000 gross in 1982. These increases were causing lost sales and market share, the PMA attested, leading to the shutdown of several domestic manufacturers. According to Robert Waller of WIMA, his association filed a petition with the U.S. Department of Commerce and the International Trade Commission and proved their case of injury. As of May 1994, Waller said his group, WIMA, was waiting for duties to be imposed on low-priced pencils from Asia.

RESEARCH AND TECHNOLOGY

Responding to rising environmental consciousness on the part of the pencil consumer, Faber-Castell Corp. introduced a pencil made of recycled materials in 1992. Instead of the traditional wood casing, Faber-Castell said its American EcoWriter would offer a pencil shaft made from reprocessed newspapers and cardboard boxes. The project, two years in the making, was challenging, a company spokesman told the *Christian Science Monitor,* because it involved developing a material that could be sharpened as easily as a wood pencil. Faber developed the material with Lydall Inc., the company that reprocesses the paper into slats used by Faber in manufacturing. The EcoWriter was Faber-Castell's second environmental contribution, following the American Natural, introduced in 1991 to highlight Faber's use of ''sustained yield'' cedar supplies—meaning no more wood would be harvested than could be replaced by new planting.

Crayons became politically correct in January 1992, when Crayola crayon maker Binney & Smith separated out eight skin-tone crayons, which reflected the colors of all races, into their own box. Teachers and children from the Montgomery County school district in Maryland, near Washington, D.C., had complained that Crayola's practice of packing flesh-colored hues (apricot to mahogany) in a 64-crayon pack made the crayons inaccessible for the children's small hands.

INDUSTRY INFORMATION SOURCES

Allen, Frank Edward, ''This Might Be Politically Correct, But Will It Be Good to Chew On?'' *Wall Street Journal,* April 22, 1992, B1.

''Amid Furor, Importers Drop Syringe Pencil,'' *New York Times,* August 11, 1991.

Dun's Million Dollar Disc, Dun & Bradstreet, 1994.

Ecenbarger, William, ''The Pencil Industry: Its History & People/Companies that Shaped It,'' Marlton, NJ: Pencil Makers Association, 1989.

Trumball, Mark, '''Eco' Pencils: A Tree-Sparing Option,'' *Christian Science Monitor,* May 13, 1992, 12.

''U.S. Pencil Makers Point to Thai, Chinese Imports,'' *Wall Street Journal,* November 24, 1993, C11.

Waller, Robert, Executive Director of the Writing Instruments Manufacturers Association, interview by Joan Oleck, May 20, 1994.

''We Are the World; We Are the Crayons,'' *New York Times,* January 16, 1992, C3.

Winerip, Michael, ''No. 2 Pencil Fades as Graduate Exam Moves to Computer,'' *New York Times,* November 15, 1993, A1.

—Joan Oleck

SIC 3953

MARKING DEVICES

This category covers establishments primarily engaged in manufacturing stencils for use in painting or marking, steel letters and figures, and rubber and metal hand-stamps, dies, and seals. Establishments primarily engaged in manufacturing felt tip markers are covered in **SIC 3951: Pens, Mechanical Pencils, and Parts.**

As of 1993, leaders in this category were: Weber Marking Systems Inc. of Arlington Heights, Illinois; Diagraph Corp. of Earth City, Missouri; Cosco Industries Inc., Consolidated Stamp of Chicago of Harwood Heights, Illinois; GM Nameplate Inc. of Seattle, Washington; and Pannier Corp. of Pittsburgh, Pennsylvania.

Several of the devices in this category date from antiquity and have changed relatively little over the centuries. But technological innovations have also made a key difference in some cases. The introduction of the mass-production automobile assembly line, for instance, led to notable advances in die-casting technology, and to the very precise formation of even the most tiny metal parts.

The introduction of stenciling has been dated to eighth century China, and this technique of reproducing designs has long been recognized as well-suited for metal or cardboard cut to simple shapes. Only with the introduction of silk-screen printing, however, was it possible to overcome the inherent limitations of stencils' great simplicity. The stencil does not permit the reproduction of one design enclosing another (as in the case of a figure eight), unless the it is halved to prevent the necessarily unattached central sections from dropping out. The fine meshes used in silk screen printing were substantial enough to support the unattached elements of a stencil, without posing a barrier to the passage of the dye or paint being forced through a water-soluble glue into the desired design. A variant to this blockout-stencil or glue-cut-out-stencil method

was the film-stencil method, whereby designs were cut into a colored lacquer laminated to a sheet of glassine paper, so the whole assemblage could be mounted on a screen before the removal of the uncut paper backing and subsequent printing.

The advances made possible by computer technology were transforming many features of office life in the United States near the end of the twentieth century, including the use of certain numbering and lettering devices. However, such age-old implements as hand presses, stamps, and seals remained widely used as a means of officially marking paperwork of various sorts. Indeed, the increasing automation of offices had given a new lease on life to such marking devices: highly sophisticated photocopying machines, for instance, could reproduce documents with such great fidelity as to make forgeries easy in the absence of, say, the unreproducible physical impression left by the impact of a notary public's or government official's seal.

INDUSTRY INFORMATION SOURCES

Rothman, Raymond C. *Notary Public Practices & Glossary,* Woodland Hills, California: National Notary Association, 1978.

Seals and Other Devices in Use at the Government Printing Office, Washington, D.C.: U.S. Government Printing Office, n.d.

—Richard Hillyer

SIC 3955

CARBON PAPER AND INKED RIBBONS

This industry contains establishments primarily engaged in manufacturing carbon paper, spirit or gelatin process and other stencil paper, and inked or carbon ribbons for business machines.

The value of shipments in the industry in 1991, a peak year, was $926 million, up from $779 million in 1982. There were about 125 establishments in the industry in 1991. Fifty-five percent of these establishments had 20 or more employees. Average firm size as measured by the number of production workers per establishment was 36 percent larger than that for the manufacturing sector as a whole. Annual capital investments were $13 million in 1991, down from a peak of $23 million invested in 1982. The top products by share in the industry in 1987 were inked ribbons (70 percent) and carbon and stencil paper (25 percent).

The carbon paper and inked ribbons industry employed 5,700 production workers in 1991, up from 5,200 in 1982. A peak year for employment was 1989, with 6,500 production workers employed. The industry was relatively labor-intensive, having only 43 percent as much investment per production worker as that for the manufacturing sector as a whole. Annual hours worked by production workers in the industry were about the same as those worked in the manufacturing sector as a whole, but hourly wages were 35 percent lower.

Of the top 30 firms by sales in the industry, 77 percent were private independents. The capital requirements for the industry were relatively low, with average investment per establishment 59 percent of that for the manufacturing sector as a whole.

The top three firms in the carbon paper and inked ribbons industry were Frye Copysystems Inc. of Des Moines, Iowa, Pelikan Inc. of Franklin, Tennessee, and the Barouh Eaton Allen Corp. of Brooklyn, New York. Together these firms accounted for 21 percent of total sales for the industry. Frye Copysystems had $75 million in sales and 283 employees in 1992. The privately held firm, founded in 1912, manufactures carbon paper. Pelikan Inc. had $70 million in sales and 400 employees in 1992. Founded in 1978, the firm produces both carbon paper and inked ribbons. Barouh Eaton Allen had $50 million in sales and 370 employees in 1992. The privately held firm manufactures thermal printer ribbons, cartridges, and wide ribbons.

The states ranking in the top ten by number of establishments in the industry were California with 22, New York with 15, Pennsylvania with 9, New Jersey with 9, Illinois with 8, Ohio with 7, North Carolina with 6, Tennessee with 5, Colorado with 4, and Georgia with 4. Together these ten states accounted for 82 percent of total employment in the industry.

The top industries and sectors buying the outputs of the carbon paper and inked ribbons industry included businesses buying manifold business forms, state and local government purchases for education and hospitals, exports, banking, and the retail trade.

INDUSTRY INFORMATION SOURCES

Annual Survey of Manufactures, Washington, DC: U.S. Census Bureau, 1991.

Darnay, Arsen J., ed., *Manufacturing USA: Industry Analysis, Statistics, and Leading Companies,* 3rd edition, Detroit: Gale Research, Inc., 1993.

U.S. Industrial Outlook 1994, Washington, DC: U.S. Department of Commerce, January 1994.

Ward's Business Directory of U.S. Private and Public Companies, Detroit: Gale Research, Inc., 1993.

—David Kucera

SIC 3961

COSTUME JEWELRY AND COSTUME NOVELTIES, EXCEPT PRECIOUS METALS

This category encompasses businesses primarily engaged in manufacturing costume jewelry, costume novelties, and ornaments made of all materials, except precious metal, precious or semiprecious stones, and rolled gold paste and gold-filled materials. The products manufactured within this category include such items as necklaces, rings, artificial pearls, compacts, cuff-links, and rosaries. Businesses primarily engaged in manufacturing jewelry of precious and semiprecious material are classified in **SIC 3911: Jewelry, Precious Metal;** those manufacturing leather compacts and vanity cases are classified in **SIC 3172: Personal Leather Goods, Except Women's Handbags and Purses;** and those manufacturing synthetic stones for gem stone and industrial use are classified in **SIC 3299: Nonmetallic Mineral Products, Not Elsewhere Classified.**

INDUSTRY SNAPSHOT

More than 600 firms are currently active in the manufacture of costume jewelry in the United States, many of the older ones based in Rhode Island. The combined value of all goods produced by these companies totaled $1.3 billion in 1992. Nearly ten percent of the industry's total production is exported to other countries, including Canada and Mexico. Some of the firms are only involved in the manufacture of pieces using purchased components. The items are then sold to costume jewelry retailers, especially department stores. Other firms, however, both fabricate and market their own product lines.

The government has begun to play an increasingly significant role in the industry. Costume jewelry manufacturers have found it necessary to upgrade their facilities in order to comply with environmental legislation. While such measures have meant increased costs, the industry remains healthy and expects to benefit from recent free trade arrangements signed by the government.

ORGANIZATION AND STRUCTURE

American costume jewelry companies manufacture their goods by various methods, primarily using base metals, including tin and lead, to fashion such findings as clasps and pin-backs, the basic components of a finished piece. One process by which this takes place is stamping, a more labor-intensive method that produces a finer, more polished piece of metal. The more typical method in the shaping of metal for costume jewelry is casting, which involves pouring molten metal into a mold. This process lends itself more readily to mass-production of the jewelry. Manufacturers also utilize relatively recent methods of centrifugal casting and injection-molding of plastic. The findings produced from these processes are then used to fabricate finished pieces or sold to individual costume jewelry houses. Another integral function is electroplating, the electrolytic process of coating base metals with a small amount of a precious metal to give the jewelry its gold or silver appearance.

Most of the large costume jewelry companies sell their wares through department stores, an innovative marketing strategy that evolved in the 1950s. Earrings are one of the biggest sellers, followed in volume by necklaces and pins. One-third of all costume jewelry purchased in the U.S. is bought as a gift—Christmas, Mother's Day, and Valentine's Day are the peak selling seasons. Two-thirds is purchased for individual use. Costume jewelry is also a popular product on the novel home-shopping networks found on cable channels.

BACKGROUND AND DEVELOPMENT

The industry is centered today around the city of Providence, Rhode Island, which originally attracted fine jewelry artisans in the eighteenth century. A craftsperson by the name of Nehemiah Dodge introduced gold-plating technology to the area in the late 1700s. The costume jewelry industry benefited from the nineteenth century's great advances in industrial technology, including the development of new machinery that allowed inexpensive jewelry to be mass-produced, and by 1900 the items had found a significant domestic market. Portuguese immigrants skilled in the necessary handiwork accounted for a large part of the labor pool and proved influential in the rise of Rhode Island as a base for costume jewelry manufacturers.

The term costume jewelry was first used in a 1933 article in the New Yorker. The development of the modern industry was directly influenced by such European fashion designers as Elsa Schiaparelli and Coco Chanel. These designers commissioned original pieces that were clearly meant to be fake and whose sole purpose was to complement the sartorial ensemble. Many of the early examples of costume jewelry were larger-than-life imitations of fine jewelry, but the burgeoning industry soon spawned innovative artisans who experimented with a variety of shapes, materials, and color palettes. Designers of costume jewelry then, as now, were often freed by the disposable nature of the product to wildly experiment and inject a good dose of imagination into their work, an attitude not often found within the realm of more traditional fine jewelry.

In the early decades of the twentieth century, costume jewelry manufacturers primarily used cut-glass stones, imitation pearls, and enamel. Costume jewelry became overwhelmingly popular during the social upheavals of the 1920s, and the materials of choice for fashionable flappers were the glass materials of jet and crystal. The Great Depression that choked the American economy during the 1930s brought many new customers to the costume jewelry market, as those who lost fortunes could no longer afford fine jewelry. White metal became the most common material in inexpensive metal jewelry, but World War II restrictions on the use of metals was manifested in the proliferation of gold- and silver-plated pieces. In addition, the war caused American manufacturers to be cut off from their Czechoslovakian and Japanese suppliers of cut glass and pearls.

The 1950s saw the rise in popularity of ornate gilt pieces and the continued use of crystal, jet, and inexpensive stones. An important court decision at that time was instrumental in solidifying the respectability of the creators and manufacturers of costume jewelry. When First Lady Mamie Eisenhower wore Trifari pieces to both presidential inaugural balls in 1952 and 1956, the much-publicized act spawned legions of copycat pieces. Trifari successfully filed suit to protect the copyright of their designs.

Innovative uses of materials and forms was the hallmark of costume jewelry styles in the 1960s. After a profitable synthetics industry burgeoned in the aftermath of World War II, molded plastics such as Perspex became commonplace as a material for inexpensive jewelry that could be easily transformed into daring shapes and colors complementing the outrageous fashions of the decade. In 1971 the U.S. gold market was deregulated, and this set off waves of sizable prices increases over the next decade that raised the cost of fine jewelry. This had a beneficial effect upon costume jewelry manufacturers, as more consumers turned to higher-end costume pieces from upscale designers, including Kenneth Jay Lane and Robert Lee Morris, rather than purchasing the genuine article from fine jewelers. Sterling silver also became a popular material during the late 1960s and early 1970s.

The British punk movement of the late 1970s even exerted its influence on costume jewelry trends of the 1980s as the "creative salvage" look, utilizing leather and rubber, became popular. The legions of women that began entering the workforce in the 1970s were also influential in the development of costume jewelry styles. The working woman's choice of clothing was often restricted to conservative styles that fit into a business environment, and thus costume jewelry became a way of personalizing a wardrobe. In the 1990s, an interest in multiculturalism was evident in the use of motifs and materials inspired by indigenous cultures and natural elements, a prime example of which was the popularity of faux-ivory materials.

CURRENT CONDITIONS

Recent costume jewelry sales have been noteworthy, as consumers hit hard by the recession of the late 1980s have been less likely to purchase fine jewelry. Indeed, some of the largest U.S. fine jewelry firms have suffered severe financial setbacks in the early 1990s, a fate which has not befallen costume jewelry companies. A newly popular niche in the market is the "fakes" category that markets relatively inexpensive pieces that look amazingly similar to the genuine article. Industry analysts noted that the recent economic downturn, while affecting overall consumer spending, has had relatively little effect on the overall health of the industry.

The projected forecast for the future of the industry is positive. As disposable personal income for Americans is expected to rise during the final decade of the twentieth century, costume jewelry sales are also expected to increase. In addition, industry experts predict that costume jewelry shipments to other countries will increase three percent annually.

Recent legislation regarding environmental issues has had an adverse effect on the industry, however. Clean air and water laws enacted in the 1990s have presented challenges to manufacturers, particularly those firms involved in electroplating, causing the cost of the process to increase significantly. Such establishments are now generally required to have wastewater treatment facilities that remove harmful chemicals and metals from discharge water, and some manufacturers have also been required to install air scrubbers to clean exhaust.

INDUSTRY LEADERS

The top company involved in the costume jewelry industry in the United States is the Illinois-based Artra Group, a publicly-held conglomerate founded in 1933. Artra holds many subsidiaries, including the number-two firm, Lori Corp. Third in line is the Napier Company, whose origins can be traced back to 1875, making it the oldest costume jewelry manufacturer in the United States. The New York City-based firm of Trifari Krussman and Fischel, Inc. is the fourth in production and sales, with origins that date back to the early 1920s. Industry leaders in the Rhode Island area include Victoria Creations, Inc., Swarovski Jewelry U.S. Ltd., and Monet Jewelers.

WORK FORCE

Employment figures for the costume jewelry industry declined to a five-year low of 166,000 by the close of 1992. However, average hourly wages for production workers in the field increased to a high of $7.20 an hour. In addition, the increase in public awareness of such repetitive-injury afflictions as carpal-tunnel syndrome has resulted in improved working conditions for costume jewelry industry employees.

AMERICA AND THE WORLD

Nearly a tenth of the goods produced by American costume jewelry manufacturers are exported to foreign markets, most notably Japan, Canada, and Mexico. In 1992 the total value of all exports within the industry reached $133 million. Costume jewelry manufacturers face stiff competition from South Korea, Taiwan, Austria, and China, as figures for the same year show $665 million in costume jewelry imports from these nations. The North American Free Trade Agreement (NAFTA) should prove beneficial to the industry, since much of what is imported from Mexico is exempt from U.S. import tariffs; under NAFTA, U.S. costume jewelry exports south of the border will be subject to a decreased tariff structure.

INDUSTRY INFORMATION SOURCES

Gonzalez, Crissy, "Costume Jewelers' Sales Sparkle While Results at Fine Gem Retailers Lag," *Los Angeles Times,* February 5, 1992.

Mulvagh, Jane, *Costume Jewelry in Vogue,* New York: Thames & Hudson, 1988.

Nemy, Enid, "Self-Proclaimed King of Junque Brings His Jewelry to the Masses," *New York Times,* June 27, 1993.

Shields, Jody, *All That Glitters: The Glory of Costume Jewelry,* New York: Rizzoli, 1987.

Sloane, Leonard, "Costume Jewelry: A Buyer's Guide," *New York Times,* February 3, 1990.

—Carol A. Brennan

SIC 3965

FASTENERS, BUTTONS, NEEDLES, AND PINS

This industry includes establishments primarily engaged in manufacturing notions, such as slide and snap fasteners and zippers, machine and hand needles, pins, hooks and eyes, buckles, buttons, button parts, and button blanks. Establishments primarily engaged in manufacturing these products from precious metals or from precious or semiprecious stones are classified in **SIC 3911: Jewelry, Precious Metals**.

Needles, pins and fasteners, made from metals and both natural and manmade fibers comprised the largest share of the industry's output. Zippers and slide fasteners made from plastics and metals, and buttons and parts made with metals and plastics, constituted the other less dominant but still significant categories of industry output. Close to 90 percent of the industry's output re-enters as inputs into other manufacturing industries. Of these, apparel, shoes, knitting mills, and household furniture manufacturers figured most prominently. Personal consumption expenditures make up for the remainder.

In 1982 approximately 356 establishments were active in the industry. By 1990 their number fell to 237, a 33.7 percent decline. Over the same period total employment plummeted from 16,100 in 1982, of which 12,700 were classified as production workers, to 9,000 in 1990, of which 7,100 were classified as production workers. To a large extent, the combined weight of two economic trends underlie the industry's establishment and employment declines. First, industry-wide, average productivity per production worker steadily rose, going from $35,200 in 1982 to $66,400 by 1990. This meant that those establishments which failed to keep pace with the industry's average lost out on the side of maintaining competitive per unit cost advantages. Conversely, within the surviving industry establishments, the same trend translated into doing more with less, leaving some industry workers redundant. Second, throughout the 1980s and early 1990s, reeling from import pressures, the U.S. apparel sector underwent a particularly acute downsizing phase. Being the principal purchasing source of the industry's output, the fall-off in apparel demand burdened the industry with high levels of unused capacity.

According to Bureau of Labor Statistics (BLS) data, assemblers and fabricators comprised the industry's largest occupational job category, accounting for 15.6 percent of all occupations. Clustered around a range of four percent were occupational categories covering blue collar work supervisors, hand packers and packagers, and sales and sales related workers. A BLS survey projecting the growth of the industry's occupational categories to the year 2005 indicated that the leading category of assemblers and fabricators was expected to decline by 18.7 percent. The same scenario was forecasted for occupational categories related to machine operators, tenders and setters, and hand workers not elsewhere classified. And, although accounting for only 1.1 percent of all occupational categories, electrical and electrical assemblers were expected to experience the steepest percentage decline, registering 41.7 percent.

Fasteners, buttons, needles, and pins are primarily manufactured in the northeast region of the United States. New York state, with 82 establishments, and Connecticut with 25, lead the nation in the number of establishment per state. In 1992 Talon Inc., Coats and Clark Inc., YKK (U.S.A.) Inc., and Medalist Ind. Inc., were the industry's leading manufacturers. In an effort to substitute lower for higher cost materials, some of the industry's leading companies were experimenting with material made from ceramic processes.

INDUSTRY INFORMATION SOURCES

Manufacturing U.S.A., 3rd Edition, Detroit: Gale Research Inc., 1993.

—Daniel E. King

SIC 3991

BROOMS AND BRUSHES

This category covers establishments primarily engaged in manufacturing household, industrial, and street sweeping brooms; and brushes, such as paintbrushes, toothbrushes, toilet brushes, and household and industrial brushes.

Broom and brush manufacturers generated consistently over $1.2 billion in annual shipments in the early 1990s. Brooms accounted for 14 percent of total sales, with paint and varnish brushes accounting for 28 percent and the remaining 58 percent divided between personal brushes, such as toothbrushes and hair-brushes, maintenance brushes, and artists brushes.

Manufacturers range from small, family-owned businesses to large corporations for whom broom or brush manufacture is one of many interests. The 1980s and early 1990s were characterized by a series of acquisitions of smaller firms by larger corporations. Empire Brush Company of Greenville, North Carolina, acquired six companies in that period and reported a 100 percent increase in sales. Two of the largest makers of "stick goods," O-Cedar and Vining Industries, merged in 1993.

The vast majority of companies are privately owned. The industry is most heavily concentrated in the Midwest and Mid-Atlantic states, with Ohio, New York and Wisconsin responsible for over 30 percent of shipments. Illinois is considered the center of the broom industry in the United States.

Until the mid-twentieth century, brushes were made of natural materials such as hog bristles, horse hairs, and Tampico fibers. Brooms were made of birch and willow twigs until replaced in the early 1800s by broomcorn straw (actually a type of sorghum). In 1906, the entire brush industry generated $19 million in sales. The innovative sales techniques of the Fuller Brush Company helped revitalize the industry, so when founder Alfred Fuller turned operations over to his son Howard in 1946, Fuller Brush alone earned $41 million. Fuller Brush, a division of the Sara Lee Corporation, saw its importance as an industry leader diminish from 1968 through 1989.

The replacement of original materials with longer-lasting synthetic fibers and metal alloys caused a major change in the industry. This, combined with advances in mass production techniques following World War II, decreased production costs and allowed for greater profit margins. Broom-making was also affected by mass production. Plastic brooms became more common, although over half of all brooms are still made of broomcorn.

Industry growth in the 1980s continued slightly but steady. Profit margins in the early 1990s were above average compared to other manufacturing industries. This was due largely to increased sales caused by new designs. Oral-B Laboratories of Redwood City, California, led the nation in the development of new toothbrush designs. While the majority of manufacturing industries showed declines in shipment values, the number of employees, and production hours in 1991, the broom and brush industry surpassed its 1990 figures in these and other categories.

Broom manufacturers in particular became concerned with the potential threat caused by the North American Free Trade Agreement (NAFTA). Before NAFTA, the American industry was protected by a 32 percent tariff on imports, due to phase out over an 11-year period. Mexico, already the largest supplier of brooms, stood poised at the end of 1993 to reap the benefit of relaxed trade controls.

INDUSTRY INFORMATION SOURCES

Barmash, Isadore. "Fuller Industries Picks Executive from Avon," *The New York Times,* February 13, 1991.

Feder, Barnaby. "Tiny Industry Fears NAFTA's Reach," *The New York Times,* September 24, 1993.

Fischman, Carol. "Better Brushes Expanding Oral Care Sales," *Supermarket News,* June 5, 1989.

Fuller, Alfred Carl. *A Foot in the Door,* New York: McGraw Hill, Inc., 1960.

"How Many Broom-Makers Does It Take to Kill a Trade Pact?" *Business Week,* July 20, 1992.

Huyser-Honig, Joan. "A Bounteous Crop of Broom," *Americana,* October 1991.

Muirhead, Greg. "Brush Strokes: New Toothbrushes Designed to Promote Better Hygiene Are Creating Opportunities for Growth," *Supermarket News,* November 16, 1992.

"Oral-B Plans Upgrades, New Products," *ADWEEK Eastern Edition* October 12, 1992.

"Sweeping Sales: Brushes Produce Better than Average Margins," *Industrial Distribution,* February 1993.

Underwood, Elaine. "The Modern Trials of the Fuller Brush Man," *Adweek's Marketing Week,* September 9, 1993.

—Michael Maschinot

SIC 3993

SIGNS AND ADVERTISING SPECIALTIES

This category covers establishments primarily engaged in manufacturing electrical, mechanical, cutout, or plate signs and advertising displays, including neon signs, and advertising specialties. Sign painting shops doing business on a custom basis are classified in **SIC 7389: Business Services, Not Elsewhere Classified.** Establishments primarily engaged in manufacturing electric signal equipment are classified in **SIC 3669: Communications Equipment, Not Elsewhere Classified,** and those manufacturing commercial lighting fixtures are classified in **SIC 3646: Commercial, Industrial, and Institutional Electric Lighting Fixtures.**

INDUSTRY SNAPSHOT

Over 3,500 establishments were engaged in the manufacture of signs and advertising displays in 1992, producing industry sales of $3.12 billion. The industry grew at a healthy pace throughout the 1980s, spurred largely by developments in computer technology. In 1990 and 1991, it followed the national economic downturn with consecutive eight percent decreases in sales volume, but rebounded with a four percent increase in 1992.

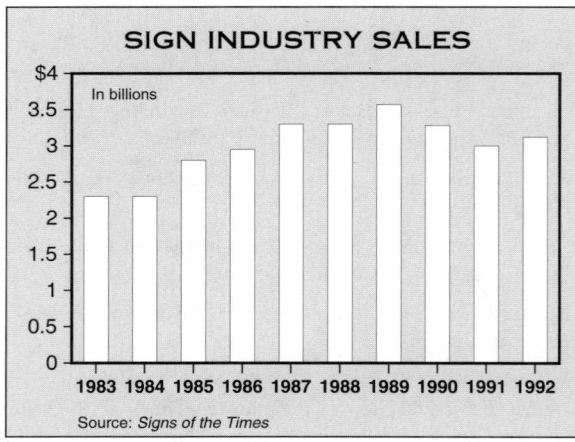

SIGN INDUSTRY SALES

In billions

Source: *Signs of the Times*

Throughout its history, and especially in recent years, the industry has fought against perceptions of signs as visual pollutants, which must be controlled or even banned except when conveying "vital information." These perceptions were often countered with new stylistic designs and aggressive government lobbying.

In 1990, electric signs made up 37 percent of all specified types of signs and advertising displays. Forty percent of these used fluorescent lamps, 24 percent used luminous tubing (neon, argon, hydrogen, etc.), and nine percent used incandescent bulbs. The most common materials in nonelectric signs (48 percent of the total product output) were polymers and plastics (including vinyl), followed by metal and wood. Advertising specialties accounted for less than 15 percent of the total output.

ORGANIZATION AND STRUCTURE

A sign shop is the establishment where signs and advertising specialties are manufactured. Sign shops are located throughout the country, with the greatest number of establishments (about 475) in the state of California. In general, though, the largest amount of shipments and the greatest number of employees occur in the midwest and eastern seaboard states. In 1990, New York's 324 establishments accounted for $454 million in shipments, 10.6 percent of the U.S. total. Shipments from New York, Illinois, Ohio, Texas and Michigan made up 37.6 percent of the 1990 U.S. total, and 35.6 percent of all U.S. employees worked in those states. A 1992 state-of-the-industry survey reported a significant increase in the percentage of shops doing business in the central, midwest, southern and eastern regions. Also, the average sign shop expanded its operations to serve a wider geographic base. This expansion may be the result of a trend toward larger shops, whose greater output quantities and increased sales forces allow them to serve larger areas.

The largest buyer of signs and advertising specialties was the gross private fixed investment industry (68.5 percent of total buying outputs in 1990). The next largest were highway and street construction, eating and drinking places, and wholesale trade.

Size of establishments ranges from single-person sign shops to industry leaders such as Actmedia, Inc., Giltspur, Inc. and Everbrite, Inc., each with sales estimated at over $100 million. An estimated 75 percent of sales volume in 1992 was generated by less than 10 percent of all sign shops. This top-heaviness may continue due to the increased volume of signage and the prevalence of quantity orders over custom or finely-crafted work. The development of computer technology decreases the need for specialized skills and gives rise to rapid-sign franchises, which facilitate same-day construction of signs. According to the 1992 survey, large sign shops (those generating more than $5,000,000 in sales) employed an average 36.7 employees.

BACKGROUND AND DEVELOPMENT

In the nineteenth century, signs and advertising displays were a common sight in residential as well as commercial neighborhoods. Since the electronic media had not yet developed, outdoor advertisements played a more crucial role in name recognition than they do today. Advertisements were often painted on empty brick walls, storefronts, or barns. The growth of cities reduced the amount and visibility of available space and necessitated free-hanging signs made of wood or metal. The advent of the automobile also increased the amount of road and traffic signs.

The public perception of advertising signs as eyesores was slow to develop. If it existed at all in the first half of the 20th century, it was not evidenced by the popularity of such cultural icons as the Burma Shave signs. With the ascendancy of television, the use of signs as part of nationwide advertising campaigns diminished.

Regulation and zoning have been recurring trends throughout the latter part of the century. Long considered the province of local governments, limitation of signs became a federal issue during the Johnson administration, with the passage of the 1965 Highway Beautification Act. Again in 1990, the introduction of the Visual Pollution Control Act by Republican Senator John H. Chafee of Rhode Island reflected a national concern for removing many highway signs by making it easier for governments to compensate owners. Funds earmarked for highway construction and maintenance were to be used for sign removal. Up to $428 million was allocated to the Federal Highway Administration to compensate sign owners who had erected signs before laws were passed making them illegal. Federal regulation of sign display has been opposed by active lobbying, as well as by publications such as the *Wall Street Journal*. For the most part, control of sign proliferation has remained on the community level. The potential negative impact to the industry caused by the reduction of advertising signs has been offset by an increased demand for signs of other types.

Electric Signs and Luminous Tubing. At the end of the 19th century, luminous signs were a new phenomenon. The hazardous and expensive gaslit method of lighting quickly gave way to electricity. In 1898, Sir William Ramsay and Morris William Travers discovered neon. In 1910, French physicist Georges Claude experimented with sending an electric discharge through a neon-filled tube. The charge produced a bright red light whose color and luminosity could be modified by altering the current. The subsequent development of luminous tubing using inert gases provided a relatively safe method of lighting. Though too expensive for general purposes, its brightness made it ideal for advertising and other special uses. Increased production of hydroelectric power under the Roosevelt administration lowered the cost involved in electric sign manufacture and use, and expanded the use of neon as an advertising tool and as an art form. Two of the best-known neon-using locales, Las Vegas and the Times Square area of New York, were developed during this neon heyday of the 1930s and 1940s. Artkraft Strauss Company, the original manufacturer of virtually all of Broadway's electric signs, continues to be the major supplier for the area, and to redevelop and renovate signs which are now considered historic landmarks (such as Times Square's famous Coca-Cola sign).

Neon reached the peak of its popularity in the 1950s. In the 1960s, regarded as an example of the opulent decadence of the previous generation, it gave way to inexpensive plastics as the advertising medium of choice. Electric signs in general continued to thrive. Electric advertising displays with moving mechanical parts proved to be attention-getting, point-of-purchase devices. Computer software also allowed for the programming of changeable messages on road signs, advertisements and architectural signage.

The industry has also been spurred by changes in signage on roadways and other public places. As travel becomes easier and tourism from non-English-speaking countries grows, a trend toward universal symbols to replace or augment public signs has increased demand. The National Park Service has been at the forefront of a movement to make recreational signs easier to read.

CURRENT CONDITIONS

The most important development in the industry since the early 1980s has been the introduction of computer technology in the manufacture of signs and displays. The ability to program sign design and manufacture through software greatly reduces turnaround time, often to less than a day. It also increases quantitative capabilities and reduces the amount of craftsmanship necessary in production.

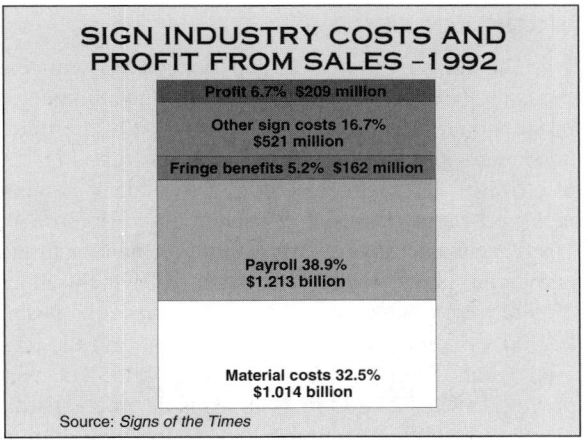

SIGN INDUSTRY COSTS AND PROFIT FROM SALES –1992

Profit 6.7% $209 million

Other sign costs 16.7% $521 million

Fringe benefits 5.2% $162 million

Payroll 38.9% $1.213 billion

Material costs 32.5% $1.014 billion

Source: *Signs of the Times*

At the same time, however, there has been a resurgence of hand craftsmanship in signmaking (perhaps in response to the stylistic standardization caused by computer technology). Major consumers such as Disney and MGM have ordered signs made of ornately handcarved gold leaf. In addition, neon has regained much of its former popularity.

Another important industry development is the response to the Americans With Disabilities Act (ADA).

Its enactment in 1992 required that all public buildings display architectural signs (including exit signs, emergency instructions, elevator signs, etc.) which are readable by disabled persons, including the blind and visually impaired. In practice, this entails creating signs with raised characters at least three inches high which are accessible by touch. Since many architectural signs were originally engraved, replacing them with raised-letter signs would necessitate complete retooling.

The expected increase in sales caused by the ADA had not occurred by the end of 1993. Consumers were slow to enact the required changes, and the federal government was slow to enforce them. In the absence of a test case, the government was unwilling to provide its own interpretation of the act, so businesses, building managers, and architectural firms were uncertain as to exactly what changes were required.

For the first time in the history of the sign industry, over $1 billion was spent on materials in 1992, a year in which the industry posted total sales of $3.12 billion and profits of $209 million. The ratio of payroll costs to sales increased by 6.4 percent from 1990 to 1992. During the same period, profit margin dropped from 7.4 percent to 6.7 percent. The median sales volume per sign shop in 1992 was $652,000, an increase over previous years which reflects the increase in size of the average shop.

WORK FORCE

The industry as a whole experienced reductions in total number of employees, payroll, and number of production workers in the early 1990s. On the other hand, sales per employee reached an all-time high of $97,700 in 1991, which indicated that many companies were involved in streamlining their work force. In 1991, signs and advertising specialties manufacturers employed about 62,200 workers, of which about 39,500 were production workers. This was down from 69,500 workers (44,400 production workers) the previous year. Total payroll of roughly $1,453,900 was down from $1,525,800 in 1990. This decline is paralleled by a similar reduction in the category of miscellaneous manufacturing industries as a whole, and reflects the stagnant national economy of the early 1990s. The 1992 state-of-the-industry survey showed that the average number of full-time employees per firm jumped from 23.5 in 1991 to 36.7 in 1992. Of this average, 25.8 were production workers, 4.9 were sales staff, and 6.0 were administrative and clerical staff.

By far the largest production group employed by the industry consists of assemblers and fabricators. These workers made up 15.6 percent of the entire work force in 1990. The next largest groups were sales

workers at 4.3 percent, production supervisors at 4.2 percent and hand packers and packagers at 4.1 percent. The Bureau of Labor Statistics estimates that by the year 2005, the number of assemblers, fabricators, machine operators and hand workers as a percentage of the total work force will be reduced by 18.7 percent. Automation may be chiefly responsible for this decline. During the same time span, the sales force will increase by 30.1. This may be explained by the expanded size and geographical clientele base of the average sign shop. Precision workers, sheet metal workers and duct installers are predicted to increase by 16.2 percent.

RESEARCH AND TECHNOLOGY

The American industry started the revolution in computer-aided signmaking in 1983. The most important innovation gave an operator the ability to key instructions to a CAD-based knife plotter, an instrument which cuts a pressure-sensitive design (such as a logo or lettering) from a sheet of perforated vinyl. This vinyl substrate (the material on which the actual sign information is contained) can then be attached to a signboard, or directly to another surface such as a store window or truck door.

Most large and mid-sized sign companies now have computerized systems, and it has been estimated that up to 90 percent of handlettering jobs have been taken over by computers. Startup costs for computer systems range from $6,000 to $35,000, but the increased speed of production reduces turnaround time and employee hours. Orders which previously took six weeks to complete are now done in a single day. The demand for quickly made signs has spawned a number of rapid-sign franchises. Fastsigns, a national vinyl-graphics chain, had 165 stores nationwide by mid-1992.

Another computer-based innovation is the electronic message sign programmable through software. Traffic signs benefit from this innovation, as do supermarkets and retail stores. In 1989, Videocart introduced a video screen mounted on the handle of a shopping cart. As the cart passes electronic sensors placed in the store, a message appears onscreen relating to a specific item or promotion. At the checkout counter the screen displays news and entertainment features. The Videocart and other electronic merchandising, such as electronic coupon machines, were slow to gain acceptance in the marketplace in the early 1990s, however. *Progressive Grocer* reported that only 12 percent of chain groceries used electronic media in 1990 and 1991.

Though Norway, Germany and Japan added important contributions to computer-aided signmaking, America was still the leader in the field at the end of 1993. Calcomp, Xerox, and Hewlett Packard Corporations pioneered in four-color imaging, a process which produces a color image directly onto the substrate by a method similar to that of a laser printer. This technique will bring more color and versatility to computerized sign design.

Advances in the area of luminous sign manufacture have served primarily to increase safety. A solid-state transformer has been developed to replace the core-and-coil construction previously used in neon lighting.

In response to a growing public concern over the rights of disabled people, a "talking sign" has been developed which may satisfy the requirements of the Americans with Disabilities Act. This small, hand-held device, when pointed in the direction of a sign, would activate a sensor which converts the sign's information to a voiced message. The talking sign's limitation is that it only works with signs equipped with the sensors; however, it has applications in public arenas, government offices, rapid rail systems and other large venues.

INDUSTRY INFORMATION SOURCES

Chafee, John H. and John Lewis, "Signs of the Billboard Lobby," *The Washington Post,* June 11, 1991.

Colford, Steven W., "Feds Set Fund to Ax Outdoor Boards," *Advertising Age,* March 16, 1992.

Cunningham, Peter, "Entrepreneur Clicks with Neon Design Firm," *Crain's Chicago Business,* April 10, 1989.

Fensholt, Carol, "Electronic In-store Media: A Sign of the Times?" *Supermarket Business Magazine,* October 1991.

Fingersh, Julie, "Rotating Courtside Signage Rolling in Controversy," *Amusement Business,* July 6, 1992.

Garry, Michael, "Waste or Windfall?" *Progressive Grocer,* September 1992.

Graebner, Lynn, "Rapid-sign Franchises, Armed with Artful Computers, Popping Up Fast," *The Business Journal Serving Greater Sacramento,* February 5, 1990.

Hildebrand, Carol, "Sign Maker Glitters with IS Gear," *Computerworld,* March 11, 1991.

"Interview with Terry Wike, Editor," *Sign Business Magazine.*

Korman, Richard, "Next Generation of Starrs in the 'New' Times Square," *ENR,* June 7, 1990.

Kueny, Barbara, "Everbrite's Future Shines in Flashing Neon, Despite Signs of Dull '91," *The Business Journal-Milwaukee,* May 27, 1991.

McWilliams, James E. and Ken Jensen, "The Writing on the Wall," *American School & University,* August 1992.

O'Dwyer, Jessica, "When Neon Signs Were Art," *Americana,* May-June 1989.

O'Harrow, Robert, Jr., "Guerilla War Waged to Save Rural Aesthetics," *The Washington Post,* May 8, 1993.

Pierson, John, "Disabilities Act Stymies Many Sign Designers," *The Wall Street Journal,* August 31, 1992.

Pierson, John, "Sign Rules May Not Foster Communication," *The Wall Street Journal,* April 26, 1991.

Pierson, John, "Signs to Make Clear Opportunities for Fun," *The Wall Street Journal,* January 8, 1992.

Riggs, Carol R., "They Light Up Broadway," *D & B Reports,* May-June 1990.

Souhrada, Paul, "Sign of the Times: Neon Maker Rides Revived Popularity," *Cincinnati Business Courier,* January 30, 1989.

Stage, Wm., *Ghost Signs: Brick Wall Signs in America,* Cincinnati: ST Publications, Inc.

Swormstedt, Wade, ed., "The 1992 State-of-the-Industry Report," *Signs of the Times,* July 1993.

"Tech Tips: Showing Energy Wasters the Exit," *Black Enterprise,* August 1989.

Thomas, G. Scott., "'Ultimate Business Card' Makes First Impression," *Business First of Buffalo,* August 24, 1992.

United States Congress Senate Committee on Public Works, *Visual Pollution Control Act of 1990: Report Together With Minority Views,* Washington: U.S. Government Printing Office, 1990.

—Michael Maschinot

SIC 3995

BURIAL CASKETS

This classifications includes establishments primarily engaged in manufacturing burial caskets and cases, including shipping cases of wood or other material except concrete.

The burial casket industry tends to be stable in terms of employment and shipments. Between 1982 and 1988 the dollar value of shipments for the industry has steadily increased; however, this is probably a reflection of inflation rather than increased deaths. The average wage for an employee in this industry was $8.76 in 1988. While this may appear low when compared to other manufacturing industries, it was an increase of 6.3 percent from the year before. Ohio manufacturers paid workers far above other states with an average wage of $13.50 per hour. Florida manufacturers paid well below the average with $5.33 per hour compensation.

Selected ratios for the industry imply that companies which manufacture burial caskets rank below other types of manufacturers in terms of employees per establishment, pay, cost, investment, and shipment volumes. However, cost as a percentage of shipments is comparatively low in this industry, implying higher profit margins may be experienced. While most of the firms in 1988 employed more than 20 people, all but the three top industry leaders employed 500 people or less. Most burial casket manufacturers employ 100 or fewer people. As of 1991, the top 30 manufacturers employed 17,700 people total and had combined sales of $1.7 billion.

The largest manufacturer of burial caskets is Batesville Casket Company Inc., a subsidiary of Hillenbrand Industries Inc. located in Batesville, Indiana.

Metal caskets in adult sizes create the most market demand, garnering 62 percent of the total market in 1987. While steel caskets are the most popular, other specialty metals, such as copper, bronze, and stainless steel, claim 12 percent of the total market. Hardwood caskets claim 18 percent of the market, while softwoods account for less than two percent of sales. Metal burial vaults also claim less than two percent of the industry's market share.

INDUSTRY INFORMATION SOURCES

Brown, Don, "Offbeat Marketing," *Sales & Marketing Management,* June 1993.

Lubove, Seth, "Dancing on Graves," *Forbes,* February 28, 1994.

—Valerie Wilson

SIC 3996

LINOLEUM, ASPHALTED-FELT-BASE, AND OTHER HARD SURFACE FLOOR COVERINGS, NOT ELSEWHERE CLASSIFIED

This category covers establishments primarily engaged in manufacturing linoleum, asphalted-felt-base, and other hard surface floor coverings, not elsewhere classified. Establishments primarily engaged in manufacturing rubber floor coverings are classified in **SIC 3069: Fabricated Rubber Products, Not Elsewhere Classified,** and those manufacturing cork floor and wall tile are classified in **SIC 2499: Wood Products, Not Elsewhere Classified.**

Companies in the hard surface floor coverings industry supply flooring primarily for residential homes, which accounted for almost 60 percent of the market in the early 1990s. Coverings used in apartment buildings represented 10 percent of industry sales. Other major consumers of hard surface flooring, in order of industry purchases, include office buildings, mobile homes, hospitals, industrial facilities, hotels and motels, stores, and restaurants.

Much of the flooring manufactured in this industry is made with synthetic materials, such as plastic and rubber. Other materials, including some tiles, are made with portland cement or paperboard products; wooden, rubber, and cork flooring are classified elsewhere, as is wall tile. Linoleum, a traditionally popular industry offering, is made in sheets by pressing a mixture of heated linseed oil, rosin, powdered cork, and pigments onto a textile backing, such as burlap or canvas. Synthetic coverings similar to linoleum are created with mixtures of resins, elastomers, and plasticizers. These newer types of flooring are often more moisture resistant, durable, and workable than linoleum.

The linoleum production process was invented in 1860 by Frederick Walton of England. The use of linoleum and similar floor coverings expanded greatly during the 1920s. Asphalt tiles were developed in 1930, and vinyl floor was invented in 1945. But it was not until the 1960s, when flat concrete subsurfaces became standard in U.S. homes, that hard surface coverings exploded in popularity. A profusion of synthetic flooring products during the 1960s and 1970s sharply increased industry sales. By the early 1980s, manufacturers were shipping about $600 million worth of flooring each year and employing about 4,000 workers.

Steady market growth and the development of new and better floor coverings more than doubled industry revenues during the 1980s. Advanced polymer technology and new plasticizers allowed the introduction of less expensive materials with higher performance. By 1989, industry participants were enjoying sales of $1.4 billion. Although a recession in the construction sector and general U.S. economic malaise countered growth trends in the late 1980s, a market upswing going into the mid-1990s buoyed profit margins for many manufacturers. The long-term outlook for this industry seemed generally positive.

The hard surface flooring industry is extremely consolidated—only 19 companies participated in 1989. The largest producer in the early 1990s was Armstrong World Industries, Inc., of Pennsylvania. Armstrong had 1991 sales of $2.5 billion from its diversified operations, and employed 25,000 workers. Mannington Mills Inc., of New Jersey, was the second-largest industry participant, with sales of $150 million and 1,800 employees. Other industry leaders included American Biltrite Inc., of New Jersey, and Vinyl Plastics Inc., of Wisconsin.

Increased manufacturing efficiency, achieved through automation and restructuring, will inhibit employment growth in this industry in the long term. However, increased demand for new synthetic coverings will create opportunities for some occupations. The number of sales positions, for example, is expected to rise 30 percent for the miscellaneous manufacturing sector between 1990 and 2005, according to the Bureau of Labor Statistics. About 5,500 workers served this industry going into the early 1990s. The average labor wage was about $14 per hour—25 percent higher than average for all U.S. manufacturing industries.

INDUSTRY INFORMATION SOURCES

Darnay, Arsen J., editor, *Manufacturing USA: Industry Analyses, Statistics, and Leading Companies,* Detroit: Gale Research Inc., 1993.

Encyclopedia Britannica, Chicago: Encyclopedia Britannica, Inc., 1993.

Grolier's Encyclopedia, Danbury, CT: Grolier's Inc., 1993.

—Dave Mote

SIC 3999

MANUFACTURING INDUSTRIES, NOT ELSEWHERE CLASSIFIED

This category covers establishments primarily engaged in manufacturing miscellaneous fabricated products, including beauty shop and barber shop equipment; hair work; tobacco pipes and cigarette holders; coin-operated amusement machines; matches; candles; lamp shades; feathers; artificial trees and flowers made from all materials, except glass; dressed and dyed furs; umbrellas, parasols, and canes; and other articles, not elsewhere classified.

The miscellaneous manufacturing industry is a testament to the complication involved in trying to delineate every U.S. manufacturer into a succinct group. Even if each segment of this cluttered industry was given its own classification, the need for new categories would likely emerge within a few months. A sample of the goods produced in this industry includes: hand grenades, lamp shade frames, nonelectric

cigar lighters, matches, doll wigs, combs (except hard rubber), framed calendars, bric-a-brac, beach umbrellas, artificial wreaths, walnut shell flour, electric vibrators, tinsel, feather plumes, and fingerprint equipment.

Despite its obscurity and fragmentation, the miscellaneous manufacturing industry sports a few major product groups. Coin-operated amusement machines, for example, accounted for a leading 7.5 percent of industry output in the late 1980s. Portable fire extinguishing equipment and related parts represented about 7.3 percent of the market for miscellaneous items. Candles made up 4.5 percent of sales, and artificial Christmas trees provided 2.4 percent of revenues. Other major categories included: artificial wreaths, fruit, and flowers (2.2 percent); dressed and dyed furs (1.5 percent); umbrellas and parasols (1.2 percent); hair clippers (1.1 percent); and fake feathers and plumes (.9 percent).

The profile of miscellaneous manufactured goods consumers mimicked that of the manufacturing sector at large in the early 1990s. About 45 percent of industry consumption was classified as private fixed investment (for use in other for-profit businesses). Personal consumption expenditures made up about 15 percent of sales. Four percent of output was exported, and state and local governments received about four percent of shipments. The remainder of the market was highly fragmented.

While some industry offerings have probably existed since before recorded history, such as fly swatters and marionettes, other items, like slot machines and tear gas canisters, are more recent inventions. Industry growth during the 20th century pushed sales of items classified in this sector to about $4.3 billion by the early 1980s. Inconsistent growth during the 1980s lagged inflation, as aggregate sales climbed about 22 percent by the end of the decade, to $5.5 billion. During the same period, the number of competitors declined from 3,900 to about 3,200, and employment rose only six percent. Rising foreign competition contributed to sluggish sales growth and consolidation.

The industry is dominated by small companies. The average industry participant had annual sales of only $374,000 in the late 1980s, compared to an average of $1.4 million for all other U.S. manufacturers. The largest company was Bally Manufacturing Corp., a maker of pinball machines and other entertainment equipment. This Chicago-based concern had 1991 sales of $2.1 billion from its diversified operations and employed 33,300 workers. Carbon/Graphite Group Inc., of Pennsylvania, was the second-largest player with sales of $220 million and about 1,500 employees.

Other industry leaders included International Game Technology Inc., of Nevada, and WMS Industries, Inc., of Illinois.

While this industry's job outlook varies by sector, the general forecast is grim. Jobs for fabricators and assemblers, which made up 16 percent of this classification's work force in the early 1990s, will fall 16 percent between 1990 and 2005, according to the Bureau of Labor Statistics. Likewise, most unskilled labor positions will diminish at a fairly rapid pace. On the other hand, workers with sales and engineering skills will see opportunities increase 20 percent to 30 percent by the year 2005. And jobs for sheet metal designers and carpenters should grow about 15 percent.

INDUSTRY INFORMATION SOURCES

Darnay, Arsen J., editor, *Manufacturing USA: Industry Analyses, Statistics, and Leading Companies,* Detroit: Gale Research Inc., 1993.

Occupational Outlook Handbook, 1992-1993 Edition, Washington, D.C.: U.S. Department of Labor, 1992.

—Dave Mote

General Index

This index contains references to companies, associations, government agencies, and specific legislation cited in the *Encyclopedia*. Citations are followed by the volume number and page number(s) in which the company, association, agency, or legislative act is discussed.

A

A. C. Dellovade, Inc.   **2:** 271
A-C Equipment   **1:** 881
A. Klein and Co.   **1:** 305
A. P. Green Industries   **1:** 674
A. P. Plant Co.   **1:** 829
A. T. Cross Co.   **1:** 1327–1328
A. T. Kearney, Inc.   **2:** 1388
AA   *See* Alcoholics Anonymous
AAA   *See* American Automobile Association
AAAS   *See* American Association for the Advancement of Science
AAFRC   *See* American Association of Fund Raising Counsel Trust for Philanthropy
AAMA   *See* American Architectural Manufacturers Association
AAMA   *See* American Automobile Manufacturers Association
Aancor Holdings Inc.   **1:** 696
A&M   **1:** 1078–1079
A&P   **1:** 75; **2:** 558, 612–613, 616–617
AAR Corp.   **2:** 540–541
Aaron Spelling Entertainment   **2:** 1169
Aaron's Furniture Warehouse   **2:** 753
AB   *See* Aid to the Blind
A.B. Carter Inc.   **1:** 177, 938
AB Dick Co. Inc.   **1:** 946, 970
AB Plastics Corporation   **1:** 327
ABA   *See* American Bar Association
ABA   *See* American Basketball Association
ABA   *See* American Booksellers Association
ABB Power T and D Co. Inc.   **1:** 1022
ABB Traction, Inc.   **1:** 1213
Abbey Healthcare Group   **2:** 1260

Abbey Healthcare, Inc.   **2:** 1261
Abbott Laboratories   **1:** 24–25, 498
Abboud, Joseph   **2:** 555
ABC   *See* American Bowling Congress
ABC   *See* American Broadcasting Company
ABC Appliance Inc.   **2:** 1131
ABC Carpet Company Inc.   **2:** 681
ABC Liquors Inc.   **2:** 719
ABC Rail Company   **1:** 737
Abex Corp.   **1:** 878
Abitibi-Price Inc.   **2:** 552
ABL   *See* American Basketball League
ABM   *See* American Building Maintenance Industries, Inc.
ABMA   *See* American Boiler Manufacturers' Association
Abrasive Engineering Society   **1:** 699
Abrasive Grain Association   **1:** 699
ABX Air, Inc.   **2:** 387
A.C. Monk   **1:** 170
AC Nielsen Co.   **2:** 1376
ACA   *See* American Camping Association
ACA   *See* American Collectors Association
Academy Entertainment   **2:** 1152
Academy Lines Inc.   **2:** 302
ACB   *See* Associated Credit Bureaus
Accessory Lady   **2:** 665
Acco International   **1:** 873
Acco USA, Inc.   **1:** 441
Accreditation Board for Engineering and Technology   **2:** 1357
Ace Hardware Corp.   **2:** 533, 589–590
Acme   **2:** 616
Acme Brick Company/Justin Industries   **1:** 670
Acme-Cleveland   **1:** 920

Anthony Farms, Inc. **2:** 16
Anthony Industries **1:** 383
Anthracite Task Force **2:** 158
Anti-Friction Bearing Manufacturers
  Association **1:** 958–959
Antwerp Diamond Distributing Inc. **1:** 1309
A.O. Smith Corp. **1:** 1059
AP *See* Associated Press
AP-Dow Jones News Service **2:** 1092
AP Holdings **2:** 1110
APAC Oklahoma **2:** 213
APCOA Inc. **2:** 1110
Apex **1:** 264
Apex Travel **2:** 411
APFC *See* Association of Physical Fitness Centers
APHA *See* American Public Health Association
Apogee Enterprises Inc. **1:** 667; **2:** 683
Appaloosa Horse Club **2:** 69
Apple Computer Inc. **1:** 976, 979, 981, 988, 994, 1093,
  1119; **2:** 434, 522, 992, 1053–1056, 1058
Appleton Electric Co. **1:** 1066
Appleton Papers, Inc. **1:** 378
Applied Energy Services **2:** 96
Applied Graphics Technology Inc. **2:** 1027
Applied Materials Inc. **1:** 952
Applied Power Inc. **1:** 865
Applied Theory Associates **1:** 941
APTA *See* American Public Transit Association
APTD *See* Aid to the Permanently and Totally Disabled
APV Consolidated Incorporated **1:** 948
APWU *See* American Postal Workers Union
Aqua Glass Corp. **1:** 619
ARA Group Inc. **2:** 974, 988
Aratex Services Inc. **2:** 974, 977
ARB Group **2:** 247
Arbitron Co. **2:** 445–446, 1376
ARC *See* American Recreation Centers, Inc.
Arcadian Partners, L.P. **1:** 550
Arcata Graphics Co. **1:** 420, 432
Arcata Redwood **1:** 420
Archer Daniels Midland Co. **1:** 109; **2:** 319
Archer Daniels Midland Flour Milling **1:** 59
Archibald Candy Corp. **1:** 90
Archive Films Inc. **2:** 1159
Arco Coal **2:** 146, 152
Arco Pipe Line Co. **2:** 406
ARCO Transportation Co. **2:** 337, 405
Arctco, Inc. **1:** 1237
Arctic Alaska Corporation **2:** 99
Arctic Alaska Fisheries Corp. **1:** 15, 139
Areal Technology Inc. **1:** 987
Argonne National Laboratory **1:** 1116; **2:** 1376
Arianespace **1:** 1225
Ariens Co. **1:** 890
Aris **1:** 629
Arista **1:** 1079
Aristokraft Inc. **1:** 299
Arizona Inc. **2:** 1123
Arjo Wiggins Appleton **1:** 378
Arkansas Best Corp. **2:** 312, 1118

Arly Merchandise Corporation **1:** 276
Armani Fashion Corp., Giorgio **2:** 554
Armco Inc. **1:** 716
Armco Steel **2:** 1451
Armco Worldwide Grinding Systems Inc. **1:** 701
Armed Forces Medical Library **2:** 1433
Armor All Corporation **2:** 553
Armour Food Company **1:** 5
Armour Pharmaceutical Company **2:** 1267
Armour Swift-Eckrich, Inc. **1:** 8, 10
Armstrong Contracting & Supply Corporation **1:** 704
Armstrong World Industries, Inc. **1:** 672, 1342
Army Appropriation Act **2:** 1432
Army Ballistic Missile Agency **2:** 1483
Army Corps of Engineers, U.S. **2:** 248, 250–251, 342,
  345, 465
Army Guard, U.S. **2:** 1490
Army, U.S. **1:** 1232–1234; **2:** 1489–1490, 1492–1493,
  1495
Arnold Engineering **1:** 682
Arnotts Ltd. **1:** 80–82
Arrears Act **2:** 1443
Arrowhead Construction **2:** 89
Arrowhead Landscaping **2:** 89
Art Instruction Schools **2:** 1296
Art Stone Theatrical Inc. **1:** 275
ARTBA *See* American Road and Transportation
  Builders Association
Artco, Inc. **2:** 651
Arthur Andersen & Company **2:** 531, 540, 1373
Arthur D. Little, Inc. **2:** 975, 1384, 1389, 1396
Arthur Murray International **2:** 1171
Artistic Shower Door & Mirror Company Inc. **1:** 667
Artkraft Strauss Company **1:** 1339
Arundel Corporation **2:** 196
ARVC *See* National Association of RV Parks &
  Campgrounds
Arvin-Calspan Corporation **2:** 1375
Arwood Corporation **1:** 735
ASA *See* American Standards Association
ASA *See* American Supply Association
Asarco Inc. **1:** 738–739; **2:** 109–111, 114, 123
The Asbestos Institute **1:** 703
ASCAP *See* American Society of Composers, Authors,
  and Publishers
ASE *See* National Institute for Automotive Service
  Excellence
Asea Brown Boveri **1:** 880
Asgrow Seed Co. **2:** 29
Ashland Chemical Company **2:** 574
Ashland Oil, Inc. **1:** 557, 567; **2:** 574
ASHRAE 90.2 Bill **1:** 654
ASI Holding Corp. **1:** 1009
Asian Art Museum **2:** 1325
Ask Group Inc. **2:** 1063
ASME *See* American Society of Mechanical Engineers
Asplundh Tree Expert Co. Inc. **2:** 90
Asset Investors Corporation **2:** 951
Assicurazioni Generali **2:** 859
Associated Builders and Contractors **2:** 267

Bachman **2:** 597

Backer Spielvogel Bates Worldwide **2:** 993

Badger Meter Inc. **1:** 1258

Baghdad Carpet Cleaning Company Inc. **2:** 976

BAI *See* Bureau of Animal Industry

Bairnco Corp. **1:** 797

Bakelite **1:** 604

Baker & McKenzie **2:** 1272–1273

Baker & Taylor Inc. **2:** 547

Baker & Taylor Video **2:** 547

Baker Brothers, Inc. **2:** 536

Baker Commodities, Inc. **1:** 100

Baker Concrete Construction Inc. **2:** 273

Baker Hughes Inc. **1:** 899–900; **2:** 1037

Baker Industries Inc. **2:** 1087, 1090

Baker Truck Rental **2:** 1098

Bakers Falls Iron Machine Works **1:** 941–942

Bakers/Leeds **2:** 677

Bakewell and Company **1:** 663

Balanced Budget and Emergency Deficit Control Act of 1985 **1:** 1234; **2:** 1420

Baldor Electric Co. **1:** 971

Baldwin Locomotive Works **1:** 1212

Baldwin Piano and Organ Co. **1:** 1312

Baldwin Technology Company Inc. **1:** 946

Bali Co. **1:** 258, 260

Ball Corp. **1:** 660, 789–790

Ball-Incon Glass Packaging **1:** 660

Ball Players Protective Association **2:** 1182–1183

Bally Gaming International **2:** 1201

Bally Health & Tennis Corporation **2:** 1198

Bally Manufacturing Corp. **1:** 1343; **2:** 1198

Bally's Health & Tennis Corp. **2:** 1197

Baltimore and Ohio Railroad Company **2:** 284, 856

Baltimore Gas and Electric Company **2:** 488

Bandag Inc. **2:** 1118

B&K Industries **1:** 803

Bando Manufacturing of America **1:** 586

Bandolino **1:** 633

Bangor Punta Corporation **1:** 859

Bank Executives Network **2:** 1041

Bank Holding Company Act **2:** 802–803, 805, 807, 921, 925

Bank Insurance Fund **2:** 787, 789

Bank of America **2:** 781, 830

Bank of Bermuda Ltd. **2:** 808

Bank of California **2:** 802

Bank of Credit and Commerce International **2:** 773, 801

Bank of North America **2:** 780

Bank of the United States **2:** 784

Bank Securities Association **2:** 931

BankAmerica Corp. **2:** 924

Bankers Trust Co. **2:** 940, 944

Bankers Trust New York Corp. **2:** 785, 891

Banking Act of 1933 **2:** 780, 921

Banking Act of 1935 **2:** 772

Bankruptcy Code, U.S. **1:** 704

Banner Radio **2:** 1001

Banque National de Paris **2:** 782

Banques Populaires **2:** 799

Banquet Frozen Foods **1:** 5

Bantam Doubleday Dell Publishing Group Inc. **1:** 414–416, 420; **2:** 714

Barbee Orchards **2:** 26

Barbers, Beauticians and Allied Industries International Association **2:** 982

Barbers Hairstyling for Men and Women, Inc. **2:** 982

Barclays Bank PLC **2:** 782

Barco NV **1:** 177

Barefoot, Inc. **2:** 89

Barnes & Noble, Inc. **2:** 727, 731, 733

Barnes Group, Inc. **1:** 871

Baroid Drilling Fluids Inc. **2:** 209

Barone Cosmetics **1:** 529

Barouh Eaton Allen Corp. **1:** 1333

Barrett-Cravens Co. **1:** 915

Barry Blau & Partners, Inc. **2:** 1018

Barry's Jewelers Inc. **2:** 737

Barton Beers Ltd. **1:** 107

Barton/Gambrinus **1:** 101

BASF Corp. **1:** 179, 464, 486, 489, 534, 557, 560, 848, 1138, 1141–1142

BASF Group **1:** 554, 1142

BASF Information Systems **1:** 1142

Basic American, Inc. **1:** 48

Basketball Association of America **2:** 1187

Basler Electric Co. **1:** 1115–1116

Bass PLC **2:** 960

Bass Pro Shops Inc. **2:** 725

Basset Bookstores **2:** 733

BAT Industries **2:** 880

Bath Iron Works **1:** 1204

Battelle Memorial Institute **2:** 1375

Battle Mountain Gold Co. **2:** 119, 128

Bausch & Lomb Inc. **1:** 1295–1296; **2:** 71

Baxter Healthcare Corp. **1:** 508, 1274, 1280

Baxter International Inc. **1:** 1274, 1280; **2:** 716, 1260, 1267

Bayer Group **1:** 464, 498, 554

Bayer USA Inc. **1:** 547

Baywood International Inc. **1:** 70

BBDO Worldwide **2:** 990, 997

BBDO Worldwide Network **2:** 992

BBM Photocopy **1:** 1299

BCA *See* British Car Auction Group

BCCI *See* Bank of Credit and Commerce International

BDB Corporation **2:** 727, 733

BDO Seidman **2:** 1373

BE Aerospace **1:** 335

BEA *See* Bureau of Economic Analysis

Bearings, Inc. **2:** 539

Beatitudes Campus of Care **2:** 1239

Beatrice Co. **1:** 5; **2:** 1104

Beatrix **1:** 527

Beaulieu Group **1:** 200–201

Beaumont Methanol **1:** 544

Beaver Excavation **2:** 278

Beaver Falls China Company **1:** 685–686

Beazer USA Inc. **2:** 191, 196

Bechtel Group, Inc. **2:** 231, 251, 1356, 1363, 1380

GENERAL INDEX

GENERAL INDEX

Depository Institutions Deregulation and Monetary
  Control Act **2:** 789, 795, 797, 922
Depository Institutions Deregulation Committee **2:** 797
DES Tobacco Corp. **2:** 763
Desco Corporation **1:** 841
Desert Land Act of 1877 **2:** 32
DesiLu Productions **2:** 1145
Detroit Aircraft **1:** 1179
Detroit Athletic Club **2:** 1204
Detroit Automobile Company **1:** 1153
Detroit Coke Co. **1:** 576
Detroit Diesel **1:** 882
Detroit Free Press **1:** 400–401
Detroit News **1:** 400
Detroit Newspaper Agency **1:** 400
Detroit Osteopathic Hospital Corp. **2:** 1254–1255
Detroit Tool & Engineering **1:** 936
Detroit Tool Metal Products **2:** 1138
Deutche Grammophone **1:** 1075, 1079
Deutsche Aerospace AG **1:** 1246
Deutsche Airbus **1:** 1183
Deutsche Bank, AG **2:** 782
Development Dimensions International **2:** 1298
DeVRY Inc. **2:** 1296
Dewberry & Davis **2:** 1364
Dexter Corporation **1:** 557, 564, 616
Dexter Shoe Co. **1:** 634
Deza **1:** 562
DeZurik Incorporated **1:** 862
DHL Airways Inc. **2:** 317, 384, 388
DHL Worldwide Express **2:** 316, 388
Diagnostic Technology Inc. **2:** 1258
Diagraph Corp. **1:** 1332
Dial-A-Messenger **2:** 315
Dial Corp. **1:** 515; **2:** 396–397, 766
DIALOG Information Services **1:** 401; **2:** 1069,
  1072–1073
Diamond Cruise Ltd. **2:** 354
Diamond Plastics Corporation **1:** 606
Diamond Shamrock, Inc. **1:** 567
Diamond State Fibre **1:** 604
Diamond Walnut Growers, Inc. **2:** 23, 77
The Diana Corporation **2:** 565
Diaper Dan's Delivery Inc. **2:** 978
Diasonics Inc. **1:** 1287
Diatomite Corporation of America **2:** 211
Dibrell Brothers **1:** 169–171
Dick AB Co. Inc. **1:** 946, 970
DIDC *See* Depository Institutions Deregulation
  Committee
DIDMCA *See* Depository Institutions Deregulation and
  Monetary Control Act of 1980
Digital Equipment Corporation **1:** 978–980, 985, 987,
  989, 994, 1086; **2:** 1053
Dillard Department Stores **2:** 604
Dillard Paper Co. **2:** 552
Dilling Harris Inc. **2:** 1128
Dillmeier Industries Inc. **1:** 667
Dillon Food Stores **2:** 616
Dillon, Read & Co. **2:** 172–173

DIMAC Direct **2:** 1015, 1018
Dior **2:** 554
Direct Container Line, Inc. **2:** 365
Direct Mail Advertising Association **2:** 1015
Direct Marketing Group **2:** 1018
DISA *See* Defense Information Systems Agency
Disability Insurance and Supplemental Security Income
  program **2:** 1441
Disclosure Incorporated **1:** 424
Discount Car Wash Inc. **2:** 1129
Disney Store Inc. **2:** 744
Distilled Spirits Council of the United States **1:** 103
Distributor Productivity Reports **2:** 533
Distributors USA Inc. **1:** 299
District Banks for Cooperatives **2:** 824
Diversified Agency Services **2:** 992
Diversified Industries Inc. **2:** 846
Diversified Metals Corp. **2:** 846
Division of State Relations **2:** 1432
Dixie Drive-It-Yourself System **2:** 1098
Dixie-Narco Inc. **1:** 1001–1002
Dixie Yarn Mills **1:** 206
Dixon Group PLC **2:** 689
DKM Building Enterprises L.P. **1:** 316
DMAA *See* Direct Mail Advertising Association
DMC Financial Corp. **2:** 836
Do-All Gas Company **2:** 760
Dobbs International **2:** 396–397
Dobbs Subsidiaries **2:** 396
Dobbs Tire and Auto Center Inc. **2:** 1125
Dobson Park Industries **1:** 933
DOC *See* U.S. Department of Commerce
Docktor Pet Centers **2:** 768
DOE *See* Department of Energy
Doe Run Company **2:** 114
DOE *See* U.S. Department of Energy
Doehler-Jarvis **1:** 777
DOI *See* Department of the Interior, U.S.
DOL *See* Department of Labor, U.S.
Dole Citrus Co. **2:** 77
Dole Dried Fruit and Nut Co. **1:** 48, 97
Dole Food Company Inc. **1:** 46, 97; **2:** 18, 77
Dolese Co. **2:** 193
Dollar General Stores **2:** 607
Dollar-Rent-a-Car, Inc. **2:** 1100–1102
Dolly Madison **1:** 29
Dologenes, Newman & Cronin **2:** 1272
Dolphin Incorporated **1:** 735
Dolphin Protection Consumer Information Act **1:** 135
DomanTurist AB **2:** 971
Dome Mines **2:** 119
Dome Petroleum Ltd. **2:** 182
Domestic Petroleum Council **2:** 481
Dominicks **2:** 762
Dominion Textiles **1:** 205, 207
Domino Sugar Corp. **1:** 87
Dominos Pizza **2:** 708
Domtar Industries, Inc. **2:** 209
Donaldson, Lufkin and Jenrette Inc. **2:** 702, 843
Donato Levi & Sons **2:** 554

Lucas Industries **1:** 1197
Lucasfilm, Ltd. **2:** 1151
Luck Stone Corp. **2:** 192
Lucky Supermarkets **2:** 615–616
Ludlow Corp. **1:** 206
Lufkin Foundry and Machine Company **1:** 900
Lufkin Industries **1:** 900
Lufthansa **2:** 388
Lycoming Foundry and Machine Shop **1:** 1186–1189, 1193
Lydall Inc. **1:** 1331
Lykes Bros., Inc. **2:** 25, 74
Lynn-Edwards Corp. **2:** 549
Lynx Express Delivery **2:** 318
Lyondell Petrochemical **1:** 543–544

M

M & M Clays Inc. **2:** 201
M. Aron Corp. **1:** 229
M-I Drilling Fluids **2:** 209
M. Lowenstein **1:** 173
MAACO **2:** 1112
Macalloy **2:** 126
MacDonald's Industrial **1:** 784
Macfield **1:** 205
MacFrugal's **2:** 606
MacGregor Golf **1:** 1323
Mack International **1:** 1163
Mack Trucks, Inc. **1:** 1162, 1165–1166
Maclean Hunter Ltd. **2:** 453, 458
MacMillan Bloedel Inc. **1:** 303
Macmillan, Inc. **1:** 414; **2:** 1295
MacNeal-Schwendler Corp. **2:** 1063
Macy & Co., Inc., R. H. **2:** 605, 662
Maersk Inc. **2:** 371
Magic Chef **1:** 1050
Magic Circle Corporation **2:** 89
Magikist Rug Cleaners **2:** 977
Magma Copper Co. **1:** 739; **2:** 109–111, 127
Magma Power Co. **2:** 505
Magnavox Co. **1:** 1071–1072, 1140, 1318
Magnavox Government **1:** 1123
Magnuson Act *See* Magnuson Fishery Conservation and Management Act
Magnuson Fishery Conservation and Management Act **2:** 98, 100
Maidenform, Inc. **1:** 254, 258, 260
Mail-Well Envelope Co. **1:** 392
Major League Baseball **2:** 1179–1181, 1183–1185, 1189
Major League Baseball Players Association **2:** 1180, 1184–1185
Makita Corp. **1:** 933
Malapai Resources **2:** 133
Malaysian Air **2:** 393
Mallard Coach Company, Inc. **1:** 1230
Mallinckrodt Speciality Chemicals Company **1:** 131
Mallory and Church Corp. **1:** 229
Malt Beverage Interbrand Competition Act **1:** 102
Malvem **2:** 911
Malvern Minerals Company Inc. **2:** 209

Management Recruiters International **2:** 1041
Management Training Corporation **2:** 1307
Manhattan Electric **2:** 687
Manhattan Industries **1:** 221
Manheim **2:** 509
Manistique, Marquette and Northern Railroad Company **2:** 359
Mann Industries **1:** 179
Manned Space Systems **1:** 1230
Mannesman Mobilfunk **2:** 434
Mannesmann Capital Corp. **1:** 1018
Mannington Mills Inc. **1:** 1343
Manor Care's Choice Hotels International **2:** 960
Manpower, Inc. **2:** 1043–1045, 1047–1048
Manuel Diaz Farms, Inc. **2:** 90
Manufactured Home Communities Inc. **2:** 907
Manufactured Housing Communities Inc. **2:** 910
Manufacturers Aircraft Association **1:** 1187
Manufacturers Hanover **2:** 781, 924
Manufacturers Hanover Trust Co. **2:** 781
Manufacturers Railway Company **1:** 105
Manufacturing Chemists Association **1:** 462
Manville Corp. **1:** 704, 707
Mapelli Brothers Company **2:** 566
Mapelli Food Distribution Company **2:** 563, 565
MARAD *See* Maritime Administration
Marantz **1:** 1072
Marathon Oil Co. **2:** 169, 181
Marathon Pipe Line Company **2:** 405
Marble Institute of America **2:** 264
Marcade Group Inc. **1:** 240
Marina Operators Association of America **2:** 374
Marine Corps, U.S. **2:** 1489–1491, 1493
Marine Hospital Fund **2:** 1430
Marine Hospital Service **2:** 1430–1431
Marine Mammal Protection Act **1:** 135; **2:** 98, 104
Marine Medical Service **2:** 1431
Marine Midland Bank **2:** 802
Marine Placement **2:** 1040
MarineSafety International **2:** 1297
Marion Merrell Dow **1:** 501
Maritime Administration **2:** 332, 336, 1474
Maritz Inc. **2:** 1297, 1397
Mark Controls Corp. **1:** 862–863
Mark Travel Corporation **2:** 417
Mark VII Equipment Inc. **2:** 1128
Markem Corp. **1:** 946
Market Facts Inc. **2:** 1376
Market News Service **2:** 1480
Market Research Corporation of America **1:** 218
Markey's Audio-Visual Inc. **2:** 1131
Marlin Firearms Co. **1:** 858
Marlin Rockwell Corporation **1:** 858
Marmac Corp. **2:** 376
Marmon Group Inc. **1:** 758
Marriott Corp. **2:** 396, 957, 960
Mars Inc. **1:** 88–90, 1002
Marsh **1:** 1217
Marsh and McLennan Companies, Inc. **2:** 899
Marshall and Williams **1:** 939

Millipore Corp. **1:** 1265

Mills Farm & Fleet **1:** 237

Milton Bradley **1:** 1317, 1319

Milwhite Inc. **2:** 211

Mine Safety and Health Administration **2:** 158–159, 162, 1481

Mineral Leasing Act of 1920 **2:** 150

Mineral Management Service and Bureau of Land Management **2:** 1481

Mineral Reagents International **1:** 701

Mineral Resources of the United States **2:** 193

Minerals Technologies Inc. **1:** 706; **2:** 190

Mingo Logan Coal Company **2:** 160

Mini-Mart **2:** 616

Minit Lube **2:** 634

Minneapolis Grain Exchange **2:** 848

Minnesota Malting Co. **1:** 109

Minnesota Mining & Manufacturing *See* 3M Co.

Minntac **2:** 107

Minolta Camera Co., Ltd. **2:** 518

Minolta Corporation **2:** 518

Minute Maid Corp. **1:** 53, 125

MIPS Computer Systems **2:** 1051

Miracle Auto Painting Inc. **2:** 1113

Mirage Imports **1:** 1331

Miramax **2:** 1152, 1155

Miss Elaine, Inc. **1:** 272

Mission Clay Products Corporation **1:** 675

Mission Insurance Co. **2:** 1311

Mississippi Chemical Company **2:** 205

Mississippi Power **2:** 469

Missouri Pacific Trailways **2:** 298

Mitel Corporation **1:** 1084

Mitre Corp. **2:** 1375

Mitsubishi Corp. **1:** 1159, 1188; **2:** 482, 627

Mitsubishi Fuso Truck of America **1:** 1166

Mitsubishi Heavy Industries Ltd. **1:** 916; **2:** 244

Mitsubishi Kasei Corporation **2:** 207

Mitsubishi Motor Sales of America **2:** 1101

Mitsui & Co. **1:** 764; **2:** 388

Mitutoyo **1:** 927

MJB Farming Co. **2:** 26

MLB *See* Major League Baseball

MLBPA *See* Major League Baseball Players Association

MMI Products, Incorporated **1:** 873

Mobil Chemical Co. **1:** 380, 601

Mobil Corp. **1:** 146, 465, 567, 569–570; **2:** 166, 168, 180–181, 927, 1324

Mobil Exploration & Producing **2:** 927

Mobil Land Development Corporation **2:** 927

Mobil Pipe Line Company **2:** 399, 401, 405

Mobile Home Communities **2:** 970

Moderna Shuch Center **2:** 677

Modified Final Judgement of 1984 **2:** 436

Moen, Inc. **1:** 803–804

Mohasco Corporation **1:** 323

Mohican Mills Inc. **1:** 191

Mojave Pipeline Company **2:** 489

Molex Inc. **1:** 1117–1118

Molnlycke **1:** 389

Molycorp Inc. **2:** 127

Monarch and Mayer **1:** 189

Monarch Design Systems **1:** 189

Monarch Industries Inc. **1:** 672

Monarch Knitting Machine Corp. **1:** 189

Monet Jewelers. **1:** 1335

Monetary Control Act of 1980 **2:** 798

Monfort, Inc. **1:** 10; **2:** 39, 565–566

Monk-Austin **1:** 169–170

Monotype, Inc. **1:** 943

Monro Muffler Brake Inc. **2:** 1114, 1116–1117

The Monroney Act **2:** 626

Monsanto Co. **1:** 179, 473, 489, 541, 554–555, 862

Montana **2:** 554

Montana Resources **2:** 109, 111

Montana Resources Inc. **2:** 127

Montana Talc Company **2:** 213

Montblanc **1:** 1327

Montenay International Inc. **2:** 280

Monterey Mushrooms Inc. **2:** 29

Montgomery Elevator Company **1:** 904

Montgomery Ward and Company Inc. **1:** 432, 890; **2:** 600, 672, 751, 753

Montreal Protocol **1:** 614; **2:** 1134

Moody's Investors Service **1:** 424

Moorco International Inc. **1:** 1258

Moore Dry Kiln Co. **1:** 941

Moore Ltd. **2:** 755

Moorman Manufacturing Co. **1:** 70

Mor-Flo Industries, Inc. **1:** 1059

Moran Towing Corporation **2:** 371

Morgan Bank **2:** 840

Morgan Construction Co. **1:** 934

Morgan Guaranty Trust Company **2:** 785

Mori-Nu **1:** 156

The Morie Company **2:** 199

Morrill Act **2:** 1424

Morrison-Knudsen Corp. **1:** 1210, 1213–1214; **2:** 242

Morton International Inc. **1:** 557–558, 564; **2:** 209

Morton-Norwich Products, Inc. **1:** 1228

Morton Thiokol, Inc. **1:** 1228; **2:** 1487–1488

Mostek **1:** 1102

Mothercare **2:** 323

Mothers Against Drunk Drivers **2:** 711–712

Mother's Cake and Cookie Company **1:** 81

Mothers Pensions programs **2:** 1439

Motif **1:** 994

Motion Picture Association of America **2:** 1148

The Motion Picture Patents Company **2:** 1143, 1153

Motion Picture Producers and Distributors of America **2:** 1143–1145

Moto Photo **2:** 1093

Motor Carrier Act **2:** 299, 308, 316, 427

Motor Carrier Safety Assistance Program **2:** 427

Motor Equipment Manufacturers Association **1:** 1168

Motor Transit Corporation **2:** 298

Motor Vehicle Air Pollution Control Act **2:** 1449

Motor Vehicle Manufacturers Association **1:** 1152

Motorcycle Industry Council **2:** 650

Motorola Inc.   **1:** 994, 1071, 1081, 1086–1087, 1090–1091, 1093, 1102, 1104, 1123, 1262; **2:** 432, 464

Motown   **1:** 1075, 1078–1079

Moving Picture Machine Operators of the United States and Canada   **2:** 1150

MPAA   *See* Motion Picture Association of America

MPPC   *See* The Motion Picture Patents Company

MPPDA   *See* Motion Picture Producers and Distributors of America

Mr. How   **2:** 592

Mrs. Field's Inc.   **1:** 79, 81; **2:** 622

Mrs. Smith's Frozen Foods Co.   **1:** 63, 83

MSHA   *See* Mine Safety and Health Administration

MTD Products Inc.   **1:** 887

MTU of North America Inc.   **1:** 1192

MTV   *See* Music Television

Mueller Company   **1:** 862

Mueller Industries Inc.   **1:** 758

Mullite Company of America Inc.   **2:** 201

Multifiber Arrangement   **1:** 229, 252

Multifoods Corp.   **2:** 564

Multiple-Use Sustained-Yield Act of 1960   **2:** 94

Munecas y Juguetes Ensueno S.A.   **2:** 544

Munsingwear Inc.   **1:** 254

Munters Moisture Control Services   **2:** 251

Murata Erie North America Inc.   **1:** 1108, 1111–1112

Murata Erie North America Inc. State College Division   **1:** 1106, 1108

Murata Manufacturing Co., Ltd.   **1:** 1108, 1112

Muratec   **1:** 1085

Murphy Brothers Inc.   **2:** 246

Murphy of Iowa Inc.   **2:** 51

Murphy Oil Corp.   **2:** 87

Murray Ohio Manufacturing Co.   **1:** 889–890, 1217–1218

Mushroom Council   **2:** 30

Music & Arts Center Inc.   **2:** 1297

Music Teachers National Conference   **1:** 1311

Music Television   **2:** 1147

Musicland Group Inc.   **2:** 699–702

Mutual Benefit Life   **2:** 863, 866

MVMA   *See* Motor Vehicle Manufacturers Association

Myers Co., L.E.   **2:** 258

Myers Container Corporation   **1:** 791

Myron Manufacturing   **2:** 755

Mystic Color Lab   **2:** 1093

N

N/S Corp   **2:** 1128

N. Schlumberger & Cie   **1:** 183

N. W. Ayer & Son   **2:** 989

NAA   *See* Neckwear Association of America

NAAG   *See* National Association of Attorneys General

Nabisco Foods Group   **1:** 45, 79–82, 97, 101, 165

NACA   *See* National Advisory Committee for Aeronautics

NACCB   *See* National Association of Computer Consultant Businesses

NACM *See* National Association of Credit Management

Naco West   **2:** 970

NACSA   *See* North American Computer Service Association

NADA   *See* National Automobile Dealers Association

NADCA   *See* North American Die Casting Association

NAFTA   *See* North American Free Trade Agreement

NAIC   *See* National Association of Investment Clubs

NAISE   *See* National Institute for Automotive Service Excellence

Nalco Chemical Co.   **1:** 370, 564; **2:** 494, 497

NALCO   *See* National Association of Letter Carriers

Nanjing Deep Well Company   **1:** 956

NAPA   *See* North American Parts Association

Napier Company   **1:** 1335

NASA Ames Research Center   **2:** 397

NASA, Life and Microgravity Sciences and Applications   **2:** 1482–1483

NASA   *See* National Aeronautics and Space Administration

NASA, Office of Advanced Concepts and Technology   **2:** 1482–1483

NASA, Office of Aeronautics   **2:** 1482

NASA, Office of Mission to Planet Earth   **2:** 1482–1483

NASA, Office of Space Communications   **2:** 1482–1483

NASA, Office of Space Flight   **2:** 1482–1483

NASA, Office of Space Science   **2:** 1482

NASA, Office of Space System Development   **2:** 1482–1483

NASCAR   *See* National Association of Stock Car Auto Racing

Nash   **1:** 1154, 1187, 1195

Nashua Corp.   **2:** 1094

NASMI   *See* National Association of Secondary Material Industries

Nastasi-White Inc.   **2:** 263

NATA   *See* North American Telecommunications Association

NATEF   *See* National Automotive Technicians Education Foundation

Nation-Wide Stores   **2:** 558

National Academy of Engineering   **2:** 1354

National Academy of Science   **1:** 553

National Advisory Committee for Aeronautics   **2:** 1482, 1485

National Aeronautics and Space Act   **2:** 1485

National Aeronautics and Space Administration   **1:** 1147, 1181, 1183, 1222–1228, 1240, 1243; **2:** 462, 1069, 1474, 1482–1488

National Aeronautics and Space Agency   **2:** 1485

National Agricultural Library   **2:** 1291

National AIDS Program   **2:** 1428, 1430, 1436

National Air Pollution Control Administration   **2:** 1450

National Air Transport Company   **1:** 1179

National Alliance for Infusion Therapy   **2:** 1259

National Appliance Energy Conservation Act   **1:** 1040, 1058

National Archives   **2:** 1291

National Association for the Advancement of Colored People   **2:** 1269, 1413

National Association for the Education of Young Children   **2:** 1309

Octir and Ommi **1:** 183
October Films **2:** 1152
O.F. Mossberg & Sons, Inc. **1:** 857
Office Depot **1:** 998; **2:** 519, 680, 735–736
Office for Civil Rights **2:** 1437
Office Max **2:** 519, 608, 736
Office of Anthracite **2:** 158
Office of Business, Industry, and Governmental
  Affairs **2:** 1407
Office of Child Care and Development
  Programs **2:** 1407
Office of Defense Transportation **2:** 1099
Office of Disease Prevention and Health
  Promotion **2:** 1430, 1435
Office of Education **2:** 1432
Office of Environmental Health Sciences **2:** 1448
Office of Malaria Control **2:** 1433
Office of Malaria Control in War Areas **2:** 1433
Office of Management and Budget **1:** 1241;
  2: 1420–1421, 1463
Office of Personnel Management **2:** 1407–1408
Office of Population Affairs **2:** 1429
Office of Prevention, Pesticides, and Toxic
  Substances **2:** 1448
Office of Production Management **2:** 132
Office of Public Roads **2:** 235
Office of Refugee Resettlement **2:** 1299
Office of Road Inquiry **2:** 235
Office of Science and Technology **2:** 1449
Office of Solid Waste and Emergency Response **2:** 1448
Office of Solid Waste Management **1:** 753
Office of Space Commerce **2:** 1482
Office of Surface Mining Reclamation and
  Enforcement **2:** 1481
Office of Technology Assessment **2:** 1304
Office of the Assistant Secretary for
  Health **2:** 1428–1429, 1435
Office of the Comptroller of the Currency **2:** 779, 1481
Office of the President **2:** 1421
Office of the Surgeon General **2:** 1433
Office of Thrift Supervision **2:** 771, 787–788, 790–791,
  1481
Office of Water **2:** 1448
Offices of Defense Transportation **1:** 1212
Offshore Pipelines Inc. **2:** 246
Ogden Aviation Services **2:** 397
Ogden Corporation **2:** 366, 397, 1395
Ogden Projects Inc. **1:** 972–973
Ogilvy & Mather **2:** 991–992
Ogilvy & Mather Worldwide **2:** 992–993
Oglebay Norton Company **2:** 199, 344
Ohio Auto Diesel Technical School **2:** 1296
Ohmite Manufacturing **1:** 1116
Ohmtek Inc. **1:** 1112
Oil-Dri Corporation of America **2:** 204
Oil Pollution Act of 1990 **2:** 335, 337, 343
Oil Pollution and Liability Act **2:** 165
Oil Pollution Liability Act of 1990 **2:** 401
Oil Pollution Liability and Compensation act of
  1990 **2:** 181

Oiltanking, Inc. **2:** 325
Okleelanta Corp. **1:** 85
Old-Age Assistance **2:** 1437
Old Deerfield Fabrics Inc. **1:** 194
Old Dominion Box Co. **1:** 365
Olde Discount **2:** 839
Olds Motor Vehicle Company **1:** 1153
Olds Motor Works **1:** 1153
Olga **1:** 260
Olin Corporation **1:** 783, 853–854, 858
Olive Garden **1:** 63; **2:** 704–705
Oliver B. Cannon and Son Inc. **2:** 255
Olivetti **1:** 979, 1093
Olofsson Corporation **1:** 936
Olsen Corp. **2:** 1260
Olsen Health Care Services **2:** 1260
Olsson Roofing Co., Inc. **2:** 271
Olsten **2:** 1044
Olympia & York Developments Ltd. **2:** 552
Olympic Sales Inc. **2:** 645
OMB *See* Office of Management and Budget
Omega Environmental Control **2:** 305
Omni Films International Inc. **2:** 1163
Omni Services Inc. **2:** 977
Omnibus Budget Reconciliation Act **2:** 165, 1231–1232,
  1239
Omnibus Corporation **2:** 1100, 1103
Omnibus Reconciliation Act of 1987 **2:** 889
Omnibus Reconciliation Act of 1993 **1:** 170
Omnicom Group Inc. **2:** 990, 992, 1392
Omnicom PR Network **2:** 1392
Omnilife Systems **2:** 1239
On Cue **2:** 702
Oneida **1:** 680–681, 1308
Onyx **2:** 396
OOEC *See* Organization of Oil Exporting Countries
OPEC *See* Organization of Petroleum Exporting
  Countries
Opel **1:** 1158
Operations Management Inc. **1:** 128
Operative Plasters' and Cement Masons' International
  Association **2:** 274
OPI International Inc. **2:** 246
OPM *See* Office of Personnel Management
Opportunities Industrialization **2:** 1296
OptiRay **2:** 525
Optoelectronic Technology Consortium **1:** 983, 989–990
Oracle Corp. **2:** 1053, 1058
Oracle Systems Corporation **2:** 1058
Oral-B Laboratories **1:** 1337
Orange-Co Inc. **2:** 25
ORBIT Online **2:** 1069
Orchard Yarn and Thread Company Inc. **2:** 582
Ore-Ida **1:** 50, 53
Oregon Steam Navigation Company **2:** 347
Organic Act **2:** 1424
Organization for Economic Cooperation and
  Development **2:** 813
Organization of Oil Exporting Countries **2:** 164,
  167–168

GENERAL INDEX

GENERAL INDEX

Pharmaceutical Manufacturers Association   **1:** 499–500, 504; **2:** 1255
Pharmacy Management Services, Inc.,   **2:** 1379
Phelps & Spafford   **1:** 941
Phelps Dodge Corporation   **1:** 738–739; **2:** 109–111
PHH Car Plan   **2:** 1106
PHH Corporation   **2:** 1107–1108
PHH FleetAmerica   **2:** 1105–1108
PHH Group, Inc.   **2:** 1108
Phi Beta Kappa   **2:** 971
Philadelphia and Reading Coal and Iron Company   **2:** 157
Philadelphia and Reading Railroad Company   **2:** 157
Philadelphia Board of Trade   **2:** 848
Philadelphia Depository Trust Co.   **2:** 854
Philadelphia Electric   **2:** 470
Philadelphia Reserve Supply Co.   **2:** 516
Philanthropic Advisory Service of the Council of Better Business Bureaus   **2:** 1320
Philco   **1:** 1071
Philip Carey Corporation   **1:** 704
Philip Morris Companies Inc.   **1:** 7, 9, 18, 51, 76, 82, 106, 159, 162–165, 170; **2:** 65
Philip Morris Inc.   **1:** 106, 126
Philip Morris International Inc.   **1:** 161, 164
Philips Consumer Electronics Co.   **1:** 326, 1073, 1079–1080
Philips Display Components Company   **1:** 1097
Philips Home Products Corp.   **1:** 1056
Philips N.V.   **1:** 1079
Phillip Holzmann U.S.A. Inc.   **2:** 231
Phillips 66 Natural Gas Company   **2:** 172
Phillips Driscopipe, Inc.   **1:** 606
Phillips Fibers Corp.   **1:** 179
Phillips Industries Inc.   **1:** 812
Phillips Petroleum Company   **2:** 172
Phillips Puerto Rico Core Inc.   **1:** 576
Phillips-Van Heusen   **1:** 221; **2:** 654
Phoenix Closures Inc.   **1:** 839
Phoenix Group, Inc.   **2:** 697
Phoenix Iron Works   **1:** 927
Photo Finishers Association of America   *See* Photo Marketing Association International
Photo Marketing Association International   **2:** 518, 742, 978, 1093
Physicians Weight Loss Centers   **2:** 988
Picanol N.V.   **1:** 175, 183
Picker International Inc.   **1:** 1292
Pickle Packers International, Inc.   **1:** 50
Pickwick Transportation   **2:** 298
Pier Operating Associates Limited   **2:** 374
Pietro Beretta Fabbrica Amri   **1:** 854, 857
Pig Improvement Company Inc.   **2:** 51
PIG   *See* Pork Industry Group
Pike Nurseries   **2:** 597
Pikes Peak Mining   **2:** 134
Pilch Inc.   **2:** 72
Pilgrim's Pride Corp.   **1:** 15; **2:** 63
Pilkington Aerospace Inc.   **1:** 667
Pilkington Brothers PLC   **1:** 653

Pilkington Glass Ltd.   **1:** 656, 668
Pilkington Holdings Inc.   **1:** 667
Pillsbury Co.   **1:** 29, 51, 56, 59, 145; **2:** 708
Pinkerton Tobacco Co.   **1:** 168
Pinkerton's, Inc.   **2:** 1087
Pinnacle Worldwide   **2:** 1392
Pioneer   **1:** 271
Pioneer Asphalt Corporation   **1:** 561
Pioneer Electronics (USA) Inc.   **1:** 1072
Pioneer-Standard Electronics   **2:** 1135
Piper   **1:** 1180–1181, 1184
Pirelli   **1:** 580
Pirelli S.p.A.   **1:** 586
Pismo Village   **2:** 970
Piston Ring Company   **1:** 1015
Pitney Bowes   **1:** 999
Pittsburg Tank & Tower Co.   **2:** 276
Pittsburgh and Boston Company   **2:** 110
Pittsburgh Corning Corporation   **1:** 703
Pittsburgh Plate Glass   **1:** 533
Pittston Company   **2:** 1087
Pittway Corporation   **1:** 1095
Pizza Hut   **2:** 704–705, 708–709
PKG Industries Inc.   **2:** 69
Placer Development   **2:** 119
Placer Dome Inc.   **2:** 119, 123
Plains Cooperative Oil Mill Inc.   **1:** 98
Planned Parenthood Federation of America   **2:** 1320
Planned Parenthood-World Population   **2:** 1264
Planning and Control Inc.   **2:** 1295
Planning Research Corporation   **2:** 1062
Plantation Pipe Line Company   **2:** 404
Planters   **1:** 96–97
Planter's Cotton Oil Mill Inc.   **1:** 98
Plastic Coatings and Film Association   **1:** 598
Plastic Containers, Inc.   **1:** 840
Plastic Engineered Components Inc.   **1:** 925–926
Plateau Resources   **2:** 134
Platt-Saco-Lowell Corporation   **1:** 938
Play It Again Sam   **2:** 722
Playtex Apparel Inc.   **1:** 258, 260
Playtogs   **2:** 611
PLS International   **2:** 483
Pluess-Staufer Industries Inc.   **1:** 698
Plumbing Manufacturers Institute   **1:** 618
Ply Gem Industries   **1:** 301
Plywood Panels Inc.   **1:** 301
PMA   *See* Pencil Makers Association
PMA   *See* Pharmaceutical Manufacturers Association
PMA   *See* Photo Marketing Association
PMA   *See* Photo Marketing Association International
PMC Inc.   **1:** 612
PMI Food Equipment Group   **1:** 948
PMI Mortgage Insurance Co.   **2:** 886
Pneumo Abex Corp.   **1:** 1230
Polaris Industries, L.P.   **1:** 1236–1237; **2:** 651
Polaroid Corporation   **1:** 1299, 1301–1302
Polident   **1:** 1284
Polishing Plus Inc.   **2:** 1129
Polk, R. L.   **2:** 1018

GENERAL INDEX

Warner Communications Inc.   **1:** 1080, 1318;
  2: 1146–1147
Warner-Jenkinson   **1:** 130
Warner-Lambert Co.   **1:** 76, 89, 91, 93, 95, 500, 504
Warner Records   **1:** 1077
Warner Western   **1:** 1075, 1080
Warner's   **1:** 259–260
Warner's Music Sound Exchange   **1:** 1077
Warrantech Corp.   **2:** 894
Warren Equities   **2:** 758
Warren Petroleum Company   **2:** 172
Warsaw Pact   **1:** 1234
Washburn Crosby Company   **1:** 61
Washington Bulb Co.   **2:** 29
Washington Duke & Sons Co.   **1:** 160
Washington Energy Co.   **1:** 1038–1039
Washington Post   **1:** 397, 400
Washington State Dental Association   **1:** 1283
Washington State Ferry System   **2:** 359
Waste Management, Inc.   **2:** 502, 504, 546, 1031
Waste Stream Technology Inc.   **2:** 73
Water Bank Act of 1970   **2:** 492
Water Facilities Act of 1937   **2:** 492, 496
Water Pollution Control Act   **2:** 373, 492, 1378, 1448,
  1452
Water Pollution Control Administration   **2:** 1449
Water Pollution Control Advisory Board   **2:** 1450
Water Quality Act   **2:** 496, 1449
Water Resources Act   **2:** 246, 250
Water Resources Development Act   **2:** 343
Water Resources Planning Act   **2:** 492
Water Resources Research Act   **2:** 492, 496
Water Supply Act   **2:** 492
Waterhouse Properties Inc.   **2:** 742
Waterman S.A.   **1:** 1328
Watsco Inc.   **2:** 1041
Wattie's Ltd.   **1:** 82
Watts Industries   **1:** 865; **2:** 494
Watts Regulator Company   **1:** 865
Waupaca Foundry Incorporated   **1:** 727
Wausau Homes, Inc.   **1:** 316
Wavetek   **1:** 1112
Wayne Poultry   **1:** 15
WB Johnson Properties Inc.   **2:** 918
W.B. Saunders   **1:** 415
WBA   *See* Workingmen's Benevolent Association
WCC   *See* Warner Cable Corporation
WEA   **2:** 701
Wean Inc.   **1:** 922, 934
Weatherford International Inc.   **2:** 273
Weber Aircraft, Inc.   **1:** 335
Weber Marking Systems Inc.   **1:** 1332
Wee Three Record Shops, Inc.   **2:** 702
Weebok   **1:** 640
Weekley Homes Inc.   **2:** 227, 229
Weight-Tronix Inc.   **1:** 1018
Weight Watchers International Inc.   **2:** 988
Weirton Steel Corp.   **1:** 789
Weldun International Incorporated   **1:** 936
Welex   **2:** 183, 185

Welfare   *See* Aid to Families with Dependent Children;
  Food Stamp Program
Wellington Puritan Cordage Mills   **1:** 210
Wells and Wade Fruit Co.   **2:** 26
Wells Fargo Armored Service Corp.   **2:** 1087
Wells Fargo Bank   **2:** 781
Wells Fargo Guard Services   **2:** 1087
Wells Lamont   **1:** 271
Wemco Inc.   **1:** 229
Wendy's   **2:** 705, 708–709
Werner Company Inc., R. D.   **1:** 878
Werner Enterprises   **2:** 310
Wesray Corporation   **2:** 1104
West Bend   **1:** 948
West Coast Video   **2:** 1169
West End Diaper Service Co.   **2:** 978
West Marine Products, Inc.   **2:** 645
West Publishing Co.   **2:** 1073
Westat Inc.   **2:** 1376
Western Auto Leasing, Inc.   **2:** 1108
Western Auto Supply Company   **2:** 636–637, 639
Western Cooperative Fertilizer Ltd.   **2:** 207
Western Electric Co.   **1:** 337, 775, 1104; **2:** 546, 687
Western Electric Manufacturing Company   **2:** 532
Western Empire Publishing   **1:** 409
Western Farmco Inc.   **2:** 578
Western Forestry and Conservation Association   **2:** 94
Western Gas Resources, Inc.   **2:** 483
Western Girl   **2:** 1044
The Western Group   **2:** 260–261
Western, Gulf   **1:** 414; **2:** 1146–1147
Western International Media   **2:** 1003
Western Mining Corporation   **2:** 127
Western Organization of Resource Councils   **2:** 37
Western Organization Resource Council   **2:** 571
Western Publishing   **1:** 414, 420
Western Resources   **2:** 489–490
Western Union Corporation   **2:** 443
Western Union Telegraph Company   **2:** 437
Western Video Market   **2:** 571
Western Waste Industries   **2:** 502, 504
Western Wood Products Association   **1:** 290
Westinghouse Broadcasting Company, Inc.   **2:** 446
Westinghouse Commercial Systems   **1:** 765
Westinghouse Electric Corp.   **1:** 327, 604, 815, 880, 959,
  1009, 1022, 1028, 1044, 1052, 1071, 1119, 1122, 1189,
  1243–1245; **2:** 446, 471, 1452
Westminster Lace   **2:** 683
Westmoreland Coal Company   **2:** 527
Westmoreland Coal Sales Company   **2:** 527
WestPoint Pepperell   **1:** 173–174
WestPoint Stevens   **1:** 174
Westrec Properties Inc.   **2:** 374
Westvaco Corp.   **1:** 371, 374, 392
Wet Seal   **2:** 660
Wetterau Inc.   **2:** 560
Weyerhaeuser Co.   **1:** 286–287, 291, 349, 356, 368;
  2: 90, 515, 1453
Weyerhaeuser Timber Co.   **2:** 93–94, 96
WGBH Learningsmith   **2:** 727

INDUSTRY INDEX

This index contains more than 19,000 references to products and services offered by business and government establishments currently operating in the United States. Each reference is preceded by the four-digit Standard Industrial Classification (SIC) code under which the U.S. government has placed the tracking of that particular economic activity. SICs 2000-3999, which cover manufacturing industries, are discussed in Volume One of the *Encyclopedia*. All other SIC numbers refer to service and other non-manufacturing industries and are covered in Volume Two of the *Encyclopedia*. Bold citations in this index indicate titles of entries; other citations refer to subcategories within the four digit SIC headings.

A

3842 Abdominal supporters, braces, and trusses (Vol. 1)
3829 Abrasion testing machines (Vol. 1)
3291 Abrasive buffs, bricks, cloth, paper, sticks, stones, wheels, etc. (Vol. 1)
3291 Abrasive-coated products (Vol. 1)
3291 Abrasive grains, natural and artificial (Vol. 1)
3843 Abrasive points, wheels, and disks: dental (Vol. 1)
3291 Abrasive Products (Vol. 1)
1446 Abrasive sand mining (Vol. 2)
3291 Abrasives, aluminous (Vol. 1)
5085 Abrasives—wholesale (Vol. 2)
3842 Absorbent cotton, sterilized (Vol. 1)
2621 Absorbent paper (Vol. 1)
3443 Absorbers, gas (Vol. 1)
3823 Absorption analyzers, industrial process type: e.g., infrared, X-ray (Vol. 1)
6541 Abstract companies, title (Vol. 2)
1622 Abutment construction-general contractors (Vol. 2)
2389 Academic caps and gowns (Vol. 1)
8211 Academies, elementary and secondary schools (Vol. 2)
8221 Academies, service (college) (Vol. 2)
3699 Accelerating waveguide structures (Vol. 1)
3812 Acceleration indicators and systems components, aerospace types (Vol. 1)
2869 Accelerators, rubber processing: cyclic and acyclic (Vol. 1)
3829 Accelerometers, except aerospace type (Vol. 1)
6321 Accident and Health Insurance (Vol. 2)

3931 Accordions and parts (Vol. 1)
2782 Account books (Vol. 1)
8721 Accounting, Auditing and Bookkeeping Services (Vol. 2)
3578 Accounting machines, operator paced (Vol. 1)
5044 Accounting machines—wholesale (Vol. 2)
8721 Accounting service (Vol. 2)
3443 Accumulators (industrial pressure vessels) (Vol. 1)
2821 Acetal resins (Vol. 1)
2869 Acetaldehyde (Vol. 1)
2221 Acetate broadwoven fabrics (Vol. 1)
2821 Acetate, cellulose (plastics) (Vol. 1)
2823 Acetate fibers (Vol. 1)
2282 Acetate filament yarn: throwing, twisting, winding, or spooling (Vol. 1)
2861 Acetate of lime, natural (Vol. 1)
2281 Acetate yarn, made from purchased staple: spun (Vol. 1)
2869 Acetates, except natural acetate of lime (Vol. 1)
2869 Acetic acid, synthetic (Vol. 1)
2869 Acetic anhydride (Vol. 1)
2869 Acetin (Vol. 1)
2861 Acetone, natural (Vol. 1)
2869 Acetone, synthetic (Vol. 1)
3443 Acetylene cylinders (Vol. 1)
2813 Acetylene (Vol. 1)
2899 Acid, battery (Vol. 1)
3069 Acid bottles, rubber (Vol. 1)
2865 Acid dyes, synthetic (Vol. 1)
2869 Acid esters and amines (Vol. 1)

2911 Acid oil, produced in petroleum refineries (Vol. 1)
2861 Acid, pyroligneous (Vol. 1)
2899 Acid resist for etching (Vol. 1)
4953 Acid waste, collection and disposal of (Vol. 2)
1389 Acidizing wells on a contract basis (Vol. 2)
2026 Acidophilus milk (Vol. 1)
2865 Acids, coal tar: derived from coal tar distillation (Vol. 1)
2899 Acids, fatty: oleic, margaric, and stearic (Vol. 1)
2819 Acids, inorganic: except nitric or phosphoric (Vol. 1)
2911 Acids, naphthenic: produced in petroleum refineries (Vol. 1)
2865 Acids, naphtholsulfonic (Vol. 1)
2869 Acids, organic (Vol. 1)
5169 Acids—wholesale (Vol. 2)
3296 Acoustical board and tile, mineral wool (Vol. 1)
3275 Acoustical plaster, gypsum (Vol. 1)
3446 Acoustical suspension systems, metal (Vol. 1)
7349 Acoustical tile cleaning service (Vol. 2)
1742 Acoustical work-contractors (Vol. 2)
2869 Acrolein (Vol. 1)
2822 Acrylate-butadiene rubbers (Vol. 1)
2822 Acrylate type rubbers (Vol. 1)
2282 Acrylic and modacrylic filament yarn: throwing, winding, or spooling (Vol. 1)
2221 Acrylic broadwoven fabrics (Vol. 1)
2824 Acrylic fibers (Vol. 1)
2821 Acrylic resins (Vol. 1)
2822 Acrylic rubbers (Vol. 1)
2281 Acrylic yarn, made from purchased staple: spun (Vol. 1)
2821 Acrylonitrile-butadiene-styrene resins (Vol. 1)
2824 Acrylonitrile fibers (Vol. 1)
2869 Acrylonitrile (Vol. 1)
3829 Actinometers, meteorological (Vol. 1)
2819 Activated carbon and charcoal (Vol. 1)
8322 Activity centers, elderly or handicapped (Vol. 2)
7929 Actors (Vol. 2)
7929 Actresses (Vol. 2)
8999 Actuaries, consulting (Vol. 2)
3593 Actuators, fluid power: hydraulic and pneumatic (Vol. 1)
8049 Acupuncturists, except M.D.: offices of (Vol. 2)
3728 Adapter assemblies, hydromatic propeller (Vol. 1)
3483 Adapters, bombcluster (Vol. 1)
3537 Adapters for multiweapon rack loading on aircraft (Vol. 1)
2679 Adding machine rolls, paper (Vol. 1)
3578 Adding machines (Vol. 1)
5044 Adding machines—wholesale (Vol. 2)
3313 Additive alloys, except copper (Vol. 1)
3579 Address labeling machines (Vol. 1)
7331 Address list compilers (Vol. 2)
3579 Addressing machines, plates and plate embossers (Vol. 1)
5044 Addressing machines—wholesale (Vol. 2)
7331 Addressing service (Vol. 2)
3842 Adhesive tape and plasters, medicated or nonmedicated (Vol. 1)

2891 Adhesives and Sealants (Vol. 1)
2891 Adhesives (Vol. 1)
2891 Adhesives, plastics (Vol. 1)
2869 Adipic acid esters (Vol. 1)
2869 Adipic acid (Vol. 1)
2869 Adiponitrile (Vol. 1)
2822 Adiprene (Vol. 1)
7322 Adjustment and Collection Services (Vol. 2)
7322 Adjustment bureaus, except insurance adjustment agencies (Vol. 2)
6411 Adjustment services, insurance (Vol. 2)
1542 Administration building construction-general contractors (Vol. 2)
9411 Administration of Educational Programs (Vol. 2)
9611 Administration of General Economic Programs (Vol. 2)
9531 Administration of Housing Programs (Vol. 2)
9431 Administration of Public Health Programs (Vol. 2)
9441 Administration of Social, Human Resource and Income Maintenance Programs (Vol. 2)
9532 Administration of Urban Planning and Community and Rural Development (Vol. 2)
9451 Administration of Veterans' Affairs Except Health and Insurance (Vol. 2)
8742 Administrative management consultants (Vol. 2)
8741 Administrative management services (Vol. 2)
6733 Administrators of private estates (nonoperating) (Vol. 2)
3259 Adobe brick (Vol. 1)
8322 Adoption services (Vol. 2)
2833 Adrenal derivatives: bulk, uncompounded (Vol. 1)
2834 Adrenal pharmaceutical preparations (Vol. 1)
8322 Adult day care centers (Vol. 2)
2791 Advertisement typesetting (Vol. 1)
7319 Advertising, aerial (Vol. 2)
7311 Advertising Agencies (Vol. 2)
3555 Advertising and newspaper mats (Vol. 1)
7312 Advertising, billboard (Vol. 2)
7311 Advertising consultants (agencies) (Vol. 2)
8999 Advertising copy, writers of (Vol. 2)
3999 Advertising curtains (Vol. 1)
7331 Advertising, direct mail (Vol. 2)
3993 Advertising displays, except printed (Vol. 1)
7319 Advertising Not Elsewhere Classified (Vol. 2)
2752 Advertising posters, lithographed (Vol. 1)
7312 Advertising service, outdoor (Vol. 2)
3993 Advertising specialties (Vol. 1)
5199 Advertising specialties—wholesale (Vol. 2)
9111 Advisory commissions, executive (Vol. 2)
9121 Advisory commissions, legislative (Vol. 2)
8399 Advocacy groups (Vol. 2)
3423 Adzes (Vol. 1)
3565 Aerating machines, for beverages (Vol. 1)
7319 Aerial advertising (Vol. 2)
3861 Aerial cameras (Vol. 1)
0721 Aerial dusting and spraying (Vol. 2)
1382 Aerial geophysical exploration, oil and gas field: on a contract basis (Vol. 2)

7335 Aerial photographic service, except mapmaking (Vol. 2)

7999 Aerial tramways, amusement or scenic (Vol. 2)

4119 Aerial tramways, except amusement and scenic (Vol. 2)

3531 Aerial work platforms, hydraulic or electric truck or carrier mounted (Vol. 1)

7991 Aerobic dance and exercise classes (Vol. 2)

5088 Aeronautical equipment and supplies—wholesale (Vol. 2)

3499 Aerosol valves, metal (Vol. 1)

3443 Aftercooler shells (Vol. 1)

3443 Aftercoolers, steam jet (Vol. 1)

2833 Agar-agar (ground) (Vol. 1)

2836 Agar culture media, except in vitro and in vivo (Vol. 1)

1499 Agate mining (Vol. 2)

6081 Agencies of foreign banks (Vol. 2)

7389 Agents and brokers for authors and nonperforming artists (Vol. 2)

6163 Agents, farm or business loan (Vol. 2)

6211 Agents for mutual funds (Vol. 2)

7922 Agents or managers for entertainers (Vol. 2)

6531 Agents, real estate (Vol. 2)

7212 Agents, retail: for laundries and drycleaners (Vol. 2)

4731 Agents, shipping (Vol. 2)

7922 Agents, talent: theatrical (Vol. 2)

3531 Aggregate spreaders (Vol. 1)

5032 Aggregate—wholesale (Vol. 2)

2836 Aggressins, except in vitro and in vivo (Vol. 1)

6082 Agreement Corporations (Vol. 2)

5191 Agricultural chemicals—wholesale (Vol. 2)

0722 Agricultural; Combining, (Vol. 2)

8748 Agricultural consulting (Vol. 2)

6331 Agricultural (crop and livestock) insurance (Vol. 2)

2879 Agricultural disinfectants (Vol. 1)

3423 Agricultural edge tools, hand (Vol. 1)

0721 Agricultural; Entomological service, (Vol. 2)

7699 Agricultural equipment repair (Vol. 2)

3275 Agricultural gypsum (Vol. 1)

3523 Agricultural hand sprayers (Vol. 1)

3423 Agricultural handtools: hoes, rakes, spades, hay forks, etc. (Vol. 1)

3523 Agricultural implements and machinery (Vol. 1)

3274 Agricultural lime (Vol. 1)

1422 Agricultural limestone, ground (Vol. 2)

5191 Agricultural limestone—wholesale (Vol. 2)

6159 Agricultural loan companies (Vol. 2)

5083 Agricultural machinery—wholesale (Vol. 2)

2879 Agricultural pesticides (Vol. 1)

6519 Agricultural properties, lessors of (Vol. 2)

8731 Agricultural research, commercial (Vol. 2)

9641 Agriculture extension services (Vol. 2)

9641 Agriculture fair boards-government (Vol. 2)

8322 Aid to families with dependent children (AFDC) (Vol. 2)

3728 Ailerons, aircraft (Vol. 1)

3827 Aiming circles (fire control equipment) (Vol. 1)

3563 Air and Gas Compressors (Vol. 1)

9511 Air and Water Resource and Solid Waste Management (Vol. 2)

3052 Air brake and air line hose, rubber or rubberized fabric (Vol. 1)

3714 Air brakes, motor vehicle (Vol. 1)

3743 Air brakes, railway (Vol. 1)

4522 Air cargo carriers, nonscheduled (Vol. 2)

4512 Air cargo carriers, scheduled (Vol. 2)

3613 Air circuit breakers (Vol. 1)

3564 Air cleaning systems (Vol. 1)

7539 Air-conditioner repair, automotive (Vol. 2)

7623 Air-conditioner repair, self-contained units: except automotive (Vol. 2)

3585 Air-conditioners, motor vehicle (Vol. 1)

3585 Air-conditioning and heating combination units (Vol. 1)

3585 Air-Conditioning and Warm Air Heating Equipment and Commercial and Industrial Refrigeration Equipment (Vol. 1)

3585 Air-conditioning compressors (Vol. 1)

3585 Air-conditioning condensers and condensing units (Vol. 1)

5531 Air conditioning equipment, automobile: sale and installation—retail (Vol. 2)

5075 Air-conditioning equipment, except room units—wholesale (Vol. 2)

5722 Air-conditioning room units, self-contained—retail (Vol. 2)

5064 Air-conditioning room units, self-contained—wholesale (Vol. 2)

4961 Air-conditioning supply services (Vol. 2)

3585 Air-conditioning units, complete: domestic and industrial (Vol. 1)

1711 Air-conditioning, with or without sheet metalwork-contractors (Vol. 2)

4513 Air Courier Services (Vol. 2)

3444 Air cowls, scoops, or airports (ship ventilators), sheet metal (Vol. 1)

2394 Air cushions, canvas (Vol. 1)

5039 Air ducts, sheet metal—wholesale (Vol. 2)

3822 Air flow controllers, air-conditioning and refrigeration: except valves (Vol. 1)

9711 Air Force (Vol. 2)

3599 Air intake filters, internal combustion engine: except motor vehicle (Vol. 1)

3089 Air mattresses, plastics (Vol. 1)

4522 Air passenger carriers, nonscheduled (Vol. 2)

4512 Air passenger carriers, scheduled (Vol. 2)

9511 Air pollution control agencies (Vol. 2)

5075 Air pollution control equipment and supplies—wholesale (Vol. 2)

3443 Air preheaters, nonrotating: plate type (Vol. 1)

3564 Air purification and dust collection equipment (Vol. 1)

3634 Air purifiers, portable (Vol. 1)

3443 Air receiver tanks, metal plate (Vol. 1)

3724 Air scoops, aircraft (Vol. 1)

3569 Air separators (machinery) (Vol. 1)

3069 Air supported rubber structures (Vol. 1)

5181 Ale—wholesale (Vol. 2)

2048 Alfalfa, cubed (Vol. 1)

0139 Alfalfa farms (Vol. 2)

2048 Alfalfa, prepared as feed for animals (Vol. 1)

5191 Alfalfa—wholesale (Vol. 2)

2869 Algin products (Vol. 1)

3829 Alidades, surveying (Vol. 1)

3728 Alighting assemblies (landing gear), aircraft (Vol. 1)

2819 Alkali metals (Vol. 1)

2812 Alkalies and Chlorine (Vol. 1)

2812 Alkalies, not produced at mines (Vol. 1)

5169 Alkalies—wholesale (Vol. 2)

3691 Alkaline cell storage batteries (Vol. 1)

2833 Alkaloids and salts (Vol. 1)

2821 Alkyd resins (Vol. 1)

2865 Alkylated diphenylamines, mixed (Vol. 1)

2865 Alkylated phenol, mixed (Vol. 1)

2911 Alkylates, produced in petroleum refineries (Vol. 1)

3799 All terrain vehicles (ATV) (Vol. 1)

5571 All-terrain vehicles—retail (Vol. 2)

2836 Allergenic extracts, except in vitro and in vivo (Vol. 1)

2836 Allergens (Vol. 1)

1611 Alley construction-general contractors (Vol. 2)

0279 Alligator farms (Vol. 2)

3325 Alloy steel castings, except investment (Vol. 1)

2821 Allyl resins (Vol. 1)

0173 Almond groves and farms (Vol. 2)

0723 Almond hulling and shelling (Vol. 2)

2099 Almond pastes (Vol. 1)

2211 Alpacas, cotton (Vol. 1)

2231 Alpacas, mohair: woven (Vol. 1)

3281 Altars, cut stone (Vol. 1)

2531 Altars, except stone and concrete (Vol. 1)

7219 Alterations and garment repair (Vol. 2)

3825 Alternator and generator testers (Vol. 1)

3694 Alternators, motor vehicle (Vol. 1)

3812 Altimeters, aeronautical (Vol. 1)

3569 Altitude testing chambers (Vol. 1)

1474 Alum mining (Vol. 2)

3297 Alumina fused refractories (Vol. 1)

2819 Alumina (Vol. 1)

3264 Alumina porcelain insulators (Vol. 1)

3291 Aluminous abrasives (Vol. 1)

3365 Aluminum and aluminum-base alloy castings, except die-castings (Vol. 1)

3399 Aluminum atomized powder (Vol. 1)

5051 Aluminum bars, rods, ingots, sheets, pipes, plates, etc.—wholesale (Vol. 2)

2819 Aluminum chloride (Vol. 1)

3479 Aluminum coating of metal products for trade not done in rolling mills (Vol. 1)

2819 Aluminum compounds (Vol. 1)

3363 Aluminum die-casting, including alloys (Vol. 1)

3363 Aluminum Die-Castings (Vol. 1)

3354 Aluminum Extruded Products (Vol. 1)

3341 Aluminum extrusion ingot, secondary (Vol. 1)

3463 Aluminum forgings, not made in hot-rolling mills (Vol. 1)

3365 Aluminum Foundries (Vol. 1)

3365 Aluminum foundries (Vol. 1)

2819 Aluminum hydroxide (alumina trihydrate) (Vol. 1)

3334 Aluminum ingots and primary production shapes, from bauxite or alumina (Vol. 1)

1099 Aluminum ore mining (Vol. 2)

3291 Aluminum oxide (fused) abrasives (Vol. 1)

2819 Aluminum oxide (Vol. 1)

1541 Aluminum plant construction-general contractors (Vol. 2)

3355 Aluminum Rolling and Drawing Not Elsewhere Classified (Vol. 1)

3353 Aluminum Sheet, Plate & Foil (Vol. 1)

3341 Aluminum smelting and refining, secondary (Vol. 1)

2819 Aluminum sulfate (Vol. 1)

5719 Aluminumware stores—retail (Vol. 2)

5023 Aluminumware—wholesale (Vol. 2)

8641 Alumni associations and clubs (Vol. 2)

2819 Alums (Vol. 1)

1479 Alunite mining (Vol. 2)

3532 Amalgamators (metallurgical and mining machinery) (Vol. 1)

3843 Amalgams, dental (Vol. 1)

5065 Amateur radio communications equipment— wholesale (Vol. 2)

2892 Amatol (explosives) (Vol. 1)

1479 Amblygonite mining (Vol. 2)

3713 Ambulance bodies (Vol. 1)

4119 Ambulance service, road (Vol. 2)

4522 Ambulance services, air (Vol. 2)

3711 Ambulances (motor vehicles) (Vol. 1)

5012 Ambulances—wholesale (Vol. 2)

8011 Ambulatory surgical centers (Vol. 2)

1499 Amethyst mining (Vol. 2)

2869 Amines of polyhydric alcohols, and of fatty and other acids (Vol. 1)

3826 Amino acid analyzers, laboratory type (Vol. 1)

2865 Aminoanthraquinone (Vol. 1)

2865 Aminoazobenzene (Vol. 1)

2865 Aminoazotoluene (Vol. 1)

2865 Aminophenol (Vol. 1)

3825 Ammeters (Vol. 1)

2819 Ammonia alum (Vol. 1)

2873 Ammonia, anhydrous (Vol. 1)

3523 Ammonia applicators and attachments (agricultural machinery) (Vol. 1)

5169 Ammonia, except for fertilizer—wholesale (Vol. 2)

2842 Ammonia, household (Vol. 1)

2873 Ammonia liquor (Vol. 1)

2819 Ammonium chloride, hydroxide, and molybdate (Vol. 1)

2819 Ammonium compounds, except for fertilizer (Vol. 1)

2873 Ammonium nitrate and sulfate (Vol. 1)

2819 Ammonium perchlorate (Vol. 1)

2874 Ammonium phosphates (Vol. 1)

2819 Ammonium thiosulfate (Vol. 1)

3483 Ammunition and component parts, more than 30 mm. (or more than 1.18 inch) (Vol. 1)

8999 Announcers, radio and television service (Vol. 2)

3823 Annunciators, relay and solid-state types: industrial display (Vol. 1)

5051 Anode metal—wholesale (Vol. 2)

3559 Anodizing equipment (except rolling mill lines) (Vol. 1)

3471 Anodizing of metals and formed products, for the trade (Vol. 1)

5064 Answering machines, telephone—wholesale (Vol. 2)

2879 Ant poisons (Vol. 1)

2834 Antacids (Vol. 1)

1799 Antenna installation, except household type-contractors (Vol. 2)

5731 Antenna stores, household—retail (Vol. 2)

7622 Antennas, household: installation and service (Vol. 2)

3679 Antennas, receiving: automobile, home, and portable (Vol. 1)

3679 Antennas, satellite: home type (Vol. 1)

3663 Antennas, transmitting and communications (Vol. 1)

2834 Anthelmintics (Vol. 1)

2865 Anthracene (Vol. 1)

1241 Anthracite mine tunneling: on a contrast basis (Vol. 2)

1231 Anthracite Mining (Vol. 2)

1241 Anthracite mining services on a contract basis (Vol. 2)

2865 Anthraquinone dyes (Vol. 1)

2836 Anti-hog-cholera serums (Vol. 1)

3489 Antiaircraft artillery (Vol. 1)

2833 Antibiotics: bulk uncompounded (Vol. 1)

2834 Antibiotics, packaged (Vol. 1)

2899 Antifreeze compounds, except industrial alcohol (Vol. 1)

3339 Antifriction bearing metals, lead-base: primary (Vol. 1)

2836 Antigens (Vol. 1)

2834 Antihistamine preparations (Vol. 1)

3341 Antimonial lead refining, secondary (Vol. 1)

1099 Antimony ore mining (Vol. 2)

3339 Antimony refining, primary (Vol. 1)

2869 Antioxidants, rubber processing: cyclic and acyclic (Vol. 1)

8399 Antipoverty boards (Vol. 2)

2834 Antipyretics (Vol. 1)

7532 Antique and classic automobile restoration (Vol. 2)

5521 Antique autos—retail (Vol. 2)

7641 Antique furniture repair and restoration (Vol. 2)

5932 Antique furniture—retail (Vol. 2)

5932 Antique home furnishings—retail (Vol. 2)

7699 Antique repair and restoration, except furniture and automotive (Vol. 2)

5932 Antique stores—retail (Vol. 2)

2899 Antiscaling compounds, boiler (Vol. 1)

2834 Antiseptics, medicinal (Vol. 1)

5122 Antiseptics—wholesale (Vol. 2)

2836 Antiserums (Vol. 1)

3496 Antisubmarine and torpedo nets, made from purchased wire (Vol. 1)

3489 Antisubmarine projectors (ordnance) (Vol. 1)

3489 Antitank rocket launchers (Vol. 1)

2836 Antitoxins (Vol. 1)

2836 Antivenin (Vol. 1)

3462 Anvils, forged: not made in rolling mills (Vol. 1)

1522 Apartment building construction-general contractors (Vol. 2)

6513 Apartment Building Operators (Vol. 2)

6513 Apartment buildings (five or more housing units), operators of (Vol. 2)

6513 Apartment hotels, operators of (Vol. 2)

1475 Apatite mining (Vol. 2)

0279 Apiaries (Vol. 2)

1459 Aplite mining (Vol. 2)

5912 Apothecaries—retail (Vol. 2)

3357 Apparatus wire and cord: made in wiredrawing plants (Vol. 1)

5611 Apparel accessory stores, men's and boys'—retail (Vol. 2)

5632 Apparel accessory stores, women's—retail (Vol. 2)

2389 Apparel and Accessories Not Elsewhere Classified (Vol. 1)

2387 Apparel Belts (Vol. 1)

5136 Apparel belts, men's and boys'—wholesale (Vol. 2)

5137 Apparel belts: women's and children's—wholesale (Vol. 2)

2299 Apparel filling: cotton mill waste, kapok, and related materials (Vol. 1)

2396 Apparel findings and trimmings (Vol. 1)

2371 Apparel, fur (Vol. 1)

7389 Apparel pressing service for the trade (Vol. 2)

2241 Apparel webbing (Vol. 1)

0175 Apple orchards and farms (Vol. 2)

2085 Applejack (Vol. 1)

3699 Appliance cords for e.g., electric irons, grills, waffle irons (Vol. 1)

3061 Appliance mechanical rubber goods: molded, extruded, and lathe-cut (Vol. 1)

3469 Appliance parts, porcelain enameled (Vol. 1)

3822 Appliance regulators, except switches (Vol. 1)

7359 Appliance rental and leasing (Vol. 2)

7629 Appliance repair, electrical (Vol. 2)

3873 Appliance timers (Vol. 1)

0711 Application for crops; Fertilizer (Vol. 2)

7372 Applications software, computer: prepackaged (Vol. 2)

7371 Applications software programming, custom (Vol. 2)

3842 Applicators, cotton tipped (Vol. 1)

2499 Applicators, wood (Vol. 1)

2395 Appliqueing, for the trade (Vol. 1)

6411 Appraisal of damaged cars-by independent adjusters (Vol. 2)

7389 Appraisers, except real estate appraisers (Vol. 2)

6531 Appraisers, real estate (Vol. 2)

0175 Apricot orchards and farms (Vol. 2)

7213 Apron supply service (Vol. 2)

5511 Automobiles, new and used—retail (Vol. 2)

5521 Automobiles, used cars only—retail (Vol. 2)

5012 Automobiles—wholesale (Vol. 2)

5013 Automotive accessories—wholesale (Vol. 2)

5075 Automotive air-conditioners—wholesale (Vol. 2)

3825 Automotive ammeters and voltmeters (Vol. 1)

3357 Automotive and aircraft wire and cable, nonferrous (Vol. 1)

7532 Automotive body shops (Vol. 2)

5599 Automotive Dealers Not Elsewhere Classified (Vol. 2)

7539 Automotive electrical service (battery and ignition repair) (Vol. 2)

5013 Automotive engines, new—wholesale (Vol. 2)

2211 Automotive fabrics, cotton (Vol. 1)

2221 Automotive fabrics, manmade fiber (Vol. 1)

3462 Automotive forgings, ferrous: not made in rolling mills (Vol. 1)

3463 Automotive forgings, nonferrous: not made in hot-rolling mills (Vol. 1)

7536 Automotive glass replacement and repair service (Vol. 2)

7536 Automotive Glass Replacement Shops (Vol. 2)

7549 Automotive inspection and diagnostic service (Vol. 2)

7532 Automotive interior shops (Vol. 2)

3647 Automotive lighting fixtures (Vol. 1)

3061 Automotive mechanical rubber goods: molded, extruded, and lathe-cut (Vol. 1)

7533 Automotive mufflers, sale and installation (Vol. 2)

7532 Automotive paint shops (Vol. 2)

5013 Automotive parts, new —wholesale (Vol. 2)

7622 Automotive radio repair shops (Vol. 2)

7538 Automotive repair shops, general (Vol. 2)

7539 Automotive Repair Shops Not Elsewhere Classified (Vol. 2)

7549 Automotive Services Not Elsewhere Classified (Vol. 2)

7539 Automotive springs, rebuilding and repair (Vol. 2)

3465 Automotive Stampings (Vol. 1)

3465 Automotive stampings: e.g., fenders, tops, hub caps, body parts, trim (Vol. 1)

5013 Automotive stampings—wholesale (Vol. 2)

7539 Automotive starter and generator repair (Vol. 2)

5013 Automotive supplies—wholesale (Vol. 2)

7532 Automotive tops (canvas or plastic), installation, repair, or sales and installation (Vol. 2)

7549 Automotive towing service (Vol. 2)

7537 Automotive Transmission Repair Shops (Vol. 2)

7532 Automotive trim shops (Vol. 2)

2396 Automotive Trimmings, Apparel Findings and Related Products (Vol. 1)

7532 Automotive upholstery and trim shops (Vol. 2)

7542 Automotive washing and polishing (Vol. 2)

3714 Automotive wiring harness sets, except ignition (Vol. 1)

5093 Automotive wrecking for scrap—wholesale (Vol. 2)

3931 Autophones (organs with perforated music rolls) (Vol. 1)

3799 Autos, midget: power driven (Vol. 1)

3612 Autotransformers, electric (power transformers) (Vol. 1)

3612 Autotransformers for switchboards, except telephone switchboards (Vol. 1)

3661 Autotransformers for telephone switchboards (Vol. 1)

3572 Auxiliary computer storage units (Vol. 1)

0279 Aviaries (e.g., parakeet, canary, love birds) (Vol. 2)

7997 Aviation clubs, membership (Vol. 2)

8249 Aviation schools, excluding flying instruction (Vol. 2)

0179 Avocado orchards and farms (Vol. 2)

3423 Awls (Vol. 1)

1799 Awning installation-contractors (Vol. 2)

7699 Awning repair shops (Vol. 2)

5999 Awning shops—retail (Vol. 2)

2211 Awning stripes, cotton (Vol. 1)

2394 Awnings, fabric (Vol. 1)

3089 Awnings, fiberglass and plastics combination (Vol. 1)

3444 Awnings, sheet metal (Vol. 1)

5039 Awnings—wholesale (Vol. 2)

2431 Awnings, wood (Vol. 1)

3423 Axes (Vol. 1)

3714 Axle housings and shafts, motor vehicle (Vol. 1)

7539 Axle straightening, automotive (Vol. 2)

3714 Axles, motor vehicle (Vol. 1)

3462 Axles, railroad: forged-not made in rolling mills (Vol. 1)

3312 Axles, rolled or forged: made in steel works or rolling mills (Vol. 1)

2273 Axminster carpets (Vol. 1)

2892 Azides (explosives) (Vol. 1)

2865 Azine dyes (Vol. 1)

2865 Azo dyes (Vol. 1)

2865 Azobenzene (Vol. 1)

2865 Azoic dyes (Vol. 1)

B

3339 Babbitt metal, primary (Vol. 1)

3341 Babbitt metal smelting and refining, secondary (Vol. 1)

5999 Baby carriages—retail (Vol. 2)

2032 Baby foods (including meats), canned (Vol. 1)

2023 Baby formula: fresh, processed, and bottled (Vol. 1)

5137 Baby goods—wholesale (Vol. 2)

3069 Baby pants, vulcanized rubber and rubberized fabric (Vol. 1)

2844 Baby powder (Vol. 1)

3596 Baby scales (Vol. 1)

7299 Babysitting bureaus (Vol. 2)

8811 Babysitting (private households employing babysitters in the home) (Vol. 2)

3531 Backfillers, self-propelled (Vol. 1)

3432 Backflow preventors (Vol. 1)

3531 Backhoes (Vol. 1)

5941 Backpacking, hiking, and mountaineering equipment—retail (Vol. 2)

5947 Balloon shops—retail (Vol. 2)

3069 Balloons, advertising and toy: rubber (Vol. 1)

3721 Balloons (aircraft) (Vol. 1)

3069 Balloons, metal foil laminated with rubber (Vol. 1)

3089 Balloons, plastics (Vol. 1)

7911 Ballroom operation (Vol. 2)

3949 Balls: baseball, basketball, football, golf, tennis, pool, and bowling (Vol. 1)

3069 Balls, rubber: except athletic equipment (Vol. 1)

3399 Balls, steel (Vol. 1)

0831 Balsam needles, gathering of (Vol. 2)

3677 Baluns (Vol. 1)

0179 Banana farms (Vol. 2)

5148 Banana ripening for the trade—wholesale (Vol. 2)

2389 Band uniforms (Vol. 1)

2399 Bandage, cheese (Vol. 1)

2211 Bandage cloths, cotton (Vol. 1)

3842 Bandages and dressings, surgical and orthopedic (Vol. 1)

3842 Bandages: plastics, muslin, and plaster of paris (Vol. 1)

5122 Bandages—wholesale (Vol. 2)

2342 Bandeaux (Vol. 1)

2241 Banding, spindle (Vol. 1)

2399 Bandoleers (Vol. 1)

7929 Bands, dance (Vol. 2)

7929 Bands, Orchestras, Actors and Other Entertainers and Entertainment Groups (Vol. 2)

3089 Bands, plastics (Vol. 1)

3351 Bands, shell: copper and copper alloy-made in copper rolling mills (Vol. 1)

3553 Bandsaws, woodworking (Vol. 1)

3931 Banjos and parts (Vol. 1)

3812 Bank and turn indicators and components (aeronautical instruments) (Vol. 1)

5044 Bank automatic teller machines—wholesale (Vol. 2)

1542 Bank building construction-general contractors (Vol. 2)

6512 Bank buildings, operation of (Vol. 2)

3499 Bank chests, metal (Vol. 1)

6399 Bank deposit insurance (Vol. 2)

3446 Bank fixtures, ornamental metal (Vol. 1)

6712 Bank holding companies (Vol. 2)

6211 Bankers, investment (Vol. 2)

9651 Banking regulatory agencies-government (Vol. 2)

8249 Banking schools (training in banking) (Vol. 2)

2759 Banknotes, engraved (Vol. 1)

6021 Banks, commercial: national (Vol. 2)

6029 Banks, commercial: not chartered (Vol. 2)

6022 Banks, commercial: state (Vol. 2)

6011 Banks, Federal Reserve (Vol. 2)

6111 Banks for cooperatives (Vol. 2)

6035 Banks, savings: Federal (Vol. 2)

6036 Banks, savings: not federally chartered (Vol. 2)

3944 Banks, toy (Vol. 1)

5999 Banner shops—retail (Vol. 2)

2399 Banners, made from fabric (Vol. 1)

3446 Bannisters, railings, guards, etc.: made from metal pipe (Vol. 1)

3281 Baptismal fonts, cut stone (Vol. 1)

8621 Bar associations (Vol. 2)

2542 Bar fixtures, except wood (Vol. 1)

2541 Bar fixtures, wood (Vol. 1)

2599 Bar furniture (Vol. 1)

5021 Bar furniture—wholesale (Vol. 2)

3547 Bar mills (Vol. 1)

2033 Barbecue sauce (Vol. 1)

3631 Barbecues, grills, and braziers for outdoor cooking (Vol. 1)

3315 Barbed and twisted wire: made in wiredrawing plants (Vol. 1)

3496 Barbed wire, made from purchased wire (Vol. 1)

7231 Barber and beauty shops, combined (Vol. 2)

7241 Barber colleges (Vol. 2)

5087 Barber shop equipment and supplies—wholesale (Vol. 2)

3999 Barber shop equipment (Vol. 1)

7241 Barber Shops (Vol. 2)

3999 Barbers' clippers, hand and electric (Vol. 1)

3421 Barbers' scissors (Vol. 1)

2326 Barbers' service apparel, washable (Vol. 1)

2833 Barbituric acid and derivatives: bulk, uncompounded (Vol. 1)

2834 Barbituric acid pharmaceutical preparations (Vol. 1)

3441 Barge sections, prefabricated metal (Vol. 1)

3731 Barges, building and repairing (Vol. 1)

3295 Barite, ground or otherwise treated (Vol. 1)

1479 Barite mining (Vol. 2)

2819 Barium compounds (Vol. 1)

2835 Barium diagnostic agents (Vol. 1)

3295 Barium, ground or otherwise treated (Vol. 1)

1479 Barium ore mining (Vol. 2)

2816 Barium sulfate, precipitated (blanc fixe) (Vol. 1)

2211 Bark cloth, cotton (Vol. 1)

0831 Barks, gathering of (Vol. 2)

0119 Barley farms (Vol. 2)

5153 Barley—wholesale (Vol. 2)

2258 Barmen laces (Vol. 1)

3523 Barn cleaners (Vol. 1)

3523 Barn stanchions and standards (Vol. 1)

3829 Barographs (Vol. 1)

3829 Barometers, mercury and aneroid types (Vol. 1)

3443 Barometric condensers (Vol. 1)

2429 Barrel heading and staves, sawed or split (Vol. 1)

3484 Barrels, gun: 30 mm. (or 1.18 inch) or less (Vol. 1)

3489 Barrels, gun: more than 30 mm. (or more than 1.18 inch) (Vol. 1)

5085 Barrels, new and reconditioned—wholesale (Vol. 2)

3412 Barrels, shipping: steel and other metal (Vol. 1)

2449 Barrels, wood: coopered (Vol. 1)

3499 Barricades, metal (Vol. 1)

5813 Bars (alcoholic beverage drinking places) (Vol. 2)

3354 Bars, aluminum: extruded (Vol. 1)

3355 Bars, aluminum: rolled (Vol. 1)

8641 Bars and restaurants owned and operated for members of organizations only (Vol. 2)

2064   Bars, candy: including chocolate covered bars (Vol. 1)

2066   Bars, candy: solid chocolate (Vol. 1)

3449   Bars, concrete reinforcing: fabricated steel (Vol. 1)

5051   Bars, concrete reinforcing—wholesale (Vol. 2)

3351   Bars, copper and copper alloy (Vol. 1)

3312   Bars, iron: made in steel works or rolling mills (Vol. 1)

3356   Bars: lead, magnesium, nickel, tin, titanium, zinc, and their alloys (Vol. 1)

5051   Bars, metal—wholesale (Vol. 2)

3423   Bars, prying (handtools) (Vol. 1)

3331   Bars, refinery: primary copper (Vol. 1)

3316   Bars, steel: cold-rolled-not made in hot-rolling mills (Vol. 1)

3312   Bars, steel: made in steel works or hot-rolling mills (Vol. 1)

7389   Bartering services for businesses (Vol. 2)

7299   Bartering services for individuals (Vol. 2)

3229   Barware, glass (Vol. 1)

2816   Barytes pigments (Vol. 1)

1429   Basalt, crushed and broken-quarrying (Vol. 2)

1411   Basalt, dimension-quarrying (Vol. 2)

8744   Base maintenance (providing personnel on continuing basis) (Vol. 2)

2353   Baseball caps, except plastics (Vol. 1)

7997   Baseball clubs, except professional and semiprofessional (Vol. 2)

7941   Baseball clubs, professional or semiprofessional (Vol. 2)

3949   Baseball equipment and supplies, except uniforms and footwear (Vol. 1)

7999   Baseball instruction schools (Vol. 2)

2329   Baseball uniforms: men's and boys' (Vol. 1)

2431   Baseboards, floor: wood (Vol. 1)

3442   Baseboards, metal (Vol. 1)

3949   Bases, baseball (Vol. 1)

2844   Bases, perfume: blending and compounding (Vol. 1)

2211   Basket weave fabrics, cotton (Vol. 1)

7941   Basketball clubs, professional or semiprofessional (Vol. 2)

7999   Basketball instruction schools (Vol. 2)

2329   Basketball uniforms: men's and boys' (Vol. 1)

3949   Basketballs and basketball equipment and supplies, except uniforms and footwear (Vol. 1)

2499   Baskets, except fruit, vegetable, fish, and bait: (e.g., rattan, reed, straw) (Vol. 1)

3949   Baskets, fish and bait (Vol. 1)

2449   Baskets, fruit and vegetable: e.g., till, berry, climax, round stave (Vol. 1)

3496   Baskets, made from purchased wire (Vol. 1)

5199   Baskets: reed, rattan, willow, and wood—wholesale (Vol. 2)

3315   Baskets, steel: made in wiredrawing plants (Vol. 1)

3944   Baskets, toy (Vol. 1)

2519   Bassinets, reed and rattan (Vol. 1)

3931   Bassoons (Vol. 1)

1099   Bastnasite ore mining (Vol. 2)

3531   Batching plants, bituminous (Vol. 1)

3531   Batching plants, for aggregate concrete and bulk cement (Vol. 1)

7999   Bath houses, independently operated (Vol. 2)

2392   Bath mitts (washcloths) (Vol. 1)

2844   Bath salts (Vol. 1)

3069   Bath sprays, rubber (Vol. 1)

1799   Bath tub refinishing-contractors (Vol. 2)

7997   Bathing beaches, membership (Vol. 2)

7999   Bathing beaches, public (Vol. 2)

3069   Bathing caps and suits, rubber (Vol. 1)

5699   Bathing suit stores—retail (Vol. 2)

2369   Bathing suits: girls', children's, and infants' (Vol. 1)

2329   Bathing suits: men's and boys' (Vol. 1)

2253   Bathing suits (Vol. 1)

2339   Bathing suits: women's, misses', and juniors' (Vol. 1)

2273   Bathmats and sets, textile (Vol. 1)

2211   Bathmats, cotton: made in weaving mills (Vol. 1)

3069   Bathmats, rubber (Vol. 1)

2273   Bathmats, textile fiber (Vol. 1)

2369   Bathrobes: girls', children's, and infants' (Vol. 1)

2384   Bathrobes, men's, boys', and women's (Vol. 1)

2253   Bathrobes (Vol. 1)

3261   Bathroom accessories, vitreous china and earthenware (Vol. 1)

3431   Bathroom fixtures: enameled iron, cast iron, and pressed metal (Vol. 1)

3088   Bathroom fixtures, plastics (Vol. 1)

3596   Bathroom scales (Vol. 1)

7299   Baths, turkish (Vol. 2)

5047   Baths, whirlpool—wholesale (Vol. 2)

3272   Bathtubs, concrete (Vol. 1)

3431   Bathtubs: enameled iron, cast iron, and pressed metal (Vol. 1)

3088   Bathtubs, plastics (Vol. 1)

3089   Bathware, plastics: except plumbing fixtures (Vol. 1)

7389   Batik work (handprinting on textiles) (Vol. 2)

2211   Batiste, cotton (Vol. 1)

8299   Baton instruction (Vol. 2)

3949   Bats, game: e.g., baseball, softball, cricket (Vol. 1)

5013   Batteries, automotive—wholesale (Vol. 2)

5063   Batteries, except automotive—wholesale (Vol. 2)

3692   Batteries, primary: dry or wet (Vol. 1)

3691   Batteries, rechargeable (Vol. 1)

3691   Batteries, storage (Vol. 1)

2899   Battery acid (Vol. 1)

3069   Battery boxes, jars, and parts: hard rubber (Vol. 1)

3694   Battery cable wiring sets for internal combustion engines (Vol. 1)

3089   Battery cases, plastics (Vol. 1)

3629   Battery chargers, rectifying or nonrotating (Vol. 1)

3694   Battery charging generators for internal combustion engines (Vol. 1)

5531   Battery dealers, automobile—retail (Vol. 2)

3229   Battery jars, glass (Vol. 1)

3356   Battery metal (Vol. 1)

2891   Battery sealing compounds (Vol. 1)

2499   Battery separators, wood (Vol. 1)

7539 Battery service, automotive (Vol. 2)

3825 Battery testers, electrical (Vol. 1)

3272 Battery wells and boxes, concrete (Vol. 1)

2299 Batts and batting: cotton mill waste, kapok, and related materials (Vol. 1)

2679 Batts, insulating: paper (Vol. 1)

3297 Bauxite brick (Vol. 1)

1099 Bauxite mining (Vol. 2)

2819 Bauxite, refined (Vol. 1)

2899 Bay oil (Vol. 1)

2844 Bay rum (Vol. 1)

7999 Beach chairs and accessories, rental (Vol. 2)

7997 Beach clubs, membership (Vol. 2)

4959 Beach maintenance cleaning (Vol. 2)

3021 Beach sandals, rubber (Vol. 1)

3999 Beach umbrellas (Vol. 1)

7999 Beaches, bathing: public (Vol. 2)

3728 Beaching gear, aircraft (Vol. 1)

2369 Beachwear: girls', children's, and infants' (Vol. 1)

5136 Beachwear, men's and boys'—wholesale (Vol. 2)

2253 Beachwear (Vol. 1)

2339 Beachwear: women's, misses', and juniors' (Vol. 1)

3999 Beaded novelties (Vol. 1)

3542 Beaders, metal (machines) (Vol. 1)

3231 Beads, glass reflector: for highway signs and other reflectors (Vol. 1)

3999 Beads, unassembled (Vol. 1)

3552 Beaming machines, textile (Vol. 1)

2282 Beaming yarns for the trade (Vol. 1)

0723 Bean cleaning (Vol. 2)

4221 Bean elevators, except sales (Vol. 2)

0161 Bean farms (bush and pole); Snap (Vol. 2)

0119 Bean farms, dry field and seed (Vol. 2)

0161 Bean farms, except dry beans (Vol. 2)

0161 Bean farms; Green lima (Vol. 2)

2032 Bean sprouts, canned (Vol. 1)

0182 Bean sprouts grown under cover (Vol. 2)

5812 Beaneries (Vol. 2)

2032 Beans, baked: with or without meat-canned (Vol. 1)

5153 Beans, dry: bulk—wholesale (Vol. 2)

5153 Beans, inedible—wholesale (Vol. 2)

5153 Beans, unshelled—wholesale (Vol. 2)

3463 Bearing and bearing race forgings, nonferrous: not made in hot-rolling mills (Vol. 1)

5051 Bearing piles, iron and steel—wholesale (Vol. 2)

3423 Bearing pullers, handtools (Vol. 1)

3562 Bearings, ball and roller (Vol. 1)

3714 Bearings, motor vehicle: except ball and roller (Vol. 1)

3568 Bearings, plain (Vol. 1)

3089 Bearings, plastics (Vol. 1)

5085 Bearings—wholesale (Vol. 2)

2499 Bearings, wood (Vol. 1)

7231 Beauticians (Vol. 2)

7231 Beauty and barber shops, combined (Vol. 2)

7231 Beauty culture schools (Vol. 2)

5087 Beauty parlor equipment and supplies—wholesale (Vol. 2)

3999 Beauty shop equipment (Vol. 1)

7231 Beauty Shops (Vol. 2)

7231 Beauty shops or salons (Vol. 2)

7011 Bed and breakfast inns (Vol. 2)

0711 Bed preparation; Seed (Vol. 2)

2258 Bed sets, lace (Vol. 1)

2211 Bed tickings, cotton (Vol. 1)

3634 Bedcoverings, electric (Vol. 1)

0181 Bedding plants, growing of (Vol. 2)

0181 Bedding plants, growing of; Vegetable (Vol. 2)

5719 Bedding (sheets, blankets, spreads, and pillows)—retail (Vol. 2)

2341 Bedjackets: women's, misses', and juniors' (Vol. 1)

5712 Beds and springs—retail (Vol. 2)

2599 Beds, hospital (Vol. 1)

5047 Beds, hospital—wholesale (Vol. 2)

2514 Beds, including folding and cabinet beds: household-metal (Vol. 1)

2511 Beds, including folding and cabinet beds: household-wood (Vol. 1)

2515 Beds, sleep-system ensembles: flotation and adjustable (Vol. 1)

2515 Beds, sofa and chair: on frames of any material (Vol. 1)

2211 Bedsheeting, cotton (Vol. 1)

2511 Bedside stands, wood (Vol. 1)

2392 Bedspreads and bed sets (Vol. 1)

2211 Bedspreads, cotton: made in weaving mills (Vol. 1)

2258 Bedspreads, lace: made on lace machines (Vol. 1)

2259 Bedspreads (Vol. 1)

2221 Bedspreads, silk and manmade fiber (Vol. 1)

5023 Bedspreads—wholesale (Vol. 2)

2514 Bedspring frames, metal (Vol. 1)

2511 Bedspring frames, wood (Vol. 1)

2515 Bedsprings, assembled (Vol. 1)

5021 Bedsprings—wholesale (Vol. 2)

0279 Bee farms (Vol. 2)

0212 Beef Cattle Except Feedlots (Vol. 2)

0212 Beef cattle farms, except feedlots (Vol. 2)

0211 Beef Cattle Feedlots (Vol. 2)

2013 Beef (Vol. 1)

2011 Beef (Vol. 1)

2013 Beef stew (Vol. 1)

3312 Beehive coke oven products (Vol. 1)

3999 Beekeeping supplies, except wood (Vol. 1)

5191 Beekeeping supplies—wholesale (Vol. 2)

2499 Beekeeping supplies, wood (Vol. 1)

4812 Beeper (radio pager) communications services (Vol. 2)

2082 Beer (alcoholic beverage) (Vol. 1)

5181 Beer and Ale (Vol. 2)

5181 Beer and other fermented malt liquors—wholesale (Vol. 2)

2086 Beer, birch and root: bottled or canned (Vol. 1)

3411 Beer cans, metal (Vol. 1)

3585 Beer dispensing equipment (Vol. 1)

5813 Beer gardens (drinking places) (Vol. 2)

5921 Beer, packaged—retail (Vol. 2)

5813 Beer parlors (tap rooms) (Vol. 2)

7699 Beer pump coil cleaning and repair service (Vol. 2)

5813 Beer taverns (Vol. 2)

3578 Billing machines (Vol. 1)

2298 Binder and baler twine (Vol. 1)

2631 Binders' board (Vol. 1)

2899 Binders (chemical foundry supplies) (Vol. 1)

2782 Binders, looseleaf (Vol. 1)

3579 Binding machines, plastics and adhesive: for store or office use (Vol. 1)

2789 Binding only: books, pamphlets, magazines, etc. (Vol. 1)

5131 Binding, textile—wholesale (Vol. 2)

2396 Bindings, bias (Vol. 1)

2396 Bindings, cap and hat (Vol. 1)

2241 Bindings, textile (Vol. 1)

3944 Bingo boards (games) (Vol. 1)

7999 Bingo parlors (Vol. 2)

3161 Binocular cases (Vol. 1)

7699 Binoculars and other optical goods repair (Vol. 2)

3827 Binoculars (Vol. 1)

5999 Binoculars—retail (Vol. 2)

3443 Bins, prefabricated metal plate (Vol. 1)

3444 Bins, prefabricated: sheet metal (Vol. 1)

8093 Biofeedback centers (Vol. 2)

2836 Biological and allied products: antitoxins, bacterins, vaccines, viruses, except in vitro and in vivo (Vol. 1)

8071 Biological laboratories (not manufacturing) (Vol. 2)

2836 Biological Products Except Diagnostic Substances (Vol. 1)

8731 Biological research, commercial (Vol. 2)

8733 Biological research, noncommercial (Vol. 2)

2865 Biological stains (Vol. 1)

5122 Biologicals and allied products—wholesale (Vol. 2)

3841 Biopsy instruments and equipment (Vol. 1)

2086 Birch beer, bottled or canned (Vol. 1)

3496 Bird cages, made from purchased wire (Vol. 1)

2048 Bird food, prepared (Vol. 1)

7342 Bird proofing (Vol. 2)

2211 Bird's-eye diaper cloth, cotton (Vol. 1)

7299 Birth certificate agencies (Vol. 2)

8093 Birth control clinics (family planning) (Vol. 2)

2771 Birthday cards, except hand painted (Vol. 1)

3556 Biscuit cutters (machines) (Vol. 1)

2041 Biscuit dough, canned (Vol. 1)

2045 Biscuit mixes and doughs (Vol. 1)

2051 Biscuits, baked: baking powder and raised (Vol. 1)

2052 Biscuits, baked: dry, except baking powder and raised (Vol. 1)

3339 Bismuth refining, primary (Vol. 1)

3423 Bits (edge tools for woodworking) (Vol. 1)

3545 Bits for use on lathes, planers, shapers, etc. (Vol. 1)

3532 Bits, rock: except oil and gas field tools (Vol. 1)

3533 Bits, rock: oil and gas field tools (Vol. 1)

2087 Bitters (flavoring concentrates) (Vol. 1)

1499 Bitumens (native) mining (Vol. 2)

3531 Bituminous batching plants (Vol. 1)

1221 Bituminous Coal and Lignite Surface Mining (Vol. 2)

1221 Bituminous coal cleaning plants (Vol. 2)

1221 Bituminous coal crushing (Vol. 2)

1241 Bituminous coal mining services on a contract basis (Vol. 2)

1221 Bituminous coal screening plants (Vol. 2)

1222 Bituminous coal stripping: except on a contract, fee, or other basis (Vol. 2)

1241 Bituminous coal stripping service: on a contract basis (Vol. 2)

1222 Bituminous Coal Underground Mining (Vol. 2)

1221 Bituminous coal washeries (Vol. 2)

1499 Bituminous limestone quarrying (Vol. 2)

1241 Bituminous or lignite auger mining service: on a contract basis (Vol. 2)

2851 Bituminous paints (Vol. 1)

5082 Bituminous processing equipment—wholesale (Vol. 2)

1499 Bituminous sandstone quarrying (Vol. 2)

2816 Black pigments, except carbon black (Vol. 1)

5051 Black plate, iron and steel—wholesale (Vol. 2)

0171 Blackberry farms (Vol. 2)

3281 Blackboards, slate (Vol. 1)

2531 Blackboards, wood (Vol. 1)

2842 Blackings (Vol. 1)

3312 Blackplate (Vol. 1)

7699 Blacksmith shops (Vol. 2)

3199 Blacksmiths' aprons, leather (Vol. 1)

2061 Blackstrap molasses (Vol. 1)

1771 Blacktop work: private driveways and private parking areas-contractors (Vol. 2)

3728 Blades, aircraft propeller: metal or wood (Vol. 1)

3531 Blades for graders, scrapers, dozers, and snowplows (Vol. 1)

3421 Blades, knife and razor (Vol. 1)

3425 Blades, saw: for hand or power saws (Vol. 1)

2816 Blanc fixe (barium sulfate, precipitated) (Vol. 1)

3482 Blank cartridges, 30 mm. (or 1.18 inch) or less (Vol. 1)

2782 Blankbook making (Vol. 1)

2782 Blankbooks, Looseleaf Binders and Devices (Vol. 1)

5112 Blankbooks—wholesale (Vol. 2)

2392 Blanket bags, plastic (Vol. 1)

2221 Blanketings, manmade fiber (Vol. 1)

2211 Blankets and blanketings, cotton (Vol. 1)

2231 Blankets and blanketings, wool and similar animal fibers (Vol. 1)

3292 Blankets, asbestos (Vol. 1)

3634 Blankets, electric (Vol. 1)

2399 Blankets, horse (Vol. 1)

3292 Blankets, insulating for aircraft: asbestos (Vol. 1)

2679 Blankets, insulating: paper (Vol. 1)

2392 Blankets (Vol. 1)

3069 Blankets, printers': rubber (Vol. 1)

5023 Blankets—wholesale (Vol. 2)

3965 Blanks, button (Vol. 1)

3545 Blanks, cutting tool (Vol. 1)

3229 Blanks for electric light bulbs, glass (Vol. 1)

3545 Blanks, tips and inserts: cutting tools (Vol. 1)

5084 Blanks, tips and inserts—wholesale (Vol. 2)

2426 Blanks, wood: for bowling pins, handles, and textile machinery accessories (Vol. 1)

3569 Blast cleaning equipment, dustless: except metalworking (Vol. 1)

3312 Blast furnace products (Vol. 1)

3295 Blast furnace slag (Vol. 1)

1446 Blast sand mining (Vol. 2)

1629 Blasting, except building demolition-contractors (Vol. 2)

2298 Blasting mats, rope (Vol. 1)

2892 Blasting powder and blasting caps (Vol. 1)

2819 Bleach (calcium hypochlorite), industrial (Vol. 1)

2819 Bleach (sodium hypochlorite), industrial (Vol. 1)

2531 Bleacher seating, portable (Vol. 1)

2844 Bleaches, hair (Vol. 1)

2842 Bleaches, household: liquid or dry (Vol. 1)

2819 Bleaches, industrial (Vol. 1)

3999 Bleaching and dyeing of sponges (Vol. 1)

2261 Bleaching cotton broadwoven fabrics (Vol. 1)

2261 Bleaching, kier: continuous machine (Vol. 1)

3552 Bleaching machinery, textile (Vol. 1)

2262 Bleaching manmade fiber and silk broadwoven fabrics (Vol. 1)

2819 Bleaching powder, industrial (Vol. 1)

2269 Bleaching raw stock, yarn, and narrow fabrics: except knit and wool (Vol. 1)

2231 Bleaching yarn and fabrics, wool and similar animal fibers: except knit (Vol. 1)

3825 Bleed control cabinets (engine testers) (Vol. 1)

1031 Blende (zinc) mining (Vol. 2)

2045 Blended flour (Vol. 1)

3634 Blenders, electric (Vol. 1)

2844 Blending and compounding perfume bases (Vol. 1)

2099 Blending tea (Vol. 1)

3721 Blimps (Vol. 1)

2431 Blinds (shutters), wood (Vol. 1)

2591 Blinds, venetian (Vol. 1)

2591 Blinds, vertical (Vol. 1)

3331 Blister copper (Vol. 1)

3089 Blister packaging, plastics (Vol. 1)

2097 Block ice (Vol. 1)

5032 Blocks, building—wholesale (Vol. 2)

3271 Blocks, concrete and cinder (Vol. 1)

3331 Blocks, copper (Vol. 1)

3555 Blocks, engravers': wood (Vol. 1)

3255 Blocks, fire clay (Vol. 1)

3229 Blocks, glass (Vol. 1)

3999 Blocks, hat (Vol. 1)

3339 Blocks, lead: primary (Vol. 1)

3281 Blocks, paving: cut stone (Vol. 1)

3299 Blocks, sand lime (Vol. 1)

3259 Blocks, segment: clay (Vol. 1)

3599 Blocks, swage (Vol. 1)

3429 Blocks, tackle: metal (Vol. 1)

2499 Blocks, tackle: wood (Vol. 1)

2499 Blocks, tailors' pressing: wood (Vol. 1)

3944 Blocks, toy (Vol. 1)

2426 Blocks, wood: for bowling pins, handles, and textile machinery accessories (Vol. 1)

3339 Blocks, zinc, primary (Vol. 1)

8071 Blood analysis laboratories (Vol. 2)

8099 Blood banks (Vol. 2)

2835 Blood derivative diagnostic reagents (Vol. 1)

2836 Blood derivatives, for human or veterinary use, except in vitro and in vivo (Vol. 1)

8099 Blood donor stations (Vol. 2)

2011 Blood meal (Vol. 1)

5122 Blood plasma—wholesale (Vol. 2)

3841 Blood pressure apparatus (Vol. 1)

7299 Blood pressure testing, coin-operated (Vol. 2)

3821 Blood testing apparatus, laboratory (Vol. 1)

3841 Blood transfusion equipment (Vol. 1)

3547 Blooming and slabbing mills (Vol. 1)

3312 Blooms (Vol. 1)

2621 Blotting paper (Vol. 1)

5632 Blouse stores—retail (Vol. 2)

2321 Blouses, boys' (Vol. 1)

2361 Blouses: girls', children's, and infants' (Vol. 1)

2253 Blouses (Vol. 1)

5137 Blouses—wholesale (Vol. 2)

2331 Blouses: women's, misses', and juniors' (Vol. 1)

3423 Blow torches (Vol. 1)

3564 Blower filter units (furnace blowers) (Vol. 1)

3523 Blowers and cutters, ensilage (Vol. 1)

3564 Blowers, commercial and industrial (Vol. 1)

3523 Blowers, forage (Vol. 1)

3931 Blowers, pipe organ (Vol. 1)

3634 Blowers, portable: electric (Vol. 1)

3524 Blowers, residential lawn (Vol. 1)

2035 Blue cheese dressing (Vol. 1)

4925 Blue gas, carbureted: production and distribution (Vol. 2)

0171 Blueberry farms (Vol. 2)

0912 Bluefish, catching of (Vol. 2)

3861 Blueprint cloth or paper, sensitized (Vol. 1)

3861 Blueprint reproduction machines and equipment (Vol. 1)

5044 Blueprinting equipment—wholesale (Vol. 2)

7334 Blueprinting service (Vol. 2)

1411 Bluestone, dimension-quarrying (Vol. 2)

2899 Bluing (Vol. 1)

3296 Board, acoustical: mineral wool (Vol. 1)

2952 Board, asphalt saturated (Vol. 1)

2493 Board, bagasse (Vol. 1)

2675 Board, chip: pasted (Vol. 1)

3275 Board, gypsum (Vol. 1)

2493 Board, particle (Vol. 1)

0752 Boarding horses (Vol. 2)

7021 Boarding houses, except organization (Vol. 2)

7041 Boarding houses, fraternity and sorority (Vol. 2)

7041 Boarding houses operated by organizations for members only (Vol. 2)

0752 Boarding kennels (Vol. 2)

8211 Boarding schools (Vol. 2)

2499 Boards, bulletin: wood and cork (Vol. 1)

2499 Boards: clip, ironing, meat, and pastry-wood (Vol. 1)

3952 Boards, drawing: artists' (Vol. 1)

9121 Boards of supervisors (Vol. 2)

8611 Boards of trade, other than security and commodity exchanges (Vol. 2)

5942 Book stores selling new books and magazines—retail (Vol. 2)

3251 Book tile, clay (Vol. 1)

3111 Bookbinders' leather (Vol. 1)

3555 Bookbinders' machines (Vol. 1)

2789 Bookbinding and Related Work (Vol. 1)

2789 Bookbinding: edition, job, library, and trade (Vol. 1)

2514 Bookcases, household: metal (Vol. 1)

2511 Bookcases, household: wood (Vol. 1)

2522 Bookcases, office: except wood (Vol. 1)

2521 Bookcases, office: wood (Vol. 1)

7999 Bookies (Vol. 2)

7829 Booking agencies, motion picture (Vol. 2)

7922 Booking agencies, theatrical: except motion picture (Vol. 2)

8721 Bookkeeping and billing service (Vol. 2)

3578 Bookkeeping machines (Vol. 1)

7999 Bookmakers, race (Vol. 2)

5961 Books, mail-order—retail (Vol. 2)

2678 Books, memorandum: except printed (Vol. 1)

2732 Books, music: printing or printing and binding, not publishing (Vol. 1)

2731 Books, music: publishing and printing, or publishing only (Vol. 1)

5192 Books, Periodicals and Newspapers (Vol. 2)

2732 Books: printing or printing and binding, not publishing (Vol. 1)

2731 Books: publishing and printing, or publishing only (Vol. 1)

2731 Books—Publishing, or Publishing and Printing (Vol. 1)

5192 Books—wholesale (Vol. 2)

3949 Boomerangs (Vol. 1)

8641 Booster clubs (Vol. 2)

3483 Boosters and bursters (Vol. 1)

3612 Boosters, feeder voltage (electric transformers) (Vol. 1)

3131 Boot and Shoe Cut Stock and Findings (Vol. 1)

3131 Boot and shoe cut stock and findings (Vol. 1)

5087 Boot and shoe cut stock and findings—wholesale (Vol. 2)

2499 Boot and shoe lasts, regardless of material (Vol. 1)

3559 Boot making and repairing machinery (Vol. 1)

7251 Bootblack parlors (Vol. 2)

3444 Booths, spray: prefabricated sheet metal (Vol. 1)

2542 Booths, telephone: except wood (Vol. 1)

2541 Booths, telephone: wood (Vol. 1)

3143 Boots, dress and casual: men's (Vol. 1)

3199 Boots, horse (Vol. 1)

3021 Boots, plastics (Vol. 1)

3021 Boots, rubber or rubber soled fabric (Vol. 1)

3144 Boots: women's canvas and leather-except athletic (Vol. 1)

1474 Borate compounds mining (Vol. 2)

1474 Borax, crude: ground and pulverized (Vol. 2)

1474 Borax mining (Vol. 2)

2819 Borax (sodium tetraborate) (Vol. 1)

2879 Bordeaux mixture (Vol. 1)

3827 Borescopes (Vol. 1)

2819 Boric acid (Vol. 1)

3541 Boring, drilling, and milling machine combinations (Vol. 1)

1799 Boring for building construction-contractors (Vol. 2)

3545 Boring machine attachments (machine tool accessories) (Vol. 1)

3541 Boring machine tools, metalworking (Vol. 1)

3541 Boring mills (Vol. 1)

1081 Boring test holes for metal mining: on a contract basis (Vol. 2)

1481 Boring test holes for nonmetallic minerals, except fuels: on a contract basis (Vol. 2)

3291 Boron carbide abrasives (Vol. 1)

2819 Boron compounds, not produced at mines (Vol. 1)

1474 Boron mineral mining (Vol. 2)

2819 Borosilicate (Vol. 1)

3291 Bort, crushing (Vol. 1)

5085 Bort—wholesale (Vol. 2)

2834 Botanical extracts: powdered, pilular, solid, and fluid, except diagnostics (Vol. 1)

8422 Botanical gardens (Vol. 2)

2833 Botanical products, medicinal: ground, graded, and milled (Vol. 1)

2631 Bottle cap board (Vol. 1)

2675 Bottle caps and tops, die-cut from purchased paper or paperboard (Vol. 1)

3466 Bottle caps and tops, stamped metal (Vol. 1)

3089 Bottle caps, molded plastics (Vol. 1)

5813 Bottle clubs (drinking places) (Vol. 2)

2499 Bottle corks (Vol. 1)

2499 Bottle covers: willow, rattan, and reed (Vol. 1)

7389 Bottle exchanges (Vol. 2)

3496 Bottle openers, made from purchased wire (Vol. 1)

3469 Bottle openers, stamped metal (Vol. 1)

3634 Bottle warmers, household: electric (Vol. 1)

3089 Bottle warmers, plastics (Vol. 1)

2086 Bottled and Canned Soft Drinks and Carbonated Waters (Vol. 1)

5984 Bottled gas—retail (Vol. 2)

5085 Bottlers' supplies: caps, bottles, etc.—wholesale (Vol. 2)

3221 Bottles for packing, bottling, and canning: glass (Vol. 1)

5085 Bottles, glass or plastics—wholesale (Vol. 2)

2655 Bottles, paper fiber (Vol. 1)

3085 Bottles, plastics (Vol. 1)

3069 Bottles, rubber (Vol. 1)

3429 Bottles, vacuum (Vol. 1)

5093 Bottles, waste—wholesale (Vol. 2)

3565 Bottling machinery: washing, sterilizing, filling, capping, and labeling (Vol. 1)

5149 Bottling mineral or spring water—wholesale (Vol. 2)

5182 Bottling wines and liquors—wholesale (Vol. 2)

3645 Boudoir lamps (Vol. 1)

2099 Bouillon cubes (Vol. 1)

1429 Boulder, crushed and broken-quarrying (Vol. 2)

2999 Boulets (fuel bricks), made with petroleum binder (Vol. 1)

3999 Boutiquing: for the trade (decorating gift items) (Vol. 1)
2323 Bow ties: men's and boys' (Vol. 1)
3089 Bowl covers, plastics (Vol. 1)
1799 Bowling alley installation and service-contractors (Vol. 2)
3949 Bowling alleys and accessories (Vol. 1)
2599 Bowling center furniture (Vol. 1)
7933 Bowling Centers (Vol. 2)
5941 Bowling equipment and supplies—retail (Vol. 2)
5091 Bowling equipment—wholesale (Vol. 2)
7999 Bowling instruction (Vol. 2)
7997 Bowling leagues or teams, except professional and semiprofessional (Vol. 2)
2426 Bowling pin blanks (Vol. 1)
3949 Bowling pin machines, automatic (Vol. 1)
3949 Bowling pins (Vol. 1)
7699 Bowling pins, refinishing or repair (Vol. 2)
3229 Bowls, glass (Vol. 1)
2499 Bowls, wood: turned and shaped (Vol. 1)
3949 Bows, archery (Vol. 1)
3131 Bows, shoe (Vol. 1)
2441 Box cleats, wood (Vol. 1)
2421 Box lumber (Vol. 1)
5812 Box lunch stands (Vol. 2)
2099 Box lunches for sale off premises (Vol. 1)
3554 Box making machines for paper boxes (Vol. 1)
3553 Box making machines for wooden boxes (Vol. 1)
2441 Box shook (Vol. 1)
5085 Box shooks—wholesale (Vol. 2)
2515 Box springs, assembled (Vol. 1)
3131 Box toes, leather (shoe cut stock) (Vol. 1)
2631 Boxboard (Vol. 1)
2011 Boxed beef (Vol. 1)
3499 Boxes, ammunition: metal (Vol. 1)
5063 Boxes and fittings, electrical—wholesale (Vol. 2)
3443 Boxes, annealing (Vol. 1)
3469 Boxes, cash and stamp: stamped metal (Vol. 1)
2441 Boxes, cigar: wood and part wood (Vol. 1)
3443 Boxes, condenser: metal plate (Vol. 1)
2653 Boxes, corrugated and solid fiber (Vol. 1)
5085 Boxes, crates, etc., other than paper—wholesale (Vol. 2)
3644 Boxes, electric wiring: junction, outlet, switch, and fuse (Vol. 1)
2657 Boxes, folding paperboard (Vol. 1)
3499 Boxes for packing and shipping, metal (Vol. 1)
3069 Boxes, hard rubber (Vol. 1)
3161 Boxes, hat: except paper or paperboard (Vol. 1)
3199 Boxes, leather (Vol. 1)
2652 Boxes, newsboard: metal edged (Vol. 1)
5113 Boxes, paperboard and disposable plastics—wholesale (Vol. 2)
3089 Boxes, plastics (Vol. 1)
2652 Boxes, setup paperboard (Vol. 1)
3952 Boxes, sketching and paint (Vol. 1)
2655 Boxes, vulcanized fiber (Vol. 1)
5093 Boxes, waste—wholesale (Vol. 2)
2441 Boxes, wood: plain or fabric covered, nailed or lock corner (Vol. 1)

2449 Boxes, wood: wirebound (Vol. 1)
3949 Boxing equipment (Vol. 1)
7032 Boys' camps (Vol. 2)
2252 Boys' hosiery (Vol. 1)
8361 Boys' towns (Vol. 2)
2341 Bra-slips: women's and misses' (Vol. 1)
3842 Braces, elastic (Vol. 1)
3842 Braces, orthopedic (Vol. 1)
0721 Bracing of orchard trees and vines (Vol. 2)
0721 Bracing, spraying, removal, and surgery; Trees, orchard: planting, pruning, (Vol. 2)
3299 Brackets, architectural: plaster-factory production only (Vol. 1)
3429 Brackets, iron and steel (Vol. 1)
2431 Brackets, wood (Vol. 1)
3399 Brads, nonferrous metal (including wire) (Vol. 1)
3315 Brads, steel: wire or cut (Vol. 1)
5072 Brads—wholesale (Vol. 2)
2269 Braided goods, except wool: bleaching, dyeing, printing, and other finishing (Vol. 1)
3552 Braiding machines, textile (Vol. 1)
3999 Braids, puffs, switches, wigs, etc.-made of hair or other fiber (Vol. 1)
2241 Braids, textile (Vol. 1)
2241 Braids, tubular nylon and plastics (Vol. 1)
3569 Brake burnishing and washing machines (Vol. 1)
3714 Brake drums (Vol. 1)
2992 Brake fluid, hydraulic (Vol. 1)
3292 Brake lining, asbestos (Vol. 1)
3069 Brake lining, rubber (Vol. 1)
7539 Brake linings, sale and installation (Vol. 2)
3292 Brake pads, asbestos (Vol. 1)
7539 Brake repairing, automotive (Vol. 2)
3321 Brake shoes, railroad: cast iron (Vol. 1)
3728 Brakes, aircraft (Vol. 1)
3714 Brakes and brake parts, motor vehicle (Vol. 1)
3751 Brakes, bicycle: friction clutch and other (Vol. 1)
3625 Brakes, electromagnetic (Vol. 1)
3542 Brakes, metal forming (Vol. 1)
3743 Brakes, railway: air and vacuum (Vol. 1)
2041 Bran and middlings, except rice (Vol. 1)
2044 Bran, rice (Vol. 1)
6081 Branches and Agencies of Foreign Banks (Vol. 2)
6081 Branches of foreign banks (Vol. 2)
3953 Branding irons, for marking purposes (Vol. 1)
5182 Brandy and brandy spirits—wholesale (Vol. 2)
2084 Brandy (Vol. 1)
2084 Brandy spirits (Vol. 1)
3364 Brass die castings (Vol. 1)
3366 Brass foundries (Vol. 1)
3432 Brass goods, plumbers' (Vol. 1)
5074 Brass goods, plumbers'—wholesale (Vol. 2)
3351 Brass rolling and drawing (Vol. 1)
3341 Brass smelting and refining, secondary (Vol. 1)
2342 Brassieres, Girdles and Allied Garments (Vol. 1)
2342 Brassieres (Vol. 1)
3446 Brasswork, ornamental: structural (Vol. 1)
3631 Braziers, barbecue (Vol. 1)
2861 Brazilwood extract (Vol. 1)

2899 Brazing fluxes (Vol. 1)

3398 Brazing (hardening) metal for the trade (Vol. 1)

7692 Brazing (welding) (Vol. 2)

2045 Bread and bread-type roll mixes (Vol. 1)

2041 Bread and bread-type roll mixes (Vol. 1)

2051 Bread and Other Bakery Products Except Cookies and Crackers (Vol. 1)

2051 Bread, brown: Boston and other-canned (Vol. 1)

2099 Bread crumbs, not made in bakeries (Vol. 1)

5142 Bread, frozen: packaged—wholesale (Vol. 2)

2051 Bread, including frozen (Vol. 1)

3556 Bread slicing machines (Vol. 1)

2754 Bread wrappers: gravure printing (Vol. 1)

2752 Bread wrappers, lithographed (Vol. 1)

2759 Bread wrappers, printed: except lithographed or gravure (Vol. 1)

2671 Bread wrappers, waxed or laminated (Vol. 1)

3565 Bread wrapping machines (Vol. 1)

3694 Breaker point sets, internal combustion engine (Vol. 1)

1231 Breakers, anthracite (Vol. 2)

3532 Breakers, coal (Vol. 1)

3531 Breakers, paving (Vol. 1)

3432 Breakers, vacuum: plumbing (Vol. 1)

2064 Breakfast bars (Vol. 1)

5149 Breakfast cereals—wholesale (Vol. 2)

2043 Breakfast foods, cereal (Vol. 1)

2514 Breakfast sets (furniture), metal (Vol. 1)

2511 Breakfast sets (furniture), wood (Vol. 1)

1629 Breakwater construction-general contractors (Vol. 2)

2399 Breast aprons (harness) (Vol. 1)

3443 Breechings, metal plate (Vol. 1)

0279 Breeding and raising own stock; Kennels, (Vol. 2)

0752 Breeding of animals, other than cattle, hogs, sheep, goats, and poultry (Vol. 2)

0751 Breeding of livestock (Vol. 2)

0751 Breeding services; Livestock (Vol. 2)

2082 Breweries (Vol. 1)

3556 Brewers' and maltsers' machinery (Vol. 1)

2082 Brewers' grain (Vol. 1)

2861 Brewers' pitch, product of softwood distillation (Vol. 1)

3999 Bric-a-brac (Vol. 1)

3291 Brick, abrasive (Vol. 1)

3259 Brick, adobe (Vol. 1)

3251 Brick and Structural Clay Tile (Vol. 1)

5211 Brick and tile dealers—retail (Vol. 2)

3297 Brick, bauxite (Vol. 1)

3297 Brick, carbon (Vol. 1)

3255 Brick, clay refractory: fire clay and high alumina (Vol. 1)

3251 Brick: common, face, glazed, vitrified, and hollow-clay (Vol. 1)

3271 Brick, concrete (Vol. 1)

5032 Brick, except refractory—wholesale (Vol. 2)

3229 Brick, glass (Vol. 1)

3255 Brick, ladle: clay (Vol. 1)

3559 Brick making machines (Vol. 1)

3297 Brick, refractory: chrome, magnesite, silica, and other nonclay (Vol. 1)

3299 Brick, sand lime (Vol. 1)

2952 Brick siding, asphalt (Vol. 1)

3297 Brick, silicon carbide (Vol. 1)

5032 Brick, Stone and Related Construction Materials (Vol. 2)

1741 Bricklaying-contractors (Vol. 2)

2335 Bridal dresses or gowns: women's, misses', and juniors' (Vol. 1)

5621 Bridal shops, except custom—retail (Vol. 2)

2396 Bridal veils (Vol. 1)

3569 Bridge and gate machinery, hydraulic (Vol. 1)

7997 Bridge clubs, membership (Vol. 2)

7999 Bridge clubs, nonmembership (Vol. 2)

1622 Bridge construction-general contractors (Vol. 2)

7999 Bridge instruction (Vol. 2)

1721 Bridge painting-contractors (Vol. 2)

3441 Bridge sections, highway: prefabricated metal (Vol. 1)

2392 Bridge sets (cloths and napkins) (Vol. 1)

2514 Bridge sets (furniture), metal (Vol. 1)

2511 Bridge sets (furniture), wood (Vol. 1)

1622 Bridge, Tunnel and Elevated Highway Construction (Vol. 2)

2491 Bridges and trestles, wood: treated (Vol. 1)

3949 Bridges, billiard and pool (Vol. 1)

3825 Bridges, electrical: e.g., Kelvin, Wheatstone, vacuum tube, and megohm (Vol. 1)

4785 Bridges, highway: operation of (Vol. 2)

3931 Bridges, piano (Vol. 1)

3111 Bridle leather (Vol. 1)

1629 Bridle path construction-general contractors (Vol. 2)

3161 Briefcases, regardless of material (Vol. 1)

2322 Briefs, underwear: men's and boys' (Vol. 1)

2254 Briefs, underwear (Vol. 1)

2341 Briefs: women's, misses', children's, and infants' (Vol. 1)

1479 Brimstone mining (Vol. 2)

2819 Brine (Vol. 1)

2035 Brining of fruits and vegetables (Vol. 1)

2999 Briquettes (fuel bricks): made with petroleum binder (Vol. 1)

2499 Briquettes, sawdust or bagasse: nonpetroleum binder (Vol. 1)

3999 Bristles, dressing of (Vol. 1)

5159 Bristles—wholesale (Vol. 2)

2631 Bristols, bogus (Vol. 1)

2621 Bristols, except bogus (Vol. 1)

3356 Britannia metal, rolling and drawing (Vol. 1)

3843 Broaches, dental (Vol. 1)

3545 Broaches (machine tool accessories) (Vol. 1)

5084 Broaches—wholesale (Vol. 2)

3541 Broaching machines (Vol. 1)

3663 Broadcast equipment (including studio), radio and television (Vol. 1)

4832 Broadcasting stations, radio (Vol. 2)

4833 Broadcasting stations, television (Vol. 2)

2211 Broadcloth, cotton (Vol. 1)

2211 Broadwoven Fabric Mills—Cotton (Vol. 1)

2221 Broadwoven Fabric Mills—Manmade Fiber and Silk (Vol. 1)

2231 Broadwoven Fabric Mills—Wool Including Dyeing and Finishing (Vol. 1)

2211 Broadwoven fabrics, cotton (Vol. 1)

2299 Broadwoven fabrics: linen, jute, hemp, and ramie (Vol. 1)

2221 Broadwoven fabrics, silk and manmade fiber (Vol. 1)

5131 Broadwoven fabrics—wholesale (Vol. 2)

2211 Brocade, cotton (Vol. 1)

2211 Brocatelle, cotton (Vol. 1)

0161 Broccoli farms (Vol. 2)

0251 Broiler chickens, raising of (Vol. 2)

0251 Broiler, Fryer and Roaster Chickens (Vol. 2)

3634 Broilers, electric (Vol. 1)

7389 Brokers, business (buying and selling business enterprises) (Vol. 2)

6221 Brokers, commodity contract (Vol. 2)

4731 Brokers, custom house (Vol. 2)

6163 Brokers, farm or business loan (Vol. 2)

6411 Brokers, insurance (Vol. 2)

6531 Brokers of manufactured homes, on site (Vol. 2)

6531 Brokers, real estate (Vol. 2)

6211 Brokers, security (Vol. 2)

4731 Brokers, shipping (Vol. 2)

4731 Brokers, transportation (Vol. 2)

2819 Bromine, elemental (Vol. 1)

2869 Bromochloromethane (Vol. 1)

3845 Bronchoscopes, electromedical (Vol. 1)

3841 Bronchoscopes, except electromedical (Vol. 1)

3952 Bronze, artists': mixtures, powders, paints, etc. (Vol. 1)

3364 Bronze die castings (Vol. 1)

3366 Bronze foundries (Vol. 1)

2893 Bronze ink (Vol. 1)

3351 Bronze rolling and drawing (Vol. 1)

3341 Bronze smelting and refining, secondary (Vol. 1)

3555 Bronzing and dusting machines for the printing trade (Vol. 1)

7389 Bronzing baby shoes (Vol. 2)

2789 Bronzing books, cards, or paper (Vol. 1)

3523 Brooders (Vol. 1)

3559 Broom making machinery (Vol. 1)

5199 Broom, mop, and paint handles—wholesale (Vol. 2)

0139 Broomcorn farms (Vol. 2)

5159 Broomcorn—wholesale (Vol. 2)

3991 Brooms and Brushes (Vol. 1)

3991 Brooms, hand and machine: bamboo, wire, fiber, splint, or other material (Vol. 1)

3711 Brooms, powered (motor vehicles) (Vol. 1)

5719 Brooms—retail (Vol. 2)

2032 Broth, except seafood: canned (Vol. 1)

2051 Brown bread, Boston and other: canned (Vol. 1)

1221 Brown coal mining (Vol. 2)

1011 Brown ore mining (Vol. 2)

3861 Brownprint paper and cloth, sensitized (Vol. 1)

3861 Brownprint reproduction machines and equipment (Vol. 1)

5044 Brownprinting equipment—wholesale (Vol. 2)

2833 Brucine and derivatives (Vol. 1)

1459 Brucite mining (Vol. 2)

3624 Brush blocks, carbon or molded graphite (Vol. 1)

2426 Brush blocks, wood: turned and shaped (Vol. 1)

1629 Brush clearing or cutting-contractors (Vol. 2)

3089 Brush handles, plastics (Vol. 1)

3952 Brushes, air: artists' (Vol. 1)

3624 Brushes and brush stock contacts: carbon and graphite-electric (Vol. 1)

3991 Brushes for vacuum cleaners, carpet sweepers, and other rotary machines (Vol. 1)

5963 Brushes, house-to-house or party plan selling—retail (Vol. 2)

3991 Brushes, household and industrial (Vol. 1)

5719 Brushes—retail (Vol. 2)

3069 Brushes, rubber (Vol. 1)

3541 Brushing machines (metalworking machinery) (Vol. 1)

3089 Bubble formed packaging, plastics (Vol. 1)

3443 Bubble towers (Vol. 1)

3432 Bubblers, drinking fountain (Vol. 1)

3531 Bucket and scarifier teeth (Vol. 1)

3535 Bucket type conveyor systems for general industrial use (Vol. 1)

3535 Buckets, elevator or conveyor for general industrial use (Vol. 1)

3531 Buckets, excavating: e.g., clamshell, concrete, dragline, drag scraper, shovel (Vol. 1)

3949 Buckets, fish and bait (Vol. 1)

3089 Buckets, plastics (Vol. 1)

2449 Buckets, wood: coopered (Vol. 1)

3965 Buckle blanks and molds (Vol. 1)

3965 Buckles and buckle parts, except shoe buckles (Vol. 1)

3131 Buckles, shoe (Vol. 1)

2211 Buckram (Vol. 1)

2295 Buckram: varnished, waxed, and impregnated (Vol. 1)

0119 Buckwheat farms (Vol. 2)

2041 Buckwheat flour (Vol. 1)

9311 Budget agencies-government (Vol. 2)

5812 Buffets (eating places) (Vol. 2)

2511 Buffets (furniture) (Vol. 1)

3541 Buffing and polishing machines (machine tools) (Vol. 1)

3291 Buffing and polishing wheels, abrasive and nonabrasive (Vol. 1)

3471 Buffing, for the trade (Vol. 1)

3546 Buffing machines, hand: electric (Vol. 1)

3111 Buffings, russet (Vol. 1)

3931 Bugles and parts (musical instruments) (Vol. 1)

3429 Builders' hardware, including locks and lock sets (Vol. 1)

5251 Builders' hardware—retail (Vol. 2)

5072 Builders' hardware—wholesale (Vol. 2)

1531 Builders, operative: on own account (Vol. 2)

1531 Builders, speculative (Vol. 2)

7922 Burlesque companies (Vol. 2)

1459 Burley mining (Vol. 2)

2231 Burling and mending wool cloth for the trade (Vol. 1)

2411 Burls, wood (Vol. 1)

5074 Burners, fuel oil and distillate oil—wholesale (Vol. 2)

3433 Burners, gas: domestic (Vol. 1)

3433 Burners, oil: domestic and industrial (Vol. 1)

3398 Burning metal for the trade (Vol. 1)

3952 Burnishers and cushions, gilders' (Vol. 1)

3569 Burnishing and washing machines, brake (Vol. 1)

2842 Burnishing ink (Vol. 1)

3541 Burnishing machines (machine tools) (Vol. 1)

3199 Burnt leather goods for the trade (Vol. 1)

2087 Burnt sugar (food color) (Vol. 1)

3999 Burnt wood articles (Vol. 1)

0272 Burro farms (Vol. 2)

1499 Burrstone quarrying (Vol. 2)

3843 Burs, dental (Vol. 1)

3613 Bus bar structures (Vol. 1)

5063 Bus bars and trolley ducts—wholesale (Vol. 2)

3643 Bus bars (electrical conductors) (Vol. 1)

3713 Bus bodies, motor vehicle (Vol. 1)

7319 Bus card advertising (Vol. 2)

4142 Bus Charter Service Except Local (Vol. 2)

4141 Bus charter service, local (Vol. 2)

4111 Bus line operation, local (Vol. 2)

4131 Bus lines, intercity (Vol. 2)

4173 Bus terminal operation (Vol. 2)

4729 Bus ticket offices, not operated by transportation companies (Vol. 2)

3715 Bus trailers, tractor type (Vol. 1)

3462 Bus, truck and trailer forgings, ferrous: not made in rolling mills (Vol. 1)

7542 Bus washing (Vol. 2)

3711 Buses, motor: except trackless trolley (Vol. 1)

4151 Buses, school: operation of (Vol. 2)

4119 Buses, sightseeing: operation of (Vol. 2)

3743 Buses, trackless trolley (Vol. 1)

5012 Buses—wholesale (Vol. 2)

3423 Bush hooks (Vol. 1)

3366 Bushings and bearings, except die-castings: brass, bronze, and copper (Vol. 1)

3325 Bushings, cast steel: except investment (Vol. 1)

3069 Bushings, rubber (Vol. 1)

2499 Bushings, wood (Vol. 1)

8244 Business and Secretarial Schools (Vol. 2)

8611 Business Associations (Vol. 2)

8611 Business associations, other than civic and social (Vol. 2)

7389 Business brokers (buying and selling business enterprises) (Vol. 2)

8244 Business colleges and schools, not of college grade (Vol. 2)

8748 Business Consulting Services Not Elsewhere Classified (Vol. 2)

6153 Business credit institutions, short-term (Vol. 2)

8732 Business economists, commercial (Vol. 2)

2754 Business forms, except manifold: gravure printing (Vol. 1)

2752 Business forms, except manifold: lithographed (Vol. 1)

2759 Business forms, except manifold, lithographed or gravure printed (Vol. 1)

2761 Business forms, manifold (Vol. 1)

5112 Business forms—wholesale (Vol. 2)

7629 Business machine repair, electrical (Vol. 2)

8741 Business management services (Vol. 2)

8732 Business research, commercial (Vol. 2)

2741 Business service newsletters: publishing and printing, or publishing only (Vol. 1)

7389 Business Services Not Elsewhere Classified (Vol. 2)

8641 Businesspersons clubs, civic and social (Vol. 2)

2822 Butadiene-acrylonitrile copolymers (more than 50 percent butadiene) (Vol. 1)

2821 Butadiene copolymers, containing less than 50 percent butadiene (Vol. 1)

2869 Butadiene, made in chemical plants (Vol. 1)

2911 Butadiene, produced in petroleum refineries (Vol. 1)

2822 Butadiene rubbers (Vol. 1)

2822 Butadiene-styrene copolymers (more than 50 percent butadiene) (Vol. 1)

5984 Butane gas, bottled—retail (Vol. 2)

5172 Butane gas, except bulk stations and terminals—wholesale (Vol. 2)

1321 Butane (natural) production (Vol. 2)

3421 Butchers' knives (Vol. 1)

2542 Butchers' store fixtures, except wood (Vol. 1)

2541 Butchers' store fixtures, wood (Vol. 1)

5451 Butter and other dairy product stores—retail (Vol. 2)

2211 Butter cloths (Vol. 1)

2449 Butter crates, wood: wirebound (Vol. 1)

2021 Butter, creamery and whey (Vol. 1)

3556 Butter making and butter working machinery (Vol. 1)

2021 Butter oil (Vol. 1)

2021 Butter powder (Vol. 1)

2099 Butter, renovated and processed (Vol. 1)

5143 Butter—wholesale (Vol. 2)

2021 Butterfat, anhydrous (Vol. 1)

0751 Butterfat; Milk testing for (Vol. 2)

2023 Buttermilk: concentrated, condensed, dried, evaporated, and powdered (Vol. 1)

2026 Buttermilk, cultured (Vol. 1)

2048 Buttermilk emulsion for animal food (Vol. 1)

2033 Butters, fruit (Vol. 1)

3965 Button backs and parts (Vol. 1)

3965 Button blanks and molds (Vol. 1)

3965 Button coloring for the trade (Vol. 1)

3639 Buttonhole and eyelet machines and attachments, household (Vol. 1)

3559 Buttonhole and eyelet machines and attachments, industrial (Vol. 1)

2395 Buttonhole making, except fur: for the trade (Vol. 1)

5169 Carbon black—wholesale (Vol. 2)

3297 Carbon brick (Vol. 1)

2813 Carbon dioxide (Vol. 1)

3955 Carbon Paper and Inked Ribbons (Vol. 1)

3955 Carbon paper (Vol. 1)

5112 Carbon paper—wholesale (Vol. 2)

2899 Carbon removing solvent (Vol. 1)

3624 Carbon specialties for electrical use (Vol. 1)

2869 Carbon tetrachloride (Vol. 1)

2086 Carbonated beverages, nonalcoholic: bottled or canned (Vol. 1)

2812 Carbonates, potassium and sodium: not produced at mines (Vol. 1)

2299 Carbonized rags (Vol. 1)

3552 Carbonizing equipment (wool processing machinery) (Vol. 1)

2299 Carbonizing of wool, mohair, and similar fibers (Vol. 1)

3624 Carbons, electric (Vol. 1)

3624 Carbons, lighting (Vol. 1)

3221 Carboys, glass (Vol. 1)

7539 Carburetor repair (Vol. 2)

3592 Carburetors, all types (Vol. 1)

3592 Carburetors, Pistons, Piston Rings and Valves (Vol. 1)

7319 Card advertising (Vol. 2)

3172 Card cases, except precious metal (Vol. 1)

3552 Card clothing for textile machines (Vol. 1)

2675 Card cutting (Vol. 1)

3577 Card punching and sorting machines (Vol. 1)

7999 Card rooms (Vol. 2)

3577 Card-type conversion equipment, computer peripheral equipment (Vol. 1)

5113 Cardboard and products—wholesale (Vol. 2)

2675 Cardboard foundations and cutouts (Vol. 1)

2631 Cardboard (Vol. 1)

2675 Cardboard panels and cutouts (Vol. 1)

2675 Cardboard: pasted, laminated, lined, and surface coated (Vol. 1)

3292 Carded fiber, asbestos (Vol. 1)

2281 Carded yarn, cotton (Vol. 1)

3552 Carding machines, textile (Vol. 1)

3845 Cardiodynameter (Vol. 1)

3845 Cardiographs (Vol. 1)

3845 Cardiophone, electric (Vol. 1)

3845 Cardioscope (Vol. 1)

3845 Cardiotachometer (Vol. 1)

2789 Cards: beveling, bronzing, deckling, edging, and gilding (Vol. 1)

2675 Cards, cut and designed: unprinted (Vol. 1)

2759 Cards, except greeting cards: engraving of (Vol. 1)

2754 Cards, except greeting: gravure printing (Vol. 1)

2771 Cards, greeting, except hand painted (Vol. 1)

2675 Cards, index: die-cut (Vol. 1)

2675 Cards, jacquard (Vol. 1)

2675 Cards, jewelers (Vol. 1)

2752 Cards, lithographed (Vol. 1)

2675 Cards, plain paper: die-cut or rotary-cut from purchased materials (Vol. 1)

2759 Cards, playing: except lithographed or gravure (Vol. 1)

2754 Cards, playing: gravure printing (Vol. 1)

2759 Cards, printed: except greeting, lithographed or gravure (Vol. 1)

2675 Cards, tabulating and time recording: die-cut from purchased paperboard (Vol. 1)

4785 Cargo checkers and surveyors, marine (Vol. 2)

2298 Cargo nets (cordage) (Vol. 1)

4499 Cargo salvaging, from distressed vessels (Vol. 2)

3731 Cargo vessels, building and repairing (Vol. 1)

3931 Carillon bells (Vol. 1)

3599 Carnival amusement rides (Vol. 1)

5087 Carnival and amusement park equipment— wholesale (Vol. 2)

7999 Carnival operation (Vol. 2)

1094 Carnotite mining (Vol. 2)

3599 Carousels (merry-go-rounds) (Vol. 1)

3423 Carpenters' handtools, except saws (Vol. 1)

1751 Carpentry Work (Vol. 2)

1751 Carpentry work-contractors (Vol. 2)

7217 Carpet and furniture cleaning on location (Vol. 2)

7217 Carpet and Upholstery Cleaning (Vol. 2)

7217 Carpet cleaning and repairing plants (Vol. 2)

7217 Carpet cleaning on customers' premises (Vol. 2)

1752 Carpet laying or removal service-contractors (Vol. 2)

2299 Carpet linings, felt: except woven (Vol. 1)

2392 Carpet linings, textile: except felt (Vol. 1)

5713 Carpet stores—retail (Vol. 2)

3589 Carpet sweepers, except household electric vacuum sweepers (Vol. 1)

2281 Carpet yarn, cotton (Vol. 1)

2281 Carpet yarn: wool, mohair, or similar animal fibers (Vol. 1)

2273 Carpets and Rugs (Vol. 1)

3996 Carpets, asphalted-felt-base (linoleum) (Vol. 1)

2499 Carpets, cork (Vol. 1)

2273 Carpets, textile fiber (Vol. 1)

2273 Carpets: twisted paper, grass, reed, coir, sisal, jute, and rag (Vol. 1)

5023 Carpets—wholesale (Vol. 2)

3448 Carports, prefabricated: metal (Vol. 1)

3944 Carriages, baby (Vol. 1)

3944 Carriages, doll (Vol. 1)

3489 Carriages, gun: for artillery more than 30 mm. (or more than 1.18 inch) (Vol. 1)

4789 Carriages, horse-drawn: for hire (Vol. 2)

2542 Carrier cases and tables, mail: except wood (Vol. 1)

3663 Carrier equipment, radio communications (Vol. 1)

3661 Carrier equipment, telephone and telegraph (Vol. 1)

2441 Carrier trays, wood (Vol. 1)

3531 Carriers, crane (Vol. 1)

5812 Carry-out restaurants (Vol. 2)

3743 Cars and car equipment, freight or passenger (Vol. 1)

3711 Cars, armored (Vol. 1)

3711 Cars, electric: for highway use (Vol. 1)

3799 Cars, electric: off-highway (Vol. 1)

3443 Cars for hot metal (Vol. 1)

3537 Cars, industrial: except automotive cars and trucks and mining cars (Vol. 1)

3532 Cars, mining (Vol. 1)

5511 Cars, new and used—retail (Vol. 2)

3944 Cars, play (children's vehicles) (Vol. 1)

5521 Cars, used only—retail (Vol. 2)

4212 Carting, by truck or horse drawn wagon (Vol. 2)

3565 Carton packing machines (Vol. 1)

2657 Cartons, folding, except milk cartons: paperboard (Vol. 1)

7812 Cartoon motion picture production (Vol. 2)

3546 Cartridge-activated hand power tools (Vol. 1)

3949 Cartridge belts, sporting type (Vol. 1)

3482 Cartridge cases for ammunition, 30 mm. (or 1.18 inch) or less (Vol. 1)

3351 Cartridge cups, discs, and sheets: copper and copper alloy (Vol. 1)

3482 Cartridges, 30 mm. (or 1.18 inch) or less (Vol. 1)

3951 Cartridges, refill: for ballpoint pens (Vol. 1)

3949 Carts, caddy (Vol. 1)

3944 Carts, doll (Vol. 1)

3524 Carts for lawn and garden use (Vol. 1)

3949 Carts, golf: hand (Vol. 1)

3496 Carts, grocery: made from purchased wire (Vol. 1)

3484 Carts, machine gun and machine gun ammunition (Vol. 1)

2599 Carts, restaurant (Vol. 1)

2499 Carved and turned wood (except furniture) (Vol. 1)

3553 Carving machine, woodworking (Vol. 1)

3421 Carving sets: except all metal (Vol. 1)

3914 Carving sets, with metal handles and blades (Vol. 1)

2426 Carvings, furniture: wood (Vol. 1)

5087 Carwash equipment and supplies—wholesale (Vol. 2)

7542 Carwashes (Vol. 2)

3589 Carwashing machinery, including coin-operated (Vol. 1)

3111 Case leather (Vol. 1)

2023 Casein, dry and wet (Vol. 1)

2824 Casein fibers (Vol. 1)

2821 Casein plastics (Vol. 1)

3089 Casein products, molded for the trade (Vol. 1)

2211 Casement cloth, cotton (Vol. 1)

3442 Casements, aluminum (Vol. 1)

3911 Cases: cigar, cigarette, and vanity-precious metal (Vol. 1)

2522 Cases, filing: except wood (Vol. 1)

2521 Cases, filing: wood (Vol. 1)

3873 Cases for watches (Vol. 1)

3949 Cases, gun and rod (sporting equipment) (Vol. 1)

3172 Cases, jewelry: regardless of material (Vol. 1)

3161 Cases, luggage (Vol. 1)

2655 Cases, mailing: paper fiber (metal-end or all-fiber) (Vol. 1)

3161 Cases, musical instrument (Vol. 1)

2441 Cases, packing: wood-nailed or lock corner (Vol. 1)

3089 Cases, plastics (Vol. 1)

2517 Cases: radio, phonograph, and sewing machine-wood (Vol. 1)

2441 Cases, shipping: wood-nailed or lock corner (Vol. 1)

2449 Cases, shipping: wood-wirebound (Vol. 1)

3585 Cases, show and display: refrigerated (Vol. 1)

3469 Cash and stamp boxes, stamped metal (Vol. 1)

0119 Cash grain farms: except wheat, rice, corn, and soybeans (Vol. 2)

0119 Cash Grains Not Elsewhere Classified (Vol. 2)

3578 Cash registers, including adding machines with cash drawers (Vol. 1)

5044 Cash registers—wholesale (Vol. 2)

3443 Casing, boiler: metal plate (Vol. 1)

2869 Casing fluids for curing fruits, spices, and tobacco (Vol. 1)

1321 Casing-head butane and propane production (Vol. 2)

3769 Casings for missiles and missile components shipping and storage (Vol. 1)

3443 Casings, scroll (Vol. 1)

3444 Casings, sheet metal (Vol. 1)

7011 Casino hotels (Vol. 2)

3429 Casket hardware (Vol. 1)

5087 Caskets, burial—wholesale (Vol. 2)

3995 Caskets, metal and wood (Vol. 1)

2449 Casks, wood: coopered (Vol. 1)

3634 Casseroles, electric (Vol. 1)

5099 Cassettes, prerecorded: audio—wholesale (Vol. 2)

5065 Cassettes, recording—wholesale (Vol. 2)

3321 Cast iron pipe (Vol. 1)

5051 Cast iron pipe—wholesale (Vol. 2)

3325 Cast steel railroad car wheels (Vol. 1)

3272 Cast stone, concrete (Vol. 1)

3255 Castable refractories, clay (Vol. 1)

3297 Castable refractories, nonclay (Vol. 1)

3429 Casters, furniture (Vol. 1)

3429 Casters, industrial (Vol. 1)

7922 Casting agencies, theatrical: except motion picture (Vol. 2)

7819 Casting bureaus, motion picture (Vol. 2)

7922 Casting bureaus, theatrical: except motion picture (Vol. 2)

3089 Casting of plastics for the trade, except foam plastics (Vol. 1)

3365 Castings, aluminum: except die-castings (Vol. 1)

3321 Castings, compacted graphite iron (Vol. 1)

3369 Castings, except die-castings and castings of aluminum and copper (Vol. 1)

3366 Castings, except die-castings: brass, bronze, copper, and copper-base alloy (Vol. 1)

3321 Castings, gray iron and semisteel (Vol. 1)

3322 Castings, malleable iron (Vol. 1)

3369 Castings, precision, except die-castings: industrial and aircraft use-cobalt-chromium (Vol. 1)

5051 Castings, rough: iron and steel—wholesale (Vol. 2)

3069 Castings, rubber (Vol. 1)

3325 Castings, steel: except investment (Vol. 1)

2076 Castor oil and pomace (Vol. 1)

3143 Casual shoes, men's: except athletic and rubber footwear (Vol. 1)

6531 Casualty insurance and reinsurance (Vol. 2)

0279 Cat farms (Vol. 2)

2047 Cat food (Vol. 1)

5961 Catalog and Mail-Order Houses (Vol. 2)

5961 Catalog (order taking) offices of mail-order houses—retail (Vol. 2)

2621 Catalog paper (Vol. 1)

5399 Catalog showrooms, general merchandise: except catalog mail-order—retail (Vol. 2)

2754 Catalogs: gravure printing (not publishing) (Vol. 1)

2759 Catalogs, printed: except lithographed or gravure (not publishing) (Vol. 1)

2741 Catalogs: publishing and printing, or publishing only (Vol. 1)

2819 Catalysts, chemical (Vol. 1)

7533 Catalytic converters, automotive: installation, repair, or sales and installation (Vol. 2)

3489 Catapult guns (Vol. 1)

3599 Catapults (Vol. 1)

7699 Catch basin cleaning (Vol. 2)

3272 Catch basin covers, concrete (Vol. 1)

9431 Categorical health program administration-government (Vol. 2)

5812 Caterers (Vol. 2)

0273 Catfish farms (Vol. 2)

3211 Cathedral glass (Vol. 1)

3841 Catheters (Vol. 1)

5065 Cathode ray picture tubes—wholesale (Vol. 2)

3575 Cathode ray tube (CRT) teleprinter, multistation (Vol. 1)

3671 Cathode ray tubes (Vol. 1)

1499 Catlinite mining (Vol. 2)

5199 Cats—wholesale (Vol. 2)

2033 Catsup (Vol. 1)

2879 Cattle dips (Vol. 1)

0212 Cattle Except Feedlots; Beef (Vol. 2)

0241 Cattle farm; Milk production, dairy (Vol. 2)

0212 Cattle farms, except feedlots; Beef (Vol. 2)

0211 Cattle feeding farms (Vol. 2)

3523 Cattle feeding, handling, and watering equipment (Vol. 1)

0211 Cattle feedlot operations (Vol. 2)

0211 Cattle; Feedlots, (Vol. 2)

0211 Cattle Feedlots; Beef (Vol. 2)

0751 Cattle, hogs, sheep, goats, and poultry; Pedigree record services for (Vol. 2)

0751 Cattle, hogs, sheep, goats, and poultry; Showing of (Vol. 2)

3523 Cattle oilers (farm equipment) (Vol. 1)

0212 Cattle raising farms (Vol. 2)

0212 Cattle ranches (Vol. 2)

2011 Cattle slaughtering plants (Vol. 1)

0751 Cattle spraying (Vol. 2)

0211 Cattle; Stockyards, exclusively for fattening (Vol. 2)

5154 Cattle—wholesale (Vol. 2)

0161 Cauliflower farms (Vol. 2)

2891 Caulking compounds (Vol. 1)

1799 Caulking (construction)-contractors (Vol. 2)

3423 Caulking guns (Vol. 1)

3546 Caulking hammers (Vol. 1)

3423 Caulking tools, hand (Vol. 1)

1622 Causeway construction on structural supports-general contractors (Vol. 2)

2812 Caustic potash (Vol. 1)

2812 Caustic soda (Vol. 1)

5169 Caustic soda—wholesale (Vol. 2)

7999 Cave operation (Vol. 2)

2091 Caviar, canned (Vol. 1)

2511 Cedar chests (Vol. 1)

2421 Ceiling lumber, dressed (Vol. 1)

3272 Ceiling squares, concrete (Vol. 1)

3089 Ceiling tile, unsupported plastics (Vol. 1)

1742 Ceilings, acoustical installation-contractors (Vol. 2)

1761 Ceilings, metal: erection and repair-contractors (Vol. 2)

3829 Ceilometers (Vol. 1)

0161 Celery farms (Vol. 2)

1479 Celestite mining (Vol. 2)

2672 Cellophane adhesive tape (Vol. 1)

3931 Cellos and parts (Vol. 1)

3663 Cellular radio telephones (Vol. 1)

4812 Cellular telephone services (Vol. 2)

3089 Celluloid products, molded for the trade (Vol. 1)

2823 Cellulose acetate monofilament, yarn, staple, or tow (Vol. 1)

2821 Cellulose acetate (plastics) (Vol. 1)

2869 Cellulose acetate, unplasticized (Vol. 1)

2823 Cellulose fibers, manmade (Vol. 1)

2823 Cellulose fibers, regenerated (Vol. 1)

2821 Cellulose nitrate resins (Vol. 1)

2821 Cellulose propionate (plastics) (Vol. 1)

3089 Cellulose, regenerated: except fibers (Vol. 1)

2823 Cellulosic Manmade Fibers (Vol. 1)

3081 Cellulosic plastics film and sheet, unsupported (Vol. 1)

2674 Cement bags (Vol. 1)

2891 Cement (cellulose nitrate base) (Vol. 1)

3255 Cement, clay refractory (Vol. 1)

3843 Cement, dental (Vol. 1)

3297 Cement: high temperature, refractory (nonclay) (Vol. 1)

3241 Cement—Hydraulic (Vol. 1)

3241 Cement, hydraulic: portland, natural, masonry, and pozzolana (Vol. 1)

3275 Cement, Keene's (Vol. 1)

3559 Cement kilns, rotary (Vol. 1)

2891 Cement, linoleum (Vol. 1)

3297 Cement, magnesia (Vol. 1)

3559 Cement making machinery (Vol. 1)

5084 Cement making machinery—wholesale (Vol. 2)

2891 Cement, mending (Vol. 1)

1422 Cement rock, crushed and broken-quarrying (Vol. 2)

2952 Cement, roofing: asphalt, fibrous plastics (Vol. 1)

2891 Cement, rubber (Vol. 1)

3531 Cement silos (batch plant) (Vol. 1)

5032 Cement—wholesale (Vol. 2)

2051 Charlotte Russe (bakery product), except frozen (Vol. 1)

8299 Charm schools (Vol. 2)

7336 Chart and graph design (Vol. 2)

2782 Chart and graph paper, ruled (Vol. 1)

4499 Chartering of commercial boats (Vol. 2)

3545 Chasers (machine tool accessories) (Vol. 1)

3555 Chases and galleys, printers' (Vol. 1)

3479 Chasing on metals for the trade, for purposes other than printing (Vol. 1)

3799 Chassis, automobile trailer: except mobile home and travel trailer (Vol. 1)

3792 Chassis for travel and camping trailers (Vol. 1)

3711 Chassis, motor vehicle (Vol. 1)

3469 Chassis, radio and television: stamped metal (Vol. 1)

7361 Chauffeur registries (Vol. 2)

2353 Chauffeurs' hats and caps, cloth (Vol. 1)

6099 Check cashing agencies (Vol. 2)

6099 Check clearinghouse associations (Vol. 2)

7389 Check validation service (Vol. 2)

3579 Check writing, endorsing, signing, numbering, and protecting machines (Vol. 1)

3172 Checkbook covers, regardless of material (Vol. 1)

2782 Checkbooks (Vol. 1)

3944 Checkers and checkerboards (Vol. 1)

7299 Checkroom concessions or services (Vol. 2)

2022 Cheese analogs (Vol. 1)

2399 Cheese bandages (Vol. 1)

2026 Cheese, cottage (Vol. 1)

2096 Cheese curls and puffs (Vol. 1)

2022 Cheese, except cottage cheese (Vol. 1)

2022 Cheese, imitation or substitutes (Vol. 1)

5961 Cheese, mail-order—retail (Vol. 2)

3556 Cheese making machinery (Vol. 1)

2022 Cheese, natural: except cottage cheese (Vol. 1)

2022 Cheese, processed (Vol. 1)

2022 Cheese products, imitation or substitutes (Vol. 1)

2022 Cheese spreads, pastes, and cheese-like preparations (Vol. 1)

5451 Cheese stores—retail (Vol. 2)

4222 Cheese warehouses (Vol. 2)

5143 Cheese—wholesale (Vol. 2)

2211 Cheesecloth (Vol. 1)

5131 Cheesecloth—wholesale (Vol. 2)

1479 Chemical and Fertilizer Mineral Mining Not Elsewhere Classified (Vol. 2)

5169 Chemical bulk stations and terminals—wholesale (Vol. 2)

2819 Chemical catalysts (Vol. 1)

1629 Chemical complex or facilities construction-general contractors (Vol. 2)

2899 Chemical cotton (processed cotton linters) (Vol. 1)

3542 Chemical explosives metal forming machines (Vol. 1)

3821 Chemical fume hoods (Vol. 1)

2865 Chemical indicators (Vol. 1)

3559 Chemical kilns (Vol. 1)

8731 Chemical laboratories, commercial research: except testing (Vol. 2)

3559 Chemical machinery and equipment (Vol. 1)

3599 Chemical milling job shops (Vol. 1)

3541 Chemical milling machines (Vol. 1)

3269 Chemical porcelain (Vol. 1)

3312 Chemical recovery coke oven products (Vol. 1)

3269 Chemical stoneware (pottery products) (Vol. 1)

2899 Chemical supplies for foundries (Vol. 1)

0721 Chemical; Thinning of crops, mechanical and (Vol. 2)

0711 Chemical treatment of soil for crops (Vol. 2)

2869 Chemical warfare gases (Vol. 1)

3483 Chemical warfare projectiles and components (Vol. 1)

1389 Chemically treating wells on a contract basis (Vol. 2)

5191 Chemicals, agricultural—wholesale (Vol. 2)

5169 Chemicals and Allied Products Not Elsewhere Classified (Vol. 2)

2899 Chemicals and Chemical Preparations Not Elsewhere Classified (Vol. 1)

5169 Chemicals, industrial and heavy—wholesale (Vol. 2)

2819 Chemicals, laboratory: inorganic (Vol. 1)

2833 Chemicals, medicinal: organic and inorganic-bulk, uncompounded (Vol. 1)

3861 Chemicals, photographic: prepared (Vol. 1)

2341 Chemises: women's, misses', children's, and infants' (Vol. 1)

8071 Chemists, biological: (not manufacturing) laboratories of (Vol. 2)

8999 Chemists, consulting: not connected with business service laboratories (Vol. 2)

2273 Chenille rugs (Vol. 1)

2211 Chenilles, tufted textile (Vol. 1)

2035 Cherries, brined (Vol. 1)

2033 Cherries, maraschino (Vol. 1)

0831 Cherry gum, gathering of (Vol. 2)

0175 Cherry orchards and farms (Vol. 2)

3944 Chessmen and chessboards (Vol. 1)

2861 Chestnut extract (Vol. 1)

0831 Chestnut gum, gathering of (Vol. 2)

2511 Chests, cedar (Vol. 1)

3499 Chests, fire or burglary resistive: metal (Vol. 1)

2441 Chests for tools, wood (Vol. 1)

3999 Chests, money: steel (Vol. 1)

3999 Chests, musical (Vol. 1)

3499 Chests, safe deposit: metal (Vol. 1)

2511 Chests, silverware: wood (floor standing) (Vol. 1)

2211 Cheviots, cotton (Vol. 1)

2131 Chewing and Smoking Tobacco and Snuff (Vol. 1)

2064 Chewing candy, except chewing gum (Vol. 1)

2067 Chewing Gum (Vol. 1)

2067 Chewing gum base (Vol. 1)

3556 Chewing gum machinery (Vol. 1)

2067 Chewing gum (Vol. 1)

5145 Chewing gum—wholesale (Vol. 2)

2131 Chewing tobacco (Vol. 1)

5194 Chewing tobacco—wholesale (Vol. 2)

3523 Chicken brooders (Vol. 1)

3999 Christmas trees, artificial (Vol. 1)

5199 Christmas trees, including artificial—wholesale (Vol. 2)

5261 Christmas trees (natural)—retail (Vol. 2)

2819 Chromates and bichromates (Vol. 1)

3826 Chromatographic instruments, laboratory type (Vol. 1)

3823 Chromatographs, industrial process type (Vol. 1)

2816 Chrome pigments: chrome green, chrome yellow, chrome orange, and zinc yellow (Vol. 1)

2819 Chromic acid (Vol. 1)

1061 Chromite mining (Vol. 2)

2819 Chromium compounds, inorganic (Vol. 1)

1061 Chromium ore mining (Vol. 2)

3471 Chromium plating of metals and formed products, for the trade (Vol. 1)

3339 Chromium refining, primary (Vol. 1)

2819 Chromium salts (Vol. 1)

8069 Chronic disease hospitals (Vol. 2)

3873 Chronographs, spring wound (Vol. 1)

3829 Chronometers, electronic (Vol. 1)

3873 Chronometers, spring wound (Vol. 1)

3826 Chronoscopes (Vol. 1)

3541 Chucking machines, automatic (Vol. 1)

3545 Chucks: drill, lathe, and magnetic (machine tool accessories) (Vol. 1)

3272 Church furniture, concrete (Vol. 1)

3281 Church furniture, cut stone (Vol. 1)

2531 Church furniture, except stone or concrete (Vol. 1)

5021 Church pews—wholesale (Vol. 2)

1542 Church, synagogue, and related building construction-general contractors (Vol. 2)

8661 Churches (Vol. 2)

3443 Chutes, metal plate (Vol. 1)

2099 Cider, nonalcoholic (Vol. 1)

3556 Cider presses (Vol. 1)

3999 Cigar and cigarette holders (Vol. 1)

2441 Cigar boxes, wood and part wood (Vol. 1)

3172 Cigar cases, except precious metal (Vol. 1)

3911 Cigar cases, precious metal (Vol. 1)

3634 Cigar lighters, electric (Vol. 1)

3999 Cigar lighters, except precious metal and electric (Vol. 1)

3911 Cigar lighters, precious metal or based metal clad with precious metal (Vol. 1)

5993 Cigar stores and stands—retail (Vol. 2)

3559 Cigarette and cigar making machines (Vol. 1)

3172 Cigarette cases, except precious metal (Vol. 1)

3911 Cigarette cases, precious metal (Vol. 1)

3999 Cigarette filters, not made in chemical plants (Vol. 1)

3069 Cigarette holder mouthpieces, molded rubber (Vol. 1)

3999 Cigarette lighter flints (Vol. 1)

3634 Cigarette lighters, electric (Vol. 1)

3999 Cigarette lighters, except precious metal and electric (Vol. 1)

3911 Cigarette lighters, precious metal (Vol. 1)

2679 Cigarette paper, book (Vol. 1)

2621 Cigarette paper (Vol. 1)

2823 Cigarette tow, cellulosic fiber (Vol. 1)

2111 Cigarettes (Vol. 1)

2111 Cigarettes (Vol. 1)

5962 Cigarettes, sale by vending machine—retail (Vol. 2)

5194 Cigarettes—wholesale (Vol. 2)

2121 Cigarillos (Vol. 1)

2121 Cigars (Vol. 1)

2121 Cigars (Vol. 1)

5194 Cigars—wholesale (Vol. 2)

2833 Cinchona and derivatives (Vol. 1)

3271 Cinder block, concrete (Vol. 1)

5032 Cinders—wholesale (Vol. 2)

3827 Cinetheodolites (Vol. 1)

1099 Cinnabar mining (Vol. 2)

3672 Circuit boards, television and radio: printed (Vol. 1)

3613 Circuit breakers, air (Vol. 1)

3613 Circuit breakers, power (Vol. 1)

5063 Circuit breakers—wholesale (Vol. 2)

8741 Circuit management services for motion picture theaters (Vol. 2)

7319 Circular distributing service (Vol. 2)

2257 Circular knit fabrics (Vol. 1)

5131 Circular knit fabrics—wholesale (Vol. 2)

2754 Circulars: gravure printing (Vol. 1)

2752 Circulars, lithographed (Vol. 1)

2759 Circulars, printed: except lithographed or gravure (Vol. 1)

8231 Circulating libraries (Vol. 2)

7999 Circus companies (Vol. 2)

7622 Citizens' band (CB) antennas, installation of (Vol. 2)

3663 Citizens' band (CB) radios (Vol. 1)

5065 Citizens' band radios—wholesale (Vol. 2)

8641 Citizens' unions (Vol. 2)

2869 Citral (Vol. 1)

2869 Citrates (Vol. 1)

2869 Citric acid (Vol. 1)

2899 Citronella oil (Vol. 1)

2869 Citronellal (Vol. 1)

0174 Citrus Fruits (Vol. 2)

0721 Citrus grove cultivation services (Vol. 2)

0762 Citrus grove management and maintenance, with or without crop services (Vol. 2)

0174 Citrus groves and farms (Vol. 2)

5084 Citrus processing machinery—wholesale (Vol. 2)

2048 Citrus seed meal (Vol. 1)

4111 City and suburban bus line operation (Vol. 2)

9121 City and town councils (Vol. 2)

9111 City and town managers' offices (Vol. 2)

8748 City planners, except professional engineering (Vol. 2)

8641 Civic associations (Vol. 2)

1542 Civic center construction-general contractors (Vol. 2)

8641 Civic, Social and Fraternal Associations (Vol. 2)

9199 Civil rights commissions-government (Vol. 2)

9199 Civil service commissions-government (Vol. 2)

8299 Civil service schools (Vol. 2)

9211 Civilian courts (Vol. 2)

6411 Claim adjusters insurance: not employed by insurance companies (Vol. 2)

2091 Clam bouillon, broth, chowder, juice: bottled or canned (Vol. 1)

3423 Clamps, hand (Vol. 1)

3429 Clamps, hose (Vol. 1)

3545 Clamps, machine tool (Vol. 1)

3429 Clamps, metal (Vol. 1)

3841 Clamps, surgical (Vol. 1)

0913 Clams, digging of (Vol. 2)

3532 Clarifying machinery, mineral (Vol. 1)

3931 Clarinets and parts (Vol. 1)

3131 Clasps, shoe (Vol. 1)

7929 Classical music groups or artists (Vol. 2)

3532 Classifiers, metallurgical and mining (Vol. 1)

1459 Clay, Ceramic and Refractory Minerals Not Elsewhere Classified (Vol. 2)

2631 Clay coated board (Vol. 1)

5032 Clay construction materials, except refractory—wholesale (Vol. 2)

3295 Clay for petroleum refining, chemically processed (Vol. 1)

3295 Clay, ground or otherwise treated (Vol. 1)

3952 Clay, modeling (Vol. 1)

3255 Clay Refractories (Vol. 1)

3255 Clay refractories (Vol. 1)

1459 Clays (common) quarrying-not in conjunction with manufacturing (Vol. 2)

3559 Clayworking and tempering machines (Vol. 1)

7218 Clean room apparel supply service (Vol. 2)

1541 Clean room construction-general contractors (Vol. 2)

3714 Cleaners, air: motor vehicle (Vol. 1)

3599 Cleaners, boiler tube (Vol. 1)

2844 Cleaners, denture (Vol. 1)

3635 Cleaners, electric: vacuum-household (Vol. 1)

3589 Cleaners, electric vacuum: industrial (Vol. 1)

7212 Cleaners, not operating own drycleaning plants (Vol. 2)

2851 Cleaners, paintbrush (Vol. 1)

3999 Cleaners, pipe and cigarette holder (Vol. 1)

3471 Cleaning and descaling metal products, for the trade (Vol. 1)

7216 Cleaning and dyeing plants, except rug cleaning (Vol. 2)

7212 Cleaning and laundry pickup stations, not owned by laundries or cleaners (Vol. 2)

7542 Cleaning and polishing (detailing) new autos for dealers on a contract or fee basis (Vol. 2)

2044 Cleaning and polishing of rice (Vol. 1)

2842 Cleaning and polishing preparations (Vol. 1)

7699 Cleaning and reglazing of baking pans (Vol. 2)

7217 Cleaning and repairing plants, rug and carpet (Vol. 2)

0723 Cleaning; Bean (Vol. 2)

7699 Cleaning bricks (Vol. 2)

1799 Cleaning building exteriors-contractors (Vol. 2)

3699 Cleaning equipment, ultrasonic: except medical and dental (Vol. 1)

0723 Cleaning; Grain (Vol. 2)

1389 Cleaning lease tanks, oil and gas field: on a contract basis (Vol. 2)

3547 Cleaning lines, electrolytic (rolling mill equipment) (Vol. 1)

3532 Cleaning machinery, mineral (Vol. 1)

3523 Cleaning machines for fruits, grains, and vegetables: farm (Vol. 1)

1799 Cleaning new buildings after construction-contractors (Vol. 2)

5149 Cleaning of dry foods and spices—wholesale (Vol. 2)

4741 Cleaning of railroad cars (Vol. 2)

1221 Cleaning plants, bituminous coal (Vol. 2)

0751 Cleaning poultry coops (Vol. 2)

4789 Cleaning railroad ballasts (Vol. 2)

0723 Cleaning; Seed (Vol. 2)

1389 Cleaning wells on a contract basis (Vol. 2)

2621 Cleansing tissue stock (Vol. 1)

2676 Cleansing tissues (Vol. 1)

3647 Clearance lamps and reflectors, motor vehicle (Vol. 1)

1629 Clearing of land-general contractors (Vol. 2)

6099 Clearinghouse associations: bank or check (Vol. 2)

6289 Clearinghouses, commodity exchange (Vol. 2)

6289 Clearinghouses, security exchange (Vol. 2)

3264 Cleats, porcelain (Vol. 1)

3421 Cleavers (Vol. 1)

2389 Clergy's vestments (Vol. 1)

2449 Climax baskets (Vol. 1)

2835 Clinical chemistry reagents (including toxicology) (Vol. 1)

2835 Clinical chemistry standards and controls (including toxicology) (Vol. 1)

3829 Clinical thermometers, including digital (Vol. 1)

8093 Clinics, alcohol and drug treatment: outpatient (Vol. 2)

8093 Clinics, mental health: outpatient (Vol. 2)

8041 Clinics of chiropractors (Vol. 2)

8021 Clinics of dentists (Vol. 2)

8042 Clinics of optometrists (Vol. 2)

8031 Clinics of osteopathic physicians (Vol. 2)

8011 Clinics of physicians (M.D.) (Vol. 2)

8043 Clinics of podiatrists (Vol. 2)

3229 Clip cups, glass (Vol. 1)

2499 Clipboards, wood (Vol. 1)

3421 Clippers, fingernail and toenail (Vol. 1)

3523 Clippers, hair: for animal use-hand and electric (Vol. 1)

3999 Clippers, hair: for human use-hand and electric (Vol. 1)

3496 Clips and fasteners, made from purchased wire (Vol. 1)

3484 Clips, gun: 30 mm. (or 1.18 inch) or less (Vol. 1)

3069 Cloaks, vulcanized rubber and rubberized fabric (Vol. 1)

3873 Clock materials and parts, except crystals and jewels (Vol. 1)

3651 Clock radio and telephone combinations (Vol. 1)

3651 Clock radios (Vol. 1)

7631 Clock repair shops (Vol. 2)

3495 Clock springs, precision: made from purchased wire (Vol. 1)

3873 Clocks, assembling of (Vol. 1)

3873 Clocks, except timeclocks (Vol. 1)

5944 Clocks, including custom made—retail (Vol. 2)

5094 Clocks—wholesale (Vol. 2)

3663 Closed circuit television equipment (Vol. 1)

4841 Closed circuit television services (Vol. 2)

3261 Closet bowls, vitreous china (Vol. 1)

5113 Closures, paper and disposable plastics—wholesale (Vol. 2)

3089 Closures, plastics (Vol. 1)

3466 Closures, stamped metal (Vol. 1)

3291 Cloth, abrasive (Vol. 1)

3292 Cloth, asbestos (Vol. 1)

2257 Cloth, circular knit (Vol. 1)

7389 Cloth: cutting to length, bolting, or winding for textile distributors (Vol. 2)

3291 Cloth: garnet, emery, aluminum oxide, and silicon carbide coated (Vol. 1)

2672 Cloth-lined paper (Vol. 1)

2269 Cloth mending, except wool: for the trade (Vol. 1)

3861 Cloth, photographic: sensitized (Vol. 1)

3552 Cloth spreading machines (Vol. 1)

3552 Cloth stripping machines (Vol. 1)

3952 Cloth, tracing (drafting material) (Vol. 1)

2295 Cloth, varnished glass (Vol. 1)

2258 Cloth, warp knit (Vol. 1)

2499 Cloth winding reels, wood (Vol. 1)

2231 Cloth, wool: mending for the trade (Vol. 1)

3496 Cloth, woven wire: made from purchased wire (Vol. 1)

3822 Clothes dryer controls, including dryness controls (Vol. 1)

2499 Clothes dryers (clothes horses), wood (Vol. 1)

5064 Clothes dryers, household: electric and gas—wholesale (Vol. 2)

2499 Clothes drying frames, wood (Vol. 1)

3089 Clothes hangers, plastics (Vol. 1)

5199 Clothes hangers—wholesale (Vol. 2)

2499 Clothes horses, wood (Vol. 1)

2499 Clothes poles, wood (Vol. 1)

3089 Clothespins, plastics (Vol. 1)

2499 Clothespins, wood (Vol. 1)

5137 Clothing accessories: women's, children's, and infants'—wholesale (Vol. 2)

7219 Clothing alteration and repair shops (Vol. 2)

3942 Clothing, doll (Vol. 1)

3699 Clothing, electrically heated (Vol. 1)

3842 Clothing, fire resistant and protective (Vol. 1)

2371 Clothing, fur (Vol. 1)

2386 Clothing, leather or sheep-lined (Vol. 1)

5136 Clothing, men's and boys'—wholesale (Vol. 2)

5621 Clothing, ready-to-wear: women's—retail (Vol. 2)

7299 Clothing rental, except industrial launderers and linen supply (Vol. 2)

5651 Clothing stores, family—retail (Vol. 2)

5611 Clothing stores, men's and boys'—retail (Vol. 2)

5932 Clothing stores, secondhand—retail (Vol. 2)

3069 Clothing, vulcanized rubber and rubberized fabric (Vol. 1)

2385 Clothing, waterproof (Vol. 1)

5137 Clothing: women's, children's, and infants'—wholesale (Vol. 2)

2394 Cloths, drop: fabric (Vol. 1)

2842 Cloths, dusting and polishing: chemically treated (Vol. 1)

2392 Cloths, lunch (Vol. 1)

2399 Cloths, saddle (Vol. 1)

8999 Cloud seeding (Vol. 2)

0139 Clover farms (Vol. 2)

2514 Clubroom furniture, metal (Vol. 1)

2511 Clubroom furniture, wood (Vol. 1)

3949 Clubs: golf, Indian, etc. (sporting goods) (Vol. 1)

7991 Clubs, health (Vol. 2)

7997 Clubs, membership: sports and recreation, except physical fitness (Vol. 2)

2499 Clubs, police: wood (Vol. 1)

3292 Clutch facings, asbestos (Vol. 1)

3568 Clutches, except motor vehicle (Vol. 1)

2835 Coagulation diagnostic reagents (Vol. 1)

2836 Coagulation products (Vol. 1)

3532 Coal breakers, cutters, and pulverizers (Vol. 1)

3444 Coal chutes, prefabricated sheet metal (Vol. 1)

5989 Coal dealers—retail (Vol. 2)

3312 Coal gas, derived from chemical recovery coke ovens (Vol. 1)

1311 Coal gasification at the mine site (Vol. 2)

1311 Coal liquefaction at the mine site (Vol. 2)

1231 Coal mining, anthracite (Vol. 2)

1221 Coal mining, bituminous: surface (Vol. 2)

1222 Coal mining, bituminous-underground (Vol. 2)

1221 Coal mining-brown (Vol. 2)

1241 Coal Mining Services (Vol. 2)

5052 Coal, Other Minerals and Ores (Vol. 2)

4619 Coal pipeline operation (Vol. 2)

1221 Coal preparation plants, bituminous or lignite (Vol. 2)

1311 Coal pyrolysis at the mine site (Vol. 2)

3312 Coal tar crudes, derived from chemical recovery coke ovens (Vol. 1)

2865 Coal tar crudes, derived from coal tar distillation (Vol. 1)

2865 Coal tar distillates (Vol. 1)

2865 Coal tar intermediates (Vol. 1)

2951 Coal tar paving materials, not made in petroleum refineries (Vol. 1)

5169 Coal tar products, primary and intermediate—wholesale (Vol. 2)

2821 Coal tar resins (Vol. 1)

5052 Coal—wholesale (Vol. 2)

3751 Coaster brakes, bicycle (Vol. 1)

4424 Coastwise transportation of freight (Vol. 2)

2369 Coat and legging sets: girls' and children's (Vol. 1)

3496 Coat hangers, made from purchased wire (Vol. 1)

2396 Coat linings, fronts, and pads: for men's coats (Vol. 1)

2371 Coat linings, fur (Vol. 1)

7213 Coat supply service (Vol. 2)

2396 Coat trimmings fabric (Vol. 1)

2672 Coated and Laminated Paper Not Elsewhere Classified (Vol. 1)

2295 Coated Fabrics—Not Rubberized (Vol. 1)

5131 Coated fabrics—wholesale (Vol. 2)

2671 Coated paper for packaging (Vol. 1)

2851 Coating, air curing (Vol. 1)

3554 Coating and finishing machinery, paper (Vol. 1)

2295 Coating and impregnating of fabrics, except rubberizing (Vol. 1)

3479 Coating and wrapping steel pipe (Vol. 1)

2952 Coating compounds, tar (Vol. 1)

3479 Coating, Engraving and Allied Services Not Elsewhere Classified (Vol. 1)

3479 Coating (hot dipping) of metals and formed products, for the trade (Vol. 1)

1799 Coating of concrete structures with plastics-contractors (Vol. 2)

3479 Coating of metals with plastics and resins, for the trade (Vol. 1)

3479 Coating of metals with silicon, for the trade (Vol. 1)

3479 Coating, rust preventive (Vol. 1)

2066 Coatings, chocolate (Vol. 1)

2337 Coats, except fur and raincoats: women's, misses', and juniors' (Vol. 1)

2329 Coats, except tailored or work: men's and boys' (Vol. 1)

2371 Coats, fur (Vol. 1)

2369 Coats: girls', children's, and infants' (Vol. 1)

2386 Coats, leather or sheep-lined (Vol. 1)

5136 Coats, men's and boys'—wholesale (Vol. 2)

2329 Coats, oiled fabric and blanket-lined: men's and boys' (Vol. 1)

2339 Coats, service apparel (e.g., medical and lab) (Vol. 1)

2311 Coats, tailored: men's and boys' (Vol. 1)

5137 Coats: women's, children's, and infants'—wholesale (Vol. 2)

3357 Coaxial cable, nonferrous (Vol. 1)

5063 Coaxial cable—wholesale (Vol. 2)

2819 Cobalt 60 (radioactive) (Vol. 1)

2819 Cobalt chloride (Vol. 1)

1061 Cobalt ore mining (Vol. 2)

3339 Cobalt refining, primary (Vol. 1)

2819 Cobalt sulfate (Vol. 1)

2833 Cocaine and derivatives (Vol. 1)

3432 Cocks, drain (including basin) (Vol. 1)

5813 Cocktail lounges (Vol. 2)

2087 Cocktail mixes, nonalcoholic (Vol. 1)

2085 Cocktails, alcoholic (Vol. 1)

5182 Cocktails, alcoholic: premixed—wholesale (Vol. 2)

2066 Cocoa butter (Vol. 1)

2066 Cocoa mix, instant (Vol. 1)

2066 Cocoa, powdered: mixed with other substances (Vol. 1)

2099 Coconut, desiccated and shredded (Vol. 1)

2076 Coconut oil (Vol. 1)

0912 Cod, catching of (Vol. 2)

2843 Cod oil, sulfonated (Vol. 1)

3827 Coddington magnifying instruments (Vol. 1)

2833 Codeine and derivatives (Vol. 1)

2091 Codfish: smoked, salted, dried, and pickled (Vol. 1)

5963 Coffee-cart food service—retail (Vol. 2)

2095 Coffee concentrates (instant coffee) (Vol. 1)

2095 Coffee extracts (Vol. 1)

0179 Coffee farms (Vol. 2)

2087 Coffee flavorings and syrups (Vol. 1)

5149 Coffee: green, roasted, instant, freeze-dried, or extract—wholesale (Vol. 2)

2095 Coffee, ground: mixed with grain or chicory (Vol. 1)

2095 Coffee, instant and freeze-dried (Vol. 1)

3634 Coffee makers, household: electric (Vol. 1)

3556 Coffee roasting and grinding machines (Vol. 1)

2095 Coffee roasting, except by wholesale grocers (Vol. 1)

5812 Coffee shops (Vol. 2)

5499 Coffee stores—retail (Vol. 2)

2043 Coffee substitutes made from grain (Vol. 1)

2511 Coffee tables, wood (Vol. 1)

5046 Coffee urns, commercial—wholesale (Vol. 2)

3589 Coffee urns-restaurant type (Vol. 1)

1629 Cofferdam construction-general contractors (Vol. 2)

4119 Cog railways, except amusement and scenic (Vol. 2)

3549 Coil winding machines for springs (Vol. 1)

7694 Coil winding service (Vol. 2)

3677 Coil windings, electronic (Vol. 1)

3493 Coiled flat springs (Vol. 1)

3549 Coilers (metalworking machines) (Vol. 1)

3677 Coils, chokes and other inductors, electronic (Vol. 1)

5065 Coils, electronic—wholesale (Vol. 2)

3621 Coils for motors and generators (Vol. 1)

3694 Coils, ignition: internal combustion engines (Vol. 1)

3498 Coils, pipe: fabricated from purchased metal pipe (Vol. 1)

3354 Coils, rod: aluminum-extruded (Vol. 1)

3353 Coils, sheet: aluminum (Vol. 1)

3355 Coils, wire: aluminum-made in rolling mills (Vol. 1)

3578 Coin counters (Vol. 1)

7993 Coin-Operated Amusement Devices (Vol. 2)

3999 Coin-operated amusement machine, except phonographs (Vol. 1)

7215 Coin-operated drycleaning (Vol. 2)

5099 Coin-operated game machines (Vol. 2)

7215 Coin-operated laundries (Vol. 2)

7215 Coin-Operated Laundries and Dry Cleaning (Vol. 2)

7215 Coin-operated laundry and drycleaning routes (Vol. 2)

7359 Coin-operated machine rental and leasing (Vol. 2)

5962 Coin-operated machines selling merchandise (Vol. 2)

3581 Coin-operated merchandise vending machines (Vol. 1)

3651 Coin-operated phonographs (Vol. 1)

7299 Coin-operated service machine operation: scales, shoeshine, lockers, and blood pressure (Vol. 2)

3172 Coin purses, regardless of material (Vol. 1)

5999 Coin shops—retail, except mail-order (Vol. 2)

3579 Coin wrapping machines (Vol. 1)

5961 Coins, mail-order—retail (Vol. 2)

5094 Coins—wholesale (Vol. 2)

2299 Coir yarns and roving (Vol. 1)

1629 Coke oven construction-general contractors (Vol. 2)

4925 Coke oven gas, production and distribution (Vol. 2)

4925 Coke ovens, byproduct: operated for manufacture or distribution of gas (Vol. 2)

2999 Coke, petroleum: not produced in petroleum refineries (Vol. 1)

2911 Coke, petroleum: produced in petroleum refineries (Vol. 1)

3312 Coke, produced in beehive ovens (Vol. 1)

3312 Coke, produced in chemical recovery coke ovens (Vol. 1)

5052 Coke—wholesale (Vol. 2)

3585 Cold drink dispensing equipment, except coin-operated (Vol. 1)

3316 Cold-finished steel bars: not made in hot-rolling mills (Vol. 1)

3547 Cold forming type mills (rolling mill machinery) (Vol. 1)

2835 Cold kits for labeling with technetium (Vol. 1)

2834 Cold remedies (Vol. 1)

3316 Cold-Rolled Steel Sheet, Strip and Bars (Vol. 1)

3316 Cold-rolled steel strip, sheet, and bars: not made in hot-rolling mills (Vol. 1)

4222 Cold storage locker rental (Vol. 2)

5078 Cold storage machinery—wholesale (Vol. 2)

1541 Cold storage plant construction-general contractors (Vol. 2)

4222 Cold storage warehousing (Vol. 2)

2099 Cole slaw in bulk (Vol. 1)

1474 Colemanite mining (Vol. 2)

3499 Collapsible tubes for viscous products, metal (Vol. 1)

2253 Collar and cuff sets (Vol. 1)

2339 Collar and cuff sets: women's, misses' and juniors' (Vol. 1)

3965 Collar buttons, except precious metal and precious or semiprecious stones (Vol. 1)

3911 Collar buttons, precious metal and precious or semiprecious stones (Vol. 1)

3111 Collar leather (Vol. 1)

2396 Collar linings, for men's coats (Vol. 1)

3199 Collars and collar pads (harness) (Vol. 1)

3199 Collars, dog (Vol. 1)

3545 Collars (machine tool accessories) (Vol. 1)

2321 Collars, men's and boys' (Vol. 1)

3568 Collars, shaft (power transmission equipment) (Vol. 1)

3555 Collating machines for printing and bookbinding trade use (Vol. 1)

3579 Collating machines for store or office use (Vol. 1)

7211 Collecting and distributing agencies, laundry: operated by power laundries (Vol. 2)

7216 Collecting and distributing agencies operated by cleaning plants (Vol. 2)

7212 Collecting and distributing agents-laundry and drycleaning (Vol. 2)

7322 Collection agencies, accounts (Vol. 2)

8631 Collective bargaining units (Vol. 2)

3621 Collector rings for motors and generators (Vol. 1)

7299 College clearinghouses (Vol. 2)

8221 Colleges, except junior (Vol. 2)

8221 Colleges, Universities and Professional Schools (Vol. 2)

3545 Collets (machine tool accessories) (Vol. 1)

7532 Collision shops, automotive (Vol. 2)

2844 Colognes (Vol. 1)

3845 Colonscopes, electromedical (Vol. 1)

2752 Color cards, paint: offset printing (Vol. 1)

2865 Color lakes and toners (Vol. 1)

2752 Color lithography (Vol. 1)

2816 Color pigments, inorganic (Vol. 1)

2865 Color pigments, organic: except animal black and bone black (Vol. 1)

2759 Color printing: except lithographed or gravure (Vol. 1)

2754 Color printing: gravure (Vol. 1)

2796 Color separations for printing (Vol. 1)

3826 Colorimeters, laboratory type (Vol. 1)

3471 Coloring and finishing of aluminum and formed products, for the trade (Vol. 1)

3111 Coloring of leather (Vol. 1)

2087 Colorings, food: except synthetic (Vol. 1)

5198 Colors and pigments—wholesale (Vol. 2)

3952 Colors, artists': water and oxide ceramic glass (Vol. 1)

2865 Colors, dry: lakes, toners, or full strength organic colors (Vol. 1)

2865 Colors, extended (color lakes) (Vol. 1)

2865 Colors, food: synthetic (Vol. 1)

2087 Colors for bakers' and confectioners' use, except synthetic (Vol. 1)

2851 Colors in oil, except artists' (Vol. 1)

3842 Colostomy appliances (Vol. 1)

1061 Columbite mining (Vol. 2)

3339 Columbium refining, primary (Vol. 1)

3272 Columns, concrete (Vol. 1)

3443 Columns, fractionating: metal plate (Vol. 1)

3299 Columns, papier-mache or plaster of paris (Vol. 1)

3172 Comb cases, except precious metal (Vol. 1)

3999 Comb mounting, except precious metal (Vol. 1)

3731 Combat ships, building and repairing (Vol. 1)

5088 Combat vehicles, except trucks—wholesale (Vol. 2)

2281 Combed yarn, cotton (Vol. 1)

3822 Combination limit and fan controls (Vol. 1)

3822 Combination oil and hydronic controls (Vol. 1)

4939 Combination Utilities Not Elsewhere Classified (Vol. 2)

3523 Combines (harvester-threshers) (Vol. 1)

2299 Combing and converting top (Vol. 1)

3552 Combing machines, textile (Vol. 1)

0722 Combining, agricultural (Vol. 2)

3999 Combs, except hard rubber (Vol. 1)

2791 Composition, machine: e.g., linotype, monotype-for the printing trade (Vol. 1)

3089 Composition stone, plastics (Vol. 1)

2875 Compost (Vol. 1)

3843 Compounds, dental (Vol. 1)

3491 Compressed gas cylinder valves (Vol. 1)

3563 Compressors, air and gas: for general industrial use (Vol. 1)

5075 Compressors, air-conditioning—wholesale (Vol. 2)

5084 Compressors, except air-conditioning and refrigeration—wholesale (Vol. 2)

3585 Compressors for refrigeration and air-conditioning (Vol. 1)

7373 Computer-aided design (CAD) systems services (Vol. 2)

7373 Computer-aided engineering (CAE) systems services (Vol. 2)

7373 Computer-aided manufacturing (CAM) systems services (Vol. 2)

5734 Computer and Computer Software Stores (Vol. 2)

5961 Computer and peripheral equipment, mail-order—retail (Vol. 2)

7371 Computer code authors (Vol. 2)

7379 Computer consultants (Vol. 2)

7376 Computer Facilities Management Services (Vol. 2)

2761 Computer forms, manifold or continuous (excludes paper simply lined) (Vol. 1)

7377 Computer hardware rental or leasing, except finance leasing or by the manufacturer (Vol. 2)

7374 Computer input-output service (Vol. 2)

7373 Computer Integrated Systems Design (Vol. 2)

3823 Computer interface equipment for industrial process control (Vol. 1)

3674 Computer logic modules (Vol. 1)

7378 Computer Maintenance and Repair (Vol. 2)

8243 Computer operator training (Vol. 2)

3577 Computer output to microfilm units, computer peripheral equipment (Vol. 1)

3577 Computer paper tape punchers and devices, computer peripheral equipment (Vol. 1)

5112 Computer paper—wholesale (Vol. 2)

3577 Computer Peripheral Equipment Not Elsewhere Classified (Vol. 1)

7377 Computer peripheral equipment, rental and leasing (Vol. 2)

7378 Computer peripheral equipment repair and maintenance (Vol. 2)

7299 Computer photography or portraits (Vol. 2)

5734 Computer printer stores—retail (Vol. 2)

7374 Computer Processing and Data Preparation and Processing Services (Vol. 2)

7371 Computer Programming Services (Vol. 2)

7371 Computer programs or systems software development, custom (Vol. 2)

7379 Computer Related Services Not Elsewhere Classified (Vol. 2)

7377 Computer Rental and Leasing (Vol. 2)

7378 Computer repair and maintenance (Vol. 2)

8243 Computer repair training (Vol. 2)

5961 Computer software, mail-order—retail (Vol. 2)

7372 Computer software publishers, prepackaged (Vol. 2)

5734 Computer software stores—retail (Vol. 2)

7371 Computer software systems analysis and design, custom (Vol. 2)

3695 Computer software tape and disks, blank: rigid and floppy (Vol. 1)

8243 Computer software training (Vol. 2)

7371 Computer software writers, free-lance (Vol. 2)

3572 Computer Storage Devices (Vol. 1)

3572 Computer storage units (Vol. 1)

5734 Computer stores—retail (Vol. 2)

3575 Computer Terminals (Vol. 1)

3575 Computer terminals (Vol. 1)

5045 Computer terminals—wholesale (Vol. 2)

7374 Computer time brokerage (Vol. 2)

7374 Computer time-sharing (Vol. 2)

3845 Computerized axial tomography (CT/CAT scanner) apparatus (Vol. 1)

5045 Computers, Computer Peripheral Equipment and Software (Vol. 2)

3571 Computers: digital, analog, and hybrid (Vol. 1)

5045 Computers—wholesale (Vol. 2)

2087 Concentrates, drink: except frozen fruit (Vol. 1)

2087 Concentrates, flavoring (Vol. 1)

2037 Concentrates, frozen fruit juice (Vol. 1)

5052 Concentrates, metallic—wholesale (Vol. 2)

2844 Concentrates, perfume (Vol. 1)

3532 Concentration machinery (metallurgical and mining) (Vol. 1)

7929 Concert artists (Vol. 2)

7922 Concert management service (Vol. 2)

3931 Concertinas and parts (Vol. 1)

7999 Concession operators, amusement devices and rides (Vol. 2)

5812 Concession stands, prepared food (e.g., in airports and sports arenas) (Vol. 2)

5169 Concrete additives—wholesale (Vol. 2)

5211 Concrete and cinder block dealers—retail (Vol. 2)

5032 Concrete and cinder block—wholesale (Vol. 2)

3546 Concrete and masonry drilling tools, power: portable (Vol. 1)

3272 Concrete articulated mattresses for river revetment (Vol. 1)

2951 Concrete, asphaltic: not made in petroleum refineries (Vol. 1)

2951 Concrete, bituminous (Vol. 1)

3271 Concrete Block and Brick (Vol. 1)

1741 Concrete block laying-contractors (Vol. 2)

1795 Concrete breaking for streets and highways-contractors (Vol. 2)

3531 Concrete buggies, powered (Vol. 1)

5032 Concrete building products—wholesale (Vol. 2)

5087 Concrete burial vaults and boxes—wholesale (Vol. 2)

1611 Concrete construction: roads, highways, public sidewalks, and streets-contractors (Vol. 2)

2899 Concrete curing compounds (blends of pigments, waxes, and resins) (Vol. 1)

7323 Consumer credit reporting bureaus (Vol. 2)

5731 Consumer electronic equipment stores—retail (Vol. 2)

6141 Consumer finance companies (Vol. 2)

9611 Consumer protection offices-government (Vol. 2)

6331 Contact lens insurance (Vol. 2)

3851 Contact lenses (Vol. 1)

5048 Contact lenses—wholesale (Vol. 2)

3643 Contacts, electrical: except carbon and graphite (Vol. 1)

2631 Container board (Vol. 1)

3537 Containers, air cargo: metal (Vol. 1)

2653 Containers, corrugated and solid fiberboard (Vol. 1)

3497 Containers, foil: for bakery goods and frozen goods (Vol. 1)

2656 Containers, food, sanitary: except folding (Vol. 1)

3221 Containers for packing, bottling, and canning: glass (Vol. 1)

2655 Containers, laminated phenolic and vulcanized fiber (Vol. 1)

2655 Containers, liquid tight fiber (except sanitary food containers) (Vol. 1)

2449 Containers made of staves (Vol. 1)

3411 Containers, metal: food, milk, oil, beer, general line (Vol. 1)

5113 Containers, paper and disposable plastics—wholesale (Vol. 2)

3089 Containers, plastics: except foam, bottles, and bags (Vol. 1)

3412 Containers, shipping: barrels, kegs, drums, packages-liquid tight (metal) (Vol. 1)

3443 Containers, shipping: metal plate (bombs, etc.)-except missile casings (Vol. 1)

2449 Containers, veneer and plywood: except nailed and lock corner boxes (Vol. 1)

8299 Continuing education programs (Vol. 2)

2761 Continuous forms, office and business: carbonized or multiple reproduction (Vol. 1)

7213 Continuous towel supply service (Vol. 2)

3827 Contour projectors (Vol. 1)

5812 Contract feeding (Vol. 2)

8611 Contractor's associations (Vol. 2)

7389 Contractors' disbursement control (Vol. 2)

2835 Contrast media diagnostic products (e.g., iodine and barium) (Vol. 1)

3625 Control circuit devices: magnet and solid-state (Vol. 1)

3625 Control circuit relays, industrial (Vol. 1)

0721 Control, crop: after planting; Weed (Vol. 2)

0711 Control, crop: before planting; Weed (Vol. 2)

3625 Control equipment, electric (Vol. 1)

3621 Control equipment for buses and trucks (Vol. 1)

3714 Control equipment, motor vehicle: acceleration mechanisms and governors (Vol. 1)

0721 Control for crops, with or without fertilizing; Disease (Vol. 2)

0721 Control for crops, with or without fertilizing; Insect (Vol. 2)

3613 Control panels, electric power distribution (Vol. 1)

3559 Control rod drive mechanisms for use on nuclear reactors (Vol. 1)

3612 Control transformers (Vol. 1)

3492 Control valves, fluid power: metal (Vol. 1)

3674 Controlled rectifiers, solid-state (Vol. 1)

3823 Controllers for process variables: electric, electronic, and pneumatic (Vol. 1)

9311 Controllers' offices-government (Vol. 2)

5084 Controlling instruments and accessories, industrial—wholesale (Vol. 2)

3625 Controls and control accessories, industrial (Vol. 1)

3625 Controls for adjustable speed drives (Vol. 1)

3824 Controls, revolution and timing instruments (Vol. 1)

8059 Convalescent homes for psychiatric patients, with health care (Vol. 2)

8051 Convalescent homes with continuous nursing care (Vol. 2)

8059 Convalescent homes with health care (Vol. 2)

3631 Convection ovens, household: including portable (Vol. 1)

5074 Convectors—wholesale (Vol. 2)

5411 Convenience food stores—retail (Vol. 2)

3643 Convenience outlets, electric (Vol. 1)

7389 Convention bureaus (Vol. 2)

7389 Convention decorators (Vol. 2)

8661 Convents (Vol. 2)

2679 Converted Paper and Paperboard Products Not Elsewhere Classified (Vol. 1)

3621 Converters, phase and rotary: electrical equipment (Vol. 1)

2515 Convertible sofas (Vol. 1)

3111 Convertors, leather (Vol. 1)

3496 Conveyor belts, made from purchased wire (Vol. 1)

1796 Conveyor system installation-contractors (Vol. 2)

3535 Conveyor systems for general industrial use (Vol. 1)

5084 Conveyor systems—wholesale (Vol. 2)

3535 Conveyors and Conveying Equipment (Vol. 1)

3523 Conveyors, farm (agricultural machinery) (Vol. 1)

3469 Cookers, pressure: stamped or drawn (Vol. 1)

3589 Cookers, steam: restaurant type (Vol. 1)

5461 Cookie stores—retail (Vol. 2)

2052 Cookies and Crackers (Vol. 1)

2052 Cookies (Vol. 1)

5149 Cookies—wholesale (Vol. 2)

3634 Cooking appliances, household: electric, except convection and microwave ovens (Vol. 1)

3589 Cooking equipment, commercial (Vol. 1)

5046 Cooking equipment, commercial—wholesale (Vol. 2)

2079 Cooking oils, vegetable: except corn oil-refined (Vol. 1)

5149 Cooking oils—wholesale (Vol. 2)

8299 Cooking schools (Vol. 2)

3365 Cooking utensils, cast aluminum: except die-castings (Vol. 1)

3321 Cooking utensils, cast iron (Vol. 1)

3229 Cooking utensils, glass and glass ceramic (Vol. 1)

3262 Cooking ware, china (Vol. 1)

3263 Cooking ware, fine earthenware (Vol. 1)
3469 Cooking ware, porcelain enameled (Vol. 1)
3269 Cooking ware: stoneware, coarse earthenware, and
       pottery (Vol. 1)
5719 Cookware—retail (Vol. 2)
4961 Cooled air suppliers (Vol. 2)
5078 Coolers, beverage and drinking water:
       mechanical—wholesale (Vol. 2)
3585 Coolers, milk and water: electric (Vol. 1)
3086 Coolers, portable: foamed plastics (Vol. 1)
0723 Cooling; Fruit vacuum (Vol. 2)
4741 Cooling of railroad cars (Vol. 2)
3724 Cooling systems, aircraft engine (Vol. 1)
3443 Cooling towers, metal plate (Vol. 1)
3444 Cooling towers, sheet metal (Vol. 1)
2499 Cooling towers, wood or wood and sheet metal
       combination (Vol. 1)
0723 Cooling; Vegetable vacuum (Vol. 2)
2449 Cooperage (Vol. 1)
2429 Cooperage stock mills (Vol. 1)
2429 Cooperage stock: staves, heading, and hoops-sawed
       or split (Vol. 1)
5085 Cooperage stock—wholesale (Vol. 2)
1531 Cooperative apartment developers on own account
       (Vol. 2)
6531 Cooperative apartment manager (Vol. 2)
6311 Cooperative life insurance organizations (Vol. 2)
2449 Coopered tubs (Vol. 1)
0751 Coops; Cleaning poultry (Vol. 2)
5137 Coordinate sets: women's, children's, and
       infants'—wholesale (Vol. 2)
3259 Coping, wall: clay (Vol. 1)
3272 Copings, concrete (Vol. 1)
2822 Copolymers: butadiene-styrene, butadiene-
       acrylonitrile, over 50 percent butadiene (Vol. 1)
3366 Copper and copper-base alloy castings, except die-
       castings (Vol. 1)
3366 Copper and copper-base alloy foundries (Vol. 1)
2879 Copper arsenate, formulated (Vol. 1)
2819 Copper chloride (Vol. 1)
3364 Copper die-castings (Vol. 1)
3497 Copper foil, not made in rolling mills (Vol. 1)
3366 Copper Foundries (Vol. 1)
3366 Copper foundries, except die-castings (Vol. 1)
3331 Copper ingots and refinery bars, primary (Vol. 1)
2819 Copper iodide and oxide (Vol. 1)
1021 Copper ore mining (Vol. 2)
5052 Copper ore—wholesale (Vol. 2)
1021 Copper Ores (Vol. 2)
3351 Copper rolling, drawing, and extruding (Vol. 1)
5051 Copper sheets, plates, bars, rods, pipes, etc.—
       wholesale (Vol. 2)
3331 Copper smelting and refining, primary (Vol. 1)
3341 Copper smelting and refining, secondary (Vol. 1)
2819 Copper sulfate (Vol. 1)
1761 Coppersmithing, in connection with construction
       work-contractors (Vol. 2)
7699 Coppersmithing repair, except construction (Vol. 2)
3555 Copy holders, printers' (Vol. 1)
6794 Copyright buying and licensing (Vol. 2)

7389 Copyright protection service (Vol. 2)
3292 Cord, asbestos (Vol. 1)
2298 Cord, braided (Vol. 1)
3643 Cord connectors, electric (Vol. 1)
2296 Cord for reinforcing rubber tires, industrial belting,
       and fuel cells (Vol. 1)
3357 Cord sets, flexible: made in wiredrawing plants
       (Vol. 1)
2298 Cordage: abaca (Manila), sisal, henequen, hemp,
       jute, and other fibers (Vol. 1)
3552 Cordage and rope machines (Vol. 1)
2298 Cordage and Twine (Vol. 1)
5085 Cordage—wholesale (Vol. 2)
2281 Cordage yarn, cotton (Vol. 1)
2892 Cordeau detonant (explosives) (Vol. 1)
2085 Cordials, alcoholic (Vol. 1)
2087 Cordials, nonalcoholic (Vol. 1)
2892 Cordite (explosives) (Vol. 1)
2241 Cords, fabric (Vol. 1)
2211 Corduroys, cotton (Vol. 1)
5099 Cordwood—wholesale (Vol. 2)
3567 Core baking and mold drying ovens (Vol. 1)
1799 Core drilling for building construction-contractors
       (Vol. 2)
3532 Core drills (Vol. 1)
2899 Core oil and binders (Vol. 1)
2899 Core wash (Vol. 1)
2899 Core wax (Vol. 1)
3482 Cores, bullet: 30 mm. (or 1.18 inch) or less (Vol.
       1)
2655 Cores, fiber (metal-end or all-fiber) (Vol. 1)
3679 Cores, magnetic (Vol. 1)
3543 Cores, sand (foundry) (Vol. 1)
3714 Cores, tire valve (Vol. 1)
2499 Cork products (Vol. 1)
5085 Cork—wholesale (Vol. 2)
3559 Cork working machinery (Vol. 1)
2499 Corks, bottle (Vol. 1)
0115 Corn (Vol. 2)
2096 Corn chips and related corn snacks (Vol. 1)
5145 Corn chips—wholesale (Vol. 2)
2452 Corn cribs, prefabricated: wood (Vol. 1)
0721 Corn; Detasseling of (Vol. 2)
0723 Corn drying (Vol. 2)
0115 Corn farms, except sweet corn or popcorn (Vol. 2)
0161 Corn farms; Sweet (Vol. 2)
2043 Corn flakes (Vol. 1)
2041 Corn grits and flakes for brewers' use (Vol. 1)
3523 Corn heads for combines (Vol. 1)
2043 Corn, hulled (cereal breakfast food) (Vol. 1)
3423 Corn knives (Vol. 1)
2041 Corn meal and flour (Vol. 1)
2046 Corn oil cake and meal (Vol. 1)
2046 Corn oil, crude and refined (Vol. 1)
3523 Corn pickers and shellers, farm (Vol. 1)
3634 Corn poppers, electric (Vol. 1)
3589 Corn popping machines, commercial type (Vol. 1)
3556 Corn popping machines, industrial type (Vol. 1)
3842 Corn remover and bunion pads (Vol. 1)

3625 Crane and hoist controls, including metal mill (Vol. 1)

3531 Crane carriers (Vol. 1)

7353 Crane rental and leasing (Vol. 2)

3531 Cranes, construction (Vol. 1)

5082 Cranes, construction—wholesale (Vol. 2)

3531 Cranes, except industrial plant (Vol. 1)

5084 Cranes, industrial—wholesale (Vol. 2)

3537 Cranes, mobile industrial truck (Vol. 1)

3536 Cranes, overhead traveling (Vol. 1)

3599 Crankshaft and camshaft machining (Vol. 1)

3714 Crankshaft assemblies, motor vehicle: gasoline engine (Vol. 1)

3541 Crankshaft regrinding machines (Vol. 1)

3462 Crankshafts, forged steel: not made in rolling mills (Vol. 1)

2299 Crash, linen (Vol. 1)

2211 Crash toweling, cotton (Vol. 1)

2449 Crates: berry, butter, fruit, and vegetable-wood, wirebound (Vol. 1)

5085 Crates, except paper—wholesale (Vol. 2)

4783 Crating goods for shipping (Vol. 2)

0913 Crayfish, catching of (Vol. 2)

3952 Crayons: chalk, gypsum, charcoal, fusains, pastel, and wax (Vol. 1)

2026 Cream, aerated (Vol. 1)

2026 Cream, bottled (Vol. 1)

2023 Cream: dried, powdered, and canned (Vol. 1)

2869 Cream of tartar (Vol. 1)

5084 Cream separators, except farm—wholesale (Vol. 2)

3523 Cream separators, farm (Vol. 1)

5083 Cream separators, farm—wholesale (Vol. 2)

3556 Cream separators, industrial (Vol. 1)

2026 Cream, sour (Vol. 1)

5143 Cream stations—wholesale (Vol. 2)

2023 Cream substitutes (Vol. 1)

2021 Creamery Butter (Vol. 1)

2021 Creamery butter (Vol. 1)

2844 Creams, cosmetic (Vol. 1)

2844 Creams, shaving (Vol. 1)

6351 Credit and other financial responsibility insurance (Vol. 2)

7323 Credit bureaus and agencies (Vol. 2)

6153 Credit card service, collection by central agency (Vol. 2)

7389 Credit card service (collection by individual firms) (Vol. 2)

7323 Credit clearinghouses (Vol. 2)

6159 Credit institutions, agricultural (Vol. 2)

7323 Credit investigation services (Vol. 2)

7323 Credit Reporting Services (Vol. 2)

6061 Credit unions, Federal (Vol. 2)

6062 Credit Unions—Not Federally Chartered (Vol. 2)

6062 Credit unions, State: not federally chartered (Vol. 2)

3949 Creels, fish (Vol. 1)

3552 Creels, textile machinery (Vol. 1)

3569 Cremating ovens (Vol. 1)

7261 Crematories (Vol. 2)

2865 Creosote oil, made in chemical plants (Vol. 1)

2861 Creosote, wood (Vol. 1)

2491 Creosoting of wood (Vol. 1)

2679 Crepe paper (Vol. 1)

2221 Crepe satins (Vol. 1)

2211 Crepes, cotton (Vol. 1)

2821 Cresol-furfural resins (Vol. 1)

2821 Cresol resins (Vol. 1)

2865 Cresols, made in chemical plants (Vol. 1)

2865 Cresylic acid, made in chemical plants (Vol. 1)

2211 Cretonne, cotton (Vol. 1)

3731 Crew boats, building and repairing (Vol. 1)

0761 Crew leaders, farm labor: contract (Vol. 2)

2252 Crew socks (Vol. 1)

3272 Cribbing, concrete (Vol. 1)

2514 Cribs, metal (Vol. 1)

2511 Cribs, wood (Vol. 1)

3949 Cricket equipment (Vol. 1)

9229 Criminal justice statistics centers-government (Vol. 2)

2211 Crinoline (Vol. 1)

8322 Crisis centers (Vol. 2)

8322 Crisis intervention centers (Vol. 2)

2284 Crochet thread: cotton, silk, manmade fibers, and wool (Vol. 1)

2395 Crochet ware, machine-made (Vol. 1)

2281 Crochet yarn: cotton, silk, wool, and manmade staple (Vol. 1)

3634 Crock pots, electric (Vol. 1)

3269 Crockery (Vol. 1)

5719 Crockery stores—retail (Vol. 2)

5023 Crockery—wholesale (Vol. 2)

2051 Croissants, except frozen (Vol. 1)

2053 Croissants, frozen (Vol. 1)

0721 Crop: after planting; Weed control, (Vol. 2)

0711 Crop: before planting; Weed control, (Vol. 2)

3523 Crop driers, farm (Vol. 1)

0721 Crop dusting, with/without fertilizing (Vol. 2)

0191 Crop farms, general (Vol. 2)

0191 Crop; General Farms—Primarily (Vol. 2)

0722 Crop Harvesting Primarily by Machine (Vol. 2)

0721 Crop Planting, Cultivating and Protecting (Vol. 2)

0723 Crop Preparation Services for Market Except Cotton Ginning (Vol. 2)

0721 Crop spraying, with/without fertilizing (Vol. 2)

0171 Crops; Berry (Vol. 2)

0711 Crops; Chemical treatment of soil for (Vol. 2)

0139 Crops Except Cash Grains Not Elsewhere Classified; Field (Vol. 2)

0711 Crops; Fertilizer application for (Vol. 2)

0182 Crops; Greenhouses for food (Vol. 2)

0182 Crops Grown Under Cover; Food (Vol. 2)

0182 Crops, grown under cover; Hydroponic (Vol. 2)

0711 Crops; Lime spreading for (Vol. 2)

0721 Crops, mechanical and chemical; Thinning of (Vol. 2)

3199 Crops, riding (Vol. 1)

0711 Crops; Spreading lime for (Vol. 2)

0721 Crops, with or without fertilizing; Disease control for (Vol. 2)

0721 Crops, with or without fertilizing; Dusting (Vol. 2)

0721 Crops, with or without fertilizing; Insect control for (Vol. 2)

0721 Crops, with or without fertilizing; Planting (Vol. 2)

0721 Crops, with or without fertilizing; Seeding (Vol. 2)

0721 Crops, with or without fertilizing; Spraying (Vol. 2)

3949 Croquet sets (Vol. 1)

3272 Crossing slabs, concrete (Vol. 1)

2491 Crossties, treated (Vol. 1)

8072 Crowns and bridges made in dental laboratories to order for the profession (Vol. 2)

3466 Crowns and Closures (Vol. 1)

5085 Crowns and closures, metal—wholesale (Vol. 2)

3466 Crowns, jar: stamped metal (Vol. 1)

3255 Crucibles, fire clay (Vol. 1)

3297 Crucibles: graphite, magnesite, chrome, silica, or other nonclay materials (Vol. 1)

5172 Crude oil, except bulk stations and terminals— wholesale (Vol. 2)

1311 Crude oil production (Vol. 2)

1311 Crude Petroleum and Natural Gas (Vol. 2)

4612 Crude Petroleum Pipelines (Vol. 2)

1311 Crude petroleum production (Vol. 2)

0851 Cruising timber (Vol. 2)

2051 Crullers, except frozen (Vol. 1)

1423 Crushed and Broken Granite (Vol. 2)

1422 Crushed and Broken Limestone (Vol. 2)

1429 Crushed and Broken Stone Not Elsewhere Classified (Vol. 2)

3523 Crushers, feed (agricultural machinery) (Vol. 1)

3569 Crushers, ice: except household (Vol. 1)

3531 Crushers, mineral: portable (Vol. 1)

3532 Crushers, mineral: stationary (Vol. 1)

3821 Crushing and grinding apparatus, laboratory (Vol. 1)

5084 Crushing machinery and equipment, industrial— wholesale (Vol. 2)

1221 Crushing plants, bituminous coal (Vol. 2)

5082 Crushing, pulverizing and screening machinery for construction and mining—wholesale (Vol. 2)

0273 Crustacean farms (Vol. 2)

3842 Crutches and walkers (Vol. 1)

3679 Cryogenic cooling devices (e.g., cryostats) for infrared detectors and masers (Vol. 1)

3443 Cryogenic tanks, for liquids and gases: metal plate (Vol. 1)

1499 Cryolite mining (Vol. 2)

2064 Crystallized fruits and fruit peel (Vol. 1)

3679 Crystals and crystal assemblies, radio (Vol. 1)

3231 Crystals, watch: made from purchased glass (Vol. 1)

3613 Cubicles (electric switchboard equipment) (Vol. 1)

0161 Cucumber farms (Vol. 2)

3949 Cues and cue tips, billiard and pool (Vol. 1)

3965 Cuff buttons, except precious metal and precious or semiprecious stones (Vol. 1)

3911 Cuff buttons, precious metal and precious or semiprecious stones (Vol. 1)

3961 Cuff-links and studs, except precious metal and gems (Vol. 1)

3429 Cuffs, leg: iron (Vol. 1)

1231 Culm bank recovery, anthracite: except on a contract basis (Vol. 2)

1241 Culm bank recovery: bituminous coal, anthracite, and lignite on a contract basis (Vol. 2)

1221 Culm bank recovery, bituminous coal or lignite: except on a contract basis (Vol. 2)

2369 Culottes: girls' and children's (Vol. 1)

2339 Culottes: women's, misses', and juniors' (Vol. 1)

0181 Cultivated: growing of; Florists' greens, (Vol. 2)

0721 Cultivating and Protecting; Crop Planting, (Vol. 2)

5083 Cultivating machinery and equipment—wholesale (Vol. 2)

0721 Cultivation of; Trees, orchard: (Vol. 2)

0721 Cultivation services; Citrus grove (Vol. 2)

0721 Cultivation services, mechanical and flame (Vol. 2)

0721 Cultivation services; Orchard (Vol. 2)

0721 Cultivation services; Vineyard (Vol. 2)

3523 Cultivators, agricultural field and row crop (Vol. 1)

3524 Cultivators (garden tractor equipment) (Vol. 1)

3069 Culture cups, rubber (Vol. 1)

2836 Culture media or concentrates, except in vitro and in vivo (Vol. 1)

0919 Cultured pearl production (Vol. 2)

1771 Culvert construction-contractors (Vol. 2)

3272 Culvert pipe, concrete (Vol. 1)

3443 Culverts, metal plate (Vol. 1)

3444 Culverts, sheet metal (Vol. 1)

2389 Cummerbunds (Vol. 1)

3443 Cupolas, metal plate (Vol. 1)

2823 Cuprammonium fibers (Vol. 1)

1021 Cuprite mining (Vol. 2)

3086 Cups, foamed plastics (Vol. 1)

3599 Cups, oil and grease: metal (Vol. 1)

5113 Cups, paper and disposable plastics—wholesale (Vol. 2)

2656 Cups, paper: except those made from pressed or molded pulp (Vol. 1)

3089 Cups, plastics: except foam (Vol. 1)

2679 Cups, pressed and molded pulp (Vol. 1)

3351 Cups, primer and cartridge: copper and copper alloy (Vol. 1)

1771 Curb construction-contractors (Vol. 2)

3281 Curbing, granite and stone (Vol. 1)

2013 Cured meats: brined, dried, and salted (Vol. 1)

2011 Cured meats (Vol. 1)

3523 Curers, tobacco (Vol. 1)

2899 Curing compounds, concrete (blends of pigments, waxes, and resins) (Vol. 1)

0723 Curing; Potato (Vol. 2)

0723 Curing; Sweet potato (Vol. 2)

5947 Curio shops—retail (Vol. 2)

5199 Curios—wholesale (Vol. 2)

3999 Curlers, hair: designed for beauty parlors (Vol. 1)

3965 Curlers, hair: except equipment designed for beauty parlor use (Vol. 1)

3069 Curlers, hair: rubber (Vol. 1)

3999 Curling feathers, for the trade (Vol. 1)
3634 Curling irons, electric (Vol. 1)
3999 Curls, artificial (hair) (Vol. 1)
0171 Currant farms (Vol. 2)
2759 Currency, engraving of (Vol. 1)
3643 Current-Carrying Wiring Devices (Vol. 1)
3629 Current collector wheels for trolley rigging (Vol. 1)
3612 Current limiting reactors, electrical (Vol. 1)
3825 Current measuring equipment (Vol. 1)
3643 Current taps, attachment plug and screw shell types (Vol. 1)
8299 Curriculum development, educational (Vol. 2)
3111 Currying of leather (Vol. 1)
7216 Curtain cleaning and repair (Vol. 2)
2591 Curtain rods, poles, and fixtures (Vol. 1)
5714 Curtain stores—retail (Vol. 2)
2499 Curtain stretchers, wood (Vol. 1)
1791 Curtain wall installation-contractors (Vol. 2)
3449 Curtain wall, metal (Vol. 1)
3999 Curtains, advertising (Vol. 1)
2258 Curtains and curtain fabrics, lace (Vol. 1)
2391 Curtains and Draperies (Vol. 1)
2394 Curtains: dock and welding (Vol. 1)
2259 Curtains (Vol. 1)
2392 Curtains, shower (Vol. 1)
5023 Curtains—wholesale (Vol. 2)
2391 Curtains, window (Vol. 1)
2515 Cushion springs, assembled (Vol. 1)
3952 Cushions and burnishers, gilders' (Vol. 1)
3086 Cushions, carpet and rug: plastics foam (Vol. 1)
2392 Cushions, except spring and carpet cushions (Vol. 1)
2515 Cushions, spring (Vol. 1)
2024 Custard, frozen (Vol. 1)
7349 Custodians of schools on a contract or fee basis (Vol. 2)
6289 Custodians of securities (Vol. 2)
1541 Custom builders, industrial and warehouse-general contractors (Vol. 2)
1542 Custom builders, nonresidential: except industrial and warehouses-general contractors (Vol. 2)
1522 Custom builders, residential: except single-family-general contractors (Vol. 2)
1521 Custom builders, single-family houses-general contractors (Vol. 2)
3087 Custom Compounding of Purchased Plastics Resins (Vol. 1)
3087 Custom compounding of purchased resins (Vol. 1)
3069 Custom compounding of rubber materials (Vol. 1)
0751 Custom: for individuals; Slaughtering, (Vol. 2)
0723 Custom; Grain grinding, (Vol. 2)
0723 Custom; Peanut shelling, (Vol. 2)
3449 Custom roll formed products, metal (Vol. 1)
2421 Custom sawmills (Vol. 1)
5699 Custom tailors—retail (Vol. 2)
4731 Customhouse brokers (Vol. 2)
7532 Customizing automobiles, trucks or vans: except on a factory basis (Vol. 2)
9311 Customs Bureaus (Vol. 2)
4731 Customs clearance of freight (Vol. 2)

3231 Cut and engraved glassware, made from purchased glass (Vol. 1)
5992 Cut flowers—retail (Vol. 2)
5193 Cut flowers—wholesale (Vol. 2)
3131 Cut stock for boots and shoes (Vol. 1)
2421 Cut stock, softwood (Vol. 1)
3281 Cut Stone and Stone Products (Vol. 1)
3281 Cut stone products (Vol. 1)
3421 Cutlery (Vol. 1)
3421 Cutlery, except table cutlery with handles of metal (Vol. 1)
5719 Cutlery stores—retail (Vol. 2)
5072 Cutlery—wholesale (Vol. 2)
3914 Cutlery, with metal handles and blades (Vol. 1)
3541 Cutoff machines (metalworking machinery) (Vol. 1)
3993 Cutouts and displays, window and lobby (Vol. 1)
3613 Cutouts, distribution (Vol. 1)
2675 Cutouts, paper and paperboard: die-cut from purchased material (Vol. 1)
3643 Cutouts, switch and fuse (Vol. 1)
3556 Cutters, biscuit (machines) (Vol. 1)
3532 Cutters, coal (Vol. 1)
3523 Cutters, ensilage (Vol. 1)
3423 Cutters, glass (Vol. 1)
3545 Cutters, milling (Vol. 1)
3554 Cutting and folding machines, paper (Vol. 1)
3423 Cutting dies: except metal cutting (Vol. 1)
3544 Cutting dies, for cutting metal (Vol. 1)
3423 Cutting dies, paper industry (Vol. 1)
3843 Cutting instruments, dental (Vol. 1)
3541 Cutting machines, pipe (machine tools) (Vol. 1)
2675 Cutting of cards (Vol. 1)
3111 Cutting of leather (Vol. 1)
2992 Cutting oils, blending and compounding from purchased material (Vol. 1)
1629 Cutting right-of-way-general contractors (Vol. 2)
3545 Cutting tools and bits for use on lathes, planers, shapers, etc. (Vol. 1)
3545 Cutting Tools, Machine Tool Accessories and Machinists' Precision Measuring Devices (Vol. 1)
3549 Cutting up lines (Vol. 1)
3231 Cutware, made from purchased glass (Vol. 1)
2819 Cyanides (Vol. 1)
1459 Cyanite mining (Vol. 2)
1321 Cycle condensate production (natural gas) (Vol. 2)
3944 Cycles, sidewalk: children's (Vol. 1)
5169 Cyclic crudes and intermediates—wholesale (Vol. 2)
2865 Cyclic crudes, coal tar: product of coal tar distillation (Vol. 1)
2865 Cyclic intermediates, made in chemical plants (Vol. 1)
2865 Cyclic Organic Crudes and Intermediates, and Organic Dyes and Pigments (Vol. 1)
3069 Cyclo rubbers, natural (Vol. 1)
2822 Cyclo rubbers, synthetic (Vol. 1)
2865 Cyclohexane (Vol. 1)
3443 Cyclones, industrial: metal plate (Vol. 1)

2834 Cyclopropane for anesthetic use (U.S.P. par N.F.), packaged (Vol. 1)
2869 Cyclopropane (Vol. 1)
3699 Cyclotrons (Vol. 1)
3714 Cylinder heads, motor vehicle: gasoline engines (Vol. 1)
3272 Cylinder pipe, prestressed concrete (Vol. 1)
3272 Cylinder pipe, pretensioned concrete (Vol. 1)
3541 Cylinder reboring machines (Vol. 1)
3496 Cylinder wire cloth, made from purchased wire (Vol. 1)
3484 Cylinders and clips, gun: 30 mm. (or 1.18 inch) or less (Vol. 1)
3593 Cylinders, fluid power: hydraulic and pneumatic (Vol. 1)
3443 Cylinders, pressure: metal plate (Vol. 1)
3561 Cylinders, pump (Vol. 1)
3931 Cymbals and parts (Vol. 1)
3845 Cystoscopes, electromedical (Vol. 1)
3841 Cystoscopes, except electromedical (Vol. 1)
2835 Cytology and histology diagnostic products (Vol. 1)

D

5812 Dairy bars (Vol. 2)
0241 Dairy cattle farm; Milk production, (Vol. 2)
5143 Dairy depots—wholesale (Vol. 2)
3523 Dairy equipment, farm (Vol. 1)
5083 Dairy farm machinery and equipment—wholesale (Vol. 2)

0241 Dairy Farms (Vol. 2)

0241 Dairy heifer replacement farms (Vol. 2)
0751 Dairy herd improvement associations (Vol. 2)
5149 Dairy products, dried or canned—wholesale (Vol. 2)

5143 Dairy Products Except Dried or Canned (Vol. 2)

5143 Dairy products, except dried or canned—wholesale (Vol. 2)
5963 Dairy products, house-to-house—retail (Vol. 2)
3556 Dairy products machinery and equipment (Vol. 1)
5084 Dairy products manufacturing machinery—wholesale (Vol. 2)

5451 Dairy Products Stores (Vol. 2)

5451 Dairy products stores—retail (Vol. 2)
1629 Dam construction-general contractors (Vol. 2)
3441 Dam gates, metal plate (Vol. 1)
2211 Damasks, cotton (Vol. 1)
3822 Damper operators: pneumatic, thermostatic, and electric (Vol. 1)
3444 Dampers, sheet metal (Vol. 1)
1799 Dampproofing buildings-contractors (Vol. 2)
7929 Dance bands (Vol. 2)
7911 Dance hall operation (Vol. 2)
7911 Dance instructors (Vol. 2)
7911 Dance studios and schools (Vol. 2)

7911 Dance Studios, Schools and Halls (Vol. 2)

7911 Dancing schools, professional (Vol. 2)
5043 Darkroom apparatus—wholesale (Vol. 2)
2284 Darning thread: cotton, silk, manmade fibers, and wool (Vol. 1)
2281 Darning yarn: cotton, silk, wool, and manmade staple (Vol. 1)
3944 Darts and dart games (Vol. 1)
7375 Data base information retrieval services (Vol. 2)
7379 Data based developers (Vol. 2)
7374 Data entry service (Vol. 2)
3823 Data loggers, industrial process type (Vol. 1)
7379 Data processing consultants (Vol. 2)

8243 Data Processing Schools (Vol. 2)

7374 Data processing services (Vol. 2)
3661 Data sets, telephone and telegraph (Vol. 1)
4813 Data telephone communications (Vol. 2)
7374 Data verification service (Vol. 2)
0179 Date orchards and farms (Vol. 2)
3953 Date stamps, hand: with rubber or metal type (Vol. 1)
2064 Dates: chocolate covered, sugared, and stuffed (Vol. 1)
2034 Dates, dried (Vol. 1)
3579 Dating devices and machines, except rubber stamps (Vol. 1)
7299 Dating service (Vol. 2)
3536 Davits (Vol. 1)
7999 Day camps (Vol. 2)
8322 Day care centers, adult and handicapped (Vol. 2)
8351 Day care centers, child (Vol. 2)
2879 DDT (insecticide), formulated (Vol. 1)
2869 DDT, technical (Vol. 1)
6221 Dealers, commodity contract (Vol. 2)
5143 Dealers in dairy products—wholesale (Vol. 2)
5144 Dealers in poultry and poultry products—wholesale (Vol. 2)
5159 Dealers in raw farm products, except grain, field beans, and livestock—wholesale (Vol. 2)
6211 Dealers, mineral royalties or leases (Vol. 2)
6211 Dealers, security (Vol. 2)
4212 Debris removal, local carting only (Vol. 2)
7299 Debt counseling or adjustment service to individuals (Vol. 2)
3541 Deburring machines (Vol. 1)
3825 Decade boxes: capacitance, inductance, and resistance (Vol. 1)
2869 Decahydronaphthalene (Vol. 1)
3999 Decalcomania work, except on china or glass: for the trade (Vol. 1)
3269 Decalcomania work on china and glass, for the trade (Vol. 1)
2752 Decalcomanias (dry transfers), lithographed (Vol. 1)
2759 Decalcomanias, printed: except lithographed or gravure (Vol. 1)

0175 Deciduous Tree Fruits (Vol. 2)

2789 Deckling books, cards, and paper (Vol. 1)
3577 Decoders, computer peripheral equipment (Vol. 1)
3471 Decontaminating and cleaning of missile and satellite parts, for the trade (Vol. 1)
3231 Decorated glassware: e.g., chipped, engraved, etched, sandblasted-made from purchased glass (Vol. 1)
3269 Decorating china, for the trade (Vol. 1)
7699 Decorating china to individual order (Vol. 2)

7389 Decoration service for special events (Vol. 2)

3648 Decorative area lighting fixtures, except residential (Vol. 1)

3229 Decorative glassware: made in glassmaking establishments (Vol. 1)

3471 Decorative plating and finishing of formed products, for the trade (Vol. 1)

2395 Decorative stitching, for the trade (Vol. 1)

7389 Decorators consulting service, interior-not painters or paperhangers (Vol. 2)

0723 Decorticating and retting; Flax (Vol. 2)

0723 Decorticating flax (Vol. 2)

3949 Decoys, duck and other game birds (Vol. 1)

3634 Deep fat fryers, household: electric (Vol. 1)

4424 Deep Sea Domestic Transportation of Freight (Vol. 2)

4481 Deep sea foreign passenger transportation (Vol. 2)

4412 Deep Sea Foreign Transportation of Freight (Vol. 2)

4481 Deep Sea of Passengers Transportation Except by Ferry (Vol. 2)

4481 Deep sea transportation of passengers (Vol. 2)

3845 Defibrilators (Vol. 1)

2874 Defluorinated phosphates (Vol. 1)

2879 Defoliants (Vol. 1)

3714 Defrosters, motor vehicle (Vol. 1)

3559 Degreasing machines, automotive (garage equipment) (Vol. 1)

3559 Degreasing machines, industrial (Vol. 1)

2842 Degreasing solvent (Vol. 1)

3634 Dehumidifiers, electric: portable (Vol. 1)

3585 Dehumidifiers, except portable: electric (Vol. 1)

2034 Dehydrated fruits, vegetables, and soups (Vol. 1)

3556 Dehydrating equipment, food processing (Vol. 1)

3728 Deicing equipment, aircraft (Vol. 1)

2899 Deicing fluid (Vol. 1)

2611 Deinking of newsprint (Vol. 1)

3679 Delay lines (Vol. 1)

0723 Delinting; Cotton seed (Vol. 2)

7319 Delivering advertising, private (Vol. 2)

3496 Delivery cases, made from purchased wire (Vol. 1)

3825 Demand meters, electric (Vol. 1)

2499 Demijohn covers: willow, rattan and reed (Vol. 1)

1795 Demolition of buildings or other structures, except marine-contractors (Vol. 2)

7389 Demonstration service, separate from sale (Vol. 2)

3715 Demountable cargo containers (Vol. 1)

2869 Denatured alcohol, industrial (nonbeverage) (Vol. 1)

2211 Denims (Vol. 1)

3826 Densitometers, analytical (Vol. 1)

3861 Densitometers (Vol. 1)

3823 Density and specific gravity instruments, industrial process type (Vol. 1)

3843 Dental alloys for amalgams (Vol. 1)

8621 Dental associations (Vol. 2)

3843 Dental chairs (Vol. 1)

3843 Dental engines (Vol. 1)

3843 Dental Equipment and Supplies (Vol. 1)

3843 Dental equipment and supplies (Vol. 1)

5047 Dental equipment—wholesale (Vol. 2)

3843 Dental hand instruments, including forceps (Vol. 1)

8049 Dental hygienists, offices of (Vol. 2)

7699 Dental instrument repair (Vol. 2)

6324 Dental insurance (providing services by contracts with health facilities) (Vol. 2)

8072 Dental Laboratories (Vol. 2)

8072 Dental laboratories, except X-ray (Vol. 2)

8071 Dental laboratories, X-ray (Vol. 2)

3843 Dental laboratory equipment (Vol. 1)

5047 Dental laboratory equipment—wholesale (Vol. 2)

3843 Dental metal (Vol. 1)

8021 Dental surgeons, offices of (Vol. 2)

2844 Dentifrices (Vol. 1)

8021 Dentists, offices and clinics of (Vol. 2)

5047 Dentists' professional supplies—wholesale (Vol. 2)

2844 Denture cleaners (Vol. 1)

3843 Denture materials (Vol. 1)

8072 Dentures made in dental laboratories to order for the profession (Vol. 2)

7342 Deodorant servicing of rest rooms (Vol. 2)

2842 Deodorants, nonpersonal (Vol. 1)

2844 Deodorants, personal (Vol. 1)

5311 Department Stores (Vol. 2)

5311 Department stores—retail (Vol. 2)

2844 Depilatories, cosmetic (Vol. 1)

7299 Depilatory salons (Vol. 2)

3471 Depolishing metal, for the trade (Vol. 1)

6099 Deposit brokers (Vol. 2)

6399 Deposit or share insurance (Vol. 2)

3842 Depressors, tongue (Vol. 1)

3489 Depth charge release pistols and projectors (Vol. 1)

3483 Depth charges and parts (ordnance) (Vol. 1)

2834 Dermatological preparations (Vol. 1)

8011 Dermatologists, offices of (Vol. 2)

1389 Derrick building, repairing, and dismantling: oil and gas-on a contract basis (Vol. 2)

3531 Derricks, except oil and gas field (Vol. 1)

3533 Derricks, oil and gas field (Vol. 1)

5084 Derricks—wholesale (Vol. 2)

3559 Desalination equipment (Vol. 1)

2899 Desalter kits, sea water (Vol. 1)

3295 Desiccants, activated: clay (Vol. 1)

2819 Desiccants, activated: silica gel (Vol. 1)

1542 Designing and erecting, combined: commercial-general contractors (Vol. 2)

1541 Designing and erecting, combined: industrial-general contractors (Vol. 2)

1522 Designing and erecting, combined: residential, except single-family-general contractors (Vol. 2)

1521 Designing and erecting combined: single-family houses-general contractors (Vol. 2)

8711 Designing: ship, boat, and machine (Vol. 2)

3634 Desk fans, electric (Vol. 1)

3646 Desk lamps, commercial (Vol. 1)

3645 Desk lamps, residential (Vol. 1)

3999 Desk pads, except paper (Vol. 1)

2678 Desk pads, paper (Vol. 1)

3281 Desk set bases, onyx (Vol. 1)

3199 Desk sets, leather (Vol. 1)

2511 Desks, household: wood (Vol. 1)

5021 Desks, including school—wholesale (Vol. 2)

2522 Desks, office: except wood (Vol. 1)

2521 Desks, office: wood (Vol. 1)

2024 Dessert pops, frozen: flavored ice, fruit, pudding, and gelatin (Vol. 1)

2024 Desserts, frozen: except bakery (Vol. 1)

2099 Desserts, ready-to-mix (Vol. 1)

3731 Destroyer tenders, building and repairing (Vol. 1)

7542 Detailing (cleaning and polishing) new autos for dealers on a contract or fee basis (Vol. 2)

0721 Detasseling of corn (Vol. 2)

7381 Detective agencies (Vol. 2)

7381 Detective, Guard and Armored Car Services (Vol. 2)

3829 Detectors, scintillation (Vol. 1)

9223 Detention centers-government (Vol. 2)

2841 Detergents, synthetic organic and inorganic alkaline (Vol. 1)

5169 Detergents—wholesale (Vol. 2)

3341 Detinning of cans (Vol. 1)

3341 Detinning of scrap (Vol. 1)

2892 Detonating caps for safety fuses (Vol. 1)

2892 Detonators (explosive compounds) (Vol. 1)

3483 Detonators for ammunition more than 30 mm. (or more than 1.18 inch) (Vol. 1)

3483 Detonators: mine, bomb, depth charge, and chemical warfare projectile (Vol. 1)

8093 Detoxification centers, outpatient (Vol. 2)

3861 Developers, prepared photographic: not made in chemical plants (Vol. 1)

7819 Developing and printing of commercial motion picture film (Vol. 2)

7384 Developing and printing of film, except commercial motion picture film (Vol. 2)

7384 Developing and processing of home movies (Vol. 2)

5043 Developing apparatus, photographic—wholesale (Vol. 2)

3861 Developing machines and equipment, still or motion picture (Vol. 1)

1799 Dewatering-contractors (Vol. 2)

0171 Dewberry farms (Vol. 2)

2046 Dextrine (Vol. 1)

2899 Dextrine sizes (Vol. 1)

2834 Dextrose and sodium chloride injection, mixed (Vol. 1)

2834 Dextrose injection (Vol. 1)

2046 Dextrose (Vol. 1)

1429 Diabase, crushed and broken-quarrying (Vol. 2)

1411 Diabase, dimension-quarrying (Vol. 2)

2835 Diagnostic agents, biological (Vol. 1)

3841 Diagnostic apparatus, physicians' (Vol. 1)

7549 Diagnostic centers, automotive (Vol. 2)

5047 Diagnostic equipment, medical—wholesale (Vol. 2)

3643 Dial light sockets, radio (Vol. 1)

3845 Dialyzers, electromedical (Vol. 1)

2874 Diammonium phosphates (Vol. 1)

3496 Diamond cloth, made from purchased wire (Vol. 1)

3915 Diamond cutting and polishing (Vol. 1)

3545 Diamond cutting tools for turning, boring, burnishing, etc. (Vol. 1)

3544 Diamond dies, metalworking (Vol. 1)

3545 Diamond dressing and wheel crushing attachments (Vol. 1)

3291 Diamond dressing wheels (Vol. 1)

1799 Diamond drilling for building construction-contractors (Vol. 2)

1499 Diamond mining, industrial (Vol. 2)

3915 Diamond points for phonograph needles (Vol. 1)

3291 Diamond powder (Vol. 1)

5094 Diamonds (gems)—wholesale (Vol. 2)

5085 Diamonds, industrial: natural and crude—wholesale (Vol. 2)

2385 Diaper covers, waterproof: except vulcanized rubber (Vol. 1)

2211 Diaper fabrics (Vol. 1)

7219 Diaper service (Vol. 2)

2676 Diapers, disposable (Vol. 1)

2399 Diapers, except disposable (Vol. 1)

5137 Diapers—wholesale (Vol. 2)

3069 Diaphragms, rubber: separate and in kits (Vol. 1)

2782 Diaries (Vol. 1)

1459 Diaspore mining (Vol. 2)

3845 Diathermy apparatus, electromedical (Vol. 1)

3845 Diathermy unit (Vol. 1)

3295 Diatomaceous earth, ground or otherwise treated (Vol. 1)

1499 Diatomaceous earth mining (Vol. 2)

1499 Diatomite mining (Vol. 2)

3861 Diazo (whiteprint) paper and cloth, sensitized (Vol. 1)

3861 Diazotype (whiteprint) reproduction machines and equipment (Vol. 1)

3944 Dice and dice cups (Vol. 1)

2869 Dichlorodifluoromethane (Vol. 1)

2819 Dichromates (Vol. 1)

2339 Dickeys: women's, misses' and juniors' (Vol. 1)

3579 Dictating machines, office types (Vol. 1)

8299 Diction schools (Vol. 2)

2821 Dicyandiamine resins (Vol. 1)

3559 Die and hub cutting equipment (jewelry manufacturing) (Vol. 1)

3537 Die and strip handlers (Vol. 1)

3542 Die-casting machines (Vol. 1)

3364 Die-casting nonferrous metals, except aluminum (Vol. 1)

3363 Die-castings, aluminum (Vol. 1)

2675 Die-Cut Paper and Paperboard and Cardboard (Vol. 1)

2675 Die-cut paper and paperboard (Vol. 1)

3554 Die-cutting and stamping machinery (paper converting machinery) (Vol. 1)

3111 Die-cutting of leather (Vol. 1)

3567 Dielectric heating equipment (Vol. 1)

3544 Dies and die holders for metal die-casting and metal cutting and forming, except threading (Vol. 1)

3556 Dies, biscuit cutting (Vol. 1)

3423 Dies, cutting: except metal cutting (Vol. 1)

3544 Dies, diamond: metalworking (Vol. 1)

3953 Dies, hand seal (Vol. 1)

3544 Dies, metalworking, except threading (Vol. 1)

5084 Dies, metalworking—wholesale (Vol. 2)

3544 Dies, plastics forming (Vol. 1)

3544 Dies, steel rule (Vol. 1)

3545 Dies, thread cutting (Vol. 1)

3519 Diesel and semidiesel engines: for stationary, marine, traction, etc. (Vol. 1)

3519 Diesel engine parts (Vol. 1)

7538 Diesel engine repair, automotive (Vol. 2)

5084 Diesel engines and engine parts, industrial—wholesale (Vol. 2)

3544 Diesets for metal stamping (presses) (Vol. 1)

3541 Diesinking machines (Vol. 1)

7299 Diet workshops (Vol. 2)

2023 Dietary supplements, dairy and nondairy base (Vol. 1)

5499 Dietetic food stores—retail (Vol. 2)

2869 Diethylcyclohexane (mixed isomers) (Vol. 1)

2869 Diethylene glycol ether (Vol. 1)

8049 Dieticians, offices of (Vol. 2)

3823 Differential pressure instruments, industrial process type (Vol. 1)

3826 Differential thermal analysis instruments (Vol. 1)

3714 Differentials and parts, motor vehicle (Vol. 1)

3443 Digesters, process: metal plate (Vol. 1)

3823 Digital displays of process variables (Vol. 1)

3663 Digital encoders (Vol. 1)

3825 Digital panel meters, electricity measuring (Vol. 1)

3825 Digital test equipment, electronic and electrical circuits and equipment (Vol. 1)

3825 Digital-to-analog converters, electronic instrumentation type (Vol. 1)

2834 Digitalis pharmaceutical preparations (Vol. 1)

2833 Digitoxin (Vol. 1)

2821 Diisocyanate resins (Vol. 1)

1629 Dike construction-general contractors (Vol. 2)

2426 Dimension, hardwood (Vol. 1)

1411 Dimension Stone (Vol. 2)

3281 Dimension stone for buildings (Vol. 1)

2869 Dimethyl divinyl acetylene (di-isopropenyl acetylene) (Vol. 1)

2869 Dimethylhydrazine, unsymmetrical (Vol. 1)

2211 Dimities (Vol. 1)

5812 Diners (eating places) (Vol. 2)

2514 Dinette sets, metal (Vol. 1)

3732 Dinghies, building and repairing (Vol. 1)

4789 Dining car operations, not performed by line-haul railroad companies (Vol. 2)

3743 Dining cars and car equipment (Vol. 1)

2511 Dining room furniture, wood (Vol. 1)

5812 Dining rooms (Vol. 2)

5812 Dinner theaters (Vol. 2)

2038 Dinners, frozen: packaged (Vol. 1)

5142 Dinners, frozen—wholesale (Vol. 2)

3089 Dinnerware, plastics: except foam (Vol. 1)

3825 Diode and transistor testers (Vol. 1)

3674 Diodes, solid-state (germanium, silicon, etc.) (Vol. 1)

5065 Diodes—wholesale (Vol. 2)

1423 Diorite, crushed and broken-quarrying (Vol. 2)

1411 Diorite, dimension-quarrying (Vol. 2)

2865 Diphenylamine (Vol. 1)

2836 Diphtheria toxin (Vol. 1)

9721 Diplomatic services-government (Vol. 2)

3469 Dippers, ice cream (Vol. 1)

0751 Dipping and shearing; Sheep (Vol. 2)

3479 Dipping metal in plastics solution as a preservative, for the trade (Vol. 1)

2879 Dips, cattle and sheep (Vol. 1)

2022 Dips, cheese-based (Vol. 1)

2099 Dips, except cheese and sour cream based (Vol. 1)

2026 Dips, sour cream based (Vol. 1)

4841 Direct broadcast satellite (DBS) services (Vol. 2)

7331 Direct mail advertising service (Vol. 2)

7331 Direct Mail Advertising Services (Vol. 2)

5963 Direct Selling Establishments (Vol. 2)

5963 Direct selling organizations (headquarters of door-to-door canvassers)—retail (Vol. 2)

6153 Direct working capital financing (Vol. 2)

1381 Directional drilling of oil and gas wells on a contract basis (Vol. 2)

3714 Directional signals, motor vehicle (Vol. 1)

2754 Directories: gravure printing (not publishing) (Vol. 1)

2759 Directories, printed: except lithographed or gravure (not publishing) (Vol. 1)

2741 Directories: publishing and printing, or publishing only (Vol. 1)

7389 Directories, telephone: distribution on a contract or fee basis (Vol. 2)

7819 Directors, motion picture: independent (Vol. 2)

3721 Dirigibles (Vol. 1)

1794 Dirt moving-contractors (Vol. 2)

3589 Dirt sweeping units, industrial (Vol. 1)

6321 Disability health insurance (Vol. 2)

9229 Disaster preparedness and management offices-government (Vol. 2)

8322 Disaster services (Vol. 2)

3651 Disc players, compact (Vol. 1)

1629 Discharging station construction, mine-general contractors (Vol. 2)

5813 Discotheques, alcoholic beverage (Vol. 2)

7911 Discotheques, except those serving alcoholic beverages (Vol. 2)

3652 Discs, laser: audio prerecorded (Vol. 1)

0721 Disease control for crops, with or without fertilizing (Vol. 2)

2599 Dish carts, restaurant (Vol. 1)

2259 Dishcloths (Vol. 1)

2392 Dishcloths, nonwoven textile (Vol. 1)

2211 Dishcloths, woven: made in weaving mills (Vol. 1)

3843 Dishes, abrasive: dental (Vol. 1)

3263 Dishes, commercial and household: fine earthenware (whiteware) (Vol. 1)

3262 Dishes: commercial and household-vitreous china (Vol. 1)

5113 Dishes, paper and disposable plastics—wholesale (Vol. 2)

3942 Dolls, doll parts, and doll clothing: except wigs (Vol. 1)

3942 Dolls, miniature: collectors' (Vol. 1)

5092 Dolls—wholesale (Vol. 2)

3297 Dolomite and dolomite-magnesite brick and shapes (Vol. 1)

1422 Dolomite, crushed and broken-quarrying (Vol. 2)

3274 Dolomite, dead-burned (Vol. 1)

1411 Dolomite, dimension-quarrying (Vol. 2)

3274 Dolomitic lime (Vol. 1)

1429 Dolomitic marble, crushed and broken-quarrying (Vol. 2)

1411 Dolomitic marble, dimension-quarrying (Vol. 2)

1542 Dome construction-general contractors (Vol. 2)

3647 Dome lights, motor vehicle (Vol. 1)

4731 Domestic forwarding (Vol. 2)

4424 Domestic freight transportation, deep sea (Vol. 2)

8811 Domestic service (private households employing cooks, maids, etc.) (Vol. 2)

3561 Domestic water pumps (Vol. 1)

8059 Domiciliary care with health care (Vol. 2)

3944 Dominoes (Vol. 1)

0272 Donkey farms (Vol. 2)

3442 Door and jamb assemblies, prefabricated: metal (Vol. 1)

1751 Door and window (prefabricated) installation-contractors (Vol. 2)

3429 Door bolts and checks (Vol. 1)

5031 Door frames, all materials—wholesale (Vol. 2)

3442 Door frames and sash, metal (Vol. 1)

2431 Door frames and sash, wood and covered wood (Vol. 1)

3272 Door frames, concrete (Vol. 1)

3444 Door hoods, aluminum (Vol. 1)

2431 Door jambs, wood (Vol. 1)

3429 Door locks and lock sets (Vol. 1)

5251 Door locks and lock sets—retail (Vol. 2)

3496 Door mats, made from purchased wire (Vol. 1)

3069 Door mats, rubber (Vol. 1)

2273 Door mats: twisted paper, grass, reed, coir, sisal, jute, and rag (Vol. 1)

3699 Door opening and closing devices, electrical (Vol. 1)

3429 Door opening and closing devices, except electrical (Vol. 1)

2431 Door screens, wood (Vol. 1)

2431 Door shutters, wood (Vol. 1)

2431 Door trim, wood (Vol. 1)

2431 Door units, prehung: wood and covered wood (Vol. 1)

3612 Doorbell transformers, electric (Vol. 1)

2431 Doors, combination screen-storm: wood (Vol. 1)

1751 Doors, folding: installation-contractors (Vol. 2)

3089 Doors, folding: plastics or plastics coated fabric (Vol. 1)

1751 Doors, garage: installation or erection-contractors (Vol. 2)

3442 Doors, louver: all metal or metal frame (Vol. 1)

3231 Doors, made from purchased glass (Vol. 1)

3442 Doors, metal (Vol. 1)

5211 Doors—retail (Vol. 2)

3499 Doors, safe and vault: metal (Vol. 1)

2431 Doors, wood and covered wood (Vol. 1)

2851 Dopes, paint (Vol. 1)

3732 Dories, building and repairing (Vol. 1)

7021 Dormitories, commercially operated (Vol. 2)

1522 Dormitory construction-general contractors (Vol. 2)

8734 Dosimetry, radiation (Vol. 2)

3552 Doubling and twisting frames (textile machinery) (Vol. 1)

2045 Dough, biscuit (Vol. 1)

2041 Dough, biscuit (Vol. 1)

3556 Dough mixing machinery (Vol. 1)

2045 Doughnut mixes (Vol. 1)

5461 Doughnut shops—retail (Vol. 2)

2051 Doughnuts, except frozen (Vol. 1)

2053 Doughnuts, frozen (Vol. 1)

2045 Doughs, refrigerated or frozen (Vol. 1)

2041 Doughs, refrigerated or frozen (Vol. 1)

3553 Dovetailing machines (woodworking machinery) (Vol. 1)

3452 Dowel pins, metal (Vol. 1)

2499 Dowels, wood (Vol. 1)

3999 Down (feathers) (Vol. 1)

2329 Down-filled clothing: men's and boys' (Vol. 1)

2339 Down-filled coats, jackets, and vests: women's, misses', and juniors' (Vol. 1)

1761 Downspout installation, metal-contractors (Vol. 2)

3089 Downspouts, plastics (Vol. 1)

3444 Downspouts, sheet metal (Vol. 1)

3531 Dozers, tractor mounted: material moving (Vol. 1)

3823 Draft gauges, industrial process type (Vol. 1)

7699 Drafting instrument repair (Vol. 2)

3829 Drafting instruments and machines (Vol. 1)

5049 Drafting instruments and tables—wholesale (Vol. 2)

3952 Drafting materials, except instruments (Vol. 1)

7389 Drafting service, except temporary help (Vol. 2)

7363 Drafting service (temporary employees) (Vol. 2)

3531 Draglines, powered (Vol. 1)

2861 Dragon's blood (Vol. 1)

3523 Drags (agricultural equipment) (Vol. 1)

3531 Drags, road (construction and road maintenance equipment) (Vol. 1)

7948 Dragstrip operation (Vol. 2)

3432 Drain cocks (Vol. 1)

2842 Drain pipe solvents and cleaners (Vol. 1)

3499 Drain plugs, magnetic: metal (Vol. 1)

3259 Drain tile, clay (Vol. 1)

3272 Drain tile, concrete (Vol. 1)

1629 Drainage project construction-general contractors (Vol. 2)

1711 Drainage system installation, cesspool and septic tank-contractors (Vol. 2)

2541 Drainboards, plastics laminated (Vol. 1)

1241 Draining or pumping of bituminous coal, anthracite, or lignite mines on a contract basis (Vol. 2)

1081 Draining or pumping of metal mines: on a contract basis (Vol. 2)

1481 Draining or pumping of nonmetallic minerals
      mines, except fuels: on a contract basis (Vol. 2)
3432 Drains, plumbers' (Vol. 1)
8299 Drama schools (Vol. 2)
2211 Draperies and drapery fabrics, cotton (Vol. 1)
2221 Draperies and drapery fabrics, manmade fiber and
      silk (Vol. 1)
2391 Draperies, plastics and textile (Vol. 1)
5023 Draperies—wholesale (Vol. 2)
5714 Drapery, Curtain and Upholstery Stores (Vol. 2)
7216 Drapery drycleaning plants (Vol. 2)
2591 Drapery Hardware and Window Blinds &
      Shades (Vol. 1)
5131 Drapery material—wholesale (Vol. 2)
2591 Drapery rods, poles, and fixtures (Vol. 1)
5714 Drapery stores—retail (Vol. 2)
3842 Drapes, surgical: cotton (Vol. 1)
3549 Draw benches (Vol. 1)
7389 Drawback service, customs (Vol. 2)
2254 Drawers, apparel (Vol. 1)
2322 Drawers: men's and boys' (Vol. 1)
3357 Drawing and Insulating of Nonferrous Wire
      (Vol. 1)
3552 Drawing frames, textile (Vol. 1)
3952 Drawing inks, blacks and colored (Vol. 1)
3549 Drawing machinery and equipment, except
      wiredrawing dies (Vol. 1)
3952 Drawing tables and boards, artists' (Vol. 1)
3423 Drawknives (Vol. 1)
4212 Draying, local: without storage (Vol. 2)
5082 Dredges and draglines, except ships—wholesale
      (Vol. 2)
3731 Dredges, building and repairing (Vol. 1)
1231 Dredging, anthracite (Vol. 2)
1629 Dredging-general contractors (Vol. 2)
3531 Dredging machinery (Vol. 1)
2259 Dress and semidress gloves, knit (Vol. 1)
3151 Dress and semidress gloves, leather (Vol. 1)
2381 Dress and Work Gloves Except Knit and All-
      Leather (Vol. 1)
2211 Dress fabrics, cotton (Vol. 1)
2221 Dress fabrics, manmade fiber and silk (Vol. 1)
2396 Dress linings (Vol. 1)
3069 Dress shields, vulcanized rubber and rubberized
      fabric (Vol. 1)
3143 Dress shoes, men's (Vol. 1)
5621 Dress shops—retail (Vol. 2)
7299 Dress suit rental (Vol. 2)
2396 Dress trimmings, fabric (Vol. 1)
2392 Dresser scarves (Vol. 1)
3545 Dressers, abrasive wheel: diamond point and other
      (Vol. 1)
2511 Dressers (Vol. 1)
3942 Dresses, doll (Vol. 1)
2361 Dresses: girls', children's, and infants' (Vol. 1)
2253 Dresses, hand-knit (Vol. 1)
5699 Dresses made to order—retail (Vol. 2)
2253 Dresses (Vol. 1)
2335 Dresses, paper, cut and sewn: women's, misses',
      and juniors' (Vol. 1)

5137 Dresses—wholesale (Vol. 2)
2335 Dresses: women's, misses', and juniors' (Vol. 1)
2384 Dressing gowns, men's and women's (Vol. 1)
3999 Dressing of furs: bleaching, blending, currying,
      scraping, and tanning (Vol. 1)
2511 Dressing tables (Vol. 1)
2844 Dressings, cosmetic (Vol. 1)
2842 Dressings for fabricated leather and other materials
      (Vol. 1)
3842 Dressings, surgical (Vol. 1)
5699 Dressmakers' shops, custom—retail (Vol. 2)
7219 Dressmaking services on material owned by
      individual customers (Vol. 2)
2034 Dried and Dehydrated Fruits, Vegetables and
      Soup Mixes (Vol. 1)
5159 Dried beet pulp—wholesale (Vol. 2)
2037 Dried citrus pulp (Vol. 1)
2034 Dried fruits and vegetables (Vol. 1)
0723 Dried fruits and vegetables; Packaging fresh or
      farm- (Vol. 2)
2013 Dried meats (Vol. 1)
2011 Dried meats (Vol. 1)
3567 Driers and redriers, industrial process (Vol. 1)
3569 Driers and reel, firehose (Vol. 1)
3523 Driers: grain, hay, and seed (agricultural
      implements) (Vol. 1)
3999 Driers, hair: designed for beauty parlors (Vol. 1)
2851 Driers, paint (Vol. 1)
3861 Driers, photographic (Vol. 1)
3812 Driftmeters, aeronautical (Vol. 1)
3545 Drill bits, metalworking (Vol. 1)
3423 Drill bits, woodworking (Vol. 1)
3545 Drill bushings (drilling jig) (Vol. 1)
3541 Drill presses (machine tools) (Vol. 1)
3533 Drill rigs, all types (Vol. 1)
3499 Drill stands, metal (Vol. 1)
3731 Drilling and production platforms, floating, oil and
      gas (Vol. 1)
5084 Drilling bits—wholesale (Vol. 2)
1241 Drilling for bituminous coal, anthracite, and lignite
      on a contract basis (Vol. 2)
1081 Drilling for metal mining: on a contract basis (Vol.
      2)
1481 Drilling for nonmetallic minerals, except fuels: on a
      contract basis (Vol. 2)
3545 Drilling machine attachments and accessories
      (machine tool accessories) (Vol. 1)
3541 Drilling machine tools (metal cutting) (Vol. 1)
2899 Drilling mud (Vol. 1)
5169 Drilling mud—wholesale (Vol. 2)
1381 Drilling of oil and gas wells: on a contract basis
      (Vol. 2)
3915 Drilling of pearls (Vol. 1)
1381 Drilling Oil and Gas Wells (Vol. 2)
1381 Drilling, service well: on a contract basis (Vol. 2)
3533 Drilling tools for gas, oil, or water wells (Vol. 1)
3546 Drilling tools, masonry and concrete: power
      (portable) (Vol. 1)
1381 Drilling water intake wells: on a contract basis
      (Vol. 2)

1781 Drilling water wells-contractors (Vol. 2)
3532 Drills and drilling equipment, mining: except oil and gas field (Vol. 1)
3532 Drills, core (Vol. 1)
2211 Drills, cotton (Vol. 1)
3843 Drills, dental (Vol. 1)
3546 Drills (except rock drilling and coring), portable: electric and pneumatic (Vol. 1)
3546 Drills, hand: electric (Vol. 1)
3423 Drills, hand: except power (Vol. 1)
3545 Drills (machine tool accessories) (Vol. 1)
3532 Drills, rock: portable (Vol. 1)
2087 Drink powders and concentrates (Vol. 1)
2656 Drinking cups, paper: except those made from pressed or molded pulp (Vol. 1)
3431 Drinking fountains, except mechanically refrigerated: metal (Vol. 1)
3088 Drinking fountains, except mechanically refrigerated: plastics (Vol. 1)
3585 Drinking fountains, mechanically refrigerated (Vol. 1)
3261 Drinking fountains, vitreous china (Vol. 1)
5813 Drinking Places—Alcoholic Beverages (Vol. 2)
2656 Drinking straws, except glass or plastics (Vol. 1)
3229 Drinking straws, glass (Vol. 1)
5078 Drinking water coolers, mechanical—wholesale (Vol. 2)
2086 Drinks, fruit: bottled, canned, or fresh (Vol. 1)
7389 Drive-a-way automobile service (Vol. 2)
3568 Drive chains, bicycle and motorcycle (Vol. 1)
7833 Drive-In Motion Picture Theaters (Vol. 2)
5812 Drive-in restaurants (Vol. 2)
7833 Drive-in theaters (Vol. 2)
3714 Drive shafts, motor vehicle (Vol. 1)
3545 Drivers, drill and cutters (machine tool accessories) (Vol. 1)
3572 Drives, computer: disk and drum (Vol. 1)
3566 Drives, high-speed industrial: except hydrostatic (Vol. 1)
3594 Drives, hydrostatic transmissions (Vol. 1)
1629 Driving piling-general contractors (Vol. 2)
2411 Driving timber (Vol. 1)
2394 Drop cloths, fabric (Vol. 1)
3462 Drop forgings, iron and steel: not made in rolling mills (Vol. 1)
3542 Drop hammers, for forging and shaping metal (Vol. 1)
8069 Drug addiction rehabilitation hospitals (Vol. 2)
2865 Drug dyes, synthetic (Vol. 1)
2833 Drug grading, grinding, and milling (Vol. 1)
5122 Drug proprietaries—wholesale (Vol. 2)
8361 Drug rehabilitation centers, residential: with health care incidental (Vol. 2)
5912 Drug Stores and Proprietary Stores (Vol. 2)
5912 Drug stores—retail (Vol. 2)
8093 Drug treatment, outpatient clinics (Vol. 2)
3069 Druggists' sundries, rubber (Vol. 1)
5122 Druggists' sundries—wholesale (Vol. 2)
5122 Drugs, Drug Proprietaries and Druggists' Sundries (Vol. 2)

5122 Drugs—wholesale (Vol. 2)
7929 Drum and bugle corps (drill teams) (Vol. 2)
3537 Drum cradles (Vol. 1)
3572 Drum drives, computer (Vol. 1)
3931 Drummers' traps (Vol. 1)
2655 Drums, fiber (metal-end or all-fiber) (Vol. 1)
5085 Drums, new and reconditioned—wholesale (Vol. 2)
3931 Drums, parts, and accessories (musical instruments) (Vol. 1)
3089 Drums, plastics (containers) (Vol. 1)
2449 Drums, plywood (Vol. 1)
3412 Drums, shipping: metal (Vol. 1)
2449 Drums, shipping: wood-wirebound (Vol. 1)
3944 Drums, toy (Vol. 1)
3692 Dry cell batteries, single and multiple cell (Vol. 1)
7216 Dry Cleaning Plants Except Rug Cleaninq (Vol. 2)
2023 Dry, Condensed and Evaporated Dairy Products (Vol. 1)
2621 Dry felts, except textile (Vol. 1)
0119 Dry field and seed; Bean farms, (Vol. 2)
0119 Dry field and seed; Pea farms, (Vol. 2)
2813 Dry ice (solid carbon dioxide) (Vol. 1)
5169 Dry ice—wholesale (Vol. 2)
3556 Dry milk processing machinery (Vol. 1)
2023 Dry milk products: whole milk, nonfat milk, buttermilk, whey, and cream (Vol. 1)
3634 Dry shavers (electric razors) (Vol. 1)
1711 Dry well construction, cesspool-contractors (Vol. 2)
3633 Drycleaning and laundry machines, household: including coin-operated (Vol. 1)
7215 Drycleaning, coin-operated (Vol. 2)
3582 Drycleaning equipment and machinery, commercial (Vol. 1)
1541 Drycleaning plant construction-general contractors (Vol. 2)
5087 Drycleaning plant equipment and supplies— wholesale (Vol. 2)
7216 Drycleaning plants, except rug cleaning (Vol. 2)
2842 Drycleaning preparations (Vol. 1)
3731 Drydocks, floating (Vol. 1)
5087 Dryers, beauty shop—wholesale (Vol. 2)
2499 Dryers, clothes (clothes horses): wood (Vol. 1)
5064 Dryers, clothes: electric or gas—wholesale (Vol. 2)
3582 Dryers, commercial laundry, including coin-operated (Vol. 1)
3634 Dryers: hand, face, and hair-electric (Vol. 1)
3821 Dryers, laboratory (Vol. 1)
3582 Dryers, laundry: commercial, including coin-operated (Vol. 1)
3633 Dryers, laundry: household, including coin-operated (Vol. 1)
3496 Drying belts, made from purchased wire (Vol. 1)
0723 Drying; Corn (Vol. 2)
0723 Drying; Fruit (Vol. 2)
2851 Drying japans (Vol. 1)
3559 Drying kilns, lumber (Vol. 1)
3552 Drying machines, textile: for stock, yarn, and cloth (Vol. 1)

3269 Earthenware table and kitchen articles, coarse (Vol. 1)

2048 Earthworm food and bedding (Vol. 1)

0279 Earthworm hatcheries (Vol. 2)

3952 Easels, artists' (Vol. 1)

2771 Easter cards, except hand painted (Vol. 1)

5812 Eating Places (Vol. 2)

5113 Eating utensils: forks, knives, spoons-disposable plastics—wholesale (Vol. 2)

3444 Eaves, sheet metal (Vol. 1)

3299 Ecclesiastical statuary: gypsum, clay, or papier-mache-factory production only (Vol. 1)

3281 Ecclesiastical statuary, marble (Vol. 1)

3914 Ecclesiastical ware: silver, nickel silver, pewter, and plated (Vol. 1)

8748 Economic consulting (Vol. 2)

9611 Economic development agencies-government (Vol. 2)

8732 Economic research, commercial (Vol. 2)

8733 Economic research, noncommercial (Vol. 2)

3443 Economizers (boilers) (Vol. 1)

6082 Edge Act Corporations (Vol. 2)

3423 Edge tools for woodworking: augers, bits, gimlets, countersinks, etc. (Vol. 1)

2789 Edging books, cards, or paper (Vol. 1)

2258 Edgings, lace (Vol. 1)

3861 Editing equipment, motion picture: rewinds, viewers, titlers, and splicers (Vol. 1)

7819 Editing of motion picture film (Vol. 2)

7338 Editing service (Vol. 2)

9411 Education offices, nonoperating (Vol. 2)

9411 Education statistics centers-government (Vol. 2)

8748 Educational consulting, except management (Vol. 2)

7812 Educational motion picture production (Vol. 2)

6732 Educational, Religious and Charitable Trusts (Vol. 2)

8732 Educational research, commercial (Vol. 2)

8733 Educational research, noncommercial (Vol. 2)

6732 Educational trusts, management of (Vol. 2)

0912 Eels, catching of (Vol. 2)

2834 Effervescent salts (Vol. 1)

2015 Egg albumen (Vol. 1)

2675 Egg cartons, die-cut paper and paperboard (Vol. 1)

2679 Egg cartons, molded pulp (Vol. 1)

2679 Egg case filler flats, molded pulp (Vol. 1)

2675 Egg case fillers and flats, die-cut from purchased paper or paperboard (Vol. 1)

2441 Egg cases, wood (Vol. 1)

3634 Egg cookers, electric (Vol. 1)

5499 Egg dealers—retail (Vol. 2)

0253 Egg farms and ranches; Turkey (Vol. 2)

0252 Egg farms, chicken (Vol. 2)

0259 Egg farms, poultry: except chicken and turkey (Vol. 2)

0253 Egg farms, turkey (Vol. 2)

0254 Egg hatcheries, poultry (Vol. 2)

2015 Egg substitutes made from eggs (Vol. 1)

2085 Eggnog, alcoholic (Vol. 1)

2023 Eggnog, canned: nonalcoholic (Vol. 1)

2026 Eggnog, fresh: nonalcoholic (Vol. 1)

2015 Eggs: canned, dehydrated, desiccated, frozen, and processed (Vol. 1)

0252 Eggs; Chicken (Vol. 2)

5144 Eggs: cleaning, oil treating, packing, and grading—wholesale (Vol. 2)

2015 Eggs: drying, freezing, and breaking (Vol. 1)

0259 Eggs Not Elsewhere Classified; Poultry and (Vol. 2)

0253 Eggs; Turkeys and Turkey (Vol. 2)

5144 Eggs—wholesale (Vol. 2)

3825 Elapsed time meters, electronic (Vol. 1)

2211 Elastic fabrics, cotton: more than 12 inches in width (Vol. 1)

2221 Elastic fabrics, manmade fiber and silk: more than 12 inches in width (Vol. 1)

2259 Elastic girdle blanks (Vol. 1)

3842 Elastic hosiery, orthopedic (Vol. 1)

3542 Elastic membrane metal forming machines (Vol. 1)

2241 Elastic narrow fabrics, woven or braided (Vol. 1)

2241 Elastic webbing (Vol. 1)

2824 Elastomeric fibers (Vol. 1)

2821 Elastomers, nonvulcanizable (plastics) (Vol. 1)

2822 Elastomers, vulcanizable (synthetic rubber) (Vol. 1)

3444 Elbows for conductor pipe, hot air ducts, and stovepipe: sheet metal (Vol. 1)

3494 Elbows, pipe: except pressure and soil pipe-metal (Vol. 1)

3321 Elbows, pipe: pressure and soil pipe-cast iron (Vol. 1)

3822 Electric air cleaner controls, automatic (Vol. 1)

3823 Electric and electronic controllers, industrial process type (Vol. 1)

3548 Electric and Gas Welding and Soldering Equipment (Vol. 1)

4931 Electric and Other Services Combined (Vol. 2)

4931 Electric and other services combined (electric less than 95 percent of total) (Vol. 2)

7629 Electric appliance repair (Vol. 2)

5064 Electric appliances, household—wholesale (Vol. 2)

3585 Electric comfort heating equipment (Vol. 1)

3699 Electric fence chargers (Vol. 1)

3612 Electric furnace transformers (Vol. 1)

3822 Electric heat proportioning controls, modulating controls (Vol. 1)

5722 Electric household appliance stores—retail (Vol. 2)

3634 Electric Housewares and Fans (Vol. 1)

5064 Electric housewares and household fans—wholesale (Vol. 2)

2241 Electric insulating tapes and braids, except plastic (Vol. 1)

5064 Electric irons—wholesale (Vol. 2)

3641 Electric lamp (bulb) parts (Vol. 1)

3641 Electric Lamp Bulbs and Tubes (Vol. 1)

3641 Electric lamps (Vol. 1)

3641 Electric light bulbs, complete (Vol. 1)

7694 Electric motor repair (Vol. 2)

3931 Electric musical instruments (Vol. 1)

4911 Electric power generation, transmission, or distribution (Vol. 2)

1623 Electric power line construction-general contractors (Vol. 2)

4011 Electric railroads, line-haul operating (Vol. 2)

5064 Electric ranges—wholesale (Vol. 2)

7629 Electric razor repair (Vol. 2)

5999 Electric razor shops—retail (Vol. 2)

5064 Electric razors—wholesale (Vol. 2)

3559 Electric screening equipment (Vol. 1)

4911 Electric Services (Vol. 2)

3822 Electric space heater controls, automatic (Vol. 1)

3634 Electric space heaters (Vol. 1)

7629 Electric tool repair (Vol. 2)

3585 Electric warm air furnaces (Vol. 1)

5064 Electric washing machines—wholesale (Vol. 2)

7629 Electrical and Electronic Repair Shops Not Elsewhere Classified (Vol. 2)

5063 Electrical Apparatus and Equipment, Wiring Supplies and Construction Materials (Vol. 2)

5064 Electrical Appliances—Television and Radio Sets (Vol. 2)

5013 Electrical automobile engine testing equipment—wholesale (Vol. 2)

5063 Electrical construction materials—wholesale (Vol. 2)

3541 Electrical discharge erosion machines (Vol. 1)

3541 Electrical discharge grinding machines (Vol. 1)

3599 Electrical discharge machining (EDM) (Vol. 1)

3694 Electrical Equipment for Internal Combustion Engines (Vol. 1)

5063 Electrical generators—wholesale (Vol. 2)

3629 Electrical Industrial Apparatus Not Elsewhere Classified (Vol. 1)

3229 Electrical insulators, glass (Vol. 1)

3264 Electrical insulators: pin, suspension, switch, and bus type-porcelain (Vol. 1)

3699 Electrical Machinery, Equipment and Supplies Not Elsewhere Classified (Vol. 1)

7629 Electrical measuring instrument repair and calibration (Vol. 2)

3825 Electrical power measuring equipment (Vol. 1)

1731 Electrical repair at site of construction-contractors (Vol. 2)

7629 Electrical repair shops, except radio, television, and refrigerator repair (Vol. 2)

7539 Electrical service, automotive (battery and ignition repair) (Vol. 2)

3993 Electrical signs and advertising displays (Vol. 1)

1731 Electrical Work (Vol. 2)

1731 Electrical work-contractors (Vol. 2)

3069 Electricians' gloves, rubber (Vol. 1)

3845 Electrocardiographs (Vol. 1)

3799 Electrocars for transporting golfers (Vol. 1)

3629 Electrochemical generators (fuel cells) (Vol. 1)

3541 Electrochemical milling machines (Vol. 1)

3548 Electrode holders for electric welding apparatus (Vol. 1)

3641 Electrodes, cold cathode fluorescent lamp (Vol. 1)

3548 Electrodes, electric welding (Vol. 1)

3624 Electrodes for thermal and electrolytic uses, carbon and graphite (Vol. 1)

3823 Electrodes used in industrial process measurement (Vol. 1)

3845 Electroencephalographs (Vol. 1)

3542 Electroforming machines (Vol. 1)

3829 Electrogamma ray loggers (Vol. 1)

3845 Electrogastrograph (Vol. 1)

3492 Electrohydraulic servo valves, fluid power: metal (Vol. 1)

3471 Electrolizing steel, for the trade (Vol. 1)

7299 Electrolysis (hair removal) (Vol. 2)

2835 Electrolyte diagnostic reagents (Vol. 1)

3823 Electrolytic conductivity instruments, industrial process type (Vol. 1)

3826 Electrolytic conductivity instruments, laboratory type (Vol. 1)

3541 Electrolytic metal cutting machine tools (Vol. 1)

3625 Electromagnetic brakes and clutches (Vol. 1)

3824 Electromechanical counters (Vol. 1)

3845 Electromedical and Electrotherapeutic Apparatus (Vol. 1)

3845 Electromedical apparatus (Vol. 1)

5047 Electromedical equipment—wholesale (Vol. 2)

3313 Electrometallurgical Products Except Steel (Vol. 1)

3845 Electromyographs (Vol. 1)

3671 Electron beam (beta ray) generator tubes (Vol. 1)

3699 Electron beam metal cutting, forming, and welding machines (Vol. 1)

3541 Electron-discharge metal cutting machine tools (Vol. 1)

3699 Electron linear accelerators (Vol. 1)

3826 Electron microprobes (Vol. 1)

3826 Electron microscopes (Vol. 1)

3826 Electron paramagnetic spin type apparatus (Vol. 1)

3559 Electron tube making machinery (Vol. 1)

3671 Electron tube parts, except glass blanks: bases, getters, and guns (Vol. 1)

3825 Electron tube test equipment (Vol. 1)

3671 Electron Tubes (Vol. 1)

3671 Electron tubes (Vol. 1)

3675 Electronic Capacitors (Vol. 1)

5065 Electronic coils and transformers—wholesale (Vol. 2)

3677 Electronic Coils, Transformers and Other Inductors (Vol. 1)

3679 Electronic Components Not Elsewhere Classified (Vol. 1)

3577 Electronic computer subassembly for film reader and phototheodolite (Vol. 1)

3571 Electronic Computers (Vol. 1)

3678 Electronic Connectors (Vol. 1)

5065 Electronic connectors—wholesale (Vol. 2)

1731 Electronic control system installation-contractors (Vol. 2)

3469 Electronic enclosures: stamped or pressed (Vol. 1)

7359 Electronic equipment rental and leasing, except medical and computer equipment (Vol. 2)

7629 Electronic equipment repair, except computers and computer peripheral equipment (Vol. 2)

6099 Electronic funds transfer networks, including switching (Vol. 2)

3944 Electronic game machines, except coin-operated (Vol. 1)

3651 Electronic kits for home assembly: radio and television receiving sets, and phonograph equipment (Vol. 1)

4822 Electronic mail services (Vol. 2)

3931 Electronic musical instruments (Vol. 1)

5065 Electronic Parts and Equipment Not Elsewhere Classified (Vol. 2)

5065 Electronic parts—wholesale (Vol. 2)

3676 Electronic Resistors (Vol. 1)

3825 Electronic test equipment for testing electrical characteristics (Vol. 1)

3824 Electronic totalizing counters (Vol. 1)

3944 Electronic toys (Vol. 1)

5065 Electronic tubes: receiving, transmitting, and industrial—wholesale (Vol. 2)

3826 Electrophoresis instruments (Vol. 1)

3559 Electroplating machinery and equipment, except rolling mill lines (Vol. 1)

3471 Electroplating of metals and formed products, for the trade (Vol. 1)

3471 Electroplating, Plating, Polishing, Anodizing and Coloring (Vol. 1)

1721 Electrostatic painting on site (including of lockers and fixtures)-contractors (Vol. 2)

3699 Electrostatic particle accelerators (Vol. 1)

3564 Electrostatic precipitators (Vol. 1)

3641 Electrotherapeutic lamp units for ultraviolet and infrared radiation (Vol. 1)

3845 Electrotherapy unit (Vol. 1)

2796 Electrotype plates (Vol. 1)

2796 Electrotyping for the trade (Vol. 1)

3555 Electrotyping machines (Vol. 1)

3826 Elemental analyzers (CHNOS) (Vol. 1)

8211 Elementary and Secondary Schools (Vol. 2)

8211 Elementary schools (Vol. 2)

2879 Elements, minor or trace (agricultural chemicals) (Vol. 1)

1622 Elevated highway construction-general contractors (Vol. 2)

4111 Elevated railway operation (Vol. 2)

1791 Elevator front installation, metal-contractors (Vol. 2)

3534 Elevator fronts (Vol. 1)

3446 Elevator guide rails, metal (Vol. 1)

1796 Elevator installation, conversion, and repair-contractors (Vol. 2)

3728 Elevators, aircraft (Vol. 1)

3534 Elevators and elevator equipment, passenger and freight (Vol. 1)

3534 Elevators and Moving Stairways (Vol. 1)

3523 Elevators, farm (Vol. 1)

4221 Elevators, grain: storage only (Vol. 2)

3534 Elevators, powered: nonfarm (Vol. 1)

5084 Elevators—wholesale (Vol. 2)

9721 Embassies (Vol. 2)

2395 Emblems, embroidered (Vol. 1)

2399 Emblems, made from fabrics (Vol. 1)

3199 Embossed leather goods for the trade (Vol. 1)

2261 Embossing cotton broadwoven fabrics (Vol. 1)

2269 Embossing linen broadwoven fabrics (Vol. 1)

3579 Embossing machines for store and office use (Vol. 1)

2262 Embossing manmade fiber and silk broadwoven fabrics (Vol. 1)

2789 Embossing of books (Vol. 1)

3111 Embossing of leather (Vol. 1)

2759 Embossing on paper (Vol. 1)

2796 Embossing plates for printing (Vol. 1)

2395 Embroideries: metallic, beaded, and sequined (Vol. 1)

2397 Embroideries, Schiffli machine (Vol. 1)

7389 Embroidering of advertising on shirts, etc. (Vol. 2)

3999 Embroidery kits (Vol. 1)

3552 Embroidery machines (Vol. 1)

2395 Embroidery products, except Schiffli machine (Vol. 1)

2284 Embroidery thread: cotton, silk, manmade fibers, and wool (Vol. 1)

2281 Embroidery yarn: cotton, silk, wool, and manmade staple (Vol. 1)

9229 Emergency management offices-government (Vol. 2)

8322 Emergency shelters (Vol. 2)

3291 Emery abrasives (Vol. 1)

1499 Emery mining (Vol. 2)

7549 Emissions testing service, automotive: without repair (Vol. 2)

3728 Empennage (tail) assemblies and parts, aircraft (Vol. 1)

7363 Employee leasing service (Vol. 2)

8631 Employees' associations for improvement of wages and working conditions (Vol. 2)

7361 Employment Agencies (Vol. 2)

7361 Employment agencies, except theatrical and motion picture (Vol. 2)

7819 Employment agencies, motion picture (Vol. 2)

7922 Employment agencies: theatrical, radio, and television-except motion picture (Vol. 2)

2843 Emulsifiers, except food and pharmaceutical (Vol. 1)

2834 Emulsifiers, fluorescent inspection (Vol. 1)

2099 Emulsifiers, food (Vol. 1)

2834 Emulsions, pharmaceutical (Vol. 1)

1446 Enamel sand mining (Vol. 2)

3253 Enamel tile, floor and wall: clay (Vol. 1)

3231 Enameled glass, made from purchased glass (Vol. 1)

3431 Enameled Iron and Metal Sanitary Ware (Vol. 1)

2672 Enameled paper (Vol. 1)

5031 Enameled tileboard (hardboard)—wholesale (Vol. 2)

3479 Enameling (including porcelain) of metal products, for the trade (Vol. 1)

3567 Enameling ovens (Vol. 1)

3952 Enamels, china painting (Vol. 1)

9441 Equal employment opportunity offices-government (Vol. 2)

0272 Equines; Horses and Other (Vol. 2)

7359 Equipment Rental and Leasing Not Elsewhere Classified (Vol. 2)

3952 Eraser guides and shields (Vol. 1)

3069 Erasers: rubber, or rubber and abrasive combined (Vol. 1)

1389 Erecting lease tanks, oil and gas field: on a contract basis (Vol. 2)

1799 Erection and dismantling of forms for poured concrete-contractors (Vol. 2)

3944 Erector sets, toy (Vol. 1)

2833 Ergot alkaloids (Vol. 1)

0181 Erosion-growing of; Mats, preseeded: soil (Vol. 2)

3534 Escalators, passenger and freight (Vol. 1)

7299 Escort service (Vol. 2)

6531 Escrow agents, real estate (Vol. 2)

6099 Escrow institutions other than real estate (Vol. 2)

2899 Essential oils (Vol. 1)

5169 Essential oils—wholesale (Vol. 2)

2822 Estane (Vol. 1)

8811 Estates, private (Vol. 2)

2821 Ester gum (Vol. 1)

2869 Esters of phosphoric, adipic, lauric, oleic, sebacic, and stearic acids (Vol. 1)

2869 Esters of phthalic anhydride (Vol. 1)

2869 Esters of polyhydric alcohols (Vol. 1)

0851 Estimating timber (Vol. 2)

3555 Etching machines (printing trades machinery) (Vol. 1)

2796 Etching on copper, steel, wood, or rubber plates for printing purposes (Vol. 1)

3479 Etching on metals for purposes other than printing (Vol. 1)

3479 Etching: photochemical, for the trade (Vol. 1)

1321 Ethane (natural) production (Vol. 2)

2869 Ethanol, industrial (Vol. 1)

2869 Ether (Vol. 1)

2861 Ethyl acetate, natural (Vol. 1)

2869 Ethyl acetate, synthetic (Vol. 1)

2085 Ethyl alcohol for medicinal and beverage purposes (Vol. 1)

2869 Ethyl alcohol, industrial (nonbeverage) (Vol. 1)

2869 Ethyl butyrate (Vol. 1)

2821 Ethyl cellulose plastics (Vol. 1)

2869 Ethyl cellulose, unplasticized (Vol. 1)

2869 Ethyl chloride (Vol. 1)

2869 Ethyl ether (Vol. 1)

2869 Ethyl formate (Vol. 1)

2869 Ethyl nitrite (Vol. 1)

2869 Ethyl perhydrophenanthrene (Vol. 1)

2865 Ethylbenzene (Vol. 1)

2899 Ethylene glycol antifreeze preparations (Vol. 1)

2869 Ethylene glycol ether (Vol. 1)

2869 Ethylene glycol, inhibited (Vol. 1)

2869 Ethylene glycol (Vol. 1)

2869 Ethylene, made in chemical plants (Vol. 1)

2869 Ethylene oxide (Vol. 1)

2911 Ethylene, produced in petroleum refineries (Vol. 1)

2822 Ethylene-propylene rubbers (Vol. 1)

2821 Ethylene-vinyl acetate resins (Vol. 1)

2899 Eucalyptus oil (Vol. 1)

2023 Evaporated milk (Vol. 1)

3821 Evaporation apparatus, laboratory type (Vol. 1)

3829 Evaporation meters (Vol. 1)

3585 Evaporative condensers (heat transfer equipment) (Vol. 1)

3443 Evaporators (process vessels), metal plate (Vol. 1)

5082 Excavating machinery and equipment—wholesale (Vol. 2)

1389 Excavating slush pits and cellars on a contract basis (Vol. 2)

1794 Excavation Work (Vol. 2)

1794 Excavation work-contractors (Vol. 2)

3531 Excavators: e.g., cable, clamshell, crane, derrick, dragline, power shovel (Vol. 1)

2429 Excelsior, including pads and wrappers: wood (Vol. 1)

2679 Excelsior, paper (Vol. 1)

6289 Exchange clearinghouses, commodity (Vol. 2)

6289 Exchange clearinghouses, security (Vol. 2)

3443 Exchangers, heat: industrial, scientific, and nuclear (Vol. 1)

6231 Exchanges, commodity contract (Vol. 2)

6231 Exchanges, security (Vol. 2)

3621 Exciter assemblies, motor and generator (Vol. 1)

4489 Excursion boat operations (Vol. 2)

9131 Executive and Legislative Offices Combined (Vol. 2)

9111 Executive Offices (Vol. 2)

7361 Executive placing services (Vol. 2)

5941 Exercise apparatus—retail (Vol. 2)

3949 Exercise cycles (Vol. 1)

7991 Exercise salons (Vol. 2)

3949 Exercising machines (Vol. 1)

3564 Exhaust fans, except household and kitchen (Vol. 1)

7533 Exhaust system services, automotive (Vol. 2)

3724 Exhaust systems, aircraft (Vol. 1)

3714 Exhaust systems and parts, motor vehicle (Vol. 1)

7999 Exhibition operation (Vol. 2)

3999 Exhibits and slides for classroom use, preparation of (Vol. 1)

7389 Exhibits, building of: by industrial contractors (Vol. 2)

2899 Exothermics for metal industries (Vol. 1)

3111 Exotic leathers (Vol. 1)

3441 Expansion joints (structural shapes): iron and steel (Vol. 1)

1081 Exploration for metal mining: on a contract basis (Vol. 2)

1481 Exploration for nonmetallic minerals, except fuels: on a contract basis (Vol. 2)

1382 Exploration, oil and gas field: on a contract basis (Vol. 2)

2892 Explosive cartridges for concussion forming of metal (Vol. 1)

2892 Explosive compounds (Vol. 1)

2892 Explosives (Vol. 1)

5169 Explosives, all kinds except ammunition and fireworks—wholesale (Vol. 2)

2892 Explosives (Vol. 1)

6111 Export-Import Bank (Vol. 2)

7999 Exposition operation (Vol. 2)

3861 Exposure meters, photographic (Vol. 1)

2211 Express stripes, cotton (Vol. 1)

3944 Express wagons, children's (Vol. 1)

8051 Extended care facilities (Vol. 2)

3699 Extension cords, made from purchased insulated wire (Vol. 1)

2499 Extension planks, wood (Vol. 1)

3842 Extension shoes, orthopedic (Vol. 1)

2879 Exterminating products, for household and industrial use (Vol. 1)

7342 Exterminating service (Vol. 2)

3724 External power units, aircraft: for hand-inertia starters (Vol. 1)

3999 Extinguishers, fire: portable (Vol. 1)

2082 Extract, malt (Vol. 1)

3582 Extractors and driers, commercial laundry (Vol. 1)

3531 Extractors, piling (Vol. 1)

2861 Extracts, dyeing and tanning: natural (Vol. 1)

2834 Extracts of botanicals: powdered, pilular, solid, and fluid, except diagnostics (Vol. 1)

3354 Extruded shapes, aluminum (Vol. 1)

3351 Extruded shapes, copper and copper alloy (Vol. 1)

3356 Extruded shapes, nonferrous metals and alloys, except copper and aluminum (Vol. 1)

3542 Extruding machines (machine tools), metal (Vol. 1)

3544 Extrusion dies (Vol. 1)

3355 Extrusion ingot, aluminum: made in rolling mills (Vol. 1)

3334 Extrusion ingot, aluminum: primary (Vol. 1)

8069 Eye, ear, nose, and throat hospitals: in-patient (Vol. 2)

3841 Eye examining instruments and apparatus (Vol. 1)

3172 Eyeglass cases, regardless of material (Vol. 1)

3851 Eyeglasses, lenses, and frames (Vol. 1)

2395 Eyelet making, for the trade (Vol. 1)

3965 Eyelets, metal: for clothing, fabrics, boots and shoes, and paper (Vol. 1)

3851 Eyes, glass and plastics (Vol. 1)

F

2261 Fabric finishing, cotton broadwoven fabrics (Vol. 1)

2262 Fabric finishing, manmade fiber and silk broadwoven (Vol. 1)

2231 Fabric finishing of wool, mohair, and similar animal fibers: except knit (Vol. 1)

2258 Fabric finishing, warp knit (Vol. 1)

5949 Fabric shops—retail (Vol. 2)

2842 Fabric softeners (Vol. 1)

3499 Fabricated Metal Products Not Elsewhere Classified (Vol. 1)

3498 Fabricated pipe and fittings: threading, bending, etc.-of purchased pipe (Vol. 1)

3498 Fabricated Pipe and Pipe Fittings (Vol. 1)

3443 Fabricated Plate Work—Boiler Shops (Vol. 1)

3069 Fabricated Rubber Products Not Elsewhere Classified (Vol. 1)

3441 Fabricated Structural Metal (Vol. 1)

3441 Fabricated structural steel (Vol. 1)

2399 Fabricated Textile Products Not Elsewhere Classified (Vol. 1)

2231 Fabrics, animal fiber: broadwoven wool, mohair, and similar animal fibers (Vol. 1)

2241 Fabrics, animal fiber: narrow woven (Vol. 1)

2297 Fabrics, bonded fiber: except felt (Vol. 1)

2211 Fabrics, broadwoven: cotton (Vol. 1)

2221 Fabrics, broadwoven: manmade fiber and silk (Vol. 1)

2231 Fabrics, broadwoven: wool, mohair, and similar animal fibers (Vol. 1)

2257 Fabrics, circular knit (Vol. 1)

2295 Fabrics, coated and impregnated: except rubberized (Vol. 1)

2296 Fabrics for reinforcing rubber tires, industrial belting, and fuel cells (Vol. 1)

2299 Fabrics: linen, jute, hemp, ramie (Vol. 1)

2297 Fabrics, nonwoven: except felts (Vol. 1)

2952 Fabrics, roofing: asphalt or tar saturated (Vol. 1)

3069 Fabrics, rubberized (Vol. 1)

2258 Fabrics, warp knit (Vol. 1)

2257 Fabrics, weft knit (Vol. 1)

3496 Fabrics, woven wire: made from purchased wire (Vol. 1)

6726 Face-amount certificate issuing (Vol. 2)

2844 Face creams and lotions (Vol. 1)

3644 Face plates (wiring devices) (Vol. 1)

2844 Face powders (Vol. 1)

7231 Facial salons (Vol. 2)

2621 Facial tissue stock (Vol. 1)

2676 Facial tissues (Vol. 1)

8744 Facilities management, except computer (Vol. 2)

7376 Facilities management services, computer (Vol. 2)

8744 Facilities Support Management Services (Vol. 2)

8744 Facilities support services, except computer (Vol. 2)

3541 Facing machines (Vol. 1)

3251 Facing tile, clay (Vol. 1)

2899 Facings (chemical foundry supplies) (Vol. 1)

3661 Facsimile equipment (Vol. 1)

2754 Facsimile letters: gravure printing (Vol. 1)

4822 Facsimile transmission services (Vol. 2)

6153 Factors of commercial paper (Vol. 2)

1541 Factory construction-general contractors (Vol. 2)

2599 Factory furniture: stools, work benches, tool stands, and cabinets (Vol. 1)

3253 Faience tile (Vol. 1)

2221 Failles (Vol. 1)

7999 Fairs, agricultural: operation of (Vol. 2)

2679 False faces, papier-mache (Vol. 1)

5651 Family Clothing Stores (Vol. 2)

5651 Family clothing stores—retail (Vol. 2)

8322 Family counseling services (Vol. 2)

8322 Family location services (Vol. 2)

8322 Family service agencies (Vol. 2)

3822 Fan control, temperature responsive (Vol. 1)

3599 Fan forges (Vol. 1)

3111 Fancy leathers (Vol. 1)
2672 Fancy paper, coated and glazed: except for packaging (Vol. 1)
2761 Fanfold forms (Vol. 1)
3564 Fans, except household (Vol. 1)
3634 Fans, household: electric, except attic fans (Vol. 1)
3634 Fans, household: kitchen-except attic (Vol. 1)
5084 Fans, industrial—wholesale (Vol. 2)
3829 Fare registers: e.g., for streetcars and buses (Vol. 1)
2043 Farina, cereal breakfast food (Vol. 1)
2041 Farina, except breakfast food (Vol. 1)
5083 Farm and Garden Machinery and Equipment (Vol. 2)
1542 Farm building construction, except residential-general contractors (Vol. 2)
3448 Farm buildings, prefabricated: metal (Vol. 1)
2452 Farm buildings, prefabricated or portable: wood (Vol. 1)
8699 Farm bureaus (Vol. 2)
0723 Farm-dried fruits and vegetables; Packaging fresh or (Vol. 2)
3523 Farm elevators (Vol. 1)
8699 Farm granges (Vol. 2)
8811 Farm homes, noncommercial (Vol. 2)
0761 Farm labor contractors (Vol. 2)
0761 Farm Labor Contractors and Crew Leaders (Vol. 2)
3523 Farm Machinery and Equipment (Vol. 1)
3523 Farm machinery and equipment (Vol. 1)
5083 Farm machinery and equipment—wholesale (Vol. 2)
7699 Farm machinery repair (Vol. 2)
0762 Farm Management Services (Vol. 2)
0241 Farm; Milk production, dairy cattle (Vol. 2)
0214 Farm; Milk production, goat (Vol. 2)
6159 Farm mortgage companies (Vol. 2)
5159 Farm-Product Raw Materials Not Elsewhere Classified (Vol. 2)
4221 Farm Product Warehousing and Storage (Vol. 2)
4221 Farm product warehousing and storage, other than cold storage (Vol. 2)
3443 Farm storage tanks, metal plate (Vol. 1)
5191 Farm Supplies (Vol. 2)
5191 Farm supplies—wholesale (Vol. 2)
4212 Farm to market hauling (Vol. 2)
3523 Farm tractors (Vol. 1)
3523 Farm wagons (Vol. 1)
6111 Farmers Home Administration (Vol. 2)
0139 Farms; Alfalfa (Vol. 2)
0279 Farms; Alligator (Vol. 2)
0173 Farms; Almond groves and (Vol. 2)
0214 Farms and ranches; Sheep feeding (Vol. 2)
0214 Farms and ranches; Sheep raising (Vol. 2)
0253 Farms and ranches; Turkey (Vol. 2)
0253 Farms and ranches; Turkey egg (Vol. 2)
0175 Farms; Apple orchards and (Vol. 2)
0175 Farms; Apricot orchards and (Vol. 2)
0161 Farms; Asparagus (Vol. 2)
0179 Farms; Avocado orchards and (Vol. 2)
0179 Farms; Banana (Vol. 2)

0119 Farms; Barley (Vol. 2)
0279 Farms; Bee (Vol. 2)
0171 Farms; Berry (Vol. 2)
0171 Farms; Blackberry (Vol. 2)
0171 Farms; Blueberry (Vol. 2)
0161 Farms; Bok choy (Vol. 2)
0161 Farms; Broccoli (Vol. 2)
0139 Farms; Broomcorn (Vol. 2)
0119 Farms; Buckwheat (Vol. 2)
0272 Farms; Burro (Vol. 2)
0161 Farms (bush and pole); Snap bean (Vol. 2)
0161 Farms; Cabbage (Vol. 2)
0161 Farms; Cantaloup (Vol. 2)
0279 Farms; Cat (Vol. 2)
0273 Farms; Catfish (Vol. 2)
0211 Farms; Cattle feeding (Vol. 2)
0212 Farms; Cattle raising (Vol. 2)
0161 Farms; Cauliflower (Vol. 2)
0161 Farms; Celery (Vol. 2)
0175 Farms; Cherry orchards and (Vol. 2)
0252 Farms, chicken; Egg (Vol. 2)
0271 Farms; Chinchilla (Vol. 2)
0174 Farms; Citrus groves and (Vol. 2)
0139 Farms; Clover (Vol. 2)
0179 Farms; Coffee (Vol. 2)
0251 Farms; Cornish hen (Vol. 2)
0131 Farms; Cotton (Vol. 2)
0131 Farms; Cottonseed (Vol. 2)
0119 Farms; Cowpea (Vol. 2)
0273 Farms; Crustacean (Vol. 2)
0161 Farms; Cucumber (Vol. 2)
0171 Farms; Currant (Vol. 2)
0241 Farms; Dairy (Vol. 2)
0241 Farms; Dairy heifer replacement (Vol. 2)
0179 Farms; Date orchards and (Vol. 2)
0171 Farms; Dewberry (Vol. 2)
0279 Farms; Dog (Vol. 2)
0272 Farms; Donkey (Vol. 2)
0119 Farms, dry field and seed; Bean (Vol. 2)
0119 Farms, dry field and seed; Pea (Vol. 2)
0259 Farms; Duck (Vol. 2)
0279 Farms (e.g., rats, mice, guinea pigs); Laboratory animal (Vol. 2)
0161 Farms; English pea (Vol. 2)
0161 Farms, except dry beans; Bean (Vol. 2)
0161 Farms, except dry peas; Pea (Vol. 2)
0212 Farms, except feedlots; Beef cattle (Vol. 2)
0119 Farms, except for syrup; Sorghum (Vol. 2)
0273 Farms, except hatcheries; Fish (Vol. 2)
0161 Farms, except sugar beet; Beet (Vol. 2)
0115 Farms, except sweet corn or popcorn; Corn (Vol. 2)
0134 Farms, except sweet potato and yam; Potato (Vol. 2)
0119 Farms: except wheat, rice, corn, and soybeans; Cash grain (Vol. 2)
0119 Farms: except wheat, rice, corn, and soybeans; Grain (Vol. 2)
0179 Farms; Fig orchards and (Vol. 2)
0173 Farms; Filbert groves and (Vol. 2)
0273 Farms; Finfish (Vol. 2)

5072 Fasteners, hardware—wholesale (Vol. 2)

3812 Fathometers (Vol. 1)

3829 Fatigue testing machines, industrial: mechanical (Vol. 1)

2843 Fats, sulfonated (Vol. 1)

0211 Fattening cattle; Stockyards, exclusively for (Vol. 2)

2869 Fatty acid esters and amines (Vol. 1)

2899 Fatty acids: margaric, oleic, and stearic (Vol. 1)

3261 Faucet handles, vitreous china and earthenware (Vol. 1)

3432 Faucets, metal and plastics (Vol. 1)

2499 Faucets, wood (Vol. 1)

3582 Feather cleaning and sterilizing machinery (Vol. 1)

2329 Feather-filled clothing: men's and boys' (Vol. 1)

2339 Feather-filled coats, jackets, and vests: women's, misses', and juniors' (Vol. 1)

2077 Feather meal (Vol. 1)

3999 Feathers: curling, dyeing, and renovating-for the trade (Vol. 1)

5159 Feathers—wholesale (Vol. 2)

6111 Federal and Federally-Sponsored Credit Agencies (Vol. 2)

6061 Federal credit unions (Vol. 2)

6331 Federal Crop Insurance Corporation (Vol. 2)

6399 Federal Deposit Insurance Corporation (Vol. 2)

6019 Federal Home Loan Banks (Vol. 2)

6111 Federal Home Loan Mortgage Corporation (Vol. 2)

6111 Federal Intermediate Credit Bank (Vol. 2)

6111 Federal Land Banks (Vol. 2)

6111 Federal National Mortgage Association (Vol. 2)

6011 Federal Reserve Banks (Vol. 2)

6011 Federal Reserve branches (Vol. 2)

6035 Federal savings and loan associations (Vol. 2)

6399 Federal Savings and Loan Insurance Corporation (Vol. 2)

6035 Federal savings banks (Vol. 2)

6061 Federally Chartered Credit Unions (Vol. 2)

6035 Federally Chartered Savings Institutions (Vol. 2)

5191 Feed additives, animal—wholesale (Vol. 2)

3199 Feed bags for horses (Vol. 1)

2048 Feed concentrates (Vol. 1)

5191 Feed, except unmixed grain—wholesale (Vol. 2)

2046 Feed, gluten (Vol. 1)

3523 Feed grinders, crushers, and mixers (agricultural machinery) (Vol. 1)

3523 Feed grinders-mixers (Vol. 1)

3556 Feed mixers, except agricultural machinery (Vol. 1)

2048 Feed premixes (Vol. 1)

2048 Feed supplements (Vol. 1)

3612 Feeder voltage regulators and boosters (electric transformers) (Vol. 1)

3523 Feeders, chicken (Vol. 1)

3532 Feeders, ore and aggregate (Vol. 1)

0214 Feeding farms and ranches; Sheep (Vol. 2)

0211 Feeding farms; Cattle (Vol. 2)

0211 Feedlot operations; Cattle (Vol. 2)

0211 Feedlots; Beef Cattle (Vol. 2)

0211 Feedlots, cattle (Vol. 2)

0213 Feedlots, hog (Vol. 2)

0214 Feedlots, lamb (Vol. 2)

2048 Feeds, prepared (including mineral): for animals and fowls-except dogs and cats (Vol. 1)

2048 Feeds, specialty: mice, guinea pigs, minks, etc. (Vol. 1)

2048 Feeds, stock: dry (Vol. 1)

3295 Feldspar, ground or otherwise treated (Vol. 1)

1459 Feldspar mining (Vol. 2)

2499 Fellies, wood (Vol. 1)

2299 Felt goods, except woven felts and hats: wool, hair, jute, or other fiber (Vol. 1)

3292 Felt roll roofing, asbestos (Vol. 1)

3951 Felt tip markers (Vol. 1)

5199 Felt—wholesale (Vol. 2)

3292 Felt, woven amosite: asbestos (Vol. 1)

2621 Felts, building (Vol. 1)

2299 Felts, pressed or needle loom (Vol. 1)

2952 Felts, roofing: asphalt saturated and tar saturated-roll or shingle (Vol. 1)

5033 Felts, tarred—wholesale (Vol. 2)

2231 Felts: wool, mohair, and similar animal fibers: woven (Vol. 1)

3699 Fence chargers, electric (Vol. 1)

1799 Fence construction-contractors (Vol. 2)

3496 Fence gates, made from purchased wire (Vol. 1)

3315 Fence gates, posts, and fittings: steel-made in wiredrawing plants (Vol. 1)

3312 Fence posts, iron and steel: made in steel works or rolling mills (Vol. 1)

3423 Fence stretchers (handtools) (Vol. 1)

3446 Fences and posts, ornamental iron and steel (Vol. 1)

5039 Fencing and accessories, wire—wholesale (Vol. 2)

5211 Fencing dealers—retail (Vol. 2)

3949 Fencing equipment (sporting goods) (Vol. 1)

3496 Fencing, made from purchased wire (Vol. 1)

2499 Fencing, wood: except rough pickets, poles, and rails (Vol. 1)

5031 Fencing, wood—wholesale (Vol. 2)

3465 Fenders, stamped and pressed (Vol. 1)

1061 Ferberite mining (Vol. 2)

3443 Fermenters (process vessels), metal plate (Vol. 1)

2869 Ferric ammonium oxalate (Vol. 1)

2819 Ferric chloride (Vol. 1)

2816 Ferric oxide pigments (Vol. 1)

2819 Ferric oxides, except pigments (Vol. 1)

4482 Ferries (Vol. 2)

4482 Ferries, operation of (Vol. 2)

3599 Ferris wheels (Vol. 1)

3264 Ferrite (Vol. 1)

1061 Ferroalloy Ores Except Vanadium (Vol. 2)

3313 Ferroalloys (including high percentage) (Vol. 1)

5051 Ferroalloys—wholesale (Vol. 2)

3313 Ferrochromium (Vol. 1)

2819 Ferrocyanides (Vol. 1)

3313 Ferromanganese (Vol. 1)

3313 Ferromolybdenum (Vol. 1)

3313 Ferrophosphorus (Vol. 1)

3313 Ferrosilicon (Vol. 1)

3313 Ferrotitanium (Vol. 1)

3861 Film, sensitized: motion picture, X-ray, still camera, and special purpose (Vol. 1)
7336 Film strip and slide producers (Vol. 2)
2211 Filter cloth, cotton (Vol. 1)
3569 Filter elements, fluid: hydraulic line (Vol. 1)
2679 Filter paper, converted (Vol. 1)
2621 Filter paper (Vol. 1)
3295 Filtering clays, treated purchased materials (Vol. 1)
3269 Filtering media, pottery (Vol. 1)
3564 Filters, air: for furnaces and air-conditioning equipment (Vol. 1)
3569 Filters, fluid, general line industrial: except internal combustion engine (Vol. 1)
3599 Filters, internal combustion engine: oil, gasoline, air intake, except motor vehicle engine (Vol. 1)
3714 Filters: oil, fuel, and air-motor vehicle (Vol. 1)
3569 Filters, pipeline (Vol. 1)
1446 Filtration sand mining (Vol. 2)
3483 Fin assemblies, mortar: more than 30 mm. (or more than 1.18 inch) (Vol. 1)
3483 Fin assemblies, torpedo and bomb (Vol. 1)
6159 Finance leasing of automobiles, trucks and machinery (Vol. 2)
6159 Finance leasing of equipment and vehicles (Vol. 2)
9311 Finance, Taxation and Monetary Policy (Vol. 2)
6282 Financial advice, investment (Vol. 2)
6289 Financial reporting (Vol. 2)
6351 Financial responsibility insurance (Vol. 2)
6141 Financing of automobiles, furniture, appliances, personal airplanes, etc.: not engaged in deposit banking (Vol. 2)
6153 Financing of dealers by motor vehicle manufacturers' organizations (Vol. 2)
3131 Findings, boot and shoe (Vol. 1)
3915 Findings, jewelers (Vol. 1)
5087 Findings, shoe repair—wholesale (Vol. 2)
2396 Findings, suit and coat: e.g., coat fronts, pockets (Vol. 1)
0912 Finfish (Vol. 2)
0912 Finfish, catching of (Vol. 2)
0273 Finfish farms (Vol. 2)
3069 Finger cots, rubber (Vol. 1)
3999 Fingerprint equipment, except cameras and optical equipment (Vol. 1)
7381 Fingerprint service (Vol. 2)
3531 Finishers and spreaders, construction (Vol. 1)
3531 Finishers, concrete and bituminous: powered (Vol. 1)
2261 Finishers of Broadwoven Fabrics of Cotton (Vol. 1)
2262 Finishers of Broadwoven Fabrics of Manmade Fiber and Silk (Vol. 1)
2269 Finishers of Textiles Not Elsewhere Classified (Vol. 1)
2273 Finishers of tufted carpets and rugs (Vol. 1)
2843 Finishing agents, textile and leather (Vol. 1)
3547 Finishing equipment, rolling mill (Vol. 1)
3552 Finishing machinery, textile (Vol. 1)
3471 Finishing metal products and formed products, for the trade (Vol. 1)

2257 Finishing of circular knit fabrics (Vol. 1)
2261 Finishing of cotton broadwoven fabrics (Vol. 1)
3111 Finishing of leather (Vol. 1)
2262 Finishing of manmade fiber and silk broadwoven fabrics (Vol. 1)
2269 Finishing of raw stock, yarn, and narrow fabrics: except knit and wool (Vol. 1)
2258 Finishing of warp knit fabrics (Vol. 1)
2231 Finishing of wool, mohair, and similar animal fiber fabrics: except knit (Vol. 1)
8299 Finishing schools, charm and modeling (Vol. 2)
8211 Finishing schools, secondary (Vol. 2)
2091 Finnan haddie (smoked haddock) (Vol. 1)
3728 Fins, aircraft (Vol. 1)
3469 Fins, tube: stamped metal (Vol. 1)
3669 Fire alarm apparatus, electric (Vol. 1)
1731 Fire alarm installation-contractors (Vol. 2)
7382 Fire alarm monitoring and maintenance (Vol. 2)
3255 Fire clay blocks, bricks, tile, and special shapes (Vol. 1)
1459 Fire clay mining (Vol. 2)
7699 Fire control (military) equipment repair (Vol. 2)
3711 Fire department vehicles (motor vehicles) (Vol. 1)
9224 Fire departments, including volunteer-government (Vol. 2)
3669 Fire detection systems, electric (Vol. 1)
3829 Fire detector systems, nonelectric (Vol. 1)
3442 Fire doors, metal (Vol. 1)
1799 Fire escape installation-contractors (Vol. 2)
3446 Fire escapes, metal (Vol. 1)
2899 Fire extinguisher charges (Vol. 1)
3999 Fire extinguishers, portable (Vol. 1)
7389 Fire extinguishers, service of (Vol. 2)
5099 Fire extinguishers—wholesale (Vol. 2)
3491 Fire hydrant valves (Vol. 1)
6411 Fire Insurance Underwriters' Laboratories (Vol. 2)
6411 Fire loss appraisal (Vol. 2)
6331 Fire, Marine and Casualty Insurance (Vol. 2)
9224 Fire marshals' offices-government (Vol. 2)
0851 Fire prevention, forest (Vol. 2)
9224 Fire prevention offices-government (Vol. 2)
9224 Fire Protection (Vol. 2)
2261 Fire resistance finishing of cotton broadwoven fabrics (Vol. 1)
2262 Fire resistance finishing of manmade fiber and silk broadwoven fabrics (Vol. 1)
2899 Fire retardant chemical preparations (Vol. 1)
1542 Fire station construction-general contractors (Vol. 2)
3484 Firearms, 30 mm. (or 1.18 inch) or less (Vol. 1)
5099 Firearms, except sporting—wholesale (Vol. 2)
5941 Firearms—retail (Vol. 2)
5091 Firearms, sporting—wholesale (Vol. 2)
3731 Fireboats, building and repairing (Vol. 1)
3255 Firebrick, clay (Vol. 1)
2311 Firefighters' dress uniforms, men's (Vol. 1)
3569 Firefighting apparatus, except automotive and chemical (Vol. 1)
5087 Firefighting equipment—wholesale (Vol. 2)
0851 Firefighting, forest (Vol. 2)

7389 Firefighting service, other than forestry or public (Vol. 2)

3569 Firehose, except rubber (Vol. 1)

3052 Firehose, rubber (Vol. 1)

3429 Fireplace equipment (hardware) (Vol. 1)

3433 Fireplace inserts (Vol. 1)

2999 Fireplace logs, made from coal (Vol. 1)

5719 Fireplace screens and accessories—retail (Vol. 2)

5719 Fireplace stores—retail (Vol. 2)

3272 Fireplaces, concrete (Vol. 1)

5074 Fireplaces, prefabricated—wholesale (Vol. 2)

1752 Fireproof flooring construction-contractors (Vol. 2)

1799 Fireproofing buildings-contractors (Vol. 2)

3251 Fireproofing tile, clay (Vol. 1)

2499 Firewood and fuel wood containing fuel binder (Vol. 1)

5099 Firewood—wholesale (Vol. 2)

7999 Fireworks display service (Vol. 2)

2899 Fireworks (Vol. 1)

5999 Fireworks—retail (Vol. 2)

5092 Fireworks—wholesale (Vol. 2)

3269 Firing china, for the trade (Vol. 1)

7699 Firing china to individual order (Vol. 2)

2449 Firkins and kits, wood: coopered (Vol. 1)

3842 First aid, snake bite, and burn kits (Vol. 1)

2091 Fish and seafood cakes: canned (Vol. 1)

2092 Fish and seafood cakes, frozen (Vol. 1)

5146 Fish and Seafoods (Vol. 2)

3556 Fish and shellfish processing machinery (Vol. 1)

9512 Fish and wildlife conservation-government (Vol. 2)

2091 Fish, canned and cured (Vol. 1)

2091 Fish: cured, dried, pickled, salted, and smoked (Vol. 1)

5146 Fish, cured—wholesale (Vol. 2)

2091 Fish egg bait, canned (Vol. 1)

0273 Fish farms, except hatcheries (Vol. 2)

0273 Fish farms; Tropical aquarium (Vol. 2)

2092 Fish fillets (Vol. 1)

2048 Fish food (Vol. 1)

2092 Fish: fresh and frozen, prepared (Vol. 1)

5146 Fish, fresh—wholesale (Vol. 2)

5146 Fish, frozen: except packaged—wholesale (Vol. 2)

5142 Fish, frozen: packaged—wholesale (Vol. 2)

0921 Fish hatcheries (Vol. 2)

0921 Fish Hatcheries and Preserves (Vol. 2)

2077 Fish liver oils, crude (Vol. 1)

2833 Fish liver oils, refined and concentrated for medicinal use (Vol. 1)

5421 Fish markets—retail (Vol. 2)

2077 Fish meal (Vol. 1)

2298 Fish nets and seines, made in cordage or twine mills (Vol. 1)

2077 Fish oil and fish oil meal (Vol. 1)

2092 Fish sticks (Vol. 1)

5199 Fish, tropical—wholesale (Vol. 2)

3644 Fish wire (electrical wiring tool) (Vol. 1)

0912 Fisheries, finfish (Vol. 2)

0913 Fisheries, shellfish (Vol. 2)

7999 Fishing boats, party: operation of (Vol. 2)

3732 Fishing boats, small (Vol. 1)

7032 Fishing camps (Vol. 2)

5941 Fishing equipment—retail (Vol. 2)

1389 Fishing for tools, oil and gas field: on a contract basis (Vol. 2)

3421 Fishing knives (Vol. 1)

2298 Fishing lines, nets, seines: made in cordage or twine mills (Vol. 1)

2399 Fishing nets (Vol. 1)

7999 Fishing piers and lakes, operation of (Vol. 2)

0921 Fishing preserves (Vol. 2)

3949 Fishing tackle (except lines, nets, and seines) (Vol. 1)

3731 Fishing vessels, large: seiners and trawlers-building and repairing (Vol. 1)

2819 Fissionable material production (Vol. 1)

7991 Fitness salons (Vol. 2)

3089 Fittings for pipe, plastics (Vol. 1)

3089 Fittings, plastics (Vol. 1)

5074 Fittings, plumbers'—wholesale (Vol. 2)

3321 Fittings, soil and pressure pipe: cast iron (Vol. 1)

3841 Fixation appliances, internal (Vol. 1)

4785 Fixed Facilities and Inspection and Weighing Services for Motor Vehicle Transportation (Vol. 2)

3861 Fixers, prepared photographic: not made in chemical plants (Vol. 1)

2541 Fixture tops, plastics laminated (Vol. 1)

2591 Fixtures, curtain and drapery (Vol. 1)

2542 Fixtures, display: office and store-except wood (Vol. 1)

2541 Fixtures, display: office and store-wood (Vol. 1)

2542 Fixtures, office and store: except wood (Vol. 1)

5078 Fixtures, refrigerated—wholesale (Vol. 2)

5046 Fixtures, store, not refrigerated—wholesale (Vol. 2)

5999 Flag shops—retail (Vol. 2)

7389 Flagging service (traffic control) (Vol. 2)

3446 Flagpoles, metal (Vol. 1)

2499 Flagpoles, wood (Vol. 1)

2399 Flags, fabric (Vol. 1)

1411 Flagstone mining (Vol. 2)

3281 Flagstones (Vol. 1)

2493 Flakeboard (Vol. 1)

3399 Flakes, metal (Vol. 1)

7218 Flame and heat resistant clothing supply service (Vol. 2)

0721 Flame; Cultivation services, mechanical and (Vol. 2)

3826 Flame photometers (Vol. 1)

3822 Flame safety controls for furnaces and boilers (Vol. 1)

3489 Flame throwers (ordnance) (Vol. 1)

3229 Flameware, glass and glass ceramic (Vol. 1)

3541 Flange facing machines (Vol. 1)

3562 Flange units for ball or roller bearings (Vol. 1)

3462 Flange, valve, and pipe fitting forgings, ferrous: not made in rolling mills (Vol. 1)

3463 Flange, valve and pipe fitting forgings, nonferrous: not made in hot-rolling mills (Vol. 1)

3494 Flanges and flange unions, pipe: metal (Vol. 1)

2321 Flannel shirts, except work shirts: men's, youths', and boys' (Vol. 1)
2211 Flannelette (Vol. 1)
2211 Flannels, cotton (Vol. 1)
2231 Flannels: wool, mohair, and similar animal fibers (Vol. 1)
3728 Flaps, aircraft wing (Vol. 1)
2899 Flares (Vol. 1)
3647 Flasher lights, automobile (Vol. 1)
3861 Flashlight apparatus for photographers, except bulbs (Vol. 1)
2899 Flashlight bombs (pyrotechnics) (Vol. 1)
3641 Flashlight bulbs, photographic (Vol. 1)
3648 Flashlights (Vol. 1)
5063 Flashlights—wholesale (Vol. 2)
3316 Flat bright steel strip, cold-rolled: not made in hot-rolling mills (Vol. 1)
2221 Flat crepes (Vol. 1)
3211 Flat Glass (Vol. 1)
3089 Flat panels, plastics (Vol. 1)
3493 Flat springs, sheet or strip stock (Vol. 1)
3312 Flats, iron and steel: made in steel works or hot-rolling mills (Vol. 1)
2441 Flats, wood: greenhouse (Vol. 1)
3914 Flatware, table: with metal handles and blades (Vol. 1)
2026 Flavored milk drinks (Vol. 1)
2087 Flavoring concentrates (Vol. 1)
5149 Flavoring extract, except for fountain use—wholesale (Vol. 2)
2087 Flavoring Extracts and Flavoring Syrups Not Elsewhere Classified (Vol. 1)
2087 Flavoring extracts, pastes, powders, and syrups (Vol. 1)
2869 Flavors and flavoring materials, synthetic (Vol. 1)
0723 Flax; Decorticating (Vol. 2)
0723 Flax decorticating and retting (Vol. 2)
0723 Flax; Retting (Vol. 2)
2299 Flax yarns and roving (Vol. 1)
0119 Flaxseed farms (Vol. 2)
3111 Fleshers, leather (flesh side of split leather) (Vol. 1)
3546 Flexible shaft metalworking machines, portable (Vol. 1)
2893 Flexographic ink (Vol. 1)
2796 Flexographic plates, preparation of (Vol. 1)
2759 Flexographic printing (Vol. 1)
3949 Flies, artificial: for fishing (Vol. 1)
3812 Flight instruments, aeronautical (Vol. 1)
3699 Flight simulators (training aids), electronic (Vol. 1)
1459 Flint clay mining (Vol. 2)
3295 Flint, ground or otherwise treated (Vol. 1)
3999 Flints, cigarette lighter (Vol. 1)
2421 Flitches (veneer stock), made in sawmills (Vol. 1)
3822 Float controls, residential and commercial types (Vol. 1)
3211 Float glass (Vol. 1)
3255 Floaters, glasshouse: clay (Vol. 1)
3443 Floating covers, metal plate (Vol. 1)
7389 Floats, decoration of (Vol. 2)
3949 Floats for fish lines (Vol. 1)

2261 Flock printing of cotton broadwoven fabrics (Vol. 1)
2262 Flock printing of manmade fiber and silk broadwoven fabrics (Vol. 1)
2269 Flock printing of narrow fabrics, except wool (Vol. 1)
2299 Flock (recovered textile fibers) (Vol. 1)
3999 Flocking metal products for the trade (Vol. 1)
2261 Flocking of cotton broadwoven fabrics (Vol. 1)
2262 Flocking of manmade fiber and silk broadwoven fabrics (Vol. 1)
1629 Flood control project construction-general contractors (Vol. 2)
3648 Floodlights (Vol. 1)
3251 Floor arch tile, clay (Vol. 1)
2431 Floor baseboards, wood (Vol. 1)
3299 Floor composition, magnesite (Vol. 1)
2951 Floor composition, mastic: hot and cold (Vol. 1)
5713 Floor Covering Stores (Vol. 2)
5713 Floor covering stores—retail (Vol. 2)
3996 Floor coverings, asphalted-felt-base (linoleum) (Vol. 1)
3089 Floor coverings, plastics (Vol. 1)
2273 Floor coverings, textile fiber (Vol. 1)
2273 Floor coverings, tufted (Vol. 1)
2273 Floor coverings: twisted paper, grass, reed, coir, sisal, jute, and rag (Vol. 1)
5023 Floor coverings—wholesale (Vol. 2)
3634 Floor fans, electric (Vol. 1)
3272 Floor filler tiles, concrete (Vol. 1)
3441 Floor jacks, metal (Vol. 1)
3645 Floor lamps (Vol. 1)
1752 Floor Laying and Other Floor Work Not Elsewhere Classified (Vol. 2)
1752 Floor laying, scraping, finishing, and refinishing-contractors (Vol. 2)
2392 Floor mops (Vol. 1)
3441 Floor posts, adjustable: metal (Vol. 1)
3589 Floor sanding, washing, and polishing machines: commercial type (Vol. 1)
3272 Floor slabs, precast concrete (Vol. 1)
3292 Floor tile, asphalt (Vol. 1)
3253 Floor tile, ceramic (Vol. 1)
3272 Floor tile, precast terrazzo (Vol. 1)
3469 Floor tile, stamped metal (Vol. 1)
5713 Floor tile stores—retail (Vol. 2)
6221 Floor traders, commodity contract (Vol. 2)
6211 Floor traders, security (Vol. 2)
2842 Floor wax emulsion (Vol. 1)
3639 Floor waxers and polishers, household: electric (Vol. 1)
2842 Floor waxes (Vol. 1)
7349 Floor waxing service (Vol. 2)
3251 Flooring brick, clay (Vol. 1)
3444 Flooring, cellular steel (Vol. 1)
2421 Flooring (dressed lumber), softwood (Vol. 1)
2426 Flooring, hardwood (Vol. 1)
3446 Flooring, open steel (grating) (Vol. 1)
3069 Flooring, rubber: tile or sheet (Vol. 1)
2491 Flooring, wood block: treated (Vol. 1)

1752 Flooring, wood—contractors (Vol. 2)
5211 Flooring, wood—retail (Vol. 2)
2452 Floors, prefabricated: wood (Vol. 1)
0181 Floral products; Greenhouses for (Vol. 2)
5992 Florists (Vol. 2)
3269 Florists' articles, red earthenware (Vol. 1)
3496 Florists' designs, made from purchased wire (Vol. 1)
0181 Florists' greens, cultivated: growing of (Vol. 2)
5992 Florists—retail (Vol. 2)
7389 Florists' telegraph service (Vol. 2)
5193 Florists—wholesale (Vol. 2)
6211 Flotation companies, security (Vol. 2)
3532 Flotation machinery (mining machinery) (Vol. 1)
2258 Flouncings, lace (Vol. 1)
2041 Flour & Other Grain Mill Products (Vol. 1)
2673 Flour bags, except fabric (Vol. 1)
2393 Flour bags, fabric (Vol. 1)
2045 Flour: blended or self-rising (Vol. 1)
2041 Flour: blended, prepared, or self-rising (Vol. 1)
2041 Flour: buckwheat, corn, graham, rye, and wheat (Vol. 1)
3556 Flour mill machinery (Vol. 1)
2041 Flour mills, cereals: except rice (Vol. 1)
2041 Flour mixes (Vol. 1)
2044 Flour, rice (Vol. 1)
5149 Flour—wholesale (Vol. 2)
2499 Flour, wood (Vol. 1)
3625 Flow actuated electrical switches (Vol. 1)
3823 Flow instruments, industrial process type (Vol. 1)
5191 Flower and field bulbs—wholesale (Vol. 2)
0181 Flower and vegetable: growing of; Seeds, (Vol. 2)
3299 Flower boxes, plaster of paris: factory production only (Vol. 1)
5261 Flower bulbs—retail (Vol. 2)
3089 Flower pots, plastics (Vol. 1)
3269 Flower pots, red earthenware (Vol. 1)
5193 Flowers and florists' supplies—wholesale (Vol. 2)
0181 Flowers and shrubbery, except forest shrubbery; Field nurseries: growing of (Vol. 2)
3999 Flowers, artificial, except glass (Vol. 1)
5999 Flowers, artificial—retail (Vol. 2)
5193 Flowers, artificial—wholesale (Vol. 2)
3231 Flowers, foliage, fruits and vines: artificial glass-made from purchased glass (Vol. 1)
5992 Flowers, fresh—retail (Vol. 2)
5193 Flowers, fresh—wholesale (Vol. 2)
0181 Flowers, growing of (Vol. 2)
3231 Flowers, made from purchased glass (Vol. 1)
5193 Flowers, Nursery Stock and Florists' Supplies (Vol. 2)
3999 Flowers, preserved (Vol. 1)
3259 Flue lining, clay (Vol. 1)
3444 Flues, stove and furnace: sheet metal (Vol. 1)
2026 Fluid Milk (Vol. 1)
3412 Fluid milk shipping containers, metal (Vol. 1)
3593 Fluid power actuators, hydraulic and pneumatic (Vol. 1)
3593 Fluid Power Cylinders and Actuators (Vol. 1)

3593 Fluid power cylinders, hydraulic and pneumatic (Vol. 1)
3593 Fluid power motors (Vol. 1)
3594 Fluid Power Pumps and Motors (Vol. 1)
3594 Fluid power pumps and motors (Vol. 1)
3492 Fluid power valves and fittings (Vol. 1)
3492 Fluid Power Valves and Hose Fittings (Vol. 1)
3823 Fluidic devices, circuits, and systems for process control (Vol. 1)
2899 Fluidifier (retarder) for concrete (Vol. 1)
3443 Flumes, metal plate (Vol. 1)
3444 Flumes, sheet metal (Vol. 1)
3612 Fluorescent ballasts (transformers) (Vol. 1)
2899 Fluorescent inspection oil (Vol. 1)
3641 Fluorescent lamp electrodes, cold cathode (Vol. 1)
3641 Fluorescent lamps, electric (Vol. 1)
3646 Fluorescent lighting fixtures, commercial (Vol. 1)
3645 Fluorescent lighting fixtures, residential (Vol. 1)
3612 Fluorescent lighting transformers (Vol. 1)
3643 Fluorescent starters (Vol. 1)
2869 Fluorinated hydrocarbon gases (Vol. 1)
2819 Fluorine, elemental (Vol. 1)
1479 Fluorite mining (Vol. 2)
2822 Fluoro rubbers (Vol. 1)
2822 Fluorocarbon derivative rubbers (Vol. 1)
2824 Fluorocarbon fibers (Vol. 1)
2821 Fluorohydrocarbon resins (Vol. 1)
3844 Fluoroscopes (Vol. 1)
3844 Fluoroscopic X-ray apparatus and tubes (Vol. 1)
1479 Fluorspar, ground or otherwise treated (Vol. 2)
1479 Fluorspar mining (Vol. 2)
3431 Flush tanks, metal (Vol. 1)
3088 Flush tanks, plastics (Vol. 1)
3261 Flush tanks, vitreous china (Vol. 1)
3432 Flush valves (Vol. 1)
3711 Flushers, street (motor vehicles) (Vol. 1)
3931 Flutes and parts (Vol. 1)
2899 Fluxes: brazing, soldering, galvanizing, and welding (Vol. 1)
3199 Fly nets (harness) (Vol. 1)
3496 Fly screening, made from purchased wire (Vol. 1)
2879 Fly sprays (Vol. 1)
3999 Fly swatters (Vol. 1)
3677 Flyback transformers (Vol. 1)
4522 Flying charter services (Vol. 2)
4581 Flying fields, except those maintained by aviation clubs (Vol. 2)
7997 Flying fields maintained by aviation clubs (Vol. 2)
8299 Flying instruction (Vol. 2)
2672 Flypaper (Vol. 1)
3699 Flytraps, electrical (Vol. 1)
3651 FM and AM tuners (Vol. 1)
2899 Foam charge mixtures (Vol. 1)
3069 Foam rubber (Vol. 1)
5199 Foam rubber—wholesale (Vol. 2)
3086 Foamed plastics products (Vol. 1)
3647 Fog lights, motor vehicle (Vol. 1)
2679 Foil board (Vol. 1)
3497 Foil containers for bakery goods and frozen foods, except bags and liners (Vol. 1)

3497 Foil, except aluminum: not made in rolling mills (Vol. 1)

3497 Foil, laminated to paper or other materials (Vol. 1)

3353 Foil, plain aluminum (Vol. 1)

7389 Folding and refolding service: textiles and apparel (Vol. 2)

2631 Folding boxboards (Vol. 1)

2657 Folding cartons, except milk cartons: paperboard (Vol. 1)

1751 Folding door installation-contractors (Vol. 2)

3089 Folding doors: plastic or plastic coated fabric, metal frame (Vol. 1)

3554 Folding machines, paper: except office machines (Vol. 1)

2657 Folding Paperboard Boxes Including Sanitary (Vol. 1)

5113 Folding paperboard boxes—wholesale (Vol. 2)

3999 Foliage, artificial and preserved: except glass (Vol. 1)

0181 Foliage, growing of (Vol. 2)

3231 Foliage, made from purchased glass (Vol. 1)

5169 Food additives, chemical—wholesale (Vol. 2)

5421 Food and freezer plans, meat—retail (Vol. 2)

5812 Food bars (Vol. 2)

5141 Food brokers, general line—wholesale (Vol. 2)

3089 Food casings, plastics (Vol. 1)

3556 Food choppers, grinders, mixers, and slicers: commercial type (Vol. 1)

2087 Food colorings, except synthetic (Vol. 1)

3411 Food containers, metal (Vol. 1)

2656 Food containers, nonfolding paperboard, sanitary (Vol. 1)

2656 Food containers, sanitary: except folding (Vol. 1)

2899 Food contamination testing and screening kits (Vol. 1)

0182 Food crops; Greenhouses for (Vol. 2)

0182 Food Crops Grown Under Cover (Vol. 2)

2865 Food dyes and colors, synthetic (Vol. 1)

2087 Food glace, for glazing foods (Vol. 1)

9641 Food inspection agencies-government (Vol. 2)

4222 Food lockers, rental (Vol. 2)

5961 Food, mail-order—retail (Vol. 2)

5411 Food markets—retail (Vol. 2)

3634 Food mixers, household: electric (Vol. 1)

2099 Food Preparations Not Elsewhere Classified (Vol. 1)

5084 Food product manufacturing machinery—wholesale (Vol. 2)

3556 Food Products Machinery (Vol. 1)

1541 Food products manufacturing or packing plant construction-general contractors (Vol. 2)

8731 Food research, commercial (Vol. 2)

5812 Food service, institutional (Vol. 2)

5963 Food service, mobile—retail (Vol. 2)

2032 Food specialties, canned (Vol. 1)

8734 Food testing services (Vol. 2)

2599 Food trucks, restaurant (Vol. 1)

2599 Food wagons, restaurant (Vol. 1)

3589 Food warming equipment, commercial (Vol. 1)

5046 Food warming equipment, commercial—wholesale (Vol. 2)

3639 Food waste disposal units, household (Vol. 1)

3842 Foot appliances, orthopedic (Vol. 1)

7997 Football clubs, except professional and semiprofessional (Vol. 2)

7941 Football clubs, professional or semiprofessional (Vol. 2)

3949 Footballs and football equipment and supplies, except uniforms and footwear (Vol. 1)

3021 Footholds, rubber (Vol. 1)

2389 Footlets (Vol. 1)

5139 Footwear (Vol. 2)

3149 Footwear, children's: house slippers and vulcanized rubber footwear (Vol. 1)

3149 Footwear, children's: leather or vinyl with molded or vulcanized shoes (Vol. 1)

3149 Footwear Except Rubber Not Elsewhere Classified (Vol. 1)

3143 Footwear, men's: except house slippers, athletic, and vulcanized rubber footwear (Vol. 1)

3143 Footwear, men's: leather or vinyl with molded or vulcanized soles (Vol. 1)

3021 Footwear, rubber or rubber soled fabric (Vol. 1)

5661 Footwear stores—retail (Vol. 2)

5139 Footwear—wholesale (Vol. 2)

3144 Footwear, women's: except house slippers, athletic, and vulcanized rubber footwear (Vol. 1)

3144 Footwear, women's: leather or vinyl with molded or vulcanized soles (Vol. 1)

3523 Forage blowers (Vol. 1)

3523 Forage harvesters (Vol. 1)

3843 Forceps, dental (Vol. 1)

3841 Forceps, surgical (Vol. 1)

6099 Foreign currency exchanges (Vol. 2)

4731 Foreign forwarding (Vol. 2)

9721 Foreign missions (Vol. 2)

6082 Foreign Trade and International Banking Institutions (Vol. 2)

4226 Foreign trade zone warehousing, and storage (Vol. 2)

8734 Forensic laboratories (Vol. 2)

0851 Forest management plans, preparation of (Vol. 2)

0831 Forest nurseries (Vol. 2)

0831 Forest Nurseries and Gathering of Forest Products (Vol. 2)

6519 Forest properties, lessors of (Vol. 2)

5082 Forestry equipment—wholesale (Vol. 2)

0851 Forestry Services (Vol. 2)

3599 Forges, fan (Vol. 1)

3542 Forging machinery and hammers (Vol. 1)

5051 Forgings, ferrous—wholesale (Vol. 2)

3312 Forgings, iron and steel: made in steel works or rolling mills (Vol. 1)

3462 Forgings, iron and steel: not made in rolling mills (Vol. 1)

3463 Forgings, nonferrous metal: not made in hot rolling mills (Vol. 1)

5812 Frankfurter (hot dog) stands (Vol. 2)

2013 Frankfurters, except poultry (Vol. 1)

2011 Frankfurters, except poultry (Vol. 1)

2015 Frankfurters, poultry (Vol. 1)

6321 Fraternal accident and health insurance organizations (Vol. 2)

8641 Fraternal associations, other than insurance offices (Vol. 2)

6311 Fraternal life insurance organizations (Vol. 2)

8641 Fraternal lodges (Vol. 2)

6311 Fraternal protective associations (Vol. 2)

8641 Fraternities and sororities, except residential (Vol. 2)

7041 Fraternity residential houses (Vol. 2)

8011 Freestanding emergency medical (M.D.) centers (Vol. 2)

2095 Freeze-dried coffee (Vol. 1)

5421 Freezer food plans, meat—retail (Vol. 2)

5421 Freezer provisioners, meat—retail (Vol. 2)

3632 Freezers, home and farm (Vol. 1)

5722 Freezers, household—retail (Vol. 2)

5064 Freezers, household—wholesale (Vol. 2)

3556 Freezers, ice cream: commercial (Vol. 1)

3499 Freezers, ice cream: household-metal (Vol. 1)

3821 Freezers, laboratory (Vol. 1)

4731 Freight agencies, railroad: not operated by railroad companies (Vol. 2)

4789 Freight car loading and unloading, not trucking (Vol. 2)

3743 Freight cars and car equipment (Vol. 1)

4731 Freight consolidation (Vol. 2)

4731 Freight forwarding (Vol. 2)

4783 Freight packing and crating (Vol. 2)

4731 Freight rate auditors (Vol. 2)

4731 Freight rate information service (Vol. 2)

4432 Freight Transportation on the Great Lakes and St. Lawrence Seaway (Vol. 2)

4231 Freight trucking terminals, with or without maintenance facilities (Vol. 2)

2221 French crepes (Vol. 1)

2035 French dressing (Vol. 1)

2038 French toast, frozen (Vol. 1)

3621 Frequency converters (electric generators) (Vol. 1)

3825 Frequency meters: electrical, mechanical, and electronic (Vol. 1)

3825 Frequency synthesizers (Vol. 1)

1743 Fresco work-contractors (Vol. 2)

5148 Fresh Fruits and Vegetables (Vol. 2)

0723 Fresh or farm-dried fruits and vegetables; Packaging (Vol. 2)

3931 Fretted instruments and parts (Vol. 1)

3499 Friction material, made from powdered metal (Vol. 1)

3292 Friction materials, asbestos: woven (Vol. 1)

3069 Friction tape, rubber (Vol. 1)

2241 Fringes, weaving (Vol. 1)

3952 Frisket paper (artists' material) (Vol. 1)

2899 Frit (Vol. 1)

0279 Frog farms (Vol. 2)

0919 Frogs, catching of (Vol. 2)

3312 Frogs, iron and steel: made in steel works or rolling mills (Vol. 1)

3462 Frogs, railroad: forgings not made in rolling mills (Vol. 1)

5082 Front-end loaders—wholesale (Vol. 2)

7539 Front end repair, automotive (Vol. 2)

3851 Fronts and temples, ophthalmic (Vol. 1)

2541 Fronts, store: prefabricated-wood (Vol. 1)

2099 Frosting, prepared (Vol. 1)

2053 Frozen Bakery Products Except Bread (Vol. 1)

2051 Frozen bread and bread-type rolls (Vol. 1)

2024 Frozen custard (Vol. 1)

5812 Frozen custard stands (Vol. 2)

5143 Frozen dairy desserts—wholesale (Vol. 2)

2024 Frozen desserts, except bakery (Vol. 1)

2038 Frozen dinners, packaged (Vol. 1)

2045 Frozen doughs (Vol. 1)

2041 Frozen doughs (Vol. 1)

2092 Frozen fish, packaged (Vol. 1)

5411 Frozen food and freezer plans, except meat—retail (Vol. 2)

5421 Frozen food and freezer plans, meat—retail (Vol. 2)

2673 Frozen food bags (Vol. 1)

2657 Frozen food containers, folding paperboard (Vol. 1)

2656 Frozen food containers, nonfolding paperboard (Vol. 1)

4222 Frozen food locker rental (Vol. 2)

5142 Frozen foods, packaged—wholesale (Vol. 2)

2037 Frozen Fruits, Fruit Juices and Vegetables (Vol. 1)

2037 Frozen fruits, fruit juices, and vegetables (Vol. 1)

2092 Frozen prepared fish (Vol. 1)

2038 Frozen soups, except seafood (Vol. 1)

2038 Frozen Specialties Not Elsewhere Classified (Vol. 1)

5142 Frozen vegetables—wholesale (Vol. 2)

2046 Fructose (Vol. 1)

5431 Fruit and Vegetable Markets (Vol. 2)

3231 Fruit, artificial: made from purchased glass (Vol. 1)

2449 Fruit baskets, veneer and splint (Vol. 1)

2033 Fruit butters (Vol. 1)

2449 Fruit crates, wood: wirebound (Vol. 1)

0723 Fruit drying (Vol. 2)

0179 Fruit farms; Kiwi (Vol. 2)

0179 Fruit farms; Tropical (Vol. 2)

2034 Fruit flour, meal, and powders (Vol. 1)

2086 Fruit (fresh) drinks, bottled or canned (Vol. 1)

3523 Fruit grading, cleaning, and sorting machines (Vol. 1)

3221 Fruit jars, glass (Vol. 1)

2037 Fruit juice concentrates, frozen (Vol. 1)

2033 Fruit juices: canned (Vol. 1)

2087 Fruit juices, concentrated: for fountain use (Vol. 1)

2037 Fruit juices, frozen (Vol. 1)

5142 Fruit juices, frozen—wholesale (Vol. 2)

5961 Fruit, mail-order—retail (Vol. 2)

5431 Fruit markets and stands—retail (Vol. 2)

2064 Fruit peel products: candied, glazed, glace, and crystallized (Vol. 1)

5149 Fruit peel—wholesale (Vol. 2)

2033 Fruit pie mixes (Vol. 1)

2024 Fruit pops, frozen (Vol. 1)

4741 Fruit precooling, in connection with railroad transportation (Vol. 2)

0723 Fruit precooling, not in connection with transportation (Vol. 2)

2033 Fruit purees (Vol. 1)

0723 Fruit sorting, grading, and packing (Vol. 2)

0181 Fruit stocks, growing of (Vol. 2)

5431 Fruit stores—retail (Vol. 2)

0723 Fruit vacuum cooling (Vol. 2)

3523 Fruit, vegetable, berry, and grape harvesting machines (Vol. 1)

0179 Fruits and Tree Nuts Not Elsewhere Classified (Vol. 2)

0723 Fruits, and vegetables; Drying of corn, rice, hay, (Vol. 2)

0723 Fruits and vegetables; Packaging fresh or farm-dried (Vol. 2)

0723 Fruits and vegetables; Packing (Vol. 2)

0723 Fruits and vegetables; Sorting, grading, and packing of (Vol. 2)

3999 Fruits, artificial and preserved: except glass (Vol. 1)

3999 Fruits, artificial, except glass (Vol. 1)

2064 Fruits: candied, glazed, and crystallized (Vol. 1)

2033 Fruits, canned (Vol. 1)

0174 Fruits; Citrus (Vol. 2)

2087 Fruits, crushed: for soda fountain use (Vol. 1)

0175 Fruits; Deciduous Tree (Vol. 2)

2034 Fruits, dried or dehydrated (Vol. 1)

5149 Fruits, dried—wholesale (Vol. 2)

5145 Fruits, fountain—wholesale (Vol. 2)

5431 Fruits, fresh—retail (Vol. 2)

5148 Fruits, fresh—wholesale (Vol. 2)

5142 Fruits, frozen—wholesale (Vol. 2)

0182 Fruits grown under cover (Vol. 2)

0722 Fruits, machine harvesting of (Vol. 2)

2035 Fruits, pickled and brined (Vol. 1)

2037 Fruits, quick frozen and coldpack (frozen) (Vol. 1)

2034 Fruits, sulphured (Vol. 1)

0251 Fryer and Roaster Chickens; Broiler, (Vol. 2)

3589 Fryers, commercial (Vol. 1)

3634 Fryers, household: electric (Vol. 1)

0251 Frying chickens, raising of (Vol. 2)

3229 Frying pans, glass and glass ceramic (Vol. 1)

2064 Fudge (candy) (Vol. 1)

5169 Fuel additives—wholesale (Vol. 2)

2999 Fuel briquettes or boulets, made with petroleum binder (Vol. 1)

2679 Fuel cell forms, cardboard (Vol. 1)

2296 Fuel cell reinforcement, cord and fabric (Vol. 1)

3629 Fuel cells, electrochemical generators (Vol. 1)

3069 Fuel cells, rubber (Vol. 1)

3674 Fuel cells, solid-state (Vol. 1)

5052 Fuel: coal and coke—wholesale (Vol. 2)

5984 Fuel dealers, bottled liquefied petroleum gas—retail (Vol. 2)

5989 Fuel Dealers Not Elsewhere Classified (Vol. 2)

3829 Fuel densitometers, aircraft engine (Vol. 1)

3829 Fuel mixture indicators, aircraft engine (Vol. 1)

1711 Fuel oil burner installation and servicing-contractors (Vol. 2)

5983 Fuel Oil Dealers (Vol. 2)

5983 Fuel oil dealers—retail (Vol. 2)

5172 Fuel oil, except bulk stations and terminals—wholesale (Vol. 2)

2819 Fuel propellants, solid: inorganic (Vol. 1)

2869 Fuel propellants, solid: organic (Vol. 1)

3714 Fuel pumps, motor vehicle (Vol. 1)

7539 Fuel system conversion, automotive (Vol. 2)

3829 Fuel system instruments, aircraft (Vol. 1)

7539 Fuel system repair, automotive (Vol. 2)

3714 Fuel systems and parts, motor vehicle (Vol. 1)

2899 Fuel tank and engine cleaning chemicals, automotive and aircraft (Vol. 1)

3728 Fuel tanks, aircraft: including self-sealing (Vol. 1)

3069 Fuel tanks, collapsible: rubberized fabric (Vol. 1)

3443 Fuel tanks, metal plate (Vol. 1)

3829 Fuel totalizers, aircraft engine (Vol. 1)

2411 Fuel wood harvesting (Vol. 1)

5989 Fuel wood—retail (Vol. 2)

5172 Fueling services, aircraft—wholesale (Vol. 2)

2819 Fuels, high energy: inorganic (Vol. 1)

2869 Fuels, high energy: organic (Vol. 1)

2911 Fuels, jet (Vol. 1)

2421 Fuelwood, from mill waste (Vol. 1)

3295 Fuller's earth, ground or otherwise treated (Vol. 1)

1459 Fuller's earth mining (Vol. 2)

2892 Fulminate of mercury (explosive compounds) (Vol. 1)

3821 Fume hoods, chemical (Vol. 1)

3443 Fumigating chambers, metal plate (Vol. 1)

7342 Fumigating service (Vol. 2)

0723 Fumigation; Grain (Vol. 2)

3825 Function generators (Vol. 1)

6099 Functions Related to Depository Banking Not Elsewhere Classified (Vol. 2)

7389 Fundraising on a contract or fee basis (Vol. 2)

8399 Fundraising organizations, except on a contract or fee basis (Vol. 2)

3578 Funds transfer devices (Vol. 1)

7261 Funeral directors (Vol. 2)

7261 Funeral homes or parlors (Vol. 2)

6311 Funeral insurance (Vol. 2)

7261 Funeral Services and Crematories (Vol. 2)

2879 Fungicides (Vol. 1)

3069 Funnels, rubber (Vol. 1)

2371 Fur apparel: capes, coats, hats, jackets, and neckpieces (Vol. 1)

5632 Fur apparel made to custom order—retail (Vol. 2)

0271 Fur-Bearing Animals and Rabbits (Vol. 2)

7219 Fur cleaning (Vol. 2)

5137 Fur clothing—wholesale (Vol. 2)

5093 Fur cuttings and scraps—wholesale (Vol. 2)

0271 Fur farms (Vol. 2)

2371 Fur finishers and liners for the fur goods trade: buttonhole making (Vol. 1)

7219 Fur garments: cleaning, repairing, and storage (Vol. 2)

3483 Fuses for ammunition more than 30 mm. (or more than 1.18 inch) (Vol. 1)

3483 Fuses: mine, torpedo, bomb, depth charge, and chemical warfare projectile (Vol. 1)

2892 Fuses, safety (Vol. 1)

2861 Fustic wood extract (Vol. 1)

6282 Futures advisory service (Vol. 2)

6221 Futures brokers, commodity (Vol. 2)

6221 Futures dealers, commodity (Vol. 2)

6231 Futures exchanges, contract (Vol. 2)

G

2211 Gabardine, cotton (Vol. 1)

1429 Gabbro, crushed and broken-quarrying (Vol. 2)

1411 Gabbro, dimension-quarrying (Vol. 2)

3021 Gaiters, rubber or rubber soled fabric (Vol. 1)

2211 Galatea, cotton (Vol. 1)

1031 Galena mining (Vol. 2)

2834 Galenical preparations (Vol. 1)

3555 Galleys and chases, printers' (Vol. 1)

2258 Galloons, lace (Vol. 1)

3021 Galoshes, plastics (Vol. 1)

3021 Galoshes, rubber or rubber soled fabric (Vol. 1)

3312 Galvanized hoops, pipes, plates, sheets, and strips: iron and steel (Vol. 1)

2899 Galvanizing fluxes (Vol. 1)

3547 Galvanizing lines (rolling mill equipment) (Vol. 1)

3479 Galvanizing of iron and steel and end formed products, for the trade (Vol. 1)

3825 Galvanometers, except geophysical (Vol. 1)

2861 Gambier extract (Vol. 1)

9311 Gambling control boards-government (Vol. 2)

7999 Gambling establishments not primarily operating coin-operated machines (Vol. 2)

7993 Gambling establishments primarily operating coin-operated machines (Vol. 2)

7993 Gambling machines, coin-operated: operation of (Vol. 2)

7999 Gambling machines, except coin-operated: operation of (Vol. 2)

9512 Game and inland fish agencies-government (Vol. 2)

3949 Game calls (Vol. 1)

0271 Game farms (fur-bearing animals) (Vol. 2)

5099 Game machines, coin-operated—wholesale (Vol. 2)

0971 Game management (Vol. 2)

7999 Game parlors, except coin-operated (Vol. 2)

0971 Game preserves (Vol. 2)

0971 Game propagation (Vol. 2)

0971 Game retreats, operation of (Vol. 2)

5945 Game shops—retail (Vol. 2)

2015 Game, small: fresh, frozen, canned, or cooked (Vol. 1)

2015 Game, small: slaughtering and dressing (Vol. 1)

3999 Games, coin-operated: pinball and other (Vol. 1)

7372 Games, computer software: prepackaged (Vol. 2)

3944 Games for children and adults: puzzles, bingo, marbles, poker chips, and chess (Vol. 1)

5092 Games (including electronic), except coin-operated—wholesale (Vol. 2)

7999 Games, teaching of (Vol. 2)

3944 Games, Toys and Children's Vehicles Except Dolls and Bicycles (Vol. 1)

3844 Gamma ray irradiation equipment (Vol. 1)

1429 Ganister, crushed and broken-quarrying (Vol. 2)

1542 Garage construction-general contractors (Vol. 2)

1751 Garage door installation-contractors (Vol. 2)

3442 Garage doors, overhead: metal (Vol. 1)

2431 Garage doors, overhead: wood (Vol. 1)

5211 Garage doors—retail (Vol. 2)

5013 Garage service equipment—wholesale (Vol. 2)

7521 Garages, automobile parking (Vol. 2)

7549 Garages, do-it-yourself (Vol. 2)

7538 Garages, general automotive repair and service (Vol. 2)

3448 Garages, prefabricated: metal (Vol. 1)

3272 Garbage boxes, concrete (Vol. 1)

3469 Garbage cans, stamped and pressed metal (Vol. 1)

4953 Garbage: collecting, destroying, and processing (Vol. 2)

3089 Garbage containers, plastics (Vol. 1)

3639 Garbage disposal units, household (Vol. 1)

5064 Garbage disposals, electric—wholesale (Vol. 2)

3589 Garbage disposers, commercial (Vol. 1)

5722 Garbage disposers, electric—retail (Vol. 2)

4212 Garbage, local collecting and transporting: without disposal (Vol. 2)

2519 Garden furniture: except wood, metal, stone, and concrete (Vol. 1)

2514 Garden furniture, metal (Vol. 1)

2511 Garden furniture, wood (Vol. 1)

3423 Garden handtools (Vol. 1)

3052 Garden hose, plastics or rubber (Vol. 1)

5083 Garden machinery and equipment—wholesale (Vol. 2)

0782 Garden maintenance (Vol. 2)

0781 Garden planning (Vol. 2)

0782 Garden planting (Vol. 2)

3269 Garden pottery (Vol. 1)

5261 Garden supplies and tools—retail (Vol. 2)

3999 Garden umbrellas (Vol. 1)

0161 Gardens; Market (Vol. 2)

3999 Garlands, wreaths and sprays; made from tree boughs, cones, etc. (Vol. 1)

7219 Garment alteration and repair shops (Vol. 2)

3496 Garment hangers, made from purchased wire (Vol. 1)

2499 Garment hangers, wood (Vol. 1)

3111 Garment leather (Vol. 1)

7212 Garment Pressing and Agents for Laundries and Drycleaners (Vol. 2)

7212 Garment pressing shops (Vol. 2)

2542 Garment racks, except wood (Vol. 1)

2541 Garment racks, wood (Vol. 1)

2673 Garment storage bags, coated paper or plastics film (Vol. 1)

2392 Garment storage bags made of materials, except paper or plastics film (Vol. 1)

2386 Garments, leather or sheep-lined (Vol. 1)

3291 Garnet abrasives (Vol. 1)

1499 Garnet mining (Vol. 2)

3291 Garnet paper (Vol. 1)

3552 Garnetting machines, textile (Vol. 1)

2299 Garnetting of textile waste and rags (Vol. 1)

2389 Garter belts (Vol. 1)

2389 Garters (Vol. 1)

3443 Gas absorbers (Vol. 1)

3826 Gas analyzers, laboratory type (Vol. 1)

3519 Gas and diesel engine rebuilding, on a factory basis (Vol. 1)

3823 Gas and liquid analysis instruments, industrial process type (Vol. 1)

4932 Gas and Other Services Combined (Vol. 2)

4932 Gas and other services combined (gas less than 95 percent of total) (Vol. 2)

3671 Gas and vapor tubes (Vol. 1)

7699 Gas appliance repair service (Vol. 2)

3822 Gas burner automatic controls, except valves (Vol. 1)

3433 Gas burners, domestic (Vol. 1)

3842 Gas capes (cold climate individual protective covers) (Vol. 1)

3826 Gas chromatographic instruments, laboratory type (Vol. 1)

3312 Gas, coal: derived from chemical recovery coke ovens (Vol. 1)

1389 Gas compressing, natural gas at the field on a contract basis (Vol. 2)

1382 Gas field exploration: on a contract basis (Vol. 2)

3823 Gas flow computers, industrial process type (Vol. 1)

3433 Gas heaters, room (Vol. 1)

3443 Gas holders, metal plate (Vol. 1)

5722 Gas household appliance stores—retail (Vol. 2)

3433 Gas infrared heating units (Vol. 1)

1799 Gas leakage detection-contractors (Vol. 2)

3648 Gas lighting fixtures (Vol. 1)

5099 Gas lighting fixtures—wholesale (Vol. 2)

5984 Gas, liquified petroleum: bottled—retail (Vol. 2)

4925 Gas, liquified petroleum: distribution through mains (Vol. 2)

1623 Gas main construction-general contractors (Vol. 2)

4925 Gas, manufactured: production and distribution (Vol. 2)

3842 Gas masks (Vol. 1)

4925 Gas, mixed natural and manufactured: production and distribution (Vol. 2)

1623 Gas (natural) compressing station construction-general contractors (Vol. 2)

4924 Gas, natural: distribution (Vol. 2)

1311 Gas (natural) production (Vol. 2)

4922 Gas, natural: transmission (Vol. 2)

4923 Gas, natural: transmission and distribution (Vol. 2)

3433 Gas-oil burners, combination (Vol. 1)

3321 Gas pipe, cast iron (Vol. 1)

3569 Gas producers (machinery) (Vol. 1)

3631 Gas ranges, domestic (Vol. 1)

2911 Gas, refinery or still oil: produced in petroleum refineries (Vol. 1)

3569 Gas separators (machinery) (Vol. 1)

7389 Gas systems, contract conversion from manufactured to natural gas (Vol. 2)

3443 Gas tanks, metal plate (Vol. 1)

3714 Gas tanks, motor vehicle (Vol. 1)

3511 Gas turbine generator set units, complete (Vol. 1)

3511 Gas turbines and parts, except aircraft type (Vol. 1)

3511 Gas turbines, mechanical drive (Vol. 1)

3491 Gas valves and parts, industrial (Vol. 1)

3548 Gas welding equipment (Vol. 1)

3496 Gas welding rods, made from purchased wire (Vol. 1)

1381 Gas well drilling: on a contract basis (Vol. 2)

3533 Gas well machinery and equipment (Vol. 1)

1389 Gas well rig building, repairing, and dismantling on a contract basis (Vol. 2)

2869 Gases, chemical warfare (Vol. 1)

5169 Gases, compressed and liquefied: except liquefied petroleum gas—wholesale (Vol. 2)

2869 Gases, fluorinated hydrocarbon (Vol. 1)

2813 Gases, industrial: compressed, liquefied, or solid (Vol. 1)

5172 Gases, liquefied petroleum: except bulk stations and terminals—wholesale (Vol. 2)

2911 Gases, liquefied petroleum: produced in petroleum refineries (Vol. 1)

3053 Gaskets, Packing and Sealing Devices (Vol. 1)

3053 Gaskets, regardless of material (Vol. 1)

5085 Gaskets—wholesale (Vol. 2)

1711 Gasline hookup-contractors (Vol. 2)

3824 Gasmeters: domestic, large capacity, and industrial (Vol. 1)

5541 Gasoline and oil—retail (Vol. 2)

2911 Gasoline blending plants (Vol. 1)

5172 Gasoline: buying in bulk and selling to farmers—wholesale (Vol. 2)

3824 Gasoline dispensing meters (except pumps) (Vol. 1)

5172 Gasoline, except bulk stations and terminals—wholesale (Vol. 2)

2911 Gasoline, except natural gasoline (Vol. 1)

5541 Gasoline filling stations—retail (Vol. 2)

3599 Gasoline filters, internal combustion engine: except motor vehicle (Vol. 1)

3586 Gasoline measuring and dispensing pumps (Vol. 1)

1321 Gasoline (natural) production (Vol. 2)

4613 Gasoline pipelines, common carriers (Vol. 2)

1799 Gasoline pump installation-contractors (Vol. 2)

5541 Gasoline Service Stations (Vol. 2)

2269 Gassing yarn (Vol. 1)

3845 Gastroscopes, electromedical (Vol. 1)

3841 Gastroscopes, except electromedical (Vol. 1)

3569 Gate and bridge machinery, hydraulic (Vol. 1)

3452 Gate hooks (Vol. 1)

3089 Gate hooks, plastics (Vol. 1)

5039 Gates and accessories, wire—wholesale (Vol. 2)

3441 Gates, dam: metal plate (Vol. 1)

3496 Gates, fence: made from purchased wire (Vol. 1)

3523 Gates, holding (farm equipment) (Vol. 1)

3446 Gates, ornamental metal (Vol. 1)

0831 Gathering, extracting, and selling of tree seeds (Vol. 2)

0831 Gathering of forest products: (e.g., gums, barks, seeds) (Vol. 2)

3545 Gauge blocks (Vol. 1)

3829 Gauges except electric, motor vehicle: oil pressure and water temperature (Vol. 1)

3545 Gauges, except optical (machine tool accessories) (Vol. 1)

3824 Gauges for computing pressure-temperature corrections (Vol. 1)

3829 Gauging instruments, thickness: ultrasonic (Vol. 1)

2211 Gauze (Vol. 1)

3842 Gauze, surgical: not made in weaving mills (Vol. 1)

2499 Gavels, wood (Vol. 1)

3541 Gear chamfering machines (machine tools) (Vol. 1)

3541 Gear cutting and finishing machines (Vol. 1)

3423 Gear pullers, handtools (Vol. 1)

3542 Gear rolling machines (Vol. 1)

3541 Gear tooth grinding machines (machine tools) (Vol. 1)

3566 Gearmotors (power transmission equipment) (Vol. 1)

3462 Gears, forged steel: not made in rolling mills (Vol. 1)

3714 Gears, motor vehicle (Vol. 1)

3751 Gears, motorcycle and bicycle (Vol. 1)

3728 Gears, power transmission: aircraft (Vol. 1)

3566 Gears, power transmission: except motor vehicle and aircraft (Vol. 1)

5085 Gears—wholesale (Vol. 2)

0259 Geese farms (Vol. 2)

2015 Geese, processed: fresh, frozen, canned, or cooked (Vol. 1)

2015 Geese: slaughtering and dressing (Vol. 1)

3829 Geiger counters (Vol. 1)

3671 Geiger Mueller tubes (Vol. 1)

2899 Gelatin capsules, empty (Vol. 1)

2099 Gelatin dessert preparations (Vol. 1)

2899 Gelatin: edible, technical, photographic, and pharmaceutical (Vol. 1)

3555 Gelatin rolls used in printing (Vol. 1)

2833 Gelatin, vegetable (agar-agar) (Vol. 1)

5169 Gelatin—wholesale (Vol. 2)

1499 Gem stone mining (Vol. 2)

5999 Gem stones, rough—retail (Vol. 2)

5094 Gem stones—wholesale (Vol. 2)

3915 Gems, real and imitation: preparation for setting (Vol. 1)

7299 Genealogical investigation service (Vol. 2)

9199 General accounting offices-government (Vol. 2)

6159 General and industrial loan institutions (Vol. 2)

0291 General; Animal specialty and livestock farms, (Vol. 2)

7538 General Automotive Repair Shops (Vol. 2)

1541 General Contractors for Industrial Buildings and Warehouses (Vol. 2)

1542 General Contractors for Nonresidential Building Except Industrial Buildings and Warehouses (Vol. 2)

1522 General Contractors for Residential Buildings other than Single-Family (Vol. 2)

1521 General Contractors for Single-Family Housing Construction (Vol. 2)

0191 General; Crop farms, (Vol. 2)

9611 General economic statistics agencies-government (Vol. 2)

0191 General Farms—Primarily Crop (Vol. 2)

0291 General Farms—Primarily Livestock and Animal Specialties (Vol. 2)

9199 General Government Not Elsewhere Classified (Vol. 2)

3569 General Industrial Machinery and Equipment Not Elsewhere Classified (Vol. 1)

3411 General line cans, metal (Vol. 1)

0291 General; Livestock and animal specialty farms, (Vol. 2)

0219 General Livestock Not Elsewhere Classified (Vol. 2)

8742 General management consultants (Vol. 2)

8062 General Medical and Surgical Hospitals (Vol. 2)

5399 General merchandise stores—retail (Vol. 2)

9199 General services departments-government (Vol. 2)

5399 General stores—retail (Vol. 2)

4225 General Warehousing and Storage (Vol. 2)

3621 Generating apparatus and parts, electrical: except internal combustion engine and arc-welding (Vol. 1)

4911 Generation of electric power (Vol. 2)

7539 Generator and starter repair, automotive (Vol. 2)

3613 Generator control and metering panels (Vol. 1)

3511 Generator set units, turbine: complete-steam, gas, and hydraulic (Vol. 1)

3621 Generator sets: gasoline, diesel, and dual fuel (Vol. 1)

3612 Generator voltage regulators, electric induction and step type (Vol. 1)

3694 Generators, aircraft and motor vehicle (Vol. 1)

3621 Generators and sets, electric: except internal combustion engine, welding, and turbogenerators (Vol. 1)

5063 Generators, electrical—wholesale (Vol. 2)

3621 Generators for gas-electric and oil-electric vehicles (Vol. 1)

3621 Generators for storage battery chargers, except internal combustion engine and aircraft (Vol. 1)

3569 Generators, gas (Vol. 1)

3548 Generators (separate) for arc-welders (Vol. 1)

3489 Generators, smoke (ordinance) (Vol. 1)

3569 Generators: steam, liquid oxygen, and nitrogen (Vol. 1)

3844 Generators, X-ray (Vol. 1)

2452 Geodesic domes, prefabricated: wood (Vol. 1)

1382 Geological exploration, oil and gas field: on a contract basis (Vol. 2)

8999 Geologists, consulting: not connected with business service laboratories (Vol. 2)

1382 Geophysical exploration, oil and gas field: on a contract basis (Vol. 2)

1081 Geophysical exploration services, for metal mining: on a contract basis (Vol. 2)

1481 Geophysical exploration services, for nonmetallic minerals, except fuels: on a contract basis (Vol. 2)

2221 Georgettes (Vol. 1)

1781 Geothermal drilling-contractors (Vol. 2)

4961 Geothermal steam production (Vol. 2)

2869 Geraniol, synthetic (Vol. 1)

3339 Germanium refining, primary (Vol. 1)

3341 Germanium refining, secondary (Vol. 1)

8999 Ghost writing (Vol. 2)

5947 Gift, Novelty and Souvenir Shops (Vol. 2)

5947 Gift shops—retail (Vol. 2)

2679 Gift wrap paper (Vol. 1)

5199 Gifts and novelties—wholesale (Vol. 2)

2789 Gilding books, cards, or paper (Vol. 1)

1499 Gilsonite mining (Vol. 2)

3423 Gimlets (edge tools) (Vol. 1)

2241 Gimps (Vol. 1)

2085 Gin (alcoholic beverage) (Vol. 1)

2086 Ginger ale, bottled or canned (Vol. 1)

2045 Gingerbread mixes (Vol. 1)

2211 Ginghams (Vol. 1)

0724 Ginning; Cotton (Vol. 2)

3559 Ginning machines, cotton (Vol. 1)

0723 Ginning; Moss (Vol. 2)

0724 Gins, cotton: operation of (Vol. 2)

0831 Ginseng, gathering of (Vol. 2)

2259 Girdle blanks, elastic (Vol. 1)

2259 Girdles (elastic) and other foundation garments (Vol. 1)

2342 Girdles, women's and misses' (Vol. 1)

7032 Girls' camps (Vol. 2)

2361 Girls', Children's and Infants' Dresses, Blouses and Shirts (Vol. 1)

2369 Girls', Children's and Infants' Outerwear Not Elsewhere Classified (Vol. 1)

2252 Girls' hosiery (Vol. 1)

2064 Glace fruits and nuts (Vol. 1)

2833 Gland derivatives: bulk, uncompounded (Vol. 1)

3229 Glass and glassware made in glassmaking establishments: for industrial, scientific, and technical use (Vol. 1)

1793 Glass and Glazing Work (Vol. 2)

3229 Glass blanks for electric light bulbs (Vol. 1)

5085 Glass bottles—wholesale (Vol. 2)

3229 Glass brick (Vol. 1)

2221 Glass broadwoven fabrics (Vol. 1)

3211 Glass, colored: cathedral and antique (Vol. 1)

3221 Glass Containers (Vol. 1)

3231 Glass: cut, ground, leaded, laminated, ornamented, and tinted (Vol. 1)

3851 Glass eyes (Vol. 1)

5039 Glass, flat: except automotive—wholesale (Vol. 2)

3211 Glass, flat (Vol. 1)

1793 Glass installation, except automotive-contractors (Vol. 2)

3559 Glass making machinery: blowing, molding, forming, grinding, etc. (Vol. 1)

5122 Glass, medical—wholesale (Vol. 2)

2241 Glass narrow fabrics (Vol. 1)

3231 Glass Products Made of Purchased Glass (Vol. 1)

7536 Glass replacement and repair, automotive (Vol. 2)

1446 Glass sand mining (Vol. 2)

3231 Glass, scientific apparatus: for druggists', hospitals, laboratories-made from purchased glass (Vol. 1)

3231 Glass, sheet: bent-made from purchased glass (Vol. 1)

5231 Glass stores—retail (Vol. 2)

2296 Glass tire cord and tire cord fabrics (Vol. 1)

2211 Glass toweling, cotton (Vol. 1)

2842 Glass window cleaning preparations (Vol. 1)

3296 Glass wool (Vol. 1)

1793 Glass work, except automotive-contractors (Vol. 2)

3827 Glasses, field or opera (Vol. 1)

3851 Glasses, sun or glare (Vol. 1)

3255 Glasshouse refractories (Vol. 1)

2674 Glassine bags, uncoated paper (Vol. 1)

2621 Glassine wrapping paper (Vol. 1)

5932 Glassware, antique—retail (Vol. 2)

3229 Glassware: art, decorative, and novelty (Vol. 1)

3231 Glassware, cut and engraved-made from purchased glass (Vol. 1)

3231 Glassware, cutting and engraving (Vol. 1)

3231 Glassware, decorated: e.g., chipped, engraved, sandblasted, etched-made from purchased glass (Vol. 1)

3229 Glassware, except glass containers for packing, bottling, and canning (Vol. 1)

3221 Glassware for packing, bottling and home canning (Vol. 1)

5023 Glassware, household—wholesale (Vol. 2)

5199 Glassware, novelty—wholesale (Vol. 2)

5719 Glassware stores—retail (Vol. 2)

2819 Glauber's salt (Vol. 1)

1474 Glauber's salt mining (Vol. 2)

7699 Glazing and cleaning baking pans (Vol. 2)

2371 Glazing furs (Vol. 1)

1799 Glazing of concrete surfaces-contractors (Vol. 2)

3089 Glazing panels, plastics (Vol. 1)

1793 Glazing work-contractors (Vol. 2)

3812 Glide slope instrumentation (Vol. 1)

3721 Gliders (aircraft) (Vol. 1)

2514 Gliders (furniture), metal (Vol. 1)

2741 Globe covers (maps): publishing and printing, or publishing only (Vol. 1)

3999 Globes, geographical (Vol. 1)

2211 Glove fabrics, cotton (Vol. 1)

3111 Glove leather (Vol. 1)

2241 Glove lining fabrics (Vol. 1)

2381 Glove linings, except fur (Vol. 1)

2371 Glove linings, fur (Vol. 1)

2399 Glove mending on factory basis (Vol. 1)

5136 Gloves (all materials), men's and boys'—wholesale (Vol. 2)

5137 Gloves, (all materials): women's, children's, and infants'—wholesale (Vol. 2)

3089 Gloves and mittens, plastics (Vol. 1)

2381 Gloves and mittens, woven or knit (Vol. 1)

3069 Gloves: e.g., surgeons', electricians', household-rubber (Vol. 1)

3151 Gloves, leather (Vol. 1)

2259 Gloves (Vol. 1)

3842 Gloves, safety: all material (Vol. 1)

3949 Gloves, sport and athletic: e.g., boxing, baseball, racketball, handball (Vol. 1)

3641 Glow lamp bulbs (Vol. 1)

2046 Glucose (Vol. 1)

3843 Glue, dental (Vol. 1)

2891 Glue, except dental: animal, vegetable, fish, casein, and synthetic resin (Vol. 1)

2899 Glue size (Vol. 1)

5169 Glue—wholesale (Vol. 2)

2046 Gluten feed (Vol. 1)

2046 Gluten meal (Vol. 1)

2841 Glycerin, crude and refined: from fats-except synthetic (Vol. 1)

2869 Glycerin, except from fats (synthetic) (Vol. 1)

2833 Glycosides (Vol. 1)

1423 Gneiss, crushed and broken-quarrying (Vol. 2)

1411 Gneiss, dimension-quarrying (Vol. 2)

0214 Goat farm; Milk production, (Vol. 2)

0214 Goat farms (Vol. 2)

0751 Goats, and poultry; Pedigree record services for cattle, hogs, sheep, (Vol. 2)

0751 Goats, and poultry; Showing of cattle, hogs, sheep, (Vol. 2)

0214 Goats' milk production (Vol. 2)

0214 Goats; Sheep and (Vol. 2)

5154 Goats—wholesale (Vol. 2)

3229 Goblets, glass (Vol. 1)

7999 Gocart raceway operation (Vol. 2)

7999 Gocart rentals (Vol. 2)

3944 Gocarts, children's (Vol. 1)

3799 Gocarts, except children's (Vol. 1)

5599 Gocarts—retail (Vol. 2)

5091 Gocarts—wholesale (Vol. 2)

3851 Goggles: sun, safety, industrial, and underwater (Vol. 1)

3356 Gold and gold alloy bars, sheets, strip, and tubing (Vol. 1)

3497 Gold beating (manufacturing of gold leaf and foil) (Vol. 1)

3843 Gold, dental (Vol. 1)

3497 Gold foil and leaf, not made in rolling mills (Vol. 1)

2893 Gold ink (Vol. 1)

1041 Gold lode mining (Vol. 2)

3952 Gold or bronze mixtures, powders, paints, and sizes: artists' (Vol. 1)

5052 Gold ore—wholesale (Vol. 2)

1041 Gold Ores (Vol. 2)

1041 Gold placer mining (Vol. 2)

3471 Gold plating, for the trade (Vol. 1)

3339 Gold refining, primary (Vol. 1)

3356 Gold rolling and drawing (Vol. 1)

3341 Gold smelting and refining, secondary (Vol. 1)

3999 Gold stamping for the trade, except books (Vol. 1)

2789 Gold stamping on books (Vol. 1)

0273 Goldfish farms (Vol. 2)

5091 Golf carts, except self-propelled—wholesale (Vol. 2)

3949 Golf carts, hand (Vol. 1)

3799 Golf carts, powered (Vol. 1)

5088 Golf carts, self-propelled—wholesale (Vol. 2)

5088 Golf clubs, membership (Vol. 2)

7997 Golf clubs, membership (Vol. 2)

7992 Golf clubs, nonmembership (Vol. 2)

1629 Golf course construction-general contractors (Vol. 2)

7999 Golf courses, miniature: operation of (Vol. 2)

7992 Golf courses, public: operation of (Vol. 2)

7999 Golf driving ranges (Vol. 2)

5091 Golf equipment—wholesale (Vol. 2)

5941 Golf goods and equipment—retail (Vol. 2)

7999 Golf, pitch-n-putt (Vol. 2)

7999 Golf professionals not operating retail stores (Vol. 2)

5941 Golf professionals operating retail stores (Vol. 2)

3949 Golfing equipment: e.g., caddy carts and bags, clubs, tees, balls (Vol. 1)

3699 Gongs, electric (Vol. 1)

3423 Gouges, woodworking (Vol. 1)

6111 Government National Mortgage Association (Vol. 2)

6726 Government National Mortgage Association (GNMA) pools (Vol. 2)

3728 Governors, aircraft propeller feathering (Vol. 1)

3519 Governors, diesel engine (Vol. 1)

3714 Governors, motor vehicle (Vol. 1)

9111 Governors' offices (Vol. 2)

3519 Governors, pump: for gas engines (Vol. 1)

3511 Governors, steam (Vol. 1)

7213 Gown supply service, uniform (Vol. 2)

2389 Gowns: academic, choir, clerical (Vol. 1)

2335 Gowns, formal: women's, misses', and juniors' (Vol. 1)

2389 Gowns, hospital: surgical and patient (Vol. 1)

2254 Gowns, night (Vol. 1)

2335 Gowns, wedding: women's, misses', and juniors' (Vol. 1)

3531 Grader attachments, elevating (Vol. 1)

5082 Graders, motor—wholesale (Vol. 2)

3531 Graders, road (construction machinery) (Vol. 1)

0723 Grading, and packing; Fruit sorting, (Vol. 2)

0723 Grading, and packing of fruits and vegetables; Sorting, (Vol. 2)

0723 Grading, and packing; Vegetable sorting, (Vol. 2)

3523 Grading, cleaning, and sorting machines: fruit, grain, and vegetable (Vol. 1)

1794 Grading: except for highways, streets, and airport runways-contractors (Vol. 2)

1611 Grading for highways, streets, and airport runways-contractors (Vol. 2)

2833 Grading of drugs and herbs (Vol. 1)

1389 Grading oil and gas well foundations on a contract basis (Vol. 2)

0723 Grading; Tobacco (Vol. 2)

3822 Gradual switches, pneumatic (Vol. 1)

3842 Grafts, artificial: for surgery-made of braided or mesh artificial fibers (Vol. 1)

2041 Graham flour (Vol. 1)

1499 Grahamite mining (Vol. 2)

2085 Grain alcohol for medicinal and beverage purposes (Vol. 1)

2869 Grain alcohol, industrial (nonbeverage) (Vol. 1)

5153 Grain and Field Beans (Vol. 2)

2082 Grain, brewers' (Vol. 1)

2041 Grain cereals, cracked (Vol. 1)

0723 Grain cleaning (Vol. 2)

3523 Grain drills, including legume planters (agricultural machinery) (Vol. 1)

1541 Grain elevator construction-general contractors (Vol. 2)

5153 Grain elevators, except storage only—wholesale (Vol. 2)

4221 Grain elevators, storage only (Vol. 2)

0119 Grain farms: except wheat, rice, corn, and soybeans (Vol. 2)

0119 Grain farms: except wheat, rice, corn, and soybeans; Cash (Vol. 2)

0723 Grain fumigation (Vol. 2)

3523 Grain grading, cleaning, and sorting machines (Vol. 1)

0723 Grain grinding, custom (Vol. 2)

4741 Grain leveling in railroad cars (Vol. 2)

0722 Grain, machine harvesting of (Vol. 2)

2499 Grain measures, wood: turned and shaped (Vol. 1)

3556 Grain mill machinery (Vol. 1)

3523 Grain stackers (Vol. 1)

5039 Grain storage bins—wholesale (Vol. 2)

4741 Grain trimming service for railroad shipment (Vol. 2)

5153 Grain—wholesale (Vol. 2)

3291 Grains, abrasive: natural and artificial (Vol. 1)

0119 Grains Not Elsewhere Classified; Cash (Vol. 2)

5032 Granite building stone—wholesale (Vol. 2)

1423 Granite, crushed and broken-quarrying (Vol. 2)

3281 Granite, cut and shaped (Vol. 1)

1411 Granite, dimension-quarrying (Vol. 2)

2064 Granola bars and clusters (Vol. 1)

2043 Granola, except bars and clusters (Vol. 1)

2041 Granular wheat flour (Vol. 1)

2063 Granulated beet sugar (Vol. 1)

3821 Granulators, laboratory (Vol. 1)

0172 Grape farms (Vol. 2)

0174 Grapefruit groves and farms (Vol. 2)

2899 Grapefruit oil (Vol. 1)

0172 Grapes (Vol. 2)

2782 Graph paper, ruled (Vol. 1)

7336 Graphic arts and related design (Vol. 2)

3861 Graphic arts plates, sensitized (Vol. 1)

3577 Graphic displays, except graphic terminals: computer peripheral equipment (Vol. 1)

3825 Graphic recording meters-electric (Vol. 1)

3624 Graphite electrodes and contacts, electric (Vol. 1)

1499 Graphite mining (Vol. 2)

3295 Graphite, natural: ground, pulverized, refined, or blended (Vol. 1)

3531 Grapples: rock, wood, etc. (Vol. 1)

3524 Grass catchers, lawnmower (Vol. 1)

3423 Grass hooks (Vol. 1)

0139 Grass seed farms (Vol. 2)

3999 Grasses, artificial and preserved: except glass (Vol. 1)

3231 Grasses, artificial: made from purchased glass (Vol. 1)

3827 Gratings, diffraction (Vol. 1)

3446 Gratings (open steel flooring) (Vol. 1)

3446 Gratings, tread: fabricated metal (Vol. 1)

1799 Grave excavation-contractors (Vol. 2)

3272 Grave markers, concrete (Vol. 1)

3272 Grave vaults, concrete (Vol. 1)

3995 Grave vaults, metal (Vol. 1)

1442 Gravel mining (Vol. 2)

3299 Gravel painting (Vol. 1)

5032 Gravel—wholesale (Vol. 2)

5999 Gravestones, finished—retail (Vol. 2)

2893 Gravure ink (Vol. 1)

2796 Gravure plates and cylinders, preparation of (Vol. 1)

3555 Gravure presses (Vol. 1)

2754 Gravure printing (Vol. 1)

2099 Gravy mixes, dry (Vol. 1)

3321 Gray and Ductile Iron Foundries (Vol. 1)

3321 Gray iron castings (Vol. 1)

3321 Gray iron foundries (Vol. 1)

3599 Grease cups, metal (Vol. 1)

3586 Grease guns (lubricators) (Vol. 1)

2077 Grease rendering, inedible (Vol. 1)

3053 Grease retainers, leather (Vol. 1)

3053 Grease seals, asbestos (Vol. 1)

3272 Grease traps, concrete (Vol. 1)

2299 Grease, wool (Vol. 1)

2621 Greaseproof wrapping paper (Vol. 1)

5199 Greases, animal and vegetable—wholesale (Vol. 2)

2992 Greases, lubricating (Vol. 1)

2911 Greases, lubricating: produced in petroleum refineries (Vol. 1)

2843 Greases, sulfonated (Vol. 1)

4432 Great Lakes and St. Lawrence Seaway freight transportation (Vol. 2)

0161 Green lima bean farms (Vol. 2)

0161 Green pea farms (Vol. 2)

0181 Greenhouses for floral products (Vol. 2)

0182 Greenhouses for food crops (Vol. 2)

3448 Greenhouses, prefabricated: metal (Vol. 1)

0181 Greens, cultivated: growing of; Florists' (Vol. 2)

3523 Greens mowing equipment (Vol. 1)

1499 Greensand mining (Vol. 2)

1411 Greenstone, dimension-quarrying (Vol. 2)

5947 Greeting card shops—retail (Vol. 2)

2771 Greeting Cards (Vol. 1)

2771 Greeting cards, except hand painted (Vol. 1)

8999 Greeting cards, hand painting of (Vol. 2)

5112 Greeting cards—wholesale (Vol. 2)

3484 Grenade launchers (Vol. 1)

3483 Grenades and parts (Vol. 1)

3999 Grenades, hand (fire extinguishers) (Vol. 1)

3634 Griddles and grills, household: electric (Vol. 1)

3699 Grids, electric (Vol. 1)

3496 Grilles and grillework, woven wire: made from purchased wire (Vol. 1)

3446 Grillework, ornamental metal (Vol. 1)

5812 Grills (eating places) (Vol. 2)

3523 Grinders and crushers, feed (agricultural machinery) (Vol. 1)

3556 Grinders, food: commercial types (Vol. 1)

3546 Grinders, pneumatic and electric: portable (metalworking machinery) (Vol. 1)

3546 Grinders, snagging (Vol. 1)

3531 Grinders, stone: portable (Vol. 1)

3532 Grinders, stone: stationary (Vol. 1)

3291 Grinding balls, ceramic (Vol. 1)

3599 Grinding castings for the trade (Vol. 1)

0723 Grinding, custom; Grain (Vol. 2)

3541 Grinding machines, metalworking (Vol. 1)

3269 Grinding media, pottery (Vol. 1)

2833 Grinding of drugs and herbs (Vol. 1)

1499 Grinding peat (Vol. 2)

3999 Grinding purchased nut shells (Vol. 1)

1446 Grinding sand mining (Vol. 2)

1499 Grindstone quarrying (Vol. 2)

3291 Grindstones, artificial (Vol. 1)

3069 Grips and handles, rubber (Vol. 1)

3291 Grit, steel (Vol. 1)

2041 Grits and flakes, corn: for brewers' use (Vol. 1)

1429 Grits mining (crushed stone) (Vol. 2)

5149 Groceries and Related Products Not Elsewhere Classified (Vol. 2)

5141 Groceries—General Line (Vol. 2)

5141 Groceries, general line—wholesale (Vol. 2)

2674 Grocers' bags and sacks, uncoated paper (Vol. 1)

3496 Grocery carts, made from purchased wire (Vol. 1)

5411 Grocery Stores (Vol. 2)

5411 Grocery stores, with or without fresh meat—retail (Vol. 2)

3069 Grommets, rubber (Vol. 1)

5085 Grommets—wholesale (Vol. 2)

3541 Grooving machines (machine tools) (Vol. 1)

2211 Grosgrain, cotton (Vol. 1)

3643 Ground clamps (electric wiring devices) (Vol. 1)

3231 Ground glass, made from purchased glass (Vol. 1)

3523 Grounds mowing equipment (Vol. 1)

2621 Groundwood paper (Vol. 1)

8351 Group day care centers, child (Vol. 2)

8361 Group foster homes (Vol. 2)

6324 Group hospitalization plans (Vol. 2)

2899 Grouting material (concrete mending compound) (Vol. 1)

1771 Grouting work-contractors (Vol. 2)

0721 Grove cultivation services; Citrus (Vol. 2)

0173 Groves and farms; Almond (Vol. 2)

0174 Groves and farms; Citrus (Vol. 2)

0173 Groves and farms; Filbert (Vol. 2)

0174 Groves and farms; Grapefruit (Vol. 2)

0174 Groves and farms; Lemon (Vol. 2)

0174 Groves and farms; Lime (Vol. 2)

0173 Groves and farms; Macadamia (Vol. 2)

0173 Groves and farms; Nut (tree) (Vol. 2)

0179 Groves and farms; Olive (Vol. 2)

0174 Groves and farms; Orange (Vol. 2)

0173 Groves and farms; Pecan (Vol. 2)

0173 Groves and farms; Pistachio (Vol. 2)

0174 Groves and farms; Tangerine (Vol. 2)

0173 Groves and farms; Tree nut (Vol. 2)

0173 Groves and farms; Walnut (Vol. 2)

3089 Grower pots, plastics (Vol. 1)

8611 Growers' associations, not engaged in contract buying or selling (Vol. 2)

8611 Growers' marketing advisory services (Vol. 2)

0181 Growers; Rose (Vol. 2)

0181 Growing of; Bedding plants, (Vol. 2)

0181 Growing of; Flowers, (Vol. 2)

0181 Growing of flowers and shrubbery, except forest shrubbery; Field nurseries: (Vol. 2)

0181 Growing of; Foliage, (Vol. 2)

0181 Growing of; Fruit stocks, (Vol. 2)

0181 Growing of; Mats, preseeded: soil erosion- (Vol. 2)

0182 Growing of; Mushrooms, (Vol. 2)

0181 Growing of; Nursery stock, (Vol. 2)

0181 Growing of; Plants, ornamental: (Vol. 2)

0181 Growing of; Plants, potted: (Vol. 2)

0181 Growing of; Seeds, flower and vegetable: (Vol. 2)

0181 Growing of; Shrubberies, except forest shrubbery: (Vol. 2)

0181 Growing of; Vegetable bedding plants, (Vol. 2)

0182 Grown under cover; Bean sprouts (Vol. 2)

0182 Grown Under Cover; Food Crops (Vol. 2)

0182 Grown under cover; Fruits (Vol. 2)

0182 Grown under cover; Hydroponic crops, (Vol. 2)

0182 Grown under cover; Rhubarb (Vol. 2)

0182 Grown under cover; Seaweed (Vol. 2)

0182 Grown under cover; Tomatoes (Vol. 2)

0182 Grown under cover; Truffles (Vol. 2)

0182 Grown under cover; Vegetables (Vol. 2)

2879 Growth regulants, agricultural (Vol. 1)

1479 Guano mining (Vol. 2)

6361 Guaranty of titles (Vol. 2)

7381 Guard service (Vol. 2)

1611 Guardrail construction on highways-contractors (Vol. 2)

3444 Guardrails, highway: sheet metal (Vol. 1)

3446 Guards, bannisters, railings, etc.: made from metal pipe (Vol. 1)

3949 Guards: e.g., football, basketball, soccer, lacrosse (Vol. 1)

3496 Guards, made from purchased wire (Vol. 1)

3769 Guided Missile and Space Vehicle Parts and Auxiliary Equipment Not Elsewhere Classified (Vol. 1)

3764 Guided Missile and Space Vehicle Propulsion Units and Propulsion Unit Parts (Vol. 1)

3761 Guided Missiles and Space Vehicles (Vol. 1)

5088 Guided missiles and space vehicles—wholesale (Vol. 2)

3761 Guided missiles, complete (Vol. 1)

7999 Guides, hunting (Vol. 2)

2741 Guides: publishing and printing, or publishing only (Vol. 1)

7999 Guides, tourist (Vol. 2)

3931 Guitars and parts, electric and nonelectric (Vol. 1)

2861 Gum and Wood Chemicals (Vol. 1)

5169 Gum and wood chemicals—wholesale (Vol. 2)

2861 Gum naval stores, processing but not gathering or warehousing (Vol. 1)

2899 Gum sizes (Vol. 1)

2759 Gummed labels and seals, printed: except lithographed or gravure (Vol. 1)

2672 Gummed paper (Vol. 1)

2672 Gummed tape, cloth and paper base (Vol. 1)

3579 Gummed tape moisteners for store and office use (Vol. 1)

0831 Gums, gathering of (Vol. 2)

3484 Gun barrels, 30 mm. (or 1.18 inch) or less (Vol. 1)

3949 Gun cases (sporting equipment) (Vol. 1)

7997 Gun clubs, membership (Vol. 2)

3312 Gun forgings, iron and steel: made in steel works or rolling mills (Vol. 1)

3489 Gun limbers (Vol. 1)

3484 Gun magazines, 30 mm. (or 1.18 inch) or less (Vol. 1)

7699 Gun parts made to individual order (Vol. 2)

3484 Gun sights, except optical: 30 mm. (or 1.18 inch) or less (Vol. 1)

3827 Gun sights, optical (Vol. 1)

2899 Gun slushing compounds (Vol. 1)

3495 Gun springs, precision: made from purchased wire (Vol. 1)

2426 Gun stocks, wood (Vol. 1)

3429 Gun trigger locks (Vol. 1)

3489 Gun turrets and parts for artillery more than 30 mm. (or more than 1.18 inch) (Vol. 1)

1771 Gunite work-contractors (Vol. 2)

3674 Gunn effect devices (Vol. 1)

3297 Gunning mixes, nonclay (Vol. 1)

2892 Gunpowder (Vol. 1)

3484 Guns, 30 mm. (or 1.18 inch) or less (Vol. 1)

3484 Guns: BB and pellet (Vol. 1)

3489 Guns, catapult (Vol. 1)

3423 Guns, caulking (Vol. 1)

3484 Guns, dart: except toy (Vol. 1)

3586 Guns, grease (lubricators) (Vol. 1)

3489 Guns, more than 30 mm. (or more than 1.18 inch) (Vol. 1)

3546 Guns, pneumatic: chip removal (Vol. 1)

3944 Guns, toy (Vol. 1)

7699 Gunsmith shops (Vol. 2)

3842 Gut sutures, surgical (Vol. 1)

3069 Gutta percha compounds (Vol. 1)

1761 Gutter installation, metal-contractors (Vol. 2)

3089 Gutters, plastics: glass fiber reinforced (Vol. 1)

3444 Gutters, sheet metal (Vol. 1)

3949 Gymnasium and playground equipment (Vol. 1)

2329 Gymnasium clothing: men's and boys' (Vol. 1)

5941 Gymnasium equipment—retail (Vol. 2)

7991 Gymnasiums (Vol. 2)

7999 Gymnastics instruction (Vol. 2)

3842 Gynecological supplies and appliances (Vol. 1)

8011 Gynecologists, offices of (Vol. 2)

1499 Gypsite mining (Vol. 2)

1499 Gypsum mining (Vol. 2)

3275 Gypsum Products (Vol. 1)

3275 Gypsum products: e.g., block, board, plaster, lath, rock, tile (Vol. 1)

3812 Gyrocompasses (Vol. 1)

3812 Gyrogimbals (Vol. 1)

3812 Gyropilots (Vol. 1)

3812 Gyroscopes (Vol. 1)

H

5611 Haberdashery stores—retail (Vol. 2)

0912 Haddock, catching of (Vol. 2)

5131 Hair accessories—wholesale (Vol. 2)

5159 Hair, animal—wholesale (Vol. 2)

3523 Hair clippers for animal use, hand and electric (Vol. 1)

3999 Hair clippers for human use, hand and electric (Vol. 1)

2844 Hair coloring preparations (Vol. 1)

2299 Hair, curled: for upholstery, pillow, and quilt filling (Vol. 1)

3999 Hair curlers, designed for beauty parlors (Vol. 1)

3634 Hair curlers, electric (Vol. 1)

3965 Hair curlers, except equipment designed for beauty parlor use (Vol. 1)

3069 Hair curlers, rubber (Vol. 1)

3999 Hair, dressing of, for the trade (Vol. 1)

3999 Hair dryers, designed for beauty parlors (Vol. 1)

3634 Hair dryers, electric: except equipment designed for beauty parlor use (Vol. 1)

3999 Hair goods: braids, nets, switches, toupees, and wigs (Vol. 1)

3999 Hair nets (Vol. 1)

3991 Hair pencils (artists' brushes) (Vol. 1)

2844 Hair preparations: dressings, rinses, tonics, and scalp conditioners (Vol. 1)

5122 Hair preparations—wholesale (Vol. 2)

7299 Hair removal (electrolysis) (Vol. 2)

7241 Hair stylists, men's (Vol. 2)

7299 Hair weaving or replacement service (Vol. 2)

5199 Hairbrushes—wholesale (Vol. 2)

2231 Haircloth: wool, mohair, and similar animal fibers (Vol. 1)

7231 Hairdressers (Vol. 2)

2844 Hairdressings, dyes, bleaches, tonics, and removers (Vol. 1)

3999 Hairpin mountings (Vol. 1)

3965 Hairpins, except rubber (Vol. 1)

3069 Hairpins, rubber (Vol. 1)

3495 Hairsprings, made from purchased wire (Vol. 1)

2026 Half and half (Vol. 1)

2759 Halftones, engraved (Vol. 1)

8361 Halfway group homes for persons with social or personal problems (Vol. 2)

8361 Halfway homes for delinquents and offenders (Vol. 2)

3674 Hall effect devices (Vol. 1)

5063   Hardware, pole line—wholesale (Vol. 2)
5072   Hardware, shelf or light—wholesale (Vol. 2)
3999   Hardware, stage (Vol. 1)
5251   Hardware Stores (Vol. 2)
5251   Hardware stores—retail (Vol. 2)
2426   Hardwood Dimension and Flooring Mills (Vol. 1)
2426   Hardwood dimension (Vol. 1)
2861   Hardwood distillates (Vol. 1)
1752   Hardwood flooring-contractors (Vol. 2)
2435   Hardwood plywood composites (Vol. 1)
2435   Hardwood Veneer and Plywood (Vol. 1)
2435   Hardwood veneer or plywood (Vol. 1)
3931   Harmonicas (Vol. 1)
3679   Harness assemblies for electronic use: wire and cable (Vol. 1)
3199   Harness, dog (Vol. 1)
2842   Harness dressing (Vol. 1)
5191   Harness equipment—wholesale (Vol. 2)
3429   Harness hardware (Vol. 1)
3111   Harness leather (Vol. 1)
5191   Harness made to individual order—wholesale (Vol. 2)
7699   Harness repair shops (Vol. 2)
3694   Harness wiring sets for internal combustion engines (Vol. 1)
3199   Harnesses and harness parts (Vol. 1)
3931   Harps and parts (Vol. 1)
3931   Harpsichords (Vol. 1)
3523   Harrows: disc, spring, and tine (Vol. 1)
2353   Harvest hats, straw (Vol. 1)
5083   Harvesting machinery and equipment—wholesale (Vol. 2)
3523   Harvesting machines (Vol. 1)
0722   Harvesting of; Berries, machine (Vol. 2)
0722   Harvesting of; Cotton, machine (Vol. 2)
0722   Harvesting of; Fruits, machine (Vol. 2)
0722   Harvesting of; Grain, machine (Vol. 2)
0722   Harvesting of; Nuts, machine (Vol. 2)
0722   Harvesting of; Peanuts, machine (Vol. 2)
0722   Harvesting of; Sugar beets, machine (Vol. 2)
0722   Harvesting of; Sugarcane, machine (Vol. 2)
0722   Harvesting of; Vegetables, machine (Vol. 2)
0722   Harvesting Primarily by Machine; Crop (Vol. 2)
3634   Hassock fans, electric (Vol. 1)
2392   Hassocks, textile (Vol. 1)
5131   Hat and cap material—wholesale (Vol. 2)
2241   Hat band fabrics (Vol. 1)
3999   Hat blocks and display forms (Vol. 1)
2353   Hat bodies: fur-felt, straw, and wool-felt (Vol. 1)
3161   Hat boxes, except paper or paperboard (Vol. 1)
2396   Hat findings, men's (Vol. 1)
2396   Hat linings and trimmings, men's (Vol. 1)
3559   Hat making and hat renovating machinery (Vol. 1)
5611   Hat stores, men's and boys'—retail (Vol. 2)
0254   Hatcheries; Chicken (Vol. 2)
0279   Hatcheries; Earthworm (Vol. 2)
0921   Hatcheries, fish (Vol. 2)
0254   Hatcheries; Poultry (Vol. 2)
0254   Hatcheries, poultry; Egg (Vol. 2)

3423   Hatchets (Vol. 1)
7251   Hatcleaning and blocking shops (Vol. 2)
2353   Hats, Caps and Millinery (Vol. 1)
3942   Hats, doll (Vol. 1)
2353   Hats: fur-felt, straw, and wool-felt (Vol. 1)
2371   Hats, fur (Vol. 1)
2386   Hats, leather (Vol. 1)
5136   Hats, men's and boys'—wholesale (Vol. 2)
2253   Hats (Vol. 1)
2679   Hats, paper (Vol. 1)
2353   Hats: textiles, straw, fur-felt, and wool-felt (Vol. 1)
2353   Hats, trimmed (Vol. 1)
5137   Hats: women's, children's, and infants'—wholesale (Vol. 2)
2396   Hatters' fur (Vol. 1)
4212   Hauling, by dump truck (Vol. 2)
4212   Hauling, farm to market (Vol. 2)
4212   Hauling live animals, local (Vol. 2)
3523   Hay balers and presses, farm (Vol. 1)
2048   Hay, cubed (Vol. 1)
0139   Hay farms (Vol. 2)
3423   Hay forks (Vol. 1)
0723   Hay, fruits, and vegetables; Drying of corn, rice, (Vol. 2)
3423   Hay knives (Vol. 1)
0722   Hay mowing, raking, baling, and chopping (Vol. 2)
5191   Hay—wholesale (Vol. 2)
5083   Haying machinery—wholesale (Vol. 2)
3523   Haying machines: mowers, rakes, loaders, stackers, balers, presses, etc. (Vol. 1)
4953   Hazardous waste material disposal sites (Vol. 2)
2044   Head rice (Vol. 1)
8351   Head Start centers, except in conjunction with schools (Vol. 2)
2511   Headboards, wood (Vol. 1)
2013   Headcheese (Vol. 1)
3542   Headers (Vol. 1)
2429   Heading, barrel (cooperage stock): sawed or split (Vol. 1)
2411   Heading bolts, wood: hewn (Vol. 1)
3647   Headlights (fixtures), vehicular (Vol. 1)
3679   Headphones, radio (Vol. 1)
3931   Heads, banjo and drum (Vol. 1)
3679   Heads, recording for speech and musical equipment (Vol. 1)
3812   Heads-up display (HUD) systems, aeronautical (Vol. 1)
3661   Headsets, telephone (Vol. 1)
2369   Headwear: girls', children's, and infants' (Vol. 1)
2253   Headwear (Vol. 1)
6321   Health and accident insurance (Vol. 2)
8099   Health and Allied Services Not Elsewhere Classified (Vol. 2)
8399   Health and welfare councils (Vol. 2)
5499   Health food stores—retail (Vol. 2)
5149   Health foods—wholesale (Vol. 2)
6411   Health insurance coverage consulting service (Vol. 2)
6399   Health insurance for pets (Vol. 2)

6321 Health insurance, indemnity plans: except medical service (Vol. 2)

3641 Health lamps, infrared and ultraviolet-radiation (Vol. 1)

8099 Health screening service (Vol. 2)

9431 Health statistics centers-government (Vol. 2)

8399 Health systems agencies (Vol. 2)

7629 Hearing aid repair (Vol. 2)

3842 Hearing aids (Vol. 1)

5999 Hearing aids—retail (Vol. 2)

5047 Hearing aids—wholesale (Vol. 2)

8099 Hearing testing service (Vol. 2)

3713 Hearse bodies (Vol. 1)

4119 Hearse rental with drivers (Vol. 2)

7514 Hearse rental, without drivers (Vol. 2)

7514 Hearses and limousines, rental without drivers (Vol. 2)

3711 Hearses (motor vehicles) (Vol. 1)

3845 Heart-lung machine (Vol. 1)

5084 Heat exchange equipment, industrial—wholesale (Vol. 2)

3443 Heat exchangers: industrial, scientific, and nuclear (Vol. 1)

2899 Heat insulating compounds (Vol. 1)

3292 Heat insulating materials except felt: for covering boilers, pipes, etc. (Vol. 1)

3585 Heat pumps, electric (Vol. 1)

3861 Heat sensitized paper made from purchased paper (Vol. 1)

3443 Heat transfer drives (finned tubing) (Vol. 1)

3398 Heat treating of metal for the trade (Vol. 1)

3567 Heat treating ovens (Vol. 1)

2899 Heat treating salts (Vol. 1)

3052 Heater hose, plastics or rubber (Vol. 1)

3269 Heater parts, pottery (Vol. 1)

3255 Heater radiants, clay (Vol. 1)

3634 Heaters, immersion: household-electric (Vol. 1)

3714 Heaters, motor vehicle (Vol. 1)

3634 Heaters, space: electric (Vol. 1)

3433 Heaters, space: except electric (Vol. 1)

3569 Heaters, swimming pool: electric (Vol. 1)

3433 Heaters, swimming pool: oil or gas (Vol. 1)

3634 Heaters, tape (Vol. 1)

3585 Heating and air conditioning combination units (Vol. 1)

3433 Heating apparatus, except electric or warm air (Vol. 1)

3433 Heating Equipment Except Electric and Warm Air Furnaces (Vol. 1)

3567 Heating equipment, induction (Vol. 1)

1711 Heating equipment installation-contractors (Vol. 2)

4741 Heating of railroad cars (Vol. 2)

3634 Heating pads, electric (Vol. 1)

4961 Heating systems, steam (suppliers of heat) (Vol. 2)

3567 Heating units and devices, industrial: electric (Vol. 1)

3634 Heating units, baseboard or wall: electric (radiant heating element) (Vol. 1)

3634 Heating units for electric appliances (Vol. 1)

1711 Heating, with or without sheet metalwork-contractors (Vol. 2)

7353 Heavy Construction Equipment Rental and Leasing (Vol. 2)

1629 Heavy Construction Not Elsewhere Classified (Vol. 2)

2819 Heavy water (Vol. 1)

3552 Heddles for loom harnesses, wire (Vol. 1)

3421 Hedge shears and trimmers, except power (Vol. 1)

3524 Hedge trimmers, power (Vol. 1)

3131 Heel caps, leather or metal (Vol. 1)

3131 Heel lifts, leather (Vol. 1)

3131 Heels, boot and shoe: finished wood or leather (Vol. 1)

3089 Heels, boot and shoe: plastics (Vol. 1)

3069 Heels, boot and shoe: rubber, composition, and fiber (Vol. 1)

0241 Heifer replacement farms; Dairy (Vol. 2)

3493 Helical springs, hot wound: for railroad equipment and vehicles (Vol. 1)

4522 Helicopter carriers (Vol. 2)

3721 Helicopters (Vol. 1)

2813 Helium (Vol. 1)

3949 Helmets, athletic (Vol. 1)

3199 Helmets, except athletic: leather (Vol. 1)

2353 Helmets, jungle-cloth: wool-lined (Vol. 1)

3842 Helmets, space (Vol. 1)

3469 Helmets, steel (Vol. 1)

7363 Help supply service (Vol. 2)

7363 Help Supply Services (Vol. 2)

8322 Helping hand services (Vol. 2)

1011 Hematite mining (Vol. 2)

2835 Hematology diagnostic reagents (Vol. 1)

2836 Hematology products, except in vitro and in vivo reagents (Vol. 1)

2861 Hemlock extract (Vol. 1)

0831 Hemlock gum, gathering of (Vol. 2)

3841 Hemodialysis apparatus (Vol. 1)

2299 Hemp yarn, thread, roving, and textiles (Vol. 1)

2395 Hemstitching, for the trade (Vol. 1)

0251 Hen farms; Cornish (Vol. 2)

2833 Herb grinding, grading, and milling (Vol. 1)

2879 Herbicides (Vol. 1)

0751 Herd improvement associations; Dairy (Vol. 2)

3679 Hermetic seals for electronic equipment (Vol. 1)

7694 Hermetics repair (Vol. 2)

2091 Herring: smoked, salted, dried, and pickled (Vol. 1)

2869 Hexamethylenediamine (Vol. 1)

2869 Hexamethylenetetramine (Vol. 1)

2211 Hickory stripes, cotton (Vol. 1)

2011 Hides and skins, cured or uncured (Vol. 1)

5159 Hides (may include curing)—wholesale (Vol. 2)

3111 Hides: tanning, currying, and finishing (Vol. 1)

2511 High chairs, children's: wood (Vol. 1)

3542 High energy rate metal forming machines (Vol. 1)

2892 High explosives (Vol. 1)

5731 High fidelity (hi-fi) equipment—retail (Vol. 2)

5064 High fidelity (hi-fi) equipment—wholesale (Vol. 2)

2046 High fructose syrup (Vol. 1)

3313 High percentage ferroalloys (Vol. 1)

3313 High percentage nonferrous additive alloys, except copper (Vol. 1)

2819 High purity grade chemicals, inorganic: refined from technical grades (Vol. 1)

2869 High purity grade chemicals, organic: refined from technical grades (Vol. 1)

8211 High schools (Vol. 2)

3297 High temperature mortar, nonclay (Vol. 1)

3443 High vacuum coaters, metal plate (Vol. 1)

1611 Highway and Street Construction Except Elevated Highways (Vol. 2)

3441 Highway bridge sections, prefabricated metal (Vol. 1)

4785 Highway bridges, operation of (Vol. 2)

1622 Highway construction, elevated-general contractors (Vol. 2)

1611 Highway construction, except elevated-general contractors (Vol. 2)

2899 Highway fusees (Vol. 1)

3444 Highway guardrails, sheet metal (Vol. 1)

1731 Highway lighting and electrical signal construction-contractors (Vol. 2)

9221 Highway patrols (Vol. 2)

3669 Highway signals, electric (Vol. 1)

1611 Highway signs, installation of-contractors (Vol. 2)

3429 Hinge tubes (Vol. 1)

3429 Hinges (Vol. 1)

8699 Historical clubs, other than professional (Vol. 2)

3799 Hitches, trailer (Vol. 1)

5092 Hobby kits—wholesale (Vol. 2)

5945 Hobby shops—retail (Vol. 2)

5945 Hobby, Toy and Game Shops (Vol. 2)

3944 Hobbyhorses (Vol. 1)

3545 Hobs (Vol. 1)

5084 Hobs—wholesale (Vol. 2)

7997 Hockey clubs, except professional and semiprofessional (Vol. 2)

3949 Hockey equipment, except uniforms and footwear (Vol. 1)

0721 Hoeing (Vol. 2)

3423 Hoes, garden and masons' (Vol. 1)

0213 Hog farms (Vol. 2)

3523 Hog feeding, handling, and watering equipment (Vol. 1)

0213 Hog; Feedlots, (Vol. 2)

3496 Hog rings, made from purchased wire (Vol. 1)

2011 Hog slaughtering plants (Vol. 1)

0213 Hogs (Vol. 2)

0751 Hogs, sheep, goats, and poultry; Pedigree record services for cattle, (Vol. 2)

0751 Hogs, sheep, goats, and poultry; Showing of cattle, (Vol. 2)

5154 Hogs—wholesale (Vol. 2)

2449 Hogsheads, wood: coopered (Vol. 1)

3537 Hoists, aircraft loading (Vol. 1)

3536 Hoists, except aircraft loading and automobile wrecker hoists (Vol. 1)

3536 Hoists, hand (Vol. 1)

3536 Hoists, overhead (Vol. 1)

5084 Hoists—wholesale (Vol. 2)

3999 Holders, cigar and cigarette (Vol. 1)

3952 Holders, pencil (Vol. 1)

3861 Holders: photographic film, plate, and paper (Vol. 1)

3089 Holders, plastics: papertowel, grocery bag, dust mop and broom (Vol. 1)

3841 Holders, surgical needle (Vol. 1)

6719 Holding companies, except bank (Vol. 2)

3914 Hollowware, silver, nickel silver, pewter, stainless steel, and plated (Vol. 1)

3199 Holsters, leather (Vol. 1)

8082 Home Health Care Services (Vol. 2)

1522 Home improvements, residential: except single-family-general contractors (Vol. 2)

1521 Home improvements, single-family-general contractors (Vol. 2)

2844 Home permanent kits (Vol. 1)

7221 Home photographers (Vol. 2)

3651 Home tape recorders: cassette, cartridge, and reel (Vol. 1)

3541 Home workshop machine tools, metalworking (Vol. 1)

5932 Homefurnishing stores, secondhand—retail (Vol. 2)

5023 Homefurnishings (Vol. 2)

5932 Homefurnishings, antique—retail (Vol. 2)

5023 Homefurnishings—wholesale (Vol. 2)

8322 Homemaker's service, primarily nonmedical (Vol. 2)

8641 Homeowner associations, except property management (Vol. 2)

8361 Homes for children, with health care incidental (Vol. 2)

8361 Homes for destitute men and women (Vol. 2)

8361 Homes for the aged, with health care incidental (Vol. 2)

8361 Homes for the deaf or blind, with health care incidental (Vol. 2)

8361 Homes for the emotionally disturbed, with health care incidental (Vol. 2)

8361 Homes for the mentally handicapped, with health care incidental (Vol. 2)

8059 Homes for the mentally retarded with health care, except skilled and intermediate care facilities (Vol. 2)

8361 Homes for the physically handicapped, with health care incidental (Vol. 2)

2033 Hominy, canned (Vol. 1)

2041 Hominy grits, except breakfast food (Vol. 1)

2043 Hominy grits prepared as cereal breakfast food (Vol. 1)

3556 Homogenizing machinery: dairy, fruit, vegetable, and other foods (Vol. 1)

3291 Hones (Vol. 1)

0279 Honey production (Vol. 2)

2099 Honey, strained and bottled (Vol. 1)

0752 Honey straining on the farm (Vol. 2)

5149 Honey—wholesale (Vol. 2)

2679 Honeycomb core and board (Vol. 1)

3999 Honeycomb foundations (beekeepers' supplies) (Vol. 1)

3469 Honeycombed metal (Vol. 1)

3541 Honing and lapping machines (Vol. 1)

3545 Honing heads (Vol. 1)

9223 Honor camps-government (Vol. 2)

3443 Hoods, industrial: metal plate (Vol. 1)

3714 Hoods, motor vehicle (Vol. 1)

3444 Hoods, range: sheet metal (Vol. 1)

2273 Hooked rugs (Vol. 1)

3965 Hooks and eyes (Vol. 1)

3423 Hooks: bush, grass, baling, and husking (Vol. 1)

3443 Hooks, crane: laminated plate (Vol. 1)

3965 Hooks, crochet (Vol. 1)

3949 Hooks, fishing (Vol. 1)

3452 Hooks, gate (Vol. 1)

3452 Hooks, screw (Vol. 1)

3312 Hoops, galvanized iron and steel (Vol. 1)

3312 Hoops, iron and steel: made in steel works or hot-rolling mills (Vol. 1)

3499 Hoops, metal: other than wire (Vol. 1)

2429 Hoops, wood: for tight or slack cooperage-sawed or split (Vol. 1)

5149 Hop extract—wholesale (Vol. 2)

0139 Hop farms (Vol. 2)

3545 Hopper feed devices (Vol. 1)

3537 Hoppers, end dump (Vol. 1)

3443 Hoppers, metal plate (Vol. 1)

3444 Hoppers, sheet metal (Vol. 1)

5159 Hops—wholesale (Vol. 2)

3812 Horizon situation instrumentation (Vol. 1)

2834 Hormone preparations, except diagnostics (Vol. 1)

2833 Hormones and derivatives (Vol. 1)

2879 Hormones, plant (Vol. 1)

3714 Horns, motor vehicle (Vol. 1)

3944 Horns, toy (Vol. 1)

3429 Horse bits (Vol. 1)

2399 Horse blankets (Vol. 1)

3199 Horse boots and muzzles (Vol. 1)

0272 Horse farms (Vol. 2)

7999 Horse shows (Vol. 2)

2824 Horsehair, artificial: nylon (Vol. 1)

2823 Horsehair, artificial: rayon (Vol. 1)

2048 Horsemeat, except for human consumption (Vol. 1)

2011 Horsemeat for human consumption (Vol. 1)

2035 Horseradish, prepared (Vol. 1)

0272 Horses and Other Equines (Vol. 2)

0752 Horses, boarding or training (except racehorses) (Vol. 2)

7948 Horses, race: owners of (Vol. 2)

7948 Horses, race: training (Vol. 2)

7948 Horses, racing of (Vol. 2)

5159 Horses—wholesale (Vol. 2)

3462 Horseshoe calks, forged: not made in rolling mills (Vol. 1)

3315 Horseshoe nails (Vol. 1)

7699 Horseshoeing (Vol. 2)

3462 Horseshoes, not made in rolling mills (Vol. 1)

0781 Horticultural advisory or counseling services (Vol. 2)

5085 Hose, belting, and packing: industrial—wholesale (Vol. 2)

3429 Hose clamps (Vol. 1)

3052 Hose: cotton fabric, rubber lined (Vol. 1)

3429 Hose couplings (Vol. 1)

2241 Hose fabrics, tubular (Vol. 1)

3569 Hose, fire: except rubber (Vol. 1)

3492 Hose fittings and assemblies, fluid power: metal (Vol. 1)

3599 Hose, flexible metallic (Vol. 1)

3052 Hose, plastics or rubber (Vol. 1)

3842 Hosiery, elastic: orthopedic (Vol. 1)

2252 Hosiery, except women's and misses' full-length and knee-length (Vol. 1)

3999 Hosiery kits, sewing and mending (Vol. 1)

3552 Hosiery machines (Vol. 1)

5136 Hosiery, men's and boys'—wholesale (Vol. 2)

2252 Hosiery Not Elsewhere Classified (Vol. 1)

7389 Hosiery pairing on a contract or fee basis (Vol. 2)

5632 Hosiery stores—retail (Vol. 2)

3842 Hosiery, support (Vol. 1)

5137 Hosiery: women's, children's, and infants'—wholesale (Vol. 2)

2251 Hosiery, women's full-length and knee-length, except socks (Vol. 1)

6324 Hospital and Medical Service Plans (Vol. 2)

2599 Hospital beds (Vol. 1)

1542 Hospital construction-general contractors (Vol. 2)

3537 Hospital dollies (Vol. 1)

5047 Hospital equipment—wholesale (Vol. 2)

5047 Hospital furniture—wholesale (Vol. 2)

5137 Hospital gowns: women's and children's—wholesale (Vol. 2)

2326 Hospital service apparel, washable: men's (Vol. 1)

2392 Hospital sheets, nonwoven textiles (Vol. 1)

3365 Hospital utensils, cast aluminum: except die-castings (Vol. 1)

3469 Hospital utensils, porcelain enameled (Vol. 1)

0741 Hospitals for livestock; Animal (Vol. 2)

0742 Hospitals for pets and other animal specialties; Animal (Vol. 2)

0742 Hospitals; Pet (Vol. 2)

8069 Hospitals, specialty: except psychiatric (Vol. 2)

3089 Hospitalware, plastics: except foam (Vol. 1)

7011 Hostels (Vol. 2)

3479 Hot dip coating of metals and formed products, for the trade (Vol. 1)

5812 Hot dog (frankfurter) stands (Vol. 2)

1389 Hot oil treating of oil field tanks: on a contract basis (Vol. 2)

3312 Hot-rolled iron and steel products (Vol. 1)

1389 Hot shot service: on a contract basis (Vol. 2)

3547 Hot strip mill machinery (Vol. 1)

3255 Hot top refractories, clay (Vol. 1)

3297 Hot top refractories, nonclay (Vol. 1)

2449 Hot tubs, coopered (Vol. 1)

3088 Hot tubs, plastics or fiberglass (Vol. 1)

5999 Hot tubs—retail (Vol. 2)

5091 Hot tubs—wholesale (Vol. 2)

0161 Hot (vegetables); Pepper farms, sweet and (Vol. 2)

3639 Hot water heaters, household: including nonelectric (Vol. 1)

3493   Hot wound springs, except wire springs (Vol. 1)

1522   Hotel construction-general contractors (Vol. 2)

7389   Hotel reservation service (Vol. 2)

3262   Hotel tableware and kitchen articles, vitreous china (Vol. 1)

7011   Hotels and Motels (Vol. 2)

7011   Hotels, except residential (Vol. 2)

7041   Hotels operated by organizations for members only (Vol. 2)

6513   Hotels, residential: operators (Vol. 2)

7011   Hotels, seasonal (Vol. 2)

8322   Hotlines (Vol. 2)

3634   Hotplates, electric (Vol. 1)

3821   Hotplates, laboratory (Vol. 1)

1521   House construction, single-family-general contractors (Vol. 2)

5963   House delivery of purchased milk—retail (Vol. 2)

8712   House designers (Vol. 2)

1799   House moving-contractors (Vol. 2)

1721   House painting-contractors (Vol. 2)

1521   House: shell erection, single-family-general contractors (Vol. 2)

3142   House Slippers (Vol. 1)

3142   House slippers (Vol. 1)

5963   House-to-house selling of coffee, soda, beer, bottled water, or other products—retail (Vol. 2)

7519   House trailer rental (Vol. 2)

7999   Houseboat rentals (Vol. 2)

3732   Houseboats, building and repairing (Vol. 1)

2384   Housecoats, except children's and infants' (Vol. 1)

2369   Housecoats: girls', children's, and infants' (Vol. 1)

2253   Housecoats (Vol. 1)

2335   Housedresses: women's, misses', and juniors' (Vol. 1)

2392   Housefurnishings Except Curtains and Draperies (Vol. 1)

2392   Housefurnishings, except curtains and draperies (Vol. 1)

5722   Household Appliance Stores (Vol. 2)

5722   Household appliance stores, electric or gas—retail (Vol. 2)

3639   Household Appliances Not Elsewhere Classified (Vol. 1)

3651   Household Audio and Video Equipment (Vol. 1)

2842   Household bleaches, dry or liquid (Vol. 1)

3991   Household brooms and brushes (Vol. 1)

3631   Household Cooking Equipment (Vol. 1)

3263   Household earthenware, semivitreous (Vol. 1)

2519   Household furniture, glass and plastics (Vol. 1)

2519   Household Furniture Not Elsewhere Classified (Vol. 1)

2519   Household furniture: rattan, reed, malacca, fiber, willow, and wicker (Vol. 1)

5712   Household furniture—retail (Vol. 2)

2512   Household furniture upholstered on wood frames, except dual-purpose sleep furniture (Vol. 1)

5021   Household furniture—wholesale (Vol. 2)

2511   Household furniture, wood: except upholstered (Vol. 1)

3069   Household gloves, rubber (Vol. 1)

4214   Household goods moving, local: combined with storage (Vol. 2)

4226   Household goods warehousing and storage, without local trucking (Vol. 2)

2879   Household insecticides (Vol. 1)

3633   Household Laundry Equipment (Vol. 1)

3632   Household Refrigerators and Home and Farm Freezers (Vol. 1)

3262   Household tableware and kitchen articles, vitreous china (Vol. 1)

2899   Household tints and dyes (Vol. 1)

3365   Household utensils, cast aluminum: except die-castings (Vol. 1)

3469   Household utensils, porcelain enameled (Vol. 1)

3469   Household utensils, stamped and pressed metal (Vol. 1)

3635   Household Vacuum Cleaners (Vol. 1)

2499   Household woodenware (Vol. 1)

8811   Households, private: employing cooks, maids, chauffeurs, gardeners, etc. (Vol. 2)

7349   Housekeeping (cleaning service) on a contract or fee basis (Vol. 2)

9223   Houses of correction-government (Vol. 2)

2452   Houses, portable: prefabricated wood-except mobile homes (Vol. 1)

3448   Houses, prefabricated: metal (Vol. 1)

3792   Housetrailers, except as permanent dwellings (Vol. 1)

5963   Housewares: house-to-house, telephone or party plan selling—retail (Vol. 2)

5719   Housewares stores—retail (Vol. 2)

9531   Housing agencies, nonoperating-government (Vol. 2)

9531   Housing authorities, nonoperating-government (Vol. 2)

6531   Housing authorities, operating (Vol. 2)

3443   Housing cabinets for radium, metal plate (Vol. 1)

3272   Housing components, prefabricated: concrete (Vol. 1)

3444   Housings for business machines, sheet metal: except stamped (Vol. 1)

3469   Housings for business machines, stamped metal (Vol. 1)

3443   Housings, pressure (Vol. 1)

3489   Howitzers, more than 30 mm. (or more than 1.18 inch) (Vol. 1)

3559   Hub and die-cutting machines (jewelers) (Vol. 1)

3465   Hub caps, automotive: stamped (Vol. 1)

3728   Hubs, aircraft propeller (Vol. 1)

2499   Hubs, wood (Vol. 1)

2211   Huck toweling (Vol. 1)

0831   Huckleberry greens, gathering of (Vol. 2)

5963   Hucksters—retail (Vol. 2)

1061   Huebnerite mining (Vol. 2)

0723   Hulling and shelling; Almond (Vol. 2)

0723   Hulling and shelling; Filbert (Vol. 2)

0723   Hulling and shelling; Nut (Vol. 2)

0723   Hulling and shelling of tree nuts (Vol. 2)

0723   Hulling and shelling; Pecan (Vol. 2)

0723   Hulling and shelling; Walnut (Vol. 2)

3523 Hulling machinery, agricultural (Vol. 1)
8742 Human resource consultants (Vol. 2)
8699 Humane societies, animal (Vol. 2)
5075 Humidifiers and dehumidifiers, except portable—wholesale (Vol. 2)
5064 Humidifiers and dehumidifiers, portable—wholesale (Vol. 2)
3634 Humidifiers, electric: portable (Vol. 1)
3585 Humidifying equipment, except portable (Vol. 1)
3822 Humidistats: wall, duct, and skeleton (Vol. 1)
3822 Humidity controls, air-conditioning types (Vol. 1)
3829 Humidity instruments, except industrial process and air-conditioning type (Vol. 1)
3823 Humidity instruments, industrial process type (Vol. 1)
7997 Hunt clubs, membership (Vol. 2)
5941 Hunters' equipment—retail (Vol. 2)
7032 Hunting camps (Vol. 2)
0971 Hunting carried on as a business enterprise (Vol. 2)
2329 Hunting coats and vests, men's (Vol. 1)
7999 Hunting guides (Vol. 2)
3421 Hunting knives (Vol. 1)
0971 Hunting preserves, operation of (Vol. 2)
0971 Hunting, Trapping and Game Propagation (Vol. 2)
3423 Husking hooks (Vol. 1)
3674 Hybrid integrated circuits (Vol. 1)
2819 Hydrated alumina silicate powder (Vol. 1)
3274 Hydrated lime (Vol. 1)
5085 Hydraulic and pneumatic pistons and valves—wholesale (Vol. 2)
3593 Hydraulic cylinders, fluid power (Vol. 1)
3714 Hydraulic fluid power pumps for automotive steering mechanisms (Vol. 1)
2992 Hydraulic fluids (Vol. 1)
2869 Hydraulic fluids, synthetic base (Vol. 1)
1389 Hydraulic fracturing wells on a contract basis (Vol. 2)
3492 Hydraulic hose assemblies (Vol. 1)
3594 Hydraulic pumps, aircraft (Vol. 1)
3511 Hydraulic turbine generator set units, complete (Vol. 1)
3511 Hydraulic turbines (Vol. 1)
3492 Hydraulic valves, including aircraft: fluid power-metal (Vol. 1)
2819 Hydrazine (Vol. 1)
2911 Hydrocarbon fluid, produced in petroleum refineries (Vol. 1)
2869 Hydrocarbon gases, fluorinated (Vol. 1)
2819 Hydrochloric acid (Vol. 1)
2819 Hydrocyanic acid (Vol. 1)
1629 Hydroelectric plant construction-general contractors (Vol. 2)
2899 Hydrofluoric acid compound, for etching and polishing glass (Vol. 1)
2819 Hydrofluoric acid (Vol. 1)
3732 Hydrofoil boats (Vol. 1)
3731 Hydrofoil vessels (Vol. 1)
2813 Hydrogen (Vol. 1)
2819 Hydrogen peroxide (Vol. 1)

2819 Hydrogen sulfide (Vol. 1)
3561 Hydrojet marine engine units (Vol. 1)
2046 Hydrol (Vol. 1)
3829 Hydrometers, except industrial process type (Vol. 1)
3823 Hydrometers, industrial process type (Vol. 1)
3822 Hydronic circulator control, automatic (Vol. 1)
5074 Hydronic heating equipment and supplies—wholesale (Vol. 2)
3822 Hydronic limit control (Vol. 1)
3822 Hydronic pressure and temperature controls (Vol. 1)
3812 Hydrophones (Vol. 1)
3443 Hydropneumatic tanks, metal plate (Vol. 1)
0182 Hydroponic crops, grown under cover (Vol. 2)
2865 Hydroquinone (Vol. 1)
3594 Hydrostatic drives (transmissions) (Vol. 1)
8734 Hydrostatic testing laboratories (Vol. 2)
3594 Hydrostatic transmissions (Vol. 1)
2819 Hydrosulfites (Vol. 1)
3842 Hydrotherapy equipment (Vol. 1)
3829 Hygrometers, except industrial process type (Vol. 1)
3829 Hygrothermographs (Vol. 1)
2822 Hypalon (Vol. 1)
8299 Hypnosis schools (Vol. 2)
8049 Hypnotists, offices of (Vol. 2)
3841 Hypodermic needles and syringes (Vol. 1)
2819 Hypophosphites (Vol. 1)

I

3069 Ice bags, rubber or rubberized fabric (Vol. 1)
3822 Ice bank controls (Vol. 1)
3632 Ice boxes, household (Vol. 1)
3585 Ice boxes, industrial (Vol. 1)
3089 Ice buckets, plastics: except foam (Vol. 1)
3429 Ice chests or coolers, portable, except insulated foam plastics (Vol. 1)
3086 Ice chests or coolers, portable: foamed plastics (Vol. 1)
3089 Ice chests or coolers, portable, plastics: except insulated or foam plastics (Vol. 1)
2024 Ice Cream and Frozen Desserts (Vol. 1)
5143 Ice cream and ices—wholesale (Vol. 2)
5078 Ice cream cabinets—wholesale (Vol. 2)
3411 Ice cream cans, metal (Vol. 1)
2052 Ice cream cones and wafers (Vol. 1)
2657 Ice cream containers, folding paperboard (Vol. 1)
2656 Ice cream containers, nonfolding paperboard (Vol. 1)
3469 Ice cream dippers (Vol. 1)
2024 Ice cream: e.g., bulk, packaged, molded, on sticks (Vol. 1)
3499 Ice cream freezers, household, nonelectric: metal (Vol. 1)
3556 Ice cream manufacturing machinery (Vol. 1)
2023 Ice cream mix, unfrozen: liquid or dry (Vol. 1)
5451 Ice cream (packaged) stores—retail (Vol. 2)
5812 Ice cream stands (Vol. 2)
5963 Ice cream wagons—retail (Vol. 2)

3634 Ice crushers, electric (Vol. 1)
3569 Ice crushers, except household (Vol. 1)
2097 Ice cubes (Vol. 1)
5999 Ice dealers—retail (Vol. 2)
7941 Ice hockey clubs, professional or semiprofessional (Vol. 2)
3822 Ice maker controls (Vol. 1)
3585 Ice making machinery (Vol. 1)
5078 Ice making machines—wholesale (Vol. 2)
2097 Ice, manufactured or artificial: except dry ice (Vol. 1)
5199 Ice, manufactured or natural—wholesale (Vol. 2)
2024 Ice milk: e.g., bulk, packaged, molded, on sticks (Vol. 1)
2023 Ice milk mix, unfrozen: liquid or dry (Vol. 1)
2097 Ice plants, operated by public utilities (Vol. 1)
3949 Ice skates (Vol. 1)
7999 Ice skating rink operation (Vol. 2)
2086 Iced tea, bottled or canned (Vol. 1)
1499 Iceland spar mining (optical grade calcite) (Vol. 2)
2024 Ices and sherbets (Vol. 1)
4741 Icing of railroad cars (Vol. 2)
7389 Identification engraving service (Vol. 2)
3999 Identification plates (Vol. 1)
3999 Identification tags, except paper (Vol. 1)
5043 Identity recorders for photographing checks and fingerprints—wholesale (Vol. 2)
2899 Igniter grains, boron potassium nitrate (Vol. 1)
3483 Igniters, tracer: for ammunition more than 30 mm. (or more than 1.18 inch) (Vol. 1)
3694 Ignition apparatus for internal combustion engines (Vol. 1)
3694 Ignition cable sets or wire assemblies for internal combustion engines (Vol. 1)
3822 Ignition controls for gas appliances and furnaces, automatic (Vol. 1)
7539 Ignition service, automotive (Vol. 2)
3694 Ignition systems, high frequency (Vol. 1)
3825 Ignition testing instruments (Vol. 1)
3612 Ignition transformers (Vol. 1)
3229 Illuminating glass: light shades, reflectors, lamp chimneys, and globes (Vol. 1)
2911 Illuminating oil, produced in petroleum refineries (Vol. 1)
1099 Ilmenite mining (Vol. 2)
3299 Images, small: gypsum, clay, or papier-mache-factory production only (Vol. 1)
3634 Immersion heaters, household: electric (Vol. 1)
9721 Immigration services-government (Vol. 2)
9431 Immunization program administration-government (Vol. 2)
3679 Impedance conversion units, high frequency (Vol. 1)
3825 Impedance measuring equipment (Vol. 1)
3824 Impeller and counter driven flow meters (Vol. 1)
3842 Implants, surgical (Vol. 1)
1389 Impounding and storing salt water in connection with petroleum production (Vol. 2)
4971 Impounding reservoirs, irrigation (Vol. 2)

2295 Impregnating and coating of fabrics, except rubberizing (Vol. 1)
3843 Impression material, dental (Vol. 1)
2759 Imprinting, except lithographed or gravure (Vol. 1)
2754 Imprinting: gravure (Vol. 1)
0751 Improvement associations; Dairy herd (Vol. 2)
3822 In-built thermostats, filled system and bimetal types (Vol. 1)
2835 In Vitro and In Vivo Diagnostic Substances (Vol. 1)
2835 In vitro diagnostics (Vol. 1)
2835 In vivo diagnostics (Vol. 1)
2835 In vivo radioactive reagents (Vol. 1)
3641 Incandescent filament lamp bulbs, complete (Vol. 1)
3559 Incandescent lamp making machinery (Vol. 1)
2899 Incense (Vol. 1)
3822 Incinerator control systems, residential and commercial types (Vol. 1)
1796 Incinerator installation, small-contractors (Vol. 2)
4953 Incinerator operation (Vol. 2)
3272 Incinerators, concrete (Vol. 1)
3567 Incinerators, metal: domestic and commercial (Vol. 1)
7291 Income tax return preparation services without accounting, auditing, or bookkeeping services (Vol. 2)
3523 Incubators, except laboratory and infant (Vol. 1)
3842 Incubators, infant (Vol. 1)
3821 Incubators, laboratory (Vol. 1)
2675 Index and other cut cards (Vol. 1)
3952 India ink (Vol. 1)
3949 Indian clubs (Vol. 1)
5084 Indicating instruments and accessories—wholesale (Vol. 2)
3825 Indicating instruments, electric (Vol. 1)
3829 Indicator testers, turntable (Vol. 1)
2865 Indicators, chemical (Vol. 1)
2819 Indium chloride (Vol. 1)
8322 Individual and Family Social Services (Vol. 2)
0751 Individuals; Slaughtering, custom: for (Vol. 2)
3567 Induction heating equipment (Vol. 1)
3677 Inductors, electronic (Vol. 1)
2869 Industrial alcohol denatured (nonbeverage) (Vol. 1)
6512 Industrial and commercial buildings, operators of (Vol. 2)
3564 Industrial and Commercial Fans and Blowers and Air Purification Equipment (Vol. 1)
3599 Industrial and Commercial Machinery and Equipment Not Elsewhere Classified (Vol. 1)
5113 Industrial and Personal Service Paper (Vol. 2)
2296 Industrial belting reinforcement, cord and fabric (Vol. 1)
3991 Industrial brooms and brushes (Vol. 1)
1541 Industrial building construction-general contractors (Vol. 2)
5169 Industrial chemicals—wholesale (Vol. 2)
3625 Industrial controls: push button, selector switches, and pilot (Vol. 1)

2816 Inorganic Pigments (Vol. 1)

2816 Inorganic pigments (Vol. 1)

3577 Input/output equipment, computer: except terminals (Vol. 1)

0721 Insect control for crops, with or without fertilizing (Vol. 2)

2879 Insect powder, household (Vol. 1)

3496 Insect screening, woven wire: made from purchased wire (Vol. 1)

2879 Insecticides, agricultural (Vol. 1)

2879 Insecticides, household (Vol. 1)

5191 Insecticides—wholesale (Vol. 2)

0751 Insemination services: livestock; Artificial (Vol. 2)

3545 Inserts, cutting tool (Vol. 1)

3999 Insignia, military: except textile (Vol. 1)

2399 Insignia, military: textile (Vol. 1)

9651 Inspection for labor standards-government (Vol. 2)

7389 Inspection of commodities, not connected with transportation (Vol. 2)

2899 Inspection oil, fluorescent (Vol. 1)

7549 Inspection service, automotive (Vol. 2)

4785 Inspection services connected with transportation (Vol. 2)

1796 Installation of machinery and other industrial equipment-contractors (Vol. 2)

1796 Installing or Erection of Building Equipment Not Elsewhere Classified (Vol. 2)

6153 Installment notes, buying of (Vol. 2)

6153 Installment paper dealer (Vol. 2)

6141 Installment sales finance, other than banks (Vol. 2)

2095 Instant coffee (Vol. 1)

2752 Instant printing, except photocopy service (Vol. 1)

1542 Institutional building construction, nonresidential-general contractors (Vol. 2)

3646 Institutional lighting fixtures (Vol. 1)

3714 Instrument board assemblies, motor vehicle (Vol. 1)

3812 Instrument landing system instrumentation, airborne or airport (Vol. 1)

3827 Instrument lenses (Vol. 1)

3728 Instrument panel mockups: aircraft training units (Vol. 1)

3825 Instrument relays, all types (Vol. 1)

3825 Instrument shunts (Vol. 1)

3495 Instrument springs, precision: made from purchased wire (Vol. 1)

3612 Instrument transformers, except portable (Vol. 1)

3829 Instrumentation for reactor controls, auxiliary (Vol. 1)

3695 Instrumentation type tape, blank (Vol. 1)

3841 Instruments and apparatus, except electromedical: medical, surgical, ophthalmic, and veterinary (Vol. 1)

3825 Instruments, electric: for testing electrical characteristics (Vol. 1)

3823 Instruments for industrial process control (Vol. 1)

3825 Instruments for Measuring and Testing of Electricity and Electrical Signals (Vol. 1)

3825 Instruments for measuring electrical quantities (Vol. 1)

3952 Instruments, lettering: artists' (Vol. 1)

3841 Instruments, microsurgical: except electromedical (Vol. 1)

3931 Instruments, musical (Vol. 1)

3861 Instruments, photographic (Vol. 1)

3357 Insulated wire and cable, nonferrous (Vol. 1)

2679 Insulating batts, fills, and blankets: paper (Vol. 1)

2899 Insulating compounds (Vol. 1)

3255 Insulating firebrick and shapes, clay (Vol. 1)

3211 Insulating glass, sealed units (Vol. 1)

2499 Insulating materials, cork (Vol. 1)

3292 Insulating materials for covering boilers and pipes (Vol. 1)

3275 Insulating plaster, gypsum (Vol. 1)

2493 Insulating siding, board (Vol. 1)

2952 Insulating siding, impregnated (Vol. 1)

2241 Insulating tapes and braids, electric, except plastics (Vol. 1)

3086 Insulation and cushioning: foamed plastics (Vol. 1)

2493 Insulation board, cellular fiber or hard pressed (without gypsum) (Vol. 1)

2679 Insulation, cellulose (Vol. 1)

1742 Insulation installation, buildings-contractors (Vol. 2)

5211 Insulation material, building—retail (Vol. 2)

3292 Insulation, molded asbestos (Vol. 1)

1799 Insulation of pipes and boilers-contractors (Vol. 2)

3296 Insulation: rock wool, fiberglass, slag, and silica minerals (Vol. 1)

5033 Insulation, thermal—wholesale (Vol. 2)

2298 Insulator pads, cordage (Vol. 1)

3644 Insulators, electrical: except glass and ceramic (Vol. 1)

3229 Insulators, electrical: glass (Vol. 1)

5063 Insulators, electrical—wholesale (Vol. 2)

3264 Insulators, porcelain (Vol. 1)

2833 Insulin: bulk, uncompounded (Vol. 1)

2834 Insulin preparations (Vol. 1)

3299 Insulsleeves (foundry materials) (Vol. 1)

6321 Insurance, accident and health (Vol. 2)

6411 Insurance adjusters (Vol. 2)

6411 Insurance advisory services (Vol. 2)

6411 Insurance agents (Vol. 2)

6411 Insurance Agents, Brokers and Service (Vol. 2)

6341 Insurance and Diversified Financial Companies (Vol. 2)

6399 Insurance, bank deposit or share (Vol. 2)

6411 Insurance brokers (Vol. 2)

6512 Insurance buildings, operation of (Vol. 2)

6321 Insurance carriers, accident (Vol. 2)

6331 Insurance carriers: fire, marine, and casualty (Vol. 2)

6321 Insurance carriers, health (Vol. 2)

6311 Insurance carriers, life (Vol. 2)

6399 Insurance Carriers Not Elsewhere Classified (Vol. 2)

6411 Insurance claim adjusters, not employed by insurance companies (Vol. 2)

9651 Insurance commissions-government (Vol. 2)

6351 Insurance, credit or other financial responsibility (Vol. 2)

6411 Insurance educational services (Vol. 2)

6351 Insurance, fidelity (Vol. 2)

6331 Insurance: fire, marine, and casualty (Vol. 2)

6411 Insurance information bureaus (Vol. 2)

6411 Insurance inspection and investigation services (Vol. 2)

6311 Insurance, life (Vol. 2)

6411 Insurance loss prevention services (Vol. 2)

6411 Insurance patrol services (Vol. 2)

8099 Insurance physical examination service, except by physicians (Vol. 2)

6411 Insurance professional standards services (Vol. 2)

6411 Insurance rate making services (Vol. 2)

6411 Insurance reporting services (Vol. 2)

6411 Insurance research services (Vol. 2)

6411 Insurance services (Vol. 2)

6351 Insurance, surety (Vol. 2)

6361 Insurance, title protection (Vol. 2)

2851 Intaglio ink vehicle (Vol. 1)

2754 Intaglio printing (Vol. 1)

3825 Integrated-circuit testers (Vol. 1)

3674 Integrated microcircuits (Vol. 1)

3825 Integrating electricity meters (Vol. 1)

3824 Integrating meters, nonelectric (Vol. 1)

3432 Interceptors, plumbers' (Vol. 1)

4131 Intercity and Rural Bus Transportation (Vol. 2)

4131 Intercity bus lines (Vol. 2)

4424 Intercoastal transportation of freight (Vol. 2)

3669 Intercommunication systems, electric (Vol. 1)

5065 Intercommunications equipment, electronic—wholesale (Vol. 2)

1731 Intercommunications equipment installation-contractors (Vol. 2)

7622 Intercommunications equipment repair (Vol. 2)

3443 Intercooler shells (Vol. 1)

3827 Interferometers (Vol. 1)

7389 Interior decorating consulting service, except painters and paperhangers (Vol. 2)

7389 Interior designing service, except painters and paperhangers (Vol. 2)

2211 Interlining material, cotton (Vol. 1)

2396 Interlinings: for suits and coats-men's and boys' (Vol. 1)

2396 Interlinings, pockets, belt loops, etc.-men's and boys' (Vol. 1)

8052 Intermediate Care Facilities (Vol. 2)

6159 Intermediate investment banks' (Vol. 2)

2865 Intermediates, cyclic (coal tar) (Vol. 1)

3825 Internal combustion engine analyzers, to test electrical characteristics (Vol. 1)

3462 Internal combustion engine (stationary and mobile) forgings, ferrous: not made in rolling mills (Vol. 1)

3519 Internal combustion engines, except aircraft and nondiesel automotive (Vol. 1)

3519 Internal Combustion Engines Not Elsewhere Classified (Vol. 1)

9721 International Affairs (Vol. 2)

4131 Interstate bus lines (Vol. 2)

3555 Intertype machines (Vol. 1)

4131 Interurban bus lines (Vol. 2)

3743 Interurban cars and car equipment (Vol. 1)

4011 Interurban railways (Vol. 2)

3851 Intra ocular lenses (Vol. 1)

4449 Intracoastal freight transportation (Vol. 2)

3842 Intrauterine devices (Vol. 1)

2834 Intravenous solutions (Vol. 1)

7352 Invalid supplies rental and leasing (Vol. 2)

8999 Inventors (Vol. 2)

2782 Inventory blankbooks (Vol. 1)

7389 Inventory computing service (Vol. 2)

2062 Invert sugar (Vol. 1)

3629 Inverters, nonrotating: electrical (Vol. 1)

3621 Inverters, rotating: electrical (Vol. 1)

7381 Investigators, private (Vol. 2)

6282 Investment Advice (Vol. 2)

6282 Investment advisory service (Vol. 2)

6211 Investment bankers (Vol. 2)

3324 Investment castings, steel (Vol. 1)

6211 Investment certificates, sale of (Vol. 2)

6799 Investment clubs (Vol. 2)

6159 Investment companies, small business (Vol. 2)

6282 Investment counselors (Vol. 2)

6211 Investment firm-general brokerage (Vol. 2)

6726 Investment funds, closed-end: management of (Vol. 2)

6722 Investment funds (management) open-end (Vol. 2)

6719 Investment holding companies, except bank (Vol. 2)

3843 Investment material, dental (Vol. 1)

6282 Investment research (Vol. 2)

6726 Investment trusts, unit (Vol. 2)

6799 Investors Not Elsewhere Classified (Vol. 2)

6726 Investors' syndicates (Vol. 2)

2759 Invitations, engraved (Vol. 1)

2819 Iodides (Vol. 1)

2835 Iodinated diagnostic agents (Vol. 1)

2819 Iodine, elemental (Vol. 1)

2819 Iodine, resublimed (Vol. 1)

2834 Iodine, tincture of (Vol. 1)

3829 Ion chambers (Vol. 1)

2821 Ion exchange resins (Vol. 1)

2821 Ionomer resins (Vol. 1)

2869 Ionone (Vol. 1)

1099 Iridium ore mining (Vol. 2)

3339 Iridium refining, primary (Vol. 1)

3341 Iridium smelting and refining, secondary (Vol. 1)

0134 Irish; Potato farms, (Vol. 2)

0134 Irish Potatoes (Vol. 2)

1011 Iron agglomerate and pellet production (Vol. 2)

5051 Iron and steel flat products—wholesale (Vol. 2)

3462 Iron and Steel Forgings (Vol. 1)

5093 Iron and steel scrap—wholesale (Vol. 2)

5051 Iron and steel semifinished products—wholesale (Vol. 2)

2816 Iron blue pigments (Vol. 1)

3321 Iron castings, ductile and nodular (Vol. 1)

2891 Iron cement, household (Vol. 1)

2816 Iron colors (Vol. 1)

3842 Iron lungs (Vol. 1)

1011 Iron ore, blocked: mining (Vol. 2)

1011   Iron ore dressing (beneficiation) plants (Vol. 2)
1011   Iron ore mining (Vol. 2)
3399   Iron ore, recovery from open hearth slag (Vol. 1)
5052   Iron ore—wholesale (Vol. 2)
1011   Iron Ores (Vol. 2)
2816   Iron oxide, black (Vol. 1)
2816   Iron oxide, magnetic (Vol. 1)
2816   Iron oxide, yellow (Vol. 1)
3312   Iron, pig (Vol. 1)
5051   Iron, pig—wholesale (Vol. 2)
3399   Iron, powdered (Vol. 1)
3312   Iron sinter, made in steel mills (Vol. 1)
2819   Iron sulphate (Vol. 1)
1799   Iron work, ornamental-contractors (Vol. 2)
1791   Iron work, structural-contractors (Vol. 2)
3469   Ironer parts, porcelain enameled (Vol. 1)
3633   Ironers and mangles, household, except portable irons (Vol. 1)
3582   Ironers, commercial laundry and drycleaning (Vol. 1)
5064   Ironers, household: electric—wholesale (Vol. 2)
2392   Ironing board pads (Vol. 1)
3499   Ironing boards, metal (Vol. 1)
2499   Ironing boards, wood (Vol. 1)
3634   Irons, domestic: electric (Vol. 1)
3953   Irons, marking or branding (Vol. 1)
3423   Ironworkers' handtools (Vol. 1)
3844   Irradiation equipment (Vol. 1)
9631   Irrigation districts-nonoperating (Vol. 2)
3523   Irrigation equipment, self-propelled (Vol. 1)
5083   Irrigation equipment—wholesale (Vol. 2)
3272   Irrigation pipe, concrete (Vol. 1)
3444   Irrigation pipe, sheet metal (Vol. 1)
1629   Irrigation projects construction-general contractors (Vol. 2)
4971   Irrigation system operation (Vol. 2)
0721   Irrigation system operation services (not providing water) (Vol. 2)
4971   Irrigation Systems (Vol. 2)
1321   Isobutane (natural) production (Vol. 2)
2822   Isobutylene-isoprene rubbers (Vol. 1)
2821   Isobutylene polymers (Vol. 1)
2822   Isocyanate type rubber (Vol. 1)
2865   Isocyanates (Vol. 1)
3612   Isolation transformers (Vol. 1)
2822   Isoprene rubbers, synthetic (Vol. 1)
2869   Isopropyl alcohol (Vol. 1)
2819   Isotopes, radioactive (Vol. 1)
6726   Issuing of face-amount installment certificates (Vol. 2)
2032   Italian foods, canned (Vol. 1)
3841   IV transfusion apparatus (Vol. 1)

J

3569   Jack screws (Vol. 1)
3482   Jackets, bullet: 30 mm. (or 1.18 inch) or less (Vol. 1)
2371   Jackets, fur (Vol. 1)
2369   Jackets: girls', children's, and infants' (Vol. 1)
3443   Jackets, industrial: metal plate (Vol. 1)

2386   Jackets, leather (except welders') or sheep-lined (Vol. 1)
2253   Jackets (Vol. 1)
2329   Jackets, nontailored except work: men's and boys' (Vol. 1)
2339   Jackets, not tailored: women's, misses', and juniors' (Vol. 1)
2326   Jackets, overall and work: men's and boys' (Vol. 1)
2339   Jackets, service apparel (e.g., medical and lab) (Vol. 1)
2339   Jackets, ski: women's, misses' and juniors' (Vol. 1)
2384   Jackets, smoking: men's (Vol. 1)
2329   Jackets, sport, nontailored: men's and boys' (Vol. 1)
2337   Jackets, tailored, except fur, sheep-lined, and leather: women's, misses', and juniors' (Vol. 1)
2311   Jackets, tailored suit-type: men's and boys' (Vol. 1)
3199   Jackets, welders': leather (Vol. 1)
3569   Jacks, hydraulic: for general industrial use (Vol. 1)
2499   Jacks, ladder: wood (Vol. 1)
3423   Jacks: lifting, screw, and ratchet (handtools) (Vol. 1)
3531   Jacks, mud (Vol. 1)
3552   Jacquard card cutting machines (Vol. 1)
2675   Jacquard cards (Vol. 1)
3552   Jacquard loom parts and attachments (Vol. 1)
2211   Jacquard woven fabrics, cotton (Vol. 1)
2221   Jacquard woven fabrics, manmade fiber and silk (Vol. 1)
1499   Jade mining (Vol. 2)
9223   Jails-government (Vol. 2)
8744   Jails, privately operated (Vol. 2)
3442   Jalousies, all metal or metal frame (Vol. 1)
2431   Jalousies, glass: wood frame (Vol. 1)
2033   Jams, including imitation (Vol. 1)
4581   Janitorial service on airplanes (Vol. 2)
7349   Janitorial services on a contract or fee basis (Vol. 2)
3589   Janitors' carts (Vol. 1)
5087   Janitors' supplies—wholesale (Vol. 2)
3111   Japanning of leather (Vol. 1)
3479   Japanning of metal (Vol. 1)
3567   Japanning ovens (Vol. 1)
2851   Japans, baking and drying (Vol. 1)
3466   Jar crowns and tops, stamped metal (Vol. 1)
3069   Jar rings, rubber (Vol. 1)
3069   Jars, battery: hard rubber (Vol. 1)
3221   Jars for packing, bottling, and canning: glass (Vol. 1)
3089   Jars, plastics (Vol. 1)
7929   Jazz music groups or artists (Vol. 2)
2325   Jean-cut casual slacks: men's and boys' (Vol. 1)
2339   Jean-cut casual slacks: women's, misses', and juniors' (Vol. 1)
2211   Jean fabrics, cotton (Vol. 1)
2369   Jeans: girls', children's, and infants' (Vol. 1)
2325   Jeans: men's and boys' (Vol. 1)
5651   Jeans stores—retail (Vol. 2)
2339   Jeans: women's, misses', and juniors' (Vol. 1)
2033   Jellies, edible: including imitation (Vol. 1)

INDUSTRY INDEX

1459 Kyanite mining (Vol. 2)

L

3565 Label moisteners, industrial type (Vol. 1)

7389 Labeling bottles, cans, cartons, etc. for the trade: not printing (Vol. 2)

3565 Labeling machinery, industrial type (Vol. 1)

3579 Labeling machines, address (Vol. 1)

2269 Labels, cotton: printed (Vol. 1)

2754 Labels: gravure printing (Vol. 1)

2752 Labels, lithographed (Vol. 1)

2759 Labels, printed: except lithographed or gravure (Vol. 1)

2241 Labels, woven (Vol. 1)

5131 Labels, woven—wholesale (Vol. 2)

7361 Labor contractors (employment agencies), except farm labor (Vol. 2)

9651 Labor-management negotiations boards-government (Vol. 2)

8631 Labor organizations (Vol. 2)

7363 Labor pools (Vol. 2)

8631 Labor unions (Vol. 2)

8631 Labor Unions and Similar Labor Organizations (Vol. 2)

8071 Laboratories: biological, medical, and X-ray (picture and treatment) (Vol. 2)

8072 Laboratories, dental-X-ray (Vol. 2)

8731 Laboratories, industrial: commercial research, except testing (Vol. 2)

7819 Laboratories, motion picture (Vol. 2)

8734 Laboratories, product testing: not manufacturing auxiliaries (Vol. 2)

8731 Laboratories, research: commercial (Vol. 2)

3826 Laboratory Analytical Instruments (Vol. 1)

0279 Laboratory animal farms (e.g., rats, mice, guinea pigs) (Vol. 2)

3821 Laboratory Apparatus and Furniture (Vol. 1)

2819 Laboratory chemicals, inorganic (Vol. 1)

2869 Laboratory chemicals, organic (Vol. 1)

2326 Laboratory coats: men's (Vol. 1)

5047 Laboratory equipment, dental and medical— wholesale (Vol. 2)

5049 Laboratory equipment, except medical or dental— wholesale (Vol. 2)

3821 Laboratory equipment: fume hoods, distillation racks, benches, and cabinets (Vol. 1)

3231 Laboratory glassware, made from purchased glass (Vol. 1)

7699 Laboratory instrument repair, except electric (Vol. 2)

8731 Laboratory (physical) research and development (Vol. 2)

3825 Laboratory standards, electric: resistance, inductance, and capacitance (Vol. 1)

3069 Laboratory sundries: e.g., cases, covers, funnels, cups, bottles-rubber (Vol. 1)

3089 Laboratoryware, plastics (Vol. 1)

0831 Lac production (Vol. 2)

3552 Lace and net machines (Vol. 1)

2258 Lace and Warp Knit Fabric Mills (Vol. 1)

2241 Lace, auto wind (Vol. 1)

2395 Lace, burnt-out (Vol. 1)

5131 Lace fabrics—wholesale (Vol. 2)

2258 Lace goods: curtains, bedspreads, table covers, flouncings, and insertions (Vol. 1)

2258 Lace, knit (Vol. 1)

3111 Lace leather (Vol. 1)

3552 Lace machine bobbins, wood or metal (Vol. 1)

2675 Lace, paper: die-cut from purchased materials (Vol. 1)

2258 Laces: Barmen, bobbinet, levers, and Nottingham (Vol. 1)

3131 Laces, boot and shoe: leather (Vol. 1)

2241 Laces, corset and shoe: textile (Vol. 1)

2241 Lacings (Vol. 1)

2851 Lacquer bases and dopes (Vol. 1)

2851 Lacquer, clear and pigmented (Vol. 1)

2851 Lacquer thinner (Vol. 1)

3479 Lacquering of metal products, for the trade (Vol. 1)

3567 Lacquering ovens (Vol. 1)

2851 Lacquers, plastics (Vol. 1)

5198 Lacquers—wholesale (Vol. 2)

3949 Lacrosse equipment (Vol. 1)

2023 Lactose, edible (Vol. 1)

3499 Ladder assemblies, combination workstand: metal (Vol. 1)

3531 Ladder ditchers, vertical boom or wheel (Vol. 1)

3429 Ladder jacks, metal (Vol. 1)

2499 Ladder jacks, wood (Vol. 1)

2426 Ladder round (Vol. 1)

2426 Ladder rounds or rungs, hardwood (Vol. 1)

3446 Ladders, chain: metal (Vol. 1)

3446 Ladders, for permanent installation: metal (Vol. 1)

3499 Ladders, metal: portable (Vol. 1)

3089 Ladders, plastics (Vol. 1)

5084 Ladders—wholesale (Vol. 2)

2499 Ladders, wood (Vol. 1)

5137 Ladies' handkerchiefs—wholesale (Vol. 2)

5137 Ladies' purses—wholesale (Vol. 2)

3443 Ladle bails (Vol. 1)

3255 Ladle brick, clay (Vol. 1)

3443 Ladles, metal plate (Vol. 1)

4449 Lake freight transportation, except on the Great Lakes (Vol. 2)

2865 Lake red C toners (Vol. 1)

2865 Lakes, color (Vol. 1)

0214 Lamb; Feedlots, (Vol. 2)

2011 Lamb (Vol. 1)

2013 Lamb stew, (Vol. 1)

2679 Laminated building paper (Vol. 1)

2675 Laminated cardboard (Vol. 1)

3211 Laminated glass, made from glass produced in the same establishment (Vol. 1)

3231 Laminated glass, made from purchased glass (Vol. 1)

3083 Laminated plastics plate, rods, and tubes and sheet, except flexible packaging (Vol. 1)

3083 Laminated Plastics Plate, Sheet and Profile Shapes (Vol. 1)

2891 Laminating compounds (Vol. 1)

2295 Laminating of fabrics (Vol. 1)
7389 Laminating of photographs (coating photographs with plastics) (Vol. 2)
3399 Laminating steel for the trade (Vol. 1)
5719 Lamp and shade shops—retail (Vol. 2)
3281 Lamp bases, onyx (Vol. 1)
3089 Lamp bases, plastics (Vol. 1)
3269 Lamp bases, pottery (Vol. 1)
2816 Lamp black (Vol. 1)
3641 Lamp (bulb) parts, electric (Vol. 1)
3641 Lamp bulbs and tubes, electric: incandescent filament, fluorescent, and vapor (Vol. 1)
3641 Lamp bulbs and tubes, health: infrared and ultraviolet radiation (Vol. 1)
5063 Lamp bulbs —wholesale (Vol. 2)
3648 Lamp fixtures, infrared (Vol. 1)
3496 Lamp frames, wire: made from purchased wire (Vol. 1)
3559 Lamp making machinery, incandescent (Vol. 1)
3229 Lamp parts, glass (Vol. 1)
3446 Lamp posts, metal (Vol. 1)
3999 Lamp shade frames (Vol. 1)
3999 Lamp shades: except metal and glass (Vol. 1)
3229 Lamp shades, glass (Vol. 1)
3645 Lamp shades, metal (Vol. 1)
3089 Lamp shades, plastics (Vol. 1)
3643 Lamp sockets and receptacles (electric wiring devices) (Vol. 1)
5023 Lamps: floor, boudoir, desk—wholesale (Vol. 2)
3641 Lamps, glow (Vol. 1)
3699 Lamps, insect: electric (Vol. 1)
3645 Lamps (lighting fixtures), residential: electric (Vol. 1)
3647 Lamps, marker and clearance: motor vehicle (Vol. 1)
3641 Lamps, sealed beam (Vol. 1)
3841 Lamps, slit (ophthalmic goods) (Vol. 1)
3844 Lamps, X-ray (Vol. 1)
1629 Land clearing-contractors (Vol. 2)
1629 Land drainage-contractors (Vol. 2)
1629 Land leveling (irrigation)-contractors (Vol. 2)
9512 Land management agencies-government (Vol. 2)
9512 Land, Mineral, Wildlife and Forest Conservation (Vol. 2)
5083 Land preparation machinery, agricultural—wholesale (Vol. 2)
1629 Land reclamation-contractors (Vol. 2)
3523 Land rollers and levelers (agricultural machinery) (Vol. 1)
6552 Land Subdividers and Developers Except Cemeteries (Vol. 2)
8713 Land surveying (Vol. 2)
4953 Landfill, sanitary: operation of (Vol. 2)
6519 Landholding offices (Vol. 2)
3728 Landing gear, aircraft (Vol. 1)
3449 Landing mats, aircraft: metal (Vol. 1)
3731 Landing ships, building and repairing (Vol. 1)
3728 Landing skis and tracks, aircraft (Vol. 1)
0781 Landscape architects (Vol. 2)
0781 Landscape counseling (Vol. 2)

0781 Landscape Counseling and Planning (Vol. 2)
0781 Landscape planning (Vol. 2)
8299 Language schools (Vol. 2)
3229 Lantern globes, glass: pressed or blown (Vol. 1)
3861 Lantern slide plates, sensitized (Vol. 1)
3648 Lanterns: electric, gas, carbide, kerosene, and gasoline (Vol. 1)
2679 Lanterns, halloween: papier mache (Vol. 1)
5085 Lapidary equipment—wholesale (Vol. 2)
3915 Lapidary work, contract and other (Vol. 1)
3541 Lapping machines (Vol. 1)
2013 Lard (Vol. 1)
2011 Lard (Vol. 1)
5147 Lard—wholesale (Vol. 2)
3674 Laser diodes (Vol. 1)
3845 Laser systems and equipment, medical (Vol. 1)
3699 Laser welding, drilling and cutting equipment (Vol. 1)
3199 Lashes (whips) (Vol. 1)
2411 Last blocks, wood: hewn or riven (Vol. 1)
2499 Last sole patterns, regardless of material (Vol. 1)
2499 Lasts, boot and shoe: regardless of material (Vol. 1)
3069 Latex, foamed (Vol. 1)
3449 Lath, expanded metal (Vol. 1)
2493 Lath, fiber (Vol. 1)
3275 Lath, gypsum (Vol. 1)
2421 Lath, made in sawmills and lathmills (Vol. 1)
3496 Lath, woven wire: made from purchased wire (Vol. 1)
3545 Lathe attachments and cutting tools (machine tool accessories) (Vol. 1)
3541 Lathes, metal cutting (Vol. 1)
3541 Lathes, metal polishing (Vol. 1)
3542 Lathes, spinning (Vol. 1)
3553 Lathes, wood turning: including accessories (Vol. 1)
1742 Lathing-contractors (Vol. 2)
3111 Latigo leather (Vol. 1)
7218 Laundered mat and rug supply service (Vol. 2)
7218 Launderers, industrial (Vol. 2)
2399 Launderers' nets (Vol. 1)
7215 Launderettes (Vol. 2)
7542 Laundries, automotive (Vol. 2)
7219 Laundries, except power and coin-operated (Vol. 2)
7211 Laundries, power: family and commercial (Vol. 2)
7215 Laundromats (Vol. 2)
7219 Laundry and Garment Services Not Elsewhere Classified (Vol. 2)
7211 Laundry collecting and distributing outlets operated by power laundries (Vol. 2)
3537 Laundry containers on wheels (Vol. 1)
5087 Laundry equipment and supplies—wholesale (Vol. 2)
2211 Laundry fabrics, cotton (Vol. 1)
3444 Laundry hampers, sheet metal (Vol. 1)
7215 Laundry machine routes, coin-operated (Vol. 2)
3582 Laundry machinery and equipment, commercial, including coin-operated (Vol. 1)

7389 Lecture bureaus (Vol. 2)
8999 Lecturers (Vol. 2)
2782 Ledgers and ledger sheets (Vol. 1)
2252 Leg warmers (Vol. 1)
8111 Legal aid services (Vol. 2)
9222 Legal Counsel and Prosecution (Vol. 2)
9222 Legal counsel offices-government (Vol. 2)
6311 Legal reserve life insurance (Vol. 2)
8111 Legal Services (Vol. 2)
2369 Leggings: girls', children's, and infants' (Vol. 1)
3199 Leggings, welders': leather (Vol. 1)
9131 Legislative and executive office combinations (Vol. 2)
9121 Legislative assemblies (Vol. 2)
9121 Legislative Bodies (Vol. 2)
7922 Legitimate theater producers (Vol. 2)
0174 Lemon groves and farms (Vol. 2)
2899 Lemon oil (Vol. 1)
2086 Lemonade: bottled, canned, or fresh (Vol. 1)
8231 Lending libraries (Vol. 2)
2211 Leno fabrics, cotton (Vol. 1)
2221 Leno fabrics, manmade fiber and silk (Vol. 1)
3229 Lens blanks, optical and ophthalmic (Vol. 1)
3827 Lens coating (Vol. 1)
3851 Lens coating, ophthalmic (Vol. 1)
3827 Lens grinding, except ophthalmic (Vol. 1)
3851 Lens grinding, ophthalmic, except prescription (Vol. 1)
3827 Lens mounts (Vol. 1)
3861 Lens shades, camera (Vol. 1)
3229 Lenses, glass: for lanterns, flashlights, headlights, and searchlights (Vol. 1)
3851 Lenses, ophthalmic (Vol. 1)
5048 Lenses, ophthalmic—wholesale (Vol. 2)
3827 Lenses, optical: photographic, magnifying, projection, and instrument (Vol. 1)
3089 Lenses, plastics: except ophthalmic or optical (Vol. 1)
0119 Lentil farms (Vol. 2)
2369 Leotards: girls', children's, and infants' (Vol. 1)
2253 Leotards (Vol. 1)
2339 Leotards: women's, misses', and juniors' (Vol. 1)
1479 Lepidolite mining (Vol. 2)
6512 Lessors of piers, docks, and associated buildings and facilities (Vol. 2)
6519 Lessors of property, except railroad, buildings, or mobile home sites (Vol. 2)
6517 Lessors of railroad property (Vol. 2)
4513 Letter delivery, private: air (Vol. 2)
4215 Letter delivery, private: except air (Vol. 2)
3579 Letter folding, stuffing, and sealing machines (Vol. 1)
3545 Letter pins (gauging and measuring) (Vol. 1)
7338 Letter writing service (Vol. 2)
3952 Lettering instruments, artists' (Vol. 1)
7389 Lettering service (Vol. 2)
2893 Letterpress ink (Vol. 1)
2796 Letterpress plates, preparation of (Vol. 1)
2759 Letterpress printing (Vol. 1)
2675 Letters, cardboard (Vol. 1)

2759 Letters, circular and form: except lithographed or gravure printed (Vol. 1)
2754 Letters, circular and form: gravure printing (Vol. 1)
2752 Letters, circular and form: lithographed (Vol. 1)
3993 Letters for signs, metal (Vol. 1)
3953 Letters (marking devices), metal (Vol. 1)
2499 Letters, wood (Vol. 1)
0161 Lettuce farms (Vol. 2)
1629 Levee construction-general contractors (Vol. 2)
3823 Level and bulk measuring instruments, industrial process type (Vol. 1)
3829 Level gauges, radiation type (Vol. 1)
3229 Level vials for instruments, glass (Vol. 1)
3547 Levelers, roller (rolling mill equipment) (Vol. 1)
3829 Levels and tapes, surveying (Vol. 1)
3423 Levels, carpenters' (Vol. 1)
6351 Liability insurance (Vol. 2)
8231 Libraries (Vol. 2)
8231 Libraries, except motion picture film (Vol. 2)
8231 Libraries, printed matter (Vol. 2)
2782 Library binders, looseleaf (Vol. 1)
2675 Library cards, paperboard (Vol. 1)
9621 Licensing and inspection of transportation facilities and services-government (Vol. 2)
9631 Licensing and inspection of utilities (Vol. 2)
9651 Licensing and permit for professional occupations-government (Vol. 2)
9651 Licensing and permit for retail trade-government (Vol. 2)
2064 Licorice candy (Vol. 1)
7381 Lie detection service (Vol. 2)
6311 Life Insurance (Vol. 2)
6411 Life insurance agents (Vol. 2)
6311 Life insurance funds, savings bank (Vol. 2)
2499 Life preservers, cork (Vol. 1)
3842 Life preservers, except cork and inflatable (Vol. 1)
6311 Life reinsurance (Vol. 2)
3732 Lifeboats, building and repairing (Vol. 1)
7999 Lifeguard service (Vol. 2)
3069 Lifejackets: inflatable rubberized fabric (Vol. 1)
3089 Lifejackets, plastics (Vol. 1)
3732 Liferafts, except inflatable (rubber and plastics) (Vol. 1)
3089 Liferafts, nonrigid: plastics (Vol. 1)
3069 Liferafts, rubber (Vol. 1)
3537 Lift trucks, industrial: fork, platform, straddle, etc. (Vol. 1)
5084 Lift trucks—wholesale (Vol. 2)
3534 Lifts (elevators), passenger and freight (Vol. 1)
3131 Lifts, heel: leather (Vol. 1)
3842 Ligatures, medical (Vol. 1)
1629 Light and power plant construction-general contractors (Vol. 2)
3641 Light bulbs, electric: complete (Vol. 1)
5063 Light bulbs, electric—wholesale (Vol. 2)
3663 Light communications equipment (Vol. 1)
3674 Light emitting diodes (Vol. 1)
3861 Light meters, photographic (Vol. 1)
3812 Light reconnaissance and surveillance systems and equipment (Vol. 1)

Industry Index

3671 Light sensing and emitting tubes (Vol. 1)

3674 Light sensitive devices, solid-state (Vol. 1)

3229 Light shades, glass: pressed or blown (Vol. 1)

3645 Light shades, metal (Vol. 1)

3827 Light sources, standard (Vol. 1)

2899 Lighter fluid (Vol. 1)

4499 Lighterage (Vol. 2)

3999 Lighters, cigar and cigarette: except precious metal and electric (Vol. 1)

5199 Lighters, cigar and cigarette—wholesale (Vol. 2)

3731 Lighters, marine: building and repairing (Vol. 1)

3731 Lighthouse tenders, building and repairing (Vol. 1)

3624 Lighting carbons (Vol. 1)

3648 Lighting Equipment Not Elsewhere Classified (Vol. 1)

3648 Lighting fixtures, airport: runway, approach, taxi, and ramp (Vol. 1)

3646 Lighting fixtures, commercial (Vol. 1)

3647 Lighting fixtures, motor vehicle (Vol. 1)

5063 Lighting fixtures: residential, commercial, and industrial—wholesale (Vol. 2)

3645 Lighting fixtures, residential, electric: e.g., garden, patio, walkway, yard (Vol. 1)

3645 Lighting fixtures, residential: electric (Vol. 1)

3648 Lighting fixtures, residential, except electric (Vol. 1)

3647 Lighting fixtures, vehicular (Vol. 1)

3229 Lighting glassware, pressed or blown (Vol. 1)

7349 Lighting maintenance service (bulb replacement and cleaning) (Vol. 2)

3612 Lighting transformers, fluorescent (Vol. 1)

3612 Lighting transformers, street and airport (Vol. 1)

3643 Lightning arrestors and coils (Vol. 1)

1799 Lightning conductor erection-contractors (Vol. 2)

3643 Lightning protection equipment (Vol. 1)

3645 Lights, yard: electric (Vol. 1)

2821 Lignin plastics (Vol. 1)

1221 Lignite mining (Vol. 2)

1241 Lignite mining services on a contract basis (Vol. 2)

0161 Lima bean farms; Green (Vol. 2)

3489 Limbers, gun and caisson (Vol. 1)

3842 Limbs, artificial (Vol. 1)

3274 Lime (Vol. 1)

5191 Lime, agricultural—wholesale (Vol. 2)

5211 Lime and plaster dealers—retail (Vol. 2)

2819 Lime bleaching compounds (Vol. 1)

2869 Lime citrate (Vol. 1)

5032 Lime, except agricultural—wholesale (Vol. 2)

0711 Lime for crops; Spreading (Vol. 2)

0174 Lime groves and farms (Vol. 2)

3274 Lime plaster (Vol. 1)

1422 Lime rock, ground (Vol. 2)

0711 Lime spreading for crops (Vol. 2)

2879 Lime-sulfur, dry and solution (Vol. 1)

3281 Limestone, cut and shaped (Vol. 1)

1411 Limestone, dimension-quarrying (Vol. 2)

1422 Limestone, except bituminous: crushed and broken-quarrying (Vol. 2)

5032 Limestone—wholesale (Vol. 2)

3822 Limit controls, residential and commercial heating types (Vol. 1)

5331 Limited price variety stores—retail (Vol. 2)

1011 Limonite mining (Vol. 2)

4119 Limousine rental with drivers (Vol. 2)

7514 Limousine rental, without drivers (Vol. 2)

2879 Lindane, formulated (Vol. 1)

3531 Line markers, self-propelled (Vol. 1)

3822 Line or limit control for electric heat (Vol. 1)

3494 Line strainers, for use in piping systems-metal (Vol. 1)

3612 Line voltage regulators (Vol. 1)

3699 Linear accelerators (Vol. 1)

3824 Linear counters (Vol. 1)

2824 Linear esters fibers (Vol. 1)

2796 Linecuts (Vol. 1)

3842 Linemen's safety belts (Vol. 1)

2269 Linen fabrics: dyeing, finishing, and printing (Vol. 1)

5131 Linen piece goods—wholesale (Vol. 2)

5719 Linen shops—retail (Vol. 2)

7213 Linen Supply (Vol. 2)

7213 Linen supply service (Vol. 2)

5023 Linens—wholesale (Vol. 2)

2631 Liner board, kraft and jute (Vol. 1)

3259 Liner brick and plates, for lining sewers, tanks, etc.: vitrified clay (Vol. 1)

3069 Liner strips, rubber (Vol. 1)

2394 Liners and covers, fabric: pond, pit, and landfill (Vol. 1)

2675 Liners for freight car doors: reinforced with metal strip (Vol. 1)

3443 Liners, industrial: metal plate (Vol. 1)

5632 Lingerie stores—retail (Vol. 2)

5137 Lingerie—wholesale (Vol. 2)

2834 Liniments (Vol. 1)

2221 Lining fabrics, manmade fiber and silk: except glove lining fabrics (Vol. 1)

3111 Lining leather (Vol. 1)

2621 Lining paper (Vol. 1)

3259 Lining, stove and flue: clay (Vol. 1)

3131 Linings, boot and shoe: leather (Vol. 1)

2299 Linings, carpet: felt except woven (Vol. 1)

2392 Linings, carpet: textile, except felt (Vol. 1)

2396 Linings: e.g., suit, coat, shirt, skirt, dress, necktie, millinery (Vol. 1)

2396 Linings, handbag or pocketbook (Vol. 1)

2396 Linings, hat: men's (Vol. 1)

2396 Linings, luggage (Vol. 1)

2221 Linings, rayon or silk (Vol. 1)

3499 Linings, safe and vault: metal (Vol. 1)

2259 Linings, shoe (Vol. 1)

3069 Linings, vulcanizable elastomeric: rubber (Vol. 1)

3728 Link trainers (aircraft training mechanisms) (Vol. 1)

3484 Links, for ammunition 30 mm. (or 1.18 inch) or less (Vol. 1)

3489 Links for ammunition more than 30 mm. (or more than 1.18 inch) (Vol. 1)

2851 Linoleates, paint driers (Vol. 1)

3996 Linoleum, Asphalted-Felt-Base and Other Hard Surface Floor Coverings Not Elsewhere Classified (Vol. 1)

1752 Linoleum installation-contractors (Vol. 2)

3996 Linoleum (Vol. 1)

5713 Linoleum stores—retail (Vol. 2)

5023 Linoleum—wholesale (Vol. 2)

3555 Linotype machines (Vol. 1)

2076 Linseed oil, cake, and meal (Vol. 1)

5199 Linseed oil—wholesale (Vol. 2)

3272 Lintels, concrete (Vol. 1)

3446 Lintels, light gauge steel (Vol. 1)

2834 Lip balms (Vol. 1)

2844 Lipsticks (Vol. 1)

5984 Liquefied Petroleum Gas Dealers (Vol. 2)

1321 Liquefied petroleum gases (natural) production (Vol. 2)

5984 Liquefied petroleum (LP) gas delivered to customers' premises—retail (Vol. 2)

4925 Liquefied petroleum (LP) gas, distribution through mains (Vol. 2)

3823 Liquid analysis instruments, industrial process type (Vol. 1)

3826 Liquid chromatographic instruments, laboratory type (Vol. 1)

3823 Liquid concentration instruments, industrial process type (Vol. 1)

3679 Liquid crystal displays (Vol. 1)

3822 Liquid level controls, residential and commercial heating types (Vol. 1)

3823 Liquid level instruments, industrial process type (Vol. 1)

3443 Liquid oxygen tanks, metal plate (Vol. 1)

7389 Liquidators of merchandise on a contract or fee basis (Vol. 2)

5921 Liquor, packaged—retail (Vol. 2)

5921 Liquor Stores (Vol. 2)

2085 Liquors: distilled and blended-except brandy (Vol. 1)

5182 Liquors, distilled—wholesale (Vol. 2)

2082 Liquors, malt (Vol. 1)

3579 List finders, automatic (Vol. 1)

3523 Listers (Vol. 1)

6531 Listing service, real estate (Vol. 2)

2816 Litharge (Vol. 1)

2819 Lithium compounds (Vol. 1)

2819 Lithium metal (Vol. 1)

1479 Lithium mineral mining (Vol. 2)

2621 Lithograph paper (Vol. 1)

2893 Lithographic ink (Vol. 1)

2796 Lithographic plates, positives or negatives: preparation of (Vol. 1)

3555 Lithographic stones (Vol. 1)

2851 Lithographic varnishes (Vol. 1)

2752 Lithographing on metal or paper (Vol. 1)

2865 Lithol rubine lakes and toners (Vol. 1)

2816 Lithopone (Vol. 1)

3845 Lithotripters (Vol. 1)

2672 Litmus paper (Vol. 1)

3489 Livens projectors (ordnance) (Vol. 1)

5154 Livestock (Vol. 2)

0291 Livestock and Animal Specialties; General Farms—Primarily (Vol. 2)

0291 Livestock and animal specialty farms, general (Vol. 2)

0741 Livestock; Animal hospitals for (Vol. 2)

0751 Livestock; Artificial insemination services: (Vol. 2)

0751 Livestock; Breeding of (Vol. 2)

0751 Livestock breeding services (Vol. 2)

0751 Livestock, except by veterinarians; Vaccinating (Vol. 2)

5154 Livestock, except horses and mules—wholesale (Vol. 2)

0291 Livestock farms, general; Animal specialty and (Vol. 2)

2048 Livestock feeds, supplements, and concentrates (Vol. 1)

6159 Livestock loan companies (Vol. 2)

0219 Livestock Not Elsewhere Classified; General (Vol. 2)

0751 Livestock Services Except Veterinary (Vol. 2)

0741 Livestock; Veterinarians for (Vol. 2)

0741 Livestock; Veterinary Services for (Vol. 2)

2512 Living room furniture, upholstered on wood frames, except convertible beds (Vol. 1)

3523 Loaders, farm type (general utility) (Vol. 1)

3524 Loaders (garden tractor equipment) (Vol. 1)

3531 Loaders, shovel (Vol. 1)

3483 Loading and assembling bombs, powder bags, and shells: more than 30 mm. (or more than 1.18 inch) (Vol. 1)

3532 Loading machines, underground: mobile (Vol. 1)

1629 Loading station construction, mine-general contractors (Vol. 2)

4491 Loading vessels (Vol. 2)

3679 Loads, electronic (Vol. 1)

6163 Loan agents (Vol. 2)

6163 Loan Brokers (Vol. 2)

6141 Loan companies, small: licensed (Vol. 2)

6162 Loan correspondents (Vol. 2)

6159 Loan institutions, general and industrial (Vol. 2)

6141 Loan societies, remedial (Vol. 2)

8743 Lobbyists (Vol. 2)

0913 Lobsters, catching of (Vol. 2)

4111 Local and Suburban Transit (Vol. 2)

7373 Local area network (LAN) systems integrators (Vol. 2)

4141 Local Bus Charter Service (Vol. 2)

4119 Local Passenger Transportation Not Elsewhere Classified (Vol. 2)

4111 Local railway passenger operation (Vol. 2)

4813 Local telephone communications, except radio telephone (Vol. 2)

4214 Local Trucking With Storage (Vol. 2)

4212 Local Trucking Without Storage (Vol. 2)

1629 Lock and waterway construction-general contractors (Vol. 2)

7699 Lock parts made to individual order (Vol. 2)

3452 Lock washers (Vol. 1)

3089 Lock washers, plastics (Vol. 1)

7299 Locker rental, except cold storage (Vol. 2)

2542 Lockers, not refrigerated: except wood (Vol. 1)

5046 Lockers, not refrigerated—wholesale (Vol. 2)

2541 Lockers, not refrigerated: wood (Vol. 1)

3585 Lockers, refrigerated (Vol. 1)

3429 Locks and lock sets: except safe, vault, and coin-operated (Vol. 1)

5072 Locks and related materials—wholesale (Vol. 2)

3581 Locks, coin-operated (Vol. 1)

3499 Locks, safe and vault: metal (Vol. 1)

3429 Locks, trigger, for guns (Vol. 1)

7699 Locksmith shops (Vol. 2)

3647 Locomotive and railroad car lights (Vol. 1)

3531 Locomotive cranes (Vol. 1)

3462 Locomotive wheels, forged: not made in rolling mills (Vol. 1)

3743 Locomotives, locomotive frames, and parts (Vol. 1)

1041 Lode gold mining (Vol. 2)

7021 Lodging houses, except organization (Vol. 2)

7041 Lodging houses operated by organizations for members only (Vol. 2)

2452 Log cabins, prefabricated: wood (Vol. 1)

4449 Log rafting and towing (Vol. 2)

3531 Log splitters (Vol. 1)

4212 Log trucking (Vol. 2)

0171 Loganberry farms (Vol. 2)

2411 Logging (Vol. 1)

2411 Logging contractors (Vol. 1)

3531 Logging equipment (Vol. 1)

5082 Logging equipment—wholesale (Vol. 2)

4013 Logging railroads (Vol. 2)

1389 Logging wells on a contract basis (Vol. 2)

3825 Logic circuit testers (Vol. 1)

3699 Logs, fireplace: electric (Vol. 1)

3433 Logs, fireplace: gas (Vol. 1)

5099 Logs, hewn ties, posts, and poles—wholesale (Vol. 2)

2411 Logs (Vol. 1)

2861 Logwood extract (Vol. 1)

2211 Long cloth, cotton (Vol. 1)

4813 Long distance telephone communications (Vol. 2)

4213 Long-distance trucking (Vol. 2)

3552 Loom bobbins, wood or metal (Vol. 1)

3552 Looms (textile machinery) (Vol. 1)

3552 Loopers (textile machinery) (Vol. 1)

2395 Looping, for the trade (Vol. 1)

5112 Looseleaf binders—wholesale (Vol. 2)

2782 Looseleaf devices and binders (Vol. 1)

2678 Looseleaf fillers and ream paper in filler sizes, except printed (Vol. 1)

2782 Looseleaf forms and fillers, pen ruled or printed only (Vol. 1)

3851 Lorgnettes (Vol. 1)

7999 Lotteries, operation of (Vol. 2)

7999 Lottery clubs and ticket sales to individuals (Vol. 2)

9311 Lottery control boards-government (Vol. 2)

3651 Loudspeakers, electrodynamic and magnetic (Vol. 1)

5813 Lounges, cocktail (Vol. 2)

2384 Lounging robes and dressing gowns, men's, boys', and women's (Vol. 1)

2369 Lounging robes: girls', children's, and infants' (Vol. 1)

2253 Lounging robes (Vol. 1)

3442 Louver windows, all metal or metal frame (Vol. 1)

2431 Louver windows and doors, glass with wood frame (Vol. 1)

3444 Louvers, sheet metal (Vol. 1)

3914 Loving cups, silver, nickel silver, pewter, and plated (Vol. 1)

2064 Lozenges, candy: nonmedicated (Vol. 1)

2834 Lozenges, pharmaceutical (Vol. 1)

2992 Lubricating greases and oils (Vol. 1)

2992 Lubricating Oils and Greases (Vol. 1)

5172 Lubricating oils and greases—wholesale (Vol. 2)

2992 Lubricating oils, re-refining (Vol. 1)

7549 Lubricating service, automotive (Vol. 2)

3724 Lubricating systems, aircraft (Vol. 1)

3569 Lubricating systems, centralized (Vol. 1)

3569 Lubrication equipment, industrial (Vol. 1)

3569 Lubrication machinery, automatic (Vol. 1)

3714 Lubrication systems and parts, motor vehicle (Vol. 1)

3743 Lubrication systems, locomotive (Vol. 1)

3161 Luggage (Vol. 1)

5948 Luggage and Leather Goods Stores (Vol. 2)

5948 Luggage and leather goods stores—retail (Vol. 2)

2211 Luggage fabrics, cotton (Vol. 1)

3429 Luggage hardware (Vol. 1)

2396 Luggage linings (Vol. 1)

3429 Luggage racks, car top (Vol. 1)

3161 Luggage, regardless of material (Vol. 1)

7699 Luggage repair shops (Vol. 2)

5099 Luggage—wholesale (Vol. 2)

5063 Lugs and connectors, electrical—wholesale (Vol. 2)

5211 Lumber and building materials dealers—retail (Vol. 2)

5211 Lumber and Other Building Materials Dealers (Vol. 2)

5211 Lumber and planing mill product dealers—retail (Vol. 2)

2426 Lumber, hardwood dimension (Vol. 1)

2421 Lumber, kiln drying of (Vol. 1)

5031 Lumber, Plywood, Millwork and Wood Panels (Vol. 2)

5031 Lumber: rough, dressed, and finished—wholesale (Vol. 2)

2421 Lumber: rough, sawed, or planed (Vol. 1)

2421 Lumber stacking or sticking (Vol. 1)

4226 Lumber terminals, storage for hire (Vol. 2)

2329 Lumberjackets: men's and boys' (Vol. 1)

2819 Luminous compounds, radium (Vol. 1)

3646 Luminous panel ceilings (Vol. 1)

3612 Luminous tube transformers (Vol. 1)

5812 Lunch bars (Vol. 2)

3469 Lunch boxes, stamped metal (Vol. 1)

2392 Lunch cloths (Vol. 1)

5812 Lunch counters (Vol. 2)

5963 Lunch wagons, mobile—retail (Vol. 2)

2013 Luncheon meat, except poultry (Vol. 1)
2011 Luncheon meat, except poultry (Vol. 1)
2015 Luncheon meat, poultry (Vol. 1)
5812 Luncheonettes (Vol. 2)
2542 Lunchroom fixtures, except wood (Vol. 1)
2541 Lunchroom fixtures, wood (Vol. 1)
5812 Lunchrooms (Vol. 2)
3827 Lupes magnifying instruments, optical (Vol. 1)
2842 Lye, household (Vol. 1)

M

0173 Macadamia groves and farms (Vol. 2)
2098 Macaroni and products, dry: e.g., alphabets, rings, seashells (Vol. 1)
2032 Macaroni, canned (Vol. 1)
3556 Macaroni machinery: for making macaroni, spaghetti, and noodles (Vol. 1)
2098 Macaroni, Spaghetti, Vermicelli and Noodles (Vol. 1)
5149 Macaroni—wholesale (Vol. 2)
3423 Machetes (Vol. 1)
3499 Machine bases, metal (Vol. 1)
3915 Machine chain, platinum or karat gold (Vol. 1)
0722 Machine; Crop Harvesting Primarily by (Vol. 2)
3444 Machine guards, sheet metal (Vol. 1)
3484 Machine gun belts, metallic: 30 mm. (or 1.18 inch) or less (Vol. 1)
3484 Machine guns and parts, 30 mm. (or 1.18 inch) or less (Vol. 1)
3489 Machine guns, more than 30 mm. (or more than 1.18 inch) (Vol. 1)
5099 Machine guns—wholesale (Vol. 2)
0722 Machine harvesting of; Berries, (Vol. 2)
0722 Machine harvesting of; Cotton, (Vol. 2)
0722 Machine harvesting of; Fruits, (Vol. 2)
0722 Machine harvesting of; Grain, (Vol. 2)
0722 Machine harvesting of; Nuts, (Vol. 2)
0722 Machine harvesting of; Peanuts, (Vol. 2)
0722 Machine harvesting of; Sugar beets, (Vol. 2)
0722 Machine harvesting of; Sugarcane, (Vol. 2)
0722 Machine harvesting of; Vegetables, (Vol. 2)
3452 Machine keys (Vol. 1)
3423 Machine knives, except metal cutting (Vol. 1)
3545 Machine knives, metalworking (Vol. 1)
3089 Machine nuts, plastics (Vol. 1)
3469 Machine parts, stamped and pressed metal (Vol. 1)
1796 Machine rigging-contractors (Vol. 2)
3599 Machine shops, jobbing and repair (Vol. 1)
5084 Machine tool accessories—wholesale (Vol. 2)
3545 Machine tool attachments and accessories (Vol. 1)
8711 Machine tool designers (Vol. 2)
3541 Machine tool replacement and repair parts, metal cutting types (Vol. 1)
3612 Machine tool transformers (Vol. 1)
3541 Machine tools, metal cutting: e.g., exotic, chemical, explosive (Vol. 1)
3541 Machine Tools—Metal Cutting Types (Vol. 1)
3542 Machine Tools—Metal Forming Types (Vol. 1)
3542 Machine tools, metal forming types: including rebuilding (Vol. 1)

5084 Machine tools—wholesale (Vol. 2)
6159 Machinery and equipment finance leasing (Vol. 2)
3365 Machinery castings, aluminum: except die-castings (Vol. 1)
3366 Machinery castings: brass, copper, and copper-base alloy-except die-castings (Vol. 1)
3369 Machinery castings, nonferrous: except aluminum, copper, copper alloys, and die-castings (Vol. 1)
7699 Machinery cleaning (Vol. 2)
3462 Machinery forgings, ferrous: not made in rolling mills (Vol. 1)
3463 Machinery forgings, nonferrous: not made in hot-rolling mills (Vol. 1)
5084 Machinists' precision measuring tools—wholesale (Vol. 2)
3812 Machmeters (Vol. 1)
0912 Mackerel, catching of (Vol. 2)
2091 Mackerel: smoked, salted, dried, and pickled (Vol. 1)
2329 Mackinaws: men's and boys' (Vol. 1)
2511 Magazine racks, wood (Vol. 1)
5994 Magazine stands—retail (Vol. 2)
5963 Magazine subscription sales, except mail-order—retail (Vol. 2)
2789 Magazines, binding only (Vol. 1)
2754 Magazines: gravure printing (not publishing) (Vol. 1)
3484 Magazines, gun: 30 mm. (or 1.18 inch) or less (Vol. 1)
5963 Magazines, house-to-house selling (Vol. 2)
5961 Magazines, mail-order—retail (Vol. 2)
2759 Magazines, printed: except lithographed or gravure (not publishing) (Vol. 1)
2721 Magazines: publishing and printing, or publishing only (Vol. 1)
5192 Magazines—wholesale (Vol. 2)
3944 Magic lanterns (toys) (Vol. 1)
7929 Magicians (Vol. 2)
3295 Magnesite, crude: ground, calcined, or dead-burned (Vol. 1)
1459 Magnesite mining (Vol. 2)
3356 Magnesium and magnesium alloy bars, rods, shapes, sheets, strip, and tubing (Vol. 1)
3497 Magnesium and magnesium base alloy foil, not made in rolling mills (Vol. 1)
2819 Magnesium carbonate (Vol. 1)
3369 Magnesium castings, except die-castings (Vol. 1)
2819 Magnesium chloride (Vol. 1)
2819 Magnesium compounds, inorganic (Vol. 1)
3364 Magnesium die-castings (Vol. 1)
3339 Magnesium refining, primary (Vol. 1)
3356 Magnesium rolling, drawing, and extruding (Vol. 1)
3341 Magnesium smelting and refining, secondary (Vol. 1)
3357 Magnet wire, insulated (Vol. 1)
3695 Magnetic and Optical Recording Media (Vol. 1)
3674 Magnetic bubble memory device (Vol. 1)
3824 Magnetic counters (Vol. 1)
3823 Magnetic flow meters, industrial process type (Vol. 1)

3542 Magnetic forming machines (Vol. 1)

3577 Magnetic ink recognition devices, computer peripheral equipment (Vol. 1)

2899 Magnetic inspection oil and powder (Vol. 1)

3695 Magnetic recording tape, blank: reels, cassettes, and disks (Vol. 1)

5065 Magnetic recording tape—wholesale (Vol. 2)

3845 Magnetic resonance imaging device (diagnostic), nuclear (Vol. 1)

3826 Magnetic resonance imaging type apparatus, except diagnostic (Vol. 1)

3572 Magnetic storage devices for computers (Vol. 1)

3652 Magnetic tape, audio: prerecorded (Vol. 1)

1011 Magnetite mining (Vol. 2)

3674 Magnetohydrodynamic (MHD) devices (Vol. 1)

3829 Magnetometers (Vol. 1)

3671 Magnetron tubes (Vol. 1)

3264 Magnets, permanent: ceramic or ferrite (Vol. 1)

3499 Magnets, permanent: metallic (Vol. 1)

3851 Magnifiers (readers and simple magnifiers) (Vol. 1)

3827 Magnifying instruments, optical (Vol. 1)

7361 Maid registries (Vol. 2)

7349 Maid service on a contract or fee basis (Vol. 2)

7331 Mail advertising service (Vol. 2)

3469 Mail boxes, except collection boxes (Vol. 1)

4212 Mail carriers, bulk, contract: local (Vol. 2)

3444 Mail chutes, sheet metal (Vol. 1)

3444 Mail collection or storage boxes, sheet metal (Vol. 1)

4215 Mail delivery, private: except air (Vol. 2)

5961 Mail-order houses—retail (not including retail outlets) (Vol. 2)

2542 Mail pouch racks, except wood (Vol. 1)

3579 Mail tying (bundling) machines (Vol. 1)

4822 Mailgram services (Vol. 2)

2655 Mailing cases and tubes, paper fiber (metal-end or all-fiber) (Vol. 1)

7331 Mailing list compilers (Vol. 2)

3579 Mailing machines (Vol. 1)

5044 Mailing machines—wholesale (Vol. 2)

2542 Mailing racks, postal service: except wood (Vol. 1)

7331 Mailing service (Vol. 2)

3571 Mainframe computers (Vol. 1)

7349 Maintenance, building: except repairs (Vol. 2)

4173 Maintenance facilities for motor vehicle passenger transportation (Vol. 2)

2519 Malacca furniture (Vol. 1)

4959 Malaria control (Vol. 2)

2865 Maleic anhydride (Vol. 1)

3322 Malleable Iron Foundries (Vol. 1)

3423 Mallets, printers' (Vol. 1)

3069 Mallets, rubber (Vol. 1)

3949 Mallets, sports: e.g., polo, croquet (Vol. 1)

2499 Mallets, wood (Vol. 1)

2869 Malononitrile, technical grade (Vol. 1)

2083 Malt (Vol. 1)

2083 Malt: barley, rye, wheat, and corn (Vol. 1)

2082 Malt Beverages (Vol. 1)

2083 Malt byproducts (Vol. 1)

2082 Malt extract, liquors, and syrups (Vol. 1)

5149 Malt extract—wholesale (Vol. 2)

3556 Malt mills (Vol. 1)

5149 Malt—wholesale (Vol. 2)

2023 Malted milk (Vol. 1)

2083 Malthouses (Vol. 1)

8742 Management Consulting Services (Vol. 2)

8742 Management engineering consultants (Vol. 2)

8742 Management information systems consultants (Vol. 2)

6726 Management investment funds, closed-end (Vol. 2)

6722 Management investment funds, open-end (Vol. 2)

6722 Management Investment Offices—Open-End (Vol. 2)

8741 Management Services (Vol. 2)

0762 Management services, farm (Vol. 2)

6282 Manager of mutual funds, contract or fee basis (Vol. 2)

7941 Managers of individual professional athletes (Vol. 2)

6211 Managers or agents for mutual funds (Vol. 2)

6531 Managers, real estate (Vol. 2)

3931 Mandolins and parts (Vol. 1)

3545 Mandrels (Vol. 1)

2819 Manganese dioxide powder, synthetic (Vol. 1)

3313 Manganese metal (Vol. 1)

1061 Manganese ore mining (Vol. 2)

1011 Manganiferous ore mining, valued chiefly for iron content (Vol. 2)

1061 Manganite mining (Vol. 2)

2861 Mangrove extract (Vol. 1)

1623 Manhole construction-contractors (Vol. 2)

3272 Manhole covers and frames, concrete (Vol. 1)

3321 Manhole covers, metal (Vol. 1)

7231 Manicure and pedicure salons (Vol. 2)

2844 Manicure preparations (Vol. 1)

2761 Manifold Business Forms (Vol. 1)

5112 Manifold business forms—wholesale (Vol. 2)

3714 Manifolds, motor vehicle: gasoline engine (Vol. 1)

3498 Manifolds, pipe: fabricated from purchased metal pipe (Vol. 1)

2675 Manila folders (Vol. 1)

2631 Manila lined board (Vol. 1)

2621 Manila wrapping paper (Vol. 1)

2284 Manmade fiber thread (Vol. 1)

5169 Manmade fibers—wholesale (Vol. 2)

2824 Manmade Organic Fibers Except Cellulosic (Vol. 1)

2281 Manmade staple fiber yarn, spun (Vol. 1)

7389 Mannequin decorating service (Vol. 2)

5046 Mannequins—wholesale (Vol. 2)

3999 Mannikins and display forms (Vol. 1)

3823 Manometers, industrial process type (Vol. 1)

7363 Manpower pools (Vol. 2)

8331 Manpower training (Vol. 2)

1743 Mantel work-contractors (Vol. 2)

3272 Mantels, concrete (Vol. 1)

4925 Manufactured gas production and distribution (Vol. 2)

2097 Manufactured Ice (Vol. 1)

8611 Manufacturers' institutes (Vol. 2)

3999 Manufacturing Industries Not Elsewhere Classified (Vol. 1)

8742 Manufacturing management consultants (Vol. 2)

5932 Manuscripts, rare—retail (Vol. 2)

7389 Map drafting service (Vol. 2)

3829 Map plotting instruments (Vol. 1)

0831 Maple sap, gathering of (Vol. 2)

7389 Mapmaking, including aerial (Vol. 2)

2759 Maps, engraved (Vol. 1)

2754 Maps: gravure printing (not publishing) (Vol. 1)

2752 Maps, lithographed (Vol. 1)

2759 Maps, printed: except lithographed or gravure (not publishing) (Vol. 1)

2741 Maps: publishing and printing, or publishing only (Vol. 1)

3281 Marble, building: cut and shaped (Vol. 1)

5032 Marble building stone—wholesale (Vol. 2)

1429 Marble, crushed and broken-quarrying (Vol. 2)

1411 Marble, dimension-quarrying (Vol. 2)

1743 Marble installation, interior: including finishing-contractors (Vol. 2)

1741 Marble work, exterior construction-contractors (Vol. 2)

1479 Marcasite mining (Vol. 2)

2899 Margaric acid (Vol. 1)

2079 Margarine-butter blend (Vol. 1)

2079 Margarine, including imitation (Vol. 1)

2079 Margarine oil, except corn (Vol. 1)

5149 Margarine—wholesale (Vol. 2)

3931 Marimbas (Vol. 1)

4493 Marinas (Vol. 2)

2452 Marinas, prefabricated: wood (Vol. 1)

3625 Marine and navy auxiliary controls (Vol. 1)

4493 Marine basins, operation of (Vol. 2)

4491 Marine Cargo Handling (Vol. 2)

1629 Marine construction-general contractors (Vol. 2)

9711 Marine Corps (Vol. 2)

8711 Marine engineering services (Vol. 2)

3519 Marine engines: diesel, semidiesel, and other internal combustion (Vol. 1)

3429 Marine hardware (Vol. 1)

3499 Marine horns, compressed air or steam: metal (Vol. 1)

3669 Marine horns, electric (Vol. 1)

2851 Marine paints (Vol. 1)

5088 Marine propulsion machinery and equipment—wholesale (Vol. 2)

3663 Marine radio communications equipment (Vol. 1)

4499 Marine railways for drydocking, operation of (Vol. 2)

3731 Marine rigging (Vol. 1)

4499 Marine salvaging (Vol. 2)

5541 Marine service stations—retail (Vol. 2)

5088 Marine supplies (dunnage)—wholesale (Vol. 2)

5551 Marine supply dealers—retail (Vol. 2)

4499 Marine surveyors, except cargo (Vol. 2)

4492 Marine towing (Vol. 2)

4499 Marine wrecking: ships for scrap (Vol. 2)

3999 Marionettes (puppets) (Vol. 1)

3647 Marker lamps, motor vehicle (Vol. 1)

3951 Markers, soft tip: e.g., felt, fabric, plastics (Vol. 1)

2499 Market baskets, except fruit and vegetable: veneer and splint (Vol. 1)

2449 Market baskets, fruit and vegetable: veneer and splint (Vol. 1)

0723 Market Except Cotton Ginning; Crop Preparation Services for (Vol. 2)

0161 Market gardens (Vol. 2)

8732 Market research, commercial (Vol. 2)

9641 Marketing and consumer services-government (Vol. 2)

8742 Marketing consultants (Vol. 2)

3953 Marking Devices (Vol. 1)

5112 Marking devices—wholesale (Vol. 2)

3549 Marking machines, metalworking (Vol. 1)

1422 Marl, crushed and broken-quarrying (Vol. 2)

2033 Marmalade (Vol. 1)

2499 Marquetry, wood (Vol. 1)

2211 Marquisettes, cotton (Vol. 1)

2221 Marquisettes, manmade fiber (Vol. 1)

7299 Marriage bureaus (Vol. 2)

8322 Marriage counseling services (Vol. 2)

9221 Marshals' offices, police (Vol. 2)

2099 Marshmallow creme (Vol. 1)

2064 Marshmallows (Vol. 1)

2064 Marzipan (candy) (Vol. 1)

3699 Maser amplifiers (Vol. 1)

2499 Mashers, potato: wood (Vol. 1)

2672 Masking tape (Vol. 1)

2679 Masks, papier-mache (Vol. 1)

3949 Masks, sports: e.g., baseball, fencing, hockey (Vol. 1)

3546 Masonry and concrete drilling tools, power: portable (Vol. 1)

1741 Masonry-contractors (Vol. 2)

1741 Masonry, Stone Setting and Other Stonework (Vol. 2)

3423 Masons' handtools (Vol. 1)

3274 Masons' lime (Vol. 1)

5032 Masons' materials—wholesale (Vol. 2)

3826 Mass spectrometers (Vol. 1)

3826 Mass spectroscopy instrumentation (Vol. 1)

3999 Massage machines, electric: designed for beauty and barber shops (Vol. 1)

3634 Massage machines, electric: except designed for beauty and barber shop (Vol. 1)

7299 Massage parlors (Vol. 2)

2951 Mastic floor composition, hot and cold (Vol. 1)

2952 Mastic roofing composition (Vol. 1)

2499 Masts, wood (Vol. 1)

3999 Matches and match books (Vol. 1)

5199 Matches—wholesale (Vol. 2)

2211 Matelasse, cotton (Vol. 1)

5084 Materials handling equipment—wholesale (Vol. 2)

9431 Maternity and child health program administration-government (Vol. 2)

2342 Maternity bras and corsets (Vol. 1)

8069 Maternity hospitals (Vol. 2)

5621 Maternity shops—retail (Vol. 2)

2631 Matrix board (Vol. 1)

7629 Medical equipment repair, electrical (Vol. 2)
7699 Medical equipment repair, except electric (Vol. 2)
5047 Medical equipment—wholesale (Vol. 2)
5047 Medical glass—wholesale (Vol. 2)
6411 Medical insurance claims, processing of: contract or fee basis (Vol. 2)
8071 Medical Laboratories (Vol. 2)
8071 Medical laboratories, clinical (Vol. 2)
8099 Medical photography and art (Vol. 2)
8733 Medical research, noncommercial (Vol. 2)
5122 Medical rubber goods—wholesale (Vol. 2)
6324 Medical service plans (Vol. 2)
3069 Medical sundries, rubber (Vol. 1)
2326 Medical uniforms, men's (Vol. 1)
2833 Medicinal Chemicals and Botanical Products (Vol. 1)
5122 Medicinals and botanicals—wholesale (Vol. 2)
3221 Medicine bottles, glass (Vol. 1)
5122 Medicine cabinet sundries—wholesale (Vol. 2)
3231 Medicine droppers, made from purchased glass (Vol. 1)
2834 Medicines, capsuled or ampuled (Vol. 1)
2493 Medium density fiberboard (MDF) (Vol. 1)
5031 Medium density fiberboard—wholesale (Vol. 2)
1499 Meerschaum mining or quarrying (Vol. 2)
2821 Melamine resins (Vol. 1)
2024 Mellorine (Vol. 1)
0161 Melon farms (Vol. 2)
3821 Melting point apparatus, laboratory (Vol. 1)
3443 Melting pots, for metal (Vol. 1)
3255 Melting pots, glasshouse: clay (Vol. 1)
2329 Melton jackets: men's and boys' (Vol. 1)
8699 Membership Organizations Not Elsewhere Classified (Vol. 2)
7997 Membership Sports and Recreation Clubs (Vol. 2)
2678 Memorandum books, except printed (Vol. 1)
2782 Memorandum books, printed (Vol. 1)
3674 Memories, solid-state (Vol. 1)
0912 Menhaden, catching of (Vol. 2)
5611 Men's and Boys' Clothing and Accessory Stores (Vol. 2)
5136 Men's and Boys' Clothing and Furnishings (Vol. 2)
2329 Men's and Boys' Clothing Not Elsewhere Classified (Vol. 1)
2323 Men's and Boys' Neckwear (Vol. 1)
2325 Men's and Boys' Separate Trousers and Slacks (Vol. 1)
2321 Men's and Boys' Shirts Except Work Shirts (Vol. 1)
2311 Men's and Boys' Suits, Coats and Overcoats (Vol. 1)
2322 Men's and Boys' Underwear and Nightwear (Vol. 1)
2326 Men's and Boys' Work Clothing (Vol. 1)
3143 Men's Footwear Except Athletic (Vol. 1)
2252 Men's hosiery (Vol. 1)
5611 Men's wearing apparel—retail (Vol. 2)
9431 Mental health agencies-government (Vol. 2)
8063 Mental hospitals, except for the mentally retarded (Vol. 2)
8051 Mental retardation hospitals (Vol. 2)
2759 Menus, except lithographed or gravure printed (Vol. 1)
2754 Menus: gravure printing (Vol. 1)
2752 Menus, lithographed (Vol. 1)
7323 Mercantile credit reporting bureaus (Vol. 2)
6153 Mercantile financing (Vol. 2)
2261 Mercerizing cotton broadwoven fabrics (Vol. 1)
3552 Mercerizing machinery (Vol. 1)
2269 Mercerizing yarn, braided goods, and narrow fabrics: except knit and wool (Vol. 1)
2673 Merchandise bags, plastics (Vol. 1)
2674 Merchandise bags, uncoated paper (Vol. 1)
5962 Merchandising, automatic (sale of products through vending machines) (Vol. 2)
3581 Merchandising machines, automatic (Vol. 1)
5046 Merchandising machines, automatic—wholesale (Vol. 2)
5699 Merchant tailors—retail (Vol. 2)
8611 Merchants' associations, not engaged in credit investigations (Vol. 2)
5159 Merchants of raw farm products, except grain, field beans, and livestock—wholesale (Vol. 2)
3629 Mercury arc rectifiers (electrical apparatus) (Vol. 1)
2892 Mercury azide (explosives) (Vol. 1)
2819 Mercury chlorides (calomel, corrosive sublimate), except U.S.P. (Vol. 1)
2833 Mercury chlorides, U.S.P. (Vol. 1)
2819 Mercury compounds, inorganic (Vol. 1)
2833 Mercury compounds, medicinal: organic and inorganic (Vol. 1)
1099 Mercury ore mining (Vol. 2)
2819 Mercury oxides (Vol. 1)
2819 Mercury, redistilled (Vol. 1)
5051 Mercury—wholesale (Vol. 2)
3496 Mesh, made from purchased wire (Vol. 1)
3661 Message concentrators (Vol. 1)
7389 Message service, telephone answering: except beeper service (Vol. 2)
3841 Metabolism apparatus (Vol. 1)
2835 Metabolite diagnostic reagents (Vol. 1)
5039 Metal buildings—wholesale (Vol. 2)
3411 Metal Cans (Vol. 1)
5169 Metal cyanides—wholesale (Vol. 2)
3542 Metal deposit forming machines (Vol. 1)
5031 Metal doors, sash and trim—wholesale (Vol. 2)
3442 Metal Doors, Sash, Frames, Molding and Trim (Vol. 1)
2899 Metal drawing compound lubricants (Vol. 1)
3429 Metal fasteners, spring and cold-rolled steel, not made in rolling mills (Vol. 1)
3559 Metal finishing equipment for plating, except rolling mill lines (Vol. 1)
3497 Metal Foil and Leaf (Vol. 1)
1791 Metal furring-contractors (Vol. 2)
3398 Metal Heat Treating (Vol. 1)
2514 Metal Household Furniture (Vol. 1)
3567 Metal melting furnaces, industrial (Vol. 1)

2311 Military uniforms, tailored: men's and boys' (Vol. 1)
2026 Milk, acidophilus (Vol. 1)
5143 Milk and cream, fluid—wholesale (Vol. 2)
5451 Milk and other dairy products stores—retail (Vol. 2)
2026 Milk, bottled (Vol. 1)
3221 Milk bottles, glass (Vol. 1)
5149 Milk, canned or dried—wholesale (Vol. 2)
3411 Milk cans, metal (Vol. 1)
2631 Milk carton board (Vol. 1)
2656 Milk cartons, paperboard (Vol. 1)
2023 Milk: concentrated, condensed, dried, evaporated, and powdered (Vol. 1)
5143 Milk cooling stations, operated by farm assemblers (Vol. 2)
5963 Milk delivery and sale of purchased milk, without processing—retail (Vol. 2)
5143 Milk depots—wholesale (Vol. 2)
2675 Milk filter disks, die-cut from purchased paper (Vol. 1)
2621 Milk filter disks (Vol. 1)
2026 Milk, flavored (Vol. 1)
3412 Milk (fluid) shipping containers, metal (Vol. 1)
3556 Milk processing machinery (Vol. 1)
2026 Milk processing (pasteurizing, homogenizing, vitaminizing, bottling) (Vol. 1)
0241 Milk production, dairy cattle farm (Vol. 2)
2026 Milk production, except farm (Vol. 1)
0214 Milk production, goat farm (Vol. 2)
0214 Milk production; Goats' (Vol. 2)
5084 Milk products manufacturing machinery and equipment—wholesale (Vol. 2)
2026 Milk, reconstituted (Vol. 1)
0751 Milk testing for butterfat (Vol. 2)
2026 Milk, ultra-high temperature (Vol. 1)
2023 Milk, whole: canned (Vol. 1)
5083 Milking machinery and equipment—wholesale (Vol. 2)
3523 Milking machines (Vol. 1)
2023 Milkshake mix (Vol. 1)
5949 Mill end stores—retail (Vol. 2)
2269 Mill enders, contract: cotton, silk, and manmade fiber (Vol. 1)
2231 Mill menders, contract: wool, mohair, and similar animal fibers (Vol. 1)
3199 Mill strapping for textile mills, leather (Vol. 1)
5085 Mill supplies—wholesale (Vol. 2)
3547 Mill tables (rolling mill equipment) (Vol. 1)
3292 Millboard, asbestos (Vol. 1)
2353 Millinery (Vol. 1)
5632 Millinery stores—retail (Vol. 2)
5131 Millinery supplies—wholesale (Vol. 2)
2396 Millinery trimmings (Vol. 1)
5137 Millinery—wholesale (Vol. 2)
3545 Milling machine attachments (machine tool accessories) (Vol. 1)
3541 Milling machines (machine tools) (Vol. 1)
2041 Milling of grains, dry, except rice (Vol. 1)
2044 Milling of rice (Vol. 1)

3556 Mills and presses: beet, cider, and sugarcane (Vol. 1)
1499 Millstone quarrying (Vol. 2)
2431 Millwork (Vol. 1)
5211 Millwork and lumber dealers—retail (Vol. 2)
2431 Millwork products (Vol. 1)
2491 Millwork, treated (Vol. 1)
5031 Millwork—wholesale (Vol. 2)
1796 Millwrights (Vol. 2)
0119 Milo farms (Vol. 2)
5044 Mimeograph equipment—wholesale (Vol. 2)
5112 Mimeograph paper—wholesale (Vol. 2)
7334 Mimeographing service (Vol. 2)
2032 Mincemeat, canned (Vol. 1)
3535 Mine conveyors (Vol. 1)
1081 Mine development for metal mining: on a contract basis (Vol. 2)
1481 Mine development for nonmetallic minerals, except fuels: on a contract basis (Vol. 2)
1629 Mine loading and discharging station construction-general contractors (Vol. 2)
2491 Mine props, treated (Vol. 1)
2491 Mine ties, wood: treated (Vol. 1)
2411 Mine timbers, hewn (Vol. 1)
5082 Mineral beneficiation machinery—wholesale (Vol. 2)
2816 Mineral colors and pigments (Vol. 1)
2048 Mineral feed supplements (Vol. 1)
2911 Mineral jelly, produced in petroleum refineries (Vol. 1)
6211 Mineral leases, dealers in (Vol. 2)
2911 Mineral oils, natural: produced in petroleum refineries (Vol. 1)
1479 Mineral pigment mining (Vol. 2)
6211 Mineral royalties, dealers in (Vol. 2)
5191 Mineral supplements, animal—wholesale (Vol. 2)
2086 Mineral water, carbonated: bottled or canned (Vol. 1)
2911 Mineral waxes, natural: produced in petroleum refineries (Vol. 1)
3296 Mineral Wool (Vol. 1)
5033 Mineral wool insulation materials—wholesale (Vol. 2)
3296 Mineral wool roofing mats (Vol. 1)
3295 Minerals and Earths—Ground or Otherwise Treated (Vol. 1)
3648 Miners' lamps (Vol. 1)
3483 Mines and parts (ordnance) (Vol. 1)
3571 Minicomputers (Vol. 1)
9651 Minimum wage program administration-government (Vol. 2)
1629 Mining appurtenance construction-general contractors (Vol. 2)
3532 Mining cars and trucks (dollies) (Vol. 1)
3532 Mining equipment, except oil and gas field: rebuilding on a factory basis (Vol. 1)
3743 Mining locomotives and parts (Vol. 1)
3532 Mining Machinery and Equipment Except Oil and Gas Field Machinery and Equipment (Vol. 1)

3532 Mining machinery and equipment, except oil and gas field (Vol. 1)

5082 Mining machinery and equipment, except petroleum—wholesale (Vol. 2)

2816 Minium (pigments) (Vol. 1)

4225 Miniwarehouse warehousing (Vol. 2)

0271 Mink farms (Vol. 2)

0273 Minnow farms (Vol. 2)

0139 Mint farms (Vol. 2)

7699 Mirror repair shops (Vol. 2)

3231 Mirrors, framed or unframed: made from purchased glass (Vol. 1)

3827 Mirrors, optical (Vol. 1)

5719 Mirrors —retail (Vol. 2)

3231 Mirrors, transportation equipment: made from purchased glass (Vol. 1)

5699 Miscellaneous Apparel and Accessory Stores (Vol. 2)

6159 Miscellaneous Business Credit Institutions (Vol. 2)

3496 Miscellaneous Fabricated Wire Products (Vol. 1)

5499 Miscellaneous Food Stores (Vol. 2)

5399 Miscellaneous General Merchandise Store (Vol. 2)

5719 Miscellaneous Home Furnishings Stores (Vol. 2)

0919 Miscellaneous Marine Products (Vol. 2)

1499 Miscellaneous Nonmetallic Minerals Except Fuels (Vol. 2)

7299 Miscellaneous Personal Services Not Elsewhere Classified (Vol. 2)

2741 Miscellaneous Publishing (Vol. 1)

5999 Miscellaneous Retail Stores Not Elsewhere Classified (Vol. 2)

3449 Miscellaneous Structural Metal Work (Vol. 1)

1629 Missile facilities construction-general contractors (Vol. 2)

3462 Missile forgings, ferrous: not made in rolling mills (Vol. 1)

3463 Missile forgings, nonferrous: not made in hot-rolling mills (Vol. 1)

3812 Missile guidance systems and equipment (Vol. 1)

3443 Missile silos and components, metal plate (Vol. 1)

3483 Missile warheads (Vol. 1)

3423 Mitre boxes, metal (Vol. 1)

2211 Mitten flannel, cotton (Vol. 1)

3151 Mittens, leather (Vol. 1)

5136 Mittens, men's and boys'—wholesale (Vol. 2)

2259 Mittens (Vol. 1)

3069 Mittens, rubber (Vol. 1)

5137 Mittens: women's, children's, and infants'—wholesale (Vol. 2)

2819 Mixed acid (Vol. 1)

4925 Mixed, Manufactured or Liquefied Petroleum Gas Production and/or Distribution Not Elsewhere Classified (Vol. 2)

3556 Mixers and whippers, electric: for food manufacturing industries (Vol. 1)

5082 Mixers, construction and mining—wholesale (Vol. 2)

3531 Mixers: e.g., concrete, ore, sand, slag, plaster, mortar, bituminous (Vol. 1)

3556 Mixers, feed: except agricultural machinery (Vol. 1)

3556 Mixers, food: commercial types (Vol. 1)

3443 Mixers for hot metal (Vol. 1)

2045 Mixes, flour: e.g., pancake, cake, biscuit, doughnut (Vol. 1)

2041 Mixes, flour: e.g., pancake, cake, biscuit, doughnut (Vol. 1)

2451 Mobile buildings for commercial use (e.g., offices, banks) (Vol. 1)

2451 Mobile classrooms (Vol. 1)

3663 Mobile communications equipment (Vol. 1)

2451 Mobile dwellings (Vol. 1)

5271 Mobile Home Dealers (Vol. 2)

5271 Mobile home equipment—retail (Vol. 2)

5271 Mobile home parts and accessories—retail (Vol. 2)

7519 Mobile home rental, except on site (Vol. 2)

1521 Mobile home repair, on site-general contractors (Vol. 2)

1799 Mobile home site setup and tie down-contractors (Vol. 2)

2451 Mobile Homes (Vol. 1)

2451 Mobile homes, except recreational (Vol. 1)

5271 Mobile homes, new and used—retail (Vol. 2)

5039 Mobile homes—wholesale (Vol. 2)

3711 Mobile lounges (motor vehicle) (Vol. 1)

3537 Mobile straddle carriers (Vol. 1)

3149 Moccasins (Vol. 1)

2221 Modacrylic broadwoven fabrics (Vol. 1)

2824 Modacrylic fibers (Vol. 1)

2281 Modacrylic yarn, made from purchased staple: spun (Vol. 1)

5092 Model kits—wholesale (Vol. 2)

7361 Model registries (Vol. 2)

3952 Modeling clay (Vol. 1)

8299 Modeling schools, clothes (Vol. 2)

7363 Modeling service (Vol. 2)

3842 Models, anatomical (Vol. 1)

3999 Models, except toy and hobby (Vol. 1)

3944 Models, toy and hobby: e.g., airplane, boat, ship, railroad equipment (Vol. 1)

3661 Modems (Vol. 1)

5065 Modems—wholesale (Vol. 2)

2522 Modular furniture systems, office: except wood (Vol. 1)

2521 Modular furniture systems, office, wood (Vol. 1)

1521 Modular housing, single-family (assembled on site)-general contractors (Vol. 2)

3674 Modules, solid-state (Vol. 1)

0214 Mohair production (Vol. 2)

5159 Mohair, raw—wholesale (Vol. 2)

2282 Mohair yarn: twisting, winding, or spooling (Vol. 1)

3579 Moisteners, gummed tape: for store and office use (Vol. 1)

3826 Moisture analysers, laboratory type (Vol. 1)

3823 Moisture meters, industrial process type (Vol. 1)

2063 Molasses beet pulp (Vol. 1)

5043 Motion picture studio and theater equipment—wholesale (Vol. 2)

7833 Motion picture theaters, drive-in (Vol. 2)

7832 Motion Picture Theaters Except Drive-In (Vol. 2)

3711 Motor buses, except trackless trolley (Vol. 1)

9621 Motor carrier licensing and inspection offices-government (Vol. 2)

3625 Motor control accessories, including overload relays (Vol. 1)

3625 Motor control centers (Vol. 1)

3625 Motor controls, electric (Vol. 1)

5063 Motor controls, electric—wholesale (Vol. 2)

3621 Motor generator sets, except automotive and turbogenerators (Vol. 1)

5561 Motor home dealers—retail (Vol. 2)

7519 Motor home rental (Vol. 2)

3716 Motor Homes (Vol. 1)

3716 Motor homes, self-contained: made on purchased chassis (Vol. 1)

3711 Motor homes, self-contained (Vol. 1)

5012 Motor homes—wholesale (Vol. 2)

3621 Motor housings (Vol. 1)

7538 Motor repair, automotive (Vol. 2)

3751 Motor scooters and parts (Vol. 1)

5571 Motor scooters—retail (Vol. 2)

5012 Motor scooters—wholesale (Vol. 2)

3625 Motor starters, contactors, and controllers, industrial (Vol. 1)

3596 Motor truck scales (Vol. 1)

3715 Motor truck trailers (Vol. 1)

3711 Motor trucks, except off-highway (Vol. 1)

5511 Motor vehicle dealers, new and used cars—retail (Vol. 2)

5521 Motor vehicle dealers, used cars only—retail (Vol. 2)

3714 Motor vehicle gasoline engine rebuilding on a factory basis (Vol. 1)

3429 Motor vehicle hardware (Vol. 1)

9621 Motor vehicle licensing and inspection offices-government (Vol. 2)

3714 Motor Vehicle Parts and Accessories (Vol. 1)

3714 Motor vehicle parts and accessories, except motor vehicle stampings (Vol. 1)

5015 Motor Vehicle Parts—Used (Vol. 2)

5015 Motor vehicle parts, used—wholesale or retail (Vol. 2)

5064 Motor vehicle radios—wholesale (Vol. 2)

5013 Motor Vehicle Supplies and New Parts (Vol. 2)

5014 Motor vehicle tires and tubes—wholesale (Vol. 2)

3711 Motor Vehicles and Passenger Car Bodies (Vol. 1)

5012 Motor vehicles, commercial—wholesale (Vol. 2)

3711 Motor vehicles, including amphibian (Vol. 1)

3751 Motorbikes and parts (Vol. 1)

5551 Motorboat dealers—retail (Vol. 2)

3732 Motorboats, inboard and outboard: building and repairing (Vol. 1)

5571 Motorcycle Dealers (Vol. 2)

5571 Motorcycle dealers—retail (Vol. 2)

3647 Motorcycle lamps (Vol. 1)

5571 Motorcycle parts—retail (Vol. 2)

5013 Motorcycle parts—wholesale (Vol. 2)

7948 Motorcycle racing (Vol. 2)

7999 Motorcycle rental (Vol. 2)

7699 Motorcycle repair service (Vol. 2)

3751 Motorcycles and parts (Vol. 1)

3751 Motorcycles, Bicycles and Parts (Vol. 1)

5012 Motorcycles—wholesale (Vol. 2)

3594 Motors, air or hydraulic (fluid power) (Vol. 1)

3621 Motors and Generators (Vol. 1)

3621 Motors, electric: except engine starting motors and gear motors (Vol. 1)

5063 Motors, electric—wholesale (Vol. 2)

3566 Motors, gear (Vol. 1)

3594 Motors, pneumatic (Vol. 1)

3694 Motors, starting: motor vehicle and aircraft (Vol. 1)

2371 Mounting heads on fur neckpieces (Vol. 1)

7389 Mounting merchandise on cards on a contract or fee basis (Vol. 2)

2789 Mounting of maps and samples, for the trade (Vol. 1)

3999 Mountings, comb and hairpin: except precious metal (Vol. 1)

3851 Mountings, eyeglass and spectacle (Vol. 1)

3911 Mountings, gold and silver: for pens, leather goods, and umbrellas (Vol. 1)

3484 Mounts for guns, 30 mm. (or 1.18 inch) or less (Vol. 1)

3931 Mouthpieces for musical instruments (Vol. 1)

3069 Mouthpieces for pipes and cigarette holders, rubber (Vol. 1)

2844 Mouthwashes (Vol. 1)

3873 Movements, watch or clock (Vol. 1)

3523 Mowers and mower-conditioners, hay (Vol. 1)

5083 Mowers, power—wholesale (Vol. 2)

0782 Mowing highway center strips and edges (Vol. 2)

0722 Mowing, raking, baling, and chopping; Hay (Vol. 2)

2891 Mucilage (Vol. 1)

3531 Mud jacks (Vol. 1)

1389 Mud service, oil field drilling: on a contract basis (Vol. 2)

7533 Mufflers, automotive: installation, repair, or sales and installation (Vol. 2)

3714 Mufflers, exhaust: motor vehicle (Vol. 1)

2323 Mufflers: men's and boys' (Vol. 1)

5136 Mufflers, men's and boys'—wholesale (Vol. 2)

2253 Mufflers (Vol. 1)

3524 Mulchers, residential lawn and garden (Vol. 1)

0272 Mule farms (Vol. 2)

5159 Mules—wholesale (Vol. 2)

7334 Multigraphing service (Vol. 2)

7334 Multilithing service (Vol. 2)

2741 Multimedia educational kits: publishing and printing, or publishing only (Vol. 1)

3825 Multimeters (Vol. 1)

3231 Multiple-glazed insulating units, made from purchased glass (Vol. 1)

3211 Multiple-glazed insulating units (Vol. 1)

6531 Multiple listing services, real estate (Vol. 2)
3663 Multiplex equipment, radio (Vol. 1)
3661 Multiplex equipment, telephone and telegraph (Vol. 1)
4841 Multipoint distribution systems (MDS) services (Vol. 2)
8322 Multiservice centers, neighborhood (Vol. 2)
3575 Multistation CRT/teleprinters (Vol. 1)
2674 Multiwall bags, paper (Vol. 1)
2819 Muriate of potash, not produced at mines (Vol. 1)
3841 Muscle exercise apparatus, ophthalmic (Vol. 1)
1499 Muscovite mining (Vol. 2)
1542 Museum construction-general contractors (Vol. 2)
8412 Museums (Vol. 2)
8412 Museums and Art Galleries (Vol. 2)
0182 Mushroom spawn, production of (Vol. 2)
2033 Mushrooms, canned (Vol. 1)
0182 Mushrooms, growing of (Vol. 2)
8999 Music arrangers (Vol. 2)
2732 Music books: printing or printing and binding, not publishing (Vol. 1)
2731 Music books: publishing and printing, or publishing only (Vol. 1)
3999 Music boxes (Vol. 1)
3651 Music distribution apparatus, except records or tape (Vol. 1)
7993 Music distribution systems, coin-operated (Vol. 2)
7389 Music distribution systems, except coin-operated (Vol. 2)
6794 Music licensing to radio stations (Vol. 2)
3931 Music rolls, perforated (Vol. 1)
6794 Music royalties, sheet and record (Vol. 2)
8299 Music schools (Vol. 2)
2759 Music, sheet: except lithographed or gravure (not publishing) (Vol. 1)
2754 Music, sheet: gravure printing (not publishing) (Vol. 1)
2741 Music, sheet: publishing and printing, or publishing only (Vol. 1)
3931 Music stands (Vol. 1)
7812 Music video production (Vol. 2)
3999 Musical chests (Vol. 1)
3931 Musical instrument accessories: e.g., reeds, mouthpieces, stands, traps (Vol. 1)
3651 Musical instrument amplifiers (Vol. 1)
3161 Musical instrument cases (Vol. 1)
7699 Musical instrument repair shops (Vol. 2)
5736 Musical instrument stores—retail (Vol. 2)
5932 Musical instrument stores, secondhand—retail (Vol. 2)
3931 Musical Instruments (Vol. 1)
3931 Musical instruments, including electric and electronic (Vol. 1)
5736 Musical Instruments Stores (Vol. 2)
3944 Musical instruments, toy (Vol. 1)
5099 Musical instruments—wholesale (Vol. 2)
7929 Musicians (Vol. 2)
2211 Muslin, cotton (Vol. 1)
0913 Mussels, taking of (Vol. 2)
2869 Mustard gas (Vol. 1)

2035 Mustard, prepared (wet) (Vol. 1)
0119 Mustard seed farms (Vol. 2)
2011 Mutton (Vol. 1)
6321 Mutual accident associations (Vol. 2)
6141 Mutual benefit associations (Vol. 2)
6331 Mutual fire, marine, and casualty insurance (Vol. 2)
6211 Mutual fund agents (Vol. 2)
6722 Mutual fund sales on own account (Vol. 2)
6211 Mutual funds, selling by independent salesperson (Vol. 2)
2861 Myrobalans extract (Vol. 1)

N

2833 N-methylpiperazine (Vol. 1)
2822 N-type rubber (Vol. 1)
3728 Nacelles, aircraft (Vol. 1)
3542 Nail heading machines (Vol. 1)
2441 Nailed and Lock Corner Wood Boxes and Shook (Vol. 1)
3399 Nails, nonferrous metal (including wire) (Vol. 1)
3315 Nails, steel: wire or cut (Vol. 1)
5051 Nails—wholesale (Vol. 2)
2211 Nainsook, cotton (Vol. 1)
3479 Nameplates: engraved and etched (Vol. 1)
3993 Nameplates, metal: except e.g., engraved, etched, chased (Vol. 1)
2899 Napalm (Vol. 1)
5172 Naphtha, except bulk stations and terminals—wholesale (Vol. 2)
2911 Naphtha, produced in petroleum refineries (Vol. 1)
2865 Naphtha, solvent: made in chemical plants (Vol. 1)
2865 Naphthalene chips and flakes (Vol. 1)
2865 Naphthalene, made in chemical plants (Vol. 1)
2869 Naphthalene sulfonic acid condensates (Vol. 1)
2851 Naphthanate driers (Vol. 1)
2869 Naphthenic acid soaps (Vol. 1)
2911 Naphthenic acids, produced in petroleum refineries (Vol. 1)
2865 Naphthol, alpha and beta (Vol. 1)
2865 Naphtholsulfonic acids (Vol. 1)
2621 Napkin stock, paper (Vol. 1)
2392 Napkins, fabric and nonwoven textiles (Vol. 1)
2676 Napkins, paper (Vol. 1)
5113 Napkins, paper—wholesale (Vol. 2)
2676 Napkins, sanitary (Vol. 1)
3552 Napping machines (textile machinery) (Vol. 1)
2261 Napping of cotton broadwoven fabrics (Vol. 1)
2262 Napping of manmade fiber and silk broadwoven fabrics (Vol. 1)
2231 Napping of wool, mohair, and similar animal fiber fabrics (Vol. 1)
2241 Narrow Fabric and Other Smallwares Mills—Cotton, Wool, Silk and Manmade Fiber (Vol. 1)
2231 Narrow fabrics, dyeing and finishing: wool, mohair, and similar animal fibers (Vol. 1)
2241 Narrow fabrics, elastic: woven or braided (Vol. 1)
2269 Narrow fabrics, except knit and wool: bleaching, dyeing, and finishing (Vol. 1)
5131 Narrow fabrics—wholesale (Vol. 2)

2241 Narrow woven fabrics: cotton, rayon, wool, silk, glass, and manmade fiber (Vol. 1)

2299 Narrow woven fabrics: linen, jute, hemp, and ramie (Vol. 1)

6021 National Commercial Banks (Vol. 2)

6111 National Consumer Cooperative Bank (Vol. 2)

6019 National Credit Union Administration (NCUA) (Vol. 2)

9711 National Guard (Vol. 2)

9711 National Security (Vol. 2)

2032 Nationality specialty foods, canned (Vol. 1)

2032 Native foods, canned (Vol. 1)

2038 Native foods, frozen (Vol. 1)

1499 Natural abrasives mining (except sand) (Vol. 2)

1623 Natural gas compressing station construction-general contractors (Vol. 2)

4924 Natural Gas Distribution (Vol. 2)

1321 Natural Gas Liquids (Vol. 2)

1321 Natural gas liquids production (Vol. 2)

1311 Natural gas production (Vol. 2)

4922 Natural gas storage (Vol. 2)

4922 Natural Gas Transmission (Vol. 2)

4923 Natural Gas Transmission and Distribution (Vol. 2)

1321 Natural gasoline production (Vol. 2)

2022 Natural, Processed and Imitation Cheese (Vol. 1)

7999 Natural wonders, tourist attraction: commercial (Vol. 2)

8049 Naturopaths, offices of (Vol. 2)

7699 Nautical and navigational instrument repair, except electric (Vol. 2)

3812 Nautical instruments (Vol. 1)

3489 Naval artillery (Vol. 1)

3731 Naval ships, building and repairing (Vol. 1)

2861 Naval stores, gum: processing but not gathering or warehousing (Vol. 1)

5169 Naval stores—wholesale (Vol. 2)

2861 Naval stores, wood (Vol. 1)

3812 Navigational instruments (Vol. 1)

9711 Navy (Vol. 2)

2082 Near beer (Vol. 1)

2371 Neckpieces, fur (Vol. 1)

2221 Necktie fabrics, manmade fiber and silk: broadwoven (Vol. 1)

2396 Necktie linings, cutting of (Vol. 1)

2323 Neckties: men's and boys' (Vol. 1)

2253 Neckties (Vol. 1)

2323 Neckwear: men's and boys' (Vol. 1)

5136 Neckwear, men's and boys'—wholesale (Vol. 2)

2339 Neckwear: women's, misses' and juniors' (Vol. 1)

0175 Nectarine orchards and farms (Vol. 2)

2033 Nectars, fruit (Vol. 1)

3841 Needle holders, surgical (Vol. 1)

3965 Needles, hand and machine (Vol. 1)

3841 Needles, hypodermic (Vol. 1)

3841 Needles, suture (Vol. 1)

2395 Needlework, art (Vol. 1)

5949 Needlework stores—retail (Vol. 2)

2254 Negligees (Vol. 1)

2341 Negligees: women's, children's, and infants' (Vol. 1)

2341 Negligees: women's, misses', children's, and infants' (Vol. 1)

8322 Neighborhood centers (Vol. 2)

2813 Neon (Vol. 1)

3993 Neon signs (Vol. 1)

5046 Neon signs—wholesale (Vol. 2)

2822 Neoprene (Vol. 1)

1459 Nepheline syenite quarrying (Vol. 2)

3826 Nephelometers, except meteorological (Vol. 1)

3829 Nephoscopes (Vol. 1)

3552 Net and lace machines (Vol. 1)

5131 Net goods—wholesale (Vol. 2)

2211 Nets and nettings (Vol. 1)

3949 Nets: e.g., badminton, basketball, tennis-not made in weaving mills (Vol. 1)

2399 Nets, fishing (Vol. 1)

3999 Nets, hair (Vol. 1)

2399 Nets, launderers' and dyers' (Vol. 1)

2298 Nets, rope (Vol. 1)

2258 Netting, knit (Vol. 1)

2258 Netting made on a lace or net machine (Vol. 1)

3089 Netting, plastics (Vol. 1)

3496 Netting, woven wire: made from purchased wire (Vol. 1)

3825 Network analyzers (Vol. 1)

7373 Network systems integration, computer (Vol. 2)

8011 Neurologists, offices of (Vol. 2)

2084 Neutral fruit spirits and neutral brandy (Vol. 1)

2085 Neutral spirits for beverage purposes, except fruit (Vol. 1)

5182 Neutral spirits—wholesale (Vol. 2)

3826 Neutron activation analysis instruments (Vol. 1)

5511 New and Used Motor Vehicle Dealers (Vol. 2)

2431 Newel posts, wood (Vol. 1)

7383 News correspondents, independent (Vol. 2)

5994 News Dealers and Newsstands (Vol. 2)

5994 News dealers—retail (Vol. 2)

7383 News feature syndicates (Vol. 2)

7383 News pictures, gathering and distributing (Vol. 2)

7383 News reporting services for newspapers and periodicals (Vol. 2)

7383 News Syndicates (Vol. 2)

2621 News tablet paper (Vol. 1)

7383 News ticker services (Vol. 2)

2631 Newsboard (Vol. 1)

2675 Newsboard, pasted (Vol. 1)

7313 Newspaper advertising representatives, not auxiliary to publishing (Vol. 2)

5192 Newspaper agencies—wholesale (Vol. 2)

2711 Newspaper branch offices, editorial and advertising (Vol. 1)

8999 Newspaper columnists (Vol. 2)

2754 Newspapers: gravure printing (not publishing) (Vol. 1)

5963 Newspapers, home delivery: except by newspaper printers or publishers (Vol. 2)

2752 Newspapers, lithographed: not published (Vol. 1)

2759 Newspapers, printed: except lithographed or gravure (not publishing) (Vol. 1)

2711 Newspapers: publishing and printing, or publishing only (Vol. 1)

2711 Newspapers—Publishing, or Publishing and Printing (Vol. 1)

2621 Newsprint (Vol. 1)

2678 Newsprint tablets and pads (Vol. 1)

5994 Newsstands—retail (Vol. 2)

3951 Nibs (pen points): gold, steel, or other metal (Vol. 1)

2819 Nickel ammonium sulfate (Vol. 1)

3356 Nickel and nickel alloy pipe, plates, sheets, strips, and tubing (Vol. 1)

3691 Nickel cadmium storage batteries (Vol. 1)

2819 Nickel carbonate (Vol. 1)

2819 Nickel compounds, inorganic (Vol. 1)

3497 Nickel foil, not made in rolling mills (Vol. 1)

1061 Nickel ore mining (Vol. 2)

3339 Nickel refining, primary (Vol. 1)

3341 Nickel smelting and refining, secondary (Vol. 1)

2819 Nickel sulfate (Vol. 1)

2879 Nicotine and salts (Vol. 1)

2879 Nicotine bearing insecticides (Vol. 1)

5813 Night clubs (Vol. 2)

2254 Nightgowns (Vol. 1)

2341 Nightgowns: women's, misses', children's, and infants' (Vol. 1)

2322 Nightshirts: men's and boys' (Vol. 1)

2322 Nightwear: men's and boys' (Vol. 1)

5136 Nightwear, men's and boys'—wholesale (Vol. 2)

2254 Nightwear (Vol. 1)

5137 Nightwear: women's, children's, and infants'—wholesale (Vol. 2)

2341 Nightwear: women's, misses', children's, and infants' (Vol. 1)

3498 Nipples, metal pipe: except pressure and soil pipe (Vol. 1)

3321 Nipples, pipe: pressure and soil pipe-cast iron (Vol. 1)

3069 Nipples, rubber (Vol. 1)

2821 Nitrate resins: cellulose (Vol. 1)

2892 Nitrated carbohydrates (explosives) (Vol. 1)

2873 Nitric acid (Vol. 1)

2822 Nitrile-butadiene rubbers (Vol. 1)

2822 Nitrile-chloroprene rubbers (Vol. 1)

2822 Nitrile type rubber (Vol. 1)

2865 Nitro dyes (Vol. 1)

2865 Nitroaniline (Vol. 1)

2865 Nitrobenzene (Vol. 1)

2823 Nitrocellulose fibers (Vol. 1)

2821 Nitrocellulose plastics (pyroxylin) (Vol. 1)

2892 Nitrocellulose powder (explosives) (Vol. 1)

2834 Nitrofuran preparations (Vol. 1)

2813 Nitrogen (Vol. 1)

2873 Nitrogen solutions (fertilizer) (Vol. 1)

2873 Nitrogenous Fertilizers (Vol. 1)

2892 Nitroglycerin (explosives) (Vol. 1)

2892 Nitromannitol (explosives) (Vol. 1)

2865 Nitrophenol (Vol. 1)

2865 Nitroso dyes (Vol. 1)

2892 Nitrostarch (explosives) (Vol. 1)

2892 Nitrosugars (explosives) (Vol. 1)

2869 Nitrous ether (Vol. 1)

2813 Nitrous oxide (Vol. 1)

3321 Nodular iron castings (Vol. 1)

2299 Noils, wool and mohair (Vol. 1)

5159 Noils, wool—wholesale (Vol. 2)

3842 Noise protectors, personal (Vol. 1)

9999 Nonclassifiable Establishments (Vol. 2)

3297 Nonclay Refractories (Vol. 1)

3297 Nonclay refractories (Vol. 1)

8733 Noncommercial Research Organizations (Vol. 2)

3644 Noncurrent-Carrying Wiring Devices (Vol. 1)

6091 Nondeposit trust companies (Vol. 2)

6091 Nondeposit Trust Facilities (Vol. 2)

5199 Nondurable Goods Not Elsewhere Classified (Vol. 2)

3313 Nonferrous additive alloys, high percentage: except copper (Vol. 1)

3364 Nonferrous Die-Castings Except Aluminum (Vol. 1)

3463 Nonferrous Forgings (Vol. 1)

3463 Nonferrous forgings, not made in hot-rolling mills (Vol. 1)

3366 Nonferrous foundries: brass, bronze, copper, and copper base alloy (Vol. 1)

3369 Nonferrous Foundries Except Aluminum and Copper (Vol. 1)

3369 Nonferrous foundries: except aluminum, copper, and copper alloys (Vol. 1)

5051 Nonferrous metal, except precious: e.g., sheets, bars, rods—wholesale (Vol. 2)

3369 Nonferrous metal foundries, except aluminum, copper, and die-castings (Vol. 1)

3369 Nonferrous metal machinery castings: except aluminum, copper, and die-castings (Vol. 1)

3341 Nonferrous metal smelting and refining, secondary (Vol. 1)

5093 Nonferrous metals scrap—wholesale (Vol. 2)

3339 Nonferrous refining, primary: except copper and aluminum (Vol. 1)

3356 Nonferrous rolling, drawing, and extruding: except copper and aluminum (Vol. 1)

3339 Nonferrous smelting, primary: except copper and aluminum (Vol. 1)

3299 Nonmetallic Mineral Products Not Elsewhere Classified (Vol. 1)

5052 Nonmetallic minerals and concentrates, crude: except petroleum—wholesale (Vol. 2)

1481 Nonmetallic Minerals Services Except Fuels (Vol. 2)

6512 Nonresidential Building Operators (Vol. 2)

6512 Nonresidential buildings, operators of (Vol. 2)

7812 Nontheatrical motion picture production (Vol. 2)

2297 Nonwoven Fabrics (Vol. 1)

2297 Nonwoven fabrics, except felt (Vol. 1)

2098 Noodles: egg, plain, and water (Vol. 1)

2099 Noodles, fried (e.g., Chinese) (Vol. 1)

2099 Noodles, uncooked: packaged with other ingredients (Vol. 1)

2869 Normal hexyl decalin (Vol. 1)

3769 Nose cones, guided missile (Vol. 1)

3842 Nose plugs (Vol. 1)

7389 Notaries public (Vol. 2)

6211 Note brokers (Vol. 2)

2678 Notebooks, including mechanically bound by wire, plastics, etc. (Vol. 1)

5949 Notion stores—retail (Vol. 2)

5131 Notions—wholesale (Vol. 2)

2258 Nottingham lace (Vol. 1)

3993 Novelties, advertising (Vol. 1)

3499 Novelties and specialties, metal: except advertising novelties (Vol. 1)

3999 Novelties: bone, beaded, and shell (Vol. 1)

3961 Novelties, costume: except precious metal and gems (Vol. 1)

3231 Novelties, glass: e.g., fruit, foliage, flowers, animals, made from purchased glass (Vol. 1)

3199 Novelties, leather (Vol. 1)

2679 Novelties, paper (Vol. 1)

5199 Novelties, paper—wholesale (Vol. 2)

2499 Novelties, wood fiber (Vol. 1)

2514 Novelty furniture, metal (Vol. 1)

3229 Novelty glassware: made in glassmaking plants (Vol. 1)

5961 Novelty merchandise, mail-order—retail (Vol. 2)

5947 Novelty shops—retail (Vol. 2)

2395 Novelty stitching, for the trade (Vol. 1)

3429 Nozzles, fire fighting (Vol. 1)

3432 Nozzles, lawn hose (Vol. 1)

3432 Nozzles, plumbers' (Vol. 1)

3499 Nozzles, spray: aerosol paint, and insecticides (Vol. 1)

3443 Nuclear core structurals, metal plate (Vol. 1)

2819 Nuclear cores, inorganic (Vol. 1)

9631 Nuclear energy inspection and regulation offices (Vol. 2)

2819 Nuclear fuel reactor cores, inorganic (Vol. 1)

2819 Nuclear fuel scrap reprocessing (Vol. 1)

2869 Nuclear fuels, organic (Vol. 1)

3829 Nuclear instrument modules (Vol. 1)

3844 Nuclear irradiation equipment (Vol. 1)

3462 Nuclear power plant forgings, ferrous: not made in rolling mills (Vol. 1)

3829 Nuclear radiation detection and monitoring instruments (Vol. 1)

1629 Nuclear reactor containment structure construction-general contractors (Vol. 2)

3559 Nuclear reactor control rod drive mechanisms (Vol. 1)

3823 Nuclear reactor controls (Vol. 1)

3443 Nuclear reactors, military and industrial (Vol. 1)

3443 Nuclear shielding, metal plate (Vol. 1)

7032 Nudist camps (Vol. 2)

3579 Numbering machines, office and store: mechanical (Vol. 1)

3953 Numbering stamps, with rubber type: hand (Vol. 1)

3625 Numerical controls (Vol. 1)

3541 Numerically controlled metal cutting machine tools (Vol. 1)

5999 Numismatist shops—retail (Vol. 2)

0831 Nurseries, forest (Vol. 2)

0181 Nurseries: growing of flowers and shrubbery, except forest shrubbery; Field (Vol. 2)

2514 Nursery furniture, metal (Vol. 1)

2511 Nursery furniture, wood (Vol. 1)

0181 Nursery Products; Ornamental (Vol. 2)

8351 Nursery schools (Vol. 2)

0181 Nursery stock, growing of (Vol. 2)

5261 Nursery stock, seeds and bulbs—retail (Vol. 2)

5193 Nursery stock—wholesale (Vol. 2)

8049 Nurses, registered and practical: offices of, except home health care services (Vol. 2)

7361 Nurses' registries (Vol. 2)

8059 Nursing and Personal Care Facilities Not Elsewhere Classified (Vol. 2)

8059 Nursing homes except skilled and intermediate care facilities (Vol. 2)

8052 Nursing homes, intermediate care (Vol. 2)

8051 Nursing homes, skilled (Vol. 2)

8249 Nursing schools, practical (Vol. 2)

3429 Nut crackers and pickers, metal (Vol. 1)

0173 Nut groves and farms; Tree (Vol. 2)

0723 Nut hulling and shelling (Vol. 2)

2079 Nut margarine (Vol. 1)

3312 Nut rods, iron and steel: made in steel works or rolling mills (Vol. 1)

3523 Nut shellers (agricultural machinery) (Vol. 1)

5441 Nut stores—retail (Vol. 2)

0173 Nut (tree) groves and farms (Vol. 2)

8049 Nutritionists, offices of (Vol. 2)

2064 Nuts, candy covered (Vol. 1)

2068 Nuts, dehydrated or dried (Vol. 1)

2064 Nuts, glace (Vol. 1)

0723 Nuts; Hulling and shelling of tree (Vol. 2)

0722 Nuts, machine harvesting of (Vol. 2)

3452 Nuts, metal (Vol. 1)

0179 Nuts Not Elsewhere Classified; Fruits and Tree (Vol. 2)

3089 Nuts, plastics (Vol. 1)

5145 Nuts, salted or roasted—wholesale (Vol. 2)

2068 Nuts: salted, roasted, cooked, or canned (Vol. 1)

0173 Nuts; Tree (Vol. 2)

5159 Nuts, unprocessed or shelled only—wholesale (Vol. 2)

2221 Nylon broadwoven fabrics (Vol. 1)

2824 Nylon fibers and bristles (Vol. 1)

5131 Nylon piece goods—wholesale (Vol. 2)

2821 Nylon resins (Vol. 1)

2284 Nylon thread (Vol. 1)

2281 Nylon yarn, spinning of staple (Vol. 1)

2282 Nylon yarn: throwing, twisting, winding, or spooling (Vol. 1)

2252 Nylons, except women's full-length and knee-length (Vol. 1)

2251 Nylons, women's full-length and knee-length (Vol. 1)

2221 Nytril broadwoven fabrics (Vol. 1)

O

2861 Oak extract (Vol. 1)

2299 Oakum (Vol. 1)

2499 Oars, wood (Vol. 1)

0119 Oat farms (Vol. 2)

2043 Oatmeal (cereal breakfast food) (Vol. 1)

2048 Oats: crimped, pulverized, and rolled: except breakfast food (Vol. 1)

2043 Oats, rolled (cereal breakfast food) (Vol. 1)

5153 Oats—wholesale (Vol. 2)

5932 Objects of art, antique—retail (Vol. 2)

3931 Oboes (Vol. 1)

7999 Observation tower operation (Vol. 2)

8011 Obstetricians, offices of (Vol. 2)

3931 Ocarinas (Vol. 1)

8049 Occupational therapists, offices of (Vol. 2)

1479 Ocher mining (Vol. 2)

2816 Ochers (Vol. 1)

3931 Octophones (Vol. 1)

8011 Oculists, offices of (Vol. 2)

3824 Odometers (Vol. 1)

3489 Oerlikon guns (Vol. 1)

3061 Off-highway machinery and equipment mechanical rubber goods: molded, extruded, and lathe-cut (Vol. 1)

7999 Off-track betting (Vol. 2)

8322 Offender rehabilitation agencies (Vol. 2)

8322 Offender self-help agencies (Vol. 2)

2542 Office and Store Fixtures, Partitions, Shelving and Lockers Except Wood (Vol. 1)

7373 Office automation, computer systems integration (Vol. 2)

1542 Office building construction-general contractors (Vol. 2)

7349 Office cleaning service (Vol. 2)

5044 Office Equipment (Vol. 2)

2542 Office fixtures, except wood (Vol. 1)

2541 Office fixtures, wood (Vol. 1)

2522 Office Furniture Except Wood (Vol. 1)

2522 Office furniture, except wood (Vol. 1)

5021 Office furniture—wholesale (Vol. 2)

2521 Office furniture, wood (Vol. 1)

7363 Office help supply service (Vol. 2)

7359 Office machine rental and leasing, except computers (Vol. 2)

7629 Office machine repair, electrical: except typewriters, computers, and computer peripheral equipment (Vol. 2)

3579 Office Machines Not Elsewhere Classified (Vol. 1)

8741 Office management services (Vol. 2)

5112 Office supplies—wholesale (Vol. 2)

8041 Offices and Clinics of Chiropractors (Vol. 2)

8021 Offices and Clinics of Dentists (Vol. 2)

8049 Offices and Clinics of Health Practitioners Not Elsewhere Classified (Vol. 2)

8011 Offices and Clinics of Medical Doctors (Vol. 2)

8042 Offices and Clinics of Optometrists (Vol. 2)

8043 Offices and Clinics of Podiatrists (Vol. 2)

8031 Offices and Offices of Osteopathic Physicians (Vol. 2)

6712 Offices of Bank Holding Companies (Vol. 2)

6719 Offices of Holding Companies Not Elsewhere Classified (Vol. 2)

2893 Offset ink (Vol. 1)

2621 Offset paper (Vol. 1)

2796 Offset plates, positives or negatives: preparation of (Vol. 1)

2752 Offset printing (Vol. 1)

3731 Offshore supply boats, building and repairing (Vol. 1)

3825 Ohmmeters (Vol. 1)

2911 Oil, acid: produced in petroleum refineries (Vol. 1)

5169 Oil additives—wholesale (Vol. 2)

1382 Oil and Gas Exploration Services (Vol. 2)

3533 Oil and Gas Field Machinery and Equipment (Vol. 1)

3061 Oil and gas field machinery and equipment mechanical rubber goods: molded, extruded, and lathe-cut (Vol. 1)

3533 Oil and gas field machinery and equipment (Vol. 1)

1389 Oil and Gas Field Services Not Elsewhere Classified (Vol. 2)

6211 Oil and gas lease brokers (Vol. 2)

4226 Oil and gasoline storage caverns for hire (Vol. 2)

2077 Oil and meal, fish (Vol. 1)

2865 Oil, aniline (Vol. 1)

3433 Oil burners, domestic and industrial (Vol. 1)

5074 Oil burners—wholesale (Vol. 2)

3411 Oil cans, metal (Vol. 1)

2046 Oil, corn: crude and refined (Vol. 1)

2074 Oil, cottonseed (Vol. 1)

2865 Oil, creosote: product of coal tar distillation (Vol. 1)

1311 Oil (crude) production (Vol. 2)

3599 Oil cups, metal (Vol. 1)

5169 Oil drilling muds—wholesale (Vol. 2)

7359 Oil field equipment rental and leasing (Vol. 2)

1382 Oil field exploration: on a contract basis (Vol. 2)

3599 Oil filters, internal combustion engine: except motor vehicle (Vol. 1)

3714 Oil filters, motor vehicle (Vol. 1)

2079 Oil, hydrogenated: edible (Vol. 1)

5159 Oil kernels—wholesale (Vol. 2)

6792 Oil leases, buying and selling on own account (Vol. 2)

3586 Oil measuring and dispensing pumps (Vol. 1)

5159 Oil nuts—wholesale (Vol. 2)

2079 Oil, olive (Vol. 1)

2851 Oil paints (Vol. 1)

2079 Oil, partially hydrogenated: edible (Vol. 1)

2861 Oil, pine: produced by distillation of pine gum or pine wood (Vol. 1)

3829 Oil pressure gauges, motor vehicle (Vol. 1)

6519 Oil properties, lessors of (Vol. 2)

2899 Oil, red (oleic acid) (Vol. 1)

1629 Oil refinery construction-general contractors (Vol. 2)

6514 Operators of residential buildings (four or fewer housing units) (Vol. 2)

6513 Operators of residential hotels (Vol. 2)

6513 Operators of retirement hotels (Vol. 2)

3229 Ophthalmic glass, except flat (Vol. 1)

3211 Ophthalmic glass, flat (Vol. 1)

5048 Ophthalmic Goods (Vol. 2)

3851 Ophthalmic Goods (Vol. 1)

5048 Ophthalmic goods—wholesale (Vol. 2)

3841 Ophthalmic instruments and apparatus (Vol. 1)

3229 Ophthalmic lens blanks (Vol. 1)

3851 Ophthalmic lens grinding, except prescription (Vol. 1)

8011 Ophthalmologists, offices of (Vol. 2)

3841 Ophthalmometers and ophthalmoscopes (Vol. 1)

8732 Opinion research, commercial (Vol. 2)

2833 Opium derivatives (Vol. 1)

3827 Optical alignment and display instruments, except photographic (Vol. 1)

3827 Optical comparators (Vol. 1)

3695 Optical disks and tape, blank (Vol. 1)

3229 Optical glass blanks (Vol. 1)

3211 Optical glass, flat (Vol. 1)

5995 Optical goods—retail (Vol. 2)

5995 Optical Goods Stores (Vol. 2)

3851 Optical grinding service for the trade (Vol. 1)

3827 Optical Instruments and Lenses (Vol. 1)

3674 Optical isolators (Vol. 1)

3229 Optical lens blanks (Vol. 1)

3559 Optical lens machinery (Vol. 1)

3577 Optical readers and scanners (Vol. 1)

7374 Optical scanning data service (Vol. 2)

3577 Optical scanning devices, computer peripheral equipment (Vol. 1)

3572 Optical storage devices for computers (Vol. 1)

3827 Optical test and inspection equipment (Vol. 1)

5995 Opticians—retail (Vol. 2)

6211 Option dealers, stock (Vol. 2)

6231 Option exchanges, stock (Vol. 2)

3841 Optometers (Vol. 1)

5048 Optometric equipment and supplies—wholesale (Vol. 2)

8042 Optometrists, offices and clinics of (Vol. 2)

8021 Oral pathologists, offices of (Vol. 2)

0174 Orange groves and farms (Vol. 2)

2899 Orange oil (Vol. 1)

0721 Orchard: cultivation of; Trees, (Vol. 2)

0721 Orchard cultivation services (Vol. 2)

0762 Orchard management and maintenance, with or without crop services (Vol. 2)

0721 Orchard: planting, pruning, bracing, spraying, removal, and surgery; Trees, (Vol. 2)

0721 Orchard trees and vines; Bracing of (Vol. 2)

0721 Orchard trees and vines; Pruning of (Vol. 2)

0721 Orchard trees and vines; Surgery on (Vol. 2)

0175 Orchards and farms; Apple (Vol. 2)

0175 Orchards and farms; Apricot (Vol. 2)

0179 Orchards and farms; Avocado (Vol. 2)

0175 Orchards and farms; Cherry (Vol. 2)

0179 Orchards and farms; Date (Vol. 2)

0179 Orchards and farms; Fig (Vol. 2)

0175 Orchards and farms; Nectarine (Vol. 2)

0175 Orchards and farms; Peach (Vol. 2)

0175 Orchards and farms; Pear (Vol. 2)

0175 Orchards and farms; Persimmon (Vol. 2)

0175 Orchards and farms; Plum (Vol. 2)

0175 Orchards and farms; Pomegranate (Vol. 2)

0175 Orchards and farms; Prune (Vol. 2)

0175 Orchards and farms; Quince (Vol. 2)

7929 Orchestras (Vol. 2)

5961 Order taking offices of mail-order houses—retail (Vol. 2)

3489 Ordnance and Accessories Not Elsewhere Classified (Vol. 1)

3462 Ordnance forgings, ferrous: not made in rolling mills (Vol. 1)

3463 Ordnance forgings, nonferrous: not made in hot-rolling mills (Vol. 1)

3569 Ordnance testing chambers (Vol. 1)

3532 Ore and aggregate feeders (Vol. 1)

3532 Ore crushing, washing, screening, and loading machinery (Vol. 1)

3429 Organ hardware (Vol. 1)

3931 Organ parts and materials, except organ hardware (Vol. 1)

7699 Organ tuning and repair (Vol. 2)

2211 Organdy, cotton (Vol. 1)

2869 Organic acid esters (Vol. 1)

2869 Organic chemicals, acyclic (Vol. 1)

5169 Organic chemicals, synthetic—wholesale (Vol. 2)

2865 Organic colors, full strength (Vol. 1)

2824 Organic fibers, synthetic: except cellulosic (Vol. 1)

2833 Organic medicinal chemicals: bulk (Vol. 1)

2865 Organic pigments (lakes and toners) (Vol. 1)

7041 Organization Hotels and Lodging Houses on Membership Basis (Vol. 2)

3089 Organizers for closets, drawers, and shelves: plastics (Vol. 1)

3931 Organs, all types: e.g., pipe, reed, hand, street, barrel, electronic, player (Vol. 1)

2493 Oriented strandboard (Vol. 1)

3446 Ornamental and architectural metalwork (Vol. 1)

3299 Ornamental and architectural plaster work: e.g., mantels and columns (Vol. 1)

0783 Ornamental bush planting, pruning, bracing, spraying, removal, and surgery (Vol. 2)

0181 Ornamental: growing of; Plants, (Vol. 2)

1799 Ornamental metalwork-contractors (Vol. 2)

0181 Ornamental Nursery Products (Vol. 2)

0783 Ornamental Shrub and Tree Services (Vol. 2)

0783 Ornamental tree planting, pruning, bracing, spraying, removal, and surgery (Vol. 2)

2431 Ornamental woodwork: e.g., cornices and mantels (Vol. 1)

3231 Ornamented glass, made from purchased glass (Vol. 1)

3699 Ornaments, Christmas tree: electric (Vol. 1)

3999 Ornaments, Christmas tree: except glass and electric (Vol. 1)

3229 Ornaments, Christmas tree: glass (Vol. 1)

3231 Ornaments, Christmas tree: made from purchased glass (Vol. 1)

3961 Ornaments, costume: except precious metal and gems (Vol. 1)

3131 Ornaments, shoe (Vol. 1)

8361 Orphanages (Vol. 2)

2899 Orris oil (Vol. 1)

2865 Orthodichlorobenzene (Vol. 1)

8072 Orthodontic appliances made in dental laboratories to order for the profession (Vol. 2)

3843 Orthodontic appliances (Vol. 1)

8021 Orthodontists, offices of (Vol. 2)

5999 Orthopedic and artificial limb stores—retail (Vol. 2)

3842 Orthopedic devices and materials (Vol. 1)

5047 Orthopedic equipment—wholesale (Vol. 2)

3842 Orthopedic hosiery, elastic (Vol. 1)

8069 Orthopedic hospitals (Vol. 2)

8011 Orthopedic physicians, offices of (Vol. 2)

3275 Orthopedic plaster, gypsum (Vol. 1)

3842 Orthopedic, Prosthetic and Surgical Appliances and Supplies (Vol. 1)

3149 Orthopedic shoes, children's: except extension shoes (Vol. 1)

3842 Orthopedic shoes, extension (Vol. 1)

3143 Orthopedic shoes, men's: except extension shoes (Vol. 1)

3144 Orthopedic shoes, women's: except extension shoes (Vol. 1)

3069 Orthopedic sundries, molded rubber (Vol. 1)

3825 Oscillators, audiofrequency and radiofrequency (instrument types) (Vol. 1)

3679 Oscillators, except laboratory type (Vol. 1)

3825 Oscillographs and oscilloscopes (Vol. 1)

1099 Osmium ore mining (Vol. 2)

3826 Osmometers (Vol. 1)

2211 Osnaburgs (Vol. 1)

2899 Ossein (Vol. 1)

8031 Osteopathic physicians, offices and clinics of (Vol. 2)

8099 Osteoperosis centers (Vol. 2)

3999 Ostrich feathers: curling, dyeing, and renovating for the trade (Vol. 1)

3845 Otoscopes, electromedical (Vol. 1)

3841 Otoscopes, except electromedical (Vol. 1)

5551 Outboard motor dealers—retail (Vol. 2)

3699 Outboard motors, electric (Vol. 1)

3519 Outboard motors, except electric (Vol. 1)

5091 Outboard motors—wholesale (Vol. 2)

7312 Outdoor advertising service (Vol. 2)

7312 Outdoor Advertising Services (Vol. 2)

5712 Outdoor furniture—retail (Vol. 2)

2253 Outerwear handknitted: for the trade (Vol. 1)

5136 Outerwear, men's and boys'—wholesale (Vol. 2)

5137 Outerwear: women's, children's, and infants'—wholesale (Vol. 2)

2211 Outing flannel, cotton (Vol. 1)

3644 Outlet boxes (electric wiring devices) (Vol. 1)

3643 Outlets, convenience: electric (Vol. 1)

8093 Outpatient detoxification centers (Vol. 2)

8093 Outpatient mental health clinics (Vol. 2)

8093 Outpatient treatment clinics for alcoholism and drug addiction (Vol. 2)

8322 Outreach programs (Vol. 2)

1629 Oven construction, bakers'-general contractors (Vol. 2)

1629 Oven construction for industrial plants-general contractors (Vol. 2)

3822 Oven temperature controls, nonindustrial (Vol. 1)

3556 Ovens, bakery (Vol. 1)

3589 Ovens, cafeteria food warming: portable (Vol. 1)

3631 Ovens, household: excluding portable appliances other than microwave and convection (Vol. 1)

3634 Ovens, household: portable: except microwave and convection ovens (Vol. 1)

3567 Ovens, industrial process: except bakery (Vol. 1)

3821 Ovens, laboratory (Vol. 1)

5046 Ovens, microwave: commercial—wholesale (Vol. 2)

3589 Ovens, microwave (cooking equipment): commercial (Vol. 1)

5064 Ovens, microwave: household—wholesale (Vol. 2)

3567 Ovens, sherardizing (Vol. 1)

3569 Ovens, surveillance: for aging and testing powder (Vol. 1)

3229 Ovenware, glass (Vol. 1)

3089 Ovenware, plastics (Vol. 1)

4213 Over-the-road trucking (Vol. 2)

2326 Overall jackets: men's and boys' (Vol. 1)

2326 Overalls, work: men's and boys' (Vol. 1)

1241 Overburden removal for bituminous coal, anthracite, and lignite on a contract basis (Vol. 2)

1081 Overburden removal for metal mining: on a contract basis (Vol. 2)

1481 Overburden removal for nonmetallic minerals, except fuels: on a contract basis (Vol. 2)

2231 Overcoatings: wool, mohair, and similar animal fibers (Vol. 1)

2311 Overcoats: men's and boys' (Vol. 1)

5136 Overcoats, men's and boys'—wholesale (Vol. 2)

3535 Overhead conveyor systems for general industrial use (Vol. 1)

3536 Overhead Traveling Cranes, Hoists and Monorail Systems (Vol. 1)

1622 Overpass construction-general contractors (Vol. 2)

2262 Overprinting manmade fiber and silk broadwoven fabric (Vol. 1)

3021 Overshoes, plastics (Vol. 1)

3021 Overshoes, rubber or rubber soled fabric (Vol. 1)

2833 Ox bile salts and derivatives: bulk, uncompounded (Vol. 1)

2869 Oxalates (Vol. 1)

2869 Oxalic acid and metallic salts (Vol. 1)

2211 Oxfords (cotton fabrics) (Vol. 1)

2819 Oxidation catalyst made from porcelain (Vol. 1)

2899 Oxidizers, inorganic (Vol. 1)

2813 Oxygen, compressed and liquefied (Vol. 1)

3728 Oxygen systems for aircraft (Vol. 1)

8099 Oxygen tent service (Vol. 2)

3841 Oxygen tents (Vol. 1)

5812 Oyster bars (Vol. 2)

0913 Oyster beds (Vol. 2)

2048 Oyster shells, ground: used as feed for animals and fowls (Vol. 1)

2091 Oysters, canned and cured (Vol. 1)

0913 Oysters, dredging or tonging of (Vol. 2)

2092 Oysters, fresh: shucking and packing in nonsealed containers (Vol. 1)

1499 Ozokerite mining (Vol. 2)

3559 Ozone machines (Vol. 1)

P

3845 Pacemakers (Vol. 1)

3069 Pacifiers, rubber (Vol. 1)

7999 Pack trains for amusement (Vol. 2)

4513 Package delivery, private: air (Vol. 2)

4215 Package delivery, private: except air (Vol. 2)

5142 Packaged Frozen Foods (Vol. 2)

7389 Packaging and labeling service (not packing and crating) (Vol. 2)

3086 Packaging foamed plastics (Vol. 1)

0723 Packaging fresh or farm-dried fruits and vegetables (Vol. 2)

3565 Packaging Machinery (Vol. 1)

3565 Packaging machinery (Vol. 1)

2671 Packaging Paper and Plastics Film—Coated and Laminated (Vol. 1)

3411 Packers' cans, metal (Vol. 1)

2899 Packers' salt (Vol. 1)

3221 Packers' ware (containers), glass (Vol. 1)

4783 Packing and Crating (Vol. 2)

2441 Packing cases, wood: nailed or lock corner (Vol. 1)

3053 Packing: cup, U-valve, etc.-leather (Vol. 1)

3053 Packing for steam engines, pipe joints, air compressors, etc. (Vol. 1)

0723 Packing; Fruit sorting, grading, and (Vol. 2)

0723 Packing fruits and vegetables (Vol. 2)

4783 Packing goods for shipping (Vol. 2)

5085 Packing, hose, and belting: industrial—wholesale (Vol. 2)

5084 Packing machinery and equipment—wholesale (Vol. 2)

3053 Packing, metallic (Vol. 1)

0723 Packing of fruits and vegetables; Sorting, grading, and (Vol. 2)

3053 Packing, rubber (Vol. 1)

2299 Packing, twisted jute (Vol. 1)

0723 Packing; Vegetable sorting, grading, and (Vol. 2)

3559 Packup assemblies (wheel overhaul) (Vol. 1)

3021 Pacs, rubber or rubber soled fabric (Vol. 1)

2299 Padding and wadding, textile (Vol. 1)

3429 Padlocks (Vol. 1)

2299 Pads and padding, felt: except woven (Vol. 1)

2392 Pads and padding, table: except asbestos, felt, rattan, reed, and willow (Vol. 1)

3949 Pads, athletic: e.g., football, basketball, soccer, lacrosse (Vol. 1)

2653 Pads, corrugated and solid fiberboard (Vol. 1)

2678 Pads, desk: paper (Vol. 1)

2429 Pads, excelsior: wood (Vol. 1)

2299 Pads, fiber: henequen, sisal, istle (Vol. 1)

3842 Pads, incontinent and bed (Vol. 1)

3953 Pads, inking and stamping (Vol. 1)

3069 Pads, kneeling: rubber (Vol. 1)

3999 Pads, permanent waving (Vol. 1)

3291 Pads, scouring: soap impregnated (Vol. 1)

2396 Pads, shoulder: e.g., for coats and suits (Vol. 1)

2499 Pads, table: rattan, reed, and willow (Vol. 1)

3663 Pagers (one-way) (Vol. 1)

4812 Paging services: radiotelephone (Vol. 2)

3549 Pail mills (Vol. 1)

3411 Pails, except shipping and stamped: metal (Vol. 1)

2657 Pails, folding sanitary food: paperboard (Vol. 1)

5085 Pails, metal—wholesale (Vol. 2)

3089 Pails, plastics (Vol. 1)

2449 Pails, plywood (Vol. 1)

3412 Pails, shipping: metal-except tinned (Vol. 1)

3469 Pails, stamped and pressed metal: except tinned and shipping type (Vol. 1)

2449 Pails, wood: coopered (Vol. 1)

2842 Paint and wallpaper cleaners (Vol. 1)

1799 Paint and wallpaper stripping-contractors (Vol. 2)

3567 Paint baking and drying ovens (Vol. 1)

5198 Paint brushes, rollers, and sprayers—wholesale (Vol. 2)

2851 Paint driers (Vol. 1)

5231 Paint, Glass and Wallpaper Stores (Vol. 2)

3952 Paint, gold or bronze (Vol. 1)

3559 Paint making machinery (Vol. 1)

2816 Paint pigments, inorganic (Vol. 1)

2865 Paint pigments, organic (Vol. 1)

2851 Paint primers (Vol. 1)

2851 Paint removers (Vol. 1)

3991 Paint rollers (Vol. 1)

3944 Paint sets, children's (Vol. 1)

7532 Paint shops, automotive (Vol. 2)

5084 Paint spray equipment, industrial—wholesale (Vol. 2)

3563 Paint sprayers (Vol. 1)

2499 Paint sticks, wood (Vol. 1)

5231 Paint stores—retail (Vol. 2)

2851 Paintbrush cleaners (Vol. 1)

3991 Paintbrushes (Vol. 1)

1721 Painting and Paper Hanging (Vol. 2)

3479 Painting (enameling and varnishing) of metal products, for the trade (Vol. 1)

3999 Painting instrument dials, for the trade (Vol. 1)

1721 Painting of buildings and other structures, except roofs-contractors (Vol. 2)

1721 Painting ships-contractors (Vol. 2)

1721 Painting traffic lanes-contractors (Vol. 2)

3952 Paints, artists' (Vol. 1)

2851 Paints, asphalt and bituminous (Vol. 1)

3952 Paints for burnt wood or leather work, platinum (Vol. 1)

3952 Paints for china painting (Vol. 1)

2851 Paints: oil and alkyd vehicle, and water thinned (Vol. 1)

2851 Paints, plastics texture: paste and dry (Vol. 1)

5198 Paints, Varnishes and Supplies (Vol. 2)

5111 Paper, fine or printing and writing—wholesale (Vol. 2)

3952 Paper, frisket (artists' material) (Vol. 1)

3291 Paper: garnet, emery, aluminum oxide, and silicon carbide coated (Vol. 1)

1721 Paper hanging-contractors (Vol. 2)

3861 Paper, heat sensitized: made from purchased paper (Vol. 1)

3554 Paper Industries Machinery (Vol. 1)

3496 Paper machine wire cloth, made from purchased wire (Vol. 1)

5084 Paper manufacturing machinery—wholesale (Vol. 2)

3554 Paper mill machinery: e.g., plating, slitting, waxing (Vol. 1)

2621 Paper Mills (Vol. 1)

2621 Paper mills (Vol. 1)

2621 Paper (Vol. 1)

2676 Paper napkins, (Vol. 1)

3861 Paper, photographic: sensitized (Vol. 1)

3554 Paper product machines, except printing machines (Vol. 1)

1541 Paper pulp mill construction-general contractors (Vol. 2)

3579 Paper punches, hand (Vol. 1)

3555 Paper ruling and sewing machines (bookbinders' machinery) (Vol. 1)

2782 Paper ruling (Vol. 1)

3482 Paper shells, 30 mm. (or 1.18 inch) or less (Vol. 1)

3953 Paper stencils (Vol. 1)

5093 Paper, waste—wholesale (Vol. 2)

5113 Paperboard and products, except office supplies—wholesale (Vol. 2)

2657 Paperboard backs for blister or skin packages (Vol. 1)

2675 Paperboard die-cut, from purchased materials (Vol. 1)

2631 Paperboard, except building board (Vol. 1)

2631 Paperboard Mills (Vol. 1)

2631 Paperboard mills, except building board mills (Vol. 1)

2675 Paperboard: pasted, lined, laminated, or surface coated (Vol. 1)

2231 Papermakers' felts, woven: wool, mohair, and similar animal fibers (Vol. 1)

2678 Papeteries (Vol. 1)

2679 Papier-mache articles, except statuary and art goods (Vol. 1)

2221 Parachute fabrics (Vol. 1)

3429 Parachute hardware (Vol. 1)

7999 Parachute training for pleasure (Vol. 2)

2399 Parachutes (Vol. 1)

2911 Paraffin wax, produced in petroleum refineries (Vol. 1)

7389 Paralegal service (Vol. 2)

8049 Paramedics, offices of (Vol. 2)

3679 Parametric amplifiers (Vol. 1)

3674 Parametric diodes (Vol. 1)

3999 Parasols and frames: handles, parts, and trimmings-except precious metal (Vol. 1)

4513 Parcel delivery, private: air (Vol. 2)

4215 Parcel delivery, private: except air (Vol. 2)

7389 Parcel packing service (packaging) (Vol. 2)

3111 Parchment leather (Vol. 1)

2621 Parchment paper (Vol. 1)

8641 Parent-teacher associations (Vol. 2)

2834 Parenteral solutions (Vol. 1)

2024 Parfait (Vol. 1)

6159 Pari-mutuel totalizator equipment finance leasing and maintenance (Vol. 2)

2879 Paris green (insecticide) (Vol. 1)

3479 Parkerizing, for the trade (Vol. 1)

3647 Parking lights, automotive (Vol. 1)

1771 Parking lot construction-contractors (Vol. 2)

7521 Parking lots (Vol. 2)

3824 Parking meters (Vol. 1)

7521 Parking structures (Vol. 2)

7299 Parking, valet (Vol. 2)

1611 Parkway construction-general contractors (Vol. 2)

4789 Parlor car operations, not performed by line-haul railroad companies (Vol. 2)

8211 Parochial schools, elementary and secondary (Vol. 2)

8322 Parole offices (Vol. 2)

1752 Parquet flooring-contractors (Vol. 2)

2426 Parquet flooring, hardwood (Vol. 1)

3699 Particle accelerators, high voltage (Vol. 1)

3826 Particle size analyzers (Vol. 1)

3821 Particle size reduction apparatus, laboratory (Vol. 1)

2493 Particleboard (Vol. 1)

5031 Particleboard—wholesale (Vol. 2)

2899 Parting compounds (chemical foundry supplies) (Vol. 1)

3251 Partition tile, clay (Vol. 1)

3496 Partitions and grillework, made from purchased wire (Vol. 1)

3446 Partitions and grillework, ornamental metal (Vol. 1)

2653 Partitions, corrugated and solid fiberboard (Vol. 1)

2522 Partitions, office: not for floor attachment-except wood (Vol. 1)

2521 Partitions, office: not for floor attachment-wood (Vol. 1)

2542 Partitions, prefabricated: except wood and free-standing (Vol. 1)

2541 Partitions, prefabricated: wood-for floor attachment (Vol. 1)

5046 Partitions—wholesale (Vol. 2)

5963 Party-plan merchandising—retail (Vol. 2)

7359 Party supplies rental and leasing (Vol. 2)

2782 Passbooks (Vol. 1)

2396 Passementeries (Vol. 1)

1542 Passenger and freight terminal building construction-general contractors (Vol. 2)

3711 Passenger automobile bodies (Vol. 1)

3535 Passenger baggage belt loaders (Vol. 1)

7515 Passenger Car Leasing (Vol. 2)

7515 Passenger car leasing, except finance leasing: without drivers (Vol. 2)

7514 Passenger Car Rental (Vol. 2)

7514 Passenger car rental, without drivers (Vol. 2)

3731 Passenger-cargo vessels, building and repairing (Vol. 1)

4111 Passenger transportation, regular route, road or rail: between airports and terminals (Vol. 2)

4489 Passenger water transportation on rivers and canals (Vol. 2)

3679 Passive repeaters (Vol. 1)

7221 Passport photographers (Vol. 2)

2032 Pasta, canned (Vol. 1)

2099 Pasta, uncooked: packaged with other ingredients (Vol. 1)

2891 Paste, adhesive (Vol. 1)

3399 Paste, metal (Vol. 1)

3952 Pastels, artists' (Vol. 1)

2099 Pastes, almond (Vol. 1)

2033 Pastes, fruit and vegetable (Vol. 1)

3556 Pasteurizing equipment, dairy and other food (Vol. 1)

2013 Pastrami (Vol. 1)

2051 Pastries, except frozen: e.g., Danish, French (Vol. 1)

2499 Pastry boards, wood (Vol. 1)

2899 Patching plaster, household (Vol. 1)

7389 Patent brokers (Vol. 2)

6794 Patent buying and licensing (Vol. 2)

2631 Patent coated paperboard (Vol. 1)

6794 Patent leasing (Vol. 2)

3111 Patent leather (Vol. 1)

5122 Patent medicines—wholesale (Vol. 2)

6794 Patent Owners and Lessors (Vol. 2)

8111 Patent solicitors' offices (Vol. 2)

8071 Pathological laboratories (Vol. 2)

8011 Pathologists (M.D.), offices of (Vol. 2)

8021 Pathologists, oral: offices of (Vol. 2)

3845 Patient monitoring equipment: intensive care/coronary care unit (Vol. 1)

5047 Patient monitoring equipment—wholesale (Vol. 2)

1771 Patio construction, concrete-contractors (Vol. 2)

3731 Patrol boats, building and repairing (Vol. 1)

7389 Patrol of electric transmission or gas lines (Vol. 2)

3711 Patrol wagons (motor vehicles) (Vol. 1)

3553 Pattern makers' machinery (woodworking) (Vol. 1)

3543 Patterns, industrial (Vol. 1)

2499 Patterns, last sole: regardless of material (Vol. 1)

3469 Patterns on metal (Vol. 1)

2741 Patterns, paper, including clothing patterns: publishing and printing, or publishing only (Vol. 1)

5113 Patterns, paper—wholesale (Vol. 2)

3999 Patterns, shoe (Vol. 1)

3531 Pavers (Vol. 1)

5082 Pavers—wholesale (Vol. 2)

2951 Paving blocks and mixtures (except brick, concrete, and cut stone), (Vol. 1)

3271 Paving blocks, concrete (Vol. 1)

3281 Paving blocks, cut stone (Vol. 1)

3531 Paving breakers (Vol. 1)

3251 Paving brick, clay (Vol. 1)

1611 Paving construction-contractors (Vol. 2)

3272 Paving materials, prefabricated concrete, except blocks (Vol. 1)

5032 Paving mixtures—wholesale (Vol. 2)

5932 Pawnshops (Vol. 2)

8721 Payroll accounting service (Vol. 2)

3661 PBX equipment, manual and automatic (Vol. 1)

3714 PCV valves (Vol. 1)

0119 Pea farms, dry field and seed (Vol. 2)

0161 Pea farms; English (Vol. 2)

0161 Pea farms, except dry peas (Vol. 2)

0161 Pea farms; Green (Vol. 2)

0175 Peach orchards and farms (Vol. 2)

2865 Peacock blue lake (Vol. 1)

2099 Peanut butter (Vol. 1)

3523 Peanut combines, diggers, packers, and threshers (agricultural equipment) (Vol. 1)

2079 Peanut cooking and salad oil (Vol. 1)

0139 Peanut farms (Vol. 2)

2076 Peanut oil, cake, and meal (Vol. 1)

3556 Peanut roasting machines (Vol. 1)

0723 Peanut shelling, custom (Vol. 2)

5159 Peanuts, bulk: unprocessed or shelled only—wholesale (Vol. 2)

0722 Peanuts, machine harvesting of (Vol. 2)

0175 Pear orchards and farms (Vol. 2)

2816 Pearl essence (Vol. 1)

7631 Pearl restringing for the trade (Vol. 2)

3322 Pearlitic castings, malleable iron (Vol. 1)

3961 Pearls, artificial (Vol. 1)

0919 Pearls, cultured: production of (Vol. 2)

3915 Pearls: drilling, sawing, or peeling of (Vol. 1)

5094 Pearls—wholesale (Vol. 2)

1499 Peat grinding (Vol. 2)

1499 Peat humus mining (Vol. 2)

1499 Peat mining (Vol. 2)

3423 Peavies (handtools) (Vol. 1)

1442 Pebble mining (Vol. 2)

0173 Pecan groves and farms (Vol. 2)

0723 Pecan hulling and shelling (Vol. 2)

5159 Pecan—wholesale (Vol. 2)

2099 Pectin (Vol. 1)

3281 Pedestals, marble (Vol. 1)

3299 Pedestals, statuary: plaster of paris or papier-mache-factory production only (Vol. 1)

2541 Pedestals, statuary: wood (Vol. 1)

3669 Pedestrian traffic control equipment (Vol. 1)

8011 Pediatricians, offices of (Vol. 2)

0751 Pedigree record services for cattle, hogs, sheep, goats, and poultry (Vol. 2)

0752 Pedigree record services for pets and other animal specialties (Vol. 2)

3824 Pedometers (Vol. 1)

2411 Peeler logs (Vol. 1)

1459 Pegmatite (feldspar) mining (Vol. 2)

3131 Pegs, shoe (Vol. 1)

3532 Pellet mills (mining machinery) (Vol. 1)

2892 Pellet powder (explosives) (Vol. 1)

3482 Pellets, ammunition: pistol and air rifle (Vol. 1)

3999 Pelts: scraping, currying, tanning, bleaching, and dyeing (Vol. 1)

5159 Pelts—wholesale (Vol. 2)

3841 Pelvimeters (Vol. 1)

5943 Pen and pencil shops—retail (Vol. 2)

3952 Pencil holders (Vol. 1)

3952 Pencil lead: black, indelible, or colored (Vol. 1)

3579 Pencil sharpeners (Vol. 1)

2499 Pencil slats (Vol. 1)

3951 Pencils and pencil parts, mechanical (Vol. 1)

3952 Pencils, except mechanical (Vol. 1)

3991 Pencils, hair (artists' brushes) (Vol. 1)

5112 Pencils—wholesale (Vol. 2)

3646 Pendant lamps: commercial, industrial, and institutional (Vol. 1)

2899 Penetrants, inspection (Vol. 1)

2843 Penetrants (Vol. 1)

3951 Penholders and parts (Vol. 1)

2833 Penicillin: bulk, uncompounded (Vol. 1)

2834 Penicillin preparations (Vol. 1)

9223 Penitentiaries-government (Vol. 2)

2399 Pennants (Vol. 1)

3951 Penpoints: gold, steel, or other metal (Vol. 1)

3951 Pens and pen parts: fountain, stylographic, and ballpoint (Vol. 1)

3951 Pens, Mechanical Pencils and Parts (Vol. 1)

5112 Pens, writing—wholesale (Vol. 2)

6411 Pension and retirement plan consultants (Vol. 2)

6371 Pension funds (Vol. 2)

6371 Pension, Health and Welfare Funds (Vol. 2)

3443 Penstocks, metal plate (Vol. 1)

2865 Pentachlorophenol (Vol. 1)

2869 Pentaerythritol (Vol. 1)

2892 Pentolite (explosives) (Vol. 1)

0161 Pepper farms; Sweet (Vol. 2)

0161 Pepper farms, sweet and hot (vegetables) (Vol. 2)

2099 Pepper (Vol. 1)

2899 Peppermint oil (Vol. 1)

2211 Percale (Vol. 1)

2211 Percaline, cotton (Vol. 1)

3827 Percentage correctors (Vol. 1)

2819 Perchloric acid (Vol. 1)

2869 Perchloroethylene (Vol. 1)

3634 Percolators, electric (Vol. 1)

5064 Percolators, electric—wholesale (Vol. 2)

3482 Percussion caps, for ammunition of 30 mm. (or 1.18 inch) or less (Vol. 1)

3931 Percussion musical instruments (Vol. 1)

3469 Perforated metal, stamped (Vol. 1)

3443 Perforating on heavy metal (Vol. 1)

3469 Perforating on light metal (Vol. 1)

1389 Perforating well casings on a contract basis (Vol. 2)

3579 Perforators (office machines) (Vol. 1)

6794 Performance rights, publishing and licensing of (Vol. 2)

7929 Performing artists (Vol. 2)

7922 Performing arts center productions (Vol. 2)

2844 Perfume bases, blending and compounding (Vol. 1)

2869 Perfume materials, synthetic (Vol. 1)

2844 Perfumes, Cosmetics and Other Toilet Preparations (Vol. 1)

2844 Perfumes, natural and synthetic (Vol. 1)

5122 Perfumes—wholesale (Vol. 2)

2754 Periodicals: gravure printing (not publishing) (Vol. 1)

2752 Periodicals, lithographed: not published (Vol. 1)

2759 Periodicals, printed: except lithographed or gravure (not publishing) (Vol. 1)

2721 Periodicals: publishing and printing, or publishing only (Vol. 1)

2721 Periodicals—Publishing, or Publishing and Printing (Vol. 1)

5192 Periodicals—wholesale (Vol. 2)

8021 Periodontists, offices of (Vol. 2)

5734 Peripheral equipment, computer stores—retail (Vol. 2)

5045 Peripheral equipment, computer—wholesale (Vol. 2)

3827 Periscopes (Vol. 1)

3295 Perlite aggregate (Vol. 1)

3295 Perlite, expanded (Vol. 1)

1499 Perlite mining (Vol. 2)

2395 Permanent pleating and pressing, for the trade (Vol. 1)

3999 Permanent wave equipment and machines (Vol. 1)

2892 Permissible explosives (Vol. 1)

2819 Peroxides, inorganic (Vol. 1)

2865 Persian orange lake (Vol. 1)

0175 Persimmon orchards and farms (Vol. 2)

8811 Personal affairs management (Vol. 2)

8059 Personal care facilities with health care (Vol. 2)

8059 Personal care homes with health care (Vol. 2)

3571 Personal computers (Vol. 1)

6141 Personal Credit Institutions (Vol. 2)

8299 Personal development schools (Vol. 2)

6141 Personal finance companies, small loan: licensed (Vol. 2)

6719 Personal holding companies, except bank (Vol. 2)

6733 Personal investment trusts, management of (Vol. 2)

3172 Personal Leather Goods Except Women's Handbags and Purses (Vol. 1)

3172 Personal leather goods, small (Vol. 1)

3842 Personal safety appliances and equipment (Vol. 1)

7299 Personal shopping service (Vol. 2)

9199 Personnel agencies-government (Vol. 2)

3711 Personnel carriers, for highway use (Vol. 1)

3829 Personnel dosimetry devices (Vol. 1)

8742 Personnel management consultants, except employment service (Vol. 2)

0851 Pest control, forest (Vol. 2)

7342 Pest control in structures (Vol. 2)

2879 Pesticides, agricultural (Vol. 1)

2879 Pesticides and Agricultural Chemicals Not Elsewhere Classified (Vol. 1)

2879 Pesticides, household (Vol. 1)

5191 Pesticides—wholesale (Vol. 2)

2048 Pet food, except dog and cat: canned, frozen, and dry (Vol. 1)

5999 Pet food stores—retail (Vol. 2)

5149 Pet food—wholesale (Vol. 2)

0742 Pet hospitals (Vol. 2)

5999 Pet shops—retail (Vol. 2)

2499 Photograph frames, wood or metal (Vol. 1)
4822 Photograph transmission services (Vol. 2)
7221 Photographers, portrait: still or video (Vol. 2)
7221 Photographers, school (Vol. 2)
5043 Photographic cameras, projectors, equipment and supplies—wholesale (Vol. 2)
3861 Photographic chemicals, packaged (Vol. 1)
3861 Photographic equipment and accessories (Vol. 1)
3861 Photographic Equipment and Supplies (Vol. 1)
5043 Photographic Equipment and Supplies (Vol. 2)
3861 Photographic instruments, electronic (Vol. 1)
7384 Photographic laboratories, except for the motion picture industry (Vol. 2)
3827 Photographic lenses (Vol. 1)
7389 Photographic library service, still (Vol. 2)
3081 Photographic, micrographic, and X-ray plastics, sheet, and film: unsupported (Vol. 1)
3861 Photographic paper and cloth, sensitized (Vol. 1)
3861 Photographic sensitized goods (Vol. 1)
7335 Photographic studios, commercial (Vol. 2)
7221 Photographic Studios—Portrait (Vol. 2)
5946 Photographic supply stores—retail (Vol. 2)
7336 Photography, aerial: except map making (Vol. 2)
7389 Photography brokers (Vol. 2)
7335 Photography, commercial (Vol. 2)
2754 Photogravure printing (Vol. 1)
2752 Photolithographing (Vol. 1)
3229 Photomask blanks, glass (Vol. 1)
3826 Photometers, except photographic exposure meters (Vol. 1)
3671 Photomultiplier tubes (Vol. 1)
3829 Photopitometers (Vol. 1)
3861 Photoreconnaissance systems (Vol. 1)
3861 Photosensitized paper (Vol. 1)
3827 Phototheodolites (Vol. 1)
3663 Phototransmission equipment (Vol. 1)
2791 Phototypesetting (Vol. 1)
3674 Photovoltaic devices, solid-state (Vol. 1)
7999 Phrenologists (Vol. 2)
2869 Phthalates (Vol. 1)
2821 Phthalic alkyd resins (Vol. 1)
2865 Phthalic anhydride (Vol. 1)
2821 Phthalic anhydride resins (Vol. 1)
2865 Phthalocyanine toners (Vol. 1)
8742 Physical distribution consultants (Vol. 2)
8099 Physical examination service, except by physicians (Vol. 2)
7991 Physical fitness centers (Vol. 2)
7991 Physical Fitness Facilities (Vol. 2)
3829 Physical properties testing and inspection equipment (Vol. 1)
8731 Physical research, commercial (Vol. 2)
8733 Physical research, noncommercial (Vol. 2)
8049 Physical therapists, offices of (Vol. 2)
8049 Physicians' assistants, offices of (Vol. 2)
5047 Physicians' equipment—wholesale (Vol. 2)
8011 Physicians (M.D.), including specialists: offices and clinics of (Vol. 2)
8031 Physicians, osteopathic: offices and clinics of (Vol. 2)

5047 Physicians' supplies—wholesale (Vol. 2)
8999 Physicists, consulting: not connected with business service laboratories (Vol. 2)
3841 Physiotherapy equipment, electrical (Vol. 1)
2833 Physostigmine and derivatives (Vol. 1)
2879 Phytoactin (Vol. 1)
3429 Piano hardware (Vol. 1)
3931 Piano parts and materials, except piano hardware (Vol. 1)
7359 Piano rental and leasing (Vol. 2)
5736 Piano stores—retail (Vol. 2)
7699 Piano tuning and repair (Vol. 2)
3931 Pianos, all types: e.g., vertical, grand, spinet, player, coin-operated (Vol. 1)
3931 Piccolos and parts (Vol. 1)
3552 Picker machines (textile machinery) (Vol. 1)
2426 Picker stick blanks (Vol. 1)
3552 Picker sticks for looms (Vol. 1)
0724 Pickery; Cotton (Vol. 2)
2411 Pickets and paling: round or split (Vol. 1)
2092 Picking of crab meat (Vol. 1)
2035 Pickled Fruits and Vegetables, Vegetable Sauces and Seasonings, and Salad Dressings (Vol. 1)
3547 Picklers and pickling lines, sheet and strip (rolling mill equipment) (Vol. 1)
2035 Pickles and pickle salting (Vol. 1)
5149 Pickles, preserves, jellies, jams, and sauces—wholesale (Vol. 2)
3423 Picks (handtools) (Vol. 1)
7212 Pickup and delivery station laundry not operated by laundries (Vol. 2)
3792 Pickup coaches (campers), for mounting on pickup trucks (Vol. 1)
3792 Pickup covers, canopies or caps (Vol. 1)
3651 Pickup heads, phonograph (Vol. 1)
5511 Pickups and vans, new and used—retail (Vol. 2)
5521 Pickups and vans, used only—retail (Vol. 2)
7999 Picnic grounds operation (Vol. 2)
3089 Picnic jugs, plastics (Vol. 1)
2892 Picric acid (explosives) (Vol. 1)
3812 Pictorial situation instrumentation (Vol. 1)
2499 Picture frame moldings, finished (Vol. 1)
5999 Picture frames, ready-made—retail (Vol. 2)
2499 Picture frames, wood or metal (Vol. 1)
7699 Picture framing, custom (Vol. 2)
7699 Picture framing to individual order, not connected with retail art stores (Vol. 2)
3211 Picture glass (Vol. 1)
3999 Picture plaques, laminated (Vol. 1)
2759 Picture post cards: except lithographed or gravure (Vol. 1)
2752 Picture postcards, lithographed (Vol. 1)
3671 Picture tube reprocessing (Vol. 1)
2099 Pie fillings, except fruits, vegetables and meat (Vol. 1)
5131 Piece Goods, Notions and Other Dry Goods (Vol. 2)
5949 Piece goods—retail (Vol. 2)
5131 Piece goods—wholesale (Vol. 2)
1629 Pier construction-general contractors (Vol. 2)

3272 Pier footings, prefabricated concrete (Vol. 1)

7996 Piers, amusement (Vol. 2)

4491 Piers, including buildings and facilities: operation and maintenance (Vol. 2)

2051 Pies, bakery, except frozen (Vol. 1)

2053 Pies, bakery, frozen (Vol. 1)

5142 Pies, fruit: frozen—wholesale (Vol. 2)

2032 Pies, meat: canned (Vol. 1)

3679 Piezoelectric crystals (Vol. 1)

3312 Pig iron (Vol. 1)

5051 Pig iron—wholesale (Vol. 2)

0259 Pigeon farms (Vol. 2)

3949 Pigeons, clay (targets) (Vol. 1)

2865 Pigment scarlet lake (Vol. 1)

5198 Pigments and colors—wholesale (Vol. 2)

2816 Pigments, inorganic (Vol. 1)

2865 Pigments, organic: except animal black and bone black (Vol. 1)

3334 Pigs, aluminum (Vol. 1)

3331 Pigs, copper (Vol. 1)

2013 Pigs' feet, cooked and pickled (Vol. 1)

3339 Pigs, lead (Vol. 1)

3339 Pigs, primary: nonferrous metals, except copper and aluminum (Vol. 1)

0912 Pilchard, catching of (Vol. 2)

1629 Pile driving-contractors (Vol. 2)

3531 Pile-driving equipment (Vol. 1)

2257 Pile fabrics, circular knit (Vol. 1)

2211 Pile fabrics, cotton (Vol. 1)

2221 Pile fabrics, manmade fiber and silk (Vol. 1)

2258 Pile fabrics, warp knit (Vol. 1)

3443 Pile shells, metal plate (Vol. 1)

3444 Pile shells, sheet metal (Vol. 1)

2491 Piles, foundation and marine construction: treated (Vol. 1)

1629 Piling, driving-general contractors (Vol. 2)

3531 Piling extractors (Vol. 1)

5051 Piling, iron and steel—wholesale (Vol. 2)

3272 Piling, prefabricated concrete (Vol. 1)

2491 Piling, wood: treated (Vol. 1)

2411 Piling, wood: untreated (Vol. 1)

3312 Pilings, sheet, plain: iron and steel (Vol. 1)

3562 Pillow block units for ball or roller bearings (Vol. 1)

3562 Pillow blocks, with ball or roller bearings (Vol. 1)

3568 Pillow blocks, with plain bearings (Vol. 1)

7219 Pillow cleaning and renovating (Vol. 2)

2299 Pillow filling: curled hair (e.g., cotton waste, moss, hemp tow, kapok) (Vol. 1)

2211 Pillow tubing (Vol. 1)

2392 Pillowcases (Vol. 1)

2211 Pillowcases (Vol. 1)

5023 Pillowcases—wholesale (Vol. 2)

2392 Pillows, bed (Vol. 1)

3069 Pillows, sponge rubber (Vol. 1)

3651 Pillows, stereo (Vol. 1)

2834 Pills, pharmaceutical (Vol. 1)

4499 Piloting vessels in and out of harbors (Vol. 2)

3812 Pilots, automatic, aircraft (Vol. 1)

2211 Pin checks, cotton (Vol. 1)

3915 Pin stems (jewelry findings) (Vol. 1)

2211 Pin stripes, cotton (Vol. 1)

2679 Pin tickets, paper (Vol. 1)

3999 Pinball machines (Vol. 1)

7993 Pinball machines, operation of (Vol. 2)

0831 Pine gum, extraction of (Vol. 2)

2861 Pine oil, produced by distillation of pine gum or pine wood (Vol. 1)

0179 Pineapple farms (Vol. 2)

7999 Ping pong parlors (Vol. 2)

1459 Pinite mining (Vol. 2)

3961 Pins, costume jewelry: except precious metal and gems (Vol. 1)

3965 Pins, except jewelry: toilet, safety, hatpins, and hairpins-steel or brass (Vol. 1)

3911 Pins, precious metal (Vol. 1)

3949 Pinsetters for bowling, automatic (Vol. 1)

3354 Pipe, aluminum: extruded (Vol. 1)

3292 Pipe and boiler covering, except felt (Vol. 1)

2299 Pipe and boiler covering, felt (Vol. 1)

5074 Pipe and boiler covering—wholesale (Vol. 2)

1799 Pipe and boilers, insulation of: contractors (Vol. 2)

3498 Pipe and fittings, fabricated from purchased metal pipe (Vol. 1)

2679 Pipe and fittings, molded pulp (Vol. 1)

3321 Pipe and fittings, soil and pressure: cast iron (Vol. 1)

3547 Pipe and tube mills (Vol. 1)

5051 Pipe and tubing, steel—wholesale (Vol. 2)

3446 Pipe bannisters, railings, and guards (Vol. 1)

5051 Pipe, cast iron—wholesale (Vol. 2)

3259 Pipe, chimney: clay (Vol. 1)

3999 Pipe cleaners (Vol. 1)

3272 Pipe, concrete (Vol. 1)

3498 Pipe couplings: fabricated from purchased metal pipe (Vol. 1)

1799 Pipe covering-contractors (Vol. 2)

3292 Pipe covering (insulation), laminated asbestos paper (Vol. 1)

3541 Pipe cutting and threading machines (machine tools) (Vol. 1)

3351 Pipe, extruded and drawn: brass, bronze, and copper (Vol. 1)

3498 Pipe, fabricated from purchased metal pipe (Vol. 1)

3494 Pipe fittings, except plumbers' brass goods: metal (Vol. 1)

3494 Pipe hangers, metal (Vol. 1)

3498 Pipe headers, welded: fabricated from purchased metal pipe (Vol. 1)

3312 Pipe, iron and steel: made in steel works or rolling mills (Vol. 1)

3443 Pipe, large diameter: metal plate-made by plate fabricators (Vol. 1)

3356 Pipe: lead, magnesium, nickel, tin, zinc, and their alloys (Vol. 1)

3272 Pipe, lined with concrete (Vol. 1)

3069 Pipe mouthpieces, molded rubber (Vol. 1)

3084 Pipe, plastics (Vol. 1)

3292 Pipe, pressure: asbestos cement (Vol. 1)

2891 Pipe sealing compounds (Vol. 1)

3842 Plasters, adhesive: medicated or nonmedicated (Vol. 1)

3479 Plastic coating of metals for the trade (Vol. 1)

1459 Plastic fire clay mining (Vol. 2)

8011 Plastic surgeons, offices of (Vol. 2)

2869 Plasticizers, organic: cyclic and acyclic (Vol. 1)

2851 Plastics base paints and varnishes (Vol. 1)

5162 Plastics basic shapes—wholesale (Vol. 2)

3085 Plastics Bottles (Vol. 1)

3089 Plastics casting, for the trade (Vol. 1)

2295 Plastics coated fabrics (Vol. 1)

3081 Plastics film and sheet, unsupported (Vol. 1)

2671 Plastics film, coated or laminated: for packaging (Vol. 1)

5162 Plastics film—wholesale (Vol. 2)

3255 Plastics fire clay bricks (Vol. 1)

3086 Plastics Foam Products (Vol. 1)

5199 Plastics foam—wholesale (Vol. 2)

2673 Plastics, Foil and Coated Paper Bags (Vol. 1)

2385 Plastics gowns (Vol. 1)

2541 Plastics laminated over particleboard (fixture tops) (Vol. 1)

3083 Plastics, laminated: plate, rods, tubes, profiles and sheet, except flexible packaging (Vol. 1)

5162 Plastics Materials and Basic Shapes (Vol. 2)

2821 Plastics Materials, Synthetic Resins and Nonvulcanizable Elastomers (Vol. 1)

5162 Plastics materials—wholesale (Vol. 2)

3089 Plastics molding, for the trade (Vol. 1)

3084 Plastics Pipe (Vol. 1)

3088 Plastics Plumbing Fixtures (Vol. 1)

3089 Plastics Products Not Elsewhere Classified (Vol. 1)

3255 Plastics refractories, clay (Vol. 1)

3297 Plastics refractories, nonclay (Vol. 1)

3087 Plastics resins, custom compounding of (Vol. 1)

5162 Plastics resins—wholesale (Vol. 2)

5093 Plastics scrap—wholesale (Vol. 2)

5162 Plastics sheet and rods—wholesale (Vol. 2)

1799 Plastics wall tile installation-contractors (Vol. 2)

3559 Plastics working machinery (Vol. 1)

2851 Plastisol coating compound (Vol. 1)

3211 Plate glass blanks for optical or ophthalmic uses (Vol. 1)

6331 Plate glass insurance (Vol. 2)

3211 Plate glass, polished and rough (Vol. 1)

5039 Plate glass—wholesale (Vol. 2)

3861 Plate holders, photographic (Vol. 1)

3083 Plate, laminated plastics (Vol. 1)

2759 Plate printing (Vol. 1)

3547 Plate rolling mill machinery (Vol. 1)

3443 Plate work, fabricated: cutting, punching, bending, and shaping (Vol. 1)

3914 Plated ware: flatware, hollow ware, toilet ware, ecclesiastical ware, etc. (Vol. 1)

2759 Plateless engraving (Vol. 1)

2796 Platemaking and Related Services (Vol. 1)

3069 Platens, except printers': solid or covered rubber (Vol. 1)

3579 Plates, addressing (Vol. 1)

3353 Plates, aluminum (Vol. 1)

2796 Plates and cylinders, rotogravure printing: preparation of (Vol. 1)

3841 Plates, bone (Vol. 1)

3351 Plates, copper and copper alloy (Vol. 1)

3089 Plates, dinnerware, plastics: except foam (Vol. 1)

3644 Plates, face (wiring devices) (Vol. 1)

3086 Plates, foamed plastics (Vol. 1)

2796 Plates for printing, embossing of (Vol. 1)

3356 Plates: lead, magnesium, nickel, zinc, and their alloys (Vol. 1)

2796 Plates, lithographic: preparation of (Vol. 1)

3312 Plates, made in steel works or rolling mills (Vol. 1)

3555 Plates, metal: engravers' (Vol. 1)

5051 Plates, metal—wholesale (Vol. 2)

2656 Plates, paper: except those made from pressed or molded pulp (Vol. 1)

2796 Plates, photoengraving (Vol. 1)

3861 Plates, photographic: sensitized (Vol. 1)

2679 Plates, pressed and molded pulp (Vol. 1)

3555 Plates, printers': of all materials (Vol. 1)

2796 Plates, printing: preparation of (Vol. 1)

3537 Platforms, cargo: metal (Vol. 1)

2899 Plating compounds (Vol. 1)

3471 Plating of metals and formed products, for the trade (Vol. 1)

3356 Platinum and platinum alloy sheets and tubing (Vol. 1)

3497 Platinum and platinum base alloy foil (Vol. 1)

3339 Platinum-group metals refining, primary (Vol. 1)

3356 Platinum-group metals rolling, drawing, and extruding (Vol. 1)

3341 Platinum-group metals smelting and refining, secondary (Vol. 1)

1099 Platinum group ore mining (Vol. 2)

3949 Playground equipment (Vol. 1)

5941 Playground equipment—retail (Vol. 2)

2754 Playing cards: gravure printing (Vol. 1)

2752 Playing cards, lithographed (Vol. 1)

2759 Playing cards, printed: except lithographed or gravure (Vol. 1)

5092 Playing cards—wholesale (Vol. 2)

2514 Playpens, children's: metal (Vol. 1)

2511 Playpens, children's: wood (Vol. 1)

7922 Plays (road companies and stock companies) (Vol. 2)

2369 Playsuits: girls', children's, and infants' (Vol. 1)

2339 Playsuits: women's, misses', and juniors' (Vol. 1)

7389 Playwrights' brokers (Vol. 2)

2395 Pleating, Decorative and Novelty Stitching and Tucking for the Trade (Vol. 1)

2395 Pleating, for the trade (Vol. 1)

3843 Pliers, dental (Vol. 1)

3423 Pliers (handtools) (Vol. 1)

3271 Plinth blocks, precast terrazzo (Vol. 1)

2673 Pliofilm bags (Vol. 1)

2211 Plisse crepe, cotton (Vol. 1)

2261 Plisse printing of cotton broadwoven fabrics (Vol. 1)

2262 Plisse printing of manmade fiber and silk broadwoven fabrics (Vol. 1)

3577 Plotter controllers, computer peripheral equipment (Vol. 1)

3577 Plotters, computer (Vol. 1)

3827 Plotting boards (sighting and fire control equipment) (Vol. 1)

0711 Plowing (Vol. 2)

3523 Plows, agricultural: disc, moldboard, chisel, etc. (Vol. 1)

3532 Plows, coal (Vol. 1)

3531 Plows, construction: excavating and grading (Vol. 1)

3524 Plows (garden tractor equipment) (Vol. 1)

3711 Plows, snow (motor vehicles) (Vol. 1)

1389 Plugging and abandoning wells on a contract basis (Vol. 2)

3499 Plugs, drain: magnetic-metal (Vol. 1)

3842 Plugs, ear and nose (Vol. 1)

3643 Plugs, electric (Vol. 1)

2499 Plugs, wood (Vol. 1)

0175 Plum orchards and farms (Vol. 2)

2032 Plum pudding (Vol. 1)

3295 Plumbago: ground, refined, or blended (Vol. 1)

5074 Plumbers' brass goods, fittings, and valves—wholesale (Vol. 2)

3432 Plumbers' brass goods (Vol. 1)

3423 Plumbers' handtools (Vol. 1)

3069 Plumbers' rubber goods (Vol. 1)

1711 Plumbing and heating-contractors (Vol. 2)

3494 Plumbing and heating valves, metal (Vol. 1)

5074 Plumbing and heating valves—wholesale (Vol. 2)

5074 Plumbing and Hydronic Heating Equipment and Supplies (Vol. 2)

3432 Plumbing fixture fittings and trim (Vol. 1)

3463 Plumbing fixture forgings, nonferrous: not made in hot-rolling mills (Vol. 1)

3431 Plumbing fixtures: enameled iron, cast iron, and pressed metal (Vol. 1)

5074 Plumbing fixtures, equipment, and supplies—wholesale (Vol. 2)

3432 Plumbing Fixtures Fittings and Trim (Vol. 1)

3088 Plumbing fixtures, plastics (Vol. 1)

3261 Plumbing fixtures, vitreous china (Vol. 1)

1711 Plumbing, Heating and Air-Conditioning (Vol. 2)

1711 Plumbing repair-contractors (Vol. 2)

1711 Plumbing, with or without sheet metalwork-contractors (Vol. 2)

3999 Plumes, feather (Vol. 1)

2211 Plushes, cotton (Vol. 1)

2221 Plushes, manmade fiber and silk (Vol. 1)

2435 Plywood, hardwood or hardwood faced (Vol. 1)

2436 Plywood, softwood (Vol. 1)

5031 Plywood—wholesale (Vol. 2)

3011 Pneumatic casings (rubber tires) (Vol. 1)

3823 Pneumatic controllers, industrial process type (Vol. 1)

3593 Pneumatic cylinders, fluid power (Vol. 1)

3492 Pneumatic hose assemblies (Vol. 1)

3052 Pneumatic hose, rubber or rubberized fabric: e.g., air brake and air line (Vol. 1)

2394 Pneumatic mattresses (Vol. 1)

3822 Pneumatic relays, air-conditioning type (Vol. 1)

3535 Pneumatic tube conveyor systems for general industrial use (Vol. 1)

1796 Pneumatic tube system installation-contractors (Vol. 2)

3492 Pneumatic valves, including aircraft: fluid power-metal (Vol. 1)

3421 Pocket knives (Vol. 1)

3999 Pocketbook frames (Vol. 1)

2396 Pocketbook linings (Vol. 1)

7699 Pocketbook repair shops (Vol. 2)

3172 Pocketbooks, men's: regardless of material (Vol. 1)

3171 Pocketbooks, women's: of all materials, except precious metal (Vol. 1)

2211 Pocketing twill, cotton (Vol. 1)

2396 Pockets for men's and boys' suits and coats (Vol. 1)

8043 Podiatrists, offices and clinics of (Vol. 2)

8699 Poetry associations (Vol. 2)

3578 Point-of-sale devices (Vol. 1)

3541 Pointing, chamfering, and burring machines (Vol. 1)

2371 Pointing furs (Vol. 1)

3843 Points, abrasive: dental (Vol. 1)

2879 Poison: ant, rat, roach, and rodent-household (Vol. 1)

3944 Poker chips (Vol. 1)

3826 Polariscopes (Vol. 1)

3826 Polarizers (Vol. 1)

3826 Polarographic equipment (Vol. 1)

2411 Pole cutting contractors (Vol. 1)

1623 Pole line construction-general contractors (Vol. 2)

3462 Pole line hardware forgings, ferrous: not made in rolling mills (Vol. 1)

3463 Pole line hardware forgings, nonferrous: not made in hot-rolling mills (Vol. 1)

3644 Pole line hardware (Vol. 1)

5063 Pole line hardware—wholesale (Vol. 2)

2491 Poles and pole crossarms, treated (Vol. 1)

3272 Poles, concrete (Vol. 1)

2591 Poles, curtain and drapery (Vol. 1)

2491 Poles, cutting and preserving (Vol. 1)

2499 Poles, wood: e.g., clothesline, tent, flag (Vol. 1)

2411 Poles, wood: untreated (Vol. 1)

9221 Police departments (Vol. 2)

2353 Police hats and caps, except protective head gear (Vol. 1)

2499 Police officer's clubs, wood (Vol. 1)

9221 Police Protection (Vol. 2)

5999 Police supply stores—retail (Vol. 2)

2311 Police uniforms, men's (Vol. 1)

6411 Policyholders' consulting service (Vol. 2)

2842 Polishes: furniture, automobile, metal, shoe, and stove (Vol. 1)

5169 Polishes: furniture, automobile, metal, shoe, etc.—wholesale (Vol. 2)

3431 Portable chemical toilets (metal) (Vol. 1)
3088 Portable chemical toilets, plastics (Vol. 1)
3825 Portable test meters (Vol. 1)
2082 Porter (alcoholic beverage) (Vol. 1)
7299 Porter service (Vol. 2)
5181 Porter—wholesale (Vol. 2)
3241 Portland cement (Vol. 1)
7221 Portrait photographers (Vol. 2)
5099 Portraits—wholesale (Vol. 2)
3812 Position indicators, airframe equipment: e.g., for landing gear, stabilizers (Vol. 1)
3824 Positive displacement meters (Vol. 1)
3845 Positron emission tomography (PET scanner) (Vol. 1)
3423 Post hole diggers, hand (Vol. 1)
3531 Post hole diggers, powered (Vol. 1)
3444 Post office collection boxes (Vol. 1)
1542 Post office construction-general contractors (Vol. 2)
7389 Post office contract stations (Vol. 2)
3579 Postage meters (Vol. 1)
3496 Postal screen wire equipment (Vol. 1)
2542 Postal service lock boxes, except wood (Vol. 1)
4311 Postal Service, U.S. (Vol. 2)
2759 Postcards, picture: except lithographed or gravure printed (Vol. 1)
2754 Postcards, picture: gravure printing (Vol. 1)
2752 Postcards, picture: lithographed (Vol. 1)
7312 Poster advertising service, outdoor (Vol. 2)
7319 Poster advertising services, except outdoor (Vol. 2)
2621 Poster paper (Vol. 1)
2754 Posters: gravure printing (Vol. 1)
2759 Posters, including billboard: except lithographed or gravure (Vol. 1)
2752 Posters, lithographed (Vol. 1)
1799 Posthole digging-contractors (Vol. 2)
3462 Posts, bumping: railroad-forged (not made in rolling mills) (Vol. 1)
3272 Posts, concrete (Vol. 1)
2411 Posts, wood: hewn, round, or split (Vol. 1)
2491 Posts, wood: treated (Vol. 1)
2026 Pot cheese (Vol. 1)
2819 Potash alum (Vol. 1)
2812 Potash, caustic (Vol. 1)
1474 Potash mining (Vol. 2)
1474 Potash, Soda and Borate Minerals (Vol. 2)
2819 Potassium aluminum sulfate (Vol. 1)
2819 Potassium bichromate and chromate (Vol. 1)
2869 Potassium bitartrate (Vol. 1)
2819 Potassium bromide (Vol. 1)
2812 Potassium carbonate (Vol. 1)
2819 Potassium chlorate (Vol. 1)
2819 Potassium chloride (Vol. 1)
2819 Potassium compounds, inorganic: except potassium hydroxide and carbonate (Vol. 1)
1474 Potassium compounds mining (Vol. 2)
2819 Potassium cyanide (Vol. 1)
2812 Potassium hydroxide (Vol. 1)
2819 Potassium hypochlorate (Vol. 1)
2819 Potassium iodide (Vol. 1)
2819 Potassium metal (Vol. 1)

2819 Potassium nitrate and sulfate (Vol. 1)
2819 Potassium permanganate (Vol. 1)
4221 Potato cellars (Vol. 2)
2096 Potato chips and related corn snacks (Vol. 1)
2096 Potato Chips, Corn Chips and Similar Snacks (Vol. 1)
5145 Potato chips—wholesale (Vol. 2)
0723 Potato curing (Vol. 2)
0723 Potato curing; Sweet (Vol. 2)
3523 Potato diggers, harvesters, and planters (agricultural machinery) (Vol. 1)
0134 Potato farms, except sweet potato and yam (Vol. 2)
0134 Potato farms, Irish (Vol. 2)
0139 Potato farms; Sweet (Vol. 2)
0139 Potato farms, yam (Vol. 2)
2034 Potato flakes, granules, and other dehydrated potato products (Vol. 1)
3496 Potato mashers, made from purchased wire (Vol. 1)
2499 Potato mashers, wood (Vol. 1)
3556 Potato peelers, electric (Vol. 1)
3421 Potato peelers, hand (Vol. 1)
2046 Potato starch (Vol. 1)
2096 Potato sticks (Vol. 1)
2099 Potatoes, dried: packaged with other ingredients (Vol. 1)
5148 Potatoes, fresh—wholesale (Vol. 2)
0134 Potatoes; Irish (Vol. 2)
2099 Potatoes, peeled for the trade (Vol. 1)
3825 Potentiometric instruments, except industrial process type (Vol. 1)
3823 Potentiometric self-balancing instruments, except X-Y plotters (Vol. 1)
3443 Pots: annealing, melting, and smelting (Vol. 1)
3255 Pots, melting: glass house-clay (Vol. 1)
0181 Potted: growing of; Plants, (Vol. 2)
2013 Potted meats (Vol. 1)
5992 Potted plants—retail (Vol. 2)
3269 Pottery: art, garden, decorative, industrial, and laboratory (Vol. 1)
3559 Pottery making machinery (Vol. 1)
3269 Pottery Products Not Elsewhere Classified (Vol. 1)
5719 Pottery stores—retail (Vol. 2)
2875 Potting soil, mixed (Vol. 1)
3172 Pouches, tobacco: regardless of material (Vol. 1)
2834 Poultry and animal remedies (Vol. 1)
5499 Poultry and egg dealers—retail (Vol. 2)
0259 Poultry and Eggs Not Elsewhere Classified (Vol. 2)
5144 Poultry and Poultry Products (Vol. 2)
3523 Poultry brooders, feeders, and waterers (Vol. 1)
0751 Poultry coops; Cleaning (Vol. 2)
5499 Poultry dealers—retail (Vol. 2)
0254 Poultry; Egg hatcheries, (Vol. 2)
5083 Poultry equipment—wholesale (Vol. 2)
0259 Poultry: except chicken and turkey; Egg farms, (Vol. 2)
2048 Poultry feeds, supplements, and concentrates (Vol. 1)
5142 Poultry, frozen: packaged—wholesale (Vol. 2)

INDUSTRY INDEX

0254 **Poultry Hatcheries (Vol. 2)**

5144 Poultry: live, dressed, or frozen (except packaged)—wholesale (Vol. 2)

3496 Poultry netting, made from purchased wire (Vol. 1)

0751 Poultry; Pedigree record services for cattle, hogs, sheep, goats, and (Vol. 2)

5142 Poultry pies, frozen—wholesale (Vol. 2)

2015 Poultry, processed: fresh, frozen, canned, or cooked (Vol. 1)

5144 Poultry products—wholesale (Vol. 2)

0751 Poultry; Showing of cattle, hogs, sheep, goats, and (Vol. 2)

2015 Poultry: slaughtering and dressing (Vol. 1)

2015 **Poultry Slaughtering and Processing (Vol. 1)**

3523 Poultry vision control devices (Vol. 1)

3546 Powder-actuated hand tools (Vol. 1)

2844 Powder: baby, face, talcum, and toilet (Vol. 1)

3483 Powder bag loading (Vol. 1)

2892 Powder, blasting (Vol. 1)

2892 Powder, explosive: pellet, smokeless, and sporting (Vol. 1)

3399 Powder, metal: except artists' materials (Vol. 1)

3499 Powder metal products, custom molding (Vol. 1)

2399 Powder puffs and mitts (Vol. 1)

3569 Powder testing chambers (Vol. 1)

2087 Powders, drink (Vol. 1)

2834 Powders, pharmaceutical (Vol. 1)

3443 Power boilers, industrial and marine (Vol. 1)

3613 Power circuit breakers (Vol. 1)

3613 Power connectors (Vol. 1)

3629 Power conversion units, a.c. to d.c.: static-electric (Vol. 1)

3531 Power cranes, draglines, and shovels (Vol. 1)

3612 **Power, Distribution and Specialty Transformers (Vol. 1)**

3546 **Power-Driven Handtools (Vol. 1)**

4911 Power, electric: generation, transmission, or distribution (Vol. 2)

3825 Power factor meters (Vol. 1)

3613 Power fuses devices, 600 volts and over (Vol. 1)

1796 Power generating equipment installation-contractors (Vol. 2)

3621 Power generators (Vol. 1)

5072 Power handtools—wholesale (Vol. 2)

7211 **Power Laundries—Family and Commercial (Vol. 2)**

1623 Power line construction-general contractors (Vol. 2)

3825 Power measuring equipment, electrical (Vol. 1)

5261 Power mowers—retail (Vol. 2)

1629 Power plant construction-general contractors (Vol. 2)

5084 Power plant machinery, except electrical—wholesale (Vol. 2)

3679 Power supplies, static, and variable frequency (Vol. 1)

3613 Power switchboards (Vol. 1)

3613 Power switching equipment (Vol. 1)

5251 Power tools—retail (Vol. 2)

3612 Power transformers, electric (Vol. 1)

3728 Power transmission equipment, aircraft (Vol. 1)

5063 Power transmission equipment, electric—wholesale (Vol. 2)

3714 Power transmission equipment, motor vehicle (Vol. 1)

5085 Power transmission supplies, mechanical—wholesale (Vol. 2)

3241 Pozzolana cement (Vol. 1)

1499 Pozzolana mining (Vol. 2)

2389 Prayer shawls (Vol. 1)

5094 Precious metal mill shapes—wholesale (Vol. 2)

3339 Precious metal refining, primary (Vol. 1)

3341 Precious metal smelting and refining, secondary (Vol. 1)

5094 Precious metals—wholesale (Vol. 2)

5094 Precious stones (gems)—wholesale (Vol. 2)

1499 Precious stones mining (Vol. 2)

3564 Precipitators, electrostatic (Vol. 1)

3443 Precipitators (process vessels), metal plate (Vol. 1)

7699 Precision instrument repair (Vol. 2)

3545 Precision tools, machinists' (Vol. 1)

5084 Precision tools, machinists'—wholesale (Vol. 2)

0723 Precooling, not in connection with transportation; Fruit (Vol. 2)

0723 Precooling, not in connection with transportation; Vegetable (Vol. 2)

4741 Precooling of fruits and vegetables in connection with transportation (Vol. 2)

3824 Predetermined counters (Vol. 1)

1541 Prefabricated building erection, industrial-general contractors (Vol. 2)

1542 Prefabricated building erection, nonresidential: except industrial and warehouses-general contractors (Vol. 2)

1522 Prefabricated building erection, residential: except single-family-general contractors (Vol. 2)

3448 Prefabricated buildings, metal (Vol. 1)

5211 Prefabricated buildings—retail (Vol. 2)

5039 Prefabricated buildings—wholesale (Vol. 2)

2452 Prefabricated buildings, wood (Vol. 1)

3448 **Prefabricated Metal Buildings and Components (Vol. 1)**

1521 Prefabricated single-family houses erection-general contractors (Vol. 2)

2452 **Prefabricated Wood Buildings and Components (Vol. 1)**

2435 Prefinished hardwood plywood (Vol. 1)

2835 Pregnancy test kits (Vol. 1)

1521 Premanufactured housing, single-family (assembled on site)-general contractors (Vol. 2)

7372 **Prepackaged Software (Vol. 2)**

3999 Preparation of slides and exhibits, for classroom use (Vol. 1)

1231 Preparation plants, anthracite (Vol. 2)

1221 Preparation plants, bituminous coal or lignite (Vol. 2)

0711 Preparation; Seed bed (Vol. 2)

0723 **Preparation Services for Market Except Cotton Ginning; Crop (Vol. 2)**

0711 **Preparation Services; Soil (Vol. 2)**

8211 Preparatory schools (Vol. 2)

2048 Prepared Feeds and Feed Ingredients for Animals and Fowls Except Dogs and Cats (Vol. 1)

2045 Prepared Flour Mixes and Doughs (Vol. 1)

2092 Prepared Fresh or Frozen Fish and Seafoods (Vol. 1)

2299 Preparing textile fibers for spinning (scouring and combing) (Vol. 1)

3652 Prerecorded audio magnetic tape (Vol. 1)

8351 Preschool centers (Vol. 2)

0181 Preseeded: soil erosion-growing of; Mats, (Vol. 2)

2033 Preserves, including imitation (Vol. 1)

2491 Preserving of wood (creosoting) (Vol. 1)

2261 Preshrinking cotton broadwoven fabrics for the trade (Vol. 1)

2262 Preshrinking manmade fiber and silk broadwoven fabrics for the trade (Vol. 1)

2231 Preshrinking wool broad woven fabrics for the trade (Vol. 1)

9111 President's office (Vol. 2)

2841 Presoaks (Vol. 1)

7389 Presorting mail service (Vol. 2)

3542 Press brakes (Vol. 1)

7389 Press clipping service (Vol. 2)

2211 Press cloth (Vol. 1)

3462 Press forgings, iron and steel: not made in rolling mills (Vol. 1)

7383 Press services (news syndicates) (Vol. 2)

7212 Press shops for garments (Vol. 2)

2631 Pressboard (Vol. 1)

3229 Pressed and Blown Glass and Glassware Not Elsewhere Classified (Vol. 1)

5113 Pressed and molded pulp goods—wholesale (Vol. 2)

2299 Pressed felts (Vol. 1)

2499 Pressed logs of sawdust and other wood particles, nonpetroleum binder (Vol. 1)

3469 Pressed metal products (stampings) (Vol. 1)

2679 Pressed products from wood pulp (Vol. 1)

3523 Presses and balers, farm: hay, cotton, etc. (Vol. 1)

3542 Presses, arbor (Vol. 1)

3556 Presses: cheese, beet, cider, and sugarcane (Vol. 1)

3582 Presses, finishing: commercial laundry and drycleaning (Vol. 1)

3542 Presses: forming, stamping, punching, and shearing (machine tools) (Vol. 1)

3542 Presses: hydraulic and pneumatic, mechanical and manual (Vol. 1)

3569 Presses, metal baling (Vol. 1)

3555 Presses, printing (Vol. 1)

3553 Presses, woodworking: particleboard, hardboard, medium density fiberboard (MDF), and plywood (Vol. 1)

2499 Pressing blocks, tailors': wood (Vol. 1)

3582 Pressing machines, commercial laundry and drycleaning (Vol. 1)

3829 Pressure and vacuum indicators, aircraft engine (Vol. 1)

3492 Pressure control valves, fluid power: metal (Vol. 1)

3822 Pressure controllers, air-conditioning system type (Vol. 1)

3365 Pressure cookers, domestic: cast aluminum, except die-castings (Vol. 1)

3469 Pressure cookers, stamped or drawn (Vol. 1)

3589 Pressure cookers, steam: commercial (Vol. 1)

3823 Pressure gauges, dial and digital (Vol. 1)

3823 Pressure instruments, industrial process type (Vol. 1)

3321 Pressure pipe, cast iron (Vol. 1)

3272 Pressure pipe, reinforced concrete (Vol. 1)

2672 Pressure sensitive paper and tape, except rubber backed (Vol. 1)

5113 Pressure sensitive tape—wholesale (Vol. 2)

3829 Pressure transducers (Vol. 1)

3491 Pressure valves, industrial: except power transfer (Vol. 1)

3443 Pressure vessels, industrial: metal plate-made in boiler shops (Vol. 1)

3443 Pressurizers and auxiliary equipment, nuclear: metal plate (Vol. 1)

3272 Prestressed concrete products (Vol. 1)

5461 Pretzel stores and stands—retail (Vol. 2)

2052 Pretzels (Vol. 1)

5149 Pretzels—wholesale (Vol. 2)

9651 Price control agencies-government (Vol. 2)

0191 Primarily Crop; General Farms— (Vol. 2)

3692 Primary Batteries—Dry and Wet (Vol. 1)

3692 Primary batteries, dry and wet (Vol. 1)

8011 Primary care medical (M.D.) clinics (Vol. 2)

3823 Primary elements for process flow measurement: orifice plates (Vol. 1)

3399 Primary Metal Products Not Elsewhere Classified (Vol. 1)

3822 Primary oil burner controls, including stack controls and cadmium cells (Vol. 1)

3334 Primary Production of Aluminum (Vol. 1)

3334 Primary production of aluminum (Vol. 1)

3339 Primary refining of nonferrous metal: except copper and aluminum (Vol. 1)

3331 Primary Smelting and Refining of Copper (Vol. 1)

3331 Primary smelting and refining of copper (Vol. 1)

3339 Primary Smelting and Refining of Nonferrous Metals Except Copper and Aluminum (Vol. 1)

3339 Primary smelting of nonferrous metal: except copper and aluminum (Vol. 1)

3351 Primer cups, copper and copper alloy (Vol. 1)

3483 Primers for ammunition, more than 30 mm. (or more than 1.18 inch) (Vol. 1)

2851 Primers, paint (Vol. 1)

2211 Print cloths, cotton (Vol. 1)

3672 Printed Circuit Boards (Vol. 1)

3672 Printed circuit boards (Vol. 1)

7389 Printed circuitry graphic layout (Vol. 2)

3672 Printed circuits (Vol. 1)

3089 Printer acoustic covers, plastics (Vol. 1)

3069 Printers' blankets, rubber (Vol. 1)

3577 Printers, computer (Vol. 1)

5045 Printers, computer—wholesale (Vol. 2)

3861 Projectors, still and motion picture: silent and sound (Vol. 1)

3253 Promenade tile, clay (Vol. 1)

7389 Promoters of home shows and flower shows (Vol. 2)

7941 Promoters, sports events (Vol. 2)

7338 Proofreading service (Vol. 2)

5984 Propane gas, bottled—retail (Vol. 2)

1321 Propane (natural) production (Vol. 2)

2819 Propellants for missiles, solid: inorganic (Vol. 1)

2869 Propellants for missiles, solid: organic (Vol. 1)

3728 Propeller adapter assemblies, hydromatic (Vol. 1)

3728 Propeller alining tables (Vol. 1)

3634 Propeller fans, window-type (household) (Vol. 1)

3549 Propeller straightening presses (Vol. 1)

3824 Propeller type meters with registers (Vol. 1)

3599 Propellers, ship and boat: machined (Vol. 1)

3366 Propellers, ship and screw: cast brass, bronze, copper, and copper-base-except die-castings (Vol. 1)

3728 Propellers, variable and fixed pitch and parts-aircraft (Vol. 1)

6331 Property damage insurance (Vol. 2)

9311 Property tax assessors' offices (Vol. 2)

3069 Prophylactics, rubber (Vol. 1)

2834 Proprietary drug products (Vol. 1)

5912 Proprietary (nonprescription medicines) stores—retail (Vol. 2)

5122 Proprietary (patent) medicines—wholesale (Vol. 2)

3764 Propulsion units for guided missiles and space vehicles (Vol. 1)

2869 Propylene glycol (Vol. 1)

2869 Propylene, made in chemical plants (Vol. 1)

2911 Propylene, produced in petroleum refineries (Vol. 1)

1081 Prospect drilling for metal mining: on a contract basis (Vol. 2)

1481 Prospect drilling for nonmetallic minerals except fuels: on a contract basis (Vol. 2)

3842 Prosthetic appliances and supplies (Vol. 1)

8021 Prosthodontists, offices of (Vol. 2)

0721 Protecting; Crop Planting, Cultivating and (Vol. 2)

6289 Protective committees, security holders (Vol. 2)

7381 Protective service, guard (Vol. 2)

3579 Protectors, check (machine) (Vol. 1)

3851 Protectors, eye (Vol. 1)

3949 Protectors, sports: e.g., baseball, basketball, hockey (Vol. 1)

3826 Protein analyzers, laboratory type (Vol. 1)

2824 Protein fibers (Vol. 1)

2821 Protein plastics (Vol. 1)

0175 Prune orchards and farms (Vol. 2)

2034 Prunes, dried (Vol. 1)

0721 Pruning, bracing, spraying, removal, and surgery; Trees, orchard: planting, (Vol. 2)

0721 Pruning of orchard trees and vines (Vol. 2)

3423 Pruning tools (Vol. 1)

2816 Prussian blue pigments (Vol. 1)

3423 Prying bars (handtools) (Vol. 1)

1061 Psilomelane mining (Vol. 2)

8063 Psychiatric Hospitals (Vol. 2)

8059 Psychiatric patient's convalescent homes (Vol. 2)

8049 Psychiatric social workers, offices of (Vol. 2)

8011 Psychiatrists, offices of (Vol. 2)

8011 Psychoanalysts, offices of (Vol. 2)

8049 Psychologists, clinical: offices of (Vol. 2)

8999 Psychologists, industrial (Vol. 2)

8049 Psychotherapists, except M.D.: offices of (Vol. 2)

8721 Public accountants, certified (Vol. 2)

5065 Public address equipment—wholesale (Vol. 2)

7622 Public address system repair (Vol. 2)

3651 Public address systems (Vol. 1)

2531 Public Building and Related Furniture (Vol. 1)

2531 Public building fixtures (Vol. 1)

5021 Public building furniture—wholesale (Vol. 2)

9222 Public defenders' offices (Vol. 2)

7992 Public Golf Courses (Vol. 2)

9431 Public health agencies-nonoperating (Vol. 2)

8732 Public opinion research (Vol. 2)

9229 Public Order and Safety Not Elsewhere Classified (Vol. 2)

9222 Public prosecutors' offices (Vol. 2)

8743 Public Relations Services (Vol. 2)

9229 Public safety bureaus-government (Vol. 2)

9229 Public safety statistics centers-government (Vol. 2)

9631 Public service commissions, except transportation (Vol. 2)

8299 Public speaking schools (Vol. 2)

8611 Public utility associations (Vol. 2)

9631 Public utility commissions (Vol. 2)

6719 Public utility holding companies (Vol. 2)

6519 Public utility property, lessors of (Vol. 2)

9441 Public welfare administration, nonoperating (Vol. 2)

8322 Public welfare centers, offices of (Vol. 2)

2621 Publication paper (Vol. 1)

7313 Publishers' representatives, advertising (Vol. 2)

2731 Publishing and printing, books and pamphlets (Vol. 1)

2741 Publishing and printing maps, guides, directories, atlases, and sheet music (Vol. 1)

2711 Publishing and printing, or publishing only: newspapers (Vol. 1)

2721 Publishing and printing, or publishing only: periodicals (Vol. 1)

2731 Publishing only, books and pamphlets (Vol. 1)

2741 Publishing without printing: maps (Vol. 1)

2024 Pudding pops, frozen (Vol. 1)

2032 Puddings, except meat: canned (Vol. 1)

2013 Puddings, meat (Vol. 1)

3423 Pullers: wheel, gear, and bearing (handtools) (Vol. 1)

0252 Pullet farms; Started (Vol. 2)

3429 Pulleys, metal: except power transmission equipment (Vol. 1)

3568 Pulleys, power transmission (Vol. 1)

2499 Pulleys, wood (Vol. 1)

1389 Pulling oil well casing: on a contract basis (Vol. 2)

2865 Pulp colors, organic (Vol. 1)

Q

0259 Quail farms (Vol. 2)

3253 Quarry tile, clay (Vol. 1)

5082 Quarrying machinery and equipment—wholesale (Vol. 2)

3131 Quarters (shoe cut stock) (Vol. 1)

1499 Quartz crystal mining (pure) (Vol. 2)

3679 Quartz crystals for electronic application (Vol. 1)

1429 Quartzite, crushed and broken-quarrying (Vol. 2)

1411 Quartzite, dimension-quarrying (Vol. 2)

2861 Quebracho extract (Vol. 1)

2861 Quercitron extract (Vol. 1)

2752 Quick printing, except photocopy service (Vol. 1)

3274 Quicklime (Vol. 1)

1099 Quicksilver (mercury) ore mining (Vol. 2)

2299 Quilt filling: curled hair (e.g., cotton waste, moss, hemp tow, kapok) (Vol. 1)

2395 Quilted fabrics or cloth (Vol. 1)

7299 Quilting for individuals (Vol. 2)

2395 Quilting, for the trade (Vol. 1)

5949 Quilting materials and supplies—retail (Vol. 2)

2221 Quilts, manmade fiber and silk (Vol. 1)

2392 Quilts (Vol. 1)

0175 Quince orchards and farms (Vol. 2)

2833 Quinine and derivatives (Vol. 1)

2865 Quinoline dyes (Vol. 1)

2869 Quinuclidinol ester of benzylic acid (Vol. 1)

6289 Quotation service, stock (Vol. 2)

R

0271 Rabbit farms (Vol. 2)

0271 Rabbits; Fur-Bearing Animals and (Vol. 2)

2015 Rabbits, processed: fresh, frozen, canned, or cooked (Vol. 1)

2015 Rabbits, slaughtering and dressing (Vol. 1)

7948 Race car drivers and owners (Vol. 2)

2741 Race track programs: publishing and printing, or publishing only (Vol. 1)

3562 Races, ball and roller bearing (Vol. 1)

7389 Racetrack cleaning, except buildings (Vol. 2)

7948 Racetrack operation: e.g., horse, dog, auto (Vol. 2)

3644 Raceways (Vol. 1)

2741 Racing forms: publishing and printing, or publishing only (Vol. 1)

7948 Racing Including Track Operations (Vol. 2)

7948 Racing stables, operation of (Vol. 2)

3949 Rackets and frames, sports: e.g., tennis, badminton, squash, racketball, lacrosse (Vol. 1)

2511 Racks, book and magazine: wood (Vol. 1)

2499 Racks, for drying clothes: wood (Vol. 1)

2542 Racks: mail pouch, mailing, mail sorting, etc., except wood (Vol. 1)

2542 Racks, merchandise display and storage: except wood (Vol. 1)

2541 Racks, merchandise display: wood (Vol. 1)

3443 Racks, trash: metal plate (Vol. 1)

3496 Racks without rigid framework, made from purchased wire (Vol. 1)

7997 Racquetball clubs, membership (Vol. 2)

7999 Racquetball courts, except membership clubs (Vol. 2)

4899 Radar station operation (Vol. 2)

3812 Radar systems and equipment (Vol. 1)

3825 Radar testing instruments, electric (Vol. 1)

3731 Radar towers, floating (Vol. 1)

3829 Radiac equipment (radiation measuring and detecting) (Vol. 1)

3567 Radiant heating systems, industrial process: e.g., dryers, cookers' (Vol. 1)

8734 Radiation dosimetry laboratories (Vol. 2)

3829 Radiation measuring and detecting (radiac) equipment (Vol. 1)

7218 Radiation protective garments supply service (Vol. 2)

3842 Radiation shielding aprons, gloves, and sheeting (Vol. 1)

7539 Radiator repair shops, automotive (Vol. 2)

3444 Radiator shields and enclosures, sheet metal (Vol. 1)

5074 Radiators and parts, heating: nonelectric—wholesale (Vol. 2)

3714 Radiators and radiator shells and cores, motor vehicle (Vol. 1)

3634 Radiators, electric (Vol. 1)

3433 Radiators, except electric (Vol. 1)

3651 Radio and phonograph combinations (Vol. 1)

4832 Radio and Television Broadcasting Stations (Vol. 2)

3469 Radio and television chassis, stamped (Vol. 1)

7622 Radio and television receiver installation (Vol. 2)

3663 Radio and television switching equipment (Vol. 1)

3441 Radio and television tower sections, prefabricated metal (Vol. 1)

1623 Radio and television transmitting tower construction-general contractors (Vol. 2)

3663 Radio and T.V. Broadcasting and Communications Equipment (Vol. 1)

7622 Radio and T.V. Repair (Vol. 2)

3825 Radio apparatus analyzers for testing electrical characteristics (Vol. 1)

7389 Radio broadcasting music checkers (Vol. 2)

4899 Radio broadcasting operated by cab companies (Vol. 2)

4832 Radio broadcasting stations (Vol. 2)

2517 Radio cabinets and cases, wood (Vol. 1)

2519 Radio cabinets, plastics (Vol. 1)

8999 Radio commentators (Vol. 2)

8748 Radio consultants (Vol. 2)

3671 Radio electron tubes (Vol. 1)

3812 Radio magnetic instrumentation (RMI) (Vol. 1)

5065 Radio parts and accessories—wholesale (Vol. 2)

5731 Radio-phonograph stores—retail (Vol. 2)

7922 Radio programs, including commercials: producers of (Vol. 2)

3663 Radio receiver networks (Vol. 1)

5065 Radio receiving and transmitting tubes—wholesale (Vol. 2)

3651 Radio receiving sets (Vol. 1)

7622 Radio repair shops (Vol. 2)

7313 Radio representatives, advertising: not auxiliary to radio broadcasting (Vol. 2)

3825 Radio set analyzers, electrical (Vol. 1)

5731 Radio stores—retail (Vol. 2)

4822 Radio telegraph services (Vol. 2)

5731 Radio, Television and Consumer Electronics Stores (Vol. 2)

7389 Radio transcription service (Vol. 2)

3663 Radio transmitting and communications antennas and ground equipment (Vol. 1)

1623 Radio transmitting tower construction-general contractors (Vol. 2)

3825 Radio tube checkers, electrical (Vol. 1)

7313 Radio, T.V. and Publishers' Advertising Representatives (Vol. 2)

2835 Radioactive diagnostic substances (Vol. 1)

2819 Radioactive isotopes (Vol. 1)

4953 Radioactive waste materials, disposal of (Vol. 2)

3825 Radiofrequency measuring equipment (Vol. 1)

3825 Radiofrequency oscillators (Vol. 1)

3844 Radiographic X-ray apparatus and tubes: medical, industrial, and research (Vol. 1)

8734 Radiographing welded joints on pipes and fittings (Vol. 2)

8011 Radiologists, offices of (Vol. 2)

5064 Radios, receiving only, household and automotive—wholesale (Vol. 2)

4812 Radiotelephone Communications (Vol. 2)

4812 Radiotelephone services (Vol. 2)

2819 Radium chloride (Vol. 1)

3844 Radium equipment (Vol. 1)

2819 Radium luminous compounds (Vol. 1)

1094 Radium ore mining (Vol. 2)

3089 Rafts, life: nonrigid-plastics (Vol. 1)

3069 Rafts, life: rubber (Vol. 1)

2273 Rag rugs (Vol. 1)

2299 Rags, carbonized (Vol. 1)

5093 Rags—wholesale (Vol. 2)

3643 Rail bonds, electric: for propulsion and signal circuits (Vol. 1)

3312 Rail joints and fastenings, made in steel works or rolling mills (Vol. 1)

3531 Rail laying and tamping equipment (Vol. 1)

3446 Railings, bannisters, guards, etc.: made from metal pipe (Vol. 1)

3446 Railings, prefabricated metal (Vol. 1)

2431 Railings, stair: wood (Vol. 1)

9621 Railroad and warehouse commissions-nonoperating (Vol. 2)

3321 Railroad brake shoes, cast iron (Vol. 1)

3462 Railroad bumping posts, forged: not made in rolling mills (Vol. 1)

4741 Railroad car cleaning, icing, ventilating, and heating (Vol. 2)

3568 Railroad car journal bearings, plain (Vol. 1)

3743 Railroad car rebuilding (Vol. 1)

4741 Railroad car rental (Vol. 2)

4789 Railroad car repair, on a contract or fee basis (Vol. 2)

3321 Railroad car wheels, chilled cast iron (Vol. 1)

3743 Railroad cars and car equipment (Vol. 1)

1629 Railroad construction-general contractors (Vol. 2)

2491 Railroad cross bridge and switch ties, treated (Vol. 1)

3312 Railroad crossings, iron and steel: made in steel works or rolling mills (Vol. 1)

3743 Railroad Equipment (Vol. 1)

5088 Railroad equipment and supplies—wholesale (Vol. 2)

3493 Railroad equipment springs (Vol. 1)

4482 Railroad ferries (Vol. 2)

4731 Railroad freight agencies, not operated by railroad companies (Vol. 2)

2899 Railroad fusees (Vol. 1)

3429 Railroad hardware (Vol. 1)

3743 Railroad locomotives and parts (Vol. 1)

3999 Railroad models, except toy and hobby models (Vol. 1)

3944 Railroad models: toy and hobby (Vol. 1)

6517 Railroad Property Lessors (Vol. 2)

6517 Railroad property, lessors of (Vol. 2)

2531 Railroad seats (Vol. 1)

3669 Railroad signaling devices, electric (Vol. 1)

4013 Railroad switching (Vol. 2)

4013 Railroad Switching and Terminal Establishments (Vol. 2)

4013 Railroad terminals (Vol. 2)

4729 Railroad ticket offices, not operated by transportation companies (Vol. 2)

2421 Railroad ties, sawed (Vol. 1)

2899 Railroad torpedoes (Vol. 1)

3596 Railroad track scales (Vol. 1)

3462 Railroad wheels, axles, frogs, and related equipment: forged (Vol. 1)

4013 Railroads, belt line (Vol. 2)

4011 Railroads, electric: line-haul (Vol. 2)

4011 Railroads—Line-Haul Operating (Vol. 2)

4013 Railroads, logging (Vol. 2)

3355 Rails, aluminum: rolled and drawn (Vol. 1)

5051 Rails and accessories—wholesale (Vol. 2)

2411 Rails, fence: round or split (Vol. 1)

3312 Rails, iron and steel (Vol. 1)

3312 Rails, rerolled or renewed (Vol. 1)

3351 Rails, rolled and drawn: brass, bronze, and copper (Vol. 1)

3441 Railway bridge sections, prefabricated metal (Vol. 1)

2491 Railway crossties, wood: treated (Vol. 1)

3743 Railway maintenance cars (Vol. 1)

3743 Railway motor cars (Vol. 1)

3621 Railway motors and control equipment, electric (Vol. 1)

4111 Railway operation, local (Vol. 2)

1629 Railway roadbed construction-general contractors (Vol. 2)

3531 Railway track equipment: e.g., rail layers, ballast distributors (Vol. 1)

4011 Railways, interurban (Vol. 2)

3829 Rain gauges (Vol. 1)

5699 Raincoat stores—retail (Vol. 2)

2385 Raincoats, except vulcanized rubber (Vol. 1)

5136 Raincoats, men's and boys'—wholesale (Vol. 2)

5137 Raincoats: women's and children's—wholesale (Vol. 2)

0214 Raising farms and ranches; Sheep (Vol. 2)

0212 Raising farms; Cattle (Vol. 2)

0251 Raising for slaughter; Chicken farms or ranches, (Vol. 2)

0251 Raising of; Broiler chickens, (Vol. 2)

0251 Raising of; Frying chickens, (Vol. 2)

0251 Raising of; Roasting chickens, (Vol. 2)

0279 Raising own stock; Kennels, breeding and (Vol. 2)

2034 Raisins (Vol. 1)

3423 Rakes, handtools (Vol. 1)

3523 Rakes, hay (agricultural machinery) (Vol. 1)

3531 Rakes, land clearing: mechanical (Vol. 1)

0722 Raking, baling, and chopping; Hay mowing, (Vol. 2)

2299 Ramie yarn, thread, roving, and textiles (Vol. 1)

3297 Ramming mixes, nonclay (Vol. 1)

3537 Ramps, aircraft-loading (Vol. 1)

3537 Ramps, loading: portable, adjustable, and hydraulic (Vol. 1)

3448 Ramps, prefabricated: metal (Vol. 1)

0212 Ranches; Cattle (Vol. 2)

0251 Ranches, raising for slaughter; Chicken farms or (Vol. 2)

0214 Ranches; Sheep feeding farms and (Vol. 2)

0214 Ranches; Sheep raising farms and (Vol. 2)

0253 Ranches; Turkey egg farms and (Vol. 2)

0253 Ranches; Turkey farms and (Vol. 2)

3674 Random access memories (RAMS) (Vol. 1)

3131 Rands (shoe cut stock) (Vol. 1)

3433 Range boilers, galvanized iron and nonferrous metal (Vol. 1)

3861 Range finders, photographic (Vol. 1)

3589 Ranges, cooking: commercial (Vol. 1)

3631 Ranges, cooking: household (Vol. 1)

5064 Ranges, electric—wholesale (Vol. 2)

5074 Ranges, except electric—wholesale (Vol. 2)

5722 Ranges, gas and electric—retail (Vol. 2)

3631 Ranges, household cooking: electric and gas (Vol. 1)

3743 Rapid transit cars and equipment (Vol. 1)

5932 Rare book stores—retail (Vol. 2)

2819 Rare earth metal salts (Vol. 1)

1099 Rare-earths ore mining (Vol. 2)

0171 Raspberry farms (Vol. 2)

3423 Rasps, including recutting and resharpening (Vol. 1)

2879 Rat poisons (Vol. 1)

6411 Rate making organizations, insurance (Vol. 2)

3812 Rate-of-climb instrumentation (Vol. 1)

4731 Rate services, transportation (Vol. 2)

2211 Ratine, cotton (Vol. 1)

3612 Ratio transformers (Vol. 1)

2499 Rattan ware, except furniture (Vol. 1)

0279 Rattlesnake farms (Vol. 2)

2032 Ravioli, canned (Vol. 1)

2231 Raw stock dyeing and finishing: wool, mohair, and similar animal fibers (Vol. 1)

2269 Raw stock dyeing and other finishing, except wool (Vol. 1)

3111 Rawhide (Vol. 1)

2221 Rayon broadwoven fabrics (Vol. 1)

5131 Rayon piece goods—wholesale (Vol. 2)

2823 Rayon primary products: fibers, straw, strips, and yarn (Vol. 1)

2611 Rayon pulp (Vol. 1)

2284 Rayon thread (Vol. 1)

2299 Rayon tops, combing and converting (Vol. 1)

2282 Rayon yarn, filament: throwing, twisting, winding (Vol. 1)

2281 Rayon yarn, made from purchased staple: spun (Vol. 1)

2823 Rayon yarn, made in chemical plants (Vol. 1)

5199 Rayon yarns—wholesale (Vol. 2)

0912 Rays, catching of (Vol. 2)

3316 Razor blade strip steel, cold-rolled: not made in hot-rolling mills (Vol. 1)

3421 Razor blades (Vol. 1)

5122 Razor blades—wholesale (Vol. 2)

3199 Razor strops (Vol. 1)

3634 Razors, electric (Vol. 1)

5064 Razors, electric—wholesale (Vol. 2)

5122 Razors, nonelectric—wholesale (Vol. 2)

3421 Razors: safety and straight (Vol. 1)

2892 RDX (explosives) (Vol. 1)

2842 Re-refining drycleaning fluid (Vol. 1)

2992 Re-refining lubricating oils and greases (Vol. 1)

3443 Reactor containment vessels, metal plate (Vol. 1)

3612 Reactors, current limiting (Vol. 1)

3443 Reactors, nuclear: military and industrial (Vol. 1)

3674 Read only memories (ROMS) (Vol. 1)

3861 Readers, microfilm (Vol. 1)

8699 Reading rooms, religious materials (Vol. 2)

8299 Reading schools (Vol. 2)

3273 Ready-Mixed Concrete (Vol. 1)

3273 Ready-mixed concrete, production and distribution (Vol. 1)

5621 Ready-to-wear stores, women's—retail (Vol. 2)

2819 Reagent grade chemicals, inorganic: refined from technical grades (Vol. 1)

2869 Reagent grade chemicals, organic: refined from technical grades, except diagnostic and substances (Vol. 1)

6531 Real Estate Agents and Managers (Vol. 2)

6531 Real estate agents, brokers and managers (Vol. 2)

6531 Real estate appraisers (Vol. 2)

6531 Real estate auctions (Vol. 2)

8611 Real estate boards (Vol. 2)

6798 Real Estate Investment Trusts (Vol. 2)

6798 Real estate investment trusts (REIT'S) (Vol. 2)

8249 Real estate schools (Vol. 2)

6361 Real estate title insurance (Vol. 2)

6519 Real Property Lessors Not Elsewhere Classified (Vol. 2)

6553 Real property subdividers and developers, cemetery lots only (Vol. 2)

6552 Real property subdividers and developers, except of cemetery lots (Vol. 2)

6798 Realty investment trusts (Vol. 2)

6798 Realty trusts (Vol. 2)

3545 Reamers, machine tool (Vol. 1)

5084 Reamers—wholesale (Vol. 2)

3541 Reaming machines (Vol. 1)

3714 Rear axle housings, motor vehicle (Vol. 1)

7699 Rebabbitting (Vol. 2)

2789 Rebinding books, magazines, or pamphlets (Vol. 1)

7534 Rebuilding and retreading tires for the trade (Vol. 2)

3714 Rebuilding motor vehicle gasoline engines and transmissions on a factory basis (Vol. 1)

7694 Rebuilding motors, other than automotive (Vol. 2)

7534 Rebuilding tires (Vol. 2)

3541 Rebuilt machine tools, metal cutting types (Vol. 1)

3542 Rebuilt machine tools, metal forming types (Vol. 1)

5084 Recapping machinery for tires—wholesale (Vol. 2)

7534 Recapping tires (Vol. 2)

2782 Receipt books (Vol. 1)

3663 Receiver-transmitter units (transceivers) (Vol. 1)

3663 Receivers, radio communications (Vol. 1)

3651 Receiving sets, radio and television: household (Vol. 1)

3671 Receiving type electron tubes (Vol. 1)

5063 Receptacles, electrical—wholesale (Vol. 2)

3471 Rechroming auto bumpers, for the trade (Vol. 1)

6321 Reciprocal interinsurance exchanges, accident and health insurance (Vol. 2)

6331 Reciprocal interinsurance exchanges: fire, marine, and casualty insurance (Vol. 2)

6351 Reciprocal interinsurance exchanges, surety and fidelity insurance (Vol. 2)

3069 Reclaimed rubber (reworked by manufacturing processes) (Vol. 1)

3399 Reclaiming ferrous metals from clay (Vol. 1)

5093 Reclaiming iron and steel scrap from slag—wholesale (Vol. 2)

1629 Reclamation projects construction-general contractors (Vol. 2)

2512 Recliners, upholstered on wood frames (Vol. 1)

3484 Recoil mechanisms for guns, 30 mm. (or 1.18 inch) or less (Vol. 1)

3489 Recoil mechanisms for guns more than 30 mm. (or more than 1.18 inch) (Vol. 1)

3489 Recoilless rifles (Vol. 1)

2493 Reconstituted wood panels (Vol. 1)

2493 Reconstituted Wood Products (Vol. 1)

2782 Record albums (Vol. 1)

5735 Record and Prerecorded Tape Stores (Vol. 2)

3652 Record blanks, phonograph (Vol. 1)

5961 Record clubs, mail-order—retail (Vol. 2)

0751 Record services for cattle, hogs, sheep, goats, and poultry; Pedigree (Vol. 2)

5735 Record stores—retail (Vol. 2)

3651 Recorders, home tape: cassette, cartridge, and reel (Vol. 1)

3825 Recorders, oscillographic (Vol. 1)

3572 Recorders, tape: for computers (Vol. 1)

3679 Recording and playback heads, magnetic (Vol. 1)

3679 Recording heads for speech and musical equipment (Vol. 1)

5084 Recording instruments and accessories—wholesale (Vol. 2)

3651 Recording machines, music and speech: except dictation and telephone answering machines (Vol. 1)

7389 Recording studios on a contract or fee basis (Vol. 2)

3652 Records, phonograph (Vol. 1)

3341 Recovering and refining of nonferrous metals (Vol. 1)

2299 Recovering textile fibers from clippings and rags (Vol. 1)

3399 Recovery of iron ore from open hearth slag (Vol. 1)

3341 Recovery of silver from used photographic film (Vol. 1)

7997 Recreation and sports clubs, membership: except physical fitness (Vol. 2)

7032 Recreational camps (Vol. 2)

7011 Recreational hotels (Vol. 2)

9512 Recreational program administration-government (Vol. 2)

5561 Recreational Vehicle Dealers (Vol. 2)

5561 Recreational vehicle dealers—retail (Vol. 2)

7033 Recreational vehicle parks (Vol. 2)

7033 Recreational Vehicle Parks and Campsites (Vol. 2)

5561 Recreational vehicle parts and accessories—retail (Vol. 2)

5012 Recreational vehicles—wholesale (Vol. 2)

3612 Rectifier transformers (Vol. 1)

3629 Rectifiers (electrical apparatus) (Vol. 1)

3679 Rectifiers, electronic: except solid-state (Vol. 1)

5065 Rectifiers, electronic—wholesale (Vol. 2)

3674 Rectifiers, solid-state (Vol. 1)

2816 Red lead pigments (Vol. 1)

2899 Red oil (oleic acid) (Vol. 1)

7389 Redemption of trading stamps (Vol. 2)

9532 Redevelopment land agencies-government (Vol. 2)

3826 Redox (oxidation-reduction potential) instruments (Vol. 1)

1381 Redrilling oil and gas wells on a contract basis (Vol. 2)

2141 Redrying and stemming of tobacco (Vol. 1)

3494 Reducer returns, pipe: metal (Vol. 1)

3566 Reducers, speed (Vol. 1)

7991 Reducing facilities, physical fitness, without lodging (Vol. 2)

3566 Reduction gears and gear units for turbines, except automotive and aircraft (Vol. 1)

2519 Reed furniture (Vol. 1)

1499 Reed peat mining (Vol. 2)

2499 Reed ware, except furniture (Vol. 1)

3931 Reedboards, organ (Vol. 1)

3931 Reeds for musical instruments (Vol. 1)

3552 Reeds, loom (Vol. 1)

3569 Reels and racks, firehose (Vol. 1)

3499 Reels, cable: metal (Vol. 1)

2499 Reels, cloth winding: wood (Vol. 1)

3861 Reels, film (Vol. 1)

3949 Reels, fishing (Vol. 1)

2499 Reels, for drying clothes: wood (Vol. 1)

2499 Reels, plywood (Vol. 1)

2655 Reels, textile: fiber (Vol. 1)

1741 Refactory brick construction-contractors (Vol. 2)

8111 Referees in bankruptcy (Vol. 2)

8322 Referral services for personal and social problems (Vol. 2)

4613 Refined Petroleum Pipelines (Vol. 2)

2062 Refineries, cane sugar (Vol. 1)

2911 Refineries, petroleum (Vol. 1)

2911 Refinery gas produced in petroleum refineries (Vol. 1)

3339 Refining of lead, primary (Vol. 1)

3339 Refining of nonferrous metal, primary: except copper and aluminum (Vol. 1)

3341 Refining of nonferrous metals and alloys, secondary (Vol. 1)

3339 Refining of zinc, primary (Vol. 1)

2231 Refinishing and sponging cloths: wool, mohair, and similar animal fibers, for the trade (Vol. 1)

2261 Refinishing and sponging cotton broadwoven fabrics for the trade (Vol. 1)

2262 Refinishing of manmade fiber and silk broadwoven fabrics (Vol. 1)

3825 Reflectometers, sliding shorts (Vol. 1)

3231 Reflector glass beads, for highway signs and other reflectors: made from purchased glass (Vol. 1)

3647 Reflectors, clearance: vehicular (Vol. 1)

3229 Reflectors for lighting equipment, glass: pressed or blown (Vol. 1)

3648 Reflectors for lighting equipment: metal (Vol. 1)

3827 Reflectors, optical (Vol. 1)

3827 Reflectors, searchlight (Vol. 1)

0851 Reforestation (Vol. 2)

9223 Reformatories-government (Vol. 2)

3823 Refractometers, industrial process type (Vol. 1)

3826 Refractometers, laboratory (Vol. 1)

3297 Refractories, castable: nonclay (Vol. 1)

3255 Refractories, clay (Vol. 1)

3297 Refractories, graphite: carbon bond or ceramic bond (Vol. 1)

3297 Refractories, nonclay (Vol. 1)

3255 Refractory cement and mortars, clay (Vol. 1)

3297 Refractory cement, nonclay (Vol. 1)

5085 Refractory material—wholesale (Vol. 2)

5812 Refreshment stands (Vol. 2)

4222 Refrigerated warehousing (Vol. 2)

4222 Refrigerated Warehousing and Storage (Vol. 2)

3822 Refrigeration/air-conditioning defrost controls (Vol. 1)

7623 Refrigeration and Air-Conditioning Service and Repair Shops (Vol. 2)

1711 Refrigeration and freezer work-contractors (Vol. 2)

3585 Refrigeration compressors (Vol. 1)

3822 Refrigeration controls, pressure (Vol. 1)

5078 Refrigeration Equipment and Supplies (Vol. 2)

3585 Refrigeration machinery and equipment, industrial (Vol. 1)

7623 Refrigeration repair service, electric (Vol. 2)

3822 Refrigeration thermostats (Vol. 1)

3632 Refrigerator cabinets, household (Vol. 1)

3229 Refrigerator dishes and jars, glass (Vol. 1)

3469 Refrigerator parts, porcelain enameled (Vol. 1)

7623 Refrigerator repair service, electric (Vol. 2)

5722 Refrigerators and related electric and gas appliances—retail (Vol. 2)

5078 Refrigerators, commercial: reach-in and walk-in—wholesale (Vol. 2)

5064 Refrigerators, household: electric and gas—wholesale (Vol. 2)

3632 Refrigerators, mechanical and absorption: household (Vol. 1)

3728 Refueling equipment, airplane: for use in flight (Vol. 1)

8322 Refugee services (Vol. 2)

4212 Refuse, local collecting and transporting: without disposal (Vol. 2)

4953 Refuse Systems (Vol. 2)

2389 Regalia (Vol. 1)

2823 Regenerated cellulose fibers (Vol. 1)

6099 Regional clearinghouse associations (Vol. 2)

8399 Regional planning organizations, for social services (Vol. 2)

8049 Registered nurses, offices of: except home care services (Vol. 2)

3446 Registers, air: metal (Vol. 1)

3579 Registers, autographic (Vol. 1)

3578 Registers, credit account (Vol. 1)

3829 Registers, fare: for streetcars, buses, etc. (Vol. 1)

3824 Registers, linear tallying (Vol. 1)

7361 Registries, nurses' (Vol. 2)

3541 Regrinding machines, crankshaft (Vol. 1)

9631 Regulation and Administration of Communications, Electric, Gas and Other Utilities (Vol. 2)

9621 Regulation and Administration of Transportation Programs (Vol. 2)

9641 Regulation and inspection of agricultural products-government (Vol. 2)

9651 Regulation, Licensing and Inspection of Miscellaneous Commercial Sectors (Vol. 2)

9641 Regulation of Agricultural Marketing and Commodities (Vol. 2)

9631 Regulation of utilities (Vol. 2)

3612 Regulators, feeder voltage (electric transformers) (Vol. 1)

3613 Regulators, power (Vol. 1)

3612 Regulators, transmission and distribution voltage (Vol. 1)

3694 Regulators, voltage: motor vehicle (Vol. 1)

8093 Rehabilitation centers, outpatient (medical treatment) (Vol. 2)

8361 Rehabilitation centers, residential: with health care incidental (Vol. 2)

8331 Rehabilitation counseling and training, vocational (Vol. 2)

8069 Rehabilitation hospitals: drug addiction and alcoholism (Vol. 2)

5051 Reinforcement mesh, wire—wholesale (Vol. 2)

3496 Reinforcing mesh concrete: made from purchased wire (Vol. 1)

6321 Reinsurance carriers, accident and health (Vol. 2)

6311 Reinsurance carriers, life (Vol. 2)

6311 Reinsurance, life (Vol. 2)

3625 Relays and Industrial Controls (Vol. 1)

3825 Relays, instrument: all types (Vol. 1)

3625 Relays (Vol. 1)

5063 Relays—wholesale (Vol. 2)

8322 Relief services, temporary (Vol. 2)

5942 Religious book stores—retail (Vol. 2)

5999 Religious goods stores (other than books)—retail (Vol. 2)

8661 Religious instruction, provided by religious organizations (Vol. 2)

7812 Religious motion picture production (Vol. 2)

8661 Religious Organizations (Vol. 2)

6732 Religious trusts, management of (Vol. 2)

2035 Relishes, fruit and vegetable (Vol. 1)

2834 Remedies, human and animal (Vol. 1)

5949 Remnant stores—retail (Vol. 2)

1541 Remodeling buildings, industrial and warehouse-general contractors (Vol. 2)

1542 Remodeling buildings, nonresidential: except industrial and warehouses-general contractors (Vol. 2)

1522 Remodeling buildings, residential: except single-family-general contractors (Vol. 2)

1521 Remodeling buildings, single-family-general contractors (Vol. 2)

7375 Remote data base information retrieval services (Vol. 2)

0721 Removal, and surgery; Trees, orchard: planting, pruning, bracing, spraying, (Vol. 2)

1389 Removal of condensate gasoline from field gathering lines: on a contract basis (Vol. 2)

1241 Removal of overburden for anthracite: on a contract basis (Vol. 2)

1241 Removal of overburden for bituminous coal: on a contract basis (Vol. 2)

1081 Removal of overburden for metal mining: on a contract basis (Vol. 2)

1481 Removal of overburden for nonmetallic minerals except fuels: on a contract basis (Vol. 2)

2077 Rendering plants, inedible grease and tallow (Vol. 1)

7699 Reneedling work (Vol. 2)

5199 Rennet—wholesale (Vol. 2)

1541 Renovating buildings, industrial and warehouse-general contractors (Vol. 2)

1542 Renovating buildings, nonresidential: except industrial and warehouses-general contractors (Vol. 2)

1522 Renovating buildings, residential: except single-family-general contractors (Vol. 2)

1521 Renovating buildings, single-family-general contractors (Vol. 2)

3999 Renovating feathers, for the trade (Vol. 1)

9651 Rent control agencies-government (Vol. 2)

6531 Rental agents for real estate (Vol. 2)

7359 Rental and leasing of dishes, silverware, and tables (Vol. 2)

7359 Rental and servicing of electronic equipment, except computers (Vol. 2)

7514 Rental of automobiles, without drivers (Vol. 2)

7999 Rental of beach chairs and accessories (Vol. 2)

7999 Rental of bicycles (Vol. 2)

8231 Rental of books (Vol. 2)

7359 Rental of coin-operated machines (Vol. 2)

4222 Rental of cold storage lockers (Vol. 2)

7374 Rental of computer time (Vol. 2)

7377 Rental of computers, except finance leasing or by the manufacturer (Vol. 2)

7353 Rental of construction equipment (Vol. 2)

7021 Rental of furnished rooms (Vol. 2)

7359 Rental of furniture (Vol. 2)

7999 Rental of golf carts (Vol. 2)

4119 Rental of hearses and limousines, with drivers (Vol. 2)

7819 Rental of motion picture equipment (Vol. 2)

7822 Rental of motion picture film (Vol. 2)

7359 Rental of oil field equipment (Vol. 2)

4119 Rental of passenger automobiles, with drivers (Vol. 2)

4741 Rental of Railroad Cars (Vol. 2)

7999 Rental of rowboats and canoes (Vol. 2)

7999 Rental of saddle horses (Vol. 2)

7922 Rental of theatrical scenery (Vol. 2)

7359 Rental of tools (Vol. 2)

7519 Rental of trailers (Vol. 2)

4212 Rental of trucks with drivers (Vol. 2)

7513 Rental of trucks, without drivers (Vol. 2)

7519 Renting automobile utility trailers (Vol. 2)

7519 Renting travel, camping, or recreational trailers (Vol. 2)

2211 Rep, cotton (Vol. 1)

5014 Repair materials, tire and tube—wholesale (Vol. 2)

7692 Repair of cracked castings (welding service) (Vol. 2)

7641 Repair of furniture upholstery (Vol. 2)

7219 Repair of furs and other garments for individuals (Vol. 2)

7699 Repair of optical instruments (Vol. 2)

7699 Repair of photographic equipment (Vol. 2)

1761 Repair of roofs-contractors (Vol. 2)

7699 Repair of service station equipment (Vol. 2)

7699 Repair of speedometers (Vol. 2)

7699 Repair Shops and Related Services Not Elsewhere Classified (Vol. 2)

7538 Repair shops, automotive: general (Vol. 2)

7217 Repairing and cleaning plants, rug and carpet (Vol. 2)

2789 Repairing books (bookbinding) (Vol. 1)

1541 Repairing buildings, industrial and warehouse-general contractors (Vol. 2)

1542 Repairing buildings, nonresidential: except industrial and warehouses-general contractors (Vol. 2)

1522 Repairing buildings, residential: except single-family-general contractors (Vol. 2)

1521 Repairing buildings, single-family-general contractors (Vol. 2)

1389 Repairing lease tanks, oil field: on a contract basis (Vol. 2)

3661 Repeater equipment, telephone and telegraph (Vol. 1)

7922 Repertory or stock companies, theatrical (Vol. 2)

5065 Replacement parts, electronic—wholesale (Vol. 2)

7389 Repossession service (Vol. 2)

6099 Representative offices of foreign banks, excluding agents and branches (Vol. 2)

8422 Reptile exhibits (Vol. 2)

7379 Requirements analysis, computer hardware (Vol. 2)

2421 Resawing lumber into smaller dimensions (Vol. 1)

8731 Research and development of computer and related hardware (Vol. 2)

3721 Research and development on aircraft by the manufacturer (Vol. 1)

3724 Research and development on aircraft engines and engine parts by the manufacturer (Vol. 1)

3728 Research and development on aircraft parts and auxiliary equipment by the manufacturer (Vol. 1)

3769 Research and development on guided missile and space vehicle components, by the manufacturer (Vol. 1)

3764 Research and development on guided missile and space vehicle engines, by the manufacturer (Vol. 1)

3761 Research and development on guided missiles and space vehicles, by the manufacturer (Vol. 1)

8731 Research and development, physical and biological: commercial (Vol. 2)

8732 Research: economic, sociological, and educational-commercial (Vol. 2)

8733 Research, noncommercial (Vol. 2)

2833 Reserpines (Vol. 1)

7389 Reservation service, hotel (Vol. 2)

1629 Reservoir construction-general contractors (Vol. 2)

7041 Residence clubs operated by organizations for members only (Vol. 2)

6514 Residential building, operators of (four or fewer housing units) (Vol. 2)

8361 Residential Care (Vol. 2)

1522 Residential construction, except single-family-general contractors (Vol. 2)

1521 Residential construction, single-family-general contractors (Vol. 2)

3645 Residential Electric Lighting Fixtures (Vol. 1)

8811 Residential farms, noncommercial (Vol. 2)

6513 Residential hotels, operators of (Vol. 2)

6515 Residential Mobile Home Site Operators (Vol. 2)

1752 Resilient floor laying-contractors (Vol. 2)

2295 Resin coated fabrics (Vol. 1)

2851 Resinate driers (Vol. 1)

2672 Resinous impregnated paper, except for packaging (Vol. 1)

2671 Resinous impregnated paper for packaging (Vol. 1)

2821 Resins, phenolic (Vol. 1)

5162 Resins, plastics—wholesale (Vol. 2)

5162 Resins, synthetic: except rubber—wholesale (Vol. 2)

2821 Resins, synthetic (Vol. 1)

5169 Resins, synthetic rubber—wholesale (Vol. 2)

3825 Resistance measuring equipment (Vol. 1)

3823 Resistance thermometers and bulbs, industrial process type (Vol. 1)

3548 Resistance welders, electric (Vol. 1)

3676 Resistor networks (Vol. 1)

3676 Resistors, electronic (Vol. 1)

5065 Resistors, electronic—wholesale (Vol. 2)

3621 Resolvers (Vol. 1)

3679 Resonant reed devices, electronic (Vol. 1)

2865 Resorcinol (Vol. 1)

7011 Resort hotels (Vol. 2)

3842 Respirators (Vol. 1)

3845 Respiratory analysis equipment, electromedical (Vol. 1)

3842 Respiratory protection equipment, personal (Vol. 1)

8093 Respiratory therapy clinics (Vol. 2)

8059 Rest homes with health care (Vol. 2)

8361 Rest homes, with health care incidental (Vol. 2)

7342 Rest room cleaning service (Vol. 2)

7299 Rest room operation (Vol. 2)

1542 Restaurant construction-general contractors (Vol. 2)

2599 Restaurant furniture (Vol. 1)

8249 Restaurant operation schools (Vol. 2)

7389 Restaurant reservation service (Vol. 2)

3444 Restaurant sheet metalwork (Vol. 1)

5812 Restaurants (Vol. 2)

5812 Restaurants, carry-out (Vol. 2)

5812 Restaurants, fast food (Vol. 2)

3829 Restitution apparatus, photogrammetrical (Vol. 1)

7641 Restoration and repair of antique furniture (Vol. 2)

7699 Restoration and repair of antiques, except furniture and automobiles (Vol. 2)

3842 Restraints, patient (Vol. 1)

7338 Resume writing service (Vol. 2)

1611 Resurfacing streets and highways-contractors (Vol. 2)

5461 Retail Bakeries (Vol. 2)

6512 Retail establishments, property operation only (Vol. 2)

5261 Retail Nurseries, Lawn and Garden Stores (Vol. 2)

1741 Retaining wall construction: block, stone, or brick-contractors (Vol. 2)

3479 Retinning of cans and utensils, not done in rolling mills (Vol. 1)

3845 Retinoscopes, electromedical (Vol. 1)

3841 Retinoscopes, except electromedical (Vol. 1)

6513 Retirement hotels, operators of (Vol. 2)

3297 Retorts, graphite (Vol. 1)

3443 Retorts, industrial (Vol. 1)

3443 Retorts, smelting (Vol. 1)

3841   Retractors (Vol. 1)
3011   Retreading materials, tire (Vol. 1)
7534   Retreading tires (Vol. 2)
0723   Retting flax (Vol. 2)
0723   Retting; Flax decorticating and (Vol. 2)
7641   Reupholstery and Furniture Repair (Vol. 2)
7641   Reupholstery shops (Vol. 2)
1629   Revetment construction-general contractors (Vol. 2)
3484   Revolvers and parts (Vol. 1)
1796   Revolving door installation-contractors (Vol. 2)
7219   Reweaving textiles (mending service) (Vol. 2)
2282   Rewinding of yarn (Vol. 1)
7694   Rewinding stators (Vol. 2)
3861   Rewinds, motion picture film (Vol. 1)
1381   Reworking oil and gas wells on a contract basis (Vol. 2)
3663   RF power amplifiers, and IF amplifiers: sold separately (Vol. 1)
3339   Rhenium refining, primary (Vol. 1)
3679   Rheostats, electronic (Vol. 1)
3625   Rheostats, industrial control (Vol. 1)
1099   Rhodium ore mining (Vol. 2)
1061   Rhodochrosite mining (Vol. 2)
0182   Rhubarb grown under cover (Vol. 2)
2655   Ribbon blocks, fiber (Vol. 1)
2297   Ribbon, nonwoven (yarn bonded by plastics) (Vol. 1)
5131   Ribbon, textile—wholesale (Vol. 2)
2396   Ribbons and bows, cut and sewed (Vol. 1)
3955   Ribbons, inked: e.g., typewriter, adding machine, cash register (Vol. 1)
5112   Ribbons, inked—wholesale (Vol. 2)
2241   Ribbons (Vol. 1)
0112   Rice (Vol. 2)
2044   Rice bran, flour, and meal (Vol. 1)
2043   Rice breakfast foods (Vol. 1)
2044   Rice, brewers' (Vol. 1)
2044   Rice, brown (Vol. 1)
2044   Rice cleaning and polishing (Vol. 1)
0723   Rice drying (Vol. 2)
0112   Rice farms (Vol. 2)
0723   Rice, hay, fruits, and vegetables; Drying of corn, (Vol. 2)
2044   Rice Milling (Vol. 1)
2044   Rice polish (Vol. 1)
5149   Rice, polished—wholesale (Vol. 2)
2046   Rice starch (Vol. 1)
2099   Rice, uncooked: packaged with other ingredients (Vol. 1)
5153   Rice, unpolished—wholesale (Vol. 2)
2044   Rice, vitamin and mineral enriched (Vol. 1)
2241   Rickrack braid (Vol. 1)
3599   Riddles, sand (hand sifting or screening apparatus) (Vol. 1)
7999   Riding academies and schools (Vol. 2)
5699   Riding apparel stores—retail (Vol. 2)
2329   Riding clothes: men's and boys' (Vol. 1)
7997   Riding clubs, membership (Vol. 2)
3199   Riding crops (Vol. 1)
5941   Riding goods and equipment—retail (Vol. 2)

2339   Riding habits: women's, misses', and juniors' (Vol. 1)
7999   Riding stables (Vol. 2)
2899   Rifle bore cleaning compounds (Vol. 1)
3541   Rifle working machines (machine tools) (Vol. 1)
3484   Rifles and parts, 30 mm. (or 1.18 inch) or less (Vol. 1)
3484   Rifles: BB and pellet (Vol. 1)
3841   Rifles for propelling hypodermics into animals (Vol. 1)
3484   Rifles, high compression pneumatic: 30 mm. (or 1.18 inch) or less (Vol. 1)
3484   Rifles: pneumatic, spring loaded, and compressed air-except toy (Vol. 1)
3489   Rifles, recoilless (Vol. 1)
3944   Rifles, toy (Vol. 1)
1389   Rig building, repairing, and dismantling: on a contract basis (Vol. 2)
3469   Rigidizing metal (Vol. 1)
3714   Rims, wheel: motor vehicle (Vol. 1)
3961   Rings, finger: gold-plated wire (Vol. 1)
3255   Rings, glasshouse: clay (Vol. 1)
3592   Rings, piston (Vol. 1)
3911   Rings, precious metal (Vol. 1)
1429   Riprap quarrying, except limestone or granite (Vol. 2)
4449   River freight transportation, except on the St. Lawrence Seaway (Vol. 2)
7999   River rafting, operation of (Vol. 2)
3546   Riveting hammers (Vol. 1)
3542   Riveting machines (Vol. 1)
3452   Rivets, metal (Vol. 1)
3089   Rivets, plastics (Vol. 1)
2879   Roach poisons (Vol. 1)
7922   Road companies, theatrical (Vol. 2)
3531   Road construction and maintenance machinery (Vol. 1)
5082   Road construction and maintenance machinery— wholesale (Vol. 2)
1611   Road construction, except elevated-general contractors (Vol. 2)
2951   Road materials, bituminous: not made in petroleum refineries (Vol. 1)
2911   Road materials, bituminous: produced in petroleum refineries (Vol. 1)
3711   Road oilers (motor vehicles) (Vol. 1)
2911   Road oils, produced in petroleum refineries (Vol. 1)
7549   Road service, automotive (Vol. 2)
4785   Roads, toll: operation of (Vol. 2)
2095   Roasted Coffee (Vol. 1)
0251   Roaster Chickens; Broiler, Fryer and (Vol. 2)
3634   Roasters, electric (Vol. 1)
0251   Roasting chickens, raising of (Vol. 2)
3556   Roasting machinery: coffee, peanut, etc. (Vol. 1)
2384   Robes and Dressing Gowns (Vol. 1)
5137   Robes and gowns: women's and children's— wholesale (Vol. 2)
2369   Robes, lounging: children's (Vol. 1)
2369   Robes, lounging: girls', children's, and infants' (Vol. 1)

2384 Robes, lounging: men's, boys', and women's (Vol. 1)

2253 Robes, lounging (Vol. 1)

5136 Robes, men's and boys'—wholesale (Vol. 2)

3535 Robotic conveyors for general industrial use (Vol. 1)

3541 Robots for drilling and cutting-machine type, metalworking (Vol. 1)

3569 Robots for general industrial use (Vol. 1)

3541 Robots for grinding, polishing, and deburring-metalworking (Vol. 1)

3542 Robots for metal forming: e.g., pressing, hammering, extruding (Vol. 1)

3563 Robots for spraying, painting-industrial (Vol. 1)

3548 Robots for welding, soldering, or brazing (Vol. 1)

3559 Robots, plastics: for molding and forming (Vol. 1)

5999 Rock and stone specimens—retail (Vol. 2)

3531 Rock crushing machinery, portable (Vol. 1)

3532 Rock crushing machinery, stationary (Vol. 1)

3532 Rock drills, portable (Vol. 1)

3275 Rock, gypsum (Vol. 1)

1629 Rock removal, underwater-contractors (Vol. 2)

1479 Rock salt mining (Vol. 2)

2512 Rockers, upholstered on wood frames (Vol. 1)

2511 Rockers, wood: except upholstered (Vol. 1)

2869 Rocket engine fuel, organic (Vol. 1)

3489 Rocket launchers, hand-held (Vol. 1)

3724 Rocket motors, aircraft (Vol. 1)

3764 Rocket motors, guided missile (Vol. 1)

3443 Rocket transportation casings (Vol. 1)

3483 Rockets (ammunition) (Vol. 1)

3761 Rockets (guided missiles), space and military: complete (Vol. 1)

2899 Rockets, pyrotechnic (Vol. 1)

3944 Rocking horses (Vol. 1)

3269 Rockingham earthenware (Vol. 1)

3547 Rod mills (rolling mill equipment) (Vol. 1)

2879 Rodent poisons (Vol. 1)

2879 Rodenticides (Vol. 1)

7999 Rodeo animal rental (Vol. 2)

7999 Rodeos, operation of (Vol. 2)

3354 Rods, aluminum: extruded (Vol. 1)

3355 Rods, aluminum: rolled (Vol. 1)

3949 Rods and rod parts, fishing (Vol. 1)

3351 Rods, copper and copper alloy (Vol. 1)

2591 Rods, curtain and drapery (Vol. 1)

3496 Rods, gas welding: made from purchased wire (Vol. 1)

3069 Rods, hard rubber (Vol. 1)

3312 Rods, iron and steel: made in steel works or rolling mills (Vol. 1)

3083 Rods, laminated plastics (Vol. 1)

3356 Rods: lead, magnesium, nickel, tin, titanium, and their alloys (Vol. 1)

5051 Rods, metal—wholesale (Vol. 2)

3829 Rods, surveyors' (Vol. 1)

3082 Rods, unsupported plastics (Vol. 1)

3069 Roll coverings: rubber for papermill; industrial, steelmills, printers' (Vol. 1)

3562 Roller bearings and parts (Vol. 1)

3069 Roller covers, printers': rubber (Vol. 1)

3111 Roller leather (Vol. 1)

3547 Roller levelers (rolling mill machinery) (Vol. 1)

2261 Roller printing of cotton broadwoven fabrics (Vol. 1)

2262 Roller printing of manmade fiber and silk broadwoven fabrics (Vol. 1)

3949 Roller skates (Vol. 1)

7999 Roller skating rink operation (Vol. 2)

2591 Rollers and fittings, window shade (Vol. 1)

3523 Rollers and levelers, land (agricultural machinery) (Vol. 1)

3991 Rollers, paint (Vol. 1)

3531 Rollers, road (Vol. 1)

3531 Rollers, sheepsfoot and vibratory (Vol. 1)

2499 Rollers, wood (Vol. 1)

3442 Rolling doors for industrial buildings and warehouses, metal (Vol. 1)

3351 Rolling, Drawing and Extruding of Copper (Vol. 1)

3351 Rolling, drawing, and extruding of copper and copper alloys (Vol. 1)

3356 Rolling, Drawing and Extruding of Nonferrous Metals Except Copper and Aluminum (Vol. 1)

3542 Rolling machines, thread and spline (Vol. 1)

3547 Rolling Mill Machinery and Equipment (Vol. 1)

3547 Rolling mill machinery and equipment (Vol. 1)

3321 Rolling mill rolls, iron: not machined (Vol. 1)

3325 Rolling mill rolls, steel: not machined (Vol. 1)

2499 Rolling pins, wood (Vol. 1)

2051 Rolls, bread-type, including frozen (Vol. 1)

3547 Rolls for rolling mill machinery, machined (Vol. 1)

2679 Rolls, paper: adding machine, telegraph tape, etc. (Vol. 1)

3321 Rolls, rolling mill: iron-not machined (Vol. 1)

3325 Rolls, rolling mill: steel-not machined (Vol. 1)

3069 Rolls, solid or covered rubber (Vol. 1)

2051 Rolls, sweet, except frozen (Vol. 1)

0161 Romaine farms (Vol. 2)

2369 Rompers: infants' (Vol. 1)

3841 Rongeurs, bone (Vol. 1)

2952 Roof cement: asphalt, fibrous, and plastics (Vol. 1)

2952 Roof coatings and cements: liquid and plastics (Vol. 1)

3444 Roof deck, sheet metal (Vol. 1)

1761 Roof spraying, painting, or coating-contractors (Vol. 2)

2439 Roof trusses, wood (Vol. 1)

3292 Roofing, asbestos felt roll (Vol. 1)

5033 Roofing, asphalt and sheet metal—wholesale (Vol. 2)

2952 Roofing, asphalt or tar saturated felt: built-up, roll, and shingle (Vol. 1)

2621 Roofing felt stock (Vol. 1)

2952 Roofing felts, cements, and coatings: asphalt, tar, and composition (Vol. 1)

3295 Roofing granules (Vol. 1)

5211 Roofing material dealers—retail (Vol. 2)

2952 Roofing pitch, coal tar: not made in byproduct coke ovens (Vol. 1)

3444 Roofing, sheet metal (Vol. 1)
5033 Roofing, Siding and Insulation Materials (Vol. 2)
1761 Roofing, Siding and Sheet Metal Work (Vol. 2)
3069 Roofing, single ply membrane: rubber (Vol. 1)
3281 Roofing, slate (Vol. 1)
3272 Roofing tile and slabs, concrete (Vol. 1)
3259 Roofing tile, clay (Vol. 1)
1761 Roofing work, including repairing-contractors (Vol. 2)
3585 Room coolers, portable (Vol. 1)
2511 Room dividers, household: wood (Vol. 1)
3433 Room heaters, except electric (Vol. 1)
3634 Room heaters, space: electric (Vol. 1)
3822 Room thermostats (Vol. 1)
7021 Rooming and Boarding Houses (Vol. 2)
7021 Rooming houses, except organization (Vol. 2)
7041 Rooming houses, fraternity and sorority (Vol. 2)
7041 Rooming houses operated by organizations for members only (Vol. 2)
2086 Root beer, bottled or canned (Vol. 1)
2046 Root starch, edible (Vol. 1)
3552 Rope and cordage machines (Vol. 1)
2621 Rope and jute wrapping paper (Vol. 1)
3292 Rope, asbestos (Vol. 1)
2298 Rope, except asbestos and wire (Vol. 1)
5085 Rope, except wire rope—wholesale (Vol. 2)
3429 Rope fittings (Vol. 1)
3496 Rope, uninsulated wire: made from purchased wire (Vol. 1)
5051 Rope, wire: not insulated—wholesale (Vol. 2)
3961 Rosaries and other small religious articles, except precious metal (Vol. 1)
3911 Rosaries and other small religious articles, precious metal (Vol. 1)
1094 Roscoelite (vanadium hydromica) mining (Vol. 2)
0181 Rose growers (Vol. 2)
2821 Rosin modified resins (Vol. 1)
2861 Rosin, produced by distillation of pine gum or pine wood (Vol. 1)
2899 Rosin sizes (Vol. 1)
5169 Rosin—wholesale (Vol. 2)
3621 Rotary converters (electrical equipment) (Vol. 1)
3523 Rotary hoes (agricultural machinery) (Vol. 1)
2754 Rotary photogravure printing (Vol. 1)
3549 Rotary slitters (metalworking machines) (Vol. 1)
3545 Rotary tables, indexing (Vol. 1)
3824 Rotary type meters, consumption registering (Vol. 1)
3351 Rotating bands, copper and copper alloy (Vol. 1)
2879 Rotenone bearing preparations (Vol. 1)
2879 Rotenone concentrates (Vol. 1)
3728 Roto-blades for helicopters (Vol. 1)
2621 Rotogravure paper (Vol. 1)
2754 Rotogravure printing (Vol. 1)
2796 Rotogravure printing plates and cylinders (Vol. 1)
3621 Rotor retainers and housings (Vol. 1)
3621 Rotors for motors (Vol. 1)
3524 Rototillers (garden machinery) (Vol. 1)
2844 Rouge, cosmetic (Vol. 1)
3291 Rouge, polishing (Vol. 1)

3523 Roughage mills (agricultural machinery) (Vol. 1)
2449 Round stave baskets, for fruits and vegetables (Vol. 1)
2426 Rounds or rungs, ladder and furniture: hardwood (Vol. 1)
3312 Rounds, tube (Vol. 1)
5099 Roundwood—wholesale (Vol. 2)
1389 Roustabout service: on a contract basis (Vol. 2)
3553 Routing machines, woodworking (Vol. 1)
2299 Roves, flax and jute (Vol. 1)
3552 Roving machines (textile machinery) (Vol. 1)
7999 Rowboat rental (Vol. 2)
3732 Rowboats, building and repairing (Vol. 1)
1521 Rowhouse (single-family) construction-general contractors (Vol. 2)
3949 Rowing machines (Vol. 1)
6792 Royalty companies, oil (Vol. 2)
6289 Royalty owners protective associations (Vol. 2)
3021 Rubber and Plastics Footwear (Vol. 1)
3052 Rubber and Plastics Hose and Belting (Vol. 1)
2891 Rubber cement (Vol. 1)
1455 Rubber clay mining (Vol. 2)
3069 Rubber-covered motor mounting rings (rubber bonded) (Vol. 1)
5199 Rubber, crude—wholesale (Vol. 2)
3567 Rubber curing ovens (Vol. 1)
3061 Rubber goods, mechanical: molded, extruded, and lathe-cut (Vol. 1)
5085 Rubber goods, mechanical—wholesale (Vol. 2)
5122 Rubber goods, medical—wholesale (Vol. 2)
3069 Rubber heels, soles, and soling strips (Vol. 1)
0831 Rubber plantations (Vol. 2)
2869 Rubber processing chemicals, organic: accelerators and antioxidants (Vol. 1)
2899 Rubber processing preparations (Vol. 1)
3559 Rubber products machinery (Vol. 1)
3069 Rubber, reclaimed and reworked by manufacturing processes (Vol. 1)
5093 Rubber scrap—wholesale (Vol. 2)
2891 Rubber sealing compounds, synthetic (Vol. 1)
5999 Rubber stamp stores—retail (Vol. 2)
2822 Rubber, synthetic (Vol. 1)
2241 Rubber thread and yarns, fabric covered (Vol. 1)
3559 Rubber working machinery (Vol. 1)
3069 Rubberbands (Vol. 1)
3069 Rubberized fabrics (Vol. 1)
1499 Rubbing stone quarrying (Vol. 2)
3291 Rubbing stones, artificial (Vol. 1)
4953 Rubbish collection and disposal (Vol. 2)
1411 Rubble mining (Vol. 2)
2819 Rubidium metal (Vol. 1)
1499 Ruby mining (Vol. 2)
3728 Rudders, aircraft (Vol. 1)
2395 Ruffling, for the trade (Vol. 1)
3069 Rug backing compounds, latex (Vol. 1)
7389 Rug binding for the trade (Vol. 2)
3582 Rug cleaning, drying, and napping machines: commercial laundry (Vol. 1)
7217 Rug cleaning, dyeing, and repairing plants (Vol. 2)

7699 Rug repair shops, not combined with cleaning (Vol. 2)

5713 Rug stores—retail (Vol. 2)

2842 Rug, upholstery, and drycleaning detergents and spotters (Vol. 1)

2299 Rugbacking, jute or other fiber (Vol. 1)

2273 Rugs, except rubber or plastics (Vol. 1)

5023 Rugs—wholesale (Vol. 2)

3423 Rules and rulers: metal, except slide (Vol. 1)

2499 Rules and rulers: wood, except slide (Vol. 1)

3555 Rules, printers' (Vol. 1)

3829 Rules, slide (Vol. 1)

2782 Ruling of paper (Vol. 1)

2085 Rum (Vol. 1)

1389 Running, cutting, and pulling casings, tubes, and rods: oil and gas field (Vol. 2)

6111 Rural Electrification Administration (Vol. 2)

2052 Rusk (Vol. 1)

2035 Russian dressing (Vol. 1)

2992 Rust arresting compounds, animal and vegetable oil base (Vol. 1)

3479 Rust proofing (hot dipping) of metals and formed products, for the trade (Vol. 1)

2842 Rust removers (Vol. 1)

2899 Rust resisting compounds (Vol. 1)

5169 Rustproofing chemicals—wholesale (Vol. 2)

7549 Rustproofing service, automotive (Vol. 2)

1099 Ruthenium ore mining (Vol. 2)

1099 Rutile mining (Vol. 2)

0119 Rye farms (Vol. 2)

2041 Rye flour (Vol. 1)

S

2822 S-type rubber (Vol. 1)

2869 Saccharin (Vol. 1)

2844 Sachet (Vol. 1)

2674 Sacks, multiwall or heavy-duty shipping sack (Vol. 1)

2399 Saddle cloths (Vol. 1)

2842 Saddle soap (Vol. 1)

2499 Saddle trees, wood (Vol. 1)

3429 Saddlery hardware (Vol. 1)

3111 Saddlery leather (Vol. 1)

7699 Saddlery repair shops (Vol. 2)

5941 Saddlery stores—retail (Vol. 2)

3199 Saddles and parts (Vol. 1)

3751 Saddles, motorcycle and bicycle (Vol. 1)

3499 Safe deposit boxes and chests, metal (Vol. 1)

6099 Safe deposit companies (Vol. 2)

3499 Safe doors and linings, metal (Vol. 1)

4212 Safe moving, local (Vol. 2)

3499 Safes, metal (Vol. 1)

3842 Safety appliances and equipment, personal (Vol. 1)

3199 Safety belts, leather (Vol. 1)

2892 Safety fuses (Vol. 1)

3231 Safety glass, made from purchased glass (Vol. 1)

7218 Safety glove supply service (Vol. 2)

3842 Safety gloves, all materials (Vol. 1)

7389 Safety inspection service, except automotive (Vol. 2)

3965 Safety pins (Vol. 1)

3421 Safety razor blades (Vol. 1)

3421 Safety razors (Vol. 1)

2399 Safety strap assemblies, automobile: except leather (Vol. 1)

5063 Safety switches—wholesale (Vol. 2)

0119 Safflower farms (Vol. 2)

2076 Safflower oil (Vol. 1)

3255 Saggers (Vol. 1)

3949 Sailboards (Vol. 1)

3732 Sailboats, building and repairing (Vol. 1)

5091 Sailboats—wholesale (Vol. 2)

2211 Sailcloth (Vol. 1)

3731 Sailing vessels, commercial: building and repairing (Vol. 1)

2394 Sails (Vol. 1)

2812 Sal soda (washing soda) (Vol. 1)

2099 Salad dressing mixes, dry (Vol. 1)

5149 Salad dressing—wholesale (Vol. 2)

2035 Salad dressings, except dry mixes (Vol. 1)

2079 Salad oils, vegetable: except corn oil-refined (Vol. 1)

2099 Salads, fresh or refrigerated (Vol. 1)

3433 Salamanders, coke and gas burning (Vol. 1)

6211 Sale of partnership shares in real estate syndicates (Vol. 2)

5112 Sales and receipt books—wholesale (Vol. 2)

5999 Sales barns—retail (Vol. 2)

2761 Sales books (Vol. 1)

2833 Salicylic acid derivatives, medicinal grade (Vol. 1)

1474 Salines mining, except common salt (Vol. 2)

0912 Salmon, catching of (Vol. 2)

2091 Salmon: smoked, salted, dried, canned, and pickled (Vol. 1)

5813 Saloons (drinking places) (Vol. 2)

2819 Salt cake (sodium sulfate) (Vol. 1)

5149 Salt, evaporated—wholesale (Vol. 2)

2899 Salt (Vol. 1)

1479 Salt mining, common (Vol. 2)

1389 Salt water, impounding (in connection with petroleum products) (Vol. 2)

2068 Salted and Roasted Nuts and Seeds (Vol. 1)

5145 Salted nuts—wholesale (Vol. 2)

2052 Saltines (Vol. 1)

2834 Salts, effervescent (Vol. 1)

2899 Salts, heat treating (Vol. 1)

5169 Salts, industrial—wholesale (Vol. 2)

5169 Salts, metal—wholesale (Vol. 2)

2819 Salts of rare earth metals (Vol. 1)

7389 Salvaging of damaged merchandise, not engaged in sales (Vol. 2)

2782 Sample books (Vol. 1)

3161 Sample cases, regardless of material (Vol. 1)

3829 Sample changers, nuclear radiation (Vol. 1)

2789 Sample mounting for the trade (Vol. 1)

3821 Sample preparation apparatus, laboratory type (Vol. 1)

7319 Samples, distribution of (Vol. 2)

7389 Sampling of commodities, not connected with transportation (Vol. 2)

3546 Saws, portable hand held: power-driven-woodworking or metalworking (Vol. 1)

3553 Saws, power: bench and table (woodworking machinery)-except portable (Vol. 1)

3541 Saws, power: metal cutting (Vol. 1)

3841 Saws, surgical (Vol. 1)

3931 Saxophones and parts (Vol. 1)

1799 Scaffolding construction-contractors (Vol. 2)

5082 Scaffolding—wholesale (Vol. 2)

3446 Scaffolds, metal (mobile or stationary) (Vol. 1)

2499 Scaffolds, wood (Vol. 1)

7699 Scale repair service (Vol. 2)

3579 Scalers for gummed tape: hand (Vol. 1)

3829 Scalers, nuclear radiation (Vol. 1)

3596 Scales and Balances Except Laboratory (Vol. 1)

7299 Scales, coin-operated: operation of (Vol. 2)

3596 Scales, except laboratory (Vol. 1)

5046 Scales, except laboratory—wholesale (Vol. 2)

3545 Scales, measuring (machinists' precision tools) (Vol. 1)

7699 Scaling, ship-contractors (Vol. 2)

2395 Scalloping, for the trade (Vol. 1)

7299 Scalp treatment service (Vol. 2)

2819 Scandium (Vol. 1)

3553 Scarfing machines (woodworking machinery) (Vol. 1)

2253 Scarfs (Vol. 1)

3531 Scarifiers, road (Vol. 1)

2865 Scarlet 2 R lake (Vol. 1)

2392 Scarves: e.g., table, dresser (Vol. 1)

2339 Scarves, hoods, and headbands: women's, misses', and juniors' (Vol. 1)

2323 Scarves: men's and boys' (Vol. 1)

5136 Scarves, men's and boys'—wholesale (Vol. 2)

5137 Scarves: women's, children's and infant's—wholesale (Vol. 2)

2273 Scatter rugs, except rubber or plastics (Vol. 1)

5093 Scavengering—wholesale (Vol. 2)

7922 Scenery design, theatrical (Vol. 2)

3999 Scenery for theaters, opera houses, halls, and schools (Vol. 1)

7922 Scenery, rental: theatrical (Vol. 2)

7999 Scenic railroads for amusement (Vol. 2)

2759 Schedules, transportation: except lithographed or gravure (Vol. 1)

2754 Schedules, transportation: gravure printing (Vol. 1)

2752 Schedules, transportation: lithographed (Vol. 1)

1061 Scheelite mining (Vol. 2)

2397 Schiffli Machine Embroideries (Vol. 1)

2397 Schiffli machine embroideries (Vol. 1)

1411 Schist, dimension-quarrying (Vol. 2)

1542 School building construction-general contractors (Vol. 2)

4151 School Buses (Vol. 2)

5021 School desks—wholesale (Vol. 2)

2531 School furniture, except stone and concrete (Vol. 1)

2531 School furniture (Vol. 1)

7221 School photographers (Vol. 2)

5943 School supplies—retail (Vol. 2)

7999 Schools and camps, sports instructional (Vol. 2)

8299 Schools and Educational Services Not Elsewhere Classified (Vol. 2)

8249 Schools, correspondence: including branch offices and solicitors (Vol. 2)

7911 Schools, dance: including children's, and professionals' (Vol. 2)

8211 Schools, elementary and secondary (Vol. 2)

8211 Schools for the physically handicapped, elementary and secondary (Vol. 2)

8211 Schools for the retarded (Vol. 2)

7999 Schools, riding (Vol. 2)

8249 Schools, vocational, except high schools, data processing, or business (Vol. 2)

3674 Schottky diodes (Vol. 1)

3944 Science kits: microscopes, chemistry sets, and natural science sets (Vol. 1)

3231 Scientific apparatus glass, made from purchased glass (Vol. 1)

3231 Scientific glassware, made from purchased glass (Vol. 1)

3229 Scientific glassware, pressed or blown: made in glassmaking plants (Vol. 1)

7699 Scientific instrument repair, except electric (Vol. 2)

5049 Scientific instruments—wholesale (Vol. 2)

8621 Scientific membership associations (Vol. 2)

8733 Scientific research, noncommercial (Vol. 2)

3829 Scintillation detectors (Vol. 1)

3421 Scissors: barbers', manicure, pedicure, tailors' and household (Vol. 1)

3634 Scissors, electric (Vol. 1)

3421 Scissors, hand (Vol. 1)

3949 Scoops, crab and fish (Vol. 1)

3423 Scoops, hand: metal (Vol. 1)

2499 Scoops, wood (Vol. 1)

3944 Scooters, children's (Vol. 1)

3993 Scoreboards, electric (Vol. 1)

1499 Scoria mining (Vol. 2)

2841 Scouring compounds (Vol. 1)

3559 Scouring machines, tannery (Vol. 1)

2299 Scouring of wool, mohair, and similar fibers (Vol. 1)

3291 Scouring pads, soap impregnated (Vol. 1)

3731 Scows, building and repairing (Vol. 1)

5093 Scrap and Waste Materials (Vol. 2)

5093 Scrap and waste materials—wholesale (Vol. 2)

5093 Scrap, rubber—wholesale (Vol. 2)

7389 Scrap steel cutting on a contract or fee basis (Vol. 2)

2782 Scrapbooks (Vol. 1)

5112 Scrapbooks—wholesale (Vol. 2)

3532 Scraper loaders, underground (Vol. 1)

3531 Scrapers, construction (Vol. 1)

3423 Scrapers, woodworking: hand (Vol. 1)

2013 Scrapple (Vol. 1)

3531 Screeds and screeding machines (Vol. 1)

3442 Screen doors, metal (Vol. 1)

2261 Screen printing of cotton broadwoven fabrics (Vol. 1)

2262 Screen printing of manmade fiber and silk broadwoven fabrics (Vol. 1)

2759 Screen printing on glass, plastics, paper, and metal, including highway signs (Vol. 1)
2893 Screen process ink (Vol. 1)
3531 Screeners, portable (Vol. 1)
3532 Screeners, stationary (Vol. 1)
3569 Screening and sifting machines for general industrial use (Vol. 1)
5084 Screening machinery and equipment, industrial—wholesale (Vol. 2)
1499 Screening peat (Vol. 2)
1231 Screening plants, anthracite (Vol. 2)
1221 Screening plants, bituminous coal (Vol. 2)
3089 Screening, window: plastics (Vol. 1)
3496 Screening, woven wire: made from purchased wire (Vol. 1)
3442 Screens, door and window: metal frame (Vol. 1)
2431 Screens, door and window: wood (Vol. 1)
2511 Screens, privacy: wood (Vol. 1)
3861 Screens, projection (Vol. 1)
3953 Screens, textile printing (Vol. 1)
3541 Screw and nut slotting machines (Vol. 1)
3423 Screw drivers (Vol. 1)
3452 Screw eyes, metal (Vol. 1)
3089 Screw eyes, plastics (Vol. 1)
3452 Screw hooks (Vol. 1)
3451 Screw Machine Products (Vol. 1)
3451 Screw machine products: produced on a job or order basis (Vol. 1)
3541 Screw machines, automatic (Vol. 1)
3366 Screw propellers: cast brass, bronze, copper, and copper base (Vol. 1)
3549 Screwdowns and boxes (Vol. 1)
3549 Screwdriving machines (Vol. 1)
3841 Screws, bone (Vol. 1)
3569 Screws, jack (Vol. 1)
3452 Screws, metal (Vol. 1)
2211 Scrim, cotton (Vol. 1)
3443 Scroll casings (Vol. 1)
2211 Scrub cloths (Vol. 1)
3589 Scrubbing machines (Vol. 1)
3089 Scrubbing pads, plastics (Vol. 1)
7999 Scuba and skin diving instruction (Vol. 2)
3949 Scuba diving equipment, except clothing (Vol. 1)
8999 Sculptors' studios (Vol. 2)
3299 Sculptures, architectural: gypsum, clay, or papier-mache-factory production only (Vol. 1)
3423 Scythes (Vol. 1)
1499 Scythestone quarrying (Vol. 2)
3291 Scythestones, artificial (Vol. 1)
0912 Sea herring, catching of (Vol. 2)
0919 Sea urchins, catching of (Vol. 2)
5421 Seafood markets—retail (Vol. 2)
2091 Seafood products, canned and cured (Vol. 1)
2092 Seafoods, fresh and frozen (Vol. 1)
5142 Seafoods, frozen: packaged—wholesale (Vol. 2)
5146 Seafoods, not canned or frozen packaged—wholesale (Vol. 2)
3953 Seal presses, notary, hand (Vol. 1)
5169 Sealants—wholesale (Vol. 2)
2851 Sealers, wood (Vol. 1)

2891 Sealing compounds for pipe threads and joints (Vol. 1)
2891 Sealing compounds, synthetic rubber and plastics (Vol. 1)
2295 Sealing or insulating tape for pipe, fiberglass coated with tar or asphalt (Vol. 1)
2891 Sealing wax (Vol. 1)
3953 Seals, corporation (Vol. 1)
5085 Seals, gaskets, and packing—wholesale (Vol. 2)
2754 Seals: gravure printing (Vol. 1)
3953 Seals, hand (dies) (Vol. 1)
3679 Seals, hermetic: for electronic equipment (Vol. 1)
2752 Seals, lithographed (Vol. 1)
2759 Seals: printing except lithographic or gravure (Vol. 1)
3548 Seam welding apparatus, gas and electric (Vol. 1)
3812 Search, Detection, Navigation, Guidance, Aeronautical and Nautical Systems, Instruments and Equipment (Vol. 1)
3827 Searchlight mirrors and reflectors (Vol. 1)
3648 Searchlights (Vol. 1)
7011 Seasonal hotels (Vol. 2)
2099 Seasonings, meat: except sauces (Vol. 1)
2033 Seasonings (prepared sauces), tomato (Vol. 1)
2035 Seasonings (prepared sauces), vegetable: except tomato and dry (Vol. 1)
2399 Seat belts, automobile and aircraft: except leather (Vol. 1)
5013 Seat belts, automotive—wholesale (Vol. 2)
2211 Seat cover cloth, automobile: cotton (Vol. 1)
2399 Seat covers, automobile (Vol. 1)
5013 Seat covers, automotive—wholesale (Vol. 2)
2499 Seat covers, rattan (Vol. 1)
3728 Seat ejector devices, aircraft (Vol. 1)
3751 Seat posts, motorcycle and bicycle (Vol. 1)
3199 Seatbelts, leather (Vol. 1)
2531 Seats: automobile, vans, aircraft, railroad, and other public conveyances (Vol. 1)
2426 Seats, chair: hardwood (Vol. 1)
2514 Seats for metal household furniture (Vol. 1)
2531 Seats, railroad (Vol. 1)
2499 Seats, toilet: wood (Vol. 1)
0919 Seaweed, gathering of (Vol. 2)
0182 Seaweed grown under cover (Vol. 2)
2869 Sebacic acid esters (Vol. 1)
2869 Sebacic acid (Vol. 1)
3341 Secondary refining and smelting of nonferrous metals (Vol. 1)
8211 Secondary schools (Vol. 2)
3341 Secondary Smelting and Refining of Nonferrous Metals (Vol. 1)
5932 Secondhand book stores—retail (Vol. 2)
5932 Secondhand clothing and shoe stores—retail (Vol. 2)
5932 Secondhand furniture stores—retail (Vol. 2)
7338 Secretarial and Court Reporting (Vol. 2)
8244 Secretarial schools (Vol. 2)
7338 Secretarial service (Vol. 2)
2511 Secretaries, household: wood (Vol. 1)
3448 Sections for prefabricated metal buildings (Vol. 1)

2452 Sections for prefabricated wood buildings (Vol. 1)

3498 Sections, pipe: fabricated from purchased metal pipe (Vol. 1)

9651 Securities regulation commissions (Vol. 2)

6231 Security and Commodity Exchanges (Vol. 2)

6211 Security brokers (Vol. 2)

6211 Security Brokers, Dealers and Flotation Companies (Vol. 2)

2759 Security certificates, engraved (Vol. 1)

6289 Security custodians (Vol. 2)

6211 Security dealers (Vol. 2)

6231 Security exchanges (Vol. 2)

6211 Security flotation companies (Vol. 2)

7381 Security guard service (Vol. 2)

6289 Security holders protective committees (Vol. 2)

6799 Security speculators for own account (Vol. 2)

7382 Security systems devices, burglar and fire alarm: monitoring and maintenance (Vol. 2)

7382 Security Systems Services (Vol. 2)

6211 Security traders (Vol. 2)

6211 Security underwriters (Vol. 2)

1499 Sedge peat mining (Vol. 2)

3532 Sedimentation machinery, mineral (Vol. 1)

0119 Seed; Bean farms, dry field and (Vol. 2)

0711 Seed bed preparation (Vol. 2)

0723 Seed cleaning (Vol. 2)

0723 Seed delinting; Cotton (Vol. 2)

0139 Seed farms; Grass (Vol. 2)

0119 Seed farms; Mustard (Vol. 2)

0119 Seed; Pea farms, dry field and (Vol. 2)

8734 Seed testing laboratories (Vol. 2)

3523 Seeders (agricultural machinery) (Vol. 1)

3524 Seeders, residential lawn and garden (Vol. 1)

0721 Seeding crops, with or without fertilizing (Vol. 2)

0782 Seeding highway strips (Vol. 2)

0782 Seeding lawns (Vol. 2)

0721 Seeding of sprouts and twigs (Vol. 2)

5261 Seeds, bulbs, and nursery stock—retail (Vol. 2)

5191 Seeds: field, garden, and flower—wholesale (Vol. 2)

0181 Seeds, flower and vegetable: growing of (Vol. 2)

2068 Seeds: salted, roasted, cooked, or canned (Vol. 1)

2211 Seersuckers, cotton (Vol. 1)

3259 Segment block, clay (Vol. 1)

3731 Seiners, building and repairing (Vol. 1)

1382 Seismograph surveys, oil and gas field: on a contract basis (Vol. 2)

3829 Seismographs (Vol. 1)

3829 Seismometers (Vol. 1)

3829 Seismoscopes (Vol. 1)

1499 Selenite mining (Vol. 2)

3339 Selenium refining, primary (Vol. 1)

3341 Selenium refining, secondary (Vol. 1)

3716 Self-contained motor homes: made on purchased chassis (Vol. 1)

8361 Self-help group homes for persons with social or personal problems (Vol. 2)

8322 Self-help organizations for alcoholics and gamblers (Vol. 2)

2045 Self-rising flour (Vol. 1)

7215 Self-service laundry and drycleaning (Vol. 2)

6531 Selling agents for real estate (Vol. 2)

5159 Semen, bovine—wholesale (Vol. 2)

1222 Semianthracite mining-underground (Vol. 2)

1221 Semianthracite surface mining (Vol. 2)

1221 Semibituminous coal surface mining (Vol. 2)

1222 Semibituminous coal underground mining (Vol. 2)

3674 Semiconductor circuit networks (solid-state integrated circuits) (Vol. 1)

3674 Semiconductor devices (Vol. 1)

5065 Semiconductor devices—wholesale (Vol. 2)

3559 Semiconductor manufacturing machinery (Vol. 1)

3825 Semiconductor test equipment (Vol. 1)

3674 Semiconductors and Related Devices (Vol. 1)

3519 Semidiesel engines for stationary, marine, traction, or other uses (Vol. 1)

8211 Seminaries, below university grade (Vol. 2)

8221 Seminaries, theological (Vol. 2)

1499 Semiprecious stones mining (Vol. 2)

3321 Semisteel castings (Vol. 1)

3321 Semisteel foundries (Vol. 1)

3715 Semitrailers for missile transportation (Vol. 1)

3715 Semitrailers for truck tractors (Vol. 1)

3263 Semivitreous or Fine Earthenware Table and Kitchen Articles (Vol. 1)

2041 Semolina (flour) (Vol. 1)

8322 Senior citizens associations (Vol. 2)

3861 Sensitometers, photographic (Vol. 1)

3845 Sentinel, cardiac (Vol. 1)

3532 Separating machinery, mineral (Vol. 1)

3069 Separators, battery: rubber (Vol. 1)

2499 Separators, battery: wood (Vol. 1)

3523 Separators, cream: farm (Vol. 1)

3556 Separators, cream: industrial (Vol. 1)

3569 Separators for steam, gas, vapor, and air (machinery) (Vol. 1)

3523 Separators, grain and berry: farm (Vol. 1)

3443 Separators, industrial process: metal plate (Vol. 1)

7699 Septic tank cleaning service (Vol. 2)

1711 Septic tank installation-contractors (Vol. 2)

3272 Septic tanks, concrete (Vol. 1)

3443 Septic tanks, metal plate (Vol. 1)

3089 Septic tanks, plastics (Vol. 1)

5039 Septic tanks—wholesale (Vol. 2)

3822 Sequencing controls for electric heat (Vol. 1)

2221 Serges, manmade fiber (Vol. 1)

2231 Serges of wool, mohair, and similar animal fibers (Vol. 1)

3629 Series capacitors, except electronic (Vol. 1)

2836 Serobacterins (Vol. 1)

1429 Serpentine, crushed and broken-quarrying (Vol. 2)

1411 Serpentine, dimension-quarrying (Vol. 2)

2836 Serums, except in vitro and in vivo (Vol. 1)

8221 Service academies (college) (Vol. 2)

0721 Service, agricultural; Entomological (Vol. 2)

1799 Service and repair of broadcasting stations-contractors (Vol. 2)

2339 Service apparel, washable: e.g., nurses', maids', waitresses', laboratory uniforms: women's, misses', and juniors' (Vol. 1)

1459   Shale (common) quarrying-not in conjunction with manufacturing (Vol. 2)
3295   Shale, expanded (Vol. 1)
2844   Shampoos, hair (Vol. 1)
3131   Shanks, shoe (Vol. 1)
2221   Shantungs, manmade fiber and silk (Vol. 1)
3541   Shapers and slotters, metal cutting (Vol. 1)
3553   Shapers, woodworking machinery (Vol. 1)
3545   Shaping tools (machine tool accessories) (Vol. 1)
0912   Sharks, catching of (Vol. 2)
7699   Sharpening and repairing knives, saws, and tools (Vol. 2)
1499   Sharpening stone quarrying (Vol. 2)
3991   Shaving brushes (Vol. 1)
3541   Shaving machines (metalworking) (Vol. 1)
2844   Shaving preparations: e.g., cakes, creams, lotions, powders, tablets (Vol. 1)
2253   Shawls (Vol. 1)
3545   Shear knives (Vol. 1)
3542   Shearing machines, power (Vol. 1)
0751   Shearing; Sheep dipping and (Vol. 2)
3111   Shearling (prepared sheepskin) (Vol. 1)
3421   Shears, hand (Vol. 1)
3421   Shears, hedge: except power (Vol. 1)
3421   Shears, metal cutting: hand (Vol. 1)
3523   Shears, sheep: power (Vol. 1)
2952   Sheathing, asphalt saturated (Vol. 1)
2621   Sheathing paper (Vol. 1)
0214   Sheep and Goats (Vol. 2)
0751   Sheep dipping and shearing (Vol. 2)
2879   Sheep dips, chemical (Vol. 1)
0214   Sheep feeding farms and ranches (Vol. 2)
0751   Sheep, goats, and poultry; Pedigree record services for cattle, hogs, (Vol. 2)
0751   Sheep, goats, and poultry; Showing of cattle, hogs, (Vol. 2)
0214   Sheep raising farms and ranches (Vol. 2)
3523   Sheep shears, power (Vol. 1)
2011   Sheep slaughtering plants (Vol. 1)
5154   Sheep—wholesale (Vol. 2)
3292   Sheet, asbestos cement: flat or corrugated (Vol. 1)
3211   Sheet glass blanks for optical or ophthalmic uses (Vol. 1)
3211   Sheet glass (Vol. 1)
3083   Sheet, laminated plastics, except flexible packaging (Vol. 1)
3444   Sheet metal specialties, not stamped (Vol. 1)
3444   Sheet Metal Work (Vol. 1)
1711   Sheet metalwork combined with heating or air-conditioning-contractors (Vol. 2)
3444   Sheet metalwork: cornices, ventilators, skylights, gutters, tanks, etc. (Vol. 1)
1761   Sheet metalwork: except plumbing, heating, or air-conditioning-contractors (Vol. 2)
3542   Sheet metalworking machines (Vol. 1)
2754   Sheet music: gravure printing (not publishing) (Vol. 1)
2759   Sheet music, printing (not publishing): except lithographed or gravure (Vol. 1)
5736   Sheet music stores—retail (Vol. 2)

5199   Sheet music—wholesale (Vol. 2)
3312   Sheet pilings, plain: iron and steel-made in steel works or rolling mills (Vol. 1)
3081   Sheet, plastics: unsupported (Vol. 1)
3316   Sheet steel, cold-rolled: not made in hot-rolling mills (Vol. 1)
2211   Sheeting, cotton (Vol. 1)
3069   Sheeting, rubber or rubberized fabric (Vol. 1)
3353   Sheets, aluminum (Vol. 1)
2211   Sheets and sheetings, cotton (Vol. 1)
3351   Sheets, copper and copper alloy (Vol. 1)
2653   Sheets, corrugated and solid fiberboard (Vol. 1)
2392   Sheets, fabric (Vol. 1)
5051   Sheets, galvanized or other coated—wholesale (Vol. 2)
3069   Sheets, hard rubber (Vol. 1)
2392   Sheets, hospital: nonwoven textile (Vol. 1)
5051   Sheets, metal—wholesale (Vol. 2)
3312   Sheets, steel: made in steel works or hot-rolling mills (Vol. 1)
5023   Sheets, textile—wholesale (Vol. 2)
5072   Shelf or light hardware—wholesale (Vol. 2)
2048   Shell crushing for feed (Vol. 1)
3351   Shell discs, copper and copper alloy (Vol. 1)
3483   Shell loading and assembly plants, for ammunition more than 30 mm. (Vol. 1)
1499   Shell mining (Vol. 2)
3999   Shell novelties (Vol. 1)
3312   Shell slugs, steel: made in steel works or rolling mills (Vol. 1)
2851   Shellac, protective coating (Vol. 1)
5198   Shellac—wholesale (Vol. 2)
3523   Shellers, nut (agricultural machinery) (Vol. 1)
0913   Shellfish (Vol. 2)
2091   Shellfish, canned and cured (Vol. 1)
0913   Shellfish, catching of (Vol. 2)
2092   Shellfish, fresh and frozen (Vol. 1)
2092   Shellfish, fresh: shucked, picked, or packed (Vol. 1)
0723   Shelling; Almond hulling and (Vol. 2)
0723   Shelling; Corn (Vol. 2)
0723   Shelling, custom; Peanut (Vol. 2)
0723   Shelling; Filbert hulling and (Vol. 2)
0723   Shelling; Nut hulling and (Vol. 2)
0723   Shelling of tree nuts; Hulling and (Vol. 2)
0723   Shelling; Pecan hulling and (Vol. 2)
0723   Shelling; Walnut hulling and (Vol. 2)
3483   Shells, artillery: more than 30 mm. (or more than 1.18 inch) (Vol. 1)
3482   Shells, small arms: 30 mm. (or 1.18 inch) or less (Vol. 1)
8331   Sheltered workshops (Vol. 2)
2542   Shelving angles and slotted bars, except wood (Vol. 1)
2542   Shelving, office and store: except wood (Vol. 1)
2541   Shelving, office and store: wood (Vol. 1)
5046   Shelving—wholesale (Vol. 2)
3496   Shelving without rigid framework, made from purchased wire (Vol. 1)
3479   Sherardizing of metals and metal products, for the trade (Vol. 1)

3149 Shoes, children's and infants': except house slippers and rubber footwear (Vol. 1)
3942 Shoes, doll (Vol. 1)
3842 Shoes, extension: orthopedic (Vol. 1)
3143 Shoes, men's: except house slippers, athletic, rubber, and extension shoes (Vol. 1)
3021 Shoes, plastics soles molded to fabric uppers (Vol. 1)
3021 Shoes, rubber or rubber soled fabric uppers (Vol. 1)
5139 Shoes—wholesale (Vol. 2)
3144 Shoes, women's: except house slippers, athletic, and rubber footwear (Vol. 1)
7251 Shoeshine parlors (Vol. 2)
2441 Shook, box (Vol. 1)
7997 Shooting clubs, membership (Vol. 2)
7999 Shooting galleries (Vol. 2)
7999 Shooting ranges, operation of (Vol. 2)
1389 Shooting wells on a contract basis (Vol. 2)
2674 Shopping bags, uncoated paper (Vol. 1)
1542 Shopping center construction-general contractors (Vol. 2)
6512 Shopping centers, property operation only (Vol. 2)
7319 Shopping news advertising and distributing service (Vol. 2)
2741 Shopping news: publishing and printing, or publishing only (Vol. 1)
7299 Shopping service for individuals (Vol. 2)
1799 Shoring and underpinning work-contractors (Vol. 2)
6153 Short-Term Business Credit Institutions Except Agricultural (Vol. 2)
2079 Shortening, Table Oils, Margarine and Other Edible Fats and Oils Not Elsewhere Classified (Vol. 1)
5149 Shortening, vegetable—wholesale (Vol. 2)
2079 Shortenings, compound and vegetable (Vol. 1)
3579 Shorthand machines (Vol. 1)
2254 Shorts (Vol. 1)
2369 Shorts, outerwear: girls' and children's (Vol. 1)
2329 Shorts, outerwear: men's and boys' (Vol. 1)
2339 Shorts, outerwear: women's, misses', and juniors' (Vol. 1)
2322 Shorts, underwear: men's and boys' (Vol. 1)
2254 Shorts, underwear (Vol. 1)
3482 Shot, BB (Vol. 1)
1389 Shot-hole drilling service, oil and gas field: on a contract basis (Vol. 2)
3482 Shot, lead (Vol. 1)
3398 Shot peening-treating steel to reduce fatigue (Vol. 1)
3482 Shot, pellet (Vol. 1)
3482 Shot, steel ammunition (Vol. 1)
3482 Shotgun ammunition (Vol. 1)
3484 Shotguns and parts (Vol. 1)
2396 Shoulder pads: for coats, suits, etc. (Vol. 1)
5131 Shoulder pads—wholesale (Vol. 2)
2396 Shoulder straps, for women's underwear (Vol. 1)
2253 Shoulderettes (Vol. 1)
3531 Shovel loaders (Vol. 1)
3423 Shovels, hand (Vol. 1)
3531 Shovels, power (Vol. 1)

5082 Shovels, power—wholesale (Vol. 2)
5078 Show cases, refrigerated—wholesale (Vol. 2)
7389 Showcard painting (Vol. 2)
2542 Showcases, not refrigerated: except wood (Vol. 1)
2541 Showcases, not refrigerated: wood (Vol. 1)
3585 Showcases, refrigerated (Vol. 1)
2392 Shower curtains (Vol. 1)
3231 Shower doors: made from purchased glass (Vol. 1)
3272 Shower receptors, concrete (Vol. 1)
3431 Shower receptors, metal (Vol. 1)
3432 Shower rods (Vol. 1)
3021 Shower sandals or slippers, rubber (Vol. 1)
3431 Shower stalls, metal (Vol. 1)
3088 Shower stalls, plastics (Vol. 1)
0751 Showing of cattle, hogs, sheep, goats, and poultry (Vol. 2)
0752 Showing of pets and other animal specialties (Vol. 2)
3523 Shredders (agricultural machinery) (Vol. 1)
1499 Shredding peat (Vol. 2)
2091 Shrimp, canned and cured (Vol. 1)
0913 Shrimp, catching of (Vol. 2)
2092 Shrimp, fresh and frozen (Vol. 1)
8661 Shrines, religious (Vol. 2)
3273 Shrink-mixed concrete (Vol. 1)
2231 Shrinking cloth of wool, mohair, and similar animal fibers: for the trade (Vol. 1)
2261 Shrinking cotton broadwoven fabrics for the trade (Vol. 1)
2262 Shrinking manmade fiber and silk broadwoven fabrics for the trade (Vol. 1)
7389 Shrinking textiles for tailors and dressmakers (Vol. 2)
0181 Shrubberies, except forest shrubbery: growing of (Vol. 2)
0181 Shrubbery, except forest shrubbery; Field nurseries: growing of flowers and (Vol. 2)
3825 Shunts, instrument (Vol. 1)
3861 Shutters, camera (Vol. 1)
3442 Shutters, door and window: metal (Vol. 1)
2431 Shutters, door and window: wood and covered wood (Vol. 1)
3089 Shutters, plastics (Vol. 1)
2426 Shuttle blocks: hardwood (Vol. 1)
3532 Shuttle cars, underground (Vol. 1)
3552 Shuttles for textile weaving (Vol. 1)
6321 Sick benefit associations, mutual (Vol. 2)
3423 Sickles, hand (Vol. 1)
1011 Siderite mining (Vol. 2)
1771 Sidewalk construction, except public-contractors (Vol. 2)
1611 Sidewalk construction, public-contractors (Vol. 2)
3292 Siding, asbestos cement (Vol. 1)
2952 Siding, asphalt brick (Vol. 1)
1761 Siding-contractors (Vol. 2)
2421 Siding, dressed lumber (Vol. 1)
5033 Siding, except wood—wholesale (Vol. 2)
2952 Siding, insulating: impregnated (Vol. 1)
2621 Siding, insulating: paper, impregnated or not (Vol. 1)

3142 Socks, slipper: made from purchased socks (Vol. 1)
2252 Socks, slipper (Vol. 1)
3842 Socks, stump (Vol. 1)
0181 Sod farms (Vol. 2)
0782 Sod laying (Vol. 2)
5261 Sod—retail (Vol. 2)
2819 Soda alum (Vol. 1)
1474 Soda ash mining (Vol. 2)
2812 Soda ash, not produced at mines (Vol. 1)
2812 Soda, caustic (Vol. 1)
5046 Soda fountain fixtures, except refrigerated—wholesale (Vol. 2)
5078 Soda fountain fixtures, refrigerated—wholesale (Vol. 2)
5812 Soda fountains (Vol. 2)
3585 Soda fountains, parts, and accessories (Vol. 1)
2656 Soda straws, except glass or plastics (Vol. 1)
2869 Sodium acetate (Vol. 1)
2869 Sodium alginate (Vol. 1)
2819 Sodium aluminate (Vol. 1)
2819 Sodium aluminum sulfate (Vol. 1)
2819 Sodium antimoniate (Vol. 1)
2879 Sodium arsenite (formulated) (Vol. 1)
2819 Sodium arsenite, technical (Vol. 1)
2869 Sodium benzoate (Vol. 1)
2812 Sodium bicarbonate, not produced at mines (Vol. 1)
2819 Sodium bichromate and chromate (Vol. 1)
2819 Sodium borates (Vol. 1)
2819 Sodium borohydride (Vol. 1)
2819 Sodium bromide, not produced at mines (Vol. 1)
2812 Sodium carbonate (soda ash), not produced at mines (Vol. 1)
2819 Sodium chlorate (Vol. 1)
2899 Sodium chloride, refined (Vol. 1)
2834 Sodium chloride solution for injection, U.S.P. (Vol. 1)
2819 Sodium compounds, inorganic (Vol. 1)
1474 Sodium compounds mining, except common salt (Vol. 2)
2819 Sodium cyanide (Vol. 1)
2869 Sodium glutamate (Vol. 1)
2819 Sodium hydrosulfite (Vol. 1)
2812 Sodium hydroxide (caustic soda) (Vol. 1)
2842 Sodium hypochlorite (household bleach) (Vol. 1)
2819 Sodium, metallic (Vol. 1)
2819 Sodium molybdate (Vol. 1)
2869 Sodium pentachlorophenate (Vol. 1)
2819 Sodium perborate (Vol. 1)
2819 Sodium peroxide (Vol. 1)
2819 Sodium phosphate (Vol. 1)
2819 Sodium polyphosphate (Vol. 1)
2834 Sodium salicylate tablets (Vol. 1)
2843 Sodium salts of sulfonated oils, fats, or greases (Vol. 1)
2819 Sodium silicate (Vol. 1)
2819 Sodium silicofluoride (Vol. 1)
2819 Sodium stannate (Vol. 1)
2819 Sodium sulfate-bulk or tablets (Vol. 1)
2869 Sodium sulfoxalate formaldehyde (Vol. 1)
2819 Sodium tetraborate, not produced at mines (Vol. 1)

2819 Sodium thiosulfate (Vol. 1)
2819 Sodium tungstate (Vol. 1)
2819 Sodium uranate (Vol. 1)
2515 Sofas, convertible (Vol. 1)
2512 Sofas, upholstered on wood frames, except convertible beds (Vol. 1)
3089 Soffit, plastics (siding) (Vol. 1)
5812 Soft drink stands (Vol. 2)
2086 Soft drinks, bottled or canned (Vol. 1)
5149 Soft drinks—wholesale (Vol. 2)
2298 Soft fiber cordage and twine (Vol. 1)
2843 Softeners (textile assistants) (Vol. 1)
7372 Software, computer: prepackaged (Vol. 2)
5045 Software, computer—wholesale (Vol. 2)
7371 Software programming, custom (Vol. 2)
7371 Software systems analysis and design, custom (Vol. 2)
2861 Softwood distillates (Vol. 1)
2436 Softwood plywood composites (Vol. 1)
2436 Softwood Veneer and Plywood (Vol. 1)
2436 Softwood veneer or plywood (Vol. 1)
1629 Soil compacting service-contractors (Vol. 2)
3531 Soil compactors: vibratory (Vol. 1)
2879 Soil conditioners (Vol. 1)
9512 Soil conservation services-government (Vol. 2)
0181 Soil erosion-growing of; Mats, preseeded: (Vol. 2)
0711 Soil for crops; Chemical treatment of (Vol. 2)
3321 Soil pipe, cast iron (Vol. 1)
0711 Soil Preparation Services (Vol. 2)
3523 Soil pulverizers and packers (agricultural machinery) (Vol. 1)
2899 Soil testing kits (Vol. 1)
5261 Soil, top—retail (Vol. 2)
3674 Solar cells (Vol. 1)
3433 Solar energy collectors, liquid or gas (Vol. 1)
3433 Solar heaters (Vol. 1)
1711 Solar heating apparatus-contractors (Vol. 2)
5074 Solar heating panels and equipment—wholesale (Vol. 2)
3511 Solar powered turbine-generator sets (Vol. 1)
1742 Solar reflecting insulation film-contractors (Vol. 2)
3829 Solarimeters (Vol. 1)
3341 Solder (base metal), pig and ingot: secondary (Vol. 1)
3356 Solder wire, bar: acid core and rosin core (Vol. 1)
3548 Soldering equipment, except soldering irons (Vol. 1)
2899 Soldering fluxes (Vol. 1)
3915 Soldering for the jewelry trade (Vol. 1)
3423 Soldering guns and tools, hand: electric (Vol. 1)
3423 Soldering iron tips and tiplets (Vol. 1)
3423 Soldering irons and coppers (Vol. 1)
3643 Solderless connectors (electric wiring devices) (Vol. 1)
3111 Sole leather (Vol. 1)
3625 Solenoid switches, industrial (Vol. 1)
3492 Solenoid valves, fluid power: metal (Vol. 1)
3679 Solenoids for electronic applications (Vol. 1)
3131 Soles, boot and shoe: except rubber, composition, plastics, and fiber (Vol. 1)

Industry Index

3089 Soles, boot and shoe: plastics (Vol. 1)
3069 Soles, boot and shoe: rubber, composition, and fiber (Vol. 1)
5087 Soles, shoe—wholesale (Vol. 2)
2819 Solid fuel propellants, inorganic (Vol. 1)
2869 Solid fuel propellants, organic (Vol. 1)
3674 Solid-state electronic devices (Vol. 1)
3089 Soling strips, boot and shoe: plastics (Vol. 1)
3069 Soling strips, boot and shoe: rubber, composition, and fiber (Vol. 1)
3295 Solite, ground or otherwise treated (Vol. 1)
2843 Soluble oils and greases (Vol. 1)
2834 Solutions, pharmaceutical (Vol. 1)
2865 Solvent naphtha, made in chemical plants (Vol. 1)
2899 Solvents, carbon (Vol. 1)
2842 Solvents, degreasing (Vol. 1)
2842 Solvents, drain pipe (Vol. 1)
2869 Solvents, organic (Vol. 1)
2911 Solvents, produced in petroleum refineries (Vol. 1)
7389 Solvents recovery service on a contract or fee basis (Vol. 2)
3812 Sonabuoys (Vol. 1)
3812 Sonar fish finders (Vol. 1)
3812 Sonar systems and equipment (Vol. 1)
8999 Song writers (Vol. 2)
2869 Sorbitol (Vol. 1)
0119 Sorghum farms, except for syrup (Vol. 2)
2041 Sorghum grain flour (Vol. 1)
2099 Sorghum, including custom refining (Vol. 1)
8641 Sororities, except residential (Vol. 2)
7041 Sorority residential houses (Vol. 2)
3579 Sorters, filing: office (Vol. 1)
3577 Sorters, punch card (Vol. 1)
0723 Sorting, grading, and packing; Fruit (Vol. 2)
0723 Sorting, grading, and packing of fruits and vegetables (Vol. 2)
0723 Sorting, grading, and packing; Vegetable (Vol. 2)
3577 Sorting machines, card (Vol. 1)
3523 Sorting machines for agricultural products (Vol. 1)
2542 Sorting racks, mail: except wood (Vol. 1)
1731 Sound equipment installation-contractors (Vol. 2)
3861 Sound recording and reproducing equipment, motion picture (Vol. 1)
5142 Soup, frozen—wholesale (Vol. 2)
2034 Soup mixes (Vol. 1)
2034 Soup powders (Vol. 1)
2034 Soups, dehydrated (Vol. 1)
5149 Soups, except frozen—wholesale (Vol. 2)
2032 Soups, except seafood: canned (Vol. 1)
2091 Soups, fish and seafood: canned (Vol. 1)
2092 Soups, fish and seafood: frozen (Vol. 1)
2038 Soups, frozen: except seafood (Vol. 1)
2026 Sour cream (Vol. 1)
2759 Souvenir cards: except lithographed or gravure (Vol. 1)
2754 Souvenir cards: gravure printing (Vol. 1)
2752 Souvenir cards, lithographed (Vol. 1)
5947 Souvenir shops—retail (Vol. 2)
2035 Soy sauce (Vol. 1)
2851 Soyate driers (Vol. 1)

2079 Soybean cooking and salad oil (Vol. 1)
0116 Soybean farms (Vol. 2)
2824 Soybean fibers (manmade textile materials) (Vol. 1)
2075 Soybean flour and grits (Vol. 1)
2075 Soybean oil, cake, and meal (Vol. 1)
2075 Soybean oil, deodorized (Vol. 1)
2075 Soybean Oil Mills (Vol. 1)
2821 Soybean plastics (Vol. 1)
2075 Soybean protein concentrates (Vol. 1)
2075 Soybean protein isolates (Vol. 1)
0116 Soybeans (Vol. 2)
5153 Soybeans—wholesale (Vol. 2)
3769 Space capsules (Vol. 1)
4789 Space flight operations, except government (Vol. 2)
9661 Space flight operations-government (Vol. 2)
3433 Space heaters, except electric (Vol. 1)
5088 Space propulsion units and parts—wholesale (Vol. 2)
9661 Space research and development-government (Vol. 2)
9661 Space Research and Technology (Vol. 2)
3663 Space satellite communications equipment (Vol. 1)
3443 Space simulation chambers, metal plate (Vol. 1)
3842 Space suits (Vol. 1)
3812 Space vehicle guidance systems and equipment (Vol. 1)
3761 Space vehicles, complete (Vol. 1)
3423 Spades, hand (Vol. 1)
2038 Spaghetti and meatballs, frozen (Vol. 1)
2032 Spaghetti, canned (Vol. 1)
2098 Spaghetti, dry (Vol. 1)
2033 Spaghetti sauce (Vol. 1)
5149 Spaghetti—wholesale (Vol. 2)
2221 Spandex broadwoven fabrics (Vol. 1)
3272 Spanish floor tile, concrete (Vol. 1)
2032 Spanish foods, canned (Vol. 1)
0831 Spanish moss, gathering of (Vol. 2)
3295 Spar, ground or otherwise treated (Vol. 1)
3825 Spark plug testing instruments, electric (Vol. 1)
3694 Spark plugs for internal combustion engines (Vol. 1)
3264 Spark plugs, porcelain (Vol. 1)
2499 Spars, wood (Vol. 1)
7991 Spas, health fitness: except resort lodges (Vol. 2)
3199 Spats (Vol. 1)
3069 Spatulas, rubber (Vol. 1)
0182 Spawn, production of; Mushroom (Vol. 2)
3651 Speaker systems (Vol. 1)
7389 Speakers' bureaus (Vol. 2)
3949 Spearguns (Vol. 1)
2899 Spearmint oil (Vol. 1)
3949 Spears, fishing (Vol. 1)
3544 Special Dies and Tools, Die Sets, Jigs and Fixtures and Industrial Molds (Vol. 1)
2631 Special food board (Vol. 1)
3559 Special Industry Machinery Not Elsewhere Classified (Vol. 1)
2429 Special Product Sawmills Not Elsewhere Classified (Vol. 1)

1799 Special Trade Contractors Not Elsewhere Classified (Vol. 2)

4226 Special Warehousing and Storage Not Elsewhere Classified (Vol. 2)

0742 Specialties; Animal hospitals for pets and other animal (Vol. 2)

0291 Specialties; General Farms—Primarily Livestock and Animal (Vol. 2)

0279 Specialties Not Elsewhere Classified; Animal (Vol. 2)

0742 Specialties; Veterinarians for pets and other animal (Vol. 2)

0742 Specialties; Veterinary Services for Animal (Vol. 2)

0742 Specialties; Veterinary services for pets and other animal (Vol. 2)

0291 Specialty and livestock farms, general; Animal (Vol. 2)

2842 Specialty Cleaning, Polishing and Sanitation Preparations (Vol. 1)

0291 Specialty farms, general; Livestock and animal (Vol. 2)

8069 Specialty Hospitals Except Psychiatric (Vol. 2)

3111 Specialty leathers (Vol. 1)

8093 Specialty Outpatient Facilities Not Elsewhere Classified (Vol. 2)

3612 Specialty transformers (Vol. 1)

3826 Specific ion measuring instruments, laboratory type (Vol. 1)

3211 Spectacle glass (Vol. 1)

3851 Spectacles (Vol. 1)

1799 Spectator seating installation-contractors (Vol. 2)

3826 Spectrofluorometers (Vol. 1)

3826 Spectrographs (Vol. 1)

3826 Spectrometers: electron diffraction, mass, nmr, raman, x-ray (Vol. 1)

3829 Spectrometers, liquid scintillation and nuclear (Vol. 1)

3826 Spectrophotometers: atomic absorption, atomic emission, flame, fluorescence, infrared, raman, visible, ultraviolet (Vol. 1)

3825 Spectrum analyzers (Vol. 1)

1531 Speculative builders (Vol. 2)

3841 Speculums (Vol. 1)

8049 Speech clinicians, offices of (Vol. 2)

8049 Speech pathologists, offices of (Vol. 2)

3566 Speed Changers, Industrial High-Speed Drives and Gears (Vol. 1)

3566 Speed changers (power transmission equipment) (Vol. 1)

3824 Speed indicators and recorders, vehicle (Vol. 1)

8299 Speed reading courses (Vol. 2)

3566 Speed reducers (power transmission equipment) (Vol. 1)

5531 Speed shops—retail (Vol. 2)

3824 Speedometers (Vol. 1)

7948 Speedway operation (Vol. 2)

3339 Spelter (zinc), primary (Vol. 1)

8099 Sperm banks (Vol. 2)

0831 Sphagnum moss, gathering of (Vol. 2)

1031 Sphalerite mining (Vol. 2)

3443 Spheres, for liquids or gas: metal plate (Vol. 1)

3841 Sphygmomanometers (Vol. 1)

5499 Spice and herb stores—retail (Vol. 2)

2099 Spices, including grinding (Vol. 1)

5149 Spices—wholesale (Vol. 2)

3313 Spiegeleisen (Vol. 1)

3432 Spigots, metal and plastics (Vol. 1)

2499 Spigots, wood (Vol. 1)

3312 Spike rods, made in steel works or rolling mills (Vol. 1)

3399 Spikes, nonferrous metal (including wire) (Vol. 1)

3315 Spikes, steel: wire or cut (Vol. 1)

2241 Spindle banding (Vol. 1)

3552 Spindles, textile (Vol. 1)

3728 Spinners, aircraft propeller (Vol. 1)

3542 Spinning lathes (Vol. 1)

3542 Spinning machines, metal (Vol. 1)

3552 Spinning machines, textile (Vol. 1)

3469 Spinning metal, for the trade (Vol. 1)

2284 Spinning thread: cotton, silk, manmade fibers, and wool (Vol. 1)

2281 Spinning wool carpet and rug yarn: wool, mohair, or animal fiber (Vol. 1)

2281 Spinning yarn: cotton, silk, wool, and manmade staple (Vol. 1)

3496 Spiral cloth, made from purchased wire (Vol. 1)

2899 Spirit duplicating fluid (Vol. 1)

2085 Spirits, neutral, except fruit-for beverage purposes (Vol. 1)

2834 Spirits, pharmaceutical (Vol. 1)

5182 Spirits—wholesale (Vol. 2)

3861 Splicers, motion picture film (Vol. 1)

3542 Spline rolling machines (Vol. 1)

2449 Splint baskets, for fruits and vegetables (Vol. 1)

3842 Splints, pneumatic and wood (Vol. 1)

3111 Splits, leather (Vol. 1)

1479 Spodumene mining (Vol. 2)

2499 Spokes, wood (Vol. 1)

2051 Sponge goods, bakery, except frozen (Vol. 1)

3312 Sponge iron (Vol. 1)

3069 Sponge rubber and sponge rubber products (Vol. 1)

3999 Sponges, bleaching and dyeing of (Vol. 1)

0919 Sponges, gathering of (Vol. 2)

3089 Sponges, plastics (Vol. 1)

3069 Sponges, rubber (Vol. 1)

3291 Sponges, scouring: metallic (Vol. 1)

3842 Sponges, surgical (Vol. 1)

5199 Sponges—wholesale (Vol. 2)

2231 Sponging and refinishing cloth: wool and similar animal fiber for the trade (Vol. 1)

7389 Sponging textiles for tailors and dressmakers (Vol. 2)

2426 Spool blocks and blanks, wood (Vol. 1)

2282 Spooling yarn: cotton, silk, and manmade fiber continuous filament (Vol. 1)

2282 Spooling yarn: wool, mohair, or similar animal fibers (Vol. 1)

2499 Spools, except for textile machinery: wood (Vol. 1)

2655 Spools, fiber (metal-end or all-fiber) (Vol. 1)

6311 Stock life insurance (Vol. 2)
6289 Stock transfer agents (Vol. 2)
3842 Stockinette, surgical (Vol. 1)
2259 Stockinettes (Vol. 1)
2252 Stockings, except women's and misses' full-length and knee-length (Vol. 1)
2251 Stockings, women's full-length and knee-length, except socks (Vol. 1)
0181 Stocks, growing of; Fruit (Vol. 2)
0211 Stockyards, exclusively for fattening cattle (Vol. 2)
4789 Stockyards, not primarily for fattening or selling livestock (Vol. 2)
2121 Stogies (Vol. 1)
3433 Stokers, mechanical: domestic and industrial (Vol. 1)
5032 Stone, building—wholesale (Vol. 2)
3272 Stone, cast concrete (Vol. 1)
5032 Stone, crushed or broken—wholesale (Vol. 2)
3281 Stone, cut and shaped (Vol. 1)
3423 Stone forks (handtools) (Vol. 1)
3532 Stone pulverizers, stationary (Vol. 1)
3281 Stone, quarrying and processing of own stone products (Vol. 1)
1741 Stone setting-contractors (Vol. 2)
3559 Stone tumblers (Vol. 1)
3559 Stone working machinery (Vol. 1)
3423 Stonecutters' handtools (Vol. 1)
3291 Stones, abrasive (Vol. 1)
5999 Stones, crystalline: rough—retail (Vol. 2)
3915 Stones: preparation of real and imitation gems for settings (Vol. 1)
3299 Stones, synthetic: for gem stones and industrial use (Vol. 1)
3269 Stoneware, chemical (pottery products) (Vol. 1)
1459 Stoneware clay mining (Vol. 2)
1741 Stonework erection-contractors (Vol. 2)
2599 Stools, factory (Vol. 1)
2514 Stools, household: metal (Vol. 1)
2511 Stools, household: wood (Vol. 1)
2599 Stools, metal: with casters-not household or office (Vol. 1)
2522 Stools, office: rotating-except wood (Vol. 1)
2521 Stools, office: wood (Vol. 1)
3272 Stools, precast terrazzo (Vol. 1)
3494 Stop cocks, except drain: metal (Vol. 1)
3432 Stopcocks (plumbers' supplies) (Vol. 1)
2499 Stoppers, cork (Vol. 1)
3842 Stoppers, ear (Vol. 1)
3255 Stoppers, glasshouse: clay (Vol. 1)
3069 Stoppers, rubber (Vol. 1)
7219 Storage and repair of fur and other garments for individuals (Vol. 2)
3691 Storage Batteries (Vol. 1)
5063 Storage batteries, industrial—wholesale (Vol. 2)
3691 Storage batteries (Vol. 1)
3621 Storage battery chargers, engine generator type (Vol. 1)
2511 Storage chests, household: wood (Vol. 1)
3572 Storage devices, computer (Vol. 1)
2542 Storage fixtures, except wood (Vol. 1)

2541 Storage fixtures, wood (Vol. 1)
4222 Storage, frozen or refrigerated goods (Vol. 2)
4226 Storage, furniture: without local trucking (Vol. 2)
4225 Storage, general (Vol. 2)
7219 Storage of furs and other garments for individuals (Vol. 2)
4226 Storage of goods at foreign trade zones (Vol. 2)
4214 Storage of household goods: combined with local trucking (Vol. 2)
4226 Storage of household goods: without local trucking (Vol. 2)
4922 Storage of natural gas (Vol. 2)
4221 Storage other than cold storage, farm product (Vol. 2)
4226 Storage, special: except farm products and cold storage (Vol. 2)
3272 Storage tanks, concrete (Vol. 1)
1791 Storage tanks, metal: erection-contractors (Vol. 2)
3443 Storage tanks, metal plate (Vol. 1)
1542 Store construction-general contractors (Vol. 2)
1751 Store fixture installation-contractors (Vol. 2)
1791 Store front installation, metal-contractors (Vol. 2)
3469 Store fronts, porcelain enameled (Vol. 1)
3442 Store fronts, prefabricated: metal, except porcelain enameled (Vol. 1)
2541 Store fronts, prefabricated: wood (Vol. 1)
3442 Storm doors and windows, metal (Vol. 1)
5211 Storm windows and sash, wood or metal—retail (Vol. 2)
2431 Storm windows, wood (Vol. 1)
2082 Stout (alcoholic beverage) (Vol. 1)
3444 Stove boards, sheet metal (Vol. 1)
3259 Stove lining, clay (Vol. 1)
3469 Stove parts, porcelain enameled (Vol. 1)
3444 Stove pipe and flues, sheet metal (Vol. 1)
2842 Stove polish (Vol. 1)
7699 Stove repair shops (Vol. 2)
5722 Stoves and related electric and gas appliances—retail (Vol. 2)
3589 Stoves, commercial (Vol. 1)
5074 Stoves, cooking: except electric—wholesale (Vol. 2)
5064 Stoves, cooking or heating, household: electric—wholesale (Vol. 2)
3631 Stoves, disk (Vol. 1)
3631 Stoves, household: cooking (Vol. 1)
3433 Stoves, household: heating-except electric (Vol. 1)
3433 Stoves, wood and coal burning (Vol. 1)
5074 Stoves, wood burning—wholesale (Vol. 2)
3537 Straddle carriers, mobile (Vol. 1)
3421 Straight razors (Vol. 1)
3547 Straightening machinery (rolling mill equipment) (Vol. 1)
3674 Strain gages, solid-state (Vol. 1)
3494 Strainers, line: for use in piping systems-metal (Vol. 1)
3714 Strainers, oil: motor vehicle (Vol. 1)
3569 Strainers, pipeline (Vol. 1)
3496 Strand, uninsulated wire: made from purchased wire (Vol. 1)

2493 Strandboard, oriented (Vol. 1)

2399 Strap assemblies, tie down: aircraft-except leather (Vol. 1)

3111 Strap leather (Vol. 1)

3499 Strapping, metal (Vol. 1)

3423 Strapping tools, steel (Vol. 1)

2241 Strapping webs (Vol. 1)

3199 Straps, except watch straps: leather (Vol. 1)

2396 Straps, shoulder: for women's underwear (Vol. 1)

3172 Straps, watch: except precious metal (Vol. 1)

3999 Straw goods (Vol. 1)

2823 Straw, rayon (Vol. 1)

5191 Straw—wholesale (Vol. 2)

0171 Strawberry farms (Vol. 2)

2631 Strawboard, except building board (Vol. 1)

2353 Strawhats (Vol. 1)

3229 Straws, glass (Vol. 1)

2656 Straws, soda: except glass or plastics (Vol. 1)

3711 Street flushers (motor vehicles) (Vol. 1)

3648 Street lighting fixtures, except traffic signals (Vol. 1)

3612 Street lighting transformers (Vol. 1)

1611 Street maintenance or repair-contractors (Vol. 2)

1611 Street paving-contractors (Vol. 2)

4953 Street refuse systems (Vol. 2)

3711 Street sprinklers and sweepers (motor vehicles) (Vol. 1)

3991 Street sweeping brooms, hand and machine (Vol. 1)

4111 Streetcar operation (Vol. 2)

3743 Streetcars and car equipment (Vol. 1)

3829 Stress, strain, and flaw detecting and measuring equipment (Vol. 1)

2211 Stretch fabrics, cotton (Vol. 1)

2499 Stretchers, curtain: wood (Vol. 1)

3842 Stretchers (Vol. 1)

3542 Stretching machines (Vol. 1)

3949 Striking (punching) bags (Vol. 1)

3931 Stringed musical instruments and parts (Vol. 1)

3999 Stringing beads for the trade (Vol. 1)

3931 Strings, musical instrument (Vol. 1)

3931 Strings, piano (Vol. 1)

3949 Strings, tennis racket (Vol. 1)

3351 Strip, copper and copper alloy (Vol. 1)

2761 Strip forms (manifold business forms) (Vol. 1)

3356 Strip: lead, magnesium, nickel, tin, titanium, zinc, and their alloys (Vol. 1)

5051 Strip, metal—wholesale (Vol. 2)

1231 Strip mining, anthracite: except on a contract basis (Vol. 2)

1221 Strip mining, bituminous coal: except on a contract basis (Vol. 2)

1481 Strip mining for nonmetallic minerals, except fuels: on a contract basis (Vol. 2)

1221 Strip mining, lignite: except on a contract basis (Vol. 2)

1081 Strip mining, metal: on a contract basis (Vol. 2)

3316 Strip steel, cold-rolled: not made in hot-rolling mills (Vol. 1)

1241 Stripping services: bituminous coal, anthracite, and lignite on a contract basis (Vol. 2)

3312 Strips, galvanized iron and steel: made in steel works or rolling mills (Vol. 1)

3312 Strips, iron and steel: made in steel works or hot-rolling mills (Vol. 1)

3069 Strips, liner: rubber (Vol. 1)

2823 Strips, rayon (Vol. 1)

2823 Strips, viscose (Vol. 1)

3825 Stroboscopes (Vol. 1)

3641 Strobotrons (Vol. 1)

3944 Strollers, baby (vehicles) (Vol. 1)

1479 Strontianite mining (Vol. 2)

2819 Strontium carbonate, precipitated, and oxide (Vol. 1)

1479 Strontium mineral mining (Vol. 2)

2819 Strontium nitrate (Vol. 1)

3199 Strops, razor (Vol. 1)

5039 Structural assemblies, prefabricated: nonwood—wholesale (Vol. 2)

5031 Structural assemblies, prefabricated: wood—wholesale (Vol. 2)

3259 Structural Clay Products Not Elsewhere Classified (Vol. 1)

5211 Structural clay products—retail (Vol. 2)

3211 Structural glass, flat (Vol. 1)

2491 Structural lumber and timber, treated (Vol. 1)

2439 Structural members, laminated wood: arches, trusses, timbers, and parallel chord ceilings (Vol. 1)

3547 Structural mills (rolling mill machinery) (Vol. 1)

3312 Structural shapes, iron and steel (Vol. 1)

5051 Structural shapes, iron and steel—wholesale (Vol. 2)

3355 Structural shapes, rolled aluminum (Vol. 1)

1791 Structural Steel Erection (Vol. 2)

1791 Structural steel erection-contractors (Vol. 2)

3441 Structural steel, fabricated (Vol. 1)

3251 Structural tile, clay (Vol. 1)

3944 Structural toy sets (Vol. 1)

2439 Structural Wood Members Not Elsewhere Classified (Vol. 1)

2833 Strychnine and derivatives (Vol. 1)

1771 Stucco construction-contractors (Vol. 2)

3299 Stucco (Vol. 1)

5032 Stucco—wholesale (Vol. 2)

3674 Stud bases or mounts for semiconductor devices (Vol. 1)

2421 Stud mills (Vol. 1)

8299 Student exchange programs (Vol. 2)

6111 Student Loan Marketing Association (Vol. 2)

3663 Studio equipment, radio and television broadcasting (Vol. 1)

7819 Studio property rental for motion picture film production (Vol. 2)

7911 Studios, dance (Vol. 2)

7221 Studios, portrait photography (Vol. 2)

3444 Studs, sheet metal (Vol. 1)

3965 Studs, shirt: except precious metal and precious or semiprecious stones (Vol. 1)

9121 Study commissions, legislative (Vol. 2)

3942 Stuffed toys (including animals) (Vol. 1)

1711 Sump pump installation and servicing-contractors (Vol. 2)

0119 Sunflower farms (Vol. 2)

2076 Sunflower seed oil (Vol. 1)

3851 Sunglasses and goggles (Vol. 1)

2844 Sunscreen lotions and oils (Vol. 1)

2369 Sunsuits: girls', children's, and infants' (Vol. 1)

2844 Suntan lotions and oils (Vol. 1)

5411 Supermarkets, grocery—retail (Vol. 2)

2874 Superphosphates, ammoniated and not ammoniated (Vol. 1)

9199 Supply agencies-government (Vol. 2)

3842 Supports: abdominal, ankle, arch, and kneecap (Vol. 1)

2834 Suppositories (Vol. 1)

6351 Surety Insurance (Vol. 2)

2843 Surface Active Agents, Finishing Agents, Sulfonated Oils and Assistants (Vol. 1)

2843 Surface active agents (Vol. 1)

5169 Surface active agents—wholesale (Vol. 2)

3826 Surface area analyzers (Vol. 1)

3822 Surface burner controls, temperature (Vol. 1)

3531 Surfacers, concrete grinding (Vol. 1)

3553 Surfacers (woodworking machines) (Vol. 1)

3949 Surfboards (Vol. 1)

3443 Surge tanks, metal plate (Vol. 1)

3069 Surgeons' gloves, rubber (Vol. 1)

8011 Surgeons (M.D.), offices of (Vol. 2)

0721 Surgery on orchard trees and vines (Vol. 2)

0721 Surgery; Trees, orchard: planting, pruning, bracing, spraying, removal, and (Vol. 2)

3841 Surgical and Medical Instruments and Apparatus (Vol. 1)

5047 Surgical and medical instruments—wholesale (Vol. 2)

3061 Surgical and medical tubing: extruded and lathe-cut (Vol. 1)

3842 Surgical appliances and supplies, except medical instruments (Vol. 1)

5047 Surgical equipment—wholesale (Vol. 2)

2211 Surgical fabrics, cotton (Vol. 1)

7699 Surgical instrument repair (Vol. 2)

3841 Surgical instruments and apparatus, except electromedical (Vol. 1)

3841 Surgical knife blades and handles (Vol. 1)

3841 Surgical stapling devices (Vol. 1)

3845 Surgical support systems: heart-lung machines, except iron lungs and blood flow systems (Vol. 1)

3569 Surveillance ovens, for aging and testing powder (Vol. 1)

7699 Surveying instrument repair (Vol. 2)

3829 Surveying instruments (Vol. 1)

8713 Surveying: land, water, and aerial (Vol. 2)

8713 Surveying Services (Vol. 2)

1389 Surveying wells on a contract basis, except seismographic (Vol. 2)

4741 Surveyors, marine cargo (Vol. 2)

2499 Surveyors' stakes, wood (Vol. 1)

8299 Survival schools (Vol. 2)

2389 Suspenders (Vol. 1)

3842 Suspensories (Vol. 1)

3842 Sutures (Vol. 1)

1389 Swabbing wells: on a contract basis (Vol. 2)

3842 Swabs, sanitary cotton (Vol. 1)

3599 Swage blocks (Vol. 1)

3542 Swaging machines (Vol. 1)

2789 Swatches and samples, mounting for the trade (Vol. 1)

3999 Swatters, fly (Vol. 1)

2253 Sweat bands (Vol. 1)

2329 Sweat pants: men's and boys' (Vol. 1)

2253 Sweat pants (Vol. 1)

2339 Sweat pants: women's, misses', and juniors' (Vol. 1)

2361 Sweat shirts: girls', children's, and infants' (Vol. 1)

2253 Sweat shirts (Vol. 1)

2369 Sweat suits: girls', children's, and infants (Vol. 1)

3111 Sweatband leather (Vol. 1)

2396 Sweatbands, hat and cap (Vol. 1)

2329 Sweater jackets: men's and boys' (Vol. 1)

2329 Sweater vests: men's and boys' (Vol. 1)

2253 Sweaters and sweater coats (Vol. 1)

2329 Sweaters: men's and boys' (Vol. 1)

2321 Sweatshirts: men's and boys' (Vol. 1)

2331 Sweatshirts: women's, misses', and juniors' (Vol. 1)

3825 Sweep generators (Vol. 1)

3825 Sweep oscillators (Vol. 1)

3589 Sweepers, carpet: except household electric vacuum sweepers (Vol. 1)

3635 Sweepers, electric: vacuum-household (Vol. 1)

3589 Sweepers, electric: vacuum-industrial (Vol. 1)

3711 Sweepers, street (motor vehicles) (Vol. 1)

2842 Sweeping compounds, oil and water absorbent, clay or sawdust (Vol. 1)

4959 Sweeping service: road, airport, parking lot, etc. (Vol. 2)

0161 Sweet and hot (vegetables); Pepper farms, (Vol. 2)

0161 Sweet corn farms (Vol. 2)

0161 Sweet pepper farms (Vol. 2)

0723 Sweet potato curing (Vol. 2)

0139 Sweet potato farms (Vol. 2)

2051 Sweet yeast goods, except frozen (Vol. 1)

2053 Sweet yeast goods, frozen (Vol. 1)

2869 Sweetners, synthetic (Vol. 1)

7997 Swimming clubs, membership (Vol. 2)

7999 Swimming instruction (Vol. 2)

7389 Swimming pool cleaning and maintenance (Vol. 2)

1799 Swimming pool construction-contractors (Vol. 2)

2394 Swimming pool covers and blankets, fabric (Vol. 1)

3089 Swimming pool covers and blankets: plastics (Vol. 1)

3589 Swimming pool filter systems (home pools) (Vol. 1)

3648 Swimming pool lighting fixtures (Vol. 1)

5091 Swimming pools and equipment—wholesale (Vol. 2)

7999 Swimming pools, except membership (Vol. 2)

5999 Swimming pools, home: not installed—retail (Vol. 2)

3949   Swimming pools, plastics (Vol. 1)
2329   Swimsuits: men's and boys' (Vol. 1)
2253   Swimsuits (Vol. 1)
2339   Swimsuits: women's, misses', and juniors' (Vol. 1)
2329   Swimwear, men's and boys' (Vol. 1)
2514   Swings, porch: metal (Vol. 1)
2511   Swings, porch: wood (Vol. 1)
2395   Swiss loom embroideries (Vol. 1)
3644   Switch boxes, electric (Vol. 1)
3643   Switch cutouts (Vol. 1)
7389   Switchboard operation of private branch exchanges (Vol. 2)
3281   Switchboard panels, slate (Vol. 1)
3613   Switchboards and parts, power (Vol. 1)
5063   Switchboards, electrical distribution—wholesale (Vol. 2)
3661   Switchboards, telephone and telegraph (Vol. 1)
3613   Switches, electric power: except snap, push button, tumbler, and solenoid (Vol. 1)
3679   Switches, electronic (Vol. 1)
5063   Switches, except electronic—wholesale (Vol. 2)
3625   Switches, flow activated electrical (Vol. 1)
3643   Switches for electric wiring: e.g., snap, tumbler, pressure, pushbutton (Vol. 1)
3999   Switches (hair) (Vol. 1)
3822   Switches, pneumatic positioning remote (Vol. 1)
3462   Switches, railroad: forged-not made in rolling mills (Vol. 1)
3674   Switches, silicon control (Vol. 1)
3679   Switches, stepping (Vol. 1)
3822   Switches, thermostatic (Vol. 1)
3613   Switchgear and Switchboard Apparatus (Vol. 1)
3613   Switchgear and switchgear accessories (Vol. 1)
5063   Switchgear—wholesale (Vol. 2)
3613   Switching equipment power (Vol. 1)
3661   Switching equipment, telephone (Vol. 1)
3743   Switching locomotives and parts, electric and nonelectric (Vol. 1)
3949   Swivels (fishing equipment) (Vol. 1)
3421   Swords (Vol. 1)
1423   Syenite, except nepheline: crushed and broken-quarrying (Vol. 2)
1411   Syenite (except nepheline), dimension-quarrying (Vol. 2)
1459   Syenite, nepheline-quarrying (Vol. 2)
1041   Sylvanite mining (Vol. 2)
7929   Symphony orchestras (Vol. 2)
3829   Synchronizers, aircraft engine (Vol. 1)
3621   Synchronous condensers and timing motors, electric (Vol. 1)
3621   Synchros (Vol. 1)
3825   Synchroscopes (Vol. 1)
3931   Synthesizers, music (Vol. 1)
3559   Synthetic filament extruding machines (Vol. 1)
6111   Synthetic Fuels Corporation (Vol. 2)
4925   Synthetic natural gas from naphtha, production and distribution (Vol. 2)
2822   Synthetic Rubber or Vulcanizable Elastomers (Vol. 1)
5169   Synthetic rubber—wholesale (Vol. 2)

3299   Synthetic stones, for gem stones and industrial use (Vol. 1)
3069   Syringes, fountain: rubber (Vol. 1)
3841   Syringes, hypodermic (Vol. 1)
2061   Syrup, cane: made from sugarcane (Vol. 1)
2046   Syrup, corn: unmixed (Vol. 1)
2062   Syrup, made from purchased raw cane sugar or sugar syrup (Vol. 1)
2063   Syrup, made from sugar beets (Vol. 1)
2087   Syrups, beverage (Vol. 1)
2066   Syrups, chocolate (Vol. 1)
5149   Syrups, except for fountain use—wholesale (Vol. 2)
2087   Syrups, flavoring (Vol. 1)
5145   Syrups, fountain—wholesale (Vol. 2)
2082   Syrups, malt (Vol. 1)
2834   Syrups, pharmaceutical (Vol. 1)
2062   Syrups, refiners' (Vol. 1)
2099   Syrups, sweetening: honey, maple syrup, sorghum (Vol. 1)
0721   System operation services (not providing water); Irrigation (Vol. 2)
7371   Systems analysis and design, computer software (Vol. 2)
8748   Systems engineering consulting, except professional engineering or computer related (Vol. 2)
7373   Systems integration, computer (Vol. 2)

T

2253   T-shirts (Vol. 1)
2361   T-shirts, outerwear: girls', children's, and infants' (Vol. 1)
2321   T-shirts, outerwear: men's and boys' (Vol. 1)
2253   T-shirts, outerwear (Vol. 1)
2331   T-shirts, outerwear: women's, misses', and juniors' (Vol. 1)
2322   T-shirts, underwear: men's and boys' (Vol. 1)
2254   T-shirts, underwear (Vol. 1)
2341   T-shirts, underwear: women's, misses', children's, and infants' (Vol. 1)
3829   T-squares (drafting) (Vol. 1)
3914   Table and kitchen cutlery, all metal (Vol. 1)
3269   Table articles, coarse earthenware (Vol. 1)
3263   Table articles, fine earthenware (whiteware) (Vol. 1)
3262   Table articles, vitreous china (Vol. 1)
2211   Table cover fabrics, cotton (Vol. 1)
7213   Table cover supply service (Vol. 2)
2258   Table covers, lace (Vol. 1)
3914   Table cutlery, all metal (Vol. 1)
3421   Table cutlery, except table cutlery with handles of metal (Vol. 1)
2211   Table damask, cotton (Vol. 1)
3645   Table lamps (Vol. 1)
5023   Table linens—wholesale (Vol. 2)
2392   Table mats, plastics and textiles (Vol. 1)
2079   Table oils (Vol. 1)
2541   Table or counter tops, plastics laminated (Vol. 1)
3292   Table pads and padding, asbestos (Vol. 1)

3999 Tanning and currying furs (Vol. 1)
2861 Tanning extracts and materials, natural (Vol. 1)
7299 Tanning salons (Vol. 2)
1061 Tantalite mining (Vol. 2)
1061 Tantalum ore mining (Vol. 2)
3339 Tantalum refining (Vol. 1)
5813 Tap rooms (drinking places) (Vol. 2)
3842 Tape, adhesive: medicated or nonmedicated (Vol. 1)
3292 Tape, asbestos (Vol. 1)
3652 Tape, audio magnetic: prerecorded (Vol. 1)
2672 Tape, cellophane adhesive (Vol. 1)
3577 Tape cleaners, magnetic: computer peripheral equipment (Vol. 1)
7822 Tape distribution for television (Vol. 2)
3069 Tape, friction: rubber (Vol. 1)
2672 Tape, gummed: cloth and paper base (Vol. 1)
3965 Tape, hook-and-eye and snap fastener (Vol. 1)
3695 Tape, magnetic recording: blank (Vol. 1)
2672 Tape, masking (Vol. 1)
3999 Tape measures (Vol. 1)
5064 Tape players and recorders, household—wholesale (Vol. 2)
3651 Tape players, household (Vol. 1)
2672 Tape, pressure sensitive: except rubber backed (Vol. 1)
3069 Tape, pressure sensitive (including friction), rubber (Vol. 1)
3577 Tape print units, computer peripheral equipment (Vol. 1)
7812 Tape production, video or motion picture (Vol. 2)
7379 Tape recertification service (Vol. 2)
7622 Tape recorder repair (Vol. 2)
5731 Tape recorders and players—retail (Vol. 2)
3572 Tape recorders for data computers (Vol. 1)
3651 Tape recorders, household (Vol. 1)
7389 Tape slitting for the trade (cutting plastics, leather, etc. into widths) (Vol. 2)
3572 Tape storage units, computer (Vol. 1)
5735 Tape stores, audio and video—retail (Vol. 2)
2679 Tape, telegraph: paper (Vol. 1)
5131 Tape, textile—wholesale (Vol. 2)
3572 Tape transports, magnetic (Vol. 1)
2295 Tape, varnished: plastics and other coated: except magnetic (Vol. 1)
5065 Tapes, audio and video recording—wholesale (Vol. 2)
5099 Tapes, audio prerecorded—wholesale (Vol. 2)
2241 Tapes, fabric (Vol. 1)
3829 Tapes, surveyors' (Vol. 1)
7822 Tapes, video, recorded—wholesale (Vol. 2)
2211 Tapestry fabrics, cotton (Vol. 1)
2221 Tapestry fabrics, manmade fiber and silk (Vol. 1)
1742 Taping and finishing drywall-contractors (Vol. 2)
2046 Tapioca (Vol. 1)
5084 Tapping attachments—wholesale (Vol. 2)
3541 Tapping machines (Vol. 1)
3643 Taps, current: attachment plug and screw shell types (Vol. 1)
3545 Taps, machine tool (Vol. 1)

3131 Taps, shoe: regardless of material (Vol. 1)
2821 Tar acid resins (Vol. 1)
2951 Tar and asphalt mixtures for paving, not made in petroleum refineries (Vol. 1)
2861 Tar and tar oils, products of wood distillation (Vol. 1)
3312 Tar, derived from chemical recovery coke ovens (Vol. 1)
2911 Tar or residuum, produced in petroleum refineries (Vol. 1)
2621 Tar paper, building and roofing (Vol. 1)
2672 Tar paper: except building or roofing and packaging (Vol. 1)
2952 Tar paper, roofing (Vol. 1)
2865 Tar, product of coal tar distillation (Vol. 1)
1311 Tar sands mining (Vol. 2)
3728 Target drones, aircraft (Vol. 1)
3499 Target drones for use by ships, metal (Vol. 1)
3949 Target shooting equipment, except small arms and ammunition (Vol. 1)
3949 Targets, archery and rifle shooting (Vol. 1)
3949 Targets, clay (Vol. 1)
3728 Targets, trailer type: aircraft (Vol. 1)
4731 Tariff consultant (Vol. 2)
4731 Tariff rate information service (Vol. 2)
2211 Tarlatan, cotton (Vol. 1)
2394 Tarpaulins, fabric (Vol. 1)
2869 Tartaric acid and metallic salts (Vol. 1)
2869 Tartrates (Vol. 1)
2284 Tatting thread: cotton, silk, manmade fibers, and wool (Vol. 1)
7299 Tattoo parlors (Vol. 2)
5813 Taverns (drinking places) (Vol. 2)
6211 Tax certificate dealers (Vol. 2)
6099 Tax certificate sale and redemption agencies (Vol. 2)
7389 Tax collection agencies: collecting for a city, county, or State (Vol. 2)
6799 Tax liens: holding, buying, and selling (Vol. 2)
7291 Tax Return Preparation Services (Vol. 2)
7291 Tax return preparation services without accounting, auditing, or bookkeeping services (Vol. 2)
7389 Tax title dealers: agencies for city, county, or State (Vol. 2)
9311 Taxation departments (Vol. 2)
7319 Taxicab card advertising (Vol. 2)
4121 Taxicab operation (Vol. 2)
4121 Taxicabs (Vol. 2)
3711 Taxicabs (Vol. 2)
5012 Taxicabs—wholesale (Vol. 2)
7699 Taxidermists (Vol. 2)
3824 Taximeters (Vol. 1)
8641 Taxpayers' associations (Vol. 2)
2393 Tea bags, fabric (Vol. 1)
2099 Tea blending (Vol. 1)
2086 Tea, iced: bottled or canned (Vol. 1)
3634 Tea kettles, electric (Vol. 1)
3229 Tea kettles, glass and glass ceramic (Vol. 1)
5812 Tea rooms (Vol. 2)
5499 Tea stores—retail (Vol. 2)

2514 Tea wagons, metal (Vol. 1)

2511 Tea wagons, wood (Vol. 1)

5149 Tea—wholesale (Vol. 2)

0831 Teaberries, gathering of (Vol. 2)

9411 Teacher certification bureaus (Vol. 2)

7361 Teachers' registries (Vol. 2)

3699 Teaching machines and aids, electronic (Vol. 1)

3469 Teakettles, except electric: stamped metal (Vol. 1)

3999 Tear gas devices and equipment (Vol. 1)

2869 Tear gas (Vol. 1)

2261 Teaseling cotton broadwoven goods (Vol. 1)

2262 Teaseling manmade fiber and silk broadwoven fabrics (Vol. 1)

2835 Technetium products (Vol. 1)

3229 Technical glassware and glass products, pressed or blown (Vol. 1)

3231 Technical glassware, made from purchased glass (Vol. 1)

8222 Technical institutes (Vol. 2)

2741 Technical manuals and papers: publishing and printing, or publishing only (Vol. 1)

2341 Teddies: women's, misses', children's, and infants' (Vol. 1)

5699 Tee shirts, custom printed—retail (Vol. 2)

8072 Teeth, artificial: made in dental laboratories to order for the profession (Vol. 2)

3843 Teeth, artificial: not made in dental laboratories (Vol. 1)

3531 Teeth, bucket and scarifier (Vol. 1)

3069 Teething rings, rubber (Vol. 1)

1731 Telecommunications equipment installation-contractors (Vol. 2)

4822 Telegram services (Vol. 2)

4822 Telegraph and Other Communications (Vol. 2)

3661 Telegraph and telephone carrier and repeater equipment (Vol. 1)

4822 Telegraph cable services (Vol. 2)

5065 Telegraph equipment—wholesale (Vol. 2)

1623 Telegraph line construction-general contractors (Vol. 2)

3661 Telegraph office switching equipment (Vol. 1)

7389 Telegraph service, florists' (Vol. 2)

4822 Telegraph services (Vol. 2)

3661 Telegraph station equipment and parts, wire (Vol. 1)

2679 Telegraph tape, paper (Vol. 1)

7389 Telemarketing (telephone marketing) service on a contract or fee basis (Vol. 2)

3663 Telemetering equipment, electronic (Vol. 1)

3823 Telemetering instruments, industrial process type (Vol. 1)

3661 Telephone and Telegraph Apparatus (Vol. 1)

1731 Telephone and telephone equipment installation-contractors (Vol. 2)

7389 Telephone answering, except beeper service (Vol. 2)

3661 Telephone answering machines (Vol. 1)

7349 Telephone booths, cleaning and maintenance of (Vol. 2)

2542 Telephone booths, except wood (Vol. 1)

2541 Telephone booths, wood (Vol. 1)

3661 Telephone central office equipment, dial and manual (Vol. 1)

4813 Telephone Communications Except Radiotelephone (Vol. 2)

8322 Telephone counseling service (Vol. 2)

3661 Telephone dialing devices, automatic (Vol. 1)

2759 Telephone directories, except lithographed or gravure (not publishing) (Vol. 1)

2754 Telephone directories, gravure printing: not publishing (Vol. 1)

2741 Telephone directories: publishing and printing, or publishing only (Vol. 1)

5065 Telephone equipment—wholesale (Vol. 2)

1623 Telephone line construction-general contractors (Vol. 2)

7629 Telephone set repair (Vol. 2)

3661 Telephone sets, except cellular radio telephone (Vol. 1)

7389 Telephone solicitation service on a contract or fee basis (Vol. 2)

2511 Telephone stands, wood (Vol. 1)

3661 Telephone station equipment and parts, wire (Vol. 1)

5999 Telephone stores—retail (Vol. 2)

3663 Telephones, cellular radio (Vol. 1)

3661 Telephones, sound powered (no battery) (Vol. 1)

3661 Telephones, underwater (Vol. 1)

3575 Teleprinters (computer terminals) (Vol. 1)

3827 Telescopes (Vol. 1)

5999 Telescopes—retail (Vol. 2)

3827 Telescopic sights (Vol. 1)

2679 Teletypewriter paper, rolls with carbon (Vol. 1)

4822 Teletypewriter services (Vol. 2)

3469 Television and radio chassis: stamped metal (Vol. 1)

1799 Television and radio stations, service and repair of-contractors (Vol. 2)

7313 Television and radio time, sale of: not auxiliary to television or radio broadcasting (Vol. 2)

4833 Television Broadcasting Stations (Vol. 2)

2519 Television cabinets, plastics (Vol. 1)

2517 Television cabinets, wood (Vol. 1)

3663 Television closed-circuit equipment (Vol. 1)

7922 Television employment agencies (Vol. 2)

7812 Television film production (Vol. 2)

5961 Television, mail-order (home shopping)—retail (Vol. 2)

3663 Television monitors (Vol. 1)

7922 Television programs (including commercials): live (Vol. 2)

5065 Television receiving and transmitting tubes—wholesale (Vol. 2)

3651 Television receiving sets (Vol. 1)

7359 Television rental and leasing (Vol. 2)

7622 Television repair shops (Vol. 2)

2721 Television schedules: publishing and printing, or publishing only (Vol. 1)

5731 Television set stores—retail (Vol. 2)

5064 Television sets—wholesale (Vol. 2)

4841 Television, subscription or closed circuit (Vol. 2)

7819 Television tape services (e.g., editing and transfers) (Vol. 2)

3441 Television tower sections, prefabricated metal (Vol. 1)

3663 Television transmitting antennas and ground equipment (Vol. 1)

1623 Television transmitting tower construction-general contractors (Vol. 2)

3229 Television tube blanks, glass (Vol. 1)

3671 Television tubes (Vol. 1)

4822 Telex services (Vol. 2)

1041 Telluride (gold) mining (Vol. 2)

3339 Tellurium refining, primary (Vol. 1)

3822 Temperature controls, automatic: residential and commercial types (Vol. 1)

3823 Temperature instruments: industrial process type, except glass and bimetal (Vol. 1)

3822 Temperature sensors for motor windings (Vol. 1)

3569 Temperature testing chambers (Vol. 1)

3231 Tempered glass, made from purchased glass (Vol. 1)

3211 Tempered glass (Vol. 1)

3398 Tempering of metal for the trade (Vol. 1)

3829 Templates, drafting (Vol. 1)

8661 Temples (Vol. 2)

3851 Temples and fronts, ophthalmic (Vol. 1)

7363 Temporary help service (Vol. 2)

7933 Ten pin centers (Vol. 2)

8641 Tenant associations, except property management (Vol. 2)

3944 Tenders, baby (vehicles) (Vol. 1)

3743 Tenders, locomotive (Vol. 1)

3731 Tenders (ships), building and repairing (Vol. 1)

7997 Tennis clubs, membership (Vol. 2)

7999 Tennis clubs, nonmembership (Vol. 2)

1629 Tennis court construction, outdoor-general contractors (Vol. 2)

7999 Tennis courts, outdoor and indoor: operation of, nonmembership (Vol. 2)

5941 Tennis goods and equipment—retail (Vol. 2)

3949 Tennis goods: e.g., balls, frames, rackets (Vol. 1)

7999 Tennis professionals (Vol. 2)

2253 Tennis shirts (Vol. 1)

3553 Tenoners (woodworking machines) (Vol. 1)

3829 Tensile strength testing equipment (Vol. 1)

2499 Tent poles, wood (Vol. 1)

7699 Tent repair shops (Vol. 2)

5999 Tent shops—retail (Vol. 2)

3792 Tent-type camping trailers (Vol. 1)

2211 Tentage (Vol. 1)

2394 Tents (Vol. 1)

4231 Terminal and Joint Terminal Maintenance Facilities for Motor Freight Transportation (Vol. 2)

4173 Terminal and Service Facilities for Motor Vehicle Passenger Transportation (Vol. 2)

4013 Terminal and switching companies, railroad (Vol. 2)

4491 Terminal operation, waterfront (Vol. 2)

4581 Terminal services, coordinated: at airports (Vol. 2)

3643 Terminals and connectors for electrical devices (Vol. 1)

3575 Terminals, computer (Vol. 1)

4231 Terminals, freight trucking: with or without maintenance facilities (Vol. 2)

7342 Termite control (Vol. 2)

3312 Terneplate (Vol. 1)

5051 Terneplate—wholesale (Vol. 2)

3312 Ternes, iron and steel: long or short (Vol. 1)

2869 Terpineol (Vol. 1)

3259 Terra cotta, architectural: clay (Vol. 1)

5032 Terra cotta—wholesale (Vol. 2)

0919 Terrapins, catching of (Vol. 2)

3272 Terrazzo products, precast (Vol. 1)

1743 Terrazzo, Tile, Marble and Mosaic Work (Vol. 2)

1743 Terrazzo work-contractors (Vol. 2)

2211 Terry woven fabrics, cotton (Vol. 1)

2869 Tert-butylated bis (p-phenoxyphenyl) ether fluid (Vol. 1)

1799 Test boring for construction-contractors (Vol. 2)

8748 Test development and evaluation service, educational or personnel (Vol. 2)

1081 Test drilling for metal mining: on a contract basis (Vol. 2)

1481 Test drilling for nonmetallic minerals except fuel: on a contract basis (Vol. 2)

3825 Test equipment for electronic and electrical circuits and equipment (Vol. 1)

3423 Test plugs: plumbers' handtools (Vol. 1)

3825 Test sets, ignition harness (Vol. 1)

3231 Test tubes, made from purchased glass (Vol. 1)

3829 Testers for checking hydraulic controls on aircraft (Vol. 1)

5084 Testing and measuring equipment, electrical: except automotive—wholesale (Vol. 2)

3569 Testing chambers for altitude, temperature, ordnance, and power (Vol. 1)

3829 Testing equipment: abrasion, shearing strength, tensile strength, and torsion (Vol. 1)

5013 Testing equipment, electrical: automotive—wholesale (Vol. 2)

0751 Testing for butterfat; Milk (Vol. 2)

8734 Testing Laboratories (Vol. 2)

8734 Testing laboratories, except clinical (Vol. 2)

8071 Testing laboratories, medical: analytic or diagnostic (Vol. 2)

8748 Testing services, educational or personnel (Vol. 2)

2869 Tetrachloroethylene (Vol. 1)

2869 Tetraethyl lead (Vol. 1)

2892 Tetryl (explosives) (Vol. 1)

2621 Text paper (Vol. 1)

2732 Textbooks: printing or printing and binding, not publishing (Vol. 1)

2731 Textbooks: publishing and printing, or publishing only (Vol. 1)

2393 Textile Bags (Vol. 1)

5131 Textile converters except knit goods—wholesale (Vol. 2)

2851 Thinners, paint: prepared (Vol. 1)
0721 Thinning of crops, mechanical and chemical (Vol. 2)
2819 Thiocyanates, inorganic (Vol. 1)
2879 Thiocyanates, organic (formulated) (Vol. 1)
2869 Thioglycolic acid, for permanent wave lotions (Vol. 1)
2822 Thiol rubbers (Vol. 1)
3714 Third axle attachments or six wheel units for motor vehicles (Vol. 1)
1099 Thorium ore mining (Vol. 2)
2035 Thousand Island dressing (Vol. 1)
3292 Thread, asbestos (Vol. 1)
3545 Thread cutting dies (Vol. 1)
2241 Thread, elastic: fabric covered (Vol. 1)
2284 Thread: except flax, hemp, and ramie (Vol. 1)
5131 Thread, except industrial—wholesale (Vol. 2)
2241 Thread, fabric covered rubber (Vol. 1)
3545 Thread gauges (machinists' precision tools) (Vol. 1)
2299 Thread: linen, hemp, and ramie (Vol. 1)
3552 Thread making machines (spinning machinery), textile (Vol. 1)
2284 Thread Mills (Vol. 1)
3542 Thread rolling machines (Vol. 1)
3069 Thread, rubber: except fabric covered (Vol. 1)
5131 Thread, sewing, except industrial—wholesale (Vol. 2)
3541 Threading machines (machine tools) (Vol. 1)
3545 Threading toolholders (Vol. 1)
3545 Threading tools (machine tool accessories) (Vol. 1)
5084 Threading tools—wholesale (Vol. 2)
0722 Threshing service (Vol. 2)
3272 Thresholds, precast terrazzo (Vol. 1)
2282 Throwing, winding, or spooling of yarn: silk, wool and manmade fiber continuous filament (Vol. 1)
3829 Thrust power indicators, aircraft engine (Vol. 1)
3674 Thyristors (Vol. 1)
2834 Thyroid preparations (Vol. 1)
7922 Ticket agencies, theatrical (Vol. 2)
3579 Ticket counting machines (Vol. 1)
4729 Ticket offices, transportation: not operated by transportation companies (Vol. 2)
7999 Ticket sales offices for sporting events, contract (Vol. 2)
2754 Tickets: gravure printing (Vol. 1)
2752 Tickets, lithographed (Vol. 1)
2679 Tickets, pin: paper (Vol. 1)
2759 Tickets, printed: except lithographed or gravure (Vol. 1)
2211 Tickings (Vol. 1)
3312 Tie plates, iron and steel (Vol. 1)
3714 Tie rods, motor vehicle (Vol. 1)
5611 Tie shops—retail (Vol. 2)
2241 Tie tapes, woven or braided (Vol. 1)
3315 Tie wires, made in wiredrawing plants (Vol. 1)
2449 Tierces (cooperage) (Vol. 1)
3496 Ties, bale: made from purchased wire (Vol. 1)
3599 Ties, form: metal (Vol. 1)
2323 Ties, handsewn (Vol. 1)
5136 Ties, men's and boys'—wholesale (Vol. 2)

2253 Ties (Vol. 1)
3272 Ties, railroad: concrete (Vol. 1)
2491 Ties, railroad cross bridge and switch: treated (Vol. 1)
2421 Ties, railroad: sawed (Vol. 1)
2339 Ties: women's, misses', and juniors' (Vol. 1)
2252 Tights, except women's (Vol. 1)
2251 Tights, women's (Vol. 1)
3296 Tile, acoustical: mineral wool (Vol. 1)
5211 Tile and brick dealers—retail (Vol. 2)
3253 Tile, ceramic wall and floor (Vol. 1)
3253 Tile, clay floor and wall: enameled (Vol. 1)
5032 Tile, clay or other ceramic: except refractory—wholesale (Vol. 2)
3255 Tile, clay refractory (Vol. 1)
3251 Tile, clay: structural (Vol. 1)
2499 Tile, cork (Vol. 1)
3259 Tile, filter underdrain: clay (Vol. 1)
3469 Tile, floor and wall: stamped metal (Vol. 1)
3292 Tile, floor: asphalt (Vol. 1)
3996 Tile, floor: supported plastics (Vol. 1)
3275 Tile, gypsum (Vol. 1)
1752 Tile installation, asphalt-contractors (Vol. 2)
1743 Tile installation, ceramic-contractors (Vol. 2)
1799 Tile installation, wall: plastics-contractors (Vol. 2)
3559 Tile making machines (Vol. 1)
3272 Tile, precast terrazzo or concrete (Vol. 1)
3259 Tile, roofing and drain: clay (Vol. 1)
3069 Tile, rubber (Vol. 1)
3299 Tile, sand lime (Vol. 1)
1743 Tile setting, ceramic-contractors (Vol. 2)
3259 Tile, sewer: clay (Vol. 1)
5032 Tile, structural clay—wholesale (Vol. 2)
3292 Tile, vinyl asbestos (Vol. 1)
2493 Tile, wall: fiberboard (Vol. 1)
2449 Till baskets, veneer and splint (Vol. 1)
2411 Timber (product of logging camps) (Vol. 1)
5099 Timber products, rough—wholesale (Vol. 2)
1629 Timber removal, underwater-contractors (Vol. 2)
2491 Timber, structural: treated (Vol. 1)
0811 Timber Tracts (Vol. 2)
0851 Timber valuation (Vol. 2)
2411 Timbers, mine: hewn (Vol. 1)
2439 Timbers, structural: laminated lumber (Vol. 1)
3825 Time code generators (Vol. 1)
3823 Time cycle and program controllers, industrial process type (Vol. 1)
3821 Time interval measuring equipment, electric (laboratory type) (Vol. 1)
3429 Time locks (Vol. 1)
3822 Time program controls, air-conditioning systems (Vol. 1)
2675 Time recording cards, die-cut from purchased paperboard (Vol. 1)
7389 Time-share condominium exchanges (Vol. 2)
7374 Time sharing, computer (Vol. 2)
6531 Time-sharing real estate: sales, leasing, and rentals (Vol. 2)
3579 Time-stamps: containing clock mechanisms (Vol. 1)

3559 Tobacco products machinery (Vol. 1)

5194 Tobacco products, manufactured—wholesale (Vol. 2)

7389 Tobacco sheeting service on a contract or fee basis (Vol. 2)

2141 Tobacco Stemming and Redrying (Vol. 1)

2141 Tobacco, stemming and redrying of (Vol. 1)

5993 Tobacco Stores and Stands (Vol. 2)

5993 Tobacco stores—retail (Vol. 2)

2141 Tobacco thrashing (mechanical stemming) (Vol. 1)

4221 Tobacco warehousing and storage (Vol. 2)

5993 Tobacconists—retail (Vol. 2)

3949 Toboggans (Vol. 1)

3131 Toe caps, leather or metal (Vol. 1)

2099 Tofu, except frozen desserts (Vol. 1)

2024 Tofu frozen desserts (Vol. 1)

3452 Toggle bolts, metal (Vol. 1)

3089 Toggle bolts, plastics (Vol. 1)

5122 Toilet articles—wholesale (Vol. 2)

3991 Toilet brushes (Vol. 1)

2844 Toilet creams, powders, and waters (Vol. 1)

3431 Toilet fixtures: enameled iron, cast iron, and pressed metal (Vol. 1)

3088 Toilet fixtures, plastics (Vol. 1)

3261 Toilet fixtures, vitreous china (Vol. 1)

3172 Toilet kits and cases, regardless of material (Vol. 1)

2676 Toilet paper (Vol. 1)

2844 Toilet preparations (Vol. 1)

5122 Toilet preparations—wholesale (Vol. 2)

2499 Toilet seats, wood (Vol. 1)

5122 Toilet soap—wholesale (Vol. 2)

2621 Toilet tissue stock (Vol. 1)

3499 Toilet ware, metal: except silver, nickel silver, pewter, and plated (Vol. 1)

3914 Toilet ware: silver, nickel silver, pewter, and plated (Vol. 1)

5122 Toiletries—wholesale (Vol. 2)

7359 Toilets, portable: rental and leasing (Vol. 2)

3829 Toll booths, automatic (Vol. 1)

4785 Toll bridge operation (Vol. 2)

4785 Toll roads, operation of (Vol. 2)

3661 Toll switching equipment, telephone (Vol. 1)

2865 Toluene, made in chemical plants (Vol. 1)

2865 Toluidines (Vol. 1)

0161 Tomato farms (Vol. 2)

3523 Tomato harvesters (Vol. 1)

2033 Tomato juice and cocktails, canned (Vol. 1)

2033 Tomato paste (Vol. 1)

2033 Tomato puree (Vol. 1)

2033 Tomato sauce (Vol. 1)

0182 Tomatoes grown under cover (Vol. 2)

3281 Tombstones, cut stone: not including only finishing or lettering to order (Vol. 1)

3272 Tombstones, precast terrazzo or concrete (Vol. 1)

5999 Tombstones—retail (Vol. 2)

3861 Toners, prepared photographic, packaged (Vol. 1)

2865 Toners (reduced or full strength organic colors) (Vol. 1)

3423 Tongs, oyster (Vol. 1)

3842 Tongue depressors (Vol. 1)

3131 Tongues, boot and shoe: leather (Vol. 1)

2844 Tonics, hair (Vol. 1)

3841 Tonometers, medical (Vol. 1)

3469 Tool boxes, stamped metal (Vol. 1)

2441 Tool chests, wood (Vol. 1)

7389 Tool designers (Vol. 2)

3089 Tool handles, plastics (Vol. 1)

2499 Tool handles, wood: turned and shaped (Vol. 1)

7359 Tool rental and leasing (Vol. 2)

7699 Tool sharpening and repair shops (Vol. 2)

2599 Tool stands, factory (Vol. 1)

3312 Tool steel (Vol. 1)

5084 Toolholders (e.g., chucks, turrets)—wholesale (Vol. 2)

3545 Toolholders (Vol. 1)

3545 Tools and accessories for machine tools (Vol. 1)

5013 Tools and equipment, automotive—wholesale (Vol. 2)

3423 Tools and equipment for use with sporting arms (Vol. 1)

3843 Tools, dentists' (Vol. 1)

3533 Tools: drilling, etc.-for artesian, gas, and oil wells (Vol. 1)

3423 Tools, edge: woodworking-augers, bits, gimlets, countersinks, etc. (Vol. 1)

3423 Tools, hand: except power-driven tools and saws (Vol. 1)

3546 Tools, hand: power-driven-woodworking or metalworking (Vol. 1)

3541 Tools, machine: metal cutting types (Vol. 1)

5084 Tools, machinists' precision—wholesale (Vol. 2)

5251 Tools, power and hand—retail (Vol. 2)

3634 Toothbrushes, electric (Vol. 1)

5064 Toothbrushes, electric—wholesale (Vol. 2)

3991 Toothbrushes, except electric (Vol. 1)

5122 Toothbrushes, except electric—wholesale (Vol. 2)

2844 Toothpastes and powders (Vol. 1)

2499 Toothpicks, wood (Vol. 1)

7532 Top, Body and Upholstery Repair and Paint Shops (Vol. 2)

3069 Top lift sheets, rubber (Vol. 1)

3131 Top lifts, boot and shoe (Vol. 1)

7532 Top repair, automotive (Vol. 2)

3069 Top roll covering, for textile mill machinery: rubber (Vol. 1)

1459 Topaz (nongem) mining (Vol. 2)

2311 Topcoats: men's and boys' (Vol. 1)

5145 Toppings, soda fountain—wholesale (Vol. 2)

3465 Tops, automobile: stamped metal (Vol. 1)

2675 Tops, bottle; die-cut from purchased paper or paperboard (Vol. 1)

3259 Tops, chimney: clay (Vol. 1)

2299 Tops, combing and converting (Vol. 1)

3466 Tops, jar: stamped metal (Vol. 1)

2299 Tops, manmade fiber (Vol. 1)

3714 Tops, motor vehicle: except stamped metal (Vol. 1)

3089 Tops, plastics (e.g., dispenser, shaker) (Vol. 1)

3713 Tops, truck (Vol. 1)

5159 Tops, wool—wholesale (Vol. 2)

2899 Torches (fireworks) (Vol. 1)

3489 Torpedo tubes (ordnance) (Vol. 1)

3483 Torpedoes and parts (ordnance) (Vol. 1)

2899 Torpedoes, railroad (Vol. 1)

2892 Torpedoes, well shooting (explosives) (Vol. 1)

3566 Torque converters, except motor vehicle (Vol. 1)

3621 Torque motors, electric (Vol. 1)

3493 Torsion bar springs (Vol. 1)

3829 Torsion testing equipment (Vol. 1)

2032 Tortillas, canned (Vol. 1)

2099 Tortillas, fresh or refrigerated (Vol. 1)

3824 Totalizing Fluid Meters and Counting Devices (Vol. 1)

3824 Totalizing meters, consumption registering, except aircraft (Vol. 1)

3999 Toupees (Vol. 1)

4725 Tour operation (travel) (Vol. 2)

4725 Tour Operators (Vol. 2)

4724 Tourist agencies for the arrangement of transportation, lodging, and car rental (Vol. 2)

7999 Tourist attractions, natural wonder: commercial (Vol. 2)

7011 Tourist cabins (Vol. 2)

7011 Tourist camps (Vol. 2)

7011 Tourist courts (Vol. 2)

7999 Tourist guides (Vol. 2)

7389 Tourist information bureaus (Vol. 2)

4725 Tours, except sightseeing buses, boats, and airplanes (Vol. 2)

7521 Tow-in parking lots (Vol. 2)

3728 Tow targets, aircraft (Vol. 1)

2299 Tow to top mills (Vol. 1)

3731 Towboats, building and repairing (Vol. 1)

3261 Towel bar holders, vitreous china and earthenware (Vol. 1)

7213 Towel supply service, except wiping (Vol. 2)

7218 Towel supply service, wiping (Vol. 2)

2844 Towelettes, premoistened (Vol. 1)

2621 Toweling paper (Vol. 1)

2211 Towels and toweling, cotton: made in weaving mills (Vol. 1)

2299 Towels and towelings, linen and linen-and-cotton mixtures (Vol. 1)

2392 Towels, fabric and nonwoven textiles (Vol. 1)

2259 Towels (Vol. 1)

2676 Towels, paper (Vol. 1)

5113 Towels, paper—wholesale (Vol. 2)

3441 Tower sections, transmission: prefabricated metal (Vol. 1)

3443 Towers: bubble, cooling, fractionating-metal plate (Vol. 1)

2499 Towers, cooling: wood or wood and sheet metal combination (Vol. 1)

3443 Towers, tank: metal plate (Vol. 1)

4492 Towing and Tugboat Services (Vol. 2)

3799 Towing bars and systems (Vol. 1)

7549 Towing service, automotive (Vol. 2)

4492 Towing services, marine (Vol. 2)

1521 Townhouse construction-general contractors (Vol. 2)

2836 Toxins (Vol. 1)

2836 Toxoids, except in vitro and in vivo (Vol. 1)

5945 Toy and game stores—retail (Vol. 2)

3612 Toy transformers (Vol. 1)

3942 Toys, doll (Vol. 1)

3944 Toys: except dolls, bicycles, rubber toys, and stuffed toys (Vol. 1)

5092 Toys, Hobby Goods and Supplies (Vol. 2)

5092 Toys (including electronic)—wholesale (Vol. 2)

3069 Toys, rubber: except dolls (Vol. 1)

3942 Toys, stuffed (Vol. 1)

2879 Trace elements (agricultural chemicals) (Vol. 1)

3483 Tracer igniters for ammunition more than 30 mm. (or more than 1.18 inch) (Vol. 1)

2211 Tracing cloth, cotton (Vol. 1)

3952 Tracing cloth (drafting material) (Vol. 1)

3949 Track and field athletic equipment, except apparel and footwear (Vol. 1)

5051 Track spikes—wholesale (Vol. 2)

4899 Tracking missiles by telemetry and photography on a contract basis (Vol. 2)

5082 Tracklaying equipment—wholesale (Vol. 2)

3743 Trackless trolley buses (Vol. 1)

3842 Traction apparatus (Vol. 1)

5082 Tractor-mounting equipment—wholesale (Vol. 2)

7699 Tractor repair (Vol. 2)

5083 Tractors, agricultural—wholesale (Vol. 2)

3531 Tractors, construction (Vol. 1)

5082 Tractors, construction—wholesale (Vol. 2)

3531 Tractors, crawler (Vol. 1)

3537 Tractors, industrial: for use in plants, depots, docks, and terminals (Vol. 1)

5084 Tractors, industrial—wholesale (Vol. 2)

3524 Tractors, lawn and garden (Vol. 1)

3531 Tractors, tracklaying (Vol. 1)

3711 Tractors, truck: for highway use (Vol. 1)

5012 Tractors, truck—wholesale (Vol. 2)

3523 Tractors, wheel: farm type (Vol. 1)

8611 Trade associations (Vol. 2)

2789 Trade binding services (Vol. 1)

9611 Trade commissions-government (Vol. 2)

2721 Trade journals, publishing and printing, or publishing only (Vol. 1)

8249 Trade schools (Vol. 2)

7389 Trade show arrangement (Vol. 2)

8631 Trade unions, local or national (Vol. 2)

6221 Traders, commodity contract (Vol. 2)

6211 Traders, security (Vol. 2)

6799 Trading companies, commodity contract (Vol. 2)

7389 Trading stamp promotion and sale to stores (Vol. 2)

7389 Trading stamp redemption (Vol. 2)

2754 Trading stamps: gravure printing (Vol. 1)

2752 Trading stamps, lithographed (Vol. 1)

2759 Trading stamps, printed: except lithographed or gravure (Vol. 1)

8748 Traffic consultants (Vol. 2)

1721 Traffic lane painting-contractors (Vol. 2)

3669 Traffic signals, electric (Vol. 1)

1629 Trail building-general contractors (Vol. 2)

1629 Trailer camp construction-general contractors (Vol. 2)

3799 Trailer hitches (Vol. 1)

7033 Trailer parks for transients (Vol. 2)

7519 Trailer rental (Vol. 2)

3523 Trailers and wagons, farm (Vol. 1)

3799 Trailers, boat (Vol. 1)

3792 Trailers, camping (Vol. 1)

3715 Trailers, fifth-wheel type: for transporting horses (Vol. 1)

3799 Trailers for automobiles, except travel and mobile home (Vol. 1)

5012 Trailers for passenger automobiles—wholesale (Vol. 2)

3799 Trailers for transporting horses, except fifth-wheel type (Vol. 1)

5012 Trailers for trucks, new and used—wholesale (Vol. 2)

3792 Trailers, house: except as permanent dwellings (Vol. 1)

5084 Trailers, industrial—wholesale (Vol. 2)

3715 Trailers, motor truck (Vol. 1)

3537 Trailers, truck: for use in plants, depots, docks, and terminals (Vol. 1)

5599 Trailers, utility—retail (Vol. 2)

3743 Train cars and equipment, freight or passenger (Vol. 1)

3728 Training aids, aircraft: except electronic (Vol. 1)

0752 Training horses, except racing (Vol. 2)

7812 Training motion picture production (Vol. 2)

0752 Training of pets and other animal specialties (Vol. 2)

2341 Training pants (underwear) except rubber or rubberized fabric: children's and infants' (Vol. 1)

7948 Training racehorses (Vol. 2)

8361 Training schools for delinquents (Vol. 2)

3944 Trains and equipment, toy: electric and mechanical (Vol. 1)

7999 Trampoline operation (Vol. 2)

4119 Tramways, aerial: except amusement and scenic (Vol. 2)

2834 Tranquilizers and mental drug preparations (Vol. 1)

3663 Transceivers (Vol. 1)

3845 Transcutaneous electrical nerve stimulators (TENS) (Vol. 1)

3679 Transducers for use in measuring and testing instruments and equipments (Vol. 1)

3829 Transducers, pressure (Vol. 1)

6289 Transfer agents, securities (Vol. 2)

2672 Transfer paper, gold and silver (Vol. 1)

2752 Transferring designs (lithographing) (Vol. 1)

2752 Transfers, decalcomania and dry: lithographed (Vol. 1)

3999 Transformations, hair (Vol. 1)

5063 Transformers, electric: except electronic—wholesale (Vol. 2)

3612 Transformers, electric power (Vol. 1)

3677 Transformers, electronic types (Vol. 1)

5065 Transformers, electronic—wholesale (Vol. 2)

3612 Transformers, for electronic meters (Vol. 1)

3612 Transformers, ignition: for use on domestic fuel burners (Vol. 1)

3612 Transformers, instrument: except portable (Vol. 1)

3825 Transformers, instrument: portable (Vol. 1)

3677 Transformers: power supply electronic type (Vol. 1)

3612 Transformers, reactor (Vol. 1)

3548 Transformers (separate) for arc-welders (Vol. 1)

7221 Transient photographers (Vol. 2)

3674 Transistors (Vol. 1)

5065 Transistors—wholesale (Vol. 2)

7319 Transit advertising (Vol. 2)

9621 Transit systems and authorities-nonoperating (Vol. 2)

3829 Transits, surveying (Vol. 1)

7389 Translation service (Vol. 2)

4923 Transmission and distribution of natural gas (Vol. 2)

3612 Transmission and distribution voltage regulators (Vol. 1)

3199 Transmission belting, leather (Vol. 1)

5063 Transmission equipment, electrical—wholesale (Vol. 2)

2992 Transmission fluid (Vol. 1)

3714 Transmission housings and parts, motor vehicle (Vol. 1)

1623 Transmission line construction-general contractors (Vol. 2)

4911 Transmission of electric power (Vol. 2)

4922 Transmission of natural gas (Vol. 2)

7537 Transmission repair, automotive (Vol. 2)

3441 Transmission towers (Vol. 1)

3728 Transmissions, aircraft (Vol. 1)

7537 Transmissions, automotive: installation, repair, or sale and installation (Vol. 2)

3594 Transmissions, hydrostatic drives (Vol. 1)

3714 Transmissions, motor vehicle (Vol. 1)

3663 Transmitter-receivers, radio (Vol. 1)

3823 Transmitters of process variables, standard signal conversion (Vol. 1)

5065 Transmitters—wholesale (Vol. 2)

3663 Transmitting apparatus, radio and television (Vol. 1)

3671 Transmitting electron tubes (Vol. 1)

3523 Transplanters (Vol. 1)

4731 Transport clearinghouse (Vol. 2)

3731 Transport vessels, passenger and troop: building and repairing (Vol. 1)

4731 Transportation brokerage (Vol. 2)

9621 Transportation departments-government (Vol. 2)

5088 Transportation Equipment and Supplies Except Motor Vehicles (Vol. 2)

5088 Transportation equipment and supplies, except motor vehicles—wholesale (Vol. 2)

3799 Transportation Equipment Not Elsewhere Classified (Vol. 1)

4449 Transportation of freight on bays and sounds of the oceans (Vol. 2)

4011 Transportation, railroad: line-haul (Vol. 2)

4731 Transportation rate services (Vol. 2)

9621 Transportation regulatory agencies-government (Vol. 2)

2754 Transportation schedules, gravure printing (Vol. 1)

2752 Transportation schedules, lithographed (Vol. 1)

2759 Transportation schedules, printing: except lithographed or gravure (Vol. 1)

4789 Transportation Services Not Elsewhere Classified (Vol. 2)

3949 Trap racks (clay targets) (Vol. 1)

1429 Trap rock, crushed and broken-quarrying (Vol. 2)

1411 Trap rock, dimension-quarrying (Vol. 2)

0971 Trapping carried on as a business enterprise (Vol. 2)

3496 Traps, animal and fish: made from purchased wire (Vol. 1)

3931 Traps, drummers' (Vol. 1)

3432 Traps, water (Vol. 1)

7999 Trapshooting facilities, except membership clubs (Vol. 2)

2673 Trash bags, plastics film, foil, and coated paper (Vol. 1)

3639 Trash compactors, household (Vol. 1)

3089 Trash containers, plastics (Vol. 1)

3443 Trash racks, metal plate (Vol. 1)

4724 Travel Agencies (Vol. 2)

4724 Travel bureaus (Vol. 2)

3792 Travel trailer chassis (Vol. 1)

3792 Travel Trailers and Campers (Vol. 1)

5561 Travel trailers, automobile: new and used—retail (Vol. 2)

8322 Traveler's aid centers (Vol. 2)

6099 Travelers' check issuance (Vol. 2)

3161 Traveling bags, regardless of material (Vol. 1)

3671 Traveling wave tubes (Vol. 1)

1422 Travertine, crushed and broken-quarrying (Vol. 2)

1411 Travertine, dimension-quarrying (Vol. 2)

2298 Trawl twine (Vol. 1)

3731 Trawlers, building and repairing (Vol. 1)

2599 Tray trucks, restaurant (Vol. 1)

2441 Trays, carrier: wood (Vol. 1)

3229 Trays, glass (Vol. 1)

3272 Trays, laundry: concrete (Vol. 1)

3496 Trays, made from purchased wire (Vol. 1)

3861 Trays, photographic printing and processing (Vol. 1)

3089 Trays, plastics: except foam (Vol. 1)

3069 Trays, rubber (Vol. 1)

3914 Trays: silver, nickel silver, pewter, stainless steel, and plated (Vol. 1)

3634 Trays, warming: electric (Vol. 1)

2499 Trays: wood, wicker, and bagasse (Vol. 1)

3011 Tread rubber (camelback) (Vol. 1)

3949 Treadmills (Vol. 1)

3446 Treads, stair: fabricated metal (Vol. 1)

3069 Treads, stair: rubber (Vol. 1)

9311 Treasurers' offices-government (Vol. 2)

7218 Treated mats, rugs, mops, dust tool covers, and cloth supply service (Vol. 2)

3999 Treating clock and watch dials with luminous material (Vol. 1)

2491 Treating wood products with creosote or other preservatives (Vol. 1)

0711 Treatment of soil for crops; Chemical (Vol. 2)

0811 Tree farms (Vol. 2)

0175 Tree Fruits; Deciduous (Vol. 2)

0173 Tree nut groves and farms (Vol. 2)

0173 Tree Nuts (Vol. 2)

0723 Tree nuts; Hulling and shelling of (Vol. 2)

0179 Tree Nuts Not Elsewhere Classified; Fruits and (Vol. 2)

0831 Tree seed gathering, extracting, and selling (Vol. 2)

3523 Tree shakers (nuts, soft fruits, and citrus) (Vol. 1)

0783 Tree trimming for public utility lines (Vol. 2)

0721 Trees and vines; Bracing of orchard (Vol. 2)

0721 Trees and vines; Pruning of orchard (Vol. 2)

0721 Trees and vines; Surgery on orchard (Vol. 2)

3999 Trees, Christmas, artificial (Vol. 1)

0721 Trees, orchard: cultivation of (Vol. 2)

0721 Trees, orchard: planting, pruning, bracing, spraying, removal, and surgery (Vol. 2)

0783 Trees, ornamental: planting, pruning, bracing, spraying, removal, and surgery (Vol. 2)

2431 Trellises, wood (Vol. 1)

1629 Trenching-contractors (Vol. 2)

3531 Trenching machines (Vol. 1)

1622 Trestle construction-general contractors (Vol. 2)

2491 Trestles, wood: treated (Vol. 1)

2823 Triacetate fibers (Vol. 1)

2869 Trichloroethylene (Vol. 1)

2869 Trichlorophenoxyacetic acid (Vol. 1)

2869 Trichlorotrifluoroethane tetrachlorodifluoroethane isopropyl alcohol (Vol. 1)

2258 Tricot fabrics (Vol. 1)

2869 Tricresyl phosphate (Vol. 1)

3944 Tricycles, children's (Vol. 1)

2869 Tridecyl alcohol (Vol. 1)

3465 Trim and body parts, automobile: stamped metal (Vol. 1)

1751 Trim and finish-contractors (Vol. 2)

3442 Trim and molding, except automobile: metal (Vol. 1)

5031 Trim, sheet metal—wholesale (Vol. 2)

2431 Trim, wood and covered wood (Vol. 1)

2869 Trimethyltrithiophosphite (rocket propellants) (Vol. 1)

3421 Trimmers, hedge: except power (Vol. 1)

3524 Trimmers, hedge: power (Vol. 1)

2299 Trimming felts, except woven (Vol. 1)

5131 Trimmings, apparel—wholesale (Vol. 2)

2396 Trimmings, fabric: auto, furniture, millinery, dress, coat, and suit (Vol. 1)

3999 Trimmings, feather (Vol. 1)

3999 Trimmings for canes, umbrellas, etc.: except precious metal (Vol. 1)

2371 Trimmings, fur (Vol. 1)

2396 Trimmings, hat: men's (Vol. 1)

3911 Trimmings, precious metal: e.g., for canes, umbrellas (Vol. 1)

3131 Trimmings, shoe: leather (Vol. 1)

2241 Trimmings, textile (Vol. 1)

3429 Trimmings, trunk: metal (Vol. 1)

2892 Trinitrotoluene (TNT) (Vol. 1)

2013 Tripe (Vol. 1)

2869 Triphenyl phosphate (Vol. 1)
3827 Triplet magnifying instruments, optical (Vol. 1)
3861 Tripods, camera and projector (Vol. 1)
3291 Tripoli (Vol. 1)
1499 Tripoli mining (Vol. 2)
3612 Tripping transformers (Vol. 1)
3841 Trocars (Vol. 1)
3743 Trolley buses, trackless (Vol. 1)
3643 Trolley line material, overhead (Vol. 1)
4111 Trolley operation, except amusement and scenic (Vol. 2)
3931 Trombones and parts (Vol. 1)
1474 Trona mining (Vol. 2)
3499 Trophies, metal: except silver, nickel silver, pewter, and plated (Vol. 1)
3914 Trophies: silver, nickel silver, pewter, and plated (Vol. 1)
5094 Trophies—wholesale (Vol. 2)
2499 Trophy bases, wood (Vol. 1)
5999 Trophy shops—retail (Vol. 2)
0273 Tropical aquarium fish farms (Vol. 2)
0179 Tropical fruit farms (Vol. 2)
3699 Trouble lights (Vol. 1)
3444 Troughs, elevator: sheet metal (Vol. 1)
3443 Troughs, industrial: metal plate (Vol. 1)
3523 Troughs, water (Vol. 1)
3634 Trouser pressers, electric (Vol. 1)
2211 Trouserings, cotton (Vol. 1)
2231 Trouserings: wool, mohair, and similar animal fibers (Vol. 1)
5136 Trousers, men's and boys'—wholesale (Vol. 2)
2253 Trousers (Vol. 1)
2325 Trousers (separate): men's and boys' (Vol. 1)
0273 Trout farms (Vol. 2)
3423 Trowels (Vol. 1)
1541 Truck and automobile assembly plant construction-general contractors (Vol. 2)

3713 Truck and Bus Bodies (Vol. 1)
3713 Truck beds (Vol. 1)
3713 Truck bodies, motor vehicle (Vol. 1)
3713 Truck cabs for motor vehicles (Vol. 1)
3792 Truck campers (slide-in campers) (Vol. 1)
3625 Truck controls, industrial battery (Vol. 1)
8249 Truck driving schools (Vol. 2)
7538 Truck engine repair, except industrial (Vol. 2)
0161 Truck farms (Vol. 2)
6159 Truck finance leasing (Vol. 2)
7513 Truck leasing, except industrial trucks and finance leasing: without drivers (Vol. 2)
7513 Truck leasing, without drivers: except finance (equity) leasing (Vol. 2)
3273 Truck-mixed concrete (Vol. 1)
7359 Truck rental and leasing, industrial (Vol. 2)

7513 Truck Rental and Leasing Without Drivers (Vol. 2)
7513 Truck rental, except industrial: without drivers (Vol. 2)
4212 Truck rental for local use, with drivers (Vol. 2)
7212 Truck route laundry and drycleaning, not operated by laundries or cleaners (Vol. 2)

5541 Truck stops—retail (Vol. 2)
5014 Truck tires and tubes—wholesale (Vol. 2)
3713 Truck tops (Vol. 1)
3711 Truck tractors for highway use (Vol. 1)
5012 Truck tractors—wholesale (Vol. 2)

3715 Truck Trailers (Vol. 1)
3537 Truck trailers for use in plants, depots, docks, and terminals (Vol. 1)
3715 Truck trailers (Vol. 1)
5012 Truck trailers—wholesale (Vol. 2)
4731 Truck transportation brokers (Vol. 2)
7542 Truck washing (Vol. 2)

4213 Trucking Except Local (Vol. 2)
4214 Trucking, local: combined with storage (Vol. 2)
4212 Trucking, local: without storage (Vol. 2)
4212 Trucking logs (Vol. 2)
4213 Trucking rental with drivers, except for local use (Vol. 2)
4231 Trucking terminals, freight: with or without maintenance facilities (Vol. 2)
4212 Trucking timber (Vol. 2)
3537 Trucks, industrial (except mining): for freight, baggage, etc. (Vol. 1)
5084 Trucks, industrial—wholesale (Vol. 2)
3711 Trucks, motor: except off-highway (Vol. 1)
3531 Trucks, off-highway (Vol. 1)
5012 Trucks—wholesale (Vol. 2)
0182 Truffles grown under cover (Vol. 2)
3931 Trumpets and parts (Vol. 1)
3429 Trunk hardware, including locks (Vol. 1)
2441 Trunk slats, wood (Vol. 1)
5948 Trunks, luggage—retail (Vol. 2)
3161 Trunks, regardless of material (Vol. 1)
3443 Truss plates, metal (Vol. 1)
2439 Trusses, laminated lumber (Vol. 1)
3842 Trusses: orthopedic and surgical (Vol. 1)
2439 Trusses, wood (Vol. 1)
6021 Trust companies (accepting deposits), commercial: national (Vol. 2)
6022 Trust companies (accepting deposits), commercial: state (Vol. 2)
6091 Trust companies, nondeposit (Vol. 2)
6153 Trust deeds, purchase and sale of (Vol. 2)
6733 Trustees: except for educational, religious, or charitable trusts (Vol. 2)
6732 Trusts, charitable: management of (Vol. 2)
6732 Trusts, educational: management of (Vol. 2)

6733 Trusts Except Educational, Religious and Charitable (Vol. 2)
6733 Trusts except educational, religious, and charitable: management of (Vol. 2)
6733 Trusts, personal investment: management of (Vol. 2)
6732 Trusts, religious: management of (Vol. 2)
3354 Tube, aluminum: extruded or drawn (Vol. 1)
3492 Tube and hose fittings and assemblies, fluid power: metal (Vol. 1)
3354 Tube blooms, aluminum: extruded (Vol. 1)
3498 Tube fabricating (contract bending and shaping); metal (Vol. 1)

3469 Tube fins, stamped metal (Vol. 1)

3492 Tube fittings and assemblies, fluid power: metal (Vol. 1)

3547 Tube mill machinery (Vol. 1)

3679 Tube retainers, electronic (Vol. 1)

3312 Tube rounds (Vol. 1)

3679 Tube spacers, mica (Vol. 1)

3825 Tube testers (Vol. 1)

3679 Tube transformer assemblies used in firing electronic tubes (Vol. 1)

2836 Tuberculins (Vol. 1)

8069 Tuberculosis and other respiratory illness hospitals (Vol. 2)

3671 Tubes, cathode ray (Vol. 1)

3499 Tubes, collapsible: for viscous products-tin, lead, and aluminum (Vol. 1)

3671 Tubes, electron (Vol. 1)

5065 Tubes, electronic: receiving and transmitting, and industrial—wholesale (Vol. 2)

2655 Tubes, fiber or paper (with or without metal ends) (Vol. 1)

2655 Tubes, for chemical and electrical uses: impregnated paper or fiber (Vol. 1)

3671 Tubes for operating above the X-ray spectrum (with shorter wavelength) (Vol. 1)

3069 Tubes, hard rubber (Vol. 1)

3011 Tubes, inner: airplane, automobile, bicycle, motorcycle, and tractor (Vol. 1)

3312 Tubes, iron and steel: made in steel works or rolling mills (Vol. 1)

3671 Tubes, klystron (Vol. 1)

3083 Tubes, laminated plastics (Vol. 1)

3264 Tubes, porcelain (Vol. 1)

3317 Tubes, seamless steel (Vol. 1)

3671 Tubes, television receiving type: cathode ray (Vol. 1)

3082 Tubes, unsupported plastics (Vol. 1)

3353 Tubes, welded: aluminum (Vol. 1)

3317 Tubes, wrought: welded, lock joint, and heavy riveted (Vol. 1)

3844 Tubes, X-ray (Vol. 1)

3292 Tubing, asbestos (Vol. 1)

3351 Tubing, copper and copper alloy (Vol. 1)

3599 Tubing, flexible metallic (Vol. 1)

3299 Tubing for electrical purposes, quartz (Vol. 1)

3229 Tubing, glass (Vol. 1)

3356 Tubing: lead magnesium, nickel, titanium, zinc, and their alloys (Vol. 1)

3317 Tubing, mechanical and hypodermic sizes: cold-drawn stainless steel (Vol. 1)

5051 Tubing, metal—wholesale (Vol. 2)

2211 Tubing, pillow (Vol. 1)

3069 Tubing, rubber: except extruded and lathe-cut (Vol. 1)

2211 Tubing, seamless: cotton (Vol. 1)

3312 Tubing, seamless: steel (Vol. 1)

2295 Tubing, textile: varnished (Vol. 1)

3312 Tubing, wrought: made in steel works or rolling mills (Vol. 1)

3431 Tubs, laundry and bath: enameled iron, cast iron, and pressed metal (Vol. 1)

3088 Tubs, plastics: bath, shower, and laundry (Vol. 1)

3089 Tubs, plastics (containers) (Vol. 1)

2449 Tubs, wood: coopered (Vol. 1)

1741 Tuck pointing-contractors (Vol. 2)

2395 Tucking, for the trade (Vol. 1)

3552 Tufting machines (Vol. 1)

4492 Tugboat service (Vol. 2)

3731 Tugboats, building and repairing (Vol. 1)

3229 Tumblers, glass (Vol. 1)

3089 Tumblers, plastics: except foam (Vol. 1)

3471 Tumbling (cleaning and polishing) of machine parts, for the trade (Vol. 1)

0912 Tuna, catching of (Vol. 2)

2091 Tuna fish, canned (Vol. 1)

3651 Tuners, FM and AM (Vol. 1)

2076 Tung oil (Vol. 1)

3356 Tungsten basic shapes (Vol. 1)

3291 Tungsten carbide abrasives (Vol. 1)

3313 Tungsten carbide powder by metallurgical process (Vol. 1)

2819 Tungsten carbide powder, except abrasives or by metallurgical process (Vol. 1)

1061 Tungsten ore mining (Vol. 2)

7699 Tuning of pianos and organs (Vol. 2)

1622 Tunnel construction-general contractors (Vol. 2)

3674 Tunnel diodes (Vol. 1)

3537 Tunnel kiln cars (Vol. 1)

3443 Tunnel lining, metal plate (Vol. 1)

4785 Tunnel operation, vehicular (Vol. 2)

1241 Tunneling, anthracite mine: on a contract basis (Vol. 2)

1241 Tunneling: bituminous coal, anthracite, and lignite on a contract basis (Vol. 2)

3443 Tunnels, vacuum: metal plate (Vol. 1)

3443 Tunnels, wind (Vol. 1)

3823 Turbidity instruments, industrial process type (Vol. 1)

3826 Turbidometers (Vol. 1)

3462 Turbine engine forgings, ferrous: not made in rolling mills (Vol. 1)

3823 Turbine flow meters, industrial process type (Vol. 1)

3511 Turbine generator set units, complete: steam, gas, and hydraulic (Vol. 1)

3824 Turbine meters, consumption registering (Vol. 1)

3724 Turbines, aircraft type (Vol. 1)

3511 Turbines: steam, hydraulic, and gas-except aircraft type (Vol. 1)

3724 Turbo-superchargers, aircraft (Vol. 1)

3564 Turboblowers, industrial (Vol. 1)

3511 Turbogenerators (Vol. 1)

3523 Turf equipment, commercial (Vol. 1)

0782 Turf installation, except artificial (Vol. 2)

0253 Turkey; Egg farms, (Vol. 2)

0253 Turkey egg farms and ranches (Vol. 2)

0253 Turkey Eggs; Turkeys and (Vol. 2)

0253 Turkey farms and ranches (Vol. 2)

2843 Turkey red oil (Vol. 1)

0253 Turkeys and Turkey Eggs (Vol. 2)
2015 Turkeys, processed: fresh, frozen, canned, or cooked (Vol. 1)
2015 Turkeys: slaughtering and dressing (Vol. 1)
7299 Turkish baths (Vol. 2)
3429 Turnbuckles (Vol. 1)
2499 Turned and carved wood (except furniture) (Vol. 1)
3541 Turning machines (lathes) (Vol. 1)
2426 Turnings, furniture: wood (Vol. 1)
7373 Turnkey vendors, computer systems (Vol. 2)
3829 Turnstiles, equipped with counting mechanisms (Vol. 1)
3651 Turntables, for phonographs (Vol. 1)
2861 Turpentine, produced by distillation of pine gum or pine wood (Vol. 1)
5169 Turpentine—wholesale (Vol. 2)
1499 Turquoise mining (Vol. 2)
3541 Turret lathes, metal cutting (Vol. 1)
3728 Turret test fixtures, aircraft (Vol. 1)
3728 Turrets and turret drives, aircraft (Vol. 1)
3489 Turrets, gun: for artillery more than 30 mm. (or more than 1.18 inch) (Vol. 1)
0919 Turtles, catching of (Vol. 2)
8299 Tutoring (Vol. 2)
7299 Tuxedo rental (Vol. 2)
2311 Tuxedos (Vol. 1)
0721 Twigs; Seeding of sprouts and (Vol. 2)
2211 Twills, cotton (Vol. 1)
2221 Twills, manmade fiber (Vol. 1)
2298 Twine (Vol. 1)
5085 Twine—wholesale (Vol. 2)
5084 Twist drills—wholesale (Vol. 2)
2282 Twisting yarn: silk, wool, and manmade fiber continuous filament (Vol. 1)
3555 Type: lead, steel, brass, copper faced, etc. (Vol. 1)
3069 Type, rubber (Vol. 1)
3555 Typecases, printers' (Vol. 1)
3555 Typecasting, founding, and melting machines (Vol. 1)

2791 Typesetting (Vol. 1)
2791 Typesetting, computer controlled (Vol. 1)
2791 Typesetting for the printing trade (Vol. 1)
3555 Typesetting machines: intertypes, linotypes, monotypes, etc. (Vol. 1)
7699 Typewriter repair, including electric (Vol. 2)
2211 Typewriter ribbon cloth, cotton (Vol. 1)
2221 Typewriter ribbon cloth, manmade fiber (Vol. 1)
3955 Typewriter ribbons, cloth or paper (Vol. 1)
5999 Typewriter stores—retail (Vol. 2)
3579 Typewriters (Vol. 1)
5044 Typewriters—wholesale (Vol. 2)
7338 Typing service (Vol. 2)
2791 Typographic composition (Vol. 1)
3555 Typographic numbering machines (Vol. 1)
1094 Tyuyamunite mining (Vol. 2)

U

3931 Ukuleles and parts (Vol. 1)
1474 Ulexite mining (Vol. 2)
2816 Ultramarine pigments (Vol. 1)

3541 Ultrasonic assisted grinding machines (metalworking) (Vol. 1)
3699 Ultrasonic cleaning equipment, except medical and dental (Vol. 1)
3843 Ultrasonic dental equipment (Vol. 1)
3699 Ultrasonic generators sold separately for inclusion in tools and equipment (Vol. 1)
3841 Ultrasonic medical cleaning equipment (Vol. 1)
3845 Ultrasonic medical equipment, except cleaning (Vol. 1)
3541 Ultrasonic metal cutting machine tools (Vol. 1)
3845 Ultrasonic scanning devices, medical (Vol. 1)
3829 Ultrasonic testing equipment (Vol. 1)
3699 Ultrasonic welding machines and equipment (Vol. 1)
3542 Ultrasonically assisted metal forming machines (Vol. 1)
3648 Ultraviolet lamp fixtures (Vol. 1)
3641 Ultraviolet lamps (Vol. 1)
3674 Ultraviolet sensors, solid-state (Vol. 1)
3826 Ultraviolet-type analytical instruments (Vol. 1)
1479 Umber mining (Vol. 2)
2816 Umbers (Vol. 1)
2211 Umbrella cloth, cotton (Vol. 1)
3911 Umbrella handles and trimmings, precious metal (Vol. 1)
5699 Umbrella stores—retail (Vol. 2)
3999 Umbrellas and parts, except precious metal (Vol. 1)
3999 Umbrellas: beach, garden, and wagon (Vol. 1)
5136 Umbrellas, men's and boys'—wholesale (Vol. 2)
2674 Uncoated Paper and Multiwall Bags (Vol. 1)
0182 Under cover; Bean sprouts grown (Vol. 2)
0182 Under Cover; Food Crops Grown (Vol. 2)
0182 Under cover; Fruits grown (Vol. 2)
0182 Under cover; Hydroponic crops, grown (Vol. 2)
0182 Under cover; Rhubarb grown (Vol. 2)
0182 Under cover; Seaweed grown (Vol. 2)
0182 Under cover; Tomatoes grown (Vol. 2)
0182 Under cover; Truffles grown (Vol. 2)
0182 Under cover; Vegetables grown (Vol. 2)
7549 Undercoating service, automotive (Vol. 2)
2851 Undercoatings, paint (Vol. 1)
1622 Underpass construction-general contractors (Vol. 2)
1799 Underpinning work-contractors (Vol. 2)
7261 Undertakers (Vol. 2)
5087 Undertakers' equipment and supplies—wholesale (Vol. 2)
3648 Underwater lighting fixtures (Vol. 1)
5091 Underwater sports equipment—wholesale (Vol. 2)
2221 Underwear fabrics, except knit: manmade fiber and silk (Vol. 1)
2211 Underwear fabrics, woven: cotton (Vol. 1)
2322 Underwear: men's and boys' (Vol. 1)
5136 Underwear, men's and boys'—wholesale (Vol. 2)
2254 Underwear (Vol. 1)
5137 Underwear: women's, children's, and infants'—wholesale (Vol. 2)
2341 Underwear: women's, misses', children's, and infants' (Vol. 1)
6211 Underwriters, security (Vol. 2)

4492 Undocking of ocean vessels (Vol. 2)

9441 Unemployment insurance offices-government (Vol. 2)

2353 Uniform hats and caps, except protective head gear (Vol. 1)

2321 Uniform shirts, except athletic or work: men's and boys' (Vol. 1)

7213 Uniform supply service, except industrial (Vol. 2)

2329 Uniforms, athletic and gymnasium: men's and boys' (Vol. 1)

2339 Uniforms, athletic: women's, misses', and juniors' (Vol. 1)

2389 Uniforms, band (Vol. 1)

2337 Uniforms, except athletic and service apparel: women's, misses', and juniors' (Vol. 1)

5136 Uniforms, men's and boys'—wholesale (Vol. 2)

2326 Uniforms, nontailored work type: men's (Vol. 1)

5699 Uniforms—retail (Vol. 2)

2311 Uniforms, tailored: men's and boys' (Vol. 1)

2339 Uniforms, washable service apparel (nurses', maid, waitresses', laboratory): women's, misses', and juniors' (Vol. 1)

5137 Uniforms: women's and children's—wholesale (Vol. 2)

2326 Uniforms, work: men's (Vol. 1)

2254 Union suits (Vol. 1)

6371 Union trust funds (Vol. 2)

6371 Union welfare, benefit, and health funds (Vol. 2)

3494 Unions, pipe: metal (Vol. 1)

3089 Unions, plastics (Vol. 1)

5651 Unisex clothing stores—retail (Vol. 2)

5137 Unisex clothing: women's and children's—wholesale (Vol. 2)

7231 Unisex hairdressers (Vol. 2)

3433 Unit heaters, domestic: except electric (Vol. 1)

3634 Unit heaters, household: electric (Vol. 1)

6726 Unit investment trusts (Vol. 2)

6726 Unit Investment Trusts, Face-Amount Certificate Offices and Closed-End Management Investment Offices (Vol. 2)

2761 Unit sets (manifold business forms) (Vol. 1)

5063 Unit substations—wholesale (Vol. 2)

8399 United fund councils (Vol. 2)

9721 United Nations (Vol. 2)

9222 U.S. attorneys' offices (Vol. 2)

4311 United States Postal Service (Vol. 2)

3711 Universal carriers, military (Vol. 1)

3568 Universal joints, except motor vehicle (Vol. 1)

3714 Universal joints, motor vehicle (Vol. 1)

8221 Universities (Vol. 2)

8641 University clubs (Vol. 2)

4491 Unloading vessels (Vol. 2)

3081 Unsupported Plastics Film and Sheet (Vol. 1)

3082 Unsupported Plastics Profile Shapes (Vol. 1)

2512 Upholstered furniture, household: on wood frames, except dual-purpose sleep furniture (Vol. 1)

2512 Upholstered Wood Household Furniture (Vol. 1)

5087 Upholsterers' equipment and supplies, except fabrics—wholesale (Vol. 2)

7217 Upholstery cleaning on customers' premises (Vol. 2)

2211 Upholstery fabrics, cotton (Vol. 1)

2221 Upholstery fabrics, manmade fiber and silk (Vol. 1)

2231 Upholstery fabrics, wool (Vol. 1)

5087 Upholstery filling and padding—wholesale (Vol. 2)

2299 Upholstery filling, textile (Vol. 1)

3111 Upholstery leather (Vol. 1)

5714 Upholstery materials stores—retail (Vol. 2)

7532 Upholstery repair, automotive (Vol. 2)

3495 Upholstery springs, unassembled: made from purchased wire (Vol. 1)

3111 Upper leather (Vol. 1)

3131 Uppers (shoe cut stock) (Vol. 1)

3462 Upset forgings, iron and steel: not made in rolling mills (Vol. 1)

3542 Upsetters (forging machines) (Vol. 1)

1094 Uraninite (pitchblende) mining (Vol. 2)

1094 Uranium ore mining (Vol. 2)

1094 Uranium, Radium and Vanadium Ores (Vol. 2)

2819 Uranium slug, radioactive (Vol. 1)

4111 Urban and suburban railway operation (Vol. 2)

6162 Urban mortgage companies (Vol. 2)

9532 Urban planning commissions-government (Vol. 2)

9532 Urban renewal agencies-government (Vol. 2)

2873 Urea (Vol. 1)

2821 Urea resins (Vol. 1)

2822 Urethane rubbers (Vol. 1)

3431 Urinals: enameled iron, cast iron, and pressed metal (Vol. 1)

3088 Urinals, plastics (Vol. 1)

3069 Urinals, rubber (Vol. 1)

3261 Urinals, vitreous china (Vol. 1)

8071 Urinalysis laboratories (Vol. 2)

3281 Urns, cut stone (Vol. 1)

3634 Urns, electric: household (Vol. 1)

3299 Urns, gypsum or papier-mache: factory production only (Vol. 1)

8011 Urologists, offices of (Vol. 2)

5932 Used Merchandise Stores (Vol. 2)

5521 Used Motor Vehicle Dealers (Vol. 2)

7363 Usher service (Vol. 2)

3365 Utensils, cast aluminum (Vol. 1)

3469 Utensils, metal, except cast: household, commercial, and hospital (Vol. 1)

2656 Utensils, paper: except those made from pressed or molded pulp (Vol. 1)

3469 Utensils, porcelain enameled: household, commercial, and hospital (Vol. 1)

2679 Utensils, pressed and molded pulp (Vol. 1)

3479 Utensils, retinning of: not done in rolling mills (Vol. 1)

4939 Utilities, combination of (Vol. 2)

3448 Utility buildings, prefabricated: metal (Vol. 1)

3429 Utility carriers, car top (Vol. 1)

3089 Utility containers, plastics (Vol. 1)

0783 Utility line tree trimming services (Vol. 2)

7372 Utility software, computer: prepackaged (Vol. 2)

7519 Utility Trailer and Recreational Vehicle Rental (Vol. 2)

7519 Utility trailer rental (Vol. 2)
5599 Utility trailers—retail (Vol. 2)

V

3052 V-belts, rubber or plastics (Vol. 1)
6733 Vacation funds for employees (Vol. 2)
0751 Vaccinating livestock, except by veterinarians (Vol. 2)
0752 Vaccinating pets and other animal specialties, except by veterinarians (Vol. 2)
2836 Vaccines (Vol. 1)
3429 Vacuum bottles and jugs (Vol. 1)
3714 Vacuum brakes, motor vehicle (Vol. 1)
3743 Vacuum brakes, railway (Vol. 1)
3052 Vacuum cleaner hose, plastics or rubber (Vol. 1)
5722 Vacuum cleaner stores—retail (Vol. 2)
3635 Vacuum cleaners and sweepers, electric: household (Vol. 1)
3589 Vacuum cleaners and sweepers, electric: industrial and commercial (Vol. 1)
5064 Vacuum cleaners, household—wholesale (Vol. 2)
1796 Vacuum cleaning systems, built-in-contractors (Vol. 2)
5087 Vacuum cleaning systems—wholesale (Vol. 2)
0723 Vacuum cooling; Fruit (Vol. 2)
0723 Vacuum cooling; Vegetable (Vol. 2)
3567 Vacuum furnaces and ovens (Vol. 1)
3563 Vacuum pumps, except laboratory (Vol. 1)
3821 Vacuum pumps, laboratory (Vol. 1)
3625 Vacuum relays (Vol. 1)
3443 Vacuum tanks, metal plate (Vol. 1)
3825 Vacuum tube bridges (electrical measuring instruments) (Vol. 1)
3671 Vacuum tubes (Vol. 1)
3443 Vacuum tunnels, metal plate (Vol. 1)
4959 Vacuuming of airport runways (Vol. 2)
3524 Vacuums, residential lawn (Vol. 1)
2771 Valentine cards, except hand painted (Vol. 1)
7212 Valet apparel service (Vol. 2)
7299 Valet parking (Vol. 2)
3161 Valises, regardless of material (Vol. 1)
2861 Valonia extract (Vol. 1)
7373 Value-added resellers, computer systems (Vol. 2)
3714 Valve cores, tire (Vol. 1)
3541 Valve grinding machines (Vol. 1)
3491 Valves, air ventilating (Vol. 1)
5085 Valves and fittings, except plumbers'—wholesale (Vol. 2)

3494 Valves and Pipe Fittings Not Elsewhere Classified (Vol. 1)

3492 Valves, automatic control: fluid power-metal (Vol. 1)
3491 Valves, automatic control: industrial, except fluid power (Vol. 1)
3592 Valves, engine: intake and exhaust (Vol. 1)
3069 Valves, hard rubber (Vol. 1)
3492 Valves, hydraulic and pneumatic control: fluid power-metal (Vol. 1)
3491 Valves, industrial: gate, globe, check, pop safety, and relief (Vol. 1)

3491 Valves, nuclear (Vol. 1)
3714 Valves, PCV (Vol. 1)
3494 Valves, plumbing and heating: metal (Vol. 1)
5074 Valves, plumbing and heating—wholesale (Vol. 2)
3491 Valves, power transfer: except fluid power (Vol. 1)
3491 Valves, relief: over 15 lbs. w.s.p. (Vol. 1)
3491 Valves, solenoid: except fluid power (Vol. 1)
3131 Vamps, leather (Vol. 1)
7532 Van conversions, except on a factory basis (Vol. 2)
3713 Van-type bodies, all purpose (Vol. 1)
1094 Vanadium ore mining (Vol. 2)
3599 Vanes, weather (Vol. 1)
2869 Vanillin, synthetic (Vol. 1)
2434 Vanities, bathroom, wood: to be installed (Vol. 1)
2514 Vanities, household: metal (Vol. 1)
3961 Vanity cases, except precious metal and leather (Vol. 1)
3172 Vanity cases, leather (Vol. 1)
3911 Vanity cases, precious metal (Vol. 1)
2511 Vanity dressers (Vol. 1)
4119 Vanpool operation (Vol. 2)
3716 Vans, self-propelled: conversion on a factory basis for recreational use (Vol. 1)
5012 Vans—wholesale (Vol. 2)
3822 Vapor heating controls (Vol. 1)
3641 Vapor lamps, electric (Vol. 1)
3569 Vapor separators (machinery) (Vol. 1)
3634 Vaporizers, electric: household (Vol. 1)
3674 Variable capacitance diodes (Vol. 1)
2674 Variety bags, uncoated paper (Vol. 1)
2011 Variety meats edible organs (Vol. 1)

5331 Variety Stores (Vol. 2)

5331 Variety stores, limited price—retail (Vol. 2)
3676 Varistors (Vol. 1)
3991 Varnish brushes (Vol. 1)
2851 Varnish removers (Vol. 1)
2851 Varnish stains (Vol. 1)
2851 Varnishes (Vol. 1)
5198 Varnishes—wholesale (Vol. 2)
3479 Varnishing of metal products, for the trade (Vol. 1)
2295 Varnishing of textiles (Vol. 1)
3281 Vases, cut stone (Vol. 1)
3229 Vases, glass (Vol. 1)
3299 Vases, gypsum or papier-mache: factory production only (Vol. 1)
3269 Vases, pottery (china, earthenware, and stoneware) (Vol. 1)
2262 Vat dyeing of manmade fiber and silk broadwoven fabrics (Vol. 1)
2865 Vat dyes, synthetic (Vol. 1)
3443 Vats, metal plate (Vol. 1)
3444 Vats, sheet metal (Vol. 1)
2449 Vats, wood: coopered (Vol. 1)
2499 Vats, wood: except coopered (Vol. 1)
7922 Vaudeville companies (Vol. 2)
3499 Vault doors and linings, metal (Vol. 1)
5044 Vaults and safes—wholesale (Vol. 2)
3499 Vaults, except burial vaults: metal (Vol. 1)
3272 Vaults, grave: concrete and precast terrazzo (Vol. 1)

3995 Vaults, grave: metal (Vol. 1)

2011 Veal (Vol. 1)

5431 Vegetable and fruit stands—retail (Vol. 2)

2449 Vegetable baskets, veneer and splint (Vol. 1)

0181 Vegetable bedding plants, growing of (Vol. 2)

5199 Vegetable cake and meal—wholesale (Vol. 2)

2079 Vegetable cooking and salad oils, except corn oil: refined (Vol. 1)

5149 Vegetable cooking oil—wholesale (Vol. 2)

2449 Vegetable crates, wood: wirebound (Vol. 1)

0723 Vegetable drying (Vol. 2)

0161 Vegetable farms (Vol. 2)

2034 Vegetable flour, meal, and powders (Vol. 1)

2833 Vegetable gelatin (agar-agar) (Vol. 1)

3523 Vegetable grading, cleaning and sorting machines: farm (Vol. 1)

0181 Vegetable: growing of; Seeds, flower and (Vol. 2)

2033 Vegetable juices: canned, bottled and bulk (Vol. 1)

5431 Vegetable markets and stands—retail (Vol. 2)

2076 Vegetable Oil Mills Except Corn, Cottonseed and Soybean (Vol. 1)

3556 Vegetable oil processing machinery (Vol. 1)

2833 Vegetable oils, medicinal grade: refined and concentrated (Vol. 1)

2899 Vegetable oils, vulcanized or sulfurized (Vol. 1)

2033 Vegetable pie mixes (Vol. 1)

0723 Vegetable precooling, not in connection with transportation (Vol. 2)

2033 Vegetable purees (Vol. 1)

2035 Vegetable sauces, except tomato (Vol. 1)

0723 Vegetable sorting, grading, and packing (Vol. 2)

2076 Vegetable tallow (Vol. 1)

0723 Vegetable vacuum cooling (Vol. 2)

0161 Vegetables and Melons (Vol. 2)

2033 Vegetables, canned (Vol. 1)

2034 Vegetables, dried or dehydrated (Vol. 1)

0723 Vegetables; Drying of corn, rice, hay, fruits, and (Vol. 2)

5148 Vegetables, fresh—wholesale (Vol. 2)

0182 Vegetables grown under cover (Vol. 2)

0722 Vegetables, machine harvesting of (Vol. 2)

0723 Vegetables; Packaging fresh or farm-dried fruits and (Vol. 2)

0723 Vegetables; Packing fruits and (Vol. 2)

2099 Vegetables peeled for the trade (Vol. 1)

2035 Vegetables, pickled and brined (Vol. 1)

2037 Vegetables, quick frozen and coldpack (frozen) (Vol. 1)

0723 Vegetables; Sorting, grading, and packing of fruits and (Vol. 2)

2034 Vegetables, sulphured (Vol. 1)

3429 Vehicle hardware: aircraft, automobile, railroad, etc. (Vol. 1)

2491 Vehicle lumber, treated (Vol. 1)

2426 Vehicle stock, hardwood (Vol. 1)

3824 Vehicle tank meters (Vol. 1)

5092 Vehicles, children's—wholesale (Vol. 2)

3944 Vehicles except bicycles, children's (Vol. 1)

3711 Vehicles, motor: including amphibian (Vol. 1)

3647 Vehicular Lighting Equipment (Vol. 1)

2396 Veils and veiling, hat (Vol. 1)

3999 Veils made of hair (Vol. 1)

3111 Vellum leather (Vol. 1)

2211 Velours (Vol. 1)

2211 Velveteens (Vol. 1)

2221 Velvets, manmade fiber and silk (Vol. 1)

5962 Vending machine sale of products (Vol. 2)

3581 Vending machines for merchandise: coin-operated (Vol. 1)

7359 Vending machines, rental only (Vol. 2)

5046 Vending machines—wholesale (Vol. 2)

2449 Veneer baskets, for fruits and vegetables (Vol. 1)

2411 Veneer logs (Vol. 1)

3553 Veneer mill machines (Vol. 1)

2435 Veneer mills, hardwood (Vol. 1)

2436 Veneer mills, softwood (Vol. 1)

5031 Veneer—wholesale (Vol. 2)

2499 Veneer work, inlaid (Vol. 1)

7349 Venetian blind cleaning, including work done on owners' premises (Vol. 2)

3553 Venetian blind machines (woodworking machinery) (Vol. 1)

7699 Venetian blind repair shops (Vol. 2)

5719 Venetian blind shops—retail (Vol. 2)

2431 Venetian blind slats, wood (Vol. 1)

2241 Venetian blind tapes (Vol. 1)

2591 Venetian blinds (Vol. 1)

2836 Venoms (Vol. 1)

3564 Ventilating, blowing, and exhaust fans: except household and kitchen (Vol. 1)

5075 Ventilating equipment and supplies—wholesale (Vol. 2)

3634 Ventilating fans, electric: household-kitchen (Vol. 1)

1711 Ventilating work, with or without sheet metalwork-contractors (Vol. 2)

4741 Ventilation of railroad cars (Vol. 2)

3444 Ventilators, sheet metal (Vol. 1)

6799 Venture capital companies (Vol. 2)

1429 Verde' antique, crushed and broken-quarrying (Vol. 2)

1411 Verde' antique, dimension-quarrying (Vol. 2)

3577 Verifiers (Vol. 1)

2098 Vermicelli (Vol. 1)

3295 Vermiculite, exfoliated (Vol. 1)

1499 Vermiculite mining (Vol. 2)

2834 Vermifuges (Vol. 1)

2816 Vermilion pigments (Vol. 1)

3545 Verniers (machinists' precision tools) (Vol. 1)

3541 Vertical turning and boring machines (metalworking) (Vol. 1)

3443 Vessels, pressure: industrial-metal plate (made in boiler shops) (Vol. 1)

3443 Vessels, process and storage: metal plate (made in boiler shops) (Vol. 1)

2389 Vestments, academic and clerical (Vol. 1)

2337 Vests, except tailored: women's, misses', and juniors' (Vol. 1)

2386 Vests, leather or sheep-lined (Vol. 1)

2329 Vests, nontailored including sweater-men's and boys' (Vol. 1)

2339 Vests, not tailored: women's, misses' and juniors (Vol. 1)

2311 Vests, tailored: men's and boys' (Vol. 1)

9451 Veterans' affairs offices (Vol. 2)

8641 Veterans' organizations (Vol. 2)

0741 Veterinarians for livestock (Vol. 2)

0742 Veterinarians for pets and other animal specialties (Vol. 2)

3841 Veterinarians' instruments and apparatus (Vol. 1)

2834 Veterinary pharmaceutical preparations (Vol. 1)

0742 Veterinary Services for Animal Specialties (Vol. 2)

0741 Veterinary Services for Livestock (Vol. 2)

0742 Veterinary services for pets and other animal specialties (Vol. 2)

8734 Veterinary testing laboratories (Vol. 2)

1622 Viaduct construction-general contractors (Vol. 2)

3221 Vials, glass: made in glassmaking establishments (Vol. 1)

3231 Vials, made from purchased glass (Vol. 1)

3089 Vials, plastics (Vol. 1)

3931 Vibraphones (Vol. 1)

3829 Vibration meters, analyzers, and calibrators (Vol. 1)

3999 Vibrators, electric: designed for beauty and barber shops (Vol. 1)

3531 Vibrators for concrete construction (Vol. 1)

3612 Vibrators, interrupter (Vol. 1)

3651 Video camera-audio recorders, household (Vol. 1)

5731 Video camera stores—retail (Vol. 2)

3651 Video cassette recorders/players (Vol. 1)

5064 Video disc players—wholesale (Vol. 2)

7841 Video disk rental to the general public (Vol. 2)

7993 Video game arcades (Vol. 2)

3944 Video game machines, except coin-operated (Vol. 1)

7221 Video photography, portrait (Vol. 2)

7539 Video recorder and player rental and leasing (Vol. 2)

7622 Video recorder or player repair (Vol. 2)

3695 Video recording tape, blank (Vol. 1)

7819 Video tape or disk reproduction (Vol. 2)

7812 Video tape production (Vol. 2)

5731 Video tape recorder stores—retail (Vol. 2)

7841 Video Tape Rental (Vol. 2)

7841 Video tape rental to the general public (Vol. 2)

5735 Video tape stores—retail (Vol. 2)

7822 Video tapes, recorded—wholesale (Vol. 2)

3679 Video triggers, except remote control television devices (Vol. 1)

3651 Video triggers (remote control television devices) (Vol. 1)

2013 Vienna sausage (Vol. 1)

2221 Vinal broadwoven fabrics (Vol. 1)

3523 Vine pullers (Vol. 1)

2099 Vinegar (Vol. 1)

2035 Vinegar pickles and relishes (Vol. 1)

0721 Vines; Bracing of orchard trees and (Vol. 2)

0721 Vines; Pruning of orchard trees and (Vol. 2)

0721 Vines; Surgery on orchard trees and (Vol. 2)

0721 Vineyard cultivation services (Vol. 2)

0762 Vineyard management and maintenance, with or without crop services (Vol. 2)

0172 Vineyards (Vol. 2)

2869 Vinyl acetate (Vol. 1)

3081 Vinyl and vinyl copolymer film and sheet, unsupported (Vol. 1)

3292 Vinyl asbestos tile (Vol. 1)

2295 Vinyl coated fabrics (Vol. 1)

2851 Vinyl coatings, strippable (Vol. 1)

2824 Vinyl fibers (Vol. 1)

1752 Vinyl floor tile and sheet installation-contractors (Vol. 2)

2851 Vinyl plastisol (Vol. 1)

2821 Vinyl resins (Vol. 1)

2824 Vinylidene chloride fibers (Vol. 1)

2221 Vinyon broadwoven fabrics (Vol. 1)

3931 Violas and parts (Vol. 1)

3931 Violins and parts (Vol. 1)

2835 Viral test diagnostic reagents (Vol. 1)

2836 Viruses (Vol. 1)

2823 Viscose fibers, bands, strips, and yarn (Vol. 1)

3829 Viscosimeters, except industrial process type (Vol. 1)

3823 Viscosimeters, industrial process type (Vol. 1)

3423 Vises, carpenters' (Vol. 1)

3423 Vises, except machine (Vol. 1)

3545 Vises, machine (machine tool accessories) (Vol. 1)

2754 Visiting cards: gravure printing (Vol. 1)

2752 Visiting cards, lithographed (Vol. 1)

2759 Visiting cards, printed: except lithographed or gravure (Vol. 1)

8082 Visiting nurse associations (Vol. 2)

2396 Visors, cap (Vol. 1)

2044 Vitamin and mineral enriched rice (Vol. 1)

5499 Vitamin food stores—retail (Vol. 2)

2834 Vitamin preparations (Vol. 1)

2833 Vitamins, natural and synthetic: bulk, uncompounded (Vol. 1)

5122 Vitamins—wholesale (Vol. 2)

3261 Vitreous China Plumbing Fixtures and China and Earthenware Fittings and Bathroom Accessories (Vol. 1)

3262 Vitreous China Table and Kitchen Articles (Vol. 1)

8249 Vocational apprenticeship training (Vol. 2)

8299 Vocational counseling, except rehabilitation counseling (Vol. 2)

8211 Vocational high schools (Vol. 2)

8331 Vocational rehabilitation agencies (Vol. 2)

8331 Vocational rehabilitation counseling (Vol. 2)

8249 Vocational schools: except high schools, data processing, or business (Vol. 2)

8249 Vocational Schools Not Elsewhere Classified (Vol. 2)

8331 Vocational training agencies, except schools (Vol. 2)

2085 Vodka (Vol. 1)

3679 Voice controls (Vol. 1)

4813 Voice telephone communications, except radio
        telephone (Vol. 2)
2655 Voids and pans, fiber and cardboard (Vol. 1)
2211 Voiles, cotton (Vol. 1)
2221 Voiles, manmade fiber and silk (Vol. 1)
1499 Volcanic ash mining (Vol. 2)
1429 Volcanic rock, crushed and broken-quarrying (Vol.
        2)
1411 Volcanic rock, dimension-quarrying (Vol. 2)
3825 Volt-ohm milliammeters (Vol. 1)
3612 Voltage regulating transformers, electric power
        (Vol. 1)
3694 Voltage regulators, motor vehicle (Vol. 1)
3612 Voltage regulators, transmission and distribution
        (Vol. 1)
3825 Voltmeters (Vol. 1)
3523 Volume guns (irrigation equipment) (Vol. 1)
3579 Voting machines (Vol. 1)
5087 Voting machines—wholesale (Vol. 2)
2655 Vulcanized fiber boxes (Vol. 1)
3089 Vulcanized fiber plate, sheet, rods and tubes (Vol.
        1)
2822 Vulcanized oils (Vol. 1)
7534 Vulcanizing tires and tubes (Vol. 2)

W

3949 Wading pools, plastics coated fabric (Vol. 1)
3482 Wads, ammunition: 30 mm. (or 1.18 inch) or less
        (Vol. 1)
2299 Wads and wadding, textile (Vol. 1)
2493 Waferboard (Vol. 1)
3674 Wafers (semiconductor devices) (Vol. 1)
2052 Wafers, sugar (Vol. 1)
2211 Waffle cloth, cotton (Vol. 1)
3634 Waffle irons, electric (Vol. 1)
5064 Waffle irons, electric—wholesale (Vol. 2)
2038 Waffles, frozen (Vol. 1)
9651 Wage control agencies-government (Vol. 2)
3523 Wagons and trailers, farm (Vol. 1)
3944 Wagons, children's: coaster, express, and play (Vol.
        1)
3524 Wagons for residential lawn and garden use (Vol.
        1)
5963 Wagons, ice cream—retail (Vol. 2)
3069 Wainscoting, rubber (Vol. 1)
2431 Wainscots, wood (Vol. 1)
2396 Waistbands, trouser (Vol. 1)
3944 Walkers, baby (vehicles) (Vol. 1)
3842 Walkers (Vol. 1)
3534 Walkways, moving (Vol. 1)
3272 Wall base, precast terrazzo (Vol. 1)
2522 Wall cases, office: except wood (Vol. 1)
3259 Wall coping, clay (Vol. 1)
3089 Wall coverings, plastics (Vol. 1)
3433 Wall heaters, except electric (Vol. 1)
3634 Wall heaters, household: electric (Vol. 1)
3645 Wall lamps (Vol. 1)
3272 Wall squares, concrete (Vol. 1)
3253 Wall tile, ceramic (Vol. 1)
2493 Wall tile, fiberboard (Vol. 1)

5211 Wallboard (composition) dealers—retail (Vol. 2)
3275 Wallboard, gypsum (Vol. 1)
5031 Wallboard—wholesale (Vol. 2)
2493 Wallboard, wood fiber: cellular fiber or hard
        pressed (Vol. 1)
5231 Wallcovering stores—retail (Vol. 2)
2679 Wallcoverings: paper (Vol. 1)
3069 Wallcoverings, rubber (Vol. 1)
3172 Wallets, regardless of material (Vol. 1)
2842 Wallpaper cleaners (Vol. 1)
2679 Wallpaper, embossed plastics: made on textile
        backing (Vol. 1)
2679 Wallpaper (Vol. 1)
1799 Wallpaper removal-contractors (Vol. 2)
2621 Wallpaper stock (hanging paper) (Vol. 1)
5231 Wallpaper stores—retail (Vol. 2)
5198 Wallpaper—wholesale (Vol. 2)
1741 Walls, retaining: block, stone, or brick-contractors
        (Vol. 2)
0173 Walnut groves and farms (Vol. 2)
0723 Walnut hulling and shelling (Vol. 2)
3952 Walnut oil, artists' (Vol. 1)
2076 Walnut oil (Vol. 1)
3999 Walnut shell flour (Vol. 1)
2673 Wardrobe bags (closet accessories), plastics film or
        coated paper (Vol. 1)
3161 Wardrobe bags (luggage) (Vol. 1)
2392 Wardrobe bags (Vol. 1)
7819 Wardrobe rental for motion picture film production
        (Vol. 2)
7299 Wardrobe service, except theatrical (Vol. 2)
2511 Wardrobes, household: wood (Vol. 1)
1541 Warehouse construction-general contractors (Vol. 2)
4221 Warehousing and storage, farm product: other than
        refrigerated (Vol. 2)
4222 Warehousing, cold storage or refrigerated (Vol. 2)
4225 Warehousing, general (Vol. 2)
4226 Warehousing of goods at foreign trade zones (Vol.
        2)
4226 Warehousing of household goods, without local
        trucking (Vol. 2)
4225 Warehousing, self-storage (Vol. 2)
4226 Warehousing, special: except farm products and
        cold storage (Vol. 2)
3812 Warfare countermeasures equipment (Vol. 1)
**5075 Warm Air Heating and Air-Conditioning
        Equipment and Supplies (Vol. 2)**
5075 Warm air heating and cooling equipment—
        wholesale (Vol. 2)
3089 Warmers, bottle: plastics, except foam (Vol. 1)
2253 Warmup and jogging suits (Vol. 1)
2369 Warmup suits: girls', children's, and infants' (Vol.
        1)
2329 Warmup suits: men's and boys' (Vol. 1)
2339 Warmup suits: women's, misses', and juniors' (Vol.
        1)
3552 Warp and knot tying machines (textile machinery)
        (Vol. 1)
2258 Warp (flat) knit fabrics (Vol. 1)
5131 Warp knit fabrics—wholesale (Vol. 2)

3552 Warping machines (textile machinery) (Vol. 1)

6399 Warranty insurance, automobile (Vol. 2)

6351 Warranty insurance, home (Vol. 2)

3272 Wash foundations, precast terrazzo (Vol. 1)

2326 Washable service apparel, men's: hospital, professional, barbers', etc. (Vol. 1)

2499 Washboards, wood and part wood (Vol. 1)

2392 Washcloths (Vol. 1)

2259 Washcloths (Vol. 1)

2211 Washcloths, woven: made in weaving mills (Vol. 1)

1231 Washeries, anthracite (Vol. 2)

1221 Washeries, bituminous coal or lignite (Vol. 2)

1629 Washeries construction, mining-general contractors (Vol. 2)

3532 Washers, aggregate and sand: stationary type (Vol. 1)

3565 Washers, bottle: for food products (Vol. 1)

5072 Washers, hardware—wholesale (Vol. 2)

3053 Washers, leather (Vol. 1)

3452 Washers, metal (Vol. 1)

3861 Washers, photographic print and film (Vol. 1)

3089 Washers, plastics (Vol. 1)

2844 Washes, cosmetic (Vol. 1)

7542 Washing and polishing, automotive (Vol. 2)

2841 Washing compounds (Vol. 1)

3469 Washing machine parts, porcelain enameled (Vol. 1)

7629 Washing machine repair (Vol. 2)

5064 Washing machines, household: electric—wholesale (Vol. 2)

3633 Washing machines, household: including coin-operated (Vol. 1)

3582 Washing machines, laundry: commercial, including coin-operated (Vol. 1)

2812 Washing soda (sal soda) (Vol. 1)

7342 Washroom sanitation service (Vol. 2)

2673 Waste bags, plastics film and laminated (Vol. 1)

5093 Waste bottles and boxes—wholesale (Vol. 2)

1629 Waste disposal plant construction-general contractors (Vol. 2)

9511 Waste management program administration-government (Vol. 2)

4953 Waste materials disposal at sea (Vol. 2)

5093 Waste rags—wholesale (Vol. 2)

5093 Waste, rubber—wholesale (Vol. 2)

2299 Waste, textile mill: processing of (Vol. 1)

5093 Waste, textile—wholesale (Vol. 2)

2655 Wastebaskets, fiber (metal-end or all-fiber) (Vol. 1)

3469 Wastebaskets, stamped metal (Vol. 1)

5093 Wastepaper, including paper recycling—wholesale (Vol. 2)

7631 Watch, Clock and Jewelry Repair (Vol. 2)

3231 Watch crystals, made from purchased glass (Vol. 1)

3915 Watch jewels (Vol. 1)

7631 Watch repair shops (Vol. 2)

3172 Watch straps, except metal (Vol. 1)

3961 Watchbands, base metal (Vol. 1)

3911 Watchbands, precious metal (Vol. 1)

3873 Watchcases (Vol. 1)

5094 Watchcases—wholesale (Vol. 2)

3873 Watches and parts: except crystals and jewels (Vol. 1)

5094 Watches and parts—wholesale (Vol. 2)

3873 Watches, Clocks, Clockwork Operated Devices and Parts (Vol. 1)

5944 Watches, including custom made—retail (Vol. 2)

1623 Water and Sewer Mains, Pipelines, and Communications and Power Line Construction (Vol. 2)

3221 Water bottles, glass (Vol. 1)

3069 Water bottles, rubber (Vol. 1)

3431 Water closets: enameled iron, cast iron, and pressed metal (Vol. 1)

3088 Water closets, plastics (Vol. 1)

3952 Water colors, artists' (Vol. 1)

3589 Water conditioners, for swimming pools (Vol. 1)

5074 Water conditioning equipment—wholesale (Vol. 2)

9511 Water control and quality agencies-government (Vol. 2)

3585 Water coolers, electric (Vol. 1)

2834 Water decontamination or purification tablets (Vol. 1)

2899 Water, distilled (Vol. 1)

4971 Water distribution or supply systems for irrigation (Vol. 2)

3589 Water filters and softeners, household type (Vol. 1)

2819 Water glass (Vol. 1)

3822 Water heater controls (Vol. 1)

5064 Water heaters, electric—wholesale (Vol. 2)

5074 Water heaters, except electric—wholesale (Vol. 2)

3639 Water heaters, household: including nonelectric (Vol. 1)

1381 Water intake well drilling: on a contract basis (Vol. 2)

3599 Water leak detectors (Vol. 1)

1623 Water main line construction-general contractors (Vol. 2)

5499 Water, mineral—retail (Vol. 2)

2851 Water paints (Vol. 1)

2086 Water, pasteurized: bottled or canned (Vol. 1)

3321 Water pipe, cast iron (Vol. 1)

9511 Water pollution control agencies (Vol. 2)

1629 Water power project construction-general contractors (Vol. 2)

3634 Water pulsating devices, electric (Vol. 1)

1711 Water pump installation and servicing-contractors (Vol. 2)

5084 Water pumps, industrial—wholesale (Vol. 2)

3589 Water purification equipment, household type (Vol. 1)

3823 Water quality monitoring and control systems (Vol. 1)

2261 Water repellency finishing of cotton broadwoven fabrics (Vol. 1)

7389 Water softener service (Vol. 2)

3589 Water softeners, household type (Vol. 1)

5074 Water softeners—wholesale (Vol. 2)

2834 Water, sterile: for injections (Vol. 1)

4941 Water Supply (Vol. 2)

4941 Water supply systems, except irrigation (Vol. 2)

1711 Water system balancing and testing-contractors (Vol. 2)

3443 Water tanks, metal plate (Vol. 1)

4489 Water taxis, operation of (Vol. 2)

3829 Water temperature gauges, motor vehicle (Vol. 1)

4449 Water Transportation of Freight Not Elsewhere Classified (Vol. 2)

4424 Water transportation of freight to noncontiguous territories (Vol. 2)

4489 Water Transportation of Passengers Not Elsewhere Classified (Vol. 2)

4499 Water Transportation Services Not Elsewhere Classified (Vol. 2)

3432 Water traps (Vol. 1)

2899 Water treating compounds (Vol. 1)

3589 Water treatment equipment, industrial (Vol. 1)

1629 Water treatment plant construction-general contractors (Vol. 2)

3523 Water troughs (Vol. 1)

3511 Water turbines (Vol. 1)

3494 Water valves, except plumbers' brass goods and fittings, metal (Vol. 1)

1781 Water Well Drilling (Vol. 2)

1781 Water well drilling-contractors (Vol. 2)

3533 Water well drilling machinery (Vol. 1)

3491 Water works valves (Vol. 1)

5712 Waterbeds—retail (Vol. 2)

5021 Waterbeds—wholesale (Vol. 2)

4491 Waterfront terminal operation (Vol. 2)

3089 Watering pots, plastics (Vol. 1)

0161 Watermelon farms (Vol. 2)

3824 Watermeters, consumption registering (Vol. 1)

2385 Waterproof and water-repellent outerwear, except vulcanized rubber, oiled and wool (Vol. 1)

2675 Waterproof cardboard (Vol. 1)

5136 Waterproof outergarments, men's and boys'—wholesale (Vol. 2)

5137 Waterproof outergarments: women's and children's—wholesale (Vol. 2)

2385 Waterproof Outerwear (Vol. 1)

2671 Waterproof wrapping paper (Vol. 1)

2899 Waterproofing compounds (Vol. 1)

1799 Waterproofing-contractors (Vol. 2)

7999 Waterslides, operation of (Vol. 2)

1629 Waterway construction-general contractors (Vol. 2)

3825 Watt-hour and demand meters, combined (Vol. 1)

3825 Watt-hour and time switch meters, combined (Vol. 1)

3825 Watt-hour meters, electric (Vol. 1)

2861 Wattle extract (Vol. 1)

3825 Wattmeters (Vol. 1)

7999 Wave pools, operation of (Vol. 2)

3825 Waveform measuring and/or analyzing equipment (Vol. 1)

3699 Waveguide pressurization equipment (Vol. 1)

3679 Waveguides and fittings (Vol. 1)

3952 Wax, artists' (Vol. 1)

2899 Wax, core (Vol. 1)

3843 Wax, dental (Vol. 1)

7999 Wax figure exhibitions (Vol. 2)

8412 Wax museums, commercial (Vol. 2)

2911 Wax, paraffin: produced in petroleum refineries (Vol. 1)

2842 Wax removers (Vol. 1)

2891 Wax, sealing (Vol. 1)

2672 Waxed paper, except for packaging (Vol. 1)

2671 Waxed paper for packaging (Vol. 1)

5169 Waxes, except petroleum—wholesale (Vol. 2)

2842 Waxes for wood, fabricated leather, and other materials (Vol. 1)

2999 Waxes, petroleum: not produced in petroleum refineries (Vol. 1)

7542 Waxing and polishing, automotive (Vol. 2)

2295 Waxing of cloth (Vol. 1)

8999 Weather forecasters (Vol. 2)

8999 Weather modification (rain makers) (Vol. 2)

3442 Weather strip, metal (Vol. 1)

3069 Weather strip, sponge rubber (Vol. 1)

2431 Weather strip, wood (Vol. 1)

1799 Weather stripping-contra tors (Vol. 2)

3829 Weather tracking equipment (Vol. 1)

3599 Weather vanes (Vol. 1)

3357 Weatherproof wire and cable, nonferrous (Vol. 1)

2231 Weaving mills, broadwoven fabrics: wool, mohair, and similar animal fibers (Vol. 1)

2211 Weaving mills, cotton broadwoven fabrics (Vol. 1)

2241 Weaving mills, narrow fabric: cotton, wool, silk, and manmade fibers-including glass (Vol. 1)

2281 Weaving yarn: cotton, silk, wool, and manmade staple (Vol. 1)

2499 Webbing: cane, reed, and rattan (Vol. 1)

2299 Webbing, jute (Vol. 1)

2241 Webbing, woven: except jute (Vol. 1)

2241 Webs, strapping (Vol. 1)

7299 Wedding chapels, privately operated (Vol. 2)

2335 Wedding dresses: women's, misses', and juniors' (Vol. 1)

0721 Weed control, crop: after planting (Vol. 2)

0711 Weed control, crop: before planting (Vol. 2)

3523 Weeding machines, farm (Vol. 1)

2257 Weft Knit Fabric Mills (Vol. 1)

2257 Weft knit fabrics (Vol. 1)

5131 Weft knit fabrics—wholesale (Vol. 2)

7389 Weighing foods and other commodities, not connected with transportation (Vol. 2)

3596 Weighing machines and apparatus, except laboratory (Vol. 1)

4785 Weighing services connected with transportation (Vol. 2)

7389 Welcoming service (Vol. 2)

3315 Welded steel wire fabric, made in wiredrawing plants (Vol. 1)

3199 Welders' aprons, leather (Vol. 1)

3151 Welders' gloves (Vol. 1)

3842 Welders' hoods (Vol. 1)

3199 Welders' jackets, leggings, and sleeves: leather (Vol. 1)

3548 Welding accessories, electric and gas (Vol. 1)

3548 Welding and cutting apparatus, gas or electric (Vol. 1)

1799 Welding contractors, operating at site of construction (Vol. 2)

2899 Welding fluxes (Vol. 1)

5084 Welding machinery and equipment—wholesale (Vol. 2)

3544 Welding positioners (jigs) (Vol. 1)

7692 Welding Repair (Vol. 2)

3356 Welding rods (Vol. 1)

7692 Welding shops, including automotive (Vol. 2)

3548 Welding wire, bare and coated (Vol. 1)

3443 Weldments (Vol. 1)

6371 Welfare pensions (Vol. 2)

3494 Well adapters, tipless: metal (Vol. 1)

3317 Well casing, wrought: welded, lock joint, and heavy riveted (Vol. 1)

3312 Well casings, iron and steel: made in steel works or rolling mills (Vol. 1)

3272 Well curbing, concrete (Vol. 1)

1381 Well drilling: gas, oil, and water intake-on a contract basis (Vol. 2)

1781 Well drilling, water: except oil or gas field water intake-contractors (Vol. 2)

1389 Well foundation grading, oil and gas wells: on a contract basis (Vol. 2)

3533 Well logging equipment (Vol. 1)

1389 Well logging: on a contract basis (Vol. 2)

1389 Well plugging and abandoning, oil and gas wells: on a contract basis (Vol. 2)

5082 Well points (drilling equipment)—wholesale (Vol. 2)

1389 Well pumping, oil and gas: on a contract basis (Vol. 2)

1389 Well servicing, oil and gas wells: on a contract basis (Vol. 2)

2892 Well shooting torpedoes (explosives) (Vol. 1)

3533 Well surveying machinery (Vol. 1)

3531 Wellpoint systems (Vol. 1)

3444 Wells, light: sheet metal (Vol. 1)

3131 Welting, leather (cut stock and findings) (Vol. 1)

3111 Welting leather (Vol. 1)

2399 Welts (Vol. 1)

3111 Wet blues (Vol. 1)

2046 Wet Corn Milling (Vol. 1)

5149 Wet corn milling products—wholesale (Vol. 2)

2631 Wet machine board (Vol. 1)

3069 Wet suits, rubber (Vol. 1)

2843 Wetting agents (Vol. 1)

2077 Whale oil, refined (Vol. 1)

1629 Wharf construction-general contractors (Vol. 2)

2511 Whatnot shelves, wood (Vol. 1)

0111 Wheat (Vol. 2)

0111 Wheat farms (Vol. 2)

2043 Wheat flakes (Vol. 1)

2041 Wheat flour (Vol. 1)

2041 Wheat germ (Vol. 1)

2046 Wheat gluten (Vol. 1)

2041 Wheat mill feed (Vol. 1)

2046 Wheat starch (Vol. 1)

5153 Wheat—wholesale (Vol. 2)

3825 Wheatstone bridges (electrical measuring instruments) (Vol. 1)

7539 Wheel alignment, automotive (Vol. 2)

3559 Wheel balancing equipment, automotive (Vol. 1)

3842 Wheel chairs (Vol. 1)

3559 Wheel mounting and balancing equipment, automotive (Vol. 1)

3812 Wheel position indicators and transmitters, aircraft (Vol. 1)

3423 Wheel pullers, handtools (Vol. 1)

3545 Wheel turning equipment, diamond point and other (machine tool accessories) (Vol. 1)

3799 Wheelbarrows (Vol. 1)

3843 Wheels, abrasive: dental (Vol. 1)

3291 Wheels, abrasive: except dental (Vol. 1)

3728 Wheels, aircraft (Vol. 1)

3462 Wheels, car and locomotive: forged-not made in rolling mills (Vol. 1)

3312 Wheels, car and locomotive: iron and steel (Vol. 1)

3291 Wheels, diamond abrasive (Vol. 1)

3291 Wheels, grinding: artificial (Vol. 1)

3714 Wheels, motor vehicle (Vol. 1)

5013 Wheels, motor vehicle: new—wholesale (Vol. 2)

3499 Wheels, stamped metal, disc type: wheelbarrow, stroller, lawnmower (Vol. 1)

1499 Whetstone quarrying (Vol. 2)

3291 Whetstones, artificial (Vol. 1)

2021 Whey butter (Vol. 1)

2023 Whey: concentrated, condensed, dried, evaporated, and powdered (Vol. 1)

2022 Whey, raw: liquid (Vol. 1)

2353 Whimseys and miniatures (millinery) (Vol. 1)

2026 Whipped cream (Vol. 1)

2023 Whipped topping, dry mix (Vol. 1)

2026 Whipped topping, except frozen or dry mix (Vol. 1)

2038 Whipped topping, frozen (Vol. 1)

3634 Whippers, household: electric (Vol. 1)

3199 Whips, horse (Vol. 1)

3199 Whipstocks (Vol. 1)

3842 Whirlpool baths, hydrotherapy equipment (Vol. 1)

5999 Whirlpool baths—retail (Vol. 2)

3991 Whisk brooms (Vol. 1)

2085 Whiskey: bourbon, rye, scotch type, and corn (Vol. 1)

4226 Whiskey warehousing (Vol. 2)

2816 White lead pigments (Vol. 1)

3369 White metal castings, except die-castings: lead, antimony, and tin (Vol. 1)

3861 Whiteprint (diazo) paper and cloth, sensitized (Vol. 1)

3861 Whiteprint (diazotype) reproduction machines and equipment (Vol. 1)

5044 Whiteprinting equipment—wholesale (Vol. 2)

3263 Whiteware, fine type semivitreous tableware and kitchenware (Vol. 1)

1721 Whitewashing-contractors (Vol. 2)

0912 Whiting, catching of (Vol. 2)

2816 Whiting (Vol. 1)

3316 Wire, flat: cold-rolled strip-not made in hot-rolling mills (Vol. 1)

3315 Wire garment hangers, steel: made in wiredrawing plants (Vol. 1)

5063 Wire, insulated—wholesale (Vol. 2)

3357 Wire, nonferrous: bare, insulated, or armored (Vol. 1)

3356 Wire, nonferrous except copper and aluminum: made in rolling mills (Vol. 1)

5051 Wire, not insulated—wholesale (Vol. 2)

4822 Wire or cable telegraph (Vol. 2)

3315 Wire products, ferrous: made in wiredrawing plants (Vol. 1)

3312 Wire products, iron and steel: made in steel works or rolling mills (Vol. 1)

5051 Wire rods—wholesale (Vol. 2)

2298 Wire rope centers (Vol. 1)

5063 Wire rope or cable, insulated—wholesale (Vol. 2)

5051 Wire rope or cable, not insulated—wholesale (Vol. 2)

3357 Wire screening, nonferrous: made in wiredrawing plants (Vol. 1)

5051 Wire screening—wholesale (Vol. 2)

3495 Wire Springs (Vol. 1)

3315 Wire, steel: insulated or armored (Vol. 1)

4813 Wire telephone (Vol. 2)

3496 Wire winding of purchased wire (Vol. 1)

3549 Wiredrawing and fabricating machinery and equipment, except dies (Vol. 1)

3544 Wiredrawing and straightening dies (Vol. 1)

3672 Wiring boards (Vol. 1)

5063 Wiring devices—wholesale (Vol. 2)

3714 Wiring harness sets motor vehicles: except ignition (Vol. 1)

5063 Wiring materials, interior—wholesale (Vol. 2)

5063 Wiring supplies—wholesale (Vol. 2)

1061 Wolframite mining (Vol. 2)

5632 Women's Accessory and Specialty Stores (Vol. 2)

9441 Women's bureaus (Vol. 2)

5137 Women's, Children's and Infants' Clothing and Accessories (Vol. 2)

5621 Women's Clothing Stores (Vol. 2)

3144 Women's Footwear Except Athletic (Vol. 1)

2251 Women's Full-Length and Knee-Length Hosiery Except Socks (Vol. 1)

3171 Women's Handbags and Purses (Vol. 1)

2331 Women's, Misses' and Juniors' Blouses and Shirts (Vol. 1)

2335 Women's, Misses' and Juniors' Dresses (Vol. 1)

2339 Women's, Misses' and Juniors' Outerwear Not Elsewhere Classified (Vol. 1)

2337 Women's, Misses' and Juniors' Suits, Skirts and Coats (Vol. 1)

2341 Women's, Misses', Children's and Infants' Underwear and Nightwear (Vol. 1)

2861 Wood alcohol, natural (Vol. 1)

5199 Wood carvings—wholesale (Vol. 2)

2421 Wood chips produced at mill (Vol. 1)

2411 Wood chips, produced in the field (Vol. 1)

5099 Wood chips—wholesale (Vol. 2)

2449 Wood Containers Not Elsewhere Classified (Vol. 1)

2861 Wood creosote (Vol. 1)

5989 Wood dealers, fuel—retail (Vol. 2)

2861 Wood distillates (Vol. 1)

3559 Wood drying kilns (Vol. 1)

2499 Wood, except furniture: turned and carved (Vol. 1)

2491 Wood fence: pickets, poling, rails-treated (Vol. 1)

2851 Wood fillers and sealers (Vol. 1)

1752 Wood flooring-contractors (Vol. 2)

2499 Wood flour (Vol. 1)

3131 Wood heel blocks, for sale as such (Vol. 1)

3131 Wood heels, finished (shoe findings) (Vol. 1)

2511 Wood Household Furniture Except Upholstered (Vol. 1)

2434 Wood Kitchen Cabinets (Vol. 1)

2541 Wood Office and Store Fixtures, Partitions, Shelving and Lockers (Vol. 1)

2521 Wood Office Furniture (Vol. 1)

2861 Wood oils, product of hardwood distillation (Vol. 1)

2448 Wood Pallets and Skids (Vol. 1)

2899 Wood, plastic (Vol. 1)

2491 Wood Preserving (Vol. 1)

2491 Wood products, creosoted (Vol. 1)

2499 Wood Products Not Elsewhere Classified (Vol. 1)

2611 Wood pulp (Vol. 1)

3452 Wood screws, metal (Vol. 1)

5031 Wood siding—wholesale (Vol. 2)

2851 Wood stains (Vol. 1)

2517 Wood T.V., Radio, Phonograph and Sewing Machine Cabinets (Vol. 1)

2429 Wood wool (excelsior) (Vol. 1)

5719 Woodburning stoves—retail (Vol. 2)

2499 Woodenware, kitchen and household (Vol. 1)

3931 Woodwind and brass wind musical instrument (Vol. 1)

2431 Woodwork, interior and ornamental: e.g., windows, doors, sash, and mantels (Vol. 1)

3553 Woodworking Machinery (Vol. 1)

5084 Woodworking machinery—wholesale (Vol. 2)

3553 Woodworking machines (Vol. 1)

4221 Wool and mohair warehousing (Vol. 2)

3552 Wool and worsted finishing machines (Vol. 1)

2231 Wool broad woven fabrics (Vol. 1)

2299 Wool felts, pressed or needle loom (Vol. 1)

2231 Wool felts, woven (Vol. 1)

2299 Wool grease, mohair, and similar fibers (Vol. 1)

3296 Wool, mineral: made of rock, slag, and silica minerals (Vol. 1)

2241 Wool narrow woven goods (Vol. 1)

0214 Wool production (Vol. 2)

3999 Wool pulling (Vol. 1)

5159 Wool, raw—wholesale (Vol. 2)

2299 Wool scouring and carbonizing (Vol. 1)

2299 Wool shoddy (Vol. 1)

3291 Wool, steel (Vol. 1)

5159 Wool tops and noils—wholesale (Vol. 2)

2299 Wool tops, combing and converting (Vol. 1)

2299 Wool waste processing (Vol. 1)

2299 Yarn, specialty and novelty (Vol. 1)

2281 Yarn spinning: cotton, silk, and manmade staple (Vol. 1)

2281 Yarn Spinning Mills (Vol. 1)

2281 Yarn, spun: cotton, silk, manmade fiber, wool, and animal fiber (Vol. 1)

3552 Yarn texturizing machines (Vol. 1)

2282 Yarn Texturizing, Throwing, Twisting and Winding Mills (Vol. 1)

2823 Yarn, viscose (Vol. 1)

2241 Yarns, fabric covered rubber (Vol. 1)

2295 Yarns, plastics coated: made from purchased yarns (Vol. 1)

5199 Yarns—wholesale (Vol. 2)

2741 Yearbooks: publishing and printing, or publishing only (Vol. 1)

2099 Yeast (Vol. 1)

5149 Yeast—wholesale (Vol. 2)

7999 Yoga (Vol. 2)

2026 Yogurt, except frozen (Vol. 1)

2024 Yogurt, frozen (Vol. 1)

2023 Yogurt mix (Vol. 1)

5143 Yogurt—wholesale (Vol. 2)

8641 Youth associations, except hotel units (Vol. 2)

8322 Youth centers (Vol. 2)

8322 Youth self-help organizations (Vol. 2)

Z

2824 Zein fibers (Vol. 1)

3674 Zener diodes (Vol. 1)

3356 Zinc and zinc alloy bars, plates, pipe, rods, sheets, tubing, and wire (Vol. 1)

1031 Zinc-blende (sphalerite) mining (Vol. 2)

3369 Zinc castings, except die-castings (Vol. 1)

2819 Zinc chloride (Vol. 1)

3364 Zinc die-castings (Vol. 1)

3339 Zinc dust, primary (Vol. 1)

3341 Zinc dust, reclaimed (Vol. 1)

3497 Zinc foil, not made in rolling mills (Vol. 1)

2834 Zinc ointment (Vol. 1)

1031 Zinc ore mining (Vol. 2)

5052 Zinc ore—wholesale (Vol. 2)

2851 Zinc oxide in oil, paint (Vol. 1)

2816 Zinc oxide pigments (Vol. 1)

2816 Zinc pigments: zinc yellow and zinc sulfide (Vol. 1)

3356 Zinc rolling, drawing, and extruding (Vol. 1)

3339 Zinc slabs, ingots, and refinery shapes: primary (Vol. 1)

3341 Zinc smelting and refining, secondary (Vol. 1)

5051 Zinc—wholesale (Vol. 2)

1031 Zincite mining (Vol. 2)

3559 Zipper making machinery (Vol. 1)

2241 Zipper tape (Vol. 1)

3965 Zippers (slide fasteners) (Vol. 1)

5131 Zippers—wholesale (Vol. 2)

3356 Zirconium and zirconium alloy bars, rods, billets, sheets, strip, and tubing (Vol. 1)

3339 Zirconium metal sponge and granules (Vol. 1)

1099 Zirconium ore mining (Vol. 2)

3931 Zithers and parts (Vol. 1)

9532 Zoning boards and commissions (Vol. 2)

8422 Zoological gardens (Vol. 2)

2052 Zwieback (Vol. 1)

Contributor Notes

Aaron, Sunder. Free-lance writer; MBA, University of Michigan, Ann Arbor.

Armstrong, Robin. Free-lance writer. Contributor to *Contemporary Musicians, Contemporary Black Biography,* and *International Dictionary of Opera.*

Balch, Trudy. Free-lance writer.

Baker, Suzanne. Free-lance writer; MBA, University of Michigan, Ann Arbor.

Ballard, Andrew. Free-lance writer.

Barduson, Thomas. MBA and free-lance writer and researcher.

Beard, James L. Free-lance writer. CPA and MBA candidate, Oral Roberts University. Author of essays including "The Balanced Budget Amendment: Pro and Con."

Bellenir, Karen. Free-lance writer and editor.

Bennett, William A. Free-lance business writer and researcher. Graduate student in business, University of Oregon.

Berger, Percy Lee. JD and MBA candidate, University of Michigan, Ann Arbor. Associate editor, *Michigan Journal of International Law*, free-lance writer.

Berry, Pamela. Free-lance writer and editor.

Bilas, Wendy Johnson. Free-lance writer. MBA in marketing, Wake Forest University; director of marketing for the Charlotte Symphony Orchestra.

Blumenfield, Steven. MBA candidate, University of Chicago. Managing editor, *Chicago Business.*

Bodine, Paul. Free-lance writer and editor.

Boyer, Dean. Former newspaper reporter; free-lance writer in Seattle area.

Brennan, Carol. Free-lance writer based in Detroit.

Brown, Susan. Free-lance writer.

Burke, Andrew. Free-lance writer.

Cohen, Kerstan B. Free-lance writer and French translator; editor for *Letter-Ex* poetry review.

Collins, Cheryl. Free-lance writer and researcher.

Cook, Allan R. Free-lance writer and journalist. Graduate student in English, Oakland University, Rochester, Michigan.

Costilow, Donald R. Free-lance writer; graphic artist/illustrator, Monongahela Power Company; instructor of business at Fairmont State College (community college segment), Fairmont, West Virginia.

Covell, Jeffrey L. Free-lance writer and corporate history contractor.

Creighton, Kevin. Free-lance writer; MBA, University of Michigan, Ann Arbor.

Cuene, Jim. Free-lance writer. Graduate student in American Studies, Purdue University.

Dailey, Kristine. Free-lance writer and MBA candidate, Boston College.

Daniels, Garth K. D.B.A. Business consultant in corporate strategy and new venture development. Adjunct faculty member, Westminster College, Salt Lake City, Utah.

Dorman, Evelyn. Free-lance journalist, public relations, French teacher, tutor, and graduate student. Contributor to *Brides Today, Lerner-Pulitzer* newspapers, the *Chicago Sun Times,* and St. James Press' *International Directory of Company Histories.*

Dougal, April S. Archivist and free-lance writer specializing in business and social history in Cleveland, Ohio.

Evans, Ken. Doctoral candidate in Economics, University of Michigan, Ann Arbor.

Fisher, Rogene M. Free-lance writer and editor.

Gallman, Jason. Free-lance writer and graduate student in literature, Purdue University, West Lafayette, Indian.

Gluskin, Lisa. Writer and editor based in San Francisco. Editor of *And...* magazine (a journal of San Francisco arts and culture).

Grant, Tina. Free-lance writer and editor.

Griffin, Attrices Dean. Free-lance researcher and writer. Former owner of research and technical writing firm.

Gustafson, Randy. Free-lance writer; MBA, University of Michigan, Ann Arbor.

Hedden, Heather Behn. Business periodical abstractor and indexer, Information Access Company, Foster City, California. Senior staff writer, *Middle East Times* Cairo bureau, 1991-92.

Hernandez, Rolando. Computer systems analyst, project leader, and knowledge engineer; free-lance writer.

Hillstrom, Laurie Collier. Free-lance writer and editor. MBA, University of Michigan, 1994. Former editor of *Authors and Artists for Young Adults* and *Major Authors and Illustrators for Children and Young Adults* (Gale Research Inc.).

Hillyer, Richard. Free-lance writer and editor, poet, and part-time English teacher. Ph.D. in English, University of Michigan, Ann Arbor.

Hoyt, Douglas. Free-lance writer.

Huerster, Patricia G. Free-lance writer and editor.

Ingram, Frederick C. Free-lance writer based in Sumter, South Carolina.

Isaacs, McAllister III. Editor of *Textile World*, Maclean Hunter's international textile magazine.

Jacobson, Robert R. Free-lance writer; musician.

Jeffrey, Tim. Playwright, short-story writer, and free-lance writer based in Detroit, Michigan.

Jones, J. Jacob. Graduate student in American History, Purdue University.

Kaufman, Scott. Free-lance writer.

King, Daniel. Free-lance writer working on doctorate in economics at the New School for Social Research, New York City.

Kirchner, Joseph. Free-lance writer based in Alexandria, Virginia.

Kody, John. Free-lance writer.

Kucera, David. Ph.D. candidate in Economics at New School for Social Research, New York City.

Kuhn, Karyn Bober. Free-lance writer and editor.

Leotta, Joan. Free-lance business and travel writer and story-teller in Burke, Virginia. Has published a book on writing techniques for hotel managers. Writes poetry, fiction, and nonfiction for children.

Levine, Kathie. Attorney and free-lance writer. Contributing editor, *California Employer Advisor*. Contributor to *San Francisco Business Times* and *Marin Independent Journal*.

Lewis, Scott M. Free-lance writer and editor; contributing editor, *Option*. Staff editor, *Security, Distributing and Marketing*, 1989-90.

MacFarlane, K. Thomas. Free-lance writer.

Malkin, Shula. Free-lance writer.

Maschinot, Michael. Free-lance writer.

Maxfield, Doris A. Owner of Written Expressions, an editorial services business. Contributor to numerous reference publications. Editor of *Online Database Search Services Directory*, 1983-84 and 1988, and of *Charitable Organizations of the U.S.*, 1991-93.

McDonald, Avril. Free-lance writer.

McKelvey, Paul S. Principal, McKelvey & Associates, Slidell, Louisiana. Extensive writing on international commerce, inland waterways and ports, and shipbuilding. Contributor to *WorkBoat, Sea Trade, International Coffee and Tea Journal, New Orleans CityBusiness*, and *Port of New Orleans Record*. Member of New Orleans Press Club, International Association of Business Communicators, Public Relations Society of America, and Society for Technical Communication.

Meyer, Bruce. Senior editor for Akron, Ohio-based *Rubber & Plastics News*, a weekly trade newspaper.

Miller, Steven W. Free-lance writer; MBA, University of Michigan, Ann Arbor.

Mogelonsky, Marcia. Free-lance writer.

Mote, David. Free-lance writer and editor based in Indianapolis, Indiana. President of information retrieval company Performance Database.

Mote, Michelle G. Free-lance writer and professional educator.

Motta, Paolo. Free-lance writer.

Nash, Margo. Free-lance writer.

Neubauer, Joan R. Owner, Word Wright International, Houston, Texas. Publisher, "The Last Word." Free-lance writer, public speaker, teacher. Author of *Tell Them Like It Really Was: The Five Step Method to Writing Your Story.*

Oleck, Joan. Free-lance writer in Brooklyn, New York. Contributor to *New York Times, New Woman, Washington Journalism Review,* and other regional and national business publications.

Ossip, Kathleen. Free-lance writer.

Pederson, Jay P. Free-lance writer and editor.

Pendergast, Sara. Free-lance writer and copy editor.

Pendergast, Tom. Free-lance writer and editor. Graduate student in American Studies, Purdue University.

Pitts, Lee. Executive editor, *Livestock Market Digest.* Author of several books and a syndicated humor column.

Plamondon, Scott. Free-lance writer.

Quagliana, Catherine A. Free-lance writer and editor based in Austin, Texas.

Ratcliffe, Mary. Free-lance writer and editor. Author of brochures, newsletters, press releases, and advertising copy.

Rooks, Alan. Free-lance writer.

Roy, Soumya. Free-lance writer. MBA candidate, Temple University.

Sarich, John A. Free-lance writer and editor. Graduate student in economics, New School for Social Research, New York City.

Schneider, Bob. Free-lance writer.

Sheil, Richard. Free-lance writer. MBA candidate, University of Wisconsin--Madison.

Sherman, Fran Shonfeld. Free-lance writer and editor. Assistant editor, *Compton's Encyclopedia,* 1986-92; contributing editor, *Britannica Book of the Year.*

Spencer, Dorothy. Free-lance writer and editor.

Sprinkle, David. Free-lance writer and editor.

Summers, Shannon. Free-lance writer.

Swartz, Mark. Manuscript editor for the journals division of the *University of the Chicago Press.*

Theodoroff, Mike. Free-lance writer.

Trimarco, Paola. Free-lance business and health writer based in Washington, D.C. Received Ph.D. from University of Edinburgh, Scotland.

Vecchiolla, Richard R. Free-lance writer and researcher focusing on shareholders' rights and total quality management issues; J.D. candidate, Georgetown University.

Von Heitman, Khatanga. Free-lance writer.

Waters, John K. Free-lance writer and editor based in California. Author of books including *Silicon Valley: Inventing the Future* and *The Bay Area: California Gateway to the Future.* Contributor to periodicals including *San Jose Magazine, South Bay Accent,* and *The Silicon Valley Insider.*

Westbrook, M. David. Free-lance writer.

Wilson, Valerie. Free-lance writer.

Wingett, Jeffery T. Free-lance writer. MBA from California Polytechnic State University.

Withem, Karen. Free-lance writer.

York, Leslee. Free-lance writer.

Zrinsky, Christine M. Free-lance writer and editor. Director of individual gifts, Chicago Symphony Orchestra.